Collins

Student's Dictionary

Collins
An Imprint of HarperCollins*Publishers*

first published 2004

HarperCollins Publishers
Westerhill Road, Bishopbriggs, Glasgow G64 2QT
Great Britain

www.collinsdictionaries.com

ISBN 0-00-716228-6

Acknowledgements

We would like to thank those authors and publishers who kindly gave permission for copyright material to be used in the Bank of English. We would also like to thank Times Newspapers Ltd for providing valuable data.

Note

Entered words that we have reason to believe constitute trademarks have been designated as such. However, neither the presence nor absence of such designation should be regarded as affecting the legal status of any trademark.

A catalogue record for this book is available from the British Library

Computing support and typesetting by Thomas Callan

Supplement typeset by Wordcraft

Printed in Italy by Legoprint S.P.A.

CONTENTS

BANK *of* ENGLISH

This dictionary has been compiled with constant reference to the Bank of English, a unique database containing over 524 million words of written and spoken English, enabling Collins lexicographers to analyse how the language is actually used and how it is changing. The Bank of English was set up as a joint initiative by HarperCollins Publishers and the University of Birmingham to be a resource for language research and lexicography. It contains a very wide range of material from books, newspapers, radio, TV, magazines, letters and talks, thereby reflecting the whole spectrum of English today. Its size and range make it an unequalled resource, and the purpose-built software for its analysis is unique to Collins dictionaries.

This ensures that Collins dictionaries accurately reflect English as it is used today in a way that is most helpful to the dictionary user.

EDITORIAL STAFF

Managing Editor
Elspeth Summers

Editors
Cordelia Lilly
Andrew Holmes
Jennifer Baird
Sandra Anderson
Alice Grandison

Supplement
Charlotte Hillenbrand
Cordelia Lilly
Barbara Waterfield

Publishing Director
Lorna Sinclair Knight

Publishing Manager
Elaine Higgleton

GUIDE TO THE DICTIONARY

Entry word

song *n* **1** a piece of music with words, composed for the voice. **2** the tuneful call made by certain birds or insects. **3** the act or process of singing: *he broke into song.* **4 for a song** at a bargain price. **5 make a song and dance** *Brit & NZ informal* to make an unnecessary fuss. ▷ **HISTORY** Old English *sang*

Regional label

songbird *n* any bird that has a musical call.

songololo (song-gol-**loll**-o) *n, pl* **-los** *S African* a kind of millipede. ▷ **HISTORY** Nguni (language group of southern Africa) *ukusonga* to roll up

songstress *n* a female singer of popular songs.

Definition

song thrush *n* a common thrush that repeats each note of its song.

Part of speech

sonic *adj* of, involving, or producing sound. ▷ **HISTORY** Latin *sonus* sound

sonic barrier *n* same as **sound barrier.**

Cross-reference

sonic boom *n* a loud explosive sound caused by the shock wave of an aircraft travelling at supersonic speed.

son-in-law *n, pl* **sons-in-law** the husband of one's daughter.

sonnet *n Prosody* a verse form consisting of 14 lines with a fixed rhyme scheme and rhythm pattern. ▷ **HISTORY** Old Provençal *sonet* a little poem

Usage label

sonny *n Often patronizing* a familiar term of address to a boy or man.

sonorous *adj* **1** (of a sound) deep or rich. **2** (of speech) using language that is unnecessarily complicated and difficult to understand; pompous. ▷ **HISTORY** Latin *sonor* a noise ▶ **sonority** *n*

Related word

Sense number

soon *adv* **1** in or after a short time; before long. **2 as soon as** at the very moment that: *as soon as he had closed the door.* **3 as soon ... as** used to indicate that the first alternative is slightly preferable to the second: *they'd just as soon die for him as live.* ▷ **HISTORY** Old English *sōna*

sooner *adv* **1** the comparative of **soon:** *I only wish I'd been back sooner.* **2** rather; in preference: *he would sooner leave the party than break with me.* **3 no sooner ... than** immediately after or when: *no sooner had he spoken than the stench drifted up.* **4 sooner or later** eventually.

Usage note

> ☑ **WORD TIP**
>
> *When* is sometimes used instead of *than* after *no sooner*, but this use is generally regarded as incorrect: *no sooner had he arrived than* (not *when*) *the telephone rang.*

GUIDE TO THE DICTIONARY

Subject label

stanza *n* *Prosody* a verse of a poem. ▷ **HISTORY** Italian: halting place

Pronunciation

staphylococcus (staff-ill-oh-**kok**-uss) *n, pl* **-cocci** (-**kok**-eye) a bacterium occurring in clusters and including many species that cause disease. ▷ **HISTORY** Greek *staphulē* bunch of grapes + *kokkos* berry

Spelling help

staple[1] *n* **1** a short length of wire bent into a square U-shape, used to fasten papers or secure things. ✧ *vb* **-pling, -pled** **2** to secure (things) with staples. ▷ **HISTORY** Old English *stapol* prop

Word history

staple[2] *adj* **1** of prime importance; principal: *the staple diet of a country.* ✧ *n* **2** something that forms a main part of the product, consumption, or trade of a region. **3** a main constituent of anything: *the personal reflections which make up the staple of the book.* ▷ **HISTORY** Middle Dutch *stapel* warehouse

stapler *n* a device used to fasten things together with a staple.

Related adjectives

Phrase

Example

star *n* **1** a planet or meteor visible in the clear night sky as a point of light. **2** a hot gaseous mass, such as the sun, that radiates energy as heat and light, or in some cases as radio waves and X-rays. *RELATED ADJECTIVES* ➧ **astral, sidereal, stellar** **3 stars** same as **horoscope** (sense 1). **4** an emblem with five or more radiating points, often used as a symbol of rank or an award: *the RAC awarded the hotel three stars.* **5** same as **asterisk**. **6** a famous person from the sports, acting, or music professions. **7** **see stars** to see flashes of light after a blow on the head. ✧ *vb* **starring, starred** **8** to feature (an actor or actress) or (of an actor or actress) to be featured as a star: *he's starred in dozens of films.* **9** to mark (something) with a star or stars. ▷ **HISTORY** Old English *steorra*

starboard *n* **1** the right side of an aeroplane or ship when facing forwards. ✧ *adj* **2** of or on the starboard.

Detailed word history

> **WORD HISTORY**
>
> 'Starboard' comes from Old English *steorbord*, which means 'steering side'. This is because boats were formerly steered with a paddle held over the right-hand side of the boat.

starch *n* **1** a carbohydrate forming the main food element in bread, potatoes, and rice: in solution with water it is used to stiffen fabric. **2** food containing a large amount of starch. ✧ *vb* **3** to stiffen (cloth) with starch. ▷ **HISTORY** Old English *sterced* stiffened

ABBREVIATIONS USED IN THE DICTIONARY

abbrev.	abbreviation	*Med*	Medicine
adj	adjective	*Meteorol*	Meteorology
adv	adverb(ial)	*Mil*	Military
Anat	Anatomy	*Myth*	Mythology
Anthropol	Anthropology	*n*	noun
Archaeol	Archaeology	*N*	North(ern)
Archit	Architecture	*Naut*	Nautical
Astrol	Astrology	*NE*	Northeast(ern)
Astron	Astronomy	*NW*	Northwest(ern)
Austral	Australian	*NZ*	New Zealand
Bacteriol	Bacteriology	*obs.*	obsolete
Biochem	Biochemistry	*orig.*	originally
Biol	Biology	*Ornithol*	Ornithology
Bot	Botany	*Pathol*	Pathology
Brit	British	*Pharmacol*	Pharmacology
C	Celsius	*Photog*	Photography
Canad	Canadian	*Physiol*	Physiology
cap	capital	*pl*	plural
cent.	century	*pp*	past participle
Chem	Chemistry	*prep*	preposition
comp.	comparative	*prob.*	probably
conj	conjuction	*pron*	pronoun
Crystallog	Crystallography	*Psychoanal*	Psychoanalysis
dim.	diminutive	*Psychol*	Psychology
E	East(ern)	*pt*	past tense
Econ	Economics	*RC*	Roman Catholic
esp.	especially	*rel.*	related
etc.	et cetera	*S*	South(ern)
F	Fahrenheit	*Scot*	Scottish
fem	feminine	*SE*	Southeast(ern)
foll.	followed	*sing*	singular
Geog	Geography	*SW*	Southwest(ern)
Geol	Geology	*Theol*	Theology
Geom	Geometry	*ult.*	ultimately
imit.	imitative	*US*	United States
infl.	influence(d)	*var.*	variant
interj	interjection	*vb*	verb
lit.	literally	*W*	West(ern)
masc	masculine	*Zool*	Zoology
Maths	Mathematics		

A a

a *or* **A** *n, pl* **a's, A's** *or* **As 1** the first letter of the English alphabet. **2 from A to B** from one place to another: *I just want a car that takes me from A to B.* **3 from A to Z** from start to finish.

a *adj* (*indefinite article*) **1** used preceding a singular count noun that has not been mentioned before: *a book; a great shame.* **2** used preceding a noun or adjective of quantity: *a litre of wine; a great amount has been written; I swim a lot and walk much more.* **3** each or every; per: *I saw him once a week for six weeks.*

A 1 *Music* the sixth note of the scale of C major. **2** ampere(s). **3** atomic: *an A-bomb.*

Å angstrom unit.

a- *or before a vowel* **an-** *prefix* not or without: *atonal; asocial; anaphrodisiac.* ▷ HISTORY Greek

A1, A-1, *or* **A-one** *adj Informal* first-class, excellent.

A4 *n* a standard paper size, 297 × 210 mm.

AA 1 Alcoholics Anonymous. **2** (in Britain and S Africa) Automobile Association.

AAA *Brit* (formerly) Amateur Athletic Association.

A & R artists and repertoire.

aardvark *n* a S African anteater with long ears and snout.

> **WORD HISTORY**
> 'Aardvark' is an obsolete Afrikaans word meaning 'earth pig', from *aarde*, meaning 'earth' and *vark*, meaning 'pig'. With its long ears and snout and its stout body, the aardvark does look rather like a pig, but pigs and aardvarks belong to totally separate animal families.

AB 1 able-bodied seaman. **2** Alberta.

ab- *prefix* away from or opposite to: *abnormal.* ▷ HISTORY Latin

aback *adv* **taken aback** startled or disconcerted.

abacus (**ab**-a-cuss) *n* a counting device consisting of a frame holding beads on metal rods. ▷ HISTORY Latin

abaft *adv, adj Naut* closer to the stern of a ship. ▷ HISTORY Old English *be* by + *æftan* behind

abalone (ab-a-**lone**-ee) *n* an edible sea creature with a shell lined with mother-of-pearl. ▷ HISTORY American Spanish *abulón*

abandon *vb* **1** to desert or leave: *he had already abandoned his first wife.* **2** to give up completely: *did you abandon all attempts at contact with the boy?* **3** to give oneself over completely to an emotion. ✧ *n* **4 with abandon** uninhibitedly and without restraint. ▷ HISTORY Old French *a bandon* under one's control ▶ **abandonment** *n*

abandoned *adj* **1** no longer used or occupied: *four people were found dead in an abandoned vehicle.* **2** wild and uninhibited: *that fluffy abandoned laugh.*

abase *vb* **abasing, abased abase oneself** to make oneself humble. ▷ HISTORY Old French *abaissier* ▶ **abasement** *n*

abashed *adj* embarrassed and ashamed. ▷ HISTORY Old French *esbair* to be astonished

abate *vb* **abating, abated** to make or become less strong: *the tension has abated in recent months.* ▷ HISTORY Old French *abatre* to beat down ▶ **abatement** *n*

abattoir (**ab**-a-twahr) *n* a slaughterhouse. ▷ HISTORY French *abattre* to fell

abbacy *n, pl* **-cies** the office or jurisdiction of an abbot or abbess. ▷ HISTORY Church Latin *abbatia*

abbé (**ab**-bay) *n* a French abbot or other clergyman.

abbess *n* the nun in charge of a convent. ▷ HISTORY Church Latin *abbatissa*

abbey *n* **1** a church associated with a community of monks or nuns. **2** a community of monks or nuns. **3** a building inhabited by monks or nuns. ▷ HISTORY Church Latin *abbatia* ABBACY

abbot *n* the head of an abbey of monks. ▷ HISTORY Aramaic *abbā* father

abbreviate *vb* **-ating, -ated 1** to shorten a word by leaving out some letters. **2** to cut short. ▷ HISTORY Latin *brevis* brief ▶ **abbreviation** *n*

ABC[1] *n* **1** the alphabet. **2** an alphabetical guide. **3** the basics of something.

ABC[2] Australian Broadcasting Corporation.

abdicate *vb* **-cating, -cated 1** to give up the throne formally. **2** to give up one's responsibilities. ▷ HISTORY Latin *abdicare* to disclaim ▶ **abdication** *n*

abdomen *n* the part of the body that contains the stomach and intestines. ▷ HISTORY Latin ▶ **abdominal** *adj*

abduct *vb* to remove (a person) by force; kidnap. ▷ HISTORY Latin *abducere* to lead away ▶ **abduction** *n* ▶ **abductor** *n*

abeam *adv, adj* at right angles to the length of a ship or aircraft.

Aberdeen Angus *n* a black hornless breed of beef cattle originating in Scotland.

aberrant *adj* not normal, accurate, or correct: *aberrant behaviour.*

aberration *n* **1** a sudden change from what is normal, accurate, or correct. **2** a brief lapse in control of one's thoughts or feelings: *he suddenly had a mental aberration.* ▷ HISTORY Latin *aberrare* to wander away

abet *vb* **abetting, abetted** to help or encourage in wrongdoing. ▷ HISTORY Old French *abeter* to lure on

abeyance *n* **in abeyance** put aside temporarily. ▷ HISTORY Old French *abeance*, literally: a gaping after

abhor *vb* **-horring, -horred** to detest utterly. ▷ HISTORY Latin *abhorrere* to shudder at

abhorrent *adj* hateful or disgusting. ▶ **abhorrence** *n*

abide *vb* **1** to tolerate: *I can't abide stupid people.* **2** to last or exist for a long time: *these instincts, while* *subdued in the individual, may abide in the race.* **3 abide by** to act in accordance with: *he must abide by the findings of the report.* **4** *Archaic* to live. ▷ **HISTORY** Old English *ābīdan*, from *a-* (intensive) + *bīdan* to wait

abiding *adj* lasting for ever: *an abiding interest in history.*

ability *n, pl* **-ties 1** possession of the necessary skill or power to do something. **2** great skill or competence: *his ability as a speaker was legendary.* ▷ **HISTORY** Latin *habilitas*

abiotic (ay-bye-**ott**-ik) *adj* not living or not produced by living organisms. Compare **biotic**.

abject *adj* **1** utterly miserable: *one Mexican in five lives in abject poverty.* **2** lacking all self-respect. ▷ **HISTORY** Latin *abjectus* thrown away ▶ **abjectly** *adv*

abjure *vb* **-juring, -jured** to renounce or deny under oath. ▷ **HISTORY** Latin *abjurare* ▶ **abjuration** *n*

ablation *n* **1** the surgical removal of an organ or part. **2** the wearing away of a rock or glacier. **3** the melting of a part, such as the heat shield of a space re-entry vehicle. ▷ **HISTORY** Latin *ablatus* carried away

ablaze *adj* **1** on fire. **2** brightly illuminated: *the sky was ablaze with the stars shining bright.* **3** emotionally aroused: *his eyes were ablaze with anger.*

able *adj* **1** having the necessary power, skill, or opportunity to do something. **2** capable or talented. ▷ **HISTORY** Latin *habilis* easy to hold

-able *suffix forming adjectives* able to be acted upon as specified: *washable.* ▷ **HISTORY** Latin *-abilis, -ibilis* ▶ **-ably** *suffix forming adverbs* ▶ **-ability** *suffix forming nouns*

able-bodied *adj* strong and healthy.

able-bodied seaman *or* **able seaman** *n* a seaman who is trained in certain skills.

ableism (**ay**-bel-iz-zum) *n Brit, Austral & S African* discrimination against disabled or handicapped people.

ablutions *pl n* the act of washing: *after the nightly ablutions, I settled down to read.* ▷ **HISTORY** Latin *abluere* to wash away

ably *adv* competently or skilfully.

ABM antiballistic missile.

abnormal *adj* differing from the usual or typical. ▶ **abnormality** *n* ▶ **abnormally** *adv*

aboard *adv, adj, prep* on, in, onto, or into (a ship, plane, or train).

abode *n* one's home. ▷ **HISTORY** from ABIDE

abolish *vb* to do away with (laws, regulations, or customs). ▷ **HISTORY** Latin *abolere* to destroy

abolition *n* **1** the act of doing away with something: *the abolition of slavery.* **2 Abolition** the ending of slavery. ▶ **abolitionist** *n, adj*

A-bomb *n* short for **atomic bomb**.

abominable *adj* very bad or unpleasant: *I think that what is being done here is utterly abominable.* ▶ **abominably** *adv*

abominable snowman *n* a large creature, like a man or an ape, that is said to live in the Himalayas. ▷ **HISTORY** translation of Tibetan *metohkangmi* foul snowman

abominate *vb* **-nating, -nated** to dislike intensely. ▷ **HISTORY** Latin *abominari* to regard as an ill omen ▶ **abomination** *n*

aboriginal *adj* existing in a place from the earliest known period.

Aboriginal *adj* **1** of the Aborigines of Australia. ✧ *n* **2** an Aborigine.

aborigine (ab-or-**rij**-in-ee) *n Brit, Austral & NZ* an original inhabitant of a country or region, esp. (**A-**) Australia. ▷ **HISTORY** from Latin *aborigines*, the name of the inhabitants of Latium in pre-Roman times

Aborigine *n* a member of a dark-skinned people who were already living in Australia when European settlers arrived.

abort *vb* **1** (of a pregnancy) to end before the fetus is viable. **2** to perform an abortion on a pregnant woman. **3** to end a plan or process before completion. ▷ **HISTORY** Latin *abortare*

abortion *n* **1** an operation to end pregnancy. **2** the premature ending of a pregnancy when a fetus is expelled from the womb before it can live independently. **3** the failure of a mission or project. **4** *Informal* something that is grotesque. ▶ **abortionist** *n*

abortion pill *n* a drug used to terminate a pregnancy in its earliest stage.

abortive *adj* failing to achieve its purpose.

abound *vb* **1** to exist in large numbers. **2 abound in** to have a large number of. ▷ **HISTORY** Latin *abundare* to overflow

about *prep* **1** relating to or concerning. **2** near to. **3** carried on: *I haven't any money about me.* **4** on every side of. ✧ *adv* **5** near in number, time, or degree; approximately. **6** nearby. **7** here and there: *there were some fifteen other people scattered about on the first floor.* **8** all around; on every side. **9** in or to the opposite direction. **10** in rotation: *turn and turn about.* **11** used to indicate understatement: *it's about time somebody told the truth on that subject.* **12 about to** on the point of; intending to: *she was about to get in the car.* **13 not about to** determined not to: *we're not about to help her out.* ✧ *adj* **14** active: *he was off the premises well before anyone was up and about.* ▷ **HISTORY** Old English *abūtan*, *onbūtan* on the outside of

about-turn *or US* **about-face** *n* **1** a complete change of opinion or direction. **2** a reversal of the direction in which one is facing.

above *prep* **1** higher than; over. **2** greater than in quantity or degree: *above average.* **3** superior to or higher than in quality, rank, or ability. **4** too high-minded for: *he considered himself above the task of working.* **5** too respected for; beyond: *his fleet was above suspicion.* **6** too difficult to be understood by: *a discussion that was way above my head.* **7** louder or higher than (other noise). **8** in preference to. **9 above all** most of all; especially. ✧ *adv* **10** in or to a higher place: *the hills above.* **11** in a previous place (in something written or printed). **12** higher in rank or position. ✧ *n* **13 the above** something previously mentioned. ✧ *adj* **14** appearing in a previous place (in something written or printed): *for a copy of the free brochure write to the above address.* ▷ **HISTORY** Old English *abufan*

above board *adj* completely honest and open.

> **WORD HISTORY**
> The phrase 'above board' is in origin a gambling term. It is an allusion to the fact that it is difficult for a player to cheat at cards when his hands are above the 'board' or gambling table and therefore clearly visible to the other players.

abracadabra *n* a word used in magic spells, which is supposed to possess magic powers. ▷ **HISTORY** Latin

abrasion *n* **1** a scraped area on the skin; graze. **2** *Geog* the erosion of rock by rock fragments scratching and scraping it. ▷ **HISTORY** Latin *abradere* to scrape away

abrasive *adj* **1** rude and unpleasant in manner. **2** tending to rub or scrape; rough. ✧ *n* **3** a substance used for cleaning, smoothing, or polishing.

abreast *adj* **1** alongside each other and facing in the same direction: *the two cars were abreast.* **2 abreast of** up to date with.

abridge *vb* **abridging, abridged** to shorten a written work by taking out parts. ▷ **HISTORY** Late Latin *abbreviare* ▸ **abridgment** *or* **abridgement** *n*

abroad *adv* **1** to or in a foreign country. **2** generally known or felt: *there is a new spirit abroad.*

abrogate *vb* **-gating, -gated** to cancel (a law or an agreement) formally. ▷ **HISTORY** from Latin *ab-* away + *rogare* to propose a law ▸ **abrogation** *n*

abrupt *adj* **1** sudden or unexpected: *an abrupt departure.* **2** rather rude in speech or manner. ▷ **HISTORY** Latin *abruptus* broken off ▸ **abruptly** *adv* ▸ **abruptness** *n*

abs *pl n Informal* abdominal muscles.

abscess (**ab**-sess) *n* **1** a swelling containing pus as a result of inflammation. ✧ *vb* **2** to form a swelling containing pus. ▷ **HISTORY** Latin *abscessus* literally: a throwing off ▸ **abscessed** *adj*

abscissa *n, pl* **-scissas** *or* **-scissae** *Maths* (in a two-dimensional system of Cartesian coordinates) the distance from the vertical axis measured parallel to the horizontal axis. ▷ **HISTORY** New Latin *linea abscissa* a cut-off line

abscond *vb* to run away unexpectedly. ▷ **HISTORY** Latin *abscondere* to conceal

abseil (**ab**-sale) *vb* **1** to go down a steep drop by a rope fastened at the top and tied around one's body. ✧ *n* **2** an instance of abseiling. ▷ **HISTORY** German *abseilen*

absence *n* **1** the state of being away. **2** the time during which a person or thing is away. **3** the fact of being without something.

absent *adj* **1** not present in a place or situation. **2** lacking. **3** not paying attention. ✧ *vb* **4 absent oneself** to stay away. ▷ **HISTORY** Latin *absens* ▸ **absently** *adv*

absentee *n* a person who should be present but is not.

absenteeism *n* persistent absence from work or school.

absent-minded *adj* inattentive or forgetful. ▸ **absent-mindedly** *adv*

absinthe *n* a strong, green, alcoholic drink, originally containing wormwood. ▷ **HISTORY** Greek *apsinthion* wormwood

absolute *adj* **1** total and complete: *he ordered an immediate and absolute ceasefire.* **2** with unrestricted power and authority: *she has absolute control with fifty per cent of the shares.* **3** undoubted or certain: *I was telling the absolute truth.* **4** not dependent on or relative to anything else. **5** pure; unmixed: *absolute alcohol.* ✧ *n* **6** a principle or rule believed to be unfailingly correct. **7 the Absolute** *Philosophy* that which is totally unconditioned, perfect, or complete. ▷ **HISTORY** Latin *absolutus*

absolute error *n Maths* the difference between the predicted value and the actual value of a quantity.

absolutely *adv* **1** completely or perfectly. ✧ *interj* **2** yes indeed, certainly.

absolute majority *n* a number of votes totalling over 50 per cent, such as the total number of votes that beats the combined opposition.

absolute pitch *n* the ability to identify the pitch of a note, or to sing a given note, without reference to one previously sounded.

absolute zero *n Physics* the lowest temperature theoretically possible, at which the particles that make up matter would be at rest: equivalent to −273.15°C or −459.67°F.

absolution *n Christianity* a formal forgiveness of sin pronounced by a priest.

absolutism *n* a political system in which a monarch or dictator has unrestricted power.

absolve *vb* **-solving, -solved** to declare to be free from blame or sin. ▷ **HISTORY** Latin *absolvere*

absorb *vb* **1** to soak up a liquid. **2** to engage the interest of someone. **3** to receive the force of an impact. **4** *Physics* to take in radiant energy and retain it. **5** to take in or incorporate: *this country has absorbed almost one million refugees.* ▷ **HISTORY** Latin *absorbere* to suck ▸ **absorbent** *adj* ▸ **absorbing** *adj*

absorption *n* **1** the process of absorbing something or the state of being absorbed. **2** *Physiol* the process by which nutrients enter the tissues of an animal or a plant. ▸ **absorptive** *adj*

abstain *vb* **1** to choose not to do something: *you will be asked to abstain from food prior to your general anaesthetic.* **2** to choose not to vote. ▷ **HISTORY** Latin *abstinere* ▸ **abstainer** *n*

abstemious (ab-**steem**-ee-uss) *adj* taking very little alcohol or food. ▷ **HISTORY** Latin *abstemius* ▸ **abstemiously** *adv* ▸ **abstemiousness** *n*

abstention *n* **1** the formal act of not voting. **2** the act of abstaining from something, such as drinking alcohol.

a b c d e f g h i j k l m n o p q r s t u v w x y z

A B C D E F G H I J K L M N O P Q R S T U V W X Y Z

abstinence *n* the practice of choosing not to do something one would like. ▶ **abstinent** *adj*

abstract *adj* **1** referring to ideas or qualities rather than material objects: *abstract words such as justice, equality and success.* **2** not applied or practical; theoretical: *he was frustrated by the highly abstract mathematics being taught.* **3** of art in which the subject is represented by shapes and patterns rather than by a realistic likeness. ✧ *n* **4** a summary. **5** an abstract painting or sculpture. **6** an abstract word or idea. **7 in the abstract** without referring to specific circumstances. ✧ *vb* **8** to summarize. **9** to remove or extract. ▷ HISTORY Latin *abstractus* drawn off

abstracted *adj* lost in thought; preoccupied. ▶ **abstractedly** *adv*

abstraction *n* **1** a general idea rather than a specific example: *these absurd philosophical abstractions continued to bother him.* **2** the quality of being abstract or abstracted.

abstract noun *n Grammar* a noun that refers to a quality, state, or concept, as for example *kindness*, *peace*, or *morality*, rather than to a physical object. Compare **concrete noun**.

abstruse *adj* not easy to understand. ▷ HISTORY Latin *abstrusus* concealed

absurd *adj* obviously senseless or illogical; ridiculous. ▷ HISTORY Latin *absurdus* ▶ **absurdity** *n* ▶ **absurdly** *adv*

abundance *n* **1** a great amount. **2** degree of plentifulness. **3 in abundance** in great amounts: *they had fish and fruit in abundance.* ▷ HISTORY Latin *abundare* to abound ▶ **abundant** *adj*

abundantly *adv* **1** very: *he made his disagreement with the prime minister abundantly clear.* **2** plentifully; in abundance.

abuse *n* **1** prolonged ill-treatment of or violence towards someone: *child abuse.* **2** insulting comments. **3** improper use: *an abuse of power.* ✧ *vb* **abusing, abused 4** to take advantage of dishonestly: *these two ministers had abused their position for financial gain.* **5** to ill-treat violently: *he had been sexually abused as a child.* **6** to speak insultingly or cruelly to. ▷ HISTORY Latin *abuti* to misuse ▶ **abuser** *n*

abusive *adj* rude or insulting: *he was alleged to have used abusive language towards spectators.* ▶ **abusively** *adv*

abut *vb* **abutting, abutted** to be next to or touching. ▷ HISTORY Old French *abouter*

abysmal *adj Informal* extremely bad. ▷ HISTORY Medieval Latin *abysmus* abyss ▶ **abysmally** *adv*

abyss *n* **1** a very deep hole in the ground. **2** a frightening or threatening situation: *the abyss of revolution and war ahead.* ▷ HISTORY Greek *abussos* bottomless

Ac *Chem* actinium.

AC **1** alternating current. **2** athletic club.

a/c **1** account. **2** account current.

acacia (a-**kay**-sha) *n* a shrub or tree with small yellow or white flowers. ▷ HISTORY Greek *akakia*

academic *adj* **1** relating to a college or university. **2** (of pupils) having an aptitude for study. **3** relating to studies such as languages and pure science rather than technical or professional studies. **4** of theoretical interest only: *the argument is academic.* ✧ *n* **5** a member of the teaching or research staff of a college or university. ▶ **academically** *adv*

academy *n, pl* **-mies 1** a society for the advancement of literature, art, or science. **2** a school for training in a particular skill: *sixteen hundred students would also spend their first year at the military academy.* **3** (in Scotland) a secondary school.

> **WORD HISTORY**
> The original Academy, in Greek *Akadêmeia*, was an olive grove outside ancient Athens where the philosopher Plato taught in the 4th century B.C. His school of philosophy then became known as the Academy, and this word came to be used for other bodies that promoted learning.

acanthus *n* **1** a plant with large spiny leaves and spikes of white or purplish flowers. **2** a carved ornament based on the leaves of the acanthus plant. ▷ HISTORY Greek *akantha* thorn

ACAS (in Britain) Advisory Conciliation and Arbitration Service.

acc. **1** *Grammar* accusative. **2** account.

ACC (in New Zealand) Accident Compensation Corporation.

accede *vb* **-ceding, -ceded accede to 1** to agree to. **2** to take up (an office or position): *he acceded to the throne after his Irish exile.* ▷ HISTORY Latin *accedere*

accelerando *adv Music* with increasing speed. ▷ HISTORY Italian

accelerate *vb* **-ating, -ated 1** to move or cause to move more quickly. **2** to cause to happen sooner than expected. ▷ HISTORY Latin *accelerare*

accelerated erosion *n Geol* a wearing away of soil and rocks that is faster than normal.

acceleration *n* **1** the act of increasing speed. **2** the rate of increase of speed or the rate of change of velocity.

accelerator *n* **1** a pedal in a motor vehicle that is pressed to increase speed. **2** *Physics* a machine for increasing the speed and energy of charged particles.

accent *n* **1** the distinctive style of pronunciation of a person or group from a particular area, country, or social background. **2** a mark used in writing to indicate the prominence of a syllable or the way a vowel is pronounced. **3** particular emphasis: *there will be an accent on sport and many will enjoy rowing.* **4** the stress on a syllable or musical note. ✧ *vb* **5** to lay particular emphasis on. ▷ HISTORY Latin *accentus*

accentuate *vb* **-ating, -ated** to stress or emphasize. ▶ **accentuation** *n*

accept *vb* **1** to take or receive something offered. **2** to agree to. **3** to consider something as true. **4** to tolerate or resign oneself to. **5** to take on the responsibilities of: *he asked if I would become his assistant and I accepted that position.* **6** to receive someone into a community or group. **7** to receive something as adequate or valid. ▷ **HISTORY** Latin *acceptare*

acceptable *adj* **1** able to be endured; tolerable: *in war killing is acceptable.* **2** good enough; adequate: *he found the article acceptable.* ▶ **acceptability** *n* ▶ **acceptably** *adv*

acceptance *n* **1** the act of accepting something. **2** favourable reception. **3** belief or agreement.

accepted *adj* commonly approved or recognized: *the accepted wisdom about old age.*

access *n* **1** a means of approaching or entering a place. **2** the condition of allowing entry, for example entry to a building by wheelchairs or prams. **3** the right or opportunity to use something or enter a place: *the bourgeoisie gained access to political power.* **4** the opportunity or right to see or approach someone: *my ex-wife sabotages my access to the children.* ✧ *vb* **5** to obtain information from a computer. ▷ **HISTORY** Latin *accedere* to accede

accessible *adj* **1** easy to approach, enter, or use. **2** easy to understand: *the most accessible opera by Wagner.* ▶ **accessibility** *n*

accession *n* the act of taking up an office or position: *the 40th anniversary of her accession to the throne.*

accessory *n, pl* **-ries 1** a supplementary part or object. **2** a small item, such as a bag or belt, worn or carried by someone to complete his or her outfit. **3** a person who is involved in a crime but who was not present when it took place. ▷ **HISTORY** Late Latin *accessorius*

access road *n* a road providing a way to a particular place or on to a motorway.

access time *n* the time required to retrieve a piece of stored information from a computer.

accident *n* **1** an unpleasant event that causes damage, injury, or death. **2** an unforeseen event or one without apparent cause: *they had met in town by accident.* ▷ **HISTORY** Latin *accidere* to happen

accidental *adj* **1** occurring by chance or unintentionally. ✧ *n* **2** *Music* a symbol denoting a sharp, flat, or natural that is not a part of the key signature. ▶ **accidentally** *adv*

accident-prone *adj* (of a person) often involved in accidents.

acclaim *vb* **1** to applaud or praise: *the highly acclaimed children's TV series.* **2** to acknowledge publicly: *he was immediately acclaimed the new prime minister.* ✧ *n* **3** an enthusiastic expression of approval. ▷ **HISTORY** Latin *acclamare*

acclamation *n* **1** an enthusiastic reception or display of approval. **2** *Canad* an instance of being elected without opposition. **3 by acclamation** by a majority without a ballot.

acclimatize *or* **-tise** *vb* **-tizing, -tized** *or* **-tising, -tised** to adapt to a new climate or environment. ▶ **acclimatization** *or* **-tisation** *n*

accolade *n* **1** an award, praise, or honour. **2** a touch on the shoulder with a sword conferring knighthood. ▷ **HISTORY** Latin *ad-* to + *collum* neck

accommodate *vb* **-dating, -dated 1** to provide with lodgings. **2** to have room for. **3** to do a favour for. **4** to get used to (something). ▷ **HISTORY** Latin *accommodare*

accommodating *adj* willing to help; obliging.

accommodation *n* a place in which to sleep, live, or work.

accommodation address *n Brit* an address on letters to a person who cannot or does not wish to receive mail at a permanent address.

accompaniment *n* **1** something that accompanies something else. **2** *Music* a supporting part for an instrument, a band, or an orchestra.

accompanist *n* a person who plays a musical accompaniment.

accompany *vb* **-nies, -nying, -nied 1** to go with (someone). **2** to happen or exist at the same time as. **3** to provide a musical accompaniment for. ▷ **HISTORY** Old French *accompaignier*

accomplice *n* a person who helps someone else commit a crime. ▷ **HISTORY** Late Latin *complex* partner

accomplish *vb* **1** to manage to do; achieve: *most infants accomplish it immediately.* **2** to complete. ▷ **HISTORY** Latin *complere* to fill up

accomplished *adj* **1** expert or proficient: *an accomplished liar.* **2** successfully completed.

accomplishment *n* **1** the successful completion of something. **2** something successfully completed. **3 accomplishments** personal abilities or skills.

accord *n* **1** agreement or harmony. **2** a formal agreement between groups or nations: *the Paris peace accords.* **3 of one's own accord** voluntarily or willingly. **4 with one accord** unanimously. ✧ *vb* **5** to grant: *she was at last accorded her true status.* **6 accord with** to fit in with or be consistent with. ▷ **HISTORY** Latin *ad-* to + *cor* heart

accordance *n* **in accordance with** conforming to or according to: *food is prepared in accordance with Jewish laws.*

according *adv* **1 according to a** as stated by: *according to her, they were once engaged.* **b** in conformity with: *work hours varied according to the tides.* **2 according as** depending on whether.

accordingly *adv* **1** in an appropriate manner. **2** consequently.

accordion *n* a box-shaped musical instrument played by moving the two sides apart and together, and pressing a keyboard or buttons to produce the notes. ▷ **HISTORY** German *Akkordion* ▶ **accordionist** *n*

accost *vb* to approach, stop, and speak to. ▷ **HISTORY** Latin *ad-* to + *costa* side, rib

account *n* **1** a report or description. **2** a person's money held in a bank. **3** a statement of financial transactions with the resulting balance. **4** part or behalf: *I am sorry that you suffered on my account.* **5 call someone to account** to demand an explanation from someone. **6 give a good** *or* **bad account of oneself** to perform well or fail to perform well. **7 of no account** of little importance or value. **8 on account of** because of. **9 take**

A B C D E F G H I J K L M N O P Q R S T U V W X Y Z

account of *or* **take into account** to take into consideration; allow for. ✧ *vb* **10** to consider as: *the evening was accounted a major step forward by all concerned.* ▷ **HISTORY** Old French *acont*

accountable *adj* responsible to someone or for some action. ▶ **accountability** *n*

accountant *n* a person who maintains and audits business accounts. ▶ **accountancy** *n*

account for *vb* **1** to give reasons for. **2** to explain or count up what has been spent.

accounting *n* the skill or practice of maintaining and auditing business accounts.

accoutrements (ak-**koo**-tra-ments) *or US* **accouterments** (ak-**koo**-ter-ments) *pl n* clothing and equipment for a particular activity. ▷ **HISTORY** Old French *accoustrer* to equip

accredit *vb* **1** to give official recognition to. **2** to send (a diplomat) with official credentials to a particular country. **3** to certify as meeting required standards. **4** to attribute (a quality or an action) to (a person). ▷ **HISTORY** French *accréditer* ▶ **accreditation** *n*

accretion (ak-**kree**-shun) *n* **1** a gradual increase in size, through growth or addition. **2** something added, such as an extra layer. ▷ **HISTORY** Latin *accretio*

accrue *vb* **-cruing, -crued 1** (of money or interest) to increase gradually over a period of time. **2 accrue to** to fall naturally to: *some advantage must accrue to the weaker party.* ▷ **HISTORY** Latin *accrescere*

accumulate *vb* **-lating, -lated** to gather together in an increasing quantity; collect. ▷ **HISTORY** Latin *accumulare* to heap up ▶ **accumulative** *adj*

accumulation *n* **1** something that has been collected. **2** the collecting together of things.

accumulator *n* **1** *Brit & Austral* a rechargeable device for storing electrical energy. **2** *Brit horse racing* a collective bet on successive races, with both stake and winnings being carried forward to accumulate progressively.

accuracy *n* faithful representation of the truth: *care is taken to ensure the accuracy of the content.*

accurate *adj* faithfully representing the truth: *all the information was accurate.* ▷ **HISTORY** Latin *accurare* to perform with care ▶ **accurately** *adv*

accursed (a-**curse**-id) *adj* **1** under a curse. **2** hateful or detestable.

accusation *n* **1** an allegation that a person is guilty of some wrongdoing. **2** a formal charge brought against a person. ▶ **accusatory** *adj*

accusative *or* **accusative case** *n Grammar* a grammatical case in some languages that identifies the direct object of a verb.

accuse *vb* **-cusing, -cused** to charge a person with wrongdoing. ▷ **HISTORY** Latin *accūsāre* ▶ **accuser** *n* ▶ **accusing** *adj* ▶ **accusingly** *adv*

accused *n* **the accused** *Law* the defendant appearing on a criminal charge.

accustom *vb* **accustom oneself to** to become familiar with or used to from habit or experience. ▷ **HISTORY** Old French *acostumer*

accustomed *adj* **1** usual or customary: *he parked his motorcycle in its accustomed place.* **2 accustomed to a** used to. **b** in the habit of.

ace *n* **1** a playing card with one symbol on it. **2** *Informal* an expert: *an American stock car ace.* **3** *Tennis* a winning serve that the opponent fails to reach. **4** a fighter pilot who has destroyed several enemy aircraft. ✧ *adj* **5** *Informal* superb or excellent: *an ace tennis player.* ▷ **HISTORY** Latin *as* a unit

acerbic (ass-**sir**-bik) *adj* harsh or bitter: *an acerbic critic.* ▷ **HISTORY** Latin *acerbus* sharp, sour

acerbity *n, pl* **-ties 1** bitter speech or temper. **2** bitterness of taste.

acetaldehyde (ass-it-**tal**-dee-hide) *n Chem* a colourless volatile liquid, used as a solvent.

acetate (**ass**-it-tate) *n* **1** *Chem* any salt or ester of acetic acid. **2** Also: **acetate rayon** a synthetic textile fibre made from cellulose acetate.

acetic (ass-**see**-tik) *adj Chem* of, containing, or producing acetic acid or vinegar. ▷ **HISTORY** Latin *acetum* vinegar

acetic acid *n Chem* a strong-smelling colourless liquid used to make vinegar.

acetone (**ass**-it-tone) *n Chem* a strong-smelling colourless liquid used as a solvent for paints and lacquers.

acetylene (ass-**set**-ill-een) *n Chem* a colourless soluble flammable gas used in welding metals.

ache *vb* **aching, ached 1** to feel or be the source of a continuous dull pain. **2** to suffer mental anguish. ✧ *n* **3** a continuous dull pain. ▷ **HISTORY** Old English *ācan*

achieve *vb* **achieving, achieved** to gain by hard work or effort. ▷ **HISTORY** Old French *achever* to bring to an end ▶ **achiever** *n*

achievement *n* **1** something that has been accomplished by hard work, ability, or heroism. **2** the successful completion of something.

Achilles heel (ak-**kill**-eez) *n* a small but fatal weakness. ▷ **HISTORY** *Achilles* in Greek mythology was killed by an arrow in his unprotected heel

Achilles tendon *n* the fibrous cord that connects the muscles of the calf to the heel bone.

achromatic *adj* **1** without colour. **2** refracting light without breaking it up into its component colours. **3** *Music* involving no sharps or flats. ▶ **achromatically** *adv*

acid *n* **1** *Chem* one of a class of compounds, corrosive and sour when dissolved in water, that combine with a base to form a salt. **2** *Slang* LSD. **3** a sour-tasting substance. ✧ *adj* **4** *Chem* of, from, or containing acid. **5** sharp or sour in taste. **6** sharp in speech or manner. ▷ **HISTORY** Latin *acidus* ▶ **acidly** *adv*

acidic *adj* containing acid.

acidify *vb* **-fies, -fying, -fied** to convert into acid. ▶ **acidification** *n*

acidity *n* **1** the quality of being acid. **2** the amount of acid in a solution.

acid rain *n Environmental science* rain containing pollutants released into the atmosphere by the burning of coal or oil.

acid rock *n Geol* igneous rock with a silica content of more than two thirds and containing not less than ten per cent quartz.

acid test *n* a rigorous and conclusive test of worth or value. ▷ HISTORY from the testing of gold with nitric acid

acknowledge *vb* **-edging, -edged 1** to recognize or admit the truth of a statement. **2** to show recognition of a person by a greeting or glance. **3** to make known that a letter or message has been received. **4** to express gratitude for (a favour or compliment). ▷ HISTORY Old English *oncnāwan* to recognize

acknowledgment *or* **acknowledgement** *n* **1** the act of acknowledging something or someone. **2** something done or given as an expression of gratitude.

acme (**ak**-mee) *n* the highest point of achievement or excellence. ▷ HISTORY Greek *akmē*

acne (**ak**-nee) *n* a skin disease in which pus-filled spots form on the face. ▷ HISTORY New Latin

acolyte *n* **1** a follower or attendant. **2** *Christianity* a person who assists a priest. ▷ HISTORY Greek *akolouthos*

aconite *n* **1** a poisonous plant with hoodlike flowers. **2** dried aconite root, used as a narcotic. ▷ HISTORY Greek *akoniton*

acorn *n* the fruit of the oak tree, consisting of a smooth nut in a cuplike base. ▷ HISTORY Old English *æcern*

acoustic *adj* **1** of sound, hearing, or acoustics. **2** (of a musical instrument) without electronic amplification. **3** designed to absorb sound: *acoustic tiles.* ▷ HISTORY Greek *akouein* to hear ▸ **acoustically** *adv*

acoustics *n* **1** the scientific study of sound. ✧ *pl n* **2** the characteristics of a room or auditorium determining how well sound can be heard within it.

acquaint *vb* **acquaint with** to make (someone) familiar with. ▷ HISTORY Latin *accognoscere* to know well

acquaintance *n* **1** a person whom one knows slightly. **2** slight knowledge of a person or subject. **3 make the acquaintance of** to come into social contact with. **4** the people one knows: *an actress of my acquaintance.*

acquainted *adj* **1** on terms of familiarity but not intimacy. **2 acquainted with** familiar with: *she became acquainted with the classics of Chinese literature.*

acquiesce (ak-wee-**ess**) *vb* **-escing, -esced** to agree to what someone wants. ▷ HISTORY Latin *acquiescere* ▸ **acquiescence** *n* ▸ **acquiescent** *adj*

> ☑ **WORD TIP**
> The use of *to* after *acquiesce* was formerly regarded as incorrect, but is now acceptable.

acquire *vb* **-quiring, -quired** to get or develop (something such as an object, trait, or ability). ▷ HISTORY Latin *acquirere* ▸ **acquirement** *n*

acquired taste *n* **1** a liking for something at first considered unpleasant. **2** the thing liked.

acquisition *n* **1** something acquired, often to add to a collection. **2** the act of acquiring something.

acquisitive *adj* eager to gain material possessions. ▸ **acquisitively** *adv* ▸ **acquisitiveness** *n*

acquit *vb* **-quitting, -quitted 1** to pronounce someone not guilty: *he's been acquitted of negligence.* **2** to behave in a particular way: *she acquitted herself well in the meeting.* ▷ HISTORY Old French *aquiter*

acquittal *n Law* (in a criminal case) the judgment by a court that the accused is not guilty.

acre *n* **1** a unit of area equal to 4840 square yards (4046.86 square metres). **2 acres** *Informal* a large amount: *acres of skin.* ▷ HISTORY Old English *æcer*

acreage (**ake**-er-rij) *n* land area in acres.

acrid (**ak**-rid) *adj* **1** unpleasantly strong-smelling. **2** sharp in speech or manner. ▷ HISTORY Latin *acer* sharp, sour ▸ **acridity** *n* ▸ **acridly** *adv*

acrimony *n* bitterness and resentment felt about something. ▷ HISTORY Latin *acrimonia* ▸ **acrimonious** *adj*

acrobat *n* an entertainer who performs gymnastic feats requiring skill, agility, and balance. ▷ HISTORY Greek *akrobatēs* one who walks on tiptoe ▸ **acrobatic** *adj* ▸ **acrobatically** *adv*

acrobatics *pl n* the skills or feats of an acrobat.

acronym *n* a word made from the initial letters of other words, for example *UNESCO* for the *United Nations Educational, Scientific, and Cultural Organization.* ▷ HISTORY Greek *akros* outermost + *onoma* name

acrophobia *n* abnormal fear of being at a great height. ▷ HISTORY Greek *akron* summit + *phobos* fear

acropolis (a-**crop**-pol-liss) *n* the citadel of an ancient Greek city. ▷ HISTORY Greek *akros* highest + *polis* city

acrosome *n Biol* a structure that forms the tip of a sperm cell.

across *prep* **1** from one side to the other side of. **2** on or at the other side of. ✧ *adv* **3** from one side to the other. **4** on or to the other side. ▷ HISTORY Old French *a croix* crosswise

acrostic *n* a number of lines of writing, such as a poem, in which the first or last letters form a word or proverb. ▷ HISTORY Greek *akros* outermost + *stikhos* line of verse

acrylic *adj* **1** made of acrylic. ✧ *n* **2** a man-made fibre used for clothes and blankets. **3** a kind of paint made from acrylic acid. ▷ HISTORY Latin *acer* sharp + *olere* to smell

acrylic acid *n Chem* a strong-smelling colourless corrosive liquid.

acrylic fibre *n* a man-made fibre used for clothes and blankets.

acrylic resin *n Chem* any of a group of polymers of acrylic acid, used as synthetic rubbers, in paints, and as plastics.

act *n* **1** something done. **2** a formal decision reached or law passed by a law-making body: *an act of parliament.* **3** a major division of a play or

A B C D E F G H I J K L M N O P Q R S T U V W X Y Z

opera. **4** a short performance, such as a sketch or dance. **5** a pretended attitude: *she appeared calm but it was just an act.* **6 get in on the act** *Informal* to become involved in something in order to share the benefit. **7 get one's act together** *Informal* to organize oneself. ✧ *vb* **8** to do something. **9** to perform (a part or role) in a play, film, or broadcast. **10** to present (a play) on stage. **11 act for** to be a substitute for: *Mr Lewis was acting for the head of the department.* **12 act as** to serve the function of: *she is acting as my bodyguard.* **13** to behave: *she acts as though she really hates you.* **14** to behave in an unnatural way. ▷ HISTORY Latin *actum* a thing done

ACT Australian Capital Territory.

acting *n* **1** the art of an actor. ✧ *adj* **2** temporarily performing the duties of: *the acting president has declared a state of emergency.*

actinide series *n Chem* a series of 15 radioactive elements with increasing atomic numbers from actinium to lawrencium.

actinium *n Chem* a radioactive element of the actinide series, occurring as a decay product of uranium. Symbol: Ac. ▷ HISTORY Greek *aktis* ray

action *n* **1** doing something for a particular purpose. **2** something done on a particular occasion. **3** a lawsuit. **4** movement during some physical activity. **5** the operating mechanism in a gun or machine. **6** the way in which something operates or works. **7** *Slang* the main activity in a place. **8** the events that form the plot of a story or play. **9** activity, force, or energy. **10** a minor battle. **11 actions** behaviour. **12 out of action** not functioning.

actionable *adj Law* giving grounds for legal action.

action painting *n* an art form in which paint is thrown, smeared, dripped, or spattered on the canvas.

action replay *n* the rerunning of a small section of a television tape, for example of a sporting event.

action stations *pl n* the positions taken up by individuals in preparation for battle or for some other activity.

activate *vb* **-vating, -vated 1** to make something active. **2** *Physics* to make something radioactive. **3** *Chem* to increase the rate of a reaction. ▶ **activation** *n*

activation energy *n Chem* the smallest amount of energy required for the reacting species to undergo a specific reaction.

active *adj* **1** busy and energetic. **2** energetically involved in or working hard for: *active in the peace movement.* **3** happening now and energetically: *the plan is under active discussion.* **4** functioning or causing a reaction: *the active ingredient is held within the capsule.* **5** (of a volcano) erupting periodically. **6** *Grammar* denoting a form of a verb used to indicate that it is the subject that is performing the action, for example *kicked* in *The boy kicked the football.* ✧ *n* **7** *Grammar* the active form of a verb. ▶ **actively** *adv*

active list *n Mil* a list of officers available for full duty.

active service *n* military duty in an operational area.

active voice *n Grammar* a set of verb forms used to indicate that the subject of the verb is the performer of the action, for example *discovered* in *Fleming discovered penicillin*. Compare **passive voice.**

activist *n* a person who works energetically to achieve political or social goals. ▶ **activism** *n*

activity *n* **1** the state of being active. **2** lively movement. **3** (*pl* **-ties**) any specific action or pursuit: *he was engaged in political activities abroad.*

act of God *n Law* a sudden occurrence caused by natural forces, such as a flood.

Act of Parliament *n Law* a bill that has become statute and law.

actor *or fem* **actress** *n* a person who acts in a play, film, or broadcast.

ACTU Australian Council of Trade Unions.

actual *adj* existing in reality or as a matter of fact. ▷ HISTORY Latin *actus* act

> **WORD TIP**
> The excessive use of *actual* and *actually* should be avoided. They are unnecessary in sentences such as *in actual fact, he is forty-two,* and *he did actually go to the play but did not enjoy it.*

actuality *n, pl* **-ties** reality.

actually *adv* as an actual fact; really.

actuary *n, pl* **-aries** a person qualified to calculate commercial risks and probabilities involving uncertain future events, esp. in such contexts as life assurance. ▷ HISTORY Latin *actuarius* one who keeps accounts ▶ **actuarial** *adj*

actuate *vb* **-ating, -ated 1** to start up a mechanical device. **2** to motivate someone. ▷ HISTORY Medieval Latin *actuare*

actus reus *n Law* the criminal act that must be proved if a defendant is to be found guilty. Compare **mens rea.** ▷ HISTORY Latin: guilty act

acuity (ak-**kew**-it-ee) *n* keenness of vision or thought. ▷ HISTORY Latin *acutus* acute

acumen (**ak**-yew-men) *n* the ability to make good decisions. ▷ HISTORY Latin: sharpness

acupuncture *n* a medical treatment involving the insertion of needles at various parts of the body to stimulate the nerve impulses. ▷ HISTORY Latin *acus* needle + PUNCTURE ▶ **acupuncturist** *n*

acute *adj* **1** severe or intense: *acute staff shortages.* **2** penetrating in perception or insight. **3** sensitive or keen: *it was amazing how acute your hearing got in the bush.* **4** (of a disease) sudden and severe. **5** *Maths* (of an angle) of less than 90°. **6** (of a hospital or bed) intended to accommodate short-term patients. ✧ *n* **7** an acute accent. ▷ HISTORY Latin *acutus* ▶ **acutely** *adv* ▶ **acuteness** *n*

acute accent *n* the mark (´), used in some languages to indicate that the vowel over which it is placed is pronounced in a certain way.

ad *n Informal* an advertisement.

AD (indicating years numbered from the supposed year of the birth of Christ) in the year of the Lord. ▷ **HISTORY** Latin *anno Domini*

ad- *prefix* **1** to or towards: *adverb*. **2** near or next to: *adrenal*. ▷ **HISTORY** Latin

Ada *n* a high-level computer programming language, used esp. for military systems. ▷ **HISTORY** after *Ada*, Countess of Lovelace, pioneer in computer programming

adage (**ad**-ij) *n* a traditional saying that is generally accepted as being true. ▷ **HISTORY** Latin *adagium*

adagietto *Music* ✧ *adv* **1** slowly, but more quickly than adagio. ✧ *n, pl* **-tos 2** a movement or piece to be performed fairly slowly.

adagio (ad-**dahj**-yo) *Music* ✧ *adv* **1** slowly. ✧ *n, pl* **-gios 2** a movement or piece to be performed slowly. ▷ **HISTORY** Italian

Adam *n* **1** *Bible* the first man created by God. **2 not know someone from Adam** to not know someone at all.

adamant *adj* unshakable in determination or purpose. ▷ **HISTORY** Greek *adamas* unconquerable ▶ **adamantly** *adv*

Adam's apple *n* the projecting lump of thyroid cartilage at the front of a person's neck.

adapt *vb* **1** to adjust (something or oneself) to different conditions. **2** to change something to suit a new purpose. ▷ **HISTORY** Latin *adaptare* ▶ **adaptable** *adj* ▶ **adaptability** *n*

adaptation *n* **1** something that is produced by adapting something else: *a TV adaptation of a Victorian novel*. **2** the act of adapting.

adapted feature *n Biol* an inherited or acquired modification in an organism that makes it better suited to survive and reproduce in a particular environment.

adaptor *or* **adapter** *n* **1** a device used to connect several electrical appliances to a single socket. **2** any device for connecting two parts of different sizes or types.

ADC aide-de-camp.

add *vb* **1** to combine (numbers or quantities) so as to make a larger number or quantity. **2** to join something to something else so as to increase its size, effect, or scope: *these new rules will add an extra burden on already overworked officials*. **3** to say or write something further. **4 add in** to include. ✧ See also **add up**. ▷ **HISTORY** Latin *addere*

addendum *n, pl* **-da** something added on, esp. an appendix to a book or magazine.

adder *n* a small poisonous snake with a black zigzag pattern along the back. ▷ **HISTORY** Old English *nǣdre*

addict *n* **1** a person who is unable to stop taking narcotic drugs. **2** *Informal* a person who is devoted to something: *he's a telly addict*. ▷ **HISTORY** Latin *addictus* given over ▶ **addictive** *adj*

addicted *adj* **1** dependent on a narcotic drug. **2** *Informal* devoted to something: *I'm a news freak and addicted to CNN*. ▶ **addiction** *n*

addition *n* **1** the act of adding. **2** a person or thing that is added. **3** a mathematical operation in which the total of two or more numbers or quantities is calculated. **4 in addition (to)** besides; as well (as). ▶ **additional** *adj* ▶ **additionally** *adv*

additive *n* any substance added to something, such as food, to improve it or prevent deterioration.

addled *adj* **1** confused or unable to think clearly. **2** (of eggs) rotten. ▷ **HISTORY** Old English *adela* filth

add-on *n Brit, Austral & NZ* a feature that can be added to a standard model to give increased benefits.

address *n* **1** the place at which someone lives. **2** the conventional form by which the location of a building is described. **3** a formal speech. **4** *Computers* a number giving the location of a piece of stored information. ✧ *vb* **5** to mark (a letter or parcel) with an address. **6** to speak to. **7** to direct one's attention to (a problem or an issue). **8 address oneself to a** to speak or write to. **b** to apply oneself to: *we have got to address ourselves properly to this problem*. ▷ **HISTORY** Latin *ad-* to + *directus* direct

addressee *n* a person to whom a letter or parcel is addressed.

adduce *vb* **-ducing, -duced** to mention something as evidence. ▷ **HISTORY** Latin *adducere* to lead to

add up *vb* **1** to calculate the total of (two or more numbers or quantities). **2** *Informal* to make sense: *there's something about it that doesn't add up*. **3 add up to** to amount to.

adenine *n Anat* a purine base present in tissues of all living organisms.

adenoidal *adj* having a nasal voice or impaired breathing because of enlarged adenoids.

adenoids (**ad**-in-oidz) *pl n* a mass of tissue at the back of the throat. ▷ **HISTORY** Greek *adenoeidēs* glandular

adept *adj* **1** proficient in something requiring skill. ✧ *n* **2** a person skilled in something. ▷ **HISTORY** Latin *adipisci* to attain ▶ **adeptness** *n*

adequate *adj* just enough in amount or just good enough in quality. ▷ **HISTORY** Latin *ad-* to + *aequus* equal ▶ **adequacy** *n* ▶ **adequately** *adv*

à deux (ah **duh**) *adj, adv* of or for two people. ▷ **HISTORY** French

ADH *Biochem* antidiuretic hormone.

adhere *vb* **-hering, -hered 1** to stick to. **2** to act according to (a rule or agreement). **3** to be a loyal supporter of (something). ▷ **HISTORY** Latin *adhaerere*

adherent *n* **1** a supporter or follower. ✧ *adj* **2** sticking or attached. ▶ **adherence** *n*

> **WORD TIP**
> See at **adhesion.**

adhesion *n* **1** the quality or condition of sticking together. **2** *Pathol* the joining together of two

A B C D E F G H I J K L M N O P Q R S T U V W X Y Z

structures or parts of the body that are normally separate, for example after surgery.

> **WORD TIP**
> *Adhesion* is preferred when talking about sticking or holding fast in a physical sense. *Adherence* is preferred when talking about attachment to a political party, cause, etc.

adhesive *n* **1** a substance used for sticking things together. ✧ *adj* **2** able or designed to stick to things.

ad hoc *adj, adv* for a particular purpose only. ▷ **HISTORY** Latin: to this

adieu (a-**dew**) *interj, n, pl* **adieux** *or* **adieus** (a-**dewz**) goodbye. ▷ **HISTORY** French

ad infinitum *adv* endlessly: *we would not be able to sustain the currency ad infinitum.* ▷ **HISTORY** Latin

adipose *adj* of or containing fat; fatty: *adipose tissue.* ▷ **HISTORY** Latin *adeps* fat

adj. adjective.

adjacent *adj* **1** near or next: *the schools were adjacent but there were separate doors.* **2** *Geom* (of a side of a right-angled triangle) lying between a specified angle and the right angle. ▷ **HISTORY** Latin *ad-* near + *jacere* to lie

adjacent angle *n Geom* an angle which has the same vertex and one side in common with another.

adjective *n* a word that adds information about a noun or pronoun. ▷ **HISTORY** Latin *nomen adjectivum* attributive noun ▶ **adjectival** *adj*

adjoin *vb* to be next to and joined onto. ▶ **adjoining** *adj*

adjourn *vb* **1** to close a court at the end of a session. **2** to postpone or be postponed temporarily. **3** *Informal* to go elsewhere: *can we adjourn to the dining room?* ▷ **HISTORY** Old French *ajourner* to defer to an arranged day ▶ **adjournment** *n*

adjudge *vb* **-judging, -judged** to declare someone to be something specified: *my wife was adjudged to be the guilty party.*

adjudicate *vb* **-cating, -cated 1** to give a formal decision on a dispute. **2** to serve as a judge, for example in a competition. ▷ **HISTORY** Latin *adjudicare* ▶ **adjudication** *n* ▶ **adjudicator** *n*

adjunct *n* **1** something added that is not essential. **2** a person who is subordinate to another. ▷ **HISTORY** Latin *adjunctus* adjoined

adjure *vb* **-juring, -jured 1** to command someone to do something. **2** to appeal earnestly to someone. ▷ **HISTORY** Latin *adjurare* ▶ **adjuration** *n*

adjust *vb* **1** to adapt to a new environment. **2** to alter slightly, so as to be accurate or suitable. **3** *Insurance* to determine the amount payable in settlement of a claim. ▷ **HISTORY** Old French *adjuster* ▶ **adjustable** *adj* ▶ **adjuster** *n*

adjustment *n* **1** a slight alteration. **2** the act of adjusting.

adjutant (**aj**-oo-tant) *n* an officer in an army who acts as administrative assistant to a superior. ▷ **HISTORY** Latin *adjutare* to aid

ad-lib *vb* **-libbing, -libbed 1** to improvise a speech or piece of music without preparation. ✧ *adj* **2** improvised: *ad-lib studio chat.* ✧ *n* **3** an improvised remark. ✧ *adv* **ad lib 4** spontaneously or freely. ▷ **HISTORY** short for Latin *ad libitum,* literally: according to pleasure

Adm. *Brit* Admiral.

adman *n, pl* **-men** *Informal* a man who works in advertising.

admin *n Informal* administration.

administer *vb* **1** to manage (an organization or estate). **2** to organize and put into practice: *anyone can learn to administer the test procedure.* **3** to give medicine to someone. **4** to supervise the taking of (an oath). ▷ **HISTORY** Latin *administrare*

administrate *vb* **-trating, -trated** to manage an organization.

administration *n* **1** management of the affairs of an organization. **2** the people who administer an organization. **3** a government: *the first non-communist administration in the country's history.* **4** the act of administering something, such as medicine or an oath. ▶ **administrative** *adj*

administrative law *n Law* the branch of law concerned with the duties and powers of administrative authorities.

administrative review *n Law* an examination carried out by a competent body to ascertain whether correct procedures have been followed or appropriate measures taken. Compare **judicial review**.

administrator *n* a person who administers an organization or estate.

admirable (**ad**-mer-a-bl) *adj* deserving or inspiring admiration: *the boldness of the undertaking is admirable.* ▶ **admirably** *adv*

admiral *n* **1** Also called: **admiral of the fleet** a naval officer of the highest rank. **2** any of various brightly coloured butterflies. ▷ **HISTORY** Arabic *amīr-al* commander of

Admiralty *n Brit* the former government department in charge of the Royal Navy.

admire *vb* **-miring, -mired** to respect and approve of (a person or thing). ▷ **HISTORY** Latin *admirari* to wonder at ▶ **admiration** *n* ▶ **admirer** *n* ▶ **admiring** *adj* ▶ **admiringly** *adv*

admissible *adj Law* allowed to be brought as evidence in court.

admission *n* **1** permission or the right to enter. **2** permission to join an organization. **3** the price charged for entrance. **4** a confession: *she was, by her own admission, not educated.*

admit *vb* **-mitting, -mitted 1** to confess or acknowledge (a crime or mistake). **2** to concede (the truth of something). **3** to allow (someone) to enter. **4** to take (someone) in to a hospital for treatment: *he was admitted for tests.* **5 admit to** to allow someone to participate in something. **6 admit of** to allow for: *these rules admit of no violation.* ▷ **HISTORY** Latin *admittere*

admittance *n* **1** the right to enter. **2** the act of entering a place.

admittedly *adv* it must be agreed: *my research is admittedly incomplete.*

admixture *n* **1** a mixture. **2** an ingredient.

admonish *vb* to reprimand sternly. ▷ **HISTORY** Latin *admonere* ▶ **admonition** *n* ▶ **admonitory** *adj*

ad nauseam (ad **naw**-zee-am) *adv* to a boring or sickening extent: *she went on and on ad nauseam about her divorce.* ▷ **HISTORY** Latin: to (the point of) nausea

ado *n* fuss: *without further ado.* ▷ **HISTORY** Middle English *at do* a to-do

adobe (ad-**oh**-bee) *n* **1** a sun-dried brick. **2** the claylike material from which such bricks are made. **3** a building made of such bricks. ▷ **HISTORY** Spanish

adolescence *n* the period between puberty and adulthood. ▷ **HISTORY** Latin *adolescere* to grow up

adolescent *adj* **1** of or relating to adolescence. **2** *Informal* (of behaviour) immature. ✧ *n* **3** an adolescent person.

Adonis *n* a handsome young man. ▷ **HISTORY** name of a handsome youth in Greek myth

adopt *vb* **1** *Law* to make someone else's child legally one's own. **2** to choose (a plan or method). **3** to choose (a country or name) to be one's own. ▷ **HISTORY** Latin *adoptare* ▶ **adoptee** *n*

adoption *n* **1** *Law* the act of making (someone else's child) legally one's own. **2** the choosing (of a plan or method). **3** the choosing (of a country or name).

adoptive *adj* **1** acquired or related by adoption: *an adoptive father.* **2** of or relating to adoption.

adorable *adj* very attractive; lovable.

adore *vb* **adoring, adored 1** to love intensely or deeply. **2** *Informal* to like very much: *I adore being in the country.* **3** to worship a god with religious rites. ▷ **HISTORY** Latin *adorare* ▶ **adoration** *n* ▶ **adoring** *adj* ▶ **adoringly** *adv*

adorn *vb* to decorate; increase the beauty of. ▷ **HISTORY** Latin *adornare* ▶ **adornment** *n*

ADP automatic data processing.

adrenal (ad-**reen**-al) *adj Anat* **1** on or near the kidneys. **2** of or relating to the adrenal glands. ▷ **HISTORY** Latin *ad-* near + *renes* kidneys

adrenal glands *pl n Anat* two endocrine glands covering the upper surface of the kidneys.

adrenalin *or* **adrenaline** *n Biochem* a hormone secreted by the adrenal gland in response to stress. It increases heart rate, pulse rate, and blood pressure.

adrift *adj, adv* **1** drifting. **2** without a clear purpose. **3** *Informal* off course, wrong: *it was obvious that something had gone adrift.*

adroit *adj* quick and skilful in how one behaves or thinks. ▷ **HISTORY** French *à droit* rightly ▶ **adroitly** *adv* ▶ **adroitness** *n*

adsorb *vb* (of a gas or vapour) to condense and form a thin film on a surface. ▷ **HISTORY** Latin *ad-* to + *sorbere* to drink in ▶ **adsorbent** *adj* ▶ **adsorption** *n*

adulation *n* uncritical admiration. ▷ **HISTORY** Latin *adulari* to flatter

adult *n* **1** a mature fully grown person, animal, or plant. ✧ *adj* **2** having reached maturity; fully developed. **3** suitable for or typical of adult people: *she had very adult features.* **4** sexually explicit: *adult films.* ▷ **HISTORY** Latin *adultus* grown up ▶ **adulthood** *n*

adulterate *vb* **-ating, -ated** to spoil something by adding inferior material. ▷ **HISTORY** Latin *adulterare* ▶ **adulteration** *n*

adulterer *or fem* **adulteress** *n* a person who has committed adultery.

adultery *n, pl* **-teries** sexual unfaithfulness of a husband or wife. ▷ **HISTORY** Latin *adulterium* ▶ **adulterous** *adj*

adv. adverb.

advance *vb* **-vancing, -vanced 1** to go or bring forward. **2** to make progress: *this student has advanced in reading and writing.* **3** to further a cause: *an association founded to advance the interests of ex-soldiers.* **4 advance on** to move towards someone in a threatening manner. **5** to present an idea for consideration. **6** to lend a sum of money. ✧ *n* **7** a forward movement. **8** improvement or progress: *the greatest advance in modern medicine.* **9** a loan of money. **10** a payment made before it is legally due. **11** an increase in price: *any advance on fifty pounds?* **12 in advance** beforehand: *you have to pay in advance.* **13 in advance of** ahead of in time or development. ✧ *adj* **14** done or happening before an event: *advance warning.* ✧ See also **advances**. ▷ **HISTORY** Latin *abante* from before

advanced *adj* **1** at a late stage in development. **2** not elementary: *he was taking the advanced class in economics.*

advance directive *n Chiefly Brit* same as **living will**.

Advanced level *n Brit* a formal name for **A level**.

advancement *n* promotion in rank or status.

advances *pl n* approaches made to a person with the hope of starting a romantic or sexual relationship.

advantage *n* **1** a more favourable position or state. **2** benefit or profit: *they could make this work to their advantage.* **3** *Tennis* the point scored after deuce. **4 take advantage of a** to use a person unfairly. **b** to use an opportunity. **5 to advantage** to good effect: *her hair was shaped to display to advantage her superb neck.* ▷ **HISTORY** Latin *abante* from before

advantaged *adj* in a superior social or financial position.

advantageous *adj* likely to bring benefits. ▶ **advantageously** *adv*

advection *n Physics* the transferring of heat in a horizontal stream of gas. ▷ **HISTORY** Latin *ad-* to + *vehere* to carry

advent *n* an arrival: *the advent of the personal computer.* ▷ **HISTORY** Latin *ad-* to + *venire* to come

Advent *n* the season that includes the four Sundays before Christmas.

a b c d e f g h i j k l m n o p q r s t u v w x y z

Adventist *n* a member of a Christian group that believes in the imminent return of Christ.

adventitious *adj* **1** added or appearing accidentally. **2** *Biol* (of a plant or animal part) developing in an abnormal position. ▷ **HISTORY** Latin *adventicius* coming from outside

adventure *n* **1** a risky undertaking, the ending of which is uncertain: *our African adventure.* **2** exciting or unexpected events. ▷ **HISTORY** Latin *advenire* to happen to (someone), arrive

adventure playground *n Brit, Austral & NZ* a playground for children that contains building materials and other equipment to build with or climb on.

adventurer *or fem* **adventuress** *n* **1** a person who seeks money or power by unscrupulous means. **2** a person who seeks adventure.

adventurous *adj* daring or enterprising.

adverb *n* a word that modifies a sentence, verb, adverb, or adjective, for example *easily, very,* and *happily* in *They could easily envy the very happily married couple.* ▷ **HISTORY** Latin *adverbium,* literally: added word ▶ **adverbial** *adj*

adversarial system *or* **adversary system** *n Law* a legal system in which opposing advocates use their skills to present the case for the party they represent and a judge or magistrate acts as an impartial referee; usual in countries where the legal system is based on common law. Compare **inquisitorial system**.

adversary (**ad**-verse-er-ree) *n, pl* **-saries** an opponent in a fight, disagreement, or sporting contest. ▷ **HISTORY** Latin *adversus* against

adverse *adj* **1** unfavourable to one's interests: *adverse effects.* **2** antagonistic or hostile. ▷ **HISTORY** Latin *ad-* towards + *vertere* to turn ▶ **adversely** *adv*

adversity *n, pl* **-ties** very difficult or hard circumstances.

advert *n Informal* an advertisement.

advertise *vb* **-tising, -tised 1** to present or praise (goods or a service) to the public, in order to encourage sales. **2** to make (a vacancy, an event, or an article for sale) publicly known. ▷ **HISTORY** Latin *advertere* to turn one's attention to ▶ **advertiser** *n* ▶ **advertising** *n*

advertisement *n* any public announcement designed to sell goods or publicize an event.

advertising agency *n Marketing* an organization that creates advertising material, finds space to advertise, and does market research for its clients.

advertorial *n* advertising presented as if it is editorial material. ▷ **HISTORY** ADVERT + (EDIT)ORIAL

advice *n* **1** recommendation as to an appropriate choice of action. **2** formal notification of facts. ▷ **HISTORY** Latin *ad* to + *visum* view

advisable *adj* sensible and likely to achieve the desired result. ▶ **advisability** *n*

advise *vb* **-vising, -vised 1** to offer advice to. **2** to inform or notify. ▷ **HISTORY** Latin *ad-* to + *videre* to see ▶ **adviser** *or* **advisor** *n*

advised *adj* thought-out: *ill-advised.*

advisedly (ad-**vize**-id-lee) *adv* deliberately; after careful consideration: *I use the word advisedly.*

advisory *adj* **1** able to offer advice. ✧ *n, pl* **-ries 2** a statement giving advice or a warning. **3** a person or organization that gives advice: *the Prime Minister's media advisory.*

advocaat *n* a liqueur with a raw egg base. ▷ **HISTORY** Dutch

advocacy *n* active support of a cause or course of action.

advocate *vb* **-cating, -cated 1** to recommend a course of action publicly. ✧ *n* **2** a person who upholds or defends a cause or course of action. **3** a person who speaks on behalf of another in a court of law. **4** *Scots Law* a barrister. ▷ **HISTORY** Latin *advocare* to call, summon

adze *or US* **adz** *n* a tool with a blade at right angles to the handle, used for shaping timber. ▷ **HISTORY** Old English *adesa*

AEEU (in Britain) Amalgamated Engineering and Electrical Union.

aegis (**ee**-jiss) *n* **under the aegis of** with the sponsorship or protection of. ▷ **HISTORY** Greek *aigis* shield of Zeus

aeolian (ee-**oh**-lee-an) *adj* of or relating to the wind; produced or carried by the wind. ▷ **HISTORY** after *Aeolus,* god of winds in Greek myth

aeolian deposits *pl n Geol* sediments that have been carried and left by the wind.

aeolian erosion *n Geol* erosion caused by the action of the wind.

aeolian harp *n* a musical instrument that produces sounds when the wind passes over its strings. ▷ **HISTORY** after *Aeolus,* god of winds in Greek myth

aeon *or US* **eon** (**ee**-on) *n* **1** an immeasurably long period of time. **2** the longest division of geological time. ▷ **HISTORY** Greek *aiōn*

aerate *vb* **-ating, -ated** to put gas into a liquid, for example when making a fizzy drink. ▶ **aeration** *n*

aerial *n* **1** the metal pole or wire on a television or radio which transmits or receives signals. ✧ *adj* **2** in, from, or operating in the air. **3** extending high into the air. **4** of or relating to aircraft. ▷ **HISTORY** Greek *aēr* air

aerial top dressing *n NZ* spreading of fertilizer from an aeroplane onto remote areas.

aero-, aeri-, *or* **aer-** *combining form* **1** relating to aircraft. **2** relating to air, atmosphere, or gas. ▷ **HISTORY** Greek *aēr* air

aerobatics *n* spectacular manoeuvres, such as loops or rolls, performed by aircraft. ▷ **HISTORY** AERO- + (ACRO)BATICS

aerobe *n Biol* an organism that requires oxygen to survive. ▷ **HISTORY** Greek *aēr* air + *bios* life

aerobic *adj* designed for or relating to aerobics: *aerobic exercise.*

aerobic respiration *n Biol* the process by which cells convert glucose to carbon dioxide and water.

aerobics *n* exercises to increase the amount of oxygen in the blood and strengthen the heart and lungs.
aerodrome *n* a small airport.
aerodynamics *n* the study of how air flows around moving objects. ▶ **aerodynamic** *adj* ▶ **aerodynamicist** *n*
aero engine *n* an engine for an aircraft.
aerofoil *n* a part of an aircraft, such as the wing, designed to give lift in flight.
aerogram *n* an airmail letter on a single sheet of light paper that seals to form an envelope.
aeronautics *n* the study or practice of flight through the air. ▶ **aeronautical** *adj*
aeroplane *or US & Canad* **airplane** *n* a heavier-than-air powered flying vehicle with fixed wings. ▷ **HISTORY** AERO- + Greek *planos* wandering
aerosol *n* a small metal pressurized can from which a substance can be dispensed in a fine spray. ▷ **HISTORY** AERO- + SOL(UTION)
aerospace *n* **1** the earth's atmosphere and space beyond. ✧ *adj* **2** of rockets or space vehicles: *the aerospace industry.*
aesthete *or US* **esthete** (**eess**-theet) *n* a person who has or who pretends to have a highly developed appreciation of beauty.
aesthetic *or US* **esthetic** (iss-**thet**-ik) *adj* **1** relating to the appreciation of art and beauty. ✧ *n* **2** a principle or set of principles relating to the appreciation of art and beauty. ▷ **HISTORY** Greek *aisthanomai* to perceive, feel ▶ **aesthetically** *or US* **esthetically** *adv* ▶ **aestheticism** *or US* **estheticism** *n*
aesthetics *or US* **esthetics** *n* **1** the branch of philosophy concerned with the study of the concepts of beauty and taste. **2** the study of the rules and principles of art.
aestivate *or US* **estivate** *Biol* ✧ *vb* **1** to pass the summer. **2** to pass the summer or the dry season in a dormant condition. ▶ **aestivation** *or* **estivation** *n*
aether *n* same as **ether** (senses 2, 3).
aetiology (ee-tee-**ol**-a-jee) *n* same as **etiology**.
a.f. audio frequency.
afar *n* **from afar** from or at a great distance.
affable *adj* showing warmth and friendliness. ▷ **HISTORY** Latin *affabilis* ▶ **affability** *n* ▶ **affably** *adv*
affair *n* **1** an event or happening: *the Irangate affair.* **2** a sexual relationship outside marriage. **3** a thing to be done or attended to: *my wife's career is her own affair.* **4** something previously specified: *lunch was a subdued affair.* ▷ **HISTORY** Old French *à faire* to do
affairs *pl n* **1** personal or business interests. **2** matters of public interest: *foreign affairs.*
affect[1] *vb* **1** to influence (someone or something): *the very difficult conditions continued to affect our performance.* **2** (of pain or disease) to attack: *the virus can spread to affect the heart muscle.* **3** to move someone emotionally: *the experience has affected him deeply.* ▷ **HISTORY** Latin *afficere*
affect[2] *vb* **1** to put on a show of: *he affects a certain disinterest.* **2** to wear or use by preference: *he likes to be called Captain John and affects a nautical cap.* ▷ **HISTORY** Latin *affectare* to strive after
affectation *n* an attitude or manner put on to impress others.
affected *adj* **1** behaving or speaking in a manner put on to impress others. **2** pretended: *an affected indifference.*
affection *n* **1** fondness or tenderness for a person or thing. **2** **affections** feelings of love; emotions: *I was angry with her for playing with their affections.*
affectionate *adj* having or displaying tenderness, affection, or warmth. ▶ **affectionately** *adv*
affianced (af-**fie**-anst) *adj Old-fashioned* engaged to be married. ▷ **HISTORY** Medieval Latin *affidare* to trust (oneself) to
affidavit (af-fid-**dave**-it) *n Law* a written statement made under oath. ▷ **HISTORY** Medieval Latin, literally: he declares on oath
affiliate *vb* **-ating, -ated 1** (of a group) to link up with a larger group. ✧ *n* **2** a person or organization that is affiliated with another. ▷ **HISTORY** Medieval Latin *affiliatus* adopted as a son ▶ **affiliation** *n*
affiliation order *n Brit Law* an order that the father of an illegitimate child must contribute towards the child's maintenance.
affinity *n, pl* **-ties 1** a feeling of closeness to and understanding of a person. **2** a close similarity in appearance, structure, or quality. **3** a chemical attraction. ▷ **HISTORY** Latin *affinis* bordering on, related
affinity card *n Brit* a credit card linked to a charity or organization which receives a donation each time the card is used.
affirm *vb* **1** to declare to be true. **2** to state clearly one's support for (an idea or belief). ▷ **HISTORY** Latin *ad-* to + *firmare* to make firm ▶ **affirmation** *n*
affirmative *adj* **1** indicating agreement: *an affirmative answer.* ✧ *n* **2** a word or phrase indicating agreement, such as *yes.*
affix *vb* **1** to attach or fasten. ✧ *n* **2** a word or syllable added to a word to produce a derived or inflected form, such as *-ment* in *establishment.* ▷ **HISTORY** Medieval Latin *affixare*
afflict *vb* to cause someone suffering or unhappiness. ▷ **HISTORY** Latin *affligere* to knock against
affliction *n* **1** something that causes physical or mental suffering. **2** a condition of great distress or suffering.
affluent *adj* having plenty of money. ▷ **HISTORY** Latin *ad-* to + *fluere* to flow ▶ **affluence** *n*
affluent society *n* a society in which the material benefits of prosperity are widely available.
afford *vb* **1** **can afford** to be able to do or spare something without risking financial difficulties or undesirable consequences: *she can't afford to be choosy.* **2** to give or supply: *afford me an opportunity to judge for myself.* ▷ **HISTORY** Old English *geforthian*

to further, promote ▶ **affordable** *adj* ▶ **affordability** *n*

afforest *vb* to plant trees on. ▷ HISTORY Medieval Latin *afforestare*

afforestation *n Geog* the creation of forests by planting trees.

affray *n Brit, Austral & NZ* a noisy fight in a public place. ▷ HISTORY Vulgar Latin *exfridare* (unattested) to break the peace

affront *n* **1** a deliberate insult. ✧ *vb* **2** to hurt someone's pride or dignity. ▷ HISTORY Old French *afronter* to strike in the face

afghan *n NZ* a type of biscuit.

Afghan *adj* **1** of Afghanistan. ✧ *n* **2** a person from Afghanistan. **3** the language of Afghanistan.

Afghan hound *n* a large slim dog with long silky hair.

aficionado (af-fish-yo-**nah**-do) *n, pl* **-dos** an enthusiastic fan of a sport or interest. ▷ HISTORY Spanish

afield *adv* **far afield** far away: *they used to travel as far afield as Hungary.*

aflame *adv, adj* **1** in flames. **2** deeply aroused: *his face was aflame with self-contempt and embarrassment.*

afloat *adj, adv* **1** floating. **2** free of debt: *his goal is to keep the company afloat.* **3** aboard ship; at sea.

afoot *adj, adv* happening; in operation: *I had no suspicion of what was afoot.*

aforementioned *adj* mentioned before.

aforesaid *adj* referred to previously.

aforethought *adj* premeditated: *malice aforethought.*

a fortiori (**eh** for-tee-**or**-rye) *adv* for similar but more convincing reasons. ▷ HISTORY Latin

afraid *adj* **1** feeling fear or apprehension. **2** regretful: *I'm afraid I lost my temper.* ▷ HISTORY Middle English *affraied*

afresh *adv* once more.

African *adj* **1** of Africa. ✧ *n* **2** a person from Africa.

African-American *n* **1** an American of African descent. ✧ *adj* **2** of African-Americans, their history, or their culture.

Africander *n* a breed of humpbacked cattle originally from southern Africa. ▷ HISTORY Afrikaans *Afrikander*

African time *n S African slang* unpunctuality.

African violet *n* a flowering house plant with pink or purple flowers and hairy leaves.

Afrikaans *n* one of the official languages of South Africa, descended from Dutch. ▷ HISTORY Dutch

Afrikaner *n* a White South African whose native language is Afrikaans.

Afro- *combining form* indicating Africa or African: *Afro-Caribbean.*

Afro-American *n, adj* same as **African-American**.

aft *adv, adj* at or towards the rear of a ship or aircraft. ▷ HISTORY shortened from ABAFT

after *prep* **1** following in time or place. **2** in pursuit of: *he was after my mother's jewellery.* **3** concerning: *he asked after Laura.* **4** considering: *you seem all right after what happened last night.* **5** next in excellence or importance to. **6** in imitation of; in the manner of. **7** in accordance with: *a man after his own heart.* **8** with the same name as: *the street is named after the designer of the church.* **9** *US* past (the hour of): *fifteen after twelve.* **10 after all a** in spite of everything: *I was, after all, a suspect.* **b** in spite of expectations or efforts. **11 after you** please go before me. ✧ *adv* **12** at a later time; afterwards. ✧ *conj* **13** at a time later than the time when: *she arrived after the reading had begun.* ✧ *adj* **14** *Naut* further aft: *the after cabin.* ▷ HISTORY Old English *æfter*

afterbirth *n* the placenta and fetal membranes expelled from the mother's womb after childbirth.

aftercare *n* **1** the help and support given to a person discharged from a hospital or prison. **2** the regular care required to keep something in good condition.

afterdamp *n* a poisonous gas formed after the explosion of firedamp in a coal mine.

aftereffect *n* any result occurring some time after its cause.

afterglow *n* **1** the glow left after the source of a light has disappeared, for example after sunset. **2** a pleasant feeling remaining after an enjoyable experience.

afterlife *n* life after death.

aftermath *n* effects or results of an event considered collectively: *the aftermath of the weekend violence.* ▷ HISTORY *after* + Old English *mæth* a mowing

afternoon *n* the period between noon and evening.

afterpains *pl n* pains caused by contraction of a woman's womb after childbirth.

afters *n Informal* the sweet course of a meal.

aftershave *n* a scented lotion applied to a man's face after shaving.

aftershock *n* one of a series of minor tremors occurring after the main shock of an earthquake.

afterthought *n* **1** something thought of after the opportunity to use it has passed. **2** an addition to something already completed.

afterwards *or* **afterward** *adv* later. ▷ HISTORY Old English *æfterweard*

Ag *Chem* silver. ▷ HISTORY Latin *argentum*

again *adv* **1** another or a second time: *I want to look at that atlas again.* **2** once more in a previously experienced state or condition: *he pictured her again as she used to be.* **3** in addition to the original amount: *twice as much again.* **4** on the other hand. **5** moreover or furthermore: *she is beautiful and, again, intelligent.* **6 again and again** continually or repeatedly. ▷ HISTORY Old English *ongegn* opposite to

against *prep* **1** standing or leaning beside: *he leaned against a tree.* **2** opposed to or in disagreement with. **3** in contrast to: *his complexion was a sickly white against the black stubble of his beard.* **4** coming in contact with: *rain rattled against the window.* **5** having an unfavourable effect on: *the* *system works against you when you don't have money.* **6** as a protection from: *a safeguard against bacteria.* **7** in exchange for or in return for: *the dollar has gained very slightly against the yen.* **8 as against** as opposed to; as compared with. ▷ **HISTORY** Middle English *ageines*

agape *adj* **1** (of the mouth) wide open. **2** (of a person) very surprised.

agar (**ayg**-ar) *or* **agar-agar** *n* a jelly-like substance obtained from seaweed and used as a thickener in food. ▷ **HISTORY** Malay

agaric *n* any fungus with gills on the underside of the cap, such as a mushroom. ▷ **HISTORY** Greek *agarikon*

agate (**ag**-git) *n* a hard semiprecious form of quartz with striped colouring. ▷ **HISTORY** Greek *akhatēs*

agave (a-**gave**-vee) *n* a tropical American plant with tall flower stalks and thick leaves. ▷ **HISTORY** Greek *agauos* illustrious

age *n* **1** the length of time that a person or thing has existed. **2** a period or state of human life. **3** the latter part of human life. **4** a period of history marked by some feature. **5 ages** *Informal* a long time. **6 come of age** to become legally responsible for one's actions (usually at 18 years). ✧ *vb* **ageing** *or* **aging, aged 7** to become old: *skin type changes as one ages.* **8** to appear or cause to appear older: *the years had not aged her in any way.* ▷ **HISTORY** Latin *aetas*

aged *adj* **1** (**ay**-jid) advanced in years; old. **2** (rhymes with **raged**) being at the age of: *a girl aged thirteen is missing.*

ageing *or* **aging** *n* **1** the fact or process of growing old. ✧ *adj* **2** becoming or appearing older.

ageism *or* **agism** *n* discrimination against people on the grounds of age. ▶ **ageist** *or* **agist** *n*

ageless *adj* **1** apparently never growing old. **2** seeming to have existed for ever; eternal: *an ageless profession.*

agency *n, pl* **-cies 1** an organization providing a specific service: *an advertising agency.* **2** the business or functions of an agent. **3** action or power by which something happens: *the intervention of a human agency in the sequence of events.* ▷ **HISTORY** Latin *agere* to do

agenda *n* a schedule or list of items to be attended to, for example at a meeting. ▷ **HISTORY** Latin: things to be done

agent *n* **1** a person who arranges business for other people, esp. for actors or singers. **2** a spy. **3** a substance which causes change in other substances: *an emulsifying agent.* **4** someone or something which causes an effect: *the agent of change.*

agent provocateur (**azh**-on prov-vok-at-**tur**) *n, pl* **agents provocateurs** (**azh**-on prov-vok-at-**tur**) a person employed by the authorities to tempt people to commit illegal acts and so be discredited or punished. ▷ **HISTORY** French

age-old *adj* very old; ancient.

agglomerate *vb* **-ating, -ated 1** to form or be formed into a mass. ✧ *n* **2** a volcanic rock consisting of fused angular fragments of rock. ▷ **HISTORY** Latin *agglomerare*

agglomeration *n* a confused mass or cluster.

agglutinate *vb* **-nating, -nated** to stick as if with glue. ▷ **HISTORY** Latin *agglutinare* ▶ **agglutination** *n*

aggradation *n Geol* the building up of the level of a land surface as a result of the deposition of sediment. Compare **degradation**.

aggrandize *or* **-dise** *vb* **-dizing, -dized** *or* **-dising, -dised** to make greater in size, power, or rank. ▷ **HISTORY** Old French *aggrandir* ▶ **aggrandizement** *or* **-disement** *n*

aggravate *vb* **-vating, -vated 1** to make (a disease, situation or problem) worse. **2** *Informal* to annoy. ▷ **HISTORY** Latin *aggravare* to make heavier ▶ **aggravating** *adj* ▶ **aggravation** *n*

aggregate *n* **1** an amount or total formed from separate units. **2** *Geol* a rock, such as granite, consisting of a mixture of minerals. **3** the sand and stone mixed with cement and water to make concrete. ✧ *adj* **4** formed of separate units collected into a whole. ✧ *vb* **-gating, -gated 5** to combine or be combined into a whole. **6** to amount to (a particular number). ▷ **HISTORY** Latin *aggregare* to add to a flock or herd ▶ **aggregation** *n*

aggression *n* **1** violent and hostile behaviour. **2** an unprovoked attack. ▷ **HISTORY** Latin *aggredi* to attack ▶ **aggressor** *n*

aggressive *adj* **1** full of anger or hostility. **2** forceful or determined: *an aggressive salesman.* ▶ **aggressively** *adv* ▶ **aggressiveness** *n*

aggrieved *adj* upset and angry. ▷ **HISTORY** Latin *aggravare* to aggravate

aggro *n Brit, Austral & NZ slang* aggressive behaviour. ▷ **HISTORY** from *aggravation*

aghast *adj* overcome with amazement or horror. ▷ **HISTORY** Old English *gæstan* to frighten

agile *adj* **1** quick in movement; nimble. **2** mentally quick or acute. ▷ **HISTORY** Latin *agilis* ▶ **agility** *n*

agin *prep Dialect* against or opposed to: *he gave the usual line of talk agin the government.* ▷ **HISTORY** obsolete *again* against

agitate *vb* **-tating, -tated 1** to excite, disturb, or trouble. **2** to shake or stir (a liquid). **3** to attempt to stir up public opinion for or against something. ▷ **HISTORY** Latin *agitare* ▶ **agitated** *adj* ▶ **agitatedly** *adv* ▶ **agitation** *n* ▶ **agitator** *n*

agitprop *n* political agitation and propaganda. ▷ **HISTORY** Russian *Agitpropbyuro*

aglitter *adj* sparkling or glittering.

aglow *adj* glowing.

AGM annual general meeting.

agnostic *n* **1** a person who believes that it is impossible to know whether God exists. **2** a person who claims that the answer to some specific question cannot be known with certainty. ✧ *adj* **3** of or relating to agnostics. ▷ **HISTORY** A- + *gnostic* having knowledge ▶ **agnosticism** *n*

A B C D E F G H I J K L M N O P Q R S T U V W X Y Z

ago *adv* in the past: *fifty years ago.* ▷ **HISTORY** Old English *āgān* to pass away

> **WORD TIP**
> The use of *ago* with *since* (*it's ten years ago since he wrote the novel*) is redundant and should be avoided: *it is ten years since he wrote the novel.*

agog *adj* eager or curious: *Marcia would be agog to hear his news.* ▷ **HISTORY** Old French *en gogues* in merriments

agonic line *n Geog* an imaginary line round the earth that passes through both magnetic north and true north, so that at any point along the line the compass points to both.

agonize *or* **-nise** *vb* **-nizing, -nized** *or* **-nising, -nised 1** to worry greatly. **2** to suffer agony. ▸ **agonizing** *or* **-nising** *adj* ▸ **agonizingly** *or* **-nisingly** *adv*

agony *n, pl* **-nies** acute physical or mental pain. ▷ **HISTORY** Greek *agōnia* struggle

agony aunt *n* a person who replies to readers' letters in an agony column.

agony column *n* a newspaper or magazine feature offering advice on readers' personal problems.

agoraphobia *n* a pathological fear of being in public places. ▷ **HISTORY** Greek *agora* marketplace + *phobos* fear ▸ **agoraphobic** *adj, n*

AGR advanced gas-cooled reactor.

agrarian *adj* of or relating to land or agriculture. ▷ **HISTORY** Latin *ager* field ▸ **agrarianism** *n*

Agrarian Reform Law *n History* a measure implemented by the Chinese People's Republic in 1950 to redistribute landed property.

agree *vb* **agreeing, agreed 1** to be of the same opinion. **2** to give assent; consent. **3** to reach a joint decision: *the ministers agreed on a strategy.* **4** to be consistent. **5 agree with** to be agreeable or suitable to (one's health or appearance): *marriage and motherhood must agree with you.* **6** to concede: *the unions have agreed that the results of appraisal are relevant.* **7** *Grammar* to be the same in number, gender, and case as a connected word. ▷ **HISTORY** Old French *a gre* at will

agreeable *adj* **1** pleasant and enjoyable. **2** prepared to consent: *I cannot say that she was agreeable to the project but she was resigned.* ▸ **agreeably** *adv*

agreement *n* **1** the act or state of agreeing. **2** a legally enforceable contract.

agribusiness *n* **1** the use of intensive methods to increase profits in agriculture. **2** all of the businesses that process, distribute, and support farm products. ▷ **HISTORY** *agri(culture) + business*

agriculture *n* the rearing of crops and livestock; farming. ▷ **HISTORY** Latin *ager* field + *cultura* cultivation ▸ **agricultural** *adj* ▸ **agriculturalist** *n*

agrimony *n* a plant with small yellow flowers and bitter-tasting bristly fruits. ▷ **HISTORY** Greek *argemōnē* poppy

agrochemical *n* a chemical used in agriculture.

agronomy (ag-**ron**-om-mee) *n* the science of land cultivation, soil management, and crop production. ▷ **HISTORY** Greek *agros* field + *nemein* to manage ▸ **agronomist** *n*

aground *adv* onto the bottom of shallow water: *they felt a jolt as the ship ran aground.*

ague (**aig**-yew) *n* **1** *Old-fashioned* malarial fever with shivering. **2** a fit of shivering. ▷ **HISTORY** Old French *(fievre) ague* acute fever

ah *interj* an exclamation expressing pleasure, pain, sympathy, etc.

aha *interj* an exclamation expressing triumph, surprise, etc.

ahead *adv* **1** at or in the front; before. **2** forwards: *go straight ahead.* **3 get ahead** to achieve success: *I was young and hungry to get ahead.* ✧ *adj* **4** in a leading position: *he is ahead in the polls.*

ahem *interj* a clearing of the throat, used to attract attention or express doubt.

ahoy *interj Naut* a shout made to call a ship or to attract attention.

AI 1 artificial insemination. **2** artificial intelligence.

aid *n* **1** money, equipment, or services provided for people in need; assistance. **2** a person or device that helps or assists. ✧ *vb* **3** to help financially or in other ways. ▷ **HISTORY** Latin *adjutare* to help

Aid *or* **-aid** *n combining form* denoting a charitable organization that raises money for a particular cause: *Band Aid.*

AID formerly, artificial insemination by donor.

aide *n* an assistant: *a senior aide to the Prime Minister.*

aide-de-camp (aid-de-**kom**) *n, pl* **aides-de-camp** (aid-de-**kom**) a military officer serving as personal assistant to a senior. ▷ **HISTORY** French: camp assistant

AIDS acquired immunodeficiency syndrome: a viral disease that destroys the body's ability to fight infection.

AIH artificial insemination by husband.

ail *vb Literary* **1** to trouble or afflict. **2** to feel unwell. ▷ **HISTORY** Old English *eglan*

aileron (**ale**-er-on) *n* a hinged flap on the back of an aircraft wing which controls rolling. ▷ **HISTORY** French *aile* wing

ailing *adj* unwell or unsuccessful over a long period: *an ailing company.*

ailment *n* a slight illness.

aim *vb* **1** to point (a weapon or missile) or direct (a blow or remark) at a particular person or object. **2** to propose or intend: *they aim to provide full and equal rights to all groups.* ✧ *n* **3** the action of directing something at an object. **4** intention or purpose. **5 take aim** to point a weapon or missile at a person or object. ▷ **HISTORY** Latin *aestimare* to estimate

aimless *adj* having no purpose or direction. ▸ **aimlessly** *adv*

ain't *not standard* am not, is not, are not, have not, *or* has not: *it ain't fair.*

air *n* **1** the mixture of gases that forms the earth's atmosphere. It consists chiefly of nitrogen, oxygen, argon, and carbon dioxide. **2** the space above and around the earth; sky. RELATED ADJECTIVE ➔ **aerial** **3** a distinctive quality, appearance, or manner: *I thought he had an air of elegance and celebrity about him.* **4** a simple tune. **5** transportation in aircraft: *I went off to Italy by air and train.* **6 in the air** in circulation; current: *a sense of expectation is in the air.* **7 into thin air** leaving no trace behind. **8 on the air** in the act of broadcasting on radio or television. **9 up in the air** uncertain. ✧ *vb* **10** to make known publicly: *these issues will be aired at a ministerial meeting.* **11** to expose to air to dry or ventilate. **12** (of a television or radio programme) to be broadcast. ✧ See also **airs**. ▷ HISTORY Greek *aēr*

air bag *n* a safety device in a car, consisting of a bag that inflates automatically in an accident to protect the driver or passenger.

air base *n* a centre from which military aircraft operate.

airborne *adj* **1** carried by air. **2** (of aircraft) flying; in the air.

air brake *n* a brake in heavy vehicles that is operated by compressed air.

airbrush *n* **1** an atomizer which sprays paint by means of compressed air. ✧ *vb* **2** to paint using an airbrush. **3** to improve the image of (a person or thing) by hiding defects beneath a bland exterior.

air chief marshal *n* a very senior officer in an air force.

air commodore *n* a senior officer in an air force.

air conditioning *n* a system for controlling the temperature and humidity of the air in a building. ▶ **air-conditioned** *adj* ▶ **air conditioner** *n*

aircraft *n, pl* **-craft** any machine capable of flying, such as a glider or aeroplane.

aircraft carrier *n* a warship with a long flat deck for the launching and landing of aircraft.

aircraftman *n, pl* **-men** a serviceman of the most junior rank in an air force. ▶ **aircraftwoman** *fem n*

air cushion *n* **1** an inflatable cushion. **2** the pocket of air that supports a hovercraft.

Airedale *n* a large terrier with rough tan-coloured hair and a black patch covering most of the back.

airfield *n* a place where aircraft can land and take off.

air force *n* the branch of a nation's armed services that is responsible for air warfare.

air gun *n* a gun fired by means of compressed air.

airhead *n Slang* a person who is stupid or incapable of serious thought.

air hostess *n Chiefly Brit* a female flight attendant on an airline.

airily *adv* in a light-hearted and casual manner.

airing *n* **1** exposure to air or warmth for drying or ventilation. **2** exposure to public debate: *both these notions got an airing during the campaign.*

airless *adj* lacking fresh air; stuffy.

airlift *n* **1** the transportation by air of troops or cargo when other routes are blocked. ✧ *vb* **2** to transport by an airlift.

airline *n* an organization that provides scheduled flights for passengers or cargo.

airliner *n* a large passenger aircraft.

airlock *n* **1** a bubble of air blocking the flow of liquid in a pipe. **2** an airtight chamber between places that do not have the same air pressure, such as in a spacecraft or submarine.

airmail *n* **1** the system of sending mail by aircraft. **2** mail sent by aircraft.

airman *or fem* **airwoman** *n, pl* **-men** *or* **-women** a person serving in an air force.

air marshal *n* **1** a senior Royal Air Force officer of equivalent rank to a vice admiral in the Royal Navy. **2** a Royal New Zealand Air Force officer of the highest rank when chief of defence forces.

air mass *n Meteorol* a large body of air whose temperature, pressure, and moisture content remain relatively uniform at the same altitude.

Air Miles *pl n Brit* points awarded on buying flight tickets and certain other products which can be used to pay for other flights.

airplane *n US & Canad* an aeroplane.

airplay *n* the broadcast performances of a record on radio.

air pocket *n* a small descending air current that causes an aircraft to lose height suddenly.

air pollution *n Environmental science* contamination of the air by poisonous or harmful substances.

airport *n* a landing and taking-off area for civil aircraft, with facilities for aircraft maintenance and passenger arrival and departure.

air pressure *n Physics* the force exerted on the earth by the air.

air pump *n* a device for pumping air into or out of something.

air raid *n* an attack by enemy aircraft in which bombs are dropped.

air resistance *n Aeronautics* the force produced by the air when an object is moving through it. Also called **drag**.

airs *pl n* manners put on to impress people: *we're poor and we never put on airs.*

airship *n* a lighter-than-air self-propelled aircraft.

airsick *adj* nauseated from travelling in an aircraft.

airside *n* the part of an airport nearest the aircraft.

airspace *n* the atmosphere above a particular country, regarded as its territory.

airspeed *n* the speed of an aircraft relative to the air in which it moves.

airstrip *n* a cleared area for the landing and taking-off of aircraft.

air terminal *n* a building in a city from which air passengers are transported to an airport.

airtight *adj* **1** sealed so that air cannot enter. **2** having no weak points: *your reasoning is airtight and your evidence sound.*

airtime *n* the time allocated to a particular programme, topic, or type of material on radio or television.

A B C D E F G H I J K L M N O P Q R S T U V W X Y Z

air vice-marshal *n* a senior officer in an air force.

airwaves *pl n Informal* radio waves used in radio and television broadcasting.

airway *n* an air route used regularly by aircraft.

airworthy *adj* (of an aircraft) safe to fly. ▶ **airworthiness** *n*

airy *adj* **airier, airiest 1** spacious and well ventilated. **2** light-hearted and casual. **3** having little basis in reality; fanciful: *airy assurances.*

aisle (rhymes with **mile**) *n* a passageway separating seating areas in a church, theatre, or cinema, or separating rows of shelves in a supermarket. ▷ HISTORY Latin *ala* wing

aitchbone *n* a cut of beef from the rump bone. ▷ HISTORY Middle English *nache-bone*

ajar *adj, adv* (of a door) slightly open. ▷ HISTORY Old English *cierran* to turn

AK Alaska.

akimbo *adv* **(with) arms akimbo** with hands on hips and elbows turned outwards. ▷ HISTORY Middle English *in kenebowe* in keen (i.e. sharp) bow

akin *adj* **akin to** similar or very close to: *the technique is akin to impressionist painting.*

Al *Chem* aluminium.

AL Alabama.

à la *prep* in the manner or style of: *laced with Gothic allusion à la David Lynch.* ▷ HISTORY French

alabaster *n* a kind of white stone used for making statues and vases. ▷ HISTORY Greek *alabastros*

à la carte *adj, adv* (of a menu) having dishes individually priced. ▷ HISTORY French

alacrity *n* speed or eagerness: *I accepted the invitation with alacrity.* ▷ HISTORY Latin *alacer* lively

à la mode *adj* fashionable. ▷ HISTORY French

alarm *n* **1** fear aroused by awareness of danger. **2** a noise warning of danger: *there had been no time to put on life jackets or to sound the alarm.* **3** a device that transmits a warning. **4** short for **alarm clock**. ✧ *vb* **5** to fill with fear. **6** to fit or activate a burglar alarm on (a house, car, etc.). ▷ HISTORY Old Italian *all'arme* to arms ▶ **alarming** *adj*

alarm clock *n* a clock that sounds at a set time to wake a person up.

alarmist *n* **1** a person who alarms others needlessly. ✧ *adj* **2** causing needless alarm.

alas *adv* **1** unfortunately or regrettably: *the answer, alas, is that they cannot get any for the moment.* ✧ *interj* **2** *Old-fashioned* an exclamation of grief or alarm. ▷ HISTORY Old French *ha las!*

alb *n* a long white linen robe worn by a Christian priest. ▷ HISTORY Latin *albus* white

albacore *n* a tuna found in warm seas which is valued as a food fish. ▷ HISTORY Arabic *al-bakrah*

Albanian *adj* **1** of Albania. ✧ *n* **2** a person from Albania. **3** the language of Albania.

albatross *n* **1** a large sea bird with very long wings. **2** *Golf* a score of three strokes under par for a hole. ▷ HISTORY Portuguese *alcatraz* pelican

albedo (al-**bee**-doe) *n* the ratio of the intensity of light reflected from an object, such as a planet, to that of the light it receives from the sun. ▷ HISTORY Church Latin: whiteness, from Latin *albus* white

albeit *conj* even though: *these effects occur, albeit to a lesser degree.* ▷ HISTORY Middle English *al be it* although it be (that)

albino *n, pl* **-nos** a person or animal with white or almost white hair and skin and pinkish eyes. ▷ HISTORY Latin *albus* white ▶ **albinism** *n*

Albion *n Poetic* Britain or England. ▷ HISTORY Latin

album *n* **1** a book with blank pages, for keeping photographs or stamps in. **2** a long-playing CD or record. ▷ HISTORY Latin: blank tablet

albumen *n* **1** egg white. **2** *Biochem* same as **albumin**. ▷ HISTORY Latin *albus* white

albumin *or* **albumen** *n Biochem* a water-soluble protein found in blood plasma, egg white, milk, and muscle.

alchemy *n* a medieval form of chemistry concerned with trying to change base metals into gold and to find an elixir to prolong life indefinitely. ▷ HISTORY Arabic *al* the + *kīmiyā'* transmutation ▶ **alchemist** *n*

alcheringa (al-chi-**ring**-ga) *n* another name for **Dreamtime**. ▷ HISTORY Aboriginal language

alcohol *n* **1** a colourless flammable liquid present in intoxicating drinks. **2** intoxicating drinks generally. ▷ HISTORY Arabic *al-kuhl* powdered antimony

alcoholic *n* **1** a person who is addicted to alcohol. ✧ *adj* **2** of or relating to alcohol.

alcoholism *n* a condition in which dependence on alcohol harms a person's health and everyday life.

alcopop *n Brit, Austral & S African informal* an alcoholic drink that tastes like a soft drink. ▷ HISTORY ALCO(HOL) + POP[1] (sense 9)

alcove *n* a recess in the wall of a room. ▷ HISTORY Arabic *al-qubbah* the vault

aldehyde *n Chem* any organic compound containing the group –CHO, derived from alcohol by oxidation. ▷ HISTORY New Latin *al(cohol) dehyd(rogenatum)* dehydrogenated alcohol

alder *n* a tree with toothed leaves and conelike fruits, often found in damp places. ▷ HISTORY Old English *alor*

alderman *n, pl* **-men 1** (formerly, in England and Wales) a senior member of a local council, elected by other councillors. **2** (in the US, Canada & Australia) a member of the governing body of a city. ▷ HISTORY Old English *ealdor* chief + *mann* man

ale *n* **1** a beer fermented in an open vessel using yeasts that rise to the top of the brew. **2** (formerly) an alcoholic drink that is unflavoured by hops. **3** *Brit* another word for **beer**. ▷ HISTORY Old English *alu, ealu*

alembic *n* **1** an obsolete type of container used for distillation. **2** anything that distils or purifies things. ▷ HISTORY Arabic *al-anbīq* the still

alert *adj* **1** watchful and attentive. **2 alert to** aware of. ✧ *n* **3** a warning or the period during which a warning remains in effect. **4 on the alert** watchful. ✧ *vb* **5** to warn of danger. **6** to make aware of a fact. ▷ HISTORY Italian *all'erta* on the watch ▶ **alertness** *n*

A level *n* **1** *Brit* the advanced level of a subject taken for the General Certificate of Education. **2** a pass in a subject at A level.

Alexander technique *n* a technique for improving posture by becoming more aware of it. ▷ HISTORY after Frederick Matthias *Alexander,* Australian actor

alfalfa *n* a plant widely used for feeding farm animals. ▷ HISTORY Arabic *al-fasfasah*

alfresco *adj, adv* in the open air. ▷ HISTORY Italian: in the cool

algae (**al**-jee) *pl n, sing* **alga** (**al**-ga) plants which grow in water or moist ground, and which have no true stems, roots, or leaves. ▷ HISTORY Latin *alga* seaweed

algal bloom *n Environmental science* a sudden growth in the numbers of algae in the water.

algebra *n* a branch of mathematics in which symbols are used to represent numbers. ▶ **algebraic** *adj*

WORD HISTORY

The term *al-jabr* is taken from the title of an Arabic book on mathematics by the 9th-century Muslim mathematician al-Khwārizmī, the *Kitab al-jabr wa al-muqābulah*. In Arabic *al-jabr* means 'reunion' or 'integration'. When the book was later translated into Latin, 'al-jabr' became 'algebra'.

algebraic expression *n Maths* a mathematical expression in which symbols are used to represent numbers.

ALGOL *n* an early computer programming language designed for mathematical and scientific purposes. ▷ HISTORY *alg(orithmic) o(riented) l(anguage)*

algorism *n* the Arabic or decimal system of counting. ▷ HISTORY from *al-Khuwārizmi,* 9th-century Persian mathematician

algorithm *n* a logical arithmetical or computational procedure for solving problems. ▷ HISTORY changed from ALGORISM

alias *adv* **1** also known as: *Iris florentina, alias orris root.* ✧ *n, pl* **-ases 2** a false name. ▷ HISTORY Latin: otherwise

alibi *n, pl* **-bis 1** *Law* a plea of being somewhere else when a crime was committed. **2** *Informal* an excuse. ✧ *vb* **-biing, -bied 3** to provide someone with an alibi. ▷ HISTORY Latin: elsewhere

alien *adj* **1** foreign. **2** from another world. **3 alien to** repugnant or opposed to: *these methods are alien to the world of politics.* ✧ *n* **4** a person who is a citizen of a country other than the one in which he or she lives. **5** a being from another world. **6** a person who does not seem to fit in with his or her environment. ▷ HISTORY Latin *alienus*

alienable *adj Law* able to be transferred to another owner.

alienate *vb* **-ating, -ated 1** to cause a friend to become unfriendly or hostile. **2** *Law* to transfer the ownership of property to another person. ▶ **alienation** *n*

alight[1] *vb* **alighting, alighted** *or* **alit 1** to step out of a vehicle or off a horse: *we alighted on Vladivostok station.* **2** to land: *we saw thirty goldfinches alighting on the ledge.* ▷ HISTORY Old English *ālīhtan*

alight[2] *adj, adv* **1** on fire. **2** illuminated: *the lamp on the desk was alight.*

align (a-**line**) *vb* **1** to bring (a person or group) into agreement with the policy of another. **2** to place (two objects) in a particular position in relation to each other. ▷ HISTORY Old French *à ligne* into line ▶ **alignment** *n*

alike *adj* **1** similar: *they were thought to be very alike.* ✧ *adv* **2** in the same way: *they even dressed alike.* **3** considered together: *players and spectators alike.* ▷ HISTORY Old English *gelīc*

alimentary *adj* of or relating to nutrition.

alimentary canal *n* the tubular passage in the body through which food is passed and digested.

alimony *n Law* an allowance paid under a court order by one spouse to another after separation. ▷ HISTORY Latin *alimonia* sustenance

A-line *adj* (of a skirt) slightly flared.

aliphatic *adj Chem* (of an organic compound) having an open chain structure. ▷ HISTORY Greek *aleiphar* oil

aliquant *adj Maths* denoting or belonging to a number that is not an exact divisor of a given number. ▷ HISTORY Latin *aliquantus* somewhat

aliquot *adj Maths* denoting or belonging to an exact divisor of a number. ▷ HISTORY Latin: several

alive *adj* **1** living; having life. **2** in existence: *he said that he would keep the company alive, no matter what.* **3** lively. **4 alive to** aware of. **5 alive with** swarming with: *the rocky shoreline was alive with birds.* ▷ HISTORY Old English *on līfe* in life

alkali (**alk**-a-lie) *n Chem* a substance that combines with acid and neutralizes it to form a salt. ▷ HISTORY Arabic *al-qili* the ashes (of saltwort)

alkaline *adj Chem* having the properties of or containing an alkali. ▶ **alkalinity** *n*

alkaloid *n Chem* any of a group of organic compounds containing nitrogen. Many are poisonous and some are used as drugs.

alkane *n Chem* any saturated hydrocarbon with the general formula C_nH_{2n+2}.

alkene *n Chem* any unsaturated hydrocarbon with the general formula C_nH_{2n}.

all *adj, adv* **1** the whole quantity or number (of): *all the banks agree; we're all to blame.* **2** every one of a class: *almost all animals sneeze.* **3** the greatest possible: *in all seriousness.* **4** any whatever: *I'm leaving out all question of motive for the time being.* **5 all along** since the beginning. **6 all but** nearly. **7 all in all** everything considered. **8 all over a** finished. **b** everywhere in or on: *we send them all over the world.* **c** *Informal* typically: *that's him all* *over.* **9 all the** so much (more or less) than otherwise: *the need for new drugs is all the more important.* **10 at all** used for emphasis: *my throat's no better at all.* **11 be all for** *Informal* to be strongly in favour of. **12 for all** in spite of: *for all his cynicism, he's at heart a closet idealist.* **13 in all** altogether: *there were five in all.* ✧ *adv* **14** (in scores of games) each: *the score was two all.* ✧ *n* **15 give one's all** to make the greatest possible effort. ▷ **HISTORY** Old English *eall*

Allah *n* the name of God in Islam.

allay *vb* to reduce (fear, doubt, or anger). ▷ **HISTORY** Old English *ālecgan* to put down

all clear *n* a signal indicating that danger is over.

allegation *n* an unproved assertion or accusation.

allege *vb* **-leging, -leged** to state without proof. ▷ **HISTORY** Latin *allegare* to dispatch on a mission

alleged *adj* stated but not proved: *the spot where the alleged crime took place.* ▸ **allegedly** (al-**lej**-id-lee) *adv*

allegiance *n* loyalty or dedication to a person, cause, or belief. ▷ **HISTORY** Old French *lige* liege

allegory *n, pl* **-ries** a story, poem, or picture with an underlying meaning as well as the literal one. ▷ **HISTORY** Greek *allēgorein* to speak figuratively ▸ **allegorical** *adj* ▸ **allegorize** *or* **-rise** *vb*

allegretto *Music* ✧ *adv* **1** fairly quickly or briskly. ✧ *n, pl* **-tos 2** a piece or passage to be performed fairly quickly or briskly. ▷ **HISTORY** Italian

allegro *Music* ✧ *adv* **1** in a brisk lively manner. ✧ *n, pl* **-gros 2** a piece or passage to be performed in a brisk lively manner. ▷ **HISTORY** Italian

allele (al-**leel**) *n* any of two or more genes that are responsible for alternative characteristics, such as smooth or wrinkled seeds in peas.

alleluia *interj* praise the Lord! ▷ **HISTORY** Hebrew *halleluyah*

allergen (**al**-ler-jen) *n* a substance capable of causing an allergic reaction. ▸ **allergenic** *adj*

allergic *adj* **1** having or caused by an allergy. **2 allergic to** *Informal* having a strong dislike of: *Father and son seemed to have been allergic to each other from the start.*

allergy *n, pl* **-gies 1** extreme sensitivity to a substance such as a food or pollen, which causes the body to react to any contact with it. **2** *Informal* a strong dislike for something. ▷ **HISTORY** Greek *allos* other + *ergon* activity

alleviate *vb* **-ating, -ated** to lessen (pain or suffering). ▷ **HISTORY** Latin *levis* light ▸ **alleviation** *n*

> **WORD TIP**
> See at **ameliorate.**

alley *n* **1** a narrow passage between or behind buildings. **2 a** a building containing lanes for tenpin bowling. **b** a long narrow wooden lane down which the ball is rolled in tenpin bowling. **3** a path in a garden, often lined with trees. ▷ **HISTORY** Old French *alee*

Allhallows *n* same as **All Saints' Day.**

alliance *n* **1** the state of being allied. **2** a formal relationship between two or more countries or political parties to work together. **3** the countries or parties involved. ▷ **HISTORY** Old French *alier* to ally

allied *adj* **1** united by a common aim or common characteristics: *the allied areas of telepathy and clairvoyance.* **2 Allied** *History* relating to the countries that fought against Germany and Austria-Hungary in World War I or against Germany and Japan in World War II: *the Allied bombing of German cities.*

Allies *pl n History* **the Allies a** (in World War I) the countries of the Triple Entente (France, Russia, and Britain) together with the other nations allied with them against Germany and Austria-Hungary. **b** (in World War II) the countries that fought against Germany and Japan (Britain and the Commonwealth countries, the US, the Soviet Union, France, China, and Poland).

alligator *n* a large reptile of the southern US, similar to the crocodile but with a shorter broader snout.

> **WORD HISTORY**
> The word 'alligator' comes from Spanish *el lagarto*, meaning 'the lizard'.

all in *adj* **1** *Informal* exhausted. **2** (of wrestling) with no style forbidden. ✧ *adv* **3** with all expenses included.

alliteration *n* the use of the same sound at the start of words occurring together, as in *round the rugged rock the ragged rascal ran.* ▷ **HISTORY** Latin *litera* letter ▸ **alliterative** *adj*

allocate *vb* **-cating, -cated** to assign to someone or for a particular purpose. ▷ **HISTORY** Latin *locus* a place ▸ **allocation** *n*

allopathy (al-**lop**-ath-ee) *n Med* an orthodox method of treating disease, by using drugs that produce an effect opposite to the effect of the disease being treated, as contrasted with homeopathy. ▷ **HISTORY** Greek *allos* other + *pathos* suffering ▸ **allopathic** *adj*

allot *vb* **-lotting, -lotted** to assign as a share or for a particular purpose. ▷ **HISTORY** Old French *lot* portion

allotment *n* **1** *Brit* a small piece of land rented by a person to grow vegetables on. **2** a portion allotted. **3** distribution.

allotrope *n Chem* any of two or more physical forms in which an element can exist.

allotropy *n Chem* the existence of an element in two or more physical forms. ▷ **HISTORY** Greek *allos* other + *tropos* manner ▸ **allotropic** *adj*

allow *vb* **1** to permit someone to do something. **2** to set aside: *I allowed plenty of time.* **3** to acknowledge (a point or claim). **4 allow for** to take into account. ▷ **HISTORY** Late Latin *allaudare* to extol ▸ **allowable** *adj*

allowance *n* **1** an amount of money given at regular intervals. **2** (in Britain) an amount of a person's income that is not subject to income tax. **3 make allowances for a** to treat or judge someone less severely because he or she has special problems. **b** to take into account in one's plans.

alloy *n* **1** a mixture of two or more metals. ✧ *vb* **2** to mix metals in order to obtain a substance with a desired property. ▷ HISTORY Latin *alligare* to bind

all right *adj* **1** acceptable or satisfactory: *Is everything all right?* **2** unharmed; safe: *I'm going to check if he's all right.* ✧ *interj* **3** an expression of approval or agreement. ✧ *adv* **4** satisfactorily. **5** safely. **6** without doubt: *it was him all right.*

> **WORD TIP**
> See at **alright.**

all-rounder *n* a person with many skills and abilities.

All Saints' Day *n* a Christian festival celebrated on November 1 to honour all the saints.

All Souls' Day *n RC Church* a day of prayer (November 2) for the dead in purgatory.

allspice *n* a spice used in cooking, which comes from the berries of a tropical American tree.

allude *vb* **-luding, -luded allude to** to refer indirectly to. ▷ HISTORY Latin *alludere*

> **WORD TIP**
> Avoid confusion with **elude.**

allure *n* attractiveness or appeal. ▷ HISTORY Old French *alurer* to lure

alluring *adj* extremely attractive.

allusion *n* an indirect reference.

alluvial *adj* **1** of or relating to alluvium. ✧ *n* **2** same as **alluvium.**

alluvial fan *or* **cone** *n Geol* a fan-shaped accumulation of silt, sand, gravel, and boulders deposited by fast-flowing mountain rivers when they reach flatter land.

alluvial soil *n Geol* fertile soil containing mud, silt, and sand deposited by flowing water onto flood plains.

alluvium *n, pl* **-via** a fertile soil consisting of mud, silt, and sand deposited by flowing water. ▷ HISTORY Latin

ally *n, pl* **-lies 1** a country, person, or group with an agreement to support another. ✧ *vb* **-lies, -lying, -lied 2 ally oneself with** to agree to support another country, person, or group. ▷ HISTORY Latin *ligare* to bind

alma mater *n* the school, college, or university that one attended. ▷ HISTORY Latin: bountiful mother

almanac *n* a yearly calendar with detailed information on matters like anniversaries and phases of the moon. ▷ HISTORY Late Greek *almenikhiaka*

almighty *adj* **1** having power over everything. **2** *Informal* very great: *there was an almighty bang.* ✧ *n* **3 the Almighty** God.

almond *n* an edible oval nut with a yellowish-brown shell, which grows on a small tree. ▷ HISTORY Greek *amugdalē*

almoner *n Brit* a former name for a hospital social worker. ▷ HISTORY Old French *almosne* alms

almost *adv* very nearly.

alms (**ahmz**) *pl n Old-fashioned* donations of money or goods to the poor. ▷ HISTORY Greek *eleēmosunē* pity

almshouse *n Brit* (formerly) a house, financed by charity, which offered accommodation to the poor.

aloe *n* **1** a plant with fleshy spiny leaves. **2 aloes** a bitter drug made from aloe leaves. ▷ HISTORY Greek

aloe vera *n* a plant producing a juice which is used to treat skin and hair.

aloft *adv* **1** in the air. **2** *Naut* in the rigging of a ship. ▷ HISTORY Old Norse *ā lopt*

alone *adj, adv* **1** without anyone or anything else. **2 leave someone** *or* **something alone** to refrain from annoying someone *or* interfering with something. **3 let alone** not to mention: *it looked inconceivable that he could run again, let alone be elected.* ▷ HISTORY Old English *al one* all (entirely) one

along *prep* **1** over part or all of the length of: *we were going along the railway tracks.* ✧ *adv* **2** moving forward: *they were roaring along at 40mph.* **3** in company with another or others: *let them go along for the ride.* **4 along with** together with: *I'm including the good days along with the bad.* ▷ HISTORY Old English *andlang*

> **WORD TIP**
> See at **plus.**

alongside *prep* **1** close beside. ✧ *adv* **2** near the side of something.

aloof *adj* distant or haughty in manner. ▷ HISTORY obsolete *a loof* to windward

alopecia (al-loh-**pee**-sha) *n* loss of hair, usually due to illness. ▷ HISTORY Greek *alōpekia* mange in foxes

aloud *adv* in an audible voice.

alp *n* **1** a high mountain. **2 the Alps** a high mountain range in S central Europe. ▷ HISTORY Latin *Alpes*

alpaca *n* **1** a South American mammal related to the llama, with dark shaggy hair. **2** wool or cloth made from this hair. ▷ HISTORY South American Indian *allpaca*

alpenstock *n* a strong stick with an iron tip used by hikers and mountain climbers. ▷ HISTORY German

alpha *n* **1** the first letter in the Greek alphabet (A, α). **2** *Brit* the highest grade in an examination or for a piece of academic work. **3 alpha and omega** the first and last.

alphabet *n* a set of letters in fixed conventional order, used in a writing system. ▷ HISTORY *alpha* + *beta*, the first two letters of the Greek alphabet

alphabetical *adj* in the conventional order of the letters of an alphabet. ► **alphabetically** *adv*

alphabetize *or* **-ise** *vb* **-izing, -ized** *or* **-ising, -ised** to put in alphabetical order. ► **alphabetization** *or* **-isation** *n*

alphanumeric *adj* consisting of alphabetical and numerical symbols.

A B C D E F G H I J K L M N O P Q R S T U V W X Y Z

alpha particle *n Physics* a positively charged particle, emitted during some radioactive transformations.

alpha ray *n Physics* a stream of alpha particles.

alpine *adj* **1** of high mountains. **2 Alpine** of the Alps. ✧ *n* **3** a plant grown on or native to mountains.

already *adv* **1** before the present time. **2** before an implied or expected time.

alright *adj, interj, adv Not universally accepted* same as **all right**.

> ☑ **WORD TIP**
> The form *alright,* though very common, is still considered by many people to be wrong or less acceptable than *all right.*

Alsatian *n* a large wolflike dog.

also *adv* in addition; too. ▷ **HISTORY** Old English *alswā*

also-ran *n* a loser in a race, competition, or election.

alt. *combining form Informal* alternative: *alt. rock.*

altar *n* **1** the table used for Communion in Christian churches. **2** a raised structure on which sacrifices are offered and religious rites performed. ▷ **HISTORY** Latin *altus* high

altarpiece *n* a painting or a decorated screen set above and behind the altar in a Christian church.

alter *vb* to make or become different; change. ▷ **HISTORY** Latin *alter* other

alteration *n* a change or modification.

altercation *n* a noisy argument. ▷ **HISTORY** Latin *altercari* to quarrel

alter ego *n* **1** a hidden side to one's personality. **2** a very close friend. ▷ **HISTORY** Latin: other self

alternate *vb* **-nating, -nated 1** to occur by turns. **2** to interchange regularly or in succession. ✧ *adj* **3** occurring by turns. **4** every second (one) of a series: *alternate days.* **5** being a second choice. ▷ **HISTORY** Latin *alternare* ▶ **alternately** *adv* ▶ **alternation** *n*

alternate angles *pl n Geom* two angles at opposite ends and on opposite sides of a line intersecting two other lines.

alternating current *n* an electric current that reverses direction at frequent regular intervals.

alternative *n* **1** a possibility of choice between two or more things. **2** either or any of such choices. ✧ *adj* **3** presenting a choice between two or more possibilities. **4** of a lifestyle etc. that is less conventional or materialistic than is usual. ▶ **alternatively** *adv*

alternative dispute resolution *n Law* methods for resolving disputes outside the court system, such as mediation, conciliation, arbitration, etc.

alternative energy *n* a form of energy obtained from natural resources like waves and wind.

alternative medicine *n* the treatment of disease by unconventional methods like homeopathy, and involving attention to the patient's emotional wellbeing.

alternator *n* an electrical machine that generates an alternating current.

although *conj* in spite of the fact that.

altimeter (al-**tim**-it-er) *n* an instrument that measures altitude. ▷ **HISTORY** Latin *altus* high + -METER

altitude *n* height, esp. above sea level. ▷ **HISTORY** Latin *altus* high, deep

alto *n, pl* **-tos 1** short for **contralto**. **2** the highest adult male voice. **3** a singer with an alto voice. **4** a musical instrument, for instance a saxophone, that is the second or third highest in its family. ✧ *adj* **5** denoting such an instrument, singer, or voice: *an alto flute.* ▷ **HISTORY** Italian: high

altocumulus (alt-oh-**cue**-mew-luss) *n, pl* **-li** (-lie) *Meteorol* a globular cloud at an intermediate height.

altogether *adv* **1** completely: *an altogether different message.* **2** on the whole: *this is not altogether a bad thing.* **3** in total: *altogether, 25 aircraft took part.* ✧ *n* **4 in the altogether** *Informal* naked.

altostratus (alt-oh-**stray**-tuss) *n, pl* **-ti** (-tie) *Meteorol* a layer cloud at an intermediate height.

altruism *n* unselfish concern for the welfare of others. ▷ **HISTORY** Italian *altrui* others ▶ **altruist** *n* ▶ **altruistic** *adj*

alum *n Chem* a double sulphate of aluminium and potassium, used in manufacturing and in medicine. ▷ **HISTORY** Latin *alumen*

aluminium *or US & Canad* **aluminum** *n Chem* a light malleable silvery-white metallic element that does not rust. Symbol: Al.

aluminize *or* **-ise** *vb* **-nizing, -nized** *or* **-nising, -nised** to cover with aluminium.

alumnus (al-**lumm**-nuss) *or fem* **alumna** (al-**lumm**-na) *n, pl* **-ni** (-nie) *or* **-nae** (-nee) *Chiefly US & Canad* a graduate of a school or college. ▷ **HISTORY** Latin: nursling, pupil

alveolus (al-**vee**-ol-luss) *n, pl* **-li** (-lie) any small pit, cavity, or saclike dilation, such as a honeycomb cell, a tooth socket, or the tiny air sacs in the lungs. ▷ **HISTORY** Latin: a little hollow

always *adv* **1** without exception: *she was always at the top of her form in school work.* **2** continually: *you're always shouting or whining.* **3** in any case: *they're all adults, they can always say no.* ▷ **HISTORY** Old English *ealne weg* all the way

alyssum *n* a garden plant with clusters of small white flowers. ▷ **HISTORY** Greek *alussos* curing rabies

Alzheimer's disease (**alts**-hime-erz) *n* a disorder of the brain resulting in a progressive decline in intellectual and physical abilities and eventual dementia. ▷ **HISTORY** after A. *Alzheimer,* German physician

am *vb* (used with *I*) a form of the present tense of **be**. ▷ **HISTORY** Old English *eam*

Am *Chem* americium.

AM 1 amplitude modulation. **2** (in Britain) Member of the National Assembly for Wales.

Am. America(n).

a.m. before noon. ▷ **HISTORY** Latin *ante meridiem*

amalgam *n* **1** a blend or combination. **2** an alloy of mercury with another metal: *dental amalgam.* ▷ **HISTORY** Medieval Latin *amalgama*

amalgamate *vb* **-ating, -mated 1** to combine or unite. **2** to alloy (a metal) with mercury. ▶ **amalgamation** *n*

amandla (a-**mand**-la) *n S African* a political slogan calling for power to the Black population. ▷ **HISTORY** Nguni (language group of southern Africa): power

amanuensis (am-man-yew-**en**-siss) *n, pl* **-ses** (-seez) a person who copies manuscripts or takes dictation. ▷ **HISTORY** Latin *servus a manu* slave at hand

amaranth *n* **1** *Poetic* an imaginary flower that never fades. **2** a lily-like plant with small green, red, or purple flowers. ▷ **HISTORY** Greek *a-* not + *marainein* to fade

amaryllis *n* a lily-like plant with large red or white flowers and a long stalk. ▷ **HISTORY** *Amaryllis,* Greek name for a shepherdess

amass *vb* to accumulate or collect: *the desire to amass wealth.* ▷ **HISTORY** Latin *ad-* to + *massa* mass

amateur *n* **1** a person who engages in a sport or other activity as a pastime rather than as a profession. **2** a person unskilled in a subject or activity. ✧ *adj* **3** doing something out of interest, not for money. **4** amateurish. ▷ **HISTORY** Latin *amator* lover ▶ **amateurism** *n*

amateurish *adj* lacking skill.

amatory *adj* of or relating to romantic or sexual love. ▷ **HISTORY** Latin *amare* to love

amaze *vb* **amazing, amazed** to fill with surprise; astonish. ▷ **HISTORY** Old English *āmasian* ▶ **amazement** *n* ▶ **amazing** *adj* ▶ **amazingly** *adv*

Amazon *n* **1** a strong and powerful woman. **2** *Greek myth* one of a race of women warriors of Scythia. ▷ **HISTORY** Greek ▶ **Amazonian** *adj*

ambassador *n* **1** a diplomat of the highest rank, sent to another country as permanent representative of his or her own country. **2** a representative or messenger: *he saw himself as an ambassador for the game.* ▷ **HISTORY** Old Provençal *ambaisador* ▶ **ambassadorial** *adj*

amber *n* **1** a yellow translucent fossilized resin, used in jewellery. ✧ *adj* **2** brownish-yellow. ▷ **HISTORY** Arabic *'anbar* ambergris

ambergris (**am**-ber-greece) *n* a waxy substance secreted by the sperm whale, which is used in making perfumes. ▷ **HISTORY** Old French *ambre gris* grey amber

ambidextrous *adj* able to use both hands with equal ease. ▷ **HISTORY** Latin *ambi-* both + *dexter* right hand

ambience *or* **ambiance** *n* the atmosphere of a place.

ambient *adj* **1** surrounding: *low ambient temperatures.* **2** creating a relaxing atmosphere: *ambient music.* ▷ **HISTORY** Latin *ambi-* round + *ire* to go

ambiguity *n, pl* **-ties 1** the possibility of interpreting an expression in more than one way. **2** an ambiguous situation or expression: *the ambiguities of feminine identity.*

ambiguous *adj* having more than one possible interpretation. ▷ **HISTORY** Latin *ambigere* to go around ▶ **ambiguously** *adv*

ambit *n* limits or boundary. ▷ **HISTORY** Latin *ambire* to go round

ambition *n* **1** strong desire for success. **2** something so desired; a goal. ▷ **HISTORY** Latin *ambitio* a going round (of candidates)

ambitious *adj* **1** having a strong desire for success. **2** requiring great effort or ability: *ambitious plans.*

ambivalence (am-**biv**-a-lenss) *n* the state of feeling two conflicting emotions at the same time. ▶ **ambivalent** *adj*

amble *vb* **-bling, -bled 1** to walk at a leisurely pace. ✧ *n* **2** a leisurely walk or pace. ▷ **HISTORY** Latin *ambulare* to walk

ambrosia *n* **1** something delightful to taste or smell. **2** *Classical myth* the food of the gods. ▷ **HISTORY** Greek: immortality

ambulance *n* a motor vehicle designed to carry sick or injured people. ▷ **HISTORY** Latin *ambulare* to walk

ambulatory *adj* **1** of or relating to walking. **2** able to walk. ✧ *n, pl* **-ries 3** a place for walking in, such as a cloister.

ambush *n* **1** the act of waiting in a concealed position to make a surprise attack. **2** an attack from such a position. ✧ *vb* **3** to attack suddenly from a concealed position. ▷ **HISTORY** Old French *embuschier* to position in ambush

ameliorate (am-**meal**-yor-rate) *vb* **-rating, -rated** to make (something) better. ▷ **HISTORY** Latin *melior* better ▶ **amelioration** *n*

> **WORD TIP**
> *Ameliorate* is often wrongly used where *alleviate* is meant. *Ameliorate* should be used to mean 'improve', not 'make easier to bear', so one should talk about *alleviating* pain or hardship, not *ameliorating* it.

amen *interj* so be it: used at the end of a prayer. ▷ **HISTORY** Hebrew: certainly

amenable (a-**mean**-a-bl) *adj* likely or willing to cooperate. ▷ **HISTORY** Latin *minare* to drive (cattle)

amend *vb* to make small changes to something such as a piece of writing or a contract, in order to improve it: *he has amended the basic design.* ▷ **HISTORY** Old French *amender*

amendment *n* an improvement or correction.

amends *pl n* **make amends for** to compensate for some injury or insult.

amenity *n, pl* **-ties** a useful or enjoyable feature: *all kinds of amenities including horse riding and golf.* ▷ **HISTORY** Latin *amoenus* agreeable

amenorrhoea *or esp US* **amenorrhea** (aim-men-or-**ree**-a) *n* abnormal absence of menstruation. ▷ **HISTORY** Greek *a-* not + *mēn* month + *rhein* to flow

American *adj* **1** of the United States of America or the American continent. ✧ *n* **2** a person from the United States of America or the American continent.

American football *n* a game similar to rugby, played by two teams of eleven players.

American Indian *n* **1** a member of any of the original peoples of America. ✧ *adj* **2** of any of these peoples.

Americanism *n* an expression or custom that is characteristic of the people of the United States.

Americanize *or* **-ise** *vb* **-izing, -ized** *or* **-ising, -ised** to make American in outlook or form.

americium *n Chem* a white metallic element artificially produced from plutonium. Symbol: Am. ▷ **HISTORY** from *America* (where it was first produced)

amethyst (**am**-myth-ist) *n* **1** a purple or violet variety of quartz used as a gemstone. ✧ *adj* **2** purple or violet.

> **WORD HISTORY**
> 'Amethyst' comes from Greek *amethustos* meaning 'not drunk'. It was thought in ancient times that anyone wearing or touching an amethyst would not become drunk. Wine goblets were sometimes carved from amethyst.

Amex (**aah**-mex) **1** *Trademark* American Express. **2** American Stock Exchange.

Amharic *n* the official language of Ethiopia.

amiable *adj* having a pleasant nature; friendly. ▷ **HISTORY** Latin *amicus* friend ▸ **amiability** *n* ▸ **amiably** *adv*

amicable *adj* characterized by friendliness: *ideally the parting should be amicable.* ▷ **HISTORY** Latin *amicus* friend ▸ **amicability** *n* ▸ **amicably** *adv*

amid *or* **amidst** *prep* in the middle of; among. ▷ **HISTORY** Old English *on middan* in the middle

amide *n Chem* **1** any organic compound containing the group $-CONH_2$. **2** an inorganic compound having the general formula $M(NH_2)_x$, where M is a metal atom. ▷ **HISTORY** from AMMONIA

amidships *adv Naut* at, near, or towards the centre of a ship.

amine (am-**mean**) *n Chem* an organic base formed by replacing one or more of the hydrogen atoms of ammonia by organic groups. ▷ **HISTORY** from AMMONIUM

amino acid (am-**mean**-oh) *n Chem* any of a group of organic compounds containing the **amino** group, $-NH_2$, and one or more carboxyl groups, $-COOH$, esp. one that is a component of protein.

amir (am-**meer**) *n* same as **emir.** ▷ **HISTORY** Arabic

amiss *adv* **1** wrongly or badly: *anxious not to tread amiss.* **2 take something amiss** to be offended by something. ✧ *adj* **3** wrong or faulty. ▷ **HISTORY** Middle English *a mis,* from *mis* wrong

amity *n Formal* friendship. ▷ **HISTORY** from Latin *amicus* friend

ammeter *n* an instrument for measuring an electric current in amperes. ▷ **HISTORY** *am(pere)* + -METER

ammo *n Informal* ammunition.

ammonia *n* **1** a colourless strong-smelling gas containing hydrogen and nitrogen. **2** a solution of this in water. ▷ **HISTORY** ultimately from a substance found near the shrine of the Roman-Egyptian god Jupiter *Ammon*

ammonite *n* the fossilized spiral shell of an extinct sea creature. ▷ **HISTORY** Medieval Latin *cornu Ammonis* horn of Ammon

ammonium *adj Chem* of or containing the chemical group NH_4– or the ion NH_4^+.

ammonium nitrate *n Chem* a colourless highly soluble crystalline solid, used as a fertilizer and in explosives and fireworks.

ammunition *n* **1** bullets, bombs, and shells that can be fired from or as a weapon. **2** facts that can be used in an argument. ▷ **HISTORY** Latin *munitio* fortification

amnesia *n* a partial or total loss of memory. ▷ **HISTORY** Greek: forgetfulness ▸ **amnesiac** *adj, n*

amnesty *n, pl* **-ties 1** a general pardon for offences against a government. **2** a period during which a law is suspended, to allow people to confess to crime or give up weapons without fear of prosecution. ▷ **HISTORY** Greek *a-* not + *mnasthai* to remember

amniocentesis *n, pl* **-ses** removal of amniotic fluid from the womb of a pregnant woman in order to detect possible abnormalities in the fetus. ▷ **HISTORY** *amnion* + Greek *kentēsis* a pricking

amnion *n, pl* **-nia** the innermost of two membranes enclosing an embryo. ▷ **HISTORY** Greek: a little lamb ▸ **amniotic** *adj*

amniotic fluid *n* the fluid surrounding the fetus in the womb.

amniotic sac *n Anat* the membranous bag that surrounds a fetus in the womb.

amoeba *or US* **ameba** (am-**mee**-ba) *n, pl* **-bae** (-bee) *or* **-bas** a microscopic single-cell creature that is able to change its shape. ▷ **HISTORY** Greek *ameibein* to change

amok *or* **amuck** *adv* **run amok** to run about in a violent frenzy.

> **WORD HISTORY**
> 'Amok' comes from the Malay word *amoq* meaning 'a furious assault'.

among *or* **amongst** *prep* **1** in the midst of: *she decided to dwell among the Greeks.* **2** in the group, class, or number of: *he is among the top trainers.* **3** to each of: *the stakes should be divided among the players.* **4** with one another within a group: *sort it out among yourselves.* ▷ **HISTORY** Old English *amang*

> **WORD TIP**
> See at **between.**

amoral (aim-**mor**-ral) *adj* without moral standards or principles. ▶ **amorality** *n*

> **WORD TIP**
> *Amoral* is often wrongly used where *immoral* is meant. *Immoral* should be used to talk about the breaking of moral rules, *amoral* about people who have no moral code or about places or situations where moral considerations do not apply.

amorous *adj* feeling, displaying, or relating to sexual love or desire. ▷ HISTORY Latin *amor* love

amorphous *adj* **1** lacking a definite shape. **2** of no recognizable character or type. ▷ HISTORY Greek *a-* not + *morphē* shape

amortize *or* **-tise** *vb* **-tizing, -tized** *or* **-tising, -tised** *Finance* to pay off (a debt) gradually by periodic transfers to a sinking fund. ▷ HISTORY Latin *ad* to + *mors* death

amount *n* **1** extent or quantity. ✧ *vb* **2 amount to** to be equal or add up to. ▷ HISTORY Old French *amonter* to go up

> **WORD TIP**
> The use of a plural noun after *amount of (an amount of bananas; the amount of refugees)* should be avoided: *a quantity of bananas; the number of refugees.*

amour *n* a secret love affair. ▷ HISTORY Latin *amor* love

amour-propre (am-moor-**prop**-ra) *n* self-esteem.

amp *n* **1** an ampere. **2** *Informal* an amplifier.

amperage *n* the strength of an electric current measured in amperes.

ampere (**am**-pair) *n* the basic unit of electric current. ▷ HISTORY after A. M. *Ampère*, French physicist & mathematician

ampersand *n* the character &, meaning *and.* ▷ HISTORY shortened from *and per se and,* that is, the symbol & by itself (represents) *and*

amphetamine (am-**fet**-am-mean) *n* a drug used as a stimulant. ▷ HISTORY shortened from chemical name

amphibian *n* **1** an animal, such as a newt, frog, or toad, that lives on land but breeds in water. **2** a vehicle that can travel on both water and land.

amphibious *adj* **1** living or operating both on land and in or on water. **2** relating to a military attack launched from the sea against a shore. ▷ HISTORY Greek *amphibios* having a double life

amphitheatre *or US* **amphitheater** *n* a circular or oval building without a roof, in which tiers of seats rise from a central open arena. ▷ HISTORY Greek *amphitheatron*

amphora (**am**-for-ra) *n, pl* **-phorae** (-for-ree) an ancient Greek or Roman jar with two handles and a narrow neck. ▷ HISTORY Greek *amphi-* on both sides + *phoreus* bearer

ample *adj* **1** more than sufficient: *there is already ample evidence.* **2** large: *ample helpings of stewed pomegranates and pears.* ▷ HISTORY Latin *amplus*

amplifier *n* an electronic device used to increase the strength of a current or sound signal.

amplify *vb* **-fies, -fying, -fied 1** *Electronics* to increase the strength of (a current or sound signal). **2** to explain in more detail. **3** to increase the size, extent, or effect of. ▷ HISTORY Latin *amplificare* ▶ **amplification** *n*

amplitude *n* **1** greatness of extent. **2** *Physics* the maximum displacement from the zero or mean position of a wave or oscillation. ▷ HISTORY Latin *amplus* spacious

amplitude modulation *n Electronics* a method of transmitting information using radio waves in which the amplitude of the carrier wave is varied in accordance with the amplitude of the input signal.

amply *adv* fully or generously: *she was amply rewarded for it.*

ampoule *or US* **ampule** *n Med* a small glass container in which liquids for injection are sealed. ▷ HISTORY French

ampulla *n, pl* **-pullae 1** *Anat* the dilated end part of certain tubes in the body. **2** *Christianity* a container for the wine and water, or the oil, used in church. ▷ HISTORY Latin

amputate *vb* **-tating, -tated** to cut off (a limb or part of a limb) for medical reasons. ▷ HISTORY Latin *am-* around + *putare* to prune ▶ **amputation** *n*

amputee *n* a person who has had a limb amputated.

amuck *adv* same as **amok.**

amulet *n* a trinket or jewel worn as a protection against evil. ▷ HISTORY Latin *amuletum*

amuse *vb* **amusing, amused 1** to cause to laugh or smile. **2** to entertain or keep interested. ▷ HISTORY Old French *amuser* to cause to be idle ▶ **amusing** *adj* ▶ **amusingly** *adv*

amusement *n* **1** the state of being amused. **2** something that amuses or entertains someone.

amylase *n* an enzyme present in saliva that helps to change starch into sugar.

an *adj* (*indefinite article*) same as **a:** used before an initial vowel sound: *an old man; an hour.* ▷ HISTORY Old English *ān* one

> **WORD TIP**
> *An* was formerly often used before words that begin with *h* and are unstressed on the first syllable: *an hotel; an historic meeting:* sometimes the initial *h* was not pronounced. This usage is now becoming obsolete.

an- *prefix* See **a-**.

Anabaptist *n* **1** a member of a 16th-century Protestant movement that believed in adult baptism. ✧ *adj* **2** of this movement. ▷ HISTORY Late Greek *anabaptizein* to baptize again

anabolic steroid *n* a synthetic steroid hormone used to stimulate muscle and bone growth.

anabolism *n Biol* a metabolic process in which body tissues are synthesized from food. ▷ HISTORY Greek *anabolē* a rising up

A
B
C
D
E
F
G
H
I
J
K
L
M
N
O
P
Q
R
S
T
U
V
W
X
Y
Z

anabranch *n Geog* a branch of a river or stream which splits off from the main flow to rejoin it further on.

anachronism (an-**nak**-kron-iz-zum) *n* **1** the representation of something in a historical context in which it could not have occurred or existed. **2** a person or thing that seems to belong to another time. ▷ **HISTORY** Greek *ana* against + *khronos* time ▶ **anachronistic** *adj*

anaconda *n* a large S American snake which squeezes its prey to death. ▷ **HISTORY** probably from Sinhalese *henakandayā* whip snake

anaemia *or US* **anemia** (an-**neem**-ee-a) *n* a deficiency of red blood cells or their haemoglobin content, resulting in paleness and lack of energy. ▷ **HISTORY** Greek *an* without + *haima* blood

anaemic *or US* **anemic** *adj* **1** having anaemia. **2** pale and sickly-looking. **3** lacking vitality.

anaerobe *n Biol* an organism that does not require oxygen. ▷ **HISTORY** Greek *an* not + *aēr* air + *bios* life ▶ **anaerobic** *adj*

anaerobic respiration *n Biol* the processing of glucose by cells in the absence of oxygen, producing a variety of end products such as ethanol or lactic acid.

anaesthesia *or US* **anesthesia** (an-niss-**theez**-ee-a) *n* loss of bodily feeling caused by disease or accident or by drugs such as ether: called **general anaesthesia** when consciousness is lost and **local anaesthesia** when only a specific area of the body is involved. ▷ **HISTORY** Greek

anaesthetic *or US* **anesthetic** (an-niss-**thet**-ik) *n* **1** a substance that causes anaesthesia. ✧ *adj* **2** causing anaesthesia.

anaesthetist (an-**neess**-thet-ist) *n Brit* a doctor who administers anaesthetics.

anaesthetize, anaesthetise *or US* **anesthetize** *vb* **-tizing, -tized** *or* **-tising, -tised** to cause to feel no pain by administering an anaesthetic.

anagram *n* a word or phrase made by rearranging the letters of another word or phrase. ▷ **HISTORY** Greek *anagrammatizein* to transpose letters

anal (**ain**-al) *adj* of or relating to the anus. ▷ **HISTORY** New Latin *analis*

analgesia *n* the absence of pain. ▷ **HISTORY** Greek

analgesic (an-nal-**jeez**-ik) *n* **1** a drug that relieves pain. ✧ *adj* **2** pain-relieving: *an analgesic balm.*

analog *n US & computers* same as **analogue**.

> ☑ **WORD TIP**
> The spelling *analog* is a US variant of *analogue* in all its senses, and is also the generally preferred spelling in the computer industry.

analogize *or* **-gise** *vb* **-gizing, -gized** *or* **-gising, -gised 1** to use analogy in argument. **2** to reveal analogy between (one thing and another).

analogous *adj* similar in some respects. ▷ **HISTORY** Greek *analogos* proportionate

> ☑ **WORD TIP**
> The use of *with* after *analogous* should be avoided: *swimming has no event that is analogous to* (not *with*) *the 100 metres in athletics.*

analogue *or US* **analog** *n* **1** a physical object or quantity used to measure or represent another quantity. **2** something that is analogous to something else. ✧ *adj* **3** displaying information by means of a dial: *analogue speedometers.*

> ☑ **WORD TIP**
> See at **analog.**

analogue recording *n* a type of sound recording process.

analogy *n, pl* **-gies 1** a similarity, usually in a limited number of features. **2** a comparison made to show such a similarity. ▷ **HISTORY** Greek *analogia* ▶ **analogical** *adj*

analyse *or US* **-lyze** (**an**-nal-lize) *vb* **-lysing, -lysed** *or* **-lyzing, -lyzed 1** to examine (something) in detail in order to discover its meaning or essential features. **2** to break (something) down into its components. **3** to psychoanalyse (someone).

analysis (an-**nal**-liss-iss) *n, pl* **-ses** (-seez) **1** the separation of a whole into its parts for study or interpretation. **2** a statement of the results of this. **3** short for **psychoanalysis.** ▷ **HISTORY** Greek *analusis* a dissolving

analyst *n* **1** a person who is skilled in analysis. **2** a psychoanalyst.

analytical *or* **analytic** *adj* relating to or using analysis. ▶ **analytically** *adv*

anarchism *n* a doctrine advocating the abolition of government and its replacement by a social system based on voluntary cooperation.

anarchist *n* **1** a person who advocates anarchism. **2** a person who causes disorder or upheaval. ▶ **anarchistic** *adj*

anarchy (**an**-ark-ee) *n* **1** general lawlessness and disorder. **2** the absence of government. ▷ **HISTORY** Greek *an* without + *arkh-* leader ▶ **anarchic** *adj*

anastigmat *n* a lens corrected for astigmatism. ▶ **anastigmatic** *adj*

anathema (an-**nath**-im-a) *n* a detested person or thing: *the very colour was anathema to him.* ▷ **HISTORY** Greek: something accursed

anathematize *or* **-tise** *vb* **-tizing, -tized** *or* **-tising, -tised** to curse: *he anathematized the world in general.*

anatomist *n* an expert in anatomy.

anatomy *n, pl* **-mies 1** the science of the physical structure of animals and plants. **2** the structure of an animal or plant. **3** *Informal* a person's body: *the male anatomy.* **4** a detailed analysis: *an anatomy of the massacre.* ▷ **HISTORY** Greek *ana* up + *temnein* to cut ▶ **anatomical** *adj*

ANC African National Congress: South African political movement instrumental in bringing an end to apartheid.

ancestor *n* **1** a person in former times from whom one is descended. **2** a forerunner: *the immediate ancestor of rock and roll is rhythm and blues.* ▷ HISTORY Latin *antecedere* to go before

ancestral *adj* of or inherited from ancestors.

ancestry *n, pl* **-tries 1** family descent: *of Japanese ancestry.* **2** origin or roots: *a vehicle whose ancestry dated back to the 1950s.*

anchor *n* **1** a hooked device attached to a boat by a cable and dropped overboard to fasten the boat to the sea bottom. **2** a source of stability or security: *a spiritual anchor.* **3 anchors** *Slang* the brakes of a motor vehicle: *he rammed on the anchors.* ✧ *vb* **4** to use an anchor to hold (a boat) in one place. **5** to fasten securely: *we anchored his wheelchair to a rock.* ▷ HISTORY Greek *ankura*

anchorage *n* a place where boats can be anchored.

anchoring *n* **1** (in the media) the use of captions, commentaries, and contexts to direct the viewer of a given image towards a particular interpretation of it. **2** (in psychology) the deliberate setting up of an association of ideas or feelings with a specific stimulus; similar to conditioning.

anchorite *n* a person who chooses to live in isolation for religious reasons. ▷ HISTORY Greek *anakhōrein* to retire

anchorman *or* **anchorwoman** *n* **1** a broadcaster in a central studio, who links up and presents items from outside camera units and reporters in other studios. **2** the last person to compete in a relay team.

anchovy (**an**-chov-ee) *n, pl* **-vies** a small marine food fish with a salty taste. ▷ HISTORY Spanish *anchova*

ancien régime (**on**-syan ray-**zheem**) *n* **1** the political and social system of France before the 1789 Revolution. **2** a former system. ▷ HISTORY French: old regime

ancient *adj* **1** dating from very long ago. **2** very old. **3** of the far past, esp. before the collapse of the Western Roman Empire (476 AD). ✧ *n* **4 ancients** people who lived very long ago, such as the Romans and Greeks. ▷ HISTORY Latin *ante* before

ancillary *adj* **1** supporting the main work of an organization: *hospital ancillary workers.* **2** used as an extra or supplement: *I had a small ancillary sleeping tent.* ▷ HISTORY Latin *ancilla* female servant

and *conj* **1** in addition to: *plants and birds.* **2** as a consequence: *she fell downstairs and broke her neck.* **3** afterwards: *she excused herself and left.* **4** used for emphasis or to indicate repetition or continuity: *they called again and again.* **5** used to express a contrast between instances of something: *there are jobs and jobs.* **6** *Informal* used in place of *to* in infinitives after verbs such as *try, go,* and *come*: *come and see us again.* ▷ HISTORY Old English

> ☑ **WORD TIP**
> See at **try.**

andante (an-**dan**-tay) *Music* ✧ *adv* **1** moderately slowly. ✧ *n* **2** a passage or piece to be performed moderately slowly. ▷ HISTORY Italian *andare* to walk

andantino (an-dan-**tee**-no) *Music* ✧ *adv* **1** slightly faster than andante. ✧ *n, pl* **-nos 2** a passage or piece to be performed in this way.

andiron *n* either of a pair of metal stands for supporting logs in a fireplace. ▷ HISTORY Old French *andier*

and/or *conj Not universally accepted* either one or the other or both.

> ☑ **WORD TIP**
> Many people think that *and/or* is only acceptable in legal and commercial contexts. In other contexts, it is better to use *or both: many drinkers lose their jobs or their driving licences or both* (not *their jobs and/or their driving licences*).

androecium (an-**dree**-see-um) *n, pl* **-cia** (-see-a) *Bot* the stamens of a flowering plant collectively.

androgynous *adj* having both male and female characteristics. ▷ HISTORY Greek *anēr* man + *gunē* woman

android *n* a robot resembling a human being. ▷ HISTORY Late Greek *androeidēs* manlike

andrology (an-**drol**-la-jee) *n* the branch of medicine concerned with diseases and conditions specific to men. ▷ HISTORY Greek *anēr* man + -LOGY ▶ **andrologist** *n*

anecdote *n* a short amusing account of an incident. ▷ HISTORY Greek *anekdotos* not published ▶ **anecdotal** *adj*

anemia *n US* anaemia.

anemometer *n* an instrument for recording wind speed.

anemone (an-**nem**-on-ee) *n* a flowering plant with white, purple, or red flowers. ▷ HISTORY Greek: windflower

aneroid barometer *n* a device for measuring air pressure, consisting of a partially evacuated chamber, in which variations in pressure cause a pointer on the lid to move. ▷ HISTORY Greek *a* not + *nēros* wet

anesthesia *n US* anaesthesia.

aneurysm *or* **aneurism** (**an**-new-riz-zum) *n Med* a permanent swelling of a blood vessel. ▷ HISTORY Greek *aneurunein* to dilate

anew *adv* **1** once more. **2** in a different way.

angel *n* **1** a spiritual being believed to be an attendant or messenger of God. **2** a conventional representation of an angel as a human being with wings. **3** *Informal* a person who is kind, pure, or beautiful. **4** *Informal* an investor in a theatrical production. ▷ HISTORY Greek *angelos* messenger

angelfish *n, pl* **-fish** *or* **-fishes** a South American aquarium fish with large fins.

angelic *adj* **1** very kind, pure, or beautiful. **2** of or relating to angels. ▶ **angelically** *adv*

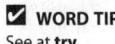

angelica (an-**jell**-ik-a) *n* a plant whose candied stalks are used in cookery. ▷ HISTORY Medieval Latin *(herba) angelica* angelic herb

Angelus (**an**-jell-uss) *n RC Church* **1** prayers recited in the morning, at midday, and in the evening. **2** the bell signalling the times of these prayers. ▷ **HISTORY** Latin *Angelus domini nuntiavit Mariae* the angel of the Lord brought tidings to Mary

anger *n* **1** a feeling of extreme annoyance or displeasure. ✧ *vb* **2** to make (someone) angry. ▷ **HISTORY** Old Norse *angr* grief

angina (an-**jine**-a) *or* **angina pectoris** (**peck**-tor-riss) *n* a sudden intense pain in the chest caused by a momentary lack of adequate blood supply to the heart muscle. ▷ **HISTORY** Greek *ankhonē* a strangling

angle[1] *n* **1** the space between or shape formed by two straight lines or surfaces that meet. **2** the divergence between two such lines or surfaces, measured in degrees. **3** a recess or corner. **4** point of view. ✧ *vb* **-gling, -gled 5** to move in or place at an angle. **6** to write (an article) from a particular point of view. ▷ **HISTORY** Latin *angulus* corner

angle[2] *vb* **-gling, -gled 1** to fish with a hook and line. **2 angle for** to try to get by hinting: *he's just angling for sympathy.* ▷ **HISTORY** Old English *angul* fish-hook

angle of depression *n Maths* (in trigonometry) a vertical angle measured below the horizontal.

angle of elevation *n Maths* (in trigonometry) a vertical angle measured above the horizontal.

angle of incidence *n Physics* the angle that a line or beam of radiation makes with a line perpendicular to the surface at the point of incidence.

angle of refraction *n Physics* the angle that a refracted beam of radiation makes with the normal to the surface between two media at the point of refraction.

angler *n* a person who fishes with a hook and line.

Angles *pl n* a race from N Germany who settled in E and N England in the 5th and 6th centuries AD. ▷ **HISTORY** Latin *Anglus* a person from Angul, Germany

Anglican *adj* **1** of or relating to the Church of England. ✧ *n* **2** a member of the Anglican Church. ▷ **HISTORY** Latin *Anglicus* English, of the Angles ▸ **Anglicanism** *n*

Anglicism *n* an expression or custom that is peculiar to the English.

anglicize *or* **-cise** *vb* **-cizing, -cized** *or* **-cising, -cised** to make or become English in outlook or form.

angling *n* the art or sport of fishing with a hook and line.

Anglo *n, pl* **-glos 1** *US* a White inhabitant of the US who is not of Latin extraction. **2** *Canad* an English-speaking Canadian.

Anglo- *combining form* English or British: *the history of Anglo-German relations.* ▷ **HISTORY** Medieval Latin *Anglii* the English

Anglo-French *adj* **1** of England and France. **2** of the Anglo-French language. ✧ *n* **3** the Norman-French language of medieval England.

Anglo-Indian *adj* **1** of England and India. **2** denoting or relating to Anglo-Indians. ✧ *n* **3** a person of mixed British and Indian descent. **4** an English person who has lived for a long time in India.

Anglo-Norman *adj* **1** of or relating to the Norman conquerors of England or their language. ✧ *n* **2** a Norman inhabitant of England after 1066. **3** the Anglo-French language.

Anglophile *n* a person who admires England or the English.

Anglo-Saxon *n* **1** a member of any of the West Germanic tribes that settled in Britain from the 5th century AD. **2** any White person whose native language is English. **3** same as **Old English**. **4** *Informal* plain, blunt, and often rude English. ✧ *adj* **5** of the Anglo-Saxons or the Old English language. **6** of the White Protestant culture of Britain and the US.

angora *n* **1** a variety of goat, cat, or rabbit with long silky hair. **2** the hair of the angora goat or rabbit. **3** cloth made from this hair. ▷ **HISTORY** *Angora,* former name of Ankara, in Turkey

Angostura Bitters *pl n Trademark* a bitter tonic, used as a flavouring in alcoholic drinks. ▷ **HISTORY** from *Angostura* in Venezuela

angry *adj* **-grier, -griest 1** feeling or expressing annoyance or rage. **2** severely inflamed: *he had angry welts on his forehead.* **3** dark and stormy: *angry waves.* ▸ **angrily** *adv*

> **WORD TIP**
>
> It was formerly considered incorrect to talk about being *angry at* a person, but this use is now acceptable.

angst *n* a feeling of anxiety. ▷ **HISTORY** German

angstrom *n* a unit of length equal to 10^{-10} metre, used to measure wavelengths. ▷ **HISTORY** after Anders J. *Ångström,* Swedish physicist

anguish *n* great mental pain. ▷ **HISTORY** Latin *angustus* narrow

anguished *adj* feeling or showing great mental pain: *anguished cries.*

angular *adj* **1** lean and bony: *his angular face.* **2** having an angle or angles. **3** measured by an angle: *angular momentum.* ▸ **angularity** *n*

anhydride *n Chem* a substance that combines with water to form an acid.

anhydrous *adj Chem* containing no water. ▷ **HISTORY** Greek *an* without + *hudōr* water

anil *n* a West Indian shrub which is a source of indigo. ▷ **HISTORY** Arabic *an-nīl,* the indigo

aniline *n Chem* a colourless oily poisonous liquid, obtained from coal tar and used for making dyes, plastics, and explosives.

animal *n* **1** *Zool* any living being that is capable of voluntary movement and possesses specialized sense organs. **2** any living being other than a human being. **3** any living being with four legs. **4** a cruel or coarse person. **5** *Facetious* a person or thing: *there's no such animal.* ✧ *adj* **6** of or from animals. **7** of or relating to physical needs or desires. ▷ **HISTORY** Latin *animalis* (adjective) living, breathing

animalcule *n* a microscopic animal.

animal husbandry *n* the science of breeding, rearing, and caring for farm animals.

animalism *n* **1** preoccupation with physical matters; sensuality. **2** the doctrine that human beings lack a spiritual nature.

animality *n* **1** the animal instincts of human beings. **2** the state of being an animal.

animal rights *pl n* the rights of animals to be protected from human abuse.

animate *vb* **-mating, -mated 1** to give life to. **2** to make lively. **3** to produce (a story) as an animated cartoon. ✧ *adj* **4** having life. ▷ **HISTORY** Latin *anima* breath, spirit

animated *adj* **1** interesting and lively. **2** (of a cartoon) made by using animation. ▸ **animatedly** *adv*

animated cartoon *n* a film produced by photographing a series of gradually changing drawings, which give the illusion of movement when the series is projected rapidly.

animation *n* **1** the techniques used in the production of animated cartoons. **2** liveliness and enthusiasm: *there's an animation in her that is new.*

animator *n* a person who makes animated cartoons.

animism *n* the belief that natural objects possess souls. ▷ **HISTORY** Latin *anima* breath, spirit ▸ **animist** *n, adj* ▸ **animistic** *adj*

animosity *n, pl* **-ties** a powerful dislike or hostility. ▷ **HISTORY** see ANIMUS

animus *n* intense dislike; hatred. ▷ **HISTORY** Latin: mind, spirit

anion (**an**-eye-on) *n* an ion with negative charge. ▷ **HISTORY** Greek *ana-* up + *ienai* to go ▸ **anionic** *adj*

anise (**an**-niss) *n* a Mediterranean plant with liquorice-flavoured seeds. ▷ **HISTORY** Greek *anison*

aniseed *n* the liquorice-flavoured seeds of the anise plant, used for flavouring.

ankle *n* **1** the joint connecting the leg and the foot. **2** the part of the leg just above the foot. ▷ **HISTORY** Old Norse

anklet *n* an ornamental chain worn round the ankle.

ankylosis (ang-kill-**loh**-siss) *n* abnormal immobility of a joint, caused by a fibrous growth within the joint. ▷ **HISTORY** Greek *ankuloun* to crook

annals *pl n* **1** yearly records of events. **2** regular reports of the work of a society or other organization. ▷ **HISTORY** Latin *(libri) annales* yearly (books) ▸ **annalist** *n*

anneal *vb* to toughen (glass or metal) by heat treatment. ▷ **HISTORY** Old English *onǣlan*

annelid *n* a worm with a segmented body, such as the earthworm. ▷ **HISTORY** Latin *anulus* ring

annex *vb* **1** to seize (territory) by conquest or occupation. **2** to take without permission. **3** to join or add (something) to something larger. ▷ **HISTORY** Latin *annectere* to attach to ▸ **annexation** *n*

annexe *or esp US* **annex** *n* **1** an extension to a main building. **2** a building used as an addition to a main one nearby.

annihilate *vb* **-lating, -lated 1** to destroy (a place or a group of people) completely. **2** *Informal* to defeat totally in an argument or a contest. ▷ **HISTORY** Latin *nihil* nothing ▸ **annihilation** *n*

anniversary *n, pl* **-ries 1** the date on which an event, such as a wedding, occurred in some previous year. **2** the celebration of this. ▷ **HISTORY** Latin *annus* year + *vertere* to turn

anno Domini *adv* in the year of our Lord.

annotate *vb* **-tating, -tated** to add critical or explanatory notes to a written work. ▷ **HISTORY** Latin *nota* mark ▸ **annotation** *n*

announce *vb* **-nouncing, -nounced 1** to make known publicly. **2** to proclaim. **3** to declare the arrival of (a person). **4** to be a sign of: *snowdrops announced the arrival of spring.* ▷ **HISTORY** Latin *annuntiare* ▸ **announcement** *n*

announcer *n* a person who introduces programmes on radio or television.

annoy *vb* **1** to irritate or displease. **2** to harass sexually. ▷ **HISTORY** Latin *in odio (esse)* (to be) hated ▸ **annoyance** *n* ▸ **annoying** *adj*

annual *adj* **1** occurring or done once a year: *the union's annual conference.* **2** lasting for a year: *the annual subscription.* ✧ *n* **3** a plant that completes its life cycle in one year. **4** a book published once every year. ▷ **HISTORY** Latin *annus* year ▸ **annually** *adv*

annuity *n, pl* **-ties** a fixed sum payable at specified intervals over a period. ▷ **HISTORY** Latin *annuus* annual

annul *vb* **-nulling, -nulled** to declare (a contract or marriage) invalid. ▷ **HISTORY** Latin *nullus* not any

annular (**an**-new-lar) *adj* ring-shaped. ▷ **HISTORY** Latin *anulus* ring

annular eclipse *n* an eclipse of the sun in which a ring of sunlight can be seen surrounding the shadow of the moon.

annulate (**an**-new-lit) *adj* having, composed of, or marked with rings. ▷ **HISTORY** Latin *anulus* ring

annulment *n* the formal declaration that a contract or marriage is invalid.

Annunciation *n* **1 the Annunciation** the announcement by the angel Gabriel to the Virgin Mary of her conception of Christ. **2** the festival commemorating this, on March 25 (Lady Day). ▷ **HISTORY** Latin *annuntiare* to announce

anode *n Electronics* the positive electrode in an electrolytic cell or in an electronic valve. ▷ **HISTORY** Greek *anodos* a way up

anodize *or* **-dise** *vb* **-dizing, -dized** *or* **-dising, -dised** *Chem* to coat (a metal) with a protective oxide film by electrolysis.

anodyne *n* **1** something that relieves pain or distress. ✧ *adj* **2** neutral. **3** capable of relieving pain or distress. ▷ **HISTORY** Greek *an-* without + *odunē* pain

anoint *vb* to smear with oil as a sign of consecration. ▷ **HISTORY** Latin *inunguere*

anointing of the sick *n RC Church* a sacrament in which a person who is dying is anointed by a priest.

anomalous *adj* different from the normal or usual order or type. ▷ **HISTORY** Greek *an-* not + *homalos* even

anomaly (an-**nom**-a-lee) *n, pl* **-lies** something that deviates from the normal; an irregularity.

anomie *or* **anomy** (**an**-oh-mee) *n Sociol* lack of social or moral standards. ▷ **HISTORY** Greek *a-* without + *nomos* law

anon *adv Old-fashioned or informal* soon: *you shall see him anon.* ▷ **HISTORY** Old English *on āne* in one, that is, immediately

anon. anonymous.

anonymous *adj* **1** by someone whose name is unknown or withheld: *an anonymous letter.* **2** having no known name: *an anonymous writer.* **3** lacking distinguishing characteristics: *an anonymous little town.* **4 Anonymous** of an organization which helps applicants who remain anonymous: *Alcoholics Anonymous.* ▷ **HISTORY** Greek *an-* without + *onoma* name ▶ **anonymity** *n*

anorak *n* **1** *Brit, Austral & S African* a waterproof hip-length jacket with a hood. **2** *Brit informal* a socially inept person with a hobby considered to be boring.

> **WORD HISTORY**
> The first people to wear anoraks were Eskimos. In the Eskimo language, *anoraq* means 'a piece of clothing' and denotes a long, hooded jacket made from fur such as sealskin or caribou skin.

anorexia *or* **anorexia nervosa** *n* a psychological disorder characterized by fear of becoming fat and refusal to eat. ▷ **HISTORY** Greek *an-* without + *orexis* appetite ▶ **anorexic** *adj, n*

another *adj* **1** one more: *they don't have the right to demand another chance.* **2** different: *you'll have to find another excuse.* ✧ *pron* **3** one more: *help yourself to another.* **4** a different one: *one way or another.* ▷ **HISTORY** originally *an other*

Anschluss (**an**-shlooss) *n History, politics* a political or economic union, used esp. of the annexation of Austria by Nazi Germany (1938). ▷ **HISTORY** German *anschliessen* to join

answer *vb* **1** to reply or respond (to) by word or act. **2** to be responsible (to a person). **3** to reply correctly to (a question). **4** to respond or react: *a dog that answers to the name of Pugg.* **5** to meet the requirements of. **6** to give a defence of (a charge). ✧ *n* **7** a reply to a question, request, letter, or article. **8** a solution to a problem. **9** a reaction or response. ▷ **HISTORY** Old English *andswaru*

answerable *adj* **answerable for** *or* **to** responsible for or accountable to.

answering machine *n* a device for answering a telephone automatically and recording messages.

ant *n* a small often wingless insect, living in highly organized colonies. ▷ **HISTORY** Old English *ǣmette*

antacid *Chem* ✧ *n* **1** a substance used to treat acidity in the stomach. ✧ *adj* **2** having the properties of this substance.

antagonism *n* openly expressed hostility.

antagonist *n* **1** an opponent or adversary. **2** *Anat* an antagonistic muscle. ▶ **antagonistic** *adj*

antagonistic muscle *n Anat* a muscle that works with another, in the opposite direction.

antagonize *or* **-nise** *vb* **-nizing, -nized** *or* **-nising, -nised** to arouse hostility in: *it was not prudent to antagonize a hired killer.* ▷ **HISTORY** Greek *anti-* against + *agōn* contest

antalkali (ant-**alk**-a-lie) *n Chem* a substance that neutralizes alkalis.

Antarctic *n* **1 the Antarctic** the area around the South Pole. ✧ *adj* **2** of this region. ▷ **HISTORY** Greek *antarktikos*

Antarctic Circle *n* the imaginary circle around the earth at latitude 66° 32′ S.

ante *n* **1** the stake put up before the deal in poker by the players. **2** *Informal* a sum of money representing a person's share. **3 up the ante** *Informal* to increase the costs or risks involved in an action. ✧ *vb* **-teing, -ted** *or* **-teed 4** to place (one's stake) in poker. **5 ante up** *Informal* to pay. ▷ **HISTORY** Latin: before

ante- *prefix* before in time or position: *antediluvian; antechamber.* ▷ **HISTORY** Latin

anteater *n* a mammal with a long snout used for eating termites.

antecedent *n* **1** an event or circumstance that happens or exists before another. **2** *Grammar* a word or phrase to which a relative pronoun, such as *who*, refers. **3 antecedents** a person's ancestors and past history. ✧ *adj* **4** preceding in time or order. ▷ **HISTORY** Latin *antecedere* to go before

antechamber *n* an anteroom.

antedate *vb* **-dating, -dated 1** to be or occur at an earlier date than. **2** to give (something) a date that is earlier than the actual date.

antediluvian *adj* **1** belonging to the ages before the biblical Flood. **2** old-fashioned. ▷ **HISTORY** Latin *ante-* before + *diluvium* flood

antelope *n, pl* **-lopes** *or* **-lope** any of a group of graceful deerlike mammals of Africa and Asia, which have long legs and horns. ▷ **HISTORY** Late Greek *antholops* a legendary beast

antenatal *adj* before birth; during pregnancy: *an antenatal clinic.*

antenna *n* **1** (*pl* **-nae**) one of a pair of mobile feelers on the heads of insects, lobsters, and certain other creatures. **2** (*pl* **-nas**) an aerial: *TV antennas.* ▷ **HISTORY** Latin: sail yard

antepenultimate *adj* **1** third from last. ✧ *n* **2** anything that is third from last.

ante-post *adj Brit* (of a bet) placed before the runners in a race are confirmed.

anterior *adj* **1** at or towards the front. **2** earlier. ▷ **HISTORY** Latin

anteroom *n* a small room leading into a larger room, often used as a waiting room.

anthem *n* **1** a song of loyalty or devotion: *a national anthem.* **2** a piece of music for a choir, usually set to words from the Bible. ▷ **HISTORY** Late Latin *antiphona* antiphon

anther *n Bot* the part of the stamen of a flower which contains the pollen. ▷ **HISTORY** Greek *anthos* flower

ant hill *n* a mound of soil built by ants around the entrance to their nest.

anthology *n, pl* **-gies** a collection of poems or other literary pieces by various authors. ▷ **HISTORY** Greek *anthos* flower + *legein* to collect ▶ **anthologist** *n*

anthracite *n* a hard coal that burns slowly with little smoke or flame but intense heat. ▷ **HISTORY** Greek *anthrax* coal

anthrax *n* a dangerous infectious disease of cattle and sheep, which can be passed to humans. ▷ **HISTORY** Greek: carbuncle

anthropocentric *adj* regarding the human being as the most important factor in the universe. ▷ **HISTORY** Greek *anthrōpos* human being + Latin *centrum* centre

anthropoid *adj* **1** resembling a human being. ✧ *n* **2** an ape, such as the chimpanzee, that resembles a human being.

anthropology *n* the study of human origins, institutions, and beliefs. ▷ **HISTORY** Greek *anthrōpos* human being + *logos* word ▶ **anthropological** *adj* ▶ **anthropologist** *n*

anthropomorphism *n* the attribution of human form or personality to a god, animal, or object. ▶ **anthropomorphic** *adj*

anti *Informal* ✧ *adj* **1** opposed to a party, policy, or attitude. ✧ *n* **2** an opponent of a party, policy, or attitude.

anti- *prefix* **1** against or opposed to: *antiwar.* **2** opposite to: *anticlimax.* **3** counteracting or neutralizing: *antifreeze.* ▷ **HISTORY** Greek

anti-aircraft *adj* for defence against aircraft attack.

antiballistic missile *n* a missile designed to destroy a ballistic missile in flight.

antibiotic *n* **1** a chemical substance capable of destroying bacteria. ✧ *adj* **2** of or relating to antibiotics.

antibody *n, pl* **-bodies** a protein produced in the blood which destroys bacteria.

Antichrist *n* **1** *New Testament* the chief enemy of Christ. **2** an enemy of Christ or Christianity.

anticipate *vb* **-pating, -pated 1** to foresee and act in advance of: *he anticipated some probing questions.* **2** to look forward to. **3** to make use of (something, such as one's salary) before receiving it. **4** to mention (part of a story) before its proper time. ▷ **HISTORY** Latin *ante-* before + *capere* to take ▶ **anticipatory** *adj*

> ☑ **WORD TIP**
> The use of *anticipate* to mean *expect* should be avoided.

anticipation *n* the act of anticipating; expectation, premonition, or foresight: *smiling in happy anticipation.*

anticlerical *adj* opposed to the power and influence of the clergy in politics.

anticlimax *n* a disappointing conclusion to a series of events. ▶ **anticlimactic** *adj*

anticline *n Geol* a fold of rock raised up into a broad arch so that the strata slope down on both sides.

anticlockwise *adv, adj* in the opposite direction to the rotation of the hands of a clock.

anticoagulant (an-tee-koh-**ag**-yew-lant) *n* a substance that prevents the clotting of blood.

antics *pl n* absurd acts or postures. ▷ **HISTORY** Italian *antico* something grotesque (from fantastic carvings found in ruins of ancient Rome)

anticyclone *n Meteorol* an area of moving air of high pressure in which the winds rotate outwards.

antidepressant *n* **1** a drug used to treat depression. ✧ *adj* **2** of or relating to such a drug.

antidote *n* **1** *Med* a substance that counteracts a poison. **2** anything that counteracts a harmful condition: *exercise may be a good antidote to insomnia.* ▷ **HISTORY** Greek *anti-* against + *didonai* to give

anti-Europeanism *n* opposition to or dislike of Europe or the European Union.

antifreeze *n* a liquid added to water to lower its freezing point, used in the radiator of a motor vehicle to prevent freezing.

antigen (**an**-tee-jen) *n* a substance, usually a toxin, that causes the body to produce antibodies. ▷ **HISTORY** *anti(body)* + *-gen* (suffix) producing

antihero *n, pl* **-roes** a central character in a novel, play, or film, who lacks the traditional heroic virtues.

antihistamine *n* a drug that neutralizes the effects of histamine, used in the treatment of allergies.

antiknock *n* a substance added to motor fuel to reduce knocking in the engine caused by too rapid combustion.

antilogarithm *n Maths* a number corresponding to a given logarithm.

antimacassar *n* a cloth put over the back of a chair to prevent it getting dirty. ▷ **HISTORY** *anti-* + *Macassar (oil)*

antimatter *n Physics* a hypothetical form of matter composed of antiparticles.

anti-microbial *adj Biochem* preventing the growth of disease-causing bacteria.

antimony (**an**-tim-mon-ee) *n Chem* a silvery-white metallic element that is added to alloys to increase their strength. Symbol: Sb. ▷ **HISTORY** Medieval Latin *antimonium*

antinomy (**an**-tin-nom-ee) *n, pl* **-mies** contradiction between two laws or principles that are reasonable in themselves. ▷ **HISTORY** Greek *anti-* against + *nomos* law

antinovel *n* a type of prose fiction in which conventional elements of the novel are rejected.

antinuclear *adj* opposed to nuclear weapons or nuclear power.

antioxidant *n Chem* a substance that slows down the process of oxidation.

antiparticle *n Nuclear physics* an elementary particle that has the same mass as its corresponding particle, but opposite charge and opposite magnetism.

antipasto *n, pl* **-tos** an appetizer in an Italian meal. ▷ HISTORY Italian: before food

antipathy (an-**tip**-a-thee) *n* a feeling of strong dislike or hostility. ▷ HISTORY Greek *anti-* against + *patheia* feeling ▸ **antipathetic** *adj*

antipersonnel *adj* (of weapons or bombs) designed to be used against people rather than equipment.

antiperspirant *n* a substance applied to the skin to reduce or prevent perspiration.

antiphon *n* a hymn sung in alternate parts by two groups of singers. ▷ HISTORY Greek *anti-* against + *phōnē* sound

antipodes (an-**tip**-pod-deez) *pl n* **1** any two places that are situated diametrically opposite one another on the earth's surface. **2 the Antipodes** *Brit* Australia and New Zealand. ▷ HISTORY Greek plural of *antipous* having the feet opposite ▸ **antipodean** *adj*

antipope *n* a pope set up in opposition to the one chosen by church laws.

antipyretic *adj* **1** reducing fever. ✧ *n* **2** a drug that reduces fever.

antiquarian *adj* **1** collecting or dealing with antiquities or rare books. ✧ *n* **2** an antiquary.

antiquary *n, pl* **-quaries** a person who collects, deals in, or studies antiques or ancient works of art.

antiquated *adj* obsolete or old-fashioned. ▷ HISTORY Latin *antiquus* ancient

antique *n* **1** a decorative object or piece of furniture, of an earlier period, that is valued for its beauty, workmanship, and age. ✧ *adj* **2** made in an earlier period. **3** *Informal* old-fashioned. ▷ HISTORY Latin *antiquus* ancient

antiquity *n, pl* **-ties 1** great age. **2** the far distant past. **3 antiquities** objects dating from ancient times.

antiracism *n* the policy of challenging racism or promoting racial tolerance. ▸ **antiracist** *n, adj*

antirrhinum *n* a two-lipped flower of various colours, such as the snapdragon. ▷ HISTORY Greek *anti-* like, imitating + *rhis* nose

antiscorbutic *adj* preventing or curing scurvy.

anti-Semitic *adj* discriminating against Jews. ▸ **anti-Semite** *n* ▸ **anti-Semitism** *n*

antiseptic *adj* **1** preventing infection by killing germs. ✧ *n* **2** an antiseptic substance.

antiserum *n* blood serum containing antibodies used to treat or provide immunity to a disease.

antisocial *adj* **1** avoiding the company of other people. **2** (of behaviour) annoying or harmful to other people.

antistatic *adj* reducing the effects of static electricity.

antistrophe *n* **1** *Drama* the movement of the chorus as it performs the second part of a choral ode in ancient Greek drama. **2** *Poetry* the second of two metrical systems used within a poem.

antitank *adj* (of weapons) designed to destroy military tanks.

antithesis (an-**tith**-iss-iss) *n, pl* **-ses** (-seez) **1** the exact opposite. **2** *Rhetoric* the placing together of contrasting ideas or words to produce an effect of balance, such as *where gods command, mere mortals must obey.* ▷ HISTORY Greek *anti-* against + *tithenai* to place ▸ **antithetical** *adj*

antitoxin *n* an antibody that acts against a toxin. ▸ **antitoxic** *adj*

antitrades *pl n* winds blowing in the opposite direction from and above the trade winds.

antitrust *adj US, Austral & S African* (of laws) opposing business monopolies.

antler *n* one of a pair of branched horns on the heads of male deer. ▷ HISTORY Old French *antoillier*

antonym *n* a word that means the opposite of another. ▷ HISTORY Greek *anti-* opposite + *onoma* name

antrum *n, pl* **-tra** *Anat* a natural cavity, esp. in a bone. ▷ HISTORY Latin: cave

Anubis *n* an Egyptian god with a jackal's head.

anus (**ain**-uss) *n* the opening at the end of the alimentary canal, through which faeces are discharged. ▷ HISTORY Latin

anvil *n* a heavy iron block on which metals are hammered into particular shapes. ▷ HISTORY Old English *anfealt*

anxiety *n, pl* **-ties 1** a state of uneasiness about what may happen. **2** eagerness: *she was uneasy with his mixture of diffidence and anxiety to please.*

anxious *adj* **1** worried and tense. **2** causing anxiety: *Sharpe faces an anxious wait for a specialist's report.* **3** intensely desiring: *both sides were anxious for a deal.* ▷ HISTORY Latin *anxius* ▸ **anxiously** *adv*

any *adj, pron* **1** one, some, or several, no matter how much or what kind: *the jar opener fits over the top of any bottle or jar; have you left me any?* **2** even the smallest amount or even one: *we can't answer any questions; don't give her any.* **3** whatever or whichever: *police may board any bus or train.* **4** an indefinite or unlimited amount or number: *he would sign cheques for any amount of money.* ✧ *adv* **5** to even the smallest extent: *the outcome wouldn't have been any different.* ▷ HISTORY Old English *ǣnig*

anybody *pron* same as **anyone**.

anyhow *adv* same as **anyway**.

anyone *pron* **1** any person: *is anyone there?* **2** a person of any importance: *is he anyone?*

anything *pron* **1** any object, event, or action whatever: *they'll do anything to please you.* ✧ *adv* **2** in any way: *it is not a computer nor anything like a computer.* **3 anything but** not at all: *the result is anything but simple.*

anyway *adv* **1** at any rate; nevertheless. **2** in any manner. **3** carelessly.

anywhere *adv* **1** in, at, or to any place. **2 get anywhere** to be successful: *we will not get anywhere by being negative.*

anzac *n NZ* a type of biscuit.

Anzac *n* (in the First World War) a soldier serving with the Australian and New Zealand Army Corps.

Anzac Day *n* 25th April, a public holiday in Australia and New Zealand commemorating the Anzac landing at Gallipoli in 1915.

AOB (on the agenda for a meeting) any other business.

aorta (eh-**or**-ta) *n* the main artery of the body, which carries oxygen-rich blood from the heart. ▷ **HISTORY** Greek *aortē* something lifted

apace *adv Literary* quickly: *repairs to the grid continued apace.*

Apache *n, pl* **Apaches** *or* **Apache** a member of a Native American people of the southwestern US and N Mexico. ▷ **HISTORY** Mexican Spanish

apart *adj, adv* **1** to or in pieces: *he took a couple of cars apart and rebuilt them.* **2** separate in time, place, or position: *my father and myself stood slightly apart from them.* **3** individual or distinct: *a nation apart.* **4** not being taken into account: *early timing difficulties apart, they encountered few problems.* **5 apart from** other than: *apart from searching the house there is little more we can do.* ▷ **HISTORY** Old French *a part* at (the) side

apartheid *n* (formerly) the official government policy of racial segregation in South Africa. ▷ **HISTORY** Afrikaans *apart* + *-heid* -hood

apartment *n* **1** any room in a building, usually one of several forming a suite, used as living accommodation. **2** *Chiefly US & Canad* a flat. ▷ **HISTORY** French *appartement*

apathy *n* lack of interest or enthusiasm. ▷ **HISTORY** Greek *a-* without + *pathos* feeling ▸ **apathetic** *adj*

ape *n* **1** an animal, such as a chimpanzee or gorilla, which is closely related to human beings and the monkeys, and which has no tail. **2** a stupid, clumsy, or ugly man. ✧ *vb* **aping, aped 3** to imitate. ▷ **HISTORY** Old English *apa* ▸ **apelike** *adj*

apeman *n, pl* **-men** an extinct primate thought to have been the forerunner of true humans.

aperient (ap-**peer**-ee-ent) *Med* ✧ *adj* **1** having a mild laxative effect. ✧ *n* **2** a mild laxative. ▷ **HISTORY** Latin *aperire* to open

aperitif (ap-per-rit-**teef**) *n* an alcoholic drink taken before a meal. ▷ **HISTORY** French

aperture *n* **1** a hole or opening. **2** an opening in a camera or telescope that controls the amount of light entering it. ▷ **HISTORY** Latin *aperire* to open

apex *n* the highest point. ▷ **HISTORY** Latin: point

APEX Advance Purchase Excursion: a reduced fare for journeys booked a specified period in advance.

aphasia *n* a disorder of the central nervous system that affects the ability to use and understand words. ▷ **HISTORY** Greek *a-* not + *phanai* to speak

aphelion (ap-**heel**-lee-on) *n, pl* **-lia** (-lee-a) *Astron* the point in the orbit of a planet or comet when it is farthest from the sun. ▷ **HISTORY** Greek *apo-* from + *hēlios* sun

aphid (**eh**-fid) *or* **aphis** (**eh**-fiss) *n, pl* **aphids** *or* **aphides** (**eh**-fid-deez) a small insect which feeds by sucking the juices from plants. ▷ **HISTORY** New Latin

aphorism *n* a short clever saying expressing a general truth. ▷ **HISTORY** Greek *aphorizein* to define

aphrodisiac (af-roh-**diz**-zee-ak) *n* **1** a substance that arouses sexual desire. ✧ *adj* **2** arousing sexual desire. ▷ **HISTORY** Greek *aphrodisios* belonging to *Aphrodite*, goddess of love

Aphrodite *n Greek myth* the goddess of love.

apiary (**ape**-yar-ee) *n, pl* **-aries** a place where bees are kept. ▷ **HISTORY** Latin *apis* bee ▸ **apiarist** *n*

apiculture *n* the breeding and care of bees. ▷ **HISTORY** Latin *apis* bee + CULTURE ▸ **apiculturist** *n*

apiece *adv* each: *they had another cocktail apiece and then went down to dinner.*

aplomb (ap-**plom**) *n* calm self-possession. ▷ **HISTORY** French: uprightness

apocalypse *n* **1** the end of the world. **2** an event of great destructive violence. ▸ **apocalyptic** *adj*

WORD HISTORY

This word comes from Greek *apokaluptein*, which means 'to reveal or disclose'. An apocalypse is a prophetic disclosure of something that is going to happen, such as the description of the end of the world given in the last book of the Bible, the 'Revelation of St John the Divine', which is also known as 'the Apocalypse'.

Apocalypse *n* **the Apocalypse** *Bible* the Book of Revelation, the last book of the New Testament.

Apocrypha (ap-**pok**-rif-fa) *pl n* **the Apocrypha** the 14 books included as an appendix to the Old Testament, which are not accepted as part of the Hebrew scriptures. ▷ **HISTORY** Late Latin *apocrypha (scripta)* hidden (writings), from Greek *apokruptein* to hide away

apocryphal *adj* of questionable authenticity: *the paranoid and clearly apocryphal story.*

apogee (**ap**-oh-jee) *n* **1** *Astron* the point in its orbit around the earth when the moon or a satellite is farthest from the earth. **2** the highest point: *the concept found its apogee in Renaissance Italy.* ▷ **HISTORY** Greek *apogaios* away from the earth

apolitical *adj* not concerned with political matters.

Apollo *n Classical myth* the god of the sun, music, and medicine.

apologetic *adj* showing or expressing regret. ▸ **apologetically** *adv*

apologetics *n* the branch of theology concerned with the reasoned defence of Christianity.

apologia *n* a formal written defence of a cause.

apologist *n* a person who offers a formal defence of a cause.

apologize *or* **-gise** *vb* **-gizing, -gized** *or* **-gising, -gised** to say that one is sorry for some wrongdoing.

apology *n, pl* **-gies 1** an expression of regret for some wrongdoing. **2** same as **apologia**. **3 an**

a b c d e f g h i j k l m n o p q r s t u v w x y z

A B C D E F G H I J K L M N O P Q R S T U V W X Y Z

apology for a poor example of: *an apology for a man.* ▷ **HISTORY** Greek *apologia* a verbal defence, speech

apoplectic *adj* **1** of apoplexy. **2** *Informal* furious.

apoplexy *n Med* a stroke. ▷ **HISTORY** Greek *apoplēssein* to cripple by a stroke

apostasy (ap-**poss**-stass-ee) *n, pl* **-sies** abandonment of one's religious faith, political party, or cause. ▷ **HISTORY** Greek *apostasis* desertion

apostate *n* **1** a person who has abandoned his or her religion, political party, or cause. ✧ *adj* **2** guilty of apostasy.

a posteriori (**eh** poss-steer-ee-**or**-rye) *adj Logic* involving reasoning from effect to cause. ▷ **HISTORY** Latin: from the latter

apostle *n* **1** one of the twelve disciples chosen by Christ to preach his gospel. **2** an ardent supporter of a cause or movement. ▷ **HISTORY** Greek *apostolos* a messenger

apostolic (ap-poss-**stoll**-ik) *adj* **1** of or relating to the Apostles or their teachings. **2** of or relating to the pope.

Apostolic See *n* the see of the pope, at Rome.

apostrophe[1] (ap-**poss**-trof-fee) *n* the punctuation mark (') used to indicate the omission of a letter or letters, such as *he's* for *he has* or *he is,* and to form the possessive, as in *John's father.* ▷ **HISTORY** Greek *apostrephein* to turn away

apostrophe[2] *n Rhetoric* a digression from a speech to address an imaginary or absent person or thing. ▷ **HISTORY** Greek: a turning away

apostrophize *or* **-phise** *vb* **-phizing, -phized** *or* **-phising, -phised** *Rhetoric* to address an apostrophe to.

apothecary *n, pl* **-caries** *Old-fashioned* a chemist. ▷ **HISTORY** Late Latin *apothecarius* warehouseman

apotheosis (ap-poth-ee-**oh**-siss) *n, pl* **-ses** (-seez) **1** a perfect example: *it was the apotheosis of elitism.* **2** elevation to the rank of a god. ▷ **HISTORY** Greek

appal *or US* **appall** *vb* **-palling, -palled** to fill with horror; terrify. ▷ **HISTORY** Old French *appalir* to turn pale

appalling *adj* **1** causing dismay, horror, or revulsion. **2** very bad. ▶ **appallingly** *adv*

apparatus *n* **1** a collection of equipment used for a particular purpose. **2** any complicated device, system, or organization: *the whole apparatus of law enforcement.* ▷ **HISTORY** Latin

apparel (ap-**par**-rel) *n Old-fashioned* clothing. ▷ **HISTORY** Latin *parare* to prepare

apparent *adj* **1** readily seen or understood; obvious. **2** seeming as opposed to real: *he frowned in apparent bewilderment.* **3** *Physics* as observed but ignoring such factors as the motion of the observer and changes in the environment: *apparent depth.* ▷ **HISTORY** Latin *apparere* to appear ▶ **apparently** *adv*

apparition *n* a ghost or ghostlike figure. ▷ **HISTORY** Latin *apparere* to appear

appeal *vb* **1** to make an earnest request. **2 appeal to** to attract, please, or interest. **3** *Law* to apply to a higher court to review (a case or issue decided by a lower court). **4** to resort to a higher authority to change a decision. **5** to call on in support of an earnest request: *he appealed for volunteers to help in relief work.* **6** *Cricket* to request the umpire to declare a batsman out. ✧ *n* **7** an earnest request for money or help. **8** the power to attract, please, or interest people. **9** *Law* a request for a review of a lower court's decision by a higher court. **10** an application to a higher authority to change a decision that has been made. **11** *Cricket* a request to the umpire to declare the batsman out. ▷ **HISTORY** Latin *appellare* to entreat

appealing *adj* attractive or pleasing.

appear *vb* **1** to come into sight. **2** to seem: *it appears that no one survived the crash.* **3** to come into existence: *a rash and small sores appeared around the shoulder and neck.* **4** to perform: *she hadn't appeared in a film for almost fifty years.* **5** to be present in court before a magistrate or judge: *two men have appeared in court in London charged with conspiracy.* **6** to be published or become available: *both books appeared in 1934.* ▷ **HISTORY** Latin *apparere*

appearance *n* **1** a sudden or unexpected arrival of someone or something at a place. **2** the introduction or invention of something: *the appearance of credit cards.* **3** an act or instance of appearing: *it will be his fiftieth appearance for his country.* **4** the way a person or thing looks: *I spotted a man of extraordinary appearance.* **5 keep up appearances** to maintain the public impression of wellbeing or normality. **6 put in an appearance** to attend an event briefly. **7 to all appearances** apparently: *to all appearances they seemed enthralled by what he was saying.*

appease *vb* **-peasing, -peased 1** to pacify (someone) by yielding to his or her demands. **2** to satisfy or relieve (a feeling). ▷ **HISTORY** Old French *apaisier*

appeasement *n* **1** the act of appeasing. **2** *History* (in the 1930s) the policy adopted by Britain and France of giving in to Hitler's demands and accepting German political and military changes in the hope of maintaining peace with Germany.

appellant *Law* ✧ *n* **1** a person who appeals to a higher court to review the decision of a lower court. ✧ *adj* **2** same as **appellate**.

appellate (ap-**pell**-it) *adj Law* **1** of appeals. **2** (of a tribunal) having the power to review appeals.

appellate jurisdiction *n Law* the authority (of a court) to hear appeals.

appellation *n Formal* a name or title.

append *vb Formal* to add as a supplement: *a series of notes appended to his translation of the poems.* ▷ **HISTORY** Latin *pendere* to hang

appendage *n* a secondary part attached to a main part.

appendicectomy *or esp US, Canad & Australia* **appendectomy** *n, pl* **-mies** surgical removal of the appendix. ▷ **HISTORY** *appendix* + Greek *tomē* a cutting

appendicitis *n* inflammation of the appendix, causing abdominal pain.

appendix (ap-**pen**-dix) *n, pl* **-dices** (-diss-seez) *or* **-dixes 1** separate additional material at the end of a book. **2** *Anat* a short thin tube, closed at one end and attached to the large intestine at the other end. ▷ HISTORY Latin

appertain *vb* **appertain to** to belong to, relate to, or be connected with. ▷ HISTORY Latin *ad-* to + *pertinere* to pertain

appetence *or* **appetency** *n, pl* **-tences** *or* **-tencies** a craving or desire. ▷ HISTORY Latin *appetentia*

appetite *n* **1** a desire for food or drink. **2** a liking or willingness: *he had an insatiable appetite for publicity.* ▷ HISTORY Latin *appetere* to desire ardently

appetizer *or* **-iser** *n* a small amount of food or drink taken at the start of a meal to stimulate the appetite.

appetizing *or* **-ising** *adj* stimulating the appetite; looking or smelling delicious.

applaud *vb* **1** to show approval of by clapping one's hands. **2** to express approval of: *we applaud her determination and ambition.* ▷ HISTORY Latin *applaudere*

applause *n* appreciation shown by clapping one's hands.

apple *n* **1** a round firm fruit with red, yellow, or green skin and crisp whitish flesh, that grows on trees. **2 apple of one's eye** a person that one loves very much. ▷ HISTORY Old English *æppel*

applet *n Computers* a computing program that runs within a page on the World Wide Web. ▷ HISTORY *app(lication program)* + *-let* small or lesser

appliance *n* a machine or device that has a specific function.

applicable *adj* appropriate or relevant.

applicant *n* a person who applies for something, such as a job or grant.

application *n* **1** a formal request, for example for a job. **2** the act of applying something to a particular use: *you can make practical application of this knowledge to everyday living.* **3** concentrated effort: *success would depend on their talent and application.* **4** the act of putting something, such as a lotion or paint, onto a surface.

applicator *n* a device for applying cosmetics, medication, or some other substance.

applied *adj* put to practical use: *applied mathematics.*

appliqué (ap-**plee**-kay) *n* a kind of decoration in which one material is cut out and sewn or fixed onto another. ▷ HISTORY French: applied

apply *vb* **-plies, -plying, -plied 1** to make a formal request for something, such as a job or a loan. **2** to put to practical use: *he applied his calligrapher's skill.* **3** to put onto a surface: *the hand lotion should be applied whenever possible throughout the day.* **4** to be relevant or appropriate: *he had been involved in research applied to flying wing aircraft.* **5 apply oneself** to concentrate one's efforts or faculties. ▷ HISTORY Latin *applicare* to attach to

appoint *vb* **1** to assign officially to a job or position. **2** to fix or decide (a time or place for an event). **3** to equip or furnish: *it was a beautifully appointed room with rows and rows of books.* ▷ HISTORY Old French *apointer* to put into a good state ▸ **appointee** *n*

appointment *n* **1** an arrangement to meet a person. **2** the act of placing someone in a job or position. **3** the person appointed. **4** the job or position to which a person is appointed. **5 appointments** fixtures or fittings.

apportion *vb* to divide out in shares.

apposite *adj* suitable or appropriate: *an apposite saying.* ▷ HISTORY Latin *ad-* near + *ponere* to put

apposition *n* a grammatical construction in which a noun or group of words is placed after another to modify its meaning, for example *my friend the mayor.*

appraisal *n* an assessment of the worth or quality of a person or thing.

appraise *vb* **-praising, -praised** to assess the worth, value, or quality of. ▷ HISTORY Old French *aprisier*

> **WORD TIP**
> *Appraise* is sometimes wrongly used where *apprise* is meant: *they had been apprised* (not *appraised*) *of my arrival.*

appreciable *adj* enough to be noticed; significant. ▸ **appreciably** *adv*

appreciate *vb* **-ating, -ated 1** to value highly: *we appreciate his music but can't afford £400 a seat.* **2** to be aware of and understand: *I can fully appreciate how desperate you must feel.* **3** to feel grateful for: *we do appreciate all you do for us.* **4** to increase in value. ▷ HISTORY Latin *pretium* price

appreciation *n* **1** gratitude. **2** awareness and understanding of a problem or difficulty. **3** sensitive recognition of good qualities, as in art. **4** an increase in value.

appreciative *adj* feeling or expressing appreciation. ▸ **appreciatively** *adv*

apprehend *vb* **1** to arrest and take into custody. **2** to grasp (something) mentally; understand. ▷ HISTORY Latin *apprehendere* to lay hold of

apprehension *n* **1** anxiety or dread. **2** the act of arresting. **3** understanding.

apprehensive *adj* fearful or anxious about the future.

apprentice *n* **1** someone who works for a skilled person for a fixed period in order to learn his or her trade. ✧ *vb* **-ticing, -ticed 2** to take or place as an apprentice. ▷ HISTORY Old French *aprendre* to learn ▸ **apprenticeship** *n*

apprise *or* **-prize** *vb* **-prising, -prised** *or* **-prizing, -prized** to make aware: *I needed to apprise* *the students of the dangers that may be involved.* ▷ **HISTORY** French *apprendre* to teach; learn

> **WORD TIP**
> See at **appraise.**

appro *n* **on appro** *Informal* on approval.
approach *vb* **1** to come close or closer to. **2** to make a proposal or suggestion to. **3** to begin to deal with (a matter). ✧ *n* **4** the act of coming close or closer. **5** a proposal or suggestion made to a person. **6** the way or means of reaching a place; access. **7** a way of dealing with a matter. **8** an approximation. **9** the course followed by an aircraft preparing for landing. ▷ **HISTORY** Latin *ad-* to + *prope* near ▶ **approachable** *adj*
approach road *n NZ & S African* a smaller road leading into a major road.
approbation *n* approval.
appropriate *adj* **1** right or suitable. ✧ *vb* **-ating, -ated 2** to take for one's own use without permission. **3** to put (money) aside for a particular purpose. ▷ **HISTORY** Latin *ad-* to + *proprius* one's own ▶ **appropriately** *adv*
appropriation *n* **1** the act of putting money aside for a particular purpose. **2** money put aside for a particular purpose.
approval *n* **1** consent. **2** a favourable opinion. **3 on approval** (of articles for sale) with an option to be returned without payment if unsatisfactory: *each volume in the collection will be sent to you on approval.*
approve *vb* **-proving, -proved 1 approve of** to consider fair, good, or right. **2** to authorize or agree to. ▷ **HISTORY** Latin *approbare*
approx. approximate or approximately.
approximate *adj* **1** almost but not quite exact. ✧ *vb* **-mating, -mated 2 approximate to a** to come close to. **b** to be almost the same as. ▷ **HISTORY** Latin *ad-* to + *proximus* nearest ▶ **approximately** *adv* ▶ **approximation** *n*
appurtenances *pl n* minor or additional features or possessions. ▷ **HISTORY** Old French *apartenance* secondary thing
APR annual percentage rate.
Apr. April.
après-ski (ap-ray-**skee**) *n* social activities after a day's skiing.
apricot *n* **1** a yellowish-orange juicy fruit which resembles a small peach. ✧ *adj* **2** yellowish-orange.

> **WORD HISTORY**
> This word has a long and interesting history. It comes originally from the Latin word *praecox*, meaning 'early ripening'. From Latin it was borrowed into Greek, and then into Arabic as *al-birqūq*, denoting the apricot, which flowers and ripens earlier than the peach. From Arabic, it came back to Europe as Portuguese *albricoque*, and from Portuguese into English as the 'apricock', later altered to 'apricot'.

April *n* the fourth month of the year. ▷ **HISTORY** Latin *Aprilis*
April fool *n* a victim of a practical joke played on the first of April (**April Fools' Day** *or* **All Fools' Day**).
a priori (**eh** pry-**or**-rye) *adj Logic* involving reasoning from cause to effect. ▷ **HISTORY** Latin: from the previous
apron *n* **1** a garment worn over the front of the body to protect one's clothes. **2** a hard-surfaced area at an airport or hangar for manoeuvring and loading aircraft. **3** the part of a stage extending in front of the curtain. **4 tied to someone's apron strings** dependent on or dominated by someone. ▷ **HISTORY** Old French *naperon* little cloth
apropos (ap-prop-**poh**) *adj* **1** appropriate. ✧ *adv* **2** by the way; incidentally. **3 apropos of** with regard to. ▷ **HISTORY** French *à propos* to the purpose
apse *n* an arched or domed recess at the east end of a church. ▷ **HISTORY** Greek *apsis* a fitting together
apsis (**ap**-siss) *n, pl* **apsides** (**ap**-sid-deez) *Astron* either of two points lying at the extremities of the elliptical orbit of a planet or satellite. ▷ **HISTORY** see APSE
apt *adj* **1** having a specified tendency: *they are apt to bend the rules.* **2** suitable or appropriate. **3** quick to learn: *she was turning out to be a more apt pupil than he had expected.* ▷ **HISTORY** Latin *aptus* fitting ▶ **aptly** *adv* ▶ **aptness** *n*
APT *Brit* Advanced Passenger Train.
apteryx *n* same as **kiwi** (sense 1). ▷ **HISTORY** Greek *a-* without + *pteron* wing
aptitude *n* natural tendency or ability.
aqua *adj* short for **aquamarine.** ▷ **HISTORY** Latin: water
aquaculture *or* **aquiculture** *n Agriculture* the cultivation of freshwater and marine organisms for human consumption or use. ▷ **HISTORY** Latin *aqua* water + *cultura* cultivation
aqua fortis *n Obsolete* nitric acid. ▷ **HISTORY** Latin: strong water
aqualung *n* an apparatus for breathing underwater, consisting of a mouthpiece attached to air cylinders.
aquamarine *n* **1** a clear greenish-blue gemstone. ✧ *adj* **2** greenish-blue. ▷ **HISTORY** Latin *aqua marina* sea water
aquaplane *n* **1** a board on which a person stands to be towed by a motorboat for sport. ✧ *vb* **-planing, -planed 2** to ride on an aquaplane. **3** (of a motor vehicle) to skim uncontrollably on a thin film of water.
aqua regia (**ak**-wa **reej**-ya) *n* a mixture of nitric acid and hydrochloric acid. ▷ **HISTORY** New Latin: royal water; referring to its use in dissolving gold, the royal metal
aquarium *n, pl* **aquariums** *or* **aquaria 1** a tank in which fish and other underwater creatures are kept. **2** a building containing such tanks. ▷ **HISTORY** Latin *aquarius* relating to water
Aquarius *n Astrol* the eleventh sign of the zodiac: the Water Carrier. ▷ **HISTORY** Latin
aquatic *adj* **1** growing or living in water. **2** *Sport* performed in or on water. ✧ *n* **3** an aquatic animal

or plant. **4 aquatics** water sports. ▷ **HISTORY** Latin *aqua* water

aquatint *n* a print like a watercolour, produced by etching copper with acid. ▷ **HISTORY** Italian *acqua tinta* dyed water

aqua vitae (**ak**-wa **vee**-tie) *n Old-fashioned* brandy. ▷ **HISTORY** Medieval Latin: water of life

aqueduct *n* a structure, often a bridge, that carries water across a valley or river. ▷ **HISTORY** Latin *aqua* water + *ducere* to convey

aqueous *adj* **1** of, like, or containing water. **2** produced by the action of water. ▷ **HISTORY** Latin *aqua* water

aqueous humour *n Physiol* the watery fluid in the eyeball, between the cornea and the lens.

aquifer *n Geol* a water-bearing layer of rock that can be used to supply wells. ▷ **HISTORY** Latin *aqua* water + *ferre* to carry

aquiline *adj* **1** (of a nose) curved like an eagle's beak. **2** of or like an eagle. ▷ **HISTORY** Latin *aquila* eagle

Ar *Chem* argon.

AR Arkansas.

Arab *n* **1** a member of a Semitic people originally from Arabia. ✧ *adj* **2** of the Arabs. ▷ **HISTORY** Arabic *'Arab*

arabesque (ar-ab-**besk**) *n* **1** a ballet position in which one leg is raised behind and the arms are extended. **2** *Arts* an elaborate design of intertwined leaves, flowers, and scrolls. **3** an ornate piece of music. ▷ **HISTORY** Italian *arabesco* in the Arabic style

Arabian *adj* **1** of Arabia or the Arabs. ✧ *n* **2** same as **Arab**.

Arabic *n* **1** the language of the Arabs. ✧ *adj* **2** of this language, the Arabs, or Arabia.

Arabic numerals *pl n* the symbols 1, 2, 3, 4, 5, 6, 7, 8, 9, 0, used to represent numbers.

arable *adj* (of land) suitable for growing crops on. ▷ **HISTORY** Latin *arare* to plough

arable farming *n Agriculture* the commercial growing of crops.

arachnid (ar-**rak**-nid) *n* an eight-legged insect-like creature, such as a spider, scorpion, or tick. ▷ **HISTORY** Greek *arakhnē* spider

arak *n* same as **arrack**.

Aramaic *n* an ancient Semitic language spoken in parts of Syria and the Lebanon.

Aran *adj* (of knitwear) knitted in a complicated pattern traditional to the Aran Islands off the west coast of Ireland.

arbiter *n* **1** a person empowered to judge in a dispute. **2** a person with influential opinions about something: *the customer must be the ultimate arbiter of quality.*

arbitrary *adj* **1** not done according to any plan or for any particular reason. **2** without consideration for the wishes of others: *the arbitrary power of the king.* ▶ **arbitrarily** *adv*

arbitrate *vb* **-trating, -trated** to settle (a dispute) by arbitration. ▷ **HISTORY** Latin *arbitrari* to give judgment ▶ **arbitrator** *n*

arbitration *n* the hearing and settlement of a dispute by an impartial referee chosen by both sides.

arbor[1] *n US* same as **arbour**.

arbor[2] *n* a revolving shaft or axle in a machine. ▷ **HISTORY** Latin: tree

arboreal (ahr-**bore**-ee-al) *adj* **1** of or resembling a tree. **2** living in or among trees.

arboretum (ahr-bore-**ee**-tum) *n, pl* **-ta** (-ta) a botanical garden where rare trees or shrubs are cultivated. ▷ **HISTORY** Latin *arbor* tree

arboriculture *n* the cultivation of trees or shrubs. ▷ **HISTORY** Latin *arbor* tree + CULTURE

arbor vitae (**ahr**-bore **vee**-tie) *n* an evergreen tree. ▷ **HISTORY** New Latin: tree of life

arbour *or US* **arbor** *n* a shelter in a garden shaded by trees or climbing plants. ▷ **HISTORY** Latin *herba* grass

arbutus (ar-**byew**-tuss) *n* an evergreen shrub with berries like strawberries. ▷ **HISTORY** Latin

arc *n* **1** something curved in shape. **2** *Maths* a section of a circle or other curve. **3** *Electricity* a stream of very bright light that forms when an electric current flows across a small gap between two electrodes. ✧ *vb* **4** to form an arc. ▷ **HISTORY** Latin *arcus* bow, arch

ARC AIDS-related complex: relatively mild symptoms suffered in the early stages of infection with the AIDS virus.

arcade *n* **1** a covered passageway lined with shops. **2** a set of arches and their supporting columns. ▷ **HISTORY** Latin *arcus* bow, arch

Arcadian *Literary* ✧ *adj* **1** rural, in an idealized way. ✧ *n* **2** a person who leads a quiet simple country life. ▷ **HISTORY** *Arcadia,* rural district of Ancient Greece

arcane *adj* very mysterious. ▷ **HISTORY** Latin *arcanus* secret

arch[1] *n* **1** a curved structure that spans an opening or supports a bridge or roof. **2** something curved. **3** the curved lower part of the foot. ✧ *vb* **4** to form an arch. ▷ **HISTORY** Latin *arcus* bow, arc

arch[2] *adj* **1** knowing or superior. **2** coyly playful: *he gave an arch smile to indicate his pride.* ▷ **HISTORY** independent use of ARCH- ▶ **archly** *adv*

arch- *or* **archi-** *combining form* chief or principal: *archbishop; archenemy.* ▷ **HISTORY** Greek *arkhein* to rule

archaeobotany *n* the study of plant remains found at archaeological sites. ▶ **archaeobotanist** *n*

archaeology *or* **archeology** *n* the study of ancient cultures by the scientific analysis of physical remains. ▷ **HISTORY** Greek *arkhaiologia* study of what is ancient ▶ **archaeological** *or* **archeological** *adj* ▶ **archaeologist** *or* **archeologist** *n*

archaeopteryx *n* an extinct primitive bird with teeth, a long tail, and well-developed wings. ▷ **HISTORY** Greek *arkhaios* ancient + *pterux* winged creature

archaeozoology *n* the study of animal remains found at archaeological sites. ▶ **archaeozoologist** *n*

A B C D E F G H I J K L M N O P Q R S T U V W X Y Z

archaic (ark-**kay**-ik) *adj* **1** of a much earlier period. **2** out of date or old-fashioned. **3** (of a word or phrase) no longer in everyday use. ▷ HISTORY Greek *arkhē* beginning ▶ **archaically** *adv*

archaism (**ark**-kay-iz-zum) *n* an archaic word or style. ▶ **archaistic** *adj*

archangel (**ark**-ain-jell) *n* an angel of the highest rank.

archbishop *n* a bishop of the highest rank.

archbishopric *n* the rank, office, or diocese of an archbishop.

archdeacon *n* a church official ranking just below a bishop. ▶ **archdeaconry** *n*

archdiocese *n* the diocese of an archbishop.

archduchess *n* **1** a woman who holds the rank of archduke. **2** the wife or widow of an archduke.

archduchy *n, pl* **-duchies** the territory ruled by an archduke or archduchess.

archduke *n* a duke of high rank, esp. one from Austria.

archenemy *n, pl* **-mies** a chief enemy.

archeology *n* same as **archaeology**.

archer *n* a person who shoots with a bow and arrow. ▷ HISTORY Latin *arcus* bow

archery *n* the art or sport of shooting with a bow and arrow.

archetype (**ark**-ee-type) *n* **1** a perfect or typical specimen. **2** an original model; prototype. ▷ HISTORY Greek *arkhetupos* first-moulded ▶ **archetypal** *adj*

archidiaconal (ark-ee-die-**ak**-on-al) *adj* of an archdeacon or his office.

archiepiscopal (ark-ee-ip-**piss**-kop-al) *adj* of an archbishop or his office.

Archimedes' principle (ark-ee-**mee**-deez) *n Physics* the principle that the apparent loss in weight of an object immersed in a fluid is equal to the weight of the displaced fluid. ▷ HISTORY after *Archimedes,* Greek mathematician & physicist

archipelago (ark-ee-**pel**-a-go) *n, pl* **-gos** *Geography* **1** a group of islands. **2** a sea full of small islands. ▷ HISTORY Greek *arkhi-* chief + *pelagos* sea

architect *n* **1** a person qualified to design and supervise the construction of buildings. **2** any planner or creator: *you will be the architect of your own future.* ▷ HISTORY Greek *arkhi-* chief + *tektōn* workman

architecture *n* **1** the style in which a building is designed and built: *Gothic architecture.* **2** the science of designing and constructing buildings. **3** the structure or design of anything: *computer architecture.* ▶ **architectural** *adj*

architrave (**ark**-ee-trave) *n Archit* **1** a beam that rests on top of columns. **2** a moulding around a doorway or window opening. ▷ HISTORY Italian, from *arch-* + *trave* beam

archive (**ark**-ive) *n* **1** a place where records or documents are kept. **2 archives** a collection of records or documents. **3** *Computers* data put on tape or disk for long-term storage. ✧ *vb* **4** to store in an archive.

archivist (**ark**-iv-ist) *n* a person in charge of archives.

archway *n* a passageway under an arch.

Arctic *n* **1 the Arctic** the area around the North Pole. ✧ *adj* **2** of this region.

> **WORD HISTORY**
>
> The word 'arctic' comes from the Greek adjective *arktikos*, meaning 'relating to a bear' (Greek *arktos*). In Greek *arktikos* also meant 'relating to the Great Bear', the constellation which can be seen in the northern sky and which points towards the Pole Star.

Arctic Circle *n* the imaginary circle around the earth at latitude 66° 32′ N.

arctic hare *n* a large hare of the Canadian Arctic whose fur turns white in winter.

arctic willow *n* a low-growing shrub of the Canadian Arctic.

arcuate delta *n Geog* a fan-shaped delta at the mouth of a river. Compare **bird's foot delta, cuspate delta**.

arc welding *n* a technique in which metal is welded by heat generated by an electric arc.

ardent *adj* **1** passionate. **2** intensely enthusiastic. ▷ HISTORY Latin *ardere* to burn ▶ **ardently** *adv*

ardour *or US* **ardor** *n* **1** emotional warmth; passion. **2** intense enthusiasm. ▷ HISTORY Latin *ardere* to burn

arduous *adj* difficult to accomplish; strenuous. ▷ HISTORY Latin *arduus* steep, difficult

are[1] *vb* the plural form of the present tense of **be:** used as the singular form with *you.* ▷ HISTORY Old English *aron*

are[2] *n* a unit of measure equal to one hundred square metres. ▷ HISTORY Latin *area* piece of ground

area *n* **1** a section, part, or region. **2** a part having a specified function: *reception area.* **3** the size of a two-dimensional surface. **4** a subject field: *the area of literature.* **5** *US & Canad* a sunken area giving access to a basement. **6** any flat, curved, or irregular expanse of a surface. **7** range or scope. ▷ HISTORY Latin: level ground, threshing floor

area school *n NZ* a school in a rural area that includes primary and post-primary classes.

arena *n* **1** a seated enclosure where sports events take place. **2** the area of an ancient Roman amphitheatre where gladiators fought. **3** a sphere of intense activity: *the political arena.* ▷ HISTORY Latin *harena* sand

aren't are not.

areola *n, pl* **-lae** *or* **-las** a small circular area, such as the coloured ring around the human nipple. ▷ HISTORY Latin

Ares *n Greek myth* the god of war.

arête *n* a sharp ridge separating valleys. ▷ HISTORY French: fishbone

Argentine *or* **Argentinian** *adj* **1** of Argentina. ✧ *n* **2** a person from Argentina.

argon *n Chem* an unreactive odourless element of the rare gas series, forming almost 1 per cent of the atmosphere. Symbol: Ar. ▷ HISTORY Greek *argos* inactive

argosy *n, pl* **-sies** *Old-fashioned or poetic* a large merchant ship, or a fleet of such ships. ▷ HISTORY Italian *Ragusea (nave)* (ship) of Ragusa, a former name for Dubrovnik

argot (**ahr**-go) *n* slang or jargon peculiar to a particular group. ▷ HISTORY French

argue *vb* **-guing, -gued 1** to try to prove by presenting reasons. **2** to debate. **3** to quarrel. **4** to persuade: *we argued her out of going.* **5** to suggest: *her looks argue despair.* ▷ HISTORY Latin *arguere* to make clear, accuse ▶ **arguable** *adj* ▶ **arguably** *adv*

argument *n* **1** a quarrel. **2** a discussion. **3** a point presented to support or oppose a proposition.

argumentation *n* the process of reasoning methodically.

argumentative *adj* likely to argue.

argy-bargy *or* **argie-bargie** *n, pl* **-bargies** *Brit informal* a squabbling argument. ▷ HISTORY Scots

aria (**ah**-ree-a) *n* an elaborate song for solo voice in an opera or choral work. ▷ HISTORY Italian

arid *adj* **1** having little or no rain. **2** uninteresting. ▷ HISTORY Latin *aridus* ▶ **aridity** *n*

Aries *n Astrol* the first sign of the zodiac: the Ram. ▷ HISTORY Latin

aright *adv* correctly or properly.

arise *vb* **arising, arose, arisen 1** to come into being: *the opportunity for action did not arise.* **2** to come into notice: *people can seek answers to their problems as and when they arise.* **3 arise from** to happen as a result of. **4** *Old-fashioned* to get or stand up. ▷ HISTORY Old English *ārīsan*

aristocracy *n, pl* **-cies 1** a class of people of high social rank. **2** government by this class. **3** a group of people considered to be outstanding in a particular sphere of activity. ▷ HISTORY Greek *aristos* best + *kratein* to rule

aristocrat *n* a member of the aristocracy.

aristocratic *adj* **1** of the aristocracy. **2** grand or elegant.

Aristotelian (ar-riss-tot-**eel**-ee-an) *adj* of Aristotle, 4th-century BC Greek philosopher, or his philosophy.

arithmetic *n* **1** the branch of mathematics concerned with numerical calculations, such as addition, subtraction, multiplication, and division. **2** calculations involving numerical operations. **3** knowledge of or skill in arithmetic: *even simple arithmetic was beyond him.* ✧ *adj also* **arithmetical 4** of or using arithmetic. ▷ HISTORY Greek *arithmos* number ▶ **arithmetically** *adv* ▶ **arithmetician** *n*

arithmetic mean *n* the average value of a set of terms, expressed as their sum divided by their number: *the arithmetic mean of 3, 4, and 8 is 5.*

arithmetic progression *n* a sequence, each term of which differs from the preceding term by a constant amount, such as 3, 6, 9, 12.

ark *n Bible* the boat built by Noah, which survived the Flood. ▷ HISTORY Latin *arca* box, chest

Ark *n Judaism* **1** Also called: **Holy Ark** the cupboard in a synagogue in which the Torah scrolls are kept. **2** Also called: **Ark of the Covenant** a chest containing the laws of the Jewish religion, regarded as the most sacred symbol of God's presence among the Hebrew people.

arm[1] *n* **1** (in humans, apes, and monkeys) either of the upper limbs from the shoulder to the wrist. **2** the sleeve of a garment. **3** the side of a chair on which one's arm can rest. **4** a subdivision or section of an organization: *the London-based arm of a Swiss bank.* **5** something resembling an arm in appearance or function: *the arm of a record player.* **6** power or authority: *the long arm of the law.* **7 arm in arm** with arms linked. **8 at arm's length** at a distance. **9 with open arms** with warmth and hospitality. ▷ HISTORY Old English

arm[2] *vb* **1** to supply with weapons. **2** to prepare (an explosive device) for use. **3** to provide (a person or thing) with something that strengthens, or protects: *you will be armed with all the information you will ever need.* ✧ See also **arms**. ▷ HISTORY Latin *arma* arms, equipment ▶ **armed** *adj*

armada *n* **1** a large number of ships. **2 the Armada** the great fleet sent by Spain against England in 1588. ▷ HISTORY Medieval Latin *armata* fleet, armed forces

armadillo *n, pl* **-los** a small S American burrowing mammal covered in strong bony plates.

> **WORD HISTORY**
> 'Armadillo' is a Spanish word meaning 'little armed man'. The animal was given this name because of its bony armour-like plates.

Armageddon *n* **1** *New Testament* the final battle between good and evil at the end of the world. **2** a catastrophic and extremely destructive conflict.

> **WORD HISTORY**
> 'Armageddon' comes from the Hebrew words *har megiddōn*, 'the mountain district of Megiddo'. Megiddo, which is in northern Israel, was the site of several battles in Old Testament times.

armament *n* **1 armaments** the weapon equipment of a military vehicle, ship, or aircraft. **2** preparation for war. ▷ HISTORY Latin *armamenta* equipment

armature *n* **1** a revolving structure in an electric motor or generator, wound with the coils that carry the current. **2** *Sculpture* a framework to support the clay or other material used in modelling. ▷ HISTORY Latin *armatura* armour, equipment

armchair *n* **1** an upholstered chair with side supports for the arms. ✧ *adj* **2** taking no active part: *we are, on the whole, a nation of armchair athletes.*

armed forces *pl n* all the military forces of a nation or nations.

armful *n* as much as can be held in the arms: *armfuls of lovely flowers.*

armhole *n* the opening in a piece of clothing through which the arm passes.

armistice (**arm**-miss-stiss) *n* an agreement between opposing armies to stop fighting. ▷ HISTORY Latin *arma* arms + *sistere* to stop

A B C D E F G H I J K L M N O P Q R S T U V W X Y Z

Armistice Day *n* the anniversary of the signing of the armistice that ended the First World War, on November 11, 1918.

armlet *n* a band or bracelet worn around the arm.

armour *or US* **armor** *n* **1** metal clothing worn by medieval warriors for protection in battle. **2** *Mil* armoured fighting vehicles in general. **3** the protective metal plates on a tank or warship. **4** protective covering, such as the shell of certain animals. **5** a quality or attitude that gives protection. ✧ *vb* **6** to equip or cover with armour. ▷ **HISTORY** Latin *armātūra* armour, equipment

armoured *or US* **armored** *adj* **1** having a protective covering. **2** consisting of armoured vehicles: *an armoured brigade.*

armourer *or US* **armorer** *n* **1** a person who makes or mends arms and armour. **2** a person in charge of small arms in a military unit.

armoury *or US* **armory** *n, pl* **-mouries** *or* **-mories 1** a secure storage place for weapons. **2** military supplies. **3** resources on which to draw: *modern medicine has a large armoury of drugs for the treatment of mental illness.*

armpit *n* **1** the hollow beneath the arm where it joins the shoulder. **2** *Slang* an extremely unpleasant place: *the armpit of the Mediterranean.*

arms *pl n* **1** weapons collectively. **2** military exploits: *prowess in arms.* **3** the heraldic symbols of a family or state. **4 take up arms** to prepare to fight. **5 under arms** armed and prepared for war. **6 up in arms** prepared to protest strongly.

army *n, pl* **-mies 1** the military land forces of a nation. **2** a large number of people or animals. ▷ **HISTORY** Medieval Latin *armata* armed forces

aroha *n NZ* love, compassion, or affection. ▷ **HISTORY** Maori

aroma *n* **1** a distinctive pleasant smell. **2** a subtle pervasive quality or atmosphere. ▷ **HISTORY** Greek: spice

aromatherapy *n* the use of fragrant essential oils as a treatment in alternative medicine, often to relieve tension.

aromatic *adj* **1** having a distinctive pleasant smell. **2** *Chem* (of an organic compound) having an unsaturated ring of atoms, usually six carbon atoms. ✧ *n* **3** something, such as a plant or drug, that gives off a fragrant smell.

arose *vb* the past tense of **arise**.

around *prep* **1** situated at various points in: *cameramen were positioned around the auditorium.* **2** from place to place in: *he had spent twenty-five minutes driving around Amsterdam.* **3** somewhere in or near. **4** approximately in: *around 1980.* ✧ *adv* **5** in all directions from a point of reference: *there wasn't a house for miles around.* **6** in the vicinity, esp. restlessly but idly: *I couldn't hang around too long.* **7** in no particular place or direction: *a few tropical fish tanks dotted around.* **8** *Informal* present in some unknown or unspecified place. **9** *Informal* available: *cancer drugs have been around for years.* **10 have been around** *Informal* to have gained considerable experience of a worldly or social nature.

> **☑ WORD TIP**
> In American English, *around* is usually used instead of *round* in adverbial and prepositional senses, except in a few fixed phrases such as *all year round.* The use of *around* in adverbial senses is less common in British English.

arouse *vb* **arousing, aroused 1** to produce (a reaction, emotion, or response). **2** to awaken from sleep. ▸ **arousal** *n*

arpeggio (arp-**pej**-ee-oh) *n, pl* **-gios** a chord whose notes are played or sung in rapid succession. ▷ **HISTORY** Italian

arrack *or* **arak** *n* a coarse alcoholic drink distilled in Eastern countries from grain or rice. ▷ **HISTORY** Arabic *'araq* sweat, sweet juice

arraign (ar-**rain**) *vb* **1** to bring (a prisoner) before a court to answer a charge. **2** to accuse. ▷ **HISTORY** Old French *araisnier* to accuse ▸ **arraignment** *n*

arrange *vb* **-ranging, -ranged 1** to plan in advance: *my parents had arranged a surprise party.* **2** to arrive at an agreement: *they had arranged to go to the cinema.* **3** to put into a proper or systematic order. **4** to adapt (a musical composition) for performance in a certain way. ▷ **HISTORY** Old French *a-* to + *rangier* to put in a row, range

arrangement *n* **1** a preparation or plan made for an event: *travel arrangements.* **2** an agreement or a plan to do something. **3** a thing composed of various ordered parts: *a flower arrangement.* **4** the form in which things are arranged. **5** an adaptation of a piece of music for performance in a certain way.

arrant *adj* utter or downright: *that's the most arrant nonsense I've ever heard.* ▷ **HISTORY** Middle English variant of *errant* (wandering, vagabond)

arras *n* a tapestry wall-hanging. ▷ **HISTORY** *Arras,* a town in N France

array *n* **1** an impressive display or collection. **2** an orderly arrangement, such as of troops in battle order. **3** *Computers* a data structure in which elements may be located by index numbers. **4** *Poetic* rich clothing. ✧ *vb* **5** to arrange in order. **6** to dress in rich clothing. ▷ **HISTORY** Old French *arayer* to arrange

arrears *pl n* **1** money owed. **2 in arrears** late in paying a debt. ▷ **HISTORY** Latin *ad* to + *retro* backwards

arrest *vb* **1** to take (a person) into custody. **2** to slow or stop the development of. **3** to catch and hold (one's attention). ✧ *n* **4** the act of taking a person into custody. **5 under arrest** being held in custody by the police. **6** the slowing or stopping of something: *a cardiac arrest.* ▷ **HISTORY** Latin *ad* at, to + *restare* to stand firm, stop

arresting *adj* attracting attention; striking.

arrival *n* **1** the act of arriving. **2** a person or thing that has just arrived. **3** *Informal* a recently born baby.

arrive *vb* **-riving, -rived 1** to reach a place or destination. **2 arrive at** to come to (a conclusion, idea, or decision). **3** to occur: *the crisis he predicted then has now arrived.* **4** *Informal* to be born. **5** *Informal* to attain success. ▷ **HISTORY** Latin *ad* to + *ripa* river bank

arrivederci (ar-reeve-a-**der**-chee) *interj* goodbye. ▷ **HISTORY** Italian

arrogant *adj* having an exaggerated opinion of one's own importance or ability. ▷ **HISTORY** Latin *arrogare* to claim as one's own ▶ **arrogance** *n* ▶ **arrogantly** *adv*

arrogate *vb* **-gating, -gated** to claim or seize without justification. ▷ **HISTORY** Latin *arrogare* ▶ **arrogation** *n*

arrow *n* **1** a long slender pointed weapon, with feathers at one end, that is shot from a bow. **2** an arrow-shaped sign or symbol used to show the direction to a place. ▷ **HISTORY** Old English *arwe*

arrowhead *n* the pointed tip of an arrow.

arrowroot *n* an easily digestible starch obtained from the root of a West Indian plant.

arse *or US & Canad* **ass** *n Taboo* the buttocks or anus. ▷ **HISTORY** Old English *ærs*

arsehole *or US & Canad* **asshole** *n Taboo* **1** the anus. **2** a stupid or annoying person.

arsenal *n* **1** a building in which arms and ammunition are made or stored. **2** a store of anything regarded as weapons: *this new weapon in the medical arsenal.*

> **WORD HISTORY**
> The word 'arsenal' came into English from Italian, but it has its origin in Arabic. In Arabic a *dār as-sinā'a* is a workshop or factory. This word was borrowed from Arabic into Italian as *arsenale*, meaning 'dockyard'. And it was in the sense of 'dockyard' that it came into English, only later coming to have the meaning of an arms and ammunition store.

arsenic *n* **1** a toxic metalloid element. Symbol: As. **2** a nontechnical name for **arsenic trioxide**, a highly poisonous compound used as a rat poison and insecticide. ✧ *adj also* **arsenical 3** of or containing arsenic. ▷ **HISTORY** Syriac *zarnīg*

arson *n* the crime of intentionally setting fire to property. ▷ **HISTORY** Latin *ardere* to burn ▶ **arsonist** *n*

art *n* **1** the creation of works of beauty or other special significance. **2** works of art collectively. **3** human creativity as distinguished from nature. **4** skill: *she was still new to the art of bargaining.* **5** any branch of the visual arts, esp. painting. **6 get something down to a fine art** to become proficient at something through practice. ✧ See also **arts**. ▷ **HISTORY** Latin *ars* craftsmanship

Art Deco (art **deck**-oh) *n* a style of design, at its height in the 1930s, characterized by geometrical shapes. ▷ **HISTORY** French *art décoratif*

artefact *or* **artifact** *n* something made by human beings, such as a tool or a work of art. ▷ **HISTORY** Latin *ars* skill + *facere* to make

Artemis *n Greek myth* the goddess of hunting.

arterial *adj* **1** of or affecting an artery. **2** being a major route: *an arterial road.*

arteriole *n Anat* a small subdivision of an artery.

arteriosclerosis (art-ear-ee-oh-skler-**oh**-siss) *n* thickening and loss of elasticity of the walls of the arteries. Nontechnical name: **hardening of the arteries**

artery *n, pl* **-teries 1** any of the tubes that carry oxygenated blood from the heart to various parts of the body. **2** a major road or means of communication. ▷ **HISTORY** Latin *arteria*

artesian well (art-**teez**-ee-en) *n Geography, engineering* a well tapping water that is under pressure in a confined aquifer with the result that the water rises naturally without the need for a pump. ▷ **HISTORY** French *artésien,* from Old French *Arteis* Artois (in N France) where such wells were common

Artex *n Trademark, Brit* a type of coating for walls and ceilings that gives a textured finish.

art form *n* a recognized mode or medium of artistic expression.

artful *adj* **1** cunning. **2** skilful in achieving a desired end. ▶ **artfully** *adv*

arthritis *n* inflammation of a joint or joints, causing pain and stiffness. ▷ **HISTORY** Greek *arthron* joint ▶ **arthritic** *adj, n*

arthropod *n* a creature, such as an insect or a spider, which has jointed legs and a hard case on its body. ▷ **HISTORY** Greek *arthron* joint + *pous* foot

artic *n Brit informal* an articulated lorry.

artichoke *n* **1** Also called: **globe artichoke** the flower head of a thistle-like plant, cooked as a vegetable. **2** same as **Jerusalem artichoke**. ▷ **HISTORY** Arabic *al-kharshūf*

article *n* **1** a written composition in a magazine or newspaper. **2** an item or object. **3** a clause in a written document. **4** *Grammar* any of the words *a, an,* or *the.* ▷ **HISTORY** Latin *articulus* small joint

articled *adj* bound by a written contract, such as one that governs a period of training: *an articled clerk.*

articular *adj* of or relating to joints. ▷ **HISTORY** Latin *articulus* small joint

articulate *adj* **1** able to express oneself fluently and coherently. **2** distinct, clear, or definite: *his amiable and articulate campaign attracted support.* **3** *Zool* possessing joints. ✧ *vb* **-lating, -lated 4** to speak clearly and distinctly. **5** to express coherently in words. ▷ **HISTORY** Latin *articulare* to divide into joints ▶ **articulately** *adv*

articulation *n* **1** the expressing of an idea in words. **2** the process of articulating a speech sound or the sound so produced. **3** a being jointed together. **4** *Zool* a joint between bones or arthropod segments.

artifact *n* same as **artefact**.

artifice *n* **1** a clever trick. **2** skill or cleverness. ▷ **HISTORY** Latin *ars* skill + *facere* to make

artificer (art-**tiff**-iss-er) *n* a skilled craftsman.

artificial *adj* **1** man-made; not occurring naturally. **2** made in imitation of a natural product: *artificial flavourings.* **3** not sincere. ▷ **HISTORY** Latin *artificialis* belonging to art ▸ **artificiality** *n* ▸ **artificially** *adv*

artificial insemination *n* introduction of semen into the womb by means other than sexual intercourse.

artificial intelligence *n* the branch of computer science aiming to produce machines which can imitate intelligent human behaviour.

artificial respiration *n* any method of restarting a person's breathing after it has stopped.

artillery *n* **1** large-calibre guns. **2** military units specializing in the use of such guns. ▷ HISTORY Old French *artillier* to equip with weapons

artisan *n* a skilled workman; craftsman. ▷ HISTORY French ▸ **artisanal** *adj*

artist *n* **1** a person who produces works of art such as paintings or sculpture. **2** a person who is skilled at something. **3** same as **artiste**. ▸ **artistic** *adj* ▸ **artistically** *adv*

artiste *n* a professional entertainer such as a singer or dancer.

artistic unity *n* the condition achieved when all the elements of a composition work together to achieve a satisfactory, integrated whole.

artistry *n* **1** artistic ability. **2** great skill.

artless *adj* **1** free from deceit or cunning: *artless generosity.* **2** natural or unpretentious. ▸ **artlessly** *adv*

Art Nouveau (ahr noo-**voh**) *n* a style of art and architecture of the 1890s, characterized by sinuous outlines and stylized natural forms. ▷ HISTORY French: new art

arts *pl n* **1 the arts** the nonscientific branches of knowledge. **2** See **fine art**. **3** cunning schemes.

artwork *n* all the photographs and illustrations in a publication.

arty *adj* **artier, artiest** *Informal* having an affected interest in art. ▸ **artiness** *n*

arum lily *n* a plant with a white funnel-shaped leaf surrounding a yellow spike of flowers.

Aryan (**air**-ree-an) *n* **1** (in Nazi ideology) a non-Jewish person of the Nordic type. **2** a person supposedly descended from the Indo-Europeans. ✧ *adj* **3** of Aryans. ▷ HISTORY Sanskrit *ārya* of noble birth

as *conj* **1** while or when: *he arrived just as the band finished the song.* **2** in the way that: *they had talked and laughed as only the best of friends can.* **3** that which; what: *George did as he was asked.* **4** (of) which fact or event (referring to the previous statement): *to become wise, as we all know, is not easy.* **5 as it were** in a way; in a manner of speaking: *he was, as it were, on probation.* **6** since; seeing that. **7** for instance. ✧ *adv, conj* **8** used to indicate amount or extent in comparisons: *he was as fat as his mum and dad.* ✧ *prep* **9** in the role of; being: *my task, as his physician, is to do the best that I can.* **10 as for** *or* **to** with reference to. **11 as if** *or* **though** as it would be if: *she felt as if she had been run over by a bulldozer.* **12 as (it) is** in the existing state of affairs. ▷ HISTORY Old English *alswā* likewise

> **☑ WORD TIP**
> See at **like.**

As *Chem* arsenic.

ASA **1** (in Britain) Amateur Swimming Association. **2** (in Britain) Advertising Standards Authority.

asafoetida *n* a strong-smelling plant resin used as a spice in Eastern cookery. ▷ HISTORY Medieval Latin *asa* gum + Latin *foetidus* evil-smelling

a.s.a.p. as soon as possible.

asbestos *n* a fibrous mineral which does not burn, formerly widely used as a heat-resistant material. ▷ HISTORY Greek: inextinguishable

asbestosis *n* inflammation of the lungs resulting from inhalation of asbestos fibre.

ascend *vb* **1** to go or move up. **2** to slope upwards. **3 ascend the throne** to become king or queen. ▷ HISTORY Latin *ascendere*

ascendancy *or* **ascendance** *n* the condition of being dominant: *when hardliners were in the ascendancy last winter.*

ascendant *or* **ascendent** *adj* **1** dominant or influential. ✧ *n* **2** *Astrol* the sign of the zodiac that is rising on the eastern horizon at a particular moment. **3 in the ascendant** increasing in power or influence.

ascension *n* the act of ascending.

Ascension Day *n Christianity* the 40th day after Easter, when the Ascension of Christ into Heaven is celebrated.

ascent *n* **1** the act of ascending. **2** an upward slope.

ascertain *vb* to find out definitely. ▷ HISTORY Old French *acertener* to make certain ▸ **ascertainment** *n*

ascetic (ass-**set**-tik) *n* **1** a person who abstains from worldly comforts and pleasures. ✧ *adj* **2** rigidly abstinent and self-denying. ▷ HISTORY Greek *askētikos*

ASCII (**ass**-kee) *n* a code for transmitting data between computers. ▷ HISTORY *A(merican) S(tandard) C(ode for) I(nformation) I(nterchange)*

ascorbic acid (ass-**core**-bik) *n* a vitamin that occurs in citrus fruits, tomatoes, and green vegetables, and which prevents and cures scurvy. Also called: **vitamin C** ▷ HISTORY A- + SCORBUTIC

ascribe *vb* **-cribing, -cribed** **1** to attribute, as to a particular origin: *headaches which may be ascribed to stress.* **2** to consider that (a particular quality) is possessed by something or someone: *specific human qualities are ascribed to each of the four elements.* ▷ HISTORY Latin *ad* in addition + *scribere* to write ▸ **ascription** *n*

> **☑ WORD TIP**
> *Ascribe* is sometimes used where *subscribe* is meant: *I do not subscribe* (not *ascribe*) *to this view.*

aseptic (eh-**sep**-tik) *adj* free from harmful bacteria.

asexual (eh-**sex**-yew-al) *adj* **1** having no apparent sex or sex organs. **2** (of reproduction) not involving sexual activity. ▶ **asexually** *adv*

ash[1] *n* **1** the powdery substance formed when something is burnt. **2** fine particles of lava thrown out by an erupting volcano. ▷ HISTORY Old English *æsce*

ash[2] *n* a tree with grey bark and winged seeds. ▷ HISTORY Old English *æsc*

ashamed *adj* **1** overcome with shame or remorse. **2** unwilling through fear of humiliation or shame: *she'd be ashamed to admit to jealousy.* ▷ HISTORY Old English *āscamod*

ashen *adj* pale with shock.

ashes *pl n* **1** remains after burning. **2** the remains of a human body after cremation.

ashlar *or* **ashler** *n* **1** a square block of cut stone for use in building. **2** a thin dressed stone used to face a wall. ▷ HISTORY Old French *aisselier* crossbeam

ashore *adv* towards or on land.

ashram *n* a religious retreat where a Hindu holy man lives. ▷ HISTORY Sanskrit *āśrama*

ashtray *n* a dish for tobacco ash and cigarette ends.

Ash Wednesday *n* the first day of Lent, named from the Christian custom of sprinkling ashes on penitents' heads.

Asian *adj* **1** of Asia. **2** *Brit* of the Indian subcontinent. ✧ *n* **3** a person from Asia. **4** *Brit* a person from the Indian subcontinent or a descendant of one.

> ☑ **WORD TIP**
> The use of *Asian* or *Asiatic* as a noun can be offensive and should be avoided.

Asian pear *n* an apple-shaped pear with crisp juicy flesh.

Asiatic *adj* Asian.

> ☑ **WORD TIP**
> See at **Asian.**

aside *adv* **1** to one side. **2** out of other people's hearing: *her mother took her aside for a serious talk.* **3** out of mind: *she pushed aside her fears of being beaten or killed.* **4** into reserve: *a certain amount must also be put aside for defence and government.* ✧ *n* **5** a remark not meant to be heard by everyone present. **6** a remark that is not connected with the subject being discussed.

asinine (**ass**-in-nine) *adj* **1** obstinate or stupid. **2** of or like an ass. ▷ HISTORY Latin *asinus* ass

ask *vb* **1** to say or write (something) in a form that requires an answer: *I asked him his name; 'do you think we'll have trouble landing?' he asked.* **2** to make a request or demand: *the chairman asked for a show of hands.* **3** to invite. **4** to inquire about: *I pretended to be lost and asked for directions.* **5** to expect: *is that too much to ask?* ▷ HISTORY Old English *āscian*

askance (ass-**kanss**) *adv* **look askance at a** to look at with an oblique glance. **b** to regard with suspicion. ▷ HISTORY origin unknown

askew *adv, adj* towards one side; crooked.

asking price *n* the price suggested by a seller.

aslant *adv* **1** at a slant. ✧ *prep* **2** slanting across.

asleep *adj* **1** in or into a state of sleep. **2** (of limbs) numb. **3** *Informal* not listening or paying attention.

ASM assistant stage manager.

asp *n* a small viper of S Europe. ▷ HISTORY Greek *aspis*

asparagus *n* the young shoots of a plant of the lily family, which can be cooked and eaten. ▷ HISTORY Greek *asparagos*

aspartame *n* an artificial sweetener.

aspect *n* **1** a distinct feature or element in a problem or situation. **2** a position facing a particular direction: *the room's east-facing aspect.* **3** appearance or look: *a room with a somewhat gloomy aspect.* ▷ HISTORY Latin *ad-* to, at + *specere* to look

aspen *n* a poplar tree whose leaves quiver in the wind. ▷ HISTORY Old English *æspe*

asperity (ass-**per**-rit-ee) *n, pl* **-ties** roughness or sharpness of temper. ▷ HISTORY Latin *asper* rough

aspersion *n* **cast aspersions on** to make disparaging or malicious remarks about. ▷ HISTORY Latin *aspergere* to sprinkle

asphalt *n* **1** a black tarlike substance used in road-surfacing and roofing materials. ✧ *vb* **2** to cover with asphalt. ▷ HISTORY Greek *asphaltos*, probably from *a-* not + *sphallein* to cause to fall; referring to its use as a binding agent

asphodel *n* a plant with clusters of yellow or white flowers.

asphyxia (ass-**fix**-ee-a) *n* unconsciousness or death caused by lack of oxygen. ▷ HISTORY Greek *a-* without + *sphuxis* pulse

asphyxiate *vb* **-ating, -ated** to smother or suffocate. ▶ **asphyxiation** *n*

aspic *n* a savoury jelly based on meat or fish stock, used as a mould for meat or vegetables. ▷ HISTORY French

aspidistra *n* a house plant with long tapered evergreen leaves. ▷ HISTORY Greek *aspis* shield

aspirant *n* a person who aspires, such as to a powerful position.

aspirate *Phonetics* ✧ *vb* **-rating, -rated 1** to pronounce (a word or syllable) with an initial *h*. ✧ *n* **2** the sound represented in English and several other languages as *h*.

aspiration *n* **1** a strong desire or aim. **2** *Phonetics* the pronunciation of an aspirated consonant. ▶ **aspirational** *adj*

aspirator *n* a device for removing fluids from a body cavity by suction.

aspire *vb* **-piring, -pired** to yearn for something or hope to do or be something: *it struck him as bizarre that somebody could aspire to be a dental technician.* ▷ HISTORY Latin *aspirare* to breathe upon ▶ **aspiring** *adj*

aspirin *n, pl* **-rin** *or* **-rins 1** a drug used to relieve pain and fever. **2** a tablet of aspirin. ▷ HISTORY German

ass[1] *n* **1** a mammal resembling the horse but with longer ears. **2** a foolish person. ▷ **HISTORY** Old English *assa*

ass[2] *n US & Canad taboo* same as **arse**. ▷ **HISTORY** Old English *ærs*

assagai *n* same as **assegai**.

assail *vb* **1** to attack violently. **2** to criticize strongly. **3** to disturb: *he was assailed by a dizzy sensation.* ▷ **HISTORY** Latin *assilire* to leap on ▶ **assailant** *n*

assassin *n* a murderer of a prominent person.

> **WORD HISTORY**
> The source of this word is the Arabic word *hashshāshīn*, meaning 'people who take hashish'. The word comes from the name of a feared medieval Muslim sect who allegedly ate or smoked hashish before embarking on missions to murder those they considered their enemies, Crusaders and Muslim leaders alike.

assassinate *vb* **-nating, -nated** to murder (a prominent person). ▶ **assassination** *n*

assault *n* **1** a violent attack, either physical or verbal. ✧ *vb* **2** to attack violently. ▷ **HISTORY** Old French *asaut*

assault and battery *n Criminal law* a threat of attack to another person followed by actual attack.

assault course *n* an obstacle course designed to give soldiers practice in negotiating hazards.

assay *vb* **1** to analyse (a substance, such as gold) to find out how pure it is. ✧ *n* **2** an analysis of the purity of an ore or precious metal. ▷ **HISTORY** Old French *assai*

assegai *or* **assagai** *n, pl* **-gais** a sharp light spear used in southern Africa. ▷ **HISTORY** Arabic *az zaghayah*

assemblage *n* **1** a collection or group of things. **2** the act of assembling.

assemble *vb* **-bling, -bled 1** to collect or gather together. **2** to put together the parts of (a machine). ▷ **HISTORY** Old French *assembler*

assembler *n* **1** a person or thing that assembles. **2** a computer program that converts a set of low-level symbolic data into machine language.

assembly *n, pl* **-blies 1** a number of people gathered together for a meeting. **2** the act of assembling.

assembly line *n* a sequence of machines and workers in a factory assembling a product.

assemblyman *n, pl* **-men** a member of a legislative assembly.

assent *n* **1** agreement, consent. ✧ *vb* **2** to agree. ▷ **HISTORY** Latin *assentiri*

assert *vb* **1** to state or declare. **2** to insist upon (one's rights, etc.). **3 assert oneself** to speak and act forcefully. ▷ **HISTORY** Latin *asserere* to join to oneself

assertion *n* **1** a positive statement, usually made without evidence. **2** the act of asserting.

assertive *adj* confident and direct in dealing with others. ▶ **assertively** *adv* ▶ **assertiveness** *n*

assess *vb* **1** to judge the worth or importance of. **2** to estimate the value of (income or property) for taxation purposes. ▷ **HISTORY** Latin *assidere* to sit beside ▶ **assessment** *n*

assessor *n* **1** a person who values property for taxation or insurance purposes. **2** a person with technical expertise called in to advise a court. **3** a person who evaluates the merits of something.

asset *n* **1** a thing or person that is valuable or useful. **2** any property owned by a person or company. ▷ **HISTORY** Latin *ad-* to + *satis* enough

asset-stripping *n Commerce* the practice of taking over a failing company at a low price and then selling the assets piecemeal. ▶ **asset-stripper** *n*

asseverate *vb* **-ating, -ated** *Formal* to declare solemnly. ▷ **HISTORY** Latin *asseverare* to do (something) earnestly ▶ **asseveration** *n*

assiduous *adj* **1** hard-working. **2** done with care. ▷ **HISTORY** Latin *assidere* to sit beside ▶ **assiduity** *n* ▶ **assiduously** *adv*

assign *vb* **1** to select (someone) for a post or task. **2** to give a task or duty (to someone). **3** to attribute to a specified cause. **4** to set apart (a place or time) for a particular function or event: *to assign a day for the meeting.* **5** *Law* to transfer (one's right, interest, or title to property) to someone else. ▷ **HISTORY** Latin *assignare*

assignation (ass-sig-**nay**-shun) *n* a secret arrangement to meet, esp. one between lovers. ▷ **HISTORY** Latin *assignatio* a marking out

assignment *n* **1** something that has been assigned, such as a task. **2** the act of assigning. **3** *Law* the transfer to another person of a right, interest, or title to property.

assignment system *n History* a system whereby convicts arriving in Australia in the first part of the 19th century were assigned to settlers as cheap labour; in force until 1840.

assimilate *vb* **-lating, -lated 1** to learn (information) and understand it thoroughly. **2** to adjust or become adjusted: *they became assimilated to German culture.* **3** to absorb (food). ▷ **HISTORY** Latin *ad-* to + *similis* like ▶ **assimilable** *adj* ▶ **assimilation** *n*

assist *vb* **1** to give help or support. ✧ *n* **2** *Sport* a pass by a player which enables another player to score a goal. ▷ **HISTORY** Latin *assistere* to stand by

assistance *n* help or support.

assistant *n* **1** a helper or subordinate. **2** same as **shop assistant**. ✧ *adj* **3** junior or deputy: *assistant manager.*

assistant referee *n Soccer* the official name for **linesman** (sense 1).

assizes *pl n Brit* (formerly in England and Wales) the sessions of the principal court in each county. ▷ **HISTORY** Latin *assidere* to sit beside

assoc. association.

associate *vb* **-ating, -ated 1** to connect in the mind. **2** to mix socially: *addicts are driven to associate with criminals.* **3 be associated** *or* **associate oneself with** to be involved with (a group) because of shared views: *she had long been* *associated with the far right.* ✧ *n* **4** a partner in business. **5** a companion or friend. ✧ *adj* **6** having partial rights or subordinate status: *an associate member.* **7** joined with in business: *an associate director.* ▷ **HISTORY** Latin *ad-* to + *sociare* to join

association *n* **1** a group of people with a common interest. **2** the act of associating or the state of being associated. **3** friendship: *their association still had to remain a secret.* **4** a mental connection of ideas or feelings: *the place contained associations for her.*

associative *adj Maths* (of an operation such as multiplication or addition) producing the same answer regardless of the way the elements are grouped, for example $(2\times 3)\times 4 = 2\times(3\times 4)$.

assonance *n* the rhyming of vowel sounds but not consonants, as in *time* and *light.* ▷ **HISTORY** Latin *assonare* to sound

assorted *adj* **1** consisting of various kinds mixed together. **2** matched: *an ill-assorted childless couple.* ▷ **HISTORY** Old French *assorter*

assortment *n* a collection of various things or sorts.

asst assistant.

assuage (ass-**wage**) *vb* **-suaging, -suaged** to relieve (grief, pain, or thirst). ▷ **HISTORY** Latin *suavis* pleasant

assume *vb* **-suming, -sumed 1** to take to be true without proof. **2** to undertake or take on: *every general staff officer was able to assume control of the army.* **3** to make a pretence of: *the man had assumed a debonair attitude.* **4** to take on: *her eyes assumed a scared haunted look.* ▷ **HISTORY** Latin *ad-* to + *sumere* to take up

assumption *n* **1** something that is taken for granted. **2** the act of assuming power or possession. ▷ **HISTORY** Latin *assumptio* a taking up

Assumption *n Christianity* the taking up of the Virgin Mary into heaven when her earthly life was ended.

assurance *n* **1** a statement or assertion intended to inspire confidence. **2** feeling of confidence; certainty. **3** insurance that provides for events that are certain to happen, such as death.

assure *vb* **-suring, -sured 1** to promise or guarantee. **2** to convince: *they assured me that they had not seen the document.* **3** to make (something) certain. **4** *Chiefly Brit* to insure against loss of life. ▷ **HISTORY** Latin *ad-* to + *securus* secure

assured *adj* **1** confident or self-assured. **2** certain to happen. **3** *Chiefly Brit* insured. ▶ **assuredly** (a-**sure**-id-lee) *adv*

Assyrian *n* an inhabitant of ancient Assyria, a kingdom of Mesopotamia.

AST Atlantic Standard Time.

astatine *n Chem* a radioactive element occurring naturally in minute amounts or artificially produced by bombarding bismuth with alpha particles. Symbol: At. ▷ **HISTORY** Greek *astatos* unstable

aster *n* a plant with white, blue, purple, or pink daisy-like flowers. ▷ **HISTORY** Greek: star

asterisk *n* **1** a star-shaped character (*) used in printing or writing to indicate a footnote etc. ✧ *vb* **2** to mark with an asterisk. ▷ **HISTORY** Greek *asteriskos* a small star

astern *adv, adj Naut* **1** at or towards the stern of a ship. **2** backwards. **3** behind a vessel.

asteroid *n* any of the small planets that orbit the sun between Mars and Jupiter. ▷ **HISTORY** Greek *asteroeidēs* starlike

asthenosphere *n Geol* a thin semifluid layer of the earth below the outer lithosphere, forming part of the mantle and thought to be able to flow vertically and horizontally, enabling sections of lithosphere to move up, down, and sideways. Compare **lithosphere**. ▷ **HISTORY** from *astheno-*, from Greek *asthenēs* weak + SPHERE

asthma (**ass**-ma) *n* an illness causing difficulty in breathing. ▷ **HISTORY** Greek ▶ **asthmatic** *adj, n*

astigmatic *adj* relating to or affected with astigmatism. ▷ **HISTORY** Greek *a-* without + *stigma* spot, focus

astigmatism (ay-**stig**-mat-tiz-zum) *n* a defect of a lens, esp. of the eye, causing it not to focus properly.

astir *adj* **1** out of bed. **2** in motion.

astonish *vb* to surprise greatly. ▷ **HISTORY** Latin *ex-* out + *tonare* to thunder ▶ **astonishing** *adj* ▶ **astonishment** *n*

astound *vb* to overwhelm with amazement. ▷ **HISTORY** Old French *estoner* ▶ **astounding** *adj*

astrakhan *n* **1** a fur made of the dark curly fleece of lambs from Astrakhan in Russia. **2** a cloth resembling this.

astral *adj* **1** relating to or resembling the stars. **2** of the spirit world. ▷ **HISTORY** Greek *astron* star

astray *adj, adv* out of the right or expected way. ▷ **HISTORY** Old French *estraier* to stray

astride *adj* **1** with a leg on either side. **2** with legs far apart. ✧ *prep* **3** with a leg on either side of.

astringent *adj* **1** causing contraction of body tissue. **2** checking the flow of blood from a cut. **3** severe or harsh. ✧ *n* **4** an astringent drug or lotion. ▷ **HISTORY** Latin *astringens* drawing together ▶ **astringency** *n*

astro- *combining form* indicating a star or stars: *astrology.* ▷ **HISTORY** Greek

astrolabe *n* an instrument formerly used to measure the altitude of stars and planets. ▷ **HISTORY** Greek *astron* star + *lambanein* to take

astrology *n* the study of the alleged influence of the stars, planets, sun, and moon on human affairs. ▷ **HISTORY** Greek *astron* star + *logos* word, account ▶ **astrologer** *or* **astrologist** *n* ▶ **astrological** *adj*

astronaut *n* a person trained for travelling in space. ▷ **HISTORY** Greek *astron* star + *nautēs* sailor

astronautics *n* the science and technology of space flight. ▶ **astronautical** *adj*

astronomical *or* **astronomic** *adj* **1** enormously large. **2** of astronomy. ▶ **astronomically** *adv*

astronomical unit *n* a unit of distance equal to the average distance between the earth and the sun (1.495×10^{11}m).

astronomy *n* the scientific study of heavenly bodies. ▷ HISTORY Greek *astron* star + *nomos* law ▸ **astronomer** *n*

astrophysics *n* the study of the physical and chemical properties of celestial bodies. ▸ **astrophysical** *adj* ▸ **astrophysicist** *n*

astute *adj* quick to notice or understand. ▷ HISTORY Latin *astutus* ▸ **astutely** *adv* ▸ **astuteness** *n*

asunder *adv, adj Literary* into parts or pieces; apart.

asylum *n* **1** refuge granted to a political refugee from a foreign country. **2** (formerly) a mental hospital. ▷ HISTORY Greek *asulon*

asymmetric bars (**ass**-sim-met-rik, **ay**-sim-met-rik) *pl n Gymnastics* a pair of bars parallel to each other but at different heights, used for various exercises.

asymmetry *n* lack of symmetry. ▸ **asymmetric** *or* **asymmetrical** *adj*

asymptote (**ass**-im-tote) *n* a straight line that is closely approached but never met by a curve. ▷ HISTORY Greek *asumptōtos* not falling together ▸ **asymptotic** *adj*

at *prep* **1** indicating location or position: *she had planted a vegetable garden at the back.* **2** towards; in the direction of: *she was staring at the wall behind him.* **3** indicating position in time: *we arrived at 12.30.* **4** engaged in: *the innocent laughter of children at play.* **5** during the passing of: *she works at night as a nurse's aide.* **6** for; in exchange for: *crude oil is selling at its lowest price since September.* **7** indicating the object of an emotion: *I'm angry at you because you were rude to me.* ▷ HISTORY Old English *æt*

At *Chem* astatine.

at. **1** atmosphere. **2** atomic.

atavism (**at**-a-viz-zum) *n* **1** the recurrence of primitive characteristics that were present in distant ancestors but not in more recent ones. **2** reversion to a former type. ▷ HISTORY Latin *atavus* great-grandfather's grandfather, ancestor ▸ **atavistic** *adj*

ataxia *n Pathol* lack of muscular coordination. ▷ HISTORY Greek ▸ **ataxic** *adj*

ate *vb* the past tense of **eat**.

-ate *suffix Chem* indicating a chemical compound containing oxygen: *zinc sulphate.*

atelier (**at**-tell-yay) *n* an artist's studio.

atheism (**aith**-ee-iz-zum) *n* the belief that there is no God. ▷ HISTORY Greek *a-* without + *theos* god ▸ **atheist** *n*

Athena *or* **Athene** *n Greek myth* the goddess of wisdom.

atheroma *n Pathol* a fatty deposit on or in the inner lining of an artery.

atherosclerosis *n, pl* **-ses** a disease in which deposits of fat cause the walls of the arteries to thicken. ▷ HISTORY Greek *athērōma* tumour + SCLEROSIS ▸ **atherosclerotic** *adj*

athlete *n* **1** a person trained to compete in sports or exercises. **2** *Chiefly Brit* a competitor in track-and-field events. ▷ HISTORY Greek *athlos* a contest

athlete's foot *n* a fungal infection of the skin of the foot.

athletic *adj* **1** physically fit or strong. **2** of or for an athlete or athletics. ▸ **athletically** *adv* ▸ **athleticism** *n*

athletics *pl n Brit & Austral* track-and-field events.

at-home *n Brit & Austral* a social gathering in a person's home.

athwart *prep* **1** across. ✧ *adv* **2** transversely; from one side to another.

Atlantic *adj* of the Atlantic Ocean, the world's second largest ocean, bounded by the Arctic, the Antarctic, America, and Europe and Africa. ▷ HISTORY Greek *(pelagos) Atlantikos* (the sea) of Atlas (so called because it lay beyond the Atlas Mountains)

Atlanticism *n* belief in close economic and military cooperation between Europe and the United States. ▸ **Atlanticist** *n*

Atlantis *n* (in ancient legend) a continent said to have sunk beneath the Atlantic west of Gibraltar.

atlas *n* a book of maps. ▷ HISTORY because *Atlas*, a Titan in Greek mythology, was shown supporting the heavens in 16th-century books of maps

atmosphere *n* **1** the mass of gases surrounding the earth or any other heavenly body. **2** the air in a particular place. **3** a pervasive feeling or mood: *the atmosphere was tense.* **4** a unit of pressure equal to the normal pressure of the air at sea level. ▷ HISTORY Greek *atmos* vapour + *sphaira* sphere ▸ **atmospheric** *adj* ▸ **atmospherically** *adv*

atmospheric circulation *n Meteorol* the movement of air in the atmosphere.

atmospheric depression *n Meteorol* a body of moving air below normal atmospheric pressure, which often brings rain.

atmospheric pressure *n Physics* the pressure exerted by the atmosphere at the earth's surface. It has an average value of 1 atmosphere.

atmospherics *pl n* radio interference caused by electrical disturbance in the atmosphere.

atoll *n* a circular coral reef surrounding a lagoon. ▷ HISTORY *atollon*, native name in the Maldive Islands

atom *n* **1 a** the smallest unit of matter which can take part in a chemical reaction. **b** this entity as a source of nuclear energy. **2** a very small amount. ▷ HISTORY Greek *atomos* that cannot be divided

atom bomb *n* same as **atomic bomb**.

atomic *adj* **1** of or using atomic bombs or atomic energy. **2** of atoms. ▸ **atomically** *adv*

atomic bomb *or* **atom bomb** *n* a type of bomb in which the energy is provided by nuclear fission.

atomic energy *n* same as **nuclear energy**.

atomic mass unit *n* a unit of mass that is equal to one twelfth of the mass of an atom of carbon-12.

atomic number *n* the number of protons in the nucleus of an atom of an element.

atomic theory *n* any theory in which matter is regarded as consisting of atoms.

atomic weight *n* the ratio of the average mass per atom of an element to one twelfth of the mass of an atom of carbon-12.

atomize *or* **-ise** *vb* **-izing, -ized** *or* **-ising, -ised** **1** to separate into free atoms. **2** to reduce to fine particles or spray. **3** to destroy by nuclear weapons.

atomizer *or* **-iser** *n* a device for reducing a liquid to a fine spray.

atonal (ay-**tone**-al) *adj* (of music) not written in an established key. ▶ **atonality** *n*

atone *vb* **atoning, atoned** to make amends (for a sin, crime, or wrongdoing).

atonement *n* **1** something done to make amends for wrongdoing. **2** *Christian theol* the reconciliation of humankind with God through the sacrificial death of Christ. ▷ **HISTORY** Middle English *at onement* in harmony

atop *prep* on top of.

atrium *n, pl* **atria 1** *Anat* the upper chamber of each half of the heart. **2** a central hall that extends through several storeys in a modern building. **3** the open main court of an ancient Roman house. ▷ **HISTORY** Latin ▶ **atrial** *adj*

atrocious *adj* **1** extremely cruel or wicked. **2** horrifying or shocking. **3** *Informal* very bad. ▷ **HISTORY** Latin *atrox* dreadful ▶ **atrociously** *adv*

atrocity *n* **1** behaviour that is wicked or cruel. **2** (*pl* **-ties**) an act of extreme cruelty.

atrophy (**at**-trof-fee) *n, pl* **-phies 1** a wasting away of a physical organ or part. **2** a failure to grow. ✧ *vb* **-phies, -phying, -phied 3** to waste away. ▷ **HISTORY** Greek *atrophos* ill-fed

atropine *n* a poisonous alkaloid obtained from deadly nightshade. ▷ **HISTORY** New Latin *atropa* deadly nightshade

attach *vb* **1** to join, fasten, or connect. **2** to attribute or ascribe: *he attaches particular importance to the proposed sale.* **3 attach oneself** *or* **be attached to** to become associated with or join. ▷ **HISTORY** Old French *atachier*

attaché (at-**tash**-shay) *n* a specialist attached to a diplomatic mission. ▷ **HISTORY** French

attaché case *n* a flat rectangular briefcase for carrying papers.

attached *adj* **1** married, engaged, or in an exclusive sexual relationship. **2 attached to** fond of.

attachment *n* **1** affection or regard for. **2** an accessory that can be fitted to a device to change what it can do.

attack *vb* **1** to launch a physical assault (against). **2** to criticize vehemently. **3** to set about (a job or problem) with vigour. **4** to affect adversely: *BSE attacks the animal's brain.* **5** to take the initiative in a game or sport. ✧ *n* **6** the act of attacking. **7** any sudden appearance of a disease or symptoms: *a bad attack of mumps.* ▷ **HISTORY** Old Italian *attaccare* ▶ **attacker** *n*

attain *vb* **1** to manage to do or get (something): *the country attained economic growth.* **2** to reach. ▷ **HISTORY** Latin *attingere* ▶ **attainable** *adj*

attainment *n* an achievement or the act of achieving something.

attar *n* a perfume made from damask roses. ▷ **HISTORY** Persian *'atir* perfumed

attempt *vb* **1** to make an effort (to do or achieve something); try. ✧ *n* **2** an endeavour to achieve something; effort. **3 attempt on someone's life** an attack on someone with the intention to kill. ▷ **HISTORY** Latin *attemptare*

> ☑ **WORD TIP**
> *Attempt* should not be used in the passive when followed by an infinitive: *attempts were made to find a solution* (not *a solution was attempted to be found*).

attempted *adj Law* (of murder, rape, theft, etc.) incomplete, although the crime would have taken place had circumstances not prevented it. Attempted crimes are legally indictable.

attend *vb* **1** to be present at (an event). **2** to go regularly to a school, college, etc. **3** to look after: *the actors lounged in their canvas chairs, attended by sycophants.* **4** to pay attention. **5 attend to** to apply oneself to: *I've a few things I must attend to.* ▷ **HISTORY** Latin *attendere* to stretch towards

attendance *n* **1** the act of attending. **2** the number of people present. **3** regularity in attending.

attendant *n* **1** a person who assists, guides, or provides a service. ✧ *adj* **2** associated: *nuclear power and its attendant dangers.* **3** being in attendance.

attention *n* **1** concentrated direction of the mind. **2** consideration, notice, or observation. **3** detailed care or treatment. **4** the alert position in military drill. **5 attentions** acts of courtesy: *the attentions of men seemed to embarrass her.*

attentive *adj* **1** paying close attention. **2** considerately helpful: *at society parties he is attentive to his wife.* ▶ **attentively** *adv* ▶ **attentiveness** *n*

attenuated *adj* **1** weakened. **2** thin and extended. ▷ **HISTORY** Latin *attenuare* to weaken ▶ **attenuation** *n*

attest *vb* **1** to affirm or prove the truth of. **2** to bear witness to (an act or event). ▷ **HISTORY** Latin *testari* to bear witness ▶ **attestation** *n*

attested *adj Brit* (of cattle) certified to be free from a disease, such as tuberculosis.

attic *n* a space or room within the roof of a house. ▷ **HISTORY** from the *Attic* style of architecture

attire *n* clothes, esp. fine or formal ones. ▷ **HISTORY** Old French *atirier* to put in order

attired *adj* dressed in a specified way.

attitude *n* **1** the way a person thinks and behaves. **2** a position of the body. **3** *Informal* a hostile manner. **4** the orientation of an aircraft or spacecraft in relation to some plane or direction. ▷ **HISTORY** Latin *aptus* apt

attorney *n* **1** a person legally appointed to act for another. **2** *US* a lawyer. ▷ **HISTORY** Old French *atourner* to direct to

A B C D E F G H I J K L M N O P Q R S T U V W X Y Z

attorney general *n, pl* **attorneys general** *or* **attorney generals** a chief law officer of some governments.

attract *vb* **1** to arouse the interest or admiration of. **2** (of a magnet) to draw (something) closer by exerting a force on it. ▷ **HISTORY** Latin *attrahere* to draw towards

attraction *n* **1** the act or quality of attracting. **2** an interesting or desirable feature: *the Scottishness of Scott is an attraction, but by no means his only merit.* **3** an object or place that people visit for interest: *this carefully preserved tourist attraction.* **4** (of a magnet) a force by which one object attracts another.

attractive *adj* appealing to the senses or mind. ▸ **attractively** *adv* ▸ **attractiveness** *n*

attribute *vb* **-uting, -uted 1 attribute to** to regard as belonging to or produced by: *a play attributed to William Shakespeare.* ✧ *n* **2** a quality or feature representative of a person or thing. ▷ **HISTORY** Latin *attribuere* to associate with ▸ **attributable** *adj* ▸ **attribution** *n*

attributive *adj Grammar* (of an adjective) coming before the noun modified.

attrition *n* constant wearing down to weaken or destroy: *a war of attrition.* ▷ **HISTORY** Latin *atterere* to weaken

attune *vb* **-tuning, -tuned** to adjust or accustom (a person or thing).

ATV all-terrain vehicle: a vehicle with wheels designed to travel on rough ground.

atypical (eh-**tip**-ik-kl) *adj* not typical. ▸ **atypically** *adv*

Au *Chem* gold. ▷ **HISTORY** Latin *aurum*

aubergine (**oh**-bur-zheen) *n Brit* the dark purple fruit of a tropical plant, cooked and eaten as a vegetable. ▷ **HISTORY** French, from Arabic *al-bādindjān*

aubrietia (aw-**bree**-sha) *n* a trailing purple-flowered rock plant. ▷ **HISTORY** after Claude *Aubriet,* painter of flowers and animals

auburn *adj* (of hair) reddish-brown. ▷ **HISTORY** (originally meaning: blond) Latin *albus* white

auction *n* **1** a public sale at which articles are sold to the highest bidder. ✧ *vb* **2** to sell by auction. ▷ **HISTORY** Latin *auctio* an increasing

auctioneer *n* a person who conducts an auction.

audacious *adj* **1** recklessly bold or daring. **2** impudent or presumptuous. ▷ **HISTORY** Latin *audax* bold ▸ **audacity** *n*

audible *adj* loud enough to be heard. ▷ **HISTORY** Latin *audire* to hear ▸ **audibility** *n* ▸ **audibly** *adv*

audience *n* **1** a group of spectators or listeners at a concert or play. **2** the people reached by a book, film, or radio or television programme. **3** a formal interview. ▷ **HISTORY** Latin *audire* to hear

audio *adj* **1** of or relating to sound or hearing. **2** of or for the transmission or reproduction of sound. ▷ **HISTORY** Latin *audire* to hear

audio frequency *n* a frequency in the range 20 hertz to 20 000 hertz, audible to the human ear.

audiometer (aw-dee-**om**-it-er) *n* an instrument for testing hearing.

audiovisual *adj* involving both hearing and sight: *audiovisual teaching aids.*

audit *n* **1** an official inspection of business accounts, conducted by an independent qualified accountant. **2** any thoroughgoing assessment or review: *an audit of their lifestyle.* ✧ *vb* **auditing, audited 3** to examine (business accounts) officially. ▷ **HISTORY** Latin *audire* to hear

audition *n* **1** a test of a performer's or musician's ability for a particular role or job. ✧ *vb* **2** to test or be tested in an audition. ▷ **HISTORY** Latin *audire* to hear

auditor *n* a person qualified to audit accounts. ▷ **HISTORY** Latin *auditor* a hearer

auditorium *n, pl* **-toriums** *or* **-toria 1** the area of a concert hall or theatre in which the audience sits. **2** *US & Canad* a building for public meetings. ▷ **HISTORY** Latin

auditory *adj* of or relating to hearing. ▷ **HISTORY** Latin *audire* to hear

au fait (oh **fay**) *adj* **1** fully informed. **2** expert. ▷ **HISTORY** French: to the point

auf Wiedersehen (owf **vee**-der-zay-en) *interj* goodbye. ▷ **HISTORY** German

Aug. August.

auger *n* a pointed tool for boring holes. ▷ **HISTORY** Old English *nafugār* nave (i.e. hub of a wheel) spear

aught *pron Old-fashioned or literary* anything whatever: *for aught I know.* ▷ **HISTORY** Old English *āwiht*

augment *vb* to make or become greater in number or strength. ▷ **HISTORY** Latin *augere* to increase ▸ **augmentation** *n*

au gratin (oh **grat**-tan) *adj* cooked with a topping of breadcrumbs and sometimes cheese. ▷ **HISTORY** French

augur *vb* to be a good or bad sign of future events: *a double fault on the opening point did not augur well.* ▷ **HISTORY** Latin: diviner of omens

augury *n* **1** the foretelling of the future. **2** (*pl* **-ries**) an omen.

august *adj* dignified and imposing. ▷ **HISTORY** Latin *augustus*

August *n* the eighth month of the year. ▷ **HISTORY** Latin, after the emperor *Augustus*

Augustan *adj* **1** *History* of the Roman emperor Augustus Caesar or the poets writing during his reign. **2** *Literature* of any literary period noted for refinement and classicism, esp. the late 17th century in France (the period of dramatists Corneille, Racine, and Molière) or the 18th century in England (the period of Swift, Pope, and Johnson).

auk *n* a northern sea bird with a heavy body, short wings, and black-and-white plumage. ▷ **HISTORY** Old Norse *ālka*

auld lang syne *n* times past. ▷ **HISTORY** Scots, literally: old long since

aunt *n* **1** a sister of one's father or mother. **2** the wife of one's uncle. **3** a child's term of address for a female friend of the parents. ▷ **HISTORY** Latin *amita* a father's sister

auntie *or* **aunty** *n, pl* **-ies** *Informal* an aunt.

Aunt Sally *n, pl* **-lies 1** a figure used in fairgrounds as a target. **2** any target for insults or criticism.

au pair *n* a young foreign woman who does housework in return for board and lodging. ▷ **HISTORY** French

aura *n, pl* **auras** *or* **aurae 1** a distinctive air or quality associated with a person or thing. **2** any invisible emanation. ▷ **HISTORY** Greek: breeze

aural *adj* of or using the ears or hearing. ▷ **HISTORY** Latin *auris* ear ▶ **aurally** *adv*

aureate *adj Literary* **1** covered with gold. **2** (of a style of writing or speaking) excessively elaborate. ▷ **HISTORY** Latin *aurum* gold

aureole *or* **aureola** *n* **1** a ring of light surrounding the head of a figure represented as holy; halo. **2** the sun's corona, visible as a faint halo during eclipses. ▷ **HISTORY** Latin *aurum* gold

au revoir (oh riv-**vwahr**) *interj* goodbye. ▷ **HISTORY** French

auric *adj* of or containing gold in the trivalent state. ▷ **HISTORY** Latin *aurum* gold

auricle *n* **1** the upper chamber of the heart. **2** the outer part of the ear. ▷ **HISTORY** Latin *auris* ear ▶ **auricular** *adj*

auricula *n, pl* **-lae** *or* **-las** an alpine primrose with leaves shaped like a bear's ear. ▷ **HISTORY** Latin *auris* ear

auriferous *adj* containing gold. ▷ **HISTORY** Latin *aurum* gold + *ferre* to bear

aurochs *n, pl* **-rochs** a recently extinct European wild ox. ▷ **HISTORY** German

aurora *n, pl* **-ras** *or* **-rae 1** an atmospheric phenomenon of bands of light sometimes seen in the polar regions. **2** *Poetic* the dawn. ▷ **HISTORY** Latin: dawn

aurora australis *n* the aurora seen around the South Pole. ▷ **HISTORY** New Latin: southern aurora

aurora borealis *n* the aurora seen around the North Pole. ▷ **HISTORY** New Latin: northern aurora

auscultation *n* the listening to of the internal sounds of the body, usually with a stethoscope, to help with medical diagnosis. ▷ **HISTORY** Latin *auscultare* to listen attentively

auspices (**aw**-spiss-siz) *pl n* **under the auspices of** with the support and approval of. ▷ **HISTORY** Latin *auspicium* augury from birds

auspicious *adj* showing the signs of future success.

> **☑ WORD TIP**
> The use of *auspicious* to mean 'very special' (as in *this auspicious occasion*) should be avoided.

Aussie *n, adj Informal* Australian.

austere *adj* **1** stern or severe: *his austere and serious attitude to events.* **2** self-disciplined or ascetic: *an extraordinarily austere and puritanical organization.* **3** severely simple or plain: *the austere backdrop of grey.* ▷ **HISTORY** Greek *austēros* astringent

austerity *n, pl* **-ties 1** the state of being austere. **2** reduced availability of luxuries and consumer goods.

austral *adj* of or from the south. ▷ **HISTORY** Latin *auster* the south wind

Austral. 1 Australasia. **2** Australia(n).

Australasian *adj* of Australia, New Zealand, and neighbouring islands.

Australia Day *n* a public holiday in Australia on 26th January.

Australian *adj* **1** of Australia. ✧ *n* **2** a person from Australia.

Austrian *adj* **1** of Austria. ✧ *n* **2** a person from Austria.

autarchy (**aw**-tar-kee) *n, pl* **-chies** absolute power or autocracy. ▷ **HISTORY** Greek *autarkhia*

autarky (**aw**-tar-kee) *n, pl* **-kies** a policy of economic self-sufficiency. ▷ **HISTORY** Greek *autarkeia*

authentic *adj* **1** of undisputed origin or authorship; genuine. **2** reliable or accurate. **3** *Music* using period instruments, scores, and playing techniques. ▷ **HISTORY** Greek *authentikos* ▶ **authentically** *adv* ▶ **authenticity** *n*

authenticate *vb* **-cating, -cated** to establish as genuine. ▶ **authentication** *n*

author *n* **1** a person who writes a book, article, or other written work. **2** an originator or creator. ▷ **HISTORY** Latin *auctor*

authoritarian *adj* **1** insisting on strict obedience to authority. ✧ *n* **2** a person who insists on strict obedience to authority. ▶ **authoritarianism** *n*

authoritative *adj* **1** recognized as being reliable: *the authoritative book on Shakespeare.* **2** possessing authority; official. ▶ **authoritatively** *adv*

authority *n, pl* **-ties 1** the power to command, control, or judge others. **2** a person or group with this power: *a third escapee turned himself in to the authorities.* **3** a decision-making organization or government department: *the local authority.* **4** an expert in a particular field. **5** official permission: *he had no authority to negotiate.* **6** a position that has the power to command, control, or judge others: *people in authority.* **7 on good authority** from reliable evidence. **8** confidence resulting from expertise. ▷ **HISTORY** Latin *auctor* author

authorize *or* **-ise** *vb* **-izing, -ized** *or* **-ising, -ised 1** to give authority to. **2** to give official permission for. ▶ **authorization** *or* **-isation** *n*

Authorized Version *n* **the Authorized Version** an English translation of the Bible published in 1611.

authorship *n* **1** the origin or originator of a written work or plan. **2** the profession of writing.

autism *n Psychiatry* abnormal self-absorption, usually affecting children, characterized by lack of response to people and limited ability to communicate. ▷ **HISTORY** Greek *autos* self ▶ **autistic** *adj*

auto *n, pl* **-tos** *US & Canad informal* short for **automobile.**

auto- *or sometimes before a vowel* **aut-** *combining form* **1** self; of or by the same one: *autobiography.* **2** self-propelling: *automobile.* ▷ **HISTORY** Greek *autos* self

autobahn *n* a motorway in German-speaking countries. ▷ **HISTORY** German, from *Auto* car + *Bahn* road

autobiography *n, pl* **-phies** an account of a person's life written by that person. ▶ **autobiographer** *n* ▶ **autobiographical** *adj*

autoclave *n* an apparatus for sterilizing objects by steam under pressure. ▷ **HISTORY** AUTO- + Latin *clavis* key

autocracy *n, pl* **-cies** government by an individual with unrestricted authority.

autocrat *n* **1** a ruler with absolute authority. **2** a dictatorial person. ▷ **HISTORY** AUTO- + Greek *kratos* power ▶ **autocratic** *adj* ▶ **autocratically** *adv*

autocross *n* a sport in which cars race over a circuit of rough grass.

Autocue *n Trademark* an electronic television prompting device displaying a speaker's script, unseen by the audience.

auto-da-fé (aw-toe-da-**fay**) *n, pl* **autos-da-fé** **1** *History* the ceremonial passing of sentence on heretics by the Spanish Inquisition. **2** the burning to death of heretics. ▷ **HISTORY** Portuguese, literally: act of the faith

autofocus *n* a camera system in which the lens is focused automatically.

autogiro *or* **autogyro** *n, pl* **-ros** a self-propelled aircraft resembling a helicopter but with an unpowered rotor.

autograph *n* **1** a handwritten signature of a famous person. ✧ *vb* **2** to write one's signature on or in. ▷ **HISTORY** AUTO- + Greek *graphein* to write

automat *n US* a vending machine.

automate *vb* **-mating, -mated** to make (a manufacturing process) automatic.

automatic *adj* **1** (of a device or mechanism) able to activate or regulate itself. **2** (of a process) performed by automatic equipment. **3** done without conscious thought. **4** (of a firearm) utilizing some of the force of each explosion to reload and fire continuously. **5** occurring as a necessary consequence: *the certificate itself carries no automatic legal benefits.* ✧ *n* **6** an automatic firearm. **7** a motor vehicle with automatic transmission. ▷ **HISTORY** Greek *automatos* acting independently ▶ **automatically** *adv*

automatic pilot *n* **1** a device that automatically maintains an aircraft on a preset course. **2 on automatic pilot** repeating an action or process without thought.

automatic transmission *n* a transmission system in a motor vehicle in which the gears change automatically.

automation *n* the use of automatic, often electronic, methods to control industrial processes.

automaton *n, pl* **-tons** *or* **-ta** **1** a mechanical device operating under its own power. **2** a person who acts mechanically. ▷ **HISTORY** Greek *automatos* spontaneous

automobile *n US* a motorcar.

automobilia *pl n* items connected with cars that are of interest to a collector.

automotive *adj* **1** relating to motor vehicles. **2** self-propelling.

autonomous *adj* **1** having self-government. **2** independent of others. ▷ **HISTORY** AUTO- + Greek *nomos* law

autonomy *n, pl* **-mies** **1** the right or state of self-government. **2** freedom to determine one's own actions and behaviour. ▷ **HISTORY** Greek *autonomia*

autopilot *n* an automatic pilot.

autopsy *n, pl* **-sies** examination of a corpse to determine the cause of death. ▷ **HISTORY** Greek *autopsia* seeing with one's own eyes

autoroute *n* a motorway in French-speaking countries. ▷ **HISTORY** French, from *auto* car + *route* road

autostrada *n* a motorway in Italian-speaking countries. ▷ **HISTORY** Italian, from *auto* car + *strada* road

autosuggestion *n* a process in which a person unconsciously supplies the means of influencing his or her own behaviour or beliefs.

autotrophic *adj Biochem* (of organisms such as green plants) able to manufacture complex organic nutritive compounds from simple inorganic sources such as carbon dioxide, water, and nitrates.

autumn *n* **1** the season of the year between summer and winter. **2** a period of late maturity followed by a decline. ▷ **HISTORY** Latin *autumnus* ▶ **autumnal** *adj*

auxiliaries *pl n* foreign troops serving another nation.

auxiliary *adj* **1** secondary or supplementary. **2** supporting. ✧ *n, pl* **-ries** **3** a person or thing that supports or supplements. ▷ **HISTORY** Latin *auxilium* help

auxiliary verb *n* a verb used to indicate the tense, voice, or mood of another verb, such as *will* in *I will go.*

auxin *n Physiol* a plant hormone that promotes growth and controls fruit and flower development.

AV (of the Bible) Authorized Version.

av. **1** average. **2** avoirdupois.

avail *vb* **1** to be of use, advantage, or assistance (to). **2 avail oneself of** to make use of. ✧ *n* **3** use or advantage: *to no avail.* ▷ **HISTORY** Latin *valere* to be strong

available *adj* **1** obtainable or accessible. **2** able to be contacted and willing to talk: *a spokesman insisted she was not available for comment.* ▶ **availability** *n* ▶ **availably** *adv*

avalanche *n* **1** a fall of large masses of snow and ice down a mountain. **2** a sudden or overwhelming quantity of anything. ▷ **HISTORY** French

avant- (av-ong) *prefix* belonging to the avant-garde of a field: *avant-jazz.*

avant-garde (av-ong-**gard**) *n* **1** those artists, writers, or musicians, whose techniques and ideas are in advance of those generally accepted. ✧ *adj* **2** using ideas or techniques in advance of those generally accepted. ▷ **HISTORY** French: vanguard

avarice (**av**-a-riss) *n* extreme greed for wealth. ▷ **HISTORY** Latin *avere* to crave ▸ **avaricious** *adj*

avast *interj Naut* stop! cease! ▷ **HISTORY** probably Dutch *hou'vast* hold fast

avatar *n Hinduism* the appearance of a god in human or animal form. ▷ **HISTORY** Sanskrit *avatāra* a going down

Ave (**ah**-vay) *or* **Ave Maria** (ma-**ree**-a) *n* same as **Hail Mary**. ▷ **HISTORY** Latin: hail, Mary!

Ave. avenue.

avenge *vb* **avenging, avenged** to inflict a punishment in retaliation for (harm done) or on behalf of (the person harmed). ▷ **HISTORY** Latin *vindicare* ▸ **avenger** *n*

> **WORD TIP**
> The use of *avenge* with a reflexive pronoun was formerly considered incorrect, but is now acceptable: *she avenged herself on the man who killed her daughter.*

avenue *n* **1** a wide street. **2** a road bordered by two rows of trees. **3** a line of approach: *the United States was exhausting every avenue to achieve a diplomatic solution.* ▷ **HISTORY** French, from *avenir* to come to

aver (av-**vur**) *vb* **averring, averred** to state to be true. ▷ **HISTORY** Latin *verus* true ▸ **averment** *n*

average *n* **1** the typical or normal amount or quality. **2** the result obtained by adding the numbers or quantities in a set and dividing the total by the number of members in the set. **3 on average** usually or typically. ✧ *adj* **4** usual or typical. **5** calculated as an average. **6** mediocre or inferior. ✧ *vb* **-aging, -aged 7** to calculate or estimate the average of. **8** to amount to or be on average. ▷ **HISTORY** Middle English *averay* loss arising from damage to ships, ultimately from Arabic *awār* damage

averse *adj* opposed: *he's not averse to publicity, of the right kind.* ▷ **HISTORY** Latin *avertere* to turn from

aversion *n* **1** extreme dislike or disinclination. **2** a person or thing that arouses this.

avert *vb* **1** to turn away: *he had to avert his eyes.* **2** to ward off: *a final attempt to avert war.* ▷ **HISTORY** Latin *avertere* to turn from

Avesta *n* a collection of sacred writings of Zoroastrianism.

avian (**aiv**-ee-an) *adj* of or like a bird: *the treatment of avian diseases.* ▷ **HISTORY** Latin *avis* bird

aviary *n, pl* **aviaries** a large enclosure in which birds are kept. ▷ **HISTORY** Latin *avis* bird

aviation *n* the art or science of flying aircraft. ▷ **HISTORY** Latin *avis* bird

aviator *n Old-fashioned* the pilot of an aircraft. ▸ **aviatrix** *fem n*

avid *adj* **1** very keen or enthusiastic: *he is an avid football fan.* **2** eager: *avid for economic development.* ▷ **HISTORY** Latin *avere* to long for ▸ **avidity** *n* ▸ **avidly** *adv*

avocado *n, pl* **-dos** a pear-shaped tropical fruit with a leathery green skin and greenish-yellow flesh.

> **WORD HISTORY**
> 'Avocado' comes from the Aztec word *ahuacatl*, meaning 'testicle' as well as 'avocado'. The fruit was given this name by the Aztecs because of its shape. The word entered Mexican Spanish as *aguacate*, and changed to 'avocado' under the influence of the Spanish word *avocado* meaning 'advocate'.

avocation *n* **1** *Brit, Austral & NZ old-fashioned* a person's regular job. **2** *Formal* a hobby. ▷ **HISTORY** Latin *avocare* to distract

avocet *n* a long-legged shore bird with a long slender upward-curving bill. ▷ **HISTORY** Italian *avocetta*

avoid *vb* **1** to refrain from doing. **2** to prevent from happening. **3** to keep out of the way of. ▷ **HISTORY** Old French *esvuidier* ▸ **avoidable** *adj* ▸ **avoidably** *adv* ▸ **avoidance** *n*

avoirdupois *or* **avoirdupois weight** (av-er-de-**poise**) *n* a system of weights based on the pound, which contains 16 ounces. ▷ **HISTORY** Old French *aver de peis* goods of weight

avow *vb* **1** to state or affirm. **2** to admit openly. ▷ **HISTORY** Latin *advocare* to call upon ▸ **avowal** *n* ▸ **avowed** *adj* ▸ **avowedly** (a-**vow**-id-lee) *adv*

avuncular *adj* (of a man) friendly, helpful, and caring towards someone younger. ▷ **HISTORY** Latin *avunculus* (maternal) uncle

await *vb* **1** to wait for. **2** to be in store for.

awake *adj* **1** not sleeping. **2** alert or aware: *awake to the danger.* ✧ *vb* **awaking, awoke** *or* **awaked, awoken** *or* **awaked 3** to emerge or rouse from sleep. **4** to become or cause to become alert. ▷ **HISTORY** Old English *awacan*

> **WORD TIP**
> See at **wake.**

awaken *vb* **1** to awake. **2** to cause to be aware of: *anxieties awakened by reunification.*

awakening *n* the start of a feeling or awareness in someone: *a picture of an emotional awakening.*

award *vb* **1** to give (something) for merit. **2** *Law* to declare to be entitled, such as by decision of a court. ✧ *n* **3** something awarded, such as a prize. **4** *Law* the decision of an arbitrator or court. ▷ **HISTORY** Old French *eswarder* to decide after investigation

aware *adj* **1 aware of** knowing about: *he's at least aware of the problem.* **2** informed: *they are becoming more politically aware every day.* ▷ **HISTORY** Old English *gewær* ▸ **awareness** *n*

awash *adv, adj* washed over by water.

away *adv* **1** from a particular place: *I saw them walk away and felt absolutely desolated.* **2** in or to another, a usual, or a proper place: *he decided to put the car away in the garage.* **3** at a distance: *keep* *away from the windows.* **4** out of existence: *the pillars rotted away.* **5** indicating motion or distance from a normal or proper place: *the child shook her head and looked away.* **6** continuously: *he continued to scribble away.* ✧ *adj* **7** not present: *he had been away from home for years.* **8** distant: *the castle was farther away than he had thought.* **9** *Sport* played on an opponent's ground. ▷ **HISTORY** Old English *on weg* on way

awe *n* **1** wonder and respect mixed with dread. ✧ *vb* **awing, awed 2** to inspire with reverence or dread. ▷ **HISTORY** Old Norse *agi*

aweigh *adj Naut* (of an anchor) no longer hooked into the bottom.

awesome *adj* **1** inspiring or displaying awe. **2** *Slang* excellent or outstanding.

awestruck *adj* overcome or filled with awe.

awful *adj* **1** very bad or unpleasant. **2** *Informal* considerable or great: *that's an awful lot of money, isn't it?* **3** *Obsolete* inspiring reverence or dread. ✧ *adv* **4** *Not standard* very: *I'm working awful hard on my lines.*

awfully *adv* **1** in an unpleasant way. **2** *Informal* very: *we were both awfully busy.*

awhile *adv* for a brief period.

awkward *adj* **1** clumsy or ungainly. **2** embarrassed: *he was awkward and nervous around girls.* **3** difficult to deal with: *the lawyer was in an awkward situation.* **4** difficult to use or handle: *it was small but heavy enough to make it awkward to carry.* **5** embarrassing: *there were several moments of awkward silence.* ▷ **HISTORY** Old Norse *öfugr* turned the wrong way round ▸ **awkwardly** *adv* ▸ **awkwardness** *n*

awl *n* a pointed hand tool for piercing wood, leather, etc. ▷ **HISTORY** Old English *ǣl*

awn *n* any of the bristles growing from the flowering parts of certain grasses and cereals. ▷ **HISTORY** Old English *agen* ear of grain

awning *n* a canvas roof supported by a frame to give protection against the weather. ▷ **HISTORY** origin unknown

awoke *vb* a past tense and (now rare or dialectal) past participle of **awake**.

awoken *vb* a past participle of **awake**.

AWOL (**eh**-woll) *adj Mil* absent without leave but without intending to desert.

awry (a-**rye**) *adv, adj* **1** with a twist to one side; askew: *my neck was really awry after the journey.* **2** amiss or faulty: *if a gear gets stuck, the whole system goes awry.* ▷ **HISTORY** Middle English *on wry*

axe *or US* **ax** *n, pl* **axes 1** a hand tool with one side of its head sharpened to a cutting edge, used for felling trees and splitting timber. **2 an axe to grind** a favourite topic one wishes to promote. **3** *Informal* a severe cut in spending or in the number of staff employed. ✧ *vb* **axing, axed 4** *Informal* to dismiss (employees), restrict (expenditure), or terminate (a project). ▷ **HISTORY** Old English *æx*

axes[1] *n* the plural of **axis**.

axes[2] *n* the plural of **axe**.

axial *adj* **1** forming or of an axis. **2** in, on, or along an axis. ▸ **axially** *adv*

axil *n* the angle where the stalk of a leaf joins a stem. ▷ **HISTORY** Latin *axilla* armpit

axiom *n* **1** a generally accepted principle. **2** a self-evident statement. ▷ **HISTORY** Greek *axios* worthy

axiomatic *adj* **1** containing axioms. **2** self-evident or obvious. ▸ **axiomatically** *adv*

axis (**ax**-iss) *n, pl* **axes** (**ax**-eez) **1** a real or imaginary line about which a body can rotate or about which an object or geometrical construction is symmetrical. **2** one of two or three reference lines used in coordinate geometry to locate a point in a plane or in space. ▷ **HISTORY** Latin

axis of symmetry *n Geom* a line about which a geometric figure is symmetrical.

axle *n* a shaft on which a wheel or pair of wheels revolves. ▷ **HISTORY** Old Norse *öxull*

axolotl *n* an aquatic salamander of N America. ▷ **HISTORY** Mexican Indian: water doll

ayatollah *n* one of a class of Islamic religious leaders in Iran. ▷ **HISTORY** Arabic *aya* sign + *allah* God

aye *or* **ay** *interj* **1** *Brit, Austral & NZ* yes. ✧ *n* **2** an affirmative vote or voter. ▷ **HISTORY** probably from *I*, expressing assent

Ayrshire *n* one of a breed of brown-and-white dairy cattle. ▷ **HISTORY** *Ayrshire*, district of Scotland

AZ Arizona.

azalea (az-**zale**-ya) *n* a garden shrub grown for its showy flowers. ▷ **HISTORY** Greek *azaleos* dry

azimuth *n* **1** the arc of the sky between the zenith and the horizon. **2** *Surveying* the horizontal angle of a bearing measured clockwise from the north. ▷ **HISTORY** Arabic *as-samt* the path

Aztec *n* **1** a member of a Mexican Indian race who established a great empire, overthrown by the Spanish in the early 16th century. **2** the language of the Aztecs. ✧ *adj* **3** of the Aztecs or their language. ▷ **HISTORY** *Aztlan*, their traditional place of origin, literally: near the cranes

azure *n* **1** the deep blue colour of a clear blue sky. **2** *Poetic* a clear blue sky. ✧ *adj* **3** deep blue. ▷ **HISTORY** Arabic *lāzaward* lapis lazuli

B b

b *or* **B** *n, pl* **b's, B's** *or* **Bs 1** the second letter of the English alphabet. **2 from A to B** See **a** (sense 2).

b *Cricket* **a** bowled. **b** bye.

B 1 *Music* the seventh note of the scale of C major. **2** the second in a series, class, or rank. **3** *Chem* boron. **4** *Chess* bishop.

Ba *Chem* barium.

BA 1 Bachelor of Arts. **2** British Airways.

baa *vb* **baaing, baaed 1** (of a sheep) to make a characteristic bleating sound. ✧ *n* **2** the cry made by a sheep.

baas *n S African* a boss. ▷ HISTORY Afrikaans

baaskap *n* (in South Africa) control by Whites of non-Whites. ▷ HISTORY Afrikaans

babaco *n* a greenish-yellow egg-shaped fruit.

babble *vb* **-bling, -bled 1** to talk in a quick, foolish, or muddled way. **2** to make meaningless sounds: *children first gurgle and babble at random.* **3** to disclose secrets carelessly. **4** *Literary* (of streams) to make a low murmuring sound. ✧ *n* **5** muddled or foolish speech. **6** a murmuring sound. ▷ HISTORY probably imitative ▶ **babbler** *n* ▶ **babbling** *n*

babe *n* **1** a baby. **2 babe in arms** *Informal* a naive or inexperienced person. **3** *Slang* a girl, esp. an attractive one.

babel (**babe**-el) *n* **1** a confusion of noises or voices. **2** a scene of noise and confusion. ▷ HISTORY from the confusion of languages on the tower of *Babel* (Genesis 11:1–10)

baboon *n* a medium-sized monkey with a long face, large teeth, and a fairly long tail. ▷ HISTORY Middle English *babewyn* gargoyle

baby *n, pl* **-bies 1** a newborn child. **2** the youngest or smallest of a family or group. **3** a recently born animal. **4** an immature person. **5** *Slang* a sweetheart. **6** a project of personal concern. **7 be left holding the baby** to be left with a responsibility. ✧ *adj* **8** comparatively small of its type: *baby carrots.* ✧ *vb* **-bies, -bying, -bied 9** to treat like a baby. ▷ HISTORY probably childish reduplication ▶ **babyhood** *n* ▶ **babyish** *adj*

baby bonus *n Canad informal* Family Allowance.

baby-sit *vb* **-sitting, -sat** to act or work as a baby-sitter. ▶ **baby-sitting** *n, adj*

baby-sitter *n* a person who takes care of a child while the parents are out.

baccalaureate (back-a-**law**-ree-it) *n* the university degree of Bachelor of Arts. ▷ HISTORY Medieval Latin *baccalarius* bachelor

baccarat (**back**-a-rah) *n* a card game in which two or more punters gamble against the banker. ▷ HISTORY French *baccara*

bacchanalian (back-a-**nail**-ee-an) *adj Literary* (of a party) unrestrained and involving a great deal of drinking and sometimes sexual activity. ▷ HISTORY from *Bacchus,* Greek & Roman god of wine

Bacchus *n Classical myth* the god of wine; Dionysus.

bach (**batch**) *NZ* ✧ *n* **1** a small holiday cottage. ✧ *vb* **2** to look after oneself when one's spouse is away.

bachelor *n* **1** an unmarried man. **2** a person who holds a first degree from a university or college. ▷ HISTORY Old French *bacheler* youth, squire ▶ **bachelorhood** *n*

Bachelor of Arts *n* a person with a first degree from a university or college, usually in the arts.

Bach flower remedy *n* an alternative medicine consisting of a distillation from various flowers. ▷ HISTORY after Dr E. *Bach,* homeopath

bacillary *adj* of or caused by bacilli.

bacillus (bass-**ill**-luss) *n, pl* **-li** (-lie) a rod-shaped bacterium, esp. one causing disease. ▷ HISTORY Latin *baculum* walking stick

back *n* **1** the rear part of the human body, from the neck to the pelvis. **2** the spinal column. **3** the part or side of an object opposite the front. **4** the part of anything less often seen or used. **5** *Ball games* a defensive player or position. **6 at the back of one's mind** not in one's conscious thoughts. **7 behind someone's back** secretly or deceitfully. **8 put** *or* **get someone's back up** to annoy someone. **9 turn one's back on someone** to refuse to help someone. ✧ *vb* **10** to move or cause to move backwards. **11** to provide money for (a person or enterprise). **12** to bet on the success of: *to back a horse.* **13** to provide (a pop singer) with a musical accompaniment. **14** (foll. by *on* or *onto*) to have the back facing (towards): *his garden backs onto a school.* **15** (of the wind) to change direction anticlockwise. ✧ *adj* **16** situated behind: *back garden.* **17** owing from an earlier date: *back rent.* **18** remote: *a back road.* ✧ *adv* **19** at, to, or towards the rear. **20** to or towards the original starting point or condition: *I went back home.* **21** in reply or retaliation: *to hit someone back.* **22** in concealment or reserve: *to keep something back.* **23 back and forth** to and fro. **24 back to front a** in reverse. **b** in disorder. ✧ See also **back down.** ▷ HISTORY Old English *bæc*

backbencher *n Brit, Austral, NZ, etc.* a Member of Parliament who does not hold office in the government or opposition.

back boiler *n Brit* a tank at the back of a fireplace for heating water.

backbone *n* **1** the spinal column. **2** strength of character. **3** *Computers* a central section that connects segments of a network.

backbreaking *adj* (of work) exhausting.

backburn *Austral & NZ* ✧ *vb* **1** to clear (an area of bush) by creating a fire that burns in the opposite direction from the wind. **2** to prevent a bush fire from spreading by clearing an area of land in front of it. ✧ *n* **3** the act or result of backburning.

backchat *n Informal* impudent replies.

A B C D E F G H I J K L M N O P Q R S T U V W X Y Z

backcloth *n* a painted curtain at the back of a stage set. Also called: **backdrop**

back country *n Austral & NZ* land far away from settled areas.

backdate *vb* **-dating, -dated** to make (a document) effective from a date earlier than its completion.

back door *n* a means of entry to a job or position that is secret or obtained through influence.

back down *vb* to withdraw an earlier claim.

back dune *n Geog* a dune that is further away from the sea than the others. Compare **foredune**.

backer *n* a person who gives financial or other support.

backfire *vb* **-firing, -fired 1** (of a plan or scheme) to fail to have the desired effect. **2** (of an internal-combustion engine) to make a loud noise as a result of an explosion of unburnt gases in the exhaust system.

backgammon *n* a game for two people played on a board with pieces moved according to throws of the dice. ▷ **HISTORY** *back* + obsolete *gammon* game

background *n* **1** the events or circumstances that help to explain something. **2** a person's social class, education, or experience. **3** the part of a scene furthest from the viewer. **4** an inconspicuous position: *in the background.* **5** the space behind the chief figures or objects in a picture.

background radiation *n* low-intensity radiation that is naturally present in the earth's surface and atmosphere.

backhand *n* **1** *Tennis etc.* a stroke made from across the body with the back of the hand facing the direction of the stroke. **2** the side on which backhand strokes are made.

backhanded *adj* **1** (of a blow or shot) performed with the arm moving from across the body. **2** ambiguous or implying criticism: *a backhanded compliment.*

backhander *n* **1** *Slang* a bribe. **2** a backhanded stroke or blow.

backing *n* **1** support. **2** something that forms or strengthens the back of something. **3** musical accompaniment for a pop singer.

backing dog *n NZ* a dog that moves a flock of sheep by jumping on their backs.

backlash *n* **1** a sudden and adverse reaction. **2** a recoil between interacting badly fitting parts in machinery.

backlog *n* an accumulation of things to be dealt with.

backlot *n* an area outside a film or television studio used for outdoor filming.

back number *n* **1** an old issue of a newspaper or magazine. **2** *Informal* a person or thing considered to be old-fashioned.

back out *vb* (often foll. by *of*) to withdraw from (an agreement).

backpack *n* **1** a rucksack. ✧ *vb* **2** to go hiking with a backpack.

back passage *n* the rectum.

back-pedal *vb* **-pedalling, -pedalled** *or US* **-pedaling, -pedaled** to retract or modify a previous opinion or statement.

back room *n* **1** a place where secret research or planning is done. ✧ *adj* **back-room 2** of or relating to secret research or planning: *back-room boys.*

back-seat driver *n Informal* a person who offers unwanted advice.

backside *n Informal* the buttocks.

backslide *vb* **-sliding, -slid** to relapse into former bad habits or vices. ▶ **backslider** *n*

backspace *vb* **-spacing, -spaced** to move a typewriter carriage or computer cursor backwards.

backspin *n Sport* a backward spin given to a ball to reduce its speed at impact.

backstage *adv* **1** behind the stage in a theatre. ✧ *adj* **2** situated backstage.

backstairs *or* **backstair** *adj* underhand: *backstairs gossip.*

backstreet *n* **1** a street in a town far from the main roads. ✧ *adj* **2** denoting secret or illegal activities: *a backstreet abortion.*

backstroke *n Swimming* a stroke performed on the back, using backward circular strokes of each arm.

backswamp *n Geog* the marshy part of a flood plain where silt settles following a flood.

backtrack *vb* **1** to go back along the same route one has just travelled. **2** to retract or reverse one's opinion or policy.

back up *vb* **1** to support. **2** *Computers* to make a copy of (a data file), esp. as a security copy. **3** (of traffic) to become jammed behind an obstruction. ✧ *n* **backup 4** a support or reinforcement. **5** a reserve or substitute. ✧ *adj* **backup 6** able to be substituted: *a backup copy.*

backward *adj* **1** directed towards the rear. **2** retarded in physical, material, or intellectual development. **3** reluctant or bashful. ✧ *adv* **4** same as **backwards**. ▶ **backwardness** *n*

backwards *or* **backward** *adv* **1** towards the rear. **2** with the back foremost. **3** in the reverse of the usual direction. **4** into a worse state: *the Gothic novel's been going backwards since Radcliffe.* **5 bend over backwards** *Informal* to make a special effort to please someone.

backwash *n* **1** water washed backwards by the motion of oars or a ship. **2** water carried back from the shore following each break of the waves. **3** an unpleasant aftereffect of an event or situation.

backwater *n* **1** an isolated or backward place or condition. **2** a body of stagnant water connected to a river.

backwoods *pl n* **1** any remote sparsely populated place. **2** partially cleared, sparsely populated forests. ▶ **backwoodsman** *n*

bacon *n* **1** meat from the back and sides of a pig, dried, salted, and often smoked. **2 bring home the bacon** *Informal* **a** to achieve success. **b** to provide material support. ▷ **HISTORY** Old French

bacteria *pl n, sing* **-rium** a large group of microorganisms, many of which cause disease. ▷ **HISTORY** Greek *baktron* rod ▶ **bacterial** *adj*

bacteriology *n* the study of bacteria. ▶ **bacteriologist** *n*

Bactrian camel *n* a two-humped camel. ▷ **HISTORY** *Bactria*, ancient country of Asia

bad *adj* **worse, worst 1** not good; of poor quality. **2** lacking skill or talent: *I'm so bad at that sort of thing.* **3** harmful: *smoking is bad for you.* **4** evil or immoral. **5** naughty or mischievous. **6** rotten or decayed: *a bad egg.* **7** severe: *a bad headache.* **8** incorrect or faulty: *bad grammar.* **9** sorry or upset: *I feel bad about saying no.* **10** unfavourable or distressing: *bad news.* **11** offensive or unpleasant: *bad language.* **12** not valid: *a bad cheque.* **13** not recoverable: *a bad debt.* **14 badder, baddest** *Slang* good; excellent. **15 not bad** *or* **not so bad** *Informal* fairly good. **16 too bad** *Informal* (often used dismissively) regrettable. ✧ *n* **17** unfortunate or unpleasant events: *you've got to take the good with the bad.* ✧ *adv* **18** *Not standard* badly: *to want something bad.* ▷ **HISTORY** Middle English ▶ **badness** *n*

bad blood *n* a feeling of intense hatred or hostility between people.

bade *or* **bad** *vb* a past tense of **bid**.

badge *n* **1** a distinguishing emblem or mark worn to show membership or achievement. **2** any revealing feature or mark. ▷ **HISTORY** Old French *bage*

badger *n* **1** a stocky burrowing mammal with a black and white striped head. ✧ *vb* **2** to pester or harass. ▷ **HISTORY** probably from *badge*

badinage (**bad**-in-nahzh) *n* playful and witty conversation. ▷ **HISTORY** French

badlands *pl n Geog* areas of arid barren land with deep ridges and gullies caused by erosion.

badly *adv* **worse, worst 1** poorly; inadequately. **2** unfavourably: *our plan worked out badly.* **3** severely: *badly damaged.* **4** very much: *he badly needed to improve his image.* **5 badly off** poor.

badminton *n* a game played with rackets and a shuttlecock which is hit back and forth across a high net. ▷ **HISTORY** *Badminton* House, Glos

Bafana bafana (bah-**fan**-na) *pl n S African* the South African national soccer team. ▷ **HISTORY** from Nguni (language group of southern Africa) *bafana* the boys

baffle *vb* **-fling, -fled 1** to perplex. ✧ *n* **2** a mechanical device to limit or regulate the flow of fluid, light, or sound. ▷ **HISTORY** origin unknown ▶ **bafflement** *n* ▶ **baffling** *adj*

bag *n* **1** a flexible container with an opening at one end. **2** the contents of such a container. **3** a piece of luggage. **4** a handbag. **5** a loose fold of skin under the eyes. **6** any sac in the body of an animal. **7** *Offensive slang* an ugly or bad-tempered woman: *an old bag.* **8** the amount of game taken by a hunter. **9 in the bag** *Slang* assured of succeeding. ✧ *vb* **bagging, bagged 10** to put into a bag. **11** to bulge or cause to bulge. **12** to capture or kill, as in hunting. **13** *Brit & NZ informal* to secure the right to do or to have: *he bagged the best chair.* ✧ See also **bags**. ▷ **HISTORY** probably Old Norse *baggi*

bagatelle *n* **1** something of little value. **2** a board game in which balls are struck into holes. **3** a short piece of music. ▷ **HISTORY** French

bagel (**bay**-gl) *n* a hard ring-shaped bread roll. ▷ **HISTORY** Yiddish *beygel*

baggage *n* **1** suitcases packed for a journey. **2** an army's portable equipment. **3** *Informal* previous knowledge or experience that may have an influence in new circumstances: *cultural baggage.* ▷ **HISTORY** Old French *bagage*

baggy *adj* **-gier, -giest** (of clothes) hanging loosely. ▶ **bagginess** *n*

bagpipes *pl n* a musical wind instrument in which sounds are produced in reed pipes by air from an inflated bag.

bags *pl n* **1** *Informal* a lot. ✧ *interj* **2** Also: **bags I** *Children's slang, Brit & NZ* an indication of the desire to do, be, or have something.

bah *interj* an expression of contempt or disgust.

bahada *n* same as **bajada**.

bail[1] *Law* ✧ *n* **1** a sum of money deposited with the court as security for a person's reappearance in court. **2** the person giving such security. **3 jump bail** to fail to reappear in court after bail has been paid. **4 stand** *or* **go bail** to act as surety for someone. ✧ *vb* **5** (foll. by *out*) to obtain the release of (a person) from custody by depositing money with the court. ▷ **HISTORY** Old French: custody

bail[2] *or* **bale** *vb* **bail out** to remove water from (a boat). See also **bail out**. ▷ **HISTORY** Old French *baille* bucket

bail[3] *n* **1** *Cricket* either of two small wooden bars across the tops of the stumps. **2** a partition between stalls in a stable or barn. **3** *Austral & NZ* a framework in a cow shed used to secure the head of a cow during milking. **4** a movable bar on a typewriter that holds the paper against the roller. ▷ **HISTORY** Old French *baile* stake

bailey *n* the outermost wall or court of a castle. ▷ **HISTORY** Old French *baille* enclosed court

Bailey bridge *n* a temporary bridge that can be rapidly assembled. ▷ **HISTORY** after Sir Donald Coleman *Bailey*, its designer

bailiff *n* **1** *Brit* a sheriff's officer who serves writs and summonses. **2** the agent of a landlord or landowner. ▷ **HISTORY** Old French *baillif*

bailiwick *n* **1** *Law* the area over which a bailiff has power. **2** a person's special field of interest. ▷ **HISTORY** *bailie* magistrate + obsolete *wick* district

bail out *or* **bale out** *vb* **1** *Informal* to help (a person or organization) out of a predicament. **2** to make an emergency parachute jump from an aircraft.

bail up *vb* **1** *Austral & NZ, informal* to confine (a cow) or (of a cow) to be confined by the head in a bail. See **bail**[3]. **2** *Austral history* (of a bushranger) to hold under guard in order to rob. **3** *Austral* to submit to robbery without offering resistance. **4** *Austral, informal* to accost or detain, esp. in conversation; buttonhole.

bairn *n Scot & N English* a child. ▷ **HISTORY** Old English *bearn*

a b c d e f g h i j k l m n o p q r s t u v w x y z

A B C D E F G H I J K L M N O P Q R S T U V W X Y Z

bait *n* **1** something edible fixed to a hook or in a trap to attract fish or animals. **2** an enticement. ✧ *vb* **3** to put a piece of food on or in (a hook or trap). **4** to persecute or tease. **5** to set dogs upon (a bear or badger). ▷ HISTORY Old Norse *beita* to hunt

> **WORD TIP**
> The phrase *with bated breath* is sometimes wrongly spelled *with baited breath.*

baize *n* a feltlike woollen fabric, usually green, which is used for the tops of billiard and card tables. ▷ HISTORY Old French *bai* reddish-brown

bajada *or* **bahada** (ba-**hah**-da) *n Geog* a sloping area of sedimentary deposits at the foot of a desert mountain range formed by the overlapping of alluvial fans. ▷ HISTORY Spanish

bake *vb* **baking, baked 1** to cook by dry heat in an oven. **2** to cook bread, pastry, or cakes. **3** to make or become hardened by heat. **4** *Informal* to be extremely hot. ▷ HISTORY Old English *bacan*

baked beans *pl n* haricot beans, baked and tinned in tomato sauce.

Bakelite (**bake**-a-lite) *n Trademark* any of a class of resins used as electric insulators and for making plastics. ▷ HISTORY after L. H. *Baekeland,* inventor

baker *n* a person who makes or sells bread, cakes, etc.

baker's dozen *n* thirteen.

bakery *n, pl* **-eries** a place where bread, cakes, etc. are made or sold.

baking powder *n* a powdered mixture that contains sodium bicarbonate and cream of tartar: used in baking as a raising agent.

bakkie (**buck**-ee) *n S African* a small truck with an enclosed cab and an open goods area at the back. ▷ HISTORY Afrikaans *bak* container

baksheesh *n* (in some Eastern countries) money given as a tip or present. ▷ HISTORY Persian *bakhshīsh*

Balaclava *or* **Balaclava helmet** *n* a close-fitting woollen hood that covers the ears and neck. ▷ HISTORY after *Balaklava,* in the Crimea

balalaika *n* a Russian musical instrument with a triangular body and three strings. ▷ HISTORY Russian

balance *n* **1** stability of mind or body: *lose one's balance.* **2** a state of being in balance. **3** harmony in the parts of a whole. **4** the power to influence or control: *the balance of power.* **5** something that remains: *the balance of what you owe.* **6** *Accounting* **a** the matching of debit and credit totals in an account. **b** a difference between such totals. **7** a weighing device. **8 in the balance** in an undecided condition. **9 on balance** after weighing up all the factors. ✧ *vb* **-ancing, -anced 10** to weigh in or as if in a balance. **11** to be or come into equilibrium. **12** to bring into or hold in equilibrium. **13** to compare the relative weight or importance of. **14** to arrange so as to create a state of harmony. **15** *Accounting* to compare or equalize the credit and debit totals of (an account). ▷ HISTORY Latin *bilanx* having two scales

balanced forces *pl n Physics* any number of forces acting on a single object and adding up to zero, so that if the object is not moving, then it will continue to stay still, and if the object is already moving, it will continue to move with a constant velocity.

balance of payments *n* the difference in value between a nation's total payments to foreign countries and its total receipts from foreign countries.

balance of power *n* the equal distribution of military and economic power among countries.

balance of probabilities *n Law* the standard of proof in a civil case, meaning that, to win a case, a claimant has only to prove that his or her version of events is the more or most likely one. Compare **beyond reasonable doubt**.

balance of trade *n* the difference in value between exports and imports of goods.

balance sheet *n* a statement that shows the financial position of a business.

balcony *n, pl* **-nies 1** a platform projecting from a building with a balustrade along its outer edge, often with access from a door. **2** an upper tier of seats in a theatre or cinema. ▷ HISTORY Italian *balcone*

bald *adj* **1** having no hair or fur, esp. of a man having no hair on the scalp. **2** lacking natural covering. **3** plain or blunt: *the bald facts.* **4** (of a tyre) having a worn tread. ▷ HISTORY Middle English *ballede* ▶ **baldly** *adv* ▶ **baldness** *n*

balderdash *n* stupid or illogical talk. ▷ HISTORY origin unknown

balding *adj* becoming bald.

bale[1] *n* **1** a large bundle of hay or goods bound by ropes or wires for storage or transportation. ✧ *vb* **baling, baled 2** to make (hay) or put (goods) into a bale or bales. ▷ HISTORY Old High German *balla* ball

bale[2] *vb* **baling, baled** same as **bail**[2].

baleen *n* whalebone. ▷ HISTORY Latin *balaena* whale

baleen whale *n* same as **whalebone whale**.

baleful *adj* harmful, menacing, or vindictive. ▶ **balefully** *adv*

balk *or* **baulk** *vb* **1** to stop short: *the horse balked at the jump.* **2** to recoil: *France balked at the parliament having a veto.* **3** to thwart, check, or foil: *he was balked in his plans.* ▷ HISTORY Old English *balca* ridge

Balkan *adj* of any of the countries of the Balkan Peninsula in SE Europe, between the Adriatic and Aegean Seas.

ball[1] *n* **1** a spherical or nearly spherical mass: *a ball of wool.* **2** a round or roundish object used in various games. **3** a single delivery of the ball in a game. **4** any more or less rounded part of the body: *the ball of the foot.* **5 have the ball at one's feet** to have the chance of doing something. **6 on the ball** *Informal* alert; informed. **7 play ball** *Informal* to cooperate. **8 set** *or* **keep the ball rolling** to initiate or maintain the progress of an action, discussion, or project. ✧ *vb* **9** to form into a ball. ✧ See also **balls**. ▷ HISTORY Old Norse *böllr*

ball[2] *n* **1** a lavish or formal social function for dancing. **2 have a ball** *Informal* to have a very enjoyable time. ▷ **HISTORY** Late Latin *ballare* to dance

ballad *n* **1** a narrative song or poem often with a chorus that is repeated. **2** a slow sentimental song. ▷ **HISTORY** Old Provençal *balada* song accompanying a dance

ballade *n* **1** *Prosody* a verse form consisting of three stanzas and an envoy, all ending with the same line. **2** *Music* a romantic instrumental composition.

ball-and-socket joint *n Anat* a joint in which a rounded head fits into a rounded cavity, allowing a wide range of movement.

ballast *n* **1** a substance, such as sand, used to stabilize a ship when it is not carrying cargo. **2** crushed rock used for the foundation of a road or railway track. ✧ *vb* **3** to give stability or weight to. ▷ **HISTORY** probably Low German

ball bearing *n* **1** an arrangement of steel balls placed between moving parts of a machine in order to reduce friction. **2** a metal ball used in such an arrangement.

ball cock *n* a device consisting of a floating ball and valve for regulating the flow of liquid into a tank or cistern.

ballerina *n* a female ballet dancer. ▷ **HISTORY** Italian

ballet *n* **1** a classical style of expressive dancing based on precise conventional steps. **2** a theatrical representation of a story performed by ballet dancers. ▷ **HISTORY** Italian *balletto* a little dance ▶ **balletic** *adj*

ballistic missile *n* a launched weapon which is guided automatically in flight but falls freely at its target.

ballistics *n* the study of the flight of projectiles, often in relation to firearms. ▷ **HISTORY** Greek *ballein* to throw ▶ **ballistic** *adj*

balloon *n* **1** an inflatable rubber bag used as a plaything or party decoration. **2** a large bag inflated with a lighter-than-air gas, designed to rise and float in the atmosphere with a basket for carrying passengers. **3** an outline containing the words or thoughts of a character in a cartoon. ✧ *vb* **4** to fly in a balloon. **5** to swell or increase rapidly in size: *the cost of health care has ballooned.* ▷ **HISTORY** Italian dialect *ballone* ball ▶ **balloonist** *n*

ballot *n* **1** the practice of selecting a representative or course of action by voting. **2** the number of votes cast in an election. **3** the actual vote or paper indicating a person's choice. ✧ *vb* **-loting, -loted 4** to vote or ask for a vote from: *we balloted the members on this issue.* **5** to vote for or decide on something by ballot.

WORD HISTORY

'Ballot' comes from Italian *ballotta* meaning 'little ball'. In medieval Venice, votes were cast by dropping black or white pebbles or balls into a box.

ballot box *n* a box into which voting papers are dropped on completion.

ballot paper *n* a paper used for voting.

ballpoint *or* **ballpoint pen** *n* a pen which has a small ball bearing as a writing point.

ballroom *n* a large hall for dancing.

balls *pl n Taboo slang* **1** the testicles. **2** nonsense. **3** courage and determination. ▶ **ballsy** *adj*

bally *adj, adv Brit old-fashioned, slang* extreme or extremely: *a bally nuisance; he's too bally charming for his own good.*

ballyhoo *n Informal* unnecessary or exaggerated fuss. ▷ **HISTORY** origin unknown

balm *n* **1** an aromatic substance obtained from certain tropical trees and used for healing and soothing. **2** something comforting or soothing: *her calmness was like a balm to my troubled mind.* **3** an aromatic herb, lemon balm. ▷ **HISTORY** Latin *balsamum* balsam

balmy *adj* **balmier, balmiest 1** (of weather) mild and pleasant. **2** same as **barmy**.

baloney *or* **boloney** *n Informal* nonsense. ▷ **HISTORY** *Bologna* (sausage)

balsa (**bawl**-sa) *n* **1** a tree of tropical America which yields light wood. **2** Also: **balsawood** the light wood of this tree, used for making rafts, models, etc. ▷ **HISTORY** Spanish: raft

balsam *n* **1** an aromatic resin obtained from various trees and shrubs and used in medicines and perfumes. **2** any plant yielding balsam. **3** a flowering plant, such as busy lizzie. ▷ **HISTORY** Greek *balsamon*

Baltic (**bawl**-tik) *adj* of the Baltic Sea in N Europe or the states bordering it.

baluster *n* a set of posts supporting a rail. ▷ **HISTORY** French *balustre*

balustrade *n* an ornamental rail supported by a set of posts. ▷ **HISTORY** French

bamboo *n* a tall treelike tropical grass with hollow stems which are used to make canes, furniture, etc. ▷ **HISTORY** probably from Malay *bambu*

bamboozle *vb* **-zling, -zled** *Informal* **1** to cheat; mislead. **2** to confuse. ▷ **HISTORY** origin unknown ▶ **bamboozlement** *n*

ban *vb* **banning, banned 1** to prohibit or forbid officially. ✧ *n* **2** an official prohibition. ▷ **HISTORY** Old English *bannan* to proclaim

banal (ban-**nahl**) *adj* lacking originality. ▶ **banality** *n*

WORD HISTORY

In Old French, the adjective *banal* referred to the mill, bakery, etc. that was owned by the local lord and that all his tenants had to use. The word 'banal' therefore came to mean 'common to everyone' and from that, 'commonplace' or 'ordinary'.

banana *n* a crescent-shaped fruit that grows on a tropical or subtropical treelike plant. ▷ **HISTORY** Spanish or Portuguese, of African origin

a b c d e f g h i j k l m n o p q r s t u v w x y z

A B C D E F G H I J K L M N O P Q R S T U V W X Y Z

banana republic *n Informal* a small politically unstable country whose economy is dominated by foreign interests.

band¹ *n* **1** a group of musicians playing together, esp. on brass or percussion instruments. **2** a group of people having a common purpose: *a band of revolutionaries.* **3** *Ethnography* (in Canada) a formally recognized group of Indians on a reserve. ✧ *vb* **4** (foll. by *together*) to unite. ▷ **HISTORY** French *bande*

band² *n* **1** a strip of some material, used to hold objects together: *a rubber band.* **2** a strip of fabric used as an ornament or to reinforce clothing. **3** a stripe of contrasting colour or texture. **4** a driving belt in machinery. **5** *Physics* a range of frequencies or wavelengths between two limits. ✧ *vb* **6** to fasten or mark with a band. ▷ **HISTORY** Old French *bende*

bandage *n* **1** a piece of material used to dress a wound or wrap an injured limb. ✧ *vb* **-aging, -aged 2** to cover or wrap with a bandage.
▷ **HISTORY** French *bande* strip

bandanna *or* **bandana** *n* a large brightly-coloured handkerchief or neckerchief.
▷ **HISTORY** Hindi *bāndhnū* tie-dyeing

B & B bed and breakfast.

bandicoot *n* **1** an Australian marsupial with a long pointed muzzle and a long tail. **2 bandicoot rat** any of three burrowing rats of S and SE Asia.
▷ **HISTORY** Telugu (language of SE India) *pandikokku*

bandit *n* a robber, esp. a member of an armed gang. ▷ **HISTORY** Italian *bandito* ▶ **banditry** *n*

bandmaster *n* the conductor of a band.

bandolier *n* a shoulder belt with small pockets for cartridges. ▷ **HISTORY** Old French *bandouliere*

band saw *n* a power-operated saw consisting of an endless toothed metal band running over two wheels.

bandsman *n, pl* **-men** a player in a musical band.

bandstand *n* a roofed outdoor platform for a band.

bandwagon *n* **jump** *or* **climb on the bandwagon** to join a popular party or movement that seems assured of success.

bandy *adj* **-dier, -diest 1** Also: **bandy-legged** having legs curved outwards at the knees. **2** (of legs) curved outwards at the knees. ✧ *vb* **-dies, -dying, -died 3** to exchange (words), sometimes in a heated manner. **4 bandy about** to use (a name, term, etc.) frequently.

> **WORD HISTORY**
> 'Bandy' comes from Old French *bander* meaning 'to hit a ball backwards and forwards in tennis'. The word 'bandy' also denotes an old form of tennis that is no longer played.

bane *n* a person or thing that causes misery or distress: *the bane of my life.* ▷ **HISTORY** Old English *bana* ▶ **baneful** *adj*

bang *n* **1** a short loud explosive noise, such as the report of a gun. **2** a hard blow or loud knock. **3** *Taboo slang* an act of sexual intercourse. **4 with a bang** successfully: *the party went with a bang.* ✧ *vb* **5** to hit or knock, esp. with a loud noise. **6** to close (a door) noisily. **7** to make or cause to make a loud noise, as of an explosion. **8** *Taboo slang* to have sexual intercourse with. ✧ *adv* **9** with a sudden impact: *the car drove bang into a lamppost.* **10** precisely: *bang in the middle.* ▷ **HISTORY** Old Norse *bang, banga* hammer

banger *n* **1** *Brit & Austral informal* an old decrepit car. **2** *Slang* a sausage. **3** a firework that explodes loudly.

Bangladeshi *adj* **1** of Bangladesh. ✧ *n* **2** a person from Bangladesh.

bangle *n* a bracelet worn round the arm or sometimes round the ankle. ▷ **HISTORY** Hindi *bangrī*

banish *vb* **1** to send into exile. **2** to drive away: *it's the only way to banish weeds from the garden.*
▷ **HISTORY** Old French *banir* ▶ **banishment** *n*

banisters *or* **bannisters** *pl n* the railing and supporting balusters on a staircase.
▷ **HISTORY** altered from BALUSTER

banjo *n, pl* **-jos** *or* **-joes** a stringed musical instrument with a long neck and a circular drumlike body. ▷ **HISTORY** US pronunciation of earlier *bandore* ▶ **banjoist** *n*

bank¹ *n* **1** an institution offering services, such as the safekeeping and lending of money at interest. **2** the building used by such an institution. **3** the funds held by a banker or dealer in some gambling games. **4** any supply, store, or reserve: *a data bank.* ✧ *vb* **5** to deposit (cash or a cheque) in a bank. **6** to transact business with a bank. ✧ See also **bank on.**
▷ **HISTORY** probably from Italian *banca* bench, moneychanger's table

bank² *n* **1** a long raised mass, esp. of earth. **2** a slope, as of a hill. **3** the sloping side and ground on either side of a river. ✧ *vb* **4** to form into a bank or mound. **5** to cover (a fire) with ashes and fuel so that it will burn slowly. **6** (of an aircraft) to tip to one side in turning. ▷ **HISTORY** Scandinavian

bank³ *n* **1** an arrangement of similar objects in a row or in tiers. ✧ *vb* **2** to arrange in a bank.
▷ **HISTORY** Old French *banc* bench

bankable *adj* likely to ensure financial success: *a bankable star.* ▶ **bankability** *n*

bank account *n* an arrangement whereby a customer deposits money at a bank and may withdraw it when it is needed.

bank card *n* any plastic card issued by a bank, such as a cash card or a cheque card.

banker¹ *n* **1** a person who owns or manages a bank. **2** the keeper of the bank in various gambling games.

banker² *n Austral & NZ informal* a stream almost overflowing its banks: *the creek was running a banker.*

banker's order *n* same as **standing order** (sense 1).

bankfull *n Environmental Science* the maximum height of water in a stream or river before it overflows its banks.

bank holiday *n* (in Britain) a public holiday when banks are closed by law.

banking *n* the business engaged in by a bank.

banknote *n* a piece of paper money issued by a central bank.

bank on *vb* to rely on.

bankrupt *n* **1** a person, declared by a court to be unable to pay his or her debts, whose property is sold and the proceeds distributed among the creditors. **2** a person no longer having a particular quality: *a spiritual bankrupt.* ✧ *adj* **3** declared insolvent. **4** financially ruined. **5** no longer having a particular quality: *morally bankrupt.* ✧ *vb* **6** to make bankrupt. ▷ HISTORY Old Italian *banca* BANK[1] + *rotta* broken ▶ **bankruptcy** *n*

banksia *n* an Australian evergreen tree or shrub.

banner *n* **1** a long strip of material displaying a slogan, advertisement, etc. **2** a placard carried in a demonstration. **3** Also called: **banner headline** a large headline in a newspaper extending across the page. ▷ HISTORY Old French *baniere*

banns *pl n* the public announcement of an intended marriage. ▷ HISTORY plural of obsolete *bann* proclamation

banquet *n* **1** an elaborate formal dinner often followed by speeches. ✧ *vb* **-queting, -queted 2** to hold or take part in a banquet. ▷ HISTORY Italian *banco* a table

banshee *n* (in Irish folklore) a female spirit whose wailing warns of a coming death. ▷ HISTORY Irish Gaelic *bean sídhe* woman of the fairy mound

bantam *n* **1** a small breed of domestic fowl. **2** a small but aggressive person. ▷ HISTORY after *Bantam*, village in Java, said to be the original home of this fowl

bantamweight *n* a professional boxer weighing up to 118 pounds (53.5 kg) or an amateur weighing up to 54 kg.

banter *vb* **1** to tease jokingly. ✧ *n* **2** teasing or joking conversation. ▷ HISTORY origin unknown

Bantu *n* **1** a group of languages of Africa. **2** (*pl* **-tu** *or* **-tus**) *Offensive* a Black speaker of a Bantu language. ✧ *adj* **3** of the Bantu languages or the peoples who speak them. ▷ HISTORY Bantu *Ba-ntu* people

Bantustan *n Offensive* formerly, an area reserved for occupation by a Black African people. Official name: **homeland** ▷ HISTORY *Bantu* + Hindi *-stan* country of

banyan *or* **banian** *n* an Indian tree whose branches grow down into the soil forming additional trunks. ▷ HISTORY Hindi *baniyā*

baobab (**bay**-oh-bab) *n* an African tree with a massive grey trunk, short angular branches, and large pulpy fruit. ▷ HISTORY probably from a native African word

bap *n Brit* a large soft bread roll. ▷ HISTORY origin unknown

baptism *n* a Christian religious rite in which a person is immersed in or sprinkled with water as a sign of being cleansed from sin and accepted as a member of the Church. ▶ **baptismal** *adj*

baptism of fire *n* **1** any introductory ordeal. **2** a soldier's first experience of battle.

Baptist *n* **1** a member of a Protestant denomination that believes in the necessity of adult baptism by immersion. **2 the Baptist** John the Baptist. ✧ *adj* **3** of the Baptist Church.

baptize *or* **-tise** *vb* **-tizing, -tized** *or* **-tising, -tised 1** *Christianity* to immerse (a person) in water or sprinkle water on (him or her) as part of the rite of baptism. **2** to give a name to. ▷ HISTORY Greek *baptein* to bathe, dip

bar[1] *n* **1** a rigid usually straight length of metal, wood, etc. used as a barrier or structural part. **2** a solid usually rectangular block of any material: *a bar of soap.* **3** anything that obstructs or prevents: *a bar to women's mobility.* **4** a counter or room where alcoholic drinks are served. **5** a narrow band or stripe, as of colour or light. **6** a heating element in an electric fire. **7** See **Bar**. **8** the place in a court of law where the accused stands during trial. **9** *Music* a group of beats that is repeated with a consistent rhythm throughout a piece of music. **10** *Football etc.* same as **crossbar**. **11** *Heraldry* a narrow horizontal line across a shield. **12 behind bars** in prison. ✧ *vb* **barring, barred 13** to secure with a bar: *to bar the door.* **14** to obstruct: *the fallen tree barred the road.* **15** to exclude: *he was barred from membership of the club.* **16** to mark with a bar or bars. ✧ *prep* **17** except for. ▷ HISTORY Old French *barre*

bar[2] *n* a unit of pressure equal to 10^5 newtons per square metre. ▷ HISTORY Greek *baros* weight

Bar *n* **1 the Bar** barristers collectively. **2 be called to the Bar** *Brit* to become a barrister.

barb *n* **1** a cutting remark. **2** a point facing in the opposite direction to the main point of a fish-hook, harpoon, etc. **3** a beardlike growth, hair, or projection. ✧ *vb* **4** to provide with a barb or barbs. ▷ HISTORY Latin *barba* beard ▶ **barbed** *adj*

barbarian *n* **1** a member of a primitive or uncivilized people. **2** a coarse or vicious person. ✧ *adj* **3** uncivilized or brutal.

barbaric *adj* primitive or brutal.

barbarism *n* **1** a brutal, coarse, or ignorant act. **2** the condition of being backward, coarse, or ignorant. **3** a substandard word or expression.

barbarity *n, pl* **-ties 1** the state of being barbaric or barbarous. **2** a vicious act.

barbarous *adj* **1** uncivilized: *a barbarous and uninhabitable jungle.* **2** brutal or cruel: *the barbarous tortures inflicted on them.* ▷ HISTORY Greek *barbaros* barbarian, non-Greek

barbecue *n* **1** a grill on which food is cooked over hot charcoal, usually out of doors. **2** food cooked over hot charcoal, usually out of doors. **3** a party or picnic at which barbecued food is served. ✧ *vb* **-cuing, -cued 4** to cook on a grill, usually over charcoal. ▷ HISTORY American Spanish *barbacoa* frame made of sticks

barbed wire *n* strong wire with sharp points protruding at close intervals.

barbel *n* **1** a long thin growth that hangs from the jaws of certain fishes, such as the carp. **2** a freshwater fish with such a growth. ▷ HISTORY Latin *barba* beard

a b c d e f g h i j k l m n o p q r s t u v w x y z

A B C D E F G H I J K L M N O P Q R S T U V W X Y Z

barber *n* a person whose business is cutting men's hair and shaving beards. ▷ HISTORY Latin *barba* beard

barberry *n, pl* **-ries** a shrub with orange or red berries. ▷ HISTORY Arabic *barbāris*

barbican *n* a walled defence to protect a gate or drawbridge of a fortification. ▷ HISTORY Old French *barbacane*

barbiturate *n* a derivative of barbituric acid used in medicine as a sedative.

barbituric acid *n* a crystalline solid used in the preparation of barbiturate drugs. ▷ HISTORY German *Barbitursäure*

barcarole *or* **barcarolle** *n* **1** a Venetian boat song. **2** an instrumental composition resembling this. ▷ HISTORY French

barchan *or* **barchan dune** *n Geog* a crescent-shaped sand dune whose gently sloping convex side is towards the wind while the steeper concave side is sheltered from the wind.

bar chart *or* **graph** *n* a diagram consisting of vertical or horizontal bars whose lengths are proportional to amounts or quantities.

bar code *n* an arrangement of numbers and parallel lines on a package, which can be electronically scanned at a checkout to give the price of the goods.

bard *n* **1** *Archaic or literary* a poet. **2 a** (formerly) an ancient Celtic poet. **b** a poet who wins a verse competition at a Welsh eisteddfod. **3 the Bard** William Shakespeare, English playwright and poet. ▷ HISTORY Scottish Gaelic

bare *adj* **1** unclothed: used esp. of a part of the body. **2** without the natural, conventional, or usual covering: *bare trees.* **3** lacking appropriate furnishings, etc.: *a bare room.* **4** simple: *the bare facts.* **5** just sufficient: *the bare minimum.* ✧ *vb* **baring, bared 6** to uncover. ▷ HISTORY Old English *bær* ▶ **bareness** *n*

bareback *adj, adv* (of horse-riding) without a saddle.

barefaced *adj* obvious or shameless: *a barefaced lie.*

barefoot *or* **barefooted** *adj, adv* with the feet uncovered.

bareheaded *adj, adv* with the head uncovered.

barely *adv* **1** only just: *barely enough.* **2** scantily: *barely furnished.*

> ☑ **WORD TIP**
> See at **hardly.**

bargain *n* **1** an agreement establishing what each party will give, receive, or perform in a transaction. **2** something acquired or received in such an agreement. **3** something bought or offered at a low price. **4 drive a hard bargain** to forcefully pursue one's own profit in a transaction. **5 into the bargain** besides. ✧ *vb* **6** to negotiate the terms of an agreement or transaction. ▷ HISTORY Old French *bargaigne*

bargain for *vb* to anticipate.

barge *n* **1** a flat-bottomed boat, used for transporting freight, esp. on canals. **2** a boat, often decorated, used in pageants, etc. ✧ *vb* **barging, barged** *Informal* **3** (foll. by *into*) to bump into. **4** to push one's way violently. **5** (foll. by *into* or *in*) to interrupt rudely: *he barged into our conversation.* ▷ HISTORY Medieval Latin *barga*

bargee *n Brit* a person in charge of a barge.

barista (bar-**ee**-sta) *n* a person who makes and sells coffee in a coffee bar.

baritone *n* **1** the second lowest adult male voice. **2** a singer with such a voice. ▷ HISTORY Greek *barus* low + *tonos* tone

barium (**bare**-ee-um) *n Chem* a soft silvery-white metallic chemical element. Symbol: Ba. ▷ HISTORY Greek *barus* heavy

barium meal *n* a preparation of barium sulphate, which is opaque to X-rays, used in X-ray examination of the alimentary canal.

bark[1] *n* **1** the loud harsh cry of a dog or certain other animals. ✧ *vb* **2** (of a dog or other animal) to make its typical cry. **3** to shout in an angry tone: *he barked an order.* **4 bark up the wrong tree** *Informal* to misdirect one's attention or efforts. ▷ HISTORY Old English *beorcan*

bark[2] *n* **1** an outer protective layer of dead corklike cells on the trunks of trees. ✧ *vb* **2** to scrape or rub off (skin), as in an injury. **3** to remove the bark from (a tree). ▷ HISTORY Old Norse *börkr*

barker *n* a person at a fairground who loudly addresses passers-by to attract customers.

barking *Slang, chiefly Brit* ✧ *adj* **1** mad or crazy. ✧ *adv* **2** extremely: *barking mad.*

barley *n* **1** a tall grasslike plant with dense bristly flower spikes, widely cultivated for grain. **2** the grain of this grass used in making beer and whisky and for soups. ▷ HISTORY Old English *bere*

barleycorn *n* a grain of barley, or barley itself.

barley sugar *n* a brittle clear amber-coloured sweet.

barley water *n* a drink made from an infusion of barley.

barmaid *n* a woman who serves in a pub.

barman *n, pl* **-men** a man who serves in a pub.

bar mitzvah *Judaism* ✧ *n* **1** a ceremony marking the 13th birthday of a boy and his assumption of religious obligations. ✧ *adj* **2** (of a Jewish boy) having undergone this ceremony. ▷ HISTORY Hebrew: son of the law

barmy *adj* **-mier, -miest** *Slang* insane. ▷ HISTORY originally, full of BARM, frothing, excited

barn *n* a large farm outbuilding, chiefly for storing grain, but also for livestock. ▷ HISTORY Old English *bere* barley + *ærn* room

barnacle *n* a marine shellfish that lives attached to rocks, ship bottoms, etc. ▷ HISTORY Old French *bernac* ▶ **barnacled** *adj*

barnacle goose *n* a goose with a black-and-white head and body. ▷ HISTORY it was formerly believed that the goose developed from a shellfish

barn dance *n* **1** *US & Canad* a party with square-dancing. **2** *Brit* a progressive round country dance.

barney *n Informal* a noisy fight or argument. ▷ **HISTORY** origin unknown

barn owl *n* an owl with a pale brown-and-white plumage and a heart-shaped face.

barnstorm *vb* **1** *Chiefly US & Canad* to tour rural districts making speeches in a political campaign. **2** to tour rural districts putting on shows. ▶ **barnstorming** *n, adj*

barnyard *n* a yard adjoining a barn.

barograph *n Meteorol* a barometer that automatically keeps a record of changes in atmospheric pressure. ▷ **HISTORY** Greek *baros* weight + *graphein* to write

barometer *n* an instrument for measuring atmospheric pressure, used to determine weather or altitude changes. ▷ **HISTORY** Greek *baros* weight + *metron* measure ▶ **barometric** *adj*

baron *n* **1** a member of the lowest rank of nobility in the British Isles. **2** a powerful businessman or financier: *a press baron.* ▷ **HISTORY** Old French ▶ **baronial** *adj*

baroness *n* **1** a woman holding the rank of baron. **2** the wife or widow of a baron.

baronet *n* a commoner who holds the lowest hereditary British title. ▶ **baronetcy** *n*

baroque (bar-**rock**) *n* **1** a highly ornate style of architecture and art, popular in Europe from the late 16th to the early 18th century. **2** a highly ornamented 17th-century style of music. ✧ *adj* **3** ornate in style. ▷ **HISTORY** French from Portuguese *barroco* imperfectly shaped pearl

barque (**bark**) *n* **1** a sailing ship, esp. one with three masts. **2** *Poetic* any boat. ▷ **HISTORY** Old Provençal *barca*

barrack[1] *vb* to house (soldiers) in barracks.

barrack[2] *vb* **1** *Brit, Austral & NZ informal* to criticize loudly or shout against (a team or speaker). **2** *Austral & NZ* (foll. by *for*) to shout encouragement for (a team). ▷ **HISTORY** Irish: to boast

barracks *pl n* **1** a building or group of buildings used to accommodate military personnel. **2** a large and bleak building. ▷ **HISTORY** French *baraque*

barracouta (bar-rack-**kew**-ta) *n* a large Pacific fish with a protruding lower jaw and strong teeth.

barracuda (bar-rack-**kew**-da) *n, pl* **-da** *or* **-das** a tropical fish which feeds on other fishes. ▷ **HISTORY** American Spanish

barrage (**bar**-rahzh) *n* **1** a continuous delivery of questions, complaints, etc. **2** *Mil* the continuous firing of artillery over a wide area. **3** a construction built across a river to control the water level. ▷ **HISTORY** French *barrer* to obstruct

barrage balloon *n* a balloon tethered by cables, often with net suspended from it, used to deter low-flying air attack.

barramundi *n* edible Australian fish.

barre (**bar**) *n* a rail at hip height used for ballet practice. ▷ **HISTORY** French

barrel *n* **1** a cylindrical container usually with rounded sides and flat ends, and held together by metal hoops. **2** a unit of capacity of varying amount in different industries. **3** the tube through which the bullet of a firearm is fired. **4 over a barrel** *Informal* powerless. ✧ *vb* **-relling, -relled** *or US* **-reling, -reled 5** to put into a barrel or barrels. ▷ **HISTORY** Old French *baril*

barrel organ *n* a musical instrument played by turning a handle.

barren *adj* **1** incapable of producing offspring. **2** unable to support the growth of crops, fruit, etc.: *barren land.* **3** unprofitable or unsuccessful: *Real Madrid have had a barren two seasons.* **4** dull. ▷ **HISTORY** Old French *brahain* ▶ **barrenness** *n*

barricade *n* **1** a barrier, esp. one erected hastily for defence. ✧ *vb* **-cading, -caded 2** to erect a barricade across (an entrance). ▷ **HISTORY** Old French *barrique* a barrel

barrier *n* **1** anything that blocks a way or separates, such as a gate. **2** anything that prevents progress: *a barrier of distrust.* **3** anything that separates or hinders union: *a language barrier.* ▷ **HISTORY** Old French *barre* bar

barrier cream *n* a cream used to protect the skin.

barrier reef *n* a long narrow ridge of coral, separated from the shore by deep water.

barrister *n* a lawyer who is qualified to plead in the higher courts. ▷ **HISTORY** from BAR[1]

barrow[1] *n* **1** same as **wheelbarrow**. **2** a handcart used by street traders. ▷ **HISTORY** Old English *bearwe*

barrow[2] *n* a heap of earth placed over a prehistoric tomb. ▷ **HISTORY** Old English *beorg*

barter *vb* **1** to trade goods or services in exchange for other goods or services, rather than for money. ✧ *n* **2** trade by the exchange of goods. ▷ **HISTORY** Old French *barater* to cheat

baryon (**bar**-ree-on) *n* an elementary particle that has a mass greater than or equal to that of the proton. ▷ **HISTORY** Greek *barus* heavy

baryta (bar-**rite**-a) *n* a compound of barium, such as barium oxide. ▷ **HISTORY** Greek *barus* heavy

barytes (bar-**rite**-eez) *n* a colourless or white mineral: a source of barium. ▷ **HISTORY** Greek *barus* heavy

basal *adj* **1** at, of, or constituting a base. **2** fundamental.

basal metabolic rate *n* the amount of energy consumed by an animal's body at rest.

basalt (**bass**-awlt) *n* a dark volcanic rock. ▷ **HISTORY** Greek *basanitēs* touchstone ▶ **basaltic** *adj*

bascule *n* a drawbridge that operates by a counterbalanced weight. ▷ **HISTORY** French: seesaw

base[1] *n* **1** the bottom or supporting part of anything. **2** the fundamental principle or part: *agriculture was the economic base of the city's growth.* **3** a centre of operations, organization, or supply. **4** a starting point: *the new discovery became the base for further research.* **5** the main ingredient of a mixture: *to use rice as a base in cookery.* **6** *Chem* a compound that combines with an acid to form a

A B C D E F G H I J K L M N O P Q R S T U V W X Y Z

salt. **7** the lower side or face of a geometric construction. **8** *Maths* the number of units in a counting system that is equivalent to one in the next higher counting place: *10 is the base of the decimal system.* **9** a starting or finishing point in any of various games. ✧ *vb* **basing, based 10** (foll. by *on* or *upon*) to use as a basis for. **11** (foll. by *at* or *in*) to station, post, or place. ▷ HISTORY Latin *basis* pedestal

base[2] *adj* **1** dishonourable or immoral: *base motives.* **2** of inferior quality or value: *a base coin.* **3** debased; counterfeit: *base currency.* ▷ HISTORY Late Latin *bassus* of low height

baseball *n* **1** a team game in which the object is to score runs by batting the ball and running round all four bases. **2** the ball used in this game.

baseless *adj* not based on fact.

base level *n Geog* the lowest level to which a river or stream bed can be eroded; equivalent to sea level in those rivers and streams that flow into the sea.

baseline *n* **1** a value or starting point on an imaginary scale with which other things are compared. **2** a line at each end of a tennis court that marks the limit of play.

basement *n* a partly or wholly underground storey of a building.

base metal *n* a common metal such as copper or lead, that is not a precious metal.

base number *n Maths* of a logarithm or exponential, a number whose powers are expressed.

base rate *n* **1** the rate of interest used by a bank as a basis for its lending rates. **2** the rate at which the Bank of England lends to other financial organizations, which effectively controls interest rates throughout the UK.

bases[1] *n* the plural of **basis**.

bases[2] *n* the plural of **base**[1].

bash *Informal* ✧ *vb* **1** to strike violently or crushingly. **2** (foll. by *into*) to crash into. ✧ *n* **3** a heavy blow. **4 have a bash** *Informal* to make an attempt. ▷ HISTORY origin unknown

bashful *adj* shy or modest. ▷ HISTORY *bash,* short for ABASH ▶ **bashfully** *adv*

-bashing *n and adj combining form Informal or slang* **a** indicating a malicious attack on members of a group: *union-bashing.* **b** indicating an activity undertaken energetically: *Bible-bashing.* ▶ **-basher** *n combining form*

basic *adj* **1** of or forming a base or basis. **2** elementary or simple: *a few basic facts.* **3** excluding additions or extras: *basic pay.* **4** *Chem* of or containing a base. ✧ *n* **5 basics** fundamental principles, facts, etc. ▶ **basically** *adv*

BASIC *n* a computer programming language that uses common English terms. ▷ HISTORY *b(eginner's) a(ll-purpose) s(ymbolic) i(nstruction) c(ode)*

basic rocks *pl n Geol* igneous rocks, such as basalt, which have a low silica content (between 45 and 52 per cent).

basic slag *n* a slag produced in steel-making, containing calcium phosphate.

basil *n* an aromatic herb used for seasoning food. ▷ HISTORY Greek *basilikos* royal

basilica *n* **1** a Roman building, used for public administration, which is rectangular with two aisles and a rounded end. **2** a Christian church of similar design. ▷ HISTORY Greek *basilikē oikia* the king's house

basilisk *n* (in classical legend) a serpent that could kill by its breath or glance. ▷ HISTORY Greek *basiliskos* royal child

basin *n* **1** a round wide container open at the top. **2** the amount a basin will hold. **3** a washbasin or sink. **4** any partially enclosed area of water where ships or boats may be moored. **5** *Geog* the catchment area of a river and its tributaries or of a lake. **6** a depression in the earth's surface. ▷ HISTORY Old French *bacin*

basis *n, pl* **bases 1** something that underlies, supports, or is essential to an idea, belief, etc. **2** a principle on which something depends. ▷ HISTORY Greek: step

bask *vb* (foll. by *in*) **1** to lie in or be exposed (to pleasant warmth or sunshine). **2** to enjoy (approval or favourable conditions). ▷ HISTORY Old Norse *bathask* to bathe

basket *n* **1** a container made of interwoven strips of wood or cane. **2** the amount a basket will hold. **3** *Basketball* **a** the high horizontal hoop through which a player must throw the ball to score points. **b** a point scored in this way. ▷ HISTORY Middle English

basketball *n* a team game in which points are scored by throwing the ball through a high horizontal hoop.

basketwork *n* same as **wickerwork**.

basking shark *n* a very large plankton-eating shark, which often floats at the sea surface.

basque *n* a tight-fitting bodice for women. ▷ HISTORY origin unknown

Basque *n* **1** a member of a people living in the W Pyrenees in France and Spain. **2** the language of the Basques. ✧ *adj* **3** of the Basques. ▷ HISTORY Latin *Vasco*

bas-relief *n* sculpture in which the figures project slightly from the background. ▷ HISTORY Italian *basso rilievo*

bass[1] (**base**) *n* **1** the lowest adult male voice. **2** a singer with such a voice. **3** *Informal* same as **bass guitar double bass**. ✧ *adj* **4** of the lowest range of musical notes: *the system is engineered to give good bass sound from very small speakers.* **5** denoting a musical instrument that is lowest or second lowest in pitch in its family: *bass trombone.* **6** of or relating to a bass guitar or double bass: *the band is unusual in that it has two bass players.* **7** of or written for a singer with the lowest adult male voice: *the bass soloist in next week's performance of Handel's 'Messiah'.* ▷ HISTORY Middle English *bas*

bass[2] (rhymes with **gas**) *n* **1** various Australian freshwater and sea fish. **2** a European spiny-finned freshwater fish. ▷ HISTORY Middle English

bass clef (**base**) *n* the clef that establishes F a fifth below middle C on the fourth line of the staff.

bass drum (**base**) *n* a large drum of low pitch.

basset hound *n* a smooth-haired dog with short legs and long ears. ▷ **HISTORY** French *bas* low

bass guitar (**base**) *n* an electric guitar with the same pitch and tuning as a double bass.

bassoon *n* a woodwind instrument that produces a range of low sounds. ▷ **HISTORY** Italian *basso* deep ▶ **bassoonist** *n*

bastard *n* **1** *Informal, offensive* an obnoxious or despicable person. **2** *Archaic or offensive* a person born of parents not married to each other. **3** *Informal* something extremely difficult or unpleasant. ✧ *adj* **4** *Archaic or offensive* illegitimate by birth. **5** counterfeit; spurious. ▷ **HISTORY** Old French *bastart* ▶ **bastardy** *n*

bastardize *or* **-ise** *vb* **-izing, -ized** *or* **-ising, -ised 1** to debase. **2** to declare illegitimate.

baste[1] *vb* **basting, basted** to sew with loose temporary stitches. ▷ **HISTORY** Old French *bastir* to build

baste[2] *vb* **basting, basted** to moisten (meat) during cooking with hot fat. ▷ **HISTORY** origin unknown

baste[3] *vb* **basting, basted** to thrash. ▷ **HISTORY** origin unknown

bastion *n* **1** a projecting part of a fortification. **2** a thing or person regarded as defending a principle or way of life: *a bastion of anti-communism*. ▷ **HISTORY** French *bastille* fortress

bat[1] *n* **1** any of various types of club used to hit the ball in certain sports. **2** *Cricket* a batsman. **3 off one's own bat a** of one's own accord. **b** by one's own unaided efforts. ✧ *vb* **batting, batted 4** to strike with or as if with a bat. **5** *Cricket etc.* to take a turn at batting. ▷ **HISTORY** Old English *batt* club

bat[2] *n* **1** a nocturnal mouselike flying animal with leathery wings. **2 blind as a bat** having extremely poor eyesight. ▷ **HISTORY** Scandinavian

bat[3] *vb* **batting, batted 1** to flutter (one's eyelids). **2 not bat an eyelid** *Informal* to show no surprise. ▷ **HISTORY** probably from obsolete *bate* flutter, beat

batch *n* **1** a group of similar objects or people dispatched or dealt with at the same time. **2** the bread, cakes, etc. produced at one baking. ✧ *vb* **3** to group (items) for efficient processing. ▷ **HISTORY** Middle English *bache*

batch processing *n* a system by which the computer programs of several users are submitted as a single batch.

batch production *n Business* the practice of manufacturing similar items in batches, resulting in a lower unit cost.

bated *adj* **with bated breath** in suspense or fear.

bath *n* **1** a large container in which to wash the body. **2** the act of washing in such a container. **3** the amount of water in a bath. **4 baths** a public swimming pool. **5 a** a liquid in which something is immersed as part of a chemical process, such as developing photographs. **b** the vessel containing such a liquid. ✧ *vb* **6** *Brit* to wash in a bath. ▷ **HISTORY** Old English *bæth*

Bath chair *n* a wheelchair for invalids.

bathe *vb* **bathing, bathed 1** to swim in open water for pleasure. **2** to apply liquid to (the skin or a wound) in order to cleanse or soothe. **3** *Chiefly US & Canad* to wash in a bath. **4** to spread over: *bathed in moonlight*. ✧ *n* **5** *Brit* a swim in open water. ▷ **HISTORY** Old English *bathian* ▶ **bather** *n*

batholith *n Geol* a very large irregular-shaped mass of igneous rock, esp. granite, formed from an intrusion of magma at great depth. ▷ **HISTORY** Greek *bathus* deep + *lithos* stone

bathos (**bay**-thoss) *n* a sudden ludicrous descent from exalted to ordinary matters in speech or writing. ▷ **HISTORY** Greek: depth ▶ **bathetic** *adj*

bathroom *n* **1** a room with a bath or shower, washbasin, and toilet. **2** *US & Canad* a toilet.

bathyscaph *or* **bathyscaphe** *n* a deep-sea diving vessel for observation. ▷ **HISTORY** Greek *bathus* deep + *skaphē* light boat

bathysphere *n* a strong steel deep-sea diving sphere, lowered by cable. ▷ **HISTORY** Greek *bathus* deep + *sphere*

batik (bat-**teek**) *n* **a** a process of printing fabric in which areas not to be dyed are covered by wax. **b** fabric printed in this way. ▷ **HISTORY** Javanese: painted

batman *n, pl* **-men** an officer's servant in the armed forces. ▷ **HISTORY** Old French *bat* packsaddle

baton *n* **1** a thin stick used by the conductor of an orchestra or choir. **2** *Athletics* a short bar transferred from one runner to another in a relay race. **3** a police officer's truncheon. ▷ **HISTORY** French

batsman *n, pl* **-men** *Cricket etc.* a person who bats or specializes in batting.

battalion *n* a military unit comprised of three or more companies. ▷ **HISTORY** French *bataillon*

batten[1] *n* **1** a strip of wood used to strengthen something or make it secure. **2** a strip of wood used for holding a tarpaulin in place over a hatch on a ship. ✧ *vb* **3** to strengthen or fasten with battens. ▷ **HISTORY** French *bâton* stick

batten[2] *vb* (foll. by *on*) to thrive at the expense of (someone else). ▷ **HISTORY** probably from Old Norse *batna* to improve

batter[1] *vb* **1** to hit repeatedly. **2** to damage or injure, as by blows, heavy wear, etc. **3** to subject (someone, usually a close relative) to repeated physical violence. ▷ **HISTORY** Middle English *bateren* ▶ **battered** *adj* ▶ **batterer** *n* ▶ **battering** *n*

batter[2] *n* a mixture of flour, eggs, and milk, used in cooking. ▷ **HISTORY** Middle English *bater*

batter[3] *n Baseball etc.* a player who bats.

battering ram *n* (esp. formerly) a large beam used to break down fortifications.

battery *n, pl* **-teries 1** two or more primary cells connected to provide a source of electric current. **2** a number of similar things occurring together: *a battery of questions*. **3** *Criminal law* unlawful beating or wounding of a person. **4** *Chiefly Brit* a series of cages for intensive rearing of poultry. **5** a fortified structure on which artillery is mounted.

A B C D E F G H I J K L M N O P Q R S T U V W X Y Z

✧ *adj* **6** kept in a series of cages for intensive rearing: *battery hens.* ▷ **HISTORY** Latin *battuere* to beat

battle *n* **1** a fight between large armed forces. **2** conflict or struggle. ✧ *vb* **-tling, -tled 3** to fight in or as if in military combat: *shop stewards battling to improve conditions at work.* **4** to struggle: *she battled through the crowd.* ▷ **HISTORY** Latin *battuere* to beat

battle-axe *n* **1** a domineering woman. **2** (formerly) a large broad-headed axe.

battle cruiser *n* a high-speed warship with lighter armour than a battleship, but of the same size.

battle cry *n* **1** a slogan used to rally the supporters of a campaign, movement, etc. **2** a shout uttered by soldiers going into battle.

battledore *n* **1** Also called: **battledore and shuttlecock** an ancient racket game. **2** a light racket used in this game. ▷ **HISTORY** Middle English *batyldoure*

battledress *n* the ordinary uniform of a soldier.

battlefield *or* **battleground** *n* the place where a battle is fought.

battlement *n* a wall with gaps, originally for firing through. ▷ **HISTORY** Old French *bataille* battle

battleship *n* a large heavily armoured warship.

batty *adj* **-tier, -tiest** *Slang* **1** crazy. **2** eccentric: *a batty OAP.* ▷ **HISTORY** from BAT²

bauble *n* a trinket of little value. ▷ **HISTORY** Old French *baubel* plaything

baud *n Computers* a unit used to measure the speed of transmission of electronic data. ▷ **HISTORY** after J. M. E. *Baudot,* inventor

bauera *n* small evergreen Australian shrub.

Bauhaus (**bow**-house) *adj* of a school of architecture and applied arts in Germany in the 1920s and 30s characterized by a functionalist approach to design. ▷ **HISTORY** German: building house

baulk *vb, n* same as **balk.**

bauxite *n* a claylike substance that is the chief source of aluminium. ▷ **HISTORY** *(Les) Baux* in southern France, where originally found

bawdy *adj* **bawdier, bawdiest** (of language, writing, etc.) containing humorous references to sex. ▶ **bawdily** *adv* ▶ **bawdiness** *n*

> **WORD HISTORY**
>
> 'Bawd' is an old word for a 'brothel keeper'. It comes from an old French word *baud* meaning 'merry' or 'lively'. Bawdy stories are therefore the sort that contain lighthearted references to sexual activity, such as might be associated with brothels.

bawl *vb* **1** to cry noisily. **2** to shout loudly. ✧ *n* **3** a loud shout or cry. ▷ **HISTORY** imitative ▶ **bawling** *n*

bay¹ *n* a stretch of shoreline that curves inwards. ▷ **HISTORY** Old French *baie*

bay² *n* **1** a recess in a wall. **2** an area set aside for a particular purpose: *a sick bay; a loading bay.* **3** same as **bay window. 4** an area off a road in which vehicles may park or unload. **5** a compartment in an aircraft: *the bomb bay.* ▷ **HISTORY** Old French *baee* gap

bay³ *n* **1** a deep howl of a hound or wolf. **2 at bay a** forced to turn and face attackers: *the stag at bay.* **b** at a safe distance: *to keep his mind blank and his despair at bay.* ✧ *vb* **3** to howl in deep prolonged tones. ▷ **HISTORY** Old French *abaiier* to bark

bay⁴ *n* **1** a Mediterranean laurel tree with glossy aromatic leaves. **2 bays** a wreath of bay leaves. ▷ **HISTORY** Latin *baca* berry

bay⁵ *adj* **1** reddish-brown. ✧ *n* **2** a reddish-brown horse. ▷ **HISTORY** Latin *badius*

bayberry *n, pl* **-ries** a tropical American tree that yields an oil used in making bay rum. Also: **bay**

bay leaf *n* the dried leaf of a laurel, used for flavouring in cooking.

bayonet *n* **1** a blade that can be attached to the end of a rifle and used as a weapon. ✧ *vb* **-neting, -neted** *or* **-netting, -netted 2** to stab or kill with a bayonet.

> **WORD HISTORY**
>
> Bayonets were first made in the 16th century in the town of *Bayonne* in southwestern France, and it is from the name of the town that they take their name.

bay rum *n* an aromatic liquid, used in medicines and cosmetics, which was originally obtained by distilling bayberry leaves with rum.

bay window *n* a window projecting from a wall.

bazaar *n* **1** a sale in aid of charity. **2** (esp. in the Orient) a market area, esp. a street of small stalls. ▷ **HISTORY** Persian *bāzār*

bazooka *n* a portable rocket launcher that fires a projectile capable of piercing armour. ▷ **HISTORY** after a pipe instrument devised by an American comedian

BB *Brit* Boys' Brigade.

BBC British Broadcasting Corporation.

BC 1 (indicating years numbered back from the supposed year of the birth of Christ) before Christ. **2** British Columbia.

BCG Bacillus Calmette-Guérin (antituberculosis vaccine).

BD Bachelor of Divinity.

BDS Bachelor of Dental Surgery.

be *vb, present sing 1st person* **am;** *2nd person* **are;** *3rd person* **is.** *present pl* **are.** *past sing 1st person* **was;** *2nd person* **were;** *3rd person* **was.** *past pl* **were.** *present participle* **being.** *past participle* **been. 1** to exist; live: *I think, therefore I am.* **2** to pay a visit; go: *have you been to Spain?* **3** to take place: *my birthday was last Thursday.* **4** used as a linking verb between the subject of a sentence and its complement: *John is a musician; honey is sweet; the dance is on Saturday.* **5** forms the progressive present tense: *the man is running.* **6** forms the passive voice of all transitive verbs: *a good film is being shown on television tomorrow.* **7** expresses intention, expectation, or obligation: *the president is to arrive at 9.30.* ▷ **HISTORY** Old English *bēon*

Be *Chem* beryllium.

BE Bachelor of Engineering.

be- *prefix forming verbs mainly from nouns* **1** to surround or cover: *befog.* **2** to affect completely: *bedazzle.* **3** to consider as or cause to be: *befriend.* **4** to provide or cover with: *bejewel.* **5** (*from verbs*) at, for, against, on, or over: *bewail.* ▷ **HISTORY** Old English *be-, bi-* by

beach *n* **1** an area of sand or pebbles sloping down to the sea or a lake. ✧ *vb* **2** to run or haul (a boat) onto a beach. ▷ **HISTORY** origin unknown

beachcomber *n* a person who searches shore debris for anything of worth.

beachhead *n Mil* an area of shore captured by an attacking army, on which troops and equipment are landed.

beach nourishment *n Building* the process of building or restoring a beach by artificial methods such as pumping sand from another location.

beacon *n* **1** a signal fire or light on a hill or tower, used formerly as a warning of invasion. **2** a lighthouse. **3** a radio or other signal marking a flight course in air navigation. **4** same as **Belisha beacon.** ▷ **HISTORY** Old English *beacen* sign

bead *n* **1** a small pierced piece of glass, wood, or plastic that may be strung with others to form a necklace, rosary, etc. **2** a small drop of moisture. **3** a small metal knob acting as the sight of a firearm. ✧ *vb* **4** to decorate with beads. ▷ **HISTORY** Old English *bed* prayer ▶ **beaded** *adj*

beading *n* a narrow rounded strip of moulding used for edging furniture.

beadle *n* **1** *Brit* (formerly) a minor parish official who acted as an usher. **2** *Scot* a church official who attends the minister. ▷ **HISTORY** Old English *bydel*

beady *adj* **beadier, beadiest** small, round, and glittering: *beady eyes.*

beagle *n* a small hound with a smooth coat, short legs, and drooping ears. ▷ **HISTORY** origin unknown

beak[1] *n* **1** the projecting horny jaws of a bird. **2** *Slang* a person's nose. ▷ **HISTORY** Latin *beccus* ▶ **beaky** *adj*

beak[2] *n Brit, Austral & NZ slang* a judge, magistrate, or headmaster. ▷ **HISTORY** originally thieves' jargon

beaker *n* **1** a tall drinking cup. **2** a lipped glass container used in laboratories. ▷ **HISTORY** Old Norse *bikarr*

beam *n* **1** a broad smile. **2** a ray of light. **3** a narrow flow of electromagnetic radiation or particles: *an electron beam.* **4** a long thick piece of wood, metal, etc. used in building. **5** the central shaft of a plough to which all the main parts are attached. **6** the breadth of a ship at its widest part. **7 off (the) beam** *Informal* mistaken or irrelevant. ✧ *vb* **8** to smile broadly. **9** to send out or radiate. **10** to divert or aim (a radio signal, light, etc.) in a certain direction: *the concert was beamed live from Geneva.* ▷ **HISTORY** Old English

bean *n* **1** the seed or pod of various climbing plants, eaten as a vegetable. **2** any of various beanlike seeds, such as coffee. **3 full of beans** *Informal* full of energy and vitality. **4 not have a bean** *Slang* to be without money. ▷ **HISTORY** Old English *bēan*

beanie *n Brit, Austral & NZ* close-fitting woollen hat.

beano *n, pl* **beanos** *Brit old-fashioned, slang* a celebration or party.

beanpole *n Slang* a tall thin person.

beansprout *n* a small edible shoot grown from a bean seed, often used in Chinese dishes.

bear[1] *vb* **bearing, bore, borne 1** to support or hold up. **2** to bring: *to bear gifts.* **3** to accept the responsibility of: *to bear a heavier burden of taxation.* **4** (**born** in passive use except when foll. by *by*) to give birth to. **5** to produce by natural growth: *to bear fruit.* **6** to tolerate or endure. **7** to stand up to; sustain: *his story does not bear scrutiny.* **8** to hold in the mind: *to bear a grudge.* **9** to show or be marked with: *he still bears the scars.* **10** to have, be, or stand in (relation or comparison): *her account bears no relation to the facts.* **11** to move in a specified direction: *bear left.* **12 bring to bear** to bring into effect. ✧ See also **bear down on.** ▷ **HISTORY** Old English *beran*

bear[2] *n, pl* **bears** *or* **bear 1** a large heavily-built mammal with a long shaggy coat. **2** a bearlike animal, such as the koala. **3** an ill-mannered person. **4** *Stock Exchange* a person who sells shares in anticipation of falling prices to make a profit on repurchase. **5 like a bear with a sore head** *Informal* bad-tempered, irritable. ▷ **HISTORY** Old English *bera*

bearable *adj* endurable; tolerable.

bear-baiting *n History* an entertainment in which dogs attacked a chained bear.

beard *n* **1** the hair growing on the lower parts of a man's face. **2** any similar growth in animals. ✧ *vb* **3** to oppose boldly: *I bearded my formidable employer in her den.* ▷ **HISTORY** Old English ▶ **bearded** *adj*

bear down on *vb* **1** to press down on. **2** to approach (someone) in a determined manner.

bearer *n* **1** a person or thing that carries, presents, or upholds something. **2** a person who presents a note or bill for payment.

bear hug *n* a rough tight embrace.

bearing *n* **1** (foll. by *on* or *upon*) relevance to: *it has no bearing on this problem.* **2** a part of a machine supporting another part, and usually reducing friction. **3** the act of producing fruit or young. **4** a person's general social conduct. **5** the angular direction of a point measured from a known position. **6** the position, as of a ship, fixed with reference to two or more known points. **7 bearings** a sense of one's relative position: *I lost my bearings in the dark.* **8** *Heraldry* a device on a heraldic shield.

bear out *vb* to show to be truthful: *the witness will bear me out.*

bearskin *n* **1** the pelt of a bear. **2** a tall fur helmet worn by certain British Army regiments.

beast *n* **1** a large wild animal. **2** a brutal or uncivilized person. **3** savage nature or characteristics: *the beast in man.* ▷ **HISTORY** Latin *bestia*

beastly *adj Informal* **-lier, -liest** unpleasant; disagreeable.

beat *vb* **beating, beat; beaten** *or* **beat 1** to strike with a series of violent blows. **2** to move (wings) up and down. **3** to throb rhythmically. **4** *Cookery* to stir or whisk vigorously. **5** to shape (metal) by repeated blows. **6** *Music* to indicate (time) by one's hand or a baton. **7** to produce (a sound) by striking a drum. **8** to overcome or defeat: *he was determined to beat his illness.* **9** to form (a path or track) by repeated use. **10** to arrive, achieve, or finish before (someone or something): *she beat her team-mate fair and square.* **11** (foll. by *back, down, off*) etc. to drive, push, or thrust. **12** to scour (woodlands or undergrowth) to rouse game for shooting. **13** *Slang* to puzzle or baffle: *it beats me.* ✧ *n* **14** a stroke or blow. **15** the sound made by a stroke or blow. **16** a regular throb. **17** an assigned route, as of a policeman. **18** the basic rhythmic unit in a piece of music. **19** pop or rock music characterized by a heavy rhythmic beat. ✧ *adj* **20** *Slang* totally exhausted. ✧ See also **beat down, beat up**. ▷ HISTORY Old English *bēatan* ▶ **beating** *n*

beat down *vb* **1** (of the sun) to shine intensely. **2** *Informal* to force or persuade (a seller) to accept a lower price.

beater *n* **1** a device used for beating: *a carpet beater.* **2** a person who rouses wild game.

beatific *adj Literary* **1** displaying great happiness. **2** having a divine aura. ▷ HISTORY Latin *beatus*

beatify (bee-**at**-if-fie) *vb* **-fies, -fying, -fied 1** *RC Church* to declare (a deceased person) to be among the blessed in heaven: the first step towards canonization. **2** to make extremely happy. ▶ **beatification** *n*

beatitude *n* supreme blessedness or happiness. ▷ HISTORY Latin *beatitudo*

Beatitude *n Christianity* any of the blessings on the poor, meek, etc., in the Sermon on the Mount.

beatnik *n* a young person in the late 1950s who rebelled against conventional attitudes and styles of dress. ▷ HISTORY BEAT (noun) + -NIK

beat up *Informal* ✧ *vb* **1** to inflict severe physical damage on (someone) by striking or kicking repeatedly. ✧ *n* **2** *Austral & NZ* a small matter deliberately exaggerated. ✧ *adj* **beat-up 3** dilapidated.

beau (**boh**) *n, pl* **beaux** *or* **beaus** (**bohz**) **1** *Chiefly US* a boyfriend. **2** a man who is greatly concerned with his appearance. ▷ HISTORY French

Beaufort scale *n Meteorol* a scale for measuring wind speeds, ranging from 0 (calm) to 12 (hurricane). ▷ HISTORY after Sir Francis *Beaufort,* who devised it

Beaujolais *n* a red or white wine from southern Burgundy in France.

beauteous *adj Poetic* beautiful.

beautician *n* a person who works in a beauty salon.

beautiful *adj* **1** being very attractive to look at. **2** highly enjoyable; very pleasant. ▶ **beautifully** *adv*

beautify *vb* **-fies, -fying, -fied** to make beautiful. ▶ **beautification** *n*

beauty *n, pl* **-ties 1** the combination of all the qualities of a person or thing that delight the senses and mind. **2** a very attractive woman. **3** *Informal* an outstanding example of its kind. **4** *Informal* an advantageous feature: *the beauty of this job is the short hours.* ▷ HISTORY Latin *bellus* handsome

beauty queen *n* a woman who has been judged the most beautiful in a contest.

beauty spot *n* **1** a place of outstanding beauty. **2** a small dark-coloured spot formerly worn on a lady's face as decoration.

beaver *n* **1** a large amphibious rodent with soft brown fur, a broad flat tail, and webbed hind feet. **2** its fur. **3** a tall hat made of this fur. ✧ *vb* **4 beaver away** to work very hard and steadily. ▷ HISTORY Old English *beofor*

becalmed *adj* (of a sailing ship) motionless through lack of wind.

became *vb* the past tense of **become**.

because *conj* **1** on account of the fact that: *because it's so cold we'll go home.* **2 because of** on account of: *I lost my job because of her.* ▷ HISTORY Middle English *bi cause*

> **☑ WORD TIP**
> See at **reason.**

beck[1] *n* **at someone's beck and call** having to be constantly available to do as someone asks. ▷ HISTORY Middle English *becnen* to beckon

beck[2] *n* (in N England) a stream. ▷ HISTORY Old English *becc*

beckon *vb* **1** to summon with a gesture. **2** to lure: *fame beckoned.* ▷ HISTORY Old English *bīecnan*

become *vb* **-coming, -came, -come 1** to come to be: *he became Prime Minister last year.* **2** (foll. by *of*) to happen to: *what became of him?* **3** to suit: *that dress becomes you.* ▷ HISTORY Old English *becuman* happen

becoming *adj* suitable or appropriate: *his conduct was not becoming to the rank of officer.*

becquerel (beck-a-**rell**) *n* the SI unit of activity of a radioactive source. ▷ HISTORY after A. H. *Becquerel,* physicist

bed *n* **1** a piece of furniture on which to sleep. **2** a plot of ground in which plants are grown. **3** the bottom of a river, lake, or sea. **4** any underlying structure or part. **5** a layer of rock. **6 get out of bed on the wrong side** *Informal* to begin the day in a bad mood. **7 go to bed with** to have sexual intercourse with. ✧ *vb* **bedding, bedded 8** (foll. by *down*) to go to or put into a place to sleep or rest. **9** to have sexual intercourse with. **10** to place firmly into position; embed: *the poles were bedded in concrete.* **11** *Geol* to form or be arranged in a distinct layer. **12** to plant in a bed of soil. ▷ HISTORY Old English *bedd*

BEd Bachelor of Education.

bed and breakfast *n Chiefly Brit* overnight accommodation and breakfast.

bedaub *vb* to smear over with something sticky or dirty.
bedbug *n* a small blood-sucking wingless insect that infests dirty houses.
bedclothes *pl n* coverings for a bed.
bedding *n* **1** bedclothes, sometimes with a mattress. **2** litter, such as straw, for animals. **3** the distinct layered deposits of rocks.
bedeck *vb* to cover with decorations.
bedevil (bid-**dev**-ill) *vb* **-illing, -illed** *or US* **-iling, -iled 1** to harass or torment. **2** to throw into confusion. ▶ **bedevilment** *n*
bedlam *n* a noisy confused situation.

> **WORD HISTORY**
> The Hospital of St. Mary of Bethlehem in London was an institution where the insane or mentally ill were cared for. Its name was colloquially shortened to *Bethlem* or *Bedlam*, from which the word 'bedlam' comes.

bedload *n Geol* the sediment carried along by a river in the form of heavy particles.
Bedouin *n* **1** (*pl* **-ins** *or* **-in**) a nomadic Arab tribesman of the deserts of Arabia, Jordan, and Syria. **2** a wanderer. ▷ HISTORY Arabic *badw* desert
bedpan *n* a shallow container used as a toilet by people who are not well enough to leave bed.
bedraggled *adj* with hair or clothing that is untidy, wet, or dirty.
bedridden *adj* unable to leave bed because of illness.
bedrock *n* **1** the solid rock beneath the surface soil. **2** basic principles or facts.
bedroom *n* **1** a room used for sleeping. ✧ *adj* **2** containing references to sex: *a bedroom comedy.*
bedsit *or* **bedsitter** *n* a furnished sitting room with a bed.
bedsore *n* an ulcer on the skin, caused by a lengthy period of lying in bed due to illness.
bedspread *n* a top cover on a bed.
bedstead *n* the framework of a bed.
bedstraw *n* a plant with small white or yellow flowers.
bed-wetting *n* involuntarily urinating in bed.
bee[1] *n* **1** a four-winged insect that collects nectar and pollen to make honey and wax. **2 have a bee in one's bonnet** to be obsessed with an idea. ▷ HISTORY Old English *bīo*
bee[2] *n* a social gathering to carry out a communal task: *quilting bee.* ▷ HISTORY probably from Old English *bēn* boon
Beeb *n* **the Beeb** *Brit informal* the BBC.
beech *n* **1** a tree with smooth greyish bark. **2** the hard wood of this tree. **3** See **copper beech**. ▷ HISTORY Old English *bēce*
beechnut *n* the small brown triangular edible nut of the beech tree.
beef *n* **1** the flesh of a cow, bull, or ox. **2** *Slang* a complaint. ✧ *vb* **3** *Slang* to complain. ✧ See also **beef up**. ▷ HISTORY Old French *boef*, from Latin *bos* ox
beefburger *n* a flat fried or grilled cake of minced beef; hamburger.
beefeater *n* a yeoman warder of the Tower of London.
beef tomato *or* **beefsteak tomato** *n* a type of large fleshy tomato.
beef up *vb Informal* to strengthen.
beefy *adj* **beefier, beefiest 1** *Informal* muscular. **2** like beef. ▶ **beefiness** *n*
beehive *n* a structure in which bees are housed.
Beelzebub (bee-**ell**-zib-bub) *n* Satan or any devil. ▷ HISTORY Hebrew *bá'al zebūb,* literally: lord of flies
been *vb* the past participle of **be**.
beep *n* **1** a high-pitched sound, like that of a car horn. ✧ *vb* **2** to make or cause to make such a noise. ▷ HISTORY imitative
beer *n* **1** an alcoholic drink brewed from malt, sugar, hops, and water. **2** a glass, can, or bottle containing this drink. ▷ HISTORY Old English *beor*
beer parlour *n Canad* a licensed place in which beer is sold and drunk.
beery *adj* **beerier, beeriest** smelling or tasting of beer.
beeswax *n* **1** a wax produced by honeybees for making honeycombs. **2** this wax after refining, used in polishes, etc.
beet *n* a plant with an edible root and leaves, such as the sugar beet and beetroot. ▷ HISTORY Old English *bēte*
beetle[1] *n* **1** an insect with a hard wing-case closed over its back for protection. ✧ *vb* **-tling, -tled 2** (foll. by *along, off*) etc. *Informal* to scuttle or scurry. ▷ HISTORY Old English *bitela*
beetle[2] *vb* **-tling, -tled** to overhang; jut: *the eaves of the roof beetled out over the windows.* ▷ HISTORY origin unknown ▶ **beetling** *adj*
beetle-browed *adj* having bushy or overhanging eyebrows.
beetroot *n* a variety of the beet plant with a dark red root that may be eaten as a vegetable, in salads, or pickled.
beet sugar *n* the sucrose obtained from sugar beet.
befall *vb* **-falling, -fell, -fallen** *Archaic or literary* to happen to. ▷ HISTORY Old English *befeallan*
befit *vb* **-fitting, -fitted** to be appropriate to or suitable for. ▶ **befitting** *adj*
before *conj* **1** earlier than the time when. **2** rather than: *she'll resign before she agrees to it.* ✧ *prep* **3** preceding in space or time; in front of; ahead of: *they stood before the altar.* **4** in the presence of: *to be brought before a judge.* **5** in preference to: *to put friendship before money.* ✧ *adv* **6** previously. **7** in front. ▷ HISTORY Old English *beforan*
beforehand *adj, adv* early; in advance.
befriend *vb* to become a friend to.
befuddled *adj* stupefied or confused, as through alcoholic drink.
beg *vb* **begging, begged 1** to ask for money or food in the street. **2** to ask formally, humbly, or earnestly: *I beg forgiveness; I beg to differ.* **3 beg the question** to put forward an argument that

A
B
C
D
E
F
G
H
I
J
K
L
M
N
O
P
Q
R
S
T
U
V
W
X
Y
Z

assumes the very point it is supposed to establish, or that depends on some other questionable assumption. **4 go begging** to be unwanted or unused. ▷ **HISTORY** probably from Old English *bedecian*

began *vb* the past tense of **begin**.

beget *vb* **-getting, -got** *or* **-gat; -gotten** *or* **-got** *Old-fashioned* **1** to cause or create: *repetition begets boredom.* **2** to father. ▷ **HISTORY** Old English *begietan*

beggar *n* **1** a person who lives by begging. **2** *Chiefly Brit* a fellow: *lucky beggar!* ✧ *vb* **3 beggar description** to be impossible to describe.
▸ **beggarly** *adj*

begin *vb* **-ginning, -gan, -gun 1** to start (something). **2** to bring or come into being. **3** to start to say or speak. **4** to have the least capacity to do something: *it doesn't even begin to address the problem.* ▷ **HISTORY** Old English *beginnan*
▸ **beginner** *n*

beginning *n* **1** a start. **2 beginnings** an early part or stage. **3** the place where or time when something starts. **4** an origin; source.

begone *interj* go away!

begonia *n* a tropical plant with ornamental leaves and waxy flowers. ▷ **HISTORY** after Michel *Bégon,* patron of science

begot *vb* a past tense and past participle of **beget**.

begotten *vb* a past participle of **beget**.

begrudge *vb* **-grudging, -grudged 1** to envy (someone) the possession of something. **2** to give or allow unwillingly: *he begrudged her an apology.*

beguile (big-**gile**) *vb* **-guiling, -guiled** to charm (someone) into doing something he or she would not normally do.

beguiling *adj* charming, often in a deceptive way.

beguine (big-**geen**) *n* **1** a dance of South American origin. **2** music for this dance.
▷ **HISTORY** French *béguin* flirtation

begum (**bay**-gum) *n* (in certain Muslim countries) a woman of high rank. ▷ **HISTORY** Turkish *begim*

begun *vb* the past participle of **begin**.

behalf *n* **on** *or US & Canad* **in behalf of** in the interest of or for the benefit of. ▷ **HISTORY** Old English *be* by + *halfe* side

behave *vb* **-having, -haved 1** to act or function in a particular way. **2** to conduct oneself in a particular way: *the baby behaved very well.* **3** to conduct oneself properly. ▷ **HISTORY** Middle English

behaviour *or US* **behavior** *n* **1** manner of behaving. **2** *Psychol* the response of an organism to a stimulus. ▸ **behavioural** *or US* ▸ **behavioral** *adj*

behavioural science *n* the scientific study of the behaviour of organisms.

behaviourism *or US* **behaviorism** *n* a school of psychology that regards objective observation of the behaviour of organisms as the only valid subject for study. ▸ **behaviourist** *or US*
▸ **behaviorist** *adj, n*

behead *vb* to remove the head from.
▷ **HISTORY** Old English *behēafdian*

beheld *vb* the past of **behold**.

behemoth (bee-**hee**-moth) *n* a huge person or thing. ▷ **HISTORY** Hebrew *bĕhēmāh* beast, name given to a huge beast in the Bible (Job 40:15)

behest *n* an order or earnest request: *I came at her behest.* ▷ **HISTORY** Old English *behǣs*

behind *prep* **1** in or to a position further back than. **2** in the past in relation to: *I want to leave the past behind me.* **3** late according to: *running behind schedule.* **4** concerning the circumstances surrounding: *the reasons behind his departure.* **5** supporting: *I'm right behind you in your application.* ✧ *adv* **6** in or to a position further back. **7** remaining after someone's departure: *she left her books behind.* **8** in arrears: *to fall behind with payments.* ✧ *adj* **9** in a position further back. ✧ *n* **10** *Informal* the buttocks. ▷ **HISTORY** Old English *behindan*

behold *vb* **-holding, -held** *Archaic or literary* to look (at); observe. ▷ **HISTORY** Old English *bihealdan*
▸ **beholder** *n*

beholden *adj* indebted; obliged: *I am beholden to you.*

behove *vb* **-hoving, -hoved** *Archaic* to be necessary or fitting for: *it behoves me to warn you.* ▷ **HISTORY** Old English *behōfian*

beige *adj* pale creamy-brown. ▷ **HISTORY** Old French

being *n* **1** the state or fact of existing. **2** essential nature; self. **3** something that exists or is thought to exist: *a being from outer space.* **4** a human being.

bel *n* a unit for comparing two power levels or measuring the intensity of a sound, equal to 10 decibels. ▷ **HISTORY** after A. G. *Bell,* scientist

belabour *or US* **belabor** *vb* to attack verbally or physically.

belated *adj* late or too late: *belated greetings.*
▸ **belatedly** *adv*

belay *vb* **-laying, -layed 1** *Naut* to secure a line to a pin or cleat. **2** *Naut* to stop. **3** *Mountaineering* to secure (a climber) by fixing a rope round a rock or piton. ▷ **HISTORY** Old English *belecgan*

belch *vb* **1** to expel wind from the stomach noisily through the mouth. **2** to expel or be expelled forcefully: *smoke belching from factory chimneys.* ✧ *n* **3** an act of belching. ▷ **HISTORY** Old English *bialcan*

beleaguered *adj* **1** struggling against difficulties or criticism: *the country's beleaguered health system.* **2** besieged by an enemy: *a ship bringing food to the beleaguered capital of Monrovia.* ▷ **HISTORY** BE- + obsolete *leaguer* a siege

belfry *n, pl* **-fries 1** the part of a tower or steeple in which bells are hung. **2** a tower or steeple.
▷ **HISTORY** Germanic

Belgian *adj* **1** of Belgium. ✧ *n* **2** a person from Belgium.

belgium sausage *n NZ* large smooth bland sausage.

Belial (**bee**-lee-al) *n* the devil or Satan.
▷ **HISTORY** Hebrew *bəlīyya'al* worthless

belie *vb* **-lying, -lied 1** to show to be untrue: *the facts belied the theory.* **2** to misrepresent: *the score belied the closeness of the match.* **3** to fail to justify:

the promises were soon belied. ▷ **HISTORY** Old English *belēogan*

belief *n* **1** trust or confidence: *belief in the free market.* **2** opinion; conviction: *it's my firm belief.* **3** a principle, etc., accepted as true, often without proof. **4** religious faith.

believe *vb* **-lieving, -lieved 1** to accept as true or real: *I believe God exists.* **2** to think, assume, or suppose: *I believe you know my father.* **3** to accept the statement or opinion of (a person) as true. **4** to have religious faith. **5 believe in** to be convinced of the truth or existence of: *I don't believe in ghosts.* ▷ **HISTORY** Old English *beliefan* ▶ **believable** *adj* ▶ **believer** *n*

Belisha beacon (bill-**lee**-sha) *n Brit* a flashing orange globe mounted on a striped post, indicating a pedestrian crossing. ▷ **HISTORY** after L. Hore-*Belisha,* politician

belittle *vb* **-tling, -tled** to treat (something or someone) as having little value or importance.

bell *n* **1** a hollow, usually metal, cup-shaped instrument that emits a ringing sound when struck. **2** the sound made by such an instrument. **3** an electrical device that rings or buzzes as a signal. **4** something shaped like a bell. **5** *Brit slang* a telephone call. **6 ring a bell** to sound familiar; recall something previously experienced. ▷ **HISTORY** Old English *belle*

belladonna *n* **1** a drug obtained from deadly nightshade. **2** same as **deadly nightshade**. ▷ **HISTORY** Italian, literally: beautiful lady; supposed to refer to its use as a cosmetic

bell-bottoms *pl n* trousers that flare from the knee. ▶ **bell-bottomed** *adj*

belle *n* a beautiful woman, esp. the most attractive woman at a function: *the belle of the ball.* ▷ **HISTORY** French

belles-lettres (bell-**let**-tra) *n* literary works, particularly essays and poetry. ▷ **HISTORY** French

bellicose *adj* warlike; aggressive. ▷ **HISTORY** Latin *bellum* war

belligerence *n* the act or quality of being belligerent or warlike.

belligerent *adj* **1** marked by readiness to fight. **2** relating to or engaged in a war. ✧ *n* **3** a person or country engaged in war. ▷ **HISTORY** Latin *bellum* war + *gerere* to wage

bell jar *n* a bell-shaped glass cover used to protect flower arrangements or cover apparatus to confine gases in experiments.

bellow *vb* **1** to make a loud deep cry like that of a bull. **2** to shout in anger. ✧ *n* **3** the characteristic noise of a bull. **4** a loud deep roar. ▷ **HISTORY** probably from Old English *bylgan*

bellows *n* **1** a device consisting of an air chamber with flexible sides that is used to create and direct a stream of air. **2** a flexible corrugated part, such as that connecting the lens system of some cameras to the body. ▷ **HISTORY** plural of Old English *belig* belly

bells and whistles *pl n* attractive but nonessential additional features. ▷ **HISTORY** from the bells and whistles which used to decorate fairground organs

belly *n, pl* **-lies 1** the part of the body of a vertebrate containing the intestines and other organs. **2** the stomach. **3** the front, lower, or inner part of something. **4 go belly up** *Informal* to die, fail, or end. ✧ *vb* **-lies, -lying, -lied 5** to swell out; bulge. ▷ **HISTORY** Old English *belig*

bellyache *n* **1** *Informal* a pain in the abdomen. ✧ *vb* **-aching, -ached 2** *Slang* to complain repeatedly.

bellybutton *n Informal* the navel.

belly flop *n* **1** a dive into water in which the body lands horizontally. ✧ *vb* **belly-flop, -flopping, -flopped 2** to perform a belly flop.

bellyful *n* **1** *Slang* more than one can tolerate. **2** as much as one wants or can eat.

belly laugh *n* a loud deep hearty laugh.

belong *vb* **1** (foll. by *to*) to be the property of. **2** (foll. by *to*) to be bound to (a person, organization, etc.) by ties of affection, association, membership, etc.: *the nations concerned belonged to NATO.* **3** (foll. by *to, under, with*) etc. to be classified with: *it belongs to a different class of comets.* **4** (foll. by *to*) to be a part of: *this lid belongs to that tin.* **5** to have a proper or usual place. **6** *Informal* to be acceptable, esp. socially. ▷ **HISTORY** Middle English *belongen*

belongings *pl n* the things that a person owns or has with him or her.

beloved *adj* **1** dearly loved. ✧ *n* **2** a person who is dearly loved.

below *prep* **1** at or to a position lower than; under. **2** less than. **3** unworthy of; beneath. ✧ *adv* **4** at or to a lower position. **5** at a later place in something written. **6** *Archaic* on earth or in hell. ▷ **HISTORY** Middle English *bilooghe*

belt *n* **1** a band of leather or cloth worn around the waist. **2** an area where a specific thing is found; zone: *a belt of high pressure.* **3** same as **seat belt**. **4** a band of flexible material between rotating shafts or pulleys to transfer motion or transmit goods: *a fan belt; a conveyer belt.* **5** *Informal* a sharp blow. **6 below the belt** *Informal* unscrupulous or cowardly. **7 tighten one's belt** to reduce expenditure. **8 under one's belt** as part of one's experience: *he had a string of successes under his belt.* ✧ *vb* **9** to fasten with or as if with a belt. **10** to hit with a belt. **11** *Slang* to give (someone) a sharp blow. **12** (foll. by *along*) *Slang* to move very fast. ▷ **HISTORY** Old English

belt out *vb Informal* to sing (a song) loudly.

beluga (bill-**loo**-ga) *n* a large white sturgeon of the Black and Caspian Seas, from which caviar and isinglass are obtained. ▷ **HISTORY** Russian *byeluga*

bemoan *vb* to lament: *he's always bemoaning his fate.*

bemused *adj* puzzled or confused.

ben *n Scot, Irish* a mountain peak: *Ben Lomond.* ▷ **HISTORY** Gaelic *beinn*

bench *n* **1** a long seat for more than one person. **2 the bench a** a judge or magistrate sitting in court. **b** judges or magistrates collectively. **3** a long and strong worktable. ▷ **HISTORY** Old English *benc*

benchmark *n* **1** a mark on a fixed object, used as a reference point in surveying. **2** a criterion by which to measure something: *the speech was a benchmark of his commitment.*

bend[1] *vb* **bending, bent 1** to form a curve. **2** to turn from a particular direction: *the road bends right.* **3** (often foll. by *down*) etc. to incline the body. **4** to submit: *to bend before public opinion.* **5** to turn or direct (one's eyes, steps, or attention). **6 bend someone's ear** *Informal* to complain (to someone) for a long time. **7 bend the rules** *Informal* to ignore or change rules to suit oneself. ✧ *n* **8** a curved part. **9** the act of bending. **10 round the bend** *Brit slang* mad. ▷ **HISTORY** Old English *bendan* ▶ **bendy** *adj*

bend[2] *n Heraldry* a diagonal line across a shield. ▷ **HISTORY** Old English: a band, strip

bends *pl n* **the bends** *Informal* decompression sickness.

bend sinister *n Heraldry* a diagonal line across a shield, indicating a bastard line.

beneath *prep* **1** below; under. **2** too trivial for: *beneath his dignity.* ✧ *adv* **3** below; underneath. ▷ **HISTORY** Old English *beneothan*

Benedictine *n* **1** a monk or nun of the Christian order of Saint Benedict. **2** a liqueur first made by Benedictine monks. ✧ *adj* **3** of Saint Benedict or his order.

benediction *n* **1** a prayer for divine blessing. **2** a Roman Catholic service in which the congregation is blessed with the sacrament. ▷ **HISTORY** Latin *benedictio* ▶ **benedictory** *adj*

benefaction *n* **1** the act of doing good, particularly donating to charity. **2** the donation or help given. ▷ **HISTORY** Latin *bene* well + *facere* to do

benefactor *n* a person who supports a person or institution by giving money. ▶ **benefactress** *fem n*

benefice *n Christianity* a Church office that provides its holder with an income. ▷ **HISTORY** Latin *beneficium* benefit

beneficent (bin-**eff**-iss-ent) *adj* charitable; generous. ▷ **HISTORY** Latin *beneficus* ▶ **beneficence** *n*

beneficial *adj* helpful or advantageous. ▷ **HISTORY** Latin *beneficium* kindness

beneficiary *n, pl* **-ciaries 1** a person who gains or benefits. **2** *Law* a person entitled to receive funds or property under a trust, will, etc.

benefit *n* **1** something that improves or promotes. **2** advantage or sake: *I'm doing this for your benefit.* **3** a payment made by an institution or government to a person who is ill, unemployed, etc. **4** a theatrical performance or sports event to raise money for a charity. ✧ *vb* **-fiting, -fited** *or US* **-fitting, -fitted 5** to do or receive good; profit. ▷ **HISTORY** Latin *bene facere* to do well

benevolence *n* **1** inclination to do good. **2** an act of kindness. ▶ **benevolent** *adj*

Bengali *n* **1** a member of a people living chiefly in Bangladesh and West Bengal. **2** the language of this people. ✧ *adj* **3** of Bengal or the Bengalis.

benighted *adj* lacking cultural, moral, or intellectual enlightenment.

benign (bin-**nine**) *adj* **1** showing kindliness. **2** favourable: *a stroke of benign fate.* **3** *Pathol* (of a tumour, etc.) able to be controlled. ▷ **HISTORY** Latin *benignus* ▶ **benignly** *adv*

benioff zone *n Geol* a narrow downward-sloping earthquake zone which is usually externally indicated by the presence of deep-sea trenches.

bent *adj* **1** not straight; curved. **2** *Slang* **a** dishonest; corrupt: *bent officials.* **b** *Brit & Austral offensive slang* homosexual. **3 bent on** determined to pursue (a course of action). ✧ *n* **4** personal inclination or aptitude: *he had a strong practical bent in his nature.*

Benthamism *n* the utilitarian philosophy of Jeremy Bentham, which holds that the ultimate goal of society should be to promote the greatest happiness of the greatest number. ▶ **Benthamite** *n, adj*

bento *or* **bento box** *n* a thin box, made of plastic or lacquered wood, divided into compartments, which contain small separate dishes comprising a Japanese meal, esp. lunch. ▷ **HISTORY** Japanese *bento* box lunch

benumb *vb* **1** to make numb or powerless. **2** to stupefy (the mind, senses, will, etc.): *the work benumbed their minds and crushed their spirits.*

benzene *n* a flammable poisonous liquid used as a solvent, insecticide, etc. ▷ **HISTORY** from *benzoin,* a fragrant resin from certain Asiatic trees

benzine *n* a volatile liquid obtained from coal tar and used as a solvent.

bequeath *vb* **1** *Law* to dispose of (property) as in a will. **2** to hand down: *the author bequeaths no solutions.* ▷ **HISTORY** Old English *becwethan*

bequest *n* **1** the act of gifting money or property in a will. **2** money or property that has been gifted in a will.

berate *vb* **-rating, -rated** to scold harshly.

Berber *n* **1** a member of a Muslim people of N Africa. **2** the language of this people. ✧ *adj* **3** of the Berbers.

berberis *n* a shrub with red berries. ▷ **HISTORY** Medieval Latin

berceuse (bare-**suhz**) *n* **1** a lullaby. **2** an instrumental piece suggestive of this. ▷ **HISTORY** French

bereaved *adj* having recently lost a close relative or friend through death. ▷ **HISTORY** Old English *bereafian* to deprive ▶ **bereavement** *n*

bereft *adj* (foll. by *of*) deprived: *a government bereft of ideas.*

beret (**ber**-ray) *n* a round flat close-fitting brimless cap. ▷ **HISTORY** French

berg[1] *n* short for **iceberg**.

berg[2] *n S African* a mountain.

bergamot *n* **1** a small Asian tree with sour pear-shaped fruit. **2 essence of bergamot** a fragrant essential oil from the fruit rind of this plant, used in perfumery. ▷ **HISTORY** French *bergamote*

bergschrund (**berk**-shroont) *n Geog* a crevasse at the head of a glacier. ▷ HISTORY German: mountain crack

beri-beri *n* a disease caused by a dietary deficiency of thiamine (vitamin B_1). ▷ HISTORY Sinhalese

berk *or* **burk** *n Brit, Austral & NZ slang* a stupid person; fool. ▷ HISTORY *Berkshire Hunt,* rhyming slang for *cunt*

berkelium *n Chem* an artificial radioactive element. Symbol: Bk. ▷ HISTORY after *Berkeley,* California, where it was discovered

Berlin Wall *n History* a wall that divided Berlin into the eastern sector and the western sector, built in 1961 to stop the flow of refugees from East Germany to West Germany, and demolished in 1989-90, when the city was reunited.

berm *n NZ* narrow grass strip between the road and the footpath in a residential area.

Bermuda shorts *pl n* shorts that come down to the knees. ▷ HISTORY after *Bermudas,* islands in NW Atlantic

Bernoulli principle *n Physics* the principle that the pressure in a moving fluid becomes less as the speed rises. ▷ HISTORY after Daniel *Bernoulli,* mathematician & physicist

berry *n, pl* **-ries** a small round fruit that grows on bushes or trees and is often edible. ▷ HISTORY Old English *berie*

berserk *adj* **go berserk** to become violent or destructive.

WORD HISTORY

'Berserk' comes from the Old Norse word *berserkr,* denoting a Viking warrior who wore a shirt (*serkr*) made from the skin of a bear (*björn*). Berserkrs worked themselves into a frenzy before going into battle, from which comes the notion of someone 'going berserk'.

berth *n* **1** a bunk in a ship or train. **2** *Naut* a place assigned to a ship at a mooring. **3** *Naut* sufficient room for a ship to manoeuvre. **4 give a wide berth to** to keep clear of. ✧ *vb* **5** *Naut* to dock (a ship). **6** to provide with a sleeping place. **7** *Naut* to pick up a mooring in an anchorage. ▷ HISTORY probably from BEAR[1]

beryl *n* a transparent hard mineral, used as a source of beryllium and as a gemstone. ▷ HISTORY Greek *bērullos*

beryllium *n* a toxic silvery-white metallic element. Symbol: Be. ▷ HISTORY Greek *bērullos*

beseech *vb* **-seeching, -sought** *or* **-seeched** to ask earnestly; beg. ▷ HISTORY Middle English; see BE-, SEEK

beset *vb* **-setting, -set 1** to trouble or harass constantly. **2** to surround or attack from all sides.

beside *prep* **1** next to; at, by, or to the side of. **2** as compared with. **3** away from: *beside the point.* **4 beside oneself** overwhelmed; overwrought: *beside oneself with grief.* ✧ *adv* **5** at, by, to, or along the side of something or someone. ▷ HISTORY Old English *be sīdan*

besides *adv* **1** in addition. ✧ *prep* **2** apart from; even considering. ✧ *conj* **3** anyway; moreover.

besiege *vb* **-sieging, -sieged 1** to surround with military forces to bring about surrender. **2** to hem in. **3** to overwhelm, as with requests.

besmirch *vb* to tarnish (someone's name or reputation).

besom *n* a broom made of a bundle of twigs tied to a handle. ▷ HISTORY Old English *besma*

besotted *adj* **1** having an irrational passion for a person or thing. **2** stupefied with alcohol.

besought *vb* a past of **beseech**.

bespatter *vb* **1** to splash with dirty water. **2** to dishonour or slander.

bespeak *vb* **-speaking, -spoke; -spoken** *or* **-spoke 1** to indicate or suggest: *imitation bespeaks admiration.* **2** to engage or ask for in advance: *she was bespoke to a family in the town.*

bespoke *adj Chiefly Brit* **1** (esp. of a suit) made to the customer's specifications. **2** making or selling such suits: *a bespoke tailor.*

best *adj* **1** the superlative of **good**. **2** most excellent of a particular group, category, etc. **3** most suitable, desirable, etc. ✧ *adv* **4** the superlative of **well**. **5** in a manner surpassing all others; most attractively, etc. ✧ *n* **6 the best** the most outstanding or excellent person, thing, or group in a category. **7** the utmost effort: *I did my best.* **8** a person's finest clothes. **9 at best a** in the most favourable interpretation. **b** under the most favourable conditions. **10 for the best a** for an ultimately good outcome. **b** with good intentions. **11 get the best of** to defeat or outwit. **12 make the best of** to cope as well as possible with. ✧ *vb* **13** to defeat. ▷ HISTORY Old English *betst*

bestial *adj* **1** brutal or savage. **2** of or relating to a beast. ▷ HISTORY Latin *bestia* beast

bestiality *n, pl* **-ties 1** brutal behaviour, character, or action. **2** sexual activity between a person and an animal.

bestiary *n, pl* **-aries** a medieval collection of descriptions of animals.

bestir *vb* **-stirring, -stirred** to cause (oneself) to become active.

best man *n* the male attendant of the bridegroom at a wedding.

bestow *vb* to present (a gift) or confer (an honour). ▶ **bestowal** *n*

bestride *vb* **-striding, -strode** to have or put a leg on either side of.

bestseller *n* a book or other product that has sold in great numbers. ▶ **bestselling** *adj*

bet *n* **1** the act of staking a sum of money or other stake on the outcome of an event. **2** the stake risked. **3** a course of action: *your best bet is to go by train.* **4** *Informal* an opinion: *my bet is that you've been up to no good.* ✧ *vb* **betting, bet** *or* **betted 5** to make or place a bet with (someone). **6** to stake (money, etc.) in a bet. **7** *Informal* to predict (a certain outcome): *I bet she doesn't turn up.* **8 you bet** *Informal* of course. ▷ HISTORY probably short for *abet*

beta *n* **1** the second letter in the Greek alphabet (Β, β). **2** the second in a group or series.

beta-blocker *n* a drug that decreases the activity of the heart: used in the treatment of high blood pressure and angina pectoris.

beta-carotene *n Biochem* the most important form of the plant pigment carotene, which occurs in milk, vegetables, and other foods and, when eaten by man and animals, is converted in the body to vitamin A.

betake *vb* **-taking, -took, -taken betake oneself** *Formal* to go or move: *he betook himself to the public house.*

beta particle *n* a high-speed electron or positron emitted by a nucleus during radioactive decay or nuclear fission.

betatron *n* a type of particle accelerator for producing high-energy beams of electrons.

betel (**bee**-tl) *n* an Asian climbing plant, the leaves and nuts of which can be chewed. ▷ **HISTORY** Malayalam (language of SW India) *vettila*

bête noire (bet **nwahr**) *n, pl* **bêtes noires** a person or thing that one particularly dislikes or dreads. ▷ **HISTORY** French, literally: black beast

betide *vb* **-tiding, -tided** to happen or happen to: *woe betide us if we're not ready on time.* ▷ **HISTORY** BE- + obsolete *tide* to happen

betoken *vb* to indicate; signify.

betray *vb* **1** to hand over or expose (one's nation, friend, etc.) treacherously to an enemy. **2** to disclose (a secret or confidence) treacherously. **3** to reveal unintentionally: *his singing voice betrays his origins.* ▷ **HISTORY** Latin *tradere* to hand over ▶ **betrayal** *n* ▶ **betrayer** *n*

betrothed *Old-fashioned* ✧ *adj* **1** engaged to be married. ✧ *n* **2** the person to whom one is engaged.

better *adj* **1** the comparative of **good**. **2** more excellent than others. **3** more suitable, attractive, etc. **4** improved or fully recovered in health. **5 the better part of** a large part of. ✧ *adv* **6** the comparative of **well**. **7** in a more excellent manner. **8** in or to a greater degree. **9 better off** in more favourable circumstances, esp. financially. **10 had better** would be sensible, etc. to: *I had better be off.* ✧ *n* **11 the better** something that is the more excellent, useful, etc. of two such things. **12 betters** people who are one's superiors, esp. in social standing. **13 get the better of** to defeat or outwit. ✧ *vb* **14** to improve upon. ▷ **HISTORY** Old English *betera*

betterment *n* improvement.

better-off *adj* reasonably wealthy: *Catalonia aims to attract better-off tourists.*

between *prep* **1** at a point intermediate to two other points in space, time, etc. **2** in combination; together: *between them, they saved enough money to buy a car.* **3** confined to: *between you and me.* **4** indicating a linking relation or comparison. **5** indicating alternatives, strictly only two alternatives. ✧ *adv also* **in between 6** between one specified thing and another. ▷ **HISTORY** Old English *betwēonum*

> **WORD TIP**
> After *distribute* and words with a similar meaning, *among* should be used rather than *between: this enterprise issued shares which were distributed among its workers.*

betwixt *prep, adv* **1** *Archaic* between. **2 betwixt and between** in an intermediate or indecisive position.

bevel *n* **1** a slanting edge. ✧ *vb* **-elling, -elled** *or US* **-eling, -eled 2** to be inclined; slope. **3** to cut a bevel on (a piece of timber, etc.). ▷ **HISTORY** Old French *baer* to gape

bevel gear *n* a toothed gear meshed with another at an angle to it.

beverage *n* any drink other than water. ▷ **HISTORY** Old French *bevrage*

beverage room *n Canad* same as **beer parlour**.

bevy *n, pl* **bevies** a flock; a group. ▷ **HISTORY** origin unknown

bewail *vb* to express great sorrow over; lament.

beware *vb* **-waring, -wared** (often foll. by *of*) to be wary (of); be on one's guard (against). ▷ **HISTORY** *be* (imperative) + obsolete *war* wary

bewilder *vb* to confuse utterly; puzzle. ▷ **HISTORY** BE- + obsolete *wilder* to lose one's way ▶ **bewildering** *adj* ▶ **bewilderment** *n*

bewitch *vb* **1** to attract and fascinate. **2** to cast a spell over. ▷ **HISTORY** Middle English *bewicchen* ▶ **bewitching** *adj*

bey *n* **1** (in modern Turkey) a title of address, corresponding to *Mr.* **2** (in the Ottoman Empire) a title given to provincial governors. ▷ **HISTORY** Turkish: lord

beyond *prep* **1** at or to a point on the other side of: *beyond those hills.* **2** outside the limits or scope of. ✧ *adv* **3** at or to the other or far side of something. **4** outside the limits of something. ✧ *n* **5 the beyond** the unknown, esp. life after death. ▷ **HISTORY** Old English *begeondan*

beyond reasonable doubt *n Law* the standard of proof in a criminal case, meaning that, before someone can be found guilty, there must not be any reasonable doubt as to their guilt in the minds of the jury or magistrate. Compare **balance of probabilities**.

bezel *n* **1** the sloping edge of a cutting tool. **2** the slanting face of a cut gem. **3** a groove holding a gem, watch crystal, etc. ▷ **HISTORY** French *biseau*

bezique *n* a card game for two or more players. ▷ **HISTORY** French *bésigue*

B/F *or* **b/f** *Book-keeping* brought forward.

BFPO British Forces Post Office.

Bh *Chem* bohrium.

bhaji *n, pl* **bhaji** *or* **bhajis** an Indian savoury made of chopped vegetables mixed in a spiced batter and deep-fried. ▷ **HISTORY** Hindi

bhang *n* a preparation of Indian hemp used as a narcotic and intoxicant. ▷ **HISTORY** Hindi

bhangra *n* a type of traditional Punjabi folk music combined with elements of Western pop music. ▷ **HISTORY** Hindi

bhp brake horsepower.

Bi *Chem* bismuth.

bi- *combining form* **1** having two: *bifocal.* **2** occurring or lasting for two: *biennial.* **3** on both sides, directions, etc.: *bilateral.* **4** occurring twice during: *biweekly.* **5** *Chem* **a** denoting a compound containing two identical cyclical hydrocarbon systems: *biphenyl.* **b** indicating an acid salt of a dibasic acid: *sodium bicarbonate.* ▷ **HISTORY** Latin *bis* twice

biannual *adj* occurring twice a year. ▸ **biannually** *adv*

bias *n* **1** mental tendency, esp. prejudice. **2** a diagonal cut across the weave of a fabric. **3** *Bowls* a bulge or weight inside one side of a bowl that causes it to roll in a curve. ✧ *vb* **-asing, -ased** *or* **-assing, -assed 4** to cause to have a bias; prejudice. ▷ **HISTORY** Old French *biais* ▸ **biased** *or* **biassed** *adj*

bias binding *n* a strip of material used for binding hems.

bib *n* **1** a piece of cloth or plastic worn to protect a very young child's clothes while eating. **2** the upper front part of some aprons, dungarees, etc. ▷ **HISTORY** Middle English *bibben* to drink

Bible *n* **1 the Bible** the sacred writings of the Christian religion, comprising the Old and New Testaments. **2 bible** a book regarded as authoritative: *this guide has long been regarded as the hill walkers' bible.* ▷ **HISTORY** Greek *biblion* book ▸ **biblical** *adj*

bibliography *n, pl* **-phies 1** a list of books on a subject or by a particular author. **2** a list of sources used in a book, etc. **3** the study of the history, etc., of literary material. ▷ **HISTORY** Greek *biblion* book + *graphein* to write ▸ **bibliographer** *n*

bibliophile *n* a person who collects or is fond of books. ▷ **HISTORY** Greek *biblion* book + *philos* loving

bibulous *adj Literary* addicted to alcohol. ▷ **HISTORY** Latin *bibere* to drink

bicameral *adj* (of a legislature) consisting of two chambers. ▷ **HISTORY** BI- + Latin *camera* chamber

bicarb *n* short for **bicarbonate of soda**.

bicarbonate *n* a salt of carbonic acid.

bicarbonate of soda *n* sodium bicarbonate used as medicine or a raising agent in baking.

bicentenary *or US* **bicentennial** *adj* **1** marking a 200th anniversary. ✧ *n, pl* **-naries 2** a 200th anniversary.

biceps *n, pl* **-ceps** *Anat* a muscle with two origins, esp. the muscle that flexes the forearm. ▷ **HISTORY** BI- + Latin *caput* head

bicker *vb* to argue over petty matters; squabble. ▷ **HISTORY** origin unknown

bicuspid *adj* **1** having two points. ✧ *n* **2** a bicuspid tooth.

bicuspid valve *n Anat* the valve between the left atrium and the left ventricle of the heart.

bicycle *n* **1** a vehicle with a metal frame and two wheels, one behind the other, pedalled by the rider. ✧ *vb* **-cling, -cled 2** to ride a bicycle. ▷ **HISTORY** BI- + Greek *kuklos* wheel

bid *vb* **bidding; bad, bade** *or* **bid; bidden** *or* **bid 1** to offer (an amount) in an attempt to buy something. **2** to say (a greeting): *to bid farewell.* **3** to order: *do as you are bid!* **4** *Bridge etc.* to declare how many tricks one expects to make. ✧ *n* **5 a** an offer of a specified amount. **b** the price offered. **6 a** the quoting by a seller of a price. **b** the price quoted. **7** an attempt, esp. to attain power. **8** *Bridge etc.* the number of tricks a player undertakes to make. ▷ **HISTORY** Old English *biddan* ▸ **bidder** *n*

biddable *adj* obedient.

bidding *n* **1** an order or command: *she had done his bidding.* **2** an invitation; summons: *he knew to knock and wait for bidding before he entered.* **3** the bids in an auction, card game, etc.

biddy-bid, biddy-biddy *n, pl* **-bids, -biddies** *NZ* a low-growing plant with hooked burrs.

bide *vb* **biding, bided** *or* **bode, bided 1** *Archaic or dialect* to remain. **2 bide one's time** to wait patiently for an opportunity. ▷ **HISTORY** Old English *bīdan*

bidet (**bee**-day) *n* a small low basin for washing the genital area. ▷ **HISTORY** French: small horse

biennial *adj* **1** occurring every two years. ✧ *n* **2** a plant that completes its life cycle in two years.

bier *n* a stand on which a corpse or a coffin rests before burial. ▷ **HISTORY** Old English *bǣr*

biff *Slang* ✧ *n* **1** a blow with the fist. ✧ *vb* **2** to give (someone) such a blow. ▷ **HISTORY** probably imitative

bifocal *adj* having two different focuses, esp. (of a lens) permitting near and distant vision.

bifocals *pl n* a pair of spectacles with bifocal lenses.

bifurcate *vb* **-cating, -cated 1** to fork into two branches. ✧ *adj* **2** forked into two branches. ▷ **HISTORY** BI- + Latin *furca* fork ▸ **bifurcation** *n*

bifurcation ratio *n Geog* in a system in which streams are ordered according to whether they have tributaries or not, the ratio of the number of streams without tributaries to the streams they flow into, or the ratio of small streams with tributaries to the next biggest streams, and so on. See also **stream order**.

big *adj* **bigger, biggest 1** of great or considerable size, weight, number, or capacity. **2** having great significance; important. **3** important through having power, wealth, etc. **4 a** elder: *my big brother.* **b** grown-up. **5** generous: *that's very big of you.* **6** extravagant; boastful: *big talk.* **7 too big for one's boots** conceited; unduly self-confident. **8** in an advanced stage of pregnancy: *big with child.* **9 in a big way** in a very grand or enthusiastic way. ✧ *adv Informal* **10** boastfully; pretentiously: *he talks big.* **11** on a grand scale: *think big.* ▷ **HISTORY** origin unknown

bigamy *n* the crime of marrying a person while still legally married to someone else. ▷ **HISTORY** BI- + Greek *gamos* marriage ▸ **bigamist** *n* ▸ **bigamous** *adj*

big-bang theory *n* a cosmological theory that suggests that the universe was created as the result of a massive explosion.

Big Brother *n* a person or organization that exercises total dictatorial control. ▷ HISTORY from the novel *1984* by George Orwell

big business *n* large commercial organizations collectively.

big end *n* the larger end of a connecting rod in an internal-combustion engine.

bighead *n Informal* a conceited person. ▶ **big-headed** *adj*

bight *n* **1** a long curved shoreline. **2** the slack part or a loop in a rope. ▷ HISTORY Old English *byht*

bigot *n* a person who is intolerant, esp. regarding religion, politics, or race. ▷ HISTORY Old French ▶ **bigoted** *adj* ▶ **bigotry** *n*

big shot *n Informal* an important person.

big top *n Informal* the main tent of a circus.

bigwig *n Informal* an important person.

bijou (**bee**-zhoo) *n, pl* **-joux** (-zhooz) **1** something small and delicately worked. ✧ *adj* **2** small but tasteful: *a bijou residence.* ▷ HISTORY French: a jewel

bike *n Informal* a bicycle or motorcycle.

biker *n* a person who rides a motorcycle.

bikini *n* a woman's brief two-piece swimming costume.

> **WORD HISTORY**
>
> The bikini takes its name from the *Bikini* Atoll in the Marshall Islands in the Pacific Ocean, where an atom-bomb was exploded in 1946. The bikini was given its name because it was said that the effect on men caused by women wearing bikinis was as explosive and devastating as the effect of the atom-bomb.

bilateral *adj* affecting or undertaken by two parties; mutual.

bilberry *n, pl* **-ries** a blue or blackish edible berry that grows on a shrub. ▷ HISTORY probably Scandinavian

bilby *n, pl* **-bies** an Australian marsupial with long pointed ears and grey fur.

Bildungsroman (**bil**-doong-sro-marn) *n Literature* a novel concerned with a person's formative years and development. ▷ HISTORY German, literally: education novel

bile *n* **1** a greenish fluid secreted by the liver to aid digestion of fats. **2** irritability or peevishness. ▷ HISTORY Latin *bilis*

bilge *n* **1** *Informal* nonsense. **2** *Naut* the bottom of a ship's hull. **3** the dirty water that collects in a ship's bilge. ▷ HISTORY probably variant of *bulge*

bilharzia (bill-**hart**-see-a) *n* a disease caused by infestation of the body with blood flukes. ▷ HISTORY after T. *Bilharz,* who discovered the blood fluke

biliary *adj* of bile, the ducts that convey bile, or the gall bladder.

bilingual *adj* **1** able to speak two languages. **2** expressed in two languages. ▶ **bilingualism** *n*

bilious *adj* **1** nauseous; sick: *a bilious attack.* **2** *Informal* bad-tempered; irritable: *the regime's most persistent and bilious critic.* **3** (of a colour) harsh and offensive. ▷ HISTORY Latin *biliosus* full of bile

bilk *vb* to cheat or deceive, esp. to avoid making payment to. ▷ HISTORY perhaps variant of *balk* ▶ **bilker** *n*

bill[1] *n* **1** a statement of money owed for goods or services supplied. **2** a draft of a proposed new law presented to a law-making body. **3** a printed notice or advertisement. **4** *US & Canad* a piece of paper money; note. **5** any list of items, events, etc. such as a theatre programme. ✧ *vb* **6** to send or present an account for payment to (a person). **7** to advertise by posters. **8** to schedule as a future programme: *next week they will discuss what are billed as new ideas for economic reform.* **9 fit** *or* **fill the bill** *Informal* to be suitable or adequate. ▷ HISTORY Late Latin *bulla* document

bill[2] *n* **1** the projecting jaws of a bird; beak. ✧ *vb* **2 bill and coo** (of lovers) to kiss and whisper amorously. ▷ HISTORY Old English *bile*

billabong *n Austral* a pool in the bed of a stream with an interrupted water flow. ▷ HISTORY Aboriginal

billboard *n* a hoarding.

billet[1] *vb* **-leting, -leted 1** to assign a lodging to (a soldier). ✧ *n* **2** accommodation, esp. for a soldier, in civilian lodgings. **3** *Austral & NZ* a person who is billeted. ▷ HISTORY Old French *billette,* from *bulle* a document

billet[2] *n* **1** a chunk of wood, esp. for fuel. **2** a small bar of iron or steel. ▷ HISTORY Old French *billette* a little log

billet-doux (**bill**-ee-**doo**) *n, pl* **billets-doux** (**bill**-ee-**dooz**) *Old-fashioned or jocular* a love letter. ▷ HISTORY French: a sweet letter

billhook *n* a tool with a hooked blade, used for chopping, etc.

billiards *n* a game in which a long cue is used to propel balls on a table. ▷ HISTORY Old French *billard* curved stick

billion *n, pl* **-lions** *or* **-lion 1** one thousand million: 1 000 000 000 or 10^9. **2** (in Britain, originally) one million million: 1 000 000 000 000 or 10^{12}. **3** (*often pl*) *Informal* an extremely large but unspecified number: *billions of dollars.* ▷ HISTORY French ▶ **billionth** *adj, n*

billionaire *n* a person who has money or property worth at least a billion pounds, dollars, etc.

bill of exchange *n* a document instructing a third party to pay a stated sum at a designated date or on demand.

bill of fare *n* a menu.

bill of lading *n* a document containing full particulars of goods shipped.

Bill of Rights *n Law* **1** an English statute of 1689 guaranteeing the rights and liberty of the individual subject. **2** the first ten amendments to the US Constitution which guarantee the liberty of the individual. **3** (*usually not caps.*) any charter of basic human rights.

billow *n* **1** a large sea wave. **2** a swelling or surging mass, as of smoke or sound. ✧ *vb* **3** to rise up or swell out. ▷ HISTORY Old Norse *bylgja* ▶ **billowing** *adj, n* ▶ **billowy** *adj*

billy *or* **billycan** *n, pl* **-lies** *or* **-lycans** a metal can or pot for boiling water etc. over a campfire. ▷ HISTORY Scots *billypot*

billy goat *n* a male goat.

biltong *n S African* strips of meat dried and cured in the sun. ▷ HISTORY Afrikaans

bimbo *n, pl* **-bos** *Slang* an attractive but empty-headed young woman. ▷ HISTORY Italian: little child

bimetallic *adj* consisting of two metals.

bimetallism *n* the use of two metals, esp. gold and silver, in fixed relative values as the standard of value and currency. ▶ **bimetallist** *n*

bimodal *adj Maths* having two modes.

bin *n* **1** a container for rubbish, etc. **2** a large container for storing something in bulk, such as coal, grain, or bottled wine. ✧ *vb* **binning, binned** **3** to put in a rubbish bin: *I bin my junk mail without reading it.* ▷ HISTORY Old English *binne* basket

binary (**bine**-a-ree) *adj* **1** composed of two parts. **2** *Maths, computers* of or expressed in a system with two as its base. **3** *Chem* containing atoms of two different elements. ✧ *n, pl* **-ries** **4** something composed of two parts. ▷ HISTORY Late Latin *binarius*

binary fission *adj Biol* reproduction in single-celled organisms by division into two similar daughter cells.

binary star *n* a system of two stars revolving around a common centre of gravity.

bind *vb* **binding, bound** **1** to make secure, such as with a rope. **2** to unite with emotional ties or commitment. **3** to place (someone) under legal or moral obligation. **4** to place under certain constraints: *bound by the rules.* **5** to stick together or cause to stick: *egg binds fat and flour.* **6** to enclose and fasten (the pages of a book) between covers. **7** to provide (a garment) with an edging. **8** (foll. by *up*) to bandage. ✧ *n* **9** *Informal* a difficult or annoying situation. ▷ HISTORY Old English *bindan*

binder *n* **1** a firm cover for holding loose sheets of paper together. **2** a person who binds books. **3** something used to fasten or tie, such as rope or twine. **4** *Obsolete* a machine for cutting and binding grain into sheaves.

binding *n* **1** anything that binds or fastens. **2** the covering of a book. ✧ *adj* **3** imposing an obligation or duty.

bind over *vb* to place (a person) under a legal obligation, esp. to keep the peace.

bindweed *n* a plant that twines around a support.

binge *n Informal* **1** a bout of excessive drinking. **2** excessive indulgence in anything. ▷ HISTORY probably dialect: to soak

bingo *n* a gambling game in which numbers called out are covered by players on their individual cards. The first to cover a given arrangement is the winner. ▷ HISTORY origin unknown

binnacle *n* a housing for a ship's compass. ▷ HISTORY Late Latin *habitaculum* dwelling-place

binocular *adj* involving or intended for both eyes: *binocular vision.* ▷ HISTORY BI- + Latin *oculus* eye

binoculars *pl n* an optical instrument for use with both eyes, consisting of two small telescopes joined together.

binomial *n* **1** a mathematical expression consisting of two terms, such as $3x + 2y$. ✧ *adj* **2** referring to two names or terms. ▷ HISTORY BI- + Latin *nomen* name

binomial theorem *n* a general mathematical formula that expresses any power of a binomial without multiplying out, as in $(a+b)^2=a^2+2ab+b^2$.

bio- *combining form* indicating: **1** life or living organisms: *biogenesis.* **2** a human life or career: *biography.* ▷ HISTORY Greek *bios* life

bioastronautics *n* the study of the effects of space flight on living organisms.

biochemistry *n* the study of the chemical compounds, reactions, etc., occurring in living organisms. ▶ **biochemical** *adj* ▶ **biochemist** *n*

biocide *n* a substance used to destroy living things. ▷ HISTORY BIO- + Latin *caedere* to kill

biocoenosis *or US* **biocenosis** (bye-oh-see-**no**-siss) *n* the relationships between animals and plants subsisting together. ▷ HISTORY BIO- + Greek *koinōsis* sharing

biodegradable *adj* (of sewage and packaging) capable of being decomposed by natural means. ▶ **biodegradability** *n*

biodiversity *n* the existence of a wide variety of plant and animal species in their natural environments.

bioengineering *n* the design and manufacture of aids, such as artificial limbs, to help people with disabilities.

biogas *n* gaseous fuel produced by the fermentation of organic waste.

biogenesis *n* the principle that a living organism must originate from a similar parent organism.

biogenic (bye-oh-**jen**-ik) *adj* originating from a living organism.

biogeochemical *adj Biol* of the study of relationships between chemical elements and the environment.

biogeography *n Biol, geog* the branch of biology concerned with the geographical distribution of plants and animals. ▶ **biogeographical** *adj* ▶ **biogeographically** *adv*

biography *n, pl* **-phies** **1** an account of a someone's life by another person. **2** such accounts collectively. ▷ HISTORY BIO- + Greek *graphein* to write ▶ **biographer** *n* ▶ **biographical** *adj*

biol. **1** biological. **2** biology.

biological *adj* **1** of or relating to biology. **2** (of a detergent) containing enzymes that remove natural stains, such as blood or grass. ▶ **biologically** *adv*

A B C D E F G H I J K L M N O P Q R S T U V W X Y Z

biological clock *n* an inherent timing mechanism that controls the rhythmic repetition of processes in living organisms, such as sleeping.

biological control *n* the control of destructive organisms, esp. insects, by nonchemical means, such as introducing a natural predator of the pest.

biological magnification *n Biol* the phenomenon whereby the higher up the food chain an animal is, the higher the concentrations of certain toxins in its body; caused by the tendency of each animal in the chain to store rather than to eliminate these toxins so that those eating other animals ingest multiple concentrations.

biological warfare *n* the use of living organisms or their toxic products to induce death or incapacity in humans.

biological weathering *pl n Geol* changes to rocks caused by living organisms such as algae, lichen, or tree roots.

biology *n* the study of living organisms. ▸ **biologist** *n*

biomass *n Biol, geog* the total number of living organisms in a given area.

biome *n Biol, geog* a major ecological community, extending over a large area and usually characterized by a dominant vegetation.

biomechanics *n* the study of the mechanics of the movement of living organisms.

biomedicine *n* **1** the medical and biological study of the effects of unusual environmental stress. **2** the study of herbal remedies.

bionic *adj* **1** of or relating to bionics. **2** (in science fiction) having physical functions augmented by electronic equipment. ▷ **HISTORY** BIO- + *(electro)nic*

bionics *n* **1** the study of biological functions in order to develop electronic equipment that operates similarly. **2** the replacement of limbs or body parts by artificial electronically powered parts.

biophysics *n* the physics of biological processes and the application of methods used in physics to biology. ▸ **biophysical** *adj* ▸ **biophysicist** *n*

biopic (**bye**-oh-pick) *n Informal* a film based on the life of a famous person. ▷ **HISTORY** *bio(graphical) + pic(ture)*

biopsy *n, pl* **-sies** examination of tissue from a living body to determine the cause or extent of a disease. ▷ **HISTORY** BIO- + Greek *opsis* sight

biorhythm *n* a complex recurring pattern of physiological states, believed to affect physical, emotional, and mental states.

bioscope *n* **1** a kind of early film projector. **2** *S African* a cinema.

biosphere *n* the part of the earth's surface and atmosphere inhabited by living things.

biosynthesis *n* the formation of complex compounds by living organisms. ▸ **biosynthetic** *adj*

biotech *n* short for **biotechnology**.

biotechnology *n* the use of microorganisms, such as cells or bacteria, in industry and technology.

bioterrorism *n* the use of viruses, bacteria, etc by terrorists. ▸ **bioterrorist** *n*

biotic *adj Biol* of or relating to living organisms or produced by living organisms. ▷ **HISTORY** Greek *biotikos,* from *bios* life Compare **abiotic**.

biotin *n* a vitamin of the B complex, abundant in egg yolk and liver. ▷ **HISTORY** Greek *biotē* life

bipartisan *adj* consisting of or supported by two political parties.

bipartite *adj* **1** consisting of or having two parts. **2** affecting or made by two parties: *a bipartite agreement.*

biped (**bye**-ped) *n* **1** any animal with two feet. ✧ *adj also* **bipedal** **2** having two feet. ▷ **HISTORY** BI- + Latin *pes* foot

biplane *n* an aeroplane with two sets of wings, one above the other.

bipolar *adj* **1** having two poles. **2** having two extremes. ▸ **bipolarity** *n*

birch *n* **1** a tree with thin peeling bark and hard close-grained wood. **2 the birch** a bundle of birch twigs or a birch rod used, esp. formerly, for flogging offenders. ✧ *vb* **3** to flog with the birch. ▷ **HISTORY** Old English *bierce*

bird *n* **1** a two-legged creature with feathers and wings, which lays eggs and can usually fly. *RELATED ADJECTIVE* ▸ **avian** **2** *Slang, chiefly Brit* a girl or young woman. **3** *Informal* a person: *he's a rare bird.* **4 a bird in the hand** something definite or certain. **5 birds of a feather** people with the same ideas or interests. **6 kill two birds with one stone** to accomplish two things with one action. ▷ **HISTORY** Old English *bridd*

birdie *n* **1** *Informal* a bird. **2** *Golf* a score of one stroke under par for a hole.

bird of paradise *n* a songbird of New Guinea, the male of which has brilliantly coloured plumage.

bird of prey *n* a bird, such as a hawk or owl, that hunts other animals for food.

bird's-eye view *n* **1** a view seen from above. **2** a general or overall impression of something.

bird's foot delta *n Geog* a delta at the mouth of a river characterized by strips of land projecting beyond the main land mass like the claws of a bird. Compare **arcuate delta, cuspate delta**.

biretta *n RC Church* a stiff square clerical cap. ▷ **HISTORY** Italian *berretta*

Biro *n, pl* **-ros** *Trademark* a kind of ballpoint pen.

birth *n* **1** the process of bearing young; childbirth. **2** the act of being born. **3** the beginning of something; origin. **4** ancestry: *of noble birth.* **5 give birth to a** to bear (offspring). **b** to produce or originate (an idea, plan, etc.). ▷ **HISTORY** Old Norse *byrth*

birth control *n* limitation of child-bearing by means of contraception.

birthday *n* **1** an anniversary of the day of one's birth. **2** the day on which a person was born.

birthmark *n* a blemish on the skin formed before birth.

birth mother *n* the woman who gives birth to a child, regardless of whether she is the genetic mother or subsequently brings up the child.

birth rate *n Sociology* the ratio of live births to population, usually expressed per 1000 population per year.
birthright *n* privileges or possessions that a person has or is believed to be entitled to as soon as he or she is born.
biscuit *n* **1** a small flat dry sweet or plain cake. **2** porcelain that has been fired but not glazed. ✧ *adj* **3** pale brown or yellowish-grey. ▷ HISTORY Old French *(pain) bescuit* twice-cooked (bread)
bisect *vb* **1** *Maths* to divide into two equal parts. **2** to cut or split into two. ▷ HISTORY BI- + Latin *secare* to cut ▶ **bisection** *n*
bisector *n Geom* a straight line or plane that bisects an angle or another line.
bisexual *adj* **1** sexually attracted to both men and women. **2** showing characteristics of both sexes. ✧ *n* **3** a bisexual person. ▶ **bisexuality** *n*
bishop *n* **1** a clergyman having spiritual and administrative powers over a diocese. **2** a chessman capable of moving diagonally. ▷ HISTORY Greek *episkopos* overseer
bishopric *n* the see, diocese, or office of a bishop.
bismuth *n Chem* a brittle pinkish-white metallic element. Some compounds are used in alloys and in medicine. Symbol: Bi. ▷ HISTORY German *Wismut*
bison *n, pl* **-son** an animal of the cattle family with a massive head, shaggy forequarters, and a humped back. ▷ HISTORY Germanic
bisque[1] *n* a thick rich soup made from shellfish. ▷ HISTORY French
bisque[2] *adj* **1** pink-to-yellowish-tan. ✧ *n* **2** *Ceramics* same as **biscuit** (sense 2). ▷ HISTORY shortened from *biscuit*
bistable *adj* (of an electronic system) having two stable states.
bistro *n, pl* **-tros** a small restaurant. ▷ HISTORY French
bit[1] *n* **1** a small piece, portion, or quantity. **2** a short time or distance. **3 a bit** rather; somewhat: *a bit stupid.* **4 a bit of** rather: *a bit of a fool.* **5 bit by bit** gradually. **6 do one's bit** to make one's expected contribution. ▷ HISTORY Old English *bite* action of biting
bit[2] *n* **1** a metal mouthpiece on a bridle for controlling a horse. **2** a cutting or drilling tool, part, or head in a brace, drill, etc. ▷ HISTORY Old English *bita*
bit[3] *vb* the past tense of **bite**.
bit[4] *n Maths, computers* **1** a single digit of binary notation, represented either by 0 or by 1. **2** the smallest unit of information, indicating the presence or absence of a single feature. ▷ HISTORY *b(inary + dig)it*
bitch *n* **1** a female dog, fox, or wolf. **2** *Slang, offensive* a malicious or spiteful woman. **3** *Informal* a difficult situation or problem. ✧ *vb* **4** *Informal* to complain; grumble. ▷ HISTORY Old English *bicce*
bitchy *adj* **bitchier, bitchiest** *Informal* spiteful or malicious. ▶ **bitchiness** *n*
bite *vb* **biting, bit, bitten 1** to grip, cut off, or tear with the teeth or jaws. **2** (of animals or insects) to injure by puncturing (the skin) with the teeth or fangs. **3** (of corrosive material) to eat away or into. **4** to smart or cause to smart; sting. **5** *Angling* (of a fish) to take the bait or lure. **6** to take firm hold of or act effectively upon: *turn the screw till it bites the wood.* **7** *Slang* to annoy or worry: *what's biting her?* ✧ *n* **8** the act of biting. **9** a thing or amount bitten off. **10** a wound or sting inflicted by biting. **11** *Angling* an attempt by a fish to take the bait or lure. **12** a snack. **13** a stinging or smarting sensation. ▷ HISTORY Old English *bītan* ▶ **biter** *n*
biting *adj* **1** piercing; keen: *a biting wind.* **2** sarcastic; incisive.
bitmap *n Computers* a picture created by colour or shading on a visual display unit.
bit part *n* a very small acting role with few lines to speak.
bitter *adj* **1** having an unpalatable harsh taste, as the peel of an orange. **2** showing or caused by hostility or resentment. **3** difficult to accept: *a bitter blow.* **4** sarcastic: *bitter words.* **5** bitingly cold: *a bitter night.* ✧ *n* **6** *Brit* beer with a slightly bitter taste. ▷ HISTORY Old English *biter* ▶ **bitterly** *adv* ▶ **bitterness** *n*
bittern *n* a large wading marsh bird with a booming call. ▷ HISTORY Old French *butor*
bitters *pl n* bitter-tasting spirits flavoured with plant extracts.
bittersweet *adj* **1** tasting of or being a mixture of bitterness and sweetness. **2** pleasant but tinged with sadness.
bitty *adj* **-tier, -tiest** lacking unity; disjointed. ▶ **bittiness** *n*
bitumen *n* a sticky or solid substance that occurs naturally in asphalt and tar and is used in road surfacing. ▷ HISTORY Latin ▶ **bituminous** *adj*
bituminous coal *n* a soft black coal that burns with a smoky yellow flame.
bivalve *n* **1** a sea creature, such as an oyster or mussel, that has a shell consisting of two hinged valves and breathes through gills. ✧ *adj* **2** of these molluscs.
bivouac *n* **1** a temporary camp, as used by soldiers or mountaineers. ✧ *vb* **-acking, -acked 2** to make a temporary camp. ▷ HISTORY French
biz *n Informal* business.
bizarre *adj* odd or unusual, esp. in an interesting or amusing way. ▷ HISTORY Italian *bizzarro* capricious
Bk *Chem* berkelium.
BL 1 *Chiefly Brit* Bachelor of Law. **2** Bachelor of Letters. **3** Barrister-at-Law.
blab *vb* **blabbing, blabbed** to divulge (secrets) indiscreetly. ▷ HISTORY Germanic
blabber *n* **1** a person who blabs. ✧ *vb* **2** to talk without thinking. ▷ HISTORY Middle English *blabberen*
black *adj* **1** having no hue, owing to the absorption of all or almost all light; of the colour of coal. **2** without light. **3** without hope; gloomy: *the future looked black.* **4** dirty or soiled. **5** angry or resentful: *black looks.* **6** unpleasant in a cynical or macabre manner: *black comedy.* **7** (of coffee or tea)

a b c d e f g h i j k l m n o p q r s t u v w x y z

A
B
C
D
E
F
G
H
I
J
K
L
M
N
O
P
Q
R
S
T
U
V
W
X
Y
Z

without milk or cream. **8** wicked or harmful: *a black lie.* ✧ *n* **9** the darkest colour; the colour of coal. **10** a dye or pigment producing this colour. **11** black clothing, worn esp. in mourning: *she was in black, as though in mourning.* **12** complete darkness: *the black of the night.* **13 in the black** in credit or without debt. ✧ *vb* **14** same as **blacken. 15** to polish (shoes or boots) with blacking. **16** *Brit, Austral & NZ* (of trade unionists) to organize a boycott of (specified goods, work, etc.). ✧ See also **blackout.** ▷ **HISTORY** Old English *blæc* ▸ **blackness** *n* ▸ **blackish** *adj*

Black *n* **1** a member of a dark-skinned race. ✧ *adj* **2** of or relating to a Black or Blacks

black-and-blue *adj* (of the skin) bruised, as from a beating.

black-and-white *n* **1** a photograph, film, etc., in black, white, and shades of grey, rather than in colour. **2 in black and white a** in print or writing. **b** in extremes: *he always sees things in black and white.*

black-backed gull *n* a large common black-and-white European gull.

blackball[1] *vb* **1** to vote against. **2** to exclude (someone) from a group, etc. ▷ **HISTORY** from *black ball,* used formerly to veto

blackball[2] *n NZ* hard boiled sweet with black-and-white stripes.

black bear *n* **1** a bear inhabiting forests of North America. **2** a bear of central and E Asia.

black belt *n Judo, karate, etc.* **a** a black belt that signifies that the wearer has reached a high standard in martial art. **b** a person entitled to wear this.

blackberry *n, pl* **-ries** a small blackish edible fruit that grows on a woody bush with thorny stems. Also called: **bramble**

blackbird *n* a common European thrush, the male of which has black plumage and a yellow bill.

blackboard *n* a hard or rigid surface made of a smooth usually dark substance, used for writing or drawing on with chalk, esp. in teaching.

black box *n Informal* a flight recorder.

blackcap *n* a brownish-grey warbler, the male of which has a black crown.

blackcock *n* the male of the black grouse.

blackcurrant *n* a very small blackish edible fruit that grows in bunches on a bush.

blackdamp *n* air that is low in oxygen content and high in carbon dioxide as a result of an explosion in a mine.

Black Death *n History* **the Black Death** a form of bubonic plague in Europe and Asia during the 14th century.

black economy *n Brit, Austral & NZ* that portion of the income of a nation that remains illegally undeclared.

blacken *vb* **1** to make or become black or dirty. **2** to damage (someone's reputation); discredit: *they planned to blacken my father's name.*

black eye *n* bruising round the eye.

Black Friar *n* a Dominican friar.

blackguard (**blag**-gard) *n* an unprincipled contemptible person. ▷ **HISTORY** originally, lowest group at court

blackhead *n* **1** a black-tipped plug of fatty matter clogging a pore of the skin. **2** a bird with black plumage on the head.

black hole *n Astron* a hypothetical region of space resulting from the collapse of a star and surrounded by a gravitational field from which neither matter nor radiation can escape.

black ice *n* a thin transparent layer of new ice on a road.

blacking *n* any preparation for giving a black finish to shoes, metals, etc.

blackjack[1] *n* pontoon or a similar card game. ▷ **HISTORY** *black + jack* (the knave)

blackjack[2] *n Chiefly US & Canad* a truncheon of leather-covered lead with a flexible shaft. ▷ **HISTORY** *black + jack* (implement)

black lead *n* same as **graphite.**

blackleg *n Brit* **1** a person who continues to work or does another's job during a strike. ✧ *vb* **-legging, -legged 2** to refuse to join a strike.

blacklist *n* **1** a list of people or organizations considered untrustworthy or disloyal. ✧ *vb* **2** to put (someone) on a blacklist.

black magic *n* magic used for evil purposes.

blackmail *n* **1** the act of attempting to obtain money by threatening to reveal shameful information. **2** the use of unfair pressure in an attempt to influence someone. ✧ *vb* **3** to obtain or attempt to obtain money by intimidation. **4** to attempt to influence (a person) by unfair pressure. ▷ **HISTORY** *black* + Old English *māl* terms ▸ **blackmailer** *n*

Black Maria (mar-**rye**-a) *n* a police van for transporting prisoners.

black market *n* a place or a system for buying or selling goods or currencies illegally, esp. in violation of controls or rationing. ▸ **black marketeer** *n*

blackout *n* **1** (in wartime) the putting out or hiding of all lights as a precaution against a night air attack. **2** a momentary loss of consciousness, vision, or memory. **3** a temporary electrical power failure. **4** the prevention of information broadcasts: *a news blackout.* ✧ *vb* **black out 5** to put out (lights). **6** to lose vision, consciousness, or memory temporarily. **7** to stop (news, a television programme, etc.) from being broadcast.

Black Power *n* a movement of Black people to obtain equality with Whites.

black pudding *n Brit* a black sausage made from pig's blood, suet, etc.

Black Rod *n* (in Britain) the chief usher of the House of Lords and of the Order of the Garter.

black sheep *n* a person who is regarded as a disgrace or failure by his or her family or peer group.

Blackshirt *n* a member of the Italian Fascist party before and during the Second World War.

blacksmith *n* a person who works iron with a furnace, anvil, and hammer.

black spot *n* **1** a place on a road where accidents frequently occur. **2** an area where a particular situation is exceptionally bad: *an unemployment black spot.*

blackthorn *n* a thorny shrub with black twigs, white flowers, and small sour plumlike fruits.

Black Thursday *n History* 24 October, 1929, the date that the American stock market crashed, marking the beginning of the Great Depression.

Black Watch *n* **the Black Watch** the Royal Highland Regiment in the British Army.

black widow *n* an American spider, the female of which is highly venomous and commonly eats its mate.

bladder *n* **1** *Anat* a membranous sac, usually containing liquid, esp. the urinary bladder. **2** a hollow bag made of leather, etc. which becomes round when filled with air or liquid. **3** a hollow saclike part in certain plants, such as seaweed. ▷ **HISTORY** Old English *blǣdre* ▶ **bladdery** *adj*

blade *n* **1** the part of a sharp weapon, tool, or knife, that forms the cutting edge. **2** the thin flattish part of a propeller, oar, or fan. **3** the flattened part of a leaf, sepal, or petal. **4** the long narrow leaf of a grass or related plant. ▷ **HISTORY** Old English *blæd*

blain *n* a blister, blotch, or sore on the skin. ▷ **HISTORY** Old English *blegen*

blame *vb* **blaming, blamed 1** to consider (someone) responsible for: *I blame her for the failure.* **2** (foll. by *on*) to put responsibility for (something) on (someone): *she blames the failure on me.* **3 be to blame** to be at fault. ✧ *n* **4** responsibility for something that is wrong: *they must take the blame for the failure.* **5** an expression of condemnation: *analysts lay the blame on party activists.* ▷ **HISTORY** Late Latin *blasphemare* to blaspheme ▶ **blamable** *or* **blameable** *adj* ▶ **blameless** *adj*

blameworthy *adj* deserving blame. ▶ **blameworthiness** *n*

blanch *vb* **1** to whiten. **2** to become pale, as with sickness or fear. **3** to prepare (meat or vegetables) by plunging them in boiling water. **4** to cause (celery, chicory, etc.) to grow white from lack of light. ▷ **HISTORY** Old French *blanc* white

blancmange (blam-**monzh**) *n* a jelly-like dessert of milk, stiffened usually with cornflour. ▷ **HISTORY** Old French *blanc manger* white food

bland *adj* **1** dull and uninteresting: *the bland predictability of the film.* **2** smooth in manner: *he looked at his visitor with a bland smile.* ▷ **HISTORY** Latin *blandus* flattering ▶ **blandly** *adv*

blandishments *pl n* flattery intended to coax or cajole.

blank *adj* **1** (of a writing surface) not written on. **2** (of a form, etc.) with spaces left for details to be filled in. **3** without ornament or break: *a blank wall.* **4** empty or void: *a blank space.* **5** showing no interest or expression: *a blank look.* **6** lacking ideas or inspiration: *his mind went blank.* ✧ *n* **7** an empty space. **8** an empty space for writing in. **9** the condition of not understanding: *my mind went a complete blank.* **10** a mark, often a dash, in place of a word. **11 draw a blank** to get no results from something. ✧ *vb* **12** (foll. by *out*) to cross out, blot, or obscure. **13** *Slang* to ignore: *the crowd blanked her for the first four numbers.* ▷ **HISTORY** Old French *blanc* white ▶ **blankly** *adv*

blank cheque *n* **1** a signed cheque on which the amount payable has not been specified. **2** complete freedom of action.

blanket *n* **1** a large piece of thick cloth for use as a bed covering. **2** a concealing cover, as of smoke, leaves, or snow. ✧ *adj* **3** applying to or covering a wide group or variety of people, conditions, situations, etc.: *a blanket ban on all supporters travelling to away matches.* ✧ *vb* **-keting, -keted 4** to cover as if with a blanket. **5** to cover a wide area; give blanket coverage to. ▷ **HISTORY** Old French *blancquete*

blank verse *n Prosody* unrhymed verse, esp. in iambic pentameters.

blare *vb* **blaring, blared 1** to sound loudly and harshly. **2** to proclaim loudly: *the newspaper headlines blared the news.* ✧ *n* **3** a loud harsh noise. ▷ **HISTORY** Middle Dutch *bleren*

blarney *n* flattering talk. ▷ **HISTORY** after the *Blarney* Stone in SW Ireland, said to endow whoever kisses it with skill in flattery

blasé (blah-**zay**) *adj* indifferent or bored, esp. through familiarity. ▷ **HISTORY** French

blaspheme *vb* **-pheming, -phemed 1** to speak disrespectfully of (God or sacred things). **2** to utter curses. ▷ **HISTORY** Greek *blasphēmos* evil-speaking ▶ **blasphemer** *n*

blasphemy *n, pl* **-mies** behaviour or language that shows disrespect for God or sacred things. ▶ **blasphemous** *adj*

blast *n* **1** an explosion, such as that caused by dynamite. **2** the charge used in a single explosion. **3** a sudden strong gust of wind or air. **4** a sudden loud sound, such as that made by a trumpet. **5** a violent verbal outburst, esp. critical. **6** *US & Austral slang* a very enjoyable or thrilling experience: *the party was a blast.* **7 at full blast** at maximum speed, volume, etc. ✧ *interj* **8** *Slang* an exclamation of annoyance. ✧ *vb* **9** to blow up (a rock, tunnel, etc.) with explosives. **10** to make or cause to make a loud harsh noise. **11** to criticize severely. ▷ **HISTORY** Old English *blǣst*

blasted *adj, adv Slang* extreme or extremely: *a blasted idiot.*

blast furnace *n* a furnace for smelting using a blast of preheated air.

blastoff *n* **1** the launching of a rocket under its own power. ✧ *vb* **blast off 2** (of a rocket) to be launched.

blastula *n Biol* an early form of an animal embryo, consisting of a sphere of cells with a central cavity.

blatant (**blay**-tant) *adj* **1** glaringly obvious: *a blatant lie.* **2** offensively noticeable: *their blatant disregard for my feelings.* ▷ **HISTORY** coined by Edmund Spenser, poet ▶ **blatantly** *adv*

blather *vb, n* same as **blether**.

blaze[1] *n* **1** a strong fire or flame. **2** a very bright light or glare. **3** an outburst (of passion, patriotism, etc.). ✧ *vb* **blazing, blazed 4** to burn fiercely. **5** to shine brightly. **6** to become stirred, as with anger or excitement. **7 blaze away** to shoot continuously. ▷ **HISTORY** Old English *blæse*

blaze² *n* **1** a mark, usually indicating a path, made on a tree. **2** a light-coloured marking on the face of an animal. ✧ *vb* **blazing, blazed 3** to mark (a tree, path, etc.) with a blaze. **4 blaze a trail** to explore new territories, areas of knowledge, etc. ▷ **HISTORY** probably from Middle Low German *bles* white marking

blaze³ *vb* **blazing, blazed blaze something abroad** to make something widely known. ▷ **HISTORY** Middle Dutch *blāsen*

blazer *n* a fairly lightweight jacket, often in the colours of a sports club, school, etc.

blazon *vb* **1** to proclaim publicly: *the newspaper photographs were blazoned on the front pages.* **2** *Heraldry* to describe or colour (heraldic arms) conventionally. ✧ *n* **3** *Heraldry* a coat of arms. ▷ **HISTORY** Old French *blason* coat of arms

bleach *vb* **1** to make or become white or colourless by exposure to sunlight, or by the action of chemical agents. ✧ *n* **2** a bleaching agent. ▷ **HISTORY** Old English *blǣcan*

bleaching powder *n* a white powder consisting of chlorinated calcium hydroxide.

bleak *adj* **1** exposed and barren. **2** cold and raw. **3** offering little hope; dismal: *a bleak future.* ▷ **HISTORY** Old English *blāc* pale ▸ **bleakly** *adv* ▸ **bleakness** *n*

bleary *adj* **blearier, bleariest 1** with eyes dimmed, by tears or tiredness: *a few bleary hacks.* **2** indistinct or unclear. ▸ **blearily** *adv*

bleat *vb* **1** (of a sheep, goat, or calf) to utter its plaintive cry. **2** to whine. ✧ *n* **3** the characteristic cry of sheep, goats, and calves. **4** a weak complaint or whine. ▷ **HISTORY** Old English *blǣtan*

bleed *vb* **bleeding, bled 1** to lose or emit blood. **2** to remove or draw blood from (a person or animal). **3** (of plants) to exude (sap or resin), esp. from a cut. **4** *Informal* to obtain money, etc., from (someone), esp. by extortion. **5** to draw liquid or gas from (a container or enclosed system). **6 my heart bleeds for you** I am sorry for you: often used ironically. ▷ **HISTORY** Old English *blēdan*

bleep *n* **1** a short high-pitched signal made by an electrical device. **2** same as **bleeper.** ✧ *vb* **3** to make a bleeping signal. **4** to call (someone) by means of a bleeper. ▷ **HISTORY** imitative

bleeper *n* a small portable radio receiver that makes a bleeping signal.

blemish *n* **1** a defect; flaw; stain. ✧ *vb* **2** to spoil or tarnish. ▷ **HISTORY** Old French *blemir* to make pale

blench *vb* to shy away, as in fear. ▷ **HISTORY** Old English *blencan* to deceive

blend *vb* **1** to mix or mingle (components). **2** to mix (different varieties of tea, whisky, etc.). **3** to look good together; harmonize. **4** (esp. of colours) to shade gradually into each other. ✧ *n* **5** a mixture produced by blending. ▷ **HISTORY** Old English *blandan*

blende *n* a mineral consisting mainly of zinc sulphide: the chief source of zinc.

blender *n* an electrical kitchen appliance for pureeing vegetables etc.

blenny *n, pl* **-nies** a small fish of coastal waters with a tapering scaleless body and long fins. ▷ **HISTORY** Greek *blennos* slime

bless *vb* **blessing, blessed** *or* **blest 1** to make holy by means of a religious rite. **2** to give honour or glory to (a person or thing) as holy. **3** to call upon God to protect. **4** to worship or adore (God). **5 be blessed with** to be endowed with: *she is blessed with immense energy.* **6 bless me!** an exclamation of surprise. **7 bless you!** said to a person who has just sneezed. ▷ **HISTORY** Old English *blǣdsian* to sprinkle with sacrificial blood

blessed *adj* **1** made holy. **2** *RC Church* (of a person) beatified by the pope. **3** bringing great happiness or good fortune: *he was blessed with good looks.* **4** *Euphemistic* damned: *I'm blessed if I know.*

blessing *n* **1** the act of invoking divine protection or aid. **2** approval; good wishes. **3** a happy event.

blether *Scot* ✧ *vb* **1** to speak foolishly at length. ✧ *n* **2** foolish talk. **3** a person who blethers. ▷ **HISTORY** Old Norse *blathr* nonsense

blew *vb* the past tense of **blow**.

blight *n* **1** a person or thing that spoils or prevents growth. **2** any plant disease characterized by withering and shrivelling without rotting. **3** a fungus or insect that causes blight in plants. **4** an ugly urban district. ✧ *vb* **5** to cause to suffer a blight. **6** to frustrate or disappoint: *blighted love.* **7** to destroy: *the event blighted her life.* ▷ **HISTORY** origin unknown

blighter *n Brit, Austral & NZ informal* a despicable or irritating person or thing.

Blighty *n Brit, Austral & NZ slang* (used esp. by troops serving abroad) **1** Britain; home. **2** (*pl* **Blighties**) (esp. in the First World War) a wound that causes the recipient to be sent home to Britain. ▷ **HISTORY** Hindi *bilāyatī* foreign land

blimey *interj Brit & NZ slang* an exclamation of surprise or annoyance. ▷ **HISTORY** short for *gorblimey* God blind me

blimp¹ *n* **1** a small nonrigid airship. **2** *Films* a soundproof cover fixed over a camera during shooting. ▷ **HISTORY** probably from *(type) B-limp*

blimp² *n Chiefly Brit* a person who is stupidly complacent and reactionary. Also called: **Colonel Blimp** ▷ **HISTORY** a cartoon character

blind *adj* **1** unable to see. **2** unable or unwilling to understand: *she is blind to his faults.* **3** not determined by reason: *blind hatred.* **4** acting or performed without control or preparation. **5** done without being able to see, relying on instruments for information. **6** hidden from sight: *a blind corner.* **7** closed at one end: *a blind alley.* **8** completely lacking awareness or consciousness: *a blind stupor.* **9** having no openings: *a blind wall.* ✧ *adv* **10** without being able to see ahead or using only instruments: *flying blind.* **11** without adequate information: *we bought the house blind.* **12 blind drunk** *Informal* very drunk. ✧ *vb* **13** to deprive of

A B C D E F G H I J K L M N O P Q R S T U V W X Y Z

sight permanently or temporarily. **14** to deprive of good sense, reason, or judgment. **15** to darken; conceal. **16** to overwhelm by showing detailed knowledge: *he tried to blind us with science.* ✧ *n* **17** a shade for a window. **18** any obstruction or hindrance to sight, light, or air. **19** a person, action, or thing that serves to deceive or conceal the truth. ▷ **HISTORY** Old English ▶ **blinding** *adj* ▶ **blindly** *adv* ▶ **blindness** *n*

> **☑ WORD TIP**
> See at **disabled.**

blind alley *n* **1** an alley open at one end only. **2** *Informal* a situation in which no further progress can be made.

blind date *n Informal* a prearranged social meeting between two people who have not met before.

blindfold *vb* **1** to prevent (a person or animal) from seeing by covering the eyes. ✧ *n* **2** a piece of cloth used to cover the eyes. ✧ *adj, adv* **3** having the eyes covered with a cloth. ▷ **HISTORY** Old English *blindfellian* to strike blind

blind man's buff *n* a game in which a blindfolded person tries to catch and identify the other players. ▷ **HISTORY** obsolete *buff* a blow

blind spot *n* **1** a small oval-shaped area of the retina which is unable to see. **2** a place where vision is obscured. **3** a subject about which a person is ignorant or prejudiced.

blindworm *n* same as **slowworm**.

blink *vb* **1** to close and immediately reopen (the eyes), usually involuntarily. **2** to shine intermittently or unsteadily. ✧ *n* **3** the act or an instance of blinking. **4** a glance; glimpse. **5 on the blink** *Slang* not working properly. ▷ **HISTORY** variant of BLENCH

blinker *vb* **1** to provide (a horse) with blinkers. **2** to obscure or be obscured with or as with blinkers.

blinkered *adj* **1** considering only a narrow point of view. **2** (of a horse) wearing blinkers.

blinkers *pl n Brit & Austral* leather side pieces attached to a horse's bridle to prevent sideways vision.

blip *n* **1** a repetitive sound, such as the kind produced by an electronic device. **2** the spot of light on a radar screen indicating the position of an object. **3** a temporary irregularity in the performance of something. ▷ **HISTORY** imitative

bliss *n* **1** perfect happiness; serene joy. **2** the joy of heaven. ▷ **HISTORY** Old English *blīths* ▶ **blissful** *adj* ▶ **blissfully** *adv*

blister *n* **1** a small bubble on the skin filled with a watery fluid. **2** a swelling containing air or liquid, such as on a painted surface. ✧ *vb* **3** to have or cause to have blisters. **4** to attack verbally with great scorn. ▷ **HISTORY** Old French *blestre* ▶ **blistering** *adj*

blithe *adj* **1** heedless; casual and indifferent. **2** very happy or cheerful. ▷ **HISTORY** Old English *blīthe* ▶ **blithely** *adv*

blithering *adj Informal* stupid; foolish: *you blithering idiot.* ▷ **HISTORY** variant of *blethering*

BLitt Bachelor of Letters. ▷ **HISTORY** Latin *Baccalaureus Litterarum*

blitz *n* **1** a violent and sustained attack by enemy aircraft. **2** any intensive attack or concerted effort. ✧ *vb* **3** to attack suddenly and intensively. ▷ **HISTORY** see BLITZKRIEG

Blitz *n* **the Blitz** the systematic bombing of Britain in 1940–41 by the German Air Force.

blitzkrieg *n* a swift intensive military attack designed to defeat the opposition quickly. ▷ **HISTORY** German: lightning war

blizzard *n* a blinding storm of wind and snow. ▷ **HISTORY** origin unknown

bloat *vb* **1** to cause to swell, as with a liquid or air. **2** to cause to be puffed up, as with conceit. **3** to cure (fish, esp. herring) by half drying in smoke. ▷ **HISTORY** Old Norse *blautr* soaked ▶ **bloated** *adj*

bloater *n Brit* a herring that has been salted in brine, smoked, and cured.

blob *n* **1** a soft mass or drop. **2** a spot of colour, ink, etc. **3** an indistinct or shapeless form or object. ▷ **HISTORY** imitative

bloc *n* a group of people or countries combined by a common interest. ▷ **HISTORY** French

block *n* **1** a large solid piece of wood, stone, etc. **2** such a piece on which particular tasks may be done, as chopping, cutting, etc. **3** a large building of offices, flats, etc. **4** a group of buildings in a city bounded by intersecting streets on each side. **5** an obstruction or hindrance: *a writer with a block.* **6** one of a set of wooden or plastic cubes as a child's toy. **7** *Slang* a person's head. **8** a piece of wood, metal, etc., engraved for printing. **9** a casing housing one or more freely rotating pulleys. See also **block and tackle**. **10** a quantity considered as a single unit. ✧ *vb* **11** to obstruct or impede by introducing an obstacle: *lorry drivers had blocked the routes to Paris.* **12** to impede, retard, or prevent (an action or procedure). **13** to stamp (a title or design) on (a book cover, etc.). **14** *Cricket* to play (a ball) defensively. ✧ See also **block out**. ▷ **HISTORY** Dutch *blok* ▶ **blockage** *n*

blockade *n* **1** *Mil* the closing off of a port or region to prevent the passage of goods. ✧ *vb* **-ading, -aded 2** to impose a blockade on.

block and tackle *n* a hoisting device in which a rope or chain is passed around a pair of blocks containing one or more pulleys.

blockbuster *n Informal* **1** a film, novel, etc. that has been or is expected to be highly successful. **2** a large bomb used to demolish extensive areas.

block disintegration *n Geol* breaking up of rocks caused by repeated expansion and contraction due to changes in temperature.

block fault *n Geol* the structure formed when faults divide the crust into blocks of different heights.

blockhead *n* a stupid person. ▶ **blockheaded** *adj*

block letter *n* a plain capital letter. Also called: **block capital**

a b c d e f g h i j k l m n o p q r s t u v w x y z

block mountain *n* See **fault-block mountain.**

block out *vb* **1** to plan or describe (something) in a general fashion. **2** to prevent the entry or consideration of (something).

blog *n* short for **weblog**.

bloke *n Brit, Austral & NZ informal* a man.
▷ HISTORY Shelta ▸ **blokeish** *or* **blokey** *adj*

blonde *or masc* **blond** *adj* **1** (of hair) fair. **2** (of a person) having fair hair and a light complexion. ✧ *n* **3** a person having light-coloured hair and skin.
▷ HISTORY Old French ▸ **blondeness** *or masc* ▸ **blondness** *n*

blood *n* **1** a reddish fluid in vertebrates that is pumped by the heart through the arteries and veins. *RELATED ADJECTIVE* ▸ **haemal 2** bloodshed, esp. when resulting in murder: *they were responsible for the spilling of blood throughout the country.* **3** life itself; lifeblood. **4** relationship through being of the same family, race, or kind; kinship. **5 the blood** royal or noble descent: *a prince of the blood.* **6 flesh and blood a** near kindred or kinship, esp. that between a parent and child. **b** human nature: *it's more than flesh and blood can stand.* **7 in one's blood** as a natural or inherited characteristic or talent. **8** newcomers viewed as an invigorating force: *new blood.* **9 in cold blood** showing no passion; ruthlessly. **10 make one's blood boil** to cause to be angry or indignant. **11 make one's blood run cold** to fill with horror. ✧ *vb* **12** *Hunting* to cause (young hounds) to taste the blood of a freshly killed quarry. **13** to initiate (a person) to war or hunting. ▷ HISTORY Old English *blōd*

blood-and-thunder *adj* denoting melodramatic behaviour.

blood bank *n* a place where blood is stored until required for transfusion.

blood bath *n* a massacre.

blood brother *n* a man or boy who has sworn to treat another as his brother, often in a ceremony in which their blood is mingled.

blood count *n* determination of the number of red and white blood corpuscles in a specific sample of blood.

bloodcurdling *adj* terrifying.

blood donor *n* a person who gives blood to be used for transfusion.

blood group *n* any one of the various groups into which human blood is classified.

blood heat *n* the normal temperature of the human body, 98.4°F or 37°C.

bloodhound *n* a large hound, formerly used in tracking and police work.

bloodless *adj* **1** without blood: *bloodless surgery.* **2** conducted without violence: *a bloodless coup.* **3** anaemic-looking; pale. **4** lacking vitality; lifeless: *the bloodless ambience of supermarkets.*

blood-letting *n* **1** bloodshed, esp. in a feud. **2** the former medical practice of removing blood.

blood money *n* **1** money obtained by ruthlessly sacrificing others. **2** money paid to a hired murderer. **3** compensation paid to the relatives of a murdered person.

blood orange *n* a variety of orange the pulp of which is dark red when ripe.

blood poisoning *n* same as **septicaemia.**

blood pressure *n* the pressure exerted by the blood on the inner walls of the blood vessels.

blood relation *or* **relative** *n* a person related by birth.

bloodshed *n* slaughter; killing.

bloodshot *adj* (of an eye) inflamed.

blood sport *n* any sport involving the killing of an animal.

bloodstained *adj* discoloured with blood.

bloodstock *n* thoroughbred horses.

bloodstream *n* the flow of blood through the vessels of a living body.

bloodsucker *n* **1** an animal that sucks blood, esp. a leech. **2** *Informal* a person who preys upon another person, esp. by extorting money.

bloodthirsty *adj* **-thirstier, -thirstiest** taking pleasure in bloodshed or violence.

blood vessel *n* a tube through which blood travels in the body.

bloody *adj* **bloodier, bloodiest 1** covered with blood. **2** marked by much killing and bloodshed: *a bloody war.* **3** cruel or murderous: *a bloody tyrant.* ✧ *adj, adv* **4** *Slang* extreme or extremely: *a bloody fool; a bloody good idea.* ✧ *vb* **bloodies, bloodying, bloodied 5** to stain with blood.

Bloody Mary *n* a drink consisting of tomato juice and vodka.

bloody-minded *adj Brit & NZ informal* deliberately obstructive and unhelpful.

bloom *n* **1** a blossom on a flowering plant. **2** the state or period when flowers open. **3** a healthy or flourishing condition; prime. **4** a youthful or healthy glow. **5** a fine whitish coating on the surface of fruits or leaves. ✧ *vb* **6** (of flowers) to open. **7** to bear flowers. **8** to flourish or grow. **9** to be in a healthy, glowing condition.
▷ HISTORY Germanic

bloomer *n Brit informal* a stupid mistake; blunder.
▷ HISTORY from BLOOMING

bloomers *pl n* **1** *Informal* women's baggy knickers. **2** (formerly) loose trousers gathered at the knee worn by women. ▷ HISTORY after Mrs A. *Bloomer,* social reformer

blooming *adv, adj Brit informal* extreme or extremely: *blooming painful.*
▷ HISTORY euphemistic for *bloody*

blossom *n* **1** the flower or flowers of a plant, esp. producing edible fruit. **2** the period of flowering. ✧ *vb* **3** (of plants) to flower. **4** to come to a promising stage. ▷ HISTORY Old English *blōstm*

blot *n* **1** a stain or spot, esp. of ink. **2** something that spoils. **3** a stain on one's character. ✧ *vb* **blotting, blotted 4** to stain or spot. **5** to cause a blemish in or on: *he blotted his copybook by missing a penalty.* **6** to soak up (excess ink, etc.) by using blotting paper. **7 blot out a** to darken or hide completely: *the mist blotted out the sea.* **b** to block from one's mind: *to blot out the memories.*
▷ HISTORY Germanic

blotch *n* **1** an irregular spot or discoloration. ✧ *vb* **2** to become or cause to become marked by such discoloration. ▷ **HISTORY** probably from *botch*, influenced by *blot* ▶ **blotchy** *adj*

blotter *n* a sheet of blotting paper.

blotting paper *n* a soft absorbent paper, used for soaking up surplus ink.

blotto *adj Brit, Austral & NZ slang* extremely drunk. ▷ **HISTORY** from *blot* (verb)

blouse *n* **1** a woman's shirtlike garment. **2** a waist-length belted jacket worn by soldiers. ✧ *vb* **blousing, bloused 3** to hang or cause to hang in full loose folds. ▷ **HISTORY** French

blouson (**blew**-zon) *n* a short loose jacket with a tight-fitting waist. ▷ **HISTORY** French

blow[1] *vb* **blowing, blew, blown 1** (of a current of air, the wind, etc.) to be or cause to be in motion. **2** to move or be carried by or as if by wind. **3** to expel (air, etc.) through the mouth or nose. **4** to breathe hard; pant. **5** to inflate with air or the breath. **6** (of wind, etc.) to make a roaring sound. **7** to cause (a musical instrument) to sound by forcing air into it. **8** (often foll. by *up, down, in*) to explode, break, or disintegrate completely. **9** *Electronics* (of a fuse or valve) to burn out because of excessive current. **10** to shape (glass, etc.) by forcing air or gas through the material when molten. **11** *Slang* to spend (money) freely. **12** *Slang* to use (an opportunity) ineffectively. **13** *Slang* to expose or betray (a secret). **14** (*past participle* **blowed**) *Informal* same as **damn. 15 blow hot and cold** *Informal* to keep changing one's attitude towards someone or something. **16 blow one's top** *Informal* to lose one's temper. ✧ *n* **17** the act or an instance of blowing. **18** the sound produced by blowing. **19** a blast of air or wind. **20** *Brit slang* cannabis. ✧ See also **blow away, blow out**, etc. ▷ **HISTORY** Old English *blāwan*

blow[2] *n* **1** a powerful or heavy stroke with the fist, a weapon, etc. **2** a sudden setback: *the scheme was dealt a blow by the introduction of martial law.* **3** an attacking action: *a blow for freedom.* **4 come to blows a** to fight. **b** to result in a fight. ▷ **HISTORY** probably Germanic

blow away *vb US slang* **1** to kill by shooting. **2** to defeat utterly.

blow-by-blow *adj* explained in great detail: *a blow-by-blow account.*

blow-dry *vb* **-dries, -drying, -dried 1** to style (the hair) while drying it with a hand-held hair dryer. ✧ *n* **2** this method of styling hair.

blower *n* **1** a mechanical device, such as a fan, that blows. **2** *Informal* a telephone.

blowfly *n, pl* **-flies** a fly that lays its eggs in meat.

blowhole *n* **1** the nostril of a whale. **2** a hole in ice through which seals, etc. breathe. **3** a vent for air or gas. **4** *Geol* a hole in a cliff top leading to a sea cave.

blowie *n Austral informal* a bluebottle.

blown *vb* a past participle of **blow**.

blow out *vb* **1** (of a flame) to extinguish or be extinguished. **2** (of a tyre) to puncture suddenly. **3** (of an oil or gas well) to lose oil or gas in an uncontrolled manner. ✧ *n* **blowout 4** a sudden burst in a tyre. **5** the uncontrolled escape of oil or gas from a well. **6** *Slang* a large filling meal. **7** *Geol* a wind-eroded depression in a land surface or sand dune.

blow over *vb* **1** to be forgotten. **2** to cease or be finished: *the crisis blew over.*

blowpipe *n* **1** a long tube from which poisoned darts, etc., are shot by blowing. **2** a tube for blowing air into a flame to intensify its heat. **3** an iron pipe used to blow glass into shape.

blowsy *adj* **blowsier, blowsiest** (of a woman) **1** slovenly or sluttish. **2** ruddy in complexion. ▷ **HISTORY** dialect *blowze* beggar girl

blowtorch *or* **blowlamp** *n* a small burner that produces a very hot flame, used to remove old paint, soften metal, etc.

blow up *vb* **1** to explode or cause to explode. **2** to inflate with air. **3** to increase the importance of (something): *an affair blown up out of all proportions.* **4** *Informal* to lose one's temper. **5** *Informal* to reprimand (someone). **6** *Informal* to enlarge (a photograph). **7** to come into existence with sudden force: *a crisis had blown up.* ✧ *n* **blow-up 8** *Informal* an enlarged photograph.

blowy *adj* **blowier, blowiest** windy.

blubber *n* **1** the fatty tissue of aquatic mammals such as the whale. **2** *Informal* flabby body fat. ✧ *vb* **3** to sob without restraint. ▷ **HISTORY** probably imitative

bludge *Austral & NZ informal* ✧ *vb* **bludging, bludged 1** (foll. by *on*) to scrounge from. **2** to evade work. ✧ *n* **3** a very easy task.

bludgeon *n* **1** a stout heavy club, typically thicker at one end. ✧ *vb* **2** to hit as if with a bludgeon. **3** to force; bully; coerce. ▷ **HISTORY** origin unknown

blue *n* **1** the colour of a clear unclouded sky. **2** anything blue, such as blue clothing or blue paint: *she is clothed in blue.* **3** a sportsman who represents or has represented Oxford or Cambridge University. **4** *Brit informal* a Tory. **5** *Austral & NZ slang* an argument or fight. **6** Also: **bluey** *Austral & NZ slang* a court summons. **7** *Austral & NZ informal* a mistake. **8 out of the blue** unexpectedly. ✧ *adj* **bluer, bluest 9** of the colour blue; of the colour of a clear unclouded sky. **10** (of the flesh) having a purple tinge from cold. **11** depressed or unhappy. **12** pornographic: *blue movies.* ✧ *vb* **blueing** *or* **bluing, blued 13** to make or become blue or bluer. **14** *Old-fashioned, informal* to spend extravagantly or wastefully: *I consoled myself by blueing my royalty cheque.* ✧ See also **blues**. ▷ **HISTORY** Old French *bleu* ▶ **blueness** *n*

blue baby *n* a baby born with a bluish tinge to the skin because of lack of oxygen in the blood.

bluebell *n* a woodland plant with blue bell-shaped flowers.

blueberry *n, pl* **-ries** a very small blackish edible fruit that grows on a North American shrub.

bluebird *n* a North American songbird with a blue plumage.

blue blood *n* royal or aristocratic descent.

bluebook *n* **1** (in Britain) a government publication, usually the report of a commission.

a b c d e f g h i j k l m n o p q r s t u v w x y z

A B C D E F G H I J K L M N O P Q R S T U V W X Y Z

2 (in Canada) an annual statement of government accounts.

bluebottle *n* **1** a large fly with a dark-blue body; blowfly. **2** *Austral & NZ informal* a Portuguese man-of-war.

blue cheese *n* cheese containing a blue mould, such as Stilton or Danish blue.

blue chip *n* **1** *Finance* a stock considered reliable. ✧ *adj* **blue-chip 2** denoting something considered to be a valuable asset.

blue-collar *adj* denoting manual industrial workers.

blue-eyed boy *n Brit, Austral & NZ informal* a favourite.

blue funk *n Slang* a state of great terror.

blue heeler *n Austral & NZ informal* a dog that controls cattle by biting their heels.

blue pencil *n* **1** deletion or alteration of the contents of a book or other work. ✧ *vb* **blue-pencil, -cilling, -cilled** *or US* **-ciling, -ciled 2** to alter or delete parts of (a book, film, etc.).

blue peter *n* a signal flag of blue with a white square at the centre, displayed by a vessel about to leave port.

blueprint *n* **1** an original description of a plan or idea that explains how it is expected to work. **2** a photographic print of plans, technical drawings, etc. consisting of white lines on a blue background.

blue ribbon *n* **1** a badge awarded as the first prize in a competition. **2** (in Britain) a badge of blue silk worn by members of the Order of the Garter.

blues *pl n* **the blues 1** a feeling of depression or deep unhappiness. **2** a type of folk song originating among Black Americans.

bluestocking *n Usually disparaging* a scholarly or intellectual woman. ▷ **HISTORY** from the blue worsted stockings worn by members of an 18th-century literary society

bluetit *n* a small European bird with a blue crown, wings, and tail and yellow underparts.

bluetongue *n* an Australian lizard with a blue tongue.

blue whale *n* a very large bluish-grey whale: the largest mammal.

bluff[1] *vb* **1** to pretend to be confident in order to influence (someone). ✧ *n* **2** deliberate deception to create the impression of a strong position. **3 call someone's bluff** to challenge someone to give proof of his or her claims. ▷ **HISTORY** Dutch *bluffen* to boast

bluff[2] *n* **1** a steep promontory, bank, or cliff. **2** *Canad* a clump of trees on the prairie; copse. ✧ *adj* **3** good-naturedly frank and hearty. ▷ **HISTORY** probably from Middle Dutch *blaf* broad

bluish *or* **blueish** *adj* slightly blue.

blunder *n* **1** a stupid or clumsy mistake. ✧ *vb* **2** to make stupid or clumsy mistakes. **3** to act clumsily; stumble. ▷ **HISTORY** Scandinavian ▶ **blundering** *n, adj*

blunderbuss *n* an obsolete gun with wide barrel and flared muzzle. ▷ **HISTORY** Dutch *donderbus* thunder gun

blunt *adj* **1** (esp. of a knife) lacking sharpness. **2** not having a sharp edge or point: *a blunt instrument.* **3** (of people, manner of speaking, etc.) straightforward and uncomplicated. ✧ *vb* **4** to make less sharp. **5** to diminish the sensitivity or perception of: *prison life has blunted his mind.* ▷ **HISTORY** Scandinavian ▶ **bluntly** *adv*

blur *vb* **blurring, blurred 1** to make or become vague or less distinct. **2** to smear or smudge. **3** to make (the judgment, memory, or perception) less clear; dim. ✧ *n* **4** something vague, hazy, or indistinct. **5** a smear or smudge. ▷ **HISTORY** perhaps variant of *blear* ▶ **blurred** *adj* ▶ **blurry** *adj*

blurb *n* a promotional description, such as on the jackets of books. ▷ **HISTORY** coined by G. Burgess, humorist & illustrator

blurt *vb* (foll. by *out*) to utter suddenly and involuntarily. ▷ **HISTORY** probably imitative

blush *vb* **1** to become suddenly red in the face, esp. from embarrassment or shame. ✧ *n* **2** a sudden reddening of the face, esp. from embarrassment or shame. **3** a rosy glow. **4** same as **rosé**. ▷ **HISTORY** Old English *blȳscan*

blusher *n* a cosmetic applied to the cheeks to give a rosy colour.

bluster *vb* **1** to speak loudly or in a bullying way. **2** (of the wind) to be gusty. ✧ *n* **3** empty threats or protests. ▷ **HISTORY** probably from Middle Low German *blüsteren* to blow violently ▶ **blustery** *adj*

BM **1** Bachelor of Medicine. **2** British Museum.

BMA British Medical Association.

B-movie *n* a film originally made as a supporting film, now considered a genre in its own right.

BMR basal metabolic rate.

BMus Bachelor of Music.

BO **1** *Informal* body odour. **2** box office.

boa *n* **1** a large nonvenomous snake of Central and South America that kills its prey by constriction. **2** a woman's long thin scarf of feathers or fur. ▷ **HISTORY** Latin

boab (**boh**-ab) *n Austral informal* short for **baobab**.

boa constrictor *n* a very large snake of tropical America and the West Indies that kills its prey by constriction.

boar *n* **1** an uncastrated male pig. **2** a wild pig. ▷ **HISTORY** Old English *bār*

board *n* **1** a long wide flat piece of sawn timber. **2** a smaller flat piece of rigid material for a specific purpose: *ironing board.* **3 a** a group of people who officially administer a company, trust, etc. **b** any other official group, such as examiners or interviewers. **4** a person's meals, provided regularly for money. **5** stiff cardboard or similar material, used for the outside covers of a book. **6** a flat thin rectangular sheet of composite material, such as chipboard. **7** *Naut* the side of a ship. **8** a portable surface for indoor games such as chess or backgammon. **9 go by the board** *Informal* to be in disuse, neglected, or lost. **10 on board** on or in a ship, aeroplane, etc. **11 the boards** the stage. ✧ *vb* **12** to go aboard (a train or other vehicle). **13** to attack (a ship) by forcing one's way aboard. **14** (foll.

by *up, in*) to cover with boards. **15** to receive meals and lodging in return for money. **16 board out** to arrange for (someone, esp. a child) to receive food and lodging away from home. **17** (in ice hockey and box lacrosse) to bodycheck an opponent against the boards. ▷ **HISTORY** Old English *bord*

boarder *n Brit* a pupil who lives at school during term time.

boarding house *n* a private house that provides accommodation and meals for paying guests.

boarding school *n* a school providing living accommodation for pupils.

boardroom *n* a room where the board of directors of a company meets.

boast *vb* **1** to speak in excessively proud terms of one's possessions, talents, etc. **2** to possess (something to be proud of): *a team which boasts five current world record holders.* ✧ *n* **3** a bragging statement. **4** something that is bragged about: *this proved to be a false boast.* ▷ **HISTORY** origin unknown

boastful *adj* tending to boast.

boat *n* **1** a small vessel propelled by oars, paddle, sails, or motor. **2** *Informal* a ship. **3 in the same boat** sharing the same problems. **4 miss the boat** to lose an opportunity. **5 rock the boat** *Informal* to cause a disturbance in the existing situation. ✧ *vb* **6** to travel or go in a boat, esp. as recreation. ▷ **HISTORY** Old English *bāt*

boater *n* a stiff straw hat with a straight brim and flat crown.

boating *n* rowing, sailing, or cruising in boats as a form of recreation.

boatman *n, pl* **-men** a man who works on, hires out, or repairs boats.

boatswain (**boh**-sn) *n Naut* same as **bosun**.

boat train *n* a train scheduled to take passengers to or from a particular ship.

bob[1] *vb* **bobbing, bobbed 1** to move or cause to move up and down repeatedly, such as while floating in water. **2** to move or cause to move with a short abrupt movement, esp. of the head. **3 bob up** to appear or emerge suddenly. ✧ *n* **4** a short abrupt movement, as of the head. ▷ **HISTORY** origin unknown

bob[2] *n* **1** a hairstyle in which the hair is cut short evenly all round the head. **2** a dangling weight on a pendulum or plumb line. ✧ *vb* **bobbing, bobbed 3** to cut (the hair) in a bob. ▷ **HISTORY** Middle English *bobbe* bunch of flowers

bob[3] *n, pl* **bob** *Brit, Austral & NZ informal* (formerly) a shilling: *two bob.* ▷ **HISTORY** origin unknown

bobbejaan *n S African* **1** a baboon. **2** a large black spider. **3** a monkey wrench. ▷ **HISTORY** Afrikaans

bobbin *n* a reel on which thread or yarn is wound. ▷ **HISTORY** Old French *bobine*

bobble *n* **1** a tufted ball, usually woollen, that is used for decoration. ✧ *vb* **-bling, -bled 2** (of a ball) to bounce erratically because of an uneven playing surface. ▷ **HISTORY** from BOB[1]

bobby *n, pl* **-bies** *Brit informal* a British policeman. ▷ **HISTORY** after *Robert* Peel, who set up the Metropolitan Police Force

bobby pin *n US, Canad, Austral & NZ* a metal hairpin.

bobotie (ba-**boot**-ee) *n S African* a traditional Cape dish of curried minced meat. ▷ **HISTORY** probably from Malay

bobsleigh *n* **1** a sledge for racing down a steeply banked ice-covered run. ✧ *vb* **2** to ride on a bobsleigh.

bobtail *n* **1** a docked tail. **2** an animal with such a tail. ✧ *adj also* **bobtailed 3** having the tail cut short.

Boche (**bosh**) *n Offensive slang* a German, esp. a German soldier. ▷ **HISTORY** French

bod *n Informal* **1** a person: *he's a queer bod.* **2** short for **body** (sense 1). ▷ **HISTORY** short for *body*

bode[1] *vb* **boding, boded** to be an omen of (good or ill); portend. ▷ **HISTORY** Old English *bodian*

bode[2] *vb* a past tense of **bide**.

bodega *n* a shop in a Spanish-speaking country that sells wine. ▷ **HISTORY** Spanish

bodge *vb* **bodging, bodged** *Brit, Austral & NZ informal* to make a mess of; botch.

bodice *n* **1** the upper part of a woman's dress, from the shoulder to the waist. **2** a tight-fitting corset worn laced over a blouse, or (formerly) as a woman's undergarment. ▷ **HISTORY** originally Scots *bodies,* plural of *body*

bodily *adj* **1** relating to the human body. ✧ *adv* **2** by taking hold of the body: *he threw him bodily from the platform.* **3** in person; in the flesh.

bodkin *n* a blunt large-eyed needle. ▷ **HISTORY** origin unknown

body *n, pl* **bodies 1** the entire physical structure of an animal or human. RELATED ADJECTIVE ▸ **corporal 2** the trunk or torso. **3** a corpse. **4** a group regarded as a single entity: *a local voluntary body.* **5** the main part of anything: *the body of a car.* **6** a separate mass of water or land. **7** the flesh as opposed to the spirit. **8** fullness in the appearance of the hair. **9** the characteristic full quality of certain wines. **10** *Informal* a person: *all the important bodies from the council were present.* **11** a woman's one-piece undergarment. **12 keep body and soul together** to manage to survive. ▷ **HISTORY** Old English *bodig*

body-board *n Austral, NZ & S African* a small polystyrene surfboard. ▸ **body-boarder** *n*

bodycheck *Ice hockey etc.* ✧ *n* **1** obstruction of another player. ✧ *vb* **2** to deliver a bodycheck to (an opponent).

body corporate *n, pl* **bodies corporate** *Law* **1** a group of persons incorporated to carry out a specific enterprise and legally recognized as a single entity. **2** *Austral* the association of apartment owners in a building in which there is common property.

body double *n* a person who substitutes for a star in the filming of a scene showing the body rather than the face.

bodyguard *n* a person or group of people employed to protect someone.

A B C D E F G H I J K L M N O P Q R S T U V W X Y Z

body language *n* the communication of one's thoughts or feelings by the position or movements of one's body rather than by words.

body politic *n* **the body politic** the people of a nation or the nation itself considered as a political entity.

body search *n* **1** a search by police, customs officials, etc., that involves examination of a prisoner's or suspect's bodily orifices. ✧ *vb* **body-search 2** to search (a prisoner or suspect) in this manner.

body shop *n* a repair yard for vehicle bodywork.

body snatcher *n* (formerly) a person who robbed graves and sold the corpses for dissection.

body stocking *n* **1** a one-piece undergarment for women, covering the torso. **2** a tightly-fitting garment covering the whole of the body, worn esp. for dancing or exercising.

bodywork *n* the external shell of a motor vehicle.

Boer *n* a descendant of any of the Dutch or Huguenot colonists who settled in South Africa. ▷ HISTORY Dutch

boere- *combining form S African* rustic or country-style. ▷ HISTORY from Afrikaans *boer* a farmer

boeremeisie (**boor**-a-may-see) *n S African* a country girl of Afrikaans stock.

boereseun (**boor**-a-see-oon) *n S African* a country boy of Afrikaans stock.

boerewors (**boor**-a-vorss) *n S African* a traditional home-made farmer's sausage.

boffin *n Brit & S African informal* a scientist or expert. ▷ HISTORY origin unknown

bog *n* **1** a wet spongy area of land. **2** *Slang* a toilet. ▷ HISTORY Gaelic *bogach* swamp ▶ **boggy** *adj* ▶ **bogginess** *n*

bog down *vb* **bogging, bogged** to impede physically or mentally.

bogey *or* **bogy** *n* **1** an evil or mischievous spirit. **2** something that worries or annoys. **3** *Golf* a score of one stroke over par on a hole. **4** *Slang* a piece of dried mucus from the nose. ▷ HISTORY probably obsolete *bug* an evil spirit

boggle *vb* **-gling, -gled 1** to be surprised, confused, or alarmed: *the mind boggles at the idea.* **2** to hesitate or be evasive when confronted with a problem. ▷ HISTORY probably Scots

bogie *or* **bogy** *n* an assembly of wheels forming a pivoted support at either end of a railway coach. ▷ HISTORY origin unknown

bogle (**boh**-gul) *n* a rhythmic dance performed to ragga music. ▷ HISTORY origin unknown

bog-standard *adj Brit & Irish slang* completely ordinary; run-of-the-mill.

bogus (**boh**-guss) *adj* not genuine. ▷ HISTORY origin unknown

bogy *n, pl* **-gies** same as **bogey, bogie**.

bohemian *n* **1** a person, esp. an artist or writer, who lives an unconventional life. ✧ *adj* **2** unconventional in appearance, behaviour, etc. ▶ **Bohemianism** *n*

bohrium *n Chem* an element artificially produced in minute quantities. Symbol: Bh. ▷ HISTORY after N. *Bohr,* physicist

boil[1] *vb* **1** to change or cause to change from a liquid to a vapour so rapidly that bubbles of vapour are formed in the liquid. **2** to reach or cause to reach boiling point. **3** to cook or be cooked by the process of boiling. **4** to bubble and be agitated like something boiling: *the sea was boiling.* **5** to be extremely angry. ✧ *n* **6** the state or action of boiling. ✧ See also **boil away, boil down**. ▷ HISTORY Latin *bullire* to bubble

boil[2] *n* a red painful swelling with a hard pus-filled core caused by infection of the skin. ▷ HISTORY Old English *bȳle*

boil away *vb* to cause (liquid) to evaporate completely by boiling or (of liquid) to evaporate completely.

boil down *vb* **1** to reduce or be reduced in quantity by boiling. **2 boil down to** to be the essential element in.

boiler *n* **1** a closed vessel in which water is heated to provide steam to drive machinery. **2** a domestic device to provide hot water, esp. for central heating.

boiler suit *n Brit* a one-piece overall.

boiling point *n* **1** the temperature at which a liquid boils. **2** *Informal* the condition of being angered or highly excited.

boisterous *adj* **1** noisy and lively; unruly. **2** (of the sea, etc.) turbulent or stormy. ▷ HISTORY Middle English *boistuous*

bold *adj* **1** courageous, confident, and fearless. **2** immodest or impudent: *she gave him a bold look.* **3** standing out distinctly; conspicuous: *a figure carved in bold relief.* **4** *Typography* in bold face. ▷ HISTORY Old English *beald* ▶ **boldly** *adv* ▶ **boldness** *n*

bold face *n Typography* type which is characterized by thick heavy lines, as the entry words in this dictionary.

bole *n* the trunk of a tree. ▷ HISTORY Old Norse *bolr*

bolero *n, pl* **-ros 1** a Spanish dance, usually in triple time. **2** music for this dance. **3** a short open jacket not reaching the waist. ▷ HISTORY Spanish

boll *n* the rounded seed capsule of flax, cotton, etc. ▷ HISTORY Dutch *bolle*

bollard *n* **1** *Brit & Austral* a small post marking a kerb or traffic island or barring cars from entering. **2** a strong wooden or metal post on a wharf, quay, etc., used for securing mooring lines. ▷ HISTORY perhaps from *bole*

bollocks *or* **ballocks** *Taboo slang* ✧ *pl n* **1** the testicles. ✧ *n* **2** nonsense; rubbish. ✧ *interj* **3** an exclamation of annoyance, disbelief, etc. ▷ HISTORY Old English *beallucas*

Bolshevik *n* **1** (formerly) a Russian Communist, especially one of the more radical members of the Russian Social Democratic Party. Compare **Menshevik**. **2** any Communist. **3** *Informal, offensive* any political radical, esp. a revolutionary. ▷ HISTORY Russian *Bol'shevik* majority ▶ **Bolshevism** *n* ▶ **Bolshevist** *adj, n*

bolshie or **bolshy** *Brit & NZ informal* ✧ *adj* **1** difficult to manage; rebellious. **2** politically radical or left-wing. ✧ *n, pl* **-shies 3** any political radical. ▷ HISTORY from BOLSHEVIK

bolson (bowl-**sown**) *n US Geog* a desert valley surrounded by mountains, with a shallow lake at the centre. ▷ HISTORY American Spanish *bolsón*, from Spanish *bolsa* purse, from Late Latin *bursa* bag

bolster *vb* **1** to support or strengthen: *the government were unwilling to bolster sterling.* ✧ *n* **2** a long narrow pillow. **3** any pad or support. ▷ HISTORY Old English

bolt[1] *n* **1** a bar that can be slid into a socket to lock a door, gate, etc. **2** a metal rod or pin that has a head and a screw thread to take a nut. **3** a flash (of lightning). **4** a sudden movement, esp. in order to escape. **5** an arrow, esp. for a crossbow. **6 a bolt from the blue** a sudden, unexpected, and usually unwelcome event. **7 shoot one's bolt** to exhaust one's efforts. ✧ *vb* **8** to run away suddenly. **9** to secure or lock with or as if with a bolt. **10** to attach firmly one thing to another by means of a nut and bolt. **11** to eat hurriedly: *bolting your food may lead to indigestion.* **12** (of a horse) to run away without control. **13** (of vegetables) to produce flowers and seeds too soon. ✧ *adv* **14 bolt upright** stiff and rigid. ▷ HISTORY Old English: arrow

bolt[2] or **boult** *vb* **1** to pass (flour, a powder, etc.) through a sieve. **2** to examine and separate. ▷ HISTORY Old French *bulter*

bolt hole *n* a place of escape.

bomb *n* **1** a hollow projectile containing explosive, incendiary, or other destructive substance. **2** an object in which an explosive device has been planted: *a car bomb.* **3** *Brit slang* a large sum of money: *it cost a bomb.* **4** *US & Canad slang* a disastrous failure: *the new play was a total bomb.* **5 like a bomb** *Brit & NZ informal* with great speed or success. **6 the bomb** a hydrogen or an atom bomb considered as the ultimate destructive weapon. ✧ *vb* **7** to attack with a bomb or bombs; drop bombs (on). **8** (foll. by *along*) *Informal* to move or drive very quickly. **9** *Chiefly US & Canad slang* to fail disastrously. **10** (foll. by *out*) *NZ informal* to fail disastrously. ▷ HISTORY Greek *bombos* booming noise ▶ **bombing** *n*

bombard *vb* **1** to attack with concentrated artillery fire or bombs. **2** to attack persistently. **3** to attack verbally, esp. with questions. **4** *Physics* to direct high-energy particles or photons against (atoms, nuclei, etc.). ▷ HISTORY Old French *bombarde* stone-throwing cannon ▶ **bombardment** *n*

bombardier *n* **1** *Brit* a noncommissioned rank in the Royal Artillery. **2** *US* the member of a bomber aircrew responsible for releasing the bombs.

Bombardier *n Canad trademark* a snow tractor, usually having caterpillar tracks at the rear and skis at the front.

bombast *n* pompous and flowery language. ▷ HISTORY Medieval Latin *bombax* cotton ▶ **bombastic** *adj*

Bombay duck *n* a fish that is eaten dried with curry dishes as a savoury. ▷ HISTORY through association with *Bombay*, port in India

bomber *n* **1** a military aircraft designed to carry out bombing missions. **2** a person who plants bombs.

bomb out *vb Informal* to fail disastrously.

bombshell *n* a shocking or unwelcome surprise.

bona fide (bone-a **fide**-ee) *adj* **1** genuine: *a bona fide manuscript.* **2** undertaken in good faith: *a bona fide agreement.* ▷ HISTORY Latin

bonanza *n* **1** sudden and unexpected luck or wealth. **2** *US & Canad* a mine or vein rich in ore. ▷ HISTORY Spanish: calm sea, hence, good luck

bonbon *n* a sweet. ▷ HISTORY French

bond *n* **1** something that binds, fastens, or holds together. **2** something that brings or holds people together; tie: *a bond of friendship.* **3 bonds** something that restrains or imprisons. **4** a written or spoken agreement, esp. a promise: *a marriage bond.* **5** *Chem* a means by which atoms are combined in a molecule. **6** *Finance* a certificate of debt issued in order to raise funds. **7** *S African* the conditional pledging of property, esp. a house, as security for the repayment of a loan. **8** *Law* a written acknowledgment of an obligation to pay a sum or to perform a contract. **9 in bond** *Commerce* securely stored until duty is paid. ✧ *vb* **10** to hold or be held together; bind. **11** to put or hold (goods) in bond. ▷ HISTORY Old Norse *band*

bondage *n* **1** slavery. **2** subjection to some influence or duty. **3** a sexual practice in which one partner is tied or chained up.

bonded *adj* **1** *Finance* consisting of, secured by, or operating under a bond or bonds. **2** *Commerce* in bond.

bondservant *n* a serf or slave.

bone *n* **1** any of the various structures that make up the skeleton in most vertebrates. **2** the porous rigid tissue of which these parts are made. **3** something consisting of bone or a bonelike substance. **4 bones** the human skeleton. **5** a thin strip of plastic, etc. used to stiffen corsets and brassieres. **6 close to** or **near the bone** risqué or indecent. **7 have a bone to pick** to have grounds for a quarrel. **8 make no bones about a** to be direct and candid about. **b** to have no scruples about. **9 the bare bones** the essentials. ✧ *vb* **boning, boned 10** to remove the bones from (meat for cooking, etc.). **11** to stiffen (a corset, etc.) by inserting bones. ▷ HISTORY Old English *bān* ▶ **boneless** *adj*

bone china *n* a type of fine porcelain containing powdered bone.

bone-dry *adj Informal* completely dry.

bone-idle *adj* extremely lazy.

bone meal *n* dried and ground animal bones, used as a fertilizer or in stock feeds.

bonfire *n* a large outdoor fire.

WORD HISTORY

A 'bonfire' is literally a 'bone-fire'. Bones were used as fuel in the Middle Ages.

bongo *n, pl* **-gos** *or* **-goes** a small bucket-shaped drum, usually one of a pair, played by beating with the fingers. ▷ **HISTORY** American Spanish

bonhomie (bon-om-**mee**) *n* exuberant friendliness. ▷ **HISTORY** French

bonito (ba-**nee**-toh) *n, pl* **-os 1** a small tunny-like marine food fish. **2** a related fish, whose flesh is dried and flaked and used in Japanese cookery.

bonk *vb Informal* **1** to have sexual intercourse. **2** to hit. ▷ **HISTORY** probably imitative ▶ **bonking** *n*

bonkbuster *n Informal* a novel featuring many graphic descriptions of sexual encounters.

bonkers *adj Brit, Austral & NZ slang* mad; crazy. ▷ **HISTORY** origin unknown

bon mot (bon **moh**) *n, pl* **bons mots** a clever and fitting remark. ▷ **HISTORY** French, literally: good word

bonnet *n* **1** the hinged metal cover over a motor vehicle's engine. **2** any of various hats tied with ribbons under the chin. **3** (in Scotland) a soft cloth cap. ▷ **HISTORY** Old French *bonet*

bonny *adj* **-nier, -niest 1** *Scot & N English dialect* beautiful: *a bonny lass.* **2** good or fine. ▷ **HISTORY** Latin *bonus*

bonsai *n, pl* **-sai** an ornamental tree or shrub grown in a small shallow pot in order to stunt its growth. ▷ **HISTORY** Japanese *bon* bowl + *sai* to plant

bonsela (bon-**sell**-a) *n S African informal* a small gift of money. ▷ **HISTORY** Zulu *ibanselo* gift

bonus *n* something given, paid, or received above what is due or expected. ▷ **HISTORY** Latin: good

bon voyage *interj* a phrase used to wish a traveller a pleasant journey. ▷ **HISTORY** French

bony *adj* **bonier, boniest 1** resembling or consisting of bone. **2** thin. **3** having many bones.

boo *interj* **1** a shout uttered to express dissatisfaction or contempt. **2** an exclamation uttered to startle someone. ✧ *vb* **booing, booed 3** to shout 'boo' at (someone or something) as an expression of disapproval.

boob *Slang* ✧ *n* **1** *Brit, Austral & NZ* an embarrassing mistake; blunder. **2** a female breast. ✧ *vb* **3** *Brit, Austral & NZ* to make a blunder. ▷ **HISTORY** from *booby*

boobook (**boo**-book) *n* a small spotted Australian brown owl.

booby *n, pl* **-bies 1** *Brit, Austral & NZ* an ignorant or foolish person. **2** a tropical marine bird related to the gannet. ▷ **HISTORY** Latin *balbus* stammering

booby prize *n* a mock prize given to the person with the lowest score in a competition.

booby trap *n* **1** a hidden explosive device primed so as to be set off by an unsuspecting victim. **2** a trap for an unsuspecting person, esp. one intended as a practical joke.

boogie *vb* **-gieing, -gied** *Slang* to dance to fast pop music. ▷ **HISTORY** origin unknown

boohai *n* **up the boohai** *NZ informal* **1** a very remote area. ✧ *adj* **2** very mistaken or astray. ▷ **HISTORY** from the remote township of *Puhoi*

book *n* **1** a number of printed pages bound together along one edge and protected by covers. **2** a written work or composition, such as a novel. **3** a number of sheets of paper bound together: *an account book.* **4 books** a record of the transactions of a business or society. **5** the libretto of an opera or musical. **6** a major division of a written composition, such as of a long novel or of the Bible. **7** a number of tickets, stamps, etc. fastened together along one edge. **8** a record of betting transactions. **9 a closed book** a subject that is beyond comprehension: *art remains a closed book to him.* **10 bring to book** to reprimand or require (someone) to give an explanation of his or her conduct. **11 by the book** according to the rules. **12 in someone's good** *or* **bad books** regarded by someone with favour (*or* disfavour). **13 throw the book at someone a** to charge someone with every relevant offence. **b** to inflict the most severe punishment on someone. ✧ *vb* **14** to reserve (a place, passage, etc.) or engage the services of (someone) in advance. **15** (of a police officer) to take the name and address of (a person) for an alleged offence with a view to prosecution. **16** (of a football referee) to take the name of (a player) who has broken the rules seriously. ✧ See also **book in.** ▷ **HISTORY** Old English *bōc*

bookcase *n* a piece of furniture containing shelves for books.

book club *n* a club that sells books at low prices to members, usually by mail order.

bookie *n Informal* short for **bookmaker**.

book in *vb Chiefly Brit & NZ* to register one's arrival at a hotel.

booking *n* **1** *Brit, Austral & NZ* a reservation, as of a table or seat. **2** *Theatre* an engagement of a performer.

bookish *adj* **1** fond of reading; studious. **2** forming opinions through reading rather than experience.

book-keeping *n* the skill or occupation of systematically recording business transactions. ▶ **book-keeper** *n*

booklet *n* a thin book with paper covers.

bookmaker *n* a person who as an occupation accepts bets, esp. on horse racing. ▶ **bookmaking** *n*

bookmark *n* **1** a strip of some material put between the pages of a book to mark a place. **2** *Computers* an identifier put on a website that enables the user to return to it quickly and easily. ✧ *vb* **3** *Computers* to identify and store a website so that one can return to it quickly and easily.

bookstall *n* a stall or stand where periodicals, newspapers, or books are sold.

bookworm *n* **1** a person devoted to reading. **2** a small insect that feeds on the binding paste of books.

Boolean algebra (**boo**-lee-an) *n* a system of symbolic logic devised to codify nonmathematical logical operations: used in computers. ▷ **HISTORY** after George *Boole,* mathematician

boom[1] *vb* **1** to make a loud deep echoing sound. **2** to prosper vigorously and rapidly: *business boomed.* ✧ *n* **3** a loud deep echoing sound. **4** a period of high economic growth. ▷ **HISTORY** imitative

boom² *n* **1** *Naut* a spar to which the foot of a sail is fastened to control its position. **2** a pole carrying an overhead microphone and projected over a film or television set. **3** a barrier across a waterway. ▷ **HISTORY** Dutch: tree

boomer *n Austral* a large male kangaroo.

boomerang *n* **1** a curved wooden missile of Australian Aborigines which can be made to return to the thrower. **2** an action or statement that recoils on its originator. ✧ *vb* **3** (of a plan) to recoil unexpectedly, harming its originator. ▷ **HISTORY** Aboriginal

boomslang *n* a large greenish venomous tree-living snake of southern Africa. ▷ **HISTORY** Afrikaans

boon¹ *n* something extremely useful, helpful, or beneficial. ▷ **HISTORY** Old Norse *bōn* request

boon² *adj* close or intimate: *boon companion.* ▷ **HISTORY** Latin *bonus* good

boongary (**boong**-gar-ree) *n, pl* **-garies** a tree kangaroo of NE Queensland, Australia.

boor *n* an ill-mannered, clumsy, or insensitive person. ▷ **HISTORY** Old English *gebūr* dweller, farmer ▶ **boorish** *adj*

boost *n* **1** encouragement or help: *a boost to morale.* **2** an upward thrust or push. **3** an increase or rise. ✧ *vb* **4** to encourage or improve: *to boost morale.* **5** to cause to rise; increase: *we significantly boosted our market share.* **6** to advertise on a big scale. ▷ **HISTORY** origin unknown

booster *n* **1** a supplementary injection of a vaccine given to ensure that the first injection will remain effective. **2** a radio-frequency amplifier to strengthen signals. **3** the first stage of a multistage rocket.

boot¹ *n* **1** an outer covering for the foot that extends above the ankle. **2** an enclosed compartment of a car for holding luggage. **3** *Informal* a kick: *he gave the door a boot.* **4 lick someone's boots** to behave flatteringly towards someone. **5 put the boot in** *Slang* **a** to kick a person when already down. **b** to finish something off with unnecessary brutality. **6 the boot** *Slang* dismissal from employment. ✧ *vb* **7** to kick. **8** to start up (a computer). **9 boot out** *Informal* **a** to eject forcibly. **b** to dismiss from employment. ▷ **HISTORY** Middle English *bote*

boot² *n* **to boot** as well; in addition. ▷ **HISTORY** Old English *bōt* compensation

boot camp *n* a centre for juvenile offenders, with strict discipline and hard physical exercise.

bootee *n* a soft boot for a baby, esp. a knitted one.

booth *n, pl* **booths 1** a small partially enclosed cubicle. **2** a stall, esp. a temporary one at a fair or market. ▷ **HISTORY** Scandinavian

bootleg *vb* **-legging, -legged 1** to make, carry, or sell (illicit goods, esp. alcohol). ✧ *adj* **2** produced, distributed, or sold illicitly. ▷ **HISTORY** smugglers carried bottles of liquor concealed in their boots ▶ **bootlegger** *n*

booty *n, pl* **-ties** any valuable article or articles obtained as plunder. ▷ **HISTORY** Old French *butin*

booze *Informal* ✧ *n* **1** alcoholic drink. ✧ *vb* **boozing, boozed 2** to drink alcohol, esp. in excess. ▷ **HISTORY** Middle Dutch *būsen* ▶ **boozy** *adj*

boozer *n Informal* **1** a person who is fond of drinking. **2** *Brit, Austral & NZ* a bar or pub.

booze-up *n Brit, Austral & NZ slang* a drinking spree.

bop *n* **1** a form of jazz with complex rhythms and harmonies. ✧ *vb* **bopping, bopped 2** *Informal* to dance to pop music. ▷ **HISTORY** from BEBOP ▶ **bopper** *n*

bora *n Austral* an Aboriginal ceremony. ▷ **HISTORY** from a native Australian language

boracic *adj* same as **boric**.

borage *n* a Mediterranean plant with star-shaped blue flowers. ▷ **HISTORY** Arabic *abū 'āraq* literally: father of sweat

borax *n* a white mineral in crystalline form used in making glass, soap, etc. ▷ **HISTORY** Persian *būrah*

Bordeaux *n* a red or white wine produced around Bordeaux in SW France.

border *n* **1** the dividing line between political or geographic regions. **2** a band or margin around or along the edge of something. **3** a design around the edge of something. **4** a narrow strip of ground planted with flowers or shrubs: *a herbaceous border.* ✧ *vb* **5** to provide with a border. **6 a** to be adjacent to; lie along the boundary of. **b** to be nearly the same as; verge on: *a story that borders on the unbelievable.* ▷ **HISTORY** Old French *bort* side of a ship

borderland *n* **1** land located on or near a boundary. **2** an indeterminate state or condition.

bore¹ *vb* **boring, bored 1** to produce (a hole) with a drill, etc. **2** to produce (a tunnel, mine shaft, etc.) by drilling. ✧ *n* **3** a hole or tunnel in the ground drilled in search of minerals, oil, etc. **4 a** the hollow of a gun barrel. **b** the diameter of this hollow; calibre. ▷ **HISTORY** Old English *borian*

bore² *vb* **boring, bored 1** to tire or make weary by being dull, repetitious, or uninteresting. ✧ *n* **2** a dull or repetitious person, activity, or state. ▷ **HISTORY** origin unknown ▶ **bored** *adj* ▶ **boring** *adj*

bore³ *n* a high wave moving up a narrow estuary, caused by the tide. ▷ **HISTORY** Old Norse *bāra*

bore⁴ *vb* the past tense of **bear¹**.

boreal (**bore**-ee-al) *adj* of or relating to the north or the north wind. ▷ **HISTORY** from Latin *boreās* the north wind

boreal forest (**bore**-ee-al) *n* the forest of northern latitudes, esp. in Scandinavia, Canada, and Siberia, consisting mainly of spruce and pine. ▷ **HISTORY** Latin *boreas* the north wind

boredom *n* the state of being bored.

boree (**baw**-ree) *n Austral* same as **myall**.

boric *adj* of or containing boron.

boric acid *n* a white soluble crystalline solid used as a mild antiseptic.

born *vb* **1** a past participle of **bear¹** (sense 4). **2 not to have been born yesterday** not to be gullible or foolish. ✧ *adj* **3** possessing certain qualities from birth: *a born musician.* **4** being in a particular social status at birth: *ignobly born.*

> **WORD TIP**
> Care should be taken not to use *born* where *borne* is intended: *he had borne* (not *born*) *his ordeal with great courage: the following points should be borne in mind.*

born-again *adj* **1** having experienced conversion, esp. to evangelical Christianity. **2** showing the enthusiasm of someone newly converted to any cause: *a born-again romantic.* ✧ *n* **3** a person with fervent enthusiasm for a newfound cause.

borne *vb* a past participle of **bear**[1].

> **WORD TIP**
> See at **born.**

boron *n Chem* a hard almost colourless crystalline metalloid element that is used in hardening steel. Symbol: B. ▷ **HISTORY** *bor(ax) + (carb)on*

boronia *n* an Australian aromatic flowering shrub.

borough *n* **1** a town, esp. (in Britain) one that forms the constituency of an MP or that was originally incorporated by royal charter. **2** any of the constituent divisions of Greater London or New York City. ▷ **HISTORY** Old English *burg*

borrow *vb* **1** to obtain (something, such as money) on the understanding that it will be returned to the lender. **2** to adopt (ideas, words, etc.) from another source. ▷ **HISTORY** Old English *borgian* ▶ **borrower** *n* ▶ **borrowing** *n*

> **WORD TIP**
> The use of *off* after *borrow* was formerly considered incorrect, but is now acceptable in informal contexts.

borscht *or* **borsch** *n* a Russian soup based on beetroot. ▷ **HISTORY** Russian *borshch*

borstal *n* (formerly in Britain) a prison for offenders aged 15 to 21. ▷ **HISTORY** after *Borstal,* village in Kent where the first institution was founded

borzoi *n* a tall dog with a narrow head and a long coat. ▷ **HISTORY** Russian: swift

bosh *n Brit, Austral & NZ informal* meaningless talk or opinions; nonsense. ▷ **HISTORY** Turkish *boş* empty

Bosnian *adj* **1** from Bosnia. ✧ *n* **2** a person from Bosnia.

bosom *n* **1** the chest or breast of a person, esp. the female breasts. **2** a protective centre or part: *the bosom of the family.* **3** the breast considered as the seat of emotions. ✧ *adj* **4** very dear: *a bosom friend.* ▷ **HISTORY** Old English *bōsm*

boss[1] *Informal* ✧ *n* **1** a person in charge of or employing others. ✧ *vb* **2** to employ, supervise, or be in charge of. **3 boss around** *or* **about** to be domineering or overbearing towards. ▷ **HISTORY** Dutch *baas* master

boss[2] *n* a raised knob or stud, esp. an ornamental one on a vault, shield, etc. ▷ **HISTORY** Old French *boce*

bossy *adj* **bossier, bossiest** *Informal* domineering, overbearing, or authoritarian. ▶ **bossiness** *n*

bosun *or* **boatswain** (**boh**-sn) *n* an officer who is responsible for the maintenance of a ship and its equipment.

bot. **1** botanical. **2** botany.

botany *n, pl* **-nies** the study of plants, including their classification, structure, etc. ▷ **HISTORY** Greek *botanē* plant ▶ **botanical** *or* **botanic** *adj* ▶ **botanist** *n*

botch *vb* **1** to spoil through clumsiness or ineptitude. **2** to repair badly or clumsily. ✧ *n also* **botch-up 3** a badly done piece of work or repair. ▷ **HISTORY** origin unknown

both *adj* **1** two considered together: *both parents were killed during the war.* ✧ *pron* **2** two considered together: *both are to blame.* ✧ *conj* **3** not just one but also the other of two (people or things): *both Darren and Keith enjoyed the match.* ▷ **HISTORY** Old Norse *bāthir*

bother *vb* **1** to take the time or trouble: *don't bother to come with me.* **2** to give annoyance, pain, or trouble to. **3** to trouble (a person) by repeatedly disturbing; pester. ✧ *n* **4** a state of worry, trouble, or confusion. **5** a person or thing that causes fuss, trouble, or annoyance. **6** *Informal* a disturbance or fight: *a spot of bother.* ✧ *interj* **7** *Brit, Austral & NZ* an exclamation of slight annoyance. ▷ **HISTORY** origin unknown

bothersome *adj* causing bother.

bothy *n, pl* **bothies** *Chiefly Scot* **1** a hut used for temporary shelter. **2** (formerly) a farm worker's quarters. ▷ **HISTORY** perhaps from *booth*

bottle *n* **1** a container, often of glass and usually cylindrical with a narrow neck, for holding liquids. **2** the amount such a container will hold. **3** *Brit slang* courage; nerve: *you don't have the bottle.* **4 the bottle** *Informal* drinking of alcohol, esp. to excess. ✧ *vb* **-tling, -tled 5** to put or place in a bottle or bottles. ✧ See also **bottle up**. ▷ **HISTORY** Late Latin *buttis* cask

bottle bank *n* a large container into which members of the public can throw glass bottles and jars for recycling.

bottle-green *adj* dark green.

bottleneck *n* **1** a narrow stretch of road or a junction at which traffic is or may be held up. **2** something that holds up progress.

bottlenose dolphin *n* a grey or greenish dolphin with a bottle-shaped snout.

bottler *n Austral & NZ old-fashioned, informal* an exceptional person or thing.

bottle shop *n Austral & NZ* a shop licensed to sell alcohol for drinking elsewhere.

bottle store *n S African* a shop licensed to sell alcohol for drinking elsewhere.

bottle tree *n* an Australian tree with a bottle-shaped swollen trunk.

bottle up *vb* to restrain (powerful emotion).

bottom *n* **1** the lowest, deepest, or farthest removed part of a thing: *the bottom of a hill.* **2** the least important or successful position: *the bottom of a class.* **3** the ground underneath a sea, lake, or river. **4** the underneath part of a thing. **5** the buttocks. **6 at bottom** in reality; basically. **7 be at the bottom of** to be the ultimate cause of. **8 get to the bottom of** to discover the real truth about. ✧ *adj* **9** lowest or last. ▷ **HISTORY** Old English *botm*

bottomless *adj* **1** unlimited; inexhaustible: *bottomless resources.* **2** very deep: *bottomless valleys.*

bottom line *n* **1** the conclusion or main point of a process, discussion, etc. **2** the last line of a financial statement that shows the net profit or loss of a company or organization.

bottom out *vb* to reach the lowest point and level out: *consumer spending has bottomed out.*

bottom-up reading *n* a text-based approach to reading and understanding based on in-depth analyses of the choice, function, and interrelationship of words. Compare **top-down reading.**

botulism *n* severe food poisoning resulting from the toxin **botulin,** produced in imperfectly preserved food. ▷ **HISTORY** Latin *botulus* sausage

bouclé *n* a curled or looped yarn or fabric giving a thick knobbly effect. ▷ **HISTORY** French: curly

boudoir (**boo**-dwahr) *n* a woman's bedroom or private sitting room. ▷ **HISTORY** French, literally: room for sulking in

bouffant (**boof**-fong) *adj* (of a hairstyle) having extra height and width through backcombing. ▷ **HISTORY** French *bouffer* to puff up

bougainvillea *n* a tropical climbing plant with flowers surrounded by showy red or purple bracts. ▷ **HISTORY** after L. A. de *Bougainville,* navigator

bough *n* any of the main branches of a tree. ▷ **HISTORY** Old English *bōg* arm, twig

bought *vb* the past of **buy**.

bouillon (**boo**-yon) *n* a thin clear broth or stock. ▷ **HISTORY** French *bouillir* to boil

boulder *n* a smooth rounded mass of rock shaped by erosion. ▷ **HISTORY** Scandinavian

boulder clay *n* an unstratified glacial deposit of fine clay, boulders, and pebbles.

boule (**boo**-ley) *n* **1** *Politics* the parliament in modern Greece. **2** *Ancient history* the senate of an ancient Greek city-state.

boulevard *n* a wide usually tree-lined road in a city. ▷ **HISTORY** Middle Dutch *bolwerc* bulwark; because originally often built on the ruins of an old rampart

bounce *vb* **bouncing, bounced 1** (of a ball, etc.) to rebound from an impact. **2** to cause (a ball, etc.) to hit a solid surface and spring back. **3** to move or cause to move suddenly; spring: *I bounced down the stairs.* **4** *Slang* (of a bank) to send (a cheque) back or (of a cheque) to be sent back unredeemed because of lack of funds in the account. ✧ *n* **5** the action of rebounding from an impact. **6** a leap or jump. **7** springiness. **8** *Informal* vitality; vigour. ▷ **HISTORY** probably imitative ▶ **bouncy** *adj*

bouncer *n* **1** *Slang* a person employed at a club, disco, etc. to prevent unwanted people from entering and to eject drunks or troublemakers. **2** *Cricket* a ball bowled so that it bounces high on pitching.

bouncing *adj* vigorous and robust: *a bouncing baby.*

bound[1] *vb* **1** the past of **bind.** ✧ *adj* **2** tied as if with a rope. **3** restricted or confined: *housebound.* **4** certain: *it's bound to happen.* **5** compelled or obliged: *they agreed to be bound by the board's recommendations.* **6** (of a book) secured within a cover or binding. **7 bound up with** closely or inextricably linked with.

bound[2] *vb* **1** to move forwards by leaps or jumps. **2** to bounce; spring away from an impact. ✧ *n* **3** a jump upwards or forwards. **4** a bounce, as of a ball. ▷ **HISTORY** Old French *bondir*

bound[3] *vb* **1** to place restrictions on; limit: *ancient art is bound by tradition.* **2** to form a boundary of. ✧ *n* **3** See **bounds.** ▷ **HISTORY** Old French *bonde* ▶ **boundless** *adj*

bound[4] *adj* going or intending to go towards: *homeward bound.* ▷ **HISTORY** Old Norse *buinn,* past participle of *būa* prepare

boundary *n, pl* **-ries 1** something that indicates the farthest limit, such as of an area. **2** *Cricket* **a** the marked limit of the playing area. **b** a stroke that hits the ball beyond this limit, scoring four or six runs.

bounder *n Old-fashioned, Brit slang* a morally reprehensible person; cad.

bounds *pl n* **1** a limit; boundary: *their jealousy knows no bounds.* **2** something that restricts or controls, esp. the standards of a society: *within the bounds of good taste.*

bountiful *or* **bounteous** *adj Literary* **1** plentiful; ample: *a bountiful harvest.* **2** giving freely; generous.

bounty *n, pl* **-ties 1** *Literary* generosity; liberality. **2** something provided in generous amounts: *nature's bounty.* **3** a reward or premium by a government. ▷ **HISTORY** Latin *bonus* good

bounty system *n History* in 19th century Australia, a system whereby settlers received grants for helping skilled immigrants come into the country.

bouquet *n* **1** a bunch of flowers, esp. a large carefully arranged one. **2** the aroma of wine. ▷ **HISTORY** French: thicket

bouquet garni *n, pl* **bouquets garnis** a bunch of herbs tied together and used for flavouring soups, stews, or stocks. ▷ **HISTORY** French

bourbon (**bur**-bn) *n* a whiskey distilled, chiefly in the US, from maize. ▷ **HISTORY** after *Bourbon* county, Kentucky, where it was first made

bourgeois (**boor**-zhwah) *Often disparaging* ✧ *adj* **1** characteristic of or comprising the middle class. **2** conservative or materialistic in outlook. **3** (in Marxist thought) dominated by capitalism. ✧ *n, pl* **-geois 4** a member of the middle class, esp. one regarded as being conservative and materialistic. ▷ **HISTORY** Old French *borjois* citizen

bourgeoisie (boor-zhwah-**zee**) *n* **the bourgeoisie 1** the middle classes. **2** (in Marxist thought) the capitalist ruling class.

bourn *n Chiefly S Brit* a stream. ▷ **HISTORY** Old French *bodne* limit

bourrée (**boor**-ray) *n* **1** a traditional French dance in fast duple time. **2** music for this dance. ▷ **HISTORY** French

Bourse (**boorss**) *n* a stock exchange, esp. of Paris. ▷ **HISTORY** French: purse

bout *n* **1 a** a period of time spent doing something, such as drinking. **b** a period of illness: *a bad bout of flu*. **2** a boxing, wrestling or fencing match. ▷ **HISTORY** obsolete *bought* turn

boutique *n* a small shop, esp. one that sells fashionable clothes. ▷ **HISTORY** French

bouzouki *n* a Greek long-necked stringed musical instrument related to the mandolin. ▷ **HISTORY** Modern Greek

bovine *adj* **1** of or relating to cattle. **2** dull, sluggish, or ugly. ▷ **HISTORY** Latin *bos* ox

bow[1] (rhymes with **cow**) *vb* **1** to lower (one's head) or bend (one's knee or body) as a sign of respect, greeting, agreement, or shame. **2** to comply or accept: *bow to the inevitable*. **3 bow and scrape** to behave in a slavish manner. ✧ *n* **4** a lowering or bending of the head or body as a mark of respect, etc. **5 take a bow** to acknowledge applause. ▷ **HISTORY** Old English *būgan*

bow[2] (rhymes with **know**) *n* **1** a decorative knot usually having two loops and two loose ends. **2** a long stick across which are stretched strands of horsehair, used for playing a violin, viola, cello, etc. **3** a weapon for shooting arrows, consisting of an arch of flexible wood, plastic, etc. bent by a string fastened at each end. **4** something that is curved, bent, or arched. ✧ *vb* **5** to form or cause to form a curve or curves. ▷ **HISTORY** Old English *boga* arch, bow

bow[3] (rhymes with **cow**) *n* **1** *Chiefly naut* the front end or part of a vessel. **2** *Rowing* the oarsman at the bow. ▷ **HISTORY** probably Low German *boog*

bowdlerize *or* **-ise** *vb* **-izing, -ized** *or* **-ising, -ised** to remove passages or words regarded as indecent from (a play, novel, etc.). ▷ **HISTORY** after Thomas *Bowdler,* editor who expurgated Shakespeare ▶ **bowdlerization** *or* **-isation** *n*

bowel *n* **1** an intestine, esp. the large intestine in man. **2 bowels** entrails. **3 bowels** the innermost part: *the bowels of the earth*. ▷ **HISTORY** Latin *botellus* a little sausage

bower *n* a shady leafy shelter in a wood or garden. ▷ **HISTORY** Old English *būr* dwelling

bowerbird *n* a brightly coloured songbird of Australia and New Guinea.

bowie knife *n* a stout hunting knife. ▷ **HISTORY** after Jim *Bowie,* Texan adventurer

bowl[1] *n* **1** a round container open at the top, used for holding liquid or serving food. **2** the amount a bowl will hold. **3** the hollow part of an object, esp. of a spoon or tobacco pipe. ▷ **HISTORY** Old English *bolla*

bowl[2] *n* **1 a** a wooden ball used in the game of bowls. **b** a large heavy ball with holes for gripping used in the game of bowling. ✧ *vb* **2** to roll smoothly or cause to roll smoothly along the ground. **3** *Cricket* **a** to send (a ball) from one's hand towards the batsman. **b** Also: **bowl out** to dismiss (a batsman) by delivering a ball that breaks his wicket. **4** to play bowls. **5 bowl along** to move easily and rapidly, as in a car. ✧ See also **bowls**. ▷ **HISTORY** French *boule*

bow-legged *adj* having legs that curve outwards at the knees.

bowler[1] *n* **1** a person who bowls in cricket. **2** a player at the game of bowls.

bowler[2] *n* a stiff felt hat with a rounded crown and narrow curved brim. ▷ **HISTORY** after John *Bowler,* hatter

bowline *n Naut* **1** a line used to keep the sail taut against the wind. **2** a knot used for securing a loop that will not slip at the end of a piece of rope. ▷ **HISTORY** probably from Middle Low German *bōlīne*

bowling *n* **1** a game in which a heavy ball is rolled down a long narrow alley at a group of wooden pins. **2** *Cricket* the act of delivering the ball to the batsman.

bowls *n* a game played on a very smooth area of grass in which opponents roll biased wooden bowls as near a small bowl (the jack) as possible.

bowsprit *n Naut* a spar projecting from the bow of a sailing ship. ▷ **HISTORY** Middle Low German *bōch* BOW[3] + *sprēt* pole

bow window *n* a curved bay window.

box[1] *n* **1** a container with a firm base and sides and sometimes a removable or hinged lid. **2** the contents of such a container. **3** a separate compartment for a small group of people, as in a theatre. **4** a compartment for a horse in a stable or a vehicle. **5** a section of printed matter on a page, enclosed by lines or a border. **6** a central agency to which mail is addressed and from which it is collected or redistributed: *a post-office box*. **7** same as **penalty box**. **8 the box** *Brit informal* television. ✧ *vb* **9** to put into a box. ✧ See also **box in**. ▷ **HISTORY** Greek *puxos* BOX[3] ▶ **boxlike** *adj*

box[2] *vb* **1** to fight (an opponent) in a boxing match. **2** to engage in boxing. **3** to hit (esp. a person's ears) with the fist. ✧ *n* **4** a punch with the fist, esp. on the ear. ▷ **HISTORY** origin unknown

box[3] *n* **1** a slow-growing evergreen tree or shrub with small shiny leaves. **2** a eucalyptus with similar timber and foliage, and with rough bark. ▷ **HISTORY** Greek *puxos*

boxer *n* **1** a person who boxes. **2** a medium-sized dog with smooth hair and a short nose.

Boxer Rebellion *n History* an unsuccessful rebellion by a Chinese secret society in 1900 against foreign interests in China. ▷ **HISTORY** rough translation of Chinese *I Ho Ch'üan,* literally: virtuous harmonious fist

boxer shorts *or* **boxers** *pl n* men's underpants shaped like shorts but with a front opening.

box in *vb* to prevent from moving freely; confine.

boxing *n* the act, art, or profession of fighting with the fists.

Boxing Day *n* the first day after Christmas (in Britain, traditionally and strictly, the first weekday), observed as a holiday. ▷ **HISTORY** from the former custom of giving Christmas boxes to tradesmen on this day

box jellyfish *n* a highly venomous jellyfish with a cuboidal body that lives in Australian tropical waters.

box junction *n* (in Britain) a road junction marked with yellow crisscross lines which vehicles may only enter when their exit is clear.

box lacrosse *n Canad* lacrosse played indoors.

box number *n* a number used as an address for mail, esp. one used by a newspaper for replies to an advertisement.

box office *n* **1** an office at a theatre, cinema, etc. where tickets are sold. **2** the public appeal of an actor or production. ✧ *adj* **box-office 3** relating to the sales at the box office: *a box-office success.*

box pleat *n* a flat double pleat made by folding under the fabric on either side of it.

boxwood *n* the hard yellow wood of the box tree, used to make tool handles, etc. See **box**³.

boy *n* **1** a male child. **2** a man regarded as immature or inexperienced. **3** *S African offensive* a Black male servant. ▷ **HISTORY** origin unknown ▶ **boyhood** *n* ▶ **boyish** *adj*

boycott *vb* **1** to refuse to deal with (an organization or country) as a protest against its actions or policy. ✧ *n* **2** an instance or the use of boycotting.

> **WORD HISTORY**
>
> Captain Charles Boycott (1832-1897) was a retired British army officer who became an estate manager in Ireland. When in 1880 he was asked to reduce his tenants' rents after a bad harvest, he refused and tried to have some of the tenants evicted. For this, the tenants refused to have anything further to do with him, and he left Ireland shortly afterwards.

boyfriend *n* a male friend with whom a person is romantically or sexually involved.

Boyle's law *n* the principle that the pressure of a gas varies inversely with its volume at constant temperature. ▷ **HISTORY** after Robert *Boyle,* scientist

BP 1 blood pressure. **2** British Pharmacopoeia.

bpi bits per inch (used of a computer tape).

Bq *Physics* becquerel.

Br *Chem* bromine.

bra *n* a woman's undergarment for covering and supporting the breasts. ▷ **HISTORY** from *brassiere*

braaivleis (**brye**-flayss) *n S African* ✧ *n* **1** a grill on which food is cooked over hot charcoal, usually outdoors. **2** an outdoor party at which food like this is served. ✧ *vb* **3** cook (food) on in this way. Also: **braai** ▷ **HISTORY** Afrikaans

brace *n* **1** something that steadies, binds, or holds up another thing. **2** a beam or prop, used to stiffen a framework. **3** a hand tool for drilling holes. **4** a pair, esp. of game birds. **5** either of a pair of characters, { }, used for connecting lines of printing or writing. **6** See **braces.** ✧ *vb* **bracing, braced 7** to steady or prepare (oneself) before an impact. **8** to provide, strengthen, or fit with a brace. ▷ **HISTORY** Latin *bracchia* arms

brace and bit *n* a hand tool for boring holes, consisting of a cranked handle into which a drilling bit is inserted.

bracelet *n* an ornamental chain or band worn around the arm or wrist. ▷ **HISTORY** Latin *bracchium* arm

braces *pl n* **1** *Brit & NZ* a pair of straps worn over the shoulders for holding up the trousers. **2** an appliance of metal bands and wires for correcting unevenness of teeth.

brachiopod (**brake**-ee-oh-pod) *n* an invertebrate sea animal with a shell consisting of two valves. ▷ **HISTORY** Greek *brakhiōn* arm + *pous* foot

brachium (**brake**-ee-um) *n, pl* **brachia** (**brake**-ee-a) *Anat* the arm, esp. the upper part. ▷ **HISTORY** Latin *bracchium* arm

bracing *adj* refreshing: *the bracing climate.*

bracken *n* **1** a fern with large fronds. **2** a clump of these ferns. ▷ **HISTORY** Scandinavian

bracket *n* **1** a pair of characters, [ ], ( ), or { }, used to enclose a section of writing or printing. **2** a group or category falling within certain defined limits: *the lower income bracket.* **3** an L-shaped or other support fixed to a wall to hold a shelf, etc. ✧ *vb* **-eting, -eted 4** to put (written or printed matter) in brackets. **5** to group or class together. ▷ **HISTORY** Latin *braca* breeches

brackish *adj* (of water) slightly salty. ▷ **HISTORY** Middle Dutch *brac*

bract *n* a leaf, usually small and scaly, growing at the base of a flower. ▷ **HISTORY** Latin *bractea* thin metal plate

brad *n* a small tapered nail with a small head. ▷ **HISTORY** Old English *brord* point

brae *n Scot* a hill or slope. ▷ **HISTORY** Middle English *bra*

brag *vb* **bragging, bragged 1** to speak arrogantly and boastfully. ✧ *n* **2** boastful talk or behaviour. **3** a card game similar to poker. ▷ **HISTORY** origin unknown

braggart *n* a person who boasts loudly or exaggeratedly.

Brahma *n* **1** a Hindu god, the Creator. **2** same as **Brahman** (sense 2).

Brahman *n, pl* **-mans 1** Also: **Brahmin** a member of the highest or priestly caste in the Hindu caste system. **2** *Hinduism* the ultimate and impersonal divine reality of the universe. ▷ **HISTORY** Sanskrit: prayer ▶ **Brahmanic** *adj*

braid *vb* **1** to interweave (hair, thread, etc.). **2** to decorate with an ornamental trim or border. ✧ *n* **3** a length of hair that has been braided. **4** narrow ornamental tape of woven silk, wool, etc. ▷ **HISTORY** Old English *bregdan* ▶ **braiding** *n*

A B C D E F G H I J K L M N O P Q R S T U V W X Y Z

braided stream *n Geog* a stream that flows in several shallow interconnected channels separated by banks of deposited material.

Braille *n* a system of writing for the blind consisting of raised dots interpreted by touch. ▷ **HISTORY** after Louis *Braille,* its inventor

brain *n* **1** the soft mass of nervous tissue within the skull of vertebrates that controls and coordinates the nervous system. **2** (*often pl*) *Informal* intellectual ability: *he's got brains.* **3** *Informal* an intelligent person. **4 on the brain** *Informal* constantly in mind: *I had that song on the brain.* **5 the brains** *Informal* a person who plans and organizes something: *the brains behind the bid.* ✧ *vb* **6** *Slang* to hit (someone) hard on the head. ▷ **HISTORY** Old English *brægen*

brainchild *n Informal* an idea or plan produced by creative thought.

braindead *adj* **1** having suffered brain death. **2** *Informal* stupid.

brain death *n* complete stoppage of breathing due to irreparable brain damage.

brain drain *n Informal* the emigration of scientists, technologists, academics, etc.

brainless *adj* stupid or foolish.

brainstorm *n* **1** *Brit informal* a sudden mental aberration. **2** a sudden and violent attack of insanity. **3** *Informal* same as **brainwave**.

brainstorming *n* a thorough discussion to solve problems or create ideas.

brains trust *n* a group of knowledgeable people who discuss topics in public or on radio or television.

brain up *vb Brit* to make (something) more intellectually demanding or sophisticated: *we need to brain up the curriculum.*

brainwash *vb* to cause (a person) to alter his or her beliefs, by methods based on isolation, sleeplessness, etc. ▶ **brainwashing** *n*

brainwave *n Informal* a sudden idea or inspiration.

brain wave *n* a fluctuation of electrical potential in the brain.

brainy *adj* **brainier, brainiest** *Informal* clever; intelligent.

braise *vb* **braising, braised** to cook (food) slowly in a closed pan with a small amount of liquid. ▷ **HISTORY** Old French *brese* live coals

brak[1] (**bruck**) *n S African* a crossbred dog; mongrel. ▷ **HISTORY** Dutch

brak[2] (**bruck**) *adj S African* (of water) slightly salty; brackish. ▷ **HISTORY** Afrikaans

brake[1] *n* **1** a device for slowing or stopping a vehicle. **2** something that slows down or stops progress: *he put a brake on my enthusiasm.* ✧ *vb* **braking, braked 3** to slow down or cause to slow down, by or as if by using a brake. ▷ **HISTORY** Middle Dutch *braeke*

brake[2] *n Brit* an area of dense undergrowth; thicket. ▷ **HISTORY** Old English *bracu*

brake horsepower *n* the rate at which an engine does work, measured by the resistance of an applied brake.

brake light *n* a red light at the rear of a motor vehicle that lights up when the brakes are applied.

brake lining *n* a renewable strip of asbestos riveted to a brake shoe to increase friction.

brake shoe *n* a curved metal casting that acts as a brake on a wheel.

bramble *n* **1** a prickly plant or shrub such as the blackberry. **2** *Scot, N English & NZ* a blackberry. ▷ **HISTORY** Old English *bræmbel* ▶ **brambly** *adj*

bran *n* husks of cereal grain separated from the flour. ▷ **HISTORY** Old French

branch *n* **1** a secondary woody stem extending from the trunk or main branch of a tree. **2** one of a number of shops, offices, or groups that belongs to a central organisation: *he was transferred to their Japanese branch.* **3** a subdivision or subsidiary section of something larger or more complex: *branches of learning.* ✧ *vb* **4** to divide, then develop in different directions. ▷ **HISTORY** Late Latin *branca* paw ▶ **branchlike** *adj*

branch out *vb* to expand or extend one's interests.

brand *n* **1** a particular product or a characteristic that identifies a particular producer. **2** a particular kind or variety. **3** an identifying mark made, usually by burning, on the skin of animals as a proof of ownership. **4** an iron used for branding animals. **5** a mark of disgrace. **6** *Archaic or poetic* a flaming torch. ✧ *vb* **7** to label, burn, or mark with or as if with a brand. **8** to label (someone): *he was branded a war criminal.* ▷ **HISTORY** Old English: fire

brand image *n Marketing* the attributes of a brand as perceived by potential and actual customers.

brandish *vb* to wave (a weapon, etc.) in a triumphant or threatening way. ▷ **HISTORY** Old French *brandir*

brand-new *adj* absolutely new.

brandy *n, pl* **-dies** an alcoholic spirit distilled from wine.

> **WORD HISTORY**
> 'Brandy' is short for 'brandywine', which comes from Dutch *brandewijn* meaning 'burnt wine' or 'distilled wine'.

brandy snap *n* a crisp sweet biscuit, rolled into a cylinder.

brash *adj* **1** tastelessly or offensively loud, or showy: *brash modernization.* **2** impudent or bold: *I thought it was very brash of her to ask me.* ▷ **HISTORY** origin unknown ▶ **brashness** *n*

brass *n* **1** an alloy of copper and zinc. **2** an object, ornament, or utensil made of brass. **3 a** the large family of wind instruments including the trumpet, trombone, etc. made of brass. **b** instruments of this family forming a section in an orchestra. **4** same as **top brass**. **5** *N English dialect* money. **6** *Brit* an engraved brass memorial tablet in a church. **7** *Informal* bold self-confidence; nerve. ▷ **HISTORY** Old English *bræs*

brass band *n* a group of musicians playing brass and percussion instruments.

brasserie *n* a bar or restaurant serving drinks and cheap meals. ▷ HISTORY French *brasser* to stir
brass hat *n Brit informal* a top-ranking official, esp. a military officer.
brassica *n* any plant of the cabbage and turnip family. ▷ HISTORY Latin: cabbage
brassiere *n* same as **bra**. ▷ HISTORY French
brass rubbing *n* an impression of an engraved brass tablet made by rubbing a paper placed over it with heelball or chalk.
brassy *adj* **brassier, brassiest 1** brazen or flashy. **2** like brass, esp. in colour. **3** (of sound) harsh and strident.
brat *n* a child, esp. one who is unruly. ▷ HISTORY origin unknown
bravado *n* an outward display of self-confidence. ▷ HISTORY Spanish *bravada*
brave *adj* **1** having or displaying courage, resolution, or daring. **2** fine; splendid: *a brave sight*. ✧ *n* **3** a warrior of a Native American tribe of N America. ✧ *vb* **braving, braved 4** to confront with resolution or courage: *she braved the 21 miles of Lake Tahoe*. ▷ HISTORY Italian *bravo* ▶ **bravery** *n*
bravo *interj* **1** well done! ✧ *n* **2** (*pl* **-vos**) a cry of 'bravo'. **3** (*pl* **-voes** *or* **-vos**) a hired killer or assassin. ▷ HISTORY Italian
bravura *n* **1** a display of boldness or daring. **2** *Music* brilliance of execution. ▷ HISTORY Italian
brawl *n* **1** a loud disagreement or fight. ✧ *vb* **2** to quarrel or fight noisily. ▷ HISTORY probably from Dutch *brallen* to boast
brawn *n* **1** strong well-developed muscles. **2** physical strength. **3** *Brit & NZ* a seasoned jellied loaf made from the head of a pig. ▷ HISTORY Old French *braon* meat ▶ **brawny** *adj*
bray *vb* **1** (of a donkey) to utter its characteristic loud harsh sound. **2** to utter something with a loud harsh sound. ✧ *n* **3** the loud harsh sound uttered by a donkey. **4** a similar loud sound. ▷ HISTORY Old French *braire*
braze *vb* **brazing, brazed** to join (two metal surfaces) by fusing brass between them. ▷ HISTORY Old French: to burn
brazen *adj* **1** shameless and bold. **2** made of or resembling brass. **3** having a ringing metallic sound. ✧ *vb* **4 brazen it out** to face and overcome a difficult or embarrassing situation boldly or shamelessly. ▶ **brazenly** *adv*
brazier[1] (**bray**-zee-er) *n* a portable metal container for burning charcoal or coal. ▷ HISTORY French *braise* live coals
brazier[2] *n* a worker in brass.
brazil *n* **1** the red wood of various tropical trees of America. **2** same as **brazil nut**. ▷ HISTORY Old Spanish *brasa* glowing coals; referring to the redness of the wood
Brazilian *adj* **1** of Brazil. ✧ *n* **2** a person from Brazil.
brazil nut *n* a large three-sided nut of a tropical American tree.
breach *n* **1** a breaking of a promise, obligation, etc. **2** any serious disagreement or separation. **3** a crack, break, or gap. ✧ *vb* **4** to break (a promise, law, etc.). **5** to break through or make an opening or hole in. ▷ HISTORY Old English *bræc*

> ☑ **WORD TIP**
> See at **breech.**

breach of contract *n Law* failure by a party to carry out obligations required under a contract.
breach of promise *n Law* (formerly) failure to carry out one's promise to marry.
breach of the peace *n Law* an offence against public order causing an unnecessary disturbance of the peace.
bread *n* **1** a food made from a dough of flour or meal mixed with water or milk, usually raised with yeast and then baked. **2** necessary food. **3** *Slang* money. ✧ *vb* **4** to cover (food) with breadcrumbs before cooking. ▷ HISTORY Old English *brēad*
breadboard *n* **1** a wooden board on which bread is sliced. **2** an experimental arrangement of electronic circuits.
breadfruit *n, pl* **-fruits** *or* **-fruit** a tree of the Pacific Islands, whose edible round fruit has a texture like bread when baked.
breadline *n* **on the breadline** impoverished; living at subsistence level.
breadth *n* **1** the extent or measurement of something from side to side. **2** openness and lack of restriction, esp. of viewpoint or interest; liberality. ▷ HISTORY Old English *brād* broad
breadwinner *n* a person supporting a family with his or her earnings.
break *vb* **breaking, broke, broken 1** to separate or become separated into two or more pieces. **2** to damage or become damaged so as not to work. **3** to burst or cut the surface of (skin). **4** to fracture (a bone) in (a limb, etc.). **5** to fail to observe (an agreement, promise, or law): *they broke their promise*. **6** to reveal or be revealed: *she broke the news gently*. **7** (foll. by *with*) to separate oneself from. **8** to stop for a rest: *to break a journey*. **9** to bring or come to an end: *the winter weather broke at last*. **10** to weaken or overwhelm or be weakened or overwhelmed, as in spirit: *he felt his life was broken by his illness*. **11** to cut through or penetrate: *silence broken by shouts*. **12** to improve on or surpass: *she broke three world records*. **13** (often foll. by *in*) to accustom (a horse) to the bridle and saddle, to being ridden, etc. **14** (foll. by *of*) to cause (a person) to give up (a habit): *this cure will break you of smoking*. **15** to weaken the impact or force of: *this net will break his fall*. **16** to decipher: *to break a code*. **17** to lose the order of: *to break ranks*. **18** to reduce to poverty or the state of bankruptcy. **19** to come into being: *light broke over the mountains*. **20** (foll. by *into*) **a** to burst into (song, laughter, etc.). **b** to change to (a faster pace). **21** to open with explosives: *to break a safe*. **22** (of waves) **a** to strike violently against. **b** to collapse into foam or surf. **23** *Snooker* to scatter the balls at the start of a game. **24** *Boxing, wrestling* (of two fighters) to separate from a clinch. **25** (of the male voice) to undergo a change in register, quality, and range at puberty. **26** to interrupt the flow of current in (an electrical circuit). **27 break camp** to pack up and

A B C D E F G H I J K L M N O P Q R S T U V W X Y Z

leave a camp. **28 break even** to make neither a profit nor a loss. **29 break the mould** to make a change that breaks an established habit or pattern. ✧ *n* **30** the act or result of breaking; fracture. **31** a brief rest. **32** a sudden rush, esp. to escape: *they made a sudden break for freedom.* **33** any sudden interruption in a continuous action. **34** *Brit & NZ* a short period between classes at school. **35** *Informal* a fortunate opportunity, esp. to prove oneself. **36** *Informal* a piece of good or bad luck. **37** *Billiards, snooker* a series of successful shots during one turn. **38** *Snooker* the opening shot that scatters the placed balls. **39** a discontinuity in an electrical circuit. **40 break of day** the dawn. ✧ See also **breakaway, break down**, etc. ▷ HISTORY Old English *brecan* ▶ **breakable** *adj*

breakage *n* **1** the act or result of breaking. **2** compensation or allowance for goods damaged while in use, transit, etc.

breakaway *n* **1** loss or withdrawal of a group of members from an association, club, etc. **2** *Austral* a stampede of cattle, esp. at the smell of water. ✧ *adj* **3** dissenting: *a breakaway faction.* ✧ *vb* **break away** **4** to leave hastily or escape. **5** to withdraw or quit.

break-bulk *adj Commerce* denoting a system of transporting goods as separate pieces rather than altogether in a container.

break down *vb* **1** to cease to function; become ineffective. **2** to give way to strong emotion or tears. **3** to crush or destroy. **4** to have a nervous breakdown. **5** to separate into component parts: *with exercise the body breaks down fat to use as fuel.* **6** to separate or cause to separate into simpler chemical elements; decompose. **7** to analyse or be subjected to analysis. ✧ *n* **breakdown 8** an act or instance of breaking down; collapse. **9** same as **nervous breakdown. 10** an analysis of something into its parts.

breaker *n* **1** a large sea wave with a white crest or one that breaks into foam on the shore. **2** a citizens' band radio operator.

break even *vb Business* to reach a point in business where there is neither profit nor loss.

breakfast *n* **1** the first meal of the day. ✧ *vb* **2** to eat breakfast. ▷ HISTORY BREAK + FAST^2

break in *vb* **1** to enter a building, illegally, esp. by force. **2** to interrupt. **3** to accustom (a person or animal) to normal duties or practice. **4** to use or wear (new shoes or new equipment) until comfortable or running smoothly. ✧ *n* **break-in 5** the act of illegally entering a building, esp. by thieves.

breakneck *adj* (of speed or pace) excessively fast and dangerous.

break off *vb* **1** to sever or detach. **2** to end (a relationship or association). **3** to stop abruptly.

break out *vb* **1** to begin or arise suddenly: *fighting broke out between the two factions.* **2** to make an escape, esp. from prison. **3 break out in** to erupt in (a rash or spots). ✧ *n* **break-out 4** an escape, esp. from prison.

break through *vb* **1** to penetrate. **2** to achieve success after lengthy efforts. ✧ *n* **breakthrough 3** a significant development or discovery.

break up *vb* **1** to separate or cause to separate. **2** to put an end to (a relationship) or (of a relationship) to come to an end. **3** to dissolve or cause to dissolve: *the meeting broke up at noon.* **4** *Brit* (of a school) to close for the holidays. ✧ *n* **break-up 5** a separation or disintegration.

breakwater *n* a massive wall built out into the sea to protect a shore or harbour from the force of waves.

bream *n, pl* **bream 1** a freshwater fish covered with silvery scales. **2** a food fish of European seas. **3** a food fish of Australasian seas. ▷ HISTORY Old French *bresme*

breast *n* **1** either of the two soft fleshy milk-secreting glands on a woman's chest. **2** the front part of the body from the neck to the abdomen; chest. **3** the corresponding part in certain other mammals. **4** the source of human emotions. **5** the part of a garment that covers the breast. **6 make a clean breast of something** to divulge truths about oneself. ✧ *vb Literary* **7** to reach the summit of: *breasting the mountain top.* **8** to confront boldly; face: *breast the storm.* ▷ HISTORY Old English *brēost*

breastbone *n* same as **sternum.**

breast-feed *vb* **-feeding, -fed** to feed (a baby) with milk from the breast; suckle.

breastplate *n* a piece of armour covering the chest.

breaststroke *n* a swimming stroke in which the arms are extended in front of the head and swept back on either side.

breastwork *n Fortifications* a temporary defensive work, usually breast-high.

breath *n* **1** the taking in and letting out of air during breathing. **2** a single instance of this. **3** the air taken in or let out during breathing. **4** the vapour, heat, or odour of air breathed out. **5** a slight gust of air. **6** a short pause or rest. **7** a suggestion or slight evidence; suspicion: *trembling at the least breath of scandal.* **8** a whisper or soft sound. **9 catch one's breath a** to rest until breathing is normal. **b** to stop breathing momentarily from excitement, fear, etc. **10 out of breath** gasping for air after exertion. **11 save one's breath** to avoid useless talk. **12 take someone's breath away** to overwhelm someone with surprise, etc. **13 under one's breath** in a quiet voice or whisper. ▷ HISTORY Old English *brǣth*

Breathalyser *or* **-lyzer** *n Brit trademark* a device for estimating the amount of alcohol in the breath. ▷ HISTORY *breath + (an)alyser* ▶ **breathalyse** *or* **-lyze** *vb*

breathe *vb* **breathing, breathed 1** to take in oxygen and give out carbon dioxide; respire. **2** to exist; be alive. **3** to rest to regain breath or composure. **4** (esp. of air) to blow lightly. **5** to exhale or emit: *the dragon breathed fire.* **6** to impart; instil: *a change that breathed new life into Polish industry.* **7** to speak softly; whisper. **8 breathe again, freely** *or* **easily** to feel relief. **9 breathe one's last** to die.

breather *n Informal* a short pause for rest.

breathing *n* **1** the passage of air into and out of the lungs to supply the body with oxygen. **2** the sound this makes.

breathless *adj* **1** out of breath; gasping, etc. **2** holding one's breath or having it taken away by excitement, etc. **3** (esp. of the atmosphere) motionless and stifling. ▶ **breathlessness** *n*

breathtaking *adj* causing awe or excitement.

breath test *n* a chemical test of a driver's breath to determine the amount of alcohol consumed.

bred *vb* the past of **breed**.

bredie (**breed**-ee) *n S African* a meat and vegetable stew. ▷ **HISTORY** Portuguese *bredo* ragout

breech *n* **1** the buttocks. **2** the part of a firearm behind the barrel. ▷ **HISTORY** Old English *brēc*, plural of *brōc* leg covering

> ☑ **WORD TIP**
> *Breech* is sometimes wrongly used as a verb where *breach* is meant: *the barrier/agreement was breached* (not *breeched*).

breech delivery *n* birth of a baby with the feet or buttocks appearing first.

breeches *pl n* trousers extending to the knee or just below, worn for riding, etc.

breed *vb* **breeding, bred 1** to produce new or improved strains of (domestic animals and plants). **2** to produce or cause to produce by mating. **3** to bear (offspring). **4** to bring up; raise: *she was city bred.* **5** to produce or be produced: *the agreement bred confidence between the two.* ✧ *n* **6** a group of animals, esp. domestic animals, within a species, that have certain clearly defined characteristics. **7** a kind, sort, or group: *he was a gentleman, a breed not greatly admired.* **8** a lineage or race. ▷ **HISTORY** Old English *brēdan* ▶ **breeder** *n*

breeder reactor *n* a nuclear reactor that produces more fissionable material than it uses.

breeding *n* **1** the process of producing plants or animals by controlled methods of reproduction. **2** the process of bearing offspring. **3** the result of good upbringing or training.

breeze[1] *n* **1** a gentle or light wind. **2** *Informal* an easy task. ✧ *vb* **breezing, breezed 3** to move quickly or casually: *he breezed into the room.* ▷ **HISTORY** probably from Old Spanish *briza*

breeze[2] *n* ashes of coal, coke, or charcoal. ▷ **HISTORY** French *braise* live coals

breeze block *n* a light building brick made from the ashes of coal, coke, etc. bonded together by cement.

breezy *adj* **breezier, breeziest 1** fresh; windy. **2** casual or carefree.

Bren gun *n* an air-cooled gas-operated light machine gun. ▷ **HISTORY** after *Br(no)*, Czech Republic, and *En(field)*, England, where it was made

brent *or esp US* **brant** *n* a small goose with dark grey plumage and a short neck.

brethren *pl n Archaic except when referring to fellow members of a religion or society* a plural of **brother**.

Breton *adj* **1** of Brittany. ✧ *n* **2** a person from Brittany. **3** the Celtic language of Brittany.

breve *n* an accent (˘), placed over a vowel to indicate that it is short or is pronounced in a specified way. ▷ **HISTORY** Latin *brevis* short

breviary *n, pl* **-ries** *RC Church* a book of psalms, hymns, prayers, etc., to be recited daily. ▷ **HISTORY** Latin *brevis* short

brevity *n* **1** a short duration; brief time. **2** lack of verbosity. ▷ **HISTORY** Latin *brevitas*

brew *vb* **1** to make (beer, ale, etc.) from malt and other ingredients by steeping, boiling, and fermentation. **2** to prepare (a drink, such as tea) by infusing. **3** to devise or plan: *to brew a plot.* **4** to be in the process of being brewed. **5** to be about to happen or forming: *a rebellion was brewing.* ✧ *n* **6** a beverage produced by brewing, esp. tea or beer. **7** an instance of brewing: *last year's brew.* ▷ **HISTORY** Old English *brēowan* ▶ **brewer** *n*

brewery *n, pl* **-eries** a place where beer, ale, etc., is brewed.

briar[1] *or* **brier** *n* **1** a shrub of S Europe, with a hard woody root (briarroot). **2** a tobacco pipe made from this root. ▷ **HISTORY** French *bruyère*

briar[2] *n* same as **brier**[1].

bribe *vb* **bribing, bribed 1** to promise, offer, or give something, often illegally, to (a person) to receive services or gain influence. ✧ *n* **2** a reward, such as money or favour, given or offered for this purpose. ▷ **HISTORY** Old French *briber* to beg ▶ **bribery** *n*

bric-a-brac *n* miscellaneous small ornamental objects.

> **WORD HISTORY**
> This word came into English from French. The French word itself comes from an obsolete phrase *à bric et à brac* meaning 'at random'.

brick *n* **1** a rectangular block of baked or dried clay, used in building construction. **2** the material used to make such blocks. **3** any rectangular block: *a brick of ice cream.* **4** bricks collectively. **5** *Informal* a reliable, trustworthy, or helpful person. **6 drop a brick** *Brit & NZ informal* to make a tactless or indiscreet remark. ✧ *vb* **7** (foll. by *in, up* or *over*) to construct, line, pave, fill, or wall up with bricks: *they bricked up access to the historic pillar.* ▷ **HISTORY** Middle Dutch *bricke*

brickbat *n* **1** blunt criticism. **2** a piece of brick used as a weapon. ▷ **HISTORY** BRICK + BAT[1]

bricklayer *n* a person who builds with bricks.

bridal *adj* of a bride or a wedding. ▷ **HISTORY** Old English *brȳdealu* bride ale

bride *n* a woman who has just been or is about to be married. ▷ **HISTORY** Old English *brȳd*

bridegroom *n* a man who has just been or is about to be married. ▷ **HISTORY** Old English *brȳdguma*

bridesmaid *n* a girl or young woman who attends a bride at her wedding.

bridge[1] *n* **1** a structure that provides a way over a railway, river, etc. **2** a platform from which a ship is piloted and navigated. **3** the hard ridge at the

A B C D E F G H I J K L M N O P Q R S T U V W X Y Z

upper part of the nose. **4** a dental plate containing artificial teeth that is secured to natural teeth. **5** a piece of wood supporting the strings of a violin, guitar, etc. ✧ *vb* **bridging, bridged 6** to build or provide a bridge over (something). **7** to connect or reduce the distance between: *talks aimed at bridging the gap between the two sides.* ▷ **HISTORY** Old English *brycg*

bridge² *n* a card game for four players, based on whist, in which the trump suit is decided by bidding between the players. ▷ **HISTORY** origin unknown

bridgehead *n Mil* a fortified or defensive position at the end of a bridge nearest to the enemy.

bridgework *n* a partial denture attached to the surrounding teeth.

bridging loan *n* a loan made to cover the period between two transactions, such as the buying of another house before the sale of the first is completed.

bridle *n* **1** headgear for controlling a horse, consisting of straps and a bit and reins. **2** something that curbs or restrains. ✧ *vb* **-dling, -dled 3** to show anger or indignation: *he bridled at the shortness of her tone.* **4** to put a bridle on (a horse). **5** to restrain; curb. ▷ **HISTORY** Old English *brigdels*

bridle path *n* a path suitable for riding or leading horses.

Brie (**bree**) *n* a soft creamy white cheese. ▷ **HISTORY** *Brie,* region in N France

brief *adj* **1** short in duration. **2** short in length or extent; scanty: *a brief bikini.* **3** terse or concise. ✧ *n* **4** a condensed statement or written synopsis. **5** *Law* a document containing all the facts and points of law of a case by which a solicitor instructs a barrister to represent a client. **6** *RC Church* a papal letter that is less formal than a bull. **7** Also called: **briefing** instructions. **8 hold a brief for** to argue for; champion. **9 in brief** in short; to sum up. ✧ *vb* **10** to prepare or instruct (someone) by giving a summary of relevant facts. **11** *English law* **a** to instruct (a barrister) by brief. **b** to retain (a barrister) as counsel. ▷ **HISTORY** Latin *brevis* ▶ **briefly** *adv*

briefcase *n* a flat portable case for carrying papers, books, etc.

briefs *pl n* men's or women's underpants without legs.

brier¹ *or* **briar** *n* any of various thorny shrubs or other plants, such as the sweetbrier. ▷ **HISTORY** Old English *brēr, brǣr*

brier² *n* same as **briar¹**.

brig¹ *n Naut* a two-masted square-rigged ship. ▷ **HISTORY** from BRIGANTINE

brig² *n Scot & N English* a bridge.

Brig. Brigadier.

brigade *n* **1** a military formation smaller than a division and usually commanded by a brigadier. **2** a group of people organized for a certain task: *a rescue brigade.* ▷ **HISTORY** Old French

brigadier *n* a senior officer in an army, usually commanding a brigade.

brigalow *n Austral* a type of acacia tree. ▷ **HISTORY** from a native Australian language

brigand *n* a bandit, esp. a member of a gang operating in mountainous areas. ▷ **HISTORY** Old French

brigantine *n* a two-masted sailing ship. ▷ **HISTORY** Old Italian *brigantino* pirate ship

bright *adj* **1** emitting or reflecting much light; shining. **2** (of colours) intense or vivid. **3** full of promise: *a bright future.* **4** lively or cheerful. **5** quick-witted or clever. ✧ *adv* **6** brightly: *the light burned bright in his office.* ▷ **HISTORY** Old English *beorht* ▶ **brightly** *adv* ▶ **brightness** *n*

brighten *vb* **1** to make or become bright or brighter. **2** to make or become cheerful.

brill *n, pl* **brill** *or* **brills** a European flatfish similar to the turbot. ▷ **HISTORY** probably Cornish *brȳthel* mackerel

brilliance *or* **brilliancy** *n* **1** great brightness. **2** excellence in physical or mental ability. **3** splendour.

brilliant *adj* **1** shining with light; sparkling. **2** (of a colour) vivid. **3** splendid; magnificent: *a brilliant show.* **4** of outstanding intelligence or intellect. ✧ *n* **5** a diamond cut with many facets to increase its sparkle. ▷ **HISTORY** French *brillant* shining

brilliantine *n* a perfumed oil used to make the hair smooth and shiny. ▷ **HISTORY** French

brim *n* **1** the upper rim of a cup, bowl, etc. **2** a projecting edge of a hat. ✧ *vb* **brimming, brimmed 3** to be full to the brim: *he saw the tears that brimmed in her eyes.* ▷ **HISTORY** Middle High German *brem* ▶ **brimless** *adj*

brimstone *n Obsolete* sulphur. ▷ **HISTORY** Old English *brynstān*

brindled *adj* brown or grey streaked with a darker colour: *a brindled dog.* ▷ **HISTORY** Middle English *brended*

brine *n* **1** a strong solution of salt and water, used for pickling. **2** *Literary* the sea or its water. ▷ **HISTORY** Old English *brīne*

bring *vb* **bringing, brought 1** to carry, convey, or take (something or someone) to a designated place or person. **2** to cause to happen: *responsibility brings maturity.* **3** to cause to come to mind: *it brought back memories.* **4** to cause to be in a certain state, position, etc.: *the punch brought him to his knees.* **5** to make (oneself): *she couldn't bring herself to do it.* **6** to sell for: *the painting brought a large sum.* **7** *Law* **a** to institute (proceedings, charges, etc.). **b** to put (evidence, etc.) before a tribunal. ✧ See also **bring about**. ▷ **HISTORY** Old English *bringan*

bring about *vb* to cause to happen: *a late harvest brought about by bad weather.*

bring-and-buy sale *n Brit & NZ* an informal sale, often for charity, to which people bring items for sale and buy those that others have brought.

bring forward *vb* **1** to move (a meeting or event) to an earlier date or time. **2** to present or introduce (a subject) for discussion. **3** *Book-keeping* to transfer (a sum) to the top of the next page or column.

bring in *vb* **1** to yield (income, profit, or cash). **2** to introduce (a legislative bill, etc.). **3** to return (a verdict).

bring off *vb* to succeed in achieving (something difficult).

bring out *vb* **1** to produce, publish, or have (a book) published. **2** to expose, reveal, or cause to be seen: *he brought out the best in me.* **3** (foll. by *in*) to cause (a person) to become covered with (a rash, spots, etc.).

bring round *vb* **1** to restore (a person) to consciousness after a faint. **2** to convince (another person) of an opinion or point of view.

bring to *vb* to restore (a person) to consciousness: *the smelling salts brought her to.*

bring up *vb* **1** to care for and train (a child); rear. **2** to raise (a subject) for discussion; mention. **3** to vomit (food).

brinjal *n S African & Indian* dark purple tropical fruit, cooked and eaten as a vegetable. ▷ HISTORY Portuguese *berinjela*

brink *n* **1** the edge or border of a steep place. **2** the land at the edge of a body of water. **3 on the brink of** very near, on the point of: *on the brink of disaster.* ▷ HISTORY Middle Dutch *brinc*

brinkmanship *n* the practice of pressing a dangerous situation to the limit of safety in order to win an advantage.

briny *adj* **brinier, briniest 1** of or like brine; salty. ✧ *n* **2 the briny** *Informal* the sea.

brio (**bree**-oh) *n* liveliness or spirit. ▷ HISTORY Italian

briquette *n* a small brick made of compressed coal dust, used for fuel. ▷ HISTORY French

brisk *adj* **1** lively and quick; vigorous: *brisk trade.* **2** invigorating or sharp: *brisk weather.* **3** practical and businesslike: *his manner was brisk.* ▷ HISTORY probably variant of BRUSQUE ▶ **briskly** *adv*

brisket *n* beef from the breast of a cow. ▷ HISTORY probably Scandinavian

brisling *n* same as **sprat**. ▷ HISTORY Norwegian

bristle *n* **1** any short stiff hair, such as on a pig's back. **2** something resembling these hairs: *toothbrush bristle.* ✧ *vb* **-tling, -tled 3** to stand up or cause to stand up like bristles. **4** to show anger or indignation: *she bristled at the suggestion.* **5** to be thickly covered or set: *the hedges bristled with blossom.* ▷ HISTORY Old English *byrst* ▶ **bristly** *adj*

Brit *n Informal* a British person.

Brit. **1** Britain. **2** British.

Britannia *n* a female warrior carrying a trident and wearing a helmet, personifying Great Britain.

Britannia metal *n* an alloy of tin with antimony and copper.

Britannic *adj* of Britain; British: *Her Britannic Majesty.*

British *adj* **1** of Britain or the British Commonwealth. **2** denoting the English language as spoken and written in Britain. ✧ *pl n* **3 the British** the people of Britain.

British Summer Time *n* a time set one hour ahead of Greenwich Mean Time: used in Britain from the end of March to the end of October, providing an extra hour of daylight in the evening. Abbrev: **BST**

Briton *n* **1** a native or inhabitant of Britain. **2** *History* any of the early Celtic inhabitants of S Britain. ▷ HISTORY of Celtic origin

brittle *adj* **1** easily cracked or broken; fragile. **2** curt or irritable: *a brittle reply.* **3** hard or sharp in quality: *a brittle laugh.* ▷ HISTORY Old English *brēotan* to break ▶ **brittly** *adv*

broach *vb* **1** to initiate or introduce (a topic) for discussion. **2** to tap or pierce (a container) to draw off (a liquid). **3** to open in order to begin to use. ✧ *n* **4** a spit for roasting meat. ▷ HISTORY Latin *brochus* projecting

broad *adj* **1** having great breadth or width. **2** of vast extent: *broad plains.* **3** not detailed; general. **4** clear and open: *broad daylight.* **5** obvious: *broad hints.* **6** tolerant: *a broad view.* **7** extensive: *broad support.* **8** vulgar or coarse. **9** strongly marked: *he spoke broad Australian English.* ✧ *n* **10** *Slang, chiefly US & Canad* a woman. **11 the Broads** in East Anglia, a group of shallow lakes connected by a network of rivers. ▷ HISTORY Old English *brād* ▶ **broadly** *adv*

B-road *n* a secondary road in Britain.

broadband *n* a telecommunications technique that uses a wide range of frequencies to allow messages to be sent simultaneously.

broad bean *n* the large edible flattened seed of a Eurasian bean plant.

broadcast *n* **1** a transmission or programme on radio or television. ✧ *vb* **-casting, -cast** *or* **-casted 2** to transmit (announcements or programmes) on radio or television. **3** to take part in a radio or television programme. **4** to make widely known throughout an area: *to broadcast news.* **5** to scatter (seed, etc.). ▶ **broadcaster** *n* ▶ **broadcasting** *n*

broaden *vb* to make or become broad or broader; widen.

broad-leaved *adj* denoting trees other than conifers; having broad rather than needle-shaped leaves.

broad-minded *adj* **1** tolerant of opposing viewpoints; liberal. **2** not easily shocked.

broadsheet *n* a newspaper in a large format.

broadside *n* **1** a strong or abusive verbal or written attack. **2** *Naval* the simultaneous firing of all the guns on one side of a ship. **3** *Naut* the entire side of a ship. ✧ *adv* **4** with a broader side facing an object.

brocade *n* **1** a rich fabric woven with a raised design. ✧ *vb* **-cading, -caded 2** to weave with such a design. ▷ HISTORY Spanish *brocado*

broccoli *n* a variety of cabbage with greenish flower heads. ▷ HISTORY Italian

brochure *n* a pamphlet or booklet, esp. one containing introductory information or advertising. ▷ HISTORY French

broderie anglaise *n* open embroidery on white cotton, fine linen, etc. ▷ HISTORY French: English embroidery

broekies (**brook**-eez) *pl n S African informal* underpants. ▷ HISTORY Afrikaans

A B C D E F G H I J K L M N O P Q R S T U V W X Y Z

brogue[1] *n* a sturdy walking shoe, often with ornamental perforations. ▷ HISTORY Irish Gaelic *bróg*

brogue[2] *n* a broad gentle-sounding dialectal accent, esp. that used by the Irish in speaking English. ▷ HISTORY origin unknown

broil *vb Austral, NZ, US & Canad* same as **grill** (sense 1). ▷ HISTORY Old French *bruillir*

broiler *n* a young tender chicken suitable for roasting.

broke *vb* **1** the past tense of **break**. ✧ *adj* **2** *Informal* having no money.

broken *vb* **1** the past participle of **break**. ✧ *adj* **2** fractured, smashed, or splintered. **3** interrupted; disturbed: *broken sleep.* **4** not functioning. **5** (of a promise or contract) violated; infringed. **6** (of the speech of a foreigner) imperfectly spoken: *broken English.* **7** Also: **broken-in** made tame by training. **8** exhausted or weakened, as through ill-health or misfortune.

broken chord *n* same as **arpeggio**.

broken-down *adj* **1** worn out, as by age or long use; dilapidated. **2** not in working order.

brokenhearted *adj* overwhelmed by grief or disappointment.

broken home *n* a family which does not live together because the parents are separated or divorced.

broker *n* **1** an agent who buys or sells goods, securities, etc.: *insurance broker.* **2** a person who deals in second-hand goods. ▷ HISTORY Anglo-French *brocour* broacher

brokerage *n* commission charged by a broker.

broker-dealer *n* same as **stockbroker**.

brolga *n* a large grey Australian crane with a trumpeting call. Also: **native companion**

brolly *n, pl* **-lies** *Brit, Austral & NZ informal* an umbrella.

bromide *n* **1** *Chem* any compound of bromine with another element or radical. **2** a dose of sodium or potassium bromide given as a sedative. **3** a boring, meaningless, or obvious remark.

bromide paper *n* a type of photographic paper coated with an emulsion of silver bromide.

bromine *n Chem* a dark red liquid chemical element that gives off a pungent vapour. Symbol: Br. ▷ HISTORY Greek *brōmos* bad smell

bromothymol blue *n Chem* an indicator with pH range of 6.0-7.6 that turns from yellow to blue in acid-alkali tartrations.

bronchial *adj* of or relating to both of the bronchi or the smaller tubes into which they divide.

bronchiole *n* any of the smallest bronchial tubes.

bronchitis *n* inflammation of the bronchial tubes, causing coughing and difficulty in breathing.

bronchus (**bronk**-uss) *n, pl* **bronchi** (**bronk**-eye) either of the two main branches of the windpipe. ▷ HISTORY Greek *bronkhos*

bronco *n, pl* **-cos** (in the US and Canada) a wild or partially tamed horse. ▷ HISTORY Mexican Spanish

brontosaurus *n* a very large plant-eating four-footed dinosaur that had a long neck and long tail. ▷ HISTORY Greek *brontē* thunder + *sauros* lizard

bronze *n* **1** an alloy of copper and smaller proportions of tin. **2** a statue, medal, or other object made of bronze. ✧ *adj* **3** made of or resembling bronze. **4** yellowish-brown. ✧ *vb* **bronzing, bronzed 5** (esp. of the skin) to make or become brown; tan. ▷ HISTORY Italian *bronzo*

Bronze Age *n* a phase of human culture, lasting in Britain from about 2000 to 500 BC during which weapons and tools were made of bronze.

bronze medal *n* a medal awarded as third prize.

brooch *n* an ornament with a hinged pin and catch, worn fastened to clothing. ▷ HISTORY Old French *broche*

brood *n* **1** a number of young animals, esp. birds, produced at one hatching. **2** all the children in a family: often used jokingly. ✧ *vb* **3** (of a bird) to sit on or hatch eggs. **4** to think long and unhappily about something: *he brooded on his failure to avert the confrontation.* ▷ HISTORY Old English *brōd*
▸ **brooding** *n, adj*

broody *adj* **broodier, broodiest 1** moody; introspective. **2** (of poultry) wishing to sit on or hatch eggs. **3** *Informal* (of a woman) wishing to have a baby.

brook[1] *n* a natural freshwater stream. ▷ HISTORY Old English *brōc*

brook[2] *vb* to bear; tolerate: *she would brook no opposition.* ▷ HISTORY Old English *brūcan*

broom *n* **1** a type of long-handled sweeping brush. **2** a yellow-flowered shrub. **3 a new broom** a newly appointed official, etc., eager to make radical changes. ▷ HISTORY Old English *brōm*

broomstick *n* the long handle of a broom.

bros. *or* **Bros.** brothers.

broth *n* a soup made by boiling meat, vegetables, etc. in water. ▷ HISTORY Old English

brothel *n* a house where men pay to have sexual intercourse with prostitutes. ▷ HISTORY short for *brothel-house*, from Middle English *brothel* useless person

brother *n* **1** a man or boy with the same parents as another person. *RELATED ADJECTIVE* ➧ **fraternal 2** a man belonging to the same group, trade union, etc. as another or others; fellow member. **3** comrade; friend. **4** *Christianity* a member of a male religious order. ▷ HISTORY Old English *brōthor*

brotherhood *n* **1** fellowship. **2** an association, such as a trade union. **3** the state of being a brother.

brother-in-law *n, pl* **brothers-in-law 1** the brother of one's wife or husband. **2** the husband of one's sister.

brotherly *adj* of or like a brother, esp. in showing loyalty and affection.

brougham (**brew**-am) *n* a horse-drawn closed carriage with a raised open driver's seat in front. ▷ HISTORY after Lord *Brougham*

brought *vb* the past of **bring**.

brouhaha *n* loud confused noise. ▷ HISTORY French

brow *n* **1** the part of the face from the eyes to the hairline; forehead. **2** same as **eyebrow**. **3** the jutting top of a hill. ▷ HISTORY Old English *brū*

browbeat *vb* **-beating, -beat, -beaten** to frighten (someone) with threats.

brown *adj* **1** of the colour of wood or the earth. **2** (of bread) made from wheatmeal or wholemeal flour. **3** deeply tanned. ✧ *n* **4** the colour of wood or the earth. **5** anything brown, such as brown paint or brown clothing: *clad in brown.* ✧ *vb* **6** to make or become brown or browner, for example as a result of cooking. ▷ HISTORY Old English *brūn* ▶ **brownish** *adj*

brown bear *n* a large ferocious brownish bear of N America, Europe and Asia.

brown coal *n* same as **lignite**.

browned-off *adj Informal, chiefly Brit* thoroughly bored and depressed.

brownfield *adj* relating to an urban area which has previously been built on: *brownfield sites.*

Brownian motion *n Physics* the random movement of particles in a fluid, caused by continuous bombardment from molecules of the fluid. ▷ HISTORY after Robert *Brown,* physicist

brownie *n* **1** (in folklore) an elf said to do helpful work, esp. household chores, at night. **2** a small square nutty chocolate cake.

Brownie Guide *or* **Brownie** *n* a member of the junior branch of the Guides.

Brownie point *n* a notional mark to one's credit for being seen to do the right thing.

brown rice *n* unpolished rice, in which the grains retain the outer yellowish-brown layer (bran).

Brown Shirt *n* **1** (in Nazi Germany) a storm trooper. **2** a member of any fascist party or group.

brown trout *n* a common brownish trout.

browse *vb* **browsing, browsed 1** to look through (a book or articles for sale) in a casual leisurely manner. **2** *Computers* to read hypertext, esp. on the World Wide Web. **3** (of deer, goats, etc.) to feed upon vegetation by continual nibbling. ✧ *n* **4** an instance of browsing. ▷ HISTORY French *broust* bud

browser *n Computers* a software package that enables a user to read hypertext, esp. on the World Wide Web.

brucellosis *n* an infectious disease of cattle, goats, and pigs, caused by bacteria and transmittable to humans. ▷ HISTORY after Sir David *Bruce,* bacteriologist

bruise *vb* **bruising, bruised 1** to injure (body tissue) without breaking the skin, usually with discoloration, or (of body tissue) to be injured in this way. **2** to hurt (someone's feelings). **3** to damage (fruit). ✧ *n* **4** a bodily injury without a break in the skin, usually with discoloration. ▷ HISTORY Old English *brӯsan*

bruiser *n Informal* a strong tough person, esp. a boxer or a bully.

brumby *n, pl* **-bies** *Austral* **1** a wild horse. **2** an unruly person. ▷ HISTORY origin unknown

brunch *n* a meal eaten late in the morning, combining breakfast with lunch. ▷ HISTORY BR(EAKFAST) + (L)UNCH

brunette *n* a girl or woman with dark brown hair. ▷ HISTORY French

brunt *n* the main force or shock of a blow, attack, etc.: *the town bore the brunt of the earthquake.*

brush¹ *n* **1** a device made of bristles, hairs, wires, etc. set into a firm back or handle: used to apply paint, groom the hair, etc. **2** the act of brushing. **3** a brief encounter, esp. an unfriendly one. **4** the bushy tail of a fox. **5** an electric conductor, esp. one made of carbon, that conveys current between stationary and rotating parts of a generator, motor, etc. ✧ *vb* **6** to clean, scrub, or paint with a brush. **7** to apply or remove with a brush or brushing movement. **8** to touch lightly and briefly. ✧ See also **brush off, brush up.** ▷ HISTORY Old French *broisse*

brush² *n* a thick growth of shrubs and small trees; scrub. ▷ HISTORY Old French *broce*

brushed *adj Textiles* treated with a brushing process to raise the nap and give a softer and warmer finish: *brushed nylon.*

brush off *Slang* ✧ *vb* **1** to dismiss and ignore (a person), esp. curtly. ✧ *n* **brushoff 2 give someone the brushoff** to reject someone.

brush turkey *n* a bird of New Guinea and Australia resembling the domestic fowl, with black plumage.

brush up *vb* **1** (often foll. by *on*) to refresh one's knowledge or memory of (a subject). ✧ *n* **brush-up 2** *Brit* the act of tidying one's appearance: *have a wash and brush-up.*

brushwood *n* **1** cut or broken-off tree branches, twigs, etc. **2** same as **brush²**.

brushwork *n* a characteristic manner of applying paint with a brush: *Rembrandt's brushwork.*

brusque *adj* blunt or curt in manner or speech. ▷ HISTORY Italian *brusco* sour ▶ **brusquely** *adv* ▶ **brusqueness** *n*

Brussels sprout *n* a vegetable like a tiny cabbage.

brutal *adj* **1** cruel; vicious; savage. **2** extremely honest or frank in speech or manner. ▶ **brutality** *n* ▶ **brutally** *adv*

brutalism *n* an austere architectural style of the 1950s on, characterized by the use of exposed concrete and angular shapes.

brutalize *or* **-ise** *vb* **-izing, -ized** *or* **-ising, -ised 1** to make or become brutal. **2** to treat (someone) brutally. ▶ **brutalization** *or* **-isation** *n*

brute *n* **1** a brutal person. **2** any animal except man; beast. ✧ *adj* **3** wholly instinctive or physical, like that of an animal: *cricket is not a game of brute force.* **4** without reason or intelligence. **5** coarse and grossly sensual. ▷ HISTORY Latin *brutus* irrational

brutish *adj* **1** of or resembling a brute; animal. **2** coarse; cruel; stupid.

bryony *n, pl* **-nies** a herbaceous climbing plant with greenish flowers and red or black berries. ▷ HISTORY Greek *bruōnia*

A B C D E F G H I J K L M N O P Q R S T U V W X Y Z

Brythonic (brith-**on**-ik) *n* **1** the S group of Celtic languages, consisting of Welsh, Cornish, and Breton. ✧ *adj* **2** of this group of languages. ▷ HISTORY Welsh *Brython* Celt

BS **1** Bachelor of Surgery. **2** British Standard(s).

BSc Bachelor of Science.

BSE bovine spongiform encephalopathy: a fatal virus disease of cattle.

BSI British Standards Institution.

BST British Summer Time.

Bt Baronet.

BT British Telecom.

btu *or* **BThU** British thermal unit.

bubble *n* **1** a small globule of air or a gas in a liquid or a solid. **2** a thin film of liquid forming a ball around air or a gas: *a soap bubble.* **3** a dome, esp. a transparent glass or plastic one. **4** an unreliable scheme or enterprise. ✧ *vb* **-bling, -bled** **5** to form bubbles. **6** to move or flow with a gurgling sound. **7 bubble over** to express an emotion freely: *she was bubbling over with excitement.* ▷ HISTORY probably Scandinavian

bubble and squeak *n Brit, Austral & NZ* a dish of boiled cabbage and potatoes fried together.

bubble car *n Brit* a small car of the 1950s with a transparent bubble-shaped top.

bubbly *adj* **-blier, -bliest** **1** lively; animated; excited. **2** full of or resembling bubbles. ✧ *n* **3** *Informal* champagne.

bubo (**byew**-boh) *n, pl* **-boes** *Pathol* inflammation and swelling of a lymph node, esp. in the armpit or groin. ▷ HISTORY Greek *boubōn* groin ▶ **bubonic** (bew-**bonn**-ik) *adj*

bubonic plague *n* an acute infectious disease characterized by the formation of buboes.

buccaneer *n* a pirate, esp. in the Caribbean in the 17th and 18th centuries. ▷ HISTORY French *boucanier*

buck[1] *n* **1** the male of the goat, hare, kangaroo, rabbit, and reindeer. **2** *Archaic* a spirited young man. **3** the act of bucking. ✧ *vb* **4** (of a horse or other animal) to jump vertically, with legs stiff and back arched. **5** (of a horse, etc.) to throw (its rider) by bucking. **6** *Informal* to resist or oppose obstinately: *bucking the system.* ✧ See also **buck up**. ▷ HISTORY Old English *bucca* he-goat

buck[2] *n US, Canad, Austral & NZ informal* a dollar. ▷ HISTORY origin unknown

buck[3] *n* **pass the buck** *Informal* to shift blame or responsibility onto another. ▷ HISTORY probably from *buckhorn knife,* placed before a player in poker to indicate that he was the next dealer

bucket *n* **1** an open-topped cylindrical container with a handle. **2** the amount a bucket will hold. **3** a bucket-like part of a machine, such as the scoop on a mechanical shovel. **4 kick the bucket** *Slang* to die. ✧ *vb* **-eting, -eted** **5** (often foll. by *down*) (of rain) to fall very heavily. ▷ HISTORY Old English *būc*

bucket shop *n* **1** *Chiefly Brit* a travel agency specializing in cheap airline tickets. **2** an unregistered firm of stockbrokers that engages in fraudulent speculation.

buckle *n* **1** a clasp for fastening together two loose ends, esp. of a belt or strap. ✧ *vb* **-ling, -led** **2** to fasten or be fastened with a buckle. **3** to bend or cause to bend out of shape, esp. as a result of pressure or heat. ▷ HISTORY Latin *buccula* cheek strap

buckle down *vb Informal* to apply oneself with determination.

buckshee *adj Brit slang* without charge; free. ▷ HISTORY from BAKSHEESH

buckshot *n* large lead pellets used for hunting game.

buckteeth *pl n* projecting upper front teeth. ▶ **buck-toothed** *adj*

buckthorn *n* a thorny shrub whose berries were formerly used as a purgative.

buck up *vb Informal* **1** to make or become more cheerful or confident. **2** to make haste.

buckwheat *n* **1** a type of small black seed used as animal fodder and in making flour. **2** the flour obtained from such seeds. ▷ HISTORY Middle Dutch *boecweite*

bucolic (byew-**koll**-ik) *adj* **1** of the countryside or country life; rustic. **2** of or relating to shepherds; pastoral. ✧ *n* **3** a pastoral poem. ▷ HISTORY Greek *boukolos* cowherd

bud *n* **1** a swelling on the stem of a plant that develops into a flower or leaf. **2** a partially opened flower: *rosebud.* **3** any small budlike outgrowth: *taste buds.* **4 nip something in the bud** to put an end to something in its initial stages. ✧ *vb* **budding, budded** **5** (of plants and some animals) to produce buds. **6** *Horticulture* to graft (a bud) from one plant onto another. ▷ HISTORY Middle English *budde*

Buddhism *n* a religion founded by the Buddha that teaches that all suffering can be brought to an end by overcoming greed, hatred, and delusion. ▶ **Buddhist** *n, adj*

budding *adj* beginning to develop or grow: *a budding actor.*

buddleia *n* a shrub which has long spikes of purple flowers. ▷ HISTORY after A. *Buddle,* botanist

buddy *n, pl* **-dies** **1** *Chiefly US & Canad informal* a friend. **2** a volunteer who helps and supports a person suffering from AIDS. ✧ *vb* **-dies, -dying, -died** **3** to act as a buddy to (a person suffering from AIDS). ▷ HISTORY probably variant of BROTHER

budge *vb* **budging, budged** **1** to move slightly: *he refuses to budge off that chair.* **2** to change or cause to change opinions: *nothing would budge him from this idea.* ▷ HISTORY Old French *bouger*

budgerigar *n* a small cage bird bred in many different-coloured varieties. ▷ HISTORY Aboriginal

budget *n* **1** a plan of expected income and expenditure over a specified period. **2** the total amount of money allocated for a specific purpose during a specified period. ✧ *adj* **3** inexpensive: *a budget hotel.* ✧ *vb* **-eting, -eted** **4** to enter or provide for in a budget. **5** to plan the expenditure of (money or time). ▷ HISTORY Latin *bulga* leather pouch ▶ **budgetary** *adj*

Budget *n* **the Budget** an annual estimate of British government expenditures and revenues and the financial plans for the following financial year.
budget deficit *n* the amount by which government spending exceeds income from taxation, etc.
budgie *n Informal* same as **budgerigar**.
buff[1] *n* **1** a soft thick flexible undyed leather. **2** a cloth or pad of material used for polishing. **3 in the buff** *Informal* completely naked. ✧ *adj* **4** dull yellowish-brown. ✧ *vb* **5** to clean or polish (a metal, floor, shoes, etc.) with a buff. ▷ **HISTORY** Late Latin *bufalus* buffalo
buff[2] *n Informal* an expert on or devotee of a given subject: *an opera buff.* ▷ **HISTORY** from the buff-coloured uniforms worn by volunteer firemen in New York City
buffalo *n, pl* **-loes** *or* **-lo 1** a type of cattle with upward-curving horns. **2** same as **water buffalo**. **3** *US & Canad* a bison. ▷ **HISTORY** Greek *bous* ox
buffer[1] *n* **1** one of a pair of spring-loaded steel pads at the ends of railway vehicles and railway tracks that reduces shock on impact. **2** a person or thing that lessens shock or protects from damaging impact, circumstances, etc. **3** *Chem* **a** a substance added to a solution to resist changes in its acidity or alkalinity. **b** Also called: **buffer solution** a solution containing such a substance. **4** *Computers* a device for temporarily storing data. ▷ **HISTORY** from BUFFET[2]
buffer[2] *n Brit informal* a stupid or bumbling person, esp. a man: *an old buffer.* ▷ **HISTORY** origin unknown
buffer state *n* a small and usually neutral state between two rival powers.
buffer zone *n* a strip of land acting as a separator between two other areas of land dedicated to incompatible uses.
buffet[1] (**boof**-fay, **buff**-ay) *n* **1** a counter where light refreshments are served. **2** a meal at which guests help themselves from a number of dishes. ▷ **HISTORY** French
buffet[2] (**buff**-it) *vb* **-feting, -feted 1** to knock against or about; batter: *the ship was buffeted by strong winds.* **2** to hit, esp. with the fist. ✧ *n* **3** a blow, esp. with a hand. ▷ **HISTORY** Old French *buffeter*
buffoon *n* a person who amuses others by silly behaviour. ▷ **HISTORY** Latin *bufo* toad ▶ **buffoonery** *n*
bug *n* **1** any of various insects having piercing and sucking mouthparts. **2** *Chiefly US & Canad* any insect. **3** *Informal* a minor illness caused by a germ or virus. **4** *Informal* an obsessive idea or hobby. **5** *Informal* a concealed microphone used for recording conversations in spying. **6** *Austral* a flattish edible shellfish. ✧ *vb* **bugging, bugged** *Informal* **7** to irritate or upset (someone). **8** to conceal a microphone in (a room or telephone). ▷ **HISTORY** origin unknown
bugbear *n* a thing that causes obsessive anxiety. ▷ **HISTORY** obsolete *bug* an evil spirit + BEAR[2]
bugger *n* **1** *Taboo slang* a person or thing considered to be unpleasant or difficult. **2** *Slang* a humorous or affectionate term for someone: *a friendly little bugger.* **3** a person who practises buggery. ✧ *vb* **4** *Slang* to tire; weary. **5** to practise buggery with. ✧ *interj* **6** *Taboo slang* an exclamation of annoyance or disappointment. ▷ **HISTORY** Medieval Latin *Bulgarus* Bulgarian heretic
bugger off *vb Taboo slang* to go away; depart.
buggery *n Brit, Austral & NZ* anal intercourse.
buggy *n, pl* **-gies 1** a light horse-drawn carriage having two or four wheels. **2** a lightweight folding pram for babies or young children. ▷ **HISTORY** origin unknown
bugle *Music* ✧ *n* **1** a brass instrument used chiefly for military calls. ✧ *vb* **-gling, -gled 2** to play or sound (on) a bugle. ▷ **HISTORY** short for *bugle horn* ox horn, from Latin *buculus* bullock ▶ **bugler** *n*
build *vb* **building, built 1** to make or construct by joining parts or materials: *more than 100 bypasses have been built in the past decade.* **2** to establish and develop: *it took ten years to build the business.* **3** to make in a particular way or for a particular purpose: *she's built for speed, not stamina.* **4** (often foll. by *up*) to increase in intensity. ✧ *n* **5** physical form, figure, or proportions: *he has an athletic build.* ▷ **HISTORY** Old English *byldan*
builder *n* a person who constructs houses and other buildings.
building *n* **1** a structure, such as a house, with a roof and walls. **2** the business of building houses, etc.
building society *n* a cooperative banking enterprise where money can be invested and mortgage loans made available.
build up *vb* **1** to construct (something) gradually, systematically, and in stages. **2** to increase by degrees: *he steadily built up a power base.* **3** to prepare for or gradually approach a climax. ✧ *n* **build-up 4** a progressive increase in number or size: *the build-up of industry.* **5** a gradual approach to a climax. **6** extravagant publicity or praise, esp. as a campaign.
built *vb* the past of **build**.
built environment *n Civil engineering* an environment that includes elements created or altered by man, such as streets, buildings, and electricity.
built-in *adj* **1** included as an essential part: *a built-in cupboard.* **2** essential: *a built-in instinct.*
built-up *adj* **1** having many buildings: *the area has become more built-up.* **2** increased by the addition of parts: *built-up heels.*
built-up area *n* an area in which there are many buildings.
bulb *n* **1** same as **light bulb**. **2** the onion-shaped base of the stem of some plants, which sends down roots. **3** a plant, such as a daffodil, which grows from a bulb. **4** any bulb-shaped thing. ▷ **HISTORY** Greek *bolbos* onion ▶ **bulbous** *adj*
Bulgarian *adj* **1** of Bulgaria. ✧ *n* **2** a person from Bulgaria. **3** the language of Bulgaria.
bulge *n* **1** a swelling or an outward curve on a normally flat surface. **2** a sudden increase in

A B C D E F G H I J K L M N O P Q R S T U V W X Y Z

number, esp. of population. ✧ *vb* **bulging, bulged** **3** to swell outwards. ▷ **HISTORY** Latin *bulga* bag ▸ **bulging** *adj*

bulimia *n* a disorder characterized by compulsive overeating followed by vomiting. ▷ **HISTORY** Greek *bous* ox + *limos* hunger ▸ **bulimic** *adj, n*

bulk *n* **1** volume or size, esp. when great. **2** the main part: *he spends the bulk of his time abroad.* **3** a large body, esp. of a person. **4** the part of food which passes unabsorbed through the digestive system. **5 in bulk** in large quantities: *how frequently do you buy food in bulk for your family?* ✧ *vb* **6 bulk large** to be or seem important or prominent. ▷ **HISTORY** Old Norse *bulki* cargo

> **WORD TIP**
> The use of a plural noun after *bulk* was formerly considered incorrect, but is now acceptable.

bulk buying *n* the purchase of goods in large amounts, often at reduced prices.

bulkhead *n* any upright partition in a ship or aeroplane. ▷ **HISTORY** probably from Old Norse *bálkr* partition + HEAD

bulky *adj* **bulkier, bulkiest** very large and massive, esp. so as to be unwieldy. ▸ **bulkiness** *n*

bull[1] *n* **1** a male of domestic cattle, esp. one that is sexually mature. **2** the male of various other animals including the elephant and whale. **3** a very large, strong, or aggressive person. **4** *Stock Exchange* a speculator who buys in anticipation of rising prices in order to make a profit on resale. **5** *Chiefly Brit* same as **bull's-eye** (senses 1, 2). **6 like a bull in a china shop** clumsy. **7 take the bull by the horns** to face and tackle a difficulty without shirking. ▷ **HISTORY** Old English *bula*

bull[2] *n* a ludicrously self-contradictory or nonsensical statement. ▷ **HISTORY** origin unknown

bull[3] *n* a formal document issued by the pope. ▷ **HISTORY** Latin *bulla* round object

bull bars *pl n* a large protective metal grille on the front of some vehicles, esp. four-wheel-drive vehicles.

bulldog *n* a thickset dog with a broad head and a muscular body.

bulldog clip *n* a clip for holding papers together, consisting of two metal clamps and a spring.

bulldoze *vb* **-dozing, -dozed 1** to move, demolish, or flatten with a bulldozer. **2** *Informal* to coerce (someone) into doing something by intimidation. ▷ **HISTORY** origin unknown

bulldozer *n* a powerful tractor fitted with caterpillar tracks and a blade at the front, used for moving earth.

bullet *n* a small metallic missile used as the projectile of a gun or rifle. ▷ **HISTORY** French *boulette* little ball

bulletin *n* **1** a broadcast summary of the news. **2** an official statement on a matter of public interest. **3** a periodical published by an organization for its members.

> **WORD HISTORY**
> A 'bull' is an edict issued by the pope, so called from the official seal (Latin *bulla*) attached to it. *Bullettino* in Italian originally meant a 'small papal bull', and came to be applied to other official announcements.

bulletin board *n* **1** *US* same as **notice board**. **2** *Computers* a type of data-exchange system by which messages can be sent and read.

bullfight *n* a public show, popular in Spain, in which a matador baits and usually kills a bull in an arena. ▸ **bullfighter** *n* ▸ **bullfighting** *n*

bullfinch *n* a common European songbird with a black head and, in the male, a pinkish breast.

bullfrog *n* any of various large frogs having a loud deep croak.

bullion *n* gold or silver in the form of bars and ingots. ▷ **HISTORY** Anglo-French: mint

bull-necked *adj* having a short thick neck.

bullock *n* a gelded bull; steer. ▷ **HISTORY** Old English *bulluc*

bull's-eye *n* **1** the small central disc of a target or a dartboard. **2** a shot hitting this. **3** *Informal* something that exactly achieves its aim. **4** a peppermint-flavoured boiled sweet. **5** a small circular window. **6** a thick disc of glass set into a ship's deck, etc. to admit light. **7** the glass boss at the centre of a sheet of blown glass. **8 a** a convex lens used as a condenser. **b** a lamp or lantern containing such a lens.

bullshit *Taboo slang* ✧ *n* **1** exaggerated or foolish talk; nonsense. ✧ *vb* **-shitting, -shitted 2** to talk bullshit to: *don't bullshit me.*

bull terrier *n* a terrier with a muscular body and a short smooth coat.

bully *n, pl* **-lies 1** a person who hurts, persecutes, or intimidates weaker people. ✧ *vb* **-lies, -lying, -lied 2** to hurt, intimidate, or persecute (a weaker or smaller person). ✧ *interj* **3 bully for you, him,** etc. *Informal* well done! bravo!: now usually used sarcastically. ▷ **HISTORY** originally, sweetheart, fine fellow, swaggering coward, probably from Middle Dutch *boele* lover

bully beef *n* canned corned beef. ▷ **HISTORY** French *bœuf bouilli* boiled beef

bully-off *Hockey* ✧ *n* **1** the method of restarting play in which two opposing players stand with the ball between them and strike their sticks together three times before trying to hit the ball. ✧ *vb* **bully off 2** to restart play with a bully-off. ▷ **HISTORY** origin unknown

bulrush *n* **1** a tall reedlike marsh plant with brown spiky flowers. **2** *Bible* same as **papyrus** (sense 1). ▷ **HISTORY** Middle English *bulrish*

bulwark *n* **1** a wall or similar structure used as a fortification; rampart. **2** a person or thing acting as a defence. ▷ **HISTORY** Middle High German *bolwerk*

bum[1] *n Brit, Austral & NZ slang* the buttocks or anus. ▷ **HISTORY** origin unknown

bum[2] *Informal* ✧ *n* **1** a disreputable loafer or idler. **2** a tramp; hobo. ✧ *vb* **bumming, bummed 3** to get by begging; cadge: *to bum a lift.* **4 bum around** to spend time to no good purpose; loaf. ✧ *adj* **5** of poor quality; useless: *he hit a bum note.* ▷ HISTORY probably from German *bummeln* to loaf

bumbag *n* a small bag worn on a belt around the waist.

bumble *vb* **-bling, -bled 1** to speak or do in a clumsy, muddled, or inefficient way. **2** to move in a clumsy or unsteady way. ▷ HISTORY origin unknown ▶ **bumbling** *adj, n*

bumblebee *n* a large hairy bee. ▷ HISTORY obsolete *bumble* to buzz

bumf *or* **bumph** *n Brit, Austral & NZ* **1** *Informal* official documents or forms. **2** *Slang* toilet paper. ▷ HISTORY short for *bumfodder*

bump *vb* **1** to knock or strike (someone or something) with a jolt. **2** to travel or proceed in jerks and jolts. **3** to hurt by knocking. ✧ *n* **4** an impact; knock; jolt; collision. **5** a dull thud from an impact or collision. **6** a lump on the body caused by a blow. **7** a raised uneven part, such as on a road surface. ✧ See also **bump into, bump off**. ▷ HISTORY probably imitative ▶ **bumpy** *adj*

bumper[1] *n* a horizontal bar attached to the front and rear of a vehicle to protect against damage from impact.

bumper[2] *n* **1** a glass or tankard, filled to the brim, esp. as a toast. **2** an unusually large or fine example of something. ✧ *adj* **3** unusually large, fine, or abundant: *a bumper crop.* ▷ HISTORY probably obsolete *bump* to bulge

bumph *n* same as **bumf**.

bump into *vb Informal* to meet (someone) by chance.

bumpkin *n* an awkward simple rustic person: *a country bumpkin.* ▷ HISTORY probably from Dutch

bump off *vb Slang* to murder (someone).

bumptious *adj* offensively self-assertive or conceited. ▷ HISTORY probably *bump* + *fractious*

bun *n* **1** a small sweetened bread roll, often containing currants or spices. **2** a small round cake. **3** a hairstyle in which long hair is gathered into a bun shape at the back of the head. ▷ HISTORY origin unknown

bunch *n* **1** a number of things growing, fastened, or grouped together: *a bunch of grapes; a bunch of keys.* **2** a collection; group: *a bunch of queries.* **3** a group or company: *a bunch of cowards.* ✧ *vb* **4** to group or be grouped into a bunch. ▷ HISTORY origin unknown

bundle *n* **1** a number of things or a quantity of material gathered or loosely bound together: *a bundle of sticks.* **2** something wrapped or tied for carrying; package. **3** *Biol* a collection of strands of specialized tissue such as nerve fibres. **4** *Bot* a strand of conducting tissue within plants. ✧ *vb* **-dling, -dled 5** (foll. by *out, off, into*) to cause (someone) to go, esp. roughly or unceremoniously: *she bundled them unceremoniously out into the garden.* **6** to push or throw (something), esp. in a quick untidy way: *the soiled items were bundled into a black plastic bag.* ▷ HISTORY probably from Middle Dutch *bundel*

bundle up *vb* to make (something) into a bundle or bundles.

bundu *n S African & Zimbabwean slang* a largely uninhabited wild region far from towns. ▷ HISTORY from a Bantu language

bun fight *n Brit, Austral & NZ slang* a tea party.

bung *n* **1** a stopper, esp. of cork or rubber, used to close something such as a cask or flask. ✧ *vb* **2** (foll. by *up*) *Informal* to close or seal (something) with or as if with a bung. **3** *Brit, Austral & NZ slang* to throw (something) somewhere in a careless manner; sling. ▷ HISTORY Middle Dutch *bonghe*

bungalow *n* a one-storey house.

WORD HISTORY

'Bungalow' comes from Hindi *banglā* meaning 'of Bengal'. A bungalow was originally a house of the style generally occupied by Europeans in Bengal, a one-storey house with a verandah round it and a thatched roof.

bungee jumping *or* **bungy jumping** *n* a sport in which a person jumps from a high bridge, tower, etc., to which he or she is connected by a rubber rope. ▷ HISTORY from *bungie,* slang word for India rubber

bungle *vb* **-gling, -gled 1** to spoil (an operation) through clumsiness or incompetence; botch. ✧ *n* **2** a clumsy or unsuccessful performance; blunder. ▷ HISTORY origin unknown ▶ **bungler** *n* ▶ **bungling** *adj, n*

bunion *n* an inflamed swelling of the first joint of the big toe. ▷ HISTORY origin unknown

bunk[1] *n* **1** a narrow shelflike bed fixed along a wall, esp. in a caravan or ship. **2** same as **bunk bed**. ▷ HISTORY probably from *bunker*

bunk[2] *n Informal* same as **bunkum**.

bunk[3] *n* **do a bunk** *Brit, Austral & NZ slang* to make a hurried and secret departure. ✧ *vb Brit, NZ & S African* be absent without permission. ▷ HISTORY origin unknown

bunk bed *n* one of a pair of beds constructed one above the other to save space.

bunker *n* **1** an obstacle on a golf course, usually a sand-filled hollow bordered by a ridge. **2** an underground shelter. **3** a large storage container for coal etc. ▷ HISTORY Scots *bonkar*

bunkum *n* empty talk; nonsense. ▷ HISTORY after *Buncombe,* North Carolina, alluded to in an inane speech by its Congressional representative

bunny *n, pl* **-nies** a child's word for **rabbit**. ▷ HISTORY Scottish Gaelic *bun* rabbit's tail

Bunsen burner *n* a gas burner consisting of a metal tube with an adjustable air valve at the base. ▷ HISTORY after R. W. *Bunsen,* chemist

bunting[1] *n* decorative flags, pennants, and streamers. ▷ HISTORY origin unknown

bunting[2] *n* a songbird with a short stout bill. ▷ HISTORY origin unknown

bunya *n* a tall dome-shaped Australian coniferous tree **bunya-bunya**

a b c d e f g h i j k l m n o p q r s t u v w x y z

A B C D E F G H I J K L M N O P Q R S T U V W X Y Z

bunyip *n Austral* a legendary monster said to live in swamps and lakes. ▷ HISTORY from a native Australian language

buoy *n* **1** a brightly coloured floating object anchored to the sea bed for marking moorings, navigable channels, or obstructions in the water. ✧ *vb* **2** (foll. by *up*) to prevent from sinking: *the life belt buoyed him up.* **3** to raise the spirits of; hearten: *exports are on the increase, buoyed by a weak dollar.* **4** *Naut* to mark (a channel or obstruction) with a buoy or buoys. ▷ HISTORY probably Germanic

buoyant *adj* **1** able to float in or rise to the surface of a liquid. **2** (of a liquid or gas) able to keep a body afloat. **3** cheerful or resilient. ▶ **buoyancy** *n*

bur *or* **burr** *n* **1** a seed case or flower head with hooks or prickles. **2** any plant that produces burs. ▷ HISTORY probably from Old Norse

burble *vb* **-bling, -bled 1** to make or utter with a bubbling sound; gurgle. **2** to talk quickly and excitedly. ▷ HISTORY probably imitative

burbot *n, pl* **-bots** *or* **-bot** a freshwater fish of the cod family that has barbels around its mouth. ▷ HISTORY Old French *bourbotte*

burden[1] *n* **1** something that is carried; load. **2** something that is difficult to bear. *RELATED ADJECTIVE* ➔ **onerous** ✧ *vb* **3** to put or impose a burden on; load. **4** to weigh down; oppress. ▷ HISTORY Old English *byrthen* ▶ **burdensome** *adj*

burden[2] *n* **1** a line of words recurring at the end of each verse of a song. **2** the theme of a speech, book, etc. ▷ HISTORY Old French *bourdon* droning sound

burden of proof *n Law* the obligation to provide evidence that will convince the court or jury of the truth of one's contention if the case is to succeed; in criminal cases, the *burden of proof* lies with the prosecution and in civil cases, it lies with the plaintiff.

burdock *n* a weed with large heart-shaped leaves, and burlike fruits. ▷ HISTORY BUR + DOCK[4]

bureau (**byew**-roe) *n, pl* **-reaus** *or* **-reaux** (-rose) **1** an office or agency, esp. one providing services for the public. **2** *US* a government department. **3** *Chiefly Brit* a writing desk with pigeonholes and drawers against which the writing surface can be closed when not in use. **4** *US* a chest of drawers. ▷ HISTORY French

bureaucracy *n, pl* **-cies 1** a rigid system of administration based upon organization into bureaus, division of labour, a hierarchy of authority, etc. **2** government by such a system. **3** government officials collectively. **4** any administration in which action is impeded by unnecessary official procedures.

bureaucrat *n* **1** an official in a bureaucracy. **2** an official who adheres rigidly to bureaucracy. ▶ **bureaucratic** *adj*

burette *or US* **buret** *n* a graduated glass tube with a stopcock on one end for dispensing known volumes of fluids. ▷ HISTORY Old French *buire* ewer

burgeon *vb* to develop or grow rapidly; flourish. ▷ HISTORY Old French *burjon*

burger *n Informal* same as **hamburger**.

burgh *n* (in Scotland until 1975) a town with a degree of self-government. ▷ HISTORY Scots form of *borough*

burgher *n Archaic* a citizen, esp. one from the Continent. ▷ HISTORY German *Bürger* or Dutch *burger*

burglar *n* a person who illegally enters a property to commit a crime. ▷ HISTORY Medieval Latin *burglator*

burglary *n, pl* **-ries** the crime of entering a building as a trespasser to commit theft or another offence.

burgle *vb* **-gling, -gled** to break into (a house, shop, etc.).

burgomaster *n* the chief magistrate of a town in Austria, Belgium, Germany, or the Netherlands. ▷ HISTORY Dutch *burgemeester*

Burgundy *n* **1** a red or white wine produced in the Burgundy region, around Dijon in France. ✧ *adj* **2 burgundy** dark purplish-red.

burial *n* the burying of a dead body.

burin (**byoor**-in) *n* a steel chisel used for engraving metal, wood, or marble. ▷ HISTORY French

burl *or* **birl** *n Informal* **1** *Scot, Austral, & NZ* an attempt; try: *give it a burl.* **2** *Austral & NZ* a ride in a car. ▷ HISTORY from Scots *birl* to spin or turn

burlesque *n* **1** an artistic work, esp. literary or dramatic, satirizing a subject by caricaturing it. **2** *US & Canad theatre* a bawdy comedy show of the late 19th and early 20th centuries. ✧ *adj* **3** of or characteristic of a burlesque. ▷ HISTORY Italian *burla* a jest

burly *adj* **-lier, -liest** large and thick of build; sturdy. ▷ HISTORY Germanic

burn[1] *vb* **burning, burnt** *or* **burned 1** to be or set on fire. **2** to destroy or be destroyed by fire. **3** to damage, injure, or mark by heat: *he burnt his hand.* **4** to die or put to death by fire. **5** to be or feel hot: *my forehead is burning.* **6** to smart or cause to smart: *brandy burns your throat.* **7** to feel strong emotion, esp. anger or passion. **8** to use for the purposes of light, heat, or power: *to burn coal.* **9** to form by or as if by fire: *to burn a hole.* **10** to char or become charred: *the toast is burning.* **11** to record data on (a compact disc). **12 burn one's bridges** *or* **boats** to commit oneself to a particular course of action with no possibility of turning back. **13 burn one's fingers** to suffer from having meddled or interfered. ✧ *n* **14** an injury caused by exposure to heat, electrical, chemical, or radioactive agents. **15** a mark caused by burning. ✧ See also **burn out**. ▷ HISTORY Old English *beornan*

burn[2] *n Scot & N English* a small stream. ▷ HISTORY Old English *burna*

burner *n* the part of a stove or lamp that produces flame or heat.

burning *adj* **1** intense; passionate. **2** urgent; crucial: *a burning problem.*

burning glass *n* a convex lens for concentrating the sun's rays to produce fire.

burnish *vb* to make or become shiny or smooth by friction; polish. ▷ **HISTORY** Old French *brunir* to make brown

burnous *n* a long circular cloak with a hood, worn esp. by Arabs. ▷ **HISTORY** Arabic *burnus*

burn out *vb* **1** to become or cause to become inoperative as a result of heat or friction: *the clutch burnt out.* ✧ *n* **burnout 2** total exhaustion and inability to work effectively as a result of excessive demands or overwork.

burnt *vb* **1** a past of **burn**[1]. ✧ *adj* **2** affected by or as if by burning; charred.

burp *n* **1** *Informal* a belch. ✧ *vb* **2** *Informal* to belch. **3** to cause (a baby) to belch. ▷ **HISTORY** imitative

burr *n* **1** the soft trilling sound given to the letter (r) in some English dialects. **2** a whirring or humming sound. **3** a rough edge left on metal or paper after cutting. **4** a small hand-operated drill. ▷ **HISTORY** origin unknown

burrawang *n* an Australian plant with fernlike leaves and an edible nut.

burrow *n* **1** a hole dug in the ground by a rabbit or other small animal. ✧ *vb* **2** to dig (a tunnel or hole) in, through, or under ground. **3** to move through a place by or as if by digging. **4** to delve deeply: *he burrowed into his coat pocket.* **5** to live in or as if in a burrow. ▷ **HISTORY** probably variant of *borough*

bursar *n* a treasurer of a school, college, or university. ▷ **HISTORY** Medieval Latin *bursarius* keeper of the purse

bursary *n, pl* **-ries 1** a scholarship or grant awarded esp. in Scottish and New Zealand schools and universities. **2** *NZ* a state examination for senior pupils at secondary school.

burst *vb* **bursting, burst 1** to break or cause to break open or apart suddenly and noisily; explode. **2** to come or go suddenly and forcibly: *he burst into the room.* **3** to be full to the point of breaking open: *bursting at the seams.* **4** (foll. by *into*) to give vent to (something) suddenly or loudly: *she burst into song.* ✧ *n* **5** an instance of breaking open suddenly; explosion. **6** a break; breach: *there was a burst in the pipe.* **7** a sudden increase of effort; spurt: *a burst of speed.* **8** a sudden and violent occurrence or outbreak: *a burst of applause.* ▷ **HISTORY** Old English *berstan*

burton *n* **go for a burton** *Brit & NZ slang* **a** to be broken, useless, or lost. **b** to die. ▷ **HISTORY** origin unknown

bury *vb* **buries, burying, buried 1** to place (a corpse) in a grave. **2** to place (something) in the earth and cover it with soil. **3** to cover (something) from sight; hide. **4** to occupy (oneself) with deep concentration: *he buried himself in his work.* **5** to dismiss (a feeling) from the mind: *they decided to bury any hard feelings.* ▷ **HISTORY** Old English *byrgan*

bus *n* **1** a large motor vehicle designed to carry passengers between stopping places along a regular route. **2** *Informal* a car or aircraft that is old and shaky. **3** *Electronics, computers* an electrical conductor used to make a common connection between several circuits. ✧ *vb* **bussing, bussed** *or* **busing, bused 4** to travel or transport by bus. **5** *Chiefly US & Canad* to transport (children) by bus from one area to another in order to create racially integrated schools. ▷ **HISTORY** short for OMNIBUS

busby *n, pl* **-bies** a tall fur helmet worn by certain British soldiers. ▷ **HISTORY** origin unknown

bush[1] *n* **1** a dense woody plant, smaller than a tree, with many branches; shrub. **2** a dense cluster of such shrubs; thicket. **3** something resembling a bush, esp. in density: *a bush of hair.* **4 the bush** an uncultivated area covered with trees or shrubs in Australia, Africa, New Zealand, and Canada. **5** *Canad* an area on a farm on which timber is grown and cut. **6 beat about the bush** to avoid the point at issue. ▷ **HISTORY** Germanic

bush[2] *n* **1** a thin metal sleeve or tubular lining serving as a bearing. ✧ *vb* **2** to fit a bush to (a casing or bearing). ▷ **HISTORY** Middle Dutch *busse* box

bushbaby *n, pl* **-babies** a small agile tree-living mammal with large eyes and a long tail.

bushed *adj Informal* extremely tired; exhausted.

bushel *n Brit* an obsolete unit of dry or liquid measure equal to 8 gallons (36.4 litres). ▷ **HISTORY** Old French *boissel*

bushman *n, pl* **-men** *Austral & NZ* a person who lives or travels in the bush.

Bushman *n, pl* **-men** a member of a hunting and gathering people of southern Africa. ▷ **HISTORY** Afrikaans *boschjesman*

bush sickness *n NZ* a disease of animals caused by mineral deficiency in old bush country. ▶ **bush-sick** *adj*

bush telegraph *n* a means of spreading rumour or gossip.

bushveld *n S African* bushy countryside. ▷ **HISTORY** Afrikaans

bushwalking *n Austral* the leisure activity of walking in the bush. ▶ **bushwalker** *n*

bushy *adj* **bushier, bushiest 1** (of hair) thick and shaggy. **2** covered or overgrown with bushes.

business *n* **1** the purchase and sale of goods and services. **2** a commercial or industrial establishment. **3** a trade or profession. **4** commercial activity; dealings: *the two countries should do business with each other.* **5** proper or rightful concern or responsibility: *mind your own business.* **6** an affair; matter: *it's a dreadful business.* **7** serious work or activity: *get down to business.* **8** a difficult or complicated matter: *it's a business trying to see him.* **9 mean business** to be in earnest. ▷ **HISTORY** Old English *bisignis* care, attentiveness

businesslike *adj* efficient and methodical.

businessman *or fem* **businesswoman** *n, pl* **-men** *or* **-women** a person engaged in commercial or industrial business, usually an owner or executive.

business park *n* an area specially designated to accommodate business offices, light industry, etc.

business rate *n* a tax levied on businesses, based on the value of their premises.

busker *n* a person who entertains for money in streets or stations. ▷ HISTORY perhaps from Spanish *buscar* to look for ▶ **busk** *vb*

bust[1] *n* **1** a woman's bosom. **2** a sculpture of the head, shoulders, and upper chest of a person. ▷ HISTORY Italian *busto* a sculpture

bust[2] *Informal* ✧ *vb* **busting, busted** *or* **bust 1** to burst or break. **2** (of the police) to raid or search (a place) or arrest (someone). **3** *US & Canad* to demote in military rank. ✧ *adj* **4** broken. **5 go bust** to become bankrupt. ▷ HISTORY from *burst*

bustard *n* a bird with long strong legs, a heavy body, a long neck, and speckled plumage.

bustle[1] *vb* **-tling, -tled 1** (often foll. by *about*) to hurry with a great show of energy or activity. ✧ *n* **2** energetic and noisy activity. ▷ HISTORY probably obsolete *buskle* to prepare ▶ **bustling** *adj*

bustle[2] *n* a cushion or framework worn by women in the late 19th century at the back in order to expand the skirt. ▷ HISTORY origin unknown

bust-up *Informal* ✧ *n* **1** a serious quarrel, esp. one ending a relationship. **2** *Brit, Austral & NZ* a disturbance or brawl. ✧ *vb* **bust up 3** to quarrel and part. **4** to disrupt (a meeting), esp. violently.

busy *adj* **busier, busiest 1** actively or fully engaged; occupied. **2** crowded with or characterized by activity. **3** (of a telephone line) in use; engaged. ✧ *vb* **busies, busying, busied 4** to make or keep (someone, esp. oneself) busy; occupy. ▷ HISTORY Old English *bisig* ▶ **busily** *adv*

busybody *n, pl* **-bodies** a meddlesome, prying, or officious person.

but *conj* **1** contrary to expectation: *he cut his hand but didn't cry.* **2** in contrast; on the contrary: *I like seafood but my husband doesn't.* **3** other than: *we can't do anything but wait.* **4** without it happening: *we never go out but it rains.* ✧ *prep* **5** except: *they saved all but one.* **6 but for** were it not for: *but for you, we couldn't have managed.* ✧ *adv* **7** only: *I can but try; he was but a child.* ✧ *n* **8** an objection: *ifs and buts.* ▷ HISTORY Old English *būtan* without, except

butane (**byew**-tane) *n* a colourless gas used in the manufacture of rubber and fuels. ▷ HISTORY from *butyl*

butch *adj Slang* (of a woman or man) markedly or aggressively masculine. ▷ HISTORY from *butcher*

butcher *n* **1** a person who sells meat. **2** a person who kills animals for meat. **3** a brutal murderer. ✧ *vb* **4** to kill and prepare (animals) for meat. **5** to kill (people) at random or brutally. **6** to make a mess of; botch. ▷ HISTORY Old French *bouchier*

butcherbird *n* an Australian magpie that impales its prey on thorns.

butchery *n, pl* **-eries 1** senseless slaughter. **2** the business of a butcher.

butler *n* the head manservant of a household, in charge of the wines, table, etc. ▷ HISTORY Old French *bouteille* bottle

butt[1] *n* **1** the thicker or blunt end of something, such as the stock of a rifle. **2** the unused end of a cigarette or cigar; stub. **3** *Chiefly US & Canad slang* the buttocks. ▷ HISTORY Middle English

butt[2] *n* **1** a person or thing that is the target of ridicule or teasing. **2** *Shooting, archery* **a** a mound of earth behind the target. **b butts** the target range. ▷ HISTORY Old French *but*

butt[3] *vb* **1** to strike (something or someone) with the head or horns. **2** (foll. by *in* or *into*) to intrude, esp. into a conversation; interfere. ✧ *n* **3** a blow with the head or horns. ▷ HISTORY Old French *boter*

butt[4] *n* a large cask for collecting or storing liquids. ▷ HISTORY Late Latin *buttis* cask

butte (**byewt**) *n US & Canad* an isolated steep flat-topped hill. ▷ HISTORY Old French *bute* mound behind a target

butter *n* **1** an edible fatty yellow solid made from cream by churning. **2** any substance with a butter-like consistency, such as peanut butter. ✧ *vb* **3** to put butter on or in (something). ✧ See also **butter up**. ▷ HISTORY Greek *bous* cow + *turos* cheese ▶ **buttery** *adj*

butter bean *n* a large pale flat edible bean.

buttercup *n* a small bright yellow flower.

butterfingers *n Informal* a person who drops things by mistake or fails to catch things.

butterflies *pl n Informal* a nervous feeling in the stomach.

butterfly *n, pl* **-flies 1** an insect with a slender body and brightly coloured wings. **2** a swimming stroke in which the arms are plunged forward together in large circular movements. **3** a person who never settles with one interest or occupation for long. ▷ HISTORY Old English *buttorflēoge*

butterfly nut *n* same as **wing nut**.

buttermilk *n* the sourish liquid remaining after the butter has been separated from milk.

butterscotch *n* a hard brittle toffee made with butter, brown sugar, etc.

butter up *vb* to flatter.

buttery *n, pl* **-teries** *Brit* (in some universities) a room in which food and drink are sold to students. ▷ HISTORY Latin *butta* cask

buttock *n* **1** either of the two large fleshy masses that form the human rump. **2** the corresponding part in some mammals. ▷ HISTORY perhaps from Old English *buttuc* round slope

button *n* **1** a disc or knob of plastic, wood, etc., attached to a garment, which fastens two surfaces together by passing through a buttonhole. **2** a small disc that operates a door bell or machine when pressed. **3** a small round object, such as a sweet or badge. **4 not worth a button** *Brit* of no value; useless. ✧ *vb* **5** to fasten (a garment) with a button or buttons. ▷ HISTORY Old French *boton*

buttonhole *n* **1** a slit in a garment through which a button is passed to fasten two surfaces together. **2** a flower worn pinned to the lapel or in the buttonhole. ✧ *vb* **-holing, -holed 3** to detain (a person) in conversation.

buttress *n* **1** a construction, usually of brick or stone, built to support a wall. **2** any support or prop. ✧ *vb* **3** to support (a wall) with a buttress. **4** to support or sustain: *his observations are buttressed by the most recent scholarly research.* ▷ HISTORY Old French *bouter* to thrust

buttress root *n Bot* a tree root that extends above ground as a platelike outgrowth of the trunk supporting the tree. Buttress roots are mainly found in trees of tropical rain forests.

butyl (**byew**-tile) *adj* of or containing any of four isomeric forms of the group C_4H_9–: *butyl rubber.* ▷ HISTORY Latin *butyrum* butter

buxom *adj* (of a woman) healthily plump, attractive, and full-bosomed. ▷ HISTORY Middle English *buhsum* compliant

buy *vb* **buying, bought 1** to acquire (something) by paying a sum of money for it; purchase. **2** to be capable of purchasing: *money can't buy love.* **3** to acquire by any exchange or sacrifice: *the rise in interest rates was just to buy time until the weekend.* **4** to bribe (someone). **5** *Slang* to accept (something) as true. **6** (foll. by *into*) to purchase shares of (a company). ✧ *n* **7** a purchase: *a good buy.* See also **buy in**. ▷ HISTORY Old English *bycgan*

> **WORD TIP**
> The use of *off* after *buy* as in *I bought this off my neighbour* was formerly considered incorrect, but is now acceptable in informal contexts.

buyer *n* **1** a person who buys; customer. **2** a person employed to buy merchandise for a shop or factory.

buy in *vb* to purchase (goods) in large quantities.

buy-out *n* **1** the purchase of a company, often by its former employees. ✧ *vb* **buy out 2** to purchase the ownership of a company or property from (someone).

buy up *vb* **1** to purchase all that is available of (something). **2** to purchase a controlling interest in (a company).

buzz *n* **1** a rapidly vibrating humming sound, such as of a bee. **2** a low sound, such as of many voices in conversation. **3** *Informal* a telephone call. **4** *Informal* a sense of excitement. ✧ *vb* **5** to make a vibrating sound like that of a prolonged *z*. **6** (of a place) to be filled with an air of excitement: *the city buzzed with the news.* **7** to summon (someone) with a buzzer. **8** *Informal* to fly an aircraft very low over (people, buildings, or another aircraft). **9 buzz about** *or* **around** to move around quickly and busily. ▷ HISTORY imitative

buzzard *n* a bird of prey with broad wings and tail and a soaring flight. ▷ HISTORY Latin *buteo* hawk

buzzer *n* an electronic device that produces a buzzing sound as a signal.

buzz off *vb Brit & Austral Informal* to go away; depart.

buzz word *n Informal* a word, originally from a particular jargon, which becomes a popular vogue word.

by *prep* **1** used to indicate the performer of the action of a passive verb: *seeds eaten by the birds.* **2** used to indicate the person responsible for a creative work: *three songs by Britten.* **3** via; through: *enter by the back door.* **4** used to indicate a means used: *he frightened her by hiding behind the door.* **5** beside; next to; near: *a tree by the stream.* **6** passing the position of; past: *I drove by the place she works.* **7** not later than; before: *return the books by Tuesday.* **8** used to indicate extent: *it is hotter by five degrees.* **9** multiplied by: *four by three equals twelve.* **10** during the passing of: *by night.* **11** placed between measurements of the various dimensions of something: *a plank fourteen inches by seven.* ✧ *adv* **12** near: *the house is close by.* **13** away; aside: *he put some money by each week.* **14** passing a point near something; past: *he drove by.* ✧ *n, pl* **byes 15** same as **bye**[1]. ▷ HISTORY Old English *bī*

by and by *adv* presently or eventually.

by and large *adv* in general; on the whole.

bye[1] *n* **1** *Sport* status of a player or team who wins a preliminary round by virtue of having no opponent. **2** *Cricket* a run scored off a ball not struck by the batsman. **3 by the bye** incidentally; by the way. ▷ HISTORY variant of *by*

bye[2] *or* **bye-bye** *interj Informal* goodbye.

by-election *or* **bye-election** *n* an election held during the life of a parliament to fill a vacant seat.

bygone *adj* past; former: *a bygone age.*

bygones *pl n* **let bygones be bygones** to agree to forget past quarrels.

bylaw *or* **bye-law** *n Law* a rule made by a local authority. ▷ HISTORY probably Scandinavian

by-line *n* **1** *Journalism* a line under the title of a newspaper or magazine article giving the author's name. **2** same as **touchline**.

BYO(G) *n Austral & NZ* an unlicensed restaurant at which diners may bring their own alcoholic drink. ▷ HISTORY *bring your own (grog)*

bypass *n* **1** a main road built to avoid a city. **2** a secondary pipe, channel, or appliance through which the flow of a substance, such as gas or electricity, is redirected. **3** a surgical operation in which the blood flow is redirected away from a diseased or blocked part of the heart. ✧ *vb* **4** to go around or avoid (a city, obstruction, problem, etc.). **5** to proceed without reference to (regulations or a superior); get round; avoid.

by-play *n* secondary action in a play, carried on apart while the main action proceeds.

by-product *n* **1** a secondary or incidental product of a manufacturing process. **2** a side effect.

byre *n Brit* a shelter for cows. ▷ HISTORY Old English *bӯre*

bystander *n* a person present but not involved; onlooker; spectator.

byte *n Computers* a group of bits processed as one unit of data. ▷ HISTORY origin unknown

byway *n* a secondary or side road, esp. in the country.

byword *n* **1** a person or thing regarded as a perfect example of something: *their name is a byword for quality.* **2** a common saying; proverb.

Byzantine *adj* **1** of Byzantium, an ancient Greek city on the Bosphorus. **2** of the Byzantine Empire, the continuation of the Roman Empire in the East. **3** of the style of architecture developed in the Byzantine Empire, with massive domes, rounded arches, and mosaics. **4** (of attitudes, methods, etc.) inflexible or complicated. ✧ *n* **5** an inhabitant of Byzantium.

C c

c 1 centi-. 2 *Cricket* caught. 3 cubic. 4 the speed of light in free space.

C 1 *Music* the first note of a major scale containing no sharps or flats (**C major**). 2 *Chem* carbon. 3 Celsius. 4 centigrade. 5 century: *C20*. 6 coulomb. 7 the Roman numeral for 100. 8 a high-level computer programming language.

c. (used preceding a date) about: *c. 1800*. ▷ HISTORY Latin *circa*

Ca *Chem* calcium.

CA 1 California. 2 Central America. 3 Chartered Accountant.

ca. (used preceding a date) about: *ca. 1930*. ▷ HISTORY Latin *circa*

cab *n* 1 a taxi. 2 the enclosed driver's compartment of a lorry, bus, or train. ▷ HISTORY from *cabriolet*

cabal (kab-**bal**) *n* 1 a small group of political plotters. 2 a secret plot or conspiracy. ▷ HISTORY French *cabale*

cabaret (**kab**-a-ray) *n* 1 a floor show of dancing and singing at a nightclub or restaurant. 2 a place providing such entertainment. ▷ HISTORY French: tavern

cabbage *n* 1 a vegetable with a large head of green or reddish-purple leaves. 2 *Informal* a person who is unable to move or think, as a result of brain damage: *he can only exist as a cabbage who must be cared for by his relatives*. ▷ HISTORY Norman French *caboche* head

cabbage tree *n NZ* a palm-like tree with a bare trunk and spiky leaves.

cabbage white *n* a large white butterfly whose larvae feed on cabbage leaves.

cabbie *or* **cabby** *n, pl* **-bies** *Informal* a taxi driver.

caber *n Scot* a heavy section of trimmed tree trunk tossed in competition at Highland games. ▷ HISTORY Gaelic *cabar* pole

cabin *n* 1 a room used as living quarters in a ship or boat. 2 a small simple dwelling: *a log cabin*. 3 the enclosed part of an aircraft in which the passengers or crew sit. ▷ HISTORY Late Latin *capanna* hut

cabin boy *n* a boy who waits on the officers and passengers of a ship.

cabin cruiser *n* a motorboat with a cabin.

cabinet *n* a piece of furniture containing shelves, cupboards, or drawers for storage or display: *a filing cabinet; a cocktail cabinet*. ▷ HISTORY Old French *cabine* cabin

Cabinet *n* a committee of senior government ministers or advisers to a president.

cabinet-maker *n* a person who makes fine furniture. ▶ **cabinet-making** *n*

cable *n* 1 a strong thick rope of twisted hemp or wire. 2 a bundle of wires covered with plastic or rubber that conducts electricity. 3 a telegram sent abroad by submarine cable or telephone line. 4 Also called: **cable stitch** a knitted design which resembles a twisted rope. ✧ *vb* **-bling, -bled** 5 to send (someone) a message by cable. ▷ HISTORY Late Latin *capulum* halter

cable car *n* a vehicle that is pulled up a steep slope by a moving cable.

cablegram *n* a more formal name for **cable** (sense 3).

cable television *n* a television service in which the subscriber's television is connected to a central receiver by cable.

caboodle *n* **the whole caboodle** *Informal* the whole lot. ▷ HISTORY origin unknown

caboose *n* 1 *US & Canad* a railway car at the rear of a train, used as quarters for the crew. 2 *Canad* a mobile building used as a cookhouse or bunkhouse for a work crew. ▷ HISTORY Dutch *cabūse*

cabriolet (kab-ree-oh-**lay**) *n* a small two-wheeled horse-drawn carriage with a folding hood. ▷ HISTORY French: a little skip; referring to the lightness of movement

cacao (kak-**kah**-oh) *n* a tropical American tree with seed pods (**cacao beans**) from which cocoa and chocolate are prepared. ▷ HISTORY Mexican Indian *cacauatl* cacao beans

cachalot *n* the sperm whale. ▷ HISTORY Portuguese *cachalote*

cache (**kash**) *n* a hidden store of weapons, provisions, or treasure. ▷ HISTORY French *cacher* to hide

cachet (**kash**-shay) *n* prestige or distinction: *a Mercedes carries a certain cachet*. ▷ HISTORY French

cachou *n* a lozenge eaten to sweeten the breath. ▷ HISTORY Malay *kāchu*

cack-handed *adj Informal* clumsy: *I open cans in a very cack-handed way*. ▷ HISTORY dialect *cack* excrement

cackle *vb* **-ling, -led** 1 to laugh shrilly. 2 (of a hen) to squawk with shrill broken notes. ✧ *n* 3 the sound of cackling. ▷ HISTORY probably imitative ▶ **cackling** *adj*

cacophony (kak-**koff**-on-ee) *n* harsh discordant sound: *a cacophony of barking*. ▷ HISTORY Greek *kakos* bad + *phōnē* sound ▶ **cacophonous** *adj*

cactoblastis (**kak**-toe-blah-stiss) *n* a type of moth; introduced into Australia to act as a biological control on the prickly pear.

cactus *n, pl* **-tuses** *or* **-ti** a thick fleshy desert plant with spines but no leaves. ▷ HISTORY Greek *kaktos* type of thistle

CAD *Computing* computer-aided design.

cad *n Old-fashioned, informal* a man who behaves dishonourably. ▷ HISTORY from *caddie* ▶ **caddish** *adj*

cadastral map *n Law, geog* an official large-scale map showing details of properties, boundaries, and ownership.

cadaver (kad-**dav**-ver) *n Med* a corpse. ▷ HISTORY Latin

cadaverous *adj* pale, thin, and haggard.

caddie *n* **1** a person who carries a golfer's clubs. ✧ *vb* **-dying, -died 2** to act as a caddie. ▷ **HISTORY** from *cadet*

caddis fly *n* an insect whose larva (the **caddis worm**) lives underwater in a protective case of silk, sand, and stones.

caddy[1] *n, pl* **-dies** *Chiefly Brit* a small container for tea. ▷ **HISTORY** Malay *kati*

caddy[2] *n, pl* **-dies**, *vb* **-dies, -dying, -died** same as **caddie**.

cadence (**kade**-enss) *n* **1** the rise and fall in the pitch of the voice. **2** the close of a musical phrase. ▷ **HISTORY** Latin *cadere* to fall

cadenza *n* a complex solo passage in a piece of music. ▷ **HISTORY** Italian

cadet *n* a young person training for the armed forces or the police. ▷ **HISTORY** French

cadge *vb* **cadging, cadged** *Informal* to get (something) from someone by taking advantage of his or her generosity. ▷ **HISTORY** origin unknown ▶ **cadger** *n*

cadi *n* a judge in a Muslim community. ▷ **HISTORY** Arabic *qādī* judge

cadmium *n Chem* bluish-white metallic element found in zinc ores and used in electroplating and alloys. Symbol: Cd. ▷ **HISTORY** Latin *cadmia* zinc ore

cadre (**kah**-der) *n* a small group of people selected and trained to form the core of a political organization or military unit. ▷ **HISTORY** Latin *quadrum* square

caecum *or US* **cecum** (**seek**-um) *n, pl* **-ca** (-ka) the pouch at the beginning of the large intestine. ▷ **HISTORY** short for Latin *intestinum caecum* blind intestine

Caenozoic *adj* same as **Cenozoic**.

Caerphilly *n* a creamy white mild-flavoured cheese.

Caesar (**seez**-ar) *n* **1** a Roman emperor. **2** any emperor or dictator. ▷ **HISTORY** after Gaius Julius *Caesar*, Roman general & statesman

Caesarean, Caesarian *or US* **Cesarean** (siz-**zair**-ee-an) *n* short for **Caesarean section**.

Caesarean section *n* surgical incision into the womb in order to deliver a baby. ▷ **HISTORY** from the belief that Julius Caesar was delivered in this way

caesium *or US* **cesium** *n Chem* a silvery-white metallic element used in photocells. Symbol: Cs. ▷ **HISTORY** Latin *caesius* bluish-grey

caesura (siz-**your**-ra) *n, pl* **-ras** *or* **-rae** (-ree) a pause in a line of verse. ▷ **HISTORY** Latin: a cutting

café *n* **1** a small or inexpensive restaurant that serves drinks and snacks or light meals. **2** *S African* a corner shop. ▷ **HISTORY** French

cafeteria *n* a self-service restaurant. ▷ **HISTORY** American Spanish: coffee shop

caffeine *n* a stimulant found in tea, coffee, and cocoa. ▷ **HISTORY** German *Kaffee* coffee

caftan *n* same as **kaftan**.

cage *n* **1** an enclosure made of bars or wires, for keeping birds or animals in. **2** the enclosed platform of a lift in a mine. ✧ *vb* **caging, caged 3** to confine in a cage. ▷ **HISTORY** Latin *cavea* enclosure ▶ **caged** *adj*

cagey *adj* **cagier, cagiest** *Informal* reluctant to go into details; wary: *he is cagey about what he paid for the business.* ▷ **HISTORY** origin unknown ▶ **cagily** *adv*

cagoule (kag-**gool**) *n Brit* a lightweight hooded waterproof jacket. ▷ **HISTORY** French

cahoots *pl n* **in cahoots** *Informal* conspiring together: *the loan sharks were in cahoots with the home-improvement companies.* ▷ **HISTORY** origin unknown

caiman *n, pl* **-mans** same as **cayman**.

cairn *n* a mound of stones erected as a memorial or marker. ▷ **HISTORY** Gaelic *carn*

cairngorm *n* a smoky yellow or brown quartz gemstone. ▷ **HISTORY** *Cairn Gorm* (blue cairn), mountain in Scotland

caisson (**kayss**-on) *n* a watertight chamber used to carry out construction work under water. ▷ **HISTORY** French

cajole *vb* **-joling, -joled** to persuade by flattery; coax: *he allowed himself to be cajoled into staying on.* ▷ **HISTORY** French *cajoler* ▶ **cajolery** *n*

cake *n* **1** a sweet food baked from a mixture of flour, sugar, eggs, etc. **2** a flat compact mass of something: *a cake of soap.* **3 have one's cake and eat it** to enjoy both of two incompatible alternatives. **4 piece of cake** *Informal* something that is easy to do. **5 sell like hot cakes** *Informal* to be sold very quickly: *commercial novels sell like hot cakes.* ✧ *vb* **caking, caked 6** to form into a hardened mass or crust: *there was blood caked an inch thick on the walls.* ▷ **HISTORY** Old Norse *kaka*

cal. calorie (small).

Cal. **1** Calorie (large). **2** California.

calabash *n* **1** a large round gourd that grows on a tropical American tree. **2** a bowl made from the dried hollow shell of a calabash. ▷ **HISTORY** obsolete French *calabasse*

calabrese (kal-lab-**bray**-zee) *n* a kind of green sprouting broccoli. ▷ **HISTORY** Italian: from Calabria (region of SW Italy)

calamine *n* a pink powder consisting chiefly of zinc oxide, used to make soothing skin lotions and ointments. ▷ **HISTORY** Medieval Latin *calamina*

calamitous *adj* resulting in or from disaster: *the country's calamitous economic decline.*

calamity *n, pl* **-ties** a disaster or misfortune. ▷ **HISTORY** Latin *calamitas*

calcareous (kal-**care**-ee-uss) *adj* of or containing calcium carbonate. ▷ **HISTORY** Latin *calx* lime

calciferol *n* a substance found in fish oils and used in the treatment of rickets. Also called: **vitamin D_2** ▷ **HISTORY** *calcif(erous + ergost)erol*, a substance in plants that is a source of vitamin D

calciferous *adj* producing salts of calcium, esp. calcium carbonate.

calcify *vb* **-fies, -fying, -fied** to harden by the depositing of calcium salts. ▷ **HISTORY** Latin *calx* lime ▶ **calcification** *n*

A B C D E F G H I J K L M N O P Q R S T U V W X Y Z

calcine *vb* **-cining, -cined** to oxidize (a substance) by heating. ▷ **HISTORY** Medieval Latin *calcinare* to heat ▶ **calcination** *n*

calcite *n* a colourless or white form of calcium carbonate.

calcium *n Chem* a soft silvery-white metallic element found in bones, teeth, limestone, and chalk. Symbol: Ca. ▷ **HISTORY** Latin *calx* lime

calcium carbonate *n* a white crystalline salt found in limestone, chalk, and pearl, used to make cement.

calcium chloride *n Chem* a white deliquescent salt which occurs naturally in seawater and is used in de-icing roads and as a drying agent.

calcium hydroxide *n* a white crystalline alkali used to make mortar and soften water.

calcium oxide *n* same as **quicklime**.

calculable *adj* able to be computed or estimated.

calculate *vb* **-lating, -lated 1** to solve or find out by a mathematical procedure or by reasoning. **2** to aim to have a particular effect: *this ad campaign is calculated to offend.*

> **WORD HISTORY**
> 'Calculate' comes from the Latin word *calculare* meaning 'to count using small stones', from *calculus*, meaning a 'stone' or 'pebble'. The Romans used pebbles to count with.

calculated *adj* **1** undertaken after considering the likelihood of success: *a calculated gamble.* **2** carefully planned: *a calculated and callous murder.*

calculating *adj* selfishly scheming.

calculation *n* **1** the act or result of calculating. **2** selfish scheming: *there was an element of calculation in her insistence on arriving after dark.*

calculator *n* a small electronic device for doing mathematical calculations.

calculus *n* **1** the branch of mathematics dealing with infinitesimal changes to a variable number or quantity. **2** (*pl* **-li**) *Pathol* same as **stone** (sense 7). ▷ **HISTORY** Latin: pebble

caldera (kal-**dare**-ruh) *n Geol* a large basin-shaped crater at the top of a volcano, formed by the collapse of the cone. ▷ **HISTORY** Spanish *caldera,* lit.: CAULDRON

Caledonian *adj* Scottish. ▷ **HISTORY** from *Caledonia,* the Roman name for Scotland

calendar *n* **1** a chart showing a year divided up into months, weeks, and days. **2** a system for determining the beginning, length, and divisions of years: *the Jewish calendar.* **3** a schedule of events or appointments: *concerts were an important part of the social calendar of the Venetian nobility.*

> **WORD HISTORY**
> This word comes from medieval Latin *kalendārium*, meaning 'account book'. The word 'kalendarium' itself comes from Latin *kalendae*, the 'calends', the first day of the month in the Roman calendar and the day on which interest on debts was due.

calender *n* **1** a machine in which paper or cloth is smoothed by passing it between rollers. ✧ *vb* **2** to smooth in such a machine. ▷ **HISTORY** French *calandre*

calends *or* **kalends** *pl n* (in the ancient Roman calendar) the first day of each month. ▷ **HISTORY** Latin *kalendae*

calendula *n* a plant with orange-and-yellow rayed flowers. ▷ **HISTORY** Medieval Latin

calf[1] *n, pl* **calves** a young cow, bull, elephant, whale, or seal. ▷ **HISTORY** Old English *cealf*

calf[2] *n, pl* **calves** the back of the leg between the ankle and the knee. ▷ **HISTORY** Old Norse *kālfi*

calf love *n* adolescent infatuation.

calibrate *vb* **-brating, -brated** to mark the scale or check the accuracy of (a measuring instrument). ▶ **calibration** *n*

calibre *or US* **caliber** (**kal**-lib-ber) *n* **1** a person's ability or worth: *a poet of Wordsworth's calibre.* **2** the diameter of the bore of a gun or of a shell or bullet. ▷ **HISTORY** Arabic *qālib* shoemaker's last, mould

calico *n* a white or unbleached cotton fabric. ▷ **HISTORY** *Calicut,* town in India

californium *n Chem* a radioactive metallic element produced artificially. Symbol: Cf. ▷ **HISTORY** after the University of *California,* where it was discovered

caliper *n US* same as **calliper**.

caliph *n Islam* the title of the successors of Mohammed as rulers of the Islamic world. ▷ **HISTORY** Arabic *khalīfa* successor

caliphate *n* the office, jurisdiction, or reign of a caliph.

call *vb* **1** to name: *a town called Eyemouth.* **2** to describe (someone or something) as being: *they called him a Hitler.* **3** to speak loudly so as to attract attention. **4** to telephone: *he left a message for Lynch to call him.* **5** to summon: *a doctor must be called immediately.* **6** to pay someone a visit: *the social worker called and she didn't answer the door.* **7** to arrange: *the meeting was called for the lunch hour.* **8 call someone's bluff** See **bluff**[1] (sense 3). ✧ *n* **9** a cry or shout. **10** the cry made by a bird or animal. **11** a communication by telephone. **12** a short visit: *I paid a call on an old friend.* **13** a summons or invitation: *the police and fire brigade continued to respond to calls.* **14** need, demand, or desire: *a call for economic sanctions.* **15** allure or fascination: *the call of the open road.* **16 on call** available when summoned: *there's a doctor on call in town.* ✧ See also **call for, call in**, etc. ▷ **HISTORY** Old English *ceallian* ▶ **caller** *n*

call box *n* a soundproof enclosure for a public telephone.

call centre *n Brit, Austral & NZ* an office where staff carry out an organization's telephone transactions.

call for *vb* **1** to require: *appendicitis calls for removal of the appendix.* **2** to come and fetch.

call girl *n* a prostitute with whom appointments are made by telephone.

calligraphy *n* beautiful handwriting. ▷ HISTORY Greek *kallos* beauty + -GRAPHY ▶ **calligrapher** *n* ▶ **calligraphic** *adj*

call in *vb* **1** to summon to one's assistance: *she called in a contractor to make the necessary repairs.* **2** to pay a brief visit. **3** to demand payment of (a loan): *if the share price continues to drop, some banks may call in their loans.*

calling *n* **1** a strong urge to follow a particular profession or occupation, esp. a caring one. **2** a profession or occupation, esp. a caring one.

Calliope *n Greek myth* the Muse of epic poetry.

calliper *or US* **caliper** *n* **1** a metal splint for supporting the leg. **2** a measuring instrument consisting of two steel legs hinged together. ▷ HISTORY variant of *calibre*

callisthenics *or* **calisthenics** *n* light exercises designed to promote general fitness. ▷ HISTORY Greek *kalli-* beautiful + *sthenos* strength ▶ **callisthenic** *or* **calisthenic** *adj*

call off *vb* **1** to cancel or abandon: *the strike has now been called off.* **2** to order (a dog or a person) to stop attacking someone.

callous *adj* showing no concern for other people's feelings. ▷ HISTORY Latin *callosus* ▶ **callously** *adv* ▶ **callousness** *n*

calloused *adj* covered in calluses.

callow *adj* young and inexperienced: *a callow youth.* ▷ HISTORY Old English *calu*

call up *vb* **1** to summon for active military service. **2** to cause one to remember. ✧ *n* **call-up 3** a general order to report for military service.

callus *n, pl* **-luses** an area of hard or thickened skin on the hand or foot. ▷ HISTORY Latin *callum* hardened skin

calm *adj* **1** not showing or not feeling agitation or excitement. **2** not ruffled by the wind: *a flat calm sea.* **3** (of weather) windless. ✧ *n* **4** a peaceful state. ✧ *vb* **5** (often foll. by *down*) to make or become calm. ▷ HISTORY Late Latin *cauma* heat, hence a rest during the heat of the day ▶ **calmly** *adv* ▶ **calmness** *n*

Calor Gas *n Trademark, Brit* butane gas liquefied under pressure in portable containers for domestic use.

caloric (kal-**or**-ik) *adj* of heat or calories.

calorie *n* **1** a unit of measure for the energy value of food. **2** Also: **small calorie** the quantity of heat required to raise the temperature of 1 gram of water by 1°C. ▷ HISTORY Latin *calor* heat

Calorie *n* **1** Also: **large calorie** a unit of heat, equal to one thousand calories. **2** the amount of a food capable of producing one calorie of energy.

calorific *adj* of calories or heat.

calumniate *vb* **-ating, -ated** to make false or malicious statements about (someone).

calumny *n, pl* **-nies** a false or malicious statement; slander. ▷ HISTORY Latin *calumnia* slander

Calvary *n Christianity* the place just outside the walls of Jerusalem where Jesus Christ was crucified. ▷ HISTORY Latin *calvaria* skull

calve *vb* **calving, calved** to give birth to a calf.

calves *n* the plural of **calf**.

Calvinism *n* the theological system of Calvin, the 16th-century French theologian, stressing predestination and salvation solely by God's grace. ▶ **Calvinist** *n, adj* ▶ **Calvinistic** *adj*

calypso *n, pl* **-sos** a West Indian song with improvised topical lyrics. ▷ HISTORY probably from *Calypso*, sea nymph in Greek mythology

calyx (**kale**-ix) *n, pl* **calyxes** *or* **calyces** (**kal**-iss-seez) the outer leaves that protect the developing bud of a flower. ▷ HISTORY Latin: shell, husk

cam *n* a part of an engine that converts a circular motion into a to-and-fro motion. ▷ HISTORY Dutch *kam* comb

camaraderie *n* familiarity and trust between friends. ▷ HISTORY French

camber *n* a slight upward curve to the centre of a road surface. ▷ HISTORY Latin *camurus* curved

Cambodian *adj* **1** of Cambodia. ✧ *n* **2** a person from Cambodia.

Cambrian *adj Geol* of the period of geological time about 600 million years ago.

cambric *n* a fine white linen fabric. ▷ HISTORY Flemish *Kamerijk* Cambrai

camcorder *n* a combined portable video camera and recorder.

came *vb* the past tense of **come**.

camel *n* either of two humped mammals, the dromedary and Bactrian camel, that can survive long periods without food or water in desert regions. ▷ HISTORY Greek *kamēlos*

camellia (kam-**meal**-ya) *n* an ornamental shrub with glossy leaves and white, pink, or red flowers. ▷ HISTORY after G. J. *Kamel*, Jesuit missionary

Camembert (**kam**-mem-bare) *n* a soft creamy cheese. ▷ HISTORY *Camembert*, village in Normandy

cameo *n, pl* **cameos 1** a brooch or ring with a profile head carved in relief. **2** a small but important part in a film or play played by a well-known actor or actress. ▷ HISTORY Italian *cammeo*

camera *n* **1** a piece of equipment used for taking photographs or pictures for television or cinema. **2 in camera** in private. ▷ HISTORY Greek *kamara* vault

camera angle *n Films, photog* the position of the camera in relation to the subject being filmed or photographed.

camera distance *n Films, photog* the distance of the camera from the subject being filmed or photographed.

cameraman *n, pl* **-men** a man who operates a camera for television or cinema.

camera obscura *n* a darkened room with an opening through which images of outside objects are projected onto a flat surface. ▷ HISTORY New Latin

camiknickers *pl n Brit* a woman's undergarment consisting of knickers attached to a camisole top.

camisole *n* a woman's bodice-like garment with shoulder straps. ▷ HISTORY French

camomile *or* **chamomile** (**kam**-mo-mile) *n* a sweet-smelling plant used to make herbal tea. ▷ **HISTORY** Greek *khamaimēlon* earth-apple (referring to the scent of the flowers)

camouflage (**kam**-moo-flahzh) *n* **1** the use of natural surroundings or artificial aids to conceal or disguise something. ✧ *vb* **-flaging, -flaged 2** to conceal by camouflage. ▷ **HISTORY** French

camp[1] *n* **1** a place where people stay in tents. **2** a collection of huts and other buildings used as temporary lodgings for military troops or for prisoners of war. **3** a group that supports a particular doctrine: *the socialist camp.* ✧ *vb* **4** to stay in a camp. ▷ **HISTORY** Latin *campus* field ▶ **camper** *n* ▶ **camping** *n*

camp[2] *Informal* ✧ *adj* **1** effeminate or homosexual. **2** consciously artificial, vulgar, or affected. ✧ *vb* **3 camp it up** to behave in a camp manner. ▷ **HISTORY** origin unknown

campaign *n* **1** a series of coordinated activities designed to achieve a goal. **2** *Mil* a number of operations aimed at achieving a single objective. ✧ *vb* **3** to take part in a campaign: *he paid tribute to all those who'd campaigned for his release.* ▷ **HISTORY** Latin *campus* field ▶ **campaigner** *n*

campanile (camp-an-**neel**-lee) *n* a bell tower, usually one not attached to another building. ▷ **HISTORY** Italian

campanology *n* the art of ringing bells. ▷ **HISTORY** Late Latin *campana* bell ▶ **campanologist** *n*

campanula *n* a plant with blue or white bell-shaped flowers. ▷ **HISTORY** New Latin: a little bell

camp follower *n* **1** a person who supports a particular group or organization without being a member of it. **2** a civilian who unofficially provides services to military personnel.

camphor *n* a sweet-smelling crystalline substance obtained from the wood of the **camphor tree**, which is used medicinally and in mothballs. ▷ **HISTORY** Arabic *kāfūr*

camphorated *adj* impregnated with camphor.

campion *n* a red, pink, or white European wild flower. ▷ **HISTORY** origin unknown

camp oven *n Austral & NZ* a heavy metal pot or box with a lid, used for baking over an open fire.

campus *n, pl* **-puses** the grounds and buildings of a university or college. ▷ **HISTORY** Latin: field

camshaft *n* a part of an engine consisting of a rod to which cams are attached.

can[1] *vb, past* **could 1** be able to: *make sure he can breathe easily.* **2** be allowed to: *you can swim in the large pool.* ▷ **HISTORY** Old English *cunnan*

> ☑ **WORD TIP**
> See at **may.**

can[2] *n* **1** a metal container, usually sealed, for food or liquids. ✧ *vb* **canning, canned 2** to put (something) into a can. ▷ **HISTORY** Old English *canne*

Canada goose *n* a greyish-brown North American goose with a black neck and head.

Canada jay *n* a grey jay of northern N America, notorious for stealing.

Canadian *adj* **1** of Canada. ✧ *n* **2** a person from Canada.

Canadian Shield *n* the wide area of Precambrian rock extending over most of central and E Canada: rich in minerals.

canal *n* **1** an artificial waterway constructed for navigation or irrigation. **2** a passage or duct in a person's body: *the alimentary canal.* ▷ **HISTORY** Latin *canna* reed

canalize *or* **-lise** *vb* **-lizing, -lized** *or* **-lising, -lised 1** to give direction to (a feeling or activity). **2** to convert into a canal. ▶ **canalization** *or* **-lisation** *n*

canapé (**kan**-nap-pay) *n* a small piece of bread or toast spread with a savoury topping. ▷ **HISTORY** French: sofa

canard *n* a false report. ▷ **HISTORY** French: a duck

canary *n, pl* **-naries** a small yellow songbird often kept as a pet.

canasta *n* a card game like rummy, played with two packs of cards. ▷ **HISTORY** Spanish: basket (because two packs, or a basketful, of cards are required)

cancan *n* a lively high-kicking dance performed by a female group. ▷ **HISTORY** French

cancel *vb* **-celling, -celled** *or US* **-celing, -celed 1** to stop (something that has been arranged) from taking place. **2** to mark (a cheque or stamp) with an official stamp to prevent further use. **3** *Maths* to eliminate numbers, quantities, or terms because they occur in both the numerator and denominator of a fraction or on opposite sides of an equation. **4 cancel out** to make ineffective by having the opposite effect: *economic vulnerability cancels out any possible political gain.* ▷ **HISTORY** Late Latin *cancellare* to strike out, make like a lattice ▶ **cancellation** *n*

cancer *n* **1** a serious disease resulting from a malignant growth or tumour, caused by abnormal and uncontrolled cell division. **2** a malignant growth or tumour. **3** an evil influence that spreads dangerously: *their country would remain a cancer of instability.* ▷ **HISTORY** Latin: crab, creeping tumour ▶ **cancerous** *adj*

Cancer *n* **1** *Astrol* the fourth sign of the zodiac; the Crab. **2 tropic of Cancer** See **tropic** (sense 1). ▷ **HISTORY** Latin

candela (kan-**dee**-la) *n* the SI unit of luminous intensity (the amount of light a source gives off in a given direction). ▷ **HISTORY** Latin: candle

candelabrum *or* **candelabra** *n, pl* **-bra, -brums** *or* **-bras** a large branched holder for candles or overhead lights. ▷ **HISTORY** Latin *candela* candle

candid *adj* honest and straightforward in speech or behaviour. ▷ **HISTORY** Latin *candere* to be white ▶ **candidly** *adv*

candidate *n* **1** a person seeking a job or position. **2** a person taking an examination. **3** a person or thing regarded as suitable or likely for a particular fate or position: *someone who smokes, drinks, or eats*

too much is a candidate for heart disease.
▶ **candidacy** *or* **candidature** *n*

WORD HISTORY
Candidatus in Latin means 'white-robed'. In ancient Rome, candidates for public office wore white togas.

candied *adj* coated with or cooked in sugar: *candied peel.*
candle *n* **1** a stick or block of wax or tallow surrounding a wick, which is burned to produce light. **2 burn the candle at both ends** to exhaust oneself by doing too much. ▷ **HISTORY** Latin *candela*
Candlemas *n Christianity* February 2, the Feast of the Purification of the Virgin Mary.
candlepower *n* the luminous intensity of a source of light: now expressed in candelas.
candlestick *or* **candleholder** *n* a holder for a candle.
candlewick *n* cotton with a tufted pattern, used to make bedspreads and dressing gowns.
candour *or US* **candor** *n* honesty and straightforwardness of speech or behaviour. ▷ **HISTORY** Latin *candor*
candy *n, pl* **-dies** *Chiefly US & Canad* a sweet or sweets. ▷ **HISTORY** Arabic *qand* cane sugar
candyfloss *n Brit* a light fluffy mass of spun sugar, held on a stick.
candy-striped *adj* having narrow coloured stripes on a white background.
candytuft *n* a garden plant with clusters of white, pink, or purple flowers.
cane *n* **1** the long flexible stems of the bamboo or any similar plant. **2** strips of such stems, woven to make wickerwork. **3** a bamboo stem tied to a garden plant to support it. **4** a flexible rod used to beat someone. **5** a slender walking stick. ✧ *vb* **caning, caned 6** to beat with a cane. ▷ **HISTORY** Greek *kanna*
cane sugar *n* the sugar that is obtained from sugar cane.
cane toad *n Biol* a large toad native to Central and South America but introduced into other countries to control pests in sugar-cane plantations.
canine (**kay**-nine) *adj* **1** of or like a dog. ✧ *n* **2** a sharp-pointed tooth between the incisors and the molars. ▷ **HISTORY** Latin *canis* dog
canister *n* a metal container for dry food. ▷ **HISTORY** Latin *canistrum* basket woven from reeds
canker *n* **1** an ulceration or ulcerous disease. **2** something evil that spreads and corrupts. ▷ **HISTORY** Latin *cancer* cancerous sore
cannabis *n* a drug obtained from the dried leaves and flowers of the hemp plant. ▷ **HISTORY** Greek *kannabis*
canned *adj* **1** preserved in a can. **2** *Informal* recorded in advance: *canned carols.*
cannelloni *or* **canneloni** *pl n* tubular pieces of pasta filled with meat or cheese. ▷ **HISTORY** Italian
cannery *n, pl* **-neries** a place where foods are canned.
cannibal *n* **1** a person who eats human flesh. **2** an animal that eats the flesh of other animals of its kind. ▷ **HISTORY** Spanish *Canibales* natives of Cuba and Haiti ▶ **cannibalism** *n*
cannibalize *or* **-ise** *vb* **-izing, -ized** *or* **-ising, -ised** to use parts from (one machine or vehicle) to repair another.
cannon *n, pl* **-nons** *or* **-non 1** a large gun consisting of a metal tube mounted on a carriage, formerly used in battles. **2** an automatic aircraft gun. **3** *Billiards* a shot in which the cue ball strikes two balls successively. ✧ *vb* **4 cannon into** to collide with. ▷ **HISTORY** Italian *canna* tube
cannonade *n* continuous heavy gunfire.
cannonball *n* a heavy metal ball fired from a cannon.
cannon fodder *n* men regarded as expendable in war.
cannot *vb* can not.
canny *adj* **-nier, -niest** shrewd or cautious. ▷ **HISTORY** from *can* (in the sense: to know how) ▶ **cannily** *adv*
canoe *n* a light narrow open boat, propelled by one or more paddles. ▷ **HISTORY** Carib ▶ **canoeist** *n*
canoeing *n* the sport of rowing or racing in a canoe.
canon[1] *n* a priest serving in a cathedral. ▷ **HISTORY** Late Latin *canonicus* person living under a rule
canon[2] *n* **1** *Christianity* a Church decree regulating morals or religious practices. **2** a general rule or standard: *the Marx-Engels canon.* **3** a list of the works of an author that are accepted as authentic: *the Yeats canon.* **4** a piece of music in which a melody in one part is taken up in one or more other parts successively. ▷ **HISTORY** Greek *kanōn* rule
canonical *adj* **1** conforming with canon law. **2** included in a canon of writings.
canonical hour *n RC Church* one of the seven prayer times appointed for each day.
canonicals *pl n* the official clothes worn by clergy when taking services.
canonize *or* **-ise** *vb* **-izing, -ized** *or* **-ising, -ised** *RC Church* to declare (a dead person) to be a saint. ▶ **canonization** *or* **-isation** *n*
canon law *n* the body of laws of a Christian Church.
canoodle *vb* **-dling, -dled** *Slang* to kiss and cuddle. ▷ **HISTORY** origin unknown
canopied *adj* covered with a canopy: *canopied niches.*
canopy *n, pl* **-pies 1** an ornamental awning above a bed or throne. **2** a rooflike covering over an altar, niche, or door. **3** any large or wide covering: *the thick forest canopy.* **4** the part of a parachute that opens out. **5** the transparent hood of an aircraft cockpit. ▷ **HISTORY** Greek *kōnōpeion* bed with a mosquito net
cant[1] *n* **1** insincere talk concerning religion or morals. **2** specialized vocabulary of a particular

A B C D E F G H I J K L M N O P Q R S T U V W X Y Z

group, such as thieves or lawyers. ✧ *vb* **3** to use cant: *canting hypocrites.* ▷ **HISTORY** probably from Latin *cantare* to sing

cant² *n* **1** a tilted position. ✧ *vb* **2** to tilt or overturn: *the engine was canted to one side.* ▷ **HISTORY** perhaps from Latin *canthus* iron hoop round a wheel

can't *vb* can not.

cantabile (kan-**tah**-bill-lay) *adv Music* flowing and melodious. ▷ **HISTORY** Italian

cantaloupe *or* **cantaloup** *n Brit* a kind of melon with sweet-tasting orange flesh. ▷ **HISTORY** *Cantaluppi,* near Rome, where first cultivated in Europe

cantankerous *adj* quarrelsome or bad-tempered. ▷ **HISTORY** origin unknown

cantata (kan-**tah**-ta) *n* a musical setting of a text, consisting of arias, duets, and choruses. ▷ **HISTORY** Italian

canteen *n* **1** a restaurant attached to a workplace or school. **2** a box containing a set of cutlery. ▷ **HISTORY** Italian *cantina* wine cellar

canter *n* **1** a gait of horses that is faster than a trot but slower than a gallop. ✧ *vb* **2** (of a horse) to move at a canter. ▷ **HISTORY** short for *Canterbury trot,* the pace at which pilgrims rode to Canterbury

canticle *n* a short hymn with words from the Bible. ▷ **HISTORY** Latin *canticulum*

cantilever *n* a beam or girder fixed at one end only. ▷ **HISTORY** origin unknown

cantilever bridge *n* a bridge made of two cantilevers which meet in the middle.

canto (**kan**-toe) *n, pl* **-tos** a main division of a long poem. ▷ **HISTORY** Italian: song

canton *n* a political division of a country, such as Switzerland. ▷ **HISTORY** Old French: corner

Cantonese *adj* **1** of Canton, a port in SE China. ✧ *n* **2** (*pl* **-nese**) a person from Canton. **3** the Chinese dialect of Canton.

cantonment (kan-**toon**-ment) *n* a permanent military camp in British India. ▷ **HISTORY** Old French *canton* corner

cantor *n Judaism* a man employed to lead synagogue services. ▷ **HISTORY** Latin: singer

canvas *n* **1** a heavy cloth of cotton, hemp, or jute, used to make tents and sails and for painting on in oils. **2** an oil painting done on canvas. **3 under canvas** in a tent: *sleeping under canvas.* ▷ **HISTORY** Latin *cannabis* hemp

canvass *vb* **1** to try to persuade (people) to vote for a particular candidate or party in an election. **2** to find out the opinions of (people) by conducting a survey. ✧ *n* **3** the activity of canvassing. ▷ **HISTORY** probably from obsolete sense of *canvas* (to toss someone in a canvas sheet, hence, to criticize) ▶ **canvasser** *n* ▶ **canvassing** *n*

canyon *n* a deep narrow steep-sided valley. ▷ **HISTORY** Spanish *cañon*

caoutchouc (**cow**-chook) *n* same as **rubber¹** (sense 1). ▷ **HISTORY** from S American Indian

cap *n* **1** a soft close-fitting covering for the head. **2** *Sport* a cap given to someone selected for a national team. **3** a small flat lid: *petrol cap.* **4** a small amount of explosive enclosed in paper and used in a toy gun. **5** a contraceptive device placed over the mouth of the womb. **6** an upper financial limit. **7 cap in hand** humbly. ✧ *vb* **capping, capped 8** to cover or top with something: *a thick cover of snow capped the cars.* **9** *Sport* to select (a player) for a national team: *Australia's most capped player.* **10** to impose an upper level on (a tax): *charge capping.* **11** *Informal* to outdo or excel: *capping anecdote with anecdote.* ▷ **HISTORY** Late Latin *cappa* hood

CAP (in the EU) Common Agricultural Policy.

cap. capital.

capability *n, pl* **-ties** the ability or skill to do something.

capable *adj* **1** having the ability or skill to do something: *a side capable of winning the championship.* **2** competent and efficient: *capable high achievers.* ▷ **HISTORY** Latin *capere* to take ▶ **capably** *adv*

capacious *adj* having a large capacity or area. ▷ **HISTORY** Latin *capere* to take

capacitance *n Physics* **1** the ability of a capacitor to store electrical charge. **2** a measure of this.

capacitor *n Physics* a device for storing a charge of electricity.

capacity *n, pl* **-ties 1** the ability to contain, absorb, or hold something. **2** the maximum amount something can contain or absorb: *filled to capacity.* **3** the ability to do something: *his capacity to elicit great loyalty.* **4** a position or function: *acting in an official capacity.* **5** the maximum output of which an industry or factory is capable: *the refinery had a capacity of three hundred thousand barrels a day.* **6** *Physics* same as **capacitance.** ✧ *adj* **7** of the maximum amount or number possible: *a capacity crowd.* ▷ **HISTORY** Latin *capere* to take

caparisoned (kap-**par**-riss-sond) *adj* (esp. of a horse) magnificently decorated or dressed. ▷ **HISTORY** Old Spanish *caparazón* saddlecloth

cape¹ *n* a short sleeveless cloak. ▷ **HISTORY** Late Latin *cappa*

cape² *n* a large piece of land that juts out into the sea. ▷ **HISTORY** Latin *caput* head

Cape *n* **the Cape 1** the Cape of Good Hope. **2** the SW region of South Africa's Cape Province.

caper *n* **1** a high-spirited escapade. ✧ *vb* **2** to skip about light-heartedly. ▷ **HISTORY** probably from CAPRIOLE

capercaillie *or* **capercailzie** (kap-per-**kale**-yee) *n* a large black European woodland grouse. ▷ **HISTORY** Scottish Gaelic *capull coille* horse of the woods

capers *pl n* the pickled flower buds of a Mediterranean shrub, used in making sauces. ▷ **HISTORY** Greek *kapparis* caper plant

capillarity *n Physics* a phenomenon caused by surface tension that results in the surface of a liquid rising or falling in contact with a solid.

capillary (kap-**pill**-a-ree) *n, pl* **-laries 1** *Anat* one of the very fine blood vessels linking the arteries and the veins. ✧ *adj* **2** (of a tube) having a fine bore. **3** *Anat* of the capillaries. ▷ **HISTORY** Latin *capillus* hair

capital[1] *n* **1** the chief city of a country, where the government meets. **2** the total wealth owned or used in business by an individual or group. **3** wealth used to produce more wealth by investment. **4 make capital out of** to gain advantage from: *to make political capital out of the hostage situation.* **5** a capital letter. ✧ *adj* **6** *Law* involving or punishable by death: *a capital offence.* **7** denoting the large letter used as the initial letter in a sentence, personal name, or place name. **8** *Brit, Austral & NZ old-fashioned* excellent or first-rate: *a capital dinner.* ▷ HISTORY Latin *caput* head

capital[2] *n* the top part of a column or pillar. ▷ HISTORY Old French *capitel*, from Latin *caput* head

capital gain *n* profit from the sale of an asset.

capital goods *pl n Econ* goods that are themselves utilized in the production of other goods.

capital-intensive *adj Econ, business* requiring large capital investments as opposed to involving a large labour force. Compare **labour-intensive**.

capitalism *n* an economic system based on the private ownership of industry.

capitalist *adj* **1** based on or supporting capitalism: *capitalist countries.* ✧ *n* **2** a supporter of capitalism. **3** a person who owns a business. ▸ **capitalistic** *adj*

capitalize *or* **-ise** *vb* **-izing, -ized** *or* **-ising, -ised** **1 capitalize on** to take advantage of: *to capitalize on the available opportunities.* **2** to write or print (words) in capital letters. **3** to convert (debt or earnings) into capital stock. ▸ **capitalization** *or* **-isation** *n*

capital levy *n* a tax on capital or property as contrasted with a tax on income.

capital punishment *n Law* the punishment of death for committing certain crimes; the death penalty.

capital stock *n* **1** the value of the total shares that a company can issue. **2** the total capital existing in an economy at a particular time.

capitation *n* a tax of a fixed amount per person. ▷ HISTORY Latin *caput* head

capitulate *vb* **-lating, -lated** to surrender under agreed conditions. ▷ HISTORY Medieval Latin *capitulare* to draw up under headings ▸ **capitulation** *n*

capo *n, pl* **-pos** a device fitted across the strings of a guitar or similar instrument so as to raise the pitch. ▷ HISTORY Italian *capo tasto* head stop

capon (**kay**-pon) *n* a castrated cock fowl fattened for eating. ▷ HISTORY Latin *capo*

cappuccino (kap-poo-**cheen**-oh) *n, pl* **-nos** coffee with steamed milk, usually sprinkled with powdered chocolate. ▷ HISTORY Italian

caprice (kap-**reess**) *n* **1** a sudden change of attitude or behaviour. **2** a tendency to have such changes. ▷ HISTORY Italian *capriccio* a shiver, caprice

capricious *adj* having a tendency to sudden unpredictable changes of attitude or behaviour. ▸ **capriciously** *adv*

Capricorn *n* **1** *Astrol* the tenth sign of the zodiac; the Goat. **2 tropic of Capricorn** See **tropic** (sense 1). ▷ HISTORY Latin *caper* goat + *cornu* horn

caps. capital letters.

capsicum *n* a kind of pepper used as a vegetable or ground to produce a spice. ▷ HISTORY Latin *capsa* box

capsize *vb* **-sizing, -sized** (of a boat) to overturn accidentally. ▷ HISTORY origin unknown

capstan *n* a vertical rotating cylinder round which a ship's rope or cable is wound. ▷ HISTORY Old Provençal *cabestan*

capsule *n* **1** a soluble gelatine case containing a dose of medicine. **2** *Bot* a plant's seed case that opens when ripe. **3** *Anat* a membrane or sac surrounding an organ or part. **4** See **space capsule**. ✧ *adj* **5** very concise: *capsule courses.* ▷ HISTORY Latin *capsa* box

Capt. Captain.

captain *n* **1** the person in charge of a ship, boat, or civil aircraft. **2** a middle-ranking naval officer. **3** a junior officer in the army. **4** the leader of a team or group. ✧ *vb* **5** to be captain of. ▷ HISTORY Latin *caput* head ▸ **captaincy** *n*

caption *n* **1** a title, brief explanation, or comment accompanying a picture. ✧ *vb* **2** to provide with a caption. ▷ HISTORY Latin *captio* a seizing

captious *adj* tending to make trivial criticisms. ▷ HISTORY Latin *captio* a seizing

captivate *vb* **-vating, -vated** to attract and hold the attention of; enchant. ▷ HISTORY Latin *captivus* captive ▸ **captivating** *adj*

captive *n* **1** a person who is kept in confinement. ✧ *adj* **2** kept in confinement. **3** (of an audience) unable to leave. ▷ HISTORY Latin *captivus*

captivity *n* the state of being kept in confinement.

captor *n* a person who captures a person or animal.

capture *vb* **-turing, -tured 1** to take by force. **2** to succeed in representing (something elusive) in words, pictures, or music: *today's newspapers capture the mood of the nation.* **3** *Physics* (of an atomic nucleus) to acquire (an additional particle). ✧ *n* **4** the act of capturing or the state of being captured. ▷ HISTORY Latin *capere* to take

capuchin (**kap**-yew-chin) *n* a S American monkey with a cowl of thick hair on the top of its head. ▷ HISTORY Italian *cappuccio* hood

Capuchin *n* **1** a friar belonging to a branch of the Franciscan Order founded in 1525. ✧ *adj* **2** of this order. ▷ HISTORY Italian *cappuccio* hood

capybara *n* the largest living rodent, found in S America.

car *n* **1** a motorized road vehicle designed to carry a small number of people. **2** the passenger compartment of a cable car, airship, lift, or balloon. **3** *US & Canad* a railway. ▷ HISTORY Latin *carra*, *carrum* two-wheeled wagon

caracal *n* a lynx with reddish fur, which inhabits deserts of N Africa and S Asia. ▷ HISTORY Turkish *kara kūlāk* black ear

A B C D E F G H I J K L M N O P Q R S T U V W X Y Z

carafe (kar-**raff**) *n* a wide-mouthed bottle for water or wine. ▷ **HISTORY** Arabic *gharrāfah* vessel
carambola *n* a yellow edible star-shaped fruit that grows on a Brazilian tree. ▷ **HISTORY** Spanish
caramel *n* **1** a chewy sweet made from sugar and milk. **2** burnt sugar, used for colouring and flavouring food. ▷ **HISTORY** French
caramelize *or* **-ise** *vb* **-izing, -ized** *or* **-ising, -ised** to turn into caramel.
carapace *n* the thick hard upper shell of tortoises and crustaceans. ▷ **HISTORY** Spanish *carapacho*
carat *n* **1** a unit of weight of precious stones, equal to 0.20 grams. **2** a measure of the purity of gold in an alloy, expressed as the number of parts of gold in 24 parts of the alloy. ▷ **HISTORY** Arabic *qīrāt* weight of four grains
caravan *n* **1** a large enclosed vehicle designed to be pulled by a car or horse and equipped to be lived in. **2** (in some Eastern countries) a company of traders or other travellers journeying together. ▷ **HISTORY** Persian *kārwān*
caravanserai *n* (in some Eastern countries, esp. formerly) a large inn enclosing a courtyard, providing accommodation for caravans. ▷ **HISTORY** Persian *kārwānsarāī* caravan inn
caraway *n* a Eurasian plant with seeds that are used as a spice in cooking. ▷ **HISTORY** Arabic *karawyā*
carbide *n Chem* a compound of carbon with a metal.
carbine *n* a type of light rifle. ▷ **HISTORY** French *carabine*
carbohydrate *n* any of a large group of energy-producing compounds, including sugars and starches, that contain carbon, hydrogen, and oxygen.
carbolic acid *n* a disinfectant derived from coal tar.
carbon *n* **1** a nonmetallic element occurring in three forms, charcoal, graphite, and diamond, and present in all organic compounds. Symbol: C. **2** short for **carbon paper, carbon copy**. ▷ **HISTORY** Latin *carbo* charcoal
carbonaceous *adj* of, resembling, or containing carbon.
carbonate *n* a salt or ester of carbonic acid.
carbonated *adj* (of a drink) containing carbon dioxide; fizzy.
carbon black *n* powdered carbon produced by partial burning of natural gas or petroleum, used in pigments and ink.
carbon copy *n* **1** a duplicate obtained by using carbon paper. **2** *Informal* a person or thing that is identical or very similar to another.
carbon cycle *n* **1** *Biol, environmental science* the circulation of carbon between living organisms and their surroundings. Carbon dioxide from the atmosphere is synthesized by plants into plant tissue, which is ingested and metabolized by animals and converted back to carbon dioxide during respiration and decay. **2** *Physics* four thermonuclear reactions believed to be the source of energy in many stars. Carbon nuclei function as catalysts in the fusion of protons to form helium nuclei.
carbon dating *n* a technique for finding the age of organic materials, such as wood, based on their content of radioactive carbon.
carbon dioxide *n* a colourless odourless incombustible gas formed during breathing, and used in fire extinguishers and in making fizzy drinks.
carbonic *adj* containing carbon.
carbonic acid *n* a weak acid formed when carbon dioxide combines with water.
carboniferous *adj* yielding coal or carbon.
Carboniferous *adj Geol* of the period of geological time about 330 million years ago, during which coal seams were formed.
carbonize *or* **-ise** *vb* **-izing, -ized** *or* **-ising, -ised** **1** to turn into carbon as a result of partial burning. **2** to coat (a substance) with carbon. ▶ **carbonization** *or* **-isation** *n*
carbon monoxide *n* a colourless odourless poisonous gas formed by the incomplete burning of carbon compounds; part of the gases that come from a vehicle's exhaust.
carbon paper *n* a thin sheet of paper coated on one side with a dark waxy pigment, containing carbon, used to make a duplicate of something as it is typed or written.
carbon tax *n* a tax on the emissions caused by the burning of coal, gas, and oil, aimed at reducing the production of greenhouse gases.
carbon tetrachloride *n* a colourless nonflammable liquid used as a solvent, cleaning fluid, and insecticide.
Carborundum *n Trademark* an abrasive material consisting of silicon carbide.
carboxyl group *or* **radical** *n Chem* the chemical group –COOH: the functional group in organic acids.
carboy *n* a large bottle protected by a basket or box. ▷ **HISTORY** Persian *qarāba*
carbuncle *n* a large painful swelling under the skin like a boil. ▷ **HISTORY** Latin *carbo* coal
carburettor *or US & Canad* **carburetor** *n* a device in an internal-combustion engine that mixes petrol with air and regulates the intake of the mixture into the engine.
carcass *or* **carcase** *n* **1** the dead body of an animal. **2** *Informal* a person's body: *ask that person to move his carcass.* ▷ **HISTORY** Old French *carcasse*
carcinogen *n* a substance that produces cancer. ▷ **HISTORY** Greek *karkinos* cancer ▶ **carcinogenic** *adj*
carcinoma *n, pl* **-mas** *or* **-mata** a malignant tumour. ▷ **HISTORY** Greek *karkinos* cancer
card[1] *n* **1** a piece of stiff paper or thin cardboard used for identification, reference, proof of membership, or sending greetings or messages: *a Christmas card.* **2** one of a set of small pieces of cardboard, marked with figures or symbols, used for playing games or for fortune-telling. **3** a small rectangle of stiff plastic with identifying numbers

for use as a credit card, cheque card, or charge card. **4** *Old-fashioned informal* a witty or eccentric person. ✧ See also **cards**. ▷ **HISTORY** Greek *khartēs* leaf of papyrus

card[2] *n* **1** a machine or tool for combing fibres of cotton or wool to disentangle them before spinning. ✧ *vb* **2** to process with such a machine or tool. ▷ **HISTORY** Latin *carduus* thistle

cardamom *n* a spice that is obtained from the seeds of a tropical plant. ▷ **HISTORY** Greek *kardamon* cress + *amōmon* an Indian spice

cardboard *n* a thin stiff board made from paper pulp.

card-carrying *adj* being an official member of an organization: *a card-carrying Conservative.*

cardiac *adj* of or relating to the heart. ▷ **HISTORY** Greek *kardia* heart

cardigan *n* a knitted jacket. ▷ **HISTORY** after 7th Earl of *Cardigan*

cardinal *n* **1** any of the high-ranking clergymen of the Roman Catholic Church who elect the pope and act as his chief counsellors. ✧ *adj* **2** fundamentally important; principal.

WORD HISTORY

The word 'cardinal' comes from Latin *cardo*, meaning 'hinge'. When something is important, other things can be said to hinge on it.

cardinal number *n* a number denoting quantity but not order in a group, for example one, two, or three.

cardinal points *pl n* the four main points of the compass: north, south, east, and west.

cardinal virtues *pl n* the most important moral qualities, traditionally justice, prudence, temperance, and fortitude.

cardiogram *n* an electrocardiogram. See **electrocardiograph**.

cardiograph *n* an electrocardiograph. ▶ **cardiographer** *n* ▶ **cardiography** *n*

cardiology *n* the branch of medicine dealing with the heart and its diseases. ▶ **cardiologist** *n*

cardiovascular *adj* of or relating to the heart and the blood vessels.

cards *n* **1** any game played with cards, or card games generally. **2 lay one's cards on the table** to declare one's intentions openly. **3 on the cards** likely to take place: *a military coup was on the cards.* **4 play one's cards right** to handle a situation cleverly.

cardsharp *or* **cardsharper** *n* a professional card player who cheats.

card vote *n Brit & NZ* a vote by delegates in which each delegate's vote counts as a vote by all his or her constituents.

care *vb* **caring, cared 1** to be worried or concerned: *he does not care what people think about him.* **2** to like (to do something): *anybody care to go out?* **3 care for a** to look after or provide for: *it is still largely women who care for dependent family members.* **b** to like or be fond of: *he did not care for his concentration to be disturbed; I don't suppose you could ever care for me seriously.* **4 I couldn't care less** I am completely indifferent. ✧ *n* **5** careful or serious attention; caution: *treat all raw meat with extreme care to avoid food poisoning.* **6** protection or charge: *the children are now in the care of a state orphanage.* **7** trouble or worry: *his mind turned towards money cares.* **8 care of** (written on envelopes) at the address of. **9 in** *or* **into care** *Brit & NZ* (of a child) made the legal responsibility of a local authority or the state by order of a court. **10 take care** to be careful. **11 take care of** to look after: *women have to take greater care of themselves during pregnancy.* ▷ **HISTORY** Old English *cearian*

careen *vb* to tilt over to one side. ▷ **HISTORY** Latin *carina* keel

career *n* **1** the series of jobs in a profession or occupation that a person has through his or her life: *a career in child psychology.* **2** the part of a person's life spent in a particular occupation or type of work: *a school career punctuated with exams.* ✧ *vb* **3** to rush in an uncontrolled way. ✧ *adj* **4** having chosen to dedicate his or her life to a particular occupation: *a career soldier.* ▷ **HISTORY** Latin *carrus* two-wheeled wagon

careerist *n* a person who seeks to advance his or her career by any means possible. ▶ **careerism** *n*

carefree *adj* without worry or responsibility.

careful *adj* **1** cautious in attitude or action. **2** very exact and thorough. ▶ **carefully** *adv* ▶ **carefulness** *n*

careless *adj* **1** done or acting with insufficient attention. **2** unconcerned in attitude or action. ▶ **carelessly** *adv* ▶ **carelessness** *n*

carer *n* a person who looks after someone who is ill or old, often a relative: *the group offers support for the carers of those with dementia.*

caress *n* **1** a gentle affectionate touch or embrace. ✧ *vb* **2** to touch gently and affectionately. ▷ **HISTORY** Latin *carus* dear

caret (**kar**-ret) *n* a symbol (‸) indicating a place in written or printed matter where something is to be inserted. ▷ **HISTORY** Latin: there is missing

caretaker *n* **1** a person employed to look after a place or thing. ✧ *adj* **2** performing the duties of an office temporarily: *a caretaker administration.*

careworn *adj* showing signs of stress or worry.

cargo *n, pl* **-goes** *or esp US* **-gos** goods carried by a ship, aircraft, or other vehicle. ▷ **HISTORY** Spanish *cargar* to load

cargo pants *or* **trousers** *pl n* loose trousers with a large external pocket on the side of each leg.

Carib *n* **1** (*pl* **-ibs** *or* **-ib**) a member of a group of Native American peoples of NE South America and the S West Indies. **2** any of the languages of these peoples. ▷ **HISTORY** Spanish *Caribe*

Caribbean *adj* of the Caribbean Sea, bounded by Central America, South America, and the West Indies, or the surrounding countries and islands.

caribou *n, pl* **-bou** *or* **-bous** a large North American reindeer. ▷ **HISTORY** from a Native American language

caricature *n* **1** a drawing or description of a person which exaggerates characteristic features

A B C D E F G H I J K L M N O P Q R S T U V W X Y Z

for comic effect. **2** a description or explanation of something that is so exaggerated or over-simplified that it is difficult to take seriously: *the classic caricature of the henpecked husband.* ✧ *vb* **-turing, -tured 3** to make a caricature of. ▷ **HISTORY** Italian *caricatura* a distortion

caries (**care**-reez) *n* tooth decay. ▷ **HISTORY** Latin: decay

carillon (kar-**rill**-yon) *n* **1** a set of bells hung in a tower and played either from a keyboard or mechanically. **2** a tune played on such bells. ▷ **HISTORY** French

caring *adj* **1** feeling or showing care and compassion for other people. **2** of or relating to professional social or medical care: *the caring professions.*

carjack *vb* to attack (a driver in a car) in order to rob the driver or to steal the car for another crime. ▷ **HISTORY** CAR + (HI)JACK

cark *vb* **cark it** *Austral & NZ slang* to die.

Carmelite *n* **1** a Christian friar or nun belonging to the order of Our Lady of Carmel. ✧ *adj* **2** of this order. ▷ **HISTORY** after Mount *Carmel,* in Palestine, where the order was founded

carminative *adj* **1** able to relieve flatulence. ✧ *n* **2** a carminative drug. ▷ **HISTORY** Latin *carminare* to card wool, comb out

carmine *adj* vivid red. ▷ **HISTORY** Arabic *qirmiz* kermes

carnage *n* extensive slaughter of people. ▷ **HISTORY** Latin *caro* flesh

carnal *adj* of a sexual or sensual nature: *carnal knowledge.* ▷ **HISTORY** Latin *caro* flesh ▶ **carnality** *n*

carnation *n* a cultivated plant with clove-scented white, pink, or red flowers. ▷ **HISTORY** Latin *caro* flesh

carnelian *n* a reddish-yellow variety of chalcedony, used as a gemstone. ▷ **HISTORY** Old French *corneline*

carnet (**kar**-nay) *n* a customs licence permitting motorists to take their cars across certain frontiers. ▷ **HISTORY** French: notebook

carnival *n* **1** a festive period with processions, music, and dancing in the street. **2** a travelling funfair. ▷ **HISTORY** Old Italian *carnelevare* a removing of meat (referring to the Lenten fast)

carnivore (**car**-niv-vore) *n* **1** a meat-eating animal. **2** *Informal* an aggressively ambitious person. ▷ **HISTORY** Latin *caro* flesh + *vorare* to consume ▶ **carnivorous** (car-**niv**-or-uss) *adj*

carob *n* the pod of a Mediterranean tree, used as a chocolate substitute. ▷ **HISTORY** Arabic *al kharrūbah*

carol *n* **1** a joyful religious song sung at Christmas. ✧ *vb* **-olling, -olled** *or US* **-oling, -oled 2** to sing carols. **3** to sing joyfully. ▷ **HISTORY** Old French

carotene *n Biochem* any of four orange-red hydrocarbons, found in many plants, converted to vitamin A in the liver. ▷ **HISTORY** from Latin *carota* carrot

carotid (kar-**rot**-id) *n* **1** either of the two arteries that supply blood to the head and neck. ✧ *adj* **2** of either of these arteries. ▷ **HISTORY** Greek *karoun* to stupefy; so named because pressure on them produced unconsciousness

carousal *n* a merry drinking party.

carouse *vb* **-rousing, -roused** to have a merry drinking party: *carousing with friends.* ▷ **HISTORY** German *(trinken) gar aus* (to drink) right out

carousel (kar-roo-**sell**) *n* **1** a revolving conveyor for luggage at an airport or for slides for a projector. **2** *US & Canad* a merry-go-round. ▷ **HISTORY** Italian *carosello*

carp[1] *n, pl* **carp** *or* **carps** a large freshwater food fish. ▷ **HISTORY** Old French *carpe*

carp[2] *vb* to complain or find fault. ▷ **HISTORY** Old Norse *karpa* to boast ▶ **carping** *adj, n*

carpal *n* a wrist bone. ▷ **HISTORY** Greek *karpos* wrist

car park *n* an area or building reserved for parking cars.

carpel *n* the female reproductive organ of a flowering plant. ▷ **HISTORY** Greek *karpos* fruit

carpenter *n* a person who makes or repairs wooden structures. ▷ **HISTORY** Latin *carpentarius* wagon-maker

carpentry *n* the skill or work of a carpenter.

carpet *n* **1** a heavy fabric for covering floors. **2** a covering like a carpet: *a carpet of leaves.* **3 on the carpet** *Informal* being or about to be reprimanded. **4 sweep something under the carpet** to conceal or keep silent about something that one does not want to be discovered. ✧ *vb* **-peting, -peted 5** to cover with a carpet or a covering like a carpet. ▷ **HISTORY** Latin *carpere* to pluck, card

carpetbagger *n* **1** a politician who seeks office in a place where he or she has no connections. **2** *Brit* a person who makes a short-term investment in a mutual savings or life-assurance organization in order to benefit from free shares issued following the organization's conversion to a public limited company.

carpet snake *or* **python** *n* a large nonvenomous Australian snake with a carpet-like pattern on its back.

car phone *n* a telephone that operates by cellular radio for use in a car.

carpus *n, pl* **-pi** the set of eight bones of the human wrist. ▷ **HISTORY** Greek *karpos*

carrageen *n* an edible red seaweed of North America and N Europe. ▷ **HISTORY** *Carragheen,* near Waterford, Ireland

carriage *n* **1** *Brit, Austral & NZ* one of the sections of a train for passengers. **2** the way a person holds and moves his or her head and body. **3** a four-wheeled horse-drawn passenger vehicle. **4** the moving part of a machine, such as a typewriter, that supports and shifts another part. **5** the charge made for conveying goods. ▷ **HISTORY** Old French *cariage*

carriageway *n* **1** *Brit* the part of a road along which traffic passes in one direction: *the westbound carriageway of the M4.* **2** *NZ* the part of a road used by vehicles.

carrier *n* **1** a person, vehicle, or organization that carries something: *armoured personnel carriers.* **2** a person or animal that, without suffering from a disease, is capable of transmitting it to others. **3** short for **aircraft carrier**.

carrier bag *n Brit* a large plastic or paper bag for carrying shopping.

carrier pigeon *n* a homing pigeon used for carrying messages.

carrion *n* dead and rotting flesh. ▷ **HISTORY** Latin *caro* flesh

carrion crow *n* a scavenging European crow with a completely black plumage and bill.

carrot *n* **1** a long tapering orange root vegetable. **2** something offered as an incentive. ▷ **HISTORY** Greek *karōton*

carroty *adj* (of hair) reddish-orange.

carry *vb* **-ries, -rying, -ried 1** to take from one place to another. **2** to have with one habitually, for example in one's pocket or handbag: *to carry a donor card.* **3** to transmit or be transmitted: *to carry disease.* **4** to have as a factor or result: *the charge of desertion carries a maximum penalty of twenty years.* **5** to be pregnant with: *women carrying Down's Syndrome babies.* **6** to hold (one's head or body) in a specified manner: *she always wears a sari and carries herself like an Indian.* **7** to secure the adoption of (a bill or motion): *the resolution was carried by fewer than twenty votes.* **8** (of a newspaper or television or radio station) to include in the contents: *several papers carried front-page pictures of the Russian president.* **9** *Maths* to transfer (a number) from one column of figures to the next. **10** to travel a certain distance or reach a specified point: *his faint voice carried no farther than the front few rows.* **11 carry the can** *Informal* to take all the blame for something. ✧ See also **carry forward**. ▷ **HISTORY** Latin *carrum* transport wagon

carrycot *n* a light portable bed for a baby, with handles and a hood, which usually also serves as the body of a pram.

carry forward *vb* to transfer (an amount) to the next column, page, or accounting period.

carrying capacity *n Ecology* the maximum number of individuals that an area of land can support.

carry on *vb* **1** to continue: *we'll carry on exactly where we left off.* **2** to do, run, or take part in: *the vast trade carried on in the city.* **3** *Informal* to cause a fuss: *I don't want to carry on and make a big scene.* ✧ *n* **carry-on 4** *Informal, chiefly Brit* a fuss.

carry out *vb* **1** to follow (an order or instruction). **2** to accomplish (a task): *to carry out repairs.*

carry over *vb* to extend from one period or situation into another: *major debts carried over from last year.*

carry through *vb* to bring to completion: *these are difficult policies to carry through.*

cart *n* **1** an open horse-drawn vehicle, usually with two wheels, used to carry goods or passengers. **2** any small vehicle that is pulled or pushed by hand. ✧ *vb* **3** to carry, usually with some effort: *men carted bricks and tiles and wooden boards.* ▷ **HISTORY** Old Norse *kartr*

carte blanche *n* complete authority: *she's got carte blanche to redecorate.* ▷ **HISTORY** French: blank paper

cartel *n* an association of competing firms formed in order to fix prices. ▷ **HISTORY** German *Kartell*

Cartesian *adj* of René Descartes, 17th-century French philosopher and mathematician, or his works. ▷ **HISTORY** *Cartesius,* Latin form of Descartes

Cartesian coordinates *pl n* a set of numbers that determine the location of a point in a plane or in space by its distance from two fixed intersecting lines.

Cartesian plane *n Maths* the two-dimensional set of axes used for plotting points and sketching graphs.

carthorse *n* a large heavily built horse kept for pulling carts or for farm work.

Carthusian *n* **1** a Christian monk or nun belonging to a strict monastic order founded in 1084. ✧ *adj* **2** of this order. ▷ **HISTORY** Latin *Carthusia* Chartreuse, near Grenoble

cartilage (**kar**-till-ij) *n* a strong flexible tissue forming part of the skeleton. ▷ **HISTORY** Latin *cartilago* ▶ **cartilaginous** *adj*

cartography *n* the art of making maps or charts. ▷ **HISTORY** French *carte* map, chart ▶ **cartographer** *n* ▶ **cartographic** *adj*

carton *n* **1** a cardboard box or container. **2** a container of waxed paper in which drinks are sold. ▷ **HISTORY** Italian *carta* card

cartoon *n* **1** a humorous or satirical drawing in a newspaper or magazine. **2** same as **comic strip**. **3** same as **animated cartoon.** ▷ **HISTORY** Italian *cartone* pasteboard ▶ **cartoonist** *n*

cartouche *n* **1** an ornamental tablet or panel in the form of a scroll. **2** (in ancient Egypt) an oblong or oval figure containing royal or divine names. ▷ **HISTORY** French: scroll, cartridge

cartridge *n* **1** a metal casing containing an explosive charge and bullet for a gun. **2** the part of the pick-up of a record player that converts the movements of the stylus into electrical signals. **3** a sealed container of film or tape, or ink for a special kind of pen. ▷ **HISTORY** from French *cartouche*

cartridge paper *n* a type of heavy rough drawing paper.

cartwheel *n* **1** a sideways somersault supported by the hands with legs outstretched. **2** the large spoked wheel of a cart.

carve *vb* **carving, carved 1** to cut in order to form something: *carving wood.* **2** to form (something) by cutting: *the statue which was carved by Michelangelo.* **3** to slice (cooked meat). ✧ See also **carve out**. ▷ **HISTORY** Old English *ceorfan* ▶ **carver** *n*

carve out *vb Informal* to make or create: *to carve out a political career.*

carving *n* a figure or design produced by carving stone or wood.

caryatid (kar-ree-**at**-id) *n* a supporting column in the shape of a female figure. ▷ **HISTORY** Greek

Karuatides priestesses of Artemis at *Karuai* (Caryae), in Laconia

Casanova *n* a promiscuous man. ▷ **HISTORY** after Giovanni *Casanova,* Italian adventurer

casbah *n* the citadel of a North African city. ▷ **HISTORY** Arabic *kasba* citadel

cascade *n* **1** a waterfall or series of waterfalls over rocks. **2** something flowing or falling like a waterfall: *a cascade of luxuriant hair.* ✧ *vb* **-cading, -caded 3** to flow or fall in a cascade: *rays of sunshine cascaded down.* ▷ **HISTORY** Italian *cascare* to fall

cascara *n* the bark of a N American shrub, used as a laxative. ▷ **HISTORY** Spanish: bark

case[1] *n* **1** a single instance or example of something: *cases of teenage pregnancies.* **2** a matter for discussion: *the case before the Ethics Committee.* **3** a specific condition or state of affairs: *a sudden-death play-off in the case of a draw.* **4** a set of arguments supporting an action or cause: *I put my case before them.* **5** a person or problem dealt with by a doctor, social worker, or solicitor. **6 a** an action or lawsuit: *a rape case.* **b** the evidence offered in court to support a claim: *he will try to show that the case against his client is largely circumstantial.* **7** *Grammar* a form of a noun, pronoun, or adjective showing its relation to other words in the sentence: *the accusative case.* **8** *Informal* an amusingly eccentric person. **9 in any case** no matter what. **10 in case** so as to allow for the possibility that: *the President has ordered a medical team to stand by in case hostages are released.* **11 in case of** in the event of: *in case of a future conflict.* ▷ **HISTORY** Old English *casus* (grammatical) case, associated with Old French *cas* a happening; both from Latin *cadere* to fall

case[2] *n* **1** a container, such as a box or chest. **2** a suitcase. **3** a protective outer covering. ✧ *vb* **casing, cased 4** *Slang* to inspect carefully (a place one plans to rob). ▷ **HISTORY** Latin *capsa* box

case-hardened *adj* having been made callous by experience: *a case-hardened senior policewoman.*

case history *n* a record of a person's background or medical history.

casein *n* a protein found in milk, which forms the basis of cheese. ▷ **HISTORY** Latin *caseus* cheese

case law *n* law established by following judicial decisions made in earlier cases.

caseload *n* the number of cases that someone like a doctor or social worker deals with at any one time.

casement *n* a window that is hinged on one side. ▷ **HISTORY** probably from Old French *encassement* frame

case study *n* an analysis of a group or person in order to make generalizations about a larger group or society as a whole.

casework *n* social work based on close study of the personal histories and circumstances of individuals and families. ▶ **caseworker** *n*

cash *n* **1** banknotes and coins, rather than cheques. **2** *Informal* money: *strapped for cash.* ✧ *adj* **3** of, for, or paid in cash: *cash hand-outs.* ✧ *vb* **4** to obtain or pay banknotes or coins for (a cheque or postal order). ✧ See also **cash in on**. ▷ **HISTORY** Old Italian *cassa* money box

cash-and-carry *adj* operating on a basis of cash payment for goods that are taken away by the purchaser: *the cash-and-carry wholesalers.*

cashback *n* **1** a discount offered in return for immediate payment. **2** a service by which a customer in a shop can draw out cash on a debit card.

cash-book *n Book-keeping* a journal in which all money transactions are recorded.

cash card *n* a card issued by a bank or building society which can be inserted into a cash dispenser in order to obtain money.

cash crop *n Agriculture* a crop produced for sale rather than for subsistence.

cash desk *n* a counter or till in a shop where purchases are paid for.

cash discount *n* a discount granted to a purchaser who pays within a specified period.

cash dispenser *n* a computerized device outside a bank which supplies cash when a special card is inserted and the user's code number keyed in.

cashew *n* an edible kidney-shaped nut. ▷ **HISTORY** S American Indian *acajū*

cash flow *n* the movement of money into and out of a business.

cashier[1] *n* a person responsible for handling cash in a bank, shop, or other business. ▷ **HISTORY** French *casse* money chest

cashier[2] *vb* to dismiss with dishonour from the armed forces. ▷ **HISTORY** Latin *quassare* to QUASH

cash in on *vb Informal* to gain profit or advantage from: *trying to cash in on the dispute.*

cashmere *n* a very fine soft wool obtained from goats. ▷ **HISTORY** from *Kashmir,* in SW central Asia

cash on delivery *n* a system involving cash payment to the carrier on delivery of merchandise. Abbrev: **COD**

cash register *n* a till that has a mechanism for displaying and adding the prices of the goods sold.

casing *n* a protective case or covering.

casino *n, pl* **-nos** a public building or room where gambling games are played. ▷ **HISTORY** Italian

cask *n* **1** a strong barrel used to hold alcoholic drink. **2** *Austral* a cubic carton containing wine, with a tap for dispensing. ▷ **HISTORY** Spanish *casco* helmet

casket *n* **1** a small box for valuables. **2** *US* a coffin. ▷ **HISTORY** probably from Old French *cassette* little box

Cassandra *n* someone whose prophecies of doom are unheeded. ▷ **HISTORY** Trojan prophetess in Greek mythology

cassava *n* a starch obtained from the root of a tropical American plant, used to make tapioca. ▷ **HISTORY** West Indian *caçábi*

casserole *n* **1** a covered dish in which food is cooked slowly, usually in an oven, and served. **2** a dish cooked and served in this way: *beef casserole.*

✧ *vb* **-roling, -roled 3** to cook in a casserole. ▷ **HISTORY** French

cassette *n* a plastic case containing a reel of film or magnetic tape. ▷ **HISTORY** French: little box

cassia *n* **1** a tropical plant whose pods yield a mild laxative. **2 cassia bark** a cinnamon-like spice obtained from the bark of a tropical Asian tree. ▷ **HISTORY** Greek *kasia*

cassock *n* an ankle-length garment, usually black, worn by some Christian priests. ▷ **HISTORY** Italian *casacca* a long coat

cassowary *n, pl* **-waries** a large flightless bird of Australia and New Guinea. ▷ **HISTORY** Malay *kĕsuari*

cast *n* **1** the actors in a play collectively. **2 a** an object made of material that has been shaped, while molten, by a mould. **b** the mould used to shape such an object. **3** *Surgery* a rigid casing made of plaster of Paris for immobilizing broken bones while they heal. **4** a sort, kind, or style: *people of an academic cast of mind.* **5** a slight squint in the eye. ✧ *vb* **casting, cast 6** to select (an actor) to play a part in a play or film. **7** to give or deposit (a vote). **8** to express (doubts or aspersions). **9** to cause to appear: *a shadow cast by the grandstand; the gloom cast by the recession.* **10 a** to shape (molten material) by pouring it into a mould. **b** to make (an object) by such a process. **11** to throw (a fishing line) into the water. **12** to throw with force: *cast into a bonfire.* **13** to direct (a glance): *he cast his eye over the horse-chestnut trees.* **14** to roll or throw (a dice). **15 cast aside** to abandon or reject: *cast aside by her lover.* **16 cast a spell a** to perform magic. **b** to have an irresistible influence. ▷ **HISTORY** Old Norse *kasta*

castanets *pl n* a musical instrument, used by Spanish dancers, consisting of curved pieces of hollow wood, held between the fingers and thumb and clicked together. ▷ **HISTORY** Spanish *castañeta*, from *castaña* chestnut

castaway *n* a person who has been shipwrecked.

caste *n* **1** any of the four major hereditary classes into which Hindu society is divided. **2** social rank. ▷ **HISTORY** Latin *castus* pure, not polluted

castellated *adj* having turrets and battlements, like a castle. ▷ **HISTORY** Medieval Latin *castellare* to fortify as a castle

caster *n* same as **castor**.

caster sugar *n* finely ground white sugar.

castigate *vb* **-gating, -gated** to find fault with or reprimand (a person) harshly. ▷ **HISTORY** Latin *castigare* to correct ▶ **castigation** *n*

casting *n* an object that has been cast in metal from a mould.

casting vote *n* the deciding vote used by the chairperson of a meeting when an equal number of votes are cast on each side.

cast iron *n* **1** iron containing so much carbon that it is brittle and must be cast into shape rather than wrought. ✧ *adj* **cast-iron 2** made of cast iron. **3** definite or unchallengeable: *cast-iron guarantees.*

castle *n* **1** a large fortified building or set of buildings, often built as a residence for a ruler or nobleman in medieval Europe. **2** same as **rook**[2]. ▷ **HISTORY** Latin: castellum

castle in the air *or* **in Spain** *n* a hope or desire unlikely to be realized.

cast-off *adj* **1** discarded because no longer wanted or needed: *cast-off clothing.* ✧ *n* **castoff 2** a person or thing that has been discarded because no longer wanted or needed. ✧ *vb* **cast off 3** to discard (something no longer wanted or needed). **4** to untie a ship from a dock. **5** to knot and remove (a row of stitches, esp. the final row) from the needle in knitting.

cast on *vb* to make (a row of stitches) on the needle in knitting.

castor *n* a small swivelling wheel fixed to a piece of furniture to enable it to be moved easily in any direction.

castor oil *n* an oil obtained from the seeds of an Indian plant, used as a lubricant and purgative.

castrate *vb* **-trating, -trated 1** to remove the testicles of. **2** to deprive of vigour or masculinity. ▷ **HISTORY** Latin *castrare* ▶ **castration** *n*

castrato *n, pl* **-ti** *or* **-tos** (in 17th- and 18th-century opera) a male singer whose testicles were removed before puberty, allowing the retention of a soprano or alto voice. ▷ **HISTORY** Italian

casual *adj* **1** being or seeming careless or nonchalant: *he was casual about security.* **2** occasional or irregular: *casual workers.* **3** shallow or superficial: *casual relationships.* **4** for informal wear: *a casual jacket.* **5** happening by chance or without planning: *a casual comment.* ✧ *n* **6** an occasional worker. ▷ **HISTORY** Latin *casus* event, chance ▶ **casually** *adv*

casualty *n, pl* **-ties 1** a person who is killed or injured in an accident or war. **2** the hospital department where victims of accidents are given emergency treatment. **3** a person or thing that has suffered as the result of a particular event or circumstance: *583 job losses with significant casualties among public-sector employees.*

casuarina (kass-yew-a-**reen**-a) *n Bot* an Australian tree with jointed green branches. ▷ **HISTORY** Malay *kĕsuari*, referring to the resemblance of the branches to the feathers of the cassowary

casuistry *n* reasoning that is misleading or oversubtle. ▷ **HISTORY** Latin *casus* case ▶ **casuist** *n*

cat *n* **1** a small domesticated mammal with thick soft fur and whiskers. **2** a wild animal related to the cat, such as the lynx, lion, or tiger. RELATED ADJECTIVE ➧ **feline 3 let the cat out of the bag** to disclose a secret. **4 raining cats and dogs** raining very heavily. **5 set the cat among the pigeons** to stir up trouble. ▷ **HISTORY** Latin *cattus* ▶ **catlike** *adj*

catabolism *n Biol* a metabolic process in which complex molecules are broken down into simple ones with the release of energy. ▷ **HISTORY** Greek *kata-* down + *ballein* to throw ▶ **catabolic** *adj*

cataclysm (**kat**-a-kliz-zum) *n* **1** a violent upheaval of a social, political, or military nature: *the cataclysm of the Second World War.* **2** a disaster such as an earthquake or a flood. ▷ HISTORY Greek *katakluzein* to flood ▶ **cataclysmic** *adj*

catacombs (**kat**-a-koomz) *pl n* an underground burial place consisting of tunnels with side recesses for tombs.

> **WORD HISTORY**
> *Catacumbas* was the name given to the underground cemetery built below the Basilica of St Sebastian near Rome. In the course of time, the name was applied to similar cemeteries elsewhere.

catafalque (**kat**-a-falk) *n* a raised platform on which a body lies in state before or during a funeral. ▷ HISTORY Italian *catafalco*

Catalan *adj* **1** of Catalonia. ✧ *n* **2** a language of Catalonia in NE Spain. **3** a person from Catalonia.

catalepsy *n* a trancelike state in which the body is rigid. ▷ HISTORY Greek *katalēpsis* a seizing ▶ **cataleptic** *adj*

catalogue *or US* **catalog** *n* **1** a book containing details of items for sale. **2** a list of all the books of a library. **3** a list of events, qualities, or things considered as a group: *a catalogue of killings.* ✧ *vb* **-loguing, -logued** *or* **-loging, -loged 4** to enter (an item) in a catalogue. **5** to list a series of (events, qualities, or things): *the report catalogues two decades of human-rights violations.* ▷ HISTORY Greek *katalegein* to list ▶ **cataloguer** *n*

catalpa *n* a tree of N America and Asia with bell-shaped whitish flowers. ▷ HISTORY Carolina Creek (a Native American language) *kutuhlpa* winged head

catalyse *or US* **-lyze** *vb* **-lysing, -lysed** *or* **-lyzing, -lyzed** to influence (a chemical reaction) by catalysis.

catalysis *n* acceleration of a chemical reaction by the action of a catalyst. ▷ HISTORY Greek *kataluein* to dissolve ▶ **catalytic** *adj*

catalyst *n* **1** a substance that speeds up a chemical reaction without itself undergoing any permanent chemical change. **2** a person or thing that causes an important change to take place: *a catalyst for peace.*

catalytic converter *n* a device which uses catalysts to reduce the quantity of poisonous substances emitted by the exhaust of a motor vehicle.

catalytic cracker *n* a unit in an oil refinery in which mineral oils are converted into fuels by a catalytic process.

catamaran *n* a boat with twin parallel hulls.

> **WORD HISTORY**
> A catamaran was originally a type of raft found in India, made by tying three logs together. The word 'catamaran' comes from Tamil *kattumaram*, which means 'tied logs'.

catapult *n* **1** a Y-shaped device with a loop of elastic fastened to the ends of the prongs, used by children for firing stones. **2** a device used to launch aircraft from a warship. ✧ *vb* **3** to shoot forwards or upwards violently: *traffic catapulted forward with a roar.* **4** to cause (someone) suddenly to be in a particular situation: *catapulted to stardom.* ▷ HISTORY Greek *kata-* down + *pallein* to hurl

cataract *n* **1** *Pathol* **a** a condition in which the lens of the eye becomes partially or totally opaque. **b** the opaque area. **2** a large waterfall. ▷ HISTORY Greek *katarassein* to dash down

catarrh (kat-**tar**) *n* excessive mucus in the nose and throat, often experienced during or following a cold. ▷ HISTORY Greek *katarrhein* to flow down ▶ **catarrhal** *adj*

catastrophe (kat-**ass**-trof-fee) *n* a great and sudden disaster or misfortune. ▷ HISTORY Greek *katastrephein* to overturn ▶ **catastrophic** *adj*

catatonia *n* a form of schizophrenia in which the sufferer experiences stupor, with outbreaks of excitement. ▷ HISTORY Greek *kata-* down + *tonos* tension ▶ **catatonic** *adj*

catcall *n* a shrill whistle or cry of disapproval or derision.

catch *vb* **catching, caught 1** to seize and hold. **2** to capture (a person or a fish or animal). **3** to surprise in an act: *two boys were caught stealing.* **4** to reach (a bus, train, or plane) in time to board it. **5** to see or hear: *you'll have to be quick if you want to catch her dj-ing.* **6** to be infected with (an illness). **7** to entangle or become entangled. **8** to attract (someone's attention, imagination, or interest). **9** to comprehend or make out: *you have to work hard to catch his tone and meaning.* **10** to reproduce (a quality) accurately in a work of art. **11** (of a fire) to start burning. **12** *Cricket* to dismiss (a batsman) by catching a ball struck by him before it touches the ground. **13 catch at a** to attempt to grasp. **b** to take advantage of (an opportunity). **14 catch it** *Informal* to be punished. ✧ *n* **15** a device such as a hook, for fastening a door, window, or box. **16** the total number of fish caught. **17** *Informal* a concealed or unforeseen drawback. **18** an emotional break in the voice. **19** *Informal* a person considered worth having as a husband or wife. **20** *Cricket* the act of catching a ball struck by a batsman before it touches the ground, resulting in him being out. ✧ See also **catch on, catch out.** ▷ HISTORY Latin *capere* to seize

catch crop *n Agriculture* a quick-growing crop planted between two regular crops grown in consecutive seasons, or between two rows of regular crops in the same season; such crops increase productivity or help make up for failed crops.

catching *adj* infectious.

catchment *n* **1** a structure in which water is collected. **2** all the people served by a school or hospital in a particular catchment area.

catchment area *n* **1** the area of land draining into a river, basin, or reservoir. **2** the area served by a particular school or hospital.

catch on *vb Informal* **1** to become popular or fashionable. **2** to understand: *I was slow to catch on to what she was trying to tell me.*

catch out *vb Informal, chiefly Brit* to trap (someone) in an error or a lie.

catchpenny *adj Brit* designed to have instant appeal without regard for quality.

catch phrase *n* a well-known phrase or slogan associated with a particular entertainer or other celebrity.

catch-22 *n* a situation in which a person is frustrated by a set of circumstances that prevent any attempt to escape from them. ▷ **HISTORY** from the title of a novel by J. Heller

catchword *n* a well-known and frequently used phrase or slogan.

catchy *adj* **catchier, catchiest** (of a tune) pleasant and easily remembered.

catechism (**kat**-tik-kiz-zum) *n* instruction on the doctrine of a Christian Church by a series of questions and answers. ▷ **HISTORY** Greek *katēkhizein* to catechize

catechize *or* **-echise** *vb* **-echizing, -echized** *or* **-echising, -echised 1** to instruct in Christianity using a catechism. **2** to question (someone) thoroughly. ▷ **HISTORY** Greek *katēkhizein* ▶ **catechist** *n*

categorical *or* **categoric** *adj* absolutely clear and certain: *he was categorical in his denial.* ▶ **categorically** *adv*

categorize *or* **-rise** *vb* **-rizing, -rized** *or* **-rising, -rised** to put in a category. ▶ **categorization** *or* **-risation** *n*

category *n, pl* **-ries** a class or group of things or people with some quality or qualities in common. ▷ **HISTORY** Greek *katēgoria* assertion

cater *vb* **1** to provide what is needed or wanted: *operating theatres that can cater for open-heart surgery.* **2** to provide food or services: *chef is pleased to cater for vegetarians and vegans.* ▷ **HISTORY** Anglo-Norman *acater* to buy

caterer *n* a person whose job is to provide food for social events such as parties and weddings.

caterpillar *n* **1** the wormlike larva of a butterfly or moth. **2** *Trademark* Also: **caterpillar track** an endless track, driven by cogged wheels, used to propel a heavy vehicle such as a bulldozer.

> **WORD HISTORY**
> Strange as it may seem, a caterpillar is, in terms of its word origins, a type of cat. The word comes from Old Norman French *catepelose*, meaning 'hairy cat'.

caterwaul *vb* **1** to make a yowling noise like a cat. ✧ *n* **2** such a noise. ▷ **HISTORY** imitative

catfish *n, pl* **-fish** *or* **-fishes** a freshwater fish with whisker-like barbels around the mouth.

catgut *n* a strong cord made from dried animals' intestines, used to string musical instruments and sports rackets.

catharsis (kath-**thar**-siss) *n* **1** the relief of strong suppressed emotions, for example through drama or psychoanalysis. **2** evacuation of the bowels, esp. with the use of a laxative. ▷ **HISTORY** Greek *kathairein* to purge, purify

cathartic *adj* **1** causing catharsis. ✧ *n* **2** a drug that causes catharsis.

Cathay *n* a literary or archaic name for China. ▷ **HISTORY** Medieval Latin *Cataya*

cathedral *n* the principal church of a diocese. ▷ **HISTORY** Greek *kathedra* seat

Catherine wheel *n* a firework that rotates, producing sparks and coloured flame. ▷ **HISTORY** after St *Catherine* of Alexandria, martyred on a spiked wheel

catheter (**kath**-it-er) *n* a slender flexible tube inserted into a body cavity to drain fluid. ▷ **HISTORY** Greek *kathienai* to insert

cathode *n Electronics* the negative electrode in an electrolytic cell or in an electronic valve or tube. ▷ **HISTORY** Greek *kathodos* a descent

cathode rays *pl n* a stream of electrons emitted from the surface of a cathode in a valve.

cathode-ray tube *n* a valve in which a beam of electrons is focused onto a fluorescent screen to produce a visible image, used in television receivers and visual display units.

catholic *adj* (of tastes or interests) covering a wide range. ▷ **HISTORY** Greek *katholikos* universal

Catholic *Christianity* ✧ *adj* **1** of the Roman Catholic Church. ✧ *n* **2** a member of the Roman Catholic Church. ▶ **Catholicism** *n*

cation (**kat**-eye-on) *n* a positively charged ion. ▷ **HISTORY** Greek *kata-* down + *ienai* to go

catkin *n* a drooping flower spike found on trees such as the birch, hazel, and willow. ▷ **HISTORY** obsolete Dutch *katteken* kitten

catmint *n* a Eurasian plant with scented leaves that attract cats. Also: **catnip**

catnap *n* **1** a short sleep or doze. ✧ *vb* **-napping, -napped 2** to sleep or doze for a short time or intermittently.

cat-o'-nine-tails *n, pl* **-tails** a rope whip with nine knotted thongs, formerly used to inflict floggings as a punishment.

catseyes *pl n Trademark, Brit, Austral & NZ* glass reflectors set into the road at intervals to indicate traffic lanes by reflecting light from vehicles' headlights.

cat's paw *n* a person used by someone else to do unpleasant things for him or her. ▷ **HISTORY** from the tale of a monkey who used a cat's paw to draw chestnuts out of a fire

cattle *pl n* domesticated cows and bulls. *RELATED ADJECTIVE* ✦ **bovine** ▷ **HISTORY** Old French *chatel* chattel

cattle-cake *n* concentrated food for cattle in the form of cakelike blocks.

cattle-grid *or NZ* **cattle-stop** *n* a grid covering a hole dug in a road to prevent livestock crossing while allowing vehicles to pass unhindered.

catty *adj* **-tier, -tiest** *Informal* spiteful: *her remarks were amusing and only slightly catty.* ▶ **cattiness** *n*

catwalk *n* **1** a narrow pathway over the stage of a theatre or along a bridge. **2** a narrow platform where models display clothes in a fashion show.

Caucasian *or* **Caucasoid** *adj* **1** of the predominantly light-skinned racial group of humankind. ✧ *n* **2** a member of this group.

A B C D E F G H I J K L M N O P Q R S T U V W X Y Z

caucus *n, pl* **-cuses 1** a local committee or faction of a political party. **2** a political meeting to decide future plans. **3** *NZ* a formal meeting of all MPs of one party. ▷ HISTORY probably of Native American origin

caudal *adj Zool* at or near the tail or back part of an animal's body. ▷ HISTORY Latin *cauda* tail

caught *vb* the past of **catch**.

caul *n Anat* a membrane sometimes covering a child's head at birth. ▷ HISTORY Old French *calotte* close-fitting cap

cauldron *or* **caldron** *n* a large pot used for boiling. ▷ HISTORY Latin *caldarium* hot bath

cauliflower *n* a vegetable with a large head of white flower buds surrounded by green leaves. ▷ HISTORY Italian *caoli fiori* cabbage flowers

cauliflower ear *n* permanent swelling and distortion of the ear, caused by repeated blows usually received in boxing.

caulk *vb* to fill in (cracks) with paste or some other material. ▷ HISTORY Latin *calcare* to trample

causal *adj* of or being a cause: *a causal connection.* ▶ **causally** *adv*

causation *or* **causality** *n* **1** the production of an effect by a cause. **2** the relationship of cause and effect.

causative *adj* producing an effect: *bright lights seem to be a causative factor in some migraines.*

cause *n* **1** something that produces a particular effect. **2** grounds for action; justification: *there is cause for concern.* **3** an aim or principle which an individual or group is interested in and supports: *the Socialist cause.* ✧ *vb* **causing, caused 4** to be the cause of. ▷ HISTORY Latin *causa* ▶ **causeless** *adj*

cause célèbre (**kawz** sill-**leb**-ra) *n, pl* **causes célèbres** (**kawz** sill-**leb**-ras) a controversial legal case, issue, or person. ▷ HISTORY French

causeway *n* a raised path or road across water or marshland. ▷ HISTORY Middle English *cauciwey* paved way

caustic *adj* **1** capable of burning or corroding by chemical action: *caustic soda.* **2** bitter and sarcastic: *caustic critics.* ✧ *n* **3** *Chem* a caustic substance. ▷ HISTORY Greek *kaiein* to burn ▶ **caustically** *adv*

caustic soda *n* same as **sodium hydroxide**.

cauterize *or* **-ise** *vb* **-izing, -ized** *or* **-ising, -ised** to burn (a wound) with heat or a caustic agent to prevent infection. ▷ HISTORY Greek *kaiein* to burn ▶ **cauterization** *or* **-isation** *n*

caution *n* **1** care or prudence, esp. in the face of danger. **2** warning: *a word of caution.* **3** *Law chiefly Brit* a formal warning given to a person suspected of an offence. ✧ *vb* **4** to warn or advise: *he cautioned against an abrupt turnaround.* ▷ HISTORY Latin *cautio* ▶ **cautionary** *adj*

cautious *adj* showing or having caution. ▶ **cautiously** *adv*

cavalcade *n* a procession of people on horseback or in cars. ▷ HISTORY Italian *cavalcare* to ride on horseback

cavalier *adj* **1** showing haughty disregard; offhand. ✧ *n* **2** *Old-fashioned* a gallant or courtly gentleman. ▷ HISTORY Late Latin *caballarius* rider

Cavalier *n* a supporter of Charles I during the English Civil War.

cavalry *n* the part of an army originally mounted on horseback, but now often using fast armoured vehicles. ▷ HISTORY Italian *cavaliere* horseman ▶ **cavalryman** *n*

cave *n* a hollow in the side of a hill or cliff, or underground. ▷ HISTORY Latin *cavus* hollow

caveat (**kav**-vee-at) *n* **1** *Law* a formal notice requesting the court not to take a certain action without warning the person lodging the caveat. **2** a caution. ▷ HISTORY Latin: let him beware

caveat emptor (**kav**-vee-at-**emp**-tor) *n Law* the principle that it is the buyer rather than the seller who must bear responsibility for checking the quality of goods purchased. ▷ HISTORY Latin: let the buyer beware

cave in *vb* **1** to collapse inwards. **2** *Informal* to yield completely under pressure: *the government caved in to the revolutionaries' demands.* ✧ *n* **cave-in 3** the sudden collapse of a roof or piece of ground.

caveman *n, pl* **-men 1** a prehistoric cave dweller. **2** *Informal* a man who is primitive or brutal in behaviour.

cavern *n* a large cave. ▷ HISTORY Latin *cavus* hollow

cavernous *adj* like a cavern in vastness, depth, or hollowness: *the cavernous building.*

caviar *or* **caviare** *n* the salted roe of the sturgeon, regarded as a delicacy and usually served as an appetizer. ▷ HISTORY Turkish *havyār*

cavil *vb* **-illing, -illed** *or US* **-iling, -iled 1** to raise annoying petty objections. ✧ *n* **2** a petty objection. ▷ HISTORY Latin *cavillari* to jeer

caving *n* the sport of climbing in and exploring caves. ▶ **caver** *n*

cavity *n, pl* **-ties 1** a hollow space. **2** *Dentistry* a decayed area on a tooth. ▷ HISTORY Latin *cavus* hollow

cavort *vb* to skip about; caper. ▷ HISTORY origin unknown

caw *n* **1** the cry of a crow, rook, or raven. ✧ *vb* **2** to make this cry. ▷ HISTORY imitative

cay *n* a small low island or bank of sand and coral fragments. ▷ HISTORY Spanish *cayo*

cayenne pepper *or* **cayenne** *n* a very hot red spice made from the dried seeds of capsicums. ▷ HISTORY S American Indian *quiynha*

cayman *or* **caiman** *n, pl* **-mans** a tropical American reptile similar to an alligator. ▷ HISTORY Carib

CB 1 Citizens' Band. **2** Commander of the Order of the Bath.

CBE Commander of the Order of the British Empire (a Brit. title).

CBI Confederation of British Industry.

cc *or* **c.c. 1** carbon copy. **2** cubic centimetre.

CC 1 County Council. **2** Cricket Club.

CCTV closed-circuit television.

cd candela.

Cd *Chem* cadmium.

CD compact disc.
CDI compact disc interactive: a system for storing a mix of software, data, audio, and compressed video for interactive use under processor control.
CD player *n* a device for playing compact discs.
Cdr Commander.
CD-R compact disk recordable.
CD-ROM compact disc read-only memory: a compact disc used with a computer system as a read-only optical disc.
CD-RW compact disk read-write.
CDT Central Daylight Time.
CD-video *n* a compact-disc player that, when connected to a television and a hi-fi, produces high-quality stereo sound and synchronized pictures from a compact disc.
Ce *Chem* cerium.
cease *vb* **ceasing, ceased 1** to bring or come to an end. ✧ *n* **2 without cease** without stopping. ▷ HISTORY Latin *cessare*
ceasefire *n* a temporary period of truce.
ceaseless *adj* without stopping. ▶ **ceaselessly** *adv*
cedar *n* **1** a coniferous tree with needle-like evergreen leaves and barrel-shaped cones. **2** the sweet-smelling wood of this tree. ▷ HISTORY Greek *kedros*
cede *vb* **ceding, ceded** to transfer or surrender (territory or legal rights). ▷ HISTORY Latin *cedere* to yield
cedilla *n* a character (¸) placed underneath a *c*, esp. in French or Portuguese, indicating that it is to be pronounced (s), not (k). ▷ HISTORY Spanish: little *z*
Ceefax *n Trademark* (in Britain) the BBC Teletext service.
ceilidh (**kay**-lee) *n* an informal social gathering in Scotland or Ireland with folk music and country dancing. ▷ HISTORY Gaelic
ceiling *n* **1** the inner upper surface of a room. **2** an upper limit set on something such as a payment or salary. **3** the upper altitude to which an aircraft can climb. ▷ HISTORY origin unknown
celandine *n* a wild plant with yellow flowers. ▷ HISTORY Greek *khelidōn* swallow; the plant's season was believed to parallel the migration of swallows
celebrant *n* a person who performs or takes part in a religious ceremony.
celebrate *vb* **-brating, -brated 1** to hold festivities to mark (a happy event, birthday, or anniversary). **2** to perform (a solemn or religious ceremony). **3** to praise publicly: *the novel is justly celebrated as a masterpiece.* ▷ HISTORY Latin *celeber* numerous, renowned ▶ **celebration** *n* ▶ **celebratory** *adj*
celebrated *adj* well known: *the celebrated musician.*
celebrity *n, pl* **-ties 1** a famous person. **2** the state of being famous.
celeriac (sill-**ler**-ree-ak) *n* a variety of celery with a large turnip-like root.
celerity (sill-**ler**-rit-tee) *n Formal* swiftness. ▷ HISTORY Latin *celeritas*
celery *n* a vegetable with long green crisp edible stalks. ▷ HISTORY Greek *selinon* parsley
celestial *adj* **1** heavenly or divine: *celestial music.* **2** of or relating to the sky or space: *celestial objects such as pulsars and quasars.* ▷ HISTORY Latin *caelum* heaven
celestial equator *n* an imaginary circle lying on the celestial sphere in a plane perpendicular to the earth's axis.
celestial sphere *n* an imaginary sphere of infinitely large radius enclosing the universe.
celibate *adj* **1** unmarried or abstaining from sex, esp. because of a religious vow of chastity. ✧ *n* **2** a celibate person. ▷ HISTORY Latin *caelebs* unmarried ▶ **celibacy** *n*
cell *n* **1** *Biol* the smallest unit of an organism that is able to function independently. **2** a small simple room in a prison, convent, or monastery. **3** any small compartment, such as a cell of a honeycomb. **4** a small group operating as the core of a larger organization: *Communist cells.* **5** a device that produces electrical energy by chemical action. ▷ HISTORY Latin *cella* room, storeroom
cellar *n* **1** an underground room, usually used for storage. **2** a place where wine is stored. **3** a stock of bottled wines. ▷ HISTORY Latin *cellarium* food store
cell membrane *n Anat* a very thin membrane that surrounds the cytoplasm of a cell.
cello (**chell**-oh) *n, pl* **-los** a large low-pitched musical instrument of the violin family, held between the knees and played with a bow. ▷ HISTORY short for *violoncello* ▶ **cellist** *n*
Cellophane *n Trademark* a thin transparent material made from cellulose that is used as a protective wrapping, esp. for food. ▷ HISTORY *cellulose* + Greek *phainein* to shine, appear
cellular *adj* **1** of, consisting of, or resembling a cell or cells: *cellular changes.* **2** woven with an open texture: *cellular blankets.* **3** designed for or using cellular radio: *cellular phones.*
cellular radio *n* radio communication, used esp. in car phones, based on a network of transmitters each serving a small area known as a cell.
cellular respiration *n Biochem* the chemical breakdown of complex organic substances, such as carbohydrates and fats, that takes place in the cells and tissues of animals and plants, during which energy is released and carbon dioxide is produced.
cellulite *n* fat deposits under the skin alleged to resist dieting.
celluloid *n* **1** a kind of plastic made from cellulose nitrate and camphor, used to make toys and, formerly, photographic film. **2** the cinema or films generally: *a Shakespeare play committed to celluloid.*
cellulose *n* the main constituent of plant cell walls, used in making paper, rayon, and plastics.
cellulose acetate *n* a nonflammable material used to make film, lacquers, and artificial fibres.

cellulose nitrate *n* a compound used in plastics, lacquers, and explosives.

cell wall *n Anat* the outer layer of a cell.

Celsius *adj* denoting a measurement on the Celsius scale. ▷ **HISTORY** after Anders *Celsius,* astronomer who invented it

Celsius scale *n* a scale of temperature in which 0° represents the melting point of ice and 100° represents the boiling point of water.

Celt (**kelt**) *n* **1** a person from Scotland, Ireland, Wales, Cornwall, or Brittany. **2** a member of a people who inhabited Britain, Gaul, and Spain in pre-Roman times. ▷ **HISTORY** Latin *Celtae* the Celts

Celtic (**kel**-tik, **sel**-tik) *n* **1** a group of languages that includes Gaelic, Welsh, and Breton. ✧ *adj* **2** of the Celts or the Celtic languages.

cement *n* **1 a** a fine grey powder made of limestone and clay, mixed with water and sand to make mortar or concrete. **b** mortar or concrete. **2** something that unites, binds, or joins things or people: *bone cement; the cement of fear and hatred of the Left.* **3** *Dentistry* a material used for filling teeth. ✧ *vb* **4** to join, bind, or cover with cement. **5** to make (a relationship) stronger: *this would cement a firm alliance between the army and rebels.* ▷ **HISTORY** Latin *caementum* stone from the quarry

cemetery *n, pl* **-teries** a place where dead people are buried: *a military cemetery.* ▷ **HISTORY** Greek *koimētērion* room for sleeping

cenotaph *n* a monument honouring soldiers who died in a war. ▷ **HISTORY** Greek *kenos* empty + *taphos* tomb

Cenozoic *or* **Caenozoic** (see-no-**zoh**-ik) *adj Geol* of the most recent geological era, beginning 65 million years ago, characterized by the development and increase of the mammals. ▷ **HISTORY** Greek *kainos* recent + *zōion* animal

censer *n* a container for burning incense.

censor *n* **1** a person authorized to examine films, letters, or publications, in order to ban or cut anything considered obscene or objectionable. ✧ *vb* **2** to ban or cut portions of (a film, letter, or publication). ▷ **HISTORY** Latin *censere* to consider

censorious *adj* harshly critical.

censorship *n* the practice or policy of censoring films, letters, or publications.

censure *n* **1** severe disapproval. ✧ *vb* **-suring, -sured 2** to criticize (someone or something) severely. ▷ **HISTORY** Latin *censere* to assess

censure motion *n Parliament* a motion expressing strong criticism (of the government, a minister, etc.).

census *n, pl* **-suses** an official periodic count of a population including such information as sex, age, and occupation. ▷ **HISTORY** Latin *censere* to assess

cent *n* a monetary unit worth one hundredth of the main unit of currency in many countries. ▷ **HISTORY** Latin *centum* hundred

cent. 1 central. **2** century.

centaur *n Greek myth* a creature with the head, arms, and torso of a man, and the lower body and legs of a horse. ▷ **HISTORY** Greek *kentauros*

centenarian *n* a person who is at least 100 years old.

centenary (sen-**teen**-a-ree) *n, pl* **-naries** *Chiefly Brit* a 100th anniversary or the celebration of one. US equivalent: **centennial** ▷ **HISTORY** Latin *centum* hundred

centesimal *n* **1** one hundredth. ✧ *adj* **2** of or divided into hundredths. ▷ **HISTORY** Latin *centum* hundred

centi- *prefix* **1** denoting one hundredth: *centimetre.* **2** a hundred: *centipede.* ▷ **HISTORY** Latin *centum* hundred

centigrade *adj* same as **Celsius**.

> **☑ WORD TIP**
> Although still used in meteorology, *centigrade,* when indicating the Celsius scale of temperature, is now usually avoided in other scientific contexts because of its possible confusion with the hundredth part of a grade.

centigram *or* **centigramme** *n* one hundredth of a gram.

centilitre *or US* **centiliter** *n* a measure of volume equivalent to one hundredth of a litre.

centime (**son**-teem) *n* a monetary unit worth one hundredth of the main unit of currency in a number of countries. ▷ **HISTORY** Latin *centum* hundred

centimetre *or US* **centimeter** *n* a unit of length equal to one hundredth of a metre.

centipede *n* a small wormlike creature with many legs.

central *adj* **1** of, at, or forming the centre of something: *eastern and central parts of the country.* **2** main or principal: *a central issue.* ▶ **centrally** *adv* ▶ **centrality** *n*

central bank *n* a national bank that acts as the government's banker, controls credit, and issues currency.

central business district *n* the main centre of a town, containing shops, businesses, and places of entertainment.

Central European Time *n* the standard time adopted by Western European countries one hour ahead of Greenwich Mean Time, corresponding to British Summer Time. Abbrev: **CET**

central government *n* the government of a whole country, as opposed to the smaller organizations that govern counties, towns, and districts.

central heating *n* a system for heating a building by means of radiators or air vents connected to a central source of heat. ▶ **centrally heated** *adj*

centralism *n* the principle of bringing a country or an organization under central control. ▶ **centralist** *adj*

centralize *or* **-ise** *vb* **-izing, -ized** *or* **-ising, -ised** to bring (a country or an organization) under central control. ▶ **centralization** *or* **-isation** *n*

central locking *n* a system by which all the doors of a motor vehicle are locked automatically when the driver's door is locked manually.

central nervous system *n* the part of the nervous system of vertebrates that consists of the brain and spinal cord.

central processing unit *n* the part of a computer that performs logical and arithmetical operations on the data.

central reservation *n Brit & NZ* the strip that separates the two sides of a motorway or dual carriageway.

centre *or US* **center** *n* **1** the middle point or part of something. **2** a place where a specified activity takes place: *a shopping centre.* **3** a person or thing that is a focus of interest: *the centre of a long-running dispute.* **4** a place of activity or influence: *the parliament building was the centre of resistance.* **5** a political party or group that favours moderation. **6** *Sport* a player who plays in the middle of the field rather than on a wing. ✧ *vb* **-tring, -tred** *or US* **-tering, -tered 7** to put in the centre of something. **8 centre on** to have as a centre or main theme: *the summit is expected to centre on expanding the role of the UN.* ▷ HISTORY Greek *kentron* needle, sharp point

centrefold *or US* **centerfold** *n* a large coloured illustration, often a photograph of a naked or scantily dressed young woman, folded to form the centre pages of a magazine.

centre forward *n Sport* the middle player in the forward line of a team.

centre half *or* **centre back** *n Soccer* a defender who plays in the middle of the defence.

centre of gravity *n* the point in an object around which its mass is evenly distributed.

centre pass *n Hockey* a push or hit made in any direction to start the game.

centre stage *n* **1** *Theatre* the centre point on a stage. **2** the main focus of attention.

centrifugal (sent-**riff**-few-gl) *adj* **1** moving or tending to move away from a centre. **2** of or operated by centrifugal force: *centrifugal extractors.* ▷ HISTORY Greek *kentron* centre + Latin *fugere* to flee

centrifugal force *n* a force that acts outwards on any body that rotates or moves along a curved path.

centrifuge *n* a machine that separates substances by the action of centrifugal force.

centripetal (sent-**rip**-it-al) *adj* moving or tending to move towards a centre. ▷ HISTORY Greek *kentron* centre + Latin *petere* to seek

centripetal force *n* a force that acts inwards on any body that rotates or moves along a curved path.

centrist *n* a person who holds moderate political views.

centromere *n Biol* the dense nonstaining region of a chromosome that attaches it to the spindle during mitosis.

centrosome *n Biol* a small protoplasmic body found near the cell nucleus.

centrosphere *n* **1** *Geol* the central part of the earth. Also called: **core 2** *Biol* another name for **centrosome**.

centurion *n* (in ancient Rome) the officer in command of a century. ▷ HISTORY Latin *centurio*

century *n, pl* **-ries 1** a period of 100 years. **2** a score of 100 runs in cricket. **3** (in ancient Rome) a unit of foot soldiers, originally consisting of 100 men. ▷ HISTORY Latin *centuria*

CEO chief executive officer.

cephalopod (**seff**-a-loh-pod) *n* a sea mollusc with a head and tentacles, such as the octopus. ▷ HISTORY Greek *kephalē* head + *pous* foot

ceramic *n* **1** a hard brittle material made by heating clay to a very high temperature. **2** an object made of this material. ✧ *adj* **3** made of ceramic: *ceramic tiles.* ▷ HISTORY Greek *keramos* potter's clay

Cerberus (**sir**-ber-uss) *n Greek myth* a three-headed dog who guarded the entrance to Hades.

cere *n* a soft waxy swelling, containing the nostrils, at the base of the upper beak of a parrot. ▷ HISTORY Latin *cera* wax

cereal *n* **1** any grass that produces an edible grain, such as oat, wheat, or rice. **2** the grain produced by such a plant. **3** a breakfast food made from this grain, usually eaten mixed with milk. ▷ HISTORY Latin *cerealis* concerning agriculture

cerebellum (serr-rib-**bell**-lum) *n, pl* **-lums** *or* **-la** (-la) the back part of the brain, which controls balance and muscular coordination. ▷ HISTORY Latin

cerebral (**serr**-rib-ral) *adj* **1** of the brain: *a cerebral haemorrhage.* **2** involving intelligence rather than emotions or instinct: *the cerebral joys of the literary world.*

cerebral palsy *n* a condition in which the limbs and muscles are permanently weak, caused by damage to the brain.

cerebrospinal *adj* of the brain and spinal cord: *a sample of cerebrospinal fluid.*

cerebrovascular (serr-rib-roh-**vass**-kew-lar) *adj* of the blood vessels and blood supply of the brain.

cerebrum (**serr**-rib-rum) *n, pl* **-brums** *or* **-bra** (-bra) the main part of the human brain, associated with thought, emotion, and personality. ▷ HISTORY Latin: the brain

ceremonial *adj* **1** of ceremony or ritual. ✧ *n* **2** a system of formal rites; ritual. ▶ **ceremonially** *adv*

ceremonious *adj* excessively polite or formal. ▶ **ceremoniously** *adv*

ceremony *n, pl* **-nies 1** a formal act or ritual performed for a special occasion: *a wedding ceremony.* **2** formally polite behaviour. **3 stand on ceremony** to insist on or act with excessive formality. ▷ HISTORY Latin *caerimonia* what is sacred

Ceres *n* the Roman goddess of agriculture.

cerise (ser-**reess**) *adj* cherry-red. ▷ HISTORY French: cherry

cerium *n Chem* a steel-grey metallic element found only in combination with other elements. Symbol: Ce. ▷ HISTORY from *Ceres* (an asteroid)

a b c d e f g h i j k l m n o p q r s t u v w x y z

CERN Conseil Européen pour la Recherche Nucléaire: a European organization for research in high-energy particle physics.

cert *n* **a dead cert** *Informal* something that is certain to happen or to be successful.

certain *adj* **1** positive and confident about something: *he was certain they would agree.* **2** definitely known: *it is by no means certain the tomb still exists.* **3** sure or bound: *the cuts are certain to go ahead.* **4** some but not much: *a certain amount.* **5** particular: *certain aspects.* **6** named but not known: *a running commentary by a certain Mr Fox.* **7 for certain** without doubt. ▷ HISTORY Latin *certus* sure

certain chance *n Maths* the point at one of the furthest ends of a likelihood scale.

certainly *adv* without doubt: *he will certainly be back.*

certainty *n* **1** the condition of being certain. **2** (*pl* **-ties**) something established as inevitable.

certifiable *adj* considered to be legally insane.

certificate *n* an official document stating the details of something such as birth, death, or completion of an academic course. ▷ HISTORY Old French *certifier* to certify

certificate of incorporation *n Company law* a signed statement that a company is duly incorporated.

certified *adj* **1** holding or guaranteed by a certificate: *a certified acupuncturist.* **2** declared legally insane.

certify *vb* **-fies, -fying, -fied 1** to confirm or attest to. **2** to guarantee (that certain required standards have been met). **3** to declare legally insane. ▷ HISTORY Latin *certus* certain + *facere* to make ▶ **certification** *n*

certitude *n Formal* confidence or certainty.

cervical smear *n Med* a smear taken from the neck (cervix) of the womb for detection of cancer.

cervix *n, pl* **cervixes** *or* **cervices 1** the lower part of the womb that extends into the vagina. **2** *Anat* the neck. ▷ HISTORY Latin ▶ **cervical** *adj*

cesium *n US* same as **caesium.**

cessation *n* an ending or pause: *a cessation of hostilities.* ▷ HISTORY Latin *cessare* to be idle

cession *n* the act of ceding territory or legal rights. ▷ HISTORY Latin *cedere* to yield

cesspool *or* **cesspit** *n* a covered tank or pit for collecting and storing sewage or waste water. ▷ HISTORY Old French *souspirail* air vent

CET Central European Time.

cetacean (sit-**tay**-shun) *n* a sea creature such as a whale or dolphin, which belongs to a family of fish-shaped mammals and breathes through a blowhole. ▷ HISTORY Greek *kētos* whale

cetane (**see**-tane) *n* a colourless liquid hydrocarbon, used as a solvent. ▷ HISTORY Latin *cetus* whale

cetane number *n* a measure of the quality of a diesel fuel expressed as the percentage of cetane in it.

cf compare. ▷ HISTORY Latin *confer*

Cf *Chem* californium.

CF Canadian Forces.

CFC chlorofluorocarbon.

CFS chronic fatigue syndrome.

cg centigram.

CGI computer-generated image(s).

cgs units *pl n* a metric system of units based on the centimetre, gram, and second: for scientific and technical purposes, replaced by SI units.

ch. **1** chapter. **2** church.

cha-cha *or* **cha-cha-cha** *n* **1** a modern ballroom dance from Latin America. **2** music for this dance. ▷ HISTORY American (Cuban) Spanish

chaconne *n* a musical form consisting of a set of variations on a repeated melodic bass line.

chad *n* the small pieces removed during the punching of holes in punch cards, printer paper, etc.

chafe *vb* **chafing, chafed 1** to make sore or worn by rubbing. **2** to be annoyed or impatient: *the lower castes are chafing against 20 years of servitude.* ▷ HISTORY Old French *chaufer* to warm

chafer *n* a large slow-moving beetle. ▷ HISTORY Old English *ceafor*

chaff[1] *n* **1** grain husks separated from the seeds during threshing. **2** something of little worth; rubbish: *you had to be a very perceptive listener to sort the wheat from the chaff of his discourse.* ▷ HISTORY Old English *ceaf*

chaff[2] *vb* to tease good-naturedly. ▷ HISTORY probably slang variant of *chafe*

chaffinch *n* a small European songbird with black-and-white wings and, in the male, a reddish body and blue-grey head. ▷ HISTORY Old English *ceaf* CHAFF[1] + *finc* finch

chagrin (**shag**-grin) *n* a feeling of annoyance and disappointment. ▷ HISTORY French

chagrined *adj* annoyed and disappointed.

chain *n* **1** a flexible length of metal links, used for fastening, binding, or connecting, or in jewellery. **2 chains** anything that restricts or restrains someone: *bound by the chains of duty.* **3** a series of connected facts or events. **4** a number of establishments, such as hotels or shops, that have the same owner or management. **5** *Chem* a number of atoms or groups bonded together so that the resulting molecule, ion, or radical resembles a chain. **6** a row of mountains or islands. ✧ *vb* **7** to restrict, fasten or bind with or as if with a chain: *the demonstrators chained themselves to railings.* ▷ HISTORY Latin *catena*

chain gang *n US* a group of convicted prisoners chained together.

chain letter *n* a letter, often with a request for or promise of money, that is sent to many people who are asked to send copies to other people.

chain mail *n* same as **mail**[2].

chain of command *n Business* a hierarchy of officials in an organization, each person reporting to the person above him or her in the hierarchy.

chain reaction *n* **1** a series of events, each of which causes the next. **2** a chemical or nuclear reaction in which the product of one step triggers the following step.

chain saw *n* a motor-driven saw in which the cutting teeth form links in a continuous chain.

chain-smoke *vb* **-smoking, -smoked** to smoke continuously, lighting one cigarette from the preceding one. ▶ **chain smoker** *n*

chair *n* **1** a seat with a back and four legs, for one person to sit on. **2** an official position of authority or the person holding it: *the chair of the Security Council.* **3** a professorship. **4 in the chair** presiding over a meeting. **5 the chair** *Informal* the electric chair. ✧ *vb* **6** to preside over (a meeting). ▷ HISTORY Greek *kathedra*

chairlift *n* a series of chairs suspended from a moving cable for carrying people up a slope.

chairman *n, pl* **-men** a person who is in charge of a company's board of directors or a meeting. ▶ **chairwoman** *fem n* ▶ **chairmanship** *n*

> **WORD TIP**
> *Chairman* can seem inappropriate when applied to a woman, while *chairwoman* can be offensive. *Chair* and *chairperson* can be applied to either a man or a woman; *chair* is generally preferred to *chairperson.*

chaise (**shaze**) *n* a light horse-drawn carriage with two wheels. ▷ HISTORY French

chaise longue (**long**) *n, pl* **chaise longues** *or* **chaises longues** a couch with a back and a single armrest. ▷ HISTORY French

chalcedony (kal-**sed**-don-ee) *n, pl* **-nies** a form of quartz composed of very fine crystals, often greyish or blue in colour. ▷ HISTORY Greek *khalkēdōn* a precious stone

chalet *n* **1** a type of Swiss wooden house with a steeply sloping roof. **2** a similar house used as a ski lodge or holiday home. ▷ HISTORY French

chalice (**chal**-liss) *n* **1** *Poetic* a drinking cup or goblet. **2** *Christianity* a gold or silver goblet containing the wine at communion. ▷ HISTORY Latin *calix* cup

chalk *n* **1** a soft white rock consisting of calcium carbonate. **2** a piece of chalk, either white or coloured, used for writing and drawing on blackboards. **3 as different as chalk and cheese** *Informal* totally different. **4 not by a long chalk** *Informal* by no means: *you haven't finished by a long chalk.* ✧ *vb* **5** to draw or mark with chalk. ▷ HISTORY Latin *calx* limestone ▶ **chalky** *adj*

chalk up *vb Informal* **1** to score or register: *the home side chalked up a 9-1 victory.* **2** to charge or credit (money) to an account.

challenge *n* **1** a demanding or stimulating situation. **2** a call to engage in a contest, fight, or argument. **3** a questioning of a statement or fact. **4** a demand by a sentry for identification or a password. **5** *Law* a formal objection to a juror. ✧ *vb* **-lenging, -lenged 6** to invite or call (someone) to take part in a contest, fight, or argument. **7** to call (a decision or action) into question. **8** to order (a person) to stop and be identified. **9** *Law* to make formal objection to (a juror). ▷ HISTORY Latin *calumnia* calumny ▶ **challenger** *n* ▶ **challenging** *adj*

challenged *adj* disabled as specified: *physically challenged; mentally challenged.*

chalybeate (kal-**lib**-bee-it) *adj* containing or impregnated with iron salts: *a natural chalybeate spring rises at the edge of the lake.* ▷ HISTORY Greek *khalups* iron

chamber *n* **1** a meeting hall, usually one used for a legislative or judicial assembly. **2** a room equipped for a particular purpose: *a decompression chamber.* **3** a legislative or judicial assembly: *the Senate, the upper chamber of Canada's parliament.* **4** *Old-fashioned or poetic* a room in a house, esp. a bedroom. **5** a compartment or cavity: *the heart chambers.* **6** a compartment for a cartridge or shell in a gun. ✧ See also **chambers.** ▷ HISTORY Greek *kamara* vault

chamberlain *n History* an officer who managed the household of a king or nobleman. ▷ HISTORY Old French *chamberlayn*

chamber magistrate *n Austral Law* a solicitor employed to provide free legal advice at a local court.

chambermaid *n* a woman employed to clean bedrooms in a hotel.

chamber music *n* classical music to be performed by a small group of musicians.

chamber pot *n* a bowl for urine, formerly used in bedrooms.

chambers *pl n* **1** a judge's room for hearing private cases not taken in open court. **2** (in England) the set of rooms used as offices by a barrister.

chameleon (kam-**meal**-yon) *n* a small lizard with long legs that is able to change colour to blend in with its surroundings.

> **WORD HISTORY**
> Although it may not much look like one, a chameleon is, in terms of its word origins, a type of lion, a 'ground lion'. The word comes from two Greek words, *khamai*, meaning 'on the ground', and *leōn*, meaning 'lion'.

chamfer (**cham**-fer) *n* **1** a bevelled surface at an edge or corner. ✧ *vb* **2** to cut a chamfer on or in. ▷ HISTORY Old French *chant* edge + *fraindre* to break

chamois *n, pl* **-ois 1** (**sham**-wah) a small mountain antelope of Europe and SW Asia. **2** (**sham**-ee) a soft suede leather made from the skin of this animal or from sheep or goats. **3** (**sham**-ee) Also: **chamois leather, shammy, chammy** a piece of such leather or similar material, used for cleaning and polishing. ▷ HISTORY Old French

chamomile (**kam**-mo-mile) *n* same as **camomile.**

champ[1] *vb* **1** to chew noisily. **2 champ at the bit** *Informal* to be restless or impatient to do something. ▷ HISTORY probably imitative

champ[2] *n Informal* short for **champion** (sense 1).

champagne *n* **1** a white sparkling wine produced around Reims and Épernay, France. ✧ *adj* **2** denoting a luxurious lifestyle: *a champagne capitalist.* ▷ **HISTORY** *Champagne,* region of France

champion *n* **1** a person, plant, or animal that has defeated all others in a competition: *the Olympic 100 metres champion.* **2** someone who defends a person or cause: *a champion of the downtrodden.* ✧ *vb* **3** to support: *he unceasingly championed equal rights and opportunities.* ✧ *adj* **4** *N English dialect* excellent. ▷ **HISTORY** Latin *campus* field ▶ **championship** *n*

chance *n* **1** the extent to which something is likely to happen; probability. **2** an opportunity or occasion to do something: *a chance to escape rural poverty.* **3** a risk or gamble: *the government is not in the mood to take any more chances.* **4** the unknown and unpredictable element that causes something to happen in one way rather than another: *in Buddhism there is no such thing as chance or coincidence.* **5 by chance** without planning: *by chance she met an old school friend.* **6 on the off chance** acting on the slight possibility: *he had called on the agents on the off chance that he might learn something of value.* ✧ *vb* **chancing, chanced 7** to risk or hazard: *a few picnickers chanced the perilous footpath.* **8** to do something without planning to: *I chanced to look down.* **9 chance on** *or* **upon** to discover by accident: *I chanced upon a copy of this book.* ▷ **HISTORY** Latin *cadere* to occur

chancel *n* the part of a church containing the altar and choir. ▷ **HISTORY** Latin *cancelli* lattice

chancellery *or* **chancellory** *n, pl* **-leries** *or* **-lories 1** *Brit & Austral* the residence or office of a chancellor. **2** *US* the office of an embassy or consulate. ▷ **HISTORY** Anglo-French *chancellerie*

chancellor *n* **1** the head of government in several European countries. **2** *US* the president of a university. **3** *Brit, Austral & Canad* the honorary head of a university. ▷ **HISTORY** Late Latin *cancellarius* porter ▶ **chancellorship** *n*

Chancellor of the Exchequer *n Brit* the cabinet minister responsible for finance.

Chancery *n* (in England) the Lord Chancellor's court, a division of the High Court of Justice. ▷ **HISTORY** shortened from CHANCELLERY

chancre (**shang**-ker) *n Pathol* a painless ulcer that develops as a primary symptom of syphilis. ▷ **HISTORY** French

chancy *adj* **chancier, chanciest** *Informal* uncertain or risky.

chandelier (shan-dill-**eer**) *n* an ornamental hanging light with branches and holders for several candles or bulbs. ▷ **HISTORY** French

chandler *n* a dealer in a specified trade or merchandise: *a ship's chandler.* ▷ **HISTORY** Old French *chandelier* dealer in candles ▶ **chandlery** *n*

change *n* **1** the fact of becoming different. **2** variety or novelty: *they wanted to print some good news for a change.* **3** a different set, esp. of clothes. **4** money exchanged for its equivalent in a larger denomination or in a different currency. **5** the balance of money when the amount paid is larger than the amount due. **6** coins of a small denomination. ✧ *vb* **changing, changed 7** to make or become different. **8** to replace with or exchange for another: *the Swedish Communist Party changed its name to the Left Party.* **9** to give and receive (something) in return: *slaves and masters changed places.* **10** to give or receive (money) in exchange for its equivalent sum in a smaller denomination or different currency. **11** to put on other clothes. **12** to get off one bus, train or airliner and on to another: *there's no direct train, so you'll need to change at York.* ✧ See also **change down, change up.** ▷ **HISTORY** Latin *cambire* to exchange, barter ▶ **changeless** *adj*

changeable *adj* changing often. ▶ **changeability** *n*

change down *vb* to select a lower gear when driving.

changeling *n* a child believed to have been exchanged by fairies for the parents' real child.

change of life *n* the menopause.

change up *vb* to select a higher gear when driving.

channel *n* **1** a band of radio frequencies assigned for the broadcasting of a radio or television signal. **2** a path for an electrical signal or computer data. **3** a means of access or communication: *reports coming through diplomatic channels.* **4** a broad strait connecting two areas of sea. **5** the bed or course of a river, stream, or canal. **6** a navigable course through an area of water. **7** a groove. ✧ *vb* **-nelling, -nelled** *or US* **-neling, -neled 8** to direct or convey through a channel or channels: *tunnels that channel the pilgrims into the area; to channel funds abroad.* ▷ **HISTORY** Latin *canalis* pipe, conduit

Channel *n* **the Channel** the English Channel.

channel-hop *vb* **-hopping, -hopped** to change television channels repeatedly using a remote control device.

chant *vb* **1** to repeat (a slogan) over and over. **2** to sing or recite (a psalm). ✧ *n* **3** a rhythmic or repetitious slogan repeated over and over, usually by more than one person. **4** a religious song with a short simple melody in which several words or syllables are sung on one note. ▷ **HISTORY** Latin *canere* to sing

chanter *n* the pipe on a set of bagpipes on which the melody is played.

chanticleer *n* a name for a cock, used in fables. ▷ **HISTORY** Old French *chanter cler* to sing clearly

chanty *n, pl* **-ties** same as **shanty**[2].

Chanukah *or* **Hanukkah** (**hah**-na-ka) *n* an eight-day Jewish festival, held in December, commemorating the rededication of the temple by Judas Maccabaeus. ▷ **HISTORY** Hebrew

chaos *n* complete disorder or confusion. ▷ **HISTORY** Greek *khaos* ▶ **chaotic** *adj* ▶ **chaotically** *adv*

chap *n Informal* a man or boy. ▷ **HISTORY** from Old English *cēapman* pedlar

chapati *or* **chapatti** *n* (in Indian cookery) a kind of flat thin unleavened bread. ▷ **HISTORY** Hindi

chapel *n* **1** a place of worship with its own altar, in a church or cathedral. **2** a similar place of worship in a large house or institution. **3** (in England and Wales) a Nonconformist place of worship. **4** (in Scotland) a Roman Catholic church. **5** the members of a trade union in a newspaper office, printing house, or publishing firm.

WORD HISTORY
According to legend, St Martin of Tours once gave half his cloak to a beggar. This cloak (Latin *cappella*) was kept as a relic and the place where it was kept also became known as the 'cappella' or, in Old French, *chapelle*. The use of this word then spread to other places of worship.

chaperone (**shap**-per-rone) *n* **1** an older person who accompanies and supervises a young person or young people on social occasions. ✧ *vb* **-oning, -oned 2** to act as a chaperone to. ▷ **HISTORY** Old French *chape* hood

chaplain *n* a clergyman attached to a chapel, military body, or institution. ▷ **HISTORY** Late Latin *cappella* chapel ▶ **chaplaincy** *n*

chaplet *n* a garland worn on the head. ▷ **HISTORY** Old French *chapelet*

chapman *n, pl* **-men** *Old-fashioned* a travelling pedlar. ▷ **HISTORY** Old English *cēapman*

chapped *adj* (of the skin) raw and cracked, through exposure to cold. ▷ **HISTORY** probably Germanic

chaps *pl n* leather leggings without a seat, worn by cowboys. ▷ **HISTORY** shortened from Spanish *chaparejos*

chapter *n* **1** a division of a book. **2** a period in a life or history: *the latest chapter in the long and complex tale of British brewing.* **3** a sequence of events: *a chapter of accidents.* **4** a branch of some societies or clubs. **5** a group of the canons of a cathedral. **6 chapter and verse** exact authority for an action or statement. ▷ **HISTORY** Latin *caput* head

char[1] *vb* **charring, charred** to blacken by partial burning. ▷ **HISTORY** short for *charcoal*

char[2] *Brit informal* ✧ *n* **1** short for **charwoman.** ✧ *vb* **charring, charred 2** to clean other people's houses as a job. ▷ **HISTORY** Old English *cerr* turn of work

char[3] *n Brit old-fashioned slang* tea. ▷ **HISTORY** Chinese *ch'a*

char[4] *n, pl* **char** *or* **chars** a troutlike fish of cold lakes and northern seas. ▷ **HISTORY** origin unknown

charabanc (**shar**-rab-bang) *n Brit old-fashioned* a coach for sightseeing. ▷ **HISTORY** French: wagon with seats

character *n* **1** the combination of qualities distinguishing an individual person, group of people, or place: *the unique charm and character of this historic town.* **2** a distinguishing quality or characteristic: *bodily movements of a deliberate character.* **3** reputation, esp. good reputation: *a man of my Dad's character and standing in the community.* **4** an attractively unusual or interesting quality: *the little town was full of life and character.* **5** a person represented in a play, film, or story. **6** an unusual or amusing person: *quite a character.* **7** *Informal* a person: *a flamboyant character.* **8** a single letter, numeral, or symbol used in writing or printing. **9 in** *or* **out of character** typical *or* not typical of the apparent character of a person. ▷ **HISTORY** Greek *kharaktēr* engraver's tool ▶ **characterless** *adj*

characteristic *n* **1** a distinguishing feature or quality. **2** *Maths* the integral part of a logarithm: *the characteristic of 2.4771 is 2.* ✧ *adj* **3** typical or representative of someone or something: *the prime minister fought with characteristic passion.* ▶ **characteristically** *adv*

characterization *or* **-isation** *n* **1** the description or portrayal of a person by an actor or writer: *a novel full of rich characterization and complex plotting.* **2** the act or an instance of characterizing.

characterize *or* **-ise** *vb* **-izing, -ized** *or* **-ising, -ised 1** to be a characteristic of: *the violence that characterized the demonstrations.* **2** to describe: *we have made what I would characterize as outstanding progress.*

characterology *n Literature* the study of the development and differences of character.

charade (shar-**rahd**) *n* an absurd pretence. ▷ **HISTORY** French

charcoal *n* **1** a black form of carbon made by partially burning wood or other organic matter. **2** a stick of this used for drawing. **3** a drawing done in charcoal. ✧ *adj* **4** Also: **charcoal-grey** very dark grey. ▷ **HISTORY** origin unknown

charge *vb* **charging, charged 1** to ask (an amount of money) as a price. **2** to enter a debit against a person's account for (a purchase). **3** to accuse (someone) formally of a crime in a court of law. **4** to make a rush at or sudden attack upon. **5** to fill (a glass). **6** to cause (an accumulator or capacitor) to take and store electricity. **7** to fill or saturate with liquid or gas: *old mine workings charged with foul gas.* **8** to fill with a feeling or mood: *the emotionally charged atmosphere.* **9** *Formal* to command or assign: *the president has charged his foreign minister with trying to open talks.* ✧ *n* **10** a price charged for something; cost. **11** a formal accusation of a crime in a court of law. **12** an onrush or attack. **13** custody or guardianship: *in the charge of the police.* **14** a person or thing committed to someone's care: *a nanny reported the cruel father of one of her charges to social workers.* **15 a** a cartridge or shell. **b** the explosive required to fire a gun. **16** *Physics* **a** the attribute of matter responsible for all electrical phenomena, existing in two forms, positive and negative. **b** the total amount of electricity stored in a capacitor or an accumulator. **17 in charge of** in control of and responsible for: *in charge of defence and foreign affairs.* ▷ **HISTORY** Old French *chargier* to load

chargeable *adj* **1** liable to be taxed or charged. **2** liable to result in a legal charge.

charge card *n* a card issued by a chain store, shop, or organization, that enables customers to obtain goods and services for which they pay later.

chargé d'affaires (**shar**-zhay daf-**fair**) *n, pl* **chargés d'affaires** (**shar**-zhay daf-**fair**) **1** the temporary head of a diplomatic mission in the

absence of the ambassador or minister. **2** the head of a small or unimportant diplomatic mission.
▷ **HISTORY** French

charger *n* **1** a device for charging a battery. **2** (in the Middle Ages) a warhorse.

chariot *n* a two-wheeled horse-drawn vehicle used in ancient times for wars and races.
▷ **HISTORY** Old French *char* car

charioteer *n* a chariot driver.

charisma (kar-**rizz**-ma) *n* the quality or power of an individual to attract, influence, or inspire people.
▷ **HISTORY** Greek *kharis* grace, favour
▶ **charismatic** (kar-rizz-**mat**-ik) *adj*

charismatic movement *n Christianity* a group that believes in divine gifts such as instantaneous healing and uttering unintelligible sounds while in a religious ecstasy.

charitable *adj* **1** kind or lenient in one's attitude towards others. **2** of or for charity: *a charitable organization.* ▶ **charitably** *adv*

charity *n* **1** (*pl* **-ties**) an organization set up to provide help to those in need. **2** the giving of help, such as money or food, to those in need. **3** help given to those in need; alms. **4** a kindly attitude towards people. ▷ **HISTORY** Latin *caritas* affection

charlady *n, pl* **-ladies** *Brit* same as **charwoman**.

charlatan (**shar**-lat-tan) *n* a person who claims expertise that he or she does not have.
▷ **HISTORY** Italian *ciarlare* to chatter

Charles' law *n Physics* the principle that the volume of a gas varies in proportion to its temperature at constant pressure. ▷ **HISTORY** after Jacques *Charles,* physicist

charleston *n* a lively dance of the 1920s.
▷ **HISTORY** after *Charleston,* South Carolina

charlock *n* a weed with hairy leaves and yellow flowers. ▷ **HISTORY** Old English *cerlic*

charlotte *n* a dessert made with fruit and bread or cake crumbs: *apple charlotte.* ▷ **HISTORY** French

charm *n* **1** the quality of attracting, fascinating, or delighting people. **2** a trinket worn on a bracelet. **3** a small object worn for supposed magical powers. **4** a magic spell. ✧ *vb* **5** to attract, fascinate, or delight. **6** to influence or obtain by personal charm: *you can easily be charmed into changing your mind.* **7** to protect as if by magic: *a charmed life.*
▷ **HISTORY** Latin *carmen* song ▶ **charmer** *n*
▶ **charmless** *adj*

charming *adj* delightful or attractive.
▶ **charmingly** *adv*

charnel house *n* (formerly) a building or vault for the bones of the dead. ▷ **HISTORY** Latin *carnalis* fleshly

chart *n* **1** a graph, table, or sheet of information in the form of a diagram. **2** a map of the sea or the stars. **3 the charts** *Informal* the weekly lists of the bestselling pop records or the most popular videos. ✧ *vb* **4** to plot the course of. **5** to make a chart of. **6** to appear in the pop charts. ▷ **HISTORY** Greek *khartēs* papyrus

charter *n* **1** a formal document granting or demanding certain rights or liberties: *a children's charter.* **2** the fundamental principles of an organization: *the UN Charter.* **3** the hire or lease of transportation for private use. ✧ *vb* **4** to lease or hire by charter. **5** to grant a charter to.
▷ **HISTORY** Latin *charta* leaf of papyrus

chartered accountant *n* (in Britain and Australia) an accountant who has passed the examinations of the Institute of Chartered Accountants.

Chartism *n English history* a movement (1838–48) for social and political reforms, demand for which was presented to Parliament in charters.
▶ **Chartist** *n, adj*

chartreuse (shar-**truhz**) *n* a green or yellow liqueur made from herbs. ▷ **HISTORY** after *La Grande Chartreuse,* monastery near Grenoble, where the liqueur is produced

charwoman *n, pl* **-women** *Brit* a woman whose job is to clean other people's houses.

chary (**chair**-ee) *adj* **charier, chariest** wary or careful: *chary of interfering.* ▷ **HISTORY** Old English *cearig*

chase[1] *vb* **chasing, chased 1** to pursue (a person or animal) persistently or quickly. **2** to force (a person or animal) to leave a place. **3** *Informal* to court (someone) in an unsubtle manner. **4** *Informal* to rush or run: *chasing around the world.* **5** *Informal* to pursue (something or someone) energetically in order to obtain results or information. ✧ *n* **6** the act or an instance of chasing a person or animal.
▷ **HISTORY** Latin *capere* to take

chase[2] *vb* **chasing, chased** to engrave or emboss (metal). ▷ **HISTORY** Old French *enchasser*

chaser *n* a drink drunk after another of a different kind, for example beer after whisky.

chasm (**kaz**-zum) *n* **1** a very deep crack in the ground. **2** a wide difference in interests or feelings: *a deep chasm separating science from politics.*
▷ **HISTORY** Greek *khasma*

chassis (**shass**-ee) *n, pl* **chassis** (**shass**-eez) the steel frame, wheels, and mechanical parts of a vehicle. ▷ **HISTORY** French

chaste *adj* **1** abstaining from sex outside marriage or from all sexual intercourse. **2** (of conduct or speech) pure, decent, or modest: *a chaste kiss on the forehead.* **3** simple in style: *chaste furniture.* ▷ **HISTORY** Latin *castus* pure ▶ **chastely** *adv* ▶ **chastity** *n*

chasten (**chase**-en) *vb* to subdue (someone) by criticism. ▷ **HISTORY** Latin *castigare*

chastise *vb* **-tising, -tised 1** to scold severely. **2** *Old-fashioned* to punish by beating.
▷ **HISTORY** Middle English *chastisen*
▶ **chastisement** *n*

chasuble (**chazz**-yew-bl) *n Christianity* a long sleeveless robe worn by a priest when celebrating Mass. ▷ **HISTORY** Late Latin *casubla* garment with a hood

chat *n* **1** an informal conversation. ✧ *vb* **chatting, chatted 2** to have an informal conversation. ✧ See also **chat up**. ▷ **HISTORY** short for *chatter*

chateau (**shat**-toe) *n, pl* **-teaux** (-toe) *or* **-teaus** a French country house or castle. ▷ **HISTORY** French

chatelaine (**shat**-tell-lane) *n* (formerly) the mistress of a large house or castle.
▷ HISTORY French

chatline *n* a telephone service enabling callers to join in general conversation with each other.

chatroom *n* a site on the Internet where users have group discussions by electronic mail.

chattels *pl n Old-fashioned* possessions.
▷ HISTORY Old French *chatel* personal property

chatter *vb* **1** to speak quickly and continuously about unimportant things. **2** (of birds or monkeys) to make rapid repetitive high-pitched noises. **3** (of the teeth) to click together rapidly through cold or fear. ✧ *n* **4** idle talk or gossip. **5** the high-pitched repetitive noise made by a bird or monkey.
▷ HISTORY imitative

chatterbox *n Informal* a person who talks a great deal, usually about unimportant things.

chattering classes *n* **the chattering classes** *Informal, often derogatory* the members of the educated sections of society who enjoy discussion of political, social, and cultural issues.

chatty *adj* **-tier, -tiest 1** (of a person) fond of friendly, informal conversation; talkative. **2** (of a letter) informal and friendly; gossipy.

chat up *vb Brit & Austral informal* to talk flirtatiously to (someone) with a view to starting a romantic or sexual relationship.

chauffeur *n* **1** a person employed to drive a car for someone. ✧ *vb* **2** to act as driver for (someone).
▷ HISTORY French: stoker ▶ **chauffeuse** *fem n*

chauvinism (**show**-vin-iz-zum) *n* an irrational belief that one's own country, race, group, or sex is superior: *male chauvinism.* ▷ HISTORY after Nicolas *Chauvin,* French soldier under Napoleon
▶ **chauvinist** *n, adj* ▶ **chauvinistic** *adj*

cheap *adj* **1** costing relatively little; inexpensive. **2** of poor quality; shoddy: *planks of cheap, splintery pine.* **3** not valued highly; not worth much: *promises are cheap.* **4** *Informal* mean or despicable: *a cheap jibe.* ✧ *n* **5 on the cheap** *Brit informal* at a low cost. ✧ *adv* **6** at a low cost. ▷ HISTORY Old English *ceap* barter, price ▶ **cheaply** *adv* ▶ **cheapness** *n*

cheapen *vb* **1** to lower the reputation of; degrade. **2** to reduce the price of.

cheap-jack *n Informal* a person who sells cheap and shoddy goods.

cheapskate *n Informal* a miserly person.

cheat *vb* **1** to act dishonestly in order to gain some advantage or profit. **2 cheat on** *Informal* to be unfaithful to (one's spouse or lover). ✧ *n* **3** a person who cheats. **4** a fraud or deception.
▷ HISTORY short for *escheat*

check *vb* **1** to examine, investigate, or make an inquiry into. **2** to slow the growth or progress of. **3** to stop abruptly. **4** to correspond or agree: *that all checks with our data here.* ✧ *n* **5** a test to ensure accuracy or progress. **6** a means to ensure against fraud or error. **7** a break in progress; stoppage. **8** *US* same as **cheque**. **9** *Chiefly US & Canad* the bill in a restaurant. **10** a pattern of squares or crossed lines. **11** a single square in such a pattern. **12** *Chess* the state or position of a king under direct attack. **13 in check** under control or restraint. ✧ *interj* **14** *Chiefly US & Canad* an expression of agreement. ✧ See also **check in, check out**, etc. ▷ HISTORY Old French *eschec* a check at chess

checked *adj* having a pattern of squares.

checkers *n US & Canad* same as **draughts**.

check in *vb* **1 a** to register one's arrival at a hotel or airport. **b** to register the arrival of (guests or passengers) at a hotel or airport. ✧ *n* **check-in 2 a** the formal registration of arrival at a hotel or airport. **b** the place where one registers one's arrival at a hotel or airport.

checkmate *n* **1** *Chess* the winning position in which an opponent's king is under attack and unable to escape. **2** utter defeat. ✧ *vb* **-mating, -mated 3** *Chess* to place the king of (one's opponent) in checkmate. **4** to thwart or defeat.

WORD HISTORY

The purpose of the game of chess may be to capture your opponent's king, but in terms of word origins, a player's aim is really to kill the king: 'checkmate' comes from the Arabic phrase *shāh māt*, meaning 'the king is dead'.

check out *vb* **1** to pay the bill and leave a hotel. **2** to investigate, examine, or look at: *he asked if he could check out the old man's theory; start the evening off by checking out one of the in bars in the city.* ✧ *n* **checkout 3** a counter in a supermarket, where customers pay.

checkup *n* a thorough examination to see if a person or thing is in good condition.

Cheddar *n* a firm orange or yellowy-white cheese. ▷ HISTORY *Cheddar,* village in Somerset, where it was originally made

cheek *n* **1** either side of the face below the eye. **2** *Informal* impudence, boldness, or lack of respect. **3** *Informal* a buttock. **4 cheek by jowl** close together. **5 turn the other cheek** to refuse to retaliate. ✧ *vb* **6** *Brit, Austral & NZ informal* to speak or behave disrespectfully to someone.
▷ HISTORY Old English *ceace*

cheekbone *n* the bone at the top of the cheek, just below the eye.

cheeky *adj* **cheekier, cheekiest** disrespectful; impudent. ▶ **cheekily** *adv* ▶ **cheekiness** *n*

cheep *n* **1** the short weak high-pitched cry of a young bird. ✧ *vb* **2** to utter a cheep.
▷ HISTORY imitative

cheer *vb* **1** to applaud or encourage with shouts. **2 cheer up** to make or become happy or hopeful; comfort or be comforted. ✧ *n* **3** a shout of applause or encouragement. **4** a feeling of cheerfulness: *the news brought little cheer.* ▷ HISTORY Middle English (in the sense: face, welcoming aspect), from Greek *kara* head

cheerful *adj* **1** having a happy disposition. **2** pleasantly bright: *a cheerful colour.* **3** ungrudging: *a cheerful giver.* ▶ **cheerfully** *adv* ▶ **cheerfulness** *n*

cheerio *interj* **1** *Informal* a farewell greeting. ✧ *n* **2** *Austral & NZ* a small red cocktail sausage.

cheerless *adj* dreary or gloomy.

A B C D E F G H I J K L M N O P Q R S T U V W X Y Z

cheers *interj Informal, chiefly Brit* **1** a drinking toast. **2** a farewell greeting. **3** an expression of gratitude.

cheery *adj* **cheerier, cheeriest** cheerful. ▶ **cheerily** *adv*

cheese[1] *n* **1** a food made from coagulated milk curd. **2** a block of this. ▷ **HISTORY** Latin *caseus*

cheese[2] *n* **big cheese** *Slang* an important person. ▷ **HISTORY** perhaps from Hindi *chiz* thing

cheeseburger *n* a hamburger with a slice of cheese melted on top of it.

cheesecake *n* **1** a dessert with a biscuit-crumb base covered with a sweet cream-cheese mixture and sometimes with a fruit topping. **2** *Slang* magazine photographs of naked or scantily dressed women.

cheesecloth *n* a light, loosely woven cotton cloth.

cheesed off *adj Brit, Austral & NZ slang* bored, disgusted, or angry. ▷ **HISTORY** origin unknown

cheeseparing *adj* **1** mean or miserly. ✧ *n* **2** meanness or miserliness.

cheesy *adj* **cheesier, cheesiest 1** like cheese. **2** *Informal* (of a smile) broad but possibly insincere. **3** *Informal* in poor taste: *a cheesy game show.*

cheetah *n* a large fast-running wild cat of Africa and SW Asia, which has a light brown coat with black spots.

WORD HISTORY

'Cheetah' comes from Hindi *cītā*, which is derived from Sanskrit *citrakāya*, meaning 'leopard', from *citra*, meaning 'bright' or 'speckled', and *kāya*, meaning 'body'.

chef *n* a cook, usually the head cook, in a restaurant or hotel. ▷ **HISTORY** French

chef-d'oeuvre (shay-**durv**) *n, pl* **chefs-d'oeuvre** (shay-**durv**) a masterpiece. ▷ **HISTORY** French

Cheka (**check**-a) *n Russian hist* the secret police set up in 1917 by the Bolshevik government. ▷ **HISTORY** from Russian, acronym of *Chrezvychainaya Komissiya* Extraordinary Commission (to combat) Counter-Revolution

chem. 1 chemical. **2** chemist. **3** chemistry.

chemical *n* **1** any substance used in or resulting from a reaction involving changes to atoms or molecules. ✧ *adj* **2** of or used in chemistry. **3** of, made from, or using chemicals: *a chemical additive found in many foods.* ▶ **chemically** *adv*

chemical energy *n Chem* the energy released by a chemical reaction.

chemical engineering *n* the applications of chemistry in industrial processes. ▶ **chemical engineer** *n*

chemical equilibrium *n Chem* a state in which a chemical reaction and its reverse reaction take place at equal rates.

chemical fertilizer *n Agriculture* a chemical substance, not derived from animal or plant matter, used as a fertilizer.

chemical reaction *n Chem* a process that involves changes in the structure and energy content of atoms, molecules, or ions, but not their nuclei. Compare **nuclear reaction**.

chemical warfare *n* warfare using weapons such as gases and poisons.

chemical weathering *n Geol* the breakdown of rocks as a result of chemical reactions which occur when they are exposed to water in the environment.

chemise (shem-**meez**) *n* a woman's old-fashioned loose-fitting slip or dress. ▷ **HISTORY** Late Latin *camisa*

chemist *n* **1** *Brit, Austral & NZ* a shop selling medicines and cosmetics. **2** *Brit, Austral & NZ* a qualified dispenser of prescribed medicines. **3** a specialist in chemistry. ▷ **HISTORY** Medieval Latin *alchimista* alchemist

chemistry *n* the branch of science concerned with the composition, properties, and reactions of substances.

chemotherapy *n* the treatment of disease, often cancer, by means of chemicals.

chenille (shen-**neel**) *n* **1** a thick soft tufty yarn. **2** a fabric made of this. ▷ **HISTORY** French

cheque *or US* **check** *n* a written order to someone's bank to pay money from his or her account to the person to whom the cheque is made out. ▷ **HISTORY** from *check* (in the sense: means of verification)

cheque book *n* a book of detachable blank cheques issued by a bank.

cheque card *n Brit* a plastic card issued by a bank guaranteeing payment of a customer's cheques.

chequer *or US* **checker** *n* a piece used in Chinese chequers. ▷ **HISTORY** Middle English: chessboard

chequered *or US* **checkered** *adj* **1** marked by varied fortunes: *a chequered career.* **2** marked with alternating squares of colour.

cherish *vb* **1** to cling to (an idea or feeling): *cherished notions.* **2** to care for. ▷ **HISTORY** Latin *carus* dear

Cherokee *n* **1** a member of a Native American people, formerly of the Appalachian mountains, now living chiefly in Oklahoma. **2** the language of this people.

cheroot (sher-**root**) *n* a cigar with both ends cut off squarely. ▷ **HISTORY** Tamil *curuttu* curl, roll

cherry *n, pl* **-ries 1** a small round soft fruit with red or blackish skin and a hard stone. **2** the tree on which this fruit grows. ✧ *adj* **3** deep red: *cherry lips.* ▷ **HISTORY** Greek *kerasios*

cherry tomato *n* a miniature tomato, slightly bigger than a cherry.

cherub *n, pl* **cherubs** *or (for sense 1)* **cherubim 1** *Christianity* an angel, often represented as a winged child. **2** an innocent or sweet child. ▷ **HISTORY** Hebrew *kērūbh* ▶ **cherubic** (chair-**roo**-bik) *adj*

chervil *n* an aniseed-flavoured herb. ▷ **HISTORY** Old English *cerfelle*

chess *n* a game of skill for two players using a chessboard on which chessmen are moved, with the object of checkmating the opponent's king. ▷ **HISTORY** Old French *esches,* plural of *eschec* check

chessman *n, pl* **-men** a piece used in chess. ▷ **HISTORY** Middle English *chessemeyne* chess company

chest *n* **1** the front of the body, from the neck to the waist. **2 get something off one's chest** *Informal* to unburden oneself of worries or secrets by talking about them. **3** a heavy box for storage or shipping: *a tea chest.* ▷ **HISTORY** Greek *kistē* box

chesterfield *n* a large couch with high padded sides and back. ▷ **HISTORY** after a 19th-century Earl of *Chesterfield*

chestnut *n* **1** a reddish-brown edible nut. **2** the tree that this nut grows on. **3** a horse of a reddish-brown colour. **4** *Informal* an old or stale joke. ✧ *adj* **5** dark reddish-brown: *chestnut hair.* ▷ **HISTORY** Greek *kastanea*

chest of drawers *n* a piece of furniture consisting of a set of drawers in a frame.

chesty *adj* **chestier, chestiest** *Brit informal* suffering from or symptomatic of chest disease: *chesty colds.* ▸ **chestiness** *n*

cheval glass (shev-**val**) *n* a full-length mirror mounted so as to swivel within a frame. ▷ **HISTORY** French *cheval* support (literally: horse)

chevalier (shev-a-**leer**) *n* **1** a member of the French Legion of Honour. **2** a chivalrous man. ▷ **HISTORY** Medieval Latin *caballarius* horseman

Cheviot *n* a large British sheep with a heavy medium-length fleece. ▷ **HISTORY** *Cheviot* Hills on borders of England & Scotland

chevron (**shev**-ron) *n* a V-shaped pattern, such as those worn on the sleeve of a military uniform to indicate rank. ▷ **HISTORY** Old French

chew *vb* **1** to work the jaws and teeth in order to grind (food). ✧ *n* **2** the act of chewing. **3** something that is chewed, such as a sweet or a piece of tobacco. ▷ **HISTORY** Old English *ceowan*

chewing gum *n* a flavoured gum which is chewed but not swallowed.

chew over *vb* to consider carefully.

chewy *adj* **chewier, chewiest** of a consistency requiring a lot of chewing.

chianti (kee-**ant**-ee) *n* a dry red wine produced in Tuscany, Italy.

chiaroscuro (kee-ah-roh-**skew**-roh) *n, pl* **-ros** the distribution of light and shade in a picture. ▷ **HISTORY** Italian *chiaro* clear + *oscuro* obscure

chic (**sheek**) *adj* **1** stylish or elegant. ✧ *n* **2** stylishness or elegance. ▷ **HISTORY** French

chicane (shik-**kane**) *n* an obstacle placed on a motor-racing circuit to slow the cars down. ▷ **HISTORY** French *chicaner* to quibble

chicanery *n* trickery or deception.

chick *n* **1** a baby bird, esp. a domestic fowl. **2** *Slang* a young woman. ▷ **HISTORY** short for *chicken*

chicken *n* **1** a domestic fowl bred for its flesh or eggs. **2** the flesh of this bird used for food. **3** *Slang* a coward. ✧ *adj* **4** *Slang* cowardly. ▷ **HISTORY** Old English *ciecen*

chicken feed *n Slang* a trifling amount of money.

chicken out *vb Informal* to fail to do something through cowardice.

chickenpox *n* an infectious viral disease, usually affecting children, which produces an itchy rash.

chickpea *n* an edible hard yellow pealike seed. ▷ **HISTORY** Latin *cicer*

chickweed *n* a common garden weed with small white flowers.

chicory *n* **1** a plant grown for its leaves, which are used in salads, and for its roots. **2** the root of this plant, roasted, dried, and used as a coffee substitute. ▷ **HISTORY** Greek *kikhōrion*

chide *vb* **chiding, chided** *Old-fashioned* to rebuke or scold. ▷ **HISTORY** Old English *cīdan*

chief *n* **1** the head of a group or body of people. **2** the head of a tribe. ✧ *adj* **3** most important: *the chief suspects.* **4** highest in rank: *the Chief Constable.* ▷ **HISTORY** Latin *caput* head

chiefly *adv* **1** especially or essentially. **2** mainly or mostly.

chief petty officer *n* a senior noncommissioned officer in a navy.

chieftain *n* the leader of a tribe or clan. ▷ **HISTORY** Late Latin *capitaneus* commander

chief technician *n* a noncommissioned officer in the Royal Air Force.

chiffchaff *n* a European warbler with a yellowish-brown plumage. ▷ **HISTORY** imitative

chiffon (**shif**-fon) *n* a fine see-through fabric of silk or nylon. ▷ **HISTORY** French *chiffe* rag

chignon (**sheen**-yon) *n* a roll or knot of long hair pinned up at the back of the head. ▷ **HISTORY** French

chigoe (**chig**-go) *n* a tropical flea that burrows into the skin. Also: **chigger** ▷ **HISTORY** Carib *chigo*

chihuahua (chee-**wah**-wah) *n* a tiny short-haired dog, originally from Mexico. ▷ **HISTORY** after *Chihuahua,* state in Mexico

chilblain *n* an inflammation of the fingers or toes, caused by exposure to cold. ▷ **HISTORY** CHILL (noun) + BLAIN

child *n, pl* **children 1** a young human being; boy or girl. **2** a son or daughter. *RELATED ADJECTIVE* ▸ **filial 3** a childish or immature person. **4** the product of an influence or environment: *a child of the Army.* **5 with child** *Old-fashioned* pregnant. ▷ **HISTORY** Old English *cild* ▸ **childless** *adj* ▸ **childlessness** *n*

child benefit *n Brit* a regular government payment to parents of children up to a certain age.

childbirth *n* the act of giving birth to a child. *RELATED ADJECTIVE* ▸ **natal**

childhood *n* the time or condition of being a child.

childish *adj* **1** immature or silly: *childish fighting over who did what.* **2** of or like a child: *childish illnesses.*

childlike *adj* like a child, for example in being innocent or trustful.

A B C D E F G H I J K L M N O P Q R S T U V W X Y Z

child minder *n* a person who looks after children whose parents are working.

children *n* the plural of **child**.

child's play *n Informal* something that is easy to do.

chill *n* **1** a feverish cold. **2** a moderate coldness. **3** a feeling of coldness resulting from a cold or damp environment or from sudden fear. ✧ *vb* **4** to make (something) cool or cold: *chilled white wine.* **5** to cause (someone) to feel cold or frightened. **6** *Informal* to calm oneself. ✧ *adj* **7** unpleasantly cold: *chill winds.* ▷ **HISTORY** Old English *ciele* ▶ **chilling** *adj* ▶ **chillingly** *adv*

chiller *n* **1** short for **spine-chiller**. **2** a cooling or refrigerating device.

chilli *or* **chili** *n, pl* **chillies** *or* **chilies** the small red or green hot-tasting pod of a type of capsicum, used in cookery, often in powdered form. ▷ **HISTORY** Mexican Indian

chilly *adj* **-lier, -liest 1** causing or feeling moderately cold. **2** without warmth; unfriendly: *a chilly reception.*

chilly bin *n NZ informal* a portable insulated container for packing food and drink in ice.

Chiltern Hundreds *pl n* (in Britain) a nominal office that an MP applies for in order to resign his seat.

chime *n* **1** the musical ringing sound made by a bell or clock. ✧ *vb* **chiming, chimed 2** (of a bell) to make a clear musical ringing sound. **3** (of a clock) to indicate (the time) by chiming. ▷ **HISTORY** Latin *cymbalum* cymbal

chimera (kime-**meer**-a) *n* **1** a wild and unrealistic dream or idea. **2** *Greek myth* a fire-breathing monster with the head of a lion, body of a goat, and tail of a serpent. ▷ **HISTORY** Greek *khimaira* she-goat

chimerical *adj* wildly fanciful or imaginary.

chimney *n* a hollow vertical structure that carries smoke or steam away from a fire or engine. ▷ **HISTORY** Greek *kaminos* oven

chimney breast *n* the walls surrounding the base of a chimney or fireplace.

chimney sweep *n* a person who cleans soot from chimneys.

chimp *n Informal* short for **chimpanzee**.

chimpanzee *n* an intelligent small black ape of central W Africa. ▷ **HISTORY** African dialect

chin *n* the front part of the face below the mouth. ▷ **HISTORY** Old English *cinn*

china[1] *n* **1** ceramic ware of a type originally from China. **2** dishes or ornamental objects made of china. ▷ **HISTORY** Persian *chīnī*

china[2] *n Brit & S African informal* a friend or companion. ▷ **HISTORY** from cockney rhyming slang *china plate* mate

china clay *n* same as **kaolin**.

Chinatown *n* a section of a town or city outside China with a mainly Chinese population.

chinchilla *n* **1** a small S American rodent bred in captivity for its soft silvery-grey fur. **2** the fur of this animal. ▷ **HISTORY** Spanish

chine *n* **1** a cut of meat including part of the backbone. ✧ *vb* **chining, chined 2** to cut (meat) along the backbone. ▷ **HISTORY** Old French *eschine*

Chinese *adj* **1** of China. ✧ *n* **2** (*pl* **-nese**) a person from China or a descendant of one. **3** any of the languages of China.

Chinese chequers *n* a game played with marbles or pegs on a six-pointed star-shaped board.

Chinese lantern *n* a collapsible lantern made of thin paper.

chink[1] *n* a small narrow opening: *a chink of light.* ▷ **HISTORY** Old English *cine* crack

chink[2] *vb* **1** to make a light ringing sound. ✧ *n* **2** a light ringing sound. ▷ **HISTORY** imitative

chinoiserie (sheen-**wahz**-a-ree) *n* **1** a style of decorative art based on imitations of Chinese motifs. **2** objects in this style. ▷ **HISTORY** French *chinois* Chinese

Chinook *n* **1** (*pl* **-nook** *or* **-nooks**) a member of a Native American people of the Pacific coast of N America. **2** the language of this people.

Chinook salmon *n* a Pacific salmon valued as a food fish.

chintz *n* a printed patterned cotton fabric with a glazed finish, used for curtains and chair coverings. ▷ **HISTORY** Hindi *chīnt*

chinwag *n Brit, Austral & NZ informal* a chat.

chip *n* **1** a thin strip of potato fried in deep fat. **2** *US, Canad, Austral & NZ* a potato crisp. **3** *Electronics* a tiny wafer of semiconductor material, such as silicon, processed to form an integrated circuit. **4** a counter used to represent money in gambling games. **5** a small piece removed by chopping, cutting, or breaking. **6** a mark left where a small piece has been broken off something. **7 chip off the old block** *Informal* a person who resembles one of his or her parents in personality. **8 have a chip on one's shoulder** *Informal* to be resentful or bear a grudge. **9 when the chips are down** *Informal* at a time of crisis. ✧ *vb* **chipping, chipped 10** to break small pieces from. ▷ **HISTORY** Old English *cipp*

chipboard *n* thin rigid board made of compressed wood particles.

chip in *vb Informal* **1** to contribute to a common fund. **2** to interrupt with a remark.

chipmunk *n* a squirrel-like striped burrowing rodent of North America and Asia. ▷ **HISTORY** from a Native American language

chipolata *n Chiefly Brit* a small sausage. ▷ **HISTORY** Italian *cipolla* onion

chiropodist (kir-**rop**-pod-ist) *n* a person who treats minor foot complaints like corns. ▶ **chiropody** *n*

chiropractic (kire-oh-**prak**-tik) *n* a system of treating bodily disorders by manipulation of the spine. ▷ **HISTORY** Greek *kheir* hand + *praktikos* practical ▶ **chiropractor** *n*

chirp *vb* **1** (of some birds and insects) to make a short high-pitched sound. **2** *Brit, Austral & NZ* to speak in a lively fashion. ✧ *n* **3** a chirping sound. ▷ **HISTORY** imitative

chirpy *adj* **chirpier, chirpiest** *Informal* lively and cheerful. ▶ **chirpiness** *n*
chirrup *vb* **1** (of some birds) to chirp repeatedly. ✧ *n* **2** a chirruping sound. ▷ **HISTORY** variant of *chirp*
chisel *n* **1** a metal tool with a sharp end for shaping wood or stone. ✧ *vb* **-elling, -elled** *or US* **-eling, -eled 2** to carve or form with a chisel. ▷ **HISTORY** Latin *caesus* cut
chit[1] *n* a short official note, such as a memorandum, requisition, or receipt. Also: **chitty** ▷ **HISTORY** Hindi *cittha* note
chit[2] *n Brit, Austral & NZ old-fashioned* a pert or impudent girl. ▷ **HISTORY** Middle English: young animal, kitten
chitchat *n* chat or gossip.
chitin (**kite**-in) *n* the tough substance forming the outer layer of the bodies of arthropods. ▷ **HISTORY** Greek *khitōn* tunic
chitterlings *pl n* the intestines of a pig or other animal prepared as food. ▷ **HISTORY** origin unknown
chivalrous *adj* gallant or courteous. ▶ **chivalrously** *adv*
chivalry *n* **1** courteous behaviour, esp. by men towards women. **2** the medieval system and principles of knighthood. ▷ **HISTORY** Old French *chevalier* knight ▶ **chivalric** *adj*
chives *pl n* the long slender hollow leaves of a small Eurasian plant, used in cooking for their onion-like flavour. ▷ **HISTORY** Latin *caepa* onion
chivvy *vb* **-vies, -vying, -vied** *Brit* to harass or nag. ▷ **HISTORY** probably from *Chevy Chase*, a Scottish ballad
chloral hydrate *n* a colourless crystalline solid used as a sedative.
chlorate *n Chem* any salt containing the ion ClO_3^-.
chloride *n Chem* **1** any compound of chlorine and another element and radical. **2** any salt or ester of hydrochloric acid.
chlorinate *vb* **-ating, -ated 1** to disinfect (water) with chlorine. **2** *Chem* to combine or treat (a substance) with chlorine: *chlorinated hydrocarbons.* ▶ **chlorination** *n*
chlorine *n* a poisonous strong-smelling greenish-yellow gaseous element, used in water purification and as a disinfectant, and, combined with sodium, to make common salt. Symbol: Cl.
chloro- *combining form* green. ▷ **HISTORY** Greek *khlōros*
chlorofluorocarbon *n Chem* any of various gaseous compounds of carbon, hydrogen, chlorine, and fluorine, used as refrigerants and aerosol propellants, some of which break down the ozone in the atmosphere.
chloroform *n* a sweet-smelling liquid, used as a solvent and cleansing agent, and formerly as an anaesthetic. ▷ **HISTORY** CHLORO- + *formyl:* see FORMIC ACID
chlorophyll *or US* **chlorophyl** *n* the green colouring matter of plants, which enables them to convert sunlight into energy. ▷ **HISTORY** CHLORO- + Greek *phullon* leaf
chloroplast *n Biol* one of the parts of a plant cell that contains chlorophyll. ▷ **HISTORY** CHLORO- + Greek *plastos* formed
chlorosis *n Pathol* a disorder marked by pale greenish-yellow skin, weakness, and palpitation, caused by insufficient iron in the body.
chock *n* **1** a block or wedge of wood used to prevent the sliding or rolling of a heavy object. ✧ *vb* **2** to fit with or secure by a chock. ▷ **HISTORY** origin unknown
chock-a-block *adj* filled to capacity.
chock-full *adj* completely full.
chocolate *n* **1** a food made from roasted ground cacao seeds, usually sweetened and flavoured. **2** a sweet or drink made from this. ✧ *adj* **3** deep brown. ▶ **chocolaty** *adj*

WORD HISTORY
Europeans were first introduced to chocolate at the court of the Aztec king Montezuma in the 16th century. 'Chocolate' or *xocoatl* was a bitter Aztec drink made from cocoa beans. The name *xocoatl* means 'bitter water', from Aztec *xococ*, meaning 'bitter', and *atl*, meaning 'water'.

choice *n* **1** the act of choosing or selecting. **2** the opportunity or power of choosing: *parental choice.* **3** a person or thing chosen or that may be chosen: *the president's choice as the new head of the CIA.* **4** an alternative action or possibility: *they had no choice but to accept.* **5** a range from which to select: *a choice of weapons.* ✧ *adj* **6** of high quality: *choice government jobs.* **7** carefully chosen: *a few choice words.* **8** vulgar: *choice language.* ▷ **HISTORY** Old French *choisir* to choose
choir *n* **1** an organized group of singers, usually for singing in church. **2** the part of a church, in front of the altar, occupied by the choir. ▷ **HISTORY** Latin *chorus*
choke *vb* **choking, choked 1** to hinder or stop the breathing of (a person or animal) by strangling or smothering. **2** to have trouble in breathing, swallowing, or speaking. **3** to block or clog up: *the old narrow streets become choked to a standstill.* **4** to hinder the growth of: *weeds would outgrow and choke the rice crop.* ✧ *n* **5** a device in a vehicle's engine that enriches the petrol-air mixture by reducing the air supply. ▷ **HISTORY** Old English *ācēocian*
choke back *vb* to suppress (tears or anger).
choker *n* a tight-fitting necklace.
choko *n, pl* **-kos** *Austral & NZ* the pear-shaped fruit of a tropical American vine, eaten as a vegetable. ▷ **HISTORY** Brazilian Indian
choler (**kol**-ler) *n Archaic* anger or bad temper. ▷ **HISTORY** Greek *kholē* bile
cholera (**kol**-ler-a) *n* a serious infectious disease causing severe diarrhoea and stomach cramps, caught from contaminated water or food. ▷ **HISTORY** Greek *kholē* bile
choleric *adj* bad-tempered.
cholesterol (kol-**lest**-er-oll) *n* a fatty alcohol found in all animal fats, tissues, and fluids, an excess of which is thought to contribute to heart and

A B C D E F G H I J K L M N O P Q R S T U V W X Y Z

artery disease. ▷ **HISTORY** Greek *kholē* bile + *stereos* solid

chomp *vb* to chew (food) noisily.

chook *n Informal, chiefly Austral & NZ* a hen or chicken.

choose *vb* **choosing, chose, chosen 1** to select (a person, thing, or course of action) from a number of alternatives. **2** to like or please: *when she did choose to reveal her secret, the group were initially hushed.* **3** to consider it desirable or proper: *I don't choose to read that sort of book.* ▷ **HISTORY** Old English *ceosan*

choosy *adj* **choosier, choosiest** *Informal* fussy; hard to please.

chop[1] *vb* **chopping, chopped 1** (often foll. by *down* or *off*) to cut (something) with a blow from an axe or other sharp tool. **2** to cut into pieces. **3** *Boxing, karate* to hit (an opponent) with a short sharp blow. **4** *Brit, Austral & NZ informal* to dispense with or reduce. **5** *Sport* to hit (a ball) sharply downwards. ✧ *n* **6** a cutting blow. **7** a slice of mutton, lamb, or pork, usually including a rib. **8** *Sport* a sharp downward blow or stroke. **9 the chop** *Slang* dismissal from employment. ▷ **HISTORY** variant of *chap:* see CHAPPED

chop[2] *vb* **chopping, chopped 1 chop and change** to change one's mind repeatedly. **2 chop logic** to use excessively subtle or involved argument. ▷ **HISTORY** Old English *ceapian* to barter

chopper *n* **1** *Informal* a helicopter. **2** *Chiefly Brit* a small hand axe. **3** a butcher's cleaver. **4** a type of bicycle or motorcycle with very high handlebars. **5** *NZ* a child's bicycle.

choppy *adj* **-pier, -piest** (of the sea) fairly rough. ▶ **choppiness** *n*

chops *pl n Brit, Austral & NZ informal* **1** the jaws or cheeks. **2 lick one's chops** to anticipate something with pleasure. ▷ **HISTORY** origin unknown

chopsticks *pl n* a pair of thin sticks of ivory, wood, or plastic, used for eating Chinese or other East Asian food. ▷ **HISTORY** pidgin English, from Chinese

chop suey *n* a Chinese-style dish of chopped meat, bean sprouts, and other vegetables in a sauce. ▷ **HISTORY** Chinese *tsap sui* odds and ends

choral *adj* of or for a choir.

chorale (kor-**rahl**) *n* **1** a slow stately hymn tune. **2** *Chiefly US* a choir or chorus. ▷ **HISTORY** German *Choralgesang* choral song

chord[1] *n* **1** *Maths* a straight line connecting two points on a curve. **2** *Anat* same as **cord. 3 strike** *or* **touch a chord** to bring about an emotional response, usually of sympathy. ▷ **HISTORY** Greek *khordē* string

chord[2] *n* the simultaneous sounding of three or more musical notes. ▷ **HISTORY** short for *accord*

chordate *n* any animal that has a long fibrous rod just above the gut to support the body, such as the vertebrates.

chore *n* **1** a small routine task. **2** an unpleasant task. ▷ **HISTORY** Old English *cerr* a turn of work

chorea (kor-**ree**-a) *n* a disorder of the nervous system characterized by uncontrollable brief jerky movements. ▷ **HISTORY** Greek *khoreia* dance

choreography *n* **1** the composition of steps and movements for ballet and other dancing. **2** the steps and movements of a ballet or dance. ▷ **HISTORY** Greek *khoreia* dance + -GRAPHY ▶ **choreographer** *n* ▶ **choreographic** *adj*

chorister *n* a singer in a church choir.

choroid *n Physiol* a brownish membrane in the eye, between the retina and the sclera.

choropleth map (**core**-uh-pleth) *n Geog* a map which presents statistical data relating to given areas using proportionally darker or lighter shading or colour to represent proportionally different numerical values.

chortle *vb* **-tling, -tled 1** to chuckle with amusement. ✧ *n* **2** an amused chuckle. ▷ **HISTORY** coined by Lewis Carroll

chorus *n, pl* **-ruses 1** a large choir. **2** a piece of music to be sung by a large choir. **3** a part of a song repeated after each verse. **4** something expressed by many people at once: *a chorus of boos.* **5** the noise made by a group of birds or small animals: *the dawn chorus.* **6** a group of singers or dancers who perform together in a show. **7** (in ancient Greece) a group of actors who commented on the action of a play. **8** (in Elizabethan drama) the actor who spoke the prologue and epilogue. **9 in chorus** in unison. ✧ *vb* **10** to sing or say together. ▷ **HISTORY** Greek *khoros*

chorus girl *n* a young woman who dances or sings in the chorus of a show or film.

chose *vb* the past tense of **choose.**

chosen *vb* **1** the past participle of **choose.** ✧ *adj* **2** selected for some special quality: *the chosen one.*

chough (**chuff**) *n* a large black bird of the crow family. ▷ **HISTORY** origin unknown

choux pastry (**shoo**) *n* a very light pastry made with eggs. ▷ **HISTORY** French *pâte choux* cabbage dough

chow *n* **1** a thick-coated dog with a curled tail, originally from China. **2** *Informal* food. ▷ **HISTORY** pidgin English

chowder *n* a thick soup containing clams or fish. ▷ **HISTORY** French *chaudière* kettle

chow mein *n* a Chinese-American dish consisting of chopped meat or vegetables fried with noodles. ▷ **HISTORY** from Chinese

chrism *n* consecrated oil used for anointing in some churches. ▷ **HISTORY** Greek *khriein* to anoint

Christ *n* **1** Jesus of Nazareth (Jesus Christ), regarded by Christians as the Messiah of Old Testament prophecies. **2** the Messiah of Old Testament prophecies. **3** an image or picture of Christ. ✧ *interj* **4** *Taboo slang* an oath expressing annoyance or surprise. ▷ **HISTORY** Greek *khristos* anointed one

christen *vb* **1** same as **baptize. 2** to give a name to (a person or thing). **3** *Informal* to use for the first time. ▷ **HISTORY** Old English *cristnian* ▶ **christening** *n*

Christendom *n* all Christian people or countries.

Christian *n* **1** a person who believes in and follows Jesus Christ. **2** *Informal* a person who displays the virtues of kindness and mercy encouraged in the teachings of Jesus Christ. ✧ *adj* **3** of Jesus Christ, Christians, or Christianity. **4** kind or good.

Christian Democrat *n* a member or supporter of political parties in Europe and Latin America that combine moderate conservatism with historic links to the church. ▸ **Christian Democratic** *adj*

Christian Era *n* the period beginning with the year of Christ's birth.

Christianity *n* **1** the religion based on the life and teachings of Christ. **2** Christian beliefs or practices. **3** same as **Christendom.**

Christianize *or* **-ise** *vb* **-izing, -ized** *or* **-ising, -ised 1** to convert to Christianity. **2** to fill with Christian principles, spirit, or outlook. ▸ **Christianization** *or* **-isation** *n*

Christian name *n* a personal name formally given to Christians at baptism: loosely used to mean a person's first name.

Christian Science *n* the religious system founded by Mary Baker Eddy (1866), which emphasizes spiritual regeneration and healing through prayer. ▸ **Christian Scientist** *n*

Christmas *n* **1 a** *Christianity* a festival commemorating the birth of Christ, held by most Churches to have occurred on Dec. 25. **b** Also: **Christmas Day** Dec. 25, as a day of secular celebrations when gifts and greetings are exchanged. ✧ *adj* **2** connected with or taking place at the time of year when this festival is celebrated: *the Christmas holidays.* ▷ HISTORY Old English *Crīstes mæsse* Mass of Christ ▸ **Christmassy** *adj*

Christmas box *n* a tip or present given at Christmas, esp. to postmen or tradesmen.

Christmas Eve *n* the evening or the whole day before Christmas Day.

Christmas pudding *n Brit & Austral* a rich steamed pudding containing suet, dried fruit, and spices.

Christmas rose *n* an evergreen plant with white or pink winter-blooming flowers.

Christmas tree *n* an evergreen tree or an imitation of one, decorated as part of Christmas celebrations.

chromate *n Chem* any salt or ester of chromic acid.

chromatic *adj* **1** of or in colour or colours. **2** *Music* **a** involving the sharpening or flattening of notes or the use of such notes. **b** of the chromatic scale. ▷ HISTORY Greek *khrōma* colour ▸ **chromatically** *adv*

chromatics *n* the science of colour.

chromatic scale *n* a twelve-note scale including all the semitones of the octave.

chromatid *n Biol* either of the two strands into which a chromosome divides during mitosis.

chromatin *n Biochem* the part of the nucleus of a cell that forms the chromosomes and can easily be dyed. ▷ HISTORY from *chrome*

chromatogram *n Chem* a column or strip of material showing the different constituents of a mixture separated by chromatography.

chromatography *n* the technique of separating and analysing the components of a mixture of liquids or gases by slowly passing it through an adsorbing material. ▷ HISTORY Greek *khrōma* colour + -GRAPHY

chrome *n* **1** same as **chromium. 2** anything plated with chromium. ✧ *vb* **chroming, chromed 3** to plate or be plated with chromium. ▷ HISTORY Greek *khrōma* colour

chromite *n* a brownish-black mineral which is the only commercial source of chromium.

chromium *n Chem* a hard grey metallic element, used in steel alloys and electroplating to increase hardness and corrosion resistance. Symbol: Cr. ▷ HISTORY from *chrome*

chromosome *n* any of the microscopic rod-shaped structures that appear in a cell nucleus during cell division, consisting of units (genes) that are responsible for the transmission of hereditary characteristics. ▷ HISTORY Greek *khrōma* colour + *sōma* body

chromosphere *n* a gaseous layer of the sun's atmosphere extending from the photosphere to the corona.

chronic *adj* **1** (of a disease) developing slowly or lasting for a long time. **2** (of a bad habit or bad behaviour) having continued for a long time; habitual: *chronic drug addiction.* **3** very serious or severe: *chronic food shortages.* **4** *Brit, Austral & NZ informal* very bad: *the play was chronic.* ▷ HISTORY Greek *khronos* time ▸ **chronically** *adv*

chronic fatigue syndrome *n* a condition characterized by painful muscles and general weakness sometimes persisting long after a viral illness.

chronicle *n* **1** a record of events in chronological order. ✧ *vb* **-cling, -cled 2** to record in or as if in a chronicle. ▷ HISTORY Greek *khronika* annals ▸ **chronicler** *n*

chronological *adj* **1** (of a sequence of events) arranged in order of occurrence. **2** relating to chronology. ▸ **chronologically** *adv*

chronology *n, pl* **-gies 1** the arrangement of dates or events in order of occurrence. **2** the determining of the proper sequence of past events. **3** a table of events arranged in order of occurrence. ▷ HISTORY Greek *khronos* time + -LOGY ▸ **chronologist** *n*

chronometer *n* a timepiece designed to be accurate in all conditions. ▷ HISTORY Greek *khronos* time + -METER

chrysalis (**kriss**-a-liss) *n* an insect in the stage between larva and adult, when it is in a cocoon. ▷ HISTORY Greek *khrusos* gold

chrysanthemum *n* a garden plant with large round flowers made up of many petals. ▷ HISTORY Greek *khrusos* gold + *anthemon* flower

A
B
C
D
E
F
G
H
I
J
K
L
M
N
O
P
Q
R
S
T
U
V
W
X
Y
Z

chub *n, pl* **chub** *or* **chubs** a common freshwater game fish of the carp family with a dark greenish body. ▷ HISTORY origin unknown

chubby *adj* **-bier, -biest** plump and round. ▷ HISTORY perhaps from *chub* ▶ **chubbiness** *n*

chuck[1] *vb* **1** *Informal* to throw carelessly. **2** *Informal* (sometimes foll. by *in* or *up*) to give up; reject: *he chucked in his job.* **3** to pat (someone) affectionately under the chin. **4** *Austral & NZ informal* to vomit. ✧ *n* **5** a throw or toss. **6** a pat under the chin. ✧ See also **chuck off**. ▷ HISTORY origin unknown

chuck[2] *n* **1** Also: **chuck steak** a cut of beef from the neck to the shoulder blade. **2** a device that holds a workpiece in a lathe or a tool in a drill. ▷ HISTORY variant of *chock*

chuck[3] *n W Canada* **1** a large body of water. **2** Also: **saltchuck** the sea. ▷ HISTORY Chinook

chuckle *vb* **-ling, -led 1** to laugh softly or to oneself. ✧ *n* **2** a partly suppressed laugh. ▷ HISTORY probably from *chuck* cluck

chuck off *vb* (often foll. by *at*) *Austral & NZ informal* to abuse or make fun of.

chuff *vb* to move while making a puffing sound, as a steam engine. ▷ HISTORY imitative

chuffed *adj Informal* pleased or delighted: *I suppose you're feeling pretty chuffed.* ▷ HISTORY origin unknown

chug *n* **1** a short dull sound like the noise of an engine. ✧ *vb* **chugging, chugged 2** (esp. of an engine) to operate or move with this sound: *lorries chug past.* ▷ HISTORY imitative

chukka *or* **chukker** *n Polo* a period of continuous play, usually $7^1/_2$ minutes. ▷ HISTORY Hindi *cakkar*

chum *n* **1** *Informal* a close friend. ✧ *vb* **chumming, chummed 2 chum up with** to form a close friendship with. ▷ HISTORY probably from *chamber fellow*

chummy *adj* **-mier, -miest** *Informal* friendly. ▶ **chummily** *adv* ▶ **chumminess** *n*

chump *n* **1** *Informal* a stupid person. **2** a thick piece of meat. **3** a thick block of wood. **4 off one's chump** *Brit slang* crazy. ▷ HISTORY origin unknown

chunk *n* **1** a thick solid piece of something. **2** a considerable amount. ▷ HISTORY variant of CHUCK[2]

chunky *adj* **chunkier, chunkiest 1** thick and short. **2** containing thick pieces. **3** *Chiefly Brit* (of clothes, esp. knitwear) made of thick bulky material. ▶ **chunkiness** *n*

church *n* **1** a building for public Christian worship. **2** religious services held in a church. **3** a particular Christian denomination. **4** Christians collectively. **5** the clergy as distinguished from the laity. **6 Church** institutional religion as a political or social force: *conflict between Church and State.* ▷ HISTORY Greek *kuriakon (dōma)* the Lord's (house)

churchgoer *n* a person who attends church regularly.

churchman *n, pl* **-men** a clergyman.

Church of England *n* the reformed established state Church in England, with the sovereign as its temporal head.

Church of Scotland *n* the established Presbyterian church in Scotland.

churchwarden *n* **1** *Church of England, Episcopal Church* a lay assistant of a parish priest. **2** an old-fashioned long-stemmed tobacco pipe made of clay.

churchyard *n* the grounds round a church, used as a graveyard.

churl *n* **1** a surly ill-bred person. **2** *Archaic* a farm labourer. ▷ HISTORY Old English *ceorl*

churlish *adj* surly and rude.

churn *n* **1** a machine in which cream is shaken to make butter. **2** a large container for milk. ✧ *vb* **3** to stir (milk or cream) vigorously in order to make butter. **4** to move about violently: *a hot tub of churning water.* ▷ HISTORY Old English *ciern*

churn out *vb Informal* to produce (something) rapidly and in large numbers.

chute[1] (**shoot**) *n* a steep sloping channel or passage down which things may be dropped. ▷ HISTORY Old French *cheoite* fallen

chute[2] *n Informal* short for **parachute**.

chutney *n* a pickle of Indian origin, made from fruit, vinegar, spices, and sugar: *mango chutney.* ▷ HISTORY Hindi *catni*

chyle *n* a milky fluid formed in the small intestine during digestion. ▷ HISTORY Greek *khulos* juice

chyme *n* the thick fluid mass of partially digested food that leaves the stomach. ▷ HISTORY Greek *khumos* juice

Ci curie.

CIA Central Intelligence Agency; a US bureau responsible for espionage and intelligence activities.

cicada (sik-**kah**-da) *n* a large broad insect, found in hot countries, that makes a high-pitched drone. ▷ HISTORY Latin

cicatrix (**sik**-a-trix) *n, pl* **cicatrices** (sik-a-**trice**-eez) the tissue that forms in a wound during healing; scar. ▷ HISTORY Latin: scar

CID (in Britain) Criminal Investigation Department; the detective division of a police force.

cider *n* an alcoholic drink made from fermented apple juice. ▷ HISTORY Hebrew *shēkhār* strong drink

cigar *n* a tube-like roll of cured tobacco leaves for smoking.

> **WORD HISTORY**
> 'Cigar' came into English from Spanish, but it probably originally comes from Mayan (a Central American language) *sicar*, meaning 'to smoke'.

cigarette *n* a thin roll of shredded tobacco in thin paper, for smoking. ▷ HISTORY French: a little cigar

cilium *n, pl* **cilia** *Biol* **1** any of the short threads projecting from a cell or organism, whose rhythmic beating causes movement. **2** an eyelash. ▷ HISTORY Latin ▶ **ciliary** *adj*

C in C *Mil* Commander in Chief.

cinch (**sinch**) *n* **1** *Informal* an easy task. **2** *Slang* a certainty. ▷ HISTORY Spanish *cincha* saddle girth

cinchona (sing-**kone**-a) *n* **1** a South American tree or shrub with medicinal bark. **2** its dried bark which yields quinine. **3** a drug made from cinchona bark. ▷ **HISTORY** after the Countess of *Chinchón*

cinder *n* **1** a piece of material that will not burn, left after burning coal or wood. **2 cinders** ashes. ▷ **HISTORY** Old English *sinder*

cinder cone *n Geol* a volcano whose sides are made entirely of loose fragments, ash, and pumice.

Cinderella *n* a poor, neglected, or unsuccessful person or thing. ▷ **HISTORY** after *Cinderella*, the heroine of a fairy tale

cine camera *n* a camera for taking moving pictures.

cinema *n* **1** a place designed for showing films. **2 the cinema a** the art or business of making films. **b** films collectively. ▷ **HISTORY** shortened from *cinematograph* ▶ **cinematic** *adj*

cinematograph *n Chiefly Brit* a combined camera, printer, and projector. ▷ **HISTORY** Greek *kinēma* motion + -GRAPH ▶ **cinematographer** *n* ▶ **cinematographic** *adj*

cinematography *n* the technique of making films: *who won an Oscar for his stunning cinematography.*

cineraria *n* a garden plant with daisy-like flowers. ▷ **HISTORY** Latin *cinis* ashes

cinerarium *n, pl* **-raria** a place for keeping the ashes of the dead after cremation. ▷ **HISTORY** Latin *cinerarius* relating to ashes ▶ **cinerary** *adj*

cinnabar *n* **1** a heavy red mineral containing mercury. **2** a large red-and-black European moth. ▷ **HISTORY** Greek *kinnabari*

cinnamon *n* the spice obtained from the aromatic bark of a tropical Asian tree. ▷ **HISTORY** Hebrew *qinnamown*

cinquefoil *n* **1** a plant with five-lobed compound leaves. **2** an ornamental carving in the form of five arcs arranged in a circle. ▷ **HISTORY** Latin *quinquefolium* plant with five leaves

Cinque Ports *pl n* an association of ports on the SE coast of England, with certain ancient duties and privileges.

cipher *or* **cypher** (**sife**-er) *n* **1** a method of secret writing using substitution of letters according to a key. **2** a secret message. **3** the key to a secret message. **4** a person or thing of no importance. **5** *Obsolete* the numeral zero. ✧ *vb* **6** to put (a message) into secret writing. ▷ **HISTORY** Arabic *sifr* zero

circa (**sir**-ka) *prep* (used with a date) approximately; about: *circa 1788.* ▷ **HISTORY** Latin

circadian *adj* of biological processes that occur regularly at 24-hour intervals. ▷ **HISTORY** Latin *circa* about + *dies* day

circle *n* **1** a curved line surrounding a central point, every point of the line being the same distance from the centre. **2** the figure enclosed by such a curve. **3** something formed or arranged in the shape of a circle: *they ran round in little circles.* **4** a group of people sharing an interest, activity, or upbringing: *his judgment is well respected in diplomatic circles.* **5** *Theatre* the section of seats above the main level of the auditorium. **6** a process or chain of events or parts that forms a connected whole; cycle. **7 come full circle** to arrive back at one's starting point. ✧ *vb* **-cling, -cled 8** to move in a circle (around). **9** to enclose in a circle. ▷ **HISTORY** Latin *circus*

circlet *n* a small circle or ring, esp. a circular ornament worn on the head. ▷ **HISTORY** Old French *cerclet* little circle

circuit *n* **1** a complete route or course, esp. one that is circular or that lies around an object. **2** a complete path through which an electric current can flow. **3 a** a periodical journey around an area, as made by judges or salesmen. **b** the places visited on such a journey. **4** a motor-racing track. **5** *Sport* a series of tournaments in which the same players regularly take part: *the professional golf circuit.* **6** a number of theatres or cinemas under one management. ▷ **HISTORY** Latin *circum* around + *ire* to go

circuit breaker *n* a device that stops the flow of current in an electrical circuit if there is a fault.

circuitous (sir-**kew**-it-uss) *adj* indirect and lengthy: *a circuitous route.*

circuitry (**sir**-kit-tree) *n* **1** the design of an electrical circuit. **2** the system of circuits used in an electronic device.

circular *adj* **1** of or in the shape of a circle. **2** travelling in a circle. **3** (of an arguments) not valid because a statement is used to prove the conclusion and the conclusion to prove the statement. **4** (of letters or announcements) intended for general distribution. ✧ *n* **5** a letter or advertisement sent to a large number of people at the same time. ▶ **circularity** *n*

circular saw *n* a power-driven saw in which a circular disc with a toothed edge is rotated at high speed.

circulate *vb* **-lating, -lated 1** to send, go, or pass from place to place or person to person: *rumours were circulating that he was about to resign.* **2** to move through a circuit or system, returning to the starting point: *regular exercise keeps the blood circulating around the body.* **3** to move around the guests at a party, talking to different people: *it wasn't like her not to circulate among all the guests.* ▷ **HISTORY** Latin *circulari* ▶ **circulatory** *adj*

circulation *n* **1** the flow of blood from the heart through the arteries, and then back through the veins to the heart, where the cycle is renewed. **2** the number of copies of a newspaper or magazine that are sold. **3** the distribution of newspapers or magazines. **4** sending or moving around: *the circulation of air.* **5 in circulation a** (of currency) being used by the public. **b** (of people) active in a social or business context.

circum- *prefix* around; on all sides: *circumlocution.* ▷ **HISTORY** Latin

circumcise *vb* **-cising, -cised 1** to remove the foreskin of (a male). **2** to cut or remove the clitoris of (a female). **3** to perform such an operation as a religious rite on (someone). ▷ **HISTORY** Latin CIRCUM- + *caedere* to cut ▶ **circumcision** *n*

A B C D E F G H I J K L M N O P Q R S T U V W X Y Z

circumference *n* **1** the boundary of a specific area or figure, esp. of a circle. **2** the distance round this. ▷ **HISTORY** Latin CIRCUM- + *ferre* to bear ▸ **circumferential** *adj*

circumflex *n* a mark (^) placed over a vowel to show that it is pronounced in a particular way, for instance as a long vowel in French. ▷ **HISTORY** Latin CIRCUM- + *flectere* to bend

circumlocution *n* **1** an indirect way of saying something. **2** an indirect expression. ▸ **circumlocutory** *adj*

circumnavigate *vb* **-gating, -gated** to sail, fly, or walk right around. ▸ **circumnavigation** *n*

circumscribe *vb* **-scribing, -scribed 1** *Formal* to limit or restrict within certain boundaries: *the President's powers are circumscribed by the Constitution.* **2** *Geom* to draw a geometric figure around (another figure) so that the two are in contact but do not intersect. ▷ **HISTORY** Latin CIRCUM- + *scribere* to write ▸ **circumscription** *n*

circumspect *adj* cautious and careful not to take risks. ▷ **HISTORY** Latin CIRCUM- + *specere* to look ▸ **circumspection** *n* ▸ **circumspectly** *adv*

circumstance *n* **1** an occurrence or condition that accompanies or influences a person or event. **2** unplanned events and situations which cannot be controlled: *a victim of circumstance.* **3 pomp and circumstance** formal display or ceremony. **4 under** *or* **in no circumstances** in no case; never. **5 under the circumstances** because of conditions. ▷ **HISTORY** Latin CIRCUM- + *stare* to stand

circumstantial *adj* **1** of or dependent on circumstances. **2** fully detailed.

circumstantial evidence *n Law* indirect evidence that suggests a conclusion but does not prove it.

circumstantiate *vb* **-ating, -ated** to prove by giving details.

circumvent *vb Formal* **1** to avoid or get round (a rule, restriction, etc.). **2** to outwit (a person). ▷ **HISTORY** Latin CIRCUM- + *venire* to come ▸ **circumvention** *n*

circus *n, pl* **-cuses 1** a travelling company of entertainers such as acrobats, clowns, trapeze artists, and trained animals. **2** a public performance given by such a company. **3** *Brit* an open place in a town where several streets meet. **4** *Informal* a hectic or well-published situation: *her second marriage turned into a media circus.* **5** (in ancient Rome) an open-air stadium for chariot races or public games. **6** a travelling group of professional sportsmen: *the Formula One circus.* ▷ **HISTORY** Greek *kirkos* ring

cirque (**sirk**) *n* a steep-sided semicircular hollow found in mountainous areas.

cirrhosis (sir-**roh**-siss) *n* a chronic progressive disease of the liver, often caused by drinking too much alcohol. ▷ **HISTORY** Greek *kirrhos* orange-coloured

cirrocumulus (sirr-oh-**kew**-myew-luss) *n, pl* **-li** (-lie) a high cloud of ice crystals grouped into small separate globular masses.

cirrostratus (sirr-oh-**strah**-tuss) *n, pl* **-ti** (-tie) a uniform layer of cloud above about 6000 metres.

cirrus *n, pl* **-ri 1** a thin wispy cloud found at high altitudes. **2** a plant tendril. **3** a slender tentacle in certain sea creatures. ▷ **HISTORY** Latin: curl

CIS Commonwealth of Independent States.

cisalpine *adj* on this (the southern) side of the Alps, as viewed from Rome.

cisco *n, pl* **-coes** *or* **-cos** a whitefish, esp. the lake herring of cold deep lakes of North America. ▷ **HISTORY** from a Native American language

Cistercian *n* **1** a Christian monk or nun belonging to an especially strict Benedictine order. ✧ *adj* **2** of or relating to this order. ▷ **HISTORY** *Cîteaux,* original home of the order

cistern *n* **1** a water tank, esp. one which holds water for flushing a toilet. **2** an underground reservoir. ▷ **HISTORY** Latin *cista* box

citadel *n* a fortress in a city. ▷ **HISTORY** Latin *civitas*

citation *n* **1** an official commendation or award, esp. for bravery. **2** the quoting of a book or author. **3** a quotation.

cite *vb* **citing, cited 1** to quote or refer to (a passage, book, or author). **2** to bring forward as proof. **3** to summon to appear before a court of law. **4** to mention or commend (someone) for outstanding bravery. **5** to enumerate: *the president cited the wonders of the American family.* ▷ **HISTORY** Old French *citer* to summon

citizen *n* **1** a native or naturalized member of a state or nation. **2** an inhabitant of a city or town.

Citizens' Band *n* a range of radio frequencies for use by the public for private communication.

citizenship *n* the condition or status of a citizen, with its rights and duties.

citrate *n* any salt or ester of citric acid.

citric *adj* of or derived from citrus fruits or citric acid.

citric acid *n* a weak acid found especially in citrus fruits and used as a flavouring (**E330**).

citron *n* **1** a lemon-like fruit of a small Asian tree. **2** the candied rind of this fruit, for decorating foods. ▷ **HISTORY** Latin *citrus* citrus tree

citronella *n* **1** a tropical Asian grass with lemon-scented leaves. **2** the aromatic oil obtained from this grass.

citrus fruit *n* juicy, sharp-tasting fruit such as oranges, lemons, or limes. ▷ **HISTORY** Latin *citrus* citrus tree

city *n, pl* **cities 1** any large town. **2** (in Britain) a town that has received this title from the Crown. **3** the people of a city collectively. **4** (in the US and Canada) a large town with its own government established by charter from the state or provincial government. ▷ **HISTORY** Latin *civis* citizen

City *n* **the City** *Brit* **1** the area in central London in which the United Kingdom's major financial business is transacted. **2** the various financial institutions in this area.

city editor *n* (on a newspaper) **1** *Brit* the editor in charge of business news. **2** *US & Canad* the editor in charge of local news.

city-state *n Ancient history* a state consisting of a sovereign city and its dependencies.

civet (**siv**-vit) *n* **1** a spotted catlike mammal of Africa and S Asia. **2** the musky fluid produced by this animal, used in perfumes. ▷ **HISTORY** Arabic *zabād* civet perfume
civic *adj* of a city or citizens. ▶ **civically** *adv*
civic centre *n Brit & NZ* a complex of public buildings, including recreational facilities and offices of local government.
civics *n* the study of the rights and responsibilities of citizenship.
civil *adj* **1** of or occurring within the state or between citizens: *civil unrest.* **2** of or relating to the citizen as an individual: *civil rights.* **3** not part of the military, legal or religious structures of a country: *civil aviation.* **4** polite or courteous: *he seemed very civil and listened politely.* ▷ **HISTORY** Latin *civis* citizen ▶ **civilly** *adv*
civil defence *n* the organizing of civilians to deal with enemy attacks and natural disasters.
civil disobedience *n* a nonviolent protest, such as a refusal to obey laws or pay taxes.
civil engineer *n* a person qualified to design and construct public works, such as roads or bridges. ▶ **civil engineering** *n*
civilian *n* **1** a person who is not a member of the armed forces or police. ✧ *adj* **2** not relating to the armed forces or police: *civilian clothes.*
civility *n, pl* **-ties 1** polite or courteous behaviour. **2 civilities** polite words or actions.
civilization *or* **-lisation** *n* **1** the total culture and way of life of a particular people, nation, region, or period. **2** a human society that has a complex cultural, political, and legal organization. **3** the races collectively who have achieved such a state. **4** cities or populated areas, as contrasted with sparsely inhabited areas. **5** intellectual, cultural, and moral refinement.
civilize *or* **-lise** *vb* **-lizing, -lized** *or* **-lising, -lised 1** to bring out of barbarism into a state of civilization. **2** to refine, educate, or enlighten. ▶ **civilized** *or* **-lised** *adj*
civil law *n Law* **1** the law of a state, relating to private and civilian affairs and rights rather than criminal offences. Compare **criminal law**. **2** the body of law in ancient Rome, esp. as applicable to private citizens. **3** a system of law based on the Roman system as distinguished from common law and canon law.
civil liberties *pl n* a person's rights to freedom of speech and action.
civil list *n* (in Britain) the annual amount given by Parliament to the royal household and the royal family.
civil marriage *n Law* a marriage performed by an official other than a clergyman.
civil rights *pl n* the personal rights of the individual citizen to have equal treatment and equal opportunities.
civil servant *n* a member of the civil service.
civil service *n* the service responsible for the public administration of the government of a country.
civil war *n* a war between people of the same country, such as the **English Civil War**, between the supporters of Charles I and those of Parliament (1642-51), the **American Civil War**, between the North and the South (1861-65), and the **Spanish Civil War**, between the nationalists and the republicans (1936-39).
civvies *pl n Brit, Austral & NZ slang* civilian clothes as opposed to uniform.
CJD Creutzfeldt-Jakob disease: a fatal virus disease that affects the central nervous system.
cl centilitre.
Cl *Chem* chlorine.
clack *n* **1** the sound made by two hard objects striking each other. ✧ *vb* **2** to make this sound. ▷ **HISTORY** imitative
clad *vb* a past of **clothe**.
cladding *n* **1** the material used to cover the outside of a building. **2** a protective metal coating attached to another metal. ▷ **HISTORY** special use of CLAD
cladistics *n* a method of grouping animals by measurable likenesses. ▷ **HISTORY** Greek *klados* branch
claim *vb* **1** to assert as a fact: *he had claimed to be too ill to return.* **2** to demand as a right or as one's property: *you can claim housing benefit to help pay your rent.* **3** to call for or need: *this problem claims our attention.* **4** to cause the death of: *violence which has claimed at least fifty lives.* **5** to succeed in obtaining; win: *she claimed her fifth European tour victory with a closing round of 64.* ✧ *n* **6** an assertion of something as true or real. **7** an assertion of a right; a demand for something as due. **8** a right or just title to something: *a claim to fame.* **9** anything that is claimed, such as a piece of land staked out by a miner. **10 a** a demand for payment in connection with an insurance policy. **b** the sum of money demanded. ▷ **HISTORY** Latin *clamare* to shout ▶ **claimant** *n*
clairvoyance *n* the alleged power of perceiving things beyond the natural range of the senses. ▷ **HISTORY** French: clear-seeing
clairvoyant *n* **1** a person claiming to have the power to foretell future events. ✧ *adj* **2** of or possessing clairvoyance.
clam *n* an edible shellfish with a hinged shell. ▷ **HISTORY** earlier *clamshell* shell that clamps
clamber *vb* **1** to climb awkwardly, using hands and feet. ✧ *n* **2** a climb performed in this manner. ▷ **HISTORY** probably variant of *climb*
clammy *adj* **-mier, -miest** unpleasantly moist and sticky. ▷ **HISTORY** Old English *clǣman* to smear ▶ **clammily** *adv* ▶ **clamminess** *n*
clamour *or US* **clamor** *n* **1** a loud protest. **2** a loud and persistent noise or outcry. ✧ *vb* **3 clamour for** to demand noisily. **4** to make a loud noise or outcry. ▷ **HISTORY** Latin *clamare* to cry out ▶ **clamorous** *adj*
clamp[1] *n* **1** a mechanical device with movable jaws for holding things together tightly. **2** See **wheel clamp**. ✧ *vb* **3** to fix or fasten with a clamp.

4 to immobilize (a car) by means of a wheel clamp. ▷ **HISTORY** Dutch or Low German *klamp*

clamp² *n* a mound of a harvested root crop, covered with straw and earth to protect it from winter weather. ▷ **HISTORY** Middle Dutch *klamp* heap

clan *n* **1** a group of families with a common surname and a common ancestor, esp. among Scottish Highlanders. **2** an extended family related by ancestry or marriage: *America's leading political clan, the Kennedys.* **3** a group of people with common characteristics, aims, or interests. ▷ **HISTORY** Scottish Gaelic *clann* ▶ **clansman** *n*

clandestine *adj Formal* secret and concealed: *a base for clandestine activities.* ▷ **HISTORY** Latin *clam* secretly ▶ **clandestinely** *adv*

clang *vb* **1** to make a loud ringing noise, as metal does when it is struck. ✧ *n* **2** a ringing metallic noise. ▷ **HISTORY** Latin *clangere*

clanger *n* **drop a clanger** *Informal* to make a very noticeable mistake.

clangour *or US* **clangor** *n* a loud continuous clanging sound. ▷ **HISTORY** Latin *clangor* ▶ **clangorous** *adj*

clank *n* **1** an abrupt harsh metallic sound. ✧ *vb* **2** to make such a sound. ▷ **HISTORY** imitative

clannish *adj* (of a group) tending to exclude outsiders: *the villagers can be very clannish.*

clap¹ *vb* **clapping, clapped 1** to applaud by striking the palms of one's hands sharply together. **2** to place or put quickly or forcibly: *in former times he would have been clapped in irons or shot.* **3** to strike (a person) lightly with an open hand as in greeting. **4** to make a sharp abrupt sound like two objects being struck together. **5 clap eyes on** *Informal* to catch sight of. ✧ *n* **6** the act or sound of clapping. **7** a sharp abrupt sound, esp. of thunder. **8** a light blow. ▷ **HISTORY** Old English *clæppan*

clap² *n Slang* gonorrhoea. ▷ **HISTORY** Old French *clapier* brothel

clapped out *adj Informal* worn out; dilapidated.

clapper *n* **1** a small piece of metal hanging inside a bell, which causes it to sound when struck against the side. **2 like the clappers** *Brit informal* extremely quickly: *he left, pedalling like the clappers.*

clapperboard *n* a pair of hinged boards clapped together during film shooting to help in synchronizing sound and picture.

claptrap *n Informal* foolish or pretentious talk: *pseudo-intellectual claptrap.*

claque *n Formal* **1** a group of people hired to applaud. **2** a group of fawning admirers. ▷ **HISTORY** French *claquer* to clap

claret (**klar**-rit) *n* **1** a dry red wine, esp. one from Bordeaux. ✧ *adj* **2** purplish-red. ▷ **HISTORY** Latin *clarus* clear

clarify *vb* **-fies, -fying, -fied 1** to make or become clear or easy to understand. **2** to make or become free of impurities, esp. by heating: *clarified butter.* ▷ **HISTORY** Latin *clarus* clear + *facere* to make ▶ **clarification** *n*

clarinet *n* a keyed woodwind instrument with a single reed. ▷ **HISTORY** French *clarinette* ▶ **clarinettist** *n*

clarion *n* **1** an obsolete high-pitched trumpet. **2** its sound. ▷ **HISTORY** Latin *clarus* clear

clarion call *n* strong encouragement to do something.

clarity *n* clearness. ▷ **HISTORY** Latin *claritas*

clash *vb* **1** to come into conflict. **2** to be incompatible. **3** (of dates or events) to coincide. **4** (of colours or styles) to look ugly or incompatible together: *patterned fabrics which combine seemingly clashing shades to great effect.* **5** to make a loud harsh sound, esp. by striking together. ✧ *n* **6** a collision or conflict. **7** a loud harsh noise. ▷ **HISTORY** imitative

clasp *n* **1** a fastening, such as a catch or hook, for holding things together. **2** a firm grasp or embrace. ✧ *vb* **3** to grasp or embrace tightly. **4** to fasten together with a clasp. ▷ **HISTORY** origin unknown

clasp knife *n* a large knife with blades which fold into the handle.

class *n* **1** a group of people sharing a similar social and economic position. **2** the system of dividing society into such groups. **3** a group of people or things sharing a common characteristic. **4 a** a group of pupils or students who are taught together. **b** a meeting of a group of students for tuition. **5** a standard of quality or attainment: *second class.* **6** *Informal* excellence or elegance, esp. in dress, design, or behaviour: *a full-bodied red wine with real class.* **7** *Biol* one of the groups into which a phylum is divided, containing one or more orders. **8 in a class of its own** *or* **in a class by oneself** without an equal for ability, talent, etc. ✧ *adj* **9** *Informal* excellent, skilful, or stylish: *a class act.* ✧ *vb* **10** to place in a class. ▷ **HISTORY** Latin *classis* class, rank

class action *n Law* a legal action undertaken by one or more people representing the interests of a large group of people with the same grievance.

class boundary *n Maths* the higher or lower limit of a class interval on a graph.

class-conscious *adj* aware of belonging to a particular social rank.

classic *adj* **1** serving as a standard or model of its kind; typical: *it is a classic symptom of iron deficiency.* **2** of lasting interest or significance because of excellence: *the classic work on Central America.* **3** characterized by simplicity and purity of form: *a classic suit.* ✧ *n* **4** an author, artist, or work of art of the highest excellence. **5** a creation or work considered as definitive. ▷ **HISTORY** Latin *classicus* of the first rank

classical *adj* **1** of or in a restrained conservative style: *it had been built in the eighteenth century in a severely classical style.* **2** *Music* **a** in a style or from a period marked by stability of form, intellectualism, and restraint. **b** denoting serious art music in general. **3** of or influenced by ancient Greek and Roman culture. **4** of the form of a language historically used for formal and literary purposes: *classical Chinese.* **5** (of an education) based on the humanities and the study of Latin and Greek. ▶ **classically** *adv*

classic car *n Chiefly Brit* a car that is more than twenty five years old.

classicism *n* **1** an artistic style based on Greek and Roman models, showing emotional restraint and regularity of form. **2** knowledge of the culture of ancient Greece and Rome. ▶ **classicist** *n*

classics *pl n* **1** the study of ancient Greek and Roman literature and culture. **2 the classics a** those works of literature regarded as great or lasting. **b** the ancient Greek and Latin languages.

classification *n* **1** placing things systematically in categories. **2** a division or category in a classifying system. ▷ HISTORY French ▶ **classificatory** *adj*

classified *adj* **1** arranged according to some system of classification. **2** *Government* (of information) not available to people outside a restricted group, esp. for reasons of national security.

classified advertisement *n Journalism* (in an advertisement column in a newspaper) a small advertisement grouped according to type, usually selling or trying to buy something.

classifier *n Grammar* a noun or adjective that categorizes a person or thing mentioned or described as being of a particular kind.

classify *vb* **-fies, -fying, -fied 1** to arrange or order by classes. **2** *Government* to declare (information) to be officially secret. ▶ **classifiable** *adj*

class interval *n Maths* one of the divisions of the base line of a bar chart or histogram.

classless *adj* **1** not belonging to a class. **2** distinguished by the absence of economic or social distinctions: *a classless society.*

classmate *n* a friend or contemporary in the same class of a school.

classroom *n* a room in a school where lessons take place.

classy *adj* **classier, classiest** *Informal* stylish and sophisticated. ▶ **classiness** *n*

clatter *vb* **1** to make a rattling noise, as when hard objects hit each other. ✧ *n* **2** a rattling sound or noise. ▷ HISTORY Old English *clatrung* clattering

clause *n* **1** a section of a legal document such as a will or contract. **2** *Grammar* a group of words, consisting of a subject and a predicate including a finite verb, that does not necessarily constitute a sentence. ▷ HISTORY Latin *clausula* conclusion ▶ **clausal** *adj*

claustrophobia *n* an abnormal fear of being in a confined space. ▷ HISTORY Latin *claustrum* cloister + -PHOBIA ▶ **claustrophobic** *adj*

clavichord *n* an early keyboard instrument with a very soft tone. ▷ HISTORY Latin *clavis* key + *chorda* string

clavicle *n* either of the two bones connecting the shoulder blades with the upper part of the breastbone; the collarbone. ▷ HISTORY Latin *clavis* key

claw *n* **1** a curved pointed nail on the foot of birds, some reptiles, and certain mammals. **2** a similar part in some invertebrates, such as a crab's pincer. ✧ *vb* **3** to scrape, tear, or dig with claws or nails: *she clawed his face with her fingernails.* **4** to achieve (something) only after overcoming great difficulties: *he clawed his way to power and wealth; settlers attempting to claw a living from the desert.* ▷ HISTORY Old English *clawu*

claw back *vb* **1** to get back (something) with difficulty. **2** to recover (a part of a grant or allowance) in the form of a tax or financial penalty.

clay *n* **1** a very fine-grained earth, soft when moist and hardening when baked, used to make bricks and pottery. **2** earth or mud. **3** *Poetic* the material of the human body. ▷ HISTORY Old English *clǣg* ▶ **clayey, clayish** *or* **claylike** *adj*

claymore *n* a large two-edged broadsword used formerly by Scottish Highlanders. ▷ HISTORY Gaelic *claidheamh mōr* great sword

clay pigeon *n* a disc of baked clay hurled into the air from a machine as a target for shooting.

Clayton's *adj Austral & NZ* acting as an imitation or substitute: *this latest ploy is simply a Clayton's resignation.* ▷ HISTORY from the trademark of a non-alcoholic drink marketed as 'the drink you have when you're not having a drink'

clean *adj* **1** free from dirt or impurities: *clean water.* **2** habitually hygienic and neat. **3** morally sound: *clean living.* **4** without objectionable language or obscenity: *good clean fun.* **5** without anything in it or on it: *a clean sheet of paper.* **6** causing little contamination or pollution: *rape seed oil may provide a clean alternative to petrol.* **7** recently washed; fresh. **8** thorough or complete: *a clean break with the past.* **9** skilful and done without fumbling; dexterous: *a clean catch.* **10** *Sport* played fairly and without fouls. **11** free from dishonesty or corruption: *clean government.* **12** simple and streamlined in design: *the clean lines and colourful simplicity of these ceramics.* **13** (esp. of a driving licence) showing or having no record of offences. **14** *Slang* **a** innocent. **b** not carrying illegal drugs, weapons, etc. ✧ *vb* **15** to make or become free of dirt: *he wanted to help me clean the room.* ✧ *adv* **16** in a clean way. **17** *Not standard* completely: *she clean forgot to face the camera.* **18 come clean** *Informal* to make a revelation or confession. ✧ *n* **19** the act or an instance of cleaning: *the fridge could do with a clean.* ▷ HISTORY Old English *clǣne*

clean-cut *adj* **1** clearly outlined. **2** wholesome in appearance.

cleaner *n* **1** a person, device, or substance that removes dirt. **2** a shop or firm that provides a dry-cleaning service. **3 take someone to the cleaners** *Informal* to rob or defraud someone.

cleanly *adv* **1** easily or smoothly. **2** in a fair manner. ✧ *adj* **-lier, -liest 3** habitually clean or neat. ▶ **cleanliness** *n*

cleanse *vb* **cleansing, cleansed 1** to remove dirt from. **2** to remove evil or guilt from. ▶ **cleanser** *n*

clean sheet *n Sport* an instance of conceding no goals or points in a match.

A B C D E F G H I J K L M N O P Q R S T U V W X Y Z

clear *adj* **1** free from doubt or confusion: *clear evidence of police thuggery.* **2** certain in the mind; sure: *I am still not clear about what they can and cannot do.* **3** easy to see or hear; distinct. **4** perceptive, alert: *clear thinking.* **5** evident or obvious: *it is not clear how he died.* **6** transparent: *clear glass doors.* **7** free from darkness or obscurity; bright. **8** (of sounds or the voice) not harsh or hoarse. **9** even and pure in tone or colour. **10** free of obstruction; open: *a clear path runs under the trees.* **11** (of weather) free from dullness or clouds. **12** without blemish or defect: *a clear skin.* **13** free of suspicion, guilt, or blame: *a clear conscience.* **14** (of money) without deduction; net. **15** free from debt or obligation. **16** without qualification or limitation; complete: *a clear lead.* ✧ *adv* **17** in a clear or distinct manner. **18** completely. **19 clear of** out of the way of: *once we were clear of the harbour we headed east.* ✧ *n* **20 in the clear** free of suspicion, guilt, or blame. ✧ *vb* **21** to free from doubt or confusion. **22** to rid of objects or obstructions. **23** to make or form (a path) by removing obstructions. **24** to move or pass by or over without contact: *he cleared the fence easily.* **25** to make or become free from darkness or obscurity. **26** to rid (one's throat) of phlegm. **27 a** (of the weather) to become free from dullness, fog, or rain. **b** (of mist or fog) to disappear. **28** (of a cheque) to pass through one's bank and be charged against one's account. **29** to free from impurity or blemish. **30** to obtain or give (clearance). **31** to prove (someone) innocent of a crime or mistake. **32** to permit (someone) to see or handle classified information. **33** to make or gain (money) as profit. **34** to discharge or settle (a debt). **35 clear the air** to sort out a misunderstanding. ✧ See also **clear off**. ▷ **HISTORY** Latin *clarus*
▸ **clearly** *adv*

clearance *n* **1** the act of clearing: *slum clearance.* **2** permission for a vehicle or passengers to proceed. **3** official permission to have access to secret information or areas. **4** space between two parts in motion.

clear-cut *adj* **1** easy to distinguish or understand: *there is no clear-cut distinction between safe and unsafe areas of the city.* **2** clearly outlined.

clearing *n* an area with few or no trees or shrubs in wooded or overgrown land.

clearing bank *n* (in Britain) any bank that makes use of the central clearing house in London.

clearing house *n* **1** *Banking* an institution where cheques and other commercial papers drawn on member banks are cancelled against each other so that only net balances are payable. **2** a central agency for the collection and distribution of information or materials.

clear off *vb Informal* to go away: often used as a command.

clear out *vb* **1** to remove and sort the contents of (a room or container). **2** *Informal* to go away: often used as a command.

clearway *n Brit & Austral* a stretch of road on which motorists may stop only in an emergency.

cleat *n* **1** a wedge-shaped block attached to a structure to act as a support. **2** a piece of wood or iron with two projecting ends round which ropes are fastened. ▷ **HISTORY** Germanic

cleavage *n* **1** the space between a woman's breasts, as revealed by a low-cut dress. **2** a division or split. **3** (of crystals) the act of splitting or the tendency to split along definite planes so as to make smooth surfaces.

cleave[1] *vb* **cleaving; cleft, cleaved** *or* **clove; cleft, cleaved** *or* **cloven 1** to split apart: *cleave the stone along the fissures.* **2** to make by or as if by cutting: *a two-lane highway that cleaved its way through the northern extremities of the Everglades.* ▷ **HISTORY** Old English *clēofan*

cleave[2] *vb* **cleaving, cleaved** to cling or stick: *a farmhouse cleaved to the hill.* ▷ **HISTORY** Old English *cleofian*

cleaver *n* a heavy knife with a square blade, used for chopping meat.

cleavers *n* a plant with small white flowers and sticky fruits. ▷ **HISTORY** Old English *clīfe*

clef *n Music* a symbol placed at the beginning of each stave indicating the pitch of the music written after it. ▷ **HISTORY** French

cleft *n* **1** a narrow opening in a rock. **2** an indentation or split. ✧ *adj* **3 in a cleft stick** in a very difficult position. ✧ *vb* **4** a past of **cleave**[1].

cleft palate *n* a congenital crack in the mid line of the hard palate.

clematis *n* a climbing plant grown for its large colourful flowers. ▷ **HISTORY** Greek *klēma* vine twig

clemency *n* mercy.

clement *adj* **1** (of the weather) mild. **2** merciful. ▷ **HISTORY** Latin *clemens* mild

clementine *n* a citrus fruit resembling a tangerine. ▷ **HISTORY** French

clench *vb* **1** to close or squeeze together (the teeth or a fist) tightly. **2** to grasp or grip firmly. ✧ *n* **3** a firm grasp or grip. ▷ **HISTORY** Old English *beclencan*

clerestory (**clear**-store-ee) *n, pl* **-ries** a row of windows in the upper part of the wall of the nave of a church above the roof of the aisle. ▷ **HISTORY** *clear + storey* ▸ **clerestoried** *adj*

clergy *n, pl* **-gies** priests and ministers as a group. ▷ **HISTORY** see CLERK

clergyman *n, pl* **-men** a member of the clergy.

cleric *n* a member of the clergy.

clerical *adj* **1** of clerks or office work: *a clerical job.* **2** of or associated with the clergy: *a Lebanese clerical leader.*

clerihew *n* a form of comic or satiric verse, consisting of two couplets and containing the name of a well-known person. ▷ **HISTORY** after E. *Clerihew* Bentley, who invented it

clerk *n* **1** an employee in an office, bank, or court who keeps records, files, and accounts. **2** *US & Canad* a hotel receptionist. **3** *Archaic* a scholar. ✧ *vb* **4** to work as a clerk. ▷ **HISTORY** Greek *klērikos* cleric, from *klēros* heritage ▸ **clerkship** *n*

clever *adj* **1** displaying sharp intelligence or mental alertness. **2** skilful with one's hands. **3** smart in a superficial way. **4** *Brit informal* sly or cunning.

▷ HISTORY Middle English *cliver* ▶ **cleverly** *adv* ▶ **cleverness** *n*

clianthus *n* a plant of Australia and New Zealand with clusters of ornamental scarlet flowers. ▷ HISTORY probably from Greek *kleos* glory + *anthos* flower

cliché (**klee**-shay) *n* an expression or idea that is no longer effective because of overuse. ▷ HISTORY French ▶ **clichéd** *or* **cliché'd** *adj*

click *n* **1** a short light often metallic sound. ✧ *vb* **2** to make a clicking sound: *cameras clicked and whirred.* **3** Also: **click on** *Computers* to press and release (a button on a mouse) or select (a particular function) by pressing and releasing a button on a mouse. **4** *Informal* to become suddenly clear: *it wasn't until I saw the photograph that everything clicked into place.* **5** *Slang* (of two people) to get on well together: *I met him at a dinner party and we clicked straight away.* **6** *Slang* to be a great success: *the film cost so much that if it hadn't clicked at the box office we'd have been totally wiped out.* ▷ HISTORY imitative

client *n* **1** someone who uses the services of a professional person or organization. **2** a customer. **3** *Computers* a program or work station that requests data from a server. ▷ HISTORY Latin *cliens* retainer

clientele (klee-on-**tell**) *n* customers or clients collectively.

cliff *n* a steep rock face, esp. along the seashore. ▷ HISTORY Old English *clif*

cliffhanger *n* a film, game, etc. which is exciting and full of suspense because its outcome is uncertain. ▶ **cliffhanging** *adj*

climacteric *n* **1** same as **menopause. 2** the period in the life of a man corresponding to the menopause, during which sexual drive and fertility diminish. ▷ HISTORY Greek *klimakter* rung of a ladder

climate *n* **1** the typical weather conditions of an area. **2** an area with a particular kind of climate. **3** a prevailing trend: *the current economic climate.* ▷ HISTORY Greek *klima* inclination, region ▶ **climatic** *adj* ▶ **climatically** *adv*

> **☑ WORD TIP**
> *Climatic* is sometimes wrongly used where *climactic* is meant. *Climatic* should be used to talk about things relating to climate; *climactic* is used to describe something which forms a climax.

climatic stress *n Biol* damage to living organisms caused by changes in weather conditions.

climatology *n Meteorol* the study of climates.

climax *n* **1** the most intense or highest point of an experience or of a series of events: *a striking climax to the year's efforts to promote tourism.* **2** a decisive moment in a dramatic or other work: *the film has a climax set atop a gale-swept lighthouse.* **3** an orgasm. ✧ *vb* **4** *Not universally accepted* to reach or bring to a climax. ▷ HISTORY Greek *klimax* ladder ▶ **climactic** *adj*

climax vegetation *n Biol, geog* the balanced plant community that will develop if a given environment is left undisturbed for long enough for the species best-equipped to flourish in it to take over.

climb *vb* **1** to go up or ascend (stairs, a mountain, etc.). **2** to move or go with difficulty: *she climbed through a window.* **3** to rise to a higher point or intensity: *I grew increasingly delirious as my temperature climbed.* **4** to increase in value or amount: *the number could eventually climb to half-a-million.* **5** to ascend in social position: *he climbed the ranks of the organization.* **6** (of plants) to grow upwards by twining, using tendrils or suckers. **7** to incline or slope upwards: *the road climbed up through the foothills.* **8 climb into** *Informal* to put on or get into: *I climbed into the van.* ✧ *n* **9** the act or an instance of climbing. **10** a place or thing to be climbed, esp. a route in mountaineering. ▷ HISTORY Old English *climban* ▶ **climbable** *adj* ▶ **climber** *n* ▶ **climbing** *n, adj*

climb down *vb* **1** to retreat (from an opinion or position). ✧ *n* **climb-down 2** a retreat from an opinion or position.

clime *n Poetic* a region or its climate.

clinch *vb* **1** to settle (an argument or agreement) decisively. **2** to secure (a nail) by bending the protruding point over. **3** to engage in a clinch, as in boxing or wrestling. ✧ *n* **4** the act of clinching. **5** *Boxing, wrestling* a movement in which one or both competitors hold on to the other to avoid punches or regain wind. **6** *Slang* a lovers' embrace. ▷ HISTORY variant of *clench*

clincher *n Informal* something decisive, such as fact, argument, or point scored.

cling *vb* **clinging, clung 1** to hold fast or stick closely. **2** to be emotionally overdependent on. **3** to continue to do or believe in: *he clings to the belief that people are capable of change.* ▷ HISTORY Old English *clingan* ▶ **clinging** *or* **clingy** *adj*

clingfilm *n Brit* a thin polythene material used for wrapping food.

clinic *n* **1** a place in which outpatients are given medical treatment or advice. **2** a similar place staffed by specialist physicians or surgeons: *I have an antenatal clinic on Friday afternoon.* **3** *Brit & NZ* a private hospital or nursing home. **4** the teaching of medicine to students at the bedside. ▷ HISTORY Greek *klinē* bed

clinical *adj* **1** of or relating to the observation and treatment of patients directly: *clinical trials of a new drug.* **2** of or relating to a clinic. **3** logical and unemotional: *they have a somewhat clinical attitude to their children's upbringing.* **4** (of a room or buildings) plain, simple, and usually unattractive. ▶ **clinically** *adv*

clinical thermometer *n* a thermometer for measuring the temperature of the body.

clink[1] *vb* **1** to make a light sharp metallic sound. ✧ *n* **2** such a sound. ▷ HISTORY perhaps from Middle Dutch *klinken*

clink[2] *n Slang* prison. ▷ HISTORY after *Clink*, a former prison in London

clinker *n* the fused coal left over in a fire or furnace. ▷ **HISTORY** Dutch *klinker* a type of brick

clinker-built *adj* (of a boat or ship) with a hull made from overlapping planks. ▷ **HISTORY** obsolete *clinker* a nailing together, probably from *clinch*

clint *n Physical geog* a section of a limestone pavement separated from adjacent sections by solution fissures.

Clio *n Greek myth* the Muse of history.

clip[1] *vb* **clipping, clipped 1** to cut or trim with scissors or shears. **2** to remove a short section from (a film or newspaper). **3** *Brit & Austral* to punch a hole in (something, esp. a ticket). **4** *Informal* to strike with a sharp, often slanting, blow. **5** to shorten (a word). **6** *Slang* to obtain (money) by cheating. ✧ *n* **7** the act of clipping. **8** a short extract from a film. **9** something that has been clipped. **10** *Informal* a sharp, often slanting, blow: *a clip on the ear.* **11** *Informal* speed: *proceeding at a smart clip.* **12** *Austral & NZ* the total quantity of wool shorn, as in one place or season. ▷ **HISTORY** Old Norse *klippa* to cut

clip[2] *n* **1** a device for attaching or holding things together. **2** an article of jewellery that can be clipped onto a dress or hat. ✧ *vb* **clipping, clipped 3** to attach or hold together with a clip. ▷ **HISTORY** Old English *clyppan* to embrace

clipboard *n* a portable writing board with a clip at the top for holding paper.

clipped *adj* (of speech) abrupt, clearly pronounced, and using as few words as possible.

clipper *n* a fast commercial sailing ship.

clippers *pl n* a tool used for clipping and cutting.

clipping *n* something cut out, esp. an article from a newspaper.

clique (**kleek**) *n* a small exclusive group of friends or associates. ▷ **HISTORY** French ▶ **cliquey, cliquy** *or* **cliquish** *adj*

clitoris (**klit**-or-riss) *n* a small sexually sensitive organ at the front of the vulva. ▷ **HISTORY** Greek *kleitoris* ▶ **clitoral** *adj*

Cllr councillor.

cloaca (kloh-**ake**-a) *n, pl* **-cae** a cavity in most animals, except higher mammals, into which the alimentary canal and the genital and urinary ducts open. ▷ **HISTORY** Latin: sewer

cloak *n* **1** a loose sleeveless outer garment, fastened at the throat and falling straight from the shoulders. **2** something that covers or conceals. ✧ *vb* **3** to hide or disguise. **4** to cover with or as if with a cloak. ▷ **HISTORY** Medieval Latin *clocca* cloak, bell

cloakroom *n* **1** a room in which coats may be left temporarily. **2** *Brit euphemistic* a toilet.

clobber[1] *vb Informal* **1** to batter. **2** to defeat utterly. **3** to criticize severely. ▷ **HISTORY** origin unknown

clobber[2] *n Brit, Austral & NZ informal* personal belongings, such as clothes. ▷ **HISTORY** origin unknown

cloche (**klosh**) *n* **1** *Brit, Austral & NZ* a small glass or plastic cover for protecting young plants. **2** a woman's close-fitting hat. ▷ **HISTORY** French: bell

clock[1] *n* **1** a device for showing the time, either through pointers that revolve over a numbered dial, or through a display of figures. **2** a device with a dial for recording or measuring. **3** the downy head of a dandelion that has gone to seed. **4** *Informal* same as **speedometer, mileometer**. **5** *Brit slang* the face. **6 round the clock** all day and all night. ✧ *vb* **7** to record (time) with a stopwatch, esp. in the calculation of speed. **8** *Brit, Austral & NZ slang* to strike, esp. on the face or head. **9** *Informal* to turn back the mileometer on (a car) illegally so that its mileage appears less. **10** *Brit slang* to see or notice. ▷ **HISTORY** Medieval Latin *clocca* bell

clock[2] *n* an ornamental design on the side of a sock. ▷ **HISTORY** origin unknown

clock in *or* **on** *vb* to register one's arrival at work on an automatic time recorder.

clock out *or* **off** *vb* to register one's departure from work on an automatic time recorder.

clock up *vb* to record or reach (a total): *he has now clocked up over 500 games for the club.*

clockwise *adv, adj* in the direction in which the hands of a clock rotate.

clockwork *n* **1** a mechanism similar to that of a spring-driven clock, as in a wind-up toy. **2 like clockwork** with complete regularity and precision.

clod *n* **1** a lump of earth or clay. **2** *Brit, Austral & NZ* a dull or stupid person. ▷ **HISTORY** Old English ▶ **cloddish** *adj*

clodhopper *n Informal* **1** a clumsy person. **2 clodhoppers** large heavy shoes.

clog *vb* **clogging, clogged 1** to obstruct or become obstructed with thick or sticky matter. **2** to encumber. **3** to stick in a mass. ✧ *n* **4** a wooden or wooden-soled shoe. ▷ **HISTORY** origin unknown

cloisonné (klwah-**zon**-nay) *n* a design made by filling in a wire outline with coloured enamel. ▷ **HISTORY** French

cloister *n* **1** a covered pillared walkway within a religious building. **2** a place of religious seclusion, such as a monastery. ✧ *vb* **3** to confine or seclude in or as if in a monastery. ▷ **HISTORY** Medieval Latin *claustrum* monastic cell, from Latin *claudere* to close

cloistered *adj* sheltered or protected.

clone *n* **1** a group of organisms or cells of the same genetic constitution that have been reproduced asexually from a single plant or animal. **2** *Informal* a person who closely resembles another. **3** *Slang* a mobile phone that has been given the electronic identity of an existing mobile phone, so that calls made on it are charged to that owner. ✧ *vb* **cloning, cloned 4** to produce as a clone. **5** *Informal* to produce near copies of (a person). **6** *Slang* to give (a mobile phone) the electronic identity of an existing mobile phone so that calls made on it are charged to that owner. ▷ **HISTORY** Greek *klōn* twig, shoot ▶ **cloning** *n*

close[1] *vb* **closing, closed 1** to shut: *he lay back and closed his eyes.* **2** to bar, obstruct, or fill up (an entrance, a hole, etc.): *the blockades had closed major roads, railways and border crossings.* **3** to cease or cause to cease giving service: *both stores closed at 9 p.m.; the Shipping Company closed its* *offices in Bangkok.* **4** to end; terminate: *'Never,' she said, so firmly that it closed the subject.* **5** (of agreements or deals) to complete or be completed successfully. **6** to come closer (to): *he was still in second place but closing fast on the leader.* **7** to take hold: *his small fingers closed around the coin.* **8** *Stock Exchange* to have a value at the end of a day's trading, as specified: *the pound closed four-and-a-half cents higher.* **9** to join the ends or edges of something: *to close a circuit.* ✧ *n* **10** the act of closing. **11** the end or conclusion: *the close of play.* **12** (rhymes with **dose**) *Brit* a courtyard or quadrangle enclosed by buildings. **13** *Scot* the entry from the street to a tenement building. ✧ See also **close down**. ▷ HISTORY Latin *claudere*

close² *adj* **1** near in space or time. **2** intimate: *we were such close friends in those days.* **3** near in relationship: *the dead man seems to have had no close relatives.* **4** careful, strict, or searching: *their research will not stand up to close scrutiny.* **5** having the parts near together: *a close formation.* **6** near to the surface; short: *an NCO's haircut, cropped close on top, shaved clean at sides and back.* **7** almost equal: *a close game.* **8** not deviating or varying greatly from something: *a close resemblance.* **9** confined or enclosed. **10** oppressive, heavy, or airless: *damp, close weather.* **11** strictly guarded: *he had been placed in close arrest.* **12** secretive or reticent. **13** miserly; not generous. **14** restricted as to public admission or membership. ✧ *adv* **15** closely; tightly. **16** near or in proximity. ▷ HISTORY Old French *clos* ▶ **closely** *adv* ▶ **closeness** *n*

closed *adj* **1** blocked against entry. **2** only admitting a selected group of people; exclusive: *he had a fairly closed circle of friends.* **3** not open to question or debate. **4** *Maths* **a** (of a curve or surface) completely enclosing an area or volume. **b** (of a set) made up of members on which a specific operation, such as addition, gives as its result another existing member of the set.

closed circuit *n* a complete electrical circuit through which current can flow.

closed-circuit television *n* a television system used within a limited area such as a building.

close down *vb* **1** to stop operating or working: *the factory closed down many years ago.* ✧ *n* **close-down 2** *Brit & NZ radio, television* the end of a period of broadcasting.

closed shop *n Brit, Austral & NZ* (formerly) a place of work in which all workers had to belong to a particular trade union.

close season *n* **1** the period of the year when it is illegal to kill certain game or fish. **2** *Sport* the period of the year when there is no domestic competition.

close shave *n Informal* a narrow escape.

closet *n* **1** *US & Austral* a small cupboard. **2** a small private room. **3** short for **water closet**. ✧ *adj* **4** private or secret: *a closet homosexual.* ✧ *vb* **-eting, -eted 5** to shut away in private, esp. in order to talk: *he was closeted with the President.* ▷ HISTORY Old French *clos* enclosure

close-up *n* **1** a photograph or film or television shot taken at close range. **2** a detailed or intimate view or examination. ✧ *vb* **close up 3** to shut entirely: *every other shop front seemed to be closed up.* **4** to draw together: *the ranks closed up and marched on.* **5** (of wounds) to heal completely.

close with *vb* to engage in battle with (an enemy).

closure *n* **1** the act of closing or the state of being closed. **2** something that closes or shuts. **3** a procedure by which a debate may be stopped and an immediate vote taken. **4** *Chiefly US* **a** a resolution of a significant event or relationship in a person's life. **b** the sense of contentment experienced after such a resolution.

clot *n* **1** a soft thick lump formed from liquid. **2** *Informal* a stupid person. ✧ *vb* **clotting, clotted 3** to form soft thick lumps. ▷ HISTORY Old English *clott*

cloth *n, pl* **cloths 1** a fabric formed by weaving, felting, or knitting fibres. **2** a piece of such fabric used for a particular purpose. **3 the cloth** the clergy. ▷ HISTORY Old English *clāth*

clothe *vb* **clothing, clothed** *or* **clad 1** to put clothes on. **2** to provide with clothes. **3** to cover or envelop (something) so as to change its appearance: *a small valley clothed in thick woodland.* ▷ HISTORY Old English *clāthian*

clothes *pl n* **1** articles of dress. **2** *Chiefly Brit* short for **bedclothes**. ▷ HISTORY Old English *clāthas,* plural of *clāth* cloth

clothier *n* a person who makes or sells clothes or cloth.

clothing *n* **1** garments collectively. **2** something that covers or clothes.

cloud *n* **1** a mass of water or ice particles visible in the sky. **2** a floating mass of smoke, dust, etc. **3** a large number of insects or other small animals in flight. **4** something that darkens, threatens, or carries gloom. **5 in the clouds** not in contact with reality. **6 on cloud nine** *Informal* elated; very happy. **7 under a cloud a** under reproach or suspicion. **b** in a state of gloom or bad temper. ✧ *vb* **8** to make or become more difficult to see through: *my glasses kept clouding up; mud clouded the water.* **9** to confuse or impair: *his judgment was no longer clouded by alcohol.* **10** to make or become gloomy or depressed: *insanity clouded the last years of his life.* ▷ HISTORY Old English *clūd* rock, hill ▶ **cloudless** *adj*

cloudburst *n* a heavy fall of rain.

cloud chamber *n Physics* an apparatus for detecting high-energy particles by observing their tracks through a chamber containing a supersaturated vapour.

cloudy *adj* **cloudier, cloudiest 1** covered with cloud or clouds. **2** (of liquids) opaque or muddy. **3** confused or unclear. ▶ **cloudily** *adv* ▶ **cloudiness** *n*

clout *n* **1** *Informal* a fairly hard blow. **2** power or influence. ✧ *vb* **3** *Informal* to hit hard. ▷ HISTORY Old English *clūt* piece of cloth

clove¹ *n* a dried closed flower bud of a tropical tree, used as a spice. ▷ HISTORY Latin *clavus* nail

A B C D E F G H I J K L M N O P Q R S T U V W X Y Z

clove[2] *n* a segment of a bulb of garlic. ▷ **HISTORY** Old English *clufu* bulb

clove[3] *vb* a past tense of **cleave**[1].

clove hitch *n* a knot used to fasten a rope to a spar or a larger rope.

cloven *vb* **1** a past participle of **cleave**[1]. ✧ *adj* **2** split or divided.

cloven hoof *or* **foot** *n* the divided hoof of a pig, goat, cow, or deer.

clover *n* **1** a plant with three-lobed leaves and dense flower heads. **2 in clover** *Informal* in ease or luxury. ▷ **HISTORY** Old English *clāfre*

clown *n* **1** a comic entertainer, usually bizarrely dressed and made up, appearing in the circus. **2** an amusing person. **3** a clumsy rude person. ✧ *vb* **4** to behave foolishly. **5** to perform as a clown. ▷ **HISTORY** origin unknown ▶ **clownish** *adj*

cloying *adj* so sweet or pleasurable that it ultimately becomes sickly: *cloying sentimentality.* ▷ **HISTORY** Middle English *cloy* originally to nail, hence, to obstruct ▶ **cloyingly** *adv*

club *n* **1** a group or association of people with common aims or interests. **2** the building used by such a group. **3** a stout stick used as a weapon. **4** a stick or bat used to strike the ball in various sports, esp. golf. **5** an establishment or regular event at which people dance to records; disco: *a new weekly club with resident DJ.* **6** a building in which members go to meet, dine, read, etc. **7** *Chiefly Brit* an organization, esp. in a shop, set up as a means of saving. **8** a playing card marked with one or more black trefoil symbols. ✧ *vb* **clubbing, clubbed 9** to beat with a club. **10 club together** to combine resources or efforts for a common purpose. ▷ **HISTORY** Old Norse *klubba*

club class *n* **1** a class of air travel which is less luxurious than first class but more luxurious than economy class. ✧ *adj* **club-class 2** of this class of air travel.

club foot *n* a congenital deformity of the foot.

club root *n* a fungal disease of cabbages and related plants, in which the roots become thickened and distorted.

cluck *n* **1** the low clicking noise made by a hen. ✧ *vb* **2** (of a hen) to make a clicking sound. **3** to express (a feeling) by making a similar sound: *the landlady was clucking feverishly behind them.* ▷ **HISTORY** imitative

clue *n* **1** something that helps to solve a problem or unravel a mystery. **2 not have a clue a** to be completely baffled. **b** to be ignorant or incompetent. ✧ *adj* **3 clued-up** shrewd and well-informed. ▷ **HISTORY** variant of *clew* ball of thread

clueless *adj Slang* helpless or stupid.

clump *n* **1** a small group of things or people together. **2** a dull heavy tread. ✧ *vb* **3** to walk or tread heavily. **4** to form into clumps. ▷ **HISTORY** Old English *clympe* ▶ **clumpy** *adj*

clumsy *adj* **-sier, -siest 1** lacking in skill or physical coordination: *an extraordinarily clumsy player.* **2** badly made or done. **3** said or done without thought or tact: *I took the clumsy hint and left.* ▷ **HISTORY** Middle English *clumse* to benumb ▶ **clumsily** *adv* ▶ **clumsiness** *n*

clung *vb* the past of **cling.**

clunk *n* **1** a dull metallic sound. ✧ *vb* **2** to make such a sound. ▷ **HISTORY** imitative

cluster *n* **1** a number of things growing, fastened, or occurring close together. **2** a number of people or things grouped together. ✧ *vb* **3** to gather or be gathered in clusters. ▷ **HISTORY** Old English *clyster*

clutch[1] *vb* **1** to seize with or as if with hands or claws. **2** to grasp or hold firmly. **3 clutch at** to attempt to get hold or possession of. ✧ *n* **4** a device that enables two revolving shafts to be joined or disconnected, esp. one that transmits the drive from the engine to the gearbox in a vehicle. **5** the pedal which operates the clutch in a car. **6** a firm grasp. **7 clutches a** hands or claws in the act of clutching: *his free kick escaped the clutches of the rival goalkeeper.* **b** power or control: *rescued from the clutches of the Gestapo.* ▷ **HISTORY** Old English *clyccan*

clutch[2] *n* **1** a set of eggs laid at the same time. **2** a group, bunch, or cluster: *a clutch of gloomy economic reports.* ▷ **HISTORY** Old Norse *klekja* to hatch

clutter *vb* **1** to scatter objects about (a place) in an untidy manner. ✧ *n* **2** an untidy heap or mass of objects. **3** a state of untidiness. ▷ **HISTORY** Middle English *clotter*

Clydesdale *n* a heavy powerful carthorse, originally from Scotland.

cm centimetre.

Cm *Chem* curium.

Cmdr Commander.

CND Campaign for Nuclear Disarmament.

CNS *Biol* central nervous system.

Co *Chem* cobalt.

CO **1** Colorado. **2** Commanding Officer.

Co.[1] *or* **co. 1** Company. **2 and co** *Informal* and the rest of them: *Harold and co.*

Co.[2] County.

co- *prefix* **1** together; joint or jointly: *coproduction.* **2** indicating partnership or equality: *co-star; copilot.* **3** to the same or a similar degree: *coextend.* **4** (in mathematics and astronomy) of the complement of an angle: *cosecant.* ▷ **HISTORY** Latin; see COM-

c/o **1** care of. **2** *Book-keeping* carried over.

coach *n* **1** a large comfortable single-decker bus used for sightseeing or long-distance travel. **2** a railway carriage. **3** a large four-wheeled enclosed carriage, usually horse-drawn. **4** a trainer or instructor: *the coach of the Mexican national team.* **5** a tutor who prepares students for examinations. ✧ *vb* **6** to train or teach. ▷ **HISTORY** from *Kocs,* village in Hungary where horse-drawn coaches were first made ▶ **coaching** *n*

coachman *n, pl* **-men** the driver of a horse-drawn coach or carriage.

coachwork *n* the body of a car.

coagulate (koh-**ag**-yew-late) *vb* **-lating, -lated** to change from a liquid into a soft semisolid mass;

clot. ▷ **HISTORY** Latin *coagulare* ▶ **coagulant** *n* ▶ **coagulation** *n*

coal *n* **1** a compact black or dark brown rock consisting largely of carbon formed from partially decomposed vegetation: a fuel and a source of coke, coal gas, and coal tar. **2** one or more lumps of coal. **3 coals to Newcastle** something supplied to a place where it is already plentiful. ▷ **HISTORY** Old English *col*

coalesce (koh-a-**less**) *vb* **-lescing, -lesced** to unite or come together in one body or mass. ▷ **HISTORY** Latin *co-* together + *alescere* to increase ▶ **coalescence** *n* ▶ **coalescent** *adj*

coalface *n* the exposed seam of coal in a mine.

coalfield *n* an area rich in deposits of coal.

coal gas *n* a mixture of gases produced by the distillation of bituminous coal and used for heating and lighting.

coalition (koh-a-**lish**-un) *n* a temporary alliance, esp. between political parties. ▷ **HISTORY** Latin *coalescere* to coalesce

coal scuttle *n* a container for holding coal for a domestic fire.

coal tar *n* a black tar, produced by the distillation of bituminous coal, used for making drugs and chemical products.

coal tit *n* a small songbird with a black head with a white patch on the nape.

coaming *n* a raised frame round a ship's hatchway for keeping out water. ▷ **HISTORY** origin unknown

coarse *adj* **1** rough in texture or structure. **2** unrefined or indecent: *coarse humour.* **3** of inferior quality. ▷ **HISTORY** origin unknown ▶ **coarsely** *adv* ▶ **coarseness** *n*

coarse fish *n Brit* a freshwater fish that is not of the salmon family. ▶ **coarse fishing** *n*

coarsen *vb* to make or become coarse.

coast *n* **1** the place where the land meets the sea. **2 the coast is clear** *Informal* the obstacles or dangers are gone. ✧ *vb* **3** to move by momentum or force of gravity, without the use of power. **4** to proceed without great effort: *they coasted to a 31-9 win in the pairs.* ▷ **HISTORY** Latin *costa* side, rib ▶ **coastal** *adj*

coastal flooding *n Geog* a raising of the level of the sea along the coastline caused by unusual tidal action or winds from tropical storms and hurricanes.

coastal plain *n Geog* a low-lying area sloping gently down to the sea, often formed as a result of sedimentary deposition.

coaster *n* **1** a small mat placed under a bottle or glass to protect a table. **2** *Brit* a small ship used for coastal trade.

coastguard *n* **1** an organization which aids shipping, saves lives at sea, and prevents smuggling. **2** a member of this.

coastline *n* the outline of a coast.

coat *n* **1** an outer garment with sleeves, covering the body from the shoulders to below the waist. **2** the hair, wool, or fur of an animal. **3** any layer that covers a surface. ✧ *vb* **4** to cover with a layer. ▷ **HISTORY** Old French *cote*

coat hanger *n* a curved piece of wood, wire or plastic, fitted with a hook and used to hang up clothes.

coating *n* a layer or film spread over a surface: *a thick coating of breadcrumbs.*

coat of arms *n* the heraldic emblem of a family or organization.

coat of mail *n History* a protective garment made of linked metal rings or plates.

coax *vb* **1** to persuade (someone) gently. **2** to obtain (something) by persistent coaxing. **3** to work on (something) carefully and patiently so as to make it function as desired: *I watched him coax the last few drops of beer out of his glass.* ▷ **HISTORY** obsolete *cokes* a fool

coaxial (koh-**ax**-ee-al) *adj* **1** *Electronics* (of a cable) transmitting by means of two concentric conductors separated by an insulator. **2** having a common axis.

cob *n* **1** a male swan. **2** a thickset type of horse. **3** the stalk of an ear of maize. **4** *Brit & Austral* a round loaf of bread. **5** *Brit* a hazel tree or hazelnut. ▷ **HISTORY** origin unknown

cobalt *n Chem* a brittle hard silvery-white metallic element used in alloys. Symbol: Co. ▷ **HISTORY** Middle High German *kobolt* goblin; from the miners' belief that goblins placed it in the silver ore

cobber *n Austral or old-fashioned NZ informal* a friend. ▷ **HISTORY** dialect *cob* to take a liking to someone

cobble *n* a cobblestone.

cobbler *n* a person who makes or mends shoes. ▷ **HISTORY** origin unknown

cobblers *pl n Brit, Austral & NZ slang* nonsense. ▷ **HISTORY** rhyming slang *cobblers' awls* balls

cobblestone *n* a rounded stone used for paving. ▷ **HISTORY** from *cob*

cobble together *vb* **-bling, -bled** to put together clumsily: *a coalition cobbled together from parties with widely differing aims.*

cobia (**koh**-bee-a) *n* a large dark-striped game fish of tropical and subtropical seas.

COBOL *n* a high-level computer programming language designed for general commercial use. ▷ **HISTORY** *co(mmon) b(usiness) o(riented) l(anguage)*

cobra *n* a highly venomous hooded snake of tropical Africa and Asia. ▷ **HISTORY** Latin *colubra* snake

cobweb *n* **1** a web spun by certain spiders. **2** a single thread of such a web. ▷ **HISTORY** Old English *(ātor)coppe* spider ▶ **cobwebbed** *adj* ▶ **cobwebby** *adj*

coca *n* the dried leaves of a S American shrub which contain cocaine. ▷ **HISTORY** S American Indian *kúka*

Coca-Cola *n Trademark* a carbonated soft drink.

cocaine *n* an addictive drug derived from coca leaves, used as a narcotic and local anaesthetic.

coccus *n, pl* **cocci** (**cock**-sigh) *Biol* a spherical or nearly spherical bacterium.

coccyx (**kok**-six) *n, pl* **coccyges** (kok-**sije**-eez) *Anat* a small triangular bone at the base of the spine in human beings and some apes. ▷ **HISTORY** Greek *kokkux* cuckoo, from its likeness to a cuckoo's beak ▶ **coccygeal** *adj*

cochineal *n* a scarlet dye obtained from a Mexican insect, used for colouring food. ▷ **HISTORY** Greek *kokkos* kermes berry

cochlea (**kok**-lee-a) *n, pl* **-leae** (-lee-ee) *Anat* the spiral tube in the internal ear, which converts sound vibrations into nerve impulses. ▷ **HISTORY** Greek *kokhlias* snail ▶ **cochlear** *adj*

cochlear implant *n* a device that stimulates the acoustic nerve in the inner ear in order to produce some form of hearing in people who are deaf from inner ear disease.

cock *n* **1** a male bird, esp. of domestic fowl. **2** a stopcock. **3** *Taboo slang* a penis. **4** the hammer of a gun. **5** *Brit informal* friend: used as a term of address. ✧ *vb* **6** to draw back the hammer of (a gun) so that it is ready to fire. **7** to lift and turn (part of the body) in a particular direction. ✧ See also **cockup**. ▷ **HISTORY** Old English *cocc*

cockabully *n* a small fresh-water fish of New Zealand. ▷ **HISTORY** Maori *kokopu*

cockade *n* a feather or rosette worn on the hat as a badge. ▷ **HISTORY** French *coq* cock

cock-a-hoop *adj Brit, Austral & NZ* in very high spirits. ▷ **HISTORY** origin unknown

cock-and-bull story *n Informal* an obviously improbable story, esp. one used as an excuse.

cockatiel, cockateel *n* a crested Australian parrot with a greyish-brown and yellow plumage.

cockatoo *n, pl* **-toos** a light-coloured crested parrot of Australia and the East Indies. ▷ **HISTORY** Malay *kakatua*

cockchafer *n* a large flying beetle. ▷ **HISTORY** COCK + *chafer* beetle

cockerel *n* a young domestic cock, less than a year old.

cocker spaniel *n* a small spaniel. ▷ **HISTORY** from *cocking* hunting woodcocks

cockeyed *adj Informal* **1** crooked or askew. **2** foolish or absurd. **3** cross-eyed.

cockie, cocky *n, pl* **-kies** *Austral & NZ informal* a cockatoo.

cockle *n* **1** an edible bivalve shellfish. **2** its shell. **3 warm the cockles of one's heart** to make one feel happy. ▷ **HISTORY** Greek *konkhule* mussel

cockleshell *n* **1** the rounded shell of the cockle. **2** a small light boat.

cockney *n* **1** a native of London, esp. of its East End. **2** the urban dialect of London or its East End. ✧ *adj* **3** characteristic of cockneys or their dialect. ▷ **HISTORY** Middle English *cokeney* cock's egg, later applied contemptuously to townsmen

cockpit *n* **1** the compartment in an aircraft for the pilot and crew. **2** the driver's compartment in a racing car. **3** *Naut* a space in a small vessel containing the wheel and tiller. **4** the site of many battles or conflicts: *the south of the country is a cockpit of conflicting interests.* **5** an enclosure used for cockfights.

cockroach *n* a beetle-like insect which is a household pest. ▷ **HISTORY** Spanish *cucaracha*

cockscomb *n* same as **coxcomb**.

cocksure *adj* overconfident or arrogant. ▷ **HISTORY** origin unknown

cocktail *n* **1** a mixed alcoholic drink. **2** an appetizer of seafood or mixed fruits. **3** any combination of diverse elements: *Central America was a cocktail of death, poverty, and destruction.* ▷ **HISTORY** origin unknown

cockup *Brit & Austral slang* ✧ *n* **1** something done badly. ✧ *vb* **cock up 2** to ruin or spoil.

cocky *adj* **cockier, cockiest** excessively proud of oneself. ▶ **cockily** *adv* ▶ **cockiness** *n*

coco *n, pl* **-cos** the coconut palm. ▷ **HISTORY** Portuguese: grimace

cocoa *or* **cacao** *n* **1** a powder made by roasting and grinding cocoa beans. **2** a hot or cold drink made from cocoa powder. ▷ **HISTORY** from CACAO

coconut *n* **1** the fruit of a type of palm tree (**coconut palm**), which has a thick fibrous oval husk and a thin hard shell enclosing edible white flesh. The hollow centre is filled with a milky fluid (**coconut milk**). **2** the flesh of the coconut.

cocoon *n* **1** a silky protective covering produced by a silkworm or other insect larva, in which the pupa develops. **2** a protective covering. ✧ *vb* **3** to wrap in or protect as if in a cocoon. ▷ **HISTORY** Provençal *coucoun* eggshell

cocotte *n* a small fireproof dish in which individual portions of food are cooked and served. ▷ **HISTORY** French

cod[1] *n, pl* **cod** *or* **cods 1** a large N Atlantic food fish. **2** any of various unrelated Australian fish, such as the Murray cod. ▷ **HISTORY** probably Germanic

cod[2] *adj Brit slang* having the character of an imitation or parody: *the chorus were dressed in exuberant cod-medieval costumes.* ▷ **HISTORY** origin unknown

COD cash (in the US collect) on delivery.

coda (**kode**-a) *n Music* the final part of a musical movement or work. ▷ **HISTORY** Italian: tail

coddle *vb* **-dling, -dled 1** to pamper or overprotect. **2** to cook (eggs) in water just below boiling point. ▷ **HISTORY** origin unknown

code *n* **1** a system of letters, symbols, or prearranged signals, by which information can be communicated secretly or briefly. **2** a set of principles or rules: *a code of practice.* **3** a system of letters or digits used for identification purposes: *area code; tax code.* **4** *Law* a body of written law. ✧ *vb* **coding, coded 5** to translate or arrange into a code. ▷ **HISTORY** Latin *codex* book, wooden block

codeine (**kode**-een) *n* a drug made mainly from morphine, used as a painkiller and sedative. ▷ **HISTORY** Greek *kōdeia* head of a poppy

codex (**koh**-dex) *n, pl* **-dices** (-diss-seez) a volume of manuscripts of an ancient text. ▷ **HISTORY** Latin: wooden block, book

codfish *n, pl* **-fish** *or* **-fishes** a cod.

codger *n Brit, Austral & NZ informal* an old man. ▷ **HISTORY** probably variant of *cadger*

codicil (**cod**-iss-ill) *n Law* an addition to a will. ▷ **HISTORY** from CODEX

codify (**kode**-if-fie) *vb* **-fies, -fying, -fied** to organize or collect together (rules or procedures) systematically. ▶ **codification** *n*

codling *n* a young cod.

cod-liver oil *n* an oil extracted from fish, rich in vitamins A and D.

codpiece *n History* a bag covering the male genitals, attached to breeches. ▷ **HISTORY** obsolete *cod* scrotum

codswallop *n Brit, Austral & NZ slang* nonsense. ▷ **HISTORY** origin unknown

coeducation *n* the education of boys and girls together. ▶ **coeducational** *adj*

coefficient *n* **1** *Maths* a number or constant placed before and multiplying another quantity: *the coefficient of the term 3xyz is 3.* **2** *Physics* a number or constant used to calculate the behaviour of a given substance under specified conditions.

coelacanth (**seel**-a-kanth) *n* a primitive marine fish, thought to be extinct until a living specimen was discovered in 1938. ▷ **HISTORY** Greek *koilos* hollow + *akanthos* spine

coelenterate (seel-**lent**-a-rate) *n* any invertebrate that has a saclike body with a single opening, such as a jellyfish or coral. ▷ **HISTORY** Greek *koilos* hollow + *enteron* intestine

coeliac disease (**seel**-ee-ak) *n* a disease which makes the digestion of food difficult. ▷ **HISTORY** Greek *koilia* belly

coenobite (**seen**-oh-bite) *n* a member of a religious order in a monastic community. ▷ **HISTORY** Greek *koinos* common + *bios* life

coequal *adj, n* equal.

coerce (koh-**urss**) *vb* **-ercing, -erced** to compel or force. ▷ **HISTORY** Latin *co-* together + *arcere* to enclose ▶ **coercion** *n*

coercive *adj* using force or authority to make a person do something against his or her will.

coeval (koh-**eev**-al) *adj, n* contemporary. ▷ **HISTORY** Latin *co-* together + *aevum* age ▶ **coevally** *adv*

coexist *vb* **1** to exist together at the same time or in the same place. **2** to exist together in peace despite differences. ▶ **coexistence** *n* ▶ **coexistent** *adj*

coextensive *adj* covering the same area, either literally or figuratively: *the concepts of 'the nation' and 'the people' are not coextensive.*

C of E Church of England.

coffee *n* **1** a drink made from the roasted and ground seeds of a tall tropical shrub. **2** Also called: **coffee beans** the beanlike seeds of this shrub. **3** the shrub yielding these seeds. ✧ *adj* **4** medium-brown.

> **WORD HISTORY**
> 'Coffee' comes, via Italian, from Turkish *kahve*, from Arabic *qahwah*, meaning 'wine' or 'coffee'.

coffee bar *n* a café; snack bar.

coffee house *n* a place where coffee is served, esp. one that was a fashionable meeting place in 18th-century London.

coffee table *n* a small low table.

coffee-table book *n* a large expensive illustrated book.

coffer *n* **1** a chest for storing valuables. **2 coffers** a store of money. **3** an ornamental sunken panel in a ceiling or dome. ▷ **HISTORY** Greek *kophinos* basket

cofferdam *n* a watertight enclosure pumped dry to enable construction work or ship repairs to be done.

coffin *n* a box in which a corpse is buried or cremated. ▷ **HISTORY** Latin *cophinus* basket

cog *n* **1** one of the teeth on the rim of a gearwheel. **2** a gearwheel, esp. a small one. **3** an unimportant person in a large organization or process. ▷ **HISTORY** Scandinavian

cogent (**koh**-jent) *adj* forcefully convincing. ▷ **HISTORY** Latin *co-* together + *agere* to drive ▶ **cogency** *n*

cogitate (**koj**-it-tate) *vb* **-tating, -tated** to think deeply about (something). ▷ **HISTORY** Latin *cogitare* ▶ **cogitation** *n* ▶ **cogitative** *adj*

cognac (**kon**-yak) *n* high-quality French brandy.

cognate *adj* **1** derived from a common original form: *cognate languages.* **2** related to or descended from a common ancestor. ✧ *n* **3** a cognate word or language. **4** a relative. ▷ **HISTORY** Latin *co-* same + *gnatus* born ▶ **cognation** *n*

cognition *n Formal* **1** the processes of getting knowledge, including perception, intuition and reasoning. **2** the results of such a process. ▷ **HISTORY** Latin *cognoscere* to learn ▶ **cognitive** *adj*

cognizance *or* **cognisance** *n Formal* **1** knowledge or understanding. **2 take cognizance of** to take notice of. **3** the range or scope of knowledge or understanding. ▷ **HISTORY** Latin *cognoscere* to learn ▶ **cognizant** *or* **cognisant** *adj*

cognomen (kog-**noh**-men) *n, pl* **-nomens** *or* **-nomina** (-**nom**-min-a) *Formal* **1** a nickname. **2** a surname. **3** an ancient Roman's third name or nickname. ▷ **HISTORY** Latin: additional name

cognoscenti (kon-yo-**shen**-tee) *pl n, sing* **-te** (-tee) connoisseurs. ▷ **HISTORY** obsolete Italian

cogwheel *n* same as **gearwheel**.

cohabit *vb* to live together as husband and wife without being married. ▷ **HISTORY** Latin *co-* together + *habitare* to live ▶ **cohabitation** *n*

cohabitation agreement *n Law* a legal agreement drawn up between some couples living together to regulate matters such as the conditions of their cohabitation as well as the division of property and any financial arrangements in the event of their splitting up.

cohere *vb* **-hering, -hered 1** to be logically connected and consistent. **2** to hold or stick firmly together. ▷ **HISTORY** Latin *co-* together + *haerere* to cling

coherent *adj* **1** logical and consistent. **2** capable of intelligible speech. **3** cohering or sticking together. **4** *Physics* (of two or more waves) having the same frequency and a constant fixed phase difference. ▶ **coherence** *n*

cohesion *n* **1** the quality of sticking together, being united and working well together. **2** *Physics* the force that holds together the atoms or molecules in a solid or liquid.

cohesive *adj* **1** characterized by sticking together, being united and working well together: *a cohesive society.* **2** causing cohesion: *they lacked a cohesive strategy.*

cohesiveness *n* **1** the quality of sticking together, being united and working well together. **2** *Grammar* the clear and logical linking of references in a text that ensures clarity and lack of ambiguity.

cohesive tie *n Grammar* a word or expression that refers back to or provides a link to a previous reference and helps ensure cohesiveness.

cohort *n* **1** a band of associates. **2** a tenth part of an ancient Roman Legion. ▷ **HISTORY** Latin *cohors* yard, company of soldiers

coif *n* **1** a close-fitting cap worn in the Middle Ages. **2** a hairstyle. ✧ *vb* **coiffing, coiffed 3** to arrange (the hair). ▷ **HISTORY** Late Latin *cofea* helmet, cap

coiffeur *n* a hairdresser. ▷ **HISTORY** French ▶ **coiffeuse** *fem n*

coiffure *n* a hairstyle. ▷ **HISTORY** French

coil[1] *vb* **1** to wind or be wound into loops. **2** to move in a winding course. ✧ *n* **3** something wound in a connected series of loops. **4** a single loop of such a series. **5** a contraceptive device in the shape of a coil, inserted in the womb. **6** an electrical conductor wound into a spiral, to provide inductance. ▷ **HISTORY** Old French *coillir* to collect together

coil[2] *n* **mortal coil** the troubles of the world. ▷ **HISTORY** coined by William Shakespeare

coin *n* **1** a metal disc used as money. **2** metal currency collectively. ✧ *vb* **3** to invent (a new word or phrase). **4** to make or stamp (coins). **5 coin it in** *or* **coin money** *Informal* to make money rapidly. ▷ **HISTORY** Latin *cuneus* wedge

coinage *n* **1** coins collectively. **2** the currency of a country. **3** a newly invented word or phrase. **4** the act of coining.

coincide *vb* **-ciding, -cided 1** to happen at the same time. **2** to agree or correspond exactly: *what she had said coincided exactly with his own thinking.* **3** to occupy the same place in space. ▷ **HISTORY** Latin *co-* together + *incidere* to occur

coincidence *n* **1** a chance occurrence of simultaneous or apparently connected events. **2** a coinciding.

coincident *adj* **1** having the same position in space or time. **2 coincident with** in exact agreement with.

coincidental *adj* resulting from coincidence; not intentional. ▶ **coincidentally** *adv*

coir *n* coconut fibre, used in making rope and matting. ▷ **HISTORY** Malayalam (a language of SW India) *kāyar* rope

coitus (**koh**-it-uss) *or* **coition** (koh-**ish**-un) *n* sexual intercourse. ▷ **HISTORY** Latin *coire* to meet ▶ **coital** *adj*

coke[1] *n* **1** a solid fuel left after gas has been distilled from coal. ✧ *vb* **coking, coked 2** to become or convert into coke. ▷ **HISTORY** probably dialect *colk* core

coke[2] *n Slang* cocaine.

Coke *n Trademark* short for **Coca-Cola**.

col *n* the lowest point of a ridge connecting two mountain peaks. ▷ **HISTORY** French: neck

Col. Colonel.

cola *n* **1** a soft drink flavoured with an extract from the nuts of a tropical tree. **2** the W African tree whose nuts contain this extract. ▷ **HISTORY** probably variant of W African *kolo* nut

colander *n* a bowl with a perforated bottom for straining or rinsing foods. ▷ **HISTORY** Latin *colum* sieve

cold *adj* **1** low in temperature: *the cold March wind; cans of cold beer.* **2** not hot enough: *eat your food before it gets cold!* **3** lacking in affection or enthusiasm. **4** not affected by emotion: *the cold truth.* **5** dead. **6** (of a trail or scent in hunting) faint. **7** (of a colour) giving the impression of coldness. **8** *Slang* unconscious. **9** *Informal* (of a seeker) far from the object of a search. **10** denoting the contacting of potential customers without previously approaching them to establish their interest: *cold mailing.* **11 cold comfort** little or no comfort. **12 have** *or* **get cold feet** to be or become fearful or reluctant. **13 in cold blood** deliberately and without mercy. **14 leave someone cold** *Informal* to fail to excite or impress someone. **15 throw cold water on** *Informal* to discourage. ✧ *n* **16** the absence of heat. **17** a viral infection of the nose and throat characterized by catarrh and sneezing. **18** the sensation caused by loss or lack of heat. **19 (out) in the cold** *Informal* neglected or ignored. ✧ *adv* **20** *Informal* unrehearsed or unprepared: *he played his part cold.* ▷ **HISTORY** Old English *ceald* ▶ **coldly** *adv* ▶ **coldness** *n*

cold-blooded *adj* **1** callous or cruel. **2** *Zool* (of all animals except birds and mammals) having a body temperature that varies according to the temperature of the surroundings.

cold chisel *n* a toughened steel chisel.

cold cream *n* a creamy preparation used for softening and cleansing the skin.

cold frame *n* an unheated wooden frame with a glass top, used to protect young plants.

cold front *n Meteorol* the boundary line between a warm air mass and the cold air pushing it from beneath and behind.

cold snap *n* a short period of cold and frosty weather.
cold sore *n* a cluster of blisters near the lips, caused by a virus.
cold sweat *n Informal* coldness and sweating as a bodily reaction to fear or nervousness.
cold war *n* **1** *Politics* a state of political hostility between two countries without actual warfare. **2** *History* **the Cold War** the state of hostility between the American and Soviet blocs after World War II.
cole *n* any of various plants such as the cabbage and rape. ▷ **HISTORY** Latin *caulis* cabbage
coleslaw *n* a salad dish of shredded raw cabbage in a dressing. ▷ **HISTORY** Dutch *koolsalade* cabbage salad
coley *n Brit* an edible fish with white or grey flesh. ▷ **HISTORY** perhaps from *coalfish*
colic *n* severe pains in the stomach and bowels. ▷ **HISTORY** Greek *kolon* COLON[2] ▶ **colicky** *adj*
colitis (koh-**lie**-tiss) *n* inflammation of the colon, usually causing diarrhoea and lower abdominal pain.
collaborate *vb* **-rating, -rated 1** to work with another or others on a joint project. **2** to cooperate with an enemy invader. ▷ **HISTORY** Latin *com-* together + *laborare* to work ▶ **collaboration** *n* ▶ **collaborative** *adj* ▶ **collaborator** *n*
collage (kol-**lahzh**) *n* **1** an art form in which various materials or objects are glued onto a surface to make a picture. **2** a picture made in this way. **3** a work, such as a piece of music, created by combining unrelated styles. ▷ **HISTORY** French ▶ **collagist** *n*
collagen *n* a protein found in cartilage and bone that yields gelatine when boiled. ▷ **HISTORY** Greek *kolla* glue
collapse *vb* **-lapsing, -lapsed 1** to fall down or cave in suddenly. **2** to fail completely: *a package holiday company which collapsed last year.* **3** to fall down from lack of strength, exhaustion, or illness: *he collapsed with an asthma attack.* **4** to sit down and rest because of tiredness or lack of energy: *she collapsed in front of the telly when she got home.* **5** to fold compactly, esp. for storage. ✧ *n* **6** the act of falling down or falling to pieces. **7** a sudden failure or breakdown. ▷ **HISTORY** Latin *collabi* to fall in ruins
collapsible *adj* able to be folded up for storage.
collar *n* **1** the part of a garment round the neck. **2** a band of leather, rope, or metal placed around an animal's neck. **3** *Biol* a ringlike marking around the neck of a bird or animal. **4** a cut of meat, esp. bacon, from the neck of an animal. **5** a ring or band around a pipe, rod, or shaft. ✧ *vb Brit, Austral & NZ informal* **6** to seize; arrest. **7** to catch in order to speak to. **8** to take for oneself. ▷ **HISTORY** Latin *collum* neck
collarbone *n* same as **clavicle**.
collate *vb* **-lating, -lated 1** to examine and compare carefully. **2** to gather together and put in order. ▷ **HISTORY** Latin *com-* together + *latus* brought ▶ **collator** *n*
collateral *n* **1** security pledged for the repayment of a loan. **2** a person, animal, or plant descended from the same ancestor as another but through a different line. ✧ *adj* **3** descended from a common ancestor but through different lines. **4** additional but subordinate: *a spokeswoman said that there was no collateral information to dispute the assurances the government had been given.* **5** situated or running side by side: *collateral ridges of mountains.* ▷ **HISTORY** Latin *com-* together + *lateralis* of the side
collateral damage *n Mil* unintentional civilian casualties or damage to civilian property caused by military action: *to minimize collateral damage maximum precision in bombing is required.*
collation *n* **1** the act or result of collating. **2** *Formal* a light meal.
colleague *n* a fellow worker, esp. in a profession. ▷ **HISTORY** Latin *collega*
collect[1] *vb* **1** to gather together or be gathered together. **2** to gather (objects, such as stamps) as a hobby or for study. **3** to go to a place to fetch (a person or thing). **4** to receive payments of (taxes, dues, or contributions). **5** to regain control of (oneself or one's emotions). ▷ **HISTORY** Latin *com-* together + *legere* to gather
collect[2] *n Christianity* a short prayer said during certain church services. ▷ **HISTORY** Medieval Latin *oratio ad collectam* prayer at the assembly
collected *adj* **1** calm and self-controlled. **2** brought together into one book or set of books: *the collected works of Dickens.*
collection *n* **1** things collected or accumulated. **2** the act or process of collecting. **3** *Art* a number of works of art such as paintings, sculptures, etc., owned by a person, organization, or museum: *the Peggy Guggenheim Collection.* **4** a selection of clothes usually presented by a particular designer. **5** a sum of money collected, as in church. **6** a regular removal of letters from a postbox.
collective *adj* **1** done by or characteristic of individuals acting as a group: *the army's collective wisdom regarding peacekeeping.* ✧ *n* **2** a group of people working together on an enterprise and sharing the benefits from it. ▶ **collectively** *adv*
collective bargaining *n* negotiation between a trade union and an employer on the wages and working conditions of the employees.
collective noun *n Grammar* a noun that is singular in form but that refers to a group of people or things, as *crowd* or *army*.

☑ **WORD TIP**

Collective nouns are usually used with singular verbs: *the family is on holiday; General Motors is mounting a big sales campaign.* In British usage, however, plural verbs are sometimes employed in this context, esp. where reference is being made to a collection of individual objects or people rather than to the group as a unit: *the family are all on holiday.* Care should be taken that the same collective noun is not treated as both singular and plural in the same sentence: *the family is well and sends its best wishes* or *the family are all well and send their best wishes,* but not *the family is well and send their best wishes.*

a b c d e f g h i j k l m n o p q r s t u v w x y z

A B C D E F G H I J K L M N O P Q R S T U V W X Y Z

collective security *n Politics* a system of maintaining world peace and security by concerted action on the part of the nations of the world.

collectivism *n* the theory that the state should own all means of production. ▶ **collectivist** *adj*

collectivize *or* **-vise** *vb* **-vizing, -vized** *or* **-vising, -vised** to organize according to the theory of collectivism. ▶ **collectivization** *or* **-visation** *n*

collector *n* **1** a person who collects objects as a hobby. **2** a person employed to collect debts, rents, or tickets.

colleen *n Irish* a girl. ▷ **HISTORY** Irish Gaelic *cailín*

college *n* **1** an institution of higher or further education that is not a university. **2** a self-governing section of certain universities. **3** *Brit & NZ* a name given to some secondary schools. **4** an organized body of people with specific rights and duties: *the president is elected by an electoral college.* **5** a body organized within a particular profession, concerned with regulating standards. **6** the staff and students of a college. ▷ **HISTORY** Latin *collega* colleague

collegian *n* a member of a college.

collegiate *adj* **1** of a college or college students. **2** (of a university) composed of various colleges.

collide *vb* **-liding, -lided 1** to crash together violently. **2** to conflict or disagree. ▷ **HISTORY** Latin *com-* together + *laedere* to strike

collie *n* a silky-haired dog used for herding sheep and cattle. ▷ **HISTORY** Scots, probably from earlier *colie* black

collier *n Chiefly Brit* **1** a coal miner. **2** a ship designed to carry coal.

colliery *n, pl* **-lieries** *Chiefly Brit* a coal mine and its buildings.

collision *n* **1** a violent crash between moving objects. **2** the conflict of opposed ideas or wishes. ▷ **HISTORY** Latin *collidere* to collide

collocate *vb* **-cating, -cated** (of words) to occur together regularly.

collocation *n Grammar* **1** the way words combine. **2** a common combination of words.

colloid *n* a mixture of particles of one substance suspended in a different substance. ▷ **HISTORY** Greek *kolla* glue ▶ **colloidal** *adj*

colloquial *adj* suitable for informal speech or writing. ▶ **colloquially** *adv*

colloquialism *n* **1** a colloquial word or phrase. **2** the use of colloquial words and phrases.

colloquium *n, pl* **-quiums** *or* **-quia** an academic conference or seminar. ▷ **HISTORY** Latin; see COLLOQUY

colloquy *n, pl* **-quies** *Formal* a conversation or conference. ▷ **HISTORY** Latin *com-* together + *loqui* to speak ▶ **colloquist** *n*

collude *vb* **-luding, -luded** to cooperate secretly or dishonestly with someone. ▷ **HISTORY** Latin *colludere* to conspire

collusion *n* secret or illegal agreement or cooperation. ▶ **collusive** *adj*

collywobbles *pl n Slang* **1** an intense feeling of nervousness. **2** an upset stomach. ▷ **HISTORY** probably from *colic* + *wobble*

cologne *n* a perfumed toilet water. ▷ **HISTORY** *Cologne,* Germany, where it was first manufactured

colon[1] *n, pl* **-lons** the punctuation mark (:) used before an explanation or an example, a list, or an extended quotation. ▷ **HISTORY** Greek *kōlon* limb, clause

colon[2] *n, pl* **-lons** *or* **-la** the part of the large intestine connected to the rectum. ▷ **HISTORY** Greek *kolon* large intestine ▶ **colonic** *adj*

colonel *n* a senior commissioned officer in the army or air force. ▷ **HISTORY** Old Italian *colonnello* column of soldiers ▶ **colonelcy** *n*

colonial *adj* **1** of or inhabiting a colony or colonies. **2** of a style of architecture popular in North America in the 17th and 18th centuries: *a colonial mansion.* **3** *Austral* of a style of architecture popular during Australia's colonial period. ✧ *n* **4** an inhabitant of a colony.

colonial goose *n NZ old-fashioned* stuffed roast mutton.

colonialism *n* the policy of acquiring and maintaining colonies, esp. for exploitation. ▶ **colonialist** *n, adj*

colonist *n* a settler in or inhabitant of a colony.

colonize *or* **-nise** *vb* **-nizing, -nized** *or* **-nising, -nised 1** to establish a colony in (an area). **2** to settle in (an area) as colonists. ▶ **colonization** *or* **-nisation** *n*

colonnade *n* a row of evenly spaced columns, usually supporting a roof. ▷ **HISTORY** French *colonne* column ▶ **colonnaded** *adj*

colony *n, pl* **-nies 1** a group of people who settle in a new country but remain under the rule of their homeland. **2** the territory occupied by such a settlement. **3** a group of people with the same nationality or interests, forming a community in a particular place: *an artists' colony.* **4** *Zool* a group of the same type of animal or plant living or growing together. **5** *Bacteriol* a group of microorganisms when grown on a culture medium. ▷ **HISTORY** Latin *colere* to cultivate, inhabit

colophon *n* a publisher's symbol on a book. ▷ **HISTORY** Greek *kolophōn* a finishing stroke

Colorado beetle *n* a black-and-yellow beetle that is a serious pest of potatoes. ▷ **HISTORY** *Colorado,* state of central US

coloration *or* **colouration** *n* arrangement of colours: *a red coloration of the eyes.*

coloratura *n Music* **1** a part for a solo singer which has much complicated ornamentation of the basic melody. **2** a soprano who specializes in such music. ▷ **HISTORY** obsolete Italian, literally: colouring

colossal *adj* **1** very large in size: *the turbulent rivers and colossal mountains of New Zealand.* **2** very serious or significant: *a colossal legal blunder.*

colossus *n, pl* **-si** *or* **-suses 1** a very large statue. **2** a huge or important person or thing. ▷ **HISTORY** Greek *kolossos*

colostomy *n, pl* **-mies** an operation to form an opening from the colon onto the surface of the body, for emptying the bowel. ▷ **HISTORY** COLON[2] + Greek *stoma* mouth

colour *or US* **color** *n* **1** a property of things that results from the particular wavelengths of light which they reflect or give out, producing a sensation in the eye. **2** a colour, such as a red or green, that possesses hue, as opposed to black, white, or grey. **3** a substance, such as a dye, that gives colour. **4** the skin complexion of a person. **5** the use of all the colours in painting, drawing, or photography. **6** the distinctive tone of a musical sound. **7** details which give vividness or authenticity: *I walked the streets and absorbed the local colour.* **8** semblance or pretext: *under colour of.* ✧ *vb* **9** to apply colour to (something). **10** to influence or distort: *anger coloured her judgment.* **11** to become red in the face, esp. when embarrassed or annoyed. **12** to give a convincing appearance to: *he coloured his account of what had happened.* ✧ See also **colours**. ▷ **HISTORY** Latin *color*

colour bar *n* racial discrimination by whites against non-whites.

colour-blind *adj* **1** unable to distinguish between certain colours, esp. red and green. **2** not discriminating on grounds of skin colour: *colour-blind policies.* ▶ **colour blindness** *n*

coloured *or US* **colored** *adj* having a colour or colours other than black or white: *coloured glass bottles; a peach-coloured outfit with matching hat.*

Coloured *or US* **Colored** *n* **1** *Offensive* a person who is not White. **2** in South Africa, a person of racially mixed parentage or descent. ✧ *adj* **3** *S African* of mixed White and non-White parentage.

colourful *or US* **colorful** *adj* **1** with bright or richly varied colours. **2** vivid or distinctive in character.

colouring *or US* **coloring** *n* **1** the application of colour. **2** something added to give colour. **3** appearance with regard to shade and colour. **4** the colour of a person's complexion.

colourless *or US* **colorless** *adj* **1** without colour: *a colourless gas.* **2** dull and uninteresting: *a colourless personality.* **3** grey or pallid in tone or hue: *a watery sun hung low in the colourless sky.*

colours *or US* **colors** *pl n* **1** the flag of a country, regiment, or ship. **2** *Brit sport* a badge or other symbol showing membership of a team, esp. at a school or college. **3 nail one's colours to the mast** to commit oneself publicly to a course of action. **4 show one's true colours** to display one's true nature or character.

colour sergeant *n* a sergeant who carries the regimental, battalion, or national colours.

colour supplement *n Brit* an illustrated magazine accompanying a newspaper.

colt *n* **1** a young male horse or pony. **2** *Sport* a young and inexperienced player. ▷ **HISTORY** Old English: young ass

coltsfoot *n, pl* **-foots** a weed with yellow flowers and heart-shaped leaves.

columbine *n* a plant that has brightly coloured flowers with five spurred petals. ▷ **HISTORY** Medieval Latin *columbina herba* dovelike plant

column *n* **1** an upright pillar usually having a cylindrical shaft, a base, and a capital. **2** a form or structure in the shape of a column: *a column of smoke.* **3** a vertical division of a newspaper page. **4** a regular feature in a paper: *a cookery column.* **5** a vertical arrangement of numbers. **6** *Mil* a narrow formation in which individuals or units follow one behind the other. ▷ **HISTORY** Latin *columna* ▶ **columnar** *adj*

columnist *n* a journalist who writes a regular feature in a newspaper.

com- *or* **con-** *prefix* used with a main word to mean together; with; jointly: *commingle.* ▷ **HISTORY** Latin, from *cum* with

coma *n* a state of unconsciousness from which a person cannot be aroused, caused by injury, disease, or drugs. ▷ **HISTORY** Greek *kōma* heavy sleep

Comanche (kom-**man**-chee) *n, pl* **-ches** *or* **-che** a member of a N American Indian people, formerly living in the plains to the east of the Rockies, now chiefly in Oklahoma.

comatose *adj* **1** in a coma. **2** sound asleep.

comb *n* **1** a toothed instrument for disentangling or arranging hair. **2** a tool or machine that cleans and straightens wool or cotton. **3** a fleshy serrated crest on the head of a domestic fowl. **4** a honeycomb. ✧ *vb* **5** to use a comb on. **6** to search with great care: *police combed the streets for the missing girl.* ▷ **HISTORY** Old English *camb*

combat *n* **1** a fight or struggle. ✧ *vb* **-bating, -bated 2** to fight: *a coordinated approach to combating the growing drugs problem.* ▷ **HISTORY** Latin *com-* with + *battuere* to beat ▶ **combative** *adj*

combatant *n* **1** a person taking part in a combat. ✧ *adj* **2** engaged in or ready for combat.

combat trousers, combats *pl n* loose casual trousers with large pockets on the legs.

combe *n* same as **coomb**.

comber *n* a long curling wave.

combination *n* **1** the act of combining or state of being combined. **2** people or things combined. **3** the set of numbers or letters that opens a combination lock. **4** a motorcycle with a sidecar. **5** *Maths* an arrangement of the members of a set into specified groups without regard to order in the group.

combine *vb* **-bining, -bined 1** to join together. **2** to form a chemical compound. ✧ *n* **3** an association of people or firms for a common purpose. **4** short for **combine harvester**. ▷ **HISTORY** Latin *com-* together + *bini* two by two

combine harvester *n* a machine used to reap and thresh grain in one process.

combining form *n* a part of a word that occurs only as part of a compound word, such as *anthropo-* in *anthropology.*

combo *n, pl* **-bos** a small group of jazz musicians.

combustible *adj* capable of igniting and burning easily.

A B C D E F G H I J K L M N O P Q R S T U V W X Y Z

combustion *n* **1** the process of burning. **2** a chemical reaction in which a substance combines with oxygen to produce heat and light. ▷ **HISTORY** Latin *comburere* to burn up

come *vb* **coming, came, come 1** to move towards a place considered near to the speaker or hearer: *come and see me as soon as you can.* **2** to arrive or reach: *turn left and continue until you come to a cattle-grid; he came to Britain in the 1920s.* **3** to occur: *Christmas comes but once a year.* **4** to happen as a result: *no good will come of this.* **5** to occur to the mind: *the truth suddenly came to me.* **6** to reach a specified point, state, or situation: *a dull brown dress that came down to my ankles; he'd come to a decision.* **7** to be produced: *it also comes in other colours.* **8 come from** to be or have been a resident or native (of): *my mother comes from Greenock.* **9** to become: *it was like a dream come true.* **10** *Slang* to have an orgasm. **11** *Brit & NZ informal* to play the part of: *don't come the innocent with me.* **12** (*subjunctive use*) when a specified time arrives: *come next August.* **13 as ... as they come** the most characteristic example of a type: *he's an arrogant swine and as devious as they come.* **14 come again?** *Informal* what did you say? **15 come to light** to be revealed. ✧ *interj* **16** an exclamation expressing annoyance or impatience: *come now!* ✧ See also **come across.** ▷ **HISTORY** Old English *cuman*

come across *vb* **1** to meet or find by accident. **2** to communicate the intended meaning or impression. **3 come across as** to give a certain impression.

comeback *n Informal* **1** a return to a former position or status. **2** a response or retaliation. ✧ *vb* **come back 3** to return, esp. to the memory. **4** to become fashionable again.

come by *vb* to find or obtain, esp. accidentally: *Graham filled him in on how he came by the envelope.*

Comecon (**kom**-meek-on) *n* (formerly) an economic league of Soviet-oriented Communist nations. ▷ **HISTORY** *Co(uncil for) M(utual) Econ(omic Aid)*

comedian *or fem* **comedienne** *n* **1** an entertainer who tells jokes. **2** a person who performs in comedy.

comedown *n* **1** a decline in status or prosperity. **2** *Informal* a disappointment. ✧ *vb* **come down 3** (of prices) to become lower. **4** to reach a decision: *a 1989 court ruling came down in favour of three councils who wanted Sunday trading banned.* **5** to be handed down by tradition or inheritance. **6 come down with** to begin to suffer from (illness). **7 come down on** to reprimand sharply. **8 come down to** to amount to: *at the end the case came down to the one simple issue.* **9 come down in the world** to lose status or prosperity.

comedy *n, pl* **-dies 1** a humorous film, play, or broadcast. **2** such works as a genre. **3** the humorous aspect of life or of events. **4** (in classical literature) a play which ends happily. ▷ **HISTORY** Greek *kōmos* village festival + *aeidein* to sing

come in *vb* **1** to prove to be: *it came in useful.* **2** to become fashionable or seasonable. **3** to finish a race (in a certain position). **4** to be received: *reports of more deaths came in today.* **5** (of money) to be received as income. **6** to be involved in a situation: *where do I come in?* **7 come in for** to be the object of: *she came in for a lot of criticism.*

come into *vb* **1** to enter. **2** to inherit.

comely *adj* **-lier, -liest** *Old-fashioned* good-looking. ▷ **HISTORY** Old English *cȳmlīc* beautiful ▶ **comeliness** *n*

come of *vb* to result from: *nothing came of it.*

come out *vb* **1** to be made public or revealed: *it was only then that the truth came out.* **2** to be published or put on sale: *their latest album which came out last month.* **3** Also: **come out of the closet** to reveal something formerly concealed, esp. that one is a homosexual. **4** *Chiefly Brit* to go on strike. **5** to declare oneself: *the report has come out in favour of maintaining child benefit.* **6** to end up or turn out: *this wine consistently came out top in our tastings; the figures came out exactly right.* **7 come out in** to become covered with (a rash or spots). **8 come out with** to say or disclose: *she came out with a remark that left me speechless.* **9** to enter society formally.

comestibles *pl n* food. ▷ **HISTORY** Latin *comedere* to eat up

comet *n* a heavenly body that travels round the sun, leaving a long bright trail behind it. ▷ **HISTORY** Greek *komētēs* long-haired

come to *vb* **1** to regain consciousness. **2** to amount to (a total figure).

come up *vb* **1** to be mentioned or arise: *we hope that the difficulties that have arisen in the past will not keep coming up.* **2** to be about to happen: *the club has important games coming up.* **3 come up against** to come into conflict with. **4 come up in the world** to rise in status. **5 come up to** to meet a standard. **6 come up with** to produce or propose: *he has a knack for coming up with great ideas.*

comeuppance *n Informal* deserved punishment. ▷ **HISTORY** from *come up* (in the sense: to appear before a court)

comfit *n* a sugar-coated sweet. ▷ **HISTORY** Latin *confectum* something prepared

comfort *n* **1** a state of physical ease or well-being. **2** relief from suffering or grief. **3** a person or thing that brings ease. **4 comforts** things that make life easier or more pleasant: *the comforts of home.* ✧ *vb* **5** to soothe or console. **6** to bring physical ease to. ▷ **HISTORY** Latin *con-* (intensive) + *fortis* strong ▶ **comforting** *adj*

comfortable *adj* **1** giving comfort; relaxing. **2** free from trouble or pain. **3** *Informal* well-off financially. **4** not afraid or embarrassed: *he was not comfortable expressing sympathy.* ▶ **comfortably** *adv*

comforter *n* **1** a person or thing that comforts. **2** *Brit* a baby's dummy. **3** *Brit* a woollen scarf.

comfrey *n* a tall plant with bell-shaped blue, purple, or white flowers. ▷ **HISTORY** Latin *conferva* water plant

comfy *adj* **-fier, -fiest** *Informal* comfortable.

comic *adj* **1** humorous; funny. **2** of or relating to comedy. ✧ *n* **3** a comedian. **4** a magazine containing comic strips. ▷ **HISTORY** Greek *kōmikos*

comical *adj* causing amusement, often because of being ludicrous or ridiculous: *an enthusiasm comical to behold.* ▶ **comically** *adv*

comic opera *n* an opera with speech and singing that tells an amusing story.

comic strip *n* a sequence of drawings in a newspaper or magazine, telling a humorous story or an adventure.

coming *adj* **1** (of time or events) approaching or next: *in the coming weeks.* **2** likely to be important in the future: *he was regarded as a coming man at the Foreign Office.* **3 have it coming to one** *Informal* to deserve what one is about to suffer. ✧ *n* **4** arrival or approach.

comity *n, pl* **-ties** *Formal* friendly politeness, esp. between different countries. ▷ **HISTORY** Latin *comis* affable

comma *n* the punctuation mark (,) indicating a slight pause and used where there is a list of items or to separate the parts of a sentence. ▷ **HISTORY** Greek *komma* clause

command *vb* **1** to order or compel. **2** to have authority over. **3** to deserve and get: *a public figure who commands almost universal respect.* **4** to look down over: *the house commands a magnificent view of the sea and the islands.* ✧ *n* **5** an authoritative instruction that something must be done. **6** the authority to command. **7** knowledge; control: *a fluent command of French.* **8** a military or naval unit with a specific function. **9** *Computers* a part of a program consisting of a coded instruction to the computer to perform a specified function. ▷ **HISTORY** Latin *com-* (intensive) + *mandare* to order

commandant *n* an officer in charge of a place or group of people.

commandeer *vb* **1** to seize for military use. **2** to take as if by right: *he commandeered the one waiting taxi outside the station.* ▷ **HISTORY** Afrikaans *kommandeer*

commander *n* **1** an officer in command of a military group or operation. **2** a middle-ranking naval officer. **3** a high-ranking member of some orders of knights.

commander-in-chief *n, pl* **commanders-in-chief** the supreme commander of a nation's armed forces.

commanding *adj* **1** being in charge: *the commanding officer.* **2** in a position or situation where success looks certain: *a commanding lead.* **3** having the air of authority: *a commanding voice.* **4** having a wide view.

commandment *n* a divine command, esp. one of the Ten Commandments in the Old Testament.

commando *n, pl* **-dos** *or* **-does a** a military unit trained to make swift raids in enemy territory. **b** a member of such a unit. ▷ **HISTORY** Dutch *commando* command

commedia dell'arte (kom-**made**-ee-a dell-**art**-tay) *n* a form of improvised comedy popular in Italy in the 16th century, with stock characters and a stereotyped plot. ▷ **HISTORY** Italian

commemorate *vb* **-rating, -rated** to honour or keep alive the memory of: *a series of events to commemorate the end of the Second World War.* ▷ **HISTORY** Latin *com-* (intensive) + *memorare* to remind ▶ **commemoration** *n* ▶ **commemorative** *adj*

commence *vb* **-mencing, -menced** to begin. ▷ **HISTORY** Latin *com-* (intensive) + *initiare* to begin

commencement *n* **1** the beginning; start. **2** *US & Canad* a graduation ceremony.

commend *vb* **1** to praise in a formal manner: *the judge commended her bravery.* **2** to recommend: *he commended the scheme warmly.* **3** to entrust: *I commend my child to your care.* ▷ **HISTORY** Latin *com-* (intensive) + *mandare* to entrust ▶ **commendable** *adj* ▶ **commendation** *n*

commensurable *adj* **1** measurable by the same standards. **2** *Maths* **a** having a common factor. **b** having units of the same dimensions and being related by whole numbers. ▶ **commensurability** *n*

commensurate *adj* **1** corresponding in degree, size, or value. **2** commensurable. ▷ **HISTORY** Latin *com-* same + *mensurare* to measure

comment *n* **1** a remark, criticism, or observation. **2** a situation or event that expresses some feeling: *a sad comment on the nature of many relationships.* **3** talk or gossip. **4** a note explaining or criticizing a passage in a text. **5 no comment** I decline to say anything about the matter. ✧ *vb* **6** to remark or express an opinion. ▷ **HISTORY** Latin *commentum* invention

commentary *n, pl* **-taries 1** a spoken accompaniment to an event, broadcast, or film. **2** a series of explanatory notes on a subject.

commentate *vb* **-tating, -tated** to act as a commentator.

> **WORD TIP**
>
> The verb *commentate,* derived from *commentator,* is sometimes used as a synonym for *comment on* or *provide a commentary for.* It is not yet fully accepted as standard, though widespread in sports reporting and journalism.

commentator *n* **1** a person who provides a spoken commentary for a broadcast, esp. of a sporting event. **2** an expert who reports on and analyses a particular subject.

commerce *n* **1** the buying and selling of goods and services. **2** *Literary* social relations. ▷ **HISTORY** Latin *commercium*

commercial *adj* **1** of or engaged in commerce: *commercial exploitation of sport.* **2** sponsored or paid for by an advertiser: *commercial radio.* **3** having profit as the main aim: *this is a more commercial, accessible album than its predecessor.* ✧ *n* **4** a radio or television advertisement.

commercial farming *n Agriculture* the cultivation of crops and rearing of livestock for the purpose of making money.

commercialism *n* **1** the principles and practices of commerce. **2** exclusive or inappropriate emphasis on profit.

commercialize *or* **-ise** *vb* **-izing, -ized** *or* **-ising, -ised 1** to make commercial. **2** to exploit for profit, esp. at the expense of quality. ▸ **commercialization** *or* **-isation** *n*

commercial traveller *n* a travelling salesman.

commie *n, pl* **-mies**, *adj Informal & offensive* Communist.

commingle *vb* **-gling, -gled** to mix or be mixed.

commis *adj Brit* (of a waiter or chef) apprentice: *the commis chef.* ▷ **HISTORY** French

commiserate *vb* **-ating, -ated** (usually foll. by *with*) to express sympathy or pity (for). ▷ **HISTORY** Latin *com-* together + *miserari* to bewail ▸ **commiseration** *n*

commissar *n* formerly, an official responsible for political education in Communist countries.

commissariat *n* a military department in charge of food supplies. ▷ **HISTORY** Medieval Latin *commissarius* commissary

commissary *n, pl* **-saries 1** *US* a shop supplying food or equipment, as in a military camp. **2** a representative or deputy. ▷ **HISTORY** Medieval Latin *commissarius* official in charge

commission *n* **1** an order for a piece of work, esp. a work of art or a piece of writing. **2** a duty given to a person or group to perform. **3** the fee or percentage paid to a salesperson for each sale made. **4** a group of people appointed to perform certain duties: *a new parliamentary commission on defence.* **5** the act of committing a sin or crime. **6** *Mil* the rank or authority officially given to an officer. **7** authority to perform certain duties. **8 in** *or* **out of commission** in *or* not in working order. ✧ *vb* **9** to place an order for: *a report commissioned by the United Nations; a new work commissioned by the BBC Symphony Orchestra.* **10** *Mil* to give a commission to. **11** to prepare (a ship) for active service. **12** to grant authority to. ▷ **HISTORY** Latin *committere* to commit

commissionaire *n Chiefly Brit* a uniformed doorman at a hotel, theatre, or cinema. ▷ **HISTORY** French

commissioned officer *n* a military officer holding a rank by a commission.

commissioner *n* **1** an appointed official in a government department or other organization. **2** a member of a commission.

commit *vb* **-mitting, -mitted 1** to perform (a crime or error). **2** to hand over or allocate: *a marked reluctance to commit new money to business.* **3** to pledge to a cause or a course of action. **4** to send (someone) to prison or hospital. **5 commit to memory** to memorize. **6 commit to paper** to write down. ▷ **HISTORY** Latin *committere* to join

commitment *n* **1** dedication to a cause or principle. **2** an obligation, responsibility, or promise that restricts freedom of action. **3** the act of committing or state of being committed.

committal *n* the official consignment of a person to a prison or mental hospital.

committal hearing *n Law* (in criminal cases) a preliminary hearing at a magistrates' court to decide whether there is enough evidence to proceed to a full trial in a higher court.

committee *n* a group of people appointed to perform a specified service or function. ▷ **HISTORY** Middle English *committen* to entrust

commode *n* **1** a chair with a hinged flap concealing a chamber pot. **2** a chest of drawers. ▷ **HISTORY** French

commodious *adj* with plenty of space. ▷ **HISTORY** Latin *commodus* convenient

commodity *n, pl* **-ties** something that can be bought or sold. ▷ **HISTORY** Latin *commoditas* suitability

commodore *n* **1** *Brit* a senior commissioned officer in the navy. **2** the president of a yacht club. ▷ **HISTORY** probably from Dutch *commandeur*

common *adj* **1** frequently encountered: *a fairly common plant; this disease is most common in kittens and young cats.* **2** widespread among people in general: *common practice.* **3** belonging to two or more people: *we share common interests.* **4** belonging to the whole community: *common property.* **5** low-class, vulgar, or coarse. **6** *Maths* belonging to two or more: *the lowest common denominator.* **7** not belonging to the upper classes: *the common people.* **8 common or garden** *Informal* ordinary. ✧ *n* **9** a piece of open land belonging to all the members of a community. **10 in common** shared, in joint use. ✧ See also **Commons.** ▷ **HISTORY** Latin *communis* general ▸ **commonly** *adv*

commonality *n, pl* **-ties 1** the sharing of common attributes. **2** the ordinary people.

commonalty *n, pl* **-ties 1** the ordinary people. **2** the members of an incorporated society.

common cold *n* same as **cold** (sense 17).

commoner *n* a person who does not belong to the nobility.

common fraction *n* same as **simple fraction.**

common law *n* **1** the body of law based on judicial decisions and custom, as distinct from statute law. ✧ *adj* **common-law 2** (of a relationship) regarded as a marriage through being long-standing.

Common Market *n* a former name for **European Union.**

common noun *n Grammar* a noun that refers to any member of a class of things sharing features in common, as for example *bird, cup,* and *tree.* Compare **proper noun.**

commonplace *adj* **1** so common or frequent as not to be worth commenting on: *foreign holidays have now become commonplace.* **2** dull or unoriginal: *a commonplace observation.* ✧ *n* **3** a cliché. **4** an ordinary thing. ▷ **HISTORY** translation of Latin *locus communis* argument of wide application

common room *n Chiefly Brit & Austral* a sitting room for students or staff in schools or colleges.

commons *pl n* **1** *Brit* shared food or rations. **2 short commons** reduced rations.

Commons *n* **the Commons** same as **House of Commons**.

common sense *n* **1** good practical understanding. ✧ *adj* **common-sense 2** inspired by or displaying this.

common time *n Music* a time signature with four crotchet beats to the bar; four-four time: *a dance in common time.*

commonwealth *n* the people of a state or nation viewed politically.

Commonwealth *n* **the Commonwealth a** Official name: **the Commonwealth of Nations** an association of sovereign states that are or at some time have been ruled by Britain. **b** the official title of the federated states of Australia.

commotion *n* noisy disturbance. ▷ **HISTORY** Latin *com-* (intensive) + *movere* to move

communal *adj* **1** belonging to or used by a community as a whole. **2** of a commune. ▶ **communally** *adv*

communautaire (kom-**myune**-aw-ter) *adj* supporting the principles of the European Union. ▷ **HISTORY** French: community

commune[1] *n* **1** a group of people living together and sharing possessions and responsibilities. **2** the smallest district of local government in Belgium, France, Italy, and Switzerland. ▷ **HISTORY** Latin *communia* things held in common

commune[2] *vb* **-muning, -muned commune with a** to experience strong emotion for: *communing with nature.* **b** to talk intimately with. ▷ **HISTORY** Old French *comuner* to hold in common

communicable *adj* **1** capable of being communicated. **2** (of a disease) capable of being passed on easily.

communicant *n Christianity* a person who receives Communion.

communicate *vb* **-cating, -cated 1** to exchange (thoughts) or make known (information or feelings) by speech, writing, or other means. **2** (usually foll. by *to*) to transmit (to): *the reaction of the rapturous audience communicated itself to the performers.* **3** to have a sympathetic mutual understanding. **4** *Christianity* to receive Communion. ▷ **HISTORY** Latin *communicare* to share ▶ **communicator** *n* ▶ **communicative** *adj*

communicating *adj* making or having a direct connection from one room to another: *the suite is made up of three communicating rooms; the communicating door.*

communication *n* **1** the exchange of information, ideas, or feelings. **2** something communicated, such as a message. **3 communications** means of travelling or sending messages.

communion *n* **1** a sharing of thoughts, emotions, or beliefs. **2 communion with** strong feelings for: *private communion with nature.* **3** a religious group with shared beliefs and practices: *the Anglican communion.* ▷ **HISTORY** Latin *communis* common

Communion *n Christianity* **1** a ritual commemorating Christ's Last Supper by the consecration of bread and wine. **2** the consecrated bread and wine. Also called: **Holy Communion**

communiqué (kom-**mune**-ik-kay) *n* an official announcement. ▷ **HISTORY** French

communism *n* the belief that private ownership should be abolished and all work and property should be shared by the community. ▷ **HISTORY** French *communisme* ▶ **communist** *n, adj*

Communism *n* **1** a political movement based upon the writings of Karl Marx that advocates communism. **2** the political and social system established in countries with a ruling Communist Party. ▶ **Communist** *n, adj*

community *n, pl* **-ties 1** all the people living in one district. **2** a group of people with shared origins or interests: *the local Jewish community.* **3** a group of countries with certain interests in common. **4** the public; society. **5** a group of interdependent plants and animals inhabiting the same region. ▷ **HISTORY** Latin *communis* common

community centre *n* a building used by a community for social gatherings or activities.

community charge *n* (in Britain) the formal name for **poll tax**.

community college *n US & Canad* a nonresidential college offering two-year courses of study.

community service *n* organized unpaid work intended for the good of the community: often used as a punishment for minor criminals.

commutative *adj Maths* giving the same result irrespective of the order of the numbers or symbols.

commutator *n* a device used to change alternating electric current into direct current.

commute *vb* **-muting, -muted 1** to travel some distance regularly between one's home and one's place of work. **2** *Law* to reduce (a sentence) to one less severe. **3** to substitute. **4** to pay (an annuity or pension) at one time, instead of in instalments. ✧ *n* **5** a journey made by commuting. ▷ **HISTORY** Latin *com-* mutually + *mutare* to change ▶ **commutable** *adj* ▶ **commutation** *n*

commuter *n* a person who regularly travels a considerable distance to work.

compact[1] *adj* **1** closely packed together. **2** neatly fitted into a restricted space. **3** concise; brief. ✧ *vb* **4** to pack closely together. ✧ *n* **5** a small flat case containing a mirror and face powder. ▷ **HISTORY** Latin *com-* together + *pangere* to fasten ▶ **compactly** *adv* ▶ **compactness** *n*

compact[2] *n* a contract or agreement. ▷ **HISTORY** Latin *com-* together + *pacisci* to contract

compact disc *n* a small digital audio disc on which the sound is read by an optical laser system.

companion *n* **1** a person who associates with or accompanies someone: *a travelling companion.* **2** a woman paid to live or travel with another woman.

A B C D E F G H I J K L M N O P Q R S T U V W X Y Z

3 a guidebook or handbook. **4** one of a pair. ▶ **companionship** *n*

> **WORD HISTORY**
> A companion was originally someone you liked enough to share a meal with. The Latin word *companio* consists of the roots *com-*, meaning 'with' or 'together', and *panis*, meaning 'bread'.

companionable *adj* friendly and pleasant to be with. ▶ **companionably** *adv*

companionway *n* a ladder from one deck to another in a ship.

company *n, pl* **-nies 1** a business organization. **2** a group of actors. **3** a small unit of troops. **4** the officers and crew of a ship. **5** the fact of being with someone: *I enjoy her company.* **6** a number of people gathered together. **7** a guest or guests. **8** a person's associates. **9 keep someone company** to accompany someone. **10 part company** to disagree or separate. ▷ **HISTORY** see COMPANION

company sergeant-major *n Mil* the senior noncommissioned officer in a company.

comparable *adj* **1** worthy of comparison. **2** able to be compared (with). ▶ **comparability** *n*

comparative *adj* **1** relative: *despite the importance of his discoveries, he died in comparative poverty.* **2** involving comparison: *comparative religion.* **3** *Grammar* the form of an adjective or adverb that indicates that the quality denoted is possessed to a greater extent. In English the comparative is marked by the suffix *-er* or the word *more*. ✧ *n* **4** the comparative form of an adjective or adverb. ▶ **comparatively** *adv*

compare *vb* **-paring, -pared 1** to examine in order to observe resemblances or differences: *the survey compared the health of three groups of children.* **2 compare to** to declare to be like: *one ambulance driver compared the carnage to an air crash.* **3** (usually foll. by *with*) to resemble: *his storytelling compares with the likes of Le Carré.* **4** to bear a specified relation when examined: *this full-flavoured white wine compares favourably with more expensive French wines.* **5 compare notes** to exchange opinions. ✧ *n* **6 beyond compare** without equal. ▷ **HISTORY** Latin *com-* together + *par* equal

comparison *n* **1** a comparing or being compared. **2** likeness or similarity: *there is no comparison at all between her and Catherine.* **3** *Grammar* the positive, comparative, and superlative forms of an adjective or adverb. **4 in comparison to** *or* **with** compared to. **5 bear** *or* **stand comparison with** to be able to be compared with (something else), esp. favourably: *his half-dozen best novels can stand comparison with anyone's.*

compartment *n* **1** one of the sections into which a railway is sometimes divided. **2** a separate section: *filing the information away in some compartment of his mind.* **3** a small storage space: *the ice-making compartment of the fridge.* ▷ **HISTORY** French *compartiment*

compass *n* **1** an instrument for finding direction, with a magnetized needle which points to magnetic north. **2** limits or range: *within the compass of a normal sized book such a comprehensive survey is not possible.* **3 compasses** an instrument used for drawing circles or measuring distances, that consists of two arms, joined at one end. ▷ **HISTORY** Latin *com-* together + *passus* step

compassion *n* a feeling of distress and pity for the suffering or misfortune of another. ▷ **HISTORY** Latin *com-* with + *pati* to suffer

compassionate *adj* showing or having compassion. ▶ **compassionately** *adv*

compass rose *n Geog* an illustration on a map showing directions as on a compass.

compatible *adj* **1** able to exist together harmoniously. **2** consistent: *his evidence is fully compatible with the other data.* **3** (of pieces of equipment) capable of being used together. ▷ **HISTORY** Late Latin *compati* to suffer with ▶ **compatibility** *n*

compatriot *n* a fellow countryman or countrywoman. ▷ **HISTORY** French *compatriote*

compel *vb* **-pelling, -pelled 1** to force (to be or do something). **2** to obtain by force: *his performance compelled attention.* ▷ **HISTORY** Latin *com-* together + *pellere* to drive

compelling *adj* **1** arousing strong interest: *a compelling new novel.* **2** convincing: *compelling evidence.*

compendious *adj* brief but comprehensive.

compendium *n, pl* **-diums** *or* **-dia 1** *Brit* a selection of different table games in one container. **2** a concise but comprehensive summary. ▷ **HISTORY** Latin: a saving, literally: something weighed

compensate *vb* **-sating, -sated 1** to make amends to (someone), esp. for loss or injury. **2** to cancel out the effects of (something): *the car's nifty handling fails to compensate for its many flaws.* **3** to serve as compensation for (injury or loss). ▷ **HISTORY** Latin *compensare* ▶ **compensatory** *adj*

compensation *n* **1** payment made as reparation for loss or injury. **2** the act of making amends for something.

compere *Brit, Austral & NZ* ✧ *n* **1** a person who introduces a stage, radio, or television show. ✧ *vb* **-pering, -pered 2** to be the compere of. ▷ **HISTORY** French: godfather

compete *vb* **-peting, -peted 1** to take part in (a contest or competition). **2** to strive (to achieve something or to be successful): *able to compete on the international market.* ▷ **HISTORY** Latin *com-* together + *petere* to seek

competence *or* **competency** *n* **1** the ability to do something well or effectively. **2** a sufficient income to live on. **3** the state of being legally competent or qualified.

competent *adj* **1** having sufficient skill or knowledge: *he was a very competent engineer.* **2** suitable or sufficient for the purpose: *it was a competent performance, but hardly a remarkable one.* **3** having valid legal authority: *lawful detention after conviction by a competent court.* ▷ **HISTORY** Latin *competens*

competition *n* **1** the act of competing; rivalry: *competition for places was keen.* **2** an event in which people compete. **3** the opposition offered by competitors. **4** people against whom one competes.

competitive *adj* **1** involving rivalry: *the increasingly competitive computer industry.* **2** characterized by an urge to compete: *her naturally competitive spirit.* **3** of good enough value to be successful against commercial rivals: *we offer worldwide flights at competitive prices.* ▶ **competitiveness** *n*

competitor *n* a person, team, or firm that competes.

compile *vb* **-piling, -piled 1** to collect and arrange (information) from various sources. **2** *Computers* to convert (commands for a computer) from the language used by the person using it into machine code suitable for the computer, using a compiler. ▷ HISTORY Latin *com-* together + *pilare* to thrust down, pack ▶ **compilation** *n*

compiler *n* **1** a person who compiles information. **2** a computer program which converts a high-level programming language into the machine language used by a computer.

complacency *n* extreme self-satisfaction. ▶ **complacent** *adj* ▶ **complacently** *adv*

complain *vb* **1** to express resentment or displeasure. **2 complain of** to state that one is suffering from a pain or illness: *he complained of breathing trouble and chest pains.* **3** to make a formal protest: *he complained to the police about his rowdy neighbours.* ▷ HISTORY Latin *com-* (intensive) + *plangere* to bewail

complainant *n Law* a plaintiff.

complaint *n* **1** the act of complaining. **2** a reason for complaining. **3** a mild illness. **4** a formal protest.

complaisant (kom-**play**-zant) *adj* willing to please or oblige. ▷ HISTORY Latin *complacere* to please greatly ▶ **complaisance** *n*

complement *n* **1** a person or thing that completes something. **2** a complete amount or number: *a full complement of staff nurses and care assistants.* **3** the officers and crew needed to man a ship. **4** *Grammar* a word or words added to the verb to complete the meaning of the predicate in a sentence, as *a fool* in *He is a fool* or *that he would come* in *I hoped that he would come.* **5** *Maths* the angle that when added to a specified angle produces a right angle. ✧ *vb* **6** to complete or form a complement to. ▷ HISTORY Latin *com-* (intensive) + *plere* to fill

> **WORD TIP**
> Avoid confusion with **compliment.**

complementary *adj* **1** forming a complete or balanced whole. **2** forming a complement.

complementary angle *n Geom* an angle that is the difference between a given angle and a right angle: *the acute angles of a right-angled triangle are complementary angles.*

complementary medicine *n* same as **alternative medicine.**

complete *adj* **1** thorough; absolute: *it was a complete shambles.* **2** perfect in quality or kind: *he is the complete modern footballer.* **3** finished. **4** having all the necessary parts. **5 complete with** having as an extra feature or part: *a mansion complete with swimming pool.* ✧ *vb* **-pleting, -pleted 6** to finish. **7** to make whole or perfect. **8 complete the square** *Maths* to write a quadratic expression in a form in which the variable appears in a squared term. ▷ HISTORY Latin *complere* to fill up ▶ **completely** *adv* ▶ **completion** *n*

complete flower *n Biol* a flower with sepals, petals, stamens, and carpels.

complex *adj* **1** made up of interconnected parts. **2** intricate or complicated. **3** *Maths* of or involving complex numbers. ✧ *n* **4** a whole made up of related parts: *a leisure complex including a gymnasium, squash courts, and a 20-metre swimming pool.* **5** *Psychoanal* a group of unconscious feelings that influences a person's behaviour. **6** *Informal* an obsession or phobia: *I have never had a complex about my height.* ▷ HISTORY Latin *com-* together + *plectere* to braid

> **WORD TIP**
> *Complex* is sometimes used where *complicated* is meant. *Complex* should be used to say only that something consists of several parts rather than that, because something consists of many parts, it is difficult to understand or analyse.

complex fraction *n Maths* a fraction in which the numerator or denominator or both contain fractions.

complexion *n* **1** the colour and general appearance of the skin of a person's face. **2** character or nature: *the political complexion of the government.* ▷ HISTORY Latin *complexio* a combination

complexity *n, pl* **-ties 1** the state or quality of being intricate or complex. **2** something complicated.

complex number *n* any number of the form $a + bi$, where a and b are real numbers and $i = \sqrt{-1}$.

complex sentence *n Grammar* a sentence containing at least one main clause and one subordinate clause, as in *call me when you get back.*

compliance *n* **1** complying. **2** a tendency to do what others want. ▶ **compliant** *adj*

complicate *vb* **-cating, -cated** to make or become complex or difficult to deal with. ▷ HISTORY Latin *complicare* to fold together

complication *n* **1** something which makes a situation more difficult to deal with: *an added complication is the growing concern for the environment.* **2** a medical condition arising as a consequence of another.

complicity *n, pl* **-ties** the fact of being an accomplice in a crime.

compliment *n* **1** an expression of praise. **2 compliments** formal greetings. ✧ *vb* **3** to express admiration for. ▷ **HISTORY** Italian *complimento*

> ☑ **WORD TIP**
> Avoid confusion with **complement.**

complimentary *adj* **1** expressing praise. **2** free of charge: *a complimentary drink.*

comply *vb* **-plies, -plying, -plied** to act in accordance (with a rule, order, or request). ▷ **HISTORY** Spanish *cumplir* to complete

component *n* **1** a constituent part or feature of a whole. **2** *Maths* one of a set of two or more vectors whose resultant is a given vector. ✧ *adj* **3** forming or functioning as a part or feature: *over 60 component parts.* ▷ **HISTORY** Latin *componere* to put together

comport *vb Formal* **1** to behave (oneself) in a specified way. **2 comport with** to suit or be appropriate to. ▷ **HISTORY** Latin *comportare* to collect ▶ **comportment** *n*

compose *vb* **-posing, -posed 1** to put together or make up. **2** to be the component elements of. **3** to create (a musical or literary work). **4** to calm (oneself). **5** to arrange artistically. **6** *Printing* to set up (type). ▷ **HISTORY** Latin *componere* to put in place

composed *adj* (of people) in control of their feelings.

composer *n* a person who writes music.

composite *adj* **1** made up of separate parts. **2** (of a plant) with flower heads made up of many small flowers, such as the dandelion. **3** *Maths* capable of being factorized: *a composite function.* ✧ *n* **4** something composed of separate parts. **5** a composite plant. ▷ **HISTORY** Latin *compositus* well arranged

Composite *adj* of a style of classical architecture which combines elements of the Ionic and Corinthian styles.

composite cone *n Geol* a steep cone-shaped volcano composed of alternate layers of viscous lava and pyroclastic material. Also called: **strato-volcano**

composite school *n Canad* a secondary school which offers both academic courses and vocational training.

composite volcano *n Geol* a cone-shaped volcano with sloping sides built by successive eruptions from a long central pipe system through which magma from a reservoir deep in the Earth's crust rises to the surface.

composition *n* **1** the act of putting together or composing. **2** something composed. **3** the things or parts which make up a whole. **4** a work of music, art, or literature. **5** the harmonious arrangement of the parts of a work of art. **6** a written exercise; an essay. **7** *Printing* the act or technique of setting up type.

compositor *n* a person who arranges type for printing.

compos mentis *adj* sane. ▷ **HISTORY** Latin

compost *n* **1** a mixture of decaying plants and manure, used as a fertilizer. **2** soil mixed with fertilizer, used for growing plants. ✧ *vb* **3** to make (vegetable matter) into compost. ▷ **HISTORY** Latin *compositus* put together

composure *n* the state of being calm or unworried.

compote *n* fruit stewed with sugar or in a syrup. ▷ **HISTORY** French

compound¹ *n* **1** *Chem* a substance that contains atoms of two or more chemical elements held together by chemical bonds. **2** any combination of two or more parts, features, or qualities. **3** a word formed from two existing words or combining forms. ✧ *vb* **4** to combine so as to create a compound. **5** to make by combining parts or features: *the film's score is compounded from surging strings, a heavenly chorus and jazzy saxophones.* **6** to intensify by an added element: *the problems of undertaking relief work are compounded by continuing civil war.* **7** *Law* to agree not to prosecute in return for payment: *to compound a crime.* ✧ *adj* **8** composed of two or more parts or elements. **9** *Music* with a time in which the number of beats per bar is a multiple of three: *such tunes are usually in a form of compound time, for example six-four.* ▷ **HISTORY** Latin *componere* to put in order ▶ **compoundable** *adj*

compound² *n* a fenced enclosure containing buildings, such as a camp for prisoners of war. ▷ **HISTORY** Malay *kampong* village

compound events *pl n Maths* (in probability) an event in which two or more items are used to generate outcome.

compound fracture *n* a fracture in which the broken bone pierces the skin.

compound interest *n* interest paid on a sum and its accumulated interest.

compound sentence *n Grammar* a sentence containing at least two independent clauses usually joined by a coordinating conjunction, as in *I love them and they love me.*

comprehend *vb* **1** to understand. **2** to include. ▷ **HISTORY** Latin *comprehendere* ▶ **comprehensible** *adj*

comprehension *n* **1** understanding. **2** inclusion.

comprehensive *adj* **1** of broad scope or content. **2** (of car insurance) providing protection against most risks, including third-party liability, fire, theft, and damage. **3** *Brit* of the comprehensive school system. ✧ *n* **4** *Brit* a comprehensive school.

comprehensive school *n Brit* a secondary school for children of all abilities.

compress *vb* **1** to squeeze together. **2** to condense. ✧ *n* **3** a cloth or pad applied firmly to some part of the body to cool inflammation or relieve pain. ▷ **HISTORY** Latin *comprimere*

compression *n* **1** the act of compressing. **2** the reduction in volume and increase in pressure of the fuel mixture in an internal-combustion engine before ignition.

compressional plate boundary *n Geol* a place where the edge of part of the earth's crust passes over the edge of another part. See also **destructive plate boundary**.

compressor *n* a device that compresses a gas.

comprise *vb* **-prising, -prised 1** to be made up of: *the group comprised six French diplomats, five Italians and three Bulgarians.* **2** to form or make up: *women comprised 57 per cent of all employees, but less than 10 per cent of managers.* ▷ **HISTORY** French *compris* included

> **WORD TIP**
> The use of *of* after *comprise* should be avoided: *the library comprises* (not *comprises of*) *500 000 books and manuscripts.*

compromise (**kom**-prom-mize) *n* **1** settlement of a dispute by concessions on each side: *everyone pleaded for compromise; the compromise was only reached after hours of hard bargaining.* **2** the terms of such a settlement. **3** something midway between different things. ✧ *vb* **-mising, -mised 4** to settle (a dispute) by making concessions. **5** to put (oneself or another person) in a dishonourable position. ✧ *adj* **6** being, or having the nature or, a compromise: *a compromise solution.* ▷ **HISTORY** Latin *compromittere* to promise at the same time ▶ **compromising** *adj*

comptroller *n* a financial controller.

compulsion *n* **1** an irresistible urge to perform some action. **2** compelling or being compelled. ▷ **HISTORY** Latin *compellere* to compel

compulsive *adj* **1** resulting from or acting from a compulsion. **2** irresistible or absorbing. ▶ **compulsively** *adv*

compulsory *adj* required by regulations or laws.

compulsory purchase *n* the enforced purchase of a property by a local authority or government department.

compunction *n* a feeling of guilt or regret. ▷ **HISTORY** Latin *compungere* to sting

computation *n* a calculation involving numbers or quantities. ▶ **computational** *adj*

compute *vb* **-puting, -puted** to calculate (an answer or result), often by using a computer. ▷ **HISTORY** Latin *computare*

computer *n* an electronic device that processes data according to a set of instructions.

computer-aided manufacture *n* *Computing* the use of computers to automate manufacturing processes.

computer game *n* a game played on a home computer by manipulating a joystick or keys in response to the graphics on the screen.

computerize *or* **-ise** *vb* **-izing, -ized** *or* **-ising, -ised 1** to equip with a computer. **2** to control or perform (operations) by means of a computer. ▶ **computerization** *or* **-isation** *n*

computing *n* **1** the activity of using computers and writing programs for them. **2** the study of computers and their application.

comrade *n* **1** a fellow member of a union or a socialist political party. **2** a companion. ▷ **HISTORY** French *camarade* ▶ **comradely** *adj* ▶ **comradeship** *n*

con[1] *Informal* ✧ *n* **1** same as **confidence trick**. ✧ *vb* **conning, conned 2** to swindle or defraud.

con[2] *n* See **pros and cons**. ▷ **HISTORY** Latin *contra* against

con[3] *n* *Slang* a convict.

Con *Politics* Conservative.

con- *prefix* See **com-**.

concatenation *n* *Formal* a series of linked events. ▷ **HISTORY** Latin *com-* together + *catena* chain

concave *adj* curving inwards like the inside surface of a ball. ▷ **HISTORY** Latin *concavus* arched ▶ **concavity** *n*

conceal *vb* **1** to cover and hide. **2** to keep secret. ▷ **HISTORY** Latin *com-* (intensive) + *celare* to hide ▶ **concealment** *n*

concede *vb* **-ceding, -ceded 1** to admit (something) as true or correct. **2** to give up or grant (something, such as a right). **3** to acknowledge defeat in (a contest or argument). ▷ **HISTORY** Latin *concedere*

conceit *n* **1** an excessively high opinion of oneself. **2** *Literary* a far-fetched or clever comparison. ▷ **HISTORY** see CONCEIVE

conceited *adj* having an excessively high opinion of oneself. ▶ **conceitedness** *n*

conceivable *adj* capable of being understood, believed, or imagined. ▶ **conceivably** *adv*

conceive *vb* **-ceiving, -ceived 1** to imagine or think. **2** to consider in a certain way: *we must do what we conceive to be right.* **3** to form in the mind. **4** to become pregnant. ▷ **HISTORY** Latin *concipere* to take in

concentrate *vb* **-trating, -trated 1** to focus all one's attention, thoughts, or efforts on something: *she tried hard to concentrate, but her mind kept flashing back to the previous night.* **2** to bring or come together in large numbers or amounts in one place: *a flawed system that concentrates power in the hands of the few.* **3** to make (a liquid) stronger by removing water from it. ✧ *n* **4** a concentrated substance. ▷ **HISTORY** Latin *com-* same + *centrum* centre ▶ **concentrated** *adj*

concentrated acid *n* *Chem* an acid with a large number of acid molecules and few water molecules.

concentration *n* **1** intense mental application. **2** the act of concentrating. **3** something that is concentrated. **4** the amount or proportion of a substance in a mixture or solution.

concentration camp *n* a prison camp for civilian prisoners, as in Nazi Germany.

concentric *adj* having the same centre: *concentric circles.* ▷ **HISTORY** Latin *com-* same + *centrum* centre

concept *n* an abstract or general idea: *one of the basic concepts of quantum theory.* ▷ **HISTORY** Latin *concipere* to conceive

conception *n* **1** a notion, idea, or plan. **2** the fertilization of an egg by a sperm in the Fallopian tube followed by implantation in the womb. **3** origin or beginning: *the gap between the*

A B C D E F G H I J K L M N O P Q R S T U V W X Y Z

conception of an invention and its production. ▷ HISTORY Latin *concipere* to conceive

conceptual *adj* of or based on concepts.

conceptualize *or* **-ise** *vb* **-izing, -ized** *or* **-ising, -ised** to form a concept or idea of. ▶ **conceptualization** *or* **-isation** *n*

concern *n* **1** anxiety or worry: *the current concern over teenage pregnancies.* **2** something that is of interest or importance to a person. **3** regard or interest: *a scrupulous concern for client confidentiality.* **4** a business or firm. ✧ *vb* **5** to worry or make anxious. **6** to involve or interest: *he had converted the building into flats without concerning himself with the niceties of planning permission.* **7** to be relevant or important to. ▷ HISTORY Latin *com-* together + *cernere* to sift

concerned *adj* **1** interested or involved: *I have spoken to the person concerned and he has no recollection of saying such a thing.* **2** worried or anxious: *we are increasingly concerned for her safety.*

concerning *prep* about; regarding.

concert *n* **1** a performance of music by players or singers in front of an audience. **2 in concert a** working together. **b** (of musicians or singers) performing live. ▷ HISTORY Latin *com-* together + *certare* strive

concerted *adj* decided or planned by mutual agreement: *a concerted effort.*

concertina *n* **1** a small musical instrument similar to an accordion. ✧ *vb* **-naing, -naed 2** to collapse or fold up like a concertina. ▷ HISTORY from *concert*

concerto (kon-**chair**-toe) *n, pl* **-tos** *or* **-ti** (-tee) a large-scale composition for an orchestra and one or more soloists. ▷ HISTORY Italian

concert pitch *n* the internationally agreed pitch to which concert instruments are tuned for performance.

concession *n* **1** any grant of rights, land, or property by a government, local authority, or company. **2** a reduction in price for a certain category of person: *fare concessions for senior citizens.* **3** the act of yielding or conceding. **4** something conceded. **5** *Canad* **a** a land subdivision in a township survey. **b** same as **concession road.** ▷ HISTORY Latin *concedere* to concede ▶ **concessionary** *adj*

concessionaire *n* someone who holds a concession.

concession road *n Canad* one of a series of roads separating concessions in a township.

conch *n, pl* **conchs** *or* **conches 1** a marine mollusc with a large brightly coloured spiral shell. **2** its shell. ▷ HISTORY Greek *konkhē* shellfish

concierge (kon-see-**airzh**) *n* (esp. in France) a caretaker in a block of flats. ▷ HISTORY French

conciliate *vb* **-ating, -ated** to try to end a disagreement with or pacify (someone). ▷ HISTORY Latin *conciliare* to bring together ▶ **conciliator** *n*

conciliation *n* **1** the act of conciliating. **2** a method of helping the parties in a dispute to reach agreement, esp. divorcing or separating couples to part amicably.

conciliatory *adj* intended to end a disagreement.

concise *adj* brief and to the point. ▷ HISTORY Latin *concidere* to cut short ▶ **concisely** *adv* ▶ **conciseness** *or* **concision** *n*

conclave *n* **1** a secret meeting. **2** *RC Church* a private meeting of cardinals to elect a new pope. ▷ HISTORY Latin *clavis* key

conclude *vb* **-cluding, -cluded 1** to decide by reasoning: *the investigation concluded that key data for the paper were faked.* **2** to come or bring to an end: *the festival concludes on December 19th.* **3** to arrange or settle finally: *officials have refused to comment on the failure to conclude an agreement.* ▷ HISTORY Latin *concludere*

conclusion *n* **1** a final decision, opinion, or judgment based on reasoning: *the obvious conclusion is that something is being covered up.* **2** end or ending. **3** outcome or result: *if you take that strategy to its logical conclusion you end up with communism.* **4 in conclusion** finally. **5 jump to conclusions** to come to a conclusion too quickly, without sufficient thought or evidence.

conclusive *adj* putting an end to doubt: *there is no conclusive proof of this.* ▶ **conclusively** *adv*

concoct *vb* **1** to make by combining different ingredients. **2** to invent or make up (a story or plan). ▷ HISTORY Latin *coquere* to cook ▶ **concoction** *n*

concomitant *adj* **1** existing or along with (something else): *the concomitant health gains.* ✧ *n* **2** something which is concomitant. ▷ HISTORY Latin *com-* with + *comes* companion

concord *n* **1** agreement or harmony. **2** peaceful relations between nations. **3** *Music* a harmonious combination of musical notes. ▷ HISTORY Latin *com-* same + *cor* heart ▶ **concordant** *adj*

concordance *n* **1** a state of harmony or agreement. **2** an alphabetical list of words in a literary work, with the context and often the meaning.

concordat *n Formal* a treaty or agreement, such as one between the Vatican and another state. ▷ HISTORY Latin *concordatum* something agreed

concourse *n* **1** a large open space in a public place, where people can meet: *a crowded concourse at Heathrow airport.* **2** a crowd. ▷ HISTORY Latin *concurrere* to run together

concrete *n* **1** a building material made of cement, sand, stone and water that hardens to a stonelike mass. ✧ *vb* **-creting, -creted 2** to cover with concrete. ✧ *adj* **3** made of concrete. **4** specific as opposed to general. **5** relating to things that can be perceived by the senses, as opposed to abstractions. ▷ HISTORY Latin *concrescere* to grow together

concrete noun *n Grammar* a noun that refers to a physical object, substance, or being, as for example *shoe, water,* or *horse,* rather than to a quality, state, or concept. Compare **abstract noun.**

concretion *n* **1** a solidified mass. **2** the act of solidifying.

concubine (**kon**-kew-bine) *n* **1** *Old-fashioned* a woman living with a man as his wife, but not married to him. **2** a secondary wife in polygamous societies. ▷ **HISTORY** Latin *concumbere* to lie together ▶ **concubinage** *n*
concupiscence (kon-**kew**-piss-enss) *n Formal* strong sexual desire. ▷ **HISTORY** Latin *concupiscere* to covet ▶ **concupiscent** *adj*
concur *vb* **-curring, -curred** to agree; be in accord. ▷ **HISTORY** Latin *concurrere* to run together
concurrence *n* **1** agreement. **2** simultaneous occurrence.
concurrent *adj* **1** taking place at the same time or place. **2** meeting at, approaching, or having a common point: *concurrent lines.* **3** in agreement. ▶ **concurrently** *adv*
concurrent power *n* **1** a power shared by two authorities. **2** (in Australia) a power that may be exercised by both the Commonwealth and the States under the Constitution.
concuss *vb* to injure (the brain) by a fall or blow. ▷ **HISTORY** Latin *concutere* to disturb greatly
concussion *n* **1** a brain injury caused by a blow or fall, usually resulting in loss of consciousness. **2** violent shaking.
concyclic *adj Geom* (of points) lying on the same circle.
condemn *vb* **1** to express strong disapproval of. **2** to pronounce sentence on in a court of law. **3** to force into a particular state: *a system that condemns most of our youngsters to failure.* **4** to judge or declare (something) unfit for use. **5** to indicate the guilt of: *everything the man had said condemned him, morally if not technically.* ▷ **HISTORY** Latin *condemnare* ▶ **condemnation** *n* ▶ **condemnatory** *adj*
condensation *n* **1** anything that has condensed from a vapour, esp. on a window. **2** the act of condensing, or the state of being condensed.
condense *vb* **-densing, -densed** **1** to express in fewer words. **2** to increase the density of; concentrate. **3** to change from a gas to a liquid or solid. ▷ **HISTORY** Latin *condensare*
condenser *n* **1** an apparatus for reducing gases to their liquid or solid form by the removal of heat. **2** same as **capacitor**. **3** a lens that concentrates light.
condescend *vb* **1** to behave patronizingly towards one's supposed inferiors. **2** to do something as if it were beneath one's dignity. ▷ **HISTORY** Church Latin *condescendere* ▶ **condescending** *adj* ▶ **condescension** *n*
condiment *n* any seasoning for food, such as salt, pepper, or sauces. ▷ **HISTORY** Latin *condire* to pickle
condition *n* **1** a particular state of being: *the human condition; the van is in very poor condition.* **2 conditions** circumstances: *worsening weather conditions; the government pledged to improve living and working conditions.* **3** a necessary requirement for something else to happen: *food is a necessary condition for survival.* **4** a restriction or a qualification. **5** a term of an agreement: *the conditions of the lease are set out.* **6** state of physical fitness, esp. good health: *she is in a serious condition in hospital; out of condition.* **7** an ailment: *a heart condition.* **8 on condition that** provided that. ✧ *vb* **9** to accustom or alter the reaction of (a person or animal) to a particular stimulus or situation. **10** to treat with a conditioner. **11** to make fit or healthy. **12** to influence or determine the form that something takes: *he argued that the failure of Latin American industry was conditioned by international economic structures.* ▷ **HISTORY** Latin *con-* together + *dicere* to say ▶ **conditioning** *n, adj*
conditional *adj* **1** depending on other factors. **2** *Grammar* expressing a condition on which something else depends, for example 'If he comes' is a conditional clause in the sentence 'If he comes I shall go'.
conditioner *n* a thick liquid used when washing to make hair or clothes feel softer.
condolence *n* sympathy expressed for someone in grief or pain. ▷ **HISTORY** Latin *com-* together + *dolere* to grieve ▶ **condole** *vb*
condom *n* a rubber sheath worn on the penis or in the vagina during sexual intercourse to prevent conception or infection. ▷ **HISTORY** origin unknown
condominium *n, pl* **-ums** **1** *Austral, US & Canad* **a** an apartment building in which each apartment is individually owned. **b** an apartment in such a building. **2** joint rule of a state by two or more other states. ▷ **HISTORY** Latin *com-* together + *dominium* ownership
condone *vb* **-doning, -doned** to overlook or forgive (an offence or wrongdoing). ▷ **HISTORY** Latin *com-* (intensive) + *donare* to donate
condor *n* a very large rare S American vulture. ▷ **HISTORY** S American Indian *kuntur*
conducive *adj* (often foll. by *to*) likely to lead to or produce (a result). ▷ **HISTORY** Latin *com-* together + *ducere* to lead
conduct *n* **1** behaviour. **2** the management or handling of an activity or business. ✧ *vb* **3** to carry out: *the police are conducting an investigation into the affair.* **4** to behave (oneself). **5** to control (an orchestra or choir) by the movements of the hands or a baton. **6** to accompany and guide (people or a party): *a conducted tour.* **7** to transmit (heat or electricity). ▷ **HISTORY** Latin *com-* together + *ducere* to lead
conductance *n* the ability of a specified body to conduct electricity.
conduction *n* the transmission of heat or electricity.
conductivity *n* the property of transmitting heat, electricity, or sound.
conductor *n* **1** a person who conducts an orchestra or choir. **2** an official on a bus who collects fares. **3** *US, Canad & NZ* a railway official in charge of a train. **4** something that conducts electricity or heat. ▶ **conductress** *fem n*
conduit (**kon**-dew-it) *n* **1** a route or system for transferring things from one place to another: *a conduit for smuggling cocaine into the United States.* **2** a channel or tube for carrying a fluid or electrical

a b c d e f g h i j k l m n o p q r s t u v w x y z

cables. **3** a means of access or communication. ▷ HISTORY Latin *conducere* to lead

cone *n* **1** a geometric solid consisting of a circular or oval base, tapering to a point. **2** a cone-shaped wafer shell used to contain ice cream. **3** the scaly fruit of a conifer tree. **4** *Brit, Austral & NZ* a plastic cone used as a temporary traffic marker on roads. **5** a type of cell in the retina, sensitive to colour and bright light. ▷ HISTORY Greek *kōnus* pine cone, geometrical cone

coney *n* same as **cony**.

confab *n Informal* a conversation.

confection *n* **1** any sweet food, such as a cake or a sweet. **2** *Old-fashioned* an elaborate piece of clothing. ▷ HISTORY Latin *confectio* a preparing

confectioner *n* a person who makes or sells confectionery.

confectionery *n, pl* **-eries 1** sweets and chocolates collectively: *a drop in confectionery sales.* **2** the art or business of a confectioner.

confederacy *n, pl* **-cies** a union of states or people joined for a common purpose. ▷ HISTORY Late Latin *confoederatio* agreement ▶ **confederal** *adj*

confederate *n* **1** a state or individual that is part of a confederacy. **2** an accomplice or conspirator. ✧ *adj* **3** united; allied. ✧ *vb* **-ating, -ated 4** to unite in a confederacy. ▷ HISTORY Late Latin *confoederare* to unite by a league

Confederate *adj* of or supporting those American states which withdrew from the USA in 1860–61, leading to the US Civil War.

confederation *n* **1** a union or alliance of states or groups. **2** confederating or being confederated. **3** a federation.

confer *vb* **-ferring, -ferred 1** to discuss together. **2** to grant or give: *the power conferred by wealth.* ▷ HISTORY Latin *com-* together + *ferre* to bring ▶ **conferment** *n* ▶ **conferrable** *adj*

conference *n* a meeting for formal consultation or discussion. ▷ HISTORY Medieval Latin *conferentia*

confess *vb* **1** to admit (a fault or crime). **2** to admit to be true, esp. reluctantly. **3** *Christianity* to declare (one's sins) to God or to a priest, so as to obtain forgiveness. ▷ HISTORY Latin *confiteri* to admit

confession *n* **1** something confessed. **2** an admission of one's faults, sins, or crimes. **3 confession of faith** a formal public statement of religious beliefs.

confessional *n* **1** *Christianity* a small room or enclosed stall in a church where a priest hears confessions. ✧ *adj* **2** of or suited to a confession.

confessor *n* **1** *Christianity* a priest who hears confessions and gives spiritual advice. **2** *History* a person who demonstrates his Christian religious faith by the holiness of his life: *Edward the Confessor.*

confetti *n* small pieces of coloured paper thrown at weddings. ▷ HISTORY Italian

confidant *or fem* **confidante** *n* a person to whom private matters are confided. ▷ HISTORY French *confident*

confide *vb* **-fiding, -fided 1 confide in** to tell (something) in confidence to. **2** *Formal* to entrust into another's keeping. ▷ HISTORY Latin *confidere*

confidence *n* **1** trust in a person or thing. **2** belief in one's own abilities. **3** trust or a trustful relationship: *she won first the confidence, then the admiration, of her bosses.* **4** something confided, such as a secret. **5 in confidence** as a secret.

confidence trick *n* a swindle in which the swindler gains the victim's trust in order to cheat him or her.

confident *adj* **1** having or showing certainty: *we are now confident that this technique works.* **2** sure of oneself. ▷ HISTORY Latin *confidere* to have complete trust in ▶ **confidently** *adv*

confidential *adj* **1** spoken or given in confidence. **2** entrusted with another's secret affairs: *a confidential secretary.* **3** suggestive of intimacy: *a halting, confidential manner.* ▶ **confidentiality** *n* ▶ **confidentially** *adv*

configuration *n* **1** the arrangement of the parts of something. **2** the form or outline of such an arrangement. ▷ HISTORY Late Latin *configurare* to model on something

confine *vb* **-fining, -fined 1** to keep within bounds. **2** to restrict the free movement of: *a nasty dose of flu which confined her to bed for days.* ✧ *n* **3 confines** boundaries or limits. ▷ HISTORY Latin *finis* boundary

confinement *n* **1** being confined. **2** the period of childbirth.

confirm *vb* **1** to prove to be true or valid. **2** to reaffirm (something), so as to make (it) more definite: *she confirmed that she is about to resign as leader of the council.* **3** to strengthen: *this cruise confirmed my first impressions of the boat's performance.* **4** to formally make valid. **5** to administer the rite of confirmation to. ▷ HISTORY Latin *confirmare*

confirmation *n* **1** the act of confirming. **2** something that confirms. **3** a rite in several Christian churches that admits a baptized person to full church membership.

confirmed *adj* long-established in a habit or condition: *a confirmed bachelor.*

confiscate *vb* **-cating, -cated** to seize (property) by authority. ▷ HISTORY Latin *confiscare* to seize for the public treasury ▶ **confiscation** *n*

conflagration *n* a large destructive fire. ▷ HISTORY Latin *com-* (intensive) + *flagrare* to burn

conflate *vb* **-flating, -flated** to combine or blend into a whole. ▷ HISTORY Latin *conflare* to blow together ▶ **conflation** *n*

conflict *n* **1** opposition between ideas or interests. **2** a struggle or battle. ✧ *vb* **3** to be incompatible. ▷ HISTORY Latin *confligere* to combat ▶ **conflicting** *adj*

confluence *n* **1** a place where rivers flow into one another. **2** a gathering. ▷ HISTORY Latin *confluere* to flow together ▶ **confluent** *adj*

conform *vb* **1** to comply with accepted standards, rules, or customs. **2** to be like or in accordance with: *people tend to absorb ideas that* *conform with their existing beliefs, and reject those that do not.* ▷ **HISTORY** Latin *confirmare* to strengthen

conformation *n* **1** the general shape of an object. **2** the arrangement of the parts of an object.

conformist *adj* **1 a** (of a person) behaving or thinking like most other people rather than in an original or unconventional way: *a shy and conformist type of boy.* **b** (of an organization or society) expecting everyone to behave in the same way: *the school was a dull, conformist place for staff and students alike.* ✧ *n* **2** a person who behaves or thinks like most other people rather than in an original or unconventional way.

conformity *n, pl* **-ities 1** compliance in actions or behaviour with certain accepted rules, customs, or standards. **2** likeness.

confound *vb* **1** to astound or bewilder. **2** to fail to distinguish between. **3 confound it!** damn it! ▷ **HISTORY** Latin *confundere* to mingle, pour together

confounded *adj* **1** *Informal* damned: *what a confounded nuisance!* **2** bewildered; confused: *her silent, utterly confounded daughter.*

confront *vb* **1** (of a problem or task) to present itself to. **2** to meet face to face in hostility or defiance. **3** to present (someone) with something, esp. in order to accuse or criticize: *she finally confronted him with her suspicions.* ▷ **HISTORY** Latin *com-* together + *frons* forehead

confrontation *n* a serious argument or fight.

Confucianism *n* the teachings of Confucius (551–479 BC), the ancient Chinese philosopher, which emphasize moral order. ▶ **Confucian** *n, adj* ▶ **Confucianist** *n*

confuse *vb* **-fusing, -fused 1** to fail to distinguish between one thing and another. **2** to perplex or disconcert. **3** to make unclear: *he confused his talk with irrelevant detail.* **4** to throw into disorder. ▷ **HISTORY** Latin *confundere* to pour together ▶ **confusing** *adj* ▶ **confusingly** *adv*

confused *adj* **1** lacking a clear understanding of something. **2** disordered and difficult to understand or make sense of: *a confused dream.*

confusion *n* **1** mistaking one person or thing for another. **2** bewilderment. **3** lack of clarity. **4** disorder.

confute *vb* **-futing, -futed** to prove to be wrong. ▷ **HISTORY** Latin *confutare* to check, silence ▶ **confutation** *n*

conga *n* **1** a Latin American dance performed by a number of people in single file. **2** a large single-headed drum played with the hands. ✧ *vb* **-gaing, -gaed 3** to dance the conga. ▷ **HISTORY** from American Spanish

congeal *vb* to change from a liquid to a semisolid state. ▷ **HISTORY** Latin *com-* together + *gelare* to freeze

congenial *adj* **1** friendly, pleasant, or agreeable: *he found the Botanic Gardens a most congenial place for strolling.* **2** having a similar disposition or tastes. ▷ **HISTORY** *con-* (same) + *genial* ▶ **congeniality** *n*

congenital *adj* (of an abnormal condition) existing at birth but not inherited: *congenital heart disease.* ▷ **HISTORY** Latin *con-* together + *genitus* born ▶ **congenitally** *adv*

conger *n* a large sea eel. ▷ **HISTORY** Greek *gongros*

congested *adj* **1** crowded to excess. **2** clogged or blocked. ▷ **HISTORY** Latin *congerere* to pile up ▶ **congestion** *n*

conglomerate *n* **1** a large corporation made up of many different companies. **2** a thing composed of several different elements. **3** a type of rock consisting of rounded pebbles or fragments held together by silica or clay. ✧ *vb* **-ating, -ated 4** to form into a mass. ✧ *adj* **5** made up of several different elements. **6** (of rock) consisting of rounded pebbles or fragments held together by silica or clay. ▷ **HISTORY** Latin *conglomerare* to roll up ▶ **conglomeration** *n*

congratulate *vb* **-lating, -lated 1** to express one's pleasure to (a person) at his or her success or good fortune. **2 congratulate oneself** to consider oneself clever or fortunate (as a result of): *she congratulated herself on her own business acumen.* ▷ **HISTORY** Latin *congratulari* ▶ **congratulatory** *adj*

congratulations *pl n, interj* expressions of pleasure or joy on another's success or good fortune.

congregate *vb* **-gating, -gated** to collect together in or as a crowd. ▷ **HISTORY** Latin *congregare* to collect into a flock

congregation *n* a group of worshippers. ▶ **congregational** *adj*

Congregationalism *n* a system of Protestant church government in which each church is self-governing. ▶ **Congregationalist** *adj, n*

congress *n* a formal meeting of representatives for discussion. ▷ **HISTORY** Latin *com-* together + *gradi* to walk ▶ **congressional** *adj*

Congress *n* the federal legislature of the US, consisting of the House of Representatives and the Senate. ▶ **Congressional** *adj* ▶ **Congressman** *n* ▶ **Congresswoman** *fem n*

congruent *adj* **1** agreeing or corresponding. **2** *Geom* identical in shape and size: *congruent triangles.* ▷ **HISTORY** Latin *congruere* to agree ▶ **congruence** *n*

conical *adj* in the shape of a cone.

conic section *n* a figure, either a circle, ellipse, parabola, or hyperbola, formed by the intersection of a plane and a cone.

conifer *n* a tree or shrub bearing cones and evergreen leaves, such as the fir or larch. ▷ **HISTORY** Latin *conus* cone + *ferre* to bear ▶ **coniferous** *adj*

coniferous forest *n* a forest of trees bearing cones and evergreen leaves, such as the fir or larch. ▷ **HISTORY** Latin *conus* cone + *ferre* to bear

conjecture *n* **1** the formation of conclusions from incomplete evidence. **2** a guess. ✧ *vb* **-turing, -tured 3** to form (an opinion or conclusion) from incomplete evidence. ▷ **HISTORY** Latin *conjicere* to throw together ▶ **conjectural** *adj*

a b c d e f g h i j k l m n o p q r s t u v w x y z

conjoined twins *pl n* the technical name for **Siamese twins.**

conjugal (**kon**-jew-gal) *adj* of marriage: *conjugal rights.* ▷ **HISTORY** Latin *conjunx* wife or husband

conjugate *vb* (**kon**-jew-gate) **-gating, -gated 1** *Grammar* to give the inflections of (a verb). **2** (of a verb) to undergo inflection according to a specific set of rules. **3** *Formal* to combine: *a country in which conjugating Marxism with Christianity has actually been tried.* ✧ *n* (**kon**-jew-git) **4** *Formal* something formed by conjugation: *haemoglobin is a conjugate of a protein with an iron-containing pigment.* ▷ **HISTORY** Latin *com-* together + *jugare* to connect

conjugation *n* **1** *Grammar* **a** inflection of a verb for person, number, tense, voice and mood. **b** the complete set of the inflections of a given verb. **2** a joining.

conjunction *n* **1** joining together. **2** simultaneous occurrence of events. **3** a word or group of words that connects words, phrases, or clauses; for example *and, if,* and *but.* **4** *Astron* the apparent nearness of two heavenly bodies to each other. ▸ **conjunctional** *adj*

conjunctiva *n, pl* **-vas** *or* **-vae** the delicate mucous membrane that covers the eyeball and inner eyelid. ▷ **HISTORY** New Latin *membrana conjunctiva* the conjunctive membrane ▸ **conjunctival** *adj*

conjunctive *adj* **1** joining or joined. **2** used as a conjunction: *a conjunctive adverb.* ✧ *n* **3** a word or words used as a conjunction. ▷ **HISTORY** Latin *conjungere* to join

conjunctivitis *n* inflammation of the conjunctiva.

conjuncture *n* a combination of events, esp. one that leads to a crisis.

conjure *vb* **-juring, -jured 1** to perform tricks that appear to be magic. **2** to summon (a spirit or demon) by magic. **3** *Formal or literary* to appeal earnestly to: *I conjure you by all which you profess: answer me!* ▷ **HISTORY** Latin *conjurare* to swear together ▸ **conjuring** *n*

conjure up *vb* **1** to create an image in the mind: *the name Versailles conjures up a past of sumptuous grandeur.* **2** to produce as if from nowhere: *he conjured up a fabulous opening goal.*

conjuror *or* **conjurer** *n* a person who performs magic tricks for people's entertainment.

conk *Brit, Austral & NZ slang* ✧ *n* **1** the head or nose. ✧ *vb* **2** to strike (someone) on the head or nose. ▷ **HISTORY** probably changed from *conch*

conker *n* same as **horse chestnut** (sense 2).

conkers *n Brit* a game in which a player swings a horse chestnut (conker), threaded onto a string, against that of another player to try to break it. ▷ **HISTORY** dialect *conker* snail shell, originally used in the game

conk out *vb Informal* **1** (of a machine or car) to break down. **2** to become tired or fall asleep suddenly. ▷ **HISTORY** origin unknown

connect *vb* **1** to link or be linked: *high blood pressure is closely connected to heart disease.* **2** to put into telephone communication with. **3** *Computing* to join pieces of equipment so that they work together: *Connect the scanner to the printer and the computer.* **4** *Computing* to put into Internet communication with. **5** (of two public vehicles) to have the arrival of one timed to occur just before the departure of the other, for the convenience of passengers. **6** to associate in the mind: *he had always connected sex with violence and attacks rather than loving and concern.* **7** to relate by birth or marriage: *she was distantly connected with the Wedgwood family.* ▷ **HISTORY** Latin *connectere* to bind together

connection *or* **connexion** *n* **1** a relationship or association. **2** a link or bond. **3** a link between two components in an electric circuit. **4 a** an opportunity to transfer from one public vehicle to another. **b** the vehicle scheduled to provide such an opportunity. **5** an influential acquaintance. **6** a relative. **7** logical sequence in thought or expression. **8** a telephone link. **9** *Computing* access to the Internet. **10** *Slang* a supplier of illegal drugs, such as heroin. **11 in connection with** with reference to: *a number of people have been arrested in connection with the explosion.*

connective *adj* **1** connecting. ✧ *n* **2** *Grammar* a conjunction; any word that connects phrases, clauses, or individual words, for example *and, if,* and *but.*

connective tissue *n* body tissue that supports organs, fills the spaces between them, and forms tendons and ligaments.

conning tower *n* the raised observation tower containing the periscope on a submarine. ▷ **HISTORY** *con* to steer a ship

connivance *n* encouragement or permission of wrongdoing.

connive *vb* **-niving, -nived 1 connive at** to allow or encourage (wrongdoing) by ignoring it. **2** to conspire. ▷ **HISTORY** Latin *connivere* to blink, hence, leave uncensured

connoisseur (kon-noss-**sir**) *n* a person with special knowledge of the arts, food, or drink. ▷ **HISTORY** French

connotation *n* an additional meaning or association implied by a word: *the German term carries a connotation of elitism.* ▷ **HISTORY** Latin *con-* + together *notare* to mark, note ▸ **connote** *vb*

connubial (kon-**new**-bee-al) *adj Formal* of marriage: *connubial bliss.* ▷ **HISTORY** Latin *conubium* marriage

conquer *vb* **1** to defeat (an opponent or opponents). **2** to overcome (a difficulty or feeling). **3** to gain possession of (a place) by force or war. ▷ **HISTORY** Latin *conquirere* to search for ▸ **conquering** *adj* ▸ **conqueror** *n*

conquest *n* **1** the act of conquering. **2** a person or thing that has been conquered. **3** a person whose affections have been won.

conquistador *n, pl* **-dors** *or* **-dores** one of the Spanish conquerors of Mexico and Peru in the 16th century. ▷ **HISTORY** Spanish: conqueror

Cons. Conservative.

conscience *n* **1** the sense of right and wrong that governs a person's thoughts and actions. **2** a feeling of guilt: *he showed no hint of conscience over the suffering he had inflicted.* **3 in (all) conscience** in fairness. **4 on one's conscience** causing feelings of guilt. ▷ **HISTORY** Latin *conscire* to know

conscience-stricken *adj* feeling guilty because of having done something wrong.

conscientious *adj* **1** painstaking or thorough in one's work. **2** governed by conscience. ▶ **conscientiously** *adv* ▶ **conscientiousness** *n*

conscientious objector *n* a person who refuses to serve in the armed forces on moral or religious grounds.

conscious *adj* **1** alert and awake. **2** aware of one's surroundings and of oneself. **3** aware (of something): *he was conscious of a need to urinate.* **4** deliberate or intentional: *a conscious attempt.* **5** of the part of the mind that is aware of a person's self, surroundings, and thoughts, and that to a certain extent determines choices of action. ✧ *n* **6** the conscious part of the mind. ▷ **HISTORY** Latin *com-* with + *scire* to know ▶ **consciously** *adv* ▶ **consciousness** *n*

conscript *n* **1** a person who is enrolled for compulsory military service. ✧ *vb* **2** to enrol (someone) for compulsory military service. ▷ **HISTORY** Latin *conscriptus* enrolled

conscription *n* compulsory military service.

consecrate *vb* **-crating, -crated 1** to make or declare sacred or for religious use. **2** to devote or dedicate (something) to a specific purpose. **3** *Christianity* to sanctify (bread and wine) to be received as the body and blood of Christ. ▷ **HISTORY** Latin *consecrare* ▶ **consecration** *n*

consecutive *adj* following in order without interruption: *three consecutive nights of rioting.* ▷ **HISTORY** Latin *consequi* to pursue ▶ **consecutively** *adv*

consensus *n* general or widespread agreement. ▷ **HISTORY** Latin *consentire* to agree

> ☑ **WORD TIP**
> Since *consensus* refers to a collective opinion, the words *of opinion* in the phrase *consensus of opinion* are redundant and should therefore be avoided.

consent *n* **1** agreement, permission, or approval. **2 age of consent** the age at which sexual intercourse is permitted by law. ✧ *vb* **3** to permit or agree (to). ▷ **HISTORY** Latin *consentire* to agree ▶ **consenting** *adj*

consequence *n* **1** a logical result or effect. **2** significance or importance: *we said little of consequence to each other; a woman of little consequence.* **3 in consequence** as a result. **4 take the consequences** to accept whatever results from one's action.

consequent *adj* **1** following as an effect. **2** following as a logical conclusion. ▷ **HISTORY** Latin *consequens* following closely

> ☑ **WORD TIP**
> See at **consequential.**

consequential *adj* **1** important or significant. **2** following as a result.

> ☑ **WORD TIP**
> Although both *consequential* and *consequent* can refer to something which happens as the result of something else, *consequent* is more common in this sense in modern English: *the new measures were put into effect, and the consequent protest led to the dismissal of those responsible.*

consequently *adv* as a result; therefore.

conservancy *n* environmental conservation.

conservation *n* **1** protection and careful management of the environment and natural resources. **2** protection from change, loss, or injury. **3** *Physics* the principle that the quantity of a specified aspect of a system, such as momentum or charge, remains constant. ▶ **conservationist** *n*

conservative *adj* **1** favouring the preservation of established customs and values, and opposing change. **2** moderate or cautious: *a conservative estimate.* **3** conventional in style: *people in this area are conservative in their tastes.* ✧ *n* **4** a conservative person. ▶ **conservatism** *n*

Conservative *adj* **1** of or supporting the Conservative Party, the major right-wing political party in Britain, which believes in private enterprise and capitalism. **2** of or supporting a similar right-wing party in other countries. ✧ *n* **3** a supporter or member of the Conservative Party.

conservatoire (kon-**serv**-a-twahr) *n* a school of music. ▷ **HISTORY** French

conservatory *n, pl* **-tories 1** a greenhouse attached to a house. **2** a conservatoire.

conserve *vb* **-serving, -served 1** to protect from harm, decay, or loss. **2** to preserve (fruit or other food) with sugar. ✧ *n* **3** fruit preserved by cooking in sugar. ▷ **HISTORY** Latin *conservare* to keep safe

consider *vb* **1** to be of the opinion that. **2** to think carefully about (a problem or decision). **3** to bear in mind: *Corsica is well worth considering for those seeking a peaceful holiday in beautiful surroundings.* **4** to have regard for or care about: *you must try to consider other people's feelings more.* **5** to discuss (something) in order to make a decision. **6** to look at: *he considered her and she forced herself to sit calmly under his gaze.* ▷ **HISTORY** Latin *considerare* to inspect closely

considerable *adj* **1** large enough to reckon with: *a considerable number of people.* **2** a lot of: *he was in considerable pain.* ▶ **considerably** *adv*

considerate *adj* thoughtful towards other people.

consideration *n* **1** careful thought. **2** a fact to be taken into account when making a decision. **3** thoughtfulness for other people. **4** payment for a service. **5 take into consideration** to bear in mind. **6 under consideration** being currently discussed.

considered *adj* **1** presented or thought out with care: *a considered opinion.* **2** thought of in a specified way: *highly considered.*

considering *conj, prep* **1** taking (a specified fact) into account: *considering the mileage the car had*

a b c d e f g h i j k l m n o p q r s t u v w x y z

done, it was lasting well. ✧ *adv* **2** *Informal* taking into account the circumstances: *it's not bad considering.*

consign *vb* **1** to give into the care or charge of. **2** to put irrevocably: *those events have been consigned to history.* **3** to put (in a specified place or situation): *only a few months ago such demands would have consigned the student leaders to prisons and labour camps.* **4** to address or deliver (goods): *a cargo of oil drilling equipment consigned to Saudi Arabia.* ▷ **HISTORY** Latin *consignare* to put one's seal to, sign ▶ **consignee** *n* ▶ **consignor** *n*

consignment *n* **1** a shipment of goods. **2** the act or an instance of consigning: *the goods are sent to Hong Kong for onward consignment to customers in the area.*

consignment note *n Commerce* a document that records details about a consignment of goods and acts as a receipt for the sender.

consist *vb* **1 consist of** to be made up of: *a match consists of seven games.* **2 consist in** to have as its main or only part: *his madness, if he is mad, consists in believing that he is a sundial.* ▷ **HISTORY** Latin *consistere* to stand firm

consistency *n, pl* **-encies 1** degree of thickness or smoothness. **2** being consistent.

consistent *adj* **1** holding to the same principles. **2** in agreement. ▶ **consistently** *adv*

consolation *n* **1** a person or thing that is a comfort in a time of sadness or distress. **2** a consoling or being consoled.

console[1] *vb* **-soling, -soled** to comfort (someone) in sadness or distress. ▷ **HISTORY** Latin *consolari* ▶ **consolable** *adj*

console[2] *n* **1** a panel of controls for electronic equipment. **2** a cabinet for a television or audio equipment. **3** an ornamental bracket used to support a wall fixture. **4** the desklike case of an organ, containing the pedals, stops, and keys. ▷ **HISTORY** Old French *consolateur* one that provides support

consolidate *vb* **-dating, -dated 1** to make or become stronger or more stable. **2** to combine into a whole. ▷ **HISTORY** Latin *consolidare* to make firm ▶ **consolidation** *n* ▶ **consolidator** *n*

consommé (kon-**som**-may) *n* a thin clear meat soup. ▷ **HISTORY** French

consonance *n Formal* agreement or harmony.

consonant *n* **1 a** a speech sound made by partially or completely blocking the breath streams, for example *b* or *f*. **b** a letter representing this. ✧ *adj* **2 consonant with** in keeping or agreement with: *an individualistic style of religion, more consonant with liberal society.* **3** harmonious: *this highly-dissonant chord is followed by a more consonant one.* ▷ **HISTORY** Latin *consonare* to sound at the same time

consort *vb* **1 consort with** to keep company with. ✧ *n* **2** a husband or wife of a reigning monarch. **3** a small group of voices or instruments. ▷ **HISTORY** Latin *consors* partner

consortium *n, pl* **-tia** an association of business firms. ▷ **HISTORY** Latin: partnership

conspectus *n Formal* a survey or summary. ▷ **HISTORY** Latin: a viewing

conspicuous *adj* **1** clearly visible. **2** noteworthy or striking: *conspicuous bravery.* ▷ **HISTORY** Latin *conspicuus* ▶ **conspicuously** *adv*

conspiracy *n, pl* **-cies 1** a secret plan to carry out an illegal or harmful act. **2** the act of making such plans.

conspire *vb* **-spiring, -spired 1** to plan a crime together in secret. **2** to act together as if by design: *the weather and the recession conspired to hit wine production and sales.* ▷ **HISTORY** Latin *conspirare* to plot together ▶ **conspirator** *n* ▶ **conspiratorial** *adj*

constable *n* a police officer of the lowest rank. ▷ **HISTORY** Late Latin *comes stabuli* officer in charge of the stable

constabulary *n, pl* **-laries** *Chiefly Brit* the police force of an area.

constant *adj* **1** continuous: *she has endured constant criticism, mockery and humiliation.* **2** unchanging: *the average speed of the winds remained constant over this period.* **3** faithful. ✧ *n* **4** *Maths, physics* a quantity or number which remains invariable: *the velocity of light is a constant.* **5** something that is unchanging. ▷ **HISTORY** Latin *constare* to be steadfast ▶ **constancy** *n* ▶ **constantly** *adv*

constellation *n* **1** a group of stars which form a pattern and are given a name. **2** a group of people or things: *the constellation of favourable circumstances.* ▷ **HISTORY** Latin *com-* together + *stella* star

consternation *n* a feeling of anxiety or dismay.

constipated *adj* unable to empty one's bowels. ▷ **HISTORY** Latin *constipare* to press closely together

constipation *n* a condition in which emptying one's bowels is difficult.

constituency *n, pl* **-cies 1** the area represented by a Member of Parliament. **2** the voters in such an area.

constituent *n* **1** a person living in an MP's constituency. **2** a component part. ✧ *adj* forming part of a whole: *the constituent parts of the universe.* ▷ **HISTORY** Latin *constituere* to constitute

constituent assembly *n Politics* a body of representatives that is elected to create or change their country's constitution.

constitute *vb* **-tuting, -tuted 1** to form or make up: *the amazing range of crags that constitute the Eglwyseg Mountains.* **2** to set up (an institution) formally. ▷ **HISTORY** Latin *com-* (intensive) + *statuere* to place

constitution *n* **1** the principles on which a state is governed. **2 the Constitution** (in certain countries) the statute embodying such principles. **3** a person's state of health. **4** the make-up or structure of something: *changes in the very constitution of society.*

constitutional *adj* **1** of a constitution. **2** authorized by or in accordance with the Constitution of a nation: *constitutional monarchy.* **3** inherent in the nature of a person or thing: *a*

constitutional sensitivity to cold. ✧ *n* **4** a regular walk taken for the good of one's health.
▶ **constitutionally** *adv*

constitutive *adj* **1** forming a part of something. **2** with the power to appoint or establish.

constrain *vb* **1** to compel or force: *he felt constrained to apologize.* **2** to limit, restrict, or inhibit: *the mobility of workers is constrained by the serious housing shortage.* ▷ HISTORY Latin *constringere* to bind together

constrained *adj* embarrassed or unnatural: *his constrained expression.*

constraint *n* **1** something that limits a person's freedom of action. **2** repression of natural feelings. **3** a forced unnatural manner.

constrict *vb* **1** to make smaller or narrower by squeezing. **2** to limit or restrict. ▷ HISTORY Latin *constringere* to tie up together ▶ **constrictive** *adj*

constriction *n* **1** a feeling of tightness in some part of the body, such as the chest. **2** a narrowing. **3** something that constricts.

constrictor *n* **1** a snake that coils around and squeezes its prey to kill it. **2** a muscle that contracts an opening.

construct *vb* **1** to build or put together. **2** *Geom* to draw (a figure) to specified requirements. **3** to compose (an argument or sentence). ✧ *n* **4** a complex idea resulting from the combination of simpler ideas. **5** something formulated or built systematically. ▷ HISTORY Latin *construere* to build ▶ **constructor** *n*

construction *n* **1** the act of constructing or manner in which a thing is constructed. **2** something that has been constructed. **3** the business or work of building houses or other structures. **4** *Formal* an interpretation: *the financial markets will put the worst possible construction on any piece of news which might affect them.* **5** *Grammar* the way in which words are arranged in a sentence, clause, or phrase. **6** *Geom* **a** the drawing of a line, angle or figure so that certain requirements are satisfied in order to solve a problem or prove a theorem. **b** the line or figure drawn. ▶ **constructional** *adj*

constructive *adj* **1** useful and helpful: *constructive criticism.* **2** *Law* deduced by inference; not openly expressed. ▶ **constructively** *adv*

constructive interference *n Physics* the effect that occurs when the crests or troughs of two waves coincide.

constructive wave *n Geog* a wave in which there is a circular motion and no friction with the seabed.

constructive waves *pl n Geog* long low waves that wash material onto the shore and build up beaches. Compare **destructive waves**.

construe *vb* **-struing, -strued 1** to interpret the meaning of (something): *her indifference was construed as rudeness.* **2** to analyse the grammatical structure of (a sentence). **3** to combine (words) grammatically. **4** *Old-fashioned* to translate literally. ▷ HISTORY Latin *construere* to build

consul *n* **1** an official representing a state in a foreign country. **2** one of the two chief magistrates in ancient Rome. ▷ HISTORY Latin ▶ **consular** *adj* ▶ **consulship** *n*

consulate *n* **1** the workplace and official home of a consul. **2** the position or period of office of a consul.

consult *vb* **1** to ask advice from or discuss matters with (someone): *he never consults his wife about what he's about to do.* **2** to refer to for information: *he consulted his watch.* ▷ HISTORY Latin *consultare*

consultant *n* **1** a specialist doctor with a senior position in a hospital. **2** a specialist who gives expert professional advice. ▶ **consultancy** *n*

consultation *n* **1** the act of consulting. **2** a meeting for discussion or the seeking of advice. ▶ **consultative** *adj*

consulting room *n* a room in which a doctor sees patients.

consume *vb* **-suming, -sumed 1** to eat or drink. **2** to use up. **3** to destroy: *the ship blew up and was consumed by flames.* **4** to obsess: *he was consumed with jealousy over the ending of their affair.* ▷ HISTORY Latin *com-* (intensive) + *sumere* to take up ▶ **consumable** *adj* ▶ **consuming** *adj*

consumer *n* **1** a person who buys goods or uses services. **2** *Biol* an organism within a community that feeds upon other plants or animals.

consumer durables *pl n* manufactured products that have a relatively long life, such as cars or televisions.

consumer goods *pl n* goods bought for personal needs rather than those required for the production of other goods or services.

consumerism *n* **1** the belief that a high level of consumer spending is desirable and beneficial to the economy: *the obsessive consumerism of the 80s.* **2** protection of the rights of consumers.

consummate *vb* (**kon**-sum-mate) **-mating, -mated 1** to make (a marriage) legal by sexual intercourse. **2** to complete or fulfil. ✧ *adj* (kon-**sum**-mit) **3** supremely skilled: *a consummate craftsman.* **4** complete or extreme: *consummate skill; consummate ignorance.* ▷ HISTORY Latin *consummare* to complete ▶ **consummation** *n*

consumption *n* **1** the quantity of something consumed or used: *for such a powerful car, fuel consumption is modest.* **2** the act of eating or drinking something: *this meat is unfit for human consumption.* **3** *Econ* purchase of goods and services for personal use. **4** *Old-fashioned* tuberculosis of the lungs.

consumptive *adj* **1** wasteful or destructive. **2** of tuberculosis of the lungs. ✧ *n* **3** a person with tuberculosis of the lungs.

cont. continued.

contact *n* **1** the state or act of communication: *the airport lost contact with the plane shortly before the crash.* **2** the state or act of touching: *rugby is a game of hard physical contact.* **3** an acquaintance who might be useful in business. **4** a connection between two electrical conductors in a circuit. **5** a person who has been exposed to a contagious disease. ✧ *vb* **6** to come or be in communication or touch with. ▷ HISTORY Latin *contingere* to touch on all sides

contact lens *n* a small lens placed on the eyeball to correct defective vision.

contact order *n Law* a court order specifying in detail the contact a child is to have with a named person or people and requiring the parent or guardian with whom he or she lives to make provision for this.

contact process *n Chem* a method of making sulphuric acid by oxidizing sulphur dioxide under the influence of a catalyst.

contagion *n* **1** the passing on of disease by contact. **2** a contagious disease. **3** a corrupting influence that tends to spread. ▷ HISTORY Latin *contagio* infection

contagious *adj* **1** (of a disease) capable of being passed on by contact. **2** (of a person) capable of passing on a transmissible disease. **3** spreading from person to person: *contagious enthusiasm.*

contain *vb* **1** to hold or be capable of holding: *the bag contained a selection of men's clothing.* **2** to have as one of its ingredients or constituents: *tea and coffee both contain appreciable amounts of caffeine.* **3** to consist of: *the book contains 13 very different and largely separate chapters.* **4** to check or restrain (feelings or behaviour). **5** to prevent from spreading or going beyond fixed limits: *the blockade was too weak to contain the French fleet.* ▷ HISTORY Latin *continere* ▶ **containable** *adj*

container *n* **1** an object used to hold or store things in. **2** a large standard-sized box for transporting cargo by lorry or ship.

containerize *or* **-ise** *vb* **-izing, -ized** *or* **-ising, -ised 1** to pack (cargo) in large standard-sized containers. **2** to fit (a port, ship, or lorry) to carry goods in standard-sized containers.
▶ **containerization** *or* **-isation** *n*

containment *n* the prevention of the spread of something harmful.

contaminate *vb* **-nating, -nated 1** to make impure; pollute. **2** to make radioactive.
▷ HISTORY Latin *contaminare* to defile
▶ **contaminant** *n* ▶ **contamination** *n*

contemn *vb Formal* to regard with contempt.
▷ HISTORY Latin *contemnere*

contemplate *vb* **-plating, -plated 1** to think deeply about. **2** to consider as a possibility. **3** to look at thoughtfully. **4** to meditate. ▷ HISTORY Latin *contemplare* ▶ **contemplation** *n*

contemplative *adj* **1** of or given to contemplation. ✧ *n* **2** a person dedicated to religious contemplation.

contemporaneous *adj* happening at the same time. ▶ **contemporaneity** *n*

contemporary *adj* **1** existing or occurring at the present time. **2** living or occurring in the same period. **3** modern in style or fashion. **4** of approximately the same age. ✧ *n, pl* **-raries 5** a person or thing living at the same time or of approximately the same age as another.
▷ HISTORY Latin *com-* together + *temporarius* relating to time

WORD TIP

Since *contemporary* can mean either of the same period or of the present period, it is best to avoid this word where ambiguity might arise as in *a production of Othello in contemporary dress. Modern dress* or *Elizabethan dress* should be used in such contexts to avoid ambiguity.

contempt *n* **1** scorn. **2 hold in contempt** to scorn or despise. **3** same as **contempt of court.**
▷ HISTORY Latin *contemnere* to scorn

contemptible *adj* deserving to be despised or hated: *a contemptible lack of courage.*

contempt of court *n Law* an action that interferes with the normal delivery of justice in court or that shows deliberate disrespect for the authority of a court of law. ▷ HISTORY Latin *contemnere* to scorn

contemptuous *adj* showing or feeling strong dislike or disrespect. ▶ **contemptuously** *adv*

contend *vb* **1 contend with** to deal with. **2** to assert. **3** to compete or fight. **4** to argue earnestly.
▷ HISTORY Latin *contendere* to strive ▶ **contender** *n*

content[1] *n* **1 contents** everything inside a container. **2 contents** a list of chapters at the front of a book. **3** the meaning or substance of a piece of writing, often as distinguished from its style or form. **4** the amount of a substance contained in a mixture: *the water vapour content of the atmosphere.* ▷ HISTORY Latin *contentus* contained

content[2] *adj* **1** satisfied with things as they are. **2** willing to accept a situation or a proposed course of action. ✧ *vb* **3** to satisfy (oneself or another person). ✧ *n* **4** peace of mind. ▷ HISTORY Latin *contentus* contented, having restrained desires
▶ **contentment** *n*

contented *adj* satisfied with one's situation or life. ▶ **contentedly** *adv* ▶ **contentedness** *n*

contention *n* **1** disagreement or dispute. **2** a point asserted in argument. **3 bone of contention** a point of dispute. ▷ HISTORY Latin *contentio*

contentious *adj* **1** causing disagreement. **2** tending to quarrel. ▶ **contentiousness** *n*

contest *n* **1** a game or match in which people or teams compete. **2** a struggle for power or control. ✧ *vb* **3** to dispute: *he has said he will not contest the verdict.* **4** to take part in (a contest or struggle for power): *all parties which meet the legal requirements will be allowed to contest the election.*
▷ HISTORY Latin *contestari* to introduce a lawsuit
▶ **contestable** *adj*

contestant *n* a person who takes part in a contest.

context *n* **1** the circumstances relevant to an event or fact. **2** the words before and after a word or passage in a piece of writing that contribute to its meaning: *taken out of context, lines like these sound ridiculous, but, as part of a scrupulously written play, they are just right.* ▷ HISTORY Latin *com-* together + *texere* to weave ▶ **contextual** *adj*

contiguous *adj Formal* very near or touching. ▷ **HISTORY** Latin *contiguus*

continent[1] *n* one of the earth's large landmasses (Asia, Australia, Africa, Europe, North and South America, and Antarctica). ▷ **HISTORY** Latin *terra continens* continuous land ▶ **continental** *adj*

continent[2] *adj* **1** able to control one's bladder and bowels. **2** sexually restrained. ▷ **HISTORY** Latin *continere* to contain, retain ▶ **continence** *n*

Continent *n* **the Continent** the mainland of Europe as distinct from the British Isles. ▶ **Continental** *adj*

continental breakfast *n* a light breakfast of coffee and rolls.

continental climate *n* a climate with hot summers, cold winters, and little rainfall, typical of the interior of a continent.

continental divide *n Geog* a watershed that divides adjacent river systems on a continent and determines in which direction they will flow and into which ocean they will empty.

continental drift *n Geol* the theory that the earth's continents drift gradually over the surface of the planet, due to currents in its mantle.

continental quilt *n Brit* a large quilt used as a bed cover in place of the top sheet and blankets.

continental shelf *n* the gently sloping shallow sea bed surrounding a continent.

contingency *n, pl* **-cies 1** an unknown or unforeseen future event or condition. **2** something dependent on a possible future event.

contingent *n* **1** a group of people with a common interest, that represents a larger group: *a contingent of European scientists.* **2** a military group that is part of a larger force: *the force includes a contingent of the Foreign Legion.* ✧ *adj* **3** (foll. by *on* or *upon*) dependent on (something uncertain). **4** happening by chance. ▷ **HISTORY** Latin *contingere* to touch, befall

continual *adj* **1** occurring without interruption. **2** recurring frequently. ▷ **HISTORY** Latin *continuus* uninterrupted ▶ **continually** *adv*

> ☑ **WORD TIP**
> See at **continuous.**

continuance *n* **1** the act of continuing. **2** duration.

continuation *n* **1** the act of continuing. **2** a part or thing added, such as a sequel. **3** a renewal of an interrupted action or process.

continue *vb* **-tinuing, -tinued 1** to remain or cause to remain in a particular condition or place. **2** to carry on (doing something): *we continued kissing; heavy fighting continued until Thursday afternoon.* **3** to resume after an interruption: *we'll continue after lunch.* **4** to go on to a further place: *the road continues on up the hill.* ▷ **HISTORY** Latin *continuare* to join together

continuity *n, pl* **-ties 1** a smooth development or sequence. **2** the arrangement of scenes in a film so that they follow each other logically and without breaks.

continuity person *n Films, television* a person whose job it is to ensure that film or TV sequences follow on logically as regards sets, props, lighting, clothing, etc.

continuo *n, pl* **-tinuos** *Music* a continuous bass accompaniment played usually on a keyboard instrument. ▷ **HISTORY** Italian

continuous *adj* **1** without end: *a continuous process.* **2** not having any breaks or gaps in it: *a continuous line of boats; continuous rain.* ▷ **HISTORY** Latin *continuus* ▶ **continuously** *adv*

> ☑ **WORD TIP**
> Both *continual* and *continuous* can be used to say that something continues without interruption, but only *continual* can correctly be used to say that something keeps happening repeatedly.

continuous data *n Statistics* data which consists of a continuum of possible values, having certain limits but not being divided into fixed class intervals. Compare **discrete data**.

continuum *n, pl* **-tinua** *or* **-tinuums** a continuous series or whole, no part of which is noticeably different from the parts immediately next to it, although the ends or extremes of it are very different from each other: *the continuum from minor misbehaviour to major crime.* ▷ **HISTORY** Latin

contort *vb* to twist or bend out of shape. ▷ **HISTORY** Latin *contortus* intricate ▶ **contortion** *n*

contortionist *n* a performer who contorts his or her body to entertain others.

contour *n* **1** an outline. **2** same as **contour line**. ✧ *vb* **3** to shape so as to form or follow the contour of something. ▷ **HISTORY** Italian *contornare* to sketch

contour line *n Geog* a line on a map or chart joining points of equal height or depth.

contour map *n Geog* a map showing topography by means of contour lines.

contour ploughing *n Agriculture* ploughing following the contours of the land, to minimize the effects of erosion.

contra- *prefix* **1** against or contrasting: *contraceptive.* **2** (in music) lower in pitch: *contrabass.* ▷ **HISTORY** Latin *contra* against

contraband *n* **1** smuggled goods. ✧ *adj* **2** (of goods) smuggled. ▷ **HISTORY** Spanish *contrabanda*

contraception *n* the deliberate use of artificial or natural means to prevent pregnancy. ▷ **HISTORY** CONTRA- + CONCEPTION

contraceptive *n* **1** a device, such as a condom, that is used to prevent pregnancy. ✧ *adj* **2** providing or relating to contraception: *the contraceptive pill.*

contract *n* **1** a formal agreement between two or more parties. **2** a document setting out a formal agreement. ✧ *vb* **3** to make a formal agreement with (a person or company) to do or deliver (something). **4** to enter into (a relationship or marriage) formally: *she had contracted an alliance with a wealthy man.* **5** to make or become smaller, narrower, or shorter. **6** to become affected by (an illness). **7** to draw (muscles) together or (of muscles) to be drawn together. **8** to shorten (a word or phrase) by omitting letters or syllables, usually indicated in writing by an apostrophe. ▷ **HISTORY** Latin *contractus* agreement ▸ **contractible** *adj*

contraction *n* **1** a contracting or being contracted. **2** a shortening of a word or group of words, often marked by an apostrophe, for example *I've come* for *I have come*. **3 contractions** *Med* temporary shortening and tensing of the uterus during pregnancy and labour.

contract of employment *n Law* a written agreement between an employer and an employee, that determines the employment relations between them.

contractor *n* a person or firm that supplies materials or labour for other companies.

contractual *adj* of or in the nature of a contract.

contradict *vb* **1** to declare the opposite of (a statement) to be true. **2** (of a fact or statement) to suggest that (another fact or statement) is wrong. ▷ **HISTORY** Latin *contra-* against + *dicere* to speak ▸ **contradiction** *n*

contradictory *adj* (of facts or statements) inconsistent.

contradistinction *n* a distinction made by contrasting different qualities. ▸ **contradistinctive** *adj*

contraflow *n* a flow of road traffic going alongside but in an opposite direction to the usual flow.

contralto *n, pl* **-tos** *or* **-ti 1** the lowest female voice. **2** a singer with such a voice. ▷ **HISTORY** Italian

contraption *n Informal* a strange-looking device or gadget. ▷ **HISTORY** origin unknown

contrapuntal *adj Music* of or in counterpoint. ▷ **HISTORY** Italian *contrappunto* counterpoint

contrariwise *adv* **1** from a contrasting point of view. **2** in the opposite way.

contrary *n, pl* **-ries 1 on** *or* **to the contrary** in opposition to what has just been said or implied. ✧ *adj* **2** opposed; completely different: *a contrary view, based on equally good information.* **3** perverse; obstinate. **4** (of the wind) unfavourable. ✧ *adv* **contrary to 5** in opposition or contrast to: *contrary to popular belief.* **6** in conflict with: *contrary to nature.* ▷ **HISTORY** Latin *contrarius* opposite ▸ **contrariness** *n*

contrast *n* **1** a difference which is clearly seen when two things are compared. **2** a person or thing showing differences when compared with another. **3** the degree of difference between the colours in a photograph or television picture. ✧ *vb* **4** to compare or be compared in order to show the differences between (things): *he contrasts that society with contemporary America.* **5 contrast with** to be very different from: *her speed of reaction contrasted with her husband's vagueness.* ▷ **HISTORY** Latin *contra-* against + *stare* to stand ▸ **contrasting** *adj*

contravene *vb* **-vening, -vened** *Formal* to break (a rule or law). ▷ **HISTORY** Latin *contra-* against + *venire* to come ▸ **contravention** *n*

contretemps (**kon**-tra-tahn) *n, pl* **-temps** an embarrassing minor disagreement. ▷ **HISTORY** French

contribute *vb* **-uting, -uted** (often foll. by *to*) **1** to give (support or money) for a common purpose or fund. **2** to supply (ideas or opinions). **3 contribute to** to be partly responsible (for): *his own unconvincing play contributed to his defeat.* **4** to write (an article) for a publication. ▷ **HISTORY** Latin *contribuere* to collect ▸ **contribution** *n* ▸ **contributory** *adj* ▸ **contributor** *n*

contrite *adj* full of guilt or regret. ▷ **HISTORY** Latin *contritus* worn out ▸ **contritely** *adv* ▸ **contrition** *n*

contrivance *n* **1** an ingenious device. **2** an elaborate or deceitful plan. **3** the act or power of contriving.

contrive *vb* **-triving, -trived 1** to make happen: *he had already contrived the murder of King Alexander.* **2** to devise or construct ingeniously: *he contrived a plausible reason to fly back to London; he contrived a hook from a bent nail.* ▷ **HISTORY** Old French *controver*

control *n* **1** power to direct something: *the province is mostly under guerrilla control.* **2** a curb or check: *import controls.* **3 controls** instruments used to operate a machine. **4** a standard of comparison used in an experiment. **5** an experiment used to verify another by having all aspects identical except for the one that is being tested. ✧ *vb* **-trolling, -trolled 6** to have power over: *the gland which controls the body's metabolic rate.* **7** to limit or restrain: *he could not control his jealousy.* **8** to regulate or operate (a machine). **9** to restrict the authorized supply of (certain drugs). ▷ **HISTORY** Old French *conteroller* to regulate ▸ **controllable** *adj*

controller *n* **1** a person who is in charge. **2** a person in charge of the financial aspects of a business.

controlling variables *n Science* the process of deciding which variables or factors will influence the outcome of an experiment, situation, or event, and deliberately controlling all recognized variables in a systematic manner.

control tower *n* a tall building at an airport from which air traffic is controlled.

control variable *n Science* a factor that remains the same in several experiments or tests.

controversy *n, pl* **-sies** argument or debate concerning a matter about which there is strong disagreement. ▷ **HISTORY** Latin *contra-* against + *vertere* to turn ▸ **controversial** *adj*

contumacy (**kon**-tume-mass-ee) *n, pl* **-cies** *Literary* obstinate disobedience. ▷ **HISTORY** Latin *contumax* obstinate ▸ **contumacious** (kon-tume-**may**-shuss) *adj*

contumely (**kon**-tume-mill-ee) *n, pl* **-lies** *Literary* **1** scornful or insulting treatment. **2** a humiliating insult. ▷ **HISTORY** Latin *contumelia*

contusion *n Formal* a bruise. ▷ **HISTORY** Latin *contusus* bruised ▸ **contuse** *vb*

conundrum *n* **1** a puzzling question or problem. **2** a riddle whose answer contains a pun. ▷ **HISTORY** origin unknown

conurbation *n* a large heavily populated urban area formed by the growth and merging of towns. ▷ HISTORY Latin *con-* together + *urbs* city

convalesce *vb* **-lescing, -lesced** to recover health after an illness or operation. ▷ HISTORY Latin *com-* (intensive) + *valescere* to grow strong

convalescence *n* **1** gradual return to health after illness or an operation. **2** the period during which such recovery occurs. ▶ **convalescent** *n, adj*

convection *n* **1** the transmission of heat caused by movement of molecules from cool regions to warmer regions of lower density. **2** *Meteorol* the process by which masses of warm air are raised into the atmosphere, often cooling and forming clouds as cooler air moves downwards. ▶ **convectional** *adj* ▷ HISTORY Latin *convehere* to bring together

convectional rain *n Meteorol* rain that occurs when hot air rises, cools, and condenses; common in equatorial regions.

convector *n* a heating device which gives out hot air.

convene *vb* **-vening, -vened** to gather or summon for a formal meeting. ▷ HISTORY Latin *convenire* to assemble

convener *or* **convenor** *n* a person who calls or chairs a meeting: *the shop stewards' convener at the factory.* ▶ **convenership** *or* **convenorship** *n*

convenience *n* **1** the quality of being suitable or convenient. **2 at your convenience** at a time suitable to you. **3** an object that is useful: *a house with every modern convenience.* **4** *Euphemistic, chiefly Brit* a public toilet.

convenient *adj* **1** suitable or opportune. **2** easy to use. **3** nearby. ▷ HISTORY Latin *convenire* to be in accord with

convent *n* **1** a building where nuns live. **2** a school in which the teachers are nuns. **3** a community of nuns. ▷ HISTORY Latin *conventus* meeting

conventicle *n Brit & US history* a secret or unauthorized religious meeting. ▷ HISTORY Latin *conventiculum*

convention *n* **1** the established view of what is thought to be proper behaviour. **2** an accepted rule or method: *a convention used by printers.* **3** a formal agreement or contract between people and nations. **4** a large formal assembly of a group with common interests. ▷ HISTORY Latin *conventio* an assembling

conventional *adj* **1** following the accepted customs and lacking originality. **2** established by accepted usage or general agreement. **3** (of weapons or warfare) not nuclear. ▶ **conventionally** *adv*

conventional current *n Electronics* a current that flows from the positive terminal to the negative terminal of a cell or battery.

conventionality *n, pl* **-ties 1** the quality of being conventional. **2** something conventional.

conventionalize *or* **-ise** *vb* **-izing, -ized** *or* **-ising, -ised** to make conventional.

converge *vb* **-verging, -verged 1** to move towards or meet at the same point. **2** (of opinions or effects) to move towards a shared conclusion or result. ▷ HISTORY Latin *com-* together + *vergere* to incline ▶ **convergence** *n* ▶ **convergent** *adj*

convergence zone *n Geol* a zone where tectonic plates collide, typified by earthquakes, mountain formation, and volcanic activity. Compare **divergence zone**.

conversant *adj* **conversant with** having knowledge or experience of. ▷ HISTORY Latin *conversari* to keep company with

conversation *n* informal talk between two or more people.

conversational *adj* **1** of or used in conversation: *conversational French.* **2** resembling informal spoken language: *the author's easy, conversational style.*

conversationalist *n* a person with a specified ability at conversation: *a brilliant conversationalist.*

conversation piece *n* something, such as an unusual object, that provokes conversation.

converse[1] *vb* **-versing, -versed** to have a conversation. ▷ HISTORY Latin *conversari* to keep company with

converse[2] *adj* **1** reversed or opposite. ✧ *n* **2** a statement or idea that is the opposite of another. ▷ HISTORY Latin *conversus* turned around ▶ **conversely** *adv*

conversion *n* **1** a change or adaptation. **2** *Maths* a calculation in which a weight, volume, or distance is worked out in a different system of measurement: *the conversion from Fahrenheit to Celsius.* **3** a change to another belief or religion. **4** *Rugby* a score made after a try by kicking the ball over the crossbar from a place kick. ▷ HISTORY Latin *conversio* a turning around

convert *vb* **1** to change or adapt. **2** to cause (someone) to change in opinion or belief. **3** to change (a measurement) from one system of units to another. **4** to change (money) into a different currency. **5** *Rugby* to make a conversion after (a try). ✧ *n* **6** a person who has been converted to another belief or religion. ▷ HISTORY Latin *convertere* to turn around, alter ▶ **converter** *or* **convertor** *n*

convertible *adj* **1** capable of being converted. **2** *Finance* (of a currency) freely exchangeable into other currencies. ✧ *n* **3** a car with a folding or removable roof.

convex *adj* curving outwards like the outside surface of a ball. ▷ HISTORY Latin *convexus* vaulted, rounded ▶ **convexity** *n*

convey *vb* **1** to communicate (information). **2** to carry or transport from one place to another. **3** (of a channel or path) to transfer or transmit. **4** *Law* to transfer (the title to property). ▷ HISTORY Old French *conveier* ▶ **conveyable** *adj* ▶ **conveyor** *n*

conveyance *n* **1** *Old-fashioned* a vehicle. **2** *Law* **a** a transfer of the legal title to property. **b** the document effecting such a transfer. **3** the act of conveying: *the conveyance of cycles on peak hour trains.* ▶ **conveyancer** *n*

conveyancing *n* the branch of law dealing with the transfer of ownership of property.

A B C D E F G H I J K L M N O P Q R S T U V W X Y Z

conveyor belt *n* an endless moving belt driven by rollers and used to transport objects, esp. in a factory.

convict *vb* **1** to declare (someone) guilty of an offence. ✧ *n* **2** a person serving a prison sentence. ▷ **HISTORY** Latin *convictus* convicted

conviction *n* **1** a firmly held belief or opinion. **2** an instance of being found guilty of a crime: *he had several convictions for petty theft.* **3** a convincing or being convinced. **4 carry conviction** to be convincing.

convictism *n History* the practice of sending convicts to a penal colony, esp. Australia, to carry out forced labour.

convince *vb* **-vincing, -vinced** to persuade by argument or evidence. ▷ **HISTORY** Latin *convincere* to demonstrate incontrovertibly ▶ **convinced** *adj* ▶ **convincible** *adj* ▶ **convincing** *adj*

convivial *adj* sociable or lively: *a convivial atmosphere; convivial company.* ▷ **HISTORY** Late Latin *convivialis* ▶ **conviviality** *n*

convocation *n Formal* a large formal meeting.

convoke *vb* **-voking, -voked** *Formal* to call together. ▷ **HISTORY** Latin *convocare*

convoluted *adj* **1** coiled or twisted. **2** (of an argument or sentence) complex and difficult to understand.

convolution *n* **1** a coil or twist. **2** an intricate or confused matter or condition. **3** a convex fold in the surface of the brain.

convolvulus *n, pl* **-luses** *or* **-li** a twining plant with funnel-shaped flowers and triangular leaves. ▷ **HISTORY** Latin: bindweed

convoy *n* a group of vehicles or ships travelling together. ▷ **HISTORY** Old French *convoier* to convey

convulse *vb* **-vulsing, -vulsed 1** to shake or agitate violently. **2** (of muscles) to undergo violent spasms. **3** *Informal* to be overcome (with laughter or rage). **4** to disrupt the normal running of: *student riots have convulsed India.* ▷ **HISTORY** Latin *con-* together + *vellere* to pluck, pull ▶ **convulsive** *adj*

convulsion *n* **1** a violent muscular spasm. **2** a violent upheaval. **3 convulsions** *Informal* uncontrollable laughter: *I was in convulsions.*

cony *or* **coney** *n, pl* **-nies** *or* **-neys** *Brit* **1** a rabbit. **2** rabbit fur. ▷ **HISTORY** Latin *cuniculus* rabbit

coo *vb* **cooing, cooed 1** (of a dove or pigeon) to make a soft murmuring sound. **2 bill and coo** to murmur softly or lovingly. ✧ *n* **3** a cooing sound. ✧ *interj* **4** *Brit slang* an exclamation of surprise or amazement. ▷ **HISTORY** imitative ▶ **cooing** *adj, n*

cooee *interj* **1** *Brit, Austral & NZ* a call used to attract attention. **2** *Austral & NZ* **within cooee** within calling distance: *the school was within cooee of our house.* ▷ **HISTORY** Aboriginal

cook *vb* **1** to prepare (food) by heating or (of food) to be prepared in this way. **2** *Slang* to alter or falsify (figures or accounts): *she had cooked the books.* ✧ *n* **3** a person who prepares food for eating. ✧ See also **cook up**. ▷ **HISTORY** Latin *coquere*

cooker *n* **1** *Chiefly Brit* an apparatus for cooking heated by gas or electricity. **2** *Brit* an apple suitable for cooking but not for eating raw.

cookery *n* the art or practice of cooking. RELATED ADJECTIVE ▶ **culinary**

cookie *n, pl* **cookies 1** *US & Canad* a biscuit. **2 that's the way the cookie crumbles** *Informal* that is how things inevitably are. **3** *Informal* a person: *a real tough cookie.* ▷ **HISTORY** Dutch *koekje* little cake

cook up *vb Informal* to invent (a story or scheme).

cool *adj* **1** moderately cold: *it should be served cool, even chilled.* **2** comfortably free of heat: *it was one of the few cool days that summer.* **3** calm and unemotional: *a cool head.* **4** indifferent or unfriendly: *the idea met with a cool response.* **5** calmly impudent. **6** *Informal* (of a large sum of money) without exaggeration: *a cool million.* **7** *Informal* sophisticated or elegant. **8** (of a colour) having violet, blue, or green predominating. **9** *Informal* marvellous. ✧ *vb* **10** to make or become cooler. **11** to calm down. ✧ *n* **12** coolness: *in the cool of the evening.* **13** *Slang* calmness; composure: *he lost his cool and wantonly kicked the ball away.* ▷ **HISTORY** Old English *cōl* ▶ **coolly** *adv* ▶ **coolness** *n*

coolant *n* a fluid used to cool machinery while it is working.

cool drink *n S African* a soft drink.

cooler *n* a container for making or keeping things cool.

coolibah *n* an Australian eucalypt that grows beside rivers. ▷ **HISTORY** Aboriginal

coolie *n Old-fashioned, offensive* an unskilled Oriental labourer. ▷ **HISTORY** Hindi *kulī*

cooling tower *n* a tall hollow structure in a factory or power station, inside which hot water cools as it trickles down.

coomb *or* **coombe** *n* a short valley or deep hollow. ▷ **HISTORY** Old English *cumb*

coon *n* **1** *Informal* short for **raccoon**. **2** *Offensive slang* a Negro or Australian Aborigine. **3** *S African offensive* a person of mixed race.

coop[1] *n* **1** a cage or pen for poultry or small animals. ✧ *vb* **2 coop up** to confine in a restricted place. ▷ **HISTORY** Latin *cupa* basket, cask

coop[2] *or* **co-op** (**koh**-op) *n Brit, Austral & NZ* a cooperative society or a shop run by a cooperative society.

cooper *n* a person who makes or repairs barrels or casks. ▷ **HISTORY** see COOP[1]

cooperate *or* **co-operate** *vb* **1** to work or act together. **2** to assist or be willing to assist. ▷ **HISTORY** Latin *co-* with + *operari* to work ▶ **cooperation** *or* **co-operation** *n*

cooperative *or* **co-operative** *adj* **1** willing to cooperate. **2** (of an enterprise or farm) owned and managed collectively. ✧ *n* **3** a cooperative organization.

cooperative society *n* a commercial enterprise owned and run by customers or workers, in which the profits are shared among the members.

coopt *or* **co-opt** (koh-**opt**) *vb* to add (someone) to a group by the agreement of the existing members. ▷ **HISTORY** Latin *cooptare* to choose, elect

coordinate *or* **co-ordinate** *vb* **-nating, -nated** **1** to bring together and cause to work together efficiently. ✧ *n* **2** *Maths* any of a set of numbers defining the location of a point with reference to a system of axes. ✧ *adj* **3** of or involving coordination. **4** of or involving the use of coordinates: *coordinate geometry.* ▷ **HISTORY** Latin *co-* together + *ordinatio* arranging ▶ **coordination** *or* **co-ordination** *n* ▶ **coordinator** *or* **co-ordinator** *n*

coordinate clause *n Grammar* one of two or more clauses in a sentence having the same status and joined by a coordinating conjunction such as *and, but,* or *or.*

coordinating conjunction *n Grammar* a conjunction that joins coordinate clauses, such as *and, but,* or *or.*

coot *n* **1** a small black water bird. **2** *Brit, Austral & NZ* a foolish person. ▷ **HISTORY** probably Low German

cop *Slang* ✧ *n* **1** a policeman. **2 not much cop** of little value or worth. ✧ *vb* **copping, copped 3** to take or seize. **4 cop it** to get into trouble or be punished: *he copped it after he was spotted driving a car without a seat belt.* ✧ See also **cop out.** ▷ **HISTORY** perhaps from Old French *caper* to seize

copal *n* a resin used in varnishes.

copartner *n* a partner or associate. ▶ **copartnership** *n*

cope[1] *vb* **coping, coped 1** to deal successfully (with): *well-nourished people cope better with stress.* **2** to tolerate or endure: *the ability to cope with his pain.* ▷ **HISTORY** Old French *coper* to strike, cut

cope[2] *n* a large ceremonial cloak worn by some Christian priests. ▷ **HISTORY** Late Latin *cappa* hooded cloak

cope[3] *vb* **coping, coped** to provide (a wall) with a coping. ▷ **HISTORY** probably from French *couper* to cut

Copernican (kop-**per**-nik-an) *adj* of the theory that the earth and the planets rotate round the sun. ▷ **HISTORY** after *Copernicus,* astronomer

copier *n* a person or machine that copies.

copilot *n* the second pilot of an aircraft.

coping *n* a layer of rounded or sloping bricks on the top of a wall.

coping saw *n* a handsaw with a U-shaped frame, used for cutting curves in wood.

copious (**kope**-ee-uss) *adj* existing or produced in large quantities. ▷ **HISTORY** Latin *copiosus* ▶ **copiously** *adv*

cop out *Slang* ✧ *vb* **1** to avoid taking responsibility or committing oneself. ✧ *n* **cop-out** **2** a way or an instance of avoiding responsibility or commitment. ▷ **HISTORY** probably from COP

copper[1] *n* **1** a soft reddish metallic element, used in such alloys as brass and bronze. Symbol: Cu. **2** *Informal* any copper or bronze coin. **3** *Chiefly Brit* a large metal container used to boil water. ✧ *adj* **4** reddish-brown. ▷ **HISTORY** Latin *Cyprium aes* Cyprian metal, from Greek *Kupris* Cyprus

copper[2] *n Brit slang* a policeman. ▷ **HISTORY** from COP (verb)

copper beech *n* a European beech with reddish leaves.

copper-bottomed *adj* financially reliable. ▷ **HISTORY** from the practice of coating the bottom of ships with copper to prevent the timbers rotting

copperhead *n* a poisonous snake with a reddish-brown head.

copperplate *n* **1** an elegant handwriting style. **2** a polished copper plate engraved for printing. **3** a print taken from such a plate.

copper sulphate *n* a blue crystalline copper salt used in electroplating and in plant sprays.

coppice *n* a small group of trees or bushes growing close together. ▷ **HISTORY** Old French *copeiz*

copra *n* the dried oil-yielding kernel of the coconut. ▷ **HISTORY** Malayalam (a language of SW India) *koppara* coconut

copse *n* same as **coppice.** ▷ **HISTORY** from COPPICE

Copt *n* **1** a member of the Coptic Church, a part of the Christian Church which was founded in Egypt. **2** an Egyptian descended from the ancient Egyptians. ▷ **HISTORY** Coptic *kyptios* Egyptian

Coptic *n* **1** the language of the Copts, descended from Ancient Egyptian and surviving only in the Coptic Church. ✧ *adj* **2** of the Copts or the Coptic Church.

copula *n, pl* **-las** *or* **-lae** a verb, such as *be,* that is used to link the subject with the complement of a sentence, as in *he became king.* ▷ **HISTORY** Latin: bond

copulate *vb* **-lating, -lated** to have sexual intercourse. ▷ **HISTORY** Latin *copulare* to join together ▶ **copulation** *n*

copy *n, pl* **copies 1** a thing made to look exactly like another. **2** a single specimen of a book, magazine, or record of which there are many others exactly the same: *my copy of 'Death on the Nile'.* **3** written material for printing. **4** the text of an advertisement. **5** *Journalism informal* suitable material for an article: *disasters are always good copy.* ✧ *vb* **copies, copying, copied 6** to make a copy (of). **7** to act or try to be like another. ▷ **HISTORY** Latin *copia* abundance

copybook *n* **1** a book of specimens of handwriting for imitation. **2 blot one's copybook** *Informal* to spoil one's reputation by a mistake or indiscretion. ✧ *adj* **3** done exactly according to the rules. **4** trite or unoriginal.

copyright *n* **1** the exclusive legal right to reproduce and control an original literary, musical, or artistic work. ✧ *vb* **2** to take out a copyright on. ✧ *adj* **3** protected by copyright.

copywriter *n* a person employed to write advertising copy.

coquette *n* a woman who flirts. ▷ **HISTORY** French ▶ **coquetry** *n* ▶ **coquettish** *adj*

coracle *n* a small round boat made of wicker covered with skins. ▷ **HISTORY** Welsh *corwgl*

coral *n* **1** the stony substance formed by the skeletons of marine animals called polyps, often forming an island or reef. **2** any of the polyps whose

skeletons form coral. ✧ *adj* **3** orange-pink.
▷ **HISTORY** Greek *korallion*

coral island *n Geog* an island formed from coral and other substances.

coral reef *n Geog* a marine ridge or reef consisting of coral and other organic material consolidated into limestone, lying just beneath the surface of the sea.

cor anglais *n, pl* **cors anglais** *Music* an alto woodwind instrument of the oboe family.
▷ **HISTORY** French: English horn

corbel *n Archit* a stone or timber support sticking out of a wall. ▷ **HISTORY** Old French: a little raven

corbie *n Scot* a raven or crow. ▷ **HISTORY** Latin *corvus*

cord *n* **1** string or thin rope made of twisted strands. **2** *Anat* a structure in the body resembling a rope: *the vocal cords.* **3** a ribbed fabric like corduroy. **4** *US, Canad, Austral & NZ* an electrical flex. **5** a unit for measuring cut wood, equal to 128 cubic feet. ✧ *adj* **6** (of fabric) ribbed. ✧ See also **cords**.
▷ **HISTORY** Greek *khordē*

cordate *adj* heart-shaped.

corded *adj* **1** tied or fastened with cord. **2** (of a fabric) ribbed: *white corded silk.* **3** (of muscles) standing out like cords.

cordial *adj* **1** warm and friendly: *a cordial atmosphere.* **2** heartfelt or sincere: *I developed a cordial dislike for the place.* ✧ *n* **3** a drink with a fruit base: *lime cordial.* ▷ **HISTORY** Latin *cor* heart
▶ **cordially** *adv*

cordiality *n* warmth of feeling.

cordite *n* a smokeless explosive used in guns and bombs. ▷ **HISTORY** from *cord,* because of its stringy appearance

cordless *adj* (of an electrical appliance such as a kettle or telephone) powered by an internal battery or kept in a holder which is connected to the mains, so that there is no cable connecting the appliance itself to the electrical mains.

cordon *n* **1** a chain of police, soldiers, or vehicles guarding an area. **2** an ornamental braid or ribbon. **3** *Horticulture* a fruit tree trained to grow as a single stem bearing fruit. ✧ *vb* **4 cordon off** to put or form a cordon round. ▷ **HISTORY** Old French: a little cord

cordon bleu (**bluh**) *adj* (of cookery or cooks) of the highest standard: *a cordon bleu chef.*
▷ **HISTORY** French: blue ribbon

cords *pl n* trousers made of corduroy.

corduroy *n* a heavy cotton fabric with a velvety ribbed surface. ▷ **HISTORY** origin unknown

core *n* **1** the central part of certain fleshy fruits, containing the seeds. **2** the central or essential part of something: *the historic core of the city.* **3** a piece of magnetic soft iron inside an electromagnet or transformer. **4** *Geol* the central part of the earth. **5** a cylindrical sample of rock or soil, obtained by the use of a hollow drill. **6** *Physics* the region of a nuclear reactor containing the fissionable material. **7** *Computers* the main internal memory of a computer. ✧ *vb* **coring, cored 8** to remove the core from (fruit). ▷ **HISTORY** origin unknown

corella *n* a white Australian cockatoo.

co-respondent *n* a person with whom someone being sued for divorce is claimed to have committed adultery.

corgi *n* a short-legged sturdy dog.
▷ **HISTORY** Welsh *cor* dwarf + *ci* dog

coriander *n* a European plant, cultivated for its aromatic seeds and leaves, used in flavouring foods. ▷ **HISTORY** Greek *koriannon*

Corinthian *adj* **1** of Corinth, a port in S Greece. **2** of a style of classical architecture characterized by a bell-shaped capital with carved leaf-shaped ornaments. ✧ *n* **3** a person from Corinth.

Coriolis effect *n Geog* the horizontal deflection of air, water, or moving objects to the right or to the left depending on whether they are in the northern or the southern hemisphere; caused by the earth's rotation. ▷ **HISTORY** after Gaspard G. *Coriolis* (1792--1843), French civil engineer

Coriolis force *n* a hypothetical force postulated to explain the deflection in the path of a body moving relative to the earth. ▷ **HISTORY** after Gaspard G. *Coriolis* (1792--1843), French civil engineer

cork *n* **1** the thick light porous outer bark of a Mediterranean oak. **2** a piece of cork used as a stopper. **3** *Bot* the outer bark of a woody plant. ✧ *vb* **4** to stop up (a bottle) with a cork.
▷ **HISTORY** probably from Arabic *qurq*

corkage *n* a charge made at a restaurant for serving wine bought elsewhere.

corked *adj* (of wine) spoiled through being stored in a bottle with a decayed cork.

corkscrew *n* **1** a device for pulling corks from bottles, usually consisting of a pointed metal spiral attached to a handle. ✧ *adj* **2** like a corkscrew in shape. ✧ *vb* **3** to move in a spiral or zigzag course.

corm *n* the scaly bulblike underground stem of certain plants. ▷ **HISTORY** Greek *kormos* tree trunk

cormorant *n* a large dark-coloured long-necked sea bird. ▷ **HISTORY** Old French *corp* raven + *mareng* of the sea

corn[1] *n* **1** a cereal plant such as wheat, oats, or barley. **2** the grain of such plants. **3** *US, Canad, Austral & NZ* maize. **4** *Slang* something unoriginal or oversentimental. ▷ **HISTORY** Old English

corn[2] *n* a painful hardening of the skin around a central point in the foot, caused by pressure.
▷ **HISTORY** Latin *cornu* horn

corn circle *n* same as **crop circle**.

corncob *n* the core of an ear of maize, to which the kernels are attached.

corncrake *n* a brown bird with a harsh grating cry.

cornea (**korn**-ee-a) *n* the transparent membrane covering the eyeball. ▷ **HISTORY** Latin *cornu* horn
▶ **corneal** *adj*

corned beef *n* cooked beef preserved in salt.

cornelian *n* same as **carnelian**.

corner *n* **1** the place or angle formed by the meeting of two converging lines or surfaces. **2** the space within the angle formed, as in a room. **3** the place where two streets meet. **4** a sharp bend in a road. **5** a remote place: *far-flung corners of the* *world.* **6** any secluded or private place. **7** *Sports* a free kick or shot taken from the corner of the field. **8 cut corners** to take the shortest or easiest way at the expense of high standards. **9 turn the corner** to pass the critical point of an illness or a difficult time. ✧ *adj* **10** on or in a corner: *a corner seat.* ✧ *vb* **11** to force (a person or animal) into a difficult or inescapable position. **12** (of a vehicle or its driver) to turn a corner. **13** to obtain a monopoly of. ▷ **HISTORY** Latin *cornu* point, horn

cornerstone *n* **1** an indispensable part or basis: *the food we eat is one of the cornerstones of good health.* **2** a stone at the corner of a wall.

cornet *n* **1** a brass instrument of the trumpet family. **2** *Brit* a cone-shaped ice-cream wafer. ▷ **HISTORY** Latin *cornu* horn ▶ **cornetist** *n*

corn exchange *n* a building where corn is bought and sold.

cornflakes *pl n* a breakfast cereal made from toasted maize.

cornflour *n* **1** a fine maize flour, used for thickening sauces. **2** *NZ* fine wheat flour.

cornflower *n* a small plant with blue flowers.

cornice (**korn**-iss) *n* **1** a decorative moulding round the top of a wall or building. **2** *Archit* the projecting mouldings at the top of a column. ▷ **HISTORY** Old French

Cornish *adj* **1** of Cornwall. ✧ *n* **2** a Celtic language of Cornwall, extinct by 1800. ✧ *pl n* **3 the Cornish** the people of Cornwall.

Cornish pasty *n* a pastry case with a filling of meat and vegetables.

cornucopia (korn-yew-**kope**-ee-a) *n* **1** a great abundance: *a cornucopia of rewards.* **2** a symbol of plenty, consisting of a horn overflowing with fruit and flowers. ▷ **HISTORY** Latin *cornu copiae* horn of plenty

corny *adj* **cornier, corniest** *Slang* unoriginal or oversentimental.

corolla *n* the petals of a flower collectively. ▷ **HISTORY** Latin: garland

corollary (kor-**oll**-a-ree) *n, pl* **-laries 1** a proposition that follows directly from another that has been proved. **2** a natural consequence. ▷ **HISTORY** Latin *corollarium* money paid for a garland

corona (kor-**rone**-a) *n, pl* **-nas** *or* **-nae** (-nee) **1** a circle of light around a luminous body, usually the moon. **2** the outermost part of the sun's atmosphere, visible as a faint halo during a total eclipse. **3** a long cigar with blunt ends. **4** *Bot* a crownlike part of some flowers on top of the seed or on the inner side of the corolla. **5** *Physics* an electrical glow appearing around the surface of a charged conductor. ▷ **HISTORY** Latin: crown

coronary (**kor**-ron-a-ree) *adj* **1** *Anat* of the arteries that supply blood to the heart. ✧ *n, pl* **-naries 2** a coronary thrombosis. ▷ **HISTORY** Latin *coronarius* belonging to a wreath or crown

coronary heart disease *n Pathol* any heart disorder caused by disease of the coronary arteries.

coronary thrombosis *n* a condition where the blood flow to the heart is blocked by a clot in a coronary artery.

coronation *n* the ceremony of crowning a monarch. ▷ **HISTORY** Latin *coronare* to crown

coroner *n* a public official responsible for the investigation of violent, sudden, or suspicious deaths. ▷ **HISTORY** Anglo-French *corouner*

coronet *n* **1** a small crown worn by princes or peers. **2** a band of jewels worn as a headdress. ▷ **HISTORY** Old French *coronete*

corpora *pl n* the plural of **corpus**.

corporal[1] *n* a noncommissioned officer in an army. ▷ **HISTORY** Old French *caporal,* from Latin *caput* head

corporal[2] *adj* of the body. ▷ **HISTORY** Latin *corpus* body

corporal punishment *n* physical punishment, such as caning.

corporate *adj* **1** relating to business corporations: *corporate finance.* **2** shared by a group. **3** forming a corporation; incorporated. ▷ **HISTORY** Latin *corpus* body

corporation *n* **1** a large business or company. **2** a city or town council. **3** *Informal* a large paunch. ▶ **corporative** *adj*

corporation tax *n Econ* a British tax on the profits of a company.

corporatism *n* organization of a state on the lines of a business enterprise, with substantial government management of the economy.

corporeal (kore-**pore**-ee-al) *adj* of the physical world rather than the spiritual. ▷ **HISTORY** Latin *corpus* body

corps (**kore**) *n, pl* **corps 1** a military unit with a specific function: *medical corps.* **2** an organized body of people: *the diplomatic corps.* ▷ **HISTORY** French

corpse *n* a dead body, esp. of a human being. ▷ **HISTORY** Latin *corpus*

corpulent *adj* fat or plump. ▷ **HISTORY** Latin *corpulentus* ▶ **corpulence** *n*

corpus *n, pl* **-pora** a collection of writings, such as one by a single author or on a specific topic: *the corpus of Marxist theory.* ▷ **HISTORY** Latin: body

corpuscle *n* a red blood cell (see **erythrocyte**) or white blood cell (see **leucocyte**). ▷ **HISTORY** Latin *corpusculum* a little body ▶ **corpuscular** *adj*

corral *US & Canad* ✧ *n* **1** an enclosure for cattle or horses. ✧ *vb* **-ralling, -ralled 2** to put in a corral. ▷ **HISTORY** Spanish

corrasion *n Geol* erosion of rocks caused by fragments transported over them by water, wind, or ice. ▷ **HISTORY** Latin *corradere* to scrape together

correct *adj* **1** free from error; true: *the correct answer.* **2** in conformity with accepted standards: *in most cultures there is a strong sense of correct sexual conduct.* ✧ *vb* **3** to make free from or put right errors. **4** to indicate the errors in (something). **5** to rebuke or punish in order to improve: *I stand corrected.* **6** to make conform to a standard. ▷ **HISTORY** Latin *corrigere* to make straight ▶ **correctly** *adv* ▶ **correctness** *n*

a b c d e f g h i j k l m n o p q r s t u v w x y z

correction *n* **1** an act or instance of correcting. **2** an alteration correcting something: *corrections to the second proofs.* **3** a reproof or punishment. ▸ **correctional** *adj*

corrective *adj* intended to put right something that is wrong: *corrective action.*

correlate *vb* **-lating, -lated 1** to place or be placed in a mutual relationship: *water consumption is closely correlated to the number of people living in a house.* ✧ *n* **2** either of two things mutually related. ▸ **correlation** *n*

correlative *adj* **1** having a mutual relationship. **2** *Grammar* (of words, usually conjunctions) corresponding to each other and occurring regularly together, for example *neither* and *nor*.

correspond *vb* **1** to be consistent or compatible (with). **2** to be similar (to). **3** to communicate (with) by letter. ▷ **HISTORY** Latin *com-* together + *respondere* to respond ▸ **corresponding** *adj* ▸ **correspondingly** *adv*

correspondence *n* **1** communication by letters. **2** the letters exchanged in this way. **3** relationship or similarity.

correspondence course *n* a course of study conducted by post.

correspondent *n* **1** a person who communicates by letter. **2** a person employed by a newspaper or news service to report on a special subject or from a foreign country.

corresponding angle *n Geom* in a diagram where two straight lines are crossed by a transversal, either of the two angles on the same side of the transversal above each straight line, or the ones below them. The corresponding angles are equal when the two straight lines are parallel.

corridor *n* **1** a passage in a building or a train. **2** a strip of land or airspace that provides access through the territory of a foreign country. **3 corridors of power** the higher levels of government or the Civil Service. ▷ **HISTORY** Old Italian *corridore,* literally: place for running

corrie *n* (in Scotland) a circular hollow on the side of a hill. ▷ **HISTORY** Gaelic *coire* cauldron

corrigendum (kor-rij-**end**-um) *n, pl* **-da** (-da) **1** an error to be corrected. **2** a slip of paper inserted into a book after printing, listing corrections. ▷ **HISTORY** Latin: that which is to be corrected

corroborate *vb* **-rating, -rated** to support (a fact or opinion) by giving proof. ▷ **HISTORY** Latin *com-* (intensive) + *roborare* to make strong ▸ **corroboration** *n* ▸ **corroborative** *adj*

corroborating evidence *n Law* evidence by another witness that supports or confirms the accuracy of evidence already given.

corroboree *n Austral* **1** an Aboriginal gathering or dance of festive or warlike character. **2** *Informal* any noisy gathering. ▷ **HISTORY** Aboriginal

corrode *vb* **-roding, -roded 1** to eat away or be eaten away by chemical action or rusting. **2** to destroy gradually: *rumours corroding the public's affection for the royal family.* ▷ **HISTORY** Latin *corrodere* to gnaw to pieces

corrosion *n* **1** the process by which something, esp. a metal, is corroded. **2** the result of corrosion. ▸ **corrosive** *adj*

corrugate *vb* **-gating, -gated** to fold into alternate grooves and ridges. ▷ **HISTORY** Latin *corrugare* ▸ **corrugation** *n*

corrugated iron *n* a thin sheet of iron or steel, formed with alternating ridges and troughs.

corrupt *adj* **1** open to or involving bribery or other dishonest practices: *corrupt practices.* **2** morally depraved. **3** (of a text or data) made unreliable by errors or alterations. ✧ *vb* **4** to make corrupt. ▷ **HISTORY** Latin *corruptus* spoiled ▸ **corruptive** *adj*

corruptible *adj* capable of being corrupted.

corruption *n* **1** dishonesty and illegal behaviour. **2** the act of corrupting morally or sexually. **3** the process of rotting or decaying. **4** an unintentional or unauthorized alteration in a text or data. **5** an altered form of a word.

corsage (kore-**sahzh**) *n* a small bouquet worn on the bodice of a dress. ▷ **HISTORY** Old French *cors* body

corsair *n* **1** a pirate. **2** a pirate ship. **3** a privateer. ▷ **HISTORY** Old French *corsaire*

corselet *n* **1** a woman's one-piece undergarment, combining corset and bra. **2** a piece of armour to cover the trunk. ▷ **HISTORY** Old French *cors* bodice

corset *n* **1** a close-fitting undergarment worn by women to shape the torso. **2** a similar garment worn by either sex to support and protect the back. ▷ **HISTORY** Old French: a little bodice ▸ **corsetry** *n*

cortege (kore-**tayzh**) *n* a funeral procession. ▷ **HISTORY** Italian *corteggio*

cortex (**kore**-tex) *n, pl* **-tices** (-tiss-seez) *Anat* the outer layer of the brain or some other internal organ. ▷ **HISTORY** Latin: bark, outer layer ▸ **cortical** *adj*

cortisone *n* a steroid hormone used in treating rheumatoid arthritis, allergies, and skin diseases. ▷ **HISTORY** *corticosterone,* a hormone

corundum *n* a hard mineral used as an abrasive, and of which the ruby and white sapphire are precious forms. ▷ **HISTORY** Tamil *kuruntam*

coruscate *vb* **-cating, -cated** *Formal* to emit flashes of light; sparkle. ▷ **HISTORY** Latin *coruscare* to flash ▸ **coruscating** *adj* ▸ **coruscation** *n*

corvette *n* a lightly armed escort warship. ▷ **HISTORY** perhaps from Middle Dutch *corf*

corymb *n Bot* a flat-topped flower cluster with the stems growing progressively shorter towards the centre. ▷ **HISTORY** Greek *korumbos* cluster

cos[1] *or* **cos lettuce** *n* a lettuce with a long slender head and crisp leaves. ▷ **HISTORY** after *Kos,* the Aegean island of its origin

cos[2] cosine.

cosec (**koh**-sek) cosecant.

cosecant (koh-**seek**-ant) *n* (in trigonometry) the ratio of the length of the hypotenuse to that of the opposite side in a right-angled triangle.

cosh *Chiefly Brit* ✧ *n* **1** a heavy blunt weapon, often made of hard rubber. ✧ *vb* **2** to hit on the head with a cosh. ▷ **HISTORY** Romany *kosh*

cosignatory *n, pl* **-ries** a person or country that signs a document jointly with others.

cosine (**koh**-sine) *n* (in trigonometry) the ratio of the length of the adjacent side to that of the hypotenuse in a right-angled triangle. ▷ **HISTORY** see CO-, SINE

cosmetic *n* **1** anything applied to the face or body in order to improve the appearance. ✧ *adj* **2** done or used to improve the appearance of the face or body. **3** improving in appearance only: *glossy brochures are part of a cosmetic exercise.* ▷ **HISTORY** Greek *kosmētikos,* from *kosmein* to arrange

cosmetic surgery *n* surgery performed to improve the appearance, rather than for medical reasons.

cosmic *adj* **1** of or relating to the whole universe: *the cosmic order.* **2** occurring in or coming from outer space: *cosmic dust.*

cosmogony *n, pl* **-nies** the study of the origin of the universe. ▷ **HISTORY** Greek *kosmos* world + *gonos* creation

cosmology *n* the study of the origin and nature of the universe. ▷ **HISTORY** Greek *kosmos* world + -LOGY ▸ **cosmological** *adj* ▸ **cosmologist** *n*

cosmonaut *n* the Russian name for an astronaut. ▷ **HISTORY** Russian *kosmonavt,* from Greek *kosmos* universe + *nautēs* sailor

cosmopolitan *adj* **1** composed of people or elements from many different countries or cultures. **2** having lived and travelled in many countries. ✧ *n* **3** a cosmopolitan person. ▷ **HISTORY** Greek *kosmos* world + *politēs* citizen ▸ **cosmopolitanism** *n*

cosmos *n* the universe considered as an ordered system. ▷ **HISTORY** Greek *kosmos* order

Cossack *n* **1** a member of a S Russian people, famous as horsemen and dancers. ✧ *adj* **2** of the Cossacks: *a Cossack dance.* ▷ **HISTORY** Russian *kazak* vagabond

cosset *vb* **-seting, -seted** to pamper or pet. ▷ **HISTORY** origin unknown

cost *n* **1** the amount of money, time, or energy required to obtain or produce something. **2** suffering or sacrifice: *these were crucial truths which rugby never grasped, to its cost.* **3** the amount paid for a commodity by its seller: *to sell at cost.* **4 costs** *Law* the expenses of a lawsuit. **5 at all costs** regardless of any cost or effort involved. **6 at the cost of** at the expense of losing: *a boat costs about a thousand dollars.* ✧ *vb* **costing, cost 7** to be obtained or obtainable in exchange for: *calls cost 36p a minute cheap rate, 48p at other times.* **8** to involve the loss or sacrifice of: *a fall which almost cost him his life.* **9** to estimate the cost of producing something. ▷ **HISTORY** Latin *constare* to stand at, cost

cost accounting *n* the recording and controlling of all the costs involved in running a business. ▸ **cost accountant** *n*

costal *adj* of the ribs.

cost-effective *adj* providing adequate financial return in relation to outlay.

costermonger *n Brit* a person who sells fruit and vegetables from a barrow in the street. ▷ **HISTORY** *costard* a kind of apple + *monger* trader

costive *adj Old-fashioned* having or causing constipation. ▷ **HISTORY** Old French *costivé*

costly *adj* **-lier, -liest 1** expensive. **2** involving great loss or sacrifice: *a bitter and costly war.* ▸ **costliness** *n*

cost of living *n* the average cost of the basic necessities of life, such as food, housing, and clothing.

costume *n* **1** a style of dressing, including all the clothes and accessories, typical of a particular country or period. **2** the clothes worn by an actor or performer: *a jester's costume.* **3** short for **swimming costume.** ✧ *vb* **-tuming, -tumed 4** to provide with a costume: *she was costumed by many of the great Hollywood designers.* ▷ **HISTORY** Italian: dress, custom ▸ **costumed** *adj*

costume jewellery *n* inexpensive but attractive jewellery.

costumier *n* a make or supplier of theatrical or fancy dress costumes.

cosy *or US* **cozy** *adj* **-sier, -siest** *or US* **-zier, -ziest 1** warm and snug. **2** intimate and friendly: *a cosy chat.* ✧ *n, pl* **-sies** *or US* **-zies 3** a cover for keeping things warm: *a tea cosy.* ▷ **HISTORY** Scots ▸ **cosiness** *or US* ▸ **coziness** *n*

cot[1] *n* **1** a bed with high sides for a baby or very young child. **2** a small portable bed. ▷ **HISTORY** Hindi *khāt* bedstead

cot[2] *n* **1** *Literary or archaic* a small cottage. **2** a cote. ▷ **HISTORY** Old English

cot[3] cotangent.

cotangent *n* (in trigonometry) the ratio of the length of the adjacent side to that of the opposite side in a right-angled triangle.

cot death *n* the unexplained sudden death of a baby while asleep.

cote *or* **cot** *n* a small shelter for birds or animals. ▷ **HISTORY** Old English

coterie (**kote**-er-ee) *n* a small exclusive group of friends or people with common interests. ▷ **HISTORY** French

cotoneaster (kot-tone-ee-**ass**-ter) *n* a garden shrub with red berries.

cottage *n* a small simple house, usually in the country. ▷ **HISTORY** from COT[2] ▸ **cottager** *n*

cottage cheese *n* a mild soft white cheese made from skimmed milk curds.

cottage industry *n* a craft industry in which employees work at home.

cottage pie *n* a dish of minced meat topped with mashed potato.

cottaging *n Brit, Austral & NZ slang* homosexual activity between men in a public lavatory. ▷ **HISTORY** from *cottage* (in the sense: a public lavatory)

cotter[1] *n Machinery* a bolt or wedge that is used to secure parts of machinery. ▷ **HISTORY** Middle English *cotterel*

cotter[2] *n Scot & history* a farm labourer occupying a cottage and land rent-free. ▷ **HISTORY** see COT[2]

cotter pin *n Machinery* a split pin used to hold parts together and fastened by having the ends spread apart after it is inserted.

cotton *n* **1** the soft white downy fibre surrounding the seeds of a plant grown in warm climates, used to make cloth and thread. **2** cloth or thread made from cotton fibres. ▷ **HISTORY** Arabic *qutn* ▶ **cottony** *adj*

cotton wool *n* absorbent fluffy cotton, used for surgical dressings and to apply creams to the skin.

cotyledon (kot-ill-**ee**-don) *n* the first leaf produced by a plant embryo. ▷ **HISTORY** Greek *kotulē* cup

couch *n* **1** a piece of upholstered furniture for seating more than one person. **2** a bed on which patients of a doctor or a psychoanalyst lie during examination or treatment. ✧ *vb* **3** to express in a particular style of language: *a proclamation couched in splendidly archaic phraseology.* **4** *Archaic* (of an animal) to crouch, as when preparing to leap. ▷ **HISTORY** Old French *coucher* to lay down

couchette (koo-**shett**) *n* a bed converted from seats on a train or ship. ▷ **HISTORY** French

couch grass *n* a grassy weed which spreads quickly.

couch potato *n Slang* a lazy person whose only hobby is watching television and videos.

cougar (**koo**-gar) *n* same as **puma**. ▷ **HISTORY** from S American Indian

cough *vb* **1** to expel air abruptly and noisily from the lungs. **2** (of an engine or other machine) to make a sound similar to this. ✧ *n* **3** an act or sound of coughing. **4** an illness which causes frequent coughing. ▷ **HISTORY** Old English *cohhetten*

cough up *vb* **1** *Informal* to give up (money or information). **2** to bring up into the mouth by coughing: *to cough up blood.*

could *vb* used: **1** to make the past tense of **can[1]**. **2** to make the subjunctive mood of **can[1]**, esp. in polite requests or conditional sentences: *could I have a word with you, please?* **3** to indicate the suggestion of a course of action: *we could make a fortune from selling players, but that would not be in the long-term interests of the club.* **4** to indicate a possibility: *it could simply be a spelling mistake.* ▷ **HISTORY** Old English *cūthe*

couldn't could not.

coulomb (**koo**-lom) *n* the SI unit of electric charge. ▷ **HISTORY** after C. A. de *Coulomb,* physicist

coulter (**kole**-ter) *n* a vertical blade on a plough in front of the ploughshare. ▷ **HISTORY** Latin *culter* ploughshare, knife

council *n* **1** a group meeting for discussion or consultation. **2** a legislative or advisory body: *the United Nations Security Council.* **3** *Brit* the local governing authority of a town or county. **4** *Austral* the local governing authority of a district or shire. ✧ *adj* **5** of or provided by a local council: *a council house.* ▷ **HISTORY** Latin *concilium* assembly

> **☑ WORD TIP**
> Avoid confusion with **counsel.**

councillor *or US* **councilor** *n* a member of a council.

> **☑ WORD TIP**
> Avoid confusion with **counsellor.**

council tax *n* (in Britain) a tax based on the relative value of property levied to fund local council services.

counsel *n* **1** advice or guidance. **2** discussion or consultation: *when it was over they took counsel of their consciences.* **3** a barrister or group of barristers who conduct cases in court and advise on legal matters. ✧ *vb* **-selling, -selled** *or US* **-seling, -seled** **4** to give advice or guidance to. **5** to recommend or urge. ▷ **HISTORY** Latin *consilium* deliberating body ▶ **counselling** *or US* ▶ **counseling** *n*

> **☑ WORD TIP**
> Avoid confusion with **council.**

counsellor *or US* **counselor** *n* **1** an adviser. **2** *US* a lawyer who conducts cases in court.

> **☑ WORD TIP**
> Avoid confusion with **councillor.**

count[1] *vb* **1** to say numbers in ascending order up to and including: *count from one to ten.* **2** to add up or check (each thing in a group) in order to find the total: *he counted the money he had left.* **3** to be important: *it's the thought that counts.* **4** to consider: *he can count himself lucky.* **5** to take into account or include: *the time he'd spent in prison on remand counted towards his sentence.* **6 not counting** excluding. **7** *Music* to keep time by counting beats. ✧ *n* **8** the act of counting. **9** the number reached by counting: *a high pollen count.* **10** *Law* one of a number of charges. **11 keep** *or* **lose count** to keep or fail to keep an accurate record of items or events. **12 out for the count** unconscious. ✧ See also **countdown**. ▷ **HISTORY** Latin *computare* to calculate ▶ **countable** *adj*

count[2] *n* a middle-ranking European nobleman. ▷ **HISTORY** Latin *comes* associate

countdown *n* the act of counting backwards to zero to time exactly an operation such as the launching of a rocket.

countenance *n* **1** *Literary* the face or facial expression. ✧ *vb* **-nancing, -nanced** **2** to support or tolerate. ▷ **HISTORY** Latin *continentia* restraint, control

counter[1] *n* **1** a long flat surface in a bank or shop, on which business is transacted. **2** a small flat disc used in board games. **3** a disc or token used as an imitation coin. **4 under the counter** (of the sale of goods) illegal. ▷ **HISTORY** Latin *computare* to compute

counter[2] *n* an apparatus for counting things.

counter[3] *vb* **1** to say or do (something) in retaliation or response. **2** to oppose or act against. **3** to return the attack of (an opponent). ✧ *adv* **4** in an opposite or opposing direction or manner. **5 run counter to** to be in direct contrast with. ✧ *adj* **6** opposing or opposite. ✧ *n* **7** something that is contrary or opposite to something else. **8** an opposing action. **9** a return attack, such as a blow in boxing. ▷ **HISTORY** Latin *contra* against

counter- *prefix* **1** against or opposite: *counterattack*. **2** complementary or corresponding: *counterpart*. ▷ **HISTORY** Latin *contra*

counteract *vb* to act against or neutralize. ▶ **counteraction** *n* ▶ **counteractive** *adj*

counterattack *n* **1** an attack in response to an attack. ✧ *vb* **2** to make a counterattack (against).

counterbalance *n* **1** a weight or influence that balances or neutralizes another. ✧ *vb* **-ancing, -anced 2** to act as a counterbalance to.

counterblast *n* an aggressive response to a verbal attack.

counterclockwise *adv, adj US & Canad* same as **anticlockwise**.

counterespionage *n* activities to counteract enemy espionage.

counterfeit *adj* **1** made in imitation of something genuine with the intent to deceive or defraud: *counterfeit currency*. **2** pretended: *counterfeit friendship*. ✧ *n* **3** an imitation designed to deceive or defraud. ✧ *vb* **4** to make a fraudulent imitation of. **5** to feign: *surprise is an easy emotion to counterfeit*. ▷ **HISTORY** Old French *contrefait*

counterfoil *n Brit* the part of a cheque or receipt kept as a record.

counterintelligence *n* activities designed to frustrate enemy espionage.

countermand *vb* to cancel (a previous order). ▷ **HISTORY** Old French *contremander*

counterpane *n* a bed covering. ▷ **HISTORY** Medieval Latin *culcita puncta* quilted mattress

counterpart *n* **1** a person or thing complementary to or corresponding to another. **2** a duplicate of a legal document.

counterpoint *n* **1** the harmonious combining of two or more parts or melodies. **2** a melody or part combined in this way. ✧ *vb* **3** to set in contrast. ▷ **HISTORY** Old French *contrepoint* an accompaniment set against the notes of a melody

counterpoise *vb* **-poising, -poised** to oppose with something of equal weight or effect: *counterpoising humour and horror*.

counterproductive *adj* having an effect opposite to the one intended.

countersign *vb* **1** to sign (a document already signed by another) as confirmation. ✧ *n* **2** the signature so written.

countersink *vb* **-sinking, -sank, -sunk** to drive (a screw) into a shaped hole so that its head is below the surface.

countertenor *n* **1** an adult male voice with an alto range. **2** a singer with such a voice.

counter urbanization *or* **urbanisation** *n Sociol* the settlement of an increasing proportion of city dwellers in rural areas.

countess *n* **1** a woman holding the rank of count or earl. **2** the wife or widow of a count or earl.

countless *adj* too many to count.

count noun *n* a noun that may be preceded by an indefinite article and can be used in the plural, such as *telephone* or *thing*.

count on *vb* to rely or depend on.

count out *vb* **1** *Informal* to exclude. **2** to declare (a boxer) defeated when he has not risen from the floor within ten seconds.

countrified *adj* having an appearance or manner associated with the countryside rather than a town.

country *n, pl* **-tries 1** an area distinguished by its people, culture, language, or government. **2** the territory of a nation or state. **3** the people of a nation or state. **4** the part of the land that is away from cities or industrial areas. **5** a person's native land. **6** same as **country and western**. **7 across country** not keeping to roads. **8 go to the country** *Brit & NZ* to dissolve Parliament and hold a general election. ▷ **HISTORY** Medieval Latin *contrata (terra)* (land) lying opposite

country and western *or* **country music** *n* popular music based on American White folk music.

countryman *n, pl* **-men 1** a person from one's own country. **2** *Brit, Austral & NZ* a person who lives in the country. ▶ **countrywoman** *fem n*

countryside *n* land away from the cities.

county *n, pl* **-ties 1** (in some countries) a division of a country. ✧ *adj* **2** *Brit informal* upper-class. ▷ **HISTORY** Old French *conté* land belonging to a count

county court *n Law* (in England) a local court exercising limited jurisdiction in civil matters.

coup (**koo**) *n* **1** a brilliant and successful action. **2** a coup d'état. ▷ **HISTORY** French

coup de grâce (**koo** de **grahss**) *n, pl* **coups de grâce** (**koo** de **grahss**) a final or decisive action. ▷ **HISTORY** French

coup d'état (**koo** day-**tah**) *n, pl* **coups d'état** (**kooz** day-**tah**) a sudden violent or illegal overthrow of a government. ▷ **HISTORY** French

coupé (**koo**-pay) *n* a sports car with two doors and a sloping fixed roof. ▷ **HISTORY** French *carrosse coupé* cut-off carriage

couple *n* **1** two people who are married or romantically involved. **2** two partners in a dance or game. **3 a couple of a** a pair of: *a couple of guys*. **b** *Informal* a few: *a couple of weeks*. ✧ *pron* **4 a couple a** two. **b** *Informal* a few: *give him a couple*. ✧ *vb* **-pling, -pled 5** to connect or link: *an ingrained sense of shame, coupled with a fear of ridicule*. **6** *Literary* to have sexual intercourse. ▷ **HISTORY** Latin *copula* a bond

couplet *n* two successive lines of verse, usually rhyming and of the same metre.

coupling *n* a device for connecting things, such as railway carriages.

A B C D E F G H I J K L M N O P Q R S T U V W X Y Z

coupon *n* **1** a piece of paper entitling the holder to a discount or free gift. **2** a detachable slip that can be used as a commercial order form. **3** *Brit* a football pools entry form. ▷ **HISTORY** Old French *colpon* piece cut off

courage *n* **1** the ability to face danger or pain without fear. **2 the courage of one's convictions** the confidence to act according to one's beliefs. ▷ **HISTORY** Latin *cor* heart

courageous *adj* showing courage. ▶ **courageously** *adv*

courgette *n* a type of small vegetable marrow. ▷ **HISTORY** French

courier *n* **1** a person who looks after and guides travellers. **2** a person paid to deliver urgent messages. ▷ **HISTORY** Latin *currere* to run

course *n* **1** a complete series of lessons or lectures: *a training course.* **2** a sequence of medical treatment prescribed for a period of time: *a course of antibiotics.* **3** an onward movement in time or space: *during the course of his career he worked with many leading actors.* **4** a route or direction taken: *the ships were blown off course by a gale.* **5** the path or channel along which a river moves. **6** an area on which a sport is played or a race is held: *a golf course.* **7** any of the successive parts of a meal. **8** a continuous, usually horizontal layer of building material, such as bricks or tiles, at one level in a building. **9** a mode of conduct or action: *the safest course of action was to do nothing.* **10** the natural development of a sequence of events: *allow the fever to run its course.* **11** a period of time: *over the course of the last two years.* **12 as a matter of course** as a natural or normal consequence or event. **13 in the course of** in the process of. **14 in due course** at the natural or appropriate time. **15 of course a** (*adv*) as expected; naturally. **b** (*interj*) certainly; definitely. ✧ *vb* **coursing, coursed 16** (of a liquid) to run swiftly. **17** to hunt with hounds that follow the quarry by sight and not scent. ▷ **HISTORY** Latin *cursus* a running

coursebook *n* a book that is used as part of an educational course.

courser[1] *n* **1** a person who courses hounds. **2** a hound trained for coursing.

courser[2] *n Literary* a swift horse; steed. ▷ **HISTORY** Old French *coursier*

coursework *n* work done by a student and assessed as part of an educational course.

court *n* **1** *Law* **a** a judicial body which hears and makes decisions on legal cases. **b** the room or building in which such a body meets. **2** a marked area used for playing a racket game. **3** an area of ground wholly or partly surrounded by walls or buildings. **4** a name given to some short street, blocks of flats, or large country houses as a part of their address: *Carlton Court.* **5** the residence or retinue of a sovereign. **6** any formal assembly held by a sovereign. **7 go to court** to take legal action. **8 hold court** to preside over a group of admirers. **9 out of court** without a trial or legal case. **10 pay court to** to give flattering attention to. ✧ *vb* **11** to attempt to gain the love of. **12** to pay attention to (someone) in order to gain favour. **13** to try to obtain (something): *he has not courted controversy, but he has certainly attracted it.* **14** to make oneself open or vulnerable to: *courting disaster.* ▷ **HISTORY** Latin *cohors* cohort

courteous *adj* polite and considerate in manner. ▷ **HISTORY** Middle English *corteis* with courtly manners ▶ **courteously** *adv* ▶ **courteousness** *n*

courtesan (kore-tiz-**zan**) *n History* a mistress or high-class prostitute. ▷ **HISTORY** Old French *courtisane*

courtesy *n, pl* **-sies 1** politeness; good manners. **2** a courteous act or remark. **3 by courtesy of** with the consent of. ▷ **HISTORY** Old French *corteis* courteous

courthouse *n* a public building in which courts of law are held.

courtier *n* an attendant at a royal court.

courtly *adj* **-lier, -liest 1** ceremoniously polite. **2** of or suitable for a royal court. ▶ **courtliness** *n*

court martial *n, pl* **court martials** *or* **courts martial 1** the trial of a member of the armed forces charged with breaking military law. ✧ *vb* **court-martial, -tialling, -tialled** *or US* **-tialing, -tialed 2** to try by court martial.

courtship *n* the courting of an intended spouse or mate.

court shoe *n* a low-cut shoe for women, without laces or straps.

courtyard *n* an open area of ground surrounded by walls or buildings.

cousin *n* the child of one's aunt or uncle. Also called: **first cousin** ▷ **HISTORY** Latin *consobrinus*

couture (koo-**toor**) *n* **1** high-fashion designing and dressmaking. ✧ *adj* **2** relating to high fashion design and dressmaking: *couture clothes.* ▷ **HISTORY** French: sewing

couturier *n* a person who designs fashion clothes for women. ▷ **HISTORY** French

covalency *or US* **covalence** *n Chem* **1** the ability to form a bond in which two atoms share a pair of electrons. **2** the number of covalent bonds which a particular atom can make with others. ▶ **covalent** *adj*

covalent bonding *n Chem* the process of forming a bond in which two atoms share a pair of electrons.

cove[1] *n* a small bay or inlet. ▷ **HISTORY** Old English *cofa*

cove[2] *n Old-fashioned, slang* a fellow; chap. ▷ **HISTORY** probably from Romany *kova*

coven (**kuv**-ven) *n* a meeting of witches. ▷ **HISTORY** Latin *convenire* to come together

covenant (**kuv**-ven-ant) *n* **1** *Chiefly Brit* a formal agreement to make an annual payment to charity. **2** *Law* a formal sealed agreement. **3** *Bible* God's promise to the Israelites and their commitment to worship him alone. ✧ *vb* **4** to agree by a legal covenant. ▷ **HISTORY** Latin *convenire* to come together, agree ▶ **covenanter** *n*

Covenanter *n Scot history* a person upholding either of two 17th-century covenants to establish and defend Presbyterianism.

Coventry *n* **send someone to Coventry** to punish someone by refusing to speak to him or her. ▷ HISTORY after *Coventry*, England

cover *vb* **1** to place something over so as to protect or conceal. **2** to put a garment on; clothe. **3** to extend over or lie thickly on the surface of: *the ground was covered with dry leaves.* **4** (sometimes foll. by *up*) to screen or conceal; hide from view. **5** to travel over. **6** to protect (an individual or group) by taking up a position from which fire may be returned if those being protected are fired upon. **7** to keep a gun aimed at. **8 a** to insure against loss or risk. **b** to provide for (loss or risk) by insurance. **9** to include or deal with: *the course covers accounting, economics, statistics, law and computer applications.* **10** to act as reporter or photographer on (a news event) for a newspaper or magazine. **11** (of a sum of money) to be enough to pay for (something). **12** *Music* to record a cover version of. **13** *Sport* to guard or obstruct (an opponent, team-mate, or area). **14 cover for** to deputize for (a person). **15** (foll. by *for* or *up for*) to provide an alibi (for): *can my men count on your friends at City Hall to cover for us?* ✧ *n* **16** anything which covers. **17** a blanket or bedspread. **18** the outside of a book or magazine. **19** a pretext or disguise: *he claimed UN resolutions were being used as a cover for planned American aggression.* **20** an envelope or other postal wrapping: *under plain cover.* **21** an individual table setting. **22** insurance. **23** a cover version. **24 the covers** *Cricket* the area roughly at right angles to the pitch on the off side and about halfway to the boundary. **25 break cover** to come out from a shelter or hiding place. **26 take cover** to make for a place of safety or shelter. **27 under cover** protected or in secret. ▷ HISTORY Latin *cooperire* to cover completely ▸ **covering** *adj, n*

coverage *n Journalism* the amount of reporting given to a subject or event.

cover charge *n* a fixed service charge added to the bill in a restaurant.

cover girl *n* an attractive woman whose picture appears on the cover of a magazine.

covering letter *n* an accompanying letter sent as an explanation.

coverlet *n* same as **bedspread**.

cover note *n Brit & Austral* a temporary certificate from an insurance company giving proof of a current policy.

covert *adj* **1** concealed or secret. ✧ *n* **2** a thicket or woodland providing shelter for game. **3** *Ornithol* any of the small feathers on the wings and tail of a bird that surround the bases of the larger feathers. ▷ HISTORY Old French: covered ▸ **covertly** *adv*

covet *vb* **-eting, -eted** to long to possess (something belonging to another person). ▷ HISTORY Latin *cupiditas* cupidity

covetous *adj* jealously longing to possess something. ▸ **covetously** *adv* ▸ **covetousness** *n*

covey (**kuv**-vee) *n* **1** a small flock of grouse or partridge. **2** a small group of people. ▷ HISTORY Old French *cover* to sit on, hatch

cow[1] *n* **1** the mature female of cattle. **2** the mature female of various other mammals, such as the elephant or whale. **3** *Not in technical use* any domestic species of cattle. **4** *Informal, offensive* a disagreeable woman. ▷ HISTORY Old English *cū*

cow[2] *vb* to frighten or subdue with threats. ▷ HISTORY Old Norse *kūga* to oppress

coward *n* a person who is easily frightened and avoids dangerous or difficult situations. ▷ HISTORY Latin *cauda* tail ▸ **cowardly** *adj*

cowardice *n* lack of courage.

cowbell *n* a bell hung around a cow's neck.

cowboy *n* **1** (in the US and Canada) a ranch worker who herds and tends cattle, usually on horseback. **2** a conventional character of Wild West folklore or films. **3** *Informal* an irresponsible or unscrupulous worker or businessman. ▸ **cowgirl** *fem n*

cow cocky *n Austral & NZ* a one-man dairy farmer.

cower *vb* to cringe or shrink in fear. ▷ HISTORY Middle Low German *kūren* to lie in wait

cowl *n* **1** a loose hood. **2** a monk's hooded robe. **3** a cover fitted to a chimney to increase ventilation and prevent draughts. ▷ HISTORY Latin *cucullus* hood ▸ **cowled** *adj*

cowling *n* a streamlined detachable metal covering around an engine.

cow parsley *n* a hedgerow plant with umbrella-shaped clusters of white flowers.

cowpat *n* a pool of cow dung.

cowpox *n* a contagious disease of cows, the virus of which is used to make smallpox vaccine.

cowrie *n, pl* **-ries** the glossy brightly-marked shell of a marine mollusc. ▷ HISTORY Hindi *kaurī*

cowslip *n* a European wild plant with yellow flowers. ▷ HISTORY Old English *cūslyppe*, from *cū* cow + *slyppe* slime, dung

cox *n* **1** a coxswain. ✧ *vb* **2** to act as coxswain of (a boat).

coxcomb *or* **cockscomb** *n* **1** the comb of a domestic cock. **2** *Informal* a conceited dandy.

coxswain (**kok**-sn) *n* the person who steers a lifeboat or rowing boat. ▷ HISTORY *cock* a ship's boat + SWAIN

coy *adj* **1** affectedly shy and modest. **2** unwilling to give information. ▷ HISTORY Latin *quietus* quiet ▸ **coyly** *adv* ▸ **coyness** *n*

coyote (koy-**ote**-ee) *n, pl* **-otes** *or* **-ote** a small wolf of the deserts and prairies of North America. ▷ HISTORY Mexican Indian *coyotl*

coypu *n, pl* **-pus** *or* **-pu** a beaver-like amphibious rodent, bred for its fur. ▷ HISTORY From a Native American language, *kóypu*

cozen *vb Literary* to cheat or trick. ▷ HISTORY originally a cant term ▸ **cozenage** *n*

Cpl Corporal.

CPU *Computers* central processing unit.

Cr *Chem* chromium.

crab *n* **1** an edible shellfish with five pairs of legs, the first pair modified into pincers. **2** short for **crab louse**. **3 catch a crab** *Rowing* to make a stroke in which the oar misses the water or digs too deeply,

A B C D E F G H I J K L M N O P Q R S T U V W X Y Z

causing the rower to fall backwards. ▷ **HISTORY** Old English *crabba*

crab apple *n* a kind of small sour apple.

crabbed *adj* **1** (of handwriting) cramped and hard to read. **2** bad-tempered. ▷ **HISTORY** probably from *crab,* because of its sideways movement & *crab apple,* because of its sourness

crab louse *n* a parasitic louse living in the pubic area of humans.

crack *vb* **1** to break or split without complete separation of the parts. **2** to break with a sudden sharp sound. **3** to make or cause to make a sudden sharp sound: *the coachman cracked his whip.* **4** (of the voice) to become harsh or change pitch suddenly. **5** *Informal* to fail or break down: *he had cracked under the strain of losing his job.* **6** to yield or cease to resist: *he had cracked under torture.* **7** to hit with a forceful or resounding blow. **8** to break into or force open: *it'll take me longer if I have to crack the safe myself.* **9** to solve or decipher (a code or problem). **10** *Informal* to tell (a joke). **11** to break (a molecule) into smaller molecules or radicals by heat or catalysis as in the distillation of petroleum. **12** to open (a bottle) for drinking. **13 crack it** *Informal* to achieve something. ✧ *n* **14** a sudden sharp noise. **15** a break or fracture without complete separation of the two parts. **16** a narrow opening or fissure. **17** *Informal* a sharp blow. **18 crack of dawn** daybreak. **19** a broken or cracked tone of voice. **20** *Informal* an attempt. **21** *Informal* a gibe or joke. **22** *Slang* a highly addictive form of cocaine. **23 a fair crack of the whip** *Informal* a fair chance or opportunity. ✧ *adj* **24** *Slang* first-class or excellent: *crack troops.* ✧ See also **crack up**. ▷ **HISTORY** Old English *cracian*

cracker *n* **1** a thin crisp unsweetened biscuit. **2** a decorated cardboard tube, pulled apart with a bang, containing a paper hat and a joke or a toy. **3** a small explosive firework. **4** *Slang* an excellent or notable thing or person.

crackers *adj Brit & NZ slang* insane.

cracking *adj* **1 get cracking** *Informal* to start doing something immediately. **2 a cracking pace** *Informal* a high speed. ✧ *adv, adj* **3** *Brit informal* first-class: *five cracking good saves.* ✧ *n* **4** the oil-refining process in which heavy oils are broken down into smaller molecules by heat or catalysis.

crackle *vb* **-ling, -led 1** to make small sharp popping noises. ✧ *n* **2** a crackling sound. ▸ **crackly** *adj*

crackling *n* **1** a series of small sharp popping noises. **2** the crisp browned skin of roast pork.

crackpot *Informal* ✧ *n* **1** an eccentric person. ✧ *adj* **2** eccentric: *crackpot philosophies.*

crack up *vb* **1** *Informal* to have a physical or mental breakdown. **2** to begin to break into pieces: *there are worrying reports of buildings cracking up as the earth dries out and foundations move.* **3 not all it is cracked up to be** *Informal* not as good as people have claimed it to be. ✧ *n* **crackup 4** *Informal* a physical or mental breakdown.

-cracy *n combining form* indicating a type of government or rule: *plutocracy; mobocracy.* See also **-crat**. ▷ **HISTORY** Greek *kratos* power

cradle *n* **1** a baby's bed on rockers. **2** a place where something originates: *the cradle of civilization.* **3** a supporting framework or structure. **4** a platform or trolley in which workmen are suspended on the side of a building or ship. ✧ *vb* **-dling, -dled 5** to hold gently as if in a cradle. ▷ **HISTORY** Old English *cradol*

craft *n* **1** an occupation requiring skill or manual dexterity. **2** skill or ability. **3** cunning or guile. **4** (*pl* **craft**) a boat, ship, aircraft, or spacecraft. ✧ *vb* **5** to make skilfully. ▷ **HISTORY** Old English *cræft* skill, strength

craftsman *or fem* **craftswoman** *n, pl* **-men** *or* **-women 1** a skilled worker. **2** a skilled artist. ▸ **craftsmanship** *n*

crafty *adj* **-tier, -tiest** skilled in deception. ▸ **craftily** *adv* ▸ **craftiness** *n*

crag *n* a steep rugged rock or peak. ▷ **HISTORY** Celtic ▸ **craggy** *adj*

crake *n Zool* a bird of the rail family, such as the corncrake. ▷ **HISTORY** Old Norse *krāka* crow or *krākr* raven

cram *vb* **cramming, crammed 1** to force (more people or things) into (a place) than it can hold. **2** to eat or feed to excess. **3** *Chiefly Brit* to study hard just before an examination. ▷ **HISTORY** Old English *crammian*

crammer *n* a person or school that prepares pupils for an examination.

cramp[1] *n* **1** a sudden painful contraction of a muscle. **2** temporary stiffness of a muscle group from overexertion: *writer's cramp.* **3** severe stomach pain. **4** a clamp for holding masonry or timber together. ✧ *vb* **5** to affect with a cramp. ▷ **HISTORY** Old French *crampe*

cramp[2] *vb* **1** to confine or restrict. **2 cramp someone's style** *Informal* to prevent someone from impressing another person or from behaving naturally: *shyness will cramp their style.* ▷ **HISTORY** Middle Dutch *crampe* hook

cramped *adj* **1** closed in. **2** (of handwriting) small and irregular.

crampon *n* a spiked iron plate strapped to a boot for climbing on ice. ▷ **HISTORY** French

cranberry *n, pl* **-ries** a sour edible red berry. ▷ **HISTORY** Low German *kraanbere* crane berry

crane *n* **1** a machine for lifting and moving heavy objects, usually by suspending them from a movable projecting arm. **2** a large wading bird with a long neck and legs. ✧ *vb* **craning, craned 3** to stretch out (the neck) in order to see something. ▷ **HISTORY** Old English *cran*

crane fly *n* a fly with long legs, slender wings, and a narrow body.

cranesbill *n* a plant with pink or purple flowers.

crane shot *n Films, television* a shot taken from a camera mounted on a crane.

cranial *adj* of or relating to the skull.

craniology *n* the scientific study of the human skull. ▷ **HISTORY** Greek *kranion* skull + -LOGY

cranium *n, pl* **-niums** *or* **-nia** *Anat* **1** the skull. **2** the part of the skull that encloses the brain. ▷ **HISTORY** Greek *kranion*

crank *n* **1** a device for transmitting or converting motion, consisting of an arm projecting at right angles from a shaft. **2** a handle incorporating a crank, used to start an engine or motor. **3** *Informal* an eccentric or odd person. ✧ *vb* **4** to turn with a crank. **5** to start (an engine) with a crank. ▷ HISTORY Old English *cranc*

crankcase *n* the metal case that encloses the crankshaft in an internal-combustion engine.

crankpin *n* a short cylindrical pin in a crankshaft, to which the connecting rod is attached.

crankshaft *n* a shaft with one or more cranks, to which the connecting rods are attached.

cranky *adj* **crankier, crankiest** *Informal* **1** eccentric. **2** bad-tempered. ▶ **crankiness** *n*

cranny *n, pl* **-nies** a narrow opening. ▷ HISTORY Old French *cran*

crap[1] *Slang* ✧ *n* **1** nonsense. **2** junk. **3** *Taboo* faeces. ✧ *vb* **crapping, crapped 4** *Taboo* to defecate. ▷ HISTORY Middle English *crappe* chaff ▶ **crappy** *adj*

crap[2] *n* same as **craps**.

crape *n* same as **crepe**.

craps *n* **1** a gambling game played with two dice. **2 shoot craps** to play this game. ▷ HISTORY probably from *crabs* lowest throw at dice

crash *n* **1** a collision involving a vehicle or vehicles. **2** a sudden descent of an aircraft as a result of which it crashes. **3** a sudden loud noise. **4** a breaking and falling to pieces. **5** the sudden collapse of a business or stock exchange. ✧ *vb* **6** to cause (a vehicle or aircraft) to collide with another vehicle, the ground, or some other object or (of vehicles or aircraft) to be involved in a collision. **7** to make or cause to make a loud smashing noise. **8** to drop with force and break into pieces with a loud noise. **9** to break or smash into pieces with a loud noise. **10** (of a business or stock exchange) to collapse or fail suddenly. **11** to move violently or noisily. **12** (of a computer system or program) to fail suddenly because of a malfunction. **13** *Brit & Austral informal* to gate-crash. ✧ *adj* **14** requiring or using great effort in order to achieve results quickly: *a crash course.* ▷ HISTORY probably Middle English *crasen* to smash + *dasshen* to strike

crash barrier *n* a safety barrier along the centre of a motorway, around a racetrack, or at the side of a dangerous road.

crash dive *n* **1** a sudden steep emergency dive by a submarine. ✧ *vb* **crash-dive, -diving, -dived 2** to perform a crash dive.

crash helmet *n* a helmet worn by motorcyclists to protect the head in case of a crash.

crash-land *vb* (of an aircraft) to land in an emergency, causing damage. ▶ **crash-landing** *n*

crash team *n* a medial team with special equipment who can arrive quickly to treat a patient having a heart attack.

crass *adj* stupid and insensitive: *the enquiry is crass and naive.* ▷ HISTORY Latin *crassus* thick ▶ **crassly** *adv* ▶ **crassness** *n*

-crat *n combining form* indicating a supporter or member of a particular form of government: *autocrat; democrat.* ▷ HISTORY Greek *-kratēs* ▶ **-cratic** *or* **-cratical** *adj combining form*

crate *n* **1** a large container made of wooden slats, used for packing goods. **2** *Slang* an old car or aeroplane. ✧ *vb* **crating, crated 3** to put in a crate. ▷ HISTORY Latin *cratis* wickerwork ▶ **crateful** *n*

crater *n* **1** the bowl-shaped opening in a volcano or a geyser. **2** a cavity made by the impact of a meteorite or an explosion. **3** a roughly circular cavity on the surface of the moon and some planets. ✧ *vb* **4** to make or form craters in (a surface, such as the ground). ▷ HISTORY Greek *kratēr* mixing bowl ▶ **cratered** *adj*

cravat *n* a scarf worn round the neck instead of a tie.

WORD HISTORY

'Cravat' came into English from French *cravate*, but ultimately comes from Serbo-Croat *Hrvat*, meaning 'Croat'. Croat mercenaries in the French army during the Thirty Years War were noted for the linen scarves they wore.

crave *vb* **craving, craved 1** to desire intensely: *a vulnerable, unhappy girl who craved affection.* **2** *Formal* to beg or plead for: *may I crave your lordship's indulgence?* ▷ HISTORY Old English *crafian* ▶ **craving** *n*

craven *adj* **1** cowardly. ✧ *n* **2** a coward. ▷ HISTORY Middle English *cravant*

craw *n* **1** the crop of a bird. **2** the stomach of an animal. **3 stick in one's craw** *Informal* to be difficult for one to agree with or accept. ▷ HISTORY Middle English

crawfish *n, pl* **-fish** *or* **-fishes** same as **crayfish**.

crawl *vb* **1** to move on one's hands and knees. **2** (of insects, worms or snakes) to creep slowly. **3** to move very slowly. **4** to act in a servile manner. **5** to be or feel as if covered with crawling creatures: *the kind of smile that made your hair stand on end and your flesh crawl.* ✧ *n* **6** a slow creeping pace or motion. **7** *Swimming* a stroke in which the feet are kicked like paddles while each arm in turn reaches forward and pulls back through the water. ▷ HISTORY probably from Old Norse *krafla*

crayfish *or esp US* **crawfish** *n, pl* **-fish** *or* **-fishes 1** an edible shellfish like a lobster. **2** an Australian freshwater crustacean. ▷ HISTORY Old French *crevice* crab

crayon *n* **1** a small stick or pencil of coloured wax or clay. ✧ *vb* **2** to draw or colour with a crayon. ▷ HISTORY Latin *creta* chalk

craze *n* **1** a short-lived fashion or enthusiasm. ✧ *vb* **crazing, crazed 2** to make mad. **3** *Ceramics, metallurgy* to develop or cause to develop fine cracks: *you must prevent the drill crazing the glazed surface of the tile.* ▷ HISTORY probably from Old Norse

crazed *adj* **1** wild and uncontrolled in behaviour. **2** (of porcelain) having fine cracks.

crazy *adj* **-zier, -ziest** *Informal* **1** ridiculous. **2 crazy about** extremely fond of: *he was crazy about me.* **3** extremely annoyed or upset. **4** insane. ▶ **crazily** *adv* ▶ **craziness** *n*

crazy paving *n Brit, Austral & NZ* a form of paving on a path, made of irregular slabs of stone.

creak *vb* **1** to make or move with a harsh squeaking sound. ✧ *n* **2** a harsh squeaking sound. ▷ HISTORY imitative ▶ **creaky** *adj* ▶ **creakiness** *n*

cream *n* **1** the fatty part of milk, which rises to the top. **2** a cosmetic or medication that resembles cream in consistency. **3** any of various foods resembling or containing cream. **4** the best part of something. **5 cream sherry** a full-bodied sweet sherry. ✧ *adj* **6** yellowish-white. ✧ *vb* **7** to beat (foodstuffs) to a light creamy consistency. **8** to remove the cream from (milk). **9** to prepare or cook (foodstuffs) with cream or milk. **10 cream off** to take away the best part of. ▷ HISTORY Late Latin *cramum* ▶ **creamy** *adj*

cream cheese *n* a type of very rich soft white cheese.

creamer *n Chiefly Brit* a powdered milk substitute for coffee.

creamery *n, pl* **-eries** a place where dairy products are made or sold.

cream of tartar *n* a purified form of the tartar produced in wine-making, an ingredient in baking powder.

crease *n* **1** a line made by folding or pressing. **2** a wrinkle or furrow, esp. on the face. **3** *Cricket* any of four lines near each wicket marking positions for the bowler or batsman. ✧ *vb* **creasing, creased** **4** to make or become wrinkled or furrowed. ▷ HISTORY Middle English *crēst* ▶ **creasy** *adj*

create *vb* **-ating, -ated** **1** to cause to come into existence. **2** to be the cause of. **3** to appoint to a new rank or position. **4** *Brit slang* to make an angry fuss. ▷ HISTORY Latin *creare*

creation *n* **1** a creating or being created. **2** something brought into existence or created.

Creation *n Christianity* **1** God's act of bringing the universe into being. **2** the universe as thus brought into being by God.

creative *adj* **1** having the ability to create. **2** imaginative or inventive. ✧ *n* **3** a creative person, esp. one who devises advertising campaigns. ▶ **creativity** *n*

creator *n* a person who creates.

Creator *n* **the Creator** God.

creature *n* **1** an animal, bird, or fish. **2** a person. **3** a person or thing controlled by another.

crèche *n* **1** a day nursery for very young children. **2** a supervised play area provided for young children for short periods. ▷ HISTORY French

credence (**kreed**-enss) *n* belief in the truth or accuracy of a statement: *the question is, how much credence to give to their accounts?* ▷ HISTORY Latin *credere* to believe

credentials *pl n* **1** something that entitles a person to credit or confidence. **2** a document giving evidence of the bearer's identity or qualifications.

credible *adj* **1** capable of being believed; convincing: *there is no credible evidence.* **2** trustworthy or reliable: *the latest claim is the only one to involve a credible witness.* ▷ HISTORY Latin *credere* to believe ▶ **credibility** *n*

credit *n* **1 a** the system of allowing customers to receive goods or services before payment. **b** the time allowed for paying for such goods or services. **2** reputation for trustworthiness in paying debts. **3 a** the positive balance in a person's bank account. **b** the sum of money that a bank makes available to a client in excess of any deposit. **4** a sum of money or equivalent purchasing power, available for a person's use. **5** *Accounting* **a** acknowledgment of a sum of money by entry on the right-hand side of an account. **b** an entry or total of entries on this side. **6** praise or approval, as for an achievement or quality: *you must give him credit for his perseverance.* **7** a person or thing who is a source of praise or approval: *he is a credit to his family.* **8** influence or reputation based on the good opinion of others: *he acquired credit within the community.* **9** belief or confidence in someone or something: *this theory is now gaining credit among the scientific community.* **10** *Education* **a** distinction awarded to an examination candidate obtaining good marks. **b** certification that a section of an examination syllabus has been satisfactorily completed. **11 on credit** with payment to be made at a future date. ✧ *vb* **-iting, -ited** **12** *Accounting* **a** to enter (an item) as a credit in an account. **b** to acknowledge (a payer) by making such an entry. **13 credit with** to attribute to: *credit us with some intelligence.* **14** to believe. ✧ See also **credits**. ▷ HISTORY Latin *credere* to believe

creditable *adj* deserving praise or honour. ▶ **creditably** *adv*

credit account *n Brit* a credit system in which shops allow customers to obtain goods and services before payment.

credit card *n* a card issued by banks or shops, allowing the holder to buy on credit.

creditor *n* a person or company to whom money is owed.

credit rating *n* an evaluation of the ability of a person or business to repay money lent.

credits *pl n* a list of people responsible for the production of a film, programme, or record.

creditworthy *adj* (of a person or a business) regarded as deserving credit on the basis of earning power and previous record of debt repayment. ▶ **creditworthiness** *n*

credo *n, pl* **-dos** a creed.

credulity *n* willingness to believe something on little evidence.

credulous *adj* **1** too willing to believe: *he has convinced only a few credulous American intellectuals.* **2** arising from or showing credulity: *credulous optimism.* ▷ HISTORY Latin *credere* to believe

creed *n* **1** a system of beliefs or principles. **2** a formal statement of the essential parts of Christian belief. ▷ HISTORY Latin *credo* I believe

creek *n* **1** a narrow inlet or bay. **2** *US, Canad, Austral & NZ* a small stream or tributary. **3 up the creek** *Slang* in a difficult position. ▷ HISTORY Old Norse *kriki* nook

creel *n* a wickerwork basket used by fishermen. ▷ **HISTORY** Scots

creep *vb* **creeping, crept 1** to move quietly and cautiously. **2** to crawl with the body near to or touching the ground. **3** to have the sensation of something crawling over the skin, from fear or disgust: *she makes my flesh creep.* **4** (of plants) to grow along the ground or over rocks. ✧ *n* **5** a creeping movement. **6** *Slang* an obnoxious or servile person. ▷ **HISTORY** Old English *crēopan*

creeper *n* **1** a plant, such as ivy, that grows by creeping. **2** *US & Canad* same as **tree creeper**.

creeps *pl n* **give someone the creeps** *Informal* to give someone a feeling of fear or disgust.

creepy *adj* **creepier, creepiest** *Informal* causing a feeling of fear or disgust. ▶ **creepiness** *n*

creepy-crawly *n, pl* **-crawlies** *Brit informal* a small crawling creature.

cremate *vb* **-mating, -mated** to burn (a corpse) to ash. ▷ **HISTORY** Latin *cremare* ▶ **cremation** *n*

crematorium *n, pl* **-riums** *or* **-ria** a building where corpses are cremated.

crème de menthe *n* a liqueur flavoured with peppermint. ▷ **HISTORY** French

crenellated *or US* **crenelated** *adj* having battlements. ▷ **HISTORY** Late Latin *crena* a notch ▶ **crenellation** *or US* ▶ **crenelation** *n*

creole *n* **1** a language developed from a mixture of different languages which has become the main language of a place. ✧ *adj* **2** of or relating to a creole. ▷ **HISTORY** Spanish

Creole *n* **1** (in the West Indies and Latin America) a native-born person of mixed European and African descent. **2** (in the Gulf States of the US) a native-born person of French descent. **3** the French creole spoken in the Gulf States. ✧ *adj* **4** of or relating to any of these peoples: *Creole cooking.*

creosote *n* **1** a thick dark liquid made from coal tar and used for preserving wood. **2** a colourless liquid made from wood tar and used as an antiseptic. ✧ *vb* **-soting, -soted 3** to treat with creosote. ▷ **HISTORY** Greek *kreas* flesh + *sōtēr* preserver

crepe (**krayp**) *n* **1** a thin light fabric with a crinkled texture. **2** a very thin pancake, often folded around a filling. **3** a type of rubber with a wrinkled surface, used for the soles of shoes. ▷ **HISTORY** French

crepe paper *n* paper with a crinkled texture, used for decorations.

crept *vb* the past of **creep**.

crepuscular *adj* **1** of or like twilight. **2** (of animals) active at twilight. ▷ **HISTORY** Latin *crepusculum* dusk

Cres. Crescent.

crescendo (krish-**end**-oh) *n, pl* **-dos 1** a gradual increase in loudness. **2** a musical passage that gradually gets louder. ✧ *adv* **3** gradually getting louder. ▷ **HISTORY** Italian

crescent *n* **1** the curved shape of the moon when in its first or last quarter. **2** *Chiefly Brit & NZ* a crescent-shaped street. ✧ *adj* **3** crescent-shaped. ▷ **HISTORY** Latin *crescere* to grow

cress *n* a plant with strong-tasting leaves, used in salads and as a garnish. ▷ **HISTORY** Old English *cressa*

crest *n* **1** the top of a mountain, hill, or wave. **2** a tuft or growth of feathers or skin on the top of a bird's or animal's head. **3** a heraldic design or figure used on a coat of arms and elsewhere. **4** an ornamental plume or emblem on top of a helmet. ✧ *vb* **5** to come or rise to a high point. **6** to lie at the top of. **7** to reach the top of (a hill or wave). ▷ **HISTORY** Latin *crista* ▶ **crested** *adj*

crestfallen *adj* disappointed or disheartened.

Cretaceous *adj Geol* of the period of geological time about 135 million years ago, at the end of which the dinosaurs died out. ▷ **HISTORY** Latin *creta* chalk

cretin *n* **1** *Informal* a very stupid person. **2** *No longer in technical use* a person who is mentally handicapped and physically deformed because of a thyroid deficiency. ▷ **HISTORY** French from Latin *Christianus* Christian, alluding to the humanity of such people despite their handicaps ▶ **cretinism** *n* ▶ **cretinous** *adj*

cretonne *n* a heavy printed cotton or linen fabric, used in furnishings. ▷ **HISTORY** French

crevasse *n* a deep open crack in a glacier. ▷ **HISTORY** French

crevice *n* a narrow crack or gap in rock. ▷ **HISTORY** Latin *crepare* to crack

crew[1] *n* **1** the people who man a ship or aircraft. **2** a group of people working together: *a film crew.* **3** *Informal* any group of people. ✧ *vb* **4** to serve as a crew member on a ship or boat. ▷ **HISTORY** Middle English *crùe* reinforcement, from Latin *crescere* to increase

crew[2] *vb Archaic* a past of **crow**[2].

crew cut *n* a closely cut haircut for men.

crewel *n* a loosely twisted worsted yarn, used in embroidery. ▷ **HISTORY** origin unknown ▶ **crewelwork** *n*

crib *n* **1** a piece of writing stolen from elsewhere. **2** a translation or list of answers used by students, often dishonestly. **3** a baby's cradle. **4** a rack or manger for fodder. **5** a model of the manger scene at Bethlehem. **6** short for **cribbage**. **7** *NZ* a small holiday house. ✧ *vb* **cribbing, cribbed 8** to copy (someone's work) dishonestly. **9** to confine in a small space. ▷ **HISTORY** Old English *cribb*

cribbage *n* a card game for two to four players, who each try to win a set number of points before the others. ▷ **HISTORY** origin unknown

crib-wall *n NZ* a retaining wall built against an earth bank.

crick *Informal* ✧ *n* **1** a painful muscle spasm or cramp in the neck or back. ✧ *vb* **2** to cause a crick in. ▷ **HISTORY** origin unknown

cricket[1] *n* **1** a game played by two teams of eleven players using a ball, bats, and wickets. **2 not cricket** *Informal* not fair play. ▷ **HISTORY** Old French *criquet* wicket ▶ **cricketer** *n*

cricket[2] *n* a jumping insect like a grasshopper, which produces a chirping sound by rubbing together its forewings. ▷ **HISTORY** Old French *criquer* to creak, imitative

cried *vb* the past of **cry**.

crier *n* an official who makes public announcements.

crime *n* **1** an act prohibited and punished by law. **2** unlawful acts collectively. **3** *Informal* a disgraceful act: *to be a woman writing music is neither a crime against nature nor a freakish rarity.* ▷ **HISTORY** Latin *crimen*

criminal *n* **1** a person guilty of a crime. ✧ *adj* **2** of or relating to crime or its punishment. **3** *Informal* senseless or disgraceful. ▶ **criminally** *adv* ▶ **criminality** *n*

criminalize *or* **-ise** *vb* **-izing, -ized** *or* **-ising, -ised 1** to make (an action or activity) criminal. **2** to treat (a person) as a criminal.

criminal law *n Law* the body of law dealing with criminal offences and offenders. Compare **civil law**.

criminology *n* the scientific study of crime. ▷ **HISTORY** Latin *crimen* crime + -LOGY ▶ **criminologist** *n*

crimp *vb* **1** to fold or press into ridges. **2** to curl (hair) tightly with curling tongs. **3** *Chiefly US informal* to restrict or hinder: *a slowdown in the US economy could crimp some big Swedish concerns' profits.* ✧ *n* **4** the act or result of crimping. ▷ **HISTORY** Old English *crympan*

crimson *adj* deep purplish-red. ▷ **HISTORY** Arabic *qirmizi* kermes (dried bodies of insects used to make a red dye)

cringe *vb* **cringing, cringed 1** to shrink or flinch in fear: *he cringed and shrank against the wall.* **2** to behave in a submissive or timid way: *women who cringe before abusive husbands.* **3** *Informal* to be very embarrassed: *I cringe every time I see that old photo of me.* ✧ *n* **4** the act of cringing.

> **WORD HISTORY**
> To 'cringe' comes from Old English *cringan* meaning 'to yield in battle'.

crinkle *vb* **-kling, -kled 1** to become slightly creased or folded. ✧ *n* **2** a crease or fold. ▷ **HISTORY** Old English *crincan* to bend ▶ **crinkly** *adj*

crinoline *n* a petticoat stiffened with hoops to make the skirt stand out. ▷ **HISTORY** Latin *crinis* hair + *lino* flax

cripple *n* **1** a person who is lame or disabled. **2** a person with a mental or social problem: *an emotional cripple.* ✧ *vb* **-pling, -pled 3** to make a cripple of. **4** to damage (something). ▷ **HISTORY** Old English *crypel* ▶ **crippled** *adj* ▶ **crippling** *adj*

crisis *n, pl* **-ses 1** a crucial stage or turning point in the course of anything. **2** a time of extreme trouble or danger. ▷ **HISTORY** Greek *krisis* decision

crisp *adj* **1** fresh and firm: *a crisp green salad.* **2** dry and brittle: *bake until crisp and golden brown.* **3** clean and neat: *crisp white cotton.* **4** (of weather) cold but invigorating: *a crisp autumn day.* **5** clear and sharp: *the telescope is designed to provide the first crisp images of distant galaxies.* **6** lively or brisk: *the service is crisp and efficient.* ✧ *n* **7** *Brit* a very thin slice of potato fried till crunchy. ✧ *vb* **8** to make or become crisp. ▷ **HISTORY** Latin *crispus* curled ▶ **crisply** *adv* ▶ **crispness** *n*

crispbread *n* a thin dry biscuit made of wheat or rye.

crispy *adj* **crispier, crispiest** hard and crunchy. ▶ **crispiness** *n*

crisscross *vb* **1** to move in or mark with a crosswise pattern. ✧ *adj* **2** (of lines) crossing one another in different directions.

criterion *n, pl* **-ria** *or* **-rions** a standard by which something can be judged or decided. ▷ **HISTORY** Greek *kritērion*

> **WORD TIP**
> *Criteria,* the plural of *criterion,* is not acceptable as a singular noun: *this criterion is not valid; these criteria are not valid.*

critic *n* **1** a professional judge of art, music, or literature. **2** a person who finds fault and criticizes. ▷ **HISTORY** Greek *kritēs* judge

critical *adj* **1** very important or dangerous: *this was a critical moment in her career.* **2** so seriously ill or injured as to be in danger of dying: *he is in a critical condition in hospital.* **3** fault-finding or disparaging: *the article is highly critical of the government.* **4** examining and judging analytically and without bias: *he submitted the plans to critical examination.* **5** of a critic or criticism. **6** *Physics* denoting a constant value at which the properties of a system undergo an abrupt change: *the critical temperature above which the material loses its superconductivity.* **7** (of a nuclear power station or reactor) having reached a state in which a nuclear chain reaction becomes self-sustaining. ▶ **critically** *adv*

critical angle *n Physics* the smallest possible angle of incidence for which light rays are totally reflected at an interface between substances of different refractive index.

criticism *n* **1** fault-finding or censure. **2** an analysis of a work of art or literature. **3** the occupation of a critic. **4** a work that sets out to analyse.

criticize *or* **-cise** *vb* **-cizing, -cized** *or* **-cising, -cised 1** to find fault with. **2** to analyse (something).

critique *n* **1** a critical essay or commentary. **2** the act or art of criticizing. ▷ **HISTORY** French

croak *vb* **1** (of a frog or crow) to make a low hoarse cry. **2** to utter or speak with a croak. **3** *Slang* to die. ✧ *n* **4** a low hoarse sound. ▷ **HISTORY** Old English *crācettan* ▶ **croaky** *adj*

Croatian (kroh-**ay**-shun) *adj* **1** of Croatia. ✧ *n* **2** a person from Croatia. **3** the dialect of Serbo-Croat spoken in Croatia.

crochet (**kroh**-shay) *vb* **-cheting, -cheted 1** to make (a piece of needlework) by looping and intertwining thread with a hooked needle. ✧ *n* **2** work made by crocheting. ▷ **HISTORY** French: small hook

crock[1] *n* an earthenware pot or jar. ▷ **HISTORY** Old English *crocc* pot

crock² *n* **old crock** *Brit, Austral & NZ slang* a person or thing that is old or broken-down. ▷ **HISTORY** Scots

crockery *n* china dishes or earthenware vessels collectively.

crocodile *n* **1** a large amphibious tropical reptile. **2** *Brit, Austral & NZ informal* a line of people, esp. schoolchildren, walking two by two. ▷ **HISTORY** Greek *krokodeilos* lizard

crocodile tears *pl n* an insincere show of grief. ▷ **HISTORY** from the belief that crocodiles wept over their prey to lure further victims

crocus *n, pl* **-cuses** a plant with white, yellow, or purple flowers in spring. ▷ **HISTORY** Greek *krokos* saffron

croft *n* a small farm worked by one family in Scotland. ▷ **HISTORY** Old English ▶ **crofter** *n* ▶ **crofting** *adj, n*

croissant (**krwah**-son) *n* a flaky crescent-shaped bread roll. ▷ **HISTORY** French

cromlech *n Brit* **1** a circle of prehistoric standing stones. **2** *No longer in technical use* a dolmen. ▷ **HISTORY** Welsh

crone *n* a witchlike old woman. ▷ **HISTORY** Old French *carogne* carrion

crony *n, pl* **-nies** a close friend. ▷ **HISTORY** Greek *khronios* long-lasting

crook *n* **1** *Informal* a dishonest person. **2** a bent or curved place or thing: *she held the puppy in the crook of her arm.* **3** a bishop's or shepherd's staff with a hooked end. **4** *Austral & NZ, informal* **a** ill. **b** of poor quality. **c** unpleasant; bad. **5 go** (**off**) **crook** *Austral & NZ, informal* to lose one's temper. **6 go crook at *or* on** *Austral & NZ, informal* to rebuke or upbraid. ✧ *vb* **7** to bend or curve. ✧ *adj* **8** *Austral & NZ slang* unwell or injured. **9 go crook** *Austral & NZ slang* to become angry. ▷ **HISTORY** Old Norse *krokr* hook

crooked *adj* **1** bent or twisted. **2** set at an angle. **3** *Informal* dishonest or illegal. ▶ **crookedly** *adv* ▶ **crookedness** *n*

croon *vb* to sing, hum, or speak in a soft low tone. ▷ **HISTORY** Middle Dutch *crōnen* to groan ▶ **crooner** *n*

crop *n* **1** a cultivated plant, such as a cereal, vegetable, or fruit plant. **2** the season's total yield of farm produce. **3** any group of things appearing at one time: *a remarkable crop of new Scottish plays.* **4** the handle of a whip. **5** a pouchlike part of the gullet of a bird, in which food is stored or prepared for digestion. **6** a short cropped hairstyle. ✧ *vb* **cropping, cropped 7** to cut (something) very short. **8** to produce or harvest as a crop. **9** (of animals) to feed on (grass). **10** to clip part of (the ear or ears) of (an animal), esp. for identification. ✧ See also **crop up**. ▷ **HISTORY** Old English *cropp*

crop circle *n* a pattern made up of ring shapes formed by the unexplained flattening of cereals growing in a field.

crop-dusting *n Agriculture* the spreading of fungicides, pesticides, etc., on crops in the form of dust, often from an aircraft.

cropper *n* **come a cropper** *Informal* **a** to fail completely. **b** to fall heavily.

crop rotation *n Agriculture* the system of growing a sequence of different crops on the same ground so as to maintain or increase its fertility.

crop-top *n* a short T-shirt or vest that reveals the wearer's midriff.

crop up *vb Informal* to occur or appear unexpectedly.

croquet (**kroh**-kay) *n* a game played on a lawn in which balls are hit through hoops. ▷ **HISTORY** French

croquette (kroh-**kett**) *n* a fried cake of mashed potato, meat, or fish. ▷ **HISTORY** French

crosier *n* same as **crozier**.

cross *vb* **1** to move or go across (something): *she crossed the street to the gallery.* **2** to meet and pass: *further south, the way is crossed by Brewer Street.* **3** *Brit & NZ* to draw two parallel lines across (a cheque) and so make it payable only into a bank account. **4** to mark with a cross or crosses. **5** to cancel or delete with a cross or with lines: *she crossed out the first three words.* **6** to place across or crosswise: *he sat down and crossed his legs.* **7** to make the sign of the cross upon as a blessing. **8** to annoy or anger someone by challenging or opposing their wishes and plans. **9** to interbreed or cross-fertilize. **10** *Football* to pass (the ball) from a wing to the middle of the field. **11** (of each of two letters in the post) to be sent before the other is received. **12** (of telephone lines) to interfere with each other so that several callers are connected together at one time. **13 cross one's fingers** to fold one finger across another in the hope of bringing good luck. **14 cross one's heart** to promise by making the sign of a cross over one's heart. **15 cross one's mind** to occur to one briefly or suddenly. ✧ *n* **16** a structure, symbol, or mark consisting of two intersecting lines. **17** an upright post with a bar across it, used in ancient times as a means of execution. **18** a representation of the Cross on which Jesus Christ was executed as an emblem of Christianity. **19** a symbol (×) used as a signature or error mark. **20 the sign of the cross** a sign made with the hand by some Christians to represent the Cross. **21** a medal or monument in the shape of a cross. **22** the place in a town or village where a cross has been set up. **23** *Biol* **a** the process of crossing; hybridization. **b** a hybrid. **24** a mixture of two things. **25** a hindrance or misfortune: *we've all got our own cross to bear.* **26** *Football* a pass of the ball from a wing to the middle of the field. ✧ *adj* **27** angry. **28** lying or placed across: *a cross beam.* ▷ **HISTORY** Latin *crux* ▶ **crossly** *adv* ▶ **crossness** *n*

Cross *n* **the Cross a** the cross on which Jesus Christ was crucified. **b** Christianity.

cross- *combining form* **1** indicating action from one individual or group to another: *cross-cultural; cross-refer.* **2** indicating movement or position across something: *crosscurrent; crosstalk.* **3** indicating a crosslike figure or intersection: *crossbones.*

crossbar *n* **1** a horizontal beam across a pair of goalposts. **2** the horizontal bar on a man's bicycle.
cross-bench *n Brit* a seat in Parliament for a member belonging to neither the government nor the opposition. ▶ **cross-bencher** *n*
crossbill *n* a finch that has a bill with crossed tips.
crossbow *n* a weapon consisting of a bow fixed across a wooden stock, which releases an arrow when the trigger is pulled.
crossbreed *vb* **-breeding, -bred 1** to produce (a hybrid animal or plant) by crossing two different species. ✧ *n* **2** a hybrid animal or plant.
cross-country *adj, adv* **1** by way of open country or fields. ✧ *n* **2** a long race held over open ground.
crosscut *vb* **-cutting, -cut 1** to cut across. ✧ *adj* **2** cut across. ✧ *n* **3** a transverse cut or course.
cross-examine *vb* **-examining, -examined 1** *Law* to question (a witness for the opposing side) in order to check his or her testimony. **2** to question closely or relentlessly. ▶ **cross-examination** *n* ▶ **cross-examiner** *n*
cross-eyed *adj* with one or both eyes turning inwards towards the nose.
cross-fertilize *or* **-lise** *vb* **-lizing, -lized** *or* **-lising, -lised** to fertilize (an animal or plant) by fusion of male and female reproductive cells from different individuals of the same species. ▶ **cross-fertilization** *or* **-lisation** *n*
crossfire *n* **1** *Mil* gunfire crossing another line of fire. **2** a lively exchange of ideas or opinions.
crosshatch *vb Drawing* to shade with two or more sets of parallel lines that cross one another.
crossing *n* **1** a place where a street, railway, or river may be crossed. **2** the place where one thing crosses another. **3** a journey across water.
cross-ply *adj* (of a tyre) having the fabric cords in the outer casing running diagonally to stiffen the sidewalls.
cross-pollination *n Bot* the transfer of pollen from the anthers of one flower to the stigma of another flower, e.g. by wind or insects.
cross-purposes *pl n* **at cross-purposes** misunderstanding each other in a discussion.
cross-reference *n* **1** a reference within a text to another part of the text. ✧ *vb* **-referencing, -referenced 2** to cross-refer.
crossroad *n US & Canad* **1** a road that crosses another road. **2** a road that connects one main road to another.
crossroads *n* **1** the point at which roads cross one another. **2 at the crossroads** at the point at which an important choice has to be made.
cross section *n* **1** *Maths* a surface formed by cutting across a solid, usually at right angles to its longest axis. **2** a diagram showing what would be visible if something were split vertically and the cut section exposed to view. **3** a random sample regarded as representative: *a cross section of society.* ▶ **cross-sectional** *adj*
crosstalk *n* **1** *Brit* rapid or witty talk. **2** unwanted signals transferred between communication channels.
crosswise *or* **crossways** *adj, adv* **1** across: *slice the celery crosswise.* **2** in the shape of a cross.
crossword puzzle *or* **crossword** *n* a puzzle in which vertically and horizontally crossing words suggested by clues are written into a grid of squares.
crotch *n* **1** the forked part of the human body between the legs. **2** the corresponding part of a pair of trousers or pants. **3** any forked part formed by the joining of two things: *the crotch of the tree.* ▷ **HISTORY** probably variant of CRUTCH ▶ **crotched** *adj*
crotchet *n Music* a note having the time value of a quarter of a semibreve. ▷ **HISTORY** Old French *crochet* little hook
crotchety *adj Informal* bad-tempered.
crouch *vb* **1** to bend low with the legs and body pulled close together. ✧ *n* **2** this position. ▷ **HISTORY** Old French *crochir* to become bent like a hook
croup[1] (**kroop**) *n* a throat disease of children, with a hoarse cough and laboured breathing. ▷ **HISTORY** Middle English: to cry hoarsely, probably imitative
croup[2] (**kroop**) *n* the hindquarters of a horse. ▷ **HISTORY** Old French *croupe*
croupier (**kroop**-ee-ay) *n* a person who collects bets and pays out winnings at a gambling table. ▷ **HISTORY** French
crouton *n* a small piece of fried or toasted bread served in soup. ▷ **HISTORY** French
crow[1] *n* **1** a large black bird with a harsh call. **2 as the crow flies** in a straight line. ▷ **HISTORY** Old English *crāwa*
crow[2] *vb* **1** (*past* **crowed** *or* **crew**) (of a cock) to utter a shrill squawking sound. **2** to boast about one's superiority. **3** (of a baby) to utter cries of pleasure. ✧ *n* **4** a crowing sound. ▷ **HISTORY** Old English *crāwan*
crowbar *n* a heavy iron bar used as a lever.
crowd *n* **1** a large number of things or people gathered together. **2** a particular group of people: *we got to know a French crowd from Lyons.* **3 the crowd** the masses. ✧ *vb* **4** to gather together in large numbers. **5** to press together into a confined space. **6** to fill or occupy fully. **7** *Informal* to make (someone) uncomfortable by coming too close. ▷ **HISTORY** Old English *crūdan* ▶ **crowded** *adj*
crown *n* **1** a monarch's ornamental headdress, usually made of gold and jewels. **2** a wreath for the head, given as an honour. **3** the highest or central point of something arched or curved: *the crown of the head.* **4 a** the enamel-covered part of a tooth projecting beyond the gum. **b** a substitute crown, usually of gold or porcelain, fitted over a decayed or broken tooth. **5** a former British coin worth 25 pence. **6** the outstanding quality or achievement: *the last piece is the crown of the evening.* ✧ *vb* **7** to put a crown on the head of (someone) to proclaim him or her monarch. **8** to put on the top of. **9** to reward. **10** to form the topmost part of. **11** to put the finishing touch to (a series of events): *he crowned a superb display with three goals.* **12** to attach a crown to (a tooth). **13** *Brit, Austral & NZ*

slang to hit over the head. **14** *Draughts* to promote (a draught) to a king by placing another draught on top of it. ▷ **HISTORY** Greek *korōnē*

Crown *n* **the Crown** the power or institution of the monarchy.

crown colony *n* a British colony controlled by the Crown.

crown court *n* a local criminal court in England and Wales.

crown jewels *pl n* the jewellery used by a sovereign on ceremonial occasions.

crown land *n Law* **1** (in the United Kingdom) land belonging to the Crown. **2** (in some dominions of the Commonwealth) public land.

crown-of-thorns *n* a starfish with a spiny outer covering that feeds on living coral.

crown prince *n* the male heir to a sovereign throne. ▶ **crown princess** *n*

crow's feet *pl n* wrinkles at the outer corners of the eye.

crow's nest *n* a lookout platform fixed at the top of a ship's mast.

crozier *or* **crosier** *n* a hooked staff carried by bishops as a symbol of office. ▷ **HISTORY** Old French *crossier* staff-bearer

crucial *adj* **1** of exceptional importance. **2** *Brit slang* very good. ▷ **HISTORY** Latin *crux* cross ▶ **crucially** *adv*

crucible *n* a pot in which metals or other substances are melted. ▷ **HISTORY** Medieval Latin *crucibulum* night lamp

crucifix *n* a model cross with a figure of Christ upon it. ▷ **HISTORY** Church Latin *crucifixus* the crucified Christ

crucifixion *n* a method of execution by fastening to a cross, normally by the hands and feet.

Crucifixion *n* **1 the Crucifixion** the crucifying of Christ. **2** a representation of this.

cruciform *adj* shaped like a cross.

crucify *vb* **-fies, -fying, -fied 1** to put to death by crucifixion. **2** to treat cruelly. **3** *Slang* to defeat or ridicule totally. ▷ **HISTORY** Latin *crux* cross + *figere* to fasten

crude *adj* **1** rough and simple: *crude farm implements.* **2** tasteless or vulgar. **3** in a natural or unrefined state. ✧ *n* **4** short for **crude oil**. ▷ **HISTORY** Latin *crudus* bloody, raw ▶ **crudely** *adv* ▶ **crudity** *or* **crudeness** *n*

crude oil *n* unrefined petroleum.

cruel *adj* **1** deliberately causing pain without pity. **2** causing pain or suffering. ▷ **HISTORY** Latin *crudelis* ▶ **cruelly** *adv* ▶ **cruelty** *n*

cruet *n* **1** a small container for pepper, salt, etc., at table. **2** a set of such containers on a stand. ▷ **HISTORY** Old French *crue* flask

cruise *n* **1** a sail taken for pleasure, stopping at various places. ✧ *vb* **cruising, cruised 2** to sail about from place to place for pleasure. **3** (of a vehicle, aircraft, or ship) to travel at a moderate and efficient speed. **4** to proceed steadily or easily: *they cruised into the final of the qualifying competition.* ▷ **HISTORY** Dutch *kruisen* to cross

cruise missile *n* a low-flying subsonic missile that is guided throughout its flight.

cruiser *n* **1** a large fast warship armed with medium-calibre weapons. **2** Also called: **cabin cruiser** a motorboat with a cabin.

cruiserweight *n* a professional boxer weighing up to 195 pounds (88.5 kg).

crumb *n* **1** a small fragment of bread or other dry food. **2** a small bit or scrap: *a crumb of comfort.* ▷ **HISTORY** Old English *cruma*

crumble *vb* **-bling, -bled 1** to break into crumbs or fragments. **2** to fall apart or decay. ✧ *n* **3** a baked pudding consisting of stewed fruit with a crumbly topping: *rhubarb crumble.* ▶ **crumbly** *adj* ▶ **crumbliness** *n*

crumby *adj* **crumbier, crumbiest 1** full of crumbs. **2** same as **crummy**.

crummy *adj* **-mier, -miest** *Slang* **1** of very bad quality: *a crummy hotel.* **2** unwell: *I felt really crummy.* ▷ **HISTORY** variant spelling of *crumby*

crumpet *n* **1** a light soft yeast cake, eaten buttered. **2** *Chiefly Brit slang* sexually attractive women collectively. ▷ **HISTORY** origin unknown

crumple *vb* **-pling, -pled 1** to crush or become crushed into untidy wrinkles or creases. **2** to collapse in an untidy heap: *her father lay crumpled on the floor.* ✧ *n* **3** an untidy crease or wrinkle. ▷ **HISTORY** obsolete *crump* to bend ▶ **crumply** *adj*

crunch *vb* **1** to bite or chew with a noisy crushing sound. **2** to make a crisp or brittle sound. ✧ *n* **3** a crunching sound. **4 the crunch** *Informal* the critical moment or situation. ▷ **HISTORY** imitative ▶ **crunchy** *adj* ▶ **crunchiness** *n*

crupper *n* **1** a strap that passes from the back of a saddle under a horse's tail. **2** the horse's rump. ▷ **HISTORY** Old French *crupiere*

crusade *n* **1** any of the medieval military expeditions undertaken by European Christians to recapture the Holy Land from the Muslims. **2** a vigorous campaign in favour of a cause. ✧ *vb* **-sading, -saded 3** to take part in a crusade. ▷ **HISTORY** Latin *crux* cross ▶ **crusader** *n*

cruse *n* a small earthenware container for liquids. ▷ **HISTORY** Old English *crūse*

crush *vb* **1** to press or squeeze so as to injure, break, or put out of shape. **2** to break or grind into small pieces. **3** to control or subdue by force. **4** to extract (liquid) by pressing: *crush a clove of garlic.* **5** to defeat or humiliate utterly. **6** to crowd together. ✧ *n* **7** a dense crowd. **8** the act of crushing. **9** *Informal* an infatuation: *I had a teenage crush on my French teacher.* **10** a drink made by crushing fruit: *orange crush.* ▷ **HISTORY** Old French *croissir*

crust *n* **1** the hard outer part of bread. **2** the baked shell of a pie or tart. **3** any hard outer layer: *a thin crust of snow.* **4** the solid outer shell of the earth. ✧ *vb* **5** to cover with or form a crust. ▷ **HISTORY** Latin *crusta* hard surface, rind

crustacean *n* **1** an animal with a hard outer shell and several pairs of legs, which usually lives in water, such as a crab or lobster. ✧ *adj* **2** of crustaceans. ▷ **HISTORY** Latin *crusta* shell

crusty *adj* **crustier, crustiest 1** having a crust. **2** rude or irritable. ▶ **crustiness** *n*

crutch *n* **1** a long staff with a rest for the armpit, used by a lame person to support the weight of the body. **2** something that supports. **3** *Brit* same as **crotch** (sense 1). ▷ HISTORY Old English *crycc*

crutchings *pl n Austral & NZ* the wool clipped from a sheep's hindquarters.

crux *n, pl* **cruxes** *or* **cruces** a crucial or decisive point. ▷ HISTORY Latin: cross

cry *vb* **cries, crying, cried 1** to shed tears. **2** to make a loud vocal sound, usually to express pain or fear or to appeal for help. **3** to utter loudly or shout. **4** (of an animal or bird) to utter loud characteristic sounds. **5 cry for** to appeal urgently for. ✧ *n, pl* **cries 6** a fit of weeping. **7** the act or sound of crying. **8** the characteristic utterance of an animal or bird. **9** an urgent appeal: *a cry for help.* **10** a public demand: *a cry for more law and order on the streets.* **11 a far cry from** something very different from. **12 in full cry a** in eager pursuit. **b** in the middle of talking or doing something. ✧ See also **cry off**. ▷ HISTORY Old French *crier*

crying *adj* **a crying shame** something that demands immediate attention.

cry off *vb Informal* to withdraw from an arrangement.

cryogenics *n* the branch of physics concerned with very low temperatures and their effects. ▷ HISTORY Greek *kruos* cold + *-genēs* born ▶ **cryogenic** *adj*

crypt *n* a vault or underground chamber, such as one beneath a church, used as a burial place. ▷ HISTORY Greek *kruptē*

cryptic *adj* having a hidden or secret meaning; puzzling: *no-one knew what he meant by that cryptic remark.* ▷ HISTORY Greek *kruptos* concealed ▶ **cryptically** *adv*

cryptogam *n Bot* a plant that reproduces by spores not seeds. ▷ HISTORY Greek *kruptos* hidden + *gamos* marriage

cryptography *n* the art of writing in and deciphering codes. ▷ HISTORY Greek *kruptos* hidden + -GRAPHY ▶ **cryptographer** *n* ▶ **cryptographic** *adj*

crystal *n* **1** a solid with a regular internal structure and symmetrical arrangement of faces. **2** a single grain of a crystalline substance. **3** a very clear and brilliant glass. **4** something made of crystal. **5** crystal glass articles collectively. **6** *Electronics* a crystalline element used in certain electronic devices, such as a detector or oscillator. ✧ *adj* **7** bright and clear: *the crystal waters of the pool.* ▷ HISTORY Greek *krustallos* ice, crystal

crystal healing *n* in alternative medicine, the use of the supposed power of crystals to affect the human energy field.

crystalline *adj* **1** of or like crystal or crystals. **2** clear.

crystallize, crystalize, *or* **-ise** *vb* **-izing, -ized** *or* **-ising, -ised 1** to make or become definite. **2** to form into crystals. **3** to preserve (fruit) in sugar. ▶ **crystallization, crystalization** *or* **-isation** *n*

crystallography *n* the science of crystal structure.

crystalloid *n* a substance that in solution can pass through a membrane.

Cs *Chem* caesium.

CSA (in Britain) Child Support Agency.

CSE (in Britain) (formerly) Certificate of Secondary Education: an examination the first grade pass of which was an equivalent to a GCE O level.

CS gas *n* a gas causing tears and painful breathing, used to control civil disturbances. ▷ HISTORY initials of its US inventors, Ben Carson and Roger Staughton

CST Central Standard Time.

CT Connecticut.

CT scanner *n* an X-ray machine that can produce cross-sectional images of the soft tissues. ▷ HISTORY *c(omputerized) t(omography) scanner*

Cu *Chem* copper. ▷ HISTORY Late Latin *cuprum*

cu. cubic.

cub *n* **1** the young of certain mammals, such as the lion or bear. **2** a young or inexperienced person. ✧ *vb* **cubbing, cubbed 3** to give birth to (cubs). ▷ HISTORY origin unknown

Cuban *adj* **1** from Cuba. ✧ *n* **2** a person from Cuba.

cubbyhole *n* a small enclosed space or room. ▷ HISTORY dialect *cub* cattle pen

cube *n* **1** an object with six equal square faces. **2** the product obtained by multiplying a number by itself twice: *the cube of 2 is 8.* ✧ *vb* **cubing, cubed 3** to find the cube of (a number). **4** to cut into cubes. ▷ HISTORY Greek *kubos*

cube root *n* the number or quantity whose cube is a given number or quantity: *2 is the cube root of 8.*

cubic *adj* **1 a** having three dimensions. **b** having the same volume as a cube with length, width, and depth each measuring the given unit: *a cubic metre.* **2** having the shape of a cube. **3** *Maths* involving the cubes of numbers.

cubicle *n* an enclosed part of a large room, screened for privacy. ▷ HISTORY Latin *cubiculum*

cubic measure *n* a system of units for the measurement of volumes.

cubic proportion *n Maths* a relationship between two variables in which one is proportional to the cube of the other.

cubism *n* a style of art, begun in the early 20th century, in which objects are represented by geometrical shapes. ▶ **cubist** *adj, n*

cubit *n* an ancient measure of length based on the length of the forearm. ▷ HISTORY Latin *cubitum* elbow, cubit

cuboid *adj* **1** shaped like a cube. ✧ *n* **2** *Maths* a geometric solid whose six faces are rectangles.

Cub Scout *or* **Cub** *n* a member of a junior branch of the Scout Association.

cuckold *Literary or old-fashioned* ✧ *n* **1** a man whose wife has been unfaithful to him. ✧ *vb* **2** to make a cuckold of. ▷ HISTORY Middle English *cukeweld*

cuckoo *n, pl* **cuckoos 1** a migratory bird with a characteristic two-note call, noted for laying its eggs in the nests of other birds. ✧ *adj* **2** *Informal* insane or foolish. ▷ **HISTORY** Old French *cucu,* imitative

cuckoopint *n* a plant with arrow-shaped leaves, purple flowers, and red berries.

cuckoo spit *n* a white frothy mass produced on plants by the larvae of some insects.

cucumber *n* **1** a long fruit with thin green rind and crisp white flesh, used in salads. **2 as cool as a cucumber** calm and self-possessed. ▷ **HISTORY** Latin *cucumis*

cud *n* **1** partially digested food which a ruminant brings back into its mouth to chew again. **2 chew the cud** to think deeply. ▷ **HISTORY** Old English *cudu*

cuddle *vb* **-dling, -dled 1** to hug or embrace fondly. **2 cuddle up** to lie close and snug. ✧ *n* **3** a fond hug. ▷ **HISTORY** origin unknown ▶ **cuddly** *adj*

cudgel *n* a short thick stick used as a weapon. ▷ **HISTORY** Old English *cycgel*

cue[1] *n* **1** a signal to an actor or musician to begin speaking or playing. **2** a signal or reminder. **3 on cue** at the right moment. ✧ *vb* **cueing, cued 4** to give a cue to. ▷ **HISTORY** perhaps from the letter *q,* used in an actor's script to represent Latin *quando* when

cue[2] *n* **1** a long tapering stick used to hit the balls in billiards, snooker, or pool. ✧ *vb* **cueing, cued 2** to hit (a ball) with a cue. ▷ **HISTORY** variant of QUEUE

cuesta (**quest**-uh) *n* a long low ridge with a steep scarp slope and a gentle back slope. ▷ **HISTORY** Spanish: shoulder, from Latin *costa* side, rib

cuff[1] *n* **1** the end of a sleeve. **2** *US, Canad, Austral & NZ* a turn-up on trousers. **3 off the cuff** *Informal* impromptu: *he delivers many speeches off the cuff.* ▷ **HISTORY** Middle English *cuffe* glove

cuff[2] *Brit, Austral & NZ* ✧ *vb* **1** to strike with an open hand. ✧ *n* **2** a blow with an open hand. ▷ **HISTORY** origin unknown

cuff link *n* one of a pair of decorative fastenings for shirt cuffs.

cuisine (quiz-**zeen**) *n* **1** a style of cooking: *Italian cuisine.* **2** the range of food served in a restaurant. ▷ **HISTORY** French

cul-de-sac *n, pl* **culs-de-sac** *or* **cul-de-sacs** a road with one end blocked off. ▷ **HISTORY** French: bottom of the bag

culinary *adj* of the kitchen or cookery. ▷ **HISTORY** Latin *culina* kitchen

cull *vb* **1** to choose or gather. **2** to remove or kill (the inferior or surplus) animals from a herd. ✧ *n* **3** the act of culling. ▷ **HISTORY** Latin *colligere* to gather together

culminate *vb* **-nating, -nated** to reach the highest point or climax: *the parade culminated in a memorial service.* ▷ **HISTORY** Latin *culmen* top ▶ **culmination** *n*

culottes *pl n* women's flared trousers cut to look like a skirt. ▷ **HISTORY** French

culpable *adj* deserving blame. ▷ **HISTORY** Latin *culpa* fault ▶ **culpability** *n*

culprit *n* the person guilty of an offence or misdeed. ▷ **HISTORY** Anglo-French *culpable* guilty + *prit* ready

cult *n* **1** a specific system of religious worship. **2** a sect devoted to the beliefs of a cult. **3** devoted attachment to a person, idea, or activity. **4** a popular fashion: *the bungee-jumping cult.* ✧ *adj* **5** very popular among a limited group of people: *a cult TV series.* ▷ **HISTORY** Latin *cultus* cultivation, refinement

cultic *adj* of a religious cult.

cultivate *vb* **-vating, -vated 1** to prepare (land) to grow crops. **2** to grow (plants). **3** to develop or improve (something) by giving special attention to it: *he tried to cultivate a reputation for fairness.* **4** to try to develop a friendship with (a person). ▷ **HISTORY** Latin *colere* to till

cultivated *adj* well-educated: *a civilized and cultivated man.*

cultivation *n* **1** the act of cultivating. **2** culture or refinement.

cultivator *n* a farm implement used to break up soil and remove weeds.

Cultural Revolution *n History* (in China) an idealistic mass movement (1965-68) intended by Mao Zedong to destroy the power of the bureaucrats but which resulted in anarchy, terror, and a huge fall in industrial and agricultural production.

culture *n* **1** the ideas, customs, and art of a particular society. **2** a particular civilization at a particular period. **3** a developed understanding of the arts. **4** development or improvement by special attention or training: *physical culture.* **5** the cultivation and rearing of plants or animals. **6** a growth of bacteria for study. ✧ *vb* **-turing, -tured 7** to grow (bacteria) in a special medium. ▷ **HISTORY** Latin *colere* to till ▶ **cultural** *adj*

cultured *adj* **1** showing good taste or manners. **2** artificially grown or synthesized.

cultured pearl *n* a pearl artificially grown in an oyster shell.

culture shock *n Sociol* the feelings of isolation and anxiety experienced by a person on first coming into contact with a culture very different from his or her own.

culvert *n* a drain or pipe that crosses under a road or railway. ▷ **HISTORY** origin unknown

cum *prep* with: *a small living-cum-dining room.* ▷ **HISTORY** Latin

cumbersome *or* **cumbrous** *adj* **1** awkward because of size or shape. **2** difficult because of complexity: *the cumbersome appeals procedure.*

cumin *or* **cummin** *n* **1** the spicy-smelling seeds of a Mediterranean herb, used in cooking. **2** the plant from which these seeds are obtained. ▷ **HISTORY** Greek *kuminon*

cummerbund *n* a wide sash worn round the waist, esp. with a dinner jacket. ▷ **HISTORY** Hindi *kamarband,* from Persian *kamar* loins + *band* band

cumquat *n* same as **kumquat**.

a b c d e f g h i j k l m n o p q r s t u v w x y z

A B C D E F G H I J K L M N O P Q R S T U V W X Y Z

cumulative (**kew**-myew-la-tiv) *adj* growing in amount, strength, or effect by small steps: *the cumulative effect of twelve years of war.*

cumulative frequency *n Statistics* the frequency of occurrence of all values of a variable either below or above a specified value.

cumulative frequency graph *n Statistics* a graph which shows the frequency of occurrence of a set of values as a cumulative total.

cumulative graph *n Statistics* a graph which shows the cumulative totals of a set of values up to each of the points on the graph.

cumulative preference shares *pl n Finance* preference shares that entitle the holder to receive any arrears of dividend before any dividend is distributed to ordinary shareholders.

cumulonimbus (kew-mew-low-**nim**-bes) *n, pl* **cumulonimbi** *or* **cumulonimbuses** *Meteorol* a towering cumulus cloud, dark-coloured at the bottom and often anvil-shaped at the top, indicating rain or hail; associated with thunderstorms.

cumulonimbus cloud *n Meteorol* a very tall cumulus cloud, the top of which often forms an anvil shape while the bottom is dark coloured, indicating rain or hail and associated with thunderstorms.

cumulus (**kew**-myew-luss) *n, pl* **-li** (-lie) a thick or billowing white or dark grey cloud. ▷ **HISTORY** Latin: mass

cuneiform (**kew**-nif-form) *n* **1** an ancient system of writing using wedge-shaped characters. ✧ *adj* **2** written in cuneiform. ▷ **HISTORY** Latin *cuneus* wedge

cunjevoi (**kun**-ji-voy) *n Austral* **1** a plant of tropical Asia and Australia, cultivated for its edible rhizome. **2** a sea squirt.

cunning *adj* **1** clever at deceiving. **2** made with skill. ✧ *n* **3** cleverness at deceiving. **4** skill or ingenuity. ▷ **HISTORY** Old English *cunnende*

cup *n* **1** a small bowl-shaped drinking container with a handle. **2** the contents of a cup. **3** something shaped like a cup: *a bra with padded cups.* **4** a cup-shaped trophy awarded as a prize. **5** a sporting contest in which a cup is awarded to the winner. **6** a mixed drink with fruit juice or wine as a base: *claret cup.* **7** one's lot in life: *his cup of bitterness was full to overflowing.* **8 someone's cup of tea** *Informal* someone's chosen or preferred thing. ✧ *vb* **cupping, cupped 9** to form (the hands) into the shape of a cup. **10** to hold in cupped hands. ▷ **HISTORY** Old English *cuppe*

cupboard *n* a piece of furniture or a recess with a door, for storage.

Cupid *n* **1** the Roman god of love, represented as a winged boy with a bow and arrow. **2** a picture or statue of Cupid. ▷ **HISTORY** Latin *cupido* desire

cupidity (kew-**pid**-it-ee) *n Formal* strong desire for wealth or possessions. ▷ **HISTORY** Latin *cupere* to long for

cupola (**kew**-pol-la) *n* **1** a domed roof or ceiling. **2** a small dome on the top of a roof. **3** an armoured revolving gun turret on a warship. ▷ **HISTORY** Latin *cupa* tub

cupreous (**kew**-pree-uss) *adj* of or containing copper. ▷ **HISTORY** Latin *cuprum* copper

cupric (**kew**-prick) *adj* of or containing copper in the divalent state.

cupronickel (kew-proh-**nik**-el) *n* a copper alloy containing up to 40 per cent nickel.

cup tie *n Brit sport* an eliminating match between two teams in a cup competition.

cur *n* **1** a vicious mongrel dog. **2** a contemptible person. ▷ **HISTORY** Middle English *kurdogge*

curable *adj* capable of being cured. ▸ **curability** *n*

curaçao (**kew**-rah-so) *n* an orange-flavoured liqueur.

curacy (**kew**-rah-see) *n, pl* **-cies** the work or position of a curate.

curare (kew-**rah**-ree) *n* a poisonous resin obtained from a South American tree, used as a muscle relaxant in medicine. ▷ **HISTORY** Carib *kurari*

curate *n* a clergyman who assists a vicar or parish priest. ▷ **HISTORY** Medieval Latin *cura* spiritual oversight

curative *adj* **1** able to cure. ✧ *n* **2** something able to cure.

curator *n* the person in charge of a museum or art gallery. ▷ **HISTORY** Latin: one who cares ▸ **curatorial** *adj* ▸ **curatorship** *n*

curb *n* **1** something that restrains or holds back. **2** a horse's bit with an attached chain or strap, used to check the horse. **3** a raised edge that strengthens or encloses. ✧ *vb* **4** to control or restrain. ✧ See also **kerb**. ▷ **HISTORY** Latin *curvus* curved

curd *n* **1** coagulated milk, used in making cheese or as a food. **2** any similar substance: *bean curd.* ▷ **HISTORY** origin unknown

curdle *vb* **-dling, -dled 1** to turn into curd; coagulate. **2 make someone's blood curdle** to fill someone with horror.

cure *vb* **curing, cured 1** to get rid of (an ailment or problem). **2** to restore (someone) to health. **3** to preserve (meat or fish) by salting or smoking. **4** to preserve (leather or tobacco) by drying. **5** to vulcanize (rubber). ✧ *n* **6** a restoration to health. **7** medical treatment that restores health. **8** a means of restoring health or improving a situation. **9** a curacy. ▷ **HISTORY** Latin *cura* care

cure-all *n* something supposed to cure all ailments or problems.

curette *or* **curet** *n* **1** a surgical instrument for scraping tissue from body cavities. ✧ *vb* **-retting, -retted 2** to scrape with a curette. ▷ **HISTORY** French ▸ **curettage** *n*

curfew *n* **1** a law which states that people must stay inside their houses after a specific time at night. **2** the time set as a deadline by such a law. **3** *History* the ringing of a bell at a fixed time, as a signal for putting out fires and lights. ▷ **HISTORY** Old French *cuevrefeu* cover the fire

Curia *n, pl* **-riae** the court and government of the Roman Catholic Church. ▷ **HISTORY** Latin ▸ **curial** *adj*

curie *n* the standard unit of radioactivity. ▷ HISTORY after Pierre *Curie*, French physicist

curio (**kew**-ree-oh) *n, pl* **-rios** a rare or unusual thing valued as a collector's item. ▷ HISTORY from *curiosity*

curiosity *n, pl* **-ties 1** eagerness to know or find out. **2** a rare or unusual thing.

curious *adj* **1** eager to learn or know. **2** eager to find out private details. **3** unusual or peculiar. ▷ HISTORY Latin *curiosus* taking pains over something ▶ **curiously** *adv*

curium (**kew**-ree-um) *n Chem* a silvery-white metallic radioactive element artificially produced from plutonium. Symbol: Cm. ▷ HISTORY after Pierre & Marie *Curie*, French physicists

curl *vb* **1** to twist (hair) or (of hair) to grow in coils or ringlets. **2** to twist into a spiral or curve. **3** to play the game of curling. **4 curl one's lip** to show contempt by raising a corner of the lip. ✧ *n* **5** a coil of hair. **6** a curved or spiral shape. ▷ HISTORY probably from Middle Dutch *crullen* ▶ **curly** *adj*

curler *n* **1** a pin or small tube for curling hair. **2** a person who plays curling.

curlew *n* a large wading bird with a long downward-curving bill. ▷ HISTORY Old French *corlieu*

curlicue *n* an intricate ornamental curl or twist. ▷ HISTORY *curly* + CUE[2]

curling *n* a game played on ice, in which heavy stones with handles are slid towards a target circle.

curmudgeon *n* a bad-tempered or mean person. ▷ HISTORY origin unknown ▶ **curmudgeonly** *adj*

currajong *n* same as **kurrajong**.

currant *n* **1** a small dried seedless raisin. **2** a small round acid berry, such as the redcurrant.

> **WORD HISTORY**
> Currants originally came from Corinth in Greece. The word 'currant' is from early English *rayson of Corannte*, which translates Norman French *raisin de Corauntz*, meaning 'grape from Corinth'.

currawong *n* an Australian songbird. ▷ HISTORY Aboriginal

currency *n, pl* **-cies 1** the system of money or the actual coins and banknotes in use in a particular country. **2** general acceptance or use: *ideas that had gained currency during the early 1960s.* ▷ HISTORY Latin *currere* to run, flow

current *adj* **1** of the immediate present: *current affairs; the current economic climate.* **2** most recent or up-to-date: *the current edition.* **3** commonly accepted: *current thinking on this issue.* **4** circulating and valid at present: *current coins.* ✧ *n* **5** a flow of water or air in a particular direction. **6** *Physics* a flow or rate of flow of electric charge through a conductor. **7** a general trend or drift: *two opposing currents of thought.* ▷ HISTORY Latin *currere* to run, flow ▶ **currently** *adv*

current account *n* a bank account from which money may be drawn at any time using a chequebook or computerized card.

current liabilities *pl n Business* business liabilities maturing within a year.

curriculum *n, pl* **-la** *or* **-lums 1** all the courses of study offered by a school or college. **2** a course of study in one subject at a school or college: *the history curriculum.* ▷ HISTORY Latin: course ▶ **curricular** *adj*

curriculum vitae (**vee**-tie) *n, pl* **curricula vitae** an outline of someone's educational and professional history, prepared for job applications. ▷ HISTORY Latin: the course of one's life

curry[1] *n, pl* **-ries 1** a dish of Indian origin consisting of meat or vegetables in a hot spicy sauce. **2** curry seasoning or sauce. **3 curry powder** a mixture of spices for making curry. ✧ *vb* **-ries, -rying, -ried 4** to prepare (food) with curry powder. ▷ HISTORY Tamil *kari* sauce, relish

curry[2] *vb* **-ries, -rying, -ried 1** to groom (a horse). **2** to dress (leather) after it has been tanned. **3 curry favour** to ingratiate oneself with an important person. ▷ HISTORY Old French *correer* to make ready

curse *vb* **cursing, cursed 1** to swear or swear at (someone). **2** to call on supernatural powers to bring harm to (someone or something). ✧ *n* **3** a profane or obscene expression, usually of anger. **4** an appeal to a supernatural power for harm to come to a person. **5** harm resulting from a curse. **6** something that causes great trouble or harm. **7 the curse** *Informal* menstruation or a menstrual period. ▷ HISTORY Old English *cursian*

cursed *adj* **1** under a curse: *he is now sick after being cursed by the witch doctor.* **2 cursed with** having (something unfortunate or unwanted): *their new-born son had been cursed with a genetic defect.*

cursive *adj* **1** of handwriting or print in which letters are joined in a flowing style. ✧ *n* **2** a cursive letter or printing type. ▷ HISTORY Medieval Latin *cursivus* running

cursor *n* **1** a movable point of light that shows a specific position on a visual display unit. **2** the sliding part of a slide rule or other measuring instrument.

cursory *adj* hasty and usually superficial. ▷ HISTORY Late Latin *cursorius* of running ▶ **cursorily** *adv*

curt *adj* so blunt and brief as to be rude. ▷ HISTORY Latin *curtus* cut short ▶ **curtly** *adv* ▶ **curtness** *n*

curtail *vb* **1** to cut short: *the opening round was curtailed by heavy rain.* **2** to restrict: *a plan to curtail drinks advertising.* ▷ HISTORY obsolete *curtal* to dock ▶ **curtailment** *n*

curtain *n* **1** a piece of material hung at an opening or window to shut out light or to provide privacy. **2** a hanging cloth that conceals all or part of a theatre stage from the audience. **3** the end of a scene or a performance in the theatre, marked by the fall or closing of the curtain. **4** the rise or opening of the curtain at the start of a performance. **5** something forming a barrier or screen: *a curtain of rain.* ✧ *vb* **6** to shut off or conceal with a curtain. **7** to provide with curtains. ▷ HISTORY Late Latin *cortina*

curtain call *n Theatre* a return to the stage by performers to receive applause.

curtain-raiser *n* **1** *Theatre* a short play performed before the main play. **2** a minor event happening before a major one.

curtains *pl n Informal* death or ruin; the end.

curtsy *or* **curtsey** *n, pl* **-sies** *or* **-seys 1** a woman's formal gesture of respect made by bending the knees and bowing the head. ✧ *vb* **-sies, -sying, -sied** *or* **-seys, -seying, -seyed 2** to make a curtsy. ▷ **HISTORY** variant of *courtesy*

curvaceous *adj Informal* having a curved shapely body.

curvature *n* the state or degree of being curved.

curve *n* **1** a continuously bending line with no straight parts. **2** something that curves or is curved. **3** curvature. **4** *Maths* a system of points whose coordinates satisfy a given equation. **5** a line representing data on a graph. ✧ *vb* **curving, curved 6** to form into or move in a curve. ▷ **HISTORY** Latin *curvare* to bend ▶ **curvy** *adj*

curvilinear *adj* consisting of or bounded by a curved line.

cuscus *n, pl* **-cuses** a large nocturnal possum of N Australia and New Guinea. ▷ **HISTORY** probably from a native word in New Guinea

cushion *n* **1** a bag filled with a soft material, used to make a seat more comfortable. **2** something that provides comfort or absorbs shock. **3** the resilient felt-covered rim of a billiard table. ✧ *vb* **4** to protect from injury or shock. **5** to lessen the effects of. **6** to provide with cushions. ▷ **HISTORY** Latin *culcita* mattress ▶ **cushiony** *adj*

cushy *adj* **cushier, cushiest** *Informal* easy: *a cushy job.* ▷ **HISTORY** Hindi *khush* pleasant

cusp *n* **1** a small point on the grinding or chewing surface of a tooth. **2** a point where two curves meet. **3** *Astrol* any division between houses or signs of the zodiac. **4** *Astron* either of the points of a crescent moon. ▷ **HISTORY** Latin *cuspis* pointed end

cuspate delta *n Geog* a type of delta whose distinguishing feature is the presence of horn-shaped pieces of land formed from sedimentary deposits at the river mouth. Compare **arcuate delta, bird's foot delta**.

cuss *Informal* ✧ *n* **1** a curse or oath. **2** an annoying person. ✧ *vb* **3** to swear or swear at.

cussed (**kuss**-id) *adj Informal* **1** obstinate: *the older she got the more cussed she became.* **2** same as **cursed.** ▶ **cussedness** *n*

custard *n* **1** a sauce made of milk and sugar thickened with cornflour. **2** a baked sweetened mixture of eggs and milk. ▷ **HISTORY** Middle English *crustade* kind of pie

custodian *n* the person in charge of a public building. ▶ **custodianship** *n*

custody *n, pl* **-dies 1** the act of keeping safe. **2** imprisonment prior to being tried. ▷ **HISTORY** Latin *custos* guard, defender ▶ **custodial** *adj*

custom *n* **1** a long-established activity, action, or festivity: *the custom of serving port after dinner.* **2** the long-established habits or traditions of a society. **3** a usual practice or habit: *she held his hand more tightly than was her custom in public.* **4** regular use of a shop or business. **5** *Law* a practice which by long-established usage has come to have the force of law. ✧ *adj* **6** made to the specifications of an individual customer: *a custom car; custom-tailored suits.* ✧ See also **customs.** ▷ **HISTORY** Latin *consuetudo*

customary *adj* **1** usual. **2** established by custom. ▶ **customarily** *adv* ▶ **customariness** *n*

customary law *n Law* law which is founded upon long-continued practices and usage rather than upon written rules.

custom-built *or* **-made** *adj* made according to the specifications of an individual customer.

customer *n* **1** a person who buys goods or services. **2** *Informal* a person with whom one has to deal: *a tricky customer.*

custom house *n* a government office where customs are collected.

customs *n* **1** duty charged on imports or exports. **2** the government department responsible for collecting this. **3** the area at a port, airport, or border where baggage and freight are examined for dutiable goods.

cut *vb* **cutting, cut 1** to open up or penetrate (a person or thing) with a sharp instrument. **2** (of a sharp instrument) to penetrate or open up (a person or thing). **3** to divide or be divided with or as if with a sharp instrument. **4** to trim. **5** to abridge or shorten. **6** to reduce or restrict: *cut your intake of fried foods.* **7** to form or shape by cutting. **8** to reap or mow. **9** *Sports* to hit (the ball) so that it spins and swerves. **10** to hurt the feelings of (a person): *her rudeness cut me to the core.* **11** *Informal* to pretend not to recognize. **12** *Informal* to absent oneself from without permission: *he found the course boring, and was soon cutting classes.* **13** to stop (doing something): *cut the nonsense.* **14** to dilute or adulterate: *heroin cut with talcum powder.* **15** to make a sharp or sudden change in direction: *the path cuts to the right just after you pass the quarry.* **16** to grow (teeth) through the gums. **17** *Films* **a** to call a halt to a shooting sequence. **b cut to** to move quickly to (another scene). **18** *Films* to edit (film). **19** to switch off (a light or engine). **20** to make (a commercial recording): *he cut his first solo album in 1971.* **21** *Cards* **a** to divide (the pack) at random into two parts after shuffling. **b** to pick cards from a spread pack to decide the dealer or who plays first. **22 cut a dash** to make a stylish impression. **23 cut a person dead** *Informal* to ignore a person completely. **24 cut and run** *Informal* to escape quickly from a difficult situation. **25 cut both ways a** to have both good and bad effects. **b** to serve both sides of an argument. **26 cut it fine** *Informal* to allow little margin of time or space. **27 cut no ice** *Informal* to fail to make an impression. **28 cut one's teeth on** *Informal* to get experience from. ✧ *n* **29** the act of cutting. **30** a stroke or incision made by cutting. **31** a piece cut off. **32** a channel or path cut or hollowed out. **33** a reduction: *a pay cut.* **34** a deletion in a text, film, or play. **35** *Informal* a portion or share. **36** the style in which hair or a garment is cut. **37** a direct route; short cut. **38** *Sports* a stroke which makes the ball spin and swerve. **39** *Films* an immediate transition from one shot to the next. **40** *Brit* a canal. **41 a cut above** *Informal* superior to; better than. ✧ *adj* **42** made or shaped by cutting. **43** reduced by cutting: *the shop has hundreds of suits, all at cut prices.* **44** adulterated or diluted. **45 cut and dried** *Informal* settled in advance. ✧ See also **cutback**. ▷ **HISTORY** probably from Old Norse

cutaneous (kew-**tane**-ee-uss) *adj* of the skin. ▷ **HISTORY** Latin *cutis* skin

cutaway *adj* (of a drawing or model) having part of the outside omitted to reveal the inside.

cutback *n* **1** a decrease or reduction. ✧ *vb* **cut back 2** to shorten by cutting. **3** to make a reduction: *we may cut back on other expenditure.*

cute *adj* **1** appealing or attractive. **2** *Informal* clever or shrewd. ▷ **HISTORY** from ACUTE ▶ **cuteness** *n*

cuticle (**kew**-tik-kl) *n* **1** hardened skin round the base of a fingernail or toenail. **2** same as **epidermis**. ▷ **HISTORY** Latin *cuticula* skin

cut in *vb* **1** to interrupt. **2** to move in front of another vehicle, leaving too little space.

cutlass *n* a curved one-edged sword formerly used by sailors. ▷ **HISTORY** French *coutelas*

cutler *n* a person who makes or sells cutlery. ▷ **HISTORY** Latin *culter* knife

cutlery *n* knives, forks, and spoons, used for eating.

cutlet *n* **1** a small piece of meat taken from the neck or ribs. **2** a flat croquette of chopped meat or fish. ▷ **HISTORY** Old French *costelette* a little rib

cut off *vb* **1** to remove or separate by cutting. **2** to stop the supply of. **3** to interrupt (a person who is speaking), esp. during a telephone conversation. **4** to bring to an end. **5** to disinherit: *cut off without a penny.* **6** to intercept so as to prevent retreat or escape. ✧ *n* **cutoff 7** the point at which something is cut off; limit. **8** *Chiefly US* a short cut. **9** a device to stop the flow of a fluid in a pipe.

cut-off meander *n Geog* a former bend of a river now by-passed by the water owing to the river having cut out a more direct course through erosion.

cut out *vb* **1** to shape by cutting. **2** to delete or remove. **3** *Informal* to stop doing (something). **4** (of an engine) to cease to operate suddenly. **5** (of an electrical device) to switch off, usually automatically. **6 be cut out for** to be suited or equipped for: *you're not cut out for this job.* **7 have one's work cut out** to have as much work as one can manage. ✧ *n* **cutout 8** a device that automatically switches off a circuit or engine as a safety device. **9** something that has been cut out from something else.

cut-price *or esp US* **cut-rate** *adj* **1** at a reduced price. **2** offering goods or services at prices below the standard price.

cutter *n* **1** a person or tool that cuts. **2** a small fast boat.

cut-throat *adj* **1** fierce or ruthless in competition: *the cut-throat world of international finance.* **2** (of a card game) played by three people: *cut-throat poker.* ✧ *n* **3** a murderer. **4** *Brit & NZ* a razor with a long blade that folds into its handle.

cutting *n* **1** an article cut from a newspaper or magazine. **2** a piece cut from a plant for rooting or grafting. **3** a passage cut through high ground for a road or railway. **4** the editing process of a film. ✧ *adj* **5** (of a remark) likely to hurt the feelings. **6** keen; piercing: *a cutting wind.* **7** designed for cutting: *the hatchet's blade is largely stone, but its cutting edge is made of copper.*

cuttlefish *n, pl* **-fish** *or* **-fishes** a flat squidlike mollusc which squirts an inky fluid when in danger. ▷ **HISTORY** Old English *cudele*

cut up *vb* **1** to cut into pieces. **2** *Informal* (of a driver) to overtake or pull in front of (another driver) in a dangerous manner. **3 be cut up** *Informal* to be very upset. **4 cut up rough** *Brit informal* to become angry or violent.

CV curriculum vitae.

cwm (**koom**) *n* (in Wales) a valley. ▷ **HISTORY** Welsh

cwt hundredweight.

cyanic acid *n* a colourless poisonous volatile liquid acid.

cyanide *n* any of a number of highly poisonous substances containing a carbon-nitrogen group of atoms.

cyanogen *n* a poisonous colourless flammable gas. ▷ **HISTORY** Greek *kuanos* dark blue

cyanosis *n Pathol* a blue discoloration of the skin, caused by a deficiency of oxygen in the blood. ▷ **HISTORY** Greek *kuanos* dark blue

cyber- *combining form* indicating computers: *cyberspace.* ▷ **HISTORY** from CYBERNETICS

cybercafé *n* a café equipped with computer terminals which customers can use to access the Internet. ▷ **HISTORY** CYBER- + CAFÉ

cybernetics *n* the branch of science in which electronic and mechanical systems are studied and compared to biological systems. ▷ **HISTORY** Greek *kubernētēs* steersman ▶ **cybernetic** *adj*

cyberpet *n* an electronic toy that mimics the actions of a pet.

cyberspace *n* the hypothetical environment which contains all the data stored in computers. ▷ **HISTORY** CYBER- + SPACE

cybersquatting *n* the practice of registering an Internet domain name that is likely to be wanted by another person or organization in the hope that it can be sold to them for a profit. ▶ **cybersquatter** *n*

cyclamen (**sik**-la-men) *n* a plant with white, pink, or red flowers, with turned-back petals. ▷ **HISTORY** Greek *kuklaminos*

cycle *vb* **-cling, -cled 1** to ride a bicycle. **2** to occur in cycles. ✧ *n* **3** *Brit, Austral & NZ* a bicycle. **4** *US* a motorcycle. **5** a complete series of recurring events. **6** the time taken or needed for one such series. **7** a single complete movement in an electrical, electronic, or mechanical process. **8** a set of plays, songs, or poems about a figure or event. ▷ **HISTORY** Greek *kuklos* ▶ **cycling** *n*

A B C D E F G H I J K L M N O P Q R S T U V W X Y Z

cyclical *or* **cyclic** *adj* **1** occurring in cycles. **2** *Chem* (of an organic compound) containing a closed ring of atoms. **3** *Geom* (of a polygon) having vertices that lie on a circle.

cyclic quadrilateral *n Geom* a quadrilateral with all its vertices lying on the circumference of a circle.

cyclist *n* a person who rides a bicycle.

cyclo- *or before a vowel* **cycl-** *combining form* **1** indicating a circle or ring: *cyclotron.* **2** *Chem* denoting a cyclical compound: *cyclopropane.* ▷ HISTORY Greek *kuklos* cycle

cyclometer (sike-**lom**-it-er) *n* a device that records the number of revolutions made by a wheel and the distance travelled.

cyclone *n* **1** a body of moving air below normal atmospheric pressure, which often brings rain. **2** a violent tropical storm. ▷ HISTORY Greek *kuklōn* a turning around ► **cyclonic** *adj*

cyclopedia *or* **cyclopaedia** *n* same as **encyclopedia**.

Cyclops *n, pl* **Cyclopes** *or* **Cyclopses** *Classical myth* one of a race of giants having a single eye in the middle of the forehead. ▷ HISTORY Greek *Kuklōps* round eye

cyclotron *n* an apparatus, used in atomic research, which accelerates charged particles by means of a strong vertical magnetic field.

cygnet *n* a young swan. ▷ HISTORY Latin *cygnus* swan

cylinder *n* **1** a solid or hollow body with circular equal ends and straight parallel sides. **2** a container or other object shaped like a cylinder. **3** the chamber in an internal-combustion engine within which the piston moves. **4** the rotating mechanism of a revolver, containing cartridge chambers. ▷ HISTORY Greek *kulindein* to roll ► **cylindrical** *adj*

cymbal *n* a percussion instrument consisting of a round brass plate which is struck against another or hit with a stick. ▷ HISTORY Greek *kumbē* something hollow ► **cymbalist** *n*

cyme *n Bot* a flower cluster which has a single flower on the end of each stem and of which the central flower blooms first. ▷ HISTORY Greek *kuma* anything swollen ► **cymose** *adj*

Cymric (**kim**-rik) *adj* **1** of Wales. ✧ *n* **2** the Celtic language of Wales.

cynic (**sin**-ik) *n* a person who believes that people always act selfishly. ▷ HISTORY Greek *kuōn* dog

Cynic *n* a member of an ancient Greek philosophical school that had contempt for worldly things. ► **Cynicism** *n*

cynical *adj* **1** believing that people always act selfishly. **2** sarcastic or sneering. ► **cynically** *adv*

cynicism *n* the attitude or beliefs of a cynic.

cynosure (**sin**-oh-zyure) *n Literary* a centre of interest or attention. ▷ HISTORY Greek *Kunosoura* dog's tail (name of the constellation of Ursa Minor)

cypher (**sife**-er) *n, vb* same as **cipher**.

cypress *n* **1** an evergreen tree with dark green leaves. **2** the wood of this tree. ▷ HISTORY Greek *kuparissos*

Cypriot *adj* **1** of Cyprus. ✧ *n* **2** a person from Cyprus. **3** the dialect of Greek spoken in Cyprus.

Cyrillic *adj* of the Slavic alphabet devised supposedly by Saint Cyril, now used primarily for Russian and Bulgarian.

cyst (**sist**) *n* **1** *Pathol* an abnormal membranous sac containing fluid or diseased matter. **2** *Anat* any normal sac in the body. ▷ HISTORY Greek *kustis* pouch, bag

cystic fibrosis *n* a congenital disease, usually affecting young children, which causes breathing disorders and malfunctioning of the pancreas.

cystitis (siss-**tite**-iss) *n* inflammation of the bladder, causing a desire to urinate frequently, accompanied by a burning sensation.

-cyte *n combining form* indicating a cell: *leucocyte.* ▷ HISTORY Greek *kutos* vessel

cytokinesis *n Biol* division of the cytoplasm of a cell contained within the cell membrane but excluding the nucleus.

cytology (site-**ol**-a-jee) *n* the study of plant and animal cells. ► **cytological** *adj* ► **cytologically** *adv* ► **cytologist** *n*

cytoplasm *n* the protoplasm of a cell excluding the nucleus. ► **cytoplasmic** *adj*

cytosine *n Biol* a white crystalline pyrimidine occurring in nucleic acids.

czar (**zahr**) *n* same as **tsar**.

Czech *adj* **1** of the Czech Republic. ✧ *n* **2** a person from the Czech Republic. **3** the language of the Czech Republic.

Czechoslovak *or* **Czechoslovakian** *adj* **1** of the former Czechoslovakia. ✧ *n* **2** a person from the former Czechoslovakia.

D d

d 1 *Physics* density. **2** deci-.

D **1** *Music* the second note of the scale of C major. **2** *Chem* deuterium. **3** the Roman numeral for 500.

d. **1** *Brit & NZ* (before decimalization) penny *or* pennies. ▷ **HISTORY** Latin *denarius* **2** died. **3** daughter.

dab[1] *vb* **dabbing, dabbed 1** to pat lightly and quickly. **2** to apply with short tapping strokes: *dabbing antiseptic on cuts.* ✧ *n* **3** a small amount of something soft or moist. **4** a light stroke or tap. **5 dabs** *Slang, chiefly Brit* fingerprints. ▷ **HISTORY** imitative

dab[2] *n* a small European flatfish covered with rough toothed scales. ▷ **HISTORY** Anglo-French *dabbe*

dabble *vb* **-bling, -bled 1** to be involved in an activity in a superficial way: *she dabbles in right-wing politics.* **2** to splash (one's toes or fingers) in water. ▷ **HISTORY** probably from Dutch *dabbelen* ▶ **dabbler** *n*

dab hand *n Informal* a person who is particularly skilled at something: *a dab hand with a needle and thread.* ▷ **HISTORY** origin unknown

dace *n, pl* **dace** *or* **daces** a European freshwater fish of the carp family. ▷ **HISTORY** Old French *dars* dart

dachshund *n* a small dog with short legs and a long body.

> **WORD HISTORY**
> 'Dachshund' is a German word meaning 'badger-dog', from *Dachs*, meaning 'badger', and *Hund*, meaning 'dog'. (*Hund* is related to the English word 'hound'.) Dachshunds were originally bred to hunt badgers.

dactyl *n Prosody* a metrical foot of three syllables, one long followed by two short. ▷ **HISTORY** Greek *daktulos* finger, comparing the finger's three joints to the three syllables ▶ **dactylic** *adj*

dad *or* **daddy** *n Informal* father. ▷ **HISTORY** from child's *da da*

Dada *or* **Dadaism** *n* an art movement of the early 20th century that systematically used arbitrary and absurd concepts. ▷ **HISTORY** French: hobbyhorse ▶ **Dadaist** *n, adj*

daddy-longlegs *n informal* **1** *Brit* crane fly. **2** a small web-spinning spider with long legs.

dado (**day**-doe) *n, pl* **-does** *or* **-dos 1** the lower part of an interior wall, often separated by a rail, that is decorated differently from the upper part. **2** *Archit* the part of a pedestal between the base and the cornice. ▷ **HISTORY** Italian: die, die-shaped pedestal

daffodil *n* **1** a spring plant with yellow trumpet-shaped flowers. ✧ *adj* **2** brilliant yellow. ▷ **HISTORY** variant of Latin *asphodelus* asphodel

daft *adj Informal, chiefly Brit* **1** foolish or crazy. **2 daft about** very enthusiastic about: *he's daft about football.*

> **WORD HISTORY**
> 'Daft' and 'deft' both come from Old English *gedæfte*, meaning 'gentle'.

dag *NZ* ✧ *n* **1** the dried dung on a sheep's rear. **2** *Informal* an amusing person. ✧ *pl n* **3 rattle one's dags** *Informal* hurry up. ✧ *vb* **4** to remove the dags from a sheep. ▷ **HISTORY** origin unknown

dagga (**duhh**-a) *n S African* a local name for marijuana. ▷ **HISTORY** probably from Khoi (language of southern Africa) *daxa*

dagger *n* **1** a short knifelike weapon with a double-edged pointed blade. **2** a character (†) used to indicate a cross-reference. **3 at daggers drawn** in a state of open hostility. **4 look daggers** to glare with hostility. ▷ **HISTORY** origin unknown

daggy *adj NZ informal* amusing.

daguerreotype (dag-**gair**-oh-type) *n* a type of early photograph produced on chemically treated silver. ▷ **HISTORY** after L. *Daguerre*, its inventor

dahlia (**day**-lya) *n* a garden plant with showy flowers. ▷ **HISTORY** after Anders *Dahl*, botanist

Dáil Éireann (doil **air**-in) *or* **Dáil** *n* (in the Republic of Ireland) the lower chamber of parliament. ▷ **HISTORY** Irish *dáil* assembly + *Éireann* of Eire

daily *adj* **1** occurring every day or every weekday: *there have been daily airdrops of food, blankets, and water.* **2** of or relating to a single day or to one day at a time: *her home help comes in on a daily basis; exercise has become part of our daily lives.* ✧ *adv* **3** every day. ✧ *n, pl* **-lies 4** *Brit & Austral* a daily newspaper. **5** *Brit informal* a woman employed to clean someone's house. ▷ **HISTORY** Old English *dæglīc*

dainty *adj* **-tier, -tiest 1** delicate, pretty, or elegant: *dainty little pink shoes.* ✧ *n, pl* **-ties 2** *Brit* a small choice cake or sweet. ▷ **HISTORY** Old French *deintié* ▶ **daintily** *adv*

daiquiri (**dak**-eer-ee) *n, pl* **-ris** an iced drink containing rum, lime juice, and sugar. ▷ **HISTORY** after *Daiquiri*, town in Cuba

dairy *n, pl* **dairies 1** a company or shop that sells milk and milk products. **2** a place where milk and cream are stored or made into butter and cheese. **3** *NZ* small shop selling groceries and milk often outside normal trading hours. ✧ *adj* **4** of milk or milk products: *dairy produce.* ▷ **HISTORY** Old English *dǣge* servant girl

dairy cattle *n* cows reared mainly for their milk.

dairy farm *n* a farm where cows are kept mainly for their milk.

dairymaid *n Brit, Austral & NZ* (formerly) a woman employed to milk cows.

dairyman *n Brit, Austral & S African* a man employed to look after cows.

dais (**day**-iss) *n* a raised platform in a hall or meeting place used by a speaker. ▷ HISTORY Old French *deis*

daisy *n, pl* **-sies** a small low-growing flower with a yellow centre and pinkish-white petals.

> **WORD HISTORY**
> 'Daisy' comes from Old English *dæges ēage*, meaning 'day's eye'. The flower was given this name because it opens in the daytime and closes at night.

daisy chain *n* a string of daisies joined together by their stems to make a necklace.

daisywheel *n* a flat disc in a word processor with radiating spokes for printing characters.

dal[1] *n* same as **dhal**.

dal[2] decalitre(s).

Dalai Lama *n* the chief lama and (until 1959) ruler of Tibet.

dale *n* an open valley. ▷ HISTORY Old English *dæl*

dalliance *n Old-fashioned* flirtation.

dally *vb* **-lies, -lying, -lied 1** *Old-fashioned* to waste time or dawdle. **2 dally with** to deal frivolously with: *to dally with someone's affections.* ▷ HISTORY Anglo-French *dalier* to gossip

Dalmatian *n* a large dog with a smooth white coat and black spots.

dam[1] *n* **1** a barrier built across a river to create a lake. **2** a lake created by such a barrier. ✧ *vb* **damming, dammed 3** to block up (a river) by a dam. ▷ HISTORY probably from Middle Low German

dam[2] *n* the female parent of an animal such as a sheep or horse. ▷ HISTORY variant of *dame*

dam[3] decametre(s).

damage *vb* **-aging, -aged 1** to harm or injure. ✧ *n* **2** injury or harm caused to a person or thing. **3** *Informal* cost: *what's the damage?* ▷ HISTORY Latin *damnum* injury, loss ▸ **damaging** *adj*

damages *pl n Law* money awarded as compensation for injury or loss.

damask *n* a heavy fabric with a pattern woven into it, used for tablecloths, curtains, etc. ▷ HISTORY *Damascus,* where fabric originally made

dame *n Slang* a woman. ▷ HISTORY Latin *domina* lady

Dame *n* (in Britain) the title of a woman who has been awarded the Order of the British Empire or another order of chivalry.

damn *interj* **1** *Slang* an exclamation of annoyance. ✧ *adv, adj also* **damned 2** *Slang* extreme or extremely: *a damn good idea.* ✧ *vb* **3** to condemn as bad or worthless. **4** to curse. **5** (of God) to condemn to hell or eternal punishment. **6** to prove (someone) guilty. **7 damn with faint praise** to praise so unenthusiastically that the effect is condemnation. ✧ *n* **8 not give a damn** *Informal* not care. ▷ HISTORY Latin *damnum* loss, injury ▸ **damning** *adj*

damnable *adj* very unpleasant or annoying. ▸ **damnably** *adv*

damnation *interj* **1** an exclamation of anger. ✧ *n* **2** *Theol* eternal punishment.

damned *adj* **1** condemned to hell. ✧ *adv, adj Slang* **2** extreme or extremely: *a damned good try.* **3** used to indicate amazement or refusal: *I'm damned if I'll do it!*

damp *adj* **1** slightly wet. ✧ *n* **2** slight wetness; moisture. ✧ *vb* **3** to make slightly wet. **4 damp down a** to reduce the intensity of (someone's emotions or reactions): *they attempted to damp down protests.* **b** to reduce the flow of air to (a fire) to make it burn more slowly. ▷ HISTORY Middle Low German: steam ▸ **damply** *adv* ▸ **dampness** *n*

damper *n* **1 put a damper on** to produce a depressing or inhibiting effect on. **2** a movable plate to regulate the draught in a stove or furnace. **3** the pad in a piano or harpsichord that deadens the vibration of each string as its key is released. **4** *Chiefly Austral & NZ* any of various unleavened loaves and scones, typically cooked on an open fire.

damsel *n Archaic or poetic* a young woman. ▷ HISTORY Old French *damoisele*

damson *n* a small blue-black edible plumlike fruit that grows on a tree. ▷ HISTORY Latin *prunum damascenum* Damascus plum

dan *n Judo, karate* **1** any of the 10 black-belt grades of proficiency. **2** a competitor entitled to dan grading. ▷ HISTORY Japanese

dance *vb* **dancing, danced 1** to move the feet and body rhythmically in time to music. **2** to perform (a particular dance): *to dance a tango.* **3** to skip or leap. **4** to move in a rhythmic way: *their reflection danced in the black waters.* **5 dance attendance on someone** to carry out someone's slightest wish in an overeager manner. ✧ *n* **6** a social meeting arranged for dancing. **7** a series of rhythmic steps and movements in time to music. **8** a piece of music in the rhythm of a particular dance. ▷ HISTORY Old French *dancier* ▸ **dancer** *n* ▸ **dancing** *n, adj*

D and C *n Med* dilatation of the cervix and curettage of the uterus: a minor operation to clear the womb or remove tissue for diagnosis.

dandelion *n* a wild plant with yellow rayed flowers and deeply notched leaves. ▷ HISTORY Old French *dent de lion* tooth of a lion, referring to its leaves

dander *n* **get one's dander up** *Brit, Austral & NZ slang* to become angry. ▷ HISTORY from *dandruff*

dandified *adj* dressed like or resembling a dandy.

dandle *vb* **-dling, -dled** to move (a young child) up and down on one's knee. ▷ HISTORY origin unknown

dandruff *n* loose scales of dry dead skin shed from the scalp. ▷ HISTORY origin unknown

dandy *n, pl* **-dies 1** a man who is greatly concerned with the elegance of his appearance. ✧ *adj* **-dier, -diest 2** *Informal* very good or fine. ▷ HISTORY origin unknown

Dane *n* a person from Denmark.

danger *n* **1** the possibility that someone may be injured or killed. **2** someone or something that may cause injury or harm. **3** a likelihood that something unpleasant will happen: *the danger of flooding.* ▷ HISTORY Middle English *daunger* power, hence power to inflict injury

danger money *n* extra money paid to compensate for the risks involved in dangerous work.

dangerous *adj* likely or able to cause injury or harm. ▶ **dangerously** *adv*

dangle *vb* **-gling, -gled 1** to hang loosely. **2** to display (something attractive) as an enticement. ▷ **HISTORY** probably imitative

Danish *adj* **1** of Denmark. ✧ *n* **2** the language of Denmark.

Danish blue *n* a white cheese with blue veins and a strong flavour.

Danish pastry *n* a rich puff pastry filled with apple, almond paste, etc. and topped with icing.

dank *adj* (esp. of cellars or caves) unpleasantly damp and chilly. ▷ **HISTORY** probably from Old Norse

dapper *adj* (of a man) neat in appearance and slight in build. ▷ **HISTORY** Middle Dutch

dappled *adj* **1** marked with spots of a different colour; mottled. **2** covered in patches of light and shadow. ▷ **HISTORY** origin unknown

dapple-grey *n* a horse with a grey coat and darker coloured spots.

Darby and Joan *n Chiefly Brit* a happily married elderly couple. ▷ **HISTORY** couple in 18th-century ballad

Darby and Joan Club *n Chiefly Brit* a club for elderly people.

dare *vb* **daring, dared 1** to be courageous enough to try (to do something). **2** to challenge (someone) to do something risky. **3 I dare say a** it is quite possible. **b** probably. ✧ *n* **4** a challenge to do something risky. ▷ **HISTORY** Old English *durran*

> ☑ **WORD TIP**
> When used negatively or interrogatively, *dare* does not usually add *-s: he dare not come; dare she come?* When used negatively in the past tense, however, *dare* usually adds -d: *he dared not come.*

daredevil *n* **1** a recklessly bold person. ✧ *adj* **2** recklessly bold or daring.

daring *adj* **1** willing to do things that may be dangerous. ✧ *n* **2** the courage to do things that may be dangerous. ▶ **daringly** *adv*

dark *adj* **1** having little or no light. **2** (of a colour) reflecting little light: *dark brown.* **3** (of hair or skin) brown or black. **4** (of thoughts or ideas) gloomy or sad. **5** sinister or evil: *a dark deed.* **6** sullen or angry: *a dark scowl.* **7** secret or mysterious: *keep it dark.* ✧ *n* **8** absence of light; darkness. **9** night or nightfall. **10 in the dark** in ignorance. ▷ **HISTORY** Old English *deorc* ▶ **darkly** *adv* ▶ **darkness** *n*

dark age *n* a period of ignorance or barbarism.

Dark Ages *n* the period of European history between 500 and 1000 AD.

darken *vb* **1** to make or become dark or darker. **2** to make gloomy, angry, or sad.

dark horse *n* a person who reveals little about himself or herself, esp. someone who has unexpected talents.

darkroom *n* a darkened room in which photographs are developed.

darling *n* **1** a person very much loved: used as a term of address. **2** a favourite: *the darling of the gossip columns.* ✧ *adj* **3** beloved. **4** pleasing: *a darling film.* ▷ **HISTORY** Old English *dēorling*

darn[1] *vb* **1** to mend a hole in (a knitted garment) with a series of interwoven stitches. ✧ *n* **2** a patch of darned work on a garment. ▷ **HISTORY** origin unknown

darn[2] *interj, adj, adv, vb, n Euphemistic* same as **damn**.

darnel *n* a weed that grows in grain fields. ▷ **HISTORY** origin unknown

dart *n* **1** a small narrow pointed missile that is thrown or shot, as in the game of darts. **2** a sudden quick movement. **3** a tapered tuck made in dressmaking. ✧ *vb* **4** to move or throw swiftly and suddenly. ▷ **HISTORY** Germanic ▶ **darting** *adj*

Darwinism *or* **Darwinian theory** *n* the theory of the origin of animal and plant species by evolution. ▷ **HISTORY** after Charles *Darwin,* English naturalist ▶ **Darwinian** *adj, n* ▶ **Darwinist** *n, adj*

dash *vb* **1** to move hastily; rush. **2** to hurl; crash: *deep-sea rollers dashing spray over jagged rocks.* **3** to frustrate: *prospects for peace have been dashed.* ✧ *n* **4** a sudden quick movement. **5** a small amount: *a dash of milk.* **6** a mixture of style and courage: *the commander's dash did not impress him.* **7** the punctuation mark (—), used to indicate a change of subject. **8** the symbol (–), used in combination with the symbol *dot* (.) in Morse code. ✧ See also **dash off**. ▷ **HISTORY** Middle English *daschen, dassen*

dashboard *n* the instrument panel in a car, boat, or aircraft.

dasher *n Canad* one of the boards surrounding an ice hockey rink.

dashing *adj* stylish and attractive: *a splendidly dashing character.*

dash off *vb* to write down or finish off hastily.

dassie *n S African* a hyrax, esp. a rock hyrax. ▷ **HISTORY** Afrikaans

dastardly *adj Old-fashioned* mean and cowardly. ▷ **HISTORY** Middle English *dastard* dullard

dasyure (**dass**-ee-your) *n* a small marsupial of Australia, New Guinea, and adjacent islands.

DAT digital audio tape.

dat. dative.

data *n* **1** a series of observations, measurements, or facts; information. **2** *Computers* the numbers, digits, characters, and symbols operated on by a computer. ▷ **HISTORY** Latin: (things) given

> ☑ **WORD TIP**
> Although now often used as a singular noun, *data* is in fact a plural.

database *n* **1** a store of information in a form that can be easily handled by a computer. **2** a large store of information: *a database of knowledge.*

data capture *n* a process for converting information into a form that can be handled by a computer.

A B C D E F G H I J K L M N O P Q R S T U V W X Y Z

data processing *n* a sequence of operations performed on data, esp. by a computer, in order to extract or interpret information.

data search *n Computing* an attempt to find information, especially by using a search engine on the Internet.

data set *n Science* information collected and organized for research purposes.

date[1] *n* **1** a specified day of the month. **2** the particular day or year when an event happened. **3 a** an appointment, esp. with a person to whom one is sexually or romantically attached. **b** the person with whom the appointment is made. **4 to date** up to now. ✧ *vb* **dating, dated 5** to mark (a letter or cheque) with the date. **6** to assign a date of occurrence or creation to. **7** to reveal the age of: *that dress dates her.* **8** to make or become old-fashioned: *it's the freshest look this year but may date quickly.* **9** *Informal, chiefly US & Canad* to be a boyfriend or girlfriend of. **10 date from** *or* **date back to** to have originated at (a specified time). ▷ **HISTORY** Latin *dare* to give, as in *epistula data Romae* letter handed over at Rome

> ☑ **WORD TIP**
> See at **year.**

date[2] *n* the dark-brown, sweet tasting fruit of the date palm. ▷ **HISTORY** Greek *daktulos* finger

dated *adj* unfashionable; outmoded.

dateline *n Journalism* information placed at the top of an article stating the time and place the article was written.

Date Line *n* short for **International Date Line**.

date palm *n* a tall palm grown in tropical regions for its fruit.

date rape *n* the act of a man raping a woman or pressuring her into having sex while they are on a date together.

dative *or* **dative case** *n Grammar* the grammatical case in certain languages that expresses the indirect object. ▷ **HISTORY** Latin *dativus*

datum *n, pl* **-ta** a single piece of information usually in the form of a fact or statistic. ▷ **HISTORY** Latin: something given

daub *vb* **1** to smear (paint or mud) quickly or carelessly over a surface. **2** to paint (a picture) clumsily or badly. ✧ *n* **3** a crude or badly done painting: *a typical child's daub.* ▷ **HISTORY** Old French *dauber* to paint

daughter *n* **1** a female child. **2** a girl or woman who comes from a certain place or is connected with a certain thing: *a daughter of the church.* ✧ *adj* **3** *Biol* denoting a cell, chromosome, etc. produced by the division of one of its own kind. **4** *Physics* (of a nuclide) formed from another nuclide by radioactive decay. ▷ **HISTORY** Old English *dohtor* ▶ **daughterly** *adj*

daughter-in-law *n, pl* **daughters-in-law** the wife of one's son.

daunting *adj* intimidating or worrying: *this project grows more daunting every day.* ▷ **HISTORY** Latin *domitare* to tame

dauntless *adj* fearless; not discouraged.

dauphin (**daw**-fin) *n* formerly, the eldest son of the king of France. ▷ **HISTORY** Old French: originally a family name

davenport *n* **1** *Chiefly Brit* a writing desk with drawers at the side. **2** *Austral, US & Canad* a large sofa. ▷ **HISTORY** sense 1 supposedly after Captain *Davenport,* who commissioned the first ones

davit (**dav**-vit) *n* a crane, usually one of a pair, on the side of a ship for lowering or hoisting a lifeboat. ▷ **HISTORY** Anglo-French *daviot,* from *Davi* David

Davy Jones's locker *n* the ocean's bottom, regarded as the grave of those lost or buried at sea. ▷ **HISTORY** origin unknown

Davy lamp *n* same as **safety lamp.** ▷ **HISTORY** after Sir Humphrey *Davy,* chemist

dawdle *vb* **-dling, -dled** to walk slowly or lag behind. ▷ **HISTORY** origin unknown

dawn *n* **1** daybreak. **2** the beginning of something. ✧ *vb* **3** to begin to grow light after the night. **4** to begin to develop or appear. **5 dawn on** *or* **upon** to become apparent (to someone). ▷ **HISTORY** Old English *dagian* to dawn

dawn chorus *n* the singing of birds at dawn.

day *n* **1** the period of 24 hours from one midnight to the next. **2** the period of light between sunrise and sunset. **3** the part of a day occupied with regular activity, esp. work. **4** a period or point in time: *in days gone by; in Shakespeare's day.* **5** a day of special observance: *Christmas Day.* **6** a time of success or recognition: *his day will come.* **7 all in a day's work** part of one's normal activity. **8 at the end of the day** in the final reckoning. **9 call it a day** to stop work or other activity. **10 day in, day out** every day without changing. **11 that'll be the day a** that is most unlikely to happen. **b** I look forward to that. *RELATED ADJECTIVE* ▸ **diurnal** ▷ **HISTORY** Old English *dæg*

daybreak *n* the time in the morning when light first appears.

day centre *n* a place that provides care where elderly or handicapped people can spend the day.

daydream *n* **1** a pleasant fantasy indulged in while awake. ✧ *vb* **2** to indulge in idle fantasy. ▶ **daydreamer** *n*

daylight *n* **1** light from the sun. **2** daytime. **3** daybreak. **4 see daylight** to realize that the end of a difficult task is approaching.

daylight robbery *n Informal* blatant overcharging.

daylight-saving time *n* time set one hour ahead of the local standard time, to provide extra daylight in the evening in summer.

Day of Atonement *n* same as **Yom Kippur**.

day release *n Brit* a system whereby workers go to college one day a week for vocational training.

day return *n* a reduced fare for a train or bus journey travelling both ways in one day.

day room *n* a communal living room in a hospital or similar institution.

day-to-day *adj* routine; everyday.

daze *vb* **dazing, dazed 1** to cause to be in a state of confusion or shock. ✧ *n* **2** a state of confusion or shock: *in a daze.* ▷ **HISTORY** Old Norse *dasa* ▶ **dazed** *adj*

dazzle *vb* **-zling, -zled 1** to impress greatly: *she was dazzled by his wit.* **2** to blind for a short time by sudden excessive light: *he passed two cars and they dazzled him with their headlights.* ✧ *n* **3** bright light that dazzles. ▷ **HISTORY** from *daze* ▶ **dazzling** *adj* ▶ **dazzlingly** *adv*

dB *or* **db** decibel(s).

Db *Chem* dubnium.

DC 1 direct current. **2** District of Columbia.

D.C. District of Columbia.

DCC digital compact cassette: a magnetic tape cassette on which sound can be recorded digitally.

DD Doctor of Divinity.

D-day *n* the day selected for the start of some operation. ▷ **HISTORY** after *D(ay)-day,* the day of the Allied invasion of Europe on June 6, 1944

DDT *n* dichlorodiphenyltrichloroëthane; an insecticide, now banned in many countries.

DE Delaware.

de- *prefix* indicating: **1** removal: *dethrone.* **2** reversal: *declassify.* **3** departure from: *decamp.* ▷ **HISTORY** Latin

deacon *n Christianity* **1** (in episcopal churches) an ordained minister ranking immediately below a priest. **2** (in some Protestant churches) a lay official who assists the minister. ▷ **HISTORY** Greek *diakonos* servant

deactivate *vb* **-vating, -vated** to make (a bomb or other explosive device) harmless.

dead *adj* **1** no longer alive. **2** no longer in use or finished: *a dead language; a dead match.* **3** unresponsive. **4** (of a limb) numb. **5** complete or absolute: *there was dead silence.* **6** *Informal* very tired. **7** (of a place) lacking activity. **8** *Electronics* **a** drained of electric charge. **b** not connected to a source of electric charge. **9** *Sport* (of a ball) out of play. **10 dead from the neck up** *Informal* stupid. **11 dead to the world** *Informal* fast asleep. ✧ *n* **12** a period during which coldness or darkness is most intense: *the dead of winter.* ✧ *adv* **13** *Informal* extremely: *dead easy.* **14** suddenly and abruptly: *stop dead.* **15 dead on** exactly right. ▷ **HISTORY** Old English *dēad*

deadbeat *n Informal* a lazy or socially undesirable person.

dead beat *adj Informal* exhausted.

deaden *vb* to make (something) less intense: *drugs deaden the pain; heavy curtains deadened the echo.* ▶ **deadening** *adj*

dead end *n* **1** a cul-de-sac. **2** a situation in which further progress is impossible: *efforts to free the hostages had reached a dead end.*

deadhead *n US & Canad* **1** *Informal* a person who does not pay on a bus, at a game, etc. **2** *Informal* a commercial vehicle travelling empty. **3** *Slang* a dull person. **4** *US & Canad* a totally or partially submerged log floating in a lake.

dead heat *n* a tie for first place between two or more participants in a race or contest.

dead letter *n* **1** a letter that cannot be delivered or returned due to lack of information. **2** a law or rule that is no longer enforced.

deadline *n* a time or date by which a job or task must be completed.

deadlock *n* a point in a dispute at which no agreement can be reached.

deadlocked *adj* having reached a deadlock.

dead loss *n Informal* a useless person or thing.

deadly *adj* **-lier, -liest 1** likely to cause death: *deadly poison.* **2** *Informal* extremely boring. ✧ *adv, adj* **3** like or suggestive of death: *deadly pale.* **4** extremely: *she was being deadly serious.*

deadly nightshade *n* a poisonous plant with purple bell-shaped flowers and black berries.

dead man's handle *or* **pedal** *n* a safety device which only allows equipment to operate when a handle or pedal is being pressed.

dead-nettle *n* a plant with leaves like nettles but without stinging hairs.

deadpan *adj, adv* with a deliberately emotionless face or manner.

dead reckoning *n* a method of establishing one's position using the distance and direction travelled.

dead set *adv* firmly decided: *he is dead set on leaving.*

dead weight *n* **1** a heavy weight or load. **2** the difference between the loaded and the unloaded weights of a ship.

dead wood *n Informal* people or things that are no longer useful.

deaf *adj* **1** unable to hear. **2 deaf to** refusing to listen or take notice of. ▷ **HISTORY** Old English *dēaf* ▶ **deafness** *n*

> ☑ **WORD TIP**
> See at **disabled.**

deaf-and-dumb *adj Offensive* unable to hear or speak.

deafblind *adj* unable to hear or see.

deafen *vb* to make deaf, esp. momentarily by a loud noise. ▶ **deafening** *adj*

deaf-mute *n* a person who is unable to hear or speak.

deal¹ *n* **1** an agreement or transaction. **2** a particular type of treatment received: *a fair deal.* **3** a large amount: *the land alone is worth a good deal.* **4** *Cards* a player's turn to distribute the cards. **5 big deal** *Slang* an important matter: often used sarcastically. ✧ *vb* **dealing, dealt** (**delt**) **6** to inflict (a blow) on. **7** *Slang* to sell any illegal drug. **8 deal in** to engage in commercially. **9 deal out** to apportion or distribute. ✧ See also **deal with.** ▷ **HISTORY** Old English *dǣlan*

deal² *n* **1** a plank of softwood timber. **2** the sawn wood of various coniferous trees. ▷ **HISTORY** Middle Low German *dele* plank

dealer *n* **1** a person or organization whose business involves buying and selling things. **2** *Slang* a person who sells illegal drugs. **3** *Cards* the person who distributes the cards.

a b c d e f g h i j k l m n o p q r s t u v w x y z

A B C D E F G H I J K L M N O P Q R S T U V W X Y Z

dealings *pl n* business relations with a person or organization.

deal with *vb* **1** to take action on: *he was not competent to deal with the legal aspects.* **2** to be concerned with: *I do not wish to deal with specifics.* **3** to do business with.

dean *n* **1** the chief administrative official of a college or university faculty. **2** *Chiefly Church of England* the chief administrator of a cathedral or collegiate church.

> **WORD HISTORY**
> 'Dean' comes, via Old French, from Latin *decanus*, meaning 'someone in charge of ten people', from Latin *decem*, meaning 'ten'. The chapter of a cathedral or collegiate church consisted of ten canons.

deanery *n, pl* **-eries 1** a place where a dean lives. **2** the parishes presided over by a rural dean.

dear *n* **1** (often used in direct address) someone regarded with affection. ✧ *adj* **2** beloved; precious. **3 a** highly priced. **b** charging high prices. **4** a form of address used at the beginning of a letter before the name of the recipient: *Dear Mr Anderson.* **5 dear to** important or close to. ✧ *interj* **6** an exclamation of surprise or dismay: *oh dear, I've broken it.* ✧ *adv* **7** dearly: *her errors have cost her dear.* ▷ **HISTORY** Old English *dēore* ▶ **dearly** *adv*

dearth (**dirth**) *n* an inadequate amount; scarcity. ▷ **HISTORY** Middle English *derthe*

death *n* **1** the permanent end of life in a person or animal. **2** an instance of this: *his sudden death.* **3** ending or destruction. **4 at death's door** likely to die soon. **5 catch one's death (of cold)** *Informal* to contract a severe cold. **6 like death warmed up** *Informal* looking or feeling very ill or very tired. **7 put to death** to execute. **8 to death a** until dead. **b** very much: *I had probably scared him to death.* ▷ **HISTORY** Old English *dēath*

deathbed *n* the bed in which a person dies or is about to die.

death certificate *n* a document signed by a doctor certifying the death of a person and stating the cause of death if known.

death duty *n* (in Britain) the former name for **inheritance tax**.

death knell *n* something that heralds death or destruction.

deathless *adj* everlasting because of fine qualities: *highbrow, deathless, and often endless prose.*

deathly *adj* **1** resembling death: *a deathly pallor.* **2** deadly.

death mask *n* a cast taken from the face of a person who has recently died.

death rate *n* the ratio of deaths in an area or group to the population of that area or group.

death row *n US* part of a prison where convicts awaiting execution are imprisoned.

death's-head *n* a human skull or a picture of one used to represent death or danger.

death trap *n* a place or vehicle considered very unsafe.

death warrant *n* **1** the official authorization for carrying out a sentence of death. **2 sign one's (own) death warrant** to cause one's own destruction.

deathwatch beetle *n* a beetle that bores into wood and produces a tapping sound.

deb *n Informal* a debutante.

debacle (day-**bah**-kl) *n* something that ends in a disastrous failure, esp. because it has not been properly planned. ▷ **HISTORY** French

debar *vb* **-barring, -barred** to prevent (someone) from doing something.

> **WORD TIP**
> See at **disbar.**

debase *vb* **-basing, -based** to lower in quality, character, or value. ▷ **HISTORY** see DE-, BASE[2] ▶ **debasement** *n*

debatable *adj* not absolutely certain: *her motives are highly debatable.*

debate *n* **1** a discussion. **2** a formal discussion, as in a parliament, in which opposing arguments are put forward. ✧ *vb* **-bating, -bated 3** to discuss (something) formally. **4** to consider (possible courses of action). ▷ **HISTORY** Old French *debatre*

debauch (dib-**bawch**) *vb* to make someone bad or corrupt, esp. sexually. ▷ **HISTORY** Old French *desbaucher* to corrupt

debauched *adj* immoral; sexually corrupt.

debauchery *n* excessive drunkenness or sexual activity.

debenture *n* a long-term bond, bearing fixed interest and usually unsecured, issued by a company or governmental agency. ▷ **HISTORY** Latin *debentur mihi* there are owed to me ▶ **debentured** *adj*

debenture stock *n* shares issued by a company, guaranteeing a fixed return at regular intervals.

debilitate *vb* **-tating, -tated** to make gradually weaker. ▷ **HISTORY** Latin *debilis* weak ▶ **debilitation** *n* ▶ **debilitating** *adj*

debility *n, pl* **-ties** a state of weakness, esp. caused by illness.

debit *n* **1** the money, or a record of the money, withdrawn from a person's bank account. **2** *Accounting* **a** acknowledgment of a sum owing by entry on the left side of an account. **b** an entry or the total of entries on this side. ✧ *vb* **-iting, -ited 3** to charge (an account) with a debt: *they had debited our account.* **4** *Accounting* to record (an item) as a debit in an account. ▷ **HISTORY** Latin *debitum* debt

debit card *n Brit, Austral & S African* a card issued by a bank or building society enabling customers to pay for goods by inserting it into a computer-controlled device at the place of sale, which is connected through the telephone network to the bank or building society.

debonair *or* **debonnaire** *adj* (of a man) confident, charming, and well-dressed. ▷ **HISTORY** Old French

debouch *vb* **1** (esp. of troops) to move into a more open space. **2** (of a river, glacier, etc.) to flow into a larger area or body. ▷ HISTORY Old French *dé-* from + *bouche* mouth ▶ **debouchment** *n*

debrief *vb* to interrogate (a soldier, diplomat, astronaut, etc.) on the completion of a mission. ▶ **debriefing** *n*

debris (**deb**-ree) *n* **1** fragments of something destroyed; rubble. **2** a mass of loose stones and earth. ▷ HISTORY French

debt *n* **1** a sum of money owed. **2 bad debt** a debt that is unlikely to be paid. **3 in debt** owing money. **4 in someone's debt** grateful to someone for his or her help: *I couldn't have managed without you – I'm in your debt.* ▷ HISTORY Latin *debitum*

debt of honour *n* a debt that is morally but not legally binding.

debtor *n* a person who owes money.

debug *vb* **-bugging, -bugged** *Informal* **1** to locate and remove defects in (a computer program). **2** to remove concealed microphones from (a room or telephone).

debunk *vb Informal* to expose the falseness of: *many commonly held myths are debunked by the book.* ▷ HISTORY DE- + BUNK[2] ▶ **debunker** *n*

debut (**day**-byoo) *n* the first public appearance of a performer. ▷ HISTORY French

debutante (**day**-byoo-tont) *n* a young upper-class woman who is formally presented to society. ▷ HISTORY French

Dec. December.

decade *n* a period of ten years. ▷ HISTORY Greek *deka* ten

decadence (**deck**-a-denss) *n* a decline in morality or culture. ▷ HISTORY Medieval Latin *decadentia* a falling away ▶ **decadent** *adj*

decaffeinated (dee-**kaf**-fin-ate-id) *adj* with the caffeine removed: *decaffeinated tea.*

decagon *n Geom* a figure with ten sides. ▷ HISTORY Greek *deka* ten + *gōnia* angle ▶ **decagonal** *adj*

decahedron (deck-a-**heed**-ron) *n* a solid figure with ten plane faces. ▷ HISTORY Greek *deka* ten + *hedra* base ▶ **decahedral** *adj*

decalitre *or US* **decaliter** *n* a measure of volume equivalent to 10 litres.

Decalogue *n* same as **Ten Commandments**. ▷ HISTORY Greek *deka* ten + *logos* word

decametre *or US* **decameter** *n* a unit of length equal to ten metres.

decamp *vb* to leave secretly or suddenly.

decant *vb* **1** to pour (a liquid, esp. wine) from one container to another. **2** *Chiefly Brit* to rehouse (people) while their homes are being renovated. ▷ HISTORY Medieval Latin *de-* from + *canthus* spout, rim

decanter *n* a stoppered bottle into which a drink is poured for serving.

decapitate *vb* **-tating, -tated** to behead. ▷ HISTORY Latin *de-* from + *caput* head ▶ **decapitation** *n*

decapod *n* **1** a creature, such as a crab, with five pairs of walking limbs. **2** a creature, such as a squid, with eight short tentacles and two longer ones. ▷ HISTORY Greek *deka* ten + *pous* foot

decarbonize *or* **-ise** *vb* **-izing, -ized** *or* **-ising, -ised** to remove carbon from (an internal-combustion engine). ▶ **decarbonization** *or* **-isation** *n*

decathlon *n* an athletic contest in which each athlete competes in ten different events. ▷ HISTORY Greek *deka* ten + *athlon* contest ▶ **decathlete** *n*

decay *vb* **1** to decline gradually in health, prosperity, or quality. **2** to rot or cause to rot. **3** *Physics* (of an atomic nucleus) to undergo radioactive disintegration. ✧ *n* **4** the process of something rotting: *too much sugar can cause tooth decay.* **5** the state brought about by this process. **6** *Physics* disintegration of a nucleus, occurring spontaneously or as a result of electron capture. ▷ HISTORY Latin *de-* from + *cadere* to fall

decease *n Formal* death. ▷ HISTORY Latin *decedere* to depart

deceased *adj Formal* **1** dead. ✧ *n* **2** a dead person: *the deceased.*

deceit *n* behaviour intended to deceive.

deceitful *adj* full of deceit.

deceive *vb* **-ceiving, -ceived** **1** to mislead by lying. **2 deceive oneself** to refuse to acknowledge something one knows to be true. **3** to be unfaithful to (one's sexual partner). ▷ HISTORY Latin *decipere* to ensnare, cheat

decelerate *vb* **-ating, -ated** to slow down. ▷ HISTORY DE- + (AC)CELERATE ▶ **deceleration** *n*

December *n* the twelfth month of the year. ▷ HISTORY Latin: the tenth month (the Roman year originally began with March)

decency *n* conformity to the prevailing standards of what is right.

decennial *adj* **1** lasting for ten years. **2** occurring every ten years.

decent *adj* **1** conforming to an acceptable standard or quality: *a decent living wage; he's made a few decent films.* **2** polite or respectable: *he's a decent man.* **3** fitting or proper: *that's the decent thing to do.* **4** conforming to conventions of sexual behaviour. **5** *Informal* kind; generous: *she was pretty decent to me.* ▷ HISTORY Latin *decens* suitable ▶ **decently** *adv*

decentralize *or* **-ise** *vb* **-izing, -ized** *or* **-ising, -ised** to reorganize into smaller local units. ▶ **decentralization** *or* **-isation** *n*

deception *n* **1** the act of deceiving someone or the state of being deceived. **2** something that deceives; trick.

deceptive *adj* likely or designed to deceive. ▶ **deceptively** *adv* ▶ **deceptiveness** *n*

deci- *combining form* denoting one tenth: *decimetre.* ▷ HISTORY Latin *decimus* tenth

decibel *n* a unit for comparing two power levels or measuring the intensity of a sound. ▷ HISTORY DECI- + BEL

A B C D E F G H I J K L M N O P Q R S T U V W X Y Z

decide *vb* **-ciding, -cided 1** to reach a decision: *we must decide on suitable action; he decided to stay on.* **2** to cause to reach a decision. **3** to settle (a question): *possible profits decided the issue.* **4** to influence the outcome of (a contest) decisively: *the goal that decided the match came just before half-time.* ▷ **HISTORY** Latin *decidere* to cut off

decided *adj* **1** definite or noticeable: *a decided improvement.* **2** strong and definite: *he has decided views on the matter.* ▶ **decidedly** *adv*

deciduous *adj* **1** (of a tree) shedding all leaves annually. **2** (of antlers or teeth) being shed at the end of a period of growth. ▷ **HISTORY** Latin *deciduus* falling off

decilitre *or US* **deciliter** *n* a measure of volume equivalent to one tenth of a litre.

decimal *n* **1** a fraction written in the form of a dot followed by one or more numbers, for example $\cdot 2 = {}^{2}/_{10}$. ✧ *adj* **2** relating to or using powers of ten. **3** expressed as a decimal. ▷ **HISTORY** Latin *decima* a tenth

decimal currency *n* a system of currency in which the units are parts or powers of ten.

decimal fraction *n Maths* same as **fraction** (sense 1).

decimalize *or* **-ise** *vb* **-izing, -ized** *or* **-ising, -ised** to change (a system or number) to the decimal system. ▶ **decimalization** *or* **-isation** *n*

decimal point *n* the dot between the unit and the fraction of a number in the decimal system.

decimal system *n* a number system with a base of ten, in which numbers are expressed by combinations of the digits 0 to 9.

decimate *vb* **-mating, -mated** to destroy or kill a large proportion of. ▷ **HISTORY** Latin *decimare* ▶ **decimation** *n*

> **WORD TIP**
> You would talk about the whole of something being *decimated,* not a part: *disease decimated the population,* not *disease decimated most of the population.*

decimetre *or US* **decimeter** *n* a unit of length equal to one tenth of a metre.

decipher *vb* **1** to make out the meaning of (something obscure or illegible). **2** to convert from code into plain text. ▶ **decipherable** *adj*

decision *n* **1** a choice or judgment made about something. **2** the act of making up one's mind. **3** the ability to make quick and definite decisions. ▷ **HISTORY** Latin *decisio* a cutting off

decisive *adj* **1** having great influence on the result of something: *the decisive goal was scored in the closing minutes.* **2** having the ability to make quick decisions. ▶ **decisively** *adv* ▶ **decisiveness** *n*

deck *n* **1** an area of a ship that forms a floor, at any level. **2** a similar area in a bus. **3** same as **tape deck**. **4** *US & Austral* a pack of playing cards. **5 clear the decks** *Informal* to prepare for action, as by removing obstacles. ✧ *vb* **6** *Slang* to knock (a person) to the ground. ▷ **HISTORY** Middle Dutch *dec* a covering

deck chair *n* a folding chair with a wooden frame and a canvas seat.

decking *n* a wooden platform in a garden, esp. for deckchairs, etc.

deck out *vb* to make more attractive by decorating: *the village was decked out in the blue-and-white flags.*

declaim *vb* **1** to speak loudly and dramatically. **2 declaim against** to protest against loudly and publicly. ▷ **HISTORY** Latin *declamare* ▶ **declamation** *n* ▶ **declamatory** *adj*

declaration *n* **1** a firm, emphatic statement. **2** an official announcement or statement. ▶ **declaratory** *adj*

declarative sentence *n Grammar* a sentence which states a fact, as in *Glasgow is in Scotland.*

declare *vb* **-claring, -clared 1** to state firmly and forcefully. **2** to announce publicly or officially: *a state of emergency has been declared.* **3** to state officially that (someone or something) is as specified: *he was declared fit to play.* **4** to acknowledge (dutiable goods or income) for tax purposes. **5** *Cards* to decide (the trump suit) by making the winning bid. **6** *Cricket* to bring an innings to an end before the last batsman is out. **7 declare for** *or* **against** to state one's support or opposition for something. ▷ **HISTORY** Latin *declarare* to make clear

declassify *vb* **-fies, -fying, -fied** to state officially that (information or a document) is no longer secret. ▶ **declassification** *n*

declension *n Grammar* changes in the form of nouns, pronouns, or adjectives to show case, number, and gender. ▷ **HISTORY** Latin *declinatio* a bending aside, hence variation

declination *n* **1** *Astron* the angular distance of a star or planet north or south from the celestial equator. **2** the angle made by a compass needle with the direction of the geographical north pole.

decline *vb* **-clining, -clined 1** to become smaller, weaker, or less important. **2** to politely refuse to accept or do (something). **3** *Grammar* to list the inflections of (a noun, pronoun, or adjective). ✧ *n* **4** a gradual weakening or loss. ▷ **HISTORY** Latin *declinare* to bend away

declivity *n, pl* **-ties** a downward slope. ▷ **HISTORY** Latin *declivitas* ▶ **declivitous** *adj*

declutch *vb* to disengage the clutch of a motor vehicle.

decoct *vb* to extract the essence from (a substance) by boiling. ▷ **HISTORY** Latin *decoquere* to boil down ▶ **decoction** *n*

decode *vb* **-coding, -coded** to convert from code into ordinary language. ▶ **decoder** *n*

decoke *vb* **-coking, -coked** same as **decarbonize**.

décolletage (day-kol-**tahzh**) *n* a low-cut dress or neckline. ▷ **HISTORY** French

décolleté (day-**kol**-tay) *adj* **1** (of a woman's garment) low-cut. ✧ *n* **2** a low-cut neckline. ▷ **HISTORY** French

decommission *vb* to dismantle or remove from service (a nuclear reactor, weapon, ship, etc. which is no longer required).

decompose *vb* **-posing, -posed 1** to rot. **2** *Chem* to break down or cause to break down into simpler chemical compounds. ▶ **decomposition** *n*

decomposer *n Biol* any organism in a community, such as a bacterium or fungus, that breaks down dead tissue into its constituent parts. See also **consumer** (sense 2) **producer** (sense 5).

decompress *vb* **1** to free from pressure. **2** to return (a diver) to normal atmospheric pressure. ▶ **decompression** *n*

decompression sickness *n* a disorder characterized by severe pain and difficulty in breathing caused by a sudden and sustained change in atmospheric pressure.

decongestant *n* a drug that relieves nasal congestion.

deconstruction *n Literature* a technique of literary analysis, developed by French philosopher Jacques Derrida, that regards meaning as resulting from the differences between words rather than their reference to the things they stand for.

decontaminate *vb* **-nating, -nated** to make (a place or object) safe by removing poisons, radioactivity, etc. ▶ **decontamination** *n*

decor (**day**-core) *n* a style or scheme of interior decoration and furnishings in a room or house. ▷ **HISTORY** French

decorate *vb* **-rating, -rated 1** to make more attractive by adding some ornament or colour. **2** to paint or wallpaper. **3** to confer a mark of distinction, esp. a medal, upon. ▷ **HISTORY** Latin *decorare* ▶ **decorative** *adj* ▶ **decorator** *n*

Decorated style *or* **architecture** *n* a 14th-century style of English architecture characterized by the ogee arch, geometrical tracery, and floral decoration.

decoration *n* **1** an addition that makes something more attractive or ornate. **2** the way in which a room or building is decorated. **3** something, esp. a medal, conferred as a mark of honour.

decorous (**deck**-or-uss) *adj* polite, calm, and sensible in behaviour. ▷ **HISTORY** Latin *decorus* ▶ **decorously** *adv* ▶ **decorousness** *n*

decorum (dik-**core**-um) *n* polite and socially correct behaviour.

decoy *n* **1** a person or thing used to lure someone into danger. **2** an image of a bird or animal, used to lure game into a trap or within shooting range. ✧ *vb* **3** to lure into danger by means of a decoy. ▷ **HISTORY** probably from Dutch *de kooi* the cage

decrease *vb* **-creasing, -creased 1** to make or become less in size, strength, or quantity. ✧ *n* **2** a lessening; reduction. **3** the amount by which something has been diminished. ▷ **HISTORY** Latin *decrescere* to grow less ▶ **decreasing** *adj* ▶ **decreasingly** *adv*

decree *n* **1** a law made by someone in authority. **2** a judgment of a court. ✧ *vb* **decreeing, decreed 3** to order by decree. ▷ **HISTORY** Latin *decretum* ordinance

decree absolute *n* the final decree in divorce proceedings, which leaves the parties free to remarry.

decree nisi *n* a provisional decree in divorce proceedings, which will later be made absolute unless cause is shown why it should not. ▷ **HISTORY** Latin *nisi* unless

decrepit *adj* weakened or worn out by age or long use. ▷ **HISTORY** Latin *crepare* to creak ▶ **decrepitude** *n*

decretal *n RC Church* a papal decree. ▷ **HISTORY** Late Latin *decretalis*

decry *vb* **-cries, -crying, -cried** to express open disapproval of. ▷ **HISTORY** Old French *descrier*

dedicate *vb* **-cating, -cated 1** to devote (oneself or one's time) wholly to a special purpose or cause. **2** to inscribe or address (a book, piece of music, etc.) to someone as a token of affection or respect. **3** to play (a record) on radio for someone as a greeting. **4** to set apart for sacred uses. ▷ **HISTORY** Latin *dedicare* to announce

dedicated *adj* **1** devoted to a particular purpose or cause. **2** *Computers* designed to fulfil one function.

dedication *n* **1** wholehearted devotion. **2** an inscription in a book dedicating it to a person.

deduce *vb* **-ducing, -duced** to reach (a conclusion) by reasoning from evidence; work out. ▷ **HISTORY** Latin *de-* away + *ducere* to lead ▶ **deducible** *adj*

deduct *vb* to subtract (a number, quantity, or part). ▷ **HISTORY** Latin *deducere* to deduce

deductible *adj* **1** capable of being deducted. **2** *US* tax-deductible.

deduction *n* **1** the act or process of subtracting. **2** something that is deducted. **3** *Logic* **a** a process of reasoning by which a conclusion necessarily follows from a set of general premises. **b** a conclusion reached by this process. ▶ **deductive** *adj*

deed *n* **1** something that is done. **2** a notable achievement. **3** action as opposed to words. **4** *Law* a legal document, esp. one concerning the ownership of property. ▷ **HISTORY** Old English *dēd*

deed box *n* a strong box in which deeds and other documents are kept.

deed of partnership *n Business* a formal agreement between business partners covering points of mutual interest, such as the amount of capital that each should provide.

deed poll *n Law* a deed made by one party only, esp. to change one's name.

deejay *n Informal* a disc jockey. ▷ **HISTORY** from the initials *DJ*

deem *vb* to judge or consider: *common sense is deemed to be a virtue.* ▷ **HISTORY** Old English *dēman*

deep *adj* **1** extending or situated far down from a surface: *a deep ditch.* **2** extending or situated far inwards, backwards, or sideways. **3** of a specified dimension downwards, inwards, or backwards: *six metres deep.* **4** coming from or penetrating to a

a b c d e f g h i j k l m n o p q r s t u v w x y z

A B C D E F G H I J K L M N O P Q R S T U V W X Y Z

great depth. **5** difficult to understand. **6** of great intensity: *deep doubts*. **7 deep in** totally absorbed in: *deep in conversation*. **8** (of a colour) intense or dark. **9** low in pitch: *a deep laugh*. **10 go off the deep end** *Informal* to lose one's temper. **11 in deep water** *Informal* in a tricky position or in trouble. ✧ *n* **12** any deep place on land or under water. **13 the deep a** *Poetic* the ocean. **b** *Cricket* the area of the field relatively far from the pitch. **14** the most profound, intense, or central part: *the deep of winter*. ✧ *adv* **15** late: *deep into the night*. **16** profoundly or intensely: *deep down I was afraid it was all my fault*. ▷ HISTORY Old English *dēop* ▸ **deeply** *adv*

deepen *vb* to make or become deeper or more intense.

deep-freeze *n* **1** same as **freezer**. ✧ *vb* **-freezing, -froze, -frozen 2** to freeze or keep in a deep-freeze.

deep-fry *vb* **-fries, -frying, -fried** to cook in hot oil deep enough to completely cover the food.

deep-rooted *or* **deep-seated** *adj* (of ideas, beliefs, etc.) firmly fixed or held.

deep-sea trench *n* same as **ocean trench**.

deep-vein thrombosis *n* a blood clot in one of the major veins, usually in the legs or pelvis.

deer *n, pl* **deer** *or* **deers** a large hoofed mammal. ▷ HISTORY Old English *dēor* beast

deerstalker *n* a cloth hat with peaks at the front and back and earflaps.

deface *vb* **-facing, -faced** to deliberately spoil the surface or appearance of. ▸ **defacement** *n*

de facto *adv* **1** in fact. ✧ *adj* **2** existing in fact, whether legally recognized or not. ▷ HISTORY Latin

defalcate *vb* **-cating, -cated** *Law* to make wrong use of funds entrusted to one. ▷ HISTORY Medieval Latin *defalcare* to cut off ▸ **defalcation** *n*

defamation *n Law* **1** the injuring of a person's good name or reputation. Compare **libel, slander**. **2** the act of defaming or state of being defamed.

defame *vb* **-faming, -famed** to attack the good reputation of. ▷ HISTORY Latin *diffamare* to spread by unfavourable report ▸ **defamatory** (dif-**fam**-a-tree) *adj*

default *n* **1** a failure to do something, esp. to meet a financial obligation or to appear in court. **2** *Computers* an instruction to a computer to select a particular option unless the user specifies otherwise. **3 by default** happening because something else has not happened: *they gained a colony by default because no other European power wanted it*. **4 in default of** in the absence of. ✧ *vb* **5** to fail to fulfil an obligation, esp. to make payment when due. ▷ HISTORY Old French *defaillir* to fail ▸ **defaulter** *n*

default judgment *n Law* a judgment in favour of the plaintiff when the defendant has failed to appear or put in a defence.

defeat *vb* **1** to win a victory over. **2** to thwart or frustrate: *this accident has defeated all his hopes of winning*. ✧ *n* **3** the act of defeating or state of being defeated. ▷ HISTORY Old French *desfaire* to undo, ruin

defeatism *n* a ready acceptance or expectation of defeat. ▸ **defeatist** *n, adj*

defecate *vb* **-cating, -cated** to discharge waste from the body through the anus. ▷ HISTORY Latin *defaecare* ▸ **defecation** *n*

defect *n* **1** an imperfection or blemish. ✧ *vb* **2** to desert one's country or cause to join the opposing forces. ▷ HISTORY Latin *deficere* to forsake, fail ▸ **defection** *n* ▸ **defector** *n*

defective *adj* imperfect or faulty: *defective hearing*.

defence *or US* **defense** *n* **1** resistance against attack. **2** something that provides such resistance. **3** an argument or piece of writing in support of something that has been criticized or questioned. **4** a country's military resources. **5** *Law* a defendant's denial of the truth of a charge. **6** *Law* the defendant and his or her legal advisers collectively. **7** *Sport* the players in a team whose function is to prevent the opposing team from scoring. **8 defences** fortifications. ▷ HISTORY Latin *defendere* to defend ▸ **defenceless** *or US* **defenseless** *adj*

defend *vb* **1** to protect from harm or danger. **2** to support in the face of criticism: *I spoke up to defend her*. **3** to represent (a defendant) in court. **4** to protect (a title or championship) against a challenge. ▷ HISTORY Latin *defendere* to ward off ▸ **defender** *n*

defendant *n* a person accused of a crime.

defensible *adj* capable of being defended because believed to be right. ▸ **defensibility** *n*

defensive *adj* **1** intended for defence. **2** guarding against criticism or exposure of one's failings: *he can be highly defensive and wary*. ✧ *n* **3 on the defensive** in a position of defence, as in being ready to reject criticism. ▸ **defensively** *adv*

defer[1] *vb* **-ferring, -ferred** to delay until a future time; postpone: *payment was deferred indefinitely*. ▷ HISTORY Old French *differer* to be different, postpone ▸ **deferment** *or* **deferral** *n*

defer[2] *vb* **-ferring, -ferred defer to** to comply with the wishes (of). ▷ HISTORY Latin *deferre* to bear down

deference *n* polite and respectful behaviour.

deferential *adj* showing respect. ▸ **deferentially** *adv*

defiance *n* open resistance to authority or opposition. ▸ **defiant** *adj*

deficiency *n, pl* **-cies 1** the state of being deficient. **2** a lack or shortage.

deficiency disease *n* any condition, such as scurvy, caused by a lack of vitamins or other essential substances.

deficient *adj* **1** lacking some essential. **2** inadequate in quantity or quality. ▷ HISTORY Latin *deficere* to fall short

deficit *n* the amount by which a sum is lower than that expected or required. ▷ HISTORY Latin: there is lacking

defile[1] *vb* **-filing, -filed 1** to make foul or dirty. **2** to make unfit for ceremonial use. ▷ HISTORY Old

French *defouler* to trample underfoot, abuse ▶ **defilement** *n*

defile[2] *n* a narrow pass or gorge: *the sandy defile of Wadi Rum.* ▷ **HISTORY** French *défiler* to file off

define *vb* **-fining, -fined 1** to describe the nature of. **2** to state precisely the meaning of. **3** to show clearly the outline of: *the picture was sharp and cleanly defined.* **4** to fix with precision; specify: *define one's duties.* ▷ **HISTORY** Latin *definire* to set bounds to ▶ **definable** *adj*

definite *adj* **1** firm, clear, and precise: *I have very definite views on this subject.* **2** having precise limits or boundaries. **3** known for certain: *it's definite that they have won.* ▷ **HISTORY** Latin *definitus* limited, distinct ▶ **definitely** *adv*

definite article *n Grammar* the word 'the'.

definition *n* **1** a statement of the meaning of a word or phrase. **2** a description of the essential qualities of something. **3** the quality of being clear and distinct. **4** sharpness of outline.

definitive *adj* **1** final and unable to be questioned or altered: *a definitive verdict.* **2** most complete, or the best of its kind: *the book was hailed as the definitive Dickens biography.* ▶ **definitively** *adv*

deflate *vb* **-flating, -flated 1** to collapse or cause to collapse through the release of gas. **2** to take away the self-esteem or conceit from. **3** to cause deflation of (an economy). ▷ **HISTORY** DE- + (IN)FLATE

deflation *n* **1** *Econ* a reduction in economic activity resulting in lower levels of output and investment. **2** a feeling of sadness following excitement. ▶ **deflationary** *adj*

deflect *vb* to turn or cause to turn aside from a course. ▷ **HISTORY** Latin *deflectere* ▶ **deflection** *n* ▶ **deflector** *n*

deflower *vb Literary* to deprive (a woman) of her virginity.

defoliate *vb* **-ating, -ated** to deprive (a plant) of its leaves. ▷ **HISTORY** Latin *de-* from + *folium* leaf ▶ **defoliant** *n* ▶ **defoliation** *n*

deforestation *n Geog* the cutting down or destruction of forests.

deform *vb* to put (something) out of shape or spoil its appearance. ▷ **HISTORY** Latin *de-* from + *forma* shape beauty

deformed *adj* disfigured or misshapen.

deformity *n, pl* **-ties 1** *Pathol* a distortion of an organ or part. **2** the state of being deformed.

defraud *vb* to cheat out of money, property, or a right to do something.

defray *vb* to provide money to cover costs or expenses. ▷ **HISTORY** Old French *deffroier* to pay expenses ▶ **defrayal** *n*

defrock *vb* to deprive (a priest) of ecclesiastical status.

defrost *vb* **1** to make or become free of frost or ice. **2** to thaw (frozen food) by removing from a deep-freeze.

deft *adj* quick and skilful in movement; dexterous. ▷ **HISTORY** Middle English variant of *daft* (in the sense: gentle) ▶ **deftly** *adv* ▶ **deftness** *n*

defunct *adj* no longer existing or working properly. ▷ **HISTORY** Latin *defungi* to discharge (one's obligations), die

defuse *or US sometimes* **defuze** *vb* **-fusing, -fused** *or* **-fuzing, -fuzed 1** to remove the fuse of (an explosive device). **2** to reduce the tension in (a difficult situation): *I said it in a bid to defuse the situation.*

> ☑ **WORD TIP**
> Avoid confusion with **diffuse.**

defy *vb* **-fies, -fying, -fied 1** to resist openly and boldly. **2** to elude in a baffling way: *his actions defy explanation.* **3** *Formal* to challenge (someone to do something). ▷ **HISTORY** Old French *desfier*

degenerate *adj* **1** having deteriorated to a lower mental, moral, or physical level. ✧ *n* **2** a degenerate person. ✧ *vb* **-ating, -ated 3** to become degenerate. ▷ **HISTORY** Latin *degener* departing from its kind, ignoble ▶ **degeneracy** *n*

degeneration *n* **1** the process of degenerating. **2** *Biol* the loss of specialization or function by organisms.

degenerative *adj* (of a disease or condition) getting steadily worse.

degradation *n* **1** a degrading or being degraded. **2** a state of degeneration or squalor. **3** some act, constraint, etc., that is degrading. **4** *Geol* the wearing down of the surface of rocks, cliffs, etc., by erosion. Compare **aggradation.**

degrade *vb* **-grading, -graded 1** to reduce to dishonour or disgrace. **2** to reduce in status or quality. **3** *Chem* to decompose into atoms or smaller molecules. ▷ **HISTORY** Latin *de-* from + *gradus* rank, degree ▶ **degrading** *adj*

degree *n* **1** a stage in a scale of relative amount or intensity: *this task involved a greater degree of responsibility.* **2** an academic award given by a university or college on successful completion of a course. **3** *Grammar* any of the forms of an adjective used to indicate relative amount or intensity. **4** a unit of temperature. Symbol: °. **5** a measure of angle equal to one three-hundred-and-sixtieth of the circumference of a circle. Symbol: °. **6** a unit of latitude or longitude. Symbol: °. **7 by degrees** little by little; gradually. ▷ **HISTORY** Latin *de-* down + *gradus* step

dehisce *vb* **-hiscing, -hisced** (of the seed capsules of some plants) to burst open spontaneously. ▷ **HISTORY** Latin *dehiscere* to split open ▶ **dehiscence** *n* ▶ **dehiscent** *adj*

dehumanize *or* **-ise** *vb* **-izing, -ized** *or* **-ising, -ised 1** to deprive of the qualities thought of as being best in human beings, such as kindness. **2** to make (an activity) mechanical or routine. ▶ **dehumanization** *or* **-isation** *n*

dehydrate *vb* **-drating, -drated 1** to remove water from (food) in order to preserve it. **2 be dehydrated** (of a person) to become weak or ill through losing too much water from the body. ▶ **dehydration** *n*

de-ice *vb* **de-icing, de-iced** to free of ice. ▶ **de-icer** *n*

a b c d e f g h i j k l m n o p q r s t u v w x y z

A B C D E F G H I J K L M N O P Q R S T U V W X Y Z

deictic *n Grammar* a term whose reference depends on the context of the utterance, such as *I, you, here, now,* or *tomorrow*.

deify (**day**-if-fie) *vb* **-fies, -fying, -fied** to treat or worship (someone or something) as a god. ▷ **HISTORY** Latin *deus* god + *facere* to make ▶ **deification** *n*

deign (**dane**) *vb* to do something that one considers beneath one's dignity: *she did not deign to reply.* ▷ **HISTORY** Latin *dignari* to consider worthy

deindustrialization *or* **-sation** *n* a decline in the importance of a country's manufacturing industry.

deism (**dee**-iz-zum) *n* belief in the existence of God based only on natural reason, without reference to revelation. ▶ **deist** *n, adj* ▶ **deistic** *adj*

deity (**dee**-it-ee) *n, pl* **-ties 1** a god or goddess. **2** the state of being divine. ▷ **HISTORY** Latin *deus* god

Deity *n* **the Deity** God.

déjà vu (**day**-zhah **voo**) *n* a feeling of having experienced before something that is happening at the present moment. ▷ **HISTORY** French: already seen

dejected *adj* in low spirits; downhearted. ▷ **HISTORY** Latin *deicere* to cast down ▶ **dejectedly** *adv* ▶ **dejection** *n*

de jure *adv* according to law. ▷ **HISTORY** Latin

dekko *n Brit, Austral & NZ slang* **have a dekko** have a look. ▷ **HISTORY** Hindi *dekhnā* to see

delay *vb* **1** to put (something) off to a later time. **2** to slow up or cause to be late. **3 a** to hesitate in doing something. **b** to deliberately take longer than necessary to do something. ✧ *n* **4** the act of delaying. **5** a period of inactivity or waiting before something happens or continues. ▷ **HISTORY** Old French *des-* off + *laier* to leave

delectable *adj* delightful or very attractive. ▷ **HISTORY** Latin *delectare* to delight

delectation *n Formal* great pleasure and enjoyment.

delegate *n* **1** a person chosen to represent others at a conference or meeting. ✧ *vb* **-gating, -gated 2** to entrust (duties or powers) to another person. **3** to appoint as a representative. ▷ **HISTORY** Latin *delegare* to send on a mission

delegated legislation *n Law* laws made under powers delegated to ministers and bodies by Parliament.

delegation *n* **1** a group chosen to represent others. **2** the act of delegating.

delete *vb* **-leting, -leted** to remove or cross out (something printed or written). ▷ **HISTORY** Latin *delere* ▶ **deletion** *n*

deleterious (del-lit-**eer**-ee-uss) *adj Formal* harmful or injurious. ▷ **HISTORY** Greek *dēlētērios*

Delft *n* tin-glazed earthenware which originated in Delft in the Netherlands, typically with blue decoration on a white ground. Also: **delftware**

deliberate *adj* **1** carefully thought out in advance; intentional. **2** careful and unhurried: *a deliberate gait.* ✧ *vb* **-ating, -ated 3** to consider (something) deeply; think over. ▷ **HISTORY** Latin *deliberare* to consider well ▶ **deliberately** *adv* ▶ **deliberative** *adj*

deliberation *n* **1** careful consideration. **2** calmness and absence of hurry. **3 deliberations** formal discussions.

delicacy *n, pl* **-cies 1** fine or subtle quality, construction, etc.: *delicacy of craftsmanship.* **2** fragile or graceful beauty. **3** something that is considered particularly nice to eat. **4** frail health. **5** refinement of feeling, manner, or appreciation: *the delicacy of the orchestra's playing.* **6** requiring careful or tactful treatment.

delicate *adj* **1** fine or subtle in quality or workmanship. **2** having a fragile beauty. **3** (of colour, smell, or taste) pleasantly subtle. **4** easily damaged; fragile. **5** precise or sensitive in action: *the delicate digestive system.* **6** requiring tact: *a delicate matter.* **7** showing consideration for the feelings of other people. ▷ **HISTORY** Latin *delicatus* affording pleasure ▶ **delicately** *adv*

delicatessen *n* a shop selling unusual or imported foods, often already cooked or prepared. ▷ **HISTORY** German *Delikatessen* delicacies

delicious *adj* **1** very appealing to taste or smell. **2** extremely enjoyable. ▷ **HISTORY** Latin *deliciae* delights ▶ **deliciously** *adv*

delight *n* **1** extreme pleasure. **2** something or someone that causes this. ✧ *vb* **3** to please greatly. **4 delight in** to take great pleasure in. ▷ **HISTORY** Latin *delectare* to please ▶ **delightful** *adj* ▶ **delightfully** *adv*

delighted *adj* greatly pleased.

delimit *vb* **-iting, -ited** to mark or lay down the limits of. ▶ **delimitation** *n*

delineate (dill-**lin**-ee-ate) *vb* **-ating, -ated 1** to show by drawing. **2** to describe in words. ▷ **HISTORY** Latin *delineare* to sketch out ▶ **delineation** *n*

delinquent *n* **1** someone, esp. a young person, who breaks the law. ✧ *adj* **2** repeatedly breaking the law. ▷ **HISTORY** Latin *delinquens* offending ▶ **delinquency** *n*

deliquesce *vb* **-quescing, -quesced** (esp. of certain salts) to dissolve in water absorbed from the air. ▷ **HISTORY** Latin *deliquescere* to melt away ▶ **deliquescence** *n* ▶ **deliquescent** *adj*

delirious *adj* **1** suffering from delirium. **2** wildly excited and happy. ▶ **deliriously** *adv*

delirium *n* **1** a state of excitement and mental confusion, often with hallucinations. **2** violent excitement. ▷ **HISTORY** Latin: madness

delirium tremens (**trem**-enz) *n* a severe condition characterized by delirium and trembling, caused by chronic alcoholism. ▷ **HISTORY** New Latin: trembling delirium

deliver *vb* **1** to carry (goods or mail) to a destination. **2** to hand over: *the tenants were asked to deliver up their keys.* **3** to aid in the birth of (offspring). **4** to present (a lecture or speech). **5** to release or rescue (from captivity or danger). **6** to strike (a blow) suddenly. **7** *Informal* Also: **deliver the goods** to produce something promised. ▷ **HISTORY** Latin *de-* from + *liberare* to free ▶ **deliverance** *n*

delivery *n, pl* **-eries 1 a** the act of delivering goods or mail. **b** something that is delivered. **2** the act of giving birth to a baby. **3** manner or style in public speaking: *her delivery was clear and humorous.* **4** *Cricket* the act or manner of bowling a ball. **5** *S African* a semi-official slogan for the provision of services to previously disadvantaged communities.

dell *n Chiefly Brit* a small wooded hollow. ▷ **HISTORY** Old English

Delphic *adj* obscure or ambiguous, like the ancient Greek oracle at Delphi.

delphinium *n, pl* **-iums** *or* **-ia** a large garden plant with spikes of blue flowers. ▷ **HISTORY** Greek *delphis* dolphin

delta *n* **1** the fourth letter in the Greek alphabet (Δ, δ). **2** the flat area at the mouth of some rivers where the main stream splits up into several branches.

delude *vb* **-luding, -luded** to make someone believe something that is not true. ▷ **HISTORY** Latin *deludere*

deluge (**del**-lyooj) *n* **1** a great flood of water. **2** torrential rain. **3** an overwhelming number. ✧ *vb* **-uging, -uged 4** to flood. **5** to overwhelm. ▷ **HISTORY** Latin *diluere* to wash away

Deluge *n* **the Deluge** same as the **Flood**.

delusion *n* **1** a mistaken idea or belief. **2** the state of being deluded. ▶ **delusive** *adj* ▶ **delusory** *adj*

de luxe *adj* rich or sumptuous; superior in quality: *a de luxe hotel.* ▷ **HISTORY** French

delve *vb* **delving, delved 1** to research deeply or intensively (for information). **2** *Old-fashioned* to dig. ▷ **HISTORY** Old English *delfan*

demagnetize *or* **-ise** *vb* **-izing, -ized** *or* **-ising, -ised** to remove magnetic properties. ▶ **demagnetization** *or* **-isation** *n*

demagogue *or US sometimes* **demagog** *n* a political agitator who attempts to win support by appealing to the prejudice and passions of the mob. ▷ **HISTORY** Greek *dēmagōgos* people's leader ▶ **demagogic** *adj* ▶ **demagogy** *n*

demand *vb* **1** to request forcefully. **2** to require as just, urgent, etc.: *the situation demands intervention.* **3** to claim as a right. ✧ *n* **4** a forceful request. **5** something that requires special effort or sacrifice: *demands upon one's time.* **6** *Econ* the amount of a commodity that consumers are willing and able to buy at a specified price. **7 in demand** sought after; popular. **8 on demand** as soon as requested: *the funds will be available on demand.* ▷ **HISTORY** Latin *demandare* to commit to

demanding *adj* requiring a lot of skill, time, or effort: *a demanding relationship.*

demarcation *n* the act of establishing limits or boundaries, esp. between the work performed by members of different trade unions. ▷ **HISTORY** Spanish *demarcar* to appoint the boundaries of

demean *vb* to do something unworthy of one's status or character: *there is no doubt that he will lose face with the boss by having to demean himself in this way.* ▷ **HISTORY** DE- + MEAN[2]

demeanour *or US* **demeanor** *n* the way a person behaves. ▷ **HISTORY** Old French *de-* (intensive) + *mener* to lead

demented *adj* mad; insane. ▷ **HISTORY** Late Latin *dementare* to drive mad ▶ **dementedly** *adv*

dementia (dim-**men**-sha) *n* a state of serious mental deterioration. ▷ **HISTORY** Latin: madness

demerara sugar *n* brown crystallized cane sugar from the West Indies. ▷ **HISTORY** after *Demerara,* a region of Guyana

demerit *n* **1** a fault or disadvantage. **2** *US & Canad* a mark given against a student for failure or misconduct.

demesne (dim-**mane**) *n* **1** land surrounding a house or manor. **2** *Property law* the possession of one's own property or land. **3** a region or district; domain. ▷ **HISTORY** Old French *demeine*

Demeter *n Greek myth* the goddess of agriculture.

demi- *combining form* **1** half: *demirelief.* **2** of less than full size, status, or rank: *demigod.* ▷ **HISTORY** Latin *dimidius* half

demigod *n* **1 a** a being who is part mortal, part god. **b** a lesser deity. **2** a godlike person.

demijohn *n* a large bottle with a short narrow neck, often encased in wickerwork. ▷ **HISTORY** probably from French *dame-jeanne*

demilitarize *or* **-rise** *vb* **-rizing, -rized** *or* **-rising, -rised** to remove all military forces from (an area): *demilitarized zone.* ▶ **demilitarization** *or* **-risation** *n*

demimonde *n* **1** (esp. in the 19th century) a class of women considered to be outside respectable society because of promiscuity. **2** any group considered not wholly respectable. ▷ **HISTORY** French: half-world

demise *n* **1** the eventual failure of something originally successful. **2** *Euphemistic, formal* death. **3** *Property law* a transfer of an estate by lease. ✧ *vb* **-mising, -mised 4** *Property law* to transfer for a limited period; lease. ▷ **HISTORY** Old French *demis* dismissed

demisemiquaver *n Music* a note with the time value of one thirty-second of a semibreve.

demist *vb* to make or become free of condensation. ▶ **demister** *n*

demo *n, pl* **-os** *Informal* **1** short for **demonstration** (sense 1). **2** a demonstration record or tape.

demob *vb* **-mobbing, -mobbed** *Brit, Austral & NZ informal* to demobilize.

demobilize *or* **-lise** *vb* **-lizing, -lized** *or* **-lising, -lised** to release from the armed forces. ▶ **demobilization** *or* **-lisation** *n*

democracy *n, pl* **-cies 1** a system of government or organization in which the citizens or members choose leaders or make other important decisions by voting. **2** a country in which the citizens choose their government by voting. ▷ **HISTORY** Greek *dēmokratia*

democrat *n* a person who believes in democracy.

A B C D E F G H I J K L M N O P Q R S T U V W X Y Z

Democrat *n US politics* a member or supporter of the Democratic Party, the more liberal of the two main political parties in the US. ▶ **Democratic** *adj*
democratic *adj* of or relating to a country, organization, or system in which leaders are chosen or decisions are made by voting. ▶ **democratically** *adv*
demodulation *n Electronics* the process by which an output wave or signal is obtained having the characteristics of the original modulating wave or signal.
demography *n* the study of population statistics, such as births and deaths. ▷ HISTORY Greek *dēmos* the populace + -GRAPHY ▶ **demographic** *adj*
demolish *vb* **1** to tear down or break up (buildings). **2** to put an end to; destroy: *I demolished her argument in seconds.* **3** *Facetious* to eat up: *he demolished the whole cake.* ▷ HISTORY Latin *demoliri* to throw down ▶ **demolisher** *n* ▶ **demolition** *n*
demon *n* **1** an evil spirit. **2** a person, obsession, etc., thought of as evil or persistently tormenting. **3** a person extremely skilful in or devoted to a given activity: *a demon at cricket.* ▷ HISTORY Greek *daimōn* spirit, fate ▶ **demonic** *adj*
demonetize *or* **-tise** *vb* **-tizing, -tized** *or* **-tising, -tised** to withdraw from use as currency. ▶ **demonetization** *or* **-tisation** *n*
demoniac *or* **demoniacal** *adj* **1** appearing to be possessed by a devil. **2** suggesting inner possession or inspiration: *the demoniac fire of genius.* **3** frantic or frenzied: *demoniac activity.* ▶ **demoniacally** *adv*
demonolatry *n* the worship of demons. ▷ HISTORY *demon* + Greek *latreia* worship
demonology *n* the study of demons or demonic beliefs. ▷ HISTORY *demon* + -LOGY
demonstrable *adj* able to be proved. ▶ **demonstrably** *adv*
demonstrate *vb* **-strating, -strated 1** to show or prove by reasoning or evidence. **2** to display and explain the workings of (a machine, product, etc.). **3** to reveal the existence of: *the adult literacy campaign demonstrated the scale of educational deprivation.* **4** to show support or opposition by public parades or rallies. ▷ HISTORY Latin *demonstrare* to point out
demonstration *n* **1** a march or public meeting to demonstrate opposition to something or support for something. **2** an explanation or demonstration showing how something works. **3** proof or evidence leading to proof.
demonstrative *adj* **1** tending to show one's feelings freely and openly. **2** *Grammar* denoting a word used to point out the person or thing referred to, such as *this* and *those*. **3 demonstrative of** giving proof of. ▶ **demonstratively** *adv*
demonstrator *n* **1** a person who demonstrates how a device or machine works. **2** a person who takes part in a public demonstration.
demoralize *or* **-ise** *vb* **-izing, -ized** *or* **-ising, -ised** to deprive (someone) of confidence or enthusiasm: *she had been demoralized and had just given up.* ▶ **demoralization** *or* **-isation** *n*
demote *vb* **-moting, -moted** to lower in rank or position. ▷ HISTORY DE- + (PRO)MOTE ▶ **demotion** *n*
demotic *adj* of or relating to the common people. ▷ HISTORY Greek *dēmotikos*
demur *vb* **-murring, -murred 1** to show reluctance; object. ✧ *n* **2 without demur** without objecting. ▷ HISTORY Latin *demorari* to linger
demure *adj* quiet, reserved, and rather shy. ▷ HISTORY perhaps from Old French *demorer* to delay, linger ▶ **demurely** *adv* ▶ **demureness** *n*
demutualize *or* **-ise** *vb* **-izing, -ized** *or* **-ising, -ised** (of a mutual savings or life-assurance organization) to convert to a public limited company. ▶ **demutualization** *or* **-isation** *n*
demystify *vb* **-fies, -fying, -fied** to remove the mystery from: *he attempted to demystify the contemporary jargon of psychology.* ▶ **demystification** *n*
den *n* **1** the home of a wild animal; lair. **2** *Chiefly US* a small secluded room in a home, often used for a hobby. **3** a place where people indulge in criminal or immoral activities: *a den of iniquity.* ▷ HISTORY Old English *denn*
denarius (din-**air**-ee-uss) *n, pl* **-narii** (-**nair**-ee-eye) a silver coin of ancient Rome, often called a penny in translation. ▷ HISTORY Latin
denary (**dean**-a-ree) *adj* calculated by tens; decimal. ▷ HISTORY Latin *denarius*
denationalize *or* **-ise** *vb* **-izing, -ized** *or* **-ising, -ised** to transfer (an industry or a service) from public to private ownership. ▶ **denationalization** *or* **-isation** *n*
denature *vb* **-turing, -tured 1** to change the nature of. **2** to make (alcohol) unfit to drink by adding another substance.
dendrology *n* the study of trees. ▷ HISTORY Greek *dendron* tree + -LOGY
dene *or* **dean** *n Chiefly Brit* a narrow wooded valley.
dengue (**deng**-gee) *n* a viral disease transmitted by mosquitoes, characterized by headache, fever, pains in the joints, and a rash. ▷ HISTORY probably of African origin
denial *n* **1** a statement that something is not true. **2** a rejection of a request. **3** *Psychol* a process by which painful thoughts are not permitted into the consciousness.
denier (**den**-yer) *n* a unit of weight used to measure the fineness of silk and man-made fibres. ▷ HISTORY Old French: coin
denigrate *vb* **-grating, -grated** to criticize (someone or something) unfairly. ▷ HISTORY Latin *denigrare* to make very black ▶ **denigration** *n* ▶ **denigrator** *n*
denim *n* **1** a hard-wearing cotton fabric used for jeans, skirts, etc. **2 denims** jeans made of denim. ▷ HISTORY French *(serge) de Nîmes* (serge) of Nîmes, in S France
denizen *n* **1** a person, animal, or plant that lives or grows in a particular place. **2** an animal or plant established in a place to which it is not native. ▷ HISTORY Old French *denzein*

denominate *vb* **-nating, -nated** to give a specific name to; designate. ▷ **HISTORY** Latin *denominare*

denomination *n* **1** a group which has slightly different beliefs from other groups within the same faith. **2** a unit in a system of weights, values, or measures: *coins of small denomination have been withdrawn.* **3** a name given to a class or group; classification. ▶ **denominational** *adj*

denominator *n* the number below the line in a fraction, as 8 in $^7/_8$.

denotation *n* the strict meaning of something. Compare **connotation**.

denote *vb* **-noting, -noted 1** to be a sign or indication of: *these contracts denote movement on the widest possible scale.* **2** (of a word or phrase) to have as a literal or obvious meaning. ▷ **HISTORY** Latin *denotare* to mark

denouement (day-**noo**-mon) *n* the final outcome or solution in a play or other work. ▷ **HISTORY** French

denounce *vb* **-nouncing, -nounced 1** to condemn openly or vehemently. **2** to give information against. ▷ **HISTORY** Latin *denuntiare* to make an official proclamation, threaten

dense *adj* **1** thickly crowded or closely packed. **2** difficult to see through: *dense clouds of smoke.* **3** *Informal* stupid or dull. **4** (of a film, book, etc.) difficult to follow or understand: *the content should be neither too dense nor too abstract.* ▷ **HISTORY** Latin *densus* thick ▶ **densely** *adv*

density *n, pl* **-ties 1** the degree to which something is filled or occupied: *an average population density.* **2** *Physics* a measure of the compactness of a substance, expressed as its mass per unit volume. **3** a measure of a physical quantity per unit of length, area, or volume.

dent *n* **1** a hollow in the surface of something. ✧ *vb* **2** to make a dent in. ▷ **HISTORY** variant of *dint*

dental *adj* of or relating to the teeth or dentistry. ▷ **HISTORY** Latin *dens* tooth

dental floss *n* a waxed thread used to remove particles of food from between the teeth.

dental surgeon *n* same as **dentist**.

dentate *adj* having teeth or toothlike notches. ▷ **HISTORY** Latin *dentatus*

dentifrice (**den**-tif-riss) *n* paste or powder for cleaning the teeth. ▷ **HISTORY** Latin *dens* tooth + *fricare* to rub

dentine (**den**-teen) *n* the hard dense tissue that forms the bulk of a tooth. ▷ **HISTORY** Latin *dens* tooth

dentist *n* a person qualified to practise dentistry. ▷ **HISTORY** French *dentiste*

dentistry *n* the branch of medicine concerned with the teeth and gums.

dentition *n* the typical arrangement, type, and number of teeth in a species. ▷ **HISTORY** Latin *dentitio* a teething

denture *n* (*often pl*) a partial or full set of artificial teeth. ▷ **HISTORY** French *dent* tooth

denudation *n* **1** the process of making something bare. **2** *Geog* the processes of erosion and weathering that wear away land and vegetation and expose rock.

denude *vb* **-nuding, -nuded 1** to make bare; strip: *the atrocious weather denuded the trees.* **2** *Geol* to expose (rock) by the erosion of the layers above.

denumerable *adj Maths* countable.

denunciation *n* open condemnation; denouncing. ▷ **HISTORY** Latin *denuntiare* to proclaim

deny *vb* **-nies, -nying, -nied 1** to declare (a statement) to be untrue. **2** to refuse to give or allow: *we have been denied permission.* **3** to refuse to acknowledge: *the baron denied his wicked son.* ▷ **HISTORY** Latin *denegare*

deodar *n* a Himalayan cedar with drooping branches. ▷ **HISTORY** Hindi

deodorant *n* a substance applied to the body to prevent or disguise the odour of perspiration.

deodorize *or* **-ise** *vb* **-izing, -ized** *or* **-ising, -ised** to remove or disguise the odour of. ▶ **deodorization** *or* **-isation** *n*

deoxygenate *vb Chem* to remove the oxygen from a substance such as water or air.

deoxyribonucleic acid *n* same as **DNA**.

depart *vb* **1** to leave. **2** to differ or deviate: *to depart from the original concept.* ▷ **HISTORY** Old French *departir*

departed *adj Euphemistic* dead.

department *n* **1** a specialized division of a large business organization, hospital, university, etc. **2** a major subdivision of the administration of a government. **3** an administrative division in several countries, such as France. **4** *Informal* a specialized sphere of activity: *wine-making is my wife's department.* ▷ **HISTORY** French *département* ▶ **departmental** *adj*

department store *n* a large shop divided into departments selling many kinds of goods.

departure *n* **1** the act of departing. **2** a divergence from previous custom, rule, etc. **3** a course of action or venture: *the album represents a new departure for them.*

depend *vb* **depend on a** to put trust (in); rely (on). **b** to be influenced or determined (by): *the answer depends on four main issues.* **c** to rely (on) for income or support. ▷ **HISTORY** Latin *dependere* to hang from

dependable *adj* reliable and trustworthy. ▶ **dependability** *n* ▶ **dependably** *adv*

dependant *n* a person who depends on another for financial support.

> **WORD TIP**
> Avoid confusion with **dependent.**

dependence *n* **1** the state of relying on something in order to be able to survive or operate properly. **2** reliance or trust: *they had a bond between them of mutual dependence and trust.*

dependency *n, pl* **-cies 1** a territory subject to a state on which it does not border. **2** *Psychol* overreliance on another person or on a drug.

A B C D E F G H I J K L M N O P Q R S T U V W X Y Z

dependent *adj* **1** depending on a person or thing for aid or support. **2** *Maths* (of a variable) dependent for its value on another variable. **3 dependent on** *or* **upon** influenced or conditioned by.

> **WORD TIP**
> Avoid confusion with **dependant.**

dependent clause *n* another term for **subordinate clause.**

dependent variable *n Maths* a variable in an equation or statement whose value depends on the value of the independent variable.

depict *vb* **1** to represent by drawing, painting, etc. **2** to describe in words. ▷ HISTORY Latin *depingere* ▶ **depiction** *n*

depilatory (dip-**pill**-a-tree) *adj* **1** able or serving to remove hair. ✧ *n, pl* **-ries 2** a chemical used to remove hair. ▷ HISTORY Latin *depilare* to pull out the hair

deplete *vb* **-pleting, -pleted 1** to use up (supplies or money). **2** to reduce in number. ▷ HISTORY Latin *deplere* to empty out ▶ **depletion** *n*

deplorable *adj* very bad or unpleasant. ▶ **deplorably** *adv*

deplore *vb* **-ploring, -plored** to express or feel strong disapproval of. ▷ HISTORY Latin *deplorare* to weep bitterly

deploy *vb* to organize (troops or resources) into a position ready for immediate and effective action. ▷ HISTORY Latin *displicare* to unfold ▶ **deployment** *n*

deponent *n Law* a person who makes a statement on oath. ▷ HISTORY Latin *deponens* putting down

depopulate *vb* **-lating, -lated** to cause to be reduced in population. ▶ **depopulation** *n*

deport *vb* **1** to remove forcibly from a country. **2 deport oneself** to behave in a specified manner. ▷ HISTORY Latin *deportare* to carry away, banish

deportation *n* the act of expelling someone from a country.

deportee *n* a person deported or awaiting deportation.

deportment *n* the way in which a person moves and stands: *she had the manners and deportment of a great lady.* ▷ HISTORY Old French *deporter* to conduct (oneself)

depose *vb* **-posing, -posed 1** to remove from an office or position of power. **2** *Law* to testify on oath. ▷ HISTORY Latin *deponere* to put aside

deposit *vb* **-iting, -ited 1** to put down. **2** to entrust (money or valuables) for safekeeping. **3** to place (money) in a bank account or other savings account. **4** to lay down naturally: *the river deposits silt.* ✧ *n* **5** a sum of money placed in a bank account or other savings account. **6** money given in part payment for goods or services. **7** an amount of a substance left on a surface as a result of chemical or geological process. ▷ HISTORY Latin *depositus* put down

deposit account *n Brit* a bank account that earns interest.

depositary *n, pl* **-taries** a person or group to whom something is entrusted for safety.

deposition *n* **1** *Law* the sworn statement of a witness used in court in his or her absence. **2** the act of deposing. **3** the act of depositing. **4** something deposited. ▷ HISTORY Late Latin *depositio* a laying down, testimony

depositor *n* a person who places or has money on deposit in a bank or similar organization: *panic-stricken depositors.*

depository *n, pl* **-ries 1** a store where furniture, valuables, etc. can be kept for safety. **2** same as **depositary**.

depot (**dep**-oh) *n* **1** a place where goods and vehicles are kept when not in use. **2** *US, Canad & NZ* a bus or railway station. ▷ HISTORY French

depraved *adj* morally bad; corrupt. ▷ HISTORY Latin *depravare* to distort, corrupt

depravity *n, pl* **-ties** moral corruption.

deprecate *vb* **-cating, -cated** to express disapproval of. ▷ HISTORY Latin *deprecari* to avert, ward off ▶ **deprecation** *n* ▶ **deprecatory** *adj*

> **WORD TIP**
> Avoid confusion with **depreciate.**

depreciate *vb* **-ating, -ated 1** to decline in value or price. **2** to deride or criticize. ▷ HISTORY Latin *de-* down + *pretium* price ▶ **depreciatory** *adj*

> **WORD TIP**
> Avoid confusion with **deprecate.**

depreciation *n* **1** *Accounting* the reduction in value of a fixed asset through use, obsolescence, etc. **2** a decrease in the exchange value of a currency. **3** the act or an instance of belittling.

depredation *n* plundering; pillage. ▷ HISTORY Latin *depraedare* to pillage

depress *vb* **1** to make sad and gloomy. **2** to lower (prices). **3** to push down. ▷ HISTORY Old French *depresser* ▶ **depressing** *adj* ▶ **depressingly** *adv*

depressant *adj* **1** *Med* able to reduce nervous or functional activity; sedative. ✧ *n* **2** a depressant drug.

depressed *adj* **1** low in spirits; downcast. **2** suffering from economic hardship, such as unemployment: *the current depressed conditions.* **3** pressed down or flattened.

depression *n* **1** a mental state in which a person has feelings of gloom and inadequacy. **2** an economic condition in which there is substantial unemployment, low output and investment; slump. **3** *Meteorol* a mass of air below normal atmospheric pressure, which often causes rain. **4** a sunken place.

Depression *n* **the Depression** the worldwide economic depression of the early 1930s.

depressive *adj* causing sadness and lack of energy.

deprive *vb* **-priving, -prived deprive of** to prevent from having or enjoying. ▷ **HISTORY** Latin *de-* from + *privare* to deprive of ▶ **deprivation** *n*

deprived *adj* lacking adequate living conditions, education, etc.: *deprived ghettos.*

dept department.

depth *n* **1** the distance downwards, backwards, or inwards. **2** intensity of emotion or feeling. **3** the quality of having a high degree of knowledge, insight, and understanding. **4** intensity of colour. **5** lowness of pitch. **6 depths a** a remote inaccessible region: *the depths of the forest.* **b** the most severe part: *the depths of depression.* **c** a low moral state. **7 out of one's depth a** in water deeper than one is tall. **b** beyond the range of one's competence or understanding. ▷ **HISTORY** Middle English *dep* deep

depth charge *n* a bomb used to attack submarines that explodes at a preset depth of water.

deputation *n* a body of people appointed to represent others.

depute *vb* **-puting, -puted** to appoint (someone) to act on one's behalf. ▷ **HISTORY** Late Latin *deputare* to assign, allot

deputize *or* **-tise** *vb* **-tizing, -tized** *or* **-tising, -tised** to act as deputy.

deputy *n, pl* **-ties** a person appointed to act on behalf of another. ▷ **HISTORY** Old French *deputer* to appoint

derail *vb* to cause (a train) to go off the rails. ▶ **derailment** *n*

derailleur (dee-**rail**-yer) *n* a type of gear-change mechanism for bicycles.

deranged *adj* **1** mad, or behaving in a wild and uncontrolled way. **2** in a state of disorder. ▷ **HISTORY** from Old French *desrengier* to disorder, disturb ▶ **derangement** *n*

derby *n, pl* **-bies** *US & Canad* a bowler hat.

Derby *n, pl* **-bies 1 the Derby** an annual horse race for three-year-olds, run at Epsom Downs, Surrey. **2 local derby** a sporting event between teams from the same area. ▷ **HISTORY** after the Earl of *Derby,* who founded the race in 1780

deregulate *vb* **-lating, -lated** to remove regulations or controls from. ▶ **deregulation** *n*

derelict *adj* **1** abandoned or unused and falling into ruins. ✧ *n* **2** a social outcast or vagrant. ▷ **HISTORY** Latin *derelinquere* to abandon

dereliction *n* **1** the state of being abandoned. **2 dereliction of duty** wilful neglect of one's duty.

derestrict *vb Brit, Austral & NZ* to make (a road) free from speed limits. ▶ **derestriction** *n*

deride *vb* **-riding, -rided** to speak of or treat with contempt or ridicule. ▷ **HISTORY** Latin *deridere* to laugh to scorn ▶ **derision** *n*

de rigueur (de rig-**gur**) *adj* required by fashion. ▷ **HISTORY** French, literally: of strictness

derisive *adj* mocking or scornful. ▶ **derisively** *adv*

derisory *adj* too small or inadequate to be considered seriously: *the shareholders have dismissed the offer as derisory.*

derivation *n* the origin or descent of something, such as a word.

derivative *adj* **1** based on other sources; not original. ✧ *n* **2** a word, idea, etc., that is derived from another. **3** *Maths* the rate of change of one quantity with respect to another.

derive *vb* **-riving, -rived** to draw or be drawn (from) in source or origin. ▷ **HISTORY** Old French *deriver* to spring from

dermatitis *n* inflammation of the skin. ▷ **HISTORY** Greek *derma* skin

dermatology *n* the branch of medicine concerned with the skin. ▷ **HISTORY** Greek *derma* skin + -LOGY ▶ **dermatologist** *n*

derogate *vb* **-gating, -gated derogate from** to cause to seem inferior; detract from. ▷ **HISTORY** Latin *derogare* to diminish ▶ **derogation** *n*

derogatory (dir-**rog**-a-tree) *adj* expressing or showing a low opinion of someone or something.

derrick *n* **1** a simple crane that has lifting tackle slung from a boom. **2** the framework erected over an oil well to enable drill tubes to be raised and lowered. ▷ **HISTORY** after *Derrick,* famous hangman

derring-do *n Archaic or literary* a daring spirit or deed. ▷ **HISTORY** Middle English *durring don* daring to do

derv *n Brit* diesel oil, when used for road transport. ▷ **HISTORY** *d(iesel) e(ngine) r(oad) v(ehicle)*

dervish *n* a member of a Muslim religious order noted for a frenzied, ecstatic, whirling dance. ▷ **HISTORY** Persian *darvīsh* mendicant monk

desalination *n* the process of removing salt, esp. from sea water.

descale *vb* to remove the hard coating which sometimes forms inside kettles, pipes, etc.

descant *n* **1** a tune played or sung above a basic melody. ✧ *adj* **2** of the highest member in a family of musical instruments: *a descant clarinet.* ▷ **HISTORY** Latin *dis-* apart + *cantus* song

descend *vb* **1** to move down (a slope, staircase, etc.). **2** to move or fall to a lower level, pitch, etc. **3 be descended from** to be connected by a blood relationship to. **4 descend on** to visit unexpectedly. **5** to stoop to (unworthy behaviour). ▷ **HISTORY** Latin *descendere*

descendant *n* a person or animal descended from an individual, race, or species.

descendent *adj* descending.

descent *n* **1** the act of descending. **2** a downward slope. **3** a path or way leading downwards. **4** derivation from an ancestor; family origin. **5** a decline or degeneration.

describe *vb* **-scribing, -scribed 1** to give an account of (something or someone) in words. **2** to trace the outline of (a circle, etc.). ▷ **HISTORY** Latin *describere* to copy off, write out

description *n* **1** a statement or account that describes someone or something. **2** the act of describing. **3** sort, kind, or variety: *antiques of every description.*

descriptive *adj* describing something: *it was a very descriptive account of the play.* ▶ **descriptively** *adv*

descry *vb* **-scries, -scrying, -scried 1** to catch sight of. **2** to discover by looking carefully. ▷ HISTORY Old French *descrier* to proclaim

desecrate *vb* **-crating, -crated** to violate the sacred character of (an object or place). ▷ HISTORY DE- + (CON)SECRATE ▶ **desecration** *n*

desegregate *vb* **-gating, -gated** to end racial segregation in (a school or other public institution). ▶ **desegregation** *n*

deselect *vb Brit politics* (of a constituency organization) to refuse to select (an MP) for re-election. ▶ **deselection** *n*

desensitize *or* **-tise** *vb* **-tizing, -tized** *or* **-tising, -tised** to make insensitive or less sensitive: *the patient was desensitized to the allergen; to desensitize photographic film.*

desert[1] *n* a region that has little or no vegetation because of low rainfall. ▷ HISTORY Church Latin *desertum*

desert[2] *vb* **1** to abandon (a person or place) without intending to return. **2** *Chiefly mil* to leave (a post or duty) with no intention of returning. ▷ HISTORY Latin *deserere* ▶ **deserted** *adj* ▶ **deserter** *n* ▶ **desertion** *n*

desertification *n* a process by which fertile land turns into desert.

desert island *n* a small uninhabited island in the tropics.

desert rat *n* **1** a jerboa, inhabiting the deserts of N Africa. **2** *History informal* an Allied soldier who took part in the desert campaigns of World War II in 1941-42. ▷ HISTORY from the jerboa symbol of the British 7th Armoured division

deserts *pl n* **get one's just deserts** get the punishment one deserves. ▷ HISTORY Old French *deserte* something deserved

deserve *vb* **-serving, -served** to be entitled to or worthy of. ▷ HISTORY Latin *deservire* to serve devotedly

deserved *adj* rightfully earned. ▶ **deservedly** (diz-**zerv**-id-lee) *adv*

deserving *adj* worthy of a reward, help, or praise.

deshabille (day-zab-**beel**) *or* **dishabille** *n* the state of being partly dressed. ▷ HISTORY French *déshabillé*

desiccate *vb* **-cating, -cated** to remove most of the water from; dry. ▷ HISTORY Latin *desiccare* to dry up ▶ **desiccated** *adj* ▶ **desiccation** *n*

design *vb* **1** to work out the structure or form of (something), by making a sketch or plans. **2** to plan and make (something) artistically. **3** to intend (something) for a specific purpose: *the move is designed to reduce travelling costs.* ✧ *n* **4** a sketch, plan, or preliminary drawing. **5** the arrangement or features of an artistic or decorative work: *he built it to his own design.* **6** a finished artistic or decorative creation. **7** the art of designing. **8** an intention; purpose. **9 have designs on** to plot to gain possession of. ▷ HISTORY Latin *designare* to mark out, describe

designate (**dez**-zig-nate) *vb* **-nating, -nated 1** to give a name to or describe as: *vessels sunk during battle are designated as war graves.* **2** to select (someone) for an office or duty; appoint. ✧ *adj* **3** appointed, but not yet in office: *a Prime Minister designate.* ▷ HISTORY Latin *designatus* marked out

designation *n* **1** something that designates, such as a name. **2** the act of designating.

designedly (dee-**zine**-id-lee) *adv* by intention.

designer *n* **1** a person who draws up original sketches or plans from which things are made. ✧ *adj* **2** designed by a well-known fashion designer: *a wardrobe full of designer clothes.* **3** having an appearance of fashionable trendiness: *designer stubble.*

designing *adj* cunning and scheming.

desirable *adj* **1** worth having or doing: *a desirable lifestyle.* **2** arousing sexual desire. ▶ **desirability** *n* ▶ **desirably** *adv*

desire *vb* **-siring, -sired 1** to want very much. **2** *Formal* to request: *we desire your company at the wedding of our daughter.* ✧ *n* **3** a wish or longing. **4** sexual appetite. **5** a person or thing that is desired. ▷ HISTORY Latin *desiderare*

desist *vb* to stop doing: *please desist from talking.* ▷ HISTORY Latin *desistere*

desk *n* **1** a piece of furniture with a writing surface and usually drawers. **2** a service counter in a public building, such as a hotel. **3** the section of a newspaper or television station responsible for a particular subject: *the picture desk.* ▷ HISTORY Medieval Latin *desca* table

desktop *adj* small enough to use at a desk: *a desktop computer.*

desktop publishing *n* a computer system which combines text and graphics and presents them in a professional-looking printed format.

desolate *adj* **1** uninhabited and bleak. **2** made uninhabitable; devastated. **3** without friends, hope, or encouragement. **4** gloomy or dismal; depressing. ✧ *vb* **-lating, -lated 5** to deprive of inhabitants. **6** to make barren; devastate. **7** to make wretched or forlorn. ▷ HISTORY Latin *desolare* to leave alone ▶ **desolately** *adv* ▶ **desolateness** *n*

desolation *n* **1** ruin or devastation. **2** solitary misery; wretchedness.

despair *n* **1** total loss of hope. ✧ *vb* **2** to lose or give up hope: *we must not despair of finding a peaceful solution.* ▷ HISTORY Old French *despoir* hopelessness

despatch *vb, n* same as **dispatch**.

desperado *n, pl* **-does** *or* **-dos** a reckless person ready to commit any violent illegal act. ▷ HISTORY probably pseudo-Spanish

desperate *adj* **1** willing to do anything to improve one's situation. **2** (of an action) undertaken as a last resort. **3** very grave: *in desperate agony.* **4** having a great need or desire: *I was desperate for a child.* ▷ HISTORY Latin *desperare* to have no hope ▶ **desperately** *adv*

desperation *n* **1** desperate recklessness. **2** the state of being desperate.

despicable *adj* deserving contempt. ▸ **despicably** *adv*

despise *vb* **-pising, -pised** to look down on with contempt. ▷ HISTORY Latin *despicere* to look down

despite *prep* in spite of. ▷ HISTORY Old French *despit*

despoil *vb Formal* to plunder. ▷ HISTORY Latin *despoliare* ▸ **despoliation** *n*

despondent *adj* dejected or depressed. ▷ HISTORY Latin *despondere* to lose heart ▸ **despondency** *n* ▸ **despondently** *adv*

despot *n* any person in power who acts tyrannically. ▷ HISTORY Greek *despotēs* lord, master ▸ **despotic** *adj* ▸ **despotically** *adv*

despotism *n* **1** absolute or tyrannical government. **2** tyrannical behaviour.

dessert *n* the sweet course served at the end of a meal. ▷ HISTORY French

dessertspoon *n* a spoon between a tablespoon and a teaspoon in size.

destination *n* the place to which someone or something is going.

destined (**dess**-tinnd) *adj* **1** certain to be or do something: *the school is destined to close this summer.* **2** heading towards a specific destination: *some of the oil was destined for Eastern Europe.* ▷ HISTORY Latin *destinare* to appoint

destiny *n, pl* **-nies 1** the future destined for a person or thing. **2** the predetermined course of events. **3** the power that predetermines the course of events. ▷ HISTORY Old French *destinee*

destitute *adj* lacking the means to live; totally impoverished. ▷ HISTORY Latin *destituere* to leave alone ▸ **destitution** *n*

destroy *vb* **1** to ruin; demolish. **2** to put an end to. **3** to kill (an animal). **4** to crush or defeat. ▷ HISTORY Latin *destruere* to pull down

destroyer *n* **1** a small heavily armed warship. **2** a person or thing that destroys.

destructible *adj* capable of being destroyed.

destruction *n* **1** the act of destroying something or state of being destroyed. **2** a cause of ruin. ▷ HISTORY Latin *destructio* a pulling down

destructive *adj* **1** causing or capable of causing harm, damage, or injury. **2** intended to discredit, esp. without positive suggestions or help: *destructive speeches against the platform.* ▸ **destructively** *adv*

destructive interference *n Physics* the effect that occurs when the crest of one wave coincides with the trough of another wave.

destructive plate boundary *n Geol* a tectonic plate boundary where an oceanic plate is forced under a continental plate.

destructive wave *n Geog* a wave in which the water moves forward and there is friction with the seabed.

destructive waves *pl n Geog* strong steep waves that drag sand and pebbles away from the shore causing erosion and destroying beaches. Compare **constructive waves**.

desuetude (diss-**syoo**-it-tude) *n Formal* the condition of not being in use. ▷ HISTORY Latin *desuescere* to lay aside a habit

desultory (**dez**-zl-tree) *adj* **1** passing or jumping from one thing to another; disconnected: *desultory conversation.* **2** occurring in a random way: *a desultory thought.* ▷ HISTORY Latin *de-* from + *salire* to jump ▸ **desultorily** *adv*

detach *vb* **1** to disengage and separate. **2** *Mil* to send (a regiment, officer, etc.) on a special assignment. ▷ HISTORY Old French *destachier* ▸ **detachable** *adj*

detached *adj* **1** *Brit, Austral & S African* separate or standing apart: *a detached farmhouse.* **2** showing no emotional involvement: *she continued to watch him in her grave and detached manner.*

detachment *n* **1** the state of not being personally involved in something. **2** *Mil* a small group of soldiers separated from the main group.

detail *n* **1** an item that is considered separately. **2** an item considered to be unimportant: *a mere detail.* **3** treatment of individual parts: *the census provides a considerable amount of detail.* **4** a small section of a work of art often enlarged to make the smaller features more distinct. **5** *Chiefly mil* **a** personnel assigned a specific duty. **b** the duty. **6 in detail** including all the important particulars. ✧ *vb* **7** to list fully. **8** *Chiefly mil* to select (personnel) for a specific duty. ▷ HISTORY Old French *detailler* to cut in pieces

detain *vb* **1** to delay (someone). **2** to force (someone) to stay: *the police detained him for questioning.* ▷ HISTORY Latin *detinere* ▸ **detainee** *n* ▸ **detainment** *n*

detect *vb* **1** to perceive or notice: *to detect a note of sarcasm.* **2** to discover the existence or presence of: *to detect alcohol in the blood.* ▷ HISTORY Latin *detegere* to uncover ▸ **detectable** *adj* ▸ **detector** *n*

detection *n* **1** the act of noticing, discovering, or sensing something. **2** the act or process of extracting information.

detective *n* **a** a police officer who investigates crimes. **b** same as **private detective**.

detente (day-**tont**) *n* the easing of tension between nations. ▷ HISTORY French

detention *n* **1** imprisonment, esp. of a suspect awaiting trial. **2** a form of punishment in which a pupil is detained after school.

detention centre *n* a place where young people may be detained for short periods of time by order of a court.

deter *vb* **-terring, -terred** to discourage or prevent (someone) from doing something by instilling fear or doubt in them. ▷ HISTORY Latin *deterrere*

detergent *n* **1** a chemical substance used for washing clothes, dishes, etc. ✧ *adj* **2** having cleansing power. ▷ HISTORY Latin *detergens* wiping off

deteriorate *vb* **-rating, -rated** to become worse. ▷ HISTORY Latin *deterior* worse ▸ **deterioration** *n*

A B C D E F G H I J K L M N O P Q R S T U V W X Y Z

determinant *adj* **1** serving to determine or affect. ✧ *n* **2** a factor that controls or influences what will happen. **3** *Maths* a square array of elements that represents the sum of certain products of these elements.

determinate *adj* definitely limited or fixed.

determination *n* **1** the condition of being determined; resoluteness. **2** the act of making a decision.

determine *vb* **-mining, -mined 1** to settle (an argument or a question) conclusively. **2** to find out the facts about (something): *the tests determined it was in fact cancer.* **3** to fix in scope, extent, etc.: *to determine the degree of the problem.* **4** to make a decision. ▷ HISTORY Latin *determinare* to set boundaries to

determined *adj* firmly decided. ▶ **determinedly** *adv*

determiner *n Grammar* a word, such as a number, article, or personal pronoun, that determines the meaning of a noun phrase.

determinism *n* the theory that human choice is not free, but is decided by past events. ▶ **determinist** *n, adj*

deterrent *n* **1** something that deters. **2** a weapon or set of weapons held by one country to deter another country attacking. ✧ *adj* **3** tending to deter. ▷ HISTORY Latin *deterrens* hindering ▶ **deterrence** *n*

detest *vb* to dislike intensely. ▷ HISTORY Latin *detestari* ▶ **detestable** *adj*

detestation *n* intense hatred.

dethrone *vb* **-throning, -throned** to remove from a throne or deprive of any high position. ▶ **dethronement** *n*

detonate *vb* **-nating, -nated** to make (an explosive device) explode or (of an explosive device) to explode. ▷ HISTORY Latin *detonare* to thunder down ▶ **detonation** *n*

detonator *n* a small amount of explosive or a device used to set off an explosion.

detour *n* a deviation from a direct route or course of action. ▷ HISTORY French

detoxify *vb* **-fies, -fying, -fied** to remove poison from. ▶ **detoxification** *n*

detract *vb* **detract from** to make (something) seem less good, valuable, or impressive: *I wouldn't want to detract from your triumph.* ▷ HISTORY Latin *detrahere* to pull away, disparage ▶ **detractor** *n* ▶ **detraction** *n*

> **WORD TIP**
>
> *Detract* is sometimes wrongly used where *distract* is meant: *a noise distracted* (not *detracted*) *my attention.*

detriment *n* disadvantage or damage. ▷ HISTORY Latin *detrimentum* a rubbing off ▶ **detrimental** *adj* ▶ **detrimentally** *adv*

detritus (dit-**trite**-uss) *n* **1** a loose mass of stones and silt worn away from rocks. **2** debris. ▷ HISTORY Latin: a rubbing away ▶ **detrital** *adj*

de trop (de **troh**) *adj* unwanted or unwelcome: *I know when I'm de trop, so I'll leave you two together.* ▷ HISTORY French

detumescence *n* the subsidence of a swelling. ▷ HISTORY Latin *detumescere* to cease swelling

deuce (**dyewss**) *n* **1** *Tennis* a tied score that requires one player to gain two successive points to win the game. **2** a playing card or dice with two spots. ▷ HISTORY Latin *duo* two

deus ex machina *n* an unlikely development introduced into a play or film to resolve the plot.

deuterium *n* a stable isotope of hydrogen. Symbol: D or ^{2}H. ▷ HISTORY Greek *deuteros* second

deuterium oxide *n* same as **heavy water**.

Deutschmark (**doytch**-mark) *or* **Deutsche Mark** (**doytch**-a) *n* a former monetary unit of Germany. ▷ HISTORY German: German mark

deutzia (**dyewt**-see-a) *n* a shrub with clusters of pink or white flowers.

devalue *vb* **-valuing, -valued 1** to reduce the exchange value of (a currency). **2** to reduce the value of (something or someone). ▶ **devaluation** *n*

devastate *vb* **-tating, -tated** to damage (a place) severely or destroy it. ▷ HISTORY Latin *devastare* ▶ **devastation** *n*

devastated *adj* shocked and extremely upset. ▶ **devastating** *adj* ▶ **devastatingly** *adv*

develop *vb* **1** to grow or bring to a later, more elaborate, or more advanced stage. **2** to come or bring into existence: *the country has developed a consumer society.* **3** to make or become gradually clearer or more widely known. **4** to follow as a result of something: *Cubism developed from attempts to give painting a more intellectual concept of form.* **5** to contract (an illness). **6** to improve the value or change the use of (land). **7** to exploit the natural resources of (a country or region). **8** *Photog* to treat (a photographic plate or film) to produce a visible image. ▷ HISTORY Old French *desveloper* to unwrap

developer *n* **1** a person who develops property. **2** *Photog* a chemical used to develop photographs or films.

developing country *n* a poor or nonindustrial country that is seeking to develop its resources by industrialization.

development *n* **1** the process of growing or developing. **2** the product of developing. **3** an event or incident that changes a situation. **4** an area of land that has been developed. ▶ **developmental** *adj*

development area *n* (in Britain) an area which has experienced economic depression and which is given government assistance to establish new industry.

deviant *adj* **1** deviating from what is considered acceptable behaviour. ✧ *n* **2** a person whose behaviour deviates from what is considered to be acceptable. ▶ **deviance** *n*

deviate *vb* **-ating, -ated 1** to differ from others in belief or thought. **2** to depart from one's usual or previous behaviour. ▷ HISTORY Late Latin *deviare* to turn aside from the direct road ▶ **deviation** *n*

device *n* **1** a machine or tool used for a particular purpose. **2** *Euphemistic* a bomb. **3** a scheme or plan. **4** a design or emblem. **5 leave someone to his** *or* **her own devices** to leave someone alone to do as he or she wishes. ▷ **HISTORY** Old French *devis* contrivance + *devise* intention

devil *n* **1** *Theol* **the Devil** the chief spirit of evil and enemy of God. **2** any evil spirit. **3** a person regarded as wicked. **4** a person: *lucky devil.* **5** a person regarded as daring: *be a devil!* **6** *Informal* something difficult or annoying. **7 between the devil and the deep blue sea** between equally undesirable alternatives. **8 give the devil his due** to acknowledge the talent or success of an unpleasant person. **9 talk of the devil!** used when an absent person who has been the subject of conversation arrives unexpectedly. **10 the devil** used as an exclamation to show surprise or annoyance: *what the devil is she doing here?* ✧ *vb* **-illing, -illed** *or US* **-iling, -iled 11** to prepare (food) by coating with a highly flavoured spiced mixture. **12** *Chiefly Brit* to do routine literary work for a lawyer or author. ▷ **HISTORY** Greek *diabolos* enemy, accuser

devilish *adj* **1** of or like a devil; fiendish. ✧ *adv, adj* **2** *Informal* extreme or extremely: *devilish good food.* ▶ **devilishly** *adv*

devil-may-care *adj* happy-go-lucky; reckless.

devilment *n* mischievous conduct.

devilry *n* **1** reckless fun or mischief. **2** wickedness.

devil's advocate *n* a person who takes an opposing or unpopular point of view for the sake of argument.

devious *adj* **1** insincere and dishonest. **2** (of a route or course of action) indirect. ▷ **HISTORY** Latin *devius* lying to one side of the road ▶ **deviously** *adv*

devise *vb* **-vising, -vised** to work out (something) in one's mind. ▷ **HISTORY** Old French *deviser* to divide

devoid *adj* **devoid of** completely lacking in a particular quality: *she was a woman totally devoid of humour.* ▷ **HISTORY** Old French *devoider* to remove

devolution *n* a transfer of authority from a central government to regional governments. ▷ **HISTORY** Medieval Latin *devolutio* a rolling down ▶ **devolutionist** *n, adj*

devolve *vb* **-volving, -volved** to pass or cause to pass to a successor or substitute, as duties or power. ▷ **HISTORY** Latin *devolvere* to roll down

Devon *n* a breed of large red cattle originally from Devon.

Devonian *adj* **1** *Geol* of the period of geological time about 405 million years ago. **2** of or relating to Devon.

devote *vb* **-voting, -voted** to apply or dedicate (one's time, money, or effort) to a particular purpose. ▷ **HISTORY** Latin *devovere* to vow

devoted *adj* feeling or demonstrating loyalty or devotion: *he was clearly devoted to his family.* ▶ **devotedly** *adv*

devotee (dev-vote-**tee**) *n* **1** a person fanatically enthusiastic about a subject or activity. **2** a zealous follower of a religion.

devotion *n* **1** strong attachment to or affection for someone or something. **2** religious zeal; piety. **3 devotions** religious observance or prayers. ▶ **devotional** *adj*

devour *vb* **1** to eat up greedily. **2** to engulf and destroy. **3** to read avidly. ▷ **HISTORY** Latin *devorare* to gulp down ▶ **devouring** *adj*

devout *adj* **1** deeply religious. **2** sincere; heartfelt: *a devout confession.* ▷ **HISTORY** Latin *devotus* faithful ▶ **devoutly** *adv*

dew *n* drops of water that form on the ground or on a cool surface at night from vapour in the air. ▷ **HISTORY** Old English *dēaw* ▶ **dewy** *adj*

dewberry *n, pl* **-berries** a type of bramble with blue-black fruits.

dewclaw *n* a nonfunctional claw on a dog's leg.

Dewey Decimal System *n* a system of library book classification with ten main subject classes. ▷ **HISTORY** after Melvil *Dewey*, educator

dewlap *n* a loose fold of skin hanging under the throat in cattle, dogs, etc. ▷ **HISTORY** Middle English *dew* + *lap* hanging flap

dew-worm *n US & Canad* a large earthworm used as fishing bait.

dewy-eyed *adj* innocent and inexperienced.

dexter *adj* of or on the right side of a shield, etc., from the bearer's point of view. ▷ **HISTORY** Latin

dexterity *n* **1** skill in using one's hands. **2** mental quickness. ▷ **HISTORY** Latin *dexteritas* aptness, readiness

dexterous *adj* possessing or done with dexterity. ▶ **dexterously** *adv*

dextrin *or* **dextrine** *n* a sticky substance obtained from starch: used as a thickening agent in food. ▷ **HISTORY** French *dextrine*

dextrose *n* a glucose occurring in fruit, honey, and in the blood of animals.

DFC (in Britain) Distinguished Flying Cross.

dg decigram.

DH *Brit* Department of Health.

dhal *or* **dal** *n* **1** the nutritious pealike seed of a tropical shrub. **2** a curry made from lentils or other pulses. ▷ **HISTORY** Hindi *dāl*

dharma *n* **1** *Hinduism* moral law or behaviour. **2** *Buddhism* ideal truth. ▷ **HISTORY** Sanskrit

dhoti *n, pl* **-tis** a long loincloth worn by men in India. ▷ **HISTORY** Hindi

DI *Brit* Donor Insemination: a method of making a woman pregnant by transferring sperm from a man other than her husband or regular partner using artificial means.

di- *prefix* **1** twice; two; double: *dicotyledon.* **2** containing two specified atoms or groups of atoms: *carbon dioxide.* ▷ **HISTORY** Greek

diabetes (die-a-**beet**-eez) *n* a medical condition in which the body is unable to control the level of sugar in the blood. ▷ **HISTORY** Greek: a passing through

diabetic *n* **1** a person who has diabetes. ✧ *adj* **2** of or having diabetes. **3** suitable for people suffering from diabetes: *diabetic chocolate.*

diabolic *adj* of the Devil; satanic. ▷ **HISTORY** Greek *diabolos* devil

diabolical *adj Informal* **1** unpleasant or annoying: *the weather was diabolical.* **2** extreme: *diabolical cheek.* **3** same as **diabolic.** ▶ **diabolically** *adv*

diabolism *n* **a** witchcraft or sorcery. **b** worship of devils. ▶ **diabolist** *n*

diaconate *n* the position or period of office of a deacon. ▷ **HISTORY** Late Latin *diaconatus* ▶ **diaconal** *adj*

diacritic *n* a sign placed above or below a character or letter to indicate phonetic value or stress. ▷ **HISTORY** Greek *diakritikos* serving to distinguish

diadem *n Old-fashioned* a small jewelled crown or headband, usually worn by royalty: *a gold diadem.* ▷ **HISTORY** Greek: royal headdress

diaeresis *or esp US* **dieresis** (die-**air**-iss-iss) *n, pl* **-ses** (-seez) the mark (¨) placed over the second of two adjacent vowels to indicate that it is to be pronounced separately, as in naïve. ▷ **HISTORY** Greek: a division

diagnose *vb* **-nosing, -nosed** to determine by diagnosis.

diagnosis (die-ag-**no**-siss) *n, pl* **-ses** (-seez) the discovery and identification of diseases from the examination of symptoms. ▷ **HISTORY** Greek: a distinguishing ▶ **diagnostic** *adj*

diagonal *adj* **1** *Maths* connecting any two vertices in a polygon that are not adjacent. **2** slanting. ✧ *n* **3** a diagonal line, plane, or pattern. ▷ **HISTORY** Greek *dia-* through + *gōnia* angle ▶ **diagonally** *adv*

diagram *n* a sketch or plan showing the form or workings of something. ▷ **HISTORY** Greek *diagraphein* to mark out ▶ **diagrammatic** *adj*

dial *n* **1** the face of a clock or watch, marked with divisions representing units of time. **2** the graduated disc on a measuring instrument. **3** the control on a radio or television set used to change the station. **4** a numbered disc on the front of some telephones. ✧ *vb* **dialling, dialled** *or US* **dialing, dialed 5** to try to establish a telephone connection with (someone) by operating the dial or buttons on a telephone. ▷ **HISTORY** Latin *dies* day

dialect *n* a form of a language spoken in a particular geographical area. ▷ **HISTORY** Greek *dialektos* speech, dialect ▶ **dialectal** *adj*

dialectic *n* **1** logical debate by question and answer to resolve differences between two views. **2** the art of logical argument. ▷ **HISTORY** Greek *dialektikē (tekhnē)* (the art) of argument ▶ **dialectical** *adj*

dialling tone *or US, Canad, Austral & NZ* **dial tone** *n* a continuous sound heard on picking up a telephone receiver, indicating that a number can be dialled.

dialogue *or US sometimes* **dialog** *n* **1** conversation between two people. **2** a conversation in a literary or dramatic work. **3** a discussion between representatives of two nations or groups. ▷ **HISTORY** Greek *dia-* between + *legein* to speak

dialysis (die-**al**-iss-iss) *n, pl* **-ses** (-seez) **1** *Med* the filtering of blood through a semipermeable membrane to remove waste products. **2** the separation of the particles in a solution by filtering through a semipermeable membrane. ▷ **HISTORY** Greek *dialuein* to tear apart, dissolve ▶ **dialyser** *or* **-lyzer** *n* ▶ **dialytic** *adj*

diamagnetism *n* the phenomenon exhibited by substances that are repelled by both poles of a magnet.

diamanté (die-a-**man**-tee) *adj* decorated with glittering bits of material, such as sequins. ▷ **HISTORY** French

diameter *n* **a** a straight line through the centre of a circle or sphere. **b** the length of such a line. ▷ **HISTORY** Greek *dia-* through + *metron* measure

diametric *or* **diametrical** *adj* **1** of or relating to a diameter. **2** completely opposed: *the diametric opposition of the two camps.* ▶ **diametrically** *adv*

diamond *n* **1** a usually colourless exceptionally hard precious stone of crystallized carbon. **2** *Geom* a figure with four sides of equal length forming two acute and two obtuse angles. **3** a playing card marked with one or more red diamond-shaped symbols. **4** *Baseball* the playing field. ✧ *adj* **5** (of an anniversary) the sixtieth: *diamond wedding.* ▷ **HISTORY** Latin *adamas* the hardest iron or steel, diamond

diapason (die-a-**pay**-zon) *n Music* **1** either of two stops found throughout the range of a pipe organ. **2** the range of an instrument or voice. ▷ **HISTORY** Greek *dia pasōn* through all (the notes)

diaper *n US & Canad* a nappy. ▷ **HISTORY** Medieval Greek *diaspros* pure white

diaphanous (die-**af**-fan-uss) *adj* (of fabrics) fine and translucent. ▷ **HISTORY** Greek *diaphanēs* transparent

diaphoretic *n* **1** a drug that causes perspiration or sweat. ✧ *adj* **2** relating to or causing perspiration or sweat.

diaphragm (**die**-a-fram) *n* **1** *Anat* the muscular partition that separates the abdominal cavity and chest cavity. **2** same as **cap** (sense 5). **3** a device to control the amount of light entering an optical instrument. **4** a thin vibrating disc which converts sound to electricity or vice versa, as in a microphone or loudspeaker. ▷ **HISTORY** Greek *dia-* across + *phragma* fence

diapositive *n* a positive transparency; slide.

diarist *n* a person who writes a diary that is subsequently published.

diarrhoea *or esp US* **diarrhea** (die-a-**ree**-a) *n* frequent discharge of abnormally liquid faeces. ▷ **HISTORY** Greek *dia-* through + *rhein* to flow

diary *n, pl* **-ries 1** a book containing a record of daily events, appointments, or observations. **2** a written record of daily events, appointments, or observations. ▷ **HISTORY** Latin *dies* day

Diaspora (die-**ass**-spore-a) *n* **1** the dispersion of the Jews after the Babylonian conquest of Palestine. **2** a dispersion of people originally belonging to one nation. ▷ **HISTORY** Greek: a scattering

diastase (**die**-ass-stayss) *n* an enzyme that converts starch into sugar. ▷ **HISTORY** Greek *diastasis* a separation ▶ **diastasic** *adj*

diastole (die-**ass**-stoh-lee) *n* dilation of the chambers of the heart. ▶ **diastolic** *adj*

diatom *n* a microscopic unicellular alga. ▷ **HISTORY** Greek *diatomos* cut in two

diatomic *adj* containing two atoms.

diatonic *adj* of or relating to any scale of five tones and two semitones produced by playing the white keys of a keyboard instrument. ▷ **HISTORY** Greek *diatonos* extending

diatribe *n* a bitter critical attack. ▷ **HISTORY** Greek *dia-* through + *tribein* to rub

dibble *n* a small hand tool used to make holes in the ground for bulbs, seeds, or roots. ▷ **HISTORY** origin unknown

dice *n, pl* **dice 1** a small cube, each of whose sides has a different number of spots (1 to 6), used in games of chance. ✧ *vb* **dicing, diced 2** to cut (food) into small cubes. **3 dice with death** to take a risk. ▷ **HISTORY** originally plural of DIE²

dicey *adj* **dicier, diciest** *Informal, chiefly Brit & NZ* dangerous or tricky.

dichotomy (die-**kot**-a-mee) *n, pl* **-mies 1** division into two opposed groups or parts. **2** *Bot* a method of branching by repeated division into two equal parts. ▷ **HISTORY** Greek *dicha* in two + *temnein* to cut ▶ **dichotomous** *adj*

> **WORD TIP**
> *Dichotomy* should always refer to a division of some kind into two groups. It is sometimes used to refer to a puzzling situation which seems to involve a contradiction, but this use is generally thought to be incorrect.

dichromatic *adj* having two colours. ▷ **HISTORY** Greek *di-* double + *khrōma* colour

dick *n Slang* **1** *Taboo* a penis. **2 clever dick** an opinionated person. ▷ **HISTORY** *Dick* familiar form of *Richard*

Dickensian *adj* **1** of Charles Dickens (1812–70), British novelist. **2** denoting poverty, distress, and exploitation, as depicted in the novels of Dickens.

dicky¹ *n, pl* **dickies** a false shirt front. ▷ **HISTORY** from *Dick,* name

dicky² *adj* **dickier, dickiest** *Brit & NZ informal* shaky or weak: *a dicky heart.* ▷ **HISTORY** origin unknown

dicky-bird *n* a child's word for a bird.

dicotyledon (die-kot-ill-**leed**-on) *n* a flowering plant with two seed leaves.

dictate *vb* **-tating, -tated 1** to say (words) aloud for another person to transcribe. **2** to seek to impose one's will on others. ✧ *n* **3** an authoritative command. **4** a guiding principle: *the dictates of reason.* ▷ **HISTORY** Latin *dictare* to say repeatedly

dictation *n* **1** the act of dictating words to be taken down in writing. **2** the words dictated.

dictator *n* **1** a ruler who has complete power. **2** a person who behaves in a tyrannical manner. ▶ **dictatorship** *n*

dictatorial *adj* **1** of or pertaining to a dictator. **2** tyrannical; overbearing. ▶ **dictatorially** *adv*

diction *n* the manner of pronouncing words and sounds. ▷ **HISTORY** Latin *dicere* to speak

dictionary *n, pl* **-aries 1 a** a book that consists of an alphabetical list of words with their meanings. **b** a similar book giving equivalent words in two languages. **2** a reference book listing terms and giving information about a particular subject. ▷ **HISTORY** Late Latin *dictio* word

dictum *n, pl* **-tums** *or* **-ta 1** a formal statement; pronouncement. **2** a popular saying or maxim. ▷ **HISTORY** Latin

did *vb* the past tense of **do¹**.

didactic *adj* intended to teach or instruct people: *an Impressionist work can be as didactic in its way as a sermon.* ▷ **HISTORY** Greek *didaktikos* skilled in teaching ▶ **didactically** *adv* ▶ **didacticism** *n*

diddle *vb* **-dling, -dled** *Informal* to swindle. ▷ **HISTORY** Jeremy *Diddler,* a scrounger in a 19th-century play ▶ **diddler** *n*

didgeridoo *n* an Australian Aboriginal deep-toned wind instrument. ▷ **HISTORY** imitative

didn't did not.

die¹ *vb* **dying, died 1** (of a person, animal, or plant) to cease all biological activity permanently. **2** (of something inanimate) to cease to exist. **3** to lose strength, power, or energy by degrees. **4** to stop working: *the engine died.* **5 be dying** to be eager (for something or to do something). **6 be dying of** *Informal* to be nearly overcome with (laughter, boredom, etc.). **7 die hard** to change or disappear only slowly: *old loyalties die hard.* **8 to die for** *Informal* highly desirable: *a salary to die for.* ✧ See also **die down, die out**. ▷ **HISTORY** Old English *dīegan*

> **WORD TIP**
> It was formerly considered incorrect to use the preposition *from* after *die,* but *of* and *from* are now both acceptable: *he died of/from his injuries.*

die² *n* **1** a shaped block used to cut or form metal. **2** a casting mould. **3** same as **dice** (sense 1). **4 the die is cast** an irrevocable decision has been taken. ▷ **HISTORY** Latin *dare* to give, play

die down *vb* **1** to lose strength or power by degrees. **2** to become calm: *the storm has died down now.*

die-hard *or* **diehard** *n* a person who resists change.

dieldrin *n* a highly toxic crystalline insecticide.

dielectric *n* **1** a substance of very low electrical conductivity; insulator. ✧ *adj* **2** having the properties of a dielectric. ▷ **HISTORY** Greek *dia-* through + ELECTRIC

die out *or* **off** *vb* to become extinct or disappear after a gradual decline.

a b c d e f g h i j k l m n o p q r s t u v w x y z

dieresis (die-**air**-iss-iss) *n, pl* **-ses** (-seez) same as **diaeresis**.

diesel *n* **1** same as **diesel engine**. **2** a vehicle driven by a diesel engine. **3** *Informal* diesel oil. ▷ **HISTORY** after R. *Diesel*, engineer

diesel engine *n* an internal-combustion engine in which oil is ignited by compression.

diesel oil *or* **fuel** *n* a fuel obtained from petroleum distillation, used in diesel engines.

diet[1] *n* **1** the food that a person or animal regularly eats. **2** a specific allowance or selection of food, to control weight or for health reasons: *a high-fibre diet*. ✧ *vb* **3** to follow a special diet so as to lose weight. ✧ *adj* **4** suitable for eating with a weight-reduction diet: *diet soft drinks*. ▷ **HISTORY** Greek *diaita* mode of living ▶ **dietary** *adj* ▶ **dieter** *n*

diet[2] *n* a legislative assembly in some countries. ▷ **HISTORY** Medieval Latin *dieta* public meeting

dietary fibre *n* the roughage in fruits and vegetables that aid digestion.

dietetic *adj* prepared for special dietary requirements.

dietetics *n* the study of diet, nutrition, and the preparation of food.

dietician *n* a person qualified to advise people about healthy eating.

differ *vb* **1** to be dissimilar in quality, nature, or degree. **2** to disagree. ▷ **HISTORY** Latin *differre* to scatter, be different

difference *n* **1** the state or quality of being unlike. **2** a disagreement or argument. **3** the result of the subtraction of one number or quantity from another. **4 make a difference** to have an effect. **5 split the difference a** to compromise. **b** to divide a remainder equally.

different *adj* **1** partly or completely unlike. **2** new or unusual. **3** not identical or the same; other: *he wears a different tie every day*. ▶ **differently** *adv*

> **WORD TIP**
> The constructions *different from, different to,* and *different than* are all found in the works of writers of English during the past. Nowadays, however, the most widely acceptable preposition to use after *different* is *from. Different to* is common in British English, but is considered by some people to be incorrect, or less acceptable. *Different than* is a standard construction in American English. As, however, this idiom is not regarded as totally acceptable in British usage, it is preferable either to use *different from: this result is only slightly different from that obtained in the US* or to rephrase the sentence: *this result differs only slightly from that in the US*.

differential *adj* **1** of, relating to, or using a difference. **2** *Maths* involving differentials. ✧ *n* **3** a factor that differentiates between two comparable things. **4** *Maths* a minute difference between values in a scale. **5** *Chiefly Brit* the difference between rates of pay for different types of labour, esp. within a company or industry.

differential calculus *n* the branch of mathematics concerned with derivatives and differentials.

differential gear *n* the gear in the driving axle of a road vehicle that permits one driving wheel to rotate faster than the other when cornering.

differentiate *vb* **-ating, -ated 1** to perceive or show the difference (between). **2** to make (one thing) distinct from other such things. **3** *Maths* to determine the derivative of a function or variable. ▶ **differentiation** *n*

difficult *adj* **1** not easy to do, understand, or solve. **2** not easily pleased or satisfied: *a difficult patient*. **3** full of hardships or trials: *he had recently had a difficult time with his job as a self-employed builder*.

difficulty *n, pl* **-ties 1** the state or quality of being difficult. **2** a task or problem that is hard to deal with. **3** a troublesome or embarrassing situation: *in financial difficulties*. **4** an objection or obstacle: *you're just making difficulties*. **5** lack of ease; awkwardness: *he could run only with difficulty*. ▷ **HISTORY** Latin *difficultas*

diffident *adj* lacking self-confidence; shy. ▷ **HISTORY** Latin *dis-* not + *fidere* to trust ▶ **diffidence** *n* ▶ **diffidently** *adv*

diffract *vb* to cause to undergo diffraction. ▶ **diffractive** *adj*

diffraction *n* **1** *Physics* a deviation in the direction of a wave at the edge of an obstacle in its path. **2** the formation of light and dark fringes by the passage of light through a small aperture. ▷ **HISTORY** Latin *diffringere* to shatter

diffuse *vb* **-fusing, -fused 1** to spread over a wide area. **2** *Physics* to cause to undergo diffusion. ✧ *adj* **3** spread out over a wide area. **4** lacking conciseness. ▷ **HISTORY** Latin *diffusus* spread abroad ▶ **diffusible** *adj* ▶ **diffuser** *n*

> **WORD TIP**
> Avoid confusion with **defuse.**

diffusion *n* **1** the act of diffusing or the fact of being diffused; dispersion. **2** *Physics* the random thermal motion of atoms and molecules in gases, liquids, and some solids. **3** *Physics* the transmission or reflection of light, in which the radiation is scattered in many directions.

dig *vb* **digging, dug 1** to cut into, break up, and turn over or remove (earth), esp. with a spade. **2** to excavate (a hole or tunnel) by digging, usually with an implement or (of animals) with claws. **3** to obtain by digging: *dig out potatoes*. **4** to find by effort or searching: *he dug out a mini cassette from his pocket*. **5** *Informal* to like or understand. **6** (foll. by *in* or *into*) to thrust or jab. ✧ *n* **7** the act of digging. **8** an archaeological excavation. **9** a thrust or poke. **10** a cutting remark. ✧ See also **dig in**. ▷ **HISTORY** Middle English *diggen*

digest *vb* **1** to subject (food) to a process of digestion. **2** to absorb mentally. ✧ *n* **3** a shortened version of a book, report, or article. ▷ **HISTORY** Latin *digerere* to divide ▶ **digestible** *adj*

digestion *n* **1** the process of breaking down food into easily absorbed substances. **2** the body's system for doing this.
digestive *adj* relating to digestion.
digger *n* a machine used for excavation.
dig in *vb* **1** to mix (compost or fertilizer) into the soil by digging. **2** *Informal* to begin to eat vigorously. **3** *Informal* (of soldiers) to dig a trench and prepare for an enemy attack. **4 dig one's heels in** *Informal* to refuse to move or be persuaded.
digit (**dij**-it) *n* **1** a finger or toe. **2** any numeral from 0 to 9. ▷ **HISTORY** Latin *digitus* toe, finger
digital *adj* **1** displaying information as numbers rather than with a dial. **2** representing data as a series of numerical values. **3** of or possessing digits. ▶ **digitally** *adv*
digital audio tape *n* magnetic tape on which sound is recorded digitally, giving high-fidelity reproduction.
digital computer *n* a computer in which the input consists of numbers, letters, and other characters that are represented internally in binary notation.
digitalis *n* a drug made from foxglove leaves: used as a heart stimulant. ▷ **HISTORY** Latin: relating to a finger (from the shape of the foxglove flowers)
digital recording *n* a sound recording process that converts audio or analogue signals into a series of pulses.
digital television *n* television in which the picture information is transmitted in digital form and decoded at the television receiver.
digitate *adj* **1** (of leaves) having leaflets in the form of a spread hand. **2** (of animals) having digits.
digitize *or* **-ise** *vb* **-izing, -ized** *or* **-ising, -ised** to transcribe (data) into a digital form for processing by a computer. ▶ **digitizer** *or* **-iser** *n*
dignify *vb* **-fies, -fying, -fied 1** to add distinction to: *the meeting was dignified by the minister.* **2** to add a semblance of dignity to by the use of a pretentious name or title: *she dignifies every plant with its Latin name.* ▷ **HISTORY** Latin *dignus* worthy + *facere* to make
dignitary *n, pl* **-taries** a person of high official position or rank.
dignity *n, pl* **-ties 1** serious, calm, and controlled behaviour or manner. **2** the quality of being worthy of honour. **3** sense of self-importance: *he considered the job beneath his dignity.* ▷ **HISTORY** Latin *dignus* worthy
digraph *n* two letters used to represent a single sound, such as *gh* in *tough*.
digress *vb* to depart from the main subject in speech or writing. ▷ **HISTORY** Latin *digressus* turned aside ▶ **digression** *n*
digs *pl n Brit, Austral & S African informal* lodgings. ▷ **HISTORY** from *diggings*, perhaps referring to where one digs or works
dihedral *adj* having or formed by two intersecting planes.
dilapidated *adj* (of a building) having fallen into ruin. ▷ **HISTORY** Latin *dilapidare* to waste ▶ **dilapidation** *n*
dilate *vb* **-lating, -lated** to make or become wider or larger: *her eyes dilated in the dark.* ▷ **HISTORY** Latin *dilatare* to spread out ▶ **dilation** *or* **dilatation** *n*
dilatory (**dill**-a-tree) *adj* tending or intended to waste time. ▷ **HISTORY** Late Latin *dilatorius* ▶ **dilatorily** *adv* ▶ **dilatoriness** *n*
dildo *n, pl* **-dos** an object used as a substitute for an erect penis. ▷ **HISTORY** origin unknown
dilemma *n* a situation offering a choice between two equally undesirable alternatives. ▷ **HISTORY** Greek *di-* double + *lēmma* proposition

> **WORD TIP**
> The use of *dilemma* to refer to a problem that seems incapable of a solution is considered by some people to be incorrect.

dilettante (dill-it-**tan**-tee) *n, pl* **-tantes** *or* **-tanti** a person whose interest in a subject is superficial rather than serious. ▷ **HISTORY** Italian ▶ **dilettantism** *n*
diligent *adj* **1** careful and persevering in carrying out tasks or duties. **2** carried out with care and perseverance: *a diligent approach to work.* ▷ **HISTORY** Latin *diligere* to value ▶ **diligence** *n* ▶ **diligently** *adv*
dill *n* a sweet-smelling herb used for flavouring. ▷ **HISTORY** Old English *dile*
dilly-dally *vb* **-lies, -lying, -lied** *Brit, Austral & NZ informal* to dawdle or waste time. ▷ **HISTORY** reduplication of *dally*
dilute *vb* **-luting, -luted 1** to make (a liquid) less concentrated by adding water or another liquid. **2** to make (someone's power, idea, or role) weaker or less effective: *socialists used their majority in parliament to dilute legislation crucial to developing a market economy.* ✧ *adj* **3** *Chem* (of a solution) having a low concentration. ▷ **HISTORY** Latin *diluere* ▶ **dilution** *n*
dilute acid *n Chem* an acid with a large number of water molecules and few acid molecules.
diluvian *or* **diluvial** *adj* of a flood, esp. the great Flood described in the Old Testament. ▷ **HISTORY** Latin *diluere* to wash away
dim *adj* **dimmer, dimmest 1** badly lit. **2** not clearly seen; faint: *a dim figure in the doorway.* **3** not seeing clearly: *eyes dim with tears.* **4** *Informal* mentally dull. **5** not clear in the mind; obscure: *a dim awareness.* **6** lacking in brightness or lustre: *a dim colour.* **7 take a dim view of** to disapprove of. ✧ *vb* **dimming, dimmed 8** to become or cause to become dim. **9** to cause to seem less bright. **10** *US & Canad* same as **dip** (sense 4). ▷ **HISTORY** Old English *dimm* ▶ **dimly** *adv* ▶ **dimness** *n*
dime *n* a coin of the US and Canada worth ten cents. ▷ **HISTORY** Latin *decem* ten
dimension *n* **1** an aspect or factor: *the attack brought a whole new dimension to the bombing campaign.* **2 dimensions** scope or extent. **3** (*often pl*) a measurement of the size of something in a particular direction. ▷ **HISTORY** Latin *dimensio* an extent ▶ **dimensional** *adj*
dimer *n Chem* a molecule made up of two identical molecules bonded together.

a b c d e f g h i j k l m n o p q r s t u v w x y z

A B C D E F G H I J K L M N O P Q R S T U V W X Y Z

dimeter *n Poetry* a line of verse consisting of two metrical feet.

diminish *vb* **1** to make or become smaller, fewer, or less. **2** *Music* to decrease (a minor interval) by a semitone. **3** to reduce in authority or status. ▷ **HISTORY** Latin *deminuere* to make smaller + archaic *minish* to lessen

diminished responsibility *n Law* a plea under which evidence of an abnormal state of mind is submitted to demonstrate lack of criminal responsibility at the time of an offence.

diminuendo *Music* ✧ *n, pl* **-dos 1 a** a gradual decrease in loudness. **b** a passage which gradually decreases in loudness. ✧ *adv* **2** gradually decreasing in loudness. ▷ **HISTORY** Italian

diminution *n* reduction in size, volume, intensity, or importance. ▷ **HISTORY** Latin *deminutio*

diminutive *adj* **1** very small; tiny. **2** *Grammar* **a** denoting an affix added to a word to convey the meaning *small* or *unimportant* or to express affection, as for example, the suffix *-ette* in French. **b** denoting a word formed by the addition of a diminutive affix. ✧ *n* **3** *Grammar* a diminutive word or affix. ▶ **diminutiveness** *n*

dimmer *n* **1** a device for dimming an electric light. **2** *US* **a** a dipped headlight on a road vehicle. **b** a parking light on a car.

dimple *n* **1** a small natural dent on the cheeks or chin. ✧ *vb* **-pling, -pled 2** to produce dimples by smiling. ▷ **HISTORY** Middle English *dympull*

dimwit *n Informal* a stupid person. ▶ **dim-witted** *adj*

din *n* **1** a loud unpleasant confused noise. ✧ *vb* **dinning, dinned 2 din something into someone** to instil something into someone by constant repetition. ▷ **HISTORY** Old English *dynn*

dinar (**dee**-nahr) *n* a monetary unit of various Balkan, Middle Eastern, and North African countries. ▷ **HISTORY** Latin *denarius* a Roman coin

dine *vb* **dining, dined 1** to eat dinner. **2 dine on** *or* **off** to make one's meal of: *the guests dined on roast beef.* ▷ **HISTORY** Old French *disner*

diner *n* **1** a person eating a meal in a restaurant. **2** *Chiefly US & Canad* a small cheap restaurant. **3** short for **dining car**.

ding *n Austral dated & NZ informal* a small dent in a vehicle.

ding-dong *n* **1** the sound of a bell. **2** a violent exchange of blows or words. ▷ **HISTORY** imitative

dinges (**ding**-uss) *n S African informal* a jocular word for something whose name is unknown or forgotten; thingumabob. ▷ **HISTORY** Dutch *ding* thing

dinghy (**ding**-ee, **ding**-gee) *n, pl* **-ghies** a small boat, powered by sail, oars, or outboard motor. ▷ **HISTORY** Hindi or Bengali *dingi*

dingle *n* a small wooded hollow or valley. ▷ **HISTORY** origin unknown

dingo *n, pl* **-goes** an Australian native wild dog. ▷ **HISTORY** Aboriginal

dingy (**din**-jee) *adj* **-gier, -giest 1** *Brit, Austral & NZ* dull, neglected, and drab: *he waited in this dingy little outer office.* **2** shabby and discoloured: *she was wearing dingy white overalls.* ▷ **HISTORY** origin unknown ▶ **dinginess** *n*

dining car *n* a railway coach in which meals are served.

dining room *n* a room where meals are eaten.

dinkum *adj Austral & NZ informal* genuine or right: *a fair dinkum offer.* ▷ **HISTORY** English dialect: work

dinky *adj* **dinkier, dinkiest** *Chiefly Brit informal* small and neat; dainty. ▷ **HISTORY** dialect *dink* neat

dinky-di *adj Austral informal* typical. ▷ **HISTORY** variant of DINKUM

dinner *n* **1** the main meal of the day, eaten either in the evening or at midday. **2** a formal social occasion at which an evening meal is served. ▷ **HISTORY** Old French *disner* to dine

dinner jacket *n* a man's semiformal black evening jacket without tails.

dinosaur *n* any of a large order of extinct prehistoric reptiles many of which were gigantic. ▷ **HISTORY** Greek *deinos* fearful + *sauros* lizard

dint *n* **by dint of** by means of: *by dint of their own efforts.* ▷ **HISTORY** Old English *dynt* a blow

diocesan *adj* of or relating to a diocese.

diocese (**die**-a-siss) *n* the district over which a bishop has control. ▷ **HISTORY** Greek *dioikēsis* administration

diode *n* **1** a semiconductor device for converting alternating current to direct current. **2** an electronic valve with two electrodes between which a current can flow only in one direction. ▷ **HISTORY** Greek *di-* double + *hodos* a way, road

dioecious (die-**eesh**-uss) *adj* (of plants) having the male and female reproductive organs on separate plants. ▷ **HISTORY** Greek *di-* twice + *oikia* house

Dionysian (die-on-**niz**-zee-an) *adj* wild or orgiastic. ▷ **HISTORY** from *Dionysus,* Greek god of wine

Dionysus *n Greek myth* the god of wine.

dioptre *or US* **diopter** (die-**op**-ter) *n* a unit for measuring the refractive power of a lens. ▷ **HISTORY** Greek *dia-* through + *opsesthai* to see

diorama *n* **1** a miniature three-dimensional scene, in which models of figures are seen against a background. **2** a picture made up of illuminated translucent curtains, viewed through an aperture. ▷ **HISTORY** Greek *dia-* through + *horama* view

dioxide *n* an oxide containing two oxygen atoms per molecule.

dip *vb* **dipping, dipped 1** to plunge or be plunged quickly or briefly into a liquid. **2** to put one's hands into something, esp. to obtain an object: *she dipped into her handbag looking for change.* **3** to slope downwards. **4** to switch (car headlights) from the main to the lower beam. **5** to undergo a slight decline, esp. temporarily: *sales dipped in November.* **6** to immerse (farm animals) briefly in a chemical to rid them of insects. **7** to lower or be lowered briefly: *she dipped her knee in a curtsy.* ✧ *n* **8** the act of dipping. **9** a brief swim. **10** a liquid chemical in which farm animals are dipped. **11** a depression, esp. in a landscape. **12** a momentary sinking down. **13** a creamy mixture into which pieces of food are dipped before being eaten. ✧ See also **dip into**. ▷ HISTORY Old English *dyppan*

Dip Ed (in Britain) Diploma in Education.

dipeptide *n Biochem* a compound consisting of two linked amino acids.

diphtheria (dif-**theer**-ree-a) *n* a contagious disease producing fever and difficulty in breathing and swallowing. ▷ HISTORY Greek *diphthera* leather; from the membrane that forms in the throat

diphthong *n* a vowel sound, occupying a single syllable, in which the speaker's tongue moves continuously from one position to another, as in the pronunciation of *a* in *late*. ▷ HISTORY Greek *di-* double + *phthongos* sound

dip into *vb* **1** to draw upon: *he dipped into his savings.* **2** to read passages at random from (a book or journal).

diploid *adj Biol* denoting a cell or organism with pairs of homologous chromosomes. ▷ HISTORY Greek *di-* double + *-ploos* -fold

diploma *n* a document conferring a qualification or recording successful completion of a course of study. ▷ HISTORY Latin: official document, literally: letter folded double

diplomacy *n* **1** the conduct of the relations between nations by peaceful means. **2** skill in the management of international relations. **3** tact or skill in dealing with people.

diplomat *n* an official, such as an ambassador, engaged in diplomacy.

diplomatic *adj* **1** of or relating to diplomacy. **2** skilled in negotiating between nations. **3** tactful in dealing with people. ▷ HISTORY French *diplomatique* concerning the documents of diplomacy; see DIPLOMA ▸ **diplomatically** *adv*

diplomatic immunity *n* the freedom from legal action and exemption from taxation which diplomats have in the country where they are working.

dipole *n* **1** two equal but opposite electric charges or magnetic poles separated by a small distance. **2** a molecule that has two such charges or poles. ▸ **dipolar** *adj*

dipper *n* **1** a ladle used for dipping. **2** a songbird that inhabits fast-flowing streams.

diprotodont (die-**pro**-toe-dont) *n* a marsupial with fewer than three upper incisor teeth on each side of the jaw.

dipsomania *n* a compulsive desire to drink alcoholic beverages. ▷ HISTORY Greek *dipsa* thirst + *mania* madness ▸ **dipsomaniac** *n, adj*

dipstick *n* a rod with notches on it dipped into a container to indicate the fluid level.

dip switch *n* a device for dipping headlights on a vehicle.

dipterous *adj* having two wings or winglike parts. ▷ HISTORY Greek *dipteros* two-winged

diptych (**dip**-tik) *n* a painting on two hinged panels. ▷ HISTORY Greek *di-* double + *ptuchē* a panel

dire *adj* disastrous, urgent, or terrible: *he was now in dire financial straits.* ▷ HISTORY Latin *dirus* ominous

direct *adj* **1** shortest; straight: *a direct route.* **2** without intervening people: *they secretly arranged direct links to their commanders.* **3** honest; frank: *he was polite but very direct.* **4** diametric: *the direct opposite.* **5** in an unbroken line of descent: *a direct descendant.* ✧ *adv* **6** directly; straight. ✧ *vb* **7** to conduct or control the affairs of. **8** to give orders with authority to (a person or group). **9** to tell (someone) the way to a place. **10** to address (a letter, parcel, etc.). **11** to address (a look or remark) at someone: *the look she directed at him was one of unconcealed hatred.* **12 a** to provide guidance to (actors, cameramen, etc.) in (a play or film). **b** to supervise the making or staging of (a film or play). ▷ HISTORY Latin *dirigere* to guide ▸ **directness** *n*

direct access *n* a method of reading data from a computer file without reading through the file from the beginning.

direct current *n* an electric current that flows in one direction only.

direct debit *n* an order given to a bank or other financial institution by an account holder to pay an amount of money from the account to a specified person or company at regular intervals.

direction *n* **1** the course or line along which a person or thing moves, points, or lies. **2** management or guidance: *the campaign was successful under his direction.* **3** the work of a stage or film director.

directional *adj* **1** of or showing direction. **2** *Electronics* (of an aerial) transmitting or receiving radio waves more effectively in some directions than in others.

directions *pl n* instructions for doing something or for reaching a place.

directive *n* an instruction; order.

directly *adv* **1** in a direct manner. **2** at once; without delay. **3** immediately or very soon: *I'll do that directly.* ✧ *conj* **4** as soon as: *we left directly the money arrived.*

direct marketing *n Marketing* selling goods directly to consumers rather than through retailers, for example by mail order or telephone selling.

direct object *n Grammar* a noun, pronoun, or other noun group denoting the person or thing receiving the direct action of a verb. For example, *a book* in *they bought Anne a book.*

director *n* **1** a person or thing that directs or controls. **2** a member of the governing board of a business, trust, etc. **3** the person responsible for the artistic and technical aspects of the making of a film or television programme. ▸ **directorial** *adj* ▸ **directorship** *n*

directorate *n* **1** a board of directors. **2** the position of director.

director-general *n, pl* **directors-general** a person in overall charge of certain large organizations.

directory *n, pl* **-ries** **1** a book listing names, addresses, and telephone numbers of individuals or business companies. **2** *Computers* an area of a disk containing the names and locations of the files it currently holds.

A B C D E F G H I J K L M N O P Q R S T U V W X Y Z

direct speech *n Grammar* the reporting of what someone has said by quoting the exact words.

direct tax *n* a tax paid by the person or organization on which it is levied.

dirge *n* **1** a chant of lamentation for the dead. **2** any mournful song. ▷ HISTORY Latin *dirige* direct (imperative), opening word of antiphon used in the office of the dead

dirigible (**dir**-rij-jib-bl) *adj* **1** able to be steered. ✧ *n* **2** same as **airship**. ▷ HISTORY Latin *dirigere* to direct

dirk *n* a dagger, formerly worn by Scottish Highlanders. ▷ HISTORY Scots *durk*

dirndl *n* **1** a woman's dress with a full gathered skirt and fitted bodice. **2** a gathered skirt of this kind. ▷ HISTORY from German

dirt *n* **1** any unclean substance, such as mud; filth. **2** loose earth; soil. **3** packed earth, cinders, etc., used to make a racetrack. **4** obscene speech or writing. **5** *Informal* harmful gossip. ▷ HISTORY Old Norse *drit* excrement

dirt-cheap *adj, adv* at an extremely low price.

dirt track *n* a racetrack made of packed earth or cinders.

dirty *adj* **dirtier, dirtiest 1** covered or marked with dirt; filthy. **2** causing one to become grimy: *a dirty job*. **3** (of a colour) not clear and bright. **4** unfair, dishonest, or unkind: *dirty tricks*. **5 a** obscene: *dirty jokes*. **b** sexually clandestine: *a dirty weekend*. **6** revealing dislike or anger: *a dirty look*. **7** (of weather) rainy or stormy. **8 dirty work** unpleasant or illicit activity. ✧ *n* **9 do the dirty on** *Informal* to behave meanly towards. ✧ *vb* **dirties, dirtying, dirtied 10** to make dirty; soil. ▸ **dirtiness** *n*

dis- *prefix* indicating: **1** reversal: *disconnect*. **2** negation or lack: *dissimilar; disgrace*. **3** removal or release: *disembowel*.

disability *n, pl* **-ties 1** a severe physical or mental illness that restricts the way a person lives his or her life. **2** something that disables someone.

disable *vb* **-abling, -abled** to make ineffective, unfit, or incapable. ▸ **disablement** *n*

disabled *adj* lacking one or more physical powers, such as the ability to walk or to coordinate one's movements.

> **WORD TIP**
> The use of *the disabled, the blind,* etc. can be offensive and should be avoided. Instead you should talk about *disabled people, blind people,* etc.

disabuse *vb* **-abusing, -abused** to rid (someone) of a mistaken idea: *Arnold felt unable to disabuse her of her prejudices*.

disaccharide (die-**sack**-a-ride) *n* a sugar, such as sucrose, whose molecules consist of two linked monosaccharides.

disadvantage *n* **1** an unfavourable or harmful circumstance. **2 at a disadvantage** in a less favourable position than other people: *he continued to insist that he was at a disadvantage at the hearings*. ▸ **disadvantageous** *adj*

disadvantaged *adj* socially or economically deprived.

disaffected *adj* having lost loyalty to or affection for someone or something; alienated: *three million disaffected voters*. ▸ **disaffection** *n*

disagree *vb* **-greeing, -greed 1** to have differing opinions or argue about (something). **2** to fail to correspond; conflict. **3** to cause physical discomfort to: *curry disagrees with me*.

disagreeable *adj* **1** (of an incident or situation) unpleasant. **2** (of a person) bad-tempered or disobliging. ▸ **disagreeably** *adv*

disagreement *n* **1** refusal or failure to agree. **2** a difference between results, totals, etc., which shows that they cannot all be true. **3** an argument.

disallow *vb* to reject as untrue or invalid; cancel.

disappear *vb* **1** to cease to be visible; vanish. **2** to go away or become lost, esp. without explanation. **3** to cease to exist: *the pain has disappeared*. ▸ **disappearance** *n*

disappoint *vb* **1** to fail to meet the expectations or hopes of; let down. **2** to prevent the fulfilment of (a plan, etc.); frustrate. ▷ HISTORY Old French *desapointier* ▸ **disappointed** *adj* ▸ **disappointing** *adj*

disappointment *n* **1** the feeling of being disappointed. **2** a person or thing that disappoints.

disapprobation *n* disapproval.

disapprove *vb* **-proving, -proved** to consider wrong or bad. ▸ **disapproval** *n* ▸ **disapproving** *adj*

disarm *vb* **1** to deprive of weapons. **2** to win the confidence or affection of. **3** (of a country) to decrease the size and capability of one's armed forces.

disarmament *n* the reduction of fighting capability by a country.

disarming *adj* removing hostility or suspicion. ▸ **disarmingly** *adv*

disarrange *vb* **-ranging, -ranged** to throw into disorder. ▸ **disarrangement** *n*

disarray *n* **1** confusion and lack of discipline. **2** extreme untidiness. ✧ *vb* **3** to throw into confusion.

disassemble *vb Technology* to take apart piece by piece.

disassociate *vb* **-ating, -ated** same as **dissociate**. ▸ **disassociation** *n*

disaster *n* **1** an accident that causes great distress or destruction. **2** something, such as a project, that fails or has been ruined. ▷ HISTORY Italian *disastro* ▸ **disastrous** *adj* ▸ **disastrously** *adv*

disavow *vb* to deny connection with or responsibility for (something). ▸ **disavowal** *n*

disband *vb* to stop or cause to stop functioning as a unit or group. ▸ **disbandment** *n*

disbar *vb* **-barring, -barred** to deprive (a barrister) of the right to practise.

> **WORD TIP**
> *Disbar* is sometimes wrongly used where *debar* is meant: *he was debarred* (not *disbarred*) *from attending meetings.*

disbelieve *vb* **-lieving, -lieved 1** to reject (a person or statement) as being untruthful. **2 disbelieve in** to have no faith or belief in: *to disbelieve in the supernatural.* ▸ **disbelief** *n*
disburse *vb* **-bursing, -bursed** to pay out. ▷ **HISTORY** Old French *desborser* ▸ **disbursement** *n*

> **WORD TIP**
> *Disburse* is sometimes wrongly used where *disperse* is meant: *the police used water cannon to disperse* (not *disburse*) *the crowd.*

disc *n* **1** a flat circular object. **2** a gramophone record. **3** *Anat* a circular flat structure in the body, esp. between the vertebrae. **4** *Computers* same as **disk.** ▷ **HISTORY** Latin *discus* discus
discard *vb* to get rid of (something or someone) as useless or undesirable. ▷ **HISTORY** DIS- + *card* (the playing card)
disc brake *n* a brake in which two pads rub against a flat disc.
discern *vb* to see or be aware of (something) clearly. ▷ **HISTORY** Latin *discernere* to divide ▸ **discernible** *adj*
discerning *adj* having or showing good judgment. ▸ **discernment** *n*
discharge *vb* **-charging, -charged 1** to release or allow to go. **2** to dismiss (someone) from duty or employment. **3** to fire (a gun). **4** to cause to pour forth: *the scar was red and swollen and began to discharge pus.* **5** to remove (the cargo) from a boat, etc.; unload. **6** to meet the demands of (a duty or responsibility). **7** to relieve oneself of (a debt). **8** *Physics* to take or supply electrical current from (a cell or battery). ✧ *n* **9** something that is discharged. **10** dismissal or release from an office, job, etc. **11** a pouring out of a fluid; emission. **12** *Physics* a conduction of electricity through a gas. **13** *Geog* the volume of water passing through an aquifer or stream at a given point during a given interval of time.
disciple (diss-**sipe**-pl) *n* **1** a follower of the doctrines of a teacher. **2** one of the personal followers of Christ during his earthly life. ▷ **HISTORY** Latin *discipulus* pupil
disciplinarian *n* a person who practises strict discipline.
disciplinary *adj* of or imposing discipline; corrective.
discipline *n* **1** the practice of imposing strict rules of behaviour on other people. **2** the ability to behave and work in a controlled manner. **3** a particular area of academic study. ✧ *vb* **-plining, -plined 4** to improve or attempt to improve the behaviour of (oneself or someone else) by training or rules. **5** to punish. ▷ **HISTORY** Latin *disciplina* teaching
disciplined *adj* able to behave and work in a controlled way.
disc jockey *n* a person who announces and plays recorded pop records on a radio programme or at a disco.
disclaim *vb* **1** to deny (responsibility for or knowledge of something). **2** to give up (any claim to).
disclaimer *n* a statement denying responsibility for or knowledge of something.
disclose *vb* **-closing, -closed 1** to make (information) known. **2** to allow to be seen: *she agreed to disclose the contents of the box.* ▸ **disclosure** *n*
disco *n, pl* **-cos 1** a nightclub for dancing to amplified pop records. **2** an occasion at which people dance to amplified pop records. **3** mobile equipment for providing music for a disco. ▷ **HISTORY** from DISCOTHEQUE
discography *n, pl* **-phies** a classified list of gramophone records.
discolour *or US* **discolor** *vb* to change in colour; fade or stain. ▸ **discoloration** *n*
discomfit *vb* **-fiting, -fited** to make uneasy or confused. ▷ **HISTORY** Old French *desconfire* to destroy ▸ **discomfiture** *n*
discomfort *n* **1** a mild pain. **2** a feeling of worry or embarrassment. **3 discomforts** conditions that cause physical uncomfortableness: *the physical discomforts of pregnancy.*
discommode *vb* **-moding, -moded** to cause inconvenience. ▷ **HISTORY** DIS- + obsolete *commode* to suit ▸ **discommodious** *adj*
discompose *vb* **-posing, -posed** to disturb or upset someone. ▸ **discomposure** *n*
disconcert *vb* to disturb the confidence or self-possession of; upset, embarrass, or take aback. ▸ **disconcerting** *adj*
disconnect *vb* **1** to undo or break the connection between (two things). **2** to stop the supply of (gas or electricity to a building). ▸ **disconnection** *n*
disconnected *adj* (of speech or ideas) not logically connected.
disconsolate *adj* sad beyond comfort. ▷ **HISTORY** Medieval Latin *disconsolatus* ▸ **disconsolately** *adv*
discontent *n* lack of contentment, as with one's condition or lot in life. ▸ **discontented** *adj* ▸ **discontentedly** *adv*
discontinue *vb* **-uing, -ued** to come or bring to an end; stop.
discontinuous *adj* characterized by interruptions; intermittent. ▸ **discontinuity** *n*
discord *n* **1** lack of agreement or harmony between people. **2** harsh confused sounds. **3** a combination of musical notes that lacks harmony. ▷ **HISTORY** Latin *discors* at variance
discordant *adj* **1** at variance; disagreeing. **2** harsh in sound; inharmonious. ▸ **discordance** *n*
discotheque *n* same as **disco.** ▷ **HISTORY** French
discount *vb* **1** to leave (something) out of account as being unreliable, prejudiced, or

A B C D E F G H I J K L M N O P Q R S T U V W X Y Z

irrelevant. **2** to deduct (an amount or percentage) from the price of something. ✧ *n* **3** a deduction from the full amount of a price. **4 at a discount** below the regular price.

discountenance *vb* **-nancing, -nanced** to make (someone) ashamed or confused.

discourage *vb* **-aging, -aged 1** to deprive of the will or enthusiasm to persist in something. **2** to oppose by expressing disapproval. ▸ **discouragement** *n* ▸ **discouraging** *adj*

discourse *n* **1** conversation. **2** a formal treatment of a subject in speech or writing. ✧ *vb* **-coursing, -coursed 3** to speak or write (about) at length. ▷ HISTORY Medieval Latin *discursus* argument

discourse analysis *n Linguistics* the study of how language is used by members of a particular speech community.

discourteous *adj* showing bad manners; rude. ▸ **discourteously** *adv* ▸ **discourtesy** *n*

discover *vb* **1** to be the first to find or find out about. **2** to learn about for the first time. **3** to find after study or search. ▸ **discoverer** *n*

discovery *n, pl* **-eries 1** the act of discovering. **2** a person, place, or thing that has been discovered.

discredit *vb* **-iting, -ited 1** to damage the reputation of (someone). **2** to cause (an idea) to be disbelieved or distrusted. ✧ *n* **3** something that causes disgrace. ▸ **discreditable** *adj*

discreet *adj* **1** careful to avoid embarrassment when dealing with secret or private matters. **2** unobtrusive: *there was a discreet entrance down a side alley.* ▷ HISTORY Old French *discret* ▸ **discreetly** *adv*

> **WORD TIP**
> Avoid confusion with **discrete.**

discrepancy *n, pl* **-cies** a conflict or variation between facts, figures, or claims. ▷ HISTORY Latin *discrepare* to differ in sound ▸ **discrepant** *adj*

> **WORD TIP**
> *Discrepancy* is sometimes wrongly used where *disparity* is meant. A *discrepancy* exists between things which ought to be the same; it can be small but is usually significant. A *disparity* is a large difference between measurable things such as age, rank, or wages.

discrete *adj* separate or distinct. ▷ HISTORY Latin *discretus* separated ▸ **discreteness** *n*

> **WORD TIP**
> Avoid confusion with **discreet.**

discrete data *n Statistics* data which has a succession of distinct values. Compare **continuous data.**

discretion (diss-**kresh**-on) *n* **1** the quality of behaving so as to avoid social embarrassment or distress. **2** freedom or authority to make judgments and to act as one sees fit: *at his discretion.* ▸ **discretionary** *adj*

discriminate *vb* **-nating, -nated 1** to make a distinction against or in favour of a particular person or group. **2** to recognize or understand a difference: *to discriminate between right and wrong.* ▷ HISTORY Latin *discriminare* to divide ▸ **discriminating** *adj*

discrimination *n* **1** unfair treatment of a person, racial group, or minority. **2** subtle appreciation in matters of taste. **3** the ability to see fine distinctions.

discriminatory *adj* based on prejudice.

discursive *adj* passing from one topic to another. ▷ HISTORY Latin *discursus* a running to and fro

discus *n Field sports* a disc-shaped object with a heavy middle, thrown by athletes. ▷ HISTORY Greek *diskos*

discuss *vb* **1** to consider (something) by talking it over. **2** to treat (a subject) in speech or writing. ▷ HISTORY Latin *discutere* to dash to pieces ▸ **discussion** *n*

discussion genre *n* a form of writing or speech in which the writer or speaker sets out facts and possible interpretations in an objective manner before offering an opinion based on the evidence.

disdain *n* **1** a feeling of superiority and dislike; contempt. ✧ *vb* **2** to refuse or reject with disdain: *he disdained domestic conventions.* ▷ HISTORY Old French *desdeign* ▸ **disdainful** *adj* ▸ **disdainfully** *adv*

disease *n* an unhealthy condition in a person, animal, or plant which is caused by bacteria or infection. ▷ HISTORY Old French *desaise* ▸ **diseased** *adj*

diseconomy *n Econ* a disadvantage, such as higher costs, resulting from the scale on which a business operates.

disembark *vb* to land or cause to land from a ship, aircraft, or other vehicle. ▸ **disembarkation** *n*

disembodied *adj* **1** lacking a body. **2** seeming not to be attached to or come from anyone. ▸ **disembodiment** *n*

disembowel *vb* **-elling, -elled** *or US* **-eling, -eled** to remove the entrails of. ▸ **disembowelment** *n*

disenchanted *adj* disappointed and disillusioned (with something). ▸ **disenchantment** *n*

disenfranchise *vb* **-chising, -chised** to deprive (someone) of the right to vote or of other rights of citizenship.

disengage *vb* **-gaging, -gaged 1** to release from a connection. **2** *Mil* to withdraw from close action. ▸ **disengagement** *n*

disentangle *vb* **-gling, -gled 1** to release from entanglement or confusion. **2** to unravel or work out. ▸ **disentanglement** *n*

disequilibrium *n* a loss or absence of stability or balance.

disestablish *vb* to deprive (a church or religion) of established status. ▸ **disestablishment** *n*

disfavour *or US* **disfavor** *n* **1** disapproval or dislike. **2** the state of being disapproved of or disliked.

disfigure *vb* **-uring, -ured** to spoil the appearance or shape of. ▶ **disfigurement** *n*

disfranchise *vb* **-chising, -chised** same as **disenfranchise**.

disgorge *vb* **-gorging, -gorged 1** to vomit. **2** to discharge (contents).

disgrace *n* **1** a condition of shame, loss of reputation, or dishonour. **2** a shameful person or thing. **3** exclusion from confidence or trust: *he was sent home in disgrace.* ✧ *vb* **-gracing, -graced 4** to bring shame upon (oneself or others). ▶ **disgraceful** *adj* ▶ **disgracefully** *adv*

disgruntled *adj* sulky or discontented: *the disgruntled home supporters.* ▷ **HISTORY** DIS- + obsolete *gruntle* to complain ▶ **disgruntlement** *n*

disguise *vb* **-guising, -guised 1** to change the appearance or manner in order to conceal the identity of (someone or something). **2** to misrepresent (something) in order to obscure its actual nature or meaning. ✧ *n* **3** a mask, costume, or manner that disguises. **4** the state of being disguised. ▷ **HISTORY** Old French *desguisier* ▶ **disguised** *adj*

disgust *n* **1** a great loathing or distaste. ✧ *vb* **2** to sicken or fill with loathing. ▷ **HISTORY** Old French *desgouster* to sicken ▶ **disgusted** *adj* ▶ **disgusting** *adj*

dish *n* **1** a container used for holding or serving food, esp. an open shallow container. **2** the food in a dish. **3** a particular kind of food. **4** short for **dish aerial**. **5** *Informal* an attractive person. ✧ See also **dish out, dish up**. ▷ **HISTORY** Old English *disc*

dishabille (diss-a-**beel**) *n* same as **deshabille**.

dish aerial *n* a large disc-shaped aerial with a concave reflector, used to receive signals in radar, radio telescopes, and satellite broadcasting.

disharmony *n* lack of agreement or harmony. ▶ **disharmonious** *adj*

dishcloth *n* a cloth for washing dishes.

dishearten *vb* to weaken or destroy the hope, courage, or enthusiasm of. ▶ **disheartened** *adj* ▶ **disheartening** *adj*

dishevelled *or US* **disheveled** *adj* (of a person's hair, clothes, or general appearance) disordered and untidy. ▷ **HISTORY** Old French *deschevelé*

dishonest *adj* not honest or fair. ▶ **dishonestly** *adv* ▶ **dishonesty** *n*

dishonour *or US* **dishonor** *vb* **1** to treat with disrespect. **2** to refuse to pay (a cheque). ✧ *n* **3** a lack of honour or respect. **4** a state of shame or disgrace. **5** something that causes a loss of honour. ▶ **dishonourable** *adj* ▶ **dishonourably** *adv*

dish out *vb* **1** *Informal* to distribute. **2 dish it out** to inflict punishment.

dish up *vb* to serve (food).

dishwasher *n* a machine for washing and drying dishes, cutlery, etc.

disillusion *vb* **1** to destroy the illusions or false ideas of (someone). ✧ *n also* **disillusionment 2** the state of being disillusioned.

disincentive *n* something that discourages someone from behaving or acting in a particular way.

disinclined *adj* unwilling or reluctant. ▶ **disinclination** *n*

disinfect *vb* to rid of harmful germs by cleaning with a chemical substance. ▶ **disinfection** *n*

disinfectant *n* a substance that destroys harmful germs.

disinformation *n* false information intended to mislead.

disingenuous *adj* dishonest and insincere. ▶ **disingenuously** *adv*

disinherit *vb* **-iting, -ited** *Law* to deprive (an heir) of inheritance. ▶ **disinheritance** *n*

disintegrate *vb* **-grating, -grated 1** to lose cohesion; break up: *the business disintegrated.* **2** (of an object) to break into fragments; shatter. **3** *Physics* **a** to undergo nuclear fission or include nuclear fission in. **b** same as **decay** (sense 3). ▶ **disintegration** *n*

disinter *vb* **-terring, -terred 1** to dig up. **2** to bring to light; expose.

disinterested *adj* **1** free from bias; objective. **2** *Not universally accepted* feeling or showing a lack of interest; uninterested. ▶ **disinterest** *n*

> **WORD TIP**
> Many people consider that the use of *disinterested* to mean not interested is incorrect and that *uninterested* should be used.

disjointed *adj* having no coherence; disconnected: *a disjointed conversation.*

disjunctive *adj* serving to disconnect or separate.

disk *n* **1** *Chiefly US & Canad* same as **disc**. **2** *Computers* a storage device, consisting of a stack of plates coated with a magnetic layer, which rotates rapidly as a single unit. ▷ **HISTORY** see DISC

disk drive *n Computers* the controller and mechanism for reading and writing data on computer disks.

dislike *vb* **-liking, -liked 1** to consider unpleasant or disagreeable. ✧ *n* **2** a feeling of not liking something or someone.

dislocate *vb* **-cating, -cated 1** to displace (a bone or joint) from its normal position. **2** to disrupt or shift out of place. ▶ **dislocation** *n*

dislodge *vb* **-lodging, -lodged** to remove (something) from a previously fixed position.

disloyal *adj* not loyal; deserting one's allegiance or duty. ▶ **disloyalty** *n*

dismal *adj* **1** gloomy and depressing. **2** *Informal* of poor quality. ▶ **dismally** *adv*

> **WORD HISTORY**
> In medieval times, 'dismal' (from Latin *dies mali*, meaning 'evil days') was the name given to the 24 days of the year (two in each month) that were believed to be unlucky.

dismantle *vb* **-tling, -tled 1** to take apart piece by piece. **2** to cause (an organization or political

a b c d e f g h i j k l m n o p q r s t u v w x y z

A B C D E F G H I J K L M N O P Q R S T U V W X Y Z

system) to stop functioning by gradually reducing its power or purpose. ▷ HISTORY Old French *desmanteler*

dismay *vb* **1** to fill with alarm or depression. ✧ *n* **2** a feeling of alarm or depression. ▷ HISTORY Old French *des-* (intensive) + *esmayer* to frighten

dismember *vb* **1** to remove the limbs of. **2** to cut to pieces. ▶ **dismemberment** *n*

dismiss *vb* **1** to remove (an employee) from a job. **2** to allow (someone) to leave. **3** to put out of one's mind; no longer think about. **4** (of a judge) to state that (a case) will not be brought to trial. **5** *Cricket* to bowl out (a side) for a particular number of runs. ▷ HISTORY Latin *dis-* from + *mittere* to send ▶ **dismissal** *n* ▶ **dismissive** *adj*

dismount *vb* to get off a horse or bicycle.

disobedient *adj* refusing to obey. ▶ **disobedience** *n*

disobey *vb* to neglect or refuse to obey (a person or an order).

disobliging *adj* unwilling to help.

disorder *n* **1** a state of untidiness and disorganization. **2** public violence or rioting. **3** an illness. ▶ **disordered** *adj*

disorderly *adj* **1** untidy and disorganized. **2** uncontrolled; unruly. **3** *Law* violating public peace.

disorganize *or* **-ise** *vb* **-izing, -ized** *or* **-ising, -ised** to disrupt the arrangement or system of. ▶ **disorganization** *or* **-isation** *n*

disorientate *or* **disorient** *vb* **-tating, -tated** *or* **-enting, -ented** to cause (someone) to lose his or her bearings. ▶ **disorientation** *n*

disown *vb* to deny any connection with (someone).

disparage *vb* **-aging, -aged** to speak contemptuously of. ▷ HISTORY Old French *desparagier* ▶ **disparagement** *n* ▶ **disparaging** *adj*

disparate *adj* utterly different in kind. ▷ HISTORY Latin *disparare* to divide ▶ **disparity** *n*

> **WORD TIP**
> See at **discrepancy.**

dispassionate *adj* not influenced by emotion; objective. ▶ **dispassionately** *adv*

dispatch *or* **despatch** *vb* **1** to send off to a destination or to perform a task. **2** to carry out (a duty or task) promptly. **3** to murder. ✧ *n* **4** an official communication or report, sent in haste. **5** a report sent to a newspaper by a correspondent. **6** murder. **7 with dispatch** quickly. ▷ HISTORY Italian *dispacciare*

dispatch rider *n Brit, Austral & NZ* a motorcyclist who carries dispatches.

dispel *vb* **-pelling, -pelled** to disperse or drive away. ▷ HISTORY Latin *dispellere*

dispensable *adj* not essential; expendable.

dispensary *n, pl* **-ries** a place where medicine is prepared and given out.

dispensation *n* **1** the act of distributing or dispensing. **2** *Chiefly RC Church* permission to dispense with an obligation of church law. **3** any exemption from an obligation. **4** the ordering of life and events by God.

dispense *vb* **-pensing, -pensed 1** to distribute in portions. **2** to prepare and distribute (medicine). **3** to administer (the law, etc.). **4 dispense with** to do away with or manage without. ▷ HISTORY Latin *dispendere* to weigh out ▶ **dispenser** *n*

> **WORD TIP**
> *Dispense with* is sometimes wrongly used where *dispose of* is meant: *this task can be disposed of* (not *dispensed with*) *quickly and easily.*

dispensing optician *n* See **optician** (sense 2).

disperse *vb* **-persing, -persed 1** to scatter over a wide area. **2** to leave or cause to leave a gathering: *police dispersed rioters.* **3** to separate (light) into its different wavelengths. **4** to separate (particles) throughout a solid, liquid, or gas. ▷ HISTORY Latin *dispergere* to scatter widely ▶ **dispersal** *or* **dispersion** *n*

> **WORD TIP**
> See at **disburse.**

dispersed settlement *n Geog* a pattern of settlement found in rural areas in which dwellings are scattered rather than clustered together. Compare **nucleated settlement**.

dispirit *vb* to make downhearted. ▶ **dispirited** *adj* ▶ **dispiriting** *adj*

displace *vb* **-placing, -placed 1** to move (something) from its usual place. **2** to remove (someone) from a post or position of authority.

displaced person *n* a person forced from his or her home or country, esp. by war or revolution.

displacement *n* **1** the act of displacing. **2** *Physics* the weight or volume of liquid displaced by an object submerged or floating in it. **3** *Maths* the distance measured in a particular direction from a reference point. Symbol: *s*.

displacement reaction *n Chemistry* a chemical reaction where one element displaces another in a compound.

display *vb* **1** to show. **2** to reveal or make evident: *to display anger.* ✧ *n* **3** the act of exhibiting or displaying. **4** something displayed. **5** an exhibition. **6** *Electronics* a device capable of representing information visually, as on a screen. **7** *Zool* a pattern of behaviour by which an animal attracts attention while courting, defending its territory, etc. ▷ HISTORY Anglo-French *despleier* to unfold

display advertisement *n* (in a magazine or newspaper) an eye-catching, often full-page, advertisement.

displease *vb* **-pleasing, -pleased** to annoy or offend (someone). ▶ **displeasure** *n*

disport *vb* **disport oneself** to indulge oneself in pleasure. ▷ HISTORY Anglo-French *desporter*

disposable *adj* **1** designed for disposal after use: *disposable cigarette lighters.* **2** available for use if needed: *disposable capital.*

disposal *n* **1** the act or means of getting rid of something. **2 at one's disposal** available for use.

dispose *vb* **-posing, -posed 1 dispose of a** to throw away. **b** to give, sell, or transfer to another. **c** to deal with or settle: *I disposed of that problem right away.* **d** to kill. **2** to arrange or place in a particular way: *around them are disposed the moulded masks of witch doctors.* ▷ **HISTORY** Latin *disponere* to set in different places

> **WORD TIP**
> See at **dispense.**

disposed *adj* **1** willing or eager (to do something): *few would feel disposed to fault his judgment.* **2** having an inclination as specified (towards someone or something): *my people aren't too well disposed towards defectors.*

disposition *n* **1** a person's usual temperament. **2** a tendency or habit. **3** arrangement; layout.

dispossess *vb* to deprive (someone) of (a possession). ▶ **dispossessed** *adj* ▶ **dispossession** *n*

disproportion *n* lack of proportion or equality.

disproportionate *adj* out of proportion. ▶ **disproportionately** *adv*

disprove *vb* **-proving, -proved** to show (an assertion or claim) to be incorrect.

dispute *n* **1** a disagreement between workers and their employer. **2** an argument between two or more people. ✧ *vb* **-puting, -puted 3** to argue or quarrel about (something). **4** to doubt the validity of. **5** to fight over possession of. **6 beyond dispute** unable to be questioned or denied: *it's beyond dispute that tensions already existed between them.* ▷ **HISTORY** Latin *disputare* to discuss ▶ **disputation** *n* ▶ **disputatious** *adj*

disqualify *vb* **-fies, -fying, -fied 1** to officially ban (someone) from doing something: *he was disqualified from driving for ten years.* **2** to make ineligible, as for entry to an examination. ▶ **disqualification** *n*

disquiet *n* **1** a feeling of anxiety or uneasiness. ✧ *vb* **2** to make (someone) anxious. ▶ **disquieting** *adj* ▶ **disquietude** *n*

disquisition *n* a formal written or oral examination of a subject.

disregard *vb* **1** to give little or no attention to; ignore. ✧ *n* **2** lack of attention or respect.

disrepair *n* the condition of being worn out or in poor working order.

disreputable *adj* having or causing a bad reputation. ▶ **disreputably** *adv*

disrepute *n* a loss or lack of good reputation.

disrespect *n* contempt or lack of respect. ▶ **disrespectful** *adj*

disrobe *vb* **-robing, -robed** *Literary* to undress.

disrupt *vb* to interrupt the progress of. ▷ **HISTORY** Latin *disruptus* burst asunder ▶ **disruption** *n* ▶ **disruptive** *adj*

dissatisfied *adj* displeased or discontented. ▶ **dissatisfaction** *n*

dissect *vb* **1** to cut open (a corpse) to examine it. **2** to examine critically and minutely: *the above conclusion causes one to dissect that policy more closely.* ▷ **HISTORY** Latin *dissecare* ▶ **dissection** *n*

dissemble *vb* **-bling, -bled** to conceal one's real motives or emotions by pretence. ▷ **HISTORY** Latin *dissimulare* ▶ **dissembler** *n*

disseminate *vb* **-nating, -nated** to spread (information, ideas, etc.) widely. ▷ **HISTORY** Latin *disseminare* ▶ **dissemination** *n*

dissension *n* disagreement and argument. ▷ **HISTORY** Latin *dissentire* to dissent

dissent *vb* **1** to disagree. **2** *Christianity* to reject the doctrines of an established church. ✧ *n* **3** a disagreement. **4** *Christianity* separation from an established church. ▷ **HISTORY** Latin *dissentire* to disagree ▶ **dissenter** *n* ▶ **dissenting** *adj*

Dissenter *n Christianity chiefly Brit* a Protestant who refuses to conform to the established church.

dissentient *adj* dissenting from the opinion of the majority.

dissertation *n* **1** a written thesis, usually required for a higher degree. **2** a long formal speech. ▷ **HISTORY** Latin *dissertare* to debate

disservice *n* a harmful action.

dissident *n* **1** a person who disagrees with a government or a powerful organization. ✧ *adj* **2** disagreeing or dissenting. ▷ **HISTORY** Latin *dissidere* to be remote from ▶ **dissidence** *n*

dissimilar *adj* not alike; different. ▶ **dissimilarity** *n*

dissimulate *vb* **-lating, -lated** to conceal one's real feelings by pretence. ▶ **dissimulation** *n*

dissipate *vb* **-pating, -pated 1** to waste or squander. **2** to scatter or break up. ▷ **HISTORY** Latin *dissipare* to disperse

dissipated *adj* showing signs of overindulgence in alcohol or other physical pleasures.

dissipation *n* **1** the process of dissipating. **2** unrestrained indulgence in physical pleasures. **3** *Physics* an undesirable loss or lessening of power, which is converted into heat.

dissociate *vb* **-ating, -ated 1 dissociate oneself from** to deny or break an association with (a person or organization). **2** to regard or treat as separate. ▶ **dissociation** *n*

dissoluble *adj* same as **soluble.** ▷ **HISTORY** Latin *dissolubilis* ▶ **dissolubility** *n*

dissolute *adj* leading an immoral life. ▷ **HISTORY** Latin *dissolutus* loose

dissolution *n* **1** the act of officially breaking up an organization or institution. **2** the act of officially ending a formal agreement, such as a marriage. **3** the formal ending of a meeting or assembly, such as a Parliament.

dissolve *vb* **-solving, -solved 1** to become or cause to become liquid; melt. **2** to officially break up (an organization or institution). **3** to formally end: *the campaign started as soon as Parliament was dissolved last month.* **4** to collapse emotionally: *she dissolved in loud tears.* **5** *Films, television* to fade out one scene and replace with another to make two scenes merge imperceptibly. ▷ HISTORY Latin *dissolvere* to make loose

dissonance *n* a lack of agreement or harmony between things: *this dissonance of colours.* ▸ **dissonant** *adj*

dissuade *vb* **-suading, -suaded** to deter (someone) by persuasion from doing something or believing in something. ▷ HISTORY Latin *dissuadere* ▸ **dissuasion** *n*

dissyllable *or* **disyllable** *n* a word of two syllables. ▸ **dissyllabic** *or* **disyllabic** *adj*

distaff *n* the rod on which flax is wound for spinning. ▷ HISTORY Old English *distæf*

distaff side *n* the female side of a family.

distance *n* **1** the space between two points or places. **2** the state of being apart. **3** a distant place. **4** remoteness in manner. **5 the distance** the most distant part of the visible scene. **6 go the distance** *Boxing* to complete a bout without being knocked out. **7 keep one's distance** to maintain a reserved attitude to another person. ✧ *vb* **-tancing, -tanced** **8 distance oneself** *or* **be distanced from** to separate oneself or be separated mentally from.

distance learning *n* a teaching system involving video and written material for studying at home.

distant *adj* **1** far apart. **2** separated by a specified distance: *five kilometres distant.* **3** apart in relationship: *a distant cousin.* **4** going to a faraway place. **5** remote in manner; aloof. **6** abstracted: *a distant look entered her eyes.* ▷ HISTORY Latin *dis-* apart + *stare* to stand ▸ **distantly** *adv*

distaste *n* a dislike of something offensive.

distasteful *adj* unpleasant or offensive. ▸ **distastefulness** *n*

distemper¹ *n* a highly contagious viral disease that can affect young dogs. ▷ HISTORY Latin *dis-* apart + *temperare* to regulate

distemper² *n* **1** paint mixed with water, glue, etc. which is used for painting walls. ✧ *vb* **2** to paint with distemper. ▷ HISTORY Latin *dis-* (intensive) + *temperare* to mingle

distend *vb* to expand by pressure from within; swell. ▷ HISTORY Latin *distendere* ▸ **distensible** *adj* ▸ **distension** *n*

distich (**diss**-stick) *n Prosody* a unit of two verse lines. ▷ HISTORY Greek *di-* two + *stikhos* row, line

distil *or US* **distill** *vb* **-tilling, -tilled** **1** to subject to or obtain by distillation. **2** to give off (a substance) in drops. **3** to extract the essence of. ▷ HISTORY Latin *de-* down + *stillare* to drip

distillation *n* **1** the process of evaporating a liquid and condensing its vapour. **2** Also: **distillate** a concentrated essence.

distiller *n* a person or company that makes spirits.

distillery *n, pl* **-eries** a place where alcoholic drinks are made by distillation.

distinct *adj* **1** not the same; different: *these two areas produce wines with distinct characteristics.* **2** clearly seen, heard, or recognized: *it is not possible to draw a distinct line between the two categories; there's a distinct smell of burning.* **3** clear and definite: *there is a distinct possibility of rain.* **4** obvious: *a distinct improvement.* ▷ HISTORY Latin *distinctus* ▸ **distinctly** *adv*

distinction *n* **1** the act of distinguishing or differentiating. **2** a distinguishing feature. **3** the state of being different or distinguishable. **4** special honour, recognition, or fame. **5** excellence of character. **6** a symbol of honour or rank.

distinctive *adj* easily recognizable; characteristic. ▸ **distinctively** *adv* ▸ **distinctiveness** *n*

distinguish *vb* **1** to make, show, or recognize a difference: *I have tried to distinguish between fact and theory.* **2** to be a distinctive feature of: *what distinguishes the good teenage reader from the less competent one?* **3** to make out by hearing, seeing, or tasting: *she listened but could distinguish nothing except the urgency of their discussion.* **4 distinguish oneself** to make oneself noteworthy. ▷ HISTORY Latin *distinguere* to separate ▸ **distinguishable** *adj* ▸ **distinguishing** *adj*

distinguished *adj* **1** dignified in appearance or behaviour. **2** highly respected: *a distinguished historian.*

distort *vb* **1** to alter or misrepresent (facts). **2** to twist out of shape; deform. **3** *Electronics* to reproduce or amplify (a signal) inaccurately. ▷ HISTORY Latin *distorquere* to turn different ways ▸ **distorted** *adj* ▸ **distortion** *n*

distract *vb* **1** to draw (a person or his or her attention) away from something. **2** to amuse or entertain. ▷ HISTORY Latin *distrahere* to pull in different directions

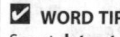

> ☑ **WORD TIP**
> See at **detract.**

distracted *adj* unable to concentrate because one's mind is on other things.

distraction *n* **1** something that diverts the attention. **2** something that serves as an entertainment. **3** mental turmoil.

distrain *vb Law* to seize (personal property) to enforce payment of a debt. ▷ HISTORY Latin *di-* apart + *stringere* to draw tight ▸ **distraint** *n*

distrait (diss-**tray**) *adj* absent-minded or abstracted. ▷ HISTORY French

distraught (diss-**trawt**) *adj* upset or agitated. ▷ HISTORY obsolete *distract*

distress *n* **1** extreme unhappiness or worry. **2** great physical pain. **3** financial trouble. ✧ *vb* **4** to upset badly. **5 in distress** in dire need of help. ▷ HISTORY Latin *districtus* divided in mind ▸ **distressing** *adj* ▸ **distressingly** *adv*

distressed *adj* **1** much troubled; upset. **2** in great physical pain. **3** in financial difficulties. **4** (of furniture or fabric) having signs of ageing artificially applied.

distributary *n, pl* **-taries** one of several outlet streams draining a river, esp. on a delta.

distribute *vb* **-uting, -uted** **1** to hand out or deliver (leaflets, mail, etc.). **2** to share (something) among the members of a particular group. ▷ HISTORY Latin *distribuere*

distribution *n* **1** the delivering of leaflets, mail, etc., to individual people or organizations. **2** the sharing out of something among a particular group. **3** the arrangement or spread of anything over an area, space, or period of time: *the unequal distribution of wealth.* **4** *Commerce* the process of satisfying the demand for goods and services.

distributive *adj* **1** of or relating to distribution. **2** *Maths* of the rule that the same result is produced when multiplication is performed on a set of numbers as when performed on the members of the set individually.

distributor *n* **1** a wholesaler who distributes goods to retailers in a specific area. **2** the device in a petrol engine that sends the electric current to the sparking plugs.

district *n* **1** an area of land regarded as an administrative or geographical unit. **2** an area which has recognizable or special features: *an upper-class residential district.* ▷ **HISTORY** Medieval Latin *districtus* area of jurisdiction

district court judge *n Austral & NZ* a judge presiding over a lower court.

district nurse *n* (in Britain) a nurse who attends to patients in their homes within a particular district.

distrust *vb* **1** to regard as untrustworthy. ✧ *n* **2** a feeling of suspicion or doubt. ▶ **distrustful** *adj*

disturb *vb* **1** to intrude on; interrupt. **2** to upset or worry. **3** to disarrange; muddle. **4** to inconvenience. ▷ **HISTORY** Latin *disturbare* ▶ **disturbing** *adj* ▶ **disturbingly** *adv*

disturbance *n* **1** an interruption or intrusion. **2** an unruly outburst in public.

disturbed *adj Psychiatry* emotionally upset, troubled, or maladjusted.

disunite *vb* **-niting, -nited** to cause disagreement among. ▶ **disunion** *n* ▶ **disunity** *n*

disuse *n* the state of being neglected or no longer used; neglect.

disused *adj* no longer used.

disyllable *n* same as **dissyllable**.

ditch *n* **1** a narrow channel dug in the earth for drainage or irrigation. ✧ *vb* **2** *Slang* to abandon or discard: *she ditched her boyfriend last month.* ▷ **HISTORY** Old English *dīc*

dither *vb* **1** *Chiefly Brit & NZ* to be uncertain or indecisive. ✧ *n* **2** *Chiefly Brit* a state of indecision or agitation. ▷ **HISTORY** Middle English *didder* ▶ **ditherer** *n* ▶ **dithery** *adj*

dithyramb *n* (in ancient Greece) a passionate choral hymn in honour of Dionysus. ▷ **HISTORY** Greek *dithurambos* ▶ **dithyrambic** *adj*

ditto *n, pl* **-tos 1** the above; the same: used in lists to avoid repetition, and represented by the mark (,,) placed under the thing repeated. ✧ *adv* **2** in the same way. ▷ **HISTORY** Italian (dialect) *detto* said

ditty *n, pl* **-ties** a short simple song or poem. ▷ **HISTORY** Latin *dictare* to say repeatedly

diuretic (die-yoor-**et**-ik) *n* a drug that increases the flow of urine. ▷ **HISTORY** Greek *dia-* through + *ourein* to urinate

diurnal (die-**urn**-al) *adj* **1** happening during the day or daily. **2** (of animals) active during the day. ▷ **HISTORY** Latin *diurnus*

diurnal range *n Meteorol* the difference between the highest and lowest temperatures over a 24-hour period.

diva *n, pl* **-vas** *or* **-ve** a distinguished female singer; prima donna. ▷ **HISTORY** Latin: a goddess

divalent *adj Chem* having two valencies or a valency of two. ▶ **divalency** *n*

divan *n* **a** a low bed with a thick base under the mattress. **b** a couch with no back or arms. ▷ **HISTORY** Turkish *dīvān*

dive *vb* **diving, dived** *or US* **dove, dived, 1** to plunge headfirst into water. **1** (of a submarine or diver) to submerge under water. **2** (of a bird or aircraft) to fly in a steep nose-down descending path. **3** to move quickly in a specified direction: *he dived for the door.* **4 dive in** *or* **into a** to put (one's hand) quickly or forcefully (into). **b** to start doing (something) enthusiastically. ✧ *n* **5** a headlong plunge into water. **6** the act of diving. **7** a steep nose-down descent of a bird or aircraft. **8** *Slang* a disreputable bar or club. ▷ **HISTORY** Old English *dȳfan*

dive bomber *n* a military aircraft designed to release bombs on a target during a dive. ▶ **dive-bomb** *vb*

diver *n* **1** a person who works or explores underwater. **2** a person who dives for sport. **3** a large diving bird of northern oceans with a straight pointed bill and webbed feet.

diverge *vb* **-verging, -verged 1** to separate and go in different directions. **2** to be at variance; differ: *the two books diverge in setting and in style.* **3** to deviate (from a prescribed course). ▷ **HISTORY** Latin *dis-* apart + *vergere* to turn ▶ **divergence** *n* ▶ **divergent** *adj*

divergence zone *n Geol* a zone where tectonic plates move apart and new crust and lithosphere are formed; characterized by earthquakes and volcanic activity. Compare **convergence zone**.

diverse *adj* **1** having variety; assorted. **2** different in kind. ▷ **HISTORY** Latin *diversus* turned in different directions

diversify *vb* **-fies, -fying, -fied 1** to create different forms of; vary. **2** *Econ* to distribute investments among several securities in order to spread risk. ▷ **HISTORY** Latin *diversus* different + *facere* to make ▶ **diversification** *n*

diversion *n* **1** *Chiefly Brit* an official detour used by traffic when a main route is closed. **2** something that distracts someone's attention or concentration. **3** the act of diverting from a specified course. **4** a pleasant or amusing pastime or activity. ▶ **diversionary** *adj*

diversity *n* **1** the quality of being different or varied. **2** a point of difference.

divert *vb* **1** to change the course or direction of (traffic). **2** to distract the attention of. **3** to entertain or amuse. ▷ **HISTORY** Latin *divertere* to turn aside

diverticulitis *n* inflammation of pouches in the wall of the colon, causing lower abdominal pain. ▷ **HISTORY** Latin *deverticulum* path, track

divertimento *n, pl* **-ti** a piece of entertaining music in several movements. ▷ **HISTORY** Italian

divest *vb* **1** to strip (of clothes). **2** to deprive of a role, function, or quality: *the chairman felt duty-bound to stay with the company after it was divested of all its aviation interests.* ▷ **HISTORY** earlier *devest*

divide *vb* **-viding, -vided 1** to separate into parts. **2** to share or be shared out in parts. **3** to disagree or cause to disagree: *experts are divided over the plan.* **4** to keep apart or be a boundary between. **5** to categorize or classify. **6** to calculate how many times one number can be contained in another. ✧ *n* **7** a division or split. **8** *Chiefly US & Canad* an area of high ground separating drainage basins. ▷ **HISTORY** Latin *dividere* to force apart

dividend *n* **1** a portion of a company's profits paid to its shareholders. **2** an extra benefit: *Saudi progressives saw a dividend to the crisis.* **3** a number to be divided by another number. ▷ **HISTORY** Latin *dividendum* what is to be divided

divider *n* a screen placed so as to divide a room into separate areas.

dividers *pl n* compasses with two pointed arms, used for measuring or dividing lines.

divination *n* the art of discovering future events as though by supernatural powers.

divine *adj* **1** of God or a god. **2** godlike. **3** *Informal* splendid or perfect. ✧ *n* **4** a priest who is learned in theology. ✧ *vb* **-vining, -vined 5** to discover (something) by intuition or guessing. ▷ **HISTORY** Latin *divus* a god ▶ **divinely** *adv* ▶ **diviner** *n*

diving bell *n* a diving apparatus with an open bottom, supplied with compressed air from above.

diving board *n* a platform from which swimmers may dive.

diving suit *n* a waterproof suit used for diving with a detachable helmet and an air supply.

divining rod *n* a forked twig said to move when held over ground in which water or metal is to be found.

divinity *n, pl* **-ties 1** the study of religion. **2** a god or goddess. **3** the state of being divine.

divisible *adj* capable of being divided. ▶ **divisibility** *n*

division *n* **1** the separation of something into two or more distinct parts. **2** the act of dividing or sharing out. **3** one of the parts into which something is divided. **4** the mathematical operation of dividing. **5** a difference of opinion. **6** a part of an organization that has been made into a unit for administrative or other reasons. **7** a formal vote in Parliament. **8** one of the groups of teams that make up a football or other sports league. **9** *Army* a major formation containing the necessary arms to sustain independent combat. **10** *Biol* one of the major groups into which the plant kingdom is divided, corresponding to a phylum. ▷ **HISTORY** Latin *dividere* to divide ▶ **divisional** *adj*

division sign *n* the symbol ÷, placed between two numbers to indicate that the first number should be divided by the second, as in $12 \div 6 = 2$.

divisive (div-**vice**-iv) *adj* tending to cause disagreement: *he played an important role in defusing potentially divisive issues.*

divisor *n* a number to be divided into another number.

divorce *n* **1** the legal ending of a marriage. **2** a separation, esp. one that is permanent. ✧ *vb* **-vorcing, -vorced 3** to separate or be separated by divorce. **4** to remove or separate. ▷ **HISTORY** Latin *divertere* to separate

divot *n* a small piece of turf.

divulge *vb* **-vulging, -vulged** to make known: *I am not permitted to divulge his name.* ▷ **HISTORY** Latin *divulgare* ▶ **divulgence** *n*

divvy¹ *vb* **-vies, -vying, -vied divvy up** *Informal* to divide and share.

divvy² *n, pl* **-vies** *Brit, dialect* a stupid person.

Diwali (duh-**wah**-lee) *n* an annual Hindu festival honouring Lakshmi, the goddess of wealth.

Dixie *n* the southern states of the US. Also called: **Dixieland** ▷ **HISTORY** origin unknown

DIY *or* **d.i.y.** *Brit, Austral & NZ* do-it-yourself.

dizzy *adj* **-zier, -ziest 1** feeling giddy. **2** unable to think clearly; confused. **3** tending to cause giddiness or confusion. ✧ *vb* **-zies, -zying, -zied 4** to cause to feel giddy or confused. ▷ **HISTORY** Old English *dysig* silly ▶ **dizzily** *adv* ▶ **dizziness** *n*

DJ *or* **dj 1** disc jockey. **2** *Brit* dinner jacket.

djinni *or* **djinny** *n, pl* **djinn** same as **jinni**.

dl decilitre(s).

DLitt *or* **DLit 1** Doctor of Letters. **2** Doctor of Literature. ▷ **HISTORY** Latin *Doctor Litterarum*

dm decimetre(s).

DM Deutschmark.

DMus Doctor of Music.

DNA deoxyribonucleic acid, the main constituent of the chromosomes of all organisms.

DNA fingerprinting *or* **profiling** *n* same as **genetic fingerprinting**.

D-notice *n Brit & Austral* an official notice sent to newspapers prohibiting the publication of certain security information. ▷ **HISTORY** from their administrative classification letter

do¹ *vb* **does, doing, did, done 1** to perform or complete (a deed or action): *we do a fair amount of entertaining.* **2** to be adequate: *it's not what I wanted but it will have to do.* **3** to provide: *this hotel only does bed and breakfast.* **4** to make tidy or elegant: *he watched her do her hair.* **5** to improve: *that style does nothing for you.* **6** to find an answer to (a problem or puzzle). **7** to conduct oneself: *do as you want.* **8** to cause or produce: *herbal teas have active ingredients that can do good.* **9** to give or grant: *do me a favour.* **10** to work at as a course of study or a job. **11** to mimic. **12** to achieve a particular speed, amount, or rate: *this computer system can do 40 different cross checks; this car can do sixty miles to the gallon.* **13** used: **a** to form questions: *do you like it?* **b** to intensify positive statements and commands: *tensions do exist.* **c** to form negative statements or commands: *do not talk while I'm talking!* **d** to replace an earlier verb: *he drinks much more than I do.* **14** *Informal* to visit (a place) as a tourist: *we plan* *to do the States this year.* **15** *Slang* to serve (a period of time) as a prison sentence. **16** *Informal* to cheat or rob: *I was done out of ten pounds.* **17** *Slang* **a** to arrest. **b** to convict of a crime: *he was done for 3 years for housebreaking.* **18** *Slang, chiefly Brit* to assault. **19** *Slang* to take or use (drugs). **20 make do** to manage with whatever is available. ✧ *n, pl* **dos** *or* **do's 21** *Informal, chiefly Brit & NZ* a party or other social event. **22 do's and don'ts** *Informal* rules. ✧ See also **do away with.** ▷ HISTORY Old English *dōn*

do² *n, pl* **dos** *Music* same as **doh.**

do away with *vb* to get rid of (someone or something).

Doberman pinscher *or* **Doberman** *n* a large dog with a glossy black-and-tan coat. ▷ HISTORY after L. *Dobermann,* dog breeder

dob in *vb* **dobbing, dobbed** *Austral & NZ informal* **1** to inform against. **2** to contribute to a fund.

doc *n Informal* same as **doctor.**

DOC (in New Zealand) Department of Conservation.

docile *adj* (of a person or animal) easily controlled. ▷ HISTORY Latin *docilis* easily taught ▶ **docilely** *adv* ▶ **docility** *n*

dock¹ *n* **1** an enclosed area of water where ships are loaded, unloaded, or repaired. **2** a wharf or pier. ✧ *vb* **3** to moor or be moored at a dock. **4** to link (two spacecraft) or (of two spacecraft) to be linked together in space. ▷ HISTORY Middle Dutch *docke*

dock² *vb* **1** to deduct (an amount) from (a person's wages). **2** to remove part of (an animal's tail) by cutting through the bone. ▷ HISTORY Middle English *dok*

dock³ *n* an enclosed space in a court of law where the accused person sits or stands. ▷ HISTORY Flemish *dok* sty

dock⁴ *n* a weed with broad leaves. ▷ HISTORY Old English *docce*

docker *n Brit* a person employed to load and unload ships.

docket *n* **1** *Chiefly Brit* a label on a package or other delivery, stating contents, delivery instructions, etc. ✧ *vb* **-eting, -eted 2** to fix a docket to (a package or other delivery). ▷ HISTORY origin unknown

dockyard *n* a place where ships are built or repaired.

doctor *n* **1** a person licensed to practise medicine. **2** a person who has been awarded a doctorate. **3** *Chiefly US & Canada* a person licensed to practise dentistry or veterinary medicine. ✧ *vb* **4** to change in order to deceive: *she confessed to having doctored the figures.* **5** to poison or drug (food or drink). **6** to castrate (an animal). ▷ HISTORY Latin: teacher ▶ **doctoral** *adj*

doctorate *n* the highest academic degree in any field of knowledge.

doctrinaire *adj* stubbornly insistent on the application of a theory without regard to practicality.

doctrine (**dock**-trin) *n* **1** a body of teachings of a religious, political, or philosophical group. **2** a principle or body of principles that is taught or advocated. ▷ HISTORY Latin *doctrina* teaching ▶ **doctrinal** *adj*

document *n* **1** a piece of paper that provides an official record of something. **2** *Computing* a computer file with text or graphics that can be altered using the appropriate software. ✧ *vb* **3** to record or report (something) in detail. **4** to support (a claim) with evidence. ▷ HISTORY Latin *documentum* a lesson

documentary *n, pl* **-ries 1** a film or television programme presenting the facts about a particular subject. ✧ *adj* **2** of or based on documents: *vital documentary evidence has been found.*

documentation *n* documents supplied as proof or evidence of something.

docu-soap *n* a television documentary series presenting the lives of the people filmed as entertainment.

dodder *vb* to move unsteadily. ▷ HISTORY variant of earlier *dadder* ▶ **dodderer** *n* ▶ **doddery** *adj*

doddle *n Brit, Austral & NZ informal* something easily accomplished: *the test turned out to be a doddle.* ▷ HISTORY origin unknown

dodecagon (doe-**deck**-a-gon) *n* a polygon with twelve sides. ▷ HISTORY Greek *dōdeka* twelve + *gōnia* angle

dodecahedron (doe-deck-a-**heed**-ron) *n* a solid figure with twelve plane faces.

dodge *vb* **dodging, dodged 1** to avoid being hit, caught, or seen by moving suddenly. **2** to evade by cleverness or trickery: *the Government will not be able to dodge the issue.* ✧ *n* **3** a cunning and deceitful trick. ▷ HISTORY origin unknown

Dodgem *n Trademark* a small electric car driven and bumped against similar cars in a rink at a funfair.

dodger *n* a person who evades a duty or obligation.

dodgy *adj* **dodgier, dodgiest** *Brit, Austral, & NZ informal* **1** dangerous, risky, or unreliable: *he's in a very dodgy political position.* **2** untrustworthy: *they considered him a very dodgy character.*

dodo *n, pl* **dodos** *or* **dodoes 1** a large extinct bird that could not fly. **2 as dead as a dodo** no longer existing. ▷ HISTORY Portuguese *duodo* stupid

do down *vb* to belittle or humiliate: *the moderate constructionist does not wish to do science down.*

doe *n, pl* **does** *or* **doe** the female of the deer, hare, or rabbit. ▷ HISTORY Old English *dā*

DOE (in Britain) Department of the Environment.

doek (rhymes with **book**) *n S African informal* a square of cloth worn on the head by women. ▷ HISTORY Afrikaans

does *vb* third person singular of the present tense of **do¹**.

doff *vb* to take off or lift (one's hat) in salutation. ▷ HISTORY Old English *dōn of*

do for *vb Informal* **1** to cause the ruin, death, or defeat of: *I'm done for if this error comes to light.* **2** to do housework for. **3 do well for oneself** to thrive or succeed.

A B C D E F G H I J K L M N O P Q R S T U V W X Y Z

dog *n* **1** a domesticated canine mammal occurring in many different breeds. **2** any other member of the dog family, such as the dingo or coyote. RELATED ADJECTIVE ▸ **canine 3** the male of animals of the dog family. **4** *Informal* a person: *you lucky dog!* **5** *US & Canad informal* something unsatisfactory or inferior. **6 a dog's life** a wretched existence. **7 dog eat dog** ruthless competition. **8 like a dog's dinner** dressed smartly and ostentatiously. ✧ *vb* **dogging, dogged 9** to follow (someone) closely. **10** to trouble: *dogged by ill health.* ✧ See also **dogs**. ▷ HISTORY Old English *docga*

dog box *n Austral & NZ informal* same as **doghouse**.

dogcart *n* a light horse-drawn two-wheeled cart.

dog collar *n* **1** a collar for a dog. **2** *Informal* a clerical collar.

dog days *pl n Brit, Austral & NZ* the hottest period of the summer. ▷ HISTORY in ancient times reckoned from the heliacal rising of the Dog Star

doge (**doje**) *n* (formerly) the chief magistrate of Venice or Genoa. ▷ HISTORY Latin *dux* leader

dog-eared *adj* **1** (of a book) having pages folded down at the corner. **2** shabby or worn.

dog-end *n Brit, Austral & NZ informal* a cigarette end.

dogfight *n* **1** close-quarters combat between fighter aircraft. **2** any rough fight.

dogfish *n, pl* **-fish** *or* **-fishes** a small shark.

dogged (**dog**-gid) *adj* obstinately determined. ▸ **doggedly** *adv* ▸ **doggedness** *n*

doggerel *n* poorly written, usually comic, verse. ▷ HISTORY Middle English *dogerel* worthless

doggo *adv* **lie doggo** *Informal* to hide and keep quiet. ▷ HISTORY probably from *dog*

doggy *or* **doggie** *n, pl* **-gies 1** a child's word for a **dog**. ✧ *adj* **-gier, -giest 2** of or like a dog. **3** fond of dogs: *I suppose dogs are all right but doggy folk can be real bores.*

doggy bag *n* a bag in which leftovers from a meal may be taken away, supposedly for the diner's dog.

doghouse *n* **1** *US & Canad* a kennel. **2 in the doghouse** *Informal* in disfavour.

dogie, dogy, *or* **dogey** (**dohg**-ee) *n, pl* **-gies** *or* **-geys** *US & Canad* a motherless calf. ▷ HISTORY from *dough-guts,* because they were fed on flour-and-water paste

dogleg *n* a sharp bend.

dogma *n* a doctrine or system of doctrines proclaimed by authority as true. ▷ HISTORY Greek: opinion

dogmatic *adj* habitually stating one's opinions in a forceful or arrogant manner. ▸ **dogmatically** *adv* ▸ **dogmatism** *n*

do-gooder *n Informal* a well-intentioned but naive or impractical person.

dog paddle *n* a swimming stroke in which the hands are paddled in imitation of a swimming dog. Also called: **doggy paddle**

dogs *pl n* **1 the dogs** *Brit & Austral informal* greyhound racing. **2 go to the dogs** *Informal* to go to ruin physically or morally. **3 let sleeping dogs lie** to leave things undisturbed.

dogsbody *n, pl* **-bodies** *Informal* a person who carries out boring or unimportant tasks for others.

dog-tired *adj Informal* exhausted.

doh *or* **do** *n Music* (in tonic sol-fa) the first note of any ascending major scale.

doily *or* **doyley** *n, pl* **-lies** *or* **-leys** a decorative lacelike paper mat laid on a plate. ▷ HISTORY after *Doily,* a London draper

do in *vb Slang* **1** to kill. **2** to exhaust.

do-it-yourself *n* the practice of constructing and repairing things oneself.

Dolby *n Trademark* a system used in tape recorders which reduces noise level on recorded or broadcast sound.

doldrums *n* **the doldrums 1 a** a feeling of depression. **b** a state of inactivity. **2** a belt of sea along the equator noted for absence of winds. ▷ HISTORY probably from Old English *dol* dull

dole *n* **1 the dole** *Brit, Austral & NZ informal* money received from the state while unemployed. **2 on the dole** *Brit, Austral & NZ informal* receiving benefit while unemployed. ✧ *vb* **doling, doled 3 dole out** to distribute in small quantities. ▷ HISTORY Old English *dāl* share

dole bludger *n Austral & NZ informal* a person who chooses to live off unemployment benefit.

doleful *adj* dreary or mournful. ▷ HISTORY from Latin *dolere* to lament ▸ **dolefully** *adv* ▸ **dolefulness** *n*

doll *n* **1** a small model of a human being, used as a toy. **2** *Slang* a pretty girl or young woman. ▷ HISTORY probably from *Doll,* pet name for *Dorothy*

dollar *n* the standard monetary unit of various countries. ▷ HISTORY Low German *daler*

dollop *n Informal* an amount of food served in a lump: *he shook the bottle and added a large dollop of ketchup.* ▷ HISTORY origin unknown

doll up *vb Slang* **get dolled up** to dress (oneself) in a stylish or showy manner.

dolly *n, pl* **-lies 1** a child's word for a **doll** (sense 1). **2** *Films, television* a wheeled support on which a camera may be mounted. **3** Also called: **dolly bird** *Slang, chiefly Brit* an attractive and fashionable girl.

dolman sleeve *n* a sleeve that is very wide at the armhole and tapers to a tight wrist. ▷ HISTORY Turkish *dolaman* a winding round

dolmen *n* a prehistoric monument consisting of a horizontal stone supported by vertical stones, thought to be a tomb. ▷ HISTORY French

dolomite *n* a mineral consisting of calcium magnesium carbonate. ▷ HISTORY after Déodat de *Dolomieu,* mineralogist

dolphin *n* a sea mammal of the whale family, with a long pointed snout. ▷ HISTORY Greek *delphis*

dolphinarium *n* an aquarium for dolphins, esp. one in which they give public displays.

dolt *n* a stupid person. ▷ HISTORY probably related to Old English *dol* stupid ▸ **doltish** *adj*

domain *n* **1** a particular area of activity or interest. **2** land under one ruler or government. **3** *Computers* a group of computers that have the same suffix in their names on the Internet, specifying the country, type of institution, etc. where they are located. **4** *NZ* public park. ▷ **HISTORY** French *domaine*

dome *n* **1** a rounded roof built on a circular base. **2** something shaped like this. ▷ **HISTORY** Latin *domus* house

domed *adj* shaped like a dome.

domestic *adj* **1** of one's own country or a specific country: *the domestic economy was generally better.* **2** of the home or family. **3** enjoying home or family life: *she was never a very domestic sort of person.* **4** intended for use in the home: *the kitchen was equipped with all the latest domestic appliances.* **5** (of an animal) bred or kept as a pet or for the supply of food. ✧ *n* **6** a household servant. ▷ **HISTORY** Latin *domesticus* belonging to the house ▶ **domestically** *adv*

domesticate *vb* **-cating, -cated 1** to bring or keep (wild animals or plants) under control or cultivation. **2** to accustom (someone) to home life. ▶ **domestication** *n*

domesticity *n, pl* **-ties 1** home life. **2** devotion to home life.

domestic science *n* the study of cooking, needlework, and other household skills.

domicile (**dom**-miss-ile) *n Formal* a person's regular dwelling place. ▷ **HISTORY** Latin *domus* house ▶ **domiciliary** *adj*

dominant *adj* **1** having control, authority, or influence: *a dominant leader.* **2** main or chief: *coal is still, worldwide, the dominant fuel.* **3** *Genetics* (in a pair of genes) designating the gene that produces a particular character in an organism. ▶ **dominance** *n*

dominate *vb* **-nating, -nated 1** to control or govern. **2** to tower above (surroundings): *the building had been designed to dominate the city skyscape.* **3** to predominate in. ▷ **HISTORY** Latin *dominari* to be lord over ▶ **dominating** *adj* ▶ **domination** *n*

dominee (**doom**-in-nee) *n S African* a minister of the Dutch Reformed Church. ▷ **HISTORY** Dutch, from Latin *dominus* master

domineering *adj* acting arrogantly or tyrannically. ▷ **HISTORY** Dutch *domineren*

Dominican *n* **1** a friar or nun of the Christian order founded by Saint Dominic. ✧ *adj* **2** of the Dominican order.

dominion *n* **1** control or authority. **2** the land governed by one ruler or government. **3** (formerly) a self-governing division of the British Empire. ▷ **HISTORY** Latin *dominium* ownership

domino[1] *n, pl* **-noes** a small rectangular block marked with dots, used in dominoes. ▷ **HISTORY** Italian, perhaps from *domino!* master!, said by the winner

domino[2] *n, pl* **-noes** *or* **-nos** a large hooded cloak worn with an eye mask at a masquerade. ▷ **HISTORY** Latin *dominus* lord, master

dominoes *n* a game in which dominoes with matching halves are laid together.

domino theory *n Politics* the theory first advanced by President Eisenhower in 1954 that if one Southeast Asian country became communist, the other countries in the region would follow.

don[1] *vb* **donning, donned** to put on (clothing). ▷ **HISTORY** Middle English

don[2] *n* **1** *Brit* a member of the teaching staff at a university or college. **2** a Spanish gentleman or nobleman. **3** (in the Mafia) the head of a family. ▷ **HISTORY** Latin *dominus* lord

donate *vb* **-nating, -nated** to give (something) to a charity or other organization.

donation *n* **1** the act of donating. **2** a contribution to a charity or other organization. ▷ **HISTORY** Latin *donum* gift

donder *S African slang* ✧ *vb* **1** to beat (someone) up. ✧ *n* **2** a wretch; swine. ▷ **HISTORY** Dutch *donderen* to swear, bully

done *vb* **1** the past participle of **do**[1]. ✧ *interj* **2** an expression of agreement: *sixty pounds seems reasonable, done!* ✧ *adj* **3** (of a task) completed. **4** (of food) cooked enough. **5** used up: *the milk is done.* **6** *Brit, Austral & NZ* socially acceptable: *the done thing.* **7** *Informal* cheated or tricked. **8 done in** *or* **up** *Informal* exhausted.

doner kebab *n* a dish of grilled minced lamb, served in a split slice of unleavened bread. ▷ **HISTORY** Turkish *döner* rotating

donjon *n* the heavily fortified central tower of a castle. ▷ **HISTORY** archaic variant of *dungeon*

Don Juan *n* a successful seducer of women. ▷ **HISTORY** after the legendary Spanish philanderer

donkey *n* **1** a long-eared member of the horse family. **2** a person who is considered to be stupid or stubborn. ▷ **HISTORY** origin unknown

donkey jacket *n Brit, Austral & NZ* a man's thick hip-length jacket with a waterproof panel across the shoulders.

donkey's years *pl n Informal* a long time.

donkey vote *n Austral Politics* a vote in which the voter's order of preference follows the order in which the candidates are listed.

donkey-work *n* uninteresting groundwork.

donnish *adj* resembling a university don; pedantic or fussy.

donor *n* **1** *Med* a person who gives blood or organs for use in the treatment of another person. **2** a person who makes a donation. ▷ **HISTORY** Latin *donare* to give

donor card *n* a card carried by someone to show that the body parts specified may be used for transplants after the person's death.

Don Quixote (**don** kee-**hoe**-tee) *n* an impractical idealist. ▷ **HISTORY** after the hero of Miguel de Cervantes' novel *Don Quixote de la Mancha*

don't do not.

doodle *vb* **-dling, -dled 1** to scribble or draw aimlessly. ✧ *n* **2** a shape or picture drawn aimlessly. ▷ **HISTORY** originally, a foolish person

doom *n* **1** death or a terrible fate. ✧ *vb* **2** to destine or condemn to death or a terrible fate.
▷ HISTORY Old English *dōm*

doomsday *or* **domesday** *n* **1** the day on which the Last Judgment will occur. **2** any dreaded day.
▷ HISTORY Old English *dōmes dæg* Judgment Day

doona *n Austral* a large quilt used as a bed cover in place of the top sheet and blankets.

door *n* **1** a hinged or sliding panel for closing the entrance to a building, room, or cupboard. **2** a doorway or entrance. **3** a means of access or escape: *the door to happiness.* **4 lay something at someone's door** to blame someone for something. **5 out of doors** in the open air.
▷ HISTORY Old English *duru*

doorjamb *n* one of the two vertical posts that form the sides of a door frame. Also called: **doorpost**

doorman *n, pl* **-men** a man employed to be on duty at the main entrance of a large building.

doormat *n* **1** a mat, placed at an entrance, for wiping dirt from shoes. **2** *Informal* a person who offers little resistance to being treated badly.

door-to-door *adj* **1** (of selling) from one house to the next. **2** (of a journey) direct.

doorway *n* an opening into a building or room.

dop *n S African informal* a tot or small drink, usually alcoholic. ▷ HISTORY Afrikaans

dope *n* **1** *Slang* an illegal drug, such as cannabis. **2** a drug administered to a person or animal to affect performance in a race or other sporting competition. **3** *Informal* a slow-witted person. **4** confidential information. **5** a thick liquid, such as a lubricant. ✧ *vb* **doping, doped 6** to administer a drug to.

> **WORD HISTORY**
> 'Dope' comes from Dutch *doop*, meaning 'a thick sauce'.

dopey *or* **dopy** *adj* **dopier, dopiest 1** *Informal* half-asleep, as when under the influence of a drug. **2** *Slang* silly.

doppelgänger (**dop**-pl-geng-er) *n Legend* a ghostly duplicate of a living person.
▷ HISTORY German *Doppelgänger* double-goer

Doppler effect *n* a change in the apparent frequency of a sound or light wave as a result of relative motion between the observer and the source. ▷ HISTORY after C. J. *Doppler,* physicist

DORA *English law* Defence of the Realm Act: a law passed in 1914 giving the state more powers.

Doric *adj* **1** of a style of classical architecture characterized by a heavy fluted column and a simple capital. ✧ *n* **2** a rustic dialect, esp. a Scots one. ▷ HISTORY *Doris,* in ancient Greece

dormant *adj* **1** temporarily quiet, inactive, or not being used. **2** *Biol* alive but in a resting condition. **3** *Geol* (of a volcano) not extinct but not recently active. ▷ HISTORY Latin *dormire* to sleep
▶ **dormancy** *n*

dormer *or* **dormer window** *n* a window that is built upright in a sloping roof. ▷ HISTORY Latin *dormitorium* dormitory

dormitory *n, pl* **-ries 1** a large room, esp. at a school, containing several beds. **2** a building, esp. at a college, providing living accommodation. ✧ *adj* **3** *Brit & Austral* denoting an area from which most of the residents commute to work: *the swelling suburban dormitory areas.* ▷ HISTORY Latin *dormitorium,* from *dormire* to sleep

Dormobile *n Trademark* a vanlike vehicle specially equipped for living in while travelling.

dormouse *n, pl* **-mice** a small rodent resembling a mouse with a furry tail. ▷ HISTORY origin unknown

dorothy dixer *n Austral Parl Informal* a prearranged question put to a minister which gives him or her the opportunity to praise the government or criticize the opposition.

dorp *n S African* a small town or village.
▷ HISTORY Dutch

dorsal *adj Anat, zool* of or on the back.
▷ HISTORY Latin *dorsum* back

dory *n, pl* **-ries** a spiny-finned food fish. Also called: **John Dory** ▷ HISTORY French *dorée* gilded

DOS *Computers* disk operating system.

dose *n* **1** a specific quantity of a medicine taken at one time. **2** *Informal* something unpleasant to experience: *a dose of the cold.* **3** the total energy of radiation absorbed. **4** *Slang* a sexually transmitted infection. ✧ *vb* **dosing, dosed 5** to administer a quantity of medicine to (someone).
▷ HISTORY Greek *dosis* a giving ▶ **dosage** *n*

dosh *n Slang* money.

dosing strip *n* (in New Zealand) an area for treating dogs suspected of having hydatid disease.

doss *vb Slang* **1 doss down** to sleep on a makeshift bed. **2** to pass time aimlessly: *I doss around a lot.* ✧ *n* **3** a task requiring little effort.
▷ HISTORY origin unknown

dosshouse *n Slang* a cheap lodging house for homeless people.

dossier (**doss**-ee-ay) *n* a collection of papers about a subject or person. ▷ HISTORY French

dot *n* **1** a small round mark. **2** the small round mark used to represent the short sound in Morse code. **3 on the dot** at exactly the arranged time. ✧ *vb* **dotting, dotted 4** to mark with a dot. **5** to scatter or intersperse: *there are numerous churches dotted around Rome.* **6 dot one's i's and cross one's t's** *Informal* to pay meticulous attention to detail. ▷ HISTORY Old English *dott* head of a boil

dotage *n* feebleness of mind as a result of old age. ▷ HISTORY Middle English *doten* to dote

dotcom *or* **dot.com** *n* a company that conducts most of its business on the Internet. ▷ HISTORY from *.com,* the domain name suffix of businesses trading on the Internet

dote *vb* **doting, doted dote on** *or* **upon** to love (someone or something) to an excessive degree.
▷ HISTORY Middle English *doten* ▶ **doting** *adj*

dot map *n Geog* a map using dots representing a particular numerical value to show the distribution of something such as population or rainfall.

dotterel *n* a shore bird with reddish-brown underparts and white bands around the head and neck. ▷ HISTORY Middle English *dotrelle*

dottle *n* the tobacco left in a pipe after smoking. ▷ HISTORY obsolete *dot* lump

dotty *adj* **-tier, -tiest** *Slang* slightly crazy. ▷ HISTORY from *dot* ▶ **dottiness** *n*

double *adj* **1** as much again in size, strength, number, etc.: *a double scotch.* **2** composed of two equal or similar parts. **3** designed for two users: *a double bed.* **4** folded in half: *the blanket had been folded double.* **5** stooping: *she was bent double over the flower bed.* **6** ambiguous: *a double meaning.* **7** false, deceitful, or hypocritical: *double standards.* **8** *Music* (of an instrument) sounding an octave lower: *a double bass.* ✧ *adv* **9** twice over: *that's double the amount requested.* ✧ *n* **10** twice the size, strength, number, etc. **11** a double measure of spirits. **12** a person who closely resembles another person. **13** a bet on two horses in different races in which any winnings from the first race are placed on the horse in the later race. **14 at** *or* **on the double** quickly or immediately. ✧ *vb* **-bling, -bled** **15** to make or become twice as much. **16** to bend or fold so that one part covers another. **17** to play two parts or serve two roles. **18** to turn sharply. **19** *Bridge* to make a call that will double certain scoring points if the preceding bid becomes the contract. **20 double for** to act as substitute. ✧ See also **doubles**. ▷ HISTORY Latin *duplus* twofold ▶ **doubler** *n*

double agent *n* a spy employed by two enemy countries at the same time.

double-barrelled *or US* **-barreled** *adj* **1** (of a gun) having two barrels. **2** *Brit* (of a surname) having hyphenated parts.

double bass *n* a stringed instrument, the largest and lowest member of the violin family.

double-breasted *adj* (of a garment) having overlapping fronts.

double-check *vb* to make certain by checking again.

double chin *n* a fold of fat under the chin.

double cream *n Brit & Austral* thick cream with a high fat content.

double-cross *vb* **1** to cheat or betray. ✧ *n* **2** an instance of double-crossing.

double-dealing *n* treacherous or deceitful behaviour.

double-decker *n* **1** *Chiefly Brit* a bus with two passenger decks one on top of the other. ✧ *adj* **2** *Informal* having two layers: *a double-decker sandwich.*

double dissolution *n Austral Parl* the simultaneous dissolution of both houses of the federal parliament, allowed for in the Australian Constitution in cases of deadlock over the approval of a law.

double Dutch *n Informal* speech or writing that is difficult to understand: *it was double Dutch to me.*

double-edged *adj* **1** (of a remark) malicious in intent though apparently complimentary. **2** (of a knife) having a cutting edge on either side of the blade.

double entendre (**doob**-bl on-**tond**-ra) *n* a word or phrase with two interpretations, esp. with one meaning that is rude. ▷ HISTORY obsolete French

double entry *n* a book-keeping system in which a transaction is entered as a debit in one account and as a credit in another.

double glazing *n* a window consisting of two layers of glass separated by a space, fitted to reduce heat loss.

double helix *n Biochem* the form of the molecular structure of DNA, consisting of two helical chains linked by hydrogen bonds and coiled around the same axis.

double jeopardy rule *n Law* the principle that a defendant cannot be prosecuted a second time for an offence for which he or she has already been tried.

double-jointed *adj* (of a person) having unusually flexible joints.

double negative *n* a grammatical construction, considered incorrect, in which two negatives are used where one is needed, for example *I wouldn't never have believed it.*

double-page spread *n Journalism* (in a newspaper or magazine) two facing pages devoted to a single article, picture, or series of related images.

double-park *vb* to park (a vehicle) alongside another vehicle, causing an obstruction.

double pneumonia *n* pneumonia affecting both lungs.

doubles *n* a game between two pairs of players.

double standard *n* a set of principles that allows greater freedom to one person or group than to another.

doublet (**dub**-lit) *n History* a man's close-fitting jacket, with or without sleeves. ▷ HISTORY Old French

double take *n* a delayed reaction by a person to a remark or situation: *she did a double take when he said he was leaving.*

double talk *n* deceptive or ambiguous talk.

double time *n* **1** *Brit, Austral & NZ* a doubled wage rate sometimes paid for overtime work. **2** *Music* two beats per bar.

double whammy *n Informal, chiefly US* a devastating setback made up of two elements.

doubloon *n* a former Spanish gold coin. ▷ HISTORY Spanish *doblón*

doubly *adv* **1** to or in a greater degree, quantity, or measure: *I have to be doubly careful.* **2** in two ways: *the defence debate was doubly complicated.*

doubt *n* **1** uncertainty about the truth, facts, or existence of something. **2** an unresolved difficulty or point. **3 give someone the benefit of the doubt** accept that someone is speaking the truth. **4 no doubt** almost certainly. ✧ *vb* **5** to be inclined to disbelieve: *I doubt that we are late.* **6** to distrust or be suspicious of: *he doubted their motives.* ▷ **HISTORY** Latin *dubitare* to hesitate ▸ **doubter** *n*

> ☑ **WORD TIP**
> Where a clause follows *doubt* in a positive sentence, it was formerly considered correct to use *whether:* (*I doubt whether he will come*), but now *if* and *that* are also acceptable. In negative statements, *doubt* is followed by *that: I do not doubt that he is telling the truth.* In such sentences, *but* (*I do not doubt but that he is telling the truth*) is redundant.

doubtful *adj* **1** unlikely or improbable: *it's doubtful that I will marry again.* **2** unsure or uncertain: *I was doubtful about some of his ideas.* ▸ **doubtfully** *adv* ▸ **doubtfulness** *n*

> ☑ **WORD TIP**
> It was formerly considered correct to use *whether* after *doubtful (it is doubtful whether he will come),* but now *if* and *that* are also acceptable.

doubtless *adv* probably or almost certainly: *somebody will know and doubtless somebody will ring us.*

douche (**doosh**) *n* **1** a stream of water directed onto or into the body for cleansing or medical purposes. **2** an instrument for applying a douche. ✧ *vb* **douching, douched 3** to cleanse or treat by means of a douche. ▷ **HISTORY** French

dough *n* **1** a thick mixture of flour and water or milk, used for making bread, pastry, or biscuits. **2** *Slang* money. ▷ **HISTORY** Old English *dāg*

doughnut *n* a small cake of sweetened dough cooked in hot fat.

doughty (**dowt**-ee) *adj* **-tier, -tiest** *Old-fashioned* brave and determined. ▷ **HISTORY** Old English *dohtig*

do up *vb* **1** to wrap and make into a bundle: *he did up the parcel.* **2** to fasten: *to do up one's blouse.* **3** to renovate or redecorate.

dour (**doo**-er, rhymes with **tower**) *adj* sullen and unfriendly. ▷ **HISTORY** probably from Latin *durus* hard ▸ **dourness** *n*

douse *or* **dowse** (rhymes with **mouse**) *vb* **dousing, doused** *or* **dowsing, dowsed 1** to drench with water or other liquid. **2** to put out (a light). ▷ **HISTORY** origin unknown

dove *n* **1** a bird with a heavy body, small head, and short legs. **2** *Politics* a person opposed to war. ▷ **HISTORY** Old English *dūfe*

dovecote *or* **dovecot** *n* a box, shelter, or part of a house built for doves or pigeons to live in.

dovetail *n* **1** Also called: **dovetail joint** a wedge-shaped joint used to fit two pieces of wood tightly together. ✧ *vb* **2** to fit together closely or neatly: *her resignation dovetails well with the new structure.*

dowager *n* a woman possessing property or a title obtained from her dead husband. ▷ **HISTORY** Old French *douagiere*

dowdy *adj* **-dier, -diest** wearing dull and unfashionable clothes. ▷ **HISTORY** Middle English *dowd* slut ▸ **dowdily** *adv* ▸ **dowdiness** *n*

dowel *n* a wooden or metal peg that fits into two corresponding holes to join larger pieces of wood or metal together. ▷ **HISTORY** Middle Low German *dövel* plug

dower *n* **1** the life interest in a part of her husband's estate allotted to a widow by law. **2** *Archaic* a dowry. ▷ **HISTORY** Latin *dos* gift

do with *vb* **1 could do with** need or would benefit from: *I could do with some royal treatment.* **2 have to do with** to be associated with: *his illness has a lot to do with his failing the exam.* **3 to do with** concerning; related to: *this book has to do with the occult.*

do without *vb* to manage without.

down[1] *prep* **1** from a higher to a lower position in or on. **2** at a lower or further level or position on, in, or along: *I wandered down the corridor.* ✧ *adv* **3** at or to a lower level or position: *he bent down.* **4** indicating lowering or destruction: *to bring down an aircraft.* **5** indicating intensity or completion: *calm down and mind your manners.* **6** immediately: *cash down.* **7** on paper: *she copied it down.* **8** away from a more important place: *he came down from head office.* **9** reduced to a state of lack: *he was down to his last pound.* **10** lacking a specified amount: *down several pounds.* **11** lower in price. **12** from an earlier to a later time: *the ring was handed down from my grandmother.* **13** to a finer state: *to grind down.* **14** *Sport* being a specified number of points or goals behind an opponent. **15** (of a person) being inactive, owing to illness: *down with the cold.* ✧ *adj* **16** depressed or unhappy: *he seems very down today.* **17** made in cash: *a down payment.* ✧ *vb* **18** *Informal* to eat or drink quickly. ✧ *n* **19 have a down on** *Informal* to feel hostile towards: *you seem to have a down on the family tonight.* ▷ **HISTORY** Old English *dūne* from the hill

down[2] *n* soft fine feathers. ▷ **HISTORY** Old Norse *dūnn* ▸ **downy** *adj*

down-and-out *n* **1** a person who is homeless and destitute. ✧ *adj* **2** without any means of support; destitute.

downbeat *adj Informal* **1** depressed or gloomy: *she was in one of her downbeat moods.* **2** casual and restrained: *the chairman's statement was decidedly downbeat.* ✧ *n* **3** *Music* the first beat of a bar.

downcast *adj* **1** sad and dejected. **2** (of the eyes) directed downwards.

downer *n Slang* **1** a barbiturate, tranquillizer, or narcotic. **2 on a downer** in a state of depression.

downfall *n* **1** a sudden loss of position or reputation. **2** the cause of this.

downgrade *vb* **-grading, -graded** to reduce in importance or value.

downhearted *adj* sad and discouraged.

downhill *adj* **1** going or sloping down. ✧ *adv* **2** towards the bottom of a hill. **3 go downhill** *Informal* to deteriorate.

Downing Street *n* the British prime minister or the British government. ▷ **HISTORY** after the street in London which contains the official residence of the prime minister and the chancellor of the exchequer

download *vb* to transfer (data) from the memory of one computer to that of another.

down-market *adj* cheap, popular, and of poor quality.

down payment *n* the deposit paid on an item purchased on hire-purchase, mortgage, etc.: *an initial down payment is usually required.*

downpour *n* a heavy continuous fall of rain.

downright *adv, adj* extreme or extremely: *it's just downright cruel.*

downs *pl n* an area of low grassy hills, esp. in S England.

downshifting *n* the practice of simplifying one's lifestyle and becoming less materialistic.

downside *n* the disadvantageous aspect of a situation: *the downside of capitalism.*

downsize *vb* **1** to reduce the number of people employed by (a company). **2** to reduce the size of or produce a smaller version of (something).

Down's syndrome *n Pathol* a genetic disorder characterized by a flat face, slanting eyes, and mental retardation. ▷ HISTORY after John *Langdon-Down,* physician

downstage *Theatre* ✧ *adv* **1** at or towards the front of the stage. ✧ *adj* **2** of or relating to the front of the stage.

downstairs *adv* **1** down the stairs; to or on a lower floor. ✧ *n* **2** a lower or ground floor.

downstream *adv, adj* in or towards the lower part of a stream; with the current.

downtime *n Commerce* time during which a computer or other machine is not working.

down-to-earth *adj* sensible or practical.

downtown *Chiefly US, Canad, & NZ* ✧ *n* **1** the central or lower part of a city, esp. the main commercial area. ✧ *adv* **2** towards, to, or into this area.

downtrodden *adj* oppressed and lacking the will to resist.

downturn *n* a drop in the success of an economy or a business.

down under *Informal* ✧ *n* **1** Australia or New Zealand. ✧ *adv* **2** in or to Australia or New Zealand.

downward *adj* **1** descending from a higher to a lower level, condition, or position. ✧ *adv* **2** same as **downwards.** ▶ **downwardly** *adv*

downwards *or* **downward** *adv* **1** from a higher to a lower level, condition, or position. **2** from an earlier time or source to a later one.

downwind *adv, adj* in the same direction towards which the wind is blowing; with the wind from behind.

dowry *n, pl* **-ries** the property brought by a woman to her husband at marriage. ▷ HISTORY Latin *dos*

dowse (rhymes with **cows**) *vb* **dowsing, dowsed** to search for underground water or minerals using a divining rod. ▷ HISTORY origin unknown ▶ **dowser** *n*

doxology *n, pl* **-gies** a hymn or verse of praise to God. ▷ HISTORY Greek *doxologos* uttering praise

doyen (**doy**-en) *n* the senior member of a group, profession, or society. ▷ HISTORY French ▶ **doyenne** (doy-**en**) *fem n*

doze *vb* **dozing, dozed 1** to sleep lightly or for a short period. **2 doze off** to fall into a light sleep. ✧ *n* **3** a short sleep. ▷ HISTORY probably from Old Norse *dūs* lull

dozen *adj, n* twelve. ▷ HISTORY Latin *duodecim* ▶ **dozenth** *adj*

dozy *adj* **dozier, doziest 1** feeling sleepy. **2** *Brit informal* stupid and slow-witted.

DP displaced person.

DPB (in New Zealand) Domestic Purposes Benefit.

DPP (in Britain) Director of Public Prosecutions.

Dr 1 Doctor. **2** Drive.

drab *adj* **drabber, drabbest 1** dull and dreary. **2** light olive-brown. ▷ HISTORY Old French *drap* cloth ▶ **drabness** *n*

drachm (**dram**) *n Brit* a unit of liquid measure equal to one eighth of a fluid ounce (3.55 ml). ▷ HISTORY variant of DRAM

drachma *n, pl* **-mas** *or* **-mae** a former monetary unit of Greece. ▷ HISTORY Greek *drakhmē* a handful

draconian *adj* severe or harsh: *draconian measures were taken by the government.* ▷ HISTORY after *Draco,* Athenian statesman

draft *n* **1** a preliminary outline of a letter, book, or speech. **2** a written order for payment of money by a bank. **3** *US & Austral* selection for compulsory military service. ✧ *vb* **4** to write a preliminary outline of a letter, book, or speech. **5** to send (personnel) from one place to another to carry out a specific job. **6** *Chiefly US* to select for compulsory military service. ✧ *n, vb* **7** *US* same as **draught**. ▷ HISTORY variant of DRAUGHT

drag *vb* **dragging, dragged 1** to pull with force along the ground. **2** to trail on the ground. **3** to persuade (someone) to go somewhere: *he didn't want to come so I had to drag him along.* **4** to move (oneself) slowly and with difficulty: *I had to drag myself out of bed this morning.* **5** to linger behind: *she dragged along behind her mother.* **6** to search (a river) with a dragnet or hook. **7** to draw (on a cigarette). **8** *Computers* to move (a graphics image) from one place to another on the screen by manipulating a mouse with its button held down. **9 drag away** *or* **from** to force (oneself) to come away from something interesting: *I was completely spellbound and couldn't drag myself away from the film.* **10 drag on** *or* **out** to last or be prolonged tediously: *winter dragged on.* **11 drag one's feet** *Informal* to act with deliberate slowness. ✧ *n* **12** a person or thing that slows up progress. **13** *Informal* a tedious or boring thing: *it was a drag having to walk 2 miles to the station every day.* **14** *Informal* a draw on a cigarette. **15** an implement, such as a dragnet, used for dragging. **16** *Aeronautics* the resistance to the motion of a body passing through air. **17 in drag** (of a man) wearing women's clothes, usually as a form of entertainment. ▷ HISTORY Old English *dragan* to draw

A B C D E F G H I J K L M N O P Q R S T U V W X Y Z

dragnet *n* a net used to scour the bottom of a pond or river when searching for something.

dragoman *n, pl* **-mans** *or* **-men** (in some Middle Eastern countries) a professional interpreter or guide. ▷ **HISTORY** Arabic *targumān*

dragon *n* **1** a mythical monster that resembles a large fire-breathing lizard. **2** *Informal* a fierce woman. **3 chase the dragon** *Slang* to smoke opium or heroin. ▷ **HISTORY** Greek *drakōn*

dragonfly *n, pl* **-flies** a brightly coloured insect with a long slender body and two pairs of wings.

dragoon *n* **1** a heavily armed cavalryman. ✧ *vb* **2** to coerce or force: *we were dragooned into participating.* ▷ **HISTORY** French *dragon*

drag race *n* a race in which specially built or modified cars or motorcycles are timed over a measured course. ▶ **drag racing** *n*

drain *n* **1** a pipe that carries off water or sewage. **2** a cause of a continuous reduction in energy or resources: *the expansion will be a drain on resources.* **3** a metal grid on a road or pavement through which rainwater flows. **4 down the drain** wasted. ✧ *vb* **5** to draw off or remove (liquid) from. **6** to flow (away) or filter (off). **7** to dry or be emptied as a result of liquid running off or flowing away. **8** to drink the entire contents of (a glass or cup). **9** to make constant demands on (energy or resources); exhaust. **10** (of a river) to carry off the surface water from (an area). ▷ **HISTORY** Old English *drēahnian*

drainage *n* **1** a system of pipes, drains, or ditches used to drain water or other liquids. **2** the process or a method of draining.

drainage basin *n Geog* the area of land that drains into a river, basin, or reservoir. Also called **catchment area**.

drainage density *n Geog* the combined length of streams per square kilometre or mile, etc., in a given area.

drainage network *n Geog* the system of interconnected streams draining a drainage basin.

drainage pattern *n Geog* the pattern of branching of streams, such as dendritic (branching like a tree), deranged (random-looking), and trellised (characterized by having branches at right angles, many with their own right-angle branches).

draining board *n* a grooved surface at the side of a sink, used for draining washed dishes.

drainpipe *n* a pipe for carrying off rainwater or sewage.

drake *n* the male of a duck. ▷ **HISTORY** origin unknown

dram *n* **1** a small amount of spirits, such as whisky. **2** a unit of weight equal to one sixteenth of an ounce (avoirdupois). ▷ **HISTORY** Greek *drakhmē*; see DRACHMA

drama *n* **1** a serious play for theatre, television, or radio. **2** plays in general, as a form of literature. **3** the art of writing, producing, or acting in a play. **4** a situation that is exciting or highly emotional. ▷ **HISTORY** Greek: something performed

dramatic *adj* **1** of or relating to drama. **2** like a drama in suddenness or effectiveness: *the government's plan has had a dramatic effect on employment in television.* **3** acting or performed in a flamboyant way: *he spread his hands in a dramatic gesture of helplessness.* ▶ **dramatically** *adv*

dramatic irony *n Theatre* the irony occurring when the implications of a situation or speech are understood by the audience but not by the characters in the play.

dramatic monologue *n Theatre, prosody* an address, especially in poetry, by a single character in which he or she reveals to the audience, seemingly unintentionally, aspects of his or her character or situation.

dramatics *n* **1** the art of acting or producing plays. ✧ *pl n* **2** exaggerated, theatrical behaviour.

dramatis personae (**drah**-mat-tiss per-**soh**-nigh) *pl n* the characters in a play. ▷ **HISTORY** New Latin

dramatist *n* a playwright: *Austria's greatest living dramatist.*

dramatize *or* **-tise** *vb* **-tizing, -tized** *or* **-tising, -tised 1** to rewrite (a book or story) in a form suitable for performing on stage. **2** to express (something) in a dramatic or exaggerated way: *he dramatizes his illness.* ▶ **dramatization** *or* **-tisation** *n*

drank *vb* the past tense of **drink**.

drape *vb* **draping, draped 1** to cover with material or fabric. **2** to hang or arrange in folds. **3** to place casually: *he draped his arm across the back of the seat.* ✧ See also **drapes**. ▷ **HISTORY** Old French *draper*

draper *n Brit* a person who sells fabrics and sewing materials.

drapery *n, pl* **-peries 1** fabric or clothing arranged and draped. **2** fabrics and cloth collectively.

drapes *pl n Austral, NZ, US & Canad* material hung at an opening or window to shut out light or to provide privacy.

drastic *adj* strong and severe: *the police are taking drastic measures against car thieves.* ▷ **HISTORY** Greek *drastikos* ▶ **drastically** *adv*

draught *or US* **draft** *n* **1** a current of cold air, usually one coming into a room or vehicle. **2** a portion of liquid to be drunk, esp. a dose of medicine. **3** a gulp or swallow: *she took a deep draught then a sip.* **4 on draught** (of beer) drawn from a cask. **5** one of the flat discs used in the game of draughts. US and Canad. equivalent: **checker** **6 feel the draught** to be short of money. ✧ *adj* **7** (of an animal) used for pulling heavy loads: *horses are specialized draught animals.* ▷ **HISTORY** probably Old Norse *drahtr*

draught beer *n* beer stored in a cask.

draughts *n* a game for two players using a draughtboard and 12 draughtsmen each. ▷ **HISTORY** plural of *draught* (in obsolete sense: a chess move)

draughtsman *or US* **draftsman** *n, pl* **-men** **1** a person employed to prepare detailed scale drawings of equipment, machinery, or buildings. **2** a person skilled in drawing. **3** US and Canad.

equivalent: **checker** *Brit* a flat disc used in the game of draughts. ▶ **draughtsmanship** *n*

draughty *or US* **drafty** *adj* **draughtier, draughtiest** *or US* **draftier, draftiest** exposed to draughts of air. ▶ **draughtily** *adv* ▶ **draughtiness** *n*

draw *vb* **drawing, drew, drawn 1** to sketch (a picture, pattern, or diagram) with a pen or pencil. **2** to cause (a person or thing) to move closer or further away from a place by pulling. **3** to bring, take, or pull (something) out of a container: *he drew a gun and laid it on the table.* **4** to take (something) from a particular source: *the inhabitants drew water from the well two miles away.* **5** to move in a specified direction: *he drew alongside me.* **6** to attract: *she drew enthusiastic audiences from all over the country.* **7** to formulate or decide: *he drew similar conclusions.* **8** to cause to flow: *the barman nodded and drew two pints.* **9** to choose or be given by lottery: *Brazil have drawn Spain in the semi-final of the Cup.* **10** (of two teams or contestants) to finish a game with an equal number of points. **11** *Archery* to bend (a bow) by pulling the string. **12** to cause (pus) to discharge from an abscess or wound. ✧ *n* **13** a raffle or lottery. **14** *Informal* a person, place, show, or event that attracts a large audience. **15** a contest or game ending in a tie. ✧ See also **drawback**. ▷ HISTORY Old English *dragan*

drawback *n* **1** a disadvantage or hindrance. ✧ *vb* **draw back 2** to move backwards: *the girl drew back as though in pain.* **3** to turn aside from an undertaking: *the prime minister drew back from his original intention.*

drawbridge *n* a bridge that may be raised to prevent access or to enable vessels to pass.

drawer *n* **1** a sliding box-shaped part of a piece of furniture used for storage. **2** a person or thing that draws.

drawers *pl n Old-fashioned* an undergarment worn on the lower part of the body.

drawing *n* **1** a picture or plan made by means of lines on a surface. **2** the art of making drawings.

drawing pin *n Brit & NZ* a short tack with a broad smooth head used for fastening papers to a drawing board or other surface.

drawing room *n* a room where visitors are received and entertained.

drawl *vb* **1** to speak slowly with long vowel sounds. ✧ *n* **2** the way of speech of someone who drawls. ▷ HISTORY probably frequentative of *draw* ▶ **drawling** *adj*

drawn *vb* **1** the past participle of **draw**. ✧ *adj* **2** haggard, tired, or tense in appearance.

draw off *vb* to cause (a liquid) to flow from something.

draw on *vb* **1** to make use of from a source or fund: *they are able to draw on a repertoire of around 400 songs.* **2** (of a period of time) to come near or pass by: *summer draws on; time draws on.*

draw out *vb* **1** (of a train) to leave a station. **2** to encourage (someone) to talk freely: *therapy groups will continue to draw her out.* **3 draw out of** to find out (information) from.

drawstring *n* a cord run through a hem around an opening, so that when it is pulled tighter, the opening closes.

draw up *vb* **1** to prepare and write out: *the signatories drew up a draft agreement.* **2** (of a vehicle) to come to a halt.

dray *n* a low cart used for carrying heavy loads. ▷ HISTORY Old English *dræge* dragnet

dread *vb* **1** to anticipate with apprehension or terror. ✧ *n* **2** great fear. ▷ HISTORY Old English *ondrædan*

dreadful *adj* **1** extremely disagreeable or shocking. **2** extreme: *there were dreadful delays.* ▶ **dreadfully** *adv*

dreadlocks *pl n* hair worn in the Rastafarian style of tightly curled strands.

dreadnought *n* a battleship armed with heavy guns.

dream *n* **1** an imagined series of events experienced in the mind while asleep. **2** a daydream: *the dream of success turning into a nightmare.* **3** a goal or aim: *Unity has been their constant dream.* **4** a wonderful person or thing: *her house is a dream.* ✧ *vb* **dreaming, dreamed** *or* **dreamt 5** to experience (a dream). **6** to indulge in daydreams. **7** to be unrealistic: *you're dreaming if you think we can win.* **8 dream of** to consider the possibility of: *she would not dream of taking his advice.* **9 dream of** *or* **about** to have an image of or fantasy about: *they often dream about what life will be like for them on the outside.* ✧ *adj* **10** beautiful or pleasing: *a dream kitchen.* ▷ HISTORY Old English *drēam* song ▶ **dreamer** *n*

dream team *n Informal* a group of people regarded as having the perfect combination of talents.

Dreamtime *n* **1** (in the mythology of Australian Aboriginal peoples) a mythical golden age of the past, when the first men were created. **2** *Austral informal* any remote period, out of touch with the realities of the present.

dream up *vb* to formulate in the imagination: *a character dreamed up by a scriptwriter.*

dreamy *adj* **dreamier, dreamiest 1** vague or impractical: *she was wild-eyed and dreamy.* **2** relaxing or gentle: *I felt this dreamy contentment.* **3** *Informal* wonderful or impressive: *he drives a dreamy Jaguar.* ▶ **dreamily** *adv* ▶ **dreaminess** *n*

dreary *adj* **drearier, dreariest** dull or uninteresting: *there are long streets of dreary red houses spreading everywhere.* ▷ HISTORY Old English *drēorig* gory ▶ **drearily** *adv* ▶ **dreariness** *n*

dredge[1] *n* **1** a machine used to scoop or suck up silt or mud from a river bed or harbour. ✧ *vb* **dredging, dredged 2** to remove silt or mud from (a river bed or harbour) by means of a dredge. **3** to search for (a submerged object) with or as if with a dredge. ▷ HISTORY origin unknown ▶ **dredger** *n*

dredge[2] *vb* **dredging, dredged** to sprinkle (food) with a substance, such as flour. ▷ HISTORY Old French *dragie* ▶ **dredger** *n*

dredge up *vb Informal* to remember (something obscure or half-forgotten): *I didn't retain you to dredge up unfortunate incidents from my past.*

a b c d e f g h i j k l m n o p q r s t u v w x y z

dregs *pl n* **1** solid particles that settle at the bottom of some liquids. **2 the dregs** the worst or most despised elements: *the dregs of colonial society.* ▷ HISTORY Old Norse *dregg*

drench *vb* **1** to make completely wet. **2** to give medicine to (an animal). ▷ HISTORY Old English *drencan* to cause to drink ▶ **drenching** *n, adj*

Dresden *or* **Dresden china** *n* delicate and decorative porcelain made near Dresden, Germany.

dress *n* **1** a one-piece garment worn by a woman or girl, with a skirt and bodice and sometimes sleeves. **2** complete style of clothing: *contemporary dress.* ✧ *adj* **3** suitable for a formal occasion: *he was wearing a dress shirt.* ✧ *vb* **4** to put clothes on. **5** to put on formal clothes. **6** to apply protective covering to (a wound). **7** to cover (a salad) with dressing. **8** to prepare (meat, poultry, or fish) for selling or cooking by cleaning or gutting. **9** to put a finish on (the surface of stone, metal, or other building material). ✧ See also **dress up**. ▷ HISTORY Old French *drecier* to arrange

dressage (**dress**-ahzh) *n* **a** the method of training horses to perform manoeuvres as a display of obedience. **b** the manoeuvres performed. ▷ HISTORY French

dress circle *n* the first gallery in a theatre.

dresser[1] *n* **1** a piece of furniture with shelves and cupboards, used for storing or displaying dishes. **2** *US* a chest of drawers. ▷ HISTORY Old French *drecier* to arrange

dresser[2] *n* **1** a person who dresses in a specified way: *Lars was a meticulous, elegant dresser.* **2** *Theatre* a person employed to assist performers with their costumes.

dressing *n* **1** a sauce for food: *salad dressing.* **2** *US & Canad* same as **stuffing** (sense 1). **3** a covering for a wound. **4** manure or fertilizer spread on land. **5** a gluey material used for stiffening paper, textiles, etc.

dressing-down *n Informal* a severe reprimand.

dressing gown *n* a loose-fitting garment worn over one's pyjamas or nightdress.

dressing room *n* a room used for changing clothes and applying make-up, esp. a backstage room in a theatre.

dressing table *n* a piece of bedroom furniture with a mirror and a set of drawers.

dressmaker *n* a person who makes clothes for women. ▶ **dressmaking** *n*

dress rehearsal *n* **1** the last rehearsal of a play, opera, or show using costumes, lighting, and other effects. **2** any full-scale practice: *astronauts are in the midst of a two day dress rehearsal of their launch countdown.*

dress up *vb* **1** to put on glamorous or stylish clothes. **2** to put fancy dress on: *the guests dressed up like cowboys.* **3** to disguise (something) to make it more attractive or acceptable: *the offer was simply an old one dressed up in new terms.*

dressy *adj* **dressier, dressiest 1** (of clothes or occasions) elegant. **2** (of people) dressing stylishly. ▶ **dressiness** *n*

drew *vb* the past tense of **draw**.

drey *or* **dray** *n Brit & Austral* a squirrel's nest. ▷ HISTORY origin unknown

dribble *vb* **-bling, -bled 1** to flow or allow to flow in a thin stream or drops. **2** to allow saliva to trickle from the mouth. **3** (in soccer, hockey, etc.) to propel (the ball) by kicking or tapping in quick succession. ✧ *n* **4** a small quantity of liquid falling in drops or flowing in a thin stream. **5** a small supply: *there's only a dribble of milk left.* **6** an act or instance of dribbling. ▷ HISTORY obsolete *drib,* variant of *drip* ▶ **dribbler** *n*

dribs and drabs *pl n Informal* small occasional amounts.

dried *vb* the past of **dry**.

drier[1] *adj* a comparative of **dry**.

drier[2] *n* same as **dryer**[1].

driest *adj* a superlative of **dry**.

drift *vb* **1** to be carried along by currents of air or water. **2** to move aimlessly from one place or activity to another. **3** to wander away from a fixed course or point. **4** (of snow) to pile up in heaps. ✧ *n* **5** something piled up by the wind or current, as a snowdrift. **6** a general movement or development: *there has been a drift away from family control.* **7** the main point of an argument or speech: *I was beginning to get his drift.* **8** the extent to which a vessel or aircraft is driven off course by winds, etc. **9** a current of water created by the wind. ▷ HISTORY Old Norse

drifter *n* **1** a person who moves aimlessly from place to place. **2** a boat used for drift-net fishing.

drift net *n* a fishing net that is allowed to drift with the tide.

driftwood *n* wood floating on or washed ashore by the sea.

drill[1] *n* **1** a machine or tool for boring holes. **2** *Mil* training in procedures or movements, as for parades. **3** strict and often repetitious training. **4** *Informal* correct procedure: *he knows the drill as well as anybody.* ✧ *vb* **5** to bore a hole in (something) with or as if with a drill. **6** to instruct or be instructed in military procedures or movements. **7** to teach by rigorous exercises or training. ▷ HISTORY Middle Dutch *drillen*

drill[2] *n* **1** a machine for planting seeds in rows. **2** a furrow in which seeds are sown. **3** a row of seeds planted by means of a drill. ✧ *vb* **4** to plant (seeds) by means of a drill. ▷ HISTORY origin unknown

drill[3] *n* a hard-wearing cotton cloth, used for uniforms. ▷ HISTORY German *Drillich*

drill[4] *n* a W African monkey, related to the mandrill. ▷ HISTORY from a West African word

drily *or* **dryly** *adv* in a dry manner.

drink *vb* **drinking, drank, drunk 1** to swallow (a liquid). **2** to consume alcohol, esp. to excess. **3** to bring (oneself) into a specified condition by consuming alcohol: *he drank himself senseless every night.* **4 drink someone's health** to wish someone health or happiness with a toast. **5 drink in** to pay close attention to: *I drank in what the speaker said.* **6 drink to** to drink a toast: *I drank to their engagement.* ✧ *n* **7** liquid suitable for drinking. **8** a portion of liquid for drinking. **9** alcohol, or the habit of drinking too much of it. ▷ HISTORY Old English *drincan* ▶ **drinkable** *adj* ▶ **drinker** *n*

drink-driving *adj Brit, Austral & NZ* of or relating to driving a car after drinking alcohol: *a drink-driving offence.*

drip *vb* **dripping, dripped 1** to fall or let fall in drops. ✧ *n* **2** the falling of drops of liquid. **3** the sound made by falling drops. **4** *Informal* a weak or foolish person. **5** *Med* a device that administers a liquid drop by drop into a vein. ▷ HISTORY Old English *dryppan*

drip-dry *adj* **1** (of clothes or fabrics) designed to dry without creases if hung up when wet. ✧ *vb* **-dries, -drying, -dried 2** to dry or become dry thus.

drip-feed *vb* **-feeding, -fed 1** to feed (someone) a liquid drop by drop, usually through a vein. ✧ *n* **drip feed 2** same as **drip** (sense 5).

dripping *n* the fat that comes from meat while it is being roasted.

drive *vb* **driving, drove, driven 1** to guide the movement of (a vehicle). **2** to transport or be transported in a vehicle. **3** to goad into a specified state: *the black despair that finally drove her to suicide.* **4** to push or propel: *he drove the nail into the wall with a hammer.* **5** *Sport* to hit (a ball) very hard and straight. **6** *Golf* to strike (the ball) with a driver. **7** to chase (game) from cover. **8 drive home** to make (a point) clearly understood by emphasis. ✧ *n* **9** a journey in a driven vehicle. **10** a road for vehicles, esp. a private road leading to a house. **11** a special effort made by a group of people for a particular purpose: *a charity drive.* **12** energy, ambition, or initiative. **13** *Psychol* a motive or interest: *sex drive.* **14** a sustained and powerful military offensive. **15** the means by which power is transmitted in a machine. **16** *Sport* a hard straight shot or stroke. ▷ HISTORY Old English *drīfan*

drive at *vb Informal* to intend or mean: *he had no idea what she was driving at.*

drive-by shooting *n* an incident in which a person is shot at by a person in a moving vehicle. Sometimes shortened to: **drive-by**

drive-in *n* **1** a cinema, restaurant, etc. offering a service where people remain in their cars while using the service provided. ✧ *adj* **2** denoting a cinema, etc. of this kind.

drivel *n* **1** foolish talk. ✧ *vb* **-elling, -elled** *or US* **-eling, -eled 2** to speak foolishly. **3** to allow (saliva) to flow from the mouth. ▷ HISTORY Old English *dreflian* to slaver

driver *n* **1** a person who drives a vehicle. **2** *Golf* a long-shafted club with a large head and steep face, used for tee shots.

drive-thru *n* **1** a takeaway restaurant, bank, etc., designed so that customers can use it without leaving their cars. ✧ *adj* **2** denoting a restaurant etc. of this kind.

drive-time *n* **1** the time of day when many people are driving to or from work, considered as a broadcasting slot. ✧ *adj* **2** of this time of day: *the daily drive-time show.*

driveway *n* a path for vehicles connecting a building to a public road.

driving licence *n* an official document authorizing a person to drive a motor vehicle.

drizzle *n* **1** very light rain. ✧ *vb* **-zling, -zled 2** to rain lightly. ▷ HISTORY Old English *drēosan* to fall ▶ **drizzly** *adj*

droll *adj* quaintly amusing. ▷ HISTORY French *drôle* scamp ▶ **drollery** *n* ▶ **drolly** *adv*

dromedary (**drom**-mid-er-ee) *n, pl* **-daries** a camel with a single hump. ▷ HISTORY Greek *dromas* running

drone[1] *n* **1** a male honeybee. **2** a person who lives off the work of others. ▷ HISTORY Old English *drān*

drone[2] *vb* **droning, droned 1** to make a monotonous low dull sound. **2 drone on** to talk in a monotonous tone without stopping. ✧ *n* **3** a monotonous low dull sound. **4** a single-reed pipe in a set of bagpipes. ▷ HISTORY related to DRONE[1]

drongo *n, pl* **-gos** a tropical songbird with a glossy black plumage, a forked tail, and a stout bill.

drool *vb* **1 drool over** to show excessive enthusiasm for or pleasure in. **2** same as **drivel** (senses 2, 3). ▷ HISTORY probably alteration of DRIVEL

droop *vb* **1** to sag, as from weakness or lack of support. **2** to be overcome by weariness: *her eyelids drooped as if she were falling asleep.* ▷ HISTORY Old Norse *drūpa* ▶ **drooping** *adj*

droopy *adj* hanging or sagging downwards: *a droopy moustache.*

drop *vb* **dropping, dropped 1** to fall or allow (something) to fall vertically. **2** to decrease in amount, strength, or value. **3** to fall to the ground, as from exhaustion. **4** to sink to a lower position, as on a scale. **5** to mention casually: *he dropped a hint.* **6** to set down (passengers or goods): *can you drop me at the hotel?* **7** *Informal* to send: *drop me a letter.* **8** to discontinue: *can we drop the subject?* **9** *Informal* to be no longer friendly with: *I dropped him when I discovered his political views.* **10** to leave out in speaking: *he has a tendency to drop his h's.* **11** (of animals) to give birth to (offspring). **12** *Sport* to omit (a player) from a team. **13** to lose (a game or point). **14 drop back** to progress more slowly than other people going in the same direction. **15 drop in** *or* **by** *Informal* to pay someone a casual visit. ✧ *n* **16** a small quantity of liquid forming a round shape. **17** a small quantity of liquid. **18** a small round sweet: *a lemon drop.* **19** a decrease in amount, strength, or value. **20** the vertical distance that anything may fall. **21** the act of unloading troops or supplies by parachute. ✧ See also **drop off, dropout, drops**. ▷ HISTORY Old English *dropian*

drop curtain *n Theatre* a curtain that can be raised and lowered onto the stage.

droplet *n* a very small drop of liquid.

drop off *vb* **1** to set down (passengers or goods). **2** *Informal* to fall asleep. **3** to decrease or decline: *sales dropped off during our period of transition.*

dropout *n* **1** a person who rejects conventional society. **2** a student who does not complete a course of study. ✧ *vb* **drop out 3** to abandon or withdraw (from an institution or group).

dropper *n* a small tube with a rubber part at one end for drawing up and dispensing drops of liquid.

A B C D E F G H I J K L M N O P Q R S T U V W X Y Z

droppings *pl n* the dung of certain animals, such as rabbits or birds.

drops *pl n* any liquid medication applied by means of a dropper.

dropsy *n* an illness in which watery fluid collects in the body. ▷ **HISTORY** Middle English *ydropesie*, from Greek *hudōr* water ▸ **dropsical** *adj*

dross *n* **1** the scum formed on the surfaces of molten metals. **2** anything of inferior quality. ▷ **HISTORY** Old English *drōs* dregs

drought (rhymes with **out**) *n* a prolonged period of time during which no rain falls. ▷ **HISTORY** Old English *drūgoth*

drove[1] *vb* the past tense of **drive**.

drove[2] *n* **1** a herd of livestock being driven together. **2** a moving crowd of people. ▷ **HISTORY** Old English *drāf* herd

drover *n* a person who drives sheep or cattle.

drown *vb* **1** to die or kill by immersion in liquid. **2** to drench thoroughly. **3** to make (a sound) impossible to hear by making a loud noise. ▷ **HISTORY** probably from Old English *druncnian*

drowse *vb* **drowsing, drowsed** to be sleepy, dull, or sluggish. ▷ **HISTORY** probably from Old English *drūsian* to sink

drowsy *adj* **drowsier, drowsiest 1** feeling sleepy. **2** peaceful and quiet: *row upon row of windows looked out over drowsy parkland.* ▸ **drowsily** *adv* ▸ **drowsiness** *n*

drubbing *n* an utter defeat, as in a contest: *the Communists received a drubbing.* ▷ **HISTORY** probably from Arabic *dáraba* to beat

drudge *n* **1** a person who works hard at an uninteresting task. ✧ *vb* **drudging, drudged 2** to work at such tasks. ▷ **HISTORY** origin unknown

drudgery *n* uninteresting work that must be done.

drug *n* **1** any substance used in the treatment, prevention, or diagnosis of disease. **2** a chemical substance, such as a narcotic, taken for the effects it produces. ✧ *vb* **drugging, drugged 3** to administer a drug to (a person or animal) in order to induce sleepiness or unconsciousness. **4** to mix a drug with (food or drink): *who drugged my wine?* ▷ **HISTORY** Old French *drogue*

druggist *n US & Canad* a pharmacist.

drugstore *n US & Canad* a pharmacy where a wide variety of goods are available.

Druid *n* a member of an ancient order of Celtic priests. ▷ **HISTORY** Latin *druides* ▸ **Druidic** *adj*

drum *n* **1** a percussion instrument sounded by striking a skin stretched across the opening of a hollow cylinder. **2** the sound produced by a drum. **3** an object shaped like a drum: *an oil drum.* **4** same as **eardrum**. ✧ *vb* **drumming, drummed 5** to play (music) on a drum. **6** to tap rhythmically or regularly: *he drummed his fingers on the desk.* **7** to fix in someone's mind by constant repetition: *my father always drummed into us how privileged we were.* ✧ See also **drum up**. ▷ **HISTORY** Middle Dutch *tromme* ▸ **drummer** *n*

drumhead *n* the part of a drum that is struck.

drum machine *n* a synthesizer programmed to reproduce the sound of percussion instruments.

drum major *n* the noncommissioned officer in the army who is in command of the drums and the band when paraded together.

drumstick *n* **1** a stick used for playing a drum. **2** the lower joint of the leg of a cooked fowl.

drum up *vb* to obtain (support or business) by making requests or canvassing.

drunk *vb* **1** the past participle of **drink**. ✧ *adj* **2** intoxicated with alcohol to the extent of losing control over normal functions. **3** overwhelmed by strong influence or emotion: *he was half drunk with satisfaction at his victory over the intruder.* ✧ *n* **4** a person who is drunk or drinks habitually to excess. ▷ **HISTORY** Old English *druncen*, past participle of *drincan* to drink

drunkard *n* a person who is frequently or habitually drunk.

drunken *adj* **1** intoxicated with alcohol. **2** habitually drunk. **3** caused by or relating to alcoholic intoxication: *a drunken argument.* ▸ **drunkenly** *adv* ▸ **drunkenness** *n*

drupe *n* a fleshy fruit with a stone, such as the peach or cherry. ▷ **HISTORY** Greek *druppa* olive

dry *adj* **drier, driest** *or* **dryer, dryest 1** lacking moisture. **2** having little or no rainfall. **3** having the water drained away or evaporated: *a dry gully for the most part of the year.* **4** not providing milk: *a dry cow.* **5** (of the eyes) free from tears. **6** *Brit, Austral & NZ informal* thirsty. **7** eaten without butter or jam: *a dry cracker.* **8** (of wine) not sweet. **9** dull and uninteresting: *a dry subject.* **10** (of humour) subtle and sarcastic. **11** prohibiting the sale of alcoholic liquor: *a dry district.* ✧ *vb* **dries, drying, dried 12** to make or become dry. **13** to preserve (food) by removing the moisture. ✧ See also **dry out, dry up**. ▷ **HISTORY** Old English *drȳge* ▸ **dryness** *n*

dryad *n, pl* **dryads** *or* **dryades** (**dry**-ad-deez) *Greek myth* a wood nymph. ▷ **HISTORY** Greek *druas*

dry battery *n* an electric battery composed of dry cells.

dry cell *n* an electric cell in which the electrolyte is in the form of a paste to prevent it from spilling.

dry-clean *vb* to clean (clothes, etc.) with a solvent other than water. ▸ **dry-cleaner** *n* ▸ **dry-cleaning** *n*

dry dock *n* a dock that can be pumped dry to permit work on a ship's bottom.

dryer[1] *n* any device that removes moisture by heating or by hot air.

dryer[2] *adj* same as **drier[1]**.

dry ice *n* solid carbon dioxide used as a refrigerant.

dryly *adv* same as **drily**.

dry out *vb* **1** to make or become dry. **2** to undergo or cause to undergo treatment for alcoholism or drug addiction.

dry rot *n* **1** crumbling and drying of timber, caused by certain fungi. **2** a fungus causing this decay.

dry run *n Informal* a rehearsal.

dry stock *n NZ* cattle raised for meat.

dry-stone *adj* (of a wall) made without mortar.

dry up *vb* **1** to make or become dry. **2** to dry (dishes, cutlery, etc.) with a tea towel after they have been washed. **3** (of a resource) to come to an end. **4** *Informal* to stop speaking: *she suddenly dried up in the middle of her speech.*

DSC (in Britain) Distinguished Service Cross.

DSO (in Britain) Distinguished Service Order.

DSS *Brit* Department of Social Security.

DSW (in New Zealand) Department of Social Welfare.

DTP *Computers* desktop publishing.

DT's *Informal* delirium tremens.

dual *adj* having two parts, functions, or aspects: *dual controls; dual nationality.* ▷ **HISTORY** Latin *duo* two ▶ **duality** *n*

dual carriageway *n Brit, Austral & NZ* a road with a central strip of grass or concrete to separate traffic travelling in opposite directions.

dual-intercept *n Maths* a method of sketching a straight line on a graph by joining the x- and y-intercepts on the x- and y-axes.

dub[1] *vb* **dubbing, dubbed** to give (a person or place) a name or nickname. ▷ **HISTORY** Old English *dubbian*

dub[2] *vb* **dubbing, dubbed 1** to provide (a film) with a new soundtrack in a different language. **2** to provide (a film or tape) with a soundtrack. ✧ *n* **3** *Music* a style of reggae record production involving exaggeration of instrumental parts, echo, etc. ▷ **HISTORY** shortened from DOUBLE

dubbin *n* a kind of thick grease applied to leather to soften it and make it waterproof. ▷ **HISTORY** *dub* to dress leather

dubious (**dew**-bee-uss) *adj* **1** not entirely honest, safe, or reliable: *this allegation was at best dubious and at worst an outright fabrication.* **2** unsure or undecided: *she felt dubious about the entire proposition.* **3** of doubtful quality or worth: *she had the dubious honour of being taken for his mother.* ▷ **HISTORY** Latin *dubius* wavering ▶ **dubiety** (dew-**by**-it-ee) *n* ▶ **dubiously** *adv*

dubnium *n Chem* an element produced in minute quantities by bombarding plutonium with high-energy neon ions. Symbol: Db. ▷ **HISTORY** after *Dubna* in Russia, where it was first reported

ducal (**duke**-al) *adj* of a duke.

ducat (**duck**-it) *n* a former European gold or silver coin. ▷ **HISTORY** Old Italian *ducato*

duchess *n* **1** a woman who holds the rank of duke. **2** the wife or widow of a duke. ▷ **HISTORY** Old French *duchesse*

duchy *n, pl* **duchies** the area of land owned or ruled by a duke or duchess. ▷ **HISTORY** Old French *duche*

duck[1] *n, pl* **ducks** *or* **duck 1** a water bird with short legs, webbed feet, and a broad blunt bill. **2** the flesh of this bird used for food. **3** the female of such a bird. **4** *Cricket* a score of nothing. **5 like water off a duck's back** without effect: *I reprimanded him but it was like water off a duck's back.* ▷ **HISTORY** Old English *dūce*

duck[2] *vb* **1** to move (the head or body) quickly downwards, to escape being seen or avoid a blow. **2** to plunge suddenly under water. **3** *Informal* to dodge (a duty or responsibility). ▷ **HISTORY** Middle English

duck-billed platypus *n* See **platypus**.

duckboard *n Building* a board or boards laid so as to form a floor or path over muddy ground.

duckling *n* a young duck.

duct *n* **1** a tube, pipe, or channel through which liquid or gas is sent. **2** a tube in the body through which liquid such as tears or bile can pass. ▷ **HISTORY** Latin *ducere* to lead

ductile *adj* (of a metal) able to be shaped into sheets or drawn out into threads. ▷ **HISTORY** Latin *ductilis* ▶ **ductility** *n*

dud *Informal* ✧ *n* **1** an ineffectual person or thing: *they had the foresight to pick on someone who was not a total dud.* ✧ *adj* **2** bad or useless: *a dud cheque.* ▷ **HISTORY** origin unknown

dude *n Informal* **1** *US & Canad* a man: *he was a black dude in his late twenties.* **2** *Chiefly US & Canad old-fashioned* a dandy. **3** *Western US & Canad* a city dweller who spends his or her holiday on a ranch. ▷ **HISTORY** origin unknown

dudgeon *n* **in high dudgeon** angry or resentful: *the scientist departed in high dudgeon.* ▷ **HISTORY** origin unknown

due *adj* **1** expected to happen, be done, or arrive at a particular time: *he is due to return on Thursday.* **2** immediately payable: *the balance is now due.* **3** owed as a debt: *they finally agreed to pay her the money she was due.* **4** fitting or proper. **5 due to** happening or existing as a direct result of someone or something else: *chronic kidney failure due to diabetes.* ✧ *n* **6** something that is owed or required. **7 give someone his** *or* **her due** to acknowledge someone's good points: *I'll give him his due, he's resourceful.* ✧ *adv* **8** directly or exactly: *due west.* ▷ **HISTORY** Latin *debere* to owe

> ☑ **WORD TIP**
> The use of *due to* as a compound preposition *(the performance has been cancelled due to bad weather)* was formerly considered incorrect, but is now acceptable.

duel *n* **1** a formal fight between two people using guns, swords, or other weapons to settle a quarrel. ✧ *vb* **duelling, duelled** *or US* **dueling, dueled 2** to fight in a duel. ▷ **HISTORY** Latin *duellum,* poetical variant of *bellum* war ▶ **duellist** *n*

duenna *n* (esp. in Spain) an elderly woman acting as chaperon to girls. ▷ **HISTORY** Spanish *dueña*

due process of law *n Law* the administration of justice in accordance with established rules and principles.

dues *pl n* membership fees paid to a club or organization: *union dues.*

duet *n* a piece of music sung or played by two people. ▷ **HISTORY** Latin *duo* two ▶ **duettist** *n*

duff *adj* **1** *Chiefly Brit informal* broken or useless: *my car had a duff clutch.* ✧ *vb* **2** *Golf informal* to bungle (a shot). **3 duff up** *Brit slang* to beat (someone) severely. ▷ **HISTORY** probably from *duffer*

duffel *or* **duffle** *n* same as **duffel coat**. ▷ **HISTORY** after *Duffel*, Belgian town

duffel bag *n* a cylinder-shaped canvas bag fastened with a drawstring.

duffel coat *n* a wool coat usually with a hood and fastened with toggles.

duffer *n Informal* a dull or incompetent person. ▷ **HISTORY** origin unknown

dug[1] *vb* the past of **dig**.

dug[2] *n* a teat or udder of a female animal. ▷ **HISTORY** Scandinavian

dugite (**doo**-gyte) *n* a medium-sized Australian venomous snake.

dugong *n* a whalelike mammal found in tropical waters. ▷ **HISTORY** Malay *duyong*

dugout *n* **1** a canoe made by hollowing out a log. **2** *Brit* (at a sports ground) the covered bench where managers and substitutes sit. **3** *Mil* a covered shelter dug in the ground to provide protection.

duiker *or* **duyker** (**dike**-er) *n, pl* **-kers** *or* **-ker** a small African antelope. ▷ **HISTORY** Dutch: diver

duke *n* **1** a nobleman of the highest rank. **2** the prince or ruler of a small principality or duchy. ▷ **HISTORY** Latin *dux* leader ▸ **dukedom** *n*

dulcet (**dull**-sit) *adj* (of a sound) soothing or pleasant: *she smiled and, in dulcet tones, told me I would be next.* ▷ **HISTORY** Latin *dulcis* sweet

dulcimer *n* a tuned percussion instrument consisting of a set of strings stretched over a sounding board and struck with hammers. ▷ **HISTORY** Old French *doulcemer*

dull *adj* **1** not interesting: *the finished article would make dull reading.* **2** slow to learn or understand. **3** (of an ache) not intense: *I have a dull ache in the middle of my back.* **4** (of weather) not bright or clear. **5** not lively or energetic: *she appeared, looking dull and apathetic.* **6** (of colour) lacking brilliance. **7** (of the blade of a knife) not sharp. **8** (of a sound) not loud or clear: *his head fell back to the carpet with a dull thud.* ✧ *vb* **9** to make or become dull. ▷ **HISTORY** Old English *dol* ▸ **dullness** *n* ▸ **dully** *adv*

dullard *n Old-fashioned* a dull or stupid person.

dulse *n* a seaweed with large red edible fronds. ▷ **HISTORY** Irish *duilesc* seaweed

duly *adv* **1** in a proper manner: *my permit was duly stamped.* **2** at the proper time: *the photographer duly arrived.*

duma *n* **1** *Russian hist* the legislative assembly established by Tsar Nicholas II in 1905 and overthrown by the Bolsheviks in 1917. **2** *Politics* the lower house of the post-Soviet Russian parliament. ▷ **HISTORY** from Russian: thought

dumb *adj* **1** lacking the power to speak. **2** lacking the power of human speech: *dumb animals.* **3** temporarily unable to speak: *I was struck dumb when I heard the news.* **4** done or performed without speech: *I looked at her in dumb puzzlement.* **5** *Informal* stupid or slow to understand. ✧ See also **dumb down**. ▷ **HISTORY** Old English ▸ **dumbly** *adv*

dumbbell *n* **1** a short bar with a heavy ball or disc at either end, used for physical exercise. **2** *Slang, chiefly US & Canad* a stupid person.

dumb down *vb* to make (something) less intellectually demanding or sophisticated: *a move to dumb down its news coverage.*

dumbfounded *adj* speechless with amazement. ▷ **HISTORY** *dumb* + *(con)found*

dumb show *n* meaningful gestures without speech.

dumbwaiter *n* **1** a lift for carrying food, etc. from one floor of a building to another. **2** *Brit* **a** a stand placed near a dining table to hold food. **b** a revolving tray placed on a table to hold food.

dumdum *or* **dumdum bullet** *n* a soft-nosed bullet that expands on impact and causes large and serious wounds. ▷ **HISTORY** after *Dum-Dum*, town near Calcutta where originally made

dummy *n, pl* **-mies 1** a large model that looks like a human being, used for displaying clothes in a shop, as a target, etc. **2** a copy of an object, often lacking some essential feature of the original. **3** *Slang* a stupid person. **4** *Bridge* **a** the hand exposed on the table by the declarer's partner and played by the declarer. **b** the declarer's partner. **5** a rubber teat for babies to suck. ✧ *adj* **6** imitation or substitute: *dummy bombs.* ▷ **HISTORY** from *dumb*

dummy run *n* a practice or test carried out to test if any problems remain: *we'll do a dummy run on the file to see if the program works.*

dump *vb* **1** to drop or let fall in a careless manner: *he dumped the books on the bed.* **2** *Informal* to abandon (someone or something) without proper care: *the unwanted babies were dumped in orphanages.* **3** to dispose of (nuclear waste). **4** *Commerce* to sell (goods) in bulk and at low prices, usually in another country, in order to keep prices high in the home market. **5** *Computers* to record (the contents of the memory) on a storage device at a series of points during a computer run. ✧ *n* **6** a place where rubbish is left. **7** *Informal* a dirty, unattractive place. **8** *Mil* a place where weapons or supplies are stored. ▷ **HISTORY** probably from Old Norse

dumpling *n* **1** a small ball of dough cooked and served with stew. **2** a round pastry case filled with fruit. ▷ **HISTORY** obsolete *dump* lump

dumps *pl n* **down in the dumps** *Informal* feeling depressed and miserable. ▷ **HISTORY** probably from Middle Dutch *domp* haze

dumpy *adj* **dumpier, dumpiest** short and plump. ▷ **HISTORY** perhaps related to DUMPLING

dun[1] *vb* **dunning, dunned 1** to press (a debtor) for payment. ✧ *n* **2** a demand for payment. ▷ **HISTORY** origin unknown

dun[2] *adj* brownish-grey. ▷ **HISTORY** Old English *dunn*

dunce *n Brit, Austral & NZ* a person who is stupid.

WORD HISTORY

In medieval times, the followers of the 13th-century theologian John Duns Scotus were called 'Dunses'. They were ridiculed by later philosophers as opponents of learning, and so the term came to be applied to those incapable of learning.

dunderhead *n Brit, Austral & NZ* a slow-witted person. ▷ **HISTORY** probably from Dutch *donder* thunder + HEAD

dune *n* a mound or ridge of drifted sand. ▷ **HISTORY** Middle Dutch

dung *n* the faeces from large animals. ▷ **HISTORY** Old English: prison

dungarees *pl n* trousers with a bib attached. ▷ **HISTORY** *Dungrī*, district of Bombay, where the fabric used originated

dungeon *n* a prison cell, often underground. ▷ **HISTORY** Old French *donjon*

dunghill *n* a heap of dung.

dunk *vb* **1** to dip (a biscuit or piece of bread) in a drink or soup before eating it. **2** to put (something) in liquid: *dunk the garment in the dye for fifteen minutes.* ▷ **HISTORY** Old High German *dunkōn*

dunlin *n* a small sandpiper, of northern and artic regions, with a brown back and a black breast. ▷ **HISTORY** from DUN²

dunnock *n* same as **hedge sparrow**. ▷ **HISTORY** from DUN²

dunny *n, pl* **-nies** *Austral or old-fashioned NZ informal* a toilet. ▷ **HISTORY** of obscure origin

duo *n, pl* **duos 1** two singers or musicians who sing or play music together as a pair. **2** *Informal* two people who have something in common or do something together. ▷ **HISTORY** Latin: two

duodecimal *adj* relating to twelve or twelfths. ▷ **HISTORY** Latin *duodecim* twelve

duodenum (dew-oh-**deen**-um) *n* the first part of the small intestine, just below the stomach. ▷ **HISTORY** Medieval Latin *intestinum duodenum digitorum* intestine of twelve fingers' length ▶ **duodenal** *adj*

duologue *or US sometimes* **duolog** *n* a part or all of a play in which the speaking roles are limited to two actors. ▷ **HISTORY** DUO + (MONO)LOGUE

DUP (in Northern Ireland) Democratic Unionist Party.

dupe *vb* **duping, duped 1** to deceive or cheat: *you duped me into doing exactly what you wanted.* ✧ *n* **2** a person who is easily deceived. ▷ **HISTORY** French

duple *adj* **1** same as **double**. **2** *Music* having two beats in a bar. ▷ **HISTORY** Latin *duplus* double

duplex *n* **1** *US & Canad* **a** an apartment on two floors. **b** *US & Austral* a semidetached house. ✧ *adj* **2** having two parts. ▷ **HISTORY** Latin: twofold

duplicate *adj* **1** copied exactly from an original: *he had a duplicate key to the front door.* ✧ *n* **2** an exact copy. **3 in duplicate** in two exact copies: *submit the draft in duplicate, please.* ✧ *vb* **-cating, -cated 4** to make an exact copy of. **5** to do again (something that has already been done). ▷ **HISTORY** Latin *duplicare* to double ▶ **duplication** *n* ▶ **duplicator** *n*

duplicity *n* deceitful behaviour. ▷ **HISTORY** Old French *duplicite*

durable *adj* strong and long-lasting: *the car's body was made of a light but durable plastic.* ▷ **HISTORY** Latin *durare* to last ▶ **durability** *n*

durable goods *pl n* goods that do not require frequent replacement. Also called: **durables**

duration *n* the length of time that something lasts. ▷ **HISTORY** Latin *durare* to last

durbar *n* (formerly) **a** the court of a native ruler or a governor in India. **b** a reception at such a court. ▷ **HISTORY** Hindi *darbār*

duress *n* physical or moral pressure used to force someone to do something: *confessions obtained under duress.* ▷ **HISTORY** Latin *durus* hard

duricrust *n Geol* a hard crust found on or in soils in arid regions.

during *prep* throughout or within the limit of (a period of time). ▷ **HISTORY** Latin *durare* to last

dusk *n* the time just before nightfall when it is almost dark. ▷ **HISTORY** Old English *dox*

dusky *adj* **duskier, duskiest 1** dark in colour: *her gold earings gleamed against her dusky cheeks.* **2** dim or shadowy: *the dusky room was crowded with absurd objects.* ▶ **duskily** *adv* ▶ **duskiness** *n*

dust *n* **1** small dry particles of earth, sand, or dirt. **2 bite the dust a** to stop functioning: *my television has finally bitten the dust.* **b** to fall down dead. **3 shake the dust off one's feet** to depart angrily. **4 throw dust in someone's eyes** to confuse or mislead someone. ✧ *vb* **5** to remove dust from (furniture) by wiping. **6** to sprinkle (something) with a powdery substance: *serve dusted with brown sugar and cinnamon.* ▷ **HISTORY** Old English *dūst*

dustbin *n* a large, usually cylindrical, container for household rubbish.

dust bowl *n* a dry area in which the surface soil is exposed to wind erosion.

dustcart *n Chiefly Brit & NZ* a lorry for collecting household rubbish.

duster *n* a cloth used for dusting.

dust jacket *or* **cover** *n* a removable paper cover used to protect a book.

dustman *n, pl* **-men** *Brit* a man whose job is to collect household rubbish.

dustpan *n* a short-handled shovel into which dust is swept from floors.

dustsheet *n* a large cloth cover used to protect furniture from dust.

dust-up *n Informal* a fight or argument.

dusty *adj* **dustier, dustiest 1** covered with dust. **2** (of a colour) tinged with grey.

Dutch *adj* **1** of the Netherlands. ✧ *n* **2** the language of the Netherlands. ✧ *pl n* **3 the Dutch** the people of the Netherlands. ✧ *adv* **4 go Dutch** *Informal* to go on an outing where each person pays his or her own expenses.

Dutch auction *n* an auction in which the price is lowered by stages until a buyer is found.

Dutch barn *n Brit* a farm building with a steel frame and a curved roof.

Dutch courage *n* false courage gained from drinking alcohol.

Dutch elm disease *n* a fungal disease of elm trees.

dutiable *adj* (of goods) requiring payment of duty.

A B C D E F G H I J K L M N O P Q R S T U V W X Y Z

dutiful *adj* doing what is expected: *she is a responsible and dutiful mother.* ▶ **dutifully** *adv*

duty *n, pl* **-ties 1** the work performed as part of one's job: *it is his duty to supervise the memorial services.* **2** a obligation to fulfil one's responsibilities: *it's my duty as a doctor to keep it confidential.* **3** a government tax on imports. **4 on** *or* **off duty** at (*or* not at) work. ▷ HISTORY Anglo-French *dueté*

duty-bound *adj* morally obliged to do something: *we are duty-bound to help.*

duty-free *adj, adv* with exemption from customs or excise duties.

duty-free shop *n* a shop, esp. at an airport, that sells duty-free goods.

duty of care *n Law* the legal obligation to take measures to avoid causing foreseeable damage to other people or their property through negligence.

duvet (**doo**-vay) *n* same as **continental quilt**. ▷ HISTORY French

DVD Digital Versatile *or* Video Disk: a type of compact disc that can store large amounts of video and audio information.

DVLA (Brit) Driver and Vehicle Licensing Agency.

dwaal *n S African* a state of absent-mindedness; a daze. ▷ HISTORY Afrikaans

dwang *n NZ & S African* a short piece of wood inserted in a timber-framed wall.

dwarf *vb* **1** to cause (someone or something) to seem small by being much larger. ✧ *adj* **2** (of an animal or plant) much below the average size for the species. ✧ *n, pl* **dwarfs** *or* **dwarves 3** a person who is smaller than average size. **4** (in folklore) a small ugly manlike creature, often possessing magical powers. ▷ HISTORY Old English *dweorg*

dwell *vb* **dwelling, dwelt** *or* **dwelled** *Formal, literary* to live as a permanent resident. ▷ HISTORY Old English *dwellan* to seduce, get lost ▶ **dweller** *n*

dwelling *n Formal, literary* a place of residence.

dwell on *or* **upon** *vb* to think, speak, or write at length about (something).

dwindle *vb* **-dling, -dled** to grow less in size, strength, or number. ▷ HISTORY Old English *dwīnan*

Dy *Chem* dysprosium.

dye *n* **1** a colouring substance. **2** the colour produced by dyeing. ✧ *vb* **dyeing, dyed 3** to colour (hair or fabric) by applying a dye. ▷ HISTORY Old English *dēag* ▶ **dyer** *n*

dyed-in-the-wool *adj* having strong and unchanging attitudes or opinions: *he's a dyed-in-the-wool communist.*

dying *vb* **1** the present participle of **die**[1]. ✧ *adj* **2** occurring at the moment of death: *in accordance with his dying wish.* **3** (of a person or animal) very ill and likely to die soon. **4** becoming less important or less current: *coal mining is a dying industry.*

dyke[1] *or esp US* **dike** *n* **1** a wall built to prevent flooding. **2** a ditch. **3** *Scot* a dry-stone wall. ▷ HISTORY Old English *dic* ditch

dyke[2] *or* **dike** *n Slang* a lesbian. ▷ HISTORY origin unknown

dynamic *adj* **1** (of a person) full of energy, ambition, or new ideas. **2** relating to a force of society, history, or the mind that produces a change: *the government needs a more dynamic policy towards the poor.* **3** *Physics* relating to energy or forces that produce motion. ▷ HISTORY Greek *dunamis* power ▶ **dynamically** *adv*

dynamic equilibrium *n* a state of ever-changing balance in a system.

dynamic equilibrium *n Chem* a state of balance between ongoing processes.

dynamics *n* **1** the branch of mechanics concerned with the forces that change or produce the motions of bodies. ✧ *pl n* **2** those forces that produce change in any field or system. **3** *Music* the various degrees of loudness in a performance.

dynamism *n* great energy or enthusiasm.

dynamite *n* **1** an explosive made of nitroglycerine. **2** *Informal* a dangerous or exciting person or thing: *she's still dynamite.* ✧ *vb* **-miting, -mited 3** to mine or blow (something) up with dynamite. ▷ HISTORY Greek *dunamis* power

dynamo *n, pl* **-mos** a device for converting mechanical energy into electricity. ▷ HISTORY short for *dynamoelectric machine*

dynamoelectric *adj* of the conversion of mechanical energy into electricity or vice versa.

dynamometer (dine-a-**mom**-it-er) *n* an instrument for measuring mechanical power.

dynast *n* a hereditary ruler. ▷ HISTORY Greek *dunasthai* to be powerful

dynasty *n, pl* **-ties 1** a series of rulers of a country from the same family. **2** a period of time during which a country is ruled by the same family. ▷ HISTORY Greek *dunastēs* dynast ▶ **dynastic** *adj*

dysentery *n* infection of the intestine which causes severe diarrhoea. ▷ HISTORY Greek *dusentera* bad bowels

dysfunction *n* **1** *Med* any disturbance or abnormality in the function of an organ or part. **2** (esp. of a family) failure to show the characteristics or fulfil the purposes accepted as normal or beneficial. ▶ **dysfunctional** *adj*

dyslexia *n* a developmental disorder that causes learning difficulty with reading, writing, and numeracy. ▷ HISTORY Greek *dus-* not + *lexis* word ▶ **dyslexic** *adj, n*

dysmenorrhoea *or esp US* **dysmenorrhea** *n* painful or difficult menstruation. ▷ HISTORY Greek *dus-* bad + *rhoia* a flowing

dyspepsia *n* indigestion. ▷ HISTORY Greek *dus-* bad + *pepsis* digestion ▶ **dyspeptic** *adj, n*

dysprosium *n Chem* a metallic element of the lanthanide series. Symbol: Dy. ▷ HISTORY Greek *dusprositos* difficult to get near

dystopia *n Literature* an imaginary place where everything is as bad as it can be. ▷ HISTORY (coined by John Stuart Mill (1806–73), English philosopher and economist): from Latin *dys-* bad + UTOPIA ▶ **dystopian** *adj, n*

dystrophy (**diss**-trof-fee) *n* See **muscular dystrophy**. ▷ HISTORY Greek *dus-* not + *trophē* food

E e

e *Maths* a number used as the base of natural logarithms. Approximate value: 2.718 282..

E **1** *Music* the third note of the scale of C major. **2** East(ern). **3** English. **4** *Physics* **a** energy. **b** electromotive force. **5** *Slang* the drug ecstasy.

e- *prefix* electronic: *e-mail; e-tailer.*

E- *prefix* used with a number following it to indicate that something, such as a food additive, conforms to an EU standard.

each *adj* **1** every one of two or more people or things considered individually: *each year.* ✧ *pron* **2** every one of two or more people or things: *each had been given one room to design.* ✧ *adv* **3** for, to, or from each person or thing: *twenty pounds each.* **4 each other** (of two or more people) each one to or at the other or others; one another: *they stared at each other.* ▷ **HISTORY** Old English *ǣlc*

> **WORD TIP**
>
> *Each* is a singular pronoun and should be used with a singular form of a verb: *each of the candidates was* (not *were*) *interviewed separately.* See also at **either.**

eager *adj* very keen to have or do something. ▷ **HISTORY** Latin *acer* sharp, keen ▶ **eagerly** *adv* ▶ **eagerness** *n*

eagle *n* **1** a large bird of prey with broad wings and strong soaring flight. **2** *Golf* a score of two strokes under par for a hole. ▷ **HISTORY** Latin *aquila*

eaglet *n* a young eagle.

ear[1] *n* **1** the part of the body with which a person or animal hears. **2** the external, visible part of the ear. **3** the ability to hear musical and other sounds and interpret them accurately: *a good ear for languages.* **4** willingness to listen: *they are always willing to lend an ear.* **5 be all ears** to be prepared to listen attentively to something. **6 fall on deaf ears** to be ignored: *his words fell on deaf ears.* **7 in one ear and out the other** heard but quickly forgotten or ignored. **8 out on one's ear** *Informal* dismissed suddenly and unpleasantly. **9 play by ear** to play without written music. **10 play it by ear** *Informal* to make up one's plan of action as one goes along. **11 turn a deaf ear to** to be deliberately unresponsive to: *many countries have turned a deaf ear to their cries for help.* **12 up to one's ears in** *Informal* deeply involved in. ▷ **HISTORY** Old English *ēare*

ear[2] *n* the part of a cereal plant, such as wheat or barley, that contains the seeds. ▷ **HISTORY** Old English *ēar*

earache *n* pain in the ear.

earbash *vb Brit, Austral & NZ informal* to talk incessantly. ▶ **earbashing** *n*

eardrum *n* the thin membrane separating the external ear from the middle ear.

earl *n* (in Britain) a nobleman ranking below a marquess and above a viscount. ▷ **HISTORY** Old English *eorl* ▶ **earldom** *n*

ear lobe *n* the soft hanging lowest part of the human ear.

early *adj, adv* **-lier, -liest 1** occurring or arriving before the correct or expected time. **2** in the first part of a period of time: *early April; early in the war.* **3** near the beginning of the development or history of something: *early Britain was very primitive; early models of this car rust easily.* ▷ **HISTORY** Old English *ǣrlīce*

Early English *n* a style of architecture used in England in the 12th and 13th centuries, characterized by narrow pointed arches and ornamental intersecting stonework in windows.

earmark *vb* **1** to set (something) aside for a specific purpose. ✧ *n* **2** a feature that enables the nature of something to be identified: *it had all the earmarks of a disaster.*

> **WORD HISTORY**
>
> The notion of 'earmarking' something comes from the practice of putting identification marks on the ears of domestic or farm animals.

earn *vb* **1** to gain or be paid (money) in return for work. **2** to acquire or deserve through one's behaviour or action: *you've earned a good night's sleep.* **3** to make (money) as interest or profit: *her savings earned 8% interest.* ▷ **HISTORY** Old English *earnian* ▶ **earner** *n*

earnest[1] *adj* **1** serious and sincere, often excessively so. ✧ *n* **2 in earnest** with serious or sincere intentions. ▷ **HISTORY** Old English *eornost* ▶ **earnestly** *adv* ▶ **earnestness** *n*

earnest[2] *n Brit, Austral & NZ old-fashioned* a part payment given in advance as a guarantee of the remainder, esp. to confirm a contract. ▷ **HISTORY** Old French *erres* pledges

earnings *pl n* money earned.

earphone *n* a small device connected to a radio or tape recorder and worn over the ear, so that a person can listen to a broadcast or tape without anyone else hearing it.

ear-piercing *adj* extremely loud or shrill.

earplug *n* a piece of soft material placed in the ear to keep out noise or water.

earring *n* a piece of jewellery worn in or hanging from the ear lobe.

earshot *n* the range within which a sound can be heard: *out of earshot.*

earth *n* **1** (*sometimes cap*) the planet that we live on, the third planet from the sun, the only one on which life is known to exist. *RELATED ADJECTIVE* ▸ **terrestrial 2** the part of the surface of this planet that is not water. **3** the soil in which plants grow. **4** the hole in which a fox lives. **5** a wire in a piece of electrical equipment through which electricity can escape into the ground if a fault develops. **6 come down to earth** to return to reality from a daydream or fantasy. **7 on earth** used for emphasis: *what on earth happened?* ✧ *vb* **8** to fit (a piece of electrical equipment) with an earth. ▷ HISTORY Old English *eorthe*

earthen *adj* made of earth or baked clay: *an earthen floor.*

earthenware *n* dishes and other objects made of baked clay: *an earthenware flowerpot.*

earthly *adj* **-lier, -liest 1** of life on earth as opposed to any heavenly or spiritual state. **2** *Informal* conceivable or possible: *what earthly reason would they have for lying?*

earthquake *n* a series of vibrations at the earth's surface caused by movement of the earth's crust.

earth science *n* any science, such as geology, concerned with the structure, age, etc., of the earth.

earthwork *n* **1** excavation of earth, as in engineering construction. **2** a fortification made of earth.

earthworm *n* a common worm that burrows in the soil.

earthy *adj* **earthier, earthiest 1** open and direct in the treatment of sex, excretion, etc. **2** of or like earth: *earthy colours.* ▶ **earthiness** *n*

earwig *n* a thin brown insect with pincers at the tip of its abdomen.

> **WORD HISTORY**
> 'Earwig' comes from Old English *earwicga*, meaning 'ear insect'. It was once believed that earwigs would creep into people's ears.

ease *n* **1** lack of difficulty. **2** freedom from discomfort or worry. **3** rest, leisure, or relaxation. **4** freedom from poverty: *a life of leisure and ease.* **5 at ease a** *Mil* (of a soldier) standing in a relaxed position with the feet apart. **b** in a relaxed attitude or frame of mind. ✧ *vb* **easing, eased 6** to make or become less difficult or severe: *the pain gradually eased.* **7** to move into or out of a place or situation slowly and carefully. **8 ease off** *or* **up** to lessen or cause to lessen in severity, pressure, tension, or strain: *the rain eased off.* ▷ HISTORY Old French *aise*

easel *n* a frame on legs, used for supporting an artist's canvas, a display, or a blackboard. ▷ HISTORY Dutch *ezel* ass

easement *n* **1** *Law* the right enjoyed by a landowner of making limited use of his neighbour's land, as by crossing it to reach his own property. **2** the act of easing or something that brings ease.

easily *adv* **1** without difficulty. **2** without doubt; by far: *easily the most senior Chinese minister to visit the West.*

> **WORD TIP**
> See at **easy.**

east *n* **1** one of the four cardinal points of the compass, at 90° clockwise from north. **2** the direction along a line of latitude towards the sunrise. **3 the east** any area lying in or towards the east. ✧ *adj* **4** situated in, moving towards, or facing the east. **5** (esp. of the wind) from the east. ✧ *adv* **6** in, to, or towards the east. ▷ HISTORY Old English *ēast*

East *n* **1 the East a** the southern and eastern parts of Asia. **b** (esp. formerly) the countries in Eastern Europe and Asia which are or have been under Communist rule. ✧ *adj* **2** of or denoting the eastern part of a country or region.

eastbound *adj* going towards the east.

Easter *n* **1** *Christianity* a festival commemorating the Resurrection of Christ. ✧ *adj* **2** taking place at the time of the year when this festival is celebrated: *the Easter holidays.*

> **WORD HISTORY**
> Although Easter is a Christian festival, its name comes from Old English *Eostre*, the name of a pre-Christian Germanic goddess whose festival was celebrated at the spring equinox.

Easter egg *n* a chocolate egg given at Easter.

easterly *adj* **1** of or in the east. ✧ *adv, adj* **2** towards the east. **3** from the east: *an easterly breeze.*

eastern *adj* **1** situated in or towards the east. **2** facing or moving towards the east. **3** (*sometimes cap*) of or characteristic of the east or East. ▶ **easternmost** *adj*

Easterner *n* a person from the east of a country or region.

eastern hemisphere *n* the half of the globe that contains Europe, Asia, Africa, and Australia.

easting *n Geog* a longitudinal grid line. Compare **northing**.

eastward *adj, adv also* **eastwards 1** towards the east. ✧ *n* **2** the eastward part or direction.

easy *adj* **easier, easiest 1** not difficult; simple: *the house is easy to keep clean.* **2** free from pain, care, or anxiety: *an easy life.* **3** tolerant and undemanding; easy-going. **4** defenceless or readily fooled: *easy prey.* **5** moderate and not involving any great effort: *an easy ride.* **6** *Informal* ready to fall in with any suggestion made: *he wanted to do something and I was easy about it.* **7** *Informal* pleasant and not involving any great effort to enjoy: *easy on the eye.* ✧ *adv* **8 go easy on a** to avoid using too much of: *he'd tried to go easy on the engines.* **b** to treat less severely than is deserved: *go easy on him, he's just a kid.* **9 take it easy** to relax and avoid stress or undue hurry. ▷ HISTORY Old French *aisié* ▶ **easiness** *n*

> **WORD TIP**
> *Easy* should only be used as an adverb in certain set phrases: *to take it easy; easy does it.* Where a fixed expression is not involved, the usual adverbial form of *easy* is preferred: *this polish goes on more easily* (not *easier*) *than the other.*

easy chair *n* a comfortable upholstered armchair.

easy-going *adj* relaxed in manner or attitude; very tolerant.

eat *vb* **eating, ate, eaten 1** to take (food) into the mouth and swallow it. **2** to have a meal: *sometimes we eat out of doors.* **3** *Informal* to make anxious or worried: *what's eating you?* **4 eat away, into** *or* **up**

to destroy or use up partly or wholly: *inflation ate into the firm's profits.* ▷ **HISTORY** Old English *etan* ▶ **eater** *n*
eatable *adj* fit or suitable for eating.
eau de Cologne (oh de kol-**lone**) *n* full form of **cologne.** ▷ **HISTORY** French: water of Cologne
eaves *pl n* the edge of a sloping roof that overhangs the walls. ▷ **HISTORY** Old English *efes*
eavesdrop *vb* **-dropping, -dropped** to listen secretly to a private conversation. ▶ **eavesdropper** *n*

WORD HISTORY
The word 'eavesdrop' comes from Old English *yfesdrype*, meaning 'water dripping from the eaves'. The 'eavesdrop' was the ground around a house where the water dripped down from the eaves, and an 'eavesdropper' was someone who would stand outside in the rain in the eavesdrop to hear what was being said inside the house.

ebb *vb* **1** (of the sea or the tide) to flow back from its highest point. **2** to fall away or decline: *her anger ebbed away.* ✧ *n* **3** the flowing back of the tide from high to low water. **4** **at a low ebb** in a weak state: *her creativity was at a low ebb.* ▷ **HISTORY** Old English *ebba* ebb-tide
ebony *n* **1** a very hard dark-coloured wood used to make furniture etc. ✧ *adj* **2** very deep black. ▷ **HISTORY** Greek *ebenos*
ebullient *adj* full of enthusiasm or excitement. ▷ **HISTORY** Latin *ebullire* to bubble forth, be boisterous ▶ **ebullience** *n*
EC **1** European Commission. **2** European Community: a former name for the European Union.
eccentric *adj* **1** unconventional or odd. **2** (of circles) not having the same centre. ✧ *n* **3** a person who behaves unconventionally or oddly. ▷ **HISTORY** Greek *ek-* away from + *kentron* centre ▶ **eccentrically** *adv*
eccentricity *n* **1** unconventional or odd behaviour. **2** (*pl* **-ties**) an unconventional or odd habit or act.
ecclesiastic *n* **1** a member of the clergy. ✧ *adj* **2** of or relating to the Christian Church or its clergy. ▷ **HISTORY** Greek *ekklēsia* assembly
ecclesiastical *adj* of or relating to the Christian Church or its clergy.
ECG electrocardiogram.
echelon (**esh**-a-lon) *n* **1** a level of power or responsibility: *the upper echelons of society.* **2** *Mil* a formation in which units follow one another but are spaced out sideways to allow each a line of fire ahead. ▷ **HISTORY** French *échelon* rung of a ladder
echidna (ik-**kid**-na) *n, pl* **-nas, -nae** (-nee) an Australian spiny egg-laying mammal. Also called: **spiny anteater**
echinoderm (ik-**kine**-oh-durm) *n* a sea creature with a five-part symmetrical body, such as a starfish or sea urchin. ▷ **HISTORY** Greek *ekhinos* sea urchin + *derma* skin
echo *n, pl* **-oes 1 a** the reflection of sound by a solid object. **b** a sound reflected by a solid object. **2** a repetition or imitation of someone else's opinions. **3** something that brings back memories: *an echo of the past.* **4** the signal reflected back to a radar transmitter by an object. ✧ *vb* **-oing, -oed** **5** (of a sound) to be reflected off an object in such a way that it can be heard again. **6** (of a place) to be filled with a sound and its echoes: *the church echoed with singing.* **7** (of people) to repeat or imitate (what someone else has said): *his conclusion echoed that of Jung.* ▷ **HISTORY** Greek *ēkhō* ▶ **echoing** *adj*
echo chamber *n* a room with walls that reflect sound, used to create an echo effect in recording and broadcasting.
echolocation *n* the discovery of an object's position by measuring the time taken for an echo to return from it.
echo sounder *n* a navigation device that determines depth by measuring the time taken for a pulse of sound to reach the sea bed and for the echo to return.
éclair *n* a finger-shaped cake of choux pastry, filled with cream and coated with chocolate. ▷ **HISTORY** French: lightning (probably because it does not last long)
eclampsia *n Pathol* a serious condition that can develop towards the end of a pregnancy, causing high blood pressure, swelling, and convulsions.
eclectic *adj* **1** composed of elements selected from a wide range of styles, ideas, or sources: *the eclectic wine list includes bottles from all round the world.* **2** selecting elements from a wide range of styles, ideas, or sources: *an eclectic approach that takes the best from all schools of psychology.* ✧ *n* **3** a person who takes an eclectic approach. ▷ **HISTORY** Greek *eklegein* to select ▶ **eclecticism** *n*
eclipse *n* **1** the obscuring of one star or planet by another. A **solar eclipse** occurs when the moon passes between the sun and the earth; a **lunar eclipse** when the earth passes between the sun and the moon. **2** a loss of importance, power, or fame: *communism eventually went into eclipse.* ✧ *vb* **eclipsing, eclipsed** **3** to overshadow or surpass. **4** (of a star or planet) to hide (another planet or star) from view. ▷ **HISTORY** Greek *ekleipsis* a forsaking
ecliptic *n Astron* the great circle on the celestial sphere representing the apparent annual path of the sun relative to the stars.
eco- *combining form* denoting ecology or ecological: *ecotourism.*
E.coli (ee-**koal**-eye) *n* a common bacterium often found in the intestines. ▷ **HISTORY** shortened from *Escherichia coli*, after Theodor *Escherich*, paediatrician
ecological *adj* **1** of or relating to ecology. **2** tending or intended to benefit or protect the environment: *an ecological approach to agriculture.* ▶ **ecologically** *adv*
ecological pyramid *n Ecology* a hierarchy of organisms shown in a diagram where the base is the producer level, and then green plants, herbivores and carnivores form the remaining tiers.
ecology *n* the study of the relationships between people, animals, and plants, and their

A B C D E F G H I J K L M N O P Q R S T U V W X Y Z

environment. ▷ **HISTORY** Greek *oikos* house ▶ **ecologist** *n*

e-commerce *or* **ecommerce** *n* business transactions conducted on the Internet.

econ. economy.

economic *adj* **1** of or relating to an economy or economics. **2** *Brit & Austral* capable of being produced or operated for profit. **3** *Informal* inexpensive or cheap.

economical *adj* **1** not requiring a lot of money to use: *low fuel consumption makes this car very economical.* **2** (of a person) spending money carefully and sensibly. **3** using no more time, effort, or resources than is necessary. **4 economical with the truth** *Euphemistic* deliberately withholding information. ▶ **economically** *adv*

economics *n* **1** the study of the production and consumption of goods and services and the commercial activities of a society. ✧ *pl n* **2** financial aspects: *the economics of health care.*

economist *n* a person who specializes in economics.

economize *or* **-mise** *vb* **-mizing, -mized** *or* **-mising, -mised** to reduce expense or waste: *people are being advised to economize on fuel use.*

economy *n, pl* **-mies 1** the system by which the production, distribution, and consumption of goods and services is organized in a country or community: *the rural economy.* **2** the ability of a country to generate wealth through business and industry: *unless the economy improves, more jobs will be lost.* **3** careful use of money or resources to save expense, time, or energy. **4** an instance of this: *we can make economies by reusing envelopes.* ✧ *adj* **5** denoting a class of air travel that is cheaper than first-class. **6** offering a larger quantity for a lower price: *an economy pack.* ▷ **HISTORY** Greek *oikos* house + *nemein* to manage

economy of scale *n Econ* a fall in average costs resulting from an increase in the scale of production.

ecosphere *n Biol* the parts of the universe, esp. on earth, where life can exist.

ecosystem *n Ecology* the system of relationships between animals and plants and their environment.

ecoterrorist *n* a person who uses violence in order to achieve environmentalist aims. ▶ **ecoterrorism** *n*

ecotone *n Environmental science* a transition zone between two major ecological communities.

ecotourism *n* tourism designed to contribute to the protection of the environment or at least minimize damage to it. ▶ **ecotourist** *n*

ecotype *n Biol* a group of organisms within a species that is adapted to particular environmental conditions and therefore exhibits behavioural, structural, or physiological differences from other members of the species.

ecru *adj* pale creamy-brown. ▷ **HISTORY** French

ecstasy *n, pl* **-sies 1** a state of extreme delight or joy. **2** *Slang* a strong drug that acts as a stimulant and can cause hallucinations. ▷ **HISTORY** Greek *ekstasis* displacement, trance ▶ **ecstatic** *adj* ▶ **ecstatically** *adv*

ECT electroconvulsive therapy: the treatment of depression and some other mental disorders by passing a current of electricity through the brain, producing a convulsion.

ectopic pregnancy (eck-**top**-ick) *n* the abnormal development of a fertilized egg outside the uterus, usually in a Fallopian tube.

ectoplasm *n* (in spiritualism) the substance that supposedly is emitted from the body of a medium during a trance. ▷ **HISTORY** Greek *ektos* outside + *plasma* something moulded

ecumenical *adj* **1** of or relating to the Christian Church throughout the world. **2** tending to promote unity among Christian churches. ▷ **HISTORY** Greek *oikoumenikos* of the inhabited world

ecumenism *or* **ecumenicism** *n* the aim of unity among Christian churches throughout the world.

eczema (**ek**-sim-a, ig-**zeem**-a) *n Pathol* a condition in which the skin becomes inflamed and itchy. ▷ **HISTORY** Greek *ek-* out + *zein* to boil

ed. **1** edition. **2** editor.

Edam *n* a round yellow Dutch cheese with a red waxy covering. ▷ **HISTORY** after *Edam,* in Holland

edaphic (ee-**dah**-fic) *adj* of or relating to the physical and chemical conditions of the soil, in relation to the plant and animal life it supports. ▷ **HISTORY** Greek *edaphos* bottom, soil

eddo (**ed**-doh) *n, pl* **eddoes** same as **taro**.

eddy *n, pl* **-dies 1** a circular movement of air, water, or smoke. ✧ *vb* **-dies, -dying, -died 2** to move with a gentle circular motion; swirl gently. ▷ **HISTORY** probably from Old Norse

edelweiss (**ade**-el-vice) *n* a small white alpine flower. ▷ **HISTORY** German: noble white

edema (id-**deem**-a) *n, pl* **-mata** same as **oedema**.

Eden *n* **1** Also called: **Garden of Eden** *Bible* the garden in which Adam and Eve were placed at the Creation. **2** a place of great delight or contentment. ▷ **HISTORY** Hebrew *'ēdhen* place of pleasure

edentate *n* **1** a mammal with few or no teeth, such as an armadillo or a sloth. ✧ *adj* **2** denoting such a mammal. ▷ **HISTORY** Latin *edentatus* lacking teeth

edge *n* **1** a border or line where something ends or begins: *the edge of the city.* **2** a line along which two faces or surfaces of a solid meet. **3** the sharp cutting side of a blade. **4** keenness, sharpness, or urgency: *there was a nervous edge to his voice.* **5 have the edge on** to have a slight advantage over. **6 on edge** nervous and irritable. **7 set someone's teeth on edge** to make someone acutely irritated. ✧ *vb* **edging, edged 8** to make, form, or be an edge or border for: *a pillow edged with lace.* **9** to move very gradually in a particular direction: *I edged through to the front of the crowd.* ▷ **HISTORY** Old English *ecg*

edgeways *or esp US & Canad* **edgewise** *adv* **1** with the edge forwards or uppermost. **2 get a**

word in edgeways to interrupt a conversation in which someone else is talking continuously.

edging *n* anything placed along an edge for decoration.

edgy *adj* **edgier, edgiest** nervous, irritable, or anxious. ▶ **edginess** *n*

edible *adj* fit to be eaten; eatable. ▷ HISTORY Latin *edere* to eat ▶ **edibility** *n*

edict (**ee**-dikt) *n* a decree or order given by any authority. ▷ HISTORY Latin *edicere* to declare

edifice (**ed**-if-iss) *n* **1** a large or impressive building. **2** an elaborate system of beliefs and institutions: *the crumbling edifice of Communist rule.* ▷ HISTORY Latin *aedificare* to build

edify (**ed**-if-fie) *vb* **-fies, -fying, -fied** to inform or instruct (someone) with a view to improving his or her morals or understanding. ▷ HISTORY Latin *aedificare* to build ▶ **edification** *n* ▶ **edifying** *adj*

edit *vb* **editing, edited 1** to prepare (text) for publication by checking and improving its accuracy or clarity. **2** to be in charge of (a newspaper or magazine). **3** to prepare (a film, tape, etc.) by rearranging or selecting material. **4 edit out** to remove (a section) from a text, film, etc.

edition *n* **1** a particular version of a book, newspaper, or magazine produced at one time: *the revised paperback edition.* **2** a single television or radio programme which forms part of a series: *the first edition goes on the air in thirty minutes.*

editor *n* **1** a person who edits. **2** a person in overall charge of a newspaper or magazine. **3** a person in charge of one section of a newspaper or magazine: *the Political Editor.* **4** a person in overall control of a television or radio programme. ▷ HISTORY Latin *edere* to publish ▶ **editorship** *n*

editorial *n* **1** an article in a newspaper expressing the opinion of the editor or publishers. ✧ *adj* **2** of editing or editors: *an editorial meeting.* **3** relating to the contents and opinions of a magazine or newspaper: *the paper's editorial policy.* ▶ **editorially** *adv*

EDP electronic data processing.

educate *vb* **-cating, -cated 1** to teach (someone) over a long period of time so that he or she acquires knowledge and understanding of a range of subjects. **2** to send (someone) to a particular educational establishment: *he was educated at mission schools.* **3** to teach (someone) about a particular matter: *a campaign to educate people to the dangers of smoking.* ▷ HISTORY Latin *educare* to rear, educate ▶ **educative** *adj*

education *n* **1** the process of acquiring knowledge and understanding. **2** knowledge and understanding acquired through study and training: *education is the key to a good job.* **3** the process of teaching, esp. at a school, college, or university. **4** the theory of teaching and learning. ▶ **educational** *adj* ▶ **educationally** *adv* ▶ **educationalist** *or* **educationist** *n*

Edwardian *adj* of or in the reign of King Edward VII of Great Britain and Ireland (1901–10).

EEC European Economic Community: a former name for the European Union.

EEG electroencephalogram.

eel *n* a slimy snakelike fish. ▷ HISTORY Old English *ǣl*

eerie *adj* **eerier, eeriest** strange and frightening. ▷ HISTORY probably from Old English *earg* cowardly ▶ **eerily** *adv*

efface *vb* **-facing, -faced 1** to obliterate or make dim: *nothing effaced the memory.* **2** to rub out or erase. **3 efface oneself** to make oneself inconspicuous. ▷ HISTORY French *effacer* to obliterate the face ▶ **effacement** *n*

effect *n* **1** a change or state of affairs caused by something or someone: *the gales have had a serious effect on the crops.* **2** power to influence or produce a result: *the wine had little effect on him.* **3** the condition of being operative: *a new law has come into effect.* **4** the overall impression: *the whole effect is one of luxury.* **5** basic meaning or purpose: *words to that effect.* **6** an impression, usually a contrived one: *he paused for effect.* **7** a physical phenomenon: *the greenhouse effect.* **8 in effect** for all practical purposes: *in effect he has no choice.* **9 take effect** to begin to produce results. ✧ *vb* **10** to cause (something) to take place: *a peace treaty was effected.* ▷ HISTORY Latin *efficere* to accomplish

effective *adj* **1** producing a desired result: *an effective vaccine against HIV.* **2** officially coming into operation: *the new rates become effective at the end of May.* **3** impressive: *a highly effective speech.* **4** in reality, although not officially or in theory: *he is in effective control of the company.* ▶ **effectively** *adv* ▶ **effectiveness** *n*

effector *n Physiol* a nerve ending that ends in a muscle or gland and provides stimulation causing contraction or secretion.

effects *pl n* **1** personal belongings. **2** lighting, sounds, etc., to accompany a stage, film, or broadcast production.

effectual *adj* **1** producing the intended result. **2** (of a document etc.) having legal force. ▶ **effectually** *adv*

effeminate *adj* (of a man) displaying characteristics regarded as typical of a woman. ▷ HISTORY Latin *femina* woman ▶ **effeminacy** *n*

effervescent *adj* **1** (of a liquid) giving off bubbles of gas. **2** (of a person) lively and enthusiastic. ▷ HISTORY Latin *effervescere* to foam up ▶ **effervescence** *n*

effete (if-**feet**) *adj* weak, powerless, and decadent. ▷ HISTORY Latin *effetus* exhausted by bearing young

efficacious *adj* producing the intended result. ▷ HISTORY Latin *efficere* to achieve ▶ **efficacy** *n*

efficient *adj* working or producing effectively without wasting effort, energy, or money. ▷ HISTORY Latin *efficiens* effecting ▶ **efficiency** *n* ▶ **efficiently** *adv*

effigy (**ef**-fij-ee) *n, pl* **-gies 1** a statue or carving of someone, often as a memorial: *a 14th-century wooden effigy of a knight.* **2** a crude representation of someone, used as a focus for contempt: *an effigy of the president was set on fire.* ▷ HISTORY Latin *effingere* to portray

efflorescence *n* **1** the blooming of flowers on a plant. **2** a brief period of high-quality artistic activity. ▷ **HISTORY** Latin *efflorescere* to blossom

effluent *n* liquid discharged as waste, for instance from a factory or sewage works. ▷ **HISTORY** Latin *effluere* to flow out

effluvium *n, pl* **-via** an unpleasant smell, such as the smell of decaying matter. ▷ **HISTORY** Latin: a flowing out

efflux *n* **1** the process of flowing out. **2** something that flows out.

effort *n* **1** physical or mental energy needed to do something. **2** a determined attempt to do something. **3** achievement or creation: *his earliest literary efforts.* **4** *Physics* an applied force acting against inertia. ▷ **HISTORY** Latin *fortis* strong ▶ **effortless** *adj* ▶ **effortlessly** *adv*

effrontery *n* insolence or boldness. ▷ **HISTORY** Late Latin *effrons* putting forth one's forehead

effusion *n* **1** an unrestrained verbal expression of emotions or ideas. **2** a sudden pouring out: *small effusions of blood.* ▷ **HISTORY** Latin *effundere* to shed

effusive *adj* enthusiastically showing pleasure, gratitude, or approval. ▶ **effusively** *adv* ▶ **effusiveness** *n*

E-FIT *n Trademark* an image generated by a computer to create the likeness of a face, used by police to trace people from witnesses' descriptions. ▷ **HISTORY** from *E*lectronic *F*acial *I*dentification *T*echnique

EFL English as a Foreign Language.

EFTA European Free Trade Association.

EFTPOS electronic funds transfer at point of sale.

e.g. for example. ▷ **HISTORY** Latin *exempli gratia*

egalitarian *adj* **1** expressing or supporting the idea that all people should be equal. ✧ *n* **2** a person who believes that all people should be equal. ▷ **HISTORY** French *égal* equal ▶ **egalitarianism** *n*

egest (ee-**jest**) *vb Physiol* to discharge waste material from the body. ▶ **egestion** *n*

egg *n* **1** the oval or round object laid by the females of birds, reptiles, and other creatures, containing a developing embryo. **2** a hen's egg used for food. **3** a type of cell produced in the body of a female animal which can develop into a baby if fertilized by a male reproductive cell. **4 have egg on one's face** *Informal* to have been made to look ridiculous. **5 put all one's eggs in one basket** to rely entirely on one action or decision, with no alternative in case of failure. ▷ **HISTORY** Old Norse

egghead *n Informal* an intellectual person.

eggplant *n US, Canad, Austral & NZ* a dark purple tropical fruit, cooked and eaten as a vegetable.

eggshell *n* **1** the hard porous outer layer of a bird's egg. ✧ *adj* **2** (of paint) having a very slight sheen.

ego *n, pl* **egos 1** the part of a person's self that is able to recognize that person as being distinct from other people and things. **2** a person's opinion of his or her own worth: *men with fragile egos.* ▷ **HISTORY** Latin: I

egocentric *adj* thinking only of one's own interests and feelings. ▶ **egocentricity** *n*

egomania *n* an obsessive concern with fulfilling one's own needs and desires, regardless of the effect on other people. ▶ **egomaniac** *n*

egotism *or* **egoism** *n* concern only for one's own interests and feelings. ▶ **egotist** *or* **egoist** *n* ▶ **egotistical, egoistical, egotistic** *or* **egoistic** *adj*

egregious (ig-**greej**-uss) *adj* shockingly bad: *egregious government waste.* ▷ **HISTORY** Latin *egregius* outstanding (literally: standing out from the herd)

egress (**ee**-gress) *n Formal* **1** the act of going out. **2** a way out or exit. ▷ **HISTORY** Latin *egredi* to come out

egret (**ee**-grit) *n* a wading bird like a heron, with long white feathery plumes. ▷ **HISTORY** Old French *aigrette*

Egyptian *adj* **1** of Egypt. **2** of the ancient Egyptians. ✧ *n* **3** a person from Egypt. **4** a member of an ancient people who established an advanced civilization in Egypt. **5** the language of the ancient Egyptians.

Egyptology *n* the study of the culture of ancient Egypt. ▶ **Egyptologist** *n*

eh *interj* an exclamation used to ask for repetition or confirmation.

eider *or* **eider duck** *n* a large sea duck of the N hemisphere. ▷ **HISTORY** Old Norse *æthr*

eiderdown *n* a thick warm cover for a bed, filled with soft feathers, originally the breast feathers of the female eider duck.

Eid-ul-Adha (**eed**-ool-**ah**-da) *n* an annual Muslim festival, marking the end of the pilgrimage to Mecca. ▷ **HISTORY** from Arabic *id ul adha* festival of sacrifice

Eid-ul-Fitr (**eed**-ool-**feet**-er) *n* an annual Muslim festival, marking the end of Ramadan. ▷ **HISTORY** from Arabic *id ul fitr* festival of fast-breaking

eight *n* **1** the cardinal number that is the sum of one and seven. **2** a numeral, 8 or VIII, representing this number. **3** something representing or consisting of eight units. **4** *Rowing* **a** a light narrow boat rowed by eight people. **b** the crew of such a boat. ✧ *adj* **5** amounting to eight: *eight apples.* ▷ **HISTORY** Old English *eahta* ▶ **eighth** *adj, n*

eighteen *n* **1** the cardinal number that is the sum of ten and eight. **2** a numeral, 18 or XVIII, representing this number. **3** something representing or consisting of 18 units. ✧ *adj* **4** amounting to eighteen: *eighteen months.* ▶ **eighteenth** *adj, n*

eightfold *adj* **1** having eight times as many or as much. **2** composed of eight parts. ✧ *adv* **3** by eight times as many or as much.

eighty *n, pl* **eighties 1** the cardinal number that is the product of ten and eight. **2** a numeral, 80 or LXXX, representing this number. **3** something representing or consisting of 80 units. ✧ *adj* **4** amounting to eighty: *eighty miles.* ▶ **eightieth** *adj, n*

eina (**ay**-na) *interj S African* an exclamation of pain. ▷ **HISTORY** Khoi (language of southern Africa)

einsteinium *n Chem* a radioactive metallic element artificially produced from plutonium. Symbol: Es. ▷ **HISTORY** after Albert *Einstein*, physicist

Eire *n* Ireland or the Republic of Ireland. ▷ **HISTORY** Irish Gaelic

EIS Educational Institute of Scotland.

eisteddfod (ice-**sted**-fod) *n* a Welsh festival with competitions in music, poetry, drama, and art. ▷ **HISTORY** Welsh: session

either *adj, pron* **1** one or the other (of two): *we were offered either fish or beef.* **2** both one and the other: *we sat at either end of a long settee.* ✧ *conj* **3** used preceding two or more possibilities joined by *or*: *it must be stored either in the fridge or in a cool place.* ✧ *adv* **4** likewise: *I don't eat meat and my husband doesn't either.* **5** used to qualify or modify a previous statement: *he wasn't exactly ugly, he wasn't an oil painting either.* ▷ **HISTORY** Old English *ǣgther*

> **☑ WORD TIP**
> *Either* should be followed by a singular verb: *either is good; either of these books is useful.* Care should be taken to avoid ambiguity when using *either* to mean *both* or *each*, as in the following sentence: *a ship could be moored on either side of the channel.* Agreement between the verb and its subject in *either...or...* constructions follows the pattern given for *neither...nor...* See at **neither.**

ejaculate *vb* **-lating, -lated 1** to discharge semen from the penis while having an orgasm. **2** *Literary* to say or shout suddenly. ▷ **HISTORY** Latin *ejaculari* to hurl out ▸ **ejaculation** *n* ▸ **ejaculatory** *adj*

eject *vb* **1** to push or send out forcefully. **2** to compel (someone) to leave a place or position. **3** to leave an aircraft rapidly in mid-flight, using an ejector seat. ▷ **HISTORY** Latin *ejicere* ▸ **ejection** *n* ▸ **ejector** *n*

ejector seat *or* **ejection seat** *n* a seat in a military aircraft that throws the pilot out in an emergency.

eke out *vb* **eking, eked 1** to make (a supply) last for a long time by using as little as possible. **2** to manage to sustain (a living) despite having barely enough food or money. ▷ **HISTORY** obsolete *eke* to enlarge

elaborate *adj* **1** very complex because of having many different parts: *elaborate equipment.* **2** having a very complicated design: *elaborate embroidery.* ✧ *vb* **-rating, -rated 3 elaborate on** to describe in more detail: *he did not elaborate on his plans.* **4** to develop (a plan or theory) in detail. ▷ **HISTORY** Latin *elaborare* to take pains ▸ **elaborately** *adv* ▸ **elaboration** *n*

élan (ale-**an**) *n* style and liveliness. ▷ **HISTORY** French

eland (**eel**-and) *n* a large spiral-horned antelope of southern Africa. ▷ **HISTORY** Dutch: elk

elapse *vb* **elapsing, elapsed** (of time) to pass by. ▷ **HISTORY** Latin *elabi* to slip away

elastic *adj* **1** capable of returning to its original shape after stretching, compression, or other distortion. **2** capable of being adapted to meet the demands of a particular situation: *an elastic interpretation of the law.* **3** made of elastic. ✧ *n* **4** tape, cord, or fabric containing flexible rubber. ▷ **HISTORY** Greek *elastikos* propellent ▸ **elastically** *adv* ▸ **elasticated** *adj* ▸ **elasticity** *n*

elastic energy *n Physics* the energy contained in an object that is capable of returning to its original shape after stretching, compression, or other distortion.

elated *adj* extremely happy and excited. ▷ **HISTORY** Latin *elatus* carried away ▸ **elatedly** *adv*

elation *n* a feeling of great happiness and excitement.

elbow *n* **1** the joint between the upper arm and the forearm. **2** the part of a garment that covers the elbow. ✧ *vb* **3** to push with one's elbow or elbows: *she elbowed him aside; he elbowed his way to the bar.* ▷ **HISTORY** Old English *elnboga*

elbow grease *n Facetious* vigorous physical labour, esp. hard rubbing.

elbow room *n* sufficient scope to move or to function.

elder¹ *adj* **1** (of one of two people) born earlier. ✧ *n* **2** an older person: *have some respect for your elders.* **3** a senior member of a tribe, who has authority. **4** (in certain Protestant Churches) a member of the church who has certain administrative, teaching, or preaching powers. ▷ **HISTORY** Old English *eldra*

elder² *n* a shrub or small tree with clusters of small white flowers and dark purple berries. ▷ **HISTORY** Old English *ellern*

elderberry *n, pl* **-ries 1** the fruit of the elder. **2** same as **elder²**.

elderly *adj* **1** rather old. ✧ *pl n* **2 the elderly** old people.

eldest *adj* (of a person, esp. a child) oldest. ▷ **HISTORY** Old English *eldesta*

El Dorado (el dor-**rah**-doe) *n* **1** a fabled city in South America, supposedly rich in treasure. **2** Also: **eldorado** any place of great riches or fabulous opportunity. ▷ **HISTORY** Spanish: the golden (place)

eldritch *adj Poetic, Scot* unearthly or weird. ▷ **HISTORY** origin unknown

elect *vb* **1** to choose (someone) to fill a position by voting for him or her: *she was elected President in 1990.* **2** to choose or decide: *those who elected to stay.* ✧ *adj* **3** voted into office but not yet having taken over from the current office-bearer: *the President elect.* ✧ *pl n* **4 the elect** any group of people specially chosen for some privilege. ▷ **HISTORY** Latin *eligere* to select ▸ **electable** *adj*

election *n* **1 a** a process whereby people vote for a person or party to fill a position: *last month's presidential election.* **b** short for **general election**. **2** the gaining of political power or taking up of a position in an organization as a result of being voted for: *he will be seeking election as the President of Romania.*

a b c d e f g h i j k l m n o p q r s t u v w x y z

A B C D E F G H I J K L M N O P Q R S T U V W X Y Z

electioneering *n* the act of taking an active part in a political campaign, for example by canvassing.

elective *adj* **1** of or based on selection by vote: *an elective office.* **2** not compulsory or necessary: *an elective hysterectomy.*

elector *n* **1** someone who is eligible to vote in an election. **2** (in the Holy Roman Empire) any of the German princes who were entitled to elect a new emperor: *the Elector of Hanover.*

electoral *adj* of or relating to elections: *the electoral system.* ▶ **electorally** *adv*

electoral register *n* the official list of all the people in an area who are eligible to vote in elections.

electorate *n* **1** all the people in an area or country who have the right to vote in an election. **2** the rank or territory of an elector of the Holy Roman Empire.

electric *adj* **1** produced by, transmitting, or powered by electricity: *an electric fire.* **2** very tense or exciting: *the atmosphere was electric.* ✧ *n* **3 electrics** *Brit* an electric circuit or electric appliances. ▷ **HISTORY** Greek *ēlektron* amber (because friction causes amber to become electrically charged)

> **WORD TIP**
> See at **electronic.**

electrical *adj* of or relating to electricity. ▶ **electrically** *adv*

> **WORD TIP**
> See at **electronic.**

electrical conductivity *n Physics* a measure of the ability of a substance to conduct electricity.

electrical energy *n Physics* electricity generated by electrons, ions, or other charged particles.

electrical engineering *n* the branch of engineering concerned with practical applications of electricity and electronics. ▶ **electrical engineer** *n*

electric blanket *n* a blanket fitted with an electric heating element, used to warm a bed.

electric chair *n* (in the US) a chair for executing criminals by passing a strong electric current through them.

electric current *n Electronics* a flow or rate of flow of electric charge through a conductor.

electric eel *n* an eel-like South American freshwater fish, which can stun or kill its prey with a powerful electric shock.

electric field *n Physics* a region of space surrounding a charged particle within which another charged particle experiences a force.

electric generator *n Physics* a device for converting mechanical energy into electricity.

electrician *n* a person trained to install and repair electrical equipment.

electricity *n* **1** a form of energy associated with stationary or moving electrons, ions, or other charged particles. **2** the supply of electricity to houses, factories, etc., for heating, lighting, etc.

> **WORD HISTORY**
> 'Electricity' comes from the Greek word *ēlektron*, meaning 'amber'. The ancient Greeks had found out that if you rub a piece of amber, it will attract small particles by the force that we now understand to be electricity.

electric shock *n* pain and muscular spasms caused by an electric current passing through the body.

electrify *vb* **-fies, -fying, -fied 1** to adapt or equip (a system or device) to work by electricity: *the whole track has now been electrified.* **2** to provide (an area) with electricity. **3** to startle or excite intensely. ▶ **electrification** *n*

electro- *combining form* electric or electrically: *electroconvulsive.* ▷ **HISTORY** Greek *ēlektron* amber; see ELECTRIC

electrocardiograph *n* an instrument for making tracings (**electrocardiograms**) recording the electrical activity of the heart.

electrocute *vb* **-cuting, -cuted** to kill or injure by an electric shock. ▷ **HISTORY** ELECTRO- + (EXE)CUTE ▶ **electrocution** *n*

electrode *n* a small piece of metal used to take an electric current to or from a power source, piece of equipment, or living body.

electrodynamics *n* the branch of physics concerned with the interactions between electrical and mechanical forces.

electroencephalograph (ill-lek-tro-en-**sef**-a-loh-graf) *n* an instrument for making tracings (**electroencephalograms**) recording the electrical activity of the brain.

electrolysis (ill-lek-**troll**-iss-iss) *n* **1** the process of passing an electric current through a liquid in order to produce a chemical reaction in the liquid. **2** the destruction of living tissue, such as hair roots, by an electric current.

electrolyte *n* a solution or molten substance that conducts electricity. ▶ **electrolytic** *adj*

electromagnet *n* a magnet consisting of a coil of wire wound round an iron core through which a current is passed.

electromagnetic *adj* **1** of or operated by an electromagnet. **2** of or relating to electromagnetism. ▶ **electromagnetically** *adv*

electromagnetic induction *n Physics* the process by which a conductor moving through an electric field creates an electric current.

electromagnetic spectrum *n Physics* the complete range of electromagnetic radiation from the longest radio waves to the shortest gamma radiation.

electromagnetic wave *n Physics* a wave of energy produced in an electromagnetic field.

electromagnetism *n* magnetism produced by an electric current.

electromotive *adj Physics* of or producing an electric current.

electromotive force *n Physics* **1** a source of energy that can cause current to flow in an electrical circuit. **2** the rate at which energy is drawn from such a source when a unit of current flows through the circuit, measured in volts.

electron *n Physics* an elementary particle in all atoms that has a negative electrical charge.

electronegative *adj Physics* **1** having a negative electric charge. **2** tending to gain or attract electrons.

electron flow *n Electronics* a continuous stream of electrons from the negative terminal to the positive terminal of a battery or cell.

electronic *adj* **1** (of a device, circuit, or system) containing transistors, silicon chips, etc., which control the current passing through it. **2** making use of electronic systems: *electronic surveillance devices.* ▶ **electronically** *adv*

> ☑ **WORD TIP**
> *Electronic* is used to refer to equipment, such as television sets, computers, etc., in which the current is controlled by transistors, valves, and similar components and also to the components themselves. *Electrical* is used in a more general sense, often to refer to the use of electricity as a whole as opposed to other forms of energy: *electrical engineering; an electrical appliance. Electric,* in many cases used interchangeably with *electrical,* is often restricted to the description of particular devices or to concepts relating to the flow of current: *electric fire; electric charge.*

electronic mail *n* See **e-mail.**

electronic publishing *n* the publication of information on discs, magnetic tape, etc., so that it can be accessed by computer.

electronics *n* the technology concerned with the development, behaviour, and applications of devices and circuits, for example televisions and computers, which make use of electronic components such as transistors or silicon chips.

electron microscope *n* a powerful microscope that uses electrons, rather than light, to produce a magnified image.

electronvolt *n Physics* a unit of energy equal to the work done on an electron accelerated through a potential difference of 1 volt.

electroplate *vb* **-plating, -plated 1** to coat (an object) with metal by dipping it in a special liquid through which an electric current is passed. ✧ *n* **2** electroplated articles collectively.

electropositive *adj Physics* **1** having a positive electric charge. **2** tending to release electrons.

electroscope *n Physics* an apparatus for detecting an electric charge, typically consisting of a rod holding two gold foils that separate when a charge is applied.

electrostatics *n* the branch of physics concerned with static electricity. ▶ **electrostatic** *adj*

elegant *adj* **1** attractive and graceful or stylish. **2** cleverly simple and clear: *an elegant summary.* ▷ **HISTORY** Latin *elegans* tasteful ▶ **elegance** *n* ▶ **elegantly** *adv*

elegiac *adj Literary* sad, mournful, or plaintive.

elegy (**el**-lij-ee) *n, pl* **-gies** a mournful poem or song, esp. a lament for the dead. ▷ **HISTORY** Greek *elegos* lament

> ☑ **WORD TIP**
> Avoid confusion with **eulogy.**

element *n* **1** one of the fundamental components making up a whole. **2** *Chem* any of the known substances that cannot be separated into simpler substances by chemical means. **3** a distinguishable section of a social group: *liberal elements in Polish society.* **4** a metal part in an electrical device, such as a kettle, that changes the electric current into heat. **5** one of the four substances (earth, air, water, and fire) formerly believed to make up the universe. **6** *Maths* any of the members of a set. **7 in one's element** in a situation in which one is happy and at ease: *she was in her element behind the wheel.* **8 elements a** the basic principles of something. **b** weather conditions, esp. wind, rain, and cold: *only 200 braved the elements.* ▷ **HISTORY** Latin *elementum*

elemental *adj* of or like basic and powerful natural forces or passions.

elementary *adj* **1** simple, basic, and straightforward: *elementary precautions.* **2** involving only the most basic principles of a subject: *elementary mathematics.*

elementary particle *n Physics* any of several entities, such as electrons, neutrons, or protons, that are less complex than atoms.

elementary school *n* **1** *Brit* same as **primary school. 2** *US & Canad* a state school for the first six to eight years of a child's education.

elephant *n* a very large four-legged animal that has a very long flexible nose called a trunk, large ears, and two ivory tusks, and lives in Africa or India. ▷ **HISTORY** Greek *elephas*

elephantiasis (el-lee-fan-**tie**-a-siss) *n Pathol* a skin disease, caused by parasitic worms, in which the affected parts of the body become extremely enlarged.

elephantine *adj* like an elephant, esp. in being huge, clumsy, or ponderous.

elevate *vb* **-vating, -vated 1** to raise in rank or status: *she had elevated flirting to an art form.* **2** to lift to a higher place: *this action elevates the upper back.* ▷ **HISTORY** Latin *elevare*

elevated *adj* **1** higher than normal: *elevated cholesterol levels.* **2** (of ideas or pursuits) on a high intellectual or moral level: *elevated discussions about postmodernism.* **3** (of land or part of a building) higher than the surrounding area.

elevation *n* **1** the act of elevating someone or something: *his elevation to the peerage.* **2** height above sea level. **3** a raised area. **4** a scale drawing of one side of a building.

elevator *n* **1** *Austral, US & Canad* a lift for carrying people. **2** a mechanical hoist.

a b c d e f g h i j k l m n o p q r s t u v w x y z

eleven *n* **1** the cardinal number that is the sum of ten and one. **2** a numeral, 11 or XI, representing this number. **3** something representing or consisting of 11 units. **4** a team of 11 players in football, cricket, etc. ✧ *adj* **5** amounting to eleven: *eleven years.* ▷ **HISTORY** Old English *endleofan* ▶ **eleventh** *adj, n*

eleven-plus *n* (in Britain, esp. formerly) an examination taken by children aged 10 or 11 that determines the type of secondary education they will be given.

elevenses *pl n Brit & S African informal* a mid-morning snack.

eleventh hour *n* **1** the latest possible time. ✧ *adj* **eleventh-hour 2** done at the latest possible time: *an eleventh-hour rescue.*

elf *n, pl* **elves** (in folklore) a small mischievous fairy. ▷ **HISTORY** Old English *ælf*

elfin *adj* **1** small and delicate: *her elfin features.* **2** of or relating to elves.

elicit *vb* **1** to bring about (a response or reaction): *her remarks elicited a sharp retort.* **2** to draw out (information) from someone: *a phone call elicited the fact that she had just awakened.* ▷ **HISTORY** Latin *elicere*

elide *vb* **eliding, elided** to omit (a syllable or vowel) from a spoken word. ▷ **HISTORY** Latin *elidere* to knock

eligible *adj* **1** meeting the requirements or qualifications needed: *he may be eligible for free legal services.* **2** *Old-fashioned* desirable as a spouse. ▷ **HISTORY** Latin *eligere* to elect ▶ **eligibility** *n*

eliminate *vb* **-nating, -nated 1** to get rid of (something or someone unwanted, unnecessary, or not meeting the requirements needed): *he can be eliminated from the list of suspects.* **2** to remove (a competitor or team) from a contest, esp. following a defeat: *they were eliminated in the third round.* **3** *Slang* to murder in cold blood: *Stalin had thousands of his former comrades eliminated.* ▷ **HISTORY** Latin *eliminare* to turn out of the house ▶ **elimination** *n*

> ☑ **WORD TIP**
> *Eliminate* is sometimes wrongly used to talk about avoiding the repetition of something undesirable: *we must prevent* (not *eliminate*) *further mistakes of this kind.*

elision *n* omission of a syllable or vowel from a spoken word. ▷ **HISTORY** Latin *elidere* to elide

elite (ill-**eet**) *n* the most powerful, rich, or gifted members of a group or community. ▷ **HISTORY** French

elitism *n* **1** the belief that society should be governed by a small group of people who are superior to everyone else. **2** pride in being part of an elite. ▶ **elitist** *n, adj*

elixir (ill-**ix**-er) *n* **1** an imaginary substance that is supposed to be capable of prolonging life and changing base metals into gold. **2** a liquid medicine mixed with syrup. ▷ **HISTORY** Arabic *al iksīr*

Elizabethan *adj* **1** of or in the reign of Queen Elizabeth I of England (1558–1603). **2** a person who lived during the reign of Queen Elizabeth I.

elk *n* a very large deer of N Europe and Asia with broad flat antlers. ▷ **HISTORY** Old English *eolh*

ellipse *n* an oval shape resembling a flattened circle.

ellipsis (ill-**lip**-siss) *n, pl* **-ses** (-seez) **1** the omission of a word or words from a sentence. **2** *Printing* three dots (...) indicating an omission. ▷ **HISTORY** Greek *elleipein* to leave out

ellipsoid *n Geom* a surface whose plane sections are ellipses or circles.

elliptical *or* **elliptic** *adj* **1** oval-shaped. **2** (of speech or writing) obscure or ambiguous.

> ☑ **WORD TIP**
> The use of *elliptical* to mean *circumlocutory* should be avoided as it may be interpreted wrongly as meaning *condensed* or *concise.*

elm *n* **1** a tall tree with broad leaves. **2** the hard heavy wood of this tree. ▷ **HISTORY** Old English

El Niño (el-**nee**-nyo) *n Meteorol* a warming of the eastern tropical Pacific that occurs every few years and disrupts weather in the region. ▷ **HISTORY** Spanish: The Child, i.e. Christ, referring to the original occurrence at Christmas time

El Niño effect *n Meteorol* unusual and often severe weather conditions set in motion by the occurrence of El Niño.

elocution *n* the art of speaking clearly in public. ▷ **HISTORY** Latin *e-* out + *loqui* to speak ▶ **elocutionist** *n*

elongate (**eel**-long-gate) *vb* **-gating, -gated** to make or become longer. ▷ **HISTORY** Latin *e-* away + *longe* (adverb) far ▶ **elongation** *n*

elope *vb* **eloping, eloped** (of two people) to run away secretly to get married. ▷ **HISTORY** Anglo-French *aloper* ▶ **elopement** *n*

eloquence *n* the ability to speak or write in a skilful and convincing way.

eloquent *adj* **1** (of speech or writing) fluent and persuasive. **2** (of a person) able to speak in a fluent and persuasive manner. **3** visibly or vividly expressive: *he raised an eloquent eyebrow.* ▷ **HISTORY** Latin *e-* out + *loqui* to speak ▶ **eloquently** *adv*

else *adv* **1** in addition or more: *what else do you want to know?* **2** other or different: *it was unlike anything else that had happened.* **3 or else a** if not, then: *tell us soon or else we shall go mad.* **b** *Informal* or something terrible will result: used as a threat: *do it our way or else.* ▷ **HISTORY** Old English *elles*

elsewhere *adv* in or to another place.

ELT English Language Teaching.

elucidate *vb* **-dating, -dated** to make (something obscure or difficult) clear. ▷ **HISTORY** Late Latin *elucidare* to enlighten ▶ **elucidation** *n*

elude *vb* **eluding, eluded 1** to avoid or escape from (someone or something). **2** to fail to be understood or remembered by: *the mysteries of* *commerce elude me.* ▷ **HISTORY** Latin *eludere* to deceive

> ☑ **WORD TIP**
> *Elude* is sometimes wrongly used where *allude* is meant: *he was alluding* (not *eluding*) *to his previous visit to the city.*

elusive *adj* **1** difficult to find or catch. **2** difficult to remember or describe. ▶ **elusiveness** *n*

> ☑ **WORD TIP**
> See at **illusory.**

elver *n* a young eel. ▷ **HISTORY** variant of *eelfare* eel-journey

elves *n* the plural of **elf**.

Elysium (ill-**liz**-zee-um) *n* **1** *Greek myth* the dwelling place of the blessed after death. **2** a state or place of perfect bliss. ▷ **HISTORY** Greek *ēlusion pedion* blessed fields ▶ **Elysian** *adj*

emaciated (im-**mace**-ee-ate-id) *adj* extremely thin through illness or lack of food. ▷ **HISTORY** Latin *macer* thin ▶ **emaciation** *n*

e-mail *or* **email** (ee-mail) *n* **1** the transmission of messages from one computer terminal to another. ✧ *vb* **2** to contact (a person) by e-mail. **3** to send (a message) by e-mail.

emanate (**em**-a-nate) *vb* **-nating, -nated** to come or seem to come from someone or something: *an aura of power emanated from him.* ▷ **HISTORY** Latin *emanare* to flow out ▶ **emanation** *n*

emancipate *vb* **-pating, -pated** to free from social, political, or legal restrictions. ▷ **HISTORY** Latin *emancipare* to give independence (to a son) ▶ **emancipation** *n*

emasculate *vb* **-lating, -lated** to deprive of power or strength. ▷ **HISTORY** Latin *emasculare* to remove the testicles of ▶ **emasculation** *n*

embalm *vb* to preserve (a corpse) by the use of chemicals and oils. ▷ **HISTORY** Old French *embaumer*

embankment *n* a man-made ridge of earth or stone that carries a road or railway or prevents a river or lake from overflowing.

embargo *n, pl* **-goes 1** an order by a government or international body prohibiting trade with a country: *the world trade embargo against Iraq.* ✧ *vb* **-going, -goed 2** to place an official prohibition on. ▷ **HISTORY** Spanish

embark *vb* **1** to go on board (a ship or aircraft). **2 embark on** to begin (a new project or venture). ▷ **HISTORY** Old Provençal *embarcar* ▶ **embarkation** *n*

embarrass *vb* **1** to make (someone) feel shy, ashamed, or guilty about something. **2** to cause political problems for (a government or party). **3** to cause to have financial difficulties. ▷ **HISTORY** Italian *imbarrare* to confine within bars ▶ **embarrassed** *adj* ▶ **embarrassing** *adj* ▶ **embarrassingly** *adv* ▶ **embarrassment** *n*

embassy *n, pl* **-sies 1** the residence or place of business of an ambassador. **2** an ambassador and his or her assistants and staff. ▷ **HISTORY** Old Provençal *ambaisada*

embattled *adj* **1** (of a country) involved in fighting a war, esp. when surrounded by enemies. **2** facing many problems and difficulties: *the embattled Mayor.*

embed *vb* **-bedding, -bedded 1** to fix firmly in a surrounding solid mass: *the boy has shrapnel embedded in his spine.* **2** to fix (an attitude or idea) in a society or in someone's mind: *corruption was deeply embedded in the ruling party.*

embedded clause *n Grammar* a clause that defines or clarifies another element in the sentence.

embedded phrase *n Grammar* a group of words, especially a prepositional phrase, that functions as a single unit and defines or clarifies another element in the sentence.

embellish *vb* **1** to make (something) more attractive by adding decorations. **2** to make (a story) more interesting by adding details which may not be true. ▷ **HISTORY** Old French *embelir* ▶ **embellishment** *n*

ember *n* a smouldering piece of coal or wood remaining after a fire has died. ▷ **HISTORY** Old English *ǣmyrge*

embezzle *vb* **-zling, -zled** to steal (money) that belongs to the company or organization that one works for. ▷ **HISTORY** Anglo-French *embeseiller* to destroy ▶ **embezzler** *n*

embezzlement *n Law* the crime of stealing money from the company or organization that one works for.

embittered *adj* feeling anger and despair as a result of misfortune: *embittered by poverty.* ▶ **embitterment** *n*

emblazon (im-**blaze**-on) *vb* **1** to decorate with a coat of arms, slogan, etc.: *a jacket emblazoned with his band's name.* **2** to proclaim or publicize: *I am not sure he would want his name emblazoned in my column.*

emblem *n* an object or design chosen to symbolize an organization or idea. ▷ **HISTORY** Greek *emblēma* insertion ▶ **emblematic** *adj*

embody *vb* **-bodies, -bodying, -bodied 1** to be an example of or express (an idea or other abstract concept). **2** to include as part of a whole: *the proposal has been embodied in a draft resolution.* ▶ **embodiment** *n*

embolden *vb* to make bold.

embolism *n Pathol* the blocking of a blood vessel by a blood clot, air bubble, etc.

embolus *n, pl* **-li** *Pathol* a blood clot, air bubble, or other stoppage that blocks a small blood vessel. ▷ **HISTORY** Greek *embolos* stopper

emboss *vb* to mould or carve a decoration on (a surface) so that it stands out from the surface. ▷ **HISTORY** Old French *embocer*

embrace *vb* **-bracing, -braced 1** to clasp (someone) with one's arms as an expression of affection or a greeting. **2** to accept eagerly: *he has embraced the Islamic faith.* **3** to include or be made up of: *a church that embraces two cultures.* ✧ *n* **4** an

A B C D E F G H I J K L M N O P Q R S T U V W X Y Z

act of embracing. ▷ **HISTORY** Latin *im-* in + *bracchia* arms

embrasure *n* **1** an opening for a door or window which is wider on the inside of the wall than on the outside. **2** an opening in a battlement or wall, for shooting through. ▷ **HISTORY** French

embrocation *n* a lotion rubbed into the skin to ease sore muscles. ▷ **HISTORY** Greek *brokhē* a moistening

embroider *vb* **1** to do decorative needlework on (a piece of cloth or a garment). **2** to add imaginary details to (a story). ▷ **HISTORY** Old French *embroder* ▶ **embroiderer** *n*

embroidery *n* **1** decorative needlework, usually on cloth or canvas. **2** the act of adding imaginary details to a story.

embroil *vb* to involve (oneself or another person) in problems or difficulties. ▷ **HISTORY** French *embrouiller* ▶ **embroilment** *n*

embryo (**em**-bree-oh) *n, pl* **-bryos 1** an unborn animal or human being in the early stages of development, in humans up to approximately the end of the second month of pregnancy. **2** something in an early stage of development: *the embryo of a serious comic novel.* ▷ **HISTORY** Greek *embruon*

embryology *n* the scientific study of embryos.

embryonic *adj* **1** of or relating to an embryo. **2** in an early stage.

emend *vb* to make corrections or improvements to (a text). ▷ **HISTORY** Latin *e-* out + *mendum* a mistake ▶ **emendation** *n*

emerald *n* **1** a green transparent variety of beryl highly valued as a gem. ✧ *adj* **2** bright green. ▷ **HISTORY** Greek *smaragdos*

emerge *vb* **emerging, emerged 1** to come into view out of something: *two men emerged from the pub.* **2** to come out of a particular state of mind or way of existence: *she emerged from the trance.* **3** to come to the end of a particular event or situation: *no party emerged from the election with a clear majority.* **4** to become apparent, esp. as the result of a discussion or investigation: *it emerged that he had been drinking.* **5** to come into existence over a long period of time: *a new style of dance music emerged in the late 1980s.* ▷ **HISTORY** Latin *emergere* to rise up from ▶ **emergence** *n* ▶ **emergent** *adj*

emergency *n, pl* **-cies 1** an unforeseen or sudden occurrence, esp. of danger demanding immediate action. **2 state of emergency** a time of crisis, declared by a government, during which normal laws and civil rights can be suspended. ✧ *adj* **3** for use in an emergency: *the emergency exit.* **4** made necessary because of an emergency: *emergency surgery.*

emeritus (im-**mer**-rit-uss) *adj* retired, but retaining one's title on an honorary basis: *a professor emeritus.* ▷ **HISTORY** Latin *merere* to deserve

emery *n* a hard greyish-black mineral used for smoothing and polishing. ▷ **HISTORY** Greek *smuris* powder for rubbing

emery board *n* a strip of cardboard coated with crushed emery, for filing one's fingernails.

emetic (im-**met**-ik) *n* **1** a substance that causes vomiting. ✧ *adj* **2** causing vomiting. ▷ **HISTORY** Greek *emetikos*

EMF electromotive force.

emigrate *vb* **-grating, -grated** to leave one's native country to settle in another country. ▷ **HISTORY** Latin *emigrare* ▶ **emigrant** *n, adj* ▶ **emigration** *n*

émigré (**em**-mig-gray) *n* someone who has left his or her native country for political reasons. ▷ **HISTORY** French

eminence *n* **1** the state of being well-known and well-respected. **2** a piece of high ground.

Eminence *n* **Your** *or* **His Eminence** a title used to address or refer to a cardinal.

eminent *adj* well-known and well-respected. ▷ **HISTORY** Latin *eminere* to stand out

eminently *adv* extremely: *eminently sensible.*

emir (em-**meer**) *n* an independent ruler in the Islamic world. ▷ **HISTORY** Arabic *'amīr* commander ▶ **emirate** *n*

emissary *n, pl* **-saries** an agent sent on a mission by a government or head of state. ▷ **HISTORY** Latin *emissarius*

emission *n* **1** the act of giving out heat, light, a smell, etc. **2** energy or a substance given out by something: *exhaust emissions from motor vehicles.*

emit *vb* **emitting, emitted 1** to give or send forth (heat, light, a smell, etc.). **2** to produce (a sound). ▷ **HISTORY** Latin *emittere* to send out

emollient *adj* **1** (of skin cream or lotion) having a softening effect. **2** helping to avoid confrontation; calming: *his emollient political style.* ✧ *n* **3** a cream or lotion that softens the skin. ▷ **HISTORY** Latin *emollire* to soften

emolument *n* fees or wages from employment. ▷ **HISTORY** Latin *emolumentum* benefit; originally fee paid to a miller

emoticon (i-**mote**-i-kon) *n Computers* same as **smiley** (sense 2). ▷ **HISTORY** EMOT(ION) + ICON

emotion *n* **1** any strong feeling, such as joy or fear. **2** the part of a person's character based on feelings rather than thought: *the conflict between emotion and logic.* ▷ **HISTORY** Latin *emovere* to disturb

emotional *adj* **1** of or relating to the emotions: *emotional abuse.* **2** influenced by feelings rather than rational thinking: *he was too emotional to be a good doctor.* **3** appealing to the emotions: *emotional appeals for public support.* **4** showing one's feelings openly, esp. when upset: *he became very emotional and burst into tears.* ▶ **emotionalism** *n* ▶ **emotionally** *adv*

emotive *adj* tending or designed to arouse emotion.

> **WORD TIP**
> *Emotional* is preferred to *emotive* when describing a display of emotion: *he was given an emotional* (not *emotive*) *welcome.*

empathize or **-thise** *vb* **-thizing, -thized** or **-thising, -thised** to sense and understand someone else's feelings as if they were one's own.

empathy *n* the ability to sense and understand someone else's feelings as if they were one's own. ▷ **HISTORY** Greek *empatheia* affection, passion ▶ **empathic** *adj*

emperor *n* a man who rules an empire. ▷ **HISTORY** Latin *imperare* to command

emperor penguin *n* a very large Antarctic penguin with orange-yellow patches on its neck.

emphasis *n, pl* **-ses 1** special importance or significance given to something, such as an object or idea. **2** stress on a particular syllable, word, or phrase in speaking. ▷ **HISTORY** Greek

emphasize or **-sise** *vb* **-sizing, -sized** or **-sising, -sised** to give emphasis or prominence to: *to emphasize her loyalty.*

emphatic *adj* **1** expressed, spoken, or done forcefully: *an emphatic denial of the allegations.* **2** forceful and positive: *he was emphatic about his desire for peace talks.* ▷ **HISTORY** Greek *emphainein* to display ▶ **emphatically** *adv*

emphysema (em-fiss-**see**-ma) *n Pathol* a condition in which the air sacs of the lungs are grossly enlarged, causing breathlessness. ▷ **HISTORY** Greek *emphusēma* a swelling up

empire *n* **1** a group of countries under the rule of a single person or sovereign state. **2** a large industrial organization that is controlled by one person: *the heiress to a jewellery empire.* ▷ **HISTORY** Latin *imperare* to command

empirical *adj* derived from experiment, experience, and observation rather than from theory or logic: *there is no empirical data to support this claim.* ▷ **HISTORY** Greek *empeirikos* practised ▶ **empirically** *adv*

empiricism *n Philosophy* the doctrine that all knowledge derives from experience. ▶ **empiricist** *n*

emplacement *n* a prepared position for an artillery gun.

employ *vb* **1** to hire (someone) to do work in return for money. **2** to keep busy or occupy: *she was busily employed cutting the grass.* **3** to use as a means: *you can employ various methods to cut your heating bills.* ✧ *n* **4 in the employ of** doing regular paid work for: *he is in the employ of The Sunday Times.* ▷ **HISTORY** Old French *emploier* ▶ **employable** *adj*

employee or *US* **employe** *n* a person who is hired to work for someone in return for payment.

employer *n* a person or company that employs workers.

employment *n* **1** the act of employing or state of being employed. **2** a person's work or occupation. **3** the availability of jobs for the population of a town, country, etc.: *the party's commitment to full employment.*

employment tribunal *n Econ* a tribunal that rules on disputes between employees and employers regarding unfair dismissal, redundancy, etc.

emporium *n, pl* **-riums** or **-ria** *Old-fashioned* a large retail shop with a wide variety of merchandise. ▷ **HISTORY** Latin, from Greek *emporos* merchant

empower *vb* to give (someone) the power or authority to do something.

empowerment *n S African* a semi-official slogan for the empowering of previously disadvantaged populations.

empress *n* **1** a woman who rules an empire. **2** the wife or widow of an emperor. ▷ **HISTORY** Latin *imperatrix*

empty *adj* **-tier, -tiest 1** containing nothing. **2** without inhabitants; unoccupied. **3** without purpose, substance, or value: *he contemplated yet another empty weekend.* **4** insincere or trivial: *empty words.* **5** *Informal* drained of energy or emotion. **6** *Maths, logic* (of a set or class) containing no members. ✧ *vb* **-ties, -tying, -tied 7** to make or become empty. **8** to remove from something: *they emptied out the remains of the tin of paint.* ✧ *n, pl* **-ties 9** an empty container, esp. a bottle. ▷ **HISTORY** Old English *æmtig* ▶ **emptiness** *n*

empyrean (em-pie-**ree**-an) *n Poetic* the sky or the heavens. ▷ **HISTORY** Greek *empuros* fiery

EMS European Monetary System: the system enabling some EU members to coordinate their exchange rates.

EMU *Econ* European Monetary Union.

emu *n* a large Australian long-legged bird that cannot fly.

> **WORD HISTORY**
> 'Emu' is from Portuguese *ema*, meaning 'ostrich'. The name was also applied to the birds we now know as the cassowary and the rhea, since emus, cassowaries and rheas all bear some resemblance to ostriches.

EMU European Monetary Union.

emulate *vb* **-lating, -lated** to imitate (someone) in an attempt to do as well as or better than him or her. ▷ **HISTORY** Latin *aemulus* competing with ▶ **emulation** *n* ▶ **emulator** *n*

emulsifier *n* a substance that helps to combine two liquids, esp. a water-based liquid and an oil.

emulsify *vb* **-fies, -fying, -fied** to make or form into an emulsion.

emulsion *n* **1** a mixture of two liquids in which particles of one are suspended evenly throughout the other. **2** *Photog* a light-sensitive coating for paper or film. **3** a type of water-based paint. ▷ **HISTORY** Latin *emulgere* to milk out

enable *vb* **-abling, -abled 1** to provide (someone) with the means or opportunity to do something. **2** to make possible: *to enable the best possible chance of cure.*

enabling act *n Law* a legislative act giving certain powers to a person or organization.

enact *vb* **1** to establish by law: *plans to enact a bill of rights.* **2** to perform (a story or play) by acting. ▶ **enactment** *n*

enamel *n* **1** a coloured glassy coating on the surface of articles made of metal, glass, or pottery.

2 an enamel-like paint or varnish. 3 the hard white substance that covers teeth. ✧ *vb* **-elling, -elled** *or US* **-eling, -eled** 4 to decorate or cover with enamel. ▷ **HISTORY** Old French *esmail*

enamoured *or US* **enamored** *adj* **enamoured of a** in love with. **b** very fond of and impressed by: *he is not enamoured of Moscow.* ▷ **HISTORY** Latin *amor* love

en bloc *adv* as a whole; all together. ▷ **HISTORY** French

encamp *vb Formal* to set up a camp. ▶ **encampment** *n*

encapsulate *vb* **-lating, -lated 1** to put in a concise form; summarize. **2** to enclose in, or as if in, a capsule. ▶ **encapsulation** *n*

encase *vb* **-casing, -cased** to enclose or cover completely: *her arms were encased in plaster.* ▶ **encasement** *n*

encephalitis (en-sef-a-**lite**-iss) *n* inflammation of the brain. ▷ **HISTORY** Greek *en-* in + *kephalē* head ▶ **encephalitic** *adj*

encephalogram *n* an electroencephalogram. ▷ **HISTORY** Greek *en-* in + *kephalē* head + *gramma* drawing

enchant *vb* **1** to delight and fascinate. **2** to cast a spell on. ▷ **HISTORY** Latin *incantare* to chant a spell ▶ **enchanted** *adj* ▶ **enchantment** *n* ▶ **enchanter** *n* ▶ **enchantress** *fem n*

enchilada (en-chill-**lah**-da) *n* a Mexican dish consisting of a tortilla filled with meat, served with chilli sauce.

encircle *vb* **-cling, -cled** to form a circle round. ▶ **encirclement** *n*

enclave *n* a part of a country entirely surrounded by foreign territory: *a Spanish enclave.* ▷ **HISTORY** Latin *in-* in + *clavis* key

enclose *vb* **-closing, -closed 1** to surround completely: *the house enclosed a courtyard.* **2** to include along with something else: *he enclosed a letter with the parcel.*

enclosure *n* **1** an area of land enclosed by a fence, wall, or hedge. **2** something, such as a cheque, enclosed with a letter.

encode *vb* **-coding, -coded** to convert (a message) into code.

encomium *n* a formal expression of praise. ▷ **HISTORY** Latin

encompass *vb* **1** to enclose within a circle; surround. **2** to include all of: *the programme encompasses the visual arts, music, literature, and drama.*

encore *interj* **1** again: used by an audience to demand a short extra performance. ✧ *n* **2** an extra song or piece performed at a concert in response to enthusiastic demand from the audience. ▷ **HISTORY** French

encounter *vb* **1** to meet (someone) unexpectedly. **2** to be faced with: *he had rarely encountered such suffering.* **3** to meet (an opponent or enemy) in a competition or battle. ✧ *n* **4** a casual or unexpected meeting. **5** a game or battle: *a fierce encounter between the army and armed rebels.* ▷ **HISTORY** Latin *in-* in + *contra* against, opposite

encourage *vb* **-aging, -aged 1** to give (someone) the confidence to do something. **2** to stimulate (something or someone) by approval or help. ▷ **HISTORY** French *encourager* ▶ **encouragement** *n* ▶ **encouraging** *adj*

encroach *vb* to intrude gradually on someone's rights or on a piece of land. ▷ **HISTORY** Old French *encrochier* to seize ▶ **encroachment** *n*

encrust *vb* to cover (a surface) with a layer of something, such as jewels or ice. ▶ **encrustation** *n*

encumber *vb* **1** to hinder or impede: *neither was greatly encumbered with social engagements.* **2** to burden with a load or with debts. ▷ **HISTORY** Old French *en-* into + *combre* a barrier

encumbrance *n* something that impedes or is burdensome.

encyclical (en-**sik**-lik-kl) *n* a letter sent by the pope to all Roman Catholic bishops. ▷ **HISTORY** Greek *kuklos* circle

encyclopedia *or* **encyclopaedia** *n* a book or set of books, often in alphabetical order, containing facts about many different subjects or about one particular subject. ▷ **HISTORY** Greek *enkuklios* general + *paideia* education

encyclopedic *or* **encyclopaedic** *adj* (of knowledge or information) very full and thorough; comprehensive.

end *n* **1** one of the two extreme points of something such as a road. **2** the surface at one of the two extreme points of an object: *a pencil with a rubber at one end.* **3** the extreme extent or limit of something: *the end of the runway.* **4** the most distant place or time that can be imagined: *the ends of the earth.* **5** the act or an instance of stopping doing something or stopping something from continuing: *I want to put an end to all the gossip.* **6** the last part of something: *at the end of the story.* **7** a remnant or fragment: *cigarette ends.* **8** death or destruction. **9** the purpose of an action: *he will only use you to achieve his own ends.* **10** *Sport* either of the two defended areas of a playing field. **11 in the end** finally. **12 make ends meet** to have just enough money to meet one's needs. **13 no end** used for emphasis: *these moments give me no end of trouble.* **14 on end** *Informal* without pause or interruption: *for months on end.* **15 the end** *Slang* the worst, esp. beyond the limits of endurance. ✧ *vb* **16** to bring or come to a finish. **17 end it all** *Informal* to commit suicide. ▷ **HISTORY** Old English *ende*

endanger *vb* to put in danger.

endangered *adj* (of a species of animal) in danger of becoming extinct.

endear *vb* to cause to be liked: *his wit endeared him to a great many people.* ▶ **endearing** *adj*

endearment *n* an affectionate word or phrase.

endeavour *or US* **endeavor** *Formal* ✧ *vb* **1** to try (to do something). ✧ *n* **2** an effort to do something. ▷ **HISTORY** Middle English *endeveren*

endemic *adj* present within a localized area or only found in a particular group of people: *he found 100 species of plant endemic to that ridge.* ▷ **HISTORY** Greek *en-* in + *dēmos* the people

ending *n* **1** the last part or conclusion of something: *the film has a happy ending.* **2** the tip or end of something: *nerve endings.*

endive *n* a plant with crisp curly leaves, used in salads. ▷ **HISTORY** Old French

endless *adj* **1** having no end; eternal or infinite. **2** continuing too long or continually recurring: *an endless stream of visitors.* ▶ **endlessly** *adv*

endnote *n* a note printed at the end of an article, chapter or book.

endocrine *adj* of or denoting a gland that secretes hormones directly into the blood stream, or a hormone secreted by such a gland. ▷ **HISTORY** Greek *endon* within + *krinein* to separate

endogenous (en-**dodge**-in-uss) *adj Biol* developing or originating from within.

endolymph *n Physiol* the fluid that fills the membranous labyrinth of the internal ear.

endometrium (end-oh-**meet**-tree-um) *n* the mucous membrane lining the womb. ▷ **HISTORY** Greek *endon* within + *mētra* womb ▶ **endometrial** *adj*

endoneurium *n Anat* the delicate connective tissue surrounding nerve fibres within a bundle.

endorphin *n* any of a group of chemicals found in the brain, which have an effect similar to morphine.

endorse *vb* **-dorsing, -dorsed 1** to give approval or support to. **2** to sign the back of (a cheque) to specify the payee. **3** *Chiefly Brit* to record a conviction on (a driving licence). ▷ **HISTORY** Old French *endosser* to put on the back ▶ **endorsement** *n*

endoskeleton *n Zool* an internal skeleton, such as the bony skeleton of vertebrates.

endothermic *adj* (of a chemical reaction) involving or requiring the absorption of heat.

endow *vb* **1** to provide with a source of permanent income, esp. by leaving money in a will. **2 endowed with** provided with or possessing (a quality or talent). ▷ **HISTORY** Old French *endouer*

endowment *n* **1** the money given to an institution, such as a hospital. **2** a natural talent or quality.

endowment assurance *or* **insurance** *n* a kind of life insurance that pays a specified sum directly to the policyholder at a designated date or to his or her beneficiary should he or she die before this date.

end product *n* the final result of a process.

endurance *n* the ability to withstand prolonged hardship.

endure *vb* **-during, -dured 1** to bear (hardship) patiently: *the children allegedly endured sexual abuse.* **2** to tolerate or put up with: *I cannot endure your disloyalty any longer.* **3** to last for a long time. ▷ **HISTORY** Latin *indurare* to harden ▶ **endurable** *adj*

enduring *adj* long-lasting.

endways *or esp US & Canad* **endwise** *adv* having the end forwards or upwards.

enema (**en**-im-a) *n Med* a quantity of fluid inserted into the rectum to empty the bowels, for example before an operation. ▷ **HISTORY** Greek: injection

enemy *n, pl* **-mies 1** a person who is hostile or opposed to a person, group, or idea. **2** a hostile nation or people. **3** something that harms or opposes something: *oil is an enemy of the environment.* RELATED ADJECTIVE ➧ **inimical** ✧ *adj* **4** of or belonging to an enemy: *enemy troops.* ▷ **HISTORY** Latin *inimicus* hostile

energetic *adj* **1** having or showing energy and enthusiasm: *an energetic campaigner for democracy.* **2** involving a lot of movement and physical effort: *energetic exercise.* ▶ **energetically** *adv*

energize *or* **-ise** *vb* **-gizing, -gized** *or* **-gising, -gised** to stimulate or enliven.

energy *n, pl* **-gies 1** capacity for intense activity; vigour. **2** intensity or vitality of action or expression; forcefulness. **3** *Physics* the capacity to do work and overcome resistance. **4** a source of power, such as electricity. ▷ **HISTORY** Greek *energeia* activity

energy drink *n* a soft drink supposed to boost the drinker's energy levels.

energy transfer *n Physics* the displacement of energy from one object or substance to another.

enervate *vb* **-vating, -vated** to deprive of strength or vitality. ▷ **HISTORY** Latin *enervare* to remove the nerves from ▶ **enervating** *adj* ▶ **enervation** *n*

enfant terrible (**on**-fon ter-**reeb**-la) *n, pl* **enfants terribles** a talented but unconventional or indiscreet person. ▷ **HISTORY** French, literally: terrible child

enfeeble *vb* **-bling, -bled** to make (someone or something) weak.

enfilade *Mil* ✧ *n* **1** a burst of gunfire sweeping from end to end along a line of troops. ✧ *vb* **-lading, -laded 2** to attack with an enfilade. ▷ **HISTORY** French *enfiler* to thread on string

enfold *vb* **1** to cover (something) by, or as if by, wrapping something round it: *darkness enfolded the city.* **2** to embrace or hug.

enforce *vb* **-forcing, -forced 1** to ensure that (a law or decision) is obeyed. **2** to impose (obedience) by, or as if by, force. ▶ **enforceable** *adj* ▶ **enforcement** *n*

enfranchise *vb* **-chising, -chised** to grant (a person or group of people) the right to vote. ▶ **enfranchisement** *n*

engage *vb* **-gaging, -gaged 1** Also: **be engaged** to take part or participate: *he engaged in criminal and illegal acts; they were engaged in espionage.* **2** to involve (a person or his or her attention) intensely: *there's nothing to engage the intellect in this film.* **3** to employ (someone) to do something. **4** to promise to do something. **5** *Mil* to begin a battle with. **6** to bring (part of a machine or other mechanism) into operation, esp. by causing components to interlock. **7 engage in conversation** to start a conversation with. ▷ **HISTORY** Old French *en-* in + *gage* a pledge

A B C D E F G H I J K L M N O P Q R S T U V W X Y Z

engaged *adj* **1** having made a promise to get married. **2** (of a telephone line or a toilet) already being used.

engagement *n* **1** a business or social appointment. **2** the period when a couple has agreed to get married but the wedding has not yet taken place. **3** a limited period of employment, esp. in the performing arts. **4** a battle.

engaging *adj* pleasant and charming. ▸ **engagingly** *adv*

engender *vb* to produce (a particular feeling, atmosphere, or situation). ▷ HISTORY Latin *ingenerare*

engine *n* **1** any machine designed to convert energy into mechanical work, esp. one used to power a vehicle. **2** a railway locomotive. ▷ HISTORY Latin *ingenium* nature, talent

engineer *n* **1** a person trained in any branch of engineering. **2** a person who repairs and maintains mechanical or electrical devices. **3** a soldier trained in engineering and construction work. **4** an officer responsible for a ship's engines. **5** *US & Canad* a train driver. ✧ *vb* **6** to cause or plan (an event or situation) in a clever or devious manner. **7** to design or construct as a professional engineer.

engineering *n* the profession of applying scientific principles to the design and construction of engines, cars, buildings, bridges, roads, and electrical machines.

English *adj* **1** of England or the English language. ✧ *n* **2** the principal language of Britain, Ireland, Australia, New Zealand, the US, Canada, and several other countries. ✧ *pl n* **3 the English** the people of England.

Englishman *or fem* **Englishwoman** *n, pl* **-men** *or* **-women** a person from England.

engorge *vb* **-gorging, -gorged** *Pathol* to clog or become clogged with blood. ▸ **engorgement** *n*

engrave *vb* **-graving, -graved 1** to carve or etch a design or inscription into (a surface). **2** to print (designs or characters) from a plate into which they have been cut or etched. **3** to fix deeply or permanently in the mind. ▷ HISTORY *en-* in + obsolete *grave* to carve ▸ **engraver** *n*

engraving *n* **1** a printing surface that has been engraved. **2** a print made from this.

engross (en-**groce**) *vb* to occupy the attention of (someone) completely. ▷ HISTORY *en-* in + Latin *grossus* thick ▸ **engrossing** *adj*

engulf *vb* **1** to immerse, plunge, or swallow up: *engulfed by flames.* **2** to overwhelm: *a terrible fear engulfed her.*

enhance *vb* **-hancing, -hanced** to improve or increase in quality, value, or power: *grilling on the barbecue enhances the flavour.* ▷ HISTORY Old French *enhaucier* ▸ **enhancement** *n* ▸ **enhancer** *n*

enigma *n* something or someone that is mysterious or puzzling. ▷ HISTORY Greek *ainissesthai* to speak in riddles ▸ **enigmatic** *adj* ▸ **enigmatically** *adv*

enjambment *or* **enjambement** (in-**jam**-ment) *n Prosody* the running over of a sentence from one line of verse into the next. ▷ HISTORY French: a straddling

enjoin *vb* **1** to order (someone) to do something. **2** to impose (a particular kind of behaviour) on someone: *the sect enjoins poverty on its members.* **3** *Law* to prohibit (someone) from doing something by an injunction. ▷ HISTORY Old French *enjoindre*

enjoy *vb* **1** to receive pleasure from. **2** to have or experience (something, esp. something good): *many fat people enjoy excellent health.* **3 enjoy oneself** to have a good time. ▷ HISTORY Old French *enjoir* ▸ **enjoyable** *adj* ▸ **enjoyably** *adv* ▸ **enjoyment** *n*

enlarge *vb* **-larging, -larged 1** to make or grow larger. **2 enlarge on** to speak or write about in greater detail. ▸ **enlargement** *n* ▸ **enlarger** *n*

enlighten *vb* to give information or understanding to. ▸ **enlightening** *adj*

enlightened *adj* **1** rational and having beneficial effects: *an enlightened approach to social welfare.* **2** (of a person) tolerant and unprejudiced.

enlightenment *n* the act of enlightening or the state of being enlightened.

enlist *vb* **1** to enter the armed forces. **2** to obtain (someone's help or support). ▸ **enlistment** *n*

enliven *vb* to make lively, cheerful, or bright. ▸ **enlivening** *adj*

en masse *adv* all together; as a group. ▷ HISTORY French

enmeshed *adj* deeply involved: *enmeshed in turmoil.*

enmity *n* a feeling of hostility or ill will. ▷ HISTORY Latin *inimicus* hostile

ennoble *vb* **-bling, -bled 1** to make (someone) a member of the nobility. **2** to make (someone or his or her life) noble or dignified: *poverty does not ennoble people.*

ennui (on-**nwee**) *n Literary* boredom and dissatisfaction resulting from lack of activity or excitement. ▷ HISTORY French

enormity *n* **1** extreme wickedness. **2** (*pl* **-ties**) an act of great wickedness. **3** the vastness or extent of a problem or difficulty.

> **WORD TIP**
> In modern English, it is common to talk about the *enormity* of something such as a task or a problem, but one should not talk about the *enormity* of an object or area: *distribution is a problem because of India's enormous size* (not *India's enormity*).

enormous *adj* unusually large in size, extent, or degree. ▷ HISTORY Latin *e-* out of, away from + *norma* rule, pattern ▸ **enormously** *adv*

enough *adj* **1** as much or as many as necessary. **2 that's enough!** used to stop someone behaving in a particular way. ✧ *pron* **3** an adequate amount or number: *I don't know enough about the subject to be able to speak about it.* ✧ *adv* **4** as much as necessary. **5** fairly or quite: *that's a common enough experience.* **6** very: used to give emphasis to the preceding word: *funnily enough, I wasn't alarmed.*

7 just adequately: *he sang well enough.*
▷ **HISTORY** Old English *genōh*

en passant (on pass-**on**) *adv* in passing: *references made en passant.* ▷ **HISTORY** French

enquire *vb* **-quiring, -quired** same as **inquire**. ▶ **enquiry** *n*

enraptured *adj* filled with delight and fascination.

enrich *vb* **1** to improve or increase the quality or value of: *his poetry has vastly enriched the English language.* **2** to improve in nutritional value, colour, or flavour: *a sauce enriched with beer.* **3** to make wealthy or wealthier. ▶ **enriched** *adj* ▶ **enrichment** *n*

enrol *or US* **enroll** *vb* **-rolling, -rolled** to become or cause to become a member. ▶ **enrolment** *or US* **enrollment** *n*

en route *adv* on or along the way.
▷ **HISTORY** French

ensconce *vb* **-sconcing, -sconced** to settle firmly or comfortably. ▷ **HISTORY** Middle English *en-* in + *sconce* fortification

ensemble (on-**som**-bl) *n* **1** all the parts of something considered as a whole. **2** the complete outfit of clothes a person is wearing. **3** a group of musicians or actors performing together. **4** *Music* a passage in which all or most of the performers are playing or singing at once. ▷ **HISTORY** French: together

enshrine *vb* **-shrining, -shrined** to contain and protect (an idea or right) in a society, legal system, etc.: *the university's independence is enshrined in its charter.*

enshroud *vb* to cover or hide (an object) completely, as if by draping something over it: *fog enshrouded the forest.*

ensign *n* **1** a flag flown by a ship to indicate its nationality. **2** any flag or banner. **3** (in the US Navy) a commissioned officer of the lowest rank. **4** (formerly, in the British infantry) a commissioned officer of the lowest rank. ▷ **HISTORY** Latin *insignia* badges

enslave *vb* **-slaving, -slaved** to make a slave of (someone). ▶ **enslavement** *n*

ensnare *vb* **-snaring, -snared 1** to trap or gain power over (someone) by dishonest or underhand means. **2** to catch (an animal) in a snare.

ensue *vb* **-suing, -sued 1** to happen next. **2** to occur as a consequence: *if glaucoma is not treated, blindness can ensue.* ▷ **HISTORY** Latin *in-* in + *sequi* to follow ▶ **ensuing** *adj*

en suite *adv* (of a bathroom) connected to a bedroom and entered directly from it.
▷ **HISTORY** French, literally: in sequence

ensure *or esp US* **insure** *vb* **-suring, -sured 1** to make certain: *we must ensure that similar accidents do not happen again.* **2** to make safe or protect: *female athletes should take extra iron to ensure against anaemia.*

ENT *Med* ear, nose, and throat.

entablature *n Archit* the part of a classical building supported by the columns, consisting of an architrave, a frieze, and a cornice.
▷ **HISTORY** Italian *intavolatura* something put on a table, hence, something laid flat

entail *vb* **1** to bring about or impose inevitably: *few women enter marriage knowing what it really entails.* **2** *Brit, Austral & NZ property law* to restrict the ability to inherit (a piece of property) to designated heirs. ▷ **HISTORY** Middle English *en-* in + *taille* limitation

entangle *vb* **-gling, -gled 1** to catch very firmly in something, such as a net or wire: *a fishing line had entangled his legs.* **2** to involve in a complicated series of problems or difficulties: *he entangles himself in contradictions.* **3** to involve in a troublesome relationship: *she kept getting entangled with unsuitable boyfriends.*
▶ **entanglement** *n*

entente (on-**tont**) *n* short for **entente cordiale**.
▷ **HISTORY** French: understanding

entente cordiale (cord-ee-**ahl**) *n* a friendly understanding between two or more countries.
▷ **HISTORY** French: cordial understanding

enter *vb* **1** to come or go into (a particular place): *he entered the room.* **2** to join (a party or organization). **3** to become involved in or take part in: *1500 schools entered the competition.* **4** to become suddenly present or noticeable in: *a note of anxiety entered his voice.* **5** to record (an item) in a journal or list. **6** *Theatre* to come on stage: used as a stage direction: *enter Joseph.* **7** to begin (a new process or period of time): *the occupation of the square has entered its eleventh day.* ▷ **HISTORY** Latin *intrare*

enteric (en-**ter**-ik) *adj* of the intestines.
▷ **HISTORY** Greek *enteron* intestine

enteritis (en-ter-**rite**-iss) *n* inflammation of the small intestine.

enterprise *n* **1** a business firm. **2** a project or undertaking, esp. one that requires boldness or effort. **3** boldness and energy. ▷ **HISTORY** Old French *entreprendre* to undertake

enterprise zone *n* an inner-city area where businesses are given incentives to create jobs.

enterprising *adj* full of boldness and initiative.
▶ **enterprisingly** *adv*

entertain *vb* **1** to provide amusement for (a person or audience). **2** to show hospitality to (guests). **3** to consider (an idea or suggestion).
▷ **HISTORY** Old French *entre-* mutually + *tenir* to hold

entertainer *n* a person who entertains, esp. professionally.

entertaining *adj* **1** interesting, amusing, and enjoyable. ✧ *n* **2** the provision of hospitality to guests: *the smart kitchen is perfect for entertaining.*

entertainment *n* **1** enjoyment and interest: *a match of top-quality entertainment and goals.* **2** an act or show that entertains, or such acts and shows collectively.

enthral *or US* **enthrall** (en-**thrawl**) *vb* **-thralling, -thralled** to hold the attention or interest of. ▶ **enthralling** *adj* ▶ **enthralment** *or US* **enthrallment** *n*

enthrone *vb* **-throning, -throned 1** to place (a person) on a throne in a ceremony to mark the beginning of his or her new role as a monarch or bishop. **2** to give an important or prominent position to (something): *the religious fundamentalism now enthroned in American life.* ▶ **enthronement** *n*

enthuse *vb* **-thusing, -thused** to feel or cause to feel enthusiasm.

enthusiasm *n* ardent and lively interest or eagerness: *your enthusiasm for literature.* ▷ HISTORY Greek *enthousiazein* to be possessed by a god

enthusiast *n* a person who is very interested in and keen on something. ▶ **enthusiastic** *adj* ▶ **enthusiastically** *adv*

entice *vb* **-ticing, -ticed** to attract (someone) away from one place or activity to another. ▷ HISTORY Old French *enticier* ▶ **enticement** *n* ▶ **enticing** *adj*

entire *adj* made up of or involving all of something, including every detail, part, or aspect. ▷ HISTORY Latin *integer* whole ▶ **entirely** *adv*

entirety *n, pl* **-ties 1** all of a person or thing: *you must follow this diet for the entirety of your life.* **2 in its entirety** as a whole.

entitle *vb* **-tling, -tled 1** to give (someone) the right to do or have something. **2** to give a name or title to (a book or film). ▶ **entitlement** *n*

entity *n, pl* **-ties** something that exists in its own right and not merely as part of a bigger thing. ▷ HISTORY Latin *esse* to be

entomb *vb* **1** to place (a corpse) in a tomb. **2** to bury or trap: *a circulatory system entombed in fat.* ▶ **entombment** *n*

entomology *n* the study of insects. ▷ HISTORY Greek *entomon* insect ▶ **entomological** *adj* ▶ **entomologist** *n*

entourage (**on**-toor-ahzh) *n* a group of people who assist or travel with an important or well-known person. ▷ HISTORY French *entourer* to surround

entozoon (en-toe-**zoe**-on) *n, pl* **-zoa** (-**zoe**-a) a parasite, such as a tapeworm, that lives inside another animal.

entrails *pl n* **1** the internal organs of a person or animal; intestines. **2** the innermost parts of anything. ▷ HISTORY Latin *interanea* intestines

entrance[1] *n* **1** something, such as a door or gate, through which it is possible to enter a place. **2** the act of coming into a place, esp. with reference to the way in which it is done: *she made a sudden startling entrance.* **3** *Theatre* the act of appearing on stage. **4** the right to enter a place: *he refused her entrance because she was carrying her Scottie dog.* **5** ability or permission to join or become involved with a group or organization: *entrance to the profession should be open to men and women alike.* ✧ *adj* **6** necessary in order to enter something: *they have paid entrance fees for English-language courses.*

entrance[2] *vb* **-trancing, -tranced** to fill with delight. ▶ **entrancement** *n* ▶ **entrancing** *adj*

entrant *n* a person who enters a university, competition, etc.

entrap *vb* **-trapping, -trapped 1** to trick (someone) into danger or difficulty. **2** to catch in a trap. ▶ **entrapment** *n*

entreat *vb* to ask (someone) earnestly to do something. ▷ HISTORY Old French *entraiter*

entreaty *n, pl* **-treaties** an earnest request or plea.

entrée (**on**-tray) *n* **1** the right to enter a place. **2** a dish served before a main course. **3** *Chiefly US* the main course. ▷ HISTORY French

entrench *vb* **1** to fix or establish firmly: *the habit had become entrenched.* **2** *Mil* to fortify (a position) by digging trenches around it. ▶ **entrenchment** *n*

entrepreneur *n* the owner of a business who attempts to make money by risk and initiative. ▷ HISTORY French ▶ **entrepreneurial** *adj*

entropy (**en**-trop-ee) *n* **1** *Formal* lack of pattern or organization. **2** *Physics* a thermodynamic quantity that represents the amount of energy present in a system that cannot be converted into work because it is tied up in the atomic structure of the system. ▷ HISTORY Greek *entropē* a turning towards

entrust *vb* **1** to give (someone) a duty or responsibility: *Miss Conway, who was entrusted with the child's education.* **2** to put (something) into the care of someone: *he stole all the money we had entrusted to him.*

> **☑ WORD TIP**
>
> It is usually considered incorrect to talk about *entrusting* someone *to do* something: *the army cannot be trusted* (not *entrusted*) *to carry out orders.*

entry *n, pl* **-tries 1** something, such as a door or gate, through which it is possible to enter a place. **2** the act of coming in to a place, esp. with reference to the way in which it is done. **3** the right to enter a place: *he was refused entry to Britain.* **4** the act of joining an organization or group: *Britain's entry into the EU.* **5** a brief note, article, or group of figures in a diary, book, or computer file. **6** a quiz form, painting, etc., submitted in an attempt to win a competition. **7** a person, horse, car, etc., entering a competition. ✧ *adj* **8** necessary in order to enter something: *entry fee.*

entry-level *adj* **1** (of a job or worker) at the most elementary level in a career structure. **2** (of a product) most appropriate for use by a beginner: *an entry-level camera.*

entwine *vb* **-twining, -twined** to twist together or round something else.

E number *n* any of a series of numbers with the prefix E- indicating a specific food additive recognized by the EU.

enumerate *vb* **-ating, -ated 1** to name or list one by one. **2** to count. **3** *Canad* to compile the voting list for an area. ▷ HISTORY Latin *e-* out + *numerare* to count ▶ **enumeration** *n* ▶ **enumerator** *n*

enunciate *vb* **-ating, -ated 1** to pronounce (words) clearly. **2** to state precisely or formally. ▷ **HISTORY** Latin *enuntiare* to declare ▶ **enunciation** *n*

enuresis (en-yoo-**reece**-iss) *n* involuntary urination, esp. during sleep. ▷ **HISTORY** Greek *en-* in + *ouron* urine

envelop *vb* to cover, surround, or enclose. ▷ **HISTORY** Old French *envoluper* ▶ **envelopment** *n*

envelope *n* **1** a flat covering of paper, that can be sealed, used to enclose a letter, etc. **2** any covering, wrapper, or enclosing structure: *an envelope of filo pastry.* **3** *Geom* a curve that is tangential to each one of a group of curves. ▷ **HISTORY** French *envelopper* to wrap round

enviable *adj* so desirable or fortunate that it is likely to cause envy. ▶ **enviably** *adv*

envious *adj* feeling, showing, or resulting from envy. ▶ **enviously** *adv*

environment (en-**vire**-on-ment) *n* **1** the external conditions or surroundings in which people live: *working in a multicultural environment.* **2** *Ecology* the natural world of land, sea, air, plants, and animals: *nuclear waste must be prevented from leaking into the environment.* ▷ **HISTORY** French *environs* surroundings ▶ **environmental** *adj*

environmentalist *n* a person concerned with the protection and preservation of the natural environment.

environs *pl n* a surrounding area, esp. the outskirts of a city.

envisage *or US* **envision** *vb* **-aging, -aged** *or* **-ioning, -ioned** to believe to be possible or likely in the future: *the commission envisages a mix of government and private funding.* ▷ **HISTORY** French *en-* in + *visage* face

> ☑ **WORD TIP**
> It was formerly considered incorrect to use a clause after *envisage* as in *it is envisaged that the new centre will cost £40 million*, but this use is now acceptable.

envoy *n* **1** a messenger or representative. **2** a diplomat ranking next below an ambassador. ▷ **HISTORY** French *envoyer* to send

envy *n, pl* **-vies 1** a feeling of discontent aroused by someone else's possessions, achievements, or qualities. **2** something that causes envy: *their standards are the envy of the world.* ✧ *vb* **-vies, -vying, -vied 3** to wish that one had the possessions, achievements, or qualities of (someone else). ▷ **HISTORY** Latin *invidia* ▶ **envyingly** *adv*

enzyme *n* any of a group of complex proteins, that act as catalysts in specific biochemical reactions. ▷ **HISTORY** Greek *en-* in + *zumē* leaven ▶ **enzymatic** *adj*

Eocene (ee-oh-seen) *adj* of the epoch of geological time about 55 million years ago. ▷ **HISTORY** Greek *ēōs* dawn + *kainos* new

Eolithic *adj* of the early period of the Stone Age, when crude stone tools were used.

EP *n* an extended-play gramophone record, which is 7 inches in diameter and has a longer recording on each side than a single does.

epaulette *n* a piece of ornamental material on the shoulder of a garment, esp. a military uniform. ▷ **HISTORY** French

epeirogeny (eh-pye-**ro**-dgi-nee) *or* **epeirogenesis** (ee-pye-ro-**ge**-ne-sis) *n Geol* the formation of continents by relatively slow displacements of the earth's crust. ▷ **HISTORY** Greek *ēpeiros* continent + *-geny*, from *-genēs* born ▶ **epeirogenic** *or* **epeirogenetic** *adj*

ephedrine (**eff**-fid-dreen) *n* an alkaloid used for the treatment of asthma and hay fever. ▷ **HISTORY** *Ephedra*, genus of plants which produce it

ephemera (if-**fem**-a-ra) *pl n* items designed to last only for a short time, such as programmes or posters.

ephemeral *adj* lasting only for a short time. ▷ **HISTORY** Greek *hēmera* day

epic *n* **1** a long exciting book, poem, or film, usually telling of heroic deeds. **2** a long narrative poem telling of the deeds of a legendary hero. ✧ *adj* **3** very large or grand: *a professional feud of epic proportions.* ▷ **HISTORY** Greek *epos* word, song

epicene *adj* (esp. of a man) having characteristics or features which are not definitely male or female. ▷ **HISTORY** Greek *epikoinos* common to many

epicentre *or US* **epicenter** *n* the point on the earth's surface immediately above the origin of an earthquake. ▷ **HISTORY** Greek *epi* above + *kentron* point

epic theatre *n Theatre* drama that creates alienation by the use of distancing devices such as narration, masks, and placards.

epicure *n* a person who enjoys good food and drink. ▷ **HISTORY** after *Epicurus*, Greek philosopher, who held that pleasure is the highest good ▶ **epicurism** *n*

epicurean *adj* **1** devoted to sensual pleasures, esp. food and drink. ✧ *n* **2** same as **epicure**. ▶ **epicureanism** *n*

epidemic *n* **1** a widespread occurrence of a disease. **2** a rapid development or spread of something: *an epidemic of rape.* ✧ *adj* **3** (esp. of a disease) affecting many people in an area: *stress has now reached epidemic proportions.* ▷ **HISTORY** Greek *epi* among + *dēmos* people

epidemiology (ep-pid-deem-ee-**ol**-a-jee) *n* the branch of medical science concerned with the occurrence and control of diseases in populations. ▶ **epidemiologist** *n*

epidermis *n* the thin protective outer layer of the skin. ▷ **HISTORY** Greek *epi* upon + *derma* skin ▶ **epidermal** *adj*

epidural (ep-pid-**dure**-al) *adj* **1** on or over the outermost membrane covering the brain and spinal cord (**dura mater**). ✧ *n* **2 a** an injection of anaesthetic into the space outside the outermost membrane enveloping the spinal cord. **b** anaesthesia produced by this method. ▷ **HISTORY** from *dura mater*

epiglottis *n* a thin flap of cartilage at the back of the mouth that covers the entrance to the larynx during swallowing. ▷ **HISTORY** Greek *epi* upon + *glōtta* tongue

epigram *n* **1** a witty remark. **2** a short poem with a witty ending. ▷ **HISTORY** Greek *epi* upon + *graphein* to write ▸ **epigrammatic** *adj*

epigraph *n* **1** a quotation at the beginning of a book. **2** an inscription on a monument or building. ▷ **HISTORY** Greek *epi* upon + *graphein* to write

epilepsy *n* a disorder of the central nervous system which causes periodic loss of consciousness and sometimes convulsions. ▷ **HISTORY** Greek *epi* upon + *lambanein* to take

epileptic *adj* **1** of or having epilepsy. ✧ *n* **2** a person who has epilepsy.

epilogue *n* a short concluding passage or speech at the end of a book or play. ▷ **HISTORY** Greek *epi* upon + *logos* word, speech

epineurium *n Anat* a sheath of connective tissue around two or more bundles of nerve fibres.

Epiphany (ip-**piff**-a-nee) *n, pl* **-nies** a Christian festival held on the 6th of January commemorating, in the Western church, the manifestation of Christ to the Magi and, in the Eastern church, the baptism of Christ. ▷ **HISTORY** Greek *epiphaneia* an appearing

epiphyte *n* a plant that grows on another plant but is not parasitic on it. ▷ **HISTORY** Greek, from *epi* upon + *phusis* growth ▸ **epiphytic, epiphytal** *or* **epiphytical** *adj*

episcopacy (ip-**piss**-kop-a-see) *n* **1** government of a Church by bishops. **2** (*pl* **-cies**) same as **episcopate**.

episcopal (ip-**piss**-kop-al) *adj* of or relating to bishops. ▷ **HISTORY** Greek *episkopos* overseer

Episcopal Church *n* (in Scotland and the US) a self-governing branch of the Anglican Church.

episcopalian *adj also* **episcopal 1** practising or advocating Church government by bishops. ✧ *n* **2** an advocate of such Church government.

Episcopalian (ip-piss-kop-**pale**-ee-an) *adj* **1** of or relating to the Episcopal Church. ✧ *n* **2** a member of this Church. ▸ **Episcopalianism** *n*

episcopate (ip-**piss**-kop-it) *n* **1** the office, status, or term of office of a bishop. **2** bishops collectively.

episiotomy (ip-peez-ee-**ot**-tom-ee) *n, pl* **-tomies** an operation involving cutting into the area between the genitals and the anus sometimes performed during childbirth to make the birth easier.

episode *n* **1** an event or series of events. **2** any of the sections into which a novel or a television or radio serial is divided. ▷ **HISTORY** Greek *epi* in addition + *eisodios* coming in

episodic *adj* **1** resembling or relating to an episode. **2** occurring at irregular and infrequent intervals.

epistemology (ip-iss-stem-**ol**-a-jee) *n* the theory of knowledge, esp. the critical study of its validity, methods, and scope. ▷ **HISTORY** Greek *epistēmē* knowledge ▸ **epistemological** *adj* ▸ **epistemologist** *n*

epistle *n* **1** *Formal or humorous* a letter. **2** a literary work in letter form, esp. a poem. ▷ **HISTORY** Greek *epistolē*

Epistle *n New Testament* any of the letters written by the apostles.

epistolary *adj* **1** of or relating to letters. **2** (of a novel) presented in the form of a series of letters.

epitaph *n* **1** a commemorative inscription on a tombstone. **2** a commemorative speech or written passage. ▷ **HISTORY** Greek *epi* upon + *taphos* tomb

epithelium *n, pl* **-lia** *Anat* a cellular tissue covering the external and internal surfaces of the body. ▷ **HISTORY** Greek *epi* upon + *thēlē* nipple ▸ **epithelial** *adj*

epithet *n* a word or short phrase used to describe someone or something: *these tracks truly deserve that overworked epithet 'classic'.* ▷ **HISTORY** Greek *epitithenai* to add

epitome (ip-**pit**-a-mee) *n* **1** a person or thing that is a typical example of a characteristic or class: *the epitome of rural tranquillity.* **2** a summary, esp. of a written work. ▷ **HISTORY** Greek *epitemnein* to abridge

epitomize *or* **-mise** *vb* **-mizing, -mized** *or* **-mising, -mised** to be or make a perfect or typical example of.

EPNS electroplated nickel silver.

epoch (**ee**-pok) *n* **1** a long period of time marked by some predominant characteristic: *the cold-war epoch.* **2** the beginning of a new or distinctive period: *the invention of nuclear weapons marked an epoch in the history of warfare.* **3** *Geol* a unit of time within a period during which a series of rocks is formed. ▷ **HISTORY** Greek *epokhē* cessation ▸ **epochal** *adj*

epoch-making *adj* very important or significant.

epode *Poetry* ✧ *n* **1** the part of a Greek lyric ode that follows the strophe and the antistrophe. **2** a type of poem composed of couplets in which a long line is followed by a shorter one.

eponymous (ip-**pon**-im-uss) *adj* **1** (of a person) being the person after whom a literary work, film, etc., is named: *the eponymous heroine in the film of Jane Eyre.* **2** (of a literary work, film, etc.) named after its central character or creator: *The Stooges' eponymous debut album.* ▷ **HISTORY** Greek *epōnumos* giving a significant name

EPOS *Brit* electronic point of sale.

epoxy *Chem* ✧ *adj* **1** of or containing an oxygen atom joined to two different groups that are themselves joined to other groups. **2** of or consisting of an epoxy resin. ✧ *n, pl* **epoxies 3** an epoxy resin. ▷ **HISTORY** Greek *epi* upon + OXY(GEN)

epoxy resin *n* a tough resistant thermosetting synthetic resin, used in laminates and adhesives.

EPROM n *Computers* erasable programmable read-only memory: a storage device that can be reprogrammed to hold different data.

Epsom salts *pl n* a medicinal preparation of hydrated magnesium sulphate, used to empty the bowels. ▷ **HISTORY** after *Epsom,* a town in England

equable (**ek**-wab-bl) *adj* **1** even-tempered and reasonable. **2** (of a climate) not varying much throughout the year, and neither very hot nor very cold. ▷ **HISTORY** Latin *aequabilis* ▶ **equably** *adv*

equal *adj* **1** identical in size, quantity, degree, or intensity. **2** having identical privileges, rights, or status. **3** applying in the same way to all people or in all circumstances: *equal rights.* **4 equal to** having the necessary strength, ability, or means for: *she was equal to any test the corporation put to her.* ✧ *n* **5** a person or thing equal to another. ✧ *vb* **equalling, equalled** *or US* **equaling, equaled 6** to be equal to; match. **7** to make or do something equal to: *he has equalled his world record in the men's 100 metres.* ▷ **HISTORY** Latin *aequalis* ▶ **equally** *adv*

> **WORD TIP**
> The use of *more equal* as in *from now on their relationship will be a more equal one* is acceptable in modern English usage. *Equally* is preferred to *equally as* in sentences such as *reassuring the victims is equally important. Just as* is preferred to *equally as* in sentences such as *their surprise was just as great as his.*

equality *n, pl* **-ties** the state of being equal.

equalize *or* **-ise** *vb* **-izing, -ized** *or* **-ising, -ised 1** to make equal or uniform. **2** (in a sport) to reach the same score as one's opponent or opponents. ▶ **equalization** *or* **-isation** *n* ▶ **equalizer** *or* **-iser** *n*

equally likely *adj, adv Maths* appearing midway along a likelihood scale.

equal opportunity *n Law* the offering of employment or promotion equally to all, without discrimination as to sex, race, colour, etc.

equanimity *n* calmness of mind or temper; composure. ▷ **HISTORY** Latin *aequus* even + *animus* mind, spirit

equate *vb* **equating, equated 1** to make or regard as equivalent. **2** *Maths* to form an equation from. ▶ **equatable** *adj*

equation *n* **1** a mathematical statement that two expressions are equal. **2** a situation or problem in which a number of different factors need to be considered: *this plan leaves human nature out of the equation.* **3** the act of equating. **4** *Chem* a representation of a chemical reaction using symbols of the elements.

equator *n* an imaginary circle around the earth at an equal distance from the North Pole and the South Pole. ▷ **HISTORY** Medieval Latin *(circulus) aequator (diei et noctis)* (circle) that equalizes (the day and night)

equatorial *adj* of, like, or existing at or near the equator.

equatorial region *n Geog* a large area of land at or near the equator.

equerry (**ek**-kwer-ee) *n, pl* **-ries** *Brit* an officer of the royal household who acts as a personal attendant to a member of the royal family. ▷ **HISTORY** Old French *escuirie* group of squires

equestrian *adj* **1** of or relating to horses and riding. **2** on horseback: *an equestrian statue of the Queen.* ▷ **HISTORY** Latin *equus* horse ▶ **equestrianism** *n*

equidistant *adj* equally distant. ▶ **equidistance** *n*

equilateral *adj* **1** having all sides of equal length. ✧ *n* **2** a geometric figure having all sides of equal length.

equilibrium *n, pl* **-ria 1** a stable condition in which forces cancel one another. **2** a state of mental and emotional balance; composure. **3** *Econ* the economic condition in which there is neither excess demand nor excess supply in a market. ▷ **HISTORY** Latin *aequi-* equal + *libra* balance

equine *adj* of or like a horse. ▷ **HISTORY** Latin *equus* horse

equinoctial *adj* **1** relating to or occurring at an equinox. ✧ *n* **2** a storm at or near an equinox.

equinox *n* either of the two occasions when day and night are of equal length, around March 21 and September 23. ▷ **HISTORY** Latin *aequi-* equal + *nox* night

equip *vb* **equipping, equipped 1** to provide with supplies, components, etc.: *the car comes equipped with a catalytic converter.* **2** to provide with abilities, understanding, etc.: *stress is something we are all equipped to cope with.* ▷ **HISTORY** Old French *eschiper* to fit out (a ship)

equipment *n* **1** a set of tools or devices used for a particular purpose: *communications equipment.* **2** an act of equipping.

equipoise *n* the state of being perfectly balanced; equilibrium.

equitable *adj* fair and reasonable. ▶ **equitably** *adv*

equitation *n* the study of riding and horsemanship. ▷ **HISTORY** Latin *equitare* to ride

equities *pl n* same as **ordinary shares**.

equity *n, pl* **-ties 1** the quality of being impartial; fairness. **2** *Law* a system of using principles of natural justice and fair conduct to reach a judgment when common law is inadequate or inappropriate. **3** the difference in value between a person's debts and the value of the property on which they are secured: *negative equity.* ▷ **HISTORY** Latin *aequus* level, equal

Equity *n Brit, Austral, & NZ* the actors' trade union.

equivalent *n* **1** something that has the same use or function as something else: *Denmark's equivalent to Silicon Valley.* ✧ *adj* **2** equal in value, quantity, significance, etc. **3** having the same or a similar effect or meaning. ▷ **HISTORY** Latin *aequi-* equal + *valere* to be worth ▶ **equivalence** *n*

equivalent fraction *n Maths* a fraction which can be reduced to the same proper fraction as another: $^2/_4$ and $^3/_6$ are equivalent fractions that can be reduced to $^1/_2$.

equivocal *adj* **1** capable of varying interpretations; ambiguous. **2** deliberately misleading or vague. **3** of doubtful character or sincerity: *the party's commitment to genuine reform is equivocal.* ▷ **HISTORY** Latin *aequi-* equal + *vox* voice ▶ **equivocally** *adv*

equivocate *vb* **-cating, -cated** to use vague or ambiguous language in order to deceive someone

A B C D E F G H I J K L M N O P Q R S T U V W X Y Z

or to avoid telling the truth. ▸ **equivocation** *n* ▸ **equivocator** *n*

er *interj* a sound made when hesitating in speech.

Er *Chem* erbium.

ER Queen Elizabeth. ▷ HISTORY Latin *Elizabeth Regina*

era *n* **1** a period of time considered as distinctive; epoch. **2** an extended period of time measured from a fixed point: *the Communist era.* **3** *Geol* a major division of time.

> **WORD HISTORY**
> In Latin *aera* means 'copper counters'. The word came to mean 'a number', and hence 'a number of years reckoned from a particular point in time'.

eradicate *vb* **-cating, -cated** to destroy or get rid of completely: *measures to eradicate racism.* ▷ HISTORY Latin *e-* out + *radix* root ▸ **eradicable** *adj* ▸ **eradication** *n* ▸ **eradicator** *n*

erase *vb* **erasing, erased 1** to destroy all traces of: *he could not erase the memory of his earlier defeat.* **2** to rub or wipe out (something written). **3** to remove sound or information from (a magnetic tape or disk). ▷ HISTORY Latin *e-* out + *radere* to scrape ▸ **erasable** *adj*

eraser *n* an object, such as a piece of rubber, for erasing something written.

erasure *n* **1** an erasing. **2** the place or mark where something has been erased.

Erato *n Greek myth* the Muse of love poetry.

erbium *n Chem* a soft silvery-white element of the lanthanide series of metals. Symbol: Er. ▷ HISTORY after *Ytterby*, Sweden

ere *conj, prep Poetic* before. ▷ HISTORY Old English *ær*

erect *vb* **1** to build. **2** to raise to an upright position. **3** to found or form: *the caricature of socialism erected by Lenin.* ✧ *adj* **4** upright in posture or position. **5** *Physiol* (of the penis, clitoris, or nipples) firm or rigid after swelling with blood, esp. as a result of sexual excitement. ▷ HISTORY Latin *erigere* to set up ▸ **erection** *n*

erectile *adj Physiol* (of an organ, such as the penis) capable of becoming erect.

eremite (**air**-rim-mite) *n* a Christian hermit. ▷ HISTORY Greek *erēmos* lonely

erg *n Geog* an area of shifting sand dunes, esp. in the Sahara Desert in N Africa. ▷ HISTORY Arabic *irj*

ergo *conj* therefore. ▷ HISTORY Latin

ergonomic *adj* **1** designed to minimize effort and discomfort. **2** of or relating to ergonomics.

ergonomics *n* the study of the relationship between workers and their environment. ▷ HISTORY Greek *ergon* work + (ECO)NOMICS

ergot *n* **1** a disease of a cereal, such as rye, caused by a fungus. **2** the dried fungus used in medicine. ▷ HISTORY French: spur (of a cock)

ermine *n, pl* **-mines** *or* **-mine 1** the stoat in northern regions, where it has a white winter coat. **2** the fur of this animal, used to trim state robes of judges, nobles, etc. ▷ HISTORY Medieval Latin *Armenius (mus)* Armenian (mouse)

erne *or* **ern** *n* a fish-eating sea eagle. ▷ HISTORY Old English *earn*

Ernie *n* (in Britain) a machine that randomly selects winning numbers of Premium Bonds. ▷ HISTORY acronym of *E*lectronic *R*andom *N*umber *I*ndicator *E*quipment

erode *vb* **eroding, eroded 1** to wear down or away. **2** to deteriorate or cause to deteriorate. ▷ HISTORY Latin *e-* away + *rodere* to gnaw

erogenous (ir-**roj**-in-uss) *adj* sensitive to sexual stimulation: *an erogenous zone.* ▷ HISTORY Greek *erōs* love + *-genēs* born

erosion *n* **1** the wearing away of rocks or soil by the action of water, ice, or wind. **2** a gradual lessening or reduction: *an erosion of national sovereignty.* ▸ **erosive** *or* **erosional** *adj*

erotic *adj* of, concerning, or arousing sexual desire or giving sexual pleasure. ▷ HISTORY Greek *erōs* love ▸ **erotically** *adv*

erotica *pl n* explicitly sexual literature or art.

eroticism *n* **1** erotic quality or nature. **2** the use of sexually arousing symbolism in literature or art. **3** sexual excitement or desire.

err *vb* **1** to make a mistake. **2** to sin. ▷ HISTORY Latin *errare*

errand *n* **1** a short trip to get or do something for someone. **2 run an errand** to make such a trip. ▷ HISTORY Old English *ǣrende*

errant *adj* **1** behaving in a way considered to be unacceptable: *an errant schoolboy.* **2** *Old-fashioned or literary* wandering in search of adventure: *a knight errant.* ▷ HISTORY Latin *iter* journey ▸ **errantry** *n*

erratic *adj* **1** irregular or unpredictable: *his increasingly erratic behaviour.* ✧ *n* **2** *Geol* a rock that has been transported by glacial action. ▷ HISTORY Latin *errare* to wander ▸ **erratically** *adv*

erratum *n, pl* **-ta** an error in writing or printing. ▷ HISTORY Latin

erroneous *adj* based on or containing an error or errors; incorrect. ▸ **erroneously** *adv*

error *n* **1** a mistake, inaccuracy, or misjudgment. **2** the act or state of being wrong or making a misjudgment: *the plane was shot down in error.* **3** the amount by which the actual value of a quantity might differ from an estimate: *a 3% margin of error.* ▷ HISTORY Latin

ersatz (**air**-zats) *adj* made in imitation of something more expensive: *ersatz coffee.* ▷ HISTORY German *ersetzen* to substitute

Erse *n, adj* Irish Gaelic. ▷ HISTORY Lowland Scots *Erisch* Irish

erstwhile *adj* **1** former. ✧ *adv* **2** *Archaic* formerly.

eruct *or* **eructate** *vb Formal* to belch. ▷ HISTORY Latin *e-* out + *ructare* to belch ▸ **eructation** *n*

erudite (**air**-rude-ite) *adj* having or showing great academic knowledge. ▷ HISTORY Latin *erudire* to polish ▸ **erudition** *n*

erupt *vb* **1** (of a volcano) to throw out molten lava, ash, and steam in a sudden and violent way. **2** to burst forth suddenly and violently: *riots erupted across the country.* **3** (of a group of people) to suddenly become angry and aggressive: *the meeting erupted in fury.* **4** (of a blemish) to appear on the skin. ▷ **HISTORY** Latin *e-* out + *rumpere* to burst ▶ **eruptive** *adj*

eruption *n* **1** an instance of erupting: *a volcanic eruption.* **2** an outbreak: *a recent eruption of violence in the capital.* **3** the flaring up of a rash or spots; also the rash itself: *acne or other skin eruptions.*

erysipelas (air-riss-**sip**-ill-ass) *n* an acute disease of the skin, with fever and raised purplish patches. ▷ **HISTORY** Greek *erusi-* red + *-pelas* skin

erythrocyte (ir-**rith**-roe-site) *n* a red blood cell that transports oxygen through the body. ▷ **HISTORY** Greek *eruthros* red + *kutos* hollow vessel

Es *Chem* einsteinium.

escalate *vb* **-lating, -lated** to increase or be increased in size, seriousness, or intensity. ▷ **HISTORY** from *escalator* ▶ **escalation** *n*

escalator *n* a moving staircase consisting of stair treads fixed to a conveyor belt. ▷ **HISTORY** Latin *scala* ladder

escalope (**ess**-kal-lop) *n* a thin slice of meat, usually veal. ▷ **HISTORY** Old French: shell

escapade *n* a mischievous act or adventure. ▷ **HISTORY** French

escape *vb* **-caping, -caped 1** to get away or break free from (confinement). **2** to manage to avoid (something dangerous, unpleasant, or difficult). **3** (of gases, liquids, etc.) to leak gradually. **4** to elude; be forgotten by: *those little round cakes whose name escapes me.* ✧ *n* **5** the act of escaping or state of having escaped. **6** a way of avoiding something difficult, dangerous, or unpleasant: *his frequent illnesses provided an escape from intolerable stress.* **7** a means of relaxation or relief: *he found temporary escape through the local cinema.* **8** a leakage of gas or liquid. ▷ **HISTORY** Late Latin *e-* out + *cappa* cloak

escapee *n* a person who has escaped from prison.

escapement *n* the mechanism in a clock or watch which connects the hands to the pendulum or balance.

escape road *n* a small road leading off a steep hill, into which a car can be driven if the brakes fail.

escape velocity *n* the minimum velocity necessary for a particle, space vehicle, etc. to escape from the gravitational field of the earth or other celestial body.

escapism *n* an inclination to retreat from unpleasant reality, for example through fantasy. ▶ **escapist** *n, adj*

escapologist *n* an entertainer who specializes in freeing himself or herself from chains, ropes, etc. ▶ **escapology** *n*

escarpment *n* the long continuous steep face of a ridge or mountain. ▷ **HISTORY** French *escarpement*

eschatology (ess-cat-**tol**-a-jee) *n* the branch of theology concerned with the end of the world. ▷ **HISTORY** Greek *eskhatos* last ▶ **eschatological** *adj*

escheat (iss-**cheat**) *Law* ✧ *n* **1** formerly, the return of property to the state in the absence of legal heirs. **2** the property so reverting. ✧ *vb* **3** to obtain (land) by escheat. ▷ **HISTORY** Old French *escheoir* to fall to the lot of

eschew (iss-**chew**) *vb* to avoid doing or being involved in (something disliked or harmful). ▷ **HISTORY** Old French *eschiver* ▶ **eschewal** *n*

escort *n* **1** people or vehicles accompanying another to protect or guard them. **2** a person who accompanies someone of the opposite sex on a social occasion. ✧ *vb* **3** to act as an escort to. ▷ **HISTORY** French *escorte*

escritoire (ess-kree-**twahr**) *n* a writing desk with compartments and drawers. ▷ **HISTORY** Medieval Latin *scriptorium* writing room in a monastery

escudo (ess-**kew**-doe) *n, pl* **-dos** a former monetary unit of Portugal. ▷ **HISTORY** Spanish: shield

escutcheon *n* **1** a shield displaying a coat of arms. **2 blot on one's escutcheon** a stain on one's honour. ▷ **HISTORY** Latin *scutum* shield

esker *or* **eskar** *n Geol* a long winding ridge of gravel, sand, etc., originally deposited by a stream of melted snow or ice running under a glacier. ▷ **HISTORY** Irish *escirridge*

Eskimo *n* **1** (*pl* **-mos** *or* **-mo**) a member of a group of peoples who live in N Canada, Greenland, Alaska, and E Siberia. **2** the language of these peoples. ✧ *adj* **3** of the Eskimos. ▷ **HISTORY** probably from Native American *esquimantsic* eaters of raw flesh

> **WORD TIP**
> The peoples native to the area from western Greenland to NW Canada prefer to be called *Inuit* rather than *Eskimo.*

ESN *Brit* educationally subnormal; formerly used to designate a child who needs special schooling.

esoteric (ee-so-**ter**-rik) *adj* understood by only a small number of people, esp. because they have special knowledge. ▷ **HISTORY** Greek *esōterō* inner ▶ **esoterically** *adv*

ESP extrasensory perception.

esp. especially.

espadrille (**ess**-pad-drill) *n* a light canvas shoe with a braided cord sole. ▷ **HISTORY** French

espalier (ess-**pal**-yer) *n* **1** a shrub or fruit tree trained to grow flat. **2** the trellis on which such plants are grown. ▷ **HISTORY** French

esparto *or* **esparto grass** *n, pl* **-tos** any of various grasses of S Europe and N Africa, used to make ropes, mats, etc. ▷ **HISTORY** Greek *spartos* a kind of rush

especial *adj Formal* same as **special**. ▷ **HISTORY** Latin *specialis* individual

> **WORD TIP**
> *Especial* and *especially* have a more limited use than *special* and *specially*. *Special* is preferred to *especial* when the sense is one of being out of the ordinary: *a special lesson; he has been specially trained*. *Special* is also used when something is referred to as being for a particular purpose: *the word was specially underlined for you*. Where an idea of pre-eminence or individuality is involved, either *especial* or *special* may be used: *he is my especial* (or *special*) *friend; he is especially* (or *specially*) *good at his job*. In informal English, however, *special* is usually preferred in all contexts.

especially *adv* **1** particularly: *people are dying, especially children and babies*. **2** more than usually: *an especially virulent disease*.

Esperanto *n* an international artificial language. ▷ **HISTORY** literally: the one who hopes, pseudonym of Dr L. L. Zamenhof, its Polish inventor ▶ **Esperantist** *n, adj*

espionage (**ess**-pyon-ahzh) *n* **1** the use of spies to obtain secret information, esp. by governments. **2** the act of spying. ▷ **HISTORY** French *espionnage*

esplanade *n* a long open level stretch of ground, esp. beside the seashore or in front of a fortified place. ▷ **HISTORY** French

espousal *n* **1** adoption or support: *his espousal of the free market*. **2** *Old-fashioned* a marriage or engagement ceremony.

espouse *vb* **-pousing, -poused 1** to adopt or give support to (a cause, ideal, etc.). **2** *Old-fashioned* (esp. of a man) to marry. ▷ **HISTORY** Latin *sponsare*

espresso *n, pl* **-sos** coffee made by forcing steam or boiling water through ground coffee. ▷ **HISTORY** Italian: pressed

esprit (ess-**pree**) *n* spirit, liveliness, or wit. ▷ **HISTORY** French

esprit de corps (de **kore**) *n* consciousness of and pride in belonging to a particular group. ▷ **HISTORY** French

espy *vb* **espies, espying, espied** to catch sight of. ▷ **HISTORY** Old French *espier*

Esq. esquire.

esquire *n* **1** *Chiefly Brit* a title of respect placed after a man's name and usually shortened to *Esq.*: *I Davies, Esquire*. **2** (in medieval times) the attendant of a knight. ▷ **HISTORY** Late Latin *scutarius* shield bearer

essay *n* **1** a short literary composition on a single subject. **2** a short piece of writing on a subject done as an exercise by a student. **3** an attempt. ✧ *vb* **4** *Formal* to attempt: *he essayed a faint smile*. ▷ **HISTORY** Old French *essai* an attempt

essayist *n* a person who writes essays.

essence *n* **1** the most important and distinctive feature of something, which determines its identity. **2** a concentrated liquid used to flavour food. **3 in essence** essentially. **4 of the essence** vitally important. ▷ **HISTORY** Latin *esse* to be

essential *adj* **1** vitally important; absolutely necessary: *it is essential to get this finished on time*. **2** basic or fundamental: *she translated the essential points of the lecture into English*. ✧ *n* **3** something fundamental or indispensable. ▶ **essentially** *adv*

essential oil *n* any of various volatile oils in plants, which have the odour or flavour of the plant from which they are extracted.

EST 1 Eastern Standard Time. **2** electric-shock treatment.

est. 1 established. **2** estimate(d).

establish *vb* **1** to create or set up (an organization, link, etc.): *the regime wants to establish better relations with neighbouring countries*. **2** to make become firmly associated with a particular activity or reputation: *the play that established him as a major dramatist*. **3** to prove: *a test to establish if your baby has any chromosomal disorder*. **4** to cause (a principle) to be accepted: *our study establishes the case for further research*. ▷ **HISTORY** Latin *stabilis* firm, stable

Established Church *n* a church, such as the Church of England, that is recognized as the official church of a country.

establishment *n* **1** the act of establishing or state of being established. **2 a** a business organization or other institution. **b** a place of business. **3** the people employed by an organization.

Establishment *n* **the Establishment** a group of people having authority within a society: usually seen as conservative.

estate *n* **1** a large piece of landed property, esp. in the country. **2** *Brit & Austral* a large area of land with houses or factories built on it: *an industrial estate*. **3** *Law* property or possessions, esp. of a deceased person. **4** *History* any of the orders or classes making up a society. ▷ **HISTORY** Latin *status* condition

estate agent *n Brit & Austral* a person whose job is to help people buy and sell houses and other property.

estate car *n Brit* a car which has a long body with a door at the back end and luggage space behind the rear seats.

estate duty *n* a former name for **inheritance tax**.

esteem *n* **1** admiration and respect. ✧ *vb* **2** to have great respect or high regard for (someone). **3** *Formal* to judge or consider: *I should esteem it a kindness*. ▷ **HISTORY** Latin *aestimare* to assess the worth of ▶ **esteemed** *adj*

ester *n Chem* a compound produced by the reaction between an acid and an alcohol. ▷ **HISTORY** German

estimable *adj* worthy of respect.

estimate *vb* **-mating, -mated 1** to form an approximate idea of (size, cost, etc.); calculate roughly. **2** to form an opinion about; judge. **3** to submit an approximate price for a job to a prospective client. ✧ *n* **4** an approximate calculation. **5** a statement of the likely charge for certain work. **6** an opinion. ▷ **HISTORY** Latin *aestimare* to assess the worth of ▸ **estimator** *n*

estimation *n* **1** a considered opinion; judgment: *overall, he went up in my estimation.* **2** the act of estimating.

Estonian *adj* **1** from Estonia. ✧ *n* **2** a person from Estonia.

estranged *adj* **1** no longer living with one's husband or wife: *his estranged wife.* **2** having quarrelled and lost touch with one's family or friends: *I am estranged from my son.* ▷ **HISTORY** from Latin *extraneus* foreign ▸ **estrangement** *n*

estuary *n, pl* **-aries** the widening channel of a river where it nears the sea. ▷ **HISTORY** Latin *aestus* tide ▸ **estuarine** *adj*

ET *Brit* Employment Training: a government scheme offering training in technology and business skills for unemployed people.

ETA estimated time of arrival.

e-tail (**ee**-tail) *n* retail conducted via the Internet.

et al. **1** and elsewhere. ▷ **HISTORY** Latin *et alibi* **2** and others. ▷ **HISTORY** Latin *et alii*

etc. et cetera.

et cetera *or* **etcetera** (et **set**-ra) *n and vb substitute* **1** and the rest; and others; and so forth. **2** or the like; or something similar. ▷ **HISTORY** Latin *et* and + *cetera* the other (things)

> **WORD TIP**
> It is unnecessary to use *and* before *etc.* as *etc.* (*et cetera*) already means *and other things.* The repetition of *etc.*, as in *he brought paper, ink, notebooks, etc., etc.,* is avoided except in informal contexts.

etceteras *pl n* miscellaneous extra things or people.

etch *vb* **1** to wear away the surface of a metal, glass, etc. by the action of an acid. **2** to cut a design or pattern into a printing plate with acid. **3** to imprint vividly: *the scene is etched on my mind.* ▷ **HISTORY** Dutch *etsen* ▸ **etcher** *n*

etching *n* **1** the art or process of preparing or printing etched designs. **2** a print made from an etched plate.

eternal *adj* **1** without beginning or end; lasting for ever. **2** unchanged by time: *eternal truths.* **3** seemingly unceasing: *his eternal whingeing.* **4** of or like God or a god: *the Eternal Buddha.* ▷ **HISTORY** Latin *aeternus* ▸ **eternally** *adv*

eternity *n, pl* **-ties** **1** endless or infinite time. **2** a seemingly endless period of time: *it seemed an eternity before he could feel his heart beating again.* **3** the timeless existence after death. **4** the state of being eternal.

eternity ring *n* a ring given as a token of lasting affection, esp. one set all around with stones to symbolize continuity.

ethane *n* a flammable gaseous alkane obtained from natural gas and petroleum: used as a fuel. ▷ **HISTORY** from *ethyl*

ethanoic acid *n* same as **acetic acid**.

ethanol *n* same as **alcohol** (sense 1).

ethene *n* same as **ethylene**.

ether *n* **1** a colourless sweet-smelling liquid used as a solvent and anaesthetic. **2** the substance formerly believed to fill all space and to transmit electromagnetic waves. **3** the upper regions of the atmosphere; clear sky. Also (for senses 2 and 3): **aether** ▷ **HISTORY** Greek *aithein* to burn

ethereal (eth-**eer**-ee-al) *adj* **1** extremely delicate or refined. **2** heavenly or spiritual. ▷ **HISTORY** Greek *aithēr* ether ▸ **ethereally** *adv*

ethic *n* a moral principle or set of moral values held by an individual or group. ▷ **HISTORY** Greek *ēthos* custom

ethical *adj* **1** of or based on a system of moral beliefs about right and wrong. **2** in accordance with principles of professional conduct. **3** of or relating to ethics. ▸ **ethically** *adv*

ethics *pl n* **1** a code of behaviour, esp. of a particular group, profession, or individual: *business ethics.* **2** the moral fitness of a decision, course of action, etc. ✧ *n* **3** the study of the moral value of human conduct.

Ethiopian *adj* **1** of Ethiopia. ✧ *n* **2** a person from Ethiopia.

ethnic *or* **ethnical** *adj* **1** of or relating to a human group with racial, religious, and linguistic characteristics in common. **2** characteristic of another culture, esp. a peasant one: *ethnic foodstuffs.* ▷ **HISTORY** Greek *ethnos* race ▸ **ethnically** *adv*

ethnic cleansing *n* the practice, by the dominant ethnic group in an area, of removing other ethnic groups by expulsion or extermination.

ethnicity *n* the condition or fact of belonging to a particular ethnic group: *harassment based on gender, race, religion, or ethnicity.*

ethnography *n* the branch of anthropology that deals with the scientific description of individual human societies. ▸ **ethnographer** *n* ▸ **ethnographic** *or* **ethnographical** *adj*

ethnology *n* the branch of anthropology that deals with races and peoples and their relations to one another. ▸ **ethnological** *adj* ▸ **ethnologist** *n*

ethos (**eeth**-oss) *n* the distinctive spirit and attitudes of a people, culture, etc. ▷ **HISTORY** Greek

ethyl (**eth**-ill) *adj* of, consisting of, or containing the monovalent group C_2H_5-. ▷ **HISTORY** from *ether*

ethyl alcohol *n* same as **alcohol** (sense 1).

ethylene *or* **ethene** *n* a colourless flammable gaseous alkene used to make polythene and other chemicals.

etiolate (**ee**-tee-oh-late) *vb* **-lating, -lated** **1** *Formal* to become or cause to become weak. **2** *Bot* to make a green plant paler through lack of sunlight. ▷ **HISTORY** French *étioler* to make pale ▸ **etiolation** *n*

etiology *n, pl* **-gies** **1** the study of causation. **2** the study of the cause of diseases. ▷ **HISTORY** Greek *aitia* cause + -LOGY ▸ **etiological** *adj*

etiquette *n* **1** the customs or rules of behaviour regarded as correct in social life. **2** a conventional

A B C D E F G H I J K L M N O P Q R S T U V W X Y Z

code of practice in certain professions.
▷ HISTORY French

étude (ay-tewd) *n Music* a short composition for a solo instrument, esp. intended to be played as an exercise or to demonstrate virtuosity.
▷ HISTORY French: study

etymology *n, pl* **-gies 1** the study of the sources and development of words. **2** an account of the source and development of a word.
▷ HISTORY Greek *etumon* basic meaning + -LOGY
▶ **etymological** *adj* ▶ **etymologist** *n*

Eu *Chem* europium.

EU European Union.

eucalyptus *or* **eucalypt** *n, pl* **-lyptuses, -lyptus** *or* **-lypts** any of a mostly Australian genus of trees, widely cultivated for timber and gum, and for the medicinal oil in their leaves (**eucalyptus oil**).
▷ HISTORY Greek *eu-* well + *kaluptos* covered

Eucharist (**yew**-kar-ist) *n* **1** the Christian sacrament commemorating Christ's Last Supper by the consecration of bread and wine. **2** the consecrated elements of bread and wine.
▷ HISTORY Greek *eukharistos* thankful
▶ **Eucharistic** *adj*

Euclidean *or* **Euclidian** (yew-**klid**-ee-an) *adj* denoting a system of geometry based on the rules of Euclid, 3rd-century BC Greek mathematician.

eugenics (yew-**jen**-iks) *n* the study of methods of improving the human race, esp. by selective breeding. ▷ HISTORY Greek *eugenēs* well-born
▶ **eugenic** *adj* ▶ **eugenically** *adv* ▶ **eugenicist** *n*

euglena *n Biol* a freshwater single-celled organism that moves by means of flagella.

eukaryotic *adj Biol* denoting cells that each have a distinct nucleus containing the genetic material.

eulogize *or* **-gise** *vb* **-gizing, -gized** *or* **-gising, -gised** to praise (a person or thing) highly in speech or writing. ▶ **eulogistic** *adj*

eulogy *n, pl* **-gies 1** a speech or piece of writing praising a person or thing, esp. a person who has recently died. **2** high praise. ▷ HISTORY Greek *eulogia* praise

> ☑ **WORD TIP**
> Avoid confusion with **elegy.**

eunuch *n* a man who has been castrated, esp. (formerly) a guard in a harem. ▷ HISTORY Greek *eunoukhos* bedchamber attendant

euphemism *n* an inoffensive word or phrase substituted for one considered offensive or upsetting, such as *departed* for *dead*.
▷ HISTORY Greek *eu-* well + *phēmē* speech
▶ **euphemistic** *adj* ▶ **euphemistically** *adv*

euphonious *adj* pleasing to the ear.

euphonium *n* a brass musical instrument with four valves, resembling a small tuba.
▷ HISTORY *euph(ony + harm)onium*

euphony *n, pl* **-nies** a pleasing sound, esp. in speech. ▷ HISTORY Greek *eu-* well + *phōnē* voice

euphoria *n* a feeling of great but often unjustified or exaggerated happiness.
▷ HISTORY Greek *eu-* well + *pherein* to bear
▶ **euphoric** *adj*

Eurasian *adj* **1** of Europe and Asia. **2** of mixed European and Asian descent. ✧ *n* **3** a person of mixed European and Asian descent.

eureka (yew-**reek**-a) *interj* an exclamation of triumph on discovering or solving something.
▷ HISTORY Greek *heurēka* I have found (it)

euro *n, pl* **euros** the unit of the European Union's single currency.

Euro- *combining form* Europe or European.

Eurocentric *adj* chiefly concerned with Europe and European culture: *a Eurocentric view of British history.*

Euroland *or* **Eurozone** *n* the geographical area containing the countries that have joined the European single currency.

European *adj* **1** of Europe. ✧ *n* **2** a person from Europe. **3** a person of European descent. **4** an advocate of closer links between the countries of Europe, esp. those in the European Union.
▶ **Europeanism** *n*

European Community *or* **European Economic Community** *n* former names for **European Union.**

European Union *n* an economic organization of W European states, which have some shared monetary, social, and political goals.

Europhile (**you**-roh-file) *n* **1** a person who admires Europe or the European Union. ✧ *adj* **2** marked by admiration of Europe or the European Union.

europium *n Chem* a silvery-white element of the lanthanide series. Symbol: Eu. ▷ HISTORY after *Europe*

Euro-sceptic (in Britain) *n* **1** a person who is opposed to closer links with the European Union. ✧ *adj* **2** opposing closer links with the European Union: *three Euro-sceptic MPs.*

Eurozone *n* same as **Euroland.**

Eustachian tube *n* a tube that connects the middle ear with the pharynx and equalizes the pressure between the two sides of the eardrum.
▷ HISTORY after Bartolomeo *Eustachio*, anatomist

Euterpe *n Greek myth* the Muse of lyric poetry.

euthanasia *n* the act of killing someone painlessly, esp. to relieve suffering from an incurable illness. ▷ HISTORY Greek: easy death

eutrophic *adj Biol* (of lakes, etc.) rich in organic and mineral nutrients and supporting an abundant plant life. ▷ HISTORY prob. from Greek *eutrophos* well-fed

eutrophication *n Biol* the process by which the number of organic and mineral nutrients builds up excessively in a body of water, favouring abundant growth of algae and consequent oxygen depletion.
▷ HISTORY prob. from Greek *eutrophos* well-fed

eV electronvolt.

evacuate *vb* **-ating, -ated 1** to send away from a dangerous place to a safe place: *200 people were evacuated from their homes because of the floods.* **2** to empty (a place) of people because it has become dangerous: *the entire street was evacuated* *until the fire was put out.* **3** *Physiol* to discharge waste from the body. ▷ **HISTORY** Latin *evacuare* to empty ▶ **evacuation** *n* ▶ **evacuee** *n*

evade *vb* **evading, evaded 1** to get away from or avoid (imprisonment, captors, etc.). **2** to get around, shirk, or dodge (the law, a duty, etc.). **3** to avoid answering (a question). ▷ **HISTORY** Latin *evadere* to go forth

evaluate *vb* **-ating, -ated** to find or judge the quality or value of something. ▷ **HISTORY** French *évaluer* ▶ **evaluation** *n*

evanescent *adj Formal* quickly fading away; ephemeral or transitory. ▶ **evanescence** *n*

evangelical *Christianity* ✧ *adj* **1** of or following from the Gospels. **2** of certain Protestant sects which emphasize salvation through faith alone and a belief in the absolute authority of the Bible. ✧ *n* **3** a member of an evangelical sect. ▷ **HISTORY** Greek *evangelion* good news ▶ **evangelicalism** *n* ▶ **evangelically** *adv*

evangelism *n* the practice of spreading the Christian gospel.

evangelist *n* a preacher, sometimes itinerant. ▶ **evangelistic** *adj*

Evangelist *n* any of the writers of the Gospels: Matthew, Mark, Luke, or John.

evangelize *or* **-lise** *vb* **-lizing, -lized** *or* **-lising, -lised** to preach the Christian gospel (to). ▶ **evangelization** *or* **-lisation** *n*

evaporate *vb* **-rating, -rated 1** to change from a liquid or solid to a vapour. **2** to become less and less and finally disappear: *faith in the government evaporated rapidly after the election.* ▷ **HISTORY** Latin *e-* out + *vapor* steam ▶ **evaporable** *adj* ▶ **evaporation** *n*

evaporated milk *n* thick unsweetened tinned milk from which some of the water has been removed.

evapotranspiration *n Environmental science* the return of water vapour to the atmosphere by evaporation from land and water surfaces and by the transpiration of vegetation.

evasion *n* **1** the act of evading something, esp. a duty or responsibility, by cunning or illegal means: *tax evasion.* **2** cunning or deception used to dodge a question, duty, etc.

evasive *adj* **1** seeking to evade; not straightforward: *an evasive answer.* **2** avoiding or seeking to avoid trouble or difficulties: *evasive action.* ▶ **evasively** *adv*

eve *n* **1** the evening or day before some special event. **2** the period immediately before an event: *on the eve of the Second World War.* **3** *Poetic or old-fashioned* evening. ▷ **HISTORY** variant of EVEN[2]

Eve *n Bible* the first woman, created by God from Adam's rib.

even[1] *adj* **1** level and regular; flat. **2** on the same level: *make sure the surfaces are even with one another.* **3** regular and unvarying: *an even pace.* **4** equally balanced between two sides. **5** equal in number, quantity, etc. **6** (of a number) divisible by two. **7** denoting alternatives, events, etc., that have an equal probability: *they have a more than even chance of winning the next election.* **8** having scored the same number of points. **9 even money** *or* **evens** a bet in which the winnings are exactly the same as the amount staked. **10 get even with** *Informal* to exact revenge on; settle accounts with. ✧ *adv* **11** used to suggest that the content of a statement is unexpected or paradoxical: *it's chilly in Nova Scotia, even in August.* **12** used to intensify a comparative adjective or adverb: *an even greater demand.* **13** used to introduce a word that is stronger and more accurate than one already used: *a normal, even inevitable aspect of ageing.* **14** used preceding a hypothesis to emphasize that whether or not the condition is fulfilled, the statement remains valid: *the remark didn't call for an answer even if he could have thought of one.* **15 even so** in spite of any assertion to the contrary; nevertheless. **16 even though** despite the fact that. ▷ **HISTORY** Old English *efen* ▶ **evenly** *adv* ▶ **evenness** *n*

even[2] *n Poetic or old-fashioned* **1** eve. **2** evening. ▷ **HISTORY** Old English *ǣfen*

evening *n* **1** the latter part of the day, esp. from late afternoon until nightfall. ✧ *adj* **2** of or in the evening: *the evening meal.* ▷ **HISTORY** Old English *ǣfnung*

evening class *n Brit, Austral & NZ* an educational class for adults, held during the evening.

evening dress *n* clothes for a formal occasion during the evening.

evening primrose *n* a plant with yellow flowers that open in the evening.

evening star *n* a planet, usually Venus, seen shining brightly just after sunset.

evensong *n Church of England* the daily evening service. Also called: **Evening Prayer**

event *n* **1** anything that takes place, esp. something important. **2** a planned and organized occasion: *the wedding was one of the social events of the year.* **3** any one contest in a sporting programme. **4 in any event** *or* **at all events** whatever happens. **5 in the event** when it came to the actual or final outcome: *in the event, neither of them turned up.* **6 in the event of** if (such a thing) happens. **7 in the event that** if it should happen that. ▷ **HISTORY** Latin *evenire* to happen

eventful *adj* full of exciting or important incidents.

eventing *n Brit, Austral & NZ* riding competitions (esp. **three-day events**), usually involving cross-country riding, jumping, and dressage.

eventual *adj* happening or being achieved at the end of a situation or process: *the Fascists' eventual victory in the Spanish Civil War.* ▶ **eventually** *adv*

eventuality *n, pl* **-ties** a possible occurrence or result: *I was utterly unprepared for such an eventuality.*

ever *adv* **1** at any time: *it was the fourth fastest time ever.* **2** always: *ever present.* **3** used to give emphasis: *tell him to put to sea as soon as ever he can.* **4 ever so** *or* **ever such** *Informal, chiefly Brit* used to give emphasis: *I'm ever so sorry.* ▷ **HISTORY** Old English *ǣfre*

evergreen *adj* **1** (of certain trees and shrubs) bearing foliage throughout the year. ✧ *n* **2** an evergreen tree or shrub.

everlasting *adj* **1** never coming to an end; eternal. **2** lasting so long or occurring so often as to become tedious. ► **everlastingly** *adv*

evermore *adv* all time to come.

every *adj* **1** each without exception: *they were winning every battle.* **2** the greatest or best possible: *there is every reason to believe in the sincerity of their commitment.* **3** each: *every 20 years.* **4** **every bit as** *Informal* just as: *she's every bit as clever as you.* **5** **every other** each alternate: *every other month.* ▷ HISTORY Old English *ǣfre* ever + *ǣlc* each

everybody *pron* every person; everyone.

> **WORD TIP**
> See at **everyone.**

everyday *adj* **1** commonplace or usual. **2** happening each day. **3** suitable for or used on ordinary days.

Everyman *n* the ordinary person; common man. ▷ HISTORY after the central figure in a medieval morality play

everyone *pron* every person; everybody.

> **WORD TIP**
> *Everyone* and *everybody* are interchangeable, as are *no one* and *nobody*, and *someone* and *somebody*. Care should be taken to distinguish between *everyone* and *someone* as single words and *every one* and *some one* as two words, the latter form correctly being used to refer to each individual person or thing in a particular group: *every one of them is wrong.*

everything *pron* **1** the whole; all things: *everything had been carefully packed.* **2** the thing that is most important: *work was everything to her.*

everywhere *adv* to or in all parts or places.

evict *vb* to expel (someone) legally from his or her home or land. ▷ HISTORY Latin *evincere* to vanquish utterly ► **eviction** *n*

evidence *n* **1** something which provides ground for belief or disbelief: *there is no evidence that depression is inherited.* **2** *Law* matter produced before a court of law in an attempt to prove or disprove a point in issue. **3** **in evidence** on display; apparent. ✧ *vb* **-dencing, -denced** **4** to show clearly; demonstrate: *you evidenced no talent for music.*

evident *adj* easy to see or understand. ▷ HISTORY Latin *videre* to see ► **evidently** *adv*

evidential *adj* of, serving as, or based on evidence. ► **evidentially** *adv*

evil *n* **1** a force or power that brings about wickedness and harm: *the battle between good and evil.* **2** a wicked or morally wrong act or thing: *the evil of racism.* ✧ *adj* **3** (of a person) deliberately causing great harm and misery; wicked: *an evil dictator.* **4** (of an act, idea, etc.) causing great harm and misery; morally wrong: *what you did was deeply evil.* **5** very unpleasant: *it was fascinating to see people vanish as if we had some very evil smell.* ▷ HISTORY Old English *yfel* ► **evilly** *adv*

evildoer *n* a person who does evil. ► **evildoing** *n*

evil eye *n* **the evil eye** a look superstitiously supposed to have the power of inflicting harm.

evince *vb* **evincing, evinced** *Formal* to show or display (a quality or feeling) clearly: *a humility which he had never evinced in earlier days.* ▷ HISTORY Latin *evincere* to overcome

> **WORD TIP**
> *Evince* is sometimes wrongly used where *evoke* is meant: *the proposal evoked* (not *evinced*) *a storm of protest.*

eviscerate *vb* **-ating, -ated** to remove the internal organs of; disembowel. ▷ HISTORY Latin *e-* out + *viscera* entrails ► **evisceration** *n*

evocation *n* the act of evoking. ► **evocative** *adj*

evoke *vb* **evoking, evoked** **1** to call or summon up (a memory or feeling) from the past. **2** to provoke or bring about: *his sacking evoked a huge public protest.* ▷ HISTORY Latin *evocare* to call forth

> **WORD TIP**
> See at **evince** and **invoke.**

evolution *n* **1** *Biol* a gradual change in the characteristics of a population of animals or plants over successive generations. **2** a gradual development, esp. to a more complex form. ▷ HISTORY Latin *evolutio* an unrolling ► **evolutionary** *adj*

evolve *vb* **evolving, evolved** **1** to develop gradually. **2** (of animal or plant species) to undergo evolution. ▷ HISTORY Latin *evolvere* to unfold

ewe *n* a female sheep. ▷ HISTORY Old English *ēowu*

ewer *n* a large jug with a wide mouth. ▷ HISTORY Latin *aqua* water

ex[1] *prep Finance* excluding or without: *ex dividend.* ▷ HISTORY Latin: out of, from

ex[2] *n, pl* **exes** *Informal* one's former wife or husband.

ex- *prefix* **1** out of, outside, or from: *exit.* **2** former: *his glamorous ex-wife.* ▷ HISTORY Latin

exacerbate (ig-**zass**-er-bate) *vb* **-bating, -bated** to make (pain, emotion, or a situation) worse. ▷ HISTORY Latin *acerbus* bitter ► **exacerbation** *n*

exact *adj* **1** correct in every detail; strictly accurate. **2** precise, as opposed to approximate. **3** based on measurement and the formulation of laws: *forecasting floods is not an exact science.* ✧ *vb* **4** to obtain or demand as a right, esp. through force or strength: *the rebels called for revenge to be exacted for the killings.* ▷ HISTORY Latin *exigere* to demand

exacting *adj* making rigorous or excessive demands.

exaction *n Formal* **1** the act of obtaining or demanding money as a right. **2** a sum or payment exacted.

exactitude *n* the quality of being exact; precision.

exactly *adv* **1** with complete accuracy and precision: *I don't know exactly where they live.* **2** in every respect: *he looks exactly like his father.* ✧ *interj* **3** just so! precisely!

exaggerate *vb* **-ating, -ated 1** to regard or represent as greater than is true. **2** to make greater or more noticeable. ▷ **HISTORY** Latin *exaggerare* to heap up ▶ **exaggerated** *adj* ▶ **exaggeratedly** *adv* ▶ **exaggeration** *n*

exalt *vb* **1** to praise highly. **2** to raise to a higher rank. ▷ **HISTORY** Latin *exaltare* to raise ▶ **exalted** *adj* ▶ **exaltation** *n*

> **WORD TIP**
> *Exalt* is sometimes wrongly used where *exult* is meant: *he was exulting* (not *exalting*) *in his win earlier that day.*

exam *n* short for **examination**.

examination *n* **1** the act of examining. **2** *Education* exercises, questions, or tasks set to test a person's knowledge and skill. **3** *Med* physical inspection of a patient. **4** *Law* the formal questioning of a person on oath.

examination in chief *n Law* the questioning (of a witness) by the side that called the witness.

examine *vb* **-ining, -ined 1** to inspect carefully or in detail; investigate. **2** *Education* to test a person's knowledge of a subject by written or oral questions. **3** *Med* to investigate a patient's state of health. **4** *Law* to formally question someone on oath. ▷ **HISTORY** Latin *examinare* to weigh ▶ **examinee** *n* ▶ **examiner** *n*

example *n* **1** a specimen that is typical of its group; sample: *a fine example of Georgian architecture.* **2** a particular event, object, or person that demonstrates a point or supports an argument, theory, etc.: *Germany is a good example of how federalism works in practice.* **3** a person, action, or thing that is worthy of imitation. **4** a punishment or the person punished regarded as a warning to others. **5 for example** as an illustration. ▷ **HISTORY** Latin *exemplum*

exasperate *vb* **-ating, -ated** to cause great irritation to. ▷ **HISTORY** Latin *exasperare* to make rough ▶ **exasperated** *adj* ▶ **exasperating** *adj* ▶ **exasperation** *n*

ex cathedra *adj, adv* **1** with the authority of one's official position. **2** *RC Church* (of doctrines of faith or morals) defined by the pope as infallibly true. ▷ **HISTORY** Latin: from the chair

excavate *vb* **-vating, -vated 1** to unearth (buried objects) methodically to discover information about the past. **2** to make a hole in something by digging into it or hollowing it out: *one kind of shrimp excavates a hole for itself.* ▷ **HISTORY** Latin *excavare* to make hollow ▶ **excavation** *n* ▶ **excavator** *n*

exceed *vb* **1** to be greater in degree or quantity. **2** to go beyond the limit of (a restriction). ▷ **HISTORY** Latin *excedere* to go beyond

exceedingly *adv* very; extremely.

excel *vb* **-celling, -celled 1** to be better than; surpass. **2 excel in** *or* **at** to be outstandingly good at. ▷ **HISTORY** Latin *excellere* to rise up

excellence *n* the quality of being exceptionally good.

Excellency *or* **Excellence** *n, pl* **-lencies** *or* **-lences Your, His** *or* **Her Excellency** a title used to address a high-ranking official, such as an ambassador.

excellent *adj* exceptionally good; outstanding.

except *prep* **1** Also: **except for** not including; apart from: *everyone except Jill laughed.* **2 except that** but for the fact that. ✧ *vb* **3** to leave out or exclude. ▷ **HISTORY** Latin *excipere* to take out

excepting *prep* except.

> **WORD TIP**
> The use of *excepting* is considered by many people to be acceptable only after *not, only, always,* or *without.* Elsewhere *except* is preferred: *every country agreed to the proposal except* (not *excepting*) *Spain; he was well again except for* (not *excepting*) *a slight pain in his chest.*

exception *n* **1** anything excluded from or not conforming to a general rule or classification. **2 take exception to** to make objections to.

exceptionable *adj* open to objection.

exceptional *adj* **1** forming an exception. **2** having much more than average intelligence, ability, or skill. ▶ **exceptionally** *adv*

excerpt *n* **1** a passage taken from a book, speech, etc.; extract. ✧ *vb* **2** to take a passage from a book, speech, etc. ▷ **HISTORY** Latin *excerptum* (something) picked out

excess *n* **1** the state or act of going beyond normal or permitted limits. **2** an immoderate or abnormal amount. **3** the amount, number, etc., by which one thing exceeds another. **4** behaviour regarded as too extreme or immoral to be acceptable: *a life of sex, drugs, and drunken excess.* **5 excesses** acts or actions that are unacceptably cruel or immoral: *one of the bloodiest excesses of a dictatorial regime.* **6 in excess of** more than. **7 to excess** to an extreme or unhealthy extent: *he had started to drink to excess.* ✧ *adj* **8** more than normal, necessary, or permitted: *excess fat.* ▷ **HISTORY** Latin *excedere* to go beyond ▶ **excessive** *adj* ▶ **excessively** *adv*

excess luggage *or* **baggage** *n* luggage that is more in weight or number of pieces than an airline etc., will carry free.

exchange *vb* **-changing, -changed 1** (of two or more people, governments, etc.) to give each other (something similar) at the same time: *they nervously exchanged smiles.* **2** to replace (one thing) with another, esp. to replace unsatisfactory goods: *could I exchange this for a larger size, please?* ✧ *n* **3** the act of exchanging. **4** anything given or received as an equivalent or substitute for something else. **5** an argument. **6** Also called: **telephone exchange** a centre in which telephone lines are interconnected. **7** a place where securities or commodities are traded, esp. by brokers or merchants. **8** a transfer of sums of money of equivalent value, as between different currencies. **9** the system by which commercial debts are settled, esp. by bills of exchange, without direct payment of money. ▷ **HISTORY** Latin *cambire* to barter ▶ **exchangeable** *adj*

exchange rate *n* the rate at which the currency unit of one country may be exchanged for that of another.

Exchequer *n Government* (in Britain and certain other countries) the accounting department of the Treasury. ▷ **HISTORY** Old French *eschequier* counting table

excise[1] *n* **1** a tax on goods, such as spirits, produced for the home market. **2** *Brit* that section of the government service responsible for the collection of excise, now the Board of Customs and Excise. ▷ **HISTORY** Latin *assidere* to sit beside, assist in judging

excise[2] *vb* **-cising, -cised 1** to delete a passage from a book. **2** to remove an organ or part surgically. ▷ **HISTORY** Latin *excidere* to cut down ▶ **excision** *n*

excitable *adj* nervous and easily excited. ▶ **excitability** *n*

excite *vb* **-citing, -cited 1** to make (a person) feel so happy that he or she is unable to relax because he or she is looking forward eagerly to something: *he was excited at the long-awaited arrival of a son.* **2** to cause or arouse (an emotion, response, etc.): *the idea strongly excited his interest.* **3** to arouse sexually. **4** *Physiol* to cause a response in (an organ, tissue, or part). **5** *Physics* to raise (an atom, molecule, etc.) to a higher energy level. ▷ **HISTORY** Latin *exciere* to stimulate ▶ **excited** *adj* ▶ **excitedly** *adv*

excitement *n* **1** the state of being excited. **2** a person or thing that excites.

exciting *adj* causing excitement; stirring; stimulating. ▶ **excitingly** *adv*

exclaim *vb* to cry out or speak suddenly or excitedly, as from surprise, delight, horror, etc. ▷ **HISTORY** Latin *exclamare*

exclamation *n* **1** an abrupt or excited cry or utterance. **2** the act of exclaiming. ▶ **exclamatory** *adj*

exclamation mark *or US* **point** *n* the punctuation mark (!) used after exclamations and forceful commands.

exclude *vb* **-cluding, -cluded 1** to keep out; prevent from entering. **2** to leave out of consideration. ▷ **HISTORY** Latin *excludere* ▶ **exclusion** *n*

exclusive *adj* **1** excluding or incompatible with anything else: *these two theories are mutually exclusive.* **2** not shared: *exclusive rights.* **3** used or lived in by a privileged minority, esp. a fashionable clique: *an exclusive skiing resort.* **4** not including the numbers, dates, etc., mentioned. **5 exclusive of** except for; not taking account of. **6 exclusive to** limited to; found only in. ✧ *n* **7** a story reported in only one newspaper. ▶ **exclusively** *adv* ▶ **exclusivity** *or* **exclusiveness** *n*

exclusive power *n Austral Law* the exclusive right of the federal parliament, as opposed to the state parliaments, to legislate on certain matters.

excommunicate *vb* **-cating, -cated** to expel (someone) from membership of a church and ban him or her from taking part in its services. ▷ **HISTORY** Late Latin *excommunicare* to exclude from the community ▶ **excommunication** *n*

excoriate *vb* **-ating, -ated 1** *Literary* to censure severely. **2** to strip skin from a person or animal. ▷ **HISTORY** Late Latin *excoriare* to strip, flay ▶ **excoriation** *n*

excrement *n* waste matter discharged from the body; faeces. ▷ **HISTORY** Latin *excernere* to sift, excrete ▶ **excremental** *adj*

excrescence *n* something that protrudes, esp. an outgrowth from a part of the body. ▷ **HISTORY** Latin *excrescrere* to grow out ▶ **excrescent** *adj*

excreta (ik-**skree**-ta) *pl n* urine and faeces discharged from the body.

excrete *vb* **-creting, -creted** to discharge waste matter, such as urine, sweat, or faeces, from the body. ▷ **HISTORY** Latin *excernere* to discharge ▶ **excretion** *n* ▶ **excretory** *adj*

excruciating *adj* **1** unbearably painful; agonizing. **2** hard to bear: *never had an afternoon passed with such excruciating slowness.* ▷ **HISTORY** Latin *excruciare* to torture ▶ **excruciatingly** *adv*

exculpate *vb* **-pating, -pated** to free from blame or guilt. ▷ **HISTORY** Latin *ex* from + *culpa* fault

excursion *n* a short outward and return journey, esp. for sightseeing, etc.; outing. ▷ **HISTORY** Latin *excurrere* to run out

excuse *n* **1** an explanation offered to justify an action which has been criticized or as a reason for not fulfilling an obligation, etc. ✧ *vb* **-cusing, -cused 2** to put forward a reason or justification for (an action, fault, or offending person). **3** to pardon (a person) or overlook (a fault). **4** to free (someone) from having to carry out a task, obligation, etc.: *a doctor's letter excusing him from games at school.* **5** to allow to leave. **6 be excused** *Euphemistic* to go to the toilet. **7 excuse me!** an expression used to catch someone's attention or to apologize for an interruption, disagreement, etc. ▷ **HISTORY** Latin *ex* out + *causa* cause, accusation ▶ **excusable** *adj*

ex-directory *adj Brit & NZ* not listed in a telephone directory by request.

execrable (**eks**-sik-rab-bl) *adj* of very poor quality. ▷ **HISTORY** see EXECRATE ▶ **execrably** *adv*

execute *vb* **-cuting, -cuted 1** to put a condemned person to death. **2** to carry out or accomplish. **3** to produce or create (a work of art). **4** *Law* to render (a deed) effective, for example by signing it. **5** to carry out the terms of (a contract, will, etc.). ▷ **HISTORY** Old French *executer* ▶ **executer** *n*

execution *n* **1** the act of executing. **2** the carrying out or undergoing of a sentence of death. **3** the manner in which something is performed; technique.

executioner *n* a person whose job is to kill people who have been sentenced to death.

executive *n* **1** a person or group responsible for the administration of a project or business. **2** the branch of government responsible for carrying out laws, decrees, etc. ✧ *adj* **3** having the function of carrying plans, orders, laws, etc., into effect: *the executive producer.* **4** of or for executives: *the executive car park.* **5** *Informal* very expensive or exclusive: *executive cars.*

Executive Council *n* (in Australia and New Zealand) a body of ministers of the Crown, presided over by the governor or governor-general, that formally approves cabinet decisions, etc.

executor *n Law* a person appointed by someone to ensure that the conditions set out in his or her will are carried out. ▶ **executorial** *adj* ▶ **executrix** *fem n*

exegesis (eks-sij-**jee**-siss) *n, pl* **-ses** (-seez) explanation of a text, esp. of the Bible. ▷ **HISTORY** Greek *exēgeisthai* to interpret

exemplar *n* **1** a person or thing to be copied; model. **2** a typical specimen; example. ▷ **HISTORY** Latin *exemplum* example

exemplary *adj* **1** so good as to be an example worthy of imitation. **2** (of a punishment) extremely harsh, so as to discourage others from committing a similar crime.

exemplify *vb* **-fies, -fying, -fied 1** to show by example. **2** to serve as an example of. ▷ **HISTORY** Latin *exemplum* example + *facere* to make ▶ **exemplification** *n*

exempt *adj* **1** not subject to an obligation, tax, etc. ✧ *vb* **2** to release (someone) from an obligation, tax, etc. ▷ **HISTORY** Latin *exemptus* removed ▶ **exemption** *n*

exequies (**eks**-sik-weez) *pl n, sing* **-quy** funeral rites. ▷ **HISTORY** Latin *exequiae*

exercise *n* **1** physical exertion, esp. for training or keeping fit. **2** an activity planned to achieve a particular purpose: *the group's meeting was mainly an exercise in mutual reassurance.* **3** a set of movements, tasks, etc., designed to improve or test one's ability or fitness. **4** the use or practice of (a right, power, or authority). **5** *Mil* a manoeuvre or simulated combat operation. ✧ *vb* **-cising, -cised 6** to put into use; make use of: *we urge all governments involved to exercise restraint.* **7** to take exercise or perform exercises. **8** to practise using in order to develop or train: *to exercise one's voice.* **9** to worry or vex: *Western governments have been exercised by the need to combat international terrorism.* **10** *Mil* to carry out simulated combat, manoeuvres, etc. ▷ **HISTORY** Latin *exercere* to drill ▶ **exerciser** *n*

exert *vb* **1** to use influence, authority, etc. forcefully or effectively. **2 exert oneself** to make a special effort. ▷ **HISTORY** Latin *exserere* to thrust out

exertion *n* **1** effort or exercise, esp. physical effort: *the sudden exertion of running for a bus.* **2** the act or an instance of using one's influence, powers, or authority: *the exertion of parental authority.*

exeunt (**eks**-see-unt) they go out: used as a stage direction. ▷ **HISTORY** Latin

exfoliate *vb* **-ating, -ated** to peel off in scales or layers. ▶ **exfoliation** *n*

exhale *vb* **-haling, -haled 1** to expel breath or smoke from the lungs; breathe out. **2** to give off or to be given off as gas, fumes, etc.: *the crater exhaled smoke.* ▷ **HISTORY** Latin *exhalare* ▶ **exhalation** *n*

exhaust *vb* **1** to tire out. **2** to use up totally. **3** to discuss a topic so thoroughly that no more remains to be said. ✧ *n* **4** gases ejected from an engine as waste products. **5** the parts of an engine through which waste gases pass. ▷ **HISTORY** Latin *exhaurire* to draw out ▶ **exhausted** *adj* ▶ **exhaustible** *adj*

exhaustible resources *pl n* Same as **non-renewable resources**.

exhaustion *n* **1** extreme tiredness. **2** the act of exhausting or state of being exhausted.

exhaustive *adj* very thorough; comprehensive. ▶ **exhaustively** *adv*

exhibit *vb* **1** to display (a work of art) to the public. **2** to show (a quality or feeling): *they exhibited extraordinary courage.* ✧ *n* **3** an object exhibited to the public. **4** *Law* a document or object produced in court as evidence. ▷ **HISTORY** Latin *exhibere* to hold forth ▶ **exhibitor** *n*

exhibition *n* **1** a public display of art, skills, etc. **2** the act of exhibiting or the state of being exhibited: *an exhibition of bad temper.* **3 make an exhibition of oneself** to behave so foolishly that one attracts public attention.

exhibitionism *n* **1** a compulsive desire to attract attention to oneself. **2** a compulsive desire to expose one's genitals publicly. ▶ **exhibitionist** *n*

exhilarate *vb* **-rating, -rated** to make (someone) feel lively and cheerful. ▷ **HISTORY** Latin *exhilarare* ▶ **exhilaration** *n*

exhort *vb Formal* to urge (someone) earnestly. ▷ **HISTORY** Latin *exhortari* ▶ **exhortation** *n*

exhume (ig-**zyume**) *vb* **-huming, -humed** *Formal* to dig up something buried, esp. a corpse. ▷ **HISTORY** Latin *ex* out + *humus* the ground ▶ **exhumation** *n*

exigency *n, pl* **-gencies** *Formal* **1** an urgent demand or need. **2** an emergency. ▷ **HISTORY** Latin *exigere* to require ▶ **exigent** *adj*

exiguous *adj Formal* scanty or meagre. ▷ **HISTORY** Latin *exiguus* ▶ **exiguity** *n*

exile *n* **1** a prolonged, usually enforced absence from one's country. **2** a person banished or living away from his or her country. ✧ *vb* **-iling, -iled 3** to expel (someone) from his or her country; banish. ▷ **HISTORY** Latin *exsilium*

exist *vb* **1** to have being or reality; be: *does God exist?* **2** to only just be able to keep oneself alive, esp. because of poverty or hunger. **3** to be living; live. **4** to be present under specified conditions or in a specified place. ▷ **HISTORY** Latin *exsistere* to step forth ▶ **existing** *adj*

existence *n* **1** the fact or state of being real, live, or actual. **2** a way of life, esp. a poor or hungry one. **3** everything that exists. ▶ **existent** *adj*

existential *adj* **1** of or relating to existence, esp. human existence. **2** of or relating to existentialism.

a b c d e f g h i j k l m n o p q r s t u v w x y z

A B C D E F G H I J K L M N O P Q R S T U V W X Y Z

existentialism *n* a philosophical movement stressing personal experience and responsibility of the individual, who is seen as a free agent. ▶ **existentialist** *adj, n*

exit *n* **1** a way out. **2** the act of going out. **3** *Theatre* the act of going offstage. **4** *Brit & Austral* a point at which vehicles may leave or join a motorway. ✧ *vb* **exiting, exited 5** to go away or out; depart. **6** *Theatre* to go offstage: used as a stage direction: *exit bleeding from the room.* ▷ **HISTORY** Latin *exire* to go out

exnuptial *adj Law* (of children) born to parents unmarried at the time of their birth.

exocrine *adj* of or denoting a gland, such as the sweat gland, that discharges its product through a duct. ▷ **HISTORY** Greek *exō* outside + *krinein* to separate

exodus (**eks**-so-duss) *n* the departure of a large number of people. ▷ **HISTORY** Greek *ex* out + *hodos* way

Exodus *n Bible* the second book of the Old Testament, containing a description of the departure of the Israelites from Egypt.

ex officio (**eks** off-**fish**-ee-oh) *adv, adj* by right of position or office. ▷ **HISTORY** Latin

exonerate *vb* **-ating, -ated** to clear (someone) of blame or a criminal charge. ▷ **HISTORY** Latin *exonerare* to free from a burden ▶ **exoneration** *n*

exorbitant *adj* (of prices, demands, etc.) excessively great or high: *an exorbitant rent.* ▷ **HISTORY** Latin *ex* out, away + *orbita* track ▶ **exorbitantly** *adv*

exorcize *or* **-cise** *vb* **-cizing, -cized** *or* **-cising, -cised** to expel (evil spirits) by prayers and religious rites. ▷ **HISTORY** Greek *ex* out + *horkos* oath ▶ **exorcism** *n* ▶ **exorcist** *n*

exoskeleton *n Zool* the protective or supporting structure covering the outside of the body of many animals, for example insects or crabs.

exosmosis *n Biol* osmosis in which the water flows from a cell or organism into the surrounding solution.

exosphere *n* the outermost layer of the earth's atmosphere.

exothermic *adj* (of a chemical reaction) involving or leading to the giving off of heat.

exotic *adj* **1** having a strange allure or beauty. **2** originating in a foreign country; not native. ✧ *n* **3** a non-native plant. ▷ **HISTORY** Greek *exō* outside ▶ **exotically** *adv*

exotica *pl n* exotic objects, esp. as a collection.

expand *vb* **1** to make or become greater in extent, size, or scope. **2** to spread out; unfold. **3 expand on** to go into more detail about (a story or subject). **4** to become increasingly relaxed, friendly, and talkative. **5** *Maths* to express a function or expression as the sum or product of terms. ▷ **HISTORY** Latin *expandere* to spread out ▶ **expandable** *adj*

expanse *n* an uninterrupted wide area; stretch: *a large expanse of water.*

expansion *n* **1** the act of expanding. **2** an increase or development, esp. in the activities of a company.

expansionism *n* the practice of expanding the economy or territory of a country. ▶ **expansionist** *n, adj*

expansive *adj* **1** wide or extensive. **2** friendly, open, and talkative. ▶ **expansiveness** *n*

expat *adj, n* short for **expatriate.**

expatiate (iks-**pay**-shee-ate) *vb* **-ating, -ated expatiate on** *Formal* to speak or write at length on (a subject). ▷ **HISTORY** Latin *exspatiari* to digress ▶ **expatiation** *n*

expatriate (eks-**pat**-ree-it) *adj* **1** living away from one's native country: *an expatriate American.* **2** exiled. ✧ *n* **3** a person living away from his or her native country. **4** an exile. ▷ **HISTORY** Latin *ex* out, away + *patria* native land ▶ **expatriation** *n*

expect *vb* **1** to regard as likely. **2** to look forward to or be waiting for. **3** to require (something) as an obligation: *he expects an answer by January.* **4 be expecting** *Informal* to be pregnant. ▷ **HISTORY** Latin *exspectare* to watch for

expectancy *n* **1** something expected, esp. on the basis of a norm: *a life expectancy of 78.* **2** anticipation or expectation.

expectant *adj* **1** expecting or hopeful. **2 a** pregnant. **b** married to or living with a woman who is pregnant: *an expectant father.* ▶ **expectantly** *adv*

expectation *n* **1** the state of expecting or of being expected. **2** something looked forward to, whether feared or hoped for. **3** belief that someone should behave in a particular way: *women with expectations of old-fashioned gallantry.*

expectorant *Med* ✧ *adj* **1** helping to bring up phlegm from the respiratory passages. ✧ *n* **2** an expectorant medicine.

expectorate *vb* **-rating, -rated** *Formal* to cough up and spit out (phlegm from the respiratory passages). ▷ **HISTORY** Latin *expectorare* to drive from the breast, expel ▶ **expectoration** *n*

expediency *or* **expedience** *n, pl* **-encies** *or* **-ences 1** the use of methods that are advantageous rather than fair or just. **2** appropriateness or suitability.

expedient (iks-**pee**-dee-ent) *n* **1** something that achieves a particular purpose: *income controls were used only as a short-term expedient.* ✧ *adj* **2** useful or advantageous in a given situation: *they only talk about human rights when it is politically expedient.* ▷ **HISTORY** Latin *expediens* setting free; see EXPEDITE

expedite *vb* **-diting, -dited** *Formal* **1** to hasten the progress of. **2** to do quickly. ▷ **HISTORY** Latin *expedire* to free the feet

expedition *n* **1** an organized journey or voyage, esp. for exploration. **2** the people and equipment comprising an expedition. **3** a pleasure trip or excursion: *an expedition to the seaside.* ▷ **HISTORY** Latin *expedire* to prepare, expedite ▶ **expeditionary** *adj*

expeditious *adj* done quickly and efficiently.

expel *vb* **-pelling, -pelled 1** to drive out with force. **2** to dismiss from a school, club, etc., permanently. ▷ **HISTORY** Latin *expellere*

expend *vb Formal* to spend or use up (time, energy, or money). ▷ **HISTORY** Latin *expendere* to weigh out, pay

expendable *adj* **1** not worth preserving. **2** able to be sacrificed to achieve an objective, esp. a military one.

expenditure *n* **1** something expended, esp. money. **2** the amount expended.

expense *n* **1** a particular payment of money; expenditure. **2** the amount of money needed to buy or do something; cost. **3 expenses** money spent in the performance of a job, etc. **4** something requiring money for its purchase or upkeep. **5 at the expense of** to the detriment of. ▷ **HISTORY** Latin *expensus* weighed out

expense account *n* **1** an arrangement by which an employee's expenses are refunded by his or her employer. **2** a record of such expenses.

expensive *adj* costing a great deal of money. ▶ **expensiveness** *n*

experience *n* **1** direct personal participation or observation of something: *his experience of prison life.* **2** a particular incident, feeling, etc., that a person has undergone. **3** accumulated knowledge, esp. of practical matters. ✧ *vb* **-encing, -enced 4** to participate in or undergo. **5** to be moved by; feel. ▷ **HISTORY** Latin *experiri* to prove

experienced *adj* skilful or knowledgeable as a result of having done something many times before.

experiential *adj Philosophy* relating to or derived from experience.

experiment *n* **1** a test or investigation to provide evidence for or against a theory: *a scientific experiment.* **2** the trying out of a new idea or method. ✧ *vb* **3** to carry out an experiment or experiments. ▷ **HISTORY** Latin *experiri* to test ▶ **experimentation** *n* ▶ **experimenter** *n*

experimental *adj* **1** relating to, based on, or having the nature of an experiment. **2** trying out new ideas or methods. ▶ **experimentally** *adv*

expert *n* **1** a person who has extensive skill or knowledge in a particular field. ✧ *adj* **2** skilful or knowledgeable. **3** of, involving, or done by an expert. ▷ **HISTORY** Latin *expertus* known by experience ▶ **expertly** *adv*

expertise (eks-per-**teez**) *n* special skill, knowledge, or judgment. ▷ **HISTORY** French

expiate *vb* **-ating, -ated** *Formal* to make amends for a sin or wrongdoing. ▷ **HISTORY** Latin *expiare* ▶ **expiation** *n*

expiration *n* **1** the finish of something; expiry. **2** the act, process, or sound of breathing out. ▶ **expiratory** *adj*

expire *vb* **-piring, -pired 1** to finish or run out; come to an end. **2** to breathe out air. **3** to die. ▷ **HISTORY** Latin *exspirare* to breathe out

expiry *n, pl* **-ries** a coming to an end, esp. of the period of a contract.

explain *vb* **1** to make something easily understandable, esp. by giving a clear and detailed account of it. **2** to justify or attempt to justify oneself by giving reasons for one's actions. **3 explain away** to offer excuses or reasons for (mistakes). ▷ **HISTORY** Latin *explanare* to flatten, make clear

explanation *n* **1** the reason or reasons why a particular event or situation happened: *there is no reasonable explanation for her behaviour.* **2** a detailed account or description: *a 90-minute explanation of his love of jazz.*

explanation genre *n* a form of writing or speech in which the writer or speaker explains how something works or happens and the sequence of processes involved.

explanatory *adj* serving or intended to serve as an explanation.

expletive (iks-**plee**-tiv) *n* an exclamation or swearword expressing emotion rather than meaning. ▷ **HISTORY** Latin *explere* to fill up

explicable *adj* capable of being explained.

explicate *vb* **-cating, -cated** *Formal* to make clear; explain. ▷ **HISTORY** Latin *explicare* to unfold ▶ **explication** *n*

explicit *adj* **1** precisely and clearly expressed, leaving nothing to implication: *an explicit commitment to democracy.* **2** leaving little to the imagination; graphically detailed: *the film contains some sexually explicit scenes.* **3** (of a person) expressing something in a precise and clear way, so as to leave no doubt about what is meant. ▷ **HISTORY** Latin *explicitus* unfolded ▶ **explicitly** *adv*

explode *vb* **-ploding, -ploded 1** to burst with great violence; blow up. **2** (of a gas) to undergo a sudden violent expansion as a result of a fast chemical or nuclear reaction. **3** to react suddenly or violently with emotion. **4** (esp. of a population) to increase rapidly. **5** to show (a theory, etc.) to be baseless. ▷ **HISTORY** Latin *explodere* to drive off by clapping

exploit *vb* **1** to take advantage of a person or situation for one's own ends. **2** to make the best use of. ✧ *n* **3** a notable deed or feat. ▷ **HISTORY** Old French: accomplishment ▶ **exploitation** *n* ▶ **exploiter** *n*

explore *vb* **-ploring, -plored 1** to examine or investigate, esp. systematically. **2** to travel into an unfamiliar region, esp. for scientific purposes. ▷ **HISTORY** Latin *ex* out + *plorare* to cry aloud ▶ **exploration** *n* ▶ **exploratory** *adj* ▶ **explorer** *n*

explosion *n* **1** an exploding. **2** a violent release of energy resulting from a rapid chemical or nuclear reaction. **3** a sudden or violent outburst of activity, noise, emotion, etc. **4** a rapid increase.

explosive *adj* **1** able or likely to explode. **2** potentially violent: *an explosive situation.* ✧ *n* **3** a substance capable of exploding. ▶ **explosiveness** *n*

expo *n, pl* **-pos** short for **exposition** (sense 3).

exponent *n* **1** a person who advocates an idea, cause, etc.: *an exponent of free speech.* **2** a person who is a skilful performer of some activity: *one of the greatest modern exponents of the blues.* **3** *Maths*

A B C D E F G H I J K L M N O P Q R S T U V W X Y Z

a number placed as a superscript to another number indicating how many times the number is to be used as a factor. ▷ **HISTORY** Latin *exponere* to expound

exponential *n* **1** *Maths* a function, curve, series, or equation containing or involving one or more numbers or quantities raised to an exponent. ✧ *adj* **2** *Maths* of or involving numbers raised to an exponent. **3** *Informal* very rapid. ▸ **exponentially** *adv*

exponential function *n Maths* a function involving numbers raised to exponents.

export *n* **1** the sale of goods and services to a foreign country: *a ban on the export of arms.* **2 exports** goods or services sold to a foreign country. ✧ *vb* **3** to sell goods or services or transport goods to a foreign country. ▷ **HISTORY** Latin *exportare* to carry away ▸ **exporter** *n*

expose *vb* **-posing, -posed 1** to uncover (something previously covered). **2** to reveal the truth about (someone or something), esp. when it is shocking or scandalous: *an MP whose private life was recently exposed in the press.* **3** to leave (a person or thing) unprotected in a potentially harmful situation: *workers were exposed to relatively low doses of radiation.* **4 expose someone to** to give someone an introduction to or experience of (something new). **5** *Photog* to subject (a film) to light. **6 expose oneself** to display one's sexual organs in public. ▷ **HISTORY** Latin *exponere* to set out

exposé (iks-**pose**-ay) *n* the bringing of a scandal, crime, etc., to public notice. ▷ **HISTORY** French

exposition *n* **1** a systematic explanation of a subject. **2** the act of expounding or setting out a viewpoint. **3** a large public exhibition. **4** *Music* the first statement of the themes of a movement. ▷ **HISTORY** Latin *exponere* to display

exposition genre *n* a form of writing or speech in which the writer or speaker puts forward an argument and backs it up with analysis and background information before summing up.

expostulate *vb* **-lating, -lated expostulate with** to reason or argue with, esp. in order to dissuade or as a protest. ▷ **HISTORY** Latin *expostulare* to require ▸ **expostulation** *n* ▸ **expostulatory** *adj*

exposure *n* **1** the state of being exposed to, or lacking protection from, something: *the body cannot cope with sudden exposure to stress.* **2** the revealing of the truth about someone or something, esp. when it is shocking or scandalous: *the exposure of a loophole in the tax laws.* **3** the harmful effect on a person's body caused by lack of shelter from the weather, esp. the cold. **4** appearance before the public, as on television. **5** *Photog* **a** the act of exposing a film to light. **b** an area on a film that has been exposed. **6** *Photog* **a** the intensity of light falling on a film multiplied by the time for which it is exposed. **b** a combination of lens aperture and shutter speed used in taking a photograph.

exposure meter *n Photog* an instrument for measuring the intensity of light so that suitable camera settings can be chosen.

expound *vb* to explain a theory, belief, etc. in detail. ▷ **HISTORY** Latin *exponere* to set forth

express *vb* **1** to state (an idea or feeling) in words; utter: *two record labels have expressed an interest in signing the band.* **2** to show (an idea or feeling): *his body and demeanour expressed distrust.* **3** to indicate through a symbol or formula. **4** to squeeze out (juice, etc.). **5 express oneself** to communicate one's thoughts or ideas. ✧ *adj* **6** explicitly stated. **7** deliberate and specific: *she came with the express purpose of causing a row.* **8** of or for rapid transportation of people, mail, etc. ✧ *n* **9** a fast train stopping at only a few stations. **10** *Chiefly US & Canad* a system for sending mail rapidly. ✧ *adv* **11** using a system for rapid transportation of people, mail, etc.: *please send this letter express: it's very urgent!* ▷ **HISTORY** Latin *exprimere* to force out ▸ **expressible** *adj*

expression *n* **1** the transforming of ideas into words. **2** a showing of emotion without words. **3** communication of emotion through music, painting, etc. **4** a look on the face that indicates mood or emotion. **5** a particular phrase used conventionally to express something. **6** *Maths* a variable, function, or some combination of these. ▸ **expressionless** *adj*

expressionism *n* an early 20th-century artistic and literary movement which sought to express emotions rather than to represent the physical world. ▸ **expressionist** *n, adj*

expression mark *n Music* one of a set of symbols indicating how a piece or passage is to be performed.

expressive *adj* **1** of or full of expression. **2 expressive of** showing or suggesting: *looks expressive of hatred and revenge.*

expressway *n Chiefly US* a motorway.

expropriate *vb* **-ating, -ated** (of a government or other official body) *Formal* to take (money or property) away from its owners. ▷ **HISTORY** Medieval Latin *expropriare* to deprive of possessions ▸ **expropriation** *n* ▸ **expropriator** *n*

expulsion *n* the act of expelling or the fact of being expelled. ▷ **HISTORY** Latin *expellere* to expel ▸ **expulsive** *adj*

expunge (iks-**sponge**) *vb* **-punging, -punged** *Formal* to remove all traces of: *he had tried to expunge his failure from his mind.* ▷ **HISTORY** Latin *expungere* to blot out

expurgate (**eks**-per-gate) *vb* **-gating, -gated** to amend a piece of writing by removing sections thought to be offensive. ▷ **HISTORY** Latin *expurgare* to clean out ▸ **expurgation** *n* ▸ **expurgator** *n*

exquisite *adj* **1** extremely beautiful or attractive. **2** showing unusual delicacy and craftsmanship. **3** sensitive or discriminating: *exquisite manners.* **4** intensely felt: *exquisite joy.* ▷ **HISTORY** Latin *exquisitus* excellent ▸ **exquisitely** *adv*

ex-serviceman *or fem* **ex-servicewoman** *n, pl* **-men** *or* **-women** a person who has served in the armed forces.

extant *adj* still in existence; surviving. ▷ HISTORY Latin *exstans* standing out

> **WORD TIP**
> *Extant* is sometimes wrongly used simply to say that something exists, without any connotation of survival: *plutonium is perhaps the deadliest element in existence* (not *the deadliest element extant*).

extemporaneous *adj* spoken or performed without preparation. ▶ **extemporaneously** *adv*

extemporize *or* **-rise** *vb* **-rizing, -rized** *or* **-rising, -rised** to perform or speak without preparation. ▶ **extemporization** *or* **-risation** *n* ▶ **extemporizer** *or* **-riser** *n*

extend *vb* **1** to make bigger or longer than before: *they extended the house by building a conservatory.* **2** to reach to a certain distance or in a certain direction: *the suburbs extend for many miles.* **3** to last for a certain time: *in Norway maternity leave extends to 52 weeks.* **4** to include or affect more people or things than before: *the law was extended to ban all guns.* **5** to make something exist or be valid for longer than before: *her visa was extended for three months.* **6** to present or offer: *a tradition of extending asylum to refugees.* **7** to straighten or stretch out (part of the body): *she extended a hand in welcome.* **8 extend oneself** to make use of all one's ability or strength, often because forced to: *she'll have to really extend herself if she wants to win.* ▷ HISTORY Latin *extendere* to stretch out ▶ **extendable** *adj*

extended family *n* a social unit in which parents, children, grandparents, and other relatives live as a family unit.

extension *n* **1** a room or rooms added to an existing building. **2** a development that includes or affects more people or things than before: *an extension of democracy within the EU.* **3** an additional telephone connected to the same line as another. **4** an extra period of time in which something continues to exist or be valid: *an extension of the contract for another 2 years.* ✧ *adj* **5** denoting something that can be extended or that extends another object: *an extension ladder.* **6** of or relating to the provision of teaching and other facilities by a school or college to people who cannot attend full-time courses.

extensive *adj* **1** covering a large area: *extensive moorland.* **2** very great in effect: *the bomb caused extensive damage.* **3** containing many details, ideas, or items on a particular subject: *an extensive collection of modern art.* ▶ **extensively** *adv*

extensive agriculture *n* farming of crops and animals that involves minimum expenditure of capital and labour but requires large areas of land. Compare **intensive agriculture**.

extensor *n* any muscle that stretches or extends an arm, leg, or other part of the body.

extent *n* **1** the length, area, or size of something. **2** the scale or seriousness of a situation or difficulty: *the extent of the damage.* **3** the degree or amount to which something applies: *to a certain extent that's true.*

extenuate *vb Formal* **-ating, -ated** to make an offence or fault less blameworthy, by giving reasons that partly excuse it. ▷ HISTORY Latin *extenuare* to make thin ▶ **extenuating** *adj* ▶ **extenuation** *n*

exterior *n* **1** a part or surface that is on the outside. **2** the outward appearance of a person: *Jim's grumpy exterior concealed a warm heart.* **3** a film scene shot outside. ✧ *adj* **4** of, situated on, or suitable for the outside. **5** coming or acting from outside or abroad. ▷ HISTORY Latin comparative of *exterus* on the outside

exterior angle *n* an angle of a polygon contained between one side extended and the adjacent side.

exterminate *vb* **-nating, -nated** to destroy a group or type of people, animals, or plants completely. ▷ HISTORY Latin *exterminare* to drive away ▶ **extermination** *n* ▶ **exterminator** *n*

external *adj* **1** of, situated on, or suitable for the outside: *there was damage to the house's external walls.* **2** coming or acting from outside: *most ill health is caused by external influences.* **3** of or involving foreign nations: *Hong Kong's external trade.* **4** *Anat* situated on or near the outside of the body: *the external ear.* **5** brought into an organization to do a task which must be done impartially, esp. one involving testing or checking: *external examiners.* **6** of or relating to someone taking a university course, but not attending a university: *an external degree.* ✧ *n* **7 externals** obvious circumstances or aspects, esp. superficial ones: *despite the war, the externals of life in the city remain normal.* ▷ HISTORY Latin *externus* ▶ **externality** *n* ▶ **externally** *adv*

external conflict *n Literature* the struggle between a character and forces, situations, or people beyond his or her control. Compare **internal conflict**.

externalize *or* **-ise** *vb* **-izing, -ized** *or* **-ising, -ised** to express (thoughts or feelings) in words or actions. ▶ **externalization** *or* **-isation** *n*

extinct *adj* **1** (of an animal or plant species) having died out. **2** no longer in existence, esp. because of social changes: *shipbuilding is virtually extinct in Scotland.* **3** (of a volcano) no longer liable to erupt. ▷ HISTORY Latin *exstinguere* to extinguish

extinction *n* **1** the dying out of a plant or animal species. **2** the end of a particular way of life or type of activity.

extinguish *vb* **1** to put out (a fire or light). **2** to remove or destroy entirely. ▷ HISTORY Latin *exstinguere* ▶ **extinguishable** *adj* ▶ **extinguisher** *n*

extirpate (**eks**-ter-pate) *vb* **-pating, -pated** to remove or destroy completely: *the Romans attempted to extirpate the Celtic religion.* ▷ HISTORY Latin *exstirpare* to root out ▶ **extirpation** *n*

extol *or US* **extoll** *vb* **-tolling, -tolled** to praise lavishly. ▷ HISTORY Latin *extollere* to elevate

extort *vb* to obtain money or favours by intimidation, violence, or the misuse of authority.

A B C D E F G H I J K L M N O P Q R S T U V W X Y Z

▷ **HISTORY** Latin *extorquere* to wrest away
▶ **extortion** *n*

extortionate *adj* (of prices, profits, etc.) much higher than is fair. ▶ **extortionately** *adv*

extra *adj* **1** more than is usual, expected or needed; additional. ✧ *n* **2** a person or thing that is additional. **3** something for which an additional charge is made. **4** *Films* a person temporarily engaged, usually for crowd scenes. **5** *Cricket* a run not scored from the bat. **6** an additional edition of a newspaper. ✧ *adv* **7** unusually; exceptionally.
▷ **HISTORY** probably from *extraordinary*

extra- *prefix* outside or beyond an area or scope: *extracellular; extraterrestrial.* ▷ **HISTORY** Latin

extract *vb* **1** to pull out or uproot by force. **2** to remove from a container. **3** to derive (pleasure, information, etc.) from some source. **4** *Informal* to obtain (money, information, etc.) from someone who is not willing to provide it: *a confession extracted by force.* **5** to obtain (a substance) from a material or the ground by mining, distillation, digestion, etc.: *oil extracted from shale.* **6** to copy out (an article, passage, etc.) from a publication. ✧ *n* **7** something extracted, such as a passage from a book, etc. **8** a preparation containing the concentrated essence of a substance.
▷ **HISTORY** Latin *extrahere* to draw out ▶ **extractive** *adj* ▶ **extractor** *n*

> **WORD TIP**
> *Extract* is sometimes wrongly used where *extricate* would be better: *he will find it difficult extricating* (not *extracting*) *himself from this situation.*

extraction *n* **1** the act or an instance of extracting. **2** the removal of a tooth by a dentist: *few patients need an extraction.* **3** the origin or ancestry of a person: *he is of German extraction.*

extractive industries *pl n* industries that involve mining or drilling to extract resources such as coal, gold, oil, or gas; sometimes extended to include any industries that harvest natural resources, such as logging and fishing.

extractor fan *n* a fan used to remove stale air from a room.

extracurricular *adj* not part of the normal courses taken by students: *her free time is devoted to extracurricular duties.*

extradite *vb* **-diting, -dited** to hand over an alleged offender to the country where the crime took place for trial: *an agreement to extradite him to Hong Kong.* ▷ **HISTORY** Latin *ex* away + *traditio* a handing over ▶ **extraditable** *adj* ▶ **extradition** *n*

extramural *adj* connected with but outside the normal courses of a university or college.
▷ **HISTORY** Latin *extra* beyond + *murus* wall

extraneous (iks-**train**-ee-uss) *adj* not essential or relevant to the situation or subject being considered. ▷ **HISTORY** Latin *extraneus* external

extraordinary *adj* **1** very unusual or surprising: *the extraordinary sight of my grandfather wearing a dress.* **2** having some special or extreme quality: *an extraordinary first novel.* **3** (of a meeting, ambassador, etc.) specially called or appointed to deal with one particular topic. ▷ **HISTORY** Latin *extraordinarius* beyond what is usual
▶ **extraordinarily** *adv*

extrapolate (iks-**trap**-a-late) *vb* **-lating, -lated** **1** to infer something not known from the known facts, using logic and reason. **2** *Maths* to estimate the value of a function or measurement beyond the known values, by the extension of a curve.
▷ **HISTORY** EXTRA- + *-polate,* as in *interpolate*
▶ **extrapolation** *n*

extrasensory *adj* of or relating to extrasensory perception.

extrasensory perception *n* the supposed ability to obtain information without the use of normal senses of sight, hearing, etc.

extravagant *adj* **1** spending more than is reasonable or affordable. **2** costing more than is reasonable or affordable: *an extravagant gift.* **3** going beyond usual or reasonable limits: *extravagant expectations.* **4** (of behaviour or gestures) extreme, esp. in order to make a particular impression: *an extravagant display of affection.* **5** very elaborate and impressive: *extravagant costumes.* ▷ **HISTORY** Latin *extra* beyond + *vagari* to wander ▶ **extravagance** *n*

extravaganza *n* **1** an elaborate and lavish entertainment. **2** any fanciful display, literary composition, etc. ▷ **HISTORY** Italian: extravagance

extravert *adj, n* same as **extrovert**.

extreme *adj* **1** of a high or the highest degree or intensity. **2** exceptionally severe or unusual: *people can survive extreme conditions.* **3** (of an opinion, political group, etc.) beyond the limits regarded as acceptable; fanatical. **4** farthest or outermost. ✧ *n* **5** either of the two limits of a scale or range. **6 go to extremes** to be unreasonable in speech or action. **7 in the extreme** to the highest or further degree: *the effect was dramatic in the extreme.*
▷ **HISTORY** Latin *extremus* outermost ▶ **extremely** *adv*

extreme sport *n* any of various sports with a high risk of injury or death.

extreme unction *n RC Church* a former name for **anointing of the sick**.

extremist *n* **1** a person who favours or uses extreme or violent methods, esp. to bring about political change. ✧ *adj* **2** holding extreme opinions or using extreme methods. ▶ **extremism** *n*

extremity *n, pl* **-ties** **1** the farthest point. **2** an unacceptable or extreme nature or degree: *the extremity of his views alienated other nationalists.* **3** an extreme condition, such as misfortune. **4 extremities** hands and feet.

extricate *vb* **-cating, -cated** to free from a difficult or complicated situation or place.
▷ **HISTORY** Latin *extricare* ▶ **extricable** *adj*
▶ **extrication** *n*

> **WORD TIP**
> See at **extract**.

extrinsic *adj* **1** not an integral or essential part. **2** originating or acting from outside.

▷ **HISTORY** Latin *exter* outward + *secus* alongside ▶ **extrinsically** *adv*

extroversion *n Psychol* the directing of one's interests outwards, esp. towards making social contacts.

extrovert *adj* **1** lively and outgoing. **2** *Psychol* concerned more with external reality than inner feelings. ✧ *n* **3** a person who has these characteristics. ▷ **HISTORY** *extro-* (variant of EXTRA-, contrasting with *intro-*) + Latin *vertere* to turn ▶ **extroverted** *adj*

extrude *vb* **-truding, -truded 1** to squeeze or force out. **2** to produce moulded sections of plastic, metal, etc. by forcing through a shaped die. ▷ **HISTORY** Latin *extrudere* to thrust out ▶ **extruded** *adj* ▶ **extrusion** *n*

extrusive *adj Geol* (of igneous rocks) formed from magma issuing from volcanoes or cracks in the earth's crust; volcanic.

exuberant *adj* **1** full of vigour and high spirits. **2** (of vegetation) growing thickly; flourishing. ▷ **HISTORY** Latin *exuberans* abounding ▶ **exuberance** *n*

exude *vb* **-uding, -uded 1** (of a liquid or smell) to seep or flow out slowly and steadily. **2** to seem to have (a quality or feeling) to a great degree: *the Chancellor exuded confidence.* ▷ **HISTORY** Latin *exsudare* ▶ **exudation** *n*

exult *vb* to be joyful or jubilant. ▷ **HISTORY** Latin *exsultare* to jump for joy ▶ **exultation** *n* ▶ **exultant** *adj*

> **WORD TIP**
> See at **exalt.**

eye *n* **1** the organ of sight in humans and animals. **2** the external part of an eye, often including the area around it. **3** (*often pl*) the ability to see or record what is happening: *the eyes of an entire nation were upon us.* **4** a look, glance, or gaze. **5** attention or observation: *his new shirt caught my eye.* **6** the ability to judge or appreciate something: *his shrewd eye for talent.* **7** (*often pl*) opinion, judgment, or authority: *in the eyes of the law.* **8** a dark spot on a potato from which new shoots can grow. **9** a small hole, such as the one at the blunt end of a sewing needle. **10** a small area of calm in the centre of a storm, hurricane, or tornado. **11 all eyes** *Informal* acutely vigilant. **12 an eye for an eye** justice consisting of an equivalent action to the original wrong or harm. **13 have eyes for** to be interested in. **14 in one's mind's eye** imagined or remembered vividly. **15 in the public eye** exposed to public curiosity. **16 keep an eye on** to take care of. **17 keep an eye open** *or* **out for** to watch with special attention for. **18 keep one's eyes peeled** *or* **skinned** to watch vigilantly. **19 look someone in the eye** to look openly and without embarrassment at someone. **20 make eyes at someone** to look at someone in an obviously attracted manner. **21 more than meets the eye** hidden motives, meanings, or facts. **22 my eye!** *Old-fashioned informal* nonsense! **23 see eye to eye with** to agree with. **24 set, lay** *or* **clap eyes on** to see: *I never laid eyes on him again.* **25 turn a blind eye to** *or* **close one's eyes to** to pretend not to notice. **26 up to one's eyes in** extremely busy with. **27 with an eye to** with the intention of. **28 with one's eyes open** in full knowledge of all the facts. ✧ *vb* **eyeing** *or* **eying, eyed 29** to look at carefully or warily. ▷ **HISTORY** Old English *ēage* ▶ **eyeless** *adj* ▶ **eyelike** *adj*

eyeball *n* **1** the entire ball-shaped part of the eye. **2 eyeball to eyeball** in close confrontation. ✧ *vb* **3** *Slang* to stare at.

eyebrow *n* **1** the bony ridge over each eye. **2** the arch of hair on this ridge. **3 raise an eyebrow** to show doubt or disapproval.

eye-catching *adj* very striking and tending to catch people's attention. ▶ **eye-catcher** *n*

eye dog *n NZ* a dog trained to control sheep by staring at them.

eyeful *n* **1** *Slang* a good look at or view of something. **2** *Slang* an attractive sight, esp. a woman. **3** an amount of liquid, dust, etc., that has got into someone's eye.

eyeglass *n* a lens for aiding defective vision.

eyelash *n* any of the short hairs that grow from the edge of the eyelids.

eyelet *n* **1** a small hole for a lace or cord to be passed through. **2** a small metal ring reinforcing such a hole.

eyelid *n* either of the two folds of skin that cover an eye when it is closed.

eyeliner *n* a cosmetic used to outline the eyes.

eye-opener *n Informal* something startling or revealing.

eyepiece *n* the lens in a microscope, telescope, etc., into which the person using it looks.

eye shadow *n* a coloured cosmetic worn on the upper eyelids.

eyesight *n* the ability to see: *poor eyesight.*

eyesore *n* something very ugly.

eyestrain *n* fatigue or irritation of the eyes, caused by tiredness or a failure to wear glasses.

eyewash *n* **1** a lotion for the eyes. **2** *Informal* nonsense; rubbish.

eyewitness *n* a person present at an event who can describe what happened.

eyrie *n* **1** the nest of an eagle, built in a high inaccessible place. **2** any high isolated place. ▷ **HISTORY** Latin *area* open field, hence, nest

F f

f[1] *Physics* frequency.

f[2], **f/,** *or* **f:** f-number.

F **1** *Music* the fourth note of the scale of C major. **2** Fahrenheit. **3** farad(s). **4** *Chem* fluorine. **5** *Physics* force. **6** franc(s).

f. *or* **F. 1** fathom(s). **2** female. **3** *Grammar* feminine. **4** (*pl* **ff.**) following (page).

fa *n Music* same as **fah**.

FA (in Britain) Football Association.

Fabian (**fay**-bee-an) *adj* **1** of the Fabian Society, which aims to establish socialism gradually and democratically. ✧ *n* **2** a member of the Fabian Society. ▷ **HISTORY** after *Fabius,* Roman general, who wore out Hannibal's strength while avoiding a pitched battle ▶ **Fabianism** *n*

fable *n* **1** a short story, often one with animals as characters, that illustrates a moral. **2** an unlikely story which is usually untrue. **3** a story about mythical characters or events. ▷ **HISTORY** Latin *fabula* story

fabled *adj* well-known from anecdotes and stories rather than experience: *the fabled Timbuktu.*

fabric *n* **1** any cloth made from yarn or fibres by weaving or knitting. **2** the structure that holds a system together: *the fabric of society.* **3** the walls, floor, and roof of a building. ▷ **HISTORY** Latin *faber* craftsman

fabricate *vb* **-cating, -cated 1** to invent a story or lie: *fabricated reports about the opposition.* **2** to make or build. ▷ **HISTORY** Latin *fabrica* workshop ▶ **fabrication** *n*

fabulous *adj* **1** *Informal* extremely good. **2** almost unbelievable: *a city of fabulous wealth.* **3** told of in fables and legends: *a fabulous horned creature.* ▷ **HISTORY** Latin *fabulosus* celebrated in fable ▶ **fabulously** *adv*

facade (fass-**sahd**) *n* **1** the front of a building. **2** a front or deceptive outer appearance. ▷ **HISTORY** French

face *n* **1** the front of the head from the forehead to the lower jaw. **2 a** one's expression: *as his eyes met hers his face sobered.* **b** a distorted expression to show disgust or defiance: *she was pulling a face at him.* **3** the front or main side of an object, building, etc. **4** the surface of a clock or watch that has the numbers or hands on it. **5** the functional side of an object, such as a tool or playing card. **6** the exposed area of a mine from which coal or metal can be mined. **7** *Brit slang* a well-known or important person. **8 in the face of** in spite of: *a determined character in the face of adversity.* **9 lose face** to lose one's credibility. **10 on the face of it** to all appearances. **11 put a good face** *or* **brave face on** to maintain a cheerful appearance despite misfortune. **12 save face** to keep one's good reputation. **13 set one's face against** to oppose with determination. **14 to someone's face** directly and openly. ✧ *vb* **facing, faced 15** to look towards. **16** to be opposite. **17** to be confronted by: *they were faced with the prospect of high inflation.* **18** to provide with a surface of a different material. ✧ See also **face up to.** ▷ **HISTORY** Latin *facies* form

faceless *adj* without individual identity or character: *faceless government officials.*

face-lift *n* **1** cosmetic surgery for tightening sagging skin and smoothing wrinkles on the face. **2** an outward improvement designed to give a more modern appearance: *the stadium was given a face-lift.*

facer *n Brit old-fashioned informal* a difficulty or problem.

face-saving *adj* preventing damage to one's reputation. ▶ **face-saver** *n*

facet *n* **1** an aspect of something, such as a personality. **2** any of the surfaces of a cut gemstone. ▷ **HISTORY** French *facette* little face

facetious (fass-**see**-shuss) *adj* joking, or trying to be amusing, esp. at inappropriate times. ▷ **HISTORY** Old French *facetie* witticism ▶ **facetiously** *adv*

face up to *vb* to accept an unpleasant fact or reality.

face value *n* apparent worth or meaning: *only a fool would take it at face value.*

facia (**fay**-shee-a) *n, pl* **-ciae** (-shee-ee) same as **fascia.**

facial *adj* **1** of the face. ✧ *n* **2** a beauty treatment for the face. ▶ **facially** *adv*

facile (**fass**-ile) *adj* **1** (of a remark, argument, etc.) overly simple and showing lack of real thought. **2** easily performed or achieved: *a facile winner of his only race this year.* ▷ **HISTORY** Latin *facilis* easy

facilitate *vb* **-tating, -tated** to make easier the progress of: *the agreement helped facilitate trade between the countries.* ▶ **facilitation** *n*

facility *n, pl* **-ties 1 facilities** the means or equipment needed for an activity: *leisure and shopping facilities.* **2** the ability to do things easily and well. **3** skill or ease: *grown human beings can forget with remarkable facility.* ▷ **HISTORY** Latin *facilis* easy

facing *n* **1** a piece of material used esp. to conceal the seam of a garment. **2 facings** contrasting collar and cuffs on a jacket. **3** an outer layer of material applied to the surface of a wall.

facsimile (fak-**sim**-ill-ee) *n* **1** an exact copy. **2** same as **fax** (senses 1, 2). ▷ **HISTORY** Latin *fac simile!* make something like it!

fact *n* **1** an event or thing known to have happened or existed. **2** a truth that can be proved from experience or observation. **3** a piece of information. **4 after** *or* **before the fact** *Criminal law* after or before the commission of the offence. **5 as a matter of fact** *or* **in fact** in reality or actuality. **6 fact of life** an inescapable truth, esp. an unpleasant one. See also **facts of life.** ▷ **HISTORY** Latin *factum* something done

faction[1] *n* **1** a small group of people within a larger body, but differing from it in certain aims and ideas. **2** strife within a group. ▷ **HISTORY** Latin *factio* a making ▶ **factional** *adj*

faction[2] *n* a dramatized presentation of actual events. ▷ **HISTORY** blend of FACT + FICTION

factious *adj* inclined to quarrel and cause divisions: *A factious political party is unelectable.*

> **☑ WORD TIP**
> See at **fractious.**

factitious *adj* artificial rather than natural. ▷ **HISTORY** Latin *facticius*

factor *n* **1** an element that contributes to a result: *reliability was an important factor in the success of the car.* **2** *Maths* any whole number that will divide exactly into a given number, for example 2 and 3 are factors of 6. **3** a quantity by which an amount is multiplied or divided to become that number of times bigger or smaller: *production increased by a factor of 3.* **4** *Med* any of several substances that participate in the clotting of blood: *factor VIII.* **5** a level on a scale of measurement: *suntan oil with a factor of 5.* **6** (in Scotland) the manager of an estate. ▷ **HISTORY** Latin: one who acts

> **☑ WORD TIP**
> *Factor* (sense 1) should only be used to refer to something which contributes to a result. It should not be used to refer to a part of something such as a plan or arrangement; instead a word such as *component* or *element* should be used.

factorial *Maths* ✧ *n* **1** the product of all the whole numbers from one to a given whole number. ✧ *adj* **2** of factorials or factors.

factorize *or* **-rise** *vb* **-izing, -ized** *or* **-ising, -ised** *Maths* to resolve a whole number or an algebraic expression into factors. ▶ **factorization** *or* **-risation** *n*

factor of production *n Econ* a resource or input entering the production of wealth, such as land or labour.

factory *n, pl* **-ries** a building where goods are manufactured in large quantities. ▷ **HISTORY** Late Latin *factorium,* from *facere* to make

factory farm *n Brit, Austral & NZ* a farm in which animals are given foods that increase the amount of meat, eggs, or milk they yield. ▶ **factory farming** *n*

factory ship *n* a vessel that processes fish supplied by a fleet.

factotum *n* a person employed to do all kinds of work. ▷ **HISTORY** Latin *fac!* do! + *totum* all

facts of life *pl n* the details of sexual behaviour and reproduction.

factual *adj* concerning facts rather than opinions or theories: *a factual report.* ▶ **factually** *adv*

faculty *n, pl* **-ties 1** one of the powers of the mind or body, such as memory, sight, or hearing. **2** any ability or power, either inborn or acquired: *his faculties of reasoning were considerable.* **3 a** a department within a university or college. **b** its staff. **c** *Chiefly US & Canad* all the teaching staff of a university, school, or college. ▷ **HISTORY** Latin *facultas* capability

fad *n Informal* **1** an intense but short-lived fashion: *the skateboard fad.* **2** a personal whim. ▷ **HISTORY** origin unknown ▶ **faddish** *adj*

faddy *adj* **-dier, -diest** unreasonably fussy, particularly about food.

fade *vb* **fading, faded 1** to lose brightness, colour, or strength. **2 fade away** *or* **out** to vanish slowly. ▷ **HISTORY** Middle English *fade* dull

faeces *or esp US* **feces** (**fee**-seez) *pl n* bodily waste matter discharged through the anus. ▷ **HISTORY** Latin: dregs ▶ **faecal** *or esp US* **fecal** (**fee**-kl) *adj*

Faeroese *or* **Faroese** (fair-oh-**eez**) *adj* **1** of the Faeroes, islands in the N Atlantic. ✧ *n* **2** (*pl* **-ese**) a person from the Faeroes. **3** the language of the Faeroes.

faff about *vb Brit & S African informal* to dither or fuss. ▷ **HISTORY** origin unknown

fag[1] *n* **1** *Informal* a boring or tiring task: *weeding was a fag.* **2** *Brit* (esp. formerly) a young public school boy who performs menial chores for an older boy. ✧ *vb* **fagging, fagged 3** *Brit* to do menial chores in a public school. ▷ **HISTORY** origin unknown

fag[2] *n Slang* a cigarette. ▷ **HISTORY** origin unknown

fag[3] *n Offensive slang, chiefly US & Canad* short for **faggot**[2].

fag end *n* **1** the last and worst part: *another dull game at the fag end of the football season.* **2** *Brit & NZ informal* the stub of a cigarette.

faggot[1] *or esp US* **fagot** *n* **1** *Brit, Austral & NZ* a ball of chopped liver bound with herbs and bread. **2** a bundle of sticks. ▷ **HISTORY** from Old French

faggot[2] *n Offensive slang* a male homosexual. ▷ **HISTORY** special use of FAGGOT[1]

fah *n Music* (in tonic sol-fa) the fourth note of any ascending major scale.

Fahrenheit (**far**-ren-hite) *adj* of or measured according to the scale of temperature in which 32° represents the melting point of ice and 212° the boiling point of water. ▷ **HISTORY** after Gabriel *Fahrenheit,* physicist

faïence (**fie**-ence) *n* tin-glazed earthenware. ▷ **HISTORY** *Faenza,* N Italy, where made

fail *vb* **1** to be unsuccessful in an attempt. **2** to stop operating. **3** to judge or be judged as being below the officially accepted standard required in a course or examination. **4** to prove disappointing or useless to someone: *the government has failed the homeless.* **5** to neglect or be unable to do something: *he failed to repair the car.* **6** to go bankrupt. ✧ *n* **7** a failure to attain the required standard. **8 without fail a** regularly or without exception: *use this shampoo once a week without fail.* **b** definitely: *they agreed to enforce the embargo without fail.* ▷ **HISTORY** Latin *fallere* to disappoint

failing *n* **1** a weak point. ✧ *prep* **2 failing that** alternatively: *your doctor will normally be able to advise you or, failing that, one of the self-help agencies.*

fail-safe *adj* **1** designed to return to a safe condition in the event of a failure or malfunction. **2** safe from failure.

failure *n* **1** the act or an instance of failing. **2** someone or something that is unsuccessful: *he couldn't help but regard his own son as a failure.* **3** the fact of something required or expected not being done or not happening: *his failure to appear at the meeting.* **4** a halt in normal operation: *heart failure.* **5** a decline or loss of something: *crop failure.* **6** the fact of not reaching the required standard in an examination or test.

fain *adv Old-fashioned* gladly or willingly. ▷ **HISTORY** Old English *fægen*

faint *adj* **1** lacking clarity, brightness, or volume: *her voice was very faint.* **2** feeling dizzy or weak. **3** lacking conviction or force: *a faint attempt to smile.* ✧ *vb* **4** to lose consciousness. ✧ *n* **5** a sudden loss of consciousness. ▷ **HISTORY** Old French *faindre* to be idle ▶ **faintly** *adv*

faint-hearted *adj* lacking courage and confidence.

fair[1] *adj* **1** reasonable and just: *a move towards fair trade.* **2** in agreement with rules. **3** light in colour: *her fair skin.* **4** *Old-fashioned* young and beautiful: *a fair maiden.* **5** quite good: *a fair attempt at making a soufflé.* **6** quite large: *they made a fair amount of money.* **7** (of the tide or wind) favourable to the passage of a ship or plane. **8** fine or cloudless. **9 fair and square** in a correct or just way. ✧ *adv* **10** in a fair way. **11** absolutely or squarely: *he was caught fair off his guard.* ▷ **HISTORY** Old English *fæger* ▶ **fairness** *n*

fair[2] *n* **1** a travelling entertainment with sideshows, rides, and amusements. **2** an exhibition of goods produced by a particular industry to promote business: *the Frankfurt book fair.* ▷ **HISTORY** Latin *feriae* holidays

fair copy *n* a neat copy, without mistakes or alterations, of a piece of writing.

fair game *n* a person regarded as a justifiable target for criticism or ridicule.

fairground *n* an open space used for a fair.

fairing *n* a metal structure fitted around parts of an aircraft, car, etc., to reduce drag. ▷ **HISTORY** *fair* to streamline

Fair Isle *n* an intricate multicoloured knitted pattern. ▷ **HISTORY** after one of the Shetland Islands where this type of pattern originated

fairly *adv* **1** to a moderate degree or extent: *in the Philippines labour is fairly cheap.* **2** to a great degree or extent: *the folder fairly bulged with documents.* **3** as deserved: *the pound was fairly valued against the Deutschmark.*

fair play *n* a conventional standard of honourable behaviour.

fair test *n Science* a test in which only one variable is changed.

fairway *n* **1** (on a golf course) the mown areas between tees and greens. **2** *Naut* a part of a river or sea on which ships may sail.

fair-weather *adj* not reliable in difficult situations: *a fair-weather friend.*

fairy *n, pl* **fairies 1** an imaginary supernatural being with magical powers. **2** *Offensive slang* a male homosexual. ▷ **HISTORY** Old French *faerie* fairyland, from *feie* fairy

fairy floss *n Austral* a light fluffy mass of spun sugar, held on a stick.

fairy godmother *n* a generous friend who appears unexpectedly and offers help in time of trouble.

fairyland *n* **1** an imaginary place where fairies live. **2** an enchanted or wonderful place.

fairy lights *pl n* small coloured electric bulbs used as decoration, esp. on a Christmas tree.

fairy penguin *n* a small penguin with a bluish head and back, found on the Australian coast.

fairy ring *n* a ring of dark grass caused by fungi.

fairy tale *or* **story** *n* **1** a story about fairies or magical events. **2** a highly improbable account: *his report was little more than a fairy tale.* ✧ *adj* **fairy-tale 3** of or like a fairy tale: *a fairy-tale wedding.* **4** highly improbable: *a fairy-tale account of his achievements.*

fait accompli (**fate** ak-**kom**-plee) *n* something already done and beyond alteration: *they had to accept the invasion as a fait accompli.* ▷ **HISTORY** French

faith *n* **1** strong belief in something, esp. without proof. **2** a specific system of religious beliefs. **3** complete confidence or trust, such as in a person or remedy. **4** allegiance to a person or cause. **5 bad faith** dishonesty. **6 good faith** honesty. ▷ **HISTORY** Latin *fides* trust, confidence

faithful *adj* **1** remaining true or loyal. **2** maintaining sexual loyalty to one's lover or spouse. **3** consistently reliable: *my old, but faithful, four cylinder car.* **4** accurate in detail: *a faithful translation of the book.* ✧ *pl n* **5 a** the believers in a religious faith. **b** loyal followers. ▶ **faithfully** *adv* ▶ **faithfulness** *n*

faithless *adj* treacherous or disloyal.

faith school *n Brit* a school that provides a general education within a framework of a specific religious belief.

fake *vb* **faking, faked 1** to cause something not genuine to appear real or more valuable by fraud. **2** to pretend to have (an illness, emotion, etc.). ✧ *n* **3** an object, person, or act that is not genuine. ✧ *adj* **4** not genuine: *fake fur.* ▷ **HISTORY** probably from Italian *facciare* to make or do

fakir (**fay**-keer) *n* **1** a Muslim religious ascetic who spurns worldy possessions. **2** a Hindu holy man. ▷ **HISTORY** Arabic *faqīr* poor

falcon *n* a type of bird of prey that can be trained to hunt other birds and small animals. ▷ **HISTORY** Late Latin *falco* hawk

falconry *n* **1** the art of training falcons to hunt. **2** the sport of hunting with falcons. ▶ **falconer** *n*

fall *vb* **falling, fell, fallen 1** to descend by the force of gravity from a higher to a lower place. **2** to drop suddenly from an upright position. **3** to collapse to the ground. **4** to become less or lower in number or quality: *inflation fell by one percentage point.* **5** to slope downwards. **6** to be badly wounded or killed. **7** to give in to attack: *in 1939 Barcelona fell to the Nationalists.* **8** to lose power or status. **9** to pass into a specified condition: *I fell asleep.* **10** to adopt a downhearted expression: *his face fell and he pouted like a child.* **11** (of night or darkness) to begin. **12** to occur at a specified time: *Christmas falls on a Sunday.* **13** to give in to temptation or sin. **14 fall apart a** to break owing to long use or poor construction: *the chassis is falling apart.* **b** to become disorganized and ineffective: *since you resigned, the office has fallen apart.* **15 fall short** to prove inadequate. **16 fall short of** to fail to reach (a standard). ✧ *n* **17** an instance of falling. **18** an amount of something, such as snow or soot, that has fallen. **19** a decrease in value or number. **20** a decline in status or importance: *the town's fall from prosperity.* **21** a capture or overthrow: *the fall of Budapest in February 1945.* **22** *Wrestling* a scoring move, pinning both shoulders of one's opponent to the floor for a specified period. **23** *Chiefly US* autumn. ✧ See also **falls**. ▷ **HISTORY** Old English *feallan*

Fall *n* **the Fall** *Theol* the state of mankind's innate sinfulness following Adam's sin of disobeying God.

fallacy *n, pl* **-cies 1** an incorrect or misleading notion based on inaccurate facts or faulty reasoning: *the fallacy underlying the government's industrial policy.* **2** reasoning that is unsound. ▷ **HISTORY** Latin *fallere* to deceive ▶ **fallacious** *adj*

fall behind *vb* **1** to fail to keep up. **2** to be in arrears, such as with a payment.

fallen *vb* **1** the past participle of **fall**. ✧ *adj* **2** *Old-fashioned* (of a woman) having had sex outside marriage. **3** killed in battle.

fall for *vb* **1** to become strongly attracted to (someone). **2** to be deceived by (a lie or trick).

fall guy *n Informal* **1** the victim of a confidence trick. **2** a person who is publicly blamed for something, though it may not be his or her fault.

fallible *adj* **1** (of a person) liable to make mistakes. **2** capable of error: *our all-too-fallible economic indicators.* ▷ **HISTORY** Latin *fallere* to deceive ▶ **fallibility** *n*

fall in *vb* **1** to collapse. **2** to get into line or formation in a display, march, or procession. **3 fall in with a** to meet and join. **b** to agree with or support (a person or a suggestion).

falling star *n Informal* a meteor.

fall on *vb* **1** to attack (an enemy). **2** to meet with (something unpleasant): *his family had fallen on hard times.* **3** to affect: *a horrified hush fell on the company.* **4 fall on one's feet** to emerge unexpectedly well from a difficult situation.

Fallopian tube *n* either of a pair of slender tubes through which eggs pass from the ovaries to the uterus in female mammals. ▷ **HISTORY** after Gabriello *Fallopio,* anatomist

fallout *n* **1** radioactive material in the atmosphere following a nuclear explosion. **2** unpleasant circumstances following an event: *the political fallout of the riots.* ✧ *vb* **fall out 3** *Informal* to disagree and quarrel: *I hope we don't fall out over this issue.* **4** to leave a military formation.

fallow[1] *adj* (of land) left unseeded after being ploughed to regain fertility for a future crop. ▷ **HISTORY** Old English *fealga*

fallow[2] *adj* light yellowish-brown. ▷ **HISTORY** Old English *fealu*

fallow deer *n* a deer that has a reddish coat with white spots in summer.

falls *pl n* a waterfall.

fall through *vb* to fail before completion: *his transfer deal fell through.*

fall to *vb* **1** to become the responsibility of: *it fell to the Prime Minister to announce the plans.* **2** to begin (some activity, such as eating, working, or fighting).

false *adj* **1** not in accordance with the truth or facts: *false allegations.* **2** not real or genuine but intended to seem so: *false teeth.* **3** misleading or deceptive: *their false promises.* **4** forced or insincere: *false cheer.* **5** based on mistaken ideas. ▷ **HISTORY** Latin *falsus* ▶ **falsely** *adv* ▶ **falseness** *n*

falsehood *n* **1** the quality of being untrue. **2** a lie.

false pretences *pl n* **under false pretences** so as to mislead people about one's true intentions.

false start *n Athletics & swimming* an occasion when one competitor starts a race before the starter's signal has been given, which means that all competitors have to be recalled and the race restarted.

falsetto *n, pl* **-tos** a voice pitch higher than one's normal range. ▷ **HISTORY** Italian

falsify *vb* **-fies, -fying, -fied** to make a report or evidence false by alteration in order to deceive. ▷ **HISTORY** Latin *falsus* false + *facere* to make ▶ **falsification** *n*

falsity *n, pl* **-ties 1** the state of being false. **2** a lie.

falter *vb* **1** to be hesitant, weak, or unsure. **2** (of a machine) to lose power or strength in an uneven way: *the engine began to falter and the plane lost height.* **3** to speak nervously and without confidence. **4** to stop moving smoothly and start moving unsteadily: *as he neared the house his steps faltered.* ▷ **HISTORY** origin unknown ▶ **faltering** *adj*

fame *n* the state of being widely known or recognized. ▷ **HISTORY** Latin *fama* report

famed *adj* extremely well-known: *a nation famed for its efficiency.*

familial *adj Formal* of or relating to the family.

familiar *adj* **1** well-known. **2** frequent or common: *it was a familiar argument.* **3 familiar with** well acquainted with. **4** friendly and informal. **5** more intimate than is acceptable. ✧ *n* **6** an animal or bird believed to share with a witch her supernatural powers. **7** a friend. ▷ **HISTORY** Latin *familia* family ▶ **familiarly** *adv* ▶ **familiarity** *n*

familiarize *or* **-rise** *vb* **-izing, -ized** *or* **-ising, -ised** to make (oneself or someone else) fully aware of a particular subject. ▶ **familiarization** *or* **-risation** *n*

family *n, pl* **-lies 1** a social group consisting of parents and their offspring. *RELATED ADJECTIVE* ▸ **familial 2** one's wife or husband and one's children. **3** one's children. **4** a group descended from a common ancestor. **5** all the people living

A B C D E F G H I J K L M N O P Q R S T U V W X Y Z

together in one household. **6** any group of related objects or beings: *a family of chemicals.* **7** *Biol* one of the groups into which an order is divided, containing one or more genera: *the cat family.* ✧ *adj* **8** of or suitable for a family or any of its members: *films for a family audience.* **9 in the family way** *Informal* pregnant. ▷ **HISTORY** Latin *familia*

family assistance *n* (in New Zealand) a tax credit given to families on the basis of their income and family size.

family court *n Law* (in some countries) a court established to deal with cases relating to family law.

family doctor *n Brit, Austral & NZ informal* same as **general practitioner**.

family law *n Law* the law as it relates to matters such as marriage, divorce, custody of children, maintenance, and adoption.

family name *n* a surname, esp. when regarded as representing a family's good reputation.

family planning *n* the control of the number of children in a family by the use of contraceptives.

family tree *n* a chart showing the relationships between individuals in a family over many generations.

famine *n* a severe shortage of food. ▷ **HISTORY** Latin *fames* hunger

famous *adj* known to or recognized by many people. ▷ **HISTORY** Latin *famosus*

famously *adv* **1** well-known: *her famously relaxed manner.* **2** very well: *the two got on famously.*

fan[1] *n* **1** any device for creating a current of air, esp. a rotating machine of blades attached to a central hub. **2** a hand-held object, usually made of paper, which creates a draught of cool air when waved. **3** something shaped like such a fan, such as the tail of certain birds. ✧ *vb* **fanning, fanned 4** to create a draught of air in the direction of someone or something. **5 fan out** to spread out in the shape of a fan: *the troops fanned out along the beach.* ▷ **HISTORY** Latin *vannus*

fan[2] *n* a person who admires or is enthusiastic about a pop star, actor, sport, or hobby: *he was a big fan of Woody Allen.* ▷ **HISTORY** from *fanatic*

fanatic *n* **1** a person whose enthusiasm for something, esp. a political or religious cause, is extreme. **2** *Informal* a person devoted to a particular hobby or pastime. ✧ *adj also* **fanatical 3** excessively enthusiastic. ▷ **HISTORY** Latin *fanaticus* belonging to a temple, hence, inspired by a god, frenzied ▸ **fanatically** *adv* ▸ **fanaticism** *n*

fanbase *n* the body of admirers of a particular pop singer, sports team, etc.

fan belt *n* the belt that drives a cooling fan in a car engine.

fancier *n* a person with a keen interest in the thing specified: *a pigeon fancier.*

fanciful *adj* **1** not based on fact. **2** made in a curious or imaginative way: *fanciful architecture.* **3** guided by unrestrained imagination: *fanciful tales of fairy folk.* ▸ **fancifully** *adv*

fancy *adj* **-cier, -ciest 1** special, unusual, and elaborate. **2** (often used ironically) superior in quality. **3** (of a price) higher than expected. ✧ *n, pl* **-cies 4** a sudden spontaneous idea. **5** a sudden or irrational liking for a person or thing. **6** *Old-fashioned or literary* a person's imagination. ✧ *vb* **-cies, -cying, -cied 7** *Brit informal* to be physically attracted to (another person). **8** *Informal* to have a wish for. **9** to picture in the imagination. **10** to think or suppose: *I fancy I am redundant here.* **11 fancy oneself** to have a high opinion of oneself. ✧ *interj* **12** Also: **fancy that!** an exclamation of surprise. ▷ **HISTORY** Middle English *fantsy* ▸ **fancily** *adv*

fancy dress *n* clothing worn for a party at which people dress up to look like a particular animal or character.

fancy-free *adj* free from commitments, esp. marriage.

fancy goods *pl n* small decorative gifts.

fandango *n, pl* **-gos 1** a lively Spanish dance. **2** music for this dance. ▷ **HISTORY** Spanish

fanfare *n* a short rousing tune played on brass instruments. ▷ **HISTORY** French

fang *n* **1** the long pointed tooth of a poisonous snake through which poison is injected. **2** the canine tooth of a meat-eating mammal. ▷ **HISTORY** Old English: what is caught, prey

fanjet *n* same as **turbofan**.

fanlight *n* a semicircular window over a door or another window.

fanny *n, pl* **-nies** *Slang* **1** *Brit & Austral taboo* the female genitals. **2** *Chiefly US & Canad* the buttocks. ▷ **HISTORY** origin unknown

fantail *n* **1** a breed of domestic pigeon with a large tail like a fan. **2** a fly-catching bird of Australia, New Zealand, and SE Asia with a broad fan-shaped tail.

fantasia *n* **1** any musical work not composed in a strict form. **2** a mixture of popular tunes arranged as a continuous whole. ▷ **HISTORY** Italian: fancy

fantasize *or* **-sise** *vb* **-sizing, -sized** *or* **-sising, -sised** to imagine pleasant but unlikely events.

fantastic *adj* **1** *Informal* excellent. **2** *Informal* very large in degree or amount: *a fantastic amount of money.* **3** strange or exotic in appearance: *fantastic costumes.* **4** difficult to believe or unlikely to happen. ▸ **fantastically** *adv*

fantasy *n, pl* **-sies 1** a far-fetched idea. **2** imagination unrestricted by reality. **3** a daydream. **4** fiction with a large fantasy content. **5** *Music* same as **fantasia**. ✧ *adj* **6** of a competition in which a participant selects players for an imaginary, ideal team and points are awarded according to the actual performances of the chosen players: *fantasy football.* ▷ **HISTORY** Greek *phantazein* to make visible

fan vaulting *n Archit* vaulting with ribs that radiate like those of a fan from the top part of a pillar.

fanzine (**fan**-zeen) *n* a magazine produced by fans of a specific interest, football club, etc., for fellow fans.

FAQ *n Computers* frequently asked question *or* questions: a text file containing basic information on a particular subject.

far farther, farthest *or* **further, furthest**, *adv* **1** at, to, or from a great distance. **2** at or to a remote time: *as far back as 1984.* **3** by a considerable degree: *far greater.* **4 as far as a** to the degree or extent that. **b** to the distance or place of. **c** *Informal* with reference to. **5 by far** by a considerable margin. **6 far and away** by a very great margin: *far and away the ugliest building in the city.* **7 far and wide** in a great many places over a large area. **8 go far a** to be successful. **b** to be sufficient or last long: *her wages didn't go far.* **9 go too far** to go beyond reasonable limits: *the press have gone too far this time.* **10 so far a** up to the present moment. **b** up to a certain point, extent, or degree. ✧ *adj* **11** distant in space or time: *the far south.* **12** extending a great distance. **13** more distant: *over in the far corner.* **14 far from** by no means: *the battle is far from over.* ▷ **HISTORY** Old English *feorr*

farad *n Physics* the SI unit of electric capacitance. ▷ **HISTORY** after Michael *Faraday,* physicist

Faraday's law *n Physics* a law that states that the current induced in a circuit is directly proportional to the rate of change of the magnetic flux linked with the circuit. ▷ **HISTORY** after Michael *Faraday,* English physicist and chemist

faraway *adj* **1** very distant. **2** dreamy or absent-minded: *a faraway look in his eyes.*

farce *n* **1** a humorous play involving characters in unlikely and ridiculous situations. **2** the style of comedy of this kind. **3** a ludicrous situation: *the game degenerated into farce.* ▷ **HISTORY** Latin *farcire* to stuff, interpolate passages (in plays) ▶ **farcical** *adj* ▶ **farcically** *adv*

fare *n* **1** the amount charged or paid for a journey in a bus, train, or plane. **2** a paying passenger. **3** a range of food and drink: *marvellous picnic fare.* ✧ *vb* **faring, fared 4** to get on (in a specified way): *he fared well in the exam.* ▷ **HISTORY** Old English *faran*

Far East *n* the countries of E Asia. ▶ **Far Eastern** *adj*

fare stage *n* **1** a section of a bus journey for which a set charge is made. **2** the bus stop marking the end of such a section.

farewell *interj* **1** *Old-fashioned* goodbye. ✧ *n* **2** the act of saying goodbye and leaving. ✧ *vb* **3** *NZ* to say goodbye. ✧ *adj* **4** parting or closing: *the President's farewell speech.*

far-fetched *adj* unlikely to be true.

far-flung *adj* **1** distributed over a wide area. **2** far distant or remote.

farinaceous *adj* containing starch or having a starchy texture. ▷ **HISTORY** Latin *far* coarse meal

farm *n* **1** a tract of land, usually with a house and buildings, cultivated as a unit or used to rear livestock. **2** a unit of land or water devoted to the growing or rearing of some particular type of fruit, animal, or fish: *a salmon farm; an ostrich farm.* ✧ *vb* **3 a** to cultivate land. **b** to rear animals or fish on a farm. **4** to do agricultural work as a way of life. **5** to collect and keep the profits from a tax district or business. ✧ See also **farm out**. ▷ **HISTORY** Old French *ferme* rented land

farmed *adj* (of fish or game) reared on a farm rather than caught in the wild.

farmer *n* a person who owns or manages a farm.

farm hand *n* a person who is hired to work on a farm.

farmhouse *n* a house attached to a farm.

farming *n* the business or skill of agriculture.

farming subsidy *n Agriculture* financial aid for farmers supplied by a government.

farmland *n* land that is used for or suitable for farming.

farm out *vb* **1** to send (work) to be done by another person or firm. **2** (of the state) to put a child into the care of a private individual.

farmstead *n* a farm and its main buildings.

farmyard *n* the small area of land enclosed by or around the farm buildings.

farrago (far-**rah**-go) *n, pl* **-gos** *or* **-goes** a hotchpotch or mixture, esp. a ridiculous or unbelievable one: *a farrago of patriotic nonsense.*

far-reaching *adj* extensive in influence, effect, or range.

farrier *n Chiefly Brit* a person who shoes horses. ▷ **HISTORY** Latin *ferrarius* smith

farrow *n* **1** a litter of piglets. ✧ *vb* **2** (of a sow) to give birth to a litter. ▷ **HISTORY** Old English *fearh*

far-sighted *adj* **1** able to look forward and plan ahead. **2** *US* long-sighted.

fart *Taboo* ✧ *n* **1** an emission of intestinal gas from the anus. ✧ *vb* **2** to break wind. ▷ **HISTORY** Middle English *farten*

farther *adv* **1** to or at a greater distance in space or time. **2** in addition. ✧ *adj* **3** more distant or remote in space or time. ▷ **HISTORY** Middle English

> ☑ **WORD TIP**
> *Farther, farthest, further,* and *furthest* can all be used to refer to literal distance, but *further* and *furthest* are regarded as more correct for figurative senses denoting greater or additional amount, time, etc.: *further to my letter. Further* and *furthest* are also preferred for figurative distance.

farthest *adv* **1** to or at the greatest distance in space or time. ✧ *adj* **2** most distant or remote in space or time. ▷ **HISTORY** Middle English *ferthest*

farthing *n* a former British coin worth a quarter of an old penny. ▷ **HISTORY** Old English *fēorthing*

farthingale *n* a hoop worn under skirts in the Elizabethan period. ▷ **HISTORY** Old Spanish *verdugo* rod

fasces (**fass**-eez) *pl n, sing* **-cis** (-siss) (in ancient Rome) a bundle of rods containing an axe with its blade pointing out; a symbol of a magistrate's power. ▷ **HISTORY** Latin

fascia *or* **facia** (**fay**-shee-a) *n, pl* **-ciae** (-shee-ee) **1** the flat surface above a shop window. **2** *Archit* a flat band or surface. **3** *Brit* the outer panel which surrounds the instruments and dials of a motor vehicle. ▷ **HISTORY** Latin: band

a b c d e f g h i j k l m n o p q r s t u v w x y z

A B C D E F G H I J K L M N O P Q R S T U V W X Y Z

fascinate *vb* **-nating, -nated** to attract and delight by arousing interest. ▷ **HISTORY** Latin *fascinum* a bewitching ▶ **fascinating** *adj* ▶ **fascinatingly** *adv* ▶ **fascination** *n*

> **WORD TIP**
> A person can be fascinated *by* or *with* another person or thing. It is correct to speak of someone's fascination *with* a person or thing; you can also say a person or thing has a fascination *for* someone.

Fascism (**fash**-iz-zum) *n* **1** the authoritarian and nationalistic political movement in Italy (1922–43). **2** any ideology or movement like this. ▷ **HISTORY** Italian *fascio* political group ▶ **Fascist** *n, adj*

fashion *n* **1** style in clothes, hairstyles, behaviour, etc., that is popular at a particular time. **2** the way that something happens or is done: *conversing in a very animated fashion.* **3 after a fashion** in some way, but not very well: *he apologized, after a fashion, for his haste.* ✧ *vb* **4** to form, make, or shape: *he had fashioned a crude musical instrument.* ▷ **HISTORY** Latin *facere* to make

fashionable *adj* **1** popular with a lot of people at a particular time. **2** popular among well-off or famous people: *the fashionable Côte d'Azur.* ▶ **fashionably** *adv*

fast[1] *adj* **1** acting or moving quickly. **2** accomplished in or lasting a short time. **3** adapted to or allowing for rapid movement: *the fast lane.* **4** (of a clock or watch) indicating a time in advance of the correct time. **5** given to a life of expensive and exciting activities: *the desire for a fast life.* **6** firmly fixed, fastened, or shut. **7** (of colours and dyes) not likely to fade. **8** *Photog* very sensitive and able to be used in low-light conditions. **9 fast friends** devoted and loyal friends. **10 pull a fast one** *Informal* play an unscrupulous trick. ✧ *adv* **11** quickly. **12 fast asleep** in a deep sleep. **13** firmly and tightly: *stuck fast.* **14 play fast and loose** to behave in an insincere or unreliable manner. ▷ **HISTORY** Old English *fæst* strong, tight

fast[2] *vb* **1** to go without food for a period of time, esp. for religious reasons. ✧ *n* **2** a period of fasting. ▷ **HISTORY** Old English *fæstan*

fast-breeder reactor *n* a nuclear reactor that produces more fissionable material (plutonium) than it consumes for the purposes of generating electricity.

fasten *vb* **1** to make or become secure or joined. **2** to close by fixing firmly in place or locking. **3 fasten on a** to direct one's attention in a concentrated way towards: *the mind needs such imagery to fasten on to.* **b** to take a firm hold on. ▷ **HISTORY** Old English *fæstnian* ▶ **fastener** *n*

fastening *n* something that fastens something, such as a clasp or lock.

fast food *n* food, such as hamburgers, that is prepared and served very quickly.

fastidious *adj* **1** paying great attention to neatness, detail, and order: *a fastidious dresser.* **2** excessively concerned with cleanliness. ▷ **HISTORY** Latin *fastidiosus* scornful ▶ **fastidiously** *adv* ▶ **fastidiousness** *n*

fast lane *n* **1** the outside lane on a motorway for overtaking or travelling fast. **2** *Informal* the quickest but most competitive route to success: *the hectic pace of life in the corporate fast lane.*

fastness *n Brit & Austral literary* a stronghold or safe place that is hard to get to.

fast-track *adj* **1** taking the quickest but most competitive route to success or personal advancement: *a fast-track marketer's dream.* ✧ *vb* **2** to speed up the progress of (a project or person).

fat *adj* **fatter, fattest 1** having more flesh on the body than is thought necessary or desirable; overweight. **2** (of meat) containing a lot of fat. **3** thick or wide: *his obligatory fat cigar.* **4** profitable or productive: *fat years for the farmers are few and far between.* **5 a fat chance** *Slang* unlikely to happen. **6 a fat lot of good** *Slang* not at all good or useful. ✧ *n* **7** extra or unwanted flesh on the body. **8** a greasy or oily substance obtained from animals or plants and used in cooking. **9 the fat is in the fire** an action has been taken from which disastrous consequences are expected. **10 the fat of the land** the best that is obtainable. ▷ **HISTORY** Old English *fætt* crammed ▶ **fatless** *adj* ▶ **fatness** *n*

fatal *adj* **1** resulting in death: *a fatal accident.* **2** resulting in unfortunate consequences: *Gorbachov's second fatal mistake.* ▷ **HISTORY** Latin *fatum* fate ▶ **fatally** *adv*

fatalism *n* the belief that all events are decided in advance by God or Fate so that human beings are powerless to alter their destiny. ▶ **fatalist** *n* ▶ **fatalistic** *adj* ▶ **fatalistically** *adv*

fatality *n, pl* **-ties** a death caused by an accident or disaster.

fate *n* **1** the ultimate force that supposedly predetermines the course of events. **2** the inevitable fortune that happens to a person or thing. **3** death or downfall: *Custer met his fate at Little Bighorn.* ▷ **HISTORY** Latin *fatum*

fated *adj* **1** certain to be or do something: *he was always fated to be a musician.* **2** doomed to death or destruction.

fateful *adj* having important, and usually disastrous, consequences. ▶ **fatefully** *adv*

Fates *pl n Classical myth* the goddesses who control human destiny.

fathead *n Informal* a stupid person. ▶ **fatheaded** *adj*

father *n* **1** a male parent. **2** a person who founds a line or family; forefather. **3** a man who starts, creates, or invents something: *the father of democracy in Costa Rica.* **4** a leader of an association or council: *the city fathers.* ✧ *vb* **5** (of a man) to be the biological cause of the conception and birth of (a child). ▷ **HISTORY** Old English *fæder* ▶ **fatherhood** *n*

Father *n* **1** God. **2** a title used for Christian priests. **3** any of the early writers on Christian doctrine.

father-in-law *n, pl* **fathers-in-law** the father of one's wife or husband.

fatherland *n* a person's native country.
fatherly *adj* kind or protective, like a father.
fathom *n* **1** a unit of length, used in navigation, equal to six feet (1.83 metres). ✧ *vb* **2** to understand by thinking carefully about: *I couldn't fathom his intentions.* ▷ **HISTORY** Old English *fæthm* ▶ **fathomable** *adj*
fathomless *adj* too deep or difficult to fathom.
fatigue (fat-**eeg**) *n* **1** extreme physical or mental tiredness. **2** the weakening of a material caused by repeated stress or movement. **3** the duties of a soldier that are not military. **4 fatigues** a soldier's clothing for nonmilitary or battlefield duties. ✧ *vb* **-tiguing, -tigued 5** to make or become weary or exhausted. ▷ **HISTORY** Latin *fatigare* to tire
fat stock *n* livestock fattened and ready for market.
fatten *vb* to grow or cause to grow fat or fatter. ▶ **fattening** *adj*
fatty *adj* **-tier, -tiest 1** containing or derived from fat. **2** greasy or oily. ✧ *n, pl* **-ties 3** *Informal* a fat person.
fatty acid *n* any of a class of organic acids some of which, such as stearic acid, are found in animal or vegetable fats.
fatuity *n, pl* **-ties 1** foolish thoughtlessness. **2** a fatuous remark.
fatuous *adj* foolish, inappropriate, and showing no thought. ▷ **HISTORY** Latin *fatuus* ▶ **fatuously** *adv*
faucet (**faw**-set) *n* **1** a tap fitted to a barrel. **2** *US & Canad* a tap. ▷ **HISTORY** Old French *fausset*
fault *n* **1** responsibility for something wrong. **2** a defect or failing: *they shut the production line to remedy a fault.* **3** a weakness in a person's character. **4** *Geol* a fracture in the earth's crust with displacement of the rocks on either side. **5** *Tennis, squash, etc.* a serve that bounces outside the proper service court or fails to get over the net. **6** (in showjumping) a penalty mark for failing to clear, or refusing, a fence. **7 at fault** to be to blame for something wrong. **8 find fault with** to seek out minor imperfections in. **9 to a fault** more than is usual or necessary: *generous to a fault.* ✧ *vb* **10** to criticize or blame. **11** *Geol* to undergo or cause to undergo a fault. ▷ **HISTORY** Latin *fallere* to fail ▶ **faultless** *adj* ▶ **faultlessly** *adv*
fault block *n Geol* a rock mass bounded by faults on at least two opposite sides.
fault-block mountain *n Geol* a mountain formed by the displacement of rock between faults.
fault-finding *n* continual criticism.
fault plane *n Geol* the plane along the fracture surface of a fault.
fault scarp *n Geol* a cliff formed as a result of vertical displacement along a fault.
faulty *adj* **faultier, faultiest** badly designed or not working properly: *a faulty toaster.*
faun *n* (in Roman legend) a creature with the head and torso of a man and the legs, ears, and horns of a goat. ▷ **HISTORY** Latin *Faunus,* god of forests
fauna *n, pl* **-nas** *or* **-nae** all the animal life of a given place or time: *the fauna of the Arctic.* ▷ **HISTORY** Late Latin *Fauna,* a goddess of living things
faux pas (foe **pah**) *n, pl* **faux pas** (foe **pahz**) a socially embarrassing action or mistake. ▷ **HISTORY** French
favour *or US* **favor** *n* **1** an approving attitude: *the company looked with favour on his plan.* **2** an act done out of goodwill or generosity. **3** bias at the expense of others: *his fellow customs officers, showing no favour, demanded to see his luggage.* **4 in** *or* **out of favour** regarded with approval *or* disapproval. **5 in favour of a** approving. **b** to the benefit of. ✧ *vb* **6** to prefer. **7** to show bias towards (someone) at the expense of others: *parents sometimes favour the youngest child in the family.* **8** to support or agree with (something): *he favours the abolition of capital punishment.* ▷ **HISTORY** Latin *favere* to protect ▶ **favoured** *or US* **favored** *adj*
favourable *or US* **favorable** *adj* **1** advantageous, encouraging, or promising: *a favourable climate for business expansion.* **2** giving consent or approval. ▶ **favourably** *or US* **favorably** *adv*
favourite *or US* **favorite** *adj* **1** most liked. ✧ *n* **2** a person or thing regarded with especial preference or liking. **3** *Sport* a competitor thought likely to win. ▷ **HISTORY** Latin *favere* to protect
favouritism *or US* **favoritism** *n* the practice of giving special treatment to a person or group: *favouritism in the allocation of government posts.*
fawn[1] *n* **1** a young deer aged under one year. ✧ *adj* **2** pale greyish-brown. ▷ **HISTORY** Latin *fetus* offspring
fawn[2] *vb* **fawn on 1** to seek attention from (someone) by insincere flattery: *it makes me sick to see the way you fawn on that awful woman.* **2** (of a dog) to try to please (someone) by a show of extreme friendliness. ▷ **HISTORY** Old English *fægnian* to be glad ▶ **fawning** *adj*
fax *n* **1** an electronic system for transmitting an exact copy of a document. **2** a document sent by this system. **3** Also called: **fax machine, facsimile machine** a machine which transmits and receives exact copies of documents. ✧ *vb* **4** to send (a document) by this system. ▷ **HISTORY** short for *facsimile*
FBI (in the US) Federal Bureau of Investigation.
FC (in Britain) Football Club.
FD Defender of the Faith: the title of the British sovereign as head of the Church of England. ▷ **HISTORY** Latin *Fidei Defensor*
Fe *Chem* iron. ▷ **HISTORY** Latin *ferrum*
fealty *n, pl* **-ties** (in feudal society) the loyalty sworn to a lord by his tenant or servant. ▷ **HISTORY** Latin *fidelitas* fidelity
fear *n* **1** a feeling of distress or alarm caused by danger or pain that is about to happen. **2** something that causes fear. **3** possibility or likelihood: *there is no fear of her agreeing to that.* **4 no fear** *Informal* certainly not. ✧ *vb* **5** to be afraid of (someone or something). **6** *Formal* to be sorry: *I fear the children were not very good yesterday.* **7 fear**

for to feel anxiety about something. ▷ HISTORY Old English *fǣr* ▶ **fearless** *adj* ▶ **fearlessly** *adv*

fearful *adj* **1** afraid and full of fear. **2** frightening or causing fear: *the ship hit a fearful storm.* **3** *Informal* very bad: *they were making a fearful noise.* ▶ **fearfully** *adv*

fearsome *adj* terrible or frightening.

feasible *adj* able to be done: *a manned journey to Mars is now feasible.* ▷ HISTORY Anglo-French *faisable* ▶ **feasibility** *n* ▶ **feasibly** *adv*

feast *n* **1** a large and special meal for many people. **2** something extremely pleasing: *a feast of colour.* **3** an annual religious celebration. ✧ *vb* **4** to take part in a feast. **5** to give a feast to. **6 feast on** to eat a large amount of: *down come hundreds of vultures to feast on the remains.* **7 feast one's eyes on** to look at (someone or something) with a great deal of attention and pleasure. ▷ HISTORY Latin *festus* joyful

Feast of Tabernacles *n* same as **Sukkoth**.

feat *n* a remarkable, skilful, or daring action: *an extraordinary feat of engineering.* ▷ HISTORY Anglo-French *fait*

feather *n* **1** any of the flat light structures that form the plumage of birds, each consisting of a shaft with soft thin hairs on either side. **2 feather in one's cap** a cause for pleasure at one's achievements. ✧ *vb* **3** to fit, cover, or supply with feathers. **4** *Rowing* to turn an oar parallel to the water between strokes, in order to lessen wind resistance. **5 feather one's nest** to collect possessions and money to make one's life comfortable, often dishonestly. ▷ HISTORY Old English *fether* ▶ **feathered** *adj* ▶ **feathery** *adj*

featherbedding *n* the practice of working in a factory or office deliberately slowly and inefficiently so that more workers are employed than are necessary.

featherweight *n* **1** a professional or an amateur boxer weighing up to 126 pounds (57 kg). **2** something very light or of little importance: *a featherweight politician.*

feature *n* **1 features** any one of the parts of the face, such as the nose, chin, or mouth. **2** a prominent or distinctive part of something: *regular debates were a feature of our final year.* **3** the main film in a cinema programme. **4** an item appearing regularly in a newspaper or magazine. **5** a prominent story in a newspaper. ✧ *vb* **-turing, -tured 6** to have as a feature or make a feature of: *this cooker features a fan-assisted oven.* **7** to give special prominence to: *the film features James Mason as Rommel.* ▷ HISTORY Anglo-French *feture* ▶ **featureless** *adj*

feature article *n Journalism* a prominent article (in a newspaper or magazine) involving in-depth research and analysis.

Feb. February.

febrile (**fee**-brile) *adj Formal* **1** very active and nervous: *increasingly febrile activity at the Stock Exchange.* **2** of or relating to fever. ▷ HISTORY Latin *febris* fever

February *n, pl* **-aries** the second month of the year. ▷ HISTORY Latin *Februarius mensis* month of expiation

feckless *adj* irresponsible and lacking character and determination: *her feckless brother was always in debt.* ▷ HISTORY obsolete *feck* value, effect

fecund *adj Literary* **1** fertile or capable of producing many offspring. **2** intellectually productive or creative: *an extraordinarily fecund year even by Mozart's standards.* ▷ HISTORY Latin *fecundus* ▶ **fecundity** *n*

fed *vb* the past of **feed**.

federal *adj* **1** of a form of government in which power is divided between one central and several regional governments. **2** of the central government of a federation. **3** *Austral* of a style of house built around the time of Federation. ▷ HISTORY Latin *foedus* league ▶ **federalism** *n* ▶ **federalist** *n, adj*

Federal *adj* of or supporting the Union government during the American Civil War.

Federal Government *n* the national government of a federated state, such as that of Canada located in Ottawa or of Australia in Canberra.

federalism *n Government & politics* **1** the principle or a system of federal union. **2** advocacy of federal union. ▶ **federalist** *n, adj* ▶ **federalistic** *adj*

federalize *or* **-ise** *vb* **-izing, -ized** *or* **-ising, -ised 1** to unite in a federal union. **2** to subject to federal control. ▶ **federalization** *or* **-isation** *n*

federate *vb* **-ating, -ated** to unite in a federal union. ▶ **federative** *adj*

federation *n* **1** the union of several provinces, states, etc. **2** any alliance or association of organizations which have freely joined together for a common purpose: *a federation of twenty regional unions.*

fed up *adj Informal* annoyed or bored.

fee *n* **1** a charge paid to be allowed to do something: *many people resent the licence fee.* **2** a payment asked by professional people for their services. **3** *Property law* an interest in land that can be inherited. The interest can be with unrestricted rights (**fee simple**) or restricted (**fee tail**). ▷ HISTORY Old French *fie*

feeble *adj* **1** lacking in physical or mental strength. **2** not effective or convincing: *feeble excuses for Aberdeen's latest defeat.* ▷ HISTORY Old French *feble* ▶ **feebly** *adv*

feeble-minded *adj* unable to think or understand effectively.

feed *vb* **feeding, fed 1** to give food to (a person or an animal). **2** to give (something) as food: *people feeding bread to their cattle.* **3** to eat food: *red squirrel feed in the pines.* **4** to supply or prepare food for. **5** to provide what is needed for the continued existence, operation, or growth of: *illustrations which will feed an older child's imagination; pools fed by waterfalls.* ✧ *n* **6** the act of feeding. **7** food, esp. that given to animals or babies. **8** *Brit, Austral & NZ informal* a meal. ▷ HISTORY Old English *fēdan*

feedback *n* **1** information in response to an inquiry or experiment: *considerable feedback from the customers.* **2** the return of part of the output of an electronic circuit to its input. **3** the return of part of the sound output of a loudspeaker to the microphone, so that a high-pitched whine is produced.

feeder *n* **1** a device used to feed an animal, child, or sick person. **2** an animal or a person who feeds: *these larvae are voracious feeders.* **3** a road, rail, or air service that links outlying areas to the main network. **4** a tributary or channel of a river.

feel *vb* **feeling, felt 1** to have a physical or emotional sensation of: *he felt a combination of shame and relief.* **2** to become aware of or examine by touching. **3** Also: **feel in one's bones** to sense by intuition. **4** to believe or think: *I felt I got off pretty lightly.* **5 feel for** to show compassion (towards). **6 feel like** to have an inclination (for something or doing something): *I feel like going to the cinema.* **7 feel up to** to be fit enough for (something or doing something). ✧ *n* **8** the act of feeling. **9** an impression: *all this mixing and matching has a French feel to it.* **10** the sense of touch. **11** an instinctive ability: *a feel for art.* ▷ **HISTORY** Old English *fēlan*

feeler *n* **1** an organ on an insect's head that is sensitive to touch. **2 put out feelers** to make informal suggestions or remarks designed to probe the reactions of others.

feeling *n* **1** an emotional reaction: *a feeling of discontent.* **2 feelings** emotional sensitivity: *I don't want to hurt your feelings.* **3** instinctive appreciation and understanding: *your feeling for language.* **4** an intuitive understanding that cannot be explained: *I began to have a sinking feeling that I was not going to get rid of her.* **5** opinion or view: *it was his feeling that the report was a misinterpretation of what had been said.* **6** capacity for sympathy or affection: *moved by feeling for his fellow citizens.* **7 a** the ability to experience physical sensations: *he has no feeling in his left arm.* **b** the sensation so experienced. **8** the impression or mood created by something: *a feeling of excitement in the air.* **9 bad feeling** resentment or anger between people, for example after an argument or an injustice: *his refusal may have triggered bad feeling between the two men.* ▶ **feelingly** *adv*

feet *n* **1** the plural of **foot**. **2 be run** *or* **rushed off one's feet** to be very busy. **3 feet of clay** a weakness that is not widely known. **4 have** *or* **keep one's feet on the ground** to be practical and reliable. **5 put one's feet up** to take a rest. **6 stand on one's own feet** to be independent. **7 sweep off one's feet** to fill with enthusiasm.

feign (**fane**) *vb* to pretend to experience (a particular feeling): *he didn't have to feign surprise.* ▷ **HISTORY** Old French *feindre* ▶ **feigned** *adj*

feint[1] (**faint**) *n* **1** a misleading movement designed to distract an opponent, such as in boxing or fencing. ✧ *vb* **2** to make a feint. ▷ **HISTORY** Old French *feindre* to feign

feint[2] (**faint**) *n Printing* paper that has pale lines across it for writing on. ▷ **HISTORY** variant of *faint*

feldspar *or* **felspar** *n* a hard mineral that is the main constituent of igneous rocks. ▷ **HISTORY** German *feldspath* ▶ **feldspathic** *or* **felspathic** *adj*

felicitations *pl n, interj* expressions of pleasure at someone's success or good fortune; congratulations.

felicitous *adj* appropriate and well-chosen: *a felicitous combination of architectural styles.*

felicity *n* **1** great happiness and pleasure. **2** the quality of being pleasant or desirable: *small moments of architectural felicity amidst acres of monotony.* **3** (*pl* **-ties**) an appropriate and well-chosen remark: *Nietzsche's verbal felicities are not lost in translation.* ▷ **HISTORY** Latin *felicitas* happiness

feline *adj* **1** of or belonging to the cat family. **2** like a cat, esp. in stealth or grace. ✧ *n* **3** any member of the cat family. ▷ **HISTORY** Latin *feles* cat ▶ **felinity** *n*

fell[1] *vb* the past tense of **fall**.

fell[2] *vb* **1** to cut down (a tree). **2** to knock down (a person), esp. in a fight. ▷ **HISTORY** Old English *fellan*

fell[3] *adj* **in one fell swoop** in one single action or on one single occasion: *they arrested all the hooligans in one fell swoop.* ▷ **HISTORY** Middle English *fel*

fell[4] *n Scot & N English* a mountain, hill, or moor. ▷ **HISTORY** Old Norse *fjall*

fell[5] *n* an animal's skin or hide with its hair. ▷ **HISTORY** Old High German *fel* skin

felloe *or* **felly** *n, pl* **-loes** *or* **-lies** a segment or the whole rim of a wooden wheel. ▷ **HISTORY** Old English *felge*

fellow *n* **1** a man or boy. **2** comrade or associate. **3** a person in the same group or condition: *he earned the respect of his fellows at Dunkirk.* **4** a member of the governing body at any of various universities or colleges. **5** (in Britain) a postgraduate research student. ✧ *adj* **6** in the same group or condition: *a conversation with a fellow passenger.* ▷ **HISTORY** Old English *fēolaga*

Fellow *n* a senior member of an academic institution.

fellow feeling *n* sympathy existing between people who have shared similar experiences.

fellowship *n* **1** the state of sharing mutual interests or activities. **2** a society of people sharing mutual interests or activities. **3** companionship or friendship. **4** *Education* a financed research post providing study facilities.

fellow traveller *n History* a person who sympathized with the Communist Party but was not a member of it.

felon *n Criminal law* (formerly) a person who committed a serious crime. ▷ **HISTORY** Old French: villain

felony *n, pl* **-nies** *Criminal law* (formerly) a serious crime, such as murder or arson. ▶ **felonious** *adj*

felspar *n* same as **feldspar**.

felt[1] *vb* the past of **feel**.

felt[2] *n* a matted fabric of wool, made by working the fibres together under pressure. ▷ **HISTORY** Old English

A B C D E F G H I J K L M N O P Q R S T U V W X Y Z

felt-tip pen *n* a pen with a writing point made from pressed fibres.

fem. 1 female. 2 feminine.

female *adj* **1** of the sex producing offspring. **2** of or characteristic of a woman. **3** (of reproductive organs such as the ovary and carpel) capable of producing reproductive cells (**gametes**) that are female. **4** (of flowers) not having parts in which pollen is produced (**stamens**). **5** (of a mechanical component) having an opening into which a projecting male component can be fitted. ✧ *n* **6** a female animal or plant. ▷ HISTORY Latin *femina* a woman

feminine *adj* **1** possessing qualities considered typical of or appropriate to a woman. **2** of women. **3** *Grammar* denoting a gender of nouns that includes some female animate things. ▷ HISTORY Latin *femina* a woman ▶ **femininity** *n*

feminism *n* a doctrine or movement that advocates equal rights for women. ▶ **feminist** *n, adj*

femme fatale (**fam** fat-**tahl**) *n, pl* **femmes fatales** (**fam** fat-**tahlz**) an alluring or seductive woman who leads men into dangerous or difficult situations by her charm. ▷ HISTORY French

femto- *combining form* denoting 10^{-15}: *femtometer.* ▷ HISTORY Danish *femten* fifteen

femur (**fee**-mer) *n, pl* **femurs** *or* **femora** (**fee**-mer-ra) the thighbone. ▷ HISTORY Latin: thigh ▶ **femoral** *adj*

fen *n Brit* low-lying flat marshy land. ▷ HISTORY Old English *fenn*

fence *n* **1** a barrier that encloses an area such as a garden or field, usually made of posts connected by wire rails or boards. **2** an obstacle for a horse to jump in steeplechasing or showjumping. **3** *Slang* a dealer in stolen property. **4** *Machinery* a guard or guide, esp. in a circular saw or plane. **5 (sit) on the fence** (to be) unwilling to commit oneself. ✧ *vb* **fencing, fenced 6** to construct a fence on or around (a piece of land). **7 fence in** *or* **off** to close in *or* separate off with or as if with a fence. **8** to fight using swords or foils. **9** to argue cleverly but evasively: *they fenced for a while, weighing each other up.* ▷ HISTORY Middle English *fens,* from *defens* defence

fencing *n* **1** the sport of fighting with swords or foils. **2** materials used for making fences.

fend *vb* **1 fend for oneself** to look after oneself; be independent. **2 fend off** to defend oneself against (verbal or physical attack). ▷ HISTORY Middle English *fenden*

fender *n* **1** a low metal barrier that stops coals from falling out of a fireplace. **2** a soft but solid object, such as a coil of rope, hung over the side of a vessel to prevent damage when docking. **3** *US & Canad* the wing of a car.

fenestration *n* the arrangement of windows in a building. ▷ HISTORY Latin *fenestra* window

feng shui (**fung shway**) *n* the Chinese art of deciding the best design or position of a grave, building, etc., in order to bring good luck. ▷ HISTORY Chinese *feng* wind + *shui* water

Fenian (**feen**-yan) *n* (formerly) a member of an Irish revolutionary organization founded to fight for an independent Ireland. ▷ HISTORY after *Fianna,* legendary band of Irish warriors ▶ **Fenianism** *n*

fenland *n Brit* an area of low-lying flat marshy land.

fennel *n* a fragrant plant whose seeds, leaves, and root are used in cookery. ▷ HISTORY Old English *fenol*

fenugreek *n* a Mediterranean plant grown for its heavily scented seeds. ▷ HISTORY Old English *fēnogrēcum*

feoff (**feef**) *n* same as **fief.** ▷ HISTORY Anglo-French

feral *adj* **1** (of animals and plants) existing in a wild state, esp. after being domestic or cultivated. **2** savage. ▷ HISTORY Latin *ferus* savage

ferment *n* **1** excitement and unrest caused by change or uncertainty. **2** any substance, such as yeast, that causes fermentation. ✧ *vb* **3** to undergo or cause to undergo fermentation. ▷ HISTORY Latin *fermentum* yeast

> **WORD TIP**
> See at **foment.**

fermentation *n* a chemical reaction in which an organic molecule splits into simpler substances, esp. the conversion of sugar to ethyl alcohol by yeast.

fermium *n Chem* an element artificially produced by neutron bombardment of plutonium. Symbol: Fm. ▷ HISTORY after Enrico *Fermi,* physicist

fern *n* a flowerless plant with roots, stems, and long feathery leaves that reproduces by releasing spores. ▷ HISTORY Old English *fearn* ▶ **ferny** *adj*

ferocious *adj* savagely fierce or cruel. ▷ HISTORY Latin *ferox* ▶ **ferocity** *n*

ferret *n* **1** a small yellowish-white animal related to the weasel and bred for hunting rats and rabbits. ✧ *vb* **-reting, -reted 2** to hunt rabbits or rats with ferrets. **3** to search around. **4 ferret out a** to drive from hiding. **b** to find by determined investigation: *she could ferret out little knowledge of his background.*

> **WORD HISTORY**
> 'Ferret' comes from Old French *furet* meaning 'little thief', from Latin *fūr,* meaning 'thief', a Latin root also found in 'furtive'.

ferric *adj* of or containing iron in the trivalent state. ▷ HISTORY Latin *ferrum* iron

Ferris wheel *n* a large vertical fairground wheel with hanging seats for riding on. ▷ HISTORY after G. W. G. *Ferris,* American engineer

ferrous *adj* of or containing iron in the divalent state. ▷ HISTORY Latin *ferrum* iron

ferruginous (fur-**rooj**-in-uss) *adj* (of a mineral or rock) containing iron. ▷ HISTORY Latin *ferrum* iron

ferrule *n* a metal ring or cap placed over the end of a stick for added strength. ▷ HISTORY Latin *viria* bracelet

ferry *n, pl* **-ries 1** a boat for transporting passengers and vehicles across a body of water, esp. as a regular service. **2** such a service. ✧ *vb* **-ries, -rying, -ried 3** to transport or go by ferry. **4** to transport (passengers or goods) on a regular basis. ▷ **HISTORY** Old English *ferian* to carry ▶ **ferryman** *n*

fertile *adj* **1** capable of producing offspring, crops, or vegetation. **2** *Biol* capable of growth and development: *fertile seeds.* **3** highly productive: *a fertile imagination.* **4** *Physics* (of a substance) able to be transformed into fissile or fissionable material. ▷ **HISTORY** Latin *fertilis* ▶ **fertility** *n*

fertilize *or* **-lise** *vb* **-lizing, -lized** *or* **-lising, -lised 1** to provide (an animal or plant) with sperm or pollen to bring about fertilization. **2** to supply (soil) with nutrients. ▶ **fertilization** *or* **-lisation** *n*

fertilizer *or* **-liser** *n* any substance, such as manure, added to soil to increase its productivity.

fervent *or* **fervid** *adj* intensely sincere and passionate. ▷ **HISTORY** Latin *fervere* to boil ▶ **fervently** *adv*

fervour *or US* **fervor** *n* great intensity of feeling or belief. ▷ **HISTORY** Latin *fervere* to boil

fescue *n* a pasture and lawn grass with stiff narrow leaves. ▷ **HISTORY** Old French *festu*

fester *vb* **1** to grow worse and increasingly hostile: *the bitterness which had been festering beneath the surface.* **2** (of a wound) to form pus. **3** to rot and decay: *rubbish festered in the heat.* ▷ **HISTORY** Old French *festre* suppurating sore

festival *n* **1** an organized series of special events and performances: *the Edinburgh Festival.* **2** a day or period set aside for celebration. ▷ **HISTORY** Latin *festivus* joyful

festive *adj* of or like a celebration. ▷ **HISTORY** Latin *festivus* joyful

festivity *n, pl* **-ties 1** happy celebration: *a spirit of joy and festivity.* **2 festivities** celebrations.

festoon *vb* **1** to drape with decorations: *Christmas trees festooned with fairy lights.* ✧ *n* **2** a decorative chain of flowers or ribbons suspended in loops. ▷ **HISTORY** Italian *festone* ornament for a feast

feta *n* a white Greek cheese made from sheep's or goat's milk. ▷ **HISTORY** Modern Greek

fetal alcohol syndrome *n* a condition in newborn babies caused by excessive alcohol intake by the mother during pregnancy: characterized by various defects including mental retardation.

fetch[1] *vb* **1** to go after and bring back. **2** to be sold for (a certain price): *Impressionist pictures fetch very high prices.* **3** *Informal* to give someone (a blow or slap). **4 fetch and carry** to perform menial tasks. ▷ **HISTORY** Old English *feccan*

fetch[2] *n* the ghost or apparition of a living person. ▷ **HISTORY** origin unknown

fetching *adj Informal* attractive: *a fetching dress.*

fetch up *vb* **1** *US & NZ informal* to arrive or end up. **2** *Slang* to vomit food.

fete (**fate**) *n* **1** an event, usually outdoors, with stalls, competitions, etc., held to raise money for charity. ✧ *vb* **feting, feted 2** to honour and entertain (someone) publicly: *the President was feted with an evening of music and dancing.* ▷ **HISTORY** French

fetid *or* **foetid** *adj* having a stale and unpleasant smell. ▷ **HISTORY** Latin *fetere* to stink

fetish *n* **1 a** a form of behaviour in which a person derives sexual satisfaction from handling an object. **b** any object that is involved in such behaviour. **2** any object, activity, etc., to which one is excessively devoted: *cleanliness is almost a fetish with her.* **3** an object that is believed to have magical powers. ▷ **HISTORY** Portuguese *feitiço* sorcery ▶ **fetishism** *n* ▶ **fetishist** *n*

fetlock *n* **1** the back part of a horse's leg, just behind the hoof. **2** the tuft of hair growing from this part. ▷ **HISTORY** Middle English *fetlak*

fetter *n* **1 fetters** checks or restraints: *free from the fetters of religion.* **2** a chain fixed around a prisoner's ankle. ✧ *vb* **3** to prevent from behaving freely and naturally: *fettered by bureaucracy.* **4** to tie up in fetters. ▷ **HISTORY** Old English *fetor*

fettle *n* **in fine fettle** in good spirits or health. ▷ **HISTORY** Old English *fetel* belt

fetus *or* **foetus** (**fee**-tuss) *n, pl* **-tuses** the embryo of a mammal in the later stages of development. ▷ **HISTORY** Latin: offspring ▶ **fetal** *or* **foetal** *adj*

feu *n Scots Law* a right to the use of land in return for a fixed annual payment (**feu duty**). ▷ **HISTORY** Old French

feud *n* **1** long and bitter hostility between two families, clans, or individuals. ✧ *vb* **2** to carry on a feud. ▷ **HISTORY** Old French *feide*

feudal *adj* of or characteristic of feudalism. ▷ **HISTORY** Medieval Latin *feudum* fief

feudalism *n History* the legal and social system in medieval Europe, in which people were given land and protection by a lord in return for which they worked and fought for him. Also called: **feudal system**

fever *n* **1** an abnormally high body temperature, accompanied by a fast pulse rate, shivering, and nausea. RELATED ADJECTIVE ➜ **febrile 2** any disease characterized by a high temperature. **3** intense nervous excitement: *she waited in a fever of anxiety.* ▷ **HISTORY** Latin *febris*

feverish *or* **fevered** *adj* **1** suffering from fever. **2** in a state of nervous excitement: *a feverish scramble to buy shares.* ▶ **feverishly** *adv*

fever pitch *n* a state of intense excitement.

few *adj* **1** hardly any: *few homes had telephones in Paris in the 1930s.* **2 a few** a small number of: *a few days ago.* **3 a good few** *Informal* several. **4 few and far between** scarce. **5 quite a few** *Informal* several. ▷ **HISTORY** Old English *fēawa*

> ☑ **WORD TIP**
> See at **less.**

fey *adj* **1** vague and whimsically strange. **2** having the ability to look into the future. ▷ **HISTORY** Old English *fæge* marked out for death

fez *n, pl* **fezzes** a round red brimless hat with a flat top and a tassel hanging from it. Formerly worn by

A B C D E F G H I J K L M N O P Q R S T U V W X Y Z

men in Turkey and some Arab countries. ▷ HISTORY Turkish

ff. and the following (pages, lines, etc.).

fiancé *or fem* **fiancée** (fee-**on**-say) *n* a person who is engaged to be married. ▷ HISTORY Old French *fiancier* to promise, betroth

fiasco *n, pl* **-cos** *or* **-coes** an action or attempt that fails completely in a ridiculous or disorganized way: *the invasion of Cuba ended in a fiasco.* ▷ HISTORY Italian: flask; sense development obscure

fiat (**fie**-at) *n* **1** an official order issued without the consultation of those expected to obey it: *the junta ruled by fiat.* **2** official permission. ▷ HISTORY Latin: let it be done

fib *n* **1** a trivial and harmless lie. ✧ *vb* **fibbing, fibbed 2** to tell such a lie. ▷ HISTORY origin unknown ▶ **fibber** *n*

fibre *or US* **fiber** *n* **1** a natural or synthetic thread that may be spun into yarn. **2** a threadlike animal or plant tissue: *a simple network of nerve fibres.* **3** a fibrous substance that helps the body digest food: *fruits, vegetables, grains, lentils, and beans are high in fibre.* **4** strength of character: *moral fibre.* **5** essential substance or nature: *my every fibre sang out in sudden relief.* ▷ HISTORY Latin *fibra* filament, entrails ▶ **fibrous** *adj*

fibreboard *n* a building material made of compressed wood.

fibreglass *n* **1** material consisting of matted fine glass fibres, used as insulation. **2** a light strong material made by bonding fibreglass with a synthetic resin, used for boats and car bodies.

fibre optics *n* the transmission of information by light along very thin flexible fibres of glass. ▶ **fibre optic** *adj*

fibril (**fibe**-rill) *n* a small fibre.

fibrillation *n* uncontrollable twitching of muscle fibres, esp. those of the heart.

fibrin *n* a white insoluble elastic protein formed when blood clots.

fibrinogen (fib-**rin**-no-jen) *n Biol* a soluble plasma protein involved in blood clotting.

fibro *n Austral* a mixture of cement and asbestos fibre, used in sheets for building. Also: **fibrocement**

fibroid (**fibe**-royd) *adj* **1** *Anat* (of structures or tissues) containing or resembling fibres. ✧ *n* **2** a harmless tumour composed of fibrous connective tissue.

fibrosis (fibe-**roh**-siss) *n* the formation of an abnormal amount of fibrous tissue.

fibrositis (fibe-roh-**site**-iss) *n* inflammation of fibrous tissue, esp. of the back muscles, causing pain and stiffness.

fibula (**fib**-yew-la) *n, pl* **-lae** (-lee) *or* **-las** the outer and thinner of the two bones between the knee and ankle of the human leg. ▷ HISTORY Latin: a clasp ▶ **fibular** *adj*

fiche (**feesh**) *n* a sheet of film for storing publications in miniature form.

fickle *adj* **1** changeable in purpose, affections, etc.: *notoriously fickle voters.* **2** (of the weather) changing often and suddenly. ▷ HISTORY Old English *ficol* deceitful ▶ **fickleness** *n*

fiction *n* **1** literary works invented by the imagination, such as novels. **2** an invented story or explanation: *the fiction that the Baltic states freely joined the USSR.* **3** *Law* something assumed to be true for the sake of convenience, though probably false. ▷ HISTORY Latin *fictio* a fashioning ▶ **fictional** *adj*

fictionalize *or* **-ise** *vb* **-izing, -ized** *or* **-ising, -ised** to make into fiction.

fictitious *adj* **1** not genuine: *rumours of false accounting and fictitious loans had surrounded the bank for years.* **2** of or in fiction.

fiddle *n* **1** *Informal or disparaging* the violin. **2** a violin played as a folk instrument. **3** *Brit & NZ informal* a dishonest action or scheme. **4 on the fiddle** *Informal* engaged in an illegal or fraudulent undertaking. **5 fit as a fiddle** *Informal* in very good health. **6 play second fiddle** *Informal* to undertake a role that is less important or powerful than someone else's. ✧ *vb* **-dling, -dled 7** to play (a tune) on the fiddle. **8** *Informal* to do (something) by illegal or dishonest means. **9** *Informal* to falsify (accounts). **10 fiddle with** to move or touch (something) restlessly or nervously. **11 fiddle about** *or* **around** *Informal* to waste time. ▷ HISTORY Old English *fithele*

fiddler *n* **1** a person who plays the fiddle. **2** a small burrowing crab. **3** *Informal* a person who dishonestly alters something or lies in order to get money.

fiddlesticks *interj* an expression of annoyance or disagreement.

fiddling *adj* small or unimportant.

fiddly *adj* **-dlier, -dliest** small and awkward to do or handle.

fidelity *n, pl* **-ties 1** faithfulness to one's spouse or lover. **2** loyalty to a person, belief, or cause. **3** accuracy in reporting detail: *an account of the invasion written with objectivity and fidelity.* **4** *Electronics* the degree to which an amplifier or radio accurately reproduces the input signal. ▷ HISTORY Latin *fides* faith

fidget *vb* **-eting, -eted 1** to move about restlessly. **2 fidget with** to make restless or uneasy movements with (something): *he broke off, fidgeting with the papers, unable to meet their gaze.* ✧ *n* **3** a person who fidgets. **4 the fidgets** a state of restlessness: *these youngsters are very highly strung and tend to get the fidgets.* ▷ HISTORY earlier *fidge* ▶ **fidgety** *adj*

fiduciary (fid-**yewsh**-ya-ree) *Law* ✧ *n* **1** a person bound to act for someone else's benefit, as a trustee. ✧ *adj* **2** of or relating to a trust or trustee. ▷ HISTORY Latin *fiducia* trust

fie *interj Obsolete or facetious* an exclamation of disapproval. ▷ HISTORY Old French *fi*

fief (**feef**) *n* (in feudal Europe) land granted by a lord in return for military service. ▷ HISTORY Old French *fie*

fiefdom *n* **1** (in Feudal Europe) the property owned by a lord. **2** an area over which a person has influence or authority.

field *n* **1** an area of uncultivated grassland; meadow. **2** a piece of cleared land used for pasture or growing crops. **3** a marked off area on which sports or athletic competitions are held. **4** an area that is rich in minerals or other natural resources: *an oil field.* **5 a** all the competitors in a competition. **b** the competitors in a competition excluding the favourite. **6** a battlefield. **7** *Cricket* the fielders collectively. **8** a wide expanse of land covered by some substance such as snow or lava. **9** an area of human activity or knowledge: *the most distinguished physicist in the field of quantum physics.* **10** a place away from the laboratory or classroom where practical work is done. **11** the surface or background of something, such as a flag. **12** *Physics* In full: **field of force** the region surrounding a body, such as a magnet, within which it can exert a force on another similar body not in contact with it. **13 play the field** *Informal* to have many romantic relationships before getting married. ✧ *adj* **14** *Mil* of equipment or personnel for operations in the field: *field guns.* ✧ *vb* **15** *Sport* to catch or return (the ball) as a fielder. **16** *Sport* to send (a player or team) onto the field to play. **17** *Sport* (of a player or team) to act or take turn as a fielder or fielders. **18** *Informal* to deal successfully with (a question or remark). ▷ **HISTORY** Old English *feld*

field day *n* **1** *Informal* an opportunity or occasion for unrestrained action, esp. if previously denied or restricted: *the revelations gave the press a field day.* **2** *Mil* a day devoted to manoeuvres or exercises.

fielder *n Cricket etc.* a member of the fielding side.

fieldfare *n* a type of large thrush. ▷ **HISTORY** Old English *feldefare*

field glasses *pl n* binoculars.

field hockey *n US & Canad* hockey played on a field, as distinguished from ice hockey.

field marshal *n* an officer holding the highest rank in certain armies.

fieldmouse *n, pl* **-mice** a nocturnal mouse that lives in woods and fields.

field officer *n* an officer holding the rank of major, lieutenant colonel, or colonel.

fieldsman *n, pl* **-men** *Cricket* a fielder.

field sports *pl n* sports carried on in the countryside, such as hunting or fishing.

field trip *n* an expedition, esp. by students, to study something at first hand.

fieldwork *n Mil* a temporary structure used in defending a place or position.

field work *n* an investigation made in the field as opposed to the classroom or laboratory. ▶ **field worker** *n*

fiend (**feend**) *n* **1** an evil spirit. **2** a cruel or wicked person. **3** *Informal* a person who is extremely interested in or fond of something: *a fitness fiend.* ▷ **HISTORY** Old English *fēond* ▶ **fiendish** *adj* ▶ **fiendishly** *adv*

Fiend *n* **the Fiend** the devil.

fierce *adj* **1** very aggressive or angry: *a fierce dog.* **2** intense or strong: *a fierce wind.* ▷ **HISTORY** Latin *ferus* ▶ **fiercely** *adv*

fiery (**fire**-ee) *adj* **fierier, fieriest 1** consisting of or like fire: *a fiery explosion.* **2** displaying strong passion, esp. anger: *a fiery speech.* **3** (of food) very spicy. ▶ **fierily** *adv* ▶ **fieriness** *n*

fiesta *n* (esp. in Spain and Latin America) a religious festival or carnival. ▷ **HISTORY** Spanish

FIFA (**fee**-fa) International Association Football Federation. ▷ **HISTORY** French *Fédération Internationale de Football Association*

fife *n* a small high-pitched flute, often used in military bands. ▷ **HISTORY** Old High German *pfīfa*

fifteen *n* **1** the cardinal number that is the sum of ten and five. **2** a numeral, 15 or XV, representing this number. **3** something representing or consisting of 15 units. **4** a Rugby Union team. ✧ *adj* **5** amounting to fifteen: *fifteen trees.* ▶ **fifteenth** *adj, n*

fifth *adj* **1** of or being number five in a series. ✧ *n* **2** one of five equal parts of something. **3** *Music* the interval between one note and the note three-and-a-half tones higher or lower than it. **4** an additional high gear fitted to some vehicles, esp. certain sports cars.

fifth column *n* any group that secretly helps the enemies of its own country or organization. ▶ **fifth columnist** *n*

fifty *n, pl* **-ties 1** the cardinal number that is the product of ten and five. **2** a numeral, 50 or L, representing this number. **3** something representing or consisting of 50 units. ✧ *adj* **4** amounting to fifty: *fifty bodies.* ▶ **fiftieth** *adj, n*

fifty-fifty *adj, adv Informal* **1** in equal parts. **2** just as likely to happen as not to happen: *a fifty-fifty chance of survival.*

fig *n* **1** a soft sweet fruit full of tiny seeds, which grows on a tree. **2 not care** *or* **give a fig** not to care at all: *he did not give a fig for his enemies.* ▷ **HISTORY** Latin *ficus* fig tree

fig. **1** figurative(ly). **2** figure.

fight *vb* **fighting, fought 1** to struggle against (an enemy) in battle or physical combat. **2** to struggle to overcome or destroy: *to fight drug trafficking.* **3** to carry on (a battle or contest). **4** to make (one's way) somewhere with difficulty: *they fought their way upstream.* **5 fight for** to uphold (a cause) by struggling: *fight for your rights.* **6 fight it out** to struggle or compete until a decisive result is obtained. **7 fight shy of** to avoid: *they fought shy of direct involvement in the conflict.* ✧ *n* **8** a battle. **9** a quarrel or contest. **10** a boxing match. **11 put up a fight** to offer resistance. ▷ **HISTORY** Old English *feohtan* ▶ **fighting** *n*

fighter *n* **1** a professional boxer. **2** a person who has determination. **3** *Mil* an armed aircraft for destroying other aircraft.

fight off *vb* **1** to drive away (an attacker). **2** to struggle to avoid: *to fight off infection.*

fig leaf *n* **1** a representation of a leaf of the fig tree used in sculpture to cover the genitals of nude figures. **2** anything used to conceal something thought to be shameful: *the agreement was a fig leaf for Hitler's violation of the treaty.*

a b c d e f g h i j k l m n o p q r s t u v w x y z

figment *n* **a figment of one's imagination** something nonexistent and only imagined by someone. ▷ **HISTORY** Latin *fingere* to shape

figuration *n* ornamentation.

figurative *adj* **1** (of language) abstract, imaginative, or symbolic; not literal. **2** (of art) involving realistic representation of people and things. ▶ **figuratively** *adv*

figure *n* **1** a written symbol for a number. **2** an amount expressed in numbers. **3 figures** calculations with numbers. **4** visible shape or form; outline. **5** a slim bodily shape: *it's not good for your figure.* **6** a well-known person: *a public figure.* **7** a representation in painting or sculpture, esp. of the human body. **8** an illustration or diagram in a text. **9** a decorative pattern. **10** a fixed set of movements in dancing or skating. **11** *Geom* any combination of points, lines, curves, or planes. **12** *Music* a characteristic short pattern of notes. **13 figure of fun** a person who is often laughed at by other people. ✧ *vb* **-uring, -ured 14** to calculate (sums or amounts). **15** *US, Canad, Austral & NZ informal* to consider. **16** to be included or play a part: *a house which figures in several of White's novels.* **17** *Informal* to be consistent with expectation: *Small-time crook, earns most of his cash as an informer. – That figures.* ▷ **HISTORY** Latin *figura* a shape

figured *adj* **1** decorated with a design: *a chair upholstered in figured velvet.* **2** *Music* ornamental.

figurehead *n* **1** a person who is formally the head of a movement or an organization, but has no real authority. **2** a carved bust on the bow of some sailing vessels.

figure of speech *n* an expression, such as a simile, in which words do not have their literal meaning.

figure out *vb Informal* to work out, solve, or understand: *I can't figure him out.*

figurine *n* a small carved or moulded figure. ▷ **HISTORY** French

filament *n* **1** the thin wire inside a light bulb that emits light. **2** *Electronics* a high-resistance wire forming the cathode in some valves. **3** a single strand of fibre. **4** *Bot* the stalk of a stamen. ▷ **HISTORY** Latin *filum* thread ▶ **filamentary** *adj*

filbert *n* the brown edible nuts of the hazel. ▷ **HISTORY** after St *Philbert,* because the nuts are ripe around his feast day, August 22

filch *vb* to steal in small amounts. ▷ **HISTORY** Middle English *filchen* to steal, attack

file[1] *n* **1** a folder or box used to keep documents in order. **2** the documents, etc., kept in this way. **3** documents or information about a specific subject or person: *the doctor handed him his file.* **4** a line of people in marching formation, one behind another. **5** *Computers* an organized collection of related records. **6 on file** recorded for reference, as in a file. ✧ *vb* **filing, filed 7** to place (a document) in a file. **8** to place (a legal document) on public or official record. **9** to bring a lawsuit, esp. for divorce. **10** to submit (a report or story) to a newspaper. **11** to march or walk in a line. ▷ **HISTORY** Latin *filum* a thread

file[2] *n* **1** a hand tool consisting of a steel blade with small cutting teeth on its faces, used for shaping or smoothing. ✧ *vb* **filing, filed 2** to shape or smooth (a surface) with a file. ▷ **HISTORY** Old English *fil*

file photograph *n Journalism & publishing* a photograph kept on file in a photograph collection for use as and when needed.

filial *adj* of or suitable to a son or daughter: *filial duty.* ▷ **HISTORY** Latin *filius* son

filibuster *n* **1** the process of obstructing legislation by means of long speeches so that time runs out and a vote cannot be taken. **2** a legislator who engages in such obstruction. ✧ *vb* **3** to obstruct (legislation) with such delaying tactics. ▷ **HISTORY** probably from Dutch *vrijbuiter* pirate

filigree *n* **1** delicate ornamental work of gold or silver wire. ✧ *adj* **2** made of filigree. ▷ **HISTORY** Latin *filum* thread + *granum* grain

filings *pl n* shavings or particles removed by a file: *iron filings.*

Filipino (fill-lip-**pee**-no) *adj* **1** of the Philippines. ✧ *n, pl* **-nos 2** Also (fem): **Filipina** a person from the Philippines.

fill *vb* (often foll. by *up*) **1** to make or become full. **2** to occupy the whole of: *their supporters filled the entire stand.* **3** to plug (a gap or crevice). **4** to meet (a requirement or need) satisfactorily: *this book fills a major gap.* **5** to cover (a page or blank space) with writing or drawing. **6** to hold and perform the duties of (an office or position). **7** to appoint or elect an occupant to (an office or position). ✧ *n* **8 one's fill** sufficient for one's needs or wants. ✧ See also **fill in.** ▷ **HISTORY** Old English *fyllan*

filler *n* **1** a paste used for filling in cracks or holes in a surface before painting. **2** *Journalism* an item to fill space between more important articles.

fillet *n* **1** a piece of boneless meat or fish. **2** a thin strip of ribbon or lace worn in the hair or around the neck. **3** *Archit* a narrow flat moulding. ✧ *vb* **-leting, -leted 4** to cut or prepare (meat or fish) as a fillet. ▷ **HISTORY** Latin *filum* thread

fill in *vb* **1** to complete (a form). **2** to act as a substitute. **3** to put material into (a hole) so as to make it level with a surface. **4** *Informal* to give (a person) fuller details.

filling *n* **1** a substance or thing used to fill something: *a sandwich filling.* **2** *Dentistry* a substance that fills a gap or cavity of a tooth. ✧ *adj* **3** (of food or a meal) substantial and satisfying.

filling station *n Chiefly Brit* a place where petrol and other supplies for motorists are sold.

fillip *n* **1** something that adds stimulation or enjoyment. **2** the action of holding a finger towards the palm with the thumb and suddenly releasing it with a snapping sound. ▷ **HISTORY** imitative

filly *n, pl* **-lies** a young female horse. ▷ **HISTORY** Old Norse *fylja*

film *n* **1 a** a sequence of images projected onto a screen, creating the illusion of movement. **b** a form of entertainment in such a sequence of images. *RELATED ADJECTIVE* ▶ **cinematic 2** a thin flexible strip of cellulose coated with a photographic emulsion, used to make negatives and slides. **3** a thin coating, covering, or layer: *a fine film of dust covered the floor.* **4** a thin sheet of any material, as of plastic for packaging. ✧ *vb* **5 a** to photograph with a movie or video camera. **b** to make a film of (a screenplay or event). **6 film over** to cover or become covered with a thin layer. ✧ *adj* **7** of or relating to films or the cinema. ▷ HISTORY Old English *filmen* membrane

filmic *adj* of or suggestive of films or the cinema. ▶ **filmically** *adv*

film star *n* a popular film actor or actress.

film strip *n* a strip of film composed of different images projected separately as slides.

filmy *adj* **filmier, filmiest** very thin and almost transparent: *a shirt of filmy black chiffon.* ▶ **filmily** *adv* ▶ **filminess** *n*

filter *n* **1** a substance, such as paper or sand, that allows fluid to pass but retains solid particles. **2** any device containing such a substance, esp. a tip on the mouth end of a cigarette. **3** any electronic or acoustic device that blocks signals of certain frequencies while allowing others to pass. **4** any transparent disc of gelatine or glass used to reduce the intensity of given frequencies from the light leaving a lamp or entering a camera. **5** *Brit* a traffic signal which permits vehicles to turn either left or right when the main signals are red. ✧ *vb* **6** Also: **filter out** to remove or separate (particles) from (a liquid or gas) by a filter. **7** Also: **filter through** to pass through a filter or something like a filter. ▷ HISTORY Medieval Latin *filtrum* piece of felt used as a filter

filter paper *n* a porous paper used for filtering liquids.

filter tip *n* **1** an attachment to the mouth end of a cigarette for trapping impurities. **2** a cigarette with such an attachment. ▶ **filter-tipped** *adj*

filth *n* **1** disgusting dirt and muck. **2** offensive material or language. ▷ HISTORY Old English *fȳlth* ▶ **filthiness** *n* ▶ **filthy** *adj*

filtrate *n* **1** a liquid or gas that has been filtered. ✧ *vb* **-trating, -trated 2** to filter. ▷ HISTORY Medieval Latin *filtrare* to filter ▶ **filtration** *n*

fin *n* **1** any of the winglike projections from a fish's body enabling it to balance and swim. **2** *Brit* a vertical surface to which the rudder is attached at the rear of an aeroplane. **3** a swimmer's flipper. ▷ HISTORY Old English *finn* ▶ **finned** *adj*

finagle (fin-**nay**-gl) *vb* **-gling, -gled** *Informal* to use or achieve by craftiness or trickery. ▷ HISTORY origin unknown

final *adj* **1** of or occurring at the end; last. **2** having no possibility of further discussion, action, or change: *a final decision.* ✧ *n* **3** a deciding contest between the winners of previous rounds in a competition. ✧ See also **finals.** ▷ HISTORY Latin *finis* limit, boundary ▶ **finality** *n* ▶ **finally** *adv*

finale (fin-**nah**-lee) *n* the concluding part of a dramatic performance or musical composition. ▷ HISTORY Italian

finalist *n* a contestant who has reached the last stage of a competition.

finalize *or* **-ise** *vb* **-izing, -ized** *or* **-ising, -ised** to put into final form; settle: *plans have yet to be finalized.* ▶ **finalization** *or* **-isation** *n*

> **WORD TIP**
> Although *finalize* has been in widespread use for some time, many speakers and writers still prefer to use *complete, conclude,* or *make final,* esp. in formal contexts.

finals *pl n* **1** the deciding part of a competition. **2** *Education Brit & S African* the last examinations in an academic course.

finance *vb* **-nancing, -nanced 1** to provide or obtain funds for (a project or large purchase). ✧ *n* **2** the system of money, credit, and investment. **3** management of money, loans, or credits: *the dangerous political arena of public-sector finance.* **4** funds or the provision of funds. **5 finances** money resources: *the company's crumbling finances.* ▷ HISTORY Old French *finer* to end, settle by payment

financial *adj* **1** of or relating to finance, finances, or people who manage money. **2** *Austral & NZ informal* having ready money. ▶ **financially** *adv*

financial market *n Econ* the buying and selling of stocks, shares, currencies, and commodities, and the results of this trade expressed in prices.

financial year *n* any annual accounting period.

financier *n* a person who is engaged in large-scale financial operations.

finch *n* a small songbird with a short strong beak. ▷ HISTORY Old English *finc*

find *vb* **finding, found 1** to discover by chance. **2** to discover by search or effort. **3** to realize or become aware: *I have found that if you make the effort then people will be more willing to help you.* **4** to consider (someone or something) to have a particular quality: *his business partner had found that odd.* **5** to experience (a particular feeling): *she found comfort in his words.* **6** *Law* to pronounce (the defendant) guilty or not guilty. **7** to reach (a target). **8** to provide, esp. with difficulty: *we'll find room for you too.* **9 find one's feet** to become capable or confident. ✧ *n* **10** a person or thing that is found, esp. a valuable discovery: *the archaeological find of the century.* ▷ HISTORY Old English *findan*

finder *n* **1** a small telescope fitted to a larger one. **2** a person or thing that finds. **3** *Photog* short for **viewfinder**.

finding *n* the conclusion reached after an inquiry or investigation.

find out *vb* **1** to learn something that one did not already know. **2 find someone out** to discover that someone has been dishonest or deceitful.

fine[1] *adj* **1** very good. **2** superior in skill: *a fine doctor.* **3** (of weather) clear and dry. **4** *Informal* quite well: *I felt fine.* **5** satisfactory: *as far as we can tell, everything is fine.* **6** of delicate or careful workmanship: *fine porcelain.* **7** subtle: *too fine a distinction.* **8** very thin or slender: *fine soft hair.* **9** very small: *fine print.* **10** (of edges or blades) sharp. **11** fancy, showy, or smart. **12** good-looking. **13** *Ironic* disappointing or terrible: *a fine mess!*

a b c d e f g h i j k l m n o p q r s t u v w x y z

✧ *adv* **14** *Informal* very well: *that's what we've always done, and it suits us just fine.* ✧ *vb* **fining, fined 15** to make (something) finer or thinner. **16 fine down** to make (a theory or criticism) more precise or exact. ▷ **HISTORY** Latin *finis* end, boundary, as in *finis honorum* the highest degree of honour ▸ **finely** *adv*

fine[2] *n* **1** a payment imposed as a penalty. ✧ *vb* **fining, fined 2** to impose a fine on. ▷ **HISTORY** Old French *fin*

fine art *n* **1** art produced chiefly to appeal to the sense of beauty. **2** any of the fields in which such art is produced, such as painting, sculpture, and engraving.

fine-drawn *adj* **1** (of arguments or distinctions) subtle. **2** (of wire) drawn out until very fine.

finery *n* elaborate or showy decoration, esp. clothing and jewellery: *the actress dressed up in her finery.*

finesse (fin-**ness**) *n* **1** elegant and delicate skill. **2** subtlety and tact in handling difficult situations: *a lack of diplomatic finesse.* **3** *Bridge, whist* an attempt to win a trick when opponents hold a high card in the suit led by playing a lower card. ✧ *vb* **-nessing, -nessed 4** to bring about with finesse. **5** *Bridge, whist* to play (a card) as a finesse. ▷ **HISTORY** Old French

fine-tune *vb* **-tuning, -tuned** to make fine adjustments to (something) so that it works really well.

finger *n* **1** one of the four long jointed parts of the hand. **2** the part of a glove made to cover a finger. **3** something that resembles a finger in shape or function. **4** a quantity of liquid in a glass as deep as a finger is wide. **5 get** or **pull one's finger out** *Brit & NZ informal* to begin or speed up activity, esp. after initial delay. **6 put one's finger on** to identify precisely. **7 put the finger on** *Informal* to inform on or identify, esp. for the police. **8 twist around one's little finger** to have easy and complete influence over. ✧ *vb* **9** to touch or manipulate with the fingers; handle. **10** to use one's fingers in playing (a musical instrument). **11** *Informal, chiefly US* to identify as a criminal or suspect. ▷ **HISTORY** Old English ▸ **fingerless** *adj*

fingerboard *n* the long strip of hard wood on a violin, guitar, etc., upon which the strings are stopped by the fingers.

finger bowl *n* a small bowl of water for rinsing the fingers at table during a meal, esp. at a formal dinner.

fingering *n* **1** the technique of using one's fingers in playing a musical instrument. **2** the numerals in a musical part indicating this.

fingernail *n* a thin hard clear plate covering part of the upper surface of the end of each finger.

fingerprint *n* **1** an impression of the pattern of ridges on the inner surface of the end of each finger and thumb. ✧ *vb* **2** to take an inked impression of the fingerprints of (a person). **3** to take a sample of the DNA of (a person).

fingerstall *n* a protective covering for a finger.

fingertip *n* **1** the end of a finger. **2 have at one's fingertips** to know thoroughly.

finicky *or* **finicking** *adj* **1** extremely fussy. **2** overelaborate or ornate: *finicky designer patterns.* ▷ **HISTORY** earlier *finical,* from FINE[1]

finis *n* the end: used at the end of books. ▷ **HISTORY** Latin

finish *vb* **1** to bring to an end; conclude or stop. **2** to be at or come to the end; use up. **3** to bring to a desired or complete condition. **4** to put a particular surface texture on (wood, cloth, or metal). **5 finish off a** to complete by doing the last part of: *he finished off his thesis last week.* **b** to destroy or defeat completely: *he finished off Faldo at the 16th hole.* **6 finish with** to end a relationship with (someone). ✧ *n* **7** the final stage or part; end. **8** death or absolute defeat. **9** the surface texture of wood, cloth, or metal. **10** a thing or event that completes. ▷ **HISTORY** Latin *finire*

finishing school *n* a private school for girls that teaches social skills and polite behaviour.

finite (**fine**-ite) *adj* **1** having limits in size, space, or time: *finite supplies of fossil fuels.* **2** *Maths, logic* having a countable number of elements. **3** *Grammar* denoting any form of a verb inflected for person, number, and tense. ▷ **HISTORY** Latin *finitus* limited

finite verb *n Grammar* a verb in an inflected form, reflecting the subject, number and tense, as opposed to an infinitive or participle.

Finn *n* a person from Finland.

Finnish *adj* **1** of Finland. ✧ *n* **2** the language of Finland.

fiord (fee-**ord**) *n* same as **fjord**.

fipple flute *n* an end-blown flute with a plug (**fipple**) at the mouthpiece, such as the recorder or flageolet.

fir *n* a pyramid-shaped tree with needle-like leaves and erect cones. ▷ **HISTORY** Old English *furh*

fire *n* **1** the state of combustion producing heat, flames, and often smoke. **2** *Brit* burning coal or wood, esp. in a hearth to heat a room. **3** a destructive uncontrolled burning that destroys building, crops, etc. **4** an electric or gas device for heating a room. **5** the act of shooting weapons. **6** passion and enthusiasm: *her questions brought new fire to the debate.* **7 catch fire** to start burning. **8 on fire a** burning. **b** ardent or eager. **9 open fire** to start firing a gun, artillery, etc. **10 play with fire** to be involved in something risky. **11 set fire to** *or* **set on fire a** to ignite. **b** to arouse or excite. **12 under fire** being attacked, such as by weapons or by harsh criticism. ✧ *vb* **firing, fired 13** to discharge (a firearm). **14** to detonate (an explosive device). **15** *Informal* to dismiss from employment. **16** to ask a lot of questions quickly in succession. **17** *Ceramics* to bake in a kiln to harden the clay. **18** to kindle or be kindled. **19** (of an internal-combustion engine) to produce an electrical spark which causes the fuel to burn and the engine to start. **20** to provide with fuel. **21** to arouse to strong emotion: *he fired his team mates with enthusiasm.* ▷ **HISTORY** Old English *fȳr*

fire alarm *n* a device to give warning of fire.

firearm *n* a weapon, such as a pistol, that fires bullets.

fireball *n* **1** ball-shaped lightning. **2** the hot ionized gas at the centre of a nuclear explosion. **3** a large bright meteor. **4** *Slang* an energetic person.

firebrand *n* a person who arouses passionate political feelings, often causing trouble.

firebreak *n* a strip of open land in a forest to stop the advance of a fire.

firebrick *n* a heat-resistant brick, used for lining furnaces, flues, and fireplaces.

fire brigade *n Brit & Austral* an organized body of firefighters.

firecracker *n* a firework which produces a loud bang.

firedamp *n Brit, Austral & NZ* an explosive mixture of hydrocarbons, chiefly methane, formed in coal mines.

fire drill *n* a rehearsal of procedures for escape from a fire.

fire-eater *n* **1** a performer who pretends to swallow flaming rods. **2** a very quarrelsome person.

fire engine *n* a vehicle that carries firefighters and firefighting equipment to a fire.

fire escape *n* a metal staircase or ladder on the outside of a building for escape in the event of fire.

fire-extinguisher *n* a portable device for spraying water, foam, or powder to extinguish a fire.

firefighter *n* a person whose job is to put out fires and rescue people endangered by them. ▶ **firefighting** *adj, n*

firefly *n, pl* **-flies** a beetle that glows in the dark.

fireguard *n* a screen made of wire mesh put before an open fire to protect against sparks.

fire hydrant *n* an outlet from a water main in the street, from which firefighters can draw water in an emergency.

fire irons *pl n* a shovel, poker, and tongs for tending a domestic fire.

fireman *n, pl* **-men 1** a man whose job is to put out fires and rescue people endangered by them. **2** (on steam trains) the man who stokes the fire.

fireplace *n* an open recess at the base of a chimney for a fire; hearth.

fireplug *n Chiefly US & NZ* same as **fire hydrant**.

fire power *n Mil* the amount of fire that can be delivered by a unit or weapon.

fire raiser *n Brit* a person who deliberately sets fire to property. ▶ **fire raising** *n*

fire ship *n History* a ship loaded with explosives, set on fire and left to drift among an enemy's warships.

fire station *n* a building where firefighting vehicles and equipment are stationed.

firewall *n Computers* a computer than prevents unauthorized access to a computer network from the Internet.

firework *n* a device containing chemicals that is ignited to produce coloured sparks and sometimes bangs.

firing *n* **1** a discharge of a firearm. **2** the process of baking ceramics in a kiln. **3** something used as fuel.

firing line *n* **1** *Mil* the positions from which fire is delivered. **2** the leading or most vulnerable position in an activity: *the manager is in the firing line after a string of bad results.*

firing squad *n* a group of soldiers appointed to shoot a condemned criminal dead.

firm[1] *adj* **1** not soft or yielding to a touch or pressure. **2** securely in position. **3** definitely established: *a firm agreement.* **4** having determination or strength: *if you are firm and consistent she will come to see things your way.* ✧ *adv* **5 stand firm** to refuse to give in. ✧ *vb* **6** to make or become firm: *to firm up flabby thighs.*
▷ **HISTORY** Latin *firmus* ▶ **firmly** *adv* ▶ **firmness** *n*

firm[2] *n* **1** a business company. **2** *Brit slang* a gang of criminals or football hooligans.
▷ **HISTORY** Spanish *firma* signature

firmament *n Literary* the sky or the heavens.
▷ **HISTORY** Late Latin *firmamentum*

first *adj* **1** earliest in time or order. **2** rated, graded, or ranked above all other levels: *the First Lord of the Admiralty.* **3** denoting the lowest forward gear in a motor vehicle. **4** *Music* denoting the highest voice part in a chorus or one of the sections of an orchestra: *the first violin.* ✧ *n* **5** the person or thing coming before all others. **6** the beginning or outset. **7** *Education chiefly Brit* an honours degree of the highest class. **8** the lowest forward gear in a motor vehicle. ✧ *adv* **9** before anything else: *I would advise you to try surgery first.* **10** for the first time: *this story first came to public attention in January 1984.* ▷ **HISTORY** Old English *fyrest*

first aid *n* immediate medical assistance given in an emergency.

first class *n* **1** the class or grade of the best or highest value, rank, or quality. ✧ *adj* **first-class 2** of the best or highest class or grade. **3** excellent. **4** denoting the most comfortable class of accommodation in a hotel, aircraft, or train. **5** denoting mail that is handled faster than second-class mail. ✧ *adv* **first-class 6** by first-class mail, transport, etc.

first-day cover *n Philately* an envelope postmarked on the first day of the issue of its stamps.

first-degree burn *n* a burn in which the skin surface is red and painful.

first-foot *Scot & NZ* ✧ *n* **1** the first person to enter a household in the New Year. ✧ *vb* **2** to visit (someone) as first-foot. ▶ **first-footing** *n*

first-hand *adj, adv* **1** (obtained) directly from the original source. **2 at first hand** directly.

firstly *adv* same as **first** (sense 9).

first mate *n* an officer second in command to the captain of a merchant ship.

First Minister *n* **1** the chief minister of the Scottish Parliament. **2** the chief minister of the Northern Ireland Assembly.

first night *n* the first public performance of a play or other production.

first offender *n* a person convicted of a criminal offence for the first time.

first officer *n* same as **first mate**.
first person *n Grammar* the form of the pronoun or verb used by the speaker to refer to himself or herself or to a group including himself or herself, as in *I see* or *we hope*.
first person narration *n Literature* a type of storytelling in which the fictional or non-fictional narrator tells his or her own story in the first person.
first-rate *adj* of the best quality; excellent.
first reading *n Parliament* the introduction of a bill in a legislative assembly.
First Secretary *n* the chief minister of the National Assembly for Wales.
firth *n* a narrow inlet of the sea, esp. in Scotland. ▷ HISTORY Old Norse *fjörthr* fjord
fiscal *adj* **1** of or relating to government finances, esp. tax revenues. ✧ *n* **2** (in Scotland) same as **procurator fiscal**. ▷ HISTORY Latin *fiscalis* concerning the state treasury
fish *n, pl* **fish** *or* **fishes 1** a cold-blooded animal with a backbone, gills, and usually fins and a skin covered in scales, that lives in water. *RELATED ADJECTIVE* ▸ **piscine 2** the flesh of fish used as food. **3 cold fish** a person who shows little emotion. **4 drink like a fish** to drink alcohol to excess. **5 have other fish to fry** to have other more important concerns. **6 like a fish out of water** ill at ease in an unfamiliar situation. ✧ *vb* **7** to attempt to catch fish. **8** to fish in (a particular area of water): *the first trawler to fish these waters.* **9** to grope for and find with some difficulty: *he fished a cigarette from his pocket.* **10 fish for** to seek (something) indirectly: *he was fishing for compliments.* ▷ HISTORY Old English *fisc*
fisherman *n, pl* **-men** a person who fishes as a profession or for sport.
fishery *n, pl* **-eries 1 a** the industry of catching, processing, and selling fish. **b** a place where this is carried on. **2** a place where fish are reared.
fish-eye lens *n Photog* a lens with a highly curved front that covers almost 180°.
fishfinger *n* an oblong piece of fish coated in breadcrumbs.
fishing *n* the occupation of catching fish.
fishmeal *n* ground dried fish used as feed for farm animals or as a fertilizer.
fishmonger *n Chiefly Brit* a seller of fish.
fishnet *n* an open mesh fabric resembling netting, sometimes used for tights or stockings.
fishplate *n* a flat piece of metal joining one rail or beam to the next, esp. on railway tracks.
fishtail *n* a nozzle having a long narrow slot at the top, placed over a Bunsen burner to produce a thin fanlike flame.
fishwife *n, pl* **-wives** a coarse or bad-tempered woman with a loud voice.
fishy *adj* **fishier, fishiest 1** of or suggestive of fish. **2** *Informal* suspicious or questionable: *something a bit fishy about his explanation.* ▸ **fishily** *adv*
fissile *adj* **1** capable of undergoing nuclear fission. **2** tending to split.
fission *n* **1** the act or process of splitting into parts. **2** *Biol* a form of asexual reproduction involving a division into two or more equal parts. **3** the splitting of atomic nuclei with the release of a large amount of energy. ▷ HISTORY Latin *fissio* a splitting ▸ **fissionable** *adj*
fissure (**fish**-er) *n* any long narrow cleft or crack, esp. in a rock. ▷ HISTORY Latin *fissus* split
fissure eruption *n Geol* a volcanic eruption in which the lava comes out through a linear crack.
fist *n* a hand with the fingers clenched into the palm. ▷ HISTORY Old English *fȳst*
fisticuffs *pl n* fighting with the fists. ▷ HISTORY probably from obsolete *fisty* with the fist + CUFF[2]
fistula (**fist**-yew-la) *n Pathol* a long narrow ulcer. ▷ HISTORY Latin: tube, ulcer
fit[1] *vb* **fitting, fitted 1** to be appropriate or suitable for. **2** to be of the correct size or shape (for). **3** to adjust in order to make appropriate. **4** to try clothes on and note any adjustments needed. **5** to make competent or ready: *the experience helped to fit him for the task.* **6** to correspond with the facts or circumstances: *this part doesn't fit in with the rest of his theory.* ✧ *adj* **fitter, fittest 7** appropriate. **8** in good health. **9** worthy or suitable: *houses fit for human habitation.* ✧ *n* **10** the manner in which something fits: *the suit was an excellent fit.* ✧ See also **fit in, fit out**. ▷ HISTORY probably from Middle Dutch *vitten* ▸ **fitly** *adv* ▸ **fitness** *n*
fit[2] *n* **1** a sudden attack or convulsion, such as an epileptic seizure. **2** a sudden short burst or spell: *fits of laughter; a fit of pique.* **3 in fits and starts** in spasmodic spells. **4 have a fit** *Informal* to become very angry. ▷ HISTORY Old English *fitt* conflict
fitful *adj* occurring in irregular spells. ▸ **fitfully** *adv*
fit in *vb* **1** to give a place or time to (someone or something). **2** to belong or conform, esp. after adjustment.
fitment *n* **1** an accessory attached to a machine. **2** *Chiefly Brit* a detachable part of the furnishings of a room.
fit out *vb* to equip: *he started to fit out a ship in secret.*
fitted *adj* **1** designed for excellent fit: *a fitted suit.* **2** (of a carpet) covering a floor completely. **3 a** (of furniture) built to fit a particular space. **b** (of a kitchen, bathroom, etc.) having equipment and furniture built or selected to suit the measurements of the room. **4** (of sheets) having ends that are elasticated to fit tightly over a mattress.
fitter *n* **1** a person who is skilled in the installation and adjustment of machinery. **2** a person who fits garments.
fitting *adj* **1** appropriate or proper. ✧ *n* **2** an accessory or part. **3** the trying-on of clothes so that they can be adjusted to fit. **4 fittings** furnishings or accessories in a building. ▸ **fittingly** *adv*
five *n* **1** the cardinal number that is the sum of one and four. **2** a numeral, 5 or V, representing this number. **3** something representing or consisting of five units. ✧ *adj* **4** amounting to five: *five years.* ✧ See also **fives**. ▷ HISTORY Old English *fif*

A B C D E F G H I J K L M N O P Q R S T U V W X Y Z

five-eighth *n Austral & NZ* a rugby player positioned between the halfbacks and three-quarters.

fivefold *adj* **1** having five times as many or as much. **2** composed of five parts. ✧ *adv* **3** by five times as many or as much.

fiver *n Brit, Austral & NZ informal* a five-pound or five-dollar note.

fives *n* a ball game similar to squash but played with bats or the hands.

fix *vb* **1** to make or become firm, stable, or secure. **2** to repair. **3** to attach or place permanently: *fix the mirror to the wall.* **4** to settle definitely or decide upon: *the meeting is fixed for the 12th.* **5** to direct (the eyes etc.) steadily: *she fixed her eyes upon the jewels.* **6** *Informal* to unfairly influence the outcome of: *the fight was fixed by the promoter.* **7** *Informal* to put a stop to the activities of (someone): *the Party was determined to fix him.* **8** *Informal* to prepare: *let me fix you a drink.* **9** *Photog* to treat (a film, plate, or paper) with fixer to make the image permanent. **10** to convert (atmospheric nitrogen) into nitrogen compounds. **11** *Slang* to inject a narcotic drug. ✧ *n* **12** *Informal* a difficult situation. **13** the reckoning of a navigational position of a ship by radar, etc. **14** *Slang* an injection of a narcotic. ✧ See also **fix up**. ▷ **HISTORY** Latin *fixus* fixed

fixation *n* **1** an obsessive interest in something. **2** *Psychol* a strong attachment of a person to another person or an object in early life. **3** *Chem* the conversion of nitrogen in the air into a compound, esp. a fertilizer. ▶ **fixated** *adj*

fixative *n* **1** a fluid sprayed over drawings to prevent smudging. **2** a liquid used to hold objects, esp. dentures, in place. **3** a substance added to a perfume to make it less volatile.

fixed *adj* **1** attached or placed so as to be immovable. **2** stable: *fixed rates.* **3** unchanging and appearing artificial: *a fixed smile.* **4** established as to relative position: *a fixed point.* **5** always at the same time. **6** (of ideas) firmly maintained. **7** *Informal* equipped or provided for, esp. with money or possessions. **8** *Informal* illegally arranged: *a fixed trial.* ▶ **fixedly** (**fix**-id-lee) *adv*

fixed star *n* an extremely distant star that appears to be almost stationary.

fixer *n* **1** *Photog* a solution used to make an image permanent. **2** *Slang* a person who makes arrangements, esp. illegally.

fixture *n* **1** an object firmly fixed in place, esp. a household appliance. **2** something or someone regarded as fixed in a particular place or position: *the diplomatic wife seems a fixture of international politics.* **3 a** a sports match. **b** the date of it.

fix up *vb* **1** to arrange. **2 fix up with** to provide with: *can you fix me up with tickets?*

fizz *vb* **1** to make a hissing or bubbling sound. **2** (of a drink) to produce bubbles of carbon dioxide. ✧ *n* **3** a hissing or bubbling sound. **4** releasing of small bubbles of gas by a liquid. **5** any effervescent drink. ▷ **HISTORY** imitative ▶ **fizzy** *adj* ▶ **fizziness** *n*

fizzle *vb* **-zling, -zled 1** to make a hissing or bubbling sound. **2 fizzle out** *Informal* to fail or die out, esp. after a promising start. ▷ **HISTORY** probably from obsolete *fist* to break wind

fjord (fee-**ord**) *n* a long narrow inlet of the sea between high cliffs, esp. in Norway. ▷ **HISTORY** Norwegian, from Old Norse *fjörthr*

FL Florida.

flab *n* unsightly or unwanted fat on the body. ▷ **HISTORY** from *flabby*

flabbergasted *adj Informal* completely astonished. ▷ **HISTORY** origin unknown

flabby *adj* **-bier, -biest 1** having flabby flesh. **2** loose or limp. **3** weak and lacking purpose: *flabby hesitant leaders.* ▷ **HISTORY** alteration of *flappy*, from *flap* ▶ **flabbiness** *n*

flaccid (**flak**-sid) *adj* soft and limp. ▷ **HISTORY** Latin *flaccidus* ▶ **flaccidity** *n*

flag[1] *n* **1** a piece of cloth often attached to a pole, used as an emblem or for signalling. **2** a code inserted into a computer file to distinguish certain information. ✧ *vb* **flagging, flagged 3** to mark with a tag or sticker. **4** *NZ* to give up an activity. **5 flag down** to signal (a vehicle) to stop. ▷ **HISTORY** origin unknown

flag[2] *n* same as **iris** (sense 2). ▷ **HISTORY** origin unknown

flag[3] *vb* **flagging, flagged 1** to lose enthusiasm or energy. **2** to become limp. ▷ **HISTORY** origin unknown ▶ **flagging** *adj*

flag[4] *n* short for **flagstone**.

flag day *n Brit* a day on which money is collected by a charity and small stickers are given to contributors.

flagellate *vb* (**flaj**-a-late) **-lating, -lated 1** to whip, esp. in religious penance or for sexual pleasure. ✧ *adj* (**flaj**-a-lit) **2** possessing one or more flagella. **3** like a whip. ▷ **HISTORY** Latin *flagellare* to whip ▶ **flagellation** *n*

flagellum (flaj-**jell**-lum) *n, pl* **-la** (-la) *or* **-lums 1** *Biol* a long whiplike outgrowth that acts as an organ of movement. **2** *Bot* a long thin shoot or runner. ▷ **HISTORY** Latin: a little whip

flageolet (flaj-a-**let**) *n* a high-pitched musical instrument of the recorder family. ▷ **HISTORY** French

flag fall *n Austral* the minimum charge for hiring a taxi, to which the rate per kilometre is added.

flagged *adj* paved with flagstones.

flag of convenience *n* a foreign flag flown by a ship registered in that country to gain financial or legal advantage.

flag of truce *n* a white flag indicating an invitation to an enemy to negotiate.

flagon *n* **1** a large bottle of wine, cider, etc. **2** a narrow-necked jug for containing liquids. ▷ **HISTORY** Late Latin *flasco* flask

flagpole *or* **flagstaff** *n* a pole on which a flag is flown.

flagrant (**flayg**-rant) *adj* openly outrageous: *flagrant violation of international law.* ▷ **HISTORY** Latin *flagrare* to blaze, burn ▶ **flagrancy** *n*

flagship *n* **1** a ship aboard which the commander of a fleet is quartered. **2** the most important ship

A B C D E F G H I J K L M N O P Q R S T U V W X Y Z

belonging to a shipping company. **3** the most modern or impressive product or asset of an organization: *the company has opened its own flagship store.*

flagstone *n* a flat slab of hard stone for paving. ▷ **HISTORY** Old Norse *flaga* slab

flail *n* **1** a tool formerly used for threshing grain by hand. ✧ *vb* **2** to wave about wildly: *arms flailing, they staggered about.* **3** to beat with or as if with a flail. ▷ **HISTORY** Latin *flagellum* whip

flair *n* **1** natural ability. **2** originality and stylishness. ▷ **HISTORY** French

flak *n* **1** anti-aircraft fire. **2** severe criticism: *most of the flak was directed at the umpire.*

WORD HISTORY
'Flak' is formed from the first letters 'fl-a-k' of the component parts of the German word for an anti-aircraft gun, *Fliegerabwehrkanone*, literally an 'aircraft defence gun'.

flake¹ *n* **1** a small thin piece chipped off an object or substance. **2** a small piece: *flakes of snow.* **3** *slang* an eccentric or unreliable person. ✧ *vb* **flaking, flaked 4** to peel or cause to peel off in flakes. **5** to break into small thin pieces: *bake for 30 minutes, or until the fish is firm and flakes easily.* ▷ **HISTORY** from Old Norse ▶ **flaky** *adj*

flake² *n* (in Australia) the commercial name for the meat of the gummy shark.

flake out *vb Informal* to collapse or fall asleep from exhaustion.

flak jacket *n* a reinforced sleeveless jacket for protection against gunfire or shrapnel.

flambé (**flahm**-bay) *vb* **flambéeing, flambéed** to cook or serve (food) in flaming brandy. ▷ **HISTORY** French

flamboyant *adj* **1** behaving in a very noticeable, extravagant way: *a flamboyant jazz pianist.* **2** very bright and showy. ▷ **HISTORY** French: flaming ▶ **flamboyance** *n*

flame *n* **1** a hot luminous body of burning gas coming in flickering streams from burning material. **2 flames** the state of burning: *half the building was in flames.* **3** intense passion: *the flame of love.* **4** *Informal* an abusive message sent by e-mail. ✧ *vb* **flaming, flamed 5** to burn brightly. **6** to become red or fiery: *colour flamed in Sally's cheeks.* **7** to become angry or excited. **8** *Informal* to send an abusive message by e-mail. ▷ **HISTORY** Latin *flamma*

flamenco *n, pl* **-cos 1** a rhythmic Spanish dance accompanied by a guitar and vocalist. **2** music for this dance. ▷ **HISTORY** Spanish

flame-thrower *n* a weapon that ejects a stream or spray of burning fluid.

flamingo *n, pl* **-gos** *or* **-goes** a large pink wading bird with a long neck and legs. ▷ **HISTORY** Portuguese *flamengo*

flammable *adj* easily set on fire; inflammable. ▶ **flammability** *n*

WORD TIP
Flammable and *inflammable* are interchangeable when used of the properties of materials. *Flammable* is, however, often preferred for warning labels as there is less likelihood of misunderstanding (*inflammable* being sometimes taken to mean *not flammable*). *Inflammable* is preferred in figurative contexts: *this could prove to be an inflammable situation.*

flan *n* an open sweet or savoury tart. ▷ **HISTORY** French

flange *n* a projecting collar or rim on an object for strengthening it or for attaching it to another object. ▷ **HISTORY** origin unknown

flank *n* **1** the side of a man or animal between the ribs and the hip. **2** a cut of beef from the flank. **3** the side of a naval or military formation. ✧ *vb* **4** to be positioned at the side of (a person or thing). ▷ **HISTORY** Old French *flanc*

flannel *n* **1** *Brit* a small piece of towelling cloth used to wash the face. **2** a soft light woollen fabric used for clothing. **3 flannels** trousers made of flannel. **4** *Brit informal* evasive talk that avoids giving any commitment or direct answer. ✧ *vb* **-nelling, -nelled** *or US* **-neling, -neled 5** *Brit informal* to flatter or talk evasively. ▷ **HISTORY** Welsh *gwlân* wool

flannelette *n* a cotton imitation of flannel, used to make sheets and nightdresses.

flap *vb* **flapping, flapped 1** to move backwards and forwards or up and down, like a bird's wings in flight. ✧ *n* **2** the action of or noise made by flapping. **3** a piece of material attached at one edge and usually used to cover an opening, such as on a pocket. **4** a hinged section of an aircraft wing that is raised or lowered to control the aircraft's speed. **5** *Informal* a state of panic or agitation. ▷ **HISTORY** probably imitative

flapjack *n* **1** *Brit* a chewy biscuit made with rolled oats. **2** *NZ* a small thick pancake.

flapper *n* (in the 1920s) a lively young woman who dressed and behaved unconventionally.

flare *vb* **flaring, flared 1** to burn with an unsteady or sudden bright flame. **2** (of temper, violence, or trouble) to break out suddenly. **3** to spread outwards from a narrow to a wider shape. ✧ *n* **4** an unsteady flame. **5** a sudden burst of flame. **6 a** a blaze of light used to illuminate, signal distress, alert, etc. **b** the device producing such a blaze. **7 flares** trousers with legs that flare out at the bottom. ▷ **HISTORY** origin unknown ▶ **flared** *adj*

flash *n* **1** a sudden short blaze of intense light or flame. **2** a sudden occurrence of a particular emotion or experience: *a flash of anger.* **3** a very brief time: *in a flash he was inside and locked the door behind him.* **4** a short unscheduled news announcement. **5** *Brit & Austral* an emblem on a uniform or vehicle to identify its military formation. **6** *Photog* short for **flashlight**. **7 flash in the pan** a project, person, etc., that enjoys only short-lived success. ✧ *adj* **8** *Informal* ostentatious or vulgar. **9** brief and rapid: *a flash fire.* ✧ *vb* **10** to burst or cause to burst suddenly into flame. **11** to shine with a bright light suddenly or repeatedly. **12** to move very fast. **13** to come rapidly (into the mind or vision). **14 a** to signal very fast: *a warning was flashed onto a computer screen in the cockpit.* **b** to signal by use of a light, such as car headlights. **15** *Informal* to display in a boastful and extravagant way: *flashing banknotes around.* **16** *Informal* to show briefly. **17** *Brit slang* to expose oneself indecently. ▷ **HISTORY** origin unknown ▶ **flasher** *n*

flashback *n* a scene in a book, play, or film that shows earlier events.

flashbulb *n Photog* a small light bulb that produces a bright flash of light.

flash flood *n* a sudden short-lived flood.

flashing *n* a weatherproof material used to cover the joins in a roof.

flashlight *n* **1** *Photog* the brief bright light emitted by a flashbulb. **2** *Chiefly US & Canad* a torch.

flash point *n* **1** a critical time beyond which a situation will inevitably erupt into violence. **2** the lowest temperature at which the vapour above a liquid can be ignited.

flask *n* **1** same as **vacuum flask**. **2** a small flat container for alcoholic drink designed to be carried in a pocket. **3** a bottle with a narrow neck, esp. used in a laboratory. ▷ **HISTORY** Medieval Latin *flasca, flasco*

flat[1] *adj* **flatter, flattest 1** horizontal or level: *roofs are now flat instead of slanted.* **2** even or smooth: *a flat surface.* **3** lying stretched out at full length. **4** (of a tyre) deflated. **5** (of shoes) having an unraised heel. **6** without qualification; total: *a flat rejection.* **7** fixed: *a flat rate.* **8** unexciting: *a picture curiously flat in tone.* **9** without variation or emotion: *a flat voice.* **10** (of drinks) no longer fizzy. **11** (of a battery) fully discharged. **12** (of paint) without gloss. **13** *Music* **a** denoting a note that has been lowered in pitch by one chromatic semitone: *B flat.* **b** (of an instrument, voice, etc.) out of tune by being too low in pitch. ✧ *adv* **14** in or into a level or flat position: *the boat was knocked almost flat.* **15** completely: *flat broke.* **16** exactly: *in three months flat.* **17** *Music* **a** lower than a standard pitch. **b** too low in pitch: *singing flat.* **18 fall flat (on one's face)** to fail to achieve a desired effect. **19 flat out** *Informal* with maximum speed and effort. ✧ *n* **20** a flat object or part. **21** low-lying land, esp. a marsh. **22** a mud bank exposed at low tide. **23** *Music* **a** an accidental that lowers the pitch of a note by one semitone. Symbol: ♭. **b** a note affected by this accidental. **24** *Theatre* a wooden frame covered with painted canvas, used to form part of a stage setting. **25** a punctured car tyre. **26 the flat** *Chiefly Brit* the season of flat racing. ▷ **HISTORY** Old Norse *flatr* ▶ **flatly** *adv*

flat[2] *n* **1** a set of rooms forming a home entirely on one floor of a building. ✧ *vb* **flatting, flatted 2** *Austral & NZ* to share a flat. **3 go flatting** *Austral & NZ* to leave home to share a flat. ▷ **HISTORY** Old English *flett* floor, hall, house

flat character *n Literature* a character in a story who lacks psychological depth, often representing a single quality such as honesty or deceit, without changing or developing as the story progresses.

flatfish *n, pl* **-fish** *or* **-fishes** a sea fish, such as the sole, which has a flat body with both eyes on the uppermost side.

flat-footed *adj* **1** having less than the usual degree of arching in the insteps of the feet. **2** *Informal* clumsy or insensitive.

flathead *n* a common Australian flatfish.

flatlet *n Brit, Austral & S African* a small flat.

flatmate *n* a person with whom one shares a flat.

flat-pack *adj* (of furniture, etc.) supplied in pieces in a flat box for assembly by the buyer.

flat racing *n* the racing of horses on racecourses without jumps.

flat spin *n* **1** an aircraft spin in which the longitudinal axis is more nearly horizontal than vertical. **2** *Informal* a state of confusion.

flatten *vb* **1** to make or become flat or flatter. **2** *Informal* **a** to knock down or injure. **b** to crush or subdue.

flatter *vb* **1** to praise insincerely, esp. in order to win favour. **2** to show to advantage: *she wore a simple green cotton dress which she knew flattered her.* **3** to make (a person) appear more attractive than in reality: *a portrait that flattered him.* **4** to cater to the vanity of (a person): *I was flattered by her praise.* **5 flatter oneself** to believe, perhaps mistakenly, something good about oneself. ▷ **HISTORY** Old French *flater* to lick, fawn upon ▶ **flatterer** *n*

flattery *n, pl* **-teries** excessive or insincere praise.

flattie *n NZ & S African informal* flat tyre.

flatulent *adj* suffering from or caused by too much gas in the stomach or intestines. ▷ **HISTORY** Latin *flatus* blowing ▶ **flatulence** *n*

flatworm *n* a worm, such as a tapeworm, with a flattened body.

flaunt *vb* to display (oneself or one's possessions) arrogantly: *flaunting his new car.* ▷ **HISTORY** origin unknown

> **☑ WORD TIP**
> *Flaunt* is sometimes wrongly used where *flout* is meant: *they must be prevented from flouting* (not *flaunting*) *the law.*

flautist (**flaw**-tist) *n* a flute player. ▷ **HISTORY** Italian *flautista*

flavour *or US* **flavor** *n* **1** taste perceived in food or liquid in the mouth. **2** a distinctive quality or atmosphere: *Rome has its own particular flavour.* ✧ *vb* **3** to give flavour to: *salmon flavoured with dill.* ▷ **HISTORY** Old French *flaour* ▶ **flavourless** *or US* **flavorless** *adj*

flavouring *or US* **flavoring** *n* a substance used to flavour food.

flaw *n* **1** an imperfection or blemish. **2** a mistake in something that makes it invalid: *a flaw in the* *system.* ▷ **HISTORY** probably from Old Norse *flaga* stone slab ▶ **flawed** *adj* ▶ **flawless** *adj*

flax *n* **1** a plant that has blue flowers and is cultivated for its seeds and the fibres of its stems. **2** its fibres, made into linen fabrics. **3** *NZ* a perennial plant producing a fibre that is used by Maoris for decorative work and weaving baskets. ▷ **HISTORY** Old English *fleax*

flaxen *adj* **1** of flax. **2** (of hair) pale yellow.

flay *vb* **1** to strip off the skin of, esp. by whipping. **2** to criticize severely. ▷ **HISTORY** Old English *flēan*

flea *n* **1** a small wingless jumping insect feeding on the blood of mammals and birds. **2 flea in one's ear** *Informal* a sharp rebuke. ▷ **HISTORY** Old English *flēah*

fleabite *n* **1** the bite of a flea. **2** a slight annoyance or discomfort.

flea-bitten *adj* **1** bitten by or infested with fleas. **2** *Informal* shabby or decrepit: *a flea-bitten hotel.*

flea market *n* an open-air market selling cheap second-hand goods.

fleapit *n Informal* a shabby cinema or theatre.

fleck *n* **1** a small marking or streak. **2** a small or tiny piece of something: *a fleck of grit.* ✧ *vb* **3** to speckle: *a grey suit flecked with white.* ▷ **HISTORY** probably from Old Norse *flekkr* stain, spot

fled *vb* the past of **flee**.

fledged *adj* **1** (of young birds) able to fly. **2** qualified and competent: *a fully fledged doctor.* ▷ **HISTORY** Old English *-flycge,* as in *unflycge* unfledged

fledgling *or* **fledgeling** *n* **1** a young bird that has grown feathers. ✧ *adj* **2** new or inexperienced: *Poland's fledgling market economy.*

flee *vb* **fleeing, fled 1** to run away from (a place, danger, etc.). **2** to run or move quickly. ▷ **HISTORY** Old English *flēon*

fleece *n* **1** the coat of wool that covers a sheep. **2** the wool removed from a sheep at one shearing. **3** sheepskin or a fabric with soft pile, used as a lining for coats, etc. **4** a warm outdoor jacket or top made from a polyester fabric with a brushed nap. **5** *Brit* a jacket or top made of this fabric. ✧ *vb* **fleecing, fleeced 6** to defraud or overcharge. **7** same as **shear** (sense 1). ▷ **HISTORY** Old English *flēos*

fleecy *adj* **1** of or resembling fleece. ✧ *n, pl* **-ies 2** *NZ informal* a person who collects fleeces after shearing and prepares them for baling.

fleet[1] *n* **1** a number of warships organized as a tactical unit. **2** all the ships of a nation or company: *the British merchant fleet.* **3** a number of vehicles under the same ownership. ▷ **HISTORY** Old English *flēot* ship, flowing water

fleet[2] *adj* rapid in movement. ▷ **HISTORY** probably from Old English *flēotan* to float

fleet chief petty officer *n* a noncommissioned officer in a navy.

fleeting *adj* rapid and soon passing: *a fleeting moment.* ▶ **fleetingly** *adv*

Fleet Street *n* **1** the street in London where many newspaper offices were formerly situated. **2** British national newspapers collectively: *Fleet Street's obsession with the Royal Family.*

Fleming *n* a person from Flanders or Flemish-speaking Belgium.

Fleming's rules *pl n Physics* two rules, assigning significance to the thumb and first and second fingers of each hand, used as mnemonics for the relationship between the directions of current flow, motion, and magnetic field in electromagnetic induction. ▷ **HISTORY** named after Sir John Ambrose *Fleming,* English electrical engineer who devised them

Flemish *adj* **1** of Flanders, in Belgium. ✧ *n* **2** one of the two official languages of Belgium. ✧ *pl n* **3 the Flemish** people from Flanders or Flemish-speaking Belgium.

flesh *n* **1** the soft part of the body of an animal or human, esp. muscular tissue. **2** *Informal* excess weight; fat. **3** the meat of animals as opposed to that of fish or, sometimes, fowl. **4** the thick soft part of a fruit or vegetable. **5 the flesh** sexuality or sensuality: *pleasures of the flesh.* RELATED ADJECTIVE ➔ **carnal 6 flesh and blood** human beings or human nature: *it is almost more than flesh and blood can bear.* **7 in the flesh** in person; actually present. **8 one's own flesh and blood** one's own family. **9 press the flesh** *Informal* to shake hands with large numbers of people, esp. in political campaigning. ▷ **HISTORY** Old English *flǣsc*

flesh-coloured *adj* yellowish-pink.

fleshly *adj* **-lier, -liest 1** relating to sexuality or sensuality: *the fleshly implications of their love.* **2** worldly as opposed to spiritual.

flesh wound *n* a wound affecting superficial tissues.

fleshy *adj* **fleshier, fleshiest 1** plump. **2** resembling flesh. **3** *Bot* (of some fruits) thick and pulpy. ▶ **fleshiness** *n*

fleur-de-lys *or* **fleur-de-lis** (**flur**-de-**lee**) *n, pl* **fleurs-de-lys** *or* **fleurs-de-lis** (**flur**-de-**leez**) a representation of a lily with three distinct petals. ▷ **HISTORY** Old French *flor de lis* lily flower

flew *vb* the past tense of **fly**[1].

flews *pl n* the fleshy hanging upper lip of a bloodhound or similar dog. ▷ **HISTORY** origin unknown

flex *n* **1** *Brit & Austral* a flexible insulated electric cable: *a coiled kettle flex.* ✧ *vb* **2** to bend. **3** to bend and stretch (a muscle). ▷ **HISTORY** Latin *flexus* bent, winding

flexible *adj* **1** able to be bent easily without breaking. **2** adaptable to changing circumstances: *flexible working arrangements.* ▶ **flexibility** *n* ▶ **flexibly** *adv*

flexitime *n* a system permitting flexibility of working hours at the beginning or end of the day, provided an agreed total is worked.

flick *vb* **1** to touch or move with the finger or hand in a quick jerky movement. **2** to move with a short sudden movement, often repeatedly: *the windscreen wipers flicked back and forth.* **3 flick through** to look at (a book or magazine) quickly or idly. ✧ *n* **4** a tap or quick stroke. ▷ **HISTORY** imitative

flicker *vb* **1** to give out an unsteady or irregular light. **2** to move quickly to and fro. ✧ *n* **3** an unsteady or brief light. **4** a brief or faint indication of emotion: *a flicker of fear in his voice.*
▷ **HISTORY** Old English *flicorian*

flick knife *n* a knife with a retractable blade that springs out when a button is pressed.

flier *n* same as **flyer**.

flight[1] *n* **1** a journey by aircraft. **2** the act or manner of flying. **3** a group of flying birds or aircraft. **4** an aircraft flying on a scheduled journey. **5** a set of stairs between one landing and the next. **6 flight of fancy** an idea that is imaginative but not practical. **7** small plastic or feather fins at the rear of an arrow or dart which make it stable in flight.
▷ **HISTORY** Old English *flyht*

flight[2] *n* **1** the act of running away, esp. from danger. **2 put to flight** to cause to run away. **3 take (to) flight** to run away. ▷ **HISTORY** Old English *flyht* (unattested)

flight attendant *n* a person who attends to the needs of passengers on a commercial flight.

flight deck *n* **1** the crew compartment in an airliner. **2** the upper deck of an aircraft carrier from which aircraft take off.

flightless *adj* (of certain birds and insects) unable to fly.

flight lieutenant *n* a junior commissioned officer in an air force.

flight recorder *n* an electronic device in an aircraft for storing information concerning its performance in flight. It is often used to determine the cause of a crash. Also called: **black box**

flight sergeant *n* a noncommissioned officer in an air force.

flighty *adj* **flightier, flightiest** frivolous and not very reliable or serious. ▸ **flightiness** *n*

flimsy *adj* **-sier, -siest 1** not strong or substantial. **2** light and thin: *a flimsy gauze mask.* **3** not very convincing: *flimsy evidence.* ▷ **HISTORY** origin unknown ▸ **flimsily** *adv* ▸ **flimsiness** *n*

flinch *vb* **1** to draw back suddenly from pain or something unpleasant. **2 flinch from** to avoid: *I wouldn't flinch from saying that to his face.*
▷ **HISTORY** Old French *flenchir*

fling *vb* **flinging, flung 1** to throw with force. **2** to move or go hurriedly or violently: *she flung her arms open wide.* **3** to put or send without warning: *they used to fling me in jail.* **4** to put (something) somewhere hurriedly or carelessly. **5 fling oneself into** to apply oneself with enthusiasm to. ✧ *n* **6** a short spell of self-indulgent enjoyment. **7** a brief romantic or sexual relationship. **8** a vigorous Scottish country dance: *a Highland fling.*
▷ **HISTORY** from Old Norse

flint *n* **1** a very hard stone that produces sparks when struck with steel. **2** any piece of flint, esp. one used as a primitive tool. **3** a small piece of an iron alloy, used in cigarette lighters. ▷ **HISTORY** Old English ▸ **flinty** *adj*

flintlock *n* an obsolete gun in which the powder was lit by a spark produced by a flint.

flip *vb* **flipping, flipped 1** to throw (something light or small) carelessly. **2** to turn (something) over: *flip the fish on its back.* **3** to turn (a device or machine) on or off by quickly pressing a switch. **4** to throw (an object such as a coin) so that it turns in the air. **5 flip through** to look at (a book or magazine) idly. **6** Also: **flip one's lid** *Slang* to fly into an emotional outburst. ✧ *n* **7** a snap or tap, usually with the fingers. ✧ *adj* **8** *Informal* flippant or pert.
▷ **HISTORY** probably imitative

flipchart *n* a large pad of paper mounted on a stand, used in giving lectures, etc.

flip-flop *n Brit & S African* a rubber-soled sandal attached to the foot by a thong between the big toe and the next toe. ▷ **HISTORY** reduplication of *flip*

flippant *adj* treating serious matters with inappropriate light-heartedness or lack of respect.
▷ **HISTORY** probably from *flip* ▸ **flippancy** *n*

flipper *n* **1** the flat broad limb of seals, whales, and other aquatic animals specialized for swimming. **2** either of a pair of rubber paddle-like devices worn on the feet as an aid in swimming.

flirt *vb* **1** to behave as if sexually attracted to someone. **2 flirt with** to consider lightly; toy with: *he had often flirted with the idea of emigrating.* ✧ *n* **3** a person who flirts. ▷ **HISTORY** origin unknown
▸ **flirtation** *n* ▸ **flirtatious** *adj*

flit *vb* **flitting, flitted 1** to fly or move along rapidly and lightly. **2** to pass quickly: *a shadow flitted across his face.* **3** *Scot & N English dialect* to move house. **4** *Brit informal* to leave hurriedly and stealthily in order to avoid debts. ✧ *n* **5** the act of flitting. **6 do a flit** *NZ informal* to abandon rented accommodation. ▷ **HISTORY** Old Norse *flytja* to carry

float *vb* **1** to rest on the surface of a fluid without sinking. **2** to move lightly or freely across a surface or through air or water. **3** to move about aimlessly, esp. in the mind: *a pleasant image floated into his mind.* **4 a** to launch (a commercial enterprise, etc.). **b** to offer for sale on the stock market. **5** *Finance* to allow (a currency) to fluctuate against other currencies. ✧ *n* **6** an inflatable object that helps people learning to swim stay afloat. **7** *Angling* an indicator attached to a baited line that moves when a fish bites. **8** a long rigid boatlike structure, of which there are usually two, attached to an aircraft instead of wheels so that it can land on and take off from water. **9** a decorated lorry that is part of a procession. **10** a small delivery vehicle: *milk floats.* **11** *Austral & NZ* a vehicle for transporting horses. **12** a sum of money used to cover small expenses or provide change. **13** the hollow floating ball of a ball cock. ▷ **HISTORY** Old English *flotian*

floatation *n* same as **flotation**.

floating *adj* **1** (of a population) moving about; not settled. **2** (of an organ or part) displaced or abnormally movable: *a floating kidney.* **3** (of a voter) not committed to one party. **4** *Finance* **a** (of capital) available for current use. **b** (of a currency) free to fluctuate against other currencies.

floating rib *n* a lower rib not attached to the breastbone.

floats *pl n Theatre* footlights.

A B C D E F G H I J K L M N O P Q R S T U V W X Y Z

flocculent *adj* like tufts of wool. ▷ **HISTORY** Latin *floccus* tuft of wool ▶ **flocculence** *n*

flock¹ *n* **1** a group of animals of one kind, esp. sheep or birds. **2** a large number of people. **3** a congregation of Christians regarded as the responsibility of a member of the clergy. ✧ *vb* **4** to gather together or move in large numbers. ▷ **HISTORY** Old English *flocc*

flock² *n* **1** waste from fabrics such as cotton or wool, used for stuffing mattresses. ✧ *adj* **2** (of wallpaper) having a velvety raised pattern. ▷ **HISTORY** Latin *floccus* tuft of wool

floe *n* a sheet of floating ice. ▷ **HISTORY** probably from Norwegian *flo* slab, layer

flog *vb* **flogging, flogged 1** to beat harshly, esp. with a whip or stick. **2** (sometimes foll. by *off*) *informal* to sell. **3** *Austral & NZ informal* to steal. **4 flog a dead horse** *Chiefly Brit* to waste one's energy. ▷ **HISTORY** probably from Latin *flagellare* ▶ **flogging** *n*

flood *n* **1** an overflowing of water on an area that is normally dry. **2** a large amount of water. **3** the rising of the tide from low to high water. *RELATED ADJECTIVES* ▶ **diluvial, diluvian 4** a large amount: *a flood of letters.* **5** *Theatre* short for **floodlight**. ✧ *vb* **6** to cover or become covered with water. **7** to fill to overflowing. **8** to put a large number of goods on sale on (a market) at the same time, often at a cheap price: *the US was flooded with cheap televisions.* **9** to flow or surge: *the memories flooded back.* **10** to supply excess petrol to (a petrol engine) so that it cannot work properly. **11** to bleed profusely from the womb. ▷ **HISTORY** Old English *flōd* ▶ **flooding** *n*

Flood *n* **the Flood** *Old Testament* the flood from which Noah and his family and livestock were saved in the ark (Genesis 7–8).

flood bank *n Civil engineering* an embankment built beside a river to prevent flooding.

floodgate *n* **1** a gate used to control the flow of water. **2 floodgates** controls against an outpouring of emotion: *it had opened the floodgates of her anxiety.*

flood irrigation *n Agriculture* a method of irrigation in which the entire soil surface of a given area is flooded with water following the opening of channels or pipes.

floodlight *n* **1** a lamp that casts a broad intense light, used in the theatre or to illuminate sports grounds or the exterior of buildings. ✧ *vb* **-lighting, -lit 2** to illuminate by floodlight.

flood plain *n Geog* a flat area beside a river that becomes flooded when the river overflows its banks.

floor *n* **1** the lower surface of a room. **2** a storey of a building. **3** a flat bottom surface: *the ocean floor.* **4** that part of a legislative hall in which debate is conducted. **5** a minimum limit: *a wages floor for low-paid employees.* **6 have the floor** to have the right to speak in a debate or discussion. ✧ *vb* **7** to knock to the ground. **8** *Informal* to disconcert or defeat. ▷ **HISTORY** Old English *flōr*

floorboard *n* one of the boards forming a floor.

floored *adj* covered with a floor: *an attic floored with pine planks.*

flooring *n* **1** the material used in making a floor: *pine flooring.* **2** a floor.

floor show *n* a series of entertainments, such as singing and dancing, in a nightclub.

floozy, floozie, *or* **floosie** *n, pl* **-zies** *or* **-sies** *Slang, old-fashioned* a woman considered to be disreputable or immoral. ▷ **HISTORY** origin unknown

flop *vb* **flopping, flopped 1** to bend, fall, or collapse loosely or carelessly. **2** *Informal* to fail: *his first big film flopped.* **3** to fall or move with a sudden noise. ✧ *n* **4** *Informal* a complete failure. **5** the act of flopping. ▷ **HISTORY** variant of *flap* ▶ **floppy** *adj*

floppy disk *n* a flexible magnetic disk that stores data in the memory of a digital computer.

flora *n* all the plant life of a given place or time. ▷ **HISTORY** *Flora,* Roman goddess of flowers

floral *adj* decorated with or consisting of flowers or patterns of flowers.

Florentine *adj* **1** of Florence, a city in central Italy. ✧ *n* **2** a person from Florence.

floret (**flaw**-ret) *n* a small flower forming part of a composite flower head. ▷ **HISTORY** Old French *florete*

floribunda *n* a type of rose whose flowers grow in large clusters. ▷ **HISTORY** New Latin *floribundus* flowering freely

florid *adj* **1** having a red or flushed complexion. **2** very ornate and extravagant: *florid prose.* ▷ **HISTORY** Latin *floridus* blooming

florin *n* a former British, Australian and New Zealand coin, equivalent to ten pence or twenty cents. ▷ **HISTORY** Old Italian *fiorino* Florentine coin

florist *n* a person or shop selling flowers.

floss *n* **1** fine silky fibres, such as those obtained from silkworm cocoons. **2** See **dental floss**. ✧ *vb* **3** to clean (between the teeth) with dental floss. ▷ **HISTORY** probably from Old French *flosche* down ▶ **flossy** *adj*

flotation *or* **floatation** *n* the launching or financing of a commercial enterprise by bond or share issues.

flotilla *n* a small fleet or a fleet of small ships. ▷ **HISTORY** Spanish *flota* fleet

flotsam *n* **1** floating wreckage from a ship. **2 flotsam and jetsam a** odds and ends. **b** *Brit* homeless or vagrant people. ▷ **HISTORY** Anglo-French *floteson*

flounce¹ *vb* **flouncing, flounced 1** to move or go with emphatic movements. ✧ *n* **2** the act of flouncing. ▷ **HISTORY** Scandinavian

flounce² *n* an ornamental frill on a garment or tablecloth. ▷ **HISTORY** Old French *froncir* to wrinkle

flounder¹ *vb* **1** to struggle to move or stay upright, esp. in water or mud. **2** to behave or speak in an awkward, confused way. ▷ **HISTORY** probably a blend of FOUNDER + BLUNDER

> **WORD TIP**
> *Flounder* is sometimes wrongly used where *founder* is meant: *the project foundered* (not *floundered*) *because of a lack of funds.*

flounder² *n, pl* **-der** *or* **-ders** an edible flatfish. ▷ **HISTORY** Scandinavian

flour *n* **1** a powder prepared by grinding grain, esp. wheat. ✧ *vb* **2** to sprinkle (food or utensils) with flour. ▷ **HISTORY** Middle English *flur* 'flower', i.e. best part ▶ **floury** *adj*

flourish *vb* **1** to be active, successful, or widespread; prosper. **2** to be at the peak of development. **3** to wave (something) dramatically. ✧ *n* **4** a dramatic waving or sweeping movement: *he created a flourish with an imaginary wand.* **5** an ornamental curly line in writing. **6** a fancy or extravagant action or part of something: *he took his tie off with a flourish.* ▷ **HISTORY** Latin *florere* to flower ▶ **flourishing** *adj*

flout (rhymes with **out**) *vb* to deliberately disobey (a rule, law, etc.). ▷ **HISTORY** probably from Middle English *flouten* to play the flute

> **WORD TIP**
> See at **flaunt.**

flow *vb* **1** (of liquids) to move in a stream. **2** (of blood, electricity, etc.) to circulate. **3** to move steadily and smoothly: *a golf club with rich-looking cars flowing into it.* **4** to be produced effortlessly: *words flowed from him in a steady stream.* **5** to hang freely: *her hair loose and flowing down her back.* **6** to be abundant: *at the buffet lunch, wine flowed like water.* **7** (of tide water) to rise. ✧ *n* **8** the act, rate, or manner of flowing: *the abundant flow of water through domestic sprinklers.* **9** a continuous stream or discharge. **10** the advancing of the tide. ▷ **HISTORY** Old English *flōwan*

flow chart *or* **sheet** *n* a diagram showing a sequence of operations in an industrial process, computer program, etc.

flower *n* **1** the part of a plant that is, usually, brightly coloured, and quickly fades, producing seeds. **2** a plant grown for its colourful flowers. RELATED ADJECTIVE ▸ **floral 3** the best or finest part: *in the flower of her youth.* **4 in flower** with flowers open. ✧ *vb* **5** to produce flowers; bloom. **6** to reach full growth or maturity: *liberty only flowers in times of peace.* ▷ **HISTORY** Latin *flos*

flowered *adj* decorated with flowers or a floral design.

flowerpot *n* a pot in which plants are grown.

flowery *adj* **1** decorated with flowers or floral patterns. **2** (of language or style) containing elaborate literary expressions. ▶ **floweriness** *n*

flown *vb* the past participle of **fly¹**.

fl. oz. fluid ounce(s).

flu *n Informal* short for **influenza**.

fluctuate *vb* **-ating, -ated** to change frequently and erratically: *share prices fluctuated wildly throughout the day.* ▷ **HISTORY** Latin *fluctus* a wave ▶ **fluctuation** *n*

flue *n* a passage or pipe in a chimney, used to carry off smoke, gas, or hot air. ▷ **HISTORY** origin unknown

fluent *adj* **1** able to speak or write with ease: *they spoke fluent English; fluent in French.* **2** spoken or written with ease. ▷ **HISTORY** Latin *fluere* to flow ▶ **fluency** *n* ▶ **fluently** *adv*

fluff *n* **1** soft light particles, such as the down of cotton or wool. **2** *Informal* a mistake, esp. in speaking or reading lines. ✧ *vb* **3** to make or become soft and puffy. **4** *Informal* to make a mistake in performing. ▷ **HISTORY** probably from earlier *flue* downy matter ▶ **fluffy** *adj* ▶ **fluffiness** *n*

fluid *n* **1** a substance, such as a liquid or gas, that can flow and has no fixed shape. ✧ *adj* **2** capable of flowing and easily changing shape. **3** constantly changing or apt to change. ▷ **HISTORY** Latin *fluere* to flow ▶ **fluidity** *n*

fluid ounce *n* **1** *Brit* a unit of liquid measure equal to one twentieth of an Imperial pint (28.4 ml). **2** *US* a unit of liquid measure equal to one sixteenth of a US pint (29.6 ml).

fluke¹ *n* an accidental stroke of luck. ▷ **HISTORY** origin unknown ▶ **fluky** *adj*

fluke² *n* **1** the flat triangular point of an anchor. **2** either of the two lobes of the tail of a whale. ▷ **HISTORY** perhaps a special use of FLUKE³ (in the sense: a flounder, flatfish)

fluke³ *n* any parasitic flatworm, such as the liver fluke. ▷ **HISTORY** Old English *flōc*

flume *n* **1** a narrow sloping channel for water. **2** an enclosed water slide at a swimming pool.

flummox *vb* to puzzle or confuse. ▷ **HISTORY** origin unknown

flung *vb* the past of **fling**.

flunk *vb US, Canad, Austral, NZ & S African Informal* to fail (an examination, course, etc.). ▷ **HISTORY** origin unknown

flunky *or* **flunkey** *n, pl* **flunkies** *or* **flunkeys 1** a manservant who wears ceremonial dress. **2** a person who performs small unimportant tasks for a powerful or important person in the hope of being rewarded. ▷ **HISTORY** origin unknown

fluor (**flew**-or) *n* same as **fluorspar**. ▷ **HISTORY** Latin: a flowing; so called from its use as a metallurgical flux

fluoresce *vb* **-rescing, -resced** to exhibit fluorescence. ▷ **HISTORY** back formation from FLUORESCENCE

fluorescence *n* **1** *Physics* the emission of light from atoms or molecules that are bombarded by particles, such as electrons, or by radiation from a separate source. **2** the radiation emitted as a result of fluorescence. ▷ **HISTORY** from *fluor* ▶ **fluorescent** *adj*

fluorescent lamp *n* a lamp in which ultraviolet radiation from an electrical gas discharge causes a thin layer of phosphor on a tube's inside surface to fluoresce.

fluoridate *vb* **-dating, -dated** to add fluoride to (water) as protection against tooth decay. ▶ **fluoridation** *n*

fluoride *n Chem* any compound containing fluorine and another element or radical.

fluorinate *vb* **-nating, -nated** to treat or combine with fluorine. ▶ **fluorination** *n*

fluorine *n Chem* a poisonous strong-smelling pale yellow gas that is the most reactive of all the elements. Symbol: F.

fluoroscopy (floor-**oss**-kop-ee) *n* same as **radioscopy**.

fluorspar, fluor *or US & Canad* **fluorite** *n* a white or colourless mineral, consisting of calcium fluoride in crystalline form: the chief ore of fluorine.

flurry *n, pl* **-ries 1** a short rush of vigorous activity or movement. **2** a light gust of wind or rain or fall of snow. ✧ *vb* **-ries, -rying, -ried 3** to confuse or bewilder. ▷ **HISTORY** obsolete *flurr* to scatter

flush[1] *vb* **1** to blush or cause to blush. **2** to send water quickly through (a pipe or a toilet) so as to clean it. **3** to elate: *she was flushed with excitement.* ✧ *n* **4** a rosy colour, esp. in the cheeks. **5** a sudden flow, such as of water. **6** a feeling of elation: *in the flush of victory.* **7** freshness: *in the first flush of youth.* ▷ **HISTORY** perhaps from FLUSH[3] ▶ **flushed** *adj*

flush[2] *adj* **1** level with another surface. **2** *Informal* having plenty of money. ✧ *adv* **3** so as to be level. ▷ **HISTORY** probably from FLUSH[1] (in the sense: spring out)

flush[3] *vb* to drive out of a hiding place. ▷ **HISTORY** Middle English *flusshen*

flush[4] *n* (in poker and similar games) a hand containing only one suit. ▷ **HISTORY** Latin *fluxus* flux

fluster *vb* **1** to make or become nervous or upset. ✧ *n* **2** a nervous or upset state. ▷ **HISTORY** from Old Norse

flute *n* **1** a wind instrument consisting of a tube of wood or metal with holes in the side stopped either by the fingers or keys. The breath is directed across a mouth hole in the side. **2** a tall narrow wineglass, used esp. for champagne. ✧ *vb* **fluting, fluted 3** to utter in a high-pitched tone. ▷ **HISTORY** Old French *flahute* ▶ **fluty** *adj*

fluted *adj* having decorated grooves.

fluting *n* a design or decoration of flutes on a column.

flutter *vb* **1** to wave rapidly. **2** (of birds or butterflies) to flap the wings. **3** to move with an irregular motion. **4** *Pathol* (of the heart) to beat abnormally rapidly. **5** to move about restlessly. ✧ *n* **6** a quick flapping or vibrating motion. **7** a state of nervous excitement or confusion. **8** excited interest. **9** *Brit informal* a modest bet. **10** *Pathol* an abnormally rapid beating of the heart. **11** *Electronics* a slow variation in pitch in a sound-reproducing system. ▷ **HISTORY** Old English *floterian* to float to and fro

fluvial (**flew**-vee-al) *adj* of or relating to a river. ▷ **HISTORY** Latin *fluvius* river

fluvioglacial *adj Geog* relating to streams flowing from melted glaciers or to deposits left by them.

flux *n* **1** continuous change or instability. **2** a flow or discharge. **3** a substance mixed with a metal oxide to assist in fusion. **4** *Physics* **a** the rate of flow of particles, energy, or a fluid. **b** the strength of a field in a given area: *magnetic flux.* ▷ **HISTORY** Latin *fluxus* a flow

fly[1] *vb* **flies, flying, flew, flown 1** to move through the air on wings or in an aircraft. **2** to control the flight of (an aircraft). **3** to float, flutter, display, or be displayed in the air: *the Red Cross flag flew at each corner of the compound.* **4** to transport or be transported through the air by aircraft, wind, etc. **5** to move very quickly or suddenly: *the front door flew open.* **6** to pass quickly: *how time flies.* **7** to escape from (an enemy or a place). **8 fly a kite** to release information or take a step in order to test public opinion. **9 fly at** to attack (someone). **10 fly high** *Informal* to have a high aim. **11 let fly** *Informal* to lose one's temper: *a young child letting fly at you in a sudden moment of temper.* ✧ *n, pl* **flies 12** Also: **flies** a closure that conceals a zip, buttons, or other fastening, as on trousers. **13** a flap forming the entrance to a tent. **14 flies** *Theatre* the space above the stage, used for storing scenery. ▷ **HISTORY** Old English *flēogan*

fly[2] *n, pl* **flies 1** a small insect with two pairs of wings. **2** any of various similar but unrelated insects, such as the dragonfly. **3** *Angling* a lure made from a fish-hook attached with feathers to resemble a fly. **4 fly in the ointment** *Informal* a slight flaw that detracts from value or enjoyment. **5 fly on the wall** a person who watches others, while not being noticed himself or herself. **6 there are no flies on him** *or* **her** *Informal* he *or* she is no fool. ▷ **HISTORY** Old English *flēoge*

fly[3] *adj Slang, chiefly Brit* sharp and cunning. ▷ **HISTORY** origin unknown

flyblown *adj* **1** covered with blowfly eggs. **2** in a dirty and bad condition.

fly-by-night *Informal* ✧ *adj* **1** unreliable or untrustworthy, esp. in money matters. ✧ *n* **2** an untrustworthy person.

flycatcher *n* a small insect-eating songbird.

flyer *or* **flier** *n* **1** a small advertising leaflet. **2** a person or thing that flies or moves very fast. **3** *Old-fashioned* an aircraft pilot.

fly-fishing *n Angling* fishing using artificial flies as lures.

flying *n* **1** the act of piloting, navigating, or travelling in an aircraft. ✧ *adj* **2** hurried and brief: *a flying visit.* **3** fast or built for speed: *Australia's flying fullback.* **4** hanging, waving, or floating freely: *flags flying proudly.*

flying boat *n* a seaplane in which the fuselage consists of a hull that provides buoyancy.

flying buttress *n* an arch and vertical column that supports a wall from the outside.

flying colours *pl n* conspicuous success; triumph: *they passed with flying colours.*

flying fish *n* a fish of warm and tropical seas, with winglike fins used for gliding above the water.

flying fox *n* **1** a large fruit bat of tropical Africa and Asia. **2** *Austral & NZ* a platform suspended from an overhead cable, used for transporting people or materials.

flying officer *n* a junior commissioned officer in an air force.

flying phalanger *n* a phalanger with black-striped greyish fur, which moves with gliding leaps.

flying saucer *n* an unidentified disc-shaped flying object alleged to come from outer space.

flying squad *n* a small group of police or soldiers ready to move into action quickly.

flying start *n* **1** any promising beginning: *a flying start to the new financial year.* **2** a start to a race in which the competitor is already travelling at speed as he or she passes the starting line.

flyleaf *n, pl* **-leaves** the inner leaf of the endpaper of a book.

flyover *n* an intersection of two roads at which one is carried over the other by a bridge.

flypaper *n* paper with a sticky and poisonous coating, hung up to trap flies.

fly-past *n* a ceremonial flight of aircraft over a given area.

flyweight *n* a professional or an amateur boxer weighing up to 112 pounds (51 kg).

flywheel *n* a heavy wheel that regulates the speed of a machine.

Fm *Chem* fermium.

FM frequency modulation.

f-number *n Photog* the ratio of the effective diameter of a lens to its focal length.

foal *n* **1** the young of a horse or related animal. ✧ *vb* **2** to give birth to (a foal). ▷ **HISTORY** Old English *fola*

foam *n* **1** a mass of small bubbles of gas formed on the surface of a liquid. **2** frothy saliva. **3** a light spongelike solid used for insulation, packing, etc. ✧ *vb* **4** to produce or cause to produce foam. **5 foam at the mouth** to be very angry. ▷ **HISTORY** Old English *fām* ▶ **foamy** *adj*

fob *n* **1** a chain by which a pocket watch is attached to a waistcoat. **2** a small pocket in a man's waistcoat, for holding a watch. ▷ **HISTORY** Germanic

f.o.b. *or* **FOB** *Commerce* free on board.

fob off *vb* **fobbing, fobbed 1** to pretend to satisfy (a person) with lies or excuses. **2** to sell or pass off (inferior goods) as valuable. ▷ **HISTORY** probably from German *foppen* to trick

focal *adj* **1** of or relating to a focus. **2** situated at or measured from the focus.

focalization *or* **-isation** *n Literature* the viewpoint from which the events of a story are presented.

focal length *n* the distance from the focal point of a lens or mirror to the surface of the mirror or the centre of the lens.

focal point *n* **1** the point where the rays of light from a lens or mirror meet. **2** the centre of attention or interest: *a focal point for the new high-technology industries.*

focus (foe-kuss) *vb* **-cusing, -cused** *or* **-cussing, -cussed 1** to adjust one's eyes or an instrument on an object so that its image is clear. **2** to concentrate. ✧ *n, pl* **-cuses** *or* **-ci** (-sigh, -kye, -kee) **3** a point of convergence of light or sound waves, or a point from which they appear to diverge. **4 in focus** (of an object or image being viewed) clear and sharp. **5 out of focus** (of an object or image being viewed) blurred and fuzzy. **6** same as **focal point** (sense 1), **focal length**. **7** *Optics* the state of an optical image when it is distinct or the state of an instrument producing this image. **8** a point upon which attention or activity is concentrated: *the focus was on health and education.* **9** *Geom* a fixed reference point on the concave side of a conic section, used when defining its eccentricity. ▷ **HISTORY** Latin: hearth, fireplace

focus group *n* a group of people gathered by a market research company to discuss and assess a product or service.

fodder *n* bulk feed for livestock, esp. hay or straw. ▷ **HISTORY** Old English *fōdor*

foe *n Formal or literary* an enemy. ▷ **HISTORY** Old English *fāh* hostile

FoE *or* **FOE** Friends of the Earth.

foetid *adj* same as **fetid**.

foetus *n, pl* **-tuses** same as **fetus**.

fog *n* **1** a mass of droplets of condensed water vapour suspended in the air, often greatly reducing visibility. **2** *Photog* a blurred area on a developed negative, print, or transparency. ✧ *vb* **fogging, fogged 3** to envelop or become enveloped with or as if with fog. ▷ **HISTORY** probably from Old Norse ▶ **foggy** *adj*

fog bank *n* a distinct mass of fog, esp. at sea.

fogbound *adj* prevented from operating by fog.

fogey *or* **fogy** *n, pl* **-geys** *or* **-gies** an extremely old-fashioned person: *a stick-in-the-mud old fogey.* ▷ **HISTORY** origin unknown ▶ **fogeyish** *or* **fogyish** *adj*

foghorn *n* a large horn sounded at intervals as a warning to ships in fog.

foible *n* a slight peculiarity or minor weakness: *he was intolerant of other people's foibles.* ▷ **HISTORY** obsolete French form of *faible* feeble

foil[1] *vb* to baffle or frustrate (a person or an attempt). ▷ **HISTORY** Middle English *foilen* to trample

foil[2] *n* **1** metal in the form of very thin sheets. **2** a person or thing setting off another thing to advantage: *mint sauce is an excellent foil to lamb.* ▷ **HISTORY** Latin *folia* leaves

foil[3] *n* a light slender flexible sword tipped by a button, used in fencing. ▷ **HISTORY** origin unknown

foist *vb* **foist on** to force (someone) to have or experience (something): *the tough economic policies which have been foisted on the developing world.* ▷ **HISTORY** probably from obsolete Dutch *vuisten* to enclose in one's hand

fold[1] *vb* **1** to bend double so that one part covers another. **2** to bring together and intertwine (the arms or legs). **3 fold up** to enclose in a surrounding material. **4** *Literary* to clasp (a person) in one's arms. **5** Also: **fold in** to mix (ingredients) by gently turning one over the other with a spoon. **6** *Informal* (of a business, organization, or project) to fail or go bankrupt. ✧ *n* **7** a piece or section that has been folded. **8** a mark, crease, or hollow made by folding. **9** a bend in stratified rocks that results from movements within the earth's crust. ▷ HISTORY Old English *fealdan*

fold² *n* **1** *Brit, Austral and S African* a small enclosure for sheep. **2** a church or the members of it. ▷ HISTORY Old English *falod*

folder *n* a binder or file for holding loose papers.

foliaceous *adj* **1** like a leaf. **2** *Geol* consisting of thin layers. ▷ HISTORY Latin *foliaceus*

foliage *n* **1** the green leaves of a plant. **2** leaves together with the stems, twigs, and branches they are attached to, esp. when used for decoration. ▷ HISTORY Old French *fuellage*

foliation *n* **1** *Bot* **a** the process of producing leaves. **b** the state of being in leaf. **2** a leaflike decoration.

folio *n, pl* **-lios 1** a sheet of paper folded in half to make two leaves for a book. **2** a book of the largest common size made up of such sheets. **3 a** a leaf of paper numbered on the front side only. **b** the page number of a book. **4** *NZ* a collection of related material. ✧ *adj* **5** of or made in the largest book size, common esp. in early centuries of European printing: *the entire series is being reissued, several in the original folio format.* ▷ HISTORY Latin *in folio* in a leaf

folk *pl n* **1** people in general, esp. those of a particular group or class: *ordinary folk.* **2** Also: **folks** *Informal* members of one's family; relatives. ✧ *n* **3** *Informal* short for **folk music**. **4** a people or tribe. ✧ *adj* **5** originating from or traditional to the common people of a country: *folk art.* ▷ HISTORY Old English *folc*

folk dance *n* **1** a traditional country dance. **2** music for such a dance.

folk etymology *n* the gradual change in the form of a word through the influence of a more familiar word, as for example *crayfish* from its Middle English form *crevis*.

folklore *n* the traditional beliefs of a people as expressed in stories and songs.

folk music *n* **1** music that is passed on from generation to generation. **2** a piece written in the style of this music.

folk song *n* **1** a song handed down among the common people. **2** a modern song like this. ▸ **folk singer** *n*

folksy *adj* **-sier, -siest** simple and unpretentious, sometimes in an artificial way.

follicle *n* any small sac or cavity in the body, esp. one from which a hair grows. ▷ HISTORY Latin *folliculus* small bag ▸ **follicular** *adj*

follow *vb* **1** to go or come after. **2** to accompany: *he followed Isabel everywhere.* **3** to be a logical or natural consequence of. **4** to keep to the course or track of. **5** to act in accordance with: *follow the rules below and it will help you a great deal.* **6** to accept the ideas or beliefs of. **7** to understand (an explanation). **8** to have a keen interest in: *he's followed the singer's career for more than 25 years.* ✧ See also **follow-on, follow through, follow up**. ▷ HISTORY Old English *folgian*

follower *n* **1** a person who accepts the teachings of another: *a follower of Nietzsche.* **2** a supporter, such as of a sport or team.

following *adj* **1** about to be mentioned. **2** next in time. **3** (of winds or currents) moving in the same direction as a vessel. ✧ *prep* **4** as a result of: *uncertainty following the collapse of communism.* ✧ *n* **5** a group of supporters or enthusiasts.

> **WORD TIP**
> The use of *following* to mean as a result of is very common in journalism, but should be avoided in other kinds of writing.

follow-on *Cricket* ✧ *n* **1** an immediate second innings forced on a team scoring a prescribed number of runs fewer than its opponents in the first innings. ✧ *vb* **follow on 2** to play a follow-on: *England had to follow on.*

follow through *vb* **1** to continue an action or series of actions until finished. **2** *Sport* to continue a stroke, kick, etc., after striking the ball. ✧ *n* **follow-through 3** *Sport* continuation of a kick, stroke, etc., after striking the ball: *Faldo's controlled follow-through.*

follow up *vb* **1** to investigate (a person, evidence, etc.) closely. **2** to continue (action) after a beginning, esp. to increase its effect. ✧ *n* **follow-up 3** something done to reinforce an initial action: *a routine follow-up to his operation.*

folly *n, pl* **-lies 1** the quality of being foolish. **2** a foolish action, idea, etc. **3** an imitation castle, temple, etc., built as a decoration in a large garden or park. ▷ HISTORY Old French *folie* madness

foment (foam-**ent**) *vb* to encourage or stir up (trouble). ▷ HISTORY Latin *fomentum* a poultice ▸ **fomentation** *n*

> **WORD TIP**
> Both *foment* and *ferment* can be used to talk about stirring up trouble: *he was accused of fomenting/fermenting unrest.* Only *ferment* can be used intransitively or as a noun: *his anger continued to ferment* (not *foment*); *rural areas were unaffected by the ferment in the cities.*

fond *adj* **1 fond of** having a liking for. **2** loving and affectionate: *his fond parents.* **3** (of hopes or wishes) cherished but unlikely to be realized. ▷ HISTORY Middle English *fonnen* to be foolish ▸ **fondly** *adv* ▸ **fondness** *n*

fondant *n* (a sweet made from) a thick flavoured paste of sugar and water. ▷ HISTORY French

fondle *vb* **-dling, -dled** to touch or stroke tenderly. ▷ HISTORY obsolete *fond* to fondle

fondue *n* a Swiss dish, consisting of melted cheese into which small pieces of bread are dipped. ▷ HISTORY French: melted

font¹ *n* a large bowl in a church for baptismal water. ▷ HISTORY Latin *fons* fountain

font² *n Printing* same as **fount²**.

fontanelle *or esp US* **fontanel** *n Anat* a soft membranous gap between the bones of a baby's skull. ▷ **HISTORY** Old French *fontanele* a little spring

food *n* any substance that can be taken into the body by a living organism and changed into energy and body tissue. *RELATED ADJECTIVE* ▸ **gastronomical** ▷ **HISTORY** Old English *fōda*

food chain *n Biol* a series of organisms in a community, each member of which is connected to another in the chain by eating or being eaten by it. Compare **food web**.

foodie *n Informal* a person with a keen interest in food and cookery.

food poisoning *n* an acute illness caused by food that is contaminated by bacteria.

food processor *n* a machine for chopping, mixing, or liquidizing food.

foodstuff *n* any substance that can be used as food.

food web *n Biol* the plants in a community together with all the primary, secondary and tertiary consumers of any organisms in this interrelated system. Compare **food chain**.

fool[1] *n* **1** a person who lacks sense or judgment. **2** a person who is made to appear ridiculous. **3** (formerly) a professional jester living in a royal or noble household. **4 play** *or* **act the fool** to deliberately act foolishly. ✧ *vb* **5** to deceive (someone), esp. in order to make them look ridiculous. **6 fool around** *or* **about with** *Informal* to act or play with irresponsibly or aimlessly. **7** to speak or act in a playful or jesting manner. ▷ **HISTORY** Latin *follis* bellows

fool[2] *n Chiefly Brit* a dessert made from a puree of fruit with cream. ▷ **HISTORY** perhaps from FOOL[1]

foolery *n* foolish behaviour.

foolhardy *adj* **-hardier, -hardiest** recklessly adventurous. ▷ **HISTORY** Old French *fol* foolish + *hardi* bold ▸ **foolhardily** *adv* ▸ **foolhardiness** *n*

foolish *adj* very silly, unwise, or absurd. ▸ **foolishly** *adv* ▸ **foolishness** *n*

foolproof *adj Informal* **1** incapable of going wrong; infallible: *a foolproof identification system.* **2** (of machines etc.) guaranteed to function as intended despite human misuse or error.

foolscap *n Chiefly Brit* a standard paper size, 34.3 × 43.2 cm. ▷ **HISTORY** from the watermark of a *fool's* (i.e. dunce's) *cap,* formerly used on it

fool's gold *n* a yellow-coloured mineral, such as pyrite, that is sometimes mistaken for gold.

fool's paradise *n* a state of happiness based on false hopes or beliefs.

foot *n, pl* **feet 1** the part of the leg below the ankle joint that is in contact with the ground during standing and walking. **2** the part of a garment covering a foot. **3** a unit of length equal to 12 inches (0.3048 metre). **4** the bottom, base, or lower end of something: *at the foot of the hill; the foot of the page.* **5** *Old-fashioned* infantry. **6** *Prosody* a group of two or more syllables in which one syllable has the major stress, forming the basic unit of poetic rhythm. **7 one foot in the grave** *Informal* near to death. **8 on foot** walking. **9 put one's best foot forward** to try to do one's best. **10 put one's foot down** *Informal* to act firmly. **11 put one's foot in it** *Informal* to make an embarrassing and tactless mistake. **12 under foot** on the ground. ✧ *vb* **13 foot it** *Informal* to travel on foot. **14 foot the bill** to pay the entire cost of something. ✧ See also **feet**. ▷ **HISTORY** Old English *fōt* ▸ **footless** *adj*

> **WORD TIP**
> In front of another noun, the plural for the unit of length is *foot: a 20-foot putt; his 70-foot ketch. Foot* can also be used instead of *feet* when mentioning a quantity and in front of words like *tall: four foot of snow; he is at least six foot tall.*

footage *n* **1** a length of film. **2** the sequences of filmed material: *footage of refugees leaving the city.*

foot-and-mouth disease *n* a highly infectious viral disease of cattle, pigs, sheep, and goats, in which blisters form in the mouth and on the feet.

football *n* **1** any of various games played with a ball in which two teams compete to kick, head, or propel the ball into each other's goal. **2** the ball used in any of these games. ▸ **footballer** *n*

football pools *pl n* same as **pools**.

footbridge *n* a narrow bridge for the use of pedestrians.

footfall *n* the sound of a footstep.

foothills *pl n Geog* relatively low hills at the foot of a mountain.

foothold *n* **1** a secure position from which further progress may be made: *a firm foothold in Europe's telecommunications market.* **2** a ledge or other place where a foot can be securely positioned, as during climbing.

footing *n* **1** basis or foundation: *on a sound financial footing.* **2** the relationship between two people or groups: *on an equal footing.* **3** a secure grip by or for the feet.

footle *vb* **-ling, -led** *Chiefly Brit informal* to loiter aimlessly. ▷ **HISTORY** probably from French *foutre* to copulate with ▸ **footling** *adj*

footlights *pl n Theatre* lights set in a row along the front of the stage floor.

footloose *adj* free to go or do as one wishes.

footloose industry *n Econ* an industry that is not tied to any particular area either by its raw materials or its market and is therefore free to relocate to take advantage of more favourable economic conditions.

footman *n, pl* **-men** a male servant in uniform.

footnote *n* a note printed at the bottom of a page.

footpad *n Old-fashioned* a highwayman, on foot rather than horseback.

footpath *n* **1** a narrow path for walkers only. **2** *Austral* a raised space alongside a road, for pedestrians.

footplate *n Chiefly Brit* a platform in the cab of a locomotive on which the crew stand to operate the controls.

A B C D E F G H I J K L M N O P Q R S T U V W X Y Z

footprint *n* an indentation or outline of the foot on a surface.

footsie *n Informal* flirtation involving the touching together of feet.

footstep *n* **1** a step in walking. **2** the sound made by walking. **3** a footmark. **4 follow in someone's footsteps** to continue the example of another.

footstool *n* a low stool used for supporting the feet of a seated person.

footwear *n* anything worn to cover the feet.

footwork *n* the way in which the feet are used, for example in sports or dancing: *nimble footwork.*

fop *n* a man who is excessively concerned with fashion. ▷ **HISTORY** perhaps from Middle English *foppe* fool ▸ **foppery** *n* ▸ **foppish** *adj*

for *prep* **1** directed or belonging to: *a bottle of beer for himself.* **2** to the advantage of: *he spelt it out for her.* **3** in the direction of: *he headed for the door.* **4** over a span of (time or distance): *she considered him coolly for a moment.* **5** in favour of: *support for the war.* **6** in order to get: *for a bit of company.* **7** designed to meet the needs of: *the instructions are for right-handed players.* **8** at a cost of: *two dishes for one.* **9** in place of: *she had to substitute for her mother because they woke late.* **10** because of: *dancing for joy.* **11** regarding the usual characteristics of: *unusually warm for the time of year.* **12** concerning: *our idea for the last scene.* **13** as being: *do you take me for an idiot?* **14** at (a specified time): *multiparty elections are planned for next year.* **15** to do or take part in: *two guests for dinner.* **16** in the duty or task of: *that's for you to decide.* **17** in relation to; as it affects: *it's too hard for me.* **18** in order to preserve or retain: *fighting for survival.* **19** as a direct equivalent to: *word for word.* **20** in order to become or enter: *training for the priesthood.* **21** in exchange for: *the cash was used to pay for medical supplies.* **22 for all** See **all** (sense 12). **23 for it** *Brit & Austral informal* liable for punishment or blame: *you'll be for it if you get caught.* ✧ *conj* **24** *Formal* because or seeing that: *implausibility cries aloud, and this is a pity, for much of the narrative is entertaining.* ▷ **HISTORY** Old English

forage (**for**-ridge) *vb* **-aging, -aged 1** to search for food. **2** to obtain by searching about: *she foraged for her shoes.* ✧ *n* **3** food for horses or cattle, esp. hay or straw. **4** the act of searching for food or provisions. ▷ **HISTORY** Old French *fourrage*

forage cap *n* a cap with a flat round crown and a visor, worn by soldiers when not in battle or on parade.

foramen (for-**ray**-men) *n, pl* **-ramina** (-**ram**-in-a) *or* **-ramens** *Anat* a natural hole, esp. one in a bone through which nerves pass. ▷ **HISTORY** Latin

foray *n* **1** a short raid or incursion. **2** a first attempt or new undertaking: *his first foray into films.* ▷ **HISTORY** Middle English *forrayen* to pillage

forbear[1] *vb* **-bearing, -bore, -borne** to cease or refrain (from doing something). ▷ **HISTORY** Old English *forberan* ▸ **forbearance** *n*

forbear[2] *n* same as **forebear**.

forbid *vb* **-bidding, -bade** *or* **-bad, -bidden** *or* **-bid** to prohibit or refuse to allow. ▷ **HISTORY** Old English *forbēodan*

> **WORD TIP**
> It was formerly considered incorrect to talk of *forbidding* someone *from* doing something, but in modern usage either *from* or *to* can be used: *he was forbidden from entering/to enter the building.*

forbidding *adj* severe and threatening in appearance or manner: *a forbidding grey sky.*

force[1] *n* **1** strength or power: *the force of the impact had thrown him into the fireplace.* **2** exertion or the use of exertion against a person or thing that resists: *they used force and repression against those who opposed their policies.* **3** *Physics* an influence that changes a body from a state of rest to one of motion or changes its rate of motion. Symbol: *F.* **4 a** intellectual or moral influence: *the Superintendent acknowledged the force of the Chief Constable's argument.* **b** a person or thing with such influence: *Hitler quickly became the decisive force behind German foreign policy.* **5** drive or intensity. **6** a group of people organized for particular duties or tasks: *a UN peacekeeping force.* **7 in force a** (of a law) having legal validity. **b** in great strength or numbers. ✧ *vb* **forcing, forced 8** to compel (a person, group, etc.) to do something through effort, superior strength, etc.: *forced into an arranged marriage.* **9** to acquire or produce through effort, superior strength, etc.: *he forced a smile.* **10** to propel or drive despite resistance. **11** to break down or open (a lock, door, etc.). **12** to impose or inflict. **13** to cause (plants or farm animals) to grow at an increased rate. ▷ **HISTORY** Latin *fortis* strong

force[2] *n* (in N England) a waterfall. ▷ **HISTORY** Old Norse *fors*

forced *adj* **1** done because of force: *forced labour.* **2** false or unnatural: *forced jollity.* **3** due to an emergency: *a forced landing.*

forced migration *n Sociol* the fact of being forced by to leave one's home, for example because of war, famine, or religious persecution.

force-feed *vb* **-feeding, -fed** to force (a person or animal) to swallow food.

forceful *adj* **1** strong, emphatic, and confident: *a forceful speech.* **2** effective. ▸ **forcefully** *adv*

forcemeat *n* a mixture of chopped ingredients used for stuffing. ▷ **HISTORY** from *force* (see FARCE) + *meat*

forceps *n, pl* **-ceps** a surgical instrument in the form of a pair of pincers. ▷ **HISTORY** Latin *formus* hot + *capere* to seize

forcible *adj* **1** involving physical force. **2** convincing or effective. ▸ **forcibly** *adv*

ford *n* **1** a shallow area in a river that can be crossed by car, on horseback, etc. ✧ *vb* **2** to cross (a river) over a shallow area. ▷ **HISTORY** Old English ▸ **fordable** *adj*

fore *adj* **1** at, in, or towards the front: *the fore foot.* ✧ *n* **2** the front part. **3 fore and aft** located at both ends of a vessel: *two double cabins fore and aft.* **4 to**

the fore to the front or prominent position. ✧ *interj* **5** a golfer's shouted warning to a person in the path of a flying ball. ▷ HISTORY Old English
fore- *prefix* **1** before in time or rank: *foregoing.* **2** at or near the front: *foreground.* ▷ HISTORY Old English
forearm[1] *n* the part of the arm from the elbow to the wrist.
forearm[2] *vb* to prepare or arm beforehand.
forebear *or* **forbear** *n* an ancestor.
foreboding *n* a strong feeling that something bad is about to happen.
forecast *vb* **-casting, -cast** *or* **-casted 1** to predict or calculate (weather, events, etc.), in advance. ✧ *n* **2** a statement predicting the weather. **3** a prediction. ▶ **forecaster** *n*
forecastle, fo'c's'le, *or* **fo'c'sle** (**foke**-sl) *n* the raised front part of a ship.
foreclose *vb* **-closing, -closed** *Law* to take possession of property bought with borrowed money because repayment has not been made. ▷ HISTORY Old French *for-* out + *clore* to close ▶ **foreclosure** *n*
forecourt *n* a courtyard in front of a building, such as one in a filling station.
foredune *n Geog* a dune that is further forward and nearer the sea than the others. Compare **back dune**.
forefather *n* an ancestor.
forefinger *n* the finger next to the thumb. Also called: **index finger**
forefoot *n, pl* **-feet** either of the front feet of an animal.
forefront *n* **1** the most active or prominent position: *at the forefront of medical research.* **2** the very front.
foregather *or* **forgather** *vb* to gather together or assemble.
forego[1] *vb* **-going, -went, -gone** to precede in time, place, etc. ▷ HISTORY Old English *foregān*
forego[2] *vb* **-going, -went, -gone** same as **forgo**.
foregoing *adj* (esp. of writing or speech) going before; preceding.
foregone conclusion *n* an inevitable result.
foreground *n* **1** the part of a view, esp. in a picture, nearest the viewer. **2** an important or prominent position.
foregrounding *n Literature* a literary device whereby particular details or passages are made to stand out thanks to the use of unexpected language, arresting images or unusual word order.
forehand *Tennis, squash, etc.* ✧ *adj* **1** (of a stroke) made so that the racket is held with the wrist facing the direction of play. ✧ *n* **2** a forehand stroke.
forehead *n* the part of the face between the natural hairline and the eyes. ▷ HISTORY Old English *forhēafod*
foreign *adj* **1** of, located in, or coming from another country, area, or people. **2** dealing or concerned with another country, area, or people: *the Foreign Minister.* **3** not familiar; strange. **4** in an abnormal place or position: *a foreign body in the food.* ▷ HISTORY Latin *foris* outside
foreigner *n* **1** a person from a foreign country. **2** an outsider.
foreign minister *or* **secretary** *n* (in Britain) a cabinet minister who is responsible for a country's dealings with other countries.
foreign office *n* (in Britain) the ministry of a country that is concerned with dealings with other states.
foreknowledge *n* knowledge of something before it actually happens.
foreleg *n* either of the front legs of an animal.
forelock *n* a lock of hair growing or falling over the forehead.
foreman *n, pl* **-men 1** a person who supervises other workmen. **2** *Law* the leader of a jury.
foremast *n* the mast nearest the bow of a ship.
foremost *adj, adv* first in time, place, or importance: *Germany's foremost conductor.* ▷ HISTORY Old English *formest*, from *forma* first
forename *n* first name.
forenoon *n* the daylight hours before noon.
forensic (for-**ren**-sik) *adj* used in or connected with a court of law. ▷ HISTORY Latin *forensis* public ▶ **forensically** *adv*
forensic medicine *n* the application of medical knowledge for the purposes of the law, such as in determining the cause of death.
foreordain *vb* to determine (events, etc.) in the future.
forepaw *n* either of the front feet of a land mammal that does not have hooves.
foreplay *n* sexual stimulation before intercourse.
forerunner *n* **1** a person or thing that existed or happened before another and is similar in some way: *a forerunner of the surrealist painters.* **2** a person or thing that is a sign of what will happen in the future.
foresail *n* the main sail on the foremast of a ship.
foresee *vb* **-seeing, -saw, -seen** to see or know beforehand. ▶ **foreseeable** *adj*
foreshadow *vb* to show, indicate, or suggest in advance.
foreshore *n* the part of the shore between high- and low-tide marks.
foreshorten *vb* to see or draw (an object) from such an angle that it appears to be shorter than it really is.
foresight *n* **1** the ability to anticipate and provide for future needs. **2** the front sight on a firearm.
foreskin *n Anat* the fold of skin covering the tip of the penis.
forest *n* **1** a large wooded area with a thick growth of trees and plants. **2** a group of narrow or tall objects standing upright: *a forest of waving arms.* **3** *NZ* an area planted with pines or other trees that are not native to the country. ▷ HISTORY Medieval Latin *forestis* unfenced woodland, from Latin *foris* outside ▶ **forested** *adj*
forestall *vb* to delay, stop, or guard against beforehand: *an action forestalling any further talks.* ▷ HISTORY Middle English *forestallen* to waylay

forestation *n* the planting of trees over a wide area.

forester *n* a person skilled in forestry or in charge of a forest.

forestry *n* the science or skill of growing and maintaining trees in a forest, esp. to obtain wood.

foretaste *n* an early but limited experience of something to come.

foretell *vb* **-telling, -told** *Literary* to correctly predict (an event, a result, etc.) beforehand.

forethought *n* thoughtful planning for future events: *a little forethought can avoid a lot of problems later.*

for ever *or* **forever** *adv* **1** without end. **2** at all times. **3** *Informal* for a long time: *I could go on for ever about similar incidents.*

forewarn *vb* to warn beforehand.

foreword *n* an introductory statement to a book.

forfeit (**for**-fit) *n* **1** something lost or given up as a penalty for a fault, mistake, etc. ✧ *vb* **2** to lose as a forfeit. ✧ *adj* **3** lost as a forfeit. ▷ **HISTORY** Old French *forfet* offence ▸ **forfeiture** *n*

forgather *vb* same as **foregather**.

forgave *vb* the past tense of **forgive**.

forge[1] *n* **1** a place in which metal is worked by heating and hammering; smithy. **2** a furnace used for heating metal. ✧ *vb* **forging, forged 3** to shape (metal) by heating and hammering. **4** to make a fraudulent imitation of (a signature, money, a painting, etc.). **5** to create (an alliance, relationship, etc.). ▷ **HISTORY** Old French *forgier* to construct ▸ **forger** *n*

forge[2] *vb* **forging, forged 1** to move at a steady pace. **2 forge ahead** to increase speed or progress; take the lead. ▷ **HISTORY** origin unknown

forgery *n, pl* **-geries 1** an illegal copy of a painting, banknote, antique, etc. **2** the crime of making a fraudulent imitation.

forget *vb* **-getting, -got, -gotten 1** to fail to remember (someone or something once known). **2** to neglect, either by mistake or on purpose. **3** to leave behind by mistake. **4 forget oneself** to act in an uncharacteristically unrestrained or unacceptable manner. ▷ **HISTORY** Old English *forgietan* ▸ **forgettable** *adj*

forgetful *adj* **1** tending to forget. **2 forgetful of** inattentive to or neglectful of: *Fiona, forgetful of the time, was still in bed.* ▸ **forgetfully** *adv*

forget-me-not *n* a low-growing plant with clusters of small blue flowers.

forgive *vb* **-giving, -gave, -given 1** to stop feeling anger and resentment towards (a person) or at (an action that has caused upset or harm). **2** to pardon (a mistake). **3** to free from (a debt). ▷ **HISTORY** Old English *forgiefan*

forgiveness *n* the act of forgiving or the state of being forgiven.

forgiving *adj* willing to forgive.

forgo *or* **forego** *vb* **-going, -went, -gone** to give up or do without. ▷ **HISTORY** Old English *forgān*

forgot *vb* **1** the past tense of **forget**. **2** *Old-fashioned or dialect* a past participle of **forget**.

forgotten *vb* a past participle of **forget**.

fork *n* **1** a small tool with long thin prongs on the end of a handle, used for lifting food to the mouth. **2** a larger similar-shaped gardening tool, used for lifting or digging. **3 forks** the part of a bicycle that links the handlebars to the front wheel. **4** (of a road, river, etc.) **a** a division into two or more branches. **b** the point where the division begins. **c** such a branch. ✧ *vb* **5** to pick up, dig, etc., with a fork. **6** to be divided into two or more branches. **7** to take one or other branch at a fork in a road, etc. ▷ **HISTORY** Latin *furca*

forked *adj* **1** having a fork or forklike parts. **2** zigzag: *forked lightning.*

fork-lift truck *n* a vehicle with two moveable arms at the front that can be raised and lowered for transporting and unloading goods.

fork out *vb Slang* to pay, esp. with reluctance.

forlorn *adj* **1** lonely, unhappy, and uncared-for. **2** (of a place) having a deserted appearance. **3** desperate and without any expectation of success. ▷ **HISTORY** Old English *forloren* lost ▸ **forlornly** *adv*

forlorn hope *n* **1** a hopeless enterprise. **2** a faint hope. ▷ **HISTORY** changed (by folk etymology) from Dutch *verloren hoop* lost troop

form *n* **1** the shape or appearance of something. **2** a visible person or animal. **3** the particular mode in which a thing or person appears: *wood in the form of paper.* **4** a type or kind: *abortion was widely used as a form of birth control.* **5** physical or mental condition. **6** a printed document, esp. one with spaces in which to fill details or answers. **7** the previous record of a horse, athlete, etc. **8** *Brit slang* a criminal record. **9** *Education chiefly Brit & NZ* a group of children who are taught together. **10** manners and etiquette: *it is considered bad form not to wear a tie.* **11** the structure and arrangement of a work of art or piece of writing as distinguished from its content. **12** a bench. **13** a hare's nest. **14** any of the various ways in which a word may be spelt or inflected. ✧ *vb* **15** to give shape to or take shape, esp. a particular shape. **16** to come or bring into existence: *glaciers dammed the valley bottoms with debris behind which lakes have formed.* **17** to make or construct or be made or constructed. **18** to train or mould by instruction or example. **19** to acquire or develop: *they've formed this impression; we formed a bond.* **20** to be an element of. ▷ **HISTORY** Latin *forma* shape, model

formal *adj* **1** of or following established conventions: *formal talks; a formal announcement.* **2** characterized by conventional forms of ceremony and behaviour: *a small formal dinner party.* **3** suitable for occasions organized according to conventional ceremony: *formal cocktail frocks.* **4** methodical and organized: *a formal approach.* **5** (of education and training) given officially at a school, college, etc.: *he had no formal training in maths.* **6** symmetrical in form: *a formal garden.* **7** relating to the form or structure of something as distinguished from its substance or content: *they addressed the formal elements of the structure of police work.* **8** *Philosophy* logically deductive rather than based on facts and observation. ▷ **HISTORY** Latin *formalis* ▶ **formally** *adv*

formaldehyde (for-**mal**-de-hide) *n* a colourless poisonous strong-smelling gas, used as formalin and in synthetic resins. Also: **methanal** ▷ **HISTORY** *form(ic) + aldehyde*

formalin *n* a solution of formaldehyde in water, used as a disinfectant and as a preservative for biological specimens.

formalism *n* concerned with outward appearances and structure at the expense of content. ▶ **formalist** *n*

formality *n, pl* **-ties 1** something done as a requirement of custom or good manners: *he dealt with the formalities regarding the cremation.* **2** a necessary procedure without real effect: *trials were often a mere formality with the verdict decided beforehand.* **3** strict observance of ceremony.

formalize *or* **-ise** *vb* **-izing, -ized** *or* **-ising, -ised 1** to make official or valid. **2** to give a definite form to. ▶ **formalization** *or* **-isation** *n*

format *n* **1** the shape, size, and general appearance of a publication. **2** style or arrangement, such as of a television programme: *a chat-show format.* **3** *Computers* the arrangement of data on disk or magnetic tape to comply with a computer's input device. ✧ *vb* **-matting, -matted 4** to arrange in a specified format. ▷ **HISTORY** Latin *formatus* formed

formation *n* **1** the act of having or taking form or existence. **2** something that is formed. **3** the manner in which something is arranged. **4** an arrangement of people or things acting as a unit, such as a troop of soldiers. **5** a series of rocks or clouds of a particular structure or shape.

formative *adj* **1** of or relating to formation, development, or growth: *formative years at school.* **2** shaping or moulding: *the formative influence on his life.*

former *adj* **1** belonging to or occurring in an earlier time: *a grotesque parody of a former greatness.* **2** having been at a previous time: *the former prime minister.* ✧ *n* **3 the former** the first or first mentioned of two.

formerly *adv* in the past.

Formica *n Trademark* a hard laminated plastic used esp. for heat-resistant surfaces.

formic acid *n* an acid derived from ants. ▷ **HISTORY** Latin *formica* ant

formidable *adj* **1** frightening because very difficult to deal with or overcome: *the Finnish winter presents formidable problems to drivers.* **2** extremely impressive: *a formidable Juventus squad.* ▷ **HISTORY** Latin *formido* fear ▶ **formidably** *adv*

formless *adj* without a definite shape or form.

formula (**form**-yew-la) *n, pl* **-las** *or* **-lae** (-lee) **1** a group of letters, numbers, or other symbols which represents a mathematical or scientific rule. **2** a plan or set of rules for doing or producing something. **3** an established form of words, as used in religious ceremonies, legal proceedings, etc. **4** a powder used to make a milky drink for babies. **5** *Motor racing* the category in which a car competes, judged according to engine size. ▷ **HISTORY** Latin *forma* form ▶ **formulaic** *adj*

formulary *n, pl* **-laries** a book of prescribed formulas.

formulate *vb* **-lating, -lated 1** to express in a formula. **2** to plan or describe precisely and clearly. ▶ **formulation** *n*

fornicate *vb* **-cating, -cated** to have sexual intercourse without being married. ▷ **HISTORY** Latin *fornix* vault, brothel situated therein ▶ **fornicator** *n*

fornication *n* voluntary sexual intercourse outside marriage.

forsake *vb* **-saking, -sook, -saken 1** to withdraw support or friendship from. **2** to give up (something valued or enjoyed). ▷ **HISTORY** Old English *forsacan*

forsooth *adv Old-fashioned* in truth or indeed. ▷ **HISTORY** Old English *forsōth*

forswear *vb* **-swearing, -swore, -sworn 1** to reject or renounce with determination. **2** to testify falsely in a court of law. ▷ **HISTORY** Old English *forswearian*

forsythia (for-**syth**-ee-a) *n* a shrub with yellow flowers which appear in spring before the leaves. ▷ **HISTORY** after William *Forsyth,* botanist

fort *n* **1** a fortified building or position. **2 hold the fort** *Informal* to keep things in operation during someone's absence. ▷ **HISTORY** Latin *fortis* strong

forte[1] (**for**-tay) *n* something at which a person excels: *cooking is his forte.* ▷ **HISTORY** Latin *fortis* strong

forte[2] *adv Music* loudly. ▷ **HISTORY** Italian

forth *adv* **1** *Formal or old-fashioned* forward, out, or away. **2 and so forth** and so on. ▷ **HISTORY** Old English

forthcoming *adj* **1** about to appear or happen: *the forthcoming elections.* **2** made available. **3** (of a person) willing to give information.

forthright *adj* direct and outspoken.

forthwith *adv* at once.

fortification *n* **1** the act of fortifying. **2 fortifications** walls, mounds, etc., used to strengthen the defences of a place.

fortify *vb* **-fies, -fying, -fied 1** to make (a place) defensible, such as by building walls. **2** to strengthen physically, mentally, or morally. **3** to increase the nutritious value of (a food), such as by adding vitamins. ▷ **HISTORY** Latin *fortis* strong + *facere* to make

fortissimo *adv Music* very loudly. ▷ **HISTORY** Italian

fortitude *n* calm and patient courage in trouble or pain. ▷ **HISTORY** Latin *fortitudo* courage

fortnight *n* a period of 14 consecutive days. ▷ **HISTORY** Old English *fēowertīene niht* fourteen nights

fortnightly *Chiefly Brit* ✧ *adj* **1** occurring or appearing once each fortnight. ✧ *adv* **2** once a fortnight.

FORTRAN *n* a high-level computer programming language designed for mathematical and scientific purposes. ▷ **HISTORY** *for(mula) tran(slation)*

A B C D E F G H I J K L M N O P Q R S T U V W X Y Z

fortress *n* a large fort or fortified town. ▷ **HISTORY** Latin *fortis* strong

fortuitous (for-**tyew**-it-uss) *adj* happening by chance, esp. by a lucky chance. ▷ **HISTORY** Latin *fortuitus* ▶ **fortuitously** *adv*

fortunate *adj* **1** having good luck. **2** occurring by good luck. ▶ **fortunately** *adv*

fortune *n* **1** luck, esp. when favourable. **2** a person's destiny. **3** a power regarded as being responsible for human affairs. **4** wealth or material prosperity. ▷ **HISTORY** Latin *fors* chance

fortune-teller *n* a person who claims to predict events in other people's lives.

forty *n, pl* **-ties 1** the cardinal number that is the product of ten and four. **2** a numeral, 40 or XL, representing this number. **3** something representing or consisting of 40 units. ✧ *adj* **4** amounting to forty: *forty pages.* ▶ **fortieth** *adj, n*

forty winks *n Informal* a short light sleep.

forum *n* **1** a meeting or medium for the open discussion of subjects of public interest. **2** (in ancient Roman cities) an open space serving as a marketplace and centre of public business. **3** (in S Africa) a pressure group of leaders and representatives. ▷ **HISTORY** Latin

forward *adj* **1** directed or moving ahead. **2** at, in, or near the front. **3** overfamiliar or disrespectful. **4** well developed or advanced. **5** of or relating to the future or favouring change. ✧ *n* **6** an attacking player in any of various sports, such as soccer. ✧ *adv* **7** same as **forwards**. ✧ *vb* **8** to send (a letter, etc.) on to an ultimate destination. **9** to advance or promote. ▷ **HISTORY** Old English *foreweard*

forward purchasing *n Commerce* the practice of buying in materials in greater quantities than current requirements demand.

forwards *or* **forward** *adv* **1** towards or at a place ahead or in advance, esp. in space but also in time. **2** towards the front.

fosse *or* **foss** *n* a ditch or moat, esp. one dug as a fortification. ▷ **HISTORY** Latin *fossa*

fossick *vb Austral & NZ* **1** to search for gold or precious stones in abandoned workings, rivers, etc. **2** to search for (something). ▷ **HISTORY** probably from English dialect *fussock* to bustle about

fossil *n* **1** remains of a plant or animal that existed in a past geological age, occurring in the form of mineralized bones, shells, etc. ✧ *adj* **2** of, like, or being a fossil. ▷ **HISTORY** Latin *fossilis* dug up

fossil fuel *n* fuel, such as coal or oil, formed from the decayed remains of prehistoric animals and plants.

fossilize *or* **-ise** *vb* **-izing, -ized** *or* **-ising, -ised 1** to convert or be converted into a fossil. **2** to become out-of-date or inflexible.

foster *adj* **1** of or involved in the bringing up of a child not one's own: *foster care.* ✧ *vb* **2** to bring up (a child not one's own). **3** to promote the growth or development of. ▷ **HISTORY** Old English *fōstrian* to feed ▶ **fostering** *n*

fought *vb* the past of **fight**.

foul *adj* **1** offensive or loathsome: *a foul deed.* **2** stinking or dirty. **3** full of dirt or offensive matter. **4** (of language) obscene or vulgar. **5** unfair: *by fair or foul means.* **6** (of weather) unpleasant. **7** very bad-tempered and irritable: *he was in a foul mood.* **8** *Informal* disgustingly bad. ✧ *n* **9** *Sport* a violation of the rules. ✧ *vb* **10** to make dirty or polluted. **11** to make or become entangled. **12** to make or become clogged. **13** *Sport* to commit a foul against (an opponent). ✧ *adv* **14 fall foul of** to come into conflict with. ▷ **HISTORY** Old English *fūl*

foul-mouthed *adj* habitually using swearwords and bad language.

foul play *n* **1** violent activity esp. murder. **2** a violation of the rules in a game.

found[1] *vb* the past of **find**.

found[2] *vb* **1** to bring into being or establish (something, such as an institution). **2** to lay the foundation of. **3 founded on** to have a basis in: *a political system founded on fear.* ▷ **HISTORY** Latin *fundus* bottom ▶ **founder** *n* ▶ **founding** *adj*

found[3] *vb* **1** to cast (metal or glass) by melting and pouring into a mould. **2** to make (articles) in this way. ▷ **HISTORY** Latin *fundere* to melt

foundation *n* **1** the basic experience, idea, or attitude on which a way of life or belief is based: *respect for the law is the foundation of commercial society.* **2** a construction below the ground that distributes the load of a building, wall, etc. **3** the base on which something stands. **4** the act of founding. **5** an endowment for the support of an institution, such as a college. **6** an institution supported by an endowment. **7** a cosmetic used as a base for make-up.

founder *vb* **1** to break down or fail: *his negotiations have foundered on economic grounds.* **2** (of a ship) to sink. **3** to sink into or become stuck in soft ground. **4** (of a horse) to stumble or go lame. ▷ **HISTORY** Old French *fondrer* to submerge

> **☑ WORD TIP**
> *Founder* is sometimes wrongly used where *flounder* is meant: *this unexpected turn of events left him floundering* (not *foundering*).

foundling *n Chiefly Brit* an abandoned baby whose parents are not known. ▷ **HISTORY** Middle English *foundeling*

foundry *n, pl* **-ries** a place where metal is melted and cast.

fount[1] *n* **1** *Poetic* a spring or fountain. **2** a source or supply: *a fount of knowledge.* ▷ **HISTORY** from *fountain*

fount[2] *n Printing chiefly Brit* a complete set of type of one style and size. ▷ **HISTORY** Old French *fonte* a founding, casting

fountain *n* **1** an ornamental feature in a pool or lake consisting of a jet of water forced into the air by a pump. **2** a jet or spray of water. **3** a natural spring of water. **4** a source or supply: *a fountain of many new ideas.* **5** a cascade of sparks, lava, etc. ▷ **HISTORY** Latin *fons* spring

fountainhead *n* a principal or original source.

fountain pen *n* a pen supplied with ink from a container inside it.

four *n* **1** the cardinal number that is the sum of one and three. **2** a numeral, 4 or IV, representing this number. **3** something representing or consisting of four units. **4** *Cricket* a score of four runs, obtained by hitting the ball so that it crosses the boundary after hitting the ground. **5** *Rowing* **a** a rowing boat propelled by four oarsmen. **b** the crew of such a rowing boat. ✧ *adj* **6** amounting to four: *four zones.* ▷ **HISTORY** Old English *fēower*

four-by-four *n* a vehicle with four-wheel drive.

fourfold *adj* **1** having four times as many or as much. **2** composed of four parts. ✧ *adv* **3** by four times as many or as much.

four-in-hand *n* a carriage drawn by four horses and driven by one driver.

four-letter word *n* any of several short English words referring to sex or excrement: regarded generally as offensive or obscene.

four-poster *n* a bed with posts at each corner supporting a canopy and curtains.

foursome *n* **1** a group of four people. **2** *Golf* a game between two pairs of players.

foursquare *adv* **1** squarely or firmly. ✧ *adj* **2** solid and strong. **3** forthright and uncompromising.

four-stroke *adj* designating an internal-combustion engine in which the piston makes four strokes for every explosion.

fourteen *n* **1** the cardinal number that is the sum of ten and four. **2** a numeral, 14 or XIV, representing this number. **3** something representing or consisting of 14 units. ✧ *adj* **4** amounting to fourteen: *fourteen points.* ▶ **fourteenth** *adj, n*

fourth *adj* **1** of or being number four in a series. **2** denoting the highest forward gear in a motor vehicle. ✧ *n* **3** the highest forward gear in a motor vehicle.

fourth dimension *n* **1** the dimension of time, which in addition to three spatial dimensions specifies the position of a point or particle. **2** the concept in science fiction of an extra dimension.

fourth estate *n* the press.

four-wheel drive *n* a system in a vehicle in which all four wheels are connected to the source of power.

fowl *n* **1** a domesticated bird such as a hen. **2** any other bird that is used as food or hunted as game. **3** the meat of fowl. **4** *Old-fashioned* a bird. ✧ *vb* **5** to hunt wild birds. ▷ **HISTORY** Old English *fugol*

fox *n, pl* **foxes** *or* **fox** **1** a doglike wild animal with a pointed muzzle and a bushy tail. **2** its reddish-brown or grey fur. **3** a person who is cunning and sly. ✧ *vb* **4** *Informal* to confuse. ▷ **HISTORY** Old English

foxglove *n* a tall plant with purple or white flowers.

foxhole *n Mil* a small pit dug to provide shelter against enemy fire.

foxhound *n* a breed of short-haired terrier, originally kept for hunting foxes.

foxtrot *n* **1** a ballroom dance with slow and quick steps. **2** music for this. ✧ *vb* **-trotting, -trotted** **3** to perform this dance.

foxy *adj* **foxier, foxiest** **1** of or resembling a fox, esp. in craftiness. **2** reddish-brown. ▶ **foxily** *adv* ▶ **foxiness** *n*

foyer (**foy**-ay) *n* an entrance hall in a hotel, theatre, or cinema. ▷ **HISTORY** French: fireplace

FP **1** fire plug. **2** freezing point.

Fr **1** *Christianity* **a** Father. **b** Frater. ▷ **HISTORY** Latin *brother* **2** *Chem* francium.

fracas (**frak**-ah) *n* a noisy quarrel or fight. ▷ **HISTORY** French

fraction *n* **1** *Maths* a numerical quantity that is not a whole number. **2** any part or subdivision. **3** a very small proportion or amount of something. **4** *Chem* a component of a mixture separated by distillation. ▷ **HISTORY** Latin *fractus* broken ▶ **fractional** *adj* ▶ **fractionally** *adv*

fractional distillation *or* **fractionation** *n Chem* the process of separating the constituents of a liquid mixture by heating it and condensing the components separately according to their different boiling points.

fractious *adj* (esp. of children) easily upset and angered, often due to tiredness. ▷ **HISTORY** obsolete *fraction* discord

> **WORD TIP**
> *Fractious* is sometimes wrongly used where *factious* is meant: *this factious* (not *fractious*) *dispute has split the party still further.*

fracture *n* **1** breaking, esp. the breaking or cracking of a bone. **2** a division, split, or breach. **3** *Geol* **a** the characteristic appearance of the surface of a freshly broken mineral or rock. **b** the way in which a mineral or rock naturally breaks. ✧ *vb* **-turing, -tured** **4** to break. ▷ **HISTORY** Latin *frangere* to break ▶ **fractural** *adj*

fracture zone *n Geol* an area where there are fractures in the rock.

fragile *adj* **1** able to be broken or damaged easily. **2** in a weakened physical state: *you're looking a bit fragile this morning.* ▷ **HISTORY** Latin *fragilis* ▶ **fragility** *n*

fragment *n* **1** a piece broken off. **2** an incomplete piece: *fragments of information.* ✧ *vb* **3** to break into small pieces or different parts. ▷ **HISTORY** Latin *fragmentum* ▶ **fragmentation** *n*

fragmentary *adj* made up of small or unconnected pieces: *fragmentary evidence to support his theory.*

fragrance *n* **1** a pleasant smell. **2** a perfume or scent.

fragrant *adj* having a pleasant smell. ▷ **HISTORY** Latin *fragrare* to emit a smell

frail *adj* **1** physically weak and delicate. **2** easily damaged: *the frail aircraft.* **3** easily tempted. ▷ **HISTORY** Old French *frele*

frailty *n* **1** physical or moral weakness. **2** (*pl* **-ties**) an inadequacy or fault resulting from moral weakness.

frame *n* **1** an open structure that gives shape and support to something, such as a building. **2** an enclosing case or border into which something is fitted: *the window frame.* **3** the system around which something is built up: *caught up in the frame of the revolution.* **4** the structure of the human body. **5** one of a series of exposures on film used in making motion pictures. **6** a television picture scanned by electron beams at a particular frequency. **7** *Snooker* **a** a single game in a match. **b** a wooden triangle used to arrange the red balls in formation before the start of a game. **8** short for **cold frame. 9** *Slang* a frame-up. **10 frame of mind** a state of mind: *in a complacent frame of mind.* ✧ *vb* **framing, framed 11** to construct by fitting parts together. **12** to create and develop (plans or a policy). **13** to construct (a statement) in a particular kind of language. **14** to provide or enclose with a frame. **15** *Slang* to conspire to incriminate (someone) on a false charge. ▷ **HISTORY** Old English *framian* to avail

frame of reference *n* **1** a set of standards that determines behaviour. **2** any set of planes or curves, such as the three coordinate axes, used to locate a point in space.

frame-up *n Slang* a conspiracy to incriminate someone on a false charge.

framework *n* **1** a particular set of beliefs, ideas, or rules referred to in order to solve a problem: *a moral framework.* **2** a structure supporting something.

franc *n* the standard monetary unit of Switzerland, various African countries, and formerly of France and Belgium. ▷ **HISTORY** Latin *Rex Francorum* King of the Franks, inscribed on 14th-century francs

franchise *n* **1** the right to vote, esp. for a member of parliament. **2** any exemption, privilege, or right granted by a public authority. **3** *Commerce* authorization granted to a distributor to sell a company's goods. ✧ *vb* **-chising, -chised 4** *Commerce* to grant (a person, etc.) a franchise. ▷ **HISTORY** Old French *franchir* to set free

franchisee *n Commerce* a person or a firm that has been granted a franchise.

franchisor *n Commerce* a person or a firm that grants franchises.

Franciscan *n* **1** a member of a Christian religious order of friars or nuns founded by Saint Francis of Assisi. ✧ *adj* **2** of this order.

francium *n Chem* an unstable radioactive element of the alkali-metal group. Symbol: Fr. ▷ **HISTORY** from *France,* because first found there

Franco- *combining form* indicating France or French: *the Franco-Prussian war.* ▷ **HISTORY** Medieval Latin *Francus*

frangipani (fran-jee-**pah**-nee) *n* **1** an Australian evergreen tree with large yellow fragrant flowers. **2** a tropical shrub with fragrant flowers.

frank *adj* **1** honest and straightforward in speech or attitude. ✧ *vb* **2** to put a mark on (a letter), ensuring free carriage. ✧ *n* **3** an official mark stamped to a letter ensuring free delivery. ▷ **HISTORY** Medieval Latin *francus* free ▶ **frankly** *adv* ▶ **frankness** *n*

Frank *n* a member of the West Germanic peoples who in the late 4th century AD gradually conquered most of Gaul. ▷ **HISTORY** Old English *Franca*

frankfurter *n* a smoked sausage of pork or beef. ▷ **HISTORY** short for German *Frankfurter Wurst* sausage from Frankfurt

frankincense *n* an aromatic gum resin burnt as incense. ▷ **HISTORY** Old French *franc* free, pure + *encens* incense

Frankish *n* **1** the ancient West Germanic language of the Franks. ✧ *adj* **2** of the Franks or their language.

frantic *adj* **1** distracted with fear, pain, joy, etc. **2** hurried and disorganized: *frantic activity.* ▷ **HISTORY** Latin *phreneticus* mad ▶ **frantically** *adv*

frappé *adj* (of drinks) chilled. ▷ **HISTORY** French

fraternal *adj* **1** of a brother; brotherly. **2** designating twins that developed from two separate fertilized ova. ▷ **HISTORY** Latin *frater* brother ▶ **fraternally** *adv*

fraternity *n, pl* **-ties 1** a body of people united in interests, aims, etc. **2** friendship between groups of people. **3** *US & Canad* a society of male students.

fraternize *or* **-nise** *vb* **-nizing, -nized** *or* **-nising, -nised** to associate on friendly terms. ▶ **fraternization** *or* **-nisation** *n*

fratricide *n* **1** the act of killing one's brother. **2** a person who kills his or her brother. ▷ **HISTORY** Latin *frater* brother + *caedere* to kill ▶ **fratricidal** *adj*

Frau (rhymes with **how**) *n, pl* **Frauen** *or* **Fraus** a German form of address equivalent to *Mrs* or *Ms.* ▷ **HISTORY** German

fraud *n* **1** deliberate deception or cheating intended to gain an advantage. **2** an act of such deception. **3** *Informal* a person who acts in a false or deceitful way. ▷ **HISTORY** Latin *fraus*

fraudulent *adj* **1** acting with intent to deceive. **2** proceeding from fraud. ▷ **HISTORY** Latin *fraudulentus* ▶ **fraudulence** *n*

fraught (**frawt**) *adj* **1 fraught with** involving or filled with: *we expected the trip to be fraught with difficulties.* **2** tense or anxious. ▷ **HISTORY** Middle Dutch *vrachten*

Fräulein (**froy**-line) *n, pl* **-lein** *or* **-leins** a German form of address equivalent to *Miss.* ▷ **HISTORY** German

fray[1] *n* **1** *Brit, Austral & NZ* a noisy quarrel or brawl. **2 the fray** any challenging conflict: *after an hour Warne entered the fray.* ▷ **HISTORY** short for *affray*

fray[2] *vb* **1** to wear away into loose threads, esp. at an edge. **2** to make or become strained or irritated. ▷ **HISTORY** French *frayer* to rub

frazil (**fray**-zil) *n* small pieces of ice that form in water moving turbulently enough to prevent the formation of a sheet of ice. ▷ **HISTORY** French *fraisil* cinders

frazzle *n Informal* the state of being exhausted: *worn to a frazzle.* ▷ **HISTORY** probably from Middle English *faselen* to fray

freak *n* **1** a person, animal, or plant that is abnormal or deformed. **2** an object, event, etc., that is abnormal: *a statistical freak.* **3** *Informal* a person whose appearance or behaviour is very unusual. **4** *Informal* a person who is very enthusiastic about something specified: *a health freak.* ✧ *adj* **5** abnormal or unusual: *a freak accident.*

A B C D E F G H I J K L M N O P Q R S T U V W X Y Z

▷ **HISTORY** origin unknown ▶ **freakish** *adj* ▶ **freaky** *adj*

freak out *vb Informal* to be or cause to be in a heightened emotional state.

freckle *n* a small brownish spot on the skin. ▷ **HISTORY** Old Norse *freknur* freckles ▶ **freckled** *adj*

free *adj* **freer, freest 1** able to act at will; not under compulsion or restraint. **2** not enslaved or confined. **3** (of a country) independent. **4** (of a translation) not exact or literal. **5** provided without charge: *free school meals.* **6** not occupied or in use; available: *is this seat free?* **7** (of a person) not busy. **8** open or available to all. **9** not fixed or joined; loose: *the free end.* **10** without obstruction or blockage: *the free flow of capital.* **11** *Chem* chemically uncombined: *free nitrogen.* **12 free and easy** casual or tolerant. **13 free from** not subject to: *free from surveillance.* **14 free with** using or giving (something) a lot: *he was free with his tongue.* **15 make free with** to behave too familiarly towards. ✧ *adv* **16** in a free manner. **17** without charge or cost. ✧ *vb* **freeing, freed 18** to release or liberate. **19** to remove obstructions or impediments from. **20** to make available or usable: *capital freed by the local authority.* **21 free of** *or* **from** to relieve or rid of (obstacles, pain, etc.). ▷ **HISTORY** Old English *frēo* ▶ **freely** *adv*

-free *adj combining form* free from: *duty-free.*

freebooter *n* a pirate. ▷ **HISTORY** Dutch *vrijbuit* booty

freeborn *adj History* not born in slavery.

Free Church *n Chiefly Brit* any Protestant Church other than the Established Church.

freedman *n, pl* **-men** *History* a man freed from slavery.

freedom *n* **1** the state of being free, esp. to enjoy political and civil liberties. **2** exemption or immunity: *freedom from government control.* **3** liberation, such as from slavery. **4** the right or privilege of unrestricted access: *freedom of the skies.* **5** self-government or independence. **6** the power to order one's own actions. **7** ease of manner.

freedom of contract *n Law* the principle that adults of full capacity are free to set up and enter into contracts and should expect to abide by the terms of the small print.

free enterprise *n* an economic system in which commercial organizations compete for profit with little state control.

free fall *n* **1** the part of a parachute descent before the parachute opens. **2** free descent of a body in which gravity is the only force acting on it.

free-for-all *n Informal* a disorganized brawl or argument involving all those present.

freehold *Property law* ✧ *n* **1** tenure of property for life without restrictions. ✧ *adj* **2** of or held by freehold. ▶ **freeholder** *n*

free house *n Brit* a public house not bound to sell only one brewer's products.

free kick *n Soccer* an unopposed kick of the ball awarded for a foul or infringement.

freelance *n* **1** a self-employed person doing specific pieces of work for various employers. ✧ *vb* **-lancing, -lanced 2** to work as a freelance. ✧ *adj, adv* **3** of or as a freelance. ▷ **HISTORY** originally applied to a mercenary soldier

freeloader *n Slang* a person who habitually depends on others for food, accommodation, etc.

freeman *n, pl* **-men** a person who has been given the freedom of a city as an honour in return for public service.

free-market *adj* denoting an economic system which allows supply and demand to regulate prices and wages.

Freemason *n* Also called: **Mason** a member of a widespread secret order whose members are pledged to help each other. ▶ **Freemasonry** *n*

free-range *adj* kept or produced in natural conditions: *free-range eggs.*

freesia *n* a plant with fragrant tubular flowers. ▷ **HISTORY** after F. H. T. *Freese,* physician

free space *n* a region that has no gravitational and electromagnetic fields.

freestanding *adj* not attached to or supported by another object.

freethinker *n* a person who forms his or her ideas independently of authority.

free trade *n* international trade that is free of such government interference as protective tariffs and import quotas.

free verse *n Prosody* unrhymed verse without a fixed rhythm.

free vote *n Parliament* a parliamentary division in which members are free to vote according to their consciences rather than as directed by their party.

freeway *n US & Austral* a motorway.

freewheel *vb* **1** to travel downhill on a bicycle without pedalling. ✧ *n* **2** a device in the rear hub of a bicycle wheel that permits it to rotate freely while the pedals are stationary.

freewheeling *adj* behaving in a relaxed spontaneous manner, without any long-term plans or commitments.

free will *n* **1** the ability to make a choice without outside coercion or pressure. **2** *Philosophy* the belief that human behaviour is an expression of personal choice and is not determined by physical forces, Fate, or God.

Free World *n* the non-Communist countries collectively.

freeze *vb* **freezing, froze, frozen 1** to change from a liquid to a solid by the reduction of temperature, such as water to ice. **2** to preserve (food) by subjection to extreme cold. **3** to cover or become covered with ice. **4** to fix fast or become fixed (to something) because of frost. **5** to feel or cause to feel the effects of extreme cold. **6** to die of extreme cold. **7** to become motionless through fear, shock, etc. **8** to cause (moving film) to stop at a particular frame. **9** to fix (prices, incomes, etc.) at a particular level. **10** to forbid by law the exchange or collection of (loans, assets, etc.). ✧ *n* **11** the act of freezing or state of being frozen. **12** *Meteorol* a spell of temperatures below freezing point. **13** the fixing of incomes, prices, etc., by legislation. ▷ HISTORY Old English *frēosan*

freeze-dry *vb* **-dries, -drying, -dried** to preserve (food) by rapid freezing and drying in a vacuum.

freezer *n* an insulated cabinet for cold-storage of perishable foods.

freeze-thaw weathering *n Geol* damage suffered by rocks as a result of surface moisture repeatedly freezing and thawing.

freezing *adj Informal* very cold.

freezing point *n* the temperature below which a liquid turns into a solid.

freezing works *n Austral & NZ* a slaughterhouse at which animals are slaughtered and carcasses frozen especially for export.

freight (**frate**) *n* **1 a** commercial transport of goods. **b** the cargo transported. **c** the cost of this. **2** *Chiefly Brit* a ship's cargo or part of it. ✧ *vb* **3** to transport (goods) by freight. **4** to load with goods for transport. ▷ HISTORY Middle Dutch *vrecht*

freighter *n* a ship or aircraft designed for transporting cargo.

French *adj* **1** of France. ✧ *n* **2** the official language of France and an official language of Switzerland, Belgium, Canada, and certain other countries. ✧ *pl n* **3 the French** the people of France. ▷ HISTORY Old English *Frencisc* French, Frankish

French bread *n* white bread in a long, thin, crusty loaf.

French chalk *n* a variety of talc used to mark cloth or remove grease stains.

French dressing *n* a salad dressing made from oil and vinegar with seasonings.

French fries *pl n Chiefly US & Canad* potato chips.

French horn *n Music* a valved brass wind instrument with a coiled tube.

French letter *n Brit & NZ slang* a condom.

Frenchman *or fem* **Frenchwoman** *n, pl* **-men** *or* **-women** a person from France.

French polish *n* a shellac varnish for wood, giving a high gloss.

frenetic (frin-**net**-ik) *adj* wild, excited, and uncontrolled. ▷ HISTORY Greek *phrenitis* insanity ▶ **frenetically** *adv*

frenzy *n, pl* **-zies 1** violent or wild and uncontrollable behaviour. **2** excited or agitated activity: *a frenzy of speculation.* ▷ HISTORY Late Latin *phrenesis* madness, from Greek *phren* mind ▶ **frenzied** *adj*

Freon *n Trademark* any of a group of gas or liquid chemical compounds of methane with chlorine and fluorine: used in propellants, aerosols, and solvents.

frequency *n, pl* **-cies 1** the number of times that an event occurs within a given period. **2** the state of being frequent. **3** *Physics* the number of times a wave repeats itself in a given time.

frequency distribution *n* statistical data arranged to show the frequency with which the possible values of a variable occur.

frequency modulation *n* a method of transmitting information by varying the frequency of the carrier wave in accordance with the amplitude of the input signal.

frequency polygon *n Maths* a graph or a frequency table where the intervals are shown on the x-axis and the number of scores in each interval is represented by the height of a point above the middle of the interval. The points are connected so that together with the x-axis they form a polygon.

frequent *adj* **1** happening often. **2** habitual. ✧ *vb* **3** to visit often. ▷ HISTORY Latin *frequens* numerous ▶ **frequently** *adv*

frequentative *Grammar* ✧ *adj* **1** denoting a verb or an affix meaning repeated action. ✧ *n* **2** a frequentative verb or affix.

fresco *n, pl* **-coes** *or* **-cos 1** a method of wall-painting using watercolours on wet plaster. **2** a painting done in this way. ▷ HISTORY Italian: fresh plaster

fresh *adj* **1** newly made, acquired, etc. **2** not thought of before; novel: *fresh ideas.* **3** most recent: *fresh allegations.* **4** further or additional: *a fresh supply.* **5** (of food) not canned or frozen. **6** (of water) not salty. **7** bright and clear: *a fresh morning.* **8** (of a wind) cold and fairly strong. **9** not tired; alert. **10** not worn or faded: *the fresh colours of spring.* **11** having a healthy or ruddy appearance. **12** having recently come (from somewhere): *cakes fresh from the oven.* **13** youthful or inexperienced. **14** *Informal* overfamiliar or disrespectful. ✧ *adv* **15** recently. ▷ HISTORY Old English *fersc* ▶ **freshly** *adv* ▶ **freshness** *n*

freshen *vb* **1** to make or become fresh or fresher. **2** (of the wind) to become stronger. **3 freshen up** to wash and tidy up one's appearance.

fresher *or* **freshman** *n, pl* **-ers** *or* **-men** *Brit & US* a first-year student at college or university.

freshet *n* **1** the sudden overflowing of a river. **2** a stream of fresh water emptying into the sea.

freshwater *adj* of or living in fresh water.

fret[1] *vb* **fretting, fretted 1** to worry: *he would fret about the smallest of problems.* **2** to rub or wear away. **3** to feel or give annoyance. ✧ *n* **4** a state of irritation or anxiety. ▷ HISTORY Old English *fretan* to eat

fret[2] *n* **1** a repetitive geometrical figure used for ornamentation. ✧ *vb* **fretting, fretted 2** to ornament with fret or fretwork. ▷ HISTORY Old French *frete* interlaced design used on a shield

fret[3] *n* a small metal bar set across the fingerboard of a musical instrument, such as a guitar, as a guide to fingering. ▷ HISTORY origin unknown

fretful *adj* irritable or upset. ▶ **fretfully** *adv*

fret saw *n* a fine-toothed saw with a long thin narrow blade, used for cutting designs in thin wood or metal.

fretwork *n* decorative geometrical carving in wood.

Freudian (**froy**-dee-an) *adj* of or relating to Sigmund Freud (1856–1939), Austrian psychiatrist, or his ideas. ▶ **Freudianism** *n*

Freudian slip *n* a slip of the tongue that may reveal an unconscious wish.

Fri. Friday.

friable (**fry**-a-bl) *adj* easily broken up. ▷ **HISTORY** Latin *friare* to crumble ▶ **friability** *n*

friar *n* a member of a male Roman Catholic religious order. ▷ **HISTORY** Latin *frater* brother

friar's balsam *n* a compound with a camphor-like smell, used as an inhalant to relieve bronchitis.

friary *n, pl* **-aries** a house of friars.

fricassee *n* stewed meat, esp. chicken or veal, served in a thick white sauce. ▷ **HISTORY** Old French

fricative *n* **1** a consonant produced by friction of breath through a partly closed mouth, such as (f) or (z). ✧ *adj* **2** relating to or being a fricative. ▷ **HISTORY** Latin *fricare* to rub

friction *n* **1** a resistance encountered when one body moves relative to another body with which it is in contact. **2** the act of rubbing one object against another. **3** disagreement or conflict. ▷ **HISTORY** Latin *fricare* to rub ▶ **frictional** *adj*

frictional force *n Physics* same as **friction** (sense 1).

Friday *n* the sixth day of the week.

> **WORD HISTORY**
> Friday, in Old English *Frigedæg*, is 'Freya's day'. Freya was the Norse goddess of love.

fridge *n* a cabinet for keeping food and drink cool. In full: **refrigerator**

fried *vb* the past of **fry**[1].

friend *n* **1** a person known well to another and regarded with liking, affection, and loyalty. **2** an ally in a fight or cause. **3** a patron or supporter. **4 make friends (with)** to become friendly (with). ▷ **HISTORY** Old English *frēond* ▶ **friendless** *adj* ▶ **friendship** *n*

Friend *n* a member of the Society of Friends; Quaker.

friendly *adj* **-lier, -liest 1** showing or expressing liking, goodwill, or trust. **2** on the same side; not hostile. **3** tending to help or support. ✧ *n, pl* **-lies 4** *Sport* a match played for its own sake and not as part of a competition. ▶ **friendliness** *n*

-friendly *adj combining form* helpful, easy, or good for the person or thing specified: *a user-friendly computer system.*

friendly society *n Brit* an association of people who pay regular dues in return for old-age pensions, sickness benefits, etc.

fries *pl n* short for **French fries**.

Friesian (**free**-zhan) *n* any of several breeds of black-and-white dairy cattle.

frieze (**freeze**) *n* **1** a sculptured or decorated band on a wall. **2** *Archit* the horizontal band between the architrave and cornice of a classical temple. ▷ **HISTORY** French *frise*

frigate (**frig**-it) *n* **1** a fast warship, smaller than a destroyer. **2** a medium-sized warship of the 18th and 19th centuries. ▷ **HISTORY** French *frégate*

fright *n* **1** sudden fear or alarm. **2** a sudden alarming shock. **3** *Informal* a very strange or unattractive person or thing. ▷ **HISTORY** Old English *fryhto*

frighten *vb* **1** to terrify or scare. **2** to force (someone) to do something from fear. ▶ **frightening** *adj*

frightful *adj* **1** very alarming or horrifying. **2** annoying or disagreeable. **3** *Informal* extreme: *a frightful mess.* ▶ **frightfully** *adv*

frigid (**frij**-id) *adj* **1** (esp. of a woman) lacking sexual responsiveness. **2** very cold: *the frigid air.* **3** formal or stiff in behaviour or temperament. ▷ **HISTORY** Latin *frigidus* cold ▶ **frigidity** *n*

Frigid Zone *n Geog* the cold regions inside the Arctic and Antarctic Circles where the sun's rays are very oblique. Compare **Temperate Zone, Torrid Zone**.

frill *n* **1** a long narrow strip of fabric with many folds in it attached at one edge of something as a decoration. **2** an unnecessary part of something added to make it more attractive or interesting. ▷ **HISTORY** origin unknown ▶ **frilly** *or* **frilled** *adj*

frilled lizard *n* a large tree-living Australian lizard with an erectile fold of skin round the neck.

fringe *n* **1** hair cut short and hanging over the forehead. **2** an ornamental edge of hanging threads, tassels, etc. **3** an outer edge: *London's southern fringe.* **4** the minor and less important parts of an activity or organization: *two agents on the fringes of espionage activity.* **5** a small group of people within a larger body, but differing from it in certain aims and ideas: *the radical fringe of the Green Party.* ✧ *adj* **6** (of theatre) unofficial or unconventional. ✧ *vb* **fringing, fringed 7** to form a border for: *sandy paths fringing the water's edge.* **8** to decorate with a fringe: *tinsel fringed the desk.* ▷ **HISTORY** Latin *fimbria* fringe, border

fringe benefit *n* a benefit given in addition to a regular salary or wage.

fringed *adj* **1** (of clothes, curtains, etc.) decorated with a fringe. **2 fringed with** *or* **by** bordered with or by: *a field fringed with trees.*

fringing reef *n Geog* a coral reef close to the shore to which it is attached, having a steep seaward edge.

frippery *n, pl* **-peries 1** showy but useless ornamentation. **2** unimportant or trivial matters. ▷ **HISTORY** Old French *frepe* frill, rag

Frisian (**free**-zhan) *n* **1** a language spoken in the NW Netherlands. **2** a speaker of this language. ✧ *adj* **3** of this language or its speakers. ▷ **HISTORY** Latin *Frisii* people of northern Germany

frisk *vb* **1** to leap, move about, or act in a playful manner. **2** *Informal* to search (someone) by feeling for concealed weapons, etc. ✧ *n* **3** a playful movement. **4** *Informal* an instance of frisking a person. ▷ **HISTORY** Old French *frisque*

frisky *adj* **friskier, friskiest** lively, high-spirited, or playful. ▶ **friskily** *adv*

frisson (**freess**-on) *n* a short sudden feeling of fear or excitement. ▷ **HISTORY** French

a b c d e f g h i j k l m n o p q r s t u v w x y z

fritter *n* a piece of food, such as apple, that is dipped in batter and fried in deep fat. ▷ **HISTORY** Latin *frigere* to fry

fritter away *vb* to waste. ▷ **HISTORY** obsolete *fitter* to break into small pieces

frivolous *adj* **1** not serious or sensible in content, attitude, or behaviour. **2** unworthy of serious or sensible treatment: *frivolous distractions.* ▷ **HISTORY** Latin *frivolus* ▶ **frivolity** *n*

frizz *vb* **1** (of hair) to form or cause (hair) to form tight curls. ✧ *n* **2** hair that has been frizzed. ▷ **HISTORY** French *friser* to curl ▶ **frizzy** *adj*

frock *n Old-fashioned* **1** a girl's or woman's dress. **2** a loose garment, formerly worn by peasants. ▷ **HISTORY** Old French *froc*

frock coat *n* a man's skirted coat, as worn in the 19th century.

frog[1] *n* **1** a smooth-skinned tailless amphibian with long back legs used for jumping. **2 a frog in one's throat** phlegm on the vocal cords, hindering speech. ▷ **HISTORY** Old English *frogga*

frog[2] *n* a military style fastening on a coat consisting of a button and a loop. ▷ **HISTORY** origin unknown ▶ **frogging** *n*

frog[3] *n* horny material in the centre of the sole of a horse's foot. ▷ **HISTORY** origin unknown

frogman *n, pl* **-men** a swimmer equipped with a rubber suit, flippers, and breathing equipment for working underwater.

frogmarch *n* **1** a method of carrying a resisting person in which each limb is held and the victim is face downwards. ✧ *vb* **2** to carry in a frogmarch or cause to move forward unwillingly.

frogspawn *n* a jelly-like substance containing a frog's eggs.

frolic *vb* **-icking, -icked 1** to run and play in a lively way. ✧ *n* **2** lively and merry behaviour. **3** a light-hearted occasion. ▷ **HISTORY** Dutch *vrolijk*

frolicsome *adj* merry and playful.

from *prep* **1** indicating the original location, situation, etc.: *from America.* **2** in a period of time starting at: *from 1950 to the current year.* **3** indicating the distance between two things or places: *60 miles from the Iraqi border.* **4** indicating a lower amount: *from 5 to 6.* **5** showing the model of: *drawn from life.* **6** used with a verbal noun to denote prohibition, etc.: *she was banned from smoking at meetings.* **7** because of: *five hundred horses collapsed from exhaustion.* ▷ **HISTORY** Old English *fram*

frond *n* **1** the compound leaf of a fern. **2** the leaf of a palm. ▷ **HISTORY** Latin *frons*

front *n* **1** that part or side that is forward, or most often seen or used. **2** a position or place directly before or ahead. **3** the beginning, opening, or first part. **4** the position of leadership. **5** a promenade at a seaside resort. **6** *Mil* **a** the total area in which opposing armies face each other. **b** the space in which a military unit is operating. **7** *Meteorol* the dividing line between two different air masses. **8** an outward appearance: *he put on a bold front.* **9** *Informal* a business or other activity serving as a respectable cover for another, usually criminal, organization. **10** Also called: **front man** a nominal leader of an organization. **11** a particular field of activity: *on the economic front.* **12** a group of people with a common goal: *the National Liberation Front.* ✧ *adj* **13** of, at, or in the front. ✧ *vb* **14** to face (onto). **15** to be a front of or for. **16** to appear as a presenter in (a television show). **17** to be the leader of (a band) on stage. ▷ **HISTORY** Latin *frons* forehead, foremost part

frontage *n* **1** the facade of a building or the front of a plot of ground. **2** the extent of the front of a shop, plot of land, etc.

frontal *adj* **1** of, at, or in the front. **2** of or relating to the forehead. ▷ **HISTORY** Latin *frons* forehead

frontal rain *n Meteorol* rain that occurs when a warm air mass meets a cooler air mass and, being lighter, is forced upwards where it cools, causing the water vapour in it to condense.

front bench *n* (in Britain) the leadership of either the Government or Opposition in the House of Commons or in various other legislative assemblies. ▶ **front-bencher** *n*

frontier *n* **1** the region of a country bordering on another or a line marking such a boundary. **2** the edge of the settled area of a country. **3 frontiers** the limit of knowledge in a particular field: *twenty years ago, laser spectroscopy was on the frontiers of chemical research.* ▷ **HISTORY** Old French *front* part which is opposite

frontispiece *n* an illustration facing the title page of a book. ▷ **HISTORY** Late Latin *frontispicium* facade

frontrunner *n Informal* the leader or a favoured contestant in a race or election.

frost *n* **1** a white deposit of ice particles. **2** an atmospheric temperature of below freezing point, producing this deposit. ✧ *vb* **3** to cover with frost. **4** to kill or damage (plants) with frost. ▷ **HISTORY** Old English

frostbite *n* destruction of tissues, esp. of the fingers, ears, toes, and nose, by freezing. ▶ **frostbitten** *adj*

frosted *adj* (of glass) having the surface roughened so that it cannot be seen through clearly.

frosting *n Chiefly US & Canad* icing.

frosty *adj* **frostier, frostiest 1** characterized by frost: *the frosty air.* **2** covered by frost. **3** unfriendly or disapproving: *a frosty reception from the bank manager.* ▶ **frostily** *adv* ▶ **frostiness** *n*

froth *n* **1** a mass of small bubbles of air or a gas in a liquid. **2** a mixture of saliva and air bubbles formed at the lips in certain diseases, such as rabies. **3** trivial but superficially attractive ideas or entertainment. ✧ *vb* **4** to produce or cause to produce froth. ▷ **HISTORY** Old Norse *frotha* ▶ **frothy** *adj*

frown *vb* **1** to wrinkle one's brows in worry, anger, or concentration. **2 frown on** to disapprove of: *smoking at work is frowned on.* ✧ *n* **3** the act of frowning. **4** a look of disapproval or displeasure. ▷ **HISTORY** Old French *froignier*

frowsty *adj* **frowstier, frowstiest** *Brit* stale or musty. ▷ **HISTORY** from *frowzy*

frowzy *or* **frowsy** *adj* **-zier, -ziest** *or* **-sier, -siest** **1** slovenly or unkempt in appearance. **2** musty and stale. ▷ **HISTORY** origin unknown

froze *vb* the past tense of **freeze**.

frozen *vb* **1** the past participle of **freeze**. ✧ *adj* **2** turned into or covered with ice. **3** killed or stiffened by extreme cold. **4** (of food) preserved by a freezing process. **5 a** (of prices or wages) officially fixed at a certain level. **b** (of business assets) not convertible into cash. **6** motionless: *she was frozen in horror.*

FRS (in Britain) Fellow of the Royal Society.

fructify *vb* **-fies, -fying, -fied** to bear or cause to bear fruit. ▷ **HISTORY** Latin *fructus* fruit + *facere* to produce

fructose *n* a crystalline sugar occurring in honey and many fruits. ▷ **HISTORY** Latin *fructus* fruit

frugal (**froo**-gl) *adj* **1** economical in the use of money or resources; thrifty. **2** meagre and inexpensive: *a frugal meal.* ▷ **HISTORY** Latin *frugi* useful, temperate ▸ **frugality** *n* ▸ **frugally** *adv*

fruit *n* **1** any fleshy part of a plant that supports the seeds and is edible, such as the strawberry. **2** *Bot* the ripened ovary of a flowering plant, containing one or more seeds. **3** any plant product useful to man, including grain and vegetables. **4 fruits** the results of an action or effort, esp. if pleasant: *they have enjoyed the fruits of a complete victory.* ✧ *vb* **5** to bear fruit. ▷ **HISTORY** Latin *fructus* enjoyment, fruit

fruiterer *n Chiefly Brit & Austral* a person who sells fruit.

fruit fly *n* **1** a small fly that feeds on and lays its eggs in plant tissues. **2** a similar fly that feeds on plant sap, decaying fruit, etc., and is widely used in genetics experiments.

fruitful *adj* **1** producing good and useful results: *a fruitful relationship.* **2** bearing much fruit. ▸ **fruitfully** *adv*

fruition (froo-**ish**-on) *n* **1** the fulfilment of something worked for or desired. **2** the act of bearing fruit. ▷ **HISTORY** Latin *frui* to enjoy

fruitless *adj* **1** producing nothing of value: *a fruitless debate.* **2** without fruit. ▸ **fruitlessly** *adv*

fruit machine *n Brit & NZ* a coin-operated gambling machine that pays out money when a particular combination of diagrams, usually of fruit, appear on a screen.

fruit sugar *n* same as **fructose**.

fruity *adj* **fruitier, fruitiest 1** of or like fruit. **2** (of a voice) mellow or rich. **3** *Informal, chiefly Brit* referring humorously to things relating to sex. ▸ **fruitiness** *n*

frump *n* a woman who dresses in a dull and old-fashioned way. ▷ **HISTORY** Middle Dutch *verrompelen* to wrinkle ▸ **frumpy** *or* **frumpish** *adj*

frustrate *vb* **-trating, -trated 1** to upset or anger (a person) by presenting difficulties that cannot be overcome: *his lack of ambition frustrated me.* **2** to hinder or prevent (the efforts, plans, or desires) of. ▷ **HISTORY** Latin *frustrare* to cheat ▸ **frustrating** *adj* ▸ **frustration** *n*

frustrated *adj* dissatisfied or unfulfilled.

frustum *n, pl* **-tums** *or* **-ta** *Geom* the part of a solid, such as a cone or pyramid, contained between the base and a plane parallel to the base that intersects the solid. ▷ **HISTORY** Latin: piece

fry[1] *vb* **fries, frying, fried 1** to cook or be cooked in fat or oil, usually over direct heat. ✧ *n, pl* **fries** **2** Also: **fry-up** *Informal* a dish of mixed fried food. ✧ See also **fries**. ▷ **HISTORY** Latin *frigere* ▸ **fryer** *or* **frier** *n*

fry[2] *pl n* **1** the young of various species of fish. **2** See **small fry**. ▷ **HISTORY** Old French *freier* to spawn

frying pan *n* **1** a long-handled shallow pan used for frying. **2 out of the frying pan into the fire** from a bad situation to a worse one.

FSH *Biol* follicle-stimulating hormone: a hormone secreted by the pituitary gland.

f-stop *n Photog* any of the lens aperture settings of a camera.

ft. foot or feet.

fuchsia (**fyew**-sha) *n* an ornamental shrub with hanging purple, red, or white flowers. ▷ **HISTORY** after Leonhard *Fuchs*, botanist

fuck *Taboo* ✧ *vb* **1** to have sexual intercourse with (someone). ✧ *n* **2** an act of sexual intercourse. **3** *Slang* a partner in sexual intercourse. **4 not give a fuck** not to care at all. ✧ *interj* **5** *Offensive* an expression of strong disgust or anger. ▷ **HISTORY** Germanic ▸ **fucking** *n, adj, adv*

fuck off *vb Offensive taboo slang* to go away.

fuck up *vb Offensive taboo slang* to make a mess of (something).

fuddle *vb* **-dling, -dled 1** to cause to be confused or intoxicated. ✧ *n* **2** a confused state. ▷ **HISTORY** origin unknown ▸ **fuddled** *adj*

fuddy-duddy *n, pl* **-dies** *Informal* a person, esp. an elderly one, who is extremely conservative or dull. ▷ **HISTORY** origin unknown

fudge[1] *n* a soft sweet made from sugar, butter, and milk. ▷ **HISTORY** origin unknown

fudge[2] *vb* **fudging, fudged 1** to make (an issue or problem) less clear deliberately. **2** to avoid making a firm statement or decision. ▷ **HISTORY** origin unknown

fuel *n* **1** any substance burned for heat or power, such as coal or petrol. **2** the material that produces energy by fission in a nuclear reactor. **3 add fuel to** to make (a difficult situation) worse. ✧ *vb* **fuelling, fuelled** *or US* **fueling, fueled 4** to supply with or receive fuel. **5** to intensify or make worse (a feeling or situation): *the move is bound to fuel speculation.* ▷ **HISTORY** Old French *feu* fire

fuel cell *n* a cell in which chemical energy is converted directly into electrical energy.

fug *n Chiefly Brit & NZ* a hot stale atmosphere. ▷ **HISTORY** origin unknown ▸ **fuggy** *adj*

fugitive (**fyew**-jit-iv) *n* **1** a person who flees, esp. from arrest or pursuit. ✧ *adj* **2** fleeing. **3** not permanent; fleeting. ▷ **HISTORY** Latin *fugere* to flee

fugue (**fyewg**) *n* a musical form consisting of a theme repeated above or below the continuing first statement. ▷ **HISTORY** French ▸ **fugal** *adj*

a b c d e f g h i j k l m n o p q r s t u v w x y z

A B C D E F G H I J K L M N O P Q R S T U V W X Y Z

Führer *n* a leader: the title used by Hitler as Nazi dictator. ▷ **HISTORY** German

-ful *adj suffix* **1** full of or characterized by: *painful; restful.* **2** able or tending to: *useful.* ✧ *n suffix* **3** as much as will fill the thing specified: *mouthful.*

fulcrum *n, pl* **-crums** *or* **-cra** the pivot about which a lever turns. ▷ **HISTORY** Latin: foot of a couch

fulfil *or US* **fulfill** *vb* **-filling, -filled 1** to bring about the achievement of (a desire or promise). **2** to carry out (a request or order). **3** to satisfy (demands or conditions). **4 fulfil oneself** to achieve one's potential. ▷ **HISTORY** Old English *fulfyllan* ▶ **fulfilment** *or US* **fulfillment** *n*

full¹ *adj* **1** holding as much or as many as possible. **2** abundant in supply: *full of enthusiasm.* **3** having consumed enough food or drink. **4** (of the face or figure) rounded or plump. **5** complete: *the full amount.* **6** with all privileges or rights: *full membership.* **7** *Music* powerful or rich in volume and sound. **8** (of a garment) containing a large amount of fabric. **9 full of** engrossed with: *she had been full of her own plans.* **10 full of oneself** full of pride or conceit. **11 full up** filled to capacity. ✧ *adv* **12** completely or entirely. **13** directly or right: *she hit him full in the face.* **14 full well** very or extremely well: *we knew full well that she was watching.* ✧ *n* **15 in full** without omitting or shortening. **16 to the full** thoroughly or fully. ▷ **HISTORY** Old English ▶ **fullness** *or esp US* **fulness** *n*

full² *vb* to make (cloth) more compact during manufacture through shrinking and beating. ▷ **HISTORY** Old French *fouler*

fullback *n Soccer, hockey, & rugby* a defensive player.

full-blooded *adj* **1** vigorous or enthusiastic. **2** (esp. of horses) having ancestors of a single race.

full-blown *adj* fully developed.

full board *n* the daily provision by a hotel of bed, breakfast, and midday and evening meals.

full-bodied *adj* having a full rich flavour or quality: *a full-bodied vintage port.*

fuller's earth *n* a natural absorbent clay used for fulling cloth.

full house *n* **1** a theatre filled to capacity. **2** (in bingo) the set of numbers needed to win.

full-length *adj* **1** (of a mirror, etc.) showing the complete human figure. **2** not abridged.

full moon *n* the phase of the moon when it is visible as a fully illuminated disc.

full-scale *adj* **1** (of a plan) of actual size. **2** using all resources; all-out.

full stop *n* the punctuation mark (.) used at the end of a sentence and after abbreviations. Also called (esp. US and Canad.): **period**

full-time *adj* **1** for all of the normal working week: *a full-time job.* ✧ *adv* **full time 2** on a full-time basis: *she worked full time until she was 72.* ✧ *n* **full time 3** *Soccer, rugby, & hockey* the end of the game.

full toss *or* **pitch** *n Cricket* a bowled ball that reaches the batsman without bouncing.

fully *adv* **1** to the greatest degree or extent. **2** amply or adequately. **3** at least: *fully a hundred people.*

fulmar *n* a heavily-built Arctic sea bird with a short tail. ▷ **HISTORY** Scandinavian

fulminate *vb* **-nating, -nated fulminate against** to criticize or denounce angrily. ▷ **HISTORY** Latin *fulmen* lightning that strikes ▶ **fulmination** *n*

fulsome *adj* **1** exaggerated and elaborate, and often sounding insincere: *fulsome praise.* **2** *Not standard* extremely complimentary.

fumarole *n Geol* a vent in or near a volcano from which hot gases, esp. steam, are emitted. ▷ **HISTORY** late Latin *fūmāriolum* smoke hole, from Latin *fūmus* smoke

fumble *vb* **-bling, -bled 1** to use the hands clumsily or grope about blindly: *fumbling for a cigarette.* **2** to say or do awkwardly. ✧ *n* **3** the act of fumbling. ▷ **HISTORY** probably Scandinavian

fume *vb* **fuming, fumed 1** to be overcome with anger or fury. **2** to give off (fumes) or (of fumes) to be given off, esp. during a chemical reaction. **3** to treat with fumes. ✧ *n* **4** a pungent or toxic vapour, gas, or smoke. ▷ **HISTORY** Latin *fumus* smoke

fumigate (**fyew**-mig-gate) *vb* **-gating, -gated** to treat (something contaminated) with fumes. ▷ **HISTORY** Latin *fumus* smoke + *agere* to drive ▶ **fumigation** *n*

fun *n* **1** pleasant, enjoyable, and light-hearted activity or amusement. **2 for** *or* **in fun** for amusement or as a joke. **3 make fun of** *or* **poke fun at** to ridicule or tease. ✧ *adj* **4** (of a person) amusing and likeable. **5** (of a place or activity) amusing and enjoyable. ▷ **HISTORY** obsolete *fon* to make a fool of

function *n* **1** the intended role or purpose of a person or thing. **2** an official or formal social gathering. **3** a factor, the precise nature of which depends upon another thing in some way. **4** *Maths* a quantity, the value of which depends on the varying value of another quantity. **5** a sequence of operations that a computer or calculator performs when a specified key is pressed. ✧ *vb* **6** to operate or work. **7 function as** to perform the action or role of (something or someone else). ▷ **HISTORY** Latin *functio*

functional *adj* **1** of or performing a function. **2** practical rather than decorative. **3** in working order. **4** *Med* affecting a function of an organ without structural change. ▶ **functionally** *adv*

functional food *n* a food containing additives which provide extra nutritional value. Also called: **nutraceutical**

functional grammar *n Grammar* a method of analysing and understanding language that examines the function of groups of words in each sentence. Compare **traditional grammar**.

functionalism *n* the theory that the form of a thing should be determined by its use. ▶ **functionalist** *n, adj*

functionary *n, pl* **-aries** a person acting in an official capacity, such as for a government; official.

function notation *n Maths* the representation of a mathematical function using a series of symbols.

fund *n* **1** a reserve of money set aside for a certain purpose. **2** a supply or store of something. ✧ *vb*

3 to provide money to. 4 *Finance* to convert (short-term debt) into long-term debt bearing fixed interest. ✧ See also **funds**. ▷ **HISTORY** Latin *fundus* the bottom, piece of land ▶ **funder** *n*

fundamental *adj* **1** essential or primary: *fundamental mathematical concepts.* **2** basic: *a fundamental error.* ✧ *n* **3 fundamentals** the most important and basic parts of a subject or activity. **4** the lowest note of a harmonic series. ▶ **fundamentally** *adv*

fundamentalism *n* **1** *Christianity* the view that the Bible is literally true. **2** *Islam* a movement favouring strict observance of Islamic law. ▶ **fundamentalist** *n, adj*

fundamental particle *n Physics* same as **elementary particle**.

fundholding *n* the system in which general practitioners may choose to receive a fixed budget from which they pay for non-urgent hospital treatment and drug costs for patients.

fundi (**foon**-dee) *n S African* an expert. ▷ **HISTORY** Nguni (language group of southern Africa) *umfindisi*

funding *n* **1** the provision of money for a project or organization. **2** the amount of money provided.

funds *pl n* money that is readily available.

fundus *n, pl* **-di** *Anat* the base of an organ.

funeral *n* **1** a ceremony at which a dead person is buried or cremated. **2 it's your funeral** *Informal* a mistake has been made and you alone will be responsible for its consequences. ✧ *adj* **3** of or for a funeral. ▷ **HISTORY** Latin *funus* ▶ **funerary** *adj*

funeral director *n* an undertaker.

funeral parlour *n* a place where the dead are prepared for burial or cremation.

funereal (fyew-**neer**-ee-al) *adj* suggestive of a funeral; gloomy or sombre. ▶ **funereally** *adv*

funfair *n Brit* an amusement park with machines to ride on and stalls.

fungicide *n* a substance used to destroy fungi. ▷ **HISTORY** FUNGUS + Latin *caedere* to kill

fungoid *adj* resembling a fungus.

fungous *adj* appearing suddenly and spreading quickly like a fungus.

fungus *n, pl* **fungi** *or* **funguses** a plant without leaves, flowers, or roots, that reproduce by spores, including moulds, yeasts, and mushrooms. ▷ **HISTORY** Latin ▶ **fungal** *adj*

funicular (fyew-**nik**-yew-lar) *n* a railway up the side of a mountain, consisting of two cars at either end of a cable passing round a driving wheel at the summit. ▷ **HISTORY** Latin *funis* rope

funk[1] *Old-fashioned, Brit* ✧ *n* **1** a state of nervousness, fear, or depression. **2** a coward. ✧ *vb* **3** to avoid doing (something) through fear. ▷ **HISTORY** origin unknown

funk[2] *n* a type of Black dance music with a strong beat. ▷ **HISTORY** from *funky*

funky *adj* **-kier, -kiest** (of jazz or pop) having a strong beat. ▷ **HISTORY** from obsolete *funk* to smoke tobacco, perhaps referring to music that is smelly, i.e. earthy

funnel *n* **1** a tube with a wide mouth tapering to a small hole, used for pouring liquids into narrow openings. **2** a chimney of a ship or steam train. ✧ *vb* **-nelling, -nelled** *or US* **-neling, -neled** **3** to move or cause to move through or as if through a funnel. ▷ **HISTORY** Old Provençal *fonilh*

funnel-web *n Austral* a large poisonous black spider that builds funnel-shaped webs.

funny *adj* **-nier, -niest** **1** causing amusement or laughter; humorous. **2** peculiar or odd. **3** *Informal* faint or ill: *this smell is making me feel a bit funny.* **4 funny business** *Informal* suspicious or dubious behaviour. ▶ **funnily** *adv* ▶ **funniness** *n*

funny bone *n* a sensitive area near the elbow where the nerve is close to the surface of the skin.

fur *n* **1** the dense coat of fine silky hairs on many mammals. **2** the skin of certain animals, with the hair left on. **3** a garment made of fur. **4 make the fur fly** to cause a scene or disturbance. **5** *Informal* a whitish coating on the tongue, caused by illness. **6** *Brit* a deposit on the insides of water pipes or kettles, caused by hard water. ✧ *vb* **furring, furred** **7** Also: **fur up** to cover or become covered with a furlike deposit. ▷ **HISTORY** Old French *fuerre* sheath

furbish *vb Formal* to brighten up or renovate. ▷ **HISTORY** Old French *fourbir* to polish

furcate *vb* **-cating, -cated** **1** to divide into two parts. ✧ *adj* **2** forked: *furcate branches.* ▷ **HISTORY** Latin *furca* a fork ▶ **furcation** *n*

Furies *pl n, sing* **Fury** *Classical myth* the goddesses of vengeance, who pursued unpunished criminals.

furious *adj* **1** extremely angry or annoyed. **2** violent or unrestrained, such as in speed or energy. ▶ **furiously** *adv*

furl *vb* to roll up (an umbrella, flag, or sail) neatly and securely. ▷ **HISTORY** Old French *ferm* tight + *lier* to bind

furlong *n* a unit of length equal to 220 yards (201.168 metres). ▷ **HISTORY** Old English *furlang*, from *furh* furrow + *lang* long

furlough (**fur**-loh) *n* leave of absence from military or other duty. ▷ **HISTORY** Dutch *verlof*

furnace *n* **1** an enclosed chamber in which heat is produced to destroy refuse or smelt ores. **2** *Informal* a very hot place. ▷ **HISTORY** Latin *fornax*

furnish *vb* **1** to provide (a house or room) with furniture, etc. **2** to supply or provide. ▷ **HISTORY** Old French *fournir* ▶ **furnished** *adj*

furnishings *pl n* furniture, carpets, and fittings with which a room or house is furnished.

furniture *n* the large movable articles, such as chairs and tables, that equip a room or house. ▷ **HISTORY** Old French *fournir* to equip

furore (fyew-**ror**-ee) *n* a very angry or excited reaction by people to something: *the furore over 'The Satanic Verses'.* ▷ **HISTORY** Latin *furor* frenzy

furrier *n* a person who makes or sells fur garments. ▷ **HISTORY** Middle English *furour*

furrow *n* **1** a long narrow trench made in the ground by a plough. **2** any long deep groove, esp. a deep wrinkle on the forehead. ✧ *vb* **3** to become wrinkled. **4** to make furrows in (land). ▷ **HISTORY** Old English *furh*

furry *adj* **-rier, -riest** like or covered with fur or something furlike.

further *adv* **1** in addition. **2** to a greater degree or extent. **3** to or at a more advanced point. **4** to or at a greater distance in time or space. ✧ *adj* **5** additional. **6** more distant or remote in time or space. ✧ *vb* **7** to assist the progress of (something). ▷ **HISTORY** Old English *furthor* ▶ **furtherance** *n*

> **WORD TIP**
> See at **farther.**

further education *n* (in Britain and Australia) formal education beyond school other than at a university or polytechnic.

furthermore *adv* in addition.

furthest *adv* **1** to the greatest degree or extent. **2** to or at the greatest distance in time or space; farthest. ✧ *adj* **3** most distant in time or space; farthest.

furtive *adj* sly, cautious, and secretive. ▷ **HISTORY** Latin *furtivus* stolen ▶ **furtively** *adv*

fury *n, pl* **-ries 1** violent anger. **2** uncontrolled violence: *the fury of the sea.* **3** an outburst of violent anger. **4** a person with a violent temper. ▷ **HISTORY** Latin *furere* to be furious

furze *n* gorse. ▷ **HISTORY** Old English *fyrs*

fuse[1] *or US* **fuze** *n* **1** a lead containing an explosive for detonating a bomb. ✧ *vb* **fusing, fused** *or US* **fuzing, fuzed 2** to equip with such a fuse. ▷ **HISTORY** Latin *fusus* spindle

fuse[2] *n* **1** a protective device for safeguarding electric circuits, containing a wire that melts and breaks the circuit when the current exceeds a certain value. ✧ *vb* **fusing, fused 2** *Brit* to fail or cause to fail as a result of a fuse blowing. **3** to equip (a plug or circuit) with a fuse. **4** to join or become combined: *the two ideas fused in his mind.* **5** to unite or become united by melting. **6** to become or cause to become liquid, esp. by the action of heat. ▷ **HISTORY** Latin *fusus* melted, cast

fuselage (**fyew**-zill-lahzh) *n* the main body of an aircraft. ▷ **HISTORY** French

fusible *adj* capable of being melted.

fusilier (fyew-zill-**leer**) *n* (formerly) an infantryman armed with a light musket: a term still used in the names of certain British regiments. ▷ **HISTORY** French

fusillade (fyew-zill-**lade**) *n* **1** a rapid continual discharge of firearms. **2** a sudden outburst of criticism, questions, etc. ▷ **HISTORY** French *fusiller* to shoot

fusion *n* **1** the act or process of melting together. **2** something produced by fusing. **3** a kind of popular music that is a blend of two or more styles, such as jazz and funk. **4** something new created by a mixture of qualities, ideas, or things. **5** See **nuclear fusion.** ✧ *adj* **6** relating to a style of cooking that combines traditional Western techniques and ingredients with those used in Eastern cuisine. ▷ **HISTORY** Latin *fusio* a melting

fuss *n* **1** needless activity and worry. **2** complaint or objection: *it was silly to make a fuss over seating arrangements.* **3** an exhibition of affection or admiration. ✧ *vb* **4** to worry unnecessarily. **5** to be excessively concerned over trivial matters. **6** to bother (a person). **7 fuss over** to show great or excessive concern or affection for. ▷ **HISTORY** origin unknown

fussy *adj* **fussier, fussiest 1** inclined to fuss. **2** very particular about detail. **3** overelaborate: *a fussy, overdecorated palace.* ▶ **fussily** *adv*

fusty *adj* **-tier, -tiest 1** smelling of damp or mould. **2** old-fashioned. ▷ **HISTORY** Middle English *fust* wine cask ▶ **fustiness** *n*

futile (**fyew**-tile) *adj* **1** useless or having no chance of success. **2** foolish and of no value: *her futile remarks began to annoy me.* ▷ **HISTORY** Latin *futtilis* pouring out easily ▶ **futility** *n*

futon (**foo**-tonn) *n* a Japanese padded quilt, laid on the floor as a bed.

future *n* **1** the time yet to come. **2** undetermined events that will occur in that time. **3** the condition of a person or thing at a later date. **4** prospects: *he had faith in its future.* **5** *Grammar* same as **future tense**. **6 in future** from now on. ✧ *adj* **7** that is yet to come or be. **8** of or expressing time yet to come. **9** destined to become. **10** *Grammar* in or denoting the future as a tense of verbs. ✧ See also **futures.** ▷ **HISTORY** Latin *futurus* about to be

future perfect *or* **future perfect tense** *n* *Grammar* a compound tense formed in English using *will have* or *shall have* plus a past participle to describe an action that will have been performed by a certain time.

futures *pl n* commodities bought or sold at an agreed price for delivery at a specified future date.

future tense *n Grammar* a tense of verbs used when the action specified has not yet taken place; in the sentence, *I'll see you later, I'll see* is the future tense.

futurism *n* an early 20th-century artistic movement making use of the characteristics of the machine age. ▶ **futurist** *n, adj*

futuristic *adj* **1** of design or technology that appears to belong to some future time. **2** of futurism.

fuzz[1] *n* a mass or covering of fine or curly hairs, fibres, etc. ▷ **HISTORY** probably from Low German *fussig* loose

fuzz[2] *n Brit, Austral & NZ slang* the police or a policeman. ▷ **HISTORY** origin unknown

fuzzy *adj* **fuzzier, fuzziest 1** of, like, or covered with fuzz. **2** unclear, blurred, or distorted: *fuzzy pictures.* **3** (of hair) tightly curled. ▶ **fuzzily** *adv* ▶ **fuzziness** *n*

fwd forward.

FX *Films informal* special effects. ▷ **HISTORY** a phonetic respelling of *effects*

A B C D E F G H I J K L M N O P Q R S T U V W X Y Z

G g

g **1** gallon(s). **2** gram(s). **3** acceleration due to gravity.
G **1** *Music* the fifth note of the scale of C major. **2** gravity. **3** good. **4** giga-. **5** *Slang* grand (a thousand pounds or dollars).
G8 Group of Eight.
Ga *Chem* gallium.
GA Georgia.
Ga. Georgia.
gab *Informal* ✧ *vb* **gabbing, gabbed 1** to talk a lot, esp. about unimportant things. ✧ *n* **2** idle talk. **3 gift of the gab** the ability to talk easily and persuasively. ▷ HISTORY probably from Irish Gaelic *gob* mouth
gabardine *or* **gaberdine** *n* **1** a strong twill cloth used esp. for raincoats. **2** a coat made of this cloth. ▷ HISTORY Old French *gauvardine* pilgrim's garment
gabble *vb* **-bling, -bled 1** to speak rapidly and indistinctly: *the interviewee started to gabble furiously.* ✧ *n* **2** rapid and indistinct speech. ▷ HISTORY Middle Dutch *gabbelen*
gabbro *n, pl* **gabbros** *Geol* a dark coarse-grained igneous rock. ▷ HISTORY Italian, probably from Latin *glaber*smooth, bald
gable *n* the triangular upper part of a wall between the sloping ends of a ridged roof. ▷ HISTORY probably from Old Norse *gafl* ▶ **gabled** *adj*
gad *vb* **gadding, gadded** (often foll. by *about* or *around*) to go about in search of pleasure. ▷ HISTORY obsolete *gadling* companion
gadabout *n Informal* a person who restlessly seeks amusement.
gadfly *n, pl* **-flies 1** a large fly that bites livestock. **2** a constantly irritating person. ▷ HISTORY obsolete *gad* sting
gadget *n* a small mechanical device or appliance. ▷ HISTORY perhaps from French *gâchette* trigger ▶ **gadgetry** *n*
gadoid (**gay**-doid) *adj* **1** of or belonging to the cod family of marine fishes. ✧ *n* **2** any gadoid fish. ▷ HISTORY New Latin *gadus* cod
gadolinium *n Chem* a silvery-white metallic element of the rare-earth group. Symbol: Gd. ▷ HISTORY after Johan *Gadolin,* mineralogist
Gael (**gayl**) *n* a Gaelic-speaker of Scotland, Ireland, or the Isle of Man. ▷ HISTORY Gaelic *Gaidheal* ▶ **Gaeldom** *n*
Gaelic (**gal**-lik, **gay**-lik) *n* **1** any of the closely related Celtic languages of Scotland, Ireland, or the Isle of Man. ✧ *adj* **2** of the Celtic people of Scotland, Ireland, or the Isle of Man, or their language.
gaff[1] *n* **1** *Angling* a pole with a hook attached for landing large fish. **2** *Naut* a spar hoisted to support a fore-and-aft sail. ▷ HISTORY Provençal *gaf* boat hook
gaff[2] *n* **blow the gaff** *Brit slang* to give away a secret. ▷ HISTORY origin unknown
gaffe *n* something said or done that is socially upsetting or incorrect. ▷ HISTORY French
gaffer *n* **1** *Informal, chiefly Brit* a boss or foreman. **2** an old man: often used affectionately. **3** *Informal* the senior electrician on a television or film set. ▷ HISTORY from *godfather*
gag[1] *vb* **gagging, gagged 1** to choke as if about to vomit or as if struggling for breath. **2** to stop up (a person's mouth), usually with a piece of cloth, to prevent them from speaking or crying out. **3** to deprive of free speech. ✧ *n* **4** something, usually a piece of cloth, stuffed into or tied across the mouth. **5** any restraint on free speech. **6** a device for keeping the jaws apart: *a dentist's gag.* ▷ HISTORY Middle English *gaggen*
gag[2] *Informal* ✧ *n* **1** a joke, usually one told by a professional comedian. ✧ *vb* **gagging, gagged 2** to tell jokes. ▷ HISTORY origin unknown
gaga (**gah**-gah) *adj Informal* **1** confused and suffering some memory loss as a result of old age. **2** foolishly doting: *she's gaga over him.* ▷ HISTORY French
gage[1] *n* (formerly) a glove or other object thrown down to indicate a challenge to fight. ▷ HISTORY Old French
gage[2] *n, vb* **gaging, gaged** *US* same as **gauge**.
gaggle *n* **1** *Informal* a group of people gathered together. **2** a flock of geese. ▷ HISTORY Germanic
Gaia hypothesis *or* **theory** *n* the theory that the earth and everything on it constitutes a single self-regulating living entity. ▷ HISTORY *Gaia,* variant of *Gaea,* Greek goddess of the earth
gaiety *n, pl* **-ties 1** a state of lively good spirits. **2** festivity; merrymaking.

> ☑ **WORD TIP**
> See at **gay.**

gaily *adv* **1** in a lively manner; cheerfully. **2** with bright colours.
gain *vb* **1** to acquire (something desirable). **2** to increase, improve, or advance: *wholesale prices gained 5.6 percent.* **3 gain on** to get nearer to or catch up on. **4** to get to; reach: *gaining the top the hill.* **5** (of a watch or clock) to become or be too fast. ✧ *n* **6** something won or acquired; profit; advantage: *a clear gain would result.* **7** an increase in size or amount. **8** *Electronics* the ratio of the output signal of an amplifier to the input signal, usually measured in decibels. ▷ HISTORY Old French *gaaignier*
gainful *adj* useful or profitable. ▶ **gainfully** *adv*
gainsay *vb* **-saying, -said** *Archaic or literary* to deny or contradict. ▷ HISTORY Middle English *gainsaien,* from *gain-* against + *saien* to say
gait *n* **1** manner of walking. **2** (of horses and dogs) the pattern of footsteps at a particular speed, such as a trot. ▷ HISTORY variant of *gate*
gal *n slang* a girl.

gala (**gah**-la) *n* **1** a special social occasion, esp. a special performance. **2** *Chiefly Brit* a sporting occasion with competitions in several events: *next week's sports gala.* ▷ **HISTORY** Old French *galer* to make merry

galactic *adj* of the Galaxy or other galaxies.

galactose *n Chem* a white water-soluble monosaccharide found in lactose.

galaxy *n, pl* **-axies 1** a star system held together by gravitational attraction. **2** a collection of brilliant people or things: *a galaxy of legal talent.* ▷ **HISTORY** Middle English (in the sense: the Milky Way); from Greek *gala* milk

Galaxy *n* **the Galaxy** the spiral galaxy that contains the solar system. Also called: **Milky Way**

gale *n* **1** a strong wind, specifically one of force 8 on the Beaufort scale. **2 gales** a loud outburst: *gales of laughter.* ▷ **HISTORY** origin unknown

galena *or* **galenite** *n* a soft bluish-grey mineral consisting of lead sulphide: the chief source of lead. ▷ **HISTORY** Latin: lead ore

gall[1] (**gawl**) *n* **1** *Informal* bold impudence: *she was stunned I had the gall to ask.* **2** a feeling of great bitterness. **3** *Physiol obsolete* same as **bile**. ▷ **HISTORY** Old Norse

gall[2] (**gawl**) *vb* **1** to annoy or irritate. **2** to make the skin sore by rubbing. ✧ *n* **3** something that causes annoyance. **4** a sore on the skin caused by rubbing. ▷ **HISTORY** Germanic

gall[3] (**gawl**) *n* an abnormal outgrowth on a tree or plant caused by parasites. ▷ **HISTORY** Latin *galla*

gallant *adj* **1** persistent and courageous in the face of overwhelming odds: *a gallant fight.* **2** (of a man) making a show of polite attentiveness to women. **3** having a reputation for bravery: *Police Medal for gallant and meritorious services.* ✧ *n* **4** *History* a young man who tried to impress women with his fashionable clothes or daring acts. ▷ **HISTORY** Old French *galer* to make merry ▸ **gallantly** *adv*

gallantry *n* **1** showy, attentive treatment of women. **2** great bravery in war or danger.

gall bladder *n* a muscular sac, attached to the liver, that stores bile.

galleon *n* a large, three-masted sailing ship used from the 15th to the 18th centuries. ▷ **HISTORY** Spanish *galeón*

gallery *n, pl* **-leries 1** a room or building for displaying works of art. **2** a balcony running along or around the inside wall of a church, hall, or other building. **3** *Theatre* **a** an upper floor that projects from the rear and contains the cheapest seats. **b** the audience seated there. **4** an underground passage in a mine or cave. **5** a group of spectators, for instance at a golf match. **6 play to the gallery** to try to gain approval by appealing to popular taste. ▷ **HISTORY** Old French *galerie*

gallery forest *n Geog* a stretch of forest along a river in an area of otherwise open country.

galley *n* **1** the kitchen of a ship, boat, or aircraft. **2** a ship propelled by oars or sails, used in ancient or medieval times. ▷ **HISTORY** Old French *galie*

galley slave *n* **1** a criminal or slave forced to row in a galley. **2** *Informal* a drudge.

Gallic *adj* **1** French. **2** of ancient Gaul or the Gauls.

Gallicism *n* a word or idiom borrowed from French.

gallinaceous *adj* of an order of birds, including poultry, pheasants, and grouse, that have a heavy rounded body. ▷ **HISTORY** Latin *gallina* hen

galling (**gawl**-ing) *adj* annoying or bitterly humiliating.

gallium *n Chem* a silvery metallic element used in high-temperature thermometers and low-melting alloys. Symbol: Ga. ▷ **HISTORY** Latin *gallus* cock, translation of French *coq* in the name of its discoverer, *Lecoq* de Boisbaudran

gallivant *vb* to go about in search of pleasure. ▷ **HISTORY** perhaps from *gallant*

gallon *n* **1** *Brit* a unit of liquid measure equal to 4.55 litres. **2** *US* a unit of liquid measure equal to 3.79 litres. ▷ **HISTORY** Old Northern French *galon*

gallop *vb* **1** (of a horse) to run fast with a two-beat stride in which all four legs are off the ground at once. **2** to ride (a horse) at a gallop. **3** to move or progress rapidly. ✧ *n* **4** the fast two-beat gait of horses. **5** a galloping. ▷ **HISTORY** Old French *galoper*

Galloway *n* a breed of black cattle originally bred in Galloway. ▷ **HISTORY** after *Galloway,* district of SW Scotland

gallows *n, pl* **-lowses** *or* **-lows 1** a wooden structure consisting of two upright posts with a crossbeam, used for hanging criminals. **2 the gallows** execution by hanging. ▷ **HISTORY** Old Norse *galgi*

gallstone *n* a small hard mass formed in the gall bladder or its ducts.

Gallup Poll *n* a sampling of the views of a representative cross section of the population, usually used to forecast voting. ▷ **HISTORY** after G. H. *Gallup,* statistician

galop *n* **1** a 19th-century dance in quick duple time. **2** music for this dance. ▷ **HISTORY** French

galore *adj* in abundance: *there were bargains galore.* ▷ **HISTORY** Irish Gaelic *go leór* to sufficiency

galoshes *pl n Brit, Austral & NZ* a pair of waterproof overshoes. ▷ **HISTORY** Old French *galoche* wooden shoe

galumph *vb Brit, Austral & NZ informal* to leap or move about clumsily or joyfully. ▷ **HISTORY** probably a blend of GALLOP + TRIUMPH

galvanic *adj* **1** of or producing an electric current by chemical means, such as in a battery. **2** *Informal* stimulating, startling, or energetic.

galvanize *or* **-nise** *vb* **-nizing, -nized** *or* **-nising, -nised 1** to stimulate into action. **2** to cover (metal) with a protective zinc coating. **3** to stimulate by an electric current. ▷ **HISTORY** after *Galvani,* physiologist ▸ **galvanization** *or* **-nisation** *n*

galvanometer *n* a sensitive instrument for detecting or measuring small electric currents.

gambit *n* **1** an opening remark or action intended to gain an advantage. **2** *Chess* an opening move in which a piece, usually a pawn, is sacrificed to gain an advantageous position. ▷ **HISTORY** Italian *gambetto* a tripping up

gamble *vb* **-bling, -bled 1** to play games of chance to win money or prizes. **2** to risk or bet (something) on the outcome of an event or sport. **3 gamble on** to act with the expectation of: *she has gambled on proving everyone wrong.* **4 gamble away** to lose by gambling. ✧ *n* **5** a risky act or venture. **6** a bet or wager. ▷ **HISTORY** probably variant of GAME[1] ▸ **gambler** *n* ▸ **gambling** *n*

gamboge (gam-**boje**) *n* a gum resin obtained from a tropical Asian tree, used as a yellow pigment and as a purgative. ▷ **HISTORY** from *Cambodia,* where first found

gambol *vb* **-bolling, -bolled** *or US* **-boling, -boled 1** to jump about playfully; frolic. ✧ *n* **2** playful jumping about; frolicking. ▷ **HISTORY** French *gambade*

game[1] *n* **1** an amusement for children. **2** a competitive activity with rules. **3** a single period of play in such an activity. **4** (in some sports) the score needed to win. **5** a single contest in a series; match. **6** short for **computer game**. **7** style or ability in playing a game: *in the second set his overall game improved markedly.* **8** an activity that seems to operate according to unwritten rules: *the political game of power.* **9** an activity undertaken in a spirit of playfulness: *people who regard life as a game.* **10** wild animals, birds, or fish, hunted for sport or food. **11** the flesh of such animals, used as food. **12** an object of pursuit: *fair game.* **13** *Informal* a trick or scheme: *what's his game?* **14 games** an event consisting of various sporting contests, usually in athletics: *Commonwealth Games.* **15 on the game** *Slang* working as a prostitute. **16 give the game away** to reveal one's intentions or a secret. **17 play the game** to behave fairly. **18 the game is up** the scheme or trick has been found out and so cannot succeed. ✧ *adj* **19** *Informal* full of fighting spirit; plucky. **20** *Informal* prepared or willing: *I'm always game for a new sensation.* ✧ *vb* **gaming, gamed 21** to play games of chance for money; gamble. ▷ **HISTORY** Old English *gamen* ▸ **gamely** *adv* ▸ **gameness** *n*

game[2] *adj Brit, Austral & NZ* lame: *he had a game leg.* ▷ **HISTORY** probably from Irish *cam* crooked

gamekeeper *n Brit* a person employed to take care of game on an estate.

gamer *n* a person who plays computer games.

gamesmanship *n Informal* the art of winning by cunning practices without actually cheating.

gamete (**gam**-eet) *n* a cell that can fuse with another in reproduction. ▷ **HISTORY** Greek *gametē* wife ▸ **gametic** *or* **gametal** *adj*

gamey *or* **gamy** *adj* **gamier, gamiest** having the smell or flavour of game.

gamin *n* a street urchin. ▷ **HISTORY** French

gamine (**gam**-een) *n* a slim and boyish girl or young woman. ▷ **HISTORY** French

gaming *n* gambling.

gamma *n* the third letter in the Greek alphabet (Γ, γ).

gamma radiation *n* electromagnetic radiation of shorter wavelength and higher energy than X-rays.

gamma rays *pl n* streams of gamma radiation.

gammon *n* **1** cured or smoked ham. **2** the hindquarter of a side of bacon. ▷ **HISTORY** Old French *gambe* leg

gammy *adj* **-mier, -miest** *Brit & NZ slang* (of the leg) lame. ▷ **HISTORY** dialect variant of GAME[2]

gamut *n* **1** entire range or scale: *a rich gamut of facial expressions.* **2** *Music* **a** a scale. **b** the whole range of notes. ▷ **HISTORY** Medieval Latin, from *gamma,* the lowest note of the hexachord as established by Guido d'Arezzo + *ut* (now, *doh*), the first of the notes of the scale *ut, re, mi, fa, sol, la, si*

gander *n* **1** a male goose. **2** *Informal* a quick look: *have a gander.* ▷ **HISTORY** Old English *gandra, ganra*

gang[1] *n* **1** a group of people who go around together, often to commit crime. **2** an organized group of workmen. ✧ *vb* **3** to become or act as a gang. ▷ **HISTORY** Old English: journey

gang[2] *vb Scot* to go or walk. ▷ **HISTORY** Old English *gangan*

gangland *n* the criminal underworld.

gangling *or* **gangly** *adj* lanky and awkward in movement. ▷ **HISTORY** see GANG[2]

ganglion *n, pl* **-glia** *or* **-glions** a collection of nerve cells outside the brain and spinal cord. ▷ **HISTORY** Greek: cystic tumour ▸ **ganglionic** *adj*

gangplank *n Naut* a portable bridge for boarding and leaving a ship.

gangrene *n* decay of body tissue caused by the blood supply being interrupted by disease or injury. ▷ **HISTORY** Greek *gangraina* an eating sore ▸ **gangrenous** *adj*

gangsta rap *n* a style of rap music portraying life in Black ghettos in the US and featuring lyrics that are anti-authority and derogatory to women. ▷ **HISTORY** phonetic rendering of GANGSTER

gangster *n* a member of an organized gang of criminals. ▸ **gangsterism**

gangue *n* valueless material in an ore. ▷ **HISTORY** German *Gang* vein of metal, course

gangway *n* **1** *Brit* an aisle between rows of seats. **2** same as **gangplank**. **3** an opening in a ship's side to take a gangplank.

gannet *n* **1** a heavily built white sea bird. **2** *Brit slang* a greedy person. ▷ **HISTORY** Old English *ganot*

ganoid *adj* **1** (of the scales of certain fishes) consisting of an inner bony layer covered with an enamel-like substance. **2** (of a fish) having such scales. ✧ *n* **3** a ganoid fish. ▷ **HISTORY** Greek *ganos* brightness

gantry *n, pl* **-tries** a large metal framework used to support something, such as a travelling crane, or to position a rocket on its launch pad. ▷ **HISTORY** Latin *cantherius* supporting frame, pack ass

gaol (**jayl**) *n, vb Brit & Austral* same as **jail**. ▸ **gaoler** *n*

gap *n* **1** a break or opening in something. **2** an interruption or interval. **3** a difference in ideas or

a b c d e f g h i j k l m n o p q r s t u v w x y z

viewpoint: *the generation gap.* ▷ **HISTORY** Old Norse: chasm ▶ **gappy** *adj*

gape *vb* **gaping, gaped 1** to stare in wonder with the mouth open. **2** to open the mouth wide, as in yawning. **3** to be or become wide open: *a hole gaped in the roof.* ▷ **HISTORY** Old Norse *gapa* ▶ **gaping** *adj*

gap year *n* a year's break between leaving school and starting further education.

garage *n* **1** a building used to keep cars. **2** a place where cars are repaired and petrol is sold. ✧ *vb* **-aging, -aged 3** to put or keep a car in a garage. ▷ **HISTORY** French

garb *n* **1** clothes, usually the distinctive dress of an occupation or group: *modern military garb.* ✧ *vb* **2** to clothe. ▷ **HISTORY** Old French *garbe* graceful contour

garbage *n* **1** *US, Austral & NZ* household waste. **2** worthless rubbish or nonsense. ▷ **HISTORY** probably from Anglo-French

garbled *adj* (of a story, message, etc.) jumbled and confused. ▷ **HISTORY** Old Italian *garbellare* to strain, sift

garden *n* **1** an area of land usually next to a house, for growing flowers, fruit, or vegetables. *RELATED ADJECTIVE* ▶ **horticultural 2** Also: **gardens** a cultivated area of land open to the public: *Kensington Gardens.* **3 lead someone up the garden path** *Informal* to mislead or deceive someone. ✧ *vb* **4** to work in or take care of a garden. ▷ **HISTORY** Old French *gardin* ▶ **gardener** *n* ▶ **gardening** *n*

garden centre *n* a place where plants and gardening tools and equipment are sold.

garden city *n Brit* a planned town of limited size surrounded by countryside.

gardenia (gar-**deen**-ya) *n* **1** a large fragrant waxy white flower. **2** the evergreen shrub on which it grows. ▷ **HISTORY** after Dr Alexander *Garden,* botanist

garfish *n* **1** a freshwater fish with a long body and very long toothed jaws. **2** a sea fish with similar characteristics.

gargantuan *adj* huge or enormous. ▷ **HISTORY** after *Gargantua,* a giant in Rabelais' *Gargantua and Pantagruel*

> ☑ **WORD TIP**
> Some people think that *gargantuan* should only be used to describe things connected with food: *a gargantuan meal; his gargantuan appetite.*

gargle *vb* **-gling, -gled 1** to rinse the mouth and throat with (a liquid) by slowly breathing out through the liquid. ✧ *n* **2** the liquid used for gargling. **3** the act or sound of gargling. ▷ **HISTORY** Old French *gargouille* throat

gargoyle *n* (on ancient buildings) a waterspout below the roof carved in the form of a grotesque face or figure. ▷ **HISTORY** Old French *gargouille* gargoyle, throat

garish *adj* crudely bright or colourful. ▷ **HISTORY** obsolete *gaure* to stare ▶ **garishly** *adv* ▶ **garishness** *n*

garland *n* **1** a wreath of flowers and leaves worn round the head or neck or hung up. ✧ *vb* **2** to decorate with a garland or garlands. ▷ **HISTORY** Old French *garlande*

garlic *n* the bulb of a plant of the onion family, with a strong taste and smell, made up of small segments which are used in cooking. ▷ **HISTORY** Old English *gārlēac* ▶ **garlicky** *adj*

garment *n* an article of clothing. ▷ **HISTORY** Old French *garniment*

garner *vb* to collect or gather: *the financial rewards garnered by his book.* ▷ **HISTORY** Latin *granum* grain

garnet *n* a red semiprecious gemstone. ▷ **HISTORY** Old French *grenat* red, from *pome grenate* pomegranate

garnish *vb* **1** to decorate (food) with something to add to its appearance or flavour. ✧ *n* **2** a decoration for food. ▷ **HISTORY** Old French *garnir* to adorn, equip

garnishee *Law* ✧ *n* **1** a person upon whom a garnishment has been served. ✧ *vb* **garnishees, garnisheeing, garnisheed 2** to seize (a debt or other property) by garnishment. **3** to serve (a person) with a garnishment.

garnishment *n* **1** decoration or embellishment. **2** Law **a** a notice or warning. **b** a notice warning a person holding money, pay, or property belonging to a debtor to hold it until directed otherwise by the court.

garret *n* an attic in a house. ▷ **HISTORY** Old French *garite* watchtower

garrison *n* **1** soldiers who guard a base or fort. **2** the place itself. ✧ *vb* **3** to station (soldiers) in (a fort or base). ▷ **HISTORY** Old French *garir* to defend

garrotte *or* **garotte** *n* **1** a Spanish method of execution by strangling. **2** a cord, wire, or iron collar, used to strangle someone. ✧ *vb* **-rotting, -rotted 3** to execute with a garrotte. ▷ **HISTORY** Spanish *garrote*

garrulous *adj* constantly chattering; talkative. ▷ **HISTORY** Latin *garrire* to chatter ▶ **garrulousness** *n*

garter *n* **1** a band, usually of elastic, worn round the leg to hold up a sock or stocking. **2** *US & Canad* a suspender. ▷ **HISTORY** Old French *gartier*

gas *n, pl* **gases** *or* **gasses 1** an airlike substance that is neither liquid nor solid at room temperature and atmospheric pressure. **2** a fossil fuel in the form of a gas, used as a source of heat. **3** an anaesthetic in the form of a gas. **4** *Mining* firedamp or the explosive mixture of firedamp and air. **5** *US, Canad, Austral, NZ* petrol. **6** a poisonous gas used in war. **7** *Informal* idle talk or boasting. **8** *Slang* an entertaining person or thing: *Monterey was a gas for musicians and fans alike.* **9** *US informal* gas generated in the alimentary canal. ✧ *vb* **gases** *or* **gasses, gassing, gassed 10** to subject to gas fumes so as to make unconscious or to suffocate. **11** *Informal* to talk a lot; chatter. ▷ **HISTORY** coined from Greek *khaos* atmosphere

gasbag *n Informal* a person who talks too much.

gas chamber *n* an airtight room which is filled with poison gas to kill people.

gaseous *adj* of or like a gas.

gash *n* **1** a long deep cut. ✧ *vb* **2** to make a long deep cut in. ▷ **HISTORY** Old French *garser* to scratch, wound

gasholder *n* a large tank for storing gas before distributing it to users.

gasify *vb* **-fies, -fying, -fied** to change into a gas. ▶ **gasification** *n*

gasket *n* a piece of paper, rubber, or metal sandwiched between the faces of a metal joint to provide a seal. ▷ **HISTORY** probably from French *garcette* rope's end

gaslight *n* **1** a lamp in which light is produced by burning gas. **2** the light produced by such a lamp.

gas mask *n* a mask fitted with a chemical filter to protect the wearer from breathing in harmful gases.

gas meter *n* a device for measuring and recording the amount of gas passed through it.

gasoline *or* **gasolene** *n US & Canad* petrol.

gasometer (gas-**som**-it-er) *n* same as **gasholder**.

gasp *vb* **1** to draw in the breath sharply or with difficulty. **2** to utter breathlessly. ✧ *n* **3** a short convulsive intake of breath. ▷ **HISTORY** Old Norse *geispa* to yawn

gas pressure *n Physics* the pressure a gas exerts on the side of its container.

gassy *adj* **-sier, -siest** filled with, containing, or like gas. ▶ **gassiness** *n*

gastric *adj* of the stomach.

gastric juice *n* a digestive fluid secreted by the stomach.

gastric ulcer *n* an ulcer on the lining of the stomach.

gastritis *n* inflammation of the lining of the stomach, causing vomiting or gastric ulcers.

gastroenteritis *n* inflammation of the stomach and intestine, causing vomiting and diarrhoea.

gastronomy *n* the art of good eating. ▷ **HISTORY** Greek *gastēr* stomach + *nomos* law ▶ **gastronomic** *adj*

gastropod *n* a mollusc, such as a snail or whelk that has a single flat muscular foot, eyes on stalks, and usually a spiral shell. ▷ **HISTORY** Greek *gastēr* stomach + *-podos* -footed

gasworks *n* a factory in which coal gas is made.

gate *n* **1** a movable barrier, usually hinged, for closing an opening in a wall or fence. **2 a** the number of people admitted to a sporting event or entertainment. **b** the total entrance money received from them. **3** an exit at an airport by which passengers get to an aircraft. **4** *Electronics* a circuit with one or more input terminals and one output terminal, the output being determined by the combination of input signals. **5** a slotted metal frame that controls the positions of the gear lever in a motor vehicle. ▷ **HISTORY** Old English *geat*

gate-crash *vb Informal* to gain entry to (a party) without invitation. ▶ **gate-crasher** *n*

gatehouse *n* a building at or above a gateway.

gateway *n* **1** an entrance that may be closed by a gate. **2** a means of entry or access: *his only gateway to the outside world.*

gather *vb* **1** to come or bring together. **2** to increase gradually in (pace, speed, or momentum). **3** to prepare oneself for a task or challenge by collecting one's thoughts, strength, or courage. **4** to learn from information given; conclude: *this is pretty important, I gather.* **5** to draw (fabric) into small folds or tucks. **6** to pick or harvest (crops). ✧ *n* **7 gathers** small folds or tucks in fabric. ▷ **HISTORY** Old English *gadrian*

gathering *n* a group of people, usually meeting for some particular purpose: *the Braemar Highland Gathering.*

GATT General Agreement on Tariffs and Trade: a former name for the World Trade Organization.

gauche (**gohsh**) *adj* socially awkward. ▷ **HISTORY** French

gaucho (**gow**-choh) *n, pl* **-chos** a cowboy of the South American pampas. ▷ **HISTORY** American Spanish

gaudy *adj* **gaudier, gaudiest** vulgarly bright or colourful. ▷ **HISTORY** from *gaud* trinket ▶ **gaudily** *adv* ▶ **gaudiness** *n*

gauge (**gayj**) *vb* **gauging, gauged 1** to estimate or judge (people's feelings or reactions). **2** to measure using a gauge. ✧ *n* **3** an instrument for measuring quantities: *a petrol gauge.* **4** a scale or standard of measurement. **5** a standard for estimating people's feelings or reactions: *a gauge of public opinion.* **6** the diameter of the barrel of a gun. **7** the distance between the rails of a railway track. ▷ **HISTORY** from Old French

Gaul *n* a native of ancient Gaul.

gaunt *adj* **1** bony and emaciated in appearance. **2** (of a place) bleak or desolate: *the gaunt disused flour mill.* ▷ **HISTORY** origin unknown ▶ **gauntness** *n*

gauntlet[1] *n* **1** a long heavy protective glove. **2** a medieval armoured glove. **3 take up the gauntlet** to accept a challenge. ▷ **HISTORY** Old French *gantelet*

gauntlet[2] *n* **run the gauntlet** to be exposed to criticism or harsh treatment. ▷ **HISTORY** Swedish *gatlopp* passageway

gauss (rhymes with **mouse**) *n, pl* **gauss** the cgs unit of magnetic flux density. ▷ **HISTORY** after K. F. *Gauss,* mathematician

gauze *n* a transparent, loosely woven cloth, often used for surgical dressings. ▷ **HISTORY** French *gaze* ▶ **gauzy** *adj*

gave *vb* the past tense of **give**.

gavel (**gav**-vl) *n* a small hammer used by a judge, auctioneer, or chairman to call for order or attention. ▷ **HISTORY** origin unknown

gavotte *n* **1** an old formal dance in quadruple time. **2** music for this dance. ▷ **HISTORY** French

gawk *vb* **1** to stare stupidly. ✧ *n* **2** a clumsy stupid person. ▷ **HISTORY** Old Danish *gaukr*

gawky *adj* **gawkier, gawkiest** clumsy and awkward.

A B C D E F G H I J K L M N O P Q R S T U V W X Y Z

gawp *vb Slang* to stare stupidly. ▷ HISTORY Middle English *galpen* ▶ **gawper** *n*

gay *adj* **1** homosexual. **2** carefree and merry: *with gay abandon.* **3** bright and cheerful: *smartly dressed in gay colours.* ✧ *n* **4** a homosexual, esp. a homosexual man: *solidarity amongst lesbians and gays.* ▷ HISTORY Old French *gai*

> **WORD TIP**
> *Gayness* is the state of being homosexual. The noun which refers to the state of being carefree and merry is *gaiety.*

gayness *n* homosexuality.

gaze *vb* **gazing, gazed 1** to look long and steadily at someone or something. ✧ *n* **2** a long steady look. ▷ HISTORY Swedish dialect *gasa* to gape at

gazebo (gaz-**zee**-boh) *n, pl* **-bos** a summerhouse or pavilion with a good view. ▷ HISTORY perhaps a pseudo-Latin coinage based on *gaze*

gazelle *n* a small graceful fawn-coloured antelope of Africa and Asia. ▷ HISTORY Arabic *ghazāl*

gazette *n* an official newspaper that gives lists of announcements, for instance in legal or military affairs. ▷ HISTORY French

gazetteer *n* a book or section of a book that lists and describes places.

gazump *vb Brit & Austral informal* to raise the price of a house after agreeing a price verbally with an intending buyer. ▷ HISTORY origin unknown

gazunder *vb Brit informal* to reduce an offer on a house immediately before exchanging contracts, having earlier agreed a higher price with (the seller). ▶ **gazunderer** *n*

GB Great Britain.

GBH (in Britain) grievous bodily harm.

GC George Cross (a Brit. award for bravery).

GCE (in Britain) **1** General Certificate of Education. **2** *Informal* a pass in a GCE examination.

GCSE (in Britain) **1** General Certificate of Secondary Education; an examination in specified subjects which replaced the GCE O level and CSE. **2** *Informal* a pass in a GCSE examination.

Gd *Chem* gadolinium.

g'day *interj Austral & NZ informal* same as **good day**.

GDP gross domestic product.

Ge *Chem* germanium.

geanticline *n Geol* a gently sloping anticline covering a large area. ▷ HISTORY Greek *gē* earth, land + ANTICLINE

gear *n* **1** a set of toothed wheels that engages with another or with a rack in order to change the speed or direction of transmitted motion. **2** a mechanism for transmitting motion by gears. **3** the setting of a gear to suit engine speed or direction: *a higher gear; reverse gear.* **4** clothing or personal belongings. **5** equipment for a particular task: *police in riot gear.* **6 in** *or* **out of gear** with the gear mechanism engaged or disengaged. ✧ *vb* **7** to prepare or organize for something: *to gear for war.* ✧ See also **gear up**. ▷ HISTORY Old Norse *gervi*

gearbox *n* the metal casing enclosing a set of gears in a motor vehicle.

gearing *n* a system of gears designed to transmit motion.

gear lever *or US & Canad* **gearshift** *n* a lever used to engage or change gears in a motor vehicle.

gear up *vb* to prepare for an activity: *to gear up for a massive relief operation.*

gearwheel *n* one of the toothed wheels in the gears of a motor vehicle.

gecko *n, pl* **geckos** a small tropical lizard. ▷ HISTORY Malay *ge'kok*

gee *interj US & Canad informal* a mild exclamation of surprise, admiration, etc. Also: **gee whizz** ▷ HISTORY euphemism for *Jesus*

geebung (**gee**-bung) *n* **1** an Australian tree or shrub with an edible but tasteless fruit. **2** the fruit of this tree.

geek *n Informal* a boring and unattractive person. ▷ HISTORY perhaps from Scottish *geck* fool ▶ **geeky** *adj*

geelbek (**heel**-bek) *n S African* an edible marine fish with yellow jaws. ▷ HISTORY Afrikaans *geel* yellow + *bek* mouth

geese *n* the plural of **goose**[1].

geezer *n Brit, Austral & NZ informal* a man. ▷ HISTORY probably dialect pronunciation of *guiser,* a mummer

Geiger counter (**guy**-ger) *or* **Geiger-Müller counter** *n* an instrument for detecting and measuring radiation. ▷ HISTORY after Hans *Geiger,* physicist

geisha (**gay**-sha) *n* a professional female companion for men in Japan, trained in music, dancing, and conversation. ▷ HISTORY Japanese

gel (**jell**) *n* **1** a thick jelly-like substance, esp. one used to keep a hairstyle in shape. ✧ *vb* **gelling, gelled 2** to become a gel. **3** same as **jell**. **4** to apply gel to (one's hair). ▷ HISTORY from *gelatine*

gelatine (**jell**-a-teen) *or* **gelatin** *n* a clear water-soluble protein made by boiling animal hides and bones, used in cooking, photography, etc. ▷ HISTORY Latin *gelare* to freeze

gelatinous (jill-**at**-in-uss) *adj* with a thick, semi-liquid consistency.

geld *vb* **gelding, gelded** *or* **gelt** to castrate (a horse or other animal). ▷ HISTORY Old Norse *gelda*

gelding *n* a castrated male horse. ▷ HISTORY Old Norse *geldingr*

gelignite *n* a type of dynamite used for blasting. ▷ HISTORY GELATINE + Latin *ignis* fire

gem *n* **1** a precious stone used for decoration. *RELATED ADJECTIVE* ▶ **lapidary 2** a person or thing regarded as precious or special: *a perfect gem of a hotel.* ▷ HISTORY Latin *gemma* bud, precious stone

gemfish *n* an Australian food fish with a delicate flavour.

Gemini *n Astrol* the third sign of the zodiac; the Twins. ▷ HISTORY Latin

gemsbok (**hemss**-bok) *n S African* same as **oryx**. ▷ HISTORY Afrikaans

gen *n Brit, Austral & NZ informal* information: *I want to get as much gen as I can about the American market.* ✧ See also **gen up on.** ▷ **HISTORY** from *gen(eral information)*

Gen. General.

gendarme (**zhahn**-darm) *n* a member of the French police force. ▷ **HISTORY** French

gender *n* **1** the state of being male, female, or neuter. **2** the classification of nouns in certain languages as masculine, feminine, or neuter. ▷ **HISTORY** Latin *genus* kind

gene (**jean**) *n* a unit composed of DNA forming part of a chromosome, by which inherited characteristics are transmitted from parent to offspring. ▷ **HISTORY** German *Gen*

genealogy (jean-ee-**al**-a-jee) *n* **1** the direct descent of an individual or group from an ancestor. **2** (*pl* **-gies**) a chart showing the descent of an individual or group. ▷ **HISTORY** Greek *genea* race ▶ **genealogical** *adj* ▶ **genealogist** *n*

genera (**jen**-er-a) *n* a plural of **genus**.

general *adj* **1** common or widespread: *general goodwill.* **2** of, affecting, or including all or most of the members of a group. **3** not specialized or specializing: *a general hospital.* **4** including various or miscellaneous items: *general knowledge.* **5** not definite; vague: *the examples used will give a general idea.* **6** highest in authority or rank: *the club's general manager.* ✧ *n* **7** a very senior military officer. **8 in general** generally; mostly or usually. ▷ **HISTORY** Latin *generalis*

general anaesthetic *n* a substance that causes general anaesthesia. See **anaesthesia**.

general election *n* an election in which representatives are chosen in all constituencies of a state.

generalissimo *n, pl* **-mos** a supreme commander of combined armed forces. ▷ **HISTORY** Italian

generality *n* **1** (*pl* **-ties**) a general principle or observation: *speaking in generalities.* **2** *Old-fashioned* the majority: *the generality of mankind.*

generalization *or* **-isation** *n* a principle or statement based on specific instances but applied generally: *the argument sinks to generalizations and name-calling.*

generalize *or* **-ise** *vb* **-izing, -ized** *or* **-ising, -ised** **1** to form general principles or conclusions from specific instances. **2** to speak in generalities. **3** to make widely used or known: *generalized violence.*

generally *adv* **1** usually; as a rule: *these protests have generally been peaceful.* **2** commonly or widely: *it's generally agreed he has performed well.* **3** not specifically; broadly: *what are your thoughts generally about the war?*

general practitioner *n* a doctor who does not specialize but has a general medical practice in which he or she treats all illnesses.

general staff *n* officers who assist commanders in the planning and execution of military operations.

general strike *n* a strike by all or most of the workers of a country.

generate *vb* **-ating, -ated** to produce or create. ▷ **HISTORY** Latin *generare* to beget

generation *n* **1** all the people of approximately the same age: *the younger generation.* **2** a successive stage in descent of people or animals: *passed on from generation to generation.* **3** the average time between two generations of a species, about 35 years for humans: *an alliance which has lasted a generation.* **4** a specified stage of development: *the next generation of fighter aircraft.* **5** production, esp. of electricity or heat.

generative *adj* capable of producing or originating something.

generator *n* a device for converting mechanical energy into electrical energy.

generic (jin-**ner**-ik) *adj* of a whole class, or group, or genus. ▷ **HISTORY** Latin *genus* kind, race ▶ **generically** *adv*

generous *adj* **1** ready to give freely; unselfish. **2** free from pettiness in character and mind. **3** large or plentiful: *a generous donation.* ▷ **HISTORY** Latin *generosus* nobly born ▶ **generously** *adv* ▶ **generosity** *n*

genesis (**jen**-iss-iss) *n, pl* **-ses** (-seez) the beginning or origin of anything. ▷ **HISTORY** Greek

Genesis *n Bible* the first book of the Old Testament, containing a description of the creation the world.

genetic (jin-**net**-tik) *adj* of genetics, genes, or the origin of something. ▷ **HISTORY** from *genesis* ▶ **genetically** *adv*

genetically modified *adj* (of an organism) having DNA which has been altered for the purpose of improvement or correction of defects.

genetic code *n Biochem* the order in which the four nucleic acid bases of DNA are arranged in the molecule for transmitting genetic information to the cells.

genetic engineering *n* alteration of the genetic structure of an organism in order to produce more desirable traits.

genetic fingerprinting *n* the use of a person's unique pattern of DNA, which can be obtained from blood, saliva, or tissue, as a means of identification. ▶ **genetic fingerprint** *n*

genetic information *n Biol* information about an individual that is carried in the genes and can be transferred to subsequent generations.

genetics *n* the study of heredity and variation in organisms. ▶ **geneticist** *n*

genial (**jean**-ee-al) *adj* cheerful, easy-going, and friendly. ▷ **HISTORY** Latin *genius* guardian deity ▶ **geniality** *n* ▶ **genially** *adv*

genie (**jean**-ee) *n* (in fairy tales) a servant who appears by magic and fulfils a person's wishes. ▷ **HISTORY** Arabic *jinni* demon

genital *adj* of the sexual organs or reproduction. ▷ **HISTORY** Latin *genitalis* concerning birth

genitals *or* **genitalia** (jen-it-**ail**-ya) *pl n* the external sexual organs.

A B C D E F G H I J K L M N O P Q R S T U V W X Y Z

genitive *or* **genitive case** *n Grammar* a grammatical case in some languages used to indicate a relation of ownership or association. ▷ **HISTORY** Latin *genetivus* relating to birth

genius (**jean**-yuss) *n, pl* **-uses 1** a person with exceptional ability in a particular subject or activity. **2** such ability. **3** a person considered as exerting influence of a certain sort: *the evil genius behind the drug-smuggling empire.* ▷ **HISTORY** Latin

genocide (**jen**-no-side) *n* the deliberate killing of a people or nation. ▷ **HISTORY** Greek *genos* race + Latin *caedere* to kill ▶ **genocidal** *adj*

genotype (**jen**-oh-type) *n Biol* the genetic constitution of an organism.

genre (**zhahn**-ra) *n* **1** a kind or type of literary, musical, or artistic work: *the mystery and supernatural genres.* **2** a kind of painting depicting incidents from everyday life. ▷ **HISTORY** French

gent *n Brit, Austral & NZ informal* short for **gentleman**.

genteel *adj* **1** overly concerned with being polite. **2** respectable, polite, and well-bred. ▷ **HISTORY** French *gentil* well-born ▶ **genteelly** *adv*

gentian (**jen**-shun) *n* a mountain plant with blue or purple flowers. ▷ **HISTORY** Latin *gentiana*

gentian violet *n* a violet-coloured solution used as an antiseptic and in the treatment of burns.

Gentile *n* **1** a person who is not a Jew. ✧ *adj* **2** not Jewish. ▷ **HISTORY** Latin *gentilis* belonging to the same tribe

gentility *n, pl* **-ties 1** noble birth or ancestry. **2** respectability and good manners. ▷ **HISTORY** Old French *gentilite*

gentle *adj* **1** kind and calm in character. **2** temperate or moderate: *gentle autumn rain.* **3** soft; not sharp or harsh: *gentle curves.* ▷ **HISTORY** Latin *gentilis* belonging to the same family ▶ **gentleness** *n* ▶ **gently** *adv*

gentlefolk *pl n Old-fashioned* people regarded as being of good breeding.

gentleman *n, pl* **-men 1** a cultured, courteous, and well-bred man. **2** a man who comes from a family of high social position. **3** a polite name for a man. ▶ **gentlemanly** *adj*

gentrification *n* a process by which the character of a traditionally working class area is made fashionable by middle class people. ▶ **gentrify** *vb*

gentry *n Brit old-fashioned* people just below the nobility in social rank. ▷ **HISTORY** Old French *genterie*

gents *n Brit & Austral informal* a men's public toilet.

genuflect *vb* to bend the knee as a sign of reverence or deference, esp. in church. ▷ **HISTORY** Latin *genu* knee + *flectere* to bend ▶ **genuflection** *n*

genuine *adj* **1** real and exactly what it appears to be: *a genuine antique.* **2** sincerely felt: *genuine concern.* **3** (of a person) honest and without pretence. ▷ **HISTORY** Latin *genuinus* inborn ▶ **genuinely** *adv* ▶ **genuineness** *n*

gen up on *vb* **genning, genned** *Brit & Austral informal* to become, or make someone else, fully informed about.

genus (**jean**-uss) *n, pl* **genera** *or* **genuses 1** *Biol* one of the groups into which a family is divided, containing one or more species. **2** a class or group. ▷ **HISTORY** Latin: race

geocentric *adj* **1** having the earth as a centre. **2** measured as from the centre of the earth.

geochemistry *n Geol* the geology and chemistry concerned with the chemical composition of, and chemical reactions taking place within, the earth's crust. ▶ **geochemical** *adj* ▶ **geochemist** *n*

geodesic *adj* **1** relating to the geometry of curved surfaces. ✧ *n* **2** the shortest line between two points on a curved surface.

geodesy *n* the study of the shape and size of the earth. ▷ **HISTORY** Greek *gē* earth + *daiein* to divide

geographic information system *or* **GIS** *n Geog* a computer system for storing, updating, accessing, analysing and manipulating geographical data indexed by map coordinates.

geography *n* **1** the study of the earth's surface, including physical features, climate, and population. **2** the physical features of a region. ▷ **HISTORY** Greek *gē* earth + -GRAPHY ▶ **geographer** *n* ▶ **geographical** *or* **geographic** *adj* ▶ **geographically** *adv*

geoisotherm *n* same as **isogeotherm**.

geological timescale *n Geol* the system used by geologists to measure time, based on time units called *aeons, eras, periods,* and *ages.*

geology *n* **1** the study of the origin, structure, and composition of the earth. **2** the geological features of an area. ▷ **HISTORY** Greek *gē* earth + -LOGY ▶ **geologist** *n* ▶ **geological** *adj* ▶ **geologically** *adv*

geometric *or* **geometrical** *adj* **1** of geometry. **2** consisting of shapes used in geometry, such as circles, triangles, and straight lines: *geometric design.* ▶ **geometrically** *adv*

geometric progression *n* a sequence of numbers, each of which differs from the succeeding one by a constant ratio, for example 1, 2, 4, 8.

geometry *n* the branch of mathematics concerned with points, lines, curves, and surfaces. ▷ **HISTORY** Greek *geōmetrein* to measure the land ▶ **geometrician** *n*

geomorphic *adj Geol* of, relating to, or resembling the earth's surface.

geomorphology *n Geol* the branch of geology that is concerned with the structure, origin, and development of the features of the earth's crust. ▶ **geomorphological** *adj*

geophysics *n* the study of the earth's physical properties and the physical forces which affect it. ▶ **geophysical** *adj* ▶ **geophysicist** *n*

Geordie *Brit* ✧ *n* **1** a person from Tyneside. **2** the Tyneside dialect. ✧ *adj* **3** of Tyneside: *a Geordie accent.*

George Cross *n* a British award for bravery, usually awarded to civilians.

georgette (jor-**jet**) *n* a thin crepe dress material. ▷ HISTORY after Mme *Georgette,* a French dressmaker

Georgian *adj* **1** of or in the reigns of any of the kings of Great Britain and Ireland called George. **2** denoting a style of architecture or furniture prevalent in Britain in the 18th century: *an elegant Georgian terrace in Edinburgh.*

geostationary *adj* (of a satellite) orbiting so as to remain over the same point on the earth's surface.

geosyncline *n Geol* a broad elongated depression in the earth's crust containing great thicknesses of sediment. ▶ **geosynclinal** *adj*

geotectonic *adj Geol* of or relating to the formation, arrangement, and structure of the rocks of the earth's crust.

geothermal *or* **geothermic** *adj* of or using the heat in the earth's interior.

geothermal energy *n Geol* power generated using steam produced by heat from the molten core of the earth.

geotropism *n Bot* the response of a plant part to the stimulus of gravity.

geranium *n* a cultivated plant with scarlet, pink, or white flowers. ▷ HISTORY Latin: cranesbill

gerbil (**jur**-bill) *n* a small rodent with long back legs, often kept as a pet. ▷ HISTORY French *gerbille*

geriatric *adj* **1** of geriatrics or old people. ✧ *n* **2** an old person, esp. as a patient.

geriatrics *n* the branch of medicine concerned with illnesses affecting old people.

germ *n* **1** a tiny living thing, esp. one that causes disease: *a diphtheria germ.* **2** the beginning from which something may develop: *the germ of a book.* ▷ HISTORY Latin *germen* sprout, seed

German *adj* **1** of Germany. ✧ *n* **2** a person from Germany. **3** the official language of Germany, Austria, and parts of Switzerland.

germane *adj* relevant: *the studies provided some evidence germane to these questions.* ▷ HISTORY Latin *germanus* of the same race

Germanic *n* **1** the ancient language from which English, German, and the Scandinavian languages developed. ✧ *adj* **2** of this ancient language or the languages that developed from it. **3** characteristic of German people or things: *Germanic-looking individuals.*

germanium *n Chem* a brittle grey metalloid element that is a semiconductor and is used in transistors. Symbol: Ge. ▷ HISTORY after *Germany*

German measles *n* same as **rubella**.

German shepherd dog *n* same as **Alsatian**.

germ cell *n* a sexual reproductive cell.

germicide *n* a substance used to destroy germs. ▷ HISTORY *germ* + Latin *caedere* to kill

germinal *adj* **1** of or in the earliest stage of development: *the germinal phases of the case.* **2** of germ cells.

germinate *vb* **-nating, -nated** to grow or cause to grow. ▷ HISTORY Latin *germinare* to sprout ▶ **germination** *n*

germ warfare *n* the military use of disease-spreading bacteria against an enemy.

gerontology *n* the scientific study of ageing and the problems of old people. ▷ HISTORY Greek *gerōn* old man + -LOGY ▶ **gerontologist** *n*

gerrymandering *n* the practice of dividing the constituencies of a voting area so as to give one party an unfair advantage. ▷ HISTORY from Elbridge *Gerry,* US politician + *(sala)mander,* from the salamander-like outline of a reshaped electoral district

gerund (**jer**-rund) *n* a noun formed from a verb, ending in *-ing,* denoting an action or state, for example *running.* ▷ HISTORY Latin *gerundum* something to be carried on

gesso (**jess**-oh) *n* plaster used for painting or in sculpture. ▷ HISTORY Italian: chalk

Gestapo *n* the secret state police of Nazi Germany. ▷ HISTORY German *Ge(heime) Sta(ats)po(lizei)* secret state police

gestation *n* **1** the process of carrying and developing babies in the womb during pregnancy, or the time during which this process takes place. **2** the process of developing a plan or idea in the mind. ▷ HISTORY Latin *gestare* to bear

gesticulate *vb* **-lating, -lated** to make expressive movements with the hands and arms, usually while talking. ▷ HISTORY Latin *gesticulari* ▶ **gesticulation** *n*

gesture *n* **1** a movement of the hands, head, or body to express or emphasize an idea or emotion. **2** something said or done to indicate intention, or as a formality: *a gesture of goodwill.* ✧ *vb* **-turing, -tured 3** to make expressive movements with the hands and arms. ▷ HISTORY Latin *gestus*

get *vb* **getting, got 1** to come into possession of. **2** to bring or fetch. **3** to catch (an illness). **4** to become: *they get frustrated and angry.* **5** to cause to be done or to happen: *he got a wart removed; to get steamed up.* **6** to hear or understand: *did you get that joke?* **7** to reach (a place or point): *we could not get to the airport in time.* **8** to catch (a bus or train). **9** to persuade: *she trying to get him to give secrets away.* **10** *Informal* to annoy: *you know what really gets me?* **11** *Informal* to baffle: *now you've got me.* **12** *Informal* to hit: *a bit of grenade got me on the left hip.* **13** *Informal* to be revenged on. **14** *Informal* to start: *we got talking about it; it got me thinking.* ▷ HISTORY Old English *gietan*

get across *vb* to make (something) understood.

get at *vb* **1** to gain access to: *to get at the information on these disks.* **2** to imply or mean: *it is hard to see quite what he is getting at.* **3** to annoy or criticize persistently: *people who know they're being got at.*

get by *vb Informal* to manage in spite of difficulties: *he saw for himself what people did to get by.*

get in *vb* **1** to arrive. **2** to be elected. **3 get in on** to join in (an activity).

A B C D E F G H I J K L M N O P Q R S T U V W X Y Z

get off *vb* **1** to leave (a bus or train or a place). **2** to escape the consequences of or punishment for an action: *the real culprits have got off scot-free.* **3 get off with** *Brit & Austral informal* to begin a romantic or sexual relationship with.

get on *vb* **1** to enter (a bus or train). **2** to have a friendly relationship: *he had a flair for getting on with people.* **3** to grow old: *he was getting on in years.* **4** (of time) to elapse: *the time was getting on.* **5** to make progress: *how are the children getting on?* **6 get on with** to continue to do: *you can get on with whatever you were doing before.* **7 getting on for** approaching (a time, age, or amount): *getting on for half a century ago.*

get out *vb* **1** to leave or escape. **2** to become known. **3** to gain something of significance or value: *that's all I got out of it.* **4 get out of** to avoid: *to get out of doing the dishes.*

get over *vb* **1** to recover from (an illness or unhappy experience). **2** to overcome (a problem). **3 get over with** to bring (something necessary but unpleasant) to an end: *better to get it over with.*

get through *vb* **1** to complete (a task or process). **2** to use up (money or supplies). **3** to succeed in (an examination or test). **4 get through to a** to succeed in making (someone) understand. **b** to contact (someone) by telephone.

geyser (**geez**-er) *n* **1** a spring that discharges steam and hot water. **2** *Brit & S African* a domestic gas water heater. ▷ HISTORY Icelandic *Geysir*

ghastly *adj* **-lier, -liest 1** *Informal* very unpleasant. **2** deathly pale. **3** horrible: *a ghastly accident.* ▷ HISTORY Old English *gāstlīc* spiritual

ghat *n* (in India) **1** stairs leading down to a river. **2** a place of cremation. **3** a mountain pass. ▷ HISTORY Hindi

ghee (**gee**) *n* clarified butter, used in Indian cookery. ▷ HISTORY Hindi *ghī*

gherkin *n* a small pickled cucumber. ▷ HISTORY Dutch *agurkkijn*

ghetto *n, pl* **-tos** *or* **-toes** an area that is inhabited by people of a particular race, religion, nationality, or class. ▷ HISTORY Italian

ghetto blaster *n Informal* a large portable CD player or cassette recorder with built-in speakers.

ghillie *n* same as **gillie**.

ghost *n* **1** the disembodied spirit of a dead person, supposed to haunt the living. **2** a faint trace: *the ghost of a smile on his face.* **3** a faint secondary image in an optical instrument or on a television screen. ✧ *vb* **4** short for **ghostwrite**. ▷ HISTORY Old English *gāst*

ghost gum *n Austral* a eucalyptus with white trunk and branches.

ghostly *adj* **-lier, -liest** frightening in appearance or effect: *ghostly noises.*

ghost town *n* a town that used to be busy but is now deserted.

ghostwrite *vb* **-writing, -wrote, -written** to write (an article or book) on behalf of a person who is then credited as author. ▶ **ghostwriter** *n*

ghoul (**gool**) *n* **1** a person who is interested in morbid or disgusting things. **2** a demon that eats corpses. ▷ HISTORY Arabic *ghūl* ▶ **ghoulish** *adj* ▶ **ghoulishly** *adv*

GHQ *Mil* General Headquarters.

GI *n, pl* **GIs** *or* **GI's** *US informal* a soldier in the US Army. ▷ HISTORY abbreviation of *government issue*

giant *n* **1** a mythical figure of superhuman size and strength. **2** a person or thing of exceptional size, ability, or importance: *industrial giants.* ✧ *adj* **3** remarkably large. **4** (of an atom or ion or its structure) having large numbers of particles present in a crystal lattice, with each particle exerting a strong force of attraction on those near to it. ▷ HISTORY Greek *gigas*

giant panda *n* See **panda**.

gibber[1] (**jib**-ber) *vb* to talk in a fast and unintelligible manner. ▷ HISTORY imitative

gibber[2] (**gib**-ber) *n Austral* a boulder. ▷ HISTORY Aboriginal

gibberish *n* rapid incomprehensible talk; nonsense.

gibber plain *n Austral Geog* barren land covered with stones. ▷ HISTORY Aboriginal

gibbet (**jib**-bit) *n* a gallows. ▷ HISTORY Old French *gibet*

gibbon (**gib**-bon) *n* a small agile ape of the forests of S Asia. ▷ HISTORY French

gibbous (**gib**-bus) *adj* (of the moon) more than half but less than fully illuminated. ▷ HISTORY Latin *gibba* hump

gibe (**jibe**) *n, vb* **gibing, gibed** same as **jibe**[1]. ▷ HISTORY perhaps from Old French *giber* to treat roughly

giblets (**jib**-lits) *pl n* the gizzard, liver, heart, and neck of a fowl. ▷ HISTORY Old French *gibelet* stew of game birds

gidday, g'day *interj Austral & NZ* an expression of greeting.

giddy *adj* **-dier, -diest 1** feeling weak and unsteady on one's feet, as if about to faint. **2** happy and excited: *a state of giddy expectation.* ▷ HISTORY Old English *gydig* mad, frenzied, possessed by God ▶ **giddiness** *n*

gift *n* **1** something given to someone: *a birthday gift.* **2** a special ability or power: *a gift for caricature.* ▷ HISTORY Old English: payment for a wife, dowry

gifted *adj* having natural talent or aptitude: *that era's most gifted director.*

gig[1] *n* **1** a single performance by jazz or pop musicians. ✧ *vb* **gigging, gigged 2** to play gigs. ▷ HISTORY origin unknown

gig[2] *n* a light open two-wheeled one-horse carriage. ▷ HISTORY origin unknown

giga- *prefix* **1** denoting 10^9: *gigavolt.* **2** *Computers* denoting 2^{30}: *gigabyte.* ▷ HISTORY Greek *gigas* giant

gigantic *adj* extremely large: *the most gigantic gold paperweight ever.* ▷ HISTORY Greek *gigantikos*

giggle *vb* **-gling, -gled 1** to laugh nervously or foolishly. ✧ *n* **2** a nervous or foolish laugh. **3** *Informal* an amusing person or thing. ▷ HISTORY imitative ▶ **giggly** *adj*

gigolo (**jig**-a-lo) *n, pl* **-los** a man who is paid by an older woman to be her escort or lover. ▷ **HISTORY** French

gigot *n Chiefly Brit* a leg of lamb or mutton. ▷ **HISTORY** French

gild *vb* **gilding, gilded** *or* **gilt 1** to cover with a thin layer of gold. **2** to make (something) appear golden: *the morning sun gilded the hills.* **3 gild the lily a** to adorn unnecessarily something already beautiful. **b** to praise someone excessively. ▷ **HISTORY** Old English *gyldan*

gill (**jill**) *n* a unit of liquid measure equal to one quarter of a pint (0.14 litres). ▷ **HISTORY** Old French *gille* vat, tub

gillie *or* **ghillie** *n Scot* a sportsman's attendant or guide for hunting or fishing. ▷ **HISTORY** Scottish Gaelic *gille* boy, servant

gills (**gillz**) *pl n* the breathing organs of fish and other water creatures. ▷ **HISTORY** from Old Norse

gilt *vb* **1** a past of **gild**. ✧ *adj* **2** covered with a thin layer of gold. ✧ *n* **3** a thin layer of gold, used as decoration.

gilt-edged *adj* denoting government securities on which interest payments and final repayments are guaranteed.

gimcrack (**jim**-krak) *adj* showy but cheap; shoddy. ▷ **HISTORY** origin unknown

gimlet (**gim**-let) *n* **1** a small hand tool with a pointed spiral tip, used for boring holes in wood. ✧ *adj* **2** penetrating or piercing: *gimlet eyes.* ▷ **HISTORY** Old French *guimbelet*

gimmick *n Informal* something designed to attract attention or publicity. ▷ **HISTORY** origin unknown ▶ **gimmicky** *adj* ▶ **gimmickry** *n*

gin[1] *n* an alcoholic drink distilled from malted grain and flavoured with juniper berries. ▷ **HISTORY** Dutch *genever* juniper

gin[2] *n* a noose of thin strong wire for catching small mammals. ▷ **HISTORY** Middle English *gyn*

gin[3] *n Austral offensive* an Aboriginal woman. ▷ **HISTORY** Aboriginal

ginger *n* **1** the root of a tropical plant, powdered and used as a spice or sugared and eaten as a sweet. ✧ *adj* **2** light reddish-brown: *ginger hair.* ▷ **HISTORY** Old French *gingivre* ▶ **gingery** *adj*

ginger ale *n* a nonalcoholic fizzy drink flavoured with ginger extract.

gingerbread *n* a moist brown cake flavoured with ginger.

ginger group *n Brit, Austral & NZ* a group within a larger group that agitates for a more active policy.

gingerly *adv* carefully or cautiously: *she sat gingerly on the edge of the chair.* ▷ **HISTORY** perhaps from Old French *gensor* dainty

ginger nut *or* **snap** *n* a hard biscuit flavoured with ginger.

gingham *n* a cotton fabric with a checked or striped design. ▷ **HISTORY** Malay *ginggang* striped cloth

gingivitis (jin-jiv-**vite**-iss) *n* inflammation of the gums. ▷ **HISTORY** Latin *gingiva* gum

ginseng (**jin**-seng) *n* the root of a plant of China and N America, believed to have tonic and energy-giving properties. ▷ **HISTORY** Mandarin Chinese *jen shen*

Gipsy *n, pl* **-sies** same as **Gypsy**.

giraffe *n* a cud-chewing African mammal with a very long neck and long legs and a spotted yellowy skin. ▷ **HISTORY** Arabic *zarāfah*

gird *vb* **girding, girded** *or* **girt 1** to put a belt or girdle around. **2 gird up one's loins** to prepare oneself for action. ▷ **HISTORY** Old English *gyrdan*

girder *n* a large steel or iron beam used in the construction of bridges and buildings.

girdle *n* **1** a woman's elastic corset that covers the stomach and hips. **2** anything that surrounds something or someone: *his girdle of supporters.* **3** *Anat* an encircling arrangement of bones: *the shoulder girdle.* ✧ *vb* **-dling, -dled 4** to surround: *a ring of volcanic ash girdling the earth.* ▷ **HISTORY** Old English *gyrdel*

girl *n* **1** a female child. **2** a young woman. ▷ **HISTORY** Middle English *girle* ▶ **girlhood** *n* ▶ **girlish** *adj*

girlfriend *n* **1** a female friend with whom a person is romantically or sexually involved. **2** any female friend.

Girl Guide *n* a former name for **Guide**.

girlie *adj Informal* **1** featuring naked or scantily dressed women: *girlie magazines.* **2** suited to or designed to appeal to young women: *a real girlie night out.*

giro (**jire**-oh) *n, pl* **-ros 1** (in some countries) a system of transferring money within a bank or post office, directly from one account into another. **2** *Brit informal* a social-security payment by giro cheque. ▷ **HISTORY** Greek *guros* circuit

girt *vb* a past of **gird**.

girth *n* **1** the measurement around something. **2** a band fastened round a horse's middle to keep the saddle in position. ▷ **HISTORY** Old Norse *gjörth* belt

GIS *n* geographic information system.

gist (**jist**) *n* the main point or meaning of something: *the gist of letter.* ▷ **HISTORY** Anglo-French, as in *cest action gist en* this action consists in

give *vb* **giving, gave, given 1** to present or hand (something) to someone. **2** to pay (an amount of money) for a purchase. **3** to grant or provide: *to give an answer.* **4** to utter (a shout or cry). **5** to perform, make, or do: *the prime minister gave a speech.* **6** to host (a party). **7** to sacrifice or devote: *comrades who gave their lives for their country.* **8** to concede: *he was very efficient, I have to give him that.* **9** to yield or break under pressure: *something has got to give.* **10 give or take** plus or minus: *about one hundred metres, give or take five.* ✧ *n* **11** a tendency to yield under pressure; elasticity. ✧ See also **give away, give in**, etc. ▷ **HISTORY** Old English *giefan* ▶ **giver** *n*

give away *vb* **1** to donate as a gift. **2** to reveal (a secret). **3** to present (a bride) formally to her husband in a marriage ceremony. **4 give something away** *NZ* to give something up. ✧ *n* **giveaway 5** something that reveals hidden feelings or intentions. ✧ *adj* **giveaway 6** very cheap or free: *a giveaway rent.*

give in *vb* to admit defeat.

given *vb* **1** the past participle of **give**. ✧ *adj* **2** specific or previously stated: *priorities within the given department.* **3** to be assumed: *any given place on the earth.* **4 given to** inclined to: *a man not given to undue optimism.*

give off *vb* to send out (heat, light, or a smell).

give out *vb* **1** to hand out: *the bloke that was giving out those tickets.* **2** to send out (heat, light, or a smell). **3** to make known: *the man who gave out the news.* **4** to fail: *the engine gave out.*

give over *vb* **1** to set aside for a specific purpose: *the amount of space given over to advertisements.* **2** *Informal* to stop doing something annoying: *tell him to give over.*

give up *vb* **1** to stop (doing something): *I did give up smoking.* **2** to resign from (a job or position). **3** to admit defeat or failure. **4** to abandon (hope). **5 give oneself up a** to surrender to the police or other authorities. **b** to devote oneself completely: *she gave herself up to her work.*

gizzard *n* the part of a bird's stomach in which hard food is broken up. ▷ **HISTORY** Old French *guisier* fowl's liver

glacé (**glass**-say) *adj* preserved in a thick sugary syrup: *glacé cherries.* ▷ **HISTORY** French: iced

glacial *adj* **1** of glaciers or ice. **2** extremely cold. **3** cold and unfriendly: *a glacial stare.*

glacial period *or* **epoch** *n Geol* **1** any period of time during which a large part of the earth's surface was covered with ice, caused by the advance of glaciers. **2** the Pleistocene epoch. ✧ Also called: **ice age**

glaciation *n* the process of covering part of the earth's surface with glaciers or masses of ice. ▶ **glaciated** *adj*

glacier *n* a slowly moving mass of ice formed by an accumulation of snow. ▷ **HISTORY** Latin *glacies* ice

glad *adj* **gladder, gladdest 1** happy and pleased. **2** very willing: *he was only too glad to help.* **3** *Archaic* causing happiness: *glad tidings.* ▷ **HISTORY** Old English *glæd* ▶ **gladly** *adv* ▶ **gladness** *n* ▶ **gladden** *vb*

glade *n* an open space in a forest: *a peaceful and sheltered glade.* ▷ **HISTORY** origin unknown

gladiator *n* (in ancient Rome) a man trained to fight in arenas to provide entertainment. ▷ **HISTORY** Latin: swordsman ▶ **gladiatorial** *adj*

gladiolus (glad-ee-**oh**-luss) *n, pl* **-li** (-lie) a garden plant with brightly coloured funnel-shaped flowers. ▷ **HISTORY** Latin: a small sword

glad rags *pl n Informal* one's best clothes.

gladwrap *Austral, NZ & S African* ✧ *n* **1** *Trademark* thin polythene material for wrapping. ✧ *vb* **2** to wrap in gladwrap.

glamorous *adj* attractive or fascinating.

glamour *or US* **glamor** *n* exciting or alluring charm or beauty. ▷ **HISTORY** Scots variant of *grammar* (hence a spell, because occult practices were popularly associated with learning) ▶ **glamorize** *or* **-ise** *vb*

glance *n* **1** a quick look. ✧ *vb* **glancing, glanced 2** to look quickly at something. **3** to be deflected off an object at an oblique angle: *the ball glanced off a spectator.* ▷ **HISTORY** Middle English *glacen* to strike obliquely ▶ **glancing** *adj*

> **☑ WORD TIP**
> *Glance* is sometimes wrongly used where *glimpse* is meant: *he caught a glimpse* (not *glance*) *of her making her way through the crowd.*

gland *n* **1** an organ that synthesizes and secretes chemical substances for the body to use or eliminate. **2** a similar organ in plants. ▷ **HISTORY** Latin *glans* acorn

glandular *adj* of or affecting a gland or glands.

glandular fever *n* an acute infectious viral disease that causes fever, sore throat, and painful swollen lymph nodes.

glare *vb* **glaring, glared 1** to stare angrily. **2** (of light or colour) to be too bright. ✧ *n* **3** an angry stare. **4** a dazzling light or brilliance. **5 in the glare of publicity** receiving a lot of attention from the media or the public. ▷ **HISTORY** Middle English

glaring *adj* conspicuous or obvious: *glaring inconsistencies.* ▶ **glaringly** *adv*

glasnost *n* a policy of public frankness and accountability, developed in the USSR in the 1980s under Mikhail Gorbachov. ▷ **HISTORY** Russian: publicity, openness

glass *n* **1** a hard brittle transparent solid, consisting of metal silicates or similar compounds. **2** a drinking vessel made of glass. **3** the amount contained in a drinking glass: *a glass of wine.* **4** objects made of glass, such as drinking glasses and bowls. ▷ **HISTORY** Old English *glæs*

glass ceiling *n* a situation in which progress, esp. promotion, appears to be possible, but restrictions or discrimination create a barrier that prevents it.

glasses *pl n* a pair of lenses for correcting faulty vision, in a frame that rests on the nose and hooks behind the ears.

glasshouse *n Brit & NZ* same as **greenhouse**.

glassy *adj* **glassier, glassiest 1** smooth, clear, and shiny, like glass: *the glassy sea.* **2** expressionless: *that glassy look.*

Glaswegian (glaz-**weej**-an) *adj* **1** of Glasgow, a city in W Scotland. ✧ *n* **2** a person from Glasgow. **3** the Glasgow dialect.

glaucoma *n* an eye disease in which increased pressure in the eyeball causes gradual loss of sight. ▷ **HISTORY** Greek *glaukos* silvery, bluish-green

glaze *vb* **glazing, glazed 1** to fit or cover with glass. **2** to cover (a piece of pottery) with a protective shiny coating. **3** to cover (food) with beaten egg or milk before cooking, in order to produce a shiny coating. ✧ *n* **4** a protective shiny coating applied to a piece of pottery. **5** a shiny coating of beaten egg or milk applied to food. ▷ **HISTORY** Middle English *glasen* ▶ **glazed** *adj* ▶ **glazing** *n*

glazier *n* a person who fits windows or doors with glass.

GLB *Maths* greatest lower bound.

gleam *n* **1** a small beam or glow of light. **2** a brief or dim indication: *a gleam of anticipation in his eye.* ✧ *vb* **3** to shine. ▷ **HISTORY** Old English *glǣm* ▶ **gleaming** *adj*

glean *vb* **1** to gather (information) bit by bit. **2** to gather the useful remnants of (a crop) after harvesting. ▷ **HISTORY** Old French *glener* ▶ **gleaner** *n*

gleanings *pl n* pieces of information that have been gleaned.

glebe *n Brit & Austral* land granted to a member of the clergy as part of his or her benefice. ▷ **HISTORY** Latin *glaeba*

glee *n* great merriment or joy, esp. caused by the misfortune of another person. ▷ **HISTORY** Old English *glēo*

gleeful *adj* merry or joyful, esp. over someone else's mistake or misfortune. ▶ **gleefully** *adv*

glen *n* a deep narrow mountain valley. ▷ **HISTORY** Scottish Gaelic *gleann*

glengarry *n, pl* **-ries** a brimless Scottish cap with a crease down the crown. ▷ **HISTORY** after *Glengarry*, Scotland

glib *adj* **glibber, glibbest** fluent and easy, often in an insincere or deceptive way: *there were no glib or easy answers.* ▷ **HISTORY** probably from Middle Low German *glibberich* slippery ▶ **glibly** *adv* ▶ **glibness** *n*

glide *vb* **gliding, glided 1** to move easily and smoothly. **2** (of an aircraft) to land without engine power. **3** to fly a glider. **4** to float on currents of air. ▷ **HISTORY** Old English *glīdan*

glider *n* **1** an aircraft that does not use an engine, but flies by floating on air currents. **2** *Austral* another name for **flying phalanger**.

glide time *n NZ* same as **flexitime**.

gliding *n* the sport of flying in a glider.

glimmer *vb* **1** (of a light) to glow faintly or flickeringly. ✧ *n* **2** a faint indication: *a glimmer of hope.* **3** a glow or twinkle. ▷ **HISTORY** Middle English

glimpse *n* **1** a brief view: *a glimpse of a rare snow leopard.* **2** a vague indication: *glimpses of insecurity.* ✧ *vb* **glimpsing, glimpsed 3** to catch sight of momentarily. ▷ **HISTORY** Germanic

> ☑ **WORD TIP**
> *Glimpse* is sometimes wrongly used where *glance* is meant: *he gave a quick glance* (not *glimpse*) *at his watch.*

glint *vb* **1** to gleam brightly. ✧ *n* **2** a bright gleam. ▷ **HISTORY** probably from Old Norse

glissade *n* **1** a gliding step in ballet. **2** a controlled slide down a snow slope. ✧ *vb* **-sading, -saded 3** to perform a glissade. ▷ **HISTORY** French

glissando *n, pl* **-dos** *Music* a slide between two notes in which all intermediate notes are played. ▷ **HISTORY** mock Italian, from French *glisser* to slide

glisten *vb* (of a wet or glossy surface) to gleam by reflecting light: *sweat glistened above his eyes.* ▷ **HISTORY** Old English *glisnian*

glitch *n* a small problem that stops something from working properly. ▷ **HISTORY** Yiddish *glitsh* a slip

glitter *vb* **1** (of a surface) to reflect light in bright flashes. **2** (of light) to be reflected in bright flashes. **3** to be brilliant in a showy way: *she glitters socially.* ✧ *n* **4** a sparkling light. **5** superficial glamour: *the trappings and glitter of the European aristocracy.* **6** tiny pieces of shiny decorative material. **7** *Canad* ice formed from freezing rain. ▷ **HISTORY** Old Norse *glitra* ▶ **glittering** *adj* ▶ **glittery** *adj*

glitzy *adj* **glitzier, glitziest** *Slang* showily attractive. ▷ **HISTORY** probably from German *glitzern* to glitter

gloaming *n Scot poetic* twilight; dusk. ▷ **HISTORY** Old English *glōmung*

gloat *vb* to regard one's own good fortune or the misfortune of others with smug or malicious pleasure. ▷ **HISTORY** probably Scandinavian

glob *n Informal* a rounded mass of thick fluid. ▷ **HISTORY** probably from *globe*, influenced by *blob*

global *adj* **1** of or applying to the whole earth: *global environmental problems.* **2** of or applying to the whole of something: *a global total for local-authority revenue.* ▶ **globally** *adv*

global circulation *n Meteorol* the circulation of winds round the earth, which results in global weather patterns.

global warming *n* an increase in the overall temperature worldwide believed to be caused by the greenhouse effect.

globe *n* **1** a sphere on which a map of the world is drawn. **2 the globe** the earth. **3** a spherical object, such as a glass lamp shade or fishbowl. **4** *S African* an electric light bulb. ▷ **HISTORY** Latin *globus*

globetrotter *n* a habitual worldwide traveller. ▶ **globetrotting** *n, adj*

globular *adj* shaped like a globe or globule.

globule *n* a small round drop of liquid. ▷ **HISTORY** Latin *globulus*

globulin *n* a simple protein found in living tissue.

glockenspiel *n* a percussion instrument consisting of tuned metal plates played with a pair of small hammers. ▷ **HISTORY** German *Glocken* bells + *Spiel* play

glomerulus (glom-**err**-oo-luss) *n, pl* **-li** (-lye) *Anat* a knot of blood vessels in the kidney projecting into the end of a urine-secreting tubule.

gloom *n* **1** depression or melancholy: *all doom and gloom.* **2** partial or total darkness. ▷ **HISTORY** Middle English *gloumben* to look sullen

gloomy *adj* **gloomier, gloomiest 1** despairing or sad. **2** causing depression or gloom: *gloomy economic forecasts.* **3** dark or dismal. ▶ **gloomily** *adv*

glorify *vb* **-fies, -fying, -fied 1** to make (something) seem more important than it really is: *computers are just glorified adding machines.* **2** to praise: *few countries have glorified success in*

a b c d e f g h i j k l m n o p q r s t u v w x y z

A B C D E F G H I J K L M N O P Q R S T U V W X Y Z

business more than the United States. **3** to worship (God). ▶ **glorification** *n*

glorious *adj* **1** brilliantly beautiful: *in glorious colour.* **2** delightful or enjoyable: *the glorious summer weather.* **3** having or full of glory: *glorious successes.* ▶ **gloriously** *adv*

glory *n, pl* **-ries** **1** fame, praise, or honour: *tales of glory.* **2** splendour: *the glory of the tropical day.* **3** something worthy of praise: *the Lady Chapel is the great glory of Lichfield.* **4** adoration or worship: *the greater glory of God.* ✧ *vb* **-ries, -rying, -ried** **5** **glory in** to take great pleasure in: *the workers were glorying in their new-found freedom.* ▷ HISTORY Latin *gloria*

glory box *n Austral & NZ old-fashioned, informal* a box in which a young woman stores her trousseau.

glory hole *n* an untidy cupboard or storeroom.

gloss[1] *n* **1** a bright shine on a surface. **2** a superficially attractive appearance. **3** a paint with a shiny finish. **4** a cosmetic used to give a shiny appearance: *lip gloss.* ✧ *vb* **5** to paint with gloss. **6** **gloss over** to conceal (an error, failing, or awkward moment) by minimizing it: *don't try to gloss over bad news.* ▷ HISTORY probably Scandinavian

gloss[2] *n* **1** an explanatory comment added to the text of a book. ✧ *vb* **2** to add a gloss or glosses to. ▷ HISTORY Latin *glossa* unusual word requiring explanatory note

glossary *n, pl* **-ries** an alphabetical list of technical or specialist words in a book, with explanations. ▷ HISTORY Late Latin *glossarium; see* GLOSS[2]

glossy *adj* **glossier, glossiest** **1** smooth and shiny: *glossy black hair.* **2** superficially attractive or sophisticated: *his glossy Manhattan flat.* **3** (of a magazine) produced on expensive shiny paper.

glottal stop *n Phonetics* a speech sound produced by tightly closing and then opening the glottis.

glottis *n* the opening at the top of the windpipe, between the vocal cords. ▷ HISTORY Greek *glōtta* tongue

glove *n* **1** a shaped covering for the hand with individual sheaths for each finger and the thumb. **2** a protective hand covering worn in sports such as boxing. ▷ HISTORY Old English *glōfe*

glove compartment *n* a small storage area in the dashboard of a car.

gloved *adj* covered by a glove or gloves: *a gloved hand.*

glow *n* **1** light produced as a result of great heat. **2** a steady light without flames. **3** brightness of complexion. **4** a feeling of wellbeing or satisfaction. ✧ *vb* **5** to produce a steady light without flames. **6** to shine intensely. **7** to experience a feeling of wellbeing or satisfaction: *she glowed with pleasure.* **8** (of the complexion) to have a strong bright colour: *his pale face glowing at the recollection.* ▷ HISTORY Old English *glōwan*

glower (rhymes with **power**) *vb* **1** to stare angrily. ✧ *n* **2** an angry stare. ▷ HISTORY origin unknown

glow-worm *n* a European beetle, the females and larvae of which have organs producing a soft greenish light.

gloxinia *n* a plant with white, red, or purple bell-shaped flowers. ▷ HISTORY after Benjamin P. *Gloxin,* botanist

glucagon *n Biochem* a hormone that stimulates the release of glucose into the blood.

glucose *n* a white crystalline sugar found in plant and animal tissues. ▷ HISTORY Greek *gleukos* sweet wine

glue *n* **1** a substance used for sticking things together. ✧ *vb* **gluing** *or* **glueing, glued** **2** to join or stick together with glue. **3** **glued to** paying full attention to: *golf fans will be glued to their televisions today for the Open Championship.* ▷ HISTORY Late Latin *glus* ▶ **gluey** *adj*

glue ear *n* an accumulation of fluid in the middle ear of children, caused by infection and causing deafness.

glue-sniffing *n* the practice of inhaling glue fumes to produce intoxicating or hallucinatory effects. ▶ **glue-sniffer** *n*

glum *adj* **glummer, glummest** gloomy and quiet, usually because of a disappointment. ▷ HISTORY variant of *gloom* ▶ **glumly** *adv*

glut *n* **1** an excessive supply. ✧ *vb* **glutting, glutted** **2** to supply (a market) with a commodity in excess of the demand for it. **3** **glut oneself** to eat or drink more than one really needs. ▷ HISTORY probably from Old French *gloutir* to swallow

gluten (**gloo**-ten) *n* a sticky protein found in cereal grains, such as wheat. ▷ HISTORY Latin: glue

glutinous (**gloo**-tin-uss) *adj* gluelike in texture.

glutton *n* **1** someone who eats and drinks too much. **2** a person who has a great capacity for something: *a glutton for work.* ▷ HISTORY Latin *gluttire* to swallow ▶ **gluttonous** *adj*

gluttony *n* the practice of eating too much.

glycerine (**gliss**-ser-reen) *or* **glycerin** *n* a nontechnical name for **glycerol**. ▷ HISTORY Greek *glukeros* sweet

glycerol (**gliss**-ser-ol) *n* a colourless odourless syrupy liquid obtained from animal and vegetable fats, used as a solvent, antifreeze, and sweetener, and in explosives.

glycogen (**glike**-oh-jen) *n* a starchlike carbohydrate stored in the liver and muscles of humans and animals.

glycolysis (glike-**kol**-iss-iss) *n Biochem* the breakdown of glucose by enzymes, with the release of energy.

glycoside *n Biochem* a substance derived from monosaccharides by replacing the hydroxyl group by another group. ▶ **glycosidic** *adj*

gm gram.

GM **1** genetically modified. **2** *Brit* grant-maintained.

G-man *n, pl* **G-men** *US slang* an FBI agent.

GMO genetically modified organism.

GMT Greenwich Mean Time.

gnarled *adj* rough, twisted, and knobbly, usually through age.

gnash *vb* to grind (the teeth) together in pain or anger. ▷ **HISTORY** probably from Old Norse

gnat *n* a small biting two-winged insect. ▷ **HISTORY** Old English *gnætt*

gnaw *vb* **1** to bite or chew constantly so as to wear away bit by bit. **2 gnaw at** to cause constant distress or anxiety to: *uneasiness gnawed at his mind.* ▷ **HISTORY** Old English *gnagan* ▶ **gnawing** *adj*

gneiss *n* a coarse-grained layered metamorphic rock. ▷ **HISTORY** German *Gneis*

gnome *n* **1** an imaginary creature in fairy tales that looks like a little old man. **2** a small statue of a gnome in a garden. ▷ **HISTORY** French

gnomic (**no**-mik) *adj Literary* of or containing short clever sayings: *gnomic pronouncements.*

Gnosticism (**noss**-tiss-siz-zum) *n* a religious movement involving belief in intuitive spiritual knowledge. ▶ **Gnostic** *n, adj*

GNP gross national product.

gnu (**noo**) *n, pl* **gnus** *or* **gnu** a sturdy African antelope with an oxlike head. ▷ **HISTORY** Xhosa *nqu*

go *vb* **going, went, gone 1** to move or proceed to or from a place: *go forward.* **2** to be in regular attendance at (work, church, or a place of learning). **3** to lead to a particular place: *the path that goes right along the bank.* **4** to be kept in a particular place: *where does this go?* **5** to do or become as specified: *he went white; the gun went bang.* **6** to be or continue to be in a specified state: *to go to sleep.* **7** to operate or function: *the car wouldn't go.* **8** to follow a specified course; fare: *I'd hate the meeting to go badly.* **9** to be allotted to a particular purpose or recipient: *a third of the total budget goes on the army.* **10** to be sold: *the portrait went for a fortune to a telephone bidder.* **11** (of words or music) to be expressed or sung: *the song goes like this.* **12** to fail or break down: *my eyesight is going; he was on lap nineteen when the engine went.* **13** to die: *he went quickly at the end.* **14** to be spent or finished: *all tension and all hope had gone.* **15** to proceed up to or beyond certain limits: *I think this is going too far.* **16** to carry authority: *what Daddy says goes.* **17** to endure or last out: *they go for eight or ten hours without resting.* **18** *Not standard* to say: *then she goes, 'shut up'.* **19 anything goes** anything is acceptable. **20 be going to** to intend or be about to: *she was afraid of what was going to happen next.* **21 let go** to relax one's hold on; release. **22 let oneself go a** to act in an uninhibited manner. **b** to lose interest in one's appearance. **23 to go** remaining: *two days to go till the holidays.* ✧ *n, pl* **goes 24** an attempt: *he had a go at the furniture business.* **25** a verbal or physical attack: *he couldn't resist having another go at me.* **26** a turn to do something in a game: *'Your go now!' I shouted.* **27** *Informal* the quality of being active and energetic: *a grand old man, full of go and determination.* **28 from the word go** *Informal* from the very beginning. **29 make a go of** *Informal* to be successful in (a business venture or a relationship). **30 on the go** *Informal* active and energetic. ▷ **HISTORY** Old English *gān*

goad *vb* **1** to provoke (someone) to take some kind of action, usually in anger. ✧ *n* **2** something that provokes someone to take some kind of action. **3** a sharp pointed stick for driving cattle. ▷ **HISTORY** Old English *gād*

go-ahead *n* **1 give the go-ahead** *Informal* to give permission to proceed. ✧ *adj* **2** enterprising or ambitious: *prosperous and go-ahead republics.*

goal *n* **1** *Sport* the space into which players try to propel the ball or puck to score. **2** *Sport* **a** a successful attempt at scoring. **b** the score so made. **3** an aim or purpose: *the goal is to get homeless people on their feet.* ▷ **HISTORY** origin unknown ▶ **goalless** *adj*

goalie *n Informal* a goalkeeper.

goalkeeper *n Sport* a player whose duty is to prevent the ball or puck from entering the goal.

goal line *n Sport* the line marking each end of the pitch, on which the goals stand.

goalpost *n* **1** either of two uprights supporting the crossbar of a goal. **2 move the goalposts** to change the aims of an activity to ensure the desired results.

goanna *n* a large Australian lizard. ▷ **HISTORY** from IGUANA

goat *n* **1** an agile cud-chewing mammal with hollow horns. **2 act the goat** *Informal* to behave in a silly manner. **3 get someone's goat** *Slang* to annoy someone. ▷ **HISTORY** Old English *gāt*

goatee *n* a small pointed beard that does not cover the cheeks.

goatherd *n* a person who looks after a herd of goats.

goatsucker *n US & Canad* same as **nightjar**.

go-away bird *n S African* a grey lourie. ▷ **HISTORY** imitative

gob¹ *n* a thick mass of a soft substance. ▷ **HISTORY** Old French *gobe* lump

gob² *n Brit, Austral & NZ slang* the mouth. ▷ **HISTORY** origin unknown

go back on *vb* to fail to fulfil (a promise): *he went back on his promise not to raise taxes.*

gobbet *n* a chunk or lump. ▷ **HISTORY** Old French *gobet*

gobble¹ *vb* **-bling, -bled** to eat quickly and greedily. ▷ **HISTORY** probably from GOB¹

gobble² *n* **1** the loud rapid gurgling sound made by a turkey. ✧ *vb* **-bling, -bled 2** to make this sound. ▷ **HISTORY** probably imitative

gobbledegook *or* **gobbledygook** *n* pretentious or unintelligible language. ▷ **HISTORY** whimsical formation from GOBBLE²

gobbler *n Informal* a turkey.

go-between *n* a person who acts as a messenger between two people or groups.

goblet *n* a drinking vessel with a base and stem but without handles. ▷ **HISTORY** Old French *gobelet* a little cup

A B C D E F G H I J K L M N O P Q R S T U V W X Y Z

goblin *n* a small grotesque creature in fairy tales that causes trouble for people. ▷ **HISTORY** Old French

gobsmacked *adj Brit, Austral & NZ slang* astonished and astounded.

goby *n, pl* **-by** *or* **-bies** a small spiny-finned fish. ▷ **HISTORY** Latin *gobius* gudgeon

go-cart *n* same as **go-kart**.

god *n* **1** a supernatural being, worshipped as the controller of the universe or some aspect of life or as the personification of some force. **2** an image of such a being. **3** a person or thing to which excessive attention is given: *the All Blacks are gods in New Zealand.* **4 the gods** the top balcony in a theatre. ▷ **HISTORY** Old English ▶ **goddess** *fem n*

God *n* **1** the sole Supreme Being, Creator and ruler of all, in religions such as Christianity, Judaism, and Islam. ✧ *interj* **2** an oath or exclamation of surprise or annoyance.

godchild *n, pl* **-children** a person who is sponsored by godparents at baptism.

goddaughter *n* a female godchild.

godetia *n* a garden plant with showy flowers. ▷ **HISTORY** after C. H. *Godet,* botanist

godfather *n* **1** a male godparent. **2** the head of a Mafia family or other criminal ring.

godforsaken *adj* desolate or dreary: *some godforsaken village in the Himalayas.*

Godhead *n* the nature and condition of being God.

godly *adj* **-lier, -liest** deeply religious. ▶ **godliness** *n*

godmother *n* a female godparent.

godparent *n* a person who promises at a person's baptism to look after his or her religious upbringing.

godsend *n* a person or thing that comes unexpectedly but is very welcome.

godson *n* a male godchild.

goer *n* a person who attends something regularly: *a church goer.*

go-faster stripe *n Informal* a decorative line suggestive of high speed on the side of a car.

go for *vb* **1** to choose: *any politician will go for the soft option.* **2** *Informal* to like very much. **3** to attack. **4** to apply equally to: *the same might go for the other woman.*

go-getter *n Informal* an ambitious enterprising person. ▶ **go-getting** *adj*

gogga (**hohh**-a) *n S African informal* an insect. ▷ **HISTORY** Nama (language of southern Africa) *xo xo*

goggle *vb* **-gling, -gled** to stare with wide-open eyes. ✧ See also **goggles**. ▷ **HISTORY** Middle English *gogelen* to look aside ▶ **goggle-eyed** *adj*

goggles *pl n* close-fitting protective spectacles.

Goidelic *n* **1** the group of Celtic languages, consisting of Irish Gaelic, Scottish Gaelic, and Manx. ✧ *adj* **2** of this group of languages. ▷ **HISTORY** Old Irish *Goidel* Celt

going *n* **1** the condition of the ground with regard to walking or riding: *the going for the cross-country is perfect.* **2** *Informal* speed or progress: *not bad going for a lad of 58.* ✧ *adj* **3** thriving: *the racecourse was a going concern.* **4** current or accepted: *this is the going rate for graduates.*

going-over *n, pl* **goings-over** *Informal* **1** a thorough examination or investigation. **2** a physical beating.

goings-on *pl n Informal* mysterious or shady activities.

goitre *or US* **goiter** (**goy**-ter) *n Pathol* a swelling of the thyroid gland in the neck. ▷ **HISTORY** French

go-kart *n* a small four-wheeled motor vehicle, used for racing.

gold *n* **1** a bright yellow precious metal, used as a monetary standard and in jewellery and plating. Symbol: Au. **2** jewellery or coins made of this metal. **3** short for **gold medal**. ✧ *adj* **4** deep yellow. ▷ **HISTORY** Old English

goldcrest *n* a small bird with a bright yellow-and-black crown.

gold-digger *n Informal* a woman who marries or has a relationship with a man for his money.

golden *adj* **1** made of gold: *golden bangles.* **2** of the colour of gold: *golden corn.* **3** *Informal* very successful or destined for success: *the golden girl of British athletics.* **4** excellent or valuable: *a golden opportunity for peace.* **5** (of an anniversary) the fiftieth: *golden wedding; Golden Jubilee.*

golden age *n* the most flourishing and outstanding period in the history of an art or nation: *the golden age of Dixieland jazz.*

golden eagle *n* a large mountain eagle of the N hemisphere with golden-brown feathers.

golden handshake *n Informal* money given to an employee either on retirement or to compensate for loss of employment.

golden hour *n* the first hour after a serious accident, when medical treatment for the victim is crucial.

golden mean *n* the middle course between extremes.

golden retriever *n* a retriever with silky wavy gold-coloured hair.

goldenrod *n* a tall plant with spikes of small yellow flowers.

golden rule *n* an important principle: *the golden rule is to start with the least difficult problems.*

golden wattle *n* an Australian plant with yellow flowers that yields a useful gum and bark.

goldfinch *n* a European finch the adult of which has yellow-and-black wings.

goldfish *n, pl* **-fish** *or* **-fishes** a gold or orange-red freshwater fish, often kept as a pet.

gold foil *n* thin gold sheet that is thicker than gold leaf.

gold leaf *n* very thin gold sheet made by rolling or hammering gold and used for gilding.

gold medal *n* a medal made of gold, awarded to the winner of a race or competition.

gold rush *n* a large-scale migration of people to a territory where gold has been found.

goldsmith *n* a person who makes gold jewellery and other articles.

gold standard *n* a monetary system in which the basic currency unit equals a specified weight of gold.

golf *n* **1** a game in which a ball is struck with clubs into a series of eighteen holes in a grassy course. ✧ *vb* **2** to play golf. ▷ **HISTORY** origin unknown
▶ **golfer** *n*

Golgi body (**goll**-jee) *n Biol* a membranous complex of vesicles, vacuoles, and flattened sacs in the cytoplasm of most cells. ▷ **HISTORY** named after Camillo *Golgi*, Italian neurologist

golliwog *n* a soft doll with a black face, usually made of cloth. ▷ **HISTORY** from a doll in a series of American children's books

golly *interj* an exclamation of mild surprise. ▷ **HISTORY** originally a euphemism for *God*

gonad *n* an organ in which reproductive cells are produced, such as a testis or ovary. ▷ **HISTORY** Greek *gonos* seed

gondola *n* **1** a long narrow flat-bottomed boat with a high ornamented stem, traditionally used on the canals of Venice. **2** a moving cabin suspended from a cable, used as a ski lift. ▷ **HISTORY** Italian

gondolier *n* a person who propels a gondola.

Gondwanaland *or* **Gondwana** *n Geol* one of the two ancient supercontinents comprising chiefly what are now Africa, South America, Australia, Antarctica, and the Indian subcontinent. ▷ **HISTORY** from *Gondwana,* region in central north India, where the rock series was orig. found

gone *vb* **1** the past participle of **go**. ✧ *adj* **2** no longer present or no longer in existence.

goner *n Slang* a person who is about to die or who is beyond help.

gong *n* **1** a flat circular metal disc that is hit with a hammer to give out a loud sound. **2** *Brit slang* a medal. ▷ **HISTORY** Malay

gonorrhoea *or esp US* **gonorrhea** (gon-or-**ree**-a) *n* a sexually transmitted disease that causes inflammation and a discharge from the genital organs. ▷ **HISTORY** Greek *gonos* semen + *rhoia* flux

good *adj* **better, best 1** having admirable, pleasing, or superior qualities: *a good listener.* **2** morally excellent; virtuous: *a good person.* **3** beneficial: *exercise is good for the heart.* **4** kindly or generous: *he is so good to us.* **5** competent or talented: *she's good at physics.* **6** obedient or well-behaved: *a good boy.* **7** reliable or recommended: *a good make.* **8** complete or thorough: *she went to have a good look round.* **9** appropriate or opportune: *a good time to clear the air.* **10** satisfying or enjoyable: *a good holiday.* **11** newest or of the best quality: *keep the good dishes for guests.* **12** fairly large, extensive, or long: *they contain a good amount of protein.* **13 as good as** virtually or practically: *the war was as good as over.* ✧ *n* **14** advantage or benefit: *what is the good of it all?* **15** positive moral qualities; virtue. **16 for good** for ever; permanently: *his political career was over for good.* ✧ See also **goods**. ▷ **HISTORY** Old English *gōd*

goodbye *interj* **1** an expression used on parting. ✧ *n* **2** the act of saying goodbye: *he said his goodbyes.* ▷ **HISTORY** from *God be with ye*

good day *interj* an expression of greeting or farewell used during the day.

good-for-nothing *n* **1** an irresponsible or worthless person. ✧ *adj* **2** irresponsible or worthless.

Good Friday *n Christianity* the Friday before Easter, observed as a commemoration of the Crucifixion of Jesus Christ.

goodies *pl n* any things considered particularly desirable.

goodly *adj* **-lier, -liest** fairly large: *a goodly number of children.*

good-natured *adj* tolerant and kindly.

goodness *n* **1** the quality of being good. ✧ *interj* **2** an exclamation of surprise.

goods *pl n* **1** articles produced to be sold: *consumer goods.* **2** movable personal property: *houses and goods are insured from fire.* **3 deliver the goods** *Informal* to do what is expected or required. **4 have the goods on someone** *US & Canad slang* to know something incriminating about someone.

Good Samaritan *n* a person who helps someone in difficulty or distress. ▷ **HISTORY** from a parable in Luke 10: 30–37

goodwill *n* **1** kindly feelings towards other people. **2** the popularity and good reputation of a well-established business, considered as a valuable asset.

goody *interj* **1** a child's exclamation of pleasure. ✧ *n, pl* **goodies 2** *Informal* the hero in a film or book. **3** See **goodies**.

goody-goody *Informal* ✧ *n, pl* **-goodies 1** a person who behaves well in order to please people in authority. ✧ *adj* **2** behaving well in order to please people in authority.

gooey *adj* **gooier, gooiest** *Informal* **1** sticky, soft, and often sweet. **2** sentimental: *one knows the whole gooey performance is an act.*

goof *vb Informal* **1** to bungle or botch. **2 goof off** *US & Canad* to spend time in a lazy or foolish way: *he's goofing off on the Costa del Sol.* ▷ **HISTORY** probably from dialect *goff* simpleton

go off *vb* **1** to stop functioning: *the heating went off.* **2** to make a sudden loud noise: *a bomb went off.* **3** to occur as specified: *the actual launch went off perfectly.* **4** *Informal* (of food) to become stale or rotten. **5** *Brit informal* to stop liking.

goofy *adj* **goofier, goofiest** *Informal* silly or ridiculous.

googly *n, pl* **-lies** *Cricket* a ball bowled like a leg break but spinning from off to leg on pitching. ▷ **HISTORY** Australian English

goon *n* **1** a stupid person. **2** *US informal* a hired thug. ▷ **HISTORY** dialect *gooney* fool; influenced by US cartoon character Alice the *goon*

go on *vb* **1** to continue or proceed. **2** to take place: *there's a war going on.* **3** to talk at length and annoyingly.

goosander *n* a duck of Europe and North America with a dark head and white body.

a b c d e f g h i j k l m n o p q r s t u v w x y z

▷ **HISTORY** probably from GOOSE[1] + Old Norse *önd* (genitive *andar*) duck

goose[1] *n, pl* **geese 1** a fairly large web-footed long-necked migratory bird. **2** the female of such a bird. **3** the flesh of the goose used for food. **4** *Informal* a silly person. ▷ **HISTORY** Old English *gōs*

goose[2] *vb* **goosing, goosed** *Slang* to prod (someone) playfully in the bottom. ▷ **HISTORY** from the jabbing of a goose's bill

gooseberry *n, pl* **-ries 1** a small edible green berry with tiny hairs on the skin. **2 play gooseberry** *Brit & NZ informal* to be an unwanted single person accompanying a couple.

goose flesh *n* the bumpy condition of the skin due to cold or fear, in which the muscles at the base of the hair follicles contract, making the hair bristle. Also: **goose pimples**

go out *vb* **1** to go to entertainments or social functions. **2 go out with** to have a romantic relationship with. **3** to be extinguished or cease to function: *the lights went out*. **4** (of information) to be released publicly. **5** (of a broadcast) to be transmitted.

go over *vb* **1** to examine very carefully. **2 go over to** to change to: *he went over to the Free Orthodox Church*.

gopher (**go**-fer) *n* an American burrowing rodent with wide cheek pouches. ▷ **HISTORY** origin unknown

gore[1] *n* blood shed from a wound. ▷ **HISTORY** Old English *gor* dirt

gore[2] *vb* **goring, gored** (of an animal) to pierce or stab (a person or another animal) with a horn or tusk. ▷ **HISTORY** probably from Old English *gār* spear

gore[3] *n* a tapering piece of material in a garment, sail, or umbrella. ▷ **HISTORY** Old English *gāra*

gorge *n* **1** a deep narrow steep-sided valley. **2 one's gorge rises** one feels disgusted or nauseated. ✧ *vb* **gorging, gorged 3** Also: **gorge oneself** to eat greedily. ▷ **HISTORY** Latin *gurges* whirlpool

gorgeous *adj* **1** strikingly beautiful or attractive. **2** *Informal* warm, sunny, and very pleasant: *a gorgeous day*. ▷ **HISTORY** Old French *gorgias* elegant ▸ **gorgeously** *adv*

Gorgon *n* **1** *Greek myth* one of three monstrous sisters who had live snakes for hair, and were so horrifying that anyone who looked at them was turned to stone. **2** *Informal* a terrifying or repulsive woman. ▷ **HISTORY** Greek *gorgos* terrible

Gorgonzola *n* a sharp-flavoured blue-veined Italian cheese. ▷ **HISTORY** after *Gorgonzola,* Italian town where it originated

gorilla *n* a very large W African ape with coarse black hair.

> **WORD HISTORY**
>
> 'Gorilla' comes from Greek *Gorillai*, the name the ancient Greeks gave to a supposed African tribe with hairy bodies.

gormless *adj Brit & NZ informal* stupid or dull-witted. ▷ **HISTORY** obsolete *gaumless*

gorse *n* an evergreen shrub with small yellow flowers and prickles, which grows wild in the countryside. ▷ **HISTORY** Old English *gors*

gory *adj* **gorier, goriest 1** horrific or bloodthirsty: *the gory details*. **2** bloody: *gory remains*.

gosh *interj* an exclamation of mild surprise or wonder. ▷ **HISTORY** euphemistic for *God*

goshawk *n* a large swift short-winged hawk. ▷ **HISTORY** Old English *gōshafoc*

gosling *n* a young goose. ▷ **HISTORY** Old Norse *gæslingr*

go-slow *n Brit & NZ* a deliberate slowing of the rate of production by workers as a tactic in industrial conflict.

gospel *n* **1 a** the teachings of Jesus Christ. **b** the story of Christ's life and teachings. **2** a doctrine held to be of great importance: *the gospel of self-help*. **3** Also called: **gospel truth** unquestionable truth: *gross inaccuracies which are sometimes taken as gospel*. ✧ *adj* **4** denoting a kind of religious music originating in the churches of the Black people in the Southern US. ▷ **HISTORY** Old English *gōdspell,* from *gōd* good + *spell* message

Gospel *n Christianity* any of the first four books of the New Testament, namely Matthew, Mark, Luke, and John, which tell the story of Jesus Christ.

gossamer *n* **1** a very fine fabric. **2** a filmy cobweb often seen on foliage or floating in the air. ▷ **HISTORY** probably Middle English *gos* goose + *somer* summer; referring to *St Martin's summer,* a period in November when goose was eaten and cobwebs abound

gossip *n* **1** idle talk, usually about other people's private lives, esp. of a disapproving or malicious nature: *office gossip*. **2** an informal conversation, esp. about other people's private lives: *to have a gossip and a giggle*. **3** a person who habitually talks about other people, usually maliciously. ✧ *vb* **4** to talk idly or maliciously, esp. about other people's private lives. ▷ **HISTORY** Old English *godsibb* godparent, applied to a woman's female friends at the birth of a child ▸ **gossipy** *adj*

got *vb* **1** the past of **get**. **2 have got** to possess. **3 have got to** must: *you have got to be prepared to work hard*.

Gothic *adj* **1** of a style of architecture used in W Europe from the 12th to the 16th centuries, characterized by pointed arches, ribbed vaults, and flying buttresses. **2** of a literary style featuring stories of gloom, horror, and the supernatural, popular in the late 18th century. **3** of or in a heavy ornate script typeface. ✧ *n* **4** Gothic architecture or art. ▷ **HISTORY** Greek *Gothoi*

go through *vb* **1** to experience (a difficult time or process). **2** to name or describe: *the president went through a list of government ministers*. **3** to qualify for the next stage of a competition: *Belgium, Spain and Uruguay all went through from Group E*. **4** to be approved: *the bill went through parliament*. **5 go through with** to bring to a successful conclusion, often by persistence.

gotten *vb Chiefly US* a past participle of **get**.

gouache *n* opaque watercolour paint bound with glue. ▷ **HISTORY** French

Gouda *n* a round mild-flavoured Dutch cheese.

gouge (**gowj**) *vb* **gouging, gouged 1** to scoop or force (something) out of its position. **2** to cut (a hole or groove) in something with a pointed object. ✧ *n* **3** a mark or groove made by gouging.
▷ **HISTORY** French

goulash (**goo**-lash) *n* a rich stew seasoned with paprika, originating in Hungary.
▷ **HISTORY** Hungarian *gulyás hus* herdsman's meat

gourd (**goord**) *n* **1** a large hard-shelled fruit similar to a cucumber or marrow. **2** a container made from a dried gourd shell. ▷ **HISTORY** Old French *gourde*

gourmand (**goor**-mand) *n* a person devoted to eating and drinking, usually to excess.
▷ **HISTORY** Old French *gourmant*

gourmet (**goor**-may) *n* an expert on good food and drink. ▷ **HISTORY** French

gout (**gowt**) *n* a disease that causes painful inflammation of certain joints, for example of the big toe. ▷ **HISTORY** Latin *gutta* a drop ▶ **gouty** *adj*

govern *vb* **1** to direct and control the policy and affairs of (a country or an organization). **2** to control or determine: *the international organizations governing athletics and rugby.* ▷ **HISTORY** Latin *gubernare* to steer ▶ **governable** *adj*

governance *n* government, control, or authority.

governess *n* a woman employed in a private household to teach the children.

government *n* **1** the executive policy-making body of a country or state. **2** the state and its administration: *the assembled heads of state and government.* **3** the system by which a country or state is ruled: *the old hard-line government.*
▶ **governmental** *adj*

governor *n* **1** the chief political administrator of a region, such as a US state or a colony. *RELATED ADJECTIVE* ✦ **gubernatorial 2** *Brit* the senior administrator of a school, prison, or other institution. **3** *Brit informal* one's employer or father.
▶ **governorship** *n*

governor general *n, pl* **governors general** *or* **governor generals** *Law* the chief representative of the British government in a Commonwealth country.

gown *n* **1** a woman's long formal dress. **2** a surgeon's overall. **3** a loose wide official robe worn by clergymen, judges, lawyers, and academics.
▷ **HISTORY** Late Latin *gunna* garment made of fur

goy *n, pl* **goyim** *or* **goys** a Jewish word for a **Gentile**. ▷ **HISTORY** Yiddish

GP general practitioner.

GPO (in Britain) general post office.

GPS Global Positioning System: a satellite-based navigation system.

Graafian follicle *n Anat* a cavity in the ovary that contains a developing egg cell. ▷ **HISTORY** after R. de *Graaf,* anatomist

grab *vb* **grabbing, grabbed 1** to seize hold of. **2** to take (food, drink, or rest) hurriedly. **3** to take (an opportunity) eagerly. **4** to seize illegally or unscrupulously: *land grabbing.* **5** *Informal* to interest or impress. ✧ *n* **6** the act of grabbing.
▷ **HISTORY** probably from Middle Dutch *grabben*

grab bag *n* **1** a collection of miscellaneous things. **2** *US, Canad, & Austral* a bag from which gifts are drawn at random.

grace *n* **1** elegance and beauty of movement, form, or expression. **2** a pleasing or charming quality: *architecture with few redeeming graces.* **3** courtesy or decency: *at least she had the grace to laugh.* **4** a delay granted for the completion of a task or payment of a debt: *another year's grace.* **5** *Christian theol* the free and unmerited favour of God shown towards humankind. **6** a short prayer of thanks for a meal. **7 airs and graces** an affected manner. **8 with bad grace** unwillingly or grudgingly: *independence was granted with bad grace.* **9 with good grace** willingly or ungrudgingly: *to accept with good grace.* ✧ *vb* **gracing, graced 10** to honour or favour: *graced by the presence of Henry Fonda.* **11** to decorate or make more attractive: *bedsit walls graced by Che Guevara and James Dean.* ▷ **HISTORY** Latin *gratia*

Grace *n* **Your, His** *or* **Her Grace** a title used to address or refer to a duke, duchess, or archbishop.

graceful *adj* having beauty of movement, style, or form. ▶ **gracefully** *adv* ▶ **gracefulness** *n*

graceless *adj* **1** lacking elegance. **2** lacking manners.

grace note *n Music* a note that ornaments a melody.

Graces *pl n Greek myth* the three sister goddesses of charm and beauty.

gracious *adj* **1** showing kindness and courtesy. **2** characterized by elegance, ease, and indulgence: *gracious living.* ✧ *interj* **3** an expression of mild surprise or wonder. ▶ **graciously** *adv*
▶ **graciousness** *n*

gradation *n* **1** a series of systematic stages; gradual progression. **2** a stage in such a series or progression.

grade *n* **1** a place on a scale of quality, rank, or size. **2** a mark or rating indicating a student's level of achievement. **3** a rank or level of importance in a company or organization. **4** *US, Canad, Austral & S African* a class or year in a school. **5 make the grade** *Informal* to be successful by reaching a required standard. ✧ *vb* **grading, graded 6** to arrange according to quality or rank: *passes are graded from A down to E.* **7** to give a grade to: *senior secretaries will need shorthand and be graded accordingly.* ▷ **HISTORY** Latin *gradus* step

gradient *n* **1** Also (esp. US): **grade** a sloping part of a railway, road, or path. **2** Also (esp. US): **grade** a measure of the steepness of such a slope. **3** a measure of the change in something, such as the angle of a curve, over a specified distance.
▷ **HISTORY** Latin *gradiens* stepping

gradual *adj* occurring, developing, or moving in small stages: *a gradual handover of power.*
▷ **HISTORY** Latin *gradus* a step ▶ **gradually** *adv*

gradualism *n* the policy of changing something gradually. ▶ **gradualist** *adj*

graduate *n* **1** a person who holds a university or college degree. **2** *US & Canad* a student who has completed a course of studies at a high school and received a diploma. **3** same as **postgraduate**. ✧ *vb* **-ating, -ated 4** to receive a degree or diploma. **5** to change by degrees: *the winds graduate from tropical storms to cyclones.* **6** to mark (a measuring flask or instrument) with units of measurement. ▷ **HISTORY** Latin *gradus* a step

graduation *n* **1** the act of graduating from university or college. **2** *US & Canad* the act of graduating from high school. **3** the ceremony at which degrees and diplomas are given to graduating students. **4** a mark indicating measure on an instrument or container.

Graeco-Roman *or esp US* **Greco-Roman** (greek-oh-**rome**-an) *adj* of, or showing the influence of, both Greek and Roman cultures.

graffiti (graf-**fee**-tee) *n* drawings or words scribbled or sprayed on walls or posters. ▷ **HISTORY** Italian: little scratches

graft[1] *n* **1** *Surgery* a piece of tissue transplanted to an area of the body in need of the tissue. **2** a small piece of tissue from one plant that is joined to another plant so that they grow together as one. ✧ *vb* **3** to transplant (tissue) to an area of the body in need of the tissue. **4** to join (part of one plant) onto another plant so that they grow together as one. **5** to attach or incorporate: *to graft Japanese production methods onto the American talent for innovation.* ▷ **HISTORY** Greek *graphein* to write

graft[2] *n* **1** *Brit informal* hard work. **2** the practice of obtaining money by taking advantage of one's position. ✧ *vb* **3** *Informal* to work hard. ▷ **HISTORY** origin unknown

grain *n* **1** the small hard seedlike fruit of a cereal plant. **2** a mass of such fruits gathered for food. **3** cereal plants in general. **4** a small hard particle: *a grain of salt.* **5** a very small amount: *a grain of compassion.* **6 a** the arrangement of the fibres, layers, or particles in wood, leather, or stone. **b** the pattern or texture resulting from this. **7 go against the grain** to be contrary to one's natural inclinations. ▷ **HISTORY** Latin *granum* ▶ **grainy** *adj*

gram *or* **gramme** *n* a metric unit of weight equal to one thousandth of a kilogram. ▷ **HISTORY** Greek *gramma* small weight

graminivorous *adj* (of an animal) grass-eating. ▷ **HISTORY** Latin *gramen* grass + *vorare* to swallow

grammar *n* **1** the rules of a language, that show how sentences are formed, or how words area inflected. **2** the way in which grammar is used: *the teacher found errors of spelling and grammar.* **3** a book on the rules of grammar. ▷ **HISTORY** Greek *gramma* letter

grammarian *n* a person who studies or writes about grammar for a living.

grammar school *n* **1** *Brit* (esp. formerly) a secondary school for children of high academic ability. **2** *US* same as **elementary school**. **3** *Austral* a private school, usually one controlled by a church.

grammatical *adj* **1** of grammar. **2** (of a sentence) following the rules of grammar. ▶ **grammatically** *adv*

gramme *n* same as **gram**.

gramophone *n* an old-fashioned type of record player. ▷ **HISTORY** inversion of *phonogram*

grampus *n, pl* **-puses** a dolphin-like mammal with a blunt snout. ▷ **HISTORY** Old French *gras* fat + *pois* fish

gran *n Brit, Austral & NZ informal* a grandmother.

grana *n Biol* plural of **granum**.

granary *n, pl* **-ries 1** a building for storing threshed grain. **2** a region that produces a large amount of grain. ▷ **HISTORY** Latin *granarium*

grand *adj* **1** large or impressive in size or appearance; magnificent: *the grand hall.* **2** ambitious or important: *grand themes.* **3** dignified or haughty. **4** *Informal* excellent or wonderful. **5** comprehensive or complete: *the grand total.* ✧ *n* **6** (*pl* **grand**) *Slang* a thousand pounds or dollars. **7** short for **grand piano**. ▷ **HISTORY** Latin *grandis* ▶ **grandly** *adv*

grand apartheid *n History* (formerly, in South Africa) a form of apartheid that involved wide-ranging racial segregation and the creation of black homelands.

grandchild *n, pl* **-children** a son or daughter of one's son or daughter.

granddaughter *n* a daughter of one's son or daughter.

grand duke *n* a prince or nobleman who rules a territory, state, or principality. ▶ **grand duchess** *fem n* ▶ **grand duchy** *n*

grandee *n* **1** a high-ranking Spanish nobleman. **2** a person who has a high rank or position: *the Party's grandees.* ▷ **HISTORY** Spanish *grande*

grandeur *n* **1** personal greatness, dignity, or nobility: *delusions of grandeur.* **2** magnificence or splendour: *cathedral-like grandeur.*

grandfather *n* the father of one's father or mother.

grandfather clock *n* an old-fashioned clock in a tall wooden case that stands on the floor.

grandiloquent *adj* using pompous or unnecessarily complicated language. ▷ **HISTORY** Latin *grandiloquus* ▶ **grandiloquence** *n*

grandiose *adj* impressive, or meant to impress: *grandiose plans for constructing a new stadium.* ▷ **HISTORY** French

grand jury *n Law chiefly US* a jury that investigates accusations of crime to decide whether the evidence is adequate to bring a prosecution.

grand mal *n* a form of epilepsy in which there is loss of consciousness and violent convulsions. ▷ **HISTORY** French: great illness

grandmother *n* the mother of one's father or mother.

grand opera *n* an opera that has a serious plot and no spoken dialogue.

grandparent *n* the father or mother of one's father or mother.

grand piano *n* a large piano in which the strings are arranged horizontally.

Grand Prix (gron **pree**) *n* **1** an international formula motor race. **2** a very important international competitive event in other sports, such as athletics. ▷ **HISTORY** French: great prize

grand slam *n* **1** the achievement of winning all the games or major tournaments in a sport in one season. **2** See **slam²**.

grandson *n* a son of one's son or daughter.

grandstand *n* the main block of seats giving the best view at a sports ground.

grand tour *n* **1** (formerly) an extended tour of continental Europe. **2** *Informal* a tour of inspection: *a grand tour of the house.*

grange *n Brit* a farmhouse or country house with its farm buildings. ▷ **HISTORY** Anglo-French *graunge*

granite (**gran**-nit) *n* a very hard rock consisting of quartz and feldspars that is widely used for building. ▷ **HISTORY** Italian *granito* grained

granivorous *adj* (of an animal) grain-eating. ▷ **HISTORY** Latin *granum* grain + *vorare* to swallow

granny *or* **grannie** *n, pl* **-nies** *Informal* a grandmother.

granny flat *n* a flat in or joined on to a house, suitable for an elderly relative to live in.

grant *vb* **1** to give (a sum of money or a right) formally: *to grant a thirty-eight per cent pay rise; only the President can grant a pardon.* **2** to consent to perform or fulfil: *granting the men's request for sanctuary.* **3** to admit that (something) is true: *I grant that her claims must be true.* **4 take for granted a** to accept that something is true without requiring proof. **b** to take advantage of (someone or something) without showing appreciation. ✧ *n* **5** a sum of money provided by a government or public fund to a person or organization for a specific purpose: *student grants.* ▷ **HISTORY** Old French *graunter*

Granth (**grunt**) *n* the sacred scripture of the Sikhs. ▷ **HISTORY** Hindi

granular *adj* of, like, or containing granules: *granular materials such as powders.*

granulated *adj* (of sugar) in the form of coarse grains.

granule *n* a small grain of something: *gravy granules.* ▷ **HISTORY** Late Latin *granulum* a small grain

granum *n, pl* **grana** *Biol* a stack of thin layers in a chloroplast that contains chlorophyll.

grape *n* a small round sweet juicy fruit with a purple or green skin, which can be eaten raw, dried to make raisins, currants, or sultanas, or used to make wine. ▷ **HISTORY** Old French *grape* bunch of grapes

grapefruit *n, pl* **-fruit** *or* **-fruits** a large round yellow juicy citrus fruit with a slightly bitter taste.

grapeshot *n* ammunition for cannons consisting of a cluster of iron balls that scatter after firing.

grapevine *n* **1** a vine grown for its grapes. **2** *Informal* an unofficial means of passing on information from person to person: *he'd doubtless heard rumours on the grapevine.*

graph *n* a diagram showing the relation between certain sets of numbers or quantities by means of a series of dots or lines plotted with reference to a set of axes. ▷ **HISTORY** short for *graphic formula*

-graph *n combining form* **1** an instrument that writes or records: *tachograph.* **2** a writing or record: *autograph.* ▷ **HISTORY** Greek *graphein* to write
▶ **-graphic** *or* **-graphical** *adj combining form*
▶ **-graphically** *adv combining form*

graphic *adj* **1** vividly described: *a graphic account of her three days in captivity.* **2** of the graphic arts: *graphic design.* **3** Also: **graphical** *Maths* of or using a graph: *a graphic presentation.* ✧ *n* **4** *Computing* a diagram or picture produced on a computer screen. ▷ **HISTORY** Greek *graphikos* ▶ **graphically** *adv*

graphic arts *pl n* the visual arts based on drawing or the use of line.

graphics *n* **1** the art of drawing in accordance with mathematical rules. ✧ *pl n* **2** the illustrations in a magazine or book, or in a television or film production. **3** *Computers* information displayed in the form of diagrams or graphs.

graphite *n* a soft black form of carbon used in pencils, as a lubricant, and in some nuclear reactors. ▷ **HISTORY** German *Graphit*

graphology *n* the study of handwriting, usually to analyse the writer's character. ▶ **graphologist** *n*

graph paper *n* paper printed with a design of small squares for drawing graphs or diagrams on.

-graphy *n combining form* indicating: **1** a form of writing or representing things: *calligraphy; photography.* **2** an art or descriptive science: *choreography; topography.* ▷ **HISTORY** Greek *graphein* to write

grapnel *n* a device with several hooks at one end, which is used to grasp or secure an object, esp. in sailing. ▷ **HISTORY** Old French *grapin* a little hook

grapple *vb* **-pling, -pled grapple with a** to try to cope with: *a difficult concept to grapple with.* **b** to come to grips with (someone) in hand-to-hand combat. ▷ **HISTORY** Old French *grappelle* a little hook

grappling iron *n* same as **grapnel**.

grasp *vb* **1** to grip firmly. **2** to understand: *his failure to grasp the gravity of the crisis.* ✧ *n* **3** a very firm grip. **4** understanding or comprehension: *a good grasp of detail.* **5 within someone's grasp** almost certain to be accomplished or won: *he now has that prize within his grasp.* ▷ **HISTORY** Low German *grapsen*

grasping *adj* greedy for money.

grass *n* **1** a very common green plant with jointed stems and long narrow leaves, eaten by animals such as sheep and cows, and used for lawns and sports fields. **2** a particular kind of grass, such as bamboo. **3** a lawn. **4** *Slang* marijuana. **5** *Brit & Austral slang* a person who informs, usually on criminals. ✧ *vb* **6 grass on** *or* **up** *Brit slang* to inform on (someone) to the police or some other authority. **7 grass over** to cover with grass. ▷ **HISTORY** Old English *græs* ▶ **grassy** *adj*

grasshopper *n* an insect with long hind legs which it uses for leaping.

A B C D E F G H I J K L M N O P Q R S T U V W X Y Z

grassland *n* **1** land covered with grass. **2** pasture land.

grass roots *pl n* **1** ordinary members of a group or organization, as distinct from its leaders. ✧ *adj* **grassroots 2** of the ordinary members of a group or organization: *the focus of a virulent grassroots campaign.*

grass snake *n* a harmless snake with a brownish-green body.

grass tree *n* an Australian plant with stiff grasslike leaves and small white flowers.

grass widow *n* a woman whose husband is regularly absent for a time. ▷ **HISTORY** perhaps an allusion to a grass bed as representing an illicit relationship

grate[1] *vb* **grating, grated 1** to reduce to shreds by rubbing against a rough surface: *grated cheese.* **2** to produce a harsh rasping sound by scraping against an object or surface: *the clutch plates grated.* **3 grate on** to annoy: *his manner always grated on me.* ▷ **HISTORY** Old French *grater*

grate[2] *n* **1** a framework of metal bars for holding coal or wood in a fireplace. **2** same as **grating**[1]. ▷ **HISTORY** Latin *cratis* hurdle

grateful *adj* feeling or showing thanks. ▷ **HISTORY** Latin *gratus* ▸ **gratefully** *adv*

grater *n* a tool with a sharp surface for grating food.

gratify *vb* **-fies, -fying, -fied 1** to satisfy or please (someone). **2** to yield to (a desire or whim): *all his wishes were to be gratified.* ▷ **HISTORY** Latin *gratus* grateful + *facere* to make ▸ **gratification** *n*

grating[1] *n* a framework of metal bars covering an opening in a wall or in the ground.

grating[2] *adj* **1** (of a sound) rough or unpleasant. **2** annoying or irritating: *his cringing obsequiousness was grating.*

gratis *adv, adj* without payment; free: *the gifts are gratis.* ▷ **HISTORY** Latin

gratitude *n* a feeling of being grateful for gifts or favours. ▷ **HISTORY** Latin *gratus* grateful

gratuitous (grat-**tyoo**-it-uss) *adj* **1** unjustified or unreasonable: *gratuitous violence.* **2** given or received without charge or obligation: *his gratuitous voluntary services.* ▷ **HISTORY** Latin *gratuitus* ▸ **gratuitously** *adv*

gratuity (grat-**tyoo**-it-ee) *n, pl* **-ties** money given for services rendered; tip.

grave[1] *adj* **1** (rhymes with **save**) serious and worrying: *grave concern.* **2** (rhymes with **save**) serious and solemn in appearance or behaviour: *the man looked grave and respectful.* **3** (rhymes with **halve**) denoting an accent (`) over a vowel in some languages, such as French, which indicates that the vowel is pronounced in a particular way. ✧ *n* (rhymes with **halve**) **4** a grave accent. ▷ **HISTORY** Latin *gravis* ▸ **gravely** *adv*

grave[2] (rhymes with **save**) *n* **1** a place where a dead person is buried. *RELATED ADJECTIVE* ➔ **sepulchral 2** death: *people are smoking themselves to an early grave.* **3 make someone turn in his** *or* **her grave** to do something that would have shocked a person who is now dead. ▷ **HISTORY** Old English *græf*

gravel *n* **1** a mixture of rock fragments and pebbles that is coarser than sand. **2** *Pathol* small rough stones in the kidneys or bladder. ✧ *vb* **-elling, -elled** *or US* **-eling, -eled 3** to cover with gravel. ▷ **HISTORY** Old French *gravele*

gravelly *adj* **1** covered with gravel. **2** (of a voice or sound) harsh and grating.

graven image *n Chiefly Bible* a carved image used as an idol.

gravestone *n* a stone marking a grave.

graveyard *n* a place where dead people are buried, esp. one by a church.

graveyard slot *n Television* the hours from late night until early morning when relatively few people are watching television.

gravid (**grav**-id) *adj Med* pregnant. ▷ **HISTORY** Latin *gravis* heavy

gravimeter (grav-**vim**-it-er) *n* **1** an instrument for measuring the force of gravity. **2** an instrument for measuring relative density. ▷ **HISTORY** French *gravimètre*

gravitate *vb* **-tating, -tated 1 gravitate towards** to be attracted or influenced by: *the mathematically inclined often gravitate towards computers.* **2** *Physics* to move under the influence of gravity.

gravitation *n Physics* **1** the force of attraction that bodies exert on one another as a result of their mass. **2** the process or result of this interaction. ▸ **gravitational** *adj*

gravitational attraction *n Physics* a mutual attraction between particles or bodies resulting from their mass.

gravitational force *n Physics* an interaction between particles or bodies resulting from their mass.

gravity *n, pl* **-ties 1** *Physics* **a** the force that attracts bodies towards the centre of the earth, a moon, or any planet. **b** same as **gravitation**. **2** seriousness or importance: *the gravity of the situation.* **3** seriousness or solemnity of appearance or behaviour: *his priestly gravity.* ▷ **HISTORY** Latin *gravitas* weight

gravy *n, pl* **-vies a** the juices that come from meat during cooking. **b** the sauce made by thickening and flavouring these juices. ▷ **HISTORY** Old French *gravé*

gray *adj, n, vb Chiefly US* grey.

graze[1] *vb* **grazing, grazed a** (of an animal) to eat (grass or other growing plants). **b** to feed (animals) on grass or other growing plants. ▷ **HISTORY** Old English *grasian*

graze[2] *vb* **grazing, grazed 1** to break the skin of (a part of the body) by scraping. **2** to brush against someone gently in passing. ✧ *n* **3** an injury on the skin caused by scraping. ▷ **HISTORY** probably special use of GRAZE[1]

grazier *n* a rancher or farmer who keeps cattle or sheep on grazing land.

grazing *n* land where grass is grown for farm animals to feed upon.

grease *n* **1** soft melted animal fat. **2** a thick oily substance, such as the kind put on machine parts to make them work smoothly. ✧ *vb* **greasing, greased 3** to apply grease to: *lightly grease a baking tin.* **4 grease someone's palm** *Slang* to bribe someone. ▷ HISTORY Latin *crassus* thick

greasepaint *n* theatrical make-up.

greasy *adj* **greasier, greasiest 1** covered with or containing grease. **2** excessively pleasant or flattering in an insincere manner. ▶ **greasiness** *n*

great *adj* **1** large in size. **2** large in number or amount: *the great majority.* **3** larger than others of its kind: *the great white whale.* **4** extreme or more than usual: *great difficulty.* **5** of importance or consequence: *a great discovery.* **6** of exceptional talents or achievements: *a great artist.* **7** skilful: *he's a great storyteller; they are great at problem solving.* **8** *Informal* excellent. ✧ *n* **9 the greats** the most successful people in a particular field: *the all-time greats of golf.* ✧ See also **Greats.** ▷ HISTORY Old English *grēat* ▶ **greatly** *adv* ▶ **greatness** *n*

great- *prefix* (in expressing relationship) one generation older or younger than: *great-grandmother.*

great auk *n* an extinct large auk that could not fly.

Great Britain *n* the mainland part of the British Isles; England, Scotland, and Wales.

great circle *n Maths* a circular section of a sphere that has a radius equal to the sphere's radius.

greatcoat *n* a heavy overcoat.

Great Dane *n* a very large dog with short smooth hair.

Greats *pl n* (at Oxford University) **1** the Honours course in classics and philosophy. **2** the final examinations at the end of this course.

Great War *n* same as **World War I.**

greave *n* a piece of armour for the shin. ▷ HISTORY Old French *greve*

grebe *n* a diving water bird. ▷ HISTORY French

Grecian (**gree**-shan) *adj* of ancient Greece.

greed *n* excessive desire for something, such as food or money.

greedy *adj* **greedier, greediest** having an excessive desire for something, such as food or money: *greedy for personal possessions.* ▷ HISTORY Old English *grǣdig* ▶ **greedily** *adv*

Greek *adj* **1** of Greece. ✧ *n* **2** a person from Greece. **3** the language of Greece.

green *adj* **1** of a colour between yellow and blue; of the colour of grass. **2** covered with grass, plants, or trees: *green fields.* **3** of or concerned with conservation and improvement of the environment: used in a political context: *green issues.* **4** (of fruit) fresh, raw, or unripe. **5** pale and sick-looking. **6** inexperienced or gullible. **7 green with envy** very envious. ✧ *n* **8** a colour between yellow and blue. **9** anything green, such as green clothing or green ink: *printed in green.* **10** a small area of grassy land: *the village green.* **11** an area of smooth turf kept for a special purpose: *putting greens.* **12 greens** the leaves and stems of certain plants, eaten as a vegetable: *turnip greens.* **13 Green** a person who supports environmentalist issues. ▷ HISTORY Old English *grēne* ▶ **greenish** *or* **greeny** *adj* ▶ **greenness** *n*

green belt *n* a protected zone of parkland or open country surrounding a town or city.

green card *n* an official permit allowing the holder permanent residence and employment, issued to foreign nationals in the US.

Green Cross Code *n Brit* a code for children giving rules on road safety.

greenery *n* green leaves or growing plants: *lush greenery.*

greenfield *adj* relating to a rural area which has not previously been built on: *greenfield factory sites.*

greenfinch *n* a European finch the male of which has olive-green feathers.

green fingers *pl n* skill in growing plants.

greenfly *n, pl* **-flies** a green aphid commonly occurring as a pest on plants.

greengage *n* a green sweet variety of plum. ▷ HISTORY after Sir W. *Gage,* botanist

greengrocer *n Brit & Austral* a shopkeeper who sells fruit and vegetables.

greenhorn *n* an inexperienced person; novice. ▷ HISTORY originally an animal with *green* (that is, young) horns

greenhouse *n* **1** a building with glass walls and roof where plants are grown under controlled conditions. ✧ *adj* **2** relating to or contributing to the greenhouse effect: *greenhouse gases such as carbon dioxide.*

greenhouse effect *n* the gradual rise in temperature in the earth's atmosphere due to heat being absorbed from the sun and being trapped by gases such as carbon dioxide in the air around the earth.

green light *n* **1** a signal to go. **2** permission to proceed with a project. ✧ *vb* **greenlight, -lighting, -lighted 3** to permit (a project) to proceed.

green paper *n* a government document containing policy proposals to be discussed.

green pepper *n* the green unripe fruit of the sweet pepper, eaten as a vegetable.

greenroom *n* (esp. formerly) a backstage room in a theatre where performers rest or receive visitors.

greenstick fracture *n* a fracture in which the bone is partly bent and splinters only on the outer side of the bend.

greenstone *n NZ* a type of green jade used for Maori carvings and ornaments.

Greenwich Mean Time (**gren**-itch) *n* the local time of the 0° meridian passing through Greenwich, England: a basis for calculating times throughout most of the world. Abbrev: **GMT**

greet[1] *vb* **1** to address or meet with expressions of friendliness or welcome. **2** to receive in a specified manner: *a direct request would be greeted coolly.* **3** to be immediately noticeable to: *the scene of devastation which greeted him.* ▷ HISTORY Old English *grētan*

A B C D E F G H I J K L M N O P Q R S T U V W X Y Z

greet[2] *vb Scot* to weep. ▷ **HISTORY** Old English *grætan*

greeting *n* the act or words of welcoming on meeting.

greetings *interj* an expression of friendly salutation.

gregarious *adj* **1** enjoying the company of others. **2** (of animals) living together in herds or in flocks. ▷ **HISTORY** Latin *grex* flock

Gregorian calendar *n* the revision of the calendar introduced in 1582 by Pope Gregory XIII and still widely used.

Gregorian chant *n* same as **plainsong**.

gremlin *n* an imaginary imp jokingly blamed for malfunctions in machinery. ▷ **HISTORY** origin unknown

grenade *n* a small bomb filled with explosive or gas, thrown by hand or fired from a rifle. ▷ **HISTORY** Spanish *grenada* pomegranate

grenadier *n Mil* **1** (in the British Army) a member of the senior regiment of infantry in the Household Brigade (the **Grenadier Guards**). **2** (formerly) a soldier trained to throw grenades. ▷ **HISTORY** French

grenadine (gren-a-**deen**) *n* a syrup made from pomegranate juice, often used as an ingredient in cocktails.

grevillea *n* any of various Australian evergreen trees and shrubs. ▷ **HISTORY** after C.F. *Greville*, botanist

grew *vb* the past tense of **grow**.

grey *or US* **gray** *adj* **1** of a colour between black and white; of the colour of ashes. **2 a** (of hair) having partly turned white. **b** (of a person) having grey hair. **3** dismal, dark, or gloomy: *a grey and misty morning.* **4** dull or boring: *in 1948 life generally was grey.* ✧ *n* **5** a colour between black and white. **6** anything grey, such as grey paint or grey clothing: *available in grey or brown.* **7** a grey or whitish horse. ▷ **HISTORY** Old English *grǣg* ▸ **greyness** *n* ▸ **greyish** *adj*

grey area *n* a situation or area that has no clearly defined characteristics or that falls somewhere between two categories.

Grey Friar *n* a Franciscan friar.

greyhound *n* a tall slender dog that can run very fast and is used for racing.

greying *adj* becoming grey: *greying hair.*

greylag *or* **greylag goose** *n* a large grey Eurasian goose. ▷ **HISTORY** GREY + LAG, because it migrates later than other species

grey matter *n Informal* intellect or brains: *those who don't have lots of grey matter.*

grey squirrel *n* a grey-furred squirrel, native to E North America but now common in Britain.

grid *n* **1** a network of crossing parallel lines on a map, plan, or graph paper for locating points. **2 the grid** the national network of cables or pipes by which electricity, gas, or water is distributed. **3** *Electronics* an electrode that controls the flow of electrons between the cathode and anode of a valve. ▷ **HISTORY** from *gridiron*

griddle *n* a thick round iron plate placed on top of a cooker and used to cook food. ▷ **HISTORY** Old French *gridil*

gridiron *n* **1** a utensil of parallel metal bars, used to grill food. **2 a** the field of play in American football. **b** *Informal* same as **American football**. ▷ **HISTORY** Middle English *gredire*

gridlock *n* **1** *Chiefly US* obstruction of traffic caused by queues of vehicles forming across junctions and so causing queues in intersecting streets. **2** a point in a dispute at which no agreement can be reached: *political gridlock.* ✧ *vb* **3** *Chiefly US* (of traffic) to obstruct (an area).

grid reference *n* a series of numbers indicating the location of a point on a map.

grief *n* **1** deep or intense sorrow. **2 come to grief** to have an unfortunate or unsuccessful end or outcome. **3** *Informal* trouble or annoyance: *people were giving me grief for leaving ten minutes early.*

grievance *n* **1** a real or imaginary cause for complaint. **2** a feeling of resentment at having been unfairly treated.

grieve *vb* **grieving, grieved** to feel or cause to feel great sorrow or distress. ▷ **HISTORY** Old French *grever* ▸ **grieved** *adj* ▸ **grieving** *adj*

grievous *adj* **1** very severe or painful: *grievous injuries.* **2** very serious or worrying: *a grievous loss.* ▸ **grievously** *adv*

grievous bodily harm *n Criminal law* serious injury caused by one person to another.

griffin, griffon, *or* **gryphon** *n* a mythical winged monster with an eagle's head and a lion's body. ▷ **HISTORY** Old French *grifon*

griffon *n* **1** a large vulture with a pale feathers and black wings. **2** a small wire-haired breed of dog. ▷ **HISTORY** French

grike *n Geol* a solution fissure that divides an exposed limestone surface into sections.

grill *vb* **1** to cook by direct heat under a grill or over a hot fire. **2** *Informal* to subject to relentless questioning: *the jury pool was grilled for signs of prejudice.* ✧ *n* **3** a device on a cooker that radiates heat downwards for grilling food. **4** a gridiron for cooking food. **5** a dish of grilled food. **6** See **grillroom**. ▷ **HISTORY** Latin *craticula* fine wickerwork ▸ **grilled** *adj* ▸ **grilling** *n*

grille *or* **grill** *n* a metal or wooden grating, used as a screen or partition. ▷ **HISTORY** Latin *craticula* fine hurdlework

grillroom *n* a restaurant specializing in grilled foods.

grilse (**grillss**) *n, pl* **grilses** *or* **grilse** a salmon on its first return from the sea to fresh water. ▷ **HISTORY** origin unknown

grim *adj* **grimmer, grimmest 1** unfavourable and worrying: *grim figures on unemployment.* **2** harsh and unpleasant: *grim conditions in the detention centres.* **3** stern or resolute: *a grim determination to fight on.* **4** *Informal* unpleasant or disagreeable. ▷ **HISTORY** Old English *grimm* ▸ **grimly** *adv* ▸ **grimness** *n*

grimace *n* **1** an ugly or distorted facial expression of disgust, pain, or displeasure. ✧ *vb* **-macing, -maced 2** to make a grimace. ▷ **HISTORY** French

grime *n* **1** ingrained dirt. ✧ *vb* **griming, grimed 2** to make very dirty: *sweat-grimed faces.* ▷ **HISTORY** Middle Dutch ▸ **grimy** *adj*

grin *vb* **grinning, grinned 1** to smile broadly, showing one's teeth. **2 grin and bear it** *Informal* to suffer hardship without complaint. ✧ *n* **3** a broad smile. ▷ **HISTORY** Old English *grennian* ▸ **grinning** *adj*

grind *vb* **grinding, ground 1** to reduce to small particles by pounding or rubbing: *grinding coffee.* **2** to smooth, sharpen, or polish by friction. **3** (of two objects) to scrape together with a harsh rasping sound. **4 an axe to grind** See **axe** (sense 2). **5 grind one's teeth** to rub one's upper and lower teeth against each other, as if chewing. **6 grind to a halt** to come to an end or a standstill: *without enzymes life would grind to a halt.* ✧ *n* **7** *Informal* hard or tedious work: *the grind of everyday life.* ▷ **HISTORY** Old English *grindan*

grinder *n* a device for grinding substances: *an electric coffee grinder.*

grindstone *n* **1** a revolving stone disc used for sharpening, grinding, or polishing things. **2 keep one's nose to the grindstone** to work hard and steadily.

grip *n* **1** a very tight hold: *he felt a grip at his throat.* **2** the style or manner of holding something, such as a golf club or tennis racket. **3** power or control over a situation, person, or activity: *rebel forces tighten their grip around the capital.* **4 get** *or* **come to grips with** to face up to and deal with (a problem or subject). **5** a travelling bag or holdall. **6** a small bent clasp used to fasten the hair. **7** a handle. **8** a person who manoeuvres the cameras in a film or television studio. ✧ *vb* **gripping, gripped 9** to take a tight hold of. **10** to affect strongly: *sudden panic gripped her.* **11** to hold the interest or attention of: *gripped by the intensity of the film; the story gripped him.* ▷ **HISTORY** Old English *gripe* grasp

gripe *vb* **griping, griped 1** *Informal* to complain persistently. **2** to cause sudden intense pain in the bowels. ✧ *n* **3** *Informal* a complaint. **4 the gripes** a sudden intense pain in the bowels. ▷ **HISTORY** Old English *grīpan*

grippe *n* a former name for **influenza**. ▷ **HISTORY** French

gripping *adj* very interesting and exciting: *a gripping story.*

grisly *adj* **-lier, -liest** causing horror or dread: *grisly murders.* ▷ **HISTORY** Old English *grislic*

> **WORD TIP**
> See at **grizzly**.

grist *n* **1** grain that is to be or that has been ground. **2 grist to the mill** anything that can be turned to profit or advantage. ▷ **HISTORY** Old English *grīst*

gristle *n* tough stringy animal tissue found in meat. ▷ **HISTORY** Old English ▸ **gristly** *adj*

grit *n* **1** small hard particles of sand, earth, or stone. **2** courage and determination. ✧ *vb* **gritting, gritted 3** to cover (an icy road) with grit. **4 grit one's teeth a** to rub one's upper and lower teeth against each other, as if chewing. **b** to decide to carry on in a difficult situation: *he urged the Cabinet to grit its teeth and continue cutting public spending.* ▷ **HISTORY** Old English *grēot*

gritter *n* a vehicle that spreads grit on the roads in icy weather.

gritty *adj* **-tier, -tiest 1** courageous and tough. **2** covered with grit.

grizzle *vb* **-zling, -zled** *Brit, Austral & NZ informal* to whine or complain. ▷ **HISTORY** Germanic

grizzled *adj* **1** (of hair) streaked or mixed with grey. **2** (of a person) having grey hair.

grizzly *n, pl* **-zlies** a large fierce greyish-brown bear of N America. In full: **grizzly bear**

> **WORD TIP**
> *Grizzly* is sometimes wrongly used where *grisly* is meant: *a grisly* (not *grizzly*) *murder.*

groan *n* **1** a long deep cry of pain, grief, or disapproval. **2** *Informal* a grumble or complaint. ✧ *vb* **3** to give a long deep cry of pain, grief, or disapproval. **4** *Informal* to complain or grumble. **5 groan under** to be weighed down by: *chemists' shelves groan under the weight of slimming aids.* ▷ **HISTORY** Old English *grānian* ▸ **groaning** *adj, n*

groat *n* a former British coin worth four old pennies. ▷ **HISTORY** Middle Dutch *groot*

groats *pl n* the crushed grain of various cereals. ▷ **HISTORY** Old English *grot* particle

grocer *n* a shopkeeper who sells food and other household supplies. ▷ **HISTORY** Old French *grossier*

groceries *pl n* food and other household supplies.

grocery *n, pl* **-ceries** the business or premises of a grocer.

grog *n* **1** an alcoholic drink, usually rum, diluted with water. **2** *Brit, Austral & NZ informal* any alcoholic drink. ▷ **HISTORY** Old *Grog*, nickname of Edward Vernon, British admiral, who in 1740 issued naval rum diluted with water

groggy *adj* **-gier, -giest** *Informal* faint, weak, or dizzy.

groin *n* **1** the part of the body where the abdomen joins the legs. **2** *Archit* a curved edge formed where two intersecting vaults meet. ▷ **HISTORY** origin unknown

grommet *n* **1** a rubber, plastic, or metal ring or eyelet. **2** *Med* a small tube inserted into the eardrum to drain fluid from the middle ear. ▷ **HISTORY** obsolete French *gourmer* bridle

groom *n* **1** a person employed to clean and look after horses. **2** short for **bridegroom**. ✧ *vb* **3** to clean and smarten (a horse or other animal). **4** to keep (oneself or one's appearance) clean and tidy: *carefully groomed hair.* **5** to train (someone) for a particular task or occupation: *groomed for future leadership.* ▷ **HISTORY** Middle English *grom* manservant ▸ **grooming** *n*

groove *n* **1** a long narrow furrow cut into a surface. **2** the spiral channel in a gramophone record. ▷ HISTORY obsolete Dutch *groeve* ▶ **grooved** *adj*

groovy *adj* **groovier, grooviest** *Slang* attractive, fashionable, or exciting.

grope *vb* **groping, groped 1** to feel about uncertainly for something. **2** to find (one's way) by groping. **3** to search uncertainly for a solution or expression: *the new democracies are groping for stability.* **4** *Slang* to fondle (someone) in a rough sexual way. ✧ *n* **5** an instance of groping. ▷ HISTORY Old English *grāpian*

gross *adj* **1** outrageously wrong: *gross violations of human rights.* **2** very coarse or vulgar: *gross bad taste.* **3** *Slang* disgusting or repulsive: *I think beards are gross.* **4** repulsively fat. **5** with no deductions for tax or the weight of the container; total: *gross income; a gross weight of 20 000 lbs.* ✧ *n* **6** (*pl* **gross**) twelve dozen (144). **7** the entire amount or weight. ✧ *vb* **8** to earn as total revenue, before deductions. ▷ HISTORY Old French *gros* large ▶ **grossly** *adv*

gross domestic product *n* the total value of all goods and services produced domestically by a nation during a year.

gross national product *n* the total value of all final goods and services produced annually by a nation: equivalent to gross domestic product plus net investment income from abroad.

gross profit *n Accounting* the difference between total revenue from sales and the total cost of purchases or materials.

grotesque (groh-**tesk**) *adj* **1** strangely distorted or bizarre: *a grotesque and pervasive personality cult.* **2** ugly or repulsive. ✧ *n* **3** a grotesque person or thing. **4** an artistic style in which parts of human, animal, and plant forms are distorted and mixed, or a work of art in this style. ▷ HISTORY Old Italian *(pittura) grottesca* cave (painting) ▶ **grotesquely** *adv*

grotto *n, pl* **-toes** *or* **-tos** a small picturesque cave. ▷ HISTORY Old Italian *grotta*

grotty *adj* **-tier, -tiest** *Brit & NZ slang* **1** nasty or unattractive. **2** in bad condition. ▷ HISTORY from *grotesque*

grouch *Informal* ✧ *vb* **1** to complain or grumble. ✧ *n* **2** a person who is always complaining. **3** a persistent complaint. ▷ HISTORY Old French *grouchier*

grouchy *adj* **grouchier, grouchiest** bad-tempered.

ground[1] *n* **1** the land surface. **2** earth or soil. **3** an area used for a particular purpose: *a cricket ground.* **4** a matter for consideration or discussion: *there is no need to cover the same ground.* **5** an advantage in an argument or competition: *neither side seems willing to give ground in this trial of strength.* **6** the background colour of a painting. **7** *US & Canad* an electrical earth. **8 grounds a** the land around a building. **b** reason or justification: *the hostages should be freed on humanitarian grounds.* **c** sediment or dregs: *coffee grounds.* **9 break new ground** to do something that has not been done before. **10 common ground** an agreed basis for identifying issues in an argument. **11 get something off the ground** to get something started: *to get the peace conference off the ground.* **12 into the ground** to exhaustion or excess: *he was running himself into the ground.* **13 suit someone down to the ground** *Brit informal* to be totally suitable or appropriate for someone. ✧ *adj* **14** on the ground: *ground troops.* ✧ *vb* **15** to confine (an aircraft or pilot) to the ground. **16** *Naut* to move (a ship) onto the bottom of shallow water, so that it cannot move. **17** to instruct in the basics of a subject: *the student who is not grounded in the elements cannot understand the advanced teaching.* **18** to provide a basis for; establish: *a scientifically grounded documentation.* **19** to forbid (a child) to go out and enjoy himself or herself as a punishment. **20** *US & Canad* to connect (a circuit or electrical device) to an earth. ▷ HISTORY Old English *grund*

ground[2] *vb* **1** the past of **grind**. ✧ *adj* **2** reduced to fine particles by grinding: *ground glass.*

ground bass *n Music* a short melodic bass line that is repeated over and over again.

ground beef *n* finely chopped beef, sometimes used to make hamburgers.

ground-breaking *adj* innovative.

ground control *n* the people and equipment on the ground that monitor the progress of aircraft or spacecraft.

ground cover *n* dense low plants that spread over the surface of the ground.

ground floor *n* the floor of a building that is level, or almost level, with the ground.

grounding *n* a foundation, esp. the basic general knowledge of a subject.

groundless *adj* without reason or justification: *the scare turned out to be groundless.*

groundnut *n Brit* a peanut.

groundsel (**grounce**-el) *n* a yellow-flowered weed. ▷ HISTORY Old English *grundeswelge*

groundsheet *n* a waterproof sheet placed on the ground in a tent to keep out damp.

groundsman *n, pl* **-men** a person employed to maintain a sports ground or park.

groundswell *n* a rapidly developing general feeling or opinion.

ground water *n* water that has seeped through from the surface and is held underground.

groundwork *n* preliminary work as a foundation or basis.

group *n* **1** a number of people or things considered as a unit. **2** a small band of players or singers, esp. of popular music. **3** an association of business firms that have the same owner. **4** *Chem* two or more atoms that are bound together in a molecule and behave as a single unit: *a methyl group* $-CH_3$. **5** *Chem* a vertical column of elements in the periodic table that all have similar properties: *the halogen group.* ✧ *vb* **6** to put into or form into a group. ▷ HISTORY French *groupe*

group captain *n* a middle-ranking officer in some air forces.

grouped data *n Maths* data which is grouped into classes. compare **discrete data**.

group therapy *n Psychol* the treatment of people by bringing them together to share their problems in group discussion.

grouse[1] *n, pl* **grouse 1** a game bird with a stocky body and feathered legs and feet. **2** the flesh of this bird used for food. ▷ HISTORY origin unknown

grouse[2] *vb* **grousing, groused 1** to complain or grumble. ✧ *n* **2** a persistent complaint. ▷ HISTORY origin unknown

grouse[3] *adj Austral & NZ slang* fine or excellent. ▷ HISTORY origin unknown

grout *n* **1** a thin mortar for filling joints between tiles or masonry. ✧ *vb* **2** to fill with grout. ▷ HISTORY Old English *grūt*

grove *n* a small wood or group of trees: *orange groves.* ▷ HISTORY Old English *grāf*

grovel (**grov**-el) *vb* **-elling, -elled** *or US* **-eling, -eled 1** to behave excessively humbly towards someone, esp. a superior, in an attempt to win his or her favour. **2** to crawl on the floor, often in search of something: *grovelling on the floor for missing cards.* ▷ HISTORY Middle English *on grufe* on the face ▶ **grovelling** *or US* **groveling** *adj, n*

grow *vb* **growing, grew, grown 1** (of a person or animal) to increase in size and develop physically. **2** (of a plant) to exist and increase in size: *an ancient meadow where wild flowers grow.* **3** to produce (a plant) by planting seeds, bulbs, or cuttings, and looking after it: *many farmers have expressed a wish to grow more cotton.* **4** to let (one's hair or nails) develop: *to grow a beard.* **5** to increase in size or degree: *the gulf between rich and poor is growing.* **6** to originate or develop: *Melbourne grew from a sheep-farming outstation and occasional port to a city.* **7** to become increasingly as specified: *as the night wore on the audience grew more intolerant.* ✧ See also **grow on**. ▷ HISTORY Old English *grōwan* ▶ **growing** *adj* ▶ **grower** *n*

growing pains *pl n* **1** pains in muscles or joints sometimes experienced by growing children. **2** difficulties experienced in the early stages of a new enterprise.

growl *vb* **1** (of a dog or other animal) to make a low rumbling sound, usually in anger. **2** to say in a gruff or angry manner: *'You're late,' he growled.* **3** to make a deep rumbling sound: *his stomach growled.* ✧ *n* **4** the act or sound of growling. ▷ HISTORY Old French *grouller* to grumble

grown *adj* developed or advanced: *fully grown; a grown man.*

grown-up *adj* **1** having reached maturity; adult. **2** of or suitable for an adult. ✧ *n* **3** an adult.

grow on *vb* to become progressively more acceptable or pleasant to: *I didn't like that programme at first but it has grown on me.*

growth *n* **1** the process of growing. **2** an increase in size, number, or significance: *the growth of drug trafficking.* **3** something grown or growing: *a thick growth of ivy.* **4** any abnormal tissue, such as a tumour. ✧ *adj* **5** of or relating to growth: *growth hormone.*

grow up *vb* to reach maturity; become adult.

groyne *n* a wall or breakwater built out from a shore to control erosion. ▷ HISTORY Old French *groign* snout

grub *n* **1** *Slang* food. **2** the short legless larva of certain insects, such as beetles. ✧ *vb* **grubbing, grubbed 3** to search carefully for something by digging or by moving things about. **4 grub up** to dig (roots or plants) out of the ground. ▷ HISTORY Germanic

grubby *adj* **-bier, -biest 1** rather dirty. **2** unsavoury or morally unacceptable: *grubby activities.* ▶ **grubbiness** *n*

grudge *n* **1** a persistent feeling of resentment against a person who has caused harm or upset. ✧ *vb* **grudging, grudged 2** to give unwillingly: *the rich men who grudged pennies for the poor.* **3** to resent or envy the success or possessions of: *none of their guests grudged them this celebration.* ✧ *adj* **4** planned or carried out in order to settle a grudge: *a grudge match.* ▷ HISTORY Old French *grouchier* to grumble

grudging *adj* felt or done unwillingly: *grudging admiration for his opponent.* ▶ **grudgingly** *adv*

gruel *n* thin porridge made by boiling oatmeal in water or milk. ▷ HISTORY Old French

gruelling *or US* **grueling** *adj* extremely severe or tiring: *a gruelling journey.* ▷ HISTORY obsolete *gruel* to punish

gruesome *adj* inspiring horror and disgust. ▷ HISTORY Scandinavian

gruff *adj* **1** rough or surly in manner or speech. **2** (of a voice) low and throaty. ▷ HISTORY Germanic ▶ **gruffly** *adv* ▶ **gruffness** *n*

grumble *vb* **-bling, -bled 1** to complain in a nagging way: *his neighbour grumbled about the long wait.* **2** to make low rumbling sounds: *the storm grumbled in the distance.* ✧ *n* **3** a complaint. **4** a low rumbling sound: *a distant grumble of artillery fire.* ▷ HISTORY Middle Low German *grommelen* ▶ **grumbling** *adj, n*

grumpy *adj* **grumpier, grumpiest** sulky and bad-tempered. ▷ HISTORY imitative ▶ **grumpily** *adv*

grunge *n* **1** a style of rock music with a fuzzy guitar sound. **2** a deliberately untidy and uncoordinated fashion style. ▷ HISTORY from US slang: dirt, rubbish

grunt *vb* **1** to make a low short gruff noise, such as the sound made by a pig, or by a person to express annoyance. **2** to express (something) gruffly: *he grunted his thanks.* ✧ *n* **3** a low short gruff noise, such as the sound made by a pig, or by a person to express annoyance. ▷ HISTORY Old English *grunnettan*

gryphon *n* same as **griffin**.

GST (in Australia, New Zealand, and Canada) Goods and Services Tax.

G-string *n* a strip of cloth worn between the legs and attached to a waistband.

G-suit *n* a close-fitting pressurized garment that is worn by the crew of high-speed aircraft. ▷ HISTORY from *g(ravity) suit*

A B C D E F G H I J K L M N O P Q R S T U V W X Y Z

GT gran turismo: a touring car, usually a fast sports car with a hard fixed roof.

guanine (**gwah**-neen) *n Biochem* a white almost insoluble compound.

guano (**gwah**-no) *n* the dried manure of sea birds, used as a fertilizer. ▷ **HISTORY** S American Indian *huano* dung

guarantee *n* **1** a formal assurance in writing that a product or service will meet certain standards or specifications. **2** something that makes a specified condition or outcome certain: *there was no guarantee that there would not be another military coup.* **3** same as **guaranty**. ✧ *vb* **-teeing, -teed** **4** to promise or make certain: *to guarantee absolute loyalty.* **5** (of a company) to provide a guarantee in writing for (a product or service). **6** to take responsibility for the debts or obligations of (another person). ▷ **HISTORY** Germanic

guarantor *n* a person who gives or is bound by a guarantee or guaranty.

guaranty *n, pl* **-ties** **1** a pledge of responsibility for fulfilling another person's obligations in case of that person's default. **2** a thing given or taken as security for a guaranty.

guard *vb* **1** to watch over or shield from danger or harm; protect: *US marines who guard the American embassy.* **2** to keep watch over (a prisoner) to prevent escape. **3** to protect (a right or privilege). **4** to take precautions: *to guard against a possible coup attempt.* ✧ *n* **5** a person or group of people who protect or watch over people or things. **6** *Brit, Austral & NZ* the official in charge of a train. **7** a device or part of a machine designed to protect the user against injury. **8** anything that provides protection: *a guard against future shocks.* **9 off guard** having one's defences down; unprepared: *England were caught off guard as the Dutch struck two telling blows.* **10 on guard** on duty to protect or watch over people or things. **11 on one's guard** prepared to face danger or difficulties: *parents have been warned to be on their guard against kidnappers.* **12 stand guard** (of a sentry) to keep watch. ▷ **HISTORY** Old French *garder* to protect

guarded *adj* cautious and avoiding any commitment: *a guarded welcome.* ▶ **guardedly** *adv*

guardhouse *or* **guardroom** *n Mil* a military police office in which prisoners can be detained.

guardian *n* **1** one who looks after, protects, or defends someone or something: *the nation's moral guardians.* **2** someone legally appointed to manage the affairs of another person, such as a child or a person who is mentally ill. ▶ **guardianship** *n*

guardsman *n, pl* **-men** *Mil* a member of a regiment responsible for ceremonial duties.

guard's van *n Brit, Austral & NZ* a small railway carriage in which the guard travels.

guava (**gwah**-va) *n* a round tropical fruit with yellow skin and pink pulp. ▷ **HISTORY** from S American Indian

gubernatorial *adj Chiefly US* of or relating to a governor. ▷ **HISTORY** Latin *gubernator* governor

gudgeon[1] *n* a small slender European freshwater fish, used as bait by anglers. ▷ **HISTORY** Old French *gougon*

gudgeon[2] *n* the socket of a hinge, which fits round the pin. ▷ **HISTORY** Old French *goujon*

Guernsey (**gurn**-zee) *n* a breed of dairy cattle that produces rich creamy milk, originating from Guernsey, in the Channel Islands.

guerrilla *or* **guerilla** *n* a member of an irregular, politically motivated, armed force that fights regular forces. ▷ **HISTORY** Spanish

guess *vb* **1** to form an estimate or conclusion about (something), without proper knowledge: *a competition to guess the weight of the cake.* **2** to arrive at a correct estimate of (something) by guessing: *I had a notion that he guessed my thoughts.* **3** *Informal* to think or suppose: *I guess he must have been a great athlete.* ✧ *n* **4** an estimate or conclusion arrived at by guessing: *we can hazard a guess at the answer.* ▷ **HISTORY** probably from Old Norse

guesswork *n* the process of arriving at conclusions or estimates by guessing.

guest *n* **1** a person who receives hospitality at someone else's home. **2** a person who is taken out socially by someone else who pays all the expenses. **3** a performer or speaker taking part in an event, show, or film by special invitation. **4** a person who is staying in a hotel. ✧ *vb* **5** to be a guest in an event, show, or film: *he guested in concert with Eric Clapton.* ▷ **HISTORY** Old English *giest* guest, stranger, enemy

guesthouse *n* a private home or boarding house offering accommodation.

guff *n Brit, Austral & NZ slang* ridiculous talk; nonsense. ▷ **HISTORY** imitative

guffaw *vb* **1** to laugh loudly and raucously. ✧ *n* **2** a loud raucous laugh. ▷ **HISTORY** imitative

guidance *n* help, advice, or instruction, usually from someone more experienced or more qualified: *marriage guidance.*

guide *n* **1** a person who conducts parties of tourists around places of interest, such as museums. **2** a person who leads travellers to a place, usually in a dangerous area: *a mountain guide.* **3** something that can be used to gauge something or to help in planning one's actions: *starting salary was not an accurate guide to future earnings.* **4** same as **guidebook**. **5** a book that explains the basics of a subject or skill: *a guide to higher education.* ✧ *vb* **guiding, guided** **6** to lead the way for (tourists or travellers). **7** to control the movement or course of; steer. **8** to direct the affairs of (a person, team, or country): *he will stay with the club he guided to promotion to the First Division.* **9** to influence (a person) in his or her actions or opinions: *to be guided by the law.* ▷ **HISTORY** Germanic ▶ **guiding** *adj*

Guide *n* a member of an organization for girls that encourages discipline and practical skills.

guidebook *n* a book which gives tourist information on a place.

guided missile *n* a missile whose course is controlled electronically.

guide dog *n* a dog that has been trained to lead a blind person.

guideline *n* a principle put forward to set standards or determine a course of action: *guidelines for arms exporting.*

guild *n* **1** an organization or club for people with shared interests. **2** (in Medieval Europe) an association of men in the same trade or craft. ▷ **HISTORY** Old Norse *gildi*

guilder *n, pl* **-ders** *or* **-der** a former monetary unit of the Netherlands. ▷ **HISTORY** Middle Dutch *gulden*

guildhall *n Brit* a hall where members of a guild meet.

guile (**gile**) *n* craftiness or deviousness. ▷ **HISTORY** Old French ▶ **guileless** *adj*

guillemot (**gil**-lee-mot) *n* a northern oceanic black-and-white diving sea bird. ▷ **HISTORY** French

guillotine *n* **1** a device formerly used, esp. in France, for beheading people, consisting of a weighted blade between two upright posts, which was dropped on the neck. **2** a device with a blade for cutting paper. ✧ *vb* **-tining, -tined 3** to behead with a guillotine. ▷ **HISTORY** after J. I. *Guillotin*, who advocated its use

guilt *n* **1** the fact or state of having done wrong: *the court was unable to establish guilt.* **2** remorse or self-reproach caused by feeling that one has done something wrong: *he feels no guilt about the planned cutbacks.* ▷ **HISTORY** Old English *gylt*

guiltless *adj* free of all responsibility for wrongdoing or crime; innocent.

guilty *adj* **guiltier, guiltiest 1** *Law* judged to have committed a crime: *she has been found guilty of drug trafficking.* **2** responsible for doing something wrong: *students who are guilty of cheating.* **3** showing, feeling, or indicating guilt: *guilty conscience.* ▶ **guiltily** *adv*

guinea *n* a former British unit of currency worth £1.05 (21 shillings), sometimes still used in quoting professional fees. ▷ **HISTORY** the coin was originally made of gold from Guinea

guinea fowl *n* a domestic bird with a heavy rounded body and speckled feathers.

guinea pig *n* **1** a tailless S American rodent, commonly kept as a pet or used in scientific experiments. **2** a person used in an experiment. ▷ **HISTORY** origin unknown

guise (rhymes with **size**) *n* **1** a false appearance: *in the guise of a wood-cutter.* **2** general appearance or form: *haricot beans are best known in Britain in their popular guise of baked beans.* ▷ **HISTORY** Old French

guitar *n* a stringed instrument with a flat back and a long neck with a fretted fingerboard, which is played by plucking or strumming. ▷ **HISTORY** Spanish *guitarra* ▶ **guitarist** *n*

Gulag *n* a system or department that silences dissidents, esp. in the former Soviet Union. ▷ **HISTORY** Russian *G(lavnoye) U(pravleniye Ispravitelno-Trudovykh) Lag(erei)* Main Administration for Corrective Labour Camps

gulch *n US & Canad* a narrow ravine with a stream running through it. ▷ **HISTORY** origin unknown

gulf *n* **1** a large deep bay. **2** something that divides or separates people, such as a lack of understanding: *gradually the gulf between father and son has lessened.* ▷ **HISTORY** Greek *kolpos*

Gulf War syndrome *n* a group of various debilitating symptoms experienced by many soldiers who served in the Gulf War of 1991, claimed to be associated with damage to the central nervous system.

gull *n* a large sea bird with white feathers tipped with black or grey. ▷ **HISTORY** Celtic

gullet *n* the muscular tube through which food passes from the throat to the stomach. ▷ **HISTORY** Latin *gula* throat

gullible *adj* easily tricked; too trusting. ▶ **gullibility** *n*

gully *or* **gulley** *n, pl* **-lies** *or* **-leys 1** a channel or small valley originally worn away by running water. **2** *Cricket* a fielding position on the off side, between the slips and point. ▷ **HISTORY** French *goulet* neck of a bottle

gully erosion *n Geog* the process whereby water run-off flows in the same narrow channels, wearing away soil and rock.

gulp *vb* **1** to swallow (a drink or food) rapidly in large mouthfuls. **2** to gasp or breathe in violently, for example when nervous or when swimming. **3 gulp back** to stifle or suppress: *he gulped back the tears as he said his goodbyes.* ✧ *n* **4** the act of gulping. **5** the quantity taken in a gulp. ▷ **HISTORY** imitative

gum[1] *n* **1** a sticky substance obtained from certain plants, which hardens on exposure to air and dissolves in water. **2** a substance used for sticking things together. **3** short for **chewing gum bubble gum**. **4** *Chiefly Brit* a gumdrop. ✧ *vb* **gumming, gummed 5** to stick with gum. ▷ **HISTORY** Old French *gomme*

gum[2] *n* the fleshy tissue that covers the bases of the teeth. ▷ **HISTORY** Old English *gōma* jaw

gum arabic *n* a gum obtained from certain acacia trees, used to make ink, food thickeners, and pills.

gumboil *n* an abscess on the gum.

gumboots *pl n Brit & NZ* long rubber boots, worn in wet or muddy conditions.

gumdrop *n* a small hard fruit-flavoured jelly-like sweet.

gummy[1] *adj* **-mier, -miest 1** sticky or tacky. **2** producing gum.

gummy[2] *adj* **-mier, -miest** toothless.

gumption *n Brit & NZ informal* common sense or initiative. ▷ **HISTORY** origin unknown

gumtree *n* **1** any of various trees that yield gum, such as the eucalyptus. **2 up a gumtree** *Brit & NZ informal* in an awkward position; in difficulties.

gun *n* **1** a weapon with a metallic tube or barrel from which a missile is fired, usually by force of an explosion. **2** a device used to force out (a substance, such as grease or paint) under pressure: *a spray gun.* **3 jump the gun** *Informal* to act prematurely. **4 stick to one's guns** *Informal* to stand by one's opinions or intentions in spite of

A B C D E F G H I J K L M N O P Q R S T U V W X Y Z

opposition. ✧ *vb* **gunning, gunned 5 gun down** to shoot (someone) with a gun. **6** to press hard on the accelerator of (a vehicle's engine). ✧ See also **gun for**. ✧ *adj* **7** *NZ slang* expert: *a gun surfer.* ▷ **HISTORY** Middle English *gonne*

gunboat *n* a small ship carrying mounted guns.

gunboat diplomacy *n* diplomacy conducted by threats of military intervention.

guncotton *n* a form of cellulose nitrate used as an explosive.

gun dog *n* **1** a dog trained to locate or retrieve birds or animals that have been shot in a hunt. **2** a dog belonging to any breed traditionally used for these activities.

gunfire *n* the repeated firing of guns.

gun for *vb Informal* to search for (someone) in order to harm him or her in some way.

gunge *n Informal* a sticky or congealed substance. ▷ **HISTORY** imitative ▶ **gungy** *adj*

gunk *n Informal* a slimy, oily, or dirty substance. ▷ **HISTORY** perhaps imitative

gunman *n, pl* **-men** a man who uses a gun to commit a crime.

gunmetal *n* **1** a type of bronze containing copper, tin, and zinc. ✧ *adj* **2** dark grey.

gunnel (**gun**-nel) *n* same as **gunwale**.

gunner *n* a member of the armed forces who works with, uses, or specializes in guns.

gunnery *n* the art and science of the efficient design and use of large guns.

gunny *n Chiefly US* a coarse hard-wearing fabric, made from jute and used for sacks. ▷ **HISTORY** Hindi *gōnī*

gunpowder *n* an explosive mixture of potassium nitrate, charcoal, and sulphur, used to make fireworks.

gunrunning *n* the practice of smuggling guns and ammunition into a country. ▶ **gunrunner** *n*

gunshot *n* **1** bullets fired from a gun. **2** the sound of a gun being fired. **3** the firing range of a gun: *within gunshot.*

gunwale *n Naut* the top of the side of a ship. ▷ **HISTORY** *wale,* ridge of planking originally supporting guns

gunyah *n Austral* a hut or shelter in the bush. ▷ **HISTORY** Aboriginal

guppy *n, pl* **-pies** a small brightly coloured tropical fish, often kept in aquariums in people's homes. ▷ **HISTORY** after R. J. L. *Guppy,* who gave specimens to the British Museum

gurgle *vb* **-gling, -gled 1** (of water) to make low bubbling noises when flowing. **2** to make low throaty bubbling noises: *the baby gurgled in delight.* ✧ *n* **3** the sound of gurgling. ▷ **HISTORY** origin unknown

Gurkha *n* **1** a member of a Hindu people living mainly in Nepal. **2** a member of a Gurkha regiment in the Indian or British Army. ▷ **HISTORY** Sanskrit

gurnard *n, pl* **-nard** *or* **-nards** a sea fish with a spiny head and long finger-like pectoral fins. ▷ **HISTORY** Old French *gornard* grunter

guru *n* **1** a Hindu or Sikh religious teacher or leader. **2** a leader or adviser of a person or group of people: *inside a team of advertising gurus are at work.* ▷ **HISTORY** Hindi

gush *vb* **1** to pour out suddenly and profusely. **2** to speak or behave in an overenthusiastic manner: *I'm not about to start gushing about raspberry coulis.* ✧ *n* **3** a sudden large flow of liquid. **4** a sudden surge of strong feeling: *she felt a gush of pure affection for her mother.* ▷ **HISTORY** probably imitative

gusher *n* **1** a person who gushes. **2** a spurting oil well.

gushing *adj* behaving in an overenthusiastic manner: *gushing television commentators.*

gusset *n* a piece of material sewn into a garment to strengthen it. ▷ **HISTORY** Old French *gousset*

gust *n* **1** a sudden blast of wind. **2** a sudden surge of strong feeling: *a gust of joviality.* ✧ *vb* **3** to blow in gusts. ▷ **HISTORY** Old Norse *gustr* ▶ **gusty** *adj*

gusto *n* vigorous enjoyment: *he downed a pint with gusto.* ▷ **HISTORY** Spanish: taste

gut *n* **1** same as **intestine**. **2** *Slang* a stomach, esp. a fat one. **3** short for **catgut**. **4** a silky fibrous substance extracted from silkworms and used in the manufacture of fishing tackle. ✧ *vb* **gutting, gutted 5** to remove the internal organs from (a dead animal or fish). **6** (of a fire) to destroy the inside of (a building): *a local pub was gutted.* ✧ *adj* **7** *Informal* basic, essential, or natural: *I have a gut feeling she's after something.* ✧ See also **guts**. ▷ **HISTORY** Old English *gutt*

gutless *adj Informal* lacking courage or determination.

guts *pl n* **1** the internal organs of a person or an animal. **2** *Informal* courage, willpower, or daring. **3** *Informal* the inner or essential part: *the new roads have torn apart the guts of the city.*

gutsy *adj* **gutsier, gutsiest** *Slang* **1** bold or courageous: *the gutsy kid who lost a leg to cancer.* **2** robust or vigorous: *a gutsy rendering of 'Bobby Shaftoe'.*

gutta-percha *n* a whitish rubber substance, obtained from a tropical Asian tree and used in electrical insulation and dentistry. ▷ **HISTORY** Malay *getah* gum + *percha* gumtree

gutted *adj Brit, Austral & NZ informal* disappointed and upset: *the supporters will be absolutely gutted if the manager leaves the club.*

gutter *n* **1** a channel on the roof of a building or alongside a kerb, used to collect and carry away rainwater. **2** *Tenpin bowling* one of the channels on either side of an alley. **3 the gutter** a poverty-stricken, degraded, or criminal environment: *he dragged himself up from the gutter.* ✧ *vb* **4** (of a candle) to flicker and be about to go out. ▷ **HISTORY** Latin *gutta* a drop ▶ **guttering** *n*

gutter press *n Informal* the section of the popular press that concentrates on the sensational aspects of the news.

guttersnipe *n Brit* a child who spends most of his or her time in the streets, usually in a slum area.

guttural (**gut**-ter-al) *adj* **1** *Phonetics* pronounced at the back of the throat. **2** harsh-sounding. ▷ HISTORY Latin *guttur* gullet

guy[1] *n* **1** *Informal* a man or boy. **2** *Informal* a person of either sex: *it's been very nice talking to you guys again.* **3** *Brit* a crude model of Guy Fawkes, that is burnt on top of a bonfire on Guy Fawkes Day (November 5). ▷ HISTORY short for *Guy* Fawkes, who plotted to blow up the Houses of Parliament

guy[2] *n* a rope or chain for steadying or securing something such as a tent. Also: **guyrope** ▷ HISTORY probably Low German

guzzle *vb* **-zling, -zled** to eat or drink quickly or greedily: *the guests guzzled their way through squid with mushrooms.* ▷ HISTORY origin unknown

gybe *or* **jibe** (**jibe**) *Naut* ✧ *vb* **gybing, gybed** *or* **jibing, jibed 1** (of a fore-and-aft sail) to swing suddenly from one side of a ship to the other. **2** to change the course of (a ship) by letting the sail gybe. ✧ *n* **3** an instance of gybing. ▷ HISTORY obsolete Dutch *gijben*

gym *n* short for **gymnasium, gymnastics**.

gymkhana (jim-**kah**-na) *n Brit, Austral & NZ* an event in which horses and riders take part in various races and contests.

> **WORD HISTORY**
>
> Originally the word 'gymkhana' did not apply to horse-riding but to other sporting and athletic activities. Hindi *gend-khānā* literally means a 'ball house' or 'racket court', and that is where sports activities were held. *Gend* was altered to 'gym' under the influence of words like 'gymnastics'.

gymnasium *n* a large room containing equipment such as bars, weights, and ropes, for physical exercise. ▷ HISTORY Greek *gumnazein* to exercise naked

gymnast *n* a person who is skilled or trained in gymnastics.

gymnastics *n* **1** practice or training in exercises that develop physical strength and agility. ✧ *pl n* **2** such exercises. ▶ **gymnastic** *adj*

gym shoes *pl n* same as **plimsolls**.

gymslip *n* a tunic formerly worn by schoolgirls as part of school uniform.

gynaecology *or US* **gynecology** (guy-nee-**kol**-la-jee) *n* the branch of medicine concerned with diseases and conditions specific to women. ▷ HISTORY Greek *gunē* woman + -LOGY ▶ **gynaecological** *or US* **gynecological** *adj* ▶ **gynaecologist** *or US* **gynecologist** *n*

gynoecium (guy-**nee**-see-um) *n, pl* **-cia** (-see-a) *Bot* the carpels of a flowering plant collectively.

gyp *or* **gip** *n* **give someone gyp** *Brit, Austral & NZ slang* to cause someone severe pain: *her back's still giving her gyp.* ▷ HISTORY probably a contraction of *gee up!*

gypsophila *n* a garden plant with small white flowers.

gypsum *n* a mineral used in making plaster of Paris. ▷ HISTORY Greek *gupsos*

Gypsy *or* **Gipsy** *n, pl* **-sies** a member of a travelling people scattered throughout Europe and North America. ▷ HISTORY from *Egyptian,* since they were thought to have come originally from Egypt

gyrate (jire-**rate**) *vb* **-rating, -rated** to turn round and round in a circle. ▷ HISTORY Greek *guros* circle ▶ **gyration** *n*

gyre *n* **1** a circular or spiral movement or path. **2** a ring, circle, or spiral. **3** *Geog* a circular current that goes clockwise (N Hemisphere) or anticlockwise (S Hemisphere) round an ocean basin due to the rotation of the earth and the Coriolis effect. ✧ *vb* **gyres, gyring, gyred. 4** to whirl. ▷ HISTORY Latin *gȳrus* circle, from Greek *guros*

gyrfalcon (**jur**-fawl-kon) *n* a very large rare falcon of northern regions. ▷ HISTORY Old French *gerfaucon*

gyro *n, pl* **-ros** short for **gyroscope**.

gyrocompass *n* a nonmagnetic compass that uses a motor-driven gyroscope to indicate true north. ▷ HISTORY Greek *guros* circle + COMPASS

gyroscope (**jire**-oh-skope) *n* a device containing a disc rotating on an axis that can turn freely in any direction, so that the disc maintains the same position regardless of the movement of the surrounding structure. ▷ HISTORY Greek *guros* circle + *skopein* to watch ▶ **gyroscopic** *adj*

H h

A B C D E F G H I J K L M N O P Q R S T U V W X Y Z

H **1** *Chem* hydrogen. **2** *Physics* henry.
ha[1] *or* **hah** *interj* an exclamation expressing triumph, surprise, or scorn.
ha[2] hectare.
Ha *Chem* hahnium.
habeas corpus (**hay**-bee-ass **kor**-puss) *n Law* a writ ordering a person to be brought before a judge, so as to decide whether his or her detention is lawful. ▷ **HISTORY** Latin: you may have the body
haberdasher *n Brit, Austral & NZ* a dealer in small articles used for sewing. ▷ **HISTORY** Anglo-French *hapertas* small items of merchandise ▶ **haberdashery** *n*
Haber process (**hah**-ber) *n Chem* a method of making ammonia by reacting nitrogen with hydrogen at high pressure in the presence of a catalyst. ▷ **HISTORY** after Fritz *Haber,* German chemist
habit *n* **1** a tendency to act in a particular way. **2** established custom or use: *the English habit of taking tea in the afternoon.* **3** an addiction to a drug. **4** mental disposition or attitude: *deference was a deeply ingrained habit of mind.* **5** the costume of a nun or monk. **6** a woman's riding costume. ▷ **HISTORY** Latin *habitus* custom
habitable *adj* fit to be lived in. ▶ **habitability** *n*
habitant *n* an early French settler in Canada or Louisiana or a descendant of one, esp. a farmer.
habitat *n* the natural home of an animal or plant. ▷ **HISTORY** Latin: it inhabits
habitation *n* **1** occupation of a dwelling place: *unfit for human habitation.* **2** *Formal* a dwelling place.
habitual *adj* **1** done regularly and repeatedly: *habitual behaviour patterns.* **2** by habit: *a habitual criminal.* ▶ **habitually** *adv*
habituate *vb* **-ating, -ated** to accustom; get used to: *habituated to failure.* ▶ **habituation** *n*
habitué (hab-**it**-yew-ay) *n* a frequent visitor to a place. ▷ **HISTORY** French
hachure (**hash**-yoor) *n* shading of short lines drawn on a map to indicate the degree of steepness of a hill. ▷ **HISTORY** French
hacienda (hass-ee-**end**-a) *n* (in Spanish-speaking countries) a ranch or large estate with a house on it. ▷ **HISTORY** Spanish
hack[1] *vb* **1** to chop roughly or violently. **2** to cut and clear (a way) through undergrowth. **3** (in sport) to foul (an opposing player) by kicking his or her shins. **4** *Brit & NZ informal* to tolerate. ✧ *n* **5** a cut or gash. **6** a tool, such as a pick. **7** a chopping blow. **8** a kick on the shins, such as in rugby. ▷ **HISTORY** Old English *haccian*
hack[2] *n* **1** a writer or journalist who produces work fast and on a regular basis. **2** a horse kept for riding, often one for hire. **3** *Brit* a country ride on horseback. ✧ *vb* **4** *Brit* to ride (a horse) cross-country for pleasure. ✧ *adj* **5** unoriginal or of a low standard: *clumsily contrived hack verse.* ▷ **HISTORY** short for *hackney*
hacker *n Slang* a computer enthusiast, esp. one who through a personal computer breaks into the computer system of a company or government. ▶ **hacking** *or* **hackery** *n*
hacking *adj* (of a cough) dry, painful and harsh-sounding.
hackles *pl n* **1 make one's hackles rise** make one feel angry or hostile. **2** the hairs or feathers on the back of the neck of certain animals or birds, which rise when they are angry. ▷ **HISTORY** Middle English *hakell*
hackney *n* **1** *Brit* a taxi. **2** same as **hack**[2] (sense 2). ▷ **HISTORY** probably after *Hackney,* London, where horses were formerly raised
hackneyed (**hak**-need) *adj* (of a word or phrase) unoriginal and overused.
hacksaw *n* a small saw for cutting metal.
had *vb* the past of **have**.
haddock *n, pl* **-dock** a North Atlantic food fish. ▷ **HISTORY** origin unknown
hadedah *or* **hadeda** (**hah**-dee-dah) *n* a large grey-green S African ibis. ▷ **HISTORY** imitative
Hades (**hay**-deez) *n Greek myth* **1** the underworld home of the souls of the dead. **2** the god of the underworld.
hadj *n* same as **hajj**.
hadji *n, pl* **hadjis** same as **hajji**.
Hadley cell *n Meteorol* the pattern of air circulation in which warm air rises near the Equator to sink around 30° latitude in each hemishere; first suggested by George Hadley in 1735 to explain trade winds.
haemal *or US* **hemal** (**heem**-al) *adj* of the blood. ▷ **HISTORY** Greek *haima* blood
haematic *or US* **hematic** (hee-**mat**-ik) *adj* relating to or containing blood.
haematite *or* **hematite** *n Geol* a red, grey, or black mineral, found as massive beds and in veins and igneous rocks. It is the chief source of iron. ▷ **HISTORY** via Latin from Greek *haimatitēs* resembling blood, from *haima* blood ▶ **haematitic** *or* **hematitic** *adj*
haematology *or US* **hematology** *n* the branch of medical science concerned with the blood. ▷ **HISTORY** Greek *haima* blood + -LOGY ▶ **haematologist** *or US* ▶ **hematologist** *n*
haemoglobin *or US* **hemoglobin** (hee-moh-**globe**-in) *n* a protein in red blood cells that carries oxygen from the lungs to the tissues. ▷ **HISTORY** Greek *haima* blood + Latin *globus* ball
haemophilia *or US* **hemophilia** (hee-moh-**fill**-lee-a) *n* a hereditary disorder, usually affecting males, in which the blood does not clot properly. ▷ **HISTORY** Greek *haima* blood + *philos* loving ▶ **haemophiliac** *n*
haemorrhage *or US* **hemorrhage** (**hem**-or-ij) *n* **1** heavy bleeding from ruptured blood vessels. ✧ *vb* **-rhaging, -rhaged 2** to bleed heavily. ▷ **HISTORY** Greek *haima* blood + *rhēgnunai* to burst

haemorrhoids *or US* **hemorrhoids** (**hem**-or-oydz) *pl n Pathol* swollen veins in the wall of the anus. ▷ **HISTORY** Greek *haimorrhoos* discharging blood

haere mai (**hire**-a-my) *interj NZ* an expression of greeting or welcome. ▷ **HISTORY** Maori

hafnium *n Chem* a metallic element found in zirconium ores. Symbol: Hf. ▷ **HISTORY** after *Hafnia,* Latin name of Copenhagen

haft *n* the handle of an axe, knife, or dagger. ▷ **HISTORY** Old English *hæft*

hag *n* **1** an unpleasant or ugly old woman. **2** a witch. ▷ **HISTORY** Old English *hægtesse* witch ▶ **haggish** *adj*

haggard *adj* looking tired and ill. ▷ **HISTORY** Old French *hagard* wild

haggis *n* a Scottish dish made from sheep's or calf's offal, oatmeal, suet, and seasonings boiled in a skin made from the animal's stomach. ▷ **HISTORY** origin unknown

haggle *vb* **-gling, -gled** to bargain or wrangle (over a price). ▷ **HISTORY** Scandinavian

hagiography *n, pl* **-phies** the writing of lives of the saints. ▷ **HISTORY** Greek *hagios* holy + *graphein* to write ▶ **hagiographer** *n*

hagiology *n, pl* **-gies** literature about the lives and legends of saints. ▷ **HISTORY** Greek *hagios* holy + -LOGY

hag-ridden *adj* distressed or worried.

ha-ha[1] *or* **haw-haw** *interj* a written representation of the sound of laughter.

ha-ha[2] *n* a wall set in a ditch so as not to interrupt a view of the landscape. ▷ **HISTORY** French

hahnium *n Chem* a transuranic element artificially produced from californium. Symbol: Ha.

haiku (**hie**-koo) *n, pl* **-ku** a Japanese verse form in 17 syllables. ▷ **HISTORY** Japanese

hail[1] *n* **1** small pellets of ice falling from thunderclouds. **2** words, ideas, missiles, etc., directed with force and in great quantity: *a hail of abuse.* ✧ *vb* **3** to fall as hail: *it's hailing.* **4** to fall like hail: *blows hailed down on him.* ▷ **HISTORY** Old English *hægl*

hail[2] *vb* **1** to call out to; greet: *a voice from behind hailed him.* **2** to praise, acclaim, or acknowledge: *his crew had been hailed as heroes.* **3** to stop (a taxi) by shouting or gesturing. **4 hail from** to come originally from: *she hails from Nova Scotia.* ✧ *n* **5 within hailing distance** within hearing range. ✧ *interj* **6** *Poetic* an exclamation of greeting. ▷ **HISTORY** Old Norse *heill* healthy

Hail Mary *n RC Church* a prayer to the Virgin Mary.

hailstone *n* a pellet of hail.

hailstorm *n* a storm during which hail falls.

hair *n* **1** any of the threadlike outgrowths on the skin of mammals. **2** a mass of such outgrowths, such as on a person's head or an animal's body. **3** *Bot* a threadlike growth from the outer layer of a plant. **4** a very small distance or margin: *he missed death by a hair.* **5 get in someone's hair** *Informal* to annoy someone. **6 hair of the dog** an alcoholic drink taken as a cure for a hangover. **7 let one's hair down** to enjoy oneself without restraint. **8 not turn a hair** to show no reaction. **9 split hairs** to make petty and unnecessary distinctions. ▷ **HISTORY** Old English *hær* ▶ **hairless** *adj*

hairclip *n NZ & S African* a small bent metal hairpin.

hairdo *n, pl* **-dos** *Informal* the style of a person's hair.

hairdresser *n* **1** a person who cuts and styles hair. RELATED ADJECTIVE ✦ **tonsorial 2** a hairdresser's premises. ▶ **hairdressing** *n*

hairgrip *n Chiefly Brit* a small bent clasp used to fasten the hair.

hairline *n* **1** the edge of hair at the top of the forehead. ✧ *adj* **2** very fine or narrow: *a hairline crack.*

hairpiece *n* a section of false hair added to a person's real hair.

hairpin *n* a thin U-shaped pin used to fasten the hair.

hairpin bend *n* a bend in the road that curves very sharply.

hair-raising *adj* very frightening or exciting.

hair's-breadth *n* an extremely small margin or distance.

hair shirt *n* a shirt made of horsehair cloth worn against the skin as a penance.

hairstyle *n* the cut and arrangement of a person's hair. ▶ **hairstylist** *n*

hairy *adj* **hairier, hairiest 1** covered with hair. **2** *Slang* dangerous, exciting, and difficult. ▶ **hairiness** *n*

hajj *or* **hadj** *n* the pilgrimage a Muslim makes to Mecca. ▷ **HISTORY** Arabic

hajji *or* **hadji** *n, pl* **hajjis** *or* **hadjis** a Muslim who has made a pilgrimage to Mecca.

haka *n NZ* **1** a Maori war chant accompanied by actions. **2** a similar chant by a sports team.

hake *n, pl* **hake** *or* **hakes 1** a northern hemisphere edible fish of the cod family. **2** *Austral* same as **barracouta**. ▷ **HISTORY** origin unknown

hakea (**hah**-kee-a) *n* an Australian tree or shrub with hard woody fruit.

halal *or* **hallal** *n* meat from animals that have been slaughtered according to Muslim law. ▷ **HISTORY** Arabic: lawful

halberd *n History* a tall spear that includes an axe blade and a pick. ▷ **HISTORY** Middle High German *helm* handle + *barde* axe

halcyon (**hal**-see-on) *adj* **1** peaceful, gentle, and calm. **2 halcyon days** a time, usually in the past, of greatest happiness or success. ▷ **HISTORY** Greek *alkuōn* kingfisher

hale *adj* healthy and robust: *hale and hearty.* ▷ **HISTORY** Old English *hæl* whole

half *n, pl* **halves 1** either of two equal or corresponding parts that together make up a whole. **2** the fraction equal to one divided by two. **3** half a pint, esp. of beer. **4** *Sport* one of two equal periods of play in a game. **5** a half-price ticket. **6 by half** to an excessive degree: *too clever by half.* **7 by halves** without being thorough: *in Italy they rarely*

A B C D E F G H I J K L M N O P Q R S T U V W X Y Z

do things by halves. **8 go halves** to share expenses. ✧ *adj* **9** denoting one of two equal parts: *a half chicken.* ✧ *adv* **10** half in degree or quantity: *half as much.* **11** partially; to an extent: *half hidden in the trees.* **12 not half** *Informal* **a** *Brit* very; indeed: *it isn't half hard to look at these charts.* **b** yes, indeed. ▷ HISTORY Old English *healf*

half-and-half *adj* half one thing and half another thing.

halfback *n Rugby* a player positioned immediately behind the forwards.

half-baked *adj Informal* poorly planned: *half-baked policies.*

half board *n Brit* the daily provision by a hotel of bed, breakfast, and evening meal.

half-breed *n Offensive* a person whose parents are of different races.

half-brother *n* the son of either one's mother or father by another partner.

half-caste *n Offensive* a person whose parents are of different races.

half-crown *or* **half-a-crown** *n* a former British coin worth two shillings and sixpence ($12^1/_2$p).

half-day *n* a day when one works only in the morning or only in the afternoon.

half-hearted *adj* without enthusiasm or determination. ▸ **half-heartedly** *adv*

half-hour *n* **1** a period of 30 minutes. **2** the point of time 30 minutes after the beginning of an hour. ▸ **half-hourly** *adv, adj*

half-life *n* the time taken for radioactive material to lose half its radioactivity.

half-mast *n* the halfway position of a flag on a mast as a sign of mourning.

half-moon *n* **1** the moon when half its face is illuminated. **2** the time at which a half-moon occurs. **3** something shaped like a half-moon.

half-nelson *n* a wrestling hold in which a wrestler places an arm under his opponent's arm from behind and exerts pressure with his palm on the back of his opponent's neck.

halfpenny *or* **ha'penny** (**hayp**-nee) *n, pl* **-pennies** a former British coin worth half a penny.

half-pie *adj NZ informal* badly planned; not properly thought out: *a half-pie scheme.* ▷ HISTORY Maori *pai* good

half-sister *n* the daughter of either one's mother or father by another partner.

half term *n Brit education* a short holiday midway through a term.

half-timbered *adj* (of a building) having an exposed timber framework filled with brick or plaster.

half-time *n Sport* an interval between the two halves of a game.

halftone *n* a photographic illustration in which the image is composed of a large number of black and white dots.

half-track *n* a vehicle with moving tracks on the rear wheels.

half volley *n Sport* **1** a stroke or shot in which the ball is hit immediately after it bounces. ✧ *vb* **half-volley 2** to hit or kick (a ball) immediately after it bounces.

halfway *adv, adj* **1** at or to half the distance. **2** at or towards the middle of a period of time or of an event or process: *he only managed to get halfway up the hill.* **3 meet someone halfway** to compromise with someone.

halfway house *n* **1** a place to rest midway on a journey. **2** the halfway stage in any process: *a halfway house between the theatre and cinema is possible.*

halfwit *n* a foolish or feeble-minded person. ▸ **halfwitted** *adj*

halibut *n* a large edible flatfish. ▷ HISTORY Middle English *hali* holy (because it was eaten on holy days) + *butte* flatfish

halitosis *n* bad-smelling breath. ▷ HISTORY Latin *halitus* breath

hall *n* **1** an entry area to other rooms in a house. **2** a building or room for public meetings, dances, etc. **3** a residential building in a college or university. **4** *Brit* a great house of an estate; manor. **5** a large dining room in a college or university. **6** the large room of a castle or stately home. ▷ HISTORY Old English *heall*

hallelujah, halleluiah (hal-ee-**loo**-ya) *or* **alleluia** *interj* an exclamation of praise to God. ▷ HISTORY Hebrew *hellēl* to praise + *yāh* the Lord

hallmark *n* **1** a typical feature: *secrecy became the hallmark of government.* **2** *Brit* an official seal stamped on gold, silver, or platinum articles to guarantee purity and date of manufacture. **3** a mark of authenticity or excellence. ✧ *vb* **4** to stamp with a hallmark. ▷ HISTORY after Goldsmiths' *Hall* in London, where items were stamped

hallo *interj, n* same as **hello**.

hallowed *adj* **1** regarded as holy: *hallowed ground.* **2** respected and revered because of age, importance, or reputation: *the hallowed pitch at Lord's.* ▷ HISTORY Old English *hālgian* to consecrate

Halloween *or* **Hallowe'en** *n* October 31, celebrated by children by dressing up as ghosts, witches, etc.

> **WORD HISTORY**
> 'Halloween' means 'holy evening', from Old English *halig*, meaning 'holy', and *æfen*, meaning 'evening'. Halloween is the evening before All Saints' Day, November 1.

hallucinate *vb* **-nating, -nated** to seem to see something that is not really there. ▷ HISTORY Latin *alucinari*

hallucination *n* the experience of seeming to see something that is not really there. ▸ **hallucinatory** *adj*

hallucinogen *n* any drug that causes hallucinations. ▸ **hallucinogenic** *adj*

halo (**hay**-loh) *n, pl* **-loes** *or* **-los 1** a ring of light around the head of a sacred figure. **2** a circle of refracted light around the sun or moon. ✧ *vb* **-loes** *or* **-los, -loing, -loed 3** to surround with a halo. ▷ HISTORY Greek *halōs* circular threshing floor

halogen (**hal**-oh-jen) *n Chem* any of the nonmetallic chemical elements fluorine, chlorine, bromine, iodine, and astatine which form salts when combined with metal. ▷ **HISTORY** Greek *hals* salt + *-genēs* born

halt *vb* **1** to come to a stop or bring (someone or something) to a stop. ✧ *n* **2** a temporary standstill. **3** a military command to stop. **4** *Chiefly Brit* a minor railway station without a building: *Deeside Halt.* **5 call a halt to** to put an end to. ▷ **HISTORY** German *halten* to stop

halter *n* **1** a strap around a horse's head with a rope to lead it with. ✧ *vb* **2** to put a halter on (a horse). ▷ **HISTORY** Old English *hælfter*

halterneck *n* a woman's top or dress which fastens behind the neck, leaving the back and arms bare.

halting *adj* hesitant or uncertain: *she spoke halting Italian.*

halve *vb* **halving, halved 1** to divide (something) into two equal parts. **2** to reduce (the size or amount of something) by half. **3** *Golf* to draw with one's opponent on (a hole or round).

halyard *n Naut* a line for hoisting or lowering a ship's sail or flag. ▷ **HISTORY** Middle English *halier*

ham[1] *n* smoked or salted meat from a pig's thigh. ▷ **HISTORY** Old English *hamm*

ham[2] *n* **1** *Informal* an amateur radio operator. **2** *Theatre informal* an actor who overacts and exaggerates the emotions and gestures of a part. ✧ *adj* **3** (of actors or their performances) exaggerated and overstated. ✧ *vb* **hamming, hammed 4 ham it up** *Informal* to overact. ▷ **HISTORY** special use of HAM[1]

hamada *n Geog* an area of desert where bedrock is exposed as a consequence of erosion.

hamba *interj S African usually offensive* go away. ▷ **HISTORY** Nguni (language group of southern Africa): to go

hamburger *n* a flat round of minced beef, often served in a bread roll.

WORD HISTORY

Hamburgers are named after their city of origin, *Hamburg* in Germany. Similarly Frankfurters are sausages from the town of Frankfurt. The word 'hamburger' has nothing to do with 'ham', but the 'burger' part has now been taken as a noun in its own right, on the basis of which we now have 'beefburgers', 'cheeseburgers', and so on.

ham-fisted *or* **ham-handed** *adj Informal* very clumsy or awkward.

hamlet *n* a small village. ▷ **HISTORY** Old French *hamelet*

hammer *n* **1** a hand tool consisting of a heavy metal head on the end of a handle, used for driving in nails, beating metal, etc. **2** the part of a gun that causes the bullet to shoot when the trigger is pulled. **3** *Athletics* **a** a heavy metal ball attached to a flexible wire: thrown in competitions. **b** the sport of throwing the hammer. **4** an auctioneer's mallet. **5** the part of a piano that hits a string when a key is pressed. **6 come** *or* **go under the hammer** to be on sale at auction. **7 hammer and tongs** with great effort or energy. ✧ *vb* **8** to hit with or as if with a hammer. **9 hammer in** *or* **into** to force (facts or ideas) into someone through repetition. **10 hammer away at** to work at (something) constantly: *the paper hammered away at the same theme all the way through the campaign.* **11** *Brit* to criticize severely. **12** *Informal* to defeat heavily. **13** to feel or sound like hammering: *his heart was hammering.* ▷ **HISTORY** Old English *hamor*

hammer and sickle *n* the emblem on the flag of the former Soviet Union, representing the industrial workers and the peasants.

hammerhead *n* a shark with a wide flattened head.

hammer out *vb* to produce (an agreement) with great effort.

hammertoe *n* a condition in which the toe is permanently bent at the joint.

hammock *n* a hanging bed made of canvas or net. ▷ **HISTORY** Spanish *hamaca*

hamper[1] *vb* to make it difficult for (someone or something) to move or progress. ▷ **HISTORY** origin unknown

hamper[2] *n* **1** a large basket with a lid. **2** *Brit* a selection of food and drink packed as a gift. ▷ **HISTORY** Middle English *hanaper* a small basket

hamster *n* a small rodent with a stocky body, short tail, and cheek pouches. ▷ **HISTORY** German

hamstring *n* **1** one of the tendons at the back of the knee. ✧ *vb* **-stringing, -strung 2** to make it difficult for someone to take any action. ▷ **HISTORY** *ham* (in the sense: leg)

hand *n* **1** the part of the body at the end of the arm, consisting of a thumb, four fingers, and a palm. *RELATED ADJECTIVE* ▸ **manual 2** a person's style of writing: *scrolls written in her own hand.* **3** the influence a person or thing has over a particular situation: *the hand of the military in shaping policy was obvious.* **4** a part in some activity: *I remember with gratitude Fortune's hand in starting my collection.* **5** assistance: *give me a hand with the rice.* **6** a round of applause: *give a big hand to the most exciting duo in the game.* **7** consent to marry someone: *he asked for her hand in marriage.* **8** a manual worker. **9** a member of a ship's crew. **10** a pointer on a dial or gauge, esp. on a clock. **11 a** the cards dealt in one round of a card game. **b** one round of a card game. **12** a position indicated by its location to the side of an object or the observer: *on the right hand.* **13** a contrasting aspect or condition: *on the other hand.* **14** source: *I had experienced at first hand many management styles.* **15** a person who creates something: *a good hand at baking.* **16** a unit of length equalling four inches, used for measuring the height of horses. **17 by hand a** by manual rather than mechanical means. **b** by messenger: *the letter was delivered by hand.* **18 from hand to mouth** with no food or money in reserve: *living from hand to mouth.* **19 hand in glove** in close association. **20 hand over fist** steadily and quickly: *losing money hand over fist.* **21 in hand a** under control. **b** receiving attention: *the business in hand.* **c** available in reserve: *Pakistan*

A B C D E F G H I J K L M N O P Q R S T U V W X Y Z

have a game in hand. **22 keep one's hand in** to continue to practise something. **23 (near) at hand** very close. **24 on hand** close by; available. **25 out of hand a** beyond control. **b** decisively, without possible reconsideration: *he dismissed the competition out of hand.* **26 show one's hand** to reveal one's plans. **27 to hand** accessible. ✧ *vb* **28** to pass or give by the hand or hands. **29 hand it to someone** to give credit to someone. ✧ See also **hand down, hands**, etc. ▷ **HISTORY** Old English ▶ **handless** *adj*

handbag *n* a woman's small bag carried to contain personal articles.

handbill *n* a small printed notice for distribution by hand.

handbook *n* a reference manual giving practical information on a subject.

handbrake *n* a brake in a motor vehicle operated by a hand lever.

handbrake turn *n* a turn sharply reversing the direction of a vehicle by applying the handbrake while turning the steering wheel.

h & c hot and cold (water).

handcart *n* a simple cart pushed or pulled by hand, used for transporting goods.

handcuff *n* **1 handcuffs** a linked pair of locking metal rings used for securing prisoners. ✧ *vb* **2** to put handcuffs on (a person).

hand down *vb* **1** to pass on (knowledge, possessions, or skills) to a younger generation. **2** to pass (outgrown clothes) on from one member of a family to a younger one. **3** *US & Canad law* to announce (a verdict).

handful *n, pl* **-fuls 1** the amount that can be held in the hand. **2** a small number: *a handful of parents.* **3** *Informal* a person or animal that is difficult to control: *as a child she was a real handful.*

handicap *n* **1** a physical or mental disability. **2** something that makes progress difficult. **3 a** a contest in which competitors are given advantages or disadvantages in an attempt to equalize their chances. **b** the advantage or disadvantage given. **4** *Golf* the number of strokes by which a player's averaged score exceeds par for the course. ✧ *vb* **-capping, -capped 5** to make it difficult for (someone) to do something. ▷ **HISTORY** probably *hand in cap,* a lottery game in which players drew forfeits from a cap

handicapped *adj* physically or mentally disabled.

handicraft *n* **1** a skill performed with the hands, such as weaving. **2** the objects produced by people with such skills.

handiwork *n* **1** the result of someone's work or activity. **2** work produced by hand.

handkerchief *n* a small square of fabric used to wipe the nose.

handle *n* **1** the part of an object that is held or operated in order that it may be used. **2** a small lever used to open and close a door or window. **3** *Slang* a person's name. **4** a reason for doing something: *trying to get a handle on why companies borrow money.* **5 fly off the handle** *Informal* to become suddenly extremely angry. ✧ *vb* **-dling, -dled 6** to hold, move, operate or touch with the hands. **7** to have responsibility for: *she handles all their affairs personally.* **8** to manage successfully: *I can handle this challenge.* **9** to discuss (a subject). **10** to deal with in a specified way: *the affair was neatly handled.* **11** to trade or deal in (specified merchandise): *we handle 1800 properties in Normandy.* **12** to react or respond in a specified way to operation or control: *it's light and handles well.* ▷ **HISTORY** Old English ▶ **handling** *n*

handlebars *pl n* a metal tube with handles at each end, used for steering a bicycle or motorcycle.

handler *n* **1** a person who trains and controls an animal. **2** a person who handles something: *a baggage handler.*

hand-out *n, pl* **hand-outs 1** clothing, food, or money given to a needy person. **2** a leaflet, free sample, etc., given out to publicize something. **3** a piece of written information given out to the audience at a talk, lecture, etc. ✧ *vb* **hand out 4** to distribute.

hand-pick *vb* to select (a person) with great care, such as for a special job. ▶ **hand-picked** *adj*

handrail *n* a rail alongside a stairway, to provide support.

hands *pl n* **1 in someone's hands** in someone's control or power: *that's in the hands of the courts.* **2 change hands** to pass from the possession of one person to another. **3 have one's hands full** to be completely occupied. **4 off one's hands** no longer one's responsibility. **5 on one's hands** for which one is responsible: *what a problem case I've got on my hands.* **6 wash one's hands of** to have nothing more to do with. **7 win hands down** to win easily.

handset *n* a telephone mouthpiece and earpiece in a single unit.

handsome *adj* **1** (esp. of a man) good-looking. **2** (of a building, garden, etc.) large, well-made, and with an attractive appearance: *a handsome building.* **3** (of an amount of money) generous or large: *a handsome dividend.* ▷ **HISTORY** obsolete *handsom* easily handled ▶ **handsomely** *adv*

hands-on *adj* involving practical experience of equipment: *Navy personnel joined the 1986 expedition for hands-on operating experience.*

handstand *n* the act of supporting the body on the hands in an upside-down position.

hand-to-hand *adj, adv* (of combat) at close quarters, with fists or knives.

hand-to-mouth *adj, adv* with barely enough money or food to live on.

handwriting *n* **1** writing by hand rather than by typing or printing. **2** a person's characteristic writing style. ▶ **handwritten** *adj*

handy *adj* **handier, handiest 1** conveniently within reach. **2** easy to handle or use. **3** good at manual work. ▶ **handily** *adv*

handyman *n, pl* **-men** a man skilled at odd jobs.

hang *vb* **hanging, hung 1** to fasten or be fastened from above. **2** to place (something) in position, for instance by a hinge, so as to allow free movement: *to hang a door.* **3** to be suspended so as to allow movement from the place where it is attached: *her long hair hung over her face.* **4** to decorate with something suspended, such as pictures. **5** (of cloth or clothing) to fall or flow in a particular way: *the fine gauge knit hangs loosely with graceful femininity.* **6** (*pt & pp* **hanged**) to suspend or be suspended by the neck until dead. **7** to hover: *clouds hung over the mountains.* **8** to fasten to a wall: *to hang wallpaper.* **9** to exhibit or be exhibited in an art gallery. **10 hang over** to threaten or overshadow: *the threat of war hung over the Middle East.* **11** (*pt & pp* **hanged**) *Slang* to damn: used in mild curses or interjections. **12 hang fire** to put off doing something. ✧ *n* **13** the way in which something hangs. **14 get the hang of something** *Informal* to understand the technique of doing something. ✧ See also **hang about, hang back**, etc. ▷ **HISTORY** Old English *hangian*

hang about *or* **around** *vb* **1** to stand about idly somewhere. **2** (foll. by *with*) to spend a lot of time in the company (of someone).

hangar *n* a large building for storing aircraft. ▷ **HISTORY** French: shed

hang back *vb* to be reluctant to do something.

hangdog *adj* dejected, ashamed, or guilty in appearance or manner.

hanger *n* same as **coat hanger**.

hanger-on *n, pl* **hangers-on** an unwanted follower, esp. of a rich or famous person.

hang-glider *n* an unpowered aircraft consisting of a large cloth wing stretched over a light framework from which the pilot hangs in a harness. ▶ **hang-gliding** *n*

hangi (**hung**-ee) *n NZ* **1** an open-air cooking pit. **2** the food cooked in it. **3** the social gathering at the resultant meal. ▷ **HISTORY** Maori

hanging *n* **1** the act or practice of putting a person to death by suspending the body by the neck. **2** a large piece of cloth hung on a wall as a decoration.

hanging valley *n Geog* a tributary valley that enters a main valley high up because the main valley has been deepened through erosion by a glacier.

hangman *n, pl* **-men** an official who carries out a sentence of hanging.

hangover *n* a feeling of sickness and headache after drinking too much alcohol.

hang up *vb* **1** to replace (a telephone receiver) at the end of a conversation. **2** to put on a hook or hanger. ✧ *n* **hang-up 3** *Informal* an emotional or psychological problem.

hank *n* a loop or coil, esp. of yarn. ▷ **HISTORY** from Old Norse

hanker *vb* (foll. by *for* or *after*) to have a great desire for. ▷ **HISTORY** probably from Dutch dialect *hankeren* ▶ **hankering** *n*

hanky *or* **hankie** *n, pl* **hankies** *Informal* short for **handkerchief**.

hanky-panky *n Informal* **1** casual sexual relations. **2** mischievous behaviour. ▷ **HISTORY** variant of *hocus-pocus*

Hanoverian (han-no-**veer**-ee-an) *adj* of or relating to the British royal house ruling from 1714 to 1901. ▷ **HISTORY** after *Hanover,* Germany

Hansard *n* the official report of the proceedings of the British or Canadian parliament. ▷ **HISTORY** after L. *Hansard,* its original compiler

Hanseatic League (han-see-**at**-ik) *n History* a commercial organization of towns in N Germany formed in the 14th century to protect and control trade.

hansom *n* formerly, a two-wheeled one-horse carriage with a fixed hood. Also called: **hansom cab** ▷ **HISTORY** after its designer J. A. *Hansom*

Hanukkah *n* same as **Chanukah**.

haphazard *adj* not organized or planned. ▷ **HISTORY** Old Norse *happ* chance, good luck + HAZARD ▶ **haphazardly** *adv*

hapless *adj* unlucky: *the hapless victim of a misplaced murder attempt.* ▷ **HISTORY** Old Norse *happ* chance, good luck

haploid *adj Biol* denoting a cell or organism with unpaired chromosomes. ▷ **HISTORY** Greek *haplous* single

happen *vb* **1** to take place; occur. **2** to chance (to be or do something): *I happen to know him.* **3** to be the case, esp. by chance: *it happens that I know him.* **4 happen to** (of some unforeseen event, such as death) to be the experience or fate of: *if anything happens to me you will know.* ▷ **HISTORY** obsolete *hap*

> ☑ **WORD TIP**
> See at **occur.**

happening *n* an event that often occurs in a way that is unexpected or hard to explain: *some strange happenings in the village recently.*

happy *adj* **-pier, -piest 1** feeling or expressing joy. **2** causing joy or gladness: *the happiest day of my life.* **3** fortunate or lucky: *it was a happy coincidence.* **4** satisfied or content: *he seems happy to let things go on as they are.* **5** willing: *I'll be happy to arrange a loan for you.* ▷ **HISTORY** Old Norse *happ* chance, good luck ▶ **happily** *adv* ▶ **happiness** *n*

happy-go-lucky *adj* carefree or easy-going.

hara-kiri *n* (formerly, in Japan) ritual suicide by disembowelment when disgraced or under sentence of death. ▷ **HISTORY** Japanese *hara* belly + *kiri* cut

harangue *vb* **-ranguing, -rangued 1** to address (a person or group) in an angry or forcefully persuasive way. ✧ *n* **2** a forceful or angry speech. ▷ **HISTORY** Old Italian *aringa* public speech

harass *vb* to trouble or annoy (someone) by repeated attacks, questions, or problems. ▷ **HISTORY** French *harasser* ▶ **harassed** *adj* ▶ **harassment** *n*

harbinger (**har**-binge-er) *n Literary* a person or thing that announces or indicates the approach of something: *a harbinger of death.* ▷ **HISTORY** Old French *herbergere*

harbour *or US* **harbor** *n* **1** a sheltered port. **2** a place of refuge or safety. ✧ *vb* **3** to maintain secretly in the mind: *he might be harbouring a death* wish. **4** to give shelter or protection to: *the government accused her of harbouring criminals.* ▷ **HISTORY** Old English *herebeorg*, from *here* army + *beorg* shelter

hard *adj* **1** firm, solid, or rigid. **2** difficult to do or understand: *a hard sum.* **3** showing or requiring a lot of effort or application: *hard work.* **4** unkind or unfeeling: *she's very hard, no pity for anyone.* **5** causing pain, sorrow, or hardship: *the hard life of a northern settler.* **6** tough or violent: *a hard man.* **7** forceful: *a hard knock.* **8** cool or uncompromising: *we took a long hard look at our profit factor.* **9** indisputable and proven to be true: *hard facts.* **10** (of water) containing calcium salts which stop soap lathering freely. **11** practical, shrewd, or calculating: *he is a hard man in business.* **12** harsh: *hard light.* **13** (of currency) high and stable in exchange value. **14** (of alcoholic drink) being a spirit rather than a wine or beer. **15** (of a drug) highly addictive. **16** hard-core. **17** *Phonetics* denoting the consonants *c* and *g* when they are pronounced as in *cat* and *got*. **18** politically extreme: *the hard left.* **19 hard of hearing** slightly deaf. **20 hard up** *Informal* in need of money. ✧ *adv* **21** with great energy or force: *they fought so hard and well in Spain.* **22** with great intensity: *thinking hard about the conversation.* **23 hard by** very close to: *Cleveland Place, hard by Bruntsfield Square.* **24 hard put (to it)** scarcely having the capacity (to do something). ✧ *n* **25 have a hard on** *Taboo slang* to have an erection of the penis. ▷ **HISTORY** Old English *heard* ▶ **hardness** *n*

hard-and-fast *adj* (of rules) fixed and not able to be changed.

hardback *n* **1** a book with stiff covers. ✧ *adj* **2** of or denoting a hardback.

hard-bitten *adj Informal* tough and determined.

hardboard *n* stiff board made in thin sheets of compressed sawdust and wood pulp.

hard-boiled *adj* **1** (of an egg) boiled until solid. **2** *Informal* tough, realistic, and unemotional.

hard cash *n* money or payment in money, as opposed to payment by cheque, credit, etc.

hard copy *n* computer output printed on paper.

hard core *n* **1** the members of a group who most resist change. **2** broken stones used to form a foundation for a road. ✧ *adj* **hard-core 3** (of pornography) showing sexual acts in explicit detail. **4** extremely committed or fanatical: *a hard-core Communist.*

hard disk *n Computers* an inflexible disk in a sealed container.

harden *vb* **1** to make or become hard; freeze, stiffen, or set. **2** to make or become tough or unfeeling: *life in the camp had hardened her considerably.* **3** to make or become stronger or firmer: *they hardened defences.* **4** to make or become more determined or resolute: *the government has hardened its attitude to the crisis.* **5** *Commerce* (of prices or a market) to cease to fluctuate.

hardened *adj* toughened by experience: *a hardened criminal.*

hardfill *n NZ & S African* a stone waste material used for landscaping.

hard-headed *adj* tough, realistic, or shrewd, esp. in business.

hardhearted *adj* unsympathetic and uncaring.

hard labour *n* difficult and tiring physical work: used as a punishment for a crime in some countries.

hard line *n* **1** an uncompromising policy: *a hard line on drugs.* ✧ *adj* **hard-line 2** tough and uncompromising: *a hard-line attitude to the refugee problem.* ▶ **hardliner** *n*

hardly *adv* **1** scarcely; barely: *he'd hardly sipped his whisky.* **2** *Ironic* not at all: *it was hardly in the Great Train Robbery league.* **3** with difficulty: *their own families would hardly recognize them.*

> **☑ WORD TIP**
>
> Since *hardly, scarcely,* and *barely* already have negative force, it is redundant to use another negative in the same clause: *he had hardly had* (not *he hadn't hardly had*) *time to think; there was scarcely any* (not *scarcely no*) *bread left.*

hard news *n* news stories based on important real events rather than analysis, interpretation, or gossip. Compare **soft news**.

hard pad *n* (in dogs) an abnormal increase in the thickness of the foot pads: a sign of distemper.

hard palate *n* the bony front part of the roof of the mouth.

hard sell *n* an aggressive insistent technique of selling.

hardship *n* **1** conditions of life that are difficult to endure. **2** something that causes suffering.

hard shoulder *n Brit & NZ* a surfaced verge running along the edge of a motorway and other roads for emergency stops.

hardware *n* **1** metal tools or implements, esp. cutlery or cooking utensils. **2** *Computers* the physical equipment used in a computer system. **3** heavy military equipment, such as tanks and missiles.

hard-wired *adj* (of a circuit or instruction) permanently wired into a computer.

hardwood *n* the wood of a deciduous tree such as oak, beech, or ash.

hardy *adj* **-dier, -diest 1** able to stand difficult conditions. **2** (of plants) able to live out of doors throughout the winter. ▷ **HISTORY** Old French *hardi* emboldened ▶ **hardiness** *n*

hare *n, pl* **hares** *or* **hare 1** a mammal like a large rabbit, with longer ears and legs. ✧ *vb* **haring, hared 2** (foll. by *off* or *after*) *Brit & Austral informal* to run fast or wildly. ▷ **HISTORY** Old English *hara*

harebell *n* a blue bell-shaped flower.

harebrained *adj* foolish or impractical: *harebrained schemes.*

harelip *n* a slight split in the mid line of the upper lip.

harem *n* **1** a Muslim man's wives and concubines collectively. **2** the part of an Oriental house reserved for wives and concubines. ▷ **HISTORY** Arabic *harīm* forbidden (place)

haricot bean *or* **haricot** (**har**-rik-oh) *n* a white edible bean, which can be dried. ▷ HISTORY French *haricot*

hark *vb Old-fashioned* to listen; pay attention: *hark, the cocks are crowing.* ▷ HISTORY Old English *heorcnian*

hark back *vb* to return (to an earlier subject in speech or thought): *he keeps harking back to his music-hall days.*

harlequin *n* **1** *Theatre* a stock comic character, usually wearing a diamond-patterned multicoloured costume and a black mask. ✧ *adj* **2** in varied colours. ▷ HISTORY Old French *Herlequin* leader of a band of demon horsemen

harlequinade *n Theatre* a play in which harlequin has a leading role.

harlot *n Literary* a prostitute. ▷ HISTORY Old French *herlot* rascal ▶ **harlotry** *n*

harm *vb* **1** to injure physically, morally, or mentally. ✧ *n* **2** physical, moral, or mental injury. ▷ HISTORY Old English *hearm*

harmful *adj* causing or tending to cause harm, esp. to a person's health.

harmless *adj* **1** safe to use, touch, or be near. **2** unlikely to annoy or worry people: *a harmless habit.*

harmonic *adj* **1** of, producing, or characterized by harmony; harmonious. ✧ *n* **2** *Music* an overtone of a musical note produced when that note is played, but not usually heard as a separate note. ✧ See also **harmonics**. ▷ HISTORY Latin *harmonicus* relating to harmony ▶ **harmonically** *adv*

harmonica *n* a small wind instrument in which reeds enclosed in a narrow oblong box are made to vibrate by blowing and sucking.

harmonics *n* the science of musical sounds.

harmonious *adj* **1** (esp. of colours or sounds) consisting of parts which blend together well. **2** showing agreement, peacefulness, and friendship: *a harmonious relationship.* **3** tuneful or melodious.

harmonium *n* a musical keyboard instrument in which air from pedal-operated bellows causes the reeds to vibrate.

harmonize *or* **-nise** *vb* **-nizing, -nized** *or* **-nising, -nised 1** to sing or play in harmony, such as with another singer or player. **2** to make or become harmonious.

harmony *n, pl* **-nies 1** a state of peaceful agreement and cooperation. **2** *Music* a pleasant combination of two or more notes sounded at the same time. **3** the way parts combine well together or into a whole. ▷ HISTORY Greek *harmonia*

harness *n* **1** an arrangement of straps for attaching a horse to a cart or plough. **2** something resembling this, for attaching something to a person's body: *a parachute harness.* **3 in harness** at one's routine work. ✧ *vb* **4** to put a harness on (a horse or other animal). **5** to control something in order to make use of it: *learning to harness the power of your own mind.* ▷ HISTORY Old French *harneis* baggage

harp *n* **1** a large upright triangular stringed instrument played by plucking the strings with the fingers. ✧ *vb* **2 harp on** to speak in a persistent and tedious manner (about a subject). ▷ HISTORY Old English *hearpe* ▶ **harpist** *n*

harpoon *n* **1** a barbed spear attached to a long rope and thrown or fired when hunting whales, etc. ✧ *vb* **2** to spear with a harpoon. ▷ HISTORY probably from Dutch *harpoen*

harpsichord *n* a keyboard instrument, resembling a small piano, with strings that are plucked mechanically. ▷ HISTORY Late Latin *harpa* harp + Latin *chorda* string ▶ **harpsichordist** *n*

harpy *n, pl* **-pies** a violent, unpleasant, or greedy woman. ▷ HISTORY Greek *Harpuiai* the Harpies, literally: snatchers (mythical birdlike female monsters)

harridan *n* a scolding old woman; nag. ▷ HISTORY origin unknown

harrier[1] *n* a cross-country runner. ▷ HISTORY from *hare*

harrier[2] *n* a bird of prey with broad wings and long legs and tail.

harrow *n* **1** an implement used to break up clods of soil. ✧ *vb* **2** to draw a harrow over (land). ▷ HISTORY from Old Norse

harrowing *adj* very upsetting or disturbing.

harry *vb* **-ries, -rying, -ried** to keep asking (someone) to do something; pester. ▷ HISTORY Old English *hergian*

harsh *adj* **1** severe and difficult to cope with: *harsh winters.* **2** unkind and showing no understanding: *the Judge was very harsh on the demonstrators.* **3** excessively hard, bright, or rough: *harsh sunlight.* **4** (of sounds) unpleasant and grating. ▷ HISTORY probably Scandinavian ▶ **harshly** *adv* ▶ **harshness** *n*

hart *n, pl* **harts** *or* **hart** the male of the deer, esp. the red deer. ▷ HISTORY Old English *heorot*

hartebeest *n* a large African antelope with curved horns and a fawn-coloured coat. ▷ HISTORY Dutch

harum-scarum *adj* **1** reckless. ✧ *adv* **2** recklessly. ✧ *n* **3** an impetuous person. ▷ HISTORY origin unknown

harvest *n* **1** the gathering of a ripened crop. **2** the crop itself. **3** the season for gathering crops. **4** the product of an effort or action. ✧ *vb* **5** to gather (a ripened crop). **6** *Chiefly US* to remove (an organ) from the body for transplantation. ▷ HISTORY Old English *hærfest*

harvester *n* **1** a harvesting machine, esp. a combine harvester. **2** a person who harvests.

harvest moon *n* the full moon occurring nearest to the autumn equinox.

harvest mouse *n* a very small reddish-brown mouse that lives in cornfields or hedgerows.

has *vb* third person singular of the present tense of **have**.

has-been *n Informal* a person who is no longer popular or successful.

hash[1] *n* **1** a dish of diced cooked meat, vegetables, etc., reheated: *corned-beef hash.* **2** a

A B C D E F G H I J K L M N O P Q R S T U V W X Y Z

reworking of old material. **3 make a hash of** *Informal* to mess up or destroy. ▷ HISTORY Old French *hacher* to chop up

hash[2] *n Slang* short for **hashish**.

hashish (**hash**-eesh) *n* a drug made from the hemp plant, smoked for its intoxicating effects. ▷ HISTORY Arabic

hasp *n* a clasp which fits over a staple and is secured by a pin, bolt, or padlock, used as a fastening. ▷ HISTORY Old English *hæpse*

hassium *n Chem* an element synthetically produced in small quantities by high-energy ion bombardment. Symbol: Hs. ▷ HISTORY Latin, from *Hesse*, the German state where it was discovered

hassle *Informal* ✧ *n* **1** a great deal of trouble. **2** a prolonged argument. ✧ *vb* **-sling, -sled 3** to cause annoyance or trouble to (someone): *stop hassling me!* ▷ HISTORY origin unknown

hassock *n* a cushion for kneeling on in church. ▷ HISTORY Old English *hassuc* matted grass

haste *n* **1** speed, esp. in an action. **2** the act of hurrying in a careless manner. **3 make haste** to hurry or rush. ✧ *vb* **hasting, hasted 4** *Poetic* to hasten. ▷ HISTORY Old French

hasten *vb* **1** to hurry or cause to hurry. **2** to be anxious (to say something).

hasty *adj* **-tier, -tiest 1** done or happening suddenly or quickly. **2** done too quickly and without thought; rash. ▶ **hastily** *adv*

hat *n* **1** a head covering, often with a brim, usually worn to give protection from the weather. **2** *Informal* a role or capacity: *I'm wearing my honorary consul's hat.* **3 keep something under one's hat** to keep something secret. **4 pass the hat round** to collect money for a cause. **5 take off one's hat to someone** to admire or congratulate someone. ▷ HISTORY Old English *hætt*

hatch[1] *vb* **1** to cause (the young of various animals, esp. birds) to emerge from the egg or (of young birds, etc.) to emerge from the egg. **2** (of eggs) to break and release the young animal within. **3** to devise (a plot or plan). ▷ HISTORY Germanic

hatch[2] *n* **1** a hinged door covering an opening in a floor or wall. **2 a** short for **hatchway**. **b** a door in an aircraft or spacecraft. **3** Also called: **serving hatch** an opening in a wall between a kitchen and a dining area. **4** *Informal* short for **hatchback**. ▷ HISTORY Old English *hæcc*

hatch[3] *vb Drawing, engraving, etc.* to mark (a figure, etc.) with fine parallel or crossed lines to indicate shading. ▷ HISTORY Old French *hacher* to chop ▶ **hatching** *n*

hatchback *n* a car with a single lifting door in the rear.

hatchet *n* **1** a short axe used for chopping wood, etc. **2 bury the hatchet** to make peace or resolve a disagreement. ✧ *adj* **3** narrow and sharp: *a hatchet face.* ▷ HISTORY Old French *hachette*

hatchet job *n Informal* a malicious verbal or written attack.

hatchet man *n Informal* a person who carries out unpleasant tasks on behalf of an employer.

hatchling *n* a young animal that has newly hatched from an egg.

hatchway *n* an opening in the deck of a vessel to provide access below.

hate *vb* **hating, hated 1** to dislike (someone or something) intensely. **2** to be unwilling (to do something): *I hate to trouble you.* ✧ *n* **3** intense dislike. **4** *Informal* a person or thing that is hated: *my own pet hate is restaurants.* ▷ HISTORY Old English *hatian* ▶ **hater** *n*

hateful *adj* causing or deserving hate.

hatred *n* intense dislike.

hat trick *n* **1** *Cricket* the achievement of a bowler in taking three wickets with three successive balls. **2** any achievement of three successive goals, victories, etc.

hauberk *n History* a long sleeveless coat of mail. ▷ HISTORY Old French *hauberc*

haughty *adj* **-tier, -tiest** having or showing excessive pride or arrogance. ▷ HISTORY Latin *altus* high ▶ **haughtily** *adv* ▶ **haughtiness** *n*

haul *vb* **1** to drag or pull (something) with effort. **2** to transport, such as in a lorry. **3** *Naut* to alter the course of (a vessel). ✧ *n* **4** the act of dragging with effort. **5** a quantity of something obtained: *a good haul of fish; a huge haul of stolen goods.* **6 long haul a** a long journey. **b** a long difficult process. ▷ HISTORY Old French *haler*

haulage *n* **1** the business of transporting goods. **2** a charge for transporting goods.

haulier *n Brit & Austral* a person or firm that transports goods by road.

haulm (**hawm**) *n* the stalks of beans, peas, or potatoes collectively. ▷ HISTORY Old English *healm*

haunch *n* **1** the human hip or fleshy hindquarter of an animal. **2** the leg and loin of an animal, used for food. ▷ HISTORY Old French *hanche*

haunt *vb* **1** to visit (a person or place) in the form of a ghost. **2** to remain in the memory or thoughts of: *it was a belief which haunted her.* **3** to visit (a place) frequently. ✧ *n* **4** a place visited frequently. ▷ HISTORY Old French *hanter*

haunted *adj* **1** (of a place) frequented or visited by ghosts. **2** (of a person) obsessed or worried.

haunting *adj* having a quality of great beauty or sadness so as to be memorable: *a haunting melody.*

hautboy (**oh**-boy) *n Old-fashioned* an oboe. ▷ HISTORY French *haut* high + *bois* wood

haute couture (**oat** koo-**ture**) *n* high fashion. ▷ HISTORY French

hauteur (oat-**ur**) *n* haughtiness. ▷ HISTORY French *haut* high

Havana *n* a hand-rolled cigar from Cuba.

have *vb* **has, having, had 1** to possess: *he has a massive collection of old movies; I have an iron constitution.* **2** to receive, take, or obtain: *I had a long letter.* **3** to hold in the mind: *she always had a yearning to be a schoolteacher.* **4** to possess a knowledge of: *I have no German.* **5** to experience or be affected by: *a good way to have a change.* **6** to suffer from: *to have a blood pressure problem.* **7** to gain control of or advantage over: *you have me on that point.* **8** *Slang* to cheat or outwit: *I've been had.*

9 to show: *have mercy on me.* **10** to take part in; hold: *I had a telephone conversation.* **11** to cause to be done: *have my shoes mended by Friday.* **12 have to** used to express compulsion or necessity: *you'd have to wait six months.* **13** to eat or drink. **14** *Taboo slang* to have sexual intercourse with. **15** to tolerate or allow: *I won't have all this noise.* **16** to receive as a guest: *we have visitors.* **17** to be pregnant with or give birth to (offspring). **18** used to form past tenses: *I have gone; I had gone.* **19 have had it** *Informal* **a** to be exhausted or killed. **b** to have lost one's last chance. **20 have it off** *Taboo, Brit slang* to have sexual intercourse. ✧ *n* **21 haves** *Informal* people who have wealth, security, etc.: *the haves and the have-nots.* ✧ See also **have on**. ▷ **HISTORY** Old English *habban*

haven *n* **1** a place of safety. **2** a harbour for shipping. ▷ **HISTORY** Old English *hæfen*

have on *vb* **1** to wear: *he'd got a long pair of trousers on.* **2** to have a commitment: *what do you have on this afternoon?* **3** *Informal* to trick or tease: *he's having you on.* **4** to have (information, esp. when incriminating) about (a person): *she's got something on him.*

haver *vb* **1** *Scot & N English dialect* to talk nonsense. **2** to be unsure and hesitant; dither. ▷ **HISTORY** origin unknown

haversack *n* a canvas bag carried on the back or shoulder. ▷ **HISTORY** French *havresac*

have up *vb* to bring to trial: *what, and get me had up for kidnapping?*

havoc *n* **1** *Informal* chaos, disorder, and confusion. **2 play havoc with** to cause a great deal of damage or confusion to. ▷ **HISTORY** Old French *havot* pillage

haw[1] *n* the fruit of the hawthorn. ▷ **HISTORY** Old English *haga*

haw[2] *vb* **hum** *or* **hem and haw** to hesitate in speaking. ▷ **HISTORY** imitative

hawk[1] *n* **1** a bird of prey with short rounded wings and a long tail. **2** a supporter or advocate of warlike policies. ✧ *vb* **3** to hunt with falcons or hawks. ▷ **HISTORY** Old English *hafoc* ▶ **hawkish** *adj* ▶ **hawklike** *adj*

hawk[2] *vb* to offer (goods) for sale in the street or door-to-door. ▷ **HISTORY** from *hawker* pedlar

hawk[3] *vb* **1** to clear the throat noisily. **2** to force (phlegm) up from the throat. ▷ **HISTORY** imitative

hawker *n* a person who travels from place to place selling goods. ▷ **HISTORY** probably from Middle Low German *hōken* to peddle

hawk-eyed *adj* having extremely keen eyesight.

hawser *n Naut* a large heavy rope. ▷ **HISTORY** Anglo-French *hauceour*

hawthorn *n* a thorny tree or shrub with white or pink flowers and reddish fruits. ▷ **HISTORY** Old English *haguthorn*

hay *n* **1** grass cut and dried as fodder. **2 hit the hay** *Slang* to go to bed. **3 make hay while the sun shines** to take full advantage of an opportunity. ▷ **HISTORY** Old English *hieg*

hay fever *n* an allergic reaction to pollen, which causes sneezing, runny nose, and watery eyes.

haystack *or* **hayrick** *n* a large pile of hay built in the open and covered with thatch.

haywire *adj* **go haywire** *Informal* to stop functioning properly.

hazard *n* **1** a thing likely to cause injury, loss, etc. **2 at hazard** at risk. **3** risk or likelihood of injury, loss, etc.: *evaluate the level of hazard in a situation.* **4** *Golf* an obstacle such as a bunker. ✧ *vb* **5** to risk: *hazarding the health of his crew.* **6 hazard a guess** to make a guess. ▷ **HISTORY** Arabic *az-zahr* the die

hazard lights *or* **hazard warning lights** *n* the indicator lights on a motor vehicle when flashing simultaneously to indicate that the vehicle is stationary.

hazardous *adj* involving great risk.

haze *n* **1** *Meteorol* reduced visibility as a result of condensed water vapour, dust, etc., in the air. **2** confused or unclear understanding or feeling. ▷ **HISTORY** from *hazy*

hazel *n* **1** a shrub with edible rounded nuts. ✧ *adj* **2** greenish-brown: *hazel eyes.* ▷ **HISTORY** Old English *hæsel*

hazelnut *n* the nut of a hazel shrub, which has a smooth shiny hard shell.

hazy *adj* **-zier, -ziest 1** (of the sky or a view) unable to be seen clearly because of dust or heat. **2** dim or vague: *my memory is a little hazy on this.* ▷ **HISTORY** origin unknown ▶ **hazily** *adv* ▶ **haziness** *n*

Hb haemoglobin.

HB *Brit & Austral* (of pencil lead) hard-black: denoting a medium-hard lead.

H-bomb *n* short for **hydrogen bomb**.

he *pron* refers to: **1** a male person or animal. **2** a person or animal of unknown or unspecified sex: *a member may vote as he sees fit.* ✧ *n* **3** a male person or animal: *a he-goat.* ▷ **HISTORY** Old English *hē*

He *Chem* helium.

HE His *or* Her Excellency.

head *n* **1** the upper or front part of the body that contains the brain, eyes, mouth, nose, and ears. **2** a person's mind and mental abilities: *I haven't any head for figures.* **3** the most forward part of a thing: *the head of a queue.* **4** the highest part of a thing; upper end: *the head of the pass.* **5** something resembling a head in form or function, such as the top of a tool. **6** the position of leadership or command. **7** the person commanding most authority within a group or an organization. **8** *Bot* the top part of a plant, where the leaves or flowers grow in a cluster. **9** a culmination or crisis: *the matter came to a head in December 1928.* **10** the froth on the top of a glass of beer. **11** the pus-filled tip of a pimple or boil. **12** part of a computer or tape recorder that can read, write, or erase information. **13** the source of a river or stream. **14** the side of a coin that usually bears a portrait of the head of a monarch, etc. **15** a headland or promontory: *Beachy Head.* **16** pressure of water or steam in an enclosed space. **17** (*pl* **head**) a person or animal considered as a unit: *the cost per head of Paris's refuse collection; six hundred head of cattle.* **18** a headline or heading. **19** *Informal* short for **headmaster, headmistress, head teacher**.

20 *Informal* short for **headache**. **21 give someone his head** to allow someone greater freedom or responsibility. **22 go to one's head a** (of an alcoholic drink) to make one slightly drunk. **b** to make one conceited: *success has gone to his head.* **23 head over heels (in love)** very much (in love). **24 keep one's head** to remain calm. **25 not make head nor tail of** not to understand (a problem, etc.). **26 off one's head** *Slang* very foolish or insane. **27 on one's own head** at a one's own risk. **28 over someone's head a** to a higher authority: *the taboo of going over the head of their immediate boss.* **b** beyond a person's understanding. **29 put our, your** *or* **their heads together** *Informal* to consult together. **30 turn someone's head** to make someone conceited. ✧ *vb* **31** to be at the front or top of: *Barnes headed the list.* **32** to be in charge of. **33** (often foll. by *for*) to go or cause to go (towards): *to head for the Channel ports.* **34** *Soccer* to propel (the ball) by striking it with the head. **35** to provide with a heading. ✧ See also **heads**. ▷ HISTORY Old English *hēafod*

headache *n* **1** a continuous pain in the head. **2** *Informal* any cause of worry, difficulty, or annoyance: *financial headaches.*

head-banger *n Brit, Austral & NZ slang* **1** a person who shakes his head violently to the beat of heavy-metal music. **2** a crazy or stupid person.

headboard *n* a vertical board at the head of a bed.

headdress *n* any decorative head covering.

header *n* **1** *Soccer* the action of striking a ball with the head. **2** *Informal* a headlong fall or dive.

head-hunting *n* **1** (of companies) the practice of actively searching for new high-level personnel, often from rival companies. **2** the practice among certain peoples of removing the heads of enemies they have killed and preserving them as trophies. ▶ **head-hunter** *n*

heading *n* **1** a title for a page, chapter, etc. **2** a main division, such as of a speech. **3** *Mining* a horizontal tunnel.

headland *n* a narrow area of land jutting out into a sea.

headlight *or* **headlamp** *n* a powerful light on the front of a vehicle.

headline *n* **1** a phrase in heavy large type at the top of a newspaper or magazine article indicating the subject. **2 headlines** the main points of a television or radio news broadcast.

headlong *adv, adj* **1** with the head foremost; headfirst. **2** with great haste and without much thought: *they rushed headlong into buying a house.*

headmaster *or fem* **headmistress** *n* the principal of a school.

head-on *adv, adj* **1** front foremost: *a head-on collision.* **2** with directness or without compromise: *a head-on confrontation with the unions.*

headphones *pl n* two small loudspeakers held against the ears, worn to listen to the radio or recorded music without other people hearing it.

headquarters *pl n* any centre from which operations are directed.

headroom *n* the space below a roof or bridge which allows an object to pass or stay underneath it without touching it.

heads *adv* with the side of a coin uppermost which has a portrait of a head on it.

headship *n* the position or state of being a leader, esp. the head teacher of a school.

headshrinker *n Slang* a psychiatrist.

head start *n* an initial advantage in a competitive situation.

headstone *n* a memorial stone at the head of a grave.

headstrong *adj* determined to do something in one's own way and ignoring the advice of others.

head teacher *n* the principal of a school.

headwaters *pl n* the tributary streams of a river in the area in which it rises.

headway *n* **1** progress towards achieving something: *have the police made any headway?* **2** motion forward: *we felt our way out to the open sea, barely making headway.* **3** same as **headroom**.

headwind *n* a wind blowing directly against the course of an aircraft or ship.

heady *adj* **headier, headiest 1** (of an experience or period of time) extremely exciting. **2** (of alcoholic drink, atmosphere, etc.) strongly affecting the physical senses: *a powerful, heady scent of cologne.* **3** rash and impetuous.

heal *vb* **1** (of a wound) to repair by natural processes, such as by scar formation. **2** to restore (someone) to health. **3** to repair (a rift in a personal relationship or an emotional wound). ▷ HISTORY Old English *hælan* ▶ **healer** *n* ▶ **healing** *n, adj*

health *n* **1** the general condition of body and mind: *better health.* **2** the state of being bodily and mentally vigorous and free from disease. **3** the condition of an organization, society, etc.: *the economic health of the republics.*

WORD HISTORY

In origin, 'health' (Old English *hælth*) is the noun related to the adjective 'hale' (as in the phrase 'hale and hearty'), in the same way as 'warmth' is related to 'warm' and 'depth' is related to 'deep'. 'Health' is 'haleness' or 'wholeness'. To drink to someone's health is to drink a toast to their wellbeing.

health camp *n NZ* a camp for children with health or behavioural problems.

health centre *n Brit* the surgery and offices of the doctors in a district.

health farm *n* a residential establishment for people wishing to improve their health by losing weight, exercising, etc.

health food *n* natural food, organically grown and free from additives.

health stamp *n NZ* a postage stamp with a small surcharge used to support health camps.

health visitor *n* (in Britain) a nurse employed to visit mothers, their preschool children, and the elderly in their homes.

healthy *adj* **healthier, healthiest 1** having or showing good health. **2** likely to produce good health: *healthy seaside air.* **3** functioning well or being sound: *this is a very healthy business to be in.* **4** *Informal* considerable: *healthy profits.* **5** sensible: *a healthy scepticism about his promises.* ▶ **healthily** *adv* ▶ **healthiness** *n*

heap *n* **1** a pile of things lying one on top of another. **2** (*often pl*) *Informal* a large number or quantity. ✧ *adv* **3 heaps** much: *he was heaps better.* ✧ *vb* **4** to collect into a pile. **5** to give freely (to): *film roles were heaped on her.* ▷ **HISTORY** Old English *hēap*

hear *vb* **hearing, heard 1** to perceive (a sound) with the sense of hearing. **2** to listen to: *I didn't want to hear what he had to say.* **3** to be informed (of something); receive information (about something): *I hear you mean to join the crusade.* **4** *Law* to give a hearing to (a case). **5 hear of** to allow: *she wouldn't hear of it.* **6 hear from** to receive a letter or telephone call from. **7 hear! hear!** an exclamation of approval. ▷ **HISTORY** Old English *hieran* ▶ **hearer** *n*

hearing *n* **1** the sense by which sound is perceived. **2** an opportunity for someone to be listened to. **3** the range within which sound can be heard; earshot. **4** the investigation of a matter by a court of law.

hearing aid *n* a small amplifier worn by a partially deaf person in or behind the ear to improve his or her hearing.

hearing dog *n* a dog that has been trained to help a deaf person by alerting him or her to various sounds.

hearsay *n* gossip or rumour.

hearse *n* a large car used to carry a coffin at a funeral. ▷ **HISTORY** Latin *hirpex* harrow

heart *n* **1** a hollow muscular organ whose contractions pump the blood throughout the body. **2** this organ considered as the centre of emotions, esp. love. **3** tenderness or pity: *my heart went out to her.* **4** courage or spirit. **5** the most central part or important part: *at the heart of Italian motor racing.* **6** (of vegetables, such as cabbage) the inner compact part. **7** the breast: *she held him to her heart.* **8** a shape representing the heart, with two rounded lobes at the top meeting in a point at the bottom. **9 a** a red heart-shaped symbol on a playing card. **b** a card with one or more of these symbols or (*when pl*) the suit of cards so marked. **10 break someone's heart** to cause someone to grieve very deeply, esp. by ending a love affair. **11 by heart** by memorizing. **12 have a change of heart** to experience a profound change of outlook or attitude. **13 have one's heart in one's mouth** to be full of apprehension, excitement, or fear. **14 have the heart** to have the necessary will or callousness (to do something): *I didn't have the heart to tell him.* **15 set one's heart on something** to have something as one's ambition. **16 take heart** to become encouraged. **17 take something to heart** to take something seriously or be upset about something. **18 wear one's heart on one's sleeve** to show one's feelings openly. **19 with all one's heart** deeply and sincerely. ▷ **HISTORY** Old English *heorte*

heartache *n* very great sadness and emotional suffering.

heart attack *n* a sudden severe malfunction of the heart.

heartbeat *n* one complete pulsation of the heart.

heartbreak *n* intense and overwhelming grief, esp. after the end of a love affair. ▶ **heartbreaking** *adj* ▶ **heartbroken** *adj*

heartburn *n* a burning sensation in the chest caused by indigestion.

hearten *vb* to encourage or make cheerful. ▶ **heartening** *adj*

heart failure *n* **1** a condition in which the heart is unable to pump an adequate amount of blood to the tissues. **2** sudden stopping of the heartbeat, resulting in death.

heartfelt *adj* sincerely and strongly felt: *heartfelt thanks.*

hearth *n* **1** the floor of a fireplace. **2** this as a symbol of the home. ▷ **HISTORY** Old English *heorth*

heartland *n* **1** the central region of a country or continent: *we headed west towards the heartland of Tibet.* **2** the area where the thing specified is most common or strongest: *Germany's industrial heartland.*

heartless *adj* unkind or cruel. ▶ **heartlessly** *adv*

heart-rending *adj* causing great sadness and pity: *a heart-rending story.*

heart-throb *n* a man, esp. a film or pop star, who is attractive to a lot of women or girls.

heart-to-heart *adj* **1** (of a talk) concerned with personal problems or intimate feelings. ✧ *n* **2** an intimate conversation.

heartwood *n* the central core of dark hard wood in tree trunks.

hearty *adj* **heartier, heartiest 1** warm, friendly, and enthusiastic. **2** strongly felt: *a hearty dislike.* **3** (of a meal) substantial and nourishing. ▶ **heartily** *adv*

heat *vb* **1** to make or become hot or warm. ✧ *n* **2** the state of being hot. **3** the energy transferred as a result of a difference in temperature. RELATED ADJECTIVES ▸ **thermal, calorific 4** hot weather: *he loves the heat of Africa.* **5** intensity of feeling: *the heat of their argument.* **6** the most intense part: *in the heat of an election campaign.* **7** pressure: *political heat on the government.* **8** *Sport* a preliminary eliminating contest in a competition. **9 on** *or* **in heat** (of some female mammals) ready for mating. ▷ **HISTORY** Old English *hǣtu* ▶ **heating** *n*

heat budget *n* the balance or imbalance of heat gain from solar radiation against heat loss through evaporation, reflection, etc.

heated *adj* impassioned or highly emotional: *a heated debate.* ▶ **heatedly** *adv*

heater *n* a device for supplying heat.

heath *n* **1** *Brit* a large open area, usually with sandy soil, low shrubs, and heather. **2** an evergreen shrub with small bell-shaped flowers. ▷ **HISTORY** Old English *hǣth*

heathen *n, pl* **-thens** *or* **-then** *Old-fashioned* **1** a person who does not believe in an established religion; pagan. ✧ *adj* **2** of or relating to heathen peoples. ▷ **HISTORY** Old English *hǣthen*

heather *n* a shrub with small bell-shaped flowers growing on heaths and mountains. ▷ **HISTORY** origin unknown

Heath Robinson *adj* (of a mechanical device) absurdly complicated in design for a simple function. ▷ **HISTORY** after William *Heath Robinson,* cartoonist

heat island *n Meteorol* the characteristically higher average temperatures to be found in a large city than in the surrounding area.

heatstroke *n* same as **sunstroke**.

heat wave *n* **1** a spell of unusually hot weather. **2** an extensive slow-moving air mass at a relatively high temperature.

heave *vb* **heaving, heaved** *or* **hove 1** to lift or move (something) with a great effort. **2** to throw (something heavy) with effort. **3** to utter (a sigh) noisily or unhappily. **4** to rise and fall heavily. **5** (*pt & pp* **hove**) *Naut* **a** to move in a specified direction: *heave her bows around and head north.* **b** (of a vessel) to pitch or roll. **6** to vomit or retch. ✧ *n* **7** the act of heaving. ▷ **HISTORY** Old English *hebban*

heaven *n* **1** the place where God is believed to live and where those leading good lives are believed to go when they die. **2** a place or state of happiness. **3 heavens** the sky. **4** Also: **heavens** God or the gods, used in exclamatory phrases: *for heaven's sake!* ▷ **HISTORY** Old English *heofon*

heavenly *adj* **1** *Informal* wonderful or very enjoyable: *a heavenly meal.* **2** of or occurring in space: *a heavenly body.* **3** of or relating to heaven.

heave to *vb* to stop (a ship) or (of a ship) to stop.

heavy *adj* **heavier, heaviest 1** of comparatively great weight. **2** with a relatively high density: *lead is a heavy metal.* **3** great in degree or amount: *heavy traffic.* **4** considerable: *heavy emphasis.* **5** hard to fulfil: *an exceptionally heavy demand for this issue.* **6** using or consuming a lot of something quickly: *a heavy drinker.* **7** deep and loud: *heavy breathing.* **8** clumsy and slow: *a heavy lumbering trot.* **9** (of a movement or action) with great downward force or pressure: *a heavy blow with a club.* **10** solid or fat: *mountain animals acquire a heavy layer of fat.* **11** not easily digestible: *a heavy meal.* **12** (of cakes or bread) insufficiently raised. **13** (of soil) with a high clay content. **14** sad or dejected: *you feel heavy or sad afterwards.* **15** (of facial features) looking sad and tired. **16** (of a situation) serious and causing anxiety or sadness. **17** cloudy or overcast: *heavy clouds obscured the sun.* **18** (of an industry) engaged in the large-scale manufacture of large objects or extraction of raw materials. **19** *Mil* (of guns, etc.) large and powerful. **20** dull and uninteresting. **21** (of music, literature, etc.) difficult to understand or not immediately appealing. **22** *Slang* (of rock music) loud and having a powerful beat. **23** *Slang* using, or prepared to use, violence or brutality. ✧ *n, pl* **heavies 24** *Slang* a large strong man hired to threaten violence or deter others by his presence. **25 a** a villainous role. **b** an actor who plays such a part. ✧ *adv* **26** heavily: *time hung heavy.* ▷ **HISTORY** Old English *hefig* ▶ **heavily** *adv* ▶ **heaviness** *n*

heavy-duty *adj* made to withstand hard wear, bad weather, etc.

heavy hydrogen *n* same as **deuterium**.

heavy industry *n Econ* the manufacturing of large products or the extraction of raw materials.

heavy metal *n* a type of very loud rock music featuring guitar riffs.

heavy water *n* water formed of oxygen and deuterium.

heavyweight *n* **1** a professional boxer weighing over 195 pounds (88.5 kg) or an amateur weighing over 91 kg. **2** a person who is heavier than average. **3** *Informal* an important person.

Heb. *or* **Hebr.** Hebrew (language).

Hebraic (hib-**ray**-ik) *adj* of the Hebrews or their language or culture.

Hebrew *n* **1** the ancient language of the Hebrews, revived as the official language of Israel. **2** a member of an ancient Semitic people; an Israelite. ✧ *adj* **3** of the Hebrews or their language. ▷ **HISTORY** Hebrew *'ibhrī* one from beyond (the river)

heckle *vb* **-ling, -led** to interrupt (a public speaker) with comments, questions, or taunts. ▷ **HISTORY** form of *hackle* ▶ **heckler** *n*

hectare *n* a unit of measure equal to one hundred ares (10 000 square metres or 2.471 acres). ▷ **HISTORY** French

hectic *adj* involving a lot of rushed activity. ▷ **HISTORY** Greek *hektikos* hectic, consumptive

hector *vb* **1** to bully or torment. ✧ *n* **2** a blustering bully. ▷ **HISTORY** after *Hector,* legendary Trojan warrior

hedge *n* **1** a row of shrubs or bushes forming a boundary. **2** a barrier or protection against something, esp. against the risk of loss on an investment. ✧ *vb* **hedging, hedged 3** to avoid making a decision by making noncommittal statements. **4 hedge against** to guard against the risk of loss in (a bet or disagreement), by supporting the opposition as well. ▷ **HISTORY** Old English *hecg*

hedgehog *n* a small mammal with a protective covering of spines.

hedgehop *vb* **-hopping, -hopped** (of an aircraft) to fly close to the ground, such as in crop spraying.

hedgerow *n* a hedge of shrubs or low trees bordering a field.

hedge sparrow *n* a small brownish songbird.

hedonism *n* the doctrine that the pursuit of pleasure is the most important thing in life. ▷ **HISTORY** Greek *hēdonē* pleasure ▶ **hedonist** *n* ▶ **hedonistic** *adj*

heed *Formal* ✧ *n* **1** careful attention: *he must have taken heed of her warning.* ✧ *vb* **2** to pay close attention to (a warning or piece of advice). ▷ **HISTORY** Old English *hēdan*

heedless *adj* taking no notice; careless or thoughtless. ▶ **heedlessly** *adv*

heel[1] *n* **1** the back part of the foot. **2** the part of a stocking or sock designed to fit the heel. **3** the part of a shoe supporting the heel. **4** *Slang* a contemptible person. **5** **at one's heels** following closely behind one. **6** **kick** *or* **cool one's heels** to be kept waiting. **7** **down at heel** untidy and in poor condition. **8** **take to one's heels** to run off. **9** **to heel** under control, such as a dog walking by a person's heel. ✧ *vb* **10** to repair or replace the heel of (a shoe or boot). ▷ **HISTORY** Old English *hēla*

heel[2] *vb* to lean to one side. ▷ **HISTORY** Old English *hieldan*

heeler *n Austral & NZ* a dog that herds cattle by biting at their heels.

hefty *adj* **heftier, heftiest** *Informal* **1** large in size, weight, or amount. **2** forceful and vigorous: *a hefty slap on the back.* **3** involving a large amount of money: *a hefty fine.*

hegemony (hig-**em**-on-ee) *n, pl* **-nies** domination of one state, country, or class within a group of others. ▷ **HISTORY** Greek *hēgemonia*

Hegira *n* the starting point of the Muslim era; the flight of Mohammed from Mecca to Medina in 622 AD, regarded as being the starting point of the Muslim era. ▷ **HISTORY** Arabic *hijrah* flight

heifer (**hef**-fer) *n* a young cow. ▷ **HISTORY** Old English *heahfore*

height *n* **1** the vertical distance from the bottom of something to the top. **2** the vertical distance of a place above sea level. **3** relatively great distance from bottom to top. **4** the topmost point; summit. **5** the period of greatest intensity: *the height of the shelling.* **6** an extreme example: *the height of luxury.* **7** **heights** extremes: *dizzy heights of success.* ▷ **HISTORY** Old English *hīehthu*

heighten *vb* to make or become higher or more intense. ▶ **heightened** *adj*

height of land *n US & Canad* a ridge of high ground dividing two river basins.

heinous *adj* evil and shocking. ▷ **HISTORY** Old French *haineus*

heir *n* the person legally succeeding to the property of a deceased person. ▷ **HISTORY** Latin *heres* ▶ **heiress** *fem n*

heir apparent *n, pl* **heirs apparent** **1** *Law* a person whose right to succeed to certain property cannot be defeated. **2** a person whose succession to a role or position is extremely likely: *heir apparent to the England captaincy.*

heirloom *n* an object that has been in a family for generations. ▷ **HISTORY** HEIR + *lome* tool

heir presumptive *n Property law* a person who expects to succeed to an estate but whose right may be defeated by the birth of an heir nearer in blood to the ancestor.

held *vb* the past of **hold**[1].

helical *adj* of or like a helix.

helicopter *n* an aircraft, powered by rotating overhead blades, that is capable of hovering, vertical flight, and horizontal flight in any direction. ▷ **HISTORY** Greek *helix* spiral + *pteron* wing

heliograph *n* an instrument with mirrors and a shutter used for sending messages in Morse code by reflecting the sun's rays. ▷ **HISTORY** Greek *hēlios* sun + -GRAPHY

heliophyte *n Bot* any plant that grows best in direct sunlight.

heliotrope *n* a plant with small fragrant purple flowers. ▷ **HISTORY** Greek *hēlios* sun + *trepein* to turn

heliport *n* an airport for helicopters. ▷ **HISTORY** *heli(copter) + port*

helium (**heel**-ee-um) *n Chem* a very light colourless odourless inert gas. Symbol: He. ▷ **HISTORY** Greek *hēlios* sun, because first detected in the solar spectrum

helix (**heel**-iks) *n, pl* **helices** (**hell**-iss-seez) *or* **helixes** a spiral. ▷ **HISTORY** Greek: spiral

hell *n* **1** (in Christianity and some other religions) the place or state of eternal punishment of the wicked after death. **2** (in various religions and cultures) the abode of the spirits of the dead. **3** *Informal* a situation that causes suffering or extreme difficulty: *war is hell.* **4** **come hell or high water** *Informal* whatever difficulties may arise. **5** **for the hell of it** *Informal* for the fun of it. **6** **from hell** *Informal* denoting a person or thing that is particularly bad or alarming: *the boss from hell.* **7** **give someone hell** *Informal* **a** to give someone a severe reprimand or punishment. **b** to be a torment to someone. **8** **hell for leather** at great speed. **9** **the hell** *Informal* **a** used for emphasis: *what the hell.* **b** an expression of strong disagreement: *the hell you do!* ✧ *interj* **10** *Informal* an exclamation of anger or surprise. ▷ **HISTORY** Old English

hellbent *adj Informal* rashly intent: *hellbent on revenge.*

hellebore *n* a plant with white flowers that bloom in winter. ▷ **HISTORY** Greek *helleboros*

Hellenic *adj* **1** of the Greeks or their language. **2** of or relating to ancient Greece during the classical period (776–323 BC).

Hellenism *n* **1** the principles and ideals of classical Greek civilization. **2** the spirit or national character of the Greeks. ▶ **Hellenist** *n*

Hellenistic *adj* of Greek civilization during the period 323–30 BC.

hellfire *n* the torment of hell, imagined as eternal fire.

hellish *adj Informal* very unpleasant.

hello, hallo, *or* **hullo** *interj* **1** an expression of greeting or surprise. **2** a call used to attract attention. ✧ *n, pl* **-los** **3** the act of saying 'hello'. ▷ **HISTORY** French *holà*

helm *n* **1** *Naut* the tiller or wheel for steering a ship. **2** **at the helm** in a position of leadership or control. ▷ **HISTORY** Old English *helma*

helmet *n* a piece of protective headgear worn by motorcyclists, soldiers, policemen, divers, etc. ▷ **HISTORY** Old French

help *vb* **1** to assist (someone to do something). **2** to contribute to: *to help Latin America's economies.* **3** to improve a situation: *a felt or rubber underlay will help.* **4** **a** to refrain from: *I couldn't help feeling foolish.* **b** to be responsible for: *you must not*

a b c d e f g h i j k l m n o p q r s t u v w x y z

A B C D E F G H I J K L M N O P Q R S T U V W X Y Z

blame him, he simply can't help it. **5** to serve (a customer). **6 help oneself** to take something, esp. food or drink, for oneself, without being served. ✧ *n* **7** the act of helping. **8** a person or thing that helps. **9** a remedy: *there's no help for it.* ✧ *interj* **10** used to call for assistance. ▷ **HISTORY** Old English *helpan* ▶ **helper** *n*

helpful *adj* giving help. ▶ **helpfully** *adv* ▶ **helpfulness** *n*

helping *n* a single portion of food.

helpless *adj* **1** unable to manage independently. **2** made weak: *it reduced her to helpless laughter.* ▶ **helplessly** *adv* ▶ **helplessness** *n*

helpline *n* a telephone line set aside for callers to contact an organization for help with a problem.

helpmate *or* **helpmeet** *n* a companion and helper, esp. a husband or wife.

helter-skelter *adj* **1** hurried or disorganized. ✧ *adv* **2** in a hurried or disorganized manner. ✧ *n* **3** *Brit* a high spiral slide at a fairground. ▷ **HISTORY** probably imitative

hem[1] *n* **1** the bottom edge of a garment, folded under and stitched down. ✧ *vb* **hemming, hemmed 2** to provide (a garment) with a hem. ✧ See also **hem in.** ▷ **HISTORY** Old English *hemm*

hem[2] *n* **1** a representation of the sound of clearing the throat, used to gain attention. ✧ *vb* **hemming, hemmed 2** to make this sound. **3 hem and haw** See **haw**[2].

he-man *n, pl* **-men** *Informal* a strong man, esp. one who shows off his strength.

hematite *or* **haematite** *n Geol* a red, grey, or black mineral, found as massive beds and in veins and igneous rocks. It is the chief source of iron. ▷ **HISTORY** via Latin from Greek *haimatitēs* resembling blood, from *haima* blood ▶ **hematitic** *or* **haematitic** *adj*

hemi- *prefix* half: *hemisphere.* ▷ **HISTORY** Greek

hem in *vb* to surround and prevent from moving.

hemipterous *or* **hemipteran** *adj* of an order of insects with sucking or piercing mouthparts. ▷ **HISTORY** Greek *hēmi* half + *pteron* wing

hemisphere *n* one half of a sphere, esp. of the earth (**northern** and **southern hemisphere**) or of the brain. ▶ **hemispherical** *adj*

hemline *n* the level to which the hem of a skirt or dress hangs: *the hemline debate.*

hemlock *n* a poisonous drug derived from a plant with spotted stems and small white flowers. ▷ **HISTORY** Old English *hymlic*

hemp *n* **1** an Asian plant with tough fibres. **2** the fibre of this plant, used to make canvas and rope. **3** a narcotic drug obtained from this plant. ▷ **HISTORY** Old English *hænep* ▶ **hempen** *adj*

hen *n* the female of any bird, esp. the domestic fowl. ▷ **HISTORY** Old English *henn*

henbane *n* a poisonous plant with sticky hairy leaves.

hence *adv* **1** for this reason; therefore. **2** from this time: *two weeks hence.* **3** *Archaic* from here. ▷ **HISTORY** Old English *hionane*

henceforth *or* **henceforward** *adv* from now on.

henchman *n, pl* **-men** a person employed by someone powerful to carry out orders. ▷ **HISTORY** Middle English *hengestman*

henge *n* a circular monument, often containing a circle of stones, dating from the Neolithic and Bronze Ages. ▷ **HISTORY** from *Stonehenge*

henna *n* **1** a reddish dye, obtained from a shrub or tree of Asia and N Africa which is used to colour hair. ✧ *vb* **2** to dye (the hair) with henna. ▷ **HISTORY** Arabic *hinnā'*

henpecked *adj* (of a man) harassed by the persistent nagging of his wife.

henry *n, pl* **-ry, -ries** *or* **-rys** the SI unit of electric inductance. ▷ **HISTORY** after Joseph *Henry,* physicist

hepatic *adj* of the liver. ▷ **HISTORY** Greek *hēpar* liver

hepatic portal vein *n Anat* a vein connecting two capillary networks in the liver.

hepatitis *n* inflammation of the liver, causing fever, jaundice, and weakness.

Hephaestus *n Greek myth* the god of fire.

hepta- *combining form* seven: *heptameter.*

heptagon *n Geom* a figure with seven sides. ▷ **HISTORY** Greek *heptagōnos* having seven angles ▶ **heptagonal** *adj*

heptathlon *n* an athletic contest for women in which athletes compete in seven different events.

her *pron* refers to: **1** a female person or animal: *he loves her.* **2** things personified as feminine, such as ships and nations. ✧ *adj* **3** of, belonging to, or associated with her: *her hair.* ▷ **HISTORY** Old English *hire*

> **WORD TIP**
> See at **me**.

Hera *or* **Here** *n Greek myth* the queen of the gods.

herald *n* **1** a person who announces important news. **2** *Often literary* a forerunner. ✧ *vb* **3** to announce or signal the approach of: *his arrival was heralded by excited barking.* ▷ **HISTORY** Germanic ▶ **heraldic** *adj*

heraldry *n, pl* **-ries** the study of coats of arms and family trees.

herb *n* **1** an aromatic plant that is used for flavouring in cookery, and in medicine. **2** *Bot* a seed-bearing plant whose parts above ground die back at the end of the growing season. ▷ **HISTORY** Latin *herba* grass, green plants ▶ **herbal** *adj* ▶ **herby** *adj*

herbaceous *adj* designating plants that are soft-stemmed rather than woody.

herbaceous border *n* a flower bed that contains perennials rather than annuals.

herbage *n* herbaceous plants collectively, esp. those on which animals graze.

herbalist *n* a person who grows or specializes in the use of medicinal herbs.

herbicide *n* a substance used to destroy plants, esp. weeds. ▷ **HISTORY** Latin *herba* plant + *caedere* to kill

herbivore (**her**-biv-vore) *n* **1** an animal that feeds only on plants. **2** *Informal* a liberal or idealistic person. ▷ HISTORY Latin *herba* plant + *vorare* to swallow ▶ **herbivorous** (her-**biv**-or-uss) *adj*

herculean (her-kew-**lee**-an) *adj* **1** (of a task) requiring tremendous effort or strength. **2** resembling Hercules, hero of classical myth, in strength or courage.

herd *n* **1** a large group of mammals, esp. cattle living and feeding together. **2** *Often disparaging* a large group of people. ✧ *vb* **3** to collect or be collected into or as if into a herd. ▷ HISTORY Old English *heord*

herd instinct *n Psychol* the inborn tendency to associate with others and follow the group's behaviour.

herdsman *n, pl* **-men** *Chiefly Brit* a man who looks after a herd of animals.

here *adv* **1** in, at, or to this place, point, case, or respect: *I am pleased to be back here.* **2 here and there** at several places in or throughout an area. **3 here's to** a convention used in proposing a toast. **4 neither here nor there** of no relevance. ✧ *n* **5** this place: *they leave here tonight.* ▷ HISTORY Old English *hēr*

hereabouts *or* **hereabout** *adv* in this region.

hereafter *adv* **1** *Formal or law* in a subsequent part of this document, matter, or case. **2** at some time in the future. ✧ *n* **3 the hereafter a** life after death. **b** the future.

hereby *adv* (used in official statements and documents) by means of or as a result of this.

hereditable *adj* same as **heritable**.

hereditary *adj* **1** passed on genetically from one generation to another. **2** *Law* passed on to succeeding generations by inheritance.

heredity (hir-**red**-it-ee) *n, pl* **-ties** the passing on from one generation to another of genetic factors that determine individual characteristics. ▷ HISTORY Latin *hereditas* inheritance

Hereford *n* a hardy breed of beef cattle which has a reddish body with white markings. ▷ HISTORY after *Hereford,* English city

herein *adv Formal or law* in this place, matter, or document.

hereinafter *adv Formal or law* from this point on in this document, matter, or case.

hereof *adv Formal or law* of or concerning this.

heresy (**herr**-iss-ee) *n, pl* **-sies 1** an opinion contrary to the principles of a religion. **2** any belief thought to be contrary to official or established theory. ▷ HISTORY Greek *hairein* to choose

heretic (**herr**-it-ik) *n* **1** *Now chiefly RC Church* a person who maintains beliefs contrary to the established teachings of the Church. **2** a person who holds unorthodox opinions in any field. ▶ **heretical** (hir-**ret**-ik-kl) *adj*

hereto *adv Formal or law* to this place, matter, or document.

heretofore *adv Formal or law* until now.

hereupon *adv* following immediately after this; at this stage.

herewith *adv Formal* together with this: *a schedule of the event is appended herewith.*

heritable *adj* capable of being inherited.

heritage *n* **1** something inherited at birth. **2** anything that has been carried over from the past or handed down by tradition. **3** the evidence of the past, such as historical sites, considered as the inheritance of present-day society.

hermaphrodite (her-**maf**-roe-dite) *n* an animal, flower, or person that has both male and female reproductive organs. ▷ HISTORY after *Hermaphroditus,* son of Hermes and Aphrodite, who merged with the nymph Salmacis to form one body ▶ **hermaphroditic** *adj*

Hermes *n Greek myth* the messenger of the gods.

hermetic *adj* sealed so as to be airtight. ▷ HISTORY after the Greek god *Hermes,* traditionally the inventor of a magic seal ▶ **hermetically** *adv*

hermit *n* a person living in solitude, esp. for religious reasons. ▷ HISTORY Greek *erēmos* lonely

hermitage *n* **1** the home of a hermit. **2** any retreat.

hermit crab *n* a small crab that lives in the empty shells of other shellfish.

hernia *n* protrusion of an organ or part through the lining of the body cavity in which it is normally situated. ▷ HISTORY Latin

hero *n, pl* **-roes 1** the principal male character in a novel, play, etc. **2** a man of exceptional courage, nobility, etc. **3** a man who is idealized for having superior qualities in any field. ▷ HISTORY Greek *hērōs*

heroic *adj* **1** brave and courageous: *heroic work by the army engineers.* **2** of, like, or befitting a hero. ▶ **heroically** *adv*

heroic couplet *n Prosody* a verse form consisting of two rhyming lines in iambic pentameter.

heroics *pl n* behaviour or language considered too melodramatic or extravagant for the particular situation in which they are used.

heroic verse *n Prosody* a type of verse suitable for epic or heroic subjects, such as the classical hexameter, the French Alexandrine, or the English iambic pentameter.

heroin *n* a highly addictive drug derived from morphine. ▷ HISTORY probably from *hero,* referring to its aggrandizing effect on the personality

heroine *n* **1** the principal female character in a novel, play, etc. **2** a woman of exceptional courage, nobility, etc. **3** a woman who is idealized for having superior qualities in any field.

heroism (**herr**-oh-izz-um) *n* great courage and bravery.

heron *n* a wading bird with a long neck, long legs, and grey or white feathers. ▷ HISTORY Old French *hairon*

heronry *n, pl* **-ries** a colony of breeding herons.

hero worship *n* admiration for heroes or idealized people.

herpes (**her**-peez) *n* any of several inflammatory skin diseases, including shingles and cold sores. ▷ HISTORY Greek *herpein* to creep

A B C D E F G H I J K L M N O P Q R S T U V W X Y Z

herpes simplex *n* an acute viral disease causing clusters of watery blisters. ▷ **HISTORY** New Latin: simple herpes

herpes zoster *n* same as **shingles**. ▷ **HISTORY** New Latin: girdle herpes

Herr (**hair**) *n, pl* **Herren** a German form of address equivalent to *Mr*. ▷ **HISTORY** German

herring *n, pl* **-rings** *or* **-ring** a food fish of northern seas, with a long silver-coloured body. ▷ **HISTORY** Old English *hǣring*

herringbone *n* a zigzag pattern consisting of short lines of V shapes, used esp. in fabrics.

herring gull *n* a common gull that has a white feathers with black-tipped wings.

hers *pron* **1** something belonging to her: *hers is the highest paid part-time job; the money which is rightfully hers.* **2 of hers** belonging to her.

herself *pron* **1 a** the reflexive form of *she* or *her*: *she busied herself at the stove.* **b** used for emphasis: *none other than The Great Mother herself.* **2** her normal self: *she hasn't been herself all week.*

hertz *n, pl* **hertz** the SI unit of frequency, equal to one cycle per second. ▷ **HISTORY** after H. R. *Hertz*, physicist

hesitant *adj* doubtful and unsure in speech or action. ▸ **hesitancy** *n* ▸ **hesitantly** *adv*

hesitate *vb* **-tating, -tated 1** to be slow and uncertain in acting. **2** to be reluctant (to do something): *I hesitate to use the word 'squandered'.* **3** to pause during speech because of uncertainty. ▷ **HISTORY** Latin *haesitare* ▸ **hesitation** *n*

hessian *n* a coarse jute fabric similar to sacking. ▷ **HISTORY** after *Hesse*, Germany

hetero- *combining form* other, another, or different: *heterosexual.* ▷ **HISTORY** Greek *heteros* other

heterodox *adj* different from established or accepted doctrines or beliefs. ▷ **HISTORY** HETERO- + Greek *doxa* opinion ▸ **heterodoxy** *n*

heterodyne *Electronics* ✧ *vb* **-dyning, -dyned 1** to combine (two alternating signals) so as to produce two signals with frequencies corresponding to the sum and the difference of the original frequencies. ✧ *adj* **2** produced or operating by heterodyning two signals. ▷ **HISTORY** HETERO- + Greek *dunamis* power

heterogeneous (het-er-oh-**jean**-ee-uss) *adj* varied in content; composed of different parts: *a heterogeneous collection of art.* ▷ **HISTORY** HETERO- + Greek *genos* sort ▸ **heterogeneity** *n*

heteromorphic *adj Biol* **1** differing from the normal form. **2** (esp. of insects) having different forms at different stages of the life cycle. ▷ **HISTORY** HETERO- + Greek *morphē* form ▸ **heteromorphism** *n*

heterosexual *n* **1** a person who is sexually attracted to members of the opposite sex. ✧ *adj* **2** (of a person) sexually attracted to members of the opposite sex. **3** (of a sexual relationship) between a man and a woman. ▸ **heterosexuality** *n*

heterotrophic *adj Biochem* (of animals and some plants) using complex organic compounds to manufacture their own organic constituents.

heterozygous *adj Biol* having two different alleles of the same gene. ▷ **HISTORY** HETERO- + Greek *zugōtos* yoked

het up *adj Informal* agitated or excited: *he was very het up about the traffic.* ▷ **HISTORY** dialect for *heated*

heuristic (**hew**-rist-ik) *adj* (of a method of teaching) allowing students to learn things for themselves by trial and error. ▷ **HISTORY** Greek *heuriskein* to discover

hew *vb* **hewing, hewed, hewed** *or* **hewn 1** to chop or cut with an axe. **2** to carve (something) from a substance: *a tunnel hewn out of the living rock.* ▷ **HISTORY** Old English *hēawan*

hex *n* **1** short for **hexadecimal notation.** ✧ *adj* **2** of or relating to hexadecimal notation: *hex code.*

hexa- *combining form* six: *hexameter.* ▷ **HISTORY** Greek *hex* six

hexadecimal notation *n* a number system with a base of 16, the numbers 10–15 being represented by the letters A–F.

hexagon *n Geom* a figure with six sides. ▸ **hexagonal** *adj*

hexagram *n Geom* a star formed by extending the sides of a regular hexagon to meet at six points.

hexameter (hek-**sam**-it-er) *n Prosody* a verse line consisting of six metrical feet.

hexose *n Chem* a monosaccharide that contains six carbon atoms per molecule.

hey *interj* **1** an expression of surprise or for catching attention. **2 hey presto!** an exclamation used by conjurors at the climax of a trick. ▷ **HISTORY** imitative

heyday *n* the time of most power, popularity, or success: *the heyday of classical composition.* ▷ **HISTORY** probably based on *hey*

Hf *Chem* hafnium.

Hg *Chem* mercury.

HGV (in Britain, formerly) heavy goods vehicle.

HH 1 His (*or* Her) Highness. **2** His Holiness (title of the pope).

hi *interj Informal* hello. ▷ **HISTORY** probably from *how are you?*

HI Hawaii.

hiatus (hie-**ay**-tuss) *n, pl* **-tuses** *or* **-tus** a pause or an interruption in continuity. ▷ **HISTORY** Latin: gap, cleft

hiatus hernia *n* protrusion of the stomach through the diaphragm at the hole for the gullet.

Hib Haemophilus influenzae type b: a vaccine against a specific type of bacterial meningitis, administered to children under four years of age.

hibernate *vb* **-nating, -nated** (of some animals) to pass the winter in a resting state in which heartbeat, temperature, and breathing rate are very low. ▷ **HISTORY** Latin *hibernare* to spend the winter ▸ **hibernation** *n*

Hibernia *n Poetic* Ireland. ▸ **Hibernian** *adj, n*

hibiscus *n, pl* **-cuses** a tropical plant with large brightly coloured flowers. ▷ **HISTORY** Greek *hibiskos* marsh mallow

hiccup *n* **1** a spasm of the breathing organs with a sharp coughlike sound. **2 hiccups** the state of having such spasms. **3** *Informal* a minor difficulty. ✧ *vb* **-cuping, -cuped** *or* **-cupping, -cupped 4** to make a hiccup or hiccups. Also: **hiccough** ▷ HISTORY imitative

hick *n US, Austral & NZ informal* an unsophisticated country person. ▷ HISTORY after *Hick,* familiar form of *Richard*

hickory *n, pl* **-ries 1** a North American tree with edible nuts. **2** the hard wood of this tree. ▷ HISTORY Native American *pawcohiccora*

hidden agenda *n* a set of motives or intentions concealed from others who might object to them.

hide[1] *vb* **hiding, hid, hidden** *or* **hid 1** to conceal (oneself or an object) from view or discovery. **2** to keep (information or one's feelings) secret. **3** to obscure or cover (something) from view. ✧ *n* **4** *Brit* a place of concealment, disguised to appear as part of its surrounding, used by hunters, bird-watchers, etc. ▷ HISTORY Old English *hȳdan*

hide[2] *n* the skin of an animal, either tanned or raw. ▷ HISTORY Old English *hȳd*

hideaway *n* a hiding place or secluded spot.

hidebound *adj* restricted by petty rules and unwilling to accept new ideas.

hideous (**hid**-ee-uss) *adj* extremely ugly or unpleasant. ▷ HISTORY Old French *hisdos*

hide-out *n* a hiding place.

hiding[1] *n* **1** a state of concealment: *in hiding.* **2 hiding place** a place of concealment.

hiding[2] *n Informal* a severe beating.

hierarchy (**hire**-ark-ee) *n, pl* **-chies 1** a system of people or things arranged in a graded order. **2 the hierarchy** the people in power in any organization. ▷ HISTORY Late Greek *hierarkhēs* high priest ▸ **hierarchical** *adj*

hieroglyphic (hire-oh-**gliff**-ik) *adj* **1** of or relating to a form of writing using picture symbols, as used in ancient Egypt. ✧ *n also* **hieroglyph 2** a symbol that is difficult to decipher. **3** a picture or symbol representing an object, idea, or sound. ▷ HISTORY Greek *hieros* holy + *gluphein* to carve

hieroglyphics *n* **1** a form of writing, as used in ancient Egypt, in which pictures or symbols are used to represent objects, ideas, or sounds. **2** writing that is difficult to decipher.

hi-fi *n Informal* **1** a set of high-quality sound-reproducing equipment. **2** short for **high fidelity**. ✧ *adj* **3** producing high-quality sound.

higgledy-piggledy *adj, adv Informal* in a muddle. ▷ HISTORY origin unknown

high *adj* **1** being a relatively great distance from top to bottom: *a high stone wall.* **2** being at a relatively great distance above sea level: *a high village.* **3** being a specified distance from top to bottom: *three feet high.* **4** coming up to a specified level: *waist-high.* **5** being at its peak: *high summer.* **6** of greater than average height: *a high ceiling.* **7** greater than usual in intensity or amount: *high blood pressure; high fees.* **8** (of a sound) acute in pitch. **9** (of food) slightly decomposed, regarded as enhancing the flavour of game. **10** towards the top of a scale of importance or quality: *high fashion.* **11** intensely emotional: *high drama.* **12** very cheerful: *high spirits.* **13** *Informal* under the influence of alcohol or drugs. **14** luxurious or extravagant: *high life.* **15** advanced in complexity: *high finance.* **16** formal and elaborate: *High Mass.* **17 high and dry** abandoned in a difficult situation. **18 high and mighty** *Informal* too confident and full of self-importance. **19 high opinion** a favourable opinion. ✧ *adv* **20** at or to a height: *flying high.* ✧ *n* **21** a high level. **22** same as **anticyclone**. **23 on a high** *Informal* **a** in a state of intoxication by alcohol or drugs. **b** in a state of great excitement and happiness. ▷ HISTORY Old English *hēah*

High Arctic *n* the regions of Canada, esp. the northern islands, within the Arctic Circle.

highball *n Chiefly US* a long iced drink consisting of whisky with soda water or ginger ale.

highbrow *adj* **1** concerned with serious, intellectual subjects. ✧ *n* **2** a person with such tastes.

highchair *n* a long-legged chair with a table-like tray, used for a child at meal times.

High Church *n* **1** the movement within the Church of England stressing the importance of ceremony and ritual. ✧ *adj* **High-Church 2** of or relating to this movement.

high commissioner *n* the senior diplomatic representative sent by one Commonwealth country to another.

high country *n* **the high country** *NZ* sheep pastures in the foothills of the Southern Alps.

High Court *n* (in England, Wales, Australia, and New Zealand) the supreme court dealing with civil and criminal law cases.

Higher *n* (in Scotland) **1** the advanced level of the Scottish Certificate of Education. **2** a pass in a subject at this level: *she has got four Highers.*

higher education *n* education and training at colleges, universities, and polytechnics.

highest common factor *n* the largest number that divides equally into each member of a group of numbers.

high explosive *n* an extremely powerful chemical explosive, such as TNT or gelignite.

highfalutin (hie-fa-**loot**-in) *adj Informal* (of behaviour) excessively grand or pompous. ▷ HISTORY *-falutin* perhaps variant of *fluting*

high fidelity *n* **1** the electronic reproduction of sound with little or no distortion. ✧ *adj* **high-fidelity 2** able to produce sound with little or no distortion: *high-fidelity stereo earphones.*

high-flown *adj* extravagant or pretentious: *high-flown language.*

high frequency *n* a radio frequency between 30 and 3 megahertz.

High German *n* the standard German language.

high-handed *adj* using authority in an unnecessarily forceful way. ▸ **high-handedness** *n*

high jump *n* **the high jump a** an athletic event in which competitors have to jump over a high bar.

b *Brit & Austral informal* a severe reprimand or punishment: *I was for the high jump again.*

Highland *adj* of or denoting the Highlands, a mountainous region of NW Scotland. ▶ **Highlander** *n*

Highland cattle *n* a breed of cattle with shaggy reddish-brown hair and long horns.

highlands *pl n* relatively high ground.

high-level language *n* a computer programming language that is close to human language.

highlight *n* **1** Also called: **high spot** the most exciting or memorable part of something. **2** an area of the lightest tone in a painting or photograph. **3** a lightened streak in the hair produced by bleaching. ✧ *vb* **4** to give emphasis to: *the prime minister repeatedly highlighted the need for lower pay.*

highly *adv* **1** extremely: *highly desirable.* **2** towards the top of a scale of importance, admiration, or respect: *highly paid doctors.*

highly strung *or US & Canad* **high-strung** *adj* tense and easily upset.

High Mass *n* a solemn and elaborate Mass.

high-minded *adj* having high moral principles.

Highness *n* (preceded by *Your, His* or *Her*) a title used to address or refer to a royal person.

high-octane *adj* **1** (of petrol) having a high octane number. **2** *Informal* dynamic or intense: *a high-octane lifestyle.*

high-powered *adj* **1** (of machinery or equipment) powerful, advanced, and sophisticated. **2** important, successful, or influential: *a high-powered business contact.*

high-pressure *adj Informal* (of selling) persuasive in an aggressive and persistent manner.

high priest *n* the head of a cult or movement. ▶ **high priestess** *fem n*

high-rise *adj* of or relating to a building that has many storeys: *a high-rise block.*

highroad *n* a main road.

high school *n* a secondary school.

high-spirited *adj* lively and wishing to have fun and excitement.

high tea *n Brit* an early evening meal consisting of a cooked dish, bread, cakes, and tea.

high technology *n* any type of sophisticated industrial process, esp. one involving electronics.

high-tension *adj* (of electricity cable) carrying a powerful current.

high tide *n* the sea at its highest level on the coast.

high time *adv Informal* the latest possible time: *it was high time she got married.*

high treason *n* a serious crime directly affecting a sovereign or state.

high-water mark *n* **1** the level reached by sea water at high tide or a river in flood. **2** the highest or most successful stage: *the premature high-water mark of his career.*

highway *n* **1** a public road that everyone may use. **2** *US, Canad, Austral & NZ* a main road, esp. one that connects towns.

Highway Code *n* (in Britain) a booklet of regulations and recommendations for all road users.

highwayman *n, pl* **-men** (formerly) a robber, usually on horseback, who held up travellers on public roads.

hijack *vb* **1** to seize control of or divert (a vehicle or aircraft) while travelling. ✧ *n* **2** an instance of hijacking. ▷ **HISTORY** origin unknown ▶ **hijacker** *n*

hike *vb* **hiking, hiked 1** to walk a long way in the country, usually for pleasure. **2** to raise (prices). **3** to pull up with a quick movement: *he hiked up his trouser legs.* ✧ *n* **4** a long walk. **5** a rise in price. ▷ **HISTORY** origin unknown ▶ **hiker** *n*

hilarious *adj* very funny. ▷ **HISTORY** Greek *hilaros* cheerful ▶ **hilariously** *adv* ▶ **hilarity** *n*

hill *n* **1** a natural elevation of the earth's surface, less high than a mountain. **2** a heap or mound. **3** an incline or slope. ▷ **HISTORY** Old English *hyll* ▶ **hilly** *adj*

hillbilly *n, pl* **-lies 1** *Usually disparaging* an unsophisticated person from the mountainous areas in the southeastern US. **2** same as **country and western**. ▷ **HISTORY** *hill* + *Billy* (the nickname)

hillock *n* a small hill or mound.

hilt *n* **1** the handle or shaft of a sword, dagger, or knife. **2 to the hilt** to the full: *he plays the role to the hilt.* ▷ **HISTORY** Old English

hilum *n, pl* **-la** *Bot* a scar on a seed marking its point of attachment to the seed vessel. ▷ **HISTORY** Latin: trifle

him *pron* refers to a male person or animal: *I greeted him at the hotel; I must send him a note of congratulation.* ▷ **HISTORY** Old English

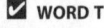

> ☑ **WORD TIP**
> See at **me.**

himself *pron* **1 a** the reflexive form of *he* or *him*: *he secretly asked himself.* **b** used for emphasis: *approved of by the Creator himself.* **2** his normal self: *he was almost himself again.*

hind¹ *adj* **hinder, hindmost** situated at the back: *a hind leg.* ▷ **HISTORY** Old English *hindan* at the back

hind² *n, pl* **hinds** *or* **hind** the female of the deer, esp. the red deer. ▷ **HISTORY** Old English

Hindenburg Line *n History* a line of strong fortifications built by the German army near the Franco-Belgian border in 1916–17 and breached by the Allies in August 1918.

hinder¹ *vb* to get in the way of (someone or something). ▷ **HISTORY** Old English *hindrian*

hinder² *adj* situated at the back. ▷ **HISTORY** Old English

Hindi *n* **1** a language or group of dialects of N central India. **2** a formal literary dialect of this language, the official language of India. ▷ **HISTORY** Old Persian *Hindu* the river Indus

hindquarters *pl n* the rear of a four-legged animal.

hindrance *n* **1** an obstruction or snag. **2** the act of hindering.

hindsight *n* the ability to understand, after something has happened, what should have been done or what caused the event.

Hindu *n, pl* **-dus 1** a person who practises Hinduism. ✧ *adj* **2** of Hinduism.

Hinduism *n* the dominant religion of India, which involves the worship of many gods and belief in reincarnation.

Hindustani *n* a group of northern Indian languages that includes Hindi and Urdu.

hinge *n* **1** a device for holding together two parts, such as a door and its frame, so that one can swing freely. ✧ *vb* **hinging, hinged 2 hinge on** to depend on. **3** to join or open (something) by means of a hinge. ▷ HISTORY probably Germanic ▶ **hinged** *adj*

hinny *n, pl* **-nies** the offspring of a male horse and a female donkey. ▷ HISTORY Greek *hinnos*

hint *n* **1** a suggestion given in an indirect or subtle manner. **2** a helpful piece of advice. **3** a small amount: *a hint of irony.* ✧ *vb* **4** (sometimes foll. by *at*) to suggest indirectly. ▷ HISTORY origin unknown

hinterland *n* **1** land lying behind a coast or the shore of a river. **2** an area near and dependent on a large city, esp. a port. ▷ HISTORY German *hinter* behind + LAND

hip¹ *n* either side of the body below the waist and above the thigh. ▷ HISTORY Old English *hype*

hip² *n* the berry-like brightly coloured fruit of a rose bush. Also called: **rosehip** ▷ HISTORY Old English *hēope*

hip³ *interj* an exclamation used to introduce cheers: *hip, hip, hurrah.* ▷ HISTORY origin unknown

hip⁴ *adj* **hipper, hippest** *Slang* aware of or following the latest trends. ▷ HISTORY variant of earlier *hep*

hipbone *n* either of the two bones that form the sides of the pelvis.

hip-hop *n* a US pop-culture movement originating in the 1980s, comprising rap music, graffiti, and break dancing.

hippie *n* same as **hippy²**.

hippo *n, pl* **-pos** *Informal* short for **hippopotamus**.

Hippocratic oath *n* an oath taken by a doctor to observe a code of medical ethics. ▷ HISTORY after *Hippocrates,* Greek physician

hippodrome *n* **1** a music hall, variety theatre, or circus. **2** (in ancient Greece or Rome) an open-air course for horse and chariot races. ▷ HISTORY Greek *hippos* horse + *dromos* race

hippopotamus *n, pl* **-muses** *or* **-mi** a very large mammal with thick wrinkled skin and short legs, which lives around the rivers of tropical Africa.

> **WORD HISTORY**
> A hippopotamus is literally a 'water horse'. The word comes from Greek *hippos*, meaning 'horse', and *potamos*, meaning 'river'.

hippy¹ *adj* **-pier, -piest** *Informal* having large hips.

hippy² *or* **hippie** *n, pl* **-pies** (esp. during the 1960s) a person whose behaviour and dress imply a rejection of conventional values. ▷ HISTORY from HIP⁴

hire *vb* **hiring, hired 1** to acquire the temporary use of (a thing) or the services of (a person) in exchange for payment. **2** to employ (a person) for wages. **3** to provide (something) or the services of (oneself or others) for payment. **4 hire out** *Chiefly Brit* to pay independent contractors for (work to be done). ✧ *n* **5** the act of hiring. **6 for hire** available to be hired. ▷ HISTORY Old English *hӯrian*

hireling *n Disparaging* a person who works only for money.

hire-purchase *n* a system in which a buyer takes possession of merchandise on payment of a deposit and completes the purchase by paying a series of instalments while the seller retains ownership until the final instalment is paid.

hirsute (**her**-suit) *adj* hairy. ▷ HISTORY Latin *hirsutus* shaggy

his *adj* **1** of, belonging to, or associated with him: *his birthday.* ✧ *pron* **2** something belonging to him: *his is on the left; that book is his.* **3 of his** belonging to him. ▷ HISTORY Old English

Hispanic *adj* **1** of or derived from Spain or the Spanish. ✧ *n* **2** *US* a US citizen of Spanish or Latin-American descent. ▷ HISTORY Latin *Hispania* Spain

hiss *n* **1** a sound like that of a prolonged *s*. **2** such a sound as an expression of dislike. ✧ *vb* **3** to utter a hiss. **4** to express with a hiss: *she hissed the name.* **5** to show dislike towards (a speaker or performer) by hissing. ▷ HISTORY imitative

histamine (**hiss**-ta-meen) *n* a chemical compound released by the body tissues in allergic reactions. ▷ HISTORY Greek *histos* tissue + *amine*

histogram *n* a statistical graph that represents the frequency of values of a quantity by vertical bars of varying heights and widths. ▷ HISTORY probably *histo(ry)* + Greek *grammē* line

histology *n* the study of the tissues of an animal or plant. ▷ HISTORY Greek *histos* tissue + -LOGY

historian *n* a person who writes or studies history.

historic *adj* important in history, or likely to be seen as important in the future.

> **WORD TIP**
> A distinction is usually made between *historic* (important, significant) and *historical* (pertaining to history): *a historic decision; a historical perspective.*

historical *adj* **1** occurring in the past. **2** describing or representing situations or people that existed in the past: *a historical novel.* **3** belonging to or typical of the study of history: *historical perspective.* ▶ **historically** *adv*

> **WORD TIP**
> See at **historic.**

historicism *n* **1** the belief that natural laws govern historical events. **2** excessive respect for historical institutions, such as traditions or laws.

A B C D E F G H I J K L M N O P Q R S T U V W X Y Z

historicity *n* historical authenticity.

historiographer *n* a historian employed to write the history of a group or public institution.

history *n, pl* **-ries 1** a record or account of past events and developments. **2** all that is preserved of the past, esp. in written form. **3** the study of interpreting past events. **4** the past events or previous experiences of a place, thing, or person. **5** a play that depicts historical events. ▷ **HISTORY** Greek *historia* inquiry

histrionic *adj* **1** very dramatic and full of exaggerated emotion: *histrionic bursts of invective.* ✧ *n* **2 histrionics** behaviour of this kind. ▷ **HISTORY** Latin *histrio* actor ▶ **histrionically** *adv*

hit *vb* **hitting, hit 1** to strike or touch (a person or thing) forcefully. **2** to come into violent contact with: *a helicopter hit a Volvo.* **3** to propel (a ball) by striking. **4** *Cricket* to score (runs). **5** to affect (a person, place, or thing) badly: *the airline says that its revenue will be hit.* **6** to reach (a point or place): *the city's crime level hit new heights.* **7 hit the bottle** *Slang* to start drinking excessive amounts of alcohol. **8 hit the road** *Informal* to set out on a journey. ✧ *n* **9** an impact or collision. **10** a shot or blow that reaches its target. **11** *Informal* a person or thing that gains wide appeal. **12** *Computers slang* a single visit to a website: *over 500 000 hits a day to its site.* ✧ See also **hit on**. ▷ **HISTORY** Old English *hittan*

hit-and-miss *adj Informal* happening in an unplanned way.

hit-and-run *adj* denoting a motor-vehicle accident in which the driver does not stop to give assistance or inform the police.

hitch *n* **1** a temporary or minor problem or difficulty. **2** a knot that can be undone by pulling against the direction of the strain that holds it. ✧ *vb* **3** *Informal* to obtain (a ride) by hitchhiking. **4** to fasten with a knot or tie. **5 get hitched** *Slang* to get married. **6 hitch up** to pull up (one's trousers etc.) with a quick jerk. ▷ **HISTORY** origin unknown

hitchhike *vb* **-hiking, -hiked** to travel by getting free lifts in motor vehicles. ▶ **hitchhiker** *n*

hi-tech *adj* using sophisticated, esp. electronic, technology.

hither *adv Old-fashioned* to or towards this place: *come hither.* ▷ **HISTORY** Old English *hider*

hitherto *adv Formal* until this time: *fundamental questions which have hitherto been ignored.*

hit man *n* a person hired to murder someone.

hit on *or* **upon** *vb* to think of (an idea).

hit-or-miss *adj Informal* unplanned or unpredictable: *hit-or-miss service.* Also: **hit-and-miss**

hit wicket *n Cricket* a batsman breaking the wicket while playing a stroke and so being out.

HIV human immunodeficiency virus, the cause of AIDS.

hive *n* **1** a structure in which bees live. **2 hive of activity** a busy place with many people working hard. ▷ **HISTORY** Old English *hȳf*

hive off *vb* to transfer (part of a business, esp. the profitable part of a nationalized industry) to new ownership.

hives *n Pathol* an allergic reaction in which itchy red or whitish raised patches develop on the skin. ▷ **HISTORY** origin unknown

HM (in Britain) Her (*or* His) Majesty.

H.M.A.S. *or* **HMAS** Her (*or* His) Majesty's Australian Ship.

HMI (in Britain) Her (*or* His) Majesty's Inspector; a government official who examines and supervises schools.

H.M.S. *or* **HMS** (in Britain) Her (*or* His) Majesty's Ship.

HMSO (in Britain) Her (*or* His) Majesty's Stationery Office.

HNC (in Britain) Higher National Certificate; a qualification recognized by many national technical and professional institutions.

HND (in Britain) Higher National Diploma; a qualification in a technical subject equivalent to an ordinary degree.

Ho *Chem* holmium.

hoar *n* short for **hoarfrost**. ▷ **HISTORY** Old English *hār*

hoard *n* **1** a store of money, food, etc., hidden away for future use. ✧ *vb* **2** to save or store (money, food, etc.). ▷ **HISTORY** Old English *hord* ▶ **hoarder** *n*

> **WORD TIP**
> *Hoard* is sometimes wrongly written where *horde* is meant: *hordes* (not *hoards*) *of tourists.*

hoarding *n* a large board at the side of a road, used for displaying advertising posters. ▷ **HISTORY** Old French *hourd* palisade

hoarfrost *n* a white layer of ice crystals formed on the ground by condensation at temperatures below freezing point.

hoarse *adj* **1** (of a voice) rough and unclear through illness or too much shouting. **2** having a rough and unclear voice. ▷ **HISTORY** from Old Norse ▶ **hoarsely** *adv* ▶ **hoarseness** *n*

hoary *adj* **hoarier, hoariest 1** having grey or white hair. **2** very old: *a hoary old problem.*

hoax *n* **1** a deception, esp. a practical joke. ✧ *vb* **2** to deceive or play a joke on (someone). ▷ **HISTORY** probably from *hocus* to trick

hob *n Brit* the flat top part of a cooker, or a separate flat surface, containing hotplates or burners. ▷ **HISTORY** perhaps from *hub*

hobble *vb* **-bling, -bled 1** to walk with a lame awkward movement. **2** to tie the legs of (a horse) together in order to restrict its movement. ▷ **HISTORY** probably from Low German

hobby *n, pl* **-bies** an activity pursued in one's spare time for pleasure or relaxation. ▷ **HISTORY** probably variant of name *Robin*

hobby farm *n* a farm run as a hobby rather than as a means of making a living.

hobbyhorse *n* **1** a favourite topic about which a person likes to talk at every opportunity. **2** a toy consisting of a stick with a figure of a horse's head at one end.

hobgoblin *n* a small, mischievous creature in fairy stories. ▷ **HISTORY** *hob,* variant of the name *Rob* + GOBLIN

hobnail boots *n Old-fashioned* heavy boots with short nails in the soles to lessen wear and tear. ▷ **HISTORY** *hob* (in archaic sense: peg)

hobnob *vb* **-nobbing, -nobbed** to socialize or talk informally: *hobnobbing with the rich.* ▷ **HISTORY** *hob or nob* to drink to one another in turns

hobo *n, pl* **-bos** *or* **-boes** *US, Canad, Austral & NZ* a tramp or vagrant. ▷ **HISTORY** origin unknown

Hobson's choice *n* the choice of taking what is offered or nothing at all. ▷ **HISTORY** after Thomas *Hobson,* liveryman who gave his customers no choice

hock[1] *n* the joint in the leg of a horse or similar animal that corresponds to the human ankle. ▷ **HISTORY** Old English *hōhsinu* heel sinew

hock[2] *n* a white wine from the German Rhine. ▷ **HISTORY** German *Hochheimer*

hock[3] *Informal* ✧ *vb* **1** to pawn or pledge. ✧ *n* **2 in hock a** in debt. **b** in pawn. ▷ **HISTORY** Dutch *hok* prison, debt

hockey *n* **1** a game played on a field by two teams of 11 players who try to hit a ball into their opponents' goal using long sticks curved at the end. **2** *US* ice hockey. ▷ **HISTORY** origin unknown

hocus-pocus *n Informal* something said or done in order to confuse or trick someone. ▷ **HISTORY** dog Latin an exclamation used by conjurors

hod *n* an open metal or plastic box attached to a pole, for carrying bricks or mortar. ▷ **HISTORY** Old French *hotte* pannier

Hodgkin's disease *n* a malignant disease that causes enlargement of the lymph nodes, spleen, and liver. ▷ **HISTORY** after Thomas *Hodgkin,* physician

hoe *n* **1** a long-handled implement used to loosen the soil or to weed. ✧ *vb* **hoeing, hoed 2** to scrape or weed with a hoe. ▷ **HISTORY** Germanic

hog *n* **1** a castrated male pig. **2** *US & Canad* any mammal of the pig family. **3** *Informal* a greedy person. **4 go the whole hog** *Slang* to do something in the most complete way possible. ✧ *vb* **hogging, hogged 5** *Slang* to take more than one's share of (something). ▷ **HISTORY** Old English *hogg*

hogback *n Geog* a narrow ridge with steep sides.

Hogmanay *n* New Year's Eve in Scotland. ▷ **HISTORY** probably from Old French *aguillanneuf* a New Year's Eve gift

hogshead *n* a large cask for storing alcoholic drinks. ▷ **HISTORY** origin unknown

hogwash *n Informal* nonsense.

ho-ho *interj* a written representation of the sound of a deep laugh.

hoick *vb* **1** to raise abruptly and sharply. **2** *NZ* to clear the throat and spit. ▷ **HISTORY** origin unknown

hoi polloi *pl n* the ordinary people when compared to the rich or well-educated. ▷ **HISTORY** Greek: the many

hoist *vb* **1** to raise or lift up, esp. by mechanical means. ✧ *n* **2** any apparatus or device for lifting things. ▷ **HISTORY** probably from Low German

hoity-toity *adj Informal* arrogant or haughty. ▷ **HISTORY** obsolete *hoit* to romp

hokey-pokey *n NZ* a brittle toffee sold in lumps.

hokum *n Slang, chiefly US & Canad* **1** nonsense; bunk. **2** obvious sentimental material in a play or film. ▷ **HISTORY** probably a blend of *hocus-pocus* + *bunkum*

hold[1] *vb* **holding, held 1** to keep (an object or a person) with or within the hands or arms. **2** to support: *a rope made from 1000 hairs would hold a large adult.* **3** to maintain in a specified state or position: *his reputation continued to hold secure.* **4** to have the capacity for: *trains designed to hold more than 400.* **5** to set aside or reserve: *they will hold our tickets until tomorrow.* **6** to restrain or keep back: *designed to hold dangerous criminals.* **7** to remain unbroken: *if the elastic holds.* **8** (of the weather) to remain dry and bright. **9** to keep (the attention of): *a writer holds a reader by his temperament.* **10** to arrange and cause to take place: *we must hold an inquiry.* **11** to have the ownership or possession of: *she holds a degree in Egyptology.* **12** to have responsibility for: *she cannot hold an elective office.* **13** to be able to control the outward effects of drinking (alcohol): *he can't hold his liquor.* **14** to (cause to) remain committed to (a promise, etc.). **15** to claim or believe: *some Sufis hold that all religious leaders were prophets.* **16** to remain valid or true: *the categories are not the same and equivalency does not hold.* **17** to consider in a specified manner: *philosophies which we hold so dear.* **18** to defend successfully: *the Russians were holding the Volga front.* **19** *Music* to sustain the sound of (a note). ✧ *n* **20** a way of holding something or the act of holding it. **21** something to hold onto for support. **22** controlling influence: *drugs will take a hold.* **23 with no holds barred** with all limitations removed. ▷ **HISTORY** Old English *healdan* ▶ **holder** *n*

hold[2] *n* the space in a ship or aircraft for storing cargo. ▷ **HISTORY** variant of *hole*

holdall *n Brit* a large strong travelling bag.

hold forth *vb* to speak for a long time.

holding *n* **1** land held under a lease. **2** property to which the holder has legal title, such as land, stocks, or shares.

holding company *n* a company that holds the controlling shares in one or more other companies.

holding paddock *n Austral & NZ* a paddock in which cattle or sheep are kept temporarily.

hold on *vb* **1** to maintain a firm grasp (of something or someone). **2 hold on to** to keep. **3** *Informal* to wait, esp. on the telephone.

hold over *vb* to postpone: *several cases had to be held over pending further investigation.*

hold-up *n* **1** an armed robbery. **2** a delay: *a traffic hold-up.* ✧ *vb* **hold up 3** to delay. **4** to support (an object). **5** to stop and rob (someone), using a weapon. **6** to exhibit or present (something) as an example: *he was held up as a model professional.*

hold with *vb* approve of: *I don't hold with divorce.*

hole *n* **1** an area hollowed out in a solid. **2** an opening in or through something. **3** an animal's burrow. **4** *Informal* a fault or error: *this points to a very big hole in parliamentary security.* **5 pick holes in** to point out faults in. **6** *Informal* an unattractive town or other place. **7 in a hole** *Slang* in a difficult and embarrassing situation. **8** (on a golf course) any one of the divisions of a course (usually 18) represented by the distance between the tee and the sunken cup on the green into which the ball is to be played. **9 make a hole in** *Informal* to use a great amount of (one's money or food supply). ✧ *vb* **holing, holed 10** to make a hole or holes in (something). **11** to hit (a golf ball) into a hole. ▷ **HISTORY** Old English *hol* ▶ **holey** *adj*

hole in the heart *n* a congenital defect of the heart, in which there is an abnormal opening in the partition between the left and right halves.

hole up *vb Informal* to go into hiding.

Holi (**holl**-lee) *n* an annual Hindu spring festival, honouring Krishna.

holiday *n* **1** a period of time spent away from home for enjoyment and relaxation. **2** (*often pl*) *Chiefly Brit & NZ* a period in which a break is taken from work or studies for rest or recreation. **3** a day on which work is suspended by law or custom, such as a bank holiday. ✧ *vb* **4** *Chiefly Brit* to spend a holiday. ▷ **HISTORY** Old English *hāligdæg* holy day

holier-than-thou *adj* offensively self-righteous.

Holiness *n* (preceded by *His* or *Your*) a title reserved for the pope.

holism *n* **1** the view that a whole is greater than the sum of its parts. **2** (in medicine) consideration of the complete person in the treatment of disease. ▷ **HISTORY** Greek *holos* whole ▶ **holistic** *adj*

holler *Informal* ✧ *vb* **1** to shout or yell. ✧ *n* **2** a shout or yell. ▷ **HISTORY** French *holà* stop!

hollow *adj* **1** having a hole or space within; not solid: *a hollow tree.* **2** curving inwards: *hollow cheeks.* **3** (of sounds) as if echoing in a hollow place. **4** without any real value or worth: *a hollow enterprise, lacking purpose, and lacking soul.* ✧ *adv* **5 beat someone hollow** *Brit & NZ informal* to defeat someone thoroughly. ✧ *n* **6** a cavity or space in something. **7** a dip in the land. ✧ *vb* **8** (often foll. by *out*) to form a hole or cavity in. ▷ **HISTORY** Old English *holh* cave ▶ **hollowly** *adv*

holly *n* an evergreen tree with prickly leaves and bright red berries, used for Christmas decorations. ▷ **HISTORY** Old English *holegn*

hollyhock *n* a tall garden plant with spikes of colourful flowers. ▷ **HISTORY** *holy* + obsolete *hock* mallow

holmium *n Chem* a silver-white metallic element, the compounds of which are highly magnetic. Symbol: Ho. ▷ **HISTORY** after *Holmia,* Latin name of Stockholm

holm oak *n* an evergreen oak tree with prickly leaves like holly.

holocaust *n* **1** destruction or loss of life on a massive scale. **2 the Holocaust** mass murder of the Jews in Europe by the Nazis (1940–45). ▷ **HISTORY** Greek *holos* whole + *kaiein* to burn

Holocene *adj* of the current geological epoch, which began about 10 000 years ago.

hologram *n* a three-dimensional photographic image produced by means of a split laser beam. ▷ **HISTORY** Greek *holos* whole + *grammē* line

holograph *n* a book or document handwritten by its author. ▷ **HISTORY** Greek *holos* whole + *graphein* to write

holography *n* the science of using lasers to produce holograms. ▷ **HISTORY** Greek *holos* whole + -GRAPHY ▶ **holographic** *adj*

hols *pl n Brit & S African school slang* holidays.

holster *n* a sheathlike leather case for a pistol, worn attached to a belt. ▷ **HISTORY** Germanic

holt *n* the lair of an otter. ▷ **HISTORY** from HOLD[2]

holy *adj* **-lier, -liest 1** of or associated with God or a deity. **2** (of a person) religious and leading a virtuous life. ▷ **HISTORY** Old English *hālig, hǣlig* ▶ **holiness** *n*

Holy Communion *n Christianity* a church service in which people take bread and wine in remembrance of Christ's Last Supper and His atonement for the sins of the world.

Holy Ghost *n* **the Holy Ghost** same as **Holy Spirit**.

Holy Grail *n* **1 the Holy Grail** (in medieval legend) the bowl used by Jesus at the Last Supper. **2** *Informal* any ambition or goal. ▷ **HISTORY** *grail* from Medieval Latin *gradalis* bowl

Holy Land *n* **the Holy Land** Palestine.

holy of holies *n* **1** any sacred place or a place considered as if it were sacred: *the holy of holies they called the Captain's Cabin.* **2** the innermost chamber of a Jewish temple.

holy orders *pl n* the status of an ordained Christian minister.

Holy See *n* **the Holy See** *RC Church* the see of the pope as bishop of Rome.

Holy Spirit *n* **the Holy Spirit** *Christianity* one of the three aspects of God.

Holy Week *n Christianity* the week before Easter Sunday.

homage *n* a public show of respect or honour towards someone or something. ▷ **HISTORY** Latin *homo* man

homburg *n* a man's soft felt with a dented crown and a stiff upturned brim.

home *n* **1** the place where one lives. **2** the country or area of one's birth. **3** a building or organization set up to care for people in a certain category, such as orphans or the aged. **4** the place where something is invented or started: *the home of the first aircraft.* **5** *Sport* a team's own ground: *the match is at home.* **6** *Baseball, rounders, etc.* the objective towards which a player runs after striking the ball. **7 at home a** in one's own home or country. **b** at ease: *he felt more at home with the Russians.* **c** receiving visitors. ✧ *adj* **8** of one's home, birthplace, or native country. **9** (of an activity) done in one's house: *home movies.* **10** *Sport* played on one's own ground: *a home game.* **11 home and dry** *Brit slang* definitely safe or successful. ✧ *adv* **12** to or at home: *I came home.* **13** to or on the point: *the*

message struck home. **14** to the fullest extent: *they drove their spears home.* **15 bring something home to someone** to make something clear to someone. ✧ *vb* **homing, homed 16 home in on** to be directed towards (a goal or target). **17** (of birds) to return home accurately from a distance.
▷ HISTORY Old English *hām*

> **WORD TIP**
> See at **hone.**

home-brew *n* beer or other alcoholic drink brewed at home.
homecoming *n* a return home, esp. after a long absence.
home economics *n* the study of diet, budgeting, child care, and other subjects concerned with running a home.
home farm *n Brit* a farm that belonged to and provided food for a large country house.
Home Guard *n* a part-time military force of volunteers recruited for the defence of the United Kingdom in the Second World War.
home help *n Brit, Austral & NZ* a person employed by a local authority to do housework in an elderly or disabled person's home.
homeland *n* **1** the country from which the ancestors of a person or group came. **2** the official name in S Africa for a **Bantustan.**
homeless *adj* **1** having nowhere to live. ✧ *pl n* **2** people who have nowhere to live: *night shelters for the homeless.* ▶ **homelessness** *n*
homely *adj* **-lier, -liest 1** simple, ordinary, and comfortable. **2** (of a person) **a** *Brit* warm and friendly. **b** *Chiefly US & Canad* plain or unattractive. ▶ **homeliness** *n*
home-made *adj* (esp. of foods) made at home or on the premises.
Home Office *n Brit government* the department responsible for law and order, immigration, and other domestic affairs.
homeopathy *or* **homoeopathy** (home-ee-**op**-ath-ee) *n* a method of treating disease by the use of small amounts of a drug that produces symptoms of the disease in healthy people. ▷ HISTORY Greek *homoios* similar + *patheia* suffering ▶ **homeopath** *or* **homoeopath** (**home**-ee-oh-path) *n* ▶ **homeopathic** *or* **homoeopathic** *adj*
homeostasis *or* **homoeostasis** (hom-ee-oh-**stass**-iss) *n* the tendency of an organism to achieve a stable metabolic state by compensating automatically for violent changes in the environment and other disruptions.
▷ HISTORY Greek *homoios* similar + *stasis* a standing
homeowner *n* a person who owns the home in which he or she lives.
home page *n Internet* the introductory information about a website with links to the information or services provided.
Homeric (home-**mer**-rik) *adj* of or relating to Homer, Greek epic poet (circa 800 BC).
home rule *n* self-government in domestic affairs.
Home Secretary *n Brit government* the head of the Home Office.
homesick *adj* depressed by being away from home and family. ▶ **homesickness** *n*
homestead *n* **1** a farmhouse and the adjoining land. **2** (in the western US & Canada) a house and adjoining tract of land (originally often 160 acres) that was granted by the government for development as a farm.
homesteader *n* (in the western US & Canada) a person who lives on and farms a homestead.
homestead law *n* (in the western US & Canada) any of various laws granting certain privileges to owners of homesteads.
home truths *pl n* unpleasant facts told to a person about himself or herself.
home unit *n Austral & NZ* a self-contained residence which is part of a block of such residences.
homeward *adj* **1** going home. ✧ *adv also* **homewards 2** towards home.
homework *n* **1** school work done at home. **2** research or preparation.
homicide *n* **1** the act of killing someone. **2** a person who kills someone. ▷ HISTORY Latin *homo* man + *caedere* to kill ▶ **homicidal** *adj*
homily *n, pl* **-lies** a moralizing talk or piece of writing. ▷ HISTORY Greek *homilia* discourse
homing *adj* **1** *Zool* denoting the ability to return home after travelling great distances. **2** (of a missile) capable of guiding itself onto a target.
homing pigeon *n* a pigeon developed for its homing instinct, used for racing.
hominid *n* **1** any member of the family of primates that includes modern man and the extinct forerunners of man. ✧ *adj* **2** of or belonging to this family. ▷ HISTORY Latin *homo* man
hominoid *adj* **1** of or like man; manlike. ✧ *n* **2** a manlike animal. ▷ HISTORY Latin *homo* man
homo- *combining form* same or like: *homologous.* ▷ HISTORY Greek *homos* same
homogeneous (home-oh-**jean**-ee-uss) *adj* having parts or members which are all the same or which consist of only one substance: *the Arabs are not a single, homogeneous nation.* ▷ HISTORY Greek *homos* same + *genos* kind ▶ **homogeneity** *n*
homogenize *or* **-nise** *vb* **-nizing, -nized** *or* **-nising, -nised 1** to break up the fat globules in (milk or cream) so that they are evenly distributed. **2** to make different elements the same or similar: *homogenized products for a mass market.*
homogenous (hom-**oj**-in-uss) *adj* having a similar structure because of common ancestry.
homograph *n* a word spelt the same as another, but having a different meaning, such as *bear* (to carry) and *bear* (the animal). ▷ HISTORY Greek *homos* same + *graphein* to write
homologous (hom-**ol**-log-uss) *adj* **1** having a related or similar position or structure. **2** *Biol* (of organs and parts) having the same origin but different functions: *the wing of a bat and the arm of a monkey are homologous.* ▷ HISTORY Greek *homos* same + *logos* ratio

homologous series *n Chem* a series of organic compounds with similar characteristics and structure but differing by a number of CH_2 groups.

homology (hom-**ol**-a-jee) *n* the condition of being homologous.

homonym *n* a word pronounced and spelt the same as another, but having a different meaning, such as *novel* (a book) and *novel* (new).

homophobia *n* intense hatred or fear of homosexuals. ▷ **HISTORY** *homo(sexual) + phobia* ▶ **homophobic** *adj*

homophone *n* a word pronounced the same as another, but having a different meaning or spelling or both, such as *bear* and *bare*. ▷ **HISTORY** Greek *homos* same + *phōnē* sound

Homo sapiens (**home**-oh **sap**-ee-enz) *n* the name for modern man as a species. ▷ **HISTORY** Latin *homo* man + *sapiens* wise

homosexual *n* **1** a person who is sexually attracted to members of the same sex. ✧ *adj* **2** (of a person) sexually attracted to members of the same sex. **3** (of a sexual relationship) between members of the same sex. ▷ **HISTORY** Greek *homos* same ▶ **homosexuality** *n*

homozygous *adj Biol* having two identical alleles of the same gene. ▷ **HISTORY** Greek *homos* same + *zugōtos* yoked

Hon. Honourable (title).

hone *vb* **honing, honed 1** to develop and improve (a quality or ability). **2** to sharpen (a tool). ✧ *n* **3** a fine whetstone used for sharpening edged tools and knives. ▷ **HISTORY** Old English *hān* stone

> ☑ **WORD TIP**
> *Hone* is sometimes wrongly used where *home* is meant: *this device makes it easier to home in on* (not *hone in on*) *the target.*

honest *adj* **1** truthful and moral in behaviour; trustworthy. **2** open and sincere in relationships and attitudes; without pretensions. **3** gained or earned fairly. ▷ **HISTORY** Latin *honos* esteem

honestly *adv* **1** in an honest manner. **2** truly.

honesty *n, pl* **-ties 1** the quality of being truthful and trustworthy. **2** a plant with flattened silvery pods which are used for indoor decoration.

honey *n* **1** a sweet edible sticky substance made by bees from nectar. **2** *Chiefly US & Canad* a term of affection. **3** *Informal, chiefly US & Canad* something very good of its kind. ▷ **HISTORY** Old English *huneg*

honeybee *n* a bee widely domesticated as a source of honey and beeswax.

honeycomb *n* a waxy structure, constructed by bees in a hive, that consists of many six-sided cells in which honey is stored.

honeydew *n* a sugary substance excreted by aphids and similar insects.

honeydew melon *n* a melon with yellow skin and sweet pale flesh.

honeyed *adj Poetic* flattering or soothing.

honeymoon *n* **1** a holiday taken by a newly married couple. **2** the early period of an undertaking or activity, such as the start of new government's term of office, when an attitude of goodwill prevails. ✧ *vb* **3** to take a honeymoon. ▷ **HISTORY** traditionally, referring to the feelings of married couples as changing with the phases of the moon ▶ **honeymooner** *n*

honeysuckle *n* **1** a climbing shrub with sweet-smelling white, yellow, or pink flowers. **2** an Australian tree or shrub with nectar-rich flowers. ▷ **HISTORY** Old English *hunigsūce*

hongi (**hong**-jee) *n NZ* a Maori greeting in which people touch noses.

honk *n* **1** the sound made by a motor horn. **2** the sound made by a goose. ✧ *vb* **3** to make or cause (something) to make a honking sound.

honorarium *n, pl* **-iums** *or* **-ia** a voluntary fee paid for a service which is usually free. ▷ **HISTORY** Latin *honorarium (donum)* honorary gift

honorary *adj* **a** held or given as a mark of respect, without the usual qualifications, payment, or work: *an honorary degree.* **b** (of a secretary, treasurer, etc.) unpaid.

honorific *adj* showing respect: *an honorific title.*

honour *or US* **honor** *n* **1** a person's good reputation and the respect they are given by other people. **2 a** fame or glory. **b** a person who wins fame or glory for his or her country, school, etc.: *he was an honour to his nation.* **3** great respect or esteem, or an outward sign of this. **4** a privilege or pleasure: *it was an honour to meet him.* **5** *Old-fashioned* a woman's virginity. **6** *Bridge, whist* any of the top four or five cards in a suit. **7** *Golf* the right to tee off first. **8 in honour of** out of respect for. **9 on one's honour** under a moral obligation. ✧ *vb* **10** to hold someone in respect. **11** to give (someone) special praise, attention, or an award. **12** to accept and then pay (a cheque or bill). **13** to keep (one's promise); fulfil (a previous agreement). ▷ **HISTORY** Latin *honor* esteem

Honour *n* (preceded by *Your, His* or *Her*) a title used to address or refer to certain judges.

honourable *or US* **honorable** *adj* worthy of respect or esteem. ▶ **honourably** *adv*

Honourable *adj* **the Honourable** a title of respect placed before a name: used of various officials, of the children of certain peers, and in Parliament by one member speaking of another.

honours *or US* **honors** *pl n* **1** (in a university degree course) a rank or mark of the highest academic standard: *an honours degree.* **2** observances of respect, esp. at a funeral. **3 do the honours** to serve as host or hostess by serving food or pouring drinks.

hooch (rhymes with **smooch**) *n Informal* alcoholic drink, esp. illegally distilled spirits. ▷ **HISTORY** from a Native American language

hood[1] *n* **1** a loose head covering either attached to a coat or made as a separate garment. **2** *US, Canad & Austral* the bonnet of a car. **3** the folding roof of a convertible car or a pram. ✧ *vb* **4** to cover with or as if with a hood. ▷ **HISTORY** Old English *hōd* ▶ **hoodlike** *adj*

hood[2] *n Slang* short for **hoodlum**.

hooded *adj* **1** (of a garment) having a hood. **2** (of eyes) having heavy eyelids that appear to be half-closed.

hooded crow *n* a crow that has a grey body and black head, wings, and tail.

hoodlum *n* a violent criminal, esp. one who is a member of a gang. ▷ **HISTORY** origin unknown

hoodoo *n, pl* **-doos 1** *Informal* bad luck. **2** *Informal* a person or thing that brings bad luck. **3** *Chiefly US* same as **voodoo**.

hoodwink *vb* to trick or deceive. ▷ **HISTORY** originally, to cover the eyes with a hood

hooey *n Slang* nonsense. ▷ **HISTORY** origin unknown

hoof *n, pl* **hooves** *or* **hoofs 1** the horny covering of the end of the foot in the horse, deer, and certain other mammals. **2 on the hoof a** (of livestock) alive. **b** in an impromptu way: *thinking on the hoof.* ✧ *vb* **3 hoof it** *Slang* to walk. ▷ **HISTORY** Old English *hōf* ▶ **hoofed** *adj*

hoo-ha *n* a noisy commotion or fuss. ▷ **HISTORY** origin unknown

hook *n* **1** a curved piece of metal or plastic used to hang, hold, or pull something. **2** something resembling a hook, such as a sharp bend in a river or a sharply curved strip of land. **3** *Boxing* a short swinging blow with the elbow bent. **4** *Cricket, golf* a shot that causes the ball to go to the player's left. **5 by hook or by crook** by any means: *get into the charts by hook or by crook.* **6 hook, line, and sinker** *Informal* completely: *we fell for it hook, line, and sinker.* **7 let someone off the hook** *Slang* to free someone from an obligation or a difficult situation. **8 sling one's hook** *Brit & Austral slang* to leave. ✧ *vb* **9** to fasten with or as if with a hook. **10** to catch (a fish) on a hook. **11** *Cricket, golf* to play (a ball) with a hook. **12** *Rugby* to obtain and pass (the ball) backwards from a scrum, using the feet. ▷ **HISTORY** Old English *hōc*

hookah *n* an oriental pipe for smoking marijuana or tobacco, with a long flexible stem connected to a container of water through which smoke is drawn and cooled. ▷ **HISTORY** Arabic *huqqah*

hooked *adj* **1** bent like a hook. **2 hooked on a** *Slang* addicted to: *hooked on drugs.* **b** obsessed with: *hooked on football.*

hooker *n* **1** *Slang* a prostitute. **2** *Rugby* a player who uses his feet to get the ball in a scrum.

Hooke's law *n Physics* the principle that a solid stretches or contracts in proportion to the force placed on it, within the limits of its elasticity. ▷ **HISTORY** after Robert *Hooke,* physicist

hook-up *n* the linking of broadcasting equipment or stations to transmit a special programme.

hookworm *n* a blood-sucking worm with hooked mouthparts.

hooligan *n Slang* a young person who behaves in a noisy and violent way in public. ▷ **HISTORY** origin unknown ▶ **hooliganism** *n*

hoon *n Austral & NZ slang* **1** a loutish youth who drives irresponsibly. ✧ *vb* **2** to drive irresponsibly.

hoop *n* **1** a rigid circular band of metal, plastic, or wood. **2** a child's toy shaped like a hoop and rolled on the ground or whirled around the body. **3** *Croquet* any of the iron arches through which the ball is driven. **4** a large ring through which performers or animals jump. **5 go** *or* **be put through the hoops** to go through an ordeal or test. ✧ *vb* **6** to surround (something) with a hoop. ▷ **HISTORY** Old English *hōp* ▶ **hooped** *adj*

hoopla *n Brit & Austral* a fairground game in which hoops are thrown over objects in an attempt to win them.

hoopoe (**hoop**-oo) *n* a bird with pinkish-brown plumage with black-and-white wings and a fanlike crest. ▷ **HISTORY** imitative

hoop pine *n* an Australian tree or shrub with flowers in dense spikes.

hooray *interj, n* same as **hurrah**.

hoot *n* **1** the sound of a car horn. **2** the cry of an owl. **3** a high-pitched noise showing disapproval. **4** *Informal* an amusing person or thing. ✧ *vb* **5** *Brit* to blow (a car horn). **6** to make a hoot. **7** to jeer or yell contemptuously at someone. **8** to drive (speakers or performers on stage) off by hooting. ▷ **HISTORY** imitative

hooter *n Chiefly Brit* **1** a device that hoots, such as a car horn. **2** *Slang* a nose.

Hoover *n* **1** *Trademark* a vacuum cleaner. ✧ *vb* **hoover 2** to vacuum-clean (a carpet). **3** (often foll. by *up*) to devour (something) quickly and completely.

hooves *n* a plural of **hoof**.

hop[1] *vb* **hopping, hopped 1** to jump forwards or upwards on one foot. **2** (of frogs, birds, etc.) to move forwards in short jumps. **3** to jump over something. **4** *Informal* to move quickly (in, on, out of, etc.): *hop into bed.* **5 hop it** *Brit & Austral slang* to go away. ✧ *n* **6** an instance of hopping. **7** *Informal* an informal dance. **8** *Informal* a short journey, usually in an aircraft. **9 on the hop** *Informal* **a** active or busy: *he keeps me on the hop.* **b** unawares or unprepared: *you caught me on the hop.* ▷ **HISTORY** Old English *hoppian*

hop[2] *n* a climbing plant with green conelike flowers. See also **hops**. ▷ **HISTORY** Middle Dutch *hoppe*

hope *vb* **hoping, hoped 1** to desire (something), usually with some possibility of fulfilment: *you would hope for their cooperation.* **2** to trust or believe: *I hope I've arranged that.* ✧ *n* **3** a feeling of desire for something, usually with confidence in the possibility of its fulfilment: *the news was greeted by some as hope for further interest rate cuts.* **4** a reasonable ground for this feeling: *there is hope for you yet.* **5** the person, thing, situation, or event that gives cause for hope or is desired: *the young are a symbol of hope for the future.* ▷ **HISTORY** Old English *hopa*

hopeful *adj* **1** having, inspiring, or expressing hope. ✧ *n* **2** a person considered to be on the brink of success: *a young hopeful.*

A B C D E F G H I J K L M N O P Q R S T U V W X Y Z

hopefully *adv* **1** in a hopeful manner. **2** *Informal* it is hoped: *hopefully I've got a long career ahead of me.*

> **WORD TIP**
> The use of *hopefully* to mean *it is hoped* used to be considered incorrect by some people but has now become acceptable in informal contexts.

hopeless *adj* **1** having or offering no hope. **2** impossible to solve. **3** *Informal* without skill or ability: *I'm hopeless at maths.* ▸ **hopelessly** *adv* ▸ **hopelessness** *n*

hopper *n* a funnel-shaped device from which solid materials can be discharged into a receptacle below.

hops *pl n* the dried flowers of the hop plant, used to give a bitter taste to beer.

hopscotch *n* a children's game in which a player throws a stone to land in one of a pattern of squares marked on the ground and then hops over to it to pick it up. ▷ **HISTORY** *hop* + obsolete *scotch* a line, scratch

horde *n* a very large crowd, often frightening or unpleasant. ▷ **HISTORY** Turkish *ordū* camp

> **WORD TIP**
> *Horde* is sometimes wrongly written where *hoard* is meant: *a hoard* (not *horde*) *of gold coins.*

horehound *n* a plant that produces a bitter juice formerly used as a cough medicine. ▷ **HISTORY** Old English *hārhūne*

horizon *n* **1** the apparent line that divides the earth and the sky. **2 horizons** the limits of a person's interests and activities. **3 on the horizon** almost certainly going to happen or be done in the future. ▷ **HISTORY** Greek *horizein* to limit

horizontal *adj* **1** flat and level with the ground or with a line considered as a base. **2** affecting or happening at one level in a system or organization: *a horizontal division of labour.* ✧ *n* **3** a horizontal plane, position, or line. ▸ **horizontally** *adv*

hormone *n* **1** a chemical substance produced in an endocrine gland and transported in the blood to a certain tissue, on which it has a specific effect. **2** a similar substance produced by a plant that is essential for growth. **3** a synthetic substance having the same effects. ▷ **HISTORY** Greek *hormōn* ▸ **hormonal** *adj*

horn *n* **1** either of a pair of permanent bony outgrowths on the heads of animals such as cattle and antelopes. **2** any hornlike projection, such as the eyestalk of a snail. **3** the antler of a deer. **4** the hard substance of which horns are made. **5** a musical wind instrument made from horn. **6** any musical instrument consisting of a pipe or tube of brass fitted with a mouthpiece. **7** a device, such as on a vehicle, for producing a warning or signalling noise. ▷ **HISTORY** Old English ▸ **horned** *adj*

hornbeam *n* a tree with smooth grey bark.

hornbill *n* a tropical bird with a bony growth on its large beak.

hornblende *n* a green-to-black mineral containing aluminium, calcium, sodium, magnesium, and iron.

hornet *n* **1** a large wasp that can inflict a severe sting. **2 hornet's nest** a very unpleasant situation that is difficult to deal with: *you'll stir up a hornet's nest.* ▷ **HISTORY** Old English *hyrnetu*

horn of plenty *n* same as **cornucopia**.

hornpipe *n* **1** a solo dance, traditionally performed by sailors. **2** music for this dance.

horny *adj* **hornier, horniest 1** of, like, or hard as horn. **2** *Slang* **a** sexually aroused. **b** provoking sexual arousal. **c** sexually eager.

horoscope *n* **1** the prediction of a person's future based on the positions of the planets, sun, and moon at the time of birth. **2** a diagram showing the positions of the planets, sun, and moon at a particular time and place.

> **WORD HISTORY**
> 'Horoscope' comes via Latin from Greek *hōroskopos*, meaning 'hour observer' or 'time observer', referring to the time of a person's birth. The word derives from *hōra*, meaning 'hour' or 'time' and *skopos*, meaning 'observer' (the same word as is seen in 'microscope', 'telescope', etc.).

horrendous *adj* very unpleasant or shocking. ▷ **HISTORY** Latin *horrendus* fearful

horrible *adj* **1** disagreeable and unpleasant: *a horrible hotel room.* **2** causing fear, shock, or disgust: *he died a horrible death.* ▷ **HISTORY** Latin *horribilis* ▸ **horribly** *adv*

horrid *adj* **1** disagreeable or unpleasant: *it had been a horrid day at school.* **2** *Informal* (of a person) unkind and nasty: *her horrid parents.* ▷ **HISTORY** Latin *horridus* prickly

horrific *adj* provoking horror: *horrific injuries.* ▸ **horrifically** *adv*

horrify *vb* **-fies, -fying, -fied** to cause feelings of horror in (someone); shock (someone) greatly.

horror *n* **1** extreme fear or terror. **2** intense hatred: *she had a horror of violence.* **3** a thing or person causing fear, loathing, or distaste. ✧ *adj* **4** having a frightening subject, usually concerned with the supernatural: *a horror film.* ▷ **HISTORY** Latin: a trembling with fear

horrors *pl n* **the horrors** *Slang* a fit of nervousness or anxiety.

hors d'oeuvre (or **durv**) *n, pl* **hors d'oeuvre** *or* **hors d'oeuvres** (or **durv**) an appetizer, usually served before the main meal. ▷ **HISTORY** French

horse *n* **1** a four-footed mammal with hooves, a mane, and a tail, used for riding and pulling carts, etc. *RELATED ADJECTIVES* ▸ **equestrian, equine 2** the adult male of this species; stallion. **3 the horses** *Informal* horse races on which bets may be placed: *an occasional flutter on the horses.* **4** *Gymnastics* a padded apparatus on legs, used for vaulting. **5 be** *or* **get on one's high horse** *Informal* to act in a haughty manner. **6 the horse's mouth** the most reliable source: *I'll tell you straight from the horse's mouth.* ▷ **HISTORY** Old English *hors*

horse around *or* **about** *vb Informal* to play roughly or boisterously.
horsebox *n Brit & Austral* a van or trailer used for transporting horses.
horse chestnut *n* **1** a tree with broad leaves and brown shiny inedible nuts enclosed in a spiky case. **2** the nut of this tree.
horseflesh *n* **1** horses collectively. **2** the flesh of a horse as food.
horsefly *n, pl* **-flies** a large fly which sucks the blood of horses, cattle, and people.
horsehair *n* hair from the tail or mane of a horse, used in upholstery.
horse latitudes *pl n Geog* the latitudes near 30°N or 30°S at sea, characterized by baffling winds, calms, and high barometric pressure. ▷ **HISTORY** referring either to the high mortality of horses on board ship in these latitudes or to *dead horse* (nautical slang: advance pay), which sailors expected to work off by this stage of a voyage
horse laugh *n* a loud and coarse laugh.
horseman *n, pl* **-men 1** a man who is skilled in riding. **2** a man riding a horse. ▶ **horsemanship** *n* ▶ **horsewoman** *fem n*
horseplay *n* rough or rowdy play.
horsepower *n* a unit of power (equivalent to 745.7 watts), used to measure the power of an engine.
horseradish *n* a plant with a white strong-tasting root, which is used to make a sauce.
horse sense *n* same as **common sense**.
horseshoe *n* **1** a piece of iron shaped like a U, nailed to the bottom of a horse's hoof to protect the foot. **2** an object of similar shape: often regarded as a symbol of good luck.
horsetail *n* a plant with small dark toothlike leaves.
horsey *or* **horsy** *adj* **horsier, horsiest 1** of or relating to horses: *a horsey smell.* **2** devoted to horses: *the horsey set.* **3** like a horse: *a horsey face.*
horst *n Geog* a ridge of land that has been forced upwards between two parallel faults. ▷ **HISTORY** German *Horst* thicket
horticulture *n* the art or science of cultivating gardens. ▷ **HISTORY** Latin *hortus* garden + CULTURE ▶ **horticultural** *adj* ▶ **horticulturalist** *or* **horticulturist** *n*
hosanna *interj* an exclamation of praise to God. ▷ **HISTORY** Hebrew *hōshi 'āh nnā* save now, we pray
hose[1] *n* **1** a flexible pipe, for conveying a liquid or gas. ✧ *vb* **hosing, hosed 2** to wash or water (a person or thing) with a hose. ▷ **HISTORY** later use of HOSE[2]
hose[2] *n* **1** *Old-fashioned* stockings, socks, and tights collectively. **2** *History* a man's garment covering the legs and reaching up to the waist. ▷ **HISTORY** Old English *hosa*
hosiery *n* stockings, socks, and knitted underclothing collectively.
hospice (**hoss**-piss) *n* **1** a nursing home that specializes in caring for the terminally ill. **2** *Archaic* a place of shelter for travellers, esp. one kept by a religious order. ▷ **HISTORY** Latin *hospes* guest
hospitable *adj* generous, friendly, and welcoming to guests or strangers: *charming and hospitable lodgings.* ▷ **HISTORY** Medieval Latin *hospitare* to receive as a guest ▶ **hospitably** *adv*
hospital *n* an institution for the medical or psychiatric care and treatment of patients. ▷ **HISTORY** Latin *hospes* guest
hospitality *n, pl* **-ties** kindness in welcoming strangers or guests.
hospitalize *or* **-ise** *vb* **-izing, -ized** *or* **-ising, -ised** to admit or send (a person) into a hospital. ▶ **hospitalization** *or* **-isation** *n*
hospitaller *or US* **hospitaler** *n* a member of a religious order dedicated to hospital work, ambulance services, etc.
host[1] *n* **1** a person who receives or entertains guests, esp. in his own home. **2** the organization or country providing the facilities for a function or event: *Barcelona, host of the 1992 Olympic Games.* **3** the compere of a radio or television programme. **4** *Biol* an animal or plant in or on which a parasite lives. **5** *Computers* a computer connected to a network and providing facilities to other computers and their users. **6** *Old-fashioned* the owner or manager of an inn. ✧ *vb* **7** to be the host of (a party, programme, or event): *he's hosting a radio show.* ▷ **HISTORY** Latin *hospes* guest, host
host[2] *n* a great number; multitude. ▷ **HISTORY** Latin *hostis* stranger
Host *n Christianity* the bread used in Holy Communion. ▷ **HISTORY** Latin *hostia* victim
hostage *n* a person who is illegally held prisoner until certain demands are met by other people. ▷ **HISTORY** Old French *hoste* guest
hostel *n* **1** a building providing overnight accommodation for homeless people. **2** a building providing cheap accommodation and meals for tourists, hikers, etc. **3** same as **youth hostel**. **4** *Brit & NZ* a supervised lodging house for nurses, students, etc. ▷ **HISTORY** Medieval Latin *hospitale* hospice ▶ **hosteller** *or US* **hosteler** *n*
hostelry *n, pl* **-ries** *Archaic or facetious* an inn.
hostel school *n Canad* same as **residential school**.
hostess *n* **1** a woman who receives and entertains guests, esp. in her own house. **2** a woman who receives and entertains patrons of a club, restaurant, or dance hall.
hostile *adj* **1** unfriendly and aggressive. **2** opposed (to): *hostile to the referendum.* **3** relating to or involving the enemies of a country. ▷ **HISTORY** Latin *hostis* enemy
hostility *n, pl* **-ties 1** unfriendly and aggressive feelings or behaviour. **2 hostilities** acts of warfare.
hot *adj* **hotter, hottest 1** having a relatively high temperature. **2** having a temperature higher than desirable. **3** spicy or causing a burning sensation on the tongue: *hot chillies.* **4** (of a temper) quick to flare up. **5** (of a contest or conflict) intense. **6** recent or new: *hot from the press.* **7** much favoured: *a hot favourite.* **8** *Informal* having a dangerously high level of radioactivity. **9** *Slang* stolen or otherwise illegally obtained. **10** (of a colour) intense; striking: *hot pink.* **11** following closely: *this LP appeared hot*

A B C D E F G H I J K L M N O P Q R S T U V W X Y Z

on the heels of the debut smash. **12** *Informal* dangerous or unpleasant: *they're making it hot for me here.* **13** (in various games) very near the answer. **14 hot on** *Informal* **a** strict about: *they are extremely hot on sloppy language.* **b** particularly knowledgeable about. **15 hot under the collar** *Informal* aroused with anger, annoyance, or resentment. **16 in hot water** *Informal* in trouble. ✧ See also **hot up**. ▷ **HISTORY** Old English *hāt*
▸ **hotly** *adv*

hot air *n Informal* empty and usually boastful talk.

hotbed *n* a place offering ideal conditions for the growth of an idea or activity: *a hotbed of resistance.*

hot-blooded *adj* passionate or excitable.

hotchpotch *or esp US & Canad* **hodgepodge** *n* a jumbled mixture. ▷ **HISTORY** Old French *hochepot* shake pot

hot-desking *n Brit, Austral & NZ* the practice of not assigning permanent desks in a workplace, so that employees may work at any available desk.

hot dog *n* a long roll split lengthways with a hot sausage inside.

hotel *n* a commercially run establishment providing lodging and meals for guests. ▷ **HISTORY** French

hotelier *n* an owner or manager of a hotel.

hotfoot *adv* with all possible speed: *hotfoot to the accident.*

hot-headed *adj* impetuous or rash.

hothouse *n* a greenhouse in which the temperature is maintained at a fixed level.

hot key *n Computers* a single key on a computer keyboard which carries out a series of commands.

hotline *n* a direct telephone link between heads of government for emergency use.

hotlink *n Computers* an instant connection from one computer file to another.

hot money *n* capital that is transferred from one financial centre to another seeking the best opportunity for short-term gain.

hotplate *n* **1** a heated metal surface on an electric cooker. **2** a portable device on which food can be kept warm.

hot pool *n NZ* a geothermally heated pool.

hotpot *n* a casserole of meat and vegetables covered with a layer of potatoes.

hot rod *n* a car with an engine that has been modified to produce increased power.

hot spot *n* **1** a place where there is a lot of exciting activity or entertainment. **2** an area where there is fighting or political unrest. **3** a small area of abnormally high temperature or radioactivity.

Hottentot *n* **1** a race of indigenous people of South Africa which is now almost extinct. **2** a member of this race. **3** Also called: **Khoi Khoi** the language of this race. ▷ **HISTORY** origin unknown

hotting *n Brit informal* the performing of high-speed stunts in a stolen car. ▸ **hotter** *n*

hot up *vb* **hotting, hotted** *Informal* to make or become more active and exciting.

hot-water bottle *n* a rubber container, designed to be filled with hot water and used for warming a bed.

hound *n* **1** a dog used for hunting: *to ride with the hounds.* **2** a despicable person. ✧ *vb* **3** to pursue, disturb, or criticize relentlessly: *hounded by the press.* ▷ **HISTORY** Old English *hund*

hour *n* **1** a period of time equal to 60 minutes; $^1/_{24}$ of a day. **2** any of the points on the face of a clock or watch that indicate intervals of 60 minutes: *in my hurry I mistook the hour.* **3** the time of day. **4** the time allowed for or used for something: *a three and a half hour test.* **5** the distance covered in an hour: *an hour from the heart of Tokyo.* **6** a special moment: *the decisive hour.* ✧ See also **hours**. ▷ **HISTORY** Latin *hora*

hourglass *n* a device consisting of two transparent sections linked by a narrow channel, containing a quantity of sand that takes an hour to trickle from one section to the other.

houri *n, pl* **-ris** (in Muslim belief) any of the nymphs of Paradise. ▷ **HISTORY** Arabic *haurā'* woman with dark eyes

hourly *adj* **1** of, occurring, or done once every hour. **2** measured by the hour: *hourly charges.* **3** frequent. ✧ *adv* **4** once every hour. **5** by the hour: *hourly paid.* **6** frequently. **7** at any moment: *the arrival of the men was hourly expected.*

hours *pl n* **1** an indefinite time: *they play on their bikes for hours.* **2** a period regularly appointed for work or business. **3** one's times of rising and going to bed: *you keep very late hours.* **4** *RC Church* prayers recited at seven specified times of the day.

Hours *pl n Classical myth* the goddesses of the seasons.

house *n, pl* **houses 1** a building used as a home; dwelling. **2** the people in a house. **3** a building for some specific purpose: *beach house.* **4** a family or dynasty: *the House of Windsor.* **5** a commercial company: *auction house.* **6** a law-making body or the hall where it meets. **7** a division of a large school: *he was captain of the house rugby team.* **8** the audience in a theatre or cinema. **9** *Astrol* any of the 12 divisions of the zodiac. **10** *Informal* a brothel. **11 get on like a house on fire** *Informal* (of people) to get on very well together. **12 on the house** (usually of drinks) paid for by the management. **13 put one's house in order** to settle or organize one's affairs. ✧ *adj* **14** (of wine) sold unnamed by a restaurant, at a lower price than wines specified on the wine list: *house red.* ✧ *vb* **housing, housed 15** to give accommodation to. **16** to contain or cover (something). ▷ **HISTORY** Old English *hūs*

house arrest *n* confinement to one's own home rather than in prison.

houseboat *n* a stationary boat used as a home.

housebound *adj* unable to leave one's house, usually because of illness.

housebreaking *n Criminal law* the act of entering a building as a trespasser for an unlawful purpose. ▸ **housebreaker** *n*

housecoat *n* a woman's loose robelike garment for casual wear.

housefly *n, pl* **-flies** a common fly often found in houses.
household *n* **1** all the people living together in one house. ✧ *adj* **2** relating to the running of a household: *household budget.*
householder *n* a person who owns or rents a house.
household name *or* **word** *n* a person or thing that is very well known.
housekeeper *n* a person employed to run someone else's household.
housekeeping *n* **1** the running of a household. **2** money allotted for this.
house lights *pl n* the lights in the auditorium of a theatre or cinema.
housemaid *n* (esp. formerly) a female servant employed to do housework.
housemaid's knee *n* a fluid-filled swelling of the kneecap.
houseman *n, pl* **-men** *Med* a junior doctor in a hospital.
house martin *n* a swallow with a slightly forked tail.
House music *or* **House** *n* a type of disco music of the late 1980s, based on funk, with fragments of other recordings edited in electronically.
House of Assembly *n* a legislative assembly or the lower chamber of such an assembly.
House of Commons *n* (in Britain and Canada) the lower chamber of Parliament.
House of Keys *n* the lower chamber of the law-making body of the Isle of Man.
House of Lords *n* (in Britain) the upper chamber of Parliament, composed of the peers of the realm.
House of Representatives *n* **1** (in the US) the lower chamber of Congress, or of many state legislatures. **2** (in Australia) the lower chamber of Parliament. **3** the sole chamber of New Zealand's Parliament.
house-proud *adj* excessively concerned with the appearance, cleanliness, and tidiness of one's house.
house-train *vb* to train (a pet) to urinate and defecate outside.
house-warming *n* a party given after moving into a new home.
housewife *n, pl* **-wives** a woman who runs her own household and does not have a paid job.
housework *n* the work of running a home, such as cleaning, cooking, and shopping.
housing *n* **1** houses collectively. **2** the job of providing people with accommodation. **3** a part designed to contain and support a component or mechanism: *the inspection panel set within the concrete housing.*
hove *vb Chiefly naut* a past of **heave**.
hovea *n* an Australian plant with purple flowers.
hovel *n* a small house or hut that is dirty or badly in need of repair. ▷ **HISTORY** origin unknown
hover *vb* **1** (of a bird, insect, or helicopter) to remain suspended in one place in the air. **2** to linger uncertainly in a place. **3** to be in an unsettled or uncertain situation or frame of mind: *hovering between two options.* ▷ **HISTORY** Middle English *hoveren*
hovercraft *n* a vehicle that is able to travel across both land and water on a cushion of air.
how *adv* **1** in what way, by what means: *how did you spend the evening?; observing how elderly people coped.* **2** to what extent: *they don't know how tough I am.* **3** how good, how well, what ... like: *how good are the copies?; so that's how things are.* **4 how about?** used to suggest something: *how about some tea?* **5 how are you?** what is your state of health? **6 how's that? a** what is your opinion?: *we'll go out for a late-night supper – how's that?* **b** *Cricket* Also written: **howzat** (an appeal to the umpire) is the batsman out? ▷ **HISTORY** Old English *hu*
howdah *n* a seat for riding on an elephant's back. ▷ **HISTORY** Hindi *haudah*
however *adv* **1** still; nevertheless: *the book does, however, almost get funny.* **2** by whatever means: *get there however you can.* **3** (*with an adjective or adverb*) no matter how: *however low we plunge, there is always hope.*
howitzer *n* a large gun that fires shells at a steep angle. ▷ **HISTORY** Czech *houfnice* stone-sling
howl *n* **1** the long, loud wailing noise made by a wolf or a dog. **2** a similar cry of pain or sorrow. **3** a loud burst of laughter. ✧ *vb* **4** to express (something) in a howl or utter such cries. **5** (of the wind, etc.) to make a wailing noise. ▷ **HISTORY** Middle English *houlen*
howler *n Informal* a glaring mistake.
how-to *adj* (of a book or guide) giving basic instructions to the lay person.
howzit *sentence substitute S African* an informal word for hello. ▷ **HISTORY** from the phrase *how is it?*
hoyden *n Old-fashioned* a wild boisterous girl; tomboy. ▷ **HISTORY** perhaps from Middle Dutch *heidijn* heathen ▶ **hoydenish** *adj*
HP *or* **h.p.** **1** *Brit* hire-purchase. **2** horsepower.
HQ *or* **h.q.** headquarters.
hr hour.
HRH Her (*or* His) Royal Highness.
HRT **1** hormone replacement therapy. **2** *Austral & NZ* high rising terminal.
Hs *Chem* hassium.
HTML *n Computers* a text description language that is used on the World Wide Web. ▷ **HISTORY** *h*yper*t*ext *m*arkup *l*anguage
hub *n* **1** the central portion of a wheel, through which the axle passes. **2** the central, most important, or active part of a place or organization. ▷ **HISTORY** probably variant of *hob*
hubble-bubble *n* **1** same as **hookah**. **2** *Archaic* turmoil or confusion. ▷ **HISTORY** imitative
hubbub *n* **1** a confused noise of many voices. **2** great confusion or excitement. ▷ **HISTORY** probably from Irish *hooboobbes*
hubby *n, pl* **-bies** *Informal* a husband.
hubcap *n* a metal disc that fits on to and protects the hub of a wheel, esp. on a car.

A B C D E F G H I J K L M N O P Q R S T U V W X Y Z

hubris (**hew**-briss) *n Formal* pride or arrogance. ▷ **HISTORY** Greek ▶ **hubristic** *adj*

huckster *n* **1** a person who uses aggressive methods of selling. **2** *Now rare* a person who sells small articles or fruit in the street. ▷ **HISTORY** probably from Middle Dutch *hoekster*

huddle *n* **1** a small group of people or things standing or lying close together. **2 go into a huddle** *Informal* to have a private conference. ✧ *vb* **-dling, -dled 3** (of a group of people) to crowd or nestle closely together. **4** to curl up one's arms and legs close to one's body through cold or fear. ▷ **HISTORY** origin unknown

hue *n* **1** the feature of colour that enables an observer to classify it as red, blue, etc. **2** a shade of a colour. ▷ **HISTORY** Old English *hīw* beauty

hue and cry *n* a loud public outcry. ▷ **HISTORY** Old French *hue* outcry

huff *n* **1** a passing mood of anger or resentment: *in a huff.* ✧ *vb* **2** to blow or puff heavily. **3** *Draughts* to remove (an opponent's draught) from the board for failure to make a capture. **4 huffing and puffing** empty threats or objections. ▷ **HISTORY** imitative ▶ **huffy** *adj* ▶ **huffily** *adv*

hug *vb* **hugging, hugged 1** to clasp (someone or something) tightly, usually with affection. **2** to keep close to (a shore or the kerb). ✧ *n* **3** a tight or fond embrace. ▷ **HISTORY** probably Scandinavian

huge *adj* extremely large. ▷ **HISTORY** Old French *ahuge* ▶ **hugely** *adv*

Huguenot (**hew**-gan-oh) *n* a French Calvinist of the 16th or 17th centuries. ▷ **HISTORY** French

huh *interj* an exclamation of derision, bewilderment, or inquiry.

hui (**hoo**-ee) *n NZ* **1** a Maori social gathering. **2** a meeting to discuss Maori matters. **3** any party. ▷ **HISTORY** Maori

hula *n* a Hawaiian dance performed by a woman. ▷ **HISTORY** Hawaiian

Hula Hoop *n Trademark* a plastic hoop swung round the body by wiggling the hips.

hulk *n* **1** the body of an abandoned ship. **2** *Disparaging* a large ungainly person or thing. ▷ **HISTORY** Old English *hulc*

hulking *adj* big and ungainly.

hull *n* **1** the main body of a boat. **2** the outer covering of a fruit or seed such as a pea or bean. **3** the leaves round the stem of a strawberry, raspberry, or similar fruit. ✧ *vb* **4** to remove the hulls from (fruit or seeds). ▷ **HISTORY** Old English *hulu*

hullabaloo *n, pl* **-loos** a loud confused noise or commotion. ▷ **HISTORY** *hallo* + Scots *baloo* lullaby

hullo *interj, n* same as **hello.**

hum *vb* **humming, hummed 1** to make a low continuous vibrating sound. **2** (of a person) to sing with the lips closed. **3** to utter an indistinct sound when hesitating. **4** *Informal* to be in a state of feverish activity: *the town hums with activity and life.* **5** *Slang* to smell unpleasant. **6 hum and haw** See **haw**[2]. ✧ *n* **7** a low continuous murmuring sound. **8** an unpleasant smell. ✧ *interj, n* **9** an indistinct sound of hesitation. ▷ **HISTORY** imitative

human *adj* **1** of or relating to people: *human occupants.* **2** having the qualities of people as opposed to animals, divine beings, or machines: *human nature.* **3** kind or considerate. ✧ *n* **4** a human being. ▷ **HISTORY** Latin *humanus*

human being *n* a man, woman, or child.

humane *adj* **1** showing kindness and sympathy. **2** inflicting as little pain as possible: *a humane method of killing minke whales.* **3** considered to have a civilizing effect on people: *the humane tradition of a literary education.* ▷ **HISTORY** variant of *human*

humanism *n* the rejection of religion in favour of a belief in the advancement of humanity by its own efforts. ▶ **humanist** *n, adj* ▶ **humanistic** *adj*

humanitarian *adj* **1** having the interests of mankind at heart. ✧ *n* **2** a person who has the interests of mankind at heart. ▶ **humanitarianism** *n*

humanity *n, pl* **-ties 1** the human race. **2** the quality of being human. **3** kindness or mercy. **4 humanities** the study of literature, philosophy, and the arts.

humanize *or* **-ise** *vb* **-izing, -ized** *or* **-ising, -ised** to make human or humane.

humankind *n* the human race; humanity.

> **☑ WORD TIP**
> See at **mankind.**

humanly *adv* by human powers or means: *as fast as is humanly possible.*

humanoid *adj* **1** like a human being in appearance. ✧ *n* **2** (in science fiction) a robot or creature resembling a human being.

human race *n* all men, women and children collectively.

human rights *pl n* the basic rights of individuals to liberty, justice, etc.

humble *adj* **1** conscious of one's failings. **2** modest and unpretentious: *humble domestic objects.* **3** ordinary or not very important: *humble beginnings.* ✧ *vb* **-bling, -bled 4** to cause to become humble; humiliate. ▷ **HISTORY** Latin *humilis* low ▶ **humbly** *adv*

humbug *n* **1** *Brit* a hard peppermint sweet with a striped pattern. **2** a speech or piece of writing that is obviously untrue, dishonest, or nonsense. **3** a dishonest person. ▷ **HISTORY** origin unknown

humdinger *n Slang* **1** something unusually large. **2** an excellent person or thing. ▷ **HISTORY** origin unknown

humdrum *adj* ordinary, dull, and uninteresting. ▷ **HISTORY** probably based on *hum*

humerus (**hew**-mer-uss) *n, pl* **-meri** (-mer-rye) the bone from the shoulder to the elbow. ▷ **HISTORY** Latin *umerus* ▶ **humeral** *adj*

humid *adj* (of the weather) damp and warm. ▷ **HISTORY** Latin *umidus*

humidex (**hew**-mid-ex) *n Canad* a system of measuring discomfort showing the combined effect of humidity and temperature.

humidify *vb* **-fies, -fying, -fied** to make the air in (a room) more humid or damp. ▶ **humidifier** *n*

humidity *n* **1** dampness. **2** a measure of the amount of moisture in the air.

humiliate *vb* **-ating, -ated** to hurt the dignity or pride of: *the English cricket team was humiliated by Australia.* ▷ HISTORY Latin *humilis* humble ▶ **humiliating** *adj* ▶ **humiliation** *n*

humility *n* the quality of being humble and modest.

hummingbird *n* a very small brightly-coloured American bird with a long slender bill, and powerful wings that hum as they vibrate.

hummock *n* a very small hill or a mound. ▷ HISTORY origin unknown

humorist *n* a person who speaks or writes in a humorous way.

humorous *adj* amusing, esp. in a witty or clever way. ▶ **humorously** *adv*

humour *or US* **humor** *n* **1** the quality of being funny. **2** the ability to appreciate or express things that are humorous: *a sense of humour.* **3** situations, speech, or writings that are humorous. **4** a state of mind; mood: *in astoundingly good humour.* **5** *Archaic* any of various fluids in the body: *aqueous humour.* ✧ *vb* **6** to be kind and indulgent to: *he decided the patient needed to be humoured.* ▷ HISTORY Latin *humor* liquid ▶ **humourless** *adj*

hump *n* **1** a rounded lump on the ground. **2** a rounded deformity of the back. **3** a rounded lump on the back of a camel or related animal. **4 the hump** *Brit informal* a fit of sulking. ✧ *vb* **5** *Slang* to carry or heave: *they were injured humping heavy gear around.* ▷ HISTORY probably from *humpbacked*

humpback *n* **1** same as **hunchback**. **2** Also called: **humpback whale** a large whalebone whale with a hump on its back. **3** Also called: **humpback bridge** *Brit* a road bridge with a sharp slope on either side. ▶ **humpbacked** *adj*

humus (**hew**-muss) *n* a dark brown or black mass of partially decomposed plant and animal matter in the soil. ▷ HISTORY Latin: soil

Hun *n, pl* **Huns** *or* **Hun 1** a member of any of several Asiatic peoples who invaded the Roman Empire in the 4th and 5th centuries AD. **2** *Offensive, informal* (esp. in World War I) a German. ▷ HISTORY Old English *Hūnas*

hunch *n* **1** a feeling or suspicion not based on facts: *she said that she had had a hunch that the coup would not succeed.* **2** same as **hump.** ✧ *vb* **3** to draw (oneself or one's shoulders) up or together. ▷ HISTORY origin unknown

hunchback *n* a person who has an abnormal curvature of the spine. ▶ **hunchbacked** *adj*

hundred *n, pl* **-dreds** *or* **-dred 1** the cardinal number that is the product of ten and ten. **2** a numeral, 100 or C, representing this number. **3** (*often pl*) a large but unspecified number. ✧ *adj* **4** amounting to a hundred: *a hundred yards.* ▷ HISTORY Old English ▶ **hundredth** *adj, n*

Hundred Flowers Campaign *n History* a period of debate in China in 1956–57, when people were encouraged to express their opinions of the government. ▷ HISTORY from the slogan 'Let a hundred flowers bloom and a hundred schools of thought contend'

hundredweight *n, pl* **-weights** *or* **-weight 1** *Brit* a unit of weight equal to 112 pounds or 50.802kg. **2** *US & Canad* a unit of weight equal to 100 pounds or 45.359kg. **3** a metric unit of weight equal to 50 kilograms.

hung *vb* **1** the past of **hang** (except in the sense of *to execute*) ✧ *adj* **2** (of a parliament or jury) with no side having a clear majority. **3 hung over** *Informal* suffering the effects of a hangover.

Hungarian *adj* **1** of Hungary. ✧ *n* **2** a person from Hungary. **3** the language of Hungary.

hunger *n* **1** a feeling of emptiness or weakness caused by lack of food. **2** a lack of food that causes suffering or death. **3** desire or craving. ✧ *vb* **4 hunger for** to have a great desire (for). ▷ HISTORY Old English *hungor*

hunger strike *n* a refusal of all food, usually by a prisoner, as a means of protest.

hungry *adj* **-grier, -griest 1** desiring food. **2** (foll. by *for*) having a craving, desire, or need for: *hungry for revenge.* **3** expressing greed, craving, or desire: *the media's hungry search for news.* ▶ **hungrily** *adv*

hunk *n* **1** a large piece: *a hunk of bread.* **2** *Slang* a well-built, sexually attractive man. ▷ HISTORY probably related to Flemish *hunke*

hunt *vb* **1** to seek out and kill (animals) for food or sport. **2 hunt for** to search for. **3 hunt down** to track in an attempt to capture (someone): *hunting down villains.* ✧ *n* **4** the act or an instance of hunting. **5** a party organized for the pursuit of wild animals for sport. **6** the members of such a party. ▷ HISTORY Old English *huntian* ▶ **hunting** *n*

huntaway *n NZ* a sheepdog trained to drive sheep by barking.

hunter *n* **1** a person or animal that seeks out and kills or captures game. **2** a person who looks carefully for something: *a house hunter.* **3** a horse or dog bred for hunting. **4** a watch with a hinged metal lid or case to protect the glass.

hunter-gatherer *n* a member of a society that lives by hunting and gathering naturally occurring resources.

huntsman *n, pl* **-men 1** a person who hunts. **2** a person who trains hounds and manages them during a hunt.

hurdle *n* **1** *Athletics* one of a number of light barriers over which runners leap in certain events. **2** a difficulty or problem: *the main technical hurdle is the environment.* **3 hurdles** a race involving hurdles. ✧ *vb* **-dling, -dled 4** to jump over (a hurdle or other obstacle). ▷ HISTORY Old English *hyrdel* ▶ **hurdler** *n*

hurdy-gurdy *n, pl* **hurdy-gurdies** a mechanical musical instrument, such as a barrel organ. ▷ HISTORY probably imitative

hurl *vb* **1** to throw (something) with great force. **2** to utter (something) with force; yell: *onlookers hurled abuse at them.* ▷ HISTORY probably imitative

hurling *or* **hurley** *n* a traditional Irish game resembling hockey.

hurly-burly *n* great noise and activity; commotion. ▷ **HISTORY** obsolete *hurling* uproar

hurrah *or* **hooray** *interj, n* a cheer of joy or victory. ▷ **HISTORY** probably from German *hurra*

hurricane *n* a severe, often destructive storm, esp. a tropical cyclone. ▷ **HISTORY** Spanish *huracán*

hurricane lamp *n* a paraffin lamp with a glass covering.

hurried *adj* done quickly or too quickly. ▸ **hurriedly** *adv* ▸ **hurriedness** *n*

hurry *vb* **-ries, -rying, -ried 1** to move or act or cause to move or act in great haste: *the umpires hurried the players off the ground.* **2** to speed up the completion or progress of: *eat a small snack rather than hurry a main meal.* ✧ *n* **3** haste. **4** urgency or eagerness. **5 in a hurry** *Informal* **a** easily: *striking old guy, not the sort you'd forget in a hurry.* **b** willingly: *he would not ease interest rates again in a hurry.* ▷ **HISTORY** probably imitative

hurt *vb* **hurting, hurt 1** to cause physical or mental injury to: *is she badly hurt?* **2** to cause someone to feel pain: *my head hurt.* **3** *Informal* to feel pain: *she was hurting.* ✧ *n* **4** physical or mental pain or suffering. ✧ *adj* **5** injured or pained: *his hurt head; a hurt expression.* ▷ **HISTORY** Old French *hurter* to knock against ▸ **hurtful** *adj*

hurtle *vb* **-ling, -led** to move very quickly or violently. ▷ **HISTORY** Middle English *hurtlen*

husband *n* **1** a woman's partner in marriage. ✧ *vb* **2** to use (resources, finances, etc.) economically. ▷ **HISTORY** Old English *hūsbonda*

husbandry *n* **1** the art or skill of farming. **2** management of resources.

hush *vb* **1** to make or be silent. ✧ *n* **2** stillness or silence. ✧ *interj* **3** a plea or demand for silence. ▷ **HISTORY** earlier *husht* quiet! ▸ **hushed** *adj*

hush-hush *adj Informal* (esp. of official work) secret and confidential.

hush money *n Slang* money given to a person to ensure that something is kept secret.

hush up *vb* to suppress information or rumours about (something).

husk *n* **1** the outer covering of certain fruits and seeds. ✧ *vb* **2** to remove the husk from. ▷ **HISTORY** probably from Middle Dutch *hūs* house

husky[1] *adj* **huskier, huskiest 1** (of a voice) slightly hoarse. **2** *Informal* (of a man) big and strong. ▷ **HISTORY** probably from *husk*, from the toughness of a corn husk ▸ **huskily** *adv*

husky[2] *n, pl* **huskies** an Arctic sledge dog with thick hair and a curled tail. ▷ **HISTORY** probably based on *eskimo*

hussar (hoo-**zar**) *n History* a member of a light cavalry regiment. ▷ **HISTORY** Hungarian *huszár*

hussy *n, pl* **-sies** *Old-fashioned* a woman considered sexually immoral or improper. ▷ **HISTORY** from *hussif* housewife

hustings *pl n* the campaigns and speeches at a parliamentary election. ▷ **HISTORY** Old Norse *hūsthing*, from *hūs* house + *thing* assembly

hustle *vb* **-tling, -tled 1** to make (someone) move by pushing or jostling them: *he hustled her away.* **2** to deal with (something) hurriedly: *they did not heedlessly hustle the tempo.* **3** *US & Canad slang* (of a prostitute) to solicit clients. ✧ *n* **4** lively activity and excitement. ▷ **HISTORY** Dutch *husselen* to shake

hut *n* a small house or shelter. ▷ **HISTORY** French *hutte*

hutch *n* a cage for small animals. ▷ **HISTORY** Old French *huche*

hyacinth *n* a plant with bell-shaped sweet-smelling flowers. ▷ **HISTORY** Greek *huakinthos*

hyaena *n* same as **hyena**.

hybrid *n* **1** an animal or plant resulting from a cross between two different types of animal or plant. **2** anything that is a mixture of two different things. ✧ *adj* **3** of mixed origin: *a hybrid electric car.* ▷ **HISTORY** Latin *hibrida*

hybridize *or* **-ise** *vb* **-izing, -ized** *or* **-ising, -ised** to produce or cause (species) to produce hybrids; crossbreed. ▸ **hybridization** *or* **-isation** *n*

hydra *n* **1** a mythical many-headed serpent. **2** a persistent problem. **3** a microscopic freshwater creature with a slender tubular body and tentacles around the mouth. ▷ **HISTORY** Greek *hudra* water serpent

hydrangea *n* an ornamental shrub with large clusters of white, pink, or blue flowers. ▷ **HISTORY** Greek *hudōr* water + *angeion* vessel

hydrant *n* an outlet from a water main, from which water can be tapped for fighting fires.

hydrate *Chem* ✧ *n* **1** a compound containing water chemically combined with a substance: *chloral hydrate.* ✧ *vb* **-drating, -drated 2** to treat (a substance) with water. ▸ **hydration** *n*

hydraulic *adj* operated by pressure transmitted through a pipe by a liquid, such as water or oil. ▷ **HISTORY** Greek *hudōr* water + *aulos* pipe ▸ **hydraulically** *adv*

hydraulic erosion *n Geog* erosion caused by moving water.

hydraulics *n* the study of the mechanical properties of fluids as they apply to practical engineering.

hydride *n Chem* a compound of hydrogen with another element.

hydro[1] *n, pl* **-dros** *Brit* a hotel offering facilities for hydropathic treatment.

hydro[2] *adj* short for **hydroelectric**.

hydro- *or before a vowel* **hydr-** *combining form* **1** indicating water or fluid: *hydrodynamics.* **2** *Chem* indicating hydrogen in a chemical compound: *hydrochloric acid.* ▷ **HISTORY** Greek *hudōr* water

hydrocarbon *n Chem* a compound containing only carbon and hydrogen.

hydrocephalus *n* accumulation of fluid in the cavities of the brain, causing enlargement of the head in children. ▷ **HISTORY** Greek *hudōr* water + *kephalē* head ▸ **hydrocephalic** *adj*

hydrochloric acid *n Chem* a solution of hydrogen chloride in water: a strong acid used in many industrial and laboratory processes.

hydrodynamics *n* the branch of science concerned with the mechanical properties of fluids.

hydroelectric *adj* **1** generated by the pressure of falling water: *hydroelectric power.* **2** of the generation of electricity by water pressure: *a hydroelectric scheme.* ▶ **hydroelectricity** *n*
hydrofoil *n* **1** a fast light vessel the hull of which is raised out of the water on one or more pairs of fins. **2** any of these fins.
hydrogen *n Chem* a colourless gas that burns easily and is the lightest element in the universe. It occurs in water and in most organic compounds. Symbol: H. ▷ **HISTORY** HYDRO- + *-gen* (producing); because its combustion produces water ▶ **hydrogenous** *adj*
hydrogenate (hide-**roj**-in-nate) *vb* **-ating, -ated** *Chem* to combine (a substance) with hydrogen: *hydrogenated vegetable oil.* ▶ **hydrogenation** *n*
hydrogen bomb *n* an extremely powerful bomb in which energy is released by fusion of hydrogen nuclei to give helium nuclei.
hydrogen peroxide *n* a colourless oily unstable liquid chemical used as a hair bleach and as an antiseptic.
hydrogen sulphide *n* a colourless poisonous gas with an odour of rotten eggs.
hydrograph *n Geog* a graph showing variations in the amount of water in a river over a period of time.
hydrography (hide-**rog**-ra-fee) *n* the study of the oceans, seas, and rivers. ▶ **hydrographic** *adj*
hydrolase *n Biochem* an enzyme that controls hydrolysis.
hydrology *n* the study of the distribution, conservation, and use of the water of the earth and its atmosphere.
hydrolysis (hide-**rol**-iss-iss) *n Chem* a process of decomposition in which a compound reacts with water to produce other compounds. ▷ **HISTORY** Greek *hudōr* water + *lusis* a loosening
hydrometer (hide-**rom**-it-er) *n* an instrument for measuring the density of a liquid.
hydropathy *n* a method of treating disease by the use of large quantities of water both internally and externally. ▷ **HISTORY** Greek *hudōr* water + *patheia* suffering ▶ **hydropathic** *adj*
hydrophilic *adj Chem* tending to dissolve in or mix with water: *a hydrophilic layer.*
hydrophobia *n* **1** same as **rabies**. **2** a fear of drinking fluids. ▶ **hydrophobic** *adj*
hydrophyte *n Bot* a plant that grows only in water or very moist soil. ▶ **hydrophytic** *adj*
hydroplane *n* **1** a motorboat that raises its hull out of the water at high speeds. **2** a fin on the hull of a submarine for controlling its vertical motion.
hydroponics *n Agriculture* a method of growing plants in gravel, etc., through which water containing the necessary nutrients is pumped. ▷ **HISTORY** HYDRO- + *(geo)ponics* science of agriculture
hydrosphere *n* the watery part of the earth's surface.
hydrostatics *n* the branch of science concerned with the properties and behaviour of fluids that are not in motion. ▶ **hydrostatic** *adj*
hydrotherapy *n Med* the treatment of certain diseases by exercise in water.
hydrotropism *n Bot* the growth of plants in response to the stimulus of water.
hydrous *adj* containing water.
hydroxide *n Chem* a compound containing a hydroxyl group or ion.
hydroxyl *adj Chem* of or containing the monovalent group –OH or the ion OH^-: *forming a hydroxyl radical.*
hyena *or* **hyaena** *n* a meat-eating doglike mammal of Africa and S Asia. ▷ **HISTORY** Greek *hus* hog
hygiene *n* **1** the principles and practices of health and cleanliness: *personal hygiene.* **2** Also called: **hygienics** the science concerned with the maintenance of health. ▷ **HISTORY** Greek *hugieinē* ▶ **hygienic** *adj* ▶ **hygienically** *adv* ▶ **hygienist** *n*
hygrometer (hie-**grom**-it-er) *n* an instrument for measuring humidity. ▷ **HISTORY** Greek *hugros* wet
hygroscope *n* any device that indicates the humidity of the air without necessarily measuring it, such as an animal or vegetable fibre which contracts with moisture. ▷ **HISTORY** Greek *hugros* wet + *skopein* to observe
hygroscopic *adj* (of a substance) tending to absorb water from the air.
hymen *n Anat* a membrane that partly covers the entrance to the vagina and is usually ruptured when sexual intercourse takes place for the first time. ▷ **HISTORY** Greek: membrane
hymenopterous *adj* of or belonging to an order of insects with two pairs of membranous wings. ▷ **HISTORY** Greek *humen* membrane + *pteron* wing
hymn *n* a Christian song of praise sung to God or a saint. ▷ **HISTORY** Greek *humnos*
hymnal *n* a book of hymns. Also: **hymn book**
hype *Slang* ✧ *n* **1** intensive or exaggerated publicity or sales promotion. ✧ *vb* **hyping, hyped** **2** to market or promote (a commodity) using intensive or exaggerated publicity. ▷ **HISTORY** origin unknown
hyper *adj Informal* overactive or overexcited.
hyper- *prefix* above, over, or in excess: *hypercritical.* ▷ **HISTORY** Greek *huper* over
hyperactive *adj* (of a person) unable to relax and always in a state of restless activity.
hyperbola (hie-**per**-bol-a) *n Geom* a curve produced when a cone is cut by a plane at a steeper angle to its base than its side. ▷ **HISTORY** Greek *huperbolē*
hyperbole (hie-**per**-bol-ee) *n* a deliberate exaggeration of speech or writing used for effect, such as *he embraced her a thousand times.* ▷ **HISTORY** Greek *huper* over + *ballein* to throw
hyperbolic *or* **hyperbolical** *adj* of a hyperbola or a hyperbole.
hyperglycaemia *or US* **hyperglycemia** (hie-per-glice-**seem**-ee-a) *n Pathol* an abnormally large amount of sugar in the blood. ▷ **HISTORY** Greek *huper* over + *glukus* sweet

a b c d e f g h i j k l m n o p q r s t u v w x y z

hyperinflation *n Econ* extremely high inflation, usually over 50% per month.
hyperlink *Computers* ✧ *n* **1** a link from a hypertext file that gives users instant access to related material in another file. ✧ *vb* **2** to link (files) in this way.
hypermarket *n* a huge self-service store. ▷ HISTORY translation of French *hypermarché*
hypersensitive *adj* **1** unduly emotionally vulnerable. **2** abnormally sensitive to an allergen, a drug, or high or low temperatures.
hypersonic *adj* having a speed of at least five times the speed of sound.
hypertension *n Pathol* abnormally high blood pressure.
hypertext *n* computer software and hardware that allows users to store and view text and move between related items easily.
hypertrophy (hie-**per**-trof-fee) *n, pl* **-phies** enlargement of an organ or part resulting from an increase in the size of the cells. ▷ HISTORY Greek *huper* over + *trophē* nourishment
hyperventilation *n* an increase in the rate of breathing at rest, sometimes resulting in cramp and dizziness. ▶ **hyperventilate** *vb*
hyphen *n* the punctuation mark (-), used to separate parts of compound words and between syllables of a word split between two consecutive lines. ▷ HISTORY Greek *huphen* together
hyphenate *vb* **-ating, -ated** to separate (words) with a hyphen. ▶ **hyphenation** *n*
hyphenated *adj* having two words or syllables connected by a hyphen.
hypnosis *n* an artificially induced state of relaxation in which the mind is more than usually receptive to suggestion.
hypnotherapy *n* the use of hypnosis in the treatment of emotional and mental problems. ▶ **hypnotherapist** *n*
hypnotic *adj* **1** of or producing hypnosis or sleep. **2** having an effect resembling hypnosis: *the film makes for hypnotic viewing.* ✧ *n* **3** a drug that induces sleep. ▷ HISTORY Greek *hupnos* sleep ▶ **hypnotically** *adv*
hypnotism *n* the practice of or process of inducing hypnosis. ▶ **hypnotist** *n*
hypnotize *or* **-tise** *vb* **-tizing, -tized** *or* **-tising, -tised 1** to induce hypnosis in (a person). **2** to hold the attention of (someone) completely; fascinate; mesmerize: *hypnotized by her beauty.*
hypo- *or before a vowel* **hyp-** *prefix* beneath; less than: *hypodermic.* ▷ HISTORY Greek *hupo* under
hypoallergenic *adj* not likely to cause an allergic reaction.
hypocaust *n* an ancient Roman heating system in which hot air circulated under the floor and between double walls. ▷ HISTORY Latin *hypocaustum*
hypochondria *n* abnormal anxiety concerning one's health. ▷ HISTORY Late Latin: abdomen, supposedly the seat of melancholy
hypochondriac *n* a person abnormally concerned about his or her health.
hypocrisy (hip-**ok**-rass-ee) *n, pl* **-sies 1** the practice of claiming to have standards or beliefs that are contrary to one's real character or actual behaviour. **2** an act or instance of this.
hypocrite (**hip**-oh-krit) *n* a person who pretends to be what he or she is not. ▷ HISTORY Greek *hupokrinein* to pretend ▶ **hypocritical** *adj*
hypodermic *adj* **1** used for injecting. ✧ *n* **2** a hypodermic syringe or needle.
hypodermic syringe *n Med* a syringe consisting of a hollow cylinder, a piston, and a hollow needle, used for withdrawing blood samples or injecting drugs under the skin.
hypotension *n Pathol* abnormally low blood pressure.
hypotenuse (hie-**pot**-a-news) *n* the side in a right-angled triangle that is opposite the right angle. ▷ HISTORY Greek *hupoteinousa grammē* subtending line
hypothermia *n Pathol* an abnormally low body temperature, as a result of exposure to cold.
hypothesis (hie-**poth**-iss-iss) *n, pl* **-ses** (-seez) a suggested explanation for a group of facts, accepted either as a basis for further verification or as likely to be true. ▷ HISTORY Greek *hupotithenai* to propose, literally: put under ▶ **hypothesize** *or* **-ise** *vb*
hypothetical *adj* based on assumption rather than fact or reality. ▶ **hypothetically** *adv*
hyrax (**hire**-ax) *n, pl* **hyraxes** *or* **hyraces** (**hire**-a-seez) a genus of hoofed rodent-like animals.
hyssop *n* **1** an aromatic plant used in herbal medicine. **2** a Biblical plant, used for sprinkling in the ritual practices of the Hebrews. ▷ HISTORY Greek *hussōpos*
hysterectomy *n, pl* **-mies** surgical removal of the womb. ▷ HISTORY Greek *hustera* womb + *tomē* a cutting
hysteria *n* **1** a mental disorder marked by emotional outbursts and, often, symptoms such as paralysis. **2** any uncontrolled emotional state, such as of panic, anger, or excitement. ▷ HISTORY Greek *hustera* womb, from the belief that hysteria in women originated in disorders of the womb
hysteric *n* a hysterical person.
hysterical *adj* **1** in a state of uncontrolled panic, anger, or excitement: *a crazy hysterical adolescent.* **2** *Informal* wildly funny. ▶ **hysterically** *adv*
hysterics *n* **1** an attack of hysteria. **2** *Informal* wild uncontrollable bursts of laughter.
Hz hertz.

I i

i the imaginary number $\sqrt{-1}$.
I[1] *pron* used by a speaker or writer to refer to himself or herself as the subject of a verb. ▷ **HISTORY** Old English *ic*
I[2] **1** *Chem* iodine. **2** the Roman numeral for one.
I. **1** Independent. **2** Institute. **3** International. **4** Island; Isle.
IA Iowa.
iamb (**eye**-am) *or* **iambus** *n, pl* **iambs** *or* **iambuses** *Prosody* a metrical foot of two syllables, a short one followed by a long one. ▷ **HISTORY** Greek *iambos*
iambic (eye-**am**-bik) *Prosody* ✧ *adj* **1** written in metrical units of one short and one long syllable. ✧ *n* **2** an iambic foot, line, or stanza.
iambic pentameter *n Prosody* (in poetry) a pattern consisting of five iambs commonly used in blank verse.
IBA (in Britain) Independent Broadcasting Authority.
Iberian *adj* **1** of Iberia, the peninsula made up of Spain and Portugal. ✧ *n* **2** a person from Iberia.
ibex (**ibe**-eks) *n, pl* **ibexes** *or* **ibex** a wild mountain goat with large backward-curving horns. ▷ **HISTORY** Latin: chamois
ibid. in the same place: used to refer to a book, page, or passage previously cited. ▷ **HISTORY** Latin *ibidem*
ibis (**ibe**-iss) *n, pl* **ibises** *or* **ibis** a large wading bird with a long thin curved bill. ▷ **HISTORY** Egyptian *hby*
Ibo (**ee**-boh) *n* **1** (*pl* **Ibos** *or* **Ibo**) a member of an African people of S Nigeria. **2** their language.
ICBM intercontinental ballistic missile.
ice *n* **1** water that has frozen and become solid. **2** *Chiefly Brit* a portion of ice cream. **3 break the ice** to relax the atmosphere, esp. between strangers. **4 on ice** in readiness or reserve. **5 on thin ice** in an dangerous situation: *he knew he was on thin ice.* **6 the Ice** *NZ informal* Antarctica. ✧ *vb* **icing, iced** **7** (foll. by *up* or *over*) to become covered with ice. **8** to cover with icing. **9** to cool or chill with ice. ▷ **HISTORY** Old English *īs*
ice age *n* **1** any period of time during which a large part of the earth's surface was covered with ice, caused by the advance of glaciers. **2** the Pleistocene epoch.
iceberg *n* **1** a large mass of ice floating in the sea. **2 tip of the iceberg** the small visible part of a problem that is much larger.

> **WORD HISTORY**
> An iceberg is an 'ice mountain'. The word is a partial translation of the Dutch word *ijsberg*, from *ijs*, meaning 'ice', and *berg*, meaning 'mountain'.

icebox *n* **1** *US & Canad* a refrigerator. **2** a compartment in a refrigerator for making or storing ice. **3** a container packed with ice for keeping food and drink cold.
icebreaker *n* a ship designed to break a channel through ice.
icecap *n* a thick mass of glacial ice that permanently covers an area.
ice cream *n* a sweet frozen food, made from cream, milk, or a custard base, flavoured in various ways.
iced *adj* **1** served very cold. **2** covered with icing.
ice field *n* a large expanse of floating sea ice.
ice floe *n* a sheet of ice floating in the sea.
ice hockey *n* a game like hockey played on ice by two teams wearing skates.
Icelander *adj* a person from Iceland.
Icelandic *adj* **1** of Iceland. ✧ *n* **2** the official language of Iceland.
ice lolly *n Brit informal* a water ice or an ice cream on a stick.
ice pack *n* **1** a bag or folded cloth containing crushed ice, applied to a part of the body to reduce swelling. **2** *Geog* same as **pack ice**.
ice skate *n* **1** a boot with a steel blade fitted to the sole which enables the wearer to glide over ice. ✧ *vb* **ice-skate, -skating, -skated** **2** to glide over ice on ice skates. ▶ **ice-skater** *n*
I Ching *n* an ancient Chinese book of divination and a source of Confucian and Taoist philosophy.
ichneumon (ik-**new**-mon) *n* a greyish-brown mongoose.
ichthyology (ik-thi-**ol**-a-jee) *n* the study of fishes. ▷ **HISTORY** Greek *ikhthus* fish + -LOGY ▶ **ichthyological** *adj* ▶ **ichthyologist** *n*
icicle *n* a tapering spike of ice hanging where water has dripped. ▷ **HISTORY** from ICE + Old English *gicel* icicle
icing *n* **1** Also (esp. US and Canad.): **frosting** a mixture of sugar and water or egg whites used to cover and decorate cakes. **2 icing on the cake** any unexpected extra or bonus. **3** the formation of ice on a ship or aircraft.
icing sugar *n Brit & Austral* a very finely ground sugar used for making icing or sweets.
icon *or* **ikon** *n* **1** a picture of Christ, the Virgin Mary, or a saint, venerated in the Orthodox Church. **2** a picture on a computer screen representing a computer function that can be activated by moving the cursor over it. **3** a person or thing regarded as a symbol of a belief or cultural movement: *a feminist icon.* ▷ **HISTORY** Greek *eikōn* image
iconoclast *n* **1** a person who attacks established or traditional ideas or principles. **2** a destroyer of religious images or objects. ▷ **HISTORY** Late Greek *eikōn* icon + *klastēs* breaker ▶ **iconoclastic** *adj* ▶ **iconoclasm** *n*
icosahedron (ike-oh-sa-**heed**-ron) *n, pl* **-drons** *or* **-dra** (-dra) a solid figure with 20 faces. ▷ **HISTORY** Greek *eikosi* twenty + *-edron* -sided

A B C D E F G H I J K L M N O P Q R S T U V W X Y Z

icy *adj* **icier, iciest 1** freezing or very cold. **2** covered with ice: *an icy runway.* **3** cold or reserved in manner. ▸ **icily** *adv* ▸ **iciness** *n*

id *n Psychoanal* the primitive instincts and energies in the unconscious mind that underlie all psychological impulses. ▷ HISTORY Latin: it

ID 1 Idaho. **2** identification.

idea *n* **1** any product of mental activity; thought. **2** a scheme, intention, or plan. **3** the thought of something: *the idea excites me.* **4** a belief or opinion. **5** a vague notion; inkling: *they had no idea of the severity of my injuries.* **6** a person's conception of something: *his idea of integrity is not the same as mine.* **7** aim or purpose: *the idea is to economize on transport.* **8** *Philosophy* (in Plato) a universal model of which all things in the same class are only imperfect imitations. ▷ HISTORY Greek: model, outward appearance

> ☑ **WORD TIP**
> It is usually considered correct to say that someone has *the idea of doing* something, rather than *the idea to do* it: *he had the idea of taking* (not *the idea to take*) *a short holiday.*

ideal *n* **1** a conception of something that is perfect. **2** a person or thing considered to represent perfection. **3** something existing only as an idea. ◇ *adj* **4** most suitable: *they seem to have adopted an ideal man as their candidate.* **5** of, involving, or existing only as an idea; imaginary: *an ideal world.* ▸ **ideally** *adv*

idealism *n* **1** belief in or striving towards ideals. **2** the tendency to represent things in their ideal forms, rather than as they are. **3** *Philosophy* the doctrine that material objects and the external world do not exist in reality, but are creations of the mind. ▸ **idealist** *n* ▸ **idealistic** *adj*

idealize *or* **-ise** *vb* **-izing, -ized** *or* **-ising, -ised** to consider or represent (something) as ideal or more nearly perfect than is true. ▸ **idealization** *or* **-isation** *n*

idem *pron, adj* the same: used to refer to an article, chapter, or book already quoted. ▷ HISTORY Latin

identical *adj* **1** that is the same: *they got the identical motel room as last year.* **2** exactly alike or equal. **3** (of twins) developed from a single fertilized ovum that has split into two, and thus of the same sex and very much alike. ▷ HISTORY Latin *idem* the same ▸ **identically** *adv*

identification parade *n* a group of people, including one suspected of a crime, assembled to discover whether a witness can identify the suspect.

identify *vb* **-fies, -fying, -fied 1** to prove or recognize as being a certain person or thing; determine the identity of. **2** (often foll. by *with*) to understand and sympathize with a person or group because one regards oneself as being similar or similarly situated. **3** to consider or treat as the same. **4** to connect or associate closely: *he was closely identified with the community charge.* ▸ **identifiable** *adj* ▸ **identification** *n*

Identikit *n Trademark* (formerly) a composite picture, assembled from descriptions given, of a person wanted by the police.

identity *n, pl* **-ties 1** the state of being a specified person or thing: *the identity of his murderers was not immediately established.* **2** the individual characteristics by which a person or thing is recognized. **3** the state of being the same. **4** *Maths* Also called: **identity element** a member of a set that when combined with any other member of the set, leaves it unchanged: the identity for multiplication of numbers is 1. ▷ HISTORY Latin *idem* the same

identity transformation *n Maths* (in transformational geometry) the process of changing the form of an identity without changing its value.

ideo- *combining form* of or indicating ideas: *ideology.* ▷ HISTORY from French *idéo-*, from Greek *idea* idea

ideogram *or* **ideograph** *n* a character or symbol that directly represents a concept or thing, rather than the sounds that form its name. ▷ HISTORY Greek *idea* idea + *gramma* a drawing

ideology *n, pl* **-gies** the body of ideas and beliefs of a person, group, or nation. ▷ HISTORY from IDEO- + -LOGY ▸ **ideological** *adj* ▸ **ideologically** *adv* ▸ **ideologist** *n*

ides *n* (in the ancient Roman calendar) the 15th day in March, May, July, and October and the 13th of the other months. ▷ HISTORY Latin *idus*

idiocy *n, pl* **-cies 1** utter stupidity. **2** a foolish act or remark.

idiolect *n Linguistics* the personal variety of language unique to an individual.

idiom *n* **1** a group of words which, when used together, have a different meaning from the one suggested by the individual words, e.g. *it was raining cats and dogs.* **2** linguistic usage that is grammatical and natural to native speakers. **3** the characteristic vocabulary or usage of a person or group. **4** the characteristic artistic style of an individual or school. ▷ HISTORY Greek *idios* private, separate ▸ **idiomatic** *adj*

idiosyncrasy *n, pl* **-sies** a personal peculiarity of mind, habit, or behaviour; quirk. ▷ HISTORY Greek *idios* private, separate + *sunkrasis* mixture ▸ **idiosyncratic** *adj*

idiot *n* **1** a foolish or senseless person. **2** *No longer in technical use* a person with severe mental retardation. ▷ HISTORY Greek *idiōtēs* private person, ignoramus ▸ **idiotic** *adj* ▸ **idiotically** *adv*

idle *adj* **1** not doing anything. **2** not operating or being used. **3** not wanting to work; lazy. **4** ineffective or useless: *it would be idle to look for a solution at this stage.* **5** frivolous or trivial: *idle pleasures.* **6** without basis; unfounded: *idle rumours.* ◇ *vb* **idling, idled 7** (often foll. by *away*) to waste or pass (time) in idleness. **8** (of an engine) to run at low speed without transmitting any power. ▷ HISTORY Old English *īdel* ▸ **idleness** *n* ▸ **idler** *n* ▸ **idly** *adv*

idol (**eye**-dl) *n* **1** an object of excessive devotion or admiration. **2** an image of a god used as an object of worship. ▷ HISTORY Greek *eidōlon* image

idolatry (ide-**ol**-a-tree) *n* **1** the worship of idols. **2** excessive devotion or reverence. ▶ **idolater** *n* ▶ **idolatrous** *adj*

idolize *or* **-ise** *vb* **-izing, -ized** *or* **-ising, -ised 1** to love or admire excessively. **2** to worship as an idol. ▶ **idolization** *or* **-isation** *n*

idyll *or US sometimes* **idyl** (**id**-ill) *n* **1** a scene or time of peace and happiness. **2** a poem or prose work describing a charming rural scene or episode. ▷ HISTORY Greek *eidullion* ▶ **idyllic** *adj*

i.e. that is to say. ▷ HISTORY Latin *id est*

if *conj* **1** in the event that, or on condition that: *if you work hard you'll succeed.* **2** used to introduce an indirect question to which the answer is either *yes* or *no*; whether: *it doesn't matter if the play is any good or not.* **3** even though: *a splendid if slightly decaying house.* **4** used to introduce an unfulfilled wish, with *only*: *if only you had told her.* ✧ *n* **5** a condition or stipulation: *there are no hidden ifs or buts.* ▷ HISTORY Old English *gif*

iffy *adj Informal* full of uncertainty.

igloo *n, pl* **-loos** a dome-shaped Eskimo house, built of blocks of solid snow. ▷ HISTORY Inuit *igdlu*

igneous (**ig**-nee-uss) *adj* **1** (of rocks) formed as molten rock cools and hardens. **2** of or like fire. ▷ HISTORY Latin *ignis* fire

ignite *vb* **-niting, -nited** to catch fire or set fire to. ▷ HISTORY Latin *ignis* fire ▶ **ignitable** *adj*

ignition *n* **1** the system used to ignite the fuel in an internal-combustion engine. **2** an igniting or the process of igniting.

ignoble *adj* **1** dishonourable. **2** of low birth or origins. ▷ HISTORY Latin *in-* not + *nobilis* noble ▶ **ignobly** *adv*

ignominy (**ig**-nom-in-ee) *n, pl* **-minies** disgrace or public shame: *the ignominy of being replaced.* ▷ HISTORY Latin *ignominia* disgrace ▶ **ignominious** *adj*

ignoramus *n, pl* **-muses** an ignorant person.

> **WORD HISTORY**
> The word 'ignoramus' comes from *Ignoramus*, the name of an uneducated lawyer in a 17th-century play of the same name written by George Ruggle. In Latin *ignoramus* means 'we do not know'.

ignorance *n* lack of knowledge or education.

ignorant *adj* **1** lacking in knowledge or education. **2** rude through lack of knowledge of good manners: *an ignorant remark.* **3 ignorant of** lacking in awareness or knowledge of: *ignorant of Asian culture.*

ignore *vb* **-noring, -nored** to refuse to notice; disregard deliberately. ▷ HISTORY Latin *ignorare* not to know

iguana *n* a large tropical tree lizard of the W Indies and S America with a spiny back. ▷ HISTORY S American Indian *iwana*

ikebana (eek-a-**bah**-na) *n* the Japanese art of flower arrangement. ▷ HISTORY Japanese

ikon *n* same as **icon**.

IL Illinois.

il- *prefix* same as **in-**[1], **in-**[2].

ileum *n* the third and lowest part of the small intestine. ▷ HISTORY Latin: flank, groin

ilex *n* **1** a genus of trees or shrubs that includes holly. **2** same as **holm oak**. ▷ HISTORY Latin

ilium *n, pl* **-ia** the uppermost and widest of the three sections of the hipbone.

ilk *n* a type or class: *three or four others of the same ilk.* ▷ HISTORY Old English *ilca* the same family

> **WORD TIP**
> Although the use of *ilk* to mean *a type or class* is sometimes condemned as being the result of a misunderstanding of a Scottish expression *of that ilk*, it is nevertheless well established and generally acceptable.

ill *adj* **worse, worst 1** not in good health. **2** bad, harmful, or hostile: *ill effects.* **3** promising an unfavourable outcome: *ill omen.* **4 ill at ease** unable to relax. ✧ *n* **5** evil or harm. ✧ *adv* **6** badly, wrongly: *the title ill befits him.* **7** with difficulty; hardly: *we can ill afford another scandal.* ▷ HISTORY Old Norse *illr* bad

ill-advised *adj* **1** (of a plan or action) badly thought out. **2** (of a person) acting without reasonable care or thought.

ill-bred *adj* lacking good manners. ▶ **ill-breeding** *n*

ill-disposed *adj* unfriendly or unsympathetic.

illegal *adj* against the law. ▶ **illegally** *adv* ▶ **illegality** *n*

illegible *adj* unable to be read or deciphered. ▶ **illegibility** *n*

illegitimate *adj* **1** born of parents who were not married to each other at the time. **2** illegal; unlawful. ▶ **illegitimacy** *n*

ill-fated *adj* doomed or unlucky.

ill-favoured *adj* ugly or unattractive.

ill-gotten *adj* obtained dishonestly or illegally: *ill-gotten gains.*

ill-health *n* the condition of being unwell.

illiberal *adj* **1** narrow-minded or intolerant. **2** not generous; mean. **3** lacking in culture or refinement. ▶ **illiberality** *n*

illicit *adj* **1** same as **illegal**. **2** forbidden or disapproved of by society: *an illicit kiss.*

illiterate *adj* **1** unable to read and write. **2** uneducated or ignorant: *linguistically illiterate.* ✧ *n* **3** an illiterate person. ▶ **illiteracy** *n*

ill-mannered *adj* having bad manners.

illness *n* **1** a disease or indisposition. **2** a state of ill health.

illogical *adj* **1** senseless or unreasonable. **2** not following logical principles. ▶ **illogicality** *n* ▶ **illogically** *adv*

ill-starred *adj* very unlucky or unfortunate.

ill-tempered *adj* having a bad temper.

a b c d e f g h i j k l m n o p q r s t u v w x y z

A B C D E F G H I J K L M N O P Q R S T U V W X Y Z

ill-timed *adj* done or happening at an unsuitable time.

ill-treat *vb* to treat cruelly or harshly. ▸ **ill-treatment** *n*

illuminate *vb* **-nating, -nated 1** to light up. **2** to make easily understood; explain: *the report obscures rather than illuminates the most relevant facts.* **3** to decorate with lights. **4** to decorate (an initial letter or manuscript) with designs of gold, silver, or bright colours. ▷ HISTORY Latin *illuminare* to light up ▸ **illuminating** *adj* ▸ **illuminative** *adj*

illumination *n* **1** an illuminating or being illuminated. **2** a source of light. **3 illuminations** *Chiefly Brit* lights used as decorations in streets or towns. **4** the decoration in colours, gold, or silver used on some manuscripts.

illusion *n* **1** a false appearance or deceptive impression of reality: *her upswept hair gave the illusion of above average height.* **2** a false or misleading idea or belief: *we may suffer from the illusion that we are special.* ▷ HISTORY Latin *illusio* deceit

illusionist *n* a conjuror.

illusory *or* **illusive** *adj* seeming to be true, but actually false: *the economic benefits of such reforms were largely illusory.*

> ☑ **WORD TIP**
> *Illusive* is sometimes wrongly used where *elusive* is meant: *they fought hard, but victory remained elusive* (not *illusive*).

illustrate *vb* **-trating, -trated 1** to clarify or explain by use of examples or comparisons. **2** to provide (a book or text) with pictures. **3** to be an example of. ▷ HISTORY Latin *illustrare* to make light, explain ▸ **illustrative** *adj* ▸ **illustrator** *n*

illustration *n* **1** a picture or diagram used to explain or decorate a text. **2** an example: *an illustration of the brutality of the regime.* **3** the art of illustrating.

illustrious *adj* famous and distinguished. ▷ HISTORY Latin *illustris* bright, famous

ill will *n* unkind feeling; hostility.

im- *prefix* same as **in-**[1], **in-**[2].

image *n* **1** a mental picture of someone or something produced by the imagination or memory. **2** the appearance or impression given to the public by a person or organization. **3** a simile or metaphor. **4** a representation of a person or thing in a work of art or literature. **5** an optical reproduction of an object, formed by the lens of an eye or camera or by a mirror. **6** a person or thing that resembles another closely. **7** a personification of a specified quality; epitome: *the image of good breeding.* ✧ *vb* **-aging, -aged 8** to picture in the mind. **9** to mirror or reflect an image of. **10** to portray or describe. ▷ HISTORY Latin *imago*

image printer *n Computers* a printer which uses optical technology to produce an image of a complete page from digital input.

imagery *n, pl* **-ries 1** figurative or descriptive language in a literary work. **2** mental images. **3** images collectively, esp. statues or carvings.

imaginary *adj* **1** existing only in the imagination. **2** *Maths* relating to the square root of a negative number.

imagination *n* **1** the faculty or action of producing mental images of what is not present or in one's experience. **2** creative mental ability.

imaginative *adj* **1** produced by or showing a creative imagination. **2** having a vivid imagination.

imagine *vb* **-ining, -ined 1** to form a mental image of. **2** to think, believe, or guess: *I would imagine they'll be here soon.* ▷ HISTORY Latin *imaginari* ▸ **imaginable** *adj*

imago (im-**may**-go) *n, pl* **imagoes** *or* **imagines** (im-**maj**-in-eez) a sexually mature adult insect. ▷ HISTORY Latin: likeness

imam *n Islam* **1** a leader of congregational prayer in a mosque. **2** the title of some Muslim leaders. ▷ HISTORY Arabic

IMAX (**eye**-max) *n Trademark* a film projection process that produces an image ten times larger than standard.

imbalance *n* a lack of balance, for instance in emphasis or proportion: *a chemical imbalance in the brain.*

imbecile (**im**-biss-eel) *n* **1** *Informal* an extremely stupid person. **2** *Old-fashioned* a person of abnormally low intelligence. ✧ *adj* **3** stupid or senseless: *imbecile fanaticism.* ▷ HISTORY Latin *imbecillus* feeble ▸ **imbecility** *n*

imbed *vb* **-bedding, -bedded** same as **embed**.

imbibe *vb* **-bibing, -bibed** *Formal* **1** to drink (alcoholic drinks). **2** to take in or assimilate (ideas): *values she had imbibed as a child.* ▷ HISTORY Latin *imbibere*

imbroglio (imb-**role**-ee-oh) *n, pl* **-glios** a confusing and complicated situation. ▷ HISTORY Italian

imbue *vb* **-buing, -bued** to fill or inspire (with ideals or principles). ▷ HISTORY Latin *imbuere* to stain

IMF International Monetary Fund.

imitate *vb* **-tating, -tated 1** to copy the manner or style of or take as a model: *he remains rock's most imitated guitarist.* **2** to mimic or impersonate, esp. for amusement. **3** to make a copy or reproduction of; duplicate. ▷ HISTORY Latin *imitari* ▸ **imitable** *adj* ▸ **imitator** *n*

imitation *n* **1** a copy of an original or genuine article. **2** an instance of imitating someone: *her Coward imitations were not the best thing she did.* **3** behaviour modelled on the behaviour of someone else: *to learn by imitation.* ✧ *adj* **4** made to resemble something which is usually superior or more expensive: *imitation leather.*

imitative *adj* **1** imitating or tending to copy. **2** copying or reproducing an original, esp. in an inferior manner: *imitative painting.* **3** onomatopoeic.

immaculate *adj* **1** completely clean or tidy: *an immaculate pinstripe suit.* **2** completely flawless: *his equestrian pedigree is immaculate.* ▷ HISTORY Latin *in-* not + *macula* blemish ▸ **immaculately** *adv*

immanent *adj* **1** present within and throughout something. **2** (of God) present throughout the universe. ▷ HISTORY Latin *immanere* to remain in ▶ **immanence** *n*

immaterial *adj* **1** of no real importance or relevance. **2** not formed of matter.

immature *adj* **1** not fully grown or developed. **2** lacking wisdom, insight, or stability because of youth. ▶ **immaturity** *n*

immeasurable *adj* too great to be measured. ▶ **immeasurably** *adv*

immediate *adj* **1** taking place without delay: *an immediate cut in interest rates.* **2** next or nearest in space, time, or relationship: *our immediate neighbour.* **3** present; current: *they had no immediate plans to close it.* ▷ HISTORY Latin *in-* not + *mediare* to be in the middle ▶ **immediacy** *n* ▶ **immediately** *adv*

immemorial *adj* having existed or happened for longer than anyone can remember: *this has been the custom since time immemorial.*

immense *adj* **1** huge or vast. **2** *Informal* very great. ▷ HISTORY Latin *immensus* unmeasured ▶ **immensely** *adv* ▶ **immensity** *n*

immerse *vb* **-mersing, -mersed 1** to plunge or dip into liquid. **2** to involve deeply: *he immersed himself in the history of Rome.* **3** to baptize by dipping the whole body into water. ▷ HISTORY Latin *immergere* ▶ **immersion** *n*

immersion heater *n* an electrical device in a domestic hot-water tank for heating water.

immigrant *n* a person who comes to a foreign country in order to settle there.

immigration *n* the act of coming to a foreign country in order to settle there. ▷ HISTORY Latin *immigrare* to go into ▶ **immigrate** *vb*

imminent *adj* likely to happen soon. ▷ HISTORY Latin *imminere* to project over ▶ **imminence** *n*

immobile *adj* **1** not moving. **2** not able to move or be moved. ▶ **immobility** *n*

immobilize *or* **-lise** *vb* **-lizing, -lized** *or* **-lising, -lised** to make unable to move or work: *a device for immobilizing steering wheels.* ▶ **immobilization** *or* **-lisation** *n*

immoderate *adj* excessive or unreasonable: *immoderate consumption of alcohol.* ▶ **immoderately** *adv*

immodest *adj* **1** behaving in an indecent or improper manner. **2** behaving in a boastful or conceited manner. ▶ **immodesty** *n*

immolate *vb* **-lating, -lated** *Literary* to kill or offer as a sacrifice, esp. by fire. ▷ HISTORY Latin *immolare* ▶ **immolation** *n*

immoral *adj* **1** morally wrong; corrupt. **2** sexually depraved or promiscuous. ▶ **immorality** *n*

immortal *adj* **1** not subject to death or decay. **2** famous for all time. **3** everlasting. ✧ *n* **4** a person whose fame will last for all time. **5** an immortal being. ▶ **immortality** *n*

immortalize *or* **-ise** *vb* **-izing, -ized** *or* **-ising, -ised 1** to give everlasting fame to: *a name immortalized by countless writers.* **2** to give immortality to.

immovable *or* **immoveable** *adj* **1** unable to be moved. **2** unwilling to change one's opinions or beliefs. **3** not affected by feeling; emotionless. **4** unchanging. **5** *Law* (of property) consisting of land or houses. ▶ **immovability** *or* **immoveability** *n* ▶ **immovably** *or* **immoveably** *adv*

immune *adj* **1** protected against a specific disease by inoculation or as the result of natural resistance. **2 immune to** secure against: *football is not immune to economic recession.* **3** exempt from obligation or penalty. ▷ HISTORY Latin *immunis* exempt from a public service

immunity *n, pl* **-ties 1** the ability of an organism to resist disease. **2** freedom from prosecution, tax, etc.

immunize *or* **-nise** *vb* **-nizing, -nized** *or* **-nising, -nised** to make (someone) immune to a disease, esp. by inoculation. ▶ **immunization** *or* **-nisation** *n*

immunodeficiency *n* a deficiency in or breakdown of a person's ability to fight diseases.

immunology *n* the branch of medicine concerned with the study of immunity. ▶ **immunological** *adj* ▶ **immunologist** *n*

immure *vb* **-muring, -mured 1** *Archaic or literary* to imprison. **2** to shut (oneself) away from society. ▷ HISTORY Latin *im-* in + *murus* wall

immutable (im-**mute**-a-bl) *adj* unchangeable or unchanging: *the immutable sequence of night and day.* ▶ **immutability** *n*

imp *n* **1** a small demon. **2** a mischievous child. ▷ HISTORY Old English *impa* bud, hence offspring, child

imp. 1 imperative. **2** imperfect.

impact *n* **1** the effect or impression made by something. **2** the act of one object striking another; collision. **3** the force of a collision. ✧ *vb* **4** to press firmly against or into. ▷ HISTORY Latin *impactus* pushed against ▶ **impaction** *n*

impacted *adj* (of a tooth) unable to grow out because of being wedged against another tooth below the gum.

impair *vb* to damage or weaken in strength or quality. ▷ HISTORY Old French *empeirer* to make worse ▶ **impairment** *n*

impala (imp-**ah**-la) *n, pl* **-las** *or* **-la** an African antelope with lyre-shaped horns. ▷ HISTORY Zulu

impale *vb* **-paling, -paled** to pierce through or fix with a sharp object: *they impaled his severed head on a spear.* ▷ HISTORY Latin *im-* on + *palus* pole ▶ **impalement** *n*

impalpable *adj Formal* **1** not able to be felt by touching: *impalpable shadows.* **2** difficult to understand. ▶ **impalpability** *n*

impart *vb* **1** to communicate (information or knowledge). **2** to give (a specified quality): *flavouring to impart a sweet taste.* ▷ HISTORY Latin *im-* in + *partire* to share

impartial *adj* not favouring one side or the other. ▶ **impartiality** *n* ▶ **impartially** *adv*

impassable *adj* (of terrain or roads) not able to be travelled through or over. ▶ **impassability** *n*

A B C D E F G H I J K L M N O P Q R S T U V W X Y Z

impasse (**am**-pass) *n* a situation in which progress or escape is impossible. ▷ **HISTORY** French

impassible *adj* **1** *Rare* not susceptible to pain or injury. **2** impassive; unmoved. ▶ **impassibility** *or* **impassibleness** *n*

impassioned *adj* full of emotion: *an impassioned plea to the United Nations.*

impassive *adj* not showing or feeling emotion. ▶ **impassively** *adv* ▶ **impassivity** *n*

impasto *n* the technique of applying paint thickly, so that brush marks are evident. ▷ **HISTORY** Italian

impatient *adj* **1** irritable at any delay or difficulty. **2** restless to have or do something. ▶ **impatience** *n* ▶ **impatiently** *adv*

impeach *vb* **1** *Chiefly US* to charge (a public official) with an offence committed in office. **2** *Brit & Austral criminal law* to accuse of treason or serious crime. **3** to challenge or question (a person's honesty or honour). ▷ **HISTORY** Late Latin *impedicare* to entangle ▶ **impeachable** *adj* ▶ **impeachment** *n*

impeccable *adj* without flaw or error: *impeccable manners.* ▷ **HISTORY** Latin *in-* not + *peccare* to sin ▶ **impeccably** *adv*

impecunious *adj Formal* without money; penniless. ▷ **HISTORY** Latin *in-* not + *pecuniosus* wealthy

impedance (imp-**eed**-anss) *n Electricity* the total effective resistance in an electric circuit to the flow of an alternating current.

impede *vb* **-peding, -peded** to block or make progress or action difficult. ▷ **HISTORY** Latin *impedire*

impediment *n* **1** a hindrance or obstruction. **2** a physical disability that makes speech or walking difficult.

impedimenta *pl n* any objects that impede progress, esp. the baggage and equipment carried by an army.

impel *vb* **-pelling, -pelled 1** to urge or force (a person) to do something. **2** to push, drive, or force into motion. ▷ **HISTORY** Latin *impellere* to drive forward

impending *adj* (esp. of something bad) about to happen. ▷ **HISTORY** Latin *impendere* to overhang

impenetrable *adj* **1** impossible to get through: *an impenetrable barrier.* **2** impossible to understand. **3** not receptive to ideas or influence: *impenetrable ignorance.* ▶ **impenetrability** *n* ▶ **impenetrably** *adv*

imperative *adj* **1** extremely urgent; essential. **2** commanding or authoritative: *an imperative tone of voice.* **3** *Grammar* denoting a mood of verbs used in commands. ✧ *n* **4** *Grammar* the imperative mood. ▷ **HISTORY** Latin *imperare* to command

imperceptible *adj* too slight, subtle, or gradual to be noticed. ▶ **imperceptibly** *adv*

imperfect *adj* **1** having faults or errors. **2** not complete. **3** *Grammar* denoting a tense of verbs describing continuous, incomplete, or repeated past actions. ✧ *n* **4** *Grammar* same as **imperfect tense.** ▶ **imperfectly** *adv*

imperfection *n* **1** the state of being imperfect. **2** a fault or defect.

imperfect tense *n Grammar* a verb tense describing continuous, incomplete, or repeated past actions; in *he was having a bath when I phoned, was having* is the imperfect tense.

imperial *adj* **1** of an empire, emperor, or empress. **2** majestic; commanding. **3** exercising supreme authority; imperious. **4** (of weights or measures) conforming to the standards of a system formerly official in Great Britain. ✧ *n* **5** a wine bottle holding the equivalent of eight normal bottles. ▷ **HISTORY** Latin *imperium* authority

imperialism *n* **1** the policy or practice of extending a country's influence over other territories by conquest, colonization, or economic domination. **2** an imperial system, authority, or government. ▶ **imperialist** *adj, n* ▶ **imperialistic** *adj*

imperil *vb* **-illing, -illed** *or US* **-iling, -iled** *Formal* to put in danger.

imperious *adj* used to being obeyed; domineering. ▷ **HISTORY** Latin *imperium* power ▶ **imperiously** *adv*

impermeable *adj* (of a substance) not allowing fluid to pass through: *an impermeable layer.* ▶ **impermeability** *n*

impersonal *adj* **1** without reference to any individual person; objective: *Buddhism began as a very impersonal doctrine.* **2** without human warmth or sympathy: *an impersonal manner.* **3** *Grammar* **a** (of a verb) having no subject, as in *it is raining.* **b** (of a pronoun) not referring to a person. ▶ **impersonality** *n* ▶ **impersonally** *adv*

impersonal narrator *n Literature* an objective storyteller who is not evident as a personality but simply gives information.

impersonate *vb* **-ating, -ated 1** to pretend to be (another person). **2** to imitate the character or mannerisms of (another person) for entertainment. ▶ **impersonation** *n* ▶ **impersonator** *n*

impertinent *adj* disrespectful or rude. ▷ **HISTORY** Latin *impertinens* not belonging ▶ **impertinence** *n*

imperturbable *adj* not easily upset; calm. ▶ **imperturbability** *n* ▶ **imperturbably** *adv*

impervious *adj* **1** not letting water etc. through. **2** not influenced by a feeling, argument, etc.

impetigo (imp-it-**tie**-go) *n* a contagious skin disease causing spots or pimples. ▷ **HISTORY** Latin: scabby eruption

impetuous *adj* **1** acting without consideration. **2** done rashly or hastily. ▷ **HISTORY** Late Latin *impetuosus* violent ▶ **impetuosity** *n*

impetus (**imp**-it-uss) *n, pl* **-tuses 1** an incentive or impulse. **2** *Physics* the force that starts a body moving or that tends to resist changes in its speed or direction once it is moving. ▷ **HISTORY** Latin: attack

impi *n, pl* **-pi** *or* **-pies** a group of Zulu warriors. ▷ **HISTORY** Nguni (language group of southern Africa) *impi* regiment, army

impinge *vb* **-pinging, -pinged** to encroach, affect or restrict: *international economic forces impinging on the local economy.* ▷ **HISTORY** Latin *impingere* to dash against ▶ **impingement** *n*

impious (**imp**-euss) *adj* showing a lack of respect or religious reverence.

impish *adj* mischievous. ▶ **impishness** *n*

implacable *adj* **1** incapable of being appeased or pacified. **2** unyielding. ▶ **implacability** *n* ▶ **implacably** *adv*

implant *vb* **1** to fix firmly in the mind: *to implant sound moral principles.* **2** to plant or embed. **3** *Surgery* to graft or insert (a tissue or hormone) into the body. ✧ *n* **4** anything implanted in the body, such as a tissue graft. ▶ **implantation** *n*

implement *vb* **1** to carry out (instructions etc.): *she refused to implement the agreed plan.* ✧ *n* **2** a tool or other piece of equipment. ▷ **HISTORY** Late Latin *implementum,* literally: a filling up ▶ **implementation** *n*

implicate *vb* **-cating, -cated 1** to show (someone) to be involved, esp. in a crime. **2** to imply. ▷ **HISTORY** Latin *implicare* to involve

implication *n* **1** something that is suggested or implied. **2** an act or instance of suggesting or implying or being implied.

implicit *adj* **1** expressed indirectly: *an implicit agreement.* **2** absolute and unquestioning: *implicit trust.* **3** contained in, although not stated openly: *this view of the mind was implicit in all his work.* ▷ **HISTORY** Latin *implicitus* ▶ **implicitly** *adv*

implied term *n Law* a condition that will be assumed by the courts to be part of a contract even though it is not specified in the agreement.

implode *vb* **-ploding, -ploded** to collapse inwards. ▷ **HISTORY** *im-* in + *(ex)plode*

implore *vb* **-ploring, -plored** to beg desperately. ▷ **HISTORY** Latin *implorare*

imply *vb* **-plies, -plying, -plied 1** to express or indicate by a hint; suggest. **2** to suggest or involve as a necessary consequence: *a spending commitment implies a corresponding tax imposition.* ▷ **HISTORY** Old French *emplier*

> **WORD TIP**
> See at **infer.**

impolite *adj* discourteous; rude. ▶ **impoliteness** *n*

impolitic *adj* ill-advised; unwise.

imponderable *adj* **1** unable to be weighed or assessed. ✧ *n* **2** something difficult or impossible to assess.

import *vb* **1** to bring in (goods) from another country. **2** *Formal* to signify; mean: *to import doom.* ✧ *n* **3** something imported. **4** *Formal* importance: *his new work is of great import.* **5** meaning. **6** *Canad slang* a sportsman who is not native to the area where he plays. ▷ **HISTORY** Latin *importare* to carry in ▶ **importer** *n* ▶ **importation** *n*

important *adj* **1** of great significance, value, or consequence. **2** of social significance: *an important man in the company hierarchy.* **3** of great concern: *it was important to me to know.* ▷ **HISTORY** Medieval Latin *importare* to signify, from Latin: to carry in ▶ **importance** *n* ▶ **importantly** *adv*

> **WORD TIP**
> The use of *more importantly* as in *more importantly, the local council is opposed to this proposal* has become very common, but many people still prefer to use *more important.*

importunate *adj Formal* persistent or demanding.

importune *vb* **-tuning, -tuned** *Formal* to harass with persistent requests. ▷ **HISTORY** Latin *importunus* tiresome ▶ **importunity** *n*

impose *vb* **-posing, -posed 1** to establish (a rule, condition, etc.) as something to be obeyed or complied with. **2** to take advantage of (a person or quality): *she imposed on her kindness.* **3** to force (oneself) on others. **4** *Printing* to arrange (pages) in the correct order for printing. **5** to pass off (something) deceptively on someone. ▷ **HISTORY** Latin *imponere* to place upon

imposing *adj* grand or impressive: *an imposing building.*

imposition *n* **1** the act of imposing. **2** something imposed, esp. unfairly, on someone. **3** the arrangement of pages for printing. **4** *Old-fashioned* a task set as a school punishment.

impossibility *n, pl* **-ties 1** the state or quality of being impossible. **2** something that is impossible.

impossible *adj* **1** not able to be done or to happen. **2** absurd or unreasonable. **3** *Informal* intolerable or outrageous: *those children are impossible.* ▶ **impossibly** *adv*

imposter *or* **impostor** *n* a person who cheats or swindles by pretending to be someone else. ▷ **HISTORY** Late Latin *impostor* deceiver

imposture *n Formal* deception, esp. by pretending to be someone else.

impotent (**imp**-a-tent) *adj* **1** not having the power to influence people or events. **2** (of a man) incapable of sexual intercourse. ▶ **impotence** *n*

impound *vb* **1** to take legal possession of; confiscate. **2** to confine (an animal) in a pound.

impoverish *vb* to make (someone) poor or weaken the quality of (something). ▷ **HISTORY** Old French *empovrir* ▶ **impoverished** *adj* ▶ **impoverishment** *n*

impracticable *adj* **1** not able to be put into practice. **2** unsuitable for a desired use. ▶ **impracticability** *n*

impractical *adj* **1** not sensible or workable: *the use of force was viewed as impractical.* **2** not having practical skills. ▶ **impracticality** *n*

imprecation *n Formal* a curse. ▷ **HISTORY** Latin *imprecari* to invoke ▶ **imprecate** *vb*

impregnable *adj* **1** unable to be broken into or taken by force: *an impregnable fortress.* **2** unable to be affected or overcome: *a confident, impregnable person.* ▷ **HISTORY** Old French *imprenable* ▶ **impregnability** *n*

impregnate *vb* **-nating, -nated 1** to saturate, soak, or fill throughout. **2** to make pregnant. **3** to imbue or permeate: *the party has been impregnated*

a b c d e f g h i j k l m n o p q r s t u v w x y z

with an enthusiasm for reform. ▷ **HISTORY** Latin *in-* in + *praegnans* pregnant ▸ **impregnation** *n*

impresario *n, pl* **-sarios** a person who runs theatre performances, concerts, etc. ▷ **HISTORY** Italian

impress *vb* **1** to make a strong, lasting, or favourable impression on: *he was impressed by the standard of play.* **2** to stress or emphasize. **3** to imprint or stamp by pressure: *a pattern impressed in paint on the rock.* ✧ *n* **4** an impressing. **5** a mark produced by impressing. ▷ **HISTORY** Latin *imprimere* to press into ▸ **impressible** *adj*

impression *n* **1** an effect produced in the mind by a person or thing: *she was keen to create a relaxed impression.* **2** a vague idea or belief: *he only had a vague impression of how it worked.* **3** a strong, favourable, or remarkable effect. **4** an impersonation for entertainment. **5** an imprint or mark produced by pressing. **6** *Printing* the number of copies of a publication printed at one time.

impressionable *adj* easily impressed or influenced: *the promotion of smoking to the impressionable young.* ▸ **impressionability** *n*

Impressionism *n* a style of painting developed in 19th-century France, with the aim of reproducing the immediate impression or mood of things, especially the effects of light and atmosphere, rather than form or structure.

impressionist *n* **1 Impressionist** an artist who painted in the style of Impressionism. **2** a person who imitates the character or mannerisms of another person for entertainment.

impressive *adj* capable of impressing, esp. by size, magnificence, or importance. ▸ **impressively** *adv*

imprimatur (imp-rim-**ah**-ter) *n* official approval for something to be printed, usually given by the Roman Catholic Church. ▷ **HISTORY** New Latin: let it be printed

imprint *n* **1** a mark or impression produced by pressing, printing, or stamping. **2** the publisher's name and address, often with the date of publication, printed on the title page of a book. ✧ *vb* **3** to produce (a mark) by pressing, printing, or stamping: *T-shirts imprinted with slogans.* **4** to establish firmly; impress: *he couldn't dislodge the images imprinted on his brain.*

imprison *vb* to confine in or as if in prison. ▸ **imprisonment** *n*

improbable *adj* not likely or probable. ▸ **improbability** *n* ▸ **improbably** *adv*

improbity *n, pl* **-ties** *Formal* dishonesty or wickedness.

impromptu *adj* **1** without planning or preparation; improvised. ✧ *adv* **2** in a spontaneous or improvised way: *he spoke impromptu.* ✧ *n* **3** a short piece of instrumental music resembling improvisation. **4** something that is impromptu. ▷ **HISTORY** Latin *in promptu* in readiness

improper *adj* **1** indecent. **2** irregular or incorrect. ▸ **improperly** *adv*

improper fraction *n* a fraction in which the numerator is greater than the denominator, as $^7/_6$.

impropriety (imp-roe-**pry**-a-tee) *n, pl* **-ties** *Formal* unsuitable or slightly improper behaviour.

improve *vb* **-proving, -proved 1** to make or become better in quality. **2 improve on** to achieve a better standard or quality in comparison with: *both had improved on their previous performance.* ▷ **HISTORY** Anglo-French *emprouer* to turn to profit ▸ **improvable** *adj*

improved pasture *n Agriculture* **1** grazing land that has been sown with a mixture of introduced plant species to improve productivity. **2** such plants used for grazing.

improvement *n* **1** the act of improving or the state of being improved. **2** a change that makes something better or adds to its value: *home improvements.* **3** *Austral & NZ* a building on a piece of land, adding to its value.

improvident *adj* **1** not providing for the future. **2** incautious or rash. ▸ **improvidence** *n*

improvisation *n* the process of making up (a piece of music, speech, etc.) as one goes along; used especially of actors working without a script. ▷ **HISTORY** Latin *improvisus* unforeseen

improvise *vb* **-vising, -vised 1** to do or make quickly from whatever is available, without previous planning. **2** to make up (a piece of music, speech, etc.) as one goes along. ▷ **HISTORY** Latin *improvisus* unforeseen

imprudent *adj* not carefully thought out; rash. ▸ **imprudence** *n*

impudent *adj* impertinent or insolent. ▷ **HISTORY** Latin *impudens* shameless ▸ **impudence** *n* ▸ **impudently** *adv*

impugn (imp-**yoon**) *vb Formal* to challenge or attack as false. ▷ **HISTORY** Latin *impugnare* to fight against ▸ **impugnment** *n*

impulse *n* **1** a sudden desire or whim. **2** an instinctive drive; urge: *the mothering impulse.* **3** *Physics* **a** the product of a force acting on a body and the time for which it acts. **b** the change in the momentum of a body as a result of a force acting upon it. **4** *Physiol* a stimulus transmitted in a nerve or muscle. ▷ **HISTORY** Latin *impulsus* incitement

impulsive *adj* **1** tending to act without thinking first: *an impulsive man.* **2** done without thinking first. **3** forceful or impelling.

impunity (imp-**yoon**-it-ee) *n* **with impunity** without punishment or unpleasant consequences. ▷ **HISTORY** Latin *impunis* unpunished

impure *adj* **1** having unwanted substances mixed in. **2** immoral or obscene: *impure thoughts.* **3** dirty or unclean.

impurity *n, pl* **-ties 1** an impure element or thing: *impurities in the water.* **2** the quality of being impure.

impute *vb* **-puting, -puted 1** to attribute (blame or a crime) to a person. **2** to attribute to a source or cause: *I impute your success to nepotism.* ▷ **HISTORY** Latin *in-* in + *putare* to think ▸ **imputation** *n*

in *prep* **1** inside; within: *in the room.* **2** at a place where there is: *in the shade.* **3** indicating a state, situation, or condition: *in silence.* **4** when (a period of time) has elapsed: *come back in one year.* **5** using: *written in code.* **6** wearing: *the man in the blue suit.* **7** with regard to (a specified activity or occupation): *in journalism.* **8** while performing the action of: *in crossing the street he was run over.* **9** having as purpose: *in honour of the president.* **10** (of certain animals) pregnant with: *in calf.* **11** into: *he fell in the water.* **12 have it in one** to have the ability (to do something). **13 in that** *or* **in so far as** because or to the extent that: *it was of great help in that it gave me more confidence.* ✧ *adv* **14** in or into a particular place; indoors: *come in.* **15** at one's home or place of work: *he's not in at the moment.* **16** fashionable or popular: *long skirts are in this year.* **17** in office or power: *the Conservatives got in at the last election.* **18** so as to enclose: *block in.* **19** (in certain games) so as to take one's turn of the play: *you have to get the other side out before you go in.* **20** *Brit* (of a fire) alight. **21** indicating prolonged activity, esp. by a large number: *teach-in; sit-in.* **22 in for** about to experience (something, esp. something unpleasant): *they're in for a shock.* **23 in on** acquainted with or sharing in: *I was in on all his plans.* **24 in with** friendly with. **25 have got it in for** *Informal* to wish or intend harm towards. ✧ *adj* **26** fashionable; modish: *the in thing to do.* ✧ *n* **27 ins and outs** the detailed points or facts (of a situation). ▷ HISTORY Old English

In *Chem* indium.

IN Indiana.

in. inch(es).

in-[1], **il-, im-,** *or* **ir-** *prefix* **a** not; non: *incredible; illegal; imperfect; irregular.* **b** lack of: *inexperience.* ▷ HISTORY Latin

in-[2], **il-, im-,** *or* **ir-** *prefix* in; into; towards; within; on: *infiltrate.* ▷ HISTORY from *in*

inability *n* the fact of not being able to do something.

inaccessible *adj* **1** impossible or very difficult to reach. **2** unable to be used or seen: *his works are inaccessible to English-speaking readers.* **3** difficult to understand or appreciate: *Webern's music is still considered inaccessible.* ▶ **inaccessibility** *n*

inaccuracy *n, pl* **-cies 1** lack of accuracy; imprecision. **2** an error or mistake. ▶ **inaccurate** *adj*

inaction *n* lack of action; inertia.

inactive *adj* **1** idle; not active. **2** *Chem* (of a substance) having little or no reactivity. ▶ **inactivity** *n*

inadequacy *n, pl* **-cies 1** lack or shortage. **2** the state of being or feeling inferior. **3** a weakness or failing: *their own failures or inadequacies.*

inadequate *adj* **1** not enough; insufficient. **2** not good enough. ▶ **inadequately** *adv*

inadmissible *adj* not allowable or acceptable.

inadvertent *adj* done unintentionally. ▶ **inadvertence** *n* ▶ **inadvertently** *adv*

inalienable *adj* not able to be taken away or transferred to another: *the inalienable rights of the citizen.*

inamorata *or masc* **inamorato** *n, pl* **-tas** *or masc* **-tos** *Literary* a sweetheart or lover. ▷ HISTORY Italian *innamorata, innamorato*

inane *adj* senseless or silly: *inane remarks.* ▷ HISTORY Latin *inanis* empty ▶ **inanity** *n*

inanimate *adj* lacking the qualities of living beings: *inanimate objects.*

inanition *n Formal* exhaustion or weakness, as from lack of food. ▷ HISTORY Latin *inanis* empty

inapplicable *adj* not suitable or relevant.

inappropriate *adj* not suitable or proper. ▶ **inappropriately** *adv*

inapt *adj* **1** not apt or fitting. **2** lacking skill. ▶ **inaptitude** *n*

inarticulate *adj* unable to express oneself clearly or well.

inasmuch as *conj* **1** since; because. **2** in so far as.

inattentive *adj* not paying attention. ▶ **inattention** *n*

inaudible *adj* not loud enough to be heard. ▶ **inaudibly** *adv*

inaugural *adj* **1** of or for an inauguration. ✧ *n* **2** *US* a speech made at an inauguration.

inaugurate *vb* **-rating, -rated 1** to open or celebrate the first public use of ceremonially: *the newest electrified line was inaugurated today.* **2** to formally establish (a new leader) in office. **3** to begin officially or formally. ▷ HISTORY Latin *inaugurare* to take omens, hence to install in office after taking auguries ▶ **inauguration** *n* ▶ **inaugurator** *n*

inauspicious *adj* unlucky; suggesting an unfavourable outcome.

inboard *adj* **1** (of a boat's motor or engine) situated within the hull. **2** situated close to the fuselage of an aircraft. ✧ *adv* **3** within the sides of or towards the centre of a vessel or aircraft.

inborn *adj* existing from birth: *an inborn sense of optimism.*

inbred *adj* **1** produced as a result of inbreeding. **2** inborn or ingrained: *inbred good manners.*

inbreeding *n* breeding from closely related individuals.

inbuilt *adj* (of a quality or feeling) present from the beginning: *an inbuilt prejudice.*

Inc. *US & Austral* (of a company) incorporated.

Inca *n* **1** (*pl* **Inca** *or* **Incas**) a member of a S American indigenous people whose empire, centred on Peru, lasted until the early 1530s. **2** the language of this people.

incalculable *adj* impossible to estimate or predict. ▶ **incalculability** *n*

in camera *adv* in private session: *the proceedings were held in camera.* ▷ HISTORY Latin

incandescent *adj* **1** glowing with heat. **2** (of artificial light) produced by a glowing filament. ▷ HISTORY Latin *incandescere* to glow ▶ **incandescence** *n*

incandescent lamp *n* a lamp that contains a filament which is electrically heated to incandescence.

incantation *n* **1** ritual chanting of magic words or sounds. **2** a magic spell. ▷ HISTORY Latin *incantare* to repeat magic formulas ▶ **incantatory** *adj*

incapable *adj* **1 incapable of** lacking the ability to. **2** helpless: *drunk and incapable.*

incapacitate *vb* **-tating, -tated** to deprive (a person) of strength, power, or ability; disable.

incapacity *n, pl* **-ties 1** lack of power, strength, or ability. **2** *Law* legal disqualification or ineligibility.

incarcerate *vb* **-ating, -ated** *Formal* to confine or imprison. ▷ **HISTORY** Latin *in-* in + *carcer* prison ▸ **incarceration** *n*

incarnate *adj* **1** possessing human form: *a devil incarnate.* **2** personified or typified: *stupidity incarnate.* ✧ *vb* **-nating, -nated 3** to give a bodily or concrete form to. **4** to be representative or typical of. ▷ **HISTORY** Late Latin *incarnare* to make flesh

incarnation *n* **1** the act of embodying or state of being embodied in human form. **2** a person or thing that typifies some quality or idea.

Incarnation *n Christian theol* God's coming to earth in human form as Jesus Christ.

incendiary (in-**send**-ya-ree) *adj* **1** (of bombs etc.) designed to cause fires. **2** tending to create strife or violence. **3** relating to the illegal burning of property or goods. ✧ *n, pl* **-aries 4** a bomb that is designed to start fires. **5** a person who illegally sets fire to property or goods. ▷ **HISTORY** Latin *incendere* to kindle ▸ **incendiarism** *n*

incense¹ *n* **1** an aromatic substance burnt for its fragrant odour, esp. in religious ceremonies. **2** the odour or smoke so produced. ✧ *vb* **-censing, -censed 3** to burn incense to (a deity). **4** to perfume or fumigate with incense. ▷ **HISTORY** Church Latin *incensum*

incense² *vb* **-censing, -censed** to make very angry. ▷ **HISTORY** Latin *incensus* set on fire ▸ **incensed** *adj*

incentive *n* **1** something that encourages effort or action. **2** an additional payment made to employees to increase production. ✧ *adj* **3** encouraging greater effort: *an incentive scheme for workers.* ▷ **HISTORY** Latin *incentivus* setting the tune

inception *n* the beginning of a project. ▷ **HISTORY** Latin *incipere* to begin

incessant *adj* never stopping. ▷ **HISTORY** Latin *in-* not + *cessare* to cease ▸ **incessantly** *adv*

incest *n* sexual intercourse between two people who are too closely related to marry. ▷ **HISTORY** Latin *in-* not + *castus* chaste ▸ **incestuous** *adj*

inch *n* **1** a unit of length equal to one twelfth of a foot (2.54cm). **2** *Meteorol* the amount of rain or snow that would cover a surface to a depth of one inch. **3** a very small distance, degree, or amount: *neither side was prepared to give an inch.* **4 every inch** in every way: *she arrived looking every inch a star.* **5 inch by inch** gradually. **6 within an inch of one's life** almost to death. ✧ *vb* **7** to move very slowly or gradually: *I inched my way to the bar.* ▷ **HISTORY** Old English *ynce*

inchoate (in-**koe**-ate) *adj Formal* just begun and not yet properly developed. ▷ **HISTORY** Latin *incohare* to make a beginning

incidence *n* **1** extent or frequency of occurrence: *the rising incidence of car fires.* **2** *Physics* the arrival of a beam of light or particles at a surface. **3** *Geom* the partial overlapping of two figures or a figure and a line.

incident *n* **1** an occurrence or event, esp. a minor one. **2** a relatively insignificant event that might have serious consequences. **3** a public disturbance. ✧ *adj* **4** *Physics* (of a beam of light or particles) arriving at or striking a surface. **5 incident to** *Formal* likely to occur in connection with: *the dangers are incident to a policeman's job.* ▷ **HISTORY** Latin *incidere* to happen

incidental *adj* **1** happening in connection with or resulting from something more important. **2** secondary or minor: *incidental expenses.* ▸ **incidentally** *adv*

incidental music *n* background music for a film or play.

incident ray *n Physics* a ray of light striking a surface.

incinerate *vb* **-ating, -ated** to burn up completely. ▷ **HISTORY** Latin *in-* to + *cinis* ashes ▸ **incineration** *n*

incinerator *n* a furnace for burning rubbish.

incipient *adj Formal* just starting to be or happen. ▷ **HISTORY** Latin *incipere* to begin

incise *vb* **-cising, -cised** to cut into with a sharp tool. ▷ **HISTORY** Latin *incidere* to cut into

incised meander *n Geog* a bend in a river where the water has carved a deep steep-sided channel in the bedrock.

incision *n* a cut, esp. one made during a surgical operation.

incisive *adj* direct and forceful: *witty and incisive comments.*

incisor *n* a sharp cutting tooth at the front of the mouth.

incite *vb* **-citing, -cited** to stir up or provoke to action. ▷ **HISTORY** Latin *in-* in, on + *citare* to excite ▸ **incitement** *n*

incivility *n, pl* **-ties 1** rudeness. **2** an impolite act or remark.

inclement *adj Formal* (of weather) stormy or severe. ▸ **inclemency** *n*

inclination *n* **1** a liking, tendency, or preference: *he showed no inclination to change his routine.* **2** the degree of slope from a horizontal or vertical plane. **3** a slope or slant. **4** *Surveying* the angular distance of the horizon below the plane of observation.

incline *vb* **-clining, -clined 1** to veer from a vertical or horizontal plane; slope or slant. **2** to have or cause to have a certain tendency or disposition: *that does not incline me to think that you are right.* **3** to bend or lower (part of the body, esp. the head). **4 incline one's ear** to listen favourably. ✧ *n* **5** an inclined surface or slope. ▷ **HISTORY** Latin *inclinare* to cause to lean ▸ **inclined** *adj*

include *vb* **-cluding, -cluded 1** to have as part of the whole. **2** to put in as part of a set, group, or category. ▷ **HISTORY** Latin *in-* in + *claudere* to close

inclusion *n* **1** an including or being included. **2** something included.

inclusive *adj* **1** including everything: *capital inclusive of profit.* **2** including the limits specified: *Monday to Friday inclusive.* **3** comprehensive.

inclusive language *n* language that avoids male pronouns and the use of words such as *mankind*, on the grounds that they exclude women.

incognito (in-kog-**nee**-toe) *adv, adj* **1** under an assumed name or appearance. ✧ *n, pl* **-tos 2** a false identity. **3** a person who is incognito. ▷ **HISTORY** Latin *incognitus* unknown

incoherent *adj* **1** unable to express oneself clearly. **2** not logically connected or ordered: *an incoherent argument.* ▶ **incoherence** *n*

income *n* the total amount of money earned from work or obtained from other sources over a given period of time.

income support *n* (in Britain) an allowance paid by the government to people with a very low income.

income tax *n* a personal tax levied on annual income.

incoming *adj* **1** about to arrive. **2** about to come into office.

incommensurable *adj* **1** not able to be judged, measured, or compared. **2** *Maths* not having a common divisor other than 1, such as 2 and $\sqrt{-5}$. ▶ **incommensurability** *n*

incommode *vb* **-moding, -moded** *Formal* to bother, disturb, or inconvenience. ▷ **HISTORY** Latin *incommodus* inconvenient

incommunicado *adv, adj* not allowed to communicate with other people, for instance while in solitary confinement. ▷ **HISTORY** Spanish *incomunicado*

incomparable *adj* so excellent as to be beyond or above comparison. ▶ **incomparably** *adv*

incompatible *adj* not able to exist together in harmony; conflicting or inconsistent. ▶ **incompatibility** *n*

incompetent *adj* **1** not having the necessary ability or skill to do something. **2** *Law* not legally qualified: *an incompetent witness.* ✧ *n* **3** an incompetent person. ▶ **incompetence** *n*

incomplete *adj* not finished or whole.

incomplete flower *n Bot* a flower which lacks either the calyx or corolla, or both.

inconceivable *adj* so unlikely to be true as to be unthinkable. ▶ **inconceivability** *n*

inconclusive *adj* not giving a final decision or result.

incongruous *adj* out of place; inappropriate: *an incongruous figure among the tourists.* ▶ **incongruously** *adv* ▶ **incongruity** *n*

inconnu (**in**-kon-new) *n Canad* a whitefish of arctic waters. ▷ **HISTORY** French, literally: unknown

inconsequential *or* **inconsequent** *adj* **1** unimportant or insignificant. **2** not following logically as a consequence. ▶ **inconsequentially** *adv*

inconsiderable *adj* **1 not inconsiderable** fairly large: *he gets not inconsiderable royalties from his musicals.* **2** not worth considering; insignificant. ▶ **inconsiderably** *adv*

inconsiderate *adj* lacking in care or thought for others; thoughtless. ▶ **inconsiderateness** *n*

inconsistent *adj* **1** unstable or changeable in behaviour or mood. **2** containing contradictory elements: *an inconsistent argument.* **3** not in accordance: *actions inconsistent with high office.* ▶ **inconsistency** *n*

inconsolable *adj* very distressed. ▶ **inconsolably** *adv*

inconspicuous *adj* not easily noticed or seen.

inconstant *adj* **1** liable to change one's loyalties or opinions. **2** variable: *their household income is inconstant.* ▶ **inconstancy** *n*

incontestable *adj* impossible to deny or argue with.

incontinent *adj* **1** unable to control the bladder and bowels. **2** lacking self-restraint, esp. sexually. ▷ **HISTORY** Latin *in-* not + *continere* to restrain ▶ **incontinence** *n*

incontrovertible *adj* absolutely certain; undeniable. ▶ **incontrovertibly** *adv*

inconvenience *n* **1** a state or instance of trouble or difficulty. ✧ *vb* **-iencing, -ienced 2** to cause trouble or difficulty to (someone). ▶ **inconvenient** *adj*

incorporate *vb* **-rating, -rated 1** to include or be included as part of a larger unit. **2** to form a united whole or mass. **3** to form into a corporation. ✧ *adj* **4** incorporated. ▷ **HISTORY** Latin *in-* in + *corpus* body ▶ **incorporated** *adj* ▶ **incorporation** *n*

incorporeal *adj* without material form, substance, or existence.

incorrigible *adj* (of a person or behaviour) beyond correction or reform; incurably bad. ▶ **incorrigibility** *n* ▶ **incorrigibly** *adv*

incorruptible *adj* **1** too honest to be bribed or corrupted. **2** not prone to decay or disintegration. ▶ **incorruptibility** *n*

increase *vb* **-creasing, -creased 1** to make or become greater in size, degree, or frequency. ✧ *n* **2** a rise in size, degree, or frequency. **3** the amount by which something increases. **4 on the increase** becoming more common. ▷ **HISTORY** Latin *in-* in + *crescere* to grow ▶ **increasingly** *adv*

incredible *adj* **1** unbelievable. **2** *Informal* marvellous; amazing. ▶ **incredibility** *n* ▶ **incredibly** *adv*

incredulity *n* unwillingness to believe.

incredulous *adj* not prepared or willing to believe something.

increment *n* **1** the amount by which something increases. **2** a regular salary increase. **3** *Maths* a small positive or negative change in a variable or function. ▷ **HISTORY** Latin *incrementum* increase ▶ **incremental** *adj*

incriminate *vb* **-nating, -nated 1** to make (someone) seem guilty of a crime. **2** to charge (someone) with a crime. ▷ **HISTORY** Late Latin *incriminare* to accuse ▶ **incrimination** *n* ▶ **incriminatory** *adj*

A B C D E F G H I J K L M N O P Q R S T U V W X Y Z

incubate (**in**-cube-ate) *vb* **-bating, -bated 1** (of birds) to hatch (eggs) by sitting on them. **2** to cause (bacteria) to develop, esp. in an incubator or culture medium. **3** (of disease germs) to remain inactive in an animal or human before causing disease. **4** to develop gradually. ▷ **HISTORY** Latin *incubare* ▶ **incubation** *n*

incubator *n* **1** *Med* a heated enclosed apparatus for rearing premature babies. **2** an apparatus for hatching birds' eggs or growing bacterial cultures.

incubus (**in**-cube-uss) *n, pl* **-bi** *or* **-buses 1** a demon believed in folklore to have sexual intercourse with sleeping women. **2** a nightmarish burden or worry. ▷ **HISTORY** Latin *incubare* to lie upon

inculcate *vb* **-cating, -cated** to fix in someone's mind by constant repetition. ▷ **HISTORY** Latin *inculcare* to tread upon ▶ **inculcation** *n*

inculpate *vb* **-pating, -pated** *Formal* to incriminate. ▷ **HISTORY** Latin *in-* on + *culpare* to blame

incumbency *n, pl* **-cies** the office, duty, or tenure of an incumbent.

incumbent *Formal* ✧ *n* **1** a person who holds a particular office or position. ✧ *adj* **2** morally binding as a duty: *it is incumbent on cricketers to respect the umpire's impartiality.* ▷ **HISTORY** Latin *incumbere* to lie upon

incur *vb* **-curring, -curred** to bring (something undesirable) upon oneself. ▷ **HISTORY** Latin *incurrere* to run into

incurable *adj* **1** not able to be cured: *an incurable tumour.* **2** not able to be changed: *he is an incurable romantic.* ✧ *n* **3** a person with an incurable disease. ▶ **incurability** *n* ▶ **incurably** *adv*

incurious *adj* showing no curiosity or interest. ▶ **incuriously** *adv*

incursion *n* **1** a sudden or brief invasion. **2** an inroad or encroachment: *a successful incursion into the American book-shop market.* ▷ **HISTORY** Latin *incursio* attack ▶ **incursive** *adj*

ind. **1** independent. **2** index. **3** indicative. **4** indirect. **5** industrial.

Ind. **1** Independent. **2** India. **3** Indian. **4** Indiana. **5** Indies.

indaba (in-**dah**-ba) *n* **1** (among native peoples of southern Africa) a meeting to discuss a serious topic. **2** *S African informal* a matter of concern or for discussion. ▷ **HISTORY** Zulu

indebted *adj* **1** owing gratitude for help or favours. **2** owing money. ▶ **indebtedness** *n*

indecent *adj* **1** morally or sexually offensive. **2** unseemly or improper: *indecent haste.* ▶ **indecency** *n* ▶ **indecently** *adv*

indecent assault *n* a sexual attack which does not include rape.

indecent exposure *n* the showing of one's genitals in public.

indecipherable *adj* impossible to read.

indecisive *adj* **1** unable to make decisions. **2** not decisive or conclusive: *an indecisive argument.* ▶ **indecision** *or* **indecisiveness** *n*

indeed *adv* **1** certainly; actually: *indeed, the sea featured heavily in his poems.* **2** truly, very: *it has become a dangerous place indeed.* **3** in fact; what is more: *it is necessary, indeed indispensable.* ✧ *interj* **4** an expression of doubt or surprise.

indefatigable *adj* never getting tired or giving up: *Mitterrand was an indefatigable organizer.* ▷ **HISTORY** Latin *in-* not + *fatigare* to tire ▶ **indefatigably** *adv*

indefensible *adj* **1** (of behaviour or statements) unable to be justified or supported. **2** (of places or buildings) impossible to defend against attack. ▶ **indefensibility** *n*

indefinable *adj* difficult to describe or explain completely.

indefinite *adj* **1** without exact limits: *an indefinite number.* **2** vague or unclear. ▶ **indefinitely** *adv*

indefinite article *n Grammar* either of the words 'a' or 'an'.

indelible *adj* **1** impossible to erase or remove. **2** making indelible marks: *indelible ink.* ▷ **HISTORY** Latin *in-* not + *delere* to destroy ▶ **indelibly** *adv*

indelicate *adj* **1** offensive, embarrassing, or tasteless. **2** coarse, crude, or rough. ▶ **indelicacy** *n*

indemnify *vb* **-fies, -fying, -fied 1** to secure against loss, damage, or liability. **2** to compensate for loss or damage. ▶ **indemnification** *n*

indemnity *n, pl* **-ties 1** insurance against loss or damage. **2** compensation for loss or damage. **3** legal exemption from penalties incurred. ▷ **HISTORY** Latin *in-* not + *damnum* damage

indent *vb* **1** to start (a line of writing) further from the margin than the other lines. **2** to order (goods) using a special order form. **3** to notch (an edge or border). **4** to write out (a document) in duplicate. **5** to bind (an apprentice) by indenture. ✧ *n* **6** *Chiefly Brit* an official order for goods, esp. foreign merchandise. ▷ **HISTORY** Latin *in-* in + *dens* tooth

indentation *n* **1** a hollow, notch, or cut, as on an edge or on a coastline. **2** an indenting or being indented. **3** Also: **indention** the leaving of space or the amount of space left between a margin and the start of an indented line.

indenture *n* **1** a contract, esp. one binding an apprentice to his or her employer. ✧ *vb* **-turing, -tured 2** to bind (an apprentice) by indenture. **3** to enter into an agreement by indenture.

independent *adj* **1** free from the influence or control of others. **2** not dependent on anything else for function or validity. **3** not relying on the support, esp. financial support, of others. **4** capable of acting for oneself or on one's own. **5** of or having a private income large enough to enable one to live without working: *independent means.* **6** *Maths* (of a variable) not dependent on another variable. ✧ *n* **7** an independent person or thing. **8** a politician who does not represent any political party. ▶ **independence** *n* ▶ **independently** *adv*

independent clause *n Grammar* another term for **main clause**.

independent school *n* (in Britain and Australia) a school that is neither financed nor controlled by the government or local authorities.

independent variable *n Maths* a variable in an equation or statement whose value determines that of the dependent variable.

in-depth *adj* detailed or thorough: *an in-depth analysis.*

indescribable *adj* too intense or extreme for words. ▶ **indescribably** *adv*

indestructible *adj* not able to be destroyed.

indeterminate *adj* **1** uncertain in extent, amount, or nature. **2** left doubtful; inconclusive: *an indeterminate reply.* **3** *Maths* **a** having no numerical meaning, as $^0/_0$. **b** (of an equation) having more than one variable and an unlimited number of solutions. ▶ **indeterminable** *adj* ▶ **indeterminacy** *n*

index (**in**-dex) *n, pl* **-dexes** *or* **-dices 1** an alphabetical list of names or subjects dealt with in a book, indicating where they are referred to. **2** a file or catalogue in a library which enables a book or reference to be found. **3** a number indicating the level of wages or prices as compared with some standard value. **4** an indication or sign: *national birth rate was once an index of military power.* **5** *Maths* **a** same as **exponent**. **b** a superscript number placed to the left of a radical sign indicating the root to be extracted: *the index of* $\sqrt[3]{8}$ *is 3.* **6** a number or ratio indicating a specific characteristic or property: *refractive index.* ✧ *vb* **7** to put an index in (a book). **8** to enter (a word or item) in an index. **9** to make index-linked. ▷ **HISTORY** Latin: pointer

indexation *or* **index-linking** *n* the act of making wages, pensions, or interest rates index-linked.

index finger *n* the finger next to the thumb. Also called: **forefinger**

index-linked *adj* (of pensions, wages, or interest rates) rising and falling in line with the cost of living.

index notation *n Maths* the system of writing a small number above and to the right of a number or term to indicate how many times that number or term has to be multiplied by itself. See also **exponent**.

Indiaman *n, pl* **-men** (formerly) a merchant ship engaged in trade with India.

Indian *adj* **1** of India. **2** of the original inhabitants of the American continent. ✧ *n* **3** a person from India. **4** a person descended from the original inhabitants of the American continent.

Indian corn *n* same as **maize**.

Indian hemp *n* same as **hemp**.

Indian summer *n* **1** a period of warm sunny weather in autumn. **2** a period of tranquillity or of renewed productivity towards the end of a person's life or career.

Indic *adj* **1** of a branch of Indo-European consisting of many of the languages of India, including Sanskrit, Hindi, and Urdu. ✧ *n* **2** this group of languages.

indicate *vb* **-cating, -cated 1** to be or give a sign or symptom of: *to concede 18 goals in 7 games indicates a serious malaise.* **2** to point out or show. **3** to state briefly. **4** to switch on the indicators in a motor vehicle to show that one is changing direction. **5** (of measuring instruments) to show a reading of. **6** (*usually passive*) to recommend or require: *surgery seems to be indicated for this patient.* ▷ **HISTORY** Latin *indicare* ▶ **indication** *n*

indicative (in-**dik**-a-tiv) *adj* **1 indicative of** suggesting: *the symptoms aren't indicative of anything serious.* **2** *Grammar* denoting a mood of verbs used to make a statement. ✧ *n* **3** *Grammar* the indicative mood.

indicator *n* **1** something that acts as a sign or indication: *an indicator of the moral decline of our society.* **2** a device for indicating that a motor vehicle is about to turn left or right, esp. two pairs of lights that flash. **3** an instrument, such as a gauge, that registers or measures something. **4** *Chem* a substance used to indicate the completion of a chemical reaction, usually by a change of colour.

indices (**in**-diss-seez) *n* a plural of **index**.

indict (in-**dite**) *vb* to charge (a person) formally with a crime, esp. in writing. ▷ **HISTORY** Latin *in-* against + *dictare* to declare ▶ **indictable** *adj*

indictable offence *n Law* a serious criminal offence for which the defendant has the right to be tried by jury. Compare **summary offence**.

indictment *n* **1** *Criminal law* a formal charge of crime, esp. in writing: *the indictment contained three similar charges against each of the defendants.* **2** a serious criticism: *a scathing indictment of faith healing.*

indie *n Informal* an independent record company.

indifference *n* **1** lack of concern or interest: *elite indifference to mass opinion.* **2** lack of importance: *a matter of indifference to me.*

indifferent *adj* **1** showing no concern or interest: *he was indifferent to politics.* **2** of only average standard or quality. **3** not at all good: *she had starred in several very indifferent movies.* **4** unimportant. **5** showing or having no preferences. ▷ **HISTORY** Latin *indifferens* making no distinction

indigenous (in-**dij**-in-uss) *adj* originating or occurring naturally in a country or area: *the indigenous population is under threat.* ▷ **HISTORY** Latin *indigenus*

indigent *adj Formal* so poor as to lack even necessities: *the indigent widow of a fellow writer.* ▷ **HISTORY** Latin *indigere* to need ▶ **indigence** *n*

indigestible *adj* difficult or impossible to digest. ▶ **indigestibility** *n*

indigestion *n* difficulty in digesting food, accompanied by stomach pain, heartburn, and belching.

indignant *adj* feeling or showing indignation. ▷ **HISTORY** Latin *indignari* to be displeased with ▶ **indignantly** *adv*

indignation *n* anger aroused by something felt to be unfair or wrong.

indignity *n, pl* **-ties** embarrassing or humiliating treatment.

indigo *adj* **1** deep violet-blue. ✧ *n, pl* **-gos** *or* **-goes 2** a dye of this colour originally obtained from plants. ▷ **HISTORY** Spanish *indico,* from Greek *Indikos* of India

indirect *adj* **1** done or caused by someone or something else: *indirect benefits.* **2** not going in a direct course or line: *he took the indirect route home.* **3** not coming straight to the point: *an indirect question.* ▶ **indirectly** *adv*

indirect object *n Grammar* the person or thing indirectly affected by the action of a verb and its direct object, as *John* in the sentence *I bought John a newspaper.*

indirect speech *n Grammar* same as **reported speech**.

indirect tax *n* a tax levied on goods or services which is paid indirectly by being added to the price.

indiscernible *adj* not able or scarcely able to be seen.

indiscreet *adj* incautious or tactless in revealing secrets.

indiscretion *n* **1** the lack of discretion. **2** an indiscreet act or remark.

indiscriminate *adj* lacking discrimination or careful choice: *an indiscriminate bombing campaign.* ▶ **indiscriminately** *adv* ▶ **indiscrimination** *n*

indispensable *adj* absolutely necessary: *an indispensable guide for any traveller.* ▶ **indispensability** *n*

indisposed *adj* **1** sick or ill. **2** unwilling. ▷ **HISTORY** Latin *indispositus* disordered ▶ **indisposition** *n*

indisputable *adj* beyond doubt.

indissoluble *adj* permanent: *joining a political party is not an indissoluble marriage.*

indistinct *adj* unable to be seen or heard clearly. ▶ **indistinctly** *adv*

indium *n Chem* a rare soft silvery metallic element. Symbol: In. ▷ **HISTORY** Latin *indicum* indigo

individual *adj* **1** of, relating to, or meant for a single person or thing: *small sums from individual donors.* **2** separate or distinct from others of its kind: *please mark the individual pages.* **3** characterized by unusual and striking qualities. ✧ *n* **4** a single person, esp. when regarded as distinct from others: *respect for the individual.* **5** *Informal* a person: *a most annoying individual.* **6** *Biol* a single animal or plant, esp. as distinct from a species. ▷ **HISTORY** Latin *individuus* indivisible ▶ **individually** *adv*

individualism *n* **1** the principle of leading one's life in one's own way. **2** same as **laissez faire**. **3** egotism. ▶ **individualist** *n* ▶ **individualistic** *adj*

individuality *n, pl* **-ties 1** distinctive or unique character or personality: *a house of great individuality.* **2** the qualities that distinguish one person or thing from another. **3** a separate existence.

indivisible *adj* **1** unable to be divided. **2** *Maths* leaving a remainder when divided by a given number.

indoctrinate *vb* **-nating, -nated** to teach (someone) systematically to accept a doctrine or opinion uncritically. ▶ **indoctrination** *n*

Indo-European *adj* **1** of a family of languages spoken in most of Europe and much of Asia, including English, Russian, and Hindi. ✧ *n* **2** the Indo-European family of languages.

indolent *adj* lazy; idle. ▷ **HISTORY** Latin *indolens* not feeling pain ▶ **indolence** *n*

indomitable *adj* too strong to be defeated or discouraged: *an indomitable work ethic.* ▷ **HISTORY** Latin *indomitus* untamable

Indonesian *adj* **1** of Indonesia. ✧ *n* **2** a person from Indonesia.

indoor *adj* situated, happening, or used inside a building: *an indoor pool.*

indoors *adv, adj* inside or into a building.

indubitable (in-**dew**-bit-a-bl) *adj* beyond doubt; definite. ▷ **HISTORY** Latin *in-* not + *dubitare* to doubt ▶ **indubitably** *adv*

induce *vb* **-ducing, -duced 1** to persuade or use influence on. **2** to cause or bring about. **3** *Med* to cause (labour) to begin by the use of drugs or other means. **4** *Logic obsolete* to draw (a general conclusion) from particular instances. **5** to produce (an electromotive force or electrical current) by induction. **6** to transmit (magnetism) by induction. ▷ **HISTORY** Latin *inducere* to lead in ▶ **inducible** *adj*

inducement *n* **1** something that encourages someone to do something. **2** the act of inducing.

induct *vb* **1** to bring in formally or install in a job, rank, or position. **2** to initiate in knowledge of (a group or profession): *boys are inducted into the world of men.* ▷ **HISTORY** Latin *inductus* led in

inductance *n* the property of an electric circuit as a result of which an electromotive force is created by a change of current in the same or in a neighbouring circuit.

induction *n* **1** *Logic* a process of reasoning by which a general conclusion is drawn from particular instances. **2** *Med* the process of inducing labour. **3** the process by which electrical or magnetic properties are transferred, without physical contact, from one circuit or body to another. **4** a formal introduction or entry into an office or position. **5** (in an internal-combustion engine) the drawing in of mixed air and fuel from the carburettor to the cylinder. ▶ **inductional** *adj*

induction coil *n* a transformer for producing a high voltage from a low voltage. It consists of a soft-iron core, a primary coil of few turns, and a concentric secondary coil of many turns.

induction course *n* a training course to help familiarize someone with a new job.

inductive *adj* **1** *Logic* of or using induction: *inductive reasoning.* **2** of or operated by electrical or magnetic induction.

inductor *n* a device designed to create inductance in an electrical circuit.

indulge *vb* **-dulging, -dulged 1** (often foll. by *in*) to yield to or gratify (a whim or desire for): *to indulge in new clothes.* **2** to allow (someone) to have or do everything he or she wants: *he had given her* *too much, indulged her in everything.* **3** to allow (oneself) the pleasure of something: *he indulged himself.* **4** *Informal* to take alcoholic drink. ▷ HISTORY Latin *indulgere* to concede

indulgence *n* **1** something that is allowed because it gives pleasure; extravagance. **2** the act of indulging oneself or someone else. **3** liberal or tolerant treatment. **4** something granted as a favour or privilege. **5** *RC Church* a remission of the temporal punishment for sin after its guilt has been forgiven.

indulgent *adj* kind or lenient, often to excess. ▶ **indulgently** *adv*

industrial *adj* **1** of, used in, or employed in industry. **2** with an economy relying heavily on industry: *northern industrial cities.*

industrial action *n Brit & Austral* action, such as a strike or work-to-rule, by which workers complain about their conditions.

industrial estate *n Brit & Austral* an area of land set aside for factories and warehouses.

industrialism *n* an organization of society characterized by large-scale manufacturing industry rather than trade or farming.

industrialist *n* a person who owns or controls large amounts of money or property in industry.

industrialize *or* **-ise** *vb* **-izing, -ized** *or* **-ising, -ised** to develop industry on a large scale in (a country or region). ▶ **industrialization** *or* **-isation** *n*

industrial relations *pl n* the relations between management and workers.

Industrial Revolution *n History* **the Industrial Revolution** the transformation in the 18th and 19th centuries of Britain and other countries into industrial nations.

industrious *adj* hard-working.

industry *n, pl* **-tries 1** the work and process involved in manufacture: *Japanese industry increased output considerably last year.* **2** a branch of commercial enterprise concerned with the manufacture of a specified product: *the steel industry.* **3** the quality of working hard. ▷ HISTORY Latin *industrius* active

inebriate *n* **1** a person who is habitually drunk. ✧ *adj* **2** drunk, esp. habitually. ▷ HISTORY Latin *ebrius* drunk ▶ **inebriation** *n*

inebriated *adj* drunk.

inedible *adj* not fit to be eaten.

ineducable (in-**ed**-yuke-a-bl) *adj* incapable of being educated, esp. on account of mental retardation.

ineffable *adj* too great or intense to be expressed in words. ▷ HISTORY Latin *in-* not + *effabilis* utterable ▶ **ineffably** *adv*

ineffectual *adj* having no effect or an inadequate effect: *the raids were costly and ineffectual.*

inefficient *adj* not performing a task or function to the best advantage. ▶ **inefficiency** *n*

inelegant *adj* lacking elegance or refinement.

ineligible *adj* not qualified for or entitled to something.

ineluctable *adj Formal* impossible to avoid: *the ineluctable collapse of the coalition.* ▷ HISTORY Latin *in-* not + *eluctari* to escape

inept *adj* **1** awkward, clumsy, or incompetent. **2** not suitable or fitting; out of place. ▷ HISTORY Latin *in-* not + *aptus* fitting ▶ **ineptitude** *n*

inequality *n, pl* **-ties 1** the state or quality of being unequal. **2** an instance of this. **3** lack of smoothness or regularity of a surface. **4** *Maths* a statement indicating that the value of one quantity or expression is not equal to another.

inequation *n Maths* a mathematical statement showing that two values are not equal, but greater or less than each other.

inequitable *adj* unjust or unfair.

inequity *n, pl* **-ties 1** injustice or unfairness. **2** something which is unjust or unfair.

ineradicable *adj* impossible to remove or root out: *an ineradicable distrust of foreigners.*

inert *adj* **1** without the power to move or to resist motion. **2** inactive or lifeless. **3** having only a limited ability to react chemically. ▷ HISTORY Latin *iners* unskilled

inertia *n* **1** a feeling of unwillingness to do anything. **2** *Physics* the tendency of a body to remain still or continue moving unless a force is applied to it. ▶ **inertial** *adj*

inertia selling *n Brit* the illegal practice of sending unrequested goods to householders, followed by a bill for the goods if they do not return them.

inescapable *adj* not able to be avoided.

inestimable *adj* too great to be calculated.

inevitable *adj* **1** unavoidable; sure to happen. **2** *Informal* so regular as to be predictable: *the inevitable guitar solo.* ✧ *n* **3** (often preceded by *the*) something that is unavoidable. ▷ HISTORY Latin *in-* not + *evitare* to avoid ▶ **inevitability** *n* ▶ **inevitably** *adv*

inexorable *adj* unable to be prevented from continuing or progressing: *an inexorable trend.* ▷ HISTORY Latin *in-* not + *exorare* to prevail upon ▶ **inexorably** *adv*

inexperienced *adj* having no knowledge or experience of a particular situation, activity, etc. ▶ **inexperience** *n*

inexpert *adj* lacking skill.

inexplicable *adj* impossible to explain.

in extremis *adv* **1** in dire straits. **2** at the point of death.

inextricable *adj* **1** impossible to escape from: *an inextricable dilemma.* **2** impossible to disentangle or separate: *an inextricable mass twisted metal.* ▶ **inextricably** *adv*

inf. **1** infantry. **2** infinitive. **3** informal. **4** information.

infallible *adj* **1** incapable of error. **2** always successful: *an infallible cure.* **3** (of the Pope) incapable of error in setting forth matters of doctrine on faith and morals. ▶ **infallibility** *n* ▶ **infallibly** *adv*

A B C D E F G H I J K L M N O P Q R S T U V W X Y Z

infamous (**in**-fam-uss) *adj* well-known for something bad.

infamy *n, pl* **-mies 1** the state of being infamous. **2** an infamous act or event. ▷ **HISTORY** Latin *infamis* of evil repute

infancy *n, pl* **-cies 1** the state or period of being an infant. **2** an early stage of growth or development: *virtual reality is in its infancy.* **3** *Law* the state or period of being a minor.

infant *n* **1** a very young child; baby. **2** *Law* same as **minor** (sense 4). **3** *Brit* a young school child. ✧ *adj* **4** of, relating to, or designed for young children: *infant school.* **5** in an early stage of development: *an infant democracy.*

WORD HISTORY

An infant is literally a child who is too young to have learned to talk. The word comes from Latin *infans*, meaning 'unable to speak', from *in-*, meaning 'not', and *fārī*, meaning 'to speak'.

infanta *n* **1** (formerly) a daughter of a king of Spain or Portugal. **2** the wife of an infante. ▷ **HISTORY** Spanish and Portuguese

infante *n* (formerly) any son of a king of Spain or Portugal, except the heir to the throne. ▷ **HISTORY** Spanish and Portuguese

infanticide *n* **1** the act of killing an infant. **2** a person who kills an infant. ▷ **HISTORY** INFANT + Latin *caedere* to kill

infantile *adj* **1** childishly immature. **2** of infants or infancy.

infantile paralysis *n* same as **poliomyelitis**.

infantry *n, pl* **-tries** soldiers who fight on foot. ▷ **HISTORY** Italian *infanteria*

infant school *n* (in England and Wales) a school for children aged between 5 and 7.

infatuate *vb* **-ating, -ated** to inspire or fill with an intense and unreasoning passion. ▷ **HISTORY** Latin *infatuare* ▶ **infatuation** *n*

infatuated *adj* (often foll. by *with*) carried away by an intense and unreasoning passion for someone.

infect *vb* **1** to contaminate (a person or thing) with a germ or virus or its consequent disease. **2** to taint or contaminate. **3** to affect with an opinion or feeling as if by contagion: *even she was infected by the excitement.* ▷ **HISTORY** Latin *inficere* to stain

infection *n* **1** an infectious disease. **2** contamination of a person or thing by a germ or virus or its consequent disease.

infectious *adj* **1** (of a disease) capable of being transmitted without actual contact. **2** causing or transmitting infection. **3** spreading from one person to another: *infectious laughter.*

infectious mononucleosis *n* same as **glandular fever**.

infer *vb* **-ferring, -ferred 1** to conclude by reasoning from evidence; deduce. **2** *Not universally accepted* to imply or suggest. ▷ **HISTORY** Latin *inferre* to bring into

WORD TIP

The use of *infer* to mean *imply* is common in both speech and writing, but is regarded by many people as incorrect.

inference *n* **1** the act or process of reaching a conclusion by reasoning from evidence. **2** an inferred conclusion or deduction.

inferior *adj* **1** lower in quality, quantity, or usefulness. **2** lower in rank, position, or status. **3** of poor quality. **4** lower in position. **5** *Printing* (of a character) printed at the foot of an ordinary character. ✧ *n* **6** a person inferior to another, esp. in rank. ▷ **HISTORY** Latin: lower ▶ **inferiority** *n*

inferior court *n Law* a court of limited jurisdiction. Compare **superior court**.

inferiority complex *n Psychiatry* a disorder arising from a feeling of inferiority to others, characterized by aggressiveness or extreme shyness.

infernal *adj* **1** of or relating to hell. **2** *Informal* irritating: *stop that infernal noise.* ▷ **HISTORY** Latin *infernus* lower

inferno *n, pl* **-nos 1** an intense raging fire. **2** a place or situation resembling hell, because it is crowded and noisy. **3 the inferno** hell. ▷ **HISTORY** Late Latin *infernus* hell

infertile *adj* **1** not capable of producing offspring. **2** (of soil) not productive; barren. ▶ **infertility** *n*

infest *vb* to inhabit or overrun (a place, plant, etc.) in unpleasantly large numbers: *the area was infested with moles.* ▷ **HISTORY** Latin *infestare* to molest ▶ **infestation** *n*

infidel *n* **1** a person who has no religious belief. **2** a person who rejects a specific religion, esp. Christianity or Islam. ✧ *adj* **3** of unbelievers or unbelief. ▷ **HISTORY** Latin *infidelis* unfaithful

infidelity *n, pl* **-ties 1** sexual unfaithfulness to one's husband, wife, or lover. **2** an act or instance of unfaithfulness.

infield *n* **1** *Cricket* the area of the field near the pitch. **2** *Baseball* the area of the playing field enclosed by the base lines. ▶ **infielder** *n*

infighting *n* **1** rivalry or quarrelling between members of the same group or organization. **2** *Boxing* combat at close quarters.

infiltrate *vb* **-trating, -trated 1** to enter (an organization, area, etc.) gradually and in secret, so as to gain influence or control: *they infiltrated the party structure.* **2** to pass (a liquid or gas) through (a substance) by filtering or (of a liquid or gas) to pass through (a substance) by filtering. ▶ **infiltrator** *n*

infiltration *n* **1** the act of entering (an organization, area, etc.) gradually and in secret, so as to gain influence or control. **2** the passing (of a liquid or gas) through (a substance) by filtering. **3** *Geog* the seeping of surface water into the soil.

infinite (**in**-fin-it) *adj* **1** having no limits or boundaries in time, space, extent, or size. **2** extremely or immeasurably great or numerous:

infinite wealth. **3** *Maths* having an unlimited or uncountable number of digits, factors, or terms. ▶ **infinitely** *adv*

infinitesimal *adj* **1** extremely small: *an infinitesimal risk.* **2** *Maths* of or involving a small change in the value of a variable that approaches zero as a limit. ✧ *n* **3** *Maths* an infinitesimal quantity.

infinitive (in-**fin**-it-iv) *n Grammar* a form of the verb which in most languages is not inflected for tense or person and is used without a particular subject: in English, the infinitive usually consists of the word *to* followed by the verb.

infinity *n, pl* **-ties 1** an infinitely great number or amount. **2** endless time, space, or quantity. **3** *Maths* the concept of a value greater than any finite numerical value.

infirm *adj* physically or mentally weak, esp. from old age.

infirmary *n, pl* **-ries** a place for the treatment of the sick or injured; hospital.

infirmity *n, pl* **-ties 1** the state of being infirm. **2** physical weakness or frailty.

infix *vb* **1** to fix firmly in. **2** to instil or impress on the mind by repetition. ▶ **infixation** *or* **infixion** *n*

in flagrante delicto (in flag-**grant**-ee dee-**lick**-toe) *adv Chiefly law* while committing the offence. ▷ **HISTORY** Latin

inflame *vb* **-flaming, -flamed 1** to make angry or excited. **2** to increase or intensify; aggravate. **3** to produce inflammation in or become inflamed. **4** to set or be set on fire.

inflammable *adj* **1** liable to catch fire. **2** easily aroused to anger or passion. ▶ **inflammability** *n*

> ☑ **WORD TIP**
> See at **flammable.**

inflammation *n* **1** the reaction of living tissue to injury or infection, characterized by heat, redness, swelling, and pain. **2** an inflaming or being inflamed.

inflammatory *adj* **1** likely to provoke anger. **2** characterized by or caused by inflammation.

inflatable *adj* **1** capable of being inflated. ✧ *n* **2** a plastic or rubber object which can be inflated.

inflate *vb* **-flating, -flated 1** to expand or cause to expand by filling with gas or air. **2** to give an impression of greater importance than is justified: *something to inflate their self-esteem.* **3** to cause or undergo economic inflation. ▷ **HISTORY** Latin *inflare* to blow into

inflation *n* **1** an inflating or being inflated. **2** *Econ* a progressive increase in the general level of prices brought about by an increase in the amount of money in circulation or by increases in costs. **3** *Informal* the rate of increase of prices. ▶ **inflationary** *adj*

inflect *vb* **1** to change (the voice) in tone or pitch. **2** *Grammar* to change (the form of a word) by inflection. **3** to bend or curve. ▷ **HISTORY** Latin *inflectere* to curve, alter ▶ **inflective** *adj*

inflection *or* **inflexion** *n* **1** a change in the pitch of the voice. **2** *Grammar* a change in the form of a word, signalling change in such grammatical functions as tense or number. **3** an angle or bend. **4** an inflecting or being inflected. **5** *Maths* a change in curvature from concave to convex or vice versa. ▶ **inflectional** *or* **inflexional** *adj*

inflexible *adj* **1** unwilling to be persuaded; obstinate. **2** (of a rule etc.) firmly fixed: *inflexible schedules.* **3** incapable of being bent: *inflexible joints.* ▶ **inflexibility** *n*

inflict *vb* **1** to impose (something unpleasant) on. **2** to deliver (a blow or wound). ▷ **HISTORY** Latin *infligere* to strike (something) against ▶ **infliction** *n* ▶ **inflictor** *n*

inflorescence *n Bot* **1** the arrangement of the flowers on the stalks. **2** the part of a plant that consists of the flower-bearing stalks. **3** the process of flowering; blossoming. ▷ **HISTORY** Latin *in-* into + *florescere* to bloom

inflow *n* **1** something, such as a liquid or gas, that flows in. **2** the act of flowing in; influx.

influence *n* **1** an effect of one person or thing on another. **2** the power of a person or thing to have such an effect. **3** power resulting from ability, wealth, or position. **4** a person or thing with influence. **5 under the influence** *Informal* drunk. ✧ *vb* **-encing, -enced 6** to have an effect upon (actions or events). **7** to persuade or induce. ▷ **HISTORY** Latin *influere* to flow into

influential *adj* having or exerting influence.

influenza *n* a highly contagious viral disease characterized by fever, muscular pains, and catarrh. ▷ **HISTORY** Italian: influence, hence incursion, epidemic

influx *n* **1** the arrival or entry of many people or things. **2** the act of flowing in. ▷ **HISTORY** Latin *influere* to flow into

info *n Informal* short for **information**.

inform *vb* **1** to give information to; tell: *he informed me that he would be free after lunch.* **2** to make knowledgeable (about) or familiar (with): *he'll be informed of his rights.* **3** to give incriminating information to the police. **4** to impart some essential or formative characteristic to. **5** to animate or inspire. ▷ **HISTORY** Latin *informare* to describe ▶ **informed** *adj*

informal *adj* **1** relaxed and friendly: *an informal interview.* **2** appropriate to everyday life or use rather than formal occasions: *informal clothes.* **3** (of speech or writing) appropriate to ordinary conversation rather than to formal written language. ▶ **informality** *n* ▶ **informally** *adv*

informant *n* a person who gives information.

information *n* **1** knowledge acquired in any manner; facts. **2** *Computers* **a** the meaning given to data by the way it is interpreted. **b** same as **data** (sense 2).

information superhighway *n* the concept of a worldwide network of computers transferring information at high speed.

information technology *n* the production, storage, and communication of information using computers and electronic technology.

A B C D E F G H I J K L M N O P Q R S T U V W X Y Z

information theory *n* the study of the processes of communication and the transmission of information.
informative *adj* giving useful information.
informer *n* a person who informs to the police.
infra dig *adj Informal* beneath one's dignity. ▷ **HISTORY** Latin *infra dignitatem*
infrared *adj* **1** of or using rays with a wavelength just beyond the red end of the visible spectrum. ✧ *n* **2** the infrared part of the spectrum. ▷ **HISTORY** Latin *infra* beneath
infrasonic *adj* having a frequency below the range audible to the human ear. ▷ **HISTORY** Latin *infra* beneath
infrasound *n* infrasonic waves.
infrastructure *n* **1** the basic structure of an organization or system. **2** the stock of facilities, services, and equipment in a country, including factories, roads, and schools, that are needed for it to function properly. ▷ **HISTORY** Latin *infra* beneath
infrequent *adj* not happening often. ▶ **infrequently** *adv*
infringe *vb* **-fringing, -fringed 1** to violate or break (a law or agreement). **2 infringe on** *or* **upon** to encroach or trespass on: *the press infringed on their privacy.* ▷ **HISTORY** Latin *infringere* to break off ▶ **infringement** *n*
infuriate *vb* **-ating, -ated** to make very angry. ▷ **HISTORY** Medieval Latin *infuriare* ▶ **infuriating** *adj* ▶ **infuriatingly** *adv*
infuse *vb* **-fusing, -fused 1** to fill with (an emotion or quality). **2** to soak or be soaked in order to extract flavour. ▷ **HISTORY** Latin *infundere* to pour into
infusion *n* **1** the act of infusing. **2** a liquid obtained by infusing.
ingenious (in-**jean**-ee-uss) *adj* showing cleverness and originality: *a truly ingenious invention.* ▷ **HISTORY** Latin *ingenium* natural ability
ingenuity (in-jen-**new**-it-ee) *n* cleverness at inventing things. ▷ **HISTORY** Latin *ingenuitas* a freeborn condition; meaning influenced by INGENIOUS
ingenuous (in-**jen**-new-uss) *adj* **1** unsophisticated and trusting. **2** frank and straightforward. ▷ **HISTORY** Latin *ingenuus* freeborn, virtuous
ingest *vb* to take (food or liquid) into the body. ▷ **HISTORY** Latin *ingerere* to put into ▶ **ingestion** *n*
inglenook *n Brit* a corner by a fireplace.
inglorious *adj* dishonourable or shameful.
ingoing *adj* going in; entering.
ingot *n* a piece of metal cast in a form suitable for storage, usually a bar. ▷ **HISTORY** origin unknown
ingrained *or* **engrained** *adj* **1** (of a habit, feeling, or belief) deeply impressed or instilled. **2** (of dirt) worked into or through the fibre or pores. ▷ **HISTORY** *dyed in grain* dyed with kermes through the fibre
ingratiate *vb* **-ating, -ated** to act in order to bring (oneself) into favour (with someone). ▷ **HISTORY** Latin *in-* in + *gratia* favour ▶ **ingratiating** *adj*
ingratitude *n* lack of gratitude or thanks.
ingredient *n* a component of a mixture or compound, esp. in cooking. ▷ **HISTORY** Latin *ingrediens* going into
ingress *n Formal* **1** the act of going or coming in. **2** the right or permission to enter. ▷ **HISTORY** Latin *ingressus*
ingrowing *adj* (esp. of a toenail) growing abnormally into the flesh. ▶ **ingrown** *adj*
inhabit *vb* to live or dwell in. ▷ **HISTORY** Latin *inhabitare* ▶ **inhabitable** *adj*
inhabitant *n* a person or animal that is a permanent resident of a particular place or region.
inhalant (in-**hale**-ant) *n* a medicinal preparation inhaled to help breathing problems.
inhale *vb* **-haling, -haled** to breathe in (air, smoke, or vapour). ▷ **HISTORY** Latin *in-* in + *halare* to breathe ▶ **inhalation** *n*
inhaler *n* a container used to administer an inhalant.
inherent *adj* existing as an inseparable part. ▶ **inherently** *adv*
inherit *vb* **1** to receive money, property, or a title from someone who has died. **2** to receive (a characteristic) from an earlier generation by heredity. **3** to receive (a position or situation) from a predecessor: *he inherited a mess.* ▷ **HISTORY** Old French *enheriter* ▶ **inheritor** *n*
inheritable *adj* **1** capable of being transmitted by heredity from one generation to a later one. **2** capable of being inherited.
inheritance *n* **1** *Law* **a** hereditary succession to an estate or title. **b** the right of an heir to succeed on the death of an ancestor. **2** something inherited or to be inherited. **3** the act of inheriting. **4** the fact of receiving characteristics from an earlier generation by heredity.
inheritance tax *n* (in Britain) a tax consisting of a percentage levied on the part of an inheritance that exceeds a specified allowance.
inhibit *vb* **1** to restrain or hinder (an impulse or desire). **2** to prohibit or prevent: *an attempt to inhibit nuclear proliferation.* **3** *Chem* to stop, prevent, or decrease the rate of (a chemical reaction). ▷ **HISTORY** Latin *inhibere* ▶ **inhibited** *adj* ▶ **inhibitor** *n*
inhibition *n* **1** *Psychol* a feeling of fear or embarrassment that stops one from behaving naturally. **2** an inhibiting or being inhibited. **3** the process of stopping or retarding a chemical reaction.
inhospitable *adj* **1** not welcoming; unfriendly. **2** (of a place or climate) not easy to live in; harsh.
inhuman *adj* **1** cruel or brutal. **2** not human.
inhumane *adj* extremely cruel or brutal.
inhumanity *n, pl* **-ties 1** lack of kindness or compassion. **2** an inhumane act.
inimical *adj* **1** adverse or unfavourable: *inimical to change.* **2** unfriendly or hostile. ▷ **HISTORY** Latin *in-* not + *amicus* friendly
inimitable *adj* impossible to imitate. ▶ **inimitably** *adv*

iniquity *n, pl* **-ties 1** injustice or wickedness. **2** a wicked act. ▷ HISTORY Latin *iniquus* unfair ▶ **iniquitous** *adj*

initial *adj* **1** of or at the beginning. ✧ *n* **2** the first letter of a word, esp. a person's name. **3** *Printing* a large letter set at the beginning of a chapter or work. ✧ *vb* **-tialling, -tialled** *or US* **-tialing, -tialed 4** to sign with one's initials, esp. to indicate approval. ▷ HISTORY Latin *initium* beginning ▶ **initially** *adv*

initiate *vb* **-ating, -ated 1** to begin or set going: *more women initiate divorce today.* **2** to accept (new members) into a group, often through secret ceremonies. **3** to teach the fundamentals of a skill or knowledge to (someone). ✧ *n* **4** a person who has been initiated, esp. recently. **5** a beginner. ▷ HISTORY Latin *initiare* ▶ **initiation** *n* ▶ **initiator** *n*

initiative *n* **1** a first step; commencing move: *a peace initiative.* **2** the right or power to initiate something: *it forced local people to take the initiative.* **3** enterprise: *the drive and initiative to create new products.* **4 on one's own initiative** without being prompted.

inject *vb* **1** *Med* to put (a fluid) into the body with a syringe. **2** to introduce (a new element): *to inject a dose of realism into the assessment.* ▷ HISTORY Latin *injicere* to throw in ▶ **injection** *n*

injudicious *adj* showing poor judgment; unwise.

injunction *n* **1** *Law* a court order not to do something. **2** an authoritative command. ▷ HISTORY Latin *injungere* to enjoin ▶ **injunctive** *adj*

injure *vb* **-juring, -jured 1** to hurt physically or mentally. **2** to do wrong to (a person), esp. by an injustice: *the injured party.* **3** to damage: *an opportunity to injure your reputation.* ▶ **injured** *adj*

injurious *adj* **1** causing harm. **2** abusive, slanderous, or libellous.

injury *n, pl* **-ries 1** physical hurt. **2** a specific instance of this: *a leg injury.* **3** harm done to the feelings. **4** damage: *inflict no injury on the wealth of the nation.* ▷ HISTORY Latin *injuria* injustice

injury time *n Sport* playing time added at the end of a match to compensate for time spent treating injured players. Also called: **stoppage time**

injustice *n* **1** unfairness. **2** an unfair action.

ink *n* **1** a black or coloured liquid used for printing, writing, and drawing. **2** a dark brown fluid squirted for self-concealment by an octopus or cuttlefish. ✧ *vb* **3** to mark or cover with ink. **4 ink in** to arrange or confirm definitely. ▷ HISTORY Old French *enque*

inkling *n* a vague idea or suspicion. ▷ HISTORY Middle English *inclen* to hint at

inky *adj* **inkier, inkiest 1** dark or black, like ink. **2** stained with ink. ▶ **inkiness** *n*

inlaid *adj* **1** set in another material so that the surface is smooth, such as a design in wood. **2** made in this way: *an inlaid table-top.*

inland *adj* **1** of or in the interior of a country or region, away from a sea or border. **2** *Chiefly Brit* operating within a country or region; domestic: *inland trade.* ✧ *n* **3** the interior of a country or region. ✧ *adv* **4** towards or into the interior of a country or region.

Inland Revenue *n* (in Britain and New Zealand) a government department that collects major direct taxes, such as income tax.

inlay *vb* **-laying, -laid 1** to decorate (an article, esp. of furniture) by inserting pieces of wood, ivory, or metal so that the surfaces are smooth and flat. ✧ *n* **2** decoration made by inlaying. **3** an inlaid article. **4** *Dentistry* a filling shaped to fit a cavity.

inlet *n* **1** a narrow strip of water extending from the sea into the land. **2** a passage or valve through which a liquid or gas enters a machine.

in loco parentis (par-**rent**-iss) in place of a parent: said of a person acting for a parent. ▷ HISTORY Latin

inmate *n* a person who is confined to an institution such as a prison or hospital.

in media res *adv Literature* in or into the middle of events or a narrative; used of books which start in the middle of events and then make use of flashback. ▷ HISTORY literally: into the midst of things, taken from a passage in Horace's *Ars Poetica*

inmost *adj* same as **innermost**.

inn *n* a pub or small hotel providing food and accommodation. ▷ HISTORY Old English

innards *pl n Informal* **1** the internal organs of the body, esp. the entrails. **2** the working parts of a machine. ▷ HISTORY variant of *inwards*

innate *adj* existing from birth, rather than acquired; inborn: *his innate decency.* ▷ HISTORY Latin *innasci* to be born in ▶ **innately** *adv*

inner *adj* **1** happening or located inside or further inside: *the door to the inner office.* **2** of the mind or spirit: *her inner self.* **3** exclusive or private: *the inner sanctum of the party secretariat.* **4** more profound; less apparent: *the inner meaning.* ✧ *n* **5** *Archery* **a** the red innermost ring on a target. **b** a shot which hits this ring.

inner child *n Psychol* the part of the psyche that retains the feelings as they were experienced in childhood.

inner city *n* the parts of a city in or near its centre, where there are often social and economic problems.

innermost *adj* **1** most intimate or private: *innermost secrets.* **2** furthest within.

inner tube *n* an inflatable rubber tube inside a pneumatic tyre casing.

inning *n Baseball* a division of the game consisting of a turn at batting and a turn in the field for each side. ▷ HISTORY Old English *innung* a going in

innings *n* **1** *Cricket* **a** the batting turn of a player or team. **b** the runs scored during such a turn. **2** a period of opportunity or action.

innkeeper *n* an owner or manager of an inn.

innocence *n* the quality or state of being innocent. ▷ HISTORY Latin *innocentia* harmlessness

innocent *adj* **1** not guilty of a particular crime. **2** without experience of evil. **3** harmless or innocuous. **4 innocent of** without or lacking:

a b c d e f g h i j k l m n o p q r s t u v w x y z

innocent of prejudice. ✧ *n* **5** an innocent person, esp. a young child or a naive adult. ▶ **innocently** *adv*

innocuous *adj* having no adverse or harmful effect. ▷ HISTORY Latin *innocuus*

innovate *vb* **-vating, -vated** to introduce new ideas or methods. ▷ HISTORY Latin *innovare* to renew ▶ **innovative** *or* **innovatory** *adj* ▶ **innovator** *n*

innovation *n* **1** something newly introduced, such as a new method or device. **2** the act of innovating.

innuendo *n, pl* **-dos** *or* **-does** an indirect or subtle reference to something rude or unpleasant. ▷ HISTORY Latin: by hinting

Innuit (**in**-new-it) *n* same as **Inuit**.

innumerable *adj* too many to be counted. ▶ **innumerably** *adv*

innumerate *adj* having no understanding of mathematics or science. ▶ **innumeracy** *n*

inoculate *vb* **-lating, -lated 1** to protect against disease by injecting with a vaccine. **2** to introduce (microorganisms, esp. bacteria) into (a culture medium). ▷ HISTORY Latin *inoculare* to implant ▶ **inoculation** *n*

inoffensive *adj* causing no harm or annoyance.

inoperable *adj Surgery* unable to be safely operated on: *an inoperable tumour.*

inoperative *adj* not working or functioning: *continued shelling has rendered the ceasefire inoperative.*

inopportune *adj* badly timed or inappropriate.

inordinate *adj* **1** excessive: *an inordinate amount of time spent arguing.* **2** unrestrained, as in behaviour or emotion: *inordinate anger.* ▷ HISTORY Latin *inordinatus* disordered ▶ **inordinately** *adv*

inorganic *adj* **1** not having the structure or characteristics of living organisms. **2** *Chem* of or denoting chemical compounds that do not contain carbon. **3** not resulting from or produced by growth; artificial: *inorganic fertilizers.*

inorganic chemistry *n* the branch of chemistry concerned with the elements and compounds which do not contain carbon.

inpatient *n* a patient who stays in a hospital for treatment.

input *n* **1** resources, such as money, labour, or power, put into a project. **2** *Computers* the data fed into a computer. ✧ *vb* **-putting, -put 3** to enter (data) in a computer.

inquest *n* **1** an official inquiry into an unexplained, sudden, or violent death, held by a coroner. **2** *Informal* an investigation or discussion. ▷ HISTORY Latin *in-* into + *quaesitus* investigation

inquietude *n Formal* restlessness or anxiety.

inquire *or* **enquire** *vb* **-quiring, -quired 1** to seek information (about). **2 inquire into** to make an investigation. **3 inquire after** to ask about the health or progress of (a person). **4 inquire of** to ask (a person) for information: *I'll inquire of my aunt when she is coming.* ▷ HISTORY Latin *inquirere* ▶ **inquirer** *or* **enquirer** *n*

inquiry *or* **enquiry** *n, pl* **-ries 1** a question. **2** an investigation.

inquisition *n* **1** a thorough investigation. **2** an official inquiry, esp. one held by a jury before an officer of the Crown. ▶ **inquisitional** *adj*

Inquisition *n History* an organization within the Catholic Church (1232–1820) for suppressing heresy.

inquisitive *adj* **1** excessively curious about other people's business. **2** eager to learn. ▶ **inquisitively** *adv* ▶ **inquisitiveness** *n*

inquisitor *n* **1** a person who inquires, esp. deeply or ruthlessly. **2 Inquisitor** an officer of the Inquisition.

inquisitorial *adj* **1** of or like an inquisition or an inquisitor. **2** offensively curious. ▶ **inquisitorially** *adv*

inquisitorial system *n Law* a legal system in which it is the duty of judges to investigate cases and to try to ascertain the truth; usual in countries where the legal system is based on civil law. Compare **adversarial system**.

inquorate *adj* without enough people present to make a quorum.

in re (in **ray**) *prep* in the matter of; concerning. ▷ HISTORY Latin

INRI Jesus of Nazareth, king of the Jews (the inscription placed over Christ's head during the Crucifixion). ▷ HISTORY Latin *Iesus Nazarenus Rex Iudaeorum*

inroads *pl n* **make inroads into** to start affecting or reducing: *my gambling has made great inroads into my savings.*

ins. 1 inches. **2** insurance.

insane *adj* **1** mentally ill. **2** stupidly irresponsible: *acting on an insane impulse.* ▶ **insanely** *adv*

insanitary *adj* dirty or unhealthy.

insanity *n, pl* **-ties 1** the state of being insane. **2** stupidity.

insatiable (in-**saysh**-a-bl) *adj* impossible to satisfy. ▶ **insatiability** *n* ▶ **insatiably** *adv*

inscribe *vb* **-scribing, -scribed 1** to mark or engrave with (words, symbols, or letters). **2** to write one's name, and sometimes a brief dedication, on (a book) before giving to someone. **3** to enter (a name) on a list. **4** *Geom* to draw (a geometric construction) inside another construction so that the two are in contact at as many points as possible but do not intersect. ▷ HISTORY Latin *inscribere*

inscription *n* **1** something inscribed, esp. words carved or engraved on a coin, tomb, or ring. **2** a signature or brief dedication in a book or on a work of art.

inscrutable *adj* mysterious or enigmatic. ▷ HISTORY Latin *in-* not + *scrutari* to examine ▶ **inscrutability** *n*

insect *n* **1** a small animal that has six legs and usually has wings, such as an ant, fly or butterfly. **2** (loosely) any similar invertebrate, such as a spider, tick, or centipede. ▷ HISTORY Latin *insectum* (animal that has been) cut into

insecticide *n* a substance used to destroy insects. ▷ HISTORY *insect* + Latin *caedere* to kill

insectivore *n* **1** a small mammal, such as a hedgehog or a shrew, that eats invertebrates. **2** a plant or animal that eats insects. ▷ **HISTORY** *insect* + Latin *vorare* to swallow ▶ **insectivorous** *adj*

insecure *adj* **1** anxious or uncertain. **2** not adequately protected: *low-paid or insecure employment.* **3** unstable or shaky. ▶ **insecurity** *n*

inselberg *n Geog* an isolated rocky hill rising abruptly from a flat plain. ▷ **HISTORY** German *Insel* island + *Berg* mountain

inseminate *vb* **-nating, -nated** to impregnate (a female) with semen. ▷ **HISTORY** Latin *in-* in + *semen* seed ▶ **insemination** *n*

insensate *adj* **1** lacking sensation or consciousness. **2** insensitive or unfeeling. **3** foolish.

insensible *adj* **1** unconscious. **2** without feeling. **3 insensible of** *or* **to** unaware of or indifferent to: *insensible to suffering.* **4** imperceptible. ▶ **insensibility** *n*

insensitive *adj* unaware of or ignoring other people's feelings. ▶ **insensitivity** *n*

inseparable *adj* **1** constantly together because of mutual liking: *they became inseparable companions.* **2** too closely connected to be separated. ▶ **inseparably** *adv*

insert *vb* **1** to place or fit (something) inside something else. **2** to introduce (a clause or comment) into text or a speech. ✧ *n* **3** something inserted, esp. an advertisement in between the pages of a magazine. ▷ **HISTORY** Latin *inserere* to plant in

insertion *n* **1** the act of inserting. **2** something inserted, such as an advertisement in a newspaper.

inset *vb* **-setting, -set 1** to place in or within; insert. ✧ *n* **2** something inserted. **3** *Printing* a small map or diagram set within the borders of a larger one. ✧ *adj* **4** decorated with something inserted.

inshore *adj* **1** in or on the water, but close to the shore: *inshore fishermen.* ✧ *adv, adj* **2** towards the shore from the water: *the boat was forced inshore; an inshore wind dashes the boats.*

inside *prep* **1** in or to the interior of: *a bomb had gone off inside the parliament building.* **2** in a period of time less than: *they took the lead inside seven minutes.* ✧ *adj* **3** on or of the inside: *an article on the paper's inside pages.* **4** by or from someone within an organization, esp. illicitly: *inside information.* **5** of or being the lane in a road which is nearer the side than other lanes going in the same direction: *all the lorries were in the inside lane.* ✧ *adv* **6** on, in, or to the inside; indoors: *when the rain started we took our drinks inside.* **7** *Brit, Austral & NZ slang* in or into prison. ✧ *n* **8** the inner side, surface, or part of something. **9 inside out** with the inside facing outwards. **10 know inside out** to know thoroughly. ✧ See also **insides**.

> **WORD TIP**
> See at **outside.**

insider *n* a member of a group or organization who therefore has exclusive information about it.

insider dealing *n* the illegal practice of a person on the stock exchange or in the civil service taking advantage of early confidential information in order to deal in shares for personal profit.

insides *pl n Informal* the stomach and bowels.

insidious *adj* working in a subtle or apparently harmless way, but nevertheless dangerous or deadly: *an insidious virus.* ▷ **HISTORY** Latin *insidiae* an ambush ▶ **insidiously** *adv* ▶ **insidiousness** *n*

insight *n* **1** a penetrating understanding, as of a complex situation or problem. **2** the ability to perceive clearly or deeply the inner nature of things.

insignia (in-**sig**-nee-a) *n, pl* **-nias** *or* **-nia** a badge or emblem of membership, office, or honour. ▷ **HISTORY** Latin: badges

insignificant *adj* having little or no importance. ▶ **insignificance** *n*

insincere *adj* pretending what one does not feel. ▶ **insincerely** *adv* ▶ **insincerity** *n*

insinuate *vb* **-ating, -ated 1** to suggest indirectly by allusion, hints, or innuendo. **2** to get (someone, esp. oneself) into a position by gradual manoeuvres: *she insinuated herself into the conversation.* ▷ **HISTORY** Latin *insinuare* to wind one's way into

insinuation *n* **1** an indirect or devious hint or suggestion. **2** an act or the practice of insinuating.

insipid *adj* **1** dull and boring. **2** lacking flavour. ▷ **HISTORY** Latin *in-* not + *sapidus* full of flavour ▶ **insipidity** *n*

insist *vb* (often foll. by *on* or *upon*) **1** to make a determined demand (for): *he insisted on his rights.* **2** to express a convinced belief (in) or assertion (of): *she insisted that she had been given permission.* ▷ **HISTORY** Latin *insistere* to stand upon, urge

insistent *adj* **1** making continual and persistent demands. **2** demanding attention: *the chirruping of an insistent bird.* ▶ **insistence** *n* ▶ **insistently** *adv*

in situ *adv, adj* in the original position. ▷ **HISTORY** Latin

in so far as *or* **insofar as** *prep* to the degree or extent that.

insolation *n* **1** *Geog* the quantity of solar radiation falling upon a body or planet, esp. per unit area. **2** exposure to the sun's rays. **3** another name for **sunstroke**.

insole *n* **1** the inner sole of a shoe or boot. **2** a loose inner sole used to give extra warmth or to make a shoe fit.

insolent *adj* rude and disrespectful. ▷ **HISTORY** Latin *in-* not + *solere* to be accustomed ▶ **insolence** *n* ▶ **insolently** *adv*

insoluble *adj* **1** impossible to solve. **2** not able to be dissolved. ▶ **insolubility** *n*

insolvent *adj* **1** unable to pay one's debts. ✧ *n* **2** a person who is insolvent. ▶ **insolvency** *n*

insomnia *n* inability to sleep. ▷ **HISTORY** Latin *in-* not + *somnus* sleep ▶ **insomniac** *n, adj*

insomuch *adv* **1** (foll. by *as* or *that*) to such an extent or degree. **2** (foll. by *as*) because of the fact (that).

insouciant *adj* carefree or unconcerned. ▷ **HISTORY** French ▶ **insouciance** *n*

A B C D E F G H I J K L M N O P Q R S T U V W X Y Z

inspan *vb* **-spanning, -spanned** *Chiefly S African* **1** to harness (animals) to (a vehicle); yoke. **2** to press (people) into service. ▷ **HISTORY** Middle Dutch *inspannen*

inspect *vb* **1** to examine closely, esp. for faults or errors. **2** to examine officially. ▷ **HISTORY** Latin *inspicere* ▶ **inspection** *n*

inspector *n* **1** an official who checks that things or places meet certain regulations and standards. **2** a police officer ranking below a superintendent and above a sergeant.

inspectorate *n* **1** a group of inspectors. **2** the position or duties of an inspector.

inspiration *n* **1** stimulation of the mind or feelings to activity or creativity. **2** a person or thing that causes this state. **3** an inspired idea or action. **4** *Biol* the action of drawing air or gas into the lungs. ▶ **inspirational** *adj*

inspire *vb* **-spiring, -spired 1** to stimulate (a person) to activity or creativity. **2** to arouse (an emotion or a reaction): *he inspires confidence.* **3** *Biol* to draw air or gas into the lungs. ▷ **HISTORY** Latin *in-* into + *spirare* to breathe

inst. *Old-fashioned* instant (this month).

instability *n* lack of steadiness or reliability.

install *vb* **1** to put in and prepare (equipment) for use. **2** to place (a person) formally in a position or rank. **3** to settle (a person, esp. oneself) in a position or state: *Tony installed himself in an armchair.* ▷ **HISTORY** Medieval Latin *installare*

installation *n* **1** installing. **2** equipment that has been installed. **3** a place containing equipment for a particular purpose: *radar installation.*

installment plan *n US* same as **hire-purchase**. Also (Canad): **instalment plan**

instalment *or US* **installment** *n* **1** one of the portions into which a debt is divided for payment at regular intervals. **2** a portion of something that is issued, broadcast, or published in parts. ▷ **HISTORY** probably from Old French *estal* something fixed

instance *n* **1** a case or particular example. **2 for instance** as an example. **3 in the first instance** in the first place; initially. **4** urgent request or order: *at the instance of.* ✧ *vb* **-stancing, -stanced 5** to mention as an example. ▷ **HISTORY** Latin *instantia* a being close upon

instant *n* **1** a very brief time; moment. **2** a particular moment: *at the same instant.* ✧ *adj* **3** immediate. **4** (of foods) able to be prepared very quickly and easily: *instant coffee.* **5** urgent or pressing. **6** of the present month: *a letter of the 7th instant.* ▷ **HISTORY** Latin *instans* present, pressing closely

instantaneous *adj* happening at once: *the applause was instantaneous.* ▶ **instantaneously** *adv*

instantly *adv* immediately.

instead *adv* **1** as a replacement or substitute for the person or thing mentioned. **2 instead of** in place of or as an alternative to. ▷ **HISTORY** *in stead* in place

instep *n* **1** the middle part of the foot forming the arch between the ankle and toes. **2** the part of a shoe or stocking covering this.

instigate *vb* **-gating, -gated 1** to cause to happen: *to instigate rebellion.* **2** to urge on to some action. ▷ **HISTORY** Latin *instigare* ▶ **instigation** *n* ▶ **instigator** *n*

instil *or US* **instill** *vb* **-stilling, -stilled 1** to introduce (an idea or feeling) gradually in someone's mind. **2** *Rare* to pour in or inject drop by drop. ▷ **HISTORY** Latin *instillare* to pour in a drop at a time ▶ **instillation** *n* ▶ **instiller** *n*

instinct *n* **1** the inborn tendency to behave in a particular way without the need for thought: *maternal instinct.* **2** natural reaction: *my first instinct was to get out of the car.* **3** intuition: *Mr Barr's mother said she knew by instinct that her son was safe.* ▷ **HISTORY** Latin *instinctus* roused

instinctive *or* **instinctual** *adj* done or happening without any logical thought: *an instinctive understanding of people.* ▶ **instinctively** *or* **instinctually** *adv*

institute *n* **1** an organization set up for a specific purpose, especially research or teaching. **2** the building where such an organization is situated. **3** a rule, custom, or precedent. ✧ *vb* **-tuting, -tuted 4** to start or establish. **5** to install in a position or office. ▷ **HISTORY** Latin *instituere,* from *statuere* to place

institution *n* **1** a large important organization such as a university or bank. **2** a hospital etc. for people with special needs. **3** an established custom, law, or principle: *the institution of marriage.* **4** *Informal* a well-established person or feature: *the programme has became an institution.* **5** an instituting or being instituted.

institutional *adj* **1** of or relating to an institution: *institutional care.* **2** dull, routine, and uniform: *institutional meals.* ▶ **institutionalism** *n*

institutionalize *or* **-ise** *vb* **-izing, -ized** *or* **-ising, -ised 1** (*often passive*) to subject (a person) to institutional life, often causing apathy and dependence on routine. **2** to make or become an institution: *institutionalized religion.* **3** to place in an institution.

instruct *vb* **1** to order to do something. **2** to teach (someone) how to do something. **3** to brief (a solicitor or barrister). ▷ **HISTORY** Latin *instruere*

instruction *n* **1** a direction or order. **2** the process or act of teaching. ▶ **instructional** *adj*

instructions *pl n* information on how to do or use something: *the plane had ignored instructions from air traffic controllers.*

instructive *adj* informative or helpful.

instructor *n* **1** a person who teaches something. **2** *US & Canad* a college teacher ranking below assistant professor.

instrument *n* **1** a tool or implement, esp. one used for precision work. **2** *Music* any of various devices that can be played to produce musical sounds. **3** a measuring device to show height, speed, etc.: *the pilot's eyes never left his instruments.* **4** *Informal* a person used by another to gain an end. **5** an important factor in something: *her evidence* *was an instrument in his arrest.* **6** a formal legal document. ▷ **HISTORY** Latin *instrumentum*

instrumental *adj* **1** helping to cause. **2** played by or composed for musical instruments. **3** of or done with an instrument: *instrumental error.*

instrumentalist *n* a person who plays a musical instrument.

instrumentation *n* **1** a set of instruments in a vehicle etc. **2** the arrangement of music for instruments. **3** the list of instruments needed for a piece of music.

instrument panel *n* a panel holding the instruments in a vehicle or on a machine.

insubordinate *adj* not submissive to authority. ▶ **insubordination** *n*

insubstantial *adj* **1** flimsy, fine, or slight. **2** imaginary or unreal.

insufferable *adj* unbearable. ▶ **insufferably** *adv*

insular *adj* **1** not open to change or new ideas: *theatre tradition become rather insular.* **2** of or like an island. ▷ **HISTORY** Latin *insula* island ▶ **insularity** *n*

insulate *vb* **-lating, -lated 1** to prevent or reduce the transfer of electricity, heat, or sound by surrounding or lining with a nonconducting material. **2** to isolate or set apart. ▷ **HISTORY** Late Latin *insulatus* made into an island ▶ **insulator** *n*

insulation *n* **1** material used to insulate something. **2** the act of insulating.

insulin (**in**-syoo-lin) *n* a hormone produced in the pancreas which controls the amount of sugar in the blood. ▷ **HISTORY** Latin *insula* islet (of tissue in the pancreas)

insult *vb* **1** to treat or speak to rudely: *they insulted us and even threatened to kill us.* ✧ *n* **2** an offensive remark or action. **3** a person or thing producing the effect of an insult: *their explanation is an insult to our intelligence.* ▷ **HISTORY** Latin *insultare* to jump upon

insuperable *adj* impossible to overcome; insurmountable. ▶ **insuperability** *n*

insupportable *adj* **1** impossible to tolerate. **2** incapable of being upheld or justified: *an insupportable accusation.*

insurable interest *n Law* a financial or other interest in the life or property covered by an insurance contract, without which the contract cannot be enforced.

insurance *n* **1** the agreement by which one makes regular payments to a company who pay an agreed sum if damage, loss, or death occurs. **2** the money paid for insurance or by an insurance company. **3** a means of protection: *sensible insurance against heart attacks.*

insurance policy *n* a contract of insurance.

insure *vb* **-suring, -sured 1** to guarantee or protect (against risk or loss). **2** (often foll. by *against*) to issue (a person) with an insurance policy or take out an insurance policy (on): *the players were insured against accidents.* **3** *Chiefly US* same as **ensure**. ▶ **insurable** *adj* ▶ **insurability** *n*

insurgent *adj* **1** rebellious or in revolt against an established authority. ✧ *n* **2** a person who takes part in a rebellion. ▷ **HISTORY** Latin *insurgens* rising ▶ **insurgency** *n*

insurmountable *adj* impossible to overcome: *insurmountable problems.*

insurrection *n* the act of rebelling against an established authority. ▷ **HISTORY** Latin *insurgere* to rise up ▶ **insurrectionist** *n, adj*

int. 1 internal. **2** Also: **Int** international.

intact *adj* not changed or damaged in any way. ▷ **HISTORY** Latin *intactus*

intaglio (in-**tah**-lee-oh) *n, pl* **-lios** *or* **-li 1** a seal or gem decorated with an engraved design. **2** an engraved design. ▷ **HISTORY** Italian ▶ **intagliated** *adj*

intake *n* **1** a thing or a quantity taken in: *an intake of students.* **2** the act of taking in. **3** the opening through which fluid or gas enters a pipe or engine.

intangible *adj* **1** difficult for the mind to grasp: *intangible ideas.* **2** incapable of being felt by touch. ▶ **intangibility** *n*

integer *n* any positive or negative whole number or zero, as opposed to a number with fractions or decimals. ▷ **HISTORY** Latin: untouched

integral *adj* **1** being an essential part of a whole. **2** whole or complete. **3** *Maths* **a** of or involving an integral. **b** involving or being an integer. ✧ *n* **4** *Maths* the sum of a large number of minute quantities, summed either between stated limits (**definite integral**) or in the absence of limits (**indefinite integral**).

integral calculus *n Maths* the branch of calculus concerned with the determination of integrals and their use in solving differential equations.

integrand *n Maths* a mathematical function to be integrated.

integrate *vb* **-grating, -grated 1** to make or be made into a whole. **2** to amalgamate (a racial or religious group) with an existing community. **3** to designate (an institution) for use by all races or groups. **4** *Maths* to determine the integral of a function or variable. ▷ **HISTORY** Latin *integrare* ▶ **integration** *n*

integrated circuit *n* a tiny electronic circuit.

integrity *n* **1** honesty. **2** the quality of being whole or united: *respect for a state's territorial integrity.* **3** the quality of being unharmed or sound: *the integrity of the cell membrane.* ▷ **HISTORY** Latin *integritas*

integument *n* any natural protective covering, such as a skin, rind, or shell. ▷ **HISTORY** Latin *integumentum*

intellect *n* **1** the ability to understand, think, and reason. **2** a particular person's mind or intelligence, esp. a brilliant one: *his intellect is wasted on that job.* **3** *Informal* a person who has a brilliant mind. ▷ **HISTORY** Latin *intellectus* comprehension

intellectual *adj* **1** of, involving, or appealing to the intellect: *intellectual literature.* **2** clever or intelligent. ✧ *n* **3** a person who has a highly developed intellect. ▶ **intellectuality** *n* ▶ **intellectually** *adv*

intelligence *n* **1** the ability to understand, learn, and think things out quickly. **2** the collection of secret information, esp. for military purposes. **3** a group or department collecting military information. **4** *Old-fashioned* news or information. ▷ HISTORY Latin *intellegere* to understand, literally: to choose between

intelligence quotient *n* a measure of the intelligence of a person calculated by dividing the person's mental age by his or her actual age and multiplying the result by 100.

intelligent *adj* **1** having or showing intelligence: *an intelligent child; an intelligent guess.* **2** (of a computerized device) able to initiate or modify action in the light of ongoing events. ▶ **intelligently** *adv*

intelligentsia *n* **the intelligentsia** the educated or intellectual people in a society. ▷ HISTORY Russian *intelligentsiya*

intelligible *adj* able to be understood. ▶ **intelligibility** *n*

intemperate *adj* **1** unrestrained or uncontrolled: *intemperate remarks.* **2** drinking alcohol too much or too often. **3** extreme or severe: *an intemperate climate.* ▶ **intemperance** *n*

intend *vb* **1** to propose or plan (something or to do something). **2** to have as one's purpose. **3** to mean to express or indicate: *no criticism was intended.* **4** (often foll. by *for*) to design or destine (for a certain purpose or person): *the plane was never intended for combat.* ▷ HISTORY Latin *intendere* to stretch forth

intended *adj* **1** planned or future. ✧ *n* **2** *Informal* a person whom one is to marry.

intense *adj* **1** of very great force, strength, degree, or amount: *intense heat.* **2** characterized by deep or forceful feelings: *an intense person.* ▷ HISTORY Latin *intensus* stretched ▶ **intensely** *adv* ▶ **intenseness** *n*

> **WORD TIP**
> *Intense* is sometimes wrongly used where *intensive* is meant: *the land is under intensive* (not *intense*) *cultivation. Intensely* is sometimes wrongly used where *intently* is meant: *he listened intently* (not *intensely*).

intensifier *n* a word, esp. an adjective or adverb, that intensifies the meaning of the word or phrase that it modifies, for example, *very* or *extremely*.

intensify *vb* **-fies, -fying, -fied** to make or become intense or more intense. ▶ **intensification** *n*

intensity *n, pl* **-ties 1** the state or quality of being intense. **2** extreme force, degree, or amount. **3** *Physics* the amount or degree of strength of electricity, heat, light, or sound per unit area of volume.

intensive *adj* **1** of or needing concentrated effort or resources: *intensive training.* **2** using one specified factor more than others: *labour-intensive.* **3** *Agriculture* designed to increase production from a particular area: *intensive farming.* **4** *Grammar* of a word giving emphasis, for example, *very* in *the very same.* ▶ **intensively** *adv* ▶ **intensiveness** *n*

> **WORD TIP**
> See at **intense.**

intensive agriculture *or* **farming** *n* *Agriculture* farming that aims for maximum output from the land and involves relatively high capital or labour costs. Compare **extensive agriculture**.

intensive care *n* thorough, continuously supervised treatment of an acutely ill patient in a hospital.

intent *n* **1** something that is intended. **2** *Law* the will or purpose to commit a crime: *loitering with intent.* **3 to all intents and purposes** in almost every respect; virtually. ✧ *adj* **4** having one's attention firmly fixed: *an intent look.* **5 intent on** *or* **upon** strongly resolved on: *intent on winning the election.* ▷ HISTORY Late Latin *intentus* aim ▶ **intently** *adv* ▶ **intentness** *n*

> **WORD TIP**
> See at **intense.**

intention *n* something intended; a plan, idea, or purpose: *he had no intention of resigning.*

intentional *adj* done on purpose. ▶ **intentionally** *adv*

inter (in-**ter**) *vb* **-terring, -terred** to bury (a corpse). ▷ HISTORY Latin *in-* into + *terra* earth

inter- *prefix* **1** between or among: *international.* **2** together, mutually, or reciprocally: *interdependent.* ▷ HISTORY Latin

interact *vb* to act on or in close relation with each other. ▶ **interaction** *n*

interactive *adj Technology* allowing two-way communication between a user and a system such as a computer or television.

interbreed *vb* **-breeding, -bred 1** to breed within a related group so as to produce particular characteristics in the offspring. **2** same as **crossbreed** (sense 1).

intercede *vb* **-ceding, -ceded 1** to plead in favour of. **2** to act as a mediator in order to end a disagreement: *a policeman was watching the beatings without interceding.* ▷ HISTORY Latin *inter-* between + *cedere* to move

intercept *vb* **1** to stop or seize on the way from one place to another. **2** *Maths* to mark off or include (part of a line, curve, plane, or surface) between two points or lines. ✧ *n* **3** *Maths* **a** a point at which two figures intersect. **b** the distance from the origin to the point at which a line, curve, or surface cuts a coordinate axis. ▷ HISTORY Latin *intercipere* to seize before arrival ▶ **interception** *n* ▶ **interceptor** *n*

intercession *n* **1** the act of interceding. **2** a prayer offered to God on behalf of others. ▶ **intercessor** *n*

interchange *vb* **-changing, -changed 1** to change places or cause to change places. ✧ *n* **2** the act of interchanging. **3** a motorway junction of interconnecting roads and bridges designed to prevent streams of traffic crossing one another. ▶ **interchangeable** *adj* ▶ **interchangeably** *adv*

Intercity *adj Trademark* (in Britain) denoting a fast train (service) travelling between cities.

intercom *n* an internal communication system with loudspeakers. ▷ HISTORY short for *intercommunication*

intercommunion *n* association between Churches, involving mutual reception of Holy Communion.

intercontinental *adj* travelling between or linking continents.

intercostal *adj Anat* between the ribs: *an intercostal nerve.*

intercourse *n* **1** the act of having sex. **2** communication or dealings between individuals or groups. ▷ HISTORY Latin *intercurrere* to run between

interdenominational *adj* among or involving more than one denomination of the Christian Church.

interdict *n* **1** *Law* an official prohibition or restraint. **2** *RC Church* the exclusion of a person or place from certain sacraments, although not from communion. ✧ *vb* **3** to prohibit or forbid. ▷ HISTORY Latin *interdicere* to forbid ▶ **interdiction** *n* ▶ **interdictory** *adj*

interdisciplinary *adj* involving more than one branch of learning.

interest *n* **1** curiosity or concern about something or someone. **2** the power of causing this: *to have great interest.* **3** something in which one is interested; a hobby or pursuit. **4** (*often pl*) advantage: *in one's own interests.* **5** money paid for the use of credit or borrowed money: *she borrowed money at 25 per cent interest.* **6** (*often pl*) a right, share, or claim, esp. in a business or property. **7** (*often pl*) a group of people with common aims: *foreign interests.* ✧ *vb* **8** to arouse the curiosity or concern of. **9** to cause to become interested or involved in something. ▷ HISTORY Latin: it concerns

interested *adj* **1** showing or having interest. **2** involved in or affected by: *a consultation paper sent to interested parties.*

interesting *adj* causing interest. ▶ **interestingly** *adv*

interface *n* **1** an area where two things interact or link: *the interface between Islamic culture and Western modernity.* **2** an electrical circuit linking one device, esp. a computer, with another. **3** *Physics, chem* a surface that forms the boundary between two liquids or chemical phases that cannot be mixed. ✧ *vb* **-facing, -faced 4** to connect or be connected with by interface. ▶ **interfacial** *adj*

interfere *vb* **-fering, -fered 1** to try to influence other people's affairs where one is not involved or wanted. **2 interfere with a** to clash with or hinder: *child-bearing may interfere with your career.* **b** *Brit, Austral & NZ euphemistic* to abuse sexually. **3** *Physics* to produce or cause to produce interference. ▷ HISTORY Old French *s'entreferir* to collide ▶ **interfering** *adj*

interference *n* **1** the act of interfering. **2** any undesired signal that interferes with the reception of radio waves. **3** *Physics* the meeting of two waves which reinforce or neutralize each other depending on whether they are in or out of phase.

interferon *n Biochem* a protein made by cells that stops the development of an invading virus.

interfluve *n Geog* a ridge or area of land dividing two river valleys. ▷ HISTORY back formation from *interfluvial,* from INTER- + Latin *fluvius* river ▶ **interfluvial** *adj*

interim *adj* **1** temporary or provisional: *an interim government.* ✧ *n* **2 in the interim** during the intervening time. ▷ HISTORY Latin: meanwhile

interior *n* **1** a part or region that is on the inside: *the interior of the earth.* **2** the inside of a building or room, with respect to design and decoration. **3** the central area of a country or continent, furthest from the sea. **4** a picture of the inside of a room or building. ✧ *adj* **5** of, situated on, or suitable for the inside. **6** mental or spiritual: *interior development.* **7** coming or acting from within. **8** of a nation's domestic affairs. ▷ HISTORY Latin

interior angle *n* an angle of a polygon contained between two adjacent sides.

interj. interjection.

interject *vb* to make (a remark) suddenly or as an interruption. ▷ HISTORY Latin *interjicere* to place between

interjection *n* a word or phrase that is used on its own and which expresses sudden emotion.

interlace *vb* **-lacing, -laced** to join by lacing or weaving together: *interlaced fingers.*

interleave *vb* **-leaving, -leaved** to insert (blank leaves in a book) between other leaves.

interleukin (in-ter-**loo**-kin) *n Biochem* a substance obtained from white blood cells that stimulates their activity against infection and may by used to fight some forms of cancer.

interlink *vb* to connect together.

interlock *vb* **1** to join or be joined firmly together. ✧ *n* **2** a device used to prevent a mechanism from operating independently or unsafely.

interlocking spur *n Geog* one of a series of ridges of land that slant towards each other from alternate sides of a river valley and appear to overlap at their nearest point by the river.

interlocutor (in-ter-**lock**-yew-ter) *n Formal* a person who takes part in a conversation. ▷ HISTORY Latin *inter-* between + *loqui* to talk

interlocutory (in-ter-**lock**-yew-tree) *adj* **1** *Law* pronounced during the course of legal proceedings; provisional: *an interlocutory injunction.* **2** *Formal* of dialogue; conversational.

interloper (**in**-ter-lope-er) *n* a person in a place or situation where he or she has no right to be.

interlude *n* **1** a period of time or different activity between longer periods or events. **2 a** a pause between the acts of a play. **b** a brief piece of music or other entertainment performed during this pause. ▷ HISTORY Latin *inter-* between + *ludus* play

intermarry *vb* **-ries, -rying, -ried 1** (of different races, religions, or social groups) to become connected by marriage. **2** to marry within one's own family or tribe. ▶ **intermarriage** *n*

intermediary *n, pl* **-aries 1** a person who tries to bring about agreement between others. **2** a messenger. ◇ *adj* **3** acting as an intermediary. **4** intermediate.

intermediate *adj* **1** occurring between two points or extremes. **2** (of a class, course, etc.) suitable for learners with some level of skill or competence. ◇ *n* **3** something intermediate. **4** *Chem* a substance formed between the first and final stages of a chemical process. ▷ **HISTORY** Latin *inter-* between + *medius* middle ▶ **intermediation** *n*

interment *n* a burial.

intermezzo (in-ter-**met**-so) *n, pl* **-zos** *or* **-zi 1** a short piece of instrumental music performed between the acts of a play or opera. **2 a** a short composition between two longer movements in an extended musical work. **b** a similar composition intended for independent performance. ▷ **HISTORY** Italian

interminable *adj* seemingly endless because boring: *an interminable, rambling anecdote.* ▶ **interminably** *adv*

intermingle *vb* **-gling, -gled** to mix together.

intermission *n* an interval between parts of a play, film, etc. ▷ **HISTORY** Latin *intermittere* to leave off, cease

intermittent *adj* **1** occurring at intervals. **2** *Geol* (of an active volcano) erupting periodically. ▶ **intermittently** *adv*

intern *vb* **1** to imprison, esp. during wartime. ◇ *n* **2** *Chiefly US* a trainee doctor in a hospital. ▷ **HISTORY** Latin *internus* internal ▶ **internment** *n*

internal *adj* **1** of, situated on, or suitable for the inside. **2** *Anat* affecting or relating to the inside of the body: *internal bleeding.* **3** of a nation's domestic affairs: *internal politics.* **4** coming or acting from within an organization: *an internal reorganization.* **5** spiritual or mental: *internal conflict.* ▷ **HISTORY** Latin *internus* ▶ **internally** *adv*

internal-combustion engine *n* an engine in which power is produced by the explosion of a fuel-and-air mixture within the cylinders.

internal conflict *n Literature* the struggle between a character and his or her own emotions, beliefs, personal dilemmas, or nature. Compare **external conflict**.

internal market *n* a system in which goods and services are sold to a range of purchasers within the same organization, who compete to establish the price.

internal migration *n Sociol* the movement of people settling in another region of the same country or state.

internal rhyme *n Prosody* rhyme that occurs between words within a verse line.

international *adj* **1** of or involving two or more nations. **2** controlling or legislating for several nations: *an international court.* **3** available for use by all nations: *international waters.* ◇ *n* **4** *Sport* **a** a game or match between the national teams of different countries. **b** a member of a national team. ▶ **internationally** *adv*

International *n* any of several international socialist organizations.

International Date Line *n* the line approximately following the 180° meridian from Greenwich on the east side of which the date is one day earlier than on the west.

internationalism *n* the ideal or practice of cooperation and understanding for the good of all nations. ▶ **internationalist** *n*

international law *n Law* the body of rules generally recognized by civilized nations as governing their conduct towards each other and towards each other's subjects.

international migration *n Sociol* the movement of people settling in another country.

International Phonetic Alphabet *n* a series of signs and letters for the representation of human speech sounds.

International Style *or* **Modernism** *n* a 20th-century architectural style characterized by undecorated straight forms and the use of glass, steel, and reinforced concrete.

internecine *adj Formal* destructive to both sides: *internecine war.* ▷ **HISTORY** Latin *internecare* to destroy

internee *n* a person who is interned.

Internet *n* (*sometimes not cap*) a large public-access computer network linked to others worldwide.

internist *n* a physician who specializes in internal medicine.

interphase *n Biol* the period between two divisions of a cell.

interplanetary *adj* of or linking planets.

interplay *n* the action and reaction of things upon each other.

Interpol International Criminal Police Organization: an association of over 100 national police forces, devoted chiefly to fighting international crime.

interpolate (in-**ter**-pole-ate) *vb* **-lating, -lated 1** to insert (a comment or passage) into (a conversation or text). **2** *Maths* to estimate (a value of a function) between the values already known. ▷ **HISTORY** Latin *interpolare* to give a new appearance to ▶ **interpolation** *n*

interpose *vb* **-posing, -posed 1** to place (something) between or among other things. **2** to interrupt (with comments or questions). **3** to put forward so as to interrupt: *he ended the discussion by interposing a veto.* ▷ **HISTORY** Latin *inter-* between + *ponere* to put ▶ **interposition** *n*

interpret *vb* **1** to explain the meaning of. **2** to work out the significance of: *his remarks were widely interpreted as a promise not to raise taxes.* **3** to convey the meaning of (a poem, song, etc.) in performance. **4** to act as an interpreter. ▷ **HISTORY** Latin *interpretari* ▶ **interpretive** *adj*

interpretation *n* **1** the act or result of interpreting or explaining. **2** the particular way in which a performer expresses his or her view of a composition: *an interpretation of Mahler's fourth symphony.* **3** explanation, as of a historical site, provided by the use of original objects, visual display material, etc.

interpreter *n* **1** a person who translates orally from one language into another. **2** *Computers* a program that translates a statement in a source program to machine language and executes it before translating and executing the next statement.

interpretive centre *n* a building situated at a place of interest, such as a country park or historical site, that provides information about the site by showing videos, exhibiting objects, etc.

interquartile range *n Statistics* the difference between the value of two variables, one below which lie 25% of the population and the other below which lie 75% of the population.

interracial *adj* between or among people of different races.

interregnum *n, pl* **-nums** *or* **-na** a period between the end of one ruler's reign and the beginning of the next. ▷ **HISTORY** Latin *inter-* between + *regnum* reign ▶ **interregnal** *adj*

interrelate *vb* **-lating, -lated** to connect (two or more things) or (of two or more things) to become connected to each other. ▶ **interrelation** *n* ▶ **interrelationship** *n*

interrogate *vb* **-gating, -gated** to question (someone) closely. ▷ **HISTORY** Latin *interrogare* ▶ **interrogation** *n* ▶ **interrogator** *n*

interrogative (in-ter-**rog**-a-tiv) *adj* **1** used in asking a question: *an interrogative pronoun.* **2** of or like a question: *an interrogative look.* ✧ *n* **3** an interrogative word, phrase, sentence, or construction.

interrogative clause *n Grammar* a type of clause used to ask a question, e.g. *What's this?* or *Have you met my sister?*

interrupt *vb* **1** to break into (a conversation or discussion) by questions or comment. **2** to stop (a process or activity) temporarily. ▷ **HISTORY** Latin *inter-* between + *rumpere* to break ▶ **interrupted** *adj* ▶ **interruptive** *adj*

interrupter *or* **interruptor** *n* a device for opening and closing an electric circuit.

interruption *n* **1** something that interrupts, such as a comment or question. **2** an interval or intermission. **3** the act of interrupting or the state of being interrupted.

interscholastic *adj* occurring between two or more schools: *an interscholastic competition.*

intersect *vb* **1** (of roads or lines) to cross (each other). **2** to divide or mark off (a place, area, or surface) by passing through or across. ▷ **HISTORY** Latin *intersecare* to divide

intersection *n* **1** a point at which things intersect, esp. a road junction. **2** the act of intersecting or the state of being intersected. **3** *Maths* **a** a point or set of points common to two or more geometric figures. **b** the set of elements that are common to two sets. ▶ **intersectional** *adj*

interstellar *adj* between or among stars.

interstice (in-**ter**-stiss) *n* (*usually pl*) **1** a small gap or crack between things. **2** *Physics* the space between adjacent atoms in a crystal lattice. ▷ **HISTORY** Latin *interstitium* interval

intertextuality *n Literature* the connections between one text and others as a result of imitation, allusion, quotation, and adaptation.

intertwine *vb* **-twining, -twined** to twist together.

interval *n* **1** the period of time between two events. **2** *Brit & Austral* a short period between parts of a play, concert, etc. **3** *Music* the difference of pitch between two notes. **4 at intervals a** now and then: *turn the chicken at intervals.* **b** with a certain amount of space between: *the poles were placed at intervals of twenty metres.* ▷ **HISTORY** Latin *intervallum,* literally: space between two palisades

intervene *vb* **-vening, -vened 1** (often foll. by *in*) to involve oneself in a situation, esp. to prevent conflict. **2** to interrupt a conversation. **3** to happen so as to stop something: *he hoped to play but a serious injury intervened.* **4** to come or be among or between: *ten years had intervened since he had seen Joe.* ▷ **HISTORY** Latin *intervenire* to come between

intervention *n* the act of intervening, esp. to influence or alter a situation in some way. ▶ **interventionist** *n, adj*

interview *n* **1** a formal discussion, esp. one in which an employer assesses a job applicant. **2** a conversation in which a well-known person is asked about his or her views, career, etc., by a reporter. ✧ *vb* **3** to question (someone). ▷ **HISTORY** Old French *entrevue* ▶ **interviewee** *n* ▶ **interviewer** *n*

interwar *adj* of or happening in the period between World War I and World War II.

interweave *vb* **-weaving, -wove** *or* **-weaved, -woven** *or* **-weaved** to weave together.

intestate *adj* **1** (of a person) not having made a will. ✧ *n* **2** a person who dies without having made a will. ▷ **HISTORY** Latin *intestatus* ▶ **intestacy** *n*

intestine *n* the part of the alimentary canal between the stomach and the anus. See **large intestine, small intestine.** ▷ **HISTORY** Latin *intestinus* internal ▶ **intestinal** *adj*

intifada (in-tiff-**ah**-da) *n* the Palestinian uprising against Israel in the West Bank and Gaza Strip. ▷ **HISTORY** Arabic

intimacy *n, pl* **-cies 1** close or warm friendship. **2** (*often pl*) intimate words or acts within a close relationship.

intimate¹ *adj* **1** characterized by a close or warm personal relationship: *an intimate friend.* **2** deeply personal, private, or secret. **3** (of knowledge) extensive and detailed. **4** *Euphemistic* having sexual relations. **5** having a friendly quiet atmosphere: *an intimate nightclub.* ✧ *n* **6** a close friend. ▷ **HISTORY** Latin *intimus* innermost ▶ **intimately** *adv*

intimate² *vb* **-mating, -mated** *Formal* **1** to make (something) known in an indirect way: *he has intimated his intention to retire.* **2** to announce. ▷ **HISTORY** Late Latin *intimare* to proclaim ▶ **intimation** *n*

A B C D E F G H I J K L M N O P Q R S T U V W X Y Z

intimidate *vb* **-dating, -dated** to subdue or influence (someone) through fear. ▷ HISTORY Latin *in-* in + *timidus* fearful ▸ **intimidating** *adj* ▸ **intimidation** *n*

into *prep* **1** to the inner part of: *they went into the house.* **2** to the middle of so as to be surrounded by: *into the bushes.* **3** against; up against: *he drove into a wall.* **4** used to indicate the result of a change: *they turned the theatre into a garage.* **5** *Maths* used to indicate division: *three into six is two.* **6** *Informal* interested in: *I'm really into healthy food.*

intolerable *adj* more than can be endured. ▸ **intolerably** *adv*

intolerant *adj* refusing to accept practices and beliefs that differ from one's own. ▸ **intolerance** *n*

intonation *n* **1** the sound pattern produced by variations in the voice. **2** the act of intoning. **3** *Music* the ability to play or sing in tune. ▸ **intonational** *adj*

intone *vb* **-toning, -toned 1** to speak or recite in a monotonous tone. **2** to speak with a particular tone. ▷ HISTORY Medieval Latin *intonare*

in toto *adv* totally or entirely. ▷ HISTORY Latin

intoxicant *n* **1** something, such as an alcoholic drink, that causes intoxication. ✧ *adj* **2** causing intoxication.

intoxicate *vb* **-cating, -cated 1** (of an alcoholic drink) to make (a person) drunk. **2** to stimulate or excite to a point beyond self-control. ▷ HISTORY Latin *in-* in + *toxicum* poison ▸ **intoxicated** *adj* ▸ **intoxicating** *adj*

intoxication *n* **1** the state of being drunk. **2** great excitement and exhilaration.

intractable *adj* **1** (of a person) difficult to influence or direct. **2** (of a problem or illness) difficult to solve or cure. ▸ **intractability** *n* ▸ **intractably** *adv*

intramural *adj Chiefly US & Canad* operating within or involving those within a school or college: *intramural sports.* ▷ HISTORY Latin *intra-* inside + *murus* wall

intranet *n Computers* an internal network that makes use of Internet technology. ▷ HISTORY *intra-* + INTERNET

intransigent *adj* **1** refusing to change one's attitude. ✧ *n* **2** an intransigent person, esp. in politics. ▷ HISTORY Latin *in-* not + *transigere* to settle ▸ **intransigence** *n*

intransitive *adj* (of a verb) not taking a direct object: *'to faint' is an intransitive verb.* ▸ **intransitively** *adv*

intransitive verb *n Grammar* a verb that does not take a direct object: *'to rise' is an intransitive verb.* Compare **transitive verb**.

intrapreneur *n Brit and US* a person who while remaining within a larger organization uses entrepreneurial skills to develop new services or systems as a subsidiary of the organization. ▷ HISTORY *intra-* inside + *(entre)preneur*

intrauterine *adj* situated within the womb. ▷ HISTORY Latin *intra-* inside + *uterus* womb

intrauterine device *n* a contraceptive device in the shape of a coil, inserted into the womb.

intravenous (in-tra-**vee**-nuss) *adj Anat* into a vein: *intravenous drug users.* ▷ HISTORY Latin *intra-* inside + *vena* vein ▸ **intravenously** *adv*

intrepid *adj* fearless or bold. ▷ HISTORY Latin *in-* not + *trepidus* fearful ▸ **intrepidity** *n* ▸ **intrepidly** *adv*

intricate *adj* **1** difficult to sort out: *an intricate problem.* **2** full of complicated detail: *intricate Arab mosaics.* ▷ HISTORY Latin *intricare* to entangle ▸ **intricacy** *n* ▸ **intricately** *adv*

intrigue *vb* **-triguing, -trigued 1** to make interested or curious: *a question which has intrigued him for years.* **2** to plot secretly or dishonestly. ✧ *n* **3** secret plotting. **4** a secret love affair. ▷ HISTORY French *intriguer* ▸ **intriguing** *adj* ▸ **intriguingly** *adv*

intrinsic *adj* **1** essential to the real nature of a thing: *hedgerows are an intrinsic part of the countryside.* **2** *Anat* situated within or peculiar to a part: *intrinsic muscles.* ▷ HISTORY Latin *intrinsecus* inwardly ▸ **intrinsically** *adv*

introduce *vb* **-ducing, -duced 1** to present (someone) by name (to another person). **2** to present (a radio or television programme). **3** to present for consideration or approval: *he introduced the bill to Parliament in 1967.* **4** to bring into use: *Latvia has introduced its own currency into circulation.* **5 introduce to** to cause to experience for the first time: *his father introduced him to golf.* **6** to insert. **7 introduce with** to start: *he introduced his talk with some music.* ▷ HISTORY Latin *introducere* to bring inside ▸ **introducible** *adj*

introduction *n* **1** the act of introducing something or someone. **2** a preliminary part, as of a book or musical composition. **3** a book that explains the basic facts about a particular subject to a beginner. **4** a presentation of one person to another or others.

introductory *adj* serving as an introduction.

introit *n* **1** *RC Church* a short prayer said or sung as the celebrant is entering the sanctuary to celebrate Mass. **2** *Church of England* a hymn or psalm sung at the beginning of a service. ▷ HISTORY Latin *introitus* entrance

introspection *n* the examining of one's own thoughts, impressions, and feelings. ▷ HISTORY Latin *introspicere* to look within ▸ **introspective** *adj*

introversion *n Psychol* the directing of interest inwards towards one's own thoughts and feelings rather than towards the external world or making social contacts.

introvert *adj* **1** shy and quiet. **2** *Psychol* concerned more with inner feelings than with external reality. ✧ *n* **3** such a person. ▷ HISTORY Latin *intro-* inward + *vertere* to turn ▸ **introverted** *adj*

intrude *vb* **-truding, -truded 1** to come in or join in without being invited. **2** *Geol* to force rock material, esp. molten magma, between solid rocks. ▷ HISTORY Latin *intrudere* to thrust in

intruder *n* a person who enters a place without permission.

intrusion *n* **1** the act of intruding; an unwelcome visit, etc.: *an intrusion into her private life.* **2** *Geol* **a** the forcing of molten rock into spaces in the overlying strata. **b** molten rock formed in this way.

intrusive *adj* **1** characterized by intrusion or tending to intrude. **2** *Geog* (of igneous rocks) formed by intrusion. **3** *Phonetics* relating to or denoting a speech sound that is introduced into a word or piece of connected speech for a phonetic reason. ▸ **intrusively** *adv* ▸ **intrusiveness** *n*

intrusive narrator *n Literature* a storyteller whose thoughts or opinions are evident and an intentional part of the narrative style.

intuition *n* instinctive knowledge of or belief about something without conscious reasoning: *intuition told her something was wrong.* ▷ **HISTORY** Latin *intueri* to gaze upon ▸ **intuitional** *adj*

intuitive *adj* of, possessing, or resulting from intuition: *an intuitive understanding.* ▸ **intuitively** *adv*

Inuit *n, pl* **-it** *or* **-its** an indigenous inhabitant of North America or Greenland. ▷ **HISTORY** plural of *inuk* person

Inuktitut *n* the language of the Inuit.

inundate *vb* **-dating, -dated 1** to cover completely with water. **2** to overwhelm, as if with a flood: *the police were inundated with calls.* ▷ **HISTORY** Latin *inundare* ▸ **inundation** *n*

inured *adj* able to tolerate something unpleasant because one has become accustomed to it: *he became inured to the casual brutality of his captors.* ▷ **HISTORY** Middle English *enuren* to accustom ▸ **inurement** *n*

invade *vb* **-vading, -vaded 1** to enter (a country or territory) by military force. **2** to enter in large numbers: *the town was invaded by rugby supporters.* **3** to disturb (privacy, etc.). ▷ **HISTORY** Latin *invadere* ▸ **invader** *n*

invalid¹ *n* **1** a person who is disabled or chronically ill. ✧ *adj* **2** sick or disabled. ✧ *vb* **3** *Chiefly Brit* to dismiss (a soldier etc.) from active service because of illness. ▷ **HISTORY** Latin *in-* not + *validus* strong ▸ **invalidism** *n*

invalid² *adj* **1** having no legal force: *an invalid cheque.* **2** (of an argument, result, etc.) not valid because it has been based on a mistake. ▸ **invalidity** *n* ▸ **invalidly** *adv*

invalidate *vb* **-dating, -dated 1** to make or show (an argument) to be invalid. **2** to take away the legal force of (a contract). ▸ **invalidation** *n*

invaluable *adj* having great value that is impossible to calculate.

invariable *adj* unchanging. ▸ **invariably** *adv*

invasion *n* **1** the act of invading with armed forces. **2** any intrusion: *an invasion of privacy.* **3** *Biol* the movement of plants to a new area or to an area to which they are not native. ▸ **invasive** *adj*

invective *n* abusive speech or writing. ▷ **HISTORY** Late Latin *invectivus* scolding

inveigh (in-**vay**) *vb Formal* **inveigh against** to make harsh criticisms against. ▷ **HISTORY** Latin *invehi,* literally: to be carried in, hence assail

inveigle *vb* **-gling, -gled** to coax or manipulate (someone) into an action or situation. ▷ **HISTORY** Old French *avogler* to blind, deceive ▸ **inveiglement** *n*

invent *vb* **1** to think up or create (something new). **2** to make up (a story, excuse, etc.). ▷ **HISTORY** Latin *invenire* to find ▸ **inventor** *n*

invention *n* **1** something that is invented. **2** the act of inventing. **3** creative power; inventive skill. **4** *Euphemistic* a lie: *his story is a malicious invention.*

inventive *adj* creative and resourceful: *her inventive use of colour.*

inventory (**in**-ven-tree) *n, pl* **-tories 1** a detailed list of the objects in a particular place. ✧ *vb* **-tories, -torying, -toried 2** to make a list of. ▷ **HISTORY** Medieval Latin *inventorium*

inverse *adj* **1** opposite in effect, sequence, direction, etc. **2** *Maths* linking two variables in such a way that one increases as the other decreases. ✧ *n* **3** the exact opposite: *the inverse of this image.* **4** *Maths* an inverse element.

inverse operation *n Maths* an operation that undoes another: *addition and subtraction are inverse operations.*

inverse proportion *n Maths* a relationship between two variables in which one increases as the other decreases.

inversion *n* **1** the act of inverting or state of being inverted. **2** something inverted, esp. a reversal of order, functions, etc.: *an inversion of their previous relationship.* ▸ **inversive** *adj*

invert *vb* **1** to turn upside down or inside out. **2** to reverse in effect, sequence, or direction. ✧ *n* **3** *Old-fashioned* a homosexual. ▷ **HISTORY** Latin *in-* in + *vertere* to turn ▸ **invertible** *adj*

invertebrate *n* **1** any animal without a backbone, such as an insect, worm, or octopus. ✧ *adj* **2** of or designating invertebrates.

inverted commas *pl n* same as **quotation marks**.

invest *vb* **1** (often foll. by *in*) to put (money) into an enterprise with the expectation of profit. **2** (often foll. by *in*) to devote (time or effort to a project). **3 invest in** to buy: *she invested in some barbecue equipment.* **4** to give power or authority to: *invested with the powers of government.* **5** (often foll. by *in*) to install someone (in an official position). **6** (foll. by *with* or *in*) to credit or provide (a person with qualities): *he was invested with great common sense.* **7 invest with** *Usually poetic* to cover, as if with a coat: *when spring invests the trees with leaves.* ▷ **HISTORY** Medieval Latin *investire* to clothe ▸ **investor** *n*

investigate *vb* **-gating, -gated** to inquire into (a situation or problem) thoroughly in order to discover the truth: *the police are currently investigating the case.* ▷ **HISTORY** Latin *investigare* to search after ▸ **investigative** *adj* ▸ **investigator** *n*

investigation *n* a careful search or examination in order to discover facts.

investiture *n* the formal installation of a person in an office or rank.

a b c d e f g h i j k l m n o p q r s t u v w x y z

A B C D E F G H I J K L M N O P Q R S T U V W X Y Z

investment *n* **1** the act of investing. **2** money invested. **3** something in which money is invested.

investment trust *n* a financial enterprise that invests its subscribed capital in a wide range of securities for its investors' benefit.

inveterate *adj* **1** deep-rooted or ingrained: *an inveterate enemy of Marxism.* **2** confirmed in a habit or practice: *an inveterate gambler.* ▷ HISTORY Latin *inveteratus* of long standing ▶ **inveteracy** *n*

invidious *adj* likely to cause resentment or unpopularity. ▷ HISTORY Latin *invidia* envy

invigilate (in-**vij**-il-late) *vb* **-lating, -lated** *Brit* to supervise people who are sitting an examination. ▷ HISTORY Latin *invigilare* to watch over ▶ **invigilation** *n* ▶ **invigilator** *n*

invigorate *vb* **-ating, -ated** to give energy to or refresh. ▷ HISTORY Latin *in-* in + *vigor* vigour ▶ **invigorating** *adj*

invincible *adj* incapable of being defeated: *an army of invincible strength.* ▷ HISTORY Latin *in-* not + *vincere* to conquer ▶ **invincibility** *n* ▶ **invincibly** *adv*

inviolable *adj* that must not be broken or violated: *an inviolable oath.* ▶ **inviolability** *n*

inviolate *adj* free from harm or injury. ▶ **inviolacy** *n*

invisible *adj* **1** not able to be seen by the eye: *invisible radiation.* **2** concealed from sight. **3** *Econ* relating to services, such as insurance and freight, rather than goods: *invisible earnings.* ▶ **invisibility** *n* ▶ **invisibly** *adv*

invitation *n* **1** a request to attend a dance, meal, etc. **2** the card or paper on which an invitation is written.

invite *vb* **-viting, -vited 1** to ask (a person) in a friendly or polite way (to do something, attend an event, etc.). **2** to make a request for, esp. publicly or formally: *we invite applications for six scholarships.* **3** to bring on or provoke: *his theory invites disaster.* **4** to tempt. ✧ *n* **5** *Informal* an invitation. ▷ HISTORY Latin *invitare*

inviting *adj* tempting or attractive.

in vitro *adv, adj* (of biological processes or reactions) happening outside the body of the organism in an artificial environment. ▷ HISTORY New Latin, literally: in glass

invocation *n* **1** the act of invoking. **2** a prayer to God or another deity asking for help, forgiveness, etc. ▶ **invocatory** *adj*

invoice *n* **1** a bill for goods and services supplied. ✧ *vb* **-voicing, -voiced 2** to present (a customer) with an invoice. ▷ HISTORY Old French *envois*, plural of *envoi* message

invoke *vb* **-voking, -voked 1** to put (a law or penalty) into use: *chapter 8 of the UN charter was invoked.* **2** to bring about: *the hills invoked a feeling of serenity.* **3** to call on (God or another deity) for help, inspiration, etc. **4** to summon (a spirit) by uttering magic words. ▷ HISTORY Latin *invocare* to appeal to

> **☑ WORD TIP**
> *Invoke* is sometimes wrongly used where *evoke* is meant: *this proposal evoked* (not *invoked*) *a strong reaction.*

involuntary *adj* **1** carried out without one's conscious wishes; unintentional. **2** *Physiol* (esp. of a movement or muscle) performed or acting without conscious control. ▶ **involuntarily** *adv*

involute *adj also* **involuted 1** complex, intricate, or involved. **2** rolled inwards or curled in a spiral. ✧ *n* **3** *Geom* the curve described by the free end of a thread as it is wound around another curve on the same plane. ▷ HISTORY Latin *involutus*

involve *vb* **-volving, -volved 1** to include as a necessary part. **2** to have an effect on: *around fifty riders were involved and some were hurt.* **3** to implicate: *several people were involved in the crime.* **4** to make complicated: *the situation was further involved by her disappearance.* ▷ HISTORY Latin *in-* in + *volvere* to roll ▶ **involvement** *n*

involved *adj* **1** complicated. **2 involved in** concerned in.

invulnerable *adj* not able to be wounded or damaged. ▶ **invulnerability** *n*

inward *adj* **1** directed towards the middle of something. **2** situated within. **3** of the mind or spirit: *inward meditation.* **4** of one's own country or a specific country: *inward investment.* ✧ *adv* **5** same as **inwards**.

inwardly *adv* **1** within the private thoughts or feelings: *inwardly troubled, he kept smiling.* **2** not aloud: *to laugh inwardly.* **3** in or on the inside.

inwards *or* **inward** *adv* towards the inside or middle of something.

Io *Chem* ionium.

iodide *n Chem* a compound containing an iodine atom, such as methyl iodide.

iodine *n Chem* a bluish-black element found in seaweed and used in medicine, photography, and dyeing. Symbol: I. ▷ HISTORY Greek *iōdēs* rust-coloured, but mistakenly derived from *ion* violet

iodize *or* **-dise** *vb* **-dizing, -dized** *or* **-dising, -dised** to treat with iodine. ▶ **iodization** *or* **-disation** *n*

ion *n* an electrically charged atom or group of atoms formed by the loss or gain of one or more electrons. ▷ HISTORY Greek, literally: going

ion exchange *n* the process in which ions are exchanged between a solution and an insoluble solid. It is used to soften water.

ionic *adj* of or in the form of ions.

Ionic *adj* of a style of classical architecture characterized by fluted columns with scroll-like ornaments on the capital.

ionic bond *n Chem* a chemical bond in which one atom loses an electron to form a positive ion, the other atom gains the electron to form a negative ion, and the ions are held together by electrostatic attraction.

ionize *or* **-ise** *vb* **-izing, -ized** *or* **-ising, -ised** to change or become changed into ions. ▶ **ionization** *or* **-isation** *n*

ionosphere *n* a region of ionized layers of air in the earth's upper atmosphere, which reflects radio waves. ▶ **ionospheric** *adj*

iota (eye-**oh**-ta) *n* **1** the ninth letter in the Greek alphabet (Ι, ι). **2** a very small amount: *I don't feel one iota of guilt.*

IOU *n* a written promise or reminder to pay a debt. ▷ **HISTORY** representing *I owe you*

IOW Isle of Wight.

IPA International Phonetic Alphabet.

ipecacuanha (ip-pee-kak-yew-**ann**-a) *or* **ipecac** (**ip**-pee-kak) *n* a drug made from the dried roots of a S American plant, used to cause vomiting. ▷ **HISTORY** S American Indian *ipekaaguéne*

ipso facto *adv* by that very fact or act. ▷ **HISTORY** Latin

IQ intelligence quotient.

Ir *Chem* iridium.

IRA Irish Republican Army.

Iranian *adj* **1** of Iran. ✧ *n* **2** a person from Iran. **3** a branch of the Indo-European family of languages, including Persian.

Iraqi *adj* **1** of Iraq. ✧ *n* **2** a person from Iraq.

irascible *adj* easily angered. ▷ **HISTORY** Latin *ira* anger ▶ **irascibility** *n* ▶ **irascibly** *adv*

irate *adj* very angry. ▷ **HISTORY** Latin *iratus* enraged

ire *n Literary* anger. ▷ **HISTORY** Latin *ira*

iridaceous (ir-rid-**day**-shuss) *adj* of or belonging to the iris family.

iridescent *adj* having shimmering changing colours like a rainbow. ▷ **HISTORY** Latin *irid-* iris ▶ **iridescence** *n*

iridium *n Chem* a hard yellowish-white chemical element that occurs in platinum ores and is used as an alloy with platinum. Symbol: Ir. ▷ **HISTORY** Latin *irid-* iris

iris *n* **1** the coloured muscular membrane in the eye that surrounds and controls the size of the pupil. **2** a tall plant with long pointed leaves and large flowers. ▷ **HISTORY** Greek: rainbow

Irish *adj* **1** of Ireland. ✧ *n* **2** same as **Irish Gaelic**. **3** the dialect of English spoken in Ireland. ✧ *pl n* **4 the Irish** the people of Ireland.

Irish coffee *n* hot coffee mixed with Irish whiskey and topped with double cream.

Irish Gaelic *n* the Celtic language of Ireland.

Irishman *or fem* **Irishwoman** *n, pl* **-men** *or* **-women** a person from Ireland.

Irish moss *n* same as **carrageen**.

irk *vb* to irritate or vex. ▷ **HISTORY** Middle English *irken* to grow weary

irksome *adj* annoying or tiresome.

iron *n* **1** a strong silvery-white metallic element, widely used for structural and engineering purposes. Symbol: Fe. **2** a tool made of iron. **3** a small electrically heated device with a weighted flat bottom for pressing clothes. **4** *Golf* a club with an angled metal head. **5** a splintlike support for a malformed leg. **6** great strength or resolve: *a will of iron.* **7 strike while the iron is hot** to act at a suitable moment. ✧ *adj* **8** made of iron. **9** very hard or merciless: *iron determination.* **10** very strong: *an iron constitution.* ✧ *vb* **11** to smooth (clothes or fabric) by removing (creases) with an iron. See also **iron out, irons.** ▷ **HISTORY** Old English *irēn*

Iron Age *n* a phase of human culture that began in the Middle East about 1100 BC during which iron tools and weapons were used.

ironbark *n* an Australian eucalyptus with hard rough bark.

ironclad *adj* **1** covered or protected with iron: *an ironclad warship.* **2** unable to be contradicted: *ironclad proof.* ✧ *n* **3** *History* a large wooden 19th-century warship with armoured plating.

Iron Curtain *n History* **the Iron Curtain** (formerly) the guarded border between the countries of the Soviet bloc and the rest of Europe.

ironic *or* **ironical** *adj* of, characterized by, or using irony. ▶ **ironically** *adv*

ironing *n* clothes to be ironed.

ironing board *n* a narrow cloth-covered board, usually with folding legs, on which to iron clothes.

iron lung *n* an airtight metal cylinder enclosing the entire body up to the neck and providing artificial respiration.

iron maiden *n* a medieval instrument of torture, consisting of a hinged case (often shaped in the form of a woman) lined with iron spikes.

ironmaster *n Brit history* a manufacturer of iron.

ironmonger *n Brit* a shopkeeper or shop dealing in hardware. ▶ **ironmongery** *n*

iron out *vb* to settle (a problem or difficulty) through negotiation or discussion.

iron pyrites *n* same as **pyrite**.

iron rations *pl n* emergency food supplies, esp. for military personnel in action.

irons *pl n* **1** fetters or chains. **2 have several irons in the fire** to have several projects or plans at once.

ironstone *n* **1** any rock consisting mainly of iron ore. **2** a tough durable earthenware.

ironwood *n* **1** any of various trees, such as hornbeam, with exceptionally hard wood. **2** the wood of any of these trees.

ironworks *n* a building in which iron is smelted, cast, or wrought.

irony *n, pl* **-nies 1** the mildly sarcastic use of words to imply the opposite of what they normally mean. **2** a situation or result that is the direct opposite of what was expected or intended. ▷ **HISTORY** Greek *eirōneia*

irradiate *vb* **-ating, -ated 1** *Physics* to subject to or treat with light or other electromagnetic radiation. **2** to make clear or bright intellectually or spiritually. **3** to light up; illuminate. ▶ **irradiation** *n*

irrational *adj* **1** not based on logical reasoning. **2** incapable of reasoning. **3** *Maths* (of an equation or expression) involving radicals or fractional exponents. ▶ **irrationality** *n* ▶ **irrationally** *adv*

irrational number *n Maths* any real number that cannot be expressed as the ratio of two integers, such as π.

A B C D E F G H I J K L M N O P Q R S T U V W X Y Z

irreconcilable *adj* not able to be resolved or settled: *irreconcilable differences.* ▶ **irreconcilability** *n*

irredeemable *adj* **1** not able to be reformed, improved, or corrected. **2** (of bonds or shares) not able to be bought back directly or paid off. **3** (of paper money) not able to be converted into coin. ▶ **irredeemably** *adv*

irredentist *n* a person in favour of seizing territory that was once part of his or her country. ▷ HISTORY Italian *irredenta* unredeemed ▶ **irredentism** *n*

irreducible *adj* impossible to put in a reduced or simpler form. ▶ **irreducibility** *n*

irrefutable *adj* impossible to deny or disprove.

irregular *adj* **1** uneven in shape, position, arrangement, etc. **2** not conforming to accepted practice or routine. **3** (of a word) not following the usual pattern of formation in a language. **4** not occurring at expected or equal intervals: *an irregular pulse.* **5** (of troops) not belonging to regular forces. ✧ *n* **6** a soldier not in a regular army. ▶ **irregularity** *n* ▶ **irregularly** *adv*

irrelevant *adj* not connected with the matter in hand. ▶ **irrelevance** *or* **irrelevancy** *n*

irreligious *adj* **1** lacking religious faith. **2** indifferent or opposed to religion.

irreparable *adj* not able to be repaired or put right: *irreparable damage to his reputation.* ▶ **irreparably** *adv*

irreplaceable *adj* impossible to replace: *acres of irreplaceable moorland were devastated.*

irrepressible *adj* not capable of being repressed, controlled, or restrained. ▶ **irrepressibility** *n* ▶ **irrepressibly** *adv*

irreproachable *adj* blameless or faultless. ▶ **irreproachability** *n*

irresistible *adj* **1** not able to be resisted or refused: *irresistible pressure from the financial markets.* **2** extremely attractive: *an irresistible woman.* ▶ **irresistibility** *n* ▶ **irresistibly** *adv*

irresolute *adj* unable to make decisions. ▶ **irresolution** *n*

irresponsible *adj* **1** not showing or done with due care for the consequences of one's actions or attitudes; reckless. **2** not capable of accepting responsibility. ▶ **irresponsibility** *n* ▶ **irresponsibly** *adv*

irretrievable *adj* impossible to put right or make good. ▶ **irretrievability** *n* ▶ **irretrievably** *adv*

irreverence *n* **1** lack of due respect. **2** a disrespectful remark or act. ▶ **irreverent** *adj*

irreversible *adj* not able to be reversed or put right again: *irreversible loss of memory.* ▶ **irreversibly** *adv*

irrevocable *adj* not possible to change or undo. ▶ **irrevocably** *adv*

irrigate *vb* **-gating, -gated 1** to supply (land) with water through ditches or pipes in order to encourage the growth of crops. **2** *Med* to bathe (a wound or part of the body). ▷ HISTORY Latin *irrigare* ▶ **irrigation** *n* ▶ **irrigator** *n*

irritable *adj* **1** easily annoyed or angered. **2** *Pathol* abnormally sensitive. **3** *Biol* (of all living organisms) capable of responding to such stimuli as heat, light, and touch. ▶ **irritability** *n*

irritant *n* **1** something that annoys or irritates. **2** a substance that causes a part of the body to become tender or inflamed. ✧ *adj* **3** causing irritation.

irritate *vb* **-tating, -tated 1** to annoy or anger (someone). **2** *Pathol* to cause (an organ or part of the body) to become inflamed or tender. **3** *Biol* to stimulate (an organ) to respond in a characteristic manner. ▷ HISTORY Latin *irritare* to provoke ▶ **irritation** *n*

irrupt *vb* to enter forcibly or suddenly. ▷ HISTORY Latin *irrumpere* ▶ **irruption** *n* ▶ **irruptive** *adj*

is *vb* third person singular of the present tense of **be**. ▷ HISTORY Old English

ISA (**eye**-sa) (in Britain) individual savings account.

isallobar (ice-**sal**-oh-bar) *n* a line on a map connecting places with equal pressure changes. ▷ HISTORY Greek *isos* equal + *allos* other + *baros* weight

ISBN International Standard Book Number.

isect (**eye**-sect) *n Maths* a calculator key that is used to locate points of intersection of two graphs.

isinglass (**ize**-ing-glass) *n* **1** a gelatine made from the air bladders of freshwater fish. **2** same as **mica**. ▷ HISTORY Middle Dutch *huysenblase* sturgeon bladder

Isl. **1** Island. **2** Isle.

Islam *n* **1** the Muslim religion teaching that there is only one God and that Mohammed is his prophet. **2** Muslim countries and civilization. ▶ **Islamic** *adj* ▶ **Islamist** *adj, n*

WORD HISTORY

In Arabic, *'islām* means 'surrender (to God)', from the verb *'aslama*, meaning 'to surrender'. The same verb also underlies the word 'Muslim', which means 'someone who surrenders (to God)'.

island *n* **1** a piece of land that is completely surrounded by water. **2** something isolated, detached, or surrounded. **3** See **traffic island** *RELATED ADJECTIVE* ✦ **insular** ▷ HISTORY Old English *īgland*

islander *n* a person who lives on an island.

Islander *n NZ* a Pacific Islander.

isle *n Poetic except when part of place name* an island.

islet *n* a small island.

islets of Langerhans *pl n Anat* small groups of endocrine cells in the pancreas that secrete insulin and glucagon. ▷ HISTORY C19: named after Paul *Langerhans*, German physician

-ism *n suffix* indicating: **1** a political or religious belief: *socialism; Judaism.* **2** a characteristic quality: *heroism.* **3** an action: *exorcism.* **4** prejudice on the basis specified: *sexism.*

isn't is not.

iso- *or before a vowel* **is-** *combining form* equal or identical: *isomagnetic.* ▷ **HISTORY** Greek *isos* equal

isobar (**ice**-oh-bar) *n* **1** a line on a map connecting places of equal atmospheric pressure. **2** *Physics* any of two or more atoms that have the same mass number but different atomic numbers. ▷ **HISTORY** Greek *isobarēs* of equal weight ▶ **isobaric** *adj* ▶ **isobarism** *n*

isobath *n Geog* a line on a map connecting points of equal underwater depth. ▷ **HISTORY** Greek *isobathēs* of equal depth, from ISO- + *bathos* depth

isochronal *or* **isochronous** *adj* **1** equal in length of time. **2** occurring at equal time intervals. ▷ **HISTORY** Greek *isos* equal + *khronos* time ▶ **isochronism** *n*

isoclinal *or* **isoclinic** *adj* **1** sloping in the same direction and at the same angle. **2** *Geol* (of folds) having sides that are parallel to each other. ◇ *n* **3** *Geog* Also: **isocline, isoclinal line** an imaginary line connecting points on the earth's surface having equal angles of magnetic dip.

isocline *n* **1** *Geol* a series of rock strata with isoclinal folds. **2** *Geog* same as **isoclinal** (sense 3).

isogeotherm *n Geog* an imaginary line below the surface of the earth connecting points of equal temperature. ▶ **isogeothermal** *or* **isogeothermic** *adj*

isohel *n* a line on a map connecting places with an equal period of sunshine. ▷ **HISTORY** Greek *isos* equal + *hēlios* sun

isohyet (ice-oh-**hie**-it) *n* a line on a map connecting places having equal rainfall. ▷ **HISTORY** Greek *isos* equal + *huetos* rain

isolate *vb* **-lating, -lated 1** to place apart or alone. **2** *Chem* to obtain (a substance) in an uncombined form. **3** *Med* to quarantine (a person or animal) with a contagious disease. ▷ **HISTORY** Latin *insulatus,* literally: made into an island ▶ **isolation** *n*

isolationism *n Politics* **1** a policy of nonparticipation in international affairs; used especially of the US in the periods prior to its entry in the two world wars. **2** an attitude favouring such a policy. ▶ **isolationist** *n, adj*

isomer (**ice**-oh-mer) *n Chem* a substance whose molecules contain the same atoms as another but in a different arrangement. ▶ **isomeric** *adj*

isometric *adj* **1** having equal dimensions or measurements. **2** *Physiol* relating to muscular contraction that does not produce shortening of the muscle. **3** (of a three-dimensional drawing) having the three axes equally inclined and all lines drawn to scale. ▷ **HISTORY** Greek *isometria* equal measurement ▶ **isometrically** *adv*

isometrics *n* a system of isometric exercises.

isomorphism *n* **1** *Biol* similarity of form, as in different generations of the same life cycle. **2** *Chem* the existence of two or more substances of different composition in a similar crystalline form. **3** *Maths* a one-to-one correspondence between the elements of two or more sets. ▶ **isomorph** *n* ▶ **isomorphic** *or* **isomorphous** *adj*

isosceles triangle (ice-**soss**-ill-eez) *n* a triangle with two sides of equal length.

> **WORD HISTORY**
> 'Isosceles' comes from Greek *isos*, meaning 'equal', and *skelos*, meaning 'leg'.

isostasy *n* the state of balance which sections of the earth's lithosphere are thought to achieve when the vertical forces upon them remain unchanged. If a section is loaded as by ice, it slowly subsides. If a section is reduced in mass, as by erosion, it slowly rises. ▷ **HISTORY** ISO- +*stasy,* from Greek *stasis* a STANDING ▶ **isostatic** *adj*

isotherm (**ice**-oh-therm) *n* a line on a map linking places of equal temperature. ▷ **HISTORY** Greek *isos* equal + *thermē* heat

isotonic *adj* **1** *Physiol* (of two or more muscles) having equal tension. **2** (of a drink) designed to replace the fluid and salts lost from the body during exercise.

isotope (**ice**-oh-tope) *n* one of two or more atoms with the same number of protons in the nucleus but a different number of neutrons. ▷ **HISTORY** Greek *isos* equal + *topos* place ▶ **isotopic** *adj* ▶ **isotopy** *n*

isotropic *or* **isotropous** *adj* having uniform physical properties, such as elasticity or conduction in all directions. ▶ **isotropy** *n*

ISP Internet service provider: a business providing its customers with connection to the Internet.

Israeli *adj* **1** of Israel. ◇ *n, pl* **-lis** *or* **-li 2** a person from Israel.

Israelite *n Bible* a member of the ethnic group claiming descent from Jacob; a Hebrew.

issue *n* **1** a topic of interest or discussion. **2** an important subject requiring a decision. **3** a particular edition of a magazine or newspaper. **4** a consequence or result. **5** *Law* the descendants of a person. **6** the act of sending or giving out something. **7** the act of emerging; outflow. **8** something flowing out, such as a river. **9 at issue a** under discussion. **b** in disagreement. **10 force the issue** to compel decision on some matter. **11 join issue** to join in controversy. **12 take issue** to disagree. ◇ *vb* **-suing, -sued 13** to make (a statement etc.) publicly. **14** to supply officially (with). **15** to send out or distribute. **16** to publish. **17** to come forth or emerge. ▷ **HISTORY** Old French *eissue* way out ▶ **issuable** *adj*

isthmus (**iss**-muss) *n* a narrow strip of land connecting two relatively large land areas. ▷ **HISTORY** Greek *isthmos*

it *pron* **1** refers to a nonhuman, animal, plant, or inanimate thing, or sometimes to a small baby. **2** refers to something unspecified or implied or to a previous or understood clause, phrase, or word: *I knew it.* **3** used to represent human life or experience in respect of the present situation: *how's it going?* **4** used as the subject of impersonal verbs: *it is snowing; it's Friday.* **5** *Informal* the crucial or ultimate point: *the steering failed and I thought that was it.* ◇ *n* **6** *Informal* **a** sexual intercourse.

b sex appeal. **7** a desirable quality or ability. ▷ HISTORY Old English *hit*

IT information technology.

ITA initial teaching alphabet: a partly phonetic alphabet used to teach reading.

Italian *adj* **1** of Italy. ✧ *n* **2** a person from Italy. **3** the official language of Italy and one of the official languages of Switzerland.

italic *adj* **1** of a style of printing type in which the characters slant to the right. ✧ *pl n* **2 italics** italic type or print, used for emphasis. ▷ HISTORY Latin *Italicus* of Italy (where it was first used)

italicize *or* **-cise** *vb* **-cizing, -cized** *or* **-cising, -cised** to print (text) in italic type. ▸ **italicization** *or* **-cisation** *n*

itch *n* **1** a skin irritation causing a desire to scratch. **2** a restless desire. **3** any skin disorder, such as scabies, characterized by intense itching. ✧ *vb* **4** to feel an irritating or tickling sensation. **5** to have a restless desire (to do something): *they were itching to join the fight.* ▷ HISTORY Old English *gīccean* to itch

itchy *adj* **itchier, itchiest 1** having an itch. **2 have itchy feet** to have a desire to travel. ▸ **itchiness** *n*

item *n* **1** a single thing in a list or collection. **2** a piece of information: *a news item.* **3** *Book-keeping* an entry in an account. **4** *Informal* a couple. ▷ HISTORY Latin: in like manner

itemize *or* **-ise** *vb* **-izing, -ized** *or* **-ising, -ised** to put on a list or make a list of. ▸ **itemization** *or* **-isation** *n*

iterate *vb* **-ating, -ated** to say or do again. ▷ HISTORY Latin *iterum* again ▸ **iteration** *n* ▸ **iterative** *adj*

itinerant *adj* **1** working for a short time in various places. ✧ *n* **2** an itinerant worker or other person. ▷ HISTORY Latin *iter* a journey

itinerary *n, pl* **-aries 1** a detailed plan of a journey. **2** a record of a journey. **3** a guidebook for travellers.

-itis *suffix forming nouns* indicating inflammation of a specified part: *tonsillitis.* ▷ HISTORY Greek *-itēs* belonging to

it'll it will *or* it shall.

its *adj* **1** of or belonging to it: *its left rear wheel; I can see its logical consequence.* ✧ *pron* **2** something belonging to it: *its is over there.*

it's it is *or* it has.

itself *pron* **1 a** the reflexive form of *it*: *the cat scratched itself.* **b** used for emphasis: *even the money itself won't convince me.* **2** its normal or usual self: *my parrot doesn't seem itself these days.*

ITV (in Britain) Independent Television.

IUD intrauterine device: a coil-shaped contraceptive fitted into the womb.

I've I have.

IVF in vitro fertilization.

ivory *n, pl* **-ries 1** a hard smooth creamy white type of bone that makes up a major part of the tusks of elephants. ✧ *adj* **2** yellowish-white. ▷ HISTORY Latin *ebur* ▸ **ivory-like** *adj*

ivory tower *n* remoteness from the realities of everyday life. ▸ **ivory-towered** *adj*

IVR International Vehicle Registration.

ivy *n, pl* **ivies 1** a woody climbing or trailing plant with evergreen leaves and black berry-like fruits. **2** any of various other climbing or creeping plants, such as the poison ivy. ▷ HISTORY Old English *īfig*

iwi (**ee**-wee) *n NZ* a Maori tribe. ▷ HISTORY Maori

ixia *n* a southern African plant of the iris family with showy ornamental funnel-shaped flowers. ▷ HISTORY Greek *ixos* mistletoe

J j

J joule(s).

jab *vb* **jabbing, jabbed 1** to poke sharply. ✧ *n* **2** a quick short punch. **3** *Informal* an injection: *a flu jab.* **4** a sharp poke. ▷ **HISTORY** variant of *job*

jabber *vb* **1** to speak very quickly and excitedly; chatter. ✧ *n* **2** quick excited chatter. ▷ **HISTORY** imitative

jabiru *n* a large white-and-black Australian stork.

jacaranda *n* a tropical American tree with sweet-smelling wood and pale purple flowers. ▷ **HISTORY** from a Native American langauge

jack *n* **1** a mechanical device used to raise a motor vehicle or other heavy object. **2** a playing card with a picture of a pageboy on it. **3** *Bowls* a small white bowl at which the players aim their bowls. **4** *Electrical engineering* a socket into which a plug can be inserted. **5** a flag flown at the bow of a ship, showing nationality. **6 every man jack** everyone without exception. ✧ See also **jack in, jack up**. ▷ **HISTORY** from short form of *John*

jackal *n* a doglike wild animal of Africa and Asia, which feeds on the decaying flesh of dead animals. ▷ **HISTORY** Persian *shagāl*

jackanapes *n Brit* a mischievous child. ▷ **HISTORY** literally: Jack of the ape, nickname of first Duke of Suffolk, whose badge showed an ape's ball and chain

jackaroo, jackeroo *n, pl* **-roos** *Austral* a trainee on a sheep station. ▷ **HISTORY** from *jack* man + *(kang)aroo*

jackass *n* **1** a fool. **2** a male donkey. **3 laughing jackass** same as **kookaburra**. ▷ **HISTORY** *jack* (male) + *ass*

jackboot *n* **1** a leather military boot reaching up to the knee. **2** brutal and authoritarian rule.

jackdaw *n* a large black-and-grey crowlike bird of Europe and Asia. ▷ **HISTORY** *jack* + *daw*, obsolete name for jackdaw

jacket *n* **1** a short coat with a front opening and long sleeves. **2** the skin of a potato. **3** same as **dust jacket**. ▷ **HISTORY** Old French *jaquet*

jacket potato *n* a potato baked in its skin.

jack in *vb Brit slang* to abandon (an attempt or enterprise).

jack-in-the-box *n* a toy consisting of a box containing a figure on a compressed spring, which jumps out when the lid is opened.

jackknife *vb* **-knifing, -knifed 1** (of an articulated lorry) to go out of control in such a way that the trailer swings round at a sharp angle to the cab. ✧ *n, pl* **-knives 2** a knife with a blade that can be folded into the handle. **3** a dive in which the diver bends at the waist in midair.

jack of all trades *n, pl* **jacks of all trades** a person who can do many different kinds of work.

jackpot *n* **1** the most valuable prize that can be won in a gambling game. **2 hit the jackpot** *Informal* to be very fortunate or very successful. ▷ **HISTORY** probably from *jack* (playing card)

jack rabbit *n* a hare of W North America with very long hind legs and large ears. ▷ **HISTORY** *jackass-rabbit*, referring to its long ears

jack-up *n NZ informal* something achieved dishonestly.

jack up *vb* **1** to raise (a motor vehicle) with a jack. **2** to increase (prices or salaries). **3** *NZ informal* to organize something through unorthodox channels

Jacobean (jak-a-**bee**-an) *adj* of or in the reign of James I of England and Ireland (1603–25). ▷ **HISTORY** Latin *Jacobus* James

Jacobite *n History* a supporter of James II and his descendants. ▷ **HISTORY** Latin *Jacobus* James

Jacquard (**jak**-ard) *n* a fabric with an intricate design incorporated into the weave. ▷ **HISTORY** after J. M. *Jacquard*, its inventor

Jacuzzi (jak-**oo**-zee) *n Trademark* a large circular bath with a mechanism that swirls the water.

jade *n* **1** an ornamental semiprecious stone, usually green in colour. ✧ *adj* **2** bluish-green. ▷ **HISTORY** obsolete Spanish *piedra de ijada* colic stone, because it was believed to cure colic

jaded *adj* tired or bored from overindulgence or overwork.

Jaffa *n Brit* a large thick-skinned orange. ▷ **HISTORY** after *Jaffa*, port in W Israel

jagged (**jag**-gid) *adj* having an uneven edge with sharp points. ▷ **HISTORY** from *jag* a sharp point

jaguar *n* a large wild cat of south and central America, with a spotted coat. ▷ **HISTORY** from S American Indian

jail *or* **gaol** *n* **1** a prison. ✧ *vb* **2** to confine in prison. ▷ **HISTORY** Old French *jaiole* cage

jailbird *n Informal* a person who is or has often been in jail.

jailer *or* **gaoler** *n* a person in charge of a jail.

jake *adj* **she's jake** *Austral & NZ slang* it is all right. ▷ **HISTORY** probably from the name *Jake*

jalopy (jal-**lop**-ee) *n, pl* **-lopies** *Informal* a dilapidated old car. ▷ **HISTORY** origin unknown

jam[1] *vb* **jamming, jammed 1** to wedge (an object) into a tight space or against another object. **2** to fill (a place) with people or vehicles: *the surrounding roads were jammed for miles.* **3** to make or become stuck or locked. **4** *Radio* to prevent the clear reception of (radio communications) by transmitting other signals on the same wavelength. **5** *Slang* to play in a jam session. **6 jam on the brakes** to apply the brakes of a vehicle very suddenly. ✧ *n* **7** a situation where a large number of people or vehicles are crowded into a place: *a traffic jam.* **8** *Informal* a difficult situation. **9** same as **jam session**. ▷ **HISTORY** probably imitative

jam[2] *n* a food made from fruit boiled with sugar until the mixture sets, used for spreading on bread. ▷ **HISTORY** perhaps from JAM[1] (the act of squeezing)

Jamaican *adj* **1** of Jamaica. ✧ *n* **2** a person from Jamaica.

jamb *n* a side post of a doorframe or window frame. ▷ **HISTORY** Old French *jambe* leg, jamb

A
B
C
D
E
F
G
H
I
J
K
L
M
N
O
P
Q
R
S
T
U
V
W
X
Y
Z

jamboree *n* a large gathering or celebration. ▷ **HISTORY** origin unknown

jammy *adj* **-mier, -miest 1** covered with or tasting like jam. **2** *Brit slang* lucky.

jam-packed *adj* filled to capacity.

jam session *n Slang* an improvised performance by jazz or rock musicians. ▷ **HISTORY** probably from JAM[1]

Jan. January.

jandal *n NZ* a rubber-soled sandal attached to the foot by a thong between the big toe and the next toe.

jangle *vb* **-gling, -gled 1** to make a harsh unpleasant ringing noise. **2** to produce an irritating or unpleasant effect on: *the caffeine in coffee can jangle the nerves.* ▷ **HISTORY** Old French *jangler*

janitor *n Chiefly Scot, US, & Canad* the caretaker of a school or other building. ▷ **HISTORY** Latin: doorkeeper

January *n* the first month of the year. ▷ **HISTORY** Latin *Januarius*

japan *n* **1** a glossy black lacquer, originally from the Orient, which is used on wood or metal. ✧ *vb* **-panning, -panned 2** to varnish with japan.

Japanese *adj* **1** of Japan. ✧ *n* **2** (*pl* **-nese**) a person from Japan. **3** the language of Japan.

jape *n Old-fashioned* a joke or prank. ▷ **HISTORY** origin unknown

japonica *n* **1** a Japanese shrub with red flowers and yellowish fruit. **2** same as **camellia**. ▷ **HISTORY** New Latin *Japonia* Japan

jar[1] *n* **1** a wide-mouthed cylindrical glass container, used for storing food. **2** *Brit informal* a glass of beer. ▷ **HISTORY** Arabic *jarrah* large earthen vessel

jar[2] *vb* **jarring, jarred 1** to have an irritating or unpleasant effect: *sometimes a light remark jarred on her father.* **2** to be in disagreement or conflict: *their very different temperaments jarred.* **3** to jolt or bump. ✧ *n* **4** a jolt or shock. ▷ **HISTORY** probably imitative ▶ **jarring** *adj*

jardiniere *n* an ornamental pot or stand for plants. ▷ **HISTORY** French

jargon *n* **1** specialized language relating to a particular subject, profession, or group. **2** pretentious or unintelligible language. ▷ **HISTORY** Old French

jarrah *n* an Australian eucalypt yielding valuable timber.

jasmine *n* a shrub or climbing plant with sweet-smelling flowers. ▷ **HISTORY** Persian *yāsmīn*

jasper *n* a kind of quartz, usually red in colour, which is used as a gemstone and for ornamental decoration. ▷ **HISTORY** Greek *iaspis*

jaundice *n* yellowing of the skin and the whites of the eyes, caused by an excess of bile pigments in the blood. ▷ **HISTORY** French *jaune* yellow

jaundiced *adj* **1** bitter or cynical: *a jaundiced view.* **2** having jaundice.

jaunt *n* **1** a pleasure trip or outing. ✧ *vb* **2** to go on a jaunt. ▷ **HISTORY** origin unknown

jaunty *adj* **-tier, -tiest 1** cheerful and energetic. **2** smart and attractive: *a jaunty little hat.* ▷ **HISTORY** French *gentil* noble ▶ **jauntily** *adv*

Java *n Trademark* a computer programming language that is widely used on the Internet. ▷ **HISTORY** after *Java* coffee from the Indonesian island, allegedly drunk by its creators

Javanese *adj* **1** of the island of Java, in Indonesia. ✧ *n* **2** (*pl* **-nese**) a person from Java. **3** the language of Java.

javelin *n* a light spear thrown in a sports competition. ▷ **HISTORY** Old French *javeline*

jaw *n* **1** either of the bones that hold the teeth and frame the mouth. **2** the lower part of the face below the mouth. **3** *Slang* a long chat. ✧ *vb* **4** *Slang* to have a long chat. ▷ **HISTORY** probably Old French *joue* cheek

jawbone *n* the bone in the lower jaw of a person or animal.

jaws *pl n* **1** the mouth of a person or animal. **2** the parts of a machine or tool that grip an object. **3** the narrow opening of a gorge or valley. **4** a dangerous or threatening position: *the jaws of death.*

jay *n* a bird of Europe and Asia with a pinkish-brown body and blue-and-black wings. ▷ **HISTORY** Old French *jai*

jaywalking *n* crossing the road in a dangerous or careless manner. ▷ **HISTORY** *jay* (in sense: a foolish person) ▶ **jaywalker** *n*

jazz *n* **1** a kind of popular music of African-American origin that has an exciting rhythm and often involves improvisation. **2 and all that jazz** *Slang* and other related things. ▷ **HISTORY** origin unknown

jazz up *vb Informal* **1** to play (a piece of music) in a jazzy style. **2** to make (something) appear more interesting or lively.

jazzy *adj* **-zier, -ziest 1** colourful and modern: *jazzy shop fronts.* **2** of or like jazz.

JCB *n Trademark, Brit* a large machine used in building, that has a shovel on the front and a digger arm on the back. ▷ **HISTORY** initials of *Joseph Cyril Bamford*, its manufacturer

jealous *adj* **1** suspicious or fearful of being displaced by a rival. **2** envious: *I was jealous of the girls who had boyfriends.* **3** resulting from jealousy: *my jealous tears.* ▷ **HISTORY** Late Latin *zelus* emulation ▶ **jealously** *adv*

jealousy *n, pl* **-ousies** the state of or an instance of feeling jealous.

jeans *pl n* casual denim trousers. ▷ **HISTORY** from *jean fustian* fabric from Genoa

Jeep *n Trademark* a small road vehicle with four-wheel drive. ▷ **HISTORY** perhaps *general-purpose (vehicle),* influenced by Eugene the *Jeep,* creature in a comic strip

jeer *vb* **1** to be derisive towards (someone). ✧ *n* **2** a cry of derision. ▷ **HISTORY** origin unknown ▶ **jeering** *adj, n*

Jehovah *n* God. ▷ **HISTORY** Hebrew *Yahweh*

Jehovah's Witness *n* a member of a Christian Church whose followers believe that the end of the world is near.

jejune *adj* **1** simple and unsophisticated. **2** dull and uninteresting. ▷ **HISTORY** Latin *jejunus* empty

jejunum (jij-**june**-um) *n Anat* the part of the small intestine between the duodenum and the ileum. ▷ **HISTORY** Latin ▶ **jejunal** *adj*

Jekyll and Hyde *n* a person with two distinct personalities, one good and the other evil. ▷ **HISTORY** after the character in a novel by R. L. Stevenson

jell *vb* **1** to take on a definite form. **2** same as **gel** (sense 2). ▷ **HISTORY** from *jelly*

jellaba *n* a loose robe with a hood, worn by some Arab men. ▷ **HISTORY** Arabic *jallabah*

jellied *adj* prepared in a jelly: *jellied eels.*

jelly *n, pl* **-lies 1** a fruit-flavoured dessert set with gelatine. **2** a food made from fruit juice boiled with sugar until the mixture sets, used for spreading on bread. **3** a savoury food preparation set with gelatine. ▷ **HISTORY** Latin *gelare* to freeze

jellyfish *n, pl* **-fish** a small sea creature with a jelly-like body and trailing tentacles.

jemmy *or US* **jimmy** *n, pl* **-mies** a short steel crowbar, used by burglars to prise open doors and windows. ▷ **HISTORY** from short form of *James*

jenny *n, pl* **-nies** a female donkey, ass, or wren. ▷ **HISTORY** from the name *Jenny*

jeopardize *or* **-ise** *vb* **-izing, -ized** *or* **-ising, -ised** to put (something) at risk.

jeopardy *n* danger of harm, loss, or death: *the survival of public hospitals is in jeopardy.* ▷ **HISTORY** Old French *jeu parti,* literally: divided game, hence uncertain issue

jerboa *n* a small rodent of Asia and N Africa with long hind legs used for jumping. ▷ **HISTORY** Arabic *yarbū'*

jerepigo (jer-ree-**pee**-go) *n S African* a sweet fortified wine similar to port. ▷ **HISTORY** Portuguese *jeropiga*

jerk *vb* **1** to move with an irregular or spasmodic motion. **2** to pull or push (something) abruptly or spasmodically. ✧ *n* **3** an abrupt or spasmodic movement. **4** an irregular jolting motion. **5** *Slang, chiefly US & Canad* a stupid or ignorant person. ▷ **HISTORY** probably variant of *yerk* to pull stitches tight

jerkin *n* a short jacket. ▷ **HISTORY** origin unknown

jerky *adj* **jerkier, jerkiest** having an irregular jolting motion. ▶ **jerkily** *adv* ▶ **jerkiness** *n*

Jerry *n Old-fashioned, Brit slang* **1** (*pl* **-ries**) a German, esp. a German soldier. **2** Germans collectively.

jerry-built *adj* (of houses) built badly with cheap materials.

jerry can *n* a flat-sided can used for carrying petrol or water. ▷ **HISTORY** from *Jerry* German soldier

jersey *n* **1** a knitted garment covering the upper part of the body. **2** a soft, slightly stretchy, machine-knitted fabric. ▷ **HISTORY** after *Jersey,* because of the woollen sweaters worn by the fishermen

Jersey *n* a breed of reddish-brown dairy cattle that produces milk with a high butterfat content. ▷ **HISTORY** after *Jersey,* island in the English Channel

Jerusalem artichoke *n* a small yellowish-white vegetable that grows underground. ▷ **HISTORY** altered from Italian *girasole* sunflower

jest *n* **1** something done or said to amuse people. **2 in jest** as a joke. ✧ *vb* **3** to do or say something to amuse people. ▷ **HISTORY** variant of *gest* exploit

jester *n* a professional clown employed by a king or nobleman during the Middle Ages.

Jesuit (**jezz**-yew-it) *n* a member of the Society of Jesus, a Roman Catholic religious order. ▷ **HISTORY** New Latin *Jesuita* ▶ **Jesuitical** *adj*

Jesus *n* **1** the founder of Christianity, believed by Christians to be the Son of God. ✧ *interj* **2** *Taboo slang* an oath expressing intense anger or shock.

jet[1] *n* **1** an aircraft driven by jet propulsion. **2** a thin stream of liquid or gas forced out of a small hole. **3** an outlet or nozzle through which a stream of liquid or gas is forced. ✧ *vb* **jetting, jetted 4** to travel by jet aircraft. ▷ **HISTORY** Old French *jeter* to throw

jet[2] *n* a hard black mineral that is polished and used in jewellery. ▷ **HISTORY** Old French *jaiet*

jet-black *adj* deep black.

jetboat *n NZ* a motorboat propelled by a jet of water.

jet engine *n* an aircraft engine that uses jet propulsion for forward motion.

jet lag *n* a feeling of fatigue and disorientation often experienced by air passengers who have crossed several time zones in a short space of time.

jet-propelled *adj* driven by jet propulsion.

jet propulsion *n* a method of propulsion by which an aircraft is moved forward by the force of the exhaust gases ejected from the rear.

jetsam *n* **1** goods thrown overboard to lighten a ship during a storm. **2 flotsam and jetsam** See **flotsam** (sense 2). ▷ **HISTORY** from *jettison*

jet set *n* rich and fashionable people who travel widely for pleasure. ▶ **jet-setter** *n* ▶ **jet-setting** *adj*

jet stream *n Meteorol* a narrow belt of high-altitude winds moving east at high speeds.

jettison *vb* **1** to abandon or give up. **2** to throw overboard. ▷ **HISTORY** Latin *jactatio* a tossing about

jetty *n, pl* **-ties 1** a landing pier or dock. **2** a structure built from a shore out into the water to protect a harbour. ▷ **HISTORY** Old French *jetee* projecting part

Jew *n* **1** a person whose religion is Judaism. **2** a descendant of the ancient Hebrews. ▷ **HISTORY** Hebrew *yehūdāh* Judah

jewel *n* **1** a precious or semiprecious stone. **2** a person or thing regarded as precious or special: *a fantastic little car, a real little jewel.* **3** a gemstone used as part of the machinery of a watch. ▷ **HISTORY** Old French *jouel*

jeweller *or US* **jeweler** *n* a person who buys, sells, and repairs jewellery.

jewellery *or US* **jewelry** *n* objects such as rings, necklaces, and bracelets, worn for decoration.

A B C D E F G H I J K L M N O P Q R S T U V W X Y Z

Jewess *n Now often offensive* a woman whose religion is Judaism.
jewfish *n Austral* a freshwater catfish.
Jewish *adj* of Jews or Judaism.
Jewry *n* Jews collectively.
jew's-harp *n* a small musical instrument held between the teeth and played by plucking a metal strip with the finger.
Jezebel *n* a wicked or shameless woman. ▷ **HISTORY** after the wife of Ahab, in the Bible
jib[1] *n* **1** *Naut* a triangular sail set in front of the foremast. **2 the cut of someone's jib** a person's manner or style. ▷ **HISTORY** origin unknown
jib[2] *vb* **jibbing, jibbed** *Chiefly Brit* **1** (of an animal) to stop short and refuse to go forwards: *my animal jibbed three times.* **2 jib at** to object to: *he jibs at any suggestion that his side are the underdogs.* ▷ **HISTORY** origin unknown
jib[3] *n* the projecting arm of a crane. ▷ **HISTORY** probably from *gibbet*
jibe[1] *n* **1** an insulting or taunting remark. ✧ *vb* **jibing, jibed 2** to make insulting or taunting remarks.
jibe[2] *vb* **jibing, jibed** *Informal* to be in accord or be consistent: *their apparent devotion hardly jibed with what he had heard about them.*
jibe[3] *vb* **jibing, jibed,** *n Naut* same as **gybe**.
jiffy *n, pl* **jiffies** *Informal* a very short time: *won't be a jiffy!* ▷ **HISTORY** origin unknown
jig *n* **1** a lively folk dance. **2** music for this dance. **3** a mechanical device that holds and locates a part during machining. ✧ *vb* **jigging, jigged 4** to dance a jig. **5** to move with quick jerky movements. ▷ **HISTORY** origin unknown
jigger *n* a small whisky glass.
jiggery-pokery *n Informal, chiefly Brit* dishonest behaviour; cheating. ▷ **HISTORY** Scots dialect *joukery-pawkery*
jiggle *vb* **-gling, -gled** to move with quick jerky movements. ▷ **HISTORY** frequentative of *jig*
jigsaw *n* **1** Also called: **jigsaw puzzle** a puzzle in which the player has to put together a picture that has been cut into irregularly shaped interlocking pieces. **2** a mechanical saw with a fine steel blade for cutting along curved or irregular lines in sheets of material. ▷ **HISTORY** *jig* (to jerk up and down) + SAW[1]
jihad *n* Islamic holy war against unbelievers.
jilt *vb* to leave or reject (a lover) abruptly or callously. ▷ **HISTORY** dialect *jillet* flighty girl
jingle *n* **1** a short catchy song used to advertise a product on radio or television. **2** a light ringing sound. ✧ *vb* **-gling, -gled 3** to make a light ringing sound. ▷ **HISTORY** probably imitative
jingoism *n* excessive and aggressive patriotism. ▷ **HISTORY** after the use of *by Jingo!* in a 19th-century song ▸ **jingoistic** *or* **jingoist** *adj*
jinks *pl n* **high jinks** boisterous or mischievous behaviour. ▷ **HISTORY** origin unknown
jinni *or* **djinni** *n, pl* **jinn** *or* **djinn** a being or spirit in Muslim belief that could take on human or animal form. ▷ **HISTORY** Arabic
jinx *n* **1** someone or something believed to bring bad luck. ✧ *vb* **2** to bring bad luck to. ▷ **HISTORY** perhaps from Greek *iunx* wryneck, a bird used in magic
jitters *pl n* **the jitters** *Informal* a feeling of extreme nervousness experienced before an important event. ▷ **HISTORY** origin unknown
jittery *adj* nervous.
jive *n* **1** a lively jerky dance that was popular in the 1940s and 1950s. ✧ *vb* **jiving, jived 2** to dance the jive. ▷ **HISTORY** origin unknown ▸ **jiver** *n*
Jnr Junior.
job *n* **1** a person's occupation or paid employment. **2** a piece of work; task. **3** the performance of a task: *he made a good job of the repair.* **4** *Informal* a difficult task: *they are having a job to fill his shoes.* **5** *Brit, Austral & NZ informal* a crime, esp. a robbery. **6 just the job** *Informal* exactly what is required. **7 make the best of a bad job** to cope as well as possible in unsatisfactory circumstances. ▷ **HISTORY** origin unknown
jobbing *adj* doing individual jobs for payment: *a jobbing gardener.*
Jobcentre *or* **job centre** *n* (in Britain) a government office where advertisements of available jobs are displayed.
Jobclub *or* **job club** *n* (in Britain) a group of unemployed people which meets every weekday and is given advice on and help with jobseeking.
jobless *adj* **1** unemployed. ✧ *pl n* **2** people who are unemployed: *the young jobless.*
job lot *n* a miscellaneous collection of articles sold together.
Job's comforter *n* a person who adds to someone else's distress while pretending to be sympathetic. ▷ **HISTORY** after *Job* in the Bible
jobseeker's allowance *n* (in Britain) a social-security payment for unemployed people.
job sharing *n* an arrangement by which a job is shared by two part-time workers.
jockey *n* **1** a person who rides horses in races as a profession. ✧ *vb* **2 jockey for position** to try to obtain an advantage by skilful manoeuvring. ▷ **HISTORY** from the name *Jock*
jockstrap *n* an elasticated belt with a pouch to support the genitals, worn by male athletes. Also called: **athletic support** ▷ **HISTORY** slang *jock* penis
jocose (joke-**kohss**) *adj Old-fashioned* playful or humorous. ▷ **HISTORY** Latin *jocus* joke ▸ **jocosely** *adv*
jocular *adj* **1** (of a person) often joking; good-humoured. **2** (of a remark) meant lightly or humorously. ▷ **HISTORY** Latin *joculus* little joke ▸ **jocularity** *n* ▸ **jocularly** *adv*
jocund (**jok**-kund) *adj Literary* cheerful or merry. ▷ **HISTORY** Latin *jucundus* pleasant
jodhpurs *pl n* trousers worn for riding, which are loose-fitting around the thighs and tight-fitting below the knees.

WORD HISTORY

'Jodhpurs' are named after the town of *Jodhpur* in northwestern India.

joey *n Austral* a young kangaroo.

jog *vb* **jogging, jogged 1** to run at a gentle pace for exercise. **2** to nudge slightly. **3 jog along** to continue in a plodding way. **4 jog someone's memory** to remind someone of something. ✧ *n* **5** a slow run as a form of exercise. ▷ **HISTORY** probably variant of *shog* to shake ▶ **jogger** *n* ▶ **jogging** *n*

joggle *vb* **-gling, -gled** to shake or move with a slightly jolting motion. ▷ **HISTORY** frequentative of *jog*

john *n Slang, chiefly US & Canad* a toilet. ▷ **HISTORY** special use of the name

joie de vivre (**zhwah** de **veev**-ra) *n* enjoyment of life. ▷ **HISTORY** French, literally: joy of living

join *vb* **1** to become a member of (a club or organization). **2** to become part of (a queue or list). **3** to meet (someone) as a companion: *join me for a beer.* **4** to take part in (an activity): *join the war effort.* **5** (of two roads or rivers) to meet and come together. **6** to bring into contact: *join hands.* **7 join forces** to combine efforts with someone. ✧ *n* **8** a place where two things are joined together. ✧ See also **join in, join up**. ▷ **HISTORY** Latin *jungere* to yoke

joined-up *adj* integrated by an overall strategy: *joined-up government.*

joiner *n* a person whose job is making finished woodwork, such as window frames and stairs.

joinery *n* the skill or work of a joiner.

join in *vb* to take part in (an activity).

joint *adj* **1** shared by or belonging to two or more parties: *a joint statement.* ✧ *n* **2** *Anat* the junction between two or more bones: *a hip joint.* **3** a junction of two or more parts or objects: *a mortar joint.* **4** a piece of meat suitable for roasting. **5** *Slang* a building or place of entertainment: *strip joints.* **6** *Slang* a cannabis cigarette. **7 out of joint a** *Informal* out of order or out of keeping. **b** (of a bone) knocked out of its normal position. **8 put someone's nose out of joint** See **nose** (sense 10). ✧ *vb* **9** to provide a joint or joints. **10** to cut or divide (meat) into joints. ▶ **jointed** *adj* ▶ **jointly** *adv*

joint committee *n* a committee composed of members of both chambers of parliament.

joint-stock company *n Brit* a business firm whose capital is owned jointly by shareholders.

joint tenancy *n Law* ownership of land or property by two or more parties, each with an equal interest; upon the death of a joint tenant, the property so owned is automatically inherited by the surviving party or parties.

join up *vb* to become a member of a military organization.

joist *n* a beam made of timber, steel, or concrete, used as a support in the construction of floors and roofs. ▷ **HISTORY** Old French *giste*

jojoba (hoe-**hoe**-ba) *n* a shrub whose seeds contain an oil used in cosmetics. ▷ **HISTORY** Mexican Spanish

joke *n* **1** something that is said or done to amuse people. **2** someone or something that is ridiculous: *the country's inexperienced leaders are regarded as something of a joke.* **3 no joke** *Informal* a serious or difficult matter: *getting over mountain passes at ten thousand feet is no joke.* ✧ *vb* **joking, joked 4** to say or do something to amuse people. ▷ **HISTORY** Latin *jocus* ▶ **jokey** *adj* ▶ **jokingly** *adv*

joker *n* **1** a person who jokes a lot. **2** *Slang* a person regarded without respect: *waiting for the next jokers to sign up.* **3** an extra playing card in a pack, which can replace any other card in some games. **4** *Austral & NZ informal* a chap.

jol (**joll**) *S African slang* ✧ *n* **1** a party. ✧ *vb* **jolling, jolled 2** to have a good time. ▷ **HISTORY** Dutch

jollification *n* a merry festivity.

jollity *n* the condition of being jolly.

jolly *adj* **-lier, -liest 1** full of good humour. **2** involving a lot of fun: *big jolly birthday parties.* ✧ *adv* **3** *Brit informal* very: *I'm going to have a jolly good try.* ✧ *vb* **-lies, -lying, -lied 4 jolly along** *Informal* to try to keep (someone) cheerful by flattery or cheerful chat. ▷ **HISTORY** Old French *jolif*

jolt *n* **1** a severe shock. **2** a sudden violent movement. ✧ *vb* **3** to surprise or shock: *he was momentarily jolted by the news.* **4** to bump against (someone or something) with a sudden violent movement. **5** to move in a jerking manner. ▷ **HISTORY** origin unknown

Jonah *n* a person believed to bring bad luck to those around him or her. ▷ **HISTORY** after *Jonah* in the Bible

jonquil *n* a narcissus with sweet-smelling yellow or white flowers. ▷ **HISTORY** French *jonquille*

Jordanian *adj* **1** of Jordan. ✧ *n* **2** a person from Jordan.

josh *vb Slang* to joke or tease. ▷ **HISTORY** origin unknown

joss stick *n* a stick of incense, giving off a sweet smell when burnt. ▷ **HISTORY** *joss* (a Chinese idol) from Portuguese *deos* god

jostle *vb* **-tling, -tled 1** to bump or push roughly. **2** to compete with someone: *jostling for power.* ▷ **HISTORY** Old French *jouster* to joust

jot *vb* **jotting, jotted 1 jot down** to write a brief note of: *quickly jot down the answers to these questions.* ✧ *n* **2** the least bit: *it makes not one jot of difference.* ▷ **HISTORY** Greek *iōta* iota, smallest letter

jotter *n* a small notebook.

jottings *pl n* notes jotted down.

joule (**jool**) *n Physics* the SI unit of work or energy. ▷ **HISTORY** after J. P. *Joule,* physicist

journal *n* **1** a newspaper or magazine. **2** a daily record of events. ▷ **HISTORY** Latin *diurnalis* daily

journalese *n* a superficial style of writing regarded as typical of newspapers and magazines.

journalism *n* the profession of collecting, writing, and publishing news through newspapers and magazines or by radio and television.

journalist *n* a person who writes or edits news items for a newspaper or magazine or for radio or television. ▶ **journalistic** *adj*

journey *n* **1** the process of travelling from one place to another. **2** the time taken or distance travelled on a journey. ✧ *vb* **3** to make a journey.

▷ HISTORY Old French *journee* a day, a day's travelling

journeyman *n, pl* **-men** a qualified craftsman who works for an employer. ▷ HISTORY *journey* (in obsolete sense: a day's work)

joust *History* ✧ *n* **1** a combat with lances between two mounted knights. ✧ *vb* **2** to take part in such a tournament. ▷ HISTORY Old French *jouster*

Jove *n* **1** Jupiter (the god). **2 by Jove** *Old-fashioned* an exclamation of surprise or for emphasis.

jovial *adj* happy and cheerful. ▷ HISTORY Latin *jovialis* of (the planet) Jupiter ▶ **joviality** *n* ▶ **jovially** *adv*

jowl[1] *n* **1** the lower jaw. **2 cheek by jowl** See **cheek**. **3 jowls** cheeks. ▷ HISTORY Old English *ceafl* jaw ▶ **jowled** *adj*

jowl[2] *n* fatty flesh hanging from the lower jaw. ▷ HISTORY Old English *ceole* throat

joy *n* **1** deep happiness and contentment. **2** something that brings deep happiness: *a thing of beauty is a joy for ever.* **3** *Informal* success or satisfaction: *we checked ports and airports without any joy.* ▷ HISTORY Latin *gaudium*

joyful *adj* feeling or bringing great joy: *joyful crowds; a joyful event.* ▶ **joyfully** *adv*

joyless *adj* feeling or bringing no joy.

joyous *adj* extremely happy and enthusiastic. ▶ **joyously** *adv*

joyride *n* a drive in a car one has stolen. ▶ **joyriding** *n* ▶ **joyrider** *n*

joystick *n* the control lever of an aircraft or a computer.

JP (in Britain) Justice of the Peace.

JPEG *n Computing* **a** a standard compressed file format used for pictures. **b** a picture held in this file format.

Jr Junior.

JSA jobseeker's allowance: in Britain, a payment made to unemployed people.

jube *n Austral & NZ informal* same as **jujube**.

jubilant *adj* feeling great joy. ▷ HISTORY Latin *jubilare* to give a joyful cry ▶ **jubilantly** *adv*

jubilation *n* a feeling of great joy and celebration.

jubilee *n* a special anniversary, esp. a 25th (**silver jubilee**) or 50th one (**golden jubilee**).

> **WORD HISTORY**
> 'Jubilee' comes from the Hebrew word *yōbhēl* meaning a 'ram's horn'. In Old Testament times a 'jubilee' year among the Jews occurred every fifty years. In a jubilee year, fields and vineyards were left uncultivated, property that had been sold was returned to its original owner or his descendants, and people who had been sold as slaves were released from their bondage. The beginning of the jubilee was marked by the blowing of a ram's horn trumpet.

Judaic *adj* of Jews or Judaism.

Judaism *n* the religion of the Jews, based on the Old Testament and the Talmud.

Judas *n* a person who betrays a friend. ▷ HISTORY after *Judas* Iscariot in the Bible

judder *vb Informal, chiefly Brit* to shake or vibrate violently: *the van juddered before it moved away.* ▷ HISTORY probably blend of *jar* (jolt) + *shudder*

judder bar *n NZ* a raised strip across a road designed to slow down vehicles.

judge *n* **1** a public official with authority to hear cases and pass sentences in a court of law. **2** a person appointed to determine the result of a competition. **3** a person whose opinion on a particular subject is usually reliable: *a fine judge of men.* ✧ *vb* **judging, judged 4** to determine the result of (a competition). **5** to appraise critically: *she hopes people judge her on her work rather than her appearance.* **6** to decide (something) after inquiry: *we use a means test to judge the most needy cases.* **7** to believe or consider: *doctors judged that the benefits of such treatment outweighed the risk.* ▷ HISTORY Latin *judex*

judgment *or* **judgement** *n* **1** a decision formed after careful consideration. **2** the verdict pronounced by a court of law. **3** the ability to make critical distinctions and achieve a balanced viewpoint. **4** the formal decision of the judge of a competition. **5 against one's better judgment** contrary to what one thinks is sensible. **6 pass judgment** to give one's opinion, usually a critical one, on a matter.

judgmental *or* **judgemental** *adj* making judgments, esp. critical ones, about other people's conduct.

Judgment Day *n Christianity* the occasion of the Last Judgment by God at the end of the world.

judicial *adj* **1** of judges or the administration of justice. **2** showing or using good judgment. ▷ HISTORY Latin *judicium* judgment ▶ **judicially** *adv*

judicial review *n Law* the process by which the courts decide whether a government or other authority had the right to act as it did or whether it exceeded its power, acting illegally, irrationally, or improperly. Compare **administrative review**.

judiciary *n* the branch of the central authority in a country that administers justice.

judicious *adj* having or showing good judgment: *the judicious use of charge cards.* ▶ **judiciously** *adv*

judo *n* a sport derived from jujitsu, in which the two opponents try to throw or force each other on to the ground. ▷ HISTORY Japanese *jū* gentleness + *dō* way

jug *n* a container with a handle and a small spout, used for holding and pouring liquids. ▷ HISTORY origin unknown

jugged hare *n* hare stewed in an earthenware pot.

juggernaut *n* **1** *Brit* a very large heavy lorry. **2** any terrible force that demands complete self-sacrifice.

WORD HISTORY
Hindi *Jagannath* comes from Sanskrit *Jagannātha*, meaning 'Lord of the World', the title given to a huge idol of the god Krishna, wheeled every year on a chariot through the streets of Puri in India. It was said that devotees of Krishna would throw themselves under the chariot and be crushed to death in the hope of going to heaven, but this story is without foundation.

juggle *vb* **-gling, -gled 1** to throw and catch several objects continuously so that most are in the air at the same time. **2** to keep (several activities) in progress at the same time. **3** to manipulate (facts or figures) to suit one's purpose. ▷ **HISTORY** Old French *jogler* to perform as a jester ▶ **juggler** *n*

jugular *n* a large vein in the neck that carries blood to the heart from the head. Also called: **jugular vein** ▷ **HISTORY** Latin *jugulum* throat

juice *n* **1** a drink made from the liquid part of a fruit or vegetable. **2** *Informal* **a** petrol. **b** electricity. **3 juices a** the fluids in a person's or animal's body: *digestive juices.* **b** the liquid that comes out of meat when it is cooked. ▷ **HISTORY** Old French *jus*

juicy *adj* **juicier, juiciest 1** full of juice. **2** *Informal* interesting and exciting: *juicy details.*

jujitsu *n* the traditional Japanese system of unarmed self-defence. ▷ **HISTORY** Japanese *jū* gentleness + *jutsu* art

juju *n* **1** a magic charm or fetish used by some tribes in W Africa. **2** the power associated with a juju. ▷ **HISTORY** probably from W African *djudju* evil spirit, fetish

jujube *n* a chewy sweet made of flavoured gelatine. ▷ **HISTORY** Medieval Latin *jujuba*

jukebox *n* an automatic coin-operated record player. ▷ **HISTORY** *juke* (from a Black American language) bawdy

jukskei *n S African* a game in which a peg is thrown over a fixed distance at a stake fixed into the ground. ▷ **HISTORY** Afrikaans *juk* yoke + *skei* pin

Jul. July.

julep *n* a sweet alcoholic drink, usually garnished with sprigs of mint.

Julian calendar *n* the calendar introduced by Julius Caesar, in which leap years occur every fourth year and in every centenary year.

julienne *adj* **1** (of vegetables or meat) cut into thin shreds. ✧ *n* **2** a clear soup containing thinly shredded vegetables. ▷ **HISTORY** French

July *n, pl* **-lies** the seventh month of the year. ▷ **HISTORY** after *Julius* Caesar

jumble *n* **1** a disordered mass or state. **2** articles donated for a jumble sale. ✧ *vb* **-bling, -bled 3** to mix up. ▷ **HISTORY** origin unknown

jumble sale *n* a sale, usually of second-hand articles, often in aid of charity.

jumbo *adj* **1** *Brit, Austral & NZ informal* very large: *jumbo prawns.* ✧ *n, pl* **-bos 2** short for **jumbo jet**.

WORD HISTORY
Jumbo was the name of a famous and very large 19th-century African elephant that was used to give rides to children at London Zoo, before being sold in 1882 to Barnum and Bailey's circus.

jumbo jet *n Informal* a very large jet-propelled airliner.

jumbuck *n Austral old-fashioned slang* sheep. ▷ **HISTORY** from a native Australian language

jump *vb* **1** to move suddenly up into the air by using the muscles in the legs and feet. **2** to move quickly: *he jumps on a No. 6 bus.* **3** to jerk with astonishment or shock: *he jumped when he heard a loud noise.* **4** (of prices) to rise suddenly or abruptly. **5** to change quickly from one subject to another: *any other comments before I jump on to the next section?* **6** *Informal* to attack without warning: *the officer was jumped by three prisoners who broke his jaw.* **7 jump down someone's throat** *Informal* to speak sharply to someone. **8 jump the gun** See **gun** (sense 3). **9 jump the queue a** to take a place in a queue ahead of people who are already queuing. **b** to have an unfair advantage over other people. **10 jump to it** *Informal* to begin doing something immediately. ✧ *n* **11** the act or an instance of jumping. **12** *Sport* any of several contests that involve jumping: *the long jump.* **13** a sudden rise: *a 78% jump in taxable profits.* **14** a sudden change from one subject to another: *stunning jumps from thought to thought.* **15** a step or degree: *one jump ahead of the competition.* **16 take a running jump** *Informal* a contemptuous expression of dismissal. ✧ See also **jump at, jump on**. ▷ **HISTORY** probably imitative

jump at *vb* to accept eagerly.

jumped-up *adj Informal* having suddenly risen in significance and appearing arrogant.

jumper[1] *n* **1** *Brit & Austral* a knitted garment covering the upper part of the body. **2** *US & Canad* a pinafore dress. ▷ **HISTORY** obsolete *jump* man's loose jacket

jumper[2] *n* a person or animal that jumps.

jump jet *n Informal* a fixed-wing jet aircraft that can land and take off vertically.

jump leads *pl n* two heavy cables used to start a motor vehicle with a flat battery by connecting the flat battery to the battery of another vehicle.

jump on *vb Informal* to make a sudden physical or verbal attack on: *the press really jumped on him.*

jump-start *vb* **1** to start the engine of (a motor vehicle) by pushing or rolling it and then engaging the gears. ✧ *n* **2** the act of starting a motor vehicle in this way.

jump suit *n* a one-piece garment combining trousers and top.

jumpy *adj* **jumpier, jumpiest** nervous.

Jun. **1** June. **2** Junior.

junction *n* a place where roads or railway lines meet, link, or cross each other. ▷ **HISTORY** Latin *junctio* a joining

juncture *n* a point in time, esp. a critical one: *trade has been halted at a crucial juncture.*

A B C D E F G H I J K L M N O P Q R S T U V W X Y Z

June *n* the sixth month of the year. ▷ **HISTORY** probably from Latin *Junius* of the goddess Juno

jungle *n* **1** a forest area in a hot country with luxuriant vegetation. **2** a confused or confusing situation: *the administrative jungle.* **3** a situation where there is an intense struggle for survival: *the economic jungle.* **4** a type of fast electronic dance music. ▷ **HISTORY** Hindi *jangal*

junior *adj* **1** lower in rank or position: *junior officers.* **2** younger: *world junior champion.* **3** (in England and Wales) of school children between the ages of 7 and 11 approximately. **4** *US* of the third year of a four-year course at college or high school. ✧ *n* **5** a person holding a low rank or position. **6** a person who is younger than another person. **7** (in England and Wales) a junior school child. **8** *US* a junior student. ▷ **HISTORY** Latin: younger

juniper *n* an evergreen shrub with purple berries which are used to make gin. ▷ **HISTORY** Latin *juniperus*

junk[1] *n* **1** old or unwanted objects. **2** *Informal* rubbish. **3** *Slang* narcotic drugs, esp. heroin. ▷ **HISTORY** Middle English *jonke* old useless rope

junk[2] *n* a Chinese sailing boat with a flat bottom and square sails. ▷ **HISTORY** Portuguese *junco,* from Javanese *jon*

junket *n* **1** an excursion made by a public official and paid for out of public funds. **2** a sweet dessert made of flavoured milk set with rennet. **3** a feast. ▷ **HISTORY** Middle English: rush basket, hence custard served on rushes ▶ **junketing** *n*

junk food *n* food with a low nutritional value.

junkie *n Informal* a drug addict.

junk mail *n* unsolicited mail advertising goods or services.

Juno *n* the queen of the Roman gods.

junta *n* a group of military officers holding the power in a country after a revolution. ▷ **HISTORY** Spanish: council

Jupiter *n* **1** the king of the Roman gods. **2** the largest planet.

Jurassic *adj Geol* of the geological period about 180 million years ago, during which dinosaurs flourished. ▷ **HISTORY** after the *Jura* (Mountains) in W central Europe

juridical *adj* of law or the administration of justice. ▷ **HISTORY** Latin *jus* law + *dicere* to say

jurisdiction *n* **1** the right or power to administer justice and to apply laws. **2** the exercise or extent of such right or power. **3** authority in general. ▷ **HISTORY** Latin *jurisdictio*

jurisprudence *n* the science or philosophy of law. ▷ **HISTORY** Latin *juris prudentia*

jurist *n* a person who is an expert on law. ▷ **HISTORY** French *juriste*

juror *n* a member of a jury. ▷ **HISTORY** Old French *jurer* to take an oath

jury *n, pl* **-ries 1** a group of, usually, twelve people, sworn to deliver a true verdict according to the evidence upon a case presented in a court of law. **2** a group of people appointed to judge a competition. ▷ **HISTORY** Old French *jurer* to swear

jury box *n* an enclosure where the jury sits in a court of law.

jury-rigged *adj Chiefly naut* set up in a makeshift manner. ▷ **HISTORY** origin unknown

just *adv* **1** very recently: *the results have just been published.* **2** at this very instant or in the very near future: *news is just coming in of a nuclear explosion.* **3** no more than; only: *nothing fancy, just solid German fare.* **4** exactly: *just the opposite.* **5** barely: *the swimmers arrived just in time for the opening ceremony.* **6 just about** practically or virtually: *just about everyone.* **7 just about to** very soon going to: *it was just about to explode.* **8 just a moment, second** *or* **minute** an expression requesting someone to wait for a short time. **9 just now a** a short time ago: *as you said just now.* **b** at the present time: *all the support he can get just now.* **c** *S African informal* in a little while. **10 just so** arranged with precision: *a cottage with the gardens all just so.* ✧ *adj* **11** fair and right: *a just war.* ▷ **HISTORY** Latin *jus* justice ▶ **justly** *adv*

> **WORD TIP**
> The use of *just* with *exactly* (*it's just exactly what they want*) is redundant and should be avoided: *it's exactly what they want.*

justice *n* **1** the quality of being just. **2** the administration of law according to prescribed and accepted principles. **3** a judge. **4 bring to justice** to capture, try, and punish (a criminal). **5 do justice to** to show to full advantage: *white slacks that did full justice to her figure.* ▷ **HISTORY** Latin *justitia*

justice of the peace *n* **1** (in Britain) a magistrate who is authorized to act as a judge in a local court of law. **2** (in New Zealand) a person authorised to act in a limited judicial capacity.

justifiable *adj* having a good cause or reason: *justifiable indignation.* ▶ **justifiably** *adv*

justify *vb* **-fies, -fying, -fied 1** to prove (something) to be just or valid: *the idea of the ends justifying the means.* **2** to defend (an action) as being warranted. **3** to arrange (text) when typing or printing so that both margins are straight. ▷ **HISTORY** Latin *justificare* ▶ **justification** *n*

jute *n* a fibre that comes from the bark of an East Indian plant, used in making rope, sacks, and mats. ▷ **HISTORY** Bengali *jhuto*

juvenile *adj* **1** young; not fully adult: *juvenile offenders.* **2** of or for young people: *juvenile court.* **3** immature in behaviour. ✧ *n* **4** a young person. ▷ **HISTORY** Latin *juvenilis*

juvenile delinquent *n* a young person who is guilty of a crime. ▶ **juvenile delinquency** *n*

juvenile water *n Geol* water occurring at the earth's surface for the first time as a result of volcanic activity.

juvenilia *pl n* works produced in an artist's youth.

juxtapose *vb* **-posing, -posed** to place (two objects or ideas) close together or side by side.

juxtaposition *n* close positioning; often used to describe the placing together of contrasting elements for effect. ▷ **HISTORY** Latin *juxta* next to + POSITION

K k

K 1 kelvin(s). 2 *Chess* king. 3 *Chem* potassium. ▷ HISTORY New Latin *kalium* 4 one thousand. ▷ HISTORY from KILO- 5 *Computers* a unit of 1024 words, bits, or bytes.

Kaffir (**kaf**-fer) *n S African offensive, obsolete* a Black African. ▷ HISTORY Arabic *kāfir* infidel

kaftan *or* **caftan** *n* 1 a long loose garment worn by men in eastern countries. 2 a woman's dress resembling this. ▷ HISTORY Turkish *qaftān*

kahawai *n* a food and game fish of New Zealand. ▷ HISTORY Maori

kai *n NZ informal* food. ▷ HISTORY Maori

kail *n* same as **kale**.

kaiser (**kize**-er) *n History* a German or Austro-Hungarian emperor. ▷ HISTORY German, from Latin *Caesar* emperor

kak (**kuck**) *n S African taboo* 1 faeces. 2 rubbish. ▷ HISTORY Afrikaans

kaka *n* a parrot of New Zealand. ▷ HISTORY Maori

kakapo *n, pl* **-pos** a ground-living nocturnal New Zealand parrot that resembles an owl. ▷ HISTORY Maori

Kalashnikov *n* a Russian-made automatic rifle. ▷ HISTORY after M. *Kalashnikov,* its designer

kale *n* a type of cabbage with crinkled leaves. ▷ HISTORY Old English *cāl*

kaleidoscope *n* 1 a tube-shaped toy lined with angled mirrors and containing loose pieces of coloured paper that form intricate patterns when viewed through a hole in the end. 2 any complicated or rapidly changing set of colours, circumstances, etc.: *a kaleidoscope of shifting political groups and alliances.* ▷ HISTORY Greek *kalos* beautiful + *eidos* form + *skopein* to look at ▶ **kaleidoscopic** *adj*

kalends *pl n* same as **calends**.

kamikaze (kam-mee-**kah**-zee) *n* 1 (in World War II) a Japanese pilot who performed a suicidal mission. ✧ *adj* 2 (of an action) undertaken in the knowledge that it will result in the death or injury of the person performing it: *a kamikaze attack.*

> **WORD HISTORY**
> 'Kamikaze' comes from Japanese *kami*, meaning 'divine', and *kaze*, meaning 'wind'.

Kamloops trout *n* a bright silvery rainbow trout common in British Columbia, Canada.

kangaroo *n, pl* **-roos** a large Australian marsupial with powerful hind legs used for leaping. ▷ HISTORY probably Aboriginal

kangaroo court *n* an unofficial court set up by a group to discipline its members.

kangaroo paw *n* an Australian plant with green-and-red flowers.

kaolin *n* a fine white clay used in making porcelain and in some medicines. ▷ HISTORY *Kaoling,* Chinese mountain where supplies for Europe were first obtained

kapok *n* a fluffy fibre from a tropical tree, used for stuffing pillows and padding sleeping bags. ▷ HISTORY Malay

kaput (kap-**poot**) *adj Informal* ruined or broken: *the chronometer, incidentally, is kaput.* ▷ HISTORY German *kaputt*

karakul *n* 1 a sheep of central Asia, the lambs of which have soft curled dark hair. 2 the fur prepared from these lambs. ▷ HISTORY Russian

karaoke *n* a form of entertainment in which members of the public sing well-known songs over a prerecorded backing tape. ▷ HISTORY Japanese *kara* empty + *ōkesutora* orchestra

karate *n* a Japanese system of unarmed combat, in which punches, chops, and kicks are made with the hands, feet, elbows, and legs. ▷ HISTORY Japanese: empty hand

karma *n Hinduism, Buddhism* a person's actions affecting his or her fate in the next reincarnation. ▷ HISTORY Sanskrit: action, effect

karoo *or* **karroo** *n, pl* **-roos** *S African* an arid semidesert plateau of Southern Africa. ▷ HISTORY Khoi (language of southern Africa) *karo* dry

kaross (ka-**ross**) *n S African* a blanket made of animal skins sewn together. ▷ HISTORY Khoi (language of southern Africa) *caro-s* animal-skin blanket

karri *n, pl* **-ris** 1 an Australian eucalypt. 2 its wood, used for building.

karst *n Geol* (*modifier*) denoting the characteristic scenery of a limestone region, including underground streams, gorges, etc.: *karst landscapes and cave systems.* ▷ HISTORY C19: German, from *Karst,* limestone plateau near Trieste

kart *n* same as **go-kart**.

karyokinesis *n Biol* same as **mitosis**.

kasbah *n* same as **casbah**.

katabatic *adj Meteorol* (of winds) blowing downhill through having become denser with cooling.

katipo *n, pl* **-pos** a large New Zealand conifer that yields valuable timber and resin.

katydid *n* a large green grasshopper of North America. ▷ HISTORY imitative

kauri *n* a large New Zealand conifer grown for its valuable wood and resin. ▷ HISTORY Maori

kayak *n* 1 an Inuit canoe-like boat consisting of a frame covered with animal skins. 2 a fibreglass or canvas-covered canoe of similar design. ▷ HISTORY Inuit

kazoo *n, pl* **-zoos** a cigar-shaped metal musical instrument that produces a buzzing sound when the player hums into it. ▷ HISTORY probably imitative

KBE (in Britain) Knight (Commander of the Order) of the British Empire.

kbyte *Computers* kilobyte.

kcal kilocalorie.

A B C D E F G H I J K L M N O P Q R S T U V W X Y Z

kea *n* a large brown-green parrot of New Zealand. ▷ **HISTORY** Maori

kebab *n* a dish consisting of small pieces of meat and vegetables, usually threaded onto skewers and grilled. ▷ **HISTORY** Arabic *kabāb* roast meat

kedge *Naut* ✧ *vb* **kedging, kedged 1** to move (a ship) along by hauling in on the cable of a light anchor. ✧ *n* **2** a light anchor used for kedging. ▷ **HISTORY** Middle English *caggen* to fasten

kedgeree *n Chiefly Brit* a dish consisting of rice, fish, and eggs. ▷ **HISTORY** Hindi *khicarī*

keel *n* **1** one of the main lengthways steel or timber pieces along the base of a ship, to which the frames are fastened. **2 on an even keel** working or progressing smoothly without any sudden changes. ▷ **HISTORY** Old Norse *kjölr*

keelhaul *vb* **1** to reprimand (someone) harshly. **2** *History* to drag (someone) under the keel of a ship as a punishment.

keel over *vb* **1** (of an object) to turn upside down. **2** *Informal* (of a person) to collapse suddenly.

keen[1] *adj* **1** eager or enthusiastic: *a keen gardener.* **2 keen on** fond of; devoted to: *he is very keen on sport.* **3** intense or strong: *a keen interest in environmental issues.* **4** intelligent, quick, and perceptive: *a keen sense of humour.* **5** (of sight, smell, or hearing) capable of recognizing fine distinctions. **6** (of a knife or blade) having a sharp cutting edge. **7** very strong and cold: *a keen wind.* **8** very competitive: *keen prices.* ▷ **HISTORY** Old English *cēne* ▶ **keenly** *adv* ▶ **keenness** *n*

keen[2] *vb* **1** to lament the dead. ✧ *n* **2** a lament for the dead. ▷ **HISTORY** Irish Gaelic *caoine*

keep *vb* **keeping, kept 1** to have or retain possession of (something). **2** to have temporary charge of: *he'd kept my broken beads in his pocket for me all evening.* **3** to store in a customary place: *I keep it at the back of the drawer with my journal.* **4** to remain or cause (someone or something) to remain in a specified state or condition: *keep still.* **5** to continue or cause (someone) to continue: *keep going straight on.* **6** to stay (in, on, or at a place or position): *keep to the paths.* **7** to have as part of normal stock: *they keep a small stock of first-class German wines.* **8** to support (someone) financially. **9** to detain (someone). **10** to be faithful to (something): *to keep a promise.* **11** (of food) to stay in good condition for a certain time: *fish doesn't keep very well.* **12** to observe (a religious festival) with rites or ceremonies. **13** to maintain by writing regular records in: *he keeps a nature diary in his spare time.* **14** to look after or maintain for use, pleasure, or profit: *an old man who kept goats and cows.* **15** to associate with: *she has started keeping bad company.* **16 keep in with** to stay friendly with someone as they may be useful to you. **17 how are you keeping?** are you well? ✧ *n* **18** the cost of food and other everyday expenses: *I have to earn my keep.* **19** the main tower within the walls of a medieval castle or fortress. **20 for keeps** *Informal* permanently. ▷ **HISTORY** Old English *cēpan* to observe

keeper *n* **1** a person in charge of animals in a zoo. **2** a person in charge of a museum, collection, or section of a museum. **3** a person who supervises a person or thing: *the self-appointed keeper of the village conscience.* **4** short for **gamekeeper, goalkeeper, wicketkeeper**.

keep fit *n* exercises designed to promote physical fitness if performed regularly.

keeping *n* **1 in keeping with** suitable or appropriate to or for. **2 out of keeping with** unsuitable or inappropriate to or for.

keepsake *n* a gift kept in memory of the giver.

keep up *vb* **1** to maintain (prices, standards, or one's morale) at the present level. **2** to maintain in good condition. **3 keep up with a** to maintain a pace set by (someone). **b** to remain informed about: *he liked to think he kept up with current musical trends.* **c** to remain in contact with (someone). **4 keep up with the Joneses** *Informal* to compete with one's friends or neighbours in material possessions.

keg *n* a small barrel in which beer is transported and stored. ▷ **HISTORY** Scandinavian

Kellogg-Briand Pact *n History* a treaty for the renunciation of war, signed in Paris in 1928 by representatives of 15 nations. ▷ **HISTORY** after French Prime Minister Aristide *Briand* and US Secretary of State Frank B *Kellogg*

kelp *n* a large brown seaweed rich in iodine and potash. ▷ **HISTORY** origin unknown

kelpie *n* **1** (in Scottish folklore) a water spirit in the form of a horse. ✧ *n* **2** an Australian sheepdog with a smooth coat and upright ears. ▷ **HISTORY** origin unknown

kelt *n* a salmon that has recently spawned. ▷ **HISTORY** origin unknown

kelvin *n Physics* the basic SI unit of thermodynamic temperature. ▷ **HISTORY** after W. T. *Kelvin,* physicist

Kelvin scale *n Physics* a thermodynamic temperature scale starting at absolute zero.

ken *n* **1 beyond one's ken** beyond one's range of knowledge. ✧ *vb* **kenning, kenned** *or* **kent 2** *Scot & N English dialect* to know. ▷ **HISTORY** Old English *cennan*

kendo *n* the Japanese sport of fencing using wooden staves. ▷ **HISTORY** Japanese

kennel *n* **1** a hutlike shelter for a dog. **2 kennels** a place where dogs are bred, trained, or boarded. ✧ *vb* **-nelling, -nelled** *or US* **-neling, -neled** to keep (a dog) in a kennel. ▷ **HISTORY** Latin *canis* dog

Kenyan *adj* **1** from Kenya. ✧ *n* **2** a person from Kenya.

kept *vb* **1** the past of **keep**. **2 kept woman** *or* **man** a person financially supported by someone in return for sexual favours.

keratin *n* a fibrous protein found in the hair and nails.

kerb *or US & Canad* **curb** *n* a line of stone or concrete forming an edge between a pavement and a roadway. ▷ **HISTORY** Old French *courbe* bent

kerb crawling *n Brit* the act of driving slowly beside a kerb to pick up a prostitute. ▶ **kerb crawler** *n*

kerchief *n* a piece of cloth worn over the head or round the neck. ▷ **HISTORY** Old French *cuevrechef*

kerfuffle *n Brit & NZ informal* a noisy and disorderly incident. ▷ **HISTORY** Scots *curfuffle, carfuffle*

kermes (**kur**-meez) *n* the dried bodies of female scale insects, used as a red dyestuff. ▷ **HISTORY** Arabic *qirmiz*

kernel *n* **1** the edible seed of a nut or fruit within the shell or stone. **2** the grain of a cereal, such as wheat, consisting of the seed in a hard husk. **3** the central or essential part of something: *there is a kernel of truth in these remarks.* ▷ **HISTORY** Old English *cyrnel* a little seed

kerosene *n US, Canad, Austral, & NZ* same as **paraffin** (sense 1). ▷ **HISTORY** Greek *kēros* wax

Kerry *n, pl* **-ries** a small black breed of dairy cattle, originally from Ireland. ▷ **HISTORY** after *Kerry,* county in SW Ireland

kestrel *n* a small falcon that feeds on small animals such as mice. ▷ **HISTORY** Old French *cresserele*

ketch *n* a two-masted sailing ship. ▷ **HISTORY** Middle English *cache*

ketchup *n* a thick cold sauce, usually made of tomatoes. ▷ **HISTORY** Chinese *kōetsiap* brine of pickled fish

ketone (**kee**-tone) *n Chem* any of a class of compounds with the general formula R′COR, where R and R′ are alkyl or aryl groups. ▷ **HISTORY** German *Keton,* from *Aketon* acetone

kettle *n* **1** a metal container with a handle and spout, for boiling water. **2** any of various metal containers for heating liquid, cooking, etc. **3 a different kettle of fish** a different matter entirely. **4 a fine kettle of fish** a difficult or awkward situation. ▷ **HISTORY** Old Norse *ketill*

kettledrum *n* a large bowl-shaped metal drum that can be tuned to play specific notes.

key[1] *n* **1** a specially shaped metal instrument, for moving the bolt of a lock so as to lock or unlock a door, suitcase, etc. **2** an instrument that is turned to operate a valve, clock winding mechanism, etc. **3** any of a set of levers pressed to operate a typewriter, computer, or musical keyboard instrument. **4** a scale of musical notes that starts at one specific note. **5** something that is crucial in providing an explanation or interpretation. **6** a means of achieving a desired end: *education is the key to success in most walks of life today.* **7** a list of explanations of symbols, codes, or abbreviations. **8** pitch: *he spoke in a low key.* ✧ *adj* **9** of great importance: *key prosecution witnesses have been giving evidence.* ✧ *vb* **10** to harmonize with: *training and educational programmes uniquely keyed for local needs.* **11** to adjust or fasten (something) with a key or some similar device. **12** same as **keyboard**. ✧ See also **key in**. ▷ **HISTORY** Old English *cǣg*

key[2] *n* same as **cay**.

keyboard *n* **1** a set of keys on a typewriter, computer, or piano. **2** a musical instrument played using a keyboard. ✧ *vb* **3** to enter (text) in type using a keyboard. ▸ **keyboarder** *n*

keyed up *adj* very excited or nervous.

key grip *n* the person in charge of moving and setting up camera tracks and scenery in a film or television studio.

keyhole *n* an opening for inserting a key into a lock.

keyhole surgery *n* surgery carried out using very small instruments, performed through a narrow hole cut in the body rather than through a major incision.

key in *vb* to enter (information or instructions) into a computer by means of a keyboard.

key money *n Brit* a sum of money required from a new tenant of a house or flat before he or she moves in.

Keynesian (**cane**-zee-an) *adj* of the economic theories of J.M. Keynes, who argued that governments should fund public works to maintain full employment, accepting if necessary the consequence of inflation.

keynote *n* **1** a central or dominant idea in a speech or literary work. **2** the note on which a scale or key is based. ✧ *adj* **3** central or dominating: *his keynote speech to the party conference.*

keypad *n* a small panel with a set of buttons for operating a Teletext system, electronic calculator, etc.

keyring *n* a metal ring, often decorative, for keeping keys on.

key signature *n Music* a group of sharps or flats at the beginning of each stave line to indicate the key.

keystone *n* **1** the most important part of a process, organization, etc.: *the keystone of the government's economic policy.* **2** the central stone at the top of an arch.

keyword *n Computers* a word or phrase that a computer will search for in order to locate the information or file that the computer user has requested.

kg kilogram.

KG (in Britain) Knight of the Order of the Garter.

KGB (formerly) the Soviet secret police. ▷ **HISTORY** Russian *Komitet Gosudarstvennoi Bezopasnosti* State Security Committee

khaki *adj* **1** dull yellowish-brown. ✧ *n* **2** a hard-wearing fabric of this colour, used for military uniforms. ▷ **HISTORY** Urdu, from Persian: dusty

khan *n* a title of respect in Afghanistan and central Asia. ▷ **HISTORY** Turkish

kHz kilohertz.

kia ora *interj NZ* Maori greeting. ▷ **HISTORY** Maori

kibbutz *n, pl* **kibbutzim** a farm, factory, or other workplace in Israel, owned and run communally by its members. ▷ **HISTORY** Modern Hebrew *qibbūs* gathering

kibosh *n* **put the kibosh on** *Slang* to put a stop to. ▷ **HISTORY** origin unknown

kick *vb* **1** to drive, push, or hit with the foot or feet. **2** to strike out with the feet, as in swimming. **3** to raise a leg high, as in dancing. **4** *Rugby* to score (a conversion, drop kick, or penalty) with a kick: *he kicked his third penalty.* **5** (of a firearm) to recoil when fired. **6** *Informal* to object or resist: *school*

A B C D E F G H I J K L M N O P Q R S T U V W X Y Z

uniforms give children something to kick against. **7** *Informal* to free oneself of (an addiction): *smokers who want to kick the habit.* **8 alive and kicking** *Informal* active and in good health. **9 kick someone upstairs** to promote someone to a higher but effectively powerless position. ✧ *n* **10** a thrust or blow with the foot. **11** any of certain rhythmic leg movements used in swimming. **12** the recoil of a firearm. **13** *Informal* an exciting effect: *we get a kick out of attacking opposing fans and overturning their buses; a few small bets just for kicks.* **14** *Informal* the intoxicating effect of an alcoholic drink: *a cocktail with a kick in it.* **15 kick in the teeth** *Slang* a humiliating rebuff. ✧ See also **kick off**. ▷ HISTORY Middle English *kiken*

kickback *n* **1** part of an income paid to a person in return for an opportunity to make a profit, often by some illegal arrangement. **2** a strong reaction.

kick off *vb* **1** to start play in a game of football by kicking the ball from the centre of the field. **2** *Informal* to commence (a discussion, event, etc.). ✧ *n* **kickoff 3 a** the kick that officially starts a game of football. **b** the time when the first kick is due to take place. **4** *Informal* the time when an event is due to begin.

kick out *vb Informal* to dismiss (someone) or throw (someone) out forcefully.

kick-start *n* **1** Also: **kick-starter** a pedal on a motorcycle that is kicked downwards to start the engine. **2** an action or event that reactivates something. ✧ *vb* **3** to start (a motorcycle) with a kick-start. **4** to do something bold or drastic in order to begin or improve the performance of something: *to kick-start the economy.*

kick up *vb Informal* to cause (trouble).

kid[1] *n* **1** *Informal* a young person; child. **2** a young goat. **3** soft smooth leather made from the hide of a kid. ✧ *adj* **4** younger: *my kid sister.* ✧ *vb* **kidding, kidded 5** (of a goat) to give birth to (young). ▷ HISTORY from Old Norse

kid[2] *vb* **kidding, kidded** *Informal* **1** to tease or deceive (someone) for fun. **2** to fool (oneself) into believing something: *don't kid yourself that no-one else knows.* ▷ HISTORY probably from KID[1] ▸ **kidder** *n*

kidnap *vb* **-napping, -napped** *or US* **-naping, -naped** to capture and hold (a person), usually for ransom. ▷ HISTORY KID[1] + obsolete *nap* to steal ▸ **kidnapper** *or US* ▸ **-naper** *n* ▸ **kidnapping** *or US* ▸ **-naping** *n*

kidney *n* **1** either of two bean-shaped organs at the back of the abdominal cavity. They filter waste products from the blood, which are excreted as urine. **2** the kidneys of certain animals used as food. ▷ HISTORY origin unknown

kidney bean *n* a reddish-brown kidney-shaped bean, edible when cooked.

kidney machine *n* a machine carrying out the functions of damaged human kidneys.

kill *vb* **1** to cause the death of (a person or animal). **2** *Informal* to cause (someone) pain or discomfort: *my feet are killing me.* **3** to put an end to: *his infidelity had killed his marriage.* **4** *Informal* to quash or veto: *the main opposition party tried to kill the bill.* **5** *Informal* to overwhelm (someone) completely with laughter, attraction, or surprise: *her jokes really kill me.* **6 kill oneself** *Informal* to overexert oneself. **7 kill time** to spend time on something unimportant or trivial while waiting for something: *I'm just killing time until I can talk to the other witnesses.* **8 kill two birds with one stone** to achieve two results with one action. ✧ *n* **9** the act of causing death at the end of a hunt or bullfight. **10** the animal or animals killed during a hunt. **11 in at the kill** present when something comes to a dramatic end with unpleasant results for someone else. ▷ HISTORY Middle English *cullen* ▸ **killer** *n*

killer whale *n* a black-and-white toothed whale, most common in cold seas.

killing *adj* **1** *Informal* very tiring: *a killing pace.* **2** *Informal* extremely funny. **3** causing death; fatal. ✧ *n* **4** the act of causing death; slaying. **5 make a killing** *Informal* to have a sudden financial success.

killjoy *n* a person who spoils other people's pleasure.

kiln *n* a large oven for burning, drying, or processing pottery, bricks, etc. ▷ HISTORY Latin *culina* kitchen

kilo *n, pl* **kilos** short for **kilogram, kilometre**.

kilo- *combining form* **1** denoting one thousand (10^3): *kilometre.* **2** (in computers) denoting 2^{10} (1024): *kilobyte*. In computer usage, *kilo-* is restricted to sizes of storage (e.g. *kilobit*) when it means 1024: in other computer contexts it retains its usual meaning of 1000. ▷ HISTORY Greek *khilioi* thousand

kilobyte *n Computers* 1024 bytes.

kilocalorie *n* one thousand calories.

kilocycle *n* an old word for kilohertz.

kilogram *or* **kilogramme** *n* **1** one thousand grams. **2** the basic SI unit of mass.

kilohertz *n, pl* **kilohertz** one thousand hertz; one thousand cycles per second.

kilojoule *n* one thousand joules.

kilolitre *or US* **kiloliter** *n* a measure of volume equivalent to one thousand litres.

kilometre *or US* **kilometer** *n* a unit of length equal to one thousand metres.

kiloton *n* **1** one thousand tons. **2** an explosive power, esp. of a nuclear weapon, equal to the power of 1000 tons of TNT.

kilovolt *n* one thousand volts.

kilowatt *n* one thousand watts.

kilowatt-hour *n* a unit of energy equal to the work done by a power of 1000 watts in one hour.

kilt *n* **1** a knee-length pleated tartan skirt, worn by men in Highland dress and by women and girls. ✧ *vb* **2** to put pleats in (cloth). ▷ HISTORY Scandinavian ▸ **kilted** *adj*

kimono (kim-**moan**-no) *n, pl* **-nos 1** a loose wide-sleeved Japanese robe, fastened with a sash. **2** a European dressing gown resembling this. ▷ HISTORY Japanese: clothing

kin *n* a person's relatives collectively. ▷ HISTORY Old English *cyn*

kind[1] *adj* **1** considerate, friendly, and helpful: *a good, kind man; a few kind words.* **2** cordial;

courteous: *reprinted by kind permission.*
▷ **HISTORY** Old English *gecynde* natural, native

kind[2] *n* **1** a class or group having characteristics in common: *what kind of music do you like?* **2** essential nature or character: *differences of degree rather than of kind.* **3 in kind a** (of payment) in goods or services rather than in money. **b** with something of the same sort: *the government threatened to retaliate in kind to any use of nuclear weapons.* **4 kind of** to a certain extent; loosely: *kind of hard; a kind of socialist.* **5 of a kind** of poorer quality or standard than is wanted or expected: *a few farmers wrest subsistence of a kind from the thin topsoil.*
▷ **HISTORY** Old English *gecynd* nature

> **WORD TIP**
> The mixture of plural and singular constructions, although often used informally with *kind* and *sort*, should be avoided in serious writing: *children enjoy those kinds* (not *those kind*) *of stories; these sorts* (not *these sort*) *of distinctions are becoming blurred.*

kindergarten *n* a class or school for children under six years old. ▷ **HISTORY** from German, literally: children's garden

kind-hearted *adj* considerate and sympathetic.

kindle *vb* **-dling, -dled 1** to set (a fire) alight or (of a fire) to start to burn. **2** to arouse or be aroused: *his passions were kindled as quickly as her own.*
▷ **HISTORY** Old Norse *kynda*

kindling *n* material for starting a fire, such as dry wood or straw.

kindly *adj* **-lier, -liest 1** having a warm-hearted and caring nature. **2** pleasant or agreeable: *a kindly climate.* ✧ *adv* **3** in a considerate or humane way. **4** please: *will you kindly stop prattling on about it!* **5 not take kindly to** to react unfavourably towards. ▶ **kindliness** *n*

kindness *n* **1** the quality of being kind. **2** a kind or helpful act.

kindred *adj* **1** having similar qualities: *cholera, and other kindred diseases.* **2** related by blood or marriage. **3 kindred spirit** a person with whom one has something in common. ✧ *n* **4** relationship by blood or marriage. **5** similarity in character. **6** a person's relatives collectively. ▷ **HISTORY** Middle English *kinred*

kindy *or* **kindie** *n, pl* **-dies** *Austral & NZ informal* a kindergarten.

kine *pl n Archaic* cows or cattle. ▷ **HISTORY** Old English *cȳna* of cows

kinematics (kin-nim-**mat**-iks) *n Physics* the study of the motion of bodies without reference to mass or force. ▷ **HISTORY** Greek *kinēma* movement ▶ **kinematic** *adj*

kinetic (kin-**net**-ik) *adj* relating to or caused by motion. ▷ **HISTORY** Greek *kinein* to move ▶ **kinetically** *adv*

kinetic art *n* art, such as sculpture, that moves or has moving parts.

kinetic energy *n Physics* the energy of motion of a body equal to the work it would do if it were brought to rest.

kinetics *n Physics* the branch of mechanics concerned with the study of bodies in motion.

king *n* **1** a male ruler of a country who has inherited the throne from his parents. **2** a ruler or chief: *the king of the fairies.* **3** a person, animal, or thing considered as the best or most important of its kind: *the king of rock and roll.* **4** a playing card with a picture of a king on it. **5** a chessman, able to move one square in any direction: the object of the game is to checkmate one's opponent's king. **6** *Draughts* a piece which has moved entirely across the board and been crowned and which may therefore move backwards as well as forwards.
▷ **HISTORY** Old English *cyning* ▶ **kingship** *n*

kingcup *n Brit* a yellow-flowered plant; marsh marigold.

kingdom *n* **1** a territory or state ruled by a king or queen. **2** any of the three groups into which natural objects may be divided: the animal, plant, and mineral kingdoms. **3** a place or area considered to be under the total power and control of a person, organization, or thing: *the kingdom of God.*

kingfisher *n* a fish-eating bird with a greenish-blue and orange plumage.
▷ **HISTORY** originally *king's fisher*

kingklip *n* an edible eel-like marine fish of S Africa. ▷ **HISTORY** Afrikaans

kingpin *n* **1** the most important person in an organization: *a Mexican narcotics kingpin.* **2** a pivot pin that provides a steering joint in a motor vehicle.

king post *n Building* a vertical post connecting the apex of a triangular roof truss to the tie beam.

king prawn *n* a large prawn, fished commercially in Australian waters.

king-size *or* **king-sized** *adj* larger than a standard size.

kink *n* **1** a twist or bend in something such as a rope or hair. **2** *Informal* a flaw or quirk in someone's personality. ✧ *vb* **3** to form or cause to form a kink.
▷ **HISTORY** Dutch

kinky *adj* **kinkier, kinkiest 1** *Slang* given to unusual sexual practices. **2** tightly looped or curled.

kinsfolk *pl n* one's family or relatives.

kinship *n* **1** blood relationship. **2** the state of having common characteristics.

kinsman *n, pl* **-men** a relation by blood or marriage. ▶ **kinswoman** *fem n*

kiosk *n* **1** a small booth from which cigarettes, newspapers, and sweets are sold. **2** *Chiefly Brit* a public telephone box. ▷ **HISTORY** French *kiosque* bandstand, from Persian *kūshk* pavilion

kip *Brit slang* ✧ *n* **1** sleep: *a couple of hours' kip.* **2** a bed. ✧ *vb* **kipping, kipped 3** to sleep or take a nap. **4 kip down** to sleep in a makeshift bed.
▷ **HISTORY** origin unknown

kipper *n* **1** a herring that has been cleaned, salted, and smoked. ✧ *vb* **2** to cure (a herring) by salting and smoking it. ▷ **HISTORY** Old English *cypera*

kirk *n Scot* a church. ▷ **HISTORY** Old Norse *kirkja*

Kirsch *or* **Kirschwasser** *n* a brandy distilled from black cherries. ▷ **HISTORY** German *Kirschwasser* cherry water

A B C D E F G H I J K L M N O P Q R S T U V W X Y Z

kismet *n* fate or destiny. ▷ **HISTORY** Persian *qismat*

kiss *vb* **1** to touch with the lips as an expression of love, greeting, or respect. **2** to join lips with another person as an act of love or desire. **3** *Literary* to touch lightly: *a long, high free kick that kissed the top of the crossbar.* ✧ *n* **4** a caress with the lips. **5** a light touch. ▷ **HISTORY** Old English *cyssan* ▶ **kissable** *adj*

kissagram *n Brit, Austral & NZ* a greetings service in which a person is employed to present greetings by kissing the person celebrating.

kisser *n Slang* the mouth or face.

kissing crust *n NZ* the soft end of a loaf of bread where two loaves have been separated.

kiss of life *n* **the kiss of life** mouth-to-mouth resuscitation in which a person blows gently into the mouth of an unconscious person.

kist *n S African* a large wooden chest.

kit[1] *n* **1** a set of tools or supplies for use together or for a purpose: *a first-aid kit.* **2** the container for such a set. **3** a set of parts sold ready to be assembled: *a model aircraft kit.* **4** *NZ* a flax basket. **5** clothing and other personal effects, such as those of a soldier: *a complete set of school team kit.* ✧ See also **kit out**. ▷ **HISTORY** Middle Dutch *kitte* tankard

kit[2] *n NZ* a shopping bag made of string. ▷ **HISTORY** Maori *kete*

kitbag *n* a canvas or other bag for a serviceman's kit.

kitchen *n* a room equipped for preparing and cooking food. ▷ **HISTORY** Late Latin *coquina*

kitchenette *n* a small kitchen or part of a room equipped for use as a kitchen.

kitchen garden *n* a garden for growing vegetables, herbs, etc.

kitchen-sink drama *n Theatre* a type of drama of the 1950s depicting the sordid aspects of domestic reality.

kitchen tea *n Austral & NZ* a party held before a wedding to which guests bring kitchen equipment as presents.

kite *n* **1** a light frame covered with a thin material flown in the wind at the end of a length of string. **2** a bird of prey with a long forked tail and large wings. **3** a four-sided geometrical shape in which each side is equal in length to one of the sides joining it. ▷ **HISTORY** Old English *cȳta*

Kite mark *n Brit* the official mark in the form of a kite on articles approved by the British Standards Institution.

kith *n* **kith and kin** *Old-fashioned* one's friends and relations. ▷ **HISTORY** Old English *cȳthth*

kit out *or* **up** *vb* **kitting, kitted** *Chiefly Brit* to provide with clothes or equipment needed for a particular activity.

kitsch *n* tawdry or sentimental art or literature. ▷ **HISTORY** from German ▶ **kitschy** *adj*

kitten *n* **1** a young cat. **2 have kittens** *Informal* to react with disapproval or anxiety: *she had kittens when she discovered the price.* ▷ **HISTORY** Old French *caton*

kittenish *adj* lively and flirtatious.

kittiwake *n* a type of seagull with pale grey black-tipped wings and a square-cut tail. ▷ **HISTORY** imitative

kitty[1] *n, pl* **-ties** a diminutive or affectionate name for a **kitten cat**.

kitty[2] *n, pl* **-ties 1** any shared fund of money. **2** the pool in certain gambling games. ▷ **HISTORY** probably from KIT[1]

kiwi *n, pl* **kiwis 1** a flightless bird of New Zealand with a long beak, stout legs, and no tail. **2** *Informal except in NZ* a New Zealander. ▷ **HISTORY** Maori

kiwi fruit *n* an edible fruit with a fuzzy brown skin and green flesh.

kJ kilojoule(s).

kl kilolitre(s).

klaxon *n* a type of loud horn used on fire engines and ambulances as a warning signal. ▷ **HISTORY** former trademark

kleinhuisie (**klayn**-hay-see) *n S African* an outside toilet. ▷ **HISTORY** Afrikaans, literally: little house

kleptomania *n Psychol* a strong impulse to steal. ▷ **HISTORY** Greek *kleptein* to steal + *mania* madness ▶ **kleptomaniac** *n*

klipspringer *n* a small agile antelope of rocky regions of Africa south of the Sahara. ▷ **HISTORY** Afrikaans: rock jumper

kloof *n S African* a mountain pass or gorge. ▷ **HISTORY** Afrikaans

km kilometre(s).

knack *n* **1** a skilful way of doing something. **2** an ability to do something difficult with apparent ease. ▷ **HISTORY** probably from Middle English *knak* sharp knock

knacker *n Brit* a person who buys up old horses for slaughter. ▷ **HISTORY** origin unknown

knackered *adj Slang* **1** extremely tired: *they'd been marching for three hours and were absolutely knackered.* **2** broken or no longer functioning: *a knackered TV set.*

knapsack *n* a canvas or leather bag carried strapped on the back or shoulder. ▷ **HISTORY** Low German *knappen* to eat + *sack* bag

knapweed *n* a plant with purplish thistle-like flowers. ▷ **HISTORY** Middle English *knopwed*

knave *n* **1** *Cards* the jack. **2** *Archaic* a dishonest man. ▷ **HISTORY** Old English *cnafa* ▶ **knavish** *adj*

knead *vb* **1** to work and press (a soft substance, such as dough) into a smooth mixture with the hands. **2** to squeeze or press with the hands. ▷ **HISTORY** Old English *cnedan* ▶ **kneader** *n*

knee *n* **1** the joint of the leg between the thigh and the lower leg. **2** the area around this joint. **3** the upper surface of a sitting person's thigh: *a little girl being cuddled on her father's knee.* **4** the part of a garment that covers the knee. **5 bring someone to his knees** to force someone into submission. ✧ *vb* **kneeing, kneed 6** to strike, nudge, or push with the knee. ▷ **HISTORY** Old English *cnēow*

kneecap *n* **1** *Anat* a small flat triangular bone in front of and protecting the knee. ✧ *vb* **-capping, -capped 2** (of terrorists) to shoot (a person) in the kneecap.

knee-jerk *n* **1** *Physiol* a sudden involuntary kick of the lower leg caused by a sharp tap on the tendon just below the kneecap. ✧ *adj* **kneejerk** **2** made or occurring as a predictable and automatic response: *a kneejerk reaction.*

kneel *vb* **kneeling, knelt** *or* **kneeled 1** to rest, fall, or support oneself on one's knees. ✧ *n* **2** the act or position of kneeling. ▷ **HISTORY** Old English *cnēowlian*

knees-up *n Brit informal* a party.

knell *n* **1** the sound of a bell rung to announce a death or a funeral. **2** something that indicates death or destruction. ✧ *vb* **3** to ring a knell. **4** to proclaim by a tolling bell. ▷ **HISTORY** Old English *cnyll*

knew *vb* the past tense of **know**.

knickerbockers *pl n* loose-fitting short trousers gathered in at the knee or calf. ▷ **HISTORY** after Diedrich *Knickerbocker*, fictitious author of Washington Irving's *History of New York*

knickers *pl n* a woman's or girl's undergarment covering the lower trunk and having separate legs or leg-holes. ▷ **HISTORY** contraction of *knickerbockers*

knick-knack *n* a small ornament or trinket. ▷ **HISTORY** reduplication of obsolete *knack* a toy

knickpoint *or esp US* **nickpoint** *n Geog* a break in the slope of a river profile caused by renewed erosion by a rejuvenated river. ▷ **HISTORY** partial translation of German *Knickpunkt*, from *knicken* to bend + *Punkt* POINT

knife *n, pl* **knives 1** a cutting instrument or weapon consisting of a sharp-edged blade of metal fitted into a handle. ✧ *vb* **knifing, knifed 2** to stab or kill with a knife. ▷ **HISTORY** Old English *cnīf* ▶ **knifelike** *adj*

knife edge *n* **1** the sharp cutting edge of a knife. **2** a critical point in the development of a situation: *and at this point the election result is still poised on a knife edge.*

knight *n* **1** a man who has been given a knighthood in recognition of his achievements. **2** (in medieval Europe) **a** a person who served his lord as a mounted and heavily armed soldier. **b** a devoted male admirer of a noblewoman, esp. her champion in a jousting tournament. **3** a chessman shaped like a horse's head, able to move either two squares horizontally and one square vertically or two squares vertically and one square horizontally. ✧ *vb* **4** to make (a man) a knight. ▷ **HISTORY** Old English *cniht* servant

knight errant *n, pl* **knights errant** (esp. in medieval romance) a knight who wanders in search of deeds of courage, chivalry, etc. ▶ **knight errantry** *n*

knighthood *n* an honorary title given to a man by the British sovereign in recognition of his achievements.

knightly *adj* of, resembling, or appropriate for a knight. ▶ **knightliness** *n*

knit *vb* **knitting, knitted** *or* **knit 1** to make (a garment) by looping (wool) using long eyeless needles or a knitting machine. **2** to join together closely. **3** to draw (one's eyebrows) together. ✧ *n* **4** a fabric made by knitting. ▷ **HISTORY** Old English *cnyttan* to tie in ▶ **knitter** *n*

knitting *n* knitted work or the process of producing it.

knitwear *n* knitted clothes, such as sweaters.

knives *n* the plural of **knife**.

knob *n* **1** a rounded projection from a surface, such as a rotating switch on a radio. **2** a rounded handle of a door or drawer. **3** a small amount of butter or margarine. ▷ **HISTORY** Middle Low German *knobbe* knot in wood ▶ **knoblike** *adj*

knobbly *adj* having or covered with small bumps: *a curious knobbly root vegetable.*

knobkerrie *n S African* a club or a stick with a rounded end. ▷ **HISTORY** Khoi (language of southern Africa) *kirri* stick

knock *vb* **1** to give a blow or push to. **2** to rap sharply with the knuckles: *he knocked on the door of the guest room.* **3** to make by striking: *he knocked a hole in the wall.* **4** to collide (with). **5** to bring into a certain condition by hitting: *he was knocked unconscious in a collision.* **6** *Informal* to criticize adversely. **7** to emit a regular banging sound as a result of a fault: *the engine was knocking badly.* **8 knock on the head** to prevent the further development of (a plan). ✧ *n* **9 a** a blow, push, or rap: *he gave the table a knock.* **b** the sound so caused. **10** the sound of knocking in an engine or bearing. **11** *Informal* a misfortune, rejection, or setback. **12** *Informal* criticism. ✧ See also **knock about, knock back**, etc. ▷ **HISTORY** Old English *cnocian*

knock about *or* **around** *vb* **1** to wander or travel about: *I have knocked about the world through three continents.* **2** (foll. by *with*) to associate. **3** to treat brutally: *she looked knocked about, with bruises and cuts to her head.* **4** to consider or discuss informally. ✧ *adj* **knockabout 5** (of comedy) lively, boisterous, and physical.

knock back *vb Informal* **1** to drink quickly: *he fell over after knocking back eight pints of lager.* **2** to cost: *lunch for two here will knock you back fifty pounds.* **3** to reject or refuse: *I don't know any man who'd knock back an offer like that.* ✧ *n* **knockback** **4** *Slang* a refusal or rejection.

knock down *vb* **1** to strike to the ground with a blow, such as in boxing. **2** (in auctions) to declare an article sold. **3** to demolish. **4** *Informal* to reduce (a price). ✧ *adj* **knockdown 5** powerful: *a knockdown argument.* **6** *Chiefly Brit* (of a price) very cheap. **7** easily dismantled: *knockdown furniture.*

knocker *n* **1** a metal object attached to a door by a hinge and used for knocking. **2 knockers** *Slang* a woman's breasts.

knock-knees *pl n* legs that are bent inwards at the knees. ▶ **knock-kneed** *adj*

knock off *vb* **1** *Informal* to finish work: *around ten, the day shift knocked off.* **2** *Informal* to make or do hastily or easily: *she knocked off 600 books in all during her long life.* **3** *Informal* to take (an amount) off the price of (an article): *I'll knock off 10% if you pay cash.* **4** *Brit, Austral & NZ informal* to steal. **5** *Slang* to kill. **6** *Slang* to stop doing something; used as a command: *knock it off!*

knock-on *Rugby* ✧ *n* **1** the foul of playing the ball forward with the hand or arm. ✧ *vb* **knock on 2** to play (the ball) forward with the hand or arm.

knock-on effect *n* the indirect result of an action or decision.

knockout *n* **1** the act of rendering someone unconscious. **2** *Boxing* a blow that renders an opponent unable to continue after the referee has counted to ten. **3** a competition in which competitors are eliminated progressively. **4** *Informal* a person or thing that is very impressive or attractive: *at my youngest sister's wedding she was a knockout in navy and scarlet.* ✧ *vb* **knock out 5** to render (someone) unconscious. **6** *Boxing* to defeat (an opponent) by a knockout. **7** to destroy: *communications in many areas were knocked out by the earthquake.* **8** to eliminate from a knockout competition. **9** *Informal* to amaze: *the fantastic audience reaction knocked me out.*

knock up *vb* **1** Also: **knock together** *Informal* to make or assemble quickly: *my boyfriend can knock up a wonderful lasagne.* **2** *Brit informal* to waken: *to knock someone up early.* **3** *Slang* to make pregnant. **4** to practise before a game of tennis, squash, or badminton. ✧ *n* **knock-up 5** a practice session at tennis, squash, or badminton.

knoll *n* a small rounded hill. ▷ **HISTORY** Old English *cnoll*

knot *n* **1** a fastening formed by looping and tying pieces of rope, cord, or string. **2** a tangle, such as in hair. **3** a decorative bow, such as of ribbon. **4** a small cluster or huddled group: *a knot of passengers gathered on the platform.* **5** a bond: *to tie the knot of friendship.* **6 a** a hard mass of wood where a branch joins the trunk of a tree. **b** a cross section of this visible in timber. **7** a feeling of tightness, caused by tension or nervousness: *a dull knot of anxiety that sat in the pit of her stomach.* **8** a unit of speed used by ships and aircraft, equal to one nautical mile per hour. **9 at a rate of knots** very fast. **10 tie someone in knots** to confuse someone completely. ✧ *vb* **knotting, knotted 11** to tie or fasten in a knot. **12** to form into a knot. **13** to entangle or become entangled. ▷ **HISTORY** Old English *cnotta* ▸ **knotted** *adj* ▸ **knotless** *adj*

knotty *adj* **-tier, -tiest 1** full of knots. **2** extremely difficult or puzzling: *a knotty problem.*

know *vb* **knowing, knew, known 1** to be or feel certain of the truth or accuracy of (a fact, answer, or piece of information). **2** to be acquainted with: *I'd known him for many years, since I was seventeen.* **3** to have a grasp of or understand (a skill or language). **4** to understand or be aware of (something, or how to do or be something): *she knew how to get on with people.* **5** to experience: *you had to have known poverty before you could give money its true value, he claimed.* **6** to be intelligent, informed, or sensible enough (to do something): *how did he know to send the letter in the first place?* **7** to be able to distinguish: *I don't know one flower from another.* **8 know what's what** to know how one thing or things in general work. **9 you never know** things are uncertain. ✧ *n* **10 in the know** *Informal* aware or informed. ▷ **HISTORY** Old English *gecnāwan* ▸ **knowable** *adj*

know-all *n Informal, disparaging* a person who pretends or appears to know a lot more than other people.

know-how *n Informal* the ability to do something that is difficult or technical.

knowing *adj* **1** suggesting secret knowledge: *Paul saw the knowing look that passed between them.* **2** cunning or shrewd. **3** deliberate. ▸ **knowingly** *adv* ▸ **knowingness** *n*

knowledge *n* **1** the facts or experiences known by a person or group of people. **2** the state of knowing. **3** specific information about a subject. **4 to my knowledge** as I understand it.

knowledgeable *or* **knowledgable** *adj* intelligent or well-informed. ▸ **knowledgeably** *or* **knowledgably** *adv*

known *vb* **1** the past participle of **know**. ✧ *adj* **2** identified: *consorting with known criminals.*

knuckle *n* **1** a joint of a finger. **2** the knee joint of a calf or pig. **3 near the knuckle** *Informal* likely to offend people because of frankness or rudeness. ✧ See also **knuckle under**. ▷ **HISTORY** Middle English

knuckle-duster *n* a metal appliance worn over the knuckles to add force to a blow.

knuckle under *vb* **-ling, -led** to give way under pressure or authority.

knurl *n* a small ridge, often one of a series. ▷ **HISTORY** probably from *knur* a knot in wood

KO *or* **k.o.** *vb* **KO'ing, KO'd** *or* **k.o.'ing, k.o.'d 1** to knock out. ✧ *n, pl* **KO's** *or* **k.o.'s 2** a knockout.

koala *n* a tree-dwelling Australian marsupial with dense grey fur. ▷ **HISTORY** Aboriginal

koeksister (**kook**-sist-er) *n S African* a plaited doughnut deep-fried and soaked in syrup. ▷ **HISTORY** Afrikaans

kohanga reo *or* **kohanga** *n NZ* an infant class where children are taught in Maori. ▷ **HISTORY** Maori: language nest

kohl *n* a cosmetic powder used to darken the area around the eyes. ▷ **HISTORY** Arabic

kohlrabi (kole-**rah**-bee) *n, pl* **-bies** a type of cabbage with an edible stem. ▷ **HISTORY** Italian *cavolo* cabbage + *rapa* turnip

kokanee (coke-**can**-ee) *n* a freshwater salmon of lakes and rivers in W North America. ▷ **HISTORY** after *Kokanee* Creek, in British Columbia

kola *n* same as **cola**.

kolkhoz (kol-**hawz**) *n* (formerly) a collective farm in the Soviet Union. ▷ **HISTORY** Russian

komatik (**koh**-ma-tik) *n Canad* a sledge with wooden runners and crossbars bound with animal hides. ▷ **HISTORY** Inuit

kook *n US & Canad informal* an eccentric or foolish person. ▷ **HISTORY** probably from *cuckoo* ▸ **kooky** *or* **kookie** *adj*

kookaburra *n* a large Australian kingfisher with a cackling cry. ▷ **HISTORY** Aboriginal

koori *n, pl* **-ris** an Australian Aborigine.

kopeck *n* a former Russian monetary unit worth one hundredth of a rouble. ▷ **HISTORY** Russian *kopeika*

kopje *or* **koppie** (**kop**-ee) *n S African* a small isolated hill. ▷ **HISTORY** Afrikaans

Köppen's climate classification system *n Meteorol* a system recognizing five, and later six, main climate types from tropical humid to polar, and charted on a map co-authored by German climatologist Wladimir Köppen (1846—1940) and Rudolph Geiger.

Koran *n* the sacred book of Islam, believed by Muslims to be the infallible word of God dictated to Mohammed. ▷ **HISTORY** Arabic *qur'ān* reading, book ▶ **Koranic** *adj*

Korean *adj* **1** of Korea. ✧ *n* **2** a person from Korea. **3** the official language of North and South Korea.

kosher (**koh**-sher) *adj* **1** *Judaism* **a** conforming to religious law. **b** (of food) prepared in accordance with the dietary laws. **2** *Informal* legitimate, genuine, or proper. ✧ *n* **3** kosher food. ▷ **HISTORY** Yiddish

kowhai (**koh**-wye, **koh**-fye) *n* a small tree of New Zealand and Chile with clusters of yellow flowers. ▷ **HISTORY** Maori

kowtow *vb* **1** to be humble and very respectful (towards): *the senior editors accused each other of kowtowing to his demands.* **2** to touch the forehead to the ground in deference. ✧ *n* **3** the act of kowtowing. ▷ **HISTORY** Chinese *k'o* to strike, knock + *t'ou* head

kph kilometres per hour.

Kr *Chem* krypton.

kraal *n* **1** a Southern African hut village surrounded by a strong fence. **2** *S African* an enclosure for livestock. ▷ **HISTORY** Afrikaans, from Portuguese *curral* enclosure

krans *n S African* a sheer rock face. ▷ **HISTORY** Afrikaans

Kremlin *n* the central government of Russia and, formerly, the Soviet Union.

krill *n, pl* **krill** a small shrimplike crustacean. ▷ **HISTORY** Norwegian *kril* young fish

Krishna *n* a Hindu god, the incarnation of Vishnu.

krona *n, pl* **-nor** the standard monetary unit of Sweden. ▷ **HISTORY** Swedish, from Latin *corona* crown

krone (**kroh**-na) *n, pl* **-ner** (-ner) the standard monetary unit of Norway and Denmark. ▷ **HISTORY** Danish or Norwegian, from Latin *corona* crown

krugerrand *n* a one-ounce gold coin minted in South Africa. ▷ **HISTORY** Paul *Kruger,* Boer statesman + *rand*

krypton *n Chem* an inert gaseous element occurring in trace amounts in air and used in fluorescent lights and lasers. Symbol: Kr. ▷ **HISTORY** Greek *kruptos* hidden

KS Kansas.

kt. kiloton.

kudos (**kew**-doss) *n* personal fame or glory. ▷ **HISTORY** Greek

kudu *or* **koodoo** *n* a spiral-horned African antelope. ▷ **HISTORY** Afrikaans, from Khoi (language of southern Africa)

kugel (**koog**-el) *n S African* a rich, fashion-conscious, materialistic young Jewish woman. ▷ **HISTORY** from Yiddish *kugel*, a type of savoury pudding popular in Jewish cookery

Ku Klux Klan *n* a secret organization of White Protestant Americans who use violence against Blacks and Jews. ▷ **HISTORY** probably based on Greek *kuklos* circle + CLAN ▶ **Ku Klux Klanner** *n*

kulak *n* (formerly) a property-owning Russian peasant. ▷ **HISTORY** Russian

kumera *or* **kumara** *n NZ* a tropical root vegetable with yellow flesh. ▷ **HISTORY** Maori

kumquat (**kumm**-kwott) *n* a citrus fruit resembling a tiny orange. ▷ **HISTORY** Cantonese Chinese *kam kwat* golden orange

kung fu *n* a Chinese martial art combining techniques of karate and judo. ▷ **HISTORY** Chinese: martial art

Kuomintang (kwoh-min-**tang**) *n History* a political party dominant in China from 1928 until 1949 under the leadership of Chiang Kai-shek.

kura kaupapa Maori *n NZ* a primary school where the teaching is done in Maori.

kurrajong *n* an Australian tree or shrub with tough fibrous bark. ▷ **HISTORY** from a native Australian language

kV kilovolt.

kW kilowatt.

Kwanzaa *n* an African-American festival held from December 26 through January 1. ▷ **HISTORY** from Swahili (*matunda ya*) *kwanza* first (fruits)

kwashiorkor *n* severe malnutrition of young children, caused by not eating enough protein. ▷ **HISTORY** native word in Ghana

kWh kilowatt-hour.

KWIC *Computers* keyword in context.

KWOC *Computers* keyword out of context.

KY Kentucky.

kyle *n Scot* a narrow strait or channel: *Kyle of Lochalsh.* ▷ **HISTORY** Gaelic *caol* narrow

L l

A
B
C
D
E
F
G
H
I
J
K
L
M
N
O
P
Q
R
S
T
U
V
W
X
Y
Z

l litre(s).

L **1** large. **2** Latin. **3** learner driver. **4** Usually written: **£** pound. ▷ **HISTORY** Latin *libra* **5** the Roman numeral for 50.

L. *or* **l.** **1** lake. **2** left. **3** length. **4** (*pl* **LL** *or* **ll**) line.

la *n Music* same as **lah**.

La *Chem* lanthanum.

LA **1** Los Angeles. **2** Louisiana.

laager *n* (in Africa) a camp defended by a circular formation of wagons. ▷ **HISTORY** Afrikaans *lager*

lab *n Informal* short for **laboratory**.

Lab *Politics* Labour.

label *n* **1** a piece of card or other material attached to an object to show its contents, ownership, use, or destination. **2** a brief descriptive term given to a person, group, or school of thought: *we would need a handy label to explain the new company.* ✧ *vb* **-belling, -belled** *or US* **-beling, -beled** **3** to attach a label to. **4** to describe or classify in a word or phrase. ▷ **HISTORY** Old French: ribbon

labial (**lay**-bee-al) *adj* **1** of or near the lips. **2** *Phonetics* relating to a speech sound made using the lips. ✧ *n* **3** *Phonetics* a speech sound such as English *p* or *m*, that involves the lips. ▷ **HISTORY** Latin *labium* lip

labiate (**lay**-bee-ate) *n* **1** any of a family of plants with square stems, aromatic leaves, and a two-lipped flower, such as mint or thyme. ✧ *adj* **2** of this family. ▷ **HISTORY** Latin *labium* lip

labium (**lay**-bee-um) *n, pl* **-bia** (-bee-a) **1** a lip or liplike structure. **2** any one of the four lip-shaped folds of the vulva. ▷ **HISTORY** Latin: lip

labor *n US, Austral & sometimes Canad* same as **labour**.

laboratory *n, pl* **-ries** a building or room equipped for conducting scientific research or for teaching practical science. ▷ **HISTORY** Latin *laborare* to work

Labor Day *n* **1** (in the US and Canada) a public holiday in honour of labour, held on the first Monday in September. **2** (in Australia) a public holiday observed on different days in different states.

laborious *adj* involving great exertion or prolonged effort. ▶ **laboriously** *adv*

Labor Party *n* the main left-wing political party in Australia.

labour *or US, Austral & sometimes Canad* **labor** *n* **1** productive work, esp. physical work done for wages. **2** the people involved in this, as opposed to management. **3** the final stage of pregnancy, leading to childbirth. **4** difficult work or a difficult job. ✧ *vb* **5** to do physical work: *the girls were labouring madly on it.* **6** to work hard (for something). **7** to make one's way with difficulty: *she was now labouring down the return length.* **8** to emphasize too persistently: *I have laboured the point.* **9** (usually foll. by *under*) to be at a disadvantage because of a mistake or false belief: *she laboured under the illusion that I understood her.* ▷ **HISTORY** Latin *labor*

Labour Day *n* **1** a public holiday in honour of work, held in Britain on May 1. **2** (in New Zealand) a public holiday commemorating the introduction of the eight-hour day, held on the 4th Monday in October.

laboured *or US, Austral & sometimes Canad* **labored** *adj* undertaken with difficulty: *laboured breathing.*

labourer *or US, Austral & sometimes Canad* **laborer** *n* a person engaged in physical work.

labour-intensive *adj Econ, business* requiring a large labour force as opposed to involving large capital investments. Compare **capital-intensive**.

Labour Party *n* **1** the main left-wing political party in a number of countries including Britain and New Zealand. **2** any similar party in various other countries.

Labrador *or* **Labrador retriever** *n* a powerfully built dog with short dense usually black or golden hair.

laburnum *n* a small ornamental tree that has clusters of yellow drooping flowers. It is highly poisonous. ▷ **HISTORY** Latin

labyrinth (**lab**-er-inth) *n* **1** a mazelike network of tunnels or paths, either natural or man-made. **2** any complex or confusing system. **3** the interconnecting cavities of the internal ear. ▷ **HISTORY** Greek *laburinthos* ▶ **labyrinthine** *adj*

lac *n* a resinous substance secreted by certain insects (**lac insects**), used in the manufacture of shellac. ▷ **HISTORY** Hindi *lākh* resin

lace *n* **1** a delicate decorative fabric made from threads woven in an open web of patterns. **2** a cord or string drawn through eyelets to fasten a shoe or garment. ✧ *vb* **lacing, laced** **3** to fasten (shoes) with a lace. **4** to draw (a cord or thread) through holes as when tying shoes. **5** to add a small amount of alcohol, a drug, or poison to (food or drink). **6** to intertwine; interlace. ▷ **HISTORY** Latin *laqueus* noose

lacerate (**lass**-er-rate) *vb* **-ating, -ated** **1** to tear (the flesh) jaggedly. **2** to hurt (the feelings): *it would only lacerate an overburdened conscience.* ▷ **HISTORY** Latin *lacerare* to tear ▶ **laceration** *n*

lachrymal *adj* same as **lacrimal**.

lachrymose *adj* **1** given to weeping; tearful. **2** mournful; sad. ▷ **HISTORY** Latin *lacrima* a tear

lack *n* **1** shortage or absence of something required or desired: *a lack of confidence.* ✧ *vb* **2** (often foll. by *in*) to be short (of) or have need (of): *lacking in sparkle.* ▷ **HISTORY** related to Middle Dutch *laken* to be wanting

lackadaisical *adj* **1** lacking vitality and purpose. **2** lazy and careless in a dreamy way. ▷ **HISTORY** earlier *lackadaisy*

lackey *n* **1** a servile follower; hanger-on. **2** a liveried male servant or valet. ▷ **HISTORY** Catalan *lacayo, alacayo*

lacklustre *or US* **lackluster** *adj* lacking brilliance, force, or vitality.

laconic *adj* (of a person's speech) using few words. ▶ **laconically** *adv*

WORD HISTORY

'Laconic' comes from the Greek word *Lakōnikos*, meaning 'Laconian' or 'Spartan'. Sparta was the capital city of the region of ancient Greece known as Laconia, and the Spartans were famous for using few words.

lacquer *n* **1** a hard glossy coating made by dissolving natural or synthetic resins in a solvent that evaporates quickly. **2** a black resin, obtained from certain trees, used to give a hard glossy finish to wooden furniture. **3** a clear sticky substance for spraying onto the hair to hold a style in place. ▷ **HISTORY** Portuguese *laca* lac

lacquered *adj* coated with lacquer.

lacrimal *or* **lachrymal** (**lack**-rim-al) *adj* of tears or the glands that secrete tears. ▷ **HISTORY** Latin *lacrima* a tear

lacrosse *n* a sport in which two teams try to propel a ball into each other's goal using long-handled sticks with a pouched net at the end. ▷ **HISTORY** Canadian French: the hooked stick

lactate[1] *vb* **-tating, -tated** (of mammals) to secrete milk.

lactate[2] *n* an ester or salt of lactic acid.

lactation *n* **1** the secretion of milk from the mammary glands. **2** the period during which milk is secreted.

lacteal *adj* **1** of or like milk. **2** (of lymphatic vessels) conveying or containing chyle. ✧ *n* **3** any of the lymphatic vessels that convey chyle from the small intestine to the blood. ▷ **HISTORY** Latin *lacteus* of milk

lactic *adj* relating to or derived from milk. ▷ **HISTORY** Latin *lac* milk

lactic acid *n* a colourless syrupy acid found in sour milk and used as a preservative (**E270**) for foodstuffs.

lactose *n* a white crystalline sugar occurring in milk.

lacuna (lak-**kew**-na) *n, pl* **-nae** (-nee) a gap or space in a book or manuscript. ▷ **HISTORY** Latin: pool, cavity

lacy *adj* **lacier, laciest** of or like lace.

lad *n* **1** a boy or young man. **2** *Informal* any male. **3 the lads** *Informal* a group of males. ▷ **HISTORY** perhaps from Old Norse

ladder *n* **1** a portable frame consisting of two long parallel supports connected by steps, for climbing up or down. **2** any system thought of as having a series of ascending stages: *the career ladder.* **3** *Chiefly Brit* a line of connected stitches that have come undone in tights or stockings. ✧ *vb* **4** *Chiefly Brit* to have or cause to have a line of undone stitches. ▷ **HISTORY** Old English *hlǣdder*

laddish *adj Brit, Austral & NZ informal, often derogatory* characteristic of young men, esp. by being rowdy or immature.

lade *vb* **lading, laded, laden** *or* **laded 1** to put cargo on board (a ship) or (of a ship) to take on cargo. **2** (foll. by *with*) to burden or load. ▷ **HISTORY** Old English *hladen* to load

laden *adj* **1** loaded. **2** burdened.

la-di-da *or* **lah-di-dah** *adj Informal* affected or pretentious in speech or manners. ▷ **HISTORY** mockingly imitative of affected speech

ladies *or* **ladies' room** *n Informal* a women's public toilet.

ladle *n* **1** a long-handled spoon with a deep bowl for serving soup, stew, etc. ✧ *vb* **-dling, -dled 2** to serve out as with a ladle. ▷ **HISTORY** Old English *hlædel*

lady *n, pl* **-dies 1** a woman regarded as having the characteristics of a good family, such as dignified manners. **2** a polite name for a woman. ✧ *adj* **3** female: *a lady chef.* ▷ **HISTORY** Old English *hlǣfdīge*

Lady *n, pl* **-dies 1** (in Britain) a title borne by various classes of women of the peerage. **2 Our Lady** a title of the Virgin Mary.

ladybird *n* a small red beetle with black spots. ▷ **HISTORY** after Our *Lady*, the Virgin Mary

Lady Day *n* March 25, the feast of the Annunciation of the Virgin Mary: a quarter day in England, Wales, and Ireland.

lady-in-waiting *n, pl* **ladies-in-waiting** a lady who attends a queen or princess.

ladylike *adj* refined and fastidious.

Ladyship *n* (preceded by *Your* or *Her*) a title used to address or refer to any peeress except a duchess.

lady's-slipper *n* an orchid with reddish or purple flowers.

lag[1] *vb* **lagging, lagged 1** (often foll. by *behind*) to hang (back) or fall (behind) in movement, progress, or development. **2** to fall away in strength or intensity. ✧ *n* **3** a slowing down or falling behind. **4** the interval of time between two events, esp. between an action and its effect: *the time lag between mobilization and combat.* ▷ **HISTORY** origin unknown

lag[2] *vb* **lagging, lagged 1** to wrap (a pipe, cylinder, or boiler) with insulating material to prevent heat loss. ✧ *n* **2** the insulating casing of a steam cylinder or boiler. ▷ **HISTORY** Scandinavian

lag[3] *n* **old lag** *Brit, Austral & NZ slang* a convict or ex-convict. ▷ **HISTORY** origin unknown

lager *n* a light-bodied effervescent beer, fermented in a closed vessel using yeasts that sink to the bottom of the brew. ▷ **HISTORY** German *Lagerbier* beer for storing

laggard *n* a person who lags behind.

lagging *n* insulating material wrapped around pipes, boilers, or tanks to prevent loss of heat.

lagoon *n* a body of water cut off from the open sea by coral reefs or sand bars. ▷ **HISTORY** Latin *lacuna* pool

lah *n Music* (in tonic sol-fa) the sixth note of any ascending major scale.

laid *vb* the past of **lay**[1].

laid-back *adj* relaxed in style or character.

A B C D E F G H I J K L M N O P Q R S T U V W X Y Z

lain *vb* the past participle of **lie**[2].

lair *n* **1** the resting place of a wild animal. **2** *Informal* a place of seclusion or hiding. ▷ **HISTORY** Old English *leger*

laird *n Scot* a landowner, esp. of a large estate. ▷ **HISTORY** Scots variant of *lord*

laissez faire *or* **laisser faire** (**less**-ay **fair**) *n* the policy of nonintervention, esp. by a government in commerce. ▷ **HISTORY** French, literally: let (them) act

laity (**lay**-it-ee) *n* **1** people who are not members of the clergy. **2** all the people who do not belong to a specific profession. ▷ **HISTORY** from LAY[3]

lake[1] *n* an expanse of water entirely surrounded by land. ▷ **HISTORY** Latin *lacus*

lake[2] *n* **1** a bright pigment produced by combining organic colouring matter with an inorganic compound. **2** a red dye obtained by combining a metallic compound with cochineal. ▷ **HISTORY** variant of *lac*

lama *n* a Buddhist priest or monk in Mongolia or Tibet. ▷ **HISTORY** Tibetan *blama*

lamb *n* **1** the young of a sheep. **2** the meat of a young sheep eaten as food. **3** someone who is innocent, gentle, and good. ✧ *vb* **4** (of a ewe) to give birth. ▷ **HISTORY** Old English

Lamb *n* **the Lamb** a title given to Christ.

lambast *or* **lambaste** *vb* **1** to beat severely. **2** to reprimand severely. ▷ **HISTORY** LAM[1] + BASTE[3]

lambent *adj* **1** (of a flame or light) flickering softly over a surface. **2** (of wit or humour) light or brilliant. ▷ **HISTORY** Latin *lambere* to lick ▶ **lambency** *n*

lambing *n* **1** the birth of lambs at the end of winter. **2** the shepherd's work of tending the ewes and newborn lambs at this time.

lamb's fry *n Austral & NZ* lamb's liver for cooking.

lambskin *n* the skin of a lamb, usually with the wool still on, used to make coats, slippers, etc.

lame *adj* **1** disabled or crippled in the legs or feet. **2** weak; unconvincing: *lame arguments.* ✧ *vb* **laming, lamed 3** to make lame. ▷ **HISTORY** Old English *lama* ▶ **lamely** *adv* ▶ **lameness** *n*

lamé (**lah**-may) *n* a fabric interwoven with gold or silver threads. ▷ **HISTORY** Old French *lame* gold or silver thread

lame duck *n* a person who is unable to cope without the help of other people.

lamella *n, pl* **-lae** (-lee) *Biol* a calcified layer of which bone is formed.

lament *vb* **1** to feel or express sorrow or regret (for or over). ✧ *n* **2** an expression of sorrow. **3** a poem or song in which a death is lamented. ▷ **HISTORY** Latin *lamentum* ▶ **lamentation** *n*

lamentable *adj* very unfortunate or disappointing. ▶ **lamentably** *adv*

lamented *adj* grieved for: usually said of someone dead.

lamina *n, pl* **-nae** a thin plate, esp. of bone or mineral. ▷ **HISTORY** Latin: thin plate ▶ **laminar** *adj*

laminate *vb* **-nating, -nated 1** to make (material in sheet form) by sticking together thin sheets. **2** to cover with a thin sheet of material. **3** to split or be split into thin sheets. ✧ *n* **4** a material made by sticking sheets together. ✧ *adj* **5** composed of lamina; laminated. ▶ **lamination** *n*

laminated *adj* **1** composed of many layers stuck together. **2** covered with a thin protective layer of plastic.

lamington *n Austral & NZ* a sponge cake coated with a sweet coating.

Lammas *n* August 1, formerly observed in England as a harvest festival: a quarter day in Scotland. ▷ **HISTORY** Old English *hlāfmæsse* loaf mass

lamp *n* **1** a device that produces light: *an electric lamp; a gas lamp; an oil lamp.* **2** a device that produces radiation, esp. for therapeutic purposes: *an ultraviolet lamp.* ▷ **HISTORY** Greek *lampein* to shine

lampblack *n* a fine black soot used as a pigment in paint and ink.

lampoon *n* **1** a piece of writing ridiculing a person. ✧ *vb* **2** to ridicule and criticize (someone) in a lampoon. ▷ **HISTORY** French *lampon* ▶ **lampooner** *or* **lampoonist** *n*

lamppost *n* a metal or concrete pole supporting a lamp in a street.

lamprey *n* an eel-like fish with a round sucking mouth. ▷ **HISTORY** Late Latin *lampreda*

Lancastrian *n* **1** a person from Lancashire or Lancaster. **2** a supporter of the house of Lancaster in the Wars of the Roses (1455–85). ✧ *adj* **3** of Lancashire or Lancaster. **4** of the house of Lancaster.

lance *n* **1** a long weapon with a pointed head used by horsemen. ✧ *vb* **lancing, lanced 2** to pierce (an abscess or boil) with a lancet. **3** to pierce with or as with a lance. ▷ **HISTORY** Latin *lancea*

lance corporal *n* a noncommissioned officer of the lowest rank.

lanceolate *adj* narrow and tapering to a point at each end, like some leaves. ▷ **HISTORY** Latin *lanceola* small lance

lancer *n* (formerly) a cavalryman armed with a lance.

lancet *n* a pointed surgical knife with two sharp edges. ▷ **HISTORY** Old French *lancette* small lance

lancewood *n* a New Zealand tree with slender leaves.

land *n* **1** the solid part of the surface of the earth as distinct from seas and lake. *RELATED ADJECTIVE* ▸ **terrestrial 2** ground, esp. with reference to its use or quality: *agricultural land.* **3** rural or agricultural areas: *he couldn't leave the land.* **4** *Law* ground owned as property. **5** a country, region, or area: *to bring peace and riches to your land.* ✧ *vb* **6** to come down or bring (something) down to earth after a flight or jump. **7** to transfer (something) or go from a ship to the shore: *sacks of malt were landed from barges.* **8** to come to or touch shore. **9** *Informal* to obtain: *he landed a handsomely paid job at Lloyd's.* **10** *Angling* to retrieve (a hooked fish) from the water. **11** *Informal* to deliver (a blow or punch). ✧ See also **land up**. ▷ **HISTORY** Old English ▶ **landless** *adj*

land army *n History* a body of women recruited to do farm work in Britain during World Wars I and II.

landau (**lan**-daw) *n* a four-wheeled horse-drawn carriage with two folding hoods. ▷ HISTORY after *Landau,* a town in Germany, where first made

land breeze *n Meteorol* a breeze that blows from land to sea, usually at night, caused by the land cooling faster than the sea and cooler air from the land flowing to replace rising warmer air from the sea. Compare **sea breeze**.

land degradation *n Geog* a decline in the condition of soil, plant life, and water, often caused by human activities and soil erosion.

landed *adj* **1** owning land: *landed gentry.* **2** consisting of land: *landed property.*

landfall *n* the act of sighting or nearing land, esp. from the sea.

landfill *n* disposing of rubbish by covering it with earth.

landform *n Geol* any natural feature of the earth's surface.

land girl *n* a girl or woman who does farm work, esp. in wartime.

landing *n* **1** the floor area at the top of a flight of stairs. **2** the act of coming to land, esp. after a flight or sea voyage. **3** a place of disembarkation.

landing field *n* an area of land on which aircraft land and from which they take off.

landing gear *n* the undercarriage of an aircraft.

landlady *n, pl* **-dies 1** a woman who owns and leases property. **2** a woman who owns or runs a lodging house or pub.

landlocked *adj* (of a country) completely surrounded by land.

landlord *n* **1** a man who owns and leases property. **2** a man who owns or runs a lodging house or pub.

landlubber *n Naut* any person without experience at sea.

landmark *n* **1** a prominent object in or feature of a particular landscape. **2** an important or unique event or development: *a landmark in scientific progress.*

landmass *n* a large continuous area of land.

land mine *n Mil* an explosive device placed in the ground, usually detonated when someone steps on it or drives over it.

landscape *n* **1** an extensive area of land regarded as being visually distinct. **2** a painting, drawing, or photograph depicting natural scenery. ✧ *vb* **-scaping, -scaped 3** to improve the natural features of (an area of land). ▷ HISTORY Middle Dutch *lantscap* region

landscape gardening *n* the art of laying out grounds in imitation of natural scenery. ▶ **landscape gardener** *n*

landside *n* the part of an airport farthest from the aircraft.

landslide *n* **1** Also called: **landslip a** the sliding of a large mass of rocks and soil down the side of a mountain or cliff. **b** the material dislodged in this way. **2** an overwhelming electoral victory.

land tenure *n Law* the system of property rights under which land is held, occupied, and used.

land up *vb* to arrive at a final point or condition.

landward *adj* **1** lying, facing, or moving towards land. **2** in the direction of the land. ✧ *adv also* **landwards 3** towards land.

lane *n* **1** a narrow road, esp. in the country. **2** one of the parallel strips into which the carriageway of a major road or motorway is divided. **3** any well-defined route or course, such as for ships or aircraft. **4** one of the parallel strips into which a running track or swimming bath is divided for races. ▷ HISTORY Old English *lane, lanu*

lang. language.

language *n* **1** a system of spoken sounds or conventional symbols for communicating thought. **2** the language of a particular nation or people. **3** the ability to use words to communicate. **4** any other means of communicating: *body language.* **5** the specialized vocabulary used by a particular group: *legal language.* **6** a particular style of verbal expression: *rough language.* **7** *Computers* See **programming language**. ▷ HISTORY Latin *lingua* tongue

languid *adj* lacking energy; dreamy and inactive. ▷ HISTORY Latin *languere* to languish ▶ **languidly** *adv*

languish *vb Literary* **1** to suffer deprivation, hardship, or neglect: *she won't languish in jail for it.* **2** to lose or diminish in strength or energy: *the design languished into oblivion.* **3** (often foll. by *for*) to be listless with desire; pine. ▷ HISTORY Latin *languere* ▶ **languishing** *adj*

languor (**lang**-ger) *n Literary* a pleasant state of dreamy relaxation. ▷ HISTORY Latin *languere* to languish ▶ **languorous** *adj*

La Niña (la-**nee**-nya) *n Meteorol* a cooling of the central and eastern Pacific Ocean associated with a strengthening of tropical Pacific trade winds and wetter weather conditions in Australia. ▷ HISTORY Spanish: the girl child Compare **El Niño**.

lank *adj* **1** (of hair) straight and limp. **2** thin or gaunt: *a lank bespectacled boy.* ▷ HISTORY Old English *hlanc* loose

lanky *adj* **lankier, lankiest** ungracefully tall and thin. ▶ **lankiness** *n*

lanolin *n* a yellowish sticky substance extracted from wool: used in some ointments. ▷ HISTORY Latin *lana* wool + *oleum* oil

lantana (lan-**tay**-na) *n* a shrub with orange or yellow flowers, considered a weed in Australia.

lantern *n* **1** a light with a transparent protective case. **2** a raised part on top of a dome or roof which lets in light or air. **3** the upper part of a lighthouse that houses the light. ▷ HISTORY Greek *lampein* to shine

lantern jaw *n* a long hollow jaw that gives the face a drawn appearance. ▶ **lantern-jawed** *adj*

lanthanide series *n Chem* a class of 15 chemically related elements (**lanthanides**) with atomic numbers from 57 (lanthanum) to 71 (lutetium).

A B C D E F G H I J K L M N O P Q R S T U V W X Y Z

lanthanum *n Chem* a silvery-white metallic element of the lanthanide series: used in electronic devices and glass manufacture. Symbol: La. ▷ HISTORY Greek *lanthanein* to lie unseen

lanyard *n* **1** a cord worn round the neck to hold a whistle or knife. **2** *Naut* a line for extending or tightening rigging. ▷ HISTORY Old French *lasne* strap

lap[1] *n* **1** the area formed by the upper surface of the thighs of a seated person. **2** a protected place or environment: *in the lap of luxury*. **3** the part of a person's clothing that covers the lap. **4 drop in someone's lap** to give someone the responsibility of. ▷ HISTORY Old English *læppa* flap

lap[2] *n* **1** one circuit of a racecourse or track. **2** a stage or part of a journey. **3 a** an overlapping part. **b** the extent of overlap. ✧ *vb* **lapping, lapped 4** to overtake (an opponent) in a race so as to be one or more circuits ahead. **5** to enfold or wrap around. **6** to place or lie partly or completely over or project beyond: *deep-pile carpet that lapped against his ankles*. **7** to envelop or surround with comfort, love, or peace: *she was lapped by the luxury of Seymour House*. ▷ HISTORY probably same as LAP[1]

lap[3] *vb* **lapping, lapped 1** (of small waves) to wash against (the shore or a boat) with light splashing sounds. **2** (often foll. by *up*) (esp. of animals) to scoop (a liquid) into the mouth with the tongue. ✧ *n* **3** the act or sound of lapping. ✧ See also **lap up**. ▷ HISTORY Old English *lapian*

lapdog *n* a small pet dog.

lapel (lap-**pel**) *n* the part on the front of a jacket or coat that folds back towards the shoulders. ▷ HISTORY from LAP[1]

lapidary *n, pl* **-daries 1** a person who cuts, polishes, sets, or deals in gemstones. ✧ *adj* **2** of or relating to gemstones or the work of a lapidary. ▷ HISTORY Latin *lapidarius*, from *lapis* stone

lapis lazuli (**lap**-iss **lazz**-yew-lie) *n* a brilliant blue mineral used as a gemstone. ▷ HISTORY Latin *lapis* stone + Medieval Latin *lazulum* azure

Lapp *n* **1** Also: **Laplander** a member of a nomadic people living chiefly in N Scandinavia. **2** the language of this people. ✧ *adj* **3** of this people or their language.

lappet *n* **1** a small hanging flap or piece of lace. **2** *Zool* a flap of flesh or membrane, such as the ear lobe or a bird's wattle. ▷ HISTORY LAP[1] + *-et* (diminutive suffix)

lapse *n* **1** a temporary drop in standard as a result of forgetfulness or lack of concentration. **2** a moment or instance of bad behaviour, esp. by someone who is usually well-behaved. **3** a period of time sufficient for a change to take place: *the lapse between phone call and now*. **4** a gradual decline to a lower degree, condition, or state: *its lapse from the tradition of Disraeli*. **5** *Law* the loss of some right by neglecting to exercise or renew it. ✧ *vb* **lapsing, lapsed 6** to drop in standard or fail to maintain a standard. **7** to decline gradually in status, condition, or degree. **8** to allow to end or become no longer valid, esp. through negligence: *a bid that lapsed last July*. **9** (usually foll. by *into*) to drift (into a condition): *she appeared to lapse into a brief reverie*. **10** (often foll. by *from*) to turn away (from beliefs or standards). **11** (of time) to slip away. ▷ HISTORY Latin *lapsus* error ▶ **lapsed** *adj*

laptop *adj* (of a computer) small and light enough to be held on the user's lap.

lap up *vb* **1** to eat or drink. **2** to accept (information or attention) eagerly: *the public are lapping up the scandal*.

lapwing *n* a bird of the plover family with a crested head. Also called: **peewit** ▷ HISTORY Old English *hlēapewince* plover

larboard *n Naut* an old word for **port**[2] (sense 1). ▷ HISTORY Middle English *laddeborde*

larceny *n, pl* **-nies** *Law* theft. ▷ HISTORY Old French *larcin* ▶ **larcenist** *n*

larch *n* **1** a coniferous tree with deciduous needle-like leaves and egg-shaped cones. **2** the wood of this tree. ▷ HISTORY Latin *larix*

lard *n* **1** the soft white fat obtained from pigs and prepared for use in cooking. ✧ *vb* **2** to prepare (lean meat or poultry) by inserting small strips of bacon or fat before cooking. **3** to add unnecessary material to (speech or writing). ▷ HISTORY Latin *laridum* bacon fat

larder *n* a room or cupboard used for storing food. ▷ HISTORY Old French *lardier*

large *adj* **1** having a relatively great size, quantity, or extent; big. **2** of wide or broad scope, capacity, or range; comprehensive: *a large effect*. ✧ *n* **3 at large a** as a whole; in general: *both the Navy and the country at large*. **b** (of a dangerous criminal or wild animal) out of captivity; free. **c** in full detail. ✧ *vb* **larging, larged large it** *Brit slang* to enjoy oneself or celebrate in an extravagant way. ▷ HISTORY Latin *largus* ample ▶ **largeness** *n*

large intestine *n* the part of the alimentary canal consisting of the caecum, colon, and rectum.

largely *adv* principally; to a great extent.

large-scale *adj* **1** wide-ranging or extensive. **2** (of maps and models) constructed or drawn to a big scale.

largesse *or* **largess** (lar-**jess**) *n* the generous giving of gifts, favours, or money. ▷ HISTORY Old French

largish *adj* fairly large.

largo *Music* ✧ *adv* **1** in a slow and stately manner. ✧ *n, pl* **-gos 2** a piece or passage to be performed in a slow and stately manner. ▷ HISTORY Italian

lariat *n US & Canad* **1** a lasso. **2** a rope for tethering animals. ▷ HISTORY Spanish *la reata* the lasso

lark[1] *n* a small brown songbird, esp. the skylark. ▷ HISTORY Old English *lāwerce, lǣwerce*

lark[2] *Informal* ✧ *n* **1** a carefree adventure or frolic. **2** a harmless piece of mischief. **3** an activity or job viewed with disrespect. ✧ *vb* **4 lark about** to have a good time frolicking or playing pranks. ▷ HISTORY origin unknown ▶ **larky** *adj*

larkspur *n* a plant with blue, pink, or white flowers with slender spikes at the base. ▷ HISTORY LARK[1] + SPUR

larrikin *n Austral or NZ old-fashioned slang* a mischievous or unruly person.

larva *n, pl* **-vae** the immature form of many insects before it develops into its adult form. ▷ **HISTORY** New Latin ▶ **larval** *adj*

laryngeal *adj* of or relating to the larynx.

laryngitis *n* inflammation of the larynx, causing huskiness or loss of voice.

larynx (**lar**-rinks) *n, pl* **larynges** (lar-**rin**-jeez) *or* **larynxes** a hollow organ forming part of the air passage to the lungs: it contains the vocal cords. ▷ **HISTORY** Greek *larunx*

lasagne *or* **lasagna** (laz-**zan**-ya) *n* **1** a form of pasta in wide flat sheets. **2** a dish made from layers of lasagne, meat, and cheese. ▷ **HISTORY** Italian, from Latin *lasanum* cooking pot

lascivious (lass-**iv**-ee-uss) *adj* showing or producing sexual desire; lustful. ▷ **HISTORY** Latin *lascivia* wantonness ▶ **lasciviously** *adv*

laser (**lay**-zer) *n* a device that produces a very narrow intense beam of light, which is used for cutting very hard materials and in surgery etc. ▷ **HISTORY** from *l*ight *a*mplification by stimulated emission of *r*adiation

laser printer *n* a computer printer that uses a laser beam to produce characters which are then transferred to paper.

lash[1] *n* **1** an eyelash. **2** a sharp cutting blow from a whip. **3** the flexible end of a whip. ✧ *vb* **4** to hit (a person or thing) sharply with a whip, esp. formerly as punishment. **5** (of rain or waves) to beat forcefully against. **6** to attack (someone) with words of ridicule or scolding. **7** to flick or wave sharply to and fro: *his tail lashing in irritation.* **8** to urge as with a whip: *to lash the audience into a violent mood.* ✧ See also **lash out**. ▷ **HISTORY** perhaps imitative

lash[2] *vb* to bind or secure with rope, string, or cord. ▷ **HISTORY** Latin *laqueus* noose

lashings *pl n Brit & NZ old-fashioned, informal* large amounts; lots: *lashings of cream.*

lash out *vb* **1** to make a sudden verbal or physical attack. **2** *Informal* to spend extravagantly.

lass *n* a girl or young woman. ▷ **HISTORY** origin unknown

Lassa fever *n* a serious viral disease of Central West Africa, characterized by high fever and muscular pains. ▷ **HISTORY** after *Lassa,* the Nigerian village where it was first identified

lassie *n Scot & N English informal* a little lass; girl.

lassitude *n* physical or mental weariness. ▷ **HISTORY** Latin *lassus* tired

lasso (lass-**oo**) *n, pl* **-sos** *or* **-soes 1** a long rope with a noose at one end used for catching horses and cattle. ✧ *vb* **-soing, -soed 2** to catch as with a lasso. ▷ **HISTORY** Spanish, from Latin *laqueus* noose ▶ **lassoer** *n*

last[1] *adj* **1** being, happening, or coming at the end or after all others. **2** most recent: *last April.* **3** only remaining: *that's the last one.* **4** most extreme; utmost. **5** least suitable or likely: *China was the last place on earth he intended to go.* ✧ *adv* **6** after all others. **7** most recently: *we last saw him on Thursday night.* **8** as the last or latest item. ✧ *n* **9 the last a** a person or thing that is last. **b** the final moment; end. **10** the final appearance, mention, or occurrence: *the last of this season's visitors.* **11 at last** in the end; finally. **12 at long last** finally, after difficulty or delay. ▷ **HISTORY** variant of Old English *latest, lætest*

> **WORD TIP**
> Since *last* can mean either *after all others* or *most recent*, it is better to avoid using this word where ambiguity might arise, as in *her last novel. Final* or *latest* should be used in such contexts to avoid ambiguity.

last[2] *vb* **1** to continue to exist for a length of time: *the soccer war lasted 100 hours.* **2** to be sufficient for the needs of (a person) for a length of time: *I shall make a couple of bottles to last me until next summer.* **3** to remain fresh, uninjured, or unaltered for a certain time: *the flowers haven't lasted well.* ▷ **HISTORY** Old English *lǣstan*

last[3] *n* the wooden or metal form on which a shoe or boot is made or repaired. ▷ **HISTORY** Old English *lāst* footprint

last-ditch *adj* done as a final resort: *a last-ditch attempt.*

lasting *adj* existing or remaining effective for a long time.

Last Judgment *n* **the Last Judgment** *Theol* God's verdict on the destinies of all human beings at the end of the world.

lastly *adv* **1** at the end or at the last point. **2** finally.

last post *n Mil* **1** a bugle call used to signal the time to retire at night. **2** a similar call sounded at military funerals.

last rites *pl n Christianity* religious rites for those close to death.

last straw *n* a small incident, irritation, or setback that coming after others is too much to cope with.

Last Supper *n* **the Last Supper** the meal eaten by Christ with his disciples on the night before his Crucifixion.

lat. latitude.

latch *n* **1** a fastening for a gate or door that consists of a bar that may be slid or lowered into a groove, hole, or notch. **2** a spring-loaded door lock that can only be opened by a key from outside. ✧ *vb* **3** to fasten, fit, or be fitted with a latch. ▷ **HISTORY** Old English *læccan* to seize

latchkey child *n Brit, Austral & NZ* a child who has to let himself or herself in at home after school, as both parents are out at work.

late *adj* **1** occurring or arriving after the correct or expected time: *the plane will be late.* **2** towards or near the end: *the late afternoon.* **3** occurring or being at a relatively advanced time: *a late starter, his first novel was effectively his last.* **4** at an advanced time in the evening or at night: *it's late, I have to get back.* **5** having died recently: *her late father.* **6** recent: *recollect the late defeats which your enemies have experienced.* **7** former: *the late manager of the team.* **8 of late** recently. ✧ *adv* **9** after the correct or expected time: *Mark Wright*

a b c d e f g h i j k l m n o p q r s t u v w x y z

A B C D E F G H I J K L M N O P Q R S T U V W X Y Z

arrived late. **10** at a relatively advanced age: *coming late to motherhood.* **11** recently: *as late as in 1983, only 9 per cent of that labour force was unionized.* **12 late in the day a** at a late or advanced stage. **b** too late. ▷ **HISTORY** Old English *læt* ▶ **lateness** *n*

> **WORD TIP**
> Since *late* can mean *deceased*, many people think it is better to avoid using this word to refer to the person who held a post or position before its present holder: *the previous* (not *the late*) *editor of The Times.*

lateen *adj Naut* denoting a rig with a triangular sail bent to a yard hoisted to the head of a low mast. ▷ **HISTORY** French *voile latine* Latin sail

Late Greek *n* the Greek language from about the 3rd to the 8th centuries AD.

Late Latin *n* the form of written Latin used from the 3rd to the 7th centuries AD.

lately *adv* in recent times; of late.

latent *adj* lying hidden and not yet developed within a person or thing. ▷ **HISTORY** Latin *latere* to lie hidden ▶ **latency** *n*

latent heat *n Physics* the heat needed to turn a solid into a liquid or a liquid into a gas and released if the process is reversed.

lateral (**lat**-ter-al) *adj* of or relating to the side or sides. ▷ **HISTORY** Latin *latus* side ▶ **laterally** *adv*

lateral erosion *n Geol* erosion occurring at the sides of a stream or river that widens or changes its course.

lateral thinking *n* a way of solving problems by apparently illogical methods.

latex *n* a milky fluid produced by many plants: latex from the rubber plant is used in the manufacture of rubber. ▷ **HISTORY** Latin: liquid

lath *n* one of several thin narrow strips of wood used as a supporting framework for plaster or tiles. ▷ **HISTORY** Old English *lætt*

lathe *n* a machine for shaping metal or wood by turning it against a fixed tool. ▷ **HISTORY** perhaps from Old Norse

lather *n* **1** foam formed by soap or detergent in water. **2** foamy sweat, as produced by a horse. **3** *Informal* a state of agitation. ✧ *vb* **4** to coat or become coated with lather. **5** to form a lather. **6** *Informal* to beat; flog. ▷ **HISTORY** Old English *lēathor* soap ▶ **lathery** *adj*

Latin *n* **1** the language of ancient Rome and the Roman Empire. **2** a member of any of those peoples whose languages are derived from Latin. ✧ *adj* **3** of the Latin language. **4** of those peoples whose languages are derived from Latin. **5** of the Roman Catholic Church. ▷ **HISTORY** Latin *Latinus* of Latium

Latin America *n* those areas of South and Central America whose official languages are Spanish and Portuguese. ▶ **Latin American** *adj, n*

latish *adj, adv* rather late.

latitude *n* **1 a** an angular distance measured in degrees north or south of the equator. **b** (*often pl*) a region considered with regard to its distance from the equator. **2** scope for freedom of action and thought. ▷ **HISTORY** Latin *latus* broad ▶ **latitudinal** *adj*

latitudinarian *adj* **1** liberal, esp. in religious matters. ✧ *n* **2** a person with latitudinarian views.

latrine *n* a toilet in a barracks or camp. ▷ **HISTORY** Latin *lavatrina* bath

latter *n* **1 the latter** the second or second mentioned of two. ✧ *adj* **2** near or nearer the end: *the latter half of the season.* **3** more advanced in time or sequence; later. ▷ **HISTORY** Old English *lætra*

> **WORD TIP**
> *The latter* should only be used to refer to the second of two items: *many people choose to go by hovercraft rather than use the ferry, but I prefer the latter.* The last of three or more items can be referred to as *the last-named.*

latter-day *adj* present-day; modern.

latterly *adv* recently; lately.

lattice (**lat**-iss) *n* **1** Also called: **latticework** a framework of strips of wood or metal interlaced in a diagonal pattern. **2** a gate, screen, or fence formed of such a framework. **3** an array of atoms, ions, or molecules in a crystal or an array of points indicating their positions in space. ✧ *vb* **-ticing, -ticed 4** to make, adorn, or supply with a lattice. ▷ **HISTORY** Old French *latte* lath ▶ **latticed** *adj*

Latvian *adj* **1** from Latvia. ✧ *n* **2** a person from Latvia. **3** the language of Latvia.

laud *Literary* ✧ *vb* **1** to praise or glorify. ✧ *n* **2** praise or glorification. ▷ **HISTORY** Latin *laudare* to praise

laudable *adj* deserving praise; commendable. ▶ **laudability** *n* ▶ **laudably** *adv*

laudanum (**lawd**-a-num) *n* a sedative extracted from opium. ▷ **HISTORY** New Latin

laudatory *adj* (of speech or writing) expressing praise.

laugh *vb* **1** to express amusement or happiness by producing a series of inarticulate sounds. **2** to utter or express with laughter: *he laughed his derision at the play.* **3** to bring or force (oneself) into a certain condition by laughter: *laughing herself silly.* **4 laugh at** to make fun of; jeer at. **5 laugh up one's sleeve** to laugh secretly. ✧ *n* **6** the act or an instance of laughing. **7** *Informal* a person or thing that causes laughter: *he's a laugh, that one.* **8 the last laugh** final success after previous defeat. ✧ See also **laugh off**. ▷ **HISTORY** Old English *læhan, hliehhen* ▶ **laughingly** *adv*

laughable *adj* ridiculous because so obviously inadequate or unsuccessful.

laughing gas *n* nitrous oxide used as an anaesthetic: it may cause laughter and exhilaration when inhaled.

laughing stock *n* a person or thing that is treated with ridicule.

laugh off *vb* to treat (something serious or difficult) lightly.

laughter *n* the action or noise of laughing. ▷ **HISTORY** Old English *hleahtor*

launch[1] *vb* **1** to move (a vessel) into the water, esp. for the first time. **2 a** to start off or set in motion: *to launch an appeal.* **b** to put (a new product) on the market. **3** to set (a rocket, missile, or spacecraft) into motion. **4** to involve (oneself) totally and enthusiastically: *Francis launched himself into the transfer market with gusto.* **5 launch into** to start talking or writing about. **6** (usually foll. by *out*) to start (out) on a new enterprise. ✧ *n* **7** an act or instance of launching. ▷ **HISTORY** Late Latin *lanceare* to use a lance, hence to set in motion ▸ **launcher** *n*

launch[2] *n* an open motorboat. ▷ **HISTORY** Malay *lancharan* boat, from *lanchar* speed

launch pad *or* **launching pad** *n* a platform from which a spacecraft, rocket, or missile is launched.

launder *vb* **1** to wash and iron (clothes and linen). **2** to make (money illegally obtained) appear to be legally gained by passing it through foreign banks or legitimate enterprises. ▷ **HISTORY** Latin *lavare* to wash

Launderette *n Brit, Austral & NZ trademark* an establishment where clothes can be washed and dried, using coin-operated machines. Also called (US, Canad, Austral and NZ): **Laundromat**

laundry *n, pl* **-dries 1** the clothes or linen to be laundered or that have been laundered. **2** a place where clothes and linen are washed and ironed.

laureate (lor-ee-at) *adj* **1** *Literary* crowned with laurel leaves as a sign of honour. ✧ *n* **2** short for **poet laureate**. ▷ **HISTORY** Latin *laurea* laurel ▸ **laureateship** *n*

laurel *n* **1** a small Mediterranean evergreen tree with glossy leaves. **2 laurels** a wreath of laurel, worn on the head as an emblem of victory or honour in classical times. **3 laurels** honour, distinction, or fame. **4 rest on one's laurels** to be satisfied with what one has already achieved and stop striving for further success. **5 look to one's laurels** to be on guard against one's rivals. ▷ **HISTORY** Latin *laurus*

lava *n* **1** molten rock discharged by volcanoes. **2** any rock formed by the solidification of lava. ▷ **HISTORY** Latin *lavare* to wash

lavatory *n, pl* **-ries** same as **toilet**. ▷ **HISTORY** Latin *lavare* to wash

lavender *n* **1** a plant grown for its bluish-purple flowers and as the source of a sweet-smelling oil. **2** its dried flowers, used to perfume clothes. ✧ *adj* **3** pale bluish-purple. ▷ **HISTORY** Medieval Latin *lavendula*

lavender water *n* a light perfume made from lavender.

lavish *adj* **1** great in quantity or richness: *lavish banquets.* **2** very generous in giving. **3** extravagant; wasteful: *lavish spending habits.* ✧ *vb* **4** to give or to spend very generously or in great quantities. ▷ **HISTORY** Old French *lavasse* torrent ▸ **lavishly** *adv*

law *n* **1** a rule or set of rules regulating what may or may not be done by members of a society or community. **2** a rule or body of rules made by the legislature or other authority. *RELATED ADJECTIVES* ▸ **legal, judicial, juridical 3** the control enforced by such rules: *scant respect for the rule of law.* **4 the law a** the legal or judicial system. **b** the profession or practice of law. **c** *Informal* the police or a policeman. **5 law and order** the policy of strict enforcement of the law, esp. against crime and violence. **6** a rule of behaviour: *an unwritten law that Nanny knows best.* **7** Also called: **law of nature** a generalization based on a recurring fact or event. **8** the science or knowledge of law; jurisprudence. **9** a general principle, formula, or rule in mathematics, science, or philosophy: *the law of gravity.* **10 the Law** the laws contained in the first five books of the Old Testament. **11 go to law** to resort to legal proceedings on some matter. **12 lay down the law** to speak in an authoritative manner. ▷ **HISTORY** Old English *lagu*

law-abiding *adj* obeying the laws: *a law-abiding citizen.*

lawbreaker *n* a person who breaks the law. ▸ **lawbreaking** *n, adj*

lawful *adj* allowed, recognized, or sanctioned by law; legal. ▸ **lawfully** *adv*

lawgiver *n* **1** the giver of a code of laws. **2** Also called: **lawmaker** a maker of laws. ▸ **lawgiving** *n, adj*

lawless *adj* **1** breaking the law, esp. in a wild or violent way: *lawless butchery.* **2** not having laws. ▸ **lawlessness** *n*

Law Lords *pl n* (in Britain) members of the House of Lords who sit as the highest court of appeal.

lawn[1] *n* an area of cultivated and mown grass. ▷ **HISTORY** Old French *lande*

lawn[2] *n* a fine linen or cotton fabric. ▷ **HISTORY** probably from *Laon*, town in France where made

lawn mower *n* a hand-operated or power-operated machine for cutting grass.

lawn tennis *n* **1** tennis played on a grass court. **2** same as **tennis**.

lawrencium *n Chem* an element artificially produced from californium. Symbol: Lr. ▷ **HISTORY** after E. O. *Lawrence*, physicist

lawsuit *n* a case in a court of law brought by one person or group against another.

lawyer *n* a member of the legal profession who can advise clients about the law and represent them in court.

lax *adj* lacking firmness; not strict. ▷ **HISTORY** Latin *laxus* loose ▸ **laxity** *n*

laxative *n* **1** a medicine that induces the emptying of the bowels. ✧ *adj* **2** easing the emptying of the bowels. ▷ **HISTORY** Latin *laxare* to loosen

lay[1] *vb* **lays, laying, laid 1** to put in a low or horizontal position; cause to lie: *Mary laid a clean square of white towelling carefully on the grass.* **2** to establish as a basis: *settlers had laid their plans for rebellion.* **3** to place or be in a particular state or position: *underneath lay a key.* **4** to regard as the responsibility of: *ridiculous attempts to lay the loss at the door of the Admiralty.* **5** to put forward: *ruses by*

A B C D E F G H I J K L M N O P Q R S T U V W X Y Z

which we lay claim on one another. **6** to arrange or prepare: *she would lay her plans.* **7** to place in position: *he laid a wreath.* **8** (of birds, esp. the domestic hen) to produce (eggs). **9** to make (a bet) with (someone): *I'll lay money he's already gone home.* **10** to arrange (a table) for a meal. **11** to prepare (a fire) by arranging fuel in the grate. **12** *Taboo slang* to have sexual intercourse with. **13 lay bare** to reveal or explain: *a century of neurophysiology has now laid bare the structures of the brain.* **14 lay hold of** to seize or grasp. **15 lay oneself open** to make oneself vulnerable (to criticism or attack). **16 lay open** to reveal or disclose. **17 lay waste** to destroy completely. ✧ *n* **18** the manner or position in which something lies or is placed. **19** *Taboo, slang* **a** an act of sexual intercourse. **b** a sexual partner. ✧ See also **lay down.** ▷ **HISTORY** Old English *lecgan*

> **WORD TIP**
> In standard English, the verb *lay* can only be used with an object, and *lie* can only be used without one: *the Queen laid a wreath; he was lying on the floor.*

lay² *vb* the past tense of **lie²**.

lay³ *adj* **1** of or involving people who are not members of the clergy. **2** nonprofessional or nonspecialist. ▷ **HISTORY** Greek *laos* people

lay⁴ *n* a short narrative poem intended to be sung. ▷ **HISTORY** Old French *lai*

layabout *n* a lazy person.

lay-by *n* **1** *Brit* a place where drivers can stop by the side of a main road. **2** *Austral & NZ* a system of payment whereby a buyer pays a deposit on an article, which is reserved for him or her until he or she has paid the full price.

lay down *vb* **1** to place on the ground or a surface. **2** to sacrifice: *willing to lay down their lives for the truth.* **3** to formulate (a rule or principle). **4** to record (plans) on paper. **5** to store or stock: *the speed with which we lay down extra, unwanted fat.*

layer *n* **1** a single thickness of something, such as a cover or a coating on a surface. **2** a laying hen. **3** *Horticulture* a shoot that forms its own root while still attached to the parent plant. ✧ *vb* **4** to form or make a layer or layers. ▷ **HISTORY** from LAY¹

layette *n* a complete set of clothing, bedclothes, and other accessories for a newborn baby. ▷ **HISTORY** Middle Dutch *laege* box

lay figure *n* **1** an artist's jointed dummy, used esp. for studying effects of drapery. **2** a person considered to be subservient or unimportant. ▷ **HISTORY** Dutch *leeman,* literally: joint-man

lay in *vb* to accumulate and store: *they've already laid in five hundred bottles of great vintages.*

lay into *vb Informal* to attack or scold severely.

layman *or fem* **laywoman** *n, pl* **-men** *or* **-women 1** a person who is not a member of the clergy. **2** a person who does not have specialized knowledge of a subject: *the layman's guide to nuclear power.*

lay off *vb* **1** to suspend (staff) during a slack period at work. **2** *Informal* to leave (a person, thing, or activity) alone: *'lay off the defence counsel bit!' he snapped.* ✧ *n* **lay-off 3** a period of imposed unemployment.

lay on *vb* **1** to provide or supply: *they laid on a treat for the entourage.* **2 lay it on thick** *Slang* to exaggerate, esp. when flattering.

lay out *vb* **1** to arrange or spread out. **2** to plan or design: *the main streets were laid out on a grid system.* **3** to prepare (a corpse) for burial or cremation. **4** *Informal* to spend (money), esp. lavishly. **5** *Informal* to knock (someone) unconscious. ✧ *n* **layout 6** the arrangement or plan of something, such as a building. **7** the arrangement of printed material.

lay reader *n* **1** *Church of England* a person licensed to conduct religious services other than the Eucharist. **2** *RC Church* a layman chosen to read the epistle at Mass.

lay up *vb* **1** *Informal* to confine through illness: *laid up with a bad cold.* **2** to store for future use.

laze *vb* **lazing, lazed 1** to be idle or lazy. **2** (often foll. by *away*) to spend (time) in idleness. ✧ *n* **3** time spent lazing. ▷ **HISTORY** from *lazy*

lazy *adj* **lazier, laziest 1** not inclined to work or exert oneself. **2** done in a relaxed manner with little effort. **3** moving in a sluggish manner: *the lazy drift of the bubbles.* ▷ **HISTORY** origin unknown ▶ **lazily** *adv* ▶ **laziness** *n*

lazybones *n Informal* a lazy person.

lb 1 pound (weight). ▷ **HISTORY** Latin *libra* **2** *Cricket* leg bye.

lbw *Cricket* leg before wicket.

lc 1 in the place cited. ▷ **HISTORY** Latin *loco citato* **2** *Printing* lower case.

LCD 1 liquid crystal display. **2** Also: **lcd** lowest common denominator.

lcm *or* **LCM** lowest common multiple.

lea *n* **1** *Poetic* a meadow or field. **2** grassland. ▷ **HISTORY** Old English *lēah*

LEA (in Britain) Local Education Authority.

leach *vb* **1** to remove or be removed from a substance by a liquid passing through it. **2** to lose soluble substances by the action of a liquid passing through. ▷ **HISTORY** perhaps Old English *leccan* to water

lead¹ *vb* **leading, led 1** to show the way to (an individual or a group) by going with or ahead: *he led her into the house.* **2** to guide, control, or direct: *he dismounted and led his horse back.* **3** to influence someone to act, think, or behave in a certain way: *researching our family history has led her to correspond with relatives abroad.* **4** to have the principal part in (something): *planners led the development of policy.* **5** to go at the head of or have the top position in (something): *the pair led the field by almost two minutes.* **6** (of a road or way) to be the means of reaching a place: *the footbridge leads on to a fine promenade.* **7** to pass or spend: *I've led a happy life.* **8** to guide or be guided by physical means: *he took her firmly by the arm and led her home.* **9** to direct the course of (water, a rope, or wire) along or as if along a channel. **10** (foll. by *with*) to have as the most important item: *the Review* *leads with a critique of A Place of Greater Safety.* **11** *Brit music* to play first violin in (an orchestra). **12** to begin a round of cards by putting down the first card. ✧ *n* **13** the first or most prominent place. **14** example or leadership: *some of his children followed his lead.* **15** an advantage over others: *Essex have a lead of 24 points.* **16** an indication; clue: *we've got a lead on how the body got into the water.* **17** a length of leather, nylon, or chain used to walk or control a dog. **18** the principal role in a play, film, or other production, or the person playing such a role. **19** the most important news story in a newspaper: *the shooting makes the lead in the Times.* **20** the act of playing the first card in a round of cards or the card so played. **21** a wire, cable, or other conductor for making an electrical connection. ✧ *adj* **22** acting as a leader or lead: *lead singer.* ✧ See also **lead on**. ▷ HISTORY Old English *lǣdan*

lead² *n* **1** a heavy toxic bluish-white metallic element: used in alloys, cable sheaths, and paints, and as a radiation shield. Symbol: Pb. **2 a** graphite used for drawing. **b** a thin stick of this as the core of a pencil. **3** a lead weight suspended on a line, used to take soundings of the depth of water. **4** lead weights or shot, as used in cartridges or fishing lines. **5** a thin strip of lead for holding small panes of glass or pieces of stained glass. **6 leads a** thin sheets or strips of lead used as a roof covering. **b** a roof covered with such sheets. **7** Also called: **leading** *Printing* a thin strip of metal, formerly used for spacing between lines of type. ✧ *adj* **8** of, relating to, or containing lead. ✧ *vb* **9** to surround, cover, or secure with lead or leads. ▷ HISTORY Old English *lēad*

leaded *adj* (of windows) made from many small panes of glass held together by lead strips.

leaden *adj* **1** heavy or sluggish: *my limbs felt leaden.* **2** of a dull greyish colour: *leaden November sky.* **3** made of lead. **4** gloomy, spiritless, or lifeless: *hollow characters and leaden dialogue.*

leader *n* **1** a person who rules, guides, or inspires others; head. **2** *Brit & Austral* Also: **leading article** the leading editorial in a newspaper. **3** *Music* the principal first violinist of an orchestra who acts as the conductor's deputy. **4** the person or animal who is leading in a race. **5** the best or the most successful of its kind: *the company is a world leader in its field.* **6** the leading horse or dog in a team. **7** a strip of blank film or tape at the beginning of a reel. **8** *Bot* any of the long slender shoots that grow from the stem or branch of a tree. ▶ **leadership** *n*

lead-in *n* an introduction to a subject.

leading *adj* **1** principal or primary: *the leading designers.* **2** in the first position: *the leading driver.*

leading aircraftman *n* the rank above aircraftman in the British air force. ▶ **leading aircraftwoman** *fem n*

leading light *n* an important and influential person in an organization or campaign.

leading question *n* a question worded to suggest the desired answer, such as *What do you think of the horrible effects of pollution?*

leading rating *n* a rank in the Royal Navy comparable to a corporal in the army.

lead on *vb* to trick (someone) into believing or doing something wrong.

lead poisoning *n* acute or chronic poisoning by lead.

lead story *n Journalism, television, etc.* the story given most prominence in a newspaper or on a news programme.

lead time *n Manufacturing* the time between the design of a product and its production.

lead up to *vb* **1** to act as a preliminary or introduction to. **2** to approach (a topic) gradually or cautiously.

leaf *n, pl* **leaves 1** one of the flat usually green blades attached to the stem of a plant. **2** the foliage of a tree or plant: *shrubs have been planted for their leaf interest.* **3 in leaf** (of shrubs or trees) with all its leaves fully opened. **4** a very thin sheet of metal. **5** one of the sheets of paper in a book. **6** a hinged, sliding, or detachable part, such as an extension to a table. **7 take a leaf out of someone's book** to imitate someone in a particular course of action. **8 turn over a new leaf** to begin a new and improved course of behaviour. ✧ *vb* **9** (usually foll. by *through*) to turn pages casually or hurriedly without reading them. **10** (of plants) to produce leaves. ▷ HISTORY Old English *lēaf* ▶ **leafless** *adj*

leafage *n* the leaves of plants.

leaflet *n* **1** a sheet of printed matter distributed, usually free, for advertising or information. **2** any small leaf. **3** one of the divisions of a compound leaf. ✧ *vb* **-leting, -leted 4** to distribute leaflets (to).

leaf mould *n* a rich soil consisting of decayed leaves.

leafy *adj* **leafier, leafiest 1** covered with leaves. **2** having many trees or shrubs: *a leafy suburb.*

league¹ *n* **1** an association of people or nations formed to promote the interests of its members. **2** an association of sporting clubs that organizes matches between member teams. **3** *Informal* a class or level: *the guy is not even in the same league.* **4 in league (with)** working or planning together (with). ✧ *vb* **leaguing, leagued 5** to form or be formed into a league. ▷ HISTORY Latin *ligare* to bind

league² *n* an obsolete unit of distance of varying length: commonly equal to 3 miles (4.8 kilometres). ▷ HISTORY Late Latin *leuga, leuca*

League of Nations *n History* an international association of states, founded in 1920 with the aim of preserving world peace, and dissolved in 1946.

leak *n* **1 a** a crack or hole that allows the accidental escape or entrance of liquid, gas, radiation, etc. **b** such escaping or entering liquid, etc. **2** a disclosure of secret information. **3** the loss of current from an electrical conductor because of faulty insulation. **4** the act or an instance of leaking. **5** *Slang* urination. ✧ *vb* **6** to enter or escape or allow to enter or escape through a crack or hole. **7** to make (secret information) public, esp. deliberately. ▷ HISTORY from Old Norse ▶ **leaky** *adj*

leakage *n* the act or an instance or the result of leaking: *the leakage of 60 tonnes of oil.*

A B C D E F G H I J K L M N O P Q R S T U V W X Y Z

lean[1] *vb* **leaning; leaned** *or* **leant 1** (foll. by *against, on* or *upon*) to rest or put (something) so that it rests against a support. **2** to bend or make (something) bend from an upright position. **3** (foll. by *to* or *towards*) to have or express a tendency or preference. ✧ *n* **4** the condition of bending from an upright position. ✧ See also **lean on.** ▷ HISTORY Old English *hleonian, hlinian*

lean[2] *adj* **1** (esp. of a person) having a trim body with no surplus flesh. **2** (of meat) having little or no fat. **3** (of a period) sparse, difficult, or causing hardship: *these are lean days in Baghdad.* ✧ *n* **4** the part of meat that contains little or no fat. ▷ HISTORY Old English *hlǣne* ▶ **leanness** *n*

leaning *n* a tendency or inclination.

lean on *vb* **1** *Informal* to try to influence (someone) by using threats. **2** to depend on (someone) for help and advice.

lean-to *n, pl* **-tos** a building with a sloping roof attached to another building or a wall.

leap *vb* **leaping; leapt** *or* **leaped 1** to jump suddenly from one place to another. **2** (often foll. by *at*) to move or react quickly. **3** to jump over. ✧ *n* **4** the act of jumping. **5** an abrupt or important change or increase: *a leap to full European union.* **6 a leap in the dark** an action performed without knowledge of the consequences. **7 by leaps and bounds** with unexpectedly rapid progress. ▷ HISTORY Old English *hlēapan*

leapfrog *n* **1** a children's game in which each player in turn leaps over the others' bent backs. ✧ *vb* **-frogging, -frogged 2 a** to play leapfrog. **b** to leap over (something). **3** to advance by jumps or stages.

leap year *n* a calendar year of 366 days, February 29 (**leap day**) being the additional day, that occurs every four years.

learn *vb* **learning; learned** *or* **learnt 1** to gain knowledge (of something) or acquire skill in (some art or practice). **2** to memorize (something). **3** to gain by experience, example, or practice: *I learned everything the hard way.* **4** (often foll. by *of* or *about*) to become informed; find out: *Captain Nelson learned of the disaster from his wireless.* ▷ HISTORY Old English *leornian* ▶ **learnable** *adj* ▶ **learner** *n*

learned (**lurn**-id) *adj* **1** having great knowledge. **2** involving or characterized by scholarship: *your learned paper on the subject.*

learning *n* knowledge gained by studying.

lease *n* **1** a contract by which an owner rents buildings or land to another person for a specified period. **2 a new lease of life** a prospect of renewed energy, health, or happiness. ✧ *vb* **leasing, leased 3** to let or rent (land or buildings) by lease. ▷ HISTORY Old French *laissier* to let go

leasehold *n* **1** land or property held under a lease. **2** the holding of such property under lease. ▶ **leaseholder** *n*

leash *n* **1** a dog's lead. **2 straining at the leash** eagerly impatient to begin something. ✧ *vb* **3** to put a leash on. ▷ HISTORY Old French *laissier* to loose (hence to let a dog run on a leash)

least *adj, adv* **1 the least** the superlative of **little:** *without encountering the least sign of civilization; he is the least well-educated prime minister.* ✧ *adj* **2** of very little importance. **3** smallest. ✧ *adv* **4 at least** if nothing else: *at least I wrote.* **5 at the least** at the minimum: *at the very least you should have some self-respect.* **6 not in the least** not at all: *you're not detaining me, not in the least.* ▷ HISTORY Old English *lǣst,* superlative of *lǣssa* less

leather *n* **1** the skin of an animal made smooth and flexible by tanning and removing the hair. **2 leathers** leather clothes, esp. as worn by motorcyclists. ✧ *adj* **3** made of leather. ✧ *vb* **4** to whip as if with a leather strap. **5** to dress in leather. ▷ HISTORY Old English *lether-* (in compound words)

leatherjacket *n* **1** any of various tropical fishes having a leathery skin. **2** the tough-skinned larva of certain crane flies, which destroy the roots of grasses.

leathery *adj* looking or feeling like leather, esp. in toughness.

leave[1] *vb* **leaving, left 1** to go away (from a person or place). **2** to cause to remain behind, often by mistake, in a place: *I left the paper under the table.* **3** to cause to be or remain in a specified state: *the poll leaves the parties neck-and-neck.* **4** to stop attending or belonging to a particular organization or institution: *at seventeen she left the convent.* **5** to not eat something or not deal with something: *he left a half-eaten lunch.* **6** to result in; cause: *I have been terribly hurt by women, it leaves indelible marks.* **7** to allow (someone) to do something without interfering: *the governor left them to it for a further few hours.* **8** to be survived by (members of one's family): *he leaves a widow and one daughter.* **9** to bequeath: *her adored son left his millions to an unknown half-sister.* **10** to have as a remainder: *37 – 14 leaves 23.* **11 leave (someone) alone a** to stop annoying (someone). **b** to permit (someone) to stay or be alone. ✧ See also **leave out.** ▷ HISTORY Old English *lǣfan*

leave[2] *n* **1** permission to be absent, for instance from work: *so I asked for leave.* **2** the length of such absence: *weekend leave.* **3** permission to do something: *they were refused leave to appeal.* **4 on leave** officially excused from work or duty. **5 take (one's) leave of** to say farewell to. ▷ HISTORY Old English *lēaf*

leaven (**lev**-ven) *n also* **leavening 1** any substance, such as yeast, that produces fermentation in dough and makes it rise. **2** an influence that produces a gradual change. ✧ *vb* **3** to cause fermentation in (dough). **4** to spread through, causing a gradual change. ▷ HISTORY Latin *levare* to raise

leave out *vb* to omit or exclude: *leave out everything not necessary to living.*

leaves *n* the plural of **leaf**.

leavings *pl n* things left behind unwanted, such as food on a plate.

Lebanese *adj* **1** from the Lebanon. ✧ *n, pl* **-nese 2** a person from the Lebanon.

Lebensraum (**lay**-benz-rowm) *n* territory claimed by a nation or state because it is necessary for survival or growth. ▷ **HISTORY** German: living space

lecherous (**letch**-er-uss) *adj* (of a man) having or showing strong and uncontrolled sexual desire. ▷ **HISTORY** Old French *lechier* to lick ▶ **lecher** *n* ▶ **lechery** *n*

lecithin (**less**-sith-in) *n Biochem* a yellow-brown compound found in plant and animal tissues, esp. egg yolk: used in making cosmetics and inks, and as an emulsifier and stabilizer (**E322**) in foods. ▷ **HISTORY** Greek *lekithos* egg yolk

lectern *n* a sloping reading desk, esp. in a church. ▷ **HISTORY** Latin *legere* to read

lecture *n* **1** a talk on a particular subject delivered to an audience. **2** a lengthy scolding. ✧ *vb* **-turing, -tured 3** to deliver a lecture (to an audience or class). **4** to scold (someone) at length. ▷ **HISTORY** Latin *legere* to read ▶ **lecturer** *n* ▶ **lectureship** *n*

led *vb* the past of **lead**[1].

LED *Electronics* light-emitting diode: a semiconductor that gives out light when an electric current is applied to it.

ledge *n* **1** a narrow horizontal surface that projects from a wall or window. **2** a narrow shelflike projection on a cliff or mountain. ▷ **HISTORY** perhaps Middle English *leggen* to lay

ledger *n Book-keeping* the principal book in which the commercial transactions of a company are recorded. ▷ **HISTORY** perhaps Middle English *leggen* to lay (because kept in a specific place)

ledger line *n Music* a short line above or below the staff used to indicate the pitch of notes higher or lower than the range of the staff.

lee *n* **1** a sheltered part or side; the side away from the direction from which the wind is blowing. ✧ *adj* **2** *Naut* on, at, or towards the side away from the wind: *her lee rail was awash.* ▷ **HISTORY** Old English *hlēow* shelter

leech *n* **1** a worm which has a sucker at each end of the body and feeds on the blood or tissues of other animals. **2** a person who lives off another person; parasite. ▷ **HISTORY** Old English *lǣce*

leek *n* a vegetable of the onion family with a slender white bulb and broad flat green overlapping leaves: the national emblem of Wales. ▷ **HISTORY** Old English *lēac*

leer *vb* **1** to give a sneering or suggestive look or grin. ✧ *n* **2** such a look. ▷ **HISTORY** Old English *hlēor* cheek

leery *adj* **leerier, leeriest 1** *Slang* (foll. by *of*) suspicious or wary. **2** *Now chiefly dialect* knowing or sly. ▷ **HISTORY** perhaps obsolete sense (to look askance) of *leer*

lees *pl n* the sediment from an alcoholic drink. ▷ **HISTORY** plural of obsolete *lee*, from Old French

leet *n Scot* a list of candidates for an office. ▷ **HISTORY** perhaps Anglo-French *litte*, variant of LIST[1]

leeward *Chiefly naut* ✧ *adj* **1** of, in, or moving in the direction towards which the wind blows. ✧ *n* **2** the side towards the lee. ✧ *adv* **3** towards the lee.

leeway *n* **1** flexibility of action or expenditure: *he gave me a lot of leeway in the work I did.* **2** sideways drift of a boat or aircraft.

left[1] *adj* **1** denoting the side of something or someone that faces west when the front is turned towards the north. **2** on the left side of the body: *I grabbed it with my left hand.* **3** liberal, radical, or socialist. ✧ *adv* **4** on or in the direction of the left. ✧ *n* **5** a left side, direction, position, area, or part. **6 the left** the people in a political party or society who have more socialist or liberal views: *the biggest party of the French Left.* **7** *Boxing* **a** a blow with the left hand. **b** the left hand. ▷ **HISTORY** Old English: idle, weak

left[2] *vb* the past of **leave**[1].

left-branching sentence *n Grammar* a sentence in which much of the information precedes the main verb in the main clause, owing to a long initial noun phrase. Compare **right-branching sentence**.

left-handed *adj* **1** better at using the left hand than the right. **2** done with the left hand. **3** designed for use by the left hand. **4** awkward or clumsy. **5** ambiguous or insincere: *a left-handed compliment.* **6** turning from right to left; anticlockwise. ✧ *adv* **7** with the left hand: *I write left-handed.* ▶ **left-hander** *n*

leftist *adj* **1** of or relating to the political left or its principles. ✧ *n* **2** a person who supports the political left. ▶ **leftism** *n*

leftover *n* **1** (*often pl*) an unused portion, esp. of cooked food. ✧ *adj* **2** left as an unused portion.

left-wing *adj* **1** socialist or radical: *the party ditched many of its more left-wing policies.* **2** belonging to the more radical part of a political party: *a group of left-wing Conservatives.* ✧ *n* **left wing 3** (*often cap*) the more radical or progressive section, esp. of a political party: *the Left Wing of the Labour Party.* **4** *Sports* **a** the left-hand side of the field of play. **b** a player positioned in this area in certain games. ▶ **left-winger** *n*

lefty *n, pl* **lefties** *Brit, Austral & NZ informal* **1** a left-winger. **2** *Chiefly US & Canad* a left-handed person.

leg *n* **1** either of the two lower limbs in humans, or any similar structure in animals that is used for movement or support. **2** the part of a garment that covers the leg. **3** a lower limb of an animal, esp. the thigh, used for food: *leg of lamb.* **4** something similar to a leg in appearance or function, such as one of the supports of a chair. **5** a section of a journey. **6** a single stage, lap, or length in a relay race. **7** one of a series of games, matches, or parts of games. **8** *Cricket* the side of the field to the left of a right-handed batsman as he faces the bowler. **9 not have a leg to stand on** *Informal* to have no reasonable basis for an opinion or argument. **10 on one's last legs** worn out or exhausted. **11 to pull someone's leg** *Informal* to tease or make fun of someone. **12 shake a leg** *Informal* to hurry up. **13 stretch one's legs** to stand up or walk around, esp. after sitting for some time. ✧ *vb* **legging, legged 14 leg it** *Informal* to walk, run, or hurry. ▷ **HISTORY** Old Norse *leggr*

A B C D E F G H I J K L M N O P Q R S T U V W X Y Z

legacy *n, pl* **-cies 1** money or personal property left to someone by a will. **2** something handed down to a successor. ▷ **HISTORY** Medieval Latin *legatia* commission

legal *adj* **1** established by or permitted by law; lawful. **2** of or relating to law. **3** relating to or characteristic of lawyers. ▷ **HISTORY** Latin *legalis* ▶ **legally** *adv*

legal aid *n* financial assistance available to people who are unable to meet the full cost of legal proceedings.

legal capacity *n Law* a person's ability, dependent on age and mental competence, to exercise legal rights and responsibilities.

legalese *n* the conventional language in which legal documents are written.

legalism *n* strict adherence to the letter of the law. ▶ **legalist** *n, adj* ▶ **legalistic** *adj*

legality *n, pl* **-ties** the state or quality of being legal or lawful.

legalize *or* **-ise** *vb* **-izing, -ized** *or* **-ising, -ised** to make lawful or legal. ▶ **legalization** *or* **-isation** *n*

legal tender *n* currency that a creditor must by law accept to pay a debt.

legate *n* a messenger, esp. one representing the Pope. ▷ **HISTORY** Latin *legare* to delegate

legatee *n* the recipient of a legacy.

legation *n* **1** a diplomatic mission headed by a minister. **2** the official residence and office of a diplomatic minister.

legato (leg-**ah**-toe) *Music* ✧ *adv* **1** smoothly and evenly. ✧ *n, pl* **-tos 2** a style of playing with no gaps between notes. ▷ **HISTORY** Italian

leg before wicket *n Cricket* a dismissal on the grounds that a batsman has been struck on the leg by a bowled ball that otherwise would have hit the wicket. Abbrev: **lbw**

leg break *n Cricket* a bowled ball that spins from leg to off on pitching.

leg bye *n Cricket* a run scored after the ball has hit the batsman's leg or some other part of his body, except his hand, without touching the bat. Abbrev: **lb**

legend *n* **1** a popular story handed down from earlier times that may or may not be true. **2** such stories collectively. **3** a person whose fame makes him or her seem exceptional: *he is a living legend.* **4** modern stories about a famous person which may or may not be true: *no Garland fan could complain about sordid revelations tarnishing the legend.* **5** words written on something to explain it: *a pub mirror spelling out the legend 'Saloon Bar'.* **6** an explanation on a table, map, or chart, of the symbols used. ▷ **HISTORY** Medieval Latin *legenda* passages to be read

legendary *adj* **1** very famous: *the legendary beauty of the Alps.* **2** of or relating to legend. **3** described in legend: *the legendary birthplace of Aphrodite.*

legerdemain (lej-er-de-**main**) *n* **1** same as **sleight of hand**. **2** cunning deception. ▷ **HISTORY** Old French: light of hand

leggings *pl n* **1** an extra outer covering for the lower legs. **2** close-fitting trousers for women or children.

leggy *adj* **1** having unusually long legs. **2** (of a plant) having a long weak stem.

leghorn *n* **1** a type of Italian wheat straw that is woven into hats. **2** any hat made from this straw. ▷ **HISTORY** English name for *Livorno*, in Italy

Leghorn (leg-**gorn**) *n* a breed of domestic fowl.

legible *adj* (of handwriting) able to be read. ▷ **HISTORY** Latin *legere* to read ▶ **legibility** *n* ▶ **legibly** *adv*

legion *n* **1** any large military force: *the French Foreign Legion.* **2** (*often pl*) any very large number. **3** an infantry unit in the ancient Roman army of three to six thousand men. **4** an association of veterans. ▷ **HISTORY** Latin *legio* ▶ **legionary** *adj, n*

legionnaire *n* (*often cap*) a member of a legion.

legislate *vb* **-lating, -lated 1** to make or pass laws. **2** to bring into effect by legislation. ▷ **HISTORY** Latin *lex, legis* law + *latus,* past participle of *ferre* to bring ▶ **legislator** *n*

legislation *n* **1** the act or process of making laws. **2** the laws so made.

legislative *adj* **1** of or relating to the process of making laws. **2** having the power or function of making laws: *the election to Singapore's new legislative assembly.*

legislative assembly *n* (*often caps*) **1** the bicameral legislature in 28 states of the US. **2** the lower chamber of the bicameral state legislatures in several Commonwealth countries, such as Australia. **3** the unicameral legislature in most Canadian provinces. **4** any assembly with legislative powers.

legislative council *n* (*often caps*) **1** the upper chamber of certain bicameral legislatures, such as those of the Indian and Australian states (except Queensland). **2** the unicameral legislature of certain colonies or dependent territories. **3** (in the US) a committee of members of both chambers of a state legislature that discusses problems, constructs a legislative programme, etc.

legislature *n* a body of people authorized to make, amend, and repeal laws.

legitimate *adj* **1** authorized by or in accordance with law: *legitimate accounting practices.* **2** based on correct or acceptable principles of reasoning: *a legitimate argument.* **3** (of a child) born of parents legally married to each other. **4** of, relating to, or ruling by hereditary right: *under their legitimate ruling house.* **5** of or relating to serious drama as distinct from films, television, or vaudeville. ✧ *vb* **-mating, -mated 6** to make, pronounce, or show to be legitimate. ▷ **HISTORY** Medieval Latin *legitimatus* made legal ▶ **legitimacy** *n* ▶ **legitimately** *adv*

legitimize *or* **-mise** *vb* **-mizing, -mized** *or* **-mising, -mised** to make legitimate; legalize. ▶ **legitimization** *or* **-misation** *n*

legless *adj* **1** without legs. **2** *Slang* very drunk.

Lego *n Trademark* a construction toy consisting of plastic bricks and other components that fit together. ▷ **HISTORY** Danish *leg godt* play well

leguaan *n* a large amphibious S African lizard. ▷ **HISTORY** Dutch, from French *l'iguane* the iguana

legume *n* **1** the pod of a plant of the pea or bean family. **2** the seed from such pods, esp. beans or peas. ▷ **HISTORY** Latin *legere* to pick (a crop)

leguminous *adj* of or relating to any family of flowering plants having pods (or legumes) as fruits.

lei *n* (in Hawaii) a garland of flowers, worn around the neck. ▷ **HISTORY** Hawaiian

leisure *n* **1** time or opportunity for relaxation or hobbies. **2 at leisure a** having free time. **b** not occupied. **3 at one's leisure** when one has free time. ▷ **HISTORY** Old French *leisir* ▶ **leisured** *adj*

leisure centre *n* a building providing facilities, such as a swimming pool, gym, and café, for a range of leisure pursuits.

leisurely *adj* **1** unhurried; relaxed. ✧ *adv* **2** in a relaxed way. ▶ **leisureliness** *n*

leitmotif *or* **leitmotiv** (**lite**-mote-eef) *n* **1** *Music* a recurring melodic phrase used to suggest a character, thing, or idea. **2** *Literature* an often repeated image in a literary work. ▷ **HISTORY** German: leading motif

lekker *adj S African slang* pleasing, enjoyable, or tasty. ▷ **HISTORY** Afrikaans, from Dutch

lemming *n* **1** a small rodent of northern and arctic regions, reputed to rush into the sea in large groups and drown. **2** a member of any group following an unthinking course towards destruction. ▷ **HISTORY** Norwegian

lemon *n* **1** a yellow oval edible fruit with juicy acidic flesh that grows on an evergreen tree in warm and tropical regions. **2** *Slang* a person or thing considered to be useless or defective. ✧ *adj* **3** light yellow. ▷ **HISTORY** Arabic *laymūn* ▶ **lemony** *adj*

lemonade *n* a drink made from lemon juice, sugar, and water or from carbonated water, citric acid, and sweetener.

lemon sole *n* an edible European flatfish.

lemur *n* a nocturnal animal, related to the monkey, with a foxy face and long tail, found on Madagascar. ▷ **HISTORY** Latin *lemures* ghosts

lend *vb* **lending, lent 1** to permit the temporary use of. **2** to provide (money) temporarily, often at interest. **3** to contribute (some abstract quality): *a painted trellis lends a classical air to any garden.* **4 lend an ear** to listen. **5 lend oneself** *or* **itself** to be appropriate for: *the building lends itself to loft conversion.* ▷ **HISTORY** Old English *lǣnan* ▶ **lender** *n*

length *n* **1** the extent or measurement of something from end to end. **2** a specified distance, esp. between two positions: *the length of a cricket pitch.* **3** a period of time, as between specified limits or moments. **4** the quality, state, or fact of being long rather than short. **5** a piece of something, usually longer than it is wide: *a length of twine.* **6** (*usually pl*) the amount of trouble taken in doing something: *to go to great lengths.* **7** *Prosody, phonetics* the duration of a vowel or syllable. **8 at length a** after a long interval or period of time. **b** in great detail. ▷ **HISTORY** Old English *lengthu*

lengthen *vb* to make or become longer.

lengthways *or* **lengthwise** *adv, adj* in, according to, or along the direction of length.

lengthy *adj* **lengthier, lengthiest** very long or tiresome. ▶ **lengthily** *adv* ▶ **lengthiness** *n*

lenient (**lee**-nee-ent) *adj* tolerant, not strict or severe. ▷ **HISTORY** Latin *lenis* soft ▶ **leniency** *n* ▶ **leniently** *adv*

lens *n* **1** a piece of glass or other transparent material with a curved surface or surfaces, used to bring together or spread rays of light passing through it: used in cameras, telescopes, and spectacles. **2** *Anat* a transparent structure in the eye, behind the iris, that focuses images on the retina. ▷ **HISTORY** Latin: lentil

lent *vb* the past of **lend**.

Lent *n Christianity* the period from Ash Wednesday to Easter Saturday, during which some Christians give up doing something they enjoy. ▷ **HISTORY** Old English *lencten, lengten* spring, literally: lengthening (of hours of daylight) ▶ **Lenten** *adj*

lentil *n* any of the small edible seeds of a leguminous Asian plant. ▷ **HISTORY** Latin *lens*

lento *Music* ✧ *adv* **1** slowly. ✧ *n, pl* **-tos 2** a movement or passage performed slowly. ▷ **HISTORY** Italian

Lenz's law (**lents**-iz) *n Physics* the principle that the direction of an induced current is such that the magnetic field produced by this current will oppose the current field. ▷ **HISTORY** after H *Lenz,* German physicist

Leo *n Astrol* the fifth sign of the zodiac; the Lion. ▷ **HISTORY** Latin

leonine *adj* of or like a lion. ▷ **HISTORY** Latin *leo* lion

leopard *or fem* **leopardess** *n* a large African and Asian mammal of the cat family, which has a tawny yellow coat with black spots. Also called: **panther** ▷ **HISTORY** Greek *leōn* lion + *pardos* panther

leotard *n* a tight-fitting garment covering the body from the shoulders to the thighs and worn by acrobats, ballet dancers, and people doing exercises. ▷ **HISTORY** after Jules *Léotard,* acrobat

leper *n* **1** a person who has leprosy. **2** a person who is avoided. ▷ **HISTORY** Greek *lepros* scaly

lepidopteran *n, pl* **-terans** *or* **-tera 1** an insect that has two pairs of fragile wings and develops from a caterpillar; a butterfly or moth. ✧ *adj also* **lepidopterous 2** denoting such an insect. ▷ **HISTORY** Greek *lepis* scale + *pteron* wing

lepidopterist *n* a person who studies or collects moths and butterflies.

leprechaun *n* (in Irish folklore) a mischievous elf. ▷ **HISTORY** Irish Gaelic *leipreachān*

leprosy *n Pathol* a chronic infectious disease, characterized by painful inflamed lumps beneath the skin and disfigurement and wasting away of affected parts. ▶ **leprous** *adj*

lepton *n Physics* any of a group of elementary particles with weak interactions. ▷ **HISTORY** Greek *leptos* thin

A B C D E F G H I J K L M N O P Q R S T U V W X Y Z

lesbian *n* **1** a female homosexual. ✧ *adj* **2** of or characteristic of lesbians. ▷ **HISTORY** *Lesbos*, Greek Aegean island ▶ **lesbianism** *n*

lese-majesty (lezz-**maj**-ist-ee) *n* **1** an offence against the sovereign power in a state; treason. **2** an act of disrespect towards authority. ▷ **HISTORY** from Latin *laesa majestas* wounded majesty

lesion *n* **1** any structural change in an organ or tissue resulting from injury or disease. **2** an injury or wound. ▷ **HISTORY** Late Latin *laesio* injury

less *adj, adv* **1** the comparative of **little:** *less fibre; his sharpness will be blunted by playing less.* ✧ *adj* **2** *Not universally accepted* fewer. ✧ *adv* **3 less of** to a smaller extent or degree: *it would become less of a problem.* **4 no less** *Sometimes ironic* used to indicate admiration or surprise: *sculpted by a famous Frenchman, Rodin no less.* ✧ *prep* **5** minus: *a £2-a-week rise (less tax).* ▷ **HISTORY** Old English *lǣssa, lǣs*

> ☑ **WORD TIP**
> *Less* should not be confused with *fewer. Less* refers strictly only to quantity and not to number: *there is less water than before. Fewer* means smaller in number: *there are fewer people than before.*

lessee *n* a person to whom a lease is granted. ▷ **HISTORY** Old French *lesser* to lease

lessen *vb* to make or become less.

lesser *adj* not as great in quantity, size, or worth.

lesson *n* **1 a** a single period of instruction in a subject. **b** the content of such a period. **2** material assigned for individual study. **3** something from which useful knowledge or principles can be learned: *one could still learn an important lesson from these masters.* **4** an experience that serves as a warning or example: *the experience will prove a sobering lesson for the military.* **5** a passage of Scripture read during a church service. ▷ **HISTORY** Old French *leçon*

lessor *n* a person who grants a lease of property.

lest *conj* **1** so as to prevent any possibility that: *one grabbed it lest a neighbour got there first.* **2** for fear that: *his anxiety lest anything mar the family event.* ▷ **HISTORY** Old English *thȳ lǣs the*, literally: whereby less that

let¹ *vb* **letting, let 1** to allow: *a child lets a friend play with his favourite toy.* **2** used as an auxiliary to express: **a** a request, proposal, or command, or to convey a warning or threat: *well, let's try it; just let me catch you here again!* **b** an assumption or hypothesis: *let 'a' equal 'b'.* **c** resigned acceptance of the inevitable: *let the worst happen.* **3** to allow someone to rent (property or accommodation). **4** to cause the movement of (something) in a specified direction: *this lets aluminium creep into the brain.* **5 let alone** not to mention: *I could hardly think, let alone find words to say.* **6 let alone** *or* **be** stop annoying or interfering with: *let the poor cat alone.* **7 let go** to relax one's hold (on). **8 let loose a** to allow (a person or animal) to leave or escape. **b** *Informal* to make (a sound) suddenly: *he let loose a laugh.* **c** *Informal* to fire (ammunition) from a gun. ✧ *n* **9** *Brit & Austral* the act of letting property or accommodation. ✧ See also **let down, let off,** etc. ▷ **HISTORY** Old English *lǣtan* to permit

let² *n* **1** *Tennis, squash* etc. a minor infringement or obstruction of the ball, requiring a point to be replayed. **2 without let or hindrance** without obstruction. ▷ **HISTORY** Old English *lettan* to hinder

let down *vb* **1** to fail to satisfy the expectations of (someone); disappoint. **2** to lower. **3** to lengthen a garment by decreasing the hem. **4** to deflate: *to let down a tyre.* ✧ *n* **letdown 5** a disappointment.

lethal *adj* capable of causing death. ▷ **HISTORY** Latin *letum* death ▶ **lethally** *adv*

lethargy *n, pl* **-gies 1** sluggishness or dullness. **2** an abnormal lack of energy. ▷ **HISTORY** Greek *lēthargos* drowsy ▶ **lethargic** *adj* ▶ **lethargically** *adv*

let off *vb* **1** to excuse from (work or duties): *I'll let you off homework for a week.* **2** *Informal* to spare (someone) the expected punishment: *lots were let off because they couldn't be bothered to prosecute anybody.* **3** to explode or fire (a bomb, gun, or firework). **4** to release (liquid, air, or steam).

let on *vb Informal* **1** to reveal (a secret). **2** to pretend: *he let on that he was a pilgrim.*

let out *vb* **1** to emit: *he let out a scream.* **2** to allow to leave; release. **3** to make (property) available for people to rent. **4** to make (a garment) wider by reducing the seams. **5** to reveal (a secret). ✧ *n* **let-out 6** a chance to escape.

letter *n* **1** a written or printed message, usually enclosed in an envelope and sent by post. **2** any of a set of conventional symbols used in writing or printing a language: character of the alphabet. **3** the strict meaning of an agreement or document; exact wording: *the letter of the law.* **4 to the letter** precisely: *you have to follow treatment to the letter for it to be effective.* ✧ *vb* **5** to write or mark letters on (a sign). ▷ **HISTORY** Latin *littera* letter of the alphabet ▶ **lettering** *n*

letter bomb *n* an explosive device in an envelope or parcel that explodes when the envelope or parcel is opened.

letter box *n Chiefly Brit* **1** a slot in a door through which letters are delivered. **2** Also called: **pillar box, postbox** a public box into which letters and postcards are put for collection.

lettered *adj* **1** well educated. **2** printed or marked with letters.

letterhead *n* a printed heading on stationery giving the name and address of the sender.

letter of credit *n* a letter issued by a bank entitling the bearer to draw money from other banks.

letters *pl n* **1** literary knowledge or ability: *a man of letters.* **2** literary culture in general.

letters patent *pl n* See **patent** (senses 1, 3).

lettuce *n* a plant cultivated for its large edible leaves, which are used in salads. ▷ **HISTORY** Latin *lactuca,* from *lac* milk, because of its milky juice

let up *vb* **1** to diminish or stop. **2** (foll. by *on*) *Informal* to be less harsh (towards someone). ✧ *n*

let-up 3 *Informal* a lessening: *there has been no let-up in the war.*

leucocyte (**loo**-koh-site) *n* any of the various large white cells in the blood of vertebrates. ▷ HISTORY Greek *leukos* white + *kutos* vessel

leukaemia *or esp US* **leukemia** (loo-**kee**-mee-a) *n* an acute or chronic disease characterized by extreme overproduction of white blood cells. ▷ HISTORY Greek *leukos* white + *haima* blood

levee[1] *n US* **1** *Geog* a natural or artificial river embankment. **2** a quay. ▷ HISTORY French, from Latin *levare* to raise

levee[2] *n* a formal reception held by a sovereign just after rising from bed. ▷ HISTORY French, from Latin *levare* to raise

level *adj* **1** on a horizontal plane. **2** having an even surface. **3** being of the same height as something else: *the floor of the lean-to was level with the patio.* **4** equal to or even with (something or someone else): *Johnson was level with the overnight leader.* **5** not exceeding the upper edge of (a spoon etc.). **6** consistent or regular: *a level pulse.* **7 one's level best** the best one can do. ✧ *vb* **-elling, -elled** *or US* **-eling, -eled 8** (sometimes foll. by *off*) to make horizontal or even. **9** to make equal in position or status. **10** to direct (an accusation or criticism) emphatically at someone. **11** to focus (a look) directly at someone. **12** to aim (a weapon) horizontally. **13** to demolish completely. ✧ *n* **14** a horizontal line or plane. **15** a device, such as a spirit level, for determining whether a surface is horizontal. **16** position or status in a scale of values: *a high-level delegation.* **17** stage or degree of progress: *primary school level.* **18** a specified vertical position: *floor level.* **19** the topmost horizontal line or plane from which the height of something is calculated: *sea level.* **20** a flat even surface or area of land. **21** a degree or intensity reached on a measurable or notional scale: *noise level.* **22 on the level** *Informal* sincere or genuine. ▷ HISTORY Latin *libella*, diminutive of *libra* scales

level crossing *n Brit, Austral, & NZ* a point at which a railway line and a road cross.

level-headed *adj* calm and sensible.

lever *n* **1** a handle used to operate machinery. **2** a bar used to move a heavy object or to prise something open. **3** a rigid bar that turns on a fixed support (fulcrum) to transfer effort and motion, for instance to move a load. **4** a means of exerting pressure in order to achieve an aim: *using the hostages as a lever to gain concessions from the west.* ✧ *vb* **5** to open or move with a lever. ▷ HISTORY Latin *levare* to raise

leverage *n* **1** the mechanical advantage gained by using a lever. **2** the ability to influence people or events: *information gives leverage.*

leveraged buyout *n* a takeover bid in which a small company uses its assets, and those of the target company, to raise the loans required to finance the takeover.

leveret (**lev**-ver-it) *n* a young hare. ▷ HISTORY Latin *lepus* hare

leviathan (lev-**vie**-ath-an) *n* any huge or powerful thing. ▷ HISTORY Hebrew *liwyāthān*, a Biblical sea monster

Levis *pl n Trademark* denim jeans.

levitate *vb* **-tating, -tated** to rise or cause to rise, suspended, in the air. ▷ HISTORY Latin *levis* light ▶ **levitation** *n*

levity *n, pl* **-ties** a frivolous or too light-hearted attitude to serious matters. ▷ HISTORY Latin *levis* light

levy (**lev**-vee) *vb* **levies, levying, levied 1** to impose and collect (a tax, tariff, or fine). **2** to conscript troops for service. ✧ *n, pl* **levies 3 a** the imposition and collection of taxes, tariffs, or fines. **b** the money so raised. **4** troops conscripted for service. ▷ HISTORY Latin *levare* to raise

lewd *adj* indecently vulgar; obscene. ▷ HISTORY Old English *lǣwde* lay, ignorant ▶ **lewdly** *adv* ▶ **lewdness** *n*

lexical *adj* **1** relating to the vocabulary of a language. **2** relating to a lexicon. ▶ **lexically** *adv*

lexical chain *n Grammar* a series of semantically related words in a text.

lexicography *n* the process or profession of compiling dictionaries. ▶ **lexicographer** *n*

lexicon *n* **1** a dictionary, esp. one of an ancient language such as Greek. **2** the vocabulary of a language or of an individual. ▷ HISTORY Greek *lexis* word

lexis *n* the set of all the morphemes of a language. ▷ HISTORY Greek *lexis* word

ley *n* land temporarily under grass. ▷ HISTORY variant of *lea*

Leyden jar (**lide**-en) *n Physics* an early type of capacitor consisting of a glass jar with the lower part of the inside and outside coated with tinfoil. ▷ HISTORY from *Leiden*, city in the Netherlands

LGV (in Britain) large goods vehicle.

Li *Chem* lithium.

liability *n, pl* **-ties 1** someone or something that is a problem or embarrassment. **2** the state of being legally responsible. **3** (*often pl*) sums of money owed by an organization.

liable *adj* **1** probable or likely: *weak and liable to give way.* **2** commonly suffering a condition: *he's liable to get colds in his chest.* **3** legally obliged or responsible; answerable. ▷ HISTORY Old French *lier* to bind

> **WORD TIP**
> The use of *liable to* to mean *probable or likely* was formerly considered incorrect, but is now acceptable.

liaise *vb* **liaising, liaised** (usually foll. by *with*) to communicate and maintain contact (with).

liaison *n* **1** communication and cooperative contact between groups. **2** a secretive or adulterous sexual relationship. ▷ HISTORY Old French *lier* to bind

liana *n* a woody climbing and twining plant of tropical forests. ▷ HISTORY French

liar *n* a person who tells lies.

lib *n Informal* liberation: used in the name of certain movements: *women's lib; gay lib.*
Lib *Brit, Austral & S African politics* Liberal.
libation (lie-**bay**-shun) *n* **a** the pouring out of wine in honour of a deity. **b** the wine so poured out. ▷ **HISTORY** Latin *libare* to pour an offering of drink
libel *n* **1** *Law* the publication of something false which damages a person's reputation. **2** any damaging or unflattering representation or statement. ✧ *vb* **-belling, -belled** *or US* **-beling, -beled 3** *Law* to make or publish a false damaging statement or representation about (a person). ▷ **HISTORY** Latin *libellus* a little book ▸ **libellous** *or* **libelous** *adj*
liberal *adj* **1** having social and political views that favour progress and reform. **2** generous in temperament or behaviour. **3** tolerant of other people. **4** using or existing in large quantities; lavish: *the world's finest gadgetry, in liberal quantities.* **5** not rigid; free: *a more liberal interpretation.* **6** (of an education) designed to develop general cultural interests and intellectual ability. **7 Liberal** of or relating to a Liberal Party. ✧ *n* **8** a person who has liberal ideas or opinions. ▷ **HISTORY** Latin *liber* free ▸ **liberalism** *n* ▸ **liberally** *adv*
Liberal Democrat *n* a member or supporter of the Liberal Democrats, a British centrist political party that advocates proportional representation.
liberality *n, pl* **-ties 1** generosity. **2** the quality of being broad-minded.
liberalize *or* **-ise** *vb* **-izing, -ized** *or* **-ising, -ised** to make (a law) less strict. ▸ **liberalization** *or* **-isation** *n*
Liberal Party *n* **1** *History* a British non-Socialist political party which advocated progress and reform. **2** any similar party in various other countries. **3** the main right-wing political party in Australia.
liberate *vb* **-ating, -ated 1** to free (someone) from social prejudices or injustices. **2** to give liberty to; make free. **3** to release (a country) from enemy occupation. ▸ **liberation** *n* ▸ **liberator** *n*
liberated *adj* **1** not bound by traditional sexual and social roles: *a liberated woman.* **2** given liberty. **3** released from enemy occupation.
libertarian *n* **1** a person who believes in freedom of thought and action. ✧ *adj* **2** believing in freedom of thought and action.
libertine (**lib**-er-teen) *n* **1** a person who is promiscuous and unscrupulous. ✧ *adj* **2** promiscuous and unscrupulous. ▷ **HISTORY** Latin *libertus* freed
liberty *n, pl* **-ties 1** the freedom to choose, think, and act for oneself. **2** the right of unrestricted movement and access; freedom. **3** (*often pl*) a social action regarded as being forward or improper. **4 at liberty** free or unconfined. **5 at liberty to** unrestricted or authorized: *I am not at liberty to divulge his name.* **6 take liberties (with)** to be overfamiliar (towards someone). ▷ **HISTORY** Latin *libertas*
libidinous *adj* characterized by excessive sexual desire. ▸ **libidinously** *adv*
libido (lib-**ee**-doe) *n, pl* **-dos 1** *Psychoanal* psychic energy from the id. **2** sexual urge or desire. ▷ **HISTORY** Latin: desire ▸ **libidinal** *adj*
Libra *n Astrol* the seventh sign of the zodiac; the Scales. ▷ **HISTORY** Latin
librarian *n* a person in charge of or assisting in a library. ▸ **librarianship** *n*
library *n, pl* **-braries 1** a room or building where books and other literary materials are kept. **2** a collection of literary materials, films, tapes, or records, kept for borrowing or reference. **3** the building or institution that houses such a collection. **4** a set of books published as a series, often in a similar format. **5** *Computers* a collection of standard programs, usually stored on disk. ▷ **HISTORY** Latin *liber* book
libretto *n, pl* **-tos** *or* **-ti** a text written for an opera. ▷ **HISTORY** Italian: little book ▸ **librettist** *n*
Libyan *adj* **1** from Libya. ✧ *n* **2** a person from Libya.
lice *n* the plural of **louse**.
licence *or US* **license** *n* **1** a document giving official permission to do, use, or own something. **2** formal permission or exemption. **3** intentional disregard of conventional rules to achieve a certain effect: *poetic licence.* **4** excessive freedom. ▷ **HISTORY** Latin *licet* it is allowed
license *vb* **-censing, -censed 1** to grant a licence to or for. **2** to give permission to or for. ▸ **licensable** *adj*
licensee *n* a person who holds a licence, esp. one to sell alcoholic drink.
licentiate *n* a person who holds a certificate of competence to practise a certain profession.
licentious *adj* sexually unrestrained or promiscuous. ▷ **HISTORY** Latin *licentia* licence ▸ **licentiousness** *n*
lichee *n* same as **lychee**.
lichen *n* any of various small mossy plants that grow in patches on tree trunks, bare ground, rocks, and stone walls. ▷ **HISTORY** Greek *leikhein* to lick
licit *adj Formal* lawful; permitted. ▷ **HISTORY** Latin *licere* to be permitted
lick *vb* **1** to pass the tongue over in order to taste, wet, or clean. **2** to flicker over or round (something): *flames licked the gutters.* **3** *Informal* **a** to defeat. **b** to thrash. **4 lick into shape** to put into a satisfactory condition. **5 lick one's wounds** to retire after a defeat. ✧ *n* **6** an instance of passing the tongue over something. **7** a small amount: *a lick of paint.* **8** *Informal* a blow. **9** *Informal* a fast pace: *a pulsating rhythm taken at a lick.* **10 a lick and a promise** something hastily done, esp. a hurried wash. ▷ **HISTORY** Old English *liccian*
licorice *n US & Canad* same as **liquorice**.
lid *n* **1** a removable or hinged cover: *a saucepan lid.* **2** short for **eyelid**. **3 put the (tin) lid on** *Informal* to put an end to. ▷ **HISTORY** Old English *hlid* ▸ **lidded** *adj*
lido (**lee**-doe) *n, pl* **-dos** *Brit* an open-air swimming pool or a part of a beach used by the public for swimming and sunbathing. ▷ **HISTORY** *Lido*, island bathing beach near Venice

lie[1] *vb* **lying, lied 1** to speak untruthfully with the intention of deceiving. **2** to convey a false impression: *the camera cannot lie.* ✧ *n* **3** an untrue statement deliberately used to mislead. **4** something that is deliberately intended to deceive. **5 give the lie to a** to disprove. **b** to accuse of lying. ▷ **HISTORY** Old English *lyge, lēogan*

> **WORD TIP**
> See at **lay**[1].

lie[2] *vb* **lying, lay, lain 1** (often foll. by *down*) to place oneself or be in a horizontal position. **2** to be situated: *I left the money lying on the table; Nepal became the only country lying between China and India.* **3** to be and remain (in a particular state or condition): *others of their species lie asleep.* **4** to stretch or extend: *an enormous task lies ahead.* **5** (usually foll. by *in*) to exist or comprise: *her charm lies in her inner beauty.* **6** (foll. by *with*) to rest (with): *the fault lies with them.* ✧ *n* **7** the manner, place, or style in which something is situated. **8** an animal's lair. **9 lie of the land** the way in which a situation is developing. ✧ See also **lie in.** ▷ **HISTORY** Old English *licgan*

lied (**leed**) *n, pl* **lieder** *Music* a musical setting for solo voice and piano of a romantic or lyrical poem. ▷ **HISTORY** German: song

liege (**leej**) *adj* **1** (of a lord) owed feudal allegiance: *their liege lord.* **2** (of a vassal or subject) owing feudal allegiance: *a liege subject.* **3** faithful; loyal. ✧ *n* **4** a liege lord. **5** a subject. ▷ **HISTORY** Old French *lige*

lie in *vb* **1** to remain in bed late into the morning. ✧ *n* **lie-in 2** a long stay in bed in the morning.

lien *n Law* a right to retain possession of someone else's property until a debt is paid. ▷ **HISTORY** Latin *ligamen* bond

lieu (**lyew**) *n* **in lieu of** instead of. ▷ **HISTORY** Old French

lieutenant (lef-**ten**-ant, loo-**ten**-ant) *n* **1** a junior officer in the army, navy, or the US police force. **2** a person who acts as principal assistant. ▷ **HISTORY** Old French, literally: place-holding ▶ **lieutenancy** *n*

lieutenant colonel *n* an officer in an army, air force, or marine corps immediately junior to a colonel.

lieutenant general *n* a senior officer in an army, air force, or marine corps.

lieutenant governor *n* **1** a deputy governor. **2** (in Canada) the representative of the Crown in a province.

life *n, pl* **lives 1** the state or quality that identifies living beings, characterized chiefly by growth, reproduction, and response to stimuli. **2** the period between birth and death or between birth and the present time. **3** a living person or being: *riots which claimed 22 lives.* **4** the remainder or extent of one's life: *with that lady for the rest of her life.* **5** the process of living: *rituals gave his life stability.* **6** *Informal* a sentence of life imprisonment, usually approximating to 15 years. **7** a characteristic state or mode of existence: *country life is best.* **8** the length of time that something is active or functioning: *the life of a battery.* **9** a present condition or mode of existence: *they are leading a joyous life.* **10** a biography. **11** the sum or course of human events and activities. **12** liveliness or high spirits: *full of life.* **13** a source of strength, animation, or vitality: *he was the life of the show.* **14** all living things collectively: *there is no life on Mars; marine life.* **15 a matter of life and death** a matter of extreme urgency. **16 as large as life** *Informal* real and living. **17 not on your life** *Informal* certainly not. **18 true to life** faithful to reality. **19 to the life** (of a copy of a painting or drawing) resembling the original exactly. ▷ **HISTORY** Old English *līf*

life assurance *n* insurance that provides for a sum of money to be paid to the insured person at a certain age or to the spouse or children on the death of the insured. Also called: **life insurance**

lifeblood *n* **1** the blood vital to life. **2** something that is essential for existence, development, or success.

lifeboat *n* a boat used for rescuing people at sea.

life cycle *n* the series of changes occurring in each generation of an animal or plant.

life expectancy *n Statistics* according to statistics, the number of years a person can expect to live.

lifeguard *n* a person at a beach or pool whose job is to rescue people in danger of drowning.

lifeless *adj* **1** inanimate; dead. **2** lacking liveliness or animation. **3** unconscious.

lifelike *adj* closely resembling or representing life.

lifeline *n* **1** a single means of contact or support on which a person or an area relies. **2** a rope used for life-saving.

lifelong *adj* lasting for a lifetime.

life peer *n Brit* a peer whose title ceases at his or her death.

lifer *n Informal* a prisoner sentenced to life imprisonment.

life science *n* any of the sciences concerned with the structure and behaviour of living organisms, such as biology, botany, or zoology.

life-size *or* **life-sized** *adj* representing actual size.

lifestyle *n* a set of attitudes, habits, and possessions regarded as typical of a particular group or an individual.

life-support *adj* (of equipment or treatment) necessary to sustain life.

lifetime *n* **1** the length of time a person is alive. **2 of a lifetime** (of an opportunity or experience) the most important or memorable.

lift *vb* **1** to rise or raise upwards to a higher place: *the breakdown truck was lifting the lorry.* **2** to move upwards: *he slowly lifted his hand.* **3** to raise in status or estimation: *lifted from poverty.* **4** to revoke or cancel: *the government lifted its restrictions on imported beef.* **5** to remove (plants or underground crops) from the ground for harvesting. **6** to disappear or disperse: *the tension lifted.* **7** *Informal* to plagiarize (music or writing). ✧ *n* **8 a** a compartment raised or lowered in a vertical shaft to transport people or goods to another floor in a building. **b** See **chairlift**. **9** a ride in a car or other vehicle as a passenger. **10** a rise in morale or feeling of cheerfulness. **11** the act of lifting. **12** the force that lifts airborne objects. ▷ **HISTORY** from Old Norse

liftoff *n* the initial movement of a rocket as it leaves its launch pad.

ligament *n Anat* a band of tough tissue that connects various bones or cartilage. ▷ **HISTORY** Latin *ligare* to bind

ligature *n* **1** a link, bond, or tie. **2** *Printing* a character of two or more joined letters, such as ff. **3** *Music* a slur or the group of notes connected by it. ✧ *vb* **-turing, -tured 4** to bind with a ligature. ▷ **HISTORY** Latin *ligare* to bind

light[1] *n* **1** the natural medium, electromagnetic radiation, that makes sight possible. **2** anything that illuminates, such as a lamp or candle. **3** a particular type of light: *dim yellow light*. **4 a** daylight. **b** daybreak; dawn. **5** anything that lets in light, such as a window. **6** an aspect or view: *we have seen the world in a new light*. **7** mental understanding or spiritual insight: *suddenly he saw the light*. **8** an outstanding person: *a leading light of the movement*. **9** brightness of countenance, esp. a sparkle in the eyes. **10 a** something that ignites, such as a spark or flame. **b** something used for igniting, such as a match. **11** See **lighthouse**. **12 come to light** to become known or visible. **13 in (the) light of** taking into account. **14 see the light** to understand. **15 see the light (of day) a** to come into being. **b** to come to public notice. ✧ *adj* **16** full of light. **17** (of a colour) pale: *light blue*. ✧ *vb* **lighting, lighted** *or* **lit 18** to ignite. **19** (often foll. by *up*) to illuminate or cause to illuminate. **20** to guide by light. ✧ See also **light up**. ▷ **HISTORY** Old English *lēoht* ▶ **lightish** *adj*

light[2] *adj* **1** not heavy; weighing relatively little. **2** relatively low in density, strength, amount, degree, etc.: *light oil; light alloy*. **3** lacking sufficient weight. **4** not bulky or clumsy: *light bedclothes*. **5** not serious or difficult to understand; entertaining: *light music*. **6** graceful or agile: *light movements*. **7** without strong emphasis or serious meaning: *he gazed about with a light inattentive smile*. **8** easily digested: *a light lunch*. **9** relatively low in alcohol: *a light wine*. **10** without burdens, difficulties, or problems: *a light heart lives longest*. **11** dizzy or unclear: *a light head*. **12** (of bread or cake) spongy or well risen. **13** (of a vessel, lorry, or other transport) **a** designed to carry light loads. **b** not loaded. **14** carrying light arms or equipment: *light infantry*. **15** (of an industry) producing small consumer goods using light machinery. **16 make light of** to treat as insignificant or unimportant. ✧ *adv* **17** with little equipment or luggage: *travelling light*. ✧ *vb* **lighting, lighted** *or* **lit 18** (esp. of birds) to settle or land after flight. **19** (foll. by *on* or *upon*) to discover by chance. ✧ See also **lights**. ▷ **HISTORY** Old English *lēoht* ▶ **lightish** *adj* ▶ **lightly** *adv* ▶ **lightness** *n*

light bulb *n* a hollow rounded glass fitting containing a gas and a thin metal filament that gives out light when an electric current is passed through it.

lighten[1] *vb* **1** to make less dark. **2** to shine; glow. **3** (of lightning) to flash.

lighten[2] *vb* **1** to make or become less heavy. **2** to make or become less burdensome. **3** to make or become more cheerful or lively.

lighter[1] *n* a small portable device for lighting cigarettes, etc.

lighter[2] *n* a flat-bottomed barge used in loading or unloading a ship. ▷ **HISTORY** probably from Middle Dutch

light-fingered *adj* skilful at thieving, esp. by picking pockets.

light-headed *adj* giddy; feeling faint.

light-hearted *adj* cheerful or carefree in mood or disposition. ▶ **light-heartedly** *adv*

light heavyweight *n* a professional boxer weighing up to 175 pounds (79.5 kg) or an amateur weighing up to 81 kg.

lighthouse *n* a tower with a light to guide ships and warn of obstructions.

light industry *n Econ* the manufacturing of small products such as clothing and household goods.

lighting *n* **1** the apparatus for and design of artificial light effects to a stage, film, or television set. **2** the act or quality of illumination.

lightning *n* **1** a flash of light in the sky caused by a discharge of electricity. ✧ *adj* **2** fast and sudden: *a lightning attack*. ▷ **HISTORY** variant of *lightening*

lightning conductor *or* **rod** *n* a metal rod attached to the highest part of a building to divert lightning safely to earth.

light pen *n* a penlike photoelectric device that in conjunction with a computer can be used to draw lines or identify symbols on a VDU screen.

lights *pl n* the lungs of sheep, bullocks, and pigs, used for feeding pets. ▷ **HISTORY** because of the light weight of the lungs

lightship *n* a moored ship equipped as a lighthouse.

light up *vb* **1** to illuminate. **2** to make or become cheerful or animated: *their faces lit up and one dug the other in the ribs*. **3** to light a cigarette or pipe.

lightweight *adj* **1** not serious. **2** of relatively light weight. ✧ *n* **3** *Informal* a person of little importance or influence. **4** a person or animal of relatively light weight. **5** a professional boxer weighing up to 135 pounds (61 kg) or an amateur weighing up to 60 kg.

light year *n Astron* the distance travelled by light in one mean solar year, i.e. 9.4607×10^{15} metres.

ligneous *adj* of or like wood. ▷ **HISTORY** Latin *lignum* wood

lignite (**lig**-nite) *n* a brown sedimentary rock with a woody texture: used as a fuel.

lignum vitae (**lig**-num **vite**-ee) *n* a tropical American tree with heavy resinous wood. ▷ **HISTORY** Late Latin, literally: wood of life

like[1] *adj* **1** resembling. ✧ *prep* **2** in the manner of; similar to: *she was like a child; it looks like a traffic* *cone.* **3** such as: *a modern material, like carbon fibre.* **4** characteristic of. ✧ *adv* **5** in the manner of: *cheering like mad.* **6** *Dialect* likely. ✧ *conj* **7** *Not universally accepted* as though; as if: *I don't want to make it seem like I had this bad childhood.* **8** in the same way that: *she doesn't dance like you do.* ✧ *n* **9** the equal or counterpart of a person or thing. **10 the like** similar things: *magic, supernormal powers and the like.* **11 the likes** *or* **like of** people or things similar to (someone or something specified): *the theatre was not meant for the likes of him.* ▷ HISTORY Old English *gelīc*

> **WORD TIP**
> The use of *like* to mean *such as* was formerly thought to be undesirable in formal writing, but has now become acceptable. It was also thought that *as* rather than *like* should be used to mean *in the same way that,* but now both *as* and *like* are acceptable: *they hunt and catch fish as/like their ancestors used to.* The use of *look like* and *seem like* before a clause, although very common, is thought by many people to be incorrect or non-standard: *it looks as though he won't come* (not *it looks like he won't come*).

like[2] *vb* **liking, liked 1** to find enjoyable. **2** to be fond of. **3** to prefer or choose: *I'd like to go home.* **4** to feel disposed or inclined; choose; wish: *do as you like.* ✧ *n* **5** (*usually pl*) a favourable feeling, desire, or preference: *tell me your likes and dislikes.* ▷ HISTORY Old English *līcian* ▶ **likeable** *or* **likable** *adj*

likelihood *n* chance; probability.

likelihood scale *n Statistics* a scale giving an indication of how often an outcome is likely to happen.

likely *adj* **1** tending or inclined: *likely to win.* **2** probable: *the likely effects of the tunnel.* **3** appropriate for a purpose or activity: *a likely candidate.* ✧ *adv* **4** probably or presumably. **5 not likely** *Informal* definitely not. ▷ HISTORY Old Norse *līkligr*

> **WORD TIP**
> *Likely* as an adverb is preceded by another, intensifying adverb, as in *it will very likely rain* or *it will most likely rain.* Its use without an intensifier, as in *it will likely rain,* is regarded as unacceptable by most users of British English, though it is common in colloquial US English.

liken *vb* to compare.

likeness *n* **1** resemblance. **2** portrait. **3** an imitative appearance; semblance: *in the likeness of a dragon.*

likewise *adv* **1** in addition; also. **2** similarly.

liking *n* **1** fondness. **2** what one likes or prefers: *if it's not to your liking, do let me know.*

lilac *n* **1** a small tree with large sprays of purple or white sweet-smelling flowers. ✧ *adj* **2** pale purple. ▷ HISTORY Persian *nīlak* bluish

Lilliputian (lil-lip-**pew**-shun) *n* **1** a tiny person or being. ✧ *adj* **2** tiny; very small. ▷ HISTORY *Lilliput,* an imaginary country of tiny people in Swift's *Gulliver's Travels*

Lilo *n, pl* **-los** *Trademark* a type of inflatable plastic mattress.

lilt *n* **1** a pleasing musical quality in a speaking voice. **2** (in music) a jaunty rhythm. **3** a graceful rhythmic motion. ✧ *vb* **4** (of a voice, tune, or song) to rise and fall in a pleasant way. **5** to move gracefully and rhythmically. ▷ HISTORY origin unknown ▶ **lilting** *adj*

lily *n, pl* **lilies 1** a perennial plant, such as the tiger lily, with scaly bulbs and showy white or coloured flowers. **2** a water lily. ▷ HISTORY Latin *lilium*

lily of the valley *n, pl* **lilies of the valley** a small plant with spikes of sweet-smelling white bell-shaped flowers.

limb[1] *n* **1** an arm, leg, or wing. **2** any of the main branches of a tree. **3 out on a limb a** in a precarious or questionable position. **b** *Brit & NZ* isolated, esp. because of unpopular opinions. ▷ HISTORY Old English *lim* ▶ **limbless** *adj*

limb[2] *n* the apparent outer edge of the sun, a moon, or a planet. ▷ HISTORY Latin *limbus* edge

limber[1] *adj* **1** pliant; supple. **2** able to move or bend the body freely; agile. ▷ HISTORY origin unknown

limber[2] *n* **1** part of a gun carriage, consisting of an axle, pole, and two wheels. ✧ *vb* **2** to attach the limber (to a gun). ▷ HISTORY Middle English *lymour* shaft of a gun carriage

limbo[1] *n, pl* **-bos 1** (*often cap*) *RC Church* (formerly) the supposed region intermediate between heaven and hell for the unbaptized. **2 in limbo** not knowing the result or next stage of something and powerless to influence it.

> **WORD HISTORY**
> The word 'limbo' comes from the Latin phrase *in limbo,* meaning 'on the border' (i.e. on the border of hell).

limbo[2] *n, pl* **-bos** a West Indian dance in which dancers lean backwards and pass under a horizontal bar which is gradually lowered. ▷ HISTORY origin unknown

lime[1] *n* **1** *Agriculture* calcium hydroxide spread as a dressing on acidic land. ✧ *vb* **liming, limed 2** to spread a calcium compound upon (land). ▷ HISTORY Old English *līm*

lime[2] *n* the green oval fruit of a small Asian citrus tree with acid fleshy pulp rich in vitamin C. ▷ HISTORY Arabic *līmah*

lime[3] *n* a European linden tree planted for ornament. ▷ HISTORY Old English *lind* linden

lime-green *adj* light yellowish-green.

limelight *n* **1 the limelight** glare of publicity: *this issue will remain in the limelight.* **2 a** a type of lamp, formerly used in stage lighting, in which lime is heated to white heat. **b** brilliant white light produced in this way.

limerick (**lim**-mer-ik) *n* a form of comic verse consisting of five lines. ▷ HISTORY allegedly from *will you come up to Limerick?,* a refrain sung between nonsense verses at a party

A B C D E F G H I J K L M N O P Q R S T U V W X Y Z

limestone *n* rock consisting mainly of calcium carbonate: used as a building stone and in making cement.

lime water *n Chem* a clear colourless solution of calcium hydroxide in water.

limey *n US, Canad & Austral slang* **1** a British person. **2** a British sailor or ship. ▷ **HISTORY** from *lime-juicer,* because British sailors drank lime juice as a protection against scurvy

limit *n* **1** (*sometimes pl*) the ultimate extent or amount of something: *each soloist was stretched to his or her limit by the demands of the vocal writing.* **2** (*often pl*) the boundary of a specific area: *beyond the city limits.* **3** the largest quantity or amount allowed. **4 the limit** *Informal* a person or thing that is intolerably exasperating. ✧ *vb* **-iting, -ited 5** to restrict. ▷ **HISTORY** Latin *limes* boundary
▶ **limitable** *adj*

limitation *n* **1** a restriction or controlling of quantity, quality, or achievement. **2 limitations** the limit or extent of an ability to achieve something: *learn your own limitations.*

limited *adj* **1** having a limit; restricted. **2** without fullness or scope; narrow. **3** (of governing powers or sovereignty) restricted by a constitution, laws, or an assembly: *limited government.* **4** *Brit & NZ* (of a business enterprise) owned by shareholders whose liability for the enterprise's debts is restricted.

limited edition *n* an edition of something, such as a book, which has been restricted to a particular number of copies.

limited point of view *n Literature* a narrative style which is presented from a particular point of view, usually that of one of the characters involved in the story.

limn *vb Old-fashioned* to represent in drawing or painting. ▷ **HISTORY** Latin *inluminare* to brighten

limousine *n* any large luxurious car.
▷ **HISTORY** French, literally: cloak

limp[1] *vb* **1** to walk with an uneven step, esp. with a weak or injured leg. **2** to advance in a labouring or faltering manner. ✧ *n* **3** an uneven walk or progress. ▷ **HISTORY** Old English *lempheallt* lame
▶ **limping** *adj, n*

limp[2] *adj* **1** lacking firmness or stiffness. **2** not energetic or vital. **3** (of the binding of a book) paperback. ▷ **HISTORY** probably Scandinavian
▶ **limply** *adv*

limpet *n* **1** a conical shellfish that clings tightly to rocks with its muscular foot. ✧ *adj* **2** denoting certain weapons that are magnetically attached to their targets and resist removal: *limpet mines.*
▷ **HISTORY** Old English *lempedu*

limpid *adj* **1** clear or transparent. **2** (of speech or writing) clear and easy to understand.
▷ **HISTORY** Latin *limpidus* clear ▶ **limpidity** *n*

linage *n* **1** the number of lines in written or printed matter. **2** payment according to the number of lines.

linchpin *or* **lynchpin** *n* **1** a pin inserted through an axle to keep a wheel in position. **2** an essential person or thing: *she was the linchpin of the experiment.* ▷ **HISTORY** Old English *lynis*

linctus *n, pl* **-tuses** a soothing syrupy cough mixture. ▷ **HISTORY** Latin *lingere* to lick

linden *n* a large tree with heart-shaped leaves and fragrant yellowish flowers. See also **lime**[3].
▷ **HISTORY** Old English *linde* lime tree

line[1] *n* **1** a narrow continuous mark, such as one made by a pencil or brush. **2** a thin indented mark or wrinkle on skin. **3** a continuous length without breadth. **4** a boundary: *the United Nations established a provisional demarcation line.* **5** *Sport* **a** a white band indicating a division on a field or track. **b** a mark or imaginary mark at which a race begins or ends. **6** a boundary or limit: *the invidious dividing line between universities and polytechnics.* **7** the edge or contour of a shape: *the shoulder line.* **8** a wire or string with a particular function: *a long washing line.* **9** a telephone connection: *it was a very bad line.* **10** a conducting wire, cable, or circuit for electric-power transmission or telecommunications. **11** a system of travel or transportation: *a shipping line.* **12** a route between two points on a railway. **13** a railway track. **14** a course or direction of movement: *the birds' line of flight.* **15** a course of action or behaviour: *to adopt a more aggressive line.* **16** a policy or prescribed way of thinking: *city commentators supported the CBI line.* **17** a field of interest or activity: *heroin – that was their line.* **18** straight or orderly alignment: *stand in line.* **19** one kind of product or article: *a line of smart suits.* **20** a row of people or things. **21** a row of printed or written words. **22** a unit of verse consisting of words in a single row. **23** one of a number of narrow horizontal bands forming a television picture. **24** *Music* any of the five horizontal marks that make up the stave. **25** the most forward defensive position: *the front line.* **26** a formation of ships or soldiers abreast of each other. **27** the combatant forces of certain armies and navies. **28** *US & Canad* a queue. **29 all along the line** at every stage in a series. **30 draw the line (at)** to object (to) or set a limit (on): *I'm not a killer, I draw the line at that.* **31 drop someone a line** to send someone a short note. **32 get a line on** *Informal* to obtain information about. **33 in line for** likely to receive: *high achievers are in line for cash bonuses.* **34 in line with** conforming to. **35 lay** *or* **put on the line a** to speak frankly and directly. **b** to risk (one's career or reputation) on something. ✧ *vb* **lining, lined 36** to mark with a line or lines. **37** to be or form a border: *the square was lined with stalls selling snacks.* **38** to place in or form a row, series, or alignment. ✧ See also **lines, line-up.** ▷ **HISTORY** Old French *ligne* + Old English *līn* ▶ **lined** *adj*

line[2] *vb* **lining, lined 1** to attach an inside layer to. **2** to cover the inside of: *the works of Shakespeare lined his walls.* **3 line one's pockets** to make a lot of money, esp. dishonestly. ▷ **HISTORY** Latin *linum* flax

lineage (**lin**-ee-ij) *n* direct descent from an ancestor.

lineal *adj* **1** being in a direct line of descent from an ancestor. **2** of or derived from direct descent. **3** linear. ▷ **HISTORY** Latin *linea* line

lineament *n* (*often pl*) a facial outline or feature.
▷ **HISTORY** Latin *lineare* to draw a line

linear (**lin**-ee-er) *adj* **1** of or in lines. **2** of or relating to length. **3** represented by a line or lines. ▸ **linearity** *n*

linear measure *n* a unit or system of units for the measurement of length.

lineation (lin-ee-**ay**-shun) *n* **1** the act of marking with lines. **2** an arrangement of lines.

line dancing *n* a form of dancing performed by rows of people to country and western music.

line drawing *n* a drawing formed with lines only.

line graph *n Maths* a graph where each value is plotted as a point, joined by a straight line to the points on either side of it.

linen *n* **1** a hard-wearing fabric woven from the spun fibres of flax. **2** articles, such as sheets or tablecloths, made from linen cloth or from cotton. ▹ HISTORY Latin *linum* flax

line of best fit *n Maths* a straight line drawn on a graph, which shows the general trend of the varying values plotted there.

line printer *n* an electromechanical device that prints a line of characters at a time: used in printing and in computer systems.

liner[1] *n* **1** a passenger ship or aircraft, esp. one that is part of a commercial fleet. **2** Also called: **eyeliner** a cosmetic used to outline the eyes.

liner[2] *n* something used as a lining: *a plastic bin liner.*

lines *pl n* **1** the words of a theatrical role: *shaky sets, fluffed lines, and wooden plots.* **2** *Informal, chiefly Brit* a marriage certificate: *marriage lines.* **3** a school punishment of writing out the same sentence or phrase a specified number of times. **4 read between the lines** to find an implicit meaning in addition to the obvious one.

linesman *n, pl* **-men 1** an official who helps the referee or umpire in various sports, by indicating when the ball has gone out of play. **2** a person who maintains railway, electricity, or telephone lines.

line-up *n* **1** people or things assembled for a particular purpose: *the Christmas TV line-up.* **2** the members of such an assembly. ✧ *vb* **line up 3** to form or organize a line-up.

ling[1] *n, pl* **ling** *or* **lings** a fish with a long slender body. ▹ HISTORY probably Low German

ling[2] *n* heather. ▹ HISTORY Old Norse *lyng*

linger *vb* **1** to delay or prolong departure. **2** to survive in a weakened condition for some time before death. **3** to spend a long time doing or considering something. ▹ HISTORY Old English *lengan* prolong ▸ **lingering** *adj*

lingerie (**lan**-zher-ee) *n* women's underwear and nightwear. ▹ HISTORY French, from Latin *lineus* linen

lingo *n, pl* **-goes** *Informal* any foreign or unfamiliar language or jargon. ▹ HISTORY perhaps from LINGUA FRANCA

lingua franca *n, pl* **lingua francas** *or* **linguae francae 1** a language used for communication among people of different mother tongues. **2** any system of communication providing mutual understanding. ▹ HISTORY Italian: Frankish tongue

lingual *adj* **1** *Anat* of the tongue. **2** articulated with the tongue. **3** *Rare* of language or languages. ▸ **lingually** *adv*

linguist *n* **1** a person who is skilled in foreign languages. **2** a person who studies linguistics. ▹ HISTORY Latin *lingua* tongue

linguistic *adj* **1** of language. **2** of linguistics. ▸ **linguistically** *adv*

linguistics *n* the scientific study of language.

liniment *n* a medicated oily liquid applied to the skin to relieve pain or stiffness. ▹ HISTORY Latin *linere* to smear

lining *n* **1** material used to line a garment or curtain. **2** any interior covering: *the lining of the womb.*

link *n* **1** any of the separate rings that form a chain. **2** an emotional or logical relationship between people or things; association. **3** a connecting part or episode. **4** a type of communications connection: *a rail link; radio link.* ✧ *vb* **5** (often foll. by *up*) to connect with or as if with links. **6** to connect by association. ▹ HISTORY from Old Norse

linkage *n* **1** the act of linking or the state of being linked. **2** a system of links.

links *pl n* a golf course. ▹ HISTORY Old English *hlincas,* plural of *hlinc* ridge

link-up *n* a joining together of two systems or groups.

Linnean system *n Biol* the system of classification of plants and animals using binomial Latin names. ▹ HISTORY after Carolus *Linnaeus,* Swedish botanist

linnet *n* a brownish finch: the male has a red breast and forehead. ▹ HISTORY Old French *linotte,* from Latin *līnum* flax (because the bird feeds on flaxseeds)

lino *n* short for **linoleum**.

linocut *n* **1** a design cut in relief in linoleum mounted on a block of wood. **2** a print made from such a block.

linoleum *n* a floor covering made of hessian or jute with a smooth decorative coating of powdered cork. ▹ HISTORY Latin *linum* flax + *oleum* oil

Linotype *n Trademark* a typesetting machine that casts an entire line of text on one piece of metal.

linseed *n* the seed of the flax plant. ▹ HISTORY Old English *līn* flax + *sǣd* seed

linseed oil *n* a yellow oil extracted from flax seeds and used in making paints, inks, linoleum, and varnish.

lint *n* **1** an absorbent material with raised fibres on one side, used to dress wounds. **2** tiny shreds of yarn or cloth; fluff. ▹ HISTORY probably Latin *linteus* made of linen, from *linum* flax

lintel *n* a horizontal beam over a door or window. ▹ HISTORY probably ultimately from Latin *limes* boundary

lion *n* **1** a large animal of the cat family found in Africa and India, with a tawny yellow coat and, in the male, a shaggy mane. **2** a courageous and strong person. **3 the lion's share** the largest portion. ▹ HISTORY Latin *leo* ▸ **lioness** *fem n*

A B C D E F G H I J K L M N O P Q R S T U V W X Y Z

lion-hearted *adj* very brave; courageous.

lionize *or* **-ise** *vb* **-izing, -ized** *or* **-ising, -ised** to treat as a celebrity.

lip *n* **1** *Anat* either of the two fleshy folds surrounding the mouth. **2** any structure resembling a lip, such as the rim of a jug. **3** *Slang* impudent talk or backchat. **4 bite one's lip** to avoid showing feelings of anger or distress. **5 keep a stiff upper lip** to maintain one's composure during a time of trouble. **6 lick** *or* **smack one's lips** to anticipate or recall something with glee or relish. ▷ **HISTORY** Old English *lippa*

lipase *n Biochem* any of a group of enzymes that digest fat and are produced in the stomach and pancreas and occur in seeds.

lipid *n Biochem* any of a group of organic compounds including fats, oils, waxes, and sterols. ▷ **HISTORY** Greek *lipos* fat

liposuction *n* a cosmetic surgical operation in which fat is removed from the body by suction.

lip-read *vb* **-reading, -read** to interpret speech by lip-reading.

lip-reading *n* a method used by deaf people to understand spoken words by interpreting movements of the speaker's lips. ▶ **lip-reader** *n*

lip service *n* **pay lip service to** to appear to support or obey something publicly while actually disregarding it.

lipstick *n* a cosmetic in the form of a stick, for colouring the lips.

liquefy *vb* **-fies, -fying, -fied** (esp. of a gas) to make or become liquid. ▷ **HISTORY** Latin *liquefacere* to make liquid ▶ **liquefaction** *n*

liqueur (lik-**cure**) *n* a highly flavoured sweetened alcoholic spirit, intended to be drunk after a meal. ▷ **HISTORY** French

liquid *n* **1** a substance in a physical state which can change shape but not size. ✧ *adj* **2** of or being a liquid: *liquid medicines.* **3** shining and clear: *liquid sunlight days.* **4** flowing, fluent, or smooth. **5** (of assets) in the form of money or easily convertible into money. ▷ **HISTORY** Latin *liquere* to be fluid

liquidate *vb* **-dating, -dated 1** to settle or pay off (a debt or claim). **2** to dissolve a company and divide its assets among creditors. **3** to convert (assets) into cash. **4** to eliminate or kill.

liquidation *n* **1 a** the dissolving of a company by selling its assets to pay off its debts. **b go into liquidation** (of a business firm) to have its affairs so terminated. **2** destruction; elimination.

liquidator *n* an official appointed to liquidate a business.

liquid-crystal display *n* a display of numbers, characters, or images, esp. on a calculator, using cells containing a liquid with crystalline properties, that change their reflectivity when an electric field is applied to them.

liquidity *n* the state of being able to meet financial obligations.

liquidize *or* **-dise** *vb* **-izing, -ized** *or* **-ising, -ised 1** to make or become liquid; liquefy. **2** to process (food) in a liquidizer to make it liquid.

liquidizer *or* **-diser** *n* a kitchen appliance with blades for liquidizing food.

liquid measure *n* a unit or system of units for measuring volumes of liquids or their containers.

liquid oxygen *n* oxygen liquefied by cooling: used in rocket fuels.

liquid paraffin *n* an oily liquid obtained by petroleum distillation and used as a laxative.

liquor *n* **1** spirits or other alcoholic drinks. **2** any liquid in which food has been cooked. ▷ **HISTORY** Latin *liquere* to be liquid

liquorice *or US & Canad* **licorice** (**lik**-ker-iss) *n* **1** a chewy black sweet with a strong flavour. **2** the dried black root of a Mediterranean plant, used as a laxative and in confectionery. ▷ **HISTORY** Greek *glukus* sweet + *rhiza* root

lira *n, pl* **lire** *or* **liras 1** a former monetary unit of Italy. **2** the standard monetary unit of Turkey. ▷ **HISTORY** Italian, from Latin *libra* pound

lisle (rhymes with **mile**) *n* a strong fine cotton thread or fabric, formerly used to make stockings. ▷ **HISTORY** after *Lisle* (now Lille), in France

lisp *n* **1** a speech defect in which *s* and *z* are pronounced like the *th* sounds in English *thin* and *then* respectively. ✧ *vb* **2** to speak with a lisp. ▷ **HISTORY** Old English *wlisp* lisping (imitative)

LISP *n* a high-level computer programming language suitable for work in artificial intelligence. ▷ **HISTORY** *lis(t) p(rocessing)*

lissom *or* **lissome** *adj* slim and graceful and agile in movement. ▷ **HISTORY** variant of *lithesome,* from *lithe* + *-some* of a specific nature

list¹ *n* **1** an item-by-item record of names or things, usually written one below the other. ✧ *vb* **2** to make a list of. **3** to include in a list. ▷ **HISTORY** Old English *līste*

list² *vb* **1** (esp. of ships) to lean to one side. ✧ *n* **2** a leaning to one side: *developed a list to starboard.* ▷ **HISTORY** origin unknown

listed building *n* (in Britain and Australia) a building protected from demolition or alteration because of its special historical or architectural interest.

listen *vb* **1** to concentrate on hearing something. **2** to take heed or pay attention: *listen, let me explain.* ▷ **HISTORY** Old English *hlysnan* ▶ **listener** *n*

listen in *vb* (often foll. by *on* or *to*) to listen secretly to; eavesdrop.

listeriosis *n* a serious form of food poisoning, caused by bacteria of the genus *Listeria.* ▷ **HISTORY** after Joseph *Lister,* surgeon

listing *n* **1** a list or an entry in a list. **2 listings** lists of films, concerts, etc. printed in newspapers and magazines, and showing details such as times and venues.

listless *adj* lacking interest or energy. ▷ **HISTORY** obsolete *list* desire ▶ **listlessly** *adv*

list price *n* the selling price of merchandise as quoted in a catalogue or advertisement.

lists *pl n* **1** *History* the enclosed field of combat at a tournament. **2 enter the lists** to engage in a conflict or controversy. ▷ **HISTORY** plural of Old English *līste* border

lit *vb* a past of **light**[1], **light**[2].

litany *n, pl* **-nies 1** *Christianity* a prayer consisting of a series of invocations, each followed by the same response. **2** any tedious recital: *a litany of complaints.* ▷ HISTORY Late Greek *litaneia* prayer

litchi *n* same as **lychee**.

liter *n US* same as **litre**.

literacy *n* **1** the ability to read and write. **2** the ability to use language effectively.

literal *adj* **1** in exact accordance with the explicit meaning of a word or text. **2** word for word: *a literal translation.* **3** dull or unimaginative: *she's very, very literal and flat in how she interprets what she sees.* **4** true; actual. ✧ *n* **5** a misprint or misspelling in a text. ▷ HISTORY Latin *littera* letter ▶ **literally** *adv*

literalism *n* the tendency to take words and statements in their literal sense. ▶ **literalist** *n*

literary *adj* **1** of or characteristic of literature: *literary criticism.* **2** knowledgeable about literature. **3** (of a word) used chiefly in written work; not colloquial. ▷ HISTORY Latin *litterarius* concerning reading and writing ▶ **literariness** *n*

literary canon *n Literature* a set of works that are considered to be important and of great literary value: *the most sublime works of the English literary canon.*

literary theory *n Literature* a collective term for the many different innovative approaches to studying and analysing texts which have been advanced over the years.

literate *adj* **1** able to read and write. **2** educated. ✧ *n* **3** a literate person. ▷ HISTORY Latin *litteratus* learned

literati *pl n* literary or scholarly people. ▷ HISTORY Latin

literature *n* **1** written material such as poetry, novels, or essays. **2** the body of written work of a particular culture, people, or era: *Elizabethan literature.* **3** written or printed matter of a particular type or genre: *medical literature.* **4** the art or profession of a writer. **5** *Informal* printed matter on any subject. ▷ HISTORY Latin *litteratura* writing

lithe *adj* attractively graceful and supple in movement. ▷ HISTORY Old English *lithe* (in the sense: gentle; later: supple)

lithium *n Chem* a soft silvery element of the alkali metal series: the lightest known metal. Symbol: Li. ▷ HISTORY Greek *lithos* stone

litho *n, pl* **-thos**, *adj, adv* short for **lithography, lithograph, lithographic, lithographically**.

lithograph *n* **1** a print made by lithography. ✧ *vb* **2** to reproduce (pictures or text) by lithography. ▶ **lithographic** *adj* ▶ **lithographically** *adv*

lithography (lith-**og**-ra-fee) *n* a method of printing from a metal or stone surface on which the printing areas are made ink-receptive. ▷ HISTORY Greek *lithos* stone + *graphein* to write ▶ **lithographer** *n*

lithosphere *n Geol* the rigid outer layer of the earth, comprising the earth's crust and the solid upper part of the mantle. Compare **asthenosphere**.

Lithuanian *adj* **1** from Lithuania. ✧ *n* **2** a person from Lithuania. **3** the language of Lithuania.

litigant *n* a person involved in a lawsuit.

litigate *vb* **-gating, -gated 1** to bring or contest a lawsuit. **2** to engage in legal proceedings. ▷ HISTORY Latin *lis, lit-* lawsuit + *agere* to carry on ▶ **litigator** *n*

litigation *n* the process of bringing or contesting a lawsuit.

litigious (lit-**ij**-uss) *adj* frequently going to law.

litmus *n* a soluble powder obtained from lichens, which is turned red by acids and blue by alkalis. Paper treated with it (**litmus paper**) is used as an indicator in chemistry. ▷ HISTORY perhaps Scandinavian

litmus test *n* something that is regarded as a simple and accurate test of a particular thing, such as a person's attitude to an issue.

litotes *n, pl* **-tes** *Literature* understatement used for effect, for example 'She was not a little upset', meaning 'She was extremely upset'. ▷ HISTORY Greek *litos* small

litre *or US* **liter** *n* a measure of volume equivalent to 1 cubic decimetre. ▷ HISTORY Greek *litra* a unit of weight

litter *n* **1** small items of rubbish carelessly dropped in public places. **2** a disordered or untidy collection of objects. **3** a group of animals produced at one birth. **4** straw or hay used as bedding for animals. **5** dry material used to line a receptacle in which a domestic cat can urinate and defecate. **6** (esp. formerly) a bed or seat held between parallel poles and used for carrying people. ✧ *vb* **7** to strew with litter. **8** to scatter or be scattered in an untidy fashion. **9** (of animals) to give birth to offspring. **10** to provide (an animal) with straw or hay for bedding. ▷ HISTORY Latin *lectus* bed

little *adj* **1** of small or less than average size. **2** young: *a little boy.* **3** endearingly familiar: *he was a sweet little man.* **4** contemptible, mean, or disagreeable: *she's got one of her horrible little friends to stay.* **5** a small quantity, extent, or duration of: *there was little money circulating; I could see little evidence of it.* ✧ *adv* **6** (usually preceded by *a*) to a small extent or degree; not a lot: *to sleep a little.* **7** not at all, or hardly: *army life varied little as the years passed.* **8** not much or often: *we go there very little now.* **9 little by little** by small degrees. ✧ *n* **10 make little of** to treat as insignificant: *one episode in their history is made little of in the guide books.* **11 think little of** to have a low opinion of. ✧ See also **less, lesser, least**. ▷ HISTORY Old English *lȳtel*

little people *pl n Folklore* small supernatural beings, such as elves.

littoral *adj* **1** of or by the shore. ✧ *n* **2** a coastal region. ▷ HISTORY Latin *litus* shore

liturgy *n, pl* **-gies** the forms of public services officially prescribed by a Church. ▷ HISTORY Greek *leitourgia* ▶ **liturgical** *adj*

live[1] *vb* **living, lived 1** to show the characteristics of life; be alive. **2** to remain alive or in existence. **3** to exist in a specified way: *to live at ease.* **4** to have one's home: *he went to live in Switzerland.* **5** to continue or last: *his childhood had always lived inside him.* **6** (foll. by *on, upon* or *by*) to support one's style of life: *forest dwellers who live by extracting rubber.* **7** (foll. by *with*) to endure the effects (of a crime or mistake); tolerate. **8** to pass or spend (one's life). **9** to enjoy life to the full: *he's the kind of person who knows how to live.* **10** to put into practice in one's daily life: *the freedom to live his own life as he chooses.* **11 live and let live** to be tolerant. ✧ See also **live down**. ▷ HISTORY Old English *libban, lifian*

live² *adj* **1** alive; living. **2** *Radio, television* transmitted at the time of performance, rather than being prerecorded: *a live broadcast.* **3** actual: *I was able to speak to a real live Hurricane pilot.* **4** (of a recording) recorded during a performance. **5** connected to a source of electric power: *a live cable.* **6** of current interest; controversial: *the document has become a live political issue.* **7** loaded or capable of exploding: *a live firing exercise using a mortar cannon.* **8** (of a coal or ember) glowing or burning. ✧ *adv* **9** during, at, or in the form of a live performance. ▷ HISTORY shortened from *on live* alive

live down *vb* to withstand people's reactions to a crime or mistake until they forget it.

livelihood *n* one's job or other source of income.

livelong (**liv**-long) *adj Chiefly poetic* long or seemingly long: *all the livelong day.*

lively *adj* **-lier, -liest 1** full of life or vigour. **2** vivacious or animated. **3** vivid. ▶ **liveliness** *n*

liver¹ *n* **1** a large glandular organ which secretes bile, balances nutrients, and removes certain poisons from the body. **2** the liver of certain animals used as food. ▷ HISTORY Old English *lifer*

liver² *n* a person who lives in a specified way: *a fast liver.*

liveried *adj* wearing livery.

liverish *adj* **1** *Informal* having a disorder of the liver. **2** feeling disagreeable and slightly irritable.

Liverpudlian *adj* **1** of Liverpool, a city in NW England. ✧ *n* **2** a person from Liverpool.

liverwort *n* a plant growing in wet places and resembling green seaweeds or leafy mosses. ▷ HISTORY late Old English *liferwyrt*

livery *n, pl* **-eries 1** the identifying uniform of a servant. **2** distinctive dress or outward appearance. **3** the stabling, keeping, or hiring out of horses for money. ▷ HISTORY Old French *livrée* allocation

lives *n* the plural of **life**.

livestock *n* animals kept on a farm.

live together *vb* (of an unmarried couple) to live in the same house; cohabit.

live up to *vb* to fulfil (an expectation, obligation, or principle).

live wire *n* **1** *Informal* an energetic person. **2** a wire carrying an electric current.

livid *adj* **1** *Informal* extremely angry. **2** of a dark grey or purple colour: *livid bruises.* ▷ HISTORY Latin *livere* to be black and blue

living *adj* **1** possessing life; not dead or inanimate. **2** currently in use or valid: *a living alliance.* **3** seeming to be real: *a living doll.* **4** (of people or animals) existing in the present age. **5** very: *the living image.* **6** of or like everyday life: *living costs.* **7** of or involving those now alive: *one of our greatest living actors.* ✧ *n* **8** the condition of being alive. **9** the manner of one's life: *high living.* **10** one's financial means. **11** *Church of England* a benefice.

living room *n* a room in a private house or flat used for relaxation and entertainment.

living wage *n* a wage adequate for a worker to live on and support a family in reasonable comfort.

living will *n* a document that states that a person who becomes terminally ill does not want their life to be prolonged by artificial means.

lizard *n* a reptile with an elongated body, four limbs, and a long tail. ▷ HISTORY Latin *lacerta*

llama *n* a South American mammal of the camel family, that is used as a beast of burden and is valued for its woolly fleece. ▷ HISTORY from a Native American language

LLB Bachelor of Laws. ▷ HISTORY Latin *Legum Baccalaureus*

LLD Doctor of Laws. ▷ HISTORY Latin *Legum Doctor*

LLM Master of Laws. ▷ HISTORY Latin *Legum Magister*

lo *interj Old-fashioned* look! see!: *lo and behold!* ▷ HISTORY Old English *lā*

loach *n* a freshwater fish with a long narrow body and barbels around the mouth. ▷ HISTORY Old French *loche*

load *n* **1** something to be borne or conveyed; weight. **2** the amount borne or conveyed. **3** something that weighs down or burdens: *I have enough of a load to carry right now.* **4** *Electronics* the power delivered by a machine, generator, or circuit. **5** an external force applied to a component or mechanism. **6 a load of** *Informal* a quantity of: *a load of half-truths.* **7 get a load of** *Informal* to pay attention to. ✧ *vb* **8** to place cargo or goods upon (a ship or vehicle). **9** to burden or oppress. **10** to supply in abundance: *other treats are loaded with fat.* **11** to cause to be biased: *the dice are loaded.* **12** to put ammunition into (a firearm). **13** *Photog* to insert film in (a camera). **14** to weight or bias (a roulette wheel or dice). **15** *Computers* to transfer (a program) to a memory. ✧ See also **loads**. ▷ HISTORY Old English *lād* course; in meaning, influenced by LADE ▶ **loader** *n*

loaded *adj* **1** carrying a load. **2** charged with ammunition. **3** (of a question or statement) containing a hidden trap or implication. **4** (of dice or a roulette wheel) weighted or otherwise biased. **5** *Slang* wealthy. **6** *Slang, chiefly US & Canad* drunk.

loads *pl n Informal* (often foll. by *of*) a lot.

loadstar *n* same as **lodestar**.

loadstone *n* same as **lodestone**.

loaf¹ *n, pl* **loaves 1** a shaped mass of baked bread. **2** any shaped or moulded mass of food, such as cooked meat. **3** *Slang* the head; common sense: *use your loaf!* ▷ HISTORY Old English *hlāf*

loaf² *vb* to loiter or lounge around in an idle way. ▷ HISTORY perhaps from *loafer*

loafer *n* **1** a person who avoids work; idler. **2** a moccasin-like shoe. ▷ **HISTORY** perhaps German *Landläufer* vagabond

loam *n* fertile soil consisting of sand, clay, and decaying organic material. ▷ **HISTORY** Old English *lām* ▶ **loamy** *adj*

loan *n* **1** money lent at interest for a fixed period of time. **2** the act of lending: *I am grateful to her for the loan of her book.* **3** property lent. **4 on loan** lent out; borrowed. ✧ *vb* **5** to lend (something, esp. money). ▷ **HISTORY** Old Norse *lān*

loan shark *n* a person who lends money at an extremely high interest rate, esp. illegally.

loath *or* **loth** (rhymes with **both**) *adj* (usually foll. by *to*) reluctant or unwilling. ▷ **HISTORY** Old English *lāth* (in the sense: hostile)

loathe *vb* **loathing, loathed** to feel strong disgust for. ▷ **HISTORY** Old English *lāthiān*

loathing *n* strong disgust.

loathsome *adj* causing loathing.

loaves *n* the plural of **loaf**[1].

lob *Sport* ✧ *n* **1** a ball struck or bowled in a high arc. ✧ *vb* **lobbing, lobbed 2** to hit or kick (a ball) in a high arc. **3** *Informal* to throw. ▷ **HISTORY** probably Low German

lobar (**loh**-ber) *adj* of or affecting a lobe.

lobate *adj* with or like lobes.

lobby *n, pl* **-bies 1** a room or corridor used as an entrance hall or vestibule. **2** a group which attempts to influence legislators on behalf of a particular interest. **3** *Chiefly Brit* a hall in a legislative building used for meetings between legislators and members of the public. **4** *Chiefly Brit* one of two corridors in a legislative building in which members vote. ✧ *vb* **-bies, -bying, -bied 5** to attempt to influence (legislators) in the formulation of policy. ▷ **HISTORY** Old High German *lauba* arbor

lobbyist *n* a person who lobbies on behalf of a particular interest.

lobe *n* **1** any rounded projection. **2** the fleshy lower part of the external ear. **3** any subdivision of a bodily organ. ▷ **HISTORY** Greek *lobos* lobe of the ear or of the liver

lobelia *n* a plant with blue, red, white, or yellow five-lobed flowers. ▷ **HISTORY** Matthias de *Lobel,* botanist

lobola *n S African* an African custom by which a bridegroom's family makes a payment in cattle or cash to the bride's family shortly before the marriage. ▷ **HISTORY** Nguni (language group of southern Africa) *ukulobola* to give bride price

lobotomy *n, pl* **-mies** the surgical cutting of nerves in the frontal lobe of the brain to treat severe mental disorders. ▷ **HISTORY** Greek *lobos* lobe + *tomē* a cutting

lobster *n, pl* **-sters** *or* **-ster 1** a large edible crustacean with large pincers and a long tail, which turns red when boiled. **2** its edible flesh. ▷ **HISTORY** Old English *loppestre,* from *loppe* spider

lobster pot *n* a round basket made of open slats, used to catch lobsters.

lobule *n* a small lobe.

local *adj* **1** of or concerning a particular area. **2** restricted to a particular place. **3** *Med* of, affecting, or confined to a limited area or part: *a local anaesthetic.* **4** (of a train or bus) stopping at all stations or stops. ✧ *n* **5** an inhabitant of a specified locality: *we swim, sunbathe, meet the locals, unwind.* **6** *Brit informal* a pub close to one's home. ▷ **HISTORY** Latin *locus* place ▶ **locally** *adv*

local anaesthetic *n Med* See **anaesthesia**.

local authority *n* the governing body of a county, district, or region.

locale (loh-**kahl**) *n* the place where something happens or has happened. ▷ **HISTORY** French, from Latin *locus* place

local government *n* the government of the affairs of counties, towns, and districts by locally elected political bodies.

locality *n, pl* **-ties 1** a neighbourhood or area. **2** the site or scene of an event.

localize *or* **-ise** *vb* **-izing, -ized** *or* **-ising, -ised** to restrict (something) to a particular place.

local relief *n Geog* the difference between the highest and lowest land levels in a given area.

locate *vb* **-cating, -cated 1** to discover the whereabouts of; find. **2** to situate or build: *located around the corner from the church.* **3** to become established or settled.

location *n* **1** a site or position; situation. **2** the act of locating or the state of being located: *make their location and rescue a top priority.* **3** a place outside a studio where filming is done: *shot on location.* **4** (in South Africa) a Black African or Coloured township. ▷ **HISTORY** Latin *locare* to place

loc. cit. (in textual annotation) in the place cited. ▷ **HISTORY** Latin *loco citato*

loch *n Scot* **1** a lake. **2** a long narrow arm of the sea. ▷ **HISTORY** Gaelic

loci (**loh**-sigh) *n* the plural of **locus**.

lock[1] *n* **1** a device for fastening a door, drawer, lid, etc., and preventing unauthorized access. **2** a section of a canal or river closed off by gates between which the water level can be altered to aid boats moving from one level to the next. **3** *Brit & NZ* the extent to which a vehicle's front wheels will turn: *they adopted more steering lock.* **4** the interlocking of parts. **5** a mechanism that fires a gun. **6 lock, stock, and barrel** completely; entirely. **7** a wrestling hold. **8** Also called: **lock forward** *Rugby* a player in the second row of the scrum. ✧ *vb* **9** to fasten or become fastened to prevent entry or exit. **10** to secure (a building) by locking all doors and windows. **11** to fix or become fixed together securely. **12** to become or cause to become immovable: *just before your knees lock.* **13** to clasp or entangle in a struggle or embrace. ✧ See also **lock up**. ▷ **HISTORY** Old English *loc*

lock[2] *n* **1** a strand or curl of hair. **2 locks** *Chiefly literary* hair. ▷ **HISTORY** Old English *loc*

locker *n* a small compartment with a lock, used for temporarily storing clothes, valuables, or luggage.

a b c d e f g h i j k l m n o p q r s t u v w x y z

A B C D E F G H I J K L M N O P Q R S T U V W X Y Z

locket *n* a small hinged ornamental pendant that holds a picture or keepsake. ▷ **HISTORY** French *loquet* latch

lockjaw *n Pathol* a nontechnical name for **trismus, tetanus**.

locksmith *n* a person who makes or repairs locks.

lock up *vb* **1** to imprison. **2** to secure a building by locking all the doors and windows. ✧ *n* **lockup 3** a jail. **4** *Brit* a garage or store separate from the main premises. **5** *Brit* a small shop with no attached quarters for the owner. ✧ *adj* **lock-up 6** *Brit & NZ* (of premises) without living quarters: *a lock-up garage.*

loco[1] *n, pl* **locos** *Informal* a locomotive.

loco[2] *adj Slang, chiefly US* insane. ▷ **HISTORY** Spanish: crazy

locomotion *n* the act or power of moving. ▷ **HISTORY** Latin *loco* from a place + MOTION

locomotive *n* **1** a self-propelled engine for pulling trains. ✧ *adj* **2** of locomotion.

locule *or* **loculus** *n, pl* **locules** *or* **loculi** *Biol* **1** any of the chambers of an ovary or anther. **2** any small hollow space or chamber.

locum *n* a person who stands in temporarily for a doctor or clergyman. ▷ **HISTORY** Medieval Latin *locum tenens* (someone) holding the place (of another)

locus (**loh**-kuss) *n, pl* **loci 1** an area or place where something happens. **2** *Maths* a set of points or lines whose location satisfies or is determined by one or more specified conditions: *the locus of points equidistant from a given point is a circle.* ▷ **HISTORY** Latin

locus standi *n Law* the right of a party to appear and be heard before a court. ▷ **HISTORY** Latin: a place for standing

locust *n* **1** an African insect, related to the grasshopper, which travels in vast swarms, stripping large areas of vegetation. **2** a North American leguminous tree with prickly branches; the carob tree. ▷ **HISTORY** Latin *locusta*

lode *n* a vein of metallic ore. ▷ **HISTORY** Old English *lād* course

lodestar *n* **1** a star, esp. the North Star, used in navigation or astronomy as a point of reference. **2** something that serves as a guide.

lodestone *n* **1 a** magnetic iron ore. **b** a piece of this, used as a magnet. **2** a person or thing regarded as a focus of attraction.

lodge *n* **1** *Chiefly Brit* the gatekeeper's house at the entrance to the grounds of a country mansion. **2** a house or cabin used occasionally by hunters, skiers, etc.: *a hunting lodge.* **3** *Chiefly Brit* a room used by porters in a university or college. **4** a local branch of certain societies. **5** a beaver's home. ✧ *vb* **lodging, lodged 6** to provide or be provided with rented accommodation. **7** to live temporarily in rented accommodation. **8** to embed or be embedded: *the bullet lodged in his brain.* **9** to leave for safety or storage: *a report was lodged with the local police station.* **10** to bring (a charge or accusation) against someone: *the Brazilians lodged a complaint.* **11** (often foll. by *in* or *with*) to place (authority or power) in the control (of someone). ▷ **HISTORY** Old French *loge*

lodger *n* a person who pays rent in return for accommodation in someone else's home.

lodging *n* **1** a temporary residence: *where might I find a night's lodging?* **2 lodgings** a rented room or rooms in another person's home.

loess (**loh**-iss) *n* a fine-grained soil, found mainly in river valleys, originally deposited by the wind. ▷ **HISTORY** Swiss German *lösch* loose

loft *n* **1** the space inside a roof. **2** a gallery in a church. **3** a room over a stable used to store hay. **4** a raised house or coop in which pigeons are kept. **5** *Golf* **a** the angle of the face of the club used to elevate a ball. **b** the height reached by a struck ball. ✧ *vb* **6** *Sport* to strike or kick (a ball) high in the air. ▷ **HISTORY** Old Norse *lopt* air, ceiling

lofty *adj* **loftier, loftiest 1** of majestic or imposing height. **2** morally admirable: *lofty ideals.* **3** unpleasantly superior: *a lofty contempt.* ▶ **loftily** *adv* ▶ **loftiness** *n*

log[1] *n* **1** a section of a felled tree stripped of branches. **2 a** a detailed record of a voyage of a ship or aircraft. **b** a record of the hours flown by pilots and aircrews. **c** a book in which these records are made; logbook. **3** a device consisting of a float with an attached line, formerly used to measure the speed of a ship. **4 sleep like a log** to sleep without stirring. ✧ *vb* **logging, logged 5** to saw logs from (trees). **6** to enter (a distance or event) in a logbook or log. ✧ See also **log in, log out**. ▷ **HISTORY** origin unknown

log[2] *n* short for **logarithm**.

loganberry *n, pl* **-ries** a purplish-red fruit, similar to a raspberry, that grows on a trailing prickly plant. ▷ **HISTORY** after J. H. *Logan,* who first grew it

logarithm *n* the exponent indicating the power to which a fixed number, the base, must be raised to obtain a given number or variable. ▷ **HISTORY** Greek *logos* ratio + *arithmos* number ▶ **logarithmic** *adj*

logbook *n* **1** a book containing the official record of trips made by a ship or aircraft. **2** *Brit informal* the registration document of a car.

loggerhead *n* **1** a large-headed turtle occurring in most seas. **2 at loggerheads** engaged in dispute or confrontation. ▷ **HISTORY** probably dialect *logger* wooden block + HEAD

loggia (**loj**-ya) *n* a covered gallery on the side of a building. ▷ **HISTORY** Italian

logging *n* the work of felling, trimming, and transporting timber. ▶ **logger** *n*

logic *n* **1** the branch of philosophy that analyses the patterns of reasoning. **2** a particular system of reasoning. **3** reasoned thought or argument, as distinguished from irrationality. **4** the interdependence of a series of events or facts. **5** *Electronics, computers* the principles underlying the units in a computer system that produce results from data. ▷ **HISTORY** Greek *logikos* concerning speech or reasoning

logical *adj* **1** relating to or characteristic of logic. **2** using or deduced from the principles of logic: *a logical conclusion.* **3** capable of or using clear and valid reasoning. **4** reasonable because of facts or events: *the logical choice.* ▶ **logically** *adv*

logical relations *pl n* (in language) the logical linking of ideas and arguments by means of connectives such as *and, but, because,* and *therefore.*

logic gate *n Electronics* same as **gate** (sense 4).

logician *n* a person who specializes in or is skilled at logic.

log in *or* **on** *vb* to gain entrance to a computer system by keying in a special command.

logistics *n* the detailed planning and organization of a large complex operation, such as a military campaign. ▷ **HISTORY** French *loger* to lodge ▶ **logistical** *or* **logistic** *adj* ▶ **logistically** *adv*

log jam *n Chiefly US & Canad* **1** a blockage caused by the crowding together of logs floating in a river. **2** a deadlock.

logo (**loh**-go) *n, pl* **logos** a special design that identifies a company or an organization and appears on all its products, printed material, etc. ▷ **HISTORY** shortened from *logotype* badge, symbol

log out *or* **off** *vb* to exit from a computer system by keying in a special command.

-logy *n combining form* **1** indicating the science or study of: *musicology.* **2** indicating writing or discourse: *trilogy; phraseology.* ▷ **HISTORY** Greek *logos* word ▶ **-logical** *or* **-logic** *adj combining form* ▶ **-logist** *n combining form*

loin *n* **1** the part of the body between the pelvis and the ribs. **2** a cut of meat from this part of an animal. ✧ See also **loins.** ▷ **HISTORY** Old French *loigne*

loincloth *n* a piece of cloth covering only the loins.

loins *pl n* **1** the hips and the inner surface of the legs where they join the body. **2** *Euphemistic* the genitals.

loiter *vb* to stand or wait aimlessly or idly. ▷ **HISTORY** perhaps Middle Dutch *löteren* to wobble

Lolita (low-**lee**-ta) *n* a sexually precocious young girl. ▷ **HISTORY** after the character in Nabokov's novel *Lolita*

loll *vb* **1** to lounge in a lazy manner. **2** to hang loosely: *a wet lolling tongue; his head lolled back and forth.* ▷ **HISTORY** perhaps imitative

lollipop *n* **1** a boiled sweet stuck on a small wooden stick. **2** *Brit* an ice lolly. ▷ **HISTORY** perhaps dialect *lolly* the tongue + POP[2]

lollipop man *or* **lady** *n Brit informal* a person holding a circular sign on a pole who stops traffic to enable children to cross the road safely.

lollop *vb Chiefly Brit* to walk or run with a clumsy or relaxed bouncing movement. ▷ **HISTORY** probably *loll* + *-op,* as in *gallop*

lolly *n, pl* **-lies 1** *Informal* a lollipop. **2** *Brit* short for **ice lolly**. **3** *Brit, Austral, & NZ slang* money. **4** *Austral & NZ informal* a sweet. ▷ **HISTORY** shortened from *lollipop*

Londoner *n* a person from London.

London pride *n* a rock plant with a rosette of leaves and pink flowers.

lone *adj* **1** solitary: *a lone figure.* **2** isolated: *a lone isle guarded by the great Atlantic swell.* **3** *Brit* unmarried or widowed: *a lone parent.* ▷ **HISTORY** from the mistaken division of *alone* into *a lone*

lonely *adj* **-lier, -liest 1** unhappy as a result of solitude. **2** resulting from the state of being alone: *command can be a lonely business.* **3** isolated and not much visited by people: *a lonely beach.* ▶ **loneliness** *n*

loner *n Informal* a person who prefers to be alone.

lonesome *adj* **1** *Chiefly US & Canad* lonely. **2** causing feelings of loneliness: *it was lonesome up here on the mountain.*

long[1] *adj* **1** having relatively great length in space or time. **2** having greater than the average or expected range, extent, or duration: *a long session of talks.* **3** seeming to occupy a greater time than is really so: *she was quiet a long moment.* **4** of a specified extent or duration: *trimmed to about 2 cm long.* **5** consisting of a large number of parts: *a long list.* **6** *Phonetics, prosody* (of a vowel) of relatively considerable duration. **7** from end to end; lengthwise. **8** *Finance* having large holdings of securities or commodities in anticipation of rising prices. **9 in the long run** ultimately; after or over a period of time. **10 long on** *Informal* plentifully supplied or endowed with: *long on show-biz gossip.* ✧ *adv* **11** for a certain time or period: *how long have we got?* **12** for or during an extensive period of time: *to talk long into the night.* **13** a considerable amount of time: *long after I met you; long ago.* **14 as** *or* **so long as a** for or during the same length of time that. **b** provided that; if. ✧ *n* **15** anything that is long. **16 before long** soon. **17 for long** for a long time. **18 the long and the short of it** the essential points or facts. ▷ **HISTORY** Old English *lang* ▶ **longish** *adj*

long[2] *vb* to have a strong desire for something or to do something: *I longed for a baby; the more I think of him the more I long to see him.* ▷ **HISTORY** Old English *langian*

long. longitude.

longboat *n* **1** the largest boat carried aboard a commercial ship. **2** same as **longship**.

longbow *n* a large powerful hand-drawn bow.

long-distance *adj* **1** covering relatively long distances: *a long-distance race.* **2** (of telephone calls) connecting points relatively far apart.

longevity (lon-**jev**-it-ee) *n* long life. ▷ **HISTORY** Latin *longus* long + *aevum* age

long face *n* a glum expression.

longhand *n* ordinary handwriting, as opposed to typing or shorthand.

longhorn *n* a British breed of beef cattle with long curved horns.

longing *n* **1** a strong feeling of wanting something one is unlikely ever to have. ✧ *adj* **2** having or showing desire: *longing glances.* ▶ **longingly** *adv*

longitude *n* distance in degrees east or west of the prime meridian at 0°. ▷ **HISTORY** Latin *longitudo* length

A B C D E F G H I J K L M N O P Q R S T U V W X Y Z

longitudinal *adj* **1** of longitude or length. **2** placed or extended lengthways.

longitudinal dune *n Geog* a long dune lying parallel to the direction of the prevailing wind.

longitudinal wave *n Physics* a wave that is propagated in the same direction as the displacement of the transmitting medium.

long johns *pl n Informal* long underpants.

long jump *n* an athletic contest of jumping the greatest length from a fixed mark.

long-life *adj* (of milk, batteries, etc.) lasting longer than the regular kind.

long-lived *adj* living or lasting for a long time.

long-playing *adj Old-fashioned* of or relating to an LP.

long-range *adj* **1** of or extending into the future: *a long-range economic forecast.* **2** (of vehicles, aircraft, or weapons) capable of covering great distances.

longship *n* a narrow open boat with oars and a square sail, used by the Vikings.

longshore drift *n* the movement of material along a beach, due to waves approaching the shore at an oblique angle.

longshoreman *n, pl* **-men** *US & Canad* a docker.

long shot *n* **1** an undertaking, guess, or possibility with little chance of success. **2** a bet against heavy odds. **3 not by a long shot** not by any means: *she wasn't beaten, not by a long shot.*

long-sighted *adj* **1** able to see only distant objects in focus. **2** far-sighted.

long-standing *adj* existing for a long time.

long-suffering *adj* enduring trouble or unhappiness without complaint.

long-term *adj* **1** lasting or extending over a long time: *a long-term commitment.* ✧ *n* **long term 2 in the long term** over a long period of time: *in the long term the cost of energy will have to go up.*

long wave *n* a radio wave with a wavelength greater than 1000 metres.

longways *or US & Canad* **longwise** *adv* lengthways.

long-winded *adj* tiresomely long. ▶ **long-windedness** *n*

loo *n, pl* **loos** *Brit & NZ informal* a toilet. ▷ **HISTORY** perhaps from French *lieux d'aisance* water closet

loofah *n* a long rough-textured bath sponge made from the dried pod of a gourd. ▷ **HISTORY** Arabic *lūf*

look *vb* **1** (often foll. by *at*) to direct the eyes (towards): *he turned to look at her.* **2** (often foll. by *at*) to consider: *we shall now have a look at some problems.* **3** to give the impression of being; seem: *Luxembourg's timetable looks a winner.* **4** to face in a particular direction: *Morgan's Rock looks south.* **5** (foll. by *for*) to search or seek: *the department looks for reputable firms.* **6** (foll. by *into*) to carry out an investigation. **7** to direct a look at (someone) in a specified way: *she looks at Teresina suspiciously.* **8** to match in appearance with (something): *looking your best.* **9** to expect or hope (to do something): *we would look to derive a procedure that would account for most cases.* **10 look alive, lively, sharp** *or* **smart** to hurry up; get busy. **11 look here** an expression used to attract someone's attention or add emphasis to a statement. ✧ *n* **12** an instance of looking: *a look of icy contempt.* **13** a view or sight (of something): *take a look at my view.* **14** (*often pl*) appearance to the eye or mind; aspect: *I'm not happy with the look of things here; better than you by the looks of it.* **15** style or fashion: *the look made famous by the great Russian.* ✧ *conj* **16** an expression demanding attention or showing annoyance: *look, I won't be coming back.* ✧ See also **look after**. ▷ **HISTORY** Old English *lōcian* ▶ **looker** *n*

> **WORD TIP**
> See at **like**.

look after *vb* to take care of.

lookalike *n* a person or thing that is the double of another, often well-known, person or thing.

look forward to *vb* to anticipate with pleasure.

look-in *Informal* ✧ *n* **1** a chance to be chosen or participate: *before anyone else gets a look-in.* ✧ *vb* **look in 2** to pay a short visit.

looking glass *n* a mirror.

look on *vb* **1** to be a spectator. **2** to consider or regard: *I just looked on her as a friend.* ▶ **looker-on** *n*

lookout *n* **1** the act of watching for danger or for an opportunity: *on the lookout for attack.* **2** a person or people keeping such a watch. **3** a viewpoint from which a watch is kept. **4** *Informal* worry or concern: *that is my lookout rather than theirs.* **5** *Chiefly Brit* chances or prospect: *it's a bad lookout for Europe.* ✧ *vb* **look out 6** to be careful. **7** to watch out for: *look out particularly for oils that have been flavoured.* **8** to find and take out: *little time to look out clothes that she might need.* **9** (foll. by *on* or *over*) to face in a particular direction: *looking out over the courtyard.*

look up *vb* **1** to discover or confirm by checking in a reference book. **2** to improve: *things were looking up.* **3 look up to** to have respect for: *she looked up to him as a kind of father.* **4** to visit (a person): *I'll look you up when I'm in town.*

loom¹ *n* a machine for weaving yarn into cloth. ▷ **HISTORY** variant of Old English *gelōma* tool

loom² *vb* **1** to appear indistinctly, esp. as a tall and threatening shape. **2** (of an event) to seem ominously close. ▷ **HISTORY** perhaps East Frisian *lomen* to move slowly

loon¹ *n US & Canad* same as **diver** (sense 3). ▷ **HISTORY** Scandinavian

loon² *n Informal* a simple-minded or stupid person.

loony *Slang* ✧ *adj* **loonier, looniest 1** insane. **2** foolish or ridiculous. ✧ *n, pl* **loonies 3** a foolish or insane person. ▷ **HISTORY** shortened from *lunatic*

loop *n* **1** the rounded shape formed by a curved line that crosses itself: *a loop of the highway.* **2** any round or oval-shaped thing that is closed or nearly closed. **3** *Electronics* a closed circuit through which a signal can circulate. **4** a flight manoeuvre in which an aircraft flies vertically in a complete circle. **5** a continuous strip of film or tape. **6** *Computers* a

series of instructions in a program, performed repeatedly until some specified condition is satisfied. ✧ *vb* **7** to make into a loop. **8** to fasten or encircle with a loop. **9** Also: **loop the loop** to fly or be flown vertically in a complete circle.
▷ **HISTORY** origin unknown

loophole *n* an ambiguity or omission in the law, which enables one to evade it.

loose *adj* **1** (of clothing) not close-fitting: *the jacket loose and unbuttoned.* **2** free or released from confinement or restraint. **3** not tight, fastened, fixed, or tense. **4** not bundled, fastened, or put in a container: *loose tobacco.* **5** inexact or imprecise: *a loose translation.* **6** (of cash) accessible: *a lot of the loose money is floating around the city.* **7** *Old-fashioned* sexually promiscuous. **8** lacking a sense of propriety: *loose talk.* **9 at a loose end** bored because one has nothing to do. ✧ *n* **10 the loose** *Rugby* the part of play when the forwards close round the ball in a ruck or loose scrum. **11 on the loose** free from confinement or restraint. ✧ *adv* **12** in a loose manner; loosely. ✧ *vb* **loosing, loosed 13** to free or release from restraint or obligation: *he loosed the dogs.* **14** to unfasten or untie: *the guards loosed his arms.* **15** to make or become less strict, tight, firmly attached, or compact. **16** to let fly (a bullet, arrow, or other missile). ▷ **HISTORY** Old Norse *lauss* free ▶ **loosely** *adv* ▶ **looseness** *n*

loosebox *n* an enclosed stall with a door in which an animal can be kept.

loose-leaf *adj* (of a binder) allowing the removal and addition of pages.

loosen *vb* **1** to make or become less tight: *loosen and relax the ankle.* **2** (often foll. by *up*) to make or become less firm, compact, or rigid: *massage is used first to loosen up the muscles.* **3** to untie. **4** (often foll. by *up*) to make or become less strict: *the churches loosen up on sexual teachings.*

loot *n* **1** goods stolen in wartime or during riots; plunder. **2** *Informal* money. ✧ *vb* **3** to plunder (a city) during war or riots. **4** to steal (money or goods) during war or riots. ▷ **HISTORY** Hindi *lūt* ▶ **looter** *n*

lop *vb* **lopping, lopped** (usually foll. by *off*) **1** to cut (parts) off a tree or body. **2** to cut out or eliminate any unnecessary parts: *some parts of the legislature were lopped off.* ▷ **HISTORY** Middle English *loppe* branches cut off

lope *vb* **loping, loped 1** to move or run with a long easy stride. ✧ *n* **2** a long steady gait or stride. ▷ **HISTORY** Old Norse *hlaupa* to leap

lop-eared *adj* (of animals) having ears that droop.

lopsided *adj* greater in weight, height, or size on one side.

loquacious *adj* talkative. ▷ **HISTORY** Latin *loqui* to speak ▶ **loquacity** *n*

lord *n* **1** a person with power or authority over others, such as a monarch or master. **2** a male member of the nobility. **3** (in medieval Europe) a feudal superior. **4 my lord** a respectful form of address used to a judge, bishop, or nobleman. ✧ *vb* **5 lord it over someone** to act in a superior manner towards someone. ▷ **HISTORY** Old English *hlāford* bread keeper

Lord *n* **1** *Christianity* a title given to God or Jesus Christ. **2** *Brit* a title given to certain male peers. **3** *Brit* a title given to certain high officials and judges. ✧ *interj* **4** an exclamation of dismay or surprise: *Good Lord!*

Lord Chancellor *n Brit government* the cabinet minister who is head of the judiciary and Speaker of the House of Lords.

Lord Lieutenant *n* **1** (in Britain) the representative of the Crown in a county. **2** (formerly) the British viceroy in Ireland.

lordly *adj* **-lier, -liest 1** haughty or arrogant. **2** of or suitable to a lord. ▶ **lordliness** *n*

Lord Mayor *n* the mayor in the City of London, in certain other English boroughs, and in some Australian cities.

Lord Privy Seal *n* (in Britain) the senior cabinet minister without official duties.

Lords *n* **the Lords** short for **House of Lords**.

lordship *n* the position or authority of a lord.

Lordship *n* (preceded by *Your* or *His*) *Brit* a title used to address or refer to a bishop, a judge of the high court, or any peer except a duke.

Lord's Prayer *n* **the Lord's Prayer** the prayer taught by Jesus Christ to his disciples.

Lords Spiritual *pl n* (in Britain) the Anglican archbishops and senior bishops who are members of the House of Lords.

Lord's Supper *n* **the Lord's Supper** same as **Holy Communion**.

Lords Temporal *pl n* (in Britain) the peers other than bishops in their capacity as members of the House of Lords.

lore *n* collective knowledge or wisdom on a particular subject. ▷ **HISTORY** Old English *lār*

lorgnette (lor-**nyet**) *n* a pair of spectacles or opera glasses mounted on a long handle.
▷ **HISTORY** French, from *lorgner* to squint

lorikeet *n* a small brightly coloured Australian parrot.

lorry *n, pl* **-ries** *Brit & S African* a large motor vehicle for transporting heavy loads.
▷ **HISTORY** perhaps dialect *lurry* to pull

lose *vb* **losing, lost 1** to come to be without, through carelessness or by accident or theft. **2** to fail to keep or maintain: *to lose control.* **3** to suffer the loss of: *he will lose his redundancy money.* **4** to get rid of: *I've lost a stone this summer.* **5** to fail to get or make use of: *Lysenko never lost a chance to show his erudition.* **6** to be defeated in a fight or competition. **7** to fail to see, hear, or understand: *she lost sight of him.* **8** to waste: *so I'd lost a fortune.* **9** to go astray: *psychologists lose the trail.* **10** to allow to go astray or out of sight: *he lost, at the Gare de Lyon, a case with most of his early manuscripts.* **11** to cause the loss of: *I came in to have the gear attended to, which lost me a lap.* **12** to absorb or engross: *lost in thought.* **13** to die or cause the death of: *two lost as yacht sinks in storm.* **14** to outdistance or escape from: *there's some satisfaction in knowing that they've lost us.* **15** (of a timepiece) to run slow (by a specified amount).
▷ **HISTORY** Old English *losian* to perish

A B C D E F G H I J K L M N O P Q R S T U V W X Y Z

loser *n* **1** a person or thing that loses. **2** *Informal* a person or thing that seems destined to fail: *he's a bit of a loser.*

loss *n* **1** the act or an instance of losing. **2** the person, thing, or amount lost: *the only loss was a sleeping-bag.* **3** the disadvantage or deprivation resulting from losing: *a loss of sovereignty.* **4 at a loss a** uncertain what to do; bewildered. **b** with income less than outlay: *they cannot afford to run branches at a loss.* ▷ **HISTORY** Old English *lōsian* to be destroyed

loss leader *n* an article offered at a low price to attract customers.

lost *vb* **1** the past of **lose.** ✧ *adj* **2** unable to find one's way. **3** unable to be found or recovered. **4** confused or bewildered: *she seemed a bit lost.* **5** (sometimes foll. by *on*) not used, noticed, or understood by: *not that the propaganda value of the game was lost on the authorities.* **6** no longer possessed or existing: *lost credit.* **7** (foll. by *in*) engrossed (in): *he remained lost in his own thoughts.* **8** morally fallen: *a lost woman.* **9** damned: *a lost soul.*

lot *pron* **1 a lot** a great number or quantity: *not that there was a lot to tell; a lot of people.* ✧ *n* **2** a collection of things or people: *your lot have wasted enough time.* **3** destiny or fortune: *the refugees did not choose their lot.* **4** any object, such as a straw or slip of paper, drawn from others at random to make a selection or choice: *they could only be split by the drawing of lots; the casting by lots.* **5** the use of lots in making a choice: *chosen by lot.* **6** an item or set of items for sale in an auction. **7** *US, Canad, Austral & NZ* an area of land: *to the parking lot.* **8 a bad lot** an unpleasant or disreputable person. **9 cast** *or* **throw in one's lot with someone** to join with voluntarily and share the fortunes of someone. **10 the lot** the entire amount or number. ✧ *adv* **11** (preceded by *a*) *Informal* to a considerable extent, degree, or amount: *steroids are used a lot in weightlifting.* ✧ See also **lots.** ▷ **HISTORY** Old English *hlot*

loth (rhymes with **both**) *adj* same as **loath.**

lotion *n* a liquid preparation having a soothing, cleansing, or antiseptic action, applied to the skin. ▷ **HISTORY** Latin *lotio* a washing

lots *Informal* ✧ *pl n* **1** (often foll. by *of*) great numbers or quantities: *lots of friends; you can read lots into Nostradamus.* ✧ *adv* **2** a great deal.

lottery *n, pl* **-teries 1** a method of raising money by selling tickets by which a winner is selected at random. **2** a venture whose outcome is a matter of luck: *hospital treatment is a lottery.* ▷ **HISTORY** Middle Dutch *loterije*

lotto *n* **1** a game of chance similar to bingo. **2 Lotto** *Brit, NZ & S African* national lottery. ▷ **HISTORY** Italian

lotus *n* **1** (in Greek mythology) a fruit that induces dreamy forgetfulness in those who eat it. **2** any of several water lilies of tropical Africa and Asia, regarded as sacred. **3** a symbolic representation of such a plant. ▷ **HISTORY** Greek *lōtos*

lotus position *n* a seated cross-legged position with each foot on top of the opposite thigh, used in yoga and meditation.

loud *adj* **1** (of sound) relatively great in volume: *loud applause.* **2** making or able to make sounds of relatively great volume: *a loud voice.* **3** insistent and emphatic: *loud appeals.* **4** (of colours or patterns) harsh to look at. **5** noisy, vulgar, and offensive. ✧ *adv* **6** in a loud manner. **7 out loud** audibly. ▷ **HISTORY** Old English *hlud* ▶ **loudly** *adv* ▶ **loudness** *n*

loud-hailer *n* a portable loudspeaker with a built-in amplifier and microphone.

loudspeaker *n* a device for converting electrical signals into sounds.

lough *n Irish* **1** a lake. **2** a long narrow arm of the sea. ▷ **HISTORY** Irish *loch* lake

lounge *n* **1** a living room in a private house. **2** a communal room in a hotel, ship, or airport, used for waiting or relaxing in. **3** the act of lounging. ✧ *vb* **lounging, lounged 4** (often foll. by *about* or *around*) to sit or lie in a relaxed manner. **5** to pass time lazily or idly. ▷ **HISTORY** origin unknown

lounge suit *n* a man's suit for daytime wear.

lour *vb* same as **lower²**.

lourie (rhymes with **dowry**) *or* **loerie** *n* a type of African bird with either crimson or grey plumage. ▷ **HISTORY** Afrikaans, from Malay

louse *n* **1** (*pl* **lice**) a wingless blood-sucking insect that feeds off man and some animals. **2** (*pl* **louses**) *Slang* an unpleasant or dishonourable person. ▷ **HISTORY** Old English *lūs*

lousy *adj* **lousier, lousiest 1** *Slang* very mean or unpleasant. **2** *Slang* inferior or bad. **3** *Slang* ill or unwell. **4** infested with lice.

lout *n* a crude or oafish person; boor. ▷ **HISTORY** perhaps Old English *lūtan* to stoop ▶ **loutish** *adj*

louvre *or US* **louver** (**loo**-ver) *n* **a** any of a set of horizontal slats in a door or window, slanted to admit air but not rain. **b** the slats and frame supporting them. ▷ **HISTORY** Old French *lovier* ▶ **louvred** *or US* **louvered** *adj*

lovage *n* a European herb with greenish-white flowers. ▷ **HISTORY** Old French *luvesche,* from Latin *ligusticum,* literally: Ligurian (plant)

love *vb* **loving, loved 1** to have a great affection for a person or thing. **2** to have passionate desire for someone. **3** to like (to do something) very much. ✧ *n* **4** an intense emotion of affection towards a person or thing. **5** a deep feeling of sexual attraction. **6** wholehearted liking for or pleasure in something. **7** a beloved person: often used as an endearment. **8** *Brit informal* a commonplace term of address, not necessarily restricted to people one knows or has regard for. **9** (in tennis, squash, etc.) a score of zero. **10 fall in love** to become in love. **11 for love or money** in any circumstances. **12 in love** feeling a strong emotional and sexual attraction. **13 make love to a** to have sexual intercourse with. **b** *Now archaic* to court. ▷ **HISTORY** Old English *lufu* ▶ **lovable** *or* **loveable** *adj*

love affair *n* a romantic or sexual relationship between two people who are not married to each other.

lovebird *n* any of several small African parrots often kept as cage birds.
love child *n Euphemistic* a child whose parents have not been married to each other.
loveless *adj* without love: *a loveless marriage.*
love-lies-bleeding *n* a plant with drooping spikes of small red flowers.
love life *n* a person's romantic or sexual relationships.
lovelorn *adj* miserable because of unreturned love or unhappiness in love.
lovely *adj* **-lier, -liest 1** very attractive or beautiful. **2** highly pleasing or enjoyable: *thanks for a lovely evening.* ✧ *n, pl* **-lies 3** *Slang* an attractive woman: *curvaceous lovelies.* ▶ **loveliness** *n*
lovemaking *n* **1** sexual play and activity between lovers, including sexual intercourse. **2** *Archaic* courtship.
lover *n* **1** a person having a sexual relationship with another person outside marriage. **2** (*often pl*) either of the people involved in a love affair. **3** someone who loves a specified person or thing: *an animal-lover.*
loving *adj* feeling or showing love and affection. ▶ **lovingly** *adv*
low¹ *adj* **1** having a relatively small distance from base to top: *a low wall.* **2** of less than usual amount, degree, quality, or cost: *low score; low inflation.* **3** situated at a relatively short distance above the ground, sea level, or the horizon: *heavy weather with low driving cloud.* **4** (of numbers) small. **5** involving or containing a relatively small amount of something: *low-alcohol summer drinks.* **6** having little value or quality: *it sounds as if your self-confidence is low.* **7** coarse or vulgar: *that's a low blow.* **8** inferior in culture or status. **9** in a weakened physical or mental state. **10** with a hushed tone: *in a low, scared voice.* **11** low-necked: *a low evening gown.* **12** *Music* of or having a relatively low pitch. **13** (of latitudes) situated not far north or south of the equator. **14** having little or no money. **15** unfavourable: *he has a low opinion of Ford.* **16** deep: *a low bow.* **17** (of a gear) providing a relatively low speed. ✧ *adv* **18** in a low position, level, or degree: *the pilot flew low over the area.* **19** at a low pitch; deeply: *he's singing very low.* **20** cheaply: *the bank is having to buy high and sell low.* **21 lay low a** to make (someone) fall by a blow. **b** to overcome or destroy. **22 lie low** to keep or be concealed or quiet. ✧ *n* **23** a low position, level, or degree: *shares hit a new low.* **24** an area of low atmospheric pressure; depression. ▷ **HISTORY** Old Norse *lāgr* ▶ **lowness** *n*
low² *n* **1** Also: **lowing** the sound uttered by cattle; moo. ✧ *vb* **2** to make a mooing sound. ▷ **HISTORY** Old English *hlōwan*
lowbrow *Disparaging* ✧ *n* **1** a person with uncultivated or nonintellectual tastes. ✧ *adj* **2** of or for such a person.
Low Church *n* a section of the Church of England which stresses evangelical beliefs and practices. ▶ **Low-Church** *adj*
Low Countries *pl n* Belgium, Luxembourg, and the Netherlands.
low-down *Informal* ✧ *adj* **1** mean, underhand, and dishonest. ✧ *n* **lowdown 2 the lowdown** information.
lower¹ *adj* **1** being below one or more other things: *the lower branches.* **2** reduced in amount or value: *lower rates.* **3 Lower** *Geol* denoting the early part of a period or formation. ✧ *vb* **4** to cause or allow to move down: *she lowered her head.* **5** to behave in a way that damages one's self-respect: *she'd never lowered herself enough to make a call.* **6** to lessen or become less: *the cholesterol was lowered by medication.* **7** to make quieter or reduce the pitch of.
lower² *or* **lour** *vb* (of the sky or weather) to be overcast and menacing. ▷ **HISTORY** Middle English *louren* to scowl ▶ **lowering** *or* **louring** *adj*
lower case *n* (in printing) small letters, as opposed to capital letters. ▶ **lower-case** *adj*
lower class *n* the class with the lowest position in society. ▶ **lower-class** *adj*
lower house *n* one of the houses of a parliament that has two chambers: usually the larger and more representative.
lowest common denominator *n Maths* the smallest integer or polynomial that is exactly divisible by each denominator of a set of fractions.
lowest common multiple *n Maths* the smallest number or quantity that is exactly divisible by each member of a set of numbers or quantities.
low frequency *n* any radio frequency lying between 300 and 30 kilohertz.
Low German *n* a language of N Germany, spoken in rural areas.
low-key *or* **low-keyed** *adj* **1** restrained or subdued. **2** having a low intensity or tone.
lowland *n* **1** relatively low ground. **2** (*often pl*) a low generally flat region. ✧ *adj* **3** of a lowland or lowlands. ▶ **lowlander** *n*
Lowland *adj* of the Lowlands or the dialects of English spoken there. ▶ **Lowlander** *n*
lowly *adj* **-lier, -liest 1** humble in position or status. **2** simple and unpretentious. ▶ **lowliness** *n*
Low Mass *n* a simplified form of Mass that is spoken rather than sung.
low profile *n* a deliberate shunning of publicity: *he kept a low profile.* ▶ **low-profile** *adj*
low-spirited *adj* depressed or dejected.
low tide *n* the tide at its lowest level or the time at which it reaches this.
low water *n* **1** low tide. **2** the lowest level that a stretch of water reaches.
loyal *adj* **1** faithful to one's friends, country, or government. **2** of or expressing loyalty: *the loyal toast.* ▷ **HISTORY** Latin *legalis* legal ▶ **loyally** *adv*
loyalist *n* a patriotic supporter of the sovereign or government. ▶ **loyalism** *n*
Loyalist *n* (in Northern Ireland) any of the Protestants wishing to retain Ulster's link with Britain.
loyalty *n, pl* **-ties 1** the quality of being loyal. **2** a feeling of friendship or duty towards someone or something.

a b c d e f g h i j k l m n o p q r s t u v w x y z

loyalty card *n* a swipe card issued by a supermarket or chain store to a customer, used to record credit points awarded for money spent in the store.

lozenge *n* **1** *Med* a medicated tablet held in the mouth until it has dissolved. **2** *Geom* a rhombus. ▷ **HISTORY** Old French *losange*

LP *n* a gramophone record of 12 inches in diameter, which holds about 20 or 25 minutes of sound on each side. ▷ **HISTORY** shortened from *long player*

L-plate *n Brit & Austral* a red 'L' on a white square attached to a motor vehicle to indicate that the driver is a learner.

Lr *Chem* lawrencium.

LSD *n* lysergic acid diethylamide; an illegal hallucinogenic drug.

Lt Lieutenant.

Ltd *Brit* Limited (Liability).

Lu *Chem* lutetium.

LUB *Maths* least upper bound.

lubricant *n* a lubricating substance, such as oil.

lubricate (**loo**-brik-ate) *vb* **-cating, -cated 1** to cover with an oily substance to lessen friction. **2** to make greasy, slippery, or smooth. ▷ **HISTORY** Latin *lubricare* to make slippery ▶ **lubrication** *n*

lubricious (loo-**brish**-uss) *adj Formal or literary* lewd. ▷ **HISTORY** Latin *lubricus* slippery

lucerne *n Brit & Austral* same as **alfalfa**.

lucid *adj* **1** clear and easily understood. **2** capable of clear thought, particularly between periods of insanity or delirium. **3** shining or glowing. ▷ **HISTORY** Latin *lucidus* full of light ▶ **lucidity** *n* ▶ **lucidly** *adv*

Lucifer *n* Satan. ▷ **HISTORY** Latin: light-bearer, from *lux* light + *ferre* to bear

luck *n* **1** events that are subject to chance; fortune, good or bad. **2** success or good fortune. **3 down on one's luck** lacking good fortune to the extent of suffering hardship. **4 no such luck** *Informal* unfortunately not. **5 try one's luck** to attempt something that is uncertain. ▷ **HISTORY** Middle Dutch *luc*

luckless *adj* unfortunate or unlucky.

lucky *adj* **luckier, luckiest 1** having or bringing good fortune. **2** happening by chance, esp. as desired. ▶ **luckily** *adv*

lucky dip *n Brit, Austral, & NZ* a box filled with sawdust containing small prizes for which children search.

lucrative *adj* profitable.

lucre (**loo**-ker) *n Usually facetious* money or wealth: *filthy lucre.* ▷ **HISTORY** Latin *lucrum* gain

Luddite *n Brit history* **1** any of the textile workers opposed to mechanization, who organized machine-breaking between 1811 and 1816. **2** any opponent of industrial change or innovation. ✧ *adj* **3** of the Luddites. ▷ **HISTORY** after Ned *Ludd,* who destroyed machinery

luderick *n* an Australian fish, usu. black or dark brown in colour.

ludicrous *adj* absurd or ridiculous. ▷ **HISTORY** Latin *ludus* game ▶ **ludicrously** *adv*

ludo *n Brit & Austral* a simple board game in which players move counters forward by throwing dice. ▷ **HISTORY** Latin: I play

luff *vb* **1** *Naut* to sail (a ship) into the wind. **2** to move the jib of a crane in order to shift a load. ▷ **HISTORY** Old French *lof*

lug[1] *vb* **lugging, lugged** to carry or drag with great effort. ▷ **HISTORY** probably from Old Norse

lug[2] *n* **1** a projecting piece by which something is connected, supported, or lifted. **2** *Informal & Scot* an ear. ▷ **HISTORY** Scots: ear

luggage *n* suitcases, trunks, and bags. ▷ **HISTORY** perhaps LUG[1] + *-age*, as in *baggage*

lugger *n Naut* a small working boat with an oblong sail. ▷ **HISTORY** origin unknown

lugubrious (loo-**goo**-bree-uss) *adj* mournful or gloomy. ▷ **HISTORY** Latin *lugere* to grieve

lugworm *n* a large worm which lives in burrows on sandy shores and is often used as bait by fishermen. ▷ **HISTORY** origin unknown

lukewarm *adj* **1** (of a liquid) moderately warm; tepid. **2** lacking enthusiasm or conviction. ▷ **HISTORY** probably from Old English *hlēow* warm

lull *vb* **1** to soothe (a person or animal) by soft sounds or motions. **2** to calm (fears or suspicions) by deception. ✧ *n* **3** a short period of calm. ▷ **HISTORY** perhaps imitative of crooning sounds

lullaby *n, pl* **-bies** a quiet song to lull a child to sleep. ▷ **HISTORY** perhaps a blend of *lull* + *goodbye*

lumbago (lum-**bay**-go) *n* pain in the lower back; low backache. ▷ **HISTORY** Latin *lumbus* loin

lumbar *adj* relating to the lower back. ▷ **HISTORY** Latin *lumbus* loin

lumbar puncture *n Med* insertion of a hollow needle into the lower spinal cord to withdraw fluid for diagnosis.

lumber[1] *n* **1** *Brit* unwanted disused household articles. **2** *Chiefly US & Canad* logs; sawn timber. ✧ *vb* **3** *Informal* to burden with something unpleasant: *somebody gets lumbered with the extra costs.* **4** to fill up with useless household articles. **5** *Chiefly US & Canad* to convert trees into marketable timber. ▷ **HISTORY** perhaps from LUMBER[2]

lumber[2] *vb* to move awkwardly and heavily. ▷ **HISTORY** Middle English *lomeren* ▶ **lumbering** *adj*

lumberjack *n* (esp. in North America) a person who fells trees and prepares the timber for transport.

lumen *n, pl* **-mens** *or* **-mina** *Anat* a passage, duct, or cavity in a tubular organ.

luminary *n, pl* **-naries 1 a** a famous person. **b** an expert in a particular subject. **2** *Literary* something, such as the sun or moon, that gives off light.

luminescence *n Physics* the emission of light at low temperatures by any process other than burning. ▶ **luminescent** *adj*

luminous *adj* **1** reflecting or giving off light: *luminous colours.* **2** *Not in technical use* luminescent: *luminous sparklers.* **3** enlightening or wise. ▷ **HISTORY** Latin *lumen* light ▶ **luminosity** *n*

lump[1] *n* **1** a small solid mass without definite shape. **2** *Pathol* any small swelling or tumour. **3** *Informal* an awkward, heavy, or stupid person. **4 a lump in one's throat** a tight dry feeling in one's throat, usually caused by great emotion. **5 the lump** *Brit* self-employed workers in the building trade considered collectively. ✧ *adj* **6** in the form of a lump or lumps: *lump sugar.* ✧ *vb* **7** (often foll. by *together*) to consider as a single group, often without justification. **8** to grow into lumps or become lumpy. ▷ **HISTORY** probably related to Scandinavian dialect: block

lump[2] *vb* **lump it** *Informal* to accept something irrespective of personal preference: *if you don't like it, you can lump it.* ▷ **HISTORY** origin unknown

lumpectomy *n, pl* **-mies** surgical removal of a tumour in a breast. ▷ **HISTORY** *lump* + Greek *tomē* a cutting

lumpish *adj* stupid, clumsy, or heavy. ▶ **lumpishness** *n*

lump sum *n* a relatively large sum of money, paid at one time.

lumpy *adj* **lumpier, lumpiest** full of or having lumps. ▶ **lumpiness** *n*

lunacy *n, pl* **-cies 1** foolishness. **2** (formerly) any severe mental illness.

lunar *adj* relating to the moon: *lunar eclipse.* ▷ **HISTORY** Latin *luna* the moon

lunatic *adj* **1** foolish; eccentric. **2** *Archaic* insane. ✧ *n* **3** a foolish or annoying person. **4** *Archaic* a person who is insane. ▷ **HISTORY** Latin *luna* moon

lunatic asylum *n Offensive* a home or hospital for the mentally ill.

lunch *n* **1** a meal eaten during the middle of the day. ✧ *vb* **2** to eat lunch. ▷ **HISTORY** shortened from *luncheon*

luncheon *n* a lunch, often a formal one. ▷ **HISTORY** probably variant of *nuncheon,* from Middle English *none* noon + *schench* drink

luncheon meat *n* a ground mixture of meat (often pork) and cereal, usually tinned.

luncheon voucher *n Brit* a voucher for a specified amount issued to employees and accepted by some restaurants as payment for food.

lung *n* the part of the body that allows an animal or bird to breathe air. Humans have two lungs, contained within the chest cavity. ▷ **HISTORY** Old English *lungen*

lunge *n* **1** a sudden forward motion. **2** *Fencing* a thrust made by advancing the front foot and straightening the back leg. ✧ *vb* **lunging, lunged 3** to move with a lunge. **4** *Fencing* to make a lunge. ▷ **HISTORY** French *allonger* to stretch out (one's arm)

lungfish *n, pl* **-fish** *or* **-fishes** a freshwater fish with an air-breathing lung.

lupin *n* a garden plant with large spikes of brightly coloured flowers and flattened pods. ▷ **HISTORY** Latin *lupinus* wolfish; from the belief that it ravenously exhausted the soil

lupine *adj* of or like a wolf. ▷ **HISTORY** Latin *lupus* wolf

lupus *n* an ulcerous skin disease. ▷ **HISTORY** Latin: wolf; so called because it rapidly eats away the affected part

> **☑ WORD TIP**
> In current usage the word *lupus* alone is generally understood to signify *lupus vulgaris. Lupus erythematosus* is normally referred to in full or by the abbreviation *LE.*

lurch[1] *vb* **1** to lean or tilt suddenly to one side. **2** to stagger. ✧ *n* **3** a lurching movement. ▷ **HISTORY** origin unknown

lurch[2] *n* **leave someone in the lurch** to abandon someone in trouble. ▷ **HISTORY** French *lourche,* a game similar to backgammon

lure *vb* **luring, lured 1** (sometimes foll. by *away* or *into*) to tempt or attract by the promise of reward. ✧ *n* **2** a person or thing that lures. **3** *Angling* a brightly coloured artificial spinning bait. **4** *Falconry* a feathered decoy to which small pieces of meat can be attached. ▷ **HISTORY** Old French *loirre* falconer's lure

lurid *adj* **1** vivid in shocking detail; sensational: *magazines whose lurid covers sickened him.* **2** glaring in colour: *a lurid red tartan.* **3** horrible in savagery or violence: *reporting lurid crimes.* ▷ **HISTORY** Latin *luridus* pale yellow ▶ **luridly** *adv*

lurk *vb* **1** to move stealthily or be concealed, esp. for evil purposes. **2** to be present in an unobtrusive way; be latent. ▷ **HISTORY** probably frequentative of *lour*

luscious (**lush**-uss) *adj* **1** extremely pleasurable to taste or smell. **2** very attractive. ▷ **HISTORY** perhaps short for *delicious*

lush[1] *adj* **1** (of vegetation) growing thickly and healthily. **2** luxurious, elaborate, or opulent. ▷ **HISTORY** Latin *laxus* loose

lush[2] *n Slang* an alcoholic. ▷ **HISTORY** origin unknown

lust *n* **1** a strong sexual desire. **2** a strong desire or drive: *a lust for power.* ✧ *vb* **3** (often foll. by *after* or *for*) to have a passionate desire (for). ▷ **HISTORY** Old English ▶ **lustful** *adj* ▶ **lustfully** *adv*

lustre *or US* **luster** *n* **1** soft shining light reflected from a surface; sheen. **2** great splendour or glory. **3** a shiny metallic surface on some pottery and porcelain. ▷ **HISTORY** Latin *lustrare* to make bright ▶ **lustrous** *adj*

lusty *adj* **lustier, lustiest 1** healthy and full of strength and energy. **2** strong or invigorating. ▶ **lustily** *adv* ▶ **lustiness** *n*

lute *n* an ancient plucked stringed instrument with a long fingerboard and a body shaped like a half pear. ▷ **HISTORY** Arabic *al 'ūd,* literally: the wood

lutetium (loo-**tee**-shee-um) *n Chem* a silvery-white metallic element of the lanthanide series. Symbol: Lu. ▷ **HISTORY** *Lutetia,* ancient name of Paris

Lutheran *n* **1** a follower of Martin Luther (1483–1546), German leader of the Reformation, or a member of a Lutheran Church. ✧ *adj* **2** of or relating to Luther, his doctrines, or any of the

Churches that follow these doctrines.
▸ **Lutheranism** *n*

luvvie *or* **luvvy** *n, pl* **-vies** *Facetious* a person who is involved in acting or the theatre.

lux *n, pl* **lux** the SI unit of illumination.
▷ HISTORY Latin: light

Luxembourger *n* a person from Luxembourg.

luxuriant *adj* **1** rich and abundant; lush: *luxuriant foliage.* **2** very elaborate or ornate. ▷ HISTORY Latin *luxuriare* to abound to excess ▸ **luxuriance** *n*
▸ **luxuriantly** *adv*

> **WORD TIP**
> See at **luxurious.**

luxuriate *vb* **-ating, -ated 1 luxuriate in** to take self-indulgent pleasure in; revel in. **2** to flourish profusely.

luxurious *adj* **1** characterized by luxury. **2** enjoying or devoted to luxury. ▸ **luxuriously** *adv*

> **WORD TIP**
> *Luxurious* is sometimes wrongly used where *luxuriant* is meant: *he had a luxuriant* (not *luxurious) moustache; the walls were covered with a luxuriant growth of wisteria.*

luxury *n, pl* **-ries 1** indulgence in rich and sumptuous living. **2** something considered an indulgence rather than a necessity. ✧ *adj* **3** relating to, indicating, or supplying luxury: *a luxury hotel.*
▷ HISTORY Latin *luxuria* excess

LV (in Britain) luncheon voucher.

lx lux.

lyceum *n* (now chiefly in the names of buildings) a public building for events such as concerts and lectures. ▷ HISTORY Latin: a school in ancient Athens

lychee (lie-**chee**) *n* a Chinese fruit with a whitish juicy pulp. ▷ HISTORY Cantonese *lai chi*

lych gate *or* **lich gate** *n* a roofed gate to a churchyard, formerly used as a temporary shelter for a coffin. ▷ HISTORY Old English *līc* corpse

Lycra *n Trademark* a synthetic elastic fabric used for tight-fitting garments, such as swimsuits.

lye *n* **1** a caustic solution obtained from wood ash. **2** a concentrated solution of sodium hydroxide or potassium hydroxide. ▷ HISTORY Old English *lēag*

lying *vb* the present participle of **lie**[1], **lie**[2].

lying-in *n, pl* **lyings-in** *Old-fashioned* confinement in childbirth.

lymph *n* the almost colourless body fluid containing chiefly white blood cells.
▷ HISTORY Latin *lympha* water ▸ **lymphatic** *adj*

lymphatic system *n* a network of fine vessels by which lymph circulates throughout the body.

lymph node *n* any of many bean-shaped masses of tissue in the lymphatic system that help to protect against infection.

lymphocyte *n* a type of white blood cell.
▷ HISTORY *lymph* + Greek *kutos* vessel

lynch *vb* (of a mob) to kill (a person) for some supposed offence without a trial. ▷ HISTORY after Captain William *Lynch* of Virginia, US ▸ **lynching** *n*

lynchpin *n* same as **linchpin.**

lynx *n, pl* **lynxes** *or* **lynx** a mammal of the cat family, with grey-brown mottled fur, tufted ears, and a short tail. ▷ HISTORY Greek *lunx*

lyre *n* an ancient Greek U-shaped stringed instrument, similar to a harp but plucked with a plectrum. ▷ HISTORY Greek *lura*

lyrebird *n* an Australian bird, the male of which spreads its tail into the shape of a lyre during courtship.

lyric *adj* **1** (of poetry) **a** expressing the writer's personal feelings. **b** having the form and manner of a song. **2** of or relating to such poetry. **3** (of a singing voice) light and melodic. ✧ *n* **4** a short poem of songlike quality. **5 lyrics** the words of a popular song: *Cole invests all her lyrics with a touch of drama.* ▷ HISTORY Greek *lura* lyre ▸ **lyrically** *adv*

lyrical *adj* **1** same as **lyric** (senses 1, 2). **2** enthusiastic or effusive.

lyricism *n* **1** the quality or style of lyric poetry. **2** emotional outpouring.

lyricist *n* a person who writes the words for a song, opera, or musical.

lysozyme *n Biochem* an enzyme that occurs in tears, some body tissues, and egg whites.

A B C D E F G H I J K L M N O P Q R S T U V W X Y Z

M m

m 1 metre(s). **2** mile(s). **3** milli-. **4** million. **5** minute(s).

M 1 mach. **2** *Currency* mark(s). **3** medium. **4** mega-. **5** (in Britain) motorway. **6** the Roman numeral for 1000.

m. 1 male. **2** married. **3** masculine. **4** meridian. **5** month.

M. 1 Majesty. **2** Master. **3** (in titles) Member. **4** (*pl* **MM.** *or* **MM**) Monsieur.

ma *n* an informal word for mother.

MA 1 Massachusetts. **2** Master of Arts.

ma'am *n* short for **madam** (sense 1).

maas (**mahs**) *n S African* thick soured milk. ▷ HISTORY Nguni (language group of southern Africa) *amasi* milk

Mabo decision *n Austral Law* the 1992 decision of the High Court of Australia that abolished the legal concept of *terra nullius*.

mac *or* **mack** *n Brit informal* a mackintosh.

macabre (mak-**kahb**-ra) *adj* strange and horrible; gruesome. ▷ HISTORY French

macadam *n* a road surface made of compressed layers of small broken stones, esp. one bound together with tar or asphalt. ▷ HISTORY after John *McAdam*, engineer

macadamia (mak-a-**day**-mee-a) *n* an Australian tree with edible nuts. ▷ HISTORY after John *Macadam*, Australian chemist

macadamize *or* **-ise** *vb* **-izing, -ized** *or* **-ising, -ised** to pave a road with macadam.

macaque (mak-**kahk**) *n* any of various Asian and African monkeys with cheek pouches and either a short tail or no tail. ▷ HISTORY W African *makaku*

macaroni *n, pl* **-nis** *or* **-nies 1** pasta tubes made from wheat flour. **2** (in 18th-century Britain) a man who was excessively concerned with his clothes and appearance. ▷ HISTORY Italian (dialect) *maccarone*

macaroon *n* a sweet biscuit made of ground almonds. ▷ HISTORY French *macaron*

macaw *n* a large tropical American parrot with a long tail and brightly coloured feathers. ▷ HISTORY Portuguese *macau*

mace[1] *n* **1** a ceremonial staff carried by certain officials. **2** a club with a spiked metal head used in the Middle Ages. ▷ HISTORY probably Vulgar Latin *mattea*

mace[2] *n* a spice made from the dried outer casing of the nutmeg. ▷ HISTORY Latin *macir*

macerate (**mass**-er-ate) *vb* **-ating, -ated** to soften or be softened by soaking. ▷ HISTORY Latin *macerare* to soften ▶ **macerated** *adj* ▶ **maceration** *n*

Mach (**mak**) *n* a unit for expressing the speed of an aircraft as a multiple of the speed of sound: *an airliner capable of cruising at Mach 2*. See also **Mach number**.

machete (mash-**ett**-ee) *n* a broad heavy knife used for cutting or as a weapon. ▷ HISTORY Spanish

Machiavellian (mak-ee-a-**vel**-yan) *adj* cleverly deceitful and unscrupulous. ▷ HISTORY after *Machiavelli*, political philosopher ▶ **Machiavellianism** *n*

machinations (mak-in-**nay**-shunz) *pl n* cunning schemes or plots to gain power or harm an opponent: *the machinations of a power-hungry institution*. ▷ HISTORY Latin *machinari* to plan

machine *n* **1** an assembly of components arranged so as to perform a particular task and usually powered by electricity. **2** a vehicle, such as a car or aircraft. **3** a system within an organization that controls activities and policies: *the party machine*. ✧ *vb* **-chining, -chined 4** to shape, cut, or make something using a machine. ▷ HISTORY Latin *machina* ▶ **machinable** *adj*

machine code *or* **language** *n* instructions for a computer in binary or hexadecimal code that require no conversion or translation by the computer.

machine gun *n* **1** a rapid-firing automatic gun, using small-arms ammunition. ✧ *vb* **machine-gun, -gunning, -gunned 2** to shoot or fire at with a machine gun.

machine-readable *adj* in a form suitable for processing by a computer.

machinery *n, pl* **-eries 1** machines, machine parts, or machine systems collectively. **2** the mechanism of a machine. **3** the organization and procedures by which a system functions: *the machinery of international politics*.

machine shop *n* a workshop in which machine tools are operated.

machine tool *n* a power-driven machine, such as a lathe, for cutting and shaping metal, wood, or plastic.

machinist *n* **1** a person who operates machines to cut or process materials. **2** a maker or repairer of machines.

machismo (mak-**izz**-moh) *n* strong or exaggerated masculinity. ▷ HISTORY Spanish *macho* male

Mach number (**mak**) *n* the ratio of the speed of a body in a particular medium to the speed of sound in that medium. ▷ HISTORY after Ernst *Mach*, physicist

macho (**match**-oh) *adj* **1** strongly or exaggeratedly masculine. ✧ *n* **2** strong or exaggerated masculinity. ▷ HISTORY from *machismo*

mack *n Brit informal* same as **mac**.

mackerel *n, pl* **-rel** *or* **-rels** an edible sea fish. ▷ HISTORY Old French *maquerel*

mackintosh *or* **macintosh** *n Brit* **1** a raincoat made of rubberized cloth. **2** any raincoat. ▷ HISTORY after Charles *Macintosh*, who invented it

macramé (mak-**rah**-mee) *n* **1** the art of knotting and weaving coarse thread into patterns. **2** ornaments made in this way. ▷ HISTORY Turkish *makrama* towel

macro- *or before a vowel* **macr-** *combining form* large, long, or great: *macroscopic.* ▷ **HISTORY** Greek *makros*

macrobiotics *n* a dietary system that advocates whole grains and vegetables grown without chemical additives. ▷ **HISTORY** Greek *makros* long + *biotos* life ▸ **macrobiotic** *adj*

macrocarpa *n* a large Californian coniferous tree, used in New Zealand and elsewhere as a windbreak on farms and for rough timber. ▷ **HISTORY** Greek *makros* large + *karpos* fruit

macrocosm *n* a complex structure, such as the universe or society, regarded as a whole. ▷ **HISTORY** Greek *makros kosmos* great world

macroeconomics *n* the branch of economics concerned with the relationships between aggregates, such as consumption and investment, in a large economic system. ▸ **macroeconomic** *adj*

macromolecule *n* any very large molecule, such as a protein or synthetic polymer.

macron *n* a mark (¯) placed over a letter to represent a long vowel. ▷ **HISTORY** Greek *makros* long

macroscopic *adj* **1** large enough to be visible to the naked eye. **2** concerned with large units. ▷ **HISTORY** Greek *makros* large + *skopein* to look at

macula (**mak**-kew-la) *n, pl* **-ulae** (-yew-lee) *Anat* a small spot or area of distinct colour, such as a freckle. ▷ **HISTORY** Latin

MAD *Mil* mutually assured destruction: a theory of nuclear deterrence whereby each side in a conflict has the capacity to destroy the other in retaliation for a nuclear attack.

mad *adj* **madder, maddest 1** mentally deranged; insane. **2** extremely foolish; senseless: *that was a mad thing to do!* **3** *Informal* angry or annoyed: *he's mad at her for the unjust accusation.* **4** extremely excited or confused: *a mad rush.* **5** (of animals) **a** unusually ferocious: *a mad bear.* **b** afflicted with rabies. **6 mad about, on** *or* **over** wildly enthusiastic about or fond of. **7 like mad** *Informal* with great energy, enthusiasm, or haste. ▷ **HISTORY** Old English *gemǣded* made insane ▸ **madness** *n*

madam *n, pl* **madams 1** (*pl* **mesdames**) a polite term of address for a woman. **2** a woman who runs a brothel. **3** *Brit & Austral informal* a spoilt or pert girl: *she is a thoroughly precocious little madam if ever there was one.* ▷ **HISTORY** Old French *ma dame* my lady

madame (mad-**dam**) *n, pl* **mesdames** (may-**dam**) a French form of address equivalent to *Mrs.*

madcap *adj* **1** impulsive, reckless, or unlikely to succeed: *a madcap expansion of council bureaucracy.* ✧ *n* **2** an impulsive or reckless person.

mad cow disease *n Informal* same as **BSE**.

madden *vb* to make or become mad or angry. ▸ **maddening** *adj*

madder *n* **1** a plant with small yellow flowers and a red fleshy root. **2** a dark reddish-purple dye formerly obtained from its root. **3** an artificial pigment of this colour. ▷ **HISTORY** Old English *mædere*

made *vb* **1** the past of **make**. ✧ *adj* **2** produced or shaped as specified: *handmade.* **3 get** *or* **have it made** *Informal* to be assured of success.

Madeira (mad-**deer**-a) *n* a fortified white wine from Madeira, an island in the N Atlantic.

Madeira cake *n* a type of rich sponge cake.

mademoiselle (mad-mwah-**zel**) *n, pl* **mesdemoiselles** (maid-mwah-**zel**) **1** a French form of address equivalent to *Miss.* **2** a French teacher or governess.

made-up *adj* **1** invented or fictitious. **2** wearing make-up. **3** put together: *some made-up carpet shampoo.* **4** (of a road) surfaced with tarmac or concrete.

madhouse *n Informal* **1** a state of uproar or confusion. **2** *Old-fashioned* a mental hospital.

madly *adv* **1** in an insane or foolish manner. **2** with great speed and energy. **3** *Informal* extremely or excessively: *she was madly in love with him.*

madman *or fem* **madwoman** *n, pl* **-men** *or* **-women** a person who is insane.

Madonna *n* **1** *Chiefly RC Church* the Virgin Mary. **2** a picture or statue of the Virgin Mary. ▷ **HISTORY** Italian: my lady

madrigal *n* a type of 16th- or 17th-century part song for unaccompanied voices. ▷ **HISTORY** Medieval Latin *matricale* primitive ▸ **madrigalist** *n*

maelstrom (**male**-strom) *n* **1** a large powerful whirlpool. **2** any confused, violent, and destructive turmoil: *a maelstrom of adulterous passion.* ▷ **HISTORY** Old Dutch *malen* to whirl round + *stroom* stream

maenad (**mean**-ad) *n* **1** *Classical history* a female disciple of Dionysus, the Greek god of wine. **2** a frenzied woman. ▷ **HISTORY** Greek *mainas* madwoman

maestro (**my**-stroh) *n, pl* **-tri** *or* **-tros 1** a distinguished musician or conductor. **2** any master of an art: *Milan's maestro of minimalism.* ▷ **HISTORY** Italian: master

mae west *n Slang* an inflatable life jacket. ▷ **HISTORY** after *Mae West,* actress renowned for her large bust

Mafia *n* **the Mafia** a secret criminal organization founded in Sicily, and carried to the US by Italian immigrants. ▷ **HISTORY** Sicilian dialect, literally: hostility to the law

mafioso (maf-fee-**oh**-so) *n, pl* **-sos** *or* **-si** (-see) a member of the Mafia.

mag *n* short for **magazine** (sense 1).

magazine *n* **1** a periodic paperback publication containing written pieces and illustrations. **2** a television or radio programme made up of short nonfictional items. **3** a metal case holding several cartridges used in some firearms. **4** a rack for automatically feeding slides through a projector. **5** a place for storing weapons, explosives, or military equipment. ▷ **HISTORY** Arabic *makhāzin* storehouses

magenta (maj-**jen**-ta) *adj* deep purplish-red. ▷ **HISTORY** after *Magenta,* Italy

maggot *n* the limbless larva of various insects, esp. the housefly and blowfly. ▷ **HISTORY** earlier *mathek* ▶ **maggoty** *adj*

magi (**maje**-eye) *pl n, sing* **magus** (**may**-guss) **1** See **magus**. **2 the three Magi** *Christianity* the wise men from the East who came to worship the infant Jesus (Matthew 2:1–12). ▷ **HISTORY** see MAGUS

magic *n* **1** the supposed power to make things happen by using supernatural means. **2** tricks done to entertain; conjuring. **3** any mysterious or extraordinary quality or power: *the magic of Placido Domingo.* **4 like magic** very quickly. ✧ *adj also* **magical 5** of magic. **6** possessing or considered to possess mysterious powers. **7** unaccountably enchanting. **8** *Informal* wonderful or marvellous. ✧ *vb* **-icking, -icked 9** to transform or produce as if by magic: *he had magicked up a gourmet meal at a moment's notice.* ▷ **HISTORY** Greek *magikē* witchcraft ▶ **magically** *adv*

magician *n* **1** a conjuror. **2** a person with magic powers.

magic lantern *n* an early type of slide projector.

Maginot line (**mazh**-in-oh) *n History* a line of fortifications built by France to defend its border with Germany prior to World War II. ▷ **HISTORY** after André *Maginot*, French minister of war when fortifications were begun in 1929

magisterial *adj* **1** commanding and authoritative. **2** of a magistrate. ▷ **HISTORY** Latin *magister* master ▶ **magisterially** *adv*

magistracy *n, pl* **-cies 1** the office or function of a magistrate. **2** magistrates collectively.

magistrate *n* **1** a public officer concerned with the administration of law. **2** same as **justice of the peace**. **3** *Austral & NZ* a former name for **district court judge**. ▷ **HISTORY** Latin *magister* master

magistrates' court *n Law* a court that deals with minor crimes, certain civil actions, and preliminary hearings.

magma *n, pl* **-mas** *or* **-mata** hot molten rock within the earth's crust which sometimes finds its way to the surface, where it solidifies to form igneous rock. ▷ **HISTORY** Greek: salve made by kneading

Magna Carta *n English history* the charter granted by King John at Runnymede in 1215, recognizing the rights and privileges of the barons, church, and freemen. ▷ **HISTORY** Medieval Latin: great charter

magnanimous *adj* generous and forgiving, esp. towards a defeated enemy. ▷ **HISTORY** Latin *magnanimus* great-souled ▶ **magnanimity** *n* ▶ **magnanimously** *adv*

magnate *n* an influential or wealthy person, esp. in industry. ▷ **HISTORY** Late Latin *magnates* great men

magnesia *n* a white tasteless substance used as an antacid and laxative; magnesium oxide. ▷ **HISTORY** Greek *Magnēsia* of *Magnēs,* ancient mineral-rich region

magnesium *n Chem* a light silvery-white metallic element that burns with a very bright white flame. Symbol: Mg. ▷ **HISTORY** from *magnesia*

magnesium sulphate *n Chem* a colourless crystalline compound used in medicine, fertilizers and manufacturing.

magnet *n* **1** a piece of iron, steel, or lodestone that has the property of attracting iron to it. **2** a person or thing that exerts a great attraction: *these woods are a magnet for bird watchers.* ▷ **HISTORY** Greek *magnēs*

magnetic *adj* **1** of, producing, or operated by means of magnetism. **2** of or like a magnet. **3** capable of being made into a magnet. **4** exerting a powerful attraction: *political leaders of magnetic appeal.* ▶ **magnetically** *adv*

magnetic anomaly *n Geog* a disturbance in the strength of the earth's magnetic field owing to the magnetism of rocks in the crust.

magnetic disk *n* a computer storage disk.

magnetic field *n* an area around a magnet in which its power of attraction is felt.

magnetic field line *n Physics* one of many lines describing the structure of a magnetic field in three dimensions. Field lines converge where the magnetic force is strong, near the poles, and spread out where it is weak.

magnetic needle *n* a slender magnetized rod used in certain instruments, such as the magnetic compass, for indicating the direction of a magnetic field.

magnetic north *n* the direction in which a compass needle points, at an angle from the direction of true (geographic) north.

magnetic pole *n* either of two variable points on the earth's surface towards which a magnetic needle points.

magnetic storm *n* a sudden severe disturbance of the earth's magnetic field, caused by emission of charged particles from the sun.

magnetic tape *n* a long plastic strip coated with a magnetic substance, used to record sound or video signals or to store information in computers.

magnetism *n* **1** the property of attraction displayed by magnets. **2** powerful personal charm. **3** the branch of physics concerned with magnetic phenomena.

magnetite *n* a black magnetizable mineral that is an important source of iron.

magnetize *or* **-ise** *vb* **-izing, -ized** *or* **-ising, -ised** **1** to make a substance or object magnetic. **2** to attract strongly: *he was magnetized by her smile.* ▶ **magnetizable** *or* **-isable** *adj* ▶ **magnetization** *or* **-isation** *n*

magneto (mag-**nee**-toe) *n, pl* **-tos** a small electric generator in which the magnetic field is produced by a permanent magnet, esp. one used to provide the spark in an internal-combustion engine. ▷ **HISTORY** short for *magnetoelectric generator*

magnetron *n* an electronic valve used with a magnetic field to generate microwave oscillations, used. esp. in radar. ▷ **HISTORY** *magnet* + *electron*

Magnificat *n Christianity* the hymn of the Virgin Mary (Luke 1:46–55), used as a canticle. ▷ **HISTORY** from its opening word

A B C D E F G H I J K L M N O P Q R S T U V W X Y Z

magnification *n* **1** the act of magnifying or the state of being magnified. **2** the degree to which something is magnified. **3** a magnified copy of something.

magnificent *adj* **1** splendid or impressive in appearance. **2** superb or very fine: *a magnificent performance.* ▷ **HISTORY** Latin *magnificus* great in deeds ▶ **magnificence** *n* ▶ **magnificently** *adv*

magnify *vb* **-fies, -fying, -fied 1** to make something look bigger than it really is, for instance by using a lens or microscope. **2** to make something seem more important than it really is; exaggerate: *you are magnifying the problem out of all proportion.* **3** to make something sound louder than it really is: *the stethoscope magnifies internal body sounds.* **4** *Archaic* to glorify or praise. ▷ **HISTORY** Latin *magnificare* to praise ▶ **magnified** *adj*

magnifying glass *or* **magnifier** *n* a convex lens used to produce an enlarged image of an object.

magnitude *n* **1** relative importance: *an evil of the first magnitude.* **2** relative size or extent. **3** *Astron* the apparent brightness of a celestial body expressed on a numerical scale on which bright stars have a low value. ▷ **HISTORY** Latin *magnitudo* size

magnolia *n* an Asian and North American tree or shrub with white, pink, purple, or yellow showy flowers. ▷ **HISTORY** after Pierre *Magnol,* botanist

magnox *n* an alloy composed mainly of magnesium, used in fuel elements of some nuclear reactors (**magnox reactors**). ▷ **HISTORY** from *mag(nesium) n(o) ox(idation)*

magnum *n, pl* **-nums** a wine bottle of twice the normal size, holding 1.5 litres. ▷ **HISTORY** Latin: a big thing

magnum opus *n* a great work of art or literature, esp. the greatest single work of an artist. ▷ **HISTORY** Latin

magpie *n* **1** a bird of the crow family with black-and-white plumage, a long tail, and a chattering call. **2** any of various similar Australian birds, such as the butcherbird. **3** *Brit* a person who hoards small objects. ▷ **HISTORY** from *Mag,* diminutive of *Margaret* + *pie,* obsolete name for the magpie

magus (**may**-guss) *n, pl* **magi** (**maje**-eye) **1** a Zoroastrian priest. **2** an astrologer or magician of ancient times. ▷ **HISTORY** Old Persian: magician

Magyar *n* **1** a member of the main ethnic group of Hungary. **2** the Hungarian language. ✧ *adj* **3** of the Magyars.

maharaja *or* **maharajah** *n* the head of one of the royal families which formerly ruled parts of India. ▷ **HISTORY** Hindi: great raja

maharani *or* **maharanee** *n* the wife of a maharaja. ▷ **HISTORY** Hindi: great rani

maharishi *n Hinduism* a teacher of religious and mystical knowledge. ▷ **HISTORY** Hindi: great sage

mahatma *n* a person revered for his holiness or wisdom: often used as a title or form of address: *Mahatma Gandhi.* ▷ **HISTORY** Sanskrit *mahā* great + *ātman* soul

mah jong *or* **mah-jongg** *n* a game of Chinese origin, played using tiles bearing various designs, in which the players try to obtain a winning combination of tiles. ▷ **HISTORY** Chinese, literally: sparrows

mahogany *n, pl* **-nies 1** the hard reddish-brown wood of any of several tropical trees. ✧ *adj* **2** reddish-brown: *wonderful mahogany tones.* ▷ **HISTORY** origin unknown

mahout (ma-**howt**) *n* (in India and the East Indies) an elephant driver or keeper. ▷ **HISTORY** Hindi *mahāut*

maid *n* **1** a female servant. **2** *Archaic or literary* a young unmarried girl; maiden. ▷ **HISTORY** form of *maiden*

maiden *n* **1** *Archaic or literary* a young unmarried girl, esp. a virgin. **2** *Horse racing* a horse that has never won a race. ✧ *adj* **3** unmarried: *a maiden aunt.* **4** first or earliest: *maiden voyage.* ▷ **HISTORY** Old English *mægden* ▶ **maidenhood** *n* ▶ **maidenly** *adj*

maidenhair fern *n* a fern with delicate hairlike fronds of small pale green leaflets.

maidenhead *n* **1** the hymen. **2** virginity or maidenhood.

maiden name *n* a woman's surname before marriage.

maiden over *n Cricket* an over in which no runs are scored.

mail¹ *n* **1** letters and packages transported and delivered by the post office. **2** the postal system. **3** a single collection or delivery of mail. **4** a train, ship, or aircraft that carries mail. **5** short for **e-mail**. ✧ *vb* **6** *Chiefly US & Canad* to send by mail. **7** to contact or send by e-mail. ▷ **HISTORY** Old French *male* bag

mail² *n* flexible armour made of riveted metal rings or links. ▷ **HISTORY** Old French *maille* mesh ▶ **mailed** *adj*

mailbox *n US, Canad & Austral* a box outside a house into which the postman puts letters for the occupiers of the house.

mail coach *n History* a fast stagecoach designed primarily for carrying mail.

mailing list *n* a register of names and addresses to which information or advertising matter is sent by post or e-mail.

mail merge *n Computers* a word-processing facility that can produce personalized letters by combining data from two different files.

mail order *n* a system of buying and selling goods by post.

mailshot *n Brit* a posting of circulars, leaflets, or other advertising to a selected large number of people at once.

maim *vb* to injure badly or cruelly, with some permanent damage resulting. ▷ **HISTORY** Old French *mahaignier* to wound

main *adj* **1** chief or principal. ✧ *n* **2** a principal pipe or line in a system used to distribute water, electricity, or gas. **3** **mains** the main distribution network for water, gas, or electricity. **4** great strength or force: *with might and main.* **5** *Literary* the open ocean. **6 in the main** on the whole. ▷ **HISTORY** Old English *mægen* strength

mainbrace *n Naut* **1** the rope that controls the movement of the spar of a ship's mainsail. **2 splice the mainbrace** See **splice**.

main clause *n Grammar* a clause that can stand alone as a sentence.

mainframe *n Computers* a high-speed general-purpose computer, with a large store capacity.

mainland *n* the main part of a land mass as opposed to an island.

main line *n* **1** *Railways* the chief route between two points, usually fed by branch lines. ✧ *vb* **2** *Slang* to inject a drug into a vein.

mainly *adv* for the most part; principally.

mainmast *n Naut* the chief mast of a sailing vessel with two or more masts.

mainsail *n Naut* the largest and lowermost sail on the mainmast.

mainspring *n* **1** the chief cause or motive of something: *the mainspring of a dynamic economy.* **2** the chief spring of a watch or clock.

mainstay *n* **1** a chief support. **2** *Naut* a rope securing a mainmast.

mainstream *n* **1** the people or things representing the most common or generally accepted ideas and styles in a society, art form, etc.: *the mainstream of academic life.* **2** the main current of a river. ✧ *adj* **3** belonging to the social or cultural mainstream: *mainstream American movies.*

mainstreeting *n Canad* the practice of a politician walking about a town or city to try to gain votes.

maintain *vb* **1** to continue or keep in existence: *we must maintain good relations with them.* **2** to keep in proper or good condition: *an expensive car to maintain.* **3** to sustain or keep up a particular level or speed: *he set off at a high speed, but couldn't maintain it all the way.* **4** to enable a person to have the money, food and other things he or she needs to live: *the money maintained us for a month.* **5** to assert: *he had always maintained that he never wanted children.* **6** to defend against contradiction; uphold: *he maintained his innocence.* ▷ **HISTORY** from Latin *manu tenere* to hold in the hand

maintenance *n* **1** the act of maintaining or the state of being maintained. **2** the process of keeping a car, building, etc. in good condition. **3** *Law* financial provision ordered to be made by way of periodical payments or a lump sum, usually for a separated or divorced spouse.

maisonette *n Brit & S African* a flat with more than one floor. ▷ **HISTORY** French, diminutive of *maison* house

maize *n* a type of corn grown for its large yellow edible grains, which are used for food and as a source of oil. See also **sweet corn**. ▷ **HISTORY** Spanish *maiz*

Maj. Major.

majestic *adj* beautiful, dignified, and impressive. ▸ **majestically** *adv*

majesty *n* **1** great dignity and grandeur. **2** supreme power or authority. ▷ **HISTORY** Latin *majestas*

Majesty *n, pl* **-ties** (preceded by *Your, His* or *Her*) a title used to address or refer to a sovereign or the wife or widow of a sovereign.

Maj. Gen. Major General.

majolica *or* **maiolica** *n* a type of porous pottery glazed with bright metallic oxides. It was extensively made in Renaissance Italy. ▷ **HISTORY** Italian, from Late Latin *Majorica* Majorca

major *adj* **1** greater in size, frequency, or importance than others of the same kind: *the major political parties.* **2** very serious or significant: *a major investigation.* **3** main or principal: *a major road.* **4** *Music* (of a scale) **a** having notes separated by a whole tone, except for the third and fourth notes, and seventh and eighth notes, which are separated by a semitone. **b** of or based on the major scale: *the key of D minor.* ✧ *n* **5** a middle-ranking military officer. **6** *Music* a major key, chord, mode, or scale. **7** a person who has reached the age of legal majority. **8** *US, Canad, S African, Austral & NZ* the principal field of study of a student. ✧ *vb* **9 major in** *US, Canad, S African, Austral & NZ* to study as one's principal subject: *he majored in economics.* ▷ **HISTORY** Latin: greater

major-domo *n, pl* **-mos** the chief steward or butler of a great household. ▷ **HISTORY** Medieval Latin *major domus* head of the household

majorette *n* one of a group of girls who practise formation marching and baton twirling.

major general *n* a senior military officer.

majority *n, pl* **-ties** **1** the greater number or part of something. **2** (in an election) the number of votes or seats by which the strongest party or candidate beats the combined opposition or the runner-up. **3** the largest party or group that votes together in a meeting, council, or parliament. **4** the age at which a person legally becomes an adult. **5 in the majority** forming or part of the group of people or things made up of more than half of a larger group. ▷ **HISTORY** Medieval Latin *majoritas*

> **WORD TIP**
> *The majority of* can only refer to a number of things or people. When talking about an amount, *most of* should be used: *most of* (not *the majority of*) *the harvest was saved.*

make *vb* **making, made** **1** to create, construct, establish, or draw up; bring into being: *houses made of stone; he will have to make a will.* **2** to cause to do or be; compel or induce: *please make her go away.* **3** to bring about or produce: *don't make a noise.* **4** to carry out or perform: *he made his first trip to China in 1987; she made an obscene gesture.* **5** to appoint: *they made him caretaker manager.* **6** to come into a specified state or condition: *to make merry.* **7** to become: *she will make a good diplomat.* **8** to cause or ensure the success of: *that news has made my day.* **9** to amount to: *5 and 5 make 10.* **10** to earn or be paid: *they must be making a fortune.* **11** to have the qualities of or be suitable for: *what makes this book such a good read?* **12** to prepare for use:

she forgot to make her bed. **13** to be the essential element in: *confidence makes a good salesman.* **14** to use for a specified purpose: *they will make this town their base.* **15** to deliver: *he made a very good speech.* **16** to consider to be: *what time do you make it?* **17** to cause to seem or represent as being: *her girlish pigtails made her look younger than she was; she made the experience sound most unpleasant.* **18** to acquire: *she doesn't make friends easily.* **19** to engage in: *they made war on the Turks.* **20** to travel a certain distance or to a certain place: *we can make at least three miles before it gets dark.* **21** to arrive in time for: *he didn't make the first act of the play.* **22** to win or score: *he made a break of 125.* **23** *Informal* to gain a place or position on or in: *to make the headlines.* **24 make a day** *or* **night of it** to cause an activity to last a day or night. **25 make eyes at** *Old-fashioned* to flirt with or ogle. **26 make it** *Informal* **a** to be able to attend: *I'm afraid I can't make it to your party.* **b** to be successful. **27 make like** *Slang, chiefly US & Canad* **a** to imitate. **b** to pretend. **28 make to, as if to** *or* **as though to** to act with the intention or with a show of doing something: *she made as if to hit him.* ✧ *n* **29** a manufacturer; brand: *what make of car is that?* **30** the way in which something is made. **31 on the make** *Slang* out for profit or conquest. ✧ See also **make for**. ▷ **HISTORY** Old English *macian* ▶ **maker** *n*

make do *vb* to manage with an inferior alternative.

make for *vb* **1** to head towards. **2** to prepare to attack. **3** to help bring about: *this will make for a spectacular race.*

make out *vb* **1** to manage to see or hear. **2** to understand. **3** to write out: *how shall I make out the cheque?* **4** to attempt to establish or prove: *she made me out to be a crook.* **5** to pretend: *he made out that he could play the piano.* **6** to manage or get on: *how did you make out in the exam?*

make over *vb* **1** to renovate or remodel: *she made over the dress to fit her sister.* ✧ *n* **makeover** **2** a complete remodelling. **3** a series of alterations, including beauty treatments and new clothes, intended to make an improvement to someone's appearance.

Maker *n* a title given to God.

makeshift *adj* serving as a temporary substitute.

make-up *n* **1** cosmetics, such as powder or lipstick. **2** the cosmetics used by an actor to adapt his or her appearance. **3** the arrangement of the parts of something. **4** mental or physical constitution. ✧ *vb* **make up** **5** to form or constitute: *these arguments make up the case for the defence.* **6** to devise or compose, sometimes with the intent to deceive: *she was well known for making up stories about herself.* **7** to supply what is lacking in; complete: *I'll make up the difference.* **8** Also: **make it up** to settle differences amicably. **9 make up for** to compensate for: *one good year can make up for several bad ones.* **10** to apply cosmetics to the face. **11 make up to** *Informal* **a** to make friendly overtures to. **b** to flirt with.

makeweight *n* an unimportant person or thing added to make up a lack.

making *n* **1** the act or process of producing something. **2 be the making of** to cause the success of. **3 in the making** in the process of becoming or being made.

makings *pl n* **have the makings of** to have the potential, qualities, or materials necessary to make or become something: *it had the makings of a classic showdown.*

mako *n, pl* **makos** a powerful shark of the Atlantic and Pacific Oceans. ▷ **HISTORY** Maori

mal- *combining form* bad or badly; wrong or wrongly: *maladjusted; malfunction.* ▷ **HISTORY** Latin *malus* bad, *male* badly

malachite (**mal**-a-kite) *n* a green mineral used as a source of copper, and for making ornaments. ▷ **HISTORY** Greek *molokhitis*

maladjustment *n Psychol* a failure to meet the demands of society, such as coping with problems and social relationships. ▶ **maladjusted** *adj*

maladroit (mal-a-**droyt**) *adj* clumsy, awkward, or tactless. ▷ **HISTORY** French *mal* badly + ADROIT ▶ **maladroitly** *adv* ▶ **maladroitness** *n*

malady (**mal**-a-dee) *n, pl* **-dies** *Old-fashioned* any disease or illness. ▷ **HISTORY** Vulgar Latin *male habitus* in poor condition

malaise (mal-**laze**) *n* **1** a vague feeling of unease, illness, or depression. **2** a complex of problems affecting a country, economy, etc.: *Belgium's political malaise.* ▷ **HISTORY** Old French *mal* bad + *aise* ease

malapropism *n* the comic misuse of a word by confusion with one which sounds similar, for example *under the affluence of alcohol.* ▷ **HISTORY** after Mrs *Malaprop* in Sheridan's play *The Rivals*

malaria *n* a disease with recurring attacks of fever, caused by the bite of some types of mosquito. ▷ **HISTORY** Italian *mala aria* bad air ▶ **malarial** *adj*

Malay *n* **1** a member of a people living chiefly in Malaysia and Indonesia. **2** the language of this people. ✧ *adj* **3** of the Malays or their language.

Malayan *adj* **1** of Malaya. ✧ *n* **2** a person from Malaya.

Malaysian *adj* **1** of Malaysia. ✧ *n* **2** a person from Malaysia.

malcontent *n* a person who is discontented with the existing situation. ▷ **HISTORY** Old French

male *adj* **1** of the sex that can fertilize female reproductive cells. **2** of or characteristic of a man. **3** for or composed of men or boys: *a male choir.* **4** (of flowers) bearing stamens but lacking a pistil. **5** *Electronics, engineering* having a projecting part or parts that fit into a hollow counterpart: *a male plug.* ✧ *n* **6** a male person, animal, or plant. ▷ **HISTORY** Latin *masculus* masculine ▶ **maleness** *n*

male chauvinism *n* the belief, held by some men, that men are better and more important than women. ▶ **male chauvinist** *n, adj*

malediction (mal-lid-**dik**-shun) *n* the utterance of a curse against someone or something. ▷ **HISTORY** Latin *maledictio* a reviling ▶ **maledictory** *adj*

A B C D E F G H I J K L M N O P Q R S T U V W X Y Z

malefactor (**mal**-if-act-or) *n* a criminal or wrongdoer. ▷ HISTORY Latin *malefacere* to do evil ▶ **malefaction** *n*

malevolent (mal-**lev**-a-lent) *adj* wishing evil to others; malicious. ▷ HISTORY Latin *malevolens* ▶ **malevolence** *n* ▶ **malevolently** *adv*

malfeasance (mal-**fee**-zanss) *n Law* wrongful or illegal behaviour, esp. by a public official. ▷ HISTORY Old French *mal faisant* evil-doing

malformation *n* **1** the condition of being faulty or abnormal in form or shape. **2** *Pathol* a deformity, esp. when congenital. ▶ **malformed** *adj*

malfunction *vb* **1** to fail to function properly or fail to function at all. ✧ *n* **2** failure to function properly or failure to function at all.

malice (**mal**-iss) *n* the desire to do harm or cause mischief to others. ▷ HISTORY Latin *malus* evil ▶ **malicious** *adj* ▶ **maliciously** *adv*

malice aforethought *n Law* a deliberate intention to do something unlawful.

malign (mal-**line**) *vb* **1** to say unpleasant and untrue things about someone; slander. ✧ *adj* **2** evil in influence or effect. ▷ HISTORY Latin *malignus* spiteful

malignant (mal-**lig**-nant) *adj* **1** seeking to harm others. **2** tending to cause great harm; injurious. **3** *Pathol* (of a tumour) uncontrollable or resistant to therapy. ▷ HISTORY Late Latin *malignare* to behave spitefully ▶ **malignancy** *n*

malignity (mal-**lig**-nit-ee) *n* the condition of being malign or deadly.

malinger (mal-**ling**-ger) *vb* to pretend to be ill, or exaggerate how ill one is, to avoid work. ▷ HISTORY French *malingre* sickly ▶ **malingerer** *n*

mall (**mawl**) *n* **1** *US, Canad, Austral, & NZ* short for **shopping mall**. **2** a shaded avenue, esp. one open to the public. ▷ HISTORY after *the Mall,* an avenue in St James's Park, London

mallard *n, pl* **-lard** *or* **-lards** a common N hemisphere duck, the male of which has a dark green head. ▷ HISTORY Old French *mallart*

malleable (**mal**-lee-a-bl) *adj* **1** (esp. of metal) capable of being hammered or pressed into shape without breaking. **2** able to be influenced. ▷ HISTORY Medieval Latin *malleabilis* ▶ **malleability** *n* ▶ **malleably** *adv*

mallee *n* a low-growing eucalypt found in dry regions of Australia.

mallet *n* **1** a hammer with a large wooden head. **2** a long stick with a head like a hammer used to strike the ball in croquet or polo. ▷ HISTORY Old French *maillet* wooden hammer

mallow *n* any of a group of plants, with purple, pink, or white flowers. ▷ HISTORY Latin *malva*

malnourished *adj* physically weak due to lack of healthy food.

malnutrition *n* physical weakness resulting from insufficient food or an unbalanced diet.

malodorous (mal-**lode**-or-uss) *adj* having an unpleasant smell: *the malodorous sludge of Boston harbour.*

Malpighian body (mal-**pig**-ee-an) *n Anat* a cluster of capillaries at the end of each tubule of the kidney. ▷ HISTORY after Marcello *Malpighi*, Italian physiologist

malpractice *n* illegal, unethical, or negligent professional conduct.

malt *n* **1** grain, such as barley, that is kiln-dried after it has been germinated by soaking in water. **2** See **malt whisky**. ✧ *vb* **3** to make into or become malt. **4** to make from malt or to add malt to. ▷ HISTORY Old English *mealt* ▶ **malted** *adj* ▶ **malty** *adj*

Maltese *adj* **1** of Malta. ✧ *n* **2** (*pl* **-tese**) a person from Malta. **3** the language of Malta.

Maltese cross *n* a cross with triangular arms that taper towards the centre, sometimes with the outer sides curving in.

Malthusian (malth-**yew**-zee-an) *adj* of the theory stating that increases in population tend to exceed increases in the food supply and that therefore sexual restraint should be exercised. ▷ HISTORY after T. R. *Malthus,* economist

maltose *n* a sugar formed by the action of enzymes on starch. ▷ HISTORY *malt* + *-ose* indicating a sugar

maltreat *vb* to treat badly, cruelly, or violently. ▷ HISTORY French *maltraiter* ▶ **maltreatment** *n*

malt whisky *n* whisky made from malted barley.

mama *or esp US* **mamma** (mam-**mah**) *n Old-fashioned, informal* same as **mother**. ▷ HISTORY reduplication of childish syllable *ma*

mamba *n* a very poisonous tree snake found in tropical and Southern Africa. ▷ HISTORY Zulu *im-amba*

mambo *n, pl* **-bos** a Latin American dance resembling the rumba. ▷ HISTORY American Spanish

mammal *n* a warm-blooded animal, such as a human being, dog or whale, the female of which produces milk to feed her babies. ▷ HISTORY Latin *mamma* breast ▶ **mammalian** *adj, n*

mammary *adj* of the breasts or milk-producing glands. ▷ HISTORY Latin *mamma* breast

mammary gland *n* any of the milk-producing glands in mammals, such as a woman's breast or a cow's udder.

mammon *n* wealth regarded as a source of evil and corruption, personified in the New Testament as a false god (**Mammon**). ▷ HISTORY New Testament Greek *mammōnas* wealth

mammoth *n* **1** a large extinct elephant with a hairy coat and long curved tusks. ✧ *adj* **2** gigantic. ▷ HISTORY Russian *mamot*

man *n, pl* **men** **1** an adult male human being, as distinguished from a woman. **2** a human being of either sex; person: *all men are born equal.* **3** human beings collectively; mankind. RELATED ADJECTIVE ➧ **anthropoid** **4** a human being regarded as representative of a particular period or category: *Neanderthal man.* **5** an adult male human being with qualities associated with the male, such as courage or virility: *take it like a man.* **6** an employee, servant, or representative. **7** a member of the armed forces who is not an officer. **8** a member of a group or team. **9** a husband, boyfriend, or male lover. **10** a movable piece in various games, such as draughts. **11** *S African slang* any person: used as a term of address. **12 as one man** with unanimous action or response. **13 he's your man** he's the person needed. **14 man and boy** from childhood. **15 sort out the men from the boys** to discover who can cope with difficult or dangerous situations and who cannot. **16 to a man** without exception. ✧ *vb* **manning, manned 17** to provide with sufficient people for operation or defence. **18** to take one's place at or near in readiness for action. ▷ **HISTORY** Old English *mann* ▶ **manhood** *n*

> **WORD TIP**
> The use of words ending in *-man* is avoided as implying a male in job advertisements, where sexual discrimination is illegal, and in many other contexts where a term that is not gender-specific is available, such as *salesperson, barperson, camera operator.*

mana *n NZ* authority, influence, and prestige.

manacle (**man**-a-kl) *n* **1** a metal ring or chain put round the wrists or ankles, used to restrict the movements of a prisoner or convict. ✧ *vb* **-cling, -cled 2** to put manacles on. ▷ **HISTORY** Latin *manus* hand

manage *vb* **-aging, -aged 1** to succeed in doing something: *we finally managed to sell our old house.* **2** to be in charge of; administer: *the company is badly managed.* **3** to have room or time for: *can you manage lunch tomorrow?* **4** to keep under control: *she disapproved of taking drugs to manage stress.* **5** to struggle on despite difficulties, esp. financial ones: *most people cannot manage on a cleaner's salary.* ▷ **HISTORY** Italian *maneggiare* to train (esp. horses) ▶ **manageable** *adj*

management *n* **1** the people responsible for running an organization or business. **2** managers or employers collectively. **3** the technique or practice of managing or controlling.

manager *n* **1** a person who manages an organization or business. **2** a person in charge of a sports team. **3** a person who controls the business affairs of an entertainer. ▶ **manageress** *fem n*

managerial *adj* of a manager or management.

managing director *n* the senior director of a company, who has overall responsibility for the way it is run.

mañana (man-**yah**-na) *n, adv* **a** tomorrow. **b** some other and later time. ▷ **HISTORY** Spanish

man-at-arms *n, pl* **men-at-arms** a soldier, esp. a medieval soldier.

manatee *n* a large plant-eating mammal occurring in tropical coastal waters of the Atlantic. ▷ **HISTORY** Carib *Manattouī*

Manchu *n, pl* **-chus** *or* **-chu** a member of a Mongoloid people of Manchuria, a region of NE China, who conquered China in the 17th century, ruling until 1912.

Mancunian (man-**kew**-nee-an) *adj* **1** of Manchester, a city in NW England. ✧ *n* **2** a person from Manchester. ▷ **HISTORY** Medieval Latin *Mancunium* Manchester

mandala *n Hindu & Buddhist art* a circular design symbolizing the universe. ▷ **HISTORY** Sanskrit: circle

mandamus *n, pl* **mandamuses** *Law* an order from a superior court commanding a body or public official to carry out a public duty. ▷ **HISTORY** Latin: we command, from *mandāre*

mandarin *n* **1** (in the Chinese Empire) a member of a senior grade of the bureaucracy. **2** a high-ranking official with extensive powers. **3** a person of standing and influence, esp. in literary or intellectual circles. **4** a small citrus fruit resembling the tangerine. ▷ **HISTORY** Sanskrit *mantrin* counsellor

Mandarin Chinese *or* **Mandarin** *n* the official language of China since 1917.

mandate *n* **1** an official or authoritative command to carry out a particular task: *the UN force's mandate does not allow it to intervene.* **2** *Politics* the political authority given to a government or an elected representative through an electoral victory. **3** Also: **mandated territory** (formerly) a territory administered by one country on behalf of an international body. ✧ *vb* **-dating, -dated 4** to delegate authority to. **5** to assign territory to a nation under a mandate. ▷ **HISTORY** Latin *mandare* to command

mandatory *adj* **1** obligatory; compulsory. **2** having the nature or powers of a mandate. ▶ **mandatorily** *adv*

mandible *n* **1** the lower jawbone of a vertebrate. **2** either of the jawlike mouthparts of an insect. **3** either part of the bill of a bird, esp. the lower part. ▷ **HISTORY** Late Latin *mandibula* jaw

mandolin *n* a musical instrument with four pairs of strings stretched over a small light body, usually played with a plectrum. ▷ **HISTORY** Italian *mandolino* small lute

mandrake *n* a plant with a forked root. It was formerly thought to have magic powers and a narcotic was prepared from its root. ▷ **HISTORY** Latin *mandragoras*

mandrel *or* **mandril** *n* **1** a spindle on which the object being worked on is supported in a lathe. **2** a shaft on which a machining tool is mounted. ▷ **HISTORY** perhaps from French *mandrin* lathe

mandrill *n* a monkey of W Africa. The male has red and blue markings on its face and buttocks. ▷ **HISTORY** *man* + *drill* an Old-World monkey

mane *n* **1** the long hair that grows from the neck in such mammals as the lion and horse. **2** long thick human hair. ▷ **HISTORY** Old English *manu* ▶ **maned** *adj*

manful *adj* determined and brave. ▶ **manfully** *adv*

manganese *n Chem* a brittle greyish-white metallic element used in making steel. Symbol: Mn. ▷ **HISTORY** probably altered form of Medieval Latin *magnesia*

mange *n* a skin disease of domestic animals, characterized by itching and loss of hair. ▷ **HISTORY** Old French *mangeue* itch

mangelwurzel *n* a variety of beet with a large yellowish root. ▷ **HISTORY** German *Mangold* beet + *Wurzel* root

manger *n* a trough in a stable or barn from which horses or cattle feed. ▷ **HISTORY** Old French *maingeure*

mangetout (**mawnzh**-too) *n* a variety of garden pea with an edible pod. ▷ **HISTORY** French: eat all

mangle[1] *vb* **-gling, -gled 1** to destroy or damage by crushing and twisting. **2** to spoil. ▷ **HISTORY** Norman French *mangler* ▶ **mangled** *adj*

mangle[2] *n* **1** a machine for pressing or squeezing water out of washed clothes, consisting of two heavy rollers between which the clothes are passed. ✧ *vb* **-gling, -gled 2** to put through a mangle. ▷ **HISTORY** Dutch *mangel*

mango *n, pl* **-goes** *or* **-gos** the egg-shaped edible fruit of a tropical Asian tree, with a smooth rind and sweet juicy flesh. ▷ **HISTORY** Malay *mangā*

mangrove *n* a tropical evergreen tree or shrub with intertwining aerial roots that forms dense thickets along coasts. ▷ **HISTORY** older *mangrow* (changed through influence of *grove*), from Portuguese *mangue*

mangy *adj* **-gier, -giest 1** having mange. **2** scruffy or shabby. ▶ **mangily** *adv* ▶ **manginess** *n*

manhandle *vb* **-handling, -handled 1** to handle or push someone about roughly. **2** to move something by manpower rather than by machinery.

manhole *n* a hole with a detachable cover, through which a person can enter a sewer or pipe to inspect or repair it.

man-hour *n* a unit of work in industry, equal to the work done by one person in one hour.

manhunt *n* an organized search, usually by police, for a wanted man or fugitive.

mania *n* **1** an obsessional enthusiasm or liking. **2** a mental disorder characterized by great or violent excitement. ▷ **HISTORY** Greek: madness

-mania *n combining form* indicating extreme or abnormal excitement aroused by something: *kleptomania.*

maniac *n* **1** a wild disorderly person. **2** a person who has a great craving or enthusiasm for something. ▷ **HISTORY** Late Latin *maniacus* belonging to madness ▶ **maniacal** (man-**eye**-ak-kl) *adj*

manic *adj* **1** extremely excited or energetic; frenzied: *manic, cavorting dancers.* **2** of, involving, or affected by mania: *deep depression broken by periods of manic excitement.*

manic-depressive *Psychiatry* ✧ *adj* **1** denoting a mental disorder characterized by an alternation between extreme euphoria and deep depression. ✧ *n* **2** a person afflicted with this disorder.

manicure *n* **1** cosmetic care of the hands and fingernails. ✧ *vb* **-curing, -cured 2** to care for the fingernails and hands. ▷ **HISTORY** Latin *manus* hand + *cura* care ▶ **manicurist** *n*

manifest *adj* **1** easily noticed, obvious. ✧ *vb* **2** to reveal or display: *an additional symptom now manifested itself.* **3** to show by the way one behaves: *he manifested great personal bravery.* **4** (of a disembodied spirit) to appear in visible form. ✧ *n* **5** a customs document containing particulars of a ship and its cargo. **6** a list of the cargo and passengers on an aeroplane. ▷ **HISTORY** Latin *manifestus* plain ▶ **manifestation** *n*

manifest destiny *n History* the 19th-century doctrine that territorial expansion of the United States was both justified and divinely ordained.

manifesto *n, pl* **-tos** *or* **-toes** a public declaration of intent or policy issued by a group of people, for instance by a political party. ▷ **HISTORY** Italian

manifold *adj* **1** *Formal* numerous and varied: *her talents are manifold.* ✧ *n* **2** a pipe with a number of inlets or outlets, esp. one in a car engine. ▷ **HISTORY** Old English *manigfeald*

manikin *n* **1** a little man; dwarf or child. **2** a model of the human body. ▷ **HISTORY** Dutch *manneken*

manila *or* **manilla** *n* a strong usually brown paper used to make envelopes. ▷ **HISTORY** after *Manila,* in the Philippines

man in the street *n* the average person.

manioc *n* same as **cassava.** ▷ **HISTORY** S American Indian *mandioca*

manipulate *vb* **-lating, -lated 1** to handle or use skilfully. **2** to control something or someone cleverly or deviously. ▷ **HISTORY** Latin *manipulus* handful ▶ **manipulation** *n* ▶ **manipulator** *n* ▶ **manipulative** *adj*

mankind *n* **1** human beings collectively. **2** men collectively.

> **☑ WORD TIP**
> Some people object to the use of *mankind* to refer to all human beings and prefer the term *humankind.*

manly *adj* **-lier, -liest 1** possessing qualities, such as vigour or courage, traditionally regarded as appropriate to a man; masculine. **2** characteristic of a man. ▶ **manliness** *n*

man-made *adj* made by humans; artificial.

manna *n* **1** *Bible* the miraculous food which sustained the Israelites in the wilderness (Exodus 16:14–36). **2** a windfall: *manna from heaven.* ▷ **HISTORY** Hebrew *mān*

manned *adj* having a human staff or crew: *thirty years of manned space flight.*

mannequin *n* **1** a woman who wears the clothes displayed at a fashion show; model. **2** a life-size dummy of the human body used to fit or display clothes. ▷ **HISTORY** French

manner *n* **1** the way a thing happens or is done. **2** a person's bearing and behaviour. **3** the style or customary way of doing something: *sculpture in the Greek manner.* **4** type or kind. **5 in a manner of speaking** in a way; so to speak. **6 to the manner born** naturally fitted to a specified role or activity. ▷ **HISTORY** Old French *maniere*

mannered *adj* **1** (of speech or behaviour) unnaturally formal and put on to impress others. **2** having manners as specified: *ill-mannered.*

mannerism *n* **1** a distinctive and individual gesture way or way of speaking. **2** excessive use of a distinctive or affected manner, esp. in art or literature.

A B C D E F G H I J K L M N O P Q R S T U V W X Y Z

mannerly *adj* well-mannered and polite. ▶ **mannerliness** *n*

manners *pl n* **1** a person's social conduct viewed in the light of whether it is regarded as polite or acceptable or not: *his manners leave something to be desired; shockingly bad manners.* **2** a socially acceptable way of behaving: *it's not manners to point.*

mannish *adj* (of a woman) displaying qualities regarded as typical of a man.

manoeuvre *or US* **maneuver** (man-**noo**-ver) *vb* **-vring, -vred** *or US* **-vering, -vered 1** to move or do something with dexterity and skill: *she manoeuvred the car easily into the parking space.* **2** to manipulate a situation in order to gain some advantage. **3** to perform a manoeuvre or manoeuvres. ✧ *n* **4** a movement or action requiring dexterity and skill. **5** a contrived, complicated, and possibly deceptive plan or action. **6 manoeuvres** military or naval exercises, usually on a large scale. **7** a change in course of a ship or aircraft, esp. a complicated one. **8 room for manoeuvre** the possibility of changing one's plans or behaviour if it becomes necessary or desirable. ▷ **HISTORY** French, from Medieval Latin *manuopera* manual work ▶ **manoeuvrable** *or US* **maneuverable** *adj* ▶ **manoeuvrability** *or US* **maneuverability** *n*

man-of-war *n, pl* **men-of-war 1** a warship. **2** short for **Portuguese man-of-war**.

manor *n* **1** (in medieval Europe) the lands and property controlled by a lord. **2** *Brit* a large country house and its lands. **3** *Brit slang* an area of operation, esp. of a local police force. ▷ **HISTORY** Old French *manoir* dwelling ▶ **manorial** *adj*

manpower *n* the number of people needed or available for a job.

manqué (**mong**-kay) *adj* unfulfilled; would-be: *an actor manqué.* ▷ **HISTORY** French, literally: having missed

manse *n* the house provided for a minister of some Christian denominations. ▷ **HISTORY** Medieval Latin *mansus* dwelling

manservant *n, pl* **menservants** a male servant, esp. a valet.

mansion *n* **1** a large and imposing house. **2 Mansions** *Brit* a name given to some blocks of flats as part of their address: *18 Wilton Mansions.* ▷ **HISTORY** Latin *mansio* a remaining

manslaughter *n Law* the unlawful but not deliberately planned killing of one human being by another.

mantel *n* a wooden, stone, or iron frame around a fireplace. ▷ **HISTORY** variant of *mantle*

mantelpiece *n* a shelf above a fireplace often forming part of the mantel. Also: **mantel shelf, chimneypiece**

mantilla *n* a woman's lace or silk scarf covering the shoulders and head, worn esp. in Spain. ▷ **HISTORY** Spanish *manta* cloak

mantis *n, pl* **-tises** *or* **-tes** a carnivorous insect resembling a grasshopper, that rests with the first pair of legs raised as if in prayer. Also: **praying mantis** ▷ **HISTORY** Greek: prophet

mantissa *n* the part of a common logarithm consisting of the decimal point and the figures following it: *the mantissa of 2.4771 is .4771.* ▷ **HISTORY** Latin: something added

mantle *n* **1** *Old-fashioned* a loose wrap or cloak. **2** anything that covers completely or envelops: *a mantle of snow covered the ground.* **3** the responsibilities and duties which go with a particular job or position: *he refuses to accept the mantle of leader.* **4** a small mesh dome used to increase illumination in a gas or oil lamp by becoming incandescent. **5** *Geol* the part of the earth between the crust and the core. ✧ *vb* **-tling, -tled 6** to spread over or become spread over: *mountains mantled in lush vegetation.* ▷ **HISTORY** Latin *mantellum* little cloak

mantra *n* **1** *Hinduism, Buddhism* any sacred word or syllable used as an object of concentration. **2** *Hinduism* a Vedic psalm of praise. ▷ **HISTORY** Sanskrit: speech, instrument of thought

manual *adj* **1** of a hand or hands: *manual dexterity.* **2** physical as opposed to mental: *manual labour.* **3** operated or done by human labour rather than automatic or computer-aided means: *a manual gearbox.* ✧ *n* **4** a book of instructions or information. **5** *Music* one of the keyboards on an organ. ▷ **HISTORY** Latin *manus* hand ▶ **manually** *adv*

manufacture *vb* **-turing, -tured 1** to process or make goods on a large scale, esp. using machinery. **2** to invent or concoct evidence, an excuse, etc. ✧ *n* **3** the production of goods, esp. by industrial processes. ▷ **HISTORY** Latin *manus* hand + *facere* to make ▶ **manufacturer** *n* ▶ **manufacturing** *n, adj*

manuka (**mah**-nook-a) *n* a New Zealand tree with strong elastic wood and aromatic leaves. ▷ **HISTORY** Maori

manure *n* **1** animal excrement used as a fertilizer. ✧ *vb* **-nuring, -nured 2** to spread manure upon fields or soil. ▷ **HISTORY** Anglo-French *mainoverer*

manuscript *n* **1** a book or other document written by hand. **2** the original handwritten or typed version of a book or article submitted by an author for publication. ▷ **HISTORY** Medieval Latin *manuscriptus* handwritten

Manx *adj* **1** of the Isle of Man. ✧ *n* **2** an almost extinct Celtic language of the Isle of Man. ✧ *pl n* **3 the Manx** the people of the Isle of Man. ▷ **HISTORY** Scandinavian ▶ **Manxman** *n* ▶ **Manxwoman** *n*

Manx cat *n* a short-haired breed of cat without a tail.

many *adj* **1** a large number of; numerous: *many times; many people think the government is incompetent.* ✧ *pron* **2** a number of people or things, esp. a large one: *his many supporters; have as many as you want.* **3 many a** each of a considerable number of: *many a man.* ✧ *n* **4 the many** the majority of mankind, esp. the common people. ▷ **HISTORY** Old English *manig*

Maoism *n* Communism as interpreted in the theories and policies of Mao Tse-tung (1893–1976), Chinese statesman. ▶ **Maoist** *n, adj*

Maori *n* **1** (*pl* **-ri** *or* **-ris**) a member of the Polynesian people living in New Zealand since before the arrival of European settlers. **2** the language of this people. ✧ *adj* **3** of this people or their language.

map *n* **1** a diagrammatic representation of the earth's surface or part of it, showing the geographical distributions or positions of features such as roads, towns, relief, and rainfall. **2** a diagrammatic representation of the stars or of the surface of a celestial body. **3** *Maths* same as **function**. **4 put on the map** to make (a town or company) well-known: *William Morris put Kelmscott on the map.* ✧ *vb* **mapping, mapped 5** to make a map of. **6** *Maths* to represent or transform (a function, figure, or set). ✧ See also **map out**. ▷ **HISTORY** Latin *mappa* cloth

maple *n* **1** any of various trees or shrubs with five-pointed leaves and winged seeds borne in pairs. **2** the hard wood of any of these trees. ✧ See also **sugar maple**. ▷ **HISTORY** Old English *mapeltrēow* maple tree

maple syrup *n* a very sweet syrup made from the sap of the sugar maple.

map out *vb* to plan or design.

mapping *n Maths* same as **function**.

map projection *n Geog* a representation of or a means of representing a globe or celestial sphere or part of it on a flat map.

maquis (mah-**kee**) *n*, *pl* **-quis** (-**kee**) **1** the French underground movement that fought against the German occupying forces in World War II. **2** a type of shrubby, mostly evergreen, vegetation found in coastal regions of the Mediterranean area. ▷ **HISTORY** French

mar *vb* **marring, marred** to spoil or be the one bad feature of: *Sicily's coastline is marred by high-rise hotels.* ▷ **HISTORY** Old English *merran*

Mar. March.

marabou *n* **1** a large black-and-white African stork. **2** the soft white down of this bird, used to trim hats etc. ▷ **HISTORY** Arabic *murābit* holy man

maraca (mar-**rak**-a) *n* a shaken percussion instrument, usually one of a pair, consisting of a gourd or plastic shell filled with dried seeds or pebbles. ▷ **HISTORY** Brazilian Portuguese

marae (mar-**rye**) *n NZ* **1** an enclosed space in front of a Maori meeting house. **2** a Maori meeting house and its buildings. ▷ **HISTORY** Maori

maraschino cherry *n* a cherry preserved in maraschino.

marasmus *n Pathol* general emaciation and wasting.

marathon *n* **1** a race on foot of 26 miles 385 yards (42.195 km). **2** any long or arduous task or event. ✧ *adj* **3** of or relating to a race on foot of 26 miles 385 yards (42.195 km): *marathon runners.* **4** long and arduous: *a marathon nine hour meeting.* ▷ **HISTORY** referring to the feat of the messenger said to have run 26 miles from Marathon to Athens to bring the news of victory in 490 BC

marble *n* **1** a hard limestone rock, which usually has a mottled appearance and can be given a high polish. **2** a block of marble or work of art made of marble. **3** a small round glass ball used in playing marbles. ✧ *vb* **-bling, -bled 4** to mottle with variegated streaks in imitation of marble. ▷ **HISTORY** Greek *marmaros* ▶ **marbled** *adj*

marbling *n* **1** a mottled effect or pattern resembling marble. **2** the streaks of fat in lean meat.

marcasite *n* **1** a pale yellow form of iron pyrites used in jewellery. **2** a cut and polished form of steel used for making jewellery. ▷ **HISTORY** Arabic *marqashītā*

march[1] *vb* **1** to walk with very regular steps, like a soldier. **2** to walk in a quick and determined manner, esp. when angry: *he marched into the kitchen without knocking.* **3** to make a person or group proceed: *he was marched back to his cell.* **4** (of an army, procession, etc.) to walk as an organized group: *the demonstrators marched down the main street.* **5** to advance or progress steadily: *time marches on.* ✧ *n* **6** a regular stride. **7** a long or exhausting walk. **8** the steady development or progress of something: *the continuous march of industrial development.* **9** a distance covered by marching. **10** an organized protest in which a large group of people walk somewhere together: *a march against racial violence.* **11** a piece of music suitable for marching to. **12 steal a march on** to gain an advantage over, esp. by a trick. ▷ **HISTORY** Old French *marchier* to tread ▶ **marcher** *n* ▶ **marching** *adj*

march[2] *n* **1** a border or boundary. **2** the land lying along a border or boundary, often of disputed ownership. ▷ **HISTORY** Old French *marche*

March *n* the third month of the year. ▷ **HISTORY** Latin *Martius* (month) of Mars

March hare *n* a hare during its breeding season in March, noted for its wild and excitable behaviour.

marching girl *n NZ* a girl who does team formation marching as a sport.

marching orders *pl n* **1** *Informal* dismissal, esp. from employment. **2** military orders, giving instructions about a march.

marchioness (marsh-on-**ness**) *n* **1** a woman who holds the rank of marquis or marquess. **2** the wife or widow of a marquis or marquess. ▷ **HISTORY** Medieval Latin *marchionissa*

Mardi Gras (**mar**-dee **grah**) *n* the festival of Shrove Tuesday, celebrated in some cities with great revelry. ▷ **HISTORY** French: fat Tuesday

mare[1] *n* the adult female of a horse or zebra. ▷ **HISTORY** Old English *mere*

mare[2] (**mar**-ray) *n*, *pl* **maria** one of many huge dry plains on the surface of the moon or Mars, visible as dark markings. ▷ **HISTORY** Latin: sea

margarine *n* a butter substitute made from vegetable and animal fats. ▷ **HISTORY** Greek *margaron* pearl

marge *n Brit & Austral informal* margarine.

margin *n* **1** an edge, rim, or border: *we came to the margin of the wood; people on the margin of society.* **2** the blank space surrounding the text on a page. **3** an additional amount or one beyond the minimum necessary: *the margin of victory was seven*

a b c d e f g h i j k l m n o p q r s t u v w x y z

lengths; a small margin of error. **4** *Chiefly Austral* a payment made in addition to a basic wage, esp. for special skill or responsibility. **5** a limit beyond which something can no longer exist or function: *the margin of physical survival.* **6** *Econ* the minimum return below which an enterprise becomes unprofitable. ▷ HISTORY Latin *margo* border

marginal *adj* **1** of, in, on, or forming a margin. **2** not important; insignificant: *he remained a rather marginal political figure.* **3** close to a limit, esp. a lower limit: *marginal legal ability.* **4** *Econ* relating to goods or services produced and sold at the margin of profitability: *marginal cost.* **5** *Politics* of or designating a constituency in which elections tend to be won by small margins: *a marginal seat.* **6** designating agricultural land on the edge of fertile areas. ✧ *n* **7** *Politics chiefly Brit & NZ* a marginal constituency. ▶ **marginally** *adv*

marginalia *pl n* notes in the margin of a book, manuscript, or letter.

margrave *n* (formerly) a German nobleman ranking above a count. ▷ HISTORY Middle Dutch *markgrave* count of the frontier

marguerite *n* a garden plant with flowers resembling large daisies. ▷ HISTORY French: daisy

marigold *n* any of various plants cultivated for their yellow or orange flowers. ▷ HISTORY from *Mary* (the Virgin) + *gold*

marijuana *or* **marihuana** (mar-ree-**wah**-na) *n* the dried leaves and flowers of the hemp plant, used as a drug, esp. in cigarettes. ▷ HISTORY Mexican Spanish

marimba *n* a percussion instrument consisting of a set of hardwood plates placed over tuned metal resonators, played with soft-headed sticks. ▷ HISTORY West African

marina *n* a harbour for yachts and other pleasure boats. ▷ HISTORY Latin: marine

marinade *n* **1** a mixture of oil, wine, vinegar, etc., in which meat or fish is soaked before cooking. ✧ *vb* **-nading, -naded 2** same as **marinate**. ▷ HISTORY French

marinate *vb* **-nating, -nated** to soak in marinade. ▷ HISTORY Italian *marinare* to pickle ▶ **marinated** *adj*

marine *adj* **1** of, found in, or relating to the sea. **2** of shipping or navigation. **3** used or adapted for use at sea. ✧ *n* **4** (esp. in Britain and the US) a soldier trained for land and sea combat. **5** a country's shipping or navy collectively: *the merchant marine.* ▷ HISTORY Latin *marinus* of the sea

mariner (**mar**-in-er) *n* a sailor.

marionette *n* a puppet whose limbs are moved by strings. ▷ HISTORY French, from the name *Marion*

marital *adj* of or relating to marriage. ▷ HISTORY Latin *maritus* married ▶ **maritally** *adv*

maritime *adj* **1** of or relating to shipping. **2** of, near, or living near the sea. ▷ HISTORY Latin *maritimus* of the sea

marjoram *n* a plant with sweet-scented leaves, used for seasoning food and in salads. ▷ HISTORY Medieval Latin *marjorana*

mark¹ *n* **1** a visible impression on a surface, such as a spot or scratch. **2** a sign, symbol, or other indication that distinguishes something. **3** a written or printed symbol, as used for punctuation. **4** a letter, number, or percentage used to grade academic work. **5** a thing that indicates position; marker. **6** an indication of some quality: *a mark of respect.* **7** a target or goal. **8** impression or influence: *this book displays the mark of its author's admiration of Kafka.* **9** (in trade names) a particular model or type of a vehicle, machine, etc.: *the Ford Escort Mark Two.* **10** one of the temperature settings at which a gas oven can work: *bake at gas mark 5 for 30 minutes.* **11 make one's mark** to achieve recognition. **12 on your mark** *or* **marks** a command given to runners in a race to prepare themselves at the starting line. **13 up to the mark** meeting the desired standard. ✧ *vb* **14** to make a visible impression, trace, or stain on. **15** to have a tendency to become dirty, scratched, or damaged: *this material marks easily.* **16** to characterize or distinguish: *the gritty determination that has marked his career.* **17** to designate someone as a particular type of person: *she would now be marked as a troublemaker.* **18** to label, esp. to indicate price. **19** to celebrate or commemorate an occasion or its anniversary: *a series of concerts to mark the 200th anniversary of Mozart's death.* **20** to pay attention to: *mark my words.* **21** to observe or notice. **22** to grade or evaluate academic work. **23** *Sport* to stay close to an opponent to hamper his or her play. **24 mark off** *or* **out** to set boundaries or limits on. **25 mark time a** to move the feet alternately as in marching but without advancing. **b** to wait for something more interesting to happen. ✧ See also **markdown, mark-up**. ▷ HISTORY Old English *mearc*

mark² *n* See **Deutschmark**. ▷ HISTORY Old English *marc* unit of weight of precious metal

markdown *n* **1** a price reduction. ✧ *vb* **mark down 2** to reduce in price. **3** to make a written note of: *she marked down the number of the getaway car.*

marked *adj* **1** obvious or noticeable: *a marked improvement.* **2** singled out, esp. as the target of attack: *a marked man.* ▶ **markedly** (**mark**-id-lee) *adv*

marker *n* **1** an object used to show the position of something. **2** Also called: **marker pen** a thick felt-tipped pen used for drawing and colouring.

market *n* **1** an occasion at which people meet to buy and sell merchandise. **2** a place at which a market is held. **3** the buying and selling of goods and services, esp. when unrestrained by political or social considerations: *the market has been brought into health care.* **4** the trading opportunities provided by a particular group of people: *the youth market.* **5** demand for a particular product. **6** short for **stock market**. **7 be in the market for** to wish to buy. **8 on the market** available for purchase. **9 seller's** *or* **buyer's market** a market characterized by excess demand (or supply) and thus favourable to sellers (or buyers). ✧ *adj* **10** of, relating to, or controlled by the buying and selling of goods and services, esp. when unrestrained by political or social considerations: *a market economy.*

✧ *vb* **-keting, -keted 11** to offer or produce for sale. ▷ **HISTORY** Latin *mercari* to trade ▶ **marketable** *adj*
market forces *pl n* the effect of supply and demand on trading within a free market.
market garden *n Chiefly Brit & NZ* a place where fruit and vegetables are grown for sale. ▶ **market gardener** *n*
marketing *n* the part of a business which controls the way that goods or services are sold.
marketing mix *n Marketing* the variables, such as price, promotion, and service, managed by an organization to influence demand for a product or service.
market maker *n Stock Exchange* a dealer in securities on the London Stock Exchange who can also deal with the public as a broker.
market-oriented *adj Marketing* focusing on consumers rather than on the products.
marketplace *n* **1** a place where a public market is held. **2** the commercial world of buying and selling.
market price *n* the prevailing price at which goods may be bought or sold.
market research *n* the study of customers' wants and purchases, and of the forces influencing them.
market segmentation *n Marketing* the division of a market into identifiable groups to improve the effectiveness of a marketing strategy.
market share *n Marketing* the percentage of a total market, in terms of either value or volume, accounted for by the sales of a specific brand.
market-test *vb* to put (a section of a public-sector service) out to tender, often before full privatization.
market town *n Chiefly Brit* the main town in an agricultural area, usually one where a market is regularly held.
marking *n* **1** the arrangement of colours on an animal or plant. **2** the assessment and correction of pupils' or students' written work by teachers.
marksman *n, pl* **-men** a person skilled in shooting. ▶ **marksmanship** *n*
mark-up *n* **1** an amount added to the cost of something to provide the seller with a profit. ✧ *vb* **mark up 2** to increase the cost of something by an amount or percentage in order to make a profit.
marl *n* a fine-grained rock consisting of clay, limestone, and silt used as a fertilizer. ▷ **HISTORY** Late Latin *margila* ▶ **marly** *adj*
marlin *n, pl* **-lin** *or* **-lins** a large fish with a long spear-like upper jaw, found in warm and tropical seas. ▷ **HISTORY** after *marlinspike* (because of its long jaw)
marlinspike *or* **marlinespike** (**mar**-lin-spike) *n Naut* a pointed metal tool used in separating strands of rope. ▷ **HISTORY** Dutch *marlijn* light rope + SPIKE
marmalade *n* a jam made from citrus fruits, esp. oranges. ▷ **HISTORY** Portuguese *marmelo* quince
marmoreal (mar-**more**-ee-al) *adj* of or like marble. ▷ **HISTORY** Latin *marmoreus*
marmoset *n* a small South American monkey with a long bushy tail. ▷ **HISTORY** Old French *marmouset* grotesque figure
marmot *n* any of various burrowing rodents of Europe, Asia, and North America. They are heavily built and have coarse fur. ▷ **HISTORY** French *marmotte*
maroon[1] *vb* **1** to abandon someone in a deserted area, esp. on an island. **2** to isolate in a helpless situation: *we're marooned here until the snow stops.* ▷ **HISTORY** American Spanish *cimarrón* wild ▶ **marooned** *adj*
maroon[2] *adj* **1** dark purplish-red. ✧ *n* **2** an exploding firework or flare used as a warning signal. ▷ **HISTORY** French: chestnut
marque (**mark**) *n* a brand of product, esp. of a car. ▷ **HISTORY** French
marquee *n* a large tent used for a party, exhibition, etc. ▷ **HISTORY** invented singular form of MARQUISE
marquess (**mar**-kwiss) *n* **1** (in the British Isles) a nobleman ranking between a duke and an earl. **2** See **marquis**.
marquetry *n, pl* **-quetries** a pattern of inlaid veneers of wood or metal used chiefly as ornamentation in furniture. ▷ **HISTORY** Old French *marqueter* to inlay
marquis *n, pl* **-quises** *or* **-quis** (in various countries) a nobleman ranking above a count, corresponding to a British marquess. ▷ **HISTORY** Old French *marchis* count of the frontier
marquise (mar-**keez**) *n* **1** (in various countries) a marchioness. **2** a gemstone cut in a pointed oval shape. ▷ **HISTORY** French
marram grass *n* a grass that grows on sandy shores: often planted to stabilize sand dunes. ▷ **HISTORY** Old Norse *marálmr*
marriage *n* **1** the state or relationship of being husband and wife: *the institution of marriage.* **2** the contract made by a man and woman to live as husband and wife. *RELATED ADJECTIVES* ▶ **connubial, nuptial 3** the ceremony formalizing this union; wedding. **4** a close union or relationship: *the marriage of scientific knowledge and industry.*
marriageable *adj* suitable for marriage, usually with reference to age.
married *adj* **1** having a husband or wife. **2** of marriage or married people: *married life.* ✧ *n* **3 marrieds** married people: *young marrieds.*
marrow *n* **1** the fatty tissue that fills the cavities of bones. **2** short for **vegetable marrow**. ▷ **HISTORY** Old English *mærg*
marry[1] *vb* **-ries, -rying, -ried 1** to take (someone) as one's husband or wife. **2** to join or give in marriage. **3** Also: **marry up** to fit together or unite; join: *their playing marries Irish traditional music and rock.* ▷ **HISTORY** Latin *maritare*
marry[2] *interj Archaic* an exclamation of surprise or anger. ▷ **HISTORY** euphemistic for the Virgin *Mary*
Mars *n* **1** the Roman god of war. **2** the fourth planet from the sun.
Marseillaise (mar-say-**yaze**) *n* **the Marseillaise** the French national anthem. ▷ **HISTORY** French

a b c d e f g h i j k l m n o p q r s t u v w x y z

(chanson) marseillaise (song) of Marseilles (first sung in Paris by the battalion of Marseilles)

marsh *n* low poorly drained land that is wet, muddy, and sometimes flooded. ▷ **HISTORY** Old English *merisc* ▶ **marshy** *adj*

marshal *n* **1** (in some armies and air forces) an officer of the highest rank: *Field Marshal.* **2** an officer who organizes or controls ceremonies or public events. **3** *US* the chief police or fire officer in some states. **4** (formerly in England) an officer of the royal family or court. ✧ *vb* **-shalling, -shalled** *or US* **-shaling, -shaled 5** to arrange in order: *she marshalled her facts and came to a conclusion.* **6** to assemble and organize people or vehicles in readiness for onward movement. **7** to guide or lead, esp. in a ceremonious way: *she marshalled them towards the lecture theatre.* ▷ **HISTORY** Old French *mareschal* ▶ **marshalcy** *n*

marshalling yard *n Railways* a place where railway wagons are shunted and made up into trains.

Marshal of the Royal Air Force *n* the highest rank in the Royal Air Force.

marsh gas *n* a gas largely composed of methane formed when plants decay in the absence of air.

marshland *n* land consisting of marshes.

marshmallow *n* a spongy pink or white sweet.

marsh mallow *n* a plant that grows in salt marshes and has pale pink flowers. It was formerly used to make marshmallows.

marsupial (mar-**soop**-ee-al) *n* **1** a mammal, such as a kangaroo or an opossum, the female of which carries her babies in a pouch at the front of her body until they reach a mature state. ✧ *adj* **2** of or like a marsupial. ▷ **HISTORY** Latin *marsupium* purse

mart *n* a market or trading centre. ▷ **HISTORY** Middle Dutch: market

Martello tower *n* a round tower used for coastal defence, formerly much used in Europe. ▷ **HISTORY** after Cape *Mortella* in Corsica

marten *n, pl* **-tens** *or* **-ten 1** any of several agile weasel-like mammals with bushy tails and golden-brown to blackish fur. **2** the fur of these animals. ▷ **HISTORY** Middle Dutch *martren*

martial *adj* of or characteristic of war, soldiers, or the military life: *martial music.* ▷ **HISTORY** Latin *martialis* of Mars, god of war

martial art *n* any of various philosophies and techniques of self-defence originating in the Far East, such as judo or karate.

martial law *n* rule of law maintained by military forces in the absence of civil law.

Martian (**marsh**-an) *adj* **1** of the planet Mars. ✧ *n* **2** an inhabitant of Mars, in science fiction.

martin *n* a bird of the swallow family with a square or slightly forked tail. ▷ **HISTORY** probably after St *Martin,* because the birds were believed to migrate at Martinmas

martinet *n* a person who maintains strict discipline. ▷ **HISTORY** after General *Martinet,* drillmaster under Louis XIV

martingale *n* a strap from the reins to the girth of a horse, preventing it from carrying its head too high. ▷ **HISTORY** French

martini *n* **1** (*often cap*) *Trademark* an Italian vermouth. **2** a cocktail of gin and vermouth.

Martinmas *n* the feast of St Martin on November 11: a quarter day in Scotland.

martyr *n* **1** a person who chooses to die rather than renounce his or her religious beliefs. **2** a person who suffers greatly or dies for a cause or belief. **3 a martyr to** suffering constantly from: *a martyr to arthritis.* ✧ *vb* **4** to make a martyr of. ▷ **HISTORY** Late Greek *martur-* witness ▶ **martyrdom** *n*

marvel *vb* **-velling, -velled** *or US* **-veling, -veled 1** to be filled with surprise or wonder. ✧ *n* **2** something that causes wonder. ▷ **HISTORY** Old French *merveille*

marvellous *or US* **marvelous** *adj* **1** excellent or splendid: *a marvellous idea.* **2** causing great wonder or surprise; extraordinary: *electricity is a marvellous thing.* ▶ **marvellously** *or US* **marvelously** *adv*

Marxism *n* the economic and political theories of Karl Marx (1818–83), German political philosopher, which argue that class struggle is the basic agency of historical change, and that capitalism will be superseded by communism. ▶ **Marxist** *n, adj*

marzipan *n* a mixture made from ground almonds, sugar, and egg whites that is put on top of cakes or used to make sweets. ▷ **HISTORY** Italian *marzapane*

masc. masculine.

mascara *n* a cosmetic for darkening the eyelashes. ▷ **HISTORY** Spanish: mask

mascot *n* a person, animal, or thing considered to bring good luck. ▷ **HISTORY** French *mascotte*

masculine *adj* **1** possessing qualities or characteristics considered typical of or appropriate to a man; manly. **2** unwomanly; not feminine. **3** *Grammar* denoting a gender of nouns that includes some male animate things. **4** *Prosody* denoting a rhyme between pairs of single final stressed syllables. ▷ **HISTORY** Latin *masculinus* ▶ **masculinity** *n*

maser *n* a device for amplifying microwaves, working on the same principle as a laser. ▷ **HISTORY** *m(icrowave) a(mplification by) s(timulated) e(mission of) r(adiation)*

mash *n* **1** a soft pulpy mass. **2** *Agriculture* bran, meal, or malt mixed with warm water and used as food for horses, cattle, or poultry. **3** *Brit informal* mashed potatoes. ✧ *vb* **4** to beat or crush into a mash. ▷ **HISTORY** Old English *mæsc-* ▶ **mashed** *adj*

mask *n* **1** any covering for the whole or a part of the face worn for amusement, protection, or disguise. **2** behaviour that hides one's true feelings: *his mask of detachment.* **3** *Surgery* a sterile gauze covering for the nose and mouth worn to minimize the spread of germs. **4** a device placed over the nose and mouth to facilitate or prevent inhalation of a gas. **5** a moulded likeness of a face or head, such as a death mask. **6** the face or head of an animal such as a fox. ✧ *vb* **7** to cover with or put on a mask. **8** to hide or disguise: *a high brick wall that masked the front of the building.* **9** to cover so as to protect. ▷ **HISTORY** Arabic *maskharah* clown ▶ **masked** *adj*

masking tape *n* an adhesive tape used to protect surfaces surrounding an area to be painted.

masochism (**mass**-oh-kiz-zum) *n* **1** *Psychiatry* a condition in which pleasure, esp. sexual pleasure, is obtained from feeling pain or from being humiliated. **2** a tendency to take pleasure from one's own suffering. ▷ **HISTORY** after Leopold von Sacher *Masoch,* novelist ▶ **masochist** *n, adj* ▶ **masochistic** *adj*

WORD HISTORY

'Masochism' derives its name from the Austrian novelist Leopold von Sacher Masoch (1836–1895), who wrote about the pleasures of masochism.

mason *n* a person skilled in building with stone. ▷ **HISTORY** Old French *masson*

Masonic *adj* of Freemasons or Freemasonry.

masonry *n* **1** stonework or brickwork. **2** the craft of a mason.

masque (**mask**) *n* a dramatic entertainment of the 16th to 17th centuries, consisting of dancing, dialogue, and song. ▷ **HISTORY** variant of *mask* ▶ **masquer** *n*

masquerade (mask-er-**aid**) *vb* **-ading, -aded** **1** to pretend to be someone or something else. ✧ *n* **2** an attempt to keep secret the real identity or nature of something: *he was unable to keep up his masquerade as the war's victor.* **3** a party at which the guests wear masks and costumes. ▷ **HISTORY** Spanish *mascara* mask

mass *n* **1** a large body of something without a definite shape. **2** a collection of the component parts of something: *a mass of fibres.* **3** a large amount or number, as of people. **4** the main part or majority. **5** the size of a body; bulk. **6** *Physics* a physical quantity expressing the amount of matter in a body. **7** (in painting or drawing) an area of unified colour, shade, or intensity. ✧ *adj* **8** done or occurring on a large scale: *mass hysteria.* **9** consisting of a mass or large number, esp. of people: *a mass meeting.* ✧ *vb* **10** to join together into a mass. ✧ See also **masses.** ▷ **HISTORY** Latin *massa* ▶ **massed** *adj*

Mass *n* **1** (in the Roman Catholic Church and certain other Christian churches) a service in which bread and wine are consecrated to represent the body and blood of Christ. **2** a musical setting of parts of this service. ▷ **HISTORY** Church Latin *missa*

massacre (**mass**-a-ker) *n* **1** the wanton or savage killing of large numbers of people. **2** *Informal* an overwhelming defeat. ✧ *vb* **-cring, -cred** **3** to kill people indiscriminately in large numbers. **4** *Informal* to defeat overwhelmingly. ▷ **HISTORY** Old French

massage (**mass**-ahzh) *n* **1** the kneading or rubbing of parts of the body to reduce pain or stiffness or help relaxation. ✧ *vb* **-saging, -saged** **2** to give a massage to. **3** to manipulate (statistics or evidence) to produce a desired result. ▷ **HISTORY** French *masser* to rub

massasauga (mass-a-**saw**-ga) *n* a North American venomous snake with a horny rattle at the end of the tail. ▷ **HISTORY** after the *Missisauga* River, Ontario, Canada

masses *pl n* **1 the masses** ordinary people as a group. **2 masses of** *Informal, chiefly Brit* a great number or quantity of: *masses of food.*

masseur (mass-**ur**) *or fem* **masseuse** (mass-**uhz**) *n* a person who gives massages.

massif (**mass**-seef) *n* a series of connected masses of rock forming a mountain range. ▷ **HISTORY** French

massive *adj* **1** (of objects) large, bulky, heavy, and usually solid. **2** impressive or imposing. **3** intensive or considerable: *a massive overdose.* ▷ **HISTORY** French *massif* ▶ **massively** *adv*

mass-market *adj* of, for, or appealing to a large number of people; popular: *mass-market newspapers.*

mass media *pl n* the means of communication that reach large numbers of people, such as television, newspapers, and radio.

mass movement *n Geol* a general term for movement of rocks and sediment down a slope as a result of gravity and the action of water.

mass noun *n Grammar* a noun that refers to a substance rather than to an individual object, e.g., *water* as opposed to *lake*; mass nouns can be preceded by *some, a lot of, much,* and *more.*

mass number *n* the total number of protons and neutrons in the nucleus of an atom.

mass-produce *vb* **-producing, -produced** to manufacture standardized goods on a large scale by extensive use of machinery. ▶ **mass-produced** *adj* ▶ **mass-production** *n*

mass spectrometer *n* an instrument for analysing the composition of a sample of material, in which ions, produced from the sample, are separated by electric or magnetic fields according to their ratios of charge to mass.

mast[1] *n* **1** *Naut* a vertical pole for supporting sails, radar equipment, etc., above the deck of a ship. **2** a tall upright pole used as an aerial for radio or television broadcasting: *a television mast.* **3 before the mast** *Naut* as an apprentice seaman. ▷ **HISTORY** Old English *mæst*

mast[2] *n* the fruit of forest trees, such as beech or oak, used as food for pigs. ▷ **HISTORY** Old English *mæst*

mastectomy (mass-**tek**-tom-ee) *n, pl* **-mies** surgical removal of a breast. ▷ **HISTORY** Greek *mastos* breast + *tomē* a cutting

master *n* **1** the man who has authority over others, such as the head of a household, the employer of servants, or the owner of slaves or animals. **2** a person with exceptional skill at a certain thing: *B.B. King is a master of the blues.* **3** a person who has complete control of a situation: *the master of his portfolio.* **4** an original copy or tape from which duplicates are made. **5** a craftsman fully qualified to practise his trade and to train others: *a master builder*. **6** a player of a game, esp. chess or bridge, who has won a specified number of tournament games. **7** a highly regarded teacher or leader. **8** a graduate holding a master's degree. **9** the chief officer aboard a merchant ship. **10** *Chiefly Brit* a male teacher. **11** the superior person or side in a contest. **12** the heir apparent of a Scottish viscount or baron: *the Master of Ballantrae*. ✧ *adj* **13** overall or controlling: *master plan*. **14** designating a mechanism that controls others: *master switch*. **15** main or principal: *master bedroom*. ✧ *vb* **16** to become thoroughly proficient in. **17** to overcome or defeat. ▷ HISTORY Latin *magister* teacher

master aircrew *n* a rank in the Royal Air Force, equal to warrant officer.

masterful *adj* **1** showing great skill. **2** domineering or authoritarian. ▶ **masterfully** *adv*

master key *n* a key that opens all the locks of a set; passkey.

masterly *adj* showing great skill; expert.

mastermind *vb* **1** to plan and direct a complex task or project. ✧ *n* **2** a person who plans and directs a complex task or project.

Master of Arts *n* a degree, usually postgraduate in a nonscientific subject, or a person holding this degree.

master of ceremonies *n* a person who presides over a public ceremony, formal dinner, or entertainment, introducing the events and performers.

Master of Science *n* a degree, usually postgraduate in a scientific subject, or a person holding this degree.

Master of the Rolls *n* (in England) the senior civil judge in the country and the head of the Public Record Office.

masterpiece *or* **masterwork** *n* **1** an outstanding work or performance. **2** the most outstanding piece of work of an artist or craftsman.

masterstroke *n* an outstanding piece of strategy, skill, or talent.

mastery *n, pl* **-teries 1** outstanding skill or expertise. **2** complete power or control: *he had complete mastery over the country*.

masthead *n* **1** *Naut* the highest part of a mast. **2** the name of a newspaper or periodical printed at the top of the front page.

mastic *n* **1** an aromatic resin obtained from a Mediterranean tree and used to make varnishes and lacquers. **2** any of several putty-like substances used as a filler, adhesive, or seal. ▷ HISTORY Greek *mastikhē*

masticate *vb* **-cating, -cated** to chew food. ▷ HISTORY Greek *mastikhan* to grind the teeth ▶ **mastication** *n*

mastiff *n* a large powerful short-haired dog, usually fawn or brown with dark streaks. ▷ HISTORY Latin *mansuetus* tame

mastitis *n* inflammation of the breast.

mastodon *n* an extinct elephant-like mammal. ▷ HISTORY New Latin, literally: breast-tooth, referring to the nipple-shaped projections on the teeth

mastoid *adj* **1** shaped like a nipple or breast. ✧ *n* **2** a nipple-like projection of bone behind the ear. **3** *Informal* mastoiditis. ▷ HISTORY Greek *mastos* breast

mastoiditis *n* inflammation of the mastoid.

masturbate *vb* **-bating, -bated** to fondle one's own genitals, or those of someone else, to cause sexual pleasure. ▷ HISTORY Latin *masturbari* ▶ **masturbation** *n*

mat[1] *n* **1** a thick flat piece of fabric used as a floor covering, a place to wipe one's shoes, etc. **2** a small pad of material used to protect a surface from heat or scratches from an object placed upon it. **3** a large piece of thick padded material put on the floor as a surface for wrestling, gymnastics, etc. ✧ *vb* **matting, matted 4** to tangle or become tangled into a dense mass. ▷ HISTORY Old English *matte*

mat[2] *adj* same as **matt**. ▷ HISTORY French, literally: dead

matador *n* the bullfighter armed with a sword, who attempts to kill the bull. ▷ HISTORY Spanish, from *matar* to kill

matai *n* a New Zealand tree, the wood of which is used for timber for building. ▷ HISTORY Maori

match[1] *n* **1** a formal game or sports event in which people or teams compete. **2** a person or thing able to provide competition for another: *he has met his match*. **3** a person or thing that resembles, harmonizes with, or is equivalent to another: *the colours aren't a perfect match, but they're close enough; white wine is not a good match for steak*. **4** a person or thing that is an exact copy or equal of another. **5** a partnership between a man and a woman, as in marriage. **6** a person regarded as a possible partner in marriage: *for any number of men she would have been a good match*. ✧ *vb* **7** to fit parts together. **8** to resemble, harmonize with, or equal one another or something else: *our bedroom curtains match the bedspread; she walked at a speed that he could barely match*. **9** to find a match for. **10 match with** *or* **against a** to compare in order to determine which is the superior. **b** to arrange a competition between. ▷ HISTORY Old English *gemæcca* spouse ▶ **matching** *adj*

match[2] *n* **1** a thin strip of wood or cardboard tipped with a chemical that ignites when scraped against a rough or specially treated surface. **2** a fuse used to fire cannons' explosives. ▷ HISTORY Old French *meiche*

matchbox *n* a small box for holding matches.

match-fit *adj Sport* in good physical condition for competing in a match.

matchless *adj* unequalled.

matchmaker *n* a person who introduces people in the hope that they will form a couple. ▶ **matchmaking** *n, adj*

match play *n Golf* scoring according to the number of holes won and lost.

match point *n Sport* the final point needed to win a match.

matchstick *n* **1** the wooden part of a match. ✧ *adj* **2** (esp. of drawn figures) thin and straight: *little matchstick men.*

matchwood *n* **1** wood suitable for making matches. **2** splinters.

mate[1] *n* **1 a** *Informal, chiefly Brit, Austral, & NZ* a friend: often used as a term of address between males: *I spotted my mate Jimmy McCrae at the other end of the bar; that's all right, mate.* **b** an associate or colleague: *a classmate; the governor's running mate.* **2** the sexual partner of an animal. **3** a marriage partner. **4** *Naut* any officer below the master on a commercial ship. **5** (in some trades) an assistant: *a plumber's mate.* **6** one of a pair of matching items. ✧ *vb* **mating, mated 7** to pair (a male and female animal) or (of animals) to pair for breeding. **8** to marry. **9** to join as a pair. ▷ **HISTORY** Low German

mate[2] *n, vb* **mating, mated** *Chess* same as **checkmate**.

material *n* **1** the substance of which a thing is made. **2** cloth. **3** ideas or notes that a finished work may be based on: *the material of the story resembles an incident in his own life.* ✧ *adj* **4** concerned with or composed of physical matter or substance; not relating to spiritual or abstract things: *the material universe.* **5** of or affecting economic or physical wellbeing: *material prosperity.* **6** relevant or pertinent: *material evidence.* ✧ See also **materials**. ▷ **HISTORY** Latin *materia* matter

materialism *n* **1** excessive interest in and desire for money or possessions. **2** the belief that only the material world exists. ▶ **materialist** *n, adj* ▶ **materialistic** *adj*

materiality *n Chiefly law* the quality of being relevant to the issue before court.

materialize *or* **-ise** *vb* **-izing, -ized** *or* **-ising, -ised 1** *Not universally accepted* to become fact; actually happen: *the promised pay rise never materialized.* **2** to appear after being invisible: *trees materialized out of the gloom.* **3** to take shape: *after hours of talks, a plan began to materialize.* ▶ **materialization** *or* **-isation** *n*

materially *adv* to a significant extent: *we were not materially affected.*

material process *n Functional grammar* an action or process specified by a verb group. Compare **mental process, relational process, verbal process**.

materials *pl n* the equipment necessary for a particular activity: *building materials.*

materiel (mat-ear-ee-**ell**) *n* the materials and equipment of an organization, esp. of a military force. ▷ **HISTORY** French

maternal *adj* **1** of or characteristic of a mother. **2** related through the mother's side of the family: *his maternal uncle.* ▷ **HISTORY** Latin *mater* mother ▶ **maternally** *adv*

maternity *n* **1** motherhood. **2** motherliness. ✧ *adj* **3** relating to women during pregnancy or childbirth: *maternity leave.*

mate's rates *pl n NZ informal* reduced charges offered to a friend or colleague.

matey *adj Brit informal* friendly or intimate.

math *n US & Canad informal* short for **mathematics**.

mathematical *adj* **1** using, used in, or relating to mathematics. **2** having the precision of mathematics. ▶ **mathematically** *adv*

mathematician *n* an expert or specialist in mathematics.

mathematics *n* **1** a group of related sciences, including algebra, geometry, and calculus, which use a specialized notation to study number, quantity, shape, and space. **2** numerical calculations involved in the solution of a problem. ▷ **HISTORY** Greek *mathēma* a science

maths *n Brit & Austral informal* short for **mathematics**.

matinee (**mat**-in-nay) *n* an afternoon performance of a play or film. ▷ **HISTORY** French

matins *n* an early morning service in various Christian Churches. ▷ **HISTORY** Latin *matutinus* of the morning

matriarch (**mate**-ree-ark) *n* the female head of a tribe or family. ▷ **HISTORY** Latin *mater* mother + Greek *arkhein* to rule ▶ **matriarchal** *adj*

matriarchy *n, pl* **-chies** a form of social organization in which a female is head of the family or society, and descent and kinship are traced through the female line.

matrices (**may**-triss-seez) *n* a plural of **matrix**.

matricide *n* **1** the act of killing one's mother. **2** a person who kills his or her mother. ▷ **HISTORY** Latin *mater* mother + *caedere* to kill ▶ **matricidal** *adj*

matriculate *vb* **-lating, -lated** to enrol or be enrolled in a college or university. ▷ **HISTORY** Medieval Latin *matriculare* to register ▶ **matriculation** *n*

matrilineal (mat-rill-**in**-ee-al) *adj* relating to descent through the female line.

matrimony *n* the state of being married. ▷ **HISTORY** Latin *matrimonium* wedlock ▶ **matrimonial** *adj*

matrix (**may**-trix) *n, pl* **-trices** *or* **matrixes 1** the context or framework in which something is formed or develops: *a highly complex matrix of overlapping interests.* **2** the rock in which fossils or pebbles are embedded. **3** a mould, esp. one used in printing. **4** *Maths* a rectangular array of numbers elements set out in rows and columns. ▷ **HISTORY** Latin: womb

matron *n* **1** a staid or dignified married woman. **2** a woman in charge of the domestic or medical arrangements in an institution. **3** *Brit* (formerly) the administrative head of the nursing staff in a hospital. ▷ **HISTORY** Latin *matrona* ▶ **matronly** *adj*

matt *or* **matte** *adj* having a dull surface rather than a shiny one.

matted *adj* tangled into a thick mass.

matter *n* **1** the substance of which something, esp. a physical object, is made; material. **2** substance that occupies space and has mass, as distinguished from substance that is mental or spiritual. **3** substance of a specified type: *vegetable matter.* **4** an event, situation, or subject: *a matter of taste; the break-in is a matter for the police.* **5** a quantity or amount: *a matter of a few pounds.* **6** the content of written or verbal material as distinct from its style or form. **7** written material in general: *advertising matter.* **8** a secretion or discharge, such as pus. **9 for that matter** as regards that. **10 no matter** regardless of; irrespective of: *you have to leave, no matter what she thinks.* **11 the matter** wrong; the trouble: *there's nothing the matter.* ✧ *vb* **12** to be of importance. ✧ *interj* **no matter 13** it is unimportant. ▷ **HISTORY** Latin *materia* cause, substance

matter of fact *n* **1 as a matter of fact** actually; in fact. ✧ *adj* **matter-of-fact 2** unimaginative or emotionless: *he conducted the executions in a completely matter-of-fact manner.*

matting *n* a coarsely woven fabric used as a floor covering.

mattock *n* a type of large pick that has one flat, horizontal end to its blade, used for loosening soil. ▷ **HISTORY** Old English *mattuc*

mattress *n* a large flat cushion with a strong cover, filled with cotton, foam rubber, etc., and often including coiled springs, used as a bed. ▷ **HISTORY** Arabic *almatrah* place where something is thrown

maturation *n* the process of becoming mature.

mature *adj* **1** fully developed physically or mentally; grown-up. **2** (of plans or theories) fully considered and thought-out. **3** sensible and balanced in personality and emotional behaviour. **4** due or payable: *a mature insurance policy.* **5** (of fruit, wine, or cheese) ripe or fully aged. ✧ *vb* **-turing, -tured 6** to make or become mature. **7** (of bills or bonds) to become due for payment or repayment. ▷ **HISTORY** Latin *maturus* early, developed ▶ **maturity** *n*

matzo *n, pl* **matzos** a large very thin biscuit of unleavened bread, traditionally eaten by Jews during Passover. ▷ **HISTORY** Hebrew *matsāh*

maudlin *adj* foolishly or tearfully sentimental, esp. as a result of drinking. ▷ **HISTORY** Middle English *Maudelen* Mary Magdalene, often shown weeping

maul *vb* **1** to tear with the claws: *she was badly mauled by a lion.* **2** to criticize a play, performance, etc., severely: *the film was mauled by the critics.* **3** to handle roughly or clumsily. ✧ *n* **4** *Rugby* a loose scrum. ▷ **HISTORY** Latin *malleus* hammer

maunder *vb* to move, talk, or act aimlessly or idly. ▷ **HISTORY** origin unknown

Maundy Thursday *n Christianity* the Thursday before Easter observed as a commemoration of the Last Supper. ▷ **HISTORY** Latin *mandatum* commandment

mausoleum (maw-so-**lee**-um) *n* a large stately tomb. ▷ **HISTORY** Greek *mausōleion* the tomb of king *Mausolus*

mauve *adj* light purple. ▷ **HISTORY** Latin *malva* mallow

maverick *n* **1** a person of independent or unorthodox views. **2** (in the US and Canada) an unbranded stray calf. ✧ *adj* **3** (of a person or his or her views) independent and unorthodox. ▷ **HISTORY** after Samuel A. *Maverick,* Texas rancher

maw *n* the mouth, throat, or stomach of an animal. ▷ **HISTORY** Old English *maga*

mawkish *adj* foolishly or embarrassingly sentimental. ▷ **HISTORY** obsolete *mawk* maggot ▶ **mawkishness** *n*

max. maximum.

maxilla *n, pl* **-lae 1** the upper jawbone of a vertebrate. **2** any part of the mouth in insects and other arthropods. ▷ **HISTORY** Latin: jaw ▶ **maxillary** *adj*

maxim *n* a brief expression of a general truth, principle, or rule of conduct. ▷ **HISTORY** Latin *maxima,* in the phrase *maxima propositio* basic axiom

maximal *adj* of or being a maximum; the greatest possible.

maximize *or* **-ise** *vb* **-izing, -ized** *or* **-ising, -ised** to make as high or great as possible; increase to a maximum. ▶ **maximization** *or* **-isation** *n*

maximum *n, pl* **-mums** *or* **-ma 1** the greatest possible amount or degree: *he gave the police the maximum of cooperation.* **2** the greatest amount recorded, allowed, or reached: *keep to a maximum of two drinks a day.* ✧ *adj* **3** of, being, or showing a maximum or maximums: *maximum speed.* ▷ **HISTORY** Latin: greatest

maxwell *n* the cgs unit of magnetic flux. ▷ **HISTORY** after J. C. *Maxwell,* physicist

may[1] *vb, past* **might** used as an auxiliary to indicate or express: **1** that permission is requested by or granted to someone: *she may leave.* **2** the possibility that something could happen: *problems which may well have tragic consequences.* **3** ability or capacity, esp. in questions: *may I help you?* **4** a strong wish: *long may she reign.* ▷ **HISTORY** Old English *mæg,* from *magan* to be able

> **☑ WORD TIP**
> It was formerly considered correct to use *may* rather than *can* when referring to permission as in: *you may use the laboratory for your experiments*, but this use of *may* is now almost entirely restricted to polite questions such as: *may I open the window?* The use of *may* with *if* in constructions such as *your analysis may have been more credible if...* is generally regarded as incorrect, *might* being preferred: *your analysis might have been more credible if...*

may[2] *or* **may tree** *n Brit* same as **hawthorn**. ▷ **HISTORY** from *May*

May *n* the fifth month of the year. ▷ **HISTORY** probably from *Maia*, Roman goddess

Maya *n* **1** (*pl* **-ya** *or* **-yas**) a member of an indigenous people of Central America, who once had an advanced civilization. **2** the language of this people. ▶ **Mayan** *n, adj*

maybe *adv* perhaps.

Mayday *n* the international radio distress signal. ▷ **HISTORY** phonetic spelling of French *m'aidez* help me

mayfly *n, pl* **-flies** a short-lived insect with large transparent wings.

mayhem *n* **1** any violent destruction or confusion: *a driver caused motorway mayhem.* **2** *Law* the maiming of a person. ▷ **HISTORY** Anglo-French *mahem* injury

mayonnaise *n* a thick creamy sauce made from egg yolks, oil, and vinegar. ▷ **HISTORY** French

mayor *n* the civic head of a municipal council in many countries. ▷ **HISTORY** Latin *maior* greater ▸ **mayoral** *adj*

mayoralty *n, pl* **-ties** the office or term of office of a mayor.

mayoress *n* **1** *Chiefly Brit* the wife of a mayor. **2** a female mayor.

maypole *n* a tall pole around which people dance during May-Day celebrations.

maze *n* **1** a complex network of paths or passages designed to puzzle people who try and find their way through or out of it. **2** a puzzle in which the player must trace a path through a complex network of lines without touching or crossing any of them. **3** any confusing network or system: *a maze of regulations.* ▷ **HISTORY** from *amaze*

mazurka *n* **1** a lively Polish dance in triple time. **2** music for this dance. ▷ **HISTORY** Polish

mb millibar.

Mb *Computers* megabyte.

MB **1** Bachelor of Medicine. **2** Manitoba.

MBE (in Britain) Member of the Order of the British Empire.

MC **1** Master of Ceremonies. **2** (in the US) Member of Congress. **3** (in Britain) Military Cross.

MCC (in Britain) Marylebone Cricket Club.

MCh Master of Surgery. ▷ **HISTORY** Latin *Magister Chirurgiae*

Md *Chem* mendelevium.

MD **1** Doctor of Medicine. ▷ **HISTORY** Latin *Medicinae Doctor* **2** Managing Director. **3** Maryland.

MDF medium-density fibreboard: a wood-substitute material used in interior decoration.

MDMA methylenedioxymethamphetamine: the chemical name for the drug ecstasy.

me[1] *pron* (*objective*) **1** refers to the speaker or writer: *that hurts me.* ✧ *n* **2** *Informal* the personality of the speaker or writer or something that expresses it: *the real me.* ▷ **HISTORY** Old English *mē*

> **WORD TIP**
> It was formerly regarded as correct to use *I, he, she,* etc. rather than *me, him, her,* after the verb *to be*, as in: *it is I who told him.* Since both *I* and *me* can sound strange in a sentence like this, it is better to use a different construction: *I am the one who told him.* The use of a possessive before an *-ing* form of a verb was formerly thought to be preferable to using *me,* etc., but now both forms are acceptable: *he didn't like my/me having a job of my own.*

me[2] *or* **mi** *n Music* (in tonic sol-fa) the third note of any ascending major scale.

ME **1** Maine. **2** Middle English. **3** myalgic encephalomyelitis: see **chronic fatigue syndrome**.

mead[1] *n* a wine-like alcoholic drink made from honey, often with spices added. ▷ **HISTORY** Old English *meodu*

mead[2] *n Archaic or poetic* a meadow. ▷ **HISTORY** Old English *mǣd*

meadow *n* **1** a grassy field used for hay or for grazing animals. **2** a low-lying piece of grassland, often near a river. ▷ **HISTORY** Old English *mǣdwe*

meadowsweet *n* a plant with dense heads of small fragrant cream-coloured flowers.

meagre *or US* **meager** *adj* **1** not enough in amount or extent: *meagre wages.* **2** thin or emaciated. ▷ **HISTORY** Old French *maigre*

meal[1] *n* **1** any of the regular occasions, such as breakfast or dinner, when food is served and eaten. **2** the food served and eaten. **3** **make a meal of** *Informal* to perform (a task) with unnecessarily great effort. ▷ **HISTORY** Old English *mǣl* measure, set time, meal

meal[2] *n* **1** the edible part of a grain or bean pulse (excluding wheat) ground to a coarse powder. **2** *Scot* oatmeal. **3** *Chiefly US* maize flour. ▷ **HISTORY** Old English *melu* ▸ **mealy** *adj*

mealie *or* **mielie** *n* (*often pl*) *S African* same as **maize**. ▷ **HISTORY** Afrikaans, from Latin *milium* millet

meals-on-wheels *n* a service taking hot meals to the elderly or infirm in their own homes.

meal ticket *n Slang* a person or situation providing a source of livelihood or income. ▷ **HISTORY** from original US sense of ticket entitling holder to a meal

mealy-mouthed *adj* unwilling or afraid to speak plainly.

mean[1] *vb* **meaning, meant 1** to intend to convey or express: *what do you mean by that?* **2** to denote, represent, or signify: *a red light means 'stop!'; 'gravid' is a technical term meaning 'pregnant'.* **3** to intend: *I meant to phone you earlier, but didn't have time.* **4** to say or do in all seriousness: *the boss means what she says.* **5** to have the importance specified: *music means everything to him.* **6** to destine or design for a certain person or purpose: *those sweets weren't meant for you.* **7** to produce, cause, or result in: *major road works will mean long traffic delays.* **8** to foretell: *those black clouds mean rain.* **9** **mean well** to have good intentions. ▷ **HISTORY** Old English *mǣnan*

> **WORD TIP**
> In standard English *mean* should not be followed by *for* when expressing intention: *I didn't mean this to happen* (not *I didn't mean for this to happen*).

mean[2] *adj* **1** not willing to give or use much of something, esp. money: *she was noticeably mean; don't be mean with the butter.* **2** unkind or spiteful: *a mean trick.* **3** *Informal* ashamed: *she felt mean about not letting the children stay out late.* **4** *Informal, chiefly US, Canad & Austral* bad-tempered or vicious. **5** shabby and poor: *a mean little room.* **6** *Slang* excellent or skilful: *he plays a mean trumpet.* **7** **no mean a** of high quality: *no mean player.* **b** difficult:

no mean feat. ▷ **HISTORY** Old English *gemǣne* common ▶ **meanly** *adv* ▶ **meanness** *n*

mean³ *n* **1** the middle point, state, or course between limits or extremes. **2** *Maths* **a** the mid-point between the highest and lowest number in a set. **b** the average. ✧ *adj* **3** intermediate in size or quantity. **4** occurring halfway between extremes or limits; average. ▷ **HISTORY** Late Latin *medianus* median

meander (mee-**and**-er) *vb* **1** (of a river, road, etc.) to follow a winding course. **2** to wander without definite aim or direction. ✧ *n* **3** *Geog* a curve or bend, as in a river. **4** a winding course or movement. ▷ **HISTORY** Greek *Maiandros* the River Maeander

mean deviation *n Statistics* the difference between an observed value of a variable and its mean.

meanie *or* **meany** *n Informal* **1** *Chiefly Brit* a miserly person. **2** *Chiefly US* a nasty ill-tempered person.

meaning *n* **1** the sense or significance of a word, sentence, or symbol. **2** the inner, symbolic, or true interpretation or message: *the meaning of the New Testament.*

meaningful *adj* **1** serious and important: *a meaningful relationship.* **2** intended to express a feeling or opinion: *a meaningful pause.*

meaningless *adj* having no meaning or purpose; futile.

means *n* **1** the medium, method, or instrument used to obtain a result or achieve an end: *a means of transport.* ✧ *pl n* **2** income: *a man of means.* **3 by all means** without hesitation or doubt; certainly. **4 by means of** with the use or help of. **5 by no** *or* **not by any means** on no account; in no way.

mean sea level *n* (in the U.K.) the sea level used by the Ordnance Survey as a datum level, determined at Newlyn in Cornwall. See **sea level**.

means test *n* the checking of a person's income to determine whether he or she qualifies for financial aid. ▶ **means-tested** *adj*

meant *vb* the past of **mean¹**.

meantime *n* **1** the intervening period: *in the meantime.* ✧ *adv* **2** same as **meanwhile**.

mean time *or* **mean solar time** *n* the times, at a particular place, measured so as to give 24-hour days (mean solar days) throughout a year.

meanwhile *adv* **1** during the intervening period. **2** at the same time, esp. in another place.

measles *n* a highly contagious viral disease common in children, characterized by fever and a rash of small red spots. ✧ See also **German measles.** ▷ **HISTORY** Low German *masele* spot on the skin

measly *adj* **-slier, -sliest 1** *Informal* too small in quantity or value. **2** having or relating to measles.

measure *n* **1** the size, quantity, or degree of something, as discovered by measurement or calculation. **2** a device for measuring distance, volume, etc., such as a graduated scale or container. **3** a system or unit of measurement: *the joule is a measure of energy.* **4** an amount of alcoholic drink, esp. that served as standard in a bar. **5** degree or extent: *a measure of success.* **6** a particular action intended to achieve an effect: *radical measures are needed to cut unemployment.* **7** a legislative bill, act, or resolution. **8** *Music* same as **bar¹** (sense 9). **9** *Prosody* poetic rhythm or metre. **10** *Prosody* a metrical foot. **11** *Old-fashioned* a dance. **12 for good measure** as an extra precaution or beyond requirements. ✧ *vb* **-uring, -ured 13** to determine the size, amount, etc., of by measurement: *he measured the room for a new carpet.* **14** to indicate or record the size, speed, force, etc., of: *this dial measures the pressure in the pipe.* **15** to have the size, quantity, etc., specified: *the room measures six feet.* **16** to estimate or assess: *you cannot measure intelligence purely by exam results.* **17** to function as a measurement of: *the ohm measures electrical resistance.* **18** to bring into competition or conflict with: *he measured his strength against that of his opponent.* ✧ See also **measures.** ▷ **HISTORY** Latin *mensura* ▶ **measurable** *adj*

measured *adj* **1** slow or stately. **2** carefully considered; deliberate.

measurement *n* **1** the act or process of measuring. **2** an amount, extent, or size determined by measuring. **3** a system or unit used for measuring: *the kilometre is the standard measurement of distance in most countries.* **4 measurements** the size of a person's waist, chest, hips, etc., used when buying clothes.

measures *pl n* rock strata that contain a particular type of deposit: *coal measures.*

meat *n* **1** the flesh of animals used as food. **2** the essence or gist: *get to the meat of your lecture as quickly as possible.* ▷ **HISTORY** Old English *mete* ▶ **meatless** *adj*

meaty *adj* **meatier, meatiest 1** of, like, or full of meat. **2** heavily built; fleshy or brawny. **3** full of import or interest: *a meaty historical drama.*

Mecca *n* **1** the holy city of Islam. **2** a place that attracts many visitors.

mechanic *n* a person skilled in maintaining or operating machinery or motors. ▷ **HISTORY** Greek *mēkhanē* machine

mechanical *adj* **1** made, performed, or operated by machinery. **2** able to understand how machines work and how to repair or maintain them. **3 a** (of an action) done without thought or feeling. **b** (of a task) not requiring any thought; routine or repetitive. **4** of or involving the science of mechanics. ▶ **mechanically** *adv*

mechanical digestion *n Biol* the process of food being broken down into smaller pieces, esp. by the teeth, chewing and grinding it.

mechanical drawing *n* a drawing to scale of a machine or architectural plan from which dimensions can be taken.

mechanical engineering *n* the branch of engineering concerned with the design, construction, and operation of machines.

mechanics *n* **1** the scientific study of motion and force. **2** the science of designing, constructing, and operating machines. ✧ *pl n* **3** the technical aspects of something.

mechanism *n* **1** a system of moving parts that performs some function, esp. in a machine. **2** any mechanical device or part of such a device. **3** a process or technique: *the body's defence mechanisms.* ▶ **mechanistic** *adj*

mechanize *or* **-nise** *vb* **-nizing, -nized** *or* **-nising, -nised 1** to equip a factory or industry with machinery. **2** to make mechanical or automatic. **3** *Mil* to equip an army with armoured vehicles. ▶ **mechanization** *or* **-nisation** *n*

med. 1 medical. **2** medicine. **3** medieval. **4** medium.

MEd Master of Education.

medal *n* a small flat piece of metal bearing an inscription or image, given as an award or in commemoration of some outstanding event. ▷ HISTORY French *médaille*

medallion *n* **1** a disc-shaped ornament worn on a chain round the neck. **2** a large medal. **3** a circular decorative device used in architecture. ▷ HISTORY Italian *medaglia* medal

medallist *or US* **medalist** *n Chiefly sport* a winner of a medal or medals.

meddle *vb* **-dling, -dled** to interfere annoyingly. ▷ HISTORY Old French *medler* ▶ **meddler** *n* ▶ **meddlesome** *adj*

media *n* **1** a plural of **medium. 2 the media** the mass media collectively. ✧ *adj* **3** of or relating to the mass media: *media hype.*

> **WORD TIP**
> When *media* refers to the mass media, it is sometimes treated as a singular form, as in: *the media has shown great interest in these events.* Many people think this use is incorrect and that *media* should always be treated as a plural form: *the media have shown great interest in these events.*

mediaeval (med-ee-**eve**-al) *adj* same as **medieval**.

media event *n* an event that is staged for or exploited by the mass media.

medial (**mee**-dee-al) *adj* of or situated in the middle. ▷ HISTORY Latin *medius* middle ▶ **medially** *adv*

median *n* **1** a middle point, plane, or part. **2** *Geom* a straight line joining one corner of a triangle to the midpoint of the opposite side. **3** *Statistics* the middle value in a frequency distribution, below and above which lie values with equal total frequencies. ▷ HISTORY Latin *medius* middle

median strip *n US, Canad & NZ* the strip that separates the two sides of a motorway or dual carriageway.

mediate (**mee**-dee-ate) *vb* **-ating, -ated 1** to intervene between people or in a dispute in order to bring about agreement. **2** to resolve differences by mediation. **3** to be changed slightly by (an experience or event): *clients' attitudes to social workers have often been mediated by their past experiences.* ▷ HISTORY Late Latin *mediare* to be in the middle ▶ **mediator** *n*

mediation *n Law* the act of mediating; intercession between people, states, etc. in an attempt to reconcile disputed matters.

medic *n Informal* a doctor, medical orderly, or medical student. ▷ HISTORY from MEDICAL

medical *adj* **1** of or relating to the science of medicine or to the treatment of patients without surgery. ✧ *n* **2** *Informal* a medical examination. ▷ HISTORY Latin *medicus* physician ▶ **medically** *adv*

medical certificate *n* **1** a doctor's certificate giving evidence of a person's unfitness for work. **2** a document stating the result of a satisfactory medical examination.

medicament (mid-**dik**-a-ment) *n* a medicine.

medicate *vb* **-cating, -cated 1** to treat a patient with a medicine. **2** to add a medication to (a bandage, shampoo, etc.). ▷ HISTORY Latin *medicare* to heal ▶ **medicative** *adj*

medication *n* **1** treatment with drugs or remedies. **2** a drug or remedy.

medicinal (mid-**diss**-in-al) *adj* relating to or having therapeutic properties. ▶ **medicinally** *adv*

medicine *n* **1** any substance used in treating or alleviating the symptoms of disease. **2** the science of preventing, diagnosing, or curing disease. **3** any nonsurgical branch of medical science. **4 take one's medicine** to accept a deserved punishment. ▷ HISTORY Latin *medicina (ars)* (art) of healing

medicine man *n* (among certain peoples) a person believed to have supernatural powers of healing.

medico *n, pl* **-cos** *Informal* a doctor or medical student.

medieval *or* **mediaeval** (med-ee-**eve**-al) *adj* **1** of, relating to, or in the style of the Middle Ages. **2** *Informal* old-fashioned or primitive. ▷ HISTORY New Latin *medium aevum* the middle age ▶ **medievalist** *or* **mediaevalist** *n*

Medieval Greek *n* the Greek language from the 7th to 13th century AD.

Medieval Latin *n* the Latin language as used throughout Europe in the Middle Ages.

mediocre (mee-dee-**oak**-er) *adj* not very high quality; average or second rate. ▷ HISTORY Latin *mediocris* moderate ▶ **mediocrity** (mee-dee-**ok**-rit-ee) *n*

meditate *vb* **-tating, -tated 1** to think about something deeply: *he meditated on the problem.* **2** to reflect deeply on spiritual matters. **3** to plan, consider, or think of doing something. ▷ HISTORY Latin *meditari* to reflect upon ▶ **meditative** *adj* ▶ **meditator** *n*

meditation *n* **1** the act of meditating; reflection. **2** contemplation of spiritual matters, esp. as a religious practice.

Mediterranean *adj* of the Mediterranean Sea, lying between S Europe, N Africa, and SW Asia, or the surrounding region. ▷ HISTORY Latin *medius* middle + *terra* land

Mediterranean climate *n Geog* a climate type having long, dry, hot summers and short, humid, cool winters found around the Mediterranean and in other regions between the same latitudes.

medium *adj* **1** midway between extremes of size, amount, or degree: *fry over a medium heat; a man of medium height.* ✧ *n, pl* **-dia** *or* **-diums 2** a middle state, degree, or condition: *the happy medium.* **3** a substance which has a particular effect or can be used for a particular purpose: *linseed oil is used as a thinning medium for oil paint.* **4** a means for communicating information or news to the public. **5** a person who can supposedly communicate with the dead. **6** the substance or surroundings in which an organism naturally lives or grows. **7** *Art* the category of a work of art, as determined by its materials: *his works in the photographic medium.* ▷ **HISTORY** Latin *medius* middle

> **WORD TIP**
> See at **media.**

medium wave *n* a radio wave with a wavelength between 100 and 1000 metres.

medlar *n* the apple-like fruit of a small Eurasian tree, which is not edible until it has begun to decay. ▷ **HISTORY** Old French *medlier*

medley *n* **1** a mixture of various elements. **2** a musical composition consisting of various tunes arranged as a continuous whole. **3** *Swimming* a race in which a different stroke is used for each length. ▷ **HISTORY** Old French, from *medler* to mix, quarrel

medulla (mid-**dull**-la) *n, pl* **-las** *or* **-lae** (-lee) **1** *Anat* the innermost part of an organ or structure. **2** *Anat* the lower stalklike section of the brain. **3** *Bot* the central pith of a plant stem. ▷ **HISTORY** Latin: marrow ▶ **medullary** *adj*

medulla oblongata *n Anat* the lower stalklike section of the brain.

medusa (mid-**dew**-za) *n, pl* **-sas** *or* **-sae** (-zee) jellyfish. ▷ **HISTORY** *Medusa,* in Greek mythology, who had snakes for hair

meek *adj* quiet, and ready to do what other people say. ▷ **HISTORY** related to Old Norse *mjūkr* amenable ▶ **meekly** *adv*

meerkat *n* a South African mongoose. ▷ **HISTORY** Dutch: sea-cat

meerschaum (**meer**-shum) *n* **1** a white, heat-resistant, claylike mineral. **2** a tobacco pipe with a bowl made of this mineral. ▷ **HISTORY** German *Meerschaum,* literally: sea foam

meet[1] *vb* **meeting, met 1** to be in or come to the same place at the same time as, either by arrangement or by accident: *I met him in town.* **2** to come into contact with something or each other: *his head met the ground with a crack; the town where the Rhine and the Moselle meet.* **3** to come to or be at the place of arrival of: *he met his train at noon.* **4** to make the acquaintance of or be introduced to someone or each other. **5** (of people) to gather together for a purpose: *the board meets once a week.* **6** to compete, play, or fight against. **7** to cope with effectively; satisfy: *they were unable to meet his demands.* **8** to pay for (something): *it is difficult to meet the cost of medical insurance.* **9** Also: **meet with** to experience or suffer: *he met his death at the Somme.* **10 more to this than meets the eye** there is more involved in this than appears. ✧ *n* **11** a sports meeting. **12** *Chiefly Brit* the assembly of hounds and huntsmen prior to a hunt. ▷ **HISTORY** Old English *mētan*

meet[2] *adj Archaic* proper, fitting, or correct: *meet and proper.* ▷ **HISTORY** Old English *gemǣte*

meeting *n* **1** an act of coming together: *a meeting was fixed for the following day.* **2** an assembly or gathering of people: *the meeting voted in favour.* **3** a sporting competition, as of athletes, or of horse racing.

mega *adj Slang* extremely good, great, or successful.

mega- *combining form* **1** denoting 10^6: *megawatt.* **2** (in computer technology) denoting 2^{20} (1,048,576): *megabyte.* **3** large or great: *megalith.* **4** *Informal* very great: *megastar.* ▷ **HISTORY** Greek *megas* huge, powerful

megabyte *n Computers* 2^{20} or 1 048 576 bytes.

megadeath *n* the death of a million people, esp. in a nuclear war or attack.

megahertz *n, pl* **megahertz** one million hertz; one million cycles per second.

megajoule *n* one million joules.

megalith *n* a very large stone, esp. one forming part of a prehistoric monument. ▶ **megalithic** *adj*

megalomania *n* **1** a mental illness characterized by delusions of power. **2** *Informal* a craving for power. ▷ **HISTORY** Greek *megas* great + *mania* madness ▶ **megalomaniac** *adj, n*

megalopolis *n* an urban complex, usually comprising several large towns. ▷ **HISTORY** Greek *megas* great + *polis* city ▶ **megalopolitan** *adj, n*

megaphone *n* a funnel-shaped instrument used to make someone's voice sound louder, esp. out of doors.

megapode *n* any of various ground-living birds of Australia, New Guinea, and adjacent islands. Their eggs incubate in mounds of sand or rotting vegetation. ▷ **HISTORY** Greek *megas* great + *-podos* -footed

megaton *n* **1** one million tons. **2** an explosive power, esp. of a nuclear weapon, equal to the power of one million tons of TNT.

megavolt *n* one million volts.

megawatt *n* one million watts.

meiosis (my-**oh**-siss) *n, pl* **-ses** (-seez) a type of cell division in which reproductive cells are produced, each containing half the chromosome number of the parent nucleus. ▷ **HISTORY** Greek *meiōn* less

Meissner's corpuscle *n Anat* a tiny touch receptor in the palms, soles, and lips that is sensitive to light pressure. ▷ **HISTORY** after Georg *Meissner,* German anatomist

meitnerium *n Chem* an element artificially produced in small quantities by high-energy ion bombardment. Symbol: Mt. ▷ **HISTORY** after Lise *Meitner,* physicist

melaleuca (mel-a-**loo**-ka) *n* an Australian shrub or tree with a white trunk and black branches. ▷ **HISTORY** Greek *melas* black + *leukos* white

melamine *n* a colourless crystalline compound used in making synthetic resins. ▷ **HISTORY** German *Melamin*

melancholia (mel-an-**kole**-lee-a) *n* an old name for **depression** (sense 1).

melancholy (**mel**-an-kol-lee) *n, pl* **-cholies 1** a tendency to gloominess or depression. **2** a sad thoughtful state of mind. ✧ *adj* **3** characterized by, causing, or expressing sadness. ▷ **HISTORY** Greek *melas* black + *kholē* bile ▸ **melancholic** *adj, n*

melange (may-**lahnzh**) *n* a mixture or assortment: *a melange of historical facts and legends.* ▷ **HISTORY** French *mêler* to mix

melanin *n* a black pigment present in the hair, skin, and eyes of humans and animals. ▷ **HISTORY** Greek *melas* black

melanoma *n, pl* **-mas** *or* **-mata** *Pathol* a tumour composed of dark-coloured cells, occurring in some skin cancers. ▷ **HISTORY** Greek *melas* black + *-oma,* modelled on *carcinoma*

Melba toast *n* very thin crisp toast. ▷ **HISTORY** after Dame Nellie *Melba,* singer

mellifluous (mel-**lif**-flew-uss) *adj* (of sound) smooth and sweet. ▷ **HISTORY** Latin *mel* honey + *fluere* to flow

mellow *adj* **1** (esp. of colours, light, or sounds) soft or rich: *the mellow stillness of a sunny Sunday morning.* **2** kind-hearted, esp. through maturity or old age. **3** genial and relaxed, for instance through the effects of alcohol or good food. **4** (esp. of fruits) sweet, ripe, and full-flavoured. **5** (esp. of wine or cheese) having developed a full, smooth flavour as a result of maturing. **6** (of soil) soft and loamy. ✧ *vb* **7** to make or become mellow. **8** (foll. by *out*) to make or become calm and relaxed. ▷ **HISTORY** origin unknown

melodic (mel-**lod**-ik) *adj* **1** of or relating to melody. **2** tuneful and pleasant to the ear; melodious. ▸ **melodically** *adv*

melodious (mel-**lode**-ee-uss) *adj* **1** pleasant to the ear: *he gave a melodious chuckle.* **2** tuneful and melodic. ▸ **melodiousness** *n*

melodrama *n* **1** a play or film full of extravagant action and emotion. **2** overdramatic emotion or behaviour. ▷ **HISTORY** Greek *melos* song + *drama* drama

melodramatic *adj* characterized by or reminiscent of melodrama. ▸ **melodramatics** *pl n* ▷ **HISTORY** Greek *melos* song + *drama* drama

melody *n, pl* **-dies 1** *Music* a succession of notes forming a distinctive sequence; tune. **2** sounds that are pleasant because of their tone or arrangement, esp. words of poetry. ▷ **HISTORY** Greek *melōidia*

melon *n* any of various large edible fruits which have a hard rind and juicy flesh. ▷ **HISTORY** Greek *mēlon* apple

Melpomene (mel-**pom**-in-nee) *n Greek myth* the Muse of tragedy.

melt *vb* **1** to change from a solid into a liquid as a result of the action of heat. **2** to dissolve: *these sweets melt in the mouth.* **3** Also: **melt away** to diminish and finally disappear; fade away: *he felt his inner doubts melt away.* **4** to blend so that it is impossible to tell where one thing ends and another begins: *they melted into the trees until the gamekeeper had passed.* **5** to make or become emotional or sentimental; soften: *she melted into tears.* ▷ **HISTORY** Old English *meltan* to digest ▸ **meltingly** *adv*

meltdown *n* **1** (in a nuclear reactor) the melting of the fuel rods, with the possible escape of radioactivity. **2** *Informal* a sudden disastrous failure. **3** *Informal* a process of irreversible decline.

melting point *n* the temperature at which a solid turns into a liquid.

melting pot *n* a place or situation in which many races, ideas, etc., are mixed.

member *n* **1** a person who belongs to a group or organization such as a club or political party. **2** any part of a plant or animal, such as a limb or petal. **3** a Member of Parliament: *the member for Glasgow Central.* ✧ *adj* **4** (of a country or group) belonging to an organization or alliance: *a summit of the member countries' heads of state is due.* ▷ **HISTORY** Latin *membrum* limb, part

Member of Parliament *n* a person who has been elected to the House of Commons or the equivalent assembly in another country.

membership *n* **1** the members of an organization collectively. **2** the number of members. **3** the state of being a member.

membrane *n* a thin flexible tissue that covers, lines, or connects plant and animal organs or cells. ▷ **HISTORY** Latin *membrana* skin covering a part of the body ▸ **membranous** *adj*

memento *n, pl* **-tos** *or* **-toes** something that reminds one of past events; a souvenir. ▷ **HISTORY** Latin, imperative of *meminisse* to remember

memento mori *n, pl* **memento mori** an object intended to remind people of death. ▷ **HISTORY** Latin: remember you must die

memo *n, pl* **memos** short for **memorandum**.

memoir (**mem**-wahr) *n* a biography or historical account based on personal knowledge. ▷ **HISTORY** Latin *memoria* memory

memoirs *pl n* **1** a collection of reminiscences about a period or series of events, written from personal experience. **2** an autobiography.

memorabilia *pl n, sing* **-rabile** objects connected with famous people or events.

memorable *adj* worth remembering or easily remembered because it is very special or important. ▷ **HISTORY** Latin *memorare* to remember ▸ **memorably** *adv*

memorandum *n, pl* **-dums** *or* **-da 1** a note sent by one person or department to another within a business organization. **2** a note of things to be remembered. **3** *Law* a short written summary of the terms of a transaction. ▷ **HISTORY** Latin: (something) to be remembered

memorial *n* **1** something, such as a statue, built or displayed to preserve the memory of someone

A B C D E F G H I J K L M N O P Q R S T U V W X Y Z

or something: *a war memorial.* ✧ *adj* **2** in memory of someone or something: *a memorial service.* ▷ **HISTORY** Late Latin *memoriale* a reminder

memorize *or* **-rise** *vb* **-rizing, -rized** *or* **-rising, -rised** to commit to memory; learn by heart.

memory *n, pl* **-ries 1** the ability of the mind to store and recall past sensations, thoughts, and knowledge: *she can do it from memory.* **2** the sum of everything retained by the mind. **3** a particular recollection of an event or person: *he started awake with a sudden memory.* **4** the length of time one can remember: *my memory doesn't go that far back.* **5** commemoration: *in memory of our leader.* **6** a person's reputation after death: *a conductor of fond memory.* **7** a part of a computer in which information is stored. ▷ **HISTORY** Latin *memoria*

memsahib *n* (formerly, in India) a term of respect used for a European married woman. ▷ **HISTORY** *ma'am + sahib*

men *n* the plural of **man**.

menace *vb* **-acing, -aced 1** to threaten with violence or danger. ✧ *n* **2** a threat; a source of danger. **3** *Informal* an annoying person or thing; nuisance. ▷ **HISTORY** Latin *minax* threatening ▶ **menacing** *adj*

menagerie (min-**naj**-er-ee) *n* a collection of wild animals kept for exhibition. ▷ **HISTORY** French

mend *vb* **1** to repair something broken or not working. **2** to heal or recover: *a wound like that will take a while to mend.* **3** (esp. of behaviour) to improve; make or become better: *if you don't mend your ways you'll be in serious trouble.* ✧ *n* **4** a mended area, esp. on a garment. **5 on the mend** regaining one's health. ▷ **HISTORY** from *amend*

mendacity *n* the tendency to be untruthful. ▷ **HISTORY** Latin *mendax* untruthful ▶ **mendacious** *adj*

mendelevium *n Chem* an artificially produced radioactive element. Symbol: Md. ▷ **HISTORY** after D. I. *Mendeleyev,* chemist

Mendel's laws *pl n* the principles of heredity proposed by Gregor Mendel (1822–84), Austrian monk and botanist. ▶ **Mendelism** *n*

mendicant *adj* **1** begging. **2** (of a monk, nun, etc.) dependent on charity for food. ✧ *n* **3** a mendicant friar. **4** a beggar. ▷ **HISTORY** Latin *mendicus* beggar

menfolk *pl n* men collectively, esp. the men of a particular family.

menhir (**men**-hear) *n* a single standing stone, dating from prehistoric times. ▷ **HISTORY** Breton *men* stone + *hir* long

menial (**mean**-nee-al) *adj* **1** involving or doing boring work of low status. ✧ *n* **2** a domestic servant. ▷ **HISTORY** Old French *meinie* household

meninges (min-**in**-jeez) *pl n, sing* **meninx** (**mean**-inks) the three membranes that surround the brain and spinal cord. ▷ **HISTORY** Greek, plural of *meninx* membrane

meningitis (men-in-**jite**-iss) *n* inflammation of the meninges, caused by infection and causing severe headache, fever, and rigidity of the neck muscles.

meniscus *n, pl* **-nisci** *or* **-niscuses 1** the curved upper surface of a liquid standing in a tube, produced by the surface tension. **2** a crescent-shaped lens. ▷ **HISTORY** Greek *mēniskos* crescent

menopause *n* the period during which a woman's menstrual cycle ceases, normally at an age of 45 to 50. ▷ **HISTORY** Greek *mēn* month + *pausis* halt ▶ **menopausal** *adj*

menorah (min-**or**-a) *n Judaism* a seven-branched candelabrum used as an emblem of Judaism. ▷ **HISTORY** Hebrew: candlestick

menses (**men**-seez) *n* same as **menstruation**. ▷ **HISTORY** Latin, plural of *mensis* month

Menshevik (**men**-shiv-ick) *or* **Menshevist** *n History* a member of the moderate wing of the Russian Social Democratic Party, advocating gradual reform to achieve socialism. Compare **Bolshevik**. ▷ **HISTORY** Russian: minority, from *menshe* less, from *malo* few ▶ **Menshevism** *n*

mens rea *n Law* the criminal intent, negligence, or other legally indefensible state of mind that must be proved for a defendant to be convicted of a crime. Compare **actus reus**. ▷ **HISTORY** Latin: guilty mind

menstrual *adj* of or relating to menstruation: *the menstrual cycle.*

menstruate *vb* **-ating, -ated** to undergo menstruation. ▷ **HISTORY** Latin *menstruare,* from *mensis* month

menstruation *n* the approximately monthly discharge of blood from the womb in women of childbearing age who are not pregnant.

mensuration *n* **1** the study of the measurement of geometric magnitudes such as length. **2** the act or process of measuring. ▷ **HISTORY** Latin *mensura* measure

mental *adj* **1** of, done by, or involving the mind: *mental alertness.* **2** done in the mind without using speech or writing: *mental arithmetic.* **3** affected by mental illness: *a mental patient.* **4** concerned with mental illness: *a mental hospital.* **5** *Slang* extremely foolish or eccentric. ▷ **HISTORY** Latin *mens* mind ▶ **mentally** *adv*

mental age *n* the age which a person is considered to have reached in thinking ability, judged by comparing his or her ability with the average for people of various ages: *a twenty-one-year-old woman with a mental age of only ten.*

mental handicap *n* any intellectual disability resulting from injury to or abnormal development of the brain. ▶ **mentally handicapped** *adj*

mental illness *n* any of various disorders in which a person's thoughts, emotions, or behaviour are so abnormal as to cause suffering to himself or herself, or other people.

mentality *n, pl* **-ties** a particular attitude or way of thinking: *the traditional civil-service mentality.*

mental map *n* a person's individual perception of the world around them, both locally and much further afield, and of how one place links to another.

mental process *n Functional grammar* the process of thinking, reflecting, or feeling as specified by a verb group. Compare **material process, relational process, verbal process**.

menthol *n* an organic compound found in peppermint oil and used as an antiseptic, decongestant, and painkiller. ▷ HISTORY Latin *mentha* mint ▶ **mentholated** *adj*

mention *vb* **1** to refer to or speak about briefly or incidentally. **2** to include in a report, list etc., because of high standards or an outstanding achievement: *the hotel is mentioned in all the guidebooks; he was twice mentioned in dispatches during the war.* **3 not to mention (something)** to say nothing of (something too obvious to mention). ✧ *n* **4** a slight reference or allusion. **5** a recognition or acknowledgment of high quality or an outstanding achievement. ▷ HISTORY Latin *mentio* a calling to mind

mentor *n* an adviser or guide. ▷ HISTORY *Mentor,* adviser of Telemachus in Homer's *Odyssey*

menu *n* **1** a list of dishes served at a meal or that can be ordered in a restaurant. **2** a list of options displayed on a visual display unit from which the operator can choose. ▷ HISTORY French: small, detailed (list)

MEP (in Britain) Member of the European Parliament.

Mercalli scale *n Geol* a scale for expressing the intensity of an earthquake, ranging from 1 (rarely felt) to 12 (total destruction). Compare **Richter scale**. ▷ HISTORY after Giuseppe *Mercalli* (1850–1914), Italian volcanologist and seismologist

mercantile *adj* of trade or traders; commercial. ▷ HISTORY Italian *mercante* merchant

Mercator projection (mer-**kate**-er) *n Geog* a way of drawing maps in which latitude and longitude form a rectangular grid, scale being exaggerated with increasing distance from the equator. ▷ HISTORY after G. *Mercator,* cartographer

mercenary *n, pl* **-naries 1** a soldier who fights for a foreign army for money. ✧ *adj* **2** motivated by greed or the desire for gain: *calculating and mercenary businessmen.* **3** of or relating to a mercenary or mercenaries. ▷ HISTORY Latin *merces* wages

mercerized *or* **-ised** *adj* (of cotton) treated with an alkali to make it strong and shiny. ▷ HISTORY after John *Mercer,* maker of textiles

merchandise *n* **1** goods for buying, selling, or trading with; commodities. ✧ *vb* **-dising, -dised 2** to engage in the commercial purchase and sale of goods or services; trade.

merchandising *n* **1** the selection and display of goods in a retail outlet. **2** commercial goods, esp. ones issued to exploit the popularity of a pop group, sporting event, etc.

merchant *n* **1** a person who buys and sells goods in large quantities and usually of one type: *a wine merchant.* **2** *Chiefly Scot, US, & Canad* a person engaged in retail trade; shopkeeper. **3** *Slang* a person dealing in something undesirable: *a gossip merchant.* ✧ *adj* **4** of ships involved in commercial trade or their crews: *a merchant sailor; the British merchant fleet.* ▷ HISTORY Latin *mercari* to trade

merchant bank *n* a financial institution that deals primarily with foreign trade and business finance. ▶ **merchant banker** *n*

merchantman *n, pl* **-men** a merchant ship.

merchant navy *n* the ships or crew engaged in a nation's commercial shipping.

merciful *adj* **1** (of an act or event) giving relief from pain or suffering: *after months of illness, death came as a merciful release.* **2** showing or giving mercy; compassionate. ▶ **mercifully** *adv*

merciless *adj* without mercy; pitiless, cruel, or heartless. ▶ **mercilessly** *adv*

mercurial (mer-**cure**-ee-al) *adj* **1** lively and unpredictable: *a mercurial and temperamental chess player.* **2** of or containing mercury. ▷ HISTORY Latin *mercurialis*

mercuric *adj* of or containing mercury in the divalent state.

mercurous *adj* of or containing mercury in the monovalent state.

mercury *n, pl* **-ries** *Chem* a silvery toxic metal, the only element liquid at normal temperatures, used in thermometers, barometers, lamps, and dental amalgams. Symbol: Hg. ▷ HISTORY Latin *Mercurius,* messenger of Jupiter

Mercury *n* **1** *Roman myth* the messenger of the gods. **2** the second smallest planet and the one nearest the sun.

mercy *n, pl* **-cies 1** compassionate treatment of or attitude towards an offender or enemy who is in one's power. **2** the power to show mercy: *they threw themselves on the King's mercy.* **3** a relieving or welcome occurrence or act: *it was a mercy you turned up when you did.* **4 at the mercy of** in the power of. ✧ *adj* **5** done or undertaken in an attempt to relieve suffering or bring help: *a mercy mission.* ▷ HISTORY Latin *merces* recompense

mercy killing *n* same as **euthanasia**.

mere[1] *adj* nothing more than: *the election in Slovenia seems a mere formality.* ▷ HISTORY Latin *merus* pure ▶ **merely** *adv*

mere[2] *n Brit dialect or archaic* a lake. ▷ HISTORY Old English: sea, lake

meretricious *adj* superficially or garishly attractive but of no real value. ▷ HISTORY Latin *meretrix* prostitute

merganser (mer-**gan**-ser) *n, pl* **-sers** *or* **-ser** a large crested marine diving duck. ▷ HISTORY Latin *mergere* to plunge + *anser* goose

merge *vb* **merging, merged 1** to combine, esp. so as to become part of a larger whole: *the two airlines merged in 1983.* **2** to blend gradually, without any sudden change being apparent: *late afternoon merged imperceptibly into early evening.* ▷ HISTORY Latin *mergere* to plunge

merger *n* the act of merging, esp. the combination of two or more companies.

meridian *n* **1** one of the imaginary lines joining the north and south poles at right angles to the equator, designated by degrees of longitude from 0° at Greenwich to 180°. **2** (in acupuncture etc.) any of various channels through which vital energy is believed to circulate round the body. ▷ HISTORY Latin *meridies* midday

meridional *adj* **1** of or along a meridian. **2** of or in the south, esp. the south of Europe.

meringue (mer-**rang**) *n* **1** stiffly beaten egg whites mixed with sugar and baked. **2** a small cake made from this mixture. ▷ HISTORY French

merino *n, pl* **-nos 1** a sheep with long fine wool, originally reared in Spain. **2** the yarn made from this wool. ▷ HISTORY Spanish

meristematic tissue *n Bot* plant tissue responsible for growth, whose cells divide to form the tissues and organs of the plant.

merit *n* **1** worth or superior quality; excellence: *the film had two sequels, neither of much merit.* **2** an admirable or advantageous quality: *the relative merits of film and video as a medium of communication.* **3 have the merit of** to have a positive feature or advantage that the alternatives do not have: *the first version has the merit of being short.* **4 on its merits** on its intrinsic qualities or virtues. ✧ *vb* **-iting, -ited 5** to be worthy of; deserve: *the issue merits much fuller discussion.* ▷ HISTORY Latin *meritum* reward

meritocracy (mer-it-**tok**-rass-ee) *n, pl* **-cies** a social system in which power is held by the most talented or intelligent people. ▶ **meritocrat** *n* ▶ **meritocratic** *adj*

meritorious *adj* deserving praise for being good or worthwhile. ▷ HISTORY Latin *meritorius* earning money

merlin *n* a small falcon with dark plumage. ▷ HISTORY Old French *esmerillon*

mermaid *n* an imaginary sea creature with a woman's head and upper body and a fish's tail. ▷ HISTORY *mere* sea + *maid* ▶ **merman** *masc n*

merry *adj* **-rier, -riest 1** cheerful and jolly. **2** *Brit & Austral informal* slightly drunk. **3 make merry** to take part in noisy cheerful celebrations or fun. ▷ HISTORY Old English *merige* agreeable ▶ **merrily** *adv* ▶ **merriment** *n*

merry-go-round *n* **1** a fairground roundabout. **2** a whirl of activity.

merrymaking *n* noisy cheerful celebrations or fun. ▶ **merrymaker** *n*

mesa *n* a flat-topped hill found in arid regions. ▷ HISTORY Spanish: table

mescal (mess-**kal**) *n* **1** a globe-shaped cactus without spine found in Mexico and the southwestern US. **2** a Mexican alcoholic spirit similar to tequila. ▷ HISTORY Mexican Indian *mexcalli*

mescaline *n* a hallucinogenic drug derived from the button-like top of the mescal cactus.

mesdames (may-**dam**) *n* the plural of **madame madam** (sense 1).

mesdemoiselles (maid-mwah-**zel**) *n* the plural of **mademoiselle**.

mesembryanthemum *n* a low-growing plant with fleshy leaves and bright daisy-like flowers. ▷ HISTORY Greek *mesēmbria* noon + *anthemon* flower

mesentery *n, pl* **-teries** *Anat* the double layer of peritoneum that is attached to the back wall of the abdominal cavity.

mesh *n* **1** a material resembling a net made from intersecting strands with a space between each strand. **2** an open space between the strands of a net or network: *the minimum permitted size of fishing net mesh.* **3** (*often pl*) the strands surrounding these spaces. **4** anything that ensnares or holds like a net. ✧ *adj* **5** made from mesh: *a wire mesh fence.* ✧ *vb* **6** to entangle or become entangled. **7** (of gear teeth) to engage or interlock. **8** to fit together closely or work in harmony: *she schedules her holidays to mesh with theirs.* ▷ HISTORY probably Dutch *maesche*

mesmerize *or* **-ise** *vb* **-izing, -ized** *or* **-ising, -ised 1** to fascinate and hold spellbound: *his voice had the entire audience mesmerized.* **2** *Archaic* to hypnotize. ▶ **mesmerism** *n* ▶ **mesmerizing** *adj*

Mesolithic (mess-oh-**lith**-ik) *adj* of the middle period of the Stone Age, in Europe from about 12,000 to 3000 BC. ▷ HISTORY Greek *misos* middle + *lithos* stone

meson (**mee**-zon) *n Physics* any of a group of elementary particles that has a mass between those of an electron and a proton. ▷ HISTORY Greek *misos* middle + *-on,* indicating an elementary particle

mesophyll *n Bot* the soft chlorophyll-containing tissue of a leaf between the upper and lower layers of epidermis. ▶ **mesophyllic** *or* **mesophyllous** *adj*

mesosphere (**mess**-oh-sfeer) *n* the atmospheric layer above the stratosphere.

Mesozoic (mess-oh-**zoh**-ik) *adj Geol* of the geological era that began 225 million years ago and lasted about 155 million years, during which the dinosaurs emerged, flourished, then became extinct. ▷ HISTORY Greek *misos* middle + *zōion* animal

mess *n* **1** a state of untidiness or confusion, esp. a dirty or unpleasant one: *the house was in a mess.* **2** a confused and difficult situation; muddle: *the firm is in a terrible financial mess.* **3** *Informal* a dirty or untidy person or thing: *there was a nasty burnt mess in the saucepan.* **4** a building providing catering, and sometimes recreation, facilities for service personnel. **5** a group of service personnel who regularly eat together. **6** *Old-fashioned* a portion of soft or runny food: *a mess of pottage.* ✧ *vb* **7** (of service personnel) to eat in a group. ▷ HISTORY Old French *mes* dish of food

message *n* **1** a communication from one person or group to another. **2** an implicit meaning or moral, as in a work of art. **3** a religious or political belief that someone attempts to communicate to others: *paintings with a fierce feminist message.* **4 get the message** *Informal* to understand. ▷ HISTORY Old French, from Latin *mittere* to send

messaging *n* the sending of a message by any form of electronic communication: *text messaging.*

messenger *n* a person who takes messages from one person or group to another. ▷ HISTORY Old French *messagier*

Messiah *n* **1** *Judaism* the awaited king of the Jews, who will be sent by God to free them. **2** *Christianity* Jesus Christ, when regarded in this role. **3** a liberator of a country or people. ▷ HISTORY Hebrew *māshīach* anointed

Messianic *adj* **1** of or relating to a Messiah, or the arrival on Earth of a Messiah. **2 messianic** of or relating to the belief that someone or something will bring about a complete transformation of the existing social order: *a messianic zeal for the free market.*

messieurs (may-**syuh**) *n* the plural of **monsieur**.

mess kit *n* a soldier's eating utensils for use in the field.

Messrs (**mess**-erz) *n* the plural of **Mr**.

messy *adj* **messier, messiest 1** dirty or untidy. **2** unpleasantly confused or complicated: *the messy, uncontrollable world of real life.* ▶ **messily** *adv* ▶ **messiness** *n*

met *vb* the past of **meet**[1].

Met *adj* **1** Meteorological: *the Met Office.* ✧ *n* **2 the Met** the Metropolitan Police, who operate in London.

metabolism (met-**tab**-ol-liz-zum) *n* the chemical processes that occur in living organisms, resulting in growth, production of energy, and elimination of waste. ▷ HISTORY Greek *metaballein* to change ▶ **metabolic** *adj*

metabolize *or* **-lise** *vb* **-lizing, -lized** *or* **-lising, -lised** to produce or be produced by metabolism.

metacarpus *n, pl* **-pi** the set of five long bones in the hand between the wrist and the fingers. ▷ HISTORY Greek *meta* after + *karpos* wrist ▶ **metacarpal** *adj, n*

metafiction *n Literature* fiction that draws attention to its fictional status and the conventions and nature of fiction.

metal *n* **1 a** *Chem* a chemical element, such as iron or copper, that reflects light and can be shaped, forms positive ions, and is a good conductor of heat and electricity. **b** an alloy, such as brass or steel, containing one or more of these elements. **2** short for **road metal**. **3** *Informal* short for **heavy metal**. **4 metals** the rails of a railway. ✧ *adj* **5** made of metal. ▷ HISTORY Greek *metallon* mine

metalanguage *n* the language or system of symbols used to discuss another language or system.

metalled *or US* **metaled** *adj* (of a road) surfaced with crushed rock or small stones: *a metalled driveway.*

metallic *adj* **1** of or consisting of metal. **2** sounding like two pieces of metal hitting each other: *a metallic click.* **3** (of a voice) harsh, unpleasant, and unemotional. **4** shining like metal: *metallic paint.* **5** (of a taste) unpleasantly harsh and bitter.

metallic bond *n Chem* the covalent bonding between atoms in metals, in which the valence electrons are free to move through the crystal.

metalliferous *adj* containing a metallic element. ▷ HISTORY Latin *metallum* metal + *ferre* to bear

metallography *n* the study of the composition and structure of metals.

metalloid *n Chem* a nonmetallic element, such as arsenic or silicon, that has some of the properties of a metal.

metallurgy *n* the scientific study of the structure, properties, extraction, and refining of metals. ▷ HISTORY *metal* + Greek *-urgia,* from *ergon* work ▶ **metallurgical** *adj* ▶ **metallurgist** *n*

metal oxide *n Chemistry* the substance formed when a base metal reacts with oxygen.

metal road *n NZ* an unsealed road covered in gravel.

metalwork *n* **1** the craft of making articles from metal. **2** articles made from metal. **3** the metal part of something. ▶ **metalworker** *n*

metamorphic *adj* **1** (of rocks) altered considerably from the original structure and composition by pressure and heat. **2** of metamorphosis or metamorphism.

metamorphic rock *n Geol* rock that has been altered over time by pressure and heat.

metamorphism *n* the process by which metamorphic rocks are formed.

metamorphose *vb* **-phosing, -phosed** to change from one state or thing into something different: *the media personality metamorphosed into society hostess.*

metamorphosis (met-a-**more**-foss-is) *n, pl* **-ses** (-seez) **1** a complete change of physical form or substance. **2** a complete change of character or appearance. **3** *Zool* the change of form that accompanies transformation into an adult in certain animals, for example the butterfly or frog. ▷ HISTORY Greek: transformation, from *meta* after + *morphē* form

metaphor *n* a figure of speech in which a word or phrase is applied to an object or action that it does not literally apply to in order to imply a resemblance, for example *he is a lion in battle.* ▷ HISTORY Greek *metapherein* to transfer ▶ **metaphorical** *adj* ▶ **metaphorically** *adv*

metaphysical *adj* **1** of metaphysics. **2** abstract, abstruse, or unduly theoretical.

Metaphysical *adj* denoting certain 17th-century poets who combined intense feeling with elaborate imagery.

metaphysics *n* **1** the philosophical study of the nature of reality. **2** abstract or subtle discussion or reasoning. ▷ HISTORY Greek *ta meta ta phusika* the things after the physics, from the arrangement of subjects treated in the works of Aristotle

metastasis (mit-**tass**-tiss-iss) *n, pl* **-ses** (-seez) *Pathol* the spreading of a disease, esp. cancer, from one part of the body to another. ▷ HISTORY Greek: transition

metatarsus *n, pl* **-si** the set of five long bones in the foot between the toes and the ankle. ▷ HISTORY Greek *meta* after + *tarsos* instep ▶ **metatarsal** *adj, n*

metathesis (mit-**tath**-iss-iss) *n, pl* **-ses** (-seez) the transposition of two sounds or letters in a word. ▷ **HISTORY** Greek *metatithenai* to transpose

metazoan (met-a-**zoh**-an) *n* **1** any animal having a body composed of many cells: includes all animals except sponges and protozoans. ✧ *adj* **2** of the metazoans. ▷ **HISTORY** New Latin *Metazoa*

meteor *n* **1** a small piece of rock or metal that has entered the earth's atmosphere from space. **2** Also: **shooting star** the bright streak of light appearing in the sky due to a piece of rock or metal burning up because of friction as it falls through the atmosphere. ▷ **HISTORY** Greek *meteōros* lofty

meteoric (meet-ee-**or**-rik) *adj* **1** of or relating to meteors. **2** brilliant and very rapid: *his meteoric rise to power.* ▸ **meteorically** *adv*

meteorite *n* the rocklike remains of a meteoroid that has collided with the earth.

meteoroid *n* any of the small celestial bodies that are thought to orbit the sun. When they enter the earth's atmosphere, they become visible as meteors.

meteorol. *or* **meteor. 1** meteorological. **2** meteorology.

meteorology *n* the study of the earth's atmosphere and weather-forming processes, esp. for weather forecasting. ▸ **meteorological** *adj* ▸ **meteorologist** *n*

meter[1] *n* **1** any device that measures and records the quantity or number of units of something that was used during a specified period or is being used at that moment: *a gas meter.* **2** short for **parking meter.** ✧ *vb* **3** to measure the amount of something used or a rate of flow with a meter. ▷ **HISTORY** Old English *metan* to measure

meter[2] *n US* same as **metre**[1], **metre**[2].

-meter *n combining form* **1** indicating an instrument for measuring: *barometer.* **2** *Prosody* indicating a verse having a specified number of feet: *pentameter.* ▷ **HISTORY** Greek *metron* measure

methadone *n* a drug similar to morphine, sometimes prescribed as a heroin substitute. ▷ **HISTORY** *(di)meth(yl) + a(mino) + d(iphenyl) + -one,* indicating a ketone

methanal *n* same as **formaldehyde**.

methane *n* a colourless odourless flammable gas, the main constituent of natural gas. ▷ **HISTORY** *meth(yl) + -ane,* indicating an alkane

methane series *n* a series of saturated hydrocarbons with the general formula C_nH_{2n+2}.

methanol *n* a colourless poisonous liquid used as a solvent and fuel. Also: **methyl alcohol** ▷ **HISTORY** *methane + -ol,* indicating alcohol

methinks *vb, past* **methought** *Archaic* it seems to me that.

method *n* **1** a way of doing something, esp. a systematic or regular one. **2** orderliness of thought or action. **3** the techniques of a particular field or subject. ▷ **HISTORY** Greek *methodos,* literally: a going after

Method *n* an acting technique in which the actor bases his or her role on the inner motivation of the character played.

methodical *adj* careful, well-organized, and systematic. ▸ **methodically** *adv*

Methodist *n* **1** a member of any of the Christian Nonconformist denominations that derive from the beliefs and practices of John Wesley and his followers. ✧ *adj* **2** of or relating to Methodists or their Church. ▸ **Methodism** *n*

methodology *n, pl* **-gies 1** the system of methods and principles used in a particular discipline. **2** the philosophical study of method. ▸ **methodological** *adj*

meths *n Brit, Austral & NZ informal* methylated spirits.

methyl *adj* of or containing the monovalent saturated hydrocarbon group of atoms CH_3–: *methyl mercury.* ▷ **HISTORY** from *methylene*

methyl alcohol *n* same as **methanol**.

methylate *vb* **-ating, -ated** to mix with methanol.

methylated spirits *n* alcohol that has been rendered undrinkable by the addition of methanol and a violet dye, used as a solvent or as a fuel for small lamps or heaters. Also: **methylated spirit**

methylene *adj* of, consisting of, or containing the divalent group of atoms –CH_2–: *a methylene group or radical.* ▷ **HISTORY** Greek *methu* wine + *hulē* wood + *-ene,* indicating a double bond

meticulous *adj* very precise about details; careful and thorough. ▷ **HISTORY** Latin *meticulosus* fearful ▸ **meticulously** *adv* ▸ **meticulousness** *n*

metonymy (mit-**on**-im-ee) *n, pl* **-mies** a figure of speech in which one thing is replaced by another associated with it, for instance the use of *Downing Street* to mean *the British government.* ▷ **HISTORY** Greek *meta-,* indicating change + *onoma* name

metre[1] *or US* **meter** *n* the basic SI unit of length, equal to 100 centimetres (39.37 inches): *the majority of people are between one and a half and two metres tall.* ▷ **HISTORY** same as METRE[2]

metre[2] *or US* **meter** *n* **1** *Prosody* the rhythmic arrangement of syllables in verse, usually according to the number and kind of feet in a line. **2** *Music chiefly US* the rhythmic arrangement of the beat in a piece of music. ▷ **HISTORY** Greek *metron* measure

metre-kilogram-second *n* See **mks units**.

metric *adj* of or relating to the metre or metric system: *use either all metric or all imperial measurements.*

metrical *or* **metric** *adj* **1** of or relating to measurement. **2** of or in poetic metre. ▸ **metrically** *adv*

metric system *n* any decimal system of units based on the metre. For scientific purposes SI units are used.

metric ton *n* (not in technical use) a tonne.

metro *n, pl* **-ros** an urban, usually underground, railway system in certain cities, such as Paris. ▷ **HISTORY** French, from *chemin de fer métropolitain* metropolitan railway

metronome *n* a device which indicates the speed music should be played at by producing a clicking sound from a pendulum with an adjustable period of swing. ▷ **HISTORY** Greek *metron* measure + *nomos* law

metropolis (mit-**trop**-oh-liss) *n* the main city of a country or region. ▷ **HISTORY** Greek *mētēr* mother + *polis* city

metropolitan *adj* **1** of or characteristic of a metropolis. **2** of or consisting of a city and its suburbs: *the Tokyo metropolitan region.* **3** of or belonging to the home territories of a country, as opposed to overseas territories: *metropolitan France.* ✧ *n* **4** *Christianity* the senior clergyman, esp. an archbishop, in charge of an ecclesiastical province. **5** an inhabitant of a large city.

-metry *n combining form* indicating the process or science of measuring: *geometry.* ▷ **HISTORY** Greek *metron* measure ▶ **-metric** *adj combining form*

mettle *n* **1** courage or spirit: *the lack of mettle evident among British politicians.* **2** character or abilities: *the mettle saints are made of.* **3 on one's mettle** roused to making one's best efforts. ▷ **HISTORY** variant of *metal*

MeV million electronvolts (10^6 electronvolts).

mew[1] *n* **1** the characteristic high-pitched cry of a cat; miaow. ✧ *vb* **2** to make such a sound. ▷ **HISTORY** imitative

mew[2] *n* a seagull. ▷ **HISTORY** Old English *mǣw*

mews *Chiefly Brit* ✧ *n* **1** a yard or street lined by buildings originally used as stables but now often converted into dwellings. ✧ *adj* **2** (of a flat or house) located in a mews: *a mews cottage.* ▷ **HISTORY** plural of *mew,* originally referring to royal stables built on the site of hawks' mews (cages)

Mex. 1 Mexican. **2** Mexico.

Mexican *adj* **1** of Mexico. ✧ *n* **2** a person from Mexico.

mezzanine (**mez**-zan-een) *n* an intermediate storey, esp. one between the ground and first floor. ▷ **HISTORY** Italian *mezzano* middle

mezzo (**met**-so) *adv* **1** *Music* moderately; quite: *mezzo-forte.* ✧ *n, pl* **-zos 2** short for **mezzo-soprano**. ▷ **HISTORY** Italian: half

mezzo-soprano *n, pl* **-nos 1** a female voice lower than soprano but higher than contralto. **2** a singer with such a voice.

mezzotint (**met**-so-tint) *n* **1** a method of engraving done by scraping and burnishing the roughened surface of a copper plate. **2** a print made from a plate so treated. ▷ **HISTORY** Italian *mezzotinto* half tint

mg milligram.

Mg *Chem* magnesium.

Mgr 1 manager. **2** monseigneur. **3** monsignor.

MHz megahertz.

mi *n Music* same as **me**[2].

MI Michigan.

MI5 Military Intelligence, section five; the part of the British security services which combats spying and subversion in Britain.

MI6 Military Intelligence, section six; the part of the British security services which spies on other countries. Also called: **SIS**

miaow (mee-**ow**) *n* **1** the characteristic high-pitched cry of a cat; mew. ✧ *vb* **2** to make such a sound.

miasma (mee-**azz**-ma) *n, pl* **-mata** *or* **-mas** an unwholesome or foreboding atmosphere. ▷ **HISTORY** Greek: defilement

mica (**my**-ka) *n* any of a group of minerals consisting of flakelike crystals of aluminium or potassium silicates. They have a high resistance to electricity and heat. ▷ **HISTORY** Latin: crumb

mice *n* the plural of **mouse**.

Mich. Michigan.

Michaelmas (**mik**-kl-mass) *n* Sept 29, the feast of St Michael the archangel: one of the four quarter days in England, Ireland, and Wales.

Michaelmas daisy *n Brit* a garden plant with small daisy-shaped purple, pink, or white flowers in autumn.

mickey *n* **take the mickey (out of)** *Informal* to tease (someone). ▷ **HISTORY** origin unknown

micro *n, pl* **micros** short for **microcomputer, microprocessor**.

micro- *or* **micr-** *combining form* **1** small or minute: *microdot.* **2** involving the use of a microscope: *microscopy.* **3** denoting 10^{-6}: *microsecond.* ▷ **HISTORY** Greek *mikros* small

microbe *n* any microscopic organism, esp. a disease-causing bacterium. ▷ **HISTORY** MICRO- + Greek *bios* life ▶ **microbial** *or* **microbic** *adj*

microbiology *n* the branch of biology involving the study of microorganisms.

microchemistry *n* chemical experimentation with minute quantities of material.

microchip *n* a tiny wafer of semiconductor material, such as silicon, containing an integrated circuit. Often shortened to: **chip**

microcircuit *n* a miniature electronic circuit in which a number of permanently connected components are contained in one small chip of semiconducting material.

microclimate *n Meteorol* the atmospheric conditions affecting an individual or a small group of organisms, esp. when they differ from the climate of the rest of the community.

microcomputer *n* a compact computer in which the central processing unit is contained in one or more silicon chips.

microcosm *n* **1** a miniature representation of something: *this area is a microcosm of France as a whole.* **2** man regarded as epitomizing the universe. **3 in microcosm** on a small scale. ▷ **HISTORY** Greek *mikros kosmos* little world ▶ **microcosmic** *adj*

microdot *n* a greatly reduced photographic copy (about the size of a pinhead) of a document.

microeconomics *n* the branch of economics concerned with particular commodities, firms, or individuals and the relationships between them.

microelectronics *n* the branch of electronics concerned with microcircuits.

microfiche (**my**-kroh-feesh) *n* same as **fiche**. ▷ **HISTORY** French, from MICRO- + *fiche* small card

A B C D E F G H I J K L M N O P Q R S T U V W X Y Z

microfilm *n* **1** a strip of film on which books or documents can be recorded in miniaturized form. ✧ *vb* **2** to photograph a page or document on microfilm.

microlight *or* **microlite** *n* a very small private aircraft with large wings.

micrometer (my-**krom**-it-er) *n* an instrument for the accurate measurement of small distances or angles.

microminiaturization *or* **-isation** *n* the production and use of very small electronic components.

micron (**my**-kron) *n* a unit of length equal to one millionth of a metre. ▷ HISTORY Greek *mikros* small

microorganism *n* any organism of microscopic size, such as a virus or bacterium.

microphone *n* a device for converting sound into electrical energy.

microprocessor *n Computers* a single integrated circuit which acts as the central processing unit in a small computer.

microscope *n* **1** an optical instrument that uses a lens or combination of lenses to produce a greatly magnified image of a small, close object. **2** any instrument, such as the electron microscope, for producing a greatly magnified visual image of a small object.

microscopic *adj* **1** too small to be seen except with a microscope. **2** very small; minute. **3** of or using a microscope. ▶ **microscopically** *adv*

microscopy *n* the use of microscopes.

microsecond *n* one millionth of a second.

microstructure *n* a structure on a microscopic scale, such as that of a metal or a cell.

microsurgery *n* intricate surgery performed using a special microscope and miniature precision instruments.

microwave *n* **1** an electromagnetic wave with a wavelength of between 0.3 and 0.001 metres: used in radar and cooking. **2** short for **microwave oven**. ✧ *vb* **-waving, -waved 3** to cook in a microwave oven.

microwave oven *n* a type of cooker which uses microwaves to cook food quickly.

micturate *vb* **-rating, -rated** to urinate. ▷ HISTORY Latin *micturire* to desire to urinate ▶ **micturition** *n*

mid[1] *n Archaic* the middle. ▷ HISTORY Old English

mid[2] *or* **'mid** *prep Poetic* amid.

mid- *combining form* indicating a middle part, point, time, or position: *midday; mid-June; mid-Victorian.*

midair *n* some point above ground level, in the air.

midbrain *n Anat* the part of the brain that develops from the middle portion of the embryonic brain.

midday *n* **1** twelve o'clock in the day; noon. **2** the middle part of the day, from late morning to early afternoon: *the midday sun.*

midden *n Brit & Austral* a dunghill or pile of refuse. ▷ HISTORY from Old Norse

middle *n* **1** an area or point equal in distance from the ends or edges of a place: *a hotel in the middle of town.* **2** the time between the first part and last part of an event or period of time: *the middle of June; the film got a bit boring in the middle.* **3** the part of the body around the stomach; waist. **4 in the middle of** busy doing something: *I'm in the middle of washing the dishes.* ✧ *adj* **5** equally distant from the ends or outer edges of something; central: *the middle finger.* **6** having an equal number of elder and younger brothers and sisters: *he was the middle child of three.* **7** intermediate in status or situation: *middle management.* **8** avoiding extremes; moderate: *we must find a middle course between authoritarianism and anarchy.* ▷ HISTORY Old English *middel*

middle age *n* the period of life between youth and old age, usually considered to occur between the ages of 40 and 60. ▶ **middle-aged** *adj*

Middle Ages *n European history* **1** (broadly) the period from the fall of the W Roman Empire in 476 AD to the Italian Renaissance. **2** (narrowly) the period from about 1000 AD to the 15th century.

Middle America *n* the US middle class, esp. those groups that are politically conservative.

middle C *n Music* the note written on the first ledger line below the treble staff or the first ledger line above the bass staff. On a piano it is near the middle of the keyboard.

middle class *n* **1** the social class between the working and upper classes. It consists of business and professional people. ✧ *adj* **middle-class 2** of or characteristic of the middle class.

middle-distance *adj* **1** *Athletics* of or being a race of a length between the sprints and the distance events, esp. the 800 or 1500 metres: *a middle-distance runner.* ✧ *n* **middle distance 2** the part of a painting between the foreground and the far distance.

middle ear *n* the sound-conducting part of the ear immediately inside the eardrum.

Middle East *n* the area around the E Mediterranean, esp. Israel and the Arab countries from Turkey to North Africa and eastwards to Iran. ▶ **Middle Eastern** *adj*

Middle England *n* a characterization of a predominantly middle-class, middle-income section of British society, living mainly in suburban and rural England.

Middle English *n* the English language from about 1100 to about 1450.

Middle High German *n* High German from about 1200 to about 1500.

Middle Low German *n* Low German from about 1200 to about 1500.

middleman *n, pl* **-men 1** a trader who buys from the producer and sells to the consumer. **2** an intermediary or go-between.

middle-of-the-road *adj* **1** not extreme, esp. in political views; moderate. **2** of or denoting popular music of wide general appeal.

middle school *n* (in England and Wales) a school for children aged between 8 or 9 and 12 or 13.

middleweight *n* a professional boxer weighing up to 160 pounds (72.5 kg) or an amateur weighing up to 75 kg.
middling *adj* **1** neither very good nor very bad. **2** moderate in size. **3 fair to middling** neither good nor bad, esp. in health. ✧ *adv* **4** *Informal* moderately: *middling well.*
midfield *n Soccer* the area between the two opposing defences.
midge *n* a small mosquito-like biting insect occurring in dancing swarms, esp. near water. ▷ **HISTORY** Old English *mycge*
midget *n* **1** a dwarf whose skeleton and features are of normal proportions. ✧ *adj* **2** much smaller than normal: *a midget submarine.* ▷ **HISTORY** *midge* + *-et* small
midi- *combining form* of medium or middle size or length: *a midi-skirt.*
midi system *n* a complete set of compact hi-fi sound equipment designed as a single unit.
midland *n* the central or inland part of a country.
Midlands *n* **1 the Midlands** the central counties of England. ✧ *adj* **2** of, in, or from the central counties of England: *a Midlands engineering firm.*
midnight *n* **1** the middle of the night; 12 o'clock at night. ✧ *adj* **2** happening or apparent at midnight or in the middle of the night: *midnight Mass.* **3 burn the midnight oil** to work or study late into the night.
midnight sun *n* the sun visible at midnight during the summer inside the Arctic and Antarctic circles.
mid-ocean ridge *n Geol* a linear landform, between 200 and 20,000 km in length, found on the ocean floor at the boundary between tectonic plates.
mid-off *n Cricket* the fielding position on the off side closest to the bowler.
mid-on *n Cricket* the fielding position on the on side closest to the bowler.
midpoint *n* **1** the point on a line equally distant from either end. **2** a point in time halfway between the beginning and end of an event.
midriff *n* **1** the middle part of the human body between waist and chest. **2** *Anat* same as **diaphragm** (sense 1). ▷ **HISTORY** Old English *midhrif* mid belly
midshipman *n, pl* **-men** a naval officer of the lowest commissioned rank.
midships *adv, adj Naut* See **amidships**.
midst *n* **1 in our midst** among us. **2 in the midst of a** surrounded by. **b** at a point during.
midsummer *n* **1** the middle or height of summer. **2** same as **summer solstice**.
Midsummer's Day *or* **Midsummer Day** *n* June 24, the feast of St John the Baptist: one of the four quarter days in England, Ireland, and Wales.
midway *adj* **1** in or at the middle of the distance; halfway: *the midway point.* ✧ *adv* **2** to the middle of the distance.
mid-wicket *n Cricket* the fielding position on the on side, roughly the same distance from both wickets, and halfway towards the boundary.
midwife *n, pl* **-wives** a person qualified to deliver babies and to care for women before, during, and after childbirth. ▷ **HISTORY** Old English *mid* with + *wīf* woman ▶ **midwifery** (mid-**wiff**-fer-ree) *n*
midwinter *n* **1** the middle or depth of winter. **2** same as **winter solstice**.
mien (**mean**) *n Literary* a person's manner, bearing, or appearance. ▷ **HISTORY** probably from obsolete *demean* appearance
mifepristone (mi-**fep**-riss-tone) *n* a technical name for **abortion pill**.
miffed *adj Informal* offended or upset. ▷ **HISTORY** perhaps imitative of bad temper
might¹ *vb* used as an auxiliary: **1** the past tense or subjunctive mood of **may¹**: *he might have come.* **2** expressing possibility: *he might well have gone already.* See **may¹** (sense 2). ▷ **HISTORY** Old English *mihte*

> **WORD TIP**
> See at **may¹**.

might² *n* **1** great power, strength, or vigour. **2 with all one's might** using all one's strength and energy. **3 (with) might and main** See **main**. ▷ **HISTORY** Old English *miht*
mighty *adj* **mightier, mightiest 1** powerful or strong. **2** very great in extent or importance. ✧ *adv* **3** *Informal, chiefly US, Canad & Austral* very: *mighty hungry.* ▶ **mightily** *adv* ▶ **mightiness** *n*
mignonette (min-yon-**net**) *n* a plant with spikes of small fragrant greenish-white flowers. ▷ **HISTORY** French, diminutive of *mignon* dainty
migraine (**mee**-grain) *n* a throbbing headache usually affecting only one side of the head and commonly accompanied by nausea and visual disturbances.

> **WORD HISTORY**
> 'Migraine' comes via French from Latin *hēmicrānia*, meaning 'pain in half the head', from Greek *hemi-*, meaning 'half', and *kranion*, meaning 'cranium, skull'.

migrant *n* **1** a person or animal that moves from one place to another. ✧ *adj* **2** moving from one place to another: *migrant farm labourers.*
migrate *vb* **-grating, -grated 1** to go from one place to settle in another, esp. in a foreign country. **2** (of living creatures, esp. birds) to journey between different habitats at specific times of the year. ▷ **HISTORY** Latin *migrare* to change one's abode ▶ **migration** *n* ▶ **migratory** *adj*
mikado *n, pl* **-dos** *Archaic* the Japanese emperor. ▷ **HISTORY** Japanese
mike *n Informal* a microphone.
mil *n Photog* short for **millimetre:** *35-mil film.* ▷ **HISTORY** Latin *millesimus* thousandth
milch (**miltch**) *adj Chiefly Brit* (esp. of cattle) kept for milk. ▷ **HISTORY** Old English *-milce* (in compounds)
mild *adj* **1** (of a taste or sensation) not strong; bland. **2** gentle or temperate in character, climate, or behaviour. **3** not extreme; moderate: *mild*

a b c d e f g h i j k l m n o p q r s t u v w x y z

criticism of senior officers. **4** feeble; unassertive: *a mild protest.* ✧ *n* **5** *Brit* a dark beer flavoured with fewer hops than bitter. ▷ **HISTORY** Old English *milde*

mildew *n* **1** a disease of plants caused by a parasitic fungus. **2** same as **mould²**. ✧ *vb* **3** to affect or become affected with mildew. ▷ **HISTORY** Old English *mildēaw* honey dew ▶ **mildewy** *adj*

mild steel *n* strong tough steel containing a small quantity of carbon.

mile *n* **1** Also: **statute mile** a unit of length used in the UK, the US and certain other countries, equal to 1760 yards. 1 mile is equivalent to 1.60934 kilometres. **2** See **nautical mile**. **3** Also: **miles** *Informal* a great distance; great deal: *he missed by miles.* **4** a race extending over a mile. ✧ *adv* **5** **miles** very much: *it's miles better than their first album.*

> **WORD HISTORY**
> In Roman times, a mile was equal to a thousand paces. In Latin, 'one thousand paces' is *mīlia passuum*, from *mille*, meaning 'a thousand' (the same Latin word as is found in English words such as 'millennium' and 'millimetre').

mileage *n* **1** a distance expressed in miles. **2** the total number of miles that a motor vehicle has travelled. **3** the number of miles a motor vehicle will travel on one gallon of fuel. **4** *Informal* the usefulness or benefit of something: *the opposition is trying to make political mileage out of the issue.*

mileometer *or* **milometer** (mile-**om**-it-er) *n* *Brit* a device that records the number of miles that a vehicle has travelled.

milepost *n* *Chiefly US & Canad* a signpost that shows the distance in miles to or from a place.

milestone *n* **1** a stone pillar that shows the distance in miles to or from a place. **2** a significant event in a life or history: *a milestone in Turkish-Bulgarian relations.*

milfoil *n* same as **yarrow**. ▷ **HISTORY** Latin *mille* thousand + *folium* leaf

milieu (**meal**-yuh) *n, pl* **milieux** *or* **milieus** (**meal**-yuhz) the social and cultural environment in which a person or thing exists: *the film takes for its milieu an apparently wholesome small town.* ▷ **HISTORY** French

militant *adj* **1** very active or aggressive in the support of a cause. **2** *Formal* warring; engaged in warfare. ✧ *n* **3** a militant person. ▷ **HISTORY** Latin *militare* to be a soldier ▶ **militancy** *n* ▶ **militantly** *adv*

militarism *n* the pursuit of policies intended to create and maintain aggressive and influential armed forces. ▶ **militarist** *n, adj* ▶ **militaristic** *adj*

militarized *or* **-ised** *adj* occupied by armed forces: *one of the most heavily militarized borders in the world.* ▶ **militarization** *or* **-isation** *n*

military *adj* **1** of or relating to the armed forces or war. **2** of or characteristic of soldiers. ✧ *n* **3** **the military** the armed services, esp. the army. ▷ **HISTORY** Latin *miles* soldier ▶ **militarily** *adv*

military police *n* a corps within an army that performs police duties.

militate *vb* **-tating, -tated** (of facts or events) to have a strong influence or effect: *our position militated against counter-attacks.*

> **WORD TIP**
> See at **mitigate.**

militia (mill-**ish**-a) *n* a military force of trained civilians enlisted for use in emergency only. ▷ **HISTORY** Latin: soldiery ▶ **militiaman** *n*

milk *n* **1 a** a whitish fluid secreted by the mammary glands of mature female mammals and used for feeding their young. **b** the milk of cows, goats, etc., used by humans as a food and to make cheese, butter and yogurt. **2** any similar fluid, such as the juice of a coconut. ✧ *vb* **3** to draw milk from the udder of a cow or other animal. **4** to extract as much money, help, or value as possible from: *he was accused of milking the situation for his own ends.* ▷ **HISTORY** Old English *milc* ▶ **milker** *n* ▶ **milkiness** *n* ▶ **milky** *adj*

milk bar *n* (formerly) a snack bar at which milk drinks and light refreshments are served.

milk float *n* *Brit* a small electrically powered vehicle used to deliver milk to houses.

milkmaid *n* a girl or woman who milks cows.

milkman *n, pl* **-men** *Brit, Austral & NZ* a man who delivers milk to people's houses.

milk of magnesia *n* a suspension of magnesium hydroxide in water, used as an antacid and laxative.

milk pudding *n* *Chiefly Brit & Austral* a pudding made by cooking milk with a grain, esp. rice.

milk round *n* **1** *Brit & NZ* a route along which a milkman regularly delivers milk. **2** *Brit* a regular series of visits made by recruitment officers from industry to colleges.

milksop *n* a feeble or ineffectual man or youth.

Milky Way *n* **1** the diffuse band of light stretching across the night sky that consists of millions of distant stars in our galaxy. **2** the galaxy in which the Earth is situated. ▷ **HISTORY** translation of Latin *via lactea*

mill *n* **1** a building where grain is crushed and ground to make flour. **2** a factory, esp. one which processes raw materials: *a steel mill.* **3** any of various processing or manufacturing machines, esp. one that grinds, presses, or rolls. **4** a small device for grinding solids: *a pepper mill.* **5** **go** *or* **be put through the mill** to have an unpleasant experience or ordeal. ✧ *vb* **6** to grind, press, or process in or as if in a mill. **7** to groove or flute the edge of a coin. **8** to move about in a confused manner: *the corridor was full of people milling about.* ▷ **HISTORY** Latin *molere* to grind

millennium (mill-**en**-nee-um) *n, pl* **-nia** (-nee-a) *or* **-niums** **1** a period of one thousand years. **2** **the Millennium** *Christianity* the period of a thousand years of Christ's awaited reign upon earth. **3** a future period of peace and happiness. ▷ **HISTORY** Latin *mille* thousand + *annus* year ▶ **millennial** *adj*

millennium bug *n Computers* any software problem arising from the change in date at the start of the 21st century.
millepede *n* same as **millipede**.
miller *n History* a person who owns or operates a mill, esp. a corn mill.
miller's thumb *n* a small freshwater European fish with a flattened body. ▷ **HISTORY** from the alleged likeness of the fish's head to a thumb
millesimal (mill-**less**-im-al) *adj* **1** denoting or consisting of a thousandth. ✧ *n* **2** a thousandth part of something. ▷ **HISTORY** Latin *millesimus*
millet *n* a cereal grass cultivated for its edible grain and as animal fodder. ▷ **HISTORY** Latin *milium*
milli- *combining form* denoting 10^{-3}: *millimetre*. ▷ **HISTORY** Latin *mille* thousand
milliard *n Brit* (no longer in technical use) a thousand million. ▷ **HISTORY** French
millibar *n* a unit of atmospheric pressure equal to 100 newtons per square metre.
milligram *or* **milligramme** *n* one thousandth of a gram. ▷ **HISTORY** French
millilitre *or US* **milliliter** *n* a measure of volume equivalent to one thousandth of a litre.
millimetre *or US* **millimeter** *n* a unit of length equal to one thousandth of a metre.
milliner *n* a person who makes or sells women's hats. ▷ **HISTORY** originally *Milaner* a native of *Milan*, once famous for its fancy goods ▶ **millinery** *n*
million *n, pl* **-lions** *or* **-lion 1** the number equal to one thousand thousands: 1 000 000 or 10^6. **2** (*often pl*) *Informal* an extremely large but unspecified number: *I've got a million things to do today.* ▷ **HISTORY** early Italian *millione* ▶ **millionth** *n, adj*
millionaire *n* a person who has money or property worth at least a million pounds, dollars, etc. ▶ **millionairess** *fem n*
millipede *or* **millepede** *n* a small crawling animal with a cylindrical many-segmented body, each segment of which bears two pairs of legs. ▷ **HISTORY** Latin *mille* thousand + *pes* foot
millisecond *n* one thousandth of a second.
millstone *n* **1** one of a pair of heavy flat stones that are rotated one against the other to grind grain. **2** a heavy burden of responsibility or obligation: *the debt had become a millstone round his neck.*
millwheel *n* a water wheel that drives a mill.
milometer (mile-**om**-it-er) *n* same as **mileometer**.
milt *n* the male reproductive gland, sperm, or semen of a fish. ▷ **HISTORY** Old English *milte* spleen
mime *n* **1** an style of acting using only gesture and bodily movement and not words. **2** a performer specializing in this. **3** a performance in this style. ✧ *vb* **miming, mimed 4** to express or describe something in actions or gestures without using speech. **5** (of musicians) to pretend to be singing or playing music that is actually prerecorded. ▷ **HISTORY** Greek *mimos* imitator ▶ **mimer** *n*
mimetic (mim-**met**-ik) *adj* **1** imitating or representing something: *most photographs are mimetic representations of the real world.* **2** *Biol* of or showing mimicry. ▷ **HISTORY** Greek *mimeisthai* to imitate
mimic *vb* **-icking, -icked 1** to imitate (a person or a way of acting or speaking), esp. to entertain or make fun of. **2** to take on the appearance of: *certain flies mimic wasps.* **3** to copy closely or in a servile manner: *social climbers in the colonies began to mimic their conquerors.* ✧ *n* **4** a person or an animal, such as a parrot, that is clever at mimicking. ▷ **HISTORY** Greek *mimikos*
mimicry *n, pl* **-ries 1** the act or art of copying or imitating closely. **2** *Biol* the resemblance shown by one animal species to another dangerous or inedible one, which protects it from predators.
mimosa *n* a tropical shrub with ball-like clusters of yellow flowers and leaves sensitive to touch and light. ▷ **HISTORY** Latin *mimus* mime, because the plant's sensitivity to touch imitates the similar reaction of animals
min. **1** minimum. **2** minute *or* minutes.
Min. **1** Minister. **2** Ministry.
minaret *n* a slender tower of a mosque with one or more balconies. ▷ **HISTORY** Arabic *manārat* lamp
minatory *adj* threatening or menacing. ▷ **HISTORY** Latin *minari* to threaten
mince *vb* **mincing, minced 1** to chop, grind, or cut into very small pieces. **2** to walk or speak in an affected dainty manner. **3 not mince one's words** to be direct and to the point rather than making an effort to avoid upsetting people. ✧ *n* **4** *Chiefly Brit & NZ* minced meat. ▷ **HISTORY** Old French *mincier*, from Late Latin *minutia* smallness ▶ **minced** *adj* ▶ **mincer** *n*
mincemeat *n* **1** a mixture of dried fruit and spices used for filling pies. **2 make mincemeat of** *Informal* to defeat completely.
mince pie *n* a small round pastry tart filled with mincemeat.
mincing *adj* (of a person or their style of walking or speaking) affectedly elegant.
mind *n* **1** the part of a person responsible for thought, feelings, and intention. *RELATED ADJECTIVE* ➧ **mental 2** intelligence as opposed to feelings or wishes. **3** memory or recollection: *his name didn't spring to mind immediately.* **4** a person considered as an intellectual being: *one of Europe's greatest minds.* **5** the condition or state of a person's feelings or thoughts: *a confused state of mind.* **6** an intention or desire: *I have a mind to go.* **7** attention or thoughts: *keep your mind on the job.* **8** a sound mental state; sanity: *he's out of his mind.* **9 change one's mind** to alter one's decision or opinion. **10 give someone a piece of one's mind** to scold someone severely. **11 in two minds** undecided or wavering. **12 make up one's mind** to reach a decision. **13 on one's mind** in one's thoughts. **14 to my mind** in my opinion. ✧ *vb* **15** to take offence at: *do you mind if I open a window?* **16** to pay attention to: *to mind one's own business.* **17** to make certain; ensure: *mind you tell him.* **18** to take care of: *mind the shop.* **19** to be cautious or careful about: *mind how you go.* **20** *Dialect* to remember. ▷ **HISTORY** Old English *gemynd*

minded *adj* having a mind or inclination as specified: *commercially minded.*

minder *n* **1** *Slang* an aide or assistant, esp. one employed as a bodyguard or public relations officer for someone. **2** short for **child minder**.

mindful *adj* **mindful of** being aware of and taking into account: *the company is ever mindful of the need to find new markets.*

mindless *adj* **1** stupid or careless. **2** requiring little or no intellectual effort. **3** heedless: *mindless of the risks involved.* ▶ **mindlessly** *adv* ▶ **mindlessness** *n*

mine¹ *pron* **1** something or someone belonging to or associated with me: *that's mine.* **2 of mine** belonging to or associated with me: *it's a great favourite of mine.* ✧ *adj* **3** *Archaic* same as **my:** *mine eyes; mine host.* ▷ HISTORY Old English *mīn*

mine² *n* **1** a place where minerals, esp. coal, ores, or precious stones, are dug from the ground. **2** a type of bomb placed in water or under the ground, and designed to destroy ships, vehicles, or people passing over or near it. **3** a profitable source or abundant supply: *a mine of information.* ✧ *vb* **mining, mined 4** to dig minerals from the ground: *lead has been mined here for over three centuries.* **5** to dig a hole or tunnel, esp. in order to obtain minerals. **6** to place explosive mines in or on: *the retreating troops had mined the bridge.* ▷ HISTORY Old French

mine dump *n S African* a large mound of waste material from gold-mining operations.

minefield *n* **1** an area of ground or water containing explosive mines. **2** a subject or situation full of hidden problems.

minelayer *n* a warship or aircraft for carrying and laying mines.

miner *n* a person who works in a mine, esp. a coal mine.

mineral *n* **1** a naturally occurring solid inorganic substance with a characteristic chemical composition and structure. **2** any inorganic matter. **3** any substance obtained by mining, esp. a metal ore. **4** *Brit* a soft drink containing carbonated water and flavourings. ✧ *adj* **5** of, containing, or resembling minerals. ▷ HISTORY Medieval Latin *minera* mine, ore

mineral acid *n* any acid which can be produced from a mineral.

mineralogy (min-er-**al**-a-jee) *n* the scientific study of minerals. ▶ **mineralogical** *adj* ▶ **mineralogist** *n*

mineral water *n* water containing dissolved mineral salts or gases.

minestrone (min-ness-**strone**-ee) *n* a soup made from a variety of vegetables and pasta. ▷ HISTORY Italian, from *minestrare* to serve

minesweeper *n* a naval vessel equipped to clear mines.

Ming *adj* of or relating to Chinese porcelain from the time of the Ming dynasty, which ruled China from 1368 to 1644.

minger *n Brit informal* an unattractive person. ▶ **minging** *adj*

mingle *vb* **-gling, -gled 1** to mix or blend. **2** to associate or mix with a group of people: *the performers mingled with the audience after the show.* ▷ HISTORY Old English *mengan* to mix

mingy *adj* **-gier, -giest** *Brit & NZ informal* mean or miserly. ▷ HISTORY probably a blend of *mean* + *stingy*

mini *adj* **1** small; miniature. **2** (of a skirt or dress) very short. ✧ *n, pl* **minis 3** something very small of its kind, esp. a miniskirt.

mini- *combining form* smaller or shorter than the standard size: *minibus; miniseries.* ▷ HISTORY from *miniature* + *minimum*

miniature *n* **1** a model or representation on a very small scale. **2** a very small painting, esp. a portrait. **3** a very small bottle of whisky or other spirits, which can hold 50 millilitres. **4 in miniature** on a small scale. ✧ *adj* **5** much smaller than usual; small-scale. ▷ HISTORY Medieval Latin *miniare* to paint red (in illuminating manuscripts), from *minium* red lead ▶ **miniaturist** *n*

miniaturize *or* **-ise** *vb* **-izing, -ized** *or* **-ising, -ised** to make a very small version of something, esp. electronic components. ▶ **miniaturization** *or* **-isation** *n*

minibus *n* a small bus.

minicab *n Brit* an ordinary car used as a taxi.

minicomputer *n* a small digital computer which is more powerful than a microcomputer.

minidisc *n* a small recordable compact disc.

minim *n* **1** a unit of fluid measure equal to one sixtieth of a drachm. **2** *Music* a note with the time value of half a semibreve. ▷ HISTORY Latin *minimus* smallest

minimal *adj* of the least possible quantity or degree.

minimalism *n* **1** a type of music based on the repetition of simple elements. **2** a design or style using the simplest and fewest elements to create the maximum effect. ▶ **minimalist** *adj, n*

minimize *or* **-mise** *vb* **-mizing, -mized** *or* **-mising, -mised 1** to reduce to the lowest possible degree or amount: *these measures should help minimize our costs.* **2** to regard or treat as less important than it really is; belittle: *I don't want to minimize the importance of her contribution.*

minimum *n, pl* **-mums** *or* **-ma 1** the least possible amount, degree, or quantity: *fry the burgers in the minimum of oil.* **2** the least amount recorded, allowed, or reached: *soak the beans for a minimum of eight hours.* ✧ *adj* **3** of, being, or showing a minimum or minimums: *the minimum age.* ▷ HISTORY Latin *minimus* least

minimum lending rate *n* (formerly) the minimum rate at which the Bank of England would lend money: replaced in 1981 by the base rate.

minimum wage *n* the lowest wage that an employer is permitted to pay by law or union contract.

mining *n* **1** the act, process, or industry of extracting coal or ores from the earth. **2** *Mil* the process of laying mines.

minion *n* a servile assistant. ▷ **HISTORY** French *mignon* darling

miniseries *n, pl* **-series** a television programme in several parts that is shown on consecutive days over a short period.

miniskirt *n* a very short skirt.

minister *n* **1** (esp. in Presbyterian and some Nonconformist Churches) a member of the clergy. **2** a head of a government department. **3** a diplomat with a lower rank than an ambassador. ✧ *vb* **4 minister to** to attend to the needs of. ▷ **HISTORY** Latin: servant ▶ **ministerial** *adj*

minister of state *n* (in the British Parliament) a minister, usually below cabinet rank, appointed to assist a senior minister.

Minister of the Crown *n Brit* any Government minister of cabinet rank.

ministry *n, pl* **-tries 1** the profession or duties of a minister of religion. **2** ministers considered as a group. **3 a** a government department headed by a minister. **b** the buildings of such a department.

mink *n, pl* **mink** *or* **minks 1** a mammal of Europe, Asia, and North America, resembling a large stoat. **2** its highly valued fur. **3** a garment made of this, esp. a woman's coat or stole. ▷ **HISTORY** Scandinavian

minneola *n* a juicy citrus fruit that is a cross between a tangerine and a grapefruit.

minnow *n, pl* **-nows** *or* **-now** a small slender European freshwater fish. ▷ **HISTORY** Old English *myne*

Minoan (min-**no**-an) *adj* of or denoting the Bronze Age culture of Crete from about 3000 BC to about 1100 BC. ▷ **HISTORY** *Minos,* in Greek mythology, king of Crete

minor *adj* **1** lesser or secondary in size, frequency, or importance than others of the same kind: *a minor poet.* **2** not very serious or significant: *minor injuries.* **3** *Music* **a** (of a scale) having a semitone between the second and third and fifth and sixth notes (**natural minor**). **b** of or based on the minor scale: *his quintet in C minor; a minor third.* ✧ *n* **4** a person below the age of legal majority. **5** *US, Canad & Austral education* a subsidiary subject. **6** *Music* a minor key, chord, mode, or scale. ✧ *vb* **7 minor in** *US education* to study as a subsidiary subject: *to minor in politics.* ▷ **HISTORY** Latin: less, smaller

minority *n, pl* **-ties 1** the smaller of two parts, factions, or groups. **2** a group that is different, esp. racially or politically, from a larger group of which it is a part. **3 in the minority** forming or part of the group of people or things made up of less than half of a larger group. ✧ *adj* **4** relating to or being a minority: *a minority sport.*

Minotaur *n Greek myth* a monster with the head of a bull and the body of a man. ▷ **HISTORY** Greek *Minōtauros*

minster *n Brit* any of certain cathedrals and large churches, usually originally connected to a monastery. ▷ **HISTORY** Church Latin *monasterium* monastery

minstrel *n* **1** a medieval singer and musician. **2** a performer in a minstrel show. ▷ **HISTORY** Old French *menestral*

minstrel show *n* a theatrical entertainment consisting of songs and dances performed by actors wearing black face make-up.

mint[1] *n* **1** any of various plants with aromatic leaves used for seasoning and flavouring. **2** a sweet flavoured with mint. ▷ **HISTORY** Greek *minthē* ▶ **minty** *adj*

mint[2] *n* **1** a factory where the official coins of a country are made. **2** a very large amount of money. ✧ *adj* **3 in mint condition** in perfect condition; as if new. ✧ *vb* **4** to make coins by stamping metal. **5** to invent or create: *no-one knows who first minted the term 'yuppie'.* ▷ **HISTORY** Latin *moneta* money, mint

minuet (min-new-**wet**) *n* **1** a stately court dance of the 17th and 18th centuries in triple time. **2** music for this dance. ▷ **HISTORY** French *menuet* dainty

minus *prep* **1** reduced by the subtraction of: *six minus two equals four.* **2** *Informal* without or lacking: *he returned minus his jacket.* ✧ *adj* **3** indicating or involving subtraction: *a minus sign.* **4** Also: **negative** less than zero: *it's minus eight degrees in Montreal today.* **5** *Education* slightly below the standard of a particular grade: *a C minus for maths.* ✧ *n* **6** short for **minus sign**. **7** a negative quantity. **8** *Informal* something detrimental or negative. ▷ **HISTORY** Latin, neuter of *minor* less

minuscule (**min**-niss-skyool) *adj* very small. ▷ **HISTORY** Latin *(littera) minuscula* very small (letter)

minus sign *n* the symbol –, indicating subtraction, a negative quantity, or a negative electrical charge.

minute[1] *n* **1** 60 seconds; one sixtieth of an hour. **2** any very short period of time; moment: *I'll be with you in a minute.* **3** the distance that can be travelled in a minute: *it's about ten minutes away.* **4** a measure of angle equal to one sixtieth of a degree. **5 up to the minute** the very latest or newest. ✧ *vb* **-uting, -uted 6** to record in minutes: *the decision was minuted in 1990.* ✧ See also **minutes**. ▷ **HISTORY** Medieval Latin *minuta,* noun use of Latin *minutus* minute (small)

minute[2] *adj* **1** very small; tiny. **2** precise or detailed: *a minute examination.* ▷ **HISTORY** Latin *minutus,* past participle of *minuere* to diminish ▶ **minutely** *adv*

minutes *pl n* an official record of the proceedings of a meeting or conference.

minutiae (my-**new**-shee-eye) *pl n, sing* **-tia** trifling or precise details. ▷ **HISTORY** Late Latin, plural of *minutia* smallness

minx *n* a bold or flirtatious girl. ▷ **HISTORY** origin unknown

Miocene (**my**-oh-seen) *adj Geol* of the epoch of geological time about 25 million years ago. ▷ **HISTORY** Greek *meiōn* less + *kainos* new

miracle *n* **1** an event contrary to the laws of nature and attributed to a supernatural cause. **2** any amazing and fortunate event: *it's a miracle that no-one was killed in the accident.* **3** a marvellous example of something: *a miracle of organization.* ▷ **HISTORY** Latin *mirari* to wonder at

miracle play *n* a medieval play based on a biblical story or the life of a saint.

miraculous *adj* **1** like a miracle. **2** surprising or remarkable.

mirage (mir-**rahzh**) *n* **1** an image of a distant object or sheet of water, often inverted or distorted, caused by atmospheric refraction by hot air. **2** something illusory: *the mirage of economic recovery.* ▷ **HISTORY** French, from *(se) mirer* to be reflected

mire *n* **1** a boggy or marshy area. **2** mud, muck, or dirt. **3** an unpleasant or difficult situation that is difficult to get out of: *the country sank deeper into the economic mire.* ✧ *vb* **miring, mired 4** to sink or be stuck in a mire: *the company has been mired in financial scandal.* ▷ **HISTORY** Old Norse *mȳrr*

mirror *n* **1** a sheet of glass with a metal coating on its back, that reflects an image of an object placed in front of it. **2** a thing that reflects or depicts something else. ✧ *vb* **3** to reflect or represent faithfully: *the book inevitably mirrors my own interests.* ▷ **HISTORY** Latin *mirari* to wonder at

mirror image *n* an image or object that has left and right reversed as if seen in a mirror.

mirth *n* laughter, gaiety, or merriment. ▷ **HISTORY** Old English *myrgth* ▶ **mirthful** *adj* ▶ **mirthless** *adj*

mis- *prefix* **1** wrong or bad; wrongly or badly: *misunderstanding; mislead.* **2** lack of; not: *mistrust.* ▷ **HISTORY** Old English *mis(se)-*

misadventure *n* **1** an unlucky event; misfortune. **2** *Law* accidental death not due to crime or negligence.

misalliance *n* an unsuitable alliance or marriage.

misanthrope (**miz**-zan-thrope) *or* **misanthropist** (miz-**zan**-throp-ist) *n* a person who dislikes or distrusts people in general. ▷ **HISTORY** Greek *misos* hatred + *anthrōpos* man ▶ **misanthropic** (miz-zan-**throp**-ik) *adj* ▶ **misanthropy** (miz-**zan**-throp-ee) *n*

misapprehend *vb* to misunderstand. ▶ **misapprehension** *n*

misappropriate *vb* **-ating, -ated** to take and use money dishonestly. ▶ **misappropriation** *n*

misbehave *vb* **-having, -haved** to behave badly. ▶ **misbehaviour** *or US* **misbehavior** *n*

miscalculate *vb* **-lating, -lated** to calculate or judge wrongly: *we miscalculated the strength of the opposition.* ▶ **miscalculation** *n*

miscarriage *n* **1** spontaneous premature expulsion of a fetus from the womb, esp. before the 20th week of pregnancy. **2** an act of mismanagement or failure: *a miscarriage of justice.*

miscarry *vb* **-ries, -rying, -ried 1** to expel a fetus prematurely from the womb. **2** to fail.

miscast *vb* **-casting, -cast** to cast a role or an actor in a play or film inappropriately: *the role of the avaricious boss was miscast; she was miscast as Cassandra.*

miscegenation (miss-ij-in-**nay**-shun) *n* interbreeding of races, esp. where differences of colour are involved. ▷ **HISTORY** Latin *miscere* to mingle + *genus* race

miscellaneous (miss-sel-**lane**-ee-uss) *adj* composed of or containing a variety of things; mixed or assorted. ▷ **HISTORY** Latin *miscere* to mix

miscellany (miss-**sell**-a-nee) *n, pl* **-nies** a mixed assortment of items.

mischance *n* **1** bad luck. **2** an unlucky event or accident.

mischief *n* **1** annoying but not malicious behaviour that causes trouble or irritation. **2** an inclination to tease. **3** injury or harm caused by a person or thing. ▷ **HISTORY** Old French *meschief,* from *mes-* mis- + *chef* end

mischievous (**miss**-chiv-uss) *adj* **1** full of mischief. **2** teasing; slightly malicious. **3** intended to cause harm: *a purveyor of mischievous disinformation.* ▶ **mischievously** *adv*

miscible (**miss**-sib-bl) *adj* able to be mixed: *miscible with water.* ▷ **HISTORY** Latin *miscere* to mix ▶ **miscibility** *n*

misconceived *adj* false, mistaken, or badly thought-out: *a misconceived conception of loyalty.*

misconception *n* a false or mistaken view, idea, or belief.

misconduct *n* behaviour, such as adultery or professional negligence, that is regarded as immoral or unethical.

misconstrue *vb* **-struing, -strued** to interpret mistakenly. ▶ **misconstruction** *n*

miscreant (**miss**-kree-ant) *n* a wrongdoer or villain. ▷ **HISTORY** Old French *mescreant* unbelieving

misdeed *n* an evil or illegal action.

misdemeanour *or US* **misdemeanor** *n* **1** a minor wrongdoing. **2** *Criminal law* (formerly) an offence less serious than a felony.

misdirect *vb* to give someone wrong directions or instructions. ▶ **misdirection** *n*

mise en scène (**meez**-orn-sen) *n* **1** the arrangement of properties, scenery, etc., in a play. **2** the objects so arranged; stage setting. ▷ **HISTORY** French: putting on stage

miser *n* a person who hoards money and hates spending it: *I'm married to a miser.* ▷ **HISTORY** Latin: wretched ▶ **miserly** *adj*

miserable *adj* **1** unhappy or depressed; wretched. **2** causing misery or discomfort: *a miserable existence.* **3** sordid or squalid: *miserable living conditions.* **4** mean or ungenerous: *a miserable pension.* ▷ **HISTORY** Latin *miserabilis* ▶ **miserableness** *n* ▶ **miserably** *adv*

misericord *n* a ledge projecting from the underside of the hinged seat of a choir stall in a church, which the occupant can rest against while standing. ▷ **HISTORY** Latin *miserere* to pity + *cor* heart

misery *n, pl* **-eries 1** intense unhappiness or suffering. **2** something which causes such unhappiness. **3** squalid or poverty-stricken conditions. **4** *Brit informal* a person who is habitually depressed: *he is such a misery.* ▷ **HISTORY** Latin *miser* wretched

misfire *vb* **-firing, -fired 1** (of a firearm) to fail to fire as expected. **2** (of a motor engine or vehicle) to

A B C D E F G H I J K L M N O P Q R S T U V W X Y Z

fail to fire at the appropriate time. **3** to fail to have the intended result; go wrong: *he was injured when a practical joke misfired.* ✧ *n* **4** the act or an instance of misfiring.

misfit *n* a person who is not suited to the role, social group, etc., he or she finds himself or herself in.

misfortune *n* **1** bad luck. **2** an unfortunate event.

misgivings *pl n* feelings of uncertainty, fear, or doubt.

misgovern *vb* to govern badly. ▶ **misgovernment** *n*

misguided *adj* mistaken or unwise.

mishandle *vb* **-dling, -dled** to handle or treat badly or inefficiently.

mishap *n* a minor accident.

mishear *vb* **-hearing, -heard** to fail to hear (what someone says) correctly.

mishit *Sport* ✧ *n* **1** a faulty shot, kick, or stroke. ✧ *vb* **-hitting, -hit 2** to hit or kick (a ball) with a faulty stroke.

mishmash *n* a confused collection or mixture. ▷ **HISTORY** reduplication of *mash*

misinform *vb* to give incorrect information to. ▶ **misinformation** *n*

misinterpret *vb* to understand or represent (something) wrongly: *the press misinterpreted the President's remarks.* ▶ **misinterpretation** *n*

misjudge *vb* **-judging, -judged** to judge wrongly or unfairly. ▶ **misjudgment** *or* **misjudgement** *n*

mislay *vb* **-lays, -laying, -laid** to lose (something) temporarily, esp. by forgetting where it is.

mislead *vb* **-leading, -led** to give false or confusing information to.

misleading *adj* giving a false or confusing impression: *misleading use of statistical data.*

mismanage *vb* **-aging, -aged** to organize or run (something) badly. ▶ **mismanagement** *n*

misnomer (miss-**no**-mer) *n* **1** an incorrect or unsuitable name for a person or thing. **2** the use of the wrong name. ▷ **HISTORY** Old French *mesnommer* to misname

misogyny (miss-**oj**-in-ee) *n* hatred of women. ▷ **HISTORY** Greek *misos* hatred + *gunē* woman ▶ **misogynist** *n* ▶ **misogynous** *adj*

misplace *vb* **-placing, -placed 1** to lose something temporarily by forgetting where it was placed. **2** to put something in the wrong place.

misprint *n* **1** an error in printing. ✧ *vb* **2** to print a letter incorrectly.

misprision *n Law* the concealment of the commission of a felony or an act of treason. ▷ **HISTORY** Old French *mesprision* error

mispronounce *vb* **-nouncing, -nounced** to pronounce a word or name wrongly. ▶ **mispronunciation** *n*

misquote *vb* **-quoting, -quoted** to quote inaccurately. ▶ **misquotation** *n*

misread *vb* **-reading, -read 1** to misinterpret or misunderstand: *he misread her politeness as approval.* **2** to read incorrectly.

misrepresent *vb* to represent wrongly or inaccurately.

misrepresentation *n Law* inaccurate or untrue information given to induce someone into entering into a contract; if proved, misrepresentation is grounds for voiding the contract.

misrule *vb* **-ruling, -ruled 1** to govern inefficiently or without justice. ✧ *n* **2** inefficient or unjust government. **3** disorder or lawlessness.

miss[1] *vb* **1** to fail to notice, see, or hear: *it's right at the top of the hill, so you can't miss it; I missed what he said because I was talking at the time.* **2** to fail to hit something aimed at: *he threw a stone at the dog but missed.* **3** to fail to achieve or reach: *they narrowly missed promotion last season.* **4** to fail to take advantage of: *he never missed a chance to make money.* **5** to fail or be unable to be present: *he had missed the last three meetings.* **6** to be too late for: *we missed the bus and had to walk.* **7** to fail to take advantage of: *he never missed a chance to make money.* **8** to discover or regret the loss or absence of: *the boys miss their father when he's away on business.* **9** to escape or avoid narrowly: *it missed the helicopters rotors by inches.* ✧ *n* **10** a failure to hit, reach, etc.: *an easy miss in the second frame gave his opponent the advantage.* **11 give something a miss** to decide not to do, go to, or take part in something: *I'll give the pub a miss and have a quiet night in.* ✧ See also **miss out**. ▷ **HISTORY** Old English *missan*

miss[2] *n Informal* an unmarried woman or girl. ▷ **HISTORY** from *mistress*

Miss *n* a title of a girl or unmarried woman, usually used before the surname: *Miss Brown to you.*

missal *n RC Church* a book containing the prayers and rites of the Masses for a complete year. ▷ **HISTORY** Church Latin *missale,* from *missa* Mass

misshapen *adj* badly shaped; deformed.

missile *n* **1** a rocket with an exploding warhead, used as a weapon. **2** an object or weapon that is thrown, launched, or fired at a target. ▷ **HISTORY** Latin *mittere* to send

missing *adj* **1** not in its proper or usual place and unable to be found. **2** not able to be traced and not known to be dead: *seven men were reported missing after the raid.* **3** not included in something although it perhaps should have been: *two things are missing from the report.*

missing link *n* **1** any missing section or part in a series. **2 the missing link** a hypothetical extinct animal, formerly thought to be intermediate between the apes and man.

mission *n* **1** a specific task or duty assigned to a person or group of people. **2** a task or duty that a person believes he or she must achieve; vocation: *he felt it was his mission to pass on his knowledge to other people.* **3** a group of people representing or working for a particular country or organization in a foreign country: *the UN peacekeeping mission.* **4** a group of people sent by a church to a foreign country to do religious and social work. **5** the place in which a church or government mission is based. **6** the dispatch of aircraft or spacecraft to achieve a particular task. **7** a charitable centre that offers shelter or aid to the poor or needy. **8** *S African* a long and difficult process. ▷ **HISTORY** Latin *mittere* to send

missionary *n, pl* **-aries 1** a person sent abroad by a church to do religious and social work. ✧ *adj* **2** of or relating to missionaries: *missionary work.* **3** resulting from a desire to convert people to one's own beliefs: *missionary zeal.*

mission statement *n* an official statement of the aims and objectives of a business or other organization.

missive *n* a formal or official letter. ▷ **HISTORY** Latin *mittere* to send

miss out *vb* **1** to leave out or overlook. **2 miss out on** to fail to take part in (something enjoyable or beneficial): *she'd missed out on going to university.*

misspell *vb* **-spelling, -spelt** *or* **-spelled** to spell a word wrongly. ▶ **misspelling** *n*

missus *or* **missis** *n* **1** *Brit, Austral & NZ informal* one's wife or the wife of the person addressed or referred to: *the missus is a fabulous cook.* **2** an informal term of address for a woman. ▷ **HISTORY** spoken version of *mistress*

mist *n* **1** a thin fog. **2** a fine spray of liquid, such as that produced by an aerosol container. **3** condensed water vapour on a surface. **4** something that causes haziness or lack of clarity, such as a film of tears. ✧ *vb* **5** to cover or be covered with mist: *the windscreen has misted up again; his eyes misted over and he shook with rage.* ▷ **HISTORY** Old English ▶ **misty** *adj* ▶ **mistiness** *n*

mistake *n* **1** an error or blunder. **2** a misconception or misunderstanding. ✧ *vb* **-taking, -took, -taken 3** to misunderstand or misinterpret: *the chaplain quite mistook her meaning.* **4** to confuse a person or thing with another: *they saw the HMS Sheffield and mistook her for the Bismarck.* **5** to choose badly or incorrectly: *he mistook his path.* ▷ **HISTORY** Old Norse *mistaka* to take erroneously

mistaken *adj* **1** wrong in opinion or judgment. **2** arising from error in opinion or judgment: *a mistaken viewpoint.*

mister *n* an informal form of address for a man. ▷ **HISTORY** variant of *master*

Mister *n* the full form of **Mr**.

mistime *vb* **-timing, -timed** to do or say at the wrong time.

mistle thrush *or* **missel thrush** *n* a large European thrush with a brown back and spotted breast. ▷ **HISTORY** Old English *mistel* mistletoe

mistletoe *n* a Eurasian evergreen shrub with waxy white berries, which grows as a parasite on various trees. ▷ **HISTORY** Old English *misteltān*, from *mistel* mistletoe + *tān* twig

mistral *n* a strong cold dry northerly wind of S France. ▷ **HISTORY** Provençal, from Latin *magistralis* masterful

mistreat *vb* to treat badly. ▶ **mistreatment** *n*

mistress *n* **1** a woman who has a continuing sexual relationship with a man who is usually married to somebody else. **2** a woman in a position of authority, ownership, or control. **3** a woman having control over something specified: *she is a mistress of disguise.* **4** *Chiefly Brit* a female teacher. ▷ **HISTORY** Old French *maistresse*

mistrial *n Law* a trial which is invalid because of some error.

mistrust *vb* **1** to have doubts or suspicions about. ✧ *n* **2** lack of trust. ▶ **mistrustful** *adj* ▶ **mistrustfully** *adv*

misunderstand *vb* **-standing, -stood** to fail to understand properly.

misunderstanding *n* **1** a failure to understand properly. **2** a disagreement.

misuse *n* **1** incorrect, improper, or careless use: *misuse of drugs.* **2** cruel or inhumane treatment. ✧ *vb* **-using, -used 3** to use wrongly. **4** to treat badly or harshly.

mite[1] *n* any of numerous very small creatures of the spider family some of which live as parasites. ▷ **HISTORY** Old English *mīte*

mite[2] *n* **1** a very small creature or thing. **2** a very small sum of money. **3 a mite** *Informal* somewhat: *the main course was a mite bland.* ▷ **HISTORY** Middle Dutch *mīte*

mitigate *vb* **-gating, -gated** to make less severe or harsh. ▷ **HISTORY** Latin *mitis* mild + *agere* to make ▶ **mitigating** *adj*

> **☑ WORD TIP**
> *Mitigate* is sometimes wrongly used where *militate* is meant: *his behaviour militates* (not *mitigates*) *against his chances of promotion.*

mitigation *n* **1** the act of making something less severe or harsh. **2** *Law* **a** (in a criminal case) a plea for sentence reduction in view of certain circumstances. **b** (in a civil case) the obligation for an injured party to try to limit any losses they may suffer.

mitochondrion *n, pl* **-dria** *Biol* a small spherical or rodlike body found in the cytoplasm of most cells. ▷ **HISTORY** Greek *mitos* thread + *khondrion* grain

mitosis *n* a type of cell division in which the nucleus divides into two nuclei each containing the same number of chromosomes as the parent nucleus. ▷ **HISTORY** Greek *mitos* thread

mitre *or US* **miter** (**my**-ter) *n* **1** *Christianity* the headdress of a bishop or abbot, consisting of a tall pointed cleft cap. **2** Also: **mitre joint** a corner joint formed by cutting bevels of equal angles at the ends of each piece of material. ✧ *vb* **-tring, -tred** *or* **-tering, -tered 3** to join with a mitre joint. ▷ **HISTORY** Greek *mitra* turban

mitt *n* **1** a glovelike hand covering that does not cover the fingers. **2** short for **mitten**. **3** *Slang* a hand. **4** a baseball glove. ▷ **HISTORY** from *mitten*

mitten *n* a glove with one section for the thumb and a single section for the fingers. ▷ **HISTORY** Old French *mitaine*

mix *vb* **1** to combine or blend into one mass or substance: *mix the water, yeast, and flour into a smooth dough.* **2** to be able to combine into one substance: *oil and water do not mix.* **3** to form by combining different substances: *to mix cement.* **4** to do at the same time: *to mix business and pleasure.* **5** to be outgoing in social situations: *he mixed well.* **6** *Music* to balance and adjust individual performers' parts to make an overall sound by electronic means. ✧ *n* **7** something produced by mixing; mixture. **8** a mixture of ingredients, esp. one commercially prepared for making a cake. **9** *Music* the sound produced by mixing. ✧ See also **mix-up**. ▷ **HISTORY** Latin *miscere* ▶ **mixed** *adj*

mixed blessing *n* an event or situation with both advantages and disadvantages.

mixed doubles *pl n Tennis, badminton* a doubles game with a man and a woman as partners on each side.

mixed economy *n* an economy in which some companies are privately owned and others are owned by the government.

mixed farming *n* farming involving both the growing of crops and the keeping of livestock. ▶ **mixed farm** *n*

mixed grill *n* a dish of several kinds of grilled meat, tomatoes, and mushrooms.

mixed market *n Econ* an economic system in which there are both privately owned and government-controlled businesses.

mixed metaphor *n* a combination of incongruous metaphors, such as *when the Nazi jackboots sing their swan song.*

mixed number *n Maths* a figure that includes a whole number and a fraction.

mixer *n* **1** a kitchen appliance, usually electrical, used for mixing foods. **2** any of various other devices or machines used for mixing things: *a cement mixer.* **3** a nonalcoholic drink such as tonic water or ginger ale that is mixed with an alcoholic drink. **4** *Informal* a person considered in relation to his or her ability to mix socially: *he's not a good mixer.*

mixture *n* **1** something produced by blending or combining other things: *top with the cheese and breadcrumb mixture.* **2** a combination of different things, such as feelings: *he speaks of her with a mixture of loyalty and regret.* **3** *Chem* a substance consisting of two or more substances mixed together without any chemical bonding between them.

mix-up *n* **1** a confused condition or situation. ✧ *vb* **mix up 2** to make into a mixture. **3** to confuse: *he mixes Ryan up with Lee.* **4 mixed up in** involved in (an activity or group, esp. one that is illegal): *she's mixed up in a drugs racket.*

mizzenmast *n Naut* (on a vessel with three or more masts) the third mast from the bow. ▷ **HISTORY** Italian *mezzano* middle + MAST

MJ megajoule.

Mk (in trade names) mark.

mks units *pl n* a metric system of units based on the metre, kilogram, and second: it forms the basis of the SI units.

ml 1 millilitre(s). **2** mile(s).

MLitt Master of Letters. ▷ **HISTORY** Latin *Magister Litterarum*

Mlle *or* **Mlle.** *pl* **Mlles** *or* **Mlles.** the French equivalent of *Miss.* ▷ **HISTORY** from *Mademoiselle*

MLR minimum lending rate.

mm millimetre(s).

Mme *pl* **Mmes** the French equivalent of *Mrs.* ▷ **HISTORY** from *Madame, Mesdames*

MMR a combined vaccine against measles, mumps, and rubella, given to very young children.

Mn *Chem* manganese.

MN Minnesota.

mnemonic (nim-**on**-ik) *n* **1** something, for instance a verse, intended to help the memory. ✧ *adj* **2** aiding or meant to aid one's memory. ▷ **HISTORY** Greek *mnēmōn* mindful ▶ **mnemonically** *adv*

mo *n Informal, chiefly Brit* short for **moment** (sense 1).

Mo *Chem* molybdenum.

MO 1 Medical Officer. **2** Missouri.

m.o. *or* **MO 1** mail order. **2** money order.

moa *n* a recently extinct large flightless bird of New Zealand that resembled the ostrich. ▷ **HISTORY** Maori

moan *n* **1** a low prolonged cry of pain or suffering. **2** any similar sound, esp. that made by the wind. **3** *Informal* a grumble or complaint. ✧ *vb* **4** to make a low cry of, or talk in a way suggesting, pain or suffering: *he moaned in pain.* **5** to make a sound like a moan: *the wind moaned through the trees.* **6** *Informal* to grumble or complain. ▷ **HISTORY** Old English *mǣnan* to grieve over ▶ **moaner** *n*

moat *n* a wide ditch, originally filled with water, surrounding a fortified place such as a castle. ▷ **HISTORY** Old French *motte* mound

mob *n* **1** a riotous or disorderly crowd of people. **2** *Informal* any group of people. **3** the masses. **4** *Slang* a gang of criminals. ✧ *vb* **mobbing, mobbed 5** to attack in a group resembling a mob. **6** to surround in a crowd to acclaim or attack: *she was mobbed by her fans when she left the theatre.* ▷ **HISTORY** shortened from Latin *mobile vulgus* the fickle populace

mobile *adj* **1** able to move or be moved: *mobile toilets.* **2** changing quickly in expression: *a mobile face.* **3** *Sociol* (of individuals or social groups) moving within and between classes, occupations, and localities. ✧ *n* **4** a light structure suspended in midair with delicately balanced parts that are set in motion by air currents. **5** short for **mobile phone**. ▷ **HISTORY** Latin *mobilis* ▶ **mobility** *n*

mobile home *n* a large caravan, usually staying in one place, which people live in permanently.

mobile phone *n* a portable telephone powered by batteries.

mobilize *or* **-lise** *vb* **-lizing, -lized** *or* **-lising, -lised 1** to prepare for war or another emergency by organizing resources and the armed services. **2** to organize for a purpose: *we must mobilize local residents behind our campaign.* ▶ **mobilization** *or* **-lisation** *n*

A B C D E F G H I J K L M N O P Q R S T U V W X Y Z

moccasin *n* **1** a type of soft leather shoe traditionally worn by some Native American peoples. **2** a soft leather shoe with a raised seam at the front above the toe. ▷ **HISTORY** American Indian

mocha (**mock**-a) *n* **1** a dark brown coffee originally imported from the port of Mocha in Arabia. **2** a flavouring made from coffee and chocolate.

mock *vb* **1** to behave with scorn or contempt towards a person or thing: *her husband mocked her attempts to educate herself.* **2** to imitate or mimic, esp. in fun. **3** to defy or frustrate: *the team mocked the visitors' attempts to score.* ✧ *n* **4 mocks** *Informal* (in England and Wales) school examinations taken as practice before public exams. ✧ *adj* **5** sham or imitation: *mock Georgian windows.* **6** serving as an imitation or substitute, esp. for practice purposes: *a mock battle.* ✧ See also **mock-up**. ▷ **HISTORY** Old French *mocquer* ▶ **mocking** *n, adj*

mockers *pl n* **put the mockers on** *Brit, Austral & NZ informal* to ruin the chances of success of. ▷ **HISTORY** perhaps from *mock*

mockery *n, pl* **-eries 1** ridicule, contempt, or derision. **2** a person, thing, or action that is so worthless that it seems like a parody: *the interview was a mockery from start to finish.* **3 make a mockery of something** to make something appear worthless or foolish: *the judge's decision makes a mockery of the law.*

mock-heroic *adj Literature, Prosody* (of a literary work, esp. a poem) imitating the style of heroic poetry in order to satirize an unheroic subject.

mockingbird *n* an American songbird which can mimic the song of other birds.

mock orange *n* a shrub with white fragrant flowers like those of the orange.

mock-up *n* a working full-scale model of a machine or apparatus for test or research purposes.

mod[1] *n Brit* a member of a group of teenagers, originally in the mid-1960s, who were very clothes-conscious and rode motor scooters. ▷ **HISTORY** from *modernist*

mod[2] *n* an annual Highland Gaelic meeting with musical and literary competitions. ▷ **HISTORY** Gaelic *mōd* assembly

MOD (in Britain) Ministry of Defence.

mod. 1 moderate. **2** modern.

modal (**mode**-al) *adj* **1** of or relating to mode or manner. **2** *Grammar* (of a verb form or auxiliary verb) expressing possibility, intention, or necessity rather than actuality: 'can', 'might', and 'will' are examples of modal verbs in English. **3** *Music* of or relating to a mode.

modal class *n Statistics* the class with the highest frequency.

modality *n, pl* **-ties 1** the condition of being modal. **2** a quality, attribute, or circumstance that denotes mode, mood, or manner.

mod cons *pl n Informal* modern conveniences, such as hot water and heating.

mode *n* **1** a manner or way of doing, acting, or existing. **2** a particular fashion or style. **3** *Music* any of the various scales of notes within one octave. **4** *Maths* the most frequently occurring of a range of values. ▷ **HISTORY** Latin *modus* manner

model *n* **1** a three-dimensional representation, usually on a smaller scale, of a device or structure: *an architect's model of the proposed new housing estate.* **2** an example or pattern that people might want to follow: *her success makes her an excellent role model for other young Black women.* **3** an outstanding example of its kind: *the report is a model of clarity.* **4** a person who poses for a sculptor, painter, or photographer. **5** a person who wears clothes to display them to prospective buyers; mannequin. **6** a design or style of a particular product: *the cheapest model of this car has a 1300cc engine.* **7** a theoretical description of the way a system or process works: *a working model of the human immune system.* **8** *Maths* a simplified description of a system, used to make predictions. ✧ *adj* **9** excellent or perfect: *a model husband.* **10** being a small-scale representation of: *a model aeroplane.* ✧ *vb* **-elling, -elled** *or US* **-eling, -eled 11** to make a model of: *he modelled a plane out of balsa wood.* **12** to plan or create according to a model or models: *it had a constitution modelled on that of the United States.* **13** to display (clothing and accessories) as a mannequin. **14** to pose for a sculptor, painter, or photographer. **15** *Maths* to devise a model of a system. ▷ **HISTORY** Latin *modulus,* diminutive of *modus* mode

modem (**mode**-em) *n Computers* a device for transmitting information between two computers by a telephone line, consisting of a modulator that converts computer signals into audio signals and a corresponding demodulator. ▷ **HISTORY** from *mo(dulator) dem(odulator)*

moderate *adj* **1** not extreme or excessive: *a man of moderate views; moderate consumption of alcohol.* **2** (of a size, rate, intensity, etc.) towards the middle of the range of possible values: *a moderate-sized garden; a moderate breeze.* **3** of average quality or extent: *moderate success.* ✧ *n* **4** a person who holds moderate views, esp. in politics. ✧ *vb* **-ating, -ated 5** to make or become less extreme or violent: *he has moderated his opinions since then.* **6** to preside over a meeting, discussion, etc. ▷ **HISTORY** Latin *moderari* to restrain ▶ **moderately** *adv*

moderation *n* **1** the quality of being moderate. **2** the act of moderating. **3 in moderation** within moderate or reasonable limits.

moderato (mod-er-**ah**-toe) *adv Music* **1** at a moderate speed. **2** with restraint: *allegro moderato.* ▷ **HISTORY** Italian

moderator *n* **1** *Presbyterian Church* a minister appointed to preside over a Church court, synod, or general assembly. **2** a person who presides over at a public or legislative assembly. **3** a material, such as heavy water, used for slowing down neutrons in nuclear reactors.

modern *adj* **1** of the present or a recent time; contemporary: *there have been very few outbreaks of the disease in modern times.* **2** using the latest techniques, equipment, etc.; up-to-date: *modern and efficient railways.* **3** of contemporary styles or schools of art, literature, and music, esp. those of an experimental kind. ✧ *n* **4** a contemporary person. ▷ **HISTORY** Late Latin *modernus,* from *modus* mode ▶ **modernity** *n*

Modern English *n* the English language since about 1450.

modernism *n* a early- and mid-20th-century movement in art, literature and music that rejected traditional styles and techniques. ▶ **modernist** *n, adj*

modernize *or* **-ise** *vb* **-izing, -ized** *or* **-ising, -ised** **1** to make modern in style, methods, or equipment: *a commitment to modernizing industry.* **2** to adopt modern ways or ideas. ▶ **modernization** *or* **-isation** *n*

modern languages *pl n* the languages spoken in present-day Europe, with the exception of English.

modern pentathlon *n* an athletic contest consisting of five different events: horse riding with jumps, fencing with electric épée, freestyle swimming, pistol shooting, and cross-country running.

modest *adj* **1** having a humble opinion of oneself or one's accomplishments. **2** not extreme or excessive: *a modest increase in inflation.* **3** not ostentatious or pretentious: *a modest flat in the suburbs.* **4** shy or easily embarrassed. **5** *Old-fashioned* (esp. of clothes) not revealing much of the body: *a modest dress.* ▷ **HISTORY** Latin *modestus* moderate ▶ **modestly** *adv* ▶ **modesty** *n*

modicum *n* a small amount. ▷ **HISTORY** Latin: a little way

modifier *n Grammar* a word or phrase that makes the sense of another word more specific: for example, the noun *garage* is a modifier of *door* in *garage door.*

modify *vb* **-fies, -fying, -fied** **1** to change or alter slightly. **2** to make less extreme or uncompromising. **3** *Grammar* (of a word or phrase) to act as a modifier to another word or phrase. ▷ **HISTORY** Latin *modus* measure + *facere* to make ▶ **modification** *n*

modish (**mode**-ish) *adj* in the current fashion or style. ▶ **modishly** *adv*

modulate *vb* **-lating, -lated** **1** to change the tone, pitch, or volume of (one's voice). **2** to adjust or regulate the degree of: *the hormone which modulates the development of the sexual organs.* **3** *Music* to change from one key to another. **4** *Physics, electronics* to superimpose the amplitude, frequency, or phase of a wave or signal onto another wave or signal. ▷ **HISTORY** Latin *modulari* to modulate ▶ **modulation** *n* ▶ **modulator** *n*

module *n* **1** a standard self-contained unit, such as an assembly of electronic components or a standardized piece of furniture, that can be used in combination with other units. **2** *Astronautics* a self-contained separable unit making up a spacecraft. **3** *Education* a short course of study that together with other such courses counts towards a qualification. ▷ **HISTORY** Latin *modulus,* diminutive of *modus* mode ▶ **modular** *adj*

modulus *n, pl* **-li** *Physics* a coefficient expressing a specified property, for instance elasticity, of a specified substance. ▷ **HISTORY** Latin

modus operandi (**mode**-uss op-er-**an**-die) *n, pl* **modi operandi** (**mode**-eye) method of operating. ▷ **HISTORY** Latin

modus vivendi (**mode**-uss viv-**venn**-die) *n, pl* **modi vivendi** (**mode**-eye) a working arrangement between conflicting interests. ▷ **HISTORY** Latin: way of living

moggy *or* **mog** *n, pl* **moggies** *or* **mogs** *Brit, Austral & NZ slang* a cat. ▷ **HISTORY** dialect *mog,* originally a pet name for a cow

mogul (**moh**-gl) *n* an important or powerful person.

Mogul *adj* of or relating to a Muslim dynasty of Indian emperors established in 1526. ▷ **HISTORY** Persian *mughul* Mongolian

MOH (in Britain) Medical Officer of Health.

mohair *n* **1** the long soft silky hair of the Angora goat. **2** a fabric made from yarn of this hair and cotton or wool. ▷ **HISTORY** Arabic *mukhayyar,* literally: choice

Mohawk *n* **1** a member of a N American Indian people formerly living along the Mohawk river. **2** the language of this people.

mohican *n* a punk hairstyle in which the head is shaved at the sides and the remaining strip of hair is worn stiffly erect and often brightly coloured. ▷ **HISTORY** after the *Mohicans,* a Native American people

Mohican *n* **1** (*pl* **-cans** *or* **-can**) a member of a N American Indian people formerly living along the Hudson river. **2** the language of this people.

Mohorovičić discontinuity *n Geol* the boundary between the earth's crust and mantle, across which there is a sudden change in the velocity of seismic waves. ▷ **HISTORY** named after Andrija *Mohorovičić* (1857–1936), Croatian geologist

moiety (**moy**-it-ee) *n, pl* **-ties** *Archaic* **1** a half. **2** one of two parts or divisions of something. ▷ **HISTORY** Old French *moitié*

moiré (**mwahr**-ray) *adj* **1** having a watered or wavelike pattern. ✧ *n* **2** such a pattern, impressed on fabrics. **3** a fabric, usually silk, with such a pattern. **4** Also: **moiré pattern** a pattern seen when two geometrical patterns, such as grids, are visually superimposed. ▷ **HISTORY** French

moist *adj* slightly damp or wet. ▷ **HISTORY** Old French

moisten *vb* to make or become moist.

moisture *n* water diffused as vapour or condensed on or in objects.

moisturize *or* **-ise** *vb* **-izing, -ized** *or* **-ising, -ised** to add moisture to the air or the skin. ▶ **moisturizer** *or* **-iser** *n*

moke *n* **1** *Brit slang* a donkey. **2** *Austral & NZ* a horse of inferior quality. ▷ **HISTORY** origin unknown

mol *Chem* mole.

mol. **1** molecular. **2** molecule.

A B C D E F G H I J K L M N O P Q R S T U V W X Y Z

molar *n* **1** a large back tooth specialized for crushing and chewing food. ✧ *adj* **2** of any of these teeth. ▷ **HISTORY** Latin *mola* millstone

molasses *n* **1** the thick brown bitter syrup obtained from sugar during refining. **2** *US & Canad* same as **treacle**. ▷ **HISTORY** Portuguese *melaço*

mole[1] *n* a small dark raised spot on the skin.

mole[2] *n* **1** a small burrowing mammal with velvety dark fur and forelimbs specialized for digging. **2** *Informal* a spy who has infiltrated an organization and become a trusted member of it. ▷ **HISTORY** Middle Dutch *mol*

mole[3] *n Chem* the basic SI unit of amount of substance: the amount that contains as many elementary entities as there are atoms in 0.012 kilogram of carbon-12. ▷ **HISTORY** German *Mol,* short for *Molekül* molecule

mole[4] *n* **1** a breakwater. **2** a harbour protected by a breakwater. ▷ **HISTORY** Latin *moles* mass

molecular (mol-**lek**-yew-lar) *adj* of or relating to molecules.

molecular compound *n Chem* a compound in which the atoms are linked by covalent bonds to form molecules.

molecular formula *n Chem* a chemical formula indicating the number and type of atoms in a molecule, but not its structure: *NH_3 is the molecular formula of ammonia.*

molecular weight *n Chem* the sum of all the atomic weights of the atoms in a molecule.

molecule (**mol**-lik-kyool) *n* **1** the simplest unit of a chemical compound that can exist, consisting of two or more atoms held together by chemical bonds. **2** a very small particle. ▷ **HISTORY** New Latin *molecula,* diminutive of Latin *moles* mass

molehill *n* **1** the small mound of earth thrown up by a burrowing mole. **2 make a mountain out of a molehill** to exaggerate an unimportant matter out of all proportion.

molest *vb* **1** to accost or attack someone, esp. a woman or child with the intention of assaulting her or him sexually. **2** to disturb or injure, esp. by using or threatening violence: *killing, capturing, or molesting the local wildlife was strictly forbidden.* ▷ **HISTORY** Latin *molestare* to annoy ▶ **molestation** *n* ▶ **molester** *n*

moll *n Slang* a gangster's female accomplice or girlfriend. ▷ **HISTORY** from *Moll,* familiar form of *Mary*

mollify *vb* **-fies, -fying, -fied** to make someone less angry or upset; soothe: *he sought to mollify his critics.* ▷ **HISTORY** Latin *mollis* soft + *facere* to make ▶ **mollification** *n*

mollusc *or US* **mollusk** *n* an invertebrate with a soft unsegmented body and often a shell, such as a snail, mussel, or octopus. ▷ **HISTORY** Latin *molluscus*

mollycoddle *vb* **-coddling, -coddled** to give an excessive amount of care and protection to. ▷ **HISTORY** from *Molly,* girl's name + *coddle*

Molotov cocktail *n* a simple bomb made from a bottle filled with petrol and a cloth wick; petrol bomb. ▷ **HISTORY** after V. M. *Molotov,* Soviet statesman

molt *vb, n US* same as **moult**.

molten *adj* so hot that it has melted and formed a liquid: *molten metal.*

molto *adv Music* very: *allegro molto; molto adagio.* ▷ **HISTORY** Italian

molybdenum (mol-**lib**-din-um) *n Chem* a very hard silvery-white metallic element used in alloys, esp. to harden and strengthen steels. Symbol: Mo. ▷ **HISTORY** Greek *molubdos* lead

mom *n Informal, chiefly US, Canad & S African* same as **mother**.

moment *n* **1** a short period of time. **2** a specific instant or point in time: *at that moment the phone rang.* **3 the moment** the present point of time: *for the moment he is out of prison.* **4** importance, significance, or value: *a matter of greatest moment.* **5** *Physics* **a** a tendency to produce motion, esp. rotation about a point or axis. **b** the product of a physical quantity, such as force or mass, and its distance from a fixed reference point. ▷ **HISTORY** Latin *momentum* movement

momentary *adj* lasting for only a moment; temporary. ▶ **momentarily** *adv*

momentous (moh-**men**-tuss) *adj* of great significance. ▶ **momentousness** *n*

momentum (moh-**men**-tum) *n* **1** the impetus to go forward, develop, or get stronger: *the campaign steadily gathered support and momentum.* **2** the impetus of a moving body: *the sledge gathered momentum as it slid ever faster down the slope.* **3** *Physics* the product of a body's mass and its velocity. ▷ **HISTORY** Latin: movement

Mon. Monday.

mon- *combining form* See **mono-**.

monad *n* **1** *Philosophy* any fundamental singular metaphysical entity. **2** a single-celled organism. **3** an atom, ion, or radical with a valency of one. ▷ **HISTORY** Greek *monas* unit

monandrous *adj* **1** *Biol* having only one stamen in each flower. **2** having only one male sexual partner over a period of time. ▷ **HISTORY** Greek *monos* sole + *anēr* man

monarch *n* a sovereign head of state, esp. a king, queen, or emperor, who rules by hereditary right. ▷ **HISTORY** Greek *monos* sole + *arkhos* ruler ▶ **monarchical** *or* **monarchic** *adj*

monarchy *n, pl* **-chies 1** a form of government in which supreme authority is held by a single hereditary ruler, such as a king. **2** a country reigned over by a monarch.

monastery *n, pl* **-teries** the building or group of buildings where a community of monks lives. ▷ **HISTORY** Greek *monazein* to live alone

monastic *adj* **1** of or relating to monasteries, monks, or nuns. **2** (of a way of life) simple and austere; ascetic. ▶ **monasticism** *n*

monatomic *adj Chem* **1** (of an element) consisting of single atoms. **2** (of a compound or molecule) having only one atom or group that can be replaced in a reaction.

Monday *n* the second day of the week, and the first day of the working week. ▷ **HISTORY** Old English *mōnandæg* moon's day

monetarism *n* **1** the theory that inflation is caused by an excess quantity of money in an economy. **2** an economic policy based on this theory and a belief in the efficiency of free market forces. ▶ **monetarist** *n, adj*

monetary *adj* of money or currency. ▷ **HISTORY** Latin *moneta* money

money *n* **1** a means of payment and measure of value: *some cultures used to use shells as money.* **2** the official currency, in the form of banknotes or coins, issued by a government. **3 moneys** *or* **monies** *Law old-fashioned* a financial sum or income. **4** an unspecified amount of wealth: *money to lend.* **5** *Informal* a rich person or rich people: *he married money.* **6 for one's money** in one's opinion. **7 one's money's worth** full value for the money one has paid for something. **8 put money on** to place a bet on. *RELATED ADJECTIVE* ✦ **pecuniary** ▷ **HISTORY** Latin *moneta*

moneybags *n Informal* a very rich person.

moneychanger *n* a person engaged in the business of exchanging currencies or money.

moneyed *or* **monied** *adj* having a great deal of money; rich.

moneylender *n* a person who lends money at interest as a living.

moneymaker *n* **1** a person whose chief concern is to make money. **2** a person or thing that is or might be profitable. ▶ **moneymaking** *adj, n*

-monger *n combining form* **1** indicating a trader or dealer: *an ironmonger.* **2** indicating a promoter of something: *a warmonger.* ▷ **HISTORY** Old English *mangere*

mongol *n Offensive* (not in technical use) a person affected by Down's syndrome. ▶ **mongoloid** *n, adj*

Mongolian *adj* **1** of Mongolia. ✧ *n* **2** a person from Mongolia. **3** the language of Mongolia.

mongolism *n Offensive* a former name (not in technical use) for **Down's syndrome**. ▷ **HISTORY** the condition produces facial features similar to those of the Mongoloid peoples

Mongoloid *adj* of a major racial group of mankind, characterized by yellowish skin, straight black hair, and slanting eyes: includes most of the people of SE Asia, E Asia, and the Arctic area of N America.

mongoose *n, pl* **-gooses** a small long-tailed predatory mammal of Asia and Africa that kills snakes. ▷ **HISTORY** from Marathi (a language of India) *mangūs*

mongrel *n* **1** a dog of mixed breeding. **2** something made up of things from a variety of sources: *despite using components from three other cars, this new model is no mongrel.* ✧ *adj* **3** of mixed breeding or origin: *a mongrel race.* ▷ **HISTORY** from obsolete *mong* mixture

monied *adj* same as **moneyed**.

monies *n Law old-fashioned* a plural of **money**.

moniker *n Slang* a person's name or nickname. ▷ **HISTORY** from Shelta *munnik*, altered from Irish Gaelic *ainm* name

monism *n Philosophy* the doctrine that reality consists of only one basic substance or element, such as mind or matter. ▷ **HISTORY** Greek *monos* sole ▶ **monist** *n, adj*

monition *n* a warning or caution. ▷ **HISTORY** Latin *monere* to warn

monitor *n* **1** a person or device that warns, checks, controls, or keeps a continuous record of something. **2** *Brit, Austral & NZ* a pupil assisting a teacher with various duties. **3** a screen used to display certain kinds of information, for example in airports or television studios. **4** a large predatory lizard inhabiting warm regions of Africa, Asia, and Australia. ✧ *vb* **5** to act as a monitor of. **6** to observe or record the condition or performance of a person or thing. **7** to check (a broadcast) for acceptable quality or content. ▷ **HISTORY** Latin *monere* to advise ▶ **monitorial** *adj*

monk *n* a male member of a religious community bound by vows of poverty, chastity, and obedience. *RELATED ADJECTIVE* ✦ **monastic** ▷ **HISTORY** Greek *monos* alone ▶ **monkish** *adj*

monkey *n* **1** any long-tailed primate that is not a lemur or tarsier. **2** (loosely) any primate that is not a human. **3** a naughty or mischievous child. **4** *Slang* £500 or $500. **5 give a monkey's** *Brit slang* to care about or regard as important: *who gives a monkey's what he thinks?* ✧ *vb* **6 monkey around** *or* **about with** to meddle or tinker with. ▷ **HISTORY** origin unknown

monkey nut *n Brit* a peanut.

monkey puzzle *n* a South American coniferous tree with branches shaped like a candelabrum and stiff sharp leaves.

monkey wrench *n Chiefly Brit* a wrench with adjustable jaws.

monkshood *n* a poisonous plant with hooded blue-purple flowers.

mono *adj* **1** short for **monophonic**. ✧ *n* **2** monophonic sound.

mono- *or before a vowel* **mon-** *combining form* **1** one; single: *monorail; monolingual.* **2** *Chem* indicating that a chemical compound contains a single specified atom or group: *monoxide.* ▷ **HISTORY** Greek *monos* alone

monobasic *adj Chem* (of an acid, such as hydrogen chloride) having only one replaceable hydrogen atom per molecule.

monochromatic *adj* (of light or other electromagnetic radiation) having only one wavelength.

monochrome *adj* **1** *Photog, television* black-and-white. ✧ *n* **2** a painting or drawing done in a range of tones of a single colour. ▷ **HISTORY** Greek *monokhrōmos* of one colour

monocle (**mon**-a-kl) *n* (formerly) a lens worn for correcting defective sight in one eye only, held in position by the facial muscles. ▷ **HISTORY** MONO- + Latin *oculus* eye ▶ **monocled** *adj*

monoclinal *adj Geol* (of folds) inclining in one direction.

monocline *n Geol* a fold in stratified rocks in which the strata are inclined in one direction from the horizontal. ▷ **HISTORY** MONO- + Greek *klinein* to lean

A B C D E F G H I J K L M N O P Q R S T U V W X Y Z

monoclinic *adj Crystallog* of the crystal system characterized by three unequal axes, one pair of which are not at right angles to each other.

monoclonal antibody *n* an antibody produced from a single clone of cells grown in a culture.

monocoque (**mon**-a-cock) *n* a vehicle body moulded from a single piece of material with no separate load-bearing parts. ▷ **HISTORY** French

monocotyledon (mon-no-kot-ill-**leed**-on) *n* any flowering plant with a single embryonic seed leaf, such as the grasses, lilies, palms, and orchids.

monocular *adj* having or intended for the use of only one eye. ▷ **HISTORY** Late Latin *monoculus* one-eyed

monoculture *n* the continuous growing of one type of crop.

monody *n, pl* **-dies 1** (in Greek tragedy) an ode sung by a single actor. **2** *Music* a style of composition consisting of a single vocal part, usually with accompaniment. ▷ **HISTORY** MONO- + Greek *aeidein* to sing ▸ **monodist** *n*

monoecious (mon-**ee**-shuss) *adj* **1** (of some flowering plants) having the male and female reproductive organs in separate flowers on the same plant. **2** (of some animals and lower plants) hermaphrodite. ▷ **HISTORY** MONO- + Greek *oikos* house

monogamy *n* the state or practice of having only one husband or wife at a time. ▷ **HISTORY** MONO- + Greek *gamos* marriage ▸ **monogamous** *adj*

monogram *n* a design of one or more letters, esp. initials, on clothing, stationery, etc. ▷ **HISTORY** Greek *monogrammatos* consisting of one letter

monograph *n* a paper, book, or other work concerned with a single subject or aspect of a subject.

monolingual *adj* knowing or expressed in only one language.

monolith *n* **1** a large block of stone. **2** a statue, obelisk, or column cut from one block of stone. **3** something which can be regarded as forming one large, single, whole: *the Christian religion should not be thought of as a monolith.* ▷ **HISTORY** Greek *monolithos* made from a single stone ▸ **monolithic** *adj*

monologue *n* **1** a long speech made by one actor in a play or film; soliloquy. **2** a dramatic piece for a single performer. **3** any long speech by one person, esp. one which prevents other people talking or expressing their views. ▷ **HISTORY** Greek *monologos* speaking alone

> ☑ **WORD TIP**
> See at **soliloquy.**

monomania *n* an obsession with one thing or idea. ▸ **monomaniac** *n, adj*

monomer *n Chem* a compound whose molecules can join together to form a polymer.

monometer *n Poetry* a line of poetry consisting of one metrical foot. ▸ **monometrical** *adj*

monomial *n Maths* an expression consisting of a single term, such as *5ax*. ▷ **HISTORY** MONO- + (BIN)OMIAL

mononucleosis (mon-oh-new-klee-**oh**-siss) *n* **infectious mononucleosis** same as **glandular fever**.

monophonic *adj* (of a system of broadcasting, recording, or reproducing sound) using only one channel between source and loudspeaker. Short form: **mono**

monoplane *n* an aeroplane with only one pair of wings.

monopolize *or* **-lise** *vb* **-lizing, -lized** *or* **-lising, -lised 1** to have full control or use of, to the exclusion of others. **2** to hold exclusive control of a market or supply.

monopoly *n, pl* **-lies 1** exclusive control of the market supply of a product or service. **2 a** an enterprise exercising this control. **b** the product or service so controlled. **3** *Law* the exclusive right granted to a person or company by the state to trade in a specified commodity or area. **4** exclusive control, possession, or use of something. ▷ **HISTORY** MONO- + Greek *pōlein* to sell ▸ **monopolist** *n* ▸ **monopolistic** *adj*

monorail *n* a single-rail railway.

monosaccharide *n* a simple sugar, such as glucose, that cannot be broken down into other sugars.

monosodium glutamate *n* a substance which enhances protein flavours: used as a food additive.

monosyllable *n* a word of one syllable. ▸ **monosyllabic** *adj*

monotheism *n* the belief or doctrine that there is only one God. ▸ **monotheist** *n, adj* ▸ **monotheistic** *adj*

monotone *n* **1** a single unvaried pitch level in speech or sound. **2** a way of speaking which lacks variety of pitch or expression: *he rambled on in a dull monotone.* **3** lack of variety in style or expression. ✧ *adj* **4** unvarying.

monotonous *adj* tedious because of lack of variety. ▸ **monotonously** *adv*

monotony *n, pl* **-nies 1** wearisome routine; dullness. **2** lack of variety in pitch or tone.

monounsaturated *adj* of a group of vegetable oils, such as olive oil, that have a neutral effect on cholesterol in the body.

monovalent *adj Chem* **1** having a valency of one. **2** having only one valency. ▸ **monovalence** *or* **monovalency** *n*

monoxide *n* an oxide that contains one oxygen atom per molecule.

Monseigneur (mon-sen-**nyur**) *n, pl* **Messeigneurs** (may-sen-**nyur**) a title given to French prelates and princes. ▷ **HISTORY** French, literally: my lord

monsieur (muss-**syuh**) *n, pl* **messieurs** (may-**syuh**) a French form of address equivalent to *sir* or *Mr.* ▷ **HISTORY** French, literally: my lord

Monsignor *n, pl* **Monsignors** *or* **Monsignori** *RC Church* a title given to certain senior clergymen. ▷ **HISTORY** Italian

monsoon *n* **1** a seasonal wind of S Asia which blows from the southwest in summer and from the northeast in winter. **2** the rainy season when the SW monsoon blows, from about April to October. ▷ **HISTORY** Arabic *mawsim* season

monsoon bucket *n NZ* a large container for water carried by helicopter and used to extinguish bush and scrub fires.

mons pubis (monz **pew**-biss) *n, pl* **montes pubis** (**mon**-teez) the fatty flesh in human males over the junction of the pubic bones. ▷ **HISTORY** New Latin: hill of the pubes

monster *n* **1** an imaginary beast, usually frightening in appearance. **2** a very large person, animal, or thing. **3** an exceptionally cruel or wicked person. **4** a person, animal, or plant with a marked deformity. ▷ **HISTORY** Latin *monstrum* portent

monstrance *n RC Church* a vessel in which the consecrated Host is exposed for adoration. ▷ **HISTORY** Latin *monstrare* to show

monstrosity *n, pl* **-ties 1** an outrageous or ugly person or thing. **2** the state or quality of being monstrous.

monstrous *adj* **1** hideous or unnatural in size or character. **2** atrocious, unjust, or shocking: *the President described the invasion as monstrous.* **3** huge. **4** of or like a monster. **5** (of plants and animals) abnormal in structure. ▶ **monstrously** *adv*

mons veneris (monz **ven**-er-iss) *n, pl* **montes veneris** (**mon**-teez) the fatty flesh in human females over the junction of the pubic bones. ▷ **HISTORY** New Latin: hill of Venus

montage (**mon**-tahzh) *n* **1** a picture made by combining material from various sources, such as other pictures or photographs. **2** the technique of producing pictures in this way. **3** a method of film editing by juxtaposition or partial superimposition of several shots to form a single image. **4** a film sequence of this kind. ▷ **HISTORY** French

month *n* **1** one of the twelve divisions (**calendar months**) of the calendar year. **2** a period of time extending from one date to a corresponding date in the next calendar month. **3** a period of four weeks or of 30 days. ▷ **HISTORY** Old English *mōnath*

monthly *adj* **1** happening or payable once every month: *a monthly magazine.* **2** lasting or valid for a month: *a monthly travel pass.* ✧ *adv* **3** once a month. ✧ *n, pl* **-lies 4** a magazine published once a month.

monument *n* **1** something, such as a statue or building, erected in commemoration of a person or event. **2** an ancient building which is regarded as an important part of a country's history. **3** an exceptional example of the results of something: *the whole town is a monument to bad 60s architecture.* ▷ **HISTORY** Latin *monumentum*

monumental *adj* **1** large, impressive, or likely to last or be remembered for a long time: *a monumental three-volume biography.* **2** of or being a monument. **3** *Informal* extreme: *a monumental gamble.*

moo *n* **1** the characteristic deep long sound made by a cow. ✧ *vb* **2** to make this sound; low.

mooch *vb Slang* **1** to loiter or walk aimlessly. **2** to cadge or scrounge. ▷ **HISTORY** perhaps Old French *muchier* to skulk

mood[1] *n* **1** a temporary state of mind or temper: *a happy mood.* **2** a sullen or gloomy state of mind, esp. when temporary: *she's in a mood.* **3** a prevailing atmosphere or feeling: *the current mood of disenchantment with politics.* **4 in the mood** inclined to do or have (something). ▷ **HISTORY** Old English *mōd* mind, feeling

mood[2] *n Grammar* a form of a verb indicating whether the verb expresses a fact (indicative mood), a wish or supposition (subjunctive mood), or a command (imperative mood). ▷ **HISTORY** same as MOOD[1]

moody *adj* **moodier, moodiest 1** sullen, sulky, or gloomy. **2** temperamental or changeable. ▶ **moodily** *adv* ▶ **moodiness** *n*

Moog *n Music trademark* a type of synthesizer. ▷ **HISTORY** after Robert *Moog,* engineer

mooi *adj S African slang* pleasing or nice. ▷ **HISTORY** Afrikaans

moon *n* **1** the natural satellite of the earth. RELATED ADJECTIVE ➡ **lunar 2** this satellite as it is seen during its revolution around the earth, esp. at one of its phases: *new moon; full moon.* **3** any natural satellite of a planet. **4** a month. **5 over the moon** *Informal* extremely happy; ecstatic. ✧ *vb* **6 moon about** *or* **around** to be idle in a listless or dreamy way. ▷ **HISTORY** Old English *mōna* ▶ **moonless** *adj*

moonbeam *n* a ray of moonlight.

moonlight *n* **1** light from the sun received on earth after reflection by the moon. ✧ *adj* **2** illuminated by the moon: *a moonlight walk.* ✧ *vb* **-lighting, -lighted 3** *Informal* to work at a secondary job, esp. illegally. ▶ **moonlighter** *n*

moonlight flit *n Brit & Austral informal* a hurried departure at night to avoid paying rent.

moonlit *adj* illuminated by the moon.

moonscape *n* the surface of the moon or a picture or model of it.

moonshine *n* **1** *US & Canad* illegally distilled or smuggled whisky. **2** foolish or nonsensical talk or thought.

moonshot *n* the launching of a spacecraft to the moon.

moonstone *n* a white translucent form of feldspar, used as a gem.

moonstruck *adj* slightly mad or odd, as if affected by the moon.

moony *adj* **moonier, mooniest** *Brit, Austral & NZ informal* dreamy or listless.

moor[1] *n Brit* an expanse of open uncultivated ground covered with heather, coarse grass, and bracken. ▷ **HISTORY** Old English *mōr*

moor[2] *vb* to secure (a ship or boat) with cables, ropes, or anchors so that it remains in one place. ▷ **HISTORY** Germanic ▶ **moorage** *n*

Moor *n* a member of a Muslim people of North Africa who ruled Spain between the 8th and 15th centuries. ▷ HISTORY Greek *Mauros*

moorhen *n* a waterfowl with black plumage and a red bill.

mooring *n* a place where a ship or boat can be tied up or anchored.

moorings *pl n Naut* the ropes and anchors used in mooring a vessel.

Moorish *adj* **1** of or relating to the Moors. **2** of a style of architecture used in Spain from the 13th to the 16th century, characterized by the horseshoe arch.

moorland *n Brit* an area of moor.

moose *n, pl* **moose** a large North American deer with large flattened antlers; the American elk. ▷ HISTORY from a Native American language

moot *adj* **1** subject or open to debate: *a moot point.* ✧ *vb* **2** to suggest or bring up for debate: *a compromise proposal, involving building fewer flats, was mooted.* ✧ *n* **3** (in Anglo-Saxon England) a local administrative assembly. ▷ HISTORY Old English *gemōt*

mop *n* **1** a tool with a head made of twists of cotton or sponge and a long handle used for washing or polishing floors. **2** a similar tool, except smaller and without a long handle, used to wash dishes. **3** a thick untidy mass of hair. ✧ *vb* **mopping, mopped 4** to clean or soak up with or as if with a mop: *she mopped her brow with a handkerchief.* ✧ See also **mop up**. ▷ HISTORY Latin *mappa* napkin

mope *vb* **moping, moped 1** to be gloomy or apathetic. **2** to walk around in a gloomy and aimless manner. ▷ HISTORY perhaps from obsolete *mope* fool

moped *n* a light motorcycle not over 50cc. ▷ HISTORY *motor* + *pedal*

mopoke *n* **1** a small spotted owl of Australia and New Zealand. **2** *Austral slang* a slow or lugubrious person. ▷ HISTORY imitative of the bird's cry

mop up *vb* **1** to clean with a mop. **2** *Informal* to complete the last remaining stages of a job. **3** *Mil* to clear remaining enemy forces after a battle, by killing them or taking them prisoner.

moraine *n* a ridge or mound formed from debris deposited by a glacier. ▷ HISTORY French

moral *adj* **1** concerned with or relating to the distinction between good and bad or right and wrong behaviour: *moral sense.* **2** based on a sense of right and wrong: *moral duty.* **3** (of support or a victory) psychological rather than practical. ✧ *n* **4** a lesson about right or wrong behaviour that is shown in a fable or event. **5 morals** principles of behaviour in accordance with standards of right and wrong. ▷ HISTORY Latin *moralis* relating to morals or customs ▶ **morally** *adv*

morale (mor-**rahl**) *n* the degree of confidence or optimism of a person or group. ▷ HISTORY French

moralist *n* **1** a person who has a strong sense of right and wrong. **2** someone who criticizes other people for not doing what he or she thinks is morally correct. ▶ **moralistic** *adj*

morality *n, pl* **-ties 1** good moral conduct. **2** the degree to which something is morally acceptable: *we discussed the morality of fox-hunting.* **3** a system of moral principles.

morality play *n* a medieval type of drama concerned with the conflict between personified virtues and vices.

moralize *or* **-ise** *vb* **-izing, -ized** *or* **-ising, -ised 1** to discuss or consider something in the light of one's own moral beliefs, esp. with disapproval. **2** to interpret or explain in a moral sense. **3** to improve the morals of.

moral philosophy *n* the branch of philosophy dealing with ethics.

morass *n* **1** a tract of swampy low-lying land. **2** a disordered, confusing, or muddled state of affairs. ▷ HISTORY Old French *marais* marsh

moratorium *n, pl* **-ria** *or* **-riums 1** a legally authorized postponement of the payment of a debt. **2** an agreed suspension of activity. ▷ HISTORY Latin *mora* delay

moray *n* a large marine eel marked with brilliant colours. ▷ HISTORY Greek *muraina*

morbid *adj* **1** having an unusual interest in death or unpleasant events. **2** *Med* relating to or characterized by disease. ▷ HISTORY Latin *morbus* illness ▶ **morbidity** *n* ▶ **morbidly** *adv*

mordant *adj* **1** sarcastic or caustic: *mordant wit.* ✧ *n* **2** a substance used in dyeing to fix colours. **3** an acid or other corrosive fluid used to etch lines on a printing plate. ▷ HISTORY Latin *mordere* to bite

more *adj* **1** the comparative of **much, many:** *more joy than you know; even more are leaving the country.* **2** additional or further: *no more apples.* **3 more of** to a greater extent or degree: *more of a nuisance.* ✧ *adv* **4** used to form the comparative of some adjectives and adverbs: *more quickly.* **5** the comparative of **much:** *people listen to the radio more now.* **6 more or less a** as an estimate; approximately. **b** to an unspecified extent or degree: *the film was a disaster, more or less.* ▷ HISTORY Old English *māra*

> ☑ **WORD TIP**
> See at **most.**

morel *n* an edible mushroom with a pitted cap. ▷ HISTORY French *morille*

morello *n, pl* **-los** a variety of small very dark sour cherry. ▷ HISTORY Italian: blackish

moreover *adv* in addition to what has already been said.

morepork *n Chiefly NZ* same as **mopoke**.

mores (**more**-rayz) *pl n* the customs and conventions embodying the fundamental values of a community. ▷ HISTORY Latin: customs

Moreton Bay bug *n* an Australian flattish edible shellfish.

morganatic *adj* of or designating a marriage between a person of high rank and a person of low rank, by which the latter is not elevated to the higher rank and any children have no rights to inherit the higher party's titles or property. ▷ HISTORY Medieval Latin *morganaticum* morning-gift after consummation representing the husband's only liability

morgue *n* **1** a mortuary. **2** *Informal* a store of clippings and back numbers used for reference in a newspaper. ▷ **HISTORY** French

moribund *adj* **1** near death. **2** no longer performing effectively or usefully: *Romania's moribund economy.* ▷ **HISTORY** Latin *mori* to die

Mormon *n* **1** a member of the Church of Jesus Christ of Latter-day Saints, founded in 1830 in New York by Joseph Smith. ✧ *adj* **2** of the Mormons, their Church, or their beliefs. ▶ **Mormonism** *n*

morn *n Poetic* morning. ▷ **HISTORY** Old English *morgen*

mornay *adj* served with a cheese sauce: *haddock mornay.* ▷ **HISTORY** after Philippe de *Mornay,* Huguenot leader

morning *n* **1** the first part of the day, ending at noon. **2** daybreak; dawn. **3 the morning after** *Informal* the after effects of excess, esp. a hangover. ✧ *adj* **4** of or in the morning: *morning coffee.* ▷ **HISTORY** from *morn,* on the model of *evening*

morning dress *n* formal daytime dress for men, consisting of a frock coat with the front cut away (**morning coat**), usually with grey trousers and top hat.

morning-glory *n, pl* **-ries** a tropical climbing plant with trumpet-shaped blue, pink, or white flowers, which close in late afternoon.

morning sickness *n* nausea occurring shortly after rising in early pregnancy.

morning star *n* a planet, usually Venus, seen just before sunrise.

Moroccan *adj* **1** of Morocco. ✧ *n* **2** a person from Morocco.

morocco *n* a fine soft leather made from goatskins. ▷ **HISTORY** after *Morocco,* where it was originally made

moron *n* **1** *Informal, derogatory* a foolish or stupid person. **2** (formerly) a person having an intelligence quotient of between 50 and 70. ▷ **HISTORY** Greek *mōros* foolish ▶ **moronic** *adj*

morose (mor-**rohss**) *adj* ill-tempered, sullen, and unwilling to talk very much. ▷ **HISTORY** Latin *morosus* peevish ▶ **morosely** *adv*

morpheme *n Linguistics* a speech element having a meaning or grammatical function that cannot be subdivided into further such elements.

morphine *or* **morphia** *n* a drug extracted from opium: used in medicine as an anaesthetic and sedative. ▷ **HISTORY** *Morpheus,* in Greek mythology, the god of sleep and dreams

morphing *n* a computer technique used for graphics and in films, in which one image is gradually transformed into another image without individual changes being noticeable in the process. ▷ **HISTORY** from METAMORPHOSIS

morphology *n* the science of forms and structures of organisms or words. ▶ **morphological** *adj*

morris dance *n* an old English folk dance performed by men (**morris men**) who wear a traditional costume decorated with bells. ▷ **HISTORY** Middle English *moreys daunce* Moorish dance

morrow *n* **the morrow** *Old-fashioned or poetic* **1** the next day. **2** the morning. ▷ **HISTORY** Old English *morgen* morning

Morse code *n* a code formerly used internationally for transmitting messages, in which letters and numbers are represented by groups of dots and dashes, or by shorter and longer sounds. ▷ **HISTORY** after Samuel *Morse,* inventor

morsel *n* a small piece of something, esp. of food. ▷ **HISTORY** Old French *mors* a bite

mortal *adj* **1** (of living beings, esp. humans) destined to die sometime rather than living forever. **2** causing death; fatal: *a mortal wound.* **3** deadly or unrelenting: *he is my mortal enemy.* **4** of or resulting from the fear of death: *mortal terror.* **5** of or involving life or the world: *the hangman's noose ended his mortal existence.* **6** great or very intense: *mortal pain.* **7** *Informal* conceivable or possible: *there was no mortal reason to leave.* **8** *Slang* long and tedious: *for three mortal hours.* ✧ *n* **9** a human being. ▷ **HISTORY** Latin *mors* death ▶ **mortally** *adv*

mortality *n, pl* **-ties 1** the condition of being mortal. **2** great loss of life, as in war or disaster. **3** the number of deaths in a given period.

mortal sin *n Christianity* a sin that will lead to damnation unless repented of.

mortar *n* **1** a small cannon that fires shells in high arcs. **2** a mixture of cement or lime or both with sand and water, used to hold bricks or stones together. **3** a vessel, usually bowl-shaped, in which substances are crushed with a pestle. ✧ *vb* **4** to fire on with mortars. **5** to join bricks or stones with mortar. ▷ **HISTORY** Latin *mortarium* basin in which mortar is mixed

mortarboard *n* **1** a black tasselled academic cap with a flat square top. **2** a small square board with a handle on the underside for carrying mortar.

mortgage *n* **1** an agreement under which a person borrows money to buy property, esp. a house, and the lender can take possession of the property if the borrower fails to repay the money. **2** a loan obtained under such an agreement: *a mortgage of three times one's income.* **3** a regular repayment of money borrowed under such an agreement: *the monthly mortgage on the building.* ✧ *vb* **-gaging, -gaged 4** to pledge a house or other property as security for the repayment of a loan. ✧ *adj* **5** of or relating to a mortgage: *a mortgage payment.* ▷ **HISTORY** Old French, literally: dead pledge

mortgagee *n* the person or organization who lends money in a mortgage agreement.

mortgagor *or* **-ger** *n* the person who borrows money in a mortgage agreement.

mortice *or* **mortise** (**more**-tiss) *n* **1** a slot or recess cut into a piece of wood or stone to receive a matching projection (tenon) on another piece, or a mortice lock. ✧ *vb* **-ticing, -ticed** *or* **-tising, -tised 2** to cut a slot or recess in a piece of wood or stone. **3** to join two pieces of wood or stone by means of a mortice and tenon. ▷ **HISTORY** Old French *mortoise*

A B C D E F G H I J K L M N O P Q R S T U V W X Y Z

mortice lock *n* a lock set into the edge of a door so that the mechanism of the lock is enclosed by the door.

mortify *vb* **-fies, -fying, -fied 1** to make someone feel ashamed or embarrassed. **2** *Christianity* to subdue one's emotions, the body, etc., by self-denial. **3** (of flesh) to become gangrenous. ▷ **HISTORY** Latin *mors* death + *facere* to do ▶ **mortification** *n* ▶ **mortifying** *adj*

mortuary *n, pl* **-aries** a building or room where dead bodies are kept before cremation or burial. ▷ **HISTORY** Latin *mortuarius* of the dead

morula (**morr**-yoo-la) *n Embryology* a solid ball of cells resulting from cleavage of a fertilized ovum.

mosaic (moh-**zay**-ik) *n* a design or decoration made up of small pieces of coloured glass or stone. ▷ **HISTORY** Greek *mouseios* of the Muses

Mosaic *adj* of or relating to Moses or the laws and traditions ascribed to him.

mosey *vb* **mosey along** *or* **on** *Brit, Austral & NZ informal* to walk slowly and casually; amble. ▷ **HISTORY** origin unknown

Moslem *n, pl* **-lems** *or* **-lem**, *adj* same as **Muslim**.

mosque *n* a Muslim place of worship. ▷ **HISTORY** Arabic *masjid* temple

mosquito *n, pl* **-toes** *or* **-tos** a two-winged insect, the females of which pierce the skin of humans and animals to suck their blood. ▷ **HISTORY** Spanish, diminutive of *mosca* fly

moss *n* **1** a very small flowerless plant typically growing in dense mats on trees, rocks, or moist ground. **2** *Scot & N English* a peat bog or marsh. ▷ **HISTORY** Old English *mos* swamp ▶ **mossy** *adj*

mossie *n S African* the common sparrow. ▷ **HISTORY** Afrikaans

moss rose *n* a variety of rose that has a mossy stem and fragrant pink flowers.

most *n* **1** the greatest number or degree: *the most I can ever remember being paid.* **2** the majority: *most of his records are dreadful.* **3 at (the) most** at the maximum: *she is fifteen at the most.* **4 make the most of** to use to the best advantage: *they made the most of their chances.* ✧ *adj* **5** of or being the majority of a group of things or people or the largest part of something: *most people don't share your views.* **6 the most** the superlative of **many, much:** *he has the most talent.* ✧ *adv* **7 the most** used to form the superlative of some adjectives and adverbs: *the most beautiful women in the world.* **8** the superlative of **much:** *what do you like most about your job?* **9** very; exceedingly: *a most unfortunate accident.* ▷ **HISTORY** Old English *māst* or *mǣst*

> ☑ **WORD TIP**
> *More* and *most* should be distinguished when used in comparisons. *More* applies to cases involving two people, objects, etc., *most* to cases involving three or more: *John is the more intelligent of the two; he is the most intelligent of the students.*

mostly *adv* **1** almost entirely; generally: *the men at the party were mostly young.* **2** on many or most occasions; usually: *rattlesnakes mostly hunt at night.*

Most Reverend *n* (in Britain) a courtesy title applied to archbishops.

MOT 1 *Brit* short for **MOT test. 2** *Brit* the certificate showing that a vehicle has passed its MOT test. **3** *NZ* Ministry of Transport.

mote *n* a tiny speck. ▷ **HISTORY** Old English *mot*

motel *n* a roadside hotel for motorists. ▷ **HISTORY** blend of MOTOR + HOTEL

motet (moh-**tet**) *n* a religious song for a choir in which several voices, usually unaccompanied, sing contrasting parts simultaneously. ▷ **HISTORY** Old French, diminutive of *mot* word

moth *n* any of numerous chiefly nocturnal insects resembling butterflies, that typically have stout bodies and do not have club-shaped antennae. ▷ **HISTORY** Old English *moththe*

mothball *n* **1** a small ball of camphor or naphthalene placed in stored clothing to repel clothes moths. **2 put in mothballs** to postpone work on. ✧ *vb* **3** to take something out of operation but maintain it for future use. **4** to postpone work on.

moth-eaten *adj* **1** decayed or scruffy. **2** eaten away by or as if by moths: *a moth-eaten suit.*

mother *n* **1** a female who has given birth to offspring. **2** a person's own mother. **3** a title given to certain members of female religious orders. **4** motherly qualities, such as maternal affection: *it appealed to the mother in her.* **5 the mother of** a female or thing that creates, founds, or protects something: *the mother of modern feminism; necessity is the mother of invention.* **6 the mother of all** *Informal* the greatest example of its kind: *the mother of all parties.* ✧ *adj* **7** of or relating to a female or thing that creates, founds, or protects something: *our mother company is in New York.* **8** native or innate: *mother wit.* ✧ *vb* **9** to give birth to or produce. **10** to nurture or protect. ▷ **HISTORY** Old English *mōdor* ▶ **motherless** *adj* ▶ **motherly** *adj*

Mother Carey's chicken *n* same as **stormy petrel**. ▷ **HISTORY** origin unknown

mother country *n* **1** the original country of colonists or settlers. **2** a person's native country.

motherhood *n* the state of being a mother.

Mothering Sunday *n* **1** (in Britain and S Africa) the fourth Sunday in Lent, when mothers traditionally receive presents from their children. **2** (in Australia) the second Sunday in May, when mothers traditionally receive presents from their children. Also called: **Mother's Day**

mother-in-law *n, pl* **mothers-in-law** the mother of one's wife or husband.

motherland *n* a person's native country.

mother-of-pearl *n* a hard iridescent substance that forms the inner layer of the shells of certain molluscs, such as the oyster.

Mother's Day *n* **1** See **Mothering Sunday**. **2** *US & Canad* the second Sunday in May, observed as a day in honour of mothers.

mother superior *n, pl* **mother superiors** *or* **mothers superior** the head of a community of nuns.

mother tongue *n* the language first learned by a child.

motif (moh-**teef**) *n* **1** a distinctive idea, esp. a theme elaborated on in a piece of music or literature. **2** a recurring shape in a design. **3** a single decoration, such as a symbol or name on a piece of clothing. ▷ HISTORY French

motile *adj* capable of independent movement. ▷ HISTORY Latin *movere* to move ▶ **motility** *n*

motion *n* **1** the process of continual change in the position of an object; movement: *the motion of the earth round the sun.* RELATED ADJECTIVE ➔ **kinetic 2** a movement or gesture: *he made stabbing motions with the spear.* **3** a way or style of moving: *massage the back with steady circular motions.* **4** a formal proposal to be discussed and voted on in a debate or meeting. **5** *Brit* **a** the evacuation of the bowels. **b** excrement. **6 go through the motions** to do something mechanically or without sincerity. **7 set in motion** to make operational or start functioning. ✧ *vb* **8** to signal or direct a person by a movement or gesture: *she motioned to me to sit down.* ▷ HISTORY Latin *movere* to move ▶ **motionless** *adj*

motion picture *n US & Canad* a film; movie.

motivate *vb* **-vating, -vated 1** to give a reason or inspiration for a course of action to someone: *he was motivated purely by greed.* **2** to inspire and encourage (someone) to do something: *a good teacher must motivate her pupils.* ▶ **motivation** *n*

motive *n* **1** the reason, whether conscious or unconscious, for a certain course of action. **2** same as **motif** (sense 2). ✧ *adj* **3** of or causing motion: *a motive force.* ▷ HISTORY Late Latin *motivus* moving

motive power *n* **1** any source of energy used to produce motion. **2** the means of supplying power to an engine or vehicle.

motley *adj* **1** made up of people or things of different types: *a motley assortment of mules, donkeys, and camels.* **2** multicoloured. ✧ *n* **3** *History* the costume of a jester. ▷ HISTORY perhaps Old English *mot* speck

motocross *n* the sport of motorcycle racing across rough ground. ▷ HISTORY *moto(r)* + *cross(-country)*

motor *n* **1** the engine, esp. an internal-combustion engine, of a vehicle. **2** a machine that converts energy, esp. electrical energy, into mechanical energy. **3** *Chiefly Brit informal* a car. ✧ *adj* **4** *Chiefly Brit* of or relating to cars and other vehicles powered by petrol or diesel engines: *the motor industry.* **5** powered by or relating to a motor: *a new synthetic motor oil.* **6** *Physiol* producing or causing motion. ✧ *vb* **7** to travel by car. **8** *Informal* to move fast. ▷ HISTORY Latin *movere* to move ▶ **motorized** *or* **-ised** *adj*

motorbicycle *n* **1** a motorcycle. **2** a moped.

motorbike *n Informal* a motorcycle.

motorboat *n* any boat powered by a motor.

motorcade *n* a procession of cars carrying an important person or people. ▷ HISTORY *motor* + *(caval)cade*

motorcar *n* a more formal word for **car**.

motorcycle *n* a two-wheeled vehicle driven by an engine. ▶ **motorcyclist** *n*

motorist *n* a driver of a car.

motorman *n, pl* **-men** *Brit, Austral & NZ* the driver of an electric train.

motor scooter *n* a light motorcycle with small wheels and an enclosed engine.

motor vehicle *n* a road vehicle driven by an engine.

motorway *n Brit, Austral, & NZ* a dual carriageway for fast-moving traffic, with no stopping permitted and no crossroads.

motte *n History* a mound on which a castle was built. ▷ HISTORY Old French

MOT test *n* (in Britain) a compulsory annual test of the roadworthiness of motor vehicles over three years old.

mottled *adj* coloured with streaks or blotches of different shades. ▷ HISTORY from *motley* ▶ **mottling** *n*

motto *n, pl* **-toes** *or* **-tos 1** a short saying expressing the guiding maxim or ideal of a family or organization, esp. when part of a coat of arms. **2** a verse or maxim contained in a paper cracker. **3** a quotation prefacing a book or chapter of a book. ▷ HISTORY Italian

mould[1] *or US* **mold** *n* **1** a shaped hollow container into which a liquid material is poured so that it can set in a particular shape: *pour the mixture into a buttered mould, cover, and steam for two hours.* **2** a shape, nature, or type: *an orthodox Communist in the Stalinist mould.* **3** a framework around which something is constructed or shaped: *the heated glass is shaped round a mould inside a kiln.* **4** something, esp. a food, made in or on a mould: *salmon mould.* ✧ *vb* **5** to make in a mould. **6** to shape or form: *a figure moulded out of clay.* **7** to influence or direct: *cultural factors moulding our everyday life.* ▷ HISTORY Latin *modulus* a small measure

mould[2] *or US* **mold** *n* a coating or discoloration caused by various fungi that develop in a damp atmosphere on food, fabrics, and walls. ▷ HISTORY Northern English dialect *mowlde* mouldy

mould[3] *or US* **mold** *n* loose soil, esp. when rich in organic matter: *leaf mould.* ▷ HISTORY Old English *molde*

mouldboard *or US* **moldboard** *n* the curved blade of a plough, which turns over the furrow.

moulder *or US* **molder** *vb* to crumble or cause to crumble, as through decay: *John Brown's body lies mouldering in the grave.* ▷ HISTORY from MOULD[3]

moulding *or US* **molding** *n* a shaped ornamental edging.

mouldy *or US* **moldy** *adj* **-dier, -diest 1** covered with mould. **2** stale or musty, esp. from age or lack of use. **3** *Slang* dull or boring.

moult *or US* **molt** *vb* **1** (of birds and animals) to shed feathers, hair, or skin so that they can be replaced by a new growth. ✧ *n* **2** the periodic process of moulting. ▷ **HISTORY** Latin *mutare* to change

mound *n* **1** a heap of earth, debris, etc. **2** any heap or pile. **3** a small natural hill. ▷ **HISTORY** origin unknown

mount[1] *vb* **1** to climb or ascend: *he mounted the stairs to his flat.* **2** to get up on a horse, a platform, etc. **3** Also: **mount up** to increase or accumulate: *costs do mount up; the tension mounted.* **4** to fix onto a backing, setting, or support: *sensors mounted on motorway bridges.* **5** to organize and stage (a campaign, a play, etc.): *the Allies mounted a counterattack on the eastern front.* ✧ *n* **6** a backing, setting, or support onto which something is fixed: *a diamond set in a gold mount.* **7** a horse for riding: *none of his mounts at yesterday's race meeting finished better than third.* ▷ **HISTORY** same as MOUNT[2]

mount[2] *n* a mountain or hill: used in literature and (when cap.) in proper names: *Mount Etna.* ▷ **HISTORY** Latin *mons* mountain

mountain *n* **1** a very large, high, and steep hill: *the highest mountain in the Alps.* **2** a huge heap or mass: *a mountain of papers.* **3** a surplus of a commodity, esp. in the European Union: *a butter mountain.* ✧ *adj* **4** of, found on, or for use on a mountain or mountains: *a mountain village.* ▷ **HISTORY** Latin *mons*

mountain ash *n* a tree with clusters of small white flowers and bright red berries; rowan.

mountain bike *n* a type of bicycle with straight handlebars and heavy-duty tyres, originally designed for use over rough hilly ground.

mountain cat *n* any of various wild animals of the cat family, such as the bobcat, lynx, or puma.

mountaineer *n* **1** a person who climbs mountains. ✧ *vb* **2** to climb mountains. ▸ **mountaineering** *n*

mountain goat *n* a wild goat inhabiting mountainous regions.

mountain lion *n* a puma.

mountainous *adj* **1** having many mountains: *a mountainous region.* **2** like a mountain or mountains, esp. in size: *mountainous waves.*

mountain oyster *n NZ informal* a sheep's testicle eaten as food.

mountain range *n* a series of adjoining mountains or of lines of mountains of similar origin.

mountain sickness *n* nausea, headache, and shortness of breath caused by climbing to high altitudes.

mountebank *n* **1** (formerly) a person who sold quack medicines in public places. **2** a charlatan or fake. ▷ **HISTORY** Italian *montambanco* a climber on a bench

Mountie *or* **Mounty** *n, pl* **Mounties** *Informal* a member of the Royal Canadian Mounted Police. ▷ **HISTORY** from *mounted*

mourn *vb* to feel or express sadness for the death or loss of someone or something. ▷ **HISTORY** Old English *murnan* ▸ **mourner** *n*

mournful *adj* **1** feeling or expressing grief and sadness: *he stood by, a mournful expression on his face.* **2** (of a sound) suggestive or reminiscent of grief or sadness: *the locomotive gave a mournful bellow.* ▸ **mournfully** *adv*

mourning *n* **1** sorrow or grief, esp. over a death. **2** the conventional symbols of grief for a death, such as the wearing of black. **3** the period of time during which a death is officially mourned. ✧ *adj* **4** of or relating to mourning.

mouse *n, pl* **mice 1** a small long-tailed rodent similar to but smaller than a rat. **2** a quiet, timid, or cowardly person. **3** *Computers* a hand-held device used to control cursor movements and computing functions without keying. ✧ *vb* **mousing, moused 4** *Rare* to stalk and catch mice. ▷ **HISTORY** Old English *mūs*

mouser *n* a cat or other animal that is used to catch mice.

mousetrap *n* **1** a spring-loaded trap for killing mice. **2** *Brit informal* cheese of mediocre quality.

moussaka *n* a dish originating in the Balkan States, consisting of meat, aubergines, and tomatoes, topped with cheese sauce. ▷ **HISTORY** Modern Greek

mousse *n* **1** a light creamy dessert made with eggs, cream, and fruit set with gelatine. **2** a similar dish made from fish or meat. ▷ **HISTORY** French: froth

moustache *or US* **mustache** *n* unshaved hair growing on the upper lip. ▷ **HISTORY** French, from Italian *mostaccio*

mousy *or* **mousey** *adj* **mousier, mousiest 1** (of hair) dull light brown in colour. **2** shy or ineffectual. ▸ **mousiness** *n*

mouth *n, pl* **mouths 1** the opening through which many animals take in food and issue sounds. **2** the visible part of the mouth; lips. **3** a person regarded as a consumer of food: *three mouths to feed.* **4** a particular manner of speaking: *a foul mouth.* **5** *Informal* boastful, rude, or excessive talk: *she is all mouth.* **6** the point where a river issues into a sea or lake. **7** an opening, such as that of a bottle, tunnel, or gun. **8 down in the mouth** in low spirits. ✧ *vb* **9** to form (words) with movements of the lips but without speaking. **10** to speak or say (something) insincerely, esp. in public: *ministers mouthing platitudes.* ▷ **HISTORY** Old English *mūth*

mouthful *n, pl* **-fuls 1** the amount of food or drink put into the mouth at any one time when eating or drinking. **2** a long word, phrase, or name that is difficult to say. **3** *Brit informal* an abusive response: *I asked him to move and he just gave me a mouthful.*

mouth organ *n* same as **harmonica**.

mouthpiece *n* **1** the part of a wind instrument into which the player blows. **2** the part of a telephone receiver into which a person speaks. **3** a person or publication expressing the views of an organization.

mouthwash *n* a medicated solution for gargling and cleansing the mouth.

movable *or* **moveable** *adj* **1** able to be moved; not fixed. **2** (of a festival, esp. Easter) varying in date from year to year. ✧ *n* **3 movables** movable articles, esp. furniture.

move *vb* **moving, moved 1** to go or take from one place to another; change in position: *I moved your books off the table.* **2** to start to live or work in a different place: *I moved to Brighton from Bristol last year.* **3** to be or cause to be in motion: *the trees were moving in the wind; the car moved slowly down the road.* **4** to act or begin to act: *the government plans to move to reduce crime.* **5** to cause or prompt to do something: *public opinion moved the President to act.* **6** to change the time when something is scheduled to happen: *can I move the appointment to Friday afternoon, please?* **7** to arouse affection, pity, or compassion in; touch: *her story moved me to tears.* **8** to change, progress, or develop in a specified way: *the conversation moved to more personal matters.* **9** to suggest a proposal formally, as in a debate: *to move a motion.* **10** to spend most of one's time with a specified social group: *they both move in theatrical, arty circles.* **11** (in board games) to change the position of a piece. **12** (of machines) to work or operate. **13 a** (of the bowels) to excrete waste. **b** to cause the bowels to excrete waste. **14** (of merchandise) to be disposed of by being bought. **15** to travel quickly: *this car can really move.* **16 move heaven and earth** to do everything possible to achieve a result. ✧ *n* **17** the act of moving; movement. **18** one of a sequence of actions, usually part of a plan: *the first real move towards disarmament.* **19** the act of moving one's home or place of business. **20** (in board games) **a** a player's turn to move his piece. **b** a manoeuvre of a piece. **21 get a move on** *Informal* to hurry up. **22 make a move** *Informal* **a** to prepare or begin to leave a place to go somewhere else: *we'd better make a move if we want to be home before dark.* **b** to do something which will produce a response: *neither of us wanted to make the first move.* **23 on the move** travelling from place to place. ▷ HISTORY Latin *movere*

movement *n* **1** the act, process, or an instance of moving. **2** the manner of moving: *their movement is jerky.* **3 a** a group of people with a common ideology. **b** the organized action and campaigning of such a group: *a successful movement to abolish child labour.* **4** a trend or tendency: *a movement towards shorter working hours.* **5** *Finance* a change in the price or value of shares, a currency, etc.: *adverse currency movements.* **6** *Music* a principal self-contained section of a large-scale work, such as a symphony. **7 movements** a person's location and activities during a specific time: *police were trying to piece together the recent movements of the two men.* **8 a** the evacuation of the bowels. **b** the matter evacuated. **9** the mechanism which drives and regulates a watch or clock.

mover *n* **1** a person or animal that moves in a particular way: *a slow mover.* **2** the person who first puts forward a proposal. **3** *US & Canad* a removal firm or a person who works for one.

movie *n* **1** *Informal* a cinema film. **2 the movies** the cinema: *I want to go to the movies tonight.*

moving *adj* **1** arousing or touching the emotions: *a moving account of her son's death.* **2** changing or capable of changing position: *a moving target.* ▸ **movingly** *adv*

moving staircase *or* **stairway** *n* an escalator.

mow *vb* **mowing, mowed, mowed** *or* **mown 1** to cut down grass or crops: *a tractor chugged along, mowing hay.* **2** to cut the growing vegetation of a field or lawn: *to mow a meadow.* ▷ HISTORY Old English *māwan* ▸ **mower** *n*

mow down *vb* to kill in large numbers, esp. by gunfire.

mozzarella (mot-sa-**rel**-la) *n* a moist white curd cheese originally made in Italy from buffalo milk. ▷ HISTORY Italian

MP 1 Member of Parliament. **2** Military Police. **3** Mounted Police.

MP3 Mpeg-1 layer3: a digital compression format used to compress audio files to a fraction of their original size without loss of sound quality. ▷ HISTORY from *Motion Picture Expert Group-1, Audio Layer-3*

MPEG *n Computing* **a** a standard compressed file format used for audio and video files. **b** a file in this format. ▷ HISTORY from *Motion Picture Experts Group*

mpg miles per gallon.

mph miles per hour.

MPhil Master of Philosophy.

MPV multipurpose vehicle.

Mr *n, pl* **Messrs** a title used before a man's name or before some office that he holds: *Mr Pickwick; Mr President.* ▷ HISTORY from *mister*

Mrs *n, pl* **Mrs** *or* **Mesdames** a title used before the name of a married woman. ▷ HISTORY from *mistress*

ms millisecond(s).

Ms (**mizz**) *n* a title used before the name of a woman to avoid indicating whether she is married or not.

MS 1 Mississippi. **2** multiple sclerosis.

MS. *or* **ms.** *pl* **MSS** *or* **mss** manuscript.

MSc Master of Science.

MSG monosodium glutamate.

MSP (in Britain) Member of the Scottish Parliament.

MST Mountain Standard Time.

mt megaton.

Mt[1] Mount: *Mt Everest.*

Mt[2] *Chem* meitnerium.

MT Montana.

mt. megaton.

MTech (in the US) Master of Technology.

much *adj* **more, most 1** a large amount or degree of: *there isn't much wine left.* ✧ *n* **2** a large amount or degree. **3 a bit much** *Informal* rather excessive. **4 make much of a** to make sense of: *he couldn't make much of her letter.* **b** to give importance to: *the press made much of the story.* **5 not much of** not to any appreciable degree or extent: *he's not much of a cook.* **6 not up to much** *Informal* of a low standard: *this beer is not up to much.* ✧ *adv* **7** considerably: *I'm much better now.* **8** practically or nearly: *it's much the same.* **9** often or a great deal: *that doesn't happen much these days.* **10 (as) much as** even though; although: *much as I'd like to, I can't* come. ✧ See also **more, most.** ▷ HISTORY Old English *mycel*

muchness *n* **much of a muchness** *Brit & NZ* very similar.

mucilage (**mew**-sill-ij) *n* **1** a sticky substance used as an adhesive, such as gum or glue. **2** a glutinous substance secreted by certain plants. ▷ HISTORY Late Latin *mucilago* mouldy juice ▶ **mucilaginous** *adj*

muck *n* **1** dirt or filth. **2** farmyard dung or decaying vegetable matter. **3** *Slang, chiefly Brit & NZ* something of poor quality; rubbish: *I don't want to eat this muck.* **4 make a muck of** *Slang, chiefly Brit & NZ* to ruin or spoil. ✧ *vb* **5** to spread manure upon. ✧ See also **muck about, muck in**, etc. ▷ HISTORY probably Old Norse

muck about *or* **around** *vb Slang* **1** to waste time by misbehaving or being silly. **2 muck about with** to interfere with, annoy, or waste the time of.

muck in *vb Brit & NZ slang* to share duties or work with other people.

muck out *vb* to clean (a barn, stable, etc.).

muckraking *n* seeking out and exposing scandal relating to well-known people. ▶ **muckraker** *n*

mucksweat *n Brit informal* profuse sweat.

muck up *vb Informal* to ruin, spoil, or do very badly: *I mucked up my driving test.*

mucky *adj* **1** dirty or muddy: *don't come in here with your mucky boots on!* **2** sexually explicit; obscene: *a mucky book.*

mucosa *n* same as **mucous membrane**. ▷ HISTORY Latin *mucosus* slimy ▶ **mucosal** *adj*

mucous membrane *n* a mucus-secreting tissue that lines body cavities or passages.

mucus (**mew**-kuss) *n* the slimy protective secretion of the mucous membranes. ▷ HISTORY Latin: nasal secretions ▶ **mucosity** *n* ▶ **mucous** *adj*

mucus glands *pl n Zool* glands that produce mucus.

mud *n* **1** soft wet earth, as found on the ground after rain or at the bottom of ponds. **2 (someone's) name is mud** *Informal* (someone) is disgraced. **3 throw mud at** *Informal* to slander or vilify. ✧ *adj* **4** made from mud or dried mud: *a mud hut.* ▷ HISTORY probably Low German *mudde*

mud bath *n* **1** a medicinal bath in heated mud. **2** a dirty or muddy place, occasion, or state: *heavy rain turned the pitch into a mud bath.*

muddle *n* **1** a state of untidiness or confusion: *the files are in a terrible muddle.* **2** a state of mental confusion or uncertainty: *the government are in a muddle over the economy.* ✧ *vb* **-dling, -dled 3** Also: **muddle up** to mix up or confuse (objects or items): *you've got your books all muddled up with mine.* **4** to make (someone) confused: *don't muddle her with too many suggestions.* ▷ HISTORY perhaps Middle Dutch *moddelen* to make muddy ▶ **muddled** *adj*

muddleheaded *adj* mentally confused or vague.

muddy *adj* **-dier, -diest 1** covered or filled with mud. **2** not clear or bright: *muddy colours.* **3** cloudy: *a muddy liquid.* **4** (esp. of thoughts) confused or vague. ✧ *vb* **-dies, -dying, -died 5** to make muddy. **6** to make a situation or issue less clear: *the allegations of sexual misconduct only serve to muddy the issue.* ▶ **muddily** *adv*

mud flat *n* an area of low muddy land that is covered at high tide but not at low tide.

mudflow *n Geol* a flow of soil mixed with water down a steep unstable slope.

mudguard *n* a curved part of a bicycle or other vehicle attached above the wheels to reduce the amount of water or mud thrown up by them.

mudslinging *n* the making of malicious personal attacks on an opponent, esp. in politics. ▶ **mudslinger** *n*

muesli (**mewz**-lee) *n* a mixture of rolled oats, nuts, and dried fruit, usually eaten with milk. ▷ HISTORY Swiss German

muezzin (moo-**ezz**-in) *n Islam* the official of a mosque who calls the faithful to prayer from the minaret. ▷ HISTORY Arabic *mu'adhdhin*

muff[1] *n* a tube of fur or cloth into which the hands are placed for warmth. ▷ HISTORY probably Dutch *mof*

muff[2] *vb* **1** to do (something) badly: *I muffed my chance to make a good impression.* **2** to bungle (a shot or catch). ▷ HISTORY origin unknown

muffin *n* **1** a small cup-shaped sweet bread roll, usually eaten hot with butter. **2** a thick round baked yeast roll, usually toasted and served with butter. ▷ HISTORY origin unknown

muffle *vb* **-fling, -fled 1** to deaden (a sound or noise), esp. by wrapping the source of it in something: *the sound was muffled by the double glazing.* **2** to wrap up in a scarf or coat for warmth. **3** to censor or restrict: *an attempt to muffle criticism.* ▷ HISTORY probably Old French *moufle* mitten ▶ **muffled** *adj*

muffler *n* **1** *Brit* a thick scarf worn for warmth. **2** a device to deaden sound, esp. one on a car exhaust; silencer.

mufti *n* civilian clothes worn by a person who normally wears a military uniform. ▷ HISTORY from *Mufti,* Muslim religious leader

mug[1] *n* **1** a large drinking cup with a handle. **2** the quantity held by a mug or its contents: *a mug of coffee.* ▷ HISTORY probably Scandinavian

mug[2] *n* **1** *Slang* a person's face or mouth: *keep your ugly mug out of this.* **2** *Slang* a gullible person, esp. one who is swindled easily. **3 a mug's game** a worthless activity. ▷ HISTORY perhaps same as MUG[1]

mug[3] *vb* **mugging, mugged** to attack someone in order to rob them. ▶ **mugger** *n* ▶ **mugging** *n*

muggins *n Slang* **a** a stupid or gullible person. **b** a title used humorously to refer to oneself. ▷ HISTORY probably from surname *Muggins*

muggy *adj* **-gier, -giest** (of weather or air) unpleasantly warm and humid. ▷ HISTORY dialect *mug* drizzle ▶ **mugginess** *n*

mug shot *n Informal* a photograph of a person's face, esp. one resembling a police-file picture.

mug up *vb Brit slang* to study a subject hard, esp. for an exam. ▷ HISTORY origin unknown

mujaheddin *or* **mujahedeen** (moo-ja-hed-**deen**) *pl n* fundamentalist Muslim guerrillas. ▷ **HISTORY** Arabic *mujāhidīn* fighters

mulatto (mew-**lat**-toe) *n, pl* **-tos** *or* **-toes** a person with one Black and one White parent. ▷ **HISTORY** Spanish *mulato* young mule

mulberry *n, pl* **-ries 1** a tree with edible blackberry-like fruit, the leaves of which are used to feed silkworms. **2** the fruit of any of these trees. ✧ *adj* **3** dark purple. ▷ **HISTORY** Latin *morum*

mulch *n* **1** a mixture of half-rotten vegetable matter and peat used to protect the roots of plants or enrich the soil. ✧ *vb* **2** to cover soil with mulch. ▷ **HISTORY** obsolete *mulch* soft

mule[1] *n* **1** the sterile offspring of a male donkey and a female horse. **2** a machine that spins cotton into yarn. ▷ **HISTORY** Latin *mulus*

mule[2] *n* a backless shoe or slipper. ▷ **HISTORY** Latin *mulleus* a magistrate's shoe

muleteer *n* a person who drives mules.

mulga *n* **1** an Australian acacia shrub growing in desert regions. **2** *Austral* the outback. ▷ **HISTORY** Aboriginal

mulish *adj* stubborn; obstinate.

mull *n Scot* a promontory or headland: *the Mull of Galloway.* ▷ **HISTORY** probably Gaelic *maol*

mullah *n* (formerly) a Muslim scholar, teacher, or religious leader. ▷ **HISTORY** Arabic *mawlā* master

mulled *adj* (of wine or ale) flavoured with sugar and spices and served hot. ▷ **HISTORY** origin unknown

mullet *n, pl* **mullets** *or* **mullet** any of various marine food fishes. ▷ **HISTORY** Greek *mullos*

mulligatawny *n* a curry-flavoured soup of Anglo-Indian origin. ▷ **HISTORY** Tamil *milakutanni* pepper water

mullion *n* a slender vertical bar between the casements or panes of a window. ▷ **HISTORY** Old French *moinel* ▶ **mullioned** *adj*

mulloway *n* a large Australian sea fish, valued for sport and food.

multi- *combining form* **1** many or much: *multimillion.* **2** more than one: *multistorey.* ▷ **HISTORY** Latin *multus* much, many

multicellular *adj Biol* consisting of more than one cell.

multicoloured *adj* having many colours: *multicoloured balls of wool.*

multicultural *adj* of or for the cultures of several different races.

multifarious (mull-tee-**fare**-ee-uss) *adj* many and varied: *multifarious religious movements and political divisions sprang up around this time.* ▷ **HISTORY** Late Latin *multifarius* manifold

multiflora rose *n* a climbing rose with clusters of small fragrant flowers.

multilateral *adj* of or involving more than two nations or parties: *multilateral trade negotiations.*

multilingual *adj* **1** able to speak more than two languages. **2** written or expressed in more than two languages: *a multilingual leaflet.*

multimedia *pl n* **1** the combined use of media such as television and slides. **2** *Computers* of or relating to systems that can manipulate data in a variety of forms, such as sound, graphics, or text.

multimillionaire *n* a person who has money or property worth several million pounds, dollars, etc.

multinational *adj* **1** (of a large business company) operating in several countries. **2** involving people from several countries: *a multinational peacekeeping force.* ✧ *n* **3** a large company operating in several countries.

multiparous (mull-**tip**-a-russ) *adj* producing many offspring at one birth. ▷ **HISTORY** New Latin *multiparus*

multiple *adj* **1** having or involving more than one part, individual, or element. ✧ *n* **2** a number or polynomial which can be divided by another specified one an exact number of times: *6 is a multiple of 2.* ▷ **HISTORY** Latin *multiplus* ▶ **multiply** *adv*

multiple-choice *adj* (of a test or question) giving a number of possible answers out of which the correct one must be chosen.

multiple sclerosis *n* a chronic progressive disease of the central nervous system, resulting in speech and visual disorders, tremor, muscular incoordination, and partial paralysis.

multiplex *n, pl* **-plexes 1** a purpose-built complex containing several cinemas and usually restaurants and bars. ✧ *adj* **2** having many elements; complex. ▷ **HISTORY** Latin: having many folds

multiplicand *n* a number to be multiplied by another number (the **multiplier**).

multiplication *n* **1** a mathematical operation, equivalent to adding a number to itself a specified number of times. For instance, 4 multiplied by 3 equals 12 (i.e. 4+4+4). **2** the act of multiplying or state of being multiplied.

multiplication sign *n* the symbol ×, placed between numbers to be multiplied.

multiplication table *n* a table giving the results of multiplying two numbers together.

multiplicity *n, pl* **-ties 1** a large number or great variety. **2** the state of being multiple.

multiplier *n* a number by which another number (the **multiplicand**) is multiplied.

multiply *vb* **-plies, -plying, -plied 1** to increase or cause to increase in number, quantity, or degree. **2** to combine numbers or quantities by multiplication. **3** to increase in number by reproduction. ▷ **HISTORY** Latin *multiplicare*

multipurpose *adj* having many uses: *a giant multipurpose enterprise.*

multipurpose vehicle *n* a large car, similar to a van, designed to carry up to eight passengers.

multiracial *adj* consisting of or involving people of many races: *a multiracial society.* ▶ **multiracialism** *n*

multistage *adj* (of a rocket or missile) having several stages, each of which can be jettisoned after it has burnt out.

a b c d e f g h i j k l m n o p q r s t u v w x y z

multistorey *adj* (of a building) having many storeys.

multitrack *adj* (in sound recording) using tape containing two or more tracks.

multitude *n* **1** a large number of people or things: *a multitude of different pressure groups.* **2 the multitude** the common people. ▷ **HISTORY** Latin *multitudo* ▶ **multitudinous** *adj*

multi-user *adj* (of a computer) capable of being used by several people at once.

mum[1] *n Chiefly Brit informal* same as **mother**. ▷ **HISTORY** a child's word

mum[2] *adj* **1 keep mum** remain silent. **2 mum's the word** keep quiet (about something). ▷ **HISTORY** suggestive of closed lips

mumble *vb* **-bling, -bled 1** to speak or say something indistinctly, with the mouth partly closed: *I could hear him mumbling under his breath.* ✧ *n* **2** an indistinct or low utterance or sound. ▷ **HISTORY** Middle English *momelen,* from MUM[2]

mumbo jumbo *n* **1** meaningless language; nonsense or gibberish. **2** foolish religious ritual or incantation. ▷ **HISTORY** probably from West African *mama dyumbo,* name of a tribal god

mummer *n* one of a group of masked performers in a folk play or mime. ▷ **HISTORY** Old French *momer* to mime

mummery *n, pl* **-meries 1** a performance by mummers. **2** hypocritical or ostentatious ceremony.

mummified *adj* (of a body) preserved as a mummy. ▶ **mummification** *n*

mummy[1] *n, pl* **-mies** *Chiefly Brit* an embalmed body as prepared for burial in ancient Egypt. ▷ **HISTORY** Persian *mūm* wax

mummy[2] *n, pl* **-mies** a child's word for **mother**. ▷ **HISTORY** variant of MUM[1]

mumps *n* an infectious viral disease in which the glands below the ear become swollen and painful. ▷ **HISTORY** obsolete *mump* to grimace

munch *vb* to chew noisily and steadily. ▷ **HISTORY** imitative

mundane *adj* **1** everyday, ordinary, and therefore not very interesting. **2** relating to the world or worldly matters. ▷ **HISTORY** Latin *mundus* world

mung bean *n* an E Asian bean plant grown for its edible seeds which are used as a source of bean sprouts. ▷ **HISTORY** Tamil *mūngu*

municipal *adj* of or relating to a town or city or its local government. ▷ **HISTORY** Latin *municipium* a free town

municipality *n, pl* **-ties 1** a city, town, or district enjoying local self-government. **2** the governing body of such a unit.

munificent (mew-**niff**-fiss-sent) *adj* very generous. ▷ **HISTORY** Latin *munus* gift + *facere* to make ▶ **munificence** *n*

muniments (**mew**-nim-ments) *pl n Law* the title deeds and other documentary evidence relating to the title to land. ▷ **HISTORY** Latin *munire* to defend

munitions (mew-**nish**-unz) *pl n* military equipment and stores, esp. ammunition.

munted *adj NZ slang* **1** destroyed or ruined. **2** abnormal or peculiar.

muon (**mew**-on) *n* a positive or negative elementary particle with a mass 207 times that of an electron. ▷ **HISTORY** short for *mu meson*

mural (**myoor**-al) *n* **1** a large painting on a wall. ✧ *adj* **2** of or relating to a wall. ▷ **HISTORY** Latin *murus* wall ▶ **muralist** *n*

murder *n* **1** the unlawful intentional killing of one human being by another. **2** *Informal* something dangerous, difficult, or unpleasant: *shopping on Christmas Eve is murder.* **3 cry blue murder** *Informal* to make an outcry. **4 get away with murder** *Informal* to do as one pleases without ever being punished. ✧ *vb* **5** to kill someone intentionally and unlawfully. **6** *Informal* to ruin a piece of music or drama by performing it very badly: *he absolutely murdered that song.* **7** *Informal* to beat decisively. ▷ **HISTORY** Old English *morthor* ▶ **murderer** *n* ▶ **murderess** *fem n* ▶ **murderous** *adj*

murk *n* thick gloomy darkness. ▷ **HISTORY** Old Norse *myrkr* darkness

murky *adj* **murkier, murkiest 1** gloomy or dark. **2** cloudy or hard to see through: *a murky stagnant pond.* **3** obscure and suspicious; shady: *murky goings-on; his murky past.* ▶ **murkily** *adv* ▶ **murkiness** *n*

murmur *vb* **1** to speak or say in a quiet indistinct way. **2** to complain. ✧ *n* **3** a continuous low indistinct sound, such as that of a distant conversation. **4** an indistinct utterance: *a murmur of protest.* **5** a complaint or grumble: *he left without a murmur.* **6** *Med* any abnormal soft blowing sound heard usually over the chest: *a heart murmur.* ▷ **HISTORY** Latin *murmurare* to rumble ▶ **murmuring** *n, adj* ▶ **murmurous** *adj*

murrain (**murr**-rin) *n* any plaguelike disease in cattle. ▷ **HISTORY** Old French *morir* to die

mus. 1 museum. **2** music. **3** musical.

muscle *n* **1** a tissue in the body composed of bundles of elongated cells which produce movement in an organ or part by contracting or relaxing. **2** an organ composed of muscle tissue: *the heart is essentially just another muscle.* **3** strength or force: *we do not have the political muscle to force through these reforms.* ✧ *vb* **-cling, -cled 4 muscle in** to force one's way into a situation; intrude: *I don't like the way he's trying to muscle in here.* ▷ **HISTORY** Medical Latin *musculus* little mouse

muscle-bound *adj* having overdeveloped and inelastic muscles.

muscleman *n, pl* **-men 1** a man with highly developed muscles. **2** a henchman employed to intimidate or use violence upon victims.

Muscovite *adj* **1** of Moscow, a city in Russia. ✧ *n* **2** a person from Moscow.

muscular *adj* **1** having well-developed muscles; brawny. **2** of or consisting of muscle: *great muscular effort is needed.* **3** forceful or powerful: *a muscular account of Schumann's Fourth Symphony.* ▶ **muscularity** *n*

muscular dystrophy *n* a hereditary disease in which the muscles gradually weaken and waste away.

musculature *n* the arrangement of muscles in an organ, part, or organism.

muse[1] *vb* **musing, mused** to think deeply and at length about: *she mused unhappily on how right her sister had been.* ▷ **HISTORY** Old French *muser*

muse[2] *n* **the muse** a force or person, esp. a woman, that inspires a creative artist. ▷ **HISTORY** Greek *Mousa* a Muse

Muses *pl n Greek myth* the nine sister goddesses, each of whom was the protector of a different art or science.

museum *n* a building where objects of historical, artistic, or scientific interest are exhibited and preserved.

> **WORD HISTORY**
> 'Museum' comes from Greek *mouseion*, meaning the 'home of the Muses', the goddesses of the arts and sciences. The first building to be given this name was a university building built in Alexandria in Egypt about 300 BC.

museum piece *n Informal* a very old or old-fashioned object or building.

mush[1] *n* **1** a soft pulpy mass. **2** *Informal* cloying sentimentality. ▷ **HISTORY** obsolete *moose* porridge

mush[2] *Canad* ✧ *interj* **1** an order to dogs in a sled team to start up or go faster. ✧ *vb* **2** to travel by or drive a dogsled. ▷ **HISTORY** perhaps from imperative of French *marcher* to advance

mushroom *n* **1** an edible fungus consisting of a cap at the end of a stem. **2** something resembling a mushroom in shape or rapid growth. ✧ *vb* **3** to grow rapidly: *consumer debt mushroomed rapidly in 1989.* ▷ **HISTORY** Late Latin *mussirio*

mushroom cloud *n* the large mushroom-shaped cloud produced by a nuclear explosion.

mushy *adj* **mushier, mushiest 1** soft and pulpy. **2** *Informal* excessively sentimental.

music *n* **1** an art form consisting of sequences of sounds organized melodically, harmonically, and rhythmically. **2** such sounds, esp. when produced by singing or musical instruments. **3** any written or printed representation of musical sounds: *I can't read music.* **4** any sequence of sounds perceived as pleasing or harmonious. **5 face the music** *Informal* to confront the consequences of one's actions. **6 music to one's ears** something, such as a piece of news, that one is pleased to hear. ▷ **HISTORY** Greek *mousikē (tekhnē)* (art) in the protection of the Muses

musical *adj* **1** of or used in music. **2** talented in or fond of music. **3** pleasant-sounding; harmonious: *musical laughter.* **4** involving or set to music: *a musical biography of Judy Garland.* ✧ *n* **5** a play or film that has dialogue interspersed with songs and dances. ▶ **musicality** *n* ▶ **musically** *adv*

music centre *n Brit* a single hi-fi unit containing a turntable, radio, compact disc player, and cassette player.

music hall *n Chiefly Brit* (formerly) **1** a variety entertainment consisting of songs and comic turns. **2** a theatre at which such entertainments were staged.

musician *n* a person who plays or composes music, esp. as a profession.

musicianship *n* the technical and interpretive skills involved in singing or playing music: *the piano part is simple but performed with great musicianship.*

musicology *n* the scholarly study of music. ▶ **musicologist** *n*

musk *n* **1** a strong-smelling glandular secretion of the male musk deer, used in perfumery. **2** any similar substance produced by animals or plants, or manufactured synthetically. ▷ **HISTORY** Persian *mushk*

musk deer *n* a small central Asian mountain deer.

muskeg *n Chiefly Canad* an area of undrained boggy land. ▷ **HISTORY** Native American: grassy swamp

musket *n* a long-barrelled muzzle-loading gun fired from the shoulder, a forerunner of the rifle. ▷ **HISTORY** Italian *moschetto* arrow, earlier: sparrow hawk ▶ **musketeer** *n*

muskmelon *n* any of several varieties of melon, such as the cantaloupe and honeydew.

musk ox *n* a large ox that has a dark shaggy coat, downward-curving horns and emits a musky smell.

muskrat *n, pl* **-rats** *or* **-rat 1** a North American beaver-like amphibious rodent. **2** the brown fur of this animal.

musk rose *n* a Mediterranean rose, cultivated for its white musk-scented flowers.

musky *adj* **muskier, muskiest** having a heady sweet smell. ▶ **muskiness** *n*

Muslim *or* **Moslem** *n, pl* **-lims, -lim** *or* **-lems, -lem 1** a follower of the religion of Islam. ✧ *adj* **2** of or relating to Islam. ▷ **HISTORY** Arabic, literally: one who surrenders

muslin *n* a very fine plain-weave cotton fabric. ▷ **HISTORY** French *mousseline*

musquash *n* muskrat fur. ▷ **HISTORY** from a Native American language

mussel *n* an edible shellfish, with a dark slightly elongated hinged shell, which lives attached to rocks. ▷ **HISTORY** Latin *musculus,* diminutive of *mus* mouse

must[1] *vb* used as an auxiliary to express or indicate: **1** the need or necessity to do something: *I must go to the shops.* **2** obligation or requirement: *you must not smoke in here.* **3** the probable correctness of a statement: *he must be finished by now.* **4** inevitability: *all good things must come to an end.* **5** determination: *I must try and finish this.* **6** conviction or certainty on the part of the speaker: *you must be kidding!* ✧ *n* **7** an essential or necessary thing: *strong boots are a must for hill walking.* ▷ **HISTORY** Old English *mōste,* past tense of *mōtan* to be allowed or obliged

must[2] *n* the pressed juice of grapes or other fruit ready for fermentation. ▷ **HISTORY** Latin *mustum* new wine

a b c d e f g h i j k l m n o p q r s t u v w x y z

mustang *n* a small breed of horse, often wild or half wild, found in the southwestern US. ▷ **HISTORY** Mexican Spanish *mestengo*

mustard *n* **1** a hot, spicy paste made from the powdered seeds of any of a family of plants. **2** any of these plants, which have yellow flowers and slender pods. ✧ *adj* **3** brownish-yellow. ▷ **HISTORY** Old French *moustarde*

mustard gas *n* an oily liquid with poisonous vapour used in chemical warfare, esp. in World War I, which can cause blindness, burns, and sometimes death.

mustard plaster *n Med* a mixture of powdered black mustard seeds applied to the skin.

muster *vb* **1** to summon or gather: *I put as much disbelief in my expression as I could muster.* **2** to call or be called together for duty or inspection: *the battalion mustered on the bank of the river.* ✧ *n* **3** an assembly of military personnel for duty or inspection. **4** a collection, assembly, or gathering. **5 pass muster** to be acceptable. ▷ **HISTORY** Latin *monstrare* to show

musty *adj* **-tier, -tiest 1** smelling or tasting old, stale, or mouldy. **2** old-fashioned, dull, or hackneyed: *musty ideas.* ▷ **HISTORY** perhaps variant of obsolete *moisty* ▶ **mustily** *adv* ▶ **mustiness** *n*

mutable (**mew**-tab-bl) *adj* able to or tending to change. ▷ **HISTORY** Latin *mutare* to change ▶ **mutability** *n*

mutagen (**mew**-ta-jen) *n* any substance that can induce genetic mutation. ▷ **HISTORY** MUTATION + *-gen* (suffix) producing ▶ **mutagenic** *adj*

mutagenesis (mew-ta-**jen**-iss-iss) *n* the origin and development of a genetic mutation. ▷ **HISTORY** MUTATION + GENESIS

mutant (**mew**-tant) *n* **1** an animal, organism, or gene that has undergone mutation. ✧ *adj* **2** of or resulting from mutation.

mutate (mew-**tate**) *vb* **-tating, -tated** to undergo or cause to undergo mutation. ▷ **HISTORY** Latin *mutare* to change

mutation (mew-**tay**-shun) *n* **1** a change or alteration. **2** a change in the chromosomes or genes of a cell which may affect the structure and development of the resultant offspring. **3** a physical characteristic in an organism resulting from this type of chromosomal change.

mute *adj* **1** not giving out sound or speech; silent. **2** unable to speak; dumb. **3** unspoken or unexpressed: *she shot him a look of mute entreaty.* **4** (of a letter in a word) silent: *the 'k' in 'know' is mute.* ✧ *n* **5** a person who is unable to speak. **6** any of various devices used to soften the tone of stringed or brass instruments. ✧ *vb* **muting, muted 7** to reduce the volume or soften the tone of (a musical instrument) by means of a mute or soft pedal. **8** to reduce the volume of (a sound): *the double glazing muted the noise.* ▷ **HISTORY** Latin *mutus* silent ▶ **mutely** *adv* ▶ **muteness** *n*

muted *adj* **1** (of a sound or colour) softened: *a muted pink shirt.* **2** (of an emotion or action) subdued or restrained: *his response was muted.* **3** (of a musical instrument) being played while fitted with a mute: *muted trumpet.*

mute swan *n* the swan most commonly seen in Britain, which has a pure white plumage and an orange-red bill.

muti (**moo**-tee) *n S African* medicine, esp. herbal. ▷ **HISTORY** Zulu

mutilate (**mew**-till-ate) *vb* **-lating, -lated 1** to injure by tearing or cutting off a limb or essential part; maim. **2** to damage a book or text so as to render it unintelligible. **3** to spoil or damage severely: *why did he mutilate his favourite tapes and leave ours alone?* ▷ **HISTORY** Latin *mutilare* to cut off ▶ **mutilated** *adj* ▶ **mutilation** *n* ▶ **mutilator** *n*

mutineer *n* a person who mutinies.

mutinous *adj* **1** openly rebellious. **2** characteristic or indicative of mutiny.

mutiny (**mew**-tin-ee) *n, pl* **-nies 1** open rebellion against authority, esp. by sailors or soldiers against their officers. ✧ *vb* **-nies, -nying, -nied 2** to engage in mutiny: *soldiers who had mutinied and taken control.* ▷ **HISTORY** Old French *mutin* rebellious

mutt *n Slang* **1** a foolish or stupid person. **2** a mongrel dog. ▷ **HISTORY** from *muttonhead*

mutter *vb* **1** to say something or speak in a low and indistinct tone: *he muttered an excuse.* **2** to grumble. ✧ *n* **3** a muttered sound or complaint. ▷ **HISTORY** Middle English *moteren* ▶ **muttering** *n, adj*

mutton *n* **1** the flesh of mature sheep, used as food. **2 mutton dressed as lamb** an older woman dressed up to look young. ▷ **HISTORY** Medieval Latin *multo* sheep

mutton bird *n* **1** *Austral* a migratory sea bird with dark plumage. **2** *NZ* any of a number of migratory sea birds, the young of which are a Maori delicacy.

mutual (**mew**-chew-al) *adj* **1** experienced or expressed by each of two or more people about the other; reciprocal: *mutual respect.* **2** common to or shared by two or more people: *a mutual friend.* **3** denoting an organization, such as an insurance company, in which the policyholders or investors share the profits and expenses and there are no shareholders. ▷ **HISTORY** Latin *mutuus* reciprocal ▶ **mutuality** *n* ▶ **mutually** *adv*

WORD TIP

The use of *mutual* to mean *common to or shared by two or more people* was formerly considered incorrect, but is now acceptable. Tautologous use of *mutual* should be avoided: *cooperation* (not *mutual cooperation*) *between the two countries.*

mutually exclusive events *pl n Maths* (in probability) two events that cannot occur at the same time.

Muzak *n Trademark* recorded light music played in places such as restaurants and shops.

muzzle *n* **1** the projecting part of an animal's face, usually the jaws and nose. **2** a guard, made of plastic or strap of strong material, fitted over an animal's nose and jaws to prevent it biting or eating. **3** the front end of a gun barrel. ✧ *vb* **-zling, -zled 4** to prevent from being heard or noticed: *an* *attempt to muzzle the press.* **5** to put a muzzle on (an animal). ▷ **HISTORY** Old French *muse* snout

muzzy *adj* **-zier, -ziest 1** confused and groggy: *he felt muzzy and hung over.* **2** blurred or hazy: *the picture was muzzy and out of focus.* ▷ **HISTORY** origin unknown ▶ **muzzily** *adv* ▶ **muzziness** *n*

MV megavolt.

MW 1 megawatt. **2** *Radio* medium wave.

Mx *Physics* maxwell.

my *adj* **1** of, belonging to, or associated with the speaker or writer (me): *my own way of doing things.* **2** used in various forms of address: *my lord.* ✧ *interj* **3** an exclamation of surprise or awe: *my, how you've grown!* ▷ **HISTORY** variant of Old English *mīn*

> **WORD TIP**
> See at **me**[1].

myall *n* an Australian acacia with hard scented wood. ▷ **HISTORY** Aboriginal

mycelium (mice-**eel**-lee-um) *n, pl* **-lia** (-lee-a) the mass forming the body of a fungus. ▷ **HISTORY** Greek *mukēs* mushroom + *hēlos* nail

Mycenaean (mice-in-**ee**-an) *adj* of or relating to the Aegean civilization of Mycenae, a city in S Greece (1400–1100 BC).

mycology *n* the study of fungi. ▷ **HISTORY** Greek *mukēs* mushroom + -LOGY

myelin (**my**-ill-in) *n* a white tissue forming an insulating sheath around certain nerve fibres. ▷ **HISTORY** Greek *muelos* marrow

myeloma (my-ill-**oh**-ma) *n, pl* **-mas** *or* **-mata** (-ma-ta) a tumour of the bone marrow. ▷ **HISTORY** Greek *muelos* marrow + *-oma,* modelled on *carcinoma*

mynah *or* **myna** *n* a tropical Asian starling which can mimic human speech. ▷ **HISTORY** Hindi *mainā*

myocardium *n, pl* **-dia** the muscular tissue of the heart. ▷ **HISTORY** Greek *mus* muscle + *kardia* heart ▶ **myocardial** *adj*

myopia (my-**oh**-pee-a) *n* inability to see distant objects clearly because the images are focused in front of the retina; short-sightedness. ▷ **HISTORY** Greek *muōps* short-sighted ▶ **myopic** (my-**op**-ik) *adj*

myriad (**mir**-ree-ad) *adj* **1** innumerable: *the myriad demands of the modern world.* ✧ *n* **2** a large indefinite number: *myriads of tiny yellow flowers.* ▷ **HISTORY** Greek *murias* ten thousand

myriapod *n* an invertebrate with a long segmented body and many legs, such as a centipede. ▷ **HISTORY** Greek *murias* ten thousand + *pous* foot

myrrh (**mur**) *n* the aromatic resin of an African or Asian shrub or tree, used in perfume, incense, and medicine. ▷ **HISTORY** Greek *murrha*

myrtle (**mur**-tl) *n* an evergreen shrub with pink or white flowers and aromatic blue-black berries. ▷ **HISTORY** Greek *murtos*

myself *pron* **1** the reflexive form of *I* or *me*: *I really enjoyed myself at the party.* **2** I or me in person, as distinct from anyone else: *I myself know of no answer.* **3** my usual self: *I'm not myself today.*

mysterious *adj* **1** of unknown cause or nature: *a mysterious illness.* **2** creating a feeling of strangeness, curiosity, or wonder: *a fascinating and mysterious old woman.* ▶ **mysteriously** *adv*

mystery *n, pl* **-teries 1** an unexplained or inexplicable event or phenomenon. **2** a person or thing that arouses curiosity or suspense because of an unknown, obscure, or enigmatic quality. **3** a story or film which arouses suspense and curiosity because of facts concealed. **4** a religious rite, such as the Eucharist in Christianity. ▷ **HISTORY** Greek *mustērion* secret rites

mystery play *n* (in the Middle Ages) a type of drama based on the life of Christ.

mystic *n* **1** a person who achieves mystical experience. ✧ *adj* **2** same as **mystical**. ▷ **HISTORY** Greek *mustēs* one who has been initiated

mystical *adj* **1** relating to or characteristic of mysticism. **2** *Christianity* having a sacred significance that is beyond human understanding. **3** having occult or metaphysical significance. ▶ **mystically** *adv*

mysticism *n* **1** belief in or experience of a reality beyond normal human understanding or experience. **2** the use of prayer and meditation in an attempt to achieve direct intuitive experience of the divine.

mystify *vb* **-fies, -fying, -fied 1** to confuse, bewilder, or puzzle: *his success mystifies many in the fashion industry.* **2** to make obscure: *it is important for us not to mystify the function of the scientist.* ▶ **mystification** *n* ▶ **mystifying** *adj*

mystique (miss-**steek**) *n* an aura of mystery, power, and awe that surrounds a person or thing.

myth *n* **1 a** a story about superhuman beings of an earlier age, usually of how natural phenomena or social customs came into existence. **b** same as **mythology** (senses 1, 2). **2 a** an idea or explanation which is widely held but untrue or unproven: *the myth that the USA is a classless society.* **b** a person or thing whose existence is fictional or unproven: *the Loch Ness Monster is a myth.* ▷ **HISTORY** Greek *muthos* fable

mythical *or* **mythic** *adj* **1** of or relating to myth. **2** imaginary or fictitious. ▶ **mythically** *adv*

mythology *n, pl* **-gies 1** myths collectively, esp. those associated with a particular culture or person. **2** a body of stories about a person, institution, etc. **3** the study of myths. ▶ **mythological** *adj*

myxoedema *or US* **myxedema** (mix-id-**deem**-a) *n* a disease caused by an underactive thyroid gland, characterized by puffy eyes, face, and hands, and mental sluggishness. ▷ **HISTORY** Greek *muxa* mucus + *oidēma* swelling

myxomatosis (mix-a-mat-**oh**-siss) *n* an infectious and usually fatal viral disease of rabbits causing swellings and tumours. ▷ **HISTORY** Greek *muxa* mucus + *-ōma* denoting tumour + *-osis* denoting disease

N n

A B C D E F G H I J K L M N O P Q R S T U V W X Y Z

n[1] **1** nano-. **2** neutron.

n[2] *n* **1** *Maths* a number whose value is not stated: *two to the power n.* ✧ *adj* **2** an indefinite number of: *there are n objects in the box.* ▶ **nth** *adj*

N **1** *Chess* knight. **2** *Chem* nitrogen. **3** *Physics* newton(s). **4** North(ern). **5** nuclear: *N plant.*

n. **1** neuter. **2** noun. **3** number.

N. **1** National(ist). **2** Navy. **3** New. **4** Norse.

Na *Chem* sodium. ▷ HISTORY Latin *natrium*

NA North America.

n/a not applicable: used to indicate that a question on a form is not relevant to the person filling it in.

Naafi *n* **1** *Brit* Navy, Army, and Air Force Institutes. **2** a canteen or shop run by this organization, esp. for military personnel.

naan *n* same as **nan bread**.

naartjie (**nahr**-chee) *n S African* a tangerine. ▷ HISTORY Afrikaans

nab *vb* **nabbing, nabbed** *Informal* **1** to arrest (someone). **2** to catch (someone) doing something wrong. ▷ HISTORY perhaps Scandinavian

nabob (**nay**-bob) *n Informal* a rich or important person. ▷ HISTORY Hindi *nawwāb;* see NAWAB

nacelle (nah-**sell**) *n* a streamlined enclosure on an aircraft, esp. one housing an engine. ▷ HISTORY French: small boat

nacho *n, pl* **nachos** *Mexican cookery* a snack of a piece of tortilla topped with cheese, peppers, etc.

nacre (**nay**-ker) *n* mother-of-pearl. ▷ HISTORY Arabic *naqqārah* shell, drum ▶ **nacreous** *adj*

nadir *n* **1** the point in the sky directly below an observer and opposite the zenith. **2** the lowest or worst point of anything: *I had touched the very nadir of despair.* ▷ HISTORY Arabic *nazīr as-samt,* literally: opposite the zenith

naevus *or US* **nevus** (**nee**-vuss) *n, pl* **-vi** a birthmark or mole. ▷ HISTORY Latin

naff *adj Brit slang* in poor taste: *naff frocks and trouser suits.* ▷ HISTORY perhaps back slang from *fan,* short for FANNY ▶ **naffness** *n*

nag[1] *vb* **nagging, nagged** **1** to scold or find fault constantly. **2 nag at** to be a constant source of discomfort or worry to. ✧ *n* **3** a person who nags. ▷ HISTORY Scandinavian ▶ **nagging** *adj, n*

nag[2] *n* **1** *Often disparaging* an old horse. **2** a small riding horse. ▷ HISTORY Germanic

naiad (**nye**-ad) *n, pl* **naiads** *or* **naiades** (**nye**-ad-deez) *Greek myth* a water nymph. ▷ HISTORY Greek *nāias*

nail *n* **1** a piece of metal with a point at one end and a head at the other, hit with a hammer to join two objects together. **2** the hard covering of the upper tips of the fingers and toes. **3 hit the nail on the head** to say something exactly correct or accurate. **4 on the nail** at once: *he paid always in cash, always on the nail.* ✧ *vb* **5** to attach (something) with nails. **6** *Informal* to arrest or catch (someone). ▷ HISTORY Old English *nægl*

naive (nye-**eev**) *adj* **1** innocent and gullible. **2** simple and lacking sophistication: *naive art.* ▷ HISTORY French, from Latin *nativus* native ▶ **naively** *adv*

naivety (nye-**eev**-tee) *or* **naïveté** *n* the state or quality of being naive.

naked *adj* **1** without clothes. **2** not concealed: *naked aggression.* **3** without any covering: *it was dimly lit by naked bulbs.* **4 the naked eye** the eye unassisted by any optical instrument: *difficult to spot with the naked eye.* ▷ HISTORY Old English *nacod* ▶ **nakedly** *adv* ▶ **nakedness** *n*

namby-pamby *adj Brit, Austral & NZ* excessively sentimental or prim. ▷ HISTORY nickname of Ambrose Phillips, 18th-century pastoral poet

name *n* **1** a word or term by which a person or thing is known. *RELATED ADJECTIVE* ▶ **nominal** **2** reputation, esp. a good one: *he was making a name for himself.* **3** a famous person: *she's a big name now.* **4 call someone names** *or* **a name** to insult someone by using rude words to describe him or her. **5 in name only** not possessing the powers or status implied by one's title: *a leadership in name only.* **6 in the name of a** for the sake of: *in the name of decency.* **b** by the authority of: *in the name of the law.* **7 name of the game** the most significant or important aspect of something: *survival is the name of the game in wartime.* **8 to one's name** in one's possession: *she hasn't a penny to her name.* ✧ *vb* **naming, named** **9** to give a name to. **10** to refer to by name: *he refused to name his source.* **11** to fix or specify: *he named a time for the meeting.* **12** to appoint: *she was named Journalist of the Year.* **13** to ban (an MP) from the House of Commons by mentioning him or her formally by name as being guilty of disorderly conduct. **14 name names** to cite people in order to blame or accuse them. ▷ HISTORY Old English *nama*

name day *n RC Church* the feast day of a saint whose name one bears.

name-dropping *n Informal* the practice of referring to famous people as though they were friends, in order to impress others.

nameless *adj* **1** without a name. **2** unspecified: *the individual concerned had better remain nameless.* **3** too horrible to speak about: *the nameless dread.*

namely *adv* that is to say.

nameplate *n* a small sign on or next to a door giving the occupant's name and, sometimes, profession.

namesake *n* a person or thing with the same name as another. ▷ HISTORY probably originally *for the name's sake*

nan bread *or* **naan** *n* a slightly leavened Indian bread in a large flat leaf shape. ▷ HISTORY Hindi

nancy *n, pl* **-cies** *Brit, Austral & NZ offensive slang* an effeminate or homosexual boy or man. Also called: **nancy boy** ▷ **HISTORY** from the girl's name

nanny *n, pl* **-nies 1** a woman whose job is looking after young children. ✧ *vb* **nannies, nannying, nannied 2** to nurse or look after someone else's children. **3** to be too protective towards (someone). ▷ **HISTORY** child's name for a nurse

nanny goat *n* a female goat.

nano- *combining form* denoting one thousand millionth (10^{-9}): *nanosecond.* ▷ **HISTORY** Latin *nanus* dwarf

nap[1] *n* **1** a short sleep. ✧ *vb* **napping, napped 2** to have a short sleep. **3 catch someone napping** to catch someone unprepared: *they don't want to be caught napping when the army moves again.* ▷ **HISTORY** Old English *hnappian*

nap[2] *n* the raised fibres of velvet or similar cloth. ▷ **HISTORY** probably Middle Dutch *noppe*

nap[3] *n* **1** a card game similar to whist. **2** *Horse racing* a tipster's choice for a certain winner. ✧ *vb* **napping, napped 3** *Horse racing* to name (a horse) as a likely winner. ▷ **HISTORY** shortened from *Napoleon*

napalm *n* **1** a highly inflammable jellied petrol, used in firebombs and flame-throwers. ✧ *vb* **2** to attack (people or places) with napalm. ▷ **HISTORY** *na(phthene)* + *palm(itate)* salt of palmitic acid

nape *n* the back of the neck. ▷ **HISTORY** origin unknown

naphtha *n Chem* a liquid mixture distilled from coal tar or petroleum: used as a solvent and in petrol. ▷ **HISTORY** Greek

naphthalene *n Chem* a white crystalline substance distilled from coal tar or petroleum, used in mothballs, dyes, and explosives. ▷ **HISTORY** *naphtha* + *alcohol* + *-ene*

napkin *n* **1** a piece of cloth or paper for wiping the mouth or protecting the clothes while eating. **2** same as **sanitary towel.** ▷ **HISTORY** Latin *mappa* cloth

nappy *n, pl* **-pies** *Brit & NZ* a piece of soft absorbent material, usually disposable, wrapped around the waist and between the legs of a baby to absorb its urine and excrement. ▷ **HISTORY** from *napkin*

narcissism *n* an exceptional interest in or admiration for oneself. ▷ **HISTORY** after *Narcissus,* a youth in Greek mythology, who fell in love with his reflection ▶ **narcissistic** *adj*

narcissus (nahr-**siss**-uss) *n, pl* **-cissi** (-**siss**-eye) a yellow, orange, or white flower related to the daffodil. ▷ **HISTORY** Greek *narkissos,* perhaps from *narkē* numbness, because of narcotic properties attributed to the plant

narcosis *n* unconsciousness caused by a narcotic or general anaesthetic. ▷ **HISTORY** Greek *narkē* numbness

narcotic *n* **1** a drug, such as opium or morphine, that produces numbness and drowsiness, used medicinally but addictive. ✧ *adj* **2** of narcotics or narcosis. ▷ **HISTORY** Greek *narkē* numbness

nark *Slang* ✧ *vb* **1** to annoy. ✧ *n* **2** an informer or spy: *copper's nark.* **3** *Brit* someone who complains in an irritating or whining manner. ▷ **HISTORY** probably from Romany *nāk* nose

narky *adj* **narkier, narkiest** *Slang* irritable, complaining, or sarcastic.

narrate *vb* **-rating, -rated 1** to tell (a story); relate. **2** to speak the words accompanying and telling what is happening in a film or TV programme. ▷ **HISTORY** Latin *narrare* to recount

narration *n* **1** a narrating. **2** a narrated account or story.

narrative *n* **1** an account of events. **2** the part of a literary work that relates events. ✧ *adj* **3** telling a story. **4** of narration.

narrative genre *n Literature* a form of writing or speech in which the writer or speaker tells a story.

narrative voice *n Literature* the style or character of the person telling the story or relating events in a work of literature.

narrator *n Literature* **1** a person telling a story. **2** (in novels) the fictional character or authorial voice relating events.

narrow *adj* **1** small in breadth in comparison to length. **2** limited in range, extent, or outlook: *a narrow circle of academics.* **3** with little margin: *a narrow advantage.* ✧ *vb* **4** to make or become narrow. **5 narrow down** to restrict or limit: *the search can be narrowed down to a single room.* ✧ See also **narrows.** ▷ **HISTORY** Old English *nearu* ▶ **narrowly** *adv* ▶ **narrowness** *n*

narrow boat *n Brit* a long bargelike canal boat.

narrow-minded *adj* bigoted, intolerant, or prejudiced. ▶ **narrow-mindedness** *n*

narrows *pl n* a narrow part of a strait, river, or current.

narwhal *n* an arctic whale with a long spiral tusk. ▷ **HISTORY** Old Norse *nāhvalr,* from *nār* corpse + *hvalr* whale

NASA (in the US) National Aeronautics and Space Administration.

nasal *adj* **1** of the nose. **2** (of a sound) pronounced with air passing through the nose. **3** (of a voice) characterized by nasal sounds. ▷ **HISTORY** Latin *nasus* nose ▶ **nasally** *adv*

nascent *adj Formal* starting to grow or develop. ▷ **HISTORY** Latin *nasci* to be born

nastic movement *n Physiol* a response of plant parts that is independent of the direction of the external stimulus.

nasturtium *n* a plant with yellow, red, or orange trumpet-shaped flowers. ▷ **HISTORY** Latin: kind of cress

nasty *adj* **-tier, -tiest 1** unpleasant: *a nasty odour.* **2** dangerous or painful: *a nasty burn.* **3** (of a person) spiteful or ill-natured. ✧ *n, pl* **-ties 4** something unpleasant: *video nasties.* ▷ **HISTORY** probably related to Dutch *nestig* dirty ▶ **nastily** *adv* ▶ **nastiness** *n*

nat. **1** national. **2** nationalist.

natal (**nay**-tl) *adj* of or relating to birth. ▷ **HISTORY** Latin *natalis* of one's birth

natality *n Statistics chiefly US* same as **birth rate**.

nation *n* **1** a large body of people of one or more cultures or races, organized into a single state: *a major industrialized nation.* **2** *Ethnography* a federation of Native American tribes.
▷ HISTORY Latin *natio* birth, tribe

national *adj* **1** of or serving a nation as a whole. **2** characteristic of a particular nation: *the national character.* ✧ *n* **3** a citizen of a particular country: *Belgian nationals.* **4** a national newspaper.
▸ **nationally** *adv*

national anthem *n* a patriotic song adopted by a nation for use on public occasions.

National Curriculum *n* (in England and Wales) the curriculum of subjects taught in state schools since 1989.

national debt *n* the total outstanding borrowings of a nation's central government.

National Estate *n* **the National Estate** Australia's national inventory of places of natural or cultural interest to be protected for the future.

national grid *n Brit & NZ* **1** a network of high-voltage power lines linking major electric power stations. **2** the arrangement of vertical and horizontal lines on an ordnance survey map.

National Health Service *n* (in Britain) the system of national medical services financed mainly by taxation.

national insurance *n* (in Britain) state insurance based on contributions from employees and employers, providing payments to the unemployed, the sick, and the retired.

nationalism *n* **1** a policy of national independence. **2** patriotism, sometimes to an excessive degree. ▸ **nationalist** *n, adj*
▸ **nationalistic** *adj*

nationality *n, pl* **-ties 1** the fact of being a citizen of a particular nation. **2** a group of people of the same race: *young men of all nationalities.*

nationalize *or* **-ise** *vb* **-izing, -ized** *or* **-ising, -ised** to put (an industry or a company) under state control. ▸ **nationalization** *or* **-isation** *n*

national park *n* an area of countryside protected by a national government for its scenic or environmental importance.

national service *n Chiefly Brit* compulsory military service.

National Socialism *n German history* the doctrines and practices of the Nazis, involving the supremacy of Hitler, anti-Semitism, state control of the economy, and national expansion. ▸ **National Socialist** *n, adj*

national superannuation *n NZ* a government pension paid to people of 65 years and over; retirement pension.

nation-state *n Politics* an independent state inhabited by the people of one nation only.

nationwide *adj* covering or available to the whole of a nation.

native *adj* **1** relating to a place where a person was born: *native land.* **2** born in a specified place: *a native New Yorker.* **3 native to** originating in: *a plant native to alpine regions.* **4** natural or inborn: *native genius.* **5** relating to the original inhabitants of a country: *archaeology may uncover magnificent native artefacts.* **6 go native** (of a settler) to adopt the lifestyle of the local population. ✧ *n* **7** a person born in a specified place: *a native of Palermo.* **8** an indigenous animal or plant: *the saffron crocus is a native of Asia Minor.* **9** a member of the original race of a country, as opposed to colonial immigrants.
▷ HISTORY Latin *nativus* innate, natural, from *nasci* to be born

Native American *n* same as **American Indian**.

native bear *n Austral* same as **koala**.

native companion *n Austral* same as **brolga**.

native dog *n Austral* a dingo.

native title *n Austral Law* land title that recognizes the indigenous inhabitants as the rightful owners of the land.

nativity *n, pl* **-ties** birth or origin. ▷ HISTORY Late Latin *nativitas* birth

Nativity *n Christianity* **1** the birth of Jesus Christ. **2** the feast of Christmas celebrating this.

NATO *or* **Nato** North Atlantic Treaty Organization: an international organization established for purposes of collective security.

natter *Brit & NZ informal* ✧ *vb* **1** to talk idly and at length. ✧ *n* **2** a long idle chat. ▷ HISTORY dialect *gnatter* to grumble, imitative

natterjack *n* a greyish-brown toad with reddish warty lumps. ▷ HISTORY origin unknown

natty *adj* **-tier, -tiest** *Informal* smart and spruce.
▷ HISTORY dialect *net* neat ▸ **nattily** *adv*

natural *adj* **1** as is normal or to be expected: *the natural consequence.* **2** genuine or spontaneous. **3** of, according to, existing in, or produced by nature: *natural disasters.* **4** not acquired; inborn: *their natural enthusiasm.* **5** not created by human beings. **6** not synthetic: *natural fibres such as wool.* **7** (of a parent) not adoptive. **8** (of a child) illegitimate. **9** *Music* not sharp or flat: *F natural.* ✧ *n* **10** *Informal* a person with an inborn talent or skill: *she's a natural at bridge.* **11** *Music* a note that is neither sharp nor flat. ▸ **naturalness** *n*

natural gas *n* a gaseous mixture, consisting mainly of methane, found below ground; used widely as a fuel.

natural hazard *n* any natural event such as an earthquake, hurricane, flood, forest fire, or outbreak of disease that could threaten the lives and livelihood of those caught up in it.

natural history *n* the study of animals and plants in the wild.

naturalism *n* a movement in art and literature advocating detailed realism. ▸ **naturalistic** *adj*

naturalist *n* **1** a student of natural history. **2** a person who advocates or practises naturalism.

naturalize *or* **-ise** *vb* **-izing, -ized** *or* **-ising, -ised** **1** to give citizenship to (a person born in another country). **2** to introduce (a plant or animal) into another region. **3** to cause (a foreign word or custom) to be adopted.

natural justice *n Law* the principles and procedures that govern the adjudication of disputes between people or organizations, chief

A B C D E F G H I J K L M N O P Q R S T U V W X Y Z

among which are that the adjudication should be unbiased and given in good faith, and that each party should have equal access to the tribunal and should be aware of arguments and documents adduced by the other.

natural law *n Philosophy* **1** an ethical belief or system of beliefs supposed to be inherent in human nature and discoverable by reason rather than revelation. **2** a law of nature. **3** the philosophical doctrine that the authority of the legal system or of certain laws derives from their justifiability by reason, and that a legal system which cannot be so justified has no authority.

natural logarithm *n* a logarithm which has the irrational number e as a base.

naturally *adv* **1** of course; surely. **2** in a natural or normal way. **3** instinctively.

natural number *n* a positive integer, such as 1, 2, 3, 4, etc.

natural philosophy *n Old-fashioned* physics.

natural radiation *n Physics* radiation that occurs freely in nature.

natural resources *pl n* naturally occurring materials such as coal, oil, and minerals.

natural science *n* any of the sciences dealing with the study of the physical world, such as biology, physics, chemistry, and geology.

natural selection *n* a process by which only those creatures and plants well adapted to their environment survive.

natural wastage *n Chiefly Brit* a reduction in the number of employees through not replacing those who leave, rather than by dismissing employees or making them redundant.

nature *n* **1** the whole system of the existence, forces, and events of the physical world that are not controlled by human beings. **2** fundamental or essential qualities: *the theory and nature of science.* **3** kind or sort: *problems of a financial nature.* **4** temperament or personality: *an amiable and pleasant nature.* **5 by nature** essentially: *he was by nature a cautious man.* **6 in the nature of** essentially; by way of: *it was in the nature of a debate rather than an argument.* ▷ **HISTORY** Latin *natura,* from *nasci* to be born

nature reserve *n* an area of land that is preserved and managed in order to protect its animal and plant life.

nature study *n* the study of animals and plants by direct observation.

naturism *n* same as **nudism.** ▶ **naturist** *n, adj*

naught *n* **1** *Archaic or literary* nothing. **2** *Chiefly US* the figure 0. ✧ *adv* **3** *Archaic or literary* not at all: *I care naught.* ▷ **HISTORY** Old English *nāwiht*

naughty *adj* **-tier, -tiest 1** (of children) mischievous or disobedient. **2** mildly indecent: *naughty lingerie.* ▷ **HISTORY** (originally: needy, poor) from *naught* ▶ **naughtily** *adv* ▶ **naughtiness** *n*

nausea (**naw**-zee-a) *n* **1** the feeling of being about to vomit. **2** disgust. ▷ **HISTORY** Greek: seasickness, from *naus* ship

nauseate *vb* **-ating, -ated 1** to cause (someone) to feel sick. **2** to arouse feelings of disgust in (someone). ▶ **nauseating** *adj*

nauseous *adj* **1** as if about to be sick: *he felt nauseous.* **2** sickening.

nautical *adj* of the sea, ships, or navigation. ▷ **HISTORY** Greek *nautikos,* from *naus* ship

nautical mile *n* a unit of length, used in navigation, standardized as 6080 feet.

nautilus *n, pl* **-luses** *or* **-li** a sea creature with a shell and tentacles. ▷ **HISTORY** Greek *nautilos* sailor

naval *adj* of or relating to a navy or ships. ▷ **HISTORY** Latin *navis* ship

nave[1] *n* the long central part of a church. ▷ **HISTORY** Latin *navis* ship, from the similarity in shape

nave[2] *n* the hub of a wheel. ▷ **HISTORY** Old English *nafu, nafa*

navel *n* the slight hollow in the centre of the abdomen, where the umbilical cord was attached. ▷ **HISTORY** Old English *nafela*

navel orange *n* a sweet orange that has a navel-like hollow at the top.

navigable *adj* **1** wide, deep, or safe enough to be sailed through. **2** able to be steered.

navigate *vb* **-gating, -gated 1** to direct or plot the course or position of a ship or aircraft. **2** to travel over or through safely: *your cousin, who's just navigated the Amazon.* **3** *Informal* to direct (oneself) carefully or safely: *he navigated his unsteady way to the bar.* **4** (of a passenger in a vehicle) to read the map and give directions to the driver. ▷ **HISTORY** Latin *navis* ship + *agere* to drive ▶ **navigation** *n* ▶ **navigational** *adj* ▶ **navigator** *n*

navvy *n, pl* **-vies** *Brit & Austral informal* a labourer on a building site or road. ▷ **HISTORY** from *navigator* builder of a *navigation* (in the sense: canal)

navy *n, pl* **-vies 1** the branch of a country's armed services comprising warships with their crews, and all their supporting services. **2** the warships of a nation. ✧ *adj* **3** short for **navy-blue.** ▷ **HISTORY** Latin *navis* ship

navy-blue *adj* very dark blue. ▷ **HISTORY** from the colour of the British naval uniform

nawab (na-**wahb**) *n* (formerly) a Muslim ruler or powerful landowner in India. ▷ **HISTORY** Hindi *nawwāb,* from Arabic *nuwwāb,* plural of *na'ib* viceroy

nay *interj* **1** *Old-fashioned* no. ✧ *n* **2** a person who votes against a motion. ✧ *adv* **3** used for emphasis: *I want, nay, need to know.* ▷ **HISTORY** Old Norse *nei*

Nazarene *n* **1 the Nazarene** Jesus Christ. **2** *Old-fashioned* a Christian. **3** a person from Nazareth, a town in N Israel. ✧ *adj* **4** of Nazareth.

Nazi *n, pl* **-zis 1** a member of the fascist National Socialist German Workers' Party, which came to power in Germany in 1933 under Adolf Hitler. ✧ *adj* **2** of or relating to the Nazis. ▷ **HISTORY** German, phonetic spelling of the first two syllables of *Nationalsozialist* National Socialist ▶ **Nazism** *n*

nb *Cricket* no-ball.

Nb *Chem* niobium.

NB 1 New Brunswick. 2 note well. ▷ HISTORY Latin *nota bene*

NC 1 North Carolina. 2 *Brit education* National Curriculum.

NCO noncommissioned officer.

Nd *Chem* neodymium.

ND North Dakota.

Ne *Chem* neon.

NE 1 Nebraska. 2 northeast(ern).

ne- *combining form* same as **neo-:** *Nearctic.*

Neanderthal (nee-**ann**-der-tahl) *adj* 1 of a type of primitive man that lived in Europe before 12,000 BC. 2 *Informal* with excessively conservative views: *his notoriously Neanderthal attitude to women.* ▷ HISTORY after *Neandertal,* a valley in Germany

neap *n* short for **neap tide**. ▷ HISTORY Old English, as in *nēpflōd* neap tide

Neapolitan *adj* 1 of Naples, a city in SW Italy. ✧ *n* 2 a person from Naples. ▷ HISTORY Greek *Neapolis* new town

neap tide *n* a tide that occurs at the first and last quarter of the moon when there is the smallest rise and fall in tidal level.

near *prep* 1 at or to a place or time not far away from. ✧ *adv* 2 at or to a place or time not far away. 3 short for **nearly:** *the pain damn near crippled him.* ✧ *adj* 4 at or in a place or time not far away: *in the near future.* 5 closely connected or intimate: *a near relation.* 6 almost being the thing specified: *a mood of near rebellion.* ✧ *vb* 7 to draw close (to): *the participants are nearing agreement.* ✧ *n* 8 the left side of a horse or vehicle. ▷ HISTORY Old English *nēar,* comparative of *nēah* close ▶ **nearness** *n*

nearby *adj, adv* not far away.

Near East *n* same as **Middle East**.

nearly *adv* 1 almost. 2 **not nearly** nowhere near: *it's not nearly as easy as it looks.*

near-market research *n* scientific research that is not to develop a specific product but which has commercial value.

near miss *n* 1 any attempt that just fails to succeed. 2 an incident in which two aircraft or vehicles narrowly avoid collision. 3 a bomb or shot that does not quite hit the target.

nearside *n* 1 *Chiefly Brit* the side of a vehicle that is nearer the kerb. 2 the left side of an animal.

near-sighted *adj* same as **short-sighted**.

neat *adj* 1 clean and tidy. 2 smoothly or competently done: *a neat answer.* 3 (of alcoholic drinks) undiluted. 4 *Slang, chiefly US & Canad* admirable; excellent. ▷ HISTORY Latin *nitidus* clean ▶ **neatly** *adv* ▶ **neatness** *n*

neaten *vb* to make neat.

neb *n Archaic or dialect* the beak of a bird or the nose of an animal. ▷ HISTORY Old English *nebb*

nebula (**neb**-yew-la) *n, pl* **-lae** (-lee) *Astron* a hazy cloud of particles and gases. ▷ HISTORY Latin: mist, cloud ▶ **nebular** *adj*

nebulize *or* **-ise** *vb* **-izing, -ized** *or* **-ising, -ised** to turn (a liquid) into a fine spray.

nebulizer *or* **-iser** *n* a device which turns a drug from a liquid into a fine spray which can be inhaled.

nebulous *adj* vague and unclear: *a nebulous concept.*

NEC (in Britain) National Executive Committee.

necessaries *pl n* essential items: *the necessaries and comforts of life.*

necessarily *adv* 1 as a certainty: *the factors were not necessarily connected with one another.* 2 inevitably: *tourism is an industry that has a necessarily close connection with governments.*

necessary *adj* 1 needed in order to obtain the desired result: *the necessary skills.* 2 certain or unavoidable: *the necessary consequences.* ✧ *n* 3 **the necessary** *Informal* the money required for a particular purpose. 4 **do the necessary** *Informal* to do something that is necessary in a particular situation. ✧ See also **necessaries**. ▷ HISTORY Latin *necessarius* indispensable

necessitate *vb* **-tating, -tated** to compel or require.

necessitous *adj Literary* very needy.

necessity *n, pl* **-ties** 1 a set of circumstances that inevitably requires a certain result: *the necessity to maintain safety standards.* 2 something needed: *the daily necessities.* 3 great poverty. 4 **of necessity** inevitably.

neck *n* 1 the part of the body connecting the head with the rest of the body. 2 the part of a garment around the neck. 3 the long narrow part of a bottle or violin. 4 the length of a horse's head and neck taken as the distance by which one horse beats another in a race: *to win by a neck.* 5 *Informal* impudence. 6 **by a neck** by a very small margin: *she held on to win by a neck.* 7 **get it in the neck** *Informal* to be reprimanded or punished severely. 8 **neck and neck** absolutely level in a race or competition. 9 **neck of the woods** *Informal* a particular area: *how did they get to this neck of the woods?* 10 **stick one's neck out** *Informal* to risk criticism or ridicule by speaking one's mind. 11 **up to one's neck in** *Informal* to be deeply involved in: *he was up to his neck in the scandal.* ✧ *vb* 12 *Informal* (of two people) to kiss each other passionately. ▷ HISTORY Old English *hnecca*

neckerchief *n* a piece of cloth worn tied round the neck. ▷ HISTORY *neck* + *kerchief*

necklace *n* 1 a decorative piece of jewellery worn round the neck. 2 (in South Africa) a tyre soaked in petrol, placed round a person's neck, and set on fire in order to burn the person to death.

neckline *n* the shape or position of the upper edge of a dress or top.

necktie *n US* same as **tie** (sense 5).

necromancy (**neck**-rome-man-see) *n* 1 communication with the dead. 2 sorcery. ▷ HISTORY Greek *nekros* corpse + *mantis* prophet ▶ **necromancer** *n*

necrophilia *n* sexual attraction for or sexual intercourse with dead bodies. ▷ HISTORY Greek *nekros* corpse + *philos* loving

necropolis (neck-**rop**-pol-liss) *n* a cemetery. ▷ HISTORY Greek *nekros* dead + *polis* city

necrosis *n* 1 *Biol, med* the death of cells in the body, as from an interruption of the blood supply.

2 *Bot* death of plant tissue due to disease or frost. ▷ **HISTORY** Greek *nekros* corpse ▶ **necrotic** *adj*

nectar *n* **1** a sugary fluid produced by flowers and collected by bees. **2** *Classical myth* the drink of the gods. **3** any delicious drink. ▷ **HISTORY** Greek *nektar*

nectarine *n* a smooth-skinned variety of peach. ▷ **HISTORY** apparently from *nectar*

NEDC (formerly) National Economic Development Council. Also (informal): **Neddy**

née *prep* indicating the maiden name of a married woman: *Jane Gray (née Blandish).* ▷ **HISTORY** French, past participle (feminine) of *naître* to be born

need *vb* **1** to require or be in want of: *they desperately need success.* **2** to be obliged: *the government may need to impose a statutory levy.* **3** used to express necessity or obligation and does not add -s when used with singular nouns or pronouns: *need he go?* ✧ *n* **4** the condition of lacking something: *he has need of a new coat.* **5** a requirement: *the need for closer economic co-operation.* **6** necessity: *there was no need for an explanation.* **7** poverty or destitution: *the money will go to those areas where need is greatest.* **8** distress: *help has been given to those in need.* ✧ See also **needs**. ▷ **HISTORY** Old English *nēad, nied*

needful *adj* **1** necessary or required. ✧ *n* **2 the needful** *Informal* what is necessary, usually money.

needle *n* **1** a pointed slender piece of metal with a hole in it through which thread is passed for sewing. **2** a long pointed rod used in knitting. **3** same as **stylus**. **4** *Med* the long hollow pointed part of a hypodermic syringe, which is inserted into the body. **5** a pointer on the scale of a measuring instrument. **6** a long narrow stiff leaf: *pine needles.* **7** *Brit informal* intense rivalry or ill-feeling in a sports match. **8** short for **magnetic needle**. **9 have** *or* **get the needle** *Brit informal* to be annoyed. ✧ *vb* **-dling, -dled 10** *Informal* to goad or provoke. ▷ **HISTORY** Old English *nǣdl*

needlecord *n* a fine-ribbed corduroy fabric.

needlepoint *n* **1** embroidery done on canvas. **2** lace made by needles on a paper pattern.

needless *adj* not required; unnecessary. ▶ **needlessly** *adv*

needlework *n* sewing and embroidery.

needs *adv* **1** necessarily: *they must needs be admired.* ✧ *pl n* **2** what is required.

needy *adj* **needier, neediest** in need of financial support.

ne'er *adv Poetic* never.

ne'er-do-well *n* **1** an irresponsible or lazy person. ✧ *adj* **2** useless; worthless.

nefarious (nif-**fair**-ee-uss) *adj Literary* evil; wicked. ▷ **HISTORY** Latin *ne* not + *fas* divine law

neg. negative.

negate *vb* **-gating, -gated 1** to cause to have no value or effect: *his prejudices largely negate his accomplishments.* **2** to deny the existence of. ▷ **HISTORY** Latin *negare*

negation *n* **1** the opposite or absence of something. **2** a negative thing or condition. **3** a negating.

negative *adj* **1** expressing a refusal or denial: *a negative response.* **2** lacking positive qualities, such as enthusiasm or optimism. **3** *Med* indicating absence of the condition for which a test was made. **4** *Physics* **a** (of an electric charge) having the same electrical charge as an electron. **b** (of a body or system) having a negative electric charge; having an excess of electrons. **5** same as **minus** (sense 4). **6** measured in a direction opposite to that regarded as positive. **7** short for **electronegative**. **8** of a photographic negative. ✧ *n* **9** a statement or act of denial or refusal. **10** *Photog* a piece of photographic film, exposed and developed, bearing an image with a reversal of tones or colours, from which positive prints are made. **11** a word or expression with a negative meaning, such as *not*. **12** a quantity less than zero. **13 in the negative** indicating denial or refusal. ▶ **negatively** *adv*

negative equity *n* the holding of a property of fallen value which is worth less than the amount of mortgage still unpaid.

negativism *n* a tendency to be unconstructively critical. ▶ **negativist** *n, adj*

neglect *vb* **1** to fail to give due care or attention to: *she had neglected her child.* **2** to fail (to do something) through carelessness: *he neglected to greet his guests.* **3** to disregard: *he neglected his duty.* ✧ *n* **4** lack of due care or attention: *the city had a look of shabbiness and neglect.* **5** the state of being neglected. ▷ **HISTORY** Latin *neglegere*

neglectful *adj* not paying enough care or attention: *abusive and neglectful parents.*

negligee (**neg**-lee-zhay) *n* a woman's light, usually lace-trimmed dressing gown. ▷ **HISTORY** French

negligence *n* neglect or carelessness. ▶ **negligent** *adj* ▶ **negligently** *adv*

negligible *adj* so small or unimportant as to be not worth considering.

negotiable *adj* **1** able to be changed or agreed by discussion. **2** (of a bill of exchange or promissory note) legally transferable.

negotiate *vb* **-ating, -ated 1** to talk with others in order to reach (an agreement). **2** to succeed in passing round or over (a place or a problem). ▷ **HISTORY** Latin *negotium* business, from *nec* not + *otium* leisure ▶ **negotiation** *n* ▶ **negotiator** *n*

Negro *Old-fashioned* ✧ *n, pl* **-groes 1** a member of any of the Black peoples originating in Africa. ✧ *adj* **2** of Negroes. ▷ **HISTORY** Latin *niger* black

Negroid *adj* of or relating to the Negro race.

neigh *n* **1** the high-pitched sound made by a horse. ✧ *vb* **2** to make this sound. ▷ **HISTORY** Old English *hnǣgan*

neighbour *or US* **neighbor** *n* **1** a person who lives near or next to another. **2** a person, thing, or country near or next to another. ▷ **HISTORY** Old English *nēah* near + *būr, gebūr* dweller

neighbourhood *or US* **neighborhood** *n* **1** a district where people live. **2** the immediate environment; surroundings. **3** the people in a district. **4 in the neighbourhood of**

approximately. ✧ *adj* **5** in and for a district: *our neighbourhood cinema.*

neighbouring *or US* **neighboring** *adj* situated nearby: *the neighbouring island.*

neighbourly *or US* **neighborly** *adj* kind, friendly, and helpful.

neither *adj* **1** not one nor the other (of two): *neither enterprise went well.* ✧ *pron* **2** not one nor the other (of two): *neither completed the full term.* ✧ *conj* **3 a** (used preceding alternatives joined by *nor*) not: *sparing neither strength nor courage.* **b** same as **nor** (sense 2). ✧ *adv* **4** *Not standard* same as **either** (sense 4). ▷ HISTORY Old English *nāwther*

> **WORD TIP**
> A verb following a compound subject that uses *neither...(nor)* should be in the singular if both subjects are in the singular: *neither Jack nor John has done the work.*

nelson *n* a wrestling hold in which a wrestler places his arm or arms under his opponent's arm or arms from behind and exerts pressure with his palms on the back of his opponent's neck. ▷ HISTORY from a proper name

nematode *n* a slender unsegmented cylindrical worm. ▷ HISTORY Greek *nēma* thread + *eidos* shape

nemesis (**nem**-miss-iss) *n, pl* **-ses** (-seez) a means of retribution or vengeance. ▷ HISTORY Greek *nemein* to distribute what is due

neo- *combining form* new, recent, or a modern form of: *neoclassicism; neo-Nazi.* ▷ HISTORY Greek *neos* new

neoclassicism *n* a late 18th- and early 19th-century style of art and architecture, based on ancient Roman and Greek models. ▸ **neoclassical** *adj*

neocolonialism *n* political control wielded by one country over another through control of its economy. ▸ **neocolonial** *adj*

neodymium *n Chem* a toxic silvery-white metallic element of the lanthanide series. Symbol: Nd. ▷ HISTORY NEO- + *didymium,* a compound originally thought to be an element

Neolithic *adj* of the period that lasted in Europe from about 4000 to 2400 BC, characterized by primitive farming and the use of polished stone and flint tools and weapons. ▷ HISTORY NEO- + Greek *lithos* stone

neologism (nee-**ol**-a-jiz-zum) *n* a newly coined word, or an established word used in a new sense. ▷ HISTORY NEO- + Greek *logos* word

neon *n* **1** *Chem* a colourless odourless rare gas, used in illuminated signs and lights. Symbol: Ne. ✧ *adj* **2** of or illuminated by neon: *a flashing neon sign.* ▷ HISTORY Greek: new

neonatal *adj* relating to the first few weeks of a baby's life. ▸ **neonate** *n*

neon light *n* a glass tube containing neon, which gives a pink or red glow when a voltage is applied.

neophyte *n Formal* **1** a beginner. **2** a person newly converted to a religious faith. **3** a novice in a religious order. ▷ HISTORY Greek *neos* new + *phuton* a plant

NEP *History* New Economic Policy: an economic programme in the former Soviet Union from 1921 to 1928 that allowed limited private ownership and commerce.

Nepali (nip-**paw**-lee) *or* **Nepalese** (nep-pal-**leez**) *adj* **1** of Nepal. ✧ *n* **2** (*pl* **-pali, -palis** *or* **-palese**) a person from Nepal. **3** the language of Nepal.

nephew *n* a son of one's sister or brother. ▷ HISTORY Latin *nepos*

nephritis (nif-**frite**-tiss) *n* inflammation of the kidney. ▷ HISTORY Greek *nephros* kidney

nepotism (**nep**-a-tiz-zum) *n* favouritism shown to relatives and friends by those with power. ▷ HISTORY Italian *nepote* nephew

Neptune *n* **1** the Roman god of the sea. **2** the eighth planet from the sun.

neptunium *n Chem* a silvery metallic element synthesized in the production of plutonium. Symbol: Np. ▷ HISTORY after *Neptune,* the planet

nerd *or* **nurd** *n Slang* **1** a boring or unpopular person, esp. one who is obsessed with a particular subject: *a computer nerd.* **2** a stupid and feeble person. ▷ HISTORY origin unknown ▸ **nerdish** *or* **nurdish** *adj*

nervate *adj* (of leaves) with veins.

nerve *n* **1** a cordlike bundle of fibres that conducts impulses between the brain and other parts of the body. **2** bravery and determination. **3** *Informal* impudence: *you've got a nerve!* **4 lose one's nerve** to lose self-confidence and become afraid about what one is doing. **5 strain every nerve** to make every effort (to do something). ✧ *vb* **nerving, nerved 6 nerve oneself** to prepare oneself (to do something difficult or unpleasant). ✧ See also **nerves.** ▷ HISTORY Latin *nervus*

nerve cell *n* same as **neuron.**

nerve centre *n* **1** a place from which a system or organization is controlled. **2** a group of nerve cells associated with a specific function.

nerve gas *n* a poisonous gas which affects the nervous system.

nerveless *adj* **1** (of fingers or hands) without feeling; numb. **2** (of a person) fearless.

nerve-racking *or* **nerve-wracking** *adj* very distressing or harrowing.

nerves *pl n Informal* **1** anxiety or tension: *nerves can often be the cause of wedding-day hitches.* **2** the ability or inability to remain calm in a difficult situation: *his nerves are in a shocking state.* **3 get on someone's nerves** to irritate someone.

nervous *adj* **1** apprehensive or worried. **2** excitable; highly strung. **3** of or relating to the nerves: *the nervous system.* ▸ **nervously** *adv* ▸ **nervousness** *n*

nervous breakdown *n* a mental illness in which the sufferer ceases to function properly, and experiences symptoms including tiredness, anxiety, and deep depression.

nervous system *n* the brain, spinal column, and nerves, which together control thought, feeling, and movement. See **neuron.**

nervy *adj* **nervier, nerviest** *Brit & Austral informal* excitable or nervous.

ness *n Brit* a headland or cape. ▷ **HISTORY** Old English *næs*

-ness *n suffix* indicating state, condition, or quality: *greatness; selfishness.* ▷ **HISTORY** Old English *-nes*

nest *n* **1** a place or structure in which birds or other animals lay eggs or give birth to young. **2** a cosy or secluded place. **3** a set of things of graduated sizes designed to fit together: *a nest of tables.* ✧ *vb* **4** to make or inhabit a nest. **5** (of a set of objects) to fit one inside another. **6** *Computers* to position (data) within other data at different ranks or levels. ▷ **HISTORY** Old English

nest egg *n* a fund of money kept in reserve.

nestle *vb* **-tling, -tled 1** to snuggle or cuddle closely. **2** to be in a sheltered position. ▷ **HISTORY** Old English *nestlian*

nestling *n* a young bird not yet able to fly.

net[1] *n* **1** a very fine fabric made from intersecting strands of material with a space between each strand. **2** a piece of net, used to protect or hold things or to trap animals. **3** (in certain sports) a strip of net over which the ball or shuttlecock must be hit. **4** the goal in soccer or hockey. **5** a strategy intended to trap people: *innocent fans were caught in the police net.* **6** *Maths* the shape that a three-dimensional figure would make if it were laid out flat. **7** *Informal* short for **Internet.** ✧ *vb* **netting, netted 8** to catch (a fish or other animal) in a net. ▷ **HISTORY** Old English *net(t)*

net[2] *or* **nett** *adj* **1** remaining after all deductions, as for taxes and expenses: *net income.* **2** (of weight) excluding the weight of wrapping or container. **3** final or conclusive: *the net effect.* ✧ *vb* **netting, netted 4** to yield or earn as a clear profit. ▷ **HISTORY** French: neat

netball *n* a team game, usually played by women, in which a ball has to be thrown through a net hanging from a ring at the top of a pole.

nether *adj Old-fashioned* lower or under: *nether regions.* ▷ **HISTORY** Old English *nithera*, literally: further down

nethermost *adj* lowest.

net profit *n* gross profit minus all operating expenses such as wages and overheads.

nett *adj, vb* same as **net**[2].

netting *n* a fabric or structure made of net.

nettle *n* **1** a plant with stinging hairs on the leaves. **2 grasp the nettle** to attempt something unpleasant with boldness and courage. ▷ **HISTORY** Old English *netele*

nettled *adj* irritated or annoyed.

nettle rash *n* a skin condition, usually caused by an allergy, in which itchy red or white raised patches appear.

network *n* **1** a system of intersecting lines, roads, veins, etc. **2** an interconnecting group or system: *a network of sympathizers and safe houses.* **3** *Radio, television* a group of broadcasting stations that all transmit the same programme at the same time. **4** *Electronics, computers* a system of interconnected components or circuits. ✧ *vb* **5** *Radio, television* to broadcast (a programme) over a network.

neural *adj* of a nerve or the nervous system.

neuralgia *n* severe pain along a nerve. ▶ **neuralgic** *adj*

neuritis (nyoor-**rite**-tiss) *n* inflammation of a nerve or nerves, often causing pain and loss of function in the affected part.

neurology *n Med* the scientific study of the nervous system. ▶ **neurological** *adj* ▶ **neurologist** *n*

neuron *or* **neurone** *n* a cell specialized to conduct nerve impulses. ▷ **HISTORY** Greek

neurosis (nyoor-**oh**-siss) *n, pl* **-ses** (-seez) a mental disorder producing hysteria, anxiety, depression, or obsessive behaviour.

neurosurgery *n Med* the branch of surgery concerned with the nervous system. ▶ **neurosurgeon** *n* ▶ **neurosurgical** *adj*

neurotic *adj* **1** tending to be emotionally unstable. **2** afflicted by neurosis. ✧ *n* **3** a person afflicted with a neurosis or tending to be emotionally unstable.

neuter *adj* **1** *Grammar* denoting a gender of nouns which are neither male nor female. **2** (of animals and plants) sexually underdeveloped. ✧ *n* **3** *Grammar* **a** the neuter gender. **b** a neuter noun. **4** a sexually underdeveloped female insect, such as a worker bee. **5** a castrated animal. ✧ *vb* **6** to castrate (an animal). ▷ **HISTORY** Latin *ne* not + *uter* either (of two)

neutral *adj* **1** not taking any side in a war or dispute. **2** of or belonging to a neutral party or country. **3** not displaying any emotions or opinions. **4** (of a colour) not definite or striking. **5** *Chem* neither acidic nor alkaline. **6** *Physics* having zero charge or potential. ✧ *n* **7** a neutral person or nation. **8** the position of the controls of a gearbox that leaves the gears unconnected to the engine. ▷ **HISTORY** Latin *neutralis* of neuter gender ▶ **neutrality** *n*

neutralize *or* **-ise** *vb* **-izing, -ized** *or* **-ising, -ised 1** to make electrically or chemically neutral. **2** to make ineffective by counteracting. **3** to make (a country) neutral by international agreement.

neutrino (new-**tree**-no) *n, pl* **-nos** *Physics* an elementary particle with no mass or electrical charge. ▷ **HISTORY** Italian diminutive of *neutrone* neutron

neutron *n Physics* a neutral elementary particle of about the same mass as a proton. ▷ **HISTORY** from *neutral,* on the model of *electron*

neutron bomb *n* a nuclear weapon designed to kill people and animals while leaving buildings virtually undamaged.

never *adv* **1** at no time; not ever. **2** certainly not; not at all. **3** Also: **well I never!** surely not! ▷ **HISTORY** Old English *nǣfre*

> **☑ WORD TIP**
>
> In informal speech and writing, *never* can be used instead of *not* with the simple past tenses of certain verbs, for emphasis (*I never said that; I never realized how clever he was*), but this usage should be avoided in formal writing.

A B C D E F G H I J K L M N O P Q R S T U V W X Y Z

never-ending *adj* long and boring.

nevermore *adv Literary* never again.

never-never *n* **the never-never** *Informal* hire-purchase: *they are buying it on the never-never.*

never-never land *n* an imaginary idyllic place.

nevertheless *adv* in spite of that.

new *adj* **1** recently made, brought into being, or acquired: *a new car.* **2** of a kind never before existing; novel: *a new approach to monetary policy.* **3** recently discovered: *testing new drugs.* **4** recently introduced to or inexperienced in a place or situation: *new to this game.* **5** fresh; additional: *you can acquire new skills.* **6** unknown: *this is new to me.* **7** (of a cycle) beginning again: *a new era.* **8** (of crops) harvested early: *new potatoes.* **9** changed for the better: *she returned a new woman.* ✧ *adv* **10** recently, newly: *new-laid eggs.* ✧ See also **news.** ▷ HISTORY Old English *nīowe* ▶ **newish** *adj* ▶ **newness** *n*

New Age *n* **1** a philosophy, originating in the late 1980s, characterized by a belief in alternative medicine, astrology, and spiritualism. ✧ *adj* **2** of the New Age: *New Age therapies.* ▶ **New Ager** *n*

New Australian *n Austral* an Australian name for a recent immigrant, esp. one from Europe.

newbie *n Informal* a person new to a job, club, etc.

newborn *adj* recently or just born.

new chum *n Austral & NZ archaic informal* a recent British immigrant.

newcomer *n* a recent arrival or participant.

newel *n* **1** Also called: **newel post** the post at the top or bottom of a flight of stairs that supports the handrail. **2** the central pillar of a winding staircase. ▷ HISTORY Old French *nouel* knob

newfangled *adj* objectionably or unnecessarily modern. ▷ HISTORY Middle English *newefangel* liking new things

new-found *adj* newly or recently discovered.

New Jerusalem *n Christianity* heaven.

New Latin *n* the form of Latin used since the Renaissance, mainly for scientific names.

newly *adv* **1** recently. **2** again; anew.

newlyweds *pl n* a recently married couple.

new maths *n Brit* an approach to mathematics in which basic set theory is introduced at an elementary level.

new moon *n* the moon when it appears as a narrow crescent at the beginning of its cycle.

news *n* **1** important or interesting new happenings. **2** information about such events, reported in the mass media. **3 the news** a television or radio programme presenting such information. **4** interesting or important new information: *it's news to me.* **5** a person or thing widely reported in the mass media: *reggae is suddenly big news again.*

news agency *n* an organization that collects news reports and sells them to newspapers, magazines, and TV and radio stations.

newsagent *n Brit* a shopkeeper who sells newspapers and magazines.

newscast *n* a radio or television broadcast of the news. ▶ **newscaster** *n*

news conference *n* same as **press conference.**

newsflash *n* a brief item of important news, which interrupts a radio or television programme.

newsgroup *n Computers* a forum where subscribers exchange information about a specific subject by e-mail.

newsletter *n* a periodical bulletin issued to members of a group.

newspaper *n* a weekly or daily publication consisting of folded sheets and containing news, features, and advertisements.

newsprint *n* an inexpensive wood-pulp paper used for newspapers.

newsreader *n* a news announcer on radio or television.

newsreel *n* a short film with a commentary which presents current events.

newsroom *n* a room in a newspaper office or radio or television station where news is received and prepared for publication or broadcasting.

New Style *n* the present method of reckoning dates using the Gregorian calendar.

newsworthy *adj* sufficiently interesting to be reported as news.

newsy *adj* **newsier, newsiest** (of a letter) full of news.

newt *n* a small amphibious creature with a long slender body and tail and short legs.

> **WORD HISTORY**
>
> The newt owes its name to a mistake by speakers of English round about the 15th century, who wrongly understood 'an ewt' (from Old English *eveta* or *efeta*) to be 'a newt'. In some English dialects, this mistake did not happen and newts are called 'efts'. Interestingly, the opposite process can be seen to have taken place in the name of the adder: 'an adder' comes from 'a nadder', from Old English *nǣdre*, meaning 'snake'.

New Testament *n* the second part of the Christian Bible, dealing with the life and teachings of Christ and his followers.

newton *n* the SI unit of force that gives an acceleration of 1 metre per second per second to a mass of 1 kilogram. ▷ HISTORY after Sir Isaac *Newton,* scientist

new town *n* (in Britain) a town planned as a complete unit and built with government sponsorship.

New World *n* **the New World** the western hemisphere of the world, esp. the Americas.

New Year *n* the first day or days of the year in various calendars, usually a holiday.

New Zealander *n* a person from New Zealand.

next *adj* **1** immediately following: *the next generation.* **2** immediately adjoining: *in the next room.* **3** closest to in degree: *the next-best thing.* ✧ *adv* **4** at a time immediately to follow: *the patient* *to be examined next.* **5 next to a** adjacent to: *the house next to ours.* **b** following in degree: *next to my wife, I love you most.* **c** almost: *the evidence is next to totally useless.* ▷ HISTORY Old English *nēhst,* superlative of *nēah* near

next door *adj, adv* in, at, or to the adjacent house or flat.

nexus *n, pl* **nexus 1** a connection or link. **2** a connected group or series. ▷ HISTORY Latin, from *nectere* to bind

NF Newfoundland.

ngati (**nah**-tee) *n, pl* **ngati** *NZ* (occurring as part of the tribe name) a tribe or clan. ▷ HISTORY Maori

NH New Hampshire.

NHS (in Britain) National Health Service.

Ni *Chem* nickel.

NI 1 (in Britain) National Insurance. **2** Northern Ireland.

niacin *n* a vitamin of the B complex that occurs in milk, liver, and yeast. Also called: **nicotinic acid** ▷ HISTORY from *ni(cotinic) ac(id)* + *-in* denoting a chemical substance

nib *n* the writing point of a pen. ▷ HISTORY origin unknown

nibble *vb* **-bling, -bled 1** to take little bites (of). **2** to bite gently: *she nibbled at her lower lip.* ✧ *n* **3** a little bite. **4** a light hurried meal. ▷ HISTORY related to Low German *nibbelen*

nibs *n* **his** *or* **her nibs** *Slang* a mock title used of an important or self-important person. ▷ HISTORY origin unknown

NICAM near-instantaneous companding system: a technique for coding audio signals into digital form.

nice *adj* **1** pleasant. **2** kind: *it's really nice of you to worry about me.* **3** good or satisfactory: *a nice clean operation.* **4** subtle: *a nice distinction.* ▷ HISTORY Old French: simple, silly ▶ **nicely** *adv* ▶ **niceness** *n*

nicety *n, pl* **-ties 1** a subtle point: *the niceties of our arguments.* **2** a refinement or delicacy: *social niceties.* **3 to a nicety** precisely.

niche (**neesh**) *n* **1** a recess in a wall for a statue or ornament. **2** a position exactly suitable for the person occupying it: *perhaps I will find my niche in a desk job.* ✧ *adj* **3** of or aimed at a specialist group or market: *niche retailing ventures.* ▷ HISTORY Old French *nichier* to nest

nick *vb* **1** to make a small cut in. **2** *Chiefly Brit slang* to steal. **3** *Chiefly Brit slang* to arrest. ✧ *n* **4** a small notch or cut. **5** *Slang* a prison or police station. **6** *Informal* condition: *in good nick.* **7 in the nick of time** just in time. ▷ HISTORY perhaps Middle English *nocke* nock

nickel *n* **1** *Chem* a silvery-white metallic element that is often used in alloys. Symbol: Ni. **2** a US or Canadian coin worth five cents. ▷ HISTORY German *Kupfernickel* nickel ore, literally: copper demon; it was mistakenly thought to contain copper

nickelodeon *n US* an early type of jukebox. ▷ HISTORY *nickel* + *(mel)odeon*

nickel silver *n* an alloy containing copper, zinc, and nickel.

nicker *n, pl* **nicker** *Brit slang* a pound sterling. ▷ HISTORY origin unknown

nickname *n* **1** a familiar, pet, or derisory name given to a person or place. ✧ *vb* **-naming, -named 2** to call (a person or place) by a nickname: *Gaius Caesar Augustus Germanicus, nicknamed Caligula.* ▷ HISTORY mistaken division of *an ekename* an additional name

nickpoint *n* a variant spelling (esp. US) of **knickpoint**.

nicotine *n* a poisonous alkaloid found in tobacco. ▷ HISTORY after J. *Nicot,* who introduced tobacco into France ▶ **nicotinic** *adj*

nictitating membrane *n* (in reptiles, birds, and some mammals) a thin fold of skin under the eyelid that can be drawn across the eye.

niece *n* a daughter of one's sister or brother. ▷ HISTORY Latin *neptis* granddaughter

nifty *adj* **-tier, -tiest** *Informal* neat or smart. ▷ HISTORY origin unknown

Nigerian *adj* **1** of Nigeria. ✧ *n* **2** a person from Nigeria.

niggard *n* a stingy person. ▷ HISTORY perhaps from Old Norse

niggardly *adj* not generous: *it pays its staff on a niggardly scale.* ▶ **niggardliness** *n*

nigger *n Offensive* a Black person. ▷ HISTORY Spanish *negro*

niggle *vb* **-gling, -gled 1** to worry slightly. **2** to find fault continually. ✧ *n* **3** a small worry or doubt. **4** a trivial objection or complaint. ▷ HISTORY Scandinavian ▶ **niggling** *adj*

nigh *adj, adv, prep Archaic, poetic* near. ▷ HISTORY Old English *nēah, nēh*

night *n* **1** the period of darkness that occurs each 24 hours, between sunset and sunrise. **2** the period between sunset and bedtime; evening. **3** the time between bedtime and morning. **4** nightfall or dusk. **5** an evening designated for a specific activity: *opening night.* **6 make a night of it** to celebrate the whole evening. RELATED ADJECTIVE ➧ **nocturnal** ✧ *adj* **7** of, occurring, or working at night: *the night sky.* ▷ HISTORY Old English *niht*

nightcap *n* **1** a drink taken just before bedtime. **2** a soft cap formerly worn in bed.

nightclub *n* a place of entertainment open until late at night, offering drink and dancing.

nightdress *n* a loose dress worn in bed by women or girls.

nightfall *n* the approach of darkness; dusk.

nightgown *n* same as **nightdress**.

nightie *n Informal* short for **nightdress**.

nightingale *n* a small bird with a musical song, usually heard at night. ▷ HISTORY Old English *nihtegale,* literally: night singer

nightjar *n* a nocturnal bird with a harsh cry. ▷ HISTORY *night* + JAR^2 (so called from its harsh cry)

nightlife *n* the entertainment and social activities available at night in a town or city.

night-light *n* a dim light left on overnight.

nightly *adj* **1** happening each night. ✧ *adv* **2** each night.

nightmare *n* **1** a terrifying or deeply distressing dream. **2** a terrifying or unpleasant experience. **3** a thing that is feared: *wheels and loose straps are a baggage handler's nightmare.* ▶ **nightmarish** *adj*

> **WORD HISTORY**
> 'Nightmare' comes from *night* and Old English *mare*, meaning 'evil spirit'.

night safe *n* a safe built into the outside wall of a bank, in which customers can deposit money when the bank is closed.

night school *n* an educational institution that holds classes in the evening.

nightshade *n* a plant which produces poisonous berries with bell-shaped flowers. ▷ **HISTORY** Old English *nihtscada*

nightshirt *n* a long loose shirtlike garment worn in bed.

night-time *n* the time from sunset to sunrise.

nihilism (**nye**-ill-liz-zum) *n* a total rejection of all established authority and institutions. ▷ **HISTORY** Latin *nihil* nothing ▶ **nihilist** *n, adj* ▶ **nihilistic** *adj*

-nik *suffix forming nouns* indicating a person associated with a particular state or quality: *refusenik.* ▷ **HISTORY** Russian

nil *n* nothing: esp. as a score in games. ▷ **HISTORY** Latin

nimble *adj* **1** agile and quick in movement. **2** mentally alert or acute. ▷ **HISTORY** Old English *næmel* quick to grasp + *numol* quick at seizing ▶ **nimbly** *adv*

nimbostratus (nim-boh-**stray**-tuss) *n, pl* **-ti** (-tie) *Meteorol* a dark-coloured rain-bearing stratus cloud.

nimbus *n, pl* **-bi** *or* **-buses 1** a dark grey rain cloud. **2** a halo. ▷ **HISTORY** Latin: cloud

nincompoop *n Informal* a stupid person. ▷ **HISTORY** origin unknown

nine *n* **1** the cardinal number that is the sum of one and eight. **2** a numeral, 9 or IX, representing this number. **3** something representing or consisting of nine units. **4 dressed up to the nines** *Informal* elaborately dressed. ✧ *adj* **5** amounting to nine: *nine men.* ▷ **HISTORY** Old English *nigon* ▶ **ninth** *adj, n*

ninefold *adj* **1** having nine times as many or as much. **2** having nine parts. ✧ *adv* **3** by nine times as much or as many.

ninepins *n* the game of skittles.

nineteen *n* **1** the cardinal number that is the sum of ten and nine. **2** a numeral, 19 or XIX, representing this number. **3** something representing or consisting of nineteen units. **4 talk nineteen to the dozen** to talk very fast. ✧ *adj* **5** amounting to nineteen: *nineteen years.* ▶ **nineteenth** *adj, n*

nineteenth hole *n Golf slang* the bar in a golf clubhouse. ▷ **HISTORY** from its being the next objective after a standard 18-hole round

ninety *n, pl* **-ties 1** the cardinal number that is the product of ten and nine. **2** a numeral, 90 or XC, representing this number. **3** something representing or consisting of ninety units. **4 nineties** the numbers 90 to 99, esp. when used to refer to a year of someone's life or of a century. ✧ *adj* **5** amounting to ninety: *ninety degrees.* ▶ **ninetieth** *adj, n*

niobium *n Chem* a white superconductive metallic element. Symbol: Nb. ▷ **HISTORY** Latin after *Niobe* (daughter of Tantalus); because it occurred in tantalite

nip[1] *vb* **nipping, nipped 1** *Informal* to hurry. **2** to pinch or squeeze. **3** to bite lightly. **4** (of the cold) to affect (someone) with a stinging sensation. **5** to check the growth of (something): *a trite script nips all hope in the bud.* ✧ *n* **6** a pinch or light bite. **7** sharp coldness: *a nip in the air.* ▷ **HISTORY** perhaps from Old Norse

nip[2] *n* a small drink of spirits. ▷ **HISTORY** from *nipperkin* a vessel holding a half-pint or less

nipper *n Brit, Austral & NZ informal* a small child.

nipple *n* **1** the small projection in the centre of each breast, which in females contains the outlet of the milk ducts. **2** a small projection through which oil or grease can be put into a machine or component. ▷ **HISTORY** perhaps from *neb* peak, tip

nippy *adj* **-pier, -piest 1** (of weather) frosty or chilly. **2** *Informal* quick or nimble. **3** (of a motor vehicle) small and relatively powerful.

nirvana (near-**vah**-na) *n Buddhism, Hinduism* the ultimate state of spiritual enlightenment and bliss attained by extinction of all desires and individual existence. ▷ **HISTORY** Sanskrit: extinction

nisi (**nye**-sigh) *adj* See **decree nisi**.

Nissen hut *n Chiefly Brit* a tunnel-shaped military shelter made of corrugated steel. ▷ **HISTORY** after Lt Col. Peter *Nissen*, mining engineer

nit[1] *n* the egg or larva of a louse. ▷ **HISTORY** Old English *hnitu*

nit[2] *n Informal* short for **nitwit**.

nit-picking *Informal* ✧ *n* **1** a concern with insignificant details, usually with the intention of finding fault. ✧ *adj* **2** showing such concern.

nitrate *Chem* ✧ *n* **1** a salt or ester of nitric acid. **2** a fertilizer containing nitrate salts. ✧ *vb* **-trating, -trated 3** to treat with nitric acid or a nitrate. **4** to convert or be converted into a nitrate. ▶ **nitration** *n*

nitre *or US* **niter** *n Chem* same as **potassium nitrate**. ▷ **HISTORY** Latin *nitrum*

nitric *adj Chem* of or containing nitrogen.

nitric acid *n Chem* a colourless corrosive liquid widely used in industry.

nitride *n Chem* a compound of nitrogen with a more electropositive element.

nitrify *vb* **-fies, -fying, -fied** *Chem* **1** to treat (a substance) or cause (a substance) to react with nitrogen. **2** to treat (soil) with nitrates. **3** to convert (ammonium compounds) into nitrates by oxidation. ▶ **nitrification** *n*

nitrite *n Chem* a salt or ester of nitrous acid.

nitro- *or before a vowel* **nitr-** *combining form* indicating that: **1** a chemical compound contains

A B C D E F G H I J K L M N O P Q R S T U V W X Y Z

the univalent group, -NO_2: *nitrobenzene.* **2** a chemical compound which is a nitrate ester: *nitrocellulose.* ▷ **HISTORY** Greek *nitron* nitre

nitrogen (**nite**-roj-jen) *n Chem* a colourless odourless gas that forms four-fifths of the air and is an essential part of all animal and plant life. Symbol: N. ▶ **nitrogenous** *adj*

nitrogen cycle *n* the natural cycle by which nitrates in the soil, derived from dead organic matter, are absorbed by plants and reduced to nitrates again when the plants and the animals feeding on them die and decay.

nitrogen fixation *n* the conversion of atmospheric nitrogen into nitrogen compounds by soil bacteria.

nitroglycerine *or* **nitroglycerin** *n Chem* a thick pale yellow explosive liquid made from glycerol and nitric and sulphuric acids.

nitrous *adj Chem* derived from or containing nitrogen in a low valency state.

nitrous acid *n Chem* a weak acid known only in solution and in the form of nitrite salts.

nitrous oxide *n Chem* a colourless gas used as an anaesthetic.

nitty-gritty *n* **the nitty-gritty** *Informal* the basic facts of a matter or situation. ▷ **HISTORY** perhaps rhyming compound from *grit*

nitwit *n Informal* a stupid person. ▷ **HISTORY** perhaps NIT[1] + WIT[1]

NJ New Jersey.

nkosi (ing-**koss**-ee) *n S African* a term of address to a superior; master; chief. ▷ **HISTORY** Nguni (language group of southern Africa) *inkosi* chief

NM New Mexico.

no[1] *interj* **1** used to express denial, disagreement, or refusal. ✧ *n, pl* **noes** *or* **nos 2** an answer or vote of *no.* **3** a person who answers or votes *no.* ▷ **HISTORY** Old English *nā*

no[2] *adj* **1** not any, not a, or not one: *I have no money; no comment.* **2** not at all: *he's no exception.* **3** not: *no taller than a child.* **4 no way!** an expression of emphatic refusal or denial. ▷ **HISTORY** Old English *nān* none

No[1] *or* **Noh** *n, pl* **No** *or* **Noh** the stylized classical drama of Japan, using music and dancing. ▷ **HISTORY** Japanese *nō* talent

No[2] *Chem* nobelium.

No. *or* **no.** *pl* **Nos.** *or* **nos.** number. ▷ **HISTORY** French *numéro*

n.o. *Cricket* not out.

nob *n Chiefly Brit slang* a person of wealth or social distinction. ▷ **HISTORY** origin unknown

no-ball *n Cricket* an improperly bowled ball, for which the batting side scores a run. Abbrev: **nb**

nobble *vb* **-bling, -bled** *Brit & Austral slang* **1** to attract the attention of (someone) in order to talk to him or her. **2** to bribe or threaten. **3** to disable (a racehorse) to stop it from winning. **4** to steal. ▷ **HISTORY** *a nobbler,* a false division of *an hobbler* one who hobbles horses

nobelium *n Chem* a radioactive element produced artificially from curium. Symbol: No. ▷ **HISTORY** after *Nobel* Institute, Stockholm, where it was discovered

Nobel prize (no-**bell**) *n* a prize for outstanding contributions to chemistry, physics, physiology and medicine, literature, economics, and peace that may be awarded annually. ▷ **HISTORY** after Alfred *Nobel,* chemist and philanthropist

nobility *n* **1** the quality of being noble; dignity. **2** the class of people who hold titles and high social rank.

noble *adj* **1** having or showing high moral qualities: *a noble cause.* **2** belonging to a class of people who hold titles and high social rank. **3** impressive and magnificent: *a noble beast.* **4** *Chem* (of certain metals) resisting oxidation. ✧ *n* **5** a person who holds a title and high social rank. ▷ **HISTORY** Latin *nobilis,* originally capable of being known, hence well-known ▶ **nobly** *adv*

noble gas *n* any of the unreactive gases helium, neon, argon, krypton, xenon, and radon.

nobleman *or fem* **noblewoman** *n, pl* **-men** *or* **-women** a person of noble rank.

noblesse oblige (no-**bless** oh-**bleezh**) *n Often ironic* the supposed obligation of the nobility to be honourable and generous. ▷ **HISTORY** French, lit: nobility obliges

nobody *pron* **1** no person; no-one. ✧ *n, pl* **-bodies** **2** a person of no importance.

> **☑ WORD TIP**
> See at **everyone.**

nock *n* **1** a notch on an arrow that fits on the bowstring. **2** a groove at either end of a bow that holds the bowstring. ▷ **HISTORY** related to Swedish *nock* tip

no-claims bonus *or* **no-claim bonus** *n* a reduction in the cost of an insurance policy made if no claims have been made in a specified period.

nocturnal *adj* **1** of the night. **2** (of animals) active at night. ▷ **HISTORY** Latin *nox* night

nocturne *n* a short dreamy piece of music.

nod *vb* **nodding, nodded 1** to lower and raise (one's head) briefly, to express agreement or greeting. **2** to express by nodding: *he nodded his approval.* **3** to sway or bend forwards and back. **4** to let one's head fall forward with sleep. **5 nodding acquaintance** a slight knowledge (of a subject or person). ✧ *n* **6** a quick down-and-up movement of the head, in agreement. **7 land of Nod** an imaginary land of sleep. ▷ **HISTORY** origin unknown

noddle *n Chiefly Brit informal* the head or brains. ▷ **HISTORY** origin unknown

noddy *n, pl* **-dies 1** a tropical tern with a dark plumage. **2** a fool. ▷ **HISTORY** perhaps from obsolete *noddy* foolish, drowsy

node *n* **1** *Bot* the point on a plant stem from which the leaves grow. **2** *Maths* a point at which a curve crosses itself. **3** a knot or knob. **4** *Physics* a point in a vibrating body at which there is practically no vibration. **5** *Anat* any natural bulge or swelling: *lymph node.* **6** *Astron* either of the two points at which the orbit of a body intersects the path of the

a b c d e f g h i j k l m n o p q r s t u v w x y z

sun or the orbit of another body. ▷ **HISTORY** Latin *nodus* knot ▶ **nodal** *adj*

nod off *vb Informal* to fall asleep.

nodule *n* **1** a small rounded lump or node. **2** a rounded mineral growth on the root of a plant such as clover. ▷ **HISTORY** Latin *nodulus* ▶ **nodular** *adj*

Noel *n* same as **Christmas**. ▷ **HISTORY** French, from Latin *natalis* a birthday

nog *n* an alcoholic drink containing beaten egg. ▷ **HISTORY** origin unknown

noggin *n* **1** *Informal* the head. **2** a small quantity of spirits. ▷ **HISTORY** origin unknown

no-go area *n* a district that is barricaded off so that the police or army can enter only by force.

noise *n* **1** a sound, usually a loud or disturbing one. **2** loud shouting; din. **3** an undesired electrical disturbance in a signal. **4** unwanted or irrelevant elements in a visual image: *removing noise from pictures.* **5 noises** conventional utterances conveying a reaction: *he made the appropriate noises.* ✧ *vb* **noising, noised 6 be noised abroad** (of news or gossip) to be spread. ▷ **HISTORY** Latin *nausea* seasickness

noiseless *adj* making little or no sound. ▶ **noiselessly** *adv*

noise pollution *n* annoying or harmful noise in an environment.

noisome *adj Formal* **1** (of smells) offensive. **2** extremely unpleasant. ▷ **HISTORY** obsolete *noy*, variant of *annoy*

noisy *adj* **noisier, noisiest 1** making a lot of noise. **2** (of a place) full of noise. ▶ **noisily** *adv*

nomad *n* **1** a member of a tribe who move from place to place to find pasture and food. **2** a wanderer. ▷ **HISTORY** Greek *nomas* wandering for pasture ▶ **nomadic** *adj*

no-man's-land *n* land between boundaries, esp. an unoccupied zone between opposing forces.

nom de plume *n, pl* **noms de plume** same as **pen name**. ▷ **HISTORY** French

nomenclature (no-**men**-klatch-er) *n Formal* the system of names used in a particular subject. ▷ **HISTORY** Latin *nomenclatura* list of names

nominal *adj* **1** in name only: *nominal independence.* **2** very small in comparison with real worth: *a nominal amount of aid.* ▷ **HISTORY** Latin *nomen* name ▶ **nominally** *adv*

nominalism *n* the philosophical theory that a general word, such as *dog*, is merely a name and does not denote a real object. ▶ **nominalist** *n*

nominalization *or* **-isation** *n Grammar* the use of an abstract noun rather than the verb or adjective from which it derives, as in *he had a shave* rather than *he shaved*; also used to refer to the noun itself.

nominal value *n* same as **par value**.

nominate *vb* **-nating, -nated 1** to propose (someone) as a candidate. **2** to appoint (someone) to an office or position. ▷ **HISTORY** Latin *nomen* name ▶ **nomination** *n*

nominative *or* **nominative case** *n Grammar* a grammatical case in some languages that identifies the subject of a verb. ▷ **HISTORY** Latin *nominativus* belonging to naming

nominee *n* a person who is nominated to an office or as a candidate.

non- *prefix* indicating: **1** negation: *nonexistent.* **2** refusal or failure: *noncooperation.* **3** exclusion from a specified class: *nonfiction.* **4** lack or absence: *nonevent.* ▷ **HISTORY** Latin *non* not

nonage *n* **1** *Law* the state of being under full legal age for various actions. **2** a period of immaturity.

nonagenarian *n* a person who is from 90 to 99 years old. ▷ **HISTORY** Latin *nonaginta* ninety

nonaggression *n* the policy of not attacking other countries.

nonagon *n Geom* a figure with nine sides. ▶ **nonagonal** *adj*

nonalcoholic *adj* containing no alcohol.

nonaligned *adj* (of a country) not part of a major alliance or power bloc. ▶ **nonalignment** *n*

nonbelligerent *adj* (of a country) not taking part in a war.

nonce *n* **for the nonce** for the present. ▷ **HISTORY** a mistaken division of *for then anes*, for the once

nonce word *n* a word coined for a single occasion.

nonchalant (**non**-shall-ant) *adj* casually unconcerned or indifferent. ▷ **HISTORY** French, from *nonchaloir* to lack warmth ▶ **nonchalance** *n* ▶ **nonchalantly** *adv*

non-com *n* short for **noncommissioned officer**.

noncombatant *n* a member of the armed forces whose duties do not include fighting, such as a chaplain or surgeon.

noncommissioned officer *n* (in the armed forces) a person who is appointed as a subordinate officer, from the lower ranks, rather than by a commission.

noncommittal *adj* not committing oneself to any particular opinion.

non compos mentis *adj* of unsound mind. ▷ **HISTORY** Latin: not in control of one's mind

nonconductor *n* a substance that is a poor conductor of heat, electricity, or sound.

nonconformist *n* **1** a person who does not conform to generally accepted patterns of behaviour or thought. ✧ *adj* **2** (of behaviour or ideas) not conforming to accepted patterns. ▶ **nonconformity** *n*

Nonconformist *n* **1** a member of a Protestant group separated from the Church of England. ✧ *adj* **2** of or relating to Nonconformists.

noncontributory *adj Brit* denoting a pension scheme for employees, the premiums of which are paid entirely by the employer.

non-cooperation *n* the refusal to do more than is legally or contractually required of one.

nondescript *adj* lacking outstanding features. ▷ **HISTORY** NON- + Latin *descriptus*, past participle of *describere* to copy

none *pron* **1** not any: *none of the men was represented by a lawyer; none of it meant anything to* him. **2** no-one; nobody: *none could deny it.* **3 none the** in no degree: *her parents were none the wiser.* ▷ **HISTORY** Old English *nān,* literally: not one

> **WORD TIP**
> *None* is a singular pronoun and should be used with a singular form of a verb: *none of the students has* (not *have*) *a car.*

nonentity (non-**enn**-tit-tee) *n, pl* **-ties** an insignificant person or thing.
nonessential *adj* not absolutely necessary.
nonetheless *adv* despite that; however.
nonevent *n* a disappointing or insignificant occurrence that was expected to be important.
nonexistent *adj* not existing in a particular place. ▶ **nonexistence** *n*
nonferrous *adj* **1** denoting a metal other than iron. **2** not containing iron.
nonfiction *n* writing that deals with facts or real events.
nonflammable *adj* not easily set on fire.
nonintervention *n* refusal to intervene in the affairs of others.
noniron *adj* not requiring ironing.
non-magnetic material *n Physics* any material that cannot be magnetized.
nonmetal *n Chem* a chemical element that forms acidic oxides and is a poor conductor of heat and electricity. ▶ **nonmetallic** *adj*
non-nuclear *adj* not involving or using nuclear power or weapons.
nonpareil (non-par-**rail**) *n* a person or thing that is unsurpassed. ▷ **HISTORY** French, from NON- + *pareil* similar
nonpartisan *adj* not supporting any single political party.
nonpayment *n* failure to pay money owed.
nonplussed *or US* **nonplused** *adj* perplexed. ▷ **HISTORY** Latin *non plus* no further
non-profit-making *adj* not intended to make a profit.
nonproliferation *n* limitation of the production or spread of something such as nuclear or chemical weapons.
non-renewable resources *pl n Environmental science* resources that cannot be replaced or take millions of years to form, such as iron, copper, oil, and coal. Compare **renewable resources**.
nonrepresentational *adj Art* same as **abstract**.
nonresident *n* a person who does not live in a particular country or place.
nonsectarian *adj* not confined to any specific subdivision of a religious group.
nonsense *n* **1** something that has or makes no sense. **2** unintelligible language. **3** foolish behaviour. ▶ **nonsensical** *adj*
non sequitur (**sek**-wit-tur) *n* a statement having little or no relation to what preceded it. ▷ **HISTORY** Latin: it does not follow
nonsmoker *n* **1** a person who does not smoke. **2** a train carriage in which smoking is forbidden.
nonsmoking *or* **no-smoking** *adj* denoting an area in which smoking is forbidden.
nonstandard *adj* denoting words, expressions, or pronunciations that are not regarded as correct by educated native speakers of a language.
nonstarter *n* a person or an idea that has little chance of success.
nonstick *adj* (of cooking utensils) coated with a substance that food will not stick to when cooked.
nonstop *adj, adv* without a stop: *two weeks of nonstop rain; most days his phone rings nonstop.*
nontoxic *adj* not poisonous.
nonunion *adj* **1** (of a company) not employing trade union members: *a nonunion shop.* **2** (of a person) not belonging to a trade union.
nonviolent *adj* using peaceful methods to bring about change. ▶ **nonviolence** *n*
nonvoter *n* **1** a person who does not vote. **2** a person not eligible to vote.
nonvoting *adj Finance* (of shares in a company) not entitling the holder to vote at company meetings.
non-White *adj* **1** belonging to a race of people not European in origin. ✧ *n* **2** a member of one of these races.
noodles *pl n* ribbon-like strips of pasta. ▷ **HISTORY** German *Nudeln*
nook *n* **1** a corner or recess. **2** a secluded or sheltered place. ▷ **HISTORY** origin unknown
noon *n* the middle of the day; 12 o'clock. ▷ **HISTORY** Latin *nona (hora)* ninth hour (originally 3 p.m., the ninth hour from sunrise)
noonday *adj* happening or appearing at noon.
no-one *or* **no one** *pron* no person; nobody.

> **WORD TIP**
> See at **everyone.**

noose *n* a loop in the end of a rope, tied with a slipknot, such as one used to hang people. ▷ **HISTORY** Latin *nodus* knot
nor *conj* **1** (used to join alternatives, the first of which is preceded by *neither*) and not: *neither willing nor able.* **2** and not ... either: *he had not arrived yet, nor had any of the models.* ▷ **HISTORY** contraction of Old English *nōther*
nordic *adj Skiing* of competitions in cross-country racing and ski-jumping.
Nordic *adj* of Scandinavia or its typically tall, blond, and blue-eyed people. ▷ **HISTORY** French *nordique* of the north
norm *n* a standard that is required or regarded as normal. ▷ **HISTORY** Latin *norma* carpenter's square
normal *adj* **1** usual, regular, or typical: *the study of normal behaviour.* **2** free from mental or physical disorder. **3** *Geom* same as **perpendicular** (sense 1). ✧ *n* **4** the usual, regular, or typical state, degree, or form. **5** *Geom* a perpendicular line or plane. ▷ **HISTORY** Latin *normalis* conforming to the carpenter's square ▶ **normality** *or esp US* **normalcy** *n*

A B C D E F G H I J K L M N O P Q R S T U V W X Y Z

normal fault *n Geol* a fault in which rock on one side of the fault drops in relation to the other. Compare **reverse fault**.

normalize *or* **-ise** *vb* **-izing, -ized** *or* **-ising, -ised** **1** to make or become normal. **2** to bring into conformity with a standard.

normally *adv* **1** as a rule; usually. **2** in a normal manner.

Norman *n* **1** a person from Normandy in N France, esp. one of the people who conquered England in 1066. **2** same as **Norman French**. ✧ *adj* **3** of the Normans or their dialect of French. **4** of Normandy. **5** of a style of architecture used in Britain from the Norman Conquest until the 12th century, with rounded arches and massive masonry walls.

Norman French *n* the medieval Norman and English dialect of Old French.

normative *adj* of or establishing a norm or standard: *a normative model.*

Norn *n Norse myth* any of the three virgin goddesses of fate. ▷ **HISTORY** Old Norse

Norse *adj* **1** of ancient and medieval Scandinavia. **2** of Norway. ✧ *n* **3 a** the N group of Germanic languages spoken in Scandinavia. **b** any one of these languages, esp. in their ancient or medieval forms.

Norseman *n, pl* **-men** same as **Viking**.

north *n* **1** one of the four cardinal points of the compass, at 0° or 360°. **2** the direction along a meridian towards the North Pole. **3** the direction in which a compass needle points; magnetic north. **4 the north** any area lying in or towards the north. ✧ *adj* **5** in or towards the north. **6** (esp. of the wind) from the north. ✧ *adv* **7** in, to, or towards the north. ▷ **HISTORY** Old English

North *n* **1 the North a** the northern part of England, generally regarded as reaching the southern boundaries of Yorkshire, Derbyshire, and Cheshire. **b** (in the US) the states north of the Mason-Dixon Line that were known as the Free States during the Civil War. **c** the economically and technically advanced countries of the world. ✧ *adj* **2** of or denoting the northern part of a country or area.

northeast *n* **1** the direction midway between north and east. **2 the northeast** any area lying in or towards the northeast. ✧ *adj also* **northeastern** **3** (*sometimes cap*) of or denoting that part of a country or area which lies in the northeast. **4** situated in, moving towards, or facing the northeast. **5** (esp. of the wind) from the northeast. ✧ *adv* **6** in, to, or towards the northeast.
▸ **northeasterly** *adj, adv, n*

northeaster *n* a strong wind or storm from the northeast.

northerly *adj* **1** of or in the north. ✧ *adv, adj* **2** towards the north. **3** from the north.

northern *adj* **1** situated in or towards the north. **2** facing or moving towards the north. **3** (*sometimes cap*) of or characteristic of the north or North. ▸ **northernmost** *adj*

northern hemisphere *n Geog* that half of the globe lying north of the equator.

northern lights *pl n* same as **aurora borealis**.

northing *n Geog* a latitudinal grid line. Compare **easting**.

Northman *n, pl* **-men** same as **Viking**.

North Pole *n* the northernmost point on the earth's axis, at a latitude of 90°N, which has very low temperatures.

North Star *n* **the North Star** same as **Pole Star**.

northward *adj, adv also* **northwards** **1** towards the north. ✧ *n* **2** the northward part or direction.

northwest *n* **1** the direction midway between north and west. **2 the northwest** any area lying in or towards the northwest. ✧ *adj also* **northwestern** **3** (*sometimes cap*) of or denoting that part of a country or area which lies in the northwest. **4** situated in, moving towards, or facing the northwest. **5** (esp. of the wind) from the northwest. ✧ *adv* **6** in, to, or towards the northwest.
▸ **northwesterly** *adj, adv, n*

northwester *n* a strong wind or storm from the northwest.

Norwegian *adj* **1** of Norway. ✧ *n* **2** a person from Norway. **3** the language of Norway.

nor'wester *n NZ* a hot dry wind.

nose *n* **1** the organ situated above the mouth, used for smelling and breathing. **2** the sense of smell. **3** the front part of a vehicle. **4** the distinctive smell of a wine or perfume. **5** instinctive skill in finding something: *he had a nose for media events.* **6 get up someone's nose** *Informal* to annoy someone. **7 keep one's nose clean** to stay out of trouble. **8 look down one's nose at** *Informal* to be haughty towards. **9 pay through the nose** *Informal* to pay a high price. **10 put someone's nose out of joint** *Informal* to make someone envious by doing what he or she would have liked to do or had expected to do. **11 rub someone's nose in it** *Informal* to remind someone unkindly of a failing or error. **12 turn up one's nose at** *Informal* to show contempt for. **13 win by a nose** to win by a narrow margin. ✧ *vb* **nosing, nosed** **14** to move forward slowly and carefully. **15** to pry or snoop. **16 nose out** to discover by searching or prying. ▷ **HISTORY** Old English *nosu*

nosebag *n* a bag containing feed, fastened around the head of a horse.

nosebleed *n* bleeding from the nose.

nose cone *n* the cone-shaped front section of a missile or spacecraft.

nose dive *n* **1** (of an aircraft) a sudden plunge with the nose pointing downwards. **2** *Informal* a sudden drop: *when we fail our self-confidence takes a nose dive.* ✧ *vb* **nose-dive, -diving, -dived** **3** to take a nose dive.

nosegay *n* a small bunch of flowers. ▷ **HISTORY** *nose* + *gay* (archaic) toy

nosey *or* **nosy** *adj* **nosier, nosiest** *Informal* prying or inquisitive. ▸ **nosiness** *n*

nosey parker *n Brit & S African informal* a prying person. ▷ **HISTORY** arbitrary use of surname *Parker*

nosh *Brit, Austral & NZ slang* ✧ *n* **1** food. ✧ *vb* **2** to eat. ▷ **HISTORY** Yiddish

nosh-up *n Brit slang* a large meal.

nostalgia *n* **1** a sentimental yearning for the past. **2** homesickness. ▷ HISTORY Greek *nostos* a return home + *algios* pain ▶ **nostalgic** *adj* ▶ **nostalgically** *adv*

nostril *n* either of the two openings at the end of the nose. ▷ HISTORY Old English *nosu* nose + *thyrel* hole

nostrum *n* **1** a quack medicine. **2** a favourite remedy. ▷ HISTORY Latin: our own (make)

nosy *adj* **nosier, nosiest** same as **nosey**.

not *adv* **1** used to negate the sentence, phrase, or word that it modifies: *I will not stand for it.* **2 not that** which is not to say that: *not that I've ever heard him complain.* ▷ HISTORY Old English *nāwiht,* from *nā* no + *wiht* creature, thing

nota bene (**note**-a **ben**-nay) note well; take note. ▷ HISTORY Latin

notable (**note**-a-bl) *adj* **1** worthy of being noted; remarkable. ✧ *n* **2** a person of distinction. ▷ HISTORY Latin *notare* to note ▶ **notably** *adv*

notary *or* **notary public** (**note**-a-ree) *n, pl* **notaries** *or* **notaries public** a public official, usually a solicitor, who is legally authorized to attest and certify documents. ▷ HISTORY Latin *notarius* one who makes notes, a clerk

notation (no-**tay**-shun) *n* **1** representation of numbers or quantities in a system by a series of symbols. **2** a set of such symbols. ▷ HISTORY Latin *notare* to note

notch *n* **1** a V-shaped cut. **2** *Informal* a step or level: *the economy moved up another notch.* ✧ *vb* **3** to cut a notch in. **4 notch up** *Informal* to score or achieve: *he notched up a hat trick of wins.*

> **WORD HISTORY**
> Like 'newt', which comes from the mistaken division of 'an ewt' into 'a newt', the word 'notch' arose from the mistaken division of *an otch* (from Old French *oche,* meaning 'notch') into 'a notch'.

note *n* **1** a brief informal letter. **2** a brief record in writing for future reference. **3** a critical comment or explanation in a book. **4** an official written communication, as from a government or from a doctor. **5** short for **banknote**. **6** *Brit & NZ* a musical sound of a particular pitch. **7** a written symbol representing the pitch and duration of a musical sound. **8** *Chiefly Brit* a key on a piano, organ, or other keyboard instrument. **9** a particular feeling or atmosphere: *an optimistic note.* **10** a distinctive vocal sound, as of a type of animal. **11** a sound used as a signal or warning: *the note to retreat was sounded.* **12** short for **promissory note**. **13 of note a** distinguished or famous. **b** important: *nothing of note.* **14 strike the right note** to behave appropriately. **15 take note of** to pay attention to. ✧ *vb* **noting, noted 16** to notice; pay attention to: *such criticism should be noted.* **17** to make a written note of. **18** to remark upon: *I note that you do not wear shoes.* ▷ HISTORY Latin *nota* sign

notebook *n* a book for writing in.

notebook computer *n* a portable computer approximately the size of a sheet of A4 paper.

noted *adj* well-known: *a noted scholar.*

notelet *n* a folded card with a printed design on the front, for writing informal letters.

notepaper *n* paper used for writing letters.

noteworthy *adj* worth noting; remarkable.

nothing *pron* **1** not anything: *I felt nothing.* **2** a matter of no importance: *don't worry, it's nothing.* **3** absence of meaning, value, or worth: *the industry shrank to almost nothing.* **4** the figure 0. **5 have** *or* **be nothing to do with** to have no connection with. **6 nothing but** not something other than; only. **7 nothing doing** *Informal* an expression of dismissal or refusal. **8 nothing less than** downright: *nothing less than complete withdrawal.* **9 think nothing of something** to regard something as easy or natural. ✧ *adv* **10** not at all: *he looked nothing like his brother.* ✧ *n* **11** *Informal* a person or thing of no importance or significance. ▷ HISTORY Old English *nāthing, nān thing*

> **WORD TIP**
> *Nothing* normally takes a singular verb, but when *nothing but* is followed by a plural form of a noun, a plural verb is usually used: *it was a large room where nothing but souvenirs were sold.*

nothingness *n* **1** nonexistence. **2** total insignificance.

notice *n* **1** observation or attention: *to attract notice.* **2** a displayed placard or announcement giving information. **3** advance notification of something such as intention to end a contract of employment: *she handed in her notice.* **4** a theatrical or literary review. **5 take notice** to pay attention. **6 take no notice of** to ignore or disregard. **7 at short notice** with very little notification. ✧ *vb* **-ticing, -ticed 8** to become aware (of). **9** to point out or remark upon. ▷ HISTORY Latin *notus* known

noticeable *adj* easily seen or detected. ▶ **noticeably** *adv*

notice board *n* a board on which notices are displayed.

notifiable *adj* having to be reported to the authorities: *a notifiable disease.*

notification *n* **1** the act of notifying someone of something. **2** a formal announcement.

notify *vb* **-fies, -fying, -fied** to inform. ▷ HISTORY Latin *notus* known + *facere* to make

notion *n* **1** an idea or opinion. **2** a whim. ▷ HISTORY Latin *notio* a becoming acquainted

notional *adj* hypothetical, imaginary, or unreal: *a notional dividend payment.*

notorious *adj* well known for some bad reason. ▷ HISTORY Medieval Latin *notorius* well-known ▶ **notoriety** *n* ▶ **notoriously** *adv*

not proven *adj* a verdict in Scottish courts, given when there is insufficient evidence to convict the accused.

no-trump *Cards* ✧ *n* **1** a bid or hand without trumps. ✧ *adj* **2** (of a hand) suitable for playing without trumps.

notwithstanding *prep* **1** in spite of. ✧ *adv* **2** nevertheless.

A B C D E F G H I J K L M N O P Q R S T U V W X Y Z

nougat *n* a hard chewy pink or white sweet containing chopped nuts. ▷ **HISTORY** French, from Latin *nux* nut

nought *n* **1** the figure 0. ✧ *n, adv* **2** same as **naught.** ▷ **HISTORY** Old English *nōwiht*, from *ne* not, no + *ōwiht* something

noughties *pl n Informal* the decade from 2000 to 2009.

noun *n* a word that refers to a person, place, or thing. ▷ **HISTORY** Latin *nomen* name

noun group *or* **phrase** *n Grammar* a noun, pronoun, or group of words containing one or more of these that acts as the subject, object, or complement of a verb, or as the object of a preposition, e.g. *my late wife and I* in *my late wife and I read a lot.*

nourish *vb* **1** to provide with the food necessary for life and growth. **2** to encourage or foster (an idea or feeling). ▷ **HISTORY** Latin *nutrire* to feed
▶ **nourishing** *adj*

nourishment *n* the food needed to nourish the body.

nous *n Old-fashioned, slang* common sense. ▷ **HISTORY** Greek: mind

nouveau riche (**noo**-voh **reesh**) *n, pl* **nouveaux riches** (**noo**-voh **reesh**) a person who has become wealthy recently and is regarded as vulgar. ▷ **HISTORY** French: new rich

nouvelle cuisine (**noo**-vell kwee-**zeen**) *n* a style of preparing and presenting food with light sauces and unusual combinations of flavours. ▷ **HISTORY** French: new cooking

Nov. November.

nova *n, pl* **-vae** *or* **-vas** a star that undergoes an explosion and fast increase of brightness, then gradually decreases to its original brightness. ▷ **HISTORY** New Latin *nova (stella)* new (star)

novel[1] *n* a long fictional story in book form. ▷ **HISTORY** Latin *novella (narratio)* new (story)

novel[2] *adj* fresh, new, or original: *a novel approach.* ▷ **HISTORY** Latin *novus* new

novelette *n* a short novel, usually one regarded as trivial or sentimental.

novelist *n* a writer of novels.

novella *n, pl* **-las** a short narrative tale or short novel. ▷ **HISTORY** Italian

novelty *n, pl* **-ties 1** the quality of being new and interesting. **2** a new or unusual experience or thing. **3** a small cheap toy or trinket.

November *n* the eleventh month of the year. ▷ **HISTORY** Latin: ninth month

novena (no-**vee**-na) *n, pl* **-nas** *or* **-nae** (-nee) *RC Church* a set of prayers or services on nine consecutive days. ▷ **HISTORY** Latin *novem* nine

novice (**nov**-viss) *n* **1** a beginner. **2** a person who has entered a religious order but has not yet taken vows. ▷ **HISTORY** Latin *novus* new

novitiate *or* **noviciate** *n* **1** the period of being a novice. **2** the part of a monastery or convent where the novices live.

now *adv* **1** at or for the present time. **2** immediately: *bring it now.* **3** in these times; nowadays. **4** given the present circumstances: *now do you understand why?* **5 a** used as a hesitation word: *now, I can't really say.* **b** used for emphasis: *now listen to this.* **c** used at the end of a command: *run along now.* **6 just now a** very recently: *he left just now.* **b** very soon: *I'm going just now.* **7 now and again** *or* **then** occasionally. **8 now now!** an exclamation used to tell someone off or to calm someone. ✧ *conj* **9** Also: **now that** seeing that: *now you're here, you can help me.* ✧ *n* **10** the present time: *now is the time to go.* ▷ **HISTORY** Old English *nū*

nowadays *adv* in these times.

Nowell *n* same as **Noel.**

nowhere *adv* **1** in, at, or to no place. **2 getting nowhere** *Informal* making no progress. **3 nowhere near** far from: *the stadium is nowhere near completion.* ✧ *n* **4 in the middle of nowhere** (of a place) completely isolated.

noxious *adj* **1** poisonous or harmful. **2** extremely unpleasant. ▷ **HISTORY** Latin *noxius* harmful

nozzle *n* a projecting spout from which fluid is discharged. ▷ **HISTORY** diminutive of *nose*

Np *Chem* neptunium.

nr near.

NS 1 New Style (method of reckoning dates). **2** Nova Scotia.

NSPCC (in Britain) National Society for the Prevention of Cruelty to Children.

NSW New South Wales.

NT 1 (in Britain) National Trust. **2** New Testament. **3** Northern Territory. **4** Nunavut.

nth *adj* See **n**[2].

nuance (**new**-ahnss) *n* a subtle difference, as in colour, meaning, or tone. ▷ **HISTORY** French

nub *n* the point or gist: *this is the nub of his theory.* ▷ **HISTORY** Middle Low German *knubbe* knob

nubile (**new**-bile) *adj* (of a young woman) **1** sexually attractive. **2** old enough for marriage. ▷ **HISTORY** Latin *nubere* to marry

nuclear *adj* **1** of nuclear weapons or energy. **2** of an atomic nucleus: *nuclear fission.*

nuclear bomb *n* a bomb whose force is due to uncontrolled nuclear fusion or fission.

nuclear energy *n* energy released during a nuclear reaction as a result of fission or fusion.

nuclear family *n Sociol, anthropol* a family consisting only of parents and their offspring.

nuclear fission *n Nuclear physics* the splitting of an atomic nucleus, either spontaneously or by bombardment by a neutron: used in atomic bombs and nuclear power plants.

nuclear fusion *n Nuclear physics* the combination of two nuclei to form a heavier nucleus with the release of energy: used in hydrogen bombs.

nuclear physics *n* the branch of physics concerned with the structure of the nucleus and the behaviour of its particles.

nuclear power *n* power produced by a nuclear reactor.

nuclear reaction *n Physics* a process in which the structure and energy content of an atomic nucleus is changed by interaction with another nucleus or particle.

nuclear reactor *n Nuclear physics* a device in which a nuclear reaction is maintained and controlled to produce nuclear energy.

nuclear winter *n* a theoretical period of low temperatures and little light that has been suggested would occur after a nuclear war.

nucleate *adj* **1** having a nucleus. ✧ *vb* **-ating, -ated 2** to form a nucleus.

nucleated settlement *n* a pattern of settlement in which dwellings are clustered together as in villages and towns. Compare **dispersed settlement**.

nuclei (**new**-klee-eye) *n* the plural of **nucleus**.

nucleic acid *n Biochem* a complex compound, such as DNA or RNA, found in all living cells.

nucleolus *n, pl* **-li** *Biol* a small rounded body within a resting nucleus that is involved in protein synthesis.

nucleon *n Physics* a proton or neutron.

nucleonics *n* the branch of physics concerned with the applications of nuclear energy. ▸ **nucleonic** *adj*

nucleoplasm *n Biol* the protoplasm that makes up the nucleus of a plant or animal cell.

nucleoside *n Biochem* a compound containing a purine or pyrimidine base linked to a sugar.

nucleotide *n Biochem* a compound consisting of a nucleoside linked to phosphoric acid.

nucleus *n, pl* **-clei 1** *Physics* the positively charged centre of an atom, made of protons and neutrons, about which electrons orbit. **2** a central thing around which others are grouped. **3** a centre of growth or development: *the nucleus of a new relationship.* **4** *Biol* the part of a cell that contains the chromosomes and associated molecules that control the characteristics and growth of the cell. **5** *Chem* a fundamental group of atoms in a molecule serving as the base structure for related compounds. ▷ **HISTORY** Latin: kernel

nude *adj* **1** completely undressed. ✧ *n* **2** a naked figure in painting, sculpture, or photography. **3 in the nude** naked. ▷ **HISTORY** Latin *nudus* ▸ **nudity** *n*

nudge *vb* **nudging, nudged 1** to push (someone) gently with the elbow to get attention. **2** to push (something or someone) lightly. **3** to persuade (someone) gently. ✧ *n* **4** a gentle poke or push. ▷ **HISTORY** origin unknown

nudism *n* the practice of not wearing clothes, for reasons of health. ▸ **nudist** *n, adj*

nugatory (**new**-gat-tree) *adj Formal* **1** of little value. **2** not valid: *their rejection rendered the treaty nugatory.* ▷ **HISTORY** Latin *nugae* trifling things

nugget *n* **1** a small lump of gold in its natural state. **2** something small but valuable: *a nugget of useful knowledge.* ✧ *vb* **3** *NZ & S African* to polish footwear. ▷ **HISTORY** origin unknown

nuisance *n* **1** a person or thing that causes annoyance or bother. ✧ *adj* **2** causing annoyance or bother: *nuisance calls.* ▷ **HISTORY** Old French *nuire* to injure

NUJ (in Britain) National Union of Journalists.

nuke *Slang* ✧ *vb* **nuking, nuked 1** to attack with nuclear weapons. ✧ *n* **2** a nuclear bomb.

null *adj* **1 null and void** not legally valid. **2 null set** *Maths* a set with no members. ▷ **HISTORY** Latin *nullus* none ▸ **nullity** *n*

nulla-nulla *n* a wooden club used by Australian Aborigines.

nullify *vb* **-fies, -fying, -fied 1** to make (something) ineffective. **2** to make (something) legally void. ▷ **HISTORY** Latin *nullus* of no account + *facere* to make ▸ **nullification** *n*

numb *adj* **1** deprived of feeling through cold, shock, or fear. **2** unable to move; paralysed. ✧ *vb* **3** to make numb. ▷ **HISTORY** Middle English *nomen,* literally: taken (with paralysis) ▸ **numbly** *adv* ▸ **numbness** *n*

numbat *n* a small Australian marsupial with a long snout and tongue.

number *n* **1** a concept of quantity that is or can be derived from a single unit, a sum of units, or zero. **2** the word or symbol used to represent a number. **3** a numeral or string of numerals used to identify a person or thing: *an account number.* **4** the person or thing so identified: *he was seeded number two.* **5** a sum or quantity: *a very large number of people have telephoned.* **6** one of a series, as of a magazine. **7** a self-contained piece of pop or jazz music. **8** a group of people: *one of their number might be willing.* **9** *Informal* an admired article: *that little number is by Dior.* **10** *Grammar* classification of words depending on how many people or things are referred to. **11 any number of** many. **12 beyond** *or* **without number** innumerable. **13 have someone's number** *Informal* to have discovered someone's true character or intentions. **14 one's number is up** *Brit & Austral informal* one is about to die. ✧ *vb* **15** to count. **16** to assign a number to: *numbered seats.* **17** to add up to: *the illustrations numbered well over 50.* **18** to include in a group. **19 one's days are numbered** something unpleasant, such as death, is likely to happen to one soon. ▷ **HISTORY** Latin *numerus*

number crunching *n Computers* the large-scale processing of numerical data.

numberless *adj* too many to be counted.

number one *n* **1** *Informal* oneself: *he looks after number one.* **2** *Informal* the bestselling pop record in any one week. ✧ *adj* **3** first in importance, urgency, or quality: *he's their number one suspect.*

numberplate *n* a plate on a motor vehicle showing the registration number.

numbskull *or* **numskull** *n* a stupid person.

numeral *n* a word or symbol used to express a sum or quantity. ▷ **HISTORY** Latin *numerus* number

numerate *adj* able to do basic arithmetic. ▸ **numeracy** *n*

numeration *n* **1** the act or process of numbering or counting. **2** a system of numbering.

numerator *n Maths* the number above the line in a fraction.

numerical *or* **numeric** *adj* measured or expressed in numbers. ▸ **numerically** *adv*

numerology *n* the study of numbers and of their supposed influence on human affairs.

numerous *adj* **1** many: *they carried out numerous bombings.* **2** consisting of a large number of people or things.

numinous *adj Formal* **1** arousing spiritual or religious emotions. **2** mysterious or awe-inspiring. ▷ **HISTORY** Latin *numen* divine will

numismatics *n* the study or collection of coins or medals. ▷ **HISTORY** Greek *nomisma* piece of currency ▶ **numismatist** *n*

numskull *n* same as **numbskull**.

nun *n* a female member of a religious order. ▷ **HISTORY** Late Latin *nonna*

nunatak *n Geog* an isolated mountain peak projecting through the surface of surrounding glacial ice and supporting a distinct fauna and flora after recession of the ice. ▷ **HISTORY** via Danish from Eskimo

nuncio *n, pl* **-cios** *RC Church* a papal ambassador. ▷ **HISTORY** Latin *nuntius* messenger

nunnery *n, pl* **-neries** a convent.

nuptial *adj* relating to marriage: *a nuptial blessing.* ▷ **HISTORY** Latin *nuptiae* marriage

nuptials *pl n* a wedding.

nurd *n Slang* same as **nerd**.

nurse *n* **1** a person trained to look after sick people, usually in a hospital. ✧ *vb* **nursing, nursed** **2** to look after (a sick person). **3** to breast-feed (a baby). **4** (of a baby) to feed at its mother's breast. **5** to try to cure (an ailment). **6** to harbour or foster (a feeling). **7** to clasp fondly: *she nursed her drink.* ▷ **HISTORY** Latin *nutrire* to nourish ▶ **nursing** *n, adj*

nursery *n, pl* **-ries** **1** a room in a house where children sleep or play. **2** a place where children are taken care of when their parents are at work. **3** a place where plants are grown for sale.

nurseryman *n, pl* **-men** a person who raises plants and trees for sale.

nursery rhyme *n* a short traditional verse or song for children.

nursery school *n* a school for young children from three to five years old.

nursery slopes *pl n* gentle slopes used by beginners in skiing.

nursing home *n* a private hospital or home for people who are old or ill.

nursing officer *n* (in Britain) the administrative head of the nursing staff of a hospital.

nurture *n* **1** the act or process of promoting the development of a child or young plant. ✧ *vb* **-turing, -tured** **2** to promote or encourage the development of. ▷ **HISTORY** Latin *nutrire* to nourish

nut *n* **1** a dry one-seeded fruit that grows inside a hard shell. **2** the edible inner part of such a fruit. **3** a small piece of metal with a hole in it, that screws on to a bolt. **4** *Slang* an eccentric or insane person. **5** *Slang* the head. **6** *Slang* an enthusiast: *a health nut.* **7** *Brit* a small piece of coal. **8 do one's nut** *Brit & Austral slang* to be very angry. **9 a tough nut to crack** a person or thing that presents difficulties. ✧ See also **nuts**. ▷ **HISTORY** Old English *hnutu*

NUT (in Britain & S Africa) National Union of Teachers.

nutcracker *n* a device for cracking the shells of nuts. Also: **nutcrackers**

nuthatch *n* a songbird that feeds on insects, seeds, and nuts. ▷ **HISTORY** Middle English *notehache* nut hatchet, because it splits nuts

nutmeg *n* a spice made from the seed of a tropical tree. ▷ **HISTORY** Old French *nois muguede* musk-scented nut

nutria (**new**-tree-a) *n* the fur of the coypu. ▷ **HISTORY** Latin *lutra* otter

nutrient (**new**-tree-ent) *n* **1** a substance that provides nourishment. ✧ *adj* **2** providing nourishment. ▷ **HISTORY** Latin *nutrire* to nourish

nutriment (**new**-tree-ment) *n* the food or nourishment required by all living things to grow and stay healthy. ▷ **HISTORY** Latin *nutrimentum*

nutrition (new-**trish**-un) *n* **1** the process of taking in and absorbing nutrients. **2** the process of being nourished. **3** the study of nutrition. ▷ **HISTORY** Latin *nutrire* to nourish ▶ **nutritional** *adj* ▶ **nutritionist** *n*

nutritious *adj* providing nourishment. ▷ **HISTORY** Latin *nutrix* nurse

nutritive *adj* of nutrition; nutritious.

nuts *adj Slang* **1** insane. **2 nuts about** very fond of.

nuts and bolts *pl n Informal* the essential or practical details: *the nuts and bolts of photography.*

nutshell *n* **in a nutshell** in essence; briefly.

nutter *n Brit & NZ slang* an insane person.

nutty *adj* **-tier, -tiest** **1** containing or resembling nuts. **2** *Slang* insane or eccentric. ▶ **nuttiness** *n*

nux vomica *n* the seed of a tree, containing strychnine. ▷ **HISTORY** Medieval Latin: vomiting nut

nuzzle *vb* **-zling, -zled** to push or rub gently with the nose or snout. ▷ **HISTORY** from *nose*

NV Nevada.

nvCJD new-variant Creutzfeldt-Jakob disease.

NW northwest(ern).

NWT Northwest Territories (of Canada).

NY *or* **N.Y.** New York.

nylon *n* a synthetic material used for clothing and many other products. ▷ **HISTORY** originally a trademark

nylons *pl n* stockings made of nylon.

nymph *n* **1** *Myth* a spirit of nature, represented as a beautiful young woman. **2** the larva of certain insects, resembling the adult form. **3** *Chiefly poetic* a beautiful young woman. ▷ **HISTORY** Greek *numphē*

nymphet *n* a girl who is sexually precocious and desirable.

nymphomaniac *n* a woman with an abnormally intense sexual desire. ▷ **HISTORY** Greek *numphē* nymph + *mania* madness ▶ **nymphomania** *n*

NZ *or* **N.Z.** New Zealand.

NZE New Zealand English.

NZRFU New Zealand Rugby Football Union.

NZSE40 Index New Zealand Stock Exchange 40 Index.

A B C D E F G H I J K L M N O P Q R S T U V W X Y Z

O o

O[1] **1** *Chem* oxygen. **2** Old. **3** same as **nought**.

O[2] *interj* same as **oh**.

o. *or* **O.** old.

o' *prep Informal or old-fashioned* of: *a cup o' tea.*

OA Order of Australia.

oaf *n* a stupid or clumsy person. ▷ HISTORY variant of Old English *ælf* elf ▶ **oafish** *adj*

oak *n* **1** a large forest tree with hard wood, acorns as fruits, and leaves with rounded projections. **2** the wood of this tree, used as building timber and for making furniture. ▷ HISTORY Old English *āc* ▶ **oaken** *adj*

oak apple *or* **gall** *n* a brownish round lump or ball produced on oak trees by certain wasps.

oakum *n* loose fibre obtained by unravelling old rope, used for filling cracks in wooden ships. ▷ HISTORY Old English *ācumba,* literally: off-combings

OAM Medal of the Order of Australia.

OAP (in Britain) old age pensioner.

oar *n* **1** a long pole with a broad blade, used for rowing a boat. **2 put** *or* **stick one's oar in** to interfere or interrupt. ▷ HISTORY Old English *ār*

oarsman *or fem* **oarswoman** *n, pl* **-men** *or* **-women** a person who rows. ▶ **oarsmanship** *n*

oasis *n, pl* **-ses 1** a fertile patch in a desert. **2** a place or situation offering relief in the midst of difficulty. ▷ HISTORY Greek

oast *n Chiefly Brit* an oven for drying hops. ▷ HISTORY Old English *āst*

oast house *n Chiefly Brit* a building containing ovens for drying hops.

oat *n* **1** a hard cereal grown as food. **2 oats** the edible grain of this cereal. **3 sow one's wild oats** to have casual sexual relationships while young. ▷ HISTORY Old English *āte* ▶ **oaten** *adj*

oatcake *n* a thin unsweetened biscuit made of oatmeal.

oath *n, pl* **oaths 1** a solemn promise, esp. to tell the truth in a court of law. **2** an offensive or blasphemous expression; a swearword. **3 on** *or* **under oath** having made a solemn promise to tell the truth, esp. in a court of law. ▷ HISTORY Old English *āth*

oatmeal *n* **1** a coarse flour made by grinding oats. ✧ *adj* **2** greyish-yellow.

obbligato (ob-lig-**gah**-toe) *Music* ✧ *adj* **1** not to be omitted in performance. ✧ *n, pl* **-tos 2** an essential part or accompaniment: *an aria with bassoon obbligato.* ▷ HISTORY Italian

obdurate *adj* not to be persuaded; hardhearted or obstinate. ▷ HISTORY Latin *obdurare* to make hard ▶ **obduracy** *n*

OBE (in Britain) Officer of the Order of the British Empire.

obedient *adj* obeying or willing to obey. ▷ HISTORY Latin *oboediens* ▶ **obedience** *n* ▶ **obediently** *adv*

obeisance (oh-**bay**-sanss) *n Formal* **1** an attitude of respect or humble obedience. **2** a bow or curtsy showing this attitude. ▷ HISTORY Old French *obéissant* obeying ▶ **obeisant** *adj*

obelisk (**ob**-bill-isk) *n* **1** a four-sided stone pillar that tapers to a pyramid at the top. **2** *Printing* same as **dagger** (sense 2). ▷ HISTORY Greek *obeliskos* a little spit

obese (oh-**beess**) *adj* very fat. ▷ HISTORY Latin *obesus* ▶ **obesity** *n*

obey *vb* **1** to carry out instructions or orders; be obedient. **2** to act in accordance with one's feelings, an impulse, etc.: *I had obeyed the impulse to open the gate and had walked up the drive.* ▷ HISTORY Latin *oboedire*

obfuscate *vb* **-cating, -cated** *Formal* to make something unnecessarily difficult to understand. ▷ HISTORY Latin *ob-* (intensive) + *fuscare* to blacken ▶ **obfuscation** *n* ▶ **obfuscatory** *adj*

obiter dictum *n, pl* **obiter dicta 1** *Law* an observation by a judge on a point of law not directly in issue in the case before him and thus neither requiring his decision nor serving as a precedent, but nevertheless of persuasive authority. **2** any comment or remark made in passing. ▷ HISTORY Latin: something said in passing

obituary *n, pl* **-aries** a published announcement of a death, usually with a short biography of the dead person. ▷ HISTORY Latin *obitus* death ▶ **obituarist** *n*

obj. **1** objection. **2** *Grammar* object(ive).

object[1] *n* **1** a thing that can be touched or seen. **2** a person or thing seen as a focus for feelings, actions, or thought: *she had become for him an object of compassion.* **3** an aim or purpose: *the main object of the exercise.* **4** *Philosophy* that which can be perceived by the mind, as contrasted with the thinking subject. **5** *Grammar* a noun, pronoun, or other noun group that receives the action of a verb or is governed by a preposition, such as *the bottle* in *she threw the bottle.* **6 no object** not a hindrance or obstacle: *money's no object.* ▷ HISTORY Late Latin *objectus* something thrown before (the mind)

object[2] *vb* **1** to express disapproval or opposition: *my colleagues objected strongly to further delays.* **2** to state as one's reason for opposing: *he objected that his small staff would be unable to handle the added work.* ▷ HISTORY Latin *ob-* against + *jacere* to throw ▶ **objector** *n*

objection *n* **1** an expression or feeling of opposition or disapproval. **2** a reason for opposing something: *the planning officer had raised no objection to the proposals.*

objectionable *adj* offensive or unacceptable.

objective *n* **1** an aim or purpose: *the objective is to highlight the environmental threat to the planet.* **2** *Grammar* same as **objective case**. **3** *Optics* the lens nearest to the object observed in an optical instrument. ✧ *adj* **4** not distorted by personal feelings or bias: *I have tried to be as objective as possible in my presentation.* **5** of or relating to actual facts as opposed to thoughts or feelings: *stand back and try to take a more objective view of your life as a whole.* **6** existing independently of the mind; real. ▶ **objectival** *adj* ▶ **objectively** *adv* ▶ **objectivity** *n*

objective case *n Grammar* a grammatical case in some languages that identifies the direct object of a verb or preposition.

objective shot *n Films, television* a camera shot taken from a neutral position rather than from the angle of vision of one of the characters in the scene. Compare **subjective shot**.

object lesson *n* a practical demonstration of some principle or ideal.

objet d'art (**ob**-zhay **dahr**) *n, pl* **objets d'art** (**ob**-zhay **dahr**) a small object considered to be of artistic worth. ▷ **HISTORY** French: object of art

oblate *adj Geom* (of a sphere) flattened at the poles: *the oblate spheroid of the earth.* ▷ **HISTORY** New Latin *oblatus* lengthened

oblation *n* **1** *Christianity* the offering of bread and wine to God at Communion. **2** any offering made for religious purposes. ▷ **HISTORY** Medieval Latin *oblatus* offered ▶ **oblational** *adj*

obligated *adj* being morally or legally bound to do something: *they are obligated to provide temporary accommodation.* ▶ **obligative** *adj*

obligation *n* **1** a moral or legal duty. **2** the binding power of such a duty: *I feel under some obligation to help you with your education.* **3** a sense of being in debt because of a service or favour: *I don't want him marrying me out of obligation.*

obligatory *adj* required or compulsory because of custom or law.

oblige *vb* **obliging, obliged 1** to compel someone by legal, moral, or physical means to do something. **2** to make (someone) indebted or grateful for a favour: *I am obliged to you for your help.* **3** to do a favour to someone: *she obliged the guests with a song.* ▷ **HISTORY** Latin *ob-* towards + *ligare* to bind

obliging *adj* willing to be helpful. ▶ **obligingly** *adv*

oblique (oh-**bleak**) *adj* **1** at an angle; slanting. **2** *Geom* (of lines or planes) neither perpendicular nor parallel to one another. **3** indirect or evasive: *only oblique references have been made to the anti-government unrest.* ✧ *n* **4** same as **solidus**. ▷ **HISTORY** Latin *obliquus* ▶ **obliquely** *adv* ▶ **obliqueness** *n*

oblique angle *n* an angle that is not a right angle or any multiple of a right angle.

obliterate *vb* **-rating, -rated** to destroy every trace of; wipe out completely. ▷ **HISTORY** Latin *oblitterare* to erase ▶ **obliteration** *n*

oblivion *n* **1** the condition of being forgotten or disregarded: *the Marxist-Leninist wing of the party looks set to sink into oblivion.* **2** the state of being unaware or unconscious: *guests seemed to feel a social obligation to drink themselves into oblivion.* ▷ **HISTORY** Latin *oblivio* forgetfulness

oblivious *adj* unaware or unconscious: *oblivious of her soaking clothes; I was oblivious to the beauty.* ▶ **obliviousness** *n*

oblong *adj* **1** having an elongated, rectangular shape. ✧ *n* **2** a figure or object having this shape. ▷ **HISTORY** Latin *oblongus*

obloquy (**ob**-lock-wee) *n, pl* **-quies** *Formal* **1** abusive statements or blame: *the British press was held up to moral obloquy.* **2** disgrace brought about by this: *the punishment of lifelong public obloquy and private embarrassment.* ▷ **HISTORY** Latin *obloquium* contradiction

obnoxious *adj* extremely unpleasant. ▷ **HISTORY** Latin *obnoxius* ▶ **obnoxiousness** *n*

oboe *n* a double-reeded woodwind instrument with a penetrating nasal tone. ▶ **oboist** *n*

> **WORD HISTORY**
> 'Oboe' comes from French *haut bois*, meaning 'high wood', a reference to the instrument's relatively high pitch compared to other instruments of the woodwind family.

obscene *adj* **1** offensive to accepted standards of decency or modesty. **2** *Law* tending to deprave or corrupt: *an obscene publication.* **3** disgusting: *a great dark obscene pool of blood.* ▷ **HISTORY** Latin *obscenus* inauspicious ▶ **obscenity** *n*

obscure *adj* **1** not well-known: *the concerts feature several obscure artists.* **2** not easily understood: *the contracts are written in obscure language.* **3** unclear or indistinct. ✧ *vb* **-scuring, -scured 4** to make unclear or vague; hide: *no amount of bluster could obscure the fact that the prime minister had run out of excuses.* **5** to cover or cloud over. ▷ **HISTORY** Latin *obscurus* dark ▶ **obscuration** *n* ▶ **obscurity** *n*

obsequies (**ob**-sick-weez) *pl n, sing* **-quy** *Formal* funeral rites. ▷ **HISTORY** Medieval Latin *obsequiae*

obsequious (ob-**seek**-wee-uss) *adj* being overattentive in order to gain favour. ▷ **HISTORY** Latin *obsequiosus* compliant ▶ **obsequiousness** *n*

observance *n* **1** the observing of a law or custom. **2** a ritual, ceremony, or practice, esp. of a religion.

observant *adj* quick to notice details around one; sharp-eyed.

observation *n* **1** the act of watching or the state of being watched. **2** a comment or remark. **3** detailed examination of something before analysis, diagnosis, or interpretation: *you may be admitted to hospital for observation and rest.* **4** the facts learned from observing. **5** the ability to notice things: *she has good powers of observation.* ▶ **observational** *adj*

observatory *n, pl* **-ries** a building specially designed and equipped for studying the weather and the stars.

observe *vb* **-serving, -served 1** to see or notice: *it is worth observing that old Chinese maps and charts usually show south at the top.* **2** to watch (something) carefully. **3** to make scientific examinations of. **4** to remark: *the speaker observed that times had changed.* **5** to keep (a law or custom). ▷ **HISTORY** Latin *observare* ▶ **observable** *adj* ▶ **observer** *n*

obsessed *adj* thinking about someone or something all the time: *he had become obsessed with her.* ▷ **HISTORY** Latin *obsessus* besieged ▶ **obsessive** *adj, n*

obsession *n* **1** something that preoccupies a person to the exclusion of other things: *his principal obsession was with trying to economize.* **2** *Psychiatry* a persistent idea or impulse, often associated with anxiety and mental illness. ▶ **obsessional** *adj*

obsidian *n* a dark glassy volcanic rock. ▷ **HISTORY** after *Obsius,* the discoverer of a stone resembling obsidian

obsolescent *adj* becoming obsolete or out of date. ▶ **obsolescence** *n*

obsolete *adj* no longer used; out of date. ▷ **HISTORY** Latin *obsoletus* worn out

> **WORD TIP**
> The word *obsoleteness* is hardly ever used, *obsolescence* standing as the noun form for both *obsolete* and *obsolescent.*

obstacle *n* **1** a situation or event that prevents something being done: *there are obstacles which could slow the development of a vaccine.* **2** a person or thing that hinders movement. ▷ **HISTORY** Latin *obstaculum,* from *ob-* against + *stare* to stand

obstetrician *n* a doctor who specializes in obstetrics.

obstetrics *n* the branch of medicine concerned with pregnancy and childbirth. ▷ **HISTORY** Latin *obstetrix* a midwife ▶ **obstetric** *adj*

obstinate *adj* **1** keeping stubbornly to a particular opinion or course of action. **2** difficult to treat or deal with: *obstinate weeds.* ▷ **HISTORY** Latin *obstinatus* ▶ **obstinacy** *n* ▶ **obstinately** *adv*

obstreperous *adj* noisy and difficult to control: *her obstreperous teenage son.* ▷ **HISTORY** Latin *ob-* against + *strepere* to roar

obstruct *vb* **1** to block a way with an obstacle. **2** to make progress or activity difficult: *this government will never obstruct the course of justice.* **3** to block a clear view of. ▷ **HISTORY** Latin *obstructus* built against

obstruction *n* **1** a person or thing that obstructs. **2** the act of obstructing or being obstructed. **3** *Sport* the act of unfairly impeding an opposing player.

obstructionist *n* a person who deliberately obstructs legal or parliamentary business. ▶ **obstructionism** *n*

obstructive *adj* deliberately causing difficulties or delays. ▶ **obstructively** *adv* ▶ **obstructiveness** *n*

obtain *vb* **1** to gain possession of; get. **2** *Formal* to be customary or accepted: *silence obtains from eight in the evening.* ▷ **HISTORY** Latin *obtinere* to take hold of ▶ **obtainable** *adj*

obtrude *vb* **-truding, -truded 1** to push oneself or one's opinions on others in an unwelcome way. **2** to be or make unpleasantly noticeable. ▷ **HISTORY** Latin *obtrudere* ▶ **obtrusion** *n*

obtrusive *adj* unpleasantly noticeable: *the music should fit your mood, it shouldn't be too obtrusive.* ▶ **obtrusiveness** *n*

obtuse *adj* **1** mentally slow or emotionally insensitive. **2** *Maths* (of an angle) between 90° and 180°. **3** not sharp or pointed; blunt. ▷ **HISTORY** Latin *obtusus* dulled ▶ **obtuseness** *n*

obverse *n* **1** a counterpart or opposite: *his true personality being the obverse of his outer image.* **2** the side of a coin that bears the main design. **3** the front, top, or main surface of anything. ▷ **HISTORY** Latin *obversus* turned towards

obviate *vb* **-ating, -ated** *Formal* to avoid or prevent (a need or difficulty): *a mediator will obviate the need for independent legal advice.* ▷ **HISTORY** Latin *obviare*

> **WORD TIP**
> Only things which have not yet occurred can be *obviated.* For example, one can *obviate* a possible future difficulty, but not one which already exists.

obvious *adj* **1** easy to see or understand. ✧ *n* **2 state the obvious** to say something that is unnecessary or already known: *he is prone to stating the obvious.* ▷ **HISTORY** Latin *obvius* ▶ **obviously** *adv* ▶ **obviousness** *n*

ocarina *n* a small egg-shaped wind instrument with a mouthpiece and finger holes. ▷ **HISTORY** Italian: little goose

occasion *n* **1** a particular event or the time at which it happens. **2** a need or reason to do or be something: *we barely knew him and never had occasion to speak of him.* **3** a suitable time or opportunity to do something. **4** a special event, time, or celebration: *a wedding day is a truly special occasion.* **5 on occasion** every so often. **6 rise to the occasion** to meet the special demands of a situation. ✧ *vb* **7** *Formal* to cause, esp. incidentally. ▷ **HISTORY** Latin *occasio* a falling down

occasional *adj* happening from time to time; not frequent or regular. ▶ **occasionally** *adv*

Occident *n* the western hemisphere, esp. Europe and America. ▷ **HISTORY** Latin *occidere* to fall (with reference to the setting sun) ▶ **Occidental** *adj*

occipital lobe *n Physiol* the rear part of each hemisphere of the brain.

occiput (**ox**-sip-putt) *n Anat* the back of the head or skull. ▷ **HISTORY** Latin *ob-* at the back of + *caput* head ▶ **occipital** *adj*

occlude *vb* **-cluding, -cluded** *Formal* **1** to block or stop up a passage or opening: *the arteries are occluded by deposits of plaque.* **2** to shut in or out: *slowly occluding him from Nash's vision.* **3** *Chem* (of a solid) to absorb and retain a gas or other substance. ▷ **HISTORY** Latin *occludere* ▶ **occlusion** *n*

occluded front *n Meteorol* the front formed when the cold front of a depression overtakes a warm front, raising the warm air from ground level.

occult *adj* **1** involving mystical or supernatural phenomena or powers. **2** beyond ordinary human understanding. **3** secret or mysterious. ✧ *n* **4 the occult** the knowledge and study of occult phenomena and powers. ▷ HISTORY Latin *occultus* hidden, secret

occupancy *n, pl* **-cies 1** the act of occupying a property. **2** the period of time during which one is an occupant of a property.

occupant *n* a person occupying a property, position, or place.

occupation *n* **1** a person's job or profession. **2** any activity on which someone's time is spent: *a pleasant and rewarding occupation.* **3** the control of a country by a foreign military power. **4** the act of occupying or the state of being occupied: *the occupation of Kuwait.* ▶ **occupational** *adj*

occupational hazard *n* something unpleasant that occurs due to your job: *frequent colds are an occupational hazard in teaching.*

occupational therapy *n* treatment of people with physical, emotional, or social problems using purposeful activity to help them overcome or learn to accept their problems.

occupier *n Brit* the person who lives in a particular house, whether as owner or tenant.

occupy *vb* **-pies, -pying, -pied 1** to live, stay, or work in (a house, flat, or office). **2** to keep (someone or someone's mind) busy. **3** to take up (time or space). **4** to move in and take control of (a country or other place): *soldiers have occupied the country's television station.* **5** to fill or hold (a position or office). ▷ HISTORY Latin *occupare* to seize hold of

occur *vb* **-curring, -curred 1** to happen. **2** to be found or be present; exist. **3 occur to** to come into the mind of. ▷ HISTORY Latin *occurrere* to run up to

> ☑ **WORD TIP**
> It is usually regarded as incorrect to talk of pre-arranged events *occurring* or *happening: the wedding took place* (not *occurred* or *happened*) *in the afternoon.*

occurrence *n* **1** something that happens. **2** the fact of occurring: *the likelihood of its occurrence increases with age.*

ocean *n* **1** the vast area of salt water covering about 70 per cent of the earth's surface. **2** one of the five principal divisions of this, the Atlantic, Pacific, Indian, Arctic, and Antarctic. **3** *Informal* a huge quantity or expanse: *oceans of replies.* **4** *Literary* the sea. ▷ HISTORY from *Oceanus,* Greek god of the stream believed to flow round the earth ▶ **oceanic** *adj*

ocean current *n Geog* a movement of water in the sea in a particular direction.

ocean-going *adj* (of a ship or boat) suited for travel on the open ocean.

oceanic crust *n Geol* the solid outer shell of the earth found beneath ocean basins and composed of basalt and sedimentary layers.

oceanic plate *n Geol* part of the earth's crust that lies under the sea.

oceanography *n* the study of oceans and their environment. ▶ **oceanographer** *n* ▶ **oceanographic** *adj*

ocean trench *n Geol* a deep trench found at the edge of an ocean basin caused by the moving of tectonic plates.

ocelot (**oss**-ill-lot) *n* a large cat of Central and South America with a dark-spotted yellow-grey coat. ▷ HISTORY Mexican Indian *ocelotl* jaguar

oche (**ok**-kee) *n Darts* a mark on the floor behind which a player must stand when throwing a dart. ▷ HISTORY origin unknown

ochre *or US* **ocher** (**oak**-er) *n* **1** a yellow or reddish-brown earth used in paints or dyes. ✧ *adj* **2** moderate yellow-orange to orange. ▷ HISTORY Greek *ōkhros* pale yellow

o'clock *adv* used after a number between one and twelve to specify an hour: *five o'clock in the morning.*

OCR optical character reader *or* recognition.

Oct. October.

octagon *n* a geometric figure with eight sides. ▷ HISTORY Greek *oktagōnos* having eight angles ▶ **octagonal** *adj*

octahedron (ok-ta-**heed**-ron) *n, pl* **-drons** *or* **-dra** a solid figure with eight plane faces.

octane *n* a liquid hydrocarbon found in petroleum.

octane number *or* **rating** *n* a number indicating the quality of a petrol.

octave *n* **1 a** the musical interval between the first note and the eighth note of a major or minor scale. **b** the higher of these two notes. **c** the series of notes filling this interval. **2** *Prosody* a rhythmic group of eight lines of verse. ▷ HISTORY Latin *octo* eight

octavo *n, pl* **-vos 1** a book size resulting from folding a sheet of paper of a standard size to form eight leaves. **2** a book or sheet of this size. ▷ HISTORY New Latin *in octavo* in an eighth (of a sheet)

octet *n* **1** a group of eight instrumentalists or singers. **2** a piece of music for eight performers. ▷ HISTORY Latin *octo* eight

October *n* the tenth month of the year. ▷ HISTORY Latin *octo* eight, since it was originally the eighth month in Roman reckoning

Octobrist *n History* a member of a Russian political party favouring the constitutional reforms granted in a manifesto issued by Nicholas II in Oct. 1905.

octogenarian *n* **1** a person between 80 and 89 years old. ✧ *adj* **2** between 80 and 89 years old. ▷ HISTORY Latin *octogenarius* containing eighty

octopus *n, pl* **-puses** a sea creature with a soft oval body and eight long tentacles with suckers. ▷ HISTORY Greek *oktōpous* having eight feet

ocular *adj* of or relating to the eyes or sight. ▷ HISTORY Latin *oculus* eye

oculist *n Old-fashioned* an ophthalmologist.

OD *Informal* ✧ *n* **1** an overdose of a drug. ✧ *vb* **OD'ing, OD'd 2** to take an overdose of a drug.

odd *adj* **1** unusual or peculiar: *his increasingly odd behaviour.* **2** occasional or incidental: *the odd letter from a friend abroad, the occasional postcard from a chum.* **3** leftover or additional: *we use up odd pieces* *of fabric to make up jerseys in wild designs.* **4** (of a number) not divisible by two. **5** being part of a pair or set when the other or others are missing: *the drawer was full of odd socks.* **6** somewhat more than the round numbers specified: *I had known him for the past twenty-odd years.* **7** **odd man** *or* **one out** a person or thing excluded from others forming a group or unit. ✧ See also **odds**. ▷ HISTORY Old Norse *oddi* angle, point, third or odd number ▶ **oddly** *adv* ▶ **oddness** *n*

oddball *n Informal* a strange or eccentric person.

oddity *n, pl* **-ties** **1** an odd person or thing. **2** a peculiar characteristic. **3** the quality of being or appearing unusual or strange.

oddments *pl n* odd pieces or things; leftovers: *oddments of wool.*

odds *pl n* **1** the probability, expressed as a ratio, that something will or will not happen: *the odds against an acquittal had stabilized at six to four.* **2** the difference, expressed as a ratio, between the money placed on a bet and the amount that would be received as winning payment: *the current odds are ten to one.* **3** the likelihood that a certain state of affairs will be so: *the odds are that you are going to fail.* **4** the advantage that one contender is judged to have over another: *the odds are in his favour.* **5 it makes no odds** *Brit & Austral* it does not matter. **6 at odds** on bad terms. **7 over the odds** more than is expected or necessary.

odds and ends *pl n* small, usually unimportant, objects, jobs to be done, etc.: *I have brought a few odds and ends with me.*

ode *n* a lyric poem, usually addressed to a particular subject, with lines of varying lengths and metres. ▷ HISTORY Greek *ōidē* song

odious *adj* offensive or hateful: *I steeled myself for the odious task.* ▷ HISTORY see ODIUM ▶ **odiousness** *n*

odium (**oh**-dee-um) *n Formal* widespread dislike or disapproval of a person or action. ▷ HISTORY Latin

odometer (odd-**om**-it-er) *n US & Canad* same as **mileometer**. ▷ HISTORY Greek *hodos* way + -METER

odour *or US* **odor** *n* a particular and distinctive scent or smell. ▷ HISTORY Latin *odor* ▶ **odorous** *adj* ▶ **odourless** *adj*

odyssey (**odd**-iss-ee) *n* a long eventful journey.

> **WORD HISTORY**
> The Odyssey is one of the two great poems attributed to the Greek poet Homer. It describes the ten-year homeward journey of the Greek hero Odysseus, king of Ithaca, after the Trojan War.

OE *NZ informal* overseas experience: *he's away on his OE.*

OECD Organization for Economic Cooperation and Development.

oedema *or* **edema** (id-**deem**-a) *n, pl* **-mata** *Pathol* an abnormal accumulation of fluid in the tissues of the body, causing swelling. ▷ HISTORY Greek *oidēma* swelling

Oedipus complex (**ee**-dip-puss) *n Psychoanal* the usually unconscious sexual desire of a child, esp. a male child, for the parent of the opposite sex. ▶ **oedipal** *adj*

o'er *prep, adv Poetic* over.

oesophagus (ee-**soff**-a-guss) *n, pl* **-gi** (-guy) the tube through which food travels from the throat to the stomach; gullet. ▷ HISTORY Greek *oisophagos* ▶ **oesophageal** *adj*

oestrogen (**ee**-stra-jen) *n* a female sex hormone that controls the reproductive cycle, and prepares the body for pregnancy. ▷ HISTORY from *oestrus* + *-gen* (suffix) producing

oestrus (**ee**-struss) *n* a regularly occurring period of fertility and sexual receptivity in the reproductive cycle of most female mammals, except humans; heat. ▷ HISTORY Greek *oistros* gadfly, hence frenzy

of *prep* **1** belonging to; situated in or coming from; because of: *the inhabitants of former East Germany; I saw five people die of chronic hepatitis.* **2** used after words or phrases expressing quantities: *a pint of milk.* **3** specifying an amount or value: *we had to release the bombs at a height of 400 metres.* **4** made up of, containing, or characterized by: *a length of rope; she is a woman of enviable beauty.* **5** used to link a verbal noun with a following noun or noun phrase that is either the subject or the object of the verb: *the sudden slipping of the plates of the Earth's crust; the bombing of civilian targets.* **6** at a given distance or space of time from: *you can still find wood within a mile of the village; he had been within hours of leaving for Romania.* **7** used to specify or give more information about: *the city of Glasgow; a meeting on the subject of regional security.* **8** about or concerning: *speaking of boycotts.* **9** *US* before the hour of: *about quarter of eight in the evening.* ▷ HISTORY Old English

> **WORD TIP**
> See at **off.**

Ofcom *n* (in Britain) Office of Communications: a government body regulating the telecommunications industries.

off *prep* **1** so as to be no longer in contact with: *take the wok off the heat.* **2** so as to be no longer attached to or associated with: *making use of benefit disqualification to terrorize the unemployed off the register.* **3** away from: *he was driven off the road.* **4** situated near to or leading away from: *they were laying out a bombing range off the coast.* **5** no longer having a liking for: *she's gone off you lately.* **6** no longer using: *he was off heroin for a year.* ✧ *adv* **7** so as to deactivate or disengage: *turn off the gas supply.* **8 a** so as to get rid of: *he was flying at midnight so he had to sleep off his hangover.* **b** as a reduction in price: *she took twenty per cent off.* **9** spent away from work or other duties: *it was the assistant manager's day off.* **10** away; at a distance: *the men dashed back to their car and sped off.* **11** away in the future: *the date was six weeks off.* **12** so as to be no longer taking place: *the investigation was hastily called off.* **13** removed from contact with something: *he took the jacket off.*

14 off and on occasionally; not regularly or continuously: *we lived together off and on.* ✧ *adj* **15** not on; no longer operating: *her bedroom light was off.* **16** cancelled or postponed: *the deal is off and your deposit will be returned in full.* **17** in a specified condition, esp. regarding money or provisions: *a married man with four children is better off on the dole; how are you off for money?* **18** not up to the usual standard: *an off year for good wine.* **19** no longer on the menu: *haddock is off.* **20** (of food or drink) having gone bad or sour: *this milk is off.* ✧ *n* **21** *Cricket* the side of the field to the right of a right-handed batsman when he is facing the bowler. ▷ **HISTORY** variant of *of*

> **WORD TIP**
> In standard English, *off* is not followed by *of: he stepped off* (not *off of*) *the platform.*

offal *n* the edible internal parts of an animal, such as the heart or liver. ▷ **HISTORY** *off* + *fall,* referring to parts cut off

offal pit *or* **hole** *n NZ* a place on a farm for the disposal of animal offal.

offbeat *adj* unusual, unconventional, or eccentric.

off-break *n Cricket* a bowled ball that spins from off to leg on pitching.

off colour *adj* **1** slightly ill; unwell. **2** slightly indecent: *an off colour joke.*

offcut *n* a piece of paper, wood, or fabric remaining after the main pieces have been cut; remnant.

offence *or US* **offense** *n* **1** *Law* a breaking of a law or rule; a crime. **2** annoyance or anger. **3** a cause of annoyance or anger. **4 give offence** to cause to feel upset or angry. **5 take offence** to feel hurt or offended.

offend *vb* **1** to hurt the feelings of (a person); insult. **2** to be disagreeable to; disgust: *the lady was offended by what she saw.* **3** to commit a crime. ▷ **HISTORY** Latin *offendere* ▶ **offender** *n* ▶ **offending** *adj*

offensive *adj* **1** unpleasant or disgusting to the senses: *there was an offensive smell of beer.* **2** causing annoyance or anger; insulting. **3** for the purpose of attack rather than defence. ✧ *n* **4** an attitude or position of aggression: *to go on the offensive.* **5** an attack or hostile action: *troops had launched a major offensive against the rebel forces.* ▶ **offensively** *adv*

offer *vb* **1** to present for acceptance or rejection: *I offered her a lift.* **2** to provide: *this department offers a wide range of courses.* **3** to present itself: *if an opportunity should offer.* **4** to be willing (to do something): *his father offered to pay his tuition.* **5** to put forward (a proposal, information, or opinion) for consideration: *may I offer a different view?* **6** to present for sale. **7** to propose as payment; bid. **8** to present (a prayer or sacrifice) as an act of worship. **9** to show readiness for: *to offer resistance.* ✧ *n* **10** something that is offered. **11** the act of offering. ▷ **HISTORY** Latin *offerre* to present

offering *n* **1** something that is offered. **2** a contribution to the funds of a religious organization. **3** a sacrifice to a god.

offertory *n, pl* **-tories** *Christianity* **1** the part of a church service when the bread and wine for communion are offered for consecration. **2** the collection of money at this service. **3** the prayers said or sung while the worshippers' offerings are being brought to the altar.

offhand *adj also* **offhanded 1** curt or casual in manner: *I felt calm enough to adopt a casual offhand manner.* ✧ *adv* **2** without preparation: *I don't know offhand why that should be so.* ▶ **offhandedly** *adv* ▶ **offhandedness** *n*

office *n* **1** a room, set of rooms, or building in which business, professional duties, or clerical work are carried out. **2** a department of an organization dealing with particular business: *cheque books were sent from the printer to the bank's sorting office.* **3** the group of people working in an office: *she assured him that the office was running smoothly.* **4** a government department or agency: *Office of Fair Trading.* **5** a position of trust or authority, as in a government: *he would not seek a second term of office.* **6** a place where tickets, information, or some service can be obtained: *why don't you give the ticket office a ring?* **7** *Christianity* a religious ceremony or service. **8 good offices** the help given by someone to someone else: *Syria's good offices finally led to the release of two western hostages.* **9 in** *or* **out of office** (of a government) in *or* out of power. ▷ **HISTORY** Latin *officium* service, duty

officer *n* **1** a person in the armed services, or on a non-naval ship, who holds a position of authority. **2** a policeman or policewoman. **3** a person holding a position of authority in a government or organization.

official *adj* **1** of an office or position of authority: *I'm not here in any official capacity.* **2** approved by or derived from authority: *there has been no official announcement.* **3** formal or ceremonial: *he was speaking at an official dinner in Warsaw.* ✧ *n* **4** a person holding a position of authority. ▶ **officially** *adv*

officialdom *n* officials or bureaucrats collectively.

Official Receiver *n Brit* an officer appointed by the government to deal with the affairs of a bankrupt person or company.

officiate *vb* **-ating, -ated 1** to perform the duties of an office; act in an official capacity: *the referee will officiate at the match.* **2** to conduct a religious or other ceremony: *the priest officiated at the wedding.* ▶ **officiation** *n* ▶ **officiator** *n*

officious *adj* offering unwanted advice or services; interfering. ▷ **HISTORY** Latin *officiosus* kindly ▶ **officiousness** *n*

offing *n* **1** the part of the sea that can be seen from the shore. **2 in the offing** *Brit, Austral & NZ* not far off; likely to occur soon.

off key *adj, adv Music* out of tune.

off-licence *n Brit* a shop or a counter in a shop where alcoholic drink is sold for drinking elsewhere.

off-line *adj* (of computer equipment) not directly connected to or controlled by the central processing unit of a computer.

off-load *vb* to get rid of (something unpleasant), usually by giving it to someone else: *you take all the credit and off-load all the blame.*

off-putting *adj Informal* rather unpleasant or disturbing: *it can be very off-putting when you first visit a social security office.*

off-road *adj* (of a motor vehicle) designed for use away from public roads.

off-roader *n* a motor vehicle designed for use away from public roads.

offset *vb* **-setting, -set 1** to cancel out or compensate for. **2** to print (something) using the offset process. ✧ *n* **3** a printing method in which the impression is made onto a surface, such as a rubber roller, which transfers it to the paper. **4** *Bot* a short runner in certain plants that produces roots and shoots at the tip.

offshoot *n* **1** a shoot growing from the main stem of a plant. **2** something that has developed from something else.

offshore *adj, adv* **1** away from or at some distance from the shore. ✧ *adj* **2** sited or conducted at sea: *he reversed his position on offshore drilling.*

offside *adj, adv* **1** *Sport* (of a player) in a position illegally ahead of the ball when it is played. ✧ *n* **2** *Chiefly Brit* the side of a vehicle nearest the centre of the road.

offspring *n* **1** the immediate descendant or descendants of a person or animal. **2** a product, outcome, or result: *the women's liberation movement was the offspring of the 1960s.*

Ofgem *n* (in Britain) Office of Gas and Electricity Markets: the body which regulates the power supply industries.

Oflot *n* (in Britain) Office of the National Lottery: the body which oversees the running of the National Lottery.

Ofsted *n* (in Britain) Office for Standards in Education: the body which assesses the educational standards of schools in England and Wales.

oft *adv Old-fashioned or poetic* short for **often**. ▷ **HISTORY** Old English

often *adv* **1** frequently; much of the time. **2 as often as not** quite frequently. **3 every so often** occasionally. **4 more often than not** in more than half the instances. ▷ **HISTORY** Middle English variant of *oft*

Ofwat *n* (in Britain) Office of Water Services: the body which regulates the activities of the water companies in England and Wales.

ogee arch (**oh**-jee) *n* a pointed arch made with an S-shaped curve on each side. ▷ **HISTORY** probably from Old French

ogle *vb* **ogling, ogled** to stare at (someone) lustfully. ▷ **HISTORY** probably from Low German *oegeln*

O grade *n* (formerly) **1** the basic level of the Scottish Certificate of Education. **2** a pass in a particular subject at O grade: *she has eight O grades.*

ogre *n* **1** (in folklore) a man-eating giant. **2** any monstrous or cruel person. ▷ **HISTORY** French ▸ **ogreish** *adj* ▸ **ogress** *fem n*

oh *interj* an exclamation of surprise, pain, pleasure, fear, or annoyance.

OH Ohio.

ohm *n* the SI unit of electrical resistance. ▷ **HISTORY** after Georg Simon *Ohm*, physicist

OHMS (in Britain and the Commonwealth) On Her (*or* His) Majesty's Service.

Ohm's law *n Electronics* the principle that the electric current passing through a conductor is directly proportional to the potential difference across it, provided that the temperature remains constant. ▷ **HISTORY** named after Georg Simon *Ohm*, German physicist

oil *n* **1** any of a number of viscous liquids with a smooth sticky feel, which are usually flammable, insoluble in water, and are obtained from plants, animals, or mineral deposits by synthesis. **2** same as **petroleum**. **3** a substance derived from petroleum and used for lubrication. **4** *Brit* paraffin as a domestic fuel. **5** oil colour or paint. **6** an oil painting. ✧ *vb* **7** to lubricate with oil or apply oil to. **8 oil the wheels** to make things run smoothly. ▷ **HISTORY** Latin *oleum* (olive) oil

oilcloth *n* a cotton fabric treated with oil or a synthetic resin to make it waterproof, formerly used esp. for tablecloths.

oilfield *n* an area containing reserves of oil.

oilfired *adj* using oil as fuel.

oil paint *n* a thick paint made of pigment ground in linseed oil.

oil painting *n* **1** a picture painted with oil paints. **2** the art of painting with oil paints.

oil rig *n* a structure used as a base when drilling an oil well.

oil-seed rape *n* same as **rape**[2].

oilskin *n* **1** a thick cotton fabric treated with oil to make it waterproof. **2** a protective outer garment made of this fabric.

oil slick *n* a mass of floating oil covering an area of water.

oil well *n* a well bored into the earth or sea bed to a supply of oil.

oily *adj* **oilier, oiliest 1** soaked or covered with oil. **2** of, containing, or like oil. **3** attempting to gain favour by insincere behaviour and flattery. ▸ **oiliness** *n*

ointment *n* a smooth greasy substance applied to the skin to heal or protect, or as a cosmetic: *home-made creams and ointments.* ▷ **HISTORY** Latin *unguentum* unguent

OK Oklahoma.

O.K. *Informal* ✧ *interj* **1** an expression of approval or agreement. ✧ *adj, adv* **2** in good or satisfactory condition. ✧ *vb* **O.K.ing, O.K.ed 3** to approve or endorse. ✧ *n, pl* **O.K.s 4** approval or agreement. ▷ **HISTORY** perhaps from *o(ll) k(orrect)*, jocular alteration of *all correct*

okapi (oh-**kah**-pee) *n, pl* **-pis** *or* **-pi** an African mammal related to the giraffe, but with a shorter neck, a reddish coat, and white stripes on the legs. ▷ **HISTORY** from a Central African word

okay *interj, adj, adv, vb, n* same as **O.K.**

okra *n* a tall plant with long green pods that are used as food. ▷ **HISTORY** West African

old *adj* **1** having lived or existed for a long time: *the old woman; burning witches is one old custom I've no desire to see revived.* **2** of or relating to advanced years or a long life: *I twisted my knee as I tried to squat and cursed old age.* **3** worn with age or use: *the old bathroom fittings.* **4** having lived or existed for a specified period: *he is 60 years old.* **5** the earlier or earliest of two or more things with the same name: *the old edition; the Old Testament.* **6** designating the form of a language in which the earliest known records are written: *Old English.* **7** familiar through long acquaintance or repetition: *an old acquaintance; the legalization argument is an old and familiar one.* **8** dear: used as a term of affection or familiarity: *always rely on old Tom to turn out.* **9** out of date; unfashionable. **10** former or previous: *my old housekeeper lent me some money.* **11** of long standing: *he's an old and respected member of staff.* **12** **good old days** an earlier period of time regarded as better than the present. ✧ *n* **13** an earlier or past time: *in days of old.* ▷ **HISTORY** Old English *eald* ▶ **oldish** *adj*

old age pension *n* a former name for **retirement pension.** ▶ **old age pensioner** *n*

Old Bailey *n* the Central Criminal Court of England.

olden *adj Archaic or poetic* old: *in the olden days the girls were married young.*

Old English *n* the English language of the Anglo-Saxons, spoken from the fifth century AD to about 1100. Also called: **Anglo-Saxon**

Old English sheepdog *n* a large sheepdog with thick shaggy hair.

old-fashioned *adj* **1** in the style of a previous period; outdated: *she wore her hair in a strangely old-fashioned tight hairdo.* **2** favouring or denoting the styles or ideas of a former time: *old-fashioned values.*

old flame *n Informal, old-fashioned* a person with whom one once had a romantic relationship.

Old French *n* the French language in its earliest forms, from about the 9th century up to about 1400.

old guard *n* a group of people in an organization who have traditional values: *the company's old guard is making way for a new, more youthful team.* ▷ **HISTORY** after Napoleon's imperial guard

old hand *n* a skilled or experienced person.

old hat *adj* old-fashioned or dull.

Old High German *n* a group of West Germanic dialects that developed into modern German; High German up to about 1200.

old identity *n NZ* a well-known local person who has lived in a area for a long time.

oldie *n Informal* an old song, film, or person.

old lady *n Informal* one's mother or wife.

old maid *n* **1** a woman regarded as unlikely ever to marry; spinster. **2** *Informal* a prim, fussy, or excessively cautious person.

old man *n* **1** *Informal* one's father or husband. **2** an affectionate form of address used to a man.

old master *n* **1** one of the great European painters of the period 1500 to 1800. **2** a painting by one of these.

old moon *n* a phase of the moon between last quarter and new moon, when it appears as a waning crescent.

Old Nick *n Informal* Satan.

old school tie *n* the system of mutual help supposed to operate among the former pupils of independent schools.

Old Style *n* the former method of reckoning dates using the Julian calendar.

Old Testament *n* the first part of the Christian Bible, containing the sacred Scriptures of the Hebrews.

Old World *n* that part of the world that was known to Europeans before the discovery of the Americas; the eastern hemisphere.

oleaginous (oh-lee-**aj**-in-uss) *adj* like or producing oil; oily. ▷ **HISTORY** Latin *oleaginus*

oleander (oh-lee-**ann**-der) *n* an evergreen Mediterranean shrub with fragrant white, pink, or purple flowers. ▷ **HISTORY** Medieval Latin

O level *n* (formerly in England and Wales) **1** the basic level of the General Certificate of Education. **2** a pass in a particular subject at O level: *a very intelligent young woman with ten O levels.*

olfactory *adj* of the sense of smell. ▷ **HISTORY** Latin *olere* to smell + *facere* to make

oligarchy (**ol**-lee-gark-ee) *n, pl* **-chies** **1** government by a small group of people. **2** a state governed this way. **3** a small group of people governing such a state. ▷ **HISTORY** Greek *oligos* few + *arkhein* to rule ▶ **oligarchic** *or* **oligarchical** *adj*

Oligocene (**ol**-lig-go-seen) *adj Geol* of the epoch of geological time about 35 million years ago. ▷ **HISTORY** Greek *oligos* little + *kainos* new

oligopoly *n, pl* **-lies** *Econ* a market situation in which control over the supply of a commodity is held by a small number of producers. ▷ **HISTORY** Greek *oligos* few + *pōlein* to sell

olive *n* **1** an evergreen Mediterranean tree. **2** the small green or black bitter-tasting fruit of this tree. ✧ *adj* **3** short for **olive-green.** ▷ **HISTORY** Latin *oliva*

olive branch *n* a peace offering: *I should offer some kind of olive branch and get in touch with them.*

olive-green *adj* deep yellowish-green.

Olympiad *n* **1** a staging of the modern Olympic Games. **2** an international contest in chess or other games.

Olympian *adj* **1** of Mount Olympus or the classical Greek gods. **2** majestic or godlike. ✧ *n* **3** a competitor in the Olympic Games. **4** a god of Mount Olympus.

Olympic *adj* of the Olympic Games.

Olympic Games *n* **1** an ancient Greek festival, held every fourth year in honour of Zeus, consisting of games and festivities. **2** Also called: **the**

Olympics the modern revival of these games, consisting of international athletic and sporting contests held every four years in a selected country.

OM Order of Merit (a Brit. title).

ombudsman *n, pl* **-men** an official who investigates citizens' complaints against the government or its servants. ▷ **HISTORY** Swedish: commissioner

omega *n* **1** the 24th and last letter of the Greek alphabet (Ω, ω). **2** the ending or last of a series.

omelette *or esp US* **omelet** *n* a dish of beaten eggs cooked in a flat pan and often folded round a savoury filling. ▷ **HISTORY** French

omen *n* **1** a thing or occurrence regarded as a sign of future happiness or disaster. **2** prophetic significance: *birds of ill omen.* ▷ **HISTORY** Latin

ominous *adj* warning of evil. ▷ **HISTORY** Latin *ominosus* ▶ **ominously** *adv*

omission *n* **1** something that has been left out or passed over. **2** an act of missing out or failing to do something: *we regret the omission of these and the names of the other fine artists.*

omit *vb* **omitting, omitted 1** to fail to include; leave out. **2** to fail (to do something). ▷ **HISTORY** Latin *omittere*

omnibus *n, pl* **-buses 1** a collection of works by one author or several works on a similar topic, reprinted in one volume. **2** Also called: **omnibus edition** a television or radio programme consisting of two or more episodes of a serial broadcast earlier in the week. **3** *Old-fashioned* a bus. ✧ *adj* **4** consisting of or dealing with several different things at once: *this year's version of an omnibus crime bill.* ▷ **HISTORY** Latin, literally: for all

omnipotent (om-**nip**-a-tent) *adj* having very great or unlimited power. ▷ **HISTORY** Latin *omnipotens* all-powerful ▶ **omnipotence** *n*

omnipresent *adj* (esp. of a god) present in all places at the same time. ▷ **HISTORY** Latin *omnis* all + *praesens* present ▶ **omnipresence** *n*

omniscient (om-**niss**-ee-ent) *adj Formal* knowing or seeming to know everything. ▷ **HISTORY** Latin *omnis* all + *scire* to know ▶ **omniscience** *n*

omniscient point of view *n Literature* a narrative style where the storyteller's point of view is not limited to that of a particular character.

omnivore (**om**-niv-vore) *n* an animal that eats any type of food.

omnivorous (om-**niv**-or-uss) *adj* **1** eating any type of food. **2** taking in everything indiscriminately: *his omnivorous sociability has meant constant hard work for his wife.* ▷ **HISTORY** Latin *omnivorus* all-devouring

on *prep* **1** in contact with or at the surface of: *let the cakes stand in the tins on a wire rack; she had dirt on her dress.* **2** attached to: *a piece of paper on a clipboard.* **3** carried with: *the message found on her.* **4** near to or along the side of: *the hotel is on the coast.* **5** within the time limits of (a day or date): *they returned to Moscow on 22nd September.* **6** being performed upon or relayed through the medium of: *a construction of refined sounds played on special musical instruments; what's on television?* **7** at the occasion of: *she had received numerous letters congratulating her on her election.* **8** immediately after or at the same time as: *check with the tourist office on arrival.* **9** through the use of: *an extraordinarily vigorous man who thrives on physical activity; the program runs on the Unix operating system.* **10** regularly taking (a drug): *she's on the pill.* **11** by means of (a mode of transport): *his only way up the hill had to be on foot; they get around on bicycles.* **12** in the process or course of: *he is away on a climbing expedition; coal miners have been on strike for six weeks.* **13** concerned with or relating to: *ten million viewers watched the recent series on homelessness.* **14** (of a statement or action) having as basis or grounds: *I have it on good authority.* **15** charged to: *all drinks are on the house for the rest of the evening.* **16** staked as a bet: *I'll have a bet on the favourite.* ✧ *adv* **17** in operation; functioning: *the lights had been left on all night.* **18** attached to, surrounding, or placed in contact with something: *they escaped with nothing on except sleeveless shirts and shorts.* **19** taking place: *what do you have on tonight?* **20** continuously or persistently: *the crisis must not be allowed to drag on indefinitely.* **21** forwards or further: *they trudged on.* **22 on and off** occasionally; not regularly or continuously. **23 on and on** without ceasing; continually. ✧ *adj* **24** *Informal* performing: *who's on next?* **25** *Informal* definitely taking place: *is the party still on?* **26** *Informal* tolerable, practicable, or acceptable: *I'm not going, that's just not on.* **27 on at** *Informal* nagging: *he was always on at her to stop smoking.* ✧ *n* **28** *Cricket* the side of the field to the left of a right-handed batsman when he is facing the bowler. ▷ **HISTORY** Old English *an, on*

ON Ontario.

onager *n, pl* **-gri** *or* **-gers** a wild ass of Persia. ▷ **HISTORY** Greek *onagros*

ONC (in Britain) Ordinary National Certificate.

once *adv* **1** one time; on one occasion only. **2** at some past time, but no longer: *I was in love once.* **3** by one degree (of relationship): *he was Deirdre's cousin once removed.* **4 once and for all** conclusively; for the last time. **5 once in a while** occasionally; now and then. **6 once or twice** a few times. **7 once upon a time** used to begin fairy tales and children's stories. ✧ *conj* **8** as soon as: *once you have learned good grammar you can leave it to nature and forget it.* ✧ *n* **9** one occasion or case: *once is enough.* **10 all at once a** suddenly. **b** simultaneously. **11 at once a** immediately. **b** simultaneously. **12 for once** this time, even if at no other time. ▷ **HISTORY** Middle English *ones, anes*

once-over *n Informal* a quick examination or appraisal.

oncogene (**ong**-koh-jean) *n* a gene present in all cells, that when abnormally activated can cause cancer. ▷ **HISTORY** Greek *onkos* tumour + *-gen* (suffix) producing

oncoming *adj* coming nearer in space or time; approaching: *oncoming traffic.*

OND (in Britain) Ordinary National Diploma.

one *adj, n* **1** single or lone (person or thing); not two or more: *one civilian has died and thirty-three have been injured.* **2** only or unique (person or thing): *he is the one to make correct judgments and influence the public; she was unique, inimitable, one of a kind.* **3** a specified (person or thing) as distinct from another or others of its kind: *place one hand under the knee and the other under the ankle; which one is correct?* **4 one or two** a few. ✧ *adj* **5** a certain, indefinite, or unspecified (time): *one day he would learn the truth about her.* **6** *Informal, emphatic* a: *we're on to one hell of a story.* ✧ *pron* **7** an indefinite person regarded as typical of every person: *one can always hope that there won't be an accident.* **8** any indefinite person: *one can catch fine trout in this stream.* **9** I or me: *one only wonders what he has against the dogs.* ✧ *n* **10** the smallest natural number and first cardinal number. **11** a numeral, 1 or I, representing this number. **12** something representing or consisting of one unit. **13** *Informal* a joke or story: *have you heard the one about the actress and the bishop?* **14 (all) in one** combined or united. **15 all one** of no consequence: *leave if you want to, it's all one to me.* **16 at one with** in agreement or harmony with. **17 one and all** everyone, without exception. **18 one by one** one at a time; individually. ▷ HISTORY Old English *ān*

one-armed bandit *n Informal* a fruit machine operated by pulling down a lever at one side.

one-liner *n Informal* a short joke or witty remark.

oneness *n* **1** agreement. **2** uniqueness. **3** sameness.

one-night stand *n* **1** *Informal* a sexual encounter lasting only one evening or night. **2** a performance given only once at any one place.

one-off *n* something that happens or is made only once.

onerous (**own**-er-uss) *adj* (of a task) difficult to carry out. ▷ HISTORY Latin *onus* load ▶ **onerousness** *n*

oneself *pron* **1** the reflexive form of *one*. **2** one's normal or usual self: *one doesn't feel oneself after such an experience.*

one-sided *adj* **1** considering or favouring only one side of a matter: *it is a one-sided debate.* **2** having all the advantage on one side: *it was a one-sided match with Brazil missing a succession of chances.*

one-to-one *adj* **1** (of two or more things) corresponding exactly. **2** denoting a relationship or encounter in which someone is involved with only one other person: *one-to-one meetings.* **3** *Maths* involving the pairing of each member of one set with only one member of another set, without remainder.

one-way *adj* **1** moving or allowing travel in one direction only: *the town centre has a baffling one-way system.* **2** involving no reciprocal obligation or action: *he does not get anything back out of the one-way relationship.*

ongoing *adj* in progress; continuing: *there are still ongoing discussions about the future role of NATO.*

onion *n* **1** a vegetable with an edible bulb with a strong smell and taste. **2 know one's onions** *Brit & NZ slang* to be fully acquainted with a subject. ▷ HISTORY Latin *unio* ▶ **oniony** *adj*

onion skin peeling *n Geol* the effect that weathering can have on sedimentary rocks, where the surface is worn away to reveal successive layers.

on-line *or* **online** *adj* **1** (of computer equipment) directly connected to and controlled by the central processing unit of a computer. **2** of or relating to the Internet: *online shopping.*

onlooker *n* a person who observes without taking part. ▶ **onlooking** *adj*

only *adj* **1** alone of its or their kind: *I will be talking to the only journalist to have been inside the prison.* **2** (of a child) having no brothers or sisters. **3** unique by virtue of superiority; best: *first class is the only way to travel.* **4 one and only** incomparable: *the one and only Diana Ross.* ✧ *adv* **5** without anyone or anything else being included; alone: *only you can decide if you can abide by this compromise.* **6** merely or just: *it's only Henry.* **7** no more or no greater than: *I was talking to a priest only a minute ago.* **8** merely: *they had only to turn up to win the competition.* **9** not earlier than; not until: *I've only found out today why you wouldn't come.* **10 if only** *or* **if ... only** used to introduce a wish or hope. **11 only too** extremely: *they were only too willing to do anything to help.* ✧ *conj* **12** but or however: *those countries are going through the same cycle, only a little later than us.* ▷ HISTORY Old English *ānlīc*

> **WORD TIP**
>
> In informal English, *only* is often used as a sentence connector: *I would have phoned you, only I didn't know your number.* This use should be avoided in formal writing: *I would have phoned you if I'd known your number.* In formal speech and writing, *only* is placed directly before the word or words that it modifies: *she could interview only three applicants in the morning.* In all but the most formal contexts, however, it is generally regarded as acceptable to put *only* before the verb: *she could only interview three applicants in the morning.* Care must be taken not to create ambiguity, esp. in written English, in which intonation will not, as it does in speech, help to show to which item in the sentence *only* applies. A sentence such as *she only drinks tea in the afternoon* is capable of two interpretations and is therefore better rephrased either as *she drinks only tea in the afternoon* (i.e. no other drink) or *she drinks tea only in the afternoon* (i.e. at no other time).

o.n.o. or near(est) offer.

onomatopoeia (on-a-mat-a-**pee**-a) *n Literature* use of a word that imitates the sound it represents, such as *hiss*. ▷ HISTORY Greek *onoma* name + *poiein* to make ▶ **onomatopoeic** *or* **onomatopoetic** *adj*

onset *n* a start; beginning.

onside *adj, adv Sport* (of a player) in a legal position, for example, behind the ball or with a required number of opponents between oneself and the opposing team's goal line.

onslaught *n* a violent attack. ▷ HISTORY Middle Dutch *aenslag*

onto *or* **on to** *prep* **1** to a position that is on: *step onto the train.* **2** having discovered or become aware of: *the police are onto us.* **3** into contact with: *get onto the factory.*

> **WORD TIP**
> *Onto* is now generally accepted as a word in its own right. *On to* is still used, however, where *on* is considered to be part of the verb: *he moved on to a different town* as contrasted with *he jumped onto the stage.*

ontology *n Philosophy* the study of the nature of being. ▷ **HISTORY** Greek *ōn* being + -LOGY ▸ **ontological** *adj*

onus (**own**-uss) *n, pl* **onuses** a responsibility, task, or burden: *the courts put the onus on parents.* ▷ **HISTORY** Latin: burden

onus of proof *n, pl* **onuses** *Law* the obligation to provide evidence that will convince the court or jury of the truth of one's contention if the case is to succeed; in criminal cases, the *onus of proof* lies with the prosecution and in civil cases, it lies with the plaintiff. Also: **burden of proof** ▷ **HISTORY** Latin: burden

onward *adj* **1** directed or moving forward. ✧ *adv also* **onwards 2** continuing; progressing.

onyx *n* a kind of quartz with alternating coloured layers, used as a gemstone. ▷ **HISTORY** Greek: fingernail (so called from its veined appearance)

oodles *pl n Informal* great quantities: *he has shown he can raise oodles of cash.* ▷ **HISTORY** origin unknown

oogenesis (oh-a-**jen**-iss-iss) *n Biol* the formation and development of ova.

oolite (**oh**-a-lite) *n* a limestone made up of tiny grains of calcium carbonate. ▷ **HISTORY** New Latin *oolites,* literally: egg stone ▸ **oolitic** *adj*

oom *n S African* a title of respect used to refer to an elderly man. ▷ **HISTORY** Afrikaans, literally: uncle

oops *interj* an exclamation of surprise or of apology when someone has a slight accident or makes a mistake.

OOS occupational overuse syndrome: pain caused by repeated awkward movements while at work.

ooze[1] *vb* **oozing, oozed 1** to flow or leak out slowly; seep. **2** (of a substance) to discharge moisture. **3** to overflow with (a feeling or quality): *he oozes confidence.* ✧ *n* **4** a slow flowing or leaking. ▷ **HISTORY** Old English *wōs* juice ▸ **oozy** *adj*

ooze[2] *n* a soft thin mud, such as that found at the bottom of a lake, river, or sea. ▷ **HISTORY** Old English *wāse* mud

op. opus.

opacity (ohp-**ass**-it-tee) *n, pl* **-ties 1** the state or quality of being opaque. **2** the quality of being difficult to understand; unintelligibility.

opal *n* a precious stone, usually milky or bluish in colour, with shimmering changing reflections. ▷ **HISTORY** Greek *opallios*

opalescent *adj* having shimmering changing reflections, like opal. ▸ **opalescence** *n*

opaque *adj* **1** not able to be seen through; not transparent or translucent. **2** hard to understand; unintelligible. ▷ **HISTORY** Latin *opacus* shady

op. cit. (op **sit**) (in textual annotations) in the work cited. ▷ **HISTORY** Latin *opere citato*

OPEC Organization of Petroleum-Exporting Countries.

open *adj* **1** not closed, fastened, or blocked up: *the doctor's office was open.* **2** not enclosed, covered, or wrapped: *the parcel was open.* **3** extended, expanded, or unfolded: *an open flower.* **4** ready for business: *some of the crafts rooms and photography shops are open all night.* **5** (of a job) available: *all the positions on the council should be open to females.* **6** unobstructed by buildings or trees: *we lived in a small market town surrounded by open countryside.* **7** free to all to join in, enter, or use: *there was an open competition and I was appointed.* **8** (of a season or period) not restricted for purposes of hunting game of various kinds. **9** not decided or finalized: *the legality of these sales is still an open question.* **10** ready to consider new ideas: *I was able to approach their problem with an open mind.* **11** honest and frank. **12** generous: *she has given me love and the open hand.* **13** exposed to view; blatant: *there has never been such sustained and open criticism of the President.* **14** unprotected; susceptible: *a change of policy which would leave vulnerable youths open to exploitation.* **15** having spaces or gaps: *open ranks; an open texture.* **16** *Computers* designed to an internationally agreed standard to allow communication between computers irrespective of size or manufacturer. **17** *Music* **a** (of a string) not stopped with the finger. **b** (of a note) played on such a string. **18** *Sport* (of a goal or court) unguarded or relatively unprotected. **19** (of a wound) exposed to the air. ✧ *vb* **20** to make or become open: *it was easy to open the back door and to slip noiselessly outside; she knelt and tried to open the drawer.* **21** to set or be set in action; start: *the US will have to open talks on Palestinian rights; I want to open a dress shop.* **22** to arrange for (a bank account), usually by making an initial deposit. **23** to declare open ceremonially or officially. ✧ *n* **24 the open** any wide or unobstructed area. **25** *Sport* a competition which anyone may enter. ▷ **HISTORY** Old English ▸ **opener** *n* ▸ **openly** *adv* ▸ **openness** *n*

open air *n* the place or space where the air is unenclosed; outdoors.

opencast mining *n Brit & Austral* mining by excavating from the surface. ▷ **HISTORY** *open* + archaic *cast* ditch, cutting

open circuit *n Electronics* an incomplete electrical circuit in which no current flows.

open day *n* a special occasion on which a school, university, or other institution is open for the public to visit.

open-ended *adj* **1** without definite limits; unrestricted: *the schedule is open-ended.* **2** (of an activity) done without the aim of attaining a particular result or decision: *the dangers of open-ended military involvement.*

open-handed *adj* generous.

open-hearted *adj* **1** kind or generous. **2** willing to speak one's mind; candid.

open-heart surgery *n* surgical repair of the heart during which the heart is exposed and the blood circulation is maintained mechanically.

open house *n* a situation in which people allow friends or visitors to come to their house whenever they want to.

opening *n* **1** the beginning or first part of something. **2** the first performance of a theatrical production. **3** a chance or opportunity: *an opening into show business.* **4** a hole or gap.

opening time *n Brit & Austral* the time at which public houses can legally open for business.

open letter *n* a letter, esp. one of protest, addressed to an individual but published in a newspaper or magazine for all to read.

open market *n* a process by which prices are decided by supply and demand and goods are sold anywhere.

open-minded *adj* willing to consider new ideas; unprejudiced.

open-plan *adj* having no or few dividing walls between areas: *the house includes an open-plan living room and dining area.*

open prison *n* a prison in which the prisoners are not locked up, thus extending the range of work they can do.

open-range *adj Agriculture* of or relating to the grazing of farm animals on unfenced pasture.

Open University *n* (in Britain) a university teaching by means of television and radio lectures, correspondence courses, and summer schools.

open up *vb* **1** to make or become accessible: *the Berlin Wall came down and opened up new territory for dramatists.* **2** to speak freely or without self-restraint. **3** to start firing a gun or guns. **4** *Informal* to increase the speed of (a vehicle).

open verdict *n* a finding by a coroner's jury of death without stating the cause.

opera[1] *n* **1** a dramatic work in which most or all of the text is sung to orchestral accompaniment. **2** the branch of music or drama relating to operas. **3** a group that produces or performs operas. **4** a theatre where opera is performed. ▷ **HISTORY** Latin: work

opera[2] *n* a plural of **opus**.

operable *adj* **1** capable of being treated by a surgical operation. **2** capable of being operated or put into practice. ▶ **operability** *n*

opera glasses *pl n* small low-powered binoculars used by audiences in theatres.

operand *n Maths* a quantity, variable, or function upon which an operation is performed.

operate *vb* **-ating, -ated 1** to work. **2** to control the working of (a machine). **3** to manage, direct, or run (a business or system). **4** to perform a surgical operation (upon a person or animal). **5** to conduct military or naval operations. ▷ **HISTORY** Latin *operari* to work

operatic *adj* **1** of or relating to opera. **2** overdramatic or exaggerated: *he was about to go out with his operatic strut.*

operating system *n* the software controlling a computer.

operating theatre *or US* **room** *n* a room in which surgical operations are performed.

operation *n* **1** the act or method of operating. **2** the condition of being in action: *there are twenty teleworking centres in operation around the country.* **3** an action or series of actions done to produce a particular result: *a large-scale police operation has been in place to manage the heavy traffic.* **4** *Surgery* a surgical procedure carried out to remove, replace, or repair a diseased or damaged part of the body. **5** a military or naval manoeuvre. **6** *Maths* any procedure, such as addition, in which a number is derived from another number or numbers by applying specific rules.

operational *adj* **1** in working order and ready for use. **2** of or relating to an action done to produce a particular result.

operations research *n* the analysis of problems in business and industry. Also called: **operational research**

operative (**op**-rat-tiv) *adj* **1** in force, effect, or operation: *these pension provisions became operative from 1978.* **2** (of a word) particularly relevant or significant: *'if' is the operative word.* **3** of or relating to a surgical operation. ✧ *n* **4** a worker with a special skill.

operator *n* **1** a person who operates a machine or instrument, esp. a telephone switchboard. **2** a person who runs a business: *your tour operator will arrange a visa for you.* **3** *Informal* a person who manipulates affairs and other people: *she considered him a shrewd operator who only liked to appear to be simple.* **4** *Maths* any symbol, term, or letter used to indicate or express a specific operation or process.

operculum (oh-**perk**-yew-lum) *n, pl* **-la** (-la) *or* **-lums** a covering flap or lidlike structure in animals or plants. ▷ **HISTORY** Latin: lid

operetta *n* a type of comic or light-hearted opera.

ophiolite suite *n Geol* a group of rock types frequently found together and originating in the oceanic crust.

ophthalmia *n* inflammation of the eyeball or conjunctiva. ▷ **HISTORY** Greek *ophthalmos* eye

ophthalmic *adj* of or relating to the eye.

ophthalmic optician *n* See **optician** (sense 1).

ophthalmology *n* the branch of medicine concerned with the eye and its diseases. ▶ **ophthalmologist** *n*

ophthalmoscope *n* an instrument for examining the interior of the eye.

opiate (**oh**-pee-ate) *n* **1** a narcotic or sedative drug containing opium. **2** something that causes mental dullness or inactivity.

opine *vb* **opining, opined** *Formal* to hold or express an opinion: *he opined that the navy would have to start again from the beginning.* ▷ **HISTORY** Latin *opinari*

opinion *n* **1** belief not founded on certainty or proof but on what seems probable. **2** evaluation or estimation of a person or thing: *they seemed to share my high opinion of her.* **3** a judgment given by an expert: *medical opinion.* **4 a matter of opinion** a point open to question. ▷ **HISTORY** Latin *opinio* belief

opinionated *adj* holding very strong opinions which one is convinced are right.

opinion evidence *n Law* evidence in which a witness expresses an opinion; such evidence is only admissible in the case of expert witnesses.

opinion poll *n* same as **poll** (sense 1).

opium (**oh**-pee-um) *n* an addictive narcotic drug made from the seed capsules of the opium poppy and used in medicine as a painkiller and sedative. ▷ **HISTORY** Latin: poppy juice

opossum *n, pl* **-sums** *or* **-sum 1** a thick-furred American marsupial, with a long snout and a hairless prehensile tail. **2** *Austral & NZ* a similar Australian animal, such as a phalanger. ▷ **HISTORY** Native American *aposoum*

opponent *n* a person who opposes another in a contest, battle, or argument. ▷ **HISTORY** Latin *opponere* to oppose

opportune *adj Formal* **1** happening at a time that is suitable or advantageous: *there was an opportune knock at the door.* **2** (of time) suitable for a particular purpose: *I have arrived at a very opportune moment.* ▷ **HISTORY** Latin *opportunus,* from *ob-* to + *portus* harbour (originally: coming to the harbour, obtaining timely protection)

opportunist *n* **1** a person who adapts his or her actions to take advantage of opportunities and circumstances without regard for principles. ✧ *adj* **2** taking advantage of opportunities and circumstances in this way. ▶ **opportunism** *n* ▶ **opportunistic** *adj*

opportunity *n, pl* **-ties 1** a favourable combination of circumstances. **2** a good chance or prospect.

opportunity shop *n Austral & NZ* a shop selling second-hand clothes, sometimes for charity. Sometimes shortened to: **op-shop**

opposable *adj Zool* (of the thumb) capable of touching the tip of all the other fingers.

oppose *vb* **-posing, -posed 1** Also: **be opposed to** to be against (something or someone) in speech or action. **2 as opposed to** in strong contrast with: *I'm a realist as opposed to a theorist.* ▷ **HISTORY** Latin *opponere* ▶ **opposing** *adj*

opposite *adj* **1** situated on the other or further side. **2** facing or going in contrary directions: *he saw another small craft heading the opposite way.* **3** completely different: *I have a different, in fact, opposite view on this subject.* **4** *Maths* (of a side in a triangle) facing a specified angle. ✧ *n* **5** a person or thing that is opposite; antithesis. ✧ *prep* **6** facing; across from. ✧ *adv* **7** in an opposite position: *fragments smashed through the windows of the house opposite.*

opposition *n* **1** the act of opposing or being opposed. **2** hostility, resistance, or disagreement. **3** a person or group antagonistic or opposed to another. **4** a political party or group opposed to the ruling party or government. **5** *Astrol* a diametrically opposite position of two heavenly bodies.

oppress *vb* **1** to put down or control by cruelty or force. **2** to make anxious or uncomfortable. ▷ **HISTORY** Latin *ob-* against + *premere* to press ▶ **oppression** *n* ▶ **oppressor** *n*

oppressive *adj* **1** cruel, harsh, or tyrannical. **2** uncomfortable or depressing: *a small flat can become rather oppressive.* **3** (of weather) hot and humid. ▶ **oppressiveness** *n*

opprobrium (op-**probe**-ree-um) *n Formal* **1** the state of being abused or scornfully criticized. **2** a cause of disgrace or shame. ▷ **HISTORY** Latin *ob-* against + *probrum* a shameful act ▶ **opprobrious** *adj*

op-shop *n Austral & NZ* short for **opportunity shop.**

opt *vb* to show preference (for) or choose (to do something). ▷ **HISTORY** Latin *optare* to choose

optic *adj* of the eye or vision. ▷ **HISTORY** Greek *optos* visible

optical *adj* **1** of or involving light or optics. **2** of the eye or the sense of sight; optic. **3** (of a lens) helping vision.

optical character reader *n* a computer device enabling letters and numbers to be optically scanned and input to a storage device.

optical fibre *n* a thin flexible glass fibre used in fibre optics to transmit information.

optician *n* **1** Also called: **ophthalmic optician** a person who is qualified to examine the eyes and prescribe and supply spectacles and contact lenses. **2** Also called: **dispensing optician** a person who supplies and fits spectacle frames and lenses, but is not qualified to prescribe lenses.

optic nerve *n* a cranial nerve of vertebrates that conducts nerve impulses from the retina of the eye to the brain.

optics *n* the science dealing with light and vision.

optimal *adj* best or most favourable.

optimism *n* **1** the tendency to take the most hopeful view in all matters. **2** *Philosophy* the doctrine of the ultimate triumph of good over evil. ▷ **HISTORY** Latin *optimus* best ▶ **optimist** *n* ▶ **optimistic** *adj* ▶ **optimistically** *adv*

optimize *or* **-mise** *vb* **-mizing, -mized** *or* **-mising, -mised** to make the most of.

optimum *n, pl* **-ma** *or* **-mums 1** the most favourable conditions or best compromise possible. ✧ *adj* **2** most favourable or advantageous; best: *balance is a critical part of an optimum diet.* ▷ **HISTORY** Latin: the best (thing)

option *n* **1** the power or liberty to choose: *we have no option other than to fully comply.* **2** something that is or may be chosen: *the menu includes a vegetarian option.* **3** an exclusive right, usually for a limited period, to buy or sell something at a future date: *a producer could extend his option on the material for another six months.* **4 keep** *or* **leave one's options open** not to commit oneself. **5 soft option** an easy alternative. ✧ *vb* **6** to obtain or grant an option on: *the film rights are optioned by an* *international film director.* ▷ HISTORY Latin *optare* to choose

optional *adj* possible but not compulsory; open to choice.

optometrist (op-**tom**-met-trist) *n* a person qualified to examine the eyes and prescribe and supply spectacles and contact lenses.
▶ **optometry** *n*

opt out *vb* **1** (often foll. by *of*) to choose not to be involved (in) or part (of), used esp. of schools and hospitals that leave the public sector. ✧ *n* **opt-out** **2** the act of opting out, esp. of a local authority administration.

opulent (**op**-pew-lent) *adj* **1** having or indicating wealth. **2** abundant or plentiful. ▷ HISTORY Latin *opulens* ▶ **opulence** *n*

opus (**oh**-puss) *n, pl* **opuses** *or* **opera** an artistic creation, esp. a musical work by a particular composer, numbered in order of publication: *Beethoven's opus 61.* ▷ HISTORY Latin: a work

or *conj* used to join: **1** alternatives: *do you want to go out or stay at home?* **2** rephrasings of the same thing: *twelve, or a dozen.* ▷ HISTORY Middle English contraction of *other*

OR Oregon.

oracle *n* **1** a shrine in ancient Greece or Rome at which gods were consulted through the medium of a priest or priestess for advice or prophecy. **2** a prophecy or statement made by an oracle. **3** any person believed to indicate future action with infallible authority. ▷ HISTORY Latin *oraculum*

oracular *adj* **1** of or like an oracle. **2** wise and prophetic. **3** mysterious or ambiguous.

oral *adj* **1** spoken or verbal; using spoken words. **2** of or for use in the mouth: *an oral thermometer.* **3** (of a drug) to be taken by mouth: *an oral contraceptive.* ✧ *n* **4** an examination in which the questions and answers are spoken rather than written. ▷ HISTORY Latin *os, oris* mouth ▶ **orally** *adv*

orange *n* **1** a round reddish-yellow juicy citrus fruit. **2** the evergreen tree on which it grows. **3** a colour between red and yellow; the colour of an orange. ✧ *adj* **4** of a colour between red and yellow. ▷ HISTORY Arabic *nāranj*

orangeade *n Brit* a usually fizzy orange-flavoured drink.

orange blossom *n* the flowers of the orange tree, traditionally worn by brides.

Orangeman *n, pl* **-men** a member of a political society founded in Ireland in 1795 to uphold Protestantism. ▷ HISTORY after William, prince of *Orange,* later William III

orangery *n, pl* **-eries** a conservatory or greenhouse in which orange trees are grown in cooler climates.

orang-utan *or* **orang-utang** *n* a large ape of the forests of Sumatra and Borneo, with shaggy reddish-brown hair and long arms.
▷ HISTORY Malay *ōrang* man + *hūtan* forest

oration *n* a formal or ceremonial public speech.
▷ HISTORY Latin *oratio*

orator (**or**-rat-tor) *n* a person who gives an oration, esp. one skilled in persuasive public speaking.

oratorio (or-rat-**tor**-ee-oh) *n, pl* **-rios** a musical composition for soloists, chorus, and orchestra, based on a religious theme. ▷ HISTORY Italian

oratory[1] (**or**-rat-tree) *n* the art or skill of public speaking. ▷ HISTORY Latin *(ars) oratoria* (the art of) public speaking

oratory[2] *n, pl* **-ries** a small room or building set apart for private prayer. ▷ HISTORY Latin *orare* to pray

orb *n* **1** an ornamental sphere with a cross on top, carried by a king or queen in important ceremonies. **2** a sphere; globe. **3** *Poetic* the eye. **4** *Obsolete or poetic* a heavenly body, such as the sun. ▷ HISTORY Latin *orbis* circle, disc

orbit *n* **1** the curved path followed by something, such as a heavenly body or spacecraft, in its motion around another body. **2** a range or sphere of action or influence. **3** *Anat* the eye socket. ✧ *vb* **-biting, -bited** **4** to move around (a heavenly body) in an orbit. **5** to send (a satellite or spacecraft) into orbit.
▷ HISTORY Latin *orbis* circle ▶ **orbital** *adj*

Orcadian *n* **1** a person from the Orkneys. ✧ *adj* **2** of the Orkneys. ▷ HISTORY Latin *Orcades* the Orkney Islands

orchard *n* an area of land on which fruit trees are grown. ▷ HISTORY Old English *orceard*

orchestra *n* **1** a large group of musicians whose members play a variety of different instruments. **2** Also called: **orchestra pit** the space, in front of or under the stage, reserved for musicians in a theatre.
▷ HISTORY Greek: the space in the theatre for the chorus ▶ **orchestral** *adj*

orchestrate *vb* **-trating, -trated** **1** to score or arrange (a piece of music) for orchestra. **2** to arrange (something) in order to produce a particular result: *he had orchestrated today's meeting.* ▶ **orchestration** *n*

orchid *n* a plant having flowers of unusual shapes and beautiful colours, usually with one lip-shaped petal which is larger than the other two.
▷ HISTORY Greek *orkhis* testicle, because of the shape of its roots

ordain *vb* **1** to make (someone) a member of the clergy. **2** *Formal* to decree or order with authority.
▷ HISTORY Late Latin *ordinare* ▶ **ordainment** *n*

ordeal *n* **1** a severe or trying experience. **2** *History* a method of trial in which the accused person was subjected to physical danger. ▷ HISTORY Old English *ordāl, ordēl* verdict

order *n* **1** an instruction that must be obeyed; command. **2** a state in which everything is arranged logically, comprehensibly, or naturally: *she strove to keep more order in the house.* **3** an arrangement of things in succession; sequence: *group them by letter and then put them in numerical order.* **4** an established or customary system of society: *there is an opportunity here for a new world order.* **5** a peaceful or harmonious condition of society: *riot police were called in to restore order.* **6 a** an instruction to supply something in return for payment: *the waitress came to take their order.* **b** the thing or things supplied. **7** a written instruction to pay money: *post the coupon below with a cheque or postal order.* **8** a social class: *the result will be harmful to society as a whole and to the lower orders in particular.* **9** *Biol* one of the groups into which a class is divided, containing one or more families. **10** kind or sort: *the orchestra played superbly and the singing was of the highest order.* **11** Also called: **religious order** a religious community of monks or nuns. **12** a group of people who have been awarded a particular honour: *the Order of the Garter.* **13** the office or rank of a Christian minister: *he studied for the priesthood as a young man, but never took Holy Orders.* **14** the procedure and rules followed by an assembly or meeting: *a point of order.* **15** one of the five major classical styles of architecture, classified by the type of columns used. **16 a tall order** something difficult or demanding. **17 in order a** in sequence. **b** properly arranged: *everything is in order for your trip.* **c** appropriate or fitting. **18 in order that** so that. **19 in order to** so that it is possible to: *a healthy diet is necessary in order to keep fit.* **20 in** *or* **of the order of** amounting approximately to: *summer temperatures are usually in the order of thirty-five degrees.* **21 keep order** to ensure that people obey the law or behave in an acceptable manner. **22 on order** having been ordered but not yet delivered. **23 out of order a** not in sequence. **b** not working: *the lift was out of order, so we had to use the stairs.* **c** not following the rules or customary procedure: *the chairperson ruled the motion out of order.* **24 to order** according to a buyer's specifications. ✧ *vb* **25** to command or instruct (to do something): *she ordered her son to wash the dishes; the police ordered her into the house.* **26** to request (something) to be supplied in return for payment: *I ordered a new car three weeks ago, but it hasn't been delivered yet.* **27** to arrange (things) methodically or in their proper places. ✧ *interj* **28** an exclamation demanding that orderly behaviour be restored. ▷ **HISTORY** Latin *ordo*

ordered pair *n Maths* an ordered set of only two elements: *the ordered pair <a,b> does not equal <b,a> unless a = b.*

ordered set *n Maths* a sequence of elements, usually enclosed in angle brackets, which must appear in a particular order to maintain the same value: *<a, b, c> is an ordered set and is therefore not equal to <c, b, a>.*

orderly *adj* **1** tidy or well-organized: *they evacuated the building in an orderly manner.* **2** well-behaved; law-abiding. ✧ *n, pl* **-lies 3** *Med* a male hospital attendant. **4** *Mil* a soldier whose duty is to carry orders or perform minor tasks for a more senior officer. ▶ **orderliness** *n*

order of combinations *n Maths* (in transformational geometry) the number of members of a set organized into specified groups without regard to order in the group.

order of operations *n Maths* the conventional order in which multiple mathematical operations should be performed: brackets, exponents, division and multiplication (left to right), addition and subtraction (left to right).

order of reactivity *n Chem* a list of chemical elements arranged according to how reactive they are.

order paper *n* a list indicating the order of business, esp. in Parliament.

ordinal number *n* a number indicating position in a sequence, such as *first, second, third.*

ordinance *n* an official rule or order. ▷ **HISTORY** Latin *ordinare* to set in order

ordinarily *adv* in circumstances; usually; normally.

ordinary *adj* **1** usual or normal: *it was an ordinary working day for them.* **2** not special or different in any way: *what do ordinary Germans feel about reunification?* **3** dull or unexciting: *the restaurant charged very high prices for very ordinary cooking.* ✧ *n, pl* **-naries 4** *RC Church* the parts of the Mass that do not vary from day to day. **5 out of the ordinary** unusual. ▷ **HISTORY** Latin *ordinarius* orderly

Ordinary level *n* (in Britain) the formal name for **O level**.

ordinary rating *n* a rank in the Royal Navy equivalent to that of a private in the army.

ordinary seaman *n Brit, Austral & NZ* a seaman of the lowest rank.

ordinary shares *pl n Brit & Austral* shares issued by a company entitling their holders to a dividend according to the profits of the company and to a claim on net assets.

ordinate *n Maths* the vertical coordinate of a point in a two-dimensional system of coordinates. ▷ **HISTORY** Latin *ordinare* to arrange in order

ordination *n* the act or ceremony of making someone a member of the clergy.

ordnance *n* **1** weapons and other military supplies. **2 the ordnance** a government department dealing with military supplies. ▷ **HISTORY** variant of *ordinance*

Ordnance Survey *n* the British government organization that produces detailed maps of Britain and Ireland.

Ordovician (or-doe-**vish**-ee-an) *adj Geol* of the period of geological time about 500 million years ago. ▷ **HISTORY** Latin *Ordovices*, ancient Celtic tribe in N Wales

ordure *n* excrement; dung. ▷ **HISTORY** Old French *ord* dirty

ore *n* rock or mineral from which valuable substances such as metals can be extracted. ▷ **HISTORY** Old English *ār, ōra*

oregano (or-rig-**gah**-no) *n* a sweet-smelling herb used as seasoning. ▷ **HISTORY** Greek *origanon* an aromatic herb

organ *n* **1** a part in animals and plants that is adapted to perform a particular function, for example the heart or lungs. **2 a** a musical keyboard instrument which produces sound by forcing air through pipes of a variety of lengths. **b** Also called: **electric organ** a keyboard instrument which produces similar sounds electronically. **3** a means

a b c d e f g h i j k l m n o p q r s t u v w x y z

of communication, such as a newspaper issued by a specialist group or party. **4** *Euphemistic* a penis. ▷ **HISTORY** Greek *organon* tool

organdie *n* a fine, slightly stiff cotton fabric. ▷ **HISTORY** French *organdi*

organelle *n Chem* a structural and functional unit such as a mitochondrion, in a cell or unicellular organism.

organ-grinder *n* (formerly) an entertainer who played a barrel organ in the streets.

organic *adj* **1** of, produced by, or found in plants or animals: *the rocks were carefully searched for organic remains.* **2** not using, or grown without, artificial fertilizers or pesticides: *organic vegetables; an organic farm.* **3** *Chem* of or belonging to the class of chemical compounds that are formed from carbon. **4** (of change or development) gradual and natural rather than sudden or forced. **5** made up of many different parts which contribute to the way in which the whole society or structure works: *an organic whole.* ▶ **organically** *adv*

organic chemistry *n Chem* the branch of chemistry dealing with carbon compounds.

organic farming *n Agriculture* farming without using artificial fertilizers and pesticides.

organism *n* **1** an animal or plant. **2** anything resembling a living creature in structure, behaviour, or complexity: *cities are more complicated organisms than farming villages.*

organist *n* a person who plays the organ.

organization *or* **-isation** *n* **1** an organized group of people, such as a club, society, union, or business. **2** the act of organizing: *setting up the European tour took a lot of organization.* **3** the structure and arrangement of the different parts of something: *the report recommended radical changes in the organization of the social services department.* **4** the state of being organized: *the material in this essay lacks any sort of organization.* ▶ **organizational** *or* **-isational** *adj*

organization chart *n Business* a chart showing the structure and relationships of the positions within an organization.

organize *or* **-ise** *vb* **-izing, -ized** *or* **-ising, -ised** **1** to plan and arrange (something): *we organized a protest meeting in the village hall.* **2** to arrange systematically: *the files are organized in alphabetical order and by date.* **3** to form, join, or recruit (people) into a trade union: *the seasonal nature of tourism makes it difficult for hotel workers to organize.* ▷ **HISTORY** Medieval Latin *organizare* ▶ **organizer** *or* **-iser** *n*

organized *or* **-ised** *adj* **1** planned and controlled on a large scale and involving many people: *organized crime.* **2** orderly and efficient: *a highly organized campaign.* **3** (of the workers in a factory or office) belonging to a trade union: *socialism is especially popular among organized labour.*

orgasm *n* the most intense point of pleasure and excitement during sexual activity. ▷ **HISTORY** Greek *orgasmos* ▶ **orgasmic** *adj*

orgy *n, pl* **-gies** **1** a wild party involving promiscuous sexual activity and excessive drinking. **2** an act of immoderate or frenzied indulgence: *the rioters were engaged in an orgy of destruction.* ▷ **HISTORY** Greek *orgia* secret rites ▶ **orgiastic** *adj*

oriel window *or* **oriel** *n* a window built out from the wall of a house at an upper level. ▷ **HISTORY** Old French *oriol* gallery

orient *vb* **1** to adjust or align (oneself or one's ideas) according to surroundings or circumstances: *new employees can take some time to orient themselves to the company's procedures.* **2** to position or set (a map or chart) with relation to the points of the compass or other specific directions. **3 be oriented to** *or* **towards** to work or act with a particular aim, idea, or person in mind: *many people feel that Britain is too much oriented to the Americans.* ✧ *n* **4** *Poetic* the east. ▷ **HISTORY** Latin *oriens* rising (sun)

Orient *n* **the Orient** East Asia.

Oriental *adj* **1** of the Orient. ✧ *n* **2** a person from the Orient.

orientate *vb* **-tating, -tated** same as **orient**.

-orientated *or* **-oriented** *adj combining form* interested in or directed towards the thing specified: *career-orientated women.*

orientation *n* **1** the activities and aims that a person or organization is interested in: *the course has a practical rather than theoretical orientation.* **2** the position of an object with relation to the points of the compass or other specific directions: *the room's southerly orientation means that it receives a lot of light.* ✧ *adj* **3** of or providing information or training needed to understand a new situation or environment: *nearly every college has an orientation programme.*

orienteering *n* a sport in which contestants race on foot over a cross-country course consisting of checkpoints found with the aid of a map and compass. ▷ **HISTORY** Swedish *orientering*

orifice (**or**-rif-fiss) *n* an opening or hole through which something can pass, esp. one in the body such as the mouth or anus. ▷ **HISTORY** Latin *os* mouth + *facere* to make

origami (or-rig-**gah**-mee) *n* the art, originally Japanese, of folding paper intricately into decorative shapes. ▷ **HISTORY** Japanese *ori* a fold + *kami* paper

origin *n* **1** the point, source, or event from which something develops: *the origin of the term 'jazz' is obscure; the war had its origin in the clash between rival nationalists.* **2** the country, race, or social class of a person's parents or ancestors: *an Australian of Greek origin; he was proud of his working-class origins.* **3** *Maths* the point at which the horizontal and vertical axes intersect. ▷ **HISTORY** Latin *origo* beginning

original *adj* **1** first or earliest: *the dining room also has attractive original beams.* **2** fresh and unusual; not copied from or based on something else: *the composer's work has created some original and attractive choreography.* **3** able to think of or carry out new ideas or concepts: *he is an excitingly original writer.* **4** being the first and genuine form of something, from which a copy or translation is made: *all French recipes were translated from the* *original abridged versions.* ✧ *n* **5** the first and genuine form of something, from which others are copied or translated: *the original is in the British Museum.* **6** a person or thing used as a model in art or literature: *she claimed to be the original on whom Lawrence based Lady Chatterley.* ▶ **originality** *n* ▶ **originally** *adv*

original jurisdiction *n Law* a court's power to hear a case for the first time rather than on appeal: *it is both a court of original jurisdiction and an appellate court.*

original sin *n* a state of sin believed by some Christians to be inborn in all human beings as a result of Adam's disobedience.

originate *vb* **-nating, -nated** to come or bring (something) into existence: *humans probably originated in East Africa.* ▶ **origination** *n* ▶ **originator** *n*

oriole *n* a songbird with a long pointed bill and a mostly yellow-and-black plumage. ▷ HISTORY Latin *aureolus* golden

ormolu *n* a gold-coloured alloy of copper, tin, or zinc, used to decorate furniture and other articles. ▷ HISTORY French *or moulu* ground gold

ornament *n* **1** anything that adorns someone or something; decoration: *the room's only ornament was a dim, oily picture of the Holy Family.* **2** decorations collectively: *he had no watch, nor ornament of any kind.* **3** a small decorative object: *I hit a garden ornament while parking.* **4** a person whose character or talent makes them an asset to society or the group to which they belong: *an ornament of the firm.* **5** *Music* a note or group of notes which embellishes the melody but is not an integral part of it, for instance a trill. ✧ *vb* **6** to decorate or adorn: *the hall had a high ceiling, ornamented with plaster fruits and flowers.* ▷ HISTORY Latin *ornamentum* ▶ **ornamental** *adj* ▶ **ornamentation** *n* ▶ **ornamented** *adj*

ornate *adj* **1** heavily or elaborately decorated: *an ornate ceiling painted with allegorical figures.* **2** (of style in writing) overelaborate; using many literary expressions. ▷ HISTORY Latin *ornare* to decorate ▶ **ornately** *adv*

ornithology *n* the study of birds. ▷ HISTORY Greek *ornis* bird ▶ **ornithological** *adj* ▶ **ornithologist** *n*

orogeny *or* **orogenesis** *n Geol* the formation of mountain ranges. ▶ **orogenic** *or* **orogenetic** *adj*

orographic rain *n Meteorol* rain that results from moist air being forced to rise by the effects of hills or mountains.

orographic rainfall *n Meteorol* rainfall resulting from moist air being forced up over mountain ranges where it cools and condenses.

orphan *n* **1** a child whose parents are dead. ✧ *vb* **2** to cause (someone) to become an orphan: *she was orphaned at 16 when her parents died in a car crash.* ▷ HISTORY Greek *orphanos*

orphanage *n* a children's home for orphans and abandoned children.

orphaned *adj* having no living parents.

orrery *n, pl* **-ries** a mechanical model of the solar system in which the planets can be moved around the sun. ▷ HISTORY originally made for Earl of *Orrery*

orris *n* **1** a kind of iris that has fragrant roots. **2** Also: **orrisroot** the root of this plant prepared and used as perfume. ▷ HISTORY variant of *iris*

orthodontics *n* the branch of dentistry concerned with correcting irregularities of the teeth. ▷ HISTORY Greek *orthos* straight + *odōn* tooth ▶ **orthodontic** *adj* ▶ **orthodontist** *n*

orthodox *adj* conforming to traditional or established standards in religion, behaviour, or attitudes: *orthodox medicine; the concerto has a more orthodox structure than is usual for this composer.* ▷ HISTORY Greek *orthos* correct + *doxa* belief ▶ **orthodoxy** *n*

Orthodox *adj* **1** of the Orthodox Church of Eastern Europe. **2** of or being the form of Judaism characterized by traditional interpretation of and strict adherence to Mosaic Law: *an Orthodox Jew.*

Orthodox Church *n* the Christian Church dominant in Eastern Europe, which has the Greek Patriarch of Constantinople as its head.

orthography *n* **1** spelling considered to be correct: *British and American orthography is different in many cases.* **2** the study of spelling. ▷ HISTORY Greek *orthos* correct + *graphein* to write ▶ **orthographic** *adj*

orthopaedics *or US* **orthopedics** *n* the branch of surgery concerned with disorders of the bones and joints. ▷ HISTORY Greek *orthos* straight + *pais* child ▶ **orthopaedic** *or US* **orthopedic** *adj* ▶ **orthopaedist** *or US* **orthopedist** *n*

ortolan *n* a small European songbird eaten as a delicacy. ▷ HISTORY Latin *hortulus* a little garden

oryx *n* any of various large straight-horned African antelopes.

Os *Chem* osmium.

OS **1** (in Britain) Ordnance Survey. **2** outsize(d).

Oscar *n Trademark* an award in the form of a small gold statuette awarded annually in the US for outstanding achievements in various aspects of the film industry: *he won an Oscar for Best Supporting Actor in 1974.* ▷ HISTORY said to have been named after a remark made by an official that it reminded her of her uncle Oscar

oscillate (**oss**-ill-late) *vb* **-lating, -lated** **1** to swing repeatedly back and forth: *its wings oscillate up and down many times a second.* **2** to waver between two extremes of opinion, attitude, or behaviour: *the government oscillates between a desire for reform and a desire to keep its powers intact.* **3** *Physics* (of an electric current) to vary between minimum and maximum values. ▷ HISTORY Latin *oscillare* to swing ▶ **oscillation** *n* ▶ **oscillator** *n*

oscilloscope (oss-**sill**-oh-scope) *n* an instrument that produces a visual representation of an oscillating electric current on the screen of a cathode-ray tube.

osier (**oh**-zee-er) *n* **1** a willow tree whose flexible branches or twigs are used for making baskets and furniture. **2** a twig or branch from this tree. ▷ HISTORY Old French

A B C D E F G H I J K L M N O P Q R S T U V W X Y Z

osmium *n Chem* a very hard brittle bluish-white metal, the heaviest known element. Symbol: Os. ▷ **HISTORY** Greek *osmē* smell, from its penetrating odour

osmoregulation *n Zool* the adjustment of the osmotic pressure of a cell or organism in relation to the surrounding fluid.

osmosis *n* **1** the diffusion of liquids through a membrane until they are mixed. **2** the process by which people or ideas influence each other gradually and subtly. ▷ **HISTORY** Greek *ōsmos* push ▶ **osmotic** *adj*

osprey *n* a large fish-eating bird of prey, with a dark back and whitish head and underparts. ▷ **HISTORY** Old French *ospres,* apparently from Latin *ossifraga,* literally: bone-breaker

osseous *adj* consisting of or like bone. ▷ **HISTORY** Latin *os* bone

ossify *vb* **-fies, -fying, -fied 1** to change into bone; harden. **2** to become rigid, inflexible, or unprogressive: *ossified traditions.* ▷ **HISTORY** Latin *os* bone + *facere* to make ▶ **ossification** *n*

ostensible *adj* apparent or seeming; alleged: *our ostensible common interest is boats.* ▷ **HISTORY** Latin *ostendere* to show ▶ **ostensibly** *adv*

ostensive *adj* directly showing or pointing out: *he gave ostensive definitions to things.* ▷ **HISTORY** Latin *ostendere* to show

ostentation *n* pretentious, showy, or vulgar display: *she felt the gold taps in the bathroom were tasteless ostentation.* ▶ **ostentatious** *adj* ▶ **ostentatiously** *adv*

osteoarthritis (ost-ee-oh-arth-**rite**-iss) *n* chronic inflammation of the joints, causing pain and stiffness. ▷ **HISTORY** Greek *osteon* bone + ARTHRITIS ▶ **osteoarthritic** *adj*

osteopathy *n* a system of healing based on the manipulation of bones or muscles. ▷ **HISTORY** Greek *osteon* bone + *patheia* suffering ▶ **osteopath** *n*

osteoporosis (ost-ee-oh-pore-**oh**-siss) *n* brittleness of the bones, caused by lack of calcium. ▷ **HISTORY** Greek *osteon* bone + *poros* passage

ostinato *n, pl* **-tos** *Music* a persistently repeated phrase or rhythm. ▷ **HISTORY** Italian, from Latin *obstinatus* obstinate

ostler *n* (formerly) a stableman at an inn. ▷ **HISTORY** variant of *hostler,* from *hostel*

ostracize *or* **-cise** *vb* **-cizing, -cized** *or* **-cising, -cised** to exclude or banish (a person) from a particular group or from society: *he was ostracized from his family when his affair became known.* ▷ **HISTORY** Greek *ostrakizein* to select someone for banishment by voting on potsherds ▶ **ostracism** *n*

ostrich *n* **1** a large African bird which runs fast but cannot fly, and has a long neck, long legs, and soft dark feathers. **2** a person who refuses to recognize an unpleasant truth: *he accused the Minister of being 'an ostrich with its head stuck in the sand, while all around him unemployment soars'.* ▷ **HISTORY** Greek *strouthion*

OT Old Testament.

OTC (in Britain) Officers' Training Corps.

OTE *Chiefly Brit* (esp. in job adverts) on target earnings: the minimum amount of money a salesman is expected to make.

other *adj* **1** remaining (one or ones) in a group of which one or some have been specified: *she wasn't getting on with the other children.* **2** being a different one or ones from the one or ones already specified or understood: *other people might not be so tolerant of your behaviour; are you sure it's not in your other pocket?* **3** refers to a place or time which is not the one the speaker or writer is in: *results in other countries have been most encouraging.* **4** additional; further: *there is one other thing for the government to do.* **5 every other** every alternate: *the doctor sees me every other week.* **6 other than a** apart from: *he knew little of the country other than it was Muslim.* **b** different from: *treatment other than a hearing aid will be possible for those with inner ear deafness.* **7 or other** used to add vagueness to the preceding word or phrase: *he could take some evening course or other which could lead to an extra qualification; he was called away from the house on some pretext or other.* **8 the other day** a few days ago. ✧ *n* **9** an additional person or thing: *show me one other.* **10 others** people apart from the person who is being spoken or written about: *she devoted her entire life to helping others.* **11 the others** the people or things remaining in a group of which one or some have been specified: *I can't speak for the others.* ✧ *adv* **12** otherwise; differently: *they couldn't behave other than they do.* ▷ **HISTORY** Old English *ōther* ▶ **otherness** *n*

> ☑ **WORD TIP**
> See at **otherwise.**

other ranks *pl n Brit & Austral* (in the armed forces) all those who do not hold a commissioned rank.

otherwise *conj* **1** or else; if not, then: *I was fifty but said I was forty, otherwise I'd never have got a job.* ✧ *adv* **2** differently: *it was fruitless to pretend or to hope otherwise.* **3** in other respects: *shrewd psychological twists perk up an otherwise predictable story line.* ✧ *adj* **4** different: *circumstances beyond our control dictated that it should be otherwise.* ✧ *pron* **5 or otherwise** or not; or the opposite: *he didn't want company, talkative or otherwise.*

> ☑ **WORD TIP**
> The expression *otherwise than* means *in any other way than* and should not be followed by an adjective: *no-one taught by this method can be other than* (not *otherwise than*) *successful; you are not allowed to use the building otherwise than as a private dwelling.*

otherworldly *adj* **1** concerned with spiritual rather than practical matters: *his otherworldly manner concealed a ruthless business mind.* **2** mystical or supernatural: *this part of Italy has an otherworldly beauty.*

otiose (**oh**-tee-oze) *adj* serving no useful purpose: *such a strike is almost otiose.* ▷ **HISTORY** Latin *otiosus* leisured

OTT *Brit & S African slang* over the top.

otter *n* a small freshwater fish-eating animal with smooth brown fur, a streamlined body, and webbed feet. ▷ HISTORY Old English *otor*

ottoman *n, pl* **-mans** a storage chest with a padded lid for use as a seat. ▷ HISTORY French *ottomane,* feminine of *Ottoman*

Ottoman *adj* **1** *History* of the Ottomans or the Ottoman Empire, the Turkish empire which lasted from the late 13th century until the end of World War I, and at its height included the Balkans and much of N Africa. ✧ *n, pl* **-mans 2** a member of a Turkish people who formed the basis of this empire. ▷ HISTORY Arabic *Othmāni*

ou (**oh**) *n S African slang* a man, bloke, or chap. ▷ HISTORY Afrikaans

OU 1 the Open University. **2** Oxford University.

oubaas (**oh**-bahss) *n S African* a man in authority. ▷ HISTORY Afrikaans *ou* man + *baas* boss

oubliette (oo-blee-**ett**) *n History* a dungeon, the only entrance to which is a trap door in the ceiling. ▷ HISTORY French *oublier* to forget

ouch *interj* an exclamation of sharp sudden pain.

ought *vb* used to express: **1** duty or obligation: *she ought to tell this to the police.* **2** advisability: *we ought to get the roof repaired before the attics get any damper.* **3** probability or expectation: *a good lawyer ought to be able to fix it for you.* **4** a desire on the part of the speaker: *you ought to have a good breakfast before you hit the road.* ▷ HISTORY Old English *āhte,* past tense of *āgan* to owe

> ☑ **WORD TIP**
> In correct English, *ought* is not used with *did* or *had. I ought not to do it,* not *I didn't ought to do it; I ought not to have done it,* not *I hadn't ought to have done it.*

Ouija board *or* **Ouija** (**weej**-a) *n Trademark* a board on which are marked the letters of the alphabet. Answers to questions are spelt out by a pointer, which is supposedly guided by spirits. ▷ HISTORY French *oui* yes + German *ja* yes

ouma (**oh**-mah) *n S African* **1** grandmother, often as a title with a surname. **2** *Slang* any elderly woman. ▷ HISTORY Afrikaans

ounce *n* **1** a unit of weight equal to one sixteenth of a pound or 28.4 grams. **2** short for **fluid ounce**. **3** a small amount: *you haven't got one ounce of control over her.* ▷ HISTORY Latin *uncia* a twelfth

OUP (in Northern Ireland) Official Unionist Party.

oupa (**oh**-pah) *n S African* **1** grandfather, often as a title with a surname. **2** *Slang* any elderly man. ▷ HISTORY Afrikaans

our *adj* **1** of, belonging to, or associated with us: *our daughter.* **2** a formal word for *my* used by monarchs. ▷ HISTORY Old English *ūre*

Our Father *n* same as the **Lord's Prayer**.

ours *pron* **1** something belonging to us: *ours are smaller guns than those; the money is ours.* **2 of ours** belonging to or associated with us: *my wife and a friend of ours had both deserted me.*

ourselves *pron* **1 a** the reflexive form of *we* or *us*: *we humiliated ourselves.* **b** used for emphasis: *we ourselves will finish it.* **2** our usual selves: *we've not been feeling quite ourselves since the accident.* **3** *Not standard* used instead of *we* or *us* in compound noun phrases: *other people and ourselves.*

ousel *n* same as **ouzel**.

oust *vb* to force (someone) out of a position; expel: *the coup which ousted the President.* ▷ HISTORY Anglo-Norman *ouster*

ouster *n US* an act or instance of forcing someone out of a position: *the demonstrators called for the ouster of the police chief.*

out *adv, adj* **1** away from the inside of a place: *she took her purse out; inspection of the eggs should be done when the hen is out of the nest.* **2** away from one's home or place of work for a short time: *I called earlier but you were out; a search party is out looking for survivors.* **3** no longer burning, shining, or functioning: *he switched the light out; the living-room fire went out while we were next door eating.* **4** used up; not having any more of: *their supplies ran out after two weeks; we're out of milk.* **5** public; revealed: *our dirty little secret is out.* **6** available to the public: *her biography will be out in December.* **7** (of the sun, stars, or moon) visible. **8** in bloom: *the roses are out early this year.* **9** not in fashion or current usage: *trying to be trendy is out.* **10** excluded from consideration: *cost cutting is out of the question.* **11** not allowed: *smoking on duty is out.* **12 out for** *or* **to** wanting or intent on (something or doing something): *the young soldiers were out for revenge; they're out to get me.* **13** *Sport* (of a player in a sport like cricket or baseball) no longer batting because he or she has been dismissed by being caught, bowled, etc. **14** on strike. **15** in or into a state of unconsciousness: *he went outside and passed out in an alley.* **16** used to indicate a burst of activity as indicated by a verb: *war broke out in the Gulf.* **17** out of existence: *the mistakes were scored out.* **18** to the fullest extent: *spread out.* **19** loudly; clearly: *he cried out in shock and pain.* **20** to a conclusion; completely: *she'd worked it out for herself.* **21** existing: *the friendliest dog out.* **22** inaccurate or incorrect: *the estimate was out by sixty pounds.* **23** not in office or authority: *she was finally voted out as party leader.* **24** (of a period of time) completed: *before the year is out.* **25** openly homosexual: *I came out as a lesbian when I was still in my teens.* **26** *Old-fashioned* (of a young woman) in or into upper-class society life: *Lucinda had a large party when she came out.* **27 out of a** at or to a point outside: *the train pulled out of the station.* **b** away from; not in: *they're out of touch with reality; out of focus.* **c** because of; motivated by: *out of jealousy.* **d** from (a material or source): *made out of plastic.* **e** no longer in a specified state or condition: *out of work; out of practice.* ✧ *adj* **28** *Informal* not concealing one's homosexuality. ✧ *prep* **29** *US or not standard* out of; out through: *he ran out the door.* ✧ *interj* **30 a** an exclamation of dismissal. **b** (in signalling and radio) an expression used to signal that the speaker is signing off: *over and out!* ✧ *vb* **31** *Informal* (of homosexuals) to expose (a public figure) as being a fellow homosexual.

A B C D E F G H I J K L M N O P Q R S T U V W X Y Z

32 *Informal* to reveal something embarrassing or unknown about (a person): *he was outed as a talented goal scorer.* ▷ **HISTORY** Old English *ūt*

> **WORD TIP**
> The use of *out* as a preposition, though common in American English, is regarded as incorrect in British English: *he climbed out of* (not *out*) *a window; he went out through the door.*

out- *prefix* **1** excelling or surpassing in a particular action: *outlast; outlive.* **2** at or from a point away, outside: *outpost; outpatient.* **3** going away, outward: *outcrop; outgrowth.*

outage *n* a period of power failure.

outback *n* the remote bush country of Australia.

outbid *vb* **-bidding, -bidded** *or* **-bid** to offer a higher price than (another person).

outboard motor *n* a portable petrol engine that can be attached externally to the stern of a boat to propel it.

outbreak *n* a sudden occurrence of disease or war.

outbuilding *n* same as **outhouse**.

outburst *n* **1** a sudden strong expression of emotion, esp. of anger: *such emotional outbursts do nothing to help calm discussion of the matter.* **2** a sudden period of violent activity: *this sudden outburst of violence has come as a shock.*

outcast *n* a person who is rejected or excluded from a particular group or from society.

outclass *vb* to surpass (someone) in performance or quality.

outcome *n* the result or consequence of something.

outcrop *n* part of a rock formation that sticks out of the earth.

outcry *n, pl* **-cries** a widespread or vehement protest: *there was great popular outcry against the plan for a dual carriageway.*

outdated *adj* old-fashioned or obsolete.

outdo *vb* **-doing, -did, -done** to be more successful or better than (someone or something) in performance: *this car easily outdoes its rivals when it comes to comfort.*

outdoor *adj* **1** taking place, existing, or intended for use in the open air: *have a swim at the beach or outdoor pool; she was just taking off her outdoor clothing.* **2** fond of the outdoors: *Paul was a butch outdoor type.*

outdoors *adv* **1** in the open air; outside: *he hardly ever went outdoors.* ✧ *n* **2** the world outside or far away from buildings; the open air: *he'd forgotten his fear of the outdoors.*

outer *adj* **1** on the outside; external: *the building's outer walls were painted pale pink.* **2** further from the middle: *the outer suburbs.* ✧ *n* **3** *Archery* **a** the white outermost ring on a target. **b** a shot that hits this ring.

outermost *adj* furthest from the centre or middle.

outer space *n* space beyond the atmosphere of the earth.

outface *vb* **-facing, -faced** to subdue or disconcert (someone) by staring.

outfall *n Brit, Austral & NZ* the mouth of a river, drain, or pipe: *the survey measured pollution levels near sewer outfalls.*

outfield *n* **1** *Cricket* the area of the field far from the pitch. **2** *Baseball* the area of the playing field beyond the lines connecting first, second, and third bases. ▶ **outfielder** *n*

outfit *n* **1** a set of clothes worn together. **2** *Informal* a group of people working together as a unit. **3** a set of equipment for a particular task; kit: *a complete anti-snakebite outfit.*

outfitter *n Old-fashioned* a shop or person that sells men's clothes.

outflank *vb* **1** to go around and beyond the side of (an enemy army). **2** to get the better of (someone).

outgoing *adj* **1** leaving: *some members of the outgoing government continued to attend the peace talks.* **2** friendly and sociable.

outgoings *pl n* expenses.

outgrow *vb* **-growing, -grew, -grown 1** to grow too large for (clothes or shoes): *it's amazing how quickly children outgrow their clothes.* **2** to lose (a way of behaving or thinking) in the course of becoming more mature: *most teenagers outgrow their moodiness as they near adulthood.* **3** to grow larger or faster than (someone or something): *the weeds threatened to outgrow and choke the rice plants.*

outgrowth *n* **1** a natural development or consequence: *he argued that religion was an outgrowth of magic.* **2** a thing growing out of a main body; offshoot.

outhouse *n* a building near to, but separate from, a main building.

outing *n* **1** a trip or excursion. **2** *Informal* the naming by homosexuals of other prominent homosexuals, often against their will.

outlandish *adj* extremely unconventional; bizarre.

outlast *vb* to last longer than.

outlaw *n* **1** *History* a criminal who has been deprived of legal protection and rights. ✧ *vb* **2** to make (something) illegal: *racial discrimination was formally outlawed.* **3** *History* to make (someone) an outlaw. ▶ **outlawed** *adj*

outlay *n* the money, effort, or time spent on something.

outlet *n* **1** a means of expressing one's feelings: *the shock would give her an outlet for her own grief.* **2 a** a market for a product: *there is a huge sales outlet for personal computers.* **b** a shop or organization selling the goods of a particular producer or wholesaler or manufacturer: *her own brand is now sold to outlets throughout the world.* **3** an opening permitting escape or release: *make sure the exhaust outlet is not blocked.*

outline *n* **1** a general explanation or description of something, which does not give all the details: *the course gave a brief outline of twentieth-century music.* **2 outlines** the important features of something: *the outlines of his theory are correct, we just need to fill in the details.* **3** the general shape of something, esp. when only the profile and not the details are visible: *it was still light enough to see the outline of the distant mountains.* **4** a drawing showing only the external lines of an object. ✧ *vb* **-lining, -lined 5** to give the main features or general idea of (something): *I outlined what we had done and what we had still to do.* **6** to show the general shape of an object but not its details, as light does coming from behind an object: *we could see the towers of the city outlined against the night sky.*

outlive *vb* **-living, -lived 1** to live longer than (someone): *she only outlived her husband by a few months.* **2** to live beyond (a date or period): *the sparrow outlived the winter.* **3 outlive its usefulness** to be no longer useful or necessary: *some argued that the organization had outlived its usefulness.*

outlook *n* **1** a general attitude to life: *my whole outlook on life had changed.* **2** the probable condition or outcome of something: *the economic outlook is not good.* **3** the weather forecast for the next few days: *the outlook for the weekend.* **4** the view from a place: *a dreary outlook of chimneys and smoke.*

outlying *adj* far away from the main area.

outmanoeuvre *or US* **outmaneuver** *vb* **-vring, -vred** *or* **-vering, -vered** to gain an advantage over (someone) by skilful dealing: *the management outmanoeuvred us into accepting redundancies.*

outmoded *adj* no longer fashionable or accepted.

outnumber *vb* to exceed in number: *they were outnumbered by fifty to one.*

out-of-date *adj, adv* old-fashioned; outmoded.

out of pocket *adj* having lost or spent money: *I was ten pounds out of pocket after paying for their drinks.*

out-of-the-way *adj* remote and isolated: *an out-of-the-way village in the Bavarian Forest.*

outpatient *n* a patient who visits a hospital for treatment but does not stay there overnight.

outpost *n* a small settlement in a distant part of the country or in a foreign country, which is used for military or trading purposes.

outpouring *n* **1** a great amount of something that is produced very rapidly: *a prolific outpouring of ideas and energy.* **2** a passionate outburst: *the hysterical outpourings of fanatics.*

output *n* **1** the amount of something that is made or produced: *our weekly output has increased by 240 tonnes.* **2** *Electronics* the power, voltage, or current delivered by a circuit or component. **3** *Computers* the information produced by a computer. ✧ *vb* **-putting, -putted** *or* **-put 4** *Computers* to produce (data) at the end of a process.

outrage *n* **1** deep indignation, anger, or resentment: *she felt a sense of outrage that he should abandon her like that.* **2** an extremely vicious or cruel act; gross violation of decency, morality, or honour: *there have been reports of another bombing outrage in the capital.* ✧ *vb* **-raging, -raged 3** to cause deep indignation, anger, or resentment in (someone): *they were outraged by the news of the assassination.* ▷ HISTORY French *outré* beyond

outrageous *adj* **1** unusual and shocking: *his sense of humour made him say and do the most outrageous things.* **2** shocking and socially or morally unacceptable: *I will fight these outrageous accusations of corruption in the courts if necessary.* ▸ **outrageously** *adv*

outré (**oo**-tray) *adj* eccentric and rather shocking. ▷ HISTORY French: having gone beyond

outrider *n* a person who rides a motorcycle or horse in front of or beside an official vehicle as an attendant or guard.

outrigger *n* **1** a stabilizing framework projecting from the side of a boat or canoe. **2** a boat or canoe equipped with such a framework.

outright *adj* **1** complete; total: *he is close to an outright victory.* **2** straightforward and direct: *outright hostility.* ✧ *adv* **3** completely: *the film was banned outright.* **4** instantly: *my driver was killed outright.* **5** openly: *ask her outright why she treated you as she did.*

outrun *vb* **-running, -ran, -run 1** to run faster or further than (someone). **2** to develop faster than (something): *the population of the city is in danger of outrunning the supply of houses.*

outsell *vb* **-selling, -sold** to be sold in greater quantities than: *CDs are now outselling cassettes.*

outset *n* a start; beginning: *we never really hit it off from the outset.*

outshine *vb* **-shining, -shone** to be better than (someone) at something: *by university she had begun to outshine me in sports.*

outside *prep* **1** on or to the exterior of: *a crowd gathered outside the court.* **2** beyond the limits of: *it was outside my experience and beyond my ability.* **3** apart from; other than: *no-one knows outside us.* ✧ *adj* **4** on or of the outside: *an outside light is also a good idea.* **5** remote; unlikely: *I still had an outside chance of the title.* **6** coming from outside a particular group or organization: *the patient had been subjected to outside influences.* **7** of or being the lane in a road which is further from the side than other lanes going in the same direction: *he was doing 120 in the outside lane.* ✧ *adv* **8** outside a specified thing or place; out of doors: *we went outside to get some fresh air.* **9** *Slang* not in prison. ✧ *n* **10** the external side or surface of something. **11 at the outside** *Informal* at the very most: *I'll be away four days at the outside.*

> **WORD TIP**
> The use of *outside of* and *inside of*, although fairly common, is generally thought to be incorrect or non-standard: *she waits outside* (not *outside of*) *the school.*

outside broadcast *n Radio, television* a broadcast not made from a studio.

outsider *n* **1** a person excluded from a group. **2** a contestant thought unlikely to win.

A B C D E F G H I J K L M N O P Q R S T U V W X Y Z

outsize *adj* **1** Also: **outsized** very large or larger than normal. ✧ *n* **2** an outsize garment.

outskirts *pl n* the parts of a town or city that are furthest from the centre: *an office in the northernmost outskirts of Glasgow.*

outsmart *vb Informal* same as **outwit**.

outsource *vb* **1** to subcontract (work) to another company. **2** to buy (components for a product) rather than manufacture them.

outspan *S African* ✧ *n* **1** an area on a farm kept available for travellers to rest and refresh their animals. ✧ *vb* **-spanning, -spanned 2** to unharness or unyoke (animals). **3** to relax. ▷ **HISTORY** Afrikaans *uit* out + *spannen* to stretch

outspoken *adj* **1** saying exactly what one thinks: *an outspoken critic of human rights abuses.* **2** spoken candidly: *she is known for her outspoken views.* ▶ **outspokenness** *n*

outstanding *adj* **1** very good; excellent: *an outstanding performance.* **2** still to be dealt with or paid: *outstanding bills; a few outstanding problems have to be put right.* **3** very obvious or important: *there are significant exceptions, of which oil is the outstanding example.* ▶ **outstandingly** *adv*

outstation *n* a station or post in a remote region.

outstay *vb* same as **overstay**.

outstretched *adj* extended or stretched out as far as possible: *he pushed a wad of drachma notes into the young man's outstretched hand.*

outstrip *vb* **-stripping, -stripped 1** to surpass (someone) in a particular activity: *his newspapers outstrip all others in vulgarity.* **2** to go faster than (someone).

outtake *n* an unreleased take from a recording session, film, or television programme.

out-tray *n* a shallow basket in an office for collecting letters and documents that are to be sent out.

outvote *vb* **-voting, -voted** to defeat (someone) by getting more votes than him or her.

outward *adj* **1** apparent or superficial: *to outward appearances the house is largely unchanged today.* **2** of or relating to the outside: *outward shape.* **3** (of a journey) away from a place to which one intends to return. ✧ *adv also* **outwards 4** in an outward direction; towards the outside. ▶ **outwardly** *adv*

outweigh *vb* **1** to be more important, significant, or influential than: *these niggles are outweighed by the excellent cooking and service.* **2** to be heavier than.

outwit *vb* **-witting, -witted** to gain an advantage over (someone) by cunning or ingenuity.

outworks *pl n Mil* defences which lie outside the main fortifications of a fort etc.

outworn *adj* (of a belief or custom) old-fashioned and no longer of any use or relevance: *there is no point in pandering to outworn superstition.*

ouzel *or* **ousel** (**ooze**-el) *n* same as **dipper** (sense 2). ▷ **HISTORY** Old English *ōsle*

ouzo (**ooze**-oh) *n, pl* **ouzos** a strong aniseed-flavoured alcoholic drink from Greece. ▷ **HISTORY** Modern Greek *ouzon*

ova *n* the plural of **ovum**.

oval *adj* **1** egg-shaped. ✧ *n* **2** anything that is oval in shape, such as a sports ground. ▷ **HISTORY** Latin *ovum* egg

ovary *n, pl* **-ries 1** a reproductive organ in women and female animals in which eggs are produced. **2** *Bot* the lower part of a pistil, containing the ovules. ▷ **HISTORY** Latin *ovum* egg ▶ **ovarian** *adj*

ovate *adj* shaped like an egg: *the tree has bluish-green, ovate leaves.* ▷ **HISTORY** Latin *ovatus* egg-shaped

ovation *n* an enthusiastic round of applause. ▷ **HISTORY** Latin *ovatio* rejoicing

oven *n* **1** an enclosed heated compartment or container for baking or roasting food, or for drying or firing ceramics. ✧ *vb* **2** to cook in an oven. ▷ **HISTORY** Old English *ofen*

over *prep* **1** directly above; across the top or upper surface of: *set the frying pan over a low heat.* **2** on or to the other side of: *the pilot flew over the blue waters.* **3** during or throughout (a period of time): *over the next few months it became clear what was happening.* **4** throughout the whole extent of: *the effects are being felt all over the country now.* **5** by means of (an instrument of telecommunication): *there was an announcement over the Tannoy system.* **6** more than: *she had met him over a year ago.* **7** concerning; about: *there has been much argument over these figures.* **8** while occupied in: *I'll tell you over dinner tonight.* **9** having recovered from the effects of: *he appeared to be over his niggling injury problems.* **10 all over someone** *Informal* extremely affectionate or attentive towards someone. **11 over and above** added to; in addition to. ✧ *adv* **12** in a state, condition, or position over something: *to climb over.* **13** onto its side: *the jug toppled over.* **14** at or to a point across an intervening space: *she carried him over to the other side of the river.* **15** covering the whole area: *there's poverty the world over.* **16** from beginning to end: *to read a document over.* **17 all over a** finished. **b** over one's entire body. **c** typically: *that's him all over.* **18 over again** once more. **19 over and over (again)** repeatedly. ✧ *interj* **20** (in signalling and radio) it is now your turn to speak. ✧ *adj* **21** finished; no longer in progress: *the second round of voting is over.* ✧ *adv, adj* **22** remaining; surplus: *there wasn't any money left over.* ✧ *n* **23** *Cricket* **a** a series of six balls bowled by a bowler from the same end of the pitch. **b** the play during this. ▷ **HISTORY** Old English *ofer*

over- *prefix* **1** excessive or excessively: *overcharge; overdue.* **2** superior in rank: *overlord.* **3** indicating location or movement above: *overhang.* **4** downwards from above: *overthrow.*

overact *vb* to act in an exaggerated way.

overactive *adj* more active than is normal or desirable: *an overactive thyroid gland.*

overall *adj* **1** from one end to the other: *the overall length.* **2** including everything; total: *the overall cost.* ✧ *adv* **3** in general; on the whole: *overall, I think this is the better car.* ✧ *n* **4** *Brit & NZ* a coat-shaped work garment worn over ordinary clothes as a protection against dirt. **5 overalls** work trousers with a bib and braces or jacket attached, worn over ordinary clothes as a protection against dirt and wear.

overarm *Sport* ✧ *adj* **1** bowled, thrown, or performed with the arm raised above the shoulder. ✧ *adv* **2** with the arm raised above the shoulder.

overawe *vb* **-awing, -awed** to affect (someone) with an overpowering sense of awe: *he was overawed by the prospect of meeting the Prime Minister.*

overbalance *vb* **-ancing, -anced** to lose one's balance.

overbearing *adj* **1** imposing one's views in an unpleasant or forceful manner. **2** of particular or overriding importance: *an overbearing need.*

overblown *adj* inflated or excessive: *humiliation comes from having overblown expectations for yourself.*

overboard *adv* **1** from a boat or ship into the water: *many passengers drowned when they jumped overboard to escape the flames.* **2 go overboard** *Informal* **a** to be extremely enthusiastic. **b** to go to extremes. **3 throw overboard** to reject or abandon (an idea or a plan).

overburden *vb* to have more of something than it is possible to cope with: *the city's streets are already overburdened by rush-hour motorists.*

overcast *adj* (of the sky or weather) cloudy.

overcharge *vb* **-charging, -charged** to charge too high a price.

overcoat *n* a warm heavy coat worn in cold weather.

overcome *vb* **-coming, -came, -come 1** to deal successfully with or control (a problem or feeling): *once I'd overcome my initial nerves I discovered hang-gliding was great fun.* **2** (of an emotion or a feeling) to affect (someone) strongly or make (someone) powerless: *he was overcome by a sudden surge of jealousy.* **3** to defeat (someone) in a conflict.

overcompensate *vb* **-sating, -sated** to attempt to make up for or cancel out (something) to an unnecessary degree: *when bookings dropped slightly, the company overcompensated by slashing the price of its holidays by 50%.*

overcrowded *adj* containing more people or things than is desirable: *overcrowded commuter trains.*

overcrowding *n* the cramming of too many people into too small a space: *prison overcrowding and poor conditions.*

overdo *vb* **-doing, -did, -done 1** to do (something) to excess. **2** to exaggerate (something). **3** to cook (something) too long. **4 overdo it** *or* **things** to something to a greater degree than is advisable or healthy.

overdose *n* **1** a larger dose of a drug than is safe: *she tried to kill herself with an overdose of alcohol and drugs.* ✧ *vb* **-dosing, -dosed 2** to take more of a drug than is safe, either accidentally or deliberately: *this drug is rarely prescribed because it is easy to overdose fatally on it.*

overdraft *n* **1** the withdrawal of more money from a bank account than there is in it. **2** the amount of money withdrawn thus.

overdraw *vb* **-drawing, -drew, -drawn** to withdraw more money from a bank account than is in it.

overdrawn *adj* **1** having overdrawn one's bank account. **2** (of an account) in debit.

overdressed *adj* wearing clothes which are too elaborate or formal for the occasion.

overdrive *n* **1** a very high gear in a motor vehicle, used at high speeds to reduce wear. **2** a state of great activity or excitement: *the government propaganda machine went into overdrive to try to play down the Minister's comments.*

overdub *vb* **-dubbing, -dubbed 1** to add (new sounds) to a tape in such a way that the old and the new sounds can be heard. ✧ *n* **2** a sound or series of sounds added by this method.

overdue *adj* **1** not having arrived or happened by the time expected or desired: *a reassessment of policy on this issue is long overdue.* **2** (of money) not having been paid by the required date: *by this time his rent was three weeks overdue.* **3** (of a library book) not having been returned to the library by the required date.

overestimate *vb* **-mating, -mated** to believe something or someone to be bigger, more important, or better than is the case.
▶ **overestimation** *n*

overexposed *adj* (of a photograph) too light in colour because the film has been exposed to light for too long.

overflow *vb* **-flowing, -flowed** *or formerly* **-flown 1** to flow over (a brim). **2** to be filled beyond capacity so as to spill over. **3 overflow with** to be filled with (an emotion): *a letter overflowing with passion and ardour.* ✧ *n* **4** something that overflows, usually a liquid. **5** an outlet that enables surplus liquid to be drained off. **6** the amount by which a limit or capacity is exceeded. ✧ *adj* **7** of or being a subsidiary thing for use when there is no room left in the main one: *an overflow car park.*

overgraze *vb* **-grazing, -grazed** to graze (land) too intensively so that it is damaged and no longer provides nourishment.

overgrown *adj* covered over with plants or weeds: *they headed up the overgrown and winding trail.*

overhang *vb* **-hanging, -hung 1** to project or hang over beyond (something). ✧ *n* **2** an overhanging part or object.

overhaul *vb* **1** to examine (a system or an idea) carefully for faults. **2** to make repairs or adjustments to (a vehicle or machine). **3** to overtake (a vehicle or person). ✧ *n* **4** a thorough examination and repair.

overhead *adj, adv* above head height.

overheads *pl n* the general costs of running a business, such as rent, electricity, and stationery.

overhear *vb* **-hearing, -heard** to hear (a speaker or remark) unintentionally or without the knowledge of the speaker.

overheat *vb* **1** to make or become too hot. **2** to cause (an economy) to tend towards inflation. **3 become overheated** (of a person, discussion, etc.) to become angry or agitated: *the Colonel becomes overheated if he sees the term 'Ms' in the newspaper.*
overjoyed *adj* extremely pleased.
overkill *n* any treatment that is greater than that required: *the overkill in negative propaganda resulted in this upsurge.*
overlap *vb* **-lapping, -lapped 1** (of two things) to share part of the same space as or lie partly over (each other): *slice the meat and lay it in overlapping slices in a serving dish.* **2** to coincide partly in time or subject: *their careers have overlapped for the last ten years.* ✧ *n* **3** a part that overlaps. **4** the amount or length of something overlapping.
overlay *vb* **-laying, -laid 1** to cover (a surface) with an applied decoration: *a woollen cloth overlaid with gold and silver embroidery.* ✧ *n* **2** something that is laid over something else; a covering. **3** an applied decoration or layer, for example of gold leaf.
overleaf *adv* on the other side of the page.
overlie *vb* **-lying, -lay, -lain** to lie on or cover (something or someone): *a thin layer of black dust overlay everything.*
overload *vb* **1** to put too large a load on or in (something): *the aircraft was dangerously overloaded.* **2** to cause (a transport system) to be unable to function properly because too many people or vehicles are using it: *Heathrow Airport was already overloaded by 1972.* **3** to try to put more electricity through a system than the system can cope with. ✧ *n* **4** an excessive load.
overlook *vb* **1** to fail to notice (something). **2** to disregard or ignore (misbehaviour or a fault): *I'm prepared to overlook your failure, but don't do it again.* **3** to give a view of (something) from above: *a cliff overlooking the Atlantic.*
overly *adv* too; excessively.
overman *vb* **-manning, -manned** to provide with too many staff: *the company is not overmanned overall, but it has too many managers and not enough productive workers.* ▶ **overmanned** *adj* ▶ **overmanning** *n*
overmuch *adv, adj* too much; very much.
overnight *adv* **1** during the night. **2** in or as if in the course of one night; suddenly: *we are not saying that a change like this would happen overnight.* ✧ *adj* **3** done in, occurring in, or lasting the night: *the army has ordered an overnight curfew.* **4** staying for one night: *overnight guests.* **5** for use during a single night: *should I pack an overnight case?* **6** happening very quickly; sudden: *he doesn't expect the programme to be an overnight success.*
overpass *n* same as **flyover**.
overplay *vb* **1** to overemphasize (something). **2 overplay one's hand** to overestimate the worth or strength of one's position.
overpower *vb* **1** to conquer or subdue (someone) by superior force. **2** to have such a strong effect on (someone) as to make him or her helpless or ineffective: *I was so appalled, so overpowered by my guilt and my shame that I was unable to speak.* ▶ **overpowering** *adj*
overrate *vb* to have too high an opinion of: *the director's role was seriously overrated.*
overreach *vb* **overreach oneself** to fail by trying to be too clever or achieve too much: *he built up a successful media empire before he overreached himself and lost much of his fortune.*
overreact *vb* to react more strongly or forcefully than is necessary: *allergies happen when the body overreacts to a harmless substance.* ▶ **overreaction** *n*
override *vb* **-riding, -rode, -ridden 1** to set aside or disregard (a person or a person's decisions) by having superior authority or power: *the managing director can override any decision he doesn't like.* **2** to be more important than or replace (something): *unsurprisingly the day-to-day struggle for survival overrode all moral considerations.* ▶ **overriding** *adj*
overrule *vb* **-ruling, -ruled 1** to reverse the decision of (a person or organization with less power): *the President overruled the hardliners in the party who wanted to use force.* **2** to rule or decide against (an argument or decision): *the initial judgment was overruled by the Supreme Court.*
overrun *vb* **-running, -ran, -run 1** to conquer (territory) rapidly by force of number. **2** to spread over (a place) rapidly: *dirty tenements, overrun by lice, rats, and roaches.* **3** to extend or run beyond a set limit: *Tuesday's lunch overran by three-quarters of an hour.*
overseas *adv* **1** across the sea; abroad. ✧ *adj* **2** of, to, from, or in a distant country or countries. ✧ *n* **3** *Informal* a foreign country or foreign countries collectively.
oversee *vb* **-seeing, -saw, -seen** to watch over and direct (someone or something); supervise. ▶ **overseer** *n*
oversell *vb* **-selling, -sold** to exaggerate the merits or abilities of.
overshadow *vb* **1** to make (someone or something) seem insignificant or less important by comparison. **2** to sadden the atmosphere of: *news of their team-mate's injury overshadowed the victory celebrations.*
overshoe *n* a protective shoe worn over an ordinary shoe.
overshoot *vb* **-shooting, -shot** to go beyond (a mark or target): *the plane overshot the main runway.*
overshot *adj* (of a water wheel) driven by a flow of water that passes over the wheel.
oversight *n* a mistake caused by not noticing something.
oversleep *vb* **-sleeping, -slept** to sleep beyond the intended time for getting up.
overspill *n Brit* the rehousing of people from crowded cities in smaller towns.
overstate *vb* **-stating, -stated** to state (something) too strongly; overemphasize. ▶ **overstatement** *n*
overstay *vb* **overstay one's welcome** to stay as a guest longer than one's host or hostess would like.

overstayer *n NZ* a person who remains in New Zealand after their permit has expired.

overstep *vb* **-stepping, -stepped 1** to go beyond the limits of what is thought acceptable: *he had overstepped his authority by acting without consulting his superiors.* **2 overstep the mark** to go too far and behave in an unacceptable way.

oversubscribe *vb* **-scribing, -scribed** to apply for or try to buy more of something than is available: *the company's new share offer was heavily oversubscribed.* ▶ **oversubscription** *n*

overt *adj* done or shown in an open and obvious way: *jurors were now looking at the defendant with overt hostility.* ▷ HISTORY Old French ▶ **overtly** *adv*

overtake *vb* **-taking, -took, -taken 1** *Chiefly Brit* to move past (another vehicle or person) travelling in the same direction. **2** to do better than (someone) after catching up with him or her. **3** to come upon (someone) suddenly or unexpectedly: *a mortal tiredness overtook him.*

overtax *vb* **1** to impose too great a strain on: *a singer who had overtaxed her voice.* **2** to tax (people) too heavily.

overthrow *vb* **-throwing, -threw, -thrown 1** to defeat and replace (a ruler or government) by force. **2** to replace (standards or values). ✧ *n* **3** downfall or destruction: *the overthrow of the US-backed dictatorship.*

overtime *n* **1** work at a regular job done in addition to regular working hours. **2** pay for such work. ✧ *adv* **3** in addition to one's regular working hours: *she had been working overtime and she fell asleep at the wheel.*

overtone *n* **1** an additional meaning or hint: *I don't want to deny that from time to time there are political overtones.* **2** *Music, acoustics* any of the tones, with the exception of the principal or lowest one, that make up a musical sound.

overture *n* **1** *Music* **a** a piece of orchestral music played at the beginning of an opera, oratorio, ballet, musical comedy, or film, often containing the main musical themes of the work. **b** a one-movement orchestral piece, usually having a descriptive or evocative title: *the 1812 Overture.* **2 overtures** opening moves towards a new relationship or agreement: *the German government made a variety of friendly overtures towards the French.* ▷ HISTORY Late Latin *apertura* opening

overturn *vb* **1** to turn over or upside down. **2** to overrule or reverse (a legal decision). **3** to overthrow or destroy (a government).

overview *n* a general survey.

overweening *adj* (of opinions or qualities) excessive or immoderate: *your modesty is a cover for your overweening conceit.* ▷ HISTORY obsolete *ween* to think

overweight *adj* **1** (of a person) weighing more than is healthy. **2** weighing more than is usual or permitted.

overwhelm *vb* **1** to overpower the thoughts, emotions, or senses of (someone): *we were overwhelmed with grief.* **2** to overcome (people) with irresistible force: *gang violence has overwhelmed an ailing police force.*
▶ **overwhelming** *adj* ▶ **overwhelmingly** *adv*

overwinter *vb* **1** to spend winter in a particular place. **2** *Biol* to remain alive through winter.
▶ **overwintering** *n*

overwork *vb* **1** to work too hard or too long. **2** to use (something) too much: *the phrase 'every parent's nightmare' is an overworked platitude.* ✧ *n* **3** excessive work.

overwrought *adj* tense, nervous, and agitated.

oviduct *n Anat* the tube through which eggs are conveyed from an ovary. ▷ HISTORY Latin *ovum* egg + *ducere* to lead

oviform *adj Biol* shaped like an egg.
▷ HISTORY Latin *ovum* egg + *forma* shape

ovine *adj* of or like a sheep. ▷ HISTORY Latin *ovis* sheep

oviparous (oh-**vip**-par-uss) *adj Zool* producing eggs that hatch outside the body of the mother.
▷ HISTORY Latin *ovum* egg + *-parus* bearing

ovoid (**oh**-void) *adj* egg-shaped.

ovulate (**ov**-yew-late) *vb* **-lating, -lated** *Biol* to produce or release eggs from an ovary.
▶ **ovulation** *n*

ovule *n* **1** *Bot* the part of a plant that contains the egg cell and develops into the seed after fertilization. **2** *Zool* an immature ovum.
▷ HISTORY Latin *ovum* egg

ovum (**oh**-vum) *n, pl* **ova** an unfertilized female egg cell. ▷ HISTORY Latin: egg

owe *vb* **owing, owed 1** to be under an obligation to pay an amount of money to (someone): *he owes me a lot of money.* **2** to feel an obligation to do or give: *I think I owe you an apology.* **3 owe something to** to have something as a result of: *many serving officers owe their present position to the former president.* ▷ HISTORY Old English *āgan* to have

owl *n* a bird of prey which has a flat face, large eyes, and a small hooked beak, and which is active at night. ▷ HISTORY Old English *ūle* ▶ **owlish** *adj*

own *adj* (*preceded by a possessive*) **1** used to emphasize that something belongs to a particular person: *rely on your own instincts.* ✧ *pron* (*preceded by a possessive*) **2** the one or ones belonging to a particular person: *I had one of my own.* **3** the people that someone feels loyalty to, esp. relations: *we all look after our own around here.* **4 come into one's own** to fulfil one's potential. **5 hold one's own** to have the necessary ability to deal successfully with a situation: *he chose a partner who could hold her own with the best.* **6 on one's own a** without help: *you'll never manage to lift that on your own.* **b** by oneself; alone: *he lives on his own in a flat in town.* ✧ *vb* **7** to have (something) as one's possession: *he owns homes in four countries.* **8** Also: **own up to** to confess or admit: *I must own to a great horror of war.*
▷ HISTORY Old English *āgen* ▶ **owner** *n*
▶ **ownership** *n*

ownership flat *n NZ* a flat owned by the occupier.

own goal *n* **1** *Soccer* a goal scored by a player accidentally playing the ball into his or her own team's net. **2** *Informal* any action that results in disadvantage to the person who took it or to his or her associates: *the minister's admission was the latest in a series of own goals by the government.*

ox *n, pl* **oxen** a castrated bull used for pulling heavy loads and for meat. ▷ **HISTORY** Old English *oxa*

oxalic acid *n* a colourless poisonous acid found in many plants. ▷ **HISTORY** Latin *oxalis* garden sorrel

oxbow lake *n Geog* a crescent-shaped lake on the flood plain of a river and constituting the remnant of a former meander.

Oxbridge *n Brit* the British universities of Oxford and Cambridge considered together.

oxen *n* the plural of **ox**.

Oxfam Oxford Committee for Famine Relief.

oxidation *n* the act or process of oxidizing.

oxide *n Chem* a compound of oxygen with another element. ▷ **HISTORY** French

-oxide *suffix Chem* indicating a compound of oxygen: *carbon dioxide.*

oxidize *or* **-dise** *vb* **-dizing, -dized** *or* **-dising, -dised** *Chem* to react chemically with oxygen, as in burning or rusting. ▶ **oxidization** *or* **-disation** *n*

oxidizing agent *or* **oxidising agent** *n Chem* a substance that oxidizes another substance, being itself reduced in the process. Common oxidizing agents are oxygen, hydrogen peroxide, and ferric salts.

Oxon. (in degree titles) of Oxford University. ▷ **HISTORY** Latin *Oxoniensis*

oxyacetylene *n* a mixture of oxygen and acetylene, used in blowlamps for cutting or welding metals at high temperatures.

oxygen *n Chem* a colourless odourless gaseous element essential to life processes and to combustion. Symbol: O. ▷ **HISTORY** Greek *oxus* sharp + *-genēs* producing: from former belief that all acids contained oxygen

oxygenate *vb* **-ating, -ated** to add oxygen to: *to oxygenate blood.*

oxygen mask *n* a small bowl-shaped object which is connected via a pipe to an cylinder of oxygen and can be placed over a person's nose and mouth to help him or her breathe.

oxygen tent *n Med* a transparent enclosure covering a bedridden patient, into which oxygen is released to aid breathing.

oxymoron (ox-see-**more**-on) *n* a figure of speech that combines two apparently contradictory terms, for example *cruel kindness.* ▷ **HISTORY** Greek *oxus* sharp + *mōros* stupid

oyez *or* **oyes** *interj* a cry usually uttered three times by a public crier or court official calling for silence and attention. ▷ **HISTORY** Old French *oiez!* hear!

oyster *n* **1** an edible shellfish, some types of which produce pearls. **2 the world is your oyster** you are in a position where there is every possible chance of personal advancement and satisfaction. ✧ *adj* **3** greyish-white. ▷ **HISTORY** Greek *ostreon*

oystercatcher *n* a wading bird with black-and-white plumage and a long stout red bill.

oz *or* **oz.** ounce. ▷ **HISTORY** Italian *onza*

Oz *n Slang* Australia.

ozone *n* **1** a form of oxygen with a strong odour, formed by an electric discharge in the atmosphere. **2** *Informal* clean bracing air, as found at the seaside. ▷ **HISTORY** Greek *ozein* to smell

ozone depletion *n Science* thinning of the ozone layer caused by atmospheric pollutants.

ozone hole *n Environmental science* a severe depletion of ozone in the ozone layer above Antarctica.

ozone layer *n Environmental science* a layer of ozone in the upper atmosphere that absorbs harmful ultraviolet rays from the sun.

P p

p *or* **P** *n, pl* **p's, P's** *or* **Ps 1** the 16th letter of the English alphabet. **2 mind one's p's and q's** to be careful to behave correctly and use polite language.

p 1 *Brit, Austral & NZ* penny. **2** *Brit* pence.

P 1 *Chem* phosphorus. **2** (on road signs) parking. **3** *Chess* pawn.

p. 1 (*pl* **pp.**) page. **2** per.

pa[1] *n Informal* father.

pa[2] *n NZ* (formerly) a fortified Maori settlement.

Pa 1 *Chem* protactinium. **2** *Physics* pascal.

PA 1 Pennsylvania. **2** personal assistant. **3** public-address system.

p.a. yearly. ▷ **HISTORY** Latin *per annum*

pace[1] *n* **1 a** a single step in walking. **b** the length of a step. **2** speed of walking or running. **3** speed of doing some other activity: *efforts to accelerate the pace of change are unlikely to succeed.* **4** manner of walking. **5 keep pace with** to advance at the same speed as. **6 put someone through his** *or* **her paces** to test someone's ability. **7 set the pace** to determine the speed at which a group advances. ✧ *vb* **pacing, paced 8** to walk with regular steps, often in anxiety or impatience: *he paced up and down the foyer impatiently.* **9** to set the speed for (the competitors) in a race. **10 pace out** to measure by paces. ▷ **HISTORY** Latin *passus* step

pace[2] *prep* with due respect to: used to express polite disagreement. ▷ **HISTORY** Latin, from *pax* peace

pacemaker *n* **1** an electronic device positioned in the body, next to the heart, to regulate the heartbeat. **2** a competitor who, by leading a race, causes it to be run at a particular speed.

pachyderm (**pak**-ee-durm) *n* a large thick-skinned mammal, such as an elephant or rhinoceros. ▷ **HISTORY** Greek *pakhus* thick + *derma* skin

Pacific *adj* of the Pacific Ocean, the world's largest and deepest ocean, lying between Asia and Australia and America, or its islands.

pacifist *n* a person who is totally opposed to violence and refuses to take part in war. ▶ **pacifism** *n*

pacify *vb* **-fies, -fying, -fied** to soothe or calm. ▷ **HISTORY** Old French *pacifier;* see PACIFIC ▶ **pacification** *n*

Pacinian corpuscle *n Anat* a sensory nerve ending that is sensitive to pressure and vibration. ▷ **HISTORY** from Felippo *Pacini*, Italian anatomist

pack[1] *n* **1** a bundle or load carried on the back. **2** *Brit & NZ* a complete set of playing cards. **3** a group of animals that hunt together: *a pack of hounds.* **4** *Rugby* the forwards of a team. **5** any collection of people or things: *a pack of lies.* **6** *Chiefly US & Canad* same as **packet** (sense 1). **7** an organized group of Cub Scouts or Brownie Guides. **8** same as **rucksack backpack. 9** Also called: **face pack** a cream treatment that cleanses and tones the skin. ✧ *vb* **10** to put (articles) in a case or container for moving. **11** to roll (articles) up into a bundle. **12** to press tightly together; cram: *thousands of people packed into the city's main square.* **13** (foll. by *off*) to send away hastily: *their young son came in to say good night and was packed off to bed.* **14** *Slang* to be able to deliver a specified amount of unexpected or violent force or power: *the film's unexpected ending packs quite a punch.* **15** *US informal* to carry (a gun) habitually. **16 send someone packing** *Informal* to dismiss someone abruptly. ✧ See also **pack in, pack up.** ▷ **HISTORY** origin unknown

pack[2] *vb* to fill (a committee, jury, or audience) with one's own supporters. ▷ **HISTORY** perhaps from *pact*

package *n* **1** a small parcel. **2** Also: **package deal** a deal in which separate items are presented together as a unit. **3** *US & Canad* same as **packet** (sense 1). ✧ *vb* **-aging, -aged 4** to put (something) into a package. ▶ **packaging** *n*

package holiday *n* a holiday in which everything is arranged by one company for a fixed price.

packet *n* **1** a container, together with its contents: *a packet of crisps.* **2** a small parcel. **3** Also: **packet boat** a boat that transports mail, passengers, or goods on a fixed short route. **4** *Slang* a large sum of money: *she was paid a packet.* **5** *Computers* a unit into which a larger piece of data is broken down for more efficient transmission. ▷ **HISTORY** Old French *pacquet*

packhorse *n* a horse used to carry goods.

pack ice *n Geog* a large area of floating ice, consisting of pieces that have become massed together.

pack in *vb Informal* to stop doing (something): *I'm going to pack it in and resign.*

packing *n* material, such as paper or plastic, used to protect packed goods.

pack up *vb* **1** to put (articles) in a bag or case before leaving. **2** *Informal* to stop doing (something). **3** (of a machine) to break down.

pact *n* a formal agreement between two or more parties. ▷ **HISTORY** Latin *pactum*

pad[1] *n* **1** a thick piece of soft material used for comfort, shape, protection, or absorption. **2** a number of sheets of paper fastened together along one edge. **3** the fleshy cushioned underpart of an animal's paw. **4** a level area or flat-topped structure, from which rockets are launched or helicopters take off. **5** the floating leaf of the water lily. **6** *Slang* a person's residence. ✧ *vb* **padding, padded 7** to fill (something) out with soft material for comfort, shape, or protection. **8 pad out** to lengthen (a speech or piece of writing) with unnecessary words or pieces of information. ▷ **HISTORY** origin unknown

pad[2] *vb* **padding, padded 1** to walk with a soft or muffled step. **2** to travel (a route) on foot: *men padding the streets in cheap sneakers.* ▷ **HISTORY** Middle Dutch *pad* path

padding *n* **1** any soft material used to pad something. **2** unnecessary information put into a speech or written work to make it longer.

paddle[1] *n* **1** a short light oar with a flat blade at one or both ends. **2** a paddle wheel used to move a boat. **3** a blade of a water wheel or paddle wheel. ✧ *vb* **-dling, -dled 4** to move (a boat) with a paddle. **5** to swim with short rapid strokes, like a dog. **6** *US & Canad informal* to spank. ▷ **HISTORY** origin unknown

paddle[2] *vb* **-dling, -dled 1** to walk barefoot in shallow water. **2** to dabble (one's fingers, hands, or feet) in water. ✧ *n* **3** the act of paddling in water. ▷ **HISTORY** origin unknown

paddle steamer *n* a ship propelled by paddle wheels turned by a steam engine.

paddle wheel *n* a large wheel fitted with paddles, turned by an engine to propel a ship.

paddock *n* **1** a small enclosed field for horses. **2** (in horse racing) the enclosure in which horses are paraded and mounted before a race. **3** *Austral & NZ* any area of fenced land. ▷ **HISTORY** Old English *pearruc* enclosure

paddy[1] *n, pl* **-dies 1** Also: **paddy field** a field planted with rice. **2** rice as a growing crop or when harvested but not yet milled. ▷ **HISTORY** Malay *pādī*

paddy[2] *n, pl* **-dies** *Brit & NZ informal* a fit of temper. ▷ **HISTORY** from *Paddy,* informal name for an Irishman

pademelon, paddymelon (**pad**-ee-mel-an) *n* a small Australian wallaby.

padkos (**pudd**-koss) *n S African* snacks and provisions for a journey. ▷ **HISTORY** Afrikaans, literally: road food

padlock *n* **1** a detachable lock with a hinged hoop fastened through a ring on the object to be secured. ✧ *vb* **2** to fasten (something) with a padlock. ▷ **HISTORY** origin unknown

padre (**pah**-dray) *n Informal* a chaplain to the armed forces. ▷ **HISTORY** via Spanish or Italian from Latin *pater* father

paean (**pee**-an) *n Literary* an expression of praise or joy. ▷ **HISTORY** Greek *paian* hymn to Apollo

paediatrician *or US* **pediatrician** *n* a doctor who specializes in children's diseases.

paediatrics *or US* **pediatrics** *n* the branch of medicine concerned with children and their diseases. ▷ **HISTORY** Greek *pais, paid-* child + *iatros* physician ▶ **paediatric** *or US* ▶ **pediatric** *adj*

paedophile *or US* **pedophile** *n* a person who is sexually attracted to children.

paedophilia *or US* **pedophilia** *n* the condition of being sexually attracted to children. ▷ **HISTORY** Greek *pais, paid-* child + *philos* loving

paella (pie-**ell**-a) *n* a Spanish dish made from rice, shellfish, chicken, and vegetables. ▷ **HISTORY** Catalan

pagan *adj* **1** having, being, or relating to religious beliefs, esp. ancient ones, which are not part of any of the world's major religions: *this was the site of a pagan temple to the sun.* **2** irreligious. ✧ *n* **3** a person who does not belong to any of the world's major religions. **4** a person without any religion. ▷ **HISTORY** Church Latin *paganus* civilian (hence not a soldier of Christ) ▶ **paganism** *n*

page[1] *n* **1** one side of one of the leaves of a book, newspaper, or magazine. **2** one of the leaves of a book, newspaper, or magazine. **3** *Literary* a period or event: *a new page in the country's political history.* **4** a screenful of information from a website or teletext service. ▷ **HISTORY** Latin *pagina*

page[2] *n* **1** a small boy who attends a bride at her wedding. **2** a youth employed to run errands for the guests in a hotel or club. **3** *Medieval history* a boy in training for knighthood. ✧ *vb* **paging, paged 4** to summon (a person), by bleeper or loudspeaker, in order to pass on a message. ▷ **HISTORY** Greek *pais* child

pageant *n* **1** an outdoor show portraying scenes from history. **2** any magnificent display or procession. ▷ **HISTORY** perhaps from Latin *pagina* scene of a play

pageantry *n* spectacular display or ceremony.

pageboy *n* **1** a hairstyle in which the hair is smooth and the same medium length with the ends curled under. **2** same as **page[2]** (senses 1, 2).

pagination *n* the numbering in sequence of the pages of a book or manuscript. ▶ **paginate** *vb*

pagoda *n* a pyramid-shaped Asian temple or tower. ▷ **HISTORY** Portuguese *pagode*

paid *vb* **1** past of **pay**. **2 put paid to** to end or destroy: *a knee injury put paid to his promising sporting career.*

pail *n* **1** a bucket. **2** Also called: **pailful** the amount contained in a pail: *a pail of water.* ▷ **HISTORY** Old English *pægel*

pain *n* **1** physical hurt or discomfort caused by injury or illness. **2** emotional suffering. **3 on pain of** subject to the penalty of: *orders which their soldiers were bound to follow on pain of death.* **4** Also called: **pain in the neck** *Informal* a person or thing that is annoying or irritating. ✧ *vb* **5** to cause (a person) physical or mental suffering. **6** *Informal* to annoy; irritate. ✧ See also **pains.** ▷ **HISTORY** Latin *poena* punishment ▶ **painless** *adj*

painful *adj* **1** causing pain or distress: *painful inflammation of the joints; he began the painful task of making funeral arrangements.* **2** affected with pain: *the symptoms include fever and painful joints.* **3** tedious or difficult: *the hours passed with painful slowness.* **4** *Informal* extremely bad: *a painful so-called comedy.* ▶ **painfully** *adv*

painkiller *n* a drug that relieves pain.

pains *pl n* care or trouble: *they are at great pains to appear realistic and responsible.*

painstaking *adj* extremely careful and thorough. ▶ **painstakingly** *adv*

paint *n* **1** a coloured substance, spread on a surface with a brush or a roller, that forms a hard coating. **2** a dry film of paint on a surface. **3** *Informal* face make-up. ✧ *vb* **4** to apply paint to paper or canvas to make (a picture) of. **5** to coat (a surface) with paint. **6** to describe vividly in words: *the survey paints a dismal picture of growing hunger and disease.* **7** to apply make-up to (the face). **8** to apply (liquid) to (a surface): *paint the varnish on and leave it to dry for at least four hours.* **9 paint the town red**

Informal to celebrate in a lively way. ▷ **HISTORY** Latin *pingere* to paint

painted lady *n* a butterfly with pale brownish-red mottled wings.

painter[1] *n* **1** an artist who paints pictures. **2** a person who paints surfaces of buildings as a trade.

painter[2] *n* a rope attached to the bow of a boat for tying it up. ▷ **HISTORY** probably from Old French *penteur* strong rope

painting *n* **1** a picture produced by using paint. **2** the art of producing pictures by applying paints to paper or canvas. **3** the act of applying paint to a surface.

pair *n* **1** two identical or similar things matched for use together: *a pair of shoes.* **2** two people, animals, or things used or grouped together: *a pair of tickets.* **3** an object consisting of two identical or similar parts joined together: *a pair of jeans.* **4** a male and a female animal of the same species kept for breeding purposes. **5** *Parliament* two opposed members who both agree not to vote on a specified motion. **6** two playing cards of the same denomination. **7** one member of a matching pair: *I can't find the pair to this glove.* ✧ *vb* **8** to group (people or things) in twos. **9 pair off** to separate into groups of two. ▷ **HISTORY** Latin *par* equal

> **WORD TIP**
> Like other collective nouns, *pair* takes a singular or a plural verb according to whether it is seen as a unit or as a collection of two things: *the pair are said to dislike each other; a pair of good shoes is essential.*

paisley pattern *or* **paisley** *n* a detailed pattern of small curving shapes, used in fabric. ▷ **HISTORY** after *Paisley*, town in Scotland

pajamas *pl n US* pyjamas.

pakeha (**pah**-kee-hah) *n, pl* **pakeha** *or* **pakehas** *NZ* a person of European descent, as distinct from a Maori. ▷ **HISTORY** Maori

Pakistani *adj* **1** of Pakistan. ✧ *n* **2** a person from Pakistan.

pal *Informal, old-fashioned in NZ* ✧ *n* **1** a close friend. ✧ *vb* **palling, palled 2 pal up with** to become friends with. ▷ **HISTORY** Romany: brother

palace *n* **1** the official residence of a king, queen, president, or archbishop. **2** a large and richly furnished building. ▷ **HISTORY** Latin *Palatium* Palatine, the site of the palace of the emperors in Rome

paladin *n* **1** one of the legendary twelve peers of Charlemagne's court. **2** (formerly) a knight who did battle for a king or queen. ▷ **HISTORY** Italian *paladino*

palaeo- *or US* **paleo-** *combining form* old, ancient, or prehistoric: *palaeobotany.*

Palaeocene *or US* **Paleocene** (**pal**-ee-oh-seen) *adj Geol* of the epoch of geological time about 65 million years ago. ▷ **HISTORY** Greek *palaeo-* ancient + *kainos* new

palaeography *or US* **paleography** (pal-ee-**og**-ra-fee) *n* the study of ancient handwriting. ▷ **HISTORY** Greek *palaeo-* ancient + -GRAPHY

Palaeolithic *or US* **Paleolithic** (pal-ee-oh-**lith**-ik) *adj* of the period from about 2.5 to 3 million years ago until about 12 000 BC during which primitive man emerged and unpolished chipped stone tools were made. ▷ **HISTORY** Greek *palaeo-* ancient + *lithos* stone

palaeontology *or US* **paleontology** (pal-ee-on-**tol**-a-jee) *n* the study of past geological periods and fossils. ▷ **HISTORY** Greek *palaeo-* ancient + *ōn, ont-* being + -LOGY ▶ **palaeontologist** *or US* ▶ **paleontologist** *n*

Palaeozoic *or US* **Paleozoic** (pal-ee-oh-**zoh**-ik) *adj Geol* of the geological era that lasted from about 600 million years ago to 230 million years ago. ▷ **HISTORY** Greek *palaeo-* ancient + *zōion* animal

Palagi (pa-**lang**-gee) *n, pl* **-gis** *NZ* the Samoan name for a pakeha.

palanquin (pal-an-**keen**) *n* (formerly, in the Orient) a covered bed in which someone could be carried on the shoulders of four men. ▷ **HISTORY** Portuguese *palanquim*

palatable *adj* **1** (of food or drink) pleasant to taste. **2** (of an experience or idea) acceptable or satisfactory.

palate *n* **1** the roof of the mouth. **2** the sense of taste: *a range of dishes to tempt every palate.* ▷ **HISTORY** Latin *palatum*

> **WORD TIP**
> Avoid confusion with **palette** or **pallet**.

palatial *adj* like a palace; magnificent: *his palatial home.*

palatinate *n* a territory ruled by a palatine prince or noble or a count palatine.

palatine *adj* possessing royal prerogatives: *a count palatine.* ▷ **HISTORY** Latin *palatium* palace

palaver (pal-**lah**-ver) *n* time-consuming fuss: *all the palaver involved in obtaining a visa.* ▷ **HISTORY** Portuguese *palavra* talk

pale[1] *adj* **1** (of a colour) whitish and not very strong: *pale yellow.* **2** (of a complexion) having a whitish appearance, usually because of illness, shock, or fear. **3** lacking brightness or colour: *the pale, chill light of an October afternoon.* ✧ *vb* **paling, paled 4** to become pale or paler: *the girl paled at the news.* ▷ **HISTORY** Latin *pallidus* ▶ **paleness** *n*

pale[2] *n* **1** a wooden post used in fences. **2 a** a fence made of pales. **b** a boundary. **3 beyond the pale** outside the limits of social convention: *the destruction of forests is beyond the pale.* ▷ **HISTORY** Latin *palus* stake

Palestinian *adj* **1** of Palestine, an area in the Middle East between the Jordan River and the Mediterranean. ✧ *n* **2** an Arab from this area, esp. one living in Israel or Israeli-occupied territory or as a refugee.

palette *n* **1** a flat board used by artists to mix paints. **2** the range of colours characteristic of a particular artist or school of painting: *he uses a cool palette with no strong red.* **3** the range of colours or patterns that can be displayed on the visual display unit of a computer. ▷ HISTORY French

> ☑ **WORD TIP**
> Avoid confusion with **palate** or **pallet**.

palette knife *n* a spatula with a thin flexible blade used in painting or cookery.

palindrome *n* a word or phrase that reads the same backwards or forwards, such as *able was I ere I saw Elba*. ▷ HISTORY Greek *palindromos* running back again

paling *n* **1** a fence made of pales. **2** pales collectively. **3** a single pale.

palisade *n* **1** a fence made of stakes driven into the ground. **2** one of the stakes used in such a fence. ▷ HISTORY Latin *palus* stake

palisade cell *n Bot* a cell containing many chloroplasts, situated below the outer epidermis of a leaf blade.

pall[1] *n* **1** a cloth spread over a coffin. **2** a coffin at a funeral ceremony. **3** a dark heavy covering: *a pall of smoke and dust hung in the air.* **4** a depressing atmosphere: *a pall hung on them all after his death.* ▷ HISTORY Latin *pallium* cloak

pall[2] *vb* to become boring or uninteresting, esp. by continuing for too long: *any pleasure had palled long before the two-hour programme was over.* ▷ HISTORY variant of *appal*

Palladian *adj* of a style of architecture characterized by symmetry and the revival and development of ancient Roman styles. ▷ HISTORY after Andrea *Palladio,* Italian architect

palladium *n Chem* a rare silvery-white element of the platinum metal group, used in jewellery. Symbol: Pd. ▷ HISTORY after the asteroid *Pallas*

pallbearer *n* a person who helps to carry or who escorts the coffin at a funeral.

pallet[1] *n* a straw-filled mattress or bed. ▷ HISTORY Latin *palea* straw

pallet[2] *n* **1** a tool with a flat, sometimes flexible, blade used for shaping pottery. **2** a portable platform for storing and moving goods. ▷ HISTORY Latin *pala* spade

> ☑ **WORD TIP**
> Avoid confusion with **palate** or **palette**.

palliasse *n* a straw-filled mattress; pallet. ▷ HISTORY French *paillasse*

palliate *vb* **-ating, -ated 1** to lessen the severity of (pain or disease) without curing it. **2** to cause (an offence) to seem less serious. ▷ HISTORY Latin *pallium* a cloak

palliative *adj* **1** relieving without curing. ✧ *n* **2** something that palliates, such as a sedative drug. **3** something that alleviates or lessens a problem: *equal pay was a palliative for the growing unrest among women.*

pallid *adj* **1** lacking colour, brightness, or vigour: *a pallid autumn sun.* **2** lacking energy or vitality; insipid: *many militants find the party's socialism too pallid.* ▷ HISTORY Latin *pallidus*

pallor *n* paleness of complexion, usually because of illness, shock, or fear. ▷ HISTORY Latin: whiteness

pally *adj* **-lier, -liest** *Informal* on friendly terms.

palm[1] *n* **1** the inner surface of the hand from the wrist to the base of the fingers. **2** the part of a glove that covers the palm. **3 in the palm of one's hand** at one's mercy or command: *he had the jury in the palm of his hand.* ✧ *vb* **4** to hide (something) in the hand: *he palmed the key.* ✧ See also **palm off**. ▷ HISTORY Latin *palma*

palm[2] *or* **palm tree** *n* a tropical or subtropical tree with a straight unbranched trunk crowned with long pointed leaves. ▷ HISTORY Latin *palma,* from the likeness of its spreading fronds to a hand

palmate *adj* shaped like an open hand: *palmate leaves.*

palmcorder *n* a small camcorder which can be held in the palm of the hand.

palmetto *n, pl* **-tos** a small palm tree with fan-shaped leaves. ▷ HISTORY Spanish *palmito* a little palm

palmistry *n* fortune-telling by examining the lines and bumps of the hand. ▶ **palmist** *n*

palm off *vb* **1** to get rid of (someone or something) by passing it on to another: *the risk has to be shared with subcontractors, not simply palmed off on them.* **2** to divert (someone) by a lie or excuse: *Mark was palmed off with a series of excuses.*

palm oil *n* an oil obtained from the fruit of certain palm trees, used as an edible fat and in soap.

Palm Sunday *n* the Sunday before Easter.

palmtop *adj* (of a computer) small enough to be held in the hand.

palomino *n, pl* **-nos** a golden or cream horse with a white mane and tail. ▷ HISTORY Spanish: dovelike

palpable *adj* **1** obvious: *palpable nonsense.* **2** (of a feeling or an atmosphere) so intense that it seems capable of being touched: *an air of palpable gloom hung over him.* ▷ HISTORY Latin *palpare* to touch ▶ **palpably** *adv*

palpate *vb* **-pating, -pated** *Med* to examine (an area of the body) by touching. ▷ HISTORY Latin *palpare* to stroke ▶ **palpation** *n*

palpitate *vb* **-tating, -tated 1** (of the heart) to beat rapidly. **2** to flutter or tremble. ▷ HISTORY Latin *palpitare* ▶ **palpitation** *n*

palsy (**pawl**-zee) *n Pathol* paralysis of a specified type: *cerebral palsy.* ▷ HISTORY Old French *paralisie* ▶ **palsied** *adj*

paltry *adj* **-trier, -triest** insignificant. ▷ HISTORY Low Germanic *palter, paltrig* ragged

pampas *n* the extensive grassy plains of South America. ▷ HISTORY Native American *bamba* plain

pampas grass *n* a South American grass with large feathery silver-coloured flower branches.

pamper *vb* to treat (someone) with excessive indulgence or care; spoil. ▷ HISTORY Germanic

pamphlet *n* a thin paper-covered booklet, often on a subject of current interest. ▷ HISTORY Medieval Latin *Pamphilus,* title of a poem

pamphleteer *n* a person who writes or issues pamphlets.

pan[1] *n* **1** a wide long-handled metal container used in cooking. **2** any of various similar containers used in industry, etc. **3** either of the two dishes on a set of scales. **4** *Brit* the bowl of a lavatory. **5** a natural or artificial hollow in the ground: *a saltpan.* ✧ *vb* **panning, panned 6** to sift gold from (a river) in a shallow pan. **7** *Informal* to criticize harshly: *his first film was panned by the critics.* ✧ See also **pan out**. ▷ HISTORY Old English *panne*

pan[2] *vb* **panning, panned 1** to move (a film camera) to follow a moving object or to take in a whole scene. ✧ *n* **2** the act of panning. ▷ HISTORY from *panoramic*

pan- *combining form* including or relating to all parts or members: *Pan-American.* ▷ HISTORY Greek

panacea (pan-a-**see**-a) *n* a remedy for all diseases or problems. ▷ HISTORY Greek *pan-* all + *akēs* remedy

panache (pan-**ash**) *n* a confident and stylish manner: *the orchestra played with great panache.* ▷ HISTORY Old Italian *pennacchio* feather

panama hat *or* **panama** *n* a straw hat with a rounded crown and a wide brim.

Pan-American *adj* of North, South, and Central America collectively.

panatella *n* a long slender cigar. ▷ HISTORY American Spanish *panetela* long thin biscuit

pancake *n* **1** a thin flat circle of fried batter. **2** Also called: **pancake landing** an aircraft landing made by levelling out a few feet from the ground and then dropping onto it.

Pancake Day *n* Shrove Tuesday, when people traditionally eat pancakes.

panchromatic *adj Photog* (of an emulsion or film) sensitive to light of all colours.

pancreas (**pang**-kree-ass) *n* a large gland behind the stomach, that produces insulin and aids digestion. ▷ HISTORY Greek *pan-* all + *kreas* flesh ▶ **pancreatic** *adj*

pancreatic juice *n Physiol* the clear alkaline secretion of the pancreas.

panda *n* **1** Also called: **giant panda** a large black-and-white bearlike animal from the high mountain bamboo forests of China. **2** Also called: **lesser panda, red panda** a raccoon-like animal of the mountain forests of S Asia, with a reddish-brown coat and ringed tail. ▷ HISTORY Nepalese

panda car *n Brit* a police patrol car.

pandemic *adj* (of a disease) occurring over a wide geographical area. ▷ HISTORY Greek *pandēmos* general

pandemonium *n* wild confusion; uproar.

> **WORD HISTORY**
> *Pandemonium* is the capital of Hell in John Milton's poem 'Paradise Lost'. The word 'pandemonium' comes from Greek *pan*, meaning 'all', and *daimon*, meaning 'demon' or 'spirit'.

pander *vb* **1** (foll. by *to*) to indulge (a person or his or her desires): *he pandered to popular fears.* ✧ *n* **2** *Chiefly archaic* a person who procures a sexual partner for someone. ▷ HISTORY after *Pandarus,* in legend, the procurer of Cressida for Troilus

pandit *n Hinduism* same as **pundit** (sense 2).

p & p *Brit* postage and packing.

pane *n* a sheet of glass in a window or door. ▷ HISTORY Latin *pannus* rag

panegyric (pan-ee-**jirr**-rik) *n* a formal speech or piece of writing that praises a person or event. ▷ HISTORY Greek *panēguris* public gathering

panel *n* **1** a distinct section of a larger surface area, such as that in a door. **2** any distinct section of something formed from a sheet of material, such as part of a car body. **3** a piece of material inserted in a garment. **4** a group of people acting as a team, such as in a quiz or a discussion before an audience. **5** *Law* **a** a list of jurors. **b** the people on a jury. **6** short for **instrument panel**. ✧ *adj* **7** of a group acting as a panel: *a panel game.* ✧ *vb* **-elling, -elled** *or US* **-eling, -eled 8** to cover or decorate with panels. ▷ HISTORY Old French: portion

panel beater *n* a person who repairs damage to car bodies.

panelling *or US* **paneling** *n* panels collectively, such as on a wall or ceiling.

panellist *or US* **panelist** *n* a member of a panel, usually on radio or television.

panel van *n Austral & NZ* a small van.

pang *n* a sudden sharp feeling of pain or sadness. ▷ HISTORY Germanic

Pangaea (pan-**jee**-a) *n Geol* the ancient supercontinent, comprising all the present continents joined together.

pangolin *n* an animal of tropical countries with a scaly body and a long snout for feeding on ants and termites. Also called: **scaly anteater** ▷ HISTORY Malay *peng-gōling*

panic *n* **1** a sudden overwhelming feeling of terror or anxiety, sometimes affecting a whole group of people. ✧ *adj* **2** of or resulting from such terror: *panic measures.* ✧ *vb* **-icking, -icked 3** to feel or cause to feel panic. ▷ HISTORY Greek *panikos* emanating from *Pan*, god of the fields ▶ **panicky** *adj*

panicle *n Bot* a loose, irregularly branched cluster of flowers, such as in the oat. ▷ HISTORY Latin *panicula* tuft

panic-stricken *adj* affected by panic.

pannier *n* **1** one of a pair of bags fixed on either side of the back wheel of a bicycle or motorcycle. **2** one of a pair of large baskets slung over a beast of burden. ▷ HISTORY Old French *panier*

panoply (**pan**-a-plee) *n* a magnificent array: *ambassadors equipped with the full panoply of diplomatic bags, codes and cyphers.* ▷ HISTORY Greek *pan-* all + *hopla* armour

panorama *n* **1** a wide unbroken view in all directions: *the beautiful panorama of the Cornish coast.* **2** a wide or comprehensive survey of a subject: *the panorama of American life.* **3** a picture of a scene unrolled before spectators a part at a time so as to appear continuous. ▷ HISTORY Greek *pan-* all + *horama* view ▶ **panoramic** *adj*

A B C D E F G H I J K L M N O P Q R S T U V W X Y Z

pan out *vb* **1** *Informal* to work out; result: *Parker's research did not pan out too well.* **2** (of gravel) to yield gold by panning.

pansy *n, pl* **-sies 1** a garden plant whose flowers have rounded white, yellow, or purple velvety petals. **2** *Offensive slang* an effeminate or homosexual man or boy. ▷ HISTORY Old French *pensée* thought

pant *vb* **1** to breathe with noisy gasps after exertion. **2** to say (something) while breathing in this way. **3** (foll. by *for*) to have a frantic desire for. ✧ *n* **4** the act of panting. ▷ HISTORY Greek *phantasioun* to have visions

pantaloons *pl n* baggy trousers gathered at the ankles. ▷ HISTORY French *pantalon* trousers

pantechnicon *n Brit* a large van used for furniture removals. ▷ HISTORY Greek *pan-* all + *tekhnē* art; originally a London bazaar later used as a furniture warehouse

pantheism *n* **1** the belief that God is present in everything. **2** readiness to worship all gods. ▸ **pantheist** *n* ▸ **pantheistic** *adj*

pantheon *n* **1** (in ancient Greece or Rome) a temple built to honour all the gods. **2** all the gods of a particular creed: *the Celtic pantheon of horse gods.* **3** a group of very important people: *he deserves a place in the pantheon of social reformers.* ▷ HISTORY Greek *pan-* all + *theos* god

panther *n* a leopard, usually a black one. ▷ HISTORY Greek

panties *pl n* women's or children's underpants.

pantihose *pl n US & Austral* women's tights.

pantile *n* a roofing tile, with an S-shaped cross section. ▷ HISTORY PAN[1] + *tile*

panto *n, pl* **-tos** *Brit informal* short for **pantomime** (sense 1).

pantograph *n* **1** an instrument for copying drawings or maps to any scale. **2** a device on the roof of an electric train to carry the current from an overhead wire. ▷ HISTORY Greek *pant-* all + *graphein* to write

pantomime *n* **1** (in Britain) a play based on a fairy tale and performed at Christmas time. **2** a theatrical entertainment in which words are replaced by gestures and bodily actions. **3** *Informal, chiefly Brit* a confused or farcical situation. ▷ HISTORY Greek *pantomīmos*

pantry *n, pl* **-tries** a small room or large cupboard in which food is kept. ▷ HISTORY Latin *panis* bread

pants *pl n* **1** *Brit* an undergarment with two leg holes, covering the body from the waist or hips to the thighs. **2** *US, Canad, Austral & NZ* trousers or shorts. **3 bore** *or* **scare the pants off someone** *Informal* to bore or scare someone very much. ▷ HISTORY shortened from *pantaloons*

pantyhose *pl n NZ & Austral* women's tights.

pap[1] *n* **1** a soft food for babies or invalids. **2** worthless or oversimplified entertainment or information. **3** *S African* maize porridge. ▷ HISTORY Latin *pappare* to eat

pap[2] *n Old-fashioned, Scot & N English dialect* a nipple or teat. ▷ HISTORY from Old Norse

papa (pap-**pah**) *n Old-fashioned, informal* father. ▷ HISTORY French

papacy (**pay**-pa-see) *n, pl* **-cies 1** the office or term of office of a pope. **2** the system of government in the Roman Catholic Church that has the pope as its head. ▷ HISTORY Medieval Latin *papa* pope

papal *adj* of the pope or the papacy.

paparazzo (pap-a-**rat**-so) *n, pl* **-razzi** (-**rat**-see) a freelance photographer who specializes in taking shots of famous people without their knowledge or consent. ▷ HISTORY Italian

papaya (pap-**pie**-a) *n* a large green fruit with a sweet yellow flesh, that grows in the West Indies. ▷ HISTORY Spanish

paper *n* **1** a flexible material made in sheets from wood pulp or other fibres and used for writing on, decorating walls, or wrapping parcels. **2** short for **newspaper wallpaper**. **3 papers** documents, such as a passport, which can identify the bearer. **4** a set of examination questions. **5 papers** the collected diaries or letters of someone's private or public life. **6** a lecture or an essay on a specific subject. **7 on paper** in theory, as opposed to fact: *countless ideas which look good on paper just don't work in practice.* ✧ *adj* **8** made of paper: *paper towels; a paper bag.* **9** recorded on paper but not yet existing in practice: *a paper profit of more than $50 million.* ✧ *vb* **10** to cover (walls) with wallpaper. ▷ HISTORY Latin *papyrus* ▸ **papery** *adj*

paperback *n* **1** a book with covers made of flexible card. ✧ *adj* **2** of a paperback or publication of paperbacks: *a paperback novel.*

paperhanger *n* a person who hangs wallpaper as an occupation.

paperknife *n, pl* **-knives** a knife-shaped object with a blunt blade for opening sealed envelopes.

paper money *n* banknotes, rather than coins.

paperweight *n* a small heavy object placed on top of loose papers to prevent them from scattering.

paperwork *n* clerical work, such as the writing of reports or letters.

papier-mâché (**pap**-yay **mash**-ay) *n* **1** a hard substance made of layers of paper mixed with paste and moulded when moist. ✧ *adj* **2** made of papier-mâché. ▷ HISTORY French, literally: chewed paper

papilla (pap-**pill**-a) *n, pl* **-lae** (-lee) *Biol* a small projection of tissue at the base of a hair, tooth, or feather. ▷ HISTORY Latin: nipple ▸ **papillary** *adj*

papist *n, adj Usually offensive* same as **Roman Catholic**. ▷ HISTORY Church Latin *papa* pope

papoose *n* a Native American baby. ▷ HISTORY Native American *papoos*

paprika *n* a mild powdered seasoning made from red peppers. ▷ HISTORY Hungarian

Pap test *or* **smear** *n Med* same as **cervical smear**. ▷ HISTORY after George *Papanicolaou*, anatomist

papyrus (pap-**ire**-uss) *n, pl* **-ri** (-rye) *or* **-ruses 1** a tall water plant of Africa. **2** a kind of paper made from the stem of this plant, used by the ancient

Egyptians, Greeks, and Romans. **3** an ancient document written on this paper. ▷ **HISTORY** Greek *papuros* reed

par *n* **1** the usual or average condition: *I feel slightly below par most of the time.* **2 on a par with** equal or equivalent to: *an environmental disaster on a par with Chernobyl.* **3** *Golf* a standard score for a hole or course that a good player should make: *four under par with two holes to play.* **4** *Finance* the established value of the unit of one national currency in terms of the unit of another. **5** *Commerce* short for **par value**. **6 par for the course** to be expected: *random acts of violence were par for the course in the capital.* ▷ **HISTORY** Latin: equal

par. **1** paragraph. **2** parenthesis.

para *n Informal* **1** a paratrooper. **2** a paragraph.

para- *or before a vowel* **par-** *prefix* **1** beside or near: *parameter.* **2** beyond: *parapsychology.* **3** resembling: *paratyphoid fever.* ▷ **HISTORY** Greek

parable *n* a short story that uses familiar situations to illustrate a religious or moral point. ▷ **HISTORY** Greek *parabolē* analogy

parabola (par-**ab**-bol-a) *n Geom* an open plane curve formed by the intersection of a cone by a plane parallel to its side. ▷ **HISTORY** Greek *parabolē* a setting alongside ▶ **parabolic** *adj*

paracetamol *n* a mild pain-relieving drug. ▷ **HISTORY** from *para-acetamidophenol*

parachute *n* **1** a large fabric canopy connected by a harness, that slows the descent of a person or package from an aircraft. ✧ *vb* **-chuting, -chuted** **2** to land or to drop (supplies or troops) by parachute from an aircraft. ▷ **HISTORY** French ▶ **parachutist** *n*

parade *n* **1** an ordered march or procession. **2** a public promenade or street of shops. **3** a blatant but sometimes insincere display: *a man who made a parade of liking his own company best.* ✧ *vb* **-rading, -raded** **4** to exhibit or flaunt: *he neither paraded nor disguised his devout faith.* **5** to walk or march, esp. in a procession. ▷ **HISTORY** French: a making ready

parade ground *n* a place where soldiers assemble regularly for inspection or display.

paradigm (**par**-a-dime) *n* a model or example: *his experience is a paradigm for the young artist.* ▷ **HISTORY** Greek *paradeigma* pattern

paradise *n* **1** heaven; where the good go after death. **2** the Garden of Eden. **3** any place or condition that fulfils a person's desires. ▷ **HISTORY** Greek *paradeisos* garden

paradise duck *n* a New Zealand duck with bright feathers.

paradox *n* **1** a statement that seems self-contradictory but may be true: *it's a strange paradox that a musician must practise improvising to become a good improviser.* **2** a self-contradictory proposition, such as *I always tell lies.* **3** a person or thing that is made up of contradictory elements. ▷ **HISTORY** Greek *paradoxos* opposed to existing notions ▶ **paradoxical** *adj* ▶ **paradoxically** *adv*

paraffin *n* **1** *Brit* a liquid mixture distilled from petroleum or shale and used as a fuel or solvent. **2** *Chem* the former name for **alkane**. ▷ **HISTORY** Latin *parum* too little + *affinis* adjacent; so called from its chemical inertia

paraffin wax *n* a white waxlike substance distilled from petroleum and used to make candles and as a sealing agent.

paragon *n* a model of perfection: *a paragon of female integrity and determination.* ▷ **HISTORY** Old Italian *paragone* comparison

paragraph *n* **1** a section of a piece of writing, usually devoted to one idea, which begins on a new line and is often indented. **2** *Printing* the character ¶, used to indicate the beginning of a new paragraph. ✧ *vb* **3** to put (a piece of writing) into paragraphs. ▷ **HISTORY** Greek *paragraphos* line drawing attention to part of a text

parakeet *n* a small colourful parrot with a long tail. ▷ **HISTORY** Spanish *periquito* parrot

paralegal *n* a person trained to assist lawyers but not qualified to practise law.

parallax *n* an apparent change in an object's position due to a change in the observer's position. ▷ **HISTORY** Greek *parallaxis* change

parallel *adj* **1** separated by an equal distance at every point: *parallel lines; a path parallel to the main road.* **2** precisely corresponding: *we decide our salaries by comparison with parallel jobs in other charities.* **3** *Computers* operating on several items of information or instructions at the same time. ✧ *n* **4** *Maths* one of a set of parallel lines or planes. **5** something with similar features to another. **6** a comparison; similarity between two things: *she attempted to excuse herself by drawing a parallel between her behaviour and ours.* **7** Also called: **parallel of latitude** any of the imaginary lines around the earth parallel to the equator, marking degrees of latitude. **8** *Printing* the character ||, used as a reference mark. ✧ *vb* **9** to correspond to: *the increase in smoking is paralleled by an increase in lung cancer.* ▷ **HISTORY** Greek *parallēlos* alongside one another

parallel bars *pl n Gymnastics* a pair of wooden bars on upright posts used for various exercises.

parallel circuit *n Electronics* an electrical circuit in which the current divides into two or more paths of the same voltage, before joining to complete the circuit.

parallelepiped (par-a-lel-ee-**pipe**-ed) *n Geom* a solid shape whose six faces are parallelograms. ▷ **HISTORY** Greek *parallēlos* parallel + *epipedon* plane surface

parallelism *n* **1** the state of being parallel. **2** a close likeness.

parallelogram *n Geom* a plane figure whose opposite sides are parallel and equal in length. ▷ **HISTORY** Greek *parallēlos* parallel + *grammē* line

paralyse *or US* **-lyze** *vb* **-lysing, -lysed** *or* **-lyzing, -lyzed** **1** *Pathol* to affect with paralysis. **2** to make immobile: *he was paralysed by fear.* ▷ **HISTORY** French *paralyser*

paralysis *n* **1** *Pathol* inability to move all or part of the body due to damage to the nervous system. **2** a state of inactivity: *the economic chaos and political paralysis into which the country has sunk.*

a b c d e f g h i j k l m n o p q r s t u v w x y z

▷ **HISTORY** Greek *paralusis,* from *para-* beyond + *lusis* a loosening

paralytic *adj* **1** of or relating to paralysis. **2** *Brit informal* very drunk. ✧ *n* **3** a person who is paralysed.

paramecium (par-a-**mee**-see-um) *n, pl* **-cia** (-see-a) a single-celled animal which lives in ponds, puddles, and sewage filters and swims by means of cilia.

paramedic *n* a person, such as a member of an ambulance crew, whose work supplements that of the medical profession. ▶ **paramedical** *adj*

parameter (par-**am**-it-er) *n* **1** *Maths* an arbitrary constant that determines the specific form of a mathematical expression, such as *a* and *b* in $y = ax^2 + b$. **2** *Informal* any limiting factor: *exchange rates are allowed to fluctuate only within designated parameters.* ▷ **HISTORY** Greek *para* beside + *metron* measure

paramilitary *adj* denoting a group of people organized on military lines.

paramount *adj* of the greatest importance. ▷ **HISTORY** Old French *par* by + *-amont* above

paramour *n Old-fashioned* an adulterous lover. ▷ **HISTORY** Old French, literally: through love

paranoia *n* **1** a mental disorder which causes delusions of grandeur or of persecution. **2** *Informal* intense fear or suspicion, usually unfounded. ▷ **HISTORY** Greek *para-* beyond + *noos* mind ▶ **paranoid** *or* **paranoiac** *adj, n*

paranormal *adj* **1** beyond normal scientific explanation. ✧ *n* **2 the paranormal** paranormal happenings or matters generally.

parapet *n* **1** a low wall or railing along the edge of a balcony or roof. **2** *Mil* a mound of sandbags in front of a trench to conceal and protect troops from fire. ▷ **HISTORY** Italian *parapetto*

paraphernalia *n* various articles or bits of equipment.

> **WORD HISTORY**
> In Latin a married woman's *parapherna* or *paraphernālia* was her personal property, what she herself owned as opposed to her dowry. The words come from Greek *para,* meaning 'beside', and *pherně,* meaning 'dowry'.

paraphrase *n* **1** an expression of a statement or text in other words. ✧ *vb* **-phrasing, -phrased 2** to put (a statement or text) into other words. ▷ **HISTORY** Greek *paraphrazein* to recount

paraplegia (par-a-**pleej**-ya) *n Pathol* paralysis of the lower half of the body. ▷ **HISTORY** Greek: a blow on one side ▶ **paraplegic** *adj, n*

parapsychology *n* the study of mental phenomena such as telepathy.

Paraquat *n Trademark* an extremely poisonous weedkiller.

parasite *n* **1** an animal or plant that lives in or on another from which it obtains nourishment. **2** a person who habitually lives at the expense of others; sponger. ▶ **parasitic** *adj*

> **WORD HISTORY**
> 'Parasite' comes from Greek *parasitos,* meaning 'someone who eats at someone else's table'.

parasol *n* an umbrella-like sunshade. ▷ **HISTORY** French

paratrooper *n* a member of the paratroops.

paratroops *pl n* troops trained to be dropped by parachute into a battle area.

paratyphoid fever *n* a disease resembling but less severe than typhoid fever.

parboil *vb* to boil (food) until partially cooked. ▷ **HISTORY** Late Latin *perbullire* to boil thoroughly; modern meaning due to confusion of *par-* with *part*

parcel *n* **1** something wrapped up; a package. **2** a group of people or things sharing something in common: *a parcel of fools.* **3** a distinct portion of land: *he was the recipient of a substantial parcel of land.* ✧ *vb* **-celling, -celled** *or US* **-celing, -celed 4** (often foll. by *up*) to wrap (something) up into a parcel. **5** (foll. by *out*) to divide (something) into portions: *the children were parcelled out to relatives.* ▷ **HISTORY** Old French *parcelle*

parch *vb* **1** to deprive (something) of water; dry up: *the summer sun parched the hills.* **2** to make (someone) very thirsty: *I'm parched. Have we got any lemonade?* ▷ **HISTORY** origin unknown

parchment *n* **1** a thick smooth material made from animal skin and used for writing on. **2** a manuscript made of this material. **3** a stiff yellowish paper resembling parchment. ▷ **HISTORY** Greek *pergamēnē,* from *Pergamēnos* of Pergamum (where parchment was made)

pardon *vb* **1** to forgive or excuse: *I hope you'll pardon the wait.* ✧ *n* **2** forgiveness. **3** official release from punishment for a crime. ✧ *interj* **4** Also: **pardon me, I beg your pardon a** sorry; excuse me. **b** what did you say? ▷ **HISTORY** Medieval Latin *perdonare* to forgive freely ▶ **pardonable** *adj*

pare *vb* **paring, pared 1** to peel (the outer layer) from (something): *thinly pare the rind from the grapefruit.* **2** to trim or cut the edge of. **3** to decrease bit by bit: *the government is prepared to pare down the armed forces.* ▷ **HISTORY** Latin *parare* to make ready

parent *n* **1** a father or mother. **2** a person acting as a father or mother; guardian. **3** a plant or animal that has produced one or more plants or animals. ▷ **HISTORY** Latin *parens,* from *parere* to bring forth ▶ **parental** *adj* ▶ **parenthood** *n*

parentage *n* ancestry or family.

parent company *n* a company that owns a number of smaller companies.

parenthesis (par-**en**-thiss-iss) *n, pl* **-ses** (-seez) **1** a word or phrase inserted into a passage, and marked off by brackets or dashes. **2** Also called: **bracket** either of a pair of characters ( ), used to enclose such a phrase. ▷ **HISTORY** Greek: something placed in besides ▶ **parenthetical** *adj* ▶ **parenthetically** *adv*

parenting *n* the activity of bringing up children.

parenting order *n Law* **a** *England and Wales* an order requiring a parent or parents of a young offender or truant to attend guidance sessions. **b** *Austral* (in cases of parental disagreement) an order specifying arrangements for a child's residence, visiting rights, and other matters such as schooling.

par excellence *adv* beyond comparison: *this book justifies its claim to be a reference work par excellence.* ▷ **HISTORY** French

pariah (par-**rye**-a) *n* a social outcast: *the man they regard as a pariah.* ▷ **HISTORY** Tamil *paraiyan* drummer

parietal (par-**rye**-it-al) *adj Anat, biol* of or forming the walls of a body cavity: *the parietal bones of the skull.* ▷ **HISTORY** Latin *paries* wall

paring *n* something that has been cut off something.

parish *n* **1** an area that has its own church and a priest or pastor. *RELATED ADJECTIVE* ▸ **parochial 2** the people who live in a parish. **3** (in England and, formerly, Wales) the smallest unit of local government. ▷ **HISTORY** Greek *paroikos* neighbour

parish clerk *n* a person who assists in various church duties.

parish council *n* (in England and, formerly, Wales) the administrative body of a parish. See **parish** (sense 3).

parishioner *n* a person who lives in a particular parish.

parish register *n* a book in which the births, baptisms, marriages, and deaths in a parish are recorded.

parity *n* **1** equality, for example of rank or pay. **2** close or exact equivalence: *the company maintained parity with the competition.* **3** *Finance* equivalence between the units of currency of two countries. ▷ **HISTORY** Latin *par* equal

park *n* **1** a large area of open land for recreational use by the public. **2** a piece of open land for public recreation in a town. **3** *Brit* a large area of private land surrounding a country house. **4** an area designed to accommodate a number of related enterprises: *a science park.* **5** *US & Canad* a playing field or sports stadium. **6 the park** *Brit informal* the pitch in soccer. ✧ *vb* **7** to stop and leave (a vehicle) temporarily: *I parked between the two cars already outside; police vans were parked on every street corner.* **8** *Informal* to leave or put (someone or something) somewhere: *she parked herself on the sofa and stayed there all evening.* ▷ **HISTORY** Germanic ▸ **parking** *n*

parka *n* a long jacket with a quilted lining and a fur-trimmed hood. ▷ **HISTORY** from Aleutian (language of Aleutian Islands, off Alaska): skin

parking meter *n* a coin-operated device beside a parking space that indicates how long a vehicle may be left parked.

parking ticket *n* the notice of a fine served on a motorist for a parking offence.

Parkinson's disease *or* **Parkinsonism** *n* a progressive disorder of the central nervous system which causes tremor, rigidity, and impaired muscular coordination. ▷ **HISTORY** after J. *Parkinson,* surgeon

Parkinson's law *n* the notion that work expands to fill the time available for its completion. ▷ **HISTORY** after C. N. *Parkinson,* historian and writer

parkland *n* grassland with scattered trees.

parky *adj* **parkier, parkiest** *Brit informal* (of the weather) chilly. ▷ **HISTORY** origin unknown

parlance *n* the manner of speaking associated with a particular group or subject: *he had, in Marxist parlance, a 'petit bourgeois' mentality.* ▷ **HISTORY** French *parler* to talk

parley *Old-fashioned* ✧ *n* **1** a discussion between members of opposing sides to decide terms of agreement. ✧ *vb* **2** to have a parley. ▷ **HISTORY** French *parler* to talk

parliament *n* a law-making assembly of a country. ▷ **HISTORY** Old French *parlement,* from *parler* to speak

Parliament *n* **1** the highest law-making authority in Britain, consisting of the House of Commons, the House of Lords, and the sovereign. **2** the equivalent law-making authority in another country.

parliamentarian *n* an expert in parliamentary procedures.

parliamentary *adj* **1** of or from a parliament: *parliamentary elections.* **2** conforming to the procedures of a parliament: *parliamentary language.*

parliamentary privilege *n Parliament* the special rights enjoyed by Members of Parliament to enable them to carry out their duties; these include immunity from civil action if they make defamatory comments in Parliament.

parlour *or US* **parlor** *n* **1** *Old-fashioned* a living room for receiving visitors. **2** a room or shop equipped as a place of business: *an ice-cream parlour.* ▷ **HISTORY** Old French *parler* to speak

parlous *adj Archaic or humorous* dangerously bad; dire: *the parlous state of the economy.* ▷ **HISTORY** variant of *perilous*

Parmesan (**par**-miz-zan) *n* a hard strong-flavoured cheese used grated on pasta dishes and soups. ▷ **HISTORY** Italian *parmegiano* of Parma, Italy

parochial *adj* **1** narrow in outlook; provincial. **2** of or relating to a parish. ▷ **HISTORY** see PARISH ▸ **parochialism** *n*

parody *n, pl* **-dies 1** a piece of music or literature that mimics the style of another composer or author in a humorous way. **2** something done so badly that it seems like an intentional mockery. ✧ *vb* **-dies, -dying, -died 3** to make a parody of. ▷ **HISTORY** Greek *paroidia* satirical poem ▸ **parodist** *n*

parol *Law* ✧ *adj* **1** expressed or given by word of mouth: *parol evidence.* **2** (of a contract, lease, etc.) made orally or in writing but not under seal. ✧ *n* **3** an oral statement; word of mouth (now only in the phrase **by parol**). ▷ **HISTORY** Old French *parole* speech

parole *n Law* **1** the freeing of a prisoner before his or her sentence has run out, on condition that he or she behaves well. **2** a promise given by a prisoner to behave well if granted liberty or partial liberty. **3 on parole** conditionally released from prison. ✧ *vb* **-roling, -roled 4** to place (a person) on parole. ▷ **HISTORY** Old French *parole d'honneur* word of honour

parotid gland *n Anat* either of a pair of salivary glands in front of and below the ears. ▷ **HISTORY** Greek *para-* near + *ous* ear

paroxysm *n* **1** an uncontrollable outburst of emotion: *a paroxysm of grief.* **2** *Pathol* **a** a sudden attack or recurrence of a disease. **b** a fit or convulsion. ▷ **HISTORY** Greek *paroxunein* to goad ▸ **paroxysmal** *adj*

parquet (**par**-kay) *n* **1** a floor covering made of blocks of wood. ✧ *vb* **2** to cover (a floor) with parquetry. ▷ **HISTORY** Old French: small enclosure

parquetry (**par**-kit-tree) *n* pieces of wood arranged in a geometric pattern, used to cover floors.

parr *n* a salmon up to two years of age. ▷ **HISTORY** origin unknown

parricide *n* **1** a person who kills one of his or her parents. **2** the act of killing either of one's parents. ▷ **HISTORY** Latin *parricidium* murder of a parent or relative ▸ **parricidal** *adj*

parrot *n* **1** a tropical bird with a short hooked beak, bright plumage, and an ability to mimic human speech. **2** a person who repeats or imitates someone else's words. **3 sick as a parrot** *Usually facetious* extremely disappointed. ✧ *vb* **-roting, -roted 4** to repeat or imitate (someone else's words) without understanding them. ▷ **HISTORY** probably from French *paroquet*

parrot fever *n* same as **psittacosis.**

parrotfish a brightly coloured sea fish.

parry *vb* **-ries, -rying, -ried 1** to ward off (an attack). **2** to avoid answering (questions) in a clever way. ✧ *n, pl* **-ries 3** an instance of parrying. **4** a skilful evasion of a question. ▷ **HISTORY** French *parer* to ward off

parse (**parz**) *vb* **parsing, parsed** to analyse (a sentence or the words in a sentence) grammatically. ▷ **HISTORY** Latin *pars (orationis)* part (of speech)

parsec *n* a unit of astronomical distance equivalent to 3.0857×10^{16} metres or 3.262 light years. ▷ **HISTORY** *parallax* + *second* (of time)

parsimony *n Formal* extreme caution in spending. ▷ **HISTORY** Latin *parcimonia* ▸ **parsimonious** *adj*

parsley *n* a herb with curled pleasant-smelling leaves, used for seasoning and decorating food. ▷ **HISTORY** Middle English *persely*

parsnip *n* a long tapering cream-coloured root vegetable. ▷ **HISTORY** Latin *pastinaca*

parson *n* **1** a parish priest in the Church of England. **2** any clergyman. **3** *NZ* a nonconformist minister. ▷ **HISTORY** Latin *persona* personage

parsonage *n* the residence of a parson, provided by the parish.

parson's nose *n* the rump of a fowl when cooked.

part *n* **1** a piece or portion. **2** one of several equal divisions: *a salad dressing made with two parts oil to one part vinegar.* **3** an actor's role in a play. **4** a person's duty: *his ancestors had done their part nobly and well at Bannockburn.* **5** an involvement in or contribution to something: *he was jailed for his part in the fraud.* **6** a region or area: *he's well known in these parts; the weather in this part of the country is extreme.* **7** *Anat* an area of the body. **8** a component that can be replaced in a vehicle or machine. **9** *US, Canad & Austral* same as **parting** (sense 2). **10** *Music* a melodic line assigned to one or more instrumentalists or singers. **11 for my part** as far as I am concerned. **12 for the most part** generally. **13 in part** to some degree; partly. **14 on the part of** on behalf of. **15 part and parcel of** an essential ingredient of. **16 play a part a** to pretend to be what one is not. **b** (foll. by *in*) to have something to do with: *examinations play a large part in education and in schools.* **17 take part in** to participate in. **18 take someone's part** to support someone, for example in an argument. **19 take something in good part** to respond to (teasing or criticism) with good humour. ✧ *vb* **20** to divide or separate from one another: *her lips parted in laughter; the cord parted with a pop.* **21** to go away from one another: *we parted with handshakes all round.* **22 part with** to give up: *check carefully before you part with your cash.* **23 part from** to cause (someone) to give up: *I was astonished at the way Henry parted his audience from their money.* **24** to split: *the path parts here.* **25** to arrange (the hair) in such a way that a line of scalp is left showing. ✧ *adv* **26** to some extent; partly: *this book is part history, part travelogue.* ✧ See also **parts.** ▷ **HISTORY** Latin *pars* a part

partake *vb* **-taking, -took, -taken 1 partake of** to take (food or drink). **2 partake in** to take part in. ▷ **HISTORY** from earlier *part taker*

> **WORD TIP**
> *Partake of* is sometimes wrongly used as if it were a synonym of *eat* or *drink.* Correctly, one can only *partake of* food or drink which is available for several people to share.

parterre *n* **1** a formally patterned flower garden. **2** the pit of a theatre. ▷ **HISTORY** French

parthenocarpy *n Biol* the development of fruit without fertilization or formation of seeds.

partial *adj* **1** relating to only a part; not complete: *partial deafness.* **2** biased: *religious programmes can be as partial as they like.* **3 partial to** having a particular liking for. ▷ **HISTORY** Latin *pars* part ▸ **partiality** *n* ▸ **partially** *adv*

> **WORD TIP**
> See at **partly.**

participant *n* **1** one who takes part in something. **2** *Functional grammar* any person or thing, as specified by a noun group, that performs or is the object of an action.

participate *vb* **-pating, -pated participate in** to become actively involved in. ▷ **HISTORY** Latin *pars* part + *capere* to take ▶ **participation** *n* ▶ **participatory** *adj*

participle *n Grammar* a form of a verb that is used in compound tenses or as an adjective. See also **present participle, past participle**. ▷ **HISTORY** Latin *pars* part + *capere* to take ▶ **participial** *adj*

particle *n* **1** an extremely small piece or amount: *clean thoroughly to remove all particles of dirt.* **2** *Grammar* an uninflected part of speech, such as an interjection or preposition. **3** *Physics* a minute piece of matter, such as an electron or proton. ▷ **HISTORY** Latin *pars* part

particular *adj* **1** of, belonging to, or being one person or thing; specific: *the particular type of tuition on offer.* **2** exceptional or special: *the report voices particular concern over the state of the country's manufacturing industry.* **3** providing specific details or circumstances: *a particular account.* **4** difficult to please; fussy. ✧ *n* **5** a separate distinct item as opposed to a generalization: *moving from the general to the particular.* **6** an item of information; detail: *she refused to go into particulars.* **7 in particular** especially or exactly: *three painters in particular were responsible for these developments.* ▷ **HISTORY** Latin *particula* a small part ▶ **particularly** *adv*

particularize *or* **-ise** *vb* **-izing, -ized** *or* **-ising, -ised** to give details about (something). ▶ **particularization** *or* **-isation** *n*

parting *n* **1** a departure or leave-taking. **2** *Brit & NZ* the line of scalp showing when sections of hair are combed in opposite directions. **3** the act of dividing (something): *the parting of the Red Sea.*

partisan *n* **1** a person who supports a particular cause or party. **2** a member of an armed resistance group within occupied territory. ✧ *adj* **3** prejudiced or one-sided. ▷ **HISTORY** Old Italian *partigiano* ▶ **partisanship** *n*

partition *n* **1** a large screen or thin wall that divides a room. **2** the division of a country into two or more independent countries. ✧ *vb* **3** to separate (a room) into sections: *the shower is partitioned off from the rest of the bathroom.* **4** to divide (a country) into separate self-governing parts: *the subcontinent was partitioned into India and Pakistan.* ▷ **HISTORY** Latin *partire* to divide

partitive *Grammar* ✧ *adj* **1** (of a noun) referring to part of something. The phrase *some of the butter* is a partitive construction. ✧ *n* **2** a partitive word, such as *some* or *any*. ▷ **HISTORY** Latin *partire* to divide

partly *adv* not completely.

> **WORD TIP**
> *Partly* and *partially* are to some extent interchangeable, but *partly* should be used when referring to a part or parts of something: *the building is partly* (not *partially*) *of stone,* while *partially* is preferred for the meaning *to some extent: his mother is partially* (not *partly*) *sighted.*

partner *n* **1** either member of a couple in a relationship. **2** a member of a business partnership. **3** one of a pair of dancers or of players on the same side in a game: *her bridge partner.* **4** an ally or companion: *the country's main European trading partner.* ✧ *vb* **5** to be the partner of (someone). ▷ **HISTORY** Middle English *parcener* joint inheritor

partnership *n* **1** a relationship in which two or more people or organizations work together in a business venture. **2** the condition of being a partner.

part of speech *n Grammar* a class of words, such as a noun, verb, or adjective, sharing important syntactic or semantic features.

partridge *n, pl* **-tridges** *or* **-tridge** a game bird with an orange-brown head, greyish neck, and a short rust-coloured tail. ▷ **HISTORY** Latin *perdix*

parts *pl n Literary* abilities or talents: *a man of many parts.*

part song *n* a song composed in harmonized parts.

part-time *adj* **1** for less than the normal full working time: *a part-time job.* ✧ *adv* **part time 2** on a part-time basis: *he works part time.* ▶ **part-timer** *n*

parturient *adj Formal* giving birth. ▷ **HISTORY** Latin *parturire* to be in labour

parturition *n* the process of giving birth. ▷ **HISTORY** Latin *parturire* to be in labour

party *n, pl* **-ties 1** a social gathering for pleasure. **2** a group of people involved in the same activity: *a search party.* **3** a group of people sharing a common political aim. **4** the person or people who take part in or are involved in something, esp. a legal action or dispute: *a judge in a wig and gown who will decide who the guilty party is.* **5** *Informal, humorous* a person: *he's an odd old party.* ✧ *vb* **-ties, -tying, -tied 6** *Informal* to celebrate; have a good time. ▷ **HISTORY** Old French *partie* part

party line *n* **1** the policies of a political party. **2** a telephone line shared by two or more subscribers.

party wall *n Property law* a common wall separating two properties.

par value *n* the value printed on a share certificate or bond at the time of its issue.

parvenu *or fem* **parvenue** (**par**-ven-new) *n* a person newly risen to a position of power or wealth who is considered to lack culture or education. ▷ **HISTORY** French

pascal *n* the SI unit of pressure; the pressure exerted on an area of 1 square metre by a force of 1 newton. ▷ **HISTORY** after B. *Pascal,* mathematician & scientist

Pascal *n* a high-level computer programming language developed as a teaching language. ▷ **HISTORY** after B. *Pascal,* mathematician & scientist

paschal (**pask**-l) *adj* **1** of or relating to the Passover. **2** of or relating to Easter. ▷ **HISTORY** Hebrew *pesah* Passover

pas de deux (pah de **duh**) *n, pl* **pas de deux** *Ballet* a dance for two people. ▷ **HISTORY** French: step for two

pasha *n* (formerly) a high official of the Ottoman Empire: placed after a name when used as a title. ▷ **HISTORY** Turkish *paşa*

pas op (**pass** op) *interj S African* beware. ▷ **HISTORY** Afrikaans

paspalum (pass-**pale**-um) *n Austral & NZ* a type of grass with wide leaves.

pasqueflower *n* a small purple-flowered plant of Europe and Asia. ▷ **HISTORY** French *passefleur*, changed to *pasqueflower* Easter flower, because it blooms at Easter

pass *vb* **1** to go by or past (a person or thing). **2** to continue or extend in a particular direction: *the road to Camerino passes through some fine scenery.* **3** to go through or cause (something) to go through (an obstacle or barrier): *the bullet passed through his head.* **4** to be successful in (a test or examination). **5** to spend (time) or (of time) go by: *the time passed surprisingly quickly.* **6** to hand over or be handed over: *she passed me her glass.* **7** to be inherited by: *his mother's small estate had passed to him after her death.* **8** *Sport* to hit, kick, or throw (the ball) to another player. **9** (of a law-making body) to agree to (a law or proposal): *the bill was passed by parliament last week.* **10** to pronounce (judgment): *the court is expected to pass sentence later today.* **11** to move onwards or over: *a flicker of amusement passed over his face.* **12** to exceed: *Australia's population has just passed the seventeen million mark.* **13** to go without comment: *the insult passed unnoticed.* **14** to choose not to answer a question or not to make a bid or a play in card games. **15** to discharge (urine etc.) from the body. **16** to come to an end or disappear: *the madness will soon pass.* **17** (foll. by *for* or *as*) to be likely to be mistaken for (someone or something else): *the few sunny days that pass for summer in this country.* **18** *Old-fashioned* to take place: *what passed at the meeting?* **19** **pass away** *or* **on** *Euphemistic* to die. ✧ *n* **20** a successful result in an examination or test. **21** *Sport* the transfer of a ball from one player to another. **22** a route through a range of mountains where there is a gap between peaks. **23** a permit or licence. **24** *Mil* a document authorizing leave of absence. **25** *Bridge etc.* an instance of choosing not to answer a question or not to make a bid or a play in card games. **26** **make a pass at** *Informal* to try to persuade (someone) to have sex: *he made a pass at his secretary.* **27** **a pretty pass** a bad state of affairs. ✧ See also **pass off, pass out**, etc. ▷ **HISTORY** Latin *passus* step

> ☑ **WORD TIP**
> The past participle of *pass* is sometimes wrongly spelt *past*: *the time for recriminations has passed* (not *past*).

passable *adj* **1** adequate or acceptable: *passable if hardly faultless German.* **2** (of a road, path, etc.) capable of being travelled along: *most main roads are passable with care despite the snow.* ▶ **passably** *adv*

passage *n* **1** a channel or opening providing a way through. **2** a hall or corridor. **3** a section of a written work, speech, or piece of music. **4** a journey by ship. **5** the act of passing from one place or condition to another: *Ireland faced a tough passage to qualify for the World Cup finals.* **6** the right or freedom to pass: *the aid convoys were guaranteed safe passage through rebel-held areas.* **7** the establishing of a law by a law-making body. ▷ **HISTORY** Old French *passer* to pass

passageway *n* corridor or passage.

passbook *n* **1** a book issued by a bank or building society for recording deposits and withdrawals. **2** *S African* formerly, an official identity document.

passé (**pas**-say) *adj* out-of-date: *smoking is a bit passé these days.* ▷ **HISTORY** French

passenger *n* **1** a person travelling in a vehicle driven by someone else. **2** *Brit & NZ* a member of a team who does not take an equal share of the work: *you'll have to pull your weight – we can't afford passengers.* ▷ **HISTORY** Old French *passager* passing

passer-by *n, pl* **passers-by** a person who is walking past someone or something.

passerine *adj* **1** belonging to an order of perching birds that includes the larks, finches, and starlings. ✧ *n* **2** any bird of this order. ▷ **HISTORY** Latin *passer* sparrow

passim *adv* throughout: used to indicate that what is referred to occurs frequently in a particular piece of writing. ▷ **HISTORY** Latin

passing *adj* **1** momentary or short-lived: *a passing fad.* **2** casual or superficial: *a passing resemblance.* ✧ *n* **3** *Euphemistic* death. **4** the ending of something: *the passing of the old order in Eastern Europe.* **5** **in passing** briefly and without going into detail; incidentally: *this fact is only noted in passing.*

passion *n* **1** intense sexual love. **2** any strongly felt emotion. **3** a strong enthusiasm for something: *a passion for football.* **4** the object of an intense desire or enthusiasm: *flying is his abiding passion.* ▷ **HISTORY** Latin *pati* to suffer ▶ **passionless** *adj*

Passion *n* the sufferings of Christ from the Last Supper to his death on the cross.

passionate *adj* **1** showing intense sexual desire. **2** capable of or revealing intense emotion: *a passionate speech.* ▶ **passionately** *adv*

passionflower *n* a tropical plant with brightly coloured showy flowers. ▷ **HISTORY** parts of the flowers are said to resemble the instruments of the Crucifixion

passion fruit *n* the edible egg-shaped fruit of the passionflower.

Passion play *n* a play about the Passion of Christ.

passive *adj* **1** not taking an active part. **2** submissive and receptive to outside forces. **3** *Grammar* denoting a form of verbs used to indicate that the subject is the recipient of the action, as *was broken* in *The glass was broken by that boy over there.* **4** *Chem* (of a substance) chemically unreactive. ✧ *n* **5** *Grammar* the passive form of a verb. ▷ **HISTORY** Latin *passivus* capable of suffering ▶ **passively** *adv* ▶ **passivity** *n*

passive resistance *n* resistance to a government or the law by nonviolent acts such as fasting, peaceful demonstrations, or refusing to cooperate.

passive smoking *n* the unwilling inhalation of smoke from other people's cigarettes by a nonsmoker.

passive voice *n Grammar* a set of verb forms used to indicate that the subject is the recipient of the action, for example *was discovered* in *penicillin was discovered by Fleming*. Compare **active voice**.

passkey *n* **1** a private key. **2** same as **master key skeleton key**.

pass law *n* (formerly in South Africa) a law restricting the movement of Black Africans.

pass off *vb* **1** to present (something or oneself) under false pretences: *women who passed themselves off effectively as men.* **2** to come to a gradual end: *the effects of the gas passed off relatively peacefully.* **3** to take place: *the main demonstration passed off peacefully.*

pass out *vb* **1** *Informal* to become unconscious; faint. **2** *Brit* (of an officer cadet) to qualify for a military commission.

pass over *vb* **1** to take no notice of; disregard: *she claims she had been passed over for promotion because she is a woman.* **2** to ignore or not discuss: *this disaster can not be passed over lightly.*

Passover *n* an eight-day Jewish festival commemorating the sparing of the Israelites in Egypt. ▷ **HISTORY** *pass over,* translation of Hebrew *pesah*

passport *n* **1** an official document issued by a government, which identifies the holder and grants him or her permission to travel abroad. **2** an asset that gains a person admission or acceptance: *good qualifications are no automatic passport to a job.* ▷ **HISTORY** French *passer* to pass + *port* port

pass up *vb Informal* to let (something) go by; disregard: *am I passing up my one chance to be really happy?*

password *n* **1** a secret word or phrase that ensures admission by proving identity or membership. **2** *Computing* a sequence of keystrokes that a particular user must enter in order to access part of a computer system.

past *adj* **1** of the time before the present: *the past history of the world.* **2** no longer in existence: *past happiness.* **3** immediately previous: *the past year.* **4** former: *a past president.* **5** *Grammar* indicating a tense of verbs used to describe actions that have been begun or completed at the time of speaking. ✧ *n* **6 the past** the period of time before the present: *a familiar face from the past.* **7** the history of a person or nation. **8** an earlier disreputable period of someone's life: *a woman with a bit of a past.* **9** *Grammar* **a** the past tense. **b** a verb in the past tense. ✧ *adv* **10** at a time before the present; ago: *three years past.* ✧ *prep* **11** beyond in time: *it's past midnight.* **12** beyond in place: *a procession of mourners filed past the coffin.* **13** beyond the limit of: *riches past his wildest dreams.* **14 not put it past someone** to consider someone capable of (a particular action): *I wouldn't put it past him to double-cross us.* **15 past it** *Informal* unable to do the things one could do when younger. ▷ **HISTORY** from *pass*

pasta *n* a type of food, such as spaghetti, that is made from a dough of flour and water and formed into different shapes. ▷ **HISTORY** Italian

paste *n* **1** a soft moist mixture, such as toothpaste. **2** an adhesive made from water and flour or starch, for use with paper. **3** a smooth creamy preparation of fish, meat, or vegetables for spreading on bread: *sausage paste.* **4** *Brit & NZ* dough for making pastry. **5** a hard shiny glass used to make imitation gems. ✧ *vb* **pasting, pasted 6** to attach by paste: *she bought a scrapbook and carefully pasted in it all her clippings.* **7** *Slang* to beat or defeat (someone). ▷ **HISTORY** Greek *pastē* barley porridge

pasteboard *n* a stiff board made by pasting layers of paper together.

pastel *n* **1 a** a crayon made of ground pigment bound with gum. **b** a picture drawn with such crayons. **2** a pale delicate colour. ✧ *adj* **3** (of a colour) pale and delicate: *pastel pink.* ▷ **HISTORY** Latin *pasta* paste

pastern *n* the part of a horse's foot between the fetlock and the hoof. ▷ **HISTORY** Old French *pasture* a tether

paste-up *n Printing* a sheet of paper or board with artwork and proofs pasted on it, which is photographed prior to making a plate.

pasteurize *or* **-ise** *vb* **-izing, -ized** *or* **-ising, -ised** to destroy bacteria (in beverages or solid foods) by a special heating process. ▷ **HISTORY** after Louis *Pasteur,* chemist ▶ **pasteurization** *or* **-isation** *n*

pastiche (past-**eesh**) *n* a work of art that mixes styles or copies the style of another artist. ▷ **HISTORY** French

pastille *n* a small fruit-flavoured and sometimes medicated sweet. ▷ **HISTORY** Latin *pastillus* small loaf

pastime *n* an activity which makes time pass pleasantly.

pasting *n* **1** *Slang* a thrashing or heavy defeat. **2** *Informal* strong criticism.

past master *n* a person with a talent for or experience in a particular activity: *a past master at manipulating the media.*

pastor *n* a member of the clergy in charge of a congregation. ▷ **HISTORY** Latin: shepherd

pastoral *adj* **1** of or depicting country life or scenery. **2** (of land) used for pasture. **3** of or relating to a member of the clergy or his or her duties. **4** of or relating to shepherds or their work. ✧ *n* **5** a literary work, picture, or piece of music portraying country life. **6** a letter from a bishop to the clergy or people of his diocese. ▷ **HISTORY** Latin *pastor* shepherd

pastoral farming *n Agriculture* the rearing of sheep and cattle as a business.

pastoralism *n* a system of agriculture in dry grassland regions based on raising stock such as cattle, sheep, or goats. ▶ **pastoralist** *n*

a b c d e f g h i j k l m n o p q r s t u v w x y z

A B C D E F G H I J K L M N O P Q R S T U V W X Y Z

past participle *n Grammar* a form of verb used with an auxiliary verb to form compound past tenses and passives; also used to modify nouns: *spoken is the past participle of speak.*

past perfect *or* **past perfect tense** *n Grammar* a compound tense formed, in English, using *had* plus a past participle: *had eaten is the past perfect of eat.*

pastrami *n* highly seasoned smoked beef. ▷ **HISTORY** Yiddish

pastry *n* **1** a dough of flour, water, and fat. **2** (*pl* **-tries**) an individual cake or pie. **3** baked foods, such as tarts, made with this dough. ▷ **HISTORY** from *paste*

past tense *Grammar* a tense of verbs used when the action took place at some time in the past; in the sentence, *I telephoned her earlier, telephoned* is in a past tense.

pasturage *n* **1** the business of grazing cattle. **2** same as **pasture**.

pasture *n* **1** land covered with grass, suitable for grazing by farm animals. **2** the grass growing on this land. ▷ **HISTORY** Latin *pascere* to feed

pasty[1] (**pay**-stee) *adj* **pastier, pastiest** (of the complexion) pale and unhealthy-looking.

pasty[2] (**past**-ee) *n, pl* **pasties** a round of pastry folded over a filling of meat and vegetables. ▷ **HISTORY** Old French *pastée*

pat[1] *vb* **patting, patted 1** to tap (someone or something) lightly with the hand. **2** to shape (something) with a flat instrument or the palm of the hand. **3 pat someone on the back** *Informal* to congratulate someone. ✧ *n* **4** a gentle tap or stroke. **5** a small shaped lump of something soft, such as butter. **6 pat on the back** *Informal* an indication of approval. ▷ **HISTORY** probably imitative

pat[2] *adv* **1** Also: **off pat** thoroughly learned: *he had all his answers off pat.* **2 stand pat** *Chiefly US & Canad* to stick firmly to a belief or decision. ✧ *adj* **3** quick, ready, or glib: *a pat generalization.* ▷ **HISTORY** perhaps adverbial use ('with a light stroke') of PAT[1]

patch *n* **1** a piece of material used to cover a hole in a garment. **2** a small contrasting section: *there was a bald patch on the top of his head.* **3** a small plot of land. **4** *Med* a protective covering for an injured eye. **5** a scrap or remnant. **6** the area under someone's supervision, such as a policeman or social worker. **7 a bad patch** a difficult time. **8 not a patch on** not nearly as good as. ✧ *vb* **9** to mend (a garment) with a patch. **10 patch up a** to mend (something) hurriedly or carelessly. **b** to make up (a quarrel). **11 patch together** to produce (something) by piecing parts together hurriedly or carelessly. ▷ **HISTORY** perhaps from French *pieche* piece

patchwork *n* **1** needlework done by sewing together pieces of different materials. **2** something made up of various parts.

patchy *adj* **patchier, patchiest 1** of uneven quality or intensity: *since then her career has been patchy.* **2** having or forming patches.

pate *n Old-fashioned or humorous* the head or the crown of the head. ▷ **HISTORY** origin unknown

pâté (**pat**-ay) *n* a spread of finely minced meat, fish, or vegetables often served as a starter. ▷ **HISTORY** French

patella (pat-**tell**-a) *n, pl* **-lae** (-lee) *Anat* kneecap. ▷ **HISTORY** Latin ▶ **patellar** *adj*

paten (**pat**-in) *n* a plate, usually made of silver or gold, used for the bread at Communion. ▷ **HISTORY** Latin *patina* pan

patent *n* **1 a** an official document granting the exclusive right to make, use, and sell an invention for a limited period. **b** the right granted by such a document. **2** an invention protected by a patent. ✧ *adj* **3** open or available for inspection: *letters patent.* **4** obvious: *their scorn was patent to everyone.* **5** concerning protection of or appointment by a patent. **6** (of food, drugs, etc.) made or held under a patent. ✧ *vb* **7** to obtain a patent for (an invention). ▷ **HISTORY** Latin *patere* to lie open

> **WORD TIP**
> The pronunciation **pat**-tunt is heard in *letters patent* and *Patent Office* and is the usual US pronunciation for all senses. In Britain **pat**-tunt is sometimes heard for senses 1, 2 and 3, but **pay**-tunt is commoner and is regularly used in collocations like *patent leather.*

patent leather *n* leather processed with lacquer to give a hard glossy surface.

patently *adv* clearly and obviously: *an outdated and patently absurd promise.*

patent medicine *n* a medicine with a patent, available without a prescription.

Patent Office *n* a government department that issues patents.

paternal *adj* **1** fatherly: *paternal authority.* **2** related through one's father: *his paternal grandmother.* ▷ **HISTORY** Latin *pater* father ▶ **paternally** *adv*

paternalism *n* authority exercised in a way that limits individual responsibility. ▷ **HISTORY** Latin *pater* father ▶ **paternalistic** *adj*

paternity *n* **1** the fact or state of being a father. **2** descent or derivation from a father.

paternity suit *n* legal proceedings, usually brought by an unmarried mother, in order to gain legal recognition that a particular man is the father of her child.

Paternoster *n RC Church* the Lord's Prayer. ▷ **HISTORY** Latin *pater noster* our father

path *n, pl* **paths 1** a road or way, often a narrow trodden track. **2** a surfaced walk, such as through a garden. **3** the course or direction in which something moves: *his car skidded into the path of an oncoming lorry.* **4** a course of conduct: *the path of reconciliation and forgiveness.* ▷ **HISTORY** Old English *pæth*

pathetic *adj* **1** arousing pity or sympathy. **2** distressingly inadequate: *his pathetic attempt to maintain a stiff upper lip failed.* ▷ **HISTORY** Greek *pathos* suffering ▶ **pathetically** *adv*

pathetic fallacy *n* (in literature) the presentation of inanimate objects in nature as possessing human feelings.

pathogen *n* any agent, such as a bacterium, that can cause disease. ▷ HISTORY Greek *pathos* suffering + *-gen* (suffix) producing ▶ **pathogenic** *adj*

pathological *adj* **1** of or relating to pathology. **2** *Informal* compulsively motivated: *pathological jealousy.*

pathology *n* the branch of medicine that studies diseases. ▷ HISTORY Greek *pathos* suffering + -LOGY ▶ **pathologist** *n*

pathos *n* the power, for example in literature, of arousing feelings of pity or sorrow. ▷ HISTORY Greek: suffering

pathway *n* a path.

patience *n* **1** the capacity for calmly enduring difficult situations: *the endless patience of the nurses.* **2** the ability to wait calmly for something to happen without complaining or giving up: *he urged the international community to have patience to allow sanctions to work.* **3** *Brit & NZ* a card game for one player only. ▷ HISTORY Latin *pati* to suffer

patient *adj* **1** enduring difficult situations with an even temper. **2** persevering or diligent: *his years of patient work may finally pay off.* ✧ *n* **3** a person who is receiving medical care. ▶ **patiently** *adv*

patina *n* **1** a film formed on the surface of a metal. **2** the sheen on the surface of an old object, caused by age and much handling. ▷ HISTORY Italian: coating

patio *n, pl* **-tios 1** a paved area adjoining a house: *a barbecue on the patio.* **2** an open inner courtyard in a Spanish or Spanish-American house. ▷ HISTORY Spanish: courtyard

patois (**pat**-wah) *n, pl* **patois** (**pat**-wahz) **1** a regional dialect of a language. **2** the jargon of a particular group. ▷ HISTORY Old French: rustic speech

patrial *n* (in Britain, formerly) a person with a right by statute to live in the United Kingdom, and so not subject to immigration control. ▷ HISTORY Latin *patria* native land

patriarch *n* **1** the male head of a tribe or family. **2** *Bible* any of the men regarded as the fathers of the human race or of the Hebrew people. **3 a** *RC Church* the pope. **b** *Eastern Orthodox Church* a highest-ranking bishop. **4** an old man who is respected. ▷ HISTORY Church Latin *patriarcha* ▶ **patriarchal** *adj*

patriarchate *n* the office, jurisdiction or residence of a patriarch.

patriarchy *n* **1** a form of social organization in which males hold most of the power. **2** (*pl* **-chies**) a society governed by such a system.

patrician *n* **1** a member of the nobility of ancient Rome. **2** an aristocrat. **3** a person of refined conduct and tastes. ✧ *adj* **4** (in ancient Rome) of or relating to patricians. **5** aristocratic. ▷ HISTORY Latin *patricius* noble

patricide *n* **1** the act of killing one's father. **2** a person who kills his or her father. ▷ HISTORY Latin *pater* father + *caedere* to kill ▶ **patricidal** *adj*

patrimony *n, pl* **-nies** an inheritance from one's father or other ancestor. ▷ HISTORY Latin *patrimonium* paternal inheritance

patriot *n* a person who loves his or her country and passionately supports its interests. ▷ HISTORY Greek *patris* native land ▶ **patriotic** *adj* ▶ **patriotically** *adv* ▶ **patriotism** *n*

patrol *n* **1** the action of going round an area or building at regular intervals for purposes of security or observation. **2** a person or group that carries out such an action. **3** a group of soldiers or ships involved in patrolling a particular area. **4** a division of a troop of Scouts or Guides. ✧ *vb* **-trolling, -trolled 5** to engage in a patrol of (a place): *peacekeepers patrolled several areas of the city.* ▷ HISTORY French *patrouiller*

patrol car *n* a police car used for patrolling streets.

patron *n* **1** a person who financially supports artists, writers, musicians, or charities. **2** a regular customer of a shop, hotel, etc. ▷ HISTORY Latin *patronus* protector

patronage *n* **1** the support or custom given by a patron. **2** (in politics) the ability or power to appoint people to jobs. **3** a condescending manner.

patronize *or* **-ise** *vb* **-izing, -ized** *or* **-ising, -ised 1** to treat (someone) in a condescending way. **2** to be a patron of. ▶ **patronizing** *or* **-ising** *adj* ▶ **patronizingly** *or* **-isingly** *adv*

patron saint *n* a saint regarded as the particular guardian of a country or a group of people.

patronymic *n* a name derived from one's father's or a male ancestor. ▷ HISTORY Greek *patēr* father + *onoma* name

patter[1] *vb* **1** to make repeated light tapping sound. **2** to walk with quick soft steps. ✧ *n* **3** a quick succession of light tapping sounds, such as by feet: *the steady patter of rain against the window.* ▷ HISTORY from PAT[1]

patter[2] *n* **1** the glib rapid speech of comedians or salesmen. **2** chatter. **3** the jargon of a particular group. ✧ *vb* **4** to speak glibly and rapidly. ▷ HISTORY Latin *pater* in *Pater Noster* Our Father

pattern *n* **1** an arrangement of repeated parts or decorative designs. **2** a regular recognizable way that something is done: *I followed a normal eating pattern.* **3** a plan or diagram used as a guide to making something: *a knitting pattern.* **4** a model worthy of imitation: *a pattern of kindness.* **5** a representative sample. ✧ *vb* **6** (foll. by *after* or *on*) to model: *an orchestra patterned after Count Basie's.* ▷ HISTORY Medieval Latin *patronus* example

patterned *n* having a decorative pattern on it: *a selection of plain and patterned fabrics.*

patty *n, pl* **-ties** a small round pie filled with meat or vegetables. ▷ HISTORY French *pâté*

paua (**pah**-ooh-uh) *n* an edible shellfish of New Zealand, which has a pearly shell used for jewellery. ▷ HISTORY Maori

paucity *n Formal* **1** scarcity. **2** smallness of amount or number. ▷ **HISTORY** Latin *paucus* few

paunch *n* a protruding belly or abdomen. ▷ **HISTORY** Latin *pantices* bowels ▶ **paunchy** *adj*

pauper *n Old-fashioned* **1** a person who is extremely poor. **2** (formerly) a person supported by public charity. ▷ **HISTORY** Latin: poor

pause *vb* **pausing, paused 1** to stop doing (something) for a short time. **2** to hesitate: *she answered him without pausing.* ✧ *n* **3** a temporary stop or rest in speech or action. **4** *Music* a continuation of a note or rest beyond its normal length. **5 give someone pause** to cause someone to hesitate: *it gave him pause for reflection.* ▷ **HISTORY** Greek *pausis*

pavane (pav-**van**) *n* **1** a slow and stately dance of the 16th and 17th centuries. **2** music for this dance. ▷ **HISTORY** Spanish *pavana*

pave *vb* **paving, paved 1** to cover (a road or area of ground) with a firm surface to make it suitable for walking or travelling on. **2 pave the way for** to prepare or make easier: *the arrests paved the way for the biggest-ever Mafia trial.* ▷ **HISTORY** Old French *paver*

pavement *n* **1** a hard-surfaced path for pedestrians, alongside and a little higher than a road. **2** the material used in paving. **3** *US* the surface of a road. ▷ **HISTORY** Latin *pavimentum* hard floor

pavilion *n* **1** a building at a sports ground, esp. a cricket pitch, in which players can wash and change. **2** an open building or temporary structure used for exhibitions. **3** a summerhouse or other decorative shelter. **4** a large ornate tent. ▷ **HISTORY** Latin *papilio* butterfly, tent

paving *n* **1** a paved surface. **2** material used for a pavement.

pavlova *n* a meringue cake topped with whipped cream and fruit. ▷ **HISTORY** after Anna *Pavlova*, ballerina

paw *n* **1** a four-legged mammal's foot with claws and pads. **2** *Informal* a hand. ✧ *vb* **3** to scrape or hit with the paws. **4** *Informal* to touch or caress (someone) in a rough or overfamiliar manner. ▷ **HISTORY** Germanic

pawl *n* a pivoted lever shaped to engage with a ratchet to prevent motion in a particular direction. ▷ **HISTORY** Dutch *pal*

pawn[1] *vb* **1** to deposit (an article) as security for money borrowed. **2** to stake or risk: *I will pawn my honour on this matter.* ✧ *n* **3** an article deposited as security. **4** the condition of being so deposited: *in pawn.* ▷ **HISTORY** Old French *pan* security

pawn[2] *n* **1** a chessman of the lowest value, usually able to move only one square forward at a time. **2** a person or thing manipulated by someone else: *our city is just a pawn in their power games.* ▷ **HISTORY** Anglo-Norman *poun,* from Medieval Latin *pedo* infantryman

pawnbroker *n* a person licensed to lend money on goods deposited. ▶ **pawnbroking** *n*

Pawnee *n, pl* **Pawnees** *or* **Pawnee 1** a member of a group of Native American peoples, formerly living in Nebraska and Kansas, now chiefly in Oklahoma. **2** the language of these peoples.

pawnshop *n* the premises of a pawnbroker.

pawpaw (**paw**-paw) *n* same as **papaya**.

pax *n* **1** *Chiefly RC Church* the kiss of peace. ✧ *interj* **2** *Brit school slang* a call signalling a desire to end hostilities. ▷ **HISTORY** Latin: peace

pay *vb* **pays, paying, paid 1** to give (money) in return for goods or services: *Willie paid for the drinks; nurses are not very well paid.* **2** to settle (a debt or obligation) by giving or doing something: *he has paid his debt to society.* **3** to suffer: *she paid dearly for her mistake.* **4** to give (a compliment, regards, attention, etc.). **5** to profit or benefit (someone): *it doesn't always pay to be honest.* **6** to make (a visit or call). **7** to yield a return of: *the account pays 5% interest.* **8 pay one's way a** to contribute one's share of expenses. **b** to remain solvent without outside help. ✧ *n* **9** money given in return for work or services; a salary or wage. **10 in the pay of** employed by. ✧ See also **pay back**. ▷ **HISTORY** Latin *pacare* to appease

payable *adj* **1** (often foll. by *on*) due to be paid: *the instalments are payable on the third of each month.* **2** that is capable of being paid: *pensions are payable to those disabled during the wars.*

pay back *vb* **1** to repay (a loan). **2** to make (someone) suffer for a wrong he or she has done you: *I want to pay him back for all the suffering he's caused me.*

pay bed *n* (in Britain) a bed in a hospital used by a patient who is paying for treatment.

PAYE (in Britain, Australia and New Zealand) pay as you earn; a system by which income tax is deducted by employers and paid directly to the government.

payee *n* the person to whom a cheque or money order is made out.

paying guest *n Euphemistic* a lodger.

payload *n* **1** the amount of passengers, cargo, or bombs which an aircraft can carry. **2** the part of a cargo which earns revenue. **3** the explosive power of a warhead or bomb carried by a missile or aircraft.

paymaster *n* an official responsible for the payment of wages and salaries.

payment *n* **1** the act of paying. **2** a sum of money paid. **3** something given in return; punishment or reward.

pay off *vb* **1** to pay the complete amount of (a debt). **2** to pay (someone) all that is due in wages and dismiss him or her from employment. **3** to turn out successfully: *her persistence finally paid off.* **4** *Informal* to give a bribe to. ✧ *n* **payoff 5** *Informal* the climax or outcome of events. **6** *Informal* a bribe. **7** the final payment of a debt. **8** the final settlement, esp. in retribution: *the payoff came when the gang besieged the squealer's house.*

payola *n Informal* a bribe to secure special treatment, esp. to promote a commercial product.

pay out *vb* **1** to spend (money) on a particular thing. **2** to release (a rope) gradually, bit by bit. ✧ *n* **payout 3** a sum of money paid out.

payphone *n* a coin-operated telephone.

payroll *n* a list of employees, giving the salary or wage of each.

Pb *Chem* lead. ▷ **HISTORY** New Latin *plumbum*

pc 1 per cent. **2** postcard.

PC 1 personal computer. **2** (in Britain) Police Constable. **3** *Informal* short for **politically correct**. **4** (in Britain) Privy Council *or* Counsellor. **5** (in Canada) Progressive Conservative.

pd paid.

Pd *Chem* palladium.

PDA personal digital assistant.

PE 1 physical education. **2** Prince Edward Island.

pea *n* **1** an annual climbing plant with green pods containing green seeds. **2** the seed of this plant, eaten as a vegetable. ▷ **HISTORY** from *pease* (incorrectly assumed to be a plural)

peace *n* **1** stillness or silence. **2** absence of mental anxiety: *peace of mind.* **3** absence of war. **4** harmony between people or groups. **5** a treaty marking the end of a war. **6** law and order within a state: *a breach of the peace.* **7 at peace a** dead: *the old lady is at peace now.* **b** in a state of harmony or serenity. **8 hold** *or* **keep one's peace** to keep silent. **9 keep the peace** to maintain law and order. ▷ **HISTORY** Latin *pax*

peaceable *adj* **1** inclined towards peace. **2** tranquil or calm.

peace dividend *n* additional money available to a government from cuts in defence expenditure because of the end of a period of hostilities.

peaceful *adj* **1** not in a state of war or disagreement. **2** calm or tranquil. ▶ **peacefully** *adv*

peacemaker *n* a person who brings about peace, esp. between others.

peace offering *n* something given or said in order to restore peace: *I bought Mum some flowers as a peace offering.*

peace pipe *n* a long decorated pipe smoked by Native Americans, esp. as a token of peace.

peach *n* **1** a soft juicy fruit with a downy skin, yellowish-orange sweet flesh, and a single stone. **2** *Informal* a person or thing that is especially pleasing: *a peach of a goal.* ✧ *adj* **3** pale pinkish-orange. ▷ **HISTORY** Latin *Persicum malum* Persian apple

peacock *n, pl* **-cocks** *or* **-cock 1** a large male bird of the pheasant family with a crested head and a very large fanlike tail with blue and green eyelike spots. **2** a vain strutting person. ▷ **HISTORY** Latin *pavo* peacock + COCK ▶ **peahen** *fem n*

peafowl *n* a peacock or peahen.

peak *n* **1** a pointed tip or projection: *the peak of the roof.* **2 a** the pointed summit of a mountain. **b** a mountain with a pointed summit. **3** the point of greatest success or achievement: *the peak of his career.* **4** a projecting piece on the front of some caps. ✧ *vb* **5** to form or reach a peak. ✧ *adj* **6** of or relating to a period of greatest demand: *hotels are generally dearer in peak season.* ▷ **HISTORY** perhaps from *pike* (the weapon)

peaked *adj* having a peak.

peak load *n* the maximum load on an electrical power-supply system.

peaky *adj* **peakier, peakiest** pale and sickly. ▷ **HISTORY** origin unknown

peal *n* **1** a long loud echoing sound, such as of bells or thunder. ✧ *vb* **2** to sound with a peal or peals. ▷ **HISTORY** Middle English *pele*

peanut *n* a plant with edible nutlike seeds which ripen underground.

pear *n* **1** a sweet juicy fruit with a narrow top and a rounded base. **2 go pear-shaped** *Informal* to go wrong: *the plan started to go pear-shaped.* ▷ **HISTORY** Latin *pirum*

pearl *n* **1** a hard smooth greyish-white rounded object found inside the shell of a clam or oyster and much valued as a gem. **2** See **mother-of-pearl**. **3** a person or thing that is like a pearl in beauty or value. ✧ *adj* **4** of, made of, or set with pearl or mother-of-pearl. ✧ *vb* **5** to set with or as if with pearls. **6** to shape into or assume a pearl-like form or colour. **7** to dive for pearls. ▷ **HISTORY** Latin *perna* sea mussel

pearl barley *n* barley ground into small round grains, used in soups and stews.

pearly *adj* **pearlier, pearliest 1** resembling a pearl, esp. in lustre. **2** decorated with pearls or mother-of-pearl.

peasant *n* **1** a member of a low social class employed in agricultural labour. **2** *Informal* an uncouth or uncultured person. ▷ **HISTORY** Old French *païsant*

peasantry *n* peasants as a class.

pease *n, pl* **pease** *Archaic or dialect* same as **pea**. ▷ **HISTORY** Old English *pise, peose*

pease pudding *n* (esp. in Britain) a dish of split peas that have been soaked and boiled.

peasouper *n Informal, chiefly Brit* thick dirty yellowish fog.

peat *n* decaying vegetable matter found in uplands and bogs and used as a fuel (when dried) and as a fertilizer. ▷ **HISTORY** perhaps Celtic

pebble *n* **1** a small smooth rounded stone, esp. one worn by the action of water. ✧ *vb* **-bling, -bled 2** to cover with pebbles. ▷ **HISTORY** Old English *papolstān* pebble stone ▶ **pebbly** *adj*

pebble dash *n Brit & Austral* a finish for external walls consisting of small stones set in plaster.

pec *n Informal* a pectoral muscle: *a gigolo with flowing blond locks and rippling pecs.*

pecan (**pee**-kan) *n* a smooth oval nut with a sweet oily kernel that grows on hickory trees in the Southern US. ▷ **HISTORY** Native American *paccan*

peccadillo *n, pl* **-loes** *or* **-los** a trivial misdeed. ▷ **HISTORY** Spanish *pecadillo,* from Latin *peccare* to sin

peccary *n, pl* **-ries** *or* **-ry** a piglike animal of American forests. ▷ **HISTORY** Carib

peck[1] *vb* **1** to strike or pick up with the beak. **2** *Informal* to kiss (a person) quickly and lightly. **3 peck at** to eat slowly and reluctantly: *pecking away at your lunch.* ✧ *n* **4** a quick light blow from a bird's beak. **5** a mark made by such a blow.

6 *Informal* a quick light kiss. ▷ **HISTORY** origin unknown

peck² *n* an obsolete unit of liquid measure equal to one quarter of a bushel or 2 gallons (9.1 litres). ▷ **HISTORY** Anglo-Norman

pecker *n* **keep one's pecker up** *Brit & NZ slang* to remain cheerful.

pecking order *n* the order of seniority or power in a group: *she came from a family low in the social pecking order.*

peckish *adj Informal* feeling slightly hungry.

pectin *n Biochem* a water-soluble carbohydrate that occurs in ripe fruit: used in the manufacture of jams because of its ability to gel. ▷ **HISTORY** Greek *pēktos* congealed

pectoral *adj* **1** of or relating to the chest, breast, or thorax: *pectoral fins.* **2** worn on the breast or chest: *a pectoral cross.* ✧ *n* **3** a pectoral organ or part, esp. a muscle or fin. ▷ **HISTORY** Latin *pectus* breast

pectoral fin *n* a fin, just behind the head in fishes, that helps to control the direction of movement.

peculate *vb* **-lating, -lated** *Literary* to embezzle (public money). ▷ **HISTORY** Latin *peculari* ▶ **peculation** *n*

peculiar *adj* **1** strange or odd: *a peculiar idea.* **2** distinct or special. **3** (foll. by *to*) belonging exclusively (to): *a fish peculiar to these waters.* ▷ **HISTORY** Latin *peculiaris* concerning private property

peculiarity *n, pl* **-ties 1** a strange or unusual habit; eccentricity. **2** a distinguishing trait. **3** the state or quality of being peculiar.

pecuniary *adj* **1** of or relating to money. **2** *Law* (of an offence) involving a monetary penalty. ▷ **HISTORY** Latin *pecunia* money

pedagogue *or US sometimes* **pedagog** *n* a teacher, esp. a pedantic one. ▷ **HISTORY** Greek *pais* boy + *agōgos* leader ▶ **pedagogic** *adj*

pedagogy (**ped**-a-goj-ee) *n* the principles, practice, or profession of teaching.

pedal¹ *n* **1** a foot-operated lever used to control a vehicle or machine, or to modify the tone of a musical instrument. ✧ *vb* **-alling, -alled** *or US* **-aling, -aled 2** to propel (a bicycle) by operating the pedals. **3** to operate the pedals of an organ or piano. ▷ **HISTORY** Latin *pedalis,* from *pes* foot

pedal² *adj* of or relating to the foot or the feet. ▷ **HISTORY** Latin *pedalis,* from *pes* foot

pedant *n* a person who is concerned chiefly with insignificant detail or who relies too much on academic learning. ▷ **HISTORY** Italian *pedante* teacher ▶ **pedantic** *adj* ▶ **pedantically** *adv*

pedantry *n, pl* **-ries** the practice of being a pedant, esp. in the minute observance of petty rules or details.

peddle *vb* **-dling, -dled 1** to sell (goods) from place to place. **2** to sell illegal drugs. **3** to advocate (an idea or information) persistently: *the version of events being peddled by his opponents.* ▷ **HISTORY** from *pedlar*

pederast *or* **paederast** *n* a man who has homosexual relations with boys. ▷ **HISTORY** Greek *pais* boy + *erastēs* lover ▶ **pederasty** *or* **paederasty** *n*

pedestal *n* **1** a base that supports something, such as a statue. **2 put someone on a pedestal** to admire someone very much. ▷ **HISTORY** Old Italian *piedestallo*

pedestal rock *n Geol* an isolated rock that is wider at the top than at the bottom, sometimes resembling a mushroom.

pedestrian *n* **1** a person who travels on foot. ✧ *adj* **2** dull or commonplace: *a pedestrian performance.* ▷ **HISTORY** Latin *pes* foot

pedestrian crossing *n Brit & Austral* a path across a road marked as a crossing for pedestrians.

pedestrianize *or* **-ise** *vb* **-izing, -ized** *or* **-ising, -ised** to convert (a street or shopping area) into an area for pedestrians only.

pedestrian precinct *n Brit* an area of a town for pedestrians only, esp. an area of shops.

pedicure *n* medical or cosmetic treatment of the feet. ▷ **HISTORY** Latin *pes* foot + *curare* to care for

pedigree *n* **1** the line of descent of a purebred animal. **2** a document recording this. **3** a genealogical table, esp. one indicating pure ancestry. ▷ **HISTORY** Old French *pie de grue* crane's foot, alluding to the spreading lines used in a genealogical chart

pediment *n* a triangular part over a door, as used in classical architecture. ▷ **HISTORY** obsolete *periment,* perhaps workman's corruption of *pyramid*

pedlar *or esp US* **peddler** *n* a person who peddles. ▷ **HISTORY** Middle English *ped* basket

pedometer (pid-**dom**-it-er) *n* a device that measures the distance walked by recording the number of steps taken. ▷ **HISTORY** Latin *pes* foot + METER

peds *pl n Geol, agriculture* clusters of soil particles regarded as units in soil analysis.

peduncle *n* **1** *Bot* a plant stalk bearing a flower cluster or solitary flower. **2** *Anat, pathol* any stalklike structure. ▷ **HISTORY** Latin *pediculus* little foot ▶ **peduncular** *adj*

pee *Informal* ✧ *vb* **peeing, peed 1** to urinate. ✧ *n* **2** urine. **3** the act of urinating. ▷ **HISTORY** euphemistic for *piss*

peek *vb* **1** to glance quickly or secretly. ✧ *n* **2** such a glance. ▷ **HISTORY** Middle English *pike*

peel *vb* **1** to remove the skin or rind of (a fruit or vegetable). **2** to come off in flakes. **3** (of a person or part of the body) to shed skin in flakes as a result of sunburn. ✧ *n* **4** the skin or rind of a fruit, etc. ▷ **HISTORY** Latin *pilare* to make bald

peelings *pl n* strips of skin or rind that have been peeled off: *potato peelings.*

peel off *vb* **1** to remove or be removed by peeling: *this softens the paint, which can then be peeled off.* **2** *Slang* to take off one's clothes or a piece of clothing. **3** to leave a group of moving people, vehicles etc. by taking a course that curves away to one side: *two aircraft peeled off to attack the enemy bombers.*

peen *n* the end of a hammer head opposite the striking face, often rounded or wedge-shaped. ▷ **HISTORY** origin unknown

peep[1] *vb* **1** to look slyly or quickly, such as through a small opening or from a hidden place. **2** to appear partially or briefly: *the sun peeped through the clouds.* ✧ *n* **3** a quick or sly look. **4** the first appearance: *the peep of dawn.* ▷ **HISTORY** variant of *peek*

peep[2] *vb* **1** (esp. of young birds) to make small shrill noises. ✧ *n* **2** a peeping sound. ▷ **HISTORY** imitative

Peeping Tom *n* a man who furtively observes women undressing. ▷ **HISTORY** after the tailor who, according to legend, peeped at Lady Godiva when she rode naked through Coventry

peer[1] *n* **1** a member of a nobility. **2** a person who holds any of the five grades of the British nobility: duke, marquess, earl, viscount, and baron. **3** a person of equal social standing, rank, age, etc.: *he is greatly respected by his peers in the arts world.* ▷ **HISTORY** Latin *par* equal

peer[2] *vb* **1** to look intently or as if with difficulty: *Walter peered anxiously at his father's face.* **2** to appear dimly: *the sun peered through the fog.* ▷ **HISTORY** Flemish *pieren* to look with narrowed eyes

peerage *Brit* ✧ *n* **1** the whole body of peers; aristocracy. **2** the position, rank, or title of a peer.

peeress *n* **1** (in Britain) a woman holding the rank of a peer. **2** the wife or widow of a peer.

peer group *n* a social group composed of people of similar age and status.

peerless *adj* having no equals; unsurpassed.

peevish *adj* fretful or irritable. ▷ **HISTORY** origin unknown ▶ **peevishly** *adv*

peewee *n* a black-and-white Australian bird.

peewit *or* **pewit** *n* same as **lapwing**. ▷ **HISTORY** imitative of its call

peg *n* **1** a small pin or bolt used to join two parts together, to fasten, or to mark. **2** a hook or knob for hanging things on. **3** *Music* a pin on a stringed instrument which can be turned to tune the string wound around it. **4** Also called: **clothes peg** a split or hinged pin for fastening wet clothes to a line to dry. **5** *Brit* a small drink of spirits. **6** an opportunity or pretext for doing something: *the play's subject matter provides a perfect peg for a discussion of issues like morality and faith.* **7 bring** *or* **take (someone) down a peg** to lower the pride of (someone). **8 off the peg** *Brit & NZ* (of clothes) ready-to-wear, as opposed to tailor-made. ✧ *vb* **pegging, pegged 9** to insert a peg into. **10** to secure with pegs: *the balloon was pegged down to stop it drifting away.* **11** to mark (a score) with pegs, as in some card games. **12** *Chiefly Brit* to work steadily: *he pegged away at his job for years.* **13** to fix or maintain something, such as prices, at a particular level or value: *a fixed rate mortgage, pegged at 9.6 per cent.* ▷ **HISTORY** Low Germanic *pegge*

peggy square *n NZ* a small hand-knitted square.

peignoir (**pay**-nwahr) *n* a woman's light dressing gown. ▷ **HISTORY** French

pejorative (pij-**jor**-a-tiv) *adj* **1** (of a word or expression) having an insulting or critical sense. ✧ *n* **2** a pejorative word or expression. ▷ **HISTORY** Late Latin *pejorare* to make worse

peke *n Informal* a Pekingese dog.

Pekingese *or* **Pekinese** *n* **1** (*pl* **-ese**) a small dog with a long straight coat, curled plumed tail, and short wrinkled muzzle. **2** the dialect of Mandarin Chinese spoken in Beijing.

pelargonium *n* a plant with circular leaves and red, pink, or white flowers: includes many cultivated geraniums. ▷ **HISTORY** Greek *pelargos* stork

pelican *n* a large water bird with a pouch beneath its long bill for holding fish. ▷ **HISTORY** Greek *pelekan*

pelican crossing *n* (in Britain) a type of road crossing with a pedestrian-operated traffic-light system. ▷ **HISTORY** from *pe(destrian) li(ght) con(trolled) crossing,* with *-con* adapted to *-can* of *pelican*

pellagra *n Pathol* a disease caused by a diet lacking in vitamin B, which results in scaling of the skin, diarrhoea and mental disorder. ▷ **HISTORY** Italian, from *pelle* skin + Greek *agra* paroxysm

pellet *n* **1** a small round ball, esp. of compressed matter. **2 a** an imitation bullet used in toy guns. **b** a piece of small shot. **3** a small pill. ▷ **HISTORY** Latin *pila* ball

pell-mell *adv* **1** in a confused headlong rush: *the hounds ran pell-mell into the yard.* **2** in a disorderly manner: *the things were piled pell-mell in the room.* ▷ **HISTORY** Old French *pesle-mesle*

pellucid *adj Literary* **1** transparent or translucent. **2** extremely clear in style and meaning. ▷ **HISTORY** Latin *pellucidus*

pelmet *n* a board or piece of fabric used to conceal the curtain rail. ▷ **HISTORY** probably from French *palmette* palm-leaf decoration on cornice moulding

pelt[1] *vb* **1** to throw (missiles) at. **2** (foll. by *along*) etc. to hurry. **3** to rain heavily. ✧ *n* **4** a blow. **5 at full pelt** very quickly: *she ran down the street at full pelt.* ▷ **HISTORY** origin unknown

pelt[2] *n* the skin or fur of an animal, esp. as material for clothing or rugs: *the lucrative international trade in beaver pelts.* ▷ **HISTORY** probably from Latin *pellis* skin

pelvis *n, pl* **-vises** *or* **-ves 1** the framework of bones at the base of the spine, to which the hips are attached. **2** the bones that form this structure. ▷ **HISTORY** Latin: basin ▶ **pelvic** *adj*

pen[1] *n* **1** an instrument for writing or drawing using ink. See also **ballpoint, fountain pen**. **2 the pen** writing as an occupation. ✧ *vb* **penning, penned 3** to write or compose. ▷ **HISTORY** Latin *penna* feather

pen[2] *n* **1** an enclosure in which domestic animals are kept. **2** any place of confinement. ✧ *vb* **penning, penned** *or* **pent 3** to enclose (animals) in

a b c d e f g h i j k l m n o p q r s t u v w x y z

a pen. **4 penned in** being or feeling trapped or confined: *she stood penned in by bodies at the front of the crowd.* ▷ **HISTORY** Old English *penn*

pen³ *n US & Canad informal* short for **penitentiary** (sense 1).

pen⁴ *n* a female swan. ▷ **HISTORY** origin unknown

Pen. Peninsula.

penal (**pee**-nal) *adj* **1** of or relating to punishment. **2** used as a place of punishment: *a penal institution.* ▷ **HISTORY** Latin *poena* penalty ▶ **penally** *adv*

penal code *n* the body of laws relating to crime and punishment.

penal colony *n History* a colony established for the containment and punishment of convicted criminals and benefitting from their forced labour.

penalize *or* **-ise** *vb* **-izing, -ized** *or* **-ising, -ised** **1** to impose a penalty on (someone) for breaking a law or rule. **2** to inflict a disadvantage on: *why should I be penalized just because I'm a woman?* ▶ **penalization** *or* **-isation** *n*

penal settlement *n* a place to which convicted criminals are banished as a punishment for their crimes.

penalty *n, pl* **-ties** **1** a legal punishment for a crime or offence. **2** loss or suffering as a result of one's own action: *we are now paying the penalty for neglecting to keep our equipment up to date.* **3** *Sport, games, etc.* a handicap awarded against a player or team for illegal play, such as a free shot at goal by the opposing team. ▷ **HISTORY** Latin *poena*

penalty box *n* **1** Also called: **penalty area** *Soccer* a rectangular area in front of the goal, within which a penalty is awarded for a serious foul by the defending team. **2** *Ice hockey* a bench for players serving time penalties.

penalty corner *n Hockey* a free hit from the goal line taken by the attacking side.

penalty shoot-out *n Sport* a method of deciding the winner of a drawn match, in which players from each team attempt to score with a penalty shot.

penance *n* **1** voluntary self-punishment to make amends for a sin. **2** *RC Church* a sacrament in which repentant sinners are forgiven provided they confess their sins to a priest and perform a penance. ▷ **HISTORY** Latin *paenitentia* repentance

pence *n* a plural of **penny**.

> **WORD TIP**
> Since the decimalization of British currency and the introduction of the abbreviation *p*, as in *10p, 85p*, etc., the abbreviation has tended to replace *pence* in speech, as in *4p, 12p*, etc.

penchant (**pon**-shon) *n* strong inclination or liking: *a stylish woman with a penchant for dark glasses.* ▷ **HISTORY** French

pencil *n* **1** a rod of graphite encased in wood which is used for writing or drawing. ✧ *vb* **-cilling, -cilled** *or US* **-ciling, -ciled** **2** to draw, colour, write, or mark with a pencil. **3 pencil in** to note, arrange, or include provisionally or tentatively. ▷ **HISTORY** Latin *penicillus* painter's brush

pendant *n* **a** an ornament worn on a chain round the neck: *a beautiful pearl pendant.* **b** an ornament that hangs from a piece of jewellery. ▷ **HISTORY** Latin *pendere* to hang down

pendent *adj Literary* **1** dangling. **2** jutting. ▷ **HISTORY** see PENDANT

pending *prep* **1** while waiting for. ✧ *adj* **2** not yet decided or settled. **3** imminent: *these developments have been pending for some time.*

pendulous *adj Literary* hanging downwards and swinging freely. ▷ **HISTORY** Latin *pendere* to hang down

pendulum *n* **1** a weight suspended so it swings freely under the influence of gravity. **2** such a device used to regulate a clock mechanism. **3** a movement from one attitude or belief towards its opposite: *the pendulum has swung back to more punitive measures.*

peneplain *or* **peneplane** *n Geog* a relatively flat land surface produced by erosion. ▷ **HISTORY** Latin *paene* almost + PLAIN

penetrate *vb* **-trating, -trated** **1** to find or force a way into or through. **2** to diffuse through; permeate: *the smell of cooking penetrated through to the sitting room.* **3** to see through: *the sunlight did not penetrate the thick canopy of leaves.* **4** (of a man) to insert the penis into the vagina of (a woman). **5** to grasp the meaning of (a principle, etc.). ▷ **HISTORY** Latin *penetrare* ▶ **penetrable** *adj* ▶ **penetrative** *adj*

penetrating *adj* tending to or able to penetrate: *a penetrating mind; a penetrating voice.*

penetration *n* **1** the act or an instance of penetrating. **2** the ability or power to penetrate. **3** keen insight or perception.

pen friend *n* a person with whom one exchanges letters, often a person in another country whom one has not met.

penguin *n* a flightless black-and-white sea bird with webbed feet and wings modified as flippers for swimming. ▷ **HISTORY** origin unknown

penicillin *n* an antibiotic used to treat diseases caused by bacteria. ▷ **HISTORY** Latin *pencillus* tuft of hairs

peninsula *n* a narrow strip of land projecting from the mainland into a sea or lake. ▷ **HISTORY** Latin, literally: almost an island ▶ **peninsular** *adj*

> **WORD TIP**
> The noun *peninsula* is sometimes confused with the adjective *peninsular: the Iberian peninsula* (not *peninsular*).

penis *n, pl* **-nises** *or* **-nes** the organ of copulation in higher vertebrates, also used for urinating in many mammals. ▷ **HISTORY** Latin ▶ **penile** *adj*

penitent *adj* **1** feeling regret for one's sins; repentant. ✧ *n* **2** a person who is penitent. ▷ **HISTORY** Church Latin *paenitens* regretting ▶ **penitence** *n*

penitential *adj* of, showing, or as a penance.

penitentiary *n, pl* **-ries** **1** (in the US and Canada) a state or federal prison. ✧ *adj* **2** of or for penance.

3 used for punishment and reformation: *the penitentiary system.* ▷ **HISTORY** Latin *paenitens* penitent

penknife *n, pl* **-knives** a small knife with one or more blades that fold into the handle.

pen name *n* a name used by a writer instead of his or her real name; nom de plume.

pennant *n* **1** a long narrow flag, esp. one used by ships as identification or for signalling. **2** *Chiefly US, Canad, & Austral* a flag indicating the winning of a championship in certain sports.
▷ **HISTORY** probably a blend of *pendant* + *pennon*

penniless *adj* very poor.

pennon *n* **1** a long flag, often tapering and divided at the end, originally a knight's personal flag. **2** a small tapering or triangular flag flown by a ship or boat. ▷ **HISTORY** Latin *penna* feather

penny *n, pl* **pennies** *or* **pence 1** a British bronze coin worth one hundredth of a pound. **2** a former British and Australian coin worth one twelfth of a shilling. **3** (*pl* **pennies**) *US & Canad* a cent.
4 *Informal, chiefly Brit* the least amount of money: *I don't have a penny.* **5 a pretty penny** *Informal* a considerable sum of money. **6 spend a penny** *Brit & NZ informal* to urinate. **7 the penny dropped** *Informal* the explanation of something was finally understood. ▷ **HISTORY** Old English *penig, pening*

penny-dreadful *n, pl* **-fuls** *Brit informal* a cheap, often lurid book or magazine.

penny-farthing *n Brit* an early type of bicycle with a large front wheel and a small rear wheel.

penny-pinching *adj* **1** excessively careful with money; miserly. ✧ *n* **2** miserliness.
▶ **penny-pincher** *n*

pennyroyal *n* a Eurasian plant with hairy leaves and small mauve flowers, which provides an aromatic oil used in medicine. ▷ **HISTORY** Old French *pouliol* pennyroyal + *real* royal

pennywort *n* a Eurasian rock plant with whitish-green tubular flowers and rounded leaves.

penology (pee-**nol**-a-jee) *n* the study of the punishment of criminals and of prison management. ▷ **HISTORY** Greek *poinē* punishment

pension[1] *n* **1** a regular payment made by the state or a former employer to a person who has retired or to a widowed or disabled person. ✧ *vb* **2** to grant a pension to. ▷ **HISTORY** Latin *pensio* a payment ▶ **pensionable** *adj* ▶ **pensioner** *n*

pension[2] (**pon**-syon) *n* (in France and some other countries) a relatively cheap boarding house.
▷ **HISTORY** French: extended meaning of *pension* grant

pension off *vb* to cause (someone) to retire from a job and pay him or her a pension.

pensive *adj* deeply thoughtful, often with a tinge of sadness. ▷ **HISTORY** Latin *pensare* to consider
▶ **pensively** *adv*

penta- *combining form* five: *pentagon; pentameter.* ▷ **HISTORY** Greek *pente*

pentacle *n* same as **pentagram**.
▷ **HISTORY** Italian *pentacolo* something having five corners

pentagon *n Geom* a figure with five sides.
▶ **pentagonal** *adj*

Pentagon *n* a five-sided building that houses the headquarters of the US Department of Defense.

pentagram *n* a star-shaped figure with five points.

pentameter (pen-**tam**-it-er) *n* a line of poetry consisting of five metrical feet.

Pentateuch (**pent**-a-tyuke) *n* the first five books of the Old Testament. ▷ **HISTORY** Greek *pente* five + *teukhos* scroll case ▶ **Pentateuchal** *adj*

pentatonic scale *n Music* a scale consisting of five notes.

pentavalent *adj Chem* having a valency of five.

Pentecost *n* a Christian festival occurring on Whit Sunday celebrating the descent of the Holy Ghost to the apostles. ▷ **HISTORY** Greek *pentēkostē* fiftieth (day after the Resurrection)

Pentecostal *adj* relating to any of the Christian groups that have a charismatic and fundamentalist approach to Christianity.

penthouse *n* a luxurious flat built on the top floor or roof of a building. ▷ **HISTORY** Middle English *pentis,* later *penthouse,* from Latin *appendere* to hang from

pent-up *adj* not released; repressed: *full of pent-up emotional violence.*

penultimate *adj* second last.

penumbra *n, pl* **-brae** *or* **-bras 1** the partially shadowed region which surrounds the full shadow in an eclipse. **2** *Literary* a partial shadow.
▷ **HISTORY** Latin *paene* almost + *umbra* shadow
▶ **penumbral** *adj*

penurious *adj Formal* **1** niggardly with money. **2** lacking money or means.

penury *n Formal* **1** extreme poverty. **2** extreme scarcity. ▷ **HISTORY** Latin *penuria*

peon *n* a Spanish-American farm labourer or unskilled worker. ▷ **HISTORY** Spanish

peony *n, pl* **-nies** a garden plant with showy pink, red, white, or yellow flowers. ▷ **HISTORY** Greek *paiōnia*

people *pl n* **1** persons collectively or in general. **2** a group of persons considered together: *old people suffer from anaemia more often than younger people do.* **3** (*pl* **-ples**) the persons living in a particular country: *the American people.* **4** one's family or ancestors: *her people originally came from Skye.* **5 the people a** the mass of ordinary persons without rank or privileges. **b** the body of persons in a country who are entitled to vote. ✧ *vb* **-pling, -pled 6** to provide with inhabitants: *the centre of the continent is sparsely peopled.* ▷ **HISTORY** Latin *populus*

> ☑ **WORD TIP**
> See at **person.**

people carrier *n* same as **multipurpose vehicle**.

people mover *n Brit, Austral & NZ* same as **multipurpose vehicle**.

A B C D E F G H I J K L M N O P Q R S T U V W X Y Z

pep *n* **1** high spirits, energy, or vitality. ✧ *vb* **pepping, pepped 2 pep up** to make more lively or interesting: *the company has spent thousands trying to pep up its image.* ▷ **HISTORY** short for *pepper*

pepper *n* **1** a sharp hot condiment obtained from the fruit of an East Indian climbing plant. **2** Also called: **capsicum** a colourful tropical fruit used as a vegetable and a condiment. ✧ *vb* **3** to season with pepper. **4** to sprinkle liberally: *his speech is heavily peppered with Americanisms.* **5** to pelt with small missiles. ▷ **HISTORY** Greek *peperi*

peppercorn *n* the small dried berry of the pepper plant.

peppercorn rent *n Brit* a rent that is very low or nominal.

pepper mill *n* a small hand mill used to grind peppercorns.

peppermint *n* **1** a mint plant which produces a pungent oil, used as a flavouring. **2** a sweet flavoured with peppermint.

peppery *adj* **1** tasting of pepper. **2** irritable.

pep pill *n Informal* a tablet containing a stimulant drug.

pepsin *n* an enzyme produced in the stomach, which, when activated by acid, breaks down proteins. ▷ **HISTORY** Greek *peptein* to digest

pep talk *n Informal* a talk designed to increase confidence and enthusiasm.

peptic *adj* **1** of or relating to digestion. **2** of or caused by pepsin or the action of the digestive juices: *a peptic ulcer.* ▷ **HISTORY** Greek *peptein* to digest

peptic ulcer *n* an ulcer in the stomach or duodenum.

peptide *n Chem* a compound consisting of two or more amino acids linked by chemical bonding between the amino group of one and the carboxyl group of another.

per *prep* **1** for every: *three pence per pound; 30 pounds per week.* **2** by; through. **3 as per** according to: *proceed as per the instructions.* **4 as per usual** *or* **as per normal** *Informal* as usual. ▷ **HISTORY** Latin: by, for each

perambulate *vb* **-lating, -lated** *Formal* to walk about (a place). ▷ **HISTORY** Latin *per-* through + *ambulare* to walk ▸ **perambulation** *n*

perambulator *n Formal* same as **pram**.

per annum *adv* in each year. ▷ **HISTORY** Latin

per capita *adj, adv* of or for each person: *the average per capita wage has increased.* ▷ **HISTORY** Latin, literally: according to heads

perceive *vb* **-ceiving, -ceived 1** to become aware of (something) through the senses. **2** to understand or grasp. ▷ **HISTORY** Latin *percipere* to seize entirely ▸ **perceivable** *adj*

per cent *adv* **1** in each hundred. Symbol: %. ✧ *n also* **percent 2** a percentage or proportion. ▷ **HISTORY** Medieval Latin *per centum* out of every hundred

percentage *n* **1** proportion or rate per hundred parts. **2** any proportion in relation to the whole: *a small percentage of the population.* **3** *Informal* profit or advantage.

percentage error *n Maths* the difference between the predicted value and the actual value of a quantity, expressed as a percentage.

percentile *n* one of 99 actual or notional values of a variable dividing its distribution into 100 groups with equal frequencies.

perceptible *adj* able to be perceived; recognizable. ▸ **perceptibly** *adv*

perception *n* **1** the act of perceiving. **2** insight or intuition: *his acute perception of other people's emotions.* **3** the ability to perceive. **4** way of viewing: *advertising affects the customer's perception of a product.* ▷ **HISTORY** Latin *perceptio* comprehension ▸ **perceptual** *adj*

perceptive *adj* **1** observant. **2** able to perceive. ▸ **perceptively** *adv* ▸ **perceptiveness** *n*

perch[1] *n* **1** a branch or other resting place above ground for a bird. **2** any raised resting place: *from his perch on the bar stool.* ✧ *vb* **3** (of birds) to alight or rest on a perch: *it fluttered to the branch and perched there for a moment.* **4** to place or position precariously: *he was perched uneasily on the edge of his chair.* ▷ **HISTORY** Latin *pertica* long staff

perch[2] *n, pl* **perch** *or* **perches 1** a spiny-finned edible freshwater fish of Europe and North America. **2** any of various similar or related fishes. ▷ **HISTORY** Greek *perkē*

perchance *adv Archaic or poetic* **1** perhaps. **2** by chance. ▷ **HISTORY** Anglo-French *par chance*

percipient *adj Formal* quick at perceiving; observant. ▷ **HISTORY** Latin *percipiens* observing ▸ **percipience** *n*

percolate *vb* **-lating, -lated 1** to pass or filter through very small holes: *the light percolating through the stained-glass windows cast coloured patterns on the floor.* **2** to spread gradually: *his theories percolated through the academic community.* **3** to make (coffee) or (of coffee) to be made in a percolator. ▷ **HISTORY** Latin *per-* through + *colare* to strain ▸ **percolation** *n*

percolator *n* a coffeepot in which boiling water is forced up through a tube and filters down through the coffee grounds into a container.

percussion *n* **1** the striking of one thing against another. **2** *Music* percussion instruments collectively. ▷ **HISTORY** Latin *percutere* to hit ▸ **percussive** *adj*

percussion instrument *n* a musical instrument, such as the drums, that produces a sound when struck directly.

percussionist *n Music* a person who plays percussion instruments.

perdition *n* **1** *Christianity* final and unalterable spiritual ruin; damnation. **2** same as **hell**. ▷ **HISTORY** Late Latin *perditio* ruin

peregrine falcon *n* a European falcon with dark plumage on the back and wings and lighter underparts. ▷ **HISTORY** Latin *peregrinus* foreign

peremptory *adj* **1** urgent or commanding: *a peremptory knock on the door.* **2** expecting immediate obedience without any discussion: *he gave peremptory instructions to his son.* **3** dogmatic.

▷ **HISTORY** Latin *peremptorius* decisive
▶ **peremptorily** *adv*

perennial *adj* **1** lasting throughout the year or through many years. ✧ *n* **2** a plant that continues its growth for at least three years. ▷ **HISTORY** Latin *per-* through + *annus* year

perestroika *n* (in the late 1980s) the policy of restructuring the Soviet economy and political system. ▷ **HISTORY** Russian: reconstruction

perfect *adj* **1** having all essential elements. **2** faultless: *a perfect circle.* **3** correct or precise: *perfect timing.* **4** utter or absolute: *a perfect stranger.* **5** excellent in all respects: *a perfect day.* **6** *Maths* exactly divisible into equal integral or polynomial roots: *36 is a perfect square.* **7** *Grammar* denoting a tense of verbs used to describe a completed action. ✧ *n* **8** *Grammar* the perfect tense. ✧ *vb* **9** to improve to one's satisfaction: *he is in Paris to perfect his French.* **10** to make fully accomplished: *he perfected the system.* ▷ **HISTORY** Latin *perficere* to complete ▶ **perfectly** *adv*

WORD TIP
For most of its meanings, the adjective *perfect* describes an absolute state, i.e. one that cannot be qualified; thus something is either *perfect* or *not perfect,* and cannot be *more perfect* or *less perfect.* However when *perfect* means excellent in all respects, a comparative can be used with it without absurdity: *the next day the weather was even more perfect.*

perfect flower *n Bot* a flower with functional stamens and pistils.

perfection *n* the state or quality of being perfect. ▷ **HISTORY** Latin *perfectio* a completing

perfectionism *n* the demand for the highest standard of excellence. ▶ **perfectionist** *n, adj*

perfect tense *n* **1** same as **present perfect**. **2** one of the tenses used to refer to the time leading up either to the present or to a particular point in the past. See also **past perfect**.

perfidious *adj Literary* treacherous or deceitful. ▷ **HISTORY** Latin *perfidus* ▶ **perfidy** *n*

perforate *vb* **-rating, -rated 1** to make a hole or holes in. **2** to punch rows of holes between (stamps) for ease of separation. ▷ **HISTORY** Latin *per-* through + *forare* to pierce ▶ **perforable** *adj* ▶ **perforator** *n*

perforation *n* **1** a hole or holes made in something. **2** a series of punched holes, such as that between individual stamps.

perforce *adv Formal* of necessity. ▷ **HISTORY** Old French *par force*

perform *vb* **1** to carry out (an action): *the hospital performs more than a hundred such operations each year.* **2** to present (a play or concert): *he performed a couple of songs from his new album.* **3** to fulfil: *you have performed the first of two conditions.* ▷ **HISTORY** Old French *parfournir* ▶ **performable** *adj* ▶ **performer** *n*

performance *n* **1** the act or process of performing. **2** an artistic or dramatic production: *the concert includes the first performance of a new trumpet concerto.* **3** manner or quality of functioning: *the car's overall performance is excellent.* **4** *Informal* conduct or behaviour, esp. when distasteful: *what did you mean by that performance at the restaurant?*

perfume *n* **1** a liquid cosmetic worn for its pleasant smell. **2** a fragrant smell. ✧ *vb* **-fuming, -fumed 3** to impart a perfume to. ▷ **HISTORY** French *parfum,* from Latin *per* through + *fumare* to smoke ▶ **perfumed** *adj*

perfumer *n* a person who makes or sells perfume. ▶ **perfumery** *n*

perfunctory *adj Formal* done only as a matter of routine: *he gave his wife a perfunctory kiss.* ▷ **HISTORY** Late Latin *perfunctorius* negligent ▶ **perfunctorily** *adv* ▶ **perfunctoriness** *n*

perfuse *vb* **-fusing, -fused 1** to permeate (a liquid, colour, etc.) through or over (something). **2** *Surgery* to pass (a fluid) through tissue.

pergola *n* an arched trellis or framework that supports climbing plants. ▷ **HISTORY** Italian

perhaps *adv* **1** possibly; maybe. **2** approximately; roughly: *it would have taken perhaps three or four minutes.* ▷ **HISTORY** earlier *perhappes,* from *per* by + *happes* chance

perianth *n Bot* the outer part of a flower. ▷ **HISTORY** Greek *peri-* around + *anthos* flower

pericardium *n, pl* **-dia** the membranous sac enclosing the heart. ▷ **HISTORY** Greek *peri-* around + *kardia* heart ▶ **pericardial** *adj*

pericarp *n Bot* the part of a fruit enclosing the seed that develops from the wall of the ovary. ▷ **HISTORY** Greek *peri-* around + *karpos* fruit

perigee *n Astron* the point in its orbit around the earth when the moon or a satellite is nearest the earth. ▷ **HISTORY** Greek *peri-* near + *gea* earth

periglacial *adj Geog* relating to a region bordering a glacier: *periglacial climate.*

perihelion *n, pl* **-lia** *Astron* the point in its orbit around the sun when a planet or comet is nearest the sun. ▷ **HISTORY** Greek *peri-* near + *hēlios* sun

peril *n* great danger or jeopardy. ▷ **HISTORY** Latin *periculum* ▶ **perilous** *adj*

perilymph *n Physiol* the fluid that fills the space between the membranous and bony labyrinths of the internal ear.

perimeter (per-**rim**-it-er) *n* **1** *Maths* **a** the curve or line enclosing a plane area. **b** the length of this curve or line. **2** any boundary around something. ▷ **HISTORY** Latin *perimetros*

perinatal *adj* of or occurring in the period from about three months before to one month after birth. ▷ **HISTORY** Greek *peri-* around + Latin *natus* born

perineum (per-rin-**nee**-um) *n, pl* **-nea** (-**nee**-a) *Anat* the region of the body between the anus and the genitals. ▷ **HISTORY** Greek *perinaion* ▶ **perineal** *adj*

perineurium *n Anat* the connective tissue forming a sheath around a single bundle of nerve fibres.

period *n* **1** a portion of time: *six inches of rain fell in a 24-hour period.* **2** a portion of time specified in

a b c d e f g h i j k l m n o p q r s t u v w x y z

some way: *the President's first period of office.* **3** an occurrence of menstruation. **4** *Geol* a unit of geological time during which a system of rocks is formed: *the Jurassic period.* **5** a division of time at school, college, or university when a particular subject is taught. **6** *Physics, maths* the time taken to complete one cycle of a regularly recurring phenomenon. **7** *Chem* one of the horizontal rows of elements in the periodic table. **8** *Chiefly US & Canad* same as **full stop.** ✧ *adj* **9** dating from or in the style of an earlier time: *a performance on period instruments.* ▷ **HISTORY** Greek *periodos* circuit

periodic *adj* recurring at intervals. ▸ **periodically** *adv* ▸ **periodicity** *n*

periodical *n* **1** a publication issued at regular intervals, usually monthly or weekly. ✧ *adj* **2** of or relating to such publications. **3** periodic or occasional.

periodic law *n Chem* the principle that the chemical properties of the elements are periodic functions of their atomic numbers.

periodic table *n Chem* a table of the elements, arranged in order of increasing atomic number, based on the periodic law.

peripatetic (per-rip-a-**tet**-ik) *adj* **1** travelling from place to place. **2** *Brit* employed in two or more educational establishments and travelling from one to another: *a peripatetic violin teacher.* ✧ *n* **3** a peripatetic person. ▷ **HISTORY** Greek *peripatein* to pace to and fro

peripheral (per-**if**-er-al) *adj* **1** not relating to the most important part of something; incidental. **2** of or relating to a periphery. ✧ *n* **3** *Computers* any device, such as a disk or modem, concerned with input/output or storage.

periphery (per-**if**-er-ee) *n, pl* **-eries 1** the boundary or edge of an area or group: *slums sprouted up on the periphery of the city.* **2** fringes of a field of activity: *less developed countries on the periphery of the capitalist system.* ▷ **HISTORY** Greek *peri-* around + *pherein* to bear

periscope *n* an optical instrument used, esp. in submarines, to give a view of objects on a different level. ▷ **HISTORY** Greek *periskopein* to look around

perish *vb* **1** to be destroyed or die. **2** to cause to suffer: *we were perished with cold.* **3** to rot or cause to rot: *to prevent your swimsuit from perishing, rinse it in clean water before it dries.* ▷ **HISTORY** Latin *perire* to pass away entirely

perishable *adj* **1** liable to rot. ✧ *n* **2** (*often pl*) a perishable article, esp. food.

perishing *adj* **1** (of weather) *Informal* extremely cold. **2** *Slang* confounded or blasted: *get rid of the perishing lot!*

peristalsis (per-riss-**tal**-siss) *n, pl* **-ses** (-seez) *Physiol* the wavelike involuntary muscular contractions of the walls of the digestive tract. ▷ **HISTORY** Greek *peri-* around + *stalsis* compression ▸ **peristaltic** *adj*

peritoneum (per-rit-toe-**nee**-um) *n, pl* **-nea** (**-nee**-a) *or* **-neums** a serous sac that lines the walls of the abdominal cavity and covers the abdominal organs. ▷ **HISTORY** Greek *peritonos* stretched around ▸ **peritoneal** *adj*

peritonitis (per-rit-tone-**ite**-iss) *n* inflammation of the peritoneum, causing severe abdominal pain.

periwinkle[1] *n* same as **winkle** (sense 1). ▷ **HISTORY** origin unknown

periwinkle[2] *n* a Eurasian evergreen plant with trailing stems and blue flowers. ▷ **HISTORY** Old English *perwince*

perjure *vb* **-juring, -jured perjure oneself** *Criminal law* to deliberately give false evidence while under oath. ▷ **HISTORY** Latin *perjurare* ▸ **perjurer** *n*

perjury (**per**-jer-ee) *n, pl* **-juries** *Criminal law* the act of deliberately giving false evidence while under oath. ▷ **HISTORY** Latin *perjurium* a false oath

perk[1] *n Informal* an incidental benefit gained from a job, such as a company car. ▷ **HISTORY** short for *perquisite*

perk[2] *vb Informal* short for **percolate** (sense 3).

perk up *vb* **1** to make or become more cheerful. **2** to rise or cause to rise briskly: *the dog's ears perked up suddenly.* ▷ **HISTORY** origin unknown

perky *adj* **perkier, perkiest 1** jaunty or lively. **2** confident or spirited.

Perl *n* a computer programming language that is used for text manipulation, esp. on the World Wide Web. ▷ **HISTORY** *p*ractical *e*xtraction and *r*eport *l*anguage

perlemoen (**per**-la-moon) *n S African* same as **abalone**. ▷ **HISTORY** Afrikaans, from Dutch

perm[1] *n* **1** a hairstyle with long-lasting waves or curls produced by treating the hair with chemicals. ✧ *vb* **2** to give a perm to (hair).

perm[2] *n Informal* short for **permutation** (sense 4).

permafrost *n* ground that is permanently frozen. ▷ **HISTORY** *perma(nent)* + *frost*

permanent *adj* **1** existing or intended to exist forever: *a permanent solution.* **2** not expected to change: *a permanent condition.* ▷ **HISTORY** Latin *permanens* continuing ▸ **permanence** *n* ▸ **permanently** *adv*

permanent health insurance *n Law* a form of insurance that provides up to 75 per cent of a person's salary in case of prolonged illness or disability.

permanent magnet *n Physics* a magnet that retains its magnetism after the magnetic field producing it is removed.

permanganate *n* a salt of an acid containing manganese, used as a disinfectant.

permeability *n* **1** the state or quality of being permeable. **2** *Geol* the degree to which a substance such as sandstone or granite is capable of transmitting fluids.

permeable *adj* capable of being permeated, esp. by liquids.

permeate *vb* **-ating, -ated 1** to penetrate or spread throughout (something): *his mystical philosophy permeates everything he creates.* **2** to pass through or cause to pass through by osmosis or diffusion: *the rain permeated her anorak.* ▷ **HISTORY** Latin *permeare* ▸ **permeation** *n*

Permian *adj Geol* of the period of geological time about 280 million years ago. ▷ **HISTORY** after *Perm,* Russian port

permissible *adj* permitted or allowable. ▶ **permissibility** *n*

permission *n* authorization to do something.

permissive *adj* tolerant or lenient, esp. in sexual matters: *the so-called permissive society.* ▶ **permissiveness** *n*

permit *vb* **-mitting, -mitted 1** to allow (something) to be done or to happen: *smoking is not permitted in the office.* **2** to allow (someone) to do something: *her father does not permit her to eat sweets.* **3** to allow the possibility (of): *they saw each other as often as time and circumstances permitted.* ✧ *n* **4** an official document granting permission to do something. ▷ **HISTORY** Latin *permittere*

permutation *n* **1** *Maths* an ordered arrangement of the numbers or terms of a set into specified groups: *the permutations of a, b, and c, taken two at a time, are ab, ba, ac, ca, bc, cb.* **2** a combination of items made by reordering. **3** a transformation. **4** a fixed combination for selections of results on football pools. ▷ **HISTORY** Latin *permutare* to change thoroughly

pernicious *adj Formal* **1** wicked or malicious: *pernicious lies.* **2** causing grave harm; deadly. ▷ **HISTORY** Latin *pernicies* ruin

pernicious anaemia *n* a severe form of anaemia resulting in a reduction of the red blood cells, weakness, and a sore tongue.

pernickety *adj Informal* **1** excessively fussy about details. **2** (of a task) requiring close attention. ▷ **HISTORY** origin unknown

peroration *n Formal* the concluding part of a speech which sums up the points made previously. ▷ **HISTORY** Latin *peroratio*

peroxide *n* **1** hydrogen peroxide used as a hair bleach. **2** any of a class of metallic oxides, such as sodium peroxide, Na_2O_2. ✧ *adj* **3** bleached with or resembling peroxide: *a peroxide blonde.* ✧ *vb* **-iding, -ided 4** to bleach (the hair) with peroxide.

perpendicular *adj* **1** at right angles to a given line or surface. **2** upright; vertical. **3** denoting a style of English Gothic architecture characterized by vertical lines. ✧ *n* **4** *Geom* a line or plane perpendicular to another. ▷ **HISTORY** Latin *perpendiculum* a plumb line ▶ **perpendicularity** *n*

perpendicular bisector *n Maths* a perpendicular line or segment that passes through the midpoint of a segment.

perpetrate *vb* **-trating, -trated** to perform or be responsible for (a deception or crime). ▷ **HISTORY** Latin *perpetrare* ▶ **perpetration** *n* ▶ **perpetrator** *n*

> **WORD TIP**
> *Perpetrate* and *perpetuate* are sometimes confused: *he must answer for the crimes he has perpetrated* (not *perpetuated*)*; the book helped to perpetuate* (not *perpetrate*) *some of the myths surrounding his early life.*

perpetual *adj* **1** never ending or never changing: *Mexico's colourful scenery and nearly perpetual sunshine.* **2** continually repeated: *his mother's perpetual worries about his health.* ▷ **HISTORY** Latin *perpetualis* ▶ **perpetually** *adv*

perpetual motion *n* motion of a hypothetical mechanism that continues indefinitely without any external source of energy.

perpetuate *vb* **-ating, -ated** to cause to continue: *images that perpetuate stereotypes of Blacks as illiterate, happy-go-lucky entertainers.* ▷ **HISTORY** Latin *perpetuare* to continue without interruption ▶ **perpetuation** *n*

> **WORD TIP**
> See at **perpetrate.**

perpetuity *n, pl* **-ties 1** eternity. **2** the state of being perpetual. **3** something perpetual, such as a pension that is payable indefinitely. **4 in perpetuity** forever. ▷ **HISTORY** Latin *perpetuitas* continuity

perplex *vb* **1** to puzzle or bewilder. **2** to complicate: *this merely perplexes the issue.* ▷ **HISTORY** Latin *perplexus* entangled ▶ **perplexing** *adj*

perplexity *n, pl* **-ties 1** the state of being perplexed. **2** something that perplexes.

perquisite *n Formal* same as **perk**[1]. ▷ **HISTORY** Latin *perquirere* to seek earnestly for something

perry *n, pl* **-ries** an alcoholic drink made from fermented pear juice. ▷ **HISTORY** Old French *peré*

per se (per **say**) *adv* in itself. ▷ **HISTORY** Latin

persecute *vb* **-cuting, -cuted 1** to oppress or maltreat (someone), because of race or religion. **2** to harass (someone) persistently. ▷ **HISTORY** Latin *persequi* to take vengeance upon ▶ **persecution** *n* ▶ **persecutor** *n*

perseverance *n* continued steady belief or efforts; persistence.

persevere *vb* **-severing, -severed** (often foll. by *with* or *in*) to continue to make an effort despite difficulties. ▷ **HISTORY** Latin *perseverus* very strict

Persian *adj* **1** of ancient Persia or modern Iran. ✧ *n* **2** a person from Persia (now Iran). **3** the language of Iran or of Persia.

Persian carpet *n* a hand-made carpet or rug with flowing or geometric designs in rich colours.

Persian cat *n* a long-haired variety of domestic cat.

Persian lamb *n* **1** a black loosely curled fur from the karakul lamb. **2** a karakul lamb.

persimmon *n* a sweet red tropical fruit. ▷ **HISTORY** from a Native American language

persist *vb* **1** to continue without interruption: *if the symptoms persist, see your doctor.* **2** (often foll. by *in* or *with*) to continue obstinately despite opposition: *she persisted in using these controversial methods.* ▷ **HISTORY** Latin *persistere*

persistent *adj* **1** unrelenting: *persistent rain.* **2** showing persistence: *she was a persistent woman.* ▶ **persistence** *n* ▶ **persistently** *adv*

persistent vegetative state *n Med* an irreversible condition, resulting from brain damage, characterized by lack of consciousness, thought, and feeling, although reflex activities continue.

person *n, pl* **people** *or* **persons 1** an individual human being. **2** the body of a human being: *he was found to have a knife concealed about his person.* **3** *Grammar* a category into which pronouns and forms of verbs are subdivided to show whether they refer to the speaker, the person addressed, or some other individual or thing. **4 in person** actually doing something or being somewhere oneself: *I had the chance to hear her speak in person.* ▷ **HISTORY** Latin *persona* mask

> **WORD TIP**
> *People* is the word usually used to refer to more than one individual: *there were a hundred people at the reception. Persons* is rarely used, except in official English: *several persons were interviewed.*

-person *n combining form* sometimes used instead of *man* and *woman* or *lady*: *chairperson.*

> **WORD TIP**
> See at **man.**

persona (per-**soh**-na) *n, pl* **-nae** (-nee) the personality that a person adopts and presents to other people. ▷ **HISTORY** Latin: mask

personable *adj* pleasant in appearance and personality.

personage *n* **1** an important or distinguished person. **2** any person.

personal *adj* **1** of the private aspects of a person's life: *redundancy can put an enormous strain on personal relationships.* **2** of a person's body: *personal hygiene.* **3** belonging to, or for the sole use of, a particular individual: *he disappeared, leaving his passport, diary and other personal belongings in his flat.* **4** undertaken by an individual: *the sponsorship deal requires him to make a number of personal appearances for publicity purposes.* **5** offensive in respect of an individual's personality or intimate affairs: *he has suffered a lifetime of personal remarks about his weight.* **6** having the attributes of an individual conscious being: *a personal God.* **7** *Grammar* of person. **8** *Law* of movable property, such as money.

personal assistant *n* a person who is employed to help someone with his or her work, esp. the secretarial and administrative aspects of it.

personal column *n* a newspaper column containing personal messages and advertisements.

personal computer *n* a small computer used for word processing or computer games.

personality *n, pl* **-ties 1** *Psychol* the distinctive characteristics which make an individual unique. **2** the distinctive character of a person which makes him or her socially attractive: *some people find him lacking in personality and a bit colourless.* **3** a well-known person in a certain field; celebrity. **4** a remarkable person: *she is a personality to be reckoned with.* **5** (*often pl*) an offensive personal remark: *the argument never degenerated into personalities.*

personalize *or* **-ise** *vb* **-izing, -ized** *or* **-ising, -ised 1** to base (an argument or discussion) around people's characters rather than on abstract arguments. **2** to mark (stationery or clothing) with a person's initials or name. **3** same as **personify**.

personally *adv* **1** without the help of others: *she had seen to it personally that permission was granted.* **2** in one's own opinion: *personally, I think it's overrated.* **3** as if referring to oneself: *yes, he was rather rude but it's not worth taking it personally.* **4** as a person: *I don't like him personally, but he's fine to work with.*

personal organizer *n* **1** a diary for storing personal records, appointments, etc. **2** a pocket-sized electronic device that performs the same functions.

personal pronoun *n Grammar* a pronoun such as *I, you, he, she, it, we,* and *they* that represents a definite person or thing.

personal stereo *n Chiefly Brit* a small portable audio cassette player used with lightweight headphones.

personate *vb* **-ating, -ated** *Criminal law* to assume the identity of (another person) with intent to deceive. ▶ **personation** *n*

personification *n* **1** the attribution of human characteristics to things, abstract ideas, etc. **2** the representation of an abstract quality or idea in the form of a person, creature, etc., as in art and literature. **3** a person or thing that personifies. **4** a person or thing regarded as the embodiment of a quality: *he is the personification of optimism.*

personify *vb* **-fies, -fying, -fied 1** to give human characteristics to (a thing or abstraction). **2** to represent (an abstract quality) in human or animal form. **3** (of a person or thing) to represent (an abstract quality), as in art. **4** to be the embodiment of: *she can be charm personified.*

personnel *n* **1** the people employed in an organization or for a service. **2** the department in an organization that appoints or keeps records of employees. **3** (in the armed forces) people, as opposed to machinery or equipment. ▷ **HISTORY** French

perspective *n* **1** a way of regarding situations or facts and judging their relative importance: *the female perspective on sex and love.* **2** objectivity: *Kay's problems helped me put my minor worries into perspective.* **3** a method of drawing that gives the effect of solidity and relative distances and sizes. **4** the appearance of objects or buildings relative to each other, determined by their distance from the viewer. ▷ **HISTORY** Latin *perspiçere* to inspect carefully

Perspex *n Trademark* a clear acrylic resin used as a substitute for glass.

perspicacious *adj Formal* acutely perceptive or discerning. ▷ **HISTORY** Latin *perspicax* ▶ **perspicacity** *n*

perspiration *n* **1** the salty fluid secreted by the sweat glands of the skin; sweat. **2** the act of sweating.

perspire *vb* **-spiring, -spired** to sweat. ▷ HISTORY Latin *per-* through + *spirare* to breathe

persuade *vb* **-suading, -suaded 1** to make (someone) do something by reason or charm: *we tried to persuade him not to come up the mountain with us.* **2** to cause to believe; convince: *persuading people of the need for enforced environmental protection may be difficult.* ▷ HISTORY Latin *persuadere* ▸ **persuadable** *adj*

persuasion *n* **1** the act of persuading. **2** the power to persuade. **3** a set of beliefs; creed: *the Roman Catholic persuasion; literary intellectuals of the modernist persuasion.*

persuasive *adj* able to persuade: *a persuasive argument.* ▸ **persuasively** *adv*

persuasive language *n* a type of language in which speakers and writers try to influence others often by appealing to their feelings, desires, and prejudices.

pert *adj* **1** saucy or impudent. **2** attractive in a neat way: *pert buttocks.* ▷ HISTORY Latin *apertus* open

pertain *vb* (often foll. by *to*) **1** to have reference or relevance: *the notes pertaining to the case.* **2** to be appropriate: *the product pertains to real user needs.* **3** to belong (to) or be a part (of). ▷ HISTORY Latin *pertinere*

pertinacious *adj* **1** doggedly resolute in purpose or belief. **2** stubbornly persistent. ▷ HISTORY Latin *per-* (intensive) + *tenax* clinging ▸ **pertinacity** *n*

pertinent *adj* relating to the matter at hand; relevant. ▷ HISTORY Latin *pertinens* ▸ **pertinence** *n*

perturb *vb* **1** to disturb the composure of. **2** to throw into disorder. ▷ HISTORY Latin *perturbare* to confuse

perturbation *n Literary* anxiety or worry.

peruse *vb* **-rusing, -rused 1** to read or examine with care. **2** to browse or read in a leisurely way. ▷ HISTORY *per-* (intensive) + *use* ▸ **perusal** *n*

pervade *vb* **-vading, -vaded** to spread through or throughout (something). ▷ HISTORY Latin *per-* through + *vadere* to go ▸ **pervasion** *n* ▸ **pervasive** *adj*

perverse *adj* **1** deliberately acting in a way different from what is regarded as normal or proper. **2** wayward or contrary; obstinate. ▷ HISTORY Latin *perversus* turned the wrong way ▸ **perversely** *adv* ▸ **perversity** *n*

perversion *n* **1** any abnormal means of obtaining sexual satisfaction. **2** the act of perverting.

pervert *vb* **1** to use wrongly or badly. **2** to interpret wrongly or badly; distort. **3** to lead (someone) into abnormal behaviour, esp. sexually; corrupt. **4** to debase. ✧ *n* **5** a person who practises sexual perversion. ▷ HISTORY Latin *pervertere* to turn the wrong way ▸ **perverted** *adj*

pervious *adj* **1** able to be penetrated; permeable: *the thin walls were pervious to the slightest sound.* **2** receptive to new ideas; open-minded. ▷ HISTORY Latin *per-* through + *via* a way

Pesach *or* **Pesah** (**pay**-sahk) *n* same as **Passover**.

peseta (pess-**say**-ta) *n* a former monetary unit of Spain. ▷ HISTORY Spanish

peso (**pay**-so) *n, pl* **-sos** the standard monetary unit of Chile, Colombia, Cuba, the Dominican Republic, Mexico, the Philippines, and Uruguay. ▷ HISTORY Spanish: weight

pessary *n, pl* **-ries** *Med* **1** a device worn in the vagina, either as a support for the uterus or as a contraceptive. **2** a vaginal suppository. ▷ HISTORY Greek *pessos* plug

pessimism *n* **1** the tendency to expect the worst in all things. **2** the doctrine of the ultimate triumph of evil over good. ▷ HISTORY Latin *pessimus* worst ▸ **pessimist** *n* ▸ **pessimistic** *adj* ▸ **pessimistically** *adv*

pest *n* **1** an annoying person or thing; nuisance. **2** any organism that damages crops, or injures or irritates livestock or man. ▷ HISTORY Latin *pestis* plague

pester *vb* to annoy or nag continually. ▷ HISTORY Old French *empestrer* to hobble (a horse)

pesticide *n* a chemical used to destroy pests, esp. insects. ▷ HISTORY *pest* + Latin *caedere* to kill

pestilence *n Literary* any deadly epidemic disease, such as the plague.

pestilent *adj* **1** annoying or irritating. **2** highly destructive morally or physically. **3** likely to cause infectious disease. ▷ HISTORY Latin *pestis* plague ▸ **pestilential** *adj*

pestle *n* a club-shaped instrument for grinding or pounding substances in a mortar. ▷ HISTORY Old French *pestel*

pet[1] *n* **1** a tame animal kept for companionship or pleasure. **2** a person who is favoured or indulged: *teacher's pet.* ✧ *adj* **3** kept as a pet: *a pet hamster.* **4** of or for pet animals: *pet food.* **5** strongly felt or particularly cherished: *a pet hatred; he would not stand by and let his pet project be abandoned.* ✧ *vb* **petting, petted 6** to treat as a pet; pamper. **7** to pat or stroke affectionately. **8** *Informal* (of two people) to caress each other in an erotic manner. ▷ HISTORY origin unknown

pet[2] *n* a fit of sulkiness. ▷ HISTORY origin unknown

petal *n* any of the brightly coloured leaflike parts which form the head of a flower. ▷ HISTORY Greek *petalon* leaf ▸ **petalled** *adj*

petard *n* **1** (formerly) a device containing explosives used to break through a wall or door. **2 hoist with one's own petard** being the victim of one's own schemes. ▷ HISTORY French: firework

peter out *vb* to come gradually to an end: *the road petered out into a rutted track.* ▷ HISTORY origin unknown

pethidine (**peth**-id-een) *n* a white crystalline water-soluble drug used to relieve pain. ▷ HISTORY perhaps a blend of *piperidine* + *ethyl*

petiole *n Bot* the stalk which attaches a leaf to a plant. ▷ HISTORY Latin *petiolus* little foot

A B C D E F G H I J K L M N O P Q R S T U V W X Y Z

petit bourgeois (**pet**-ee **boor**-zhwah) *n, pl* **petits bourgeois** (**pet**-ee **boor**-zhwahz) the lower middle class. ▷ **HISTORY** French

petite (pit-**eat**) *adj* (of a woman) small and dainty. ▷ **HISTORY** French

petition *n* **1** a written document signed by a large number of people demanding some form of action from a government or other authority. **2** any formal request to a higher authority. **3** *Law* a formal application in writing made to a court asking for some specific judicial action: *she filed a petition for divorce.* ✧ *vb* **4** to address or present a petition to (a government or to someone in authority): *he petitioned the Crown for mercy.* **5** (foll. by *for*) to seek by petition: *the firm's creditors petitioned for liquidation.* ▷ **HISTORY** Latin *petere* to seek ▶ **petitioner** *n*

petit mal (**pet**-ee **mal**) *n* a mild form of epilepsy in which there are periods of loss of consciousness for up to 30 seconds. ▷ **HISTORY** French: little illness

petrel *n* a sea bird with a hooked bill and tubular nostrils, such as the albatross, storm petrel, or shearwater. ▷ **HISTORY** variant of earlier *pitteral*

Petri dish (**pet**-ree) *n* a shallow dish used in laboratories, esp. for producing cultures of bacteria. ▷ **HISTORY** after J. R. *Petri,* bacteriologist

petrify *vb* **-fies, -fying, -fied 1** to stun or daze with fear: *he was petrified of going to jail.* **2** (of organic material) to turn to stone. **3** to make or become unable to change or develop: *a society petrified by outmoded conventions.* ▷ **HISTORY** Greek *petra* stone ▶ **petrification** *n*

petrochemical *n* a substance, such as acetone, obtained from petroleum. ▶ **petrochemistry** *n*

petrodollar *n* money earned by a country by exporting petroleum.

petrol *n* a volatile flammable liquid obtained from petroleum and used as a fuel for internal-combustion engines. ▷ **HISTORY** see PETROLEUM

petrolatum (pet-rol-**late**-um) *n* a translucent jelly-like substance obtained from petroleum: used as a lubricant and in medicine as an ointment base.

petrol bomb *n* a simple grenade consisting of a bottle filled with petrol. A piece of cloth is put in the neck of the bottle and set alight just before the bomb is thrown.

petroleum *n* a dark-coloured thick flammable crude oil occurring in sedimentary rocks, consisting mainly of hydrocarbons: the source of petrol and paraffin. ▷ **HISTORY** Latin *petra* stone + *oleum* oil

petroleum jelly *n* same as **petrolatum**.

petrol station *n Brit* same as **filling station**.

petticoat *n* a woman's underskirt. ▷ **HISTORY** from *petty* + *coat*

pettifogging *adj* excessively concerned with unimportant detail. ▷ **HISTORY** origin unknown ▶ **pettifogger** *n*

petty *adj* **-tier, -tiest 1** trivial or unimportant: *petty details.* **2** small-minded: *petty spite.* **3** low in importance: *petty criminals.* ▷ **HISTORY** French *petit* little ▶ **pettily** *adv* ▶ **pettiness** *n*

petty apartheid *n* History (formerly, in South Africa) a form of apartheid as applied in trivial or everyday situations.

petty cash *n* a small cash fund for minor incidental expenses.

petty officer *n* a noncommissioned officer in the navy.

petulant *adj* unreasonably irritable or peevish. ▷ **HISTORY** Latin *petulans* bold ▶ **petulance** *n* ▶ **petulantly** *adv*

petunia *n* a tropical American plant with pink, white, or purple funnel-shaped flowers. ▷ **HISTORY** obsolete French *petun* variety of tobacco

pew *n* **1** (in a church) **a** a long benchlike seat with a back, used by the congregation. **b** an enclosed compartment reserved for the use of a family or group. **2 take a pew** take a seat. ▷ **HISTORY** Greek *pous* foot

pewter *n* **1** an alloy containing tin, lead, and sometimes copper and antimony. **2** dishes or kitchen utensils made from pewter. ▷ **HISTORY** Old French *peaultre*

PG indicating a film certified for viewing by anyone, but which contains scenes that may be unsuitable for children, for whom parental guidance is necessary.

pH *n* potential of hydrogen; a measure of the acidity or alkalinity of a solution.

phagocyte (**fag**-go-site) *n* a cell or protozoan that engulfs particles, such as microorganisms. ▷ **HISTORY** Greek *phagein* to eat + *kutos* vessel

phalanger *n* an Australian marsupial with dense fur and a long tail. ▷ **HISTORY** Greek *phalaggion* spider's web, referring to its webbed hind toes

phalanx (**fal**-lanks) *n, pl* **phalanxes** *or* **phalanges** (fal-**lan**-jeez) **1** any closely grouped mass of people: *a solid phalanx of reporters and photographers.* **2** a number of people united for a common purpose. **3** an ancient Greek battle formation of infantry in close ranks. ▷ **HISTORY** Greek

phallic *adj* of or resembling a phallus: *a phallic symbol.*

phallus (**fal**-luss) *n, pl* **-luses** *or* **-li** (-lie) **1** same as **penis**. **2** an image of the penis as a symbol of reproductive power. ▷ **HISTORY** Greek *phallos*

phantasm *n* **1** a phantom. **2** an unreal vision; illusion. ▷ **HISTORY** Greek *phantasma* ▶ **phantasmal** *adj*

phantasmagoria *n* a shifting medley of dreamlike figures. ▷ **HISTORY** probably from French *fantasmagorie* production of phantoms ▶ **phantasmagoric** *adj*

phantasy *n, pl* **-sies** *Archaic* same as **fantasy**.

phantom *n* **1** an apparition or spectre. **2** the visible representation of something abstract, such as in a dream or hallucination: *the phantom of liberty.* ✧ *adj* **3** deceptive or unreal: *she regularly took days off for what her bosses considered phantom illnesses.* ▷ **HISTORY** Latin *phantasma*

Pharaoh (**fare**-oh) *n* the title of the ancient Egyptian kings. ▷ **HISTORY** Egyptian *pr-'o* great house

Pharisee *n* **1** a member of an ancient Jewish sect teaching strict observance of Jewish traditions. **2** (*often not cap*) a self-righteous or hypocritical person. ▷ **HISTORY** Hebrew *pārūsh* separated ▶ **Pharisaic** *adj*

pharmaceutical *adj* of or relating to drugs or pharmacy.

pharmaceutics *n* same as **pharmacy** (sense 1).

pharmacist *n* a person qualified to prepare and dispense drugs.

pharmacology *n* the science or study of drugs. ▶ **pharmacological** *adj* ▶ **pharmacologist** *n*

pharmacopoeia (far-ma-koh-**pee**-a) *n* an authoritative book containing a list of medicinal drugs along with their uses, preparation and dosages. ▷ **HISTORY** Greek *pharmakopoiia* art of preparing drugs

pharmacy *n* **1** the preparation and dispensing of drugs. **2** (*pl* **-cies**) a dispensary. ▷ **HISTORY** Greek *pharmakon* drug

pharyngitis (far-rin-**jite**-iss) *n* inflammation of the pharynx, causing a sore throat.

pharynx (**far**-rinks) *n, pl* **pharynges** (far-**rin**-jeez) *or* **pharynxes** the part of the alimentary canal between the mouth and the oesophagus. ▷ **HISTORY** Greek *pharunx* throat ▶ **pharyngeal** *adj*

phase *n* **1** any distinct or characteristic stage in a sequence of events: *these two CDs sum up two distinct phases in the singer's career.* **2** *Astron* one of the recurring shapes of the portion of the moon, Mercury, or Venus illuminated by the sun. **3** *Physics* a particular stage in a periodic process or phenomenon. **4** *Physics* **in** *or* **out of phase** (of two waves or signals) reaching or not reaching corresponding phases at the same time. ✧ *vb* **phasing, phased 5** to do or introduce gradually: *the redundancies will be phased over two years.* ▷ **HISTORY** Greek *phasis* aspect

phase in *vb* to introduce in a gradual or cautious manner: *the scheme was phased in over seven years.*

PhD Doctor of Philosophy.

pheasant *n* a long-tailed bird with a brightly coloured plumage in the male: native to Asia but introduced elsewhere. ▷ **HISTORY** Latin *phasianus*

phenobarbitone *or* **phenobarbital** *n* a sedative used to treat insomnia and epilepsy.

phenol *n* a white crystalline derivative of benzene, used as an antiseptic and disinfectant and in the manufacture of resins, explosives, and pharmaceutical substances. ▷ **HISTORY** Greek *phaino-* shining; because originally prepared from illuminating gas

phenolphtalein (fee-noll-**fthal**-ee-in) *n Chem* a colourless crystalline compound used in medicine as a laxative and in chemistry as an indicator.

phenomenal *adj* **1** extraordinary or outstanding: *a phenomenal success.* **2** of or relating to a phenomenon. ▶ **phenomenally** *adv*

phenomenalism *n Philosophy* the doctrine that all knowledge comes from sense perception. ▶ **phenomenalist** *n, adj*

phenomenon *n, pl* **-ena** *or* **-enons 1** anything that can be perceived as an occurrence or fact. **2** any remarkable occurrence or person. ▷ **HISTORY** Greek *phainomenon,* from *phainesthai* to appear

> **☑ WORD TIP**
> Although *phenomena* is often treated as if it were singular, correct usage is to employ *phenomenon* with a singular construction and *phenomena* with a plural: *that is an interesting phenomenon* (not *phenomena*)*; several new phenomena were recorded in his notes.*

phenotype *n* the physical form of an organism as determined by the interaction of its genetic make-up and its environment.

phenyl (**fee**-nile) *adj* of, containing, or consisting of the monovalent group C_6H_5, derived from benzene: *a phenyl group.*

phew *interj* an exclamation of relief, surprise, disbelief, or weariness.

phial *n* a small bottle for liquid medicine. ▷ **HISTORY** Greek *phialē* wide shallow vessel

phil. 1 philharmonic. **2** philosophy.

philadelphus *n* a shrub grown for its strongly scented showy flowers. ▷ **HISTORY** Greek *philadelphon,* literally: loving one's brother

philanthropy *n, pl* **-pies 1** the practice of helping people less well-off than oneself. **2** love of mankind in general. ▷ **HISTORY** Greek *philanthrōpia* love of mankind ▶ **philanthropic** *adj* ▶ **philanthropist** *n*

philately (fill-**lat**-a-lee) *n* the collection and study of postage stamps. ▷ **HISTORY** Greek *philos* loving + *ateleia* exemption from tax ▶ **philatelist** *n*

philharmonic *adj* **1** fond of music. ✧ *n* **2** a specific choir, orchestra, or musical society: *the Vienna Philharmonic.* ▷ **HISTORY** French *philharmonique*

philippic *n* a bitter verbal attack. ▷ **HISTORY** after the orations of Demosthenes against Philip of Macedon

Philippine *adj, n* same as **Filipino**.

philistine *n* **1** a person who is hostile towards culture and the arts. ✧ *adj* **2** boorishly uncultured. ▶ **philistinism** *n*

Philistine *n* a member of the non-Semitic people who inhabited ancient Palestine.

philology *n* the science of the structure and development of languages. ▷ **HISTORY** Greek *philologia* love of language ▶ **philological** *adj* ▶ **philologist** *n*

philosopher *n* **1** a person who studies philosophy. **2** a person who remains calm and stoical in the face of difficulties or disappointments.

philosopher's stone *n* a substance thought by alchemists to be capable of changing base metals into gold.

philosophical *or* **philosophic** *adj* **1** of or relating to philosophy or philosophers. **2** calm and stoical in the face of difficulties or disappointments. ▶ **philosophically** *adv*

philosophize *or* **-phise** *vb* **-phizing, -phized** *or* **-phising, -phised** to discuss in a philosophical manner. ▶ **philosophizer** *or* **-phiser** *n*

philosophy *n, pl* **-phies 1** the academic study of knowledge, thought, and the meaning of life. **2** the particular doctrines of a specific individual or school relating to these issues: *the philosophy of John Locke.* **3** any system of beliefs or values. **4** a personal outlook or viewpoint. ▷ HISTORY Greek *philosophia* love of wisdom

philtre *or US* **philter** *n* a drink supposed to arouse desire. ▷ HISTORY Greek *philtron* love potion

phlebitis (fleb-**bite**-iss) *n* inflammation of a vein, usually in the legs. ▷ HISTORY Greek *phleps* vein ▶ **phlebitic** *adj*

phlegm (**flem**) *n* **1** the thick yellowish substance secreted by the walls of the respiratory tract. **2** apathy or stolidity. **3** calmness. ▷ HISTORY Greek *phlegma* ▶ **phlegmy** *adj*

phlegmatic (fleg-**mat**-ik) *adj* having an unemotional disposition.

phloem (**flow**-em) *n Bot* the plant tissue that acts as a path for the distribution of food substances to all parts of the plant. ▷ HISTORY Greek *phloos* bark

phlox *n, pl* **phlox** *or* **phloxes** a plant with clusters of white, red, or purple flowers. ▷ HISTORY Greek, literally: flame

phobia *n Psychiatry* an intense and irrational fear of a given situation or thing. ▷ HISTORY Greek *phobos* fear ▶ **phobic** *adj, n*

Phoenician (fon-**nee**-shun) *adj* **1** of Phoenicia, an ancient E Mediterranean country. ✧ *n* **2** a person from Phoenicia.

phoenix *n* a legendary Arabian bird said to set fire to itself and rise anew from the ashes every 500 years. ▷ HISTORY Greek *phoinix*

phone *n, vb* **phoning, phoned** short for **telephone**.

phonecard *n* a card used instead of coins to operate certain public telephones.

phone-in *n Brit, Austral & S African* a radio or television programme in which telephone questions or comments from the public are broadcast live as part of a discussion.

phoneme *n Linguistics* one of the set of speech sounds in any given language that serve to distinguish one word from another. ▷ HISTORY Greek *phōnēma* sound, speech ▶ **phonemic** *adj*

phonemics *n* the classification and analysis of the phonemes of a language.

phonetic *adj* **1** of phonetics. **2** denoting any perceptible distinction between one speech sound and another. **3** conforming to pronunciation: *phonetic spelling.* ▷ HISTORY Greek *phōnein* to make sounds, speak ▶ **phonetically** *adv*

phonetics *n* the study of speech processes, including the production, perception, and analysis of speech sounds.

phoney *or esp US* **phony** *Informal* ✧ *adj* **-nier, -niest 1** not genuine: *a phoney Belgian 50-franc coin.* **2** (of a person) insincere or pretentious. ✧ *n, pl* **-neys** *or esp US* **-nies 3** an insincere or pretentious person. **4** something that is not genuine. ▷ HISTORY origin unknown

phonics *n* (*functioning as sing*) a method of teaching people to read by training them to associate letters with their phonetic values. ▶ **phonic** *adj* ▶ **phonically** *adv*

phonograph *n* **1** an early form of record player capable of recording and reproducing sound on wax cylinders. **2** *US & Canad* a record player. ▷ HISTORY Greek *phonē* sound + *graphein* to write

phonology *n, pl* **-gies 1** the study of the sound system in a language. **2** such a sound system. ▷ HISTORY Greek *phonē* sound, voice + -LOGY ▶ **phonological** *adj*

phosgene (**foz**-jean) *n* a poisonous gas used in warfare. ▷ HISTORY Greek *phōs* light + *-genēs* born

phosphate *n* **1** any salt or ester of any phosphoric acid. **2** (*often pl*) chemical fertilizer containing phosphorous compounds. ▶ **phosphatic** *adj*

phosphor *n* a substance capable of emitting light when irradiated with particles of electromagnetic radiation. ▷ HISTORY Greek *phōsphoros* phosphorus

phosphoresce *vb* **-rescing, -resced** to exhibit phosphorescence.

phosphorescence *n* **1** *Physics* a fluorescence that persists after the bombarding radiation producing it has stopped. **2** the light emitted in phosphorescence. ▶ **phosphorescent** *adj*

phosphoric *adj* of or containing phosphorus in the pentavalent state.

phosphorous *adj* of or containing phosphorus in the trivalent state.

phosphorus *n Chem* a toxic flammable nonmetallic element which appears luminous in the dark. It exists in two forms, white and red. Symbol: P. ▷ HISTORY Greek *phōsphoros* light-bringing

photo *n, pl* **-tos** short for **photograph**.

photo- *combining form* **1** of or produced by light: *photosynthesis.* **2** indicating a photographic process: *photolithography.* ▷ HISTORY Greek *phōs, phōt-* light

photocell *n* a cell which produces a current or voltage when exposed to light or other electromagnetic radiation.

photochemical smog *n Environmental science* a kind of smog caused by chemical reactions involving light, ozone, and pollutants that occurs in big cities.

photocopier *n* a machine using light-sensitive photographic materials to reproduce written, printed, or graphic work.

photocopy *n, pl* **-copies 1** a photographic reproduction of written, printed, or graphic work. ✧ *vb* **-copies, -copying, -copied 2** to reproduce on photographic material.

photoelectric *adj* of or concerned with electric or electronic effects caused by light or other electromagnetic radiation. ▶ **photoelectricity** *n*

photo finish *n* a finish of a race in which contestants are so close that a photograph is needed to decide the result.

Photofit *n Trademark* a picture of someone wanted by the police which has been made by combining photographs of different facial features resembling those of the wanted person.

photoflash *n* same as **flashbulb**.

photoflood *n* a highly incandescent electric lamp used for indoor photography and television.

photogenic *adj* **1** (esp. of a person) always looking attractive in photographs. **2** *Biol* producing or emitting light.

photograph *n* **1** a picture made by the chemical action of light on sensitive film. ✧ *vb* **2** to take a photograph of.

photographic *adj* **1** of or like photography or a photograph. **2** (of a person's memory) able to retain facts or appearances in precise detail.
▸ **photographically** *adv*

photographic image *n* **1** a photograph. **2** the way something or someone is presented in a photograph.

photography *n* **1** the process of recording images on sensitized material by the action of light. **2** the practice of taking photographs.
▸ **photographer** *n*

photogravure *n* a process in which an etched metal plate for printing is produced by photography. ▷ **HISTORY** PHOTO- + French *gravure* engraving

photojournalism *n* journalism in which photographs are the predominant feature.
▸ **photojournalist** *n*

photolithography *n* a lithographic printing process using photographically made plates.
▸ **photolithographer** *n*

photometer (foe-**tom**-it-er) *n* an instrument used to measure the intensity of light.

photometry (foe-**tom**-it-tree) *n* the branch of physics concerned with the measurement of the intensity of light. ▸ **photometrist** *n*

photomontage (foe-toe-mon-**tahzh**) *n* **1** the combination of several photographs to produce one picture. **2** a picture produced in this way.

photon *n Physics* a quantum of electromagnetic radiation energy, such as light, having both particle and wave behaviour.

photoreceptor *n Zool, Physiol* a light-sensitive cell or organ that conveys impulses through a sensory neuron.

photosensitive *adj* sensitive to electromagnetic radiation, esp. light.

photostat *n* **1** a type of photocopying machine or process. **2** any copy made by such a machine. ✧ *vb* **-statting, -statted** *or* **-stating, -stated** **3** to make a photostat copy (of).

photosynthesis *n Biol, geog* (in plants) the process by which a green plant uses sunlight to build up carbohydrate reserves.
▸ **photosynthesize** *or* **-sise** *vb* ▸ **photosynthetic** *adj*

phototropism (foe-toe-**trope**-iz-zum) *n* the growth of plants towards a source of light.
▷ **HISTORY** PHOTO- + Greek *tropos* turn
▸ **phototropic** *adj*

phrasal verb *n* a phrase that consists of a verb plus an adverb or preposition, esp. one whose meaning cannot be deduced from its parts, such as *take in* meaning *deceive*.

phrase *n* **1** a group of words forming a unit of meaning in a sentence. **2** an idiomatic or original expression. **3** *Music* a small group of notes forming a coherent unit of melody. ✧ *vb* **phrasing, phrased** **4** to express orally or in a phrase: *I could have phrased that better.* **5** *Music* to divide (a melodic line or part) into musical phrases, esp. in performance.
▷ **HISTORY** Greek *phrasis* speech ▸ **phrasal** *adj*

phrase book *n* a book containing frequently used expressions and their equivalent in a foreign language.

phraseology *n, pl* **-gies** the manner in which words or phrases are used.

phrasing *n* **1** the exact words used to say or write something. **2** the way in which someone who is performing a piece of music or reading aloud divides up the work being performed by pausing slightly in appropriate places.

phrenology *n* (formerly) the study of the shape and size of the skull as a means of finding out a person's character and mental ability.
▷ **HISTORY** Greek *phrēn* mind + -LOGY
▸ **phrenological** *adj* ▸ **phrenologist** *n*

pH-scale *n Chem* a method of measuring the acidity or alkalinity of a solution.

phut *Informal* ✧ *n* **1** a representation of a muffled explosive sound. ✧ *adv* **2 go phut** to break down or collapse. ▷ **HISTORY** imitative

phylactery *n, pl* **-teries** *Judaism* either of the pair of square cases containing biblical passages, worn by Jewish men on the left arm and head during weekday morning prayers. ▷ **HISTORY** Greek *phulaktērion* safeguard

phylum *n, pl* **-la** *Biol* one of the major groups into which the animal and plant kingdoms are divided, containing one or more classes. ▷ **HISTORY** Greek *phulon* race

physical *adj* **1** of the body, as distinguished from the mind or spirit. **2** of material things or nature: *the physical world.* **3** of or concerned with matter and energy. **4** of or relating to physics. ▸ **physically** *adv*

physical education *n* training and practice in sports and gymnastics.

physical geography *n* the branch of geography that deals with the natural features of the earth's surface.

physical jerks *pl n Brit & Austral informal* repetitive keep-fit exercises.

physical science *n* any of the sciences concerned with nonliving matter, such as physics, chemistry, astronomy, and geology.

physical weathering *n Geol* damage such as erosion, caused to rocks as a result of being exposed to wind, water, or ice.

A B C D E F G H I J K L M N O P Q R S T U V W X Y Z

physician *n* **1** a medical doctor. **2** *Archaic* a healer. ▷ **HISTORY** Greek *phusis* nature

physicist *n* a person versed in or studying physics.

physics *n* **1** the branch of science concerned with the properties of matter and energy and the relationships between them. **2** physical properties of behaviour: *the physics of the electron.* ▷ **HISTORY** translation of Greek *ta phusika* natural things

physio *n* **1** short for **physiotherapy**. **2** (*pl* **physios**) short for **physiotherapist**.

physiognomy (fiz-ee-**on**-om-ee) *n* **1** a person's face considered as an indication of personality. **2** the outward appearance of something: *the changed physiognomy of the forests.* ▷ **HISTORY** Greek *phusis* nature + *gnōmōn* judge

physiography *n* same as **physical geography**. ▶ **physiographic** *adj* ▷ **HISTORY** Greek *phusis* nature + -GRAPHY

physiology *n* **1** the branch of science concerned with the functioning of organisms. **2** the processes and functions of all or part of an organism. ▷ **HISTORY** Greek *phusis* nature + -LOGY ▶ **physiologist** *n* ▶ **physiological** *adj*

physiotherapy *n* the treatment of disease or injury by physical means, such as massage or exercises, rather than by drugs. ▶ **physiotherapist** *n* ▷ **HISTORY** *physio-* (prefix) physical + *therapy*

physique *n* person's bodily build and muscular development. ▷ **HISTORY** French

pi *n, pl* **pis 1** the 16th letter in the Greek alphabet (Π, π). **2** *Maths* a number that is the ratio of the circumference of a circle to its diameter; approximate value: 3.141 592.. Symbol: π.

pianissimo *adj, adv Music* to be performed very quietly. ▷ **HISTORY** Italian

pianist *n* a person who plays the piano.

piano¹ *n, pl* **-anos** a musical instrument played by depressing keys that cause hammers to strike strings and produce audible vibrations. ▷ **HISTORY** short for *pianoforte*

piano² *adj, adv Music* to be performed softly. ▷ **HISTORY** Italian

Pianola (pee-an-**oh**-la) *n Trademark* a type of mechanical piano, the music for which is encoded in perforations in a paper roll.

piazza *n* **1** a large open square in an Italian town. **2** *Chiefly Brit* a covered passageway or gallery. ▷ **HISTORY** Italian: marketplace

pibroch (**pee**-brok) *n* a form of music for Scottish bagpipes, consisting of a theme and variations. ▷ **HISTORY** Gaelic *piobaireachd*

pic *n, pl* **pics** *or* **pix** *Informal* a photograph or illustration.

pica (**pie**-ka) *n* **1** a size of printer's type giving 6 lines to the inch. **2** a size of typewriter type that has 10 characters to the inch. ▷ **HISTORY** Latin *pica* magpie; sense connection obscure

picador *n Bullfighting* a horseman who wounds the bull with a lance to weaken it. ▷ **HISTORY** Spanish

picaresque *adj* of or relating to a type of fiction in which the hero, a rogue, goes through a series of episodic adventures. ▷ **HISTORY** Spanish *pícaro* a rogue

piccalilli *n* a pickle of mixed vegetables in a mustard sauce. ▷ **HISTORY** origin unknown

piccanin *n S African offensive* a Black African child. ▷ **HISTORY** variant of *piccaninny*

piccolo *n, pl* **-los** a woodwind instrument an octave higher than the flute. ▷ **HISTORY** Italian: small

pick¹ *vb* **1** to choose or select. **2** to gather (fruit, berries, or crops) from (a tree, bush, or field). **3** to remove loose particles from: *she picked some bits of fluff off her sleeve.* **4** (foll. by *at*) to nibble (at) without appetite. **5** to provoke (an argument or fight) deliberately. **6** to separate (strands or fibres), as in weaving. **7** to steal from (someone's pocket). **8** to open (a lock) with an instrument other than a key. **9** to make (one's way) carefully on foot: *they picked their way through the rubble.* **10 pick and choose** to select fastidiously or fussily. ✧ *n* **11** choice: *take your pick.* **12** the best: *the pick of the country's young cricketers.* ✧ See also **pick off, pick on**, etc. ▷ **HISTORY** Middle English *piken*

pick² *n* **1** a tool with a handle and a long curved steel head, used for loosening soil or breaking rocks. **2** any tool used for picking, such as an ice pick or toothpick. **3** a plectrum. ✧ *vb* **4** to pierce or break up (a hard surface) with a pick. ▷ **HISTORY** perhaps a variant of PIKE²

pickaxe *or US* **pickax** *n* a large pick.

picket *n* **1** a person or group standing outside a workplace to dissuade strikebreakers from entering. **2** a small unit of troops posted to give early warning of attack. **3** a pointed stake that is driven into the ground to support a fence. ✧ *vb* **-eting, -eted 4** to act as pickets outside (a workplace). ▷ **HISTORY** Old French *piquer* to prick

picket line *n* a line of people acting as pickets.

pickings *pl n* money or profits acquired easily.

pickle *n* **1** (*often pl*) food, esp. vegetables preserved in vinegar or brine. **2** a liquid or marinade, such as spiced vinegar, for preserving vegetables, meat, or fish. **3** *Informal* an awkward or difficult situation: *to be in a pickle; they are in a pickle over what to do with toxic waste.* ✧ *vb* **-ling, -led 4** to preserve or treat in a pickling liquid. ▷ **HISTORY** probably Middle Dutch *pekel*

pickled *adj* **1** (of food) preserved in a pickling liquid. **2** *Informal* drunk.

pick-me-up *n Informal* a tonic, esp. a special drink taken as a stimulant.

pick off *vb* to aim at and shoot (people or things) one by one.

pick on *vb* to continually treat someone unfairly.

pick out *vb* **1** to select for use or special consideration: *she picked out a wide gold wedding ring.* **2** to distinguish (an object from its surroundings), such as in painting: *the wall panels are light brown, with their edges picked out in gold.* **3** to recognize (a person or thing): *the culprit was picked out at a police identification parade.* **4** to play (a tune) tentatively, as by ear.

pickpocket *n* a person who steals from the pockets of others in public places.

pick up *vb* **1** to lift or raise: *he picked up his glass.* **2** to obtain or purchase: *a couple of pictures she had picked up in a flea market in Paris.* **3** to improve in health or condition: *the tourist trade has picked up after the slump caused by the Gulf War.* **4** to learn as one goes along: *she had a good ear and picked up languages quickly.* **5** to raise (oneself) after a fall or setback: *she picked herself up and got on with her life.* **6** to resume; return to. **7** to accept the responsibility for paying (a bill). **8** to collect or give a lift to (passengers or goods). **9** *Informal* to become acquainted with for a sexual purpose. **10** *Informal* to arrest. **11** to receive (sounds or signals).

pick-up *n* **1** a small truck with an open body used for light deliveries. **2** *Informal* a casual acquaintance made for a sexual purpose. **3** *Informal* **a** a stop to collect passengers or goods. **b** the people or things collected. **4** a device which converts vibrations into electrical signals, such as that to which a record player stylus is attached.

picky *adj* **pickier, pickiest** *Brit, Austral & NZ informal* fussy; finicky.

picnic *n* **1** an excursion on which people bring food to be eaten in the open air. **2** an informal meal eaten out-of-doors. **3 no picnic** *Informal* a hard or disagreeable task. ✧ *vb* **-nicking, -nicked 4** to eat or take part in a picnic. ▷ **HISTORY** French *piquenique* ▶ **picnicker** *n*

pico- *combining form* denoting 10^{-12}: *picofarad.* ▷ **HISTORY** Spanish *pico* small quantity

picot (**peek**-oh) *n* any of a pattern of small loops, for example on lace.

Pict *n* a member of any of the peoples who lived in N Britain in the first to the fourth centuries AD. ▷ **HISTORY** Late Latin *Picti* painted men ▶ **Pictish** *adj*

pictograph *n* **1** a picture or symbol standing for a word or group of words, as in written Chinese. **2** Also called: **pictogram** a chart on which symbols are used to represent values. ▷ **HISTORY** Latin *pingere* to paint ▶ **pictographic** *adj*

pictorial *adj* **1** relating to or expressed by pictures. ✧ *n* **2** a periodical containing many pictures. ▷ **HISTORY** Latin *pingere* to paint

picture *n* **1** a visual representation produced on a surface, such as in a photograph or painting. **2** a mental image: *neither had any clear picture of whom they were looking for.* **3** a description or account of a situation considered as an observable scene: *the reports do not provide an accurate picture of the spread of AIDS.* **4** a person or thing resembling another: *he is the picture of a perfect host.* **5** a person or scene typifying a particular state: *his face was a picture of dejection.* **6** the image on a television screen. **7** a cinema film. **8 the pictures** a cinema or film show. **9 in the picture** informed about a situation. ✧ *vb* **-turing, -tured 10** to visualize or imagine. **11** to describe or depict vividly: *a documentary that had pictured the police as good-natured dolts.* **12** to put in a picture or make a picture of: *the women pictured above are all the same age.* ▷ **HISTORY** Latin *pingere* to paint

picture rail *n* the rail near the top of a wall from which pictures are hung.

picturesque *adj* **1** visually pleasing, as in being striking or quaint: *a small picturesque harbour.* **2** (of language) graphic or vivid. ▷ **HISTORY** French *pittoresque*

picture window *n* a large window with a single pane of glass, usually facing a view.

piddle *vb* **-dling, -dled 1** *Informal* to urinate. **2 piddle about, around** *or* **away** to spend (one's time) aimlessly: *we have been piddling around for seven months.* ▷ **HISTORY** origin unknown

piddling *adj Informal* petty or trivial: *piddling amounts of money.*

pidgin *n* a language made up of elements of two or more languages and used between the speakers of the languages involved. ▷ **HISTORY** supposed Chinese pronunciation of *business*

pidgin English *n* a pidgin in which one of the languages involved is English.

pie *n* **1** a sweet or savoury filling baked in pastry. **2 pie in the sky** illusory hope or promise of some future good. ▷ **HISTORY** origin unknown

piebald *adj* **1** marked in two colours, esp. black and white. ✧ *n* **2** a black-and-white horse. ▷ **HISTORY** dialect *pie* magpie + BALD

piece *n* **1** a separate bit or part. **2** an instance or occurrence: *a piece of luck.* **3** an example or specimen of a style or type: *each piece of furniture is crafted from native red pine by traditional methods.* **4** a literary, musical, or artistic composition. **5** a coin: *a fifty-pence piece.* **6** a firearm or cannon. **7** a small object used in playing various games: *a chess piece.* **8 go to pieces** (of a person) to lose control of oneself; have a breakdown. ✧ *vb* **piecing, pieced 9** (often foll. by *together*) to fit or assemble bit by bit. **10** (often foll. by *up*) to patch or make up (a garment) by adding pieces. ▷ **HISTORY** Middle English *pece*

pièce de résistance (**pyess** de ray-**zeest**-onss) *n* the most outstanding item in a series. ▷ **HISTORY** French

piecemeal *adv* **1** bit by bit; gradually. ✧ *adj* **2** fragmentary or unsystematic: *a piecemeal approach.* ▷ **HISTORY** Middle English *pece* piece + *-mele* a measure

piece rate *n Business* a fixed rate paid according to the quantity produced.

piecework *n* work paid for according to the quantity produced.

pie chart *n* a circular graph divided into sectors proportional to the sizes of the quantities represented.

pied *adj* having markings of two or more colours. ▷ **HISTORY** dialect *pie* magpie

pied-à-terre (**pyay**-da-**tair**) *n, pl* **pieds-à-terre** (**pyay**-da-**tair**) a flat or other lodging for occasional use. ▷ **HISTORY** French, literally: foot on (the) ground

pie-eyed *adj Slang* drunk.

pier *n* **1** a structure with a deck that is built out over water and used as a landing place or promenade. **2** a pillar or support that bears heavy loads. **3** the part of a wall between two adjacent openings. ▷ **HISTORY** Middle English *per*

pierce *vb* **piercing, pierced 1** to make a hole in (something) with a sharp point. **2** to force (a way) through (something). **3** (of light) to shine through (darkness). **4** (of sounds or cries) to sound sharply through (the silence). **5** to penetrate: *the cold pierced the air.* ▷ **HISTORY** Old French *percer* ▶ **piercing** *adj*

Pierrot (**pier**-roe) *n* a male character from French pantomime with a whitened face, white costume, and pointed hat.

pietism *n* exaggerated piety.

piety *n, pl* **-ties 1** dutiful devotion to God and observance of religious principles. **2** the quality of being pious. **3** a pious action or saying. ▷ **HISTORY** Latin *pietas*

piezoelectric effect (pie-eez-oh-ill-**ek**-trik) *or* **piezoelectricity** *n Physics* **a** the production of electricity by applying a mechanical stress to certain crystals. **b** the converse effect in which stress is produced in a crystal as a result of an applied voltage. ▷ **HISTORY** Greek *piezein* to press

piffle *n Informal* nonsense. ▷ **HISTORY** origin unknown

pig *n* **1** a mammal with a long head, a snout, and bristle-covered skin, which is kept and killed for pork, ham, and bacon. *RELATED ADJECTIVE* ▶ **porcine** **2** *Informal* a dirty, greedy, or bad-mannered person. **3** *Offensive slang* a policeman. **4** a mass of metal cast into a simple shape. **5** *Brit informal* something that is difficult or unpleasant: *the coast is a pig for little boats.* **6 a pig in a poke** something bought or received without previous sight or knowledge. **7 make a pig of oneself** *Informal* to overeat. ✧ *vb* **pigging, pigged 8** (of a sow) to give birth. **9** (often foll. by *out*) *Slang* to eat greedily or to excess: *she had pigged out on pizza before the show.* ▷ **HISTORY** Middle English *pigge*

pigeon¹ *n* **1** a bird which has a heavy body, small head, and short legs, and is usually grey in colour. **2** *Slang* a victim or dupe. ▷ **HISTORY** Old French *pijon* young dove

pigeon² *n Informal* concern or responsibility: *this is our pigeon – there's nothing to keep you.* ▷ **HISTORY** from *pidgin*

pigeonhole *n* **1** a small compartment, such as in a bureau, for filing papers. ✧ *vb* **-holing, -holed 2** to classify or categorize. **3** to put aside.

pigeon-toed *adj* with the toes or feet turned inwards.

piggery *n, pl* **-geries** a place where pigs are kept.

piggish *adj* **1** like a pig in appetite or manners. **2** stubborn. ▶ **piggishness** *n*

piggy *n, pl* **-gies 1** a child's word for a **pig**. ✧ *adj* **-gier, -giest 2** same as **piggish**.

piggyback *or* **pickaback** *n* **1** a ride on the back and shoulders of another person. ✧ *adv, adj* **2** on the back and shoulders of another person.

piggy bank *n* a child's bank shaped like a pig with a slot for coins.

pig-headed *adj* stupidly stubborn.

pig iron *n* crude iron produced in a blast furnace and poured into moulds.

piglet *n* a young pig.

pigment *n* **1** any substance which gives colour to paint or dye. **2** a substance which occurs in plant or animal tissue and produces a characteristic colour. ▷ **HISTORY** Latin *pigmentum* ▶ **pigmentary** *adj*

pigmentation *n* colouring in plants, animals, or humans, caused by the presence of pigments.

Pigmy *n, pl* **-mies** same as **Pygmy**.

pigsty *or US & Canad* **pigpen** *n, pl* **-sties 1** a pen for pigs. **2** *Brit & Austral* an untidy place.

pigswill *n* waste food or other edible matter fed to pigs.

pigtail *n* a plait of hair or one of two plaits on either side of the face.

pike¹ *n, pl* **pike** *or* **pikes** a large predatory freshwater fish with a broad flat snout, strong teeth, and a long body covered with small scales. ▷ **HISTORY** Old English *pīc* point, from the shape of its jaw

pike² *n* a medieval weapon consisting of a metal spearhead on a long pole. ▷ **HISTORY** Old English *pīc* point ▶ **pikeman** *n*

pikelet *n Austral & NZ* a small thick pancake.

piker *n Austral & NZ slang* shirker.

pilaster *n* a shallow rectangular column attached to the face of a wall. ▷ **HISTORY** Latin *pila* pillar ▶ **pilastered** *adj*

pilau *or* **pilaf** *n* a Middle Eastern dish, consisting of rice flavoured with spices and cooked in stock, to which meat, poultry, or fish may be added. ▷ **HISTORY** Turkish *pilāw*

pilchard *n* a small edible sea fish of the herring family, with a rounded body covered with large scales. ▷ **HISTORY** origin unknown

pile¹ *n* **1** a collection of objects laid on top of one another. **2** *Informal* a large amount: *boxing has made him a pile of money; I've got piles of work to do.* **3** same as **pyre**. **4** a large building or group of buildings. **5** *Physics* a nuclear reactor. ✧ *vb* **piling, piled 6** (often foll. by *up*) to collect or be collected into a pile: *snow piled up in the drive.* **7** (foll. by *in, into, off, out*) etc. to move in a group, often in a hurried manner: *the crew piled into the van.* **8 pile it on** *Informal* to exaggerate. ▷ **HISTORY** Latin *pila* stone pier

pile² *n* a long heavy beam driven into the ground as a foundation for a structure. ▷ **HISTORY** Latin *pilum*

pile³ *n* the fibres in a fabric that stand up or out from the weave, such as in carpeting or velvet. ▷ **HISTORY** Latin *pilus* hair

pile-driver *n* a machine that drives piles into the ground.

piles *pl n* swollen veins in the rectum; haemorrhoids. ▷ **HISTORY** Latin *pilae* balls

pilfer *vb* to steal (minor items) in small quantities. ▷ **HISTORY** Old French *pelfre* booty

pilgrim *n* **1** a person who journeys to a holy place. **2** any wayfarer. ▷ **HISTORY** Latin *peregrinus* foreign

pilgrimage *n* **1** a journey to a shrine or other holy place. **2** a journey or long search made for sentimental reasons: *a sentimental pilgrimage to the poet's birthplace.*

Pilgrim Fathers *pl n* the English Puritans who founded Plymouth Colony in SE Massachusetts (1620).

pill *n* **1** a small mass of medicine intended to be swallowed whole. **2 the pill** *Informal* an oral contraceptive taken by a woman. **3** something unpleasant that must be endured: *her reinstatement was a bitter pill to swallow; the pill was sweetened by a reduction in interest.* ▷ **HISTORY** Latin *pilula* a little ball

pillage *vb* **-laging, -laged 1** to steal property violently, often in war. ✧ *n* **2** the act of pillaging. **3** something obtained by pillaging; booty. ▷ **HISTORY** Old French *piller* to despoil

pillar *n* **1** an upright support of stone, brick, or metal; column. **2** something resembling this: *a pillar of smoke.* **3** a prominent supporter or member: *a pillar of society.* **4 from pillar to post** from one place to another. ▷ **HISTORY** Latin *pila*

pillar box *n* (in Britain) a red pillar-shaped public letter box situated in the street.

pillbox *n* **1** a box for pills. **2** a small enclosed fort of reinforced concrete. **3** a small round hat.

pillion *n* **1** a seat for a passenger behind the rider of a motorcycle or horse. ✧ *adv* **2** on a pillion: *the motorbike on which he was riding pillion.* ▷ **HISTORY** from Gaelic

pillory *n, pl* **-ries 1** *Historical* a wooden frame in which offenders were locked by the neck and wrists and exposed to public abuse and ridicule. ✧ *vb* **-ries, -rying, -ried 2** to expose to public ridicule. **3** to punish by putting in a pillory. ▷ **HISTORY** Old French *pilori*

pillow *n* **1** a cloth bag stuffed with feathers, polyester fibre, or pieces of foam rubber used to support the head in bed. ✧ *vb* **2** to rest (one's head) on or as if on a pillow: *he pillowed his head in her lap.* ▷ **HISTORY** Old English *pylwe*

pillowcase *or* **pillowslip** *n* a removable washable cover for a pillow.

pilot *n* **1** a person who is qualified to fly an aircraft or spacecraft. **2** a person employed to steer a ship into or out of a port. **3** a person who acts as a guide. ✧ *adj* **4** serving as a test or trial: *a pilot scheme.* **5** serving as a guide: *a pilot beacon.* ✧ *vb* **-loting, -loted 6** to act as pilot of. **7** to guide or lead (a project or people): *the legislation was piloted through its committee stage.* ▷ **HISTORY** French *pilote*

pilot light *n* a small flame that lights the main burner of a gas appliance.

pilot officer *n* the most junior commissioned rank in certain air forces.

pimento *n, pl* **-tos** same as **allspice pimiento**. ▷ **HISTORY** Spanish *pimiento* pepper plant

pimiento (pim-**yen**-toe) *n, pl* **-tos** a Spanish pepper with a red fruit used as a vegetable. ▷ **HISTORY** variant of PIMENTO

pimp *n* **1** a man who obtains customers for a prostitute, in return for a share of his or her earnings. ✧ *vb* **2** to act as a pimp. ▷ **HISTORY** origin unknown

pimpernel *n* a plant, such as the scarlet pimpernel, typically having small star-shaped flowers. ▷ **HISTORY** Old French *pimpernelle*

pimple *n* a small swollen infected spot on the skin. ▷ **HISTORY** Middle English ▸ **pimpled** *adj* ▸ **pimply** *adj*

pin *n* **1** a short stiff straight piece of wire with a pointed end and a rounded head: used mainly for fastening. **2** short for **cotter pin, hairpin, rolling pin, safety pin**. **3** a wooden or metal peg. **4** a pin-shaped brooch. **5** (in various bowling games) a club-shaped wooden object set up in groups as a target. **6** a clip that prevents a hand grenade from exploding until it is removed or released. **7** *Golf* the flagpole marking the hole on a green. **8** *Informal* a leg. ✧ *vb* **pinning, pinned 9** to fasten with a pin or pins. **10** to seize and hold fast: *they pinned his arms behind his back.* **11 pin something on someone** *Informal* to place the blame for something on someone: *corruption charges are the easiest to pin on former dictators.* ✧ See also **pin down**. ▷ **HISTORY** Old English *pinn*

PIN Personal Identity Number: a code number used in conjunction with a bank card to enable an account holder to use certain computerized systems, such as cash dispensers.

pinafore *n* **1** *Chiefly Brit* an apron with a bib. **2** a dress with a sleeveless bodice or bib top, worn over a jumper or blouse. ▷ **HISTORY** *pin* + *afore* in front

pinball *n* an electrically operated table game in which the player shoots a small ball through several hazards.

pince-nez (panss-**nay**) *n, pl* **pince-nez** glasses that are held in place only by means of a clip over the bridge of the nose. ▷ **HISTORY** French, literally: pinch-nose

pincers *pl n* **1** a gripping tool consisting of two hinged arms and curved jaws. **2** the jointed grasping arms of crabs and lobsters. ▷ **HISTORY** Old French *pincier* to pinch

pinch *vb* **1** to squeeze (something, esp. flesh) between a finger and thumb. **2** to squeeze by being too tight: *shoes that pinch.* **3** to cause stinging pain to: *the cold pinched his face.* **4** to make thin or drawn-looking, such as from grief or cold. **5** *Informal* to steal. **6** *Informal* to arrest. **7** (usually foll. by *out* or *back*) to remove the tips of (a plant shoot) to correct or encourage growth. ✧ *n* **8** a squeeze or sustained nip. **9** the quantity that can be taken up between a thumb and finger: *a pinch of ground ginger.* **10** extreme stress or need: *most companies are feeling the pinch of recession.* **11 at a pinch** if absolutely necessary. **12 feel the pinch** to be forced to economize. ▷ **HISTORY** probably from Old French

pinchbeck *n* **1** an alloy of copper and zinc, used as imitation gold. ✧ *adj* **2** sham or cheap.

a b c d e f g h i j k l m n o p q r s t u v w x y z

▷ HISTORY after C. *Pinchbeck*, watchmaker who invented the alloy

pincushion *n* a small cushion in which pins are stuck ready for use.

pin down *vb* **1** to force (someone) to make a decision or carry out a promise. **2** to define clearly: *the courts have found it difficult to pin down what exactly obscenity is.*

pine¹ *n* **1** an evergreen tree with long needle-shaped leaves and brown cones. **2** the light-coloured wood of this tree. ▷ HISTORY Latin *pinus*

pine² *vb* **pining, pined 1** (often foll. by *for*) to feel great longing (for). **2** (often foll. by *away*) to become ill or thin through grief or longing. ▷ HISTORY Old English *pīnian* to torture

pineal gland *or* **body** (**pin**-ee-al) *n* a small cone-shaped gland at the base of the brain. ▷ HISTORY Latin *pinea* pine cone

pineapple *n* a large tropical fruit with juicy flesh and a thick hard skin. ▷ HISTORY Middle English *pinappel* pine cone

pine cone *n* the woody seed case of a pine tree.

pine marten *n* a mammal of N European and Asian coniferous woods, with dark brown fur and a creamy-yellow patch on the throat.

ping *n* **1** a short high-pitched sound, such as of a bullet striking metal. ✧ *vb* **2** to make such a noise. ▷ HISTORY imitative

pinger *n* a device that makes a pinging sound, esp. a timer.

pingo *n Geog* (in Arctic regions) a cone-shaped ice mound covered with soil and vegetation, formed by the freezing and expansion of water under the ground. ▷ HISTORY Eskimo

Ping-Pong *n Trademark* same as **table tennis**.

pinion¹ *n* **1** *Chiefly poetic* a bird's wing. **2** the outer part of a bird's wing including the flight feathers. ✧ *vb* **3** to immobilize (someone) by holding or tying his or her arms. **4** to confine. ▷ HISTORY Latin *pinna* wing

pinion² *n* a cogwheel that engages with a larger wheel or rack. ▷ HISTORY French *pignon*

pink¹ *n* **1** a colour between red and white. **2** anything pink, such as pink paint or pink clothing: *packaged in pink.* **3** a garden plant with pink, red, or white fragrant flowers. **4 in the pink** in good health. ✧ *adj* **5** of a colour between red and white. **6** *Brit, Austral & S African informal* having mild left-wing sympathies. **7** *Informal* relating to homosexuals or homosexuality: *the pink vote.* ✧ *vb* **8** same as **knock** (sense 7). ▷ HISTORY origin unknown ▶ **pinkish** *or* **pinky** *adj*

pink² *vb* to cut with pinking shears. ▷ HISTORY perhaps from Low German

pinkie *or* **pinky** *n, pl* **-ies** *Scot, US, Canad & NZ* the little finger. ▷ HISTORY Dutch *pinkje*

pinking shears *pl n* scissors with a serrated edge that give a wavy edge to material cut and so prevent fraying.

pin money *n* a small amount of extra money earned to buy small luxuries.

pinna *n Anat* the external part of the ear.

pinnace *n* a ship's boat. ▷ HISTORY French *pinace*

pinnacle *n* **1** the highest point of fame or success. **2** a towering peak of a mountain. **3** a slender spire. ▷ HISTORY Latin *pinna* wing

pinnate *adj Bot* (of compound leaves) having leaflets growing opposite each other in pairs. ▷ HISTORY Latin *pinna* feather

pinotage (**pin**-oh-tazh) *n* a red wine blended from the Pinot Noir and Hermitage grapes that is unique to South Africa.

pinpoint *vb* **1** to locate or identify exactly: *we've pinpointed the fault.* ✧ *adj* **2** exact: *pinpoint accuracy.*

pinprick *n* a small irritation or annoyance.

pins and needles *n Informal* a tingling sensation in a part of the body.

pinstripe *n* (in textiles) a very narrow stripe in fabric or the fabric itself.

pint *n* **1** *Brit* a unit of liquid measure equal to one eighth of an Imperial gallon (0.568 litre). **2** *US* a unit of liquid measure equal to one eighth of a US gallon (0.473 litre). **3** *Brit informal* a pint of beer. ▷ HISTORY Old French *pinte*

pinta *n Brit informal* a pint of milk. ▷ HISTORY phonetic rendering of *pint of*

pintail *n, pl* **-tails** *or* **-tail** a greyish-brown duck with a pointed tail.

pintle *n* a pin or bolt forming the pivot of a hinge. ▷ HISTORY Old English *pintel* penis

pinto *US & Canad* ✧ *adj* **1** marked with patches of white; piebald. ✧ *n, pl* **-tos 2** a pinto horse. ▷ HISTORY American Spanish

pin tuck *n* a narrow, ornamental fold used on shirt fronts and dress bodices.

pin-up *n* **1** *Informal* a picture of a sexually attractive person, often partially or totally undressed. **2** *Slang* a person who has appeared in such a picture: *your favourite pin-up.* **3** a photograph of a famous personality.

pinwheel *n* same as **Catherine wheel**.

Pinyin *n* a system of spelling used to represent Chinese in Roman letters.

pion *or* **pi meson** *n Physics* any of three subatomic particles which are classified as mesons.

pioneer *n* **1** an explorer or settler of a new land or region. **2** an originator or developer of something new. ✧ *vb* **3** to be a pioneer (in or of). **4** to initiate or develop: *the new technique was pioneered in France.* ▷ HISTORY Old French *paonier* infantryman

pious *adj* **1** religious or devout. **2** insincerely reverent; sanctimonious. ▷ HISTORY Latin *pius* ▶ **piousness** *n*

pip¹ *n* the seed of a fleshy fruit, such as an apple or pear. ▷ HISTORY short for *pippin*

pip² *n* **1** a short high-pitched sound used as a time signal on radio. **2** any of the spots on a playing card, dice, or domino. **3** *Informal* the emblem worn on the shoulder by junior officers in the British Army, indicating their rank. ▷ HISTORY imitative

pip³ *n* **1** a contagious disease of poultry. **2** *Facetious slang* a minor human ailment. **3 give someone the pip** *Brit, NZ & S African slang* to annoy someone: *it really gives me the pip.* **4 get** or **have**

the pip *NZ slang* to sulk. ▷ **HISTORY** Middle Dutch *pippe*

pip[4] *vb* **pipping, pipped pip someone at the post** *Brit & NZ slang* to defeat someone whose success seems certain. ▷ **HISTORY** probably from PIP[2]

pipe *n* **1** a long tube for conveying water, oil, or gas. **2 a** a tube with a small bowl at the end for smoking tobacco. **b** the amount of tobacco that fills the bowl of a pipe. **3 put that in your pipe and smoke it** *Informal* accept that fact if you can. **4** *Zool, bot* any of various hollow organs, such as the respiratory passage of certain animals. **5 a** a tubular instrument in which air vibrates and produces a musical sound. **b** any of the tubular devices on an organ. **6 the pipes** See **bagpipes**. **7** a boatswain's whistle. ✧ *vb* **piping, piped 8** to play (music) on a pipe. **9** to summon or lead by a pipe: *to pipe in the haggis.* **10 a** to signal orders to (the crew) by a boatswain's pipe. **b** to signal the arrival or departure of: *he piped his entire ship's company on deck.* **11** to utter in a shrill tone. **12** to convey (water, oil, or gas) by pipe. **13** to force cream or icing through a shaped nozzle to decorate food. ✧ See also **pipe down, pipe up**. ▷ **HISTORY** Old English *pīpe*

pipeclay *n* a fine white pure clay, used in tobacco pipes and pottery and to whiten leather and similar materials.

pipe cleaner *n* a short length of wire covered with tiny tufts of yarn: used to clean the stem of a tobacco pipe.

piped music *n* light music played as background music in public places.

pipe down *vb Informal* to stop talking or making noise.

pipe dream *n* a fanciful or impossible plan or hope. ▷ **HISTORY** alluding to dreams produced by smoking an opium pipe

pipeline *n* **1** a long pipe for transporting oil, water, or gas. **2** a means of communication. **3 in the pipeline** in preparation.

piper *n* a person who plays a pipe or bagpipes.

pipette *n* a slender glass tube for transferring or measuring out liquids. ▷ **HISTORY** French: little pipe

pipe up *vb* to speak up unexpectedly.

pipi *n, pl* **pipi** *or* **pipis 1** *Austral* an Australian mollusc of sandy beaches widely used as bait. **2** *NZ* an edible shellfish of New Zealand. ▷ **HISTORY** Maori

piping *n* **1** a system of pipes. **2** a string of icing or cream used to decorate cakes and desserts. **3** a thin strip of covered cord or material, used to edge hems or cushions. **4** the sound of a pipe or bagpipes. **5** a shrill voice or whistling sound: *a dove's cool piping.* ✧ *adj* **6** making a shrill sound. ✧ *adv* **7 piping hot** extremely hot.

pipistrelle *n* a type of small brownish bat found throughout the world. ▷ **HISTORY** Italian *pipistrello*

pipit *n* a small songbird with a brownish speckled plumage and a long tail. ▷ **HISTORY** probably imitative

pippin *n* a type of eating apple. ▷ **HISTORY** Old French *pepin*

piquant (**pee**-kant) *adj* **1** having a spicy taste. **2** stimulating to the mind: *love was a forbidden piquant secret.* ▷ **HISTORY** French, literally: prickling ▶ **piquancy** *n*

pique (**peek**) *n* **1** a feeling of resentment or irritation, such as from hurt pride. ✧ *vb* **piquing, piqued 2** to hurt (someone's) pride. **3** to excite (curiosity or interest). ▷ **HISTORY** French *piquer* to prick

piqué (**pee**-kay) *n* a stiff ribbed fabric of cotton, silk, or spun rayon. ▷ **HISTORY** French: pricked

piquet (pik-**ket**) *n* a card game for two people played with a reduced pack. ▷ **HISTORY** French

piracy *n, pl* **-cies 1** *Brit & NZ* robbery on the seas. **2** a crime, such as hijacking, committed aboard a ship or aircraft. **3** the unauthorized use of patented or copyrighted material.

piranha *n* a small fierce freshwater fish of tropical America, with strong jaws and sharp teeth. ▷ **HISTORY** S American Indian: fish with teeth

pirate *n* **1** a person who commits piracy. **2** a vessel used by pirates. **3** a person who illegally sells or publishes someone else's literary or artistic work. **4** a person or group of people who broadcast illegally. ✧ *vb* **-rating, -rated 5** to sell or reproduce (artistic work, ideas, etc.) illegally. ▷ **HISTORY** Greek *peira* an attack ▶ **piratical** *adj*

pirouette *n* **1** a body spin performed on the toes or the ball of the foot. ✧ *vb* **-etting, -etted 2** to perform a pirouette. ▷ **HISTORY** French

piscatorial *adj Formal* of or relating to fish, fishing, or fishermen. ▷ **HISTORY** Latin *piscatorius*

Pisces *n Astrol* the twelfth sign of the zodiac; the Fishes. ▷ **HISTORY** Latin

pisciculture (**piss**-ee-cult-cher) *n Formal* the rearing and breeding of fish under controlled conditions. ▷ **HISTORY** Latin *piscis* fish

piscine (**piss**-sign) *adj* of or resembling a fish. ▷ **HISTORY** Latin *piscis* fish

piss *Taboo* ✧ *vb* **1** to urinate. **2** to discharge as or in one's urine: *to piss blood.* ✧ *n* **3** an act of urinating. **4** urine. **5 take the piss** to make fun of or mock someone. ▷ **HISTORY** probably imitative

pissed *adj Brit, Austral & NZ slang* drunk.

pistachio *n, pl* **-chios** a Mediterranean nut with a hard shell and an edible green kernel. ▷ **HISTORY** Persian *pistah*

piste (**peest**) *n* a slope or course for skiing. ▷ **HISTORY** French

pistil *n* the seed-bearing part of a flower. ▷ **HISTORY** Latin *pistillum* pestle

pistillate *adj Bot* (of plants) having pistils.

pistol *n* a short-barrelled handgun. ▷ **HISTORY** Czech *pišt'ala*

piston *n* a cylindrical part that slides to and fro in a hollow cylinder: in an engine it is attached by a rod to other parts, thus its movement causes the other parts to move. ▷ **HISTORY** Old Italian *pistone*

pit[1] *n* **1** a large deep opening in the ground. **2** a coal mine. **3** *Anat* **a** a small natural depression on the surface of a body or organ. **b** the floor of any natural bodily cavity: *the pit of the stomach.* **4** *Pathol* a pockmark. **5** a concealed danger or difficulty. **6** an

A B C D E F G H I J K L M N O P Q R S T U V W X Y Z

area at the side of a motor-racing track for servicing or refuelling vehicles. **7 the pit** hell. **8** the area occupied by the orchestra in a theatre. **9** an enclosure for fighting animals or birds. **10** the back of the ground floor of a theatre. **11** same as **pitfall** (sense 2). ✧ *vb* **pitting, pitted 12** (often foll. by *against*) to match in opposition, esp. as antagonists: *sister pitted against sister.* **13** to mark with small dents or scars. **14** to place or bury in a pit. **15 pit one's wits against** to compete against in a test or contest. ✧ See also **pits.** ▷ **HISTORY** Old English *pytt*

pit² *Chiefly US & Canad* ✧ *n* **1** the stone of various fruits. ✧ *vb* **pitting, pitted 2** to remove the stone from (a fruit). ▷ **HISTORY** Dutch: kernel

pitapat *adv* **1** with quick light taps. ✧ *n* **2** such taps. ▷ **HISTORY** imitative

pit bull terrier *n* a strong muscular terrier with a short coat.

pitch¹ *vb* **1** to hurl or throw. **2** to set up (a tent or camp). **3** to slope or fall forwards or downwards: *she pitched forwards like a diver.* **4** (of a ship or plane) to dip and raise its back and front alternately. **5** to set the level or tone of: *his ambitions were pitched too high.* **6** to aim to sell (a product) to a specified market or on a specified basis. **7** *Music* to sing or play (a note or interval) accurately. ✧ *n* **8** *Chiefly Brit* (in many sports) the field of play. **9** a level of emotion: *children can wind their parents up to a pitch of anger and guilt.* **10** the degree or angle of slope. **11** the distance between corresponding points or adjacent threads on a screw thread. **12** the pitching motion of a ship or plane. **13** *Music* the highness or lowness of a note in relation to other notes: *low pitch.* **14** the act or manner of pitching a ball. **15** *Chiefly Brit* the place where a street or market trader regularly sells. **16** *Slang* a persuasive sales talk, esp. one routinely repeated. ✧ See also **pitch in, pitch into.** ▷ **HISTORY** Middle English *picchen*

pitch² *n* **1** a thick sticky substance formed from coal tar and used for paving or waterproofing. **2** any similar substance, such as asphalt, occurring as a natural deposit. ✧ *vb* **3** to apply pitch to. ▷ **HISTORY** Old English *pic*

pitch-black *adj* extremely dark; unlit: *it was a wild night, pitch-black, with howling gales.*

pitchblende *n* a blackish mineral which is the principal source of uranium and radium. ▷ **HISTORY** German *Pechblende*

pitch-dark *adj* extremely or completely dark.

pitched battle *n* a fierce fight.

pitcher¹ *n* a large jug, usually rounded with a narrow neck. ▷ **HISTORY** Old French *pichier*

pitcher² *n Baseball* the player on the fielding team who throws the ball to the batter.

pitcher plant *n* a plant with pitcher-like leaves that attract and trap insects, which are then digested.

pitchfork *n* **1** a long-handled fork with two or three long curved prongs for tossing hay. ✧ *vb* **2** to use a pitchfork on (something).

pitch in *vb* to cooperate or contribute.

pitch into *vb Informal* to attack (someone) physically or verbally.

pitch pine *n* a pine tree of North America: a source of turpentine and pitch.

piteous *adj* arousing or deserving pity: *the piteous mewing of an injured kitten.* ▸ **piteousness** *n*

pitfall *n* **1** an unsuspected difficulty or danger. **2** a trap in the form of a concealed pit, designed to catch men or wild animals. ▷ **HISTORY** Old English *pytt* pit + *fealle* trap

pith *n* **1** the soft white lining inside the rind of fruits such as the orange. **2** the essential part: *policy, though, isn't the pith of what happened yesterday.* **3** the soft spongy tissue in the centre of the stem of certain plants. ▷ **HISTORY** Old English *pitha*

pithead *n* the top of a mine shaft and the buildings and hoisting gear around it.

pith helmet *n* a lightweight hat made from the pith of the sola, an E Indian swamp plant, that is worn for protection from the sun.

pithy *adj* **pithier, pithiest 1** terse and full of meaning. **2** of, resembling, or full of pith. ▸ **pithiness** *n*

pitiable *adj* arousing or deserving pity or contempt. ▸ **pitiableness** *n*

pitiful *adj* arousing or deserving great pity or contempt. ▸ **pitifully** *adv* ▸ **pitifulness** *n*

pitiless *adj* feeling no pity or mercy. ▸ **pitilessly** *adv*

piton (**peet**-on) *n Mountaineering* a metal spike that may be driven into a crack and used to secure a rope. ▷ **HISTORY** French

pits *pl n* **the pits** *Slang* the worst possible person, place, or thing. ▷ **HISTORY** perhaps from *armpits*

pitta bread *or* **pitta** *n* a flat rounded slightly leavened bread, originally from the Middle East. ▷ **HISTORY** Modern Greek *pitta* a cake

pittance *n* a very small amount of money. ▷ **HISTORY** Old French *pietance* ration

pitter-patter *n* **1** the sound of light rapid taps or pats, such as of rain drops. ✧ *vb* **2** to make such a sound.

pituitary *or* **pituitary gland** *n* the gland at the base of the brain which secretes hormones that affect skeletal growth, development of the sex glands, and other functions of the body. ▷ **HISTORY** Late Latin *pituitarius* slimy

pity *n, pl* **pities 1** sorrow felt for the sufferings of others. **2 have** *or* **take pity on** to have sympathy or show mercy for. **3** a cause of regret: *it's a great pity he did not live longer.* ✧ *vb* **pities, pitying, pitied 4** to feel pity for. ▷ **HISTORY** Latin *pietas* duty ▸ **pitying** *adj*

pivot *n* **1** a central shaft around which something turns. **2** the central person or thing necessary for progress or success. ✧ *vb* **-oting, -oted 3** to turn on or provide with a pivot. ▷ **HISTORY** Old French

pivotal *adj* **1** of crucial importance. **2** of or acting as a pivot.

pix *n Informal* a plural of **pic.**

pixie *or* **pixy** *n, pl* **pixies** (in folklore) a fairy or elf.

pizza *n* a dish of Italian origin consisting of a baked disc of dough covered with a wide variety of savoury toppings. ▷ HISTORY Italian

pizzazz *or* **pizazz** *n Informal* an attractive combination of energy and style. ▷ HISTORY origin obscure

pizzicato (pit-see-**kah**-toe) *adj, adv Music* (in music for the violin family) to be plucked with the finger. ▷ HISTORY Italian: pinched

Pl. (in street names) Place.

plaas *n S African* a farm. ▷ HISTORY Afrikaans

placard *n* **1** a notice that is paraded in public. ✧ *vb* **2** to attach placards to. ▷ HISTORY Old French *plaquart*

placate *vb* **-cating, -cated** to calm (someone) to stop him or her feeling angry or upset. ▷ HISTORY Latin *placare* ▶ **placatory** *adj*

place *n* **1** a particular part of a space or of a surface. **2** a geographical point, such as a town or city. **3** a position or rank in a sequence or order. **4** an open square lined with houses in a city or town. **5** space or room. **6** a house or living quarters: *he's buying his own place.* **7** any building or area set aside for a specific purpose. **8** the point reached in reading or speaking: *her finger was pressed to the page as if marking her place.* **9** right or duty: *it's not my place to do their job for them.* **10** appointment, position, or job: *she won a place at university.* **11** position, condition, or state: *you know what your place in the world is.* **12** a space or seat, as at a dining table. **13** *Maths* the relative position of a digit in a number. **14 all over the place** in disorder or disarray. **15 go places** *Informal* to become successful. **16 in** *or* **out of place** in or out of the proper or customary position. **17 in place of a** instead of: *leeks can be used in place of the broccoli.* **b** in exchange for: *he gave her it in place of her ring.* **18 know one's place** to be aware of one's inferior position. **19 put someone in his** *or* **her place** to humble someone who is arrogant, conceited, etc. **20 take place** to happen or occur. **21 take the place of** to be a substitute for. ✧ *vb* **placing, placed 22** to put in a particular or appropriate place. **23** to find or indicate the place of: *I bet you the media couldn't have placed Neath on the map before the by-election.* **24** to identify or classify by linking with an appropriate context: *I felt I should know him, but could not quite place him.* **25** to make (an order or bet). **26** to find a home or job for (someone). **27** (often foll. by *with*) to put under the care (of). **28** (of a racehorse, greyhound, athlete, etc.) to arrive in first, second, third, or sometimes fourth place. ▷ HISTORY Latin *platea* courtyard

placebo (plas-**see**-bo) *n, pl* **-bos** *or* **-boes** *Med* an inactive substance given to a patient usually to compare its effects with those of a real drug but sometimes for the psychological benefit gained by the patient through believing that he or she is receiving treatment. ▷ HISTORY Latin: I shall please

place kick *n Rugby, American football, etc.* a kick in which the ball is placed in position before it is kicked.

placement *n* **1** arrangement or position. **2** a temporary job which someone is given as part of a training course: *many pupils have been on work placements with local businesses.* **3** the act or an instance of finding someone a job or a home: *the main task of the adoption agency is to find the best family placement for each child.*

placenta (plass-**ent**-a) *n, pl* **-tas** *or* **-tae** the organ formed in the womb of most mammals during pregnancy, providing oxygen and nutrients for the fetus. ▷ HISTORY Latin, from Greek *plakoeis* flat cake ▶ **placental** *adj*

place setting *n* the cutlery, crockery, and glassware laid for one person at a dining table.

placid *adj* having a calm appearance or nature: *placid waters; a placid temperament.* ▷ HISTORY Latin *placidus* peaceful ▶ **placidity** *or* **placidness** *n* ▶ **placidly** *adv*

placket *n Dressmaking* an opening at the waist of a dress or skirt for buttons or zips or for access to a pocket. ▷ HISTORY perhaps from Medieval Dutch *plackaet* breastplate

plagiarize *or* **-rise** (**play**-jer-ize) *vb* **-rizing, -rized** *or* **-rising, -rised** to steal ideas or passages from (another's work) and present them as one's own. ▷ HISTORY Latin *plagium* kidnapping ▶ **plagiarism** *n* ▶ **plagiarizer** *or* **-riser** *n*

plague *n* **1** any widespread and usually highly contagious disease with a high fatality rate. **2** an infectious disease of rodents transmitted to man by the bite of the rat flea; bubonic plague. **3** something that afflicts or harasses: *a plague of locusts.* **4** *Informal* a nuisance. ✧ *vb* **plaguing, plagued 5** to afflict or harass: *a playing career plagued by injury.* **6** *Informal* to annoy or pester. ▷ HISTORY Latin *plaga* a blow

plaice *n, pl* **plaice** *or* **plaices** an edible European flatfish with a brown body marked with red or orange spots. ▷ HISTORY Greek *platus* flat

plaid *n* **1** a long piece of tartan cloth worn over the shoulder as part of Highland costume. **2** a crisscross weave or cloth. ▷ HISTORY Scottish Gaelic *plaide*

Plaid Cymru (plide **kumm**-ree) *n* the Welsh nationalist party. ▷ HISTORY Welsh

plain *adj* **1** flat or smooth. **2** easily understood: *he made it plain what he wanted from me.* **3** honest or blunt: *the plain fact is that my mother has no time for me.* **4** without adornment: *a plain brown envelope.* **5** not good-looking. **6** (of fabric) without pattern or of simple weave. **7** lowly, esp. in social rank or education: *the plain people of Ireland.* **8** *Knitting* of or done in plain stitch. ✧ *n* **9** a level stretch of country. **10** a simple stitch in knitting made by passing the wool round the front of the needle. ✧ *adv* **11** clearly or simply: *that's just plain stupid!* ▷ HISTORY Latin *planus* level, clear ▶ **plainly** *adv* ▶ **plainness** *n*

plain clothes *pl n* ordinary clothes, as opposed to uniform, worn by a detective on duty.

plain sailing *n* **1** *Informal* smooth or easy progress. **2** *Naut* sailing in a body of water that is unobstructed; clear sailing.

plainsong *n* the style of unaccompanied choral music used in the medieval Church, esp. in

Gregorian chant. ▷ **HISTORY** translation of Medieval Latin *cantus planus*

plain speaking *n* saying exactly what one thinks. ▸ **plain-spoken** *adj*

plaint *n* **1** *Archaic* a complaint or lamentation. **2** *Law* a statement in writing of grounds of complaint made to a court of law. ▷ **HISTORY** Old French *plainte*

plaintiff *n* a person who sues in a court of law. ▷ **HISTORY** Old French *plaintif* complaining

plaintive *adj* sad and mournful. ▷ **HISTORY** Old French *plaintif* grieving ▸ **plaintively** *adv*

plait (**platt**) *n* **1** a length of hair that has been plaited. ✧ *vb* **2** to intertwine (strands or strips) in a pattern. ▷ **HISTORY** Latin *plicare* to fold

plan *n* **1** a method thought out for doing or achieving something. **2** a detailed drawing to scale of a horizontal section through a building. **3** an outline or sketch. ✧ *vb* **planning, planned 4** to form a plan (for). **5** to make a plan of (a building). **6** to intend. ▷ **HISTORY** Latin *planus* flat

plane[1] *n* **1** an aeroplane. **2** *Maths* a flat surface in which a straight line joining any two of its points lies entirely on that surface. **3** a level surface: *an inclined plane.* **4** a level of existence or attainment: *her ambition was set on a higher plane than pulling pints in a pub.* ✧ *adj* **5** level or flat. **6** *Maths* lying entirely in one plane. ✧ *vb* **planing, planed 7** to glide or skim: *they planed over the ice.* ▷ **HISTORY** Latin *planum* level surface

plane[2] *n* **1** a tool with a steel blade for smoothing timber. ✧ *vb* **planing, planed 2** to smooth (timber) using a plane. **3** (often foll. by *away* or *off*) to remove using a plane. ▷ **HISTORY** Latin *planare* to level

planet *n* any of the nine celestial bodies, Mercury, Venus, Earth, Mars, Jupiter, Saturn, Uranus, Neptune, or Pluto, that revolve around the sun in oval-shaped orbits. ▷ **HISTORY** Greek *planaein* to wander ▸ **planetary** *adj*

planetarium *n, pl* **-iums** *or* **-ia 1** an instrument for projecting images of the sun, moon, stars, and planets onto a domed ceiling. **2** a building in which such an instrument is housed.

planetoid (**plan**-it-oid) *n* See **asteroid**.

plane tree *or* **plane** *n* a tree with rounded heads of fruit and leaves with pointed lobes. ▷ **HISTORY** Greek *platos* wide (because of its broad leaves)

plangent (**plan**-jent) *adj* (of sounds) mournful and resounding.

plank *n* **1** a long flat piece of sawn timber. **2** one of the policies in a political party's programme. **3 walk the plank** to be forced by sailors to walk to one's death off the end of a plank jutting out from the side of a ship. ▷ **HISTORY** Late Latin *planca* board

plankton *n* the small drifting plants and animals on the surface layer of a sea or lake. ▷ **HISTORY** Greek *planktos* wandering

planned market *n Econ* an economic system in which the government controls the factors of production.

planner *n* **1** a person who makes plans, esp. for the development of a town, building, etc. **2** a chart for recording future appointments, etc.

planning permission *n* formal permission granted by a local authority for the construction, alteration, or change of use of a building.

plant *n* **1** a living organism that grows in the ground and lacks the power of movement. **2** the land, building, and equipment used in an industry or business. **3** a factory or workshop. **4** mobile mechanical equipment for construction or road-making. **5** *Informal* a thing positioned secretly for discovery by someone else, often in order to incriminate an innocent person. ✧ *vb* **6** to set (seeds or crops) into the ground to grow: *it's the wrong time of year for planting roses.* **7** to place firmly in position: *I planted my chair beside hers.* **8** to introduce into someone's mind: *once Wendy had planted the idea in the minds of the owners, they quite fancied selling.* **9** *Slang* to deliver (a blow or kiss). **10** *Informal* to position or hide (someone) in order to deceive or observe. **11** *Informal* to hide or secrete (something), usually for some illegal purpose or in order to incriminate someone. ▷ **HISTORY** Old English

plantae (**plahn**-tee) *pl n Bot* the plant kingdom.

plantain[1] *n* a plant with a rosette of broad leaves and a slender spike of small greenish flowers. ▷ **HISTORY** Latin *planta* sole of the foot

plantain[2] *n* **1** a large tropical fruit like a green-skinned banana. **2** the tree on which this fruit grows. ▷ **HISTORY** Spanish *platano*

plantation *n* **1** an estate, esp. in tropical countries, where cash crops such as rubber or coffee are grown on a large scale. **2** a group of cultivated trees or plants. **3** (formerly) a colony of settlers.

planter *n* **1** the owner or manager of a plantation. **2** a decorative pot for house plants.

plantigrade *adj* walking on the entire sole of the foot, as humans and bears do. ▷ **HISTORY** Latin *planta* sole of the foot + *gradus* a step

plant succession *n Geog* the natural process by which one plant community succeeds another.

plaque *n* **1** a commemorative inscribed stone or metal plate. **2** Also called: **dental plaque** a filmy deposit on teeth consisting of mucus, bacteria, and food, that causes decay. ▷ **HISTORY** French

plasma *n* **1** the clear yellowish fluid portion of blood which contains the corpuscles and cells. **2** a sterilized preparation of such fluid, taken from the blood, for use in transfusions. **3** a former name for **protoplasm**. **4** *Physics* a hot ionized gas containing positive ions and free electrons. ▷ **HISTORY** Greek: something moulded

plasmalemma *n Biol* a very thin membrane that surrounds the cytoplasm of a cell.

plasmolysis *n Biol* the shrinkage of protoplasm away from the cell walls that occurs as a result of excessive water loss.

plaster *n* **1** a mixture of lime, sand, and water that is applied to a wall or ceiling as a soft paste and dries as a hard coating. **2** *Brit, Austral, & NZ* an adhesive strip of material for dressing a cut or wound. **3** short for **mustard plaster, plaster of Paris.** ✧ *vb* **4** to coat (a wall or ceiling) with plaster. **5** to apply like plaster: *he plastered his face with shaving cream.* **6** to cause to lie flat or to adhere: *his hair was plastered to his forehead.* ▷ **HISTORY** Greek *emplastron* healing dressing ▶ **plasterer** *n*

plasterboard *n* a thin rigid board, made of plaster compressed between two layers of fibreboard, used to form or cover interior walls.

plaster cast *n Med* a casing around a limb, often made of plaster of Paris, for preventing broken bones from moving while they heal.

plastered *adj Slang* drunk.

plaster of Paris *n* a white powder that sets to a hard solid when mixed with water, used for making sculptures and casts for setting broken limbs.

plastic *n* **1** any of a large number of synthetic materials that can be moulded when soft and then set. **2** *Informal* Also called: **plastic money** credit cards etc. as opposed to cash. ✧ *adj* **3** made of plastic. **4** easily influenced. **5** capable of being moulded or formed. **6** of moulding or modelling: *the plastic arts.* **7** *Slang* superficially attractive yet artificial or false: *glamorous models with plastic smiles.* ▷ **HISTORY** Greek *plastikos* mouldable ▶ **plasticity** *n*

plastic bullet *n* a solid PVC cylinder fired by the police in riot control.

plastic explosive *n* an adhesive jelly-like explosive substance.

Plasticine *n Trademark* a soft coloured material used, esp. by children, for modelling.

plasticizer *or* **-ciser** *n* a substance added to a plastic material to soften it and improve flexibility.

plastic surgery *n* the branch of surgery concerned with the repair or reconstruction of missing, injured, or malformed tissues or parts. ▶ **plastic surgeon** *n*

plate *n* **1** a shallow dish made of porcelain, earthenware, glass, etc., on which food is served. **2** Also called: **plateful** the contents of a plate. **3** a shallow dish for receiving a collection in church. **4** flat metal of even thickness obtained by rolling. **5** a thin coating of metal usually on another metal. **6** dishes or cutlery made of gold or silver. **7** a sheet of metal, plastic, or rubber having a printing surface produced by a process such as stereotyping. **8** a print taken from such a sheet or from a woodcut. **9** a thin flat sheet of a substance, such as glass. **10** a small piece of metal or plastic with an inscription, fixed to another surface: *a brass name plate.* **11** *Photog* a sheet of glass coated with photographic emulsion on which an image can be formed by exposure to light. **12** *Informal* same as **denture**. **13** *Anat* any flat platelike structure. **14** a cup awarded to the winner of a sporting contest, esp. a horse race. **15** any of the rigid layers of the earth's crust. **16 have a lot on one's plate** to have many pressing things to deal with. **17 on a plate** acquired without trouble: *he got the job handed to him on a plate.* ✧ *vb* **plating, plated 18** to coat (a metal surface) with a thin layer of another metal. **19** to cover with metal plates, usually for protection. **20** to form (metal) into plate, usually by rolling. ▷ **HISTORY** Old French: something flat

plateau (**plat**-oh) *n, pl* **-eaus** *or* **-eaux** (-ohs) **1** a wide level area of high land. **2** a relatively long period of stability: *the body temperature rises to a plateau that it keeps until shortly before bedtime.* ✧ *vb* **3** to remain stable for a long period. ▷ **HISTORY** French

plated *adj* coated with a layer of metal.

plate glass *n* glass produced in thin sheets, used for windows and mirrors.

platelet *n* a minute particle occurring in the blood of vertebrates and involved in the clotting of the blood.

platen *n* **1** the roller on a typewriter, against which the keys strike. **2** a flat plate in a printing press that presses the paper against the type. ▷ **HISTORY** Old French *platine*

plate tectonics *n Geol* (*functioning as sing*) the study of the earth's crust with reference to the theory that the lithosphere is divided into rigid blocks (plates) that float on semimolten rock and are thus able to interact with each other at their boundaries.

platform *n* **1** a raised floor. **2** a raised area at a railway station where passengers get on or off the trains. **3** the declared aims of a political party. **4** the thick raised sole of some shoes. **5** a type of computer hardware or operating system. ▷ **HISTORY** French *plat* flat + *forme* layout

platform game *n* a type of computer game that is played by moving a figure on the screen through a series of obstacles.

plating *n* **1** a coating of metal. **2** a layer or covering of metal plates.

platinum *n* a silvery-white metallic element, very resistant to heat and chemicals: used in jewellery, laboratory apparatus, electrical contacts, dentistry, electroplating, and as a catalyst. Symbol: Pt. ▷ **HISTORY** Spanish *platina* silvery element

platinum blonde *n* a girl or woman with silvery-blonde hair.

platitude *n* a trite or unoriginal remark: *it's a platitude, but people need people.* ▷ **HISTORY** French: flatness ▶ **platitudinous** *adj*

platonic *adj* friendly or affectionate but without physical desire: *platonic love.*

> **WORD HISTORY**
> 'Platonic' comes from the name of the Greek philosopher Plato (428-347 B.C.). The concept of 'platonic love' between people of opposite sexes is based on a passage in one of his writings.

Platonic *adj* of the philosopher Plato or his teachings.

Platonism (**plate**-on-iz-zum) *n* the teachings of Plato (?427–?347 BC), Greek philosopher, and his followers. ▶ **Platonist** *n*

platoon *n Mil* a subunit of a company, usually comprising three sections of ten to twelve men. ▷ **HISTORY** French *peloton* little ball, group of men

platteland *n* **the platteland** (in South Africa) the country districts or rural areas.
▷ HISTORY Afrikaans

platter *n* a large shallow, usually oval, dish.
▷ HISTORY Anglo-Norman *plater*

platypus *or* **duck-billed platypus** *n, pl* **-puses** an Australian egg-laying amphibious mammal, with dense fur, webbed feet, and a ducklike bill. ▷ HISTORY Greek *platus* flat + *pous* foot

plausible *adj* **1** apparently reasonable or true: *a plausible excuse.* **2** apparently trustworthy or believable: *he is an extraordinarily plausible liar.*
▷ HISTORY Latin *plausibilis* worthy of applause
▶ **plausibility** *n* ▶ **plausibly** *adv*

play *vb* **1** to occupy oneself in (a sport or recreation). **2** to compete against (someone) in a sport or game: *I saw Brazil play Argentina recently.* **3** to fulfil (a particular role) in a team game: *he usually plays in midfield.* **4** (often foll. by *about* or *around*) to behave carelessly: *he's only playing with your affections, you know.* **5** to act the part (of) in a dramatic piece: *he has played Hamlet to packed Broadway houses.* **6** to perform (a dramatic piece). **7 a** to perform (music) on an instrument. **b** to be able to perform on (a musical instrument): *she plays the bassoon.* **8** to send out (water) or cause to send out water: *they played a hose across the wrecked building.* **9** to cause (a radio etc.) to emit sound. **10** to move freely or quickly: *the light played across the water.* **11** *Stock Exchange* to speculate for gain in (a market). **12** *Angling* to tire (a hooked fish) by alternately letting out and reeling in the line. **13** to put (a card) into play. **14** to gamble. **15 play fair** *or* **false with** to act fairly *or* unfairly with. **16 play for time** to gain time to one's advantage by the use of delaying tactics. **17 play into the hands of** to act unwittingly to the advantage of (an opponent). ✧ *n* **18 a** a dramatic piece written for performance by actors. **b** the performance of such a piece. **19** games or other activity undertaken for pleasure. **20** the playing of a game or the time during which a game is in progress: *rain stopped play.* **21** conduct: *fair play.* **22** gambling. **23** activity or operation: *radio allows full play to your imagination.* **24** scope for freedom of movement: *there was a lot of play in the rope.* **25** free or rapidly shifting motion: *the play of light on the water.* **26** fun or jest: *I used to throw cushions at her in play.* **27 in** *or* **out of play** (of a ball in a game) in *or* not in a position for continuing play according to the rules. **28 make a play for** *Informal* to make an obvious attempt to gain (something).
✧ See also **playback**. ▷ HISTORY Old English *plega, plegan* ▶ **playable** *adj*

playa (**plah**-ya) *n Geog* (in the US) a temporary lake, or its dry often salty bed, in a desert basin.
▷ HISTORY Spanish: shore, from Late Latin *plagia*, from Greek *plagios* slanting, from *plagos* side

playback *n* **1** the playing of a recording on magnetic tape. ✧ *vb* **play back 2** to listen to or watch (something recorded).

playbill *n* a poster or bill advertising a play.

playboy *n* a rich man who devotes himself to such pleasures as nightclubs and female company.

playcentre *n NZ* a centre for preschool children run by parents.

play down *vb* to minimize the importance of: *she played down the problems of the company.*

player *n* **1** a person who takes part in a game or sport. **2** a person who plays a musical instrument. **3** *Informal* a leading participant in a particular field or activity: *one of the key players in Chinese politics.* **4** an actor.

playful *adj* **1** good-natured and humorous: *a playful remark.* **2** full of high spirits and fun: *a playful child.* ▶ **playfully** *adv*

playgoer *n* a person who goes often to the theatre.

playground *n* **1** an outdoor area for children's play, either with swings and slides, or adjoining a school. **2** a place or activity enjoyed by a specified person or group: *they oppose turning the island into a tourist playground.*

playgroup *n* a regular meeting of infants for supervised creative play.

playhouse *n* a theatre.

playing field *n* (*sometimes pl*) *Brit & NZ* a field or open space used for sport.

play-lunch *n Austral & NZ* a child's mid-morning snack at school.

playmaker *n Sport* a player who creates scoring opportunities for his or her team-mates.

play off *vb* **1** to set (two people) against each other for one's own ends: *she delighted in playing one parent off against the other.* **2** to take part in a play-off. ✧ *n* **play-off 3** *Sport* an extra contest to decide the winner when there is a tie. **4** *Chiefly US & Canad* a contest or series of games to determine a championship.

play on *vb* to exploit (the feelings or weakness of another): *he played on my sympathy.*

play on words *n* same as **pun**.

playpen *n* a small portable enclosure in which a young child can safely be left to play.

playschool *n* a nursery group for preschool children.

plaything *n* **1** a toy. **2** a person regarded or treated as a toy.

playtime *n* a time for play or recreation, such as a school break.

play up *vb* **1** to highlight: *the temptation is to play up the sensational aspects of the story.* **2** *Brit & Austral informal* to behave in an unruly way. **3** to give (one) trouble or not be working properly: *my back's playing me up again; the photocopier's started to play up.* **4 play up to** to try to please by flattery.

playwright *n* a person who writes plays.

plaza *n* **1** an open public square, usually in Spain. **2** *Chiefly US & Canad* a modern shopping complex.
▷ HISTORY Spanish

PLC *or* **plc** (in Britain) Public Limited Company.

plea *n* **1** an emotional appeal. **2** *Law* a statement by or on behalf of a defendant. **3** an excuse: *his plea of poverty rings a little hollow.*
▷ HISTORY Anglo-Norman *plai*

plea bargaining *n Law* the process whereby the prosecution, defence, and sometimes the judge, come to an agreement in which the accused agrees to plead guilty to a lesser charge in return for more serious charges being dropped.

plead *vb* **pleading, pleaded, plead** *or esp Scot & US* **pled 1** (sometimes foll. by *with*) to ask with deep feeling. **2** to give as an excuse: *whenever she invites him to dinner, he pleads a prior engagement.* **3** *Law* to declare oneself to be (guilty or not guilty) of the charge made against one. **4** *Law* to present (a case) in a court of law. ▷ HISTORY Latin *placere* to please

pleadings *pl n Law* the formal written statements presented by the plaintiff and defendant in a lawsuit.

pleasant *adj* **1** pleasing or enjoyable: *what a pleasant surprise.* **2** having pleasing manners or appearance: *he was a pleasant boy.* ▷ HISTORY Old French *plaisant* ▶ **pleasantly** *adv*

pleasantry *n, pl* **-ries 1** (*often pl*) a polite or jocular remark: *we exchanged pleasantries about the weather.* **2** agreeable jocularity. ▷ HISTORY French *plaisanterie*

please *vb* **pleasing, pleased 1** to give pleasure or satisfaction to (a person). **2** to regard as suitable or satisfying: *he can get almost anyone he pleases to work with him.* **3 if you please** if you wish, sometimes used in ironic exclamation. **4 pleased with** happy because of. **5 please oneself** to do as one likes. ✧ *adv* **6** used in making polite requests or pleading: *please sit down.* **7 yes please** a polite phrase used to accept an offer or invitation. ▷ HISTORY Latin *placere* ▶ **pleased** *adj*

pleasing *adj* giving pleasure.

pleasurable *adj* enjoyable or agreeable. ▶ **pleasurably** *adv*

pleasure *n* **1** a feeling of happiness and contentment: *the pleasure of hearing good music.* **2** something that gives enjoyment: *his garden was his only pleasure.* **3** the activity of enjoying oneself: *business before pleasure.* **4** *Euphemistic* sexual gratification: *he took his pleasure of her.* **5** a person's preference. ▷ HISTORY Old French *plaisir*

pleat *n* **1** a fold formed by doubling back fabric and pressing or stitching into place. ✧ *vb* **2** to arrange (material) in pleats. ▷ HISTORY variant of *plait*

pleb *n Brit informal, often offensive* a common vulgar person.

plebeian (pleb-**ee**-an) *adj* **1** of the lower social classes. **2** unrefined: *plebeian tastes.* ✧ *n* **3** one of the common people, usually of ancient Rome. **4** a coarse or unrefined person. ▷ HISTORY Latin *plebs* the common people of ancient Rome

plebiscite (**pleb**-iss-ite) *n* a direct vote by all the electorate on an issue of national importance. ▷ HISTORY Latin *plebiscitum* decree of the people

plectrum *n, pl* **-trums** *or* **-tra** an implement for plucking the strings of a guitar or similar instrument. ▷ HISTORY Greek *plektron*

pledge *n* **1** a solemn promise. **2 a** something valuable given as a guarantee that a promise will be kept or a debt paid. **b** the condition of being used as security: *in pledge.* **3** a token: *a pledge of good faith.* **4** an assurance of support or goodwill, given by drinking a toast: *we drank a pledge to their success.* **5 take** *or* **sign the pledge** to vow not to drink alcohol. ✧ *vb* **pledging, pledged 6** to promise solemnly. **7** to bind by or as if by a pledge: *I was pledged to secrecy.* **8** to give (one's word or property) as a guarantee. **9** to drink a toast to (a person or cause). ▷ HISTORY Old French *plege*

Pleiocene *adj, n* same as **Pliocene**.

Pleistocene (**ply**-stow-seen) *adj Geol* of the epoch of geological time from about 1.6 million to 10 000 years ago. ▷ HISTORY Greek *pleistos* most + *kainos* recent

plenary *adj* **1** (of an assembly) attended by all the members. **2** full or complete: *plenary powers.* ▷ HISTORY Latin *plenus* full

plenipotentiary *adj* **1** (usually of a diplomat) invested with full authority. ✧ *n, pl* **-aries 2** a diplomat or representative who has full authority to transact business. ▷ HISTORY Latin *plenus* full + *potentia* power

plenitude *n Literary* **1** abundance. **2** fullness or completeness. ▷ HISTORY Latin *plenus* full

plenteous *adj Literary* **1** abundant: *a plenteous supply.* **2** producing abundantly: *a plenteous harvest.*

plentiful *adj* existing in large amounts or numbers. ▶ **plentifully** *adv*

plenty *n, pl* **-ties 1** (often foll. by *of*) a great number or amount: *plenty of time.* **2** abundance: *an age of plenty.* ✧ *adj* **3** very many: *there's plenty more fish in the sea.* ✧ *adv* **4** *Informal* more than adequately: *that's plenty fast enough for me.* ▷ HISTORY Latin *plenus* full

pleonasm *n Rhetoric* **1** the use of more words than necessary, such as *a tiny little child.* **2** an unnecessary word or phrase. ▷ HISTORY Greek *pleonasmos* excess ▶ **pleonastic** *adj*

plethora *n* an excess. ▷ HISTORY Greek *plēthōrē* fullness

pleura (**ploor**-a) *n, pl* **pleurae** (**ploor**-ee) *Anat* the thin transparent membrane enveloping the lungs. ▷ HISTORY Greek: side, rib ▶ **pleural** *adj*

pleurisy *n* inflammation of the pleura, making breathing painful. ▶ **pleuritic** *adj, n*

plexus *n, pl* **-uses** *or* **-us** a complex network of nerves or blood vessels. ▷ HISTORY Latin *plectere* to braid

pliable *adj* **1** easily bent: *pliable branches.* **2** easily influenced: *his easy and pliable nature.* ▶ **pliability** *n*

pliant *adj* **1** easily bent; supple: *pliant young willow and hazel twigs.* **2** easily influenced: *he was a far more pliant subordinate than his predecessor.* ▷ HISTORY Old French *plier* to fold ▶ **pliancy** *n*

pliers *pl n* a gripping tool consisting of two hinged arms usually with serrated jaws. ▷ HISTORY from PLY[1]

plight[1] *n* a dangerous or difficult situation: *the plight of the British hostages.* ▷ HISTORY Old French *pleit* fold, and probably influenced by Old English *pliht* peril

A B C D E F G H I J K L M N O P Q R S T U V W X Y Z

plight² *vb* **plight one's troth** *Old-fashioned* to make a promise to marry. ▷ **HISTORY** Old English *pliht* peril

Plimsoll line *n* a line on the hull of a ship showing the level that the water should reach if the ship is properly loaded. ▷ **HISTORY** after Samuel *Plimsoll,* who advocated its adoption

plimsolls *pl n Brit* light rubber-soled canvas sports shoes. ▷ **HISTORY** from the resemblance of the sole to a Plimsoll line

plinth *n* **1** a base on which a statue stands. **2** the slab that forms the base of a column or pedestal. ▷ **HISTORY** Greek *plinthos* brick

Pliocene *or* **Pleiocene** (**ply**-oh-seen) *adj Geol* of the epoch of geological time about 10 million years ago. ▷ **HISTORY** Greek *pleiōn* more + *kainos* recent

PLO Palestine Liberation Organization.

plod *vb* **plodding, plodded 1** to walk with heavy slow steps. **2** to work slowly and steadily. ✧ *n* **3** the act of plodding. **4** *Brit slang* a policeman. ▷ **HISTORY** imitative ▶ **plodder** *n*

plonk¹ *vb* **1** to put down heavily and carelessly: *he plonked himself down on the sofa.* ✧ *n* **2** the act or sound of plonking. ▷ **HISTORY** variant of *plunk*

plonk² *n Informal* cheap inferior wine. ▷ **HISTORY** origin unknown

plop *n* **1** the sound made by an object dropping into water without a splash. ✧ *vb* **plopping, plopped 2** to drop with such a sound: *a tear rolled down his cheek and plopped into his soup.* **3** to fall or be placed heavily or carelessly: *we plopped down on the bed and went straight to sleep.* ▷ **HISTORY** imitative

plosive *Phonetics* ✧ *adj* **1** pronounced with a sudden release of breath. ✧ *n* **2** a plosive consonant. ▷ **HISTORY** French *explosif* explosive

plot¹ *n* **1** a secret plan for an illegal purpose. **2** the story of a play, novel, or film. ✧ *vb* **plotting, plotted 3** to plan secretly; conspire. **4** to mark (a course) on a map. **5** to make a plan or map of. **6 a** to locate (points) on a graph by means of coordinates. **b** to draw (a curve) through these points. **7** to construct the plot of (a play, novel, or film). ▷ **HISTORY** from PLOT², influenced by obsolete *complot* conspiracy ▶ **plotter** *n*

plot² *n* a small piece of land: *there was a small vegetable plot in the garden.* ▷ **HISTORY** Old English

plough *or esp US* **plow** *n* **1** an agricultural tool for cutting or turning over the earth. **2** a similar tool used for clearing snow. ✧ *vb* **3** to turn over (the soil) with a plough. **4** to make (furrows or grooves) in (something) with or as if with a plough. **5** (sometimes foll. by *through*) to move (through something) in the manner of a plough: *the ship ploughed through the water.* **6** (foll. by *through*) to work at slowly or perseveringly. **7** to invest (money): *he ploughed the profits back into the business.* **8 plough into** (of a vehicle, plane, etc.) to run uncontrollably into (something): *the aircraft ploughed into a motorway embankment.* ▷ **HISTORY** Old English *plōg* plough land

Plough *n* **the Plough** the group of the seven brightest stars in the constellation Ursa Major.

ploughman *or esp US* **plowman** *n, pl* **-men** a man who ploughs.

ploughman's lunch *n* a snack lunch consisting of bread and cheese with pickle.

ploughshare *or esp US* **plowshare** *n* the cutting blade of a plough.

plover *n* a shore bird with a round head, straight bill, and long pointed wings. ▷ **HISTORY** Old French *plovier* rainbird

plow *n, vb US* same as **plough**.

ploy *n* a manoeuvre designed to gain an advantage in a situation: *a cheap political ploy.* ▷ **HISTORY** from obsolete noun sense of *employ,* meaning an occupation

pluck *vb* **1** to pull or pick off. **2** to pull out the feathers of (a bird for cooking). **3** (foll. by *off, away*) *Archaic* to pull (something) forcibly or violently (from something or someone). **4** to sound the strings of (a musical instrument) with the fingers or a plectrum. **5** *Slang* to swindle. ✧ *n* **6** courage. **7** a pull or tug. **8** the heart, liver, and lungs of an animal used for food. ▷ **HISTORY** Old English *pluccian*

pluck up *vb* to summon up (courage).

plucky *adj* **pluckier, pluckiest** courageous. ▶ **pluckily** *adv* ▶ **pluckiness** *n*

plug *n* **1** an object used to block up holes or waste pipes. **2** a device with one or more pins which connects an appliance to an electricity supply. **3** *Informal* a favourable mention of a product etc., for example on television, to encourage people to buy it. **4** See **spark plug**. **5** a piece of tobacco for chewing. ✧ *vb* **plugging, plugged 6** to block or seal (a hole or gap) with a plug. **7** *Informal* to make frequent favourable mentions of (a product etc.), for example on television. **8** *Slang* to shoot: *he lifted the rifle and plugged the deer.* **9** *Slang* to punch. **10** (foll. by *along, away*) etc. *Informal* to work steadily. ▷ **HISTORY** Middle Dutch *plugge*

plug in *vb* to connect (an electrical appliance) to a power source by pushing a plug into a socket.

plum *n* **1** an oval dark red or yellow fruit with a stone in the middle, that grows on a small tree. **2** a raisin, as used in a cake or pudding. **3** *Informal* something of a superior or desirable kind. ✧ *adj* **4** made from plums: *plum cake.* **5** dark reddish-purple. **6** very desirable: *plum targets for attack.* ▷ **HISTORY** Old English *plūme*

plumage *n* the feathers of a bird. ▷ **HISTORY** Old French *plume* feather

plumb *vb* **1** to understand (something obscure): *to plumb a mystery.* **2 plumb the depths** to experience the worst extremes of: *to plumb the depths of despair.* **3** to test the alignment of or make vertical with a plumb line. **4** (foll. by *in* or *into*) to connect (an appliance or fixture) to a water pipe or drainage system: *the shower should be plumbed in professionally.* ✧ *n* **5** a lead weight hanging at the end of a string and used to test the depth of water or to test whether something is vertical. **6 out of plumb** not vertical. ✧ *adv* **7** vertical or perpendicular. **8** *Informal, chiefly US* utterly: *plumb stupid.* **9** *Informal* exactly: *plumb in the centre.* ▷ **HISTORY** Latin *plumbum* lead

plumber *n* a person who fits and repairs pipes and fixtures for water, drainage, or gas systems. ▷ HISTORY Old French *plommier* worker in lead

plumbing *n* **1** the pipes and fixtures used in a water, drainage, or gas system. **2** the trade or work of a plumber.

plumb line *n* a string with a metal weight at one end, used to test the depth of water or to test whether something is vertical.

plume *n* **1** a large ornamental feather. **2** a group of feathers worn as a badge or ornament on a hat. **3** something like a plume: *a plume of smoke.* ✧ *vb* **pluming, plumed 4** to adorn with plumes. **5** (of a bird) to preen (its feathers). **6** (foll. by *on* or *upon*) to be proud of oneself or one's achievements, esp. unjustifiably: *she was pluming herself on her figure.* ▷ HISTORY Old French

plummet *vb* **-meting, -meted 1** to plunge downward. ✧ *n* **2** the weight on a plumb line or fishing line. ▷ HISTORY Old French *plommet* ball of lead

plump[1] *adj* **1** full or rounded: *until puberty I was really quite plump.* ✧ *vb* **2** (often foll. by *up* or *out*) to make (something) fuller or rounded: *she plumped up the cushions on the couch.* ▷ HISTORY Middle Dutch *plomp* blunt ▶ **plumpness** *n*

plump[2] *vb* **1** (often foll. by *down, into*) to drop or sit suddenly and heavily: *he plumped down on the seat.* **2 plump for** to choose one from a selection. ✧ *n* **3** a heavy abrupt fall or the sound of this. ✧ *adv* **4** suddenly or heavily. **5** directly: *the plane landed plump in the middle of the field.* **6** in a blunt, direct, or decisive manner. ▷ HISTORY probably imitative

plum pudding *n Brit & Austral* a boiled or steamed pudding made with flour, suet, and dried fruit.

plunder *vb* **1** to seize (valuables or goods) from (a place) by force, usually in wartime; loot. ✧ *n* **2** anything plundered; booty. **3** the act of plundering; pillage. ▷ HISTORY probably from Dutch *plunderen*

plunge *vb* **plunging, plunged 1** (usually foll. by *into*) to thrust or throw (something or oneself) forcibly or suddenly: *they plunged into the sea; he plunged the knife in to the hilt.* **2** to throw or be thrown into a certain condition: *the room was plunged into darkness.* **3** (usually foll. by *into*) to involve or become involved deeply (in). **4** to move swiftly or impetuously. **5** to descend very suddenly or steeply: *temperatures were plunging.* **6** *Informal* to gamble recklessly. ✧ *n* **7** a leap or dive. **8** *Informal* a swim. **9** a pitching motion. **10 take the plunge** *Informal* to make a risky decision which cannot be reversed later. ▷ HISTORY Old French *plongier*

plunge pool *n Geog* a pool at the base of a waterfall carved out by the action of the water.

plunger *n* **1** a rubber suction cup used to clear blocked drains. **2** a device with a plunging motion; piston.

plunk *vb* **1** to pluck the strings of (an instrument) to produce a twanging sound. **2** (often foll. by *down*) to drop or be dropped heavily. ✧ *n* **3** the act or sound of plunking. ▷ HISTORY imitative

plunket baby *n NZ* a baby brought up according to the principles of the Plunket Society. ▶ **plunket nurse** *NZ* a nurse working for the Plunket Society.

Plunket Society *n NZ* an organization for the care of mothers and babies.

pluperfect *or* **pluperfect tense** *n Grammar* same as **past perfect**. ▷ HISTORY Latin *plus quam perfectum* more than perfect

plural *adj* **1** of or consisting of more than one. **2** *Grammar* denoting a word indicating more than one. ✧ *n* **3** *Grammar* **a** the plural number. **b** a plural form. ▷ HISTORY Latin *plus* more

pluralism *n* **1** the existence and toleration in a society of a variety of groups of different ethnic origins, cultures, or religions. **2** the holding of more than one office by a person. ▶ **pluralist** *n, adj* ▶ **pluralistic** *adj*

plurality *n, pl* **-ties 1** the state of being plural. **2** *Maths* a number greater than one. **3** a large number. **4** a majority.

pluralize *or* **-ise** *vb* **-izing, -ized** *or* **-ising, -ised** to make or become plural.

plus *prep* **1** increased by the addition of: *four plus two.* **2** with the addition of: *a good salary, plus a company car.* ✧ *adj* **3** indicating addition: *a plus sign.* **4** *Maths* same as **positive** (sense 7). **5** on the positive part of a scale. **6** indicating the positive side of an electrical circuit. **7** involving advantage: *a plus factor.* **8** *Informal* having a value above the value stated: *it must be worth a thousand pounds plus.* **9** slightly above a specified standard: *he received a B plus for his essay.* ✧ *n* **10** a plus sign (+), indicating addition. **11** a positive quantity. **12** *Informal* something positive or an advantage. **13** a gain, surplus, or advantage. ▷ HISTORY Latin: more

> **WORD TIP**
> *Plus, together with,* and *along with* do not create compound subjects in the way that *and* does: the number of the verb depends on that of the subject to which *plus, together with,* or *along with* is added: *this task, plus all the others, was* (not *were*) *undertaken by the government; the doctor, together with the nurses, was* (not *were*) *waiting for the patient.*

plus fours *pl n* men's baggy knickerbockers gathered in at the knee, now only worn for hunting or golf. ▷ HISTORY because made with four inches of material to hang over at the knee

plush *n* **1** a velvety fabric with a long soft pile, used for furniture coverings. ✧ *adj* **2** Also: **plushy** *Informal* luxurious. ▷ HISTORY French *pluche*

Pluto *n* **1** *Classical myth* the god of the underworld. **2** the smallest planet and the one farthest from the sun.

plutocracy *n, pl* **-cies 1** government by the wealthy. **2** a state ruled by the wealthy. **3** a group that exercises power on account of its wealth. ▷ HISTORY Greek *ploutos* wealth + *-kratia* rule ▶ **plutocratic** *adj*

A B C D E F G H I J K L M N O **P** Q R S T U V W X Y Z

plutocrat *n* a person who is powerful because of being very rich.

plutonic *adj* (of igneous rocks) formed from molten rock that has cooled and solidified below the earth's surface. ▷ HISTORY after the Greek god *Pluto*

plutonium *n Chem* a toxic radioactive metallic element, used in nuclear reactors and weapons. Symbol: Pu. ▷ HISTORY after *Pluto,* because Pluto lies beyond Neptune and plutonium was discovered soon after neptunium

pluvial *adj Geog, geol* of or due to the action of rain. ▷ HISTORY Latin *pluvia* rain

ply[1] *vb* **plies, plying, plied 1** to work at (a job or trade). **2** to use (a tool). **3** (usually foll. by *with*) to provide (with) or subject (to) persistently: *he plied us with drink; he plied me with questions.* **4** to work steadily. **5** (of a ship) to travel regularly along (a route): *to ply the trade routes.* ▷ HISTORY Middle English *plye,* short for *aplye* to apply

ply[2] *n, pl* **plies 1** a layer or thickness, such as of fabric or wood. **2** one of the strands twisted together to make rope or yarn. ▷ HISTORY Old French *pli* fold

Plymouth Brethren *pl n* a Puritanical religious sect with no organized ministry.

plywood *n* a board made of thin layers of wood glued together under pressure, with the grain of one layer at right angles to the grain of the next.

Pm *Chem* promethium.

PM 1 Prime Minister. **2** Postmaster. **3** Paymaster.

p.m. 1 after noon. ▷ HISTORY Latin *post meridiem* **2** postmortem (examination).

PMG 1 Postmaster General. **2** Paymaster General.

PMS premenstrual syndrome.

PMT premenstrual tension.

pneumatic *adj* **1** operated by compressed air: *pneumatic drill.* **2** containing compressed air: *a pneumatic tyre.* **3** of or concerned with air, gases, or wind. ▷ HISTORY Greek *pneuma* breath, wind

pneumatics *n* the branch of physics concerned with the mechanical properties of air and other gases.

pneumonia *n* inflammation of one or both lungs. ▷ HISTORY Greek *pneumōn* lung

Po *Chem* polonium.

PO 1 Also: **p.o.** *Brit* postal order. **2** Post Office. **3** petty officer. **4** Pilot Officer.

poach[1] *vb* **1** to catch (game or fish) illegally on someone else's land. **2 a** to encroach on (someone's rights or duties). **b** to steal (an idea, employee, or player). ▷ HISTORY Old French *pocher* ▶ **poacher** *n*

poach[2] *vb* to simmer (food) very gently in liquid. ▷ HISTORY Old French *pochier* to enclose in a bag

pock *n* **1** a pus-filled blister resulting from smallpox. **2** a pockmark. ▷ HISTORY Old English *pocc*

pocket *n* **1** a small pouch sewn into clothing for carrying small articles. **2** any pouchlike container, esp. for catching balls at the edge of a snooker table. **3** a small isolated area or group: *a pocket of resistance.* **4** a cavity in the earth, such as one containing ore. **5 in one's pocket** under one's control. **6 out of pocket** having made a loss. ✧ *vb* **-eting, -eted 7** to put into one's pocket. **8** to take secretly or dishonestly. **9** *Billiards etc.* to drive (a ball) into a pocket. **10** to conceal or suppress: *he pocketed his pride and asked for help.* ✧ *adj* **11** small: *a pocket edition.* ▷ HISTORY Anglo-Norman *poket* a little bag

pocket borough *n* (before the Reform Act of 1832) an English borough constituency controlled by one person or family.

pocketknife *n, pl* **-knives** a small knife with one or more blades that fold into the handle; penknife.

pocket money *n* **1** a small weekly sum of money given to children by parents. **2** money for small personal expenses.

pockmarked *adj* **1** (of the skin) marked with pitted scars after the healing of smallpox. **2** (of a surface) covered in many small hollows: *the building is pockmarked with bullet holes.* ▶ **pockmark** *n*

pod *n* **1 a** a long narrow seedcase containing peas, beans, etc. **b** the seedcase as distinct from the seeds. ✧ *vb* **podding, podded 2** to remove the pod from. ▷ HISTORY origin unknown

podgy *adj* **podgier, podgiest** short and fat. ▷ HISTORY from *podge* a short plump person ▶ **podginess** *n*

podium *n, pl* **-diums** *or* **-dia 1** a small raised platform used by conductors or speakers. **2** a plinth that supports a colonnade or wall. ▷ HISTORY Latin: platform

podzol *or* **podsol** *n Geol* a type of soil characteristic of coniferous forest regions having a greyish-white colour in its upper layers from which certain minerals have leached. ▷ HISTORY Russian: ash ground, from *pod* ground + *zola* ashes

poem *n* **1** a literary work, often in verse, usually dealing with emotional or descriptive themes in a rhythmic form. **2** a literary work that is not in verse but deals with emotional or descriptive themes in a rhythmic form: *a prose poem.* **3** anything like a poem in beauty or effect: *his painting is a poem on creation.* ▷ HISTORY Greek *poiēma* something created

poep (**poop**) *n S African taboo* **1** an emission of intestinal gas from the anus. **2** a mean or despicable person. ▷ HISTORY Afrikaans

poesy *n Archaic* poetry.

poet *n* **1** a writer of poetry. **2** a person with great imagination and creativity. ▷ HISTORY Greek *poiētēs* maker, poet

poetaster *n* a writer of inferior verse.

poetic *or* **poetical** *adj* **1** like poetry, by being expressive or imaginative. **2** of poetry or poets. **3** recounted in verse.

poetic justice *n* an appropriate punishment or reward for previous actions.

poetic licence *n* freedom from the normal rules of language or truth, as in poetry.

poet laureate *n, pl* **poets laureate** *Brit* the poet selected by the British sovereign to write poems on important occasions.

poetry *n* **1** poems in general. **2** the art or craft of writing poems. **3** a poetic quality that prompts an emotional response: *her acting was full of poetry.* ▷ **HISTORY** Latin *poeta* poet

po-faced *adj* wearing a disapproving stern expression. ▷ **HISTORY** perhaps from PO + POKER-FACED

pogey *or* **pogy** (**pohg**-ee) *n, pl* **pogeys** *or* **pogies** *Canad slang* **1** financial or other relief given to the unemployed by the government; dole. **2** unemployment insurance. ▷ **HISTORY** from earlier *pogie* workhouse

pogo stick *n* a pole with steps for the feet and a spring at the bottom, so that the user can bounce up, down, and along on it. ▷ **HISTORY** origin unknown

pogrom *n* an organized persecution and massacre. ▷ **HISTORY** Russian: destruction

poi *n NZ* a ball of woven flax swung rhythmically by Maori women during poi dances. ▷ **HISTORY** Maori

poi dance *n NZ* a women's formation dance that involves singing and twirling a poi.

poignant *adj* **1** sharply painful to the feelings: *a poignant reminder.* **2** cutting: *poignant wit.* **3** pertinent in mental appeal: *a poignant subject.* ▷ **HISTORY** Latin *pungens* pricking ▶ **poignancy** *n*

poinsettia *n* a shrub of Mexico and Central America, widely grown for its showy scarlet bracts, which resemble petals. ▷ **HISTORY** after J. P. *Poinsett,* US Minister to Mexico

point *n* **1** the essential idea in an argument or discussion: *I agreed with the point he made.* **2** a reason or aim: *what is the point of this exercise?* **3** a detail or item. **4** a characteristic: *he has his good points.* **5** a location or position. **6** a dot or tiny mark. **7** a dot used as a decimal point or a full stop. **8** the sharp tip of anything: *the point of the spear.* **9** a headland: *the soaring cliffs at Dwerja Point in the southwest of the island.* **10** *Maths* a geometric element having a position located by coordinates, but no magnitude. **11** a specific condition or degree: *freezing point.* **12** a moment: *at that point he left.* **13** (*often pl*) any of the extremities, such as the tail, ears, or feet, of a domestic animal. **14** (*often pl*) *Ballet* the tip of the toes. **15** a single unit for measuring something such as value, or of scoring in a game. **16** *Printing* a unit of measurement equal to one twelfth of a pica. **17** *Navigation* one of the 32 direction marks on the compass. **18** *Cricket* a fielding position at right angles to the batsman on the off side. **19** either of the two electrical contacts that make or break the circuit in the distributor of a motor vehicle. **20** *Brit, Austral, & NZ* (*often pl*) a movable section of railway track used to direct a train from one line to another. **21** *Brit* short for **power point**. **22** *Boxing* a mark awarded for a scoring blow or knockdown. **23 beside the point** irrelevant. **24 make a point of a** to make a habit of (something). **b** to do (something) because one thinks it important. **25 on** *or* **at the point of** about to; on the verge of: *on the point of leaving.* **26 to the point** relevant. **27 up to a point** not completely. ✧ *vb* **28** (usually foll. by *at* or *to*) to show the position or direction of something by extending a finger or other pointed object towards it. **29** (usually foll. by *at* or *to*) to single out one person or thing from among several: *all the symptoms pointed to epilepsy.* **30** to direct or face in a specific direction: *point me in the right direction.* **31** to finish or repair the joints in brickwork with mortar or cement. **32** (of gun dogs) to show where game is lying by standing rigidly with the muzzle turned towards it. ▷ **HISTORY** Latin *pungere* to pierce

point-blank *adj* **1** fired at a very close target. **2** plain or blunt: *a point-blank refusal to discuss the matter.* ✧ *adv* **3** directly or bluntly: *the Minister was asked point-blank if he intended to resign.* ▷ **HISTORY** *point* + *blank* (centre spot of an archery target)

point duty *n* the control of traffic by a policeman at a road junction.

pointed *adj* **1** having a sharp tip. **2** cutting or incisive: *pointed wit.* **3** obviously directed at a particular person: *a pointed remark.* **4** emphasized or obvious: *pointed ignorance.* ▶ **pointedly** *adv*

pointer *n* **1** something that is a helpful indicator of how a situation has arisen or may turn out: *a significant pointer to the likely resumption of talks.* **2** an indicator on a measuring instrument. **3** a long stick used by teachers, to point out particular features on a map, chart, etc. **4** a large smooth-coated gun dog.

pointillism (**pwan**-till-iz-zum) *n* a technique used by some impressionist painters, in which dots of colour are placed side by side so that they merge when seen from a distance. ▷ **HISTORY** French ▶ **pointillist** *n, adj*

pointless *adj* without meaning or purpose.

point of order *n, pl* **points of order** an objection in a meeting to the departure from the proper procedure.

point of view *n, pl* **points of view 1** a mental viewpoint or attitude: *she refuses to see the other person's point of view.* **2** a way of considering something: *a scientific point of view.*

point-to-point *n Brit* a steeplechase organized by a hunt.

poise *n* **1** dignified manner. **2** physical balance: *the poise of a natural model.* **3** mental balance: *he recovered his poise.* ✧ *vb* **poising, poised 4** to be balanced or suspended. **5** to be held in readiness: *the cats were poised to spring on her.* ▷ **HISTORY** Old French *pois* weight

poised *adj* **1** absolutely ready. **2** behaving with or showing poise.

poison *n* **1** a substance that causes death or injury when swallowed or absorbed. **2** something that destroys or corrupts: *the poison of Nazism.* ✧ *vb* **3** to give poison to someone. **4** to add poison to something. **5** to have a harmful or evil effect on. **6** (foll. by *against*) to turn (a person's mind) against: *he poisoned her mind against me.* ▷ **HISTORY** Latin *potio* a drink, esp. a poisonous one ▶ **poisoner** *n*

poison ivy *n* a North American climbing plant that causes an itching rash if it touches the skin.

poisonous *adj* **1** of or like a poison. **2** malicious.

poison-pen letter *n* a malicious anonymous letter.

poke[1] *vb* **poking, poked 1** to jab or prod with an elbow, finger, etc. **2** to make a hole by poking. **3** (sometimes foll. by *at*) to thrust (at): *she poked at the food with her fork.* **4** (usually foll. by *in, through*) to thrust forward or out: *yellow hair poked from beneath his cap.* **5** to stir (a fire) by poking. **6** (often foll. by *about* or *around*) to search or pry. **7 poke one's nose into** to meddle in. ✧ *n* **8** a jab or prod. ▷ **HISTORY** Low German & Middle Dutch *poken*

poke[2] *n* **1** *Dialect* a pocket or bag. **2 a pig in a poke** See **pig**. ▷ **HISTORY** Old French *poque*

poker[1] *n* a metal rod with a handle for stirring a fire.

poker[2] *n* a card game of bluff and skill in which players bet on the hands dealt. ▷ **HISTORY** origin unknown

pokerwork *n* the art of producing pictures or designs on wood by burning it with a heated metal point.

poky *adj* **pokier, pokiest** (of a room) small and cramped. ▷ **HISTORY** from POKE[1] (in slang sense: to confine) ▶ **pokiness** *n*

pol. 1 political. **2** politics.

polar *adj* **1** of or near either of the earth's poles or the area inside the Arctic or Antarctic Circles. **2** of or having a pole or polarity. **3** directly opposite in tendency or nature: *polar opposites.*

polar bear *n* a white bear of coastal regions of the North Pole.

polar circle *n* the Arctic or Antarctic Circle.

polarity *n, pl* **-ties 1** the state of having two directly opposite tendencies or opinions. **2** the condition of a body which has opposing physical properties, usually magnetic poles or electric charge. **3** the particular state of a part with polarity: *an electrode with positive polarity.*

polarization *or* **-isation** *n* **1** the condition of having or giving polarity. **2** *Physics* the condition in which waves of light or other radiation are restricted to certain directions of vibration.

polarize *or* **-ise** *vb* **-izing, -ized** *or* **-ising, -ised 1** to cause people to adopt directly opposite opinions: *political opinion had polarized since the restoration of democracy.* **2** to have or give polarity or polarization.

Polaroid *n Trademark* **1** a type of plastic that polarizes light: used in sunglasses to eliminate glare. **2 Polaroid camera** a camera that produces a finished print by developing and processing it inside the camera within a few seconds. **3 Polaroids** sunglasses with Polaroid plastic lenses.

polder *n* a stretch of land reclaimed from the sea. ▷ **HISTORY** Middle Dutch *polre*

pole[1] *n* **1** a long slender rounded piece of wood, metal, or other material. **2 up the pole** *Brit, Austral & NZ informal* **a** slightly mad. **b** in a predicament. ▷ **HISTORY** Latin *palus* a stake

pole[2] *n* **1** either end of the earth's axis of rotation. See also **North Pole, South Pole**. **2** *Physics* **a** either of the opposite forces of a magnet. **b** either of two points at which there are opposite electric charges. **3** either of two directly opposite tendencies or opinions. **4 poles apart** having widely divergent opinions or tastes. ▷ **HISTORY** Greek *polos* pivot

Pole *n* a person from Poland.

poleaxe *or US* **poleax** *vb* **-axing, -axed 1** to hit or stun with a heavy blow. ✧ *n* **2** an axe formerly used in battle or used by a butcher. ▷ **HISTORY** Middle English *pollax* battle-axe

polecat *n, pl* **-cats** *or* **-cat 1** a dark brown mammal like a weasel that gives off a foul smell. **2** *US* a skunk. ▷ **HISTORY** origin unknown

polemic (pol-**em**-ik) *n* **1** a fierce attack on or defence of a particular opinion, belief, etc.: *anti-capitalist polemic.* ✧ *adj also* **polemical 2** of or involving dispute or controversy. ▷ **HISTORY** Greek *polemos* war ▶ **polemicist** *n*

polemics *n* the art of dispute.

pole position *n* **1** (in motor racing) the starting position on the inside of the front row, generally considered the best one. **2** an advantageous starting position.

Pole Star *n* **the Pole Star** the star closest to the N celestial pole.

pole vault *n* **1 the pole vault** a field event in which competitors try to clear a high bar with the aid of a very flexible long pole. ✧ *vb* **pole-vault 2** to perform or compete in the pole vault. ▶ **pole-vaulter** *n*

police *n* **1** (often preceded by *the*) the organized civil force in a state which keeps law and order. **2** the men and women who are members of such a force. **3** an organized body with a similar function: *security police.* ✧ *vb* **-licing, -liced 4** to maintain order or control by means of a police force or similar body. ▷ **HISTORY** French, from Latin *politia* administration

police dog *n* a dog trained to help the police.

policeman *or fem* **policewoman** *n, pl* **-men** *or* **-women** a member of a police force.

police procedural *n* a novel, film, or television drama that deals with police work.

police state *n* a state in which a government controls people's freedom through the police.

police station *n* the office of the police force of a district.

policy[1] *n, pl* **-cies 1** a plan of action adopted by a person, group, or government. **2** *Archaic* wisdom or prudence. ▷ **HISTORY** Old French *policie,* from Latin *politia* administration

policy[2] *n, pl* **-cies** a document containing an insurance contract. ▷ **HISTORY** Old French *police* certificate ▶ **policyholder** *n*

polio *n* short for **poliomyelitis**.

poliomyelitis (pole-ee-oh-my-el-**lite**-iss) *n* a viral disease which affects the brain and spinal cord, often causing paralysis. ▷ **HISTORY** Greek *polios* grey + *muelos* marrow

polish *vb* **1** to make smooth and shiny by rubbing. **2** to perfect or complete: *media experts he had hired to polish his image.* **3** to make or become elegant or refined: *not having polished his south London accent didn't help his career.* ✧ *n* **4** a substance used for polishing. **5** a shine or gloss.

6 elegance or refinement. ▷ **HISTORY** Latin *polire* to polish

Polish *adj* **1** of Poland. ✧ *n* **2** the language of Poland.

polished *adj* **1** accomplished: *a polished actor.* **2** done or performed well or professionally: *a polished performance.*

polish off *vb Informal* **1** to finish completely. **2** to dispose of or kill.

Politburo *n* formerly, the chief decision-making committee of a Communist country. ▷ **HISTORY** Russian

polite *adj* **1** having good manners; courteous. **2** cultivated or refined: *polite society.* **3** socially correct but insincere: *he smiled a polite response and stifled an urge to scream.* ▷ **HISTORY** Latin *politus* polished ▶ **politely** *adv* ▶ **politeness** *n*

politic *adj* **1** wise or possibly advantageous: *I didn't feel it was politic to mention it.* **2** artful or shrewd: *a politic manager.* **3** crafty; cunning: *a politic old scoundrel.* **4** *Archaic* political. See also **body politic**. ▷ **HISTORY** Old French *politique*, from Greek *polis* city

political *adj* **1** of the state, government, or public administration. **2** relating to or interested in politics: *she was always a very political person.* **3** of the parties and the partisan aspects of politics: *the government blames political opponents for fanning the unrest.* ▶ **politically** *adv*

political cartoon *n* a cartoon that satirizes or makes observations about recent political events.

politically correct *adj* displaying progressive attitudes, esp. in using vocabulary which is intended to avoid any implied prejudice.

political prisoner *n* a person imprisoned for holding particular political beliefs.

political science *n* the study of the state, government, and politics. ▶ **political scientist** *n*

politician *n* a person actively engaged in politics, esp. a member of parliament.

politicize *or* **-cise** *vb* **-cizing, -cized** *or* **-cising, -cised 1** to make political or politically aware. **2** to take part in political discussion or activity. ▶ **politicization** *or* **-cisation** *n*

politics *n* **1** (*functioning as sing*) the art and science of government. **2** (*functioning as pl*) political opinions or sympathies: *his conservative politics.* **3** (*functioning as pl*) political activities or affairs: *party politics.* **4** (*functioning as sing*) the business or profession of politics. **5** (*functioning as sing or pl*) any activity concerned with the acquisition of power: *company politics are often vicious.*

polity *n, pl* **-ties** *Formal* **1** a politically organized state, church, or society. **2** a form of government of a state, church, or society. ▷ **HISTORY** Greek *politeia* citizenship, from *polis* city

polka *n* **1** a lively 19th-century dance. **2** music for this dance. ✧ *vb* **-kaing, -kaed 3** to dance a polka. ▷ **HISTORY** Czech *pulka* half-step

polka dots *pl n* a regular pattern of small bold spots on a fabric.

poll *n* **1** Also called: **opinion poll** the questioning of a random sample of people to find out the general opinion. **2** the casting, recording, or counting of votes in an election. **3** the result of such a voting: *a marginal poll.* **4** the head. ✧ *vb* **5** to receive (a certain number of votes). **6** to record the votes of: *he polled the whole town.* **7** to question (a person, etc.) as part of an opinion poll. **8** to vote in an election. **9** to clip or shear. **10** to remove or cut short the horns of (cattle). ▷ **HISTORY** Middle Low German *polle* hair, head, top of a tree

pollack *or* **pollock** *n, pl* **-lacks, -lack, -locks** *or* **-lock** a food fish related to the cod, found in northern seas. ▷ **HISTORY** origin unknown

pollard *n* **1** an animal that has shed its horns or has had them removed. **2** a tree with its top cut off to encourage a more bushy growth. ✧ *vb* **3** to cut off the top of (a tree) to make it grow bushy. ▷ **HISTORY** see POLL ▶ **pollarded** *adj*

pollen *n* a fine powder produced by flowers to fertilize other flowers of the same species. ▷ **HISTORY** Latin: powder

pollen count *n* a measure of the amount of pollen in the air over a 24-hour period, often published as a warning to hay fever sufferers.

pollinate *vb* **-nating, -nated** to fertilize by the transfer of pollen. ▶ **pollination** *n*

polling booth *n* a compartment in which a voter can mark his or her ballot paper in private during an election.

polling station *n* a building where voters go during an election to cast their votes.

pollster *n* a person who conducts opinion polls.

poll tax *n* any tax levied per head of adult population, esp. the tax which replaced domestic rates (in Scotland from 1989 and England and Wales from 1990, until 1993).

pollutant *n* a substance that pollutes, usually the chemical waste of an industrial process.

pollute *vb* **-luting, -luted 1** to contaminate with poisonous or harmful substances. **2** to corrupt morally. ▷ **HISTORY** Latin *polluere* to defile

pollution *n* **1** *Environmental science* harmful or poisonous substances introduced into an environment. **2** the act of polluting or the state of being polluted.

polo *n* **1** a game like hockey played on horseback with long-handled mallets and a wooden ball. **2** short for **water polo**. ▷ **HISTORY** Tibetan *pulu* ball

polonaise *n* **1** a stately Polish dance. **2** music for this dance. ▷ **HISTORY** French *danse polonaise* Polish dance

polo neck *n* a sweater with a high tight turned-over collar.

polonium *n Chem* a rare radioactive element found in trace amounts in uranium ores. Symbol: Po. ▷ **HISTORY** Medieval Latin *Polonia* Poland; in honour of the nationality of its discoverer, Marie Curie

polo shirt *n* a cotton short-sleeved shirt with a collar and three-button opening at the neck.

poltergeist *n* a spirit believed to be responsible for noises and acts of mischief, such as throwing objects about. ▷ **HISTORY** German *poltern* to be noisy + *Geist* ghost

poltroon *n Obsolete* a complete coward. ▷ **HISTORY** Old Italian *poltrone* lazy good-for-nothing

poly *n, pl* **polys** *Informal* short for **polytechnic**.

poly- *combining form* many or much: *polyhedron; polysyllabic.* ▷ **HISTORY** Greek *polus*

polyandry *n* the practice of having more than one husband at the same time. ▷ **HISTORY** Greek *polus* many + *anēr* man ▶ **polyandrous** *adj*

polyanthus *n, pl* **-thuses** a hybrid garden primrose with brightly coloured flowers. ▷ **HISTORY** Greek: having many flowers

polychromatic *adj* **1** having many colours. **2** (of radiation) containing more than one wavelength.

polyester *n* a synthetic material used to make plastics and textile fibres.

polyethylene *n* same as **polythene**.

polygamy (pol-**ig**-a-mee) *n* the practice of having more than one wife or husband at the same time. ▷ **HISTORY** Greek *polus* many + *gamos* marriage ▶ **polygamist** *n* ▶ **polygamous** *adj*

polyglot *adj* **1** able to speak many languages. **2** written in or using many languages. ✧ *n* **3** a person who can speak many languages. ▷ **HISTORY** Greek *poluglōttos* many-tongued

polygon *n* a geometrical figure with three or more sides and angles. ▷ **HISTORY** Greek *polugōnon* figure with many angles ▶ **polygonal** *adj*

polygraph *n* an instrument for recording pulse rate and perspiration, often used as a lie detector. ▷ **HISTORY** Greek *polugraphos* writing copiously

polygyny *n* the practice of having more than one wife at the same time. ▷ **HISTORY** Greek *polus* many + *gunē* woman ▶ **polygynous** *adj*

polyhedron *n, pl* **-drons** *or* **-dra** a solid figure with four or more sides. ▷ **HISTORY** Greek *polus* many + *hedron* side ▶ **polyhedral** *adj*

Polyhymnia *n Greek myth* the Muse of singing, mime, and sacred dance.

polymath *n* a person of great and varied learning. ▷ **HISTORY** Greek *polumathēs* having much knowledge

polymer *n* a natural or synthetic compound with large molecules made up of simple molecules of the same kind.

polymeric *adj* of or being a polymer: *polymeric materials such as PVC.* ▷ **HISTORY** Greek *polumerēs* having many parts

polymerization *or* **-isation** *n* the process of forming a polymer. ▶ **polymerize** *or* **-ise** *vb*

polymorphous *or* **polymorphic** *adj* having, or passing through many different forms or stages. ▷ **HISTORY** Greek *polus* many + *morphē* form

Polynesian *adj* **1** of Polynesia. ✧ *n* **2** a person from Polynesia. **3** any of the languages of Polynesia.

polynomial *Maths* ✧ *adj* **1** consisting of two or more terms. ✧ *n* **2** an algebraic expression consisting of the sum of a number of terms.

polyp *n* **1** *Zool* a small sea creature that has a hollow cylindrical body with a ring of tentacles around the mouth. **2** *Pathol* a small growth on the surface of a mucous membrane. ▷ **HISTORY** Greek *polupous* having many feet

polypeptide *n Biochem* a polymer made up of amino acids chemically linked together.

polyphonic *adj Music* consisting of several melodies played together.

polyphony (pol-**if**-on-ee) *n, pl* **-nies** polyphonic style of composition or a piece of music using it. ▷ **HISTORY** Greek *poluphōnia* diversity of tones

polysaccharide *n* a carbohydrate which consists of a number of linked sugar molecules, such as starch or cellulose.

polystyrene *n* a synthetic material used esp. as white rigid foam for insulating and packing.

polysyllabic *adj* **1** having more than two syllables: *polysyllabic words.* **2** containing a marked number of words of more than two syllables: *polysyllabic language.*

polysyllable *n* a word having more than two syllables.

polytechnic *n* **1** *Brit* (in New Zealand and formerly in Britain) college offering courses in many subjects at and below degree level. ✧ *adj* **2** of or relating to technical instruction. ▷ **HISTORY** Greek *polutekhnos* skilled in many arts

polytheism *n* belief in more than one god. ▶ **polytheistic** *adj* ▶ **polytheist** *n*

polythene *n* a light plastic material made from ethylene, usually made into thin sheets or bags.

polyunsaturated *adj* of a group of fats that are less likely to contribute to the build-up of cholesterol in the body.

polyurethane *n* a synthetic material used esp. in paints.

polyvinyl chloride *n* See **PVC**.

pom *n Austral & NZ slang* person from England **pommy**

pomade *n* a perfumed oil put on the hair to make it smooth and shiny, esp. formerly. ▷ **HISTORY** French *pommade*

pomander *n* **1** a mixture of sweet-smelling substances in a container, used to perfume drawers or cupboards. **2** a container for such a mixture. ▷ **HISTORY** Medieval Latin *pomum ambrae* apple of amber

pomegranate *n* a round tropical fruit with a tough reddish rind containing many seeds in a juicy red pulp. ▷ **HISTORY** Latin *pomum* apple + *granatus* full of seeds

pomelo (**pom**-ill-oh) *n, pl* **-los** the edible yellow fruit, like a grapefruit, of a tropical tree. ▷ **HISTORY** Dutch *pompelmoes*

Pomeranian *n* a toy dog with a long straight silky coat. ▷ **HISTORY** after *Pomerania,* region of N central Europe

pomfret (**pum**-frit) *or* **pomfret-cake** *n* a small black rounded liquorice sweet. ▷ **HISTORY** from *Pomfret,* earlier form of *Pontefract,* Yorks., where originally made

pommel *n* **1** the raised part on the front of a saddle. **2** a knob at the top of a sword handle. ✧ *vb* **-melling, -melled** *or US* **-meling, -meled 3** same as **pummel**. ▷ **HISTORY** Old French *pomel* knob

pommy *n, pl* **-mies** (*sometimes cap*) *Slang* a word used by Australians and New Zealanders for a British person. Sometimes shortened to: **pom** ▷ **HISTORY** origin unknown

pomp *n* **1** stately display or ceremony. **2** ostentatious display. ▷ **HISTORY** Greek *pompē* procession

pompom *n* **1** a decorative ball of tufted silk or wool. **2** the small round flower head of some dahlias and chrysanthemums. ▷ **HISTORY** French

pompous *adj* **1** foolishly dignified or self-important. **2** foolishly grand in style: *a pompous speech.* ▸ **pomposity** *n* ▸ **pompously** *adv*

ponce *Offensive slang, chiefly Brit* ✧ *n* **1** an effeminate man. **2** same as **pimp**. ✧ *vb* **poncing, ponced 3** (often foll. by *around* or *about*) *Brit & Austral* to act stupidly or waste time. ▷ **HISTORY** from Polari, an English slang derived from the Mediterranean ports

poncho *n, pl* **-chos** a type of cloak made of a piece of cloth with a hole in the middle for the head. ▷ **HISTORY** American Spanish

pond *n* a pool of still water. ▷ **HISTORY** Middle English *ponde* enclosure

ponder *vb* (sometimes foll. by *on* or *over*) to consider thoroughly or deeply. ▷ **HISTORY** Latin *ponderare* to weigh, consider ▸ **ponderable** *adj*

ponderous *adj* **1** serious and dull: *much of the film is ponderous and pretentious.* **2** heavy or huge. **3** (of movement) slow and clumsy. ▷ **HISTORY** Latin *ponderosus* of great weight

pondok *or* **pondokkie** *n* (in southern Africa) a crudely made house or shack. ▷ **HISTORY** Malay *pondók* leaf house

pondweed *n* a plant which grows in ponds and slow streams.

pong *Brit & Austral informal* ✧ *n* **1** a strong unpleasant smell. ✧ *vb* **2** to give off a strong unpleasant smell. ▷ **HISTORY** origin unknown ▸ **pongy** *adj*

ponga (**pong**-a) *n* a tall New Zealand tree fern with large leathery leaves. ▷ **HISTORY** Maori

pons *n, pl* **pontes** *Anat* a bridge of connective tissue.

pontiff *n* the Pope. ▷ **HISTORY** Latin *pontifex* high priest

pontifical *adj* **1** of a pontiff. **2** pompous or dogmatic in manner.

pontificate *vb* **-cating, -cated 1** to speak in a dogmatic manner. **2** to officiate as a pontiff. ✧ *n* **3** the term of office of a Pope.

pontoon[1] *n* a floating platform used to support a bridge. ▷ **HISTORY** Latin *ponto* punt

pontoon[2] *n* a card game in which players try to obtain sets of cards worth 21 points. ▷ **HISTORY** probably an alteration of French *vingt-et-un* twenty-one

pony *n, pl* **-nies** a breed of small horse. ▷ **HISTORY** Scots *powney*, perhaps from Latin *pullus* young animal, foal

ponytail *n* a hairstyle in which the hair is tied in a bunch at the back of the head and hangs down like a tail.

pony trekking *n* the pastime of riding ponies cross-country.

poodle *n* a dog with curly hair, which is sometimes clipped. ▷ **HISTORY** German *Pudel*

poof *n Brit, Austral & NZ offensive slang* a male homosexual. ▷ **HISTORY** French *pouffe* puff ▸ **poofy** *adj*

pooh *interj* an exclamation of disdain, scorn, or disgust.

pooh-pooh *vb* to express disdain or scorn for.

pool[1] *n* **1** a small body of still water. **2** a small body of spilt liquid: *a pool of blood.* **3** See **swimming pool**. **4** a deep part of a stream or river. ▷ **HISTORY** Old English *pōl*

pool[2] *n* **1** a shared fund of resources or workers: *a typing pool.* **2** a billiard game in which all the balls are potted with the cue ball. **3** the combined stakes of those betting in many gambling games. **4** *Commerce* a group of producers who agree to maintain output levels and high prices. ✧ *vb* **5** to put into a common fund. ▷ **HISTORY** French *poule*, literally: hen used to signify stakes in a card game

pool and riffle sequence *n Geog* the natural alternating pattern of deep pools and fast flowing shallows found in rivers and streams.

pools *pl n* **the pools** *Chiefly Brit* a nationwide mainly postal form of gambling which bets on the results of football matches.

poop *n Naut* a raised part at the back of a sailing ship. ▷ **HISTORY** Latin *puppis*

pooped *adj US, Canad, Austral & NZ slang* exhausted or tired: *if I wasn't so pooped I'd run and have a look at it.* ▷ **HISTORY** Middle English *poupen* to blow

poor *adj* **1** having little money and few possessions. **2** less than is necessary or expected: *it was a poor reward for all his effort.* **3** (sometimes foll. by *in*) lacking in (something): *a food which is rich in energy but poor in vitamins.* **4** inferior: *poor quality.* **5** disappointing or disagreeable: *a poor play.* **6** pitiable; unlucky: *poor John is ill.* **7 poor man's (something)** a cheaper substitute for (something): *pewter, sometimes known as poor man's silver.* ▷ **HISTORY** Latin *pauper*

poorhouse *n* same as **workhouse**.

poor law *n English history* a law providing for support of the poor from parish funds.

poorly *adv* **1** badly. ✧ *adj* **2** *Informal* rather ill.

poor White *n Often offensive* a poverty-stricken White person, usually in the southern US or South Africa.

pop[1] *vb* **popping, popped 1** to make or cause to make a small explosive sound. **2** (often foll. by *in, out*) *Informal* to enter or leave briefly or suddenly: *his mother popped out to buy him an ice cream.* **3** to place suddenly or unexpectedly: *Benny popped a sweet into his mouth.* **4** to burst with a small

A B C D E F G H I J K L M N O P Q R S T U V W X Y Z

explosive sound. **5** (of the eyes) to protrude. **6** *Informal* to pawn. **7 pop the question** *Informal* to propose marriage. ✧ *n* **8** a light sharp explosive sound. **9** *Brit informal* a nonalcoholic fizzy drink. ✧ *adv* **10** with a pop. ▷ **HISTORY** imitative

pop[2] *n* **1** music of general appeal, esp. to young people, that usually has a strong rhythm and uses electrical amplification. ✧ *adj* **2** relating to pop music: *a pop concert.* **3** *Informal* short for **popular**.

pop[3] *n Informal* **1** father. **2** an old man.

pop art *n* a movement in modern art that uses the methods, styles, and themes of popular culture and mass media.

popcorn *n* grains of maize heated until they puff up and burst.

Pope *n* the bishop of Rome as head of the Roman Catholic Church. ▷ **HISTORY** Greek *pappas* father

popery (**pope**-er-ee) *n Offensive* Roman Catholicism.

popeyed *adj* **1** staring in astonishment. **2** having bulging eyes.

popinjay *n* a conceited or talkative person. ▷ **HISTORY** Arabic *babaghā* parrot

popish (**pope**-ish) *adj Offensive* relating to Roman Catholicism.

poplar *n* a tall slender tree with light soft wood, triangular leaves, and catkins. ▷ **HISTORY** Latin *populus*

poplin *n* a strong plain-woven fabric, usually of cotton, with fine ribbing. ▷ **HISTORY** French *papeline*

poppadom *or* **poppadum** *n* a thin round crisp fried Indian bread. ▷ **HISTORY** Hindi

poppet *n* a term of affection for a small child or sweetheart. ▷ **HISTORY** variant of *puppet*

popping crease *n Cricket* a line in front of and parallel with the wicket where the batsman stands. ▷ **HISTORY** from obsolete *pop* to hit

poppy *n, pl* **-pies 1** a plant with showy red, orange, or white flowers. **2** a drug, such as opium, obtained from these plants. **3** an artificial red poppy worn to mark Remembrance Sunday and in New Zealand to mark Anzac Day. ✧ *adj* **4** reddish-orange. ▷ **HISTORY** Old English *popæg*

poppycock *n Informal* nonsense. ▷ **HISTORY** Dutch dialect *pappekak,* literally: soft excrement

populace *n* the common people; masses. ▷ **HISTORY** Latin *populus*

popular *adj* **1** widely liked or admired. **2** (often foll. by *with*) liked by a particular person or group: *the bay is popular with windsurfers and water-skiers.* **3** common among the general public: *the groundswell of popular feeling.* **4** designed to appeal to a mass audience: *an attack on him in the popular press.* ▷ **HISTORY** Latin *popularis* of the people ▶ **popularity** *n* ▶ **popularly** *adv*

popular front *n* a left-wing group or party opposed to fascism.

popularize *or* **-ise** *vb* **-izing, -ized** *or* **-ising, -ised 1** to make popular. **2** to make easily understandable. ▶ **popularization** *or* **-isation** *n*

populate *vb* **-lating, -lated 1** (*often passive*) to live in: *a mountainous region populated mainly by Armenians.* **2** to provide with inhabitants. ▷ **HISTORY** Latin *populus* people ▶ **populated** *adj*

population *n* **1** all the inhabitants of a place. **2** the number of such inhabitants. **3** all the people of a particular class in a place: *the bulk of the rural population lives in poverty.* **4** *Ecology* a group of individuals of the same species inhabiting a given area: *a population of grey seals.*

population density *n Statistics* a statistic showing the number of people living within a given area.

population distribution *n Geog* the way in which people settle more or less densely in different areas.

population pyramid *n Statistics* a pyramid-shaped diagram showing the age distribution of a population: the youngest are represented by a rectangle at the base, the oldest by one at the apex.

population size *n Geog* the number of people living in a particular area.

populism *n* a political strategy based on a calculated appeal to the interests or prejudices of ordinary people: *the Islamic radicals preach a heady message of populism and religion.* ▶ **populist** *adj, n*

populous *adj* containing many inhabitants.

porangi (**pore**-ang-ee) *adj NZ informal* crazy; mad. ▷ **HISTORY** Maori

porbeagle *n* a kind of shark.

porcelain *n* **1** a delicate type of china. **2** an object or objects made of this. ▷ **HISTORY** French *porcelaine,* from Italian *porcellana* cowrie shell

porch *n* a covered approach to the entrance of a building. ▷ **HISTORY** French *porche*

porcine *adj* of or like a pig. ▷ **HISTORY** Latin *porcus* a pig

porcupine *n* a large rodent covered with long pointed quills. ▷ **HISTORY** Middle English *porc despyne* pig with spines

pore[1] *vb* **poring, pored pore over** to examine or study intently: *a wife who pored over account books and ledgers all day.* ▷ **HISTORY** Middle English *pouren*

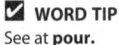

> **☑ WORD TIP**
> See at **pour.**

pore[2] *n* **1** a small opening in the skin or surface of an animal or plant. **2** any small hole, such as a tiny gap in a rock. ▷ **HISTORY** Greek *poros* passage, pore

poriferan (por-**riff**-er-an) *n Biol* a sponge. ▷ **HISTORY** from New Latin *porifer* bearing pores

pork *n* the flesh of pigs used as food. ▷ **HISTORY** Latin *porcus* pig

porker *n* a pig fattened for food.

porn *or* **porno** *n, adj Informal* short for **pornography, pornographic**.

pornography *n* writings, pictures, or films designed to be sexually exciting. ▷ **HISTORY** Greek *pornographos* writing of prostitutes ▶ **pornographer** *n* ▶ **pornographic** *adj*

porosity *n Science* the state or condition of being porous.

porous *adj* **1** allowing air and liquids to be absorbed. **2** *Biol, geol* having pores. ▷ **HISTORY** Late Latin *porus* passage, pore

porphyry (**por**-fir-ee) *n, pl* **-ries** a reddish-purple rock with large crystals of feldspar in it. ▷ **HISTORY** Greek *porphuros* purple ▶ **porphyritic** *adj*

porpoise *n, pl* **-poises** *or* **-poise** a small mammal of the whale family with a blunt snout. ▷ **HISTORY** Latin *porcus* pig + *piscis* fish

porridge *n* **1** a dish made of oatmeal or other cereal, cooked in water or milk. **2** *Chiefly Brit slang* a term of imprisonment. ▷ **HISTORY** variant of *pottage*

port[1] *n* a town with a harbour where ships can load and unload. ▷ **HISTORY** Latin *portus*

port[2] *n* **1** the left side of an aircraft or ship when facing the front of it. ✧ *vb* **2** to turn or be turned towards the port. ▷ **HISTORY** origin unknown

port[3] *n* a strong sweet fortified wine, usually dark red. ▷ **HISTORY** after *Oporto*, Portugal, from where it came originally

port[4] *n* **1** *Naut* **a** an opening with a watertight door in the side of a ship, used for loading, etc. **b** See **porthole**. **2** *Electronics* a logical circuit for the input and output of data. ▷ **HISTORY** Latin *porta* gate

port[5] *vb Computers* to change (programs) from one system to another. ▷ **HISTORY** probably from PORT[4]

portable *adj* **1** easily carried. ✧ *n* **2** an article designed to be easily carried, such as a television or typewriter. ▷ **HISTORY** Latin *portare* to carry ▶ **portability** *n*

portage *n* **1** the transporting of boats and supplies overland between navigable waterways. **2** the route used for such transport. ✧ *vb* **-taging, -taged 3** to transport (boats and supplies) in this way. ▷ **HISTORY** French

portal *n* **1** *Literary* a large and impressive gateway or doorway. **2** *Computers* an Internet site providing links to other sites. ▷ **HISTORY** Latin *porta* gate

portcullis *n* an iron grating suspended in a castle gateway, that can be lowered to bar the entrance. ▷ **HISTORY** Old French *porte coleïce* sliding gate

portend *vb* to be an omen of: *the 0.5 percent increase certainly portends higher inflation ahead.* ▷ **HISTORY** Latin *portendere* to indicate

portent *n* **1** a sign of a future event. **2** great or ominous significance: *matters of great portent.* **3** a marvel. ▷ **HISTORY** Latin *portentum* sign

portentous *adj* **1** of great or ominous significance. **2** self-important or pompous: *there was nothing portentous or solemn about him.*

porter[1] *n* **1** a man employed to carry luggage at a railway station or hotel. **2** a hospital worker who transfers patients between rooms. ▷ **HISTORY** Latin *portare* to carry ▶ **porterage** *n*

porter[2] *n Chiefly Brit* a doorman or gatekeeper of a building. ▷ **HISTORY** Latin *porta* door

porter[3] *n Brit* a dark sweet ale brewed from black malt. ▷ **HISTORY** short for *porter's ale*

porterhouse *n* a thick choice beef steak. Also called: **porterhouse steak** ▷ **HISTORY** formerly, a place that served porter, beer, and sometimes meals

portfolio *n, pl* **-os 1** a flat case for carrying maps, drawings, or papers. **2** selected examples, such as drawings or photographs, that show an artist's recent work. **3** the area of responsibility of the head of a government department: *the defence portfolio.* **4 Minister without portfolio** a cabinet minister without responsibility for a government department. **5** a list of investments held by an investor. ▷ **HISTORY** Italian *portafoglio*

porthole *n* a small round window in a ship or aircraft.

portico *n, pl* **-coes** *or* **-cos** a porch or covered walkway with columns supporting the roof. ▷ **HISTORY** Italian, from Latin *porticus*

portion *n* **1** a part of a whole. **2** a part belonging to a person or group. **3** a helping of food served to one person. **4** *Law* a dowry. **5** *Literary* someone's fate or destiny: *utter disaster was my portion.* ✧ *vb* **6** to divide (something) into shares. ▷ **HISTORY** Latin *portio*

portion out *vb* to distribute or share (something) among a group of people: *the British portioned out the oil-rich lands to various sheikhs.*

portly *adj* **-lier, -liest** stout or rather fat. ▷ **HISTORY** from *port* (in the sense: deportment)

portmanteau *n, pl* **-teaus** *or* **-teaux** *Old-fashioned* a large suitcase made of stiff leather that opens out into two compartments. ▷ **HISTORY** French: cloak carrier

portmanteau word *n* a word made by joining together the beginning and end of two other words, such as *brunch*. Also called: **blend**

portrait *n* **1** a painting, drawing, or photograph of a person, often only of the face. **2** a description. ▷ **HISTORY** French ▶ **portraitist** *n*

portraiture *n* **1** the art of making portraits. **2** a description. **3 a** a portrait. **b** portraits collectively.

portray *vb* to describe or represent (someone) by artistic means, such as in writing or on film. ▷ **HISTORY** Old French *portraire* to depict ▶ **portrayal** *n*

Portuguese *adj* **1** of Portugal. ✧ *n* **2** (*pl* **-guese**) a person from Portugal. **3** the language of Portugal and Brazil.

Portuguese man-of-war *n* a large sea creature like a jellyfish, with long stinging tentacles.

pose *vb* **posing, posed 1** to take up a particular position to be photographed or drawn. **2** to behave in an affected way in order to impress others. **3** (often foll. by *as*) to pretend to be (someone one is not). **4** to create or be (a problem, threat, etc.): *dressing complicated wounds has always posed a problem for doctors.* **5** to put forward or ask: *the question you posed earlier.* ✧ *n* **6** a position taken up for an artist or photographer. **7** behaviour adopted for effect. ▷ **HISTORY** Old French *poser* to set in place

Poseidon *n Greek myth* the god of the sea.

poser[1] *n* **1** *Brit, Austral & NZ informal* a person who likes to be seen in trendy clothes in fashionable places. **2** a person who poses.

poser[2] *n* a baffling question.

poseur *n* a person who behaves in an affected way in order to impress others. ▷ **HISTORY** French

posh *adj Informal, chiefly Brit* **1** smart or elegant. **2** upper-class. ▷ **HISTORY** probably from obsolete slang *posh* a dandy

posit (**pozz**-it) *vb* **-iting, -ited** to lay down as a basis for argument: *the archetypes posited by modern psychology.* ▷ **HISTORY** Latin *ponere* to place

position *n* **1** place or location: *the hotel is in an elevated position above the River Wye.* **2** the proper or usual place. **3** the way in which a person or thing is placed or arranged: *an upright position.* **4** point of view; attitude: *the Catholic Church's position on contraception.* **5** social status, esp. high social standing. **6** a job; appointment. **7** *Sport* a player's allotted role or place in the playing area. **8 in a position to** able to: *you were not in a position to repay the money.* **9** *Mil* a place occupied for tactical reasons. ✧ *vb* **10** to put in the proper or usual place; locate. ▷ **HISTORY** Latin *ponere* to place ▶ **positional** *adj*

positive *adj* **1** expressing certainty: *a positive answer.* **2** definite or certain: *are you absolutely positive about the date?* **3** tending to emphasize what is good; constructive: *positive thinking.* **4** tending towards progress or improvement: *investment that could have a positive impact on the company's fortunes.* **5** *Philosophy* constructive rather than sceptical. **6** *Informal* complete; downright: *a positive delight.* **7** *Maths* having a value greater than zero: *a positive number.* **8** *Grammar* denoting the unmodified form of an adjective as opposed to its comparative or superlative form. **9** *Physics* (of an electric charge) having an opposite charge to that of an electron. **10** *Physics* short for **electropositive**. **11** *Med* (of the result of an examination or test) indicating the presence of a suspected condition or organism. ✧ *n* **12** something positive. **13** *Maths* a quantity greater than zero. **14** *Photog* a print showing an image whose colours and tones correspond to those of the original subject. **15** *Grammar* the positive degree of an adjective or adverb. **16** a positive object, such as a terminal in a cell. ▷ **HISTORY** Late Latin *positivus* ▶ **positively** *adv* ▶ **positiveness** *or* **positivity** *n*

positive discrimination *n* the provision of special opportunities for a disadvantaged group.

positive vetting *n Brit* the thorough checking of all aspects of a person's life to ensure his or her suitability for a position that may involve national security.

positivism *n* a system of philosophy that accepts only things that can be seen or proved. ▶ **positivist** *n, adj*

positron *n Physics* the antiparticle of the electron, having the same mass but an equal and opposite charge. ▷ **HISTORY** *posi(tive)* + *(elec)tron*

posse (**poss**-ee) *n* **1** *US* a selected group of men on whom the sheriff may call for assistance. **2** *Informal* a group of friends or associates: *a posse of reporters.* **3** (in W Canada) a troop of horses and riders who perform at rodeos. ▷ **HISTORY** Latin: to be able

possess *vb* **1** to have as one's property; own. **2** to have as a quality or attribute: *he possessed an innate elegance, authority, and wit on screen.* **3** to gain control over or dominate: *absolute terror possessed her.* ▷ **HISTORY** Latin *possidere* ▶ **possessor** *n*

possessed *adj* **1** (foll. by *of*) owning or having: *he is possessed of a calm maturity far beyond his years.* **2** under the influence of a powerful force, such as a spirit or strong emotion: *possessed by the devil; she was possessed by a frenzied urge to get out of Moscow.*

possession *n* **1** the state of possessing; ownership: *how had this compromising picture come into the possession of the press?* **2** anything that is possessed. **3 possessions** wealth or property. **4** the state of being controlled by or as if by evil spirits. **5** the occupancy of land or property: *troops had taken possession of the airport.* **6** a territory subject to a foreign state. **7** the criminal offence of having something illegal on one's person: *arrested for drug dealing and possession.* **8** *Sport* control of the ball by a team or player: *City had most of the possession, but couldn't score.*

possessive *adj* **1** of possession. **2** desiring excessively to possess or dominate: *a possessive husband.* **3** *Grammar* denoting a form of a noun or pronoun used to convey possession, as *my* or *Harry's*: *a possessive pronoun.* ✧ *n* **4** *Grammar* **a** the possessive case. **b** a word in the possessive case. ▶ **possessiveness** *n*

possessive case *n Grammar* (in some languages) a grammatical case used to indicate a relation of ownership.

possibility *n, pl* **-ties 1** the state of being possible. **2** anything that is possible. **3** a competitor or candidate with a chance of success. **4** a future prospect or potential: *all sorts of possibilities began to open up.*

possible *adj* **1** capable of existing, happening, or proving true: *the earliest possible moment.* **2** capable of being done: *I am grateful to the library staff for making this work possible.* **3** having potential: *a possible buyer.* **4** feasible but less than probable: *it's possible that's what he meant, but I doubt it.* ✧ *n* **5** same as **possibility** (sense 3). ▷ **HISTORY** Latin *possibilis*

> ☑ **WORD TIP**
> Although it is very common to talk about something being *very possible* or *more possible*, these uses are generally thought to be incorrect, since *possible* describes an absolute state, and therefore something can only be *possible* or *not possible: it is very likely* (not *very possible*) *that he will resign; it has now become easier* (not *more possible*) *to obtain an entry visa.*

possibly *adv* **1** perhaps or maybe. **2** by any means; at all: *he can't possibly come.*

possum *n* **1** *Informal* an opossum. **2** *Austral & NZ* a phalanger. **3 play possum** to pretend to be dead, ignorant, or asleep in order to deceive an opponent.

post[1] *n* **1** an official system of mail delivery. **2** letters or packages that are transported and delivered by the Post Office; mail. **3** a single collection or delivery of mail. **4** a postbox or post office: *take this to the post.* **5** *Computers* an item of e-mail made publicly available. ✧ *vb* **6** to send by post. **7** *Computers* to make (e-mail) publicly available. **8** *Book-keeping* **a** to enter (an item) in a ledger. **b** (often foll. by *up*) to enter all paper items in (a ledger). **9 keep someone posted** to inform someone regularly of the latest news.
▷ **HISTORY** Latin *posita* something placed

post[2] *n* **1** a length of wood, metal, or concrete fixed upright to support or mark something. **2** *Horse racing* **a** either of two upright poles marking the beginning and end of a racecourse. **b** the finish of a horse race. ✧ *vb* **3** (sometimes foll. by *up*) to put up (a notice) in a public place. **4** to publish (a name) on a list. ▷ **HISTORY** Latin *postis*

post[3] *n* **1** a position to which a person is appointed; job. **2** a position to which a soldier or guard is assigned for duty. **3** a permanent military establishment. **4** *Brit* either of two military bugle calls (**first post** and **last post**) giving notice of the time to retire for the night. ✧ *vb* **5** *Brit & Austral* to send (someone) to a new place to work. **6** to assign to or station at a particular place or position: *guards were posted at the doors.* ▷ **HISTORY** French *poste,* from Latin *ponere* to place

post- *prefix* **1** after in time: *postgraduate.* **2** behind: *postdated.* ▷ **HISTORY** Latin

postage *n* the charge for sending a piece of mail by post.

postal *adj* of a Post Office or the mail-delivery service.

postal order *n Brit & Austral* a written money order sent by post and cashed at a post office by the person who receives it.

postbag *n* **1** *Chiefly Brit* a mailbag. **2** the mail received by a magazine, radio programme, or public figure.

postbox *n* same as **letter box** (sense 2).

postcard *n* a card, often with a picture on one side, for sending a message by post without an envelope.

postcode *n* a system of letters and numbers used to aid the sorting of mail.

postdate *vb* **-dating, -dated 1** to write a future date on (a cheque or document). **2** to occur at a later date than. **3** to assign a date to (an event or period) that is later than its previously assigned date.

poster *n* **1** a large notice displayed in a public place as an advertisement. **2** a large printed picture.

poste restante *n* a post-office department where mail is kept until it is called for.
▷ **HISTORY** French, literally: mail remaining

posterior *n* **1** *Formal or humorous* the buttocks. ✧ *adj* **2** at the back of or behind something: *posterior leg muscles.* **3** coming after in a series or time. ▷ **HISTORY** Latin: latter

posterity *n* **1** future generations. **2** all of one's descendants. ▷ **HISTORY** Latin *posterus* coming after

postern *n* a small back door or gate.
▷ **HISTORY** Old French *posterne*

post-free *adv, adj* **1** *Brit & Austral* with the postage prepaid. **2** free of postal charge.

postgraduate *n* **1** a person who is studying for a more advanced qualification after obtaining a degree. ✧ *adj* **2** of or for postgraduates.

posthaste *adv* with great speed.

posthumous (**poss**-tume-uss) *adj* **1** happening after one's death. **2** born after the death of one's father. **3** (of a book) published after the author's death. ▷ **HISTORY** Latin *postumus* the last
▶ **posthumously** *adv*

postie *n Scot, Austral & NZ informal* a postman.

postilion *or* **postillion** *n* (esp. formerly) a person who rides one of a pair of horses drawing a coach. ▷ **HISTORY** French *postillon*

postimpressionism *n* a movement in painting in France at the end of the 19th century which rejected Impressionism but adapted its use of pure colour to paint with greater subjective emotion. ▶ **postimpressionist** *n, adj*

posting *n* **1** a job to which someone is assigned by his or her employer which involves moving to a particular town or country: *Bonn was his third posting overseas.* **2** *Computers* an e-mail message that is publicly available.

postman *or fem* **postwoman** *n, pl* **-men** *or* **-women** a person who collects and delivers mail as a profession.

postmark *n* **1** an official mark stamped on mail, showing the place and date of posting. ✧ *vb* **2** to put such a mark on (mail).

postmaster *n* **1** Also (fem): **postmistress** an official in charge of a post office. **2** the person who manages the e-mail at a site.

postmaster general *n, pl* **postmasters general** the executive head of the postal service.

postmortem *n* **1** In full: **postmortem examination** medical examination of a dead body to discover the cause of death. **2** analysis of a recent event: *a postmortem on the party's recent appalling by-election results.* ✧ *adj* **3** occurring after death.
▷ **HISTORY** Latin, literally: after death

postnatal *adj* occurring after childbirth: *postnatal depression.*

post office *n* a building where stamps are sold and postal business is conducted.

Post Office *n* a government department responsible for postal services.

postoperative *adj* of or occurring in the period after a surgical operation.

postpone *vb* **-poning, -poned** to put off until a future time. ▷ **HISTORY** Latin *postponere* to put after
▶ **postponement** *n*

postpositive *adj Grammar* (of an adjective) placed after the word it modifies.

postscript *n* a message added at the end of a letter, after the signature. ▷ **HISTORY** Late Latin *postscribere* to write after

A B C D E F G H I J K L M N O P Q R S T U V W X Y Z

postulant *n* an applicant for admission to a religious order. ▷ **HISTORY** Latin *postulare* to ask

postulate *Formal* ✧ *vb* **-lating, -lated 1** to assume to be true as the basis of an argument or theory. **2** to ask, demand, or claim. ✧ *n* **3** something postulated. ▷ **HISTORY** Latin *postulare* to ask for ▶ **postulation** *n*

posture *n* **1** a position or way in which a person stands, walks, etc.: *good posture.* **2** a mental attitude: *a cooperative posture.* **3** an affected attitude: *an intellectual posture.* ✧ *vb* **-turing, -tured 4** to behave in an exaggerated way to attract attention. **5** to assume an affected attitude. ▷ **HISTORY** Latin *positura* ▶ **postural** *adj*

posy *n, pl* **-sies** a small bunch of flowers. ▷ **HISTORY** variant of *poesy*

pot[1] *n* **1** a round deep container, often with a handle and lid, used for cooking. **2** the amount that a pot will hold. **3** short for **flowerpot, teapot**. **4** a handmade piece of pottery. **5** *Billiards etc.* a shot by which a ball is pocketed. **6** a chamber pot. **7** the money in the pool in gambling games. **8** (*often pl*) *Informal* a large sum of money. **9** *Informal* a cup or other trophy. **10** See **potbelly**. **11 go to pot** to go to ruin. ✧ *vb* **potting, potted 12** to put (a plant) in soil in a flowerpot. **13** *Billiards etc.* to pocket (a ball). **14** to preserve (food) in a pot. **15** to shoot (game) for food rather than for sport. **16** to shoot casually or without careful aim. **17** *Informal* to capture or win. ▷ **HISTORY** Old English *pott*

pot[2] *n Slang* cannabis. ▷ **HISTORY** perhaps from Mexican Indian *potiguaya*

potable (**pote**-a-bl) *adj Formal* drinkable. ▷ **HISTORY** Latin *potare* to drink

potash *n* **1** potassium carbonate, used as fertilizer. **2** a compound containing potassium: *permanganate of potash.* ▷ **HISTORY** from *pot ashes,* because originally obtained by evaporating the lye of wood ashes in pots

potassium *n Chem* a light silvery element of the alkali metal group. Symbol: K. ▷ **HISTORY** New Latin *potassa* potash

potassium nitrate *n* a crystalline compound used in gunpowders, fertilizers, and as a preservative for foods (**E252**).

potato *n, pl* **-toes 1** a starchy vegetable that grows underground. **2** the plant from which this vegetable is obtained. ▷ **HISTORY** Spanish *patata,* from a Native American language

potato beetle *n* same as **Colorado beetle**.

potbelly *n, pl* **-lies 1** a bulging belly. **2** a person with such a belly.

potboiler *n Informal* an inferior work of art produced quickly to make money.

pot-bound *adj* (of a pot plant) having roots too big for its pot, so that it is unable to grow further.

poteen *or* **poitín** *n* (in Ireland) illegally made alcoholic drink. ▷ **HISTORY** Irish *poitín* little pot

potent *adj* **1** having great power or influence. **2** (of arguments) persuasive or forceful. **3** highly effective: *a potent poison.* **4** (of a male) capable of having sexual intercourse. ▷ **HISTORY** Latin *potens* able ▶ **potency** *n*

potentate *n* a ruler or monarch. ▷ **HISTORY** Latin *potens* powerful

potential *adj* **1 a** possible but not yet actual: *potential buyers.* **b** capable of being or becoming; latent: *potential danger.* ✧ *n* **2** ability or talent not yet in full use: *she has great potential as a painter.* **3** In full: **electric potential** the work required to transfer a unit positive electric charge from an infinite distance to a given point. ▷ **HISTORY** Latin *potentia* power ▶ **potentially** *adv*

potential difference *n* the difference in electric potential between two points in an electric field, measured in volts.

potential energy *n* the energy which an object has stored up because of its position.

potentiality *n, pl* **-ties** latent capacity for becoming or developing.

potherb *n* a plant whose leaves, flowers, or stems are used in cooking.

pothole *n* **1** a hole in the surface of a road. **2** a deep hole in a limestone area.

potholing *n* the sport of exploring underground caves. ▶ **potholer** *n*

pothook *n* **1** an S-shaped hook for suspending a pot over a fire. **2** an S-shaped mark in handwriting.

potion *n* a drink of medicine, poison, or some supposedly magic liquid. ▷ **HISTORY** Latin *potio* a drink, esp. a poisonous one

potoroo *n, pl* **-roos** an Australian leaping rodent.

potpourri (po-**poor**-ee) *n, pl* **-ris 1** a fragrant mixture of dried flower petals. **2** an assortment or medley. ▷ **HISTORY** French, literally: rotten pot

Potsdam Conference *n History* a conference held in 1945 between British, US, and Soviet leaders, to establish principles for the Allied occupation of Germany after World War II.

potsherd *n* a broken piece of pottery. ▷ **HISTORY** *pot* + *schoord* piece of broken crockery

pot shot *n* **1** a shot taken without careful aim. **2** a shot fired at an animal within easy range.

pottage *n* a thick soup or stew. ▷ **HISTORY** Old French *potage* contents of a pot

potted *adj* **1** grown in a pot: *potted plant.* **2** cooked or preserved in a pot: *potted shrimps.* **3** *Informal* shortened or abridged: *a potted history.*

potter[1] *n* a person who makes pottery.

potter[2] *or esp US & Canad* **putter** *vb* **1 potter about, around** *or* **away** to be busy in a pleasant but aimless way: *he potters away doing God knows what all day.* **2** to move with little energy or direction: *I saw him pottering off to see to his canaries.* ▷ **HISTORY** Old English *potian* to thrust

pottery *n, pl* **-teries 1** articles made from baked clay. **2** a place where such articles are made. **3** the craft of making such articles.

potting shed *n* a garden hut in which plants are put in flowerpots and potting materials are stored.

potty[1] *adj* **-tier, -tiest** *Informal* **1** slightly crazy. **2** trivial or insignificant. **3** (foll. by *about*) very keen (on). ▷ **HISTORY** origin unknown ▶ **pottiness** *n*

potty[2] *n, pl* **-ties** a bowl used as a toilet by a small child.

pouch *n* **1** a small bag. **2** a baglike pocket in various animals, such as the cheek fold in hamsters. ✧ *vb* **3** to place in or as if in a pouch. **4** to make or be made into a pouch. ▷ HISTORY Old French *poche* bag

pouf *or* **pouffe** (**poof**) *n* a large solid cushion used as a seat. ▷ HISTORY French

poulterer *n Brit* a person who sells poultry.

poultice (**pole**-tiss) *n Med* a moist dressing, often heated, applied to painful and swollen parts of the body. ▷ HISTORY Latin *puls* a thick porridge

poultry *n* domestic fowls. ▷ HISTORY Old French *pouletrie*

pounce *vb* **pouncing, pounced 1** (often foll. by *on* or *upon*) to spring upon suddenly to attack or capture. ✧ *n* **2** the act of pouncing; a spring or swoop. ▷ HISTORY origin unknown

pound[1] *n* **1** the standard monetary unit of the United Kingdom and some other countries, made up of 100 pence. Official name: **pound sterling** **2** the standard monetary unit of various other countries, such as Cyprus and Malta. **3** a unit of weight made up of 16 ounces and equal to 0.454 kilograms. ▷ HISTORY Old English *pund*

pound[2] *vb* **1** (sometimes foll. by *on* or *at*) to hit heavily and repeatedly. **2** to crush to pieces or to powder. **3** (foll. by *out*) to produce, by typing heavily. **4** (of the heart) to throb heavily. **5** to run with heavy steps. ▷ HISTORY Old English *pūnian*

pound[3] *n* an enclosure for stray dogs or officially removed vehicles. ▷ HISTORY Old English *pund-*

poundage *n* **1** a charge of so much per pound of weight. **2** a charge of so much per pound sterling.

-pounder *n combining form* **1** something weighing a specified number of pounds: *a 200-pounder.* **2** something worth a specified number of pounds: *a ten-pounder.* **3** a gun that discharges a shell weighing a specified number of pounds: *a two-pounder.*

pour *vb* **1** to flow or cause to flow out in a stream. **2** to rain heavily. **3** to be given or obtained in large amounts: *foreign aid is pouring into Iran.* **4** to move together in large numbers: *the fans poured onto the pitch.* ▷ HISTORY origin unknown

> **WORD TIP**
> The verbs *pour* and *pore* are sometimes confused: *she poured cream over her strudel; she pored* (not *poured*) *over the manuscript.*

pout *vb* **1** to thrust out (the lips) sullenly or provocatively. **2** to swell out; protrude. ✧ *n* **3** a pouting. ▷ HISTORY origin unknown

pouter *n* a breed of domestic pigeon that can puff out its crop.

poverty *n* **1** the state of lacking adequate food or money. **2** lack or scarcity: *a poverty of information.* **3** inferior quality or inadequacy: *the poverty of political debate in this country.* ▷ HISTORY Old French *poverté*

poverty-stricken *adj* extremely poor.

poverty trap *n Brit, Austral & NZ* the situation of being unable to raise one's living standard because any extra income would result in state benefits being reduced or withdrawn.

pow *interj* an exclamation to indicate that a collision or explosion has taken place.

POW prisoner of war.

powder *n* **1** a substance in the form of tiny loose particles. **2** a medicine or cosmetic in this form. ✧ *vb* **3** to cover or sprinkle with powder. ▷ HISTORY Old French *poldre,* from Latin *pulvis* dust ▶ **powdery** *adj*

powdered *adj* **1** sold in the form of a powder, esp. one which has been formed by grinding or drying the original material: *powdered milk.* **2** covered or made up with a cosmetic in the form of a powder: *liveried footmen in powdered wigs.*

powder puff *n* a soft pad used to apply cosmetic powder to the skin.

powder room *n* a ladies' cloakroom or toilet.

power *n* **1** ability to do something. **2** (*often pl*) a specific ability or faculty. **3** political, financial, or social force or authority: *men's use of power over women in a subordinate position in the workforce; economic power is the bedrock of political power.* **4** a position of control, esp. over the running of a country: *he seized power in a coup in 1966.* **5** a state with political, industrial, or military strength. **6** a person or group having authority. **7** a prerogative or privilege: *the power of veto.* **8** official or legal authority. **9** *Maths* the value of a number or quantity raised to some exponent. **10** *Physics, engineering* a measure of the rate of doing work expressed as the work done per unit time. **11** the rate at which electrical energy is fed into or taken from a device or system, measured in watts. **12** mechanical energy as opposed to manual labour. **13** a particular form of energy: *nuclear power.* **14** the magnifying capacity of a lens or optical system. **15** *Informal* a great deal: *a power of good.* **16 the powers that be** established authority. ✧ *vb* **17** to supply with power. ✧ *adj* **18** producing or using electrical energy: *a large selection of power tools.* ▷ HISTORY Anglo-Norman *poer*

power cut *n* a temporary interruption in the supply of electricity.

powerful *adj* **1** having great power. **2** extremely effective: *a powerful drug.* ▶ **powerfully** *adv* ▶ **powerfulness** *n*

powerhouse *n* **1** *Informal* a forceful person or thing. **2** an electrical generating station.

powerless *adj* without control or authority. ▶ **powerlessly** *adv* ▶ **powerlessness** *n*

power of attorney *n* **1** legal authority to act for another person. **2** the document conferring such authority.

power point *n* an electrical socket fitted into a wall for plugging in electrical appliances.

power pole *n Austral & NZ* a pole carrying an overhead power line.

power-sharing *n* a political arrangement in which opposing groups in a society participate in government.

A B C D E F G H I J K L M N O P Q R S T U V W X Y Z

power station *n* an installation for generating and distributing electricity.

power steering *n* a type of steering in vehicles in which the turning of the steering wheel is assisted by power from the engine.

power supply *n Science* a source of energy such as electricity, gas, etc.

powwow *n* **1** a talk or meeting. **2** a meeting of Native Americans of N America. ✧ *vb* **3** to hold a powwow. ▷ **HISTORY** from a Native American language

pox *n* **1** a disease in which pus-filled blisters or pimples form on the skin. **2 the pox** *Informal* syphilis. ▷ **HISTORY** changed from *pocks,* plural of *pock*

pp 1 past participle. **2** (in signing documents on behalf of someone else) by delegation to. ▷ **HISTORY** Latin *per procurationem*

> ☑ **WORD TIP**
> In formal correspondence, when Brenda Smith is signing on behalf of Peter Jones, she should write *Peter Jones pp* (or *per pro*) *Brenda Smith,* not the other way about.

pp. pages.

PPS 1 parliamentary private secretary. **2** additional postscript. ▷ **HISTORY** Latin *post postscriptum*

PPTA (in New Zealand) Post Primary Teachers Association.

PQ 1 Province of Quebec. **2** (in Canada) Parti Québecois.

pr *pl* **prs** pair.

Pr *Chem* praseodymium.

PR 1 proportional representation. **2** public relations.

pr. 1 price. **2** pronoun.

practicable *adj* **1** capable of being done. **2** usable. ▷ **HISTORY** French *praticable* ▶ **practicability** *n*

> ☑ **WORD TIP**
> See at **practical.**

practical *adj* **1** involving experience or actual use rather than theory. **2** concerned with everyday matters: *the kind of practical and emotional upheaval that divorce can bring.* **3** sensible, useful, and effective rather than fashionable or attractive: *it's a marvellous design, because it's comfortable, it's practical, and it actually looks good.* **4** involving the simple basics: *practical skills.* **5** being very close to (a state); virtual: *it's a practical certainty.* ✧ *n* **6** an examination or lesson in which something has to be made or done. ▷ **HISTORY** Greek *praktikos,* from *prassein* to experience ▶ **practicality** *n* ▶ **practically** *adv*

> ☑ **WORD TIP**
> A distinction is usually made between *practical* and *practicable. Practical* refers to a person, idea, project, etc., as being more concerned with or relevant to practice than theory: *he is a very practical person; the idea had no practical application. Practicable* refers to a project or idea as being capable of being done or put into effect: *the plan was expensive, yet practicable.*

practical joke *n* a trick intended to make someone look foolish. ▶ **practical joker** *n*

practice *n* **1** something done regularly or repeatedly. **2** repetition of an activity in order to gain skill: *regular practice is essential if you want to play an instrument well.* **3** the business or surgery of a doctor or lawyer. **4** the act of doing something: *I'm not sure how effective these methods will be when put into practice.* **5 in practice a** what actually happens as distinct from what is supposed to happen: *many ideas which look good on paper just don't work in practice.* **b** skilled in something through having had a lot of regular recent experience at it: *I still go shooting, just to keep in practice.* **6 out of practice** not having had much regular recent experience at an activity: *although out of practice, I still love playing my violin.* ▷ **HISTORY** Greek *praktikē* practical work

practise *or US* **practice** *vb* **-tising, -tised** *or US* **-ticing, -ticed 1** to do repeatedly in order to gain skill. **2** to take part in or follow (a religion etc.): *none of them practise Islam.* **3** to work at (a profession): *he originally intended to practise medicine.* **4** to do regularly: *they practise meditation.* ▷ **HISTORY** Greek *prattein* to do

practitioner *n* a person who practises a profession.

praetor (**pree**-tor) *n* (in ancient Rome) a senior magistrate ranking just below the consuls. ▷ **HISTORY** Latin ▶ **praetorian** *adj, n*

pragmatic *adj* **1** concerned with practical consequences rather than theory. **2** *Philosophy* of pragmatism. ▷ **HISTORY** Greek *pragmatikos* ▶ **pragmatically** *adv*

pragmatism *n* **1** policy dictated by practical consequences rather than by theory. **2** *Philosophy* the doctrine that the content of a concept consists only in its practical applicability. ▶ **pragmatist** *n, adj*

Prague Spring *n History* a period in 1968 when Alexander Dubček, first secretary of the Czechoslovak Communist Party, attempted to reform communism in Czechoslovakia. His reforms were brought to an end by Soviet occupation.

prairie *n* (*often pl*) a large treeless area of grassland of North America. ▷ **HISTORY** French, from Latin *pratum* meadow

prairie dog *n* a rodent that lives in burrows in the N American prairies.

praise *vb* **praising, praised 1** to express admiration or approval for. **2** to express thanks and worship to (one's God). ✧ *n* **3** the expression of admiration or approval. **4 sing someone's praises** to praise someone highly. ▷ HISTORY Latin *pretium* prize

praiseworthy *adj* deserving praise; commendable.

praline (**prah**-leen) *n* a sweet made of nuts with caramelized sugar. ▷ HISTORY French

pram *n* a four-wheeled carriage for a baby, pushed by a person on foot. ▷ HISTORY altered from *perambulator*

prance *vb* **prancing, pranced 1** to walk with exaggerated movements. **2** (of an animal) to move with high springing steps. ✧ *n* **3** the act of prancing. ▷ HISTORY origin unknown

prang *Old-fashioned slang* ✧ *n* **1** a crash in an aircraft or car. ✧ *vb* **2** to crash or damage (an aircraft or car). ▷ HISTORY perhaps imitative

prank *n* a mischievous trick. ▷ HISTORY origin unknown ▶ **prankster** *n*

praseodymium (pray-zee-oh-**dim**-ee-um) *n Chem* a silvery-white element of the lanthanide series of metals. Symbol: Pr. ▷ HISTORY New Latin

prat *n Brit, Austral & NZ slang* an incompetent or ineffectual person. ▷ HISTORY probably special use of earlier *prat* buttocks, origin unknown

prattle *vb* **-tling, -tled 1** to chatter in a foolish or childish way. ✧ *n* **2** foolish or childish talk. ▷ HISTORY Middle Low German *pratelen* to chatter

prawn *n* a small edible shellfish. ▷ HISTORY origin unknown

praxis *n* **1** practice as opposed to the theory. **2** accepted practice or custom. ▷ HISTORY Greek: deed, action

pray *vb* **1** to say prayers (to one's God). **2** to ask earnestly; beg. ✧ *adv* **3** *Archaic* I beg you; please: *pray, leave us alone.* ▷ HISTORY Latin *precari* to implore

prayer[1] *n* **1** a thanksgiving or an appeal spoken to one's God. **2** a set form of words used in praying: *the Lord's Prayer.* **3** an earnest request. **4** the practice of praying: *call the faithful to prayer.* **5** (*often pl*) a form of devotion spent mainly praying: *morning prayers.* **6** something prayed for.

prayer[2] *n* a person who prays.

prayer book *n* a book of prayers used in church or at home.

prayer mat *or* **prayer rug** *n* the small carpet on which a Muslim performs his or her daily prayers.

prayer wheel *n Buddhism* (in Tibet) a cylinder inscribed with prayers, each turning of which is counted as an uttered prayer.

praying mantis *n* same as **mantis**.

pre- *prefix* before in time or position: *predate; pre-eminent.* ▷ HISTORY Latin *prae*

preach *vb* **1** to talk on a religious theme as part of a church service. **2** to speak in support of (something) in a moralizing way. ▷ HISTORY Latin *praedicare* to proclaim

preacher *n* a person who preaches.

preamble *n* an introduction that comes before something spoken or written. ▷ HISTORY Latin *prae* before + *ambulare* to walk

prearranged *adj* arranged beforehand. ▶ **prearrangement** *n*

prebend *n* **1** the allowance paid by a cathedral or collegiate church to a canon or member of the chapter. **2** the land or tithe from which this is paid. ▷ HISTORY Old French *prébende* ▶ **prebendal** *adj*

prebendary *n, pl* **-daries** a clergyman who is a member of the chapter of a cathedral.

Precambrian *or* **Pre-Cambrian** *adj Geol* of the earliest geological era, lasting from about 4500 million years ago to 600 million years ago.

precancerous *adj* relating to cells that show signs that they may develop cancer.

precarious *adj* (of a position or situation) dangerous or insecure. ▷ HISTORY Latin *precarius* obtained by begging ▶ **precariously** *adv*

precaution *n* an action taken in advance to prevent an undesirable event. ▷ HISTORY Latin *prae* before + *cavere* to beware ▶ **precautionary** *adj*

precede *vb* **-ceding, -ceded** to go or be before (someone or something) in time, place, or rank. ▷ HISTORY Latin *praecedere*

precedence (**press**-ee-denss) *n* formal order of rank or position.

precedent *n* **1** a previous occurrence used to justify taking the same action in later similar situations. **2** *Law* a judicial decision that serves as an authority for deciding a later case. ✧ *adj* **3** preceding.

precentor *n* a person who leads the singing in church services. ▷ HISTORY Latin *prae* before + *canere* to sing

precept *n* **1** a rule of conduct. **2** a rule for morals. **3** *Law* a writ or warrant. ▷ HISTORY Latin *praeceptum* ▶ **preceptive** *adj*

preceptor *n Rare* an instructor. ▶ **preceptorial** *adj*

precession *n* **1** the act of preceding. **2** the motion of a spinning body, in which the axis of rotation sweeps out a cone. **3 precession of the equinoxes** the slightly earlier occurrence of the equinoxes each year. ▷ HISTORY Latin *praecedere* to precede

precinct *n* **1** *Brit, Austral & S African* an area in a town closed to traffic: *a shopping precinct.* **2** *Brit, Austral & S African* an enclosed area around a building. **3** *US* an administrative area of a city. ▷ HISTORY Latin *praecingere* to surround

precincts *pl n* the surrounding region.

precious *adj* **1** very costly or valuable: *precious jewellery.* **2** loved and treasured. **3** very affected in speech, manners, or behaviour. **4** *Informal* worthless: *nothing is too good for his precious dog.* ✧ *adv* **5** *Informal* very: *there's precious little to do in this town.* ▷ HISTORY Latin *pretiosus* valuable

precious metal *n* gold, silver, or platinum.

precious stone *n* a rare mineral, such as diamond, ruby, or opal, that is highly valued as a gem.

a b c d e f g h i j k l m n o p q r s t u v w x y z

A B C D E F G H I J K L M N O P Q R S T U V W X Y Z

precipice *n* the very steep face of a cliff. ▷ **HISTORY** Latin *praecipitium* steep place

precipitant *adj* **1** hasty or rash. **2** rushing or falling rapidly. ✧ *n* **3** something which helps bring about an event or condition: *stressful events are often the precipitant for a manic attack.*

precipitate *vb* **-tating, -tated 1** to cause to happen earlier than expected: *the scandal could bring the government down, precipitating a general election.* **2** to condense or cause to condense and fall as snow or rain. **3** *Chem* to cause to be deposited in solid form from a solution. **4** to throw from a height: *the encircled soldiers chose to precipitate themselves into the ocean.* ✧ *adj* **5** done rashly or hastily. **6** rushing ahead. ✧ *n* **7** *Chem* a precipitated solid. ▷ **HISTORY** Latin *praecipitare* to throw down headlong

precipitation *n* **1** the formation of a chemical precipitate. **2** *Meteorol* **a** rain, hail, snow, or sleet formed by condensation of water vapour in the atmosphere. **b** the falling of these. **3** rash haste: *they decamped with the utmost precipitation.*

precipitous *adj* **1** very steep: *precipitous cliffs.* **2** very quick and severe: *a precipitous decline.* **3** rapid and unplanned; hasty: *European governments urged the Americans not to make a precipitous decision.*

> ☑ **WORD TIP**
> The use of *precipitous* to mean *hasty* is thought by some people to be incorrect.

précis (**pray**-see) *n, pl* **précis 1** a short summary of a longer text. ✧ *vb* **2** to make a précis of. ▷ **HISTORY** French

precise *adj* **1** particular or exact: *this precise moment.* **2** strictly correct in amount or value: *precise measurements.* **3** working with total accuracy: *precise instruments.* **4** strict in observing rules or standards. ▷ **HISTORY** Latin *prae* before + *caedere* to cut ▶ **precisely** *adv*

precision *n* **1** the quality of being precise. ✧ *adj* **2** accurate: *precision engineering.*

preclude *vb* **-cluding, -cluded** *Formal* to make impossible to happen. ▷ **HISTORY** Latin *prae* before + *claudere* to close

precocious *adj* having developed or matured early or too soon. ▷ **HISTORY** Latin *prae* early + *coquere* to ripen ▶ **precocity** *n*

precognition *n Psychol* the alleged ability to foresee future events. ▷ **HISTORY** Latin *praecognoscere* to foresee

preconceived *adj* (of ideas etc.) formed without real experience or reliable information. ▶ **preconception** *n*

precondition *n* something that is necessary before something else can come about.

precursor *n* **1** something that comes before and signals something to follow; a forerunner. **2** a predecessor. ▷ **HISTORY** Latin *praecursor* one who runs in front

pred. predicate.

predacious *adj* (of animals) habitually hunting and killing other animals for food. ▷ **HISTORY** Latin *praeda* plunder

predate *vb* **-dating, -dated 1** to occur at an earlier date than. **2** to write a date on (a document) that is earlier than the actual date.

predator *n* an animal that kills and eats other animals.

predatory (**pred**-a-tree) *adj* **1** (of animals) habitually hunting and killing other animals for food. **2** eager to gain at the expense of others. ▷ **HISTORY** Latin *praedari* to pillage

predecease *vb* **-ceasing, -ceased** to die before (someone else).

predecessor *n* **1** a person who precedes another in an office or position. **2** an ancestor. **3** something that precedes something else: *the library will be more extravagant than its predecessors.* ▷ **HISTORY** Latin *prae* before + *decedere* to go away

predestination *n Christian theol* the belief that future events have already been decided by God.

predestined *adj Christian theol* determined in advance by God. ▷ **HISTORY** Latin *praedestinare* to resolve beforehand

predicable *adj* capable of being predicated.

predicament *n* an embarrassing or difficult situation. ▷ **HISTORY** see PREDICATE

predicant (**pred**-ik-ant) *adj* **1** of preaching. ✧ *n* **2** a member of a religious order founded for preaching, usually a Dominican. ▷ **HISTORY** Latin *praedicans* preaching

predicate *n* **1** *Grammar* the part of a sentence in which something is said about the subject. **2** *Logic* something that is asserted about the subject of a proposition. ✧ *vb* **-cating, -cated 3** to base or found: *political aims which are predicated upon a feminist view of women's oppression.* **4** to declare or assert: *it has been predicated that if we continue with our current sexual behaviour every family will have an AIDS victim.* **5** *Logic* to assert (something) about the subject of a proposition. ▷ **HISTORY** Latin *praedicare* to assert publicly ▶ **predication** *n* ▶ **predicative** *adj*

predict *vb* to tell about in advance; prophesy. ▷ **HISTORY** Latin *praedicere* ▶ **predictable** *adj* ▶ **predictably** *adv* ▶ **predictor** *n*

prediction *n* **1** the act of forecasting in advance. **2** something that is forecast in advance.

predictive *adj* **1** relating to or able to make predictions. **2** (of a word processer) able to complete words after only part of a word has been keyed.

predikant (pred-ik-**ant**) *n* a minister in the Dutch Reformed Church in South Africa. ▷ **HISTORY** Dutch

predilection *n Formal* a preference or liking. ▷ **HISTORY** French *prédilection*

predispose *vb* **-posing, -posed** (often foll. by *to*) **1** to influence (someone) in favour of something: *some scientists' social class background predisposes them to view the natural world in a certain way.* **2** to make (someone) susceptible to something: *a* *high-fat diet appears to predispose men towards heart disease.* ▶ **predisposition** *n*

predominant *adj* being more important or noticeable than others: *improved living conditions probably played the predominant role in reducing disease in the nineteenth century.* ▶ **predominance** *n* ▶ **predominantly** *adv*

predominate *vb* **-nating, -nated 1** to be the most important or controlling aspect or part: *the image of brutal repression that has tended to predominate since the protests were crushed.* **2** to form the greatest part or be most common: *women predominate in this gathering.* ▷ HISTORY Latin *prae* before + *dominari* to rule

pre-eminent *adj* outstanding. ▶ **pre-eminence** *n*

pre-empt *vb* to prevent an action by doing something which makes it pointless or impossible: *he pre-empted his expulsion from the party by resigning.*

pre-emption *n Law* the purchase of or right to buy property in advance of others. ▷ HISTORY Medieval Latin *praeemere* to buy beforehand

pre-emptive *adj Mil* designed to damage or destroy an enemy's attacking strength before it can be used: *a pre-emptive strike.*

preen *vb* **1** (of birds) to clean or trim (feathers) with the beak. **2** to smarten (oneself) carefully. **3** (often foll. by *on*) to be self-satisfied. ▷ HISTORY Middle English *preinen*

prefab *n* a prefabricated house.

prefabricated *adj* (of a building) made in shaped sections for quick assembly.

preface (**pref**-iss) *n* **1** an introduction to a book, usually explaining its intention or content. **2** anything introductory. ✧ *vb* **-acing, -aced 3** to say or do something before proceeding to the main part. **4** to act as a preface to. ▷ HISTORY Latin *praefari* to say in advance

prefatory *adj* concerning a preface. ▷ HISTORY Latin *praefari* to say in advance

prefect *n* **1** *Brit, Austral, & NZ* a senior pupil in a school with limited power over the behaviour of other pupils. **2** (in some countries) the chief administrative officer in a department. ▷ HISTORY Latin *praefectus* one put in charge

prefecture *n* the office or area of authority of a prefect.

prefer *vb* **-ferring, -ferred 1** to like better: *most people prefer television to reading books.* **2** *Law* to put (charges) before a court for judgment. **3** (*often passive*) to promote over another or others. ▷ HISTORY Latin *praeferre* to carry in front, prefer

> **WORD TIP**
> Normally, *to* is used after *prefer* and *preferable*, not *than*: *I prefer Brahms to Tchaikovsky; a small income is preferable to no income at all,* but *than* or *rather than* should be used to link infinitives: *I prefer to walk than/rather than to catch the train.*

preferable *adj* more desirable or suitable. ▶ **preferably** *adv*

> **WORD TIP**
> Since *preferable* already means *more desirable,* you should not say something is *more preferable* or *most preferable.* See also at **prefer.**

preference *n* **1** a liking for one thing above the rest. **2** a person or thing preferred.

preference shares *pl n Finance* shares in a company that entitle their owners to receive dividends from profits before ordinary shareholders although the rate of dividend is generally lower than that declared on ordinary shares.

preferential *adj* **1** showing preference: *preferential treatment.* **2** indicating a special favourable status in business affairs: *the President is to renew China's preferential trading status.* **3** indicating a voting system which allows voters to rank candidates in order of preference: *a multi-option referendum with preferential voting.*

preferment *n* promotion to a higher position.

prefigure *vb* **-uring, -ured 1** to represent or suggest in advance. **2** to imagine beforehand.

prefix *n* **1** *Grammar* a letter or group of letters put at the beginning of a word to make a new word, such as *un-* in *unhappy*. **2** a title put before a name, such as *Mr.* ✧ *vb* **3** *Grammar* to add (a letter or group of letters) as a prefix to the beginning of a word. **4** to put before.

pregnant *adj* **1** carrying a fetus or fetuses within the womb. **2** full of meaning or significance: *a pregnant pause.* ▷ HISTORY Latin *praegnans* ▶ **pregnancy** *n*

prehensile *adj* capable of curling round objects and grasping them: *a prehensile tail.* ▷ HISTORY Latin *prehendere* to grasp

prehistoric *adj* of man's development before the appearance of the written word. ▶ **prehistory** *n*

preindustrial *adj* of a time before the mechanization of industry.

prejudge *vb* **-judging, -judged** to judge before knowing all the facts.

prejudice *n* **1** an unreasonable or unfair dislike or preference. **2** intolerance of or dislike for people because they belong to a specific race, religion, or group: *class prejudice.* **3** the act or condition of holding such opinions. **4** harm or detriment: *conduct to the prejudice of good order and military discipline.* **5 without prejudice** *Law* without harm to an existing right or claim. ✧ *vb* **-dicing, -diced 6** to cause (someone) to have a prejudice. **7** to harm: *the incident prejudiced his campaign.* ▷ HISTORY Latin *prae* before + *judicium* sentence

prejudicial *adj* harmful; damaging.

prelacy *n, pl* **-cies 1 a** the office or status of a prelate. **b** prelates collectively. **2** *Often offensive* government of the Church by prelates.

prelate (**prel**-it) *n* a clergyman of high rank, such as a bishop. ▷ HISTORY Church Latin *praelatus,* from Latin *praeferre* to hold in special esteem

preliminary *adj* **1** occurring before or in preparation; introductory. ✧ *n, pl* **-naries 2** an action or event occurring before or in preparation for an activity: *the discussions are a preliminary to the main negotiations.* **3** a qualifying contest held before a main competition. ▷ **HISTORY** Latin *prae* before + *limen* threshold

prelims *pl n* **1** the pages of a book, such as the title page and contents, which come before the main text. **2** the first public examinations in some universities. ▷ **HISTORY** a contraction of *preliminaries*

prelude (**prel**-yewd) *n* **1 a** an introductory movement in music. **b** a short piece of music for piano or organ. **2** an event introducing or preceding the main event. ✧ *vb* **-uding, -uded 3** to act as a prelude to (something). **4** to introduce by a prelude. ▷ **HISTORY** Latin *prae* before + *ludere* to play

premarital *adj* occurring before marriage: *premarital sex.*

premature *adj* **1** happening or done before the normal or expected time: *premature ageing.* **2** impulsive or hasty: *a premature judgment.* **3** (of a baby) born weeks before the date when it was due to be born. ▷ **HISTORY** Latin *prae* in advance + *maturus* ripe ▶ **prematurely** *adv*

premedication *n Surgery* any drugs given to prepare a patient for a general anaesthetic.

premeditated *adj* planned in advance. ▶ **premeditation** *n*

premenstrual *adj* occurring or experienced before a menstrual period.

premenstrual syndrome *or* **tension** *n* symptoms, such as nervous tension, that may be experienced because of hormonal changes in the days before a menstrual period starts.

premier *n* **1** a prime minister. **2** a head of government of a Canadian province or Australian state. ✧ *adj* **3** first in importance or rank: *Torbay, Devon's premier resort.* **4** first in occurrence. ▷ **HISTORY** Latin *primus* first ▶ **premiership** *n*

premiere *n* **1** the first public performance of a film, play, or opera. ✧ *vb* **-ering, -ered 2** to give a premiere of: *the play was premiered last year in Johannesburg.* ▷ **HISTORY** French, feminine of *premier* first

premise *or* **premiss** *n Logic* a statement that is assumed to be true and is used as a basis for an argument. ▷ **HISTORY** Medieval Latin *praemissa* sent on before

premises *pl n* **1** a piece of land together with its buildings. **2** *Law* (in a deed) the matters referred to previously.

premium *n* **1** an extra sum of money added to a standard rate, price, or wage: *the superior taste persuades me to pay the premium for bottled water.* **2** the (regular) amount paid for an insurance policy. **3** the amount above the usual value at which something sells: *some even pay a premium of up to 15 per cent for the privilege.* **4** great value or regard: *we do put a very high premium on common sense.* **5 at a premium a** in great demand, usually because of scarcity. **b** at a higher price than usual. ▷ **HISTORY** Latin *praemium* prize

Premium Savings Bonds *pl n* (in Britain) savings certificates issued by the government, on which no interest is paid, but there is a monthly draw for cash prizes. Also called: **premium bonds**

premonition *n* a feeling that something unpleasant is going to happen; foreboding. ▷ **HISTORY** Latin *prae* before + *monere* to warn ▶ **premonitory** *adj*

prenatal *adj* before birth; during pregnancy.

preoccupy *vb* **-pies, -pying, -pied** to fill the thoughts or mind of (someone) to the exclusion of other things. ▷ **HISTORY** Latin *praeoccupare* to capture in advance ▶ **preoccupation** *n*

preordained *adj* decreed or determined in advance.

prep *n Brit informal* short for **preparation** (sense 4).

prep. 1 preparation. **2** preparatory. **3** preposition.

prepacked *adj* (of goods) sold already wrapped.

prepaid *adj* paid for in advance.

preparation *n* **1** the act of preparing or being prepared. **2** (*often pl*) something done in order to prepare for something else: *to make preparations for a wedding.* **3** something that is prepared, such as a medicine. **4** *Brit old-fashioned* **a** homework. **b** the period reserved for this.

preparatory (prip-**par**-a-tree) *adj* **1** preparing for: *a preparatory meeting to organize the negotiations.* **2** introductory. **3 preparatory to** before: *Jack cleared his throat preparatory to speaking.*

preparatory school *n* **1** *Brit & S African* a private school for children between the ages of 6 and 13, generally preparing pupils for public school. **2** (in the US) a private secondary school preparing pupils for college.

prepare *vb* **-paring, -pared 1** to make or get ready: *the army prepared for battle.* **2** to put together using parts or ingredients: *he had spent most of the afternoon preparing the meal.* **3** to equip or outfit, as for an expedition. **4 be prepared to** to be willing and able to: *I'm not prepared to say.* ▷ **HISTORY** Latin *prae* before + *parare* to make ready

preponderant *adj* greater in amount, force, or influence. ▶ **preponderance** *n*

preposition *n* a word used before a noun or pronoun to relate it to the other words, for example *in* in *he is in the car.* ▷ **HISTORY** Latin *praepositio* a putting before ▶ **prepositional** *adj*

> ☑ **WORD TIP**
>
> The practice of ending a sentence with a preposition (*Venice is a place I should like to go to*) was formerly regarded as incorrect, but is now acceptable and is the preferred form in many contexts.

prepossessing *adj* making a favourable impression; attractive.

preposterous *adj* utterly absurd. ▷ **HISTORY** Latin *praeposterus* reversed

prep school *n Informal* See **preparatory school**.

prepuce (**pree**-pyewss) *n* **1** the retractable fold of skin covering the tip of the penis; foreskin. **2** the retractable fold of skin covering the tip of the clitoris. ▷ HISTORY Latin *praeputium*

Pre-Raphaelite (pree-**raff**-a-lite) *n* **1** a member of a group of painters in the nineteenth century who revived the style considered typical of Italian painting before Raphael. ✧ *adj* **2** of or in the manner of Pre-Raphaelite painting and painters.

prerequisite *n* **1** something that is required before something else is possible. ✧ *adj* **2** required before something else is possible.

prerogative *n* a special privilege or right. ▷ HISTORY Latin *praerogativa* privilege

pres. 1 present (time). **2** presidential.

Pres. President.

presage (**press**-ij) *vb* **-aging, -aged 1** to be a warning or sign of something about to happen: *the windless air presaged disaster.* ✧ *n* **2** an omen. **3** a misgiving. ▷ HISTORY Latin *praesagire* to perceive beforehand

presbyopia *n Med* a gradual inability of the eye to focus on nearby objects. ▷ HISTORY Greek *presbus* old man + *ōps* eye

presbyter *n* **1** (in some episcopal Churches) an official with administrative and priestly duties. **2** (in the Presbyterian Church) an elder. ▷ HISTORY Greek *presbuteros* an older man ▶ **presbyterial** *adj*

presbyterian *adj* **1** of or designating Church government by lay elders. ✧ *n* **2** someone who supports this type of Church government. ▶ **presbyterianism** *n*

Presbyterian *adj* **1** of any of the Protestant Churches governed by lay elders. ✧ *n* **2** a member of a Presbyterian Church. ▶ **Presbyterianism** *n*

presbytery *n, pl* **-teries 1** *Presbyterian Church* a local Church court. **2** *RC Church* the residence of a parish priest. **3** elders collectively. **4** the part of a church east of the choir; a sanctuary. ▷ HISTORY see PRESBYTER

preschool *adj* of or for children below the age of five: *a preschool playgroup.*

prescience (**press**-ee-enss) *n Formal* knowledge of events before they happen. ▷ HISTORY Latin *praescire* to know beforehand ▶ **prescient** *adj*

prescribe *vb* **-scribing, -scribed 1** *Med* to recommend the use of (a medicine or other remedy). **2** to lay down as a rule. ▷ HISTORY Latin *praescribere* to write previously

prescription *n* **1 a** written instructions from a doctor for the preparation and use of a medicine. **b** the medicine prescribed. **2** written instructions from an optician specifying the lenses needed to correct bad eyesight. **3** a prescribing. ▷ HISTORY Legal Latin *praescriptio* an order

prescriptive *adj* **1** laying down rules. **2** based on tradition.

presence *n* **1** the fact of being in a specified place: *the test detects the presence of sugar in the urine.* **2** impressive personal appearance or bearing: *a person of dignified and commanding presence.* **3** the company or nearness of a person: *she seemed completely unaware of my presence.* **4** *Mil* a force stationed in another country: *the American-led military presence in the Gulf.* **5** an invisible spirit felt to be nearby: *I felt a presence in the room.* ▷ HISTORY Latin *praesentia* a being before

presence of mind *n* the ability to stay calm and act sensibly in a crisis.

present[1] *adj* **1** being in a specified place: *he had been present at the birth of his son.* **2** existing or happening now. **3** current: *the present exchange rate.* **4** *Grammar* of a verb tense used when the action described is happening now. ✧ *n* **5** *Grammar* the present tense. **6 at present** now. **7 for the present** for now; temporarily. **8 the present** the time being; now. ✧ See also **presents**. ▷ HISTORY Latin *praesens*

present[2] *n* (**prez**-int) **1** a gift. ✧ *vb* (pri-**zent**) **2** to introduce (a person) formally to another. **3** to introduce to the public: *the Museum of Modern Art is presenting a retrospective of his work.* **4** to introduce and compere (a radio or television show). **5** to show or exhibit: *they took advantage of every tax dodge that presented itself.* **6** to bring about: *the case presented a large number of legal difficulties.* **7** to put forward or submit: *they presented a petition to the Prime Minister.* **8** to give or offer formally: *he was presented with a watch to celebrate his twenty-five years with the company.* **9** to hand over for action or payment: *to present a bill.* **10** to portray in a particular way: *her lawyer presented her as a naive woman who had got into bad company.* **11** to aim (a weapon). **12 present arms** to salute with one's weapon. ▷ HISTORY Latin *praesentare* to exhibit

presentable *adj* **1** fit to be seen by or introduced to other people. **2** acceptable: *the team reached a presentable total.* ▶ **presentability** *n*

presentation *n* **1** the act of presenting or being presented. **2** the manner of presenting. **3** a formal ceremony in which an award is made. **4** a public performance, such as a play or a ballet.

presenter *n* a person who introduces a radio or television show and links the items in it.

presentiment (priz-**zen**-tim-ent) *n* a sense that something unpleasant is about to happen; premonition. ▷ HISTORY obsolete French *pressentir* to sense beforehand

presently *adv* **1** soon: *you will understand presently.* **2** *Chiefly Scot, US, & Canad* at the moment: *these methods are presently being developed.*

present participle *n Grammar* a form of verb, in English ending in *-ing*, that is used both adjectivally, to describe action happening at the same time as that of the main verb, and in continuous tenses.

present perfect *or* **present perfect tense** *n Grammar* a compound tense formed, in English, using *have* or *has* plus a past participle: *have/has eaten is the present perfect of eat.*

presents *pl n Law* used in a deed or document to refer to itself: *know all men by these presents.*

present tense *n Grammar* a verb tense used to describe action which is happening now.

preservative *n* **1** a chemical added to foods to prevent decay. ✧ *adj* **2** preventing decay.

preserve *vb* **-serving, -served 1** to keep safe from change or extinction; protect: *we are interested in preserving world peace.* **2** to protect from decay or damage: *the carefully preserved village of Cregneish.* **3** to treat (food) in order to prevent it from decaying. **4** to maintain; keep up: *the 1.2% increase in earnings needed to preserve living standards.* ✧ *n* **5** an area of interest restricted to a particular person or group: *working-class preserves such as pigeon racing.* **6** (*usually pl*) fruit preserved by cooking in sugar. **7** an area where game is kept for private hunting or fishing. ▷ **HISTORY** Latin *prae* before + *servare* to keep safe ▶ **preservation** *n*

preset *vb* **-setting, -set 1** to set the timer on a piece of equipment so that it starts to work at a specific time. ✧ *adj* **2** (of equipment) with the controls set in advance.

preshrunk *adj* (of fabric or a garment) having been shrunk during manufacture so that further shrinkage will not occur when washed.

preside *vb* **-siding, -sided 1** to chair a meeting. **2** to exercise authority: *he presided over the burning of the books.* ▷ **HISTORY** Latin *praesidere* to superintend

presidency *n, pl* **-cies** the office or term of a president.

president *n* **1** the head of state of a republic, esp. of the US. **2** the head of a company, society, or institution. **3** a person who presides over a meeting. **4** the head of certain establishments of higher education. ▷ **HISTORY** Late Latin *praesidens* ruler ▶ **presidential** *adj*

presidium *n* (in Communist countries) a permanent administrative committee. ▷ **HISTORY** Russian *prezidium*

press[1] *vb* **1** to apply weight or force to: *he pressed the button on the camera.* **2** to squeeze: *she pressed his hand.* **3** to compress to alter in shape. **4** to smooth out creases by applying pressure or heat. **5** to make (objects) from soft material by pressing with a mould. **6** to crush to force out (juice). **7** to urge (someone) insistently: *they pressed for an answer.* **8** to force or compel: *I was pressed into playing rugby at school.* **9** to plead or put forward strongly: *they intend to press their claim for damages in the courts.* **10** to be urgent: *time presses.* **11** (sometimes foll. by *on* or *forward*) to continue in a determined way: *they pressed on with their journey.* **12** to crowd; push: *shoppers press along the pavements.* **13 pressed for** short of: *pressed for time.* ✧ *n* **14** any machine that exerts pressure to form or cut materials or to extract liquids or compress solids. **15** the art or process of printing. **16 go to press** to go to be printed: *when is this book going to press?* **17 the press a** news media collectively, esp. newspapers. **b** journalists collectively. **18** the opinions and reviews in the newspapers: *the government is not receiving a good press at the moment.* **19** the act of pressing or state of being pressed: *at the press of a button.* **20** a crowd: *a press of people at the exit.* **21** a cupboard for storing clothes or linen. ▷ **HISTORY** Old French *presser*

press[2] *vb* **1** to recruit (men) forcibly for military service. **2** to use for a purpose other than intended: *press into service.* ▷ **HISTORY** from *prest* to recruit soldiers

press agent *n* a person employed to obtain favourable publicity for an individual or organization.

press box *n* a room at a sports ground reserved for reporters.

press conference *n* an interview for reporters given by a famous person.

press gallery *n* an area for newspaper reporters, esp. in a parliament.

press gang *n* **1** (formerly) a group of men used to capture men and boys and force them to join the navy. ✧ *vb* **press-gang 2** to force (a person) to join the navy by a press gang. **3** to persuade (someone) to do something that he or she does not want to do: *he was press-ganged into joining the family business.*

pressing *adj* **1** demanding immediate attention. ✧ *n* **2** a large number of gramophone records produced at one time.

press stud *n Brit* a fastener in which one part with a projecting knob snaps into a hole on another part.

press-up *n* an exercise in which the body is raised from and lowered to the floor by straightening and bending the arms.

pressure *n* **1** the state of pressing or being pressed. **2** the application of force by one body on the surface of another. **3** urgent claims or demands: *to work under pressure.* **4** a condition that is hard to bear: *the pressure of grief.* **5** *Physics* the force applied to a unit area of a surface. **6 bring pressure to bear on** to use influence or authority to persuade. ✧ *vb* **-suring, -sured 7** to persuade forcefully: *he was pressured into resignation.* ▷ **HISTORY** Late Latin *pressura* a pressing, from Latin *premere* to press

pressure cooker *n* an airtight pot which cooks food quickly by steam under pressure. ▶ **pressure-cook** *vb*

pressure gradient *n Meteorol* the decrease in atmospheric pressure per unit of horizontal distance, shown on a synoptic chart by the spacing of the isobars.

pressure group *n* a group that tries to influence policies or public opinion.

pressurize or **-ise** *vb* **-izing, -ized** or **-ising, -ised 1** to increase the pressure in (an aircraft cabin, etc.) in order to maintain approximately atmospheric pressure when the external pressure is low. **2** to make insistent demands of (someone): *do not be pressurized into making a decision.* ▶ **pressurization** or **-isation** *n*

Prestel *n Trademark* (in Britain) the Post Office public Viewdata service.

prestidigitation *n Formal* same as **sleight of hand.** ▷ **HISTORY** French ▶ **prestidigitator** *n*

prestige *n* **1** high status or respect resulting from success or achievements: *a symbol of French*

power and prestige. **2** the power to impress: *a humdrum family car with no prestige.*
▷ **HISTORY** Latin *praestigiae* tricks ▶ **prestigious** *adj*

presto *Music* ✧ *adv* **1** very fast. ✧ *n, pl* **-tos 2** a passage to be played very quickly. ▷ **HISTORY** Italian

presumably *adv* one supposes or guesses; probably: *he emerged from what was presumably the kitchen carrying a tray.*

presume *vb* **-suming, -sumed 1** to take (something) for granted: *I presume he's dead.* **2** to dare (to): *I would not presume to lecture you on medical matters, Dr Jacobs.* **3** (foll. by *on* or *upon*) to rely or depend: *don't presume on his agreement.* **4** (foll. by *on* or *upon*) to take advantage (of): *I'm afraid I presumed on Aunt Ginny's generosity.* ▷ **HISTORY** Latin *praesumere* to take in advance ▶ **presumedly** *adv* ▶ **presuming** *adj*

presumption *n* **1** the act of presuming. **2** a basis on which an assumption is made. **3** bold insolent behaviour. **4** a belief or assumption based on reasonable evidence. ▶ **presumptive** *adj*

presumptuous *adj* bold and insolent.

presuppose *vb* **-posing, -posed 1** to require as a previous condition in order to be true: *the idea of integration presupposes a disintegrated state.* **2** to take for granted. ▶ **presupposition** *n*

pretence *or US* **pretense** *n* **1** an action or claim that could mislead people into believing something which is not true: *Daniel made a pretence of carefully reading it; the pretence that many of the unemployed are on 'training schemes'.* **2** a false display; affectation: *she abandoned all pretence of work and watched me.* **3** a claim, esp. a false one, to a right, title, or distinction. **4** make-believe. **5** a pretext: *they were placed in a ghetto on the pretence that they would be safe there.*

pretend *vb* **1** to claim or give the appearance of (something untrue): *he pretended to be asleep.* **2** to make believe: *one of the actresses pretended to urinate into a bucket.* **3** (foll. by *to*) to present a claim, esp. a doubtful one: *to pretend to the throne.* ▷ **HISTORY** Latin *praetendere* to stretch forth, feign

pretender *n* a person who makes a false or disputed claim to a throne or title.

pretension *n* (*often pl*) a false claim to merit or importance.

pretentious *adj* **1** making (unjustified) claims to special merit or importance: *many critics thought her work and ideas pretentious and empty.* **2** vulgarly showy; ostentatious: *a family restaurant with no pretentious furnishing.*

preterite *or esp US* **preterit** (**pret**-er-it) *Grammar* ✧ *n* Also **preterite tense 1** a past tense of verbs, such as *jumped, swam.* **2** a verb in this tense. ✧ *adj* **3** expressing such a past tense. ▷ **HISTORY** Late Latin *praeteritum (tempus)* past (time)

preternatural *adj* beyond what is natural; supernatural. ▷ **HISTORY** Latin *praeter naturam* beyond the scope of nature

pretext *n* a false reason given to hide the real one: *delivering the book had been a good pretext for seeing her again.* ▷ **HISTORY** Latin *praetextum* disguise, from *praetexere* to weave in front

pretty *adj* **-tier, -tiest 1** attractive in a delicate or graceful way. **2** pleasant to look at. **3** *Informal, often ironic* excellent or fine: *well, this is a pretty state of affairs to have got into.* ✧ *adv* **4** *Informal* fairly: *I think he and Nicholas got on pretty well.* **5 sitting pretty** *Informal* in a favourable state. ▷ **HISTORY** Old English *prættig* clever ▶ **prettily** *adv* ▶ **prettiness** *n*

pretzel *n* a brittle salted biscuit in the shape of a knot. ▷ **HISTORY** from German

prevail *vb* **1** (often foll. by *over* or *against*) to prove superior; gain mastery: *moderate nationalists have until now prevailed over the radicals.* **2** to be the most important feature: *a casual good-natured mood prevailed.* **3** to be generally established: *this attitude has prevailed for many years.* **4 prevail on** *or* **upon** to succeed in persuading: *he had easily been prevailed upon to accept a lift.* ▷ **HISTORY** Latin *praevalere* to be superior in strength

prevailing *adj* **1** widespread: *the prevailing mood.* **2** most usual: *elsewhere, the prevailing weather will vary.*

prevailing wind *n Meteorol* the most frequent wind direction over a given period.

prevalent *adj* widespread or common. ▶ **prevalence** *n*

prevaricate *vb* **-cating, -cated** to avoid giving a direct or truthful answer. ▷ **HISTORY** Latin *praevaricari* to walk crookedly ▶ **prevarication** *n* ▶ **prevaricator** *n*

prevent *vb* **1** to keep from happening: *vitamin C prevented scurvy.* **2** (often foll. by *from*) to keep (someone from doing something): *circumstances prevented her from coming.* ▷ **HISTORY** Latin *praevenire* ▶ **preventable** *adj* ▶ **prevention** *n*

preventive *adj* **1** intended to prevent or hinder. **2** *Med* tending to prevent disease. ✧ *n* **3** something that serves to prevent. **4** *Med* any drug or agent that tends to prevent disease. Also: **preventative**

preview *n* **1** an opportunity to see a film, exhibition, or play before it is shown to the public. ✧ *vb* **2** to view in advance.

previous *adj* **1** coming or happening before. **2** *Informal* happening too soon; premature: *such criticism is a bit previous because no definite decision has yet been taken.* **3 previous to** before. ▷ **HISTORY** Latin *praevius* leading the way ▶ **previously** *adv*

prey *n* **1** an animal hunted and killed for food by another animal. **2** the victim of a hostile person, influence, emotion, or illness: *children are falling prey to the disease.* **3 bird** *or* **beast of prey** a bird *or* animal that kills and eats other birds or animals. ✧ *vb* (often foll. by *on* or *upon*) **4** to hunt and kill for food. **5** to worry or obsess: *it preyed on his conscience.* **6** to make a victim (of others), by profiting at their expense. ▷ **HISTORY** Old French *preie*

price *n* **1** the amount of money for which a thing is bought or sold. **2** the cost at which something is obtained: *the price of making the wrong decision.* **3 at any price** whatever the price or cost. **4 at a price** at a high price. **5** *Gambling* odds. **6 what price (something)?** what are the chances of (something) happening now? ✧ *vb* **pricing, priced**

a b c d e f g h i j k l m n o p q r s t u v w x y z

7 to fix the price of. **8** to discover the price of. ▷ **HISTORY** Latin *pretium*

price-fixing *n* the setting of prices by agreement among producers and distributors.

priceless *adj* **1** extremely valuable. **2** *Informal* extremely amusing.

pricey *adj* **pricier, priciest** *Informal* expensive.

prick *vb* **1** to pierce lightly with a sharp point. **2** to cause a piercing sensation (in): *a needle pricked her finger.* **3** to cause a sharp emotional pain (in): *the film pricked our consciences about the plight of the Afghan refugees.* **4 prick up one's ears a** (of a dog) to make the ears stand erect. **b** (of a person) to listen attentively. ✧ *n* **5** a sudden sharp pain caused by pricking. **6** a mark made by a sharp point. **7** a sharp emotional pain: *a prick of conscience.* **8** *Slang taboo* a penis. **9** *Slang offensive* a man who provokes contempt. ▷ **HISTORY** Old English *prica* point, puncture

prickle *n* **1** *Bot* a thorn or spike on a plant. **2** a pricking or stinging sensation. ✧ *vb* **-ling, -led 3** to feel a stinging sensation. ▷ **HISTORY** Old English *pricel*

prickly *adj* **-lier, -liest 1** having prickles. **2** tingling or stinging: *he had a prickly feeling down his back.* **3** touchy or irritable: *Canadians are notoriously prickly about being taken for Americans.*

prickly heat *n* an itchy rash that occurs in very hot moist weather.

prickly pear *n* **1** a tropical cactus with edible oval fruit. **2** the fruit of this plant.

pride *n* **1** a feeling of satisfaction about one's achievements. **2** an excessively high opinion of oneself. **3** satisfaction in one's own or another's success or achievements: *his obvious pride in his son's achievements.* **4** a sense of dignity and self-respect: *he must swallow his pride and ally himself with his political enemies.* **5** one of the better or most admirable parts of something: *the pride of the main courses is the Japanese fish and vegetable tempura.* **6** a group of lions. **7 pride and joy** the main source of pride: *the car was his pride and joy.* **8 pride of place** the most important position. ✧ *vb* **priding, prided 9** (foll. by *on* or *upon*) to take pride in (oneself) for. ▷ **HISTORY** Old English *prȳde*

priest *n* **1** (in the Christian Church) a person ordained to administer the sacraments and preach. **2** a minister of any religion. **3** an official who performs religious ceremonies. ▷ **HISTORY** Old English *prēost*, apparently from *presbyter* ▶ **priestess** *fem n* ▶ **priesthood** *n* ▶ **priestly** *adj*

prig *n* a person who is smugly self-righteous and narrow-minded. ▷ **HISTORY** origin unknown ▶ **priggish** *adj* ▶ **priggishness** *n*

prim *adj* **primmer, primmest** affectedly proper, or formal, and rather prudish. ▷ **HISTORY** origin unknown ▶ **primly** *adv*

prima ballerina *n* a leading female ballet dancer. ▷ **HISTORY** Italian: first ballerina

primacy *n, pl* **-cies 1** the state of being first in rank, grade, or order. **2** *Christianity* the office of an archbishop.

prima donna *n, pl* **prima donnas 1** a leading female opera singer. **2** *Informal* a temperamental person. ▷ **HISTORY** Italian: first lady

primaeval *adj* same as **primeval**.

prima facie (**prime**-a **fay**-shee) *adv* as it seems at first. ▷ **HISTORY** Latin

prima-facie case *n Law* a case in which the evidence against someone is sufficient for it to succeed unless the evidence can be rebutted. A finding by a magistrate that there is a prima facie case to answer means that a case will proceed to a higher court.

prima-facie evidence *n Law* evidence that is sufficient to establish a fact or to raise a presumption of the truth unless controverted.

primal *adj* **1** of basic causes or origins. **2** chief or most important. ▷ **HISTORY** Latin *primus* first

primarily *adv* **1** chiefly or mainly. **2** originally.

primary *adj* **1** first in importance. **2** first in position or time, as in a series: *he argued that the country was only in the primary stage of socialism.* **3** fundamental or basic: *the new policy will put the emphasis on primary health care rather than hospital care.* **4** being the first stage; elementary: *all new recruits participated in the same primary training courses.* **5** relating to the education of children up to the age of 11 or 12. **6** (of an industry) involving the obtaining of raw materials. **7** (of the flight feathers of a bird's wing) outer and longest. **8** being the part of an electric circuit in which a changing current causes a current in a neighbouring circuit: *a primary coil.* ✧ *n, pl* **-ries 9** a person or thing that is first in position, time, or importance. **10** (in the US) an election in which the voters of a state choose a candidate for office. Full name: **primary election 11** a primary school. **12** a primary colour. **13** any of the outer and longest flight feathers of a bird's wing. **14** a primary part of an electric circuit. ▷ **HISTORY** Latin *primarius* principal

primary accent *or* **stress** *n Linguistics* the strongest accent in a word.

primary colours *pl n* **1** *Physics* the colours red, green, and blue from which all other colours can be obtained by mixing. **2** *Art* the colours red, yellow, and blue from which all other colours can be obtained by mixing.

primary consumer *n Biol* a herbivore. Compare **primary producer, secondary consumer, tertiary consumer**.

primary differentiation *n Marketing* the real or illusory distinction between competing products in a market.

primary industry *n Econ, business* an industry concerned with the growing, collecting, or extracting of raw materials. Compare **secondary industry, tertiary industry**.

primary producer *n Biol* an organism such as a plant that converts inorganic matter into organic matter and serves as food for a primary consumer. Compare **primary consumer**.

primary production *n Econ* the process of producing raw materials for industry.

primary school *n* **1** (in England and Wales) a school for children between the ages of 5 and 11.

A B C D E F G H I J K L M N O P Q R S T U V W X Y Z

2 (in Scotland, Australia and New Zealand) a school for children between the ages of 5 and 12. **3** (in the US and Canada) a school equivalent to the first three or four grades of elementary school.

primary source *n* a document, diary, or artefact that was created at the time being studied and that offers first-hand evidence of something. Compare **secondary source**.

primate[1] *n* a mammal with flexible hands and feet and a highly developed brain, such as a monkey, an ape, or a human being.

primate[2] *n* an archbishop. ▷ **HISTORY** Latin *primas* principal

primate city *n Geog* the most important city in a country or region in population, economic, and general terms, and one that is likely to be twice the size of the next most important city.

prime *adj* **1** first in importance: *the prime aim.* **2** of the highest quality: *prime beef.* **3** typical: *a prime example.* ✧ *n* **4** the time when a thing is at its best. **5** a period of power, vigour, and activity: *he was in the prime of life.* **6** *Maths* short for **prime number**. ✧ *vb* **priming, primed 7** to give (someone) information in advance to prepare him or her. **8** to prepare (a surface) for painting. **9** to prepare (a gun or mine) before detonating or firing. **10** to fill (a pump) with its working fluid, to expel air from it before starting. **11** to prepare (something). ▷ **HISTORY** Latin *primus* first

prime meridian *n* the 0° meridian from which the other meridians are worked out, usually taken to pass through Greenwich.

Prime Minister *n* the leader of a government.

prime mover *n* a person or thing which was important in helping create an idea, situation, etc.: *he was the prime mover behind the coup.*

prime number *n* an integer that cannot be divided into other integers but is only divisible by itself or 1, such as 2, 3, 5, 7, and 11.

primer[1] *n* **1** a substance applied to a surface as a base coat or sealer. **2** a device for detonating the main charge in a gun or mine. ▷ **HISTORY** see PRIME (verb)

primer[2] *n* an introductory text, such as a school textbook. ▷ **HISTORY** Medieval Latin *primarius (liber)* a first (book)

prime stock *n NZ* livestock in peak condition and ready for killing.

primeval (prime-**ee**-val) *adj* of the earliest age of the world. ▷ **HISTORY** Latin *primus* first + *aevum* age

primitive *adj* **1** of or belonging to the beginning. **2** *Biol* of an early stage in development: *primitive amphibians.* **3** characteristic of an early simple state, esp. in being crude or basic: *a primitive dwelling.* ✧ *n* **4** a primitive person or thing. **5** a painter of any era whose work appears childlike or untrained. **6** a work by such an artist. ▷ **HISTORY** Latin *primitivus* earliest of its kind

primogeniture *n* **1** *Formal* the state of being the first-born child. **2** *Law* the right of an eldest son to inherit all the property of his parents. ▷ **HISTORY** Medieval Latin *primogenitura* birth of a first child

primordial *adj Formal* existing at or from the beginning. ▷ **HISTORY** Late Latin *primordialis* original

primrose *n* **1** a wild plant which has pale yellow flowers in spring. ✧ *adj* **2** Also: **primrose yellow** pale yellow. **3** of primroses. ▷ **HISTORY** Medieval Latin *prima rosa* first rose

primula *n* a type of primrose with brightly coloured funnel-shaped flowers. ▷ **HISTORY** Medieval Latin *primula (veris)* little first one (of the spring)

Primus *n Trademark* a portable paraffin cooking stove, used esp. by campers.

prince *n* **1** a male member of a royal family, esp. the son of the king or queen. **2** the male ruler of a small country. **3** an outstanding member of a specified group: *Dryden, that prince of poets.* ▷ **HISTORY** Latin *princeps* first man, ruler

prince consort *n* the husband of a queen, who is himself a prince.

princely *adj* **-lier, -liest 1** of or characteristic of a prince. **2** generous or lavish.

Prince of Wales *n* the eldest son of the British sovereign.

princess *n* **1** a female member of a royal family, esp. the daughter of the king or queen. **2** the wife of a prince.

Princess Royal *n* a title sometimes given to the eldest daughter of the British sovereign.

principal *adj* **1** first in importance, rank, or value: *salt is the principal source of sodium in our diets; the Republic's two principal parties.* ✧ *n* **2** the head of a school or other educational institution. **3** a person who holds one of the most important positions in an organization: *she became a principal in the home finance department.* **4** the leading actor in a play. **5** *Law* **a** a person who engages another to act as his or her agent. **b** a person who takes an active part in a crime. **c** the person held responsible for fulfilling an obligation. **6** *Finance* **a** capital or property, as contrasted with income. **b** the original amount of a debt on which interest is calculated. ▷ **HISTORY** Latin *principalis* chief ▶ **principally** *adv*

> **WORD TIP**
> See at **principle.**

principal boy *n Brit* the leading male role in a pantomime, traditionally played by a woman.

principal clause *n* the same as **main clause**.

principality *n, pl* **-ties** a territory ruled by a prince.

principal parts *pl n Grammar* the main verb forms, from which all other verb forms may be deduced.

principle *n* **1** a moral rule guiding personal conduct: *he'd stoop to anything – he has no principles.* **2** a set of such moral rules: *a man of principle.* **3** a basic or general truth: *the principle of freedom of expression.* **4** a basic law or rule underlying a particular theory or philosophy: *the government has been deceitful and has violated basic principles of democracy.* **5** a general law in science: *the principle of the conservation of mass.* **6** *Chem* a constituent of a substance that determines its characteristics. **7 in principle** in theory though not always in practice. **8 on principle** because of one's beliefs. ▷ **HISTORY** Latin *principium* beginning, basic tenet

> **WORD TIP**
> *Principle* and *principal* are often confused: *the principal* (not *principle*) *reason for his departure; the plan was approved in principle* (not *in principal*).

principle of moments *n Physics* the relationship between the forces on either side of a pivot.

print *vb* **1** to reproduce (a newspaper, book, etc.) in large quantities by mechanical or electronic means. **2** to reproduce (text or pictures) by applying ink to paper. **3** to write in letters that are not joined up. **4** to stamp (fabric) with a design. **5** to produce (a photograph) from a negative. **6** to fix in the mind or memory. ✧ *n* **7** printed content, such as newsprint. **8** a printed publication, such as a book. **9 in print a** in printed or published form. **b** (of a book) available from a publisher. **10 out of print** no longer available from a publisher. **11** a picture printed from an engraved plate or wood block. **12** printed text, with regard to the typeface: *italic print.* **13** a photograph produced from a negative. **14** a fabric with a printed design. **15** a mark made by pressing something onto a surface. **16** See **fingerprint**. ✧ See also **print out**. ▷ **HISTORY** Old French *preindre* to make an impression

printed circuit *n* an electronic circuit in which the wiring is a metallic coating printed on a thin insulating board.

printer *n* **1** a person or business engaged in printing. **2** a machine that prints. **3** *Computers* a machine that prints out results on paper.

printing *n* **1** the process of producing printed matter. **2** printed text. **3** all the copies of a book printed at one time. **4** a form of writing in which the letters are not joined together.

print out *vb* **1** *Computers* to produce (printed information). ✧ *n* **print-out, printout 2** printed information from a computer.

prior[1] *adj* **1** previous: *prior knowledge.* **2 prior to** before. ▷ **HISTORY** Latin: previous

prior[2] *n* **1** the head monk in a priory. **2** the abbot's deputy in a monastery. ▷ **HISTORY** Late Latin: head ▶ **prioress** *fem n*

priority *n, pl* **-ties 1** the most important thing that must be dealt with first. **2** the right to be or go before others.

priory *n, pl* **-ories** a religious house where certain orders of monks or nuns live.

prise *or* **prize** *vb* **prising, prised** *or* **prizing, prized** to force open or out by levering. ▷ **HISTORY** Old French *prise* a taking

prism *n* **1** a transparent block, often with triangular ends and rectangular sides, used to disperse light into a spectrum or refract it in optical instruments. **2** *Maths* a polyhedron with parallel bases and sides that are parallelograms. ▷ **HISTORY** Greek *prisma* something shaped by sawing

prismatic *adj* **1** of or shaped like a prism. **2** exhibiting bright spectral colours; rainbow-like: *prismatic light.*

prison *n* **1** a public building used to hold convicted criminals and accused people awaiting trial. **2** any place of confinement. ▷ **HISTORY** Old French *prisun,* from Latin *prensio* a capturing

prisoner *n* **1** a person kept in prison as a punishment for a crime, or while awaiting trial. **2** a person confined by any restraints: *he's a prisoner of his own past.* **3 take (someone) prisoner** to capture and hold (someone) as a prisoner.

prisoner of war *n* a serviceman captured by an enemy in wartime.

prissy *adj* **-sier, -siest** prim and prudish. ▷ **HISTORY** probably from *prim* + *sissy* ▶ **prissily** *adv*

pristine *adj* **1** completely new, clean, and pure: *pristine white plates.* **2** of or involving the original, unchanged, and unspoilt period or state: *the viewing of wild game in its pristine natural state.* ▷ **HISTORY** Latin *pristinus* primitive

privacy *n* **1** the condition of being private. **2** secrecy.

private *adj* **1** not for general or public use: *a private bathroom.* **2** confidential or secret: *a private conversation.* **3** involving someone's domestic and personal life rather than his or her work or business: *what I do in my private life is none of your business.* **4** owned or paid for by individuals rather than by the government: *private enterprise.* **5** not publicly known: *they had private reasons for the decision.* **6** having no public office, rank, or position: *the Red Cross received donations from private citizens.* **7** (of a place) quiet and secluded: *the garden is completely private.* **8** (of a person) quiet and retiring: *she was private – her life was her own.* ✧ *n* **9** a soldier of the lowest rank in the army. **10 in private** in secret. ▷ **HISTORY** Latin *privatus* belonging to one individual, withdrawn from public life ▶ **privately** *adv*

private bill *n* a bill presented to Parliament on behalf of a private individual or corporation.

private company *n* a limited company that does not issue shares for public subscription.

private detective *n* a person hired by a client to do detective work.

privateer *n* **1** a privately owned armed vessel authorized by the government to take part in a war. **2** a captain of such a ship.

private income *n* income from sources other than employment, such as investment.

private law *n Law* the branch of law that deals with the rights and duties of private individuals and the relations between them. Compare **public law**.

private member *n* a Member of Parliament who is not a government minister.

private member's bill *n Law* a law proposed by a Member of Parliament who is not a government minister.

private parts *or* **privates** *pl n Euphemistic* the genitals.

private school *n* a school controlled by a private body, accepting mostly fee-paying pupils.

private sector *n* the part of a country's economy that consists of privately owned enterprises.

privation *n Formal* loss or lack of the necessities of life. ▷ **HISTORY** Latin *privatio* deprivation

privative (**priv**-a-tiv) *adj* **1** causing privation. **2** *Grammar* expressing lack or absence, for example *-less* and *un-*.

privatize *or* **-ise** *vb* **-izing, -ized** *or* **-ising, -ised** to sell (a state-owned company) to individuals or a private company. ▶ **privatization** *or* **-isation** *n*

privet *n* a bushy evergreen shrub used for hedges. ▷ **HISTORY** origin unknown

privilege *n* **1** a benefit or advantage granted only to certain people: *a privilege of rank.* **2** the opportunity to do something which gives you great satisfaction and which most people never have the chance to do: *I had the privilege of meeting the Queen when she visited our school.* **3** the power and advantages that come with great wealth or high social class: *the use of violence to protect class privilege and thwart popular democracy.* ▷ **HISTORY** Latin *privilegium* law relevant to rights of an individual

privileged *adj* enjoying a special right or immunity.

privity of contract *n Law* the legal principle (in some countries including England) that only the parties to a contract have the right to take legal action to enforce it.

privy *adj* **privier, priviest 1 privy to** sharing in the knowledge of something secret. **2** *Archaic* secret. ✧ *n, pl* **privies 3** *Obsolete* a toilet, esp. an outside one. ▷ **HISTORY** Old French *privé* something private

Privy Council *n* **1** the private council of the British king or queen. **2** (in Canada) a formal body of advisers of the governor general. ▶ **Privy Counsellor** *n*

privy purse *n* an allowance voted by Parliament for the private expenses of the king or queen.

privy seal *n* (in Britain) a seal affixed to certain documents of state.

prize[1] *n* **1** something of value, such as a trophy, given to the winner of a contest or game. **2** something given to the winner of any game of chance, lottery, etc. **3** something striven for. ✧ *adj* **4** winning or likely to win a prize: *a prize bull.* ▷ **HISTORY** Old French *prise* a capture

prize[2] *vb* **prizing, prized** to value highly. ▷ **HISTORY** Old French *preisier* to praise

prizefight *n* a boxing match for a prize or purse. ▶ **prizefighter** *n*

pro[1] *adv* **1** in favour of a motion etc. ✧ *prep* **2** in favour of. ✧ *n, pl* **pros 3** (*usually pl*) an argument or vote in favour of a proposal or motion. ✧ See also **pros and cons**. ▷ **HISTORY** Latin: in favour of

pro[2] *n, pl* **pros**, *adj Informal* **1** short for **professional**. **2** a prostitute.

PRO public relations officer.

pro-[1] *prefix* **1** in favour of; supporting: *pro-Chinese.* **2** acting as a substitute for: *pronoun.* ▷ **HISTORY** Latin

pro-[2] *prefix* before in time or position: *proboscis.* ▷ **HISTORY** Greek

proactive *adj* tending to initiate change rather than reacting to events.

probability *n, pl* **-ties 1** the condition of being probable. **2** an event or other thing that is likely to happen or be true. **3** *Statistics* a measure of the likelihood of an event happening.

probable *adj* **1** likely to happen or be true. **2** most likely: *the probable cause of the accident.* ✧ *n* **3** a person who is likely to be chosen for a team, event, etc. ▷ **HISTORY** Latin *probabilis* that may be proved

probably *adv* in all likelihood or probability: *the wedding's probably going to be in late August.*

probate *n* **1** the process of officially proving the validity of a will. **2** the official certificate stating that a will is genuine. ▷ **HISTORY** Latin *probare* to inspect

probation *n* **1** a system of dealing with offenders, esp. juvenile ones, by placing them under supervision. **2 on probation a** under the supervision of a probation officer. **b** undergoing a test or trial period, such as at the start of a new job. ▷ **HISTORY** Latin *probare* to test ▶ **probationary** *adj*

probationer *n* a person on probation.

probation officer *n* an officer of a court who supervises offenders placed on probation.

probe *vb* **probing, probed 1** to search into closely. **2** to poke or examine (something) with or as if with a probe: *he probed carefully with his fingertips.* ✧ *n* **3** *Surgery* a slender instrument for exploring a wound etc. **4** a thorough inquiry, such as one into corrupt practices. **5** See **space probe**. ▷ **HISTORY** Latin *probare* to test

probiotic *n* **1** a bacterium that protects the body from harmful bacteria. ✧ *adj* **2** relating to probiotics: *probiotic yogurts.*

probity *n Formal* honesty; integrity. ▷ **HISTORY** Latin *probitas* honesty

problem *n* **1** something or someone that is difficult to deal with. **2** a puzzle or question set for solving. **3** *Maths* a statement requiring a solution usually by means of several operations. ✧ *adj* **4** of a literary work that deals with difficult moral questions: *a problem play.* **5** difficult to deal with or creating difficulties for others: *a problem child.* ▷ **HISTORY** Greek *problēma* something put forward

problematic *or* **problematical** *adj* difficult to solve or deal with.

proboscis (pro-**boss**-iss) *n* **1** a long flexible trunk or snout, such as an elephant's. **2** the elongated mouth part of certain insects. ▷ **HISTORY** Greek *proboskis* trunk of an elephant

procedural genre *n* a form of writing or speech in which the writer or speaker explains the procedures to follow in order to do something.

procedure *n* **1** a way of doing something, esp. an established method. **2** the established form of conducting the business of a legislature. ▶ **procedural** *adj*

proceed *vb* **1** to advance or carry on, esp. after stopping. **2** (often foll. by *with*) to start or continue doing: *he proceeded to pour himself a large whisky.* **3** *Formal* to walk or go. **4** (often foll. by *against*) to start a legal action. **5** *Formal* to arise from: *their mutual dislike proceeded from differences of political opinion.* ▷ HISTORY Latin *procedere* to advance

proceeding *n* **1** an act or course of action. **2 proceedings** the events of an occasion: *millions watched the proceedings on television.* **3 proceedings** the minutes of the meetings of a society. **4 proceedings** legal action.

proceeds *pl n* the amount of money obtained from an event or activity.

process[1] *n* **1** a series of actions or changes: *a process of genuine national reconciliation.* **2** a series of natural developments which result in an overall change: *the ageing process.* **3** a method of doing or producing something: *the various production processes use up huge amounts of water.* **4 in the process of** during or in the course of. **5 a** a summons to appear in court. **b** an action at law. **6** a natural outgrowth or projection of a part or organism. ✧ *vb* **7** to handle or prepare by a special method of manufacture. **8** *Computers* to perform operations on (data) in order to obtain the required information. ▷ HISTORY Latin *processus* an advancing

process[2] *vb* to move in an orderly or ceremonial group: *the cult members processed through the streets to the music of tambourines.*

processed *adj* (of food) treated by adding colouring, preservatives, etc., to improve its appearance or the period it will stay edible: *processed cheese.*

procession *n* **1** a line of people or vehicles moving forwards in an orderly or ceremonial manner. **2** the act of proceeding in a regular formation. ▷ HISTORY Latin *processio* a marching forwards

processional *adj* **1** of or suitable for a procession: *the processional route.* ✧ *n* **2** *Christianity* a hymn sung as the clergy enter church.

processor *n* **1** *Computers* same as **central processing unit**. **2** a person or thing that carries out a process.

proclaim *vb* **1** to announce publicly; declare: *Greece was proclaimed an independent kingdom in 1832.* **2** to indicate plainly: *the sharp hard glint in the eye proclaimed her determination.* ▷ HISTORY Latin *proclamare* to shout aloud ▶ **proclamation** *n*

proclivity *n, pl* **-ties** *Formal* a tendency or inclination. ▷ HISTORY Latin *proclivitas*

procrastinate *vb* **-nating, -nated** to put off (an action) until later; delay. ▷ HISTORY Latin *procrastinare* to postpone until tomorrow ▶ **procrastination** *n* ▶ **procrastinator** *n*

procreate *vb* **-ating, -ated** *Formal* to produce (offspring). ▷ HISTORY Latin *procreare* ▶ **procreative** *adj* ▶ **procreation** *n*

Procrustean *adj* ruthlessly enforcing uniformity. ▷ HISTORY after *Procrustes,* robber in Greek myth who fitted travellers into his bed by stretching or lopping off their limbs

proctor *n* a member of the staff of certain universities having duties including the enforcement of discipline. ▷ HISTORY syncopated variant of *procurator* ▶ **proctorial** *adj*

procurator fiscal *n* (in Scotland) a legal officer who acts as public prosecutor and coroner.

procure *vb* **-curing, -cured 1** to get or provide: *it remained very difficult to procure food and fuel.* **2** to obtain (people) to act as prostitutes. ▷ HISTORY Latin *procurare* to look after ▶ **procurement** *n*

procurer *n* a person who obtains people to act as prostitutes.

prod *vb* **prodding, prodded 1** to poke with a pointed object. **2** to rouse (someone) to action. ✧ *n* **3** the act of prodding. **4** a reminder. ▷ HISTORY origin unknown

prodigal *adj* **1** recklessly wasteful or extravagant. **2 prodigal of** lavish with: *you are prodigal of both your toil and your talent.* ✧ *n* **3** a person who squanders money. ▷ HISTORY Latin *prodigere* to squander ▶ **prodigality** *n*

prodigious *adj* **1** very large or immense. **2** wonderful or amazing. ▷ HISTORY Latin *prodigiosus* marvellous

prodigy *n, pl* **-gies 1** a person, esp. a child, with marvellous talent. **2** anything that is a cause of wonder. ▷ HISTORY Latin *prodigium* an unnatural happening

produce *vb* **-ducing, -duced 1** to bring (something) into existence. **2** to present to view: *he produced his passport.* **3** to make: *this area produces much of Spain's best wine.* **4** to give birth to. **5** to present on stage, film, or television: *the girls and boys write and produce their own plays.* **6** to act as producer of. ✧ *n* **7** food grown for sale: *farm produce.* **8** something produced. ▷ HISTORY Latin *producere* to bring forward ▶ **producible** *adj*

producer *n* **1** a person with the financial and administrative responsibility for a film or television programme. **2** *Brit & NZ* a person responsible for the artistic direction of a play. **3** a person who supervises the arrangement, performance, and mixing of a recording. **4** a person or thing that produces. **5** *Biology* an organism, esp. a green plant, that builds up its own tissues from simple inorganic compounds and is itself a food source for other organisms. Compare **consumer**.

product *n* **1** something produced. **2** a consequence: *their skill was the product of hours of training.* **3** *Maths* the result achieved by multiplication.

production *n* **1** the act of producing. **2** anything that is produced. **3** the amount produced or the rate at which it is produced. **4** *Econ* the creation or manufacture of goods and services. **5** any work created as a result of literary or artistic effort. **6** the presentation of a play, opera, etc. **7** *Brit & NZ* the artistic direction of a play. **8** the overall sound of a recording.

A B C D E F G H I J K L M N O P Q R S T U V W X Y Z

production designer *n Films, television* the person responsible for a film's look and design, which includes sets, props, costumes, and location.

production line *n* a system in a factory in which an item being manufactured is moved from machine to machine by conveyor belt, and each machine carries out one step in the manufacture of the item.

production unit *n Films, television* the director, camera crew, sound and lighting teams, and everyone else responsible for providing the necessary expertise and technical support involved in making a film or TV programme.

productive *adj* **1** producing or having the power to produce. **2** yielding favourable results. **3** *Econ* producing goods and services that have exchange value: *the country's productive capacity.* **4** (foll. by *of*) resulting in: *a period highly productive of books and ideas.* ▸ **productivity** *n*

product life-cycle *n Business* the progress of a product from its initial development, its introduction to the market, the growth and decline of its sales and its redevelopment or ultimate withdrawal from the market.

product-oriented *adj Marketing* focusing on the design and development of products.

product placement *n* the practice of a company of paying for its product to appear prominently in a film or television programme.

proem (**pro**-em) *n Formal* an introduction or preface. ▷ HISTORY Greek *pro-* before + *hoimē* song

Prof. Professor.

profane *adj* **1** showing disrespect for religion or something sacred. **2** secular. **3** coarse or blasphemous: *profane language.* ✧ *vb* **-faning, -faned 4** to treat (something sacred) with irreverence. **5** to put to an unworthy use. ▷ HISTORY Latin *profanus* outside the temple ▸ **profanation** *n*

profanity *n, pl* **-ties 1** the quality of being profane. **2** coarse or blasphemous action or speech.

profess *vb* **1** to claim (something as true), often falsely: *he professes not to want the job of prime minister.* **2** to acknowledge openly: *he professed great relief at getting some rest.* **3** to have as one's belief or religion: *most Indonesians profess the Islamic faith.* ▷ HISTORY Latin *profiteri* to confess openly ▸ **professed** *adj*

profession *n* **1** a type of work that requires special training, such as in law or medicine. **2** the people employed in such an occupation. **3** a declaration of a belief or feeling: *a profession of faith.* ▷ HISTORY Latin *professio* public acknowledgment

professional *adj* **1** of a profession. **2** taking part in an activity, such as sport or music, as a means of livelihood. **3** displaying a high level of competence or skill: *a professional and polished performance.* **4** undertaken or performed by people who are paid: *professional golf.* ✧ *n* **5** a professional person. ▸ **professionalism** *n* ▸ **professionally** *adv*

professor *n* **1** the highest rank of teacher in a university. **2** *Chiefly US & Canad* any teacher in a university or college. **3** *Rare* a person who professes his or her opinions or beliefs. ▷ HISTORY Latin: a public teacher ▸ **professorial** *adj* ▸ **professorship** *n*

proffer *vb Formal* to offer for acceptance. ▷ HISTORY Old French *proffrir*

proficient *adj* skilled; expert. ▷ HISTORY Latin *proficere* to make progress ▸ **proficiency** *n*

profile *n* **1** an outline, esp. of the human face, as seen from the side. **2** a short biographical sketch. ▷ HISTORY Italian *profilo*

profit *n* **1** (*often pl*) money gained in business or trade. **2** a benefit or advantage. ✧ *vb* **-iting, -ited 3** to gain a profit or advantage: *we do not want to profit from someone else's problems.* ▷ HISTORY Latin *proficere* to make progress

profitable *adj* making profit. ▸ **profitability** *n* ▸ **profitably** *adv*

profit and loss *n Finance* an account compiled at the end of a financial year showing that year's income and expenses and indicating gross and net profit.

profiteer *n* **1** a person who makes excessive profits at the expense of the public. ✧ *vb* **2** to make excessive profits. ▸ **profiteering** *n*

profit-sharing *n* a system in which a portion of the net profit of a business is shared among its employees.

profligate *adj* **1** recklessly extravagant. **2** shamelessly immoral. ✧ *n* **3** a profligate person. ▷ HISTORY Latin *profligatus* corrupt ▸ **profligacy** *n*

pro forma *adj* **1** laying down a set form. ✧ *adv* **2** performed in a set manner. ▷ HISTORY Latin: for form's sake

pro forma invoice *n Commerce* an invoice issued before an order is placed or before the goods are delivered, giving all the details and the cost of the goods.

profound *adj* **1** showing or needing great knowledge: *a profound knowledge of Greek literature.* **2** strongly felt; intense: *profound relief.* **3** extensive: *profound changes.* **4** situated at or having a great depth. ▷ HISTORY Latin *profundus* deep ▸ **profoundly** *adv* ▸ **profundity** *n*

profuse *adj* **1** plentiful or abundant: *he broke out in a profuse sweat.* **2** (often foll. by *in*) generous in the giving (of): *he was profuse in his apologies.* ▷ HISTORY Latin *profundere* to pour lavishly ▸ **profusely** *adv* ▸ **profusion** *n*

progenitor (pro-**jen**-it-er) *n* **1** a direct ancestor. **2** an originator or founder. ▷ HISTORY Latin: ancestor

progeny (**proj**-in-ee) *n, pl* **-nies 1** offspring; descendants. **2** an outcome. ▷ HISTORY Latin *progenies* lineage

progesterone *n* a hormone, produced in the ovary, that prepares the womb for pregnancy and prevents further ovulation. ▷ HISTORY PRO-[1] + *ge(station)* + *ster(ol)* + *-one*

prognathous *adj* having a projecting lower jaw.

prognosis *n, pl* **-noses 1** *Med* a forecast about the course or outcome of an illness. **2** any forecast. ▷ HISTORY Greek: knowledge beforehand

A B C D E F G H I J K L M N O P Q R S T U V W X Y Z

program *n* **1** a sequence of coded instructions which enables a computer to perform various tasks. ✧ *vb* **-gramming, -grammed 2** to arrange (data) so that it can be processed by a computer. **3** to feed a program into (a computer). ▶ **programmer** *n*

programmable *or* **programable** *adj* capable of being programmed for computer processing.

programme *or US* **program** *n* **1** a planned series of events. **2** a broadcast on radio or television. **3** a printed list of items or performers in an entertainment. ✧ *vb* **-gramming, -grammed** *or US* **-graming, -gramed 4** to schedule (something) as a programme. ▷ HISTORY Greek *programma* written public notice ▶ **programmatic** *adj*

programming language *n* a language system by which instructions to a computer are coded, that is understood by both user and computer.

progress *n* **1** improvement or development. **2** movement forward or advance. **3 in progress** taking place. ✧ *vb* **4** to become more advanced or skilful. **5** to move forward. ▷ HISTORY Latin *progressus* a going forwards

progression *n* **1** the act of progressing; advancement. **2** the act or an instance of moving from one thing in a sequence to the next. **3** *Maths* a sequence of numbers in which each term differs from the succeeding term by a fixed ratio.

progressive *adj* **1** favouring political or social reform. **2** happening gradually: *a progressive illness.* **3** (of a dance, card game, etc.) involving a regular change of partners. ✧ *n* **4** a person who favours political or social reform. ▶ **progressively** *adv*

prohibit *vb* **-iting, -ited 1** to forbid by law or other authority. **2** to hinder or prevent: *the paucity of information prohibits us from drawing reliable conclusions.* ▷ HISTORY Latin *prohibere* to prevent ▶ **prohibitor** *n*

prohibition *n* **1** the act of forbidding. **2** a legal ban on the sale or drinking of alcohol. **3** an order or decree that forbids. ▶ **prohibitionist** *n*

Prohibition *n* the period (1920–33) when making, selling, and transporting alcohol was banned in the US. ▶ **Prohibitionist** *n*

prohibitive *adj* **1** (esp. of prices) too high to be affordable. **2** prohibiting or tending to prohibit: *a prohibitive distance.*

project *n* **1** a proposal or plan. **2** a detailed study of a particular subject. ✧ *vb* **3** to make a prediction based on known data and observations. **4** to cause (an image) to appear on a surface. **5** to communicate (an impression): *he wants to project an image of a deep-thinking articulate gentleman.* **6** to jut out. **7** to cause (one's voice) to be heard clearly at a distance. **8** to transport in the imagination: *it's hard to project oneself into his situation.* ▷ HISTORY Latin *proicere* to throw down

projectile *n* **1** an object thrown as a weapon or fired from a gun. ✧ *adj* **2** designed to be thrown forwards. **3** projecting forwards. ▷ HISTORY New Latin *projectilis* jutting forwards

projection *n* **1** a part that juts out. **2** a forecast based on known data. **3** the process of showing film on a screen. **4** the representation on a flat surface of a three-dimensional figure or curved line.

projectionist *n* a person who operates a film projector.

projector *n* an apparatus for projecting photographic images, film, or slides onto a screen.

prokaryotic *adj Biol* denoting an organism that has cells in each of which the genetic material is in a single filament of DNA.

prolapse *Pathol* ✧ *n* **1** Also: **prolapsus** the slipping down of an internal organ of the body from its normal position. ✧ *vb* **-lapsing, -lapsed 2** (of an internal organ) to slip from its normal position. ▷ HISTORY Latin *prolabi* to slide along

prolapsed *adj Pathol* (of an internal organ) having slipped from its normal position.

prolate *adj Geom* having a polar diameter which is longer than the equatorial diameter. ▷ HISTORY Latin *prolatus* enlarged

prole *n Chiefly Brit offensive slang* a proletarian.

proletarian (pro-lit-**air**-ee-an) *adj* **1** of the proletariat. ✧ *n* **2** a member of the proletariat.

proletariat (pro-lit-**air**-ee-at) *n* the working class. ▷ HISTORY Latin *proletarius* one whose only contribution to the state was his offspring

proliferate *vb* **-ating, -ated 1** to increase rapidly in numbers. **2** to grow or reproduce (new parts, such as cells) rapidly. ▷ HISTORY Latin *proles* offspring + *ferre* to bear ▶ **proliferation** *n*

prolific *adj* **1** producing a constant creative output: *a prolific author.* **2** producing fruit or offspring in abundance. **3** (often foll. by *in* or *of*) rich or fruitful. ▷ HISTORY Latin *proles* offspring ▶ **prolifically** *adv*

prolix *adj* (of a speech or piece of writing) overlong and boring. ▷ HISTORY Latin *prolixus* stretched out widely ▶ **prolixity** *n*

prologue *or US often* **prolog** *n* **1** an introduction to a play or book. **2** an event that comes before another: *this success was a happy prologue to their transatlantic tour.* ▷ HISTORY Greek *pro-* before + *logos* discourse

prolong *vb* to make (something) last longer. ▷ HISTORY Late Latin *prolongare* ▶ **prolongation** *n*

prom *n* **1** *Brit* short for **promenade** (sense 1), **promenade concert**. **2** *US & Canad informal* a formal dance held at a high school or college.

PROM *n Computers* Programmable Read Only Memory.

promenade *n* **1** *Chiefly Brit* a paved walkway along the seafront at a holiday resort. **2** *Old-fashioned* a leisurely walk for pleasure or display. ✧ *vb* **-nading, -naded 3** *Old-fashioned* to take a leisurely walk. ▷ HISTORY French

promenade concert *n* a concert at which some of the audience stand rather than sit.

promethium (pro-**meeth**-ee-um) *n Chem* an artificial radioactive element of the lanthanide series. Symbol: Pm. ▷ HISTORY from *Prometheus,* in Greek mythology, the Titan who gave fire to mankind

prominent *adj* **1** standing out from the surroundings; noticeable. **2** widely known; famous.

3 jutting or projecting outwards: *prominent eyes.* ▷ HISTORY Latin *prominere* to jut out ▶ **prominence** *n* ▶ **prominently** *adv*

promiscuous *adj* **1** taking part in many casual sexual relationships. **2** *Formal* consisting of different elements mingled indiscriminately. ▷ HISTORY Latin *promiscuus* indiscriminate ▶ **promiscuity** *n*

promise *vb* **-ising, -ised 1** to say that one will definitely do or not do something: *I promise I'll have it finished by the end of the week.* **2** to undertake to give (something to someone): *he promised me a car for my birthday.* **3** to show signs of; seem likely: *she promises to be a fine singer.* **4** to assure (someone) of the certainty of something: *everything's fine, I promise you.* ✧ *n* **5** an undertaking to do or not do something. **6** indication of future success: *a young player who shows great promise.* ▷ HISTORY Latin *promissum* a promise

Promised Land *n* **1** *Bible* the land of Canaan. **2** any longed-for place where one expects to find greater happiness.

promising *adj* likely to succeed or turn out well.

promissory note *n Commerce chiefly US* a written promise to pay a stated sum of money to a particular person on a certain date or on demand.

promo *n, pl* **-mos** *Informal* an item produced to promote a product, esp. a video used to promote a pop record.

promontory *n, pl* **-ries** a point of high land that juts out into the sea. ▷ HISTORY Latin *promunturium* headland

promote *vb* **-moting, -moted 1** to encourage the progress or success of: *all attempts to promote a lasting ceasefire have failed.* **2** to raise to a higher rank or position. **3** to encourage the sale of (a product) by advertising. **4** to work for: *he actively promoted reform.* ▷ HISTORY Latin *promovere* to push onwards ▶ **promotion** *n* ▶ **promotional** *adj*

promoter *n* **1** a person who helps to organize and finance an event, esp. a sports one. **2** a person or thing that encourages the progress or success of: *a promoter of terrorism.*

prompt *vb* **1** to cause (an action); bring about: *the killings prompted an anti-Mafia crackdown.* **2** to motivate or cause someone to do something: *I still don't know what prompted me to go.* **3** to remind (an actor) of lines forgotten during a performance. **4** to refresh the memory of. ✧ *adj* **5** done without delay. **6** quick to act. ✧ *adv* **7** *Informal* punctually: *at 8 o'clock prompt.* ✧ *n* **8** anything that serves to remind. ▷ HISTORY Latin *promptus* evident ▶ **promptly** *adv* ▶ **promptness** *n*

prompter *n* a person offstage who reminds the actors of forgotten lines.

promulgate *vb* **-gating, -gated 1** to put (a law or decree) into effect by announcing it officially. **2** to make widely known. ▷ HISTORY Latin *promulgare* ▶ **promulgation** *n* ▶ **promulgator** *n*

pron. **1** pronoun. **2** pronunciation.

prone *adj* **1** having a tendency to be affected by or do something: *I am prone to indigestion.* **2** lying face downwards; prostrate. ▷ HISTORY Latin *pronus* bent forward

prong *n* a long pointed projection from an instrument or tool such as a fork. ▷ HISTORY Middle English

pronominal *adj Grammar* relating to or playing the part of a pronoun.

pronoun *n* a word, such as *she* or *it*, that replaces a noun or noun phrase that has already been or is about to be mentioned. ▷ HISTORY Latin *pronomen*

pronounce *vb* **-nouncing, -nounced 1** to speak (a sound or sounds), esp. clearly or in a certain way. **2** to announce or declare officially: *I now pronounce you man and wife.* **3** to declare as one's judgment: *he pronounced the wine drinkable.* ▷ HISTORY Latin *pronuntiare* to announce ▶ **pronounceable** *adj*

pronounced *adj* very noticeable: *he speaks with a pronounced lisp.*

pronouncement *n* a formal announcement.

pronto *adv Informal* at once. ▷ HISTORY Spanish: quick

pronunciation *n* **1** the recognized way to pronounce sounds in a given language. **2** the way in which someone pronounces words.

proof *n* **1** any evidence that confirms that something is true or exists. **2** *Law* the total evidence upon which a court bases its verdict. **3** *Maths, logic* a sequence of steps or statements that establishes the truth of a proposition. **4** the act of testing the truth of something. **5** an early copy of printed matter for checking before final production. **6** *Photog* a trial print from a negative. **7** (esp. formerly) a defined level of alcoholic content used as a standard measure for comparing the alcoholic strength of other liquids: *Moldavian ruby port, seventeen degrees proof.* ✧ *adj* **8** (foll. by *against*) able to withstand: *proof against tears.* **9** (esp. formerly) having a level of alcoholic content used as a standard measure for comparing the alcoholic strength of other liquids. ✧ *vb* **10** to take a proof from (type matter). **11** to render (something) proof, esp. to waterproof. ▷ HISTORY Old French *preuve* a test

proofread *vb* **-reading, -read** to read and correct (printer's proofs). ▶ **proofreader** *n*

prop[1] *vb* **propping, propped** (often foll. by *up*) **1** to support (something or someone) in an upright position: *she was propped up by pillows.* **2** to sustain or support: *the type of measures necessary to prop up the sagging US economy.* **3** (often foll. by *against*) to place or lean. ✧ *n* **4** something that gives rigid support, such as a pole. **5** a person or thing giving moral support. ▷ HISTORY perhaps from Middle Dutch *proppe*

prop[2] *n* a movable object used on the set of a film or play.

prop[3] *n Informal* a propeller.

prop. **1** proper(ly). **2** property. **3** proposition. **4** proprietor.

propaganda *n* **1** the organized promotion of information to assist or damage the cause of a government or movement. **2** such information. ▷ HISTORY Italian ▶ **propagandist** *n, adj*

propagate *vb* **-gating, -gated 1** to spread (information or ideas). **2** *Biol* to reproduce or breed. **3** *Horticulture* to produce (plants). **4** *Physics* to transmit, esp. in the form of a wave: *the electrical signal is propagated through a specialized group of conducting fibres.* ▷ HISTORY Latin *propagare* to increase (plants) by cuttings ▸ **propagation** *n* ▸ **propagator** *n*

propane *n* a flammable gas found in petroleum and used as a fuel. ▷ HISTORY from *propionic (acid)*

propel *vb* **-pelling, -pelled** to cause to move forwards. ▷ HISTORY Latin *propellere* ▸ **propellant** *n, adj*

propeller *n* a revolving shaft with blades to drive a ship or aircraft.

propene *n* same as **propylene**.

propensity *n, pl* **-ties** *Formal* a natural tendency: *his problem had always been a propensity to live beyond his means.* ▷ HISTORY Latin *propensus* inclined to

proper *adj* **1** real or genuine: *a proper home.* **2** appropriate or usual: *good wine must have the proper balance of sugar and acid.* **3** suited to a particular purpose: *they set out without any proper climbing gear.* **4** correct in behaviour: *in many societies it is not considered proper for a woman to show her legs.* **5** excessively moral: *she was very strait-laced and proper.* **6** being or forming the main or central part of something: *a suburb some miles west of the city proper.* **7** *Brit, Austral & NZ informal* complete: *you made him look a proper fool.* ▷ HISTORY Latin *proprius* special ▸ **properly** *adv*

proper fraction *n* a fraction in which the numerator has a lower absolute value than the denominator, for example $^1/_2$.

proper noun *or* **name** *n Grammar* the name of a person or place, for example *Iceland* or *Patrick*. Compare **common noun**.

property *n, pl* **-ties 1** something owned. **2** *Law* the right to possess, use, and dispose of anything. **3** possessions collectively. **4** land or buildings owned by someone. **5** a quality or attribute: *the oils have healing properties.* **6** same as **prop²**. ▷ HISTORY Latin *proprius* one's own

prophecy *n, pl* **-cies 1** a prediction. **2 a** a message revealing God's will. **b** the act of uttering such a message. **3** the function or activity of a prophet.

prophesy *vb* **-sies, -sying, -sied** to foretell.

prophet *n* **1** a person supposedly chosen by God to pass on His message. **2** a person who predicts the future: *a prophet of doom.* **3** a spokesman for, or advocate of, some cause: *a prophet of revolution.* ▷ HISTORY Greek *prophētēs* one who declares the divine will ▸ **prophetess** *fem n*

Prophet *n* **the** the main name used of Mohammed, the founder of Islam.

prophetic *adj* **1** foretelling what will happen. **2** of the nature of a prophecy. ▸ **prophetically** *adv*

prophylactic *adj* **1** preventing disease. ✧ *n* **2** a drug or device that prevents disease. **3** *Chiefly US* a condom. ▷ HISTORY Greek *prophulassein* to guard by taking advance measures

propitiate *vb* **-ating, -ated** to appease (someone, esp. a god or spirit); make well disposed. ▷ HISTORY Latin *propitiare* ▸ **propitiable** *adj* ▸ **propitiation** *n* ▸ **propitiator** *n* ▸ **propitiatory** *adj*

propitious *adj* **1** favourable or auspicious: *a propitious moment.* **2** likely to prove favourable; advantageous: *his origins were not propitious for a literary career.* ▷ HISTORY Latin *propitius* well disposed

proponent *n* a person who argues in favour of something. ▷ HISTORY Latin *proponere* to propose

proportion *n* **1** relative size or extent: *a large proportion of our revenue comes from advertisements.* **2** correct relationship between parts. **3** a part considered with respect to the whole: *the proportion of women in the total workforce.* **4 proportions** dimensions or size: *a building of vast proportions.* **5** *Maths* a relationship between four numbers in which the ratio of the first pair equals the ratio of the second pair. **6 in proportion a** comparable in size, rate of increase, etc. **b** without exaggerating. ✧ *vb* **7** to adjust in relative amount or size: *the size of the crops are very rarely proportioned to the wants of the inhabitants.* **8** to cause to be harmonious in relationship of parts. ▷ HISTORY Latin *pro portione*, literally: for (its, one's) portion

proportional *adj* **1** being in proportion. ✧ *n* **2** *Maths* an unknown term in a proportion, for example in $a/b = c/x$, x is the fourth proportional. ▸ **proportionally** *adv*

proportional representation *n* the representation of political parties in parliament in proportion to the votes they win.

proportionate *adj* being in proper proportion. ▸ **proportionately** *adv*

proposal *n* **1** the act of proposing. **2** a suggestion put forward for consideration. **3** an offer of marriage.

propose *vb* **-posing, -posed 1** to put forward (a plan) for consideration. **2** to nominate (someone) for a position. **3** to intend (to do something): *I don't propose to waste any more time discussing it.* **4** to ask people to drink a toast. **5** (often foll. by *to*) to make an offer of marriage. ▷ HISTORY Old French *proposer*, from Latin *proponere* to display

proposition *n* **1** a proposal or offer. **2** *Logic* a statement that affirms or denies something and is capable of being true or false. **3** *Maths* a statement or theorem, usually containing its proof. **4** *Informal* a person or matter to be dealt with: *even among experienced climbers the mountain is considered a tough proposition.* **5** *Informal* an invitation to engage in sexual intercourse. ✧ *vb* **6** to invite (someone) to engage in sexual intercourse. ▷ HISTORY Latin *propositio* a setting forth

propound *vb* to put forward for consideration. ▷ HISTORY Latin *proponere* to set forth

proprietary *adj* **1** denoting a product manufactured and distributed under a trade name. **2** possessive: *she watched them with a proprietary eye.* **3** privately owned and controlled. ▷ HISTORY Late Latin *proprietarius* an owner

proprietor *n* an owner of a business establishment. ▸ **proprietress** *fem n* ▸ **proprietorial** *adj*

propriety *n, pl* **-ties 1** the quality or state of being appropriate or fitting. **2** correct conduct. **3 the proprieties** the standards of behaviour considered correct by polite society. ▷ HISTORY Old French *propriété,* from Latin *proprius* one's own

propulsion *n* **1** a force that moves (something) forward. **2** the act of propelling or the state of being propelled. ▷ HISTORY Latin *propellere* to propel ▶ **propulsive** *adj*

propylene *or* **propene** *n* a gas found in petroleum and used to produce many organic compounds. ▷ HISTORY from *propionic (acid)*

pro rata *adv, adj* in proportion. ▷ HISTORY Medieval Latin

prorogue *vb* **-roguing, -rogued** to suspend (parliament) without dissolving it. ▷ HISTORY Latin *prorogare,* literally: to ask publicly ▶ **prorogation** *n*

prosaic (pro-**zay**-ik) *adj* **1** lacking imagination; dull. **2** having the characteristics of prose. ▶ **prosaically** *adv*

pros and cons *pl n* the advantages and disadvantages of a situation. ▷ HISTORY Latin *pro* for + *con(tra)* against

proscenium *n, pl* **-nia** *or* **-niums** *Theatre* the arch in a theatre separating the stage from the auditorium. ▷ HISTORY Greek *pro* before + *skēnē* scene

proscribe *vb* **-scribing, -scribed 1** to condemn or prohibit (something). **2** to outlaw or banish. ▷ HISTORY Latin *proscribere* to put up a public notice ▶ **proscription** *n* ▶ **proscriptive** *adj*

prose *n* **1** ordinary spoken or written language in contrast to poetry. **2** a passage set for translation into a foreign language. **3** commonplace or dull talk. ✧ *vb* **prosing, prosed 4** to speak or write in a tedious style. ▷ HISTORY Latin *prosa oratio* straightforward speech

prosecute *vb* **-cuting, -cuted 1** to bring a criminal charge against (someone). **2** to continue to do (something): *the business of prosecuting a cold war through propaganda.* **3 a** to seek redress by legal proceedings. **b** to institute or conduct a prosecution. ▷ HISTORY Latin *prosequi* to follow ▶ **prosecutor** *n*

prosecution *n* **1** the bringing of criminal charges against (someone). **2** the institution and conduct of legal proceedings against a person. **3** the lawyers acting for the Crown to put the case against a person. **4** the carrying out of something begun.

proselyte (**pross**-ill-ite) *n* a recent convert. ▷ HISTORY Greek *prosēlutos* recent arrival, convert ▶ **proselytism** *n*

proselytize *or* **-ise** (**pross**-ill-it-ize) *vb* **-izing, -ized** *or* **-ising, -ised** to attempt to convert (someone).

prosody (**pross**-a-dee) *n* **1** the study of poetic metre and techniques. **2** the vocal patterns in a language. ▷ HISTORY Greek *prosōidia* song set to music ▶ **prosodic** *adj* ▶ **prosodist** *n*

prospect *n* **1** (*usually pl*) a probability of future success: *a job with impossible workloads and poor career prospects.* **2** expectation, or something anticipated: *she was terrified at the prospect of bringing up two babies on her own.* **3** *Old-fashioned* a view or scene: *a prospect of spires, domes, and towers.* ✧ *vb* **4** (sometimes foll. by *for*) to search for gold or other valuable minerals. ▷ HISTORY Latin *prospectus* distant view

prospective *adj* **1** future: *prospective customers.* **2** expected or likely: *the prospective loss.* ▶ **prospectively** *adv*

prospector *n* a person who searches for gold or other valuable minerals.

prospectus *n, pl* **-tuses** a booklet produced by a university, company, etc., giving details about it and its activities.

prosper *vb* to be successful. ▷ HISTORY Latin *prosperare* to succeed

prosperity *n* success and wealth.

prosperous *adj* wealthy and successful.

prostate *n* a gland in male mammals that surrounds the neck of the bladder. Also called: **prostate gland** ▷ HISTORY Greek *prostatēs* something standing in front (of the bladder)

prosthesis (pross-**theess**-iss) *n, pl* **-ses** (-seez) *Surgery* **a** the replacement of a missing body part with an artificial substitute. **b** an artificial body part such as a limb, eye, or tooth. ▷ HISTORY Greek: an addition ▶ **prosthetic** *adj*

prostitute *n* **1** a person who offers sexual intercourse in return for payment. ✧ *vb* **-tuting, -tuted 2** to offer (oneself or another) in sexual intercourse for money. **3** to offer (oneself or one's talent) for unworthy purposes. ▷ HISTORY Latin *pro-* in public + *statuere* to cause to stand ▶ **prostitution** *n*

prostrate *adj* **1** lying face downwards. **2** physically or emotionally exhausted. ✧ *vb* **-trating, -trated 3** to lie face downwards. **4** to exhaust physically or emotionally. ▷ HISTORY Latin *prosternere* to throw to the ground ▶ **prostration** *n*

Prot. 1 Protectorate. **2** Protestant.

protactinium *n Chem* a toxic radioactive metallic element. Symbol: Pa.

protagonist *n* **1** a supporter of a cause: *a great protagonist of the ideas and principles of mutuality.* **2** the leading character in a play or story. ▷ HISTORY Greek *prōtos* first + *agōnistēs* actor

protea (**pro**-tee-a) *n* an African shrub with showy heads of flowers. ▷ HISTORY after *Proteus,* a sea god who could take many shapes

protean (pro-**tee**-an) *adj* capable of constantly changing shape or form: *he is a protean stylist who can move from blues to ballads with consummate ease.* ▷ HISTORY after *Proteus;* see PROTEA

protect *vb* **1** to defend from trouble, harm, or loss. **2** *Econ* to assist (domestic industries) by taxing imports. ▷ HISTORY Latin *protegere* to cover before

protection *n* **1** the act of protecting or the condition of being protected. **2** something that keeps (one) safe. **3 a** the charging of taxes on imports, to protect domestic industries. **b** Also called: **protectionism** the policy of such taxation. **4** *Informal* Also called: **protection money** money paid to gangsters to avoid attack or damage. ▶ **protectionism** *n* ▶ **protectionist** *n, adj*

protective *adj* **1** giving protection: *protective clothing.* **2** tending or wishing to protect someone. ▶ **protectively** *adv* ▶ **protectiveness** *n*

protector *n* **1** a person or thing that protects. **2** *History* a person who acts for the king or queen during his or her childhood, absence, or incapacity. ▶ **protectress** *fem n*

protectorate *n* **1** a territory largely controlled by a stronger state. **2** the office or term of office of a protector.

protégé *or fem* **protégée** (**pro**-tizh-ay) *n* a person who is protected and helped by another. ▷ **HISTORY** French *protéger* to protect

protein *n* any of a large group of nitrogenous compounds that are essential for life. ▷ **HISTORY** Greek *prōteios* primary

pro tempore *adv, adj* for the time being. Often shortened to: **pro tem**

protest *n* **1** public, often organized, demonstration of objection. **2** a strong objection. **3** a formal statement declaring that a debtor has dishonoured a bill. **4** the act of protesting. ✧ *vb* **5** to take part in a public demonstration to express one's support for or disapproval of an action, proposal, etc.: *the workers marched through the city to protest against the closure of their factory.* **6** to disagree or object: *'I'm OK,' she protested.* **7** to assert in a formal or solemn manner: *all three repeatedly protested their innocence.* **8** *US & NZ* to object forcefully to: *students and teachers have protested the budget reductions.* ▷ **HISTORY** Latin *protestari* to make a formal declaration ▶ **protestant** *adj, n* ▶ **protester** *n*

Protestant *n* **1** a follower of any of the Christian Churches that separated from the Roman Catholic Church in the sixteenth century. ✧ *adj* **2** of or relating to any of these Churches or their followers. ▶ **Protestantism** *n*

protestation *n Formal* a strong declaration.

protist *n Biol* an organism belonging to a kingdom that includes bacteria, algae, and fungi and that is distinct from plants and animals.

protium *n* the most common isotope of hydrogen, with a mass number of 1. ▷ **HISTORY** from Greek *prōtos* first

proto- *or sometimes before a vowel* **prot-** *combining form* **1** first: *protomartyr.* **2** original: *prototype.* ▷ **HISTORY** Greek *prōtos* first

protocol *n* **1** the rules of behaviour for formal occasions. **2** a record of an agreement in international negotiations. **3** *Computers* a standardized format for exchanging data, esp. between different computer systems. ▷ **HISTORY** Late Greek *prōtokollon* sheet glued to the front of a manuscript

proton (**pro**-ton) *n* a positively charged elementary particle, found in the nucleus of an atom. ▷ **HISTORY** Greek *prōtos* first

protoplasm *n Biol* a complex colourless substance forming the living contents of a cell. ▷ **HISTORY** Greek *prōtos* first + *plasma* form ▶ **protoplasmic** *adj*

prototype *n* **1** an early model of a product, which is tested so that the design can be changed if necessary. **2** a person or thing that serves as an example of a type.

protozoan (pro-toe-**zoe**-an) *n, pl* **-zoa** a very tiny single-celled invertebrate, such as an amoeba. Also: **protozoon** ▷ **HISTORY** Greek *prōtos* first + *zoion* animal

protract *vb* to lengthen or extend (a situation etc.). ▷ **HISTORY** Latin *protrahere* to prolong ▶ **protracted** *adj* ▶ **protraction** *n*

protractor *n* an instrument for measuring angles, usually a flat semicircular piece of plastic.

protrude *vb* **-truding, -truded** to stick out or project. ▷ **HISTORY** PRO-[2] + Latin *trudere* to thrust ▶ **protrusion** *n* ▶ **protrusive** *adj*

protuberant *adj* swelling out; bulging. ▷ **HISTORY** Late Latin *protuberare* to swell ▶ **protuberance** *n*

proud *adj* **1** feeling pleasure or satisfaction: *she was proud of her daughter's success.* **2** feeling honoured. **3** haughty or arrogant. **4** causing pride: *the city's proud history.* **5** dignified: *too proud to accept charity.* **6** (of a surface or edge) projecting or protruding. ✧ *adv* **7** **do someone proud** to entertain someone on a grand scale: *Mum did us all proud last Christmas.* ▷ **HISTORY** Old French *prud, prod* brave ▶ **proudly** *adv*

proud flesh *n* a mass of tissue formed around a healing wound.

prove *vb* **proving, proved; proved** *or* **proven** **1** to establish the validity of: *such a claim is difficult to prove scientifically.* **2** to demonstrate or test: *the autopsy proved that she had drowned.* **3** *Law* to establish the genuineness of (a will). **4** to show (oneself) to be: *he proved equal to the task.* **5** to be found to be: *it proved to be a trap.* **6** (of dough) to rise in a warm place before baking. ▷ **HISTORY** Latin *probare* to test ▶ **provable** *adj*

proven *vb* **1** a past participle of **prove**. **2** See **not proven**. ✧ *adj* **3** known from experience to work: *a proven ability to make money.*

provenance (**prov**-in-anss) *n* a place of origin. ▷ **HISTORY** French

Provençal (prov-on-**sahl**) *adj* **1** of Provence, in SE France. ✧ *n* **2** a language of Provence. **3** a person from Provence.

provender *n Old-fashioned* fodder for livestock. ▷ **HISTORY** Old French *provendre*

proverb *n* a short memorable saying that expresses a truth or gives a warning, for example *half a loaf is better than no bread.* ▷ **HISTORY** Latin *proverbium*

proverbial *adj* **1** well-known because commonly or traditionally referred to. **2** of a proverb. ▶ **proverbially** *adv*

provide *vb* **-viding, -vided** **1** to make available. **2** to afford; yield: *social activities providing the opportunity to meet new people.* **3** (often foll. by *for* or *against*) to take careful precautions: *we provide for the possibility of illness in the examination regulations.* **4** (foll. by *for*) to support financially: *both parents should be expected to provide for their children.* **5** *Formal* **provide for** (of a law, treaty, etc.) to make possible: *a bill providing for stiffer penalties* *for racial discrimination.* ▷ HISTORY Latin *providere* to provide for ▶ **provider** *n*

providence *n* **1** God or nature seen as a protective force that oversees people's lives. **2** the foresight shown by a person in the management of his or her affairs.

Providence *n Christianity* God, esp. as showing foreseeing care of his creatures.

provident *adj* **1** thrifty. **2** showing foresight. ▷ HISTORY Latin *providens* foreseeing

providential *adj* fortunate, as if through divine involvement.

provident society *n* same as **friendly society**.

providing *or* **provided** *conj* on condition (that): *the deal is on, providing he passes his medical.*

province *n* **1** a territory governed as a unit of a country or empire. **2** an area of learning, activity, etc. **3 the provinces** those parts of a country lying outside the capital. ▷ HISTORY Latin *provincia* conquered territory

provincial *adj* **1** of a province. **2** unsophisticated or narrow-minded. **3** *NZ* denoting a football team representing a province. ✧ *n* **4** an unsophisticated person. **5** a person from a province or the provinces. ▶ **provincialism** *n*

provision *n* **1** the act of supplying something. **2** something supplied. **3 provisions** food and other necessities. **4** a condition incorporated in a document. **5 make provision for** to make arrangements for beforehand: *many restaurants still make no provision for non-smokers.* ✧ *vb* **6** to supply with provisions. ▷ HISTORY Latin *provisio* a providing

provisional *adj* temporary or conditional: *a provisional diagnosis.* ▶ **provisionally** *adv*

Provisional *n* a member of the Provisional IRA or Sinn Féin.

proviso (pro-**vize**-oh) *n, pl* **-sos** *or* **-soes** a condition or stipulation. ▷ HISTORY Medieval Latin *proviso quod* it being provided that ▶ **provisory** *adj*

provocation *n* **1** the act of provoking or inciting. **2** something that causes indignation or anger.

provocative *adj* provoking or inciting, esp. to anger or sexual desire: *a provocative remark.* ▶ **provocatively** *adv*

provoke *vb* **-voking, -voked 1** to deliberately act in a way intended to anger someone: *waving a red cape, Delgado provoked the animal into charging.* **2** to incite or stimulate: *the army seems to have provoked this latest confrontation.* **3** (often foll. by *into*) to cause a person to react in a particular, often angry, way: *keeping your true motives hidden may provoke others into being just as two-faced with you.* **4** to bring about: *the case has provoked furious public debate.* ▷ HISTORY Latin *provocare* to call forth ▶ **provoking** *adj*

provost *n* **1** the head of certain university colleges or schools. **2** the chief councillor of a Scottish town. ▷ HISTORY Old English *profost*

provost marshal *n* the officer in charge of military police in a camp or city.

prow *n* the bow of a vessel. ▷ HISTORY Greek *prōra*

prowess *n* **1** superior skill or ability. **2** bravery or fearlessness. ▷ HISTORY Old French *proesce*

prowl *vb* **1** (sometimes foll. by *around* or *about*) to move stealthily around (a place) as if in search of prey or plunder. ✧ *n* **2** the act of prowling. **3 on the prowl** moving around stealthily. ▷ HISTORY origin unknown ▶ **prowler** *n*

proximate *adj* **1** next or nearest in space or time. **2** very near. **3** immediately coming before or following in a series. **4** approximate. ▷ HISTORY Latin *proximus* next

proximity *n* **1** nearness in space or time. **2** nearness or closeness in a series. ▷ HISTORY Latin *proximitas* closeness

proxy *n, pl* **proxies 1** a person authorized to act on behalf of someone else: *the firm's creditors can vote either in person or by proxy.* **2** the authority to act on behalf of someone else. ▷ HISTORY Latin *procuratio* procuration

Prozac *n Trademark* an antidepressant drug.

prude *n* a person who is excessively modest or prim, esp. regarding sex. ▷ HISTORY Old French *prode femme* respectable woman ▶ **prudery** *n* ▶ **prudish** *adj*

prudent *adj* **1** sensible and careful. **2** discreet or cautious. **3** exercising good judgment. ▷ HISTORY Latin *prudens* far-sighted ▶ **prudence** *n* ▶ **prudently** *adv*

prudential *adj Old-fashioned* showing prudence: *prudential reasons.* ▶ **prudentially** *adv*

prune[1] *n* a purplish-black partially dried plum. ▷ HISTORY Latin *prunum* plum

prune[2] *vb* **pruning, pruned 1** to cut off dead or surplus branches of (a tree or shrub). **2** to shorten or reduce. ▷ HISTORY Old French *proignier* to clip

prurient *adj* **1** excessively interested in sexual matters. **2** exciting lustfulness. ▷ HISTORY Latin *prurire* to lust after, itch ▶ **prurience** *n*

Prussian *adj* **1** of Prussia, a former German state. ✧ *n* **2** a person from Prussia.

prussic acid *n* the extremely poisonous solution of hydrogen cyanide. ▷ HISTORY French *acide prussique* Prussian acid

pry *vb* **pries, prying, pried** (often foll. by *into*) to make an impertinent or uninvited inquiry (about a private matter). ▷ HISTORY origin unknown

PS 1 Also: **ps** postscript. **2** private secretary.

PSA (in New Zealand) Public Service Association.

psalm *n* (*often cap*) any of the sacred songs that make up a book (Psalms) of the Old Testament. ▷ HISTORY Greek *psalmos* song accompanied on the harp

psalmist *n* a writer of psalms.

psalmody *n, pl* **-dies** the singing of sacred music.

Psalter *n* **1** the Book of Psalms. **2** a book containing a version of Psalms. ▷ HISTORY Greek *psaltērion* stringed instrument

psaltery *n, pl* **-teries** an ancient musical instrument played by plucking strings.

PSBR (in Britain) public sector borrowing requirement: the money needed by the public sector of the economy for items not paid for by income.

psephology (sef-**fol**-a-jee) *n* the statistical and sociological study of elections. ▷ **HISTORY** Greek *psephos* pebble, vote + -LOGY ▶ **psephologist** *n*
pseud *n Informal* a pretentious person.
pseudo *adj Informal* not genuine.
pseudo- *or sometimes before a vowel* **pseud-** *combining form* false, pretending, or unauthentic: *pseudo-intellectual.* ▷ **HISTORY** Greek *pseudēs* false
pseudonym *n* a fictitious name adopted, esp. by an author. ▷ **HISTORY** Greek *pseudēs* false + *onoma* name ▶ **pseudonymity** *n* ▶ **pseudonymous** *adj*
psittacosis *n* a viral disease of parrots that can be passed on to humans. ▷ **HISTORY** Greek *psittakos* a parrot
psoriasis (so-**rye**-a-siss) *n* a skin disease with reddish spots and patches covered with silvery scales. ▷ **HISTORY** Greek: itching disease
PST Pacific Standard Time.
PSV (in Britain, formerly) public service vehicle.
psyche *n* the human mind or soul. ▷ **HISTORY** Greek *psukhē* breath, soul
psychedelic *adj* **1** denoting a drug that causes hallucinations. **2** *Informal* having vivid colours and complex patterns similar to those experienced during hallucinations. ▷ **HISTORY** Greek *psukhē* mind + *delos* visible
psychiatry *n* the branch of medicine concerned with the study and treatment of mental disorders. ▶ **psychiatric** *adj* ▶ **psychiatrist** *n*
psychic *adj* **1** having mental powers which cannot be explained by natural laws. **2** relating to the mind. ✧ *n* **3** a person who has psychic powers. ▶ **psychical** *adj*
psycho *Informal* ✧ *n, pl* **-chos 1** same as **psychopath**. ✧ *adj* **2** same as **psychopathic**.
psycho- *or sometimes before a vowel* **psych-** *combining form* indicating the mind or mental processes: *psychology; psychosomatic.* ▷ **HISTORY** Greek *psukhē* spirit, breath
psychoactive *adj* capable of affecting mental activity: *a psychoactive drug.*
psychoanalyse *or esp US* **-lyze** *vb* **-lysing, -lysed** *or* **-lyzing, -lyzed** to examine or treat (a person) by psychoanalysis.
psychoanalysis *n* a method of treating mental and emotional disorders by discussion and analysis of the patient's thoughts and feelings. ▶ **psychoanalyst** *n* ▶ **psychoanalytical** *or* **psychoanalytic** *adj*
psychogenic *adj Psychol* (esp. of disorders or symptoms) of mental, rather than organic, origin.
psychological *adj* **1** relating to the mind or mental activity. **2** relating to psychology. **3** having its origin in the mind: *his backaches are purely psychological.* ▶ **psychologically** *adv*
psychological moment *n* the best time for achieving the desired response or effect.
psychological warfare *n* the military application of psychology, esp. to influence morale in time of war.
psychology *n, pl* **-gies 1** the scientific study of all forms of human and animal behaviour. **2** *Informal* the mental make-up of a person. ▶ **psychologist** *n*
psychopath *n* a person afflicted with a personality disorder which causes him or her to commit antisocial and sometimes violent acts. ▶ **psychopathic** *adj*
psychopathology *n* the scientific study of mental disorders.
psychopathy (sike-**op**-ath-ee) *n* any mental disorder or disease.
psychosis (sike-**oh**-siss) *n, pl* **-ses** (-seez) a severe mental disorder in which the sufferer's contact with reality becomes highly distorted: *a classic case of psychosis.* ▶ **psychotic** *adj*
psychosomatic *adj* (of a physical disorder) thought to have psychological causes, such as stress.
psychotherapy *n* the treatment of nervous disorders by psychological methods. ▶ **psychotherapeutic** *adj* ▶ **psychotherapist** *n*
psych up *vb* to prepare (oneself or another) mentally for a contest or task.
pt 1 part. **2** past tense. **3** point. **4** port. **5** pro tempore.
Pt *Chem* platinum.
PT *Old-fashioned* physical training.
pt. pint.
PTA Parent-Teacher Association.
ptarmigan (**tar**-mig-an) *n* a bird of the grouse family that turns white in winter.
Pte. *Mil* private.
pterodactyl (terr-roe-**dak**-til) *n* an extinct flying reptile with batlike wings. ▷ **HISTORY** Greek *pteron* wing + *daktulos* finger
PTO *or* **pto** please turn over.
Ptolemaic (tol-lim-**may**-ik) *adj* relating to Ptolemy, the 2nd-century AD Greek astronomer, or to his belief that the earth was in the centre of the universe.
ptomaine *or* **ptomain** (**toe**-main) *n* any of a group of poisonous alkaloids found in decaying matter. ▷ **HISTORY** Greek *ptoma* corpse
Pty *Austral & S African* Proprietary.
Pu *Chem* plutonium.
pub *n* **1** *Chiefly Brit* a building with a licensed bar where alcoholic drinks may be bought and drunk. **2** *Austral & NZ* a hotel.
pub. 1 public. **2** publication. **3** published. **4** publisher. **5** publishing.
puberty (**pew**-ber-tee) *n* the beginning of sexual maturity. ▷ **HISTORY** Latin *pubertas* maturity ▶ **pubertal** *adj*
pubes (**pew**-beez) *n, pl* **pubes 1** the region above the genitals. **2** pubic hair. **3** the plural of **pubis**. ▷ **HISTORY** Latin
pubescent *adj* **1** arriving or arrived at puberty. **2** covered with down, as some plants and animals. ▷ **HISTORY** Latin *pubescere* to reach manhood ▶ **pubescence** *n*
pubic (**pew**-bik) *adj* of or relating to the pubes or pubis: *pubic hair.*
pubis *n, pl* **-bes** one of the three sections of the hipbone that forms part of the pelvis. ▷ **HISTORY** New Latin *os pubis* bone of the pubes

public *adj* **1** relating to the people as a whole. **2** open to all: *public gardens.* **3** well-known: *a public figure.* **4** performed or made openly: *public proclamation.* **5** maintained by and for the community: *a public library.* **6** open, acknowledged, or notorious: *a public scandal.* **7 go public a** (of a private company) to offer shares for sale to the public: *few German firms have gone public in recent years.* **b** to make information, plans, etc., known: *the group would not have gone public with its suspicions unless it was fully convinced of them.* ✧ *n* **8** the community or people in general. **9** a particular section of the community: *the racing public.* ▷ HISTORY Latin *publicus* ▶ **publicly** *adv*

public-address system *n* a system of microphones, amplifiers, and loudspeakers for increasing the sound level of speech or music at public gatherings.

publican *n Brit, Austral & NZ* a person who owns or runs a public house.

publication *n* **1** the publishing of a printed work. **2** any printed work offered for sale. **3** the act of making information known to the public.

public bar *n* a bar in a hotel or pub which is cheaper and more basically furnished than the lounge or saloon bar.

public company *or* **public limited company** *n* a limited company whose shares may be purchased by the public.

public enemy *n* a notorious person who is considered a danger to the public.

public house *n* **1** *Brit* a pub. **2** *US & Canad* an inn or small hotel.

publicist *n* a person, such as a press agent or journalist, who publicizes something.

publicity *n* **1** the process or information used to arouse public attention. **2** the public interest so aroused.

publicize *or* **-cise** *vb* **-cizing, -cized** *or* **-cising, -cised** to bring to public attention.

public law *n Law* the branch of law that deals with relations between a state and its individual members. Compare **private law**.

public lending right *n* the right of authors to receive payment when their books are borrowed from public libraries.

public prosecutor *n Law* an official in charge of prosecuting important cases.

public relations *n* the practice of gaining the public's goodwill and approval for an organization.

public school *n* **1** (in England and Wales) a private independent fee-paying secondary school. **2** (in certain Canadian provinces) a public elementary school as distinguished from a separate school. **3** (in the US) any school that is part of a free local educational system.

public sector *n* the part of a country's economy that consists of state-owned industries and services.

public servant *n* **1** an elected or appointed holder of a public office. **2** *Austral & NZ* a civil servant.

public service *n Austral & NZ* the civil service.

public-spirited *adj* having or showing an active interest in the good of the community.

public utility *n* an organization that supplies water, gas, or electricity to the public.

publish *vb* **1** to produce and issue (printed matter) for sale. **2** to have one's written work issued for publication. **3** to announce formally or in public. ▷ HISTORY Latin *publicare* to make public ▶ **publishing** *n*

publisher *n* **1** a company or person that publishes books, periodicals, music, etc. **2** *US & Canad* the proprietor of a newspaper.

puce *adj* dark brownish-purple: *his face suddenly turned puce with futile rage.* ▷ HISTORY French *couleur puce* flea colour

puck[1] *n* a small disc of hard rubber used in ice hockey. ▷ HISTORY origin unknown

puck[2] *n* a mischievous or evil spirit. ▷ HISTORY Old English *pūca* ▶ **puckish** *adj*

pucker *vb* **1** to gather into wrinkles. ✧ *n* **2** a wrinkle or crease. ▷ HISTORY origin unknown

pudding *n* **1** a dessert, esp. a cooked one served hot. **2** a savoury dish with pastry or batter: *steak-and-kidney pudding.* **3** a sausage-like mass of meat: *black pudding.* ▷ HISTORY Middle English *poding*

puddle *n* **1** a small pool of water, esp. of rain. **2** a worked mixture of wet clay and sand that is impervious to water. ✧ *vb* **-dling, -dled 3** to make (clay etc.) into puddle. **4** to subject (iron) to puddling. ▷ HISTORY Middle English *podel* ▶ **puddly** *adj*

pudenda *pl n* the human genitals, esp. of a female. ▷ HISTORY Latin: the shameful (parts)

puerile *adj* silly and childish. ▷ HISTORY Latin *puer* a boy ▶ **puerility** *n*

puerperal (pew-**er**-per-al) *adj* concerning the period following childbirth. ▷ HISTORY Latin *puerperium* childbirth

puerperal fever *n* a serious, formerly widespread, form of blood poisoning caused by infection during childbirth.

puerperium (pure-**peer**-ee-um) *n* the period after childbirth.

puff *n* **1** a short quick blast of breath, wind, or smoke. **2** the amount of wind or smoke released in a puff. **3** the sound made by a puff. **4 out of puff** out of breath: *by the third flight of stairs she was out of puff.* **5** an act of inhaling and expelling cigarette smoke. **6** a light pastry usually filled with cream and jam. ✧ *vb* **7** to blow or breathe in short quick blasts. **8** (often foll. by *out*) to cause to be out of breath. **9** to take draws at (a cigarette). **10** to move with or by the emission of puffs: *the steam train puffed up the incline.* **11** (often foll. by *up* or *out*) to swell. ▷ HISTORY Old English *pyffan* ▶ **puffy** *adj*

puff adder *n* a large venomous African viper whose body swells when alarmed.

puffball *n* a ball-shaped fungus that sends out a cloud of brown spores when mature.

puffin *n* a black-and-white sea bird with a brightly coloured beak. ▷ HISTORY origin unknown

A B C D E F G H I J K L M N O P Q R S T U V W X Y Z

puff pastry *or US* **puff paste** *n* a light flaky pastry.

pug *n* a small dog with a smooth coat, lightly curled tail, and a short wrinkled nose. ▷ **HISTORY** origin unknown

pugilist (**pew**-jil-ist) *n* a boxer. ▷ **HISTORY** Latin *pugil* a boxer ▶ **pugilism** *n* ▶ **pugilistic** *adj*

pugnacious *adj* ready and eager to fight. ▷ **HISTORY** Latin *pugnax* ▶ **pugnacity** *n*

pug nose *n* a short stubby upturned nose. ▷ **HISTORY** from *pug* (the dog) ▶ **pug-nosed** *adj*

puissance *n* a showjumping competition that tests a horse's ability to jump large obstacles. ▷ **HISTORY** see PUISSANT

puke *Slang* ✧ *vb* **puking, puked 1** to vomit. ✧ *n* **2** the act of vomiting. **3** the matter vomited. ▷ **HISTORY** probably imitative

pukeko (**poo**-kek-oh) *n, pl* **-kos** a brightly coloured New Zealand wading bird. ▷ **HISTORY** Maori

pukka *adj Anglo-Indian* **1** properly done, constructed, etc. **2** genuine or real. ▷ **HISTORY** Hindi *pakkā* firm

pulchritude *n Formal or literary* physical beauty. ▷ **HISTORY** Latin *pulchritudo* ▶ **pulchritudinous** *adj*

pull *vb* **1** to exert force on (an object) to draw it towards the source of the force. **2** to strain or stretch. **3** to remove or extract: *he pulled a crumpled tenner from his pocket.* **4** *Informal* to draw out (a weapon) for use: *he pulled a knife on his attacker.* **5** *Informal* to attract: *the game is expected to pull a large crowd.* **6** *Slang* to attract a sexual partner. **7** (usually foll. by *on* or *at*) to drink or inhale deeply: *he pulled on his pipe.* **8** to possess or exercise the power to move: *this car doesn't pull well on hills.* **9** to withdraw or remove: *the board pulled their support.* **10** *Printing* to take (a proof) from type. **11** *Golf, baseball, etc.* to hit (a ball) away from the direction in which the player intended to hit it. **12** *Cricket* to hit (a ball) to the leg side. **13** to row (a boat) or take a stroke of (an oar) in rowing. **14 pull a face** to make a grimace. **15 pull a fast one** *Slang* to play a sly trick. **16 pull apart** *or* **to pieces** to criticize harshly. **17 pull (one's) punches** to limit the force of one's criticisms or blows. ✧ *n* **18** the act of pulling. **19** the force used in pulling: *the pull of the moon affects the tides.* **20** the act of taking in drink or smoke. **21** *Printing* a proof taken from type. **22** something used for pulling, such as a handle. **23** *Informal* power or influence: *his uncle is chairman of the company, so he has quite a lot of pull.* **24** *Informal* the power to attract attention or support. **25** a single stroke of an oar in rowing. **26** the act of pulling the ball in golf, cricket, etc. ✧ See also **pull in.** ▷ **HISTORY** Old English *pullian*

pullet *n* a hen less than one year old. ▷ **HISTORY** Old French *poulet* chicken

pulley *n* a wheel with a grooved rim in which a belt, chain, or piece of rope runs in order to lift weights by a downward pull. ▷ **HISTORY** Old French *polie*

pull in *vb* **1** Also: **pull over** (of a motor vehicle) to draw in to the side of the road. **2** (often foll. by *to*) to reach a destination: *the train pulled in to the station.* **3** to attract: *his appearance will pull in the crowds.* **4** *Brit, Austral & NZ slang* to arrest. **5** to earn (money): *he pulls in at least thirty thousand a year.*

Pullman *n, pl* **-mans** *Chiefly Brit* a luxurious railway coach. ▷ **HISTORY** after G. M. *Pullman,* its inventor

pull off *vb Informal* to succeed in accomplishing (something difficult): *super-heroes who pull off the impossible.*

pull out *vb* **1** (of a motor vehicle) **a** to draw away from the side of the road. **b** to move out from behind another vehicle to overtake. **2** to depart: *the train pulled out of the station.* **3** to withdraw: *several companies have pulled out of the student market.* **4** to remove by pulling. **5** to abandon a situation.

pullover *n* a sweater that is pulled on over the head.

pull through *vb* to survive or recover, esp. after a serious illness.

pull up *vb* **1** (of a motor vehicle) to stop. **2** to remove by the roots. **3** to rebuke.

pulmonary *adj* **1** of or affecting the lungs. **2** having lungs or lunglike organs. ▷ **HISTORY** Latin *pulmo* a lung

pulmonary vein *n Anat* a vein that conveys blood from the heart to the lungs.

pulp *n* **1** a soft wet substance made from matter which has been crushed or beaten: *mash the strawberries to a pulp.* **2** the soft fleshy part of a fruit or vegetable: *halve the tomatoes then scoop the seeds and pulp into a bowl.* **3** printed or recorded material with little depth or designed to shock: *pulp fiction; a tape player churned out disco pulp.* ✧ *vb* **4** to reduce a material to pulp: *he began to pulp the orange in his fingers.* ▷ **HISTORY** Latin *pulpa* ▶ **pulpy** *adj*

pulpit *n* **1** a raised platform in churches used for preaching. **2** (usually preceded by *the*) preaching or the clergy. ▷ **HISTORY** Latin *pulpitum* a platform

pulpwood *n* pine, spruce, or any other soft wood used to make paper.

pulsar *n* a very small star which emits regular pulses of radio waves. ▷ **HISTORY** from *puls(ating st)ar*

pulsate *vb* **-sating, -sated 1** to expand and contract rhythmically, like a heartbeat. **2** to quiver or vibrate: *the images pulsate with energy and light.* **3** *Physics* to vary in intensity or magnitude. ▷ **HISTORY** Latin *pulsare* to push ▶ **pulsation** *n*

pulse[1] *n* **1** *Physiol* **a** the regular beating of blood through the arteries at each heartbeat. **b** a single such beat. **2** *Physics, electronics* a sudden change in a quantity, such as a voltage, that is normally constant in a system. **3** a regular beat or vibration. **4** bustle or excitement: *the lively pulse of a city.* **5** the feelings or thoughts of a group as they can be measured: *the political pulse of the capital.* ✧ *vb* **pulsing, pulsed 6** to beat, throb, or vibrate. ▷ **HISTORY** Latin *pulsus* a beating

pulse[2] *n* the edible seeds of pod-bearing plants, such as peas, beans, and lentils. ▷ **HISTORY** Latin *puls* pottage of pulse

pulverize *or* **-ise** *vb* **-izing, -ized** *or* **-ising, -ised** **1** to reduce to fine particles by crushing or grinding. **2** to destroy completely. ▷ HISTORY Latin *pulvis* dust ▶ **pulverization** *or* **-isation** *n*

puma *n* a large American wild cat with a plain greyish-brown coat and a long tail. ▷ HISTORY S American Indian

pumice (**pumm**-iss) *n* a light porous stone used for scouring and for removing hard skin. Also called: **pumice stone** ▷ HISTORY Old French *pomis*

pummel *vb* **-melling, -melled** *or US* **-meling, -meled** to strike repeatedly with the fists. ▷ HISTORY see POMMEL

pump[1] *n* **1** a device to force a gas or liquid to move in a particular direction. ✧ *vb* **2** (sometimes foll. by *from, out*) etc. to raise or drive (air, liquid, etc.) with a pump, esp. into or from something. **3** (usually foll. by *in* or *into*) to supply in large amounts: *pumping money into the economy.* **4** to operate (a handle etc.) in the manner of a pump: *he was warmly applauded, and his hand was pumped by well-wishers.* **5** to obtain information from (someone) by persistent questioning. **6 pump iron** *Slang* to exercise with weights; do body-building exercises. ▷ HISTORY Middle Dutch *pumpe* pipe

pump[2] *n* **1** *Chiefly Brit* a shoe with a rubber sole, used in games such as tennis; plimsoll. **2** *Chiefly Brit* a low-cut low-heeled shoe, worn for dancing. ▷ HISTORY origin unknown

pumpernickel *n* a slightly sour black bread made of coarse rye flour. ▷ HISTORY from German

pumpkin *n* **1** a large round fruit with a thick orange rind, pulpy flesh, and many seeds. **2** the creeping plant that bears this fruit. ▷ HISTORY Greek *pepōn* ripe

pun *n* **1** the use of words to exploit double meanings for humorous effect, for example *my dog's a champion boxer.* ✧ *vb* **punning, punned** **2** to make puns. ▷ HISTORY origin unknown

punch[1] *vb* **1** to strike at with a clenched fist. ✧ *n* **2** a blow with the fist. **3** *Informal* point or vigour: *the jokes are mildly amusing but lack any real punch.* ▷ HISTORY probably variant of *pounce* to stamp

punch[2] *n* **1** a tool or machine for shaping, piercing, or engraving. **2** *Computers* a device for making holes in a card or paper tape. ✧ *vb* **3** to pierce, cut, stamp, shape, or drive with a punch. ▷ HISTORY Latin *pungere* to prick

punch[3] *n* a mixed drink containing fruit juice and, usually, alcoholic liquor, generally hot and spiced. ▷ HISTORY origin unknown

Punch *n* the main character in the children's puppet show, Punch and Judy.

punchbowl *n* a large bowl for serving punch.

punch-drunk *adj* dazed and confused through suffering repeated blows to the head.

punched card *or esp US* **punch card** *n* *Computers* a card on which data can be coded in the form of punched holes.

Punchinello *n, pl* **-los** *or* **-loes** a clown from Italian puppet shows, the origin of Punch. ▷ HISTORY Italian *Polecenella*

punch line *n* the last line of a joke or funny story that gives it its point.

punch-up *n Informal* a fight or brawl.

punchy *adj* **punchier, punchiest** *Informal* effective or forceful: *learn to compose short concise punchy letters.*

punctilious *adj Formal* **1** paying careful attention to correct social behaviour. **2** attentive to detail. ▷ HISTORY Latin *punctum* a point ▶ **punctiliously** *adv*

punctual *adj* **1** arriving or taking place at an arranged time. **2** (of a person) always keeping exactly to arranged times. ▷ HISTORY Medieval Latin *punctualis* concerning detail ▶ **punctuality** *n* ▶ **punctually** *adv*

punctuate *vb* **-ating, -ated** **1** to insert punctuation marks into (a written text). **2** to interrupt at frequent intervals: *the meeting was punctuated by heckling.* **3** to emphasize: *he punctuated the question by pressing the muzzle into the pilot's neck.* ▷ HISTORY Latin *pungere* to puncture

punctuation *n* **1** the use of symbols, such as commas, to indicate speech patterns and meaning not otherwise shown by the written language. **2** the symbols used for this purpose.

punctuation mark *n* any of the signs used in punctuation, such as a comma.

puncture *n* **1** a small hole made by a sharp object. **2** a tear and loss of pressure in a tyre. **3** the act of puncturing or perforating. ✧ *vb* **-turing, -tured** **4** to pierce a hole in (something) with a sharp object. **5** to cause (a tyre etc.) to lose pressure by piercing. ▷ HISTORY Latin *pungere* to prick

pundit *n* **1** an expert on a subject who often speaks or writes about it for a non-specialist audience: *Spain's leading sports pundit, who hosts two TV programmes.* **2** a Hindu scholar learned in Sanskrit, religion, philosophy, or law. ▷ HISTORY Hindi *pandit*

pungent *adj* **1** having a strong sharp bitter smell or taste. **2** (of speech or writing) biting; critical. ▷ HISTORY Latin *pungens* piercing ▶ **pungency** *n*

punish *vb* **1** to force (someone) to undergo a penalty for some crime or misbehaviour. **2** to inflict punishment for (some crime or misbehaviour). **3** to treat harshly, esp. by overexertion: *he continued to punish himself in the gym.* ▷ HISTORY Latin *punire* ▶ **punishable** *adj* ▶ **punishing** *adj*

punishment *n* **1** a penalty for a crime or offence. **2** the act of punishing or state of being punished. **3** *Informal* rough physical treatment: *the boxer's face could not withstand further punishment.*

punitive (**pew**-nit-tiv) *adj* relating to punishment: *punitive measures.*

punk *n* **1** a worthless person. **2** a youth movement of the late 1970s, characterized by anti-Establishment slogans, short spiky hair, and the wearing of worthless articles such as safety pins for decoration. **3** short for **punk rock**. **4** a follower of the punk movement or of punk rock. ✧ *adj* **5** relating to the punk youth movement of the late 1970s: *a punk band.* **6** worthless or insignificant. ▷ HISTORY origin unknown

punkah *or* **punka** *n* (in India) a ceiling fan made of a cloth stretched over a rectangular frame. ▷ **HISTORY** Hindi *pankhā*

punk rock *n* rock music of the punk youth movement of the late 1970s, characterized by energy and aggressive lyrics and performance. ▶ **punk rocker** *n*

punnet *n* a small basket for fruit. ▷ **HISTORY** origin unknown

punster *n* a person who is fond of making puns.

punt[1] *n* **1** an open flat-bottomed boat, propelled by a pole. ✧ *vb* **2** to propel (a punt) by pushing with a pole on the bottom of a river. ▷ **HISTORY** Latin *ponto*

punt[2] *n* **1** a kick in certain sports, such as rugby, in which the ball is dropped and kicked before it hits the ground. ✧ *vb* **2** to kick (a ball) using a punt. ▷ **HISTORY** origin unknown

punt[3] *Chiefly Brit* ✧ *vb* **1** to gamble or bet. ✧ *n* **2** a gamble or bet, esp. against the bank, such as in roulette. **3 take a punt at** *Austral & NZ* to make an attempt at. ▷ **HISTORY** French *ponter*

punt[4] *n* a former monetary unit of the Republic of Ireland.

punter *n* **1** a person who places a bet. **2** *Brit, Austral & NZ informal* any member of the public, esp. when a customer: *the punters are flocking into the sales.*

puny *adj* **-nier, -niest** small and weakly. ▷ **HISTORY** Old French *puisné* born later

pup *n* **1 a** a young dog; puppy. **b** the young of various other animals, such as the seal. ✧ *vb* **pupping, pupped 2** (of dogs, seals, etc.) to give birth to pups.

pupa (**pew**-pa) *n, pl* **-pae** (-pee) *or* **-pas** an insect at the stage of development between larva and adult. ▷ **HISTORY** Latin: a doll ▶ **pupal** *adj*

pupil[1] *n* a student who is taught by a teacher. ▷ **HISTORY** Latin *pupus* a child

pupil[2] *n* the dark circular opening at the centre of the iris of the eye. ▷ **HISTORY** Latin *pupilla*, diminutive of *pupa* doll; from the tiny reflections in the eye

puppet *n* **1** a small doll or figure moved by strings attached to its limbs or by the hand inserted in its cloth body. **2** a person or state that appears independent but is controlled by another: *the former cabinet ministers have denied that they are puppets of a foreign government.* ▷ **HISTORY** Latin *pupa* doll

puppeteer *n* a person who operates puppets.

puppy *n, pl* **-pies 1** a young dog. **2** *Informal, contemptuous* a brash or conceited young man. ▷ **HISTORY** Old French *popée* doll ▶ **puppyish** *adj*

puppy fat *n* fatty tissue that develops in childhood or adolescence and usually disappears with maturity.

purblind *adj* **1** partly or nearly blind. **2** lacking in understanding. ▷ **HISTORY** *pure* (that is, utterly) *blind*

purchase *vb* **-chasing, -chased 1** to obtain (goods) by payment. **2** to obtain by effort or sacrifice: *he had purchased his freedom at the expense of his principles.* ✧ *n* **3** something that is bought. **4** the act of buying. **5** the mechanical advantage achieved by a lever. **6** a firm leverage or grip. ▷ **HISTORY** Old French *porchacier* to strive to obtain ▶ **purchaser** *n*

purchasing cycle *n Commerce* the practice of consecutive purchasing.

purchasing function *n Commerce* the acquisition of the materials and services that are required in the running of a company.

purdah *n* the custom in some Muslim and Hindu communities of keeping women in seclusion, with clothing that conceals them completely when they go out. ▷ **HISTORY** Hindi *parda* veil

pure *adj* **1** not mixed with any other materials or elements: *pure wool.* **2** free from tainting or polluting matter: *pure water.* **3** innocent: *pure love.* **4** complete: *Pamela's presence on that particular flight was pure chance.* **5** (of a subject) studied in its theoretical aspects rather than for its practical applications: *pure mathematics.* **6** of unmixed descent. ▷ **HISTORY** Latin *purus* unstained ▶ **purely** *adv* ▶ **pureness** *n*

purebred *adj* denoting a pure strain obtained through many generations of controlled breeding.

puree (**pure**-ray) *n* **1** a smooth thick pulp of sieved fruit, vegetables, meat, or fish. ✧ *vb* **-reeing, -reed 2** to make (foods) into a puree. ▷ **HISTORY** French

purgative *Med* ✧ *n* **1** a medicine for emptying the bowels. ✧ *adj* **2** causing emptying of the bowels.

purgatory *n* **1** *Chiefly RC Church* a place in which the souls of those who have died undergo limited suffering for their sins on earth before they go to heaven. **2** a situation of temporary suffering or torment: *it was purgatory living in the same house as him.* ▷ **HISTORY** Latin *purgare* to purify ▶ **purgatorial** *adj*

purge *vb* **purging, purged 1** to rid (something) of undesirable qualities. **2** to rid (an organization etc.) of undesirable people: *the party was purged.* **3 a** to empty (the bowels). **b** to cause (a person) to empty his or her bowels. **4 a** *Law* to clear (a person) of a charge. **b** to free (oneself) of guilt by showing repentance. **5** to be purified. ✧ *n* **6** the act or process of purging. **7** the removal of undesirables from a state, organization, or political party. **8** a medicine that empties the bowels. ▷ **HISTORY** Latin *purgare* to purify

purify *vb* **-fies, -fying, -fied 1** to free (something) of harmful or inferior matter. **2** to free (a person) from sin or guilt. **3** to make clean, for example in a religious ceremony. ▷ **HISTORY** Latin *purus* pure + *facere* to make ▶ **purification** *n*

purism *n* strict insistence on the correct usage or style, such as in grammar or art. ▶ **purist** *adj, n* ▶ **puristic** *adj*

puritan *n* **1** a person who follows strict moral or religious principles. ✧ *adj* **2** of or like a puritan: *he maintained a streak of puritan self-denial.* ▷ **HISTORY** Late Latin *puritas* purity ▶ **puritanism** *n*

Puritan *History* ✧ *n* **1** a member of the extreme English Protestants who wished to strip the Church of England of most of its rituals. ✧ *adj* **2** of or relating to the Puritans. ▶ **Puritanism** *n*

puritanical *adj* **1** *Usually disparaging* strict in moral or religious outlook. **2** (*sometimes cap*) of or relating to a puritan or the Puritans.
▶ **puritanically** *adv*

purity *n* the state or quality of being pure.

purl[1] *n* **1** a knitting stitch made by doing a plain stitch backwards. **2** a decorative border, such as of lace. ✧ *vb* **3** to knit in purl stitch. ▷ **HISTORY** dialect *pirl* to twist into a cord

purl[2] *vb Literary* (of a stream) to flow with a gentle movement and a murmuring sound.
▷ **HISTORY** probably imitative

purlieu (**per**-lyoo) *n* **1** *English history* land on the edge of a royal forest. **2** (*usually pl*) *Literary* a neighbouring area; outskirts. **3** (*often pl*) *Literary* a place one frequents: *the committee was the purlieu of civil servants.* ▷ **HISTORY** Anglo-French *puralé* a going through

purloin *vb Formal* to steal. ▷ **HISTORY** Old French *porloigner* to put at a distance

purple *n* **1** a colour between red and blue. **2** cloth of this colour, often used to symbolize royalty or nobility. **3** the official robe of a cardinal. **4** anything purple, such as purple paint or purple clothing: *a large lady, unwisely dressed in purple.* ✧ *adj* **5** of a colour between red and blue. **6** (of writing) excessively elaborate: *purple prose.*
▷ **HISTORY** Greek *porphura* the purple fish (murex)
▶ **purplish** *adj*

purple heart *n Informal, chiefly Brit* a heart-shaped purple tablet consisting mainly of amphetamine.

Purple Heart *n* a decoration awarded to members of the US Armed Forces wounded in action.

purport *vb* **1** to claim to be or do something, esp. falsely: *painkillers may actually cause the headaches they purport to cure.* **2** (of speech or writing) to signify or imply. ✧ *n* **3** meaning or significance.
▷ **HISTORY** Old French *porporter* to convey

purpose *n* **1** the reason for which anything is done, created, or exists. **2** a fixed design or idea that is the object of an action. **3** determination: *his easy manner only lightly conceals a clear sense of purpose.* **4** practical advantage or use: *we debated senseless points of dogma for hours to no fruitful purpose.* **5 on purpose** intentionally. ✧ *vb* **-posing, -posed 6** to intend or determine to do (something).
▷ **HISTORY** Old French *porposer* to plan

purposeful *adj* with a fixed and definite purpose; determined. ▶ **purposefully** *adv*

> ☑ **WORD TIP**
> *Purposefully* is sometimes wrongly used where *purposely* is meant: *he had purposely* (not *purposefully*) *left the door unlocked.*

purposely *adv* on purpose.

> ☑ **WORD TIP**
> See at **purposeful.**

purr *vb* **1** (esp. of cats) to make a low vibrant sound, usually considered as expressing pleasure. **2** to express (pleasure) by this sound or by a sound suggestive of purring. ✧ *n* **3** a purring sound.
▷ **HISTORY** imitative

purse *n* **1** a small pouch for carrying money. **2** *US, Canad, Austral & NZ* a woman's handbag. **3** wealth or resources: *the public purse appeared bottomless.* **4** a sum of money that is offered as a prize. ✧ *vb* **pursing, pursed 5** to pull (the lips) into a small rounded shape. ▷ **HISTORY** Old English *purs*

purser *n* an officer aboard a ship who keeps the accounts.

purse strings *pl n* **hold the purse strings** to control the spending of a particular family, group, etc.

pursue *vb* **-suing, -sued 1** to follow (a person, vehicle, or animal) in order to capture or overtake. **2** to try hard to achieve (some desire or aim). **3** to follow the guidelines of (a plan or policy). **4** to apply oneself to (studies or interests). **5** to follow persistently or seek to become acquainted with: *was his desire to pursue and marry Carol based purely on her looks?* **6** to continue to discuss or argue (a point or subject). ▷ **HISTORY** Old French *poursivre*
▶ **pursuer** *n*

pursuit *n* **1** the act of pursuing. **2** an occupation or pastime.

pursuivant (**purse**-iv-ant) *n* the lowest rank of heraldic officer. ▷ **HISTORY** Old French

purulent (**pure**-yew-lent) *adj* of, relating to, or containing pus. ▷ **HISTORY** Latin *purulentus*
▶ **purulence** *n*

purvey *vb* **1** to sell or provide (foodstuffs). **2** to provide or make available: *the foreign ministry used him to purvey sensitive items of diplomatic news.*
▷ **HISTORY** Old French *porveeir* to provide
▶ **purveyor** *n*

purview *n* **1** scope of operation: *each designation falls under the purview of a different ministry.* **2** breadth or range of outlook: *he hopes that the purview of science will be widened.*
▷ **HISTORY** Anglo-Norman *purveu*

pus *n* the yellowish fluid that comes from inflamed or infected tissue. ▷ **HISTORY** Latin

push *vb* **1** (sometimes foll. by *off, away*) to apply steady force to in order to move. **2** to thrust (one's way) through something, such as a crowd. **3** (sometimes foll. by *for*) to be an advocate or promoter (of): *there are many groups you can join to push for change.* **4** to spur or drive (oneself or another person) in order to achieve more effort or better results: *you must be careful not to push your children too hard.* **5** *Informal* to sell (narcotic drugs) illegally. ✧ *n* **6** the act of pushing; thrust. **7** *Informal* drive or determination: *everything depends on him having the push to obtain the money.* **8** *Informal* a special effort to achieve something: *when this push spent itself it was obvious the bid had failed.* **9 the push** *Brit & NZ informal* dismissal from employment. ▷ **HISTORY** Latin *pulsare*

push-bike *n Brit, Austral & NZ informal* a bicycle.

A B C D E F G H I J K L M N O P Q R S T U V W X Y Z

push button *n* **1** an electrical switch operated by pressing a button. ✧ *adj* **push-button** **2** operated by a push button: *a push-button radio.*

pushchair *n Brit* a small folding chair on wheels in which a small child can be wheeled around: *escalators are difficult with pushchairs.*

pusher *n Informal* a person who sells illegal drugs.

pushover *n Informal* **1** something that is easily achieved. **2** a person, team, etc., that is easily taken advantage of or defeated.

push-start *vb* **1** to start (a motor vehicle) by pushing it, thus turning the engine. ✧ *n* **2** this process.

pushy *adj* **pushier, pushiest** *Informal* offensively assertive or ambitious.

pusillanimous *adj Formal* timid and cowardly: *pusillanimous behaviour.* ▷ **HISTORY** Latin *pusillus* weak + *animus* courage ▶ **pusillanimity** *n*

puss *n* **1** *Informal* a cat. **2** *Slang* a girl or woman. ▷ **HISTORY** probably Low German

pussy[1] *n, pl* **pussies** **1** Also called: **pussycat** *Informal* a cat. **2** *Taboo slang* the female genitals. ▷ **HISTORY** from *puss*

pussy[2] *adj* **-sier, -siest** containing or full of pus.

pussyfoot *vb Informal* **1** to move about stealthily. **2** to avoid committing oneself: *don't let's pussyfoot about naming the hit man.*

pussy willow *n* a willow tree with silvery silky catkins.

pustulate *vb* **-lating, -lated** to form into pustules.

pustule *n* a small inflamed raised area of skin containing pus. ▷ **HISTORY** Latin *pustula* a blister ▶ **pustular** *adj*

put *vb* **putting, put** **1** to cause to be (in a position or place): *he put the book on the table.* **2** to cause to be (in a state or condition): *what can be done to put things right?* **3** to lay (blame, emphasis, etc.) on a person or thing: *don't try to put the blame on someone else!* **4** to set or commit (to an action, task, or duty), esp. by force: *she put him to work weeding the garden.* **5** to estimate or judge: *I wouldn't put him in the same class as Verdi as a composer.* **6** (foll. by *to*) to utilize: *he put his culinary skills to good use when he opened a restaurant.* **7** to express: *he didn't put it quite as crudely as that.* **8** to make (an end or limit): *opponents claim the scheme will put an end to much of the sailing and boating in the area.* **9** to present for consideration; propose: *he put the question to the committee.* **10** to invest (money) in or expend (time or energy) on: *they put a lot of money into the sport.* **11** to throw or cast: *put the shot.* ✧ *n* **12** a throw, esp. in putting the shot. ✧ See also **put about, put across**, etc. ▷ **HISTORY** Middle English *puten* to push

put about *vb* **1** to make widely known: *a rumour was put about that he had been drunk.* **2** *Naut* to change course.

put across *vb* to communicate successfully: *he's not very good at putting his ideas across.*

putative (**pew**-tat-iv) *adj Formal* **1** commonly regarded as being: *the desire of the putative father to establish his possible paternity.* **2** considered to exist or have existed; inferred: *a putative earlier form.* ▷ **HISTORY** Latin *putare* to consider

put away *vb* **1** to save: *it takes a lot of discipline to put away for your old age.* **2** *Informal* to lock up in a prison, mental institution, etc.: *we have enough evidence to put him away for life.* **3** *Informal* to eat or drink in large amounts: *he put away three beers and three huge shots of brandy.*

put down *vb* **1** to make a written record of. **2** to repress: *the rising was put down with revolting cruelty.* **3** to consider: *I'd put him down as a complete fool.* **4** to attribute: *the government's defeat in the election can be put down to a general desire for change.* **5** to put (an animal) to death. **6** *Slang* to belittle or humiliate. ✧ *n* **put-down** **7** *Informal* a cruelly crushing remark.

put in *vb* **1** to devote (time or effort): *the competitors who did best were the ones who had put in some practice.* **2** (often foll. by *for*) to apply (for a job). **3** to submit: *they have put in an official complaint.* **4** *Naut* to bring a vessel into port.

put off *vb* **1** to postpone: *ministers have put off making a decision until next month.* **2** to evade (a person) by delay: *they tried to put him off, but he came anyway.* **3** to cause extreme dislike in: *he was put off by her appearance.* **4** to cause to lose interest in: *the accident put him off driving.*

put on *vb* **1** to dress oneself in. **2** to adopt (an attitude or feeling) insincerely: *I don't see why you have to put on that fake American accent.* **3** to present (a play or show). **4** to add: *I've put on nearly a stone since September.* **5** to cause (an electrical device) to function: *she put on the light.* **6** to bet (money) on a horse race or game. **7** to impose: *the government has put a tax on gas.*

put out *vb* **1 a** to annoy or anger. **b** to disturb or confuse. **2** to extinguish (a fire, light, etc.). **3** to inconvenience (someone): *I hope I'm not putting you out.* **4** to select or lay out for use: *she put out two clean cloths in the kitchen.* **5** to publish or broadcast: *she put out a statement denying the rumours.* **6** to dislocate: *he put his back out digging the garden.*

put over *vb Informal* to communicate (facts or information).

putrefy *vb* **-fies, -fying, -fied** *Formal* (of organic matter) to rot and produce an offensive smell. ▷ **HISTORY** Latin *putrefacere* ▶ **putrefaction** *n*

putrescent *adj Formal* becoming putrid; rotting: *putrescent toadstools.* ▷ **HISTORY** Latin *putrescere* to become rotten ▶ **putrescence** *n*

putrid *adj* **1** (of organic matter) rotting: *putrid meat.* **2** sickening or foul: *a putrid stench.* **3** *Informal* deficient in quality or value: *a penchant for putrid puns.* **4** morally corrupt. ▷ **HISTORY** Latin *putrere* to be rotten ▶ **putridity** *n*

putsch *n* a violent and sudden political revolt: *an attempted putsch against the general.* ▷ **HISTORY** from German

putt *Golf* ✧ *n* **1** a stroke on the green with a putter to roll the ball into or near the hole. ✧ *vb* **2** to strike (the ball) in this way. ▷ **HISTORY** Scot

putter *n Golf* a club, usually with a short shaft, for putting.

put through *vb* **1** to connect by telephone: *I'm sorry, you've been put through to the wrong extension.* **2** to carry out to a conclusion.

putting green *n* (on a golf course) the area of closely mown grass around the hole.

putty *n, pl* **-ties 1** a stiff paste used to fix glass into frames and fill cracks in woodwork. ✧ *vb* **-ties, -tying, -tied 2** to fix or fill with putty. ▷ **HISTORY** French *potée* a potful

put up *vb* **1** to build or erect: *I want to put up some shelves in the living room.* **2** to accommodate or be accommodated at: *can you put me up for tonight?* **3** to increase (prices). **4** to submit (a plan, case, etc.). **5** to offer: *the factory is being put up for sale.* **6** to give: *they put up a good fight.* **7** to provide (money) for: *they put up 35 per cent of the film's budget.* **8** to nominate or be nominated as a candidate: *the party have yet to decide whether to put up a candidate.* **9 put up to** to incite to: *I wonder who put them up to it?* **10 put up with** *Informal* to endure or tolerate. ✧ *adj* **put-up 11** *Informal* dishonestly or craftily prearranged: *a put-up job.*

puzzle *vb* **-zling, -zled 1** to baffle or bewilder. **2 puzzle out** to solve (a problem) by mental effort. **3 puzzle over** to think deeply about in an attempt to understand: *he puzzled over the squiggles and curves on the paper.* ✧ *n* **4** a problem that cannot be easily solved. **5** a toy, game, or question presenting a problem that requires skill or ingenuity for its solution. ▷ **HISTORY** origin unknown ▶ **puzzlement** *n* ▶ **puzzled** *adj* ▶ **puzzler** *n* ▶ **puzzling** *adj*

PVC polyvinyl chloride.

PVS persistent vegetative state.

PW policewoman.

PWR pressurized-water reactor.

pyaemia *or* **pyemia** *n Med* blood poisoning with pus-forming microorganisms in the blood. ▷ **HISTORY** Greek *puon* pus + *haima* blood

pye-dog *or* **pi-dog** *n* a half-wild Asian dog with no owner. ▷ **HISTORY** Hindi *pāhī* outsider

pygmy *n, pl* **-mies 1** something that is a very small example of its type. **2** an abnormally undersized person. **3** a person of little importance or significance. ✧ *adj* **4** very small: *the pygmy anteater.* ▷ **HISTORY** Greek *pugmaios* undersized

Pygmy *n, pl* **-mies** a member of one of the very short peoples of Equatorial Africa.

pyjamas *or US* **pajamas** *pl n* a loose-fitting jacket or top and trousers worn to sleep in.

> **WORD HISTORY**
> 'Pyjamas' comes from Persian *pāy jāma*, meaning 'leg clothing'.

pylon *n* a large vertical steel tower-like structure supporting high-tension electrical cables. ▷ **HISTORY** Greek *pulōn* a gateway

pylorus *n, pl* **-ri** *Anat* the small circular opening at the base of the stomach through which partially digested food passes to the duodenum.

pyorrhoea *or esp US* **pyorrhea** (pire-**ree**-a) *n Med* a discharge of pus, esp. in disease of the gums or tooth sockets. ▷ **HISTORY** Greek *puon* pus + *rhein* to flow

pyramid *n* **1** a huge stone building with a square base and four sloping triangular sides meeting in a point, such as the royal tombs built by the ancient Egyptians. **2** *Maths* a solid figure with a polygonal base and triangular sides that meet in a common vertex. ▷ **HISTORY** Greek *puramis* ▶ **pyramidal** *adj*

pyramid of numbers *n Biol* the graduated decrease in numbers at each stage in a food chain.

pyramid selling *n* the practice of selling distributors batches of goods which they then subdivide and sell to other distributors, this process continuing until the final distributors are left with a stock that is unsaleable except at a loss.

pyre *n* a pile of wood for cremating a corpse. ▷ **HISTORY** Greek *pur* fire

pyrethrum (pie-**reeth**-rum) *n* **1** a Eurasian chrysanthemum with white, pink, red, or purple flowers. **2** an insecticide prepared from dried pyrethrum flowers. ▷ **HISTORY** Greek *purethron*

pyretic (pie-**ret**-ik) *adj Pathol* of, relating to, or characterized by fever. ▷ **HISTORY** Greek *puretos* fever

Pyrex *n Trademark* a variety of heat-resistant glassware used in cookery and chemical apparatus.

pyrite (**pie**-rite) *n* a yellow mineral consisting of iron sulphide in cubic crystalline form. Formula: FeS_2. ▷ **HISTORY** Latin *pyrites* flint

pyrites (pie-**rite**-eez) *n, pl* **-tes 1** same as **pyrite**. **2** a disulphide of a metal, esp. of copper and tin.

pyroclastic *adj Geol* formed from the solid fragments ejected during a volcanic eruption: *the pyroclastic flows coming down the slope of a volcano.*

pyromania *n Psychiatry* the uncontrollable impulse and practice of setting things on fire. ▷ **HISTORY** Greek *pur* fire + *mania* madness ▶ **pyromaniac** *n, adj*

pyrotechnics *n* **1** the art of making fireworks. **2** a firework display. **3** a brilliant display of skill: *all those courtroom pyrotechnics.* ▷ **HISTORY** Greek *pur* fire + *tekhnē* art ▶ **pyrotechnic** *adj*

Pyrrhic victory (**pir**-ik) *n* a victory in which the victor's losses are as great as those of the defeated. ▷ **HISTORY** after *Pyrrhus,* who defeated the Romans in 279 BC but suffered heavy losses

Pythagoras' theorem (pie-**thag**-or-ass) *n* the theorem that in a right-angled triangle the square of the length of the hypotenuse equals the sum of the squares of the other two sides. ▷ **HISTORY** after *Pythagoras,* Greek philosopher and mathematician

python *n* a large nonpoisonous snake of Australia, Africa, and S Asia which kills its prey by crushing it with its body. ▷ **HISTORY** after *Python,* a dragon killed by Apollo

pyx *n Christianity* any receptacle in which the bread used in Holy Communion is kept. ▷ **HISTORY** Latin *pyxis* small box

a b c d e f g h i j k l m n o p q r s t u v w x y z

Q q

Q 1 *Chess* queen. 2 question.
q. 1 quart. 2 quarter. 3 question. 4 quire.
Q. 1 Queen. 2 question.
QC 1 Queen's Counsel. 2 Quebec.
QED which was to be shown or proved. ▷ **HISTORY** Latin *quod erat demonstrandum*
QLD *or* **Qld** Queensland.
QM Quartermaster.
qr. *pl* **qrs.** 1 quarter. 2 quire.
qt *pl* **qt** *or* **qts** quart.
q.t. *n* **on the q.t.** *Informal* secretly.
qua (**kwah**) *prep* in the capacity of; by virtue of being. ▷ **HISTORY** Latin
quack[1] *vb* **1** (of a duck) to utter a harsh guttural sound. **2** to make a noise like a duck. ✧ *n* **3** the sound made by a duck. ▷ **HISTORY** imitative
quack[2] *n* **1** an unqualified person who claims medical knowledge. **2** *Brit, Austral & NZ informal* a doctor. ▷ **HISTORY** short for *quacksalver,* from Dutch ▶ **quackery** *n*
quad[1] *n* short for **quadrangle** (sense 1).
quad[2] *n Informal* a quadruplet.
quad[3] *n* **1** quadraphonics. ✧ *adj* **2** quadraphonic.
quad bike *or* **quad** *n* a vehicle like a small motorcycle, with four large wheels, designed for agricultural and sporting uses.
quadrangle *n* **1** a rectangular courtyard with buildings on all four sides. **2** *Geom* a figure consisting of four points connected by four lines. ▷ **HISTORY** Late Latin *quadrangulum* ▶ **quadrangular** *adj*
quadrant *n* **1** *Geom* **a** a quarter of the circumference of a circle. **b** the area enclosed by two perpendicular radii of a circle. **c** any of the four sections into which a plane is divided by two coordinate axes. **2** a piece of a mechanism in the form of a quarter circle. **3** an instrument formerly used in astronomy and navigation for measuring the altitudes of stars. ▷ **HISTORY** Latin *quadrans* a quarter
quadraphonic *adj* using four independent channels to reproduce or record sound. ▶ **quadraphonics** *n*
quadrat *n Ecology* an area of vegetation, usually one square metre, selected at random for the study of plants in the surrounding area.
quadrate *n* **1** a cube or square, or a square or cubelike object. ✧ *vb* **-rating, -rated 2** to make square or rectangular. ▷ **HISTORY** Latin *quadrare* to make square
quadratic *Maths* ✧ *n* **1** Also called: **quadratic equation** an equation in which the variable is raised to the power of two, but nowhere raised to a higher power: *solve the quadratic equation* $2x^2-3x-6=3$. ✧ *adj* **2** of or relating to the second power.
quadratic function *n Maths* a function of the second power, which has a graph called a parabola.
quadrat sampling *n Ecology* the process of making assumptions about a large area of a habitat based on the information that can be learnt about a smaller, randomly selected area within it, usually one square metre.
quadrennial *adj* **1** occurring every four years. **2** lasting four years.
quadri- *or before a vowel* **quadr-** *combining form* four: *quadrilateral.* ▷ **HISTORY** Latin
quadriceps *n Anat* a muscle at the front of the thigh. ▷ **HISTORY** New Latin
quadrilateral *adj* **1** having four sides. ✧ *n* **2** a polygon with four sides.
quadrille *n* **1** a square dance for four couples. **2** music for this dance. ▷ **HISTORY** Spanish *cuadrilla*
quadrillion *n, pl* **-lions** *or* **-lion 1** (in Britain, France, and Germany) the number represented as one followed by 24 zeros (10^{24}). **2** (in the US and Canada) the number represented as one followed by 15 zeros (10^{15}). ▷ **HISTORY** French *quadrillon*
quadriplegia *n* paralysis of all four limbs. ▷ **HISTORY** QUADRI- + Greek *plēssein* to strike ▶ **quadriplegic** *adj, n*
quadruped (**kwod**-roo-ped) *n* an animal, esp. a mammal, that has four legs. ▷ **HISTORY** Latin *quadru-* four + *pes* foot
quadruple *vb* **-pling, -pled 1** to multiply by four. ✧ *adj* **2** four times as much or as many. **3** consisting of four parts. **4** *Music* having four beats in each bar. ✧ *n* **5** a quantity or number four times as great as another. ▷ **HISTORY** Latin *quadru-* four + *-plus* -fold
quadruplet *n* one of four children born at one birth.
quaff (**kwoff**) *vb Old-fashioned* to drink heartily or in one draught. ▷ **HISTORY** perhaps imitative
quagga *n, pl* **-gas** *or* **-ga** a recently extinct zebra, striped only on the head and shoulders. ▷ **HISTORY** Hottentot *qŭagga*
quagmire (**kwog**-mire) *n* a soft wet area of land that gives way under the feet; bog. ▷ **HISTORY** from *quag* bog + *mire*
quail[1] *n, pl* **quails** *or* **quail** a small game bird of the partridge family. ▷ **HISTORY** Old French *quaille*
quail[2] *vb* to shrink back with fear; cower. ▷ **HISTORY** origin unknown
quaint *adj* attractively unusual, esp. in an old-fashioned style. ▷ **HISTORY** Old French *cointe,* from Latin *cognitus* known
quake *vb* **quaking, quaked 1** to shake or tremble with or as if with fear. **2** to shudder because of instability. ✧ *n* **3** *Informal* an earthquake. ▷ **HISTORY** Old English *cwacian*
Quaker *n* a member of a Christian sect, the Religious Society of Friends. ▷ **HISTORY** originally an offensive nickname ▶ **Quakerism** *n*
qualification *n* **1** an official record of achievement awarded on the successful completion of a course of training or passing of an examination. **2** an ability, quality, or attribute, esp. one that fits a person to perform a particular job or task. **3** a condition that modifies or limits;

restriction. **4** the act of qualifying or being qualified.

qualified *adj* **1** having successfully completed a training course or passed the exams necessary in order to be entitled to work in a particular profession: *a qualified lawyer.* **2** having the abilities, qualities, or attributes necessary to perform a particular job or task. **3** having completed a training or degree course and gained the relevant certificates. **4** limited or restricted; not wholehearted: *the mission was only a qualified success.*

qualifier *n* **1** a person or thing that qualifies, esp. a contestant in a competition who wins a preliminary heat or contest and so earns the right to take part in the next round. **2** a preliminary heat or contest. **3** *Grammar* another word for **modifier**.

qualify *vb* **-fies, -fying, -fied 1** to have the abilities or attributes required in order to do or have something, such as a job: *he qualified as a teacher; she did not qualify for a State pension at that time.* **2** to moderate or restrict (a statement one has made). **3** to describe or be described as having a particular quality: *it was neither witty nor subtle enough to qualify as a spoof.* **4** to be successful in one stage of a competition and as a result progress to the next stage: *Lewis failed to qualify for the 100 metres.* **5** *Grammar* to modify the sense of (a word). ▷ **HISTORY** Latin *qualis* of what kind + *facere* to make

qualitative *adj* involving or relating to distinctions based on quality.

qualitative analysis *n Chem* analysis of a substance to determine its constituents.

qualitative observation *n Science* scientific study in which descriptive information is collected.

quality *n, pl* **-ties 1** degree or standard of excellence. **2** a distinguishing characteristic or attribute. **3** the basic character or nature of something. **4** a feature of personality. **5** (formerly) high social status. ✧ *adj* **6** excellent or superior: *a quality product.* ▷ **HISTORY** Latin *qualis* of what sort

quality control *n* checking of the relative quality of a manufactured product, usually by testing samples.

qualm (**kwahm**) *n* **1** a pang of conscience; scruple. **2** a sudden sensation of misgiving. **3** a sudden feeling of sickness or nausea. ▷ **HISTORY** Old English *cwealm* death or plague

quandary *n, pl* **-ries** a situation in which it is difficult to decide what to do; predicament; dilemma. ▷ **HISTORY** origin unknown

quandong (**kwon**-dong) *n* **1** a small Australian tree with edible fruit and nuts used in preserves. **2** an Australian tree with pale timber.

quango *n, pl* **-gos** *Chiefly Brit* a semipublic government-financed administrative body whose members are appointed by the government. ▷ **HISTORY** *qu(asi-)a(utonomous) n(on)g(overnmental) o(rganization)*

quangocracy *n, pl* **-cies a** the influence held by quangos. **b** quangos collectively.

quantify *vb* **-fies, -fying, -fied** to discover or express the quantity of. ▷ **HISTORY** Latin *quantus* how much + *facere* to make ▶ **quantifiable** *adj* ▶ **quantification** *n*

quantitative *adj* **1** involving considerations of amount or size. **2** capable of being measured.

quantitative analysis *n Chem* analysis of a substance to determine the proportions of its constituents.

quantitative observation *n Science* scientific study in which numerical information is collected.

quantity *n, pl* **-ties 1** a specified or definite amount or number. **2** the aspect of anything that can be measured, weighed, or counted. **3** a large amount. **4** *Maths* an entity having a magnitude that may be denoted by a numerical expression. ▷ **HISTORY** Latin *quantus* how much

> **☑ WORD TIP**
> The use of a plural noun after *quantity of* as in *a large quantity of bananas* was formerly considered incorrect, but is now acceptable.

quantity surveyor *n* a person who estimates the cost of the materials and labour necessary for a construction job.

quantum *n, pl* **-ta 1** an amount or quantity, esp. a specific amount. **2** *Physics* the smallest quantity of some physical property that a system can possess. ✧ *adj* **3** of or designating a major breakthrough or sudden advance: *a quantum leap in business computing.* ▷ **HISTORY** Latin *quantus* how much

quantum theory *n* a theory concerning the behaviour of physical systems based on the idea that they can only possess certain properties, such as energy and angular momentum, in discrete amounts (quanta).

quarantine *n* **1** a period of isolation, esp. of people or animals arriving from abroad, to prevent the spread of disease. ✧ *vb* **-tining, -tined 2** to isolate in or as if in quarantine. ▷ **HISTORY** Italian *quarantina* period of forty days

quark *n Physics* the hypothetical elementary particle supposed to be a fundamental unit of all baryons and mesons. ▷ **HISTORY** special use of a word coined by James Joyce in the novel *Finnegans Wake*

quarrel *n* **1** an angry disagreement; argument. **2** a cause of dispute; grievance. ✧ *vb* **-relling, -relled** *or US* **-reling, -reled** (often foll. by *with*) **3** to engage in a disagreement or dispute; argue. **4** to find fault; complain. ▷ **HISTORY** Latin *querella* complaint

quarrelsome *adj* inclined to quarrel or disagree.

quarry[1] *n, pl* **-ries 1** a place where stone is dug from the surface of the earth. ✧ *vb* **-ries, -rying, -ried 2** to extract (stone) from a quarry. ▷ **HISTORY** Old French *quarriere*

quarry[2] *n, pl* **-ries 1** an animal that is being hunted; prey. **2** anything pursued. ▷ **HISTORY** Middle English *quirre* entrails offered to the hounds

quart *n* a unit of liquid measure equal to one quarter of a gallon or two pints (1.136 litres). ▷ **HISTORY** Latin *quartus* fourth

a b c d e f g h i j k l m n o p q r s t u v w x y z

A B C D E F G H I J K L M N O P Q R S T U V W X Y Z

quarter *n* **1** one of four equal parts of something such as an object or quantity. **2** the fraction equal to one divided by four ($^1/_4$). **3** a fourth part of a year; three months. **4** *Brit informal* a unit of weight equal to four ounces (113.4 grams). **5** a region or district of a town or city: *the French quarter of New Orleans.* **6** a region, direction, or point of the compass. **7** *US & Canad* a coin worth 25 cents. **8** short for **quarter-hour**. **9** *Astron* **a** one fourth of the moon's period of revolution around the earth. **b** either of two phases of the moon when half of the lighted surface is visible. **10** (*sometimes pl*) an unspecified person or group of people: *it met stiff opposition in some quarters.* **11** mercy or pity shown to a defeated opponent: *no quarter was asked or given.* **12** any of the four limbs of a quadruped. ✧ *vb* **13** to divide into four equal parts. **14** (formerly) to dismember (a human body). **15** to billet or be billeted in lodgings. **16** *Heraldry* to divide (a shield) into four separate bearings. ✧ *adj* **17** being or consisting of one of four equal parts. ✧ See also **quarters**. ▷ **HISTORY** Latin *quartus* fourth

quarterback *n* a player in American football who directs attacking play.

quarter day *n Brit* any of four days in the year when certain payments become due.

quarterdeck *n Naut* the rear part of the upper deck of a ship, traditionally for official or ceremonial use.

quarterfinal *n* the round before the semifinal in a competition.

quarter-hour *n* **1** a period of 15 minutes. **2** either of the points of time 15 minutes before or after the hour.

quarterlight *n Brit* a small pivoted window in the door of a car for ventilation.

quarterly *adj* **1** occurring, done, due, or issued at intervals of three months. ✧ *n, pl* **-lies 2** a periodical issued every three months. ✧ *adv* **3** once every three months.

quartermaster *n* **1** a military officer responsible for accommodation, food, and equipment. **2** a naval officer responsible for navigation.

quarters *pl n* accommodation, esp. as provided for military personnel.

quarter sessions *n* (formerly) a court with limited jurisdiction, held four times a year.

quartet *n* **1** a group of four singers or instrumentalists. **2** a piece of music for four performers. **3** any group of four. ▷ **HISTORY** Italian *quarto* fourth

quartile *n* **1** one of three values of a variable dividing its distribution into four groups with equal frequencies. ✧ *adj* **2** of a quartile.

quarto *n, pl* **-tos** a book size resulting from folding a sheet of paper into four leaves or eight pages. ▷ **HISTORY** New Latin *in quarto* in quarter

quartz *n* a hard glossy mineral consisting of crystalline silicon dioxide. ▷ **HISTORY** German *Quarz*

quartz crystal *n* a thin plate or rod cut from a piece of quartz and ground so that it vibrates at a particular frequency.

quartzite *n Geol* **1** a very hard metamorphic rock consisting of a mosaic of intergrown quartz crystals. **2** a white or grey sandstone composed of quartz.

quasar (**kway**-zar) *n* any of a class of extremely distant starlike objects that are powerful sources of radio waves and other forms of energy. ▷ **HISTORY** *quas(i-stell)ar (radio source)*

quash *vb* **1** to officially reject (something, such as a judgment or decision) as invalid. **2** to defeat or suppress forcefully and completely. ▷ **HISTORY** Latin *quassare* to shake

quasi- (**kway**-zie) *combining form* **1** almost but not really; seemingly: *a quasi-religious cult.* **2** resembling but not actually being; so-called: *a quasi-scholar.* ▷ **HISTORY** Latin: as if

quassia (**kwosh**-a) *n* **1** a tropical American tree with bitter bark and wood. **2** the wood of this tree or a bitter compound extracted from it, used in insecticides. ▷ **HISTORY** after Graman *Quassi*, who discovered its medicinal value

quaternary *adj* **1** consisting of four parts. **2** *Economics* denoting those activities that provide the specialist knowledge and skills for the other economic sectors. ▷ **HISTORY** Latin *quaterni* by fours

Quaternary *adj Geol* of the most recent period of geological time, which started about one million years ago.

quatrain *n* a stanza or poem of four lines. ▷ **HISTORY** French, from Latin *quattuor* four

quatrefoil *n* **1** a leaf composed of four leaflets. **2** *Archit* a carved ornament of four arcs about a common centre. ▷ **HISTORY** Old French *quatre* four + *-foil* leaflet

quattrocento (kwat-roe-**chen**-toe) *n* the 15th century, esp. in reference to Renaissance Italian art. ▷ **HISTORY** Italian: four hundred (short for fourteen hundred)

quaver *vb* **1** (esp. of the voice) to quiver or tremble. **2** to say or sing (something) with a trembling voice. ✧ *n* **3** *Music* a note having the time value of an eighth of a semibreve. **4** a tremulous sound or note. ▷ **HISTORY** Germanic ▶ **quavering** *adj*

quay (**kee**) *n* a wharf built parallel to the shoreline. ▷ **HISTORY** Old French *kai*

queasy *adj* **-sier, -siest 1** having the feeling that one is about to vomit; nauseous. **2** feeling or causing uneasiness. ▷ **HISTORY** origin unknown ▶ **queasily** *adv* ▶ **queasiness** *n*

queen *n* **1** a female sovereign who is the official ruler or head of state. **2** the wife of a king. **3** a woman, thing, or place considered the best or most important of her or its kind: *the rose is considered the queen of garden flowers.* **4** *Slang* an effeminate male homosexual. **5** the only fertile female in a colony of bees, wasps, or ants. **6** a playing card with a picture of a queen on it. **7** a chessman, able to move in a straight line in any direction. ✧ *vb* **8** *Chess* to promote (a pawn) to a queen when it reaches the eighth rank. **9 queen it** *Informal* to behave in an overbearing manner: *she is more beautiful than ever and still queening it over everybody.* ▷ **HISTORY** Old English *cwēn* ▶ **queenly** *adj*

queen consort *n* the wife of a reigning king.

queen mother *n* the widow of a former king who is also the mother of the reigning sovereign.

queen post *n Building* one of a pair of vertical posts that connect the tie beam of a truss to the principal rafters of a roof.

Queensberry rules *pl n* **1** the code of rules followed in modern boxing. **2** *Informal* gentlemanly conduct, esp. in a dispute. ▷ **HISTORY** after the ninth Marquess of *Queensberry,* who originated the rules

Queen's Counsel *n* **1** (in Britain, Australia and New Zealand) a barrister or advocate appointed Counsel to the Crown. **2** (in Canada and New Zealand) an honorary title bestowed on lawyers with long experience.

Queen's English *n* correctly spoken and written British English.

queen's evidence *n English law* evidence given for the Crown against former associates in crime by an accomplice.

queen's highway *n* **1** (in Britain) any public road or right of way. **2** (in Canada) a main road maintained by the provincial government.

queer *adj* **1** not normal or usual; odd or strange. **2** dubious; shady. **3** *Brit* faint, giddy, or queasy. **4** *Informal, usually offensive* homosexual. **5** *Informal* eccentric or slightly mad. ✧ *n* **6** *Informal, usually offensive* a homosexual. ✧ *vb* **7 queer someone's pitch** *Informal* to spoil or thwart someone's chances of something. ▷ **HISTORY** origin unknown

> ☑ **WORD TIP**
> Although the term *queer* meaning homosexual is still considered derogatory when used by non-homosexuals, it is now being used by homosexuals of themselves as a positive term, as in *queer politics, queer cinema.*

quell *vb* **1** to suppress (rebellion or unrest); subdue. **2** to overcome or allay. ▷ **HISTORY** Old English *cwellan* to kill

quench *vb* **1** to satisfy (one's thirst). **2** to put out; extinguish. **3** to suppress or subdue. **4** *Metallurgy* to cool (hot metal) by plunging it into cold water. ▷ **HISTORY** Old English *ācwencan* to extinguish

quern *n* a stone hand mill for grinding corn. ▷ **HISTORY** Old English *cweorn*

querulous (**kwer**-yew-luss) *adj* complaining; whining or peevish. ▷ **HISTORY** Latin *queri* to complain ▶ **querulously** *adv*

query *n, pl* **-ries 1** a question, esp. one expressing doubt. **2** a question mark. ✧ *vb* **-ries, -rying, -ried 3** to express uncertainty, doubt, or an objection concerning (something). **4** to express as a query; ask. ▷ **HISTORY** Latin *quaere* ask!

quest *n* **1** a looking for or seeking; search. **2** the object of a search; a goal or target. ✧ *vb* **3 quest for** to go in search of. **4** (of dogs) to search for game. ▷ **HISTORY** Old French *queste*

question *n* **1** a form of words addressed to a person in order to obtain an answer; interrogative sentence. **2** a point at issue: *they were silent on the question of social justice.* **3** a difficulty or uncertainty. **4 a** an act of asking. **b** an investigation into some problem. **5** a motion presented for debate. **6 beyond (all) question** beyond (any) doubt. **7 call something into question a** to make something the subject of disagreement. **b** to cast doubt upon the validity or truth of something. **8 in question** under discussion: *the area in question was not contaminated.* **9 out of the question** beyond consideration; impossible. ✧ *vb* **10** to put a question or questions to (a person); interrogate. **11** to make (something) the subject of dispute. **12** to express uncertainty; doubt. ▷ **HISTORY** Latin *quaestio*

> ☑ **WORD TIP**
> *The question whether* should be used rather than *the question of whether* or *the question as to whether: this leaves open the question whether he acted correctly.*

questionable *adj* **1** (esp. of a person's morality or honesty) doubtful. **2** of disputable value or authority. ▶ **questionably** *adv*

question mark *n* **1** the punctuation mark (?), used at the end of questions. **2** a doubt or uncertainty: *a question mark still hangs over their success.*

question master *n Brit* the person chairing a radio or television quiz or panel game.

questionnaire *n* a set of questions on a form, used to collect statistical information or opinions from people.

question on notice *n Austral politics* a question submitted in writing to a minister and answered in writing.

question tag *n Grammar* a clause added on to another clause to invite the hearer's agreement or disagreement, such as *isn't it* in *the bread's on the table, isn't it?*

question time *n* (in some parliamentary bodies) the time set aside each day for questions to government ministers.

question without notice *n Austral politics* a question put orally to a minister usually without prior warning as to the content of it.

queue *n* **1** a line of people or vehicles waiting for something. ✧ *vb* **queuing** *or* **queueing, queued 2** (often foll. by *up*) to form or remain in a line while waiting. ▷ **HISTORY** Latin *cauda* tail

quibble *vb* **-bling, -bled 1** to make trivial objections. ✧ *n* **2** a trivial objection or equivocation, esp. one used to avoid an issue. **3** *Archaic* a pun. ▷ **HISTORY** origin unknown

quiche (**keesh**) *n* a savoury flan with an egg custard filling to which cheese, bacon, or vegetables are added. ▷ **HISTORY** French

quick *adj* **1** characterized by rapidity of movement or action; fast. **2** lasting or taking a short time. **3** immediate or prompt: *her quick action minimized the damage.* **4** eager or ready to perform (an action): *quick to condemn.* **5** responsive to stimulation; alert; lively: *they were impressed by his quick mind.* **6** easily excited or aroused: *he is impulsive and has a quick temper.* **7** nimble in one's movements or actions; deft: *she has quick hands.* ✧ *n* **8** any area of sensitive flesh, esp. that under a nail. **9 cut someone to the quick** to hurt someone's feelings deeply. **10 the quick** *Archaic* living people. ✧ *adv* **11** in a rapid manner; swiftly. ▷ **HISTORY** Old English *cwicu* living ▶ **quickly** *adv* ▶ **quickness** *n*

quick-change artist *n* an actor or entertainer who undertakes several rapid changes of costume during a performance.

quicken *vb* **1** to make or become faster; accelerate. **2** to impart to or receive vigour or enthusiasm: *science quickens the imagination.* **3 a** (of a fetus) to begin to show signs of life. **b** (of a pregnant woman) to reach the stage of pregnancy at which movements of the fetus can be felt.

quickie *Informal* ✧ *n* **1** anything made or done rapidly. ✧ *adj* **2** made or done rapidly: *a quickie divorce.*

quicklime *n* a white caustic solid, mainly composed of calcium oxide, used in the manufacture of glass and steel.

quicksand *n* a deep mass of loose wet sand that submerges anything on top of it.

quickset *Chiefly Brit* ✧ *adj* **1** (of plants or cuttings) planted so as to form a hedge. ✧ *n* **2** a hedge composed of such plants.

quicksilver *n* the metal mercury.

quickstep *n* **1** a modern ballroom dance in rapid quadruple time. **2** music for this dance.

quid[1] *n, pl* **quid** *Brit slang* **1** a pound (sterling). **2 be quids in** to be in a very favourable or advantageous position. ▷ **HISTORY** origin unknown

quid[2] *n* a piece of tobacco for chewing. ▷ **HISTORY** Old English *cwidu* chewing resin

quiddity *n, pl* **-ties 1** the essential nature of something. **2** a petty or trifling distinction. ▷ **HISTORY** Latin *quid* what

quid pro quo *n, pl* **quid pro quos** one thing, esp. an advantage or object, given in exchange for another. ▷ **HISTORY** Latin: something for something

quiescent (kwee-**ess**-ent) *adj Formal* quiet, inactive, or dormant. ▷ **HISTORY** Latin *quiescere* to rest ▶ **quiescence** *n*

quiet *adj* **1** characterized by an absence of noise. **2** calm or tranquil: *the sea is quiet today.* **3** untroubled: *a quiet life.* **4** not busy: *business is quiet this morning.* **5** private or secret: *I had a quiet word with her.* **6** free from anger, impatience, or other extreme emotion. **7** not showy: *quiet colours; a quiet wedding.* **8** modest or reserved: *quiet humour.* ✧ *n* **9** the state of being silent, peaceful, or untroubled. **10 on the quiet** without other people knowing. ✧ *vb* **11** to make or become calm or silent. ▷ **HISTORY** Latin *quies* repose ▶ **quietly** *adv* ▶ **quietness** *n*

quieten *vb Brit & NZ* **1** (often foll. by *down*) to make or become calm or silent. **2** to allay (fear or doubts).

quietism *n Formal* passivity and calmness of mind towards external events. ▶ **quietist** *n, adj*

quietude *n Formal* quietness, peace, or tranquillity.

quietus *n, pl* **-tuses 1** *Literary* a release from life; death. **2** the discharge or settlement of debts or duties. ▷ **HISTORY** Latin *quietus est,* literally: he is at rest

quiff *n Brit* a tuft of hair brushed up above the forehead. ▷ **HISTORY** origin unknown

quill *n* **1** Also called: **quill pen** a feather made into a pen. **2 a** any of the large stiff feathers of the wing or tail of a bird. **b** the hollow stem of a feather. **3** any of the stiff hollow spines of a porcupine or hedgehog. ▷ **HISTORY** origin unknown

quilt *n* **1** a cover for a bed, consisting of a soft filling sewn between two layers of material, usually with crisscross seams. **2** a continental quilt; duvet. ✧ *vb* **3** to stitch together two layers of (fabric) with padding between them. ▷ **HISTORY** Old French *coilte* mattress ▶ **quilted** *adj*

quin *n* a quintuplet.

quince *n* the acid-tasting pear-shaped fruit of an Asian tree, used in preserves. ▷ **HISTORY** Greek *kudōnion*

quincunx *n* a group of five objects arranged in the shape of a rectangle with one at each corner and the fifth in the centre. ▷ **HISTORY** Latin: five twelfths; in ancient Rome, this was a coin marked with five spots

quinine *n* a bitter drug extracted from cinchona bark, used as a tonic and formerly in malaria therapy. ▷ **HISTORY** Spanish *quina* cinchona bark

quinquennial *adj* occurring once every five years or over a period of five years.

quinquereme *n* an ancient Roman galley with five banks of oars. ▷ **HISTORY** Latin *quinque* five + *remus* oar

quinsy *n* inflammation of the tonsils and throat, with abscesses. ▷ **HISTORY** Greek *kuōn* dog + *ankhein* to strangle

quint *n US & Canad* a quintuplet.

quintain *History* ✧ *n* **1** a post or target set up for jousting practice for medieval knights. **2** the exercise of tilting at such a target.

quintal *n* **1** a unit of weight equal to (esp. in Britain) 112 pounds (50.85 kg) or (esp. in US) 100 pounds (45.36 kg). **2** a unit of weight equal to 100 kilograms. ▷ **HISTORY** Arabic *qintār*

quintessence *n* **1** the most perfect representation of a quality or state. **2** an extract of a substance containing its central nature in its most concentrated form. ▷ **HISTORY** Medieval Latin *quinta essentia* the fifth essence ▶ **quintessential** *adj*

quintet *n* **1** a group of five singers or instrumentalists. **2** a piece of music for five performers. **3** any group of five. ▷ **HISTORY** Italian *quintetto*

quintillion *n, pl* **-lions** *or* **-lion 1** (in Britain, France, and Germany) the number represented as one followed by 30 zeros (10^{30}). **2** (in the US and Canada) the number represented as one followed by 18 zeros (10^{18}). ▷ **HISTORY** Latin *quintus* fifth

quintuple *vb* **-pling, -pled 1** to multiply by five. ✧ *adj* **2** five times as much or as many. **3** consisting of five parts. ✧ *n* **4** a quantity or number five times

A B C D E F G H I J K L M N O P Q R S T U V W X Y Z

as great as another. ▷ **HISTORY** Latin *quintus* fifth + *-plus* -fold

quintuplet *n* one of five children born at one birth.

quip *n* **1** a witty saying. ✧ *vb* **quipping, quipped** **2** to make a quip. ▷ **HISTORY** probably from Latin *quippe* indeed, to be sure

quire *n* a set of 24 or 25 sheets of paper. ▷ **HISTORY** Old French *quaier*

quirk *n* **1** a peculiarity of character; mannerism or foible. **2** an unexpected twist or turn: *a strange quirk of fate.* ▷ **HISTORY** origin unknown ▶ **quirky** *adj*

quisling *n* a traitor who aids an occupying enemy force; collaborator. ▷ **HISTORY** after Vidkun *Quisling*, Norwegian collaborator with the Nazis

quit *vb* **quitting, quit** **1** to stop (doing something). **2** to resign (from): *the Prime Minister's decision to quit; he quit his job as a salesman.* **3** to leave (a place). ▷ **HISTORY** Old French *quitter* ▶ **quitter** *n*

quite *adv* **1** (*not used with a negative*) to a greater than average extent; somewhat: *he found her quite attractive.* **2** absolutely: *you're quite right.* **3** in actuality; truly. **4 quite a** *or* **an** of an exceptional kind: *she is quite a girl.* **5 quite something** a remarkable thing or person. ✧ *interj* **6** an expression used to indicate agreement. ▷ **HISTORY** adverbial use of *quite* (adjective) quit, free of

> **WORD TIP**
> See at **very.**

quits *adj Informal* **1** on an equal footing. **2 call it quits** to end a dispute or contest, agreeing that honours are even.

quittance *n* **1** release from debt or other obligation. **2** a document certifying this. ▷ **HISTORY** Old French *quitter* to release from obligation

quiver[1] *vb* **1** to shake with a tremulous movement; tremble. ✧ *n* **2** a shaking or trembling. ▷ **HISTORY** obsolete *cwiver* quick, nimble ▶ **quivering** *adj*

quiver[2] *n* a case for holding or carrying arrows. ▷ **HISTORY** Old French *cuivre*

quixotic (kwik-**sot**-ik) *adj* unrealistically optimistic or chivalrous. ▷ **HISTORY** after Don *Quixote* in Cervantes' romance ▶ **quixotically** *adv*

quiz *n, pl* **quizzes** **1** an entertainment in which the knowledge of the players is tested by a series of questions. **2** any set of quick questions designed to test knowledge. **3** an investigation by close questioning. ✧ *vb* **quizzing, quizzed** **4** to investigate by close questioning; interrogate. ▷ **HISTORY** origin unknown

quizzical *adj* questioning and mocking or supercilious: *the question elicits a quizzical expression.* ▶ **quizzically** *adv*

quod *n Brit slang* a jail. ▷ **HISTORY** origin unknown

quoin *n* **1** an external corner of a wall. **2** the stone forming the outer corner of a wall; a cornerstone. **3** a wedge. ▷ **HISTORY** variant of *coin* (in former sense of corner)

quoit *n* a large ring used in the game of quoits. ▷ **HISTORY** origin unknown

quokka *n* a small Australian wallaby.

quondam *adj Formal* of an earlier time; former: *her quondam employers.* ▷ **HISTORY** Latin

quorate *adj* having or being a quorum: *the meeting is now quorate.*

quorum *n* the minimum number of members required to be present in a meeting or assembly before any business can be transacted. ▷ **HISTORY** Latin, literally: of whom

quota *n* **1** the share that is due from, due to, or allocated to a person or group. **2** the prescribed number or quantity allowed, required, or admitted. ▷ **HISTORY** Latin *quotus* of what number

quotation *n* **1** a written or spoken passage repeated exactly in a later work, speech, or conversation, usually with an acknowledgment of its source. **2** the act of quoting. **3** an estimate of costs submitted by a contractor to a prospective client.

quotation marks *pl n* the punctuation marks used to begin and end a quotation, either " and " or ' and '.

quote *vb* **quoting, quoted** **1** to repeat (words) exactly from (an earlier work, speech, or conversation), usually with an acknowledgment of their source. **2** to state a price for goods or a job of work. **3** to put quotation marks round (words). ✧ *n* **4** *Informal* a quotation. **5 quotes** *Informal* quotation marks. ✧ *interj* **6** an expression used to indicate that the words that follow are a quotation. ▷ **HISTORY** Medieval Latin *quotare* to assign reference numbers to passages ▶ **quotable** *adj*

quoth *vb Archaic* (used before *I, he* or *she*) said. ▷ **HISTORY** Old English *cwæth*

quotidian *adj* **1** daily. **2** *Literary* commonplace. **3** (esp. of fever) recurring daily. ▷ **HISTORY** Latin *quotidianus*

quotient *n* the result of the division of one number or quantity by another. ▷ **HISTORY** Latin *quotiens* how often

Quran (koo-**rahn**) *n* same as **Koran**.

q.v. (denoting a cross-reference) which (word, item, etc.) see. ▷ **HISTORY** New Latin *quod vide*

qwerty *or* **QWERTY keyboard** *n* the standard English language typewriter or computer keyboard with the characters q, w, e, r, t, and y at the top left of the keyboard.

R r

r 1 radius. **2** ratio. **3** right. **4** *Cricket* run(s).
R **1** *Chem* radical. **2** Regina. **3** Registered Trademark. **4** *Physics, electronics* resistance. **5** Rex. **6** River. **7** *Chess* rook.
Ra *Chem* radium.
RA **1** rear admiral. **2** (in Britain) Royal Academy. **3** (in Britain) Royal Artillery.
RAAF Royal Australian Air Force.
rabbi (**rab**-bye) *n, pl* **-bis 1** the spiritual leader of a Jewish congregation. **2** an expert in or teacher of Jewish Law. ▷ **HISTORY** Hebrew: my master ▶ **rabbinical** *adj*
rabbit *n, pl* **-bits** *or* **-bit 1** a common burrowing mammal with long ears and a short fluffy tail. ✧ *vb* **-biting, -bited 2** *Informal* to talk too much: *he keeps rabbiting on about interrogation.* ▷ **HISTORY** origin unknown
rabbit ears *pl n Austral & NZ* an indoor television aerial.
rabbit fence *n Austral & NZ* a fence to prevent the spread of rabbits.
rabble *n* **1** a disorderly crowd of noisy people. **2 the rabble** *Contemptuous* the common people. ▷ **HISTORY** origin unknown
rabble-rouser *n* a person who stirs up the feelings of the mob. ▶ **rabble-rousing** *adj, n*
Rabelaisian *adj* characterized by broad, often bawdy humour and sharp satire. ▷ **HISTORY** after the work of the French writer, François *Rabelais*
rabid *adj* **1** fanatical: *a rabid separatist.* **2** having rabies. ▷ **HISTORY** Latin *rabidus* frenzied ▶ **rabidity** *n*
rabies (**ray**-beez) *n Pathol* a fatal infectious viral disease of the nervous system transmitted by dogs and certain other animals. ▷ **HISTORY** Latin: madness
RAC (in Britain) Royal Automobile Club.
raccoon *or* **racoon** *n, pl* **-coons** *or* **-coon** a small American mammal with a long striped tail. ▷ **HISTORY** from a Native American language
race[1] *n* **1** a contest of speed. **2** any competition or rivalry: *the arms race.* **3** a rapid current of water. **4** a channel of a stream: *a mill race.* **5** *Austral & NZ* a narrow passage through which sheep pass individually, as to a sheep dip. ✧ *vb* **racing, raced 6** to take part in a contest of speed with (someone). **7** to enter (an animal or vehicle) in a race: *to race greyhounds.* **8** to travel as fast as possible. **9** (of an engine) to run faster than normal. **10** (of the heart) to beat faster than normal. ✧ See also **races**. ▷ **HISTORY** Old Norse *rās* running ▶ **racer** *n* ▶ **racing** *adj, n*
race[2] *n* **1** a group of people of common ancestry with distinguishing physical features, such as skin colour or build. **2 the human race** human beings collectively. **3** a group of animals or plants having common characteristics that distinguish them from other members of the same species. ▷ **HISTORY** Italian *razza*
race caller *n Austral & NZ* a professional horse-racing commentator.
racecourse *n* a long broad track on which horses are raced.
racehorse *n* a horse specially bred for racing.
raceme (rass-**eem**) *n Bot* a cluster of flowers along a central stem, as in the foxglove. ▷ **HISTORY** Latin *racemus* bunch of grapes
race relations *pl n* the relations between members of two or more races within a single community.
race riot *n* a riot involving violence between people of different races.
races *pl n* **the races** a series of contests of speed between horses or greyhounds over a fixed course.
racetrack *n* **1** a circuit used for races between cars, bicycles, or runners. **2** *US & Canad* a racecourse.
racial *adj* **1** relating to the division of the human species into races. **2** typically associated with any such group. ▶ **racially** *adv*
racism *or* **racialism** *n* **1** hostile or oppressive behaviour towards people because they belong to a different race. **2** the belief that some races are innately superior to others because of hereditary characteristics. ▶ **racist** *or* **racialist** *n, adj*
rack[1] *n* **1** a framework for holding particular articles, such as coats or luggage. **2** a straight bar with teeth on its edge, to work with a cogwheel. **3 the rack** *History* an instrument of torture that stretched the body of the victim. ✧ *vb* **4** to cause great suffering to: *Germany was racked by food riots.* **5 rack one's brains** to try very hard to think of something. ▷ **HISTORY** probably from Middle Dutch *rec* framework

> **☑ WORD TIP**
> See at **wrack**[1].

rack[2] *n* **go to rack and ruin** to be destroyed through neglect. ▷ **HISTORY** variant of WRACK[1]
rack[3] *vb* to clear (wine or beer) by siphoning it off from the dregs.
rack[4] *n* the neck or rib part of a joint of meat.
rack-and-pinion *n* a device for converting rotary into linear motion and vice versa, in which a gearwheel (the pinion) engages with a flat toothed bar (the rack).
racket[1] *n* **1** a noisy disturbance. **2** an illegal activity done to make money. **3** *Slang* a business or occupation: *I've been in the racket since I was sixteen.* ✧ *vb* **-eting, -eted 4** to make a commotion. ▷ **HISTORY** probably imitative ▶ **rackety** *adj*
racket[2] *or* **racquet** *n* a bat consisting of an oval frame surrounding a mesh of strings, with a handle, used in tennis, badminton, and squash. ✧ See also **rackets**. ▷ **HISTORY** French *raquette*
racketeer *n* a person who makes money from illegal activities. ▶ **racketeering** *n*

rackets *n* a game similar to squash, played by two or four people.

raconteur (rak-on-**tur**) *n* a person skilled in telling stories. ▷ HISTORY French

racoon *n, pl* **-coons** *or* **-coon** same as **raccoon**.

racquet *n* same as **racket²**.

racy *adj* **racier, raciest 1** slightly shocking. **2** spirited or lively. ▶ **racily** *adv* ▶ **raciness** *n*

rad radian.

RADA (in Britain) Royal Academy of Dramatic Art.

radar *n* **1** a method of detecting the position and velocity of a distant object by bouncing a narrow beam of extremely high-frequency radio pulses off it. **2** the equipment used in this. ▷ HISTORY *ra(dio) d(etecting) a(nd) r(anging)*

raddle *vb* **-dling, -dled** *Austral & NZ* to mark (sheep) for identification.

raddled *adj* (of a person) untidy or run-down in appearance. ▷ HISTORY from *rud* red ochre

radial *adj* **1** spreading out from a common central point. **2** of a radius or ray. **3** short for **radial-ply**. **4** *Anat* of the forearm: *a radial nerve.* ✧ *n* **5** a radial-ply tyre. ▶ **radially** *adv*

radial-ply *adj* (of a tyre) having the fabric cords in the outer casing running radially to enable the sidewalls to be flexible.

radian *n* an SI unit of plane angle; the angle between two radii of a circle that cut off on the circumference an arc equal in length to the radius.

radiant *adj* **1** characterized by health and happiness: *radiant good looks.* **2** shining. **3** emitted as radiation: *radiant heat.* **4** sending out heat by radiation: *radiant heaters.* ▷ HISTORY Latin *radiare* to shine ▶ **radiance** *n* ▶ **radiantly** *adv*

radiant energy *n* energy that is emitted or propagated in the form of particles or electromagnetic radiation.

radiate *vb* **-ating, -ated 1** to spread out from a central point. **2** to show (an emotion or quality) to a great degree: *she radiated competence and composure.* **3** to emit or be emitted as radiation. ✧ *adj* **4** having rays or a radial structure. ▷ HISTORY Latin *radiare* to emit rays

radiation *n* **1** *Physics* **a** the emission of energy as particles, electromagnetic waves or sound. **b** the particles or waves emitted. **2** the process of radiating.

radiation sickness *n* illness caused by overexposure to radioactive material or X-rays.

radiator *n* **1** *Brit* a device for heating a room or building, consisting of a series of pipes containing hot water. **2** a device for cooling an internal-combustion engine, consisting of thin-walled tubes containing water. **3** *Austral & NZ* an electric fire.

radical *adj* **1** favouring fundamental change in political or social conditions: *a radical student movement.* **2** of the essential nature of a person or thing; fundamental: *a radical fault.* **3** searching or thorough: *a radical interpretation.* **4** *Maths* of or containing roots of numbers or quantities. ✧ *n* **5** a person who favours fundamental change in existing institutions or in political, social, or economic conditions. **6** *Maths* a root of a number or quantity, such as $\sqrt[3]{5}$, $\sqrt{x}$. **7** *Chem* an atom or group of atoms which acts as a unit during chemical reactions. ▷ HISTORY Latin *radix* a root ▶ **radicalism** *n* ▶ **radically** *adv*

radical sign *n* the symbol √ placed before a number or quantity to indicate the extraction of a root, esp. a square root. The value of a higher root is indicated by a raised digit in front of the symbol, as in $\sqrt[3]{}$.

radicchio (rad-**deek**-ee-oh) *n, pl* **-chios** an Italian variety of chicory, with purple leaves streaked with white that are eaten raw in salads.

radicle *n Bot* **a** the part of the embryo of seed-bearing plants that develops into the main root. **b** a very small root or rootlike part. ▷ HISTORY Latin *radix* root

radii *n* a plural of **radius**.

radio *n, pl* **-dios 1** the use of electromagnetic waves for broadcasting or two-way communication without the use of linking wires. **2** an electronic device for converting radio signals into sounds. **3** a communications device for sending and receiving messages using radio waves. **4** sound broadcasting. ✧ *vb* **5** to transmit (a message) by radio. ✧ *adj* **6** of, relating to, or using radio broadcasting or radio signals: *a radio interview.* **7** using or producing electromagnetic waves in the range used for radio signals: *radio astronomy.* ▷ HISTORY Latin *radius* ray

radio- *combining form* denoting: **1** radio. **2** radioactivity or radiation: *radiocarbon.*

radioactive *adj* showing or using radioactivity.

radioactivity *n* the spontaneous emission of radiation from atomic nuclei. The radiation can consist of alpha or beta particles, or gamma rays.

radio astronomy *n* astronomy using a radio telescope to analyse signals received from radio sources in space.

radiocarbon *n* a radioactive isotope of carbon, esp. carbon-14.

radiocarbon dating *n* same as **carbon dating**.

radiochemistry *n* the chemistry of radioactive substances.

radio-controlled *adj* controlled by signals sent by radio.

radio frequency *n* any electromagnetic frequency that lies in the range 10 kilohertz to 300,000 megahertz and can be used for broadcasting.

radiogram *n Brit* an old-fashioned combined radio and record player.

radiograph *n* an image produced on a special photographic film or plate by radiation, usually by X-rays.

radiography (ray-dee-**og**-ra-fee) *n* the production of radiographs for use in medicine or industry. ▶ **radiographer** *n*

radioisotope *n* a radioactive isotope.

radiology (ray-dee-**ol**-a-jee) *n* the use of X-rays and radioactive substances in the diagnosis and treatment of disease. ▶ **radiologist** *n*

A B C D E F G H I J K L M N O P Q R S T U V W X Y Z

radioscopy (ray-dee-**oss**-kop-ee) *n* examination of a person or object by means of a fluorescent screen and an X-ray source.

radiosonde *n* an airborne instrument to send meteorological information back to earth by radio. ▷ **HISTORY** RADIO- + French *sonde* sounding line

radiotelegraphy *n* telegraphy in which messages are transmitted by radio waves.

radiotelephone *n* a telephone which sends and receives messages using radio waves rather than wires. ▶ **radiotelephony** *n*

radio telescope *n* an instrument used in radio astronomy to pick up and analyse radio waves from space.

radiotherapy *n* the treatment of disease, esp. cancer, by radiation.

radish *n* a small hot-flavoured red root vegetable eaten raw in salads. ▷ **HISTORY** Latin *radix* root

radium *n Chem* a highly radioactive luminescent metallic element, found in pitchblende. Symbol: Ra. ▷ **HISTORY** Latin *radius* ray

radius (**ray**-dee-uss) *n, pl* **-dii** (-dee-eye) *or* **-diuses 1** a straight line joining the centre of a circle to any point on the circumference. **2** the length of this line. **3** *Anat* the outer, slightly shorter of the two bones of the forearm. **4** a circular area of a specified size round a central point: *within a seven-mile radius of the club.* ▷ **HISTORY** Latin: ray, spoke

radon (**ray**-don) *n Chem* a colourless radioactive element of the noble gas group. Symbol: Rn. ▷ **HISTORY** from *radium*

RAF (in Britain) Royal Air Force.

Rafferty *or* **Rafferty's rules** *pl n Austral & NZ slang* no rules at all. ▷ **HISTORY** origin unknown

raffia *n* a fibre obtained from the leaves of a palm tree, used for weaving. ▷ **HISTORY** Malagasy

raffish *adj* unconventional or slightly disreputable. ▷ **HISTORY** obsolete *raff* rubbish

raffle *n* **1** a lottery, often to raise money for charity, in which the prizes are goods rather than money. ✧ *vb* **-fling, -fled 2** to offer as a prize in a raffle. ▷ **HISTORY** Old French

raft *n* a floating platform of logs or planks tied together. ▷ **HISTORY** Old Norse *raptr* rafter

rafter *n* any of the parallel sloping beams that form the framework of a roof. ▷ **HISTORY** Old English

rag[1] *n* **1** a small piece of cloth. **2** *Brit, Austral & NZ informal* a newspaper. **3 rags** old tattered clothing. **4 from rags to riches** from being extremely poor to being extremely wealthy. ▷ **HISTORY** probably formed from *ragged,* from Old English *raggig*

rag[2] *Brit* ✧ *vb* **ragging, ragged 1** to tease. **2** to play rough practical jokes on. ✧ *n* **3** a boisterous practical joke. ✧ *adj* **4** (in British universities and colleges) of various events organized to raise money for charity: *a rag week.* ▷ **HISTORY** origin unknown

rag[3] *n* a piece of ragtime music.

ragamuffin *n* a ragged dirty child. ▷ **HISTORY** probably from RAG[1]

ragbag *n* a confused mixture: *the traditional ragbag of art traders.*

rage *n* **1** intense anger or passion. **2** a fashion or craze: *the dance was the rage of Europe.* **3** aggressive behaviour associated with a specified activity or environment: *road rage; school rage.* **4 all the rage** *Informal* very popular. **5** *Austral & NZ informal* a dance or party. ✧ *vb* **raging, raged 6** to feel or show intense anger. **7** to proceed violently and without restraint: *the argument was still raging.* ▷ **HISTORY** Latin *rabies* madness

ragged (**rag**-gid) *adj* **1** dressed in shabby or torn clothes. **2** (of clothes) tattered and torn. **3** having a rough or uneven surface or edge. **4** neglected or untidy: *the ragged stone-built village.*

ragged robin *n* a plant that has pink or white flowers with ragged petals.

raglan *adj* **1** (of a sleeve) joined to the garment by diagonal seams from the collar to the underarm. **2** (of a garment) with this style of sleeve. ▷ **HISTORY** after Lord *Raglan*

ragout (rag-**goo**) *n* a richly seasoned stew of meat and vegetables. ▷ **HISTORY** French

ragtime *n* a style of jazz piano music with a syncopated melody. ▷ **HISTORY** probably *ragged time*

rag trade *n Brit, Austral & NZ informal* the clothing business.

ragwort *n* a plant with ragged leaves and yellow flowers.

raid *n* **1** a sudden surprise attack: *a bombing raid.* **2** a surprise visit by police searching for people or goods: *a drugs raid.* ✧ *vb* **3** to make a raid on. **4** to sneak into (a place) in order to steal. ▷ **HISTORY** Old English *rād* military expedition ▶ **raider** *n*

rail[1] *n* **1** a horizontal bar supported by vertical posts, used as a fence or barrier. **2** a horizontal bar on which to hang things: *a curtain rail.* **3** one of a pair of parallel bars that serve as a running surface for the wheels of a train. **4** railway: *by car or by rail.* **5 go off the rails** to start behaving improperly or eccentrically. ✧ *vb* **6** to fence (an area) with rails. ▷ **HISTORY** Old French *raille* rod

rail[2] *vb* **rail against** *or* **at** to complain bitterly or loudly about. ▷ **HISTORY** Old French *railler* to mock

rail[3] *n* a small wading marsh bird. ▷ **HISTORY** Old French *raale*

railcard *n Brit* an identity card, which pensioners or young people can buy, entitling them to cheaper rail travel.

railhead *n* **1** a terminal of a railway. **2** the farthest point reached by completed track on an unfinished railway.

railing *n* a fence made of rails supported by posts.

raillery *n, pl* **-leries** good-natured teasing. ▷ **HISTORY** French *railler* to tease

railroad *n* **1** *US* a railway. ✧ *vb* **2** *Informal* to force (a person) into an action with haste or by unfair means.

railway *n* **1** a track composed of a line of parallel metal rails fixed to sleepers, on which trains run. **2** any track on which the wheels of a vehicle may run: *a cable railway.* **3** the rolling stock, buildings, and tracks used in such a transport system. **4** the organization responsible for operating a railway network.

raiment *n Archaic or poetic* clothing. ▷ HISTORY from *arrayment*

rain *n* **1 a** water falling from the sky in drops formed by the condensation of water vapour in the atmosphere. **b** a fall of rain. *RELATED ADJECTIVE* ▸ **pluvial 2** a large quantity of anything falling rapidly: *a rain of stones descended on the police.* **3 (come) rain or shine** regardless of circumstances. **4 right as rain** *Informal* perfectly all right. ✧ *vb* **5** to fall as rain: *it's raining back home.* **6** to fall rapidly and in large quantities: *steel rungs and sawdust raining down.* **7 rained off** cancelled or postponed because of rain. US and Canad term: **rained out** ✧ See also **rains**. ▷ HISTORY Old English *regn* ▸ **rainy** *adj*

rainbird *n S African* a common name for **Burchell's coucal**, a bird whose call is believed to be a sign of impending rain.

rainbow *n* an arched display in the sky of the colours of the spectrum, caused by the refraction and reflection of the sun's rays through rain.

rainbow nation *n* the South African nation.

rainbow trout *n* a freshwater trout with black spots and two red stripes.

raincoat *n* a coat made of a waterproof material.

rainfall *n* the amount of rain, hail, or snow in a specified place and time.

rainforest *n* dense forest found in tropical areas of heavy rainfall.

rain gauge *n Meteorol* an instrument for measuring rainfall or snowfall, consisting of a cylinder covered by a funnel-like lid.

rains *pl n* **the rains** the season in the tropics when there is a lot of rain.

rain shadow *n Meteorol* the relatively dry area on the leeward side of high ground in the path of rain-bearing winds.

rainstorm *n* a storm with heavy rain.

rainwater *n* water from rain.

rainy day *n* a future time of need, esp. financial need.

raise *vb* **raising, raised 1** to lift to a higher position or level. **2** to place in an upright position. **3** to increase in amount, quality, or intensity: *to raise interest rates.* **4** to collect or gather together: *to raise additional capital; to raise an army.* **5** to cause to be expressed: *to raise a smile.* **6** to stir up. **7** to bring up: *to raise a family.* **8** to grow: *to raise a crop.* **9** to put forward for consideration: *they raised controversial issues.* **10** to arouse from sleep or death. **11** to build: *to raise a barn.* **12** to bring to an end: *to raise a siege.* **13** to establish radio communications with: *we raised Moscow last night.* **14** to advance in rank; promote. **15** *Maths* to multiply (a number) by itself a specified number of times: *8 is 2 raised to the power 3.* **16** to cause (dough) to rise, as by the addition of yeast. **17** *Cards* to bet more than (the previous player). **18 raise Cain a** to create a disturbance. **b** to protest vehemently. ✧ *n* **19** *US, Canad & NZ* an increase in pay. ▷ HISTORY Old Norse *reisa*

raised *adj* higher than the surrounding area: *a small raised platform.*

raised beach *n Geog* a wave-cut platform raised above the shoreline by a relative fall in the water level.

raisin *n* a dried grape. ▷ HISTORY Old French: grape

raison d'être (**ray**-zon **det**-ra) *n, pl* **raisons d'être** (**ray**-zon **det**-ra) reason or justification for existence. ▷ HISTORY French

raita (**rye**-ta) *n* an Indian dish of chopped cucumber, mint, etc., in yogurt, served with curry. ▷ HISTORY Hindi

Raj *n* **the Raj** the British government in India before 1947. ▷ HISTORY Hindi

raja *or* **rajah** *n History* an Indian prince or ruler. ▷ HISTORY Hindi

rake[1] *n* **1** a farm or garden tool consisting of a row of teeth set in a headpiece attached to a long shaft and used for gathering leaves or straw, or for smoothing loose earth. **2** any of various implements similar in shape or function. ✧ *vb* **raking, raked 3** to scrape or gather with a rake. **4** to smooth (a surface) with a rake. **5** Also: **rake out** to clear (ashes) from (a fire). **6 rake together** *or* **up** to gather (items or people) with difficulty, as from a limited supply. **7** to search or examine carefully: *raking over the past is not always popular.* **8** to direct (gunfire) along the length of (a target): *the machine guns raked up and down their line.* **9** to scrape or graze: *he raked the tip of his shoe across the pavement.* ✧ See also **rake-off**. ▷ HISTORY Old English *raca*

rake[2] *n* an immoral man. ▷ HISTORY short for *rakehell*

rake[3] *n* **1** the degree to which an object slopes. ✧ *vb* **raking, raked 2** to slope from the vertical, esp. (of a ship's mast) towards the stern. **3** to construct with a backward slope. ▷ HISTORY origin unknown

raked *adj* (of a surface) sloping so that it is higher at the back than at the front.

rake-off *n Slang* a share of profits, esp. an illegal one.

rake up *vb* to bring back memories of (a forgotten unpleasant event): *she doesn't want to rake up the past.*

rakish[1] (**ray**-kish) *adj* dashing or jaunty: *a hat which he wore at a rakish angle.* ▷ HISTORY probably from RAKE[3]

rakish[2] *adj* immoral: *a rakish life of drinking and womanizing.* ▷ HISTORY from RAKE[2] ▸ **rakishly** *adv*

rallentando *Music* ✧ *adj, adv* **1** becoming slower. ✧ *n* **2** a passage in which the music becomes slower. ▷ HISTORY Italian

rally[1] *n, pl* **-lies 1** a large gathering of people for a meeting. **2** a marked recovery of strength, as during illness. **3** *Stock Exchange* a sharp increase in price or trading activity after a decline. **4** *Tennis, squash, etc.* an exchange of several shots before one player wins the point. **5** a car-driving competition on public roads. ✧ *vb* **-lies, -lying, -lied 6** to bring or come together after being dispersed. **7** to bring or come together for a common cause. **8** to summon up (one's strength or spirits). **9** to recover (sometimes only temporarily) from an illness. **10** *Stock Exchange* to increase sharply after a decline. ▷ HISTORY Old French *rallier*

rally² *vb* **-lies, -lying, -lied** to mock or tease (someone) in a good-natured way. ▷ HISTORY Old French *railler* to tease

rally round *vb* to group together to help someone.

ram *n* **1** an uncastrated adult male sheep. **2** a hydraulically or pneumatically driven piston. **3** the falling weight of a pile driver. **4** short for **battering ram.** ✧ *vb* **ramming, rammed 5** to strike against with force. **6** to force or drive: *he rammed his sword into the man's belly.* **7** to stuff or cram. **8 ram something home** to make something clear or obvious: *to ram home the message.* **9 ram something down someone's throat** to put forward or emphasize an argument or idea with excessive force. ▷ HISTORY Old English *ramm*

RAM *Computers* random access memory: a temporary storage space which loses its contents when the computer is switched off.

Rama *n* a Hindu god, the incarnation of Vishnu.

Ramadan *n* **1** the ninth month of the Muslim year, 30 days long, during which strict fasting is observed from sunrise to sunset. **2** the fast itself.

ramble *vb* **-bling, -bled 1** to walk for relaxation, sometimes with no particular direction. **2** to speak or write in a confused style. **3** to grow or develop in a random fashion. ✧ *n* **4** a walk, esp. in the countryside. ▷ HISTORY Middle English *romblen*

rambler *n* **1** a person who takes country walks. **2** a climbing rose.

rambling *adj* **1** long and irregularly shaped: *a rambling 14th-century church.* **2** (of speech or writing) confused and long-winded. ✧ *n* **3** the activity of going for long walks in the country.

RAMC Royal Army Medical Corps.

ramekin (**ram**-ik-in) *n* a small container for baking and serving one portion of food. ▷ HISTORY French *ramequin*

ramification *n* **1 ramifications** the consequences or complications resulting from an action. **2** a structure of branching parts.

ramp *n* **1** a slope that joins two surfaces at different levels. **2** a place where the level of a road surface changes because of road works. **3** a movable stairway by which passengers enter and leave an aircraft. **4** *Brit* a small hump on a road to make traffic slow down. ▷ HISTORY Old French *ramper* to crawl, rear

rampage *vb* **-paging, -paged 1** to rush about violently. ✧ *n* **2 on the rampage** behaving violently or destructively. ▷ HISTORY Scots

rampant *adj* **1** growing or spreading uncontrollably. **2** *Heraldry* (of a beast) standing on the hind legs, the right foreleg raised above the left: *a lion rampant.* ▷ HISTORY Old French *ramper* to crawl, rear

rampart *n* a mound of earth or wall built to protect a fort or city. ▷ HISTORY Old French

ram raid *n Informal* a raid on a shop in which a stolen car is driven into the window. ▶ **ram raider** *n*

ramrod *n* **1** a long thin rod for cleaning the barrel of a gun or forcing gunpowder into an old-fashioned gun. ✧ *adj* **2** (of someone's posture) very straight and upright.

ramshackle *adj* badly made or cared for: *a curious ramshackle building.* ▷ HISTORY obsolete *ransackle* to ransack

ran *vb* the past tense of **run**.

RAN Royal Australian Navy.

ranch *n* **1** a large cattle farm in the American West. **2** *Chiefly US & Canad* a large farm for the rearing of a particular kind of livestock or crop: *he owned a yak ranch in Tibet.* ✧ *vb* **3** to run a ranch. ▷ HISTORY Mexican Spanish *rancho* small farm ▶ **rancher** *n*

ranchslider *n NZ* a glazed sliding door usually opening onto an outside terrace.

rancid *adj* (of fatty foods) stale and having an offensive smell. ▷ HISTORY Latin *rancidus* ▶ **rancidity** *n*

rancour *or US* **rancor** *n* deep bitter hate. ▷ HISTORY Old French ▶ **rancorous** *adj*

rand *n* the standard monetary unit of the Republic of South Africa. ▷ HISTORY from *Witwatersrand,* S Transvaal, referring to the gold-mining there

R & B rhythm and blues.

R & D research and development.

random *adj* **1** lacking any definite plan or prearranged order: *a random sample.* ✧ *n* **2 at random** not following any prearranged order. ▷ HISTORY Old French *randir* to gallop ▶ **randomly** *adv* ▶ **randomness** *n*

random access *n* a method of reading data from a computer file without having to read through the file from the beginning.

randy *adj* **randier, randiest** *Informal* sexually aroused. ▷ HISTORY probably from obsolete *rand* to rant ▶ **randily** *adv* ▶ **randiness** *n*

ranee *n* same as **rani**.

rang *vb* the past tense of **ring¹**.

> **☑ WORD TIP**
> See at **ring¹**.

rangatira (rung-a-**teer**-a) *n NZ* a Maori chief of either sex. ▷ HISTORY Maori

range *n* **1** the limits within which a person or thing can function effectively: *academic ability range.* **2 a** the maximum effective distance of a projectile fired from a weapon. **b** the distance between a target and a weapon. **3** the total distance which a ship, aircraft, or vehicle can travel without taking on fresh fuel. **4** the difference in pitch between the highest and lowest note of a voice or musical instrument. **5** a whole set of related things: *a range of treatments was available.* **6** the total products of a manufacturer, designer, or stockist: *the latest skin-care range.* **7** the limits

within which something can lie: *a range of prices.* **8** *US & Canad* an extensive tract of open land on which livestock can graze. **9** a chain of mountains. **10** an area set aside for shooting practice or rocket testing. **11** a large cooking stove with one or more ovens. **12** *Maths* the set of values that a function or variable can take. ✧ *vb* **ranging, ranged 13** to vary between one point and another. **14** to cover a specified period or specified things: *attitudes ranged from sympathy to indifference.* **15** to roam (over). **16** to establish or be situated in a line or series. **17** to put into a specific category: *they ranged themselves with the opposition.*
▷ **HISTORY** Old French: row

rangefinder *n* an instrument for finding how far away an object is.

ranger *n* **1** an official in charge of a park or nature reserve. **2** *US* an armed trooper employed to police a State or district: *a Texas ranger.*

Ranger *or* **Ranger Guide** *n Brit & Austral* a member of the senior branch of the Guides.

rangy (**rain**-jee) *adj* **rangier, rangiest** having long slender limbs.

rani *or* **ranee** *n* the wife or widow of a raja.
▷ **HISTORY** Hindi

rank[1] *n* **1** a position within a social organization: *the rank of superintendent.* **2** high social or other standing: *accusations were made against people of high rank.* **3** a person's social class: *it was too grand for someone of his lowly rank.* **4** the position of an item in any ordering or sequence. **5** a line or row of people or things. **6** *Brit, NZ & S African* a place where taxis wait to be hired. **7** a line of people, esp. soldiers, positioned one beside the other. **8** any of the eight horizontal rows of squares on a chessboard. **9 close ranks** to maintain solidarity. **10 pull rank** to get one's own way by virtue of one's superior position. **11 rank and file** the ordinary people or members of a group. **12 the ranks** the common soldiers. ✧ *vb* **13** to give or hold a specific position in an organization or group. **14** to arrange in rows or lines. **15** to arrange in sequence: *it ranks a lowly 19th worldwide.* **16** to be important: *the legendary coronation stone ranks high in the hearts of patriots.* ▷ **HISTORY** Old French *ranc*

rank[2] *adj* **1** complete or absolute: *rank incompetence.* **2** smelling offensively strong. **3** growing too quickly: *rank weeds.* ▷ **HISTORY** Old English *ranc* straight, proud

rankle *vb* **-kling, -kled** to continue to cause resentment or bitterness. ▷ **HISTORY** Old French *draoncle* ulcer

rank-size rule *n Geog, sociology* the theory proposed by George Zipf in 1949 according to which a country's second city will be half the size of its primate city while its third major city will be a third of its size, and so on.

ransack *vb* **1** to search through every part of (a place or thing). **2** to plunder or pillage.
▷ **HISTORY** Old Norse *rann* house + *saka* to search

ransom *n* **1** the money demanded in return for the release of someone who has been kidnapped. **2 hold to ransom a** to keep (a prisoner) in confinement until payment is received. **b** to attempt to force (a person) to do something. ✧ *vb* **3** to pay money to obtain the release of (a prisoner). **4** to set free (a prisoner) in return for money.
▷ **HISTORY** Old French *ransoun* ▶ **ransomer** *n*

rant *vb* **1** to talk in a loud and excited way. ✧ *n* **2** loud excited speech. ▷ **HISTORY** Dutch *ranten* to rave ▶ **ranting** *adj, n*

ranunculus *n, pl* **-luses** *or* **-li** a genus of plants including the buttercup. ▷ **HISTORY** Latin *rana* frog

RAOC Royal Army Ordnance Corps.

rap[1] *vb* **rapping, rapped 1** to hit with a sharp quick blow. **2** to knock loudly and sharply. **3 rap out** to utter in sharp rapid speech: *he rapped out his address.* **4** to perform a rhythmic monologue with musical backing. **5** *Slang* to talk in a relaxed and friendly way. **6** to rebuke or criticize sharply. **7 rap over the knuckles** to reprimand. ✧ *n* **8** a sharp quick blow or the sound produced by it. **9** a fast rhythmic monologue over a musical backing. **10** a sharp rebuke or criticism. **11** *Slang* a legal charge: *a murder rap.* **12 take the rap** *Slang* to suffer the punishment for a crime, whether guilty or not.
▷ **HISTORY** probably from Old Norse ▶ **rapper** *n*

rap[2] *n* **not care a rap** to not care in the least: *she didn't care a rap for us.* ▷ **HISTORY** probably from *ropaire,* counterfeit coin formerly current in Ireland

rapacious *adj* **1** greedy or grasping. **2** (of animals or birds) living by catching prey.
▷ **HISTORY** Latin *rapax* ▶ **rapacity** *n*

rape[1] *vb* **raping, raped 1** to force (someone) to submit to sexual intercourse. ✧ *n* **2** the act of raping. **3** any violation or abuse: *the rape of the country's natural resources.* ▷ **HISTORY** Latin *rapere* to seize ▶ **rapist** *n*

rape[2] *n* a yellow-flowered plant cultivated for its seeds, **rapeseed,** which yield a useful oil, **rape oil,** and as a fodder plant. ▷ **HISTORY** Latin *rapum* turnip

rapid *adj* **1** (of an action) taking or lasting a short time. **2** acting or moving quickly: *a rapid advance.*
▷ **HISTORY** Latin *rapidus* ▶ **rapidly** *adv* ▶ **rapidity** *n*

rapid eye movement *n* the movement of the eyeballs while a person is dreaming.

rapids *pl n* part of a river where the water is very fast and turbulent.

rapier (**ray**-pyer) *n* a long narrow two-edged sword. ▷ **HISTORY** Old French *espee rapiere* rasping sword

rapine (**rap**-pine) *n* pillage or plundering.
▷ **HISTORY** Latin *rapina*

rapport (rap-**pore**) *n* a sympathetic relationship or understanding. ▷ **HISTORY** French

rapprochement (rap-**prosh**-mong) *n* a re-establishment of friendly relations: *the policy of rapprochement with Eastern Europe.*
▷ **HISTORY** French

rapscallion *n Old-fashioned* a rascal or rogue.
▷ **HISTORY** earlier *rascallion*

rapt *adj* **1** totally engrossed: *rapt attention.* **2** arising from or showing rapture: *with a rapt look on his face.* ▷ **HISTORY** Latin *raptus* carried away

raptor *n* any bird of prey. ▷ **HISTORY** Latin: robber
▶ **raptorial** *adj*

A B C D E F G H I J K L M N O P Q R S T U V W X Y Z

rapture *n* **1** extreme happiness or delight. **2 raptures** ecstatic joy: *they will be in raptures over the rugged scenery.* ▷ **HISTORY** Latin *raptus* carried away ▶ **rapturous** *adj*

rare¹ *adj* **1** uncommon or unusual: *a rare plant.* **2** not happening or done very often: *a rare appearance in London.* **3** of uncommonly high quality: *a rare beauty.* **4** (of air at high altitudes) having low density; thin. ▷ **HISTORY** Latin *rarus* sparse

rare² *adj* (of meat) very lightly cooked. ▷ **HISTORY** Old English *hrēr*

rarebit *n* short for **Welsh rarebit**.

rare earth *n Chem* **1** any oxide of a lanthanide. **2** Also called: **rare-earth element** any element of the lanthanide series.

rarefied (**rare**-if-ide) *adj* **1** highly specialized: *the rarefied world of classical ballet.* **2** (of air) thin. **3** exalted in character: *the rarefied heights of academic excellence.*

rarely *adv* **1** hardly ever. **2** to an unusual degree; exceptionally.

> **☑ WORD TIP**
> Since *rarely* means *hardly ever,* one should not say something *rarely ever* happens.

raring *adj* **raring to do something** keen and willing to do something. ▷ **HISTORY** *rare,* variant of REAR²

rarity *n, pl* **-ties 1** something that is valuable because it is unusual. **2** the state of being rare.

rascal *n* **1** a scoundrel or rogue. **2** a mischievous child. ▷ **HISTORY** Old French *rascaille* rabble ▶ **rascally** *adj*

rase *vb* **rasing, rased** same as **raze**.

rash¹ *adj* acting or done without proper thought or consideration; hasty: *rash actions.* ▷ **HISTORY** Old High German *rasc* hurried, clever ▶ **rashly** *adv* ▶ **rashness** *n*

rash² *n* **1** an outbreak of spots or patches on the skin, caused by illness or allergy. **2** an outbreak of occurrences: *a rash of censorship trials.* ▷ **HISTORY** Old French *rasche*

rasher *n* a thin slice of bacon. ▷ **HISTORY** origin unknown

rasp *n* **1** a harsh grating noise. **2** a coarse file with rows of raised teeth. ✧ *vb* **3** to say or speak in a grating voice. **4** to make a harsh grating noise. **5** to scrape or rub (something) roughly. **6** to irritate (one's nerves). ▷ **HISTORY** Old French *raspe*

raspberry *n, pl* **-ries 1** the red fruit of a prickly shrub of Europe and North America. **2** *Informal* a spluttering noise made with the tongue and lips to express contempt: *she blew a loud raspberry.* ▷ **HISTORY** origin unknown

Rastafarian *or* **Rasta** *n* **1** a believer in a religion of Jamaican origin that regards Ras Tafari, the former emperor of Ethiopia, Haile Selassie, as God. ✧ *adj* **2** of Rastafarians.

rat *n* **1** a long-tailed rodent, similar to but larger than a mouse. **2** *Informal* someone who is disloyal or treacherous. **3 smell a rat** to detect something suspicious. ✧ *vb* **ratting, ratted 4 rat on a** to betray (someone): *good friends don't rat on each other.* **b** to go back on (an agreement): *his ex-wife claims he ratted on their divorce settlement.* **5** to hunt and kill rats. ▷ **HISTORY** Old English *ræt*

ratafia (rat-a-**fee**-a) *n* **1** a liqueur made from fruit. **2** *Chiefly Brit* an almond-flavoured biscuit. ▷ **HISTORY** West Indian Creole French

rat-arsed *adj Brit & Austral slang* drunk.

ratatouille (rat-a-**twee**) *n* a vegetable casserole made of stewed tomatoes, aubergines, etc. ▷ **HISTORY** French

ratchet *n* **1** a device in which a toothed rack or wheel is engaged by a pivoted lever which permits motion in one direction only. **2** the toothed rack or wheel in such a device. ▷ **HISTORY** French *rochet*

rate¹ *n* **1** a quantity or amount considered in relation to or measured against another quantity or amount: *he was publishing at the rate of about 10 books a year.* **2** a price or charge with reference to a standard or scale: *an exchange rate.* **3** the speed of progress or change: *crime is increasing at an alarming rate.* **4** a charge made per unit for a commodity or service. **5** See **rates**. **6** relative quality: *a third-rate power.* **7 at any rate** in any case. ✧ *vb* **rating, rated 8** to assign a position on a scale of relative values: *he is rated as one of the top caterers in the country.* **9** to estimate the value of: *we rate your services highly.* **10** to consider or regard: *it could hardly be rated a success.* **11** to be worthy of: *it barely rates a mention.* **12** *Informal* to have a high opinion of: *the cognoscenti have always rated his political skills.* ▷ **HISTORY** Medieval Latin *rata*

rate² *vb* **rating, rated** to scold or criticize severely. ▷ **HISTORY** origin unknown

rateable *adj* **1** able to be rated or evaluated. **2** liable to payment of rates.

ratepayer *n* a person who pays local rates on a building.

rates *pl n* (in some countries) a tax on property levied by a local authority.

rather *adv* **1** fairly: *that was a rather narrow escape.* **2** to a limited extent: *I rather thought that was the case.* **3** more truly or appropriately: *they tend to be cat rather than dog people.* **4** more willingly: *I would rather go straight home.* ✧ *interj* **5** an expression of strong affirmation: *Is it worth seeing? Rather!* ▷ **HISTORY** Old English *hrathor,* comparative of *hrathe* ready, quick

> **☑ WORD TIP**
> Both *would* and *had* are used with *rather* in sentences such as *I would rather* (or *had rather*) *go to the film than to the play. Had rather* is less common and now widely regarded as slightly old-fashioned.

ratify *vb* **-fies, -fying, -fied** to give formal approval to. ▷ **HISTORY** Latin *ratus* fixed + *facere* to make ▶ **ratification** *n*

rating *n* **1** a valuation or assessment. **2** a classification according to order or grade. **3** a noncommissioned sailor. **4 ratings** the size of the audience for a television or radio programme.

ratio *n, pl* **-tios 1** the relationship between two numbers or amounts expressed as a proportion: *a ratio of one instructor to every five pupils.* **2** *Maths* a quotient of two numbers or quantities. ▷ HISTORY Latin: a reckoning

ratio decidendi *n Law* the legal principle on which a particular judicial decision is based. ▷ HISTORY Latin: reason for deciding

ration *n* **1** a fixed allowance of something that is scarce, such as food or petrol in wartime. **2 rations** a fixed daily allowance of food, such as that given to a soldier. ✧ *vb* **3** to restrict the distribution of (something): *the government has rationed petrol.* **4** to distribute a fixed amount of something to (each person in a group). ▷ HISTORY Latin *ratio* reckoning ▸ **rationing** *n*

rational *adj* **1** reasonable or sensible. **2** using reason or logic in thinking out a problem. **3** capable of reasoning: *man is a rational being.* **4** sane: *rational behaviour.* **5** *Maths* able to be expressed as a ratio of two integers: *a rational number.* ▷ HISTORY Latin *rationalis* ▸ **rationality** *n* ▸ **rationally** *adv*

rationale (rash-a-**nahl**) *n* the reason for an action or belief.

rationalism *n* the philosophy that regards reason as the only basis for beliefs or actions. ▸ **rationalist** *n* ▸ **rationalistic** *adj*

rationalize *or* **-ise** *vb* **-izing, -ized** *or* **-ising, -ised 1** to find reasons to justify or explain (one's actions). **2** to apply logic or reason to (something). **3** to get rid of unnecessary equipment or staff to make (a business) more efficient. ▸ **rationalization** *or* **-isation** *n*

rational number *n* any real number that can be expressed in the form *a/b*, where *a* and *b* are integers and *b* is not zero, as 7 or $^7/_3$.

ratpack *n Slang* the members of the press who pursue celebrities and give wide coverage of their private lives: *the royal ratpack.*

rat race *n* a continual routine of hectic competitive activity: *get out of the rat race for a while.*

rattan *n* a climbing palm with tough stems used for wickerwork and canes. ▷ HISTORY Malay *rōtan*

rattle *vb* **-tling, -tled 1** to make a rapid succession of short sharp sounds, such as when loose pellets are shaken in a container. **2** to send, move, or drive with such a sound: *rain rattled against the window.* **3** to shake briskly causing sharp sounds. **4** *Informal* to frighten or confuse. **5 rattle off** *or* **out** to recite perfunctorily or rapidly. **6 rattle on** *or* **away** to talk quickly and at length about something unimportant. **7 rattle through** to do (something) very quickly: *she rattled through a translation.* ✧ *n* **8** a rapid succession of short sharp sounds. **9** a baby's toy filled with small pellets that rattle when shaken. ▷ HISTORY Middle Dutch *ratelen* ▸ **rattly** *adj*

rattlesnake *n* a poisonous snake with loose horny segments on the tail that make a rattling sound.

rattling *adv Informal, old-fashioned* very: *a rattling good yarn.*

ratty *adj* **-tier, -tiest 1** *Informal* cross and irritable. **2** *Informal* (of the hair) straggly and greasy. ▸ **rattily** *adv* ▸ **rattiness** *n*

raucous *adj* loud and harsh. ▷ HISTORY Latin *raucus*

raunchy *adj* **-chier, -chiest** *Slang* sexy or earthy. ▷ HISTORY origin unknown

ravage *vb* **-aging, -aged 1** to cause extensive damage to. ✧ *n* **2 ravages** the damaging effects: *the ravages of weather and pollution.* ▷ HISTORY Old French *ravir* to snatch away

rave *vb* **raving, raved 1** to talk in a wild or incoherent manner. **2** *Informal* to write or speak (about) with great enthusiasm. ✧ *n* **3** *Informal* an enthusiastically favourable review. **4** *Slang* a professionally organized large-scale party with electronic dance music. **5** a name given to various types of dance music, such as techno, that feature a fast electronic rhythm. ▷ HISTORY probably from Old French *resver* to wander

ravel *vb* **-elling, -elled** *or US* **-eling, -eled 1** to tangle or become entangled. **2** (of a fabric) to fray out in loose ends; unravel. ▷ HISTORY Middle Dutch *ravelen*

raven *n* **1** a large bird of the crow family with shiny black feathers. ✧ *adj* **2** (of hair) shiny black. ▷ HISTORY Old English *hrǣfn*

ravening *adj* (of animals) hungrily searching for prey.

ravenous *adj* **1** very hungry. **2** ravening. ▷ HISTORY Old French *ravineux* ▸ **ravenously** *adv*

raver *n Slang* **1** *Brit, Austral & S African* a person who leads a wild or uninhibited social life. **2** a person who enjoys rave music and goes to raves.

ravine (rav-**veen**) *n* a deep narrow steep-sided valley worn by a stream. ▷ HISTORY Old French: torrent

raving *adj* **1** delirious. **2** *Informal* great or exceptional: *a raving beauty.* ✧ *adv* **3** to an excessive degree: *raving mad.* ✧ *n* **4 ravings** frenzied or wildly extravagant talk.

ravioli *pl n* small squares of pasta with a savoury filling, such as meat or cheese. ▷ HISTORY Italian

ravish *vb* **1** to enrapture or delight: *tourists ravished by our brilliant costumes.* **2** *Literary* to rape. ▷ HISTORY Latin *rapere* to seize ▸ **ravishment** *n*

ravishing *adj* lovely or delightful. ▸ **ravishingly** *adv*

raw *adj* **1** (of food) not cooked. **2** in an unfinished or unrefined state: *raw sewage.* **3** not selected or modified: *raw data.* **4** (of the skin or a wound) painful, with the surface scraped away. **5** untrained or inexperienced: *a raw recruit.* **6** (of the weather) harshly cold and damp. **7** frank or realistic: *a raw reality.* **8 raw deal** *Informal* unfair or dishonest treatment. ✧ *n* **9 in the raw a** *Informal* naked. **b** in a natural and uncivilized state: *to see life in the raw.* **10 on the raw** *Brit informal* sensitive to upset: *my nerves are on the raw today.* ▷ HISTORY Old English *hrēaw*

rawhide *n* **1** untanned hide. **2** a whip or rope made of strips of this.

a b c d e f g h i j k l m n o p q r s t u v w x y z

A B C D E F G H I J K L M N O P Q R S T U V W X Y Z

ray[1] *n* **1** a narrow beam of light. **2** any of a set of lines spreading from a central point. **3** a slight indication: *a ray of hope.* **4** *Maths* a straight line extending from a point. **5** a thin beam of electromagnetic radiation or particles. **6** any of the spines that support the fin of a fish. ▷ **HISTORY** Old French *rai*

ray[2] *n* a sea fish related to the sharks, with a flattened body and a long whiplike tail. ▷ **HISTORY** Old French *raie*

ray[3] *n Music* (in tonic sol-fa) the second note of any ascending major scale.

rayon *n* a textile fibre or fabric made from cellulose. ▷ **HISTORY** French

raze *or* **rase** *vb* **razing, razed** *or* **rasing, rased** to destroy (buildings or a town) completely. ▷ **HISTORY** Old French *raser*

razoo *n, pl* **-zoos** *Austral & NZ informal* an imaginary coin: *we haven't got a brass razoo.* ▷ **HISTORY** origin unknown

razor *n* an implement with a sharp blade, used for shaving. ▷ **HISTORY** Old French *raseor*

razorbill *n* a black-and-white sea bird with a stout sideways flattened bill.

razor shell *n* **1** a burrowing shellfish with a long narrow shell. **2** this shell.

razor wire *n* strong wire with pieces of sharp metal set across it at intervals.

razzle-dazzle *or* **razzmatazz** *n Slang* **1** noisy or showy fuss or activity. **2** a spree or frolic. ▷ **HISTORY** rhyming compound from *dazzle*

Rb *Chem* rubidium.

RC **1** Red Cross. **2** Roman Catholic.

Rd road.

re[1] *prep* with reference to. ▷ **HISTORY** Latin *res* thing

re[2] *n Music* same as **ray**[3].

Re *Chem* rhenium.

RE **1** Religious Education. **2** Royal Engineers.

re- *prefix* used with many main words to mean: **1** repetition of an action: *remarry.* **2** return to a previous condition: *renew.* ▷ **HISTORY** Latin

reach *vb* **1** to arrive at or get to (a place). **2** to make a movement (towards), as if to grasp or touch: *she reached for her bag.* **3** to succeed in touching: *I can't reach that shelf unless I stand on a chair.* **4** to make contact or communication with: *to reach a wider audience.* **5** to extend as far as (a point or place): *to reach the ceiling.* **6** to come to (a certain condition or situation): *to reach a compromise.* **7** to arrive at or amount to (an amount or value): *temperatures in Greece reached 35° yesterday.* **8** *Informal* to give (something to a person) with the outstretched hand. ✧ *n* **9** the extent or distance of reaching: *within easy reach.* **10** the range of influence or power: *it symbolized America's global reach.* **11** **reaches** a section of river, land, or sky: *the quieter reaches of the upper Thames.* ▷ **HISTORY** Old English *rǣcan* ▶ **reachable** *adj*

react *vb* **1** (of a person or thing) to act in response to another person, a stimulus, or a situation. **2** **react against** to act in an opposing or contrary manner. **3** *Chem* to undergo a chemical reaction. **4** *Physics* to exert an equal force in the opposite direction to an acting force. ▷ **HISTORY** Late Latin *reagere*

reactance *n Electricity* the resistance to the flow of an alternating current caused by the inductance or capacitance of the circuit.

reactant *n* a substance that participates in a chemical reaction.

reaction *n* **1** a physical or emotional response to a stimulus. **2** any action resisting another. **3** opposition to change. **4** *Med* any effect produced by a drug or by a substance (allergen) to which a person is allergic. **5** *Chem* a process that involves changes in the structure and energy content of atoms, molecules, or ions. **6** the equal and opposite force that acts on a body whenever it exerts a force on another body. **7** **reactions** someone's ability to act in response to something that happens.

> ☑ **WORD TIP**
> *Reaction* is used to refer both to an instant response (*her reaction was one of amazement*) and to a considered response in the form of a statement (*the Minister gave his reaction to the court's decision*). Some people think this second use is incorrect.

reactionary *adj* **1** opposed to political or social change. ✧ *n, pl* **-aries** **2** a person opposed to radical change.

reaction rate *n Physics* the rate of fission that occurs in a nuclear reactor.

reactive *adj* **1** readily taking part in chemical reactions: *ozone is a highly reactive form of oxygen gas.* **2** of or having a reactance. **3** responsive to stimulus. ▶ **reactively** *adv* ▶ **reactivity** *n*

reactor *n* short for **nuclear reactor**.

read *vb* **reading, read** **1** to look at and understand or take in (written or printed matter). **2** to look at and say aloud. **3** to have a certain wording: *the memorandum read as follows.* **4** to interpret in a specified way: *it can be read as satire.* **5** to interpret the significance or meaning of: *an astrologer who reads Tarot.* **6** to register or show: *the meter reads 100.* **7** to make out the true nature or mood of: *she had read his thoughts.* **8** to interpret (signs, characters, etc.) other than by visual means: *to read Braille.* **9** to have sufficient knowledge of (a language) to understand the written word. **10** to undertake a course of study in (a subject): *to read economics.* **11** to gain knowledge by reading: *he read about the war.* **12** to hear and understand, esp. when using a two-way radio: *we are reading you loud and clear.* **13** *Computers* to obtain (data) from a storage device, such as magnetic tape. ✧ *n* **14** matter suitable for reading: *this book is a very good read.* **15** a spell of reading. ✧ See also **read out**. ▷ **HISTORY** Old English *rǣdan* to advise, explain

readable *adj* **1** enjoyable to read. **2** (of handwriting or print) legible.

reader *n* **1** a person who reads. **2** a person who reads aloud in public. **3** a person who reads and judges manuscripts sent to a publisher. **4** a book of texts for those learning a foreign language. **5** *Brit* a member of staff below a professor but above a senior lecturer at a university. **6** a proofreader. **7** short for **lay reader**.

readership *n* all the readers collectively of a publication or author: *a new format would alienate its readership.*

reading *n* **1** the act of reading. **2** ability to read: *disputes over methods of teaching reading.* **3** material for reading. **4** a public recital of a literary work. **5** a measurement indicated by a gauge or dial. **6** *Parliamentary procedure* one of the three stages in the passage of a bill through a legislative assembly. **7** the form of a particular word or passage in a given text. **8** an interpretation of a situation or something said. ✧ *adj* **9** of or for reading: *reading glasses.*

readjust *vb* to adapt to a new situation. ▸ **readjustment** *n*

readmit *vb* **-mitting, -mitted** to let (a person or country) back into a place or organization. ▸ **readmission** *n*

read out *vb* **1** to read (something) aloud. **2** to retrieve (information) from a computer memory. ✧ *n* **read-out 3** the information retrieved from a computer memory.

read-write head *n Computers* an electromagnet that can both read and write information on a magnetic tape or disk.

ready *adj* **readier, readiest 1** prepared for use or action. **2** prompt or eager: *the ready use of corporal punishment.* **3** quick or intelligent: *a ready wit.* **4 ready to** on the point of or liable to: *ready to pounce.* **5** easily available: *his ready tears.* ✧ *n* **6** *Informal* same as **ready money**. **7 at the ready** poised for use: *with pen at the ready.* ✧ *vb* **readies, readying, readied 8** to make ready; prepare. ▷ HISTORY Old English *(ge)rǣde* ▸ **readily** *adv* ▸ **readiness** *n*

ready-made *adj* **1** for immediate use by any customer. **2** extremely convenient or ideally suited: *a ready-made audience.*

ready money *n* cash for immediate use. Also: **the ready, the readies**

reaffirm *vb* to state again. ▸ **reaffirmation** *n*

reafforest *vb* to plant new trees in (an area that was formerly forested). ▸ **reafforestation** *n*

reagent (ree-**age**-ent) *n* a chemical substance that reacts with another, used to detect the presence of the other.

real[1] *adj* **1** existing or occurring in the physical world. **2** actual: *the real agenda.* **3** important or serious: *the real challenge.* **4** rightly so called: *a real friend.* **5** genuine: *the council has no real authority.* **6** (of food or drink) made in a traditional way to ensure the best flavour. **7** *Maths* involving or containing real numbers alone. **8** relating to immovable property such as land or buildings: *real estate.* **9** *Econ* (of prices or incomes) considered in terms of purchasing power rather than nominal currency value. **10 the real thing** the genuine article, not a substitute or imitation. ▷ HISTORY Latin *res* thing

real[2] *n* a former small Spanish or Spanish-American silver coin. ▷ HISTORY Spanish, literally: royal

real ale *n Chiefly Brit* beer that has fermented in the barrel.

real depth *n Physics* the depth at which an object actually is.

real estate *n* immovable property, esp. land and houses.

realism *n* **1** awareness or acceptance of things as they are, as opposed to the abstract or ideal. **2** a style in art or literature that attempts to show the world as it really is. **3** *Philosophy* the theory that physical objects continue to exist whether they are perceived or not. ▸ **realist** *n* ▸ **realistic** *adj* ▸ **realistically** *adv*

reality *n, pl* **-ties 1** the state of things as they are or appear to be, rather than as one might wish them to be. **2** something that is real. **3** the state of being real. **4 in reality** in fact.

reality TV *n* television programmes focusing on members of the public living in conditions created especially by the programme makers.

realize *or* **-ise** *vb* **-izing, -ized** *or* **-ising, -ised 1** to be aware of or grasp the significance of. **2** to achieve (a plan or ambition). **3** to convert (property or goods) into cash. **4** (of goods or property) to sell for (a certain sum): *this table realized a large sum at auction.* **5** to produce (a complete work of art) from an idea or draft. ▸ **realizable** *or* **-isable** *adj* ▸ **realization** *or* **-isation** *n*

really *adv* **1** truly: *really boring.* **2** in reality: *it's really quite harmless.* ✧ *interj* **3** an exclamation of dismay, doubt, or surprise.

> ☑ **WORD TIP**
> See at **very.**

realm *n* **1** a kingdom. **2** a field of interest or study: *the realm of science.* ▷ HISTORY Old French *reialme*

real number *n* any rational or irrational number.

real property *n* immovable property, esp. land and houses.

real tennis *n* an ancient form of tennis played in a four-walled indoor court.

real-time *adj* (of a computer system) processing data as it is received.

realty *n* same as **real estate**.

ream *n* **1** a number of sheets of paper, now equal to 500 or 516 sheets (20 quires). **2 reams** *Informal* a large quantity (of written material): *reams of verse.* ▷ HISTORY Arabic *rizmah* bale

reap *vb* **1** to cut and gather (a harvest). **2** to receive as the result of a previous activity: *reap the benefits of our efforts.* ▷ HISTORY Old English *riopan*

reaper *n* **1** a person who reaps or a machine for reaping. **2 the grim reaper** death.

reappear *vb* to come back into view. ▸ **reappearance** *n*

reappraise *vb* **-praising, -praised** to consider or review (something) to see if changes are needed. ▸ **reappraisal** *n*

rear[1] *n* **1** the back part. **2** the area or position that lies at the back. **3** *Informal* the buttocks. **4 bring up the rear** to come last. ✧ *adj* **5** of or in the rear: *the rear carriage.* ▷ HISTORY Old French *rer*

rear[2] *vb* **1** to care for and educate (children) until maturity. **2** to breed (animals) or grow (plants). **3** (of a horse) to lift the front legs in the air and stand nearly upright. **4** to place or lift (something) upright. ▷ HISTORY Old English *rǣran*

rear admiral *n* a high-ranking naval officer.

rearguard *n* **1** the troops who protect the rear of a military formation. **2 rearguard action** an effort to prevent or postpone something that is unavoidable.

rear light *or* **rear lamp** *n* a red light, usually one of a pair, attached to the rear of a vehicle. Also called: **tail-light, tail lamp**

rearm *vb* **1** to arm again. **2** to equip with better weapons. ▶ **rearmament** *n*

rearmost *adj* nearest the back.

rearrange *vb* **-ranging, -ranged** to organize differently. ▶ **rearrangement** *n*

rear-view mirror *n* a mirror on a motor vehicle enabling the driver to see the traffic behind.

rearward *adj* **1** in the rear. ✧ *adv also* **rearwards 2** towards the rear.

reason *n* **1** a cause or motive for a belief or action: *he had two reasons for his dark mood.* **2** the ability to think or argue rationally. **3** an argument in favour of or a justification for something: *there is every reason to encourage people to keep fit.* **4** sanity. **5 by reason of** because of. **6 within reason** within moderate or justifiable bounds. **7 it stands to reason** it is logical or obvious. ✧ *vb* **8** to think logically in forming conclusions. **9 reason with** to persuade by logical arguments into doing something. **10 reason out** to work out (a problem) by reasoning. ▷ HISTORY Latin *reri* to think

> **☑ WORD TIP**
> The expression *the reason is because...* should be avoided. Instead one should say either *this is because...* or *the reason is that...*

reasonable *adj* **1** sensible. **2** not making unfair demands. **3** logical: *a reasonable explanation.* **4** moderate in price. **5** average: *a reasonable amount of luck.* ▶ **reasonably** *adv* ▶ **reasonableness** *n*

reassess *vb* to reconsider the value or importance of. ▶ **reassessment** *n*

reassure *vb* **-assuring, -assured** to relieve (someone) of anxieties. ▶ **reassurance** *n* ▶ **reassuring** *adj*

rebate[1] *n* a refund or discount. ▷ HISTORY Old French *rabattre* to beat down

rebate[2] *or* **rabbet** *n* **1** a groove cut into a piece of timber into which another piece fits. ✧ *vb* **-bating, -bated** *or* **-beting, -beted 2** to cut a rabbet in. **3** to join (pieces of timber) with a rabbet. ▷ HISTORY Old French *rabattre* to beat down

rebel *vb* **-belling, -belled 1** to fight against the ruling power. **2** to reject accepted conventions of behaviour. ✧ *n* **3** a person who rebels. **4** a person who rejects accepted conventions of behaviour. ✧ *adj* **5** rebelling: *rebel councillors.* ▷ HISTORY Latin *re-* again + *bellum* war

rebellion *n* **1** organized opposition to a government or other authority involving the use of violence. **2** nonviolent opposition to a government or other authority: *a Tory backbenchers' rebellion.* **3** rejection of accepted conventions of behaviour. ▷ HISTORY Latin *rebellio*

rebellious *adj* rebelling or showing a tendency towards rebellion. ▶ **rebelliously** *adv*

rebirth *n* a revival or renaissance: *the rebirth of their nation.*

reboot *vb* to shut down and then restart (a computer system).

rebore *or* **reboring** *n* the boring of a cylinder to restore its true shape.

reborn *adj* active again after a period of inactivity.

rebound *vb* **1** to spring back from a sudden impact. **2** (of a plan or action) to misfire so as to hurt the person responsible. ✧ *n* **3** the act of rebounding. **4 on the rebound** *Informal* while recovering from rejection: *she married him on the rebound.*

rebrand *vb* to change or update the image of (an organization or product).

rebuff *vb* **1** to snub and reject an offer or suggestion. ✧ *n* **2** a blunt refusal; snub. ▷ HISTORY Old French *rebuffer*

rebuke *vb* **-buking, -buked 1** to scold sternly. ✧ *n* **2** a stern scolding. ▷ HISTORY Old French *rebuker*

rebus (**ree**-buss) *n, pl* **-buses** a puzzle consisting of pictures and symbols representing syllables and words. ▷ HISTORY Latin: by things

rebut *vb* **-butting, -butted** to prove that (a claim) is untrue. ▷ HISTORY Old French *reboter* ▶ **rebuttal** *n*

recalcitrant *adj* wilfully disobedient. ▷ HISTORY Latin *re-* again + *calcitrare* to kick ▶ **recalcitrance** *n*

recall *vb* **1** to bring back to mind. **2** to order to return. **3** to annul or cancel. ✧ *n* **4** the ability to remember things. **5** an order to return.

recant *vb* to take back (a former belief or statement) publicly. ▷ HISTORY Latin *re-* again + *cantare* to sing ▶ **recantation** *n*

recap *Informal* ✧ *vb* **-capping, -capped 1** to recapitulate. ✧ *n* **2** a recapitulation.

recapitulate *vb* **-lating, -lated** to restate the main points of (an argument or speech). ▷ HISTORY Late Latin *recapitulare,* literally: to put back under headings

recapitulation *n* **1** the act of recapitulating. **2** *Music* the repeating of earlier themes, esp. in the final section of a movement.

recapture *vb* **-turing, -tured 1** to relive vividly (a former experience or sensation): *they recaptured some of those first feelings.* **2** to capture again. ✧ *n* **3** the act of recapturing.

recast *vb* **-casting, -cast 1** to give a new form or shape to: *he found the organization wholly recast.* **2** to change the actors or singers in (a play, musical, or opera). **3** to rework (a piece of writing or music): *she has recast most of my book.*

recce *Chiefly Brit slang* ✧ *vb* **-ceing, -ced** *or* **-ceed** **1** to reconnoitre. ✧ *n* **2** reconnaissance.

recede *vb* **-ceding, -ceded 1** to withdraw from a point or limit: *the tide had receded.* **2** to become more distant: *the threat of intervention had receded.* **3** (of a man's hair) to stop growing at the temples and above the forehead. **4** to slope backwards: *a receding chin.* ▷ HISTORY Latin *recedere* to go back

receipt *n* **1** a written acknowledgment that money or goods have been received. **2** the act of receiving. **3 receipts** money taken in over a particular period by a shop or business. ▷ HISTORY Old French *receite*

receive *vb* **-ceiving, -ceived 1** to get (something offered or sent to one). **2** to experience: *he received a knife wound.* **3** to greet (guests). **4** to have (an honour) bestowed: *he received the Order of the Garter.* **5** to admit (a person) to a society or condition: *he was received into the Church.* **6** to convert (incoming radio or television signals) into sounds or pictures. **7** to be informed of (news). **8** to react to: *the article was well received.* **9** to support or sustain (the weight of something). **10** *Tennis etc.* to play at the other end from the server. **11** *Brit & NZ* to buy and sell stolen goods. ▷ HISTORY Latin *recipere*

received *adj* generally accepted or believed: *contrary to received wisdom.*

Received Pronunciation *n* the accent of standard Southern British English.

receiver *n* **1** the detachable part of a telephone that is held to the ear. **2** the equipment in a telephone, radio, or television that converts the incoming signals into sound or pictures. **3** a person appointed by a court to manage property of a bankrupt. **4** a person who receives stolen goods knowing they have been stolen.

receivership *n Law* the state of being administered by a receiver: *the company went into receivership.*

recent *adj* **1** having happened lately. **2** new. ▷ HISTORY Latin *recens* fresh ▶ **recently** *adv*

Recent *adj* same as **Holocene**.

receptacle *n* **1** an object used to contain something. **2** *Bot* the enlarged or modified tip of the flower stalk that bears the flower. ▷ HISTORY Latin *receptaculum* store-place

reception *n* **1** an area in an office, hotel, etc., where visitors are received or reservations dealt with. **2** a formal party for guests, esp. after a wedding. **3** the manner in which something is received: *an enthusiastic reception.* **4** the act of formally welcoming. **5** *Radio, television* the quality of a received broadcast: *the reception was poor.*

receptionist *n* a person employed to receive guests or clients and deal with reservations and appointments.

reception room *n* a room in a private house suitable for entertaining guests.

receptive *adj* willing to consider and accept new ideas or suggestions. ▶ **receptivity** *or* **receptiveness** *n*

receptor *n Physiol* a sensory nerve ending that changes specific stimuli into nerve impulses.

recess *n* **1** a space, such as an alcove, set back in a wall. **2** a holiday between sessions of work. **3 recesses** secret hidden places: *the recesses of her brain.* **4** *US & Canad* a break between classes at a school. ▷ HISTORY Latin *recessus* a retreat

recessed *adj* hidden or placed in a recess.

recession *n* **1** a period of economic difficulty when little is being bought or sold. **2** the act of receding.

recessional *n* a hymn sung as the clergy and choir withdraw after a church service.

recessive *adj* **1** tending to recede. **2** *Genetics* (in a pair of genes) designating a gene that has a characteristic which will only be passed on if the other gene has the same characteristic.

recharge *vb* **-charging, -charged** to cause (a battery) to take in and store electricity again. ▶ **rechargeable** *adj*

recherché (rish-**air**-shay) *adj* **1** studiedly refined or elegant. **2** known only to connoisseurs. ▷ HISTORY French: thoroughly sought after

recidivism *n* habitual relapse into crime. ▷ HISTORY Latin *recidivus* falling back ▶ **recidivist** *n, adj*

recipe *n* **1** a list of ingredients and directions for making a particular dish. **2** a method for achieving something: *a recipe for industrial chaos.* ▷ HISTORY Latin, literally: take (it)!

recipient *n* a person who receives something.

reciprocal (ris-**sip**-pro-kl) *adj* **1** done or felt by each of two people or groups to or about the other: *a reciprocal agreement.* **2** given or done in return: *a reciprocal invitation.* **3** *Grammar* (of a pronoun) indicating that action is given and received by each subject, for example, *each other* in *they started to shout at each other.* ✧ *n* **4** Also called: **inverse** *Maths* a number or quantity that when multiplied by a given number or quantity gives a product of one: *the reciprocal of 2 is 0.5.* ▷ HISTORY Latin *reciprocus* alternating ▶ **reciprocally** *adv*

reciprocal function *n Maths* a function that includes a reciprocal.

reciprocal ratio *n Maths* the reciprocal of the ratio of two numbers or quantities.

reciprocate *vb* **-cating, -cated 1** to give or feel in return: *not everyone reciprocated his enthusiasm.* **2** (of a machine part) to move backwards and forwards. ▶ **reciprocation** *n*

reciprocity *n* **1** reciprocal action or relation. **2** a mutual exchange of commercial or other privileges.

recital (ris-**site**-al) *n* **1** a musical performance by a soloist or soloists. **2** the act of reciting something learned or prepared. **3** a narration or description: *she plagued her with the recital of constant ailments and illnesses.*

recitation *n* **1** the act of reciting poetry or prose from memory. **2** something recited.

recitative (ress-it-a-**teev**) *n* a narrative passage in an opera or oratorio, reflecting the natural rhythms of speech. ▷ HISTORY Italian *recitativo*

recite *vb* **-citing, -cited 1** to repeat (a poem or passage) aloud from memory before an audience.

2 to give a detailed account of. ▷ HISTORY Latin *recitare*

reckless *adj* **1** having no regard for danger or consequences: *reckless behaviour.* **2** *Law* carrying a serious and foreseeable risk: *she was charged with reckless driving.* ▷ HISTORY Old English *recceleās*

recklessness *n* **1** a lack of regard for danger or consequences: *it seems foolhardy to the point of recklessness.* **2** *Law* acts that are unreasonable and carry a serious foreseeable risk.

reckon *vb* **1** *Informal* to be of the opinion: *she reckoned she could find them.* **2** to consider: *he reckoned himself a failure.* **3** to calculate or compute. **4** to expect. **5 reckon with** *or* **without** to take into account or fail to take into account: *there is this ancestral hatred to reckon with.* **6 reckon on** *or* **upon** to rely on or expect: *they can't reckon on your automatic support.* ▷ HISTORY Old English *(ge)recenian* recount

reckoning *n* **1** counting or calculating: *by his reckoning, he owed him money.* **2** retribution for one's actions: *the moment of reckoning came.* **3** settlement of an account or bill.

reclaim *vb* **1** to get back possession of: *the club is now trying to reclaim the money from the blockaders.* **2** to convert (unusable or submerged land) into land suitable for farming or building on. **3** to recover (useful substances) from waste products. ▷ HISTORY Latin *reclamare* to cry out ▶ **reclamation** *n*

recline *vb* **-clining, -clined** to rest in a leaning position. ▷ HISTORY Latin *reclinare*

reclining *adj* (of a seat) with a back that can be adjusted to slope at various angles.

recluse *n* a person who lives alone and avoids people. ▷ HISTORY Late Latin *recludere* to shut away ▶ **reclusive** *adj*

recognition *n* **1** the act of recognizing. **2** acceptance or acknowledgment. **3** formal acknowledgment of a government or of the independence of a country. **4 in recognition of** as a token of thanks for.

recognizance *or* **recognisance** (rik-**og**-nizz-anss) *n Law* **a** an undertaking made before a court or magistrate to do something specified, such as to appear in court on a stated day. **b** a sum of money promised as a guarantee of this undertaking. ▷ HISTORY Old French *reconoissance*

recognize *or* **-nise** *vb* **-nizing, -nized** *or* **-nising, -nised 1** to identify (a person or thing) as someone or something already known. **2** to accept or be aware of (a fact or problem): *to recognize change.* **3** to acknowledge formally the status or legality of (something or someone): *an organization recognized by the UN.* **4** to show approval or appreciation of (something). **5** to make formal acknowledgment of (a claim or duty): *I must ask for her to be recognized as a hostile witness.* ▷ HISTORY Latin *re-* again + *cognoscere* to know ▶ **recognizable** *or* **-isable** *adj*

recoil *vb* **1** to jerk or spring back. **2** to draw back in fear or horror. **3** (of an action) to go wrong so as to hurt the person responsible. ✧ *n* **4** the backward movement of a gun when fired. **5** the act of recoiling. ▷ HISTORY Old French *reculer*

recollect *vb* to remember. ▷ HISTORY Latin *recolligere* to gather again ▶ **recollection** *n*

recombinant (ree-**kom**-bin-ant) *adj Genetics* produced by the combining of genetic material from more than one origin.

recombinant DNA *n Biol* DNA molecules extracted from different sources and chemically joined together.

recommend *vb* **1** to advise as the best course or choice. **2** to praise or commend: *I would wholeheartedly recommend his books.* **3** to make attractive or advisable: *she has everything to recommend her.* ▷ HISTORY Latin *re-* again + *commendare* to commend ▶ **recommendation** *n*

recompense *vb* **-pensing, -pensed 1** to pay or reward for work or help. **2** to compensate or make up for loss or injury. ✧ *n* **3** compensation for loss or injury. **4** reward or repayment. ▷ HISTORY Latin *re-* again + *compensare* to balance

reconcile *vb* **-ciling, -ciled 1** to make (two apparently conflicting things) compatible or consistent with each other: *in many cases science and religion are reconciled.* **2** to re-establish friendly relations with (a person or people) or between (people). **3** to accept or cause to accept (an unpleasant situation): *we reconciled ourselves to a change.* ▷ HISTORY Latin *reconciliare*

reconciliation *n* **1** the state of being reconciled. **2** the act of reconciling people or groups. **3** *S African* a political term emphasizing the need to acknowledge the wrongs of the past.

recondite *adj Formal* **1** requiring special knowledge. **2** dealing with abstruse or profound subjects. ▷ HISTORY Latin *reconditus* hidden away

recondition *vb* to restore to good condition or working order: *a reconditioned engine.* ▶ **reconditioned** *adj*

reconnaissance (rik-**kon**-iss-anss) *n* **1** the process of obtaining information about the position and movements of an enemy. **2** a preliminary inspection. ▷ HISTORY French

reconnoitre *or US* **reconnoiter** (rek-a-**noy**-ter) *vb* to make a reconnaissance of. ▷ HISTORY obsolete French *reconnoître*

reconsider *vb* to think about again, with a view to changing one's policy or course of action. ▶ **reconsideration** *n*

reconstitute *vb* **-tuting, -tuted 1** to reorganize in a slightly different form. **2** to restore (dried food) to its former state by adding water. ▶ **reconstitution** *n*

reconstruct *vb* **1** to build again. **2** to reorganize: *three works proved useful in reconstructing the training routine.* **3** to form a picture of (a past event, esp. a crime) by piecing together evidence. ▶ **reconstruction** *n*

record *n* (**rek**-ord) **1** a document or other thing that preserves information. **2 records** information or data on a subject collected over a long period: *dental records.* **3** a thin disc of a plastic material upon which sound has been recorded in a continuous spiral groove on each side. **4** the best recorded achievement in some field: *her score set a Games record.* **5** the known facts about a person's achievements. **6** a list of crimes of which an accused person has previously been convicted. **7** anything serving as evidence or as a memorial: *the First World War is a record of human folly.* **8** *Computers* a group of data or piece of information preserved as a unit in machine-readable form. **9 for the record** for the sake of strict factual accuracy. **10 go on record** to state one's views publicly. **11 have a record** to have previous criminal convictions. **12 off the record** not for publication. **13 on record a** stated in a public document. **b** publicly known. ✧ *adj* **14** the highest or lowest, or best or worst ever achieved: *record losses.* ✧ *vb* (rik-**kord**) **15** to put in writing to preserve the true facts: *to record the minutes of a meeting.* **16** to preserve (sound, TV programmes, etc.) on plastic disc, magnetic tape, etc., for reproduction on a playback device. **17** to show or register. ▷ HISTORY Latin *recordari* to remember

recorded delivery *n* a postal service by which an official receipt is obtained for the posting and delivery of a letter or parcel.

recorder *n* **1** a person or machine that records, esp. a video, cassette, or tape recorder. **2** *Music* a wind instrument, blown through the end with finger-holes and a reedlike tone. **3** (in England and Wales) a barrister or solicitor appointed to sit as a part-time judge in the crown court.

recording *n* **1** something that has been recorded. **2** the process of storing sounds or visual signals for later use.

record player *n* a device for reproducing the sounds stored on a record.

recount *vb* to tell the story or details of. ▷ HISTORY Old French *reconter*

re-count *vb* **1** to count again. ✧ *n* **2** a second or further count, esp. of votes in an election.

recount genre *n* a form of writing or speech in which the writer or speaker relates events as they happened and in chronological order.

recoup (rik-**koop**) *vb* **1** to regain or make good (a loss). **2** to reimburse or compensate (someone) for a loss. ▷ HISTORY Old French *recouper* to cut back ▶ **recoupment** *n*

recourse *n* **1** a source of help or course of action that is turned to when in difficulty. **2 have recourse to** to turn to (a source of help or course of action). ▷ HISTORY Latin *re-* back + *currere* to run

recover *vb* **1** (of a person) to regain health, spirits, or composure. **2** to regain a former and better condition: *real wages have recovered from the recession.* **3** to find again or obtain the return of (something lost). **4** to get back or make good (expense or loss). **5** to obtain (useful substances) from waste. **6** *Law* to gain (something) by the judgment of a court: *it should be possible to recover damages.* ▷ HISTORY Latin *recuperare* ▶ **recoverable** *adj*

recovery *n, pl* **-eries 1** the act of recovering from sickness, a shock, or a setback. **2** restoration to a former and better condition. **3** the regaining of something lost. **4** the extraction of useful substances from waste.

re-create *vb* **-creating, -created** to make happen or exist again. ▶ **re-creation** *n*

recreation *n* an activity done for pleasure or relaxation. ▷ HISTORY Latin *recreare* to refresh ▶ **recreational** *adj*

recreation ground *n* an area of publicly owned land where sports and games may be played.

recrimination *n* accusations made by two people or groups about each other: *bitter recrimination.* ▷ HISTORY Latin *re-* back + *criminari* to accuse ▶ **recriminatory** *adj*

recrudescence *n Literary* an outbreak of trouble or a disease after a period of quiet. ▷ HISTORY Latin *re-* again + *crudus* bloody, raw

recruit *vb* **1** to enlist (people) for military service. **2** to enrol or obtain (members or support). ✧ *n* **3** a newly joined member of a military service. **4** a new member or supporter. ▷ HISTORY French *recrute* new growth ▶ **recruitment** *n*

rectal *adj* of the rectum.

rectangle *n* an oblong shape with four straight sides and four right angles. ▷ HISTORY Latin *rectus* straight + *angulus* angle ▶ **rectangular** *adj*

rectify *vb* **-fies, -fying, -fied 1** to put right; correct. **2** *Chem* to separate (a substance) from a mixture by distillation. **3** *Electricity* to convert (alternating current) into direct current. ▷ HISTORY Latin *rectus* straight + *facere* to make ▶ **rectification** *n* ▶ **rectifier** *n*

rectilinear (rek-tee-**lin**-ee-er) *adj Formal* **1** in a straight line. **2** bounded by or formed of straight lines.

rectitude *n* moral or religious correctness: *a model of rectitude.* ▷ HISTORY Latin *rectus* right

recto *n, pl* **-tos 1** the right-hand page of a book. **2** the front of a sheet of printed paper. ▷ HISTORY Latin: on the right

rector *n* **1** *Church of England* a clergyman in charge of a parish. **2** *RC Church* a cleric in charge of a college or congregation. **3** *Chiefly Brit* the head of certain academic institutions. **4** (in Scotland) a high-ranking official in a university, elected by the students. ▷ HISTORY Latin: director ▶ **rectorship** *n*

rectory *n, pl* **-ries** the house of a rector.

rectum *n, pl* **-tums** *or* **-ta** the lower part of the alimentary canal, ending in the anus. ▷ HISTORY Latin: straight

recumbent *adj* lying down. ▷ HISTORY Latin *recumbere* to lie back

recuperate *vb* **-ating, -ated** to recover from illness or exhaustion. ▷ HISTORY Latin *recuperare* ▶ **recuperation** *n* ▶ **recuperative** *adj*

recur *vb* **-curring, -curred 1** to happen or occur again. **2** (of a thought or feeling) to come back to the mind. ▷ HISTORY Latin *re-* again + *currere* to run ▶ **recurrence** *n* ▶ **recurrent** *adj* ▶ **recurring** *adj*

recurring decimal *n* a rational number that contains a pattern of digits repeated indefinitely after the decimal point: *1 divided by 11 gives the recurring decimal 0.09090909...*

a b c d e f g h i j k l m n o p q r s t u v w x y z

recusant (rek-yew-zant) *n* **1** *History* a Roman Catholic who did not attend the services of the Church of England. **2** a person who refuses to obey authority. ▷ HISTORY Latin *recusans* refusing ▶ **recusancy** *n*

recyclable *adj* capable of being reused either in its current state or after reprocessing.

recyclable resource *n Environmental science* a resource such as a mineral, paper, or man-made substance that can be reclaimed at the end of its current use and used for or reprocessed into something else.

recycle *vb* **-cling, -cled 1** to reprocess (something already used) for further use: *public demand for recycled paper.* **2** to pass (a substance) through a system again for further use.

red *adj* **redder, reddest 1** of a colour varying from crimson to orange; of the colour of blood. **2** reddish in colour or having parts or marks that are reddish: *red deer.* **3** flushed in the face from anger or shame. **4** (of the eyes) bloodshot. **5** (of wine) made from black grapes and coloured by their skins. ✧ *n* **6** the colour red; the colour of blood. **7** anything red, such as red clothing or red paint: *she had dressed in red.* **8 in the red** *Informal* in debt. **9 see red** *Informal* to become very angry. ▷ HISTORY Old English *rēad* ▶ **redness** *n* ▶ **reddish** *adj*

Red *Informal* ✧ *n* **1** a Communist or socialist. ✧ *adj* **2** Communist or socialist.

red admiral *n* a butterfly with black wings with red and white markings.

redback spider *n* a small venomous Australian spider with a red stripe on the back of the abdomen.

red blood cell *n* same as **erythrocyte**.

red-blooded *adj Informal* vigorous or virile.

redbreast *n* a robin.

redbrick *adj* (of a university in Britain) founded in the late 19th or early 20th century.

red card *Soccer* ✧ *n* **1** a piece of red pasteboard raised by a referee to indicate that a player has been sent off. ✧ *vb* **red-card 2** to send off (a player).

red carpet *n* very special treatment given to an important guest.

redcoat *n* **1** *History* a British soldier. **2** *Canad informal* a Mountie.

Red Crescent *n* the name and symbol used by the Red Cross in Muslim countries.

Red Cross *n* an international organization (**Red Cross Society**) which helps victims of war or natural disaster.

redcurrant *n* a very small red edible fruit that grows in bunches on a bush.

red deer *n* a large deer of Europe and Asia, which has a reddish-brown coat and a short tail.

redden *vb* **1** to make or become red or redder. **2** to blush.

redeem *vb* **1** to make up for. **2** to reinstate (oneself) in someone's good opinion: *he missed a penalty but redeemed himself by setting up the winning goal.* **3** *Christianity* (of Christ as Saviour) to free (humanity) from sin by death on the Cross. **4** to buy back: *she didn't have the money to redeem it.* **5** to pay off (a loan or debt). **6** to convert (bonds or shares) into cash. **7** to exchange (coupons) for goods. **8** to fulfil (a promise): *I vowed to abide by the bill and have redeemed my pledge.* ▷ HISTORY Latin *re-* back + *emere* to buy ▶ **redeemable** *adj* ▶ **redeemer** *n*

Redeemer *n* **the Redeemer** *Christianity* Jesus Christ.

redeeming *adj* making up for faults or deficiencies: *the soundtrack is the film's only redeeming feature.*

redemption *n* **1** the act of redeeming. **2** the state of being redeemed. **3** *Christianity* deliverance from sin through the incarnation and death of Christ. ▶ **redemptive** *adj*

redeploy *vb* to assign (people) to new positions or tasks. ▶ **redeployment** *n*

redevelop *vb* to rebuild or renovate (an area or building). ▶ **redeveloper** *n* ▶ **redevelopment** *n*

redfish *n, pl* **-fish** *or* **-fishes** *Canad* same as **kokanee**.

red flag *n* **1** a symbol of revolution. **2** a warning of danger.

red-handed *adj* **catch someone red-handed** to catch someone in the act of doing something wrong or illegal.

red hat *n* the broad-brimmed crimson hat given to cardinals as the symbol of their rank.

redhead *n* a person with reddish hair. ▶ **redheaded** *adj*

red herring *n* something which diverts attention from the main issue.

red-hot *adj* **1** (of metal) glowing hot. **2** extremely hot. **3** very keen or excited. **4** furious: *one of those red-hot blazes of temper.* **5** very recent or topical: *red-hot information.*

red-hot poker *n* a garden plant with spikes of red or yellow flowers.

Red Indian *n, adj Offensive* Native American.

redirect *vb* **1** to send in a new direction or course. **2** to send (mail) to a different address.

red lead *n* a bright-red poisonous insoluble oxide of lead.

red-letter day *n* a memorably important or happy occasion. ▷ HISTORY from the red letters in ecclesiastical calendars to indicate saints' days

red light *n* **1** a traffic signal to stop. **2** a danger signal.

red-light district *n* an area where many prostitutes work.

red meat *n* meat, such as beef or lamb, that is dark brown when cooked.

redolent *adj* **redolent of** *or* **with 1** reminiscent or suggestive of: *a castle redolent of historical novels.* **2** smelling of: *the warm heavy air was redolent of sea and flowers.* ▷ HISTORY Latin *redolens* ▶ **redolence** *n*

redouble *vb* **-bling, -bled 1** to make or become much greater: *the party will have to redouble its efforts.* **2** *Bridge* to double (an opponent's double).

redoubt *n* **1** a small fort defending a hill top or pass. **2** a stronghold. ▷ HISTORY French *redoute*

redoubtable *adj* to be feared and respected: *the redoubtable Mr Brooks.* ▷ **HISTORY** Old French *redouter* to dread ▶ **redoubtably** *adv*

redound *vb* **1 redound to** to have an advantageous or disadvantageous effect on: *individual rights redound to the common good.* **2 redound on** *or* **upon** to recoil or rebound on. ▷ **HISTORY** Latin *redundare* to stream over

redox *n* a chemical reaction between two substances, in which one is oxidized and the other reduced.

red pepper *n* **1** the red ripe fruit of the sweet pepper, eaten as a vegetable. **2** same as **cayenne pepper**.

redraft *vb* to write a second copy of (a letter, proposal, essay, etc.).

red rag *n* something that infuriates or provokes: *a red rag to businessmen.* ▷ **HISTORY** so called because red objects supposedly infuriate bulls

redress *vb* **1** to make amends for. **2** to adjust in order to make fair or equal: *to redress the balance.* ✧ *n* **3** compensation or reparation. **4** the setting right of a wrong. ▷ **HISTORY** Old French *redrecier* to set up again

red salmon *n* a salmon with reddish flesh.

redshank *n* a large common European sandpiper with red legs.

red shift *n* the appearance of lines in the spectrum of distant stars nearer the red end of the spectrum than on earth: used to calculate the velocity of objects in relation to the earth.

redskin *n Informal, offensive* a Native American. ▷ **HISTORY** so called because one now extinct tribe painted themselves with red ochre

red squirrel *n* a reddish-brown squirrel of Europe and Asia.

redstart *n* **1** a European songbird of the thrush family, the male of which has an orange-brown tail and breast. **2** a North American warbler. ▷ **HISTORY** Old English *rēad* red + *steort* tail

red tape *n* time-consuming official rules or procedure. ▷ **HISTORY** from the red tape used to bind official government documents

reduce *vb* **-ducing, -duced 1** to bring down or lower: *monitoring could reduce the number of perinatal deaths.* **2** to weaken or lessen: *vegetarian diets reduce cancer risk.* **3** to bring by force or necessity to some state or action: *it reduced her to helpless laughter.* **4** to slim. **5** to set out systematically as an aid to understanding: *reducing the problem to three main issues.* **6** *Cookery* to thicken (a sauce) by boiling away some of its liquid. **7** to impoverish: *to be in reduced circumstances.* **8** *Chem* **a** to undergo a chemical reaction with hydrogen. **b** to lose oxygen atoms. **c** to increase the number of electrons. **9** *Maths* to simplify the form of (an expression or equation), esp. by substitution of one term by another. ▷ **HISTORY** Latin *reducere* to bring back ▶ **reducible** *adj*

reducing agent *n Chem* a substance that reduces another substance in a chemical reaction, being itself oxidized in the process.

reduction *n* **1** the act of reducing. **2** the amount by which something is reduced. **3** a reduced form of an original, such as a copy of a document on a smaller scale. ▶ **reductive** *adj*

reduction formula *n Maths* a formula expressing the values of a trigonometric function of any angle greater than 90° in terms of a function of an acute angle.

redundant *adj* **1** deprived of one's job because it is no longer necessary or sufficiently profitable. **2** surplus to requirements. ▷ **HISTORY** Latin *redundans* overflowing ▶ **redundancy** *n*

reduplicate *vb* **-cating, -cated** to make double; repeat.

redwood *n* a giant Californian conifer with reddish bark.

re-echo *vb* **-oing, -oed** to echo over and over again.

reed *n* **1** a tall grass that grows in swamps and shallow water. **2** a straight hollow stem of this plant. **3** *Music* **a** a thin piece of cane or metal in certain wind instruments, which vibrates producing a musical note when the instrument is blown. **b** a wind instrument or organ pipe that sounds by means of a reed. ▷ **HISTORY** Old English *hrēod*

reedy *adj* **reedier, reediest 1** harsh or thin in tone: *his reedy, hesitant voice.* **2** (of a place) full of reeds. ▶ **reedily** *adv* ▶ **reediness** *n*

reef[1] *n* **1** a ridge of rock, sand, or coral, lying just beneath the surface of the sea: *a coral reef.* **2** a vein of ore. ▷ **HISTORY** Middle Dutch *ref*

reef[2] *Naut* ✧ *n* **1** the part of a sail which can be rolled up to reduce its area. ✧ *vb* **2** to reduce the area of (sail) by taking in a reef. ▷ **HISTORY** Middle Dutch *rif*

reefer *n* **1** Also called: **reefer jacket** a man's short heavy double-breasted woollen jacket. **2** *Old-fashioned, slang* a hand-rolled cigarette containing cannabis. ▷ **HISTORY** from the cigarette's resemblance to the rolled reef of a sail

reef knot *n* a knot consisting of two overhand knots turned opposite ways.

reek *vb* **1** to give off a strong unpleasant smell. **2 reek of** to give a strong suggestion of: *the scene had reeked of insincerity.* **3** *Dialect* to give off smoke or fumes. ✧ *n* **4** a strong unpleasant smell. **5** *Dialect* smoke or steam. ▷ **HISTORY** Old English *rēocan*

reel[1] *n* **1** a cylindrical object or frame that turns on an axis and onto which film, tape, wire, or thread is wound. **2** a winding device attached to a fishing rod, used for casting and winding in the line. **3** a roll of film for projection. ✧ *vb* **4 reel in** to wind or draw in on a reel. ▷ **HISTORY** Old English *hrēol*

reel[2] *vb* **1** to move unsteadily or spin round, as if about to fall. **2** to be in a state of confusion or stress: *my mind was still reeling.* ▷ **HISTORY** probably from REEL[1]

reel[3] *n* **1** a lively Scottish dance. **2** music for this dance. ▷ **HISTORY** from REEL[2]

re-elect *vb* to vote for (someone) to retain his or her position, for example as a Member of Parliament. ▶ **re-election** *n*

reel off *vb* to recite or write fluently or quickly.

re-enter *vb* **1** to come back into (a place, esp. a country). **2** (of a spacecraft) to return into (the earth's atmosphere). ▶ **re-entry** *n*

re-entrant *n Geog* a small valley forming an indentation in a hillside.

reeve *n* **1** *English history* the local representative of the king in a shire until the early 11th century. **2** (in medieval England) a steward who supervised the daily affairs of a manor. **3** *Canad government* (in some provinces) a president of a local council. ▷ HISTORY Old English *gerēfa*

re-examine *vb* **-examining, -examined** to inspect or investigate again. ▶ **re-examination** *n*

ref *n Informal* the referee in a sport.

refectory *n, pl* **-ries** a dining hall in a religious or academic institution. ▷ HISTORY Latin *refectus* refreshed

refectory table *n* a long narrow dining table supported by two trestles.

refer *vb* **-ferring, -ferred refer to 1** to mention or allude to. **2** to be relevant or relate to: *the word 'cancer' refers to many quite specific different diseases.* **3** to seek information from: *he referred to his notes.* **4** to direct the attention of (someone) for information: *the reader is referred to the introduction.* **5** to direct (a patient or client) to another doctor or agency: *her GP referred her to a specialist.* **6** to hand over for consideration or decision: *to refer a complaint to another department.* ▷ HISTORY Latin *re-* back + *ferre* to carry ▶ **referable** *or* **referrable** *adj* ▶ **referral** *n*

> **☑ WORD TIP**
> The common practice of adding *back* to *refer* is tautologous, since this meaning is already contained in the *re-* of *refer: this refers to* (not *back to*) *what has already been said.* However, when *refer* is used in the sense of passing a document or question for further consideration to the person from whom it was received, it may be appropriate to say *he referred the matter back.*

referee *n* **1** the umpire in various sports, such as football and boxing. **2** a person who is willing to provide a reference for someone for a job. **3** a person referred to for a decision or opinion in a dispute. ✧ *vb* **-eeing, -eed 4** to act as a referee.

reference *n* **1** the act of referring. **2** a mention: *this book contains several references to the Civil War.* **3** direction to a passage elsewhere in a book or to another book. **4** a book or passage referred to. **5** a written testimonial regarding one's character or capabilities. **6** a person referred to for such a testimonial. **7** relation or restriction, esp. to or by membership of a specific group: *without reference to sex or age.* **8 with reference to** concerning. ✧ *adj* **9** containing information or facts: *reference books.* ▶ **referential** *adj*

referendum *n, pl* **-dums** *or* **-da** a direct vote of the electorate on a question of importance. ▷ HISTORY Latin: something to be carried back

refill *vb* **1** to fill (something) again. ✧ *n* **2** a second or subsequent filling: *I held out my glass for a refill.* **3** a replacement supply of something in a permanent container. ▶ **refillable** *adj*

refine *vb* **-fining, -fined 1** to make free from impurities; purify. **2** to improve: *surgical techniques are constantly being refined.* **3** to separate (a mixture) into pure constituents: *molasses is a residual syrup obtained during sugar refining.*

refined *adj* **1** cultured or polite. **2** freed from impurities. **3** highly developed and effective: *refined intelligence tests.*

refinement *n* **1** an improvement to something, such as a piece of equipment. **2** fineness of taste or manners. **3** a subtle point or distinction. **4** the act of refining.

refinery *n, pl* **-eries** a factory for purifying a raw material, such as sugar or oil.

refit *vb* **-fitting, -fitted 1** to make (a ship) ready for use again by repairing or re-equipping. ✧ *n* **2** a repair or re-equipping for further use.

reflation *n* an increase in the supply of money and credit designed to encourage economic activity. ▷ HISTORY RE- + *-flation,* as in *inflation* ▶ **reflate** *vb* ▶ **reflationary** *adj*

reflect *vb* **1** (of a surface or object) to throw back (light, heat, or sound). **2** (of a mirror) to form an image of (something) by reflection. **3** to show: *many of her books reflect her obsession with fine art.* **4** to consider carefully. **5 reflect on** *or* **upon** to cause to be regarded in a specified way: *the incident reflects very badly on me.* **6** to bring as a consequence: *the programme reflected great credit on the technicians.* ▷ HISTORY Latin *re-* back + *flectere* to bend

reflecting telescope *n* a telescope in which the initial image is formed by a concave mirror.

reflection *n* **1** the act of reflecting. **2** the return of rays of light, heat, or sound. **3** an image of a an object given back in a mirror. **4** careful or long consideration. **5 on reflection** after careful consideration or reconsideration. **6** discredit or blame: *it's a sad reflection on modern morality.* **7** *Maths* a transformation of a shape in which right and left, or top and bottom, are reversed.

reflection in the x-axis *n Maths* a reflection in which a shape is reversed along the x-axis.

reflection in the y-axis *n Maths* a reflection in which a shape is reversed along the y-axis.

reflective *adj* **1** characterized by quiet thought or contemplation. **2** capable of reflecting: *a reflective coating.*

reflector *n* **1** a polished surface for reflecting light. **2** a reflecting telescope.

reflex *n* **1** an immediate involuntary response to a given stimulus. **2** a mechanical response to a particular situation, involving no conscious decision. **3** an image produced by reflection. ✧ *adj* **4** of or caused by a reflex: *a reflex action.* **5** reflected. **6** *Maths* (of an angle) between 180° and 360°. ▷ HISTORY Latin *reflexus* bent back

reflex arc *n Physiol* the neural pathway over which impulses travel to produce a reflex action.

reflex camera *n* a camera which uses a mirror to channel light from a lens to the viewfinder, so that the image seen is the same as the image photographed.

reflexive *adj* **1** *Grammar* denoting a pronoun that refers back to the subject of a sentence or clause. Thus, in *that man thinks a great deal of himself*, the pronoun *himself* is reflexive. **2** *Grammar* denoting a verb used with a reflexive pronoun as its direct object, as in *to dress oneself*. **3** *Physiol* of or relating to a reflex. ✧ *n* **4** a reflexive pronoun or verb.

reflexology *n* foot massage as a therapy in alternative medicine. ▸ **reflexologist** *n*

reforest *vb* same as **reafforest**.

reform *n* **1** correction of abuses or malpractices: *a programme of economic reforms*. **2** improvement of morals or behaviour. ✧ *vb* **3** to improve (a law or institution) by correcting abuses. **4** to give up or cause to give up a bad habit or way of life. ▷ HISTORY Latin *reformare* to form again ▸ **reformative** *adj* ▸ **reformer** *n*

reformation (ref-fer-**may**-shun) *n* **1** a reforming. **2 the Reformation** a religious movement in 16th-century Europe that began as an attempt to reform the Roman Catholic Church and resulted in the establishment of the Protestant Churches.

reformatory *n, pl* **-ries** (formerly) a place where young offenders were sent to be reformed.

Reformed *adj* of a Protestant Church, esp. a Calvinist one.

reformist *adj* **1** advocating reform rather than abolition, esp. of a religion or a political movement. ✧ *n* **2** a person advocating reform.

refract *vb* to cause light, heat, or sound to undergo refraction. ▷ HISTORY Latin *re-* back + *frangere* to break ▸ **refractive** *adj* ▸ **refractor** *n*

refracted ray *n Physics* a ray of light that has undergone refraction.

refracting telescope *n* a type of telescope in which the image is formed by a set of lenses. Also called: **refractor**

refraction *n Physics* **1** the change in direction of a wave, such as light or sound, in passing from one medium to another in which it has a different velocity. **2** the amount by which a wave is refracted.

refractory *adj* **1** *Formal* stubborn or rebellious. **2** *Med* not responding to treatment. **3** (of a material) able to withstand high temperatures without fusion or decomposition.

refrain[1] *vb* **refrain from** to keep oneself from (doing). ▷ HISTORY Latin *refrenare* to check with a bridle

refrain[2] *n* **1** a frequently repeated part of a song. **2** a much repeated saying or idea. ▷ HISTORY Latin *refringere* to break into pieces

refrangible *adj* capable of being refracted.

refresh *vb* **1** to revive or reinvigorate, for example through rest, drink, or food. **2** to stimulate (the memory). ▷ HISTORY Old French *refreschir* ▸ **refresher** *n*

refresher course *n* a course designed to improve or update a person's knowledge of a subject.

refreshing *adj* **1** having a reviving effect. **2** pleasantly different or new: *refreshing candour*.

refreshment *n* **1** the act of refreshing. **2 refreshments** snacks and drinks served as a light meal.

refrigerant *n* **1** a fluid capable of vaporizing at low temperatures, used in refrigerators. ✧ *adj* **2** causing cooling or freezing.

refrigerate *vb* **-ating, -ated** to chill or freeze in order to preserve. ▷ HISTORY Latin *refrigerare* to make cold ▸ **refrigeration** *n*

refrigerator *n* the full name for **fridge**.

refuel *vb* **-elling, -elled** *or US* **-eling, -eled** to supply or be supplied with fresh fuel.

refuge *n* **1** shelter or protection from danger or hardship. **2** a place, person, or thing that offers protection or help. ▷ HISTORY Latin *re-* back + *fugere* to escape

refugee *n* a person who has fled from some danger, such as war or political persecution.

refulgent *adj Literary* shining brightly. ▷ HISTORY Latin *refulgere* to reflect ▸ **refulgence** *n*

refund *vb* **1** to give back (money). **2** to pay back (a person). ✧ *n* **3** return of money to a purchaser or the amount returned. ▷ HISTORY Latin *re-* back + *fundere* to pour ▸ **refundable** *adj*

refurbish *vb* to renovate and brighten up. ▸ **refurbishment** *n*

refusal *n* **1** the act of refusing. **2** the opportunity to reject or accept: *he was given first refusal on all three scripts*.

refuse[1] *vb* **-fusing, -fused 1** to be determined not (to do something): *he refuses to consider it*. **2** to decline to give or allow (something) to (someone): *if the judge refuses bail, he'll appeal*. **3** to decline to accept (something offered): *he refused the captaincy*. **4** (of a horse) to be unwilling to jump a fence. ▷ HISTORY Latin *refundere* to pour back

refuse[2] *n* anything thrown away; rubbish. ▷ HISTORY Old French *refuser* to refuse

refusenik *n* **1** (formerly) a Jew in the USSR who was refused permission to emigrate. **2** a person who refuses to obey a law or cooperate with the government because of strong beliefs.

refute *vb* **-futing, -futed** to prove (a statement or theory) to be false or incorrect. ▷ HISTORY Latin *refutare* ▸ **refutation** *n*

> **WORD TIP**
> The use of *refute* to mean *deny* is thought by many people to be incorrect.

reg *n Geol* an area of desert covered with loose stones.

regain *vb* **1** to get back or recover. **2** to reach again: *to regain the shore*.

regal *adj* **1** of or fit for a king or queen. **2** splendid and dignified; magnificent: *a luxury cruise liner on her serene and regal way around the better ports*. ▷ HISTORY Latin *regalis* ▸ **regality** *n* ▸ **regally** *adv*

regale *vb* **-galing, -galed 1** to give delight or amusement to: *she would regale her friends with* *stories.* **2** to provide with abundant food or drink. ▷ **HISTORY** French *régaler*

regalia *n* the ceremonial emblems or robes of royalty or high office. ▷ **HISTORY** Medieval Latin: royal privileges

regard *vb* **1** to look upon or think of in a specified way: *angina can therefore be regarded as heart cramp.* **2** to look closely or attentively at (something or someone). **3** to take notice of: *he has never regarded the conventions.* **4 as regards** on the subject of. ✧ *n* **5** respect or affection: *you haven't a high regard for her opinion.* **6** attention: *he eats what he wants with no regard to health.* **7** a gaze or look. **8** reference or connection: *with regard to my complaint.* **9 regards** an expression of goodwill: *give her my regards.* ▷ **HISTORY** Old French *regarder* to look at, care about

regarding *prep* on the subject of; relating to.

regardless *adj* **1 regardless of** taking no notice of: *the illness can affect anyone regardless of their social class.* ✧ *adv* **2** in spite of everything: *I carried on regardless.*

regatta *n* a series of races of boats or yachts. ▷ **HISTORY** obsolete Italian *rigatta* contest

regency *n, pl* **-cies 1** government by a regent. **2** the status of a regent. **3** a period when a regent is in power. ▷ **HISTORY** Latin *regere* to rule

Regency *adj* of the regency (1811–20) of the Prince of Wales (later George IV) or the styles of architecture or furniture produced during it.

regenerate *vb* (ri-**jen**-er-ate) **-ating, -ated 1** to undergo or cause to undergo physical, economic, or spiritual renewal. **2** to come or bring into existence once again. **3** to replace (lost or damaged tissues or organs) by new growth. ✧ *adj* (ri-**jen**-er-it) **4** physically, economically, or spiritually renewed. ▸ **regeneration** *n* ▸ **regenerative** *adj*

regent *n* **1** the ruler of a country during the childhood, absence, or illness of its monarch. **2** *US & Canad* a member of the governing board of certain schools and colleges. ✧ *adj* **3** acting as a regent: *the Prince Regent.* ▷ **HISTORY** Latin *regere* to rule

reggae *n* a type of popular music of Jamaican origin with a strong beat. ▷ **HISTORY** West Indian

regicide *n* **1** the killing of a king. **2** a person who kills a king. ▷ **HISTORY** Latin *rex* king + *caedere* to kill

regime (ray-**zheem**) *n* **1** a system of government. **2** a particular administration: *the corrupt regime.* **3** *Med* a regimen. ▷ **HISTORY** French

regimen *n* a prescribed system of diet and exercise. ▷ **HISTORY** Latin: guidance

regiment *n* **1** an organized body of troops as a unit in the army. **2** a large number or group. ▷ **HISTORY** Late Latin *regimentum* government ▸ **regimental** *adj*

regimentals *pl n* **1** the uniform and insignia of a regiment. **2** military uniform.

regimental sergeant major *n Mil* the senior warrant officer in a regiment or battalion.

regimented *adj* very strictly controlled: *the regimented confines of the school.* ▸ **regimentation** *n*

Regina *n* queen: now used chiefly in documents and inscriptions. ▷ **HISTORY** Latin

region *n* **1** an administrative division of a country. **2** an area considered as a unit for geographical or social reasons. **3** a sphere of activity or interest. **4** a part of the body: *the lumbar region.* **5 in the region of** approximately: *in the region of 100,000 troops.* **6 the regions** the parts of a country away from the capital: *discord between Moscow and the regions.* ▷ **HISTORY** Latin *regio* ▸ **regional** *adj*

regionalism *n* **1** the division of a country or organization into geographical regions each having some autonomy. **2** loyalty to one's home region.

register *n* **1** an official list recording names, events, or transactions. **2** the book in which such a list is written. **3** a device that records data, totals sums of money, etc.: *a cash register.* **4** a style of speaking or writing, such as slang, used in particular circumstances or social situations. **5** *Music* **a** the timbre characteristic of a certain manner of voice production. **b** any of the stops on an organ in respect of its tonal quality: *the flute register.* ✧ *vb* **6** to enter (an event, person's name, ownership, etc.) in a register. **7** to show on a scale or other measuring instrument. **8** to show in a person's face or bearing: *his face registered surprise.* **9** *Informal* to have an effect or make an impression: *the news did not register at first.* **10** to have a letter or parcel insured against loss by the Post Office: *registered mail.* ▷ **HISTORY** Medieval Latin *registrum* ▸ **registration** *n*

register office *n Brit* a government office where civil marriages are performed and births, marriages, and deaths are recorded.

registrar *n* **1** a person who keeps official records. **2** an official responsible for student records and enrolment in a college. **3** a hospital doctor senior to a houseman but junior to a consultant.

registration document *n Brit & Austral* a document giving identification details of a vehicle, including its owner's name.

registration number *n* a sequence of letters and numbers given to a motor vehicle when it is registered, displayed on numberplates at the front and rear.

registry *n, pl* **-tries 1** a place where official records are kept. **2** the registration of a ship's country of origin: *a ship of Liberian registry.*

registry office *n Brit & NZ* same as **register office**.

Regius professor (**reej**-yuss) *n Brit* a person appointed by the Crown to a university chair founded by a royal patron. ▷ **HISTORY** Latin *regius* royal

regolith *n Geol* the layer of loose material covering the bedrock of the earth and moon, etc., comprising soil, sand, rock fragments, volcanic ash, glacial drift, etc. ▷ **HISTORY** Greek *rhēgos* covering, blanket + *lithos* stone

regress *vb* **1** to return to a former and worse condition. ✧ *n* **2** return to a former and worse condition. ▷ **HISTORY** Latin *regredi* to go back ▶ **regressive** *adj*

regression *n* **1** the act of regressing. **2** *Psychol* the use by an adult of behaviour more appropriate to a child.

regret *vb* **-gretting, -gretted 1** to feel sorry or upset about. **2** to express apology or distress: *we regret any misunderstanding caused.* ✧ *n* **3** a feeling of repentance, guilt, or sorrow. **4 regrets** a polite expression of refusal: *she had sent her regrets.* ▷ **HISTORY** Old French *regreter* ▶ **regretful** *adj* ▶ **regretfully** *adv* ▶ **regrettable** *adj* ▶ **regrettably** *adv*

> **☑ WORD TIP**
> *Regretful* and *regretfully* are sometimes wrongly used where *regrettable* and *regrettably* are meant: *he gave a regretful smile; he smiled regretfully; this is a regrettable* (not *regretful*) *mistake; regrettably* (not *regretfully*), *I shall be unable to attend.*

regroup *vb* **1** to reorganize (military forces) after an attack or a defeat. **2** to rearrange into a new grouping.

regular *adj* **1** normal, customary, or usual. **2** symmetrical or even: *regular features.* **3** according to a uniform principle, arrangement, or order. **4** occurring at fixed or prearranged intervals: *we run regular advertisements in the press.* **5** following a set rule or normal practice. **6** *Grammar* following the usual pattern of formation in a language: *regular verbs.* **7** of or serving in the permanent military services: *the regular armed forces.* **8** *Maths* (of a polygon) having all its sides and angles the same. **9** officially qualified or recognized: *he's not a regular doctor.* **10** *Informal* not constipated: *eating fresh vegetables helps keep you regular.* **11** *US & Canad informal* likeable: *a regular guy.* **12** complete or utter: *a regular fool.* **13** subject to the rule of an established religious community: *canons regular.* ✧ *n* **14** a professional long-term serviceman in a military unit. **15** *Informal* a frequent customer or visitor. ▷ **HISTORY** Latin *regula* ruler, model ▶ **regularity** *n* ▶ **regularize** *or* **-ise** *vb* ▶ **regularly** *adv*

regulate *vb* **-lating, -lated 1** to control by means of rules: *a code of practice to regulate advertising by schools.* **2** to adjust slightly: *he had to take drugs to regulate his heartbeat.* ▷ **HISTORY** Late Latin *regulare* to control ▶ **regulatory** *adj*

regulation *n* **1** a rule that governs procedure or behaviour. **2** the act of regulating. ✧ *adj* **3** in accordance with rules or conventions: *dressed in the orchestra's regulation black tie.*

regulator *n* **1** a mechanism that automatically controls pressure, temperature, etc. **2** the mechanism by which the speed of a clock is regulated. **3** *Econ* a person or body appointed by the government to ensure that a particular industry or utility offers choice and value to consumers.

regurgitate *vb* **-tating, -tated 1** to vomit. **2** (of some birds and animals) to bring back (partly digested food) to the mouth to feed the young. **3** to reproduce (ideas or facts) without understanding them. ▷ **HISTORY** Medieval Latin *re-* back + *gurgitare* to flood ▶ **regurgitation** *n*

rehabilitate *vb* **-tating, -tated 1** to help (a person) to readapt to society after illness or imprisonment. **2** to restore to a former position or rank. **3** to restore the good reputation of. ▷ **HISTORY** Medieval Latin *rehabilitare* to restore ▶ **rehabilitation** *n*

rehash *vb* **1** to use (old or already used ideas) in a slightly different form without real improvement. ✧ *n* **2** old ideas presented in a new form. ▷ **HISTORY** *re-* again + *hash* to chop into pieces

rehearse *vb* **-hearsing, -hearsed 1** to practise (a play, concert, etc.) for public performance. **2** to repeat aloud: *he rehearsed his familiar views on the press.* **3** to train (a person) for public performance. ▷ **HISTORY** Old French *rehercier* to harrow a second time ▶ **rehearsal** *n* ▶ **rehearser** *n*

rehouse *vb* **-housing, -housed** to provide with a new and better home.

Reich (**rike**) *n* the former German state, esp. the Nazi dictatorship in Germany from 1933–45 (**Third Reich**). ▷ **HISTORY** German: kingdom

reign *n* **1** the period during which a monarch is the official ruler of a country. **2** a period during which a person or thing is dominant: *a reign of terror.* ✧ *vb* **3** to rule (a country). **4** to be supreme: *a sense of confusion reigns in the capital.* ▷ **HISTORY** Old French *reigne*

> **☑ WORD TIP**
> *Reign* is sometimes wrongly written for *rein* in certain phrases: *he gave full rein* (not *reign*) *to his feelings; it will be necessary to rein in* (not *reign in*) *public spending.*

reimburse *vb* **-bursing, -bursed** to repay (someone) for (expenses or losses). ▷ **HISTORY** Medieval Latin *imbursare* to put in a moneybag ▶ **reimbursement** *n*

rein *n* **1 reins a** long narrow straps attached to a bit to control a horse. **b** narrow straps attached to a harness to control a young child. **c** means of control: *to take up the reins of government.* **2 give (a) free rein** to allow a considerable amount of freedom. **3 keep a tight rein on** to control carefully: *we have to keep a tight rein on expenditure.* ✧ *vb* **4** to restrain or halt with reins. **5** to control or limit: *public spending was reined in.* ▷ **HISTORY** Old French *resne*

> **☑ WORD TIP**
> See at **reign.**

reincarnate *vb* **-nating, -nated** to be born again in a different body: *souls may be reincarnated in human forms.*

reincarnation *n* **1** the belief that after death the soul is reborn in another body. **2** an instance of rebirth in another body. **3** reappearance in a new form of a principle or idea: *he was the reincarnation of the old Republican Party isolationist.*

reindeer *n, pl* **-deer** *or* **-deers** a deer with large branched antlers that lives in the arctic regions. ▷ **HISTORY** Old Norse *hreindýri*

A B C D E F G H I J K L M N O P Q R S T U V W X Y Z

reinforce *vb* **-inforcing, -inforced 1** to give added emphasis to (an idea or feeling): *his tired face reinforced his own weariness.* **2** to make physically stronger or harder: *the plastic panels were reinforced with carbon fibre.* **3** to give added support to (a military force) by providing more men or equipment: *the army garrison had been reinforced with helicopters.* ▷ **HISTORY** French *renforcer* ▶ **reinforcement** *n*

reinforced concrete *n* concrete with steel bars or mesh embedded in it to strengthen it.

reinstate *vb* **-stating, -stated 1** to restore to a former rank or status. **2** to cause to exist or be important again: *reinstate some semblance of order.* ▶ **reinstatement** *n*

reiterate *vb* **-ating, -ated** *Formal* to repeat again and again. ▷ **HISTORY** Latin *reiterare* ▶ **reiteration** *n*

reject *vb* **1** to refuse to accept, use, or believe. **2** to deny to (a person) the feelings hoped for: *the boy had been rejected by his mother.* **3** to pass over or throw out as useless. **4** (of an organism) to fail to accept (a tissue graft or organ transplant). ✧ *n* **5** a person or thing rejected as not up to standard. ▷ **HISTORY** Latin *reicere* to throw back ▶ **rejection** *n*

rejig *vb* **-jigging, -jigged 1** to re-equip (a factory or plant). **2** *Informal* to rearrange or manipulate, sometimes in an unscrupulous way: *the promoter hastily rejigged the running order.*

rejoice *vb* **-joicing, -joiced** to feel or express great happiness. ▷ **HISTORY** Old French *resjoir* ▶ **rejoicing** *n*

rejoin[1] *vb* to come together with (someone or something) again.

rejoin[2] *vb* to reply in a sharp or witty way. ▷ **HISTORY** Old French *rejoindre*

rejoinder *n* a sharp or witty reply.

rejuvenate *vb* **-nating, -nated 1** to give back youth or vitality to. **2** *Geol* to cause (a river) to begin eroding more vigorously to a new lower base level, usually because of uplift of the land. ▷ **HISTORY** Latin *re-* again + *juvenis* young

rekindle *vb* **-dling, -dled** to arouse (former emotions or interests).

relapse *vb* **-lapsing, -lapsed 1** to fall back into bad habits or illness. ✧ *n* **2** the act of relapsing. **3** the return of ill health after an apparent or partial recovery. ▷ **HISTORY** Latin *re-* back + *labi* to slip

relate *vb* **-lating, -lated 1** to establish a relation between. **2** to have reference or relation to. **3** to have an understanding (of people or ideas): *the inability to relate to others.* **4** to tell (a story) or describe (an event). ▷ **HISTORY** Latin *relatus* brought back

related *adj* **1** linked by kinship or marriage. **2** connected or associated: *salts and related compounds.*

relation *n* **1** the connection between things or people. **2** a person who is connected by blood or marriage. **3** connection by blood or marriage. **4** an account or narrative. **5 in** *or* **with relation to** with reference to: *an inquiry into export controls in relation to Iraq.*

relational process *n Functional grammar* the process of being or possessing as specified by a verb group. Compare **material process, mental process, verbal process**.

relations *pl n* **1** social or political dealings between individuals or groups. **2** family or relatives. **3** *Euphemistic* sexual intercourse.

relationship *n* **1** the dealings and feelings that exist between people or groups. **2** an emotional or sexual affair. **3** the connection between two things: *the relationship between exercise and mental health.* **4** association by blood or marriage.

relative *adj* **1** true to a certain degree or extent: *a zone of relative affluence.* **2** having significance only in relation to something else: *time is relative.* **3 relative to** in proportion to: *it will benefit from high growth in earnings relative to prices.* **4** respective: *the relative qualities of speed and accuracy.* **5** relevant: *the facts relative to the enquiry.* **6** *Grammar* of a clause (**relative clause**) that modifies a noun or pronoun occurring earlier in the sentence. **7** *Grammar* of or belonging to a class of words, such as *who, which,* or *that,* which function as conjunctions introducing relative clauses. ✧ *n* **8** a person who is related by blood or marriage. ▶ **relatively** *adv*

relative atomic mass *n* same as **atomic weight**.

relative clause *n Grammar* a subordinate clause, often beginning with *who, whom, which, whose,* or *that,* that gives information about or defines the person or thing mentioned immediately before.

relative density *n Physics* the ratio of the density of a substance such as water, under specified conditions. Compare **specific gravity**.

relative frequency *n Statistics* an estimate of probability based on the ratio of the actual number of favourable events to the total possible number of events.

relative pronoun *n Grammar* one of the pronouns *who, whom, whose, which,* or *that* when they introduce additional or defining information about a person or thing just mentioned, as in the example, *the man who masterminded the campaign.*

relativity *n* **1** either of two theories developed by Albert Einstein, the **special theory of relativity**, which requires that the laws of physics shall be the same as seen by any two different observers in uniform relative motion, and the **general theory of relativity**, which considers observers with relative acceleration and leads to a theory of gravitation. **2** the state of being relative.

relax *vb* **1** to make or become less tense, looser, or less rigid. **2** to ease up from effort or attention. **3** to make (rules or discipline) less strict. **4** to become more friendly. **5** to lessen the intensity of: *he relaxed his vigilance in the lulls between attacks.* ▷ **HISTORY** Latin *relaxare* to loosen ▶ **relaxed** *adj*

relaxation *n* **1** rest after work or effort. **2** a form of recreation: *his favoured form of relaxation was walking on the local moors.* **3** the act of relaxing.

relay *n* **1** a fresh set of people or animals relieving others. **2** short for **relay race**. **3** an automatic device that controls a valve or switch, esp. one in which a small change in current or voltage controls the switching on or off of circuits. **4** *Radio* a combination of a receiver and transmitter designed to receive radio signals and retransmit them. ✧ *vb* **5** to pass on (a message). **6** to retransmit (a signal) by means of a relay. **7** *Brit* to broadcast (a performance or event) as it happens. ▷ **HISTORY** Old French *relaier* to leave behind

relay race *n* a race between teams in which each contestant covers a specified portion of the distance.

release *vb* **-leasing, -leased 1** to free (a person or animal) from captivity or imprisonment. **2** to free (someone) from obligation or duty. **3** to free (something) from (one's grip). **4** to allow news or information to be made public or available. **5** to allow (something) to move freely: *she released the handbrake.* **6** to issue (a record, film, or book) for sale or public showing: *the record was originally released six years ago.* **7** to give out (heat, energy, radiation, etc.): *the explosion released a cloud of toxic gas.* ✧ *n* **8** the act of freeing or state of being freed. **9** a statement to the press. **10** the act of issuing for sale or publication. **11** something issued for sale or public showing. ▷ **HISTORY** Old French *relesser*

relegate *vb* **-gating, -gated 1** to put in a less important position. **2** to demote (a sports team) to a lower division: *four clubs were relegated from the first division.* ▷ **HISTORY** Latin *re-* back + *legare* to send ▸ **relegation** *n*

relent *vb* **1** to change one's mind about some decision. **2** to become milder or less severe: *the weather relented.* ▷ **HISTORY** Latin *re-* back + *lentare* to bend

relentless *adj* **1** never stopping or reducing in severity: *relentless deterioration in standards.* **2** (of a person) determined and pitiless.

relevant *adj* to do with the matter in hand. ▷ **HISTORY** Medieval Latin *relevans* ▸ **relevance** *n*

reliable *adj* able to be trusted. ▸ **reliability** *n* ▸ **reliably** *adv*

reliance *n* the state of relying on or trusting (a person or thing). ▸ **reliant** *adj*

relic *n* **1** an object or custom that has survived from the past. **2** something valued for its past associations. **3 relics** remaining parts or traces. **4** *RC Church, Eastern Church* a body part or possession of a saint, venerated as holy. ▷ **HISTORY** Latin *reliquiae* remains

relict *n Archaic* **1** a relic. **2** a widow. ▷ **HISTORY** Latin *relictus* left behind

relief *n* **1** a feeling of cheerfulness that follows the removal of anxiety, pain, or distress. **2** a temporary pause in anxiety, pain, or distress. **3** money, food, or clothing given to people in special need: *disaster relief.* **4** the act of freeing a besieged town or fortress: *the relief of Mafeking.* **5** a person who replaces another at some task or duty. **6** a bus, plane, etc., that carries additional passengers when a scheduled service is full. **7** Also called: **relievo** *Sculpture, archit* the projection of a carved design from the surface. **8** any vivid effect resulting from contrast: *a welcome relief.* **9** the difference between the highest and lowest level: *study the map of relief and the rainfall map.* **10 on relief** *US & Canad* (of people) in receipt of government aid because of personal need. ▷ **HISTORY** Old French *relever* to relieve

relief map *n* a map showing the shape and height of the land surface by contours and shading.

relief rainfall *n Meteorol* rain that occurs when air has been blown over the sea and is then forced up over an area of high land. The air then cools and the moisture in the air condenses and rain falls.

relieve *vb* **-lieving, -lieved 1** to lessen (pain, distress, boredom, etc.). **2** to bring assistance to (someone in need): *a plan to relieve those facing hunger.* **3** to free (someone) from an obligation: *a further attempt to relieve the taxpayers of their burdens.* **4** to take over the duties of (someone): *the night nurse came in to relieve her.* **5** to free (a besieged town or fort). **6 relieve oneself** to urinate or defecate. **7** to set off by contrast: *painted walls are marginally relieved by some abstract prints.* **8** *Informal* to take from: *the prince had relieved him of his duties.* ▷ **HISTORY** Latin *re-* again + *levare* to lighten ▸ **relieved** *adj*

religion *n* **1** belief in or worship of a supernatural power or powers considered to be divine or to have control of human destiny. **2** any formal expression of such belief: *the Christian religion.* **3** *Chiefly RC Church* the way of life entered upon by monks and nuns: *to enter religion.* ▷ **HISTORY** Latin *religio*

religious *adj* **1** of religion. **2** pious or devout. **3** scrupulous or conscientious: *religious attention to detail.* **4** *Christianity* relating to the way of life of monks and nuns. ✧ *n* **5** *Christianity* a monk or nun. ▸ **religiously** *adv*

relinquish *vb Formal* **1** to give up: *that hope has to be relinquished.* **2** to renounce (a claim or right). **3** to release one's hold on. ▷ **HISTORY** Latin *relinquere* ▸ **relinquishment** *n*

reliquary (**rel**-lik-wer-ee) *n, pl* **-quaries** a container for relics of saints.

relish *vb* **1** to savour or enjoy (an experience) to the full. **2** to anticipate eagerly. ✧ *n* **3** liking or enjoyment: *he has an enormous relish for life.* **4** pleasurable anticipation: *his early relish for a new challenge.* **5** an appetizing or spicy food, such as a pickle, added to a main dish to improve its flavour. **6** a zestful quality: *he tells stories with great relish.* ▷ **HISTORY** earlier *reles* aftertaste

relive *vb* **-living, -lived** to experience (a sensation or event) again, esp. in the imagination.

relocate *vb* **-cating, -cated** to move or be moved to a new place of work. ▸ **relocation** *n*

reluctance *n* **1** unwillingness to do something. **2** *Physics* a measure of the resistance of a closed magnetic circuit to a magnetic flux. ▷ **HISTORY** Latin *reluctari* to resist

reluctant *adj* unwilling or disinclined. ▸ **reluctantly** *adv*

rely *vb* **-lies, -lying, -lied rely on** *or* **upon a** to be dependent on: *the organization relies on voluntary contributions.* **b** to have trust or confidence in: *you can rely on his judgment.* ▷ **HISTORY** Old French *relier* to fasten together

REM rapid eye movement.

remain *vb* **1** to continue to be: *the situation remains alarming.* **2** to stay behind or in the same place: *to remain at home.* **3** to be left after use or the passage of time. **4** to be left to be done, said, etc.: *whether this will be a long-term trend remains to be seen.* ▷ **HISTORY** Latin *remanere*

remainder *n* **1** a part or portion that is left after use or the passage of time: *we ate some biscuits and the remainder of the jam.* **2** *Maths* **a** the amount left over when one quantity cannot be exactly divided by another: *for 10 ÷ 3, the remainder is 1.* **b** the amount left over when one quantity is subtracted from another. **3** a number of copies of a book sold cheaply because it has been impossible to sell them at full price. ✧ *vb* **4** to sell (copies of a book) as a remainder.

remains *pl n* **1** parts left over from something after use or the passage of time: *the remains of the old Roman fortress.* **2** a corpse.

remand *vb* **1** *Law* to send (a prisoner or accused person) back into custody or put on bail before trial. ✧ *n* **2** the sending of a person back into custody or putting on bail before trial. **3 on remand** in custody or on bail awaiting trial. ▷ **HISTORY** Latin *re-* back + *mandare* to command

remand centre *n* (in Britain) a place where accused people are detained while awaiting trial.

remark *vb* **1** to pass a casual comment (about). **2** to say. **3** to observe or notice. ✧ *n* **4** a brief casually expressed thought or opinion. ▷ **HISTORY** Old French *remarquer* to observe

remarkable *adj* **1** worthy of note or attention: *a remarkable career.* **2** striking or extraordinary: *a thing of remarkable beauty.* ▶ **remarkably** *adv*

remarry *vb* **-ries, -rying, -ried** to marry again following a divorce or the death of one's previous spouse. ▶ **remarriage** *n*

REME Royal Electrical and Mechanical Engineers.

remedial *adj* **1** providing or intended as a remedy. **2** of special teaching for slow learners: *remedial classes.* ▶ **remedially** *adv*

remedy *n, pl* **-edies 1** a drug or treatment for curing pain or disease. **2** a way of solving a problem: *every statesman promised a remedy for unemployment.* ✧ *vb* **-edies, -edying, -edied 3** to put right or improve. ▷ **HISTORY** Latin *remedium* a cure ▶ **remediable** *adj*

remember *vb* **1** to become aware of (something forgotten) again. **2** to keep (an idea, intention, etc.) in one's mind: *remember to write.* **3** to give money to (someone), as in a will or in tipping. **4 remember to** to mention (a person's name) to another person, by way of greeting: *remember me to her.* **5** to commemorate: *we are here to remember the dead.* ▷ **HISTORY** Latin *re-* again + *memor* mindful

remembrance *n* **1** a memory. **2** a memento or keepsake. **3** the act of honouring some past event or person.

Remembrance Day *n* **1** (in Britain) Remembrance Sunday. **2** (in Canada and Australia) a statutory holiday observed on November 11 in memory of the dead of both World Wars.

Remembrance Sunday *n* (in Britain) the Sunday closest to November 11th, on which the dead of both World Wars are commemorated.

remind *vb* **1** to cause to remember: *remind her that she was on duty.* **2** to put in mind (of someone or something): *you remind me of Alice in Wonderland.*

reminder *n* **1** something that recalls the past. **2** a note to remind a person of something not done.

reminisce *vb* **-niscing, -nisced** to talk or write about old times or past experiences.

reminiscence *n* **1** the act of recalling or narrating past experiences. **2** something remembered from the past. **3 reminiscences** stories about a person's life, often presented in a book.

reminiscent *adj* **1 reminiscent of** reminding or suggestive of. **2** characterized by reminiscence. ▷ **HISTORY** Latin *reminisci* to call to mind

remiss *adj Formal* careless in attention to duty or responsibility. ▷ **HISTORY** Latin *remissus*

remission *n* **1** a reduction in the length of a prison term. **2** forgiveness for sin. **3** easing of intensity of the symptoms of a disease. **4** a release from an obligation.

remit *vb* (rim-**mitt**) **-mitting, -mitted 1** to send (money) for goods or services. **2** to cancel (a punishment or debt). **3** *Law* to send back (a case) to a lower court for further consideration. **4** to slacken or ease off. **5** *Archaic* to forgive (crime or sins). ✧ *n* (**ree**-mitt) **6** area of authority: *within the review body's remit.* ▷ **HISTORY** Latin *re-* back + *mittere* to send

remittance *n* money sent as payment.

remittent *adj* (of a disease) periodically less severe.

remix *vb* **1** to change the relative prominence of each performer's part of (a recording). ✧ *n* **2** a remixed version of a recording.

remnant *n* **1** a part left over. **2** a piece of material from the end of a roll. **3** a surviving trace or vestige: *the authorities drafted in the military to crush any remnant of protest.* ▷ **HISTORY** Old French *remenant* remaining

remonstrance *n Formal* a strong protest about something.

remonstrate *vb* **-strating, -strated** *Formal* to argue in protest or objection: *the player remonstrated loudly with the official.* ▷ **HISTORY** Latin *re-* again + *monstrare* to show ▶ **remonstration** *n*

remorse *n* a sense of deep regret and guilt for something one did. ▷ **HISTORY** Medieval Latin *remorsus* a gnawing ▶ **remorseful** *adj*

remorseless *adj* **1** constantly unkind and lacking pity: *remorseless fate.* **2** continually intense: *the superintendent's remorseless gaze.*

remote *adj* **1** far away. **2** far from civilization. **3** distant in time. **4** not relevant: *the issues seem remote from the general population.* **5** (of a person's manner) aloof or abstracted. **6** slight or faint: *a remote possibility.* **7** operated from a distance; remote-controlled: *a remote manipulator arm.*

▷ **HISTORY** Latin *remotus* far removed ▶ **remotely** *adv*

remote control *n* control of an apparatus from a distance by radio or electrical signals. ▶ **remote-controlled** *adj*

remote sensing *n* the use of an instrument, such as a radar device or camera, to scan the earth or another planet from space in order to collect data about some aspect of it. ▶ **remote-sensing** *adj*

remould *vb* **1** to change completely: *to remould the country.* **2** *Brit* to bond a new tread onto the casing of (a worn pneumatic tyre). ✧ *n* **3** *Brit* a tyre made by this process.

removable *adj* capable of being removed from a place or released from another object: *a farmer's truck with removable wooden sides.*

removal *n* **1** the act of removing or state of being removed. **2** the process of moving one's possessions from a previous address to a new one.

remove *vb* **-moving, -moved 1** to take away and place elsewhere. **2** to take (clothing) off. **3** to get rid of. **4** to dismiss (someone) from office. **5** *Formal* to change the location of one's home or place of business. ✧ *n* **6** the degree of difference: *one remove away from complete rebuttal.* **7** *Brit* (in certain schools) a class or form designed to prepare pupils for senior classes. ▷ **HISTORY** Old French *removoir*

removed *adj* **1** very different or distant: *madness seemed far removed from the sunny order of things.* **2** separated by a degree of descent: *the child of a person's first cousin is their first cousin once removed.*

remunerate *vb* **-ating, -ated** *Formal* to reward or pay for work or service. ▷ **HISTORY** Latin *remunerari* ▶ **remuneration** *n* ▶ **remunerative** *adj*

renaissance *n* a renewal of interest or creativity in an area: *a complete renaissance in maze building.* ▷ **HISTORY** French

Renaissance *n* **1 the Renaissance** the great revival of art, literature, and learning in Europe in the 14th, 15th, and 16th centuries. ✧ *adj* **2** of or from the Renaissance.

renal (**ree**-nal) *adj* of the kidneys. ▷ **HISTORY** Latin *renes* kidneys

renascent *adj Literary* becoming active or vigorous again: *renascent nationalism.* ▷ **HISTORY** Latin *renasci* to be born again ▶ **renascence** *n*

rend *vb* **rending, rent** *Literary* **1** to tear violently. **2** (of a sound) to break (the silence) with a shrill or piercing tone. ▷ **HISTORY** Old English *rendan*

render *vb* **1** to cause to become: *he was rendered unconscious by his wound.* **2** to give or provide (aid, a service, etc.). **3** *Formal* to present or submit (a bill). **4** to translate. **5** to represent in painting, music, or acting. **6** to yield or give: *he rendered up his soul to God.* **7** to cover with plaster. **8** to melt down (fat). ▷ **HISTORY** Old French *rendre* ▶ **rendering** *n*

rendezvous (**ron**-day-voo) *n, pl* **-vous** (-vooz) **1** an appointment to meet at a specified time and place. **2** a place where people meet. ✧ *vb* **3** to meet at a specified time or place. ▷ **HISTORY** French

rendition *n Formal* **1** a performance of a piece of music or a dramatic role. **2** a translation.

renegade *n* a person who deserts a cause for another. ▷ **HISTORY** Spanish *renegado*

renege (rin-**nayg**) *vb* **-neging, -neged** to go back (on an agreement or promise): *the politicians reneged on every promise.* ▷ **HISTORY** Medieval Latin *renegare* to renounce

renew *vb* **1** to begin again. **2** to take up again after a break: *they wanted to renew diplomatic ties.* **3** to make valid again: *we didn't renew the lease.* **4** to grow again. **5** to restore to a new or fresh condition. **6** to replace (an old or worn-out part or piece). **7** to restate or reaffirm (a promise). ▶ **renewal** *n*

renewable *adj* **1** able to be renewed. ✧ *pl n* **renewables 2** sources of alternative energy, such as wind and wave power.

renewable resources *pl n Environmental science* resources that can easily be replaced or that can be replaced through good management, such as quick-growing species of tree. Compare **non-renewable resources.**

rennet *n* a substance prepared from the stomachs of calves and used for curdling milk to make cheese. ▷ **HISTORY** Old English *gerinnan* to curdle

renounce *vb* **-nouncing, -nounced 1** to give up (a belief or habit) voluntarily. **2** to give up formally (a claim or right): *he would renounce his rights to the throne.* ▷ **HISTORY** Latin *renuntiare*

renovate *vb* **-vating, -vated** to restore to good condition. ▷ **HISTORY** Latin *re-* again + *novare* to make new ▶ **renovation** *n* ▶ **renovator** *n*

renown *n* widespread good reputation. ▷ **HISTORY** Old French *renom*

renowned *adj* famous.

rent[1] *vb* **1** to give or have use of (land, a building, a machine, etc.) in return for periodic payments. ✧ *n* **2** a payment made periodically for the use of land, a building, a machine, etc. ▷ **HISTORY** Old French *rente* revenue

rent[2] *n* **1** a slit made by tearing. ✧ *vb* **2** the past of **rend**.

rent-a- *prefix* **1** denoting a rental service: *rent-a-car.* **2** *Derogatory* denoting a person or group that performs a function as if hired from a rental service: *rent-a-mob.*

rental *n* **1** the amount paid or received as rent. ✧ *adj* **2** of or relating to rent.

rentier (**ron**-tee-ay) *n* a person who lives off unearned income such as rents or interest.

renunciation *n* **1** the act or an instance of renouncing. **2** a formal declaration renouncing something.

reorganize *or* **-ise** *vb* **-izing, -ized** *or* **-ising, -ised** to organize in a new and more efficient way. ▶ **reorganization** *or* **-isation** *n*

rep[1] *n Theatre* short for **repertory company**.

rep[2] *n* **1** a sales representative. **2** someone elected to represent a group of people: *the union rep.* **3** *NZ informal* a rugby player selected to represent his district.

a b c d e f g h i j k l m n o p q r s t u v w x y z

repair[1] *vb* **1** to restore (something damaged or broken) to good condition or working order. **2** to make up for (a mistake or injury). **3** to heal (a breach or division) in (something): *he is attempting to repair his country's relations with America.* ✧ *n* **4** the act, task, or process of repairing. **5** a part that has been repaired. **6** state or condition: *many museums may have to close because they are in such bad repair.* ▷ **HISTORY** Latin *re-* again + *parare* to make ready ▸ **repairable** *adj*

repair[2] *vb* **repair to** to go to (a place). ▷ **HISTORY** Latin *re-* back + *patria* fatherland

reparation *n* **1** the act of making up for loss or injury. **2 reparations** compensation paid by a defeated nation after a war for the damage and injuries it caused. ▷ **HISTORY** Latin *reparare* to repair

repartee *n* **1** conversation consisting of witty remarks. **2** a sharp witty remark made as a reply. ▷ **HISTORY** French *repartie*

repast *n Literary* a meal. ▷ **HISTORY** Old French *repaistre* to feed

repatriate *vb* **-ating, -ated 1** to send back (a person) to the country of his or her birth or citizenship. ✧ *n* **2** a person who has been repatriated: *Algerian repatriates.* ▷ **HISTORY** Latin *re-* back + *patria* fatherland ▸ **repatriation** *n*

repay *vb* **-paying, -paid 1** to refund or reimburse. **2** to make a return for (something): *to repay hospitality.* ▸ **repayable** *adj* ▸ **repayment** *n*

repeal *vb* **1** to cancel (a law) officially. ✧ *n* **2** the act of repealing: *the repeal of repressive legislation.* ▷ **HISTORY** Old French *repeler* ▸ **repealable** *adj*

repeat *vb* **1** to say, write, or do again. **2** to tell to another person (the secrets told to one by someone else). **3** to recite (a poem, etc.) from memory. **4** to occur more than once: *this pattern repeats itself many times.* **5** (of food) to be tasted again after eating as the result of belching. **6** to say (the words or sounds) uttered by someone else; echo. ✧ *n* **7** the act or an instance of repeating. **8** a word, action, pattern, etc., that is repeated. **9** *Radio, television* a broadcast of a programme which has been broadcast before. **10** *Music* a passage that is an exact restatement of the passage preceding it. ▷ **HISTORY** Latin *repetere* to seek again ▸ **repeated** *adj* ▸ **repeatedly** *adv* ▸ **repeatable** *adj*

> **WORD TIP**
> Since *again* is part of the meaning of *repeat*, one should not say something is *repeated again*.

repeater *n* **1** a gun capable of firing several shots without reloading. **2** a clock or watch which strikes the hour or quarter-hour just past, when a spring is pressed.

repeat reading *n Science* the practice of taking a measurement more than once and then using an average of those results as a value, for example on a graph.

repel *vb* **-pelling, -pelled 1** to cause (someone) to feel disgusted. **2** to force or drive back (someone or something). **3** to be effective in keeping away or controlling: *these buzzers are claimed to repel female mosquitoes.* **4** to fail to mix with or absorb: *water and oil repel each other.* **5** to reject or spurn: *she repelled his advances.* ▷ **HISTORY** Latin *re-* back + *pellere* to push

> **WORD TIP**
> See at **repulse.**

repellent *adj* **1** disgusting or distasteful. **2** resisting water etc. ✧ *n* **3** a chemical used to keep insects or other creatures away.

repent *vb* to feel regret for (something bad one has done). ▷ **HISTORY** Old French *repentir* ▸ **repentance** *n* ▸ **repentant** *adj*

repercussion *n* **1 repercussions** results or consequences of an action or event. **2** an echo or reverberation. ▷ **HISTORY** Latin *repercutere* to strike back

repertoire *n* **1** all the works that a company or performer can perform. **2** the entire stock of skills or techniques that someone or something, such as a computer, is capable of: *a superb repertoire of shots.* ▷ **HISTORY** French

repertory *n, pl* **-ries 1** same as **repertoire** (sense 2). **2** short for **repertory company**. ▷ **HISTORY** Late Latin *repertorium* storehouse

repertory company *n* a permanent theatre company producing a succession of plays.

repetition *n* **1** the act of repeating. **2** a thing that is repeated. **3** a replica or copy. ▸ **repetitious** *adj* ▸ **repetitive** *adj*

rephrase *vb* **-phrasing, -phrased** to express in different words. ▸ **rephrasing** *n*

repine *vb* **-pining, -pined** *Literary* to be worried or discontented. ▷ **HISTORY** RE- + PINE[2]

replace *vb* **-placing, -placed 1** to take the place of. **2** to substitute a person or thing for (another): *we need to replace that chair.* **3** to put (something) back in its rightful place.

replacement *n* **1** the act or process of replacing. **2** a person or thing that replaces another.

replay *n* **1** a showing again of a sequence of action immediately after it happens. **2** a second sports match played because an earlier game was drawn. ✧ *vb* **3** to play (a recording, match, etc.) again.

replenish *vb* to make full or complete again by supplying what has been used up. ▷ **HISTORY** Old French *replenir* ▸ **replenishment** *n*

replete *adj* **1** pleasantly full of food and drink. **2** well supplied: *a world replete with true horror.* ▷ **HISTORY** Latin *repletus* ▸ **repletion** *n*

replica *n* an exact copy. ▷ **HISTORY** Italian, literally: a reply

replicate *vb* **-cating, -cated** to make or be an exact copy of; reproduce. ▷ **HISTORY** Latin *replicatus* bent back ▸ **replication** *n*

reply *vb* **-plies, -plying, -plied 1** to make answer (to) in words or writing or by an action. **2** to say (something) in answer: *she replied that she did not believe him.* ✧ *n, pl* **-plies 3** an answer or response. ▷ **HISTORY** Old French *replier* to fold again

report *vb* **1** to give an account (of). **2** to give an account of the results of an investigation (into): *the* *commission is to report on global warming.* **3** to make a formal report on (a subject). **4** to make a formal complaint about. **5** to present (oneself) at an appointed place or for a specific purpose: *report to the manager's office.* **6 report to** to be responsible to and under the authority of. **7** to act as a reporter. ✧ *n* **8** an account prepared after investigation and published or broadcast. **9** an account of the discussions of a committee or other group of people: *I have the report of the mining union.* **10** a story for which there is no absolute proof: *according to report, he is not dead.* **11** *Brit & NZ* a statement on the progress of a school child. **12** a loud bang made by a gun or explosion. **13** comment on a person's character or actions: *he is of good report here.* ▷ HISTORY Latin *re-* back + *portare* to carry ▶ **reportedly** *adv*

reported speech *n Grammar* a report of what someone said that gives the content of the speech without repeating the exact words.

reporter *n* a person who gathers news for a newspaper or broadcasting organization.

report genre *n* a form of writing or speech in which the writer or speaker presents information in the form of a report.

repose[1] *n* **1** a state of quiet restfulness. **2** calmness or composure. **3** sleep. ✧ *vb* **-posing, -posed 4** to lie or lay down at rest. **5** to lie when dead. ▷ HISTORY Old French *reposer*

repose[2] *vb* **-posing, -posed** to put (trust) in a person or thing. ▷ HISTORY Latin *reponere* to store up

reposition *vb* to place in a different position.

repository *n, pl* **-ries 1** a place or container in which things can be stored for safety: *a repository for national treasures.* **2** a person to whom a secret is entrusted. ▷ HISTORY Latin *repositorium*

repossess *vb* (of a lender) to take back (property) from a customer who is behind with payments, for example mortgage repayments. ▶ **repossession** *n*

reprehend *vb* to find fault with. ▷ HISTORY Latin *reprehendere*

reprehensible *adj* deserving criticism: *Willie's reprehensible behaviour.*

represent *vb* **1** to act as the authorized delegate for (a person, country, etc.): *she represented her country at the Olympic Games.* **2** to act as a substitute for. **3** to stand as an equivalent of. **4** to be a means of expressing: *the lights are relit to represent resurrection.* **5** to display the characteristics of: *romanticism in music is represented by Liszt.* **6** to describe as having a specified character or quality: *the magical bird was often represented as having two heads.* **7** to state or explain. **8** to present an image of through a picture or sculpture. **9** to bring clearly before the mind. ▷ HISTORY Latin *repraesentare* to exhibit

representation *n* **1** the state of being represented. **2** anything that represents, such as a pictorial portrait. **3 representations** formal statements made to an official body by a person making a complaint. ▶ **representational** *adj*

representative *n* **1** a person chosen to act for or represent a group. **2** a person who tries to sell the products or services of a firm. **3** a typical example. ✧ *adj* **4** typical of a class or kind. **5** representing. **6** including examples of all the interests or types in a group. **7** acting as deputy for another. **8** of a political system in which people choose a person to make decisions on their behalf.

representative action *n Law* a legal action undertaken by one or more people representing the interests of a large group of people with the same grievance.

repress *vb* **1** to keep (feelings) under control. **2** to restrict the freedom of: *he continued to repress his people.* **3** *Psychol* to banish (unpleasant thoughts) from one's conscious mind. ▷ HISTORY Latin *reprimere* to press back ▶ **repression** *n* ▶ **repressive** *adj*

reprieve *vb* **-prieving, -prieved 1** to postpone the execution of (a condemned person). **2** to give temporary relief to. ✧ *n* **3** a postponement or cancellation of a punishment. **4** a warrant granting a postponement or cancellation. **5** a temporary relief from pain or harm. ▷ HISTORY Old French *repris* (something) taken back

reprimand *vb* **1** to blame (someone) officially for a fault. ✧ *n* **2** an instance of blaming someone officially. ▷ HISTORY French *réprimande*

reprint *vb* **1** to print further copies of (a book). ✧ *n* **2** a reprinted copy.

reprisal *n* an act of taking revenge: *many residents say they are living in fear of reprisals by the army.* ▷ HISTORY Old French *reprisaille*

reprise (rip-**preez**) *Music* ✧ *n* **1** the repeating of an earlier theme. ✧ *vb* **-prising, -prised 2** to repeat an earlier theme.

reproach *n* **1** blame or rebuke. **2** a scolding. **3 beyond reproach** beyond criticism. ✧ *vb* **4** to express disapproval (of someone's actions). ▷ HISTORY Old French *reprochier* ▶ **reproachful** *adj*

reprobate (**rep**-roh-bate) *n* **1** an unprincipled bad person. ✧ *adj* **2** morally unprincipled. ▷ HISTORY Late Latin *reprobatus* held in disfavour

reprobation *n Literary* disapproval or blame.

reproduce *vb* **-ducing, -duced 1** to make a copy or representation of. **2** *Biol* to produce offspring. **3** to re-create. ▶ **reproducible** *adj*

reproduction *n* **1** *Biol* a process by which an animal or plant produces one or more individuals similar to itself. **2** a copy of a work of art. **3** the quality of sound from an audio system. **4** the act or process of reproducing. ✧ *adj* **5** made in imitation of an earlier style: *reproduction furniture.* ▶ **reproductive** *adj*

reproof *n* a severe blaming of someone for a fault.

reprove *vb* **-proving, -proved** to speak severely to (someone) about a fault. ▷ HISTORY Old French *reprover* ▶ **reprovingly** *adv*

reptile *n* **1** a cold-blooded animal, such as a tortoise, snake, or crocodile, that has an outer covering of horny scales or plates and lays eggs. **2** a contemptible grovelling person. ▷ HISTORY Late Latin *reptilis* creeping ▶ **reptilian** *adj*

A B C D E F G H I J K L M N O P Q R S T U V W X Y Z

republic *n* **1** a form of government in which the people or their elected representatives possess the supreme power. **2** a country in which the head of state is an elected or nominated president. ▷ HISTORY Latin *respublica,* literally: the public thing

republican *adj* **1** of or supporting a republic. ✧ *n* **2** a person who supports or advocates a republic. ▶ **republicanism** *n*

Republican *adj* **1** belonging to the Republican Party, the more conservative of the two main political parties in the US. **2** belonging to the Irish Republican Army. ✧ *n* **3** a member or supporter of the Republican Party in the US. **4** a member or supporter of the Irish Republican Army. ▶ **Republicanism** *n*

repudiate (rip-**pew**-dee-ate) *vb* **-ating, -ated** **1** to reject the authority or validity of. **2** to disown (a person). **3** to refuse to acknowledge or pay (a debt). ▷ HISTORY Latin *repudium* divorce ▶ **repudiation** *n*

repugnant *adj* offensive or disgusting. ▷ HISTORY Latin *repugnans* resisting ▶ **repugnance** *n*

repulse *vb* **-pulsing, -pulsed** **1** to be disgusting to: *this act of feminist rage repulsed as many as it delighted.* **2** to drive (an army) back. **3** to reject with coldness or discourtesy: *she repulsed his advances.* ✧ *n* **4** a driving back. **5** a cold discourteous rejection or refusal. ▷ HISTORY Latin *repellere*

> **WORD TIP**
> Some people think that the use of *repulse* in sentences such as *he was repulsed by what he saw* is incorrect and that the correct word is *repel.*

repulsion *n* **1** a feeling of disgust or aversion. **2** *Physics* a force separating two objects, such as the force between two like electric charges.

repulsive *adj* **1** disgusting or distasteful. **2** *Physics* of repulsion. ▶ **repulsively** *adv*

reputable (**rep**-pew-tab-bl) *adj* trustworthy or respectable. ▶ **reputably** *adv*

reputation *n* **1** the opinion generally held of a person or thing. **2** a high opinion generally held about a person or thing. **3** notoriety or fame, esp. for some specified characteristic. ▷ HISTORY Latin *reputatio*

repute *n* good reputation: *a sculptor of international repute.* ▷ HISTORY Latin *reputare* to think over

reputed *adj* supposed or rumoured: *the island was reputed to have held a Roman temple; the reputed murderess.* ▶ **reputedly** *adv*

request *vb* **1** to ask for or politely demand: *we requested a formal meeting with the committee.* ✧ *n* **2** the act or an instance of asking for something: *a polite request.* **3** something asked for. **4 on request** if asked for: *most companies will send samples on request.* ▷ HISTORY Old French *requeste*

Requiem (**rek**-wee-em) *n* **1** *RC Church* a Mass celebrated for the dead. **2** a musical setting of this Mass. ▷ HISTORY Latin *requies* rest

require *vb* **-quiring, -quired** **1** to need. **2** to be a necessary condition: *the decision requires a logical common-sense approach.* **3** to insist upon. **4** to order or command: *family doctors are required to produce annual reports.* ▷ HISTORY Latin *requirere* to seek to know

> **WORD TIP**
> The use of *require to* as in *I require to see the manager* or *you require to complete a special form* is thought by many people to be incorrect: *I need to see the manager; you are required to complete a special form.*

requirement *n* **1** something demanded or imposed as an obligation. **2** a specific need or want.

requisite (**rek**-wizz-it) *adj* **1** absolutely essential. ✧ *n* **2** something essential. ▷ HISTORY Latin *requisitus* sought after

requisition *vb* **1** to demand and take for use, esp. for military or public use. ✧ *n* **2** a formal request or demand for the use of something. **3** the act of taking something over, esp. for military or public use. **4** a formal written demand.

requite *vb* **-quiting, -quited** to return to someone (the same treatment or feeling as received): *an Australian who requites her love.* ▷ HISTORY *re-* back + obsolete *quite* to repay ▶ **requital** *n*

reredos (**rear**-doss) *n* a screen or wall decoration at the back of an altar. ▷ HISTORY Old French *arere* behind + *dos* back

rerun *n* **1** a film or programme that is broadcast again. **2** a race that is run again. ✧ *vb* **-running, -ran, -run** **3** to put on (a film or programme) again. **4** to run (a race) again.

resale *n* the selling again of something purchased.

reschedule *vb* **-uling, -uled** **1** to change the time, date, or schedule of: *the show has been rescheduled for August.* **2** to arrange a revised schedule for repayment of (a debt).

rescind *vb* to annul or repeal. ▷ HISTORY Latin *rescindere* to cut off

rescission *n* **1** the act of rescinding. **2** *Law* the right to have a contract set aside if it has been entered into mistakenly, as a result of misrepresentation, undue influence, etc.

rescue *vb* **-cuing, -cued** **1** to bring (someone or something) out of danger or trouble. ✧ *n* **2** the act or an instance of rescuing. ▷ HISTORY Old French *rescourre* ▶ **rescuer** *n*

research *n* **1** systematic investigation to establish facts or collect information on a subject. ✧ *vb* **2** to carry out investigations into (a subject). ▷ HISTORY Old French *recercher* to search again ▶ **researcher** *n*

resemble *vb* **-bling, -bled** to be or look like. ▷ HISTORY Old French *resembler* ▶ **resemblance** *n*

resent *vb* to feel bitter or indignant about. ▷ HISTORY French *ressentir* ▶ **resentful** *adj* ▶ **resentment** *n*

reservation *n* **1** a doubt: *his only reservation was, did he have the stamina?* **2** an exception or limitation that prevents one's wholehearted acceptance: *work I admire without reservation.* **3** a seat, room, etc., that has been reserved. **4** (esp. in the US) an area of land set aside for American Indian peoples: *the Cherokee reservation.* **5** *Brit* short for **central reservation**.

reserve *vb* **-serving, -served 1** to keep back or set aside for future use. **2** to obtain by arranging beforehand: *I phoned to reserve two tickets.* **3** to keep for oneself: *the association reserves the right to charge a fee.* **4** to delay announcing (a legal judgment). ✧ *n* **5** something kept back or set aside for future use. **6** the state or condition of being reserved: *we're keeping these two in reserve.* **7** *Sport* a substitute. **8** an area of publicly owned land used for sport, etc.: *a wildlife reserve.* **9** the hiding of one's feelings and personality. **10** the part of a nation's armed services not in active service. **11 reserves** *Finance* money or assets held by a bank or business to meet future expenses. **12** *Canad* an Indian reservation. ▷ **HISTORY** Latin *reservare* to keep

reserved *adj* **1** not showing one's feelings. **2** set aside for use by a particular person.

reserve price *n* the minimum price acceptable to the owner of property being auctioned or sold.

reservist *n* a member of a nation's military reserve.

reservoir *n* **1** a natural or artificial lake for storing water for community use. **2** a large supply of something: *a vast reservoir of youthful enthusiasm.* ▷ **HISTORY** French *réservoir*

reshuffle *n* **1** a reorganization of jobs in a government or company. ✧ *vb* **-fling, -fled 2** to reorganize jobs or duties in a government or company.

reside *vb* **-siding, -sided** *Formal* **1** to live permanently (in a place): *my daughter resides in Europe.* **2** to be present (in): *desire resides in the unconscious.* ▷ **HISTORY** Latin *residere* to sit back

residence *n* **1** a person's home or house. **2** a large imposing house. **3** the fact of residing in a place. **4** a period of residing in a place. **5 in residence a** living in a particular place: *the Monarch was not in residence.* **b** (of an artist) working for a set period at a college, gallery, etc.: *composer in residence.*

residence order *n Law* a court order specifying with which party a child shall live.

resident *n* **1** a person who lives in a place. **2** a bird or animal that does not migrate. ✧ *adj* **3** living in a place. **4** living at a place in order to carry out a job: *a resident custodian.* **5** employed for one's specialized abilities: *the Museum's resident expert on 17th-century Dutch art.* **6** (of birds and animals) not in the habit of migrating.

residential *adj* **1** (of a part of a town) consisting mainly of houses. **2** providing living accommodation: *residential clubs for homeless boys.*

residential school *n* a government boarding school in N Canada for Indian and Inuit students.

residual *adj* **1** of or being a remainder. ✧ *n* **2** something left over as a residue.

residue *n* **1** what is left over after something has been removed. **2** *Law* what is left of an estate after the discharge of debts and distribution of specific gifts. ▷ **HISTORY** Latin *residuus* remaining over

residuum *n, pl* **-ua** same as **residue**.

resign *vb* **1** to give up office or a job. **2** to accept (an unpleasant fact): *he resigned himself to the inevitable.* **3** to give up (a right or claim). ▷ **HISTORY** Latin *resignare* to unseal, destroy

resignation *n* **1** the act of resigning. **2** a formal document stating one's intention to resign. **3** passive endurance of difficulties: *full of quiet resignation.*

resigned *adj* content to endure something unpleasant. ▶ **resignedly** *adv*

resilient *adj* **1** (of a person) recovering easily and quickly from misfortune or illness. **2** (of an object) capable of regaining its original shape or position after bending or stretching. ▷ **HISTORY** Latin *resilire* to jump back ▶ **resilience** *n*

resin (**rezz**-in) *n* **1** a solid or semisolid substance obtained from certain plants: *cannabis resin.* **2** a similar substance produced synthetically. ▷ **HISTORY** Latin *resina* ▶ **resinous** *adj*

resist *vb* **1** to stand firm against or oppose: *the party's old guard continue to resist economic reform.* **2** to refrain from in spite of temptation: *I couldn't resist a huge portion of almond cake.* **3** to refuse to comply with: *to resist arrest.* **4** to be proof against: *airport design should be strengthened to help resist explosion.* ▷ **HISTORY** Latin *resistere* ▶ **resistible** *adj*

resistance *n* **1** the act of resisting. **2** the capacity to withstand something, esp. the body's natural capacity to withstand disease. **3** *Electricity* the opposition to a flow of electric current through a circuit, component, or substance. **4** any force that slows or hampers movement: *wind resistance.* **5 line of least resistance** the easiest, but not necessarily the best, course of action. ▶ **resistant** *adj, n*

Resistance *n* **the Resistance** an illegal organization fighting for national liberty in a country under enemy occupation.

resistor *n* an electrical component designed to introduce a known value of resistance into a circuit.

resit *vb* **-sitting, -sat 1** to sit (an examination) again. ✧ *n* **2** an examination which one must sit again.

resolute *adj* firm in purpose or belief. ▷ **HISTORY** Latin *resolutus* ▶ **resolutely** *adv*

resolution *n* **1** firmness or determination. **2** a decision to do something. **3** a formal expression of opinion by a meeting. **4** the act of resolving. **5** *Music* the process in harmony whereby a dissonant note or chord is followed by a consonant one. **6** the ability of a television to reproduce fine detail. **7** *Physics* Also called: **resolving power** the ability of a telescope or microscope to produce separate images of closely placed objects.

resolve *vb* **-solving, -solved 1** to decide or determine firmly. **2** to express (an opinion) formally by a vote. **3** to separate or cause to separate into constituent parts. **4** to find the answer or solution to. **5** to explain away or dispel: *to resolve the controversy.* **6** *Music* to follow (a dissonant note or chord) by one producing a consonance. **7** *Physics* to distinguish between (separate parts) of (an image) as in a microscope, telescope, or other optical instrument. ✧ *n* **8** absolute determination:

a b c d e f g h i j k l m n o p q r s t u v w x y z

he spoke of his resolve to deal with the problem of terrorism. ▷ HISTORY Latin *resolvere* to unfasten, reveal

resolved *adj* determined.

resonance *n* **1** the condition or quality of being resonant. **2** sound produced by a body vibrating in sympathy with a neighbouring source of sound. ▷ HISTORY Latin *resonare* to resound

resonant *adj* **1** resounding or re-echoing. **2** producing resonance: *the resonant cavities of the mouth.* **3** full of resonance: *his voice is a resonant baritone.*

resonate *vb* **-nating, -nated** to resound or cause to resound. ▶ **resonator** *n*

resort *vb* **1 resort to** to have recourse to for help, use, etc.: *some people have resorted to begging for food.* **2** to go, esp. often or habitually: *to resort to the beach.* ✧ *n* **3** a place to which many people go for holidays. **4** the use of something as a means or aid. **5 last resort** the last possible course of action open to a person. ▷ HISTORY Old French *resortir* to come out again

resound (riz-**zownd**) *vb* **1** to ring or echo with sound. **2** (of sounds) to echo or ring. **3** to be widely known: *his fame resounded throughout India.* ▷ HISTORY Latin *resonare* to sound again

resounding *adj* **1** echoing. **2** clear and emphatic: *he won a resounding victory.* ▶ **resoundingly** *adv*

resource *n* **1 resources** sources of economic wealth, esp. of a country or business enterprise: *mineral resources.* **2 resources** money available for use. **3** something resorted to for aid or support: *he saw the university as a resource for the community.* **4** the ability to deal with problems: *a man of resource.* **5** a means of doing something: *resistance was their only resource.* ▷ HISTORY Old French *resourdre* to spring up again

resourceful *adj* capable and full of initiative. ▶ **resourcefulness** *n*

respect *n* **1** consideration: *respect for my feelings.* **2** an attitude of deference or esteem. **3** the state of being honoured or esteemed. **4** a detail or characteristic: *in virtually all respects boys develop more slowly than girls.* **5 in respect of** *or* **with respect to** in reference or relation to. **6 respects** polite greetings: *he paid his respects to her and left.* ✧ *vb* **7** to have an attitude of esteem towards: *she is the person I most respect and wish to emulate.* **8** to pay proper attention or consideration to: *he called on rebel groups to respect a cease-fire.* ▷ HISTORY Latin *respicere* to pay attention to ▶ **respecter** *n*

respectable *adj* **1** worthy of respect. **2** having good social standing or reputation. **3** relatively or fairly good: *they obtained respectable results.* **4** fit to be seen by other people. ▶ **respectability** *n* ▶ **respectably** *adv*

respectful *adj* full of or showing respect. ▶ **respectfully** *adv*

respecting *prep* on the subject of.

respective *adj* relating separately to each of several people or things: *the culprits will be repatriated to their respective countries.*

respectively *adv* (in listing things that refer to another list) separately in the order given: *Diotema and Mantinea were tutors to Pythagoras and Socrates respectively.*

respiration (ress-per-**ray**-shun) *n* **1** breathing. **2** the process in living organisms of taking in oxygen and giving out carbon dioxide. **3** the breakdown of complex organic substances that takes place in the cells of animals and plants, producing energy and carbon dioxide. ▶ **respiratory** *adj*

respirator *n* **1** a device worn over the mouth and nose to prevent the breathing in of poisonous fumes. **2** an apparatus for providing artificial respiration.

respire *vb* **-spiring, -spired 1** to breathe. **2** to undergo respiration. ▷ HISTORY Latin *respirare* to exhale

respite *n* **1** an interval of rest: *I allowed myself a six-month respite to enjoy my family.* **2** a temporary delay. ▷ HISTORY Old French *respit*

resplendent *adj* **1** brilliant or splendid in appearance. **2** shining. ▷ HISTORY Latin *re-* again + *splendere* to shine ▶ **resplendence** *n*

respond *vb* **1** to state or utter (something) in reply. **2** to act in reply: *the government must respond accordingly to our recommendations.* **3** to react favourably: *most headaches will respond to the use of relaxants.* ▷ HISTORY Old French *respondre*

respondent *n Law* a person against whom a petition is brought.

response *n* **1** the act of responding. **2** a reply or reaction. **3** a reaction to stimulation of the nervous system. **4 responses** *Christianity* the words recited or sung in reply to the priest at a church service.

responsibility *n, pl* **-ties 1** the state of being responsible. **2** a person or thing for which one is responsible.

responsible *adj* **1 a responsible for** having control or authority over. **b** being the agent or cause (of some action): *only a small number of students were responsible for the disturbances.* **2 responsible to** being accountable for one's actions and decisions to: *management should be made more responsible to shareholders.* **3** rational and accountable for one's own actions. **4** (of a position or duty) involving decision and accountability. ▷ HISTORY Latin *respondere* to respond ▶ **responsibly** *adv*

responsive *adj* reacting quickly or favourably to something. ▶ **responsiveness** *n*

respray *n* a new coat of paint applied to a vehicle.

rest[1] *n* **1** relaxation from exertion or labour. **2** a period of inactivity. **3** relief or refreshment. **4** calm. **5** death regarded as repose: *now he has gone to his eternal rest.* **6 at rest a** not moving. **b** calm. **c** dead. **d** asleep. **7** a pause or interval. **8** a mark in a musical score indicating a pause lasting a specific time. **9** a thing or place on which to put something for support or to steady it. **10 lay to rest** to bury (a dead person). ✧ *vb* **11** to become or make refreshed. **12** to position (oneself, etc.) for rest or relaxation. **13** to place for support or steadying: *he* *slumped forward to rest his head on his forearms.* **14** to depend or rely: *his presidency rested on the outcome of the crisis.* **15** to direct (one's eyes) or (of one's eyes) to be directed: *she rested her gaze on the face of the statue.* **16** to be at ease. **17** to cease or cause to cease from motion or exertion. **18** to remain without further attention or action: *she refused to let the matter rest.* **19** *Law* to finish the introduction of evidence in (a case). **20** to put (pastry) in a cool place to allow the gluten to contract. ▷ HISTORY Old English *ræst, reste*

rest² *n* **1 the rest a** something left; remainder. **b** the others: *the rest of the world.* ✧ *vb* **2** to continue to be (as specified): *your conscience can rest easy.* ▷ HISTORY Old French *rester* to remain

rest area *n Austral & NZ* a motorist's stopping place off a highway, equipped with tables and seats.

restaurant *n* a place where meals are prepared and served to customers. ▷ HISTORY French

restaurant car *n Brit & Austral* a railway coach in which meals are served.

restaurateur (rest-er-a-**tur**) *n* a person who owns or runs a restaurant.

rest-cure *n* a rest taken as part of a course of medical treatment.

restful *adj* relaxing or soothing.

restitution *n* **1** the act of giving back something that has been lost or stolen. **2** *Law* compensation for loss or injury. ▷ HISTORY Latin *restituere* to rebuild

restive *adj* **1** restless or uneasy. **2** impatient of control or authority. ▷ HISTORY Old French *restif* balky

restless *adj* **1** bored or dissatisfied. **2** unable to stay still or quiet. **3** not restful: *a restless sleep.* ▸ **restlessly** *adv* ▸ **restlessness** *n*

restoration *n* **1** the act of restoring to a former or original condition, place, etc. **2** the giving back of something lost or stolen. **3** something restored, replaced, or reconstructed. **4** a model or representation of a ruin or extinct animal. **5 the Restoration** *Brit* the re-establishment of the monarchy in 1660 or the reign of Charles II (1660–85).

restorative (rist-**or**-a-tiv) *adj* **1** giving back health or good spirits. ✧ *n* **2** a food or medicine that gives back health or good spirits.

restore *vb* **-storing, -stored 1** to return (something) to its original or former condition. **2** to bring back to health or good spirits. **3** to return (something lost or stolen) to its owner. **4** to re-enforce or re-establish: *he must restore confidence in himself and his government; they worked to restore the monarchy.* **5** to reconstruct (a ruin, extinct animal, etc.). ▷ HISTORY Latin *restaurare* to rebuild ▸ **restorer** *n*

restrain *vb* **1** to hold (someone) back from some action. **2** to limit or restrict: *restrain any tendency to impulse-buy.* **3** to deprive (someone) of liberty. ▷ HISTORY Latin *re-* back + *stringere* to draw

restrained *adj* not displaying emotion.

restraining order *n Law* a court order prohibiting a person from doing something such as making contact with a specified individual or going to a particular place.

restraint *n* **1** something that restrains. **2** the ability to control one's impulses or passions. **3** a restraining or being restrained.

restrict *vb* to confine or keep within certain limits. ▷ HISTORY Latin *restrictus* bound up ▸ **restrictive** *adj*

restriction *n* a rule or situation that limits or controls something or someone: *operating under severe financial restrictions.*

restrictive practice *n Brit & Austral* **1** a trading agreement against the public interest. **2** a practice of a union or other group tending to limit the freedom of other workers or employers.

rest room *n US, Canad & Austral* a toilet in a public building.

restructure *vb* **-turing, -tured** to organize in a different way: *to restructure the world economy.*

result *n* **1** the outcome or consequence of an action, policy, etc. **2** the final score of a sporting contest. **3** a number or value obtained by solving a mathematical problem. **4** a favourable result, esp. a victory or success: *the best chance of a result is at Cheltenham.* **5 results** the marks or grades obtained in an examination. ✧ *vb* **6 result from** to be the outcome or consequence of: *poverty resulting from high unemployment.* **7 result in** to end in (a specified way): *negotiations which resulted in the Treaty of Paris.* ▷ HISTORY Latin *resultare* to spring from

resultant *adj* **1** arising as a result: *the resultant publicity.* ✧ *n* **2** *Maths, physics* a single vector that is the vector sum of two or more other vectors, such as a force which results from two other forces acting on a single point.

resume *vb* **-suming, -sumed 1** to begin again or go on with (something interrupted). **2** to occupy again or recover: *he will resume his party posts today.* ▷ HISTORY Latin *resumere*

résumé (**rezz**-yew-may) *n* **1** a short descriptive summary. **2** *US, Canad & Austral* a curriculum vitae. ▷ HISTORY French

resumption *n* the act of resuming or beginning again.

resurgence *n* a rising again to vigour: *worldwide religious resurgence.* ▷ HISTORY Latin *resurgere* to rise again ▸ **resurgent** *adj*

resurrect *vb* **1** to bring or be brought back to life from death. **2** to bring back into use or activity.

resurrection *n* **1** a return to life by a dead person. **2** revival or renewal. **3 the Resurrection a** *Christian theol* the rising again of Christ from the tomb three days after his death. **b** the rising again from the dead of all people at the Last Judgment. ▷ HISTORY Latin *resurgere* to rise again

resuscitate (ris-**suss**-it-tate) *vb* **-tating, -tated** to restore to consciousness. ▷ HISTORY Latin *re-* again + *suscitare* to raise ▸ **resuscitation** *n*

retail *n* **1** the sale of goods individually or in small quantities to the public. ✧ *adj* **2** of or engaged in such selling: *auctioneers have been successful in cornering the retail market.* ✧ *adv* **3** in small amounts or at a retail price. ✧ *vb* **4** to sell or be sold in small quantities to the public. **5** to relate (gossip or scandal) in detail: *he gleefully retailed the story.* ▷ HISTORY Old French *re-* again + *taillier* to cut ▶ **retailer** *n*

retain *vb* **1** to keep in one's possession. **2** to be able to hold or contain: *with this method the salmon retains its flavour and texture.* **3** *Law* to engage the services of (a barrister) by payment of a preliminary fee. **4** (of a person) to be able to remember (something) without difficulty. **5** to hold in position. ▷ HISTORY Latin *retinere* to hold back

retainer *n* **1** a fee paid in advance to engage someone's services. **2** *Brit, Austral & NZ* a reduced rent paid for a room or flat to reserve it for future use. **3** a servant who has been with a family for a long time.

retake *vb* **-taking, -took, -taken 1** to recapture: *to retake Jerusalem.* **2** to take something, such as an examination or vote, again. ✧ *n* **3** *Films* a rephotographed scene.

retaliate *vb* **-ating, -ated 1** to repay some injury or wrong in kind. **2** to cast (accusations) back upon a person. ▷ HISTORY Latin *re-* back + *talis* of such kind ▶ **retaliation** *n* ▶ **retaliatory** *adj*

retard *vb* to delay or slow down (the progress or development). ▷ HISTORY Latin *retardare* ▶ **retardant** *n, adj* ▶ **retardation** *n*

retarded *adj* underdeveloped mentally.

retch *vb* **1** to undergo spasms of the stomach as if one is vomiting. ✧ *n* **2** an involuntary spasm of the stomach. ▷ HISTORY Old English *hrǣcan*

retention *n* **1** the act of retaining or state of being retained. **2** the capacity to remember. **3** *Pathol* the abnormal holding of something within the body, esp. fluid. ▶ **retentive** *adj*

rethink *vb* **-thinking, -thought 1** to think about (something) again with a view to changing one's tactics. ✧ *n* **2** the act or an instance of thinking again.

reticent *adj* not willing to say or tell much. ▷ HISTORY Latin *reticere* to keep silent ▶ **reticence** *n*

reticulate *adj* in the form of a network or having a network of parts: *a reticulate leaf.* ▷ HISTORY Late Latin *reticulatus* like a net ▶ **reticulation** *n*

retina *n, pl* **-nas** *or* **-nae** the light-sensitive inner lining of the back of the eyeball. ▷ HISTORY Medieval Latin ▶ **retinal** *adj*

retinue *n* a band of attendants accompanying an important person. ▷ HISTORY Old French *retenue*

retire *vb* **-tiring, -tired 1** to give up or to cause (a person) to give up work, esp. on reaching pensionable age. **2** to go away into seclusion. **3** to go to bed. **4** to withdraw from a sporting contest, esp. because of injury. **5** to pull back (troops) from battle or (of troops) to fall back. ▷ HISTORY French *retirer* ▶ **retired** *adj* ▶ **retirement** *n*

retirement pension *n Brit* a regular payment made by the state or a former employee to a retired person over a specified age.

retiring *adj* very shy.

retort[1] *vb* **1** to reply quickly, wittily, or angrily. **2** to use (an argument) against its originator. ✧ *n* **3** a sharp, angry, or witty reply. **4** an argument used against its originator. ▷ HISTORY Latin *re-* back + *torquere* to twist, wrench

retort[2] *n* **1** a glass vessel with a long tapering neck that is bent down, used for distillation. **2** a vessel used for heating ores in the production of metals or heating coal to produce gas. ▷ HISTORY see RETORT[1]

retouch *vb* to restore or improve (a painting or photograph) with new touches.

retrace *vb* **-tracing, -traced 1** to go back over (one's steps or a route). **2** to go over (a story) from the beginning.

retract *vb* **1** to withdraw (a statement, charge, etc.) as invalid or unjustified. **2** to go back on (a promise or agreement). **3** to draw in (a part or appendage): *the rear wheels are retracted for tight spaces.* ▷ HISTORY Latin *retractare* to withdraw ▶ **retraction** *n*

retractile *adj* capable of being drawn in: *the retractile claws of a cat.*

retread *vb* **-treading, -treaded 1** to bond a new tread onto (a worn tyre). ✧ *n* **2** a remoulded tyre.

retreat *vb* **1** *Mil* to withdraw or retire in the face of or from action with an enemy. **2** to retire or withdraw to seclusion or shelter. **3** to alter one's opinion about something. ✧ *n* **4** the act of retreating or withdrawing. **5** *Mil* **a** a withdrawal or retirement in the face of the enemy. **b** a bugle call signifying withdrawal or retirement. **6** a place to which one may retire, esp. for religious contemplation. **7** a period of seclusion, esp. for religious contemplation. **8** the act of altering one's opinion about something. ▷ HISTORY Old French *retret*

retrench *vb* to reduce expenditure. ▷ HISTORY Old French *re-* off + *trenchier* to cut ▶ **retrenchment** *n*

retrial *n* a second trial of a defendant in a court of law.

retribution *n* punishment or vengeance for evil deeds. ▷ HISTORY Latin *re-* back + *tribuere* to pay ▶ **retributive** *adj*

retrieve *vb* **-trieving, -trieved 1** to get or fetch back again. **2** to bring back to a more satisfactory state: *his attempt to retrieve the situation.* **3** to rescue or save. **4** to recover (stored information) from a computer system. **5** (of dogs) to find and fetch (shot birds and animals). **6** to remember. ✧ *n* **7** the chance of being retrieved: *beyond retrieve.* ▷ HISTORY Old French *retrover* ▶ **retrievable** *adj* ▶ **retrieval** *n*

retriever *n* a dog trained to retrieve shot birds and animals.

retro *adj* associated with or revived from the past: *swap sandals for heeled mules to complete the retro look.*

retro- *prefix* **1** back or backwards: *retroactive.* **2** located behind: *retrochoir.* ▷ HISTORY Latin

retroactive *adj* effective from a date in the past: *justice through retroactive legislation is never justice.*

A B C D E F G H I J K L M N O P Q R S T U V W X Y Z

retrograde *adj* **1** tending towards an earlier worse condition. **2** moving or bending backwards. **3** (esp. of order) reverse or inverse. ✧ *vb* **-grading, -graded 4** to go backwards or deteriorate. ▷ **HISTORY** Latin *retro-* backwards + *gradi* to walk

retrogress *vb* to go back to an earlier worse condition. ▷ **HISTORY** Latin *retrogressus* having moved backwards ▶ **retrogression** *n* ▶ **retrogressive** *adj*

retrorocket *n* a small rocket on a larger rocket or a spacecraft, that produces thrust in the opposite direction to the direction of flight in order to slow down.

retrospect *n* **in retrospect** when looking back on the past. ▷ **HISTORY** Latin *retrospicere* to look back

retrospective *adj* **1** looking back in time. **2** applying from a date in the past: *retrospective legislation.* ✧ *n* **3** an exhibition of an artist's life's work.

retroussé (rit-**troo**-say) *adj* (of a nose) turned upwards. ▷ **HISTORY** French

retsina *n* a Greek wine flavoured with resin. ▷ **HISTORY** Modern Greek

return *vb* **1** to come back to a former place or state. **2** to give, put, or send back. **3** to repay with something of equivalent value: *she returned the compliment.* **4** *Sport* to hit, throw, or play (a ball) back. **5** to recur or reappear: *as he relaxed his appetite returned.* **6** to come back or revert in thought or speech: *let's return to what he said.* **7** to earn or yield (profit or interest). **8** to answer or reply. **9** to vote into office. **10** *Law* (of a jury) to deliver (a verdict). ✧ *n* **11** the act or an instance of coming back. **12** the act of being returned. **13** replacement or restoration: *the return of law and order.* **14** something that is given or sent back. **15** *Sport* the act of playing or throwing a ball back. **16** a recurrence or reappearance: *the return of tuberculosis.* **17** the yield or profit from an investment or venture. **18** a statement of one's taxable income (a **tax return**). **19** an answer or reply. **20** *Brit, Austral, & NZ* short for **return ticket**. **21 in return** in exchange. **22 returns** statement of the votes counted at an election. **23 by return (of post)** *Brit* by the next post back to the sender. **24 many happy returns (of the day)** a conventional birthday greeting. ✧ *adj* **25** of or being a return: *the team is keen on a return match.* ▷ **HISTORY** Old French *retorner* ▶ **returnable** *adj*

returning officer *n* an official in charge of conducting an election in a constituency.

return ticket *n Brit, Austral, & NZ* a ticket allowing a passenger to travel to a place and back.

reunify *vb* **-fies, -fying, -fied** to bring together again something previously divided. ▶ **reunification** *n*

reunion *n* **1** a gathering of people who have been apart. **2** the act of coming together again.

reunite *vb* **-niting, -nited** to bring or come together again after a separation.

reuse *n* **1** the act of using something again. ✧ *vb* **-using, -used 2** to use again. ▶ **reusable** *adj*

rev *Informal* ✧ *n* **1** revolution per minute (of an engine). ✧ *vb* **revving, revved 2** to increase the speed of revolution of (an engine).

Rev. Reverend.

revalue *vb* **-valuing, -valued** to adjust the exchange value of (a currency) upwards. ▶ **revaluation** *n*

revamp *vb* to patch up or renovate.

Revd. Reverend.

reveal *vb* **1** to disclose or divulge (a secret). **2** to expose to view or show (something concealed). **3** (of God) to disclose (divine truths). ▷ **HISTORY** Latin *revelare* to unveil

revealing *adj* **1** disclosing information that one did not know: *she made several revealing remarks during the interview.* **2** (of clothes) showing more of the body than is usual.

reveille (riv-**val**-ee) *n* a signal given by a bugle or drum to awaken soldiers or sailors in the morning. ▷ **HISTORY** French *réveillez!* awake!

revel *vb* **-elling, -elled** *or US* **-eling, -eled 1 revel in** to take pleasure or wallow in: *he would revel in his victory.* **2** to take part in noisy festivities. ✧ *n* **3 revels** noisy merrymaking. ▷ **HISTORY** Old French *reveler* ▶ **reveller** *n*

revelation *n* **1** the act of making known a truth that was previously secret. **2** a fact newly made known. **3** a person or experience that proves to be different from expectations: *New York State could prove a revelation to first-time visitors.* **4** *Christianity* God's disclosure of his own nature and his purpose for mankind.

Revelation *or* **Revelations** *n Informal* the last book of the New Testament, containing visionary descriptions of heaven, and of the end of the world.

revelry *n, pl* **-ries** noisy or unrestrained merrymaking.

revenge *n* **1** vengeance for wrongs or injury received. **2** something done as a means of vengeance. ✧ *vb* **-venging, -venged 3** to inflict equivalent injury or damage for (injury received). **4** to take vengeance for (oneself or another). ▷ **HISTORY** Old French *revenger* ▶ **revengeful** *adj*

revenue *n* **1** income, esp. that obtained by a government from taxation. **2** a government department responsible for collecting taxes. ▷ **HISTORY** Old French *revenir* to return

reverberate *vb* **-ating, -ated 1** to resound or re-echo. **2** to reflect or be reflected many times. ▷ **HISTORY** Latin *re-* again + *verberare* to beat ▶ **reverberation** *n*

revere *vb* **-vering, -vered** to be in awe of and respect deeply. ▷ **HISTORY** Latin *revereri*

reverence *n* profound respect. ▶ **reverential** *adj*

Reverence *n* **Your** *or* **His Reverence** a title sometimes used for a Roman Catholic priest.

reverend *adj* **1** worthy of reverence. **2** relating to or designating a clergyman. ✧ *n* **3** *Informal* a clergyman.

Reverend *adj* a title of respect for a clergyman.

> ☑ **WORD TIP**
> *Reverend* with a surname alone (*Reverend Smith*), as a term of address (*'Yes, Reverend'*), or in the greeting of a letter (*Dear Rev. Mr Smith*) are all generally considered to be wrong usage. Preferred are (*the*) *Reverend John Smith* or *Reverend Mr Smith* and *Dear Mr Smith.*

reverent *adj* feeling or expressing reverence.

reverie *n* absent-minded daydream. ▷ **HISTORY** Old French *resverie* wildness

revers (riv-**veer**) *n, pl* **-vers** the turned-back lining of part of a garment, such as the lapel or cuff. ▷ **HISTORY** French

reverse *vb* **-versing, -versed 1** to turn or set in an opposite direction, order, or position. **2** to change into something different or contrary: *the Cabinet intends to reverse the trend of recent polls.* **3** to move backwards or in an opposite direction: *as he started to reverse the car, the bomb exploded.* **4** to run (machinery) in the opposite direction to normal. **5** to turn inside out. **6** *Law* to revoke or set aside (a judgment or decree). **7 reverse the charges** to make a telephone call at the recipient's expense. ✧ *n* **8** the opposite or contrary of something. **9** the back or rear side of something. **10** a change to an opposite position, state, or direction. **11** a change for the worse. **12** the gear by which a motor vehicle can be made to go backwards. **13** the side of a coin bearing a secondary design. **14 in reverse** in an opposite or backward direction. **15 the reverse of** not at all: *the result was the reverse of his expectations.* ✧ *adj* **16** opposite or contrary in direction, position, etc. **17** denoting the gear by which a motor vehicle can be made to go backwards. ▷ **HISTORY** Latin *reversus* turned back ▶ **reversal** *n*

reverse fault *n Geol* a fault in which rock on one side of the fault is pushed up higher than the other. Compare **normal fault**.

reversible *adj* **1** capable of being reversed: *the effect of the operation may not be reversible.* **2** (of a garment) made so that either side may be used as the outer side.

reversible reaction *n Chem, Physics* a reaction that is capable of producing either of two possible states and changing from one to the other.

reversing lights *pl n* a pair of lights on the rear of a motor vehicle that go on when the vehicle is moving backwards.

reversion *n* **1** a return to an earlier condition, practice, or belief. **2** *Biol* the return of individuals or organs to a more primitive condition or type. **3** the rightful passing of property to the owner or designated heir.

revert *vb* **1** to go back to a former state. **2** *Biol* (of individuals or organs) to return to a more primitive, earlier, or simpler condition or type. **3** to come back to a subject. **4** *Property law* (of an estate) to return to its former owner. ▷ **HISTORY** Latin *revertere*

> ☑ **WORD TIP**
> Since *back* is part of the meaning of *revert*, one should not say that someone *reverts back* to a certain type of behaviour.

review *n* **1** a critical assessment of a book, film, etc. **2** a publication containing such articles. **3** a general survey or report: *the new curriculum is to be set up a year after the conclusions of the review are due.* **4** a formal or official inspection. **5** the act or an instance of reviewing. **6** a second consideration; re-examination. **7** a retrospective survey. **8** *Law* a re-examination of a case. ✧ *vb* **9** to hold or write a review of. **10** to examine again: *the committee will review the ban in the summer.* **11** to look back upon (a period of time or sequence of events): *he reviewed his achievements with pride.* **12** to inspect formally or officially: *when he reviewed the troops they cheered him.* **13** *Law* to re-examine (a decision) judicially. ▷ **HISTORY** Latin *re-* again + *videre* to see

reviewer *n* a person who writes reviews of books, films, etc.

revile *vb* **-viling, -viled** to be abusively scornful of: *his works were reviled and admired in equal measure.* ▷ **HISTORY** Old French *reviler*

revise *vb* **-vising, -vised 1** to change or alter: *he grudgingly revised his opinion.* **2** to prepare a new edition of (a previously printed work). **3** to read (something) several times in order to learn it in preparation for an examination. ▷ **HISTORY** Latin *re-* again + *visere* to inspect

Revised Version *n* a revision of the Authorized Version of the Bible published between 1881 and 1885.

revision *n* **1** the act or process of revising. **2** a corrected or new version of a book, article, etc.

revisionism *n* **1** (in Marxist ideology) any dangerous departure from the true interpretation of Marx's teachings. **2** the advocacy of revision of some political theory. ▶ **revisionist** *n, adj*

revival *n* **1** a reviving or being revived. **2** a reawakening of religious faith. **3** a new production of a play that has not been recently performed. **4** a renewed use or interest in: *there has been an Art Deco revival.*

revivalism *n* a movement that seeks to revive religious faith. ▶ **revivalist** *n, adj*

revive *vb* **-viving, -vived 1** to make or become lively or active again. **2** to bring or be brought back to life, consciousness, or strength: *revived by a drop of whisky.* **3** *Theatre* to put on a new production of (an old play). ▷ **HISTORY** Latin *re-* again + *vivere* to live

revoke *vb* **-voking, -voked 1** to take back or cancel (an agreement, will, etc.). **2** *Cards* to break a rule by failing to follow suit when able to do so. ✧ *n* **3** *Cards* the act of revoking. ▷ **HISTORY** Latin *revocare* to call back ▶ **revocation** *n*

revolt *n* **1** a rebellion or uprising against authority. **2 in revolt** in the state of rebelling. ✧ *vb*

3 to rise up in rebellion against authority. **4** to cause to feel disgust. ▷ **HISTORY** French *révolter*

revolting *adj* horrible and disgusting.

revolution *n* **1** the overthrow of a regime or political system by the governed. **2** (in Marxist theory) the transition from one system of production in a society to the next. **3** a far-reaching and drastic change. **4 a** movement in or as if in a circle. **b** one complete turn in a circle: *33 revolutions per minute.* ▷ **HISTORY** Latin *revolvere* to revolve

revolutionary *adj* **1** of or like a revolution. **2** advocating or engaged in revolution. **3** radically new or different: *they have designed revolutionary new materials to build power stations.* ✧ *n, pl* **-aries** **4** a person who advocates or engages in revolution.

revolutionize *or* **-ise** *vb* **-izing, -ized** *or* **-ising, -ised** to bring about a radical change in.

revolve *vb* **-volving, -volved 1** to move or cause to move around a centre. **2 revolve around** to be centred or focused upon: *the campaign revolves around one man.* **3** to occur periodically or in cycles. **4** to consider or be considered. ▷ **HISTORY** Latin *revolvere* ▶ **revolvable** *adj*

revolver *n* a pistol with a revolving cylinder that allows several shots to be fired without reloading.

revolving door *n* a door with four leaves at right angles to each other, revolving about a vertical axis.

revue *n* a theatrical entertainment with topical sketches and songs. ▷ **HISTORY** French

revulsion *n* a violent feeling of disgust. ▷ **HISTORY** Latin *revulsio* a pulling away

reward *n* **1** something given in return for a service. **2** a sum of money offered for finding a criminal or missing property. **3** something received in return for good or evil: *sacrifice provided its own reward.* ✧ *vb* **4** to give something to (someone) for a service rendered. ▷ **HISTORY** Old French *rewarder* to regard

rewarding *adj* giving personal satisfaction: *my most professionally rewarding experience.*

rewarewa (ray-wa-**ray**-wa) *n* a tall New Zealand tree with reddish wood. ▷ **HISTORY** Maori

rewind *vb* **-winding, -wound** to run (a tape or film) back to an earlier point in order to replay.

rewire *vb* **-wiring, -wired** to provide (a house, engine, etc.) with new wiring.

rewrite *vb* **-writing, -wrote, -written 1** to write again in a different way. ✧ *n* **2** something rewritten.

Rex *n* king: now used chiefly in documents and inscriptions. ▷ **HISTORY** Latin

Rf *chem* rutherfordium.

RFC Rugby Football Club.

RGN (in Britain) Registered General Nurse.

Rh 1 *Chem* rhodium. **2** See **Rh factor**.

rhapsodize *or* **-dise** *vb* **-dizing, -dized** *or* **-dising, -dised** to speak or write with extravagant enthusiasm.

rhapsody *n, pl* **-dies 1** *Music* a freely structured and emotional piece of music. **2** an expression of ecstatic enthusiasm. ▷ **HISTORY** Greek *rhaptein* to sew together + *ōidē* song ▶ **rhapsodic** *adj*

rhea (**ree**-a) *n* a large fast-running flightless bird of South America, similar to the ostrich. ▷ **HISTORY** after *Rhea,* mother of Zeus

rheme *n Linguistics* everything in a sentence that is not the theme; the part of the sentence that adds most new information. Compare **theme** (sense 5). ▷ **HISTORY** Greek *rhēma* that which is said

rhenium *n Chem* a silvery-white metallic element with a high melting point. Symbol: Re. ▷ **HISTORY** Latin *Rhenus* the Rhine

rheostat *n* a variable resistor in an electrical circuit, such as one used to dim lights. ▷ **HISTORY** Greek *rheos* flow + *-statēs* stationary ▶ **rheostatic** *adj*

rhesus factor (**ree**-suss) *n* See **Rh factor**.

rhesus monkey *n* a small long-tailed monkey of S Asia. ▷ **HISTORY** Greek *Rhesos,* mythical Thracian king

rhetoric (**ret**-a-rik) *n* **1** the art of using speech or writing to persuade or influence. **2** artificial or exaggerated language: *there's been no shortage of soaring rhetoric at this summit.* ▷ **HISTORY** Greek *rhētorikē (tekhnē)* (art) of rhetoric

rhetorical (rit-**tor**-ik-kl) *adj* **1** concerned with effect or style rather than content or meaning; bombastic. **2** of or relating to rhetoric or oratory. ▶ **rhetorically** *adv*

rhetorical device *n* any device used by speakers or writers to give more impact to their speech or writing, for example the use of repetition or direct address.

rhetorical question *n* a question to which no answer is required, used for dramatic effect, for example *who knows?*

rheum (**room**) *n* a watery discharge from the eyes or nose. ▷ **HISTORY** Greek *rheuma* a flow ▶ **rheumy** *adj*

rheumatic *adj* **1** caused by or affected by rheumatism. ✧ *n* **2** a person suffering from rheumatism. ▶ **rheumatically** *adv*

rheumatic fever *n* a disease with inflammation and pain in the joints.

rheumatics *n Informal* rheumatism.

rheumatism *n* any painful disorder of joints, muscles, or connective tissue. ▷ **HISTORY** Greek *rheuma* a flow

rheumatoid *adj* (of symptoms) resembling rheumatism.

rheumatoid arthritis *n* a chronic disease causing painful swelling of the joints.

Rh factor *n* an antigen commonly found in human blood: the terms **Rh positive** and **Rh negative** are used to indicate its presence or absence. ▷ **HISTORY** after the rhesus monkey, in which it was first discovered

rhinestone *n* an imitation diamond made of glass. ▷ **HISTORY** originally made at Strasbourg, on the Rhine

rhino *n, pl* **-nos** *or* **-no** a rhinoceros.

a b c d e f g h i j k l m n o p q r s t u v w x y z

rhinoceros *n, pl* **-oses** *or* **-os** a large plant-eating mammal of SE Asia and Africa with one or two horns on the nose and a very thick skin.

WORD HISTORY
'Rhinoceros' came into English via Latin from Greek *rhinokerōs*, from *rhino-*, meaning 'of the nose', and *keras*, meaning 'horn'.

rhizome *n* a thick horizontal underground stem whose buds develop into new plants. ▷ HISTORY Greek *rhiza* a root

rhodium *n Chem* a hard silvery-white metallic element, used to harden platinum and palladium. Symbol: Rh. ▷ HISTORY Greek *rhodon* rose, from the pink colour of its compounds

rhododendron *n* an evergreen shrub with clusters of showy flowers. ▷ HISTORY Greek *rhodon* rose + *dendron* tree

rhodopsin *n Physiol* a red pigment in the rods of the retina of the eye.

rhombohedron (rom-boh-**heed**-ron) *n, pl* **-drons** *or* **-dra** (-dra) a six-sided prism whose sides are parallelograms. ▷ HISTORY RHOMBUS + Greek *-edron* -sided

rhomboid *n* **1** a parallelogram with adjacent sides of unequal length. It resembles a rectangle but does not have 90° angles. ✧ *adj also* **rhomboidal 2** having such a shape. ▷ HISTORY Greek *rhomboeidēs* shaped like a rhombus

rhombus (**rom**-buss) *n, pl* **-buses** *or* **-bi** (-bye) a parallelogram with sides of equal length but no right angles. ▷ HISTORY Greek *rhombos* something that spins ▶ **rhombic** *adj*

rhubarb *n* **1** a large-leaved plant with long green and red stalks which can be cooked and eaten. **2** a related plant of central Asia, whose root can be dried and used as a laxative or astringent. ✧ *interj, n* **3** the noise made by actors to simulate conversation, esp. by repeating the word *rhubarb*. ▷ HISTORY Old French *reubarbe*

rhyme *n* **1** sameness of the final sounds in lines of verse or in words. **2** a word that is identical to another in its final sound: *'while' is a rhyme for 'mile'*. **3** a piece of poetry with corresponding sounds at the ends of the lines. **4 rhyme or reason** sense or meaning. ✧ *vb* **rhyming, rhymed 5** (of a word) to form a rhyme with another word. **6** to compose (verse) in a metrical structure. ▷ HISTORY Old French *rime;* spelling influenced by *rhythm*

rhyme scheme *or* **pattern** *n Poetry* the system of rhymes used by a poet in a particular work.

rhymester *n* a mediocre poet.

rhyming couplet *n Poetry* two lines of verse which rhyme and usually have the same metre.

rhyming slang *n* slang in which a word is replaced by another word or phrase that rhymes with it, e.g. *apples and pears* meaning *stairs*.

rhythm *n* **1** any regular movement or beat: *the side-effects can cause changes in the rhythm of the heart beat.* **2** any regular pattern that occurs over a period of time: *the seasonal rhythm of the agricultural year.* **3 a** the arrangement of the durations of and stress on the notes of a piece of music, usually laid out in regular groups (**bars**) of beats. **b** any specific arrangement of such groupings: *waltz rhythm.* **4** (in poetry) the arrangement of words to form a regular pattern of stresses. ▷ HISTORY Greek *rhuthmos* ▶ **rhythmic** *or* **rhythmical** *adj* ▶ **rhythmically** *adv*

rhythm and blues *n* a kind of popular music of Black American origin, derived from and influenced by the blues.

rhythm method *n* a method of contraception in which intercourse is avoided at times when conception is most likely.

RI Rhode Island.

ria *n* a long narrow inlet of the sea coast, being a former valley that was submerged by the sea. ▷ HISTORY Spanish *ría* estuary

rialto *n, pl* **-tos** a market or exchange. ▷ HISTORY after the *Rialto,* the business centre of medieval Venice

rib¹ *n* **1** one of the curved bones forming the framework of the upper part of the body and attached to the spinal column. **2** a cut of meat including one or more ribs. **3** a curved supporting part, such as in the hull of a boat. **4** one of a series of raised rows in knitted fabric. ✧ *vb* **ribbing, ribbed 5** to provide or support with ribs. **6** to knit to form a rib pattern. ▷ HISTORY Old English *ribb* ▶ **ribbed** *adj*

rib² *vb* **ribbing, ribbed** *Informal* to tease or ridicule. ▷ HISTORY short for *rib-tickle* ▶ **ribbing** *n*

ribald *adj* coarse or obscene in a humorous or mocking way. ▷ HISTORY Old French *ribauld* ▶ **ribaldry** *n*

ribbing *n* **1** a pattern of ribs in knitted material. **2** a framework or structure of ribs.

ribbon *n* **1** a narrow strip of fine material used for trimming, tying, etc. **2** a long narrow strip of inked cloth or plastic used to produce print in a typewriter. **3** a small strip of coloured cloth worn as a badge or as a symbol of an award. **4** a long thin strip: *a ribbon of white water.* **5 ribbons** ragged strips or shreds: *his clothes were torn to ribbons; his credibility was shot to ribbons.* ▷ HISTORY Old French *riban*

ribbon development *n Brit & Austral* the building of houses along a main road.

ribbonwood *n* a small evergreen tree of New Zealand.

ribcage *n* the bony structure formed by the ribs that encloses the lungs.

riboflavin (rye-boe-**flay**-vin) *n* a vitamin of the B complex that occurs in green vegetables, milk, fish, eggs, liver, and kidney: used as a yellow or orange food colouring (**E101**). Also called: **vitamin B_2** ▷ HISTORY *ribose,* a sugar + Latin *flavus* yellow

ribonucleic acid *n* the full name of **RNA**.

ribosome *n Biol* a minute particle in the cytoplasm of cells that contains RNA and protein and is the site of protein synthesis. ▶ **ribosomal** *adj*

rice *n* **1** the edible grain of an erect grass that grows on wet ground in warm climates. ✧ *vb* **ricing, riced 2** *US & Canad* to sieve (potatoes or other vegetables) to a coarse mashed consistency. ▷ HISTORY Greek *orūza*

rice paper *n* **1** a thin edible paper made from rice straw. **2** a thin Chinese paper made from the rice-paper plant, the pith of which is flattened into sheets.

rich *adj* **1** owning a lot of money or property. **2** well supplied (with a desirable substance or quality): *a country rich with cultural interest.* **3** having an abundance of natural resources, minerals, etc.: *a land rich in unexploited minerals.* **4** producing abundantly: *the island is a blend of hilly moorland and rich farmland.* **5** luxuriant or prolific: *the meadows rich with corn.* **6** (of food) containing much fat or sugar. **7** having a full-bodied flavour: *a gloriously rich Cabernet-dominated wine.* **8** (of colour) intense or vivid: *her hair had a rich auburn tint.* **9** (of sound or a voice) full or resonant. **10** very amusing or ridiculous: *a rich joke.* **11** (of a fuel-air mixture) containing a relatively high proportion of fuel. ▷ HISTORY Old English *rīce* (originally of people, with sense: great, mighty) ▶ **richness** *n*

riches *pl n* valuable possessions or desirable substances: *the unexpected riches of Georgian culture.*

richly *adv* **1** in a rich or elaborate manner: *the rooms are richly decorated with a variety of classical motifs.* **2** fully and appropriately: *he left the field to a richly deserved standing ovation.*

Richter scale *n Geol* a scale for expressing the magnitude of an earthquake, ranging from 0 to over 8. Compare **Mercalli scale**. ▷ HISTORY after Charles *Richter*, seismologist

rick[1] *n* a large stack of hay or straw. ▷ HISTORY Old English *hrēac*

rick[2] *vb* **1** to wrench or sprain (a joint). ✧ *n* **2** a wrench or sprain of a joint. ▷ HISTORY variant of *wrick*

rickets *n* a disease of children, caused by a deficiency of vitamin D and characterized by softening of developing bone, and hence bow legs. ▷ HISTORY origin unknown

rickety *adj* **1** likely to collapse or break: *a rickety wooden table.* **2** resembling or afflicted with rickets. ▶ **ricketiness** *n*

rickshaw *or* **ricksha** *n* **1** a small two-wheeled passenger vehicle pulled by one or two people, used in parts of Asia. **2** a similar vehicle with three wheels, propelled by a person pedalling. ▷ HISTORY Japanese *jinrikisha*

ricochet (**rik**-osh-ay) *vb* **-cheting, -cheted** *or* **-chetting, -chetted 1** (of a bullet) to rebound from a surface. ✧ *n* **2** the motion or sound of a rebounding bullet. ▷ HISTORY French

rid *vb* **ridding, rid** *or* **ridded 1 rid of** to relieve (oneself) or make a place free of (something undesirable). **2 get rid of** to relieve or free oneself of (something undesirable). ▷ HISTORY Old Norse *rythja*

ridden *vb* **1** the past participle of **ride**. ✧ *adj* **2** afflicted or affected by the thing specified: *the police found three bullet-ridden bodies.*

riddle[1] *n* **1** a question, puzzle, or verse phrased so that ingenuity is required to find the answer or meaning. **2** a puzzling person or thing. ✧ *vb* **-dling, -dled 3** to speak in riddles. ▷ HISTORY Old English *rǣdels(e)*

riddle[2] *vb* **-dling, -dled 1** to pierce with many holes. **2** to put through a sieve. ✧ *n* **3** a coarse sieve. ▷ HISTORY Old English *hriddel* a sieve

ride *vb* **riding, rode, ridden 1** to sit on and control the movements of (a horse or other animal). **2** to sit on and propel (a bicycle or motorcycle). **3** to travel on or in a vehicle: *he rides around in a chauffeur-driven Rolls-Royce.* **4** to travel over: *they rode the countryside in search of shelter.* **5** to travel through or be carried across (sea, sky, etc.): *the moon was riding high.* **6** *US & Canad* to cause to be carried: *to ride someone out of town.* **7** (of a vessel) to lie at anchor. **8** to tyrannize over or dominate: *politicians must stop riding roughshod over voters' wishes.* **9 be riding on** to be dependent on (something) for success: *a lot is riding on the profits of the film.* **10** *Informal* to continue undisturbed: *let it ride.* **11 riding high** popular and successful. ✧ *n* **12** a journey on a bicycle, on horseback, or in a vehicle. **13** transport in a vehicle: *most of us have been told not to accept rides from strangers.* **14** the type of movement experienced in a vehicle: *a bumpy ride.* **15** a path for riding on horseback. **16 take for a ride** *Informal* to cheat or deceive. ▷ HISTORY Old English *rīdan*

ride out *vb* to survive (a period of difficulty or danger) successfully.

rider *n* **1** a person who rides. **2** an extra clause or condition added to a document.

ride up *vb* (of a garment) to move up from the proper position.

ridge *n* **1** a long narrow raised land formation with sloping sides. **2** a long narrow raised strip on a flat surface. **3** the top of a roof where the two sloping sides meet. **4** *Meteorol* an elongated area of high pressure. ▷ HISTORY Old English *hrycg* ▶ **ridged** *adj* ▶ **ridgy** *adj*

ridicule *n* **1** language or behaviour intended to humiliate or mock. ✧ *vb* **-culing, -culed 2** to make fun of or mock. ▷ HISTORY Latin *ridere* to laugh

ridiculous *adj* worthy of or causing ridicule.

riding[1] *n* the art or practice of horsemanship.

riding[2] *n* **1 Riding** any of the three former administrative divisions of Yorkshire: North Riding, East Riding, and West Riding. **2** *Canad* an electoral constituency. ▷ HISTORY Old English *thriding* a third

riesling *n* a medium-dry white wine. ▷ HISTORY from German

rife *adj* **1** widespread or common. **2 rife with** full of: *the media is rife with speculation.* ▷ HISTORY Old English *rīfe*

riff *n Jazz, rock* a short series of chords. ▷ HISTORY probably from REFRAIN[2]

riffle *vb* **-fling, -fled 1** to flick through (papers or pages) quickly: *I riffled through the rest of the memos.* ✧ *n* **2** *US & Canad* **a** a rapid in a stream. **b** a rocky shoal causing a rapid. **c** a ripple on water. **3** a riffling. ▷ HISTORY probably from *ruffle*

riffraff *n* worthless or disreputable people. ▷ HISTORY Old French *rif et raf*

rifle[1] *n* **1** a firearm having a long barrel with a spirally grooved interior, which gives the bullet a spinning motion and thus greater accuracy over a longer range. **2 Rifles** a unit of soldiers equipped with rifles: *the Burma Rifles.* ✧ *vb* **-fling, -fled 3** to cut spiral grooves inside the barrel of (a gun). ▷ HISTORY Old French *rifler* to scratch ▶ **rifled** *adj*

rifle[2] *vb* **-fling, -fled 1** to search (a house or safe) and steal from it. **2** to steal and carry off: *he rifled whatever valuables he could lay his hands on.* ▷ HISTORY Old French *rifler* to plunder, scratch

rift *n* **1** a break in friendly relations between people or groups of people. **2** a gap or space made by splitting. ▷ HISTORY Old Norse

rift valley *n* a long narrow valley resulting from the subsidence of land between two faults.

rig *vb* **rigging, rigged 1** to arrange in a dishonest way, for profit or advantage: *he claimed that the poll was rigged.* **2** to set up or prepare (something) hastily ready for use. **3** *Naut* to equip (a vessel or mast) with (sails or rigging). ✧ *n* **4** an apparatus for drilling for oil and gas. **5** *Naut* the arrangement of the sails and masts of a vessel. **6** apparatus or equipment. **7** *Informal* an outfit of clothes. **8** *US, Canad & Austral* an articulated lorry. ✧ See also **rig up**. ▷ HISTORY Scandinavian

rigging *n* the ropes and cables supporting a ship's masts and sails.

right *adj* **1** morally or legally acceptable or correct: *his conduct seemed reasonable, even right.* **2** correct or true: *the customer is always right.* **3** appropriate, suitable, or proper: *there were problems involved in finding the right candidate.* **4** most favourable or convenient: *she waited until the right moment to broach the subject.* **5** in a satisfactory condition: *things are right again now.* **6** accurate: *is that clock right?* **7** correct in opinion or judgment. **8** sound in mind or body. **9** of or on the side of something or someone that faces east when the front is turned towards the north. **10** conservative or reactionary: *it was alleged he was an agent of the right wing.* **11** *Geom* formed by or containing a line or plane perpendicular to another line or plane: *a right angle.* **12** of or on the side of cloth worn or facing outwards. **13 in one's right mind** sane. **14 she'll be right** *Austral & NZ informal* that's all right; not to worry. **15 the right side of a** in favour with: *you'd better stay on the right side of him.* **b** younger than: *he's still on the right side of fifty.* **16 too right** *Informal* an exclamation of agreement. ✧ *adv* **17** correctly: *if we change the structure of local government we must do it right.* **18** in the appropriate manner: *do it right next time!* **19** straight or directly: *let's go right to bed.* **20** in the direction of the east from the point of view of a person or thing facing north. **21** all the way: *he drove right up to the gate.* **22** without delay: *I'll be right over.* **23** exactly or precisely: *right here.* **24** fittingly: *it serves him right.* **25** to good or favourable advantage: *it all came out right in the end.* ✧ *n* **26** a freedom or power that is morally or legally due to a person: *the defendant had an absolute right to a fair trial.* **27** anything that accords with the principles of legal or moral justice. **28 in the right** the state of being in accordance with reason or truth. **29** the right side, direction, or part: *the right of the army.* **30 the Right** the supporters or advocates of conservatism or reaction: *the rise of the far Right in France.* **31** *Boxing* a punch with the right hand. **32 rights** *Finance* the privilege of a company's shareholders to subscribe for new issues of the company's shares on advantageous terms. **33 by right** *or* **rights** properly: *by rights he should have won.* **34 in one's own right** having a claim or title oneself rather than through marriage or other connection. **35 to rights** consistent with justice or orderly arrangement: *he put the matter to rights.* ✧ *vb* **36** to bring or come back to a normal or correct state. **37** to bring or come back to a vertical position: *he slipped and righted himself at once.* **38** to compensate for or redress: *there is a wrong to be righted.* **39** to make (something) accord with truth or facts. ✧ *interj* **40** an expression of agreement or compliance. ▷ HISTORY Old English *riht*

right angle *n* **1** an angle of 90° or $\pi/2$ radians. **2 at right angles** perpendicular or perpendicularly. ▶ **right-angled** *adj*

right-angled triangle *n* a triangle with one angle which is a right angle.

right away *adv* without delay.

right-branching sentence *n Grammar* a sentence in which most of the information comes after the main verb in the main clause. Compare **left-branching sentence**.

righteous (**rye**-chuss) *adj* **1** moral, just, or virtuous: *the lieutenant was a righteous cop.* **2** morally justifiable or right: *her eyes were blazing with righteous indignation.* ▷ HISTORY Old English *rihtwīs* ▶ **righteousness** *n*

rightful *adj* **1** in accordance with what is right. **2** having a legally or morally just claim: *he is the rightful heir to her fortune.* **3** held by virtue of a legal or just claim: *these moves will restore them to their rightful homes.* ▶ **rightfully** *adv* ▶ **rightfulness** *n*

right-handed *adj* **1** more adept with the right hand than with the left. **2** made for or by the right hand. **3** turning from left to right.

rightist *adj* **1** of the political right or its principles. ✧ *n* **2** a supporter of the political right. ▶ **rightism** *n*

rightly *adv* **1** in accordance with the true facts or justice. **2** with good reason: *he was rightly praised for his constancy.*

right-minded *or* **right-thinking** *adj* holding opinions or principles considered acceptable by the speaker.

right of way *n, pl* **rights of way 1** the right of one vehicle or ship to go before another. **2 a** the legal right of someone to pass over someone else's land. **b** the path used by this right.

Right Reverend *adj* (in Britain) a title of respect for a bishop.

right whale *n* a large grey or black whalebone whale with a large head. ▷ HISTORY origin unknown

right-wing *adj* **1** conservative or reactionary: *there's a very fast-growing right-wing feeling in our country.* **2** belonging to the more conservative part of a political party: *a group of right-wing Labour MPs.*

✧ *n* **right wing 3** (*often cap*) the more conservative or reactionary section, esp. of a political party: *the Right Wing of the Conservative Party.* **4** *Sports* **a** the right-hand side of the field of play. **b** a player positioned in this area in certain games. ▶ **right-winger** *n*

rigid *adj* **1** inflexible or strict: *the talks will be general without a rigid agenda.* **2** physically unyielding or stiff: *use only rigid plastic containers.* ▷ HISTORY Latin *rigidus* ▶ **rigidity** *n* ▶ **rigidly** *adv*

rigmarole *n* **1** a long complicated procedure. **2** a set of incoherent or pointless statements. ▷ HISTORY earlier *ragman roll* a list

rigor mortis *n* the stiffness of joints and muscles of a dead body. ▷ HISTORY Latin: rigidity of death

rigorous *adj* **1** harsh, strict, or severe: *rigorous enforcement of the libel laws.* **2** severely accurate: *rigorous scientific testing.*

rigour *or US* **rigor** *n* **1** a severe or cruel circumstance: *the rigours of forced labour.* **2** strictness in judgment or conduct. **3** harsh but just treatment. ▷ HISTORY Latin *rigor*

rig up *vb* to set up or build temporarily: *they rigged up a loudspeaker system.*

rile *vb* **riling, riled 1** to annoy or anger. **2** *US & Canad* to stir up (a liquid). ▷ HISTORY variant of *roil* to agitate

rill *n* a small stream. ▷ HISTORY Low German *rille*

rim *n* **1** the raised edge of an object. **2** the outer part of a wheel to which the tyre is attached. ▷ HISTORY Old English *rima* ▶ **rimless** *adj*

rime¹ *Literary* ✧ *n* **1** frost formed by the freezing of water droplets in fog onto solid objects. ✧ *vb* **riming, rimed 2** to cover with rime or something resembling it. ▷ HISTORY Old English *hrīm* ▶ **rimy** *adj*

rime² *n, vb* **riming, rimed** *Archaic* same as **rhyme**.

rind *n* a hard outer layer on fruits, bacon, or cheese. ▷ HISTORY Old English *rinde*

ring¹ *vb* **ringing, rang, rung 1** to give out a clear resonant sound, like that of a bell. **2** to cause (a bell) to give out a ringing sound or (of a bell) to give out such a sound. **3** *Chiefly Brit & NZ* to call (a person) by telephone. **4 ring for** to call by means of a bell: *ring for the maid.* **5** (of a building or place) to be filled with sound: *the church rang with singing.* **6** (of the ears) to have the sensation of humming or ringing. **7** *Slang* to change the identity of (a stolen vehicle) by using the licence plate or serial number of another, usually disused, vehicle. **8 ring a bell** to bring something to the mind or memory: *the name doesn't ring a bell.* **9 ring down the curtain a** to lower the curtain at the end of a theatrical performance. **b ring down the curtain on** to put an end to. **10 ring true** *or* **false** to give the impression of being true *or* false. ✧ *n* **11** the act of or a sound made by ringing. **12** a sound produced by or sounding like a bell. **13** *Informal, chiefly Brit & NZ* a telephone call. **14** an inherent quality: *it has the ring of possibility to it.* ✧ See also **ring in, ring off**, etc. ▷ HISTORY Old English *hringan*

> **WORD TIP**
> *Rang* and *sang* are the correct forms of the past tenses of *ring* and *sing*, although *rung* and *sung* are still heard informally and dialectally: *he rung (rang) the bell.*

ring² *n* **1** a circular band of a precious metal worn on the finger. **2** any object or mark that is circular in shape. **3** a group of people or things standing or arranged in a circle: *a ring of standing stones.* **4** a circular path or course: *crowds of people walking round in a ring.* **5** a circular enclosure where circus acts perform or livestock is sold at a market. **6** a square raised platform, marked off by ropes, in which contestants box or wrestle. **7** a group of people, usually illegal, who control a specified market: *a drugs ring.* **8** *Chem* a closed loop of atoms in a molecule. **9** one of the systems of circular bands orbiting the planets Saturn, Uranus, and Jupiter. **10 the ring** the sport of boxing. **11 throw one's hat in the ring** to announce one's intention to be a candidate or contestant. **12 run rings around** *Informal* to outclass completely. ✧ *vb* **ringing, ringed 13** to put a ring round. **14** to mark (a bird) with a ring or clip for subsequent identification. **15** to kill (a tree) by cutting the bark round the trunk. **16** to fit a ring in the nose of (a bull, etc.) so that it can be led easily. ▷ HISTORY Old English *hring* ▶ **ringed** *adj*

ring binder *n* a loose-leaf binder with metal rings that can be opened to insert perforated paper.

ringdove *n* a wood pigeon.

ringer *n* **1** *Brit, Austral & NZ* Also called: **dead ringer** a person or thing that is almost identical to another. **2** *Slang* a stolen vehicle the identity of which has been changed by the use of the licence plate or serial number of another, usually disused, vehicle.

ring finger *n* the third finger, esp. of the left hand, on which a wedding ring is worn.

ring in *vb* to report to someone by telephone.

ringleader *n* a person who leads others in illegal or mischievous actions.

ringlet *n* a lock of hair hanging down in a spiral curl. ▶ **ringleted** *adj*

ring main *n* a domestic electrical supply in which outlet sockets are connected to the mains supply through a continuous closed circuit (**ring circuit**).

ringmaster *n* the master of ceremonies in a circus.

ring off *vb Chiefly Brit & NZ* to end a telephone conversation by replacing the receiver.

ring road *n Brit, Austral & S African* a main road that bypasses a town or town centre.

ringside *n* **1** the row of seats nearest a boxing or wrestling ring. ✧ *adj* **2** providing a close uninterrupted view: *a ringside seat for the election.*

ringtail *n Austral* a possum with a curling tail used to grip branches while climbing.

A B C D E F G H I J K L M N O P Q R S T U V W X Y Z

ringtone *n* a musical tune played by a mobile phone when it receives a call.

ring up *vb* **1** to make a telephone call to. **2** to record on a cash register. **3 ring up the curtain a** to begin a theatrical performance. **b ring up the curtain on** to make a start on.

ringworm *n* a fungal infection of the skin producing itchy patches.

rink *n* **1** a sheet of ice for skating on, usually indoors. **2** an area for roller-skating on. **3** a building for ice-skating or roller-skating. **4** (in bowls or curling) **a** a strip of grass or ice on which a game is played. **b** the players on one side in a game. ▷ **HISTORY** Old French *renc* row

rinkhals (**rink**-hals) *n, pl* **-hals** *or* **-halses** a highly venomous snake of Southern Africa capable of spitting its venom accurately at its victim's eyes. ▷ **HISTORY** Afrikaans

rinse *vb* **rinsing, rinsed 1** to remove soap or shampoo from (clothes, dishes, or hair) by washing it out with clean water. **2** to wash lightly, esp. without using soap. **3** to cleanse the mouth by swirling water or mouthwash in it and then spitting the liquid out. **4** *Hairdressing* to give a light tint to (hair). ✧ *n* **5** the act or an instance of rinsing. **6** *Hairdressing* a liquid to tint hair: *a blue rinse.* ▷ **HISTORY** Old French *rincer*

riot *n* **1** a disturbance made by an unruly mob. **2** *Brit, Austral & NZ* an occasion of lively enjoyment. **3** a dazzling display: *the pansies provided the essential riot of colour.* **4** *Slang* a very amusing person or thing. **5 read the riot act** to reprimand severely. **6 run riot a** to behave without restraint. **b** (of plants) to grow profusely. ✧ *vb* **7** to take part in a riot. ▷ **HISTORY** Old French *riote* dispute ▶ **rioter** *n* ▶ **rioting** *n*

riotous *adj* **1** unrestrained and excessive: *riotous decadence.* **2** unruly or rebellious. **3** characterized by unrestrained merriment: *riotous celebration.*

rip[1] *vb* **ripping, ripped 1** to tear or be torn violently or roughly. **2** to remove hastily or roughly. **3** *Informal* to move violently or hurriedly. **4 let rip** to act or speak without restraint. ✧ *n* **5** a tear or split. ✧ See also **rip off**. ▷ **HISTORY** origin unknown

rip[2] *n* short for **riptide**.

RIP may he, she, *or* they rest in peace. ▷ **HISTORY** Latin *requiescat* or *requiescant in pace*

riparian (rip-**pair**-ee-an) *adj Formal* of or on the bank of a river. ▷ **HISTORY** Latin *ripa* river bank

ripcord *n* a cord pulled to open a parachute from its pack.

ripe *adj* **1** mature enough to be eaten or used: *a round ripe apple.* **2** fully developed in mind or body. **3** suitable: *wait until the time is ripe.* **4 ripe for** ready or eager to (undertake or undergo an action): *China was ripe for revolution.* **5 ripe old age** an elderly but healthy age. ▷ **HISTORY** Old English *rīpe*

ripen *vb* **1** to make or become ripe. **2** to mature.

rip off *Slang* ✧ *vb* **1** to cheat by overcharging. **2** to steal (something). ✧ *n* **rip-off 3** a grossly overpriced article. **4** the act of stealing or cheating.

riposte (rip-**posst**) *n* **1** a swift clever reply. **2** *Fencing* a counterattack made immediately after a successful parry. ✧ *vb* **-posting, -posted 3** to make a riposte. ▷ **HISTORY** French

ripple *n* **1** a slight wave on the surface of water. **2** a slight ruffling of a surface. **3** a sound like water flowing gently in ripples: *a ripple of applause.* **4** vanilla ice cream with stripes of another ice cream through it: *raspberry ripple.* ✧ *vb* **-pling, -pled 5** to form ripples or flow with a waving motion. **6** (of sounds) to rise and fall gently. ▷ **HISTORY** origin unknown ▶ **rippling** *adj*

rip-roaring *adj Informal* boisterous and exciting.

ripsaw *n* a handsaw for cutting along the grain of timber.

riptide *n Geog* **1** Also: **rip** a stretch of turbulent water in the sea, caused by the meeting of currents. **2** Also: **rip current** a strong current, esp. one flowing outwards from the shore.

rise *vb* **rising, rose, risen 1** to get up from a lying, sitting, or kneeling position. **2** to get out of bed, esp. to begin one's day: *she rises at 5 a.m. every day to look after her horse.* **3** to move from a lower to a higher position or place. **4** to appear above the horizon: *as the sun rises higher the mist disappears.* **5** to slope upwards: *the road crossed the valley then rose to a low ridge.* **6** to increase in height or level: *the tide rose.* **7** to swell up: *dough rises.* **8** to increase in strength or degree: *frustration is rising amongst sections of the population.* **9** to increase in amount or value: *living costs are rising at an annual rate of nine per cent.* **10** *Informal* to respond (to a challenge or remark). **11** to revolt: *the people rose against their oppressors.* **12** (of a court or parliament) to adjourn. **13** to be resurrected. **14** to become erect or rigid: *the hairs on his neck rose in fear.* **15** to originate: *that river rises in the mountains.* **16** *Angling* (of fish) to come to the surface of the water. ✧ *n* **17** the act or an instance of rising. **18** a piece of rising ground. **19** an increase in wages. **20** an increase in amount, cost, or quantity. **21** an increase in height. **22** an increase in status or position. **23** an increase in degree or intensity. **24** the vertical height of a step or of a flight of stairs. **25 get** *or* **take a rise out of** *Slang* to provoke an angry reaction from. **26 give rise to** to cause the development of. ▷ **HISTORY** Old English *rīsan*

riser *n* **1** a person who rises from bed: *an early riser.* **2** the vertical part of a step.

risible (**riz**-zib-bl) *adj Formal* ridiculous. ▷ **HISTORY** Latin *ridere* to laugh

rising *n* **1** a rebellion. ✧ *adj* **2** increasing in rank or maturity.

risk *n* **1** the possibility of bringing about misfortune or loss. **2** a person or thing considered as a potential hazard: *in parts of the world transfusions carry the risk of infection.* **3 at risk** in a dangerous situation. **4 take** *or* **run a risk** to act without regard to the danger involved. ✧ *vb* **5** to act in spite of the possibility of (injury or loss): *if they clamp down they risk a revolution.* **6** to expose to danger or loss. ▷ **HISTORY** French *risque* ▶ **risky** *adj*

risotto *n, pl* **-tos** a dish of rice cooked in stock with vegetables, meat, etc. ▷ **HISTORY** Italian

risqué (**risk**-ay) *adj* making slightly rude references to sex: *risqué humour.* ▷ **HISTORY** French *risquer* to risk

rissole *n* a mixture of minced cooked meat coated in egg and breadcrumbs and fried. ▷ **HISTORY** French

ritardando *adj, adv* same as **rallentando**. ▷ **HISTORY** Italian

rite *n* **1** a formal act which forms part of a religious ceremony: *the rite of burial.* **2** a custom that is carried out within a particular group: *the barbaric rites of public execution.* **3** a particular body of such acts, esp. of a particular Christian Church: *the traditional Anglican rite.* ▷ **HISTORY** Latin *ritus*

rite of passage *n* a ceremony or event that marks an important change in a person's life.

ritual *n* **1** a religious or other ceremony involving a series of fixed actions performed in a certain order. **2** these ceremonies collectively: *people need ritual.* **3** regular repeated action or behaviour. **4** stereotyped activity or behaviour. ✧ *adj* **5** of or like rituals. ▸ **ritually** *adv*

ritualism *n* exaggerated emphasis on the importance of rites and ceremonies. ▸ **ritualistic** *adj* ▸ **ritualistically** *adv*

ritzy *adj* **ritzier, ritziest** *Slang* luxurious or elegant. ▷ **HISTORY** after the hotels established by César *Ritz*

rival *n* **1** a person or group that competes with another for the same object or in the same field. **2** a person or thing that is considered the equal of another: *she is without rival in the field of physics.* ✧ *adj* **3** in the position of a rival. ✧ *vb* **-valling, -valled** *or US* **-valing, -valed 4** to be the equal or near equal of: *his inarticulateness was rivalled only by that of his brother.* **5** to try to equal or surpass. ▷ **HISTORY** Latin *rivalis,* literally: one who shares the same brook

rivalry *n, pl* **-ries** active competition between people or groups.

riven *adj Old-fashioned* **1** split apart: *the party is riven by factions.* **2** torn to shreds. ▷ **HISTORY** Old Norse *rīfa* to tear, rend

river *n* **1** a large natural stream of fresh water flowing along a definite course into the sea, a lake, or a larger river. *RELATED ADJECTIVE* ▸ **fluvial 2** an abundant stream or flow: *rivers of blood.* ▷ **HISTORY** Old French *riviere*

river basin *n Geog* the catchment area of a river and its tributaries.

river profile *n Geog* a cross-sectional representation mapping the height above sea level of a river at different points along its length and showing variations in slope and river bed.

river terrace *n Geog* an area of flat land that was part of an earlier higher flood plain when the river bed was higher.

rivet (**riv**-vit) *n* **1** a short metal pin for fastening metal plates, with a head at one end, the other end being hammered flat after being put through holes in the plates. ✧ *vb* **-eting, -eted 2** to join by riveting. **3** to cause a person's attention to be fixed in fascination or horror: *their eyes riveted on the protesters.* ▷ **HISTORY** Old French *river* to fasten ▸ **riveter** *n*

riveting *adj* very interesting or exciting.

rivulet *n* a small stream. ▷ **HISTORY** Latin *rivus* stream

RM 1 Royal Mail. **2** Royal Marines. **3** (in Canada) Rural Municipality. **4** (in Canada) Regional Municipality.

RME (in England and Wales) Religious and Moral Education.

Rn *Chem* radon.

RN 1 (in Canada and New Zealand) Registered Nurse. **2** (in Britain) Royal Navy.

RNA *n Biochem* ribonucleic acid: any of a group of nucleic acids, present in all living cells, that play an essential role in the synthesis of proteins.

RNZ Radio New Zealand.

RNZAF Royal New Zealand Air Force.

RNZN Royal New Zealand Navy.

roach[1] *n, pl* **roaches** *or* **roach** a European freshwater food fish. ▷ **HISTORY** Old French *roche*

roach[2] *n Chiefly US & Canad* a cockroach.

road *n* **1** a route, usually surfaced, used by travellers and vehicles to get from one place to another. **2** a street. **3** a way or course: *on the road to recovery.* **4** *Naut* same as **roadstead**. **5 one for the road** *Informal* a last alcoholic drink before leaving. **6 on the road** travelling about. ▷ **HISTORY** Old English *rād*

roadblock *n* a barrier set up across a road by the police or military, in order to stop and check vehicles.

road hog *n Informal* a selfish or aggressive driver.

roadholding *n* the extent to which a vehicle is stable and does not skid on bends or wet roads.

roadhouse *n* a pub or restaurant at the side of a road.

roadie *n Brit, Austral & NZ informal* a person who transports and sets up equipment for a band.

road metal *n Brit, Austral & NZ* crushed rock or broken stone used in building roads.

road rage *n* aggressive behaviour by a motorist in response to the actions of another road user.

road show *n* **1** *Radio* a live broadcast from a radio van taking a particular programme on a tour of the country. **2** a group of entertainers on tour.

roadside *n* **1** the edge of a road. ✧ *adj* **2** by the edge or side of a road: *a roadside café.*

roadstead *n Naut* a partly sheltered anchorage.

roadster *n* an open car with only two seats.

road tax *n* (in Britain) a tax paid on vehicles used on the roads.

road test *n* **1** a test of something, such as a vehicle in actual use. ✧ *vb* **road-test 2** to test (a vehicle etc.) in actual use.

roadway *n* the part of a road that is used by vehicles.

roadworks *pl n* repairs to a road or cable under a road, esp. when they block part of the road.

roadworthy *adj* (of a motor vehicle) mechanically sound. ▸ **roadworthiness** *n*

A B C D E F G H I J K L M N O P Q R S T U V W X Y Z

roam *vb* to walk about with no fixed purpose or direction. ▷ HISTORY origin unknown

roan *adj* **1** (of a horse) having a brown or black coat sprinkled with white hairs. ✧ *n* **2** a horse with such a coat. ▷ HISTORY Spanish *roano*

roar *vb* **1** (of lions and other animals) to make loud growling cries. **2** to shout (something) with a loud deep cry: *'Don't do that!' he roared at me.* **3** to make a very loud noise: *the engine roared.* **4** to laugh in a loud hearty manner. **5** (of a fire) to burn fiercely with a roaring sound. ✧ *n* **6** a roaring noise: *there was a roar as the train came in.* **7** a loud deep cry, uttered by a person or crowd, esp. in anger or triumph: *a roar of approval came from the crowd.* ▷ HISTORY Old English *rārian*

roaring *adj* **1 a roaring trade** a brisk and profitable business. ✧ *adv* **2 roaring drunk** noisily or boisterously drunk.

Roaring Forties *pl n* **the Roaring Forties** *Geog* the areas of ocean between 40° and 50° latitude in the S Hemisphere, noted for gale-force winds.

roast *vb* **1** to cook (food) by dry heat in an oven or over a fire. **2** to brown or dry (coffee or nuts) by exposure to heat. **3** to make or be extremely hot. **4** *Informal* to criticize severely. ✧ *n* **5** a roasted joint of meat. ✧ *adj* **6** cooked by roasting: *roast beef.* ▷ HISTORY Old French *rostir* ▸ **roaster** *n*

roasting *Informal* ✧ *adj* **1** extremely hot. ✧ *n* **2** severe criticism or scolding.

rob *vb* **robbing, robbed 1** to take something from (a person or place) illegally. **2** to deprive, esp. of something deserved: *I can't forgive him for robbing me of an Olympic gold.* ▷ HISTORY Old French *rober* ▸ **robber** *n*

robbery *n, pl* **-beries 1** *Criminal law* the stealing of property from a person by using or threatening to use force. **2** the act or an instance of robbing.

robe *n* **1** a long loose flowing garment. **2** a dressing gown or bathrobe. ✧ *vb* **robing, robed 3** to put a robe on. ▷ HISTORY Old French

robin *n* **1** Also called: **robin redbreast** a small Old World songbird with a brown back and an orange-red breast and face. **2** a North American thrush similar to but larger than the Old World robin. ▷ HISTORY arbitrary use of name *Robin*

robot *n* **1** a machine programmed to perform specific tasks in a human manner, esp. one with a human shape. **2** a person of machine-like efficiency. **3** *S African* a set of traffic lights. ▸ **robotic** *adj*

> **WORD HISTORY**
> The word 'robot' was first used by the Czech writer Karel Capek (1890–1938) in his play *R.U.R.*, published in 1920. In the play, people create manlike machines called robots. The word 'robot' comes from Czech *robota*, meaning 'work'.

robotics *n* the science of designing, building, and using robots.

robust *adj* **1** very strong and healthy. **2** sturdily built: *the new generation of robust lasers.* **3** requiring or displaying physical strength: *robust tackles.* ▷ HISTORY Latin *robur* an oak, strength

roc *n* (in Arabian legend) a bird of enormous size and power. ▷ HISTORY Persian *rukh*

rock¹ *n* **1** *Geol* the mass of mineral matter that makes up part of the earth's crust; stone. **2** a large rugged mass of stone. **3** *Chiefly US, Canad, & Austral* a stone. **4** *Brit* a hard peppermint-flavoured sweet, usually in the shape of a long stick. **5** a person or thing on which one can always depend: *your loyalty is a rock.* **6** *Slang* a precious jewel. **7 on the rocks a** (of a marriage) about to end. **b** (of an alcoholic drink) served with ice. ▷ HISTORY Old French *roche*

rock² *vb* **1** to move from side to side or backwards and forwards. **2** to shake or move (something) violently. **3** to feel or cause to feel shock: *key events have rocked both countries.* **4** to dance to or play rock music. **5** *Slang* to be very good. ✧ *n* **6** Also called: **rock music** a style of pop music with a heavy beat. **7** a rocking motion. ✧ *adj* **8** of or relating to rock music. ▷ HISTORY Old English *roccian*

rock and roll *or* **rock'n'roll** *n* a type of pop music originating in the 1950s as a blend of rhythm and blues and country and western.

rock bottom *n* the lowest possible level.

rock cake *n* a small fruit cake with a rough surface.

rock crystal *n* a pure transparent colourless quartz.

rock cycle *n Geol* the cycle of change which rocks are subjected to, including being uplifted, eroded, transported, deposited, and possibly metamorphosed.

rock dove *n* a common dove from which domestic and wild pigeons are descended.

rocker *n* **1** a rocking chair. **2** either of two curved supports on which a rocking chair stands. **3** a rock music performer or fan. **4 off one's rocker** *Slang* crazy.

rockery *n, pl* **-eries** a garden built of rocks and soil, for growing rock plants.

rocket *n* **1** a self-propelling device, usually cylindrical, which produces thrust by expelling through a nozzle the gases produced by burning fuel, such as one used as a firework or distress signal. **2** any vehicle propelled by a rocket engine, as a weapon or carrying a spacecraft. **3** *Informal* a severe reprimand: *my sister gave me a rocket for writing such dangerous nonsense.* ✧ *vb* **-eting, -eted 4** to increase rapidly: *within six years their turnover had rocketed.* **5** to attack with rockets. ▷ HISTORY Italian *rochetto* little distaff

rocketry *n* the science and technology of the design and operation of rockets.

rock garden *n* a garden featuring rocks or rockeries.

rocking chair *n* a chair set on curving supports so that the sitter may rock backwards and forwards.

rocking horse *n* a toy horse mounted on a pair of rocking supports on which a child can rock to and fro.

rock melon *n US, Austral, & NZ* same as **cantaloupe**.

rock plant *n* a plant that grows on rocks or in rocky ground.

rock salmon *n Brit* a former term for dogfish when used as a food.

rock salt *n* common salt as a naturally occurring solid mineral.

rock tripe *n Canad* any edible lichen that grows on rocks.

rocky[1] *adj* **rockier, rockiest** covered with rocks: *rocky and sandy shores.* ▶ **rockiness** *n*

rocky[2] *adj* **rockier, rockiest** shaky or unstable: *a rocky relationship.* ▶ **rockiness** *n*

rococo (rok-**koe**-koe) *adj* **1** relating to an 18th-century style of architecture, decoration, and music characterized by elaborate ornamentation. **2** excessively elaborate in style. ▷ **HISTORY** French

rod *n* **1** a thin straight pole made of wood or metal. **2** a cane used to beat people as a punishment. **3** a type of cell in the retina, sensitive to dim light. ▷ **HISTORY** Old English *rodd* ▶ **rodlike** *adj*

rode *vb* the past tense of **ride**.

rodent *n* a small mammal with teeth specialized for gnawing, such as a rat, mouse, or squirrel. ▷ **HISTORY** Latin *rodere* to gnaw ▶ **rodent-like** *adj*

rodeo *n, pl* **-deos** a display of the skills of cowboys, including bareback riding. ▷ **HISTORY** Spanish

roe[1] *n* the ovary and eggs of a female fish, sometimes eaten as food. ▷ **HISTORY** Middle Dutch *roge*

roe[2] *or* **roe deer** *n* a small graceful deer with short antlers. ▷ **HISTORY** Old English *rā(ha)*

roentgen (**ront**-gan) *n* a unit measuring a radiation dose. ▷ **HISTORY** after the German physicist *Roentgen,* who discovered X-rays

roger *interj* **1** (used in signalling) message received and understood. **2** an expression of agreement. ▷ **HISTORY** from the name *Roger,* representing *R* for *received*

rogue *n* **1** a dishonest or unprincipled person. **2** a mischievous person. **3** a crop plant which is inferior, diseased, or of a different variety. **4** an inferior or defective specimen. ✧ *adj* **5** (of a wild animal) having a savage temper and living apart from the herd: *a rogue elephant.* **6** inferior or defective: *rogue heroin.* ▷ **HISTORY** origin unknown ▶ **roguish** *adj*

roguery *n, pl* **-gueries** dishonest or immoral behaviour.

rogues' gallery *n* a collection of photographs of known criminals kept by the police for identification purposes.

roister *vb Old-fashioned* to enjoy oneself noisily and boisterously. ▷ **HISTORY** Old French *rustre* lout ▶ **roisterer** *n*

role *n* **1** a task or function: *their role in international relations.* **2** an actor's part in a production. ▷ **HISTORY** French

role model *n* a person regarded by others, esp. younger people, as a good example to follow.

role play *n* activity in which a person improvises a role or part.

roll *vb* **1** to move along by turning over and over. **2** to move along on wheels or rollers. **3** to curl or make by curling into a ball or tube. **4** to move along in an undulating movement. **5** to rotate wholly or partially: *he would snort in derision, roll his eyes, and heave a deep sigh.* **6** to spread out flat or smooth with a roller or rolling pin: *roll the pastry out thinly.* **7** (of a ship or aircraft) to turn from side to side around the longitudinal axis. **8** to operate or begin to operate: *the cameras continued to roll as she pulled up to the nightclub.* **9** to make a continuous deep reverberating sound: *the thunder rolled.* **10** to walk in a swaying manner: *the drunks came rolling home.* **11** to appear like a series of waves: *mountain ranges rolling away in every direction.* **12** to pass or elapse: *watching the time roll away.* **13** (of animals) to turn onto the back and kick. **14** to trill or cause to be trilled: *she rolled her r's.* **15** to throw (dice). ✧ *n* **16** the act or an instance of rolling. **17** anything rolled up into a tube: *a roll of paper towels.* **18** a small cake of bread for one person. **19** a flat pastry or cake rolled up with a meat, jam, or other filling. **20** an official list or register of names: *the electoral roll; the voters' roll.* **21** a complete rotation about its longitudinal axis by an aircraft. **22** a continuous deep reverberating sound: *the roll of musketry.* **23** a swaying or unsteady movement or gait. **24** a rounded mass: *rolls of fat.* **25** a very rapid beating of the sticks on a drum. **26 on a roll** *Slang* experiencing continued good luck or success. **27 strike off the roll** to expel from membership of a professional association. ▷ **HISTORY** Old French *roler*

roll call *n* the reading aloud of an official list of names, to check who is present.

rolled gold *n* a metal, such as brass, coated with a thin layer of gold.

roller *n* **1** a rotating cylinder used for smoothing, supporting a thing to be moved, spreading paint, etc. **2** a small tube around which hair may be wound in order to make it curly. **3** a long heavy wave of the sea. **4** a cylinder fitted on pivots, used to enable heavy objects to be easily moved.

Rollerblade *n Trademark* a type of roller skate in which the wheels are set in a single straight line under the boot.

roller coaster *n* (at a funfair) a narrow railway with open carriages, sharp curves, and steep slopes.

roller skate *n* **1** a shoe with four small wheels that enable the wearer to glide swiftly over a floor. ✧ *vb* **roller-skate, -skating, -skated 2** to move on roller skates. ▶ **roller skater** *n*

rollicking *adj* boisterously carefree: *a rollicking read.* ▷ **HISTORY** origin unknown

rolling *adj* **1** having gentle rising and falling slopes: *rolling hills.* **2** (of a walk) slow and swaying. **3** subject to regular review and updating: *a 10-year rolling programme.* **4** progressing by stages or in succession: *a rolling campaign.*

rolling mill *n* **1** a factory where metal ingots are passed between rollers to produce sheets or bars of the required shape. **2** a machine with rollers for doing this.

A B C D E F G H I J K L M N O P Q R S T U V W X Y Z

rolling pin *n* a cylinder with handles at both ends used for rolling pastry.

rolling stock *n* the locomotives and coaches of a railway.

rolling stone *n* a restless or wandering person.

rollmop *n* a herring fillet rolled around onion slices and pickled. ▷ **HISTORY** German *rollen* to roll + *Mops* pug dog

roll of honour *n* a list of those who have died in war for their country.

roll-on/roll-off *adj Brit, Austral & NZ* denoting a ship designed so that vehicles can be driven straight on and straight off.

roll-top *adj* (of a desk) having a slatted wooden panel that can be pulled down over the writing surface when not in use.

roll up *vb* **1** to form into a cylindrical shape: *roll up a length of black material.* **2** *Informal* to arrive. ✧ *n* **roll-up 3** *Brit informal* a cigarette made by the smoker from loose tobacco and cigarette papers.

roly-poly *adj* **1** plump or chubby. ✧ *n, pl* **-lies** **2** *Brit* a strip of suet pastry spread with jam, rolled up, and baked or steamed. ▷ **HISTORY** probably from *roll*

ROM *n Computers* read only memory: a storage device that holds data permanently and cannot be altered by the programmer.

roman *adj* **1** in or relating to the vertical style of printing type used for most printed matter. ✧ *n* **2** roman type. ▷ **HISTORY** so called because the style of letters is that used in ancient Roman inscriptions

Roman *adj* **1** of Rome, a city in Italy, or its inhabitants in ancient or modern times. **2** of Roman Catholicism or the Roman Catholic Church. ✧ *n* **3** a person from ancient or modern Rome.

Roman alphabet *n* the alphabet evolved by the ancient Romans for writing Latin, used for writing most of the languages of W Europe, including English.

Roman candle *n* a firework that produces a steady stream of coloured sparks. ▷ **HISTORY** it originated in Italy

Roman Catholic *adj* **1** of the Roman Catholic Church. ✧ *n* **2** a member of this Church. ▶ **Roman Catholicism** *n*

Roman Catholic Church *n* the Christian Church over which the pope presides.

romance *n* **1** a love affair: *a failed romance.* **2** love, esp. romantic love idealized for its purity or beauty. **3** a spirit of or inclination for adventure or mystery. **4** a mysterious or sentimental quality. **5** a story or film dealing with love, usually in an idealized way. **6** a story or film dealing with events and characters remote from ordinary life. **7** an extravagant, absurd, or fantastic account. **8** a medieval narrative dealing with adventures of chivalrous heroes. ✧ *vb* **-mancing, -manced 9** to tell extravagant or improbable lies. ▷ **HISTORY** Old French *romans*

Romance *adj* of the languages derived from Latin, such as French, Spanish, and Italian.

Romanesque *adj* of or in the style of architecture used in Europe from the 9th to the 12th century, characterized by rounded arches and massive walls.

Romanian *adj* **1** of Romania. ✧ *n* **2** a person from Romania. **3** the language of Romania.

Roman nose *n* a nose with a high prominent bridge.

Roman numerals *pl n* the letters used as numerals by the Romans, used occasionally today: I (= 1), V (= 5), X (= 10), L (= 50), C (= 100), D (= 500), and M (= 1000). VI = 6 (V + I) but IV = 4 (V – I).

romantic *adj* **1** of or dealing with love. **2** idealistic but impractical: *a romantic notion.* **3** evoking or given to thoughts and feelings of love: *romantic images.* **4 Romantic** relating to a movement in European art, music, and literature in the late 18th and early 19th centuries, characterized by an emphasis on feeling and content rather than order and form. ✧ *n* **5** a person who is idealistic or amorous. **6** a person who likes or produces artistic works in the style of Romanticism. ▶ **romantically** *adv*

romanticism *n* **1** idealistic but unrealistic thoughts and feelings. **2 Romanticism** the spirit and style of the Romantic art, music, and literature of the late 18th and early 19th centuries. ▶ **romanticist** *n*

romanticize *or* **-cise** *vb* **-cizing, -cized** *or* **-cising, -cised** to describe or regard (something or someone) in an unrealistic and idealized way: *the Victorian legacy of romanticizing family life.*

Romany *n* **1** (*pl* **-nies**) a Gypsy. **2** the language of the Gypsies. ▷ **HISTORY** Romany *romani* (adjective) Gypsy

Romeo *n, pl* **Romeos** an ardent male lover. ▷ **HISTORY** after the hero of Shakespeare's *Romeo and Juliet*

romp *vb* **1** to play or run about wildly or joyfully. **2 romp home** *or* **in** to win a race or other competition easily. **3 romp through** to do (something) quickly and easily. ✧ *n* **4** a noisy or boisterous game or prank. ▷ **HISTORY** probably from Old French *ramper* to crawl, climb

rompers *pl n* Also called: **romper suit** a one-piece baby garment combining trousers and a top.

rondavel *n S African* a small circular building with a cone-shaped roof. ▷ **HISTORY** origin unknown

rondeau (**ron**-doe) *n, pl* **-deaux** (-doe) a poem consisting of 13 or 10 lines with the opening words of the first line used as a refrain. ▷ **HISTORY** Old French

rondo *n, pl* **-dos** a piece of music with a leading theme continually returned to: often forms the last movement of a sonata or concerto. ▷ **HISTORY** Italian

roo *n, pl* **roos** *Austral informal* a kangaroo.

rood *n* **1** *Christianity* the Cross. **2** a crucifix. ▷ **HISTORY** Old English *rōd*

rood screen *n* (in a church) a screen separating the nave from the choir.

roof *n, pl* **roofs 1** a structure that covers or forms the top of a building. **2** the top covering of a vehicle, oven, or other structure. **3** the highest part of the mouth or a cave. **4 hit** *or* **go through the roof** *Informal* to get extremely angry. **5 raise the roof** *Informal* to be very noisy. ✧ *vb* **6** to put a roof on. ▷ **HISTORY** Old English *hrōf*

roof rack *n* a rack for carrying luggage attached to the roof of a car.

rooibos (**roy**-boss) *n S African* a kind of tea made from the leaves of a South African wild shrub. Also called: **rooibos tea, bush tea** ▷ **HISTORY** Afrikaans *rooi* red + *bos* bush

rooinek (**roy**-neck) *n S African* a contemptuous name for an Englishman. ▷ **HISTORY** Afrikaans *rooi* red + *nek* neck

rook[1] *n* **1** a large European black bird of the crow family. ✧ *vb* **2** *Old-fashioned, slang* to cheat or swindle. ▷ **HISTORY** Old English *hrōc*

rook[2] *n* a chessman that may move any number of unoccupied squares in a straight line, horizontally or vertically; castle. ▷ **HISTORY** Arabic *rukhkh*

rookery *n, pl* **-eries 1** a group of nesting rooks. **2** a colony of penguins or seals.

rookie *n Informal* a newcomer without much experience. ▷ **HISTORY** changed from *recruit*

room *n* **1** an area within a building enclosed by a floor, a ceiling, and walls. **2** the people present in a room: *the whole room was laughing.* **3** unoccupied or unobstructed space: *there wasn't enough room.* **4 room for** opportunity or scope for: *there was no room for acts of heroism.* **5 rooms** lodgings. ✧ *vb* **6** *US* to occupy or share a rented room: *I roomed with him for five years.* ▷ **HISTORY** Old English *rūm*

roomy *adj* **roomier, roomiest** with plenty of space inside: *a roomy entrance hall.* ▶ **roominess** *n*

roost *n* **1** a place where birds rest or sleep. ✧ *vb* **2** to rest or sleep on a roost. **3 come home to roost** to have unfavourable repercussions. **4 rule the roost** to have authority over people in a particular place. ▷ **HISTORY** Old English *hrōst*

rooster *n Chiefly US, Canad & Austral* the male of the domestic fowl; a cock.

root[1] *n* **1** the part of a plant that anchors the rest of the plant in the ground and absorbs water and mineral salts from the soil. **2** a plant with an edible root, such as a carrot. **3** *Anat* the part of a tooth, hair, or nail that is below the skin. **4 roots** a person's sense of belonging in a place, esp. the one in which he or she was brought up. **5** source or origin. **6** the essential part or nature of something: *the root of a problem.* **7** *Linguistics* the form of a word from which other words and forms are derived. **8** *Maths* a quantity that when multiplied by itself a certain number of times equals a given quantity: *what is the cube root of 1000?* **9** Also called: **solution** *Maths* a number that when substituted for the variable satisfies a given equation. **10** *Austral & NZ slang* sexual intercourse. **11 root and branch** entirely or utterly. RELATED ADJECTIVE ▸ **radical** ✧ *vb* **12** Also: **take root** to establish a root and begin to grow. **13** Also: **take root** to become established or embedded. **14** *Austral & NZ slang* to have sexual intercourse (with). ✧ See also **root out, roots.** ▷ **HISTORY** Old English *rōt*

root[2] *vb* **1** *Brit* to dig up the earth in search of food, using the snout: *dogs were rooting in the rushes for bones.* **2** *Informal* to search vigorously but unsystematically: *she was rooting around in her large untidy purse.* ▷ **HISTORY** Old English *wrōtan*

root crop *n* a crop, such as potato or turnip, cultivated for its roots.

root for *vb Informal* to give support to (a team or contestant). ▷ **HISTORY** origin unknown

rootle *vb* **-ling, -led** *Brit* same as **root**[2].

rootless *adj* having no sense of belonging: *a rootless city dweller.*

root mean square *n* the square root of the average of the squares of a set of numbers or quantities, for example *the root mean square of* 1, 2, *and* 4 *is* $\sqrt{[(1^2 + 2^2 + 4^2)/3]} = \sqrt{7}$.

root out *vb* to get rid of completely: *a major drive to root out corruption.*

rootstock *n* same as **rhizome**.

rope *n* **1** a fairly thick cord made of intertwined fibres or wire. **2** a row of objects fastened to form a line: *a 20-inch rope of pearls.* **3 know the ropes** to have a thorough understanding of a particular activity. **4 the rope a** a rope noose used for hanging someone. **b** death by hanging. ✧ *vb* **roping, roped 5** to tie with a rope. **6 rope off** to enclose or divide with a rope. ▷ **HISTORY** Old English *rāp*

rope in *vb* to persuade to take part in some activity.

ropey *or* **ropy** *adj* **ropier, ropiest** *Brit informal* **1** poor or unsatisfactory in quality: *a ropey performance.* **2** slightly unwell. ▶ **ropiness** *n*

Roquefort *n* a strong blue-veined cheese made from ewes' and goats' milk. ▷ **HISTORY** after *Roquefort,* village in S France

rorqual *n* a whalebone whale with a fin on the back. ▷ **HISTORY** Norwegian *rörhval*

Rorschach test (**ror**-shahk) *n Psychol* a personality test consisting of a number of unstructured inkblots for interpretation. ▷ **HISTORY** after H. *Rorschach,* psychiatrist

rort *Austral informal* ✧ *n* **1** a dishonest scheme. ✧ *vb* **2** to take unfair advantage of something.

rosaceous *adj* of or belonging to a family of plants typically having five-petalled flowers, which includes the rose, strawberry, and many fruit trees.

rosary *n, pl* **-saries** *RC Church* **1** a series of prayers counted on a string of beads. **2** a string of beads used to count these prayers as they are recited. ▷ **HISTORY** Latin *rosarium* rose garden

rose[1] *n* **1** a shrub or climbing plant with prickly stems and fragrant flowers. **2** the flower of any of these plants. **3** a plant similar to this, such as the Christmas rose. **4** a perforated cap fitted to a watering can or hose, causing the water to come out in a spray. **5 bed of roses** a situation of comfort or ease. ✧ *adj* **6** reddish-pink. ▷ **HISTORY** Latin *rosa*

rose[2] *vb* the past tense of **rise**.

rosé (**roe**-zay) *n* a pink wine. ▷ **HISTORY** French

roseate (**roe**-zee-ate) *adj* **1** of the colour rose or pink. **2** excessively optimistic.

rosebud *n* a rose which has not yet fully opened.

a b c d e f g h i j k l m n o p q r s t u v w x y z

A B C D E F G H I J K L M N O P Q R S T U V W X Y Z

rosehip *n* the berry-like fruit of a rose plant.

rosella *n* a type of Australian parrot.

rosemary *n, pl* **-maries** an aromatic European shrub widely cultivated for its grey-green evergreen leaves, which are used in cookery and perfumes. ▷ **HISTORY** Latin *ros* dew + *marinus* marine

rosette *n* a rose-shaped decoration, esp. a circular bunch of ribbons.

rose window *n* a circular window with spokes branching out from the centre to form a symmetrical roselike pattern.

rosewood *n* a fragrant dark wood used to make furniture.

Rosh Hashanah *or* **Rosh Hashana** *n* the festival celebrating the Jewish New Year. ▷ **HISTORY** Hebrew: beginning of the year

rosin (**rozz**-in) *n* **1** a translucent brittle substance produced from turpentine and used for treating the bows of stringed instruments. ✧ *vb* **2** to apply rosin to. ▷ **HISTORY** variant of *resin*

roster *n* **1** a list showing the order in which people are to perform a duty. ✧ *vb* **2** to place on a roster. ▷ **HISTORY** Dutch *rooster* grating or list

rostrum *n, pl* **-trums** *or* **-tra** a platform or stage. ▷ **HISTORY** Latin: beak

rosy *adj* **rosier, rosiest 1** of the colour rose or pink: *rosy cheeks.* **2** hopeful or promising: *the analysis revealed a far from rosy picture.* ▶ **rosiness** *n*

rot *vb* **rotting, rotted 1** to decay or cause to decay. **2** to deteriorate slowly, mentally and physically: *I thought he was either dead or rotting in a Chinese jail.* ✧ *n* **3** the process of rotting or the state of being rotten. **4** something decomposed. **5** short for **dry rot**. **6** a plant or animal disease which causes decay of the tissues. **7** nonsense. ▷ **HISTORY** Old English *rotian*

rota *n* a list of people who take it in turn to do a particular task. ▷ **HISTORY** Latin: a wheel

rotary *adj* **1** revolving. **2** operating by rotation. ✧ *n, pl* **-ries 3** *US & Canad* a traffic roundabout.

Rotary Club *n* a club that is part of **Rotary International**, an international association of professional and businesspeople who raise money for charity. ▶ **Rotarian** *n, adj*

rotate *vb* **-tating, -tated 1** to turn around a centre or pivot. **2** to follow or cause to follow a set sequence. **3** to regularly change the type of crop grown on a piece of land in order to preserve the fertility of the soil. ▷ **HISTORY** Latin *rota* wheel

rotation *n* **1** the act of rotating; rotary motion. **2** a regular cycle of events in a set order or sequence. **3** *Agriculture* a planned sequence of cropping according to which the crops grown in successive seasons on the same land are varied so as to make a balanced demand on its resources of fertility. **4** the spinning motion of a body, such as a planet, about an internal axis. **5** *Maths* **a** a circular motion of a configuration about a given point, without a change in shape. **b** a transformation in which the coordinate axes are rotated by a fixed angle about the origin. ▶ **rotational** *adj*

Rotavator *n Trademark* a mechanical cultivator with rotary blades.

rote *adj* **1** done by routine repetition: *rote learning.* ✧ *n* **2 by rote** by repetition: *we learned by rote.* ▷ **HISTORY** origin unknown

rotisserie *n* a rotating spit on which meat and poultry can be cooked. ▷ **HISTORY** French

rotor *n* **1** the rotating part of a machine or device, such as the revolving arm of the distributor of an internal-combustion engine. **2** a rotating device with blades projecting from a hub which produces thrust to lift a helicopter.

rotten *adj* **1** decomposing or decaying: *rotten vegetables.* **2** breaking up through age or hard use: *the window frames are rotten.* **3** *Informal* very bad: *what rotten luck!* **4** morally corrupt: *this country's politics are rotten and out of date.* **5** *Informal* miserably unwell: *I had glandular fever and spent that year feeling rotten.* **6** *Informal* distressed and embarrassed: *I'm feeling rotten as a matter of fact, rotten and guilty.* ✧ *adv* **7** *Informal* extremely; very much: *men fancy her rotten.* ▷ **HISTORY** Old Norse *rotinn*

rotter *n Chiefly Brit old-fashioned slang* a despicable person.

Rottweiler (**rot**-vile-er) *n* a large sturdy dog with a smooth black-and-tan coat and a docked tail. ▷ **HISTORY** *Rottweil,* German city where it was first bred

rotund (roe-**tund**) *adj* **1** round and plump. **2** (of speech) pompous or grand. ▷ **HISTORY** Latin *rotundus* ▶ **rotundity** *n* ▶ **rotundly** *adv*

rotunda *n* a circular building or room, esp. with a dome. ▷ **HISTORY** Italian *rotonda*

rouble *or* **ruble** (**roo**-bl) *n* the standard monetary unit of Russia and Tadzhikistan. ▷ **HISTORY** Russian *rubl*

roué (**roo**-ay) *n* a man who leads a sensual and immoral life. ▷ **HISTORY** French

rouge *n* **1** a red cosmetic for adding colour to the cheeks. ✧ *vb* **rouging, rouged 2** to apply rouge to. ▷ **HISTORY** French: red

rough *adj* **1** not smooth; uneven or irregular. **2** not using enough care or gentleness. **3** difficult or unpleasant: *tomorrow will be a rough day.* **4** approximate: *a rough guess.* **5** violent or stormy. **6** troubled by violence or crime: *he lived in a rough area.* **7** incomplete or basic: *a rough draft.* **8** lacking refinement: *a rough shelter.* **9** (of ground) covered with scrub or rubble. **10** harsh or grating to the ear. **11** harsh or sharp: *the rough interrogation of my father.* **12** unfair: *rough luck.* **13** *Informal* ill: *Feeling rough? A good stiff drink will soon fix that!* **14** shaggy or hairy: *the rough wool of her sweater.* **15** (of work etc.) requiring physical rather than mental effort: *wear gloves for any rough work.* ✧ *vb* **16** to make rough. **17 rough it** *Informal* to live without the usual comforts of life. ✧ *n* **18** rough ground. **19** a sketch or preliminary piece of artwork. **20** *Informal* a violent person. **21 in rough** in an unfinished or crude state. **22 the rough** *Golf* the part of the course beside the fairways where the grass is untrimmed. **23** the unpleasant side of something: *you have to take the rough with the smooth.* ✧ *adv*

24 roughly. **25 sleep rough** to spend the night in the open without shelter. ✧ See also **rough out**. ▷ HISTORY Old English *rūh* ▶ **roughly** *adv*

roughage *n* the coarse indigestible constituents of food, which help digestion.

rough-and-ready *adj* **1** hastily prepared but adequate for the purpose. **2** (of a person) without formality or refinement.

rough-and-tumble *n* **1** a playful fight. **2** a disorderly situation.

roughcast *n* **1** a mixture of plaster and small stones for outside walls. ✧ *vb* **-casting, -cast 2** to put roughcast on (a wall).

roughen *vb* to make or become rough.

rough-hewn *adj* roughly shaped or cut without being properly finished.

roughhouse *n Slang* rough or noisy behaviour.

roughneck *n Slang* **1** a violent person. **2** a worker on an oil rig.

rough out *vb* to prepare (a sketch or report) in preliminary form: *he offered to rough out some designs for the sets.*

roughshod *adv* **ride roughshod over** to act with complete disregard for.

roulette *n* a gambling game in which a ball is dropped onto a revolving wheel with numbered coloured slots. ▷ HISTORY French

round *adj* **1** having a flat circular shape, like a hoop. **2** having the shape of a ball. **3** curved; not angular. **4** involving or using circular motion. **5** complete. **6** *Maths* **a** forming or expressed by a whole number, with no fraction. **b** expressed to the nearest ten, hundred, or thousand: *in round figures.* ✧ *adv* **7** on all or most sides. **8** on or outside the circumference or perimeter: *ponds which are steeply sided all round.* **9** in rotation or revolution: *she swung round on me.* **10** by a circuitous route: *a four-month cruise round the Mediterranean.* **11** to all members of a group: *handing cigarettes round.* **12** to a specific place: *the boys invited him round.* **13 all year round** throughout the year. ✧ *prep* **14** surrounding or encircling: *wrap your sash round the wound.* **15** on all or most sides of: *the man turned in a circle, looking all round him.* **16** on or outside the circumference or perimeter of. **17** from place to place in: *a trip round the island in an ancient bus.* **18** reached by making a partial circuit about: *just round the corner.* **19** revolving about: *if you have two bodies in orbit, they orbit round their common centre of gravity.* ✧ *vb* **20** to move round: *as he rounded the last corner, he raised a fist.* ✧ *n* **21** a round shape or object. **22** a session: *a round of talks.* **23** a series: *the petty round of domestic matters.* **24** a series of calls: *a paper round.* **25 the daily round** the usual activities of a person's day. **26** a playing of all the holes on a golf course. **27** a stage of a competition: *the first round of the Portuguese Open.* **28** one of a number of periods in a boxing or wrestling match. **29** a single turn of play by each player in a card game. **30** a number of drinks bought at one time for a group of people. **31** a bullet or shell for a gun. **32** a single discharge by a gun. **33** *Music* a part song in which the voices follow each other at equal intervals. **34** circular movement. **35 a** a single slice of bread. **b** a serving of sandwiches made from two complete slices of bread. **36** a general outburst: *a round of applause.* **37 in the round a** in full detail. **b** *Theatre* with the audience all round the stage. **38 go the rounds** (of information or infection) to be passed around from person to person. ▷ HISTORY Old French *ront*

> **☑ WORD TIP**
> See at **around.**

roundabout *n* **1** a road junction in which traffic moves in one direction around a central island. **2** a revolving circular platform, often with seats, on which people ride for amusement. ✧ *adj* **3** not straightforward: *the roundabout sea route; she thought of asking about it in a roundabout way.* ✧ *adv, prep* **round about 4** approximately: *round about 1900.*

round character *n Literature* a character in a story who is well-developed and interesting, changing as the story progresses and therefore wholly convincing.

roundel *n* **1** a circular identifying mark on military aircraft. **2** a small circular object. ▷ HISTORY Old French *rondel* little circle

roundelay *n* a song in which a line or phrase is repeated as a refrain. ▷ HISTORY Old French *rondelet*

rounders *n Brit & NZ* a bat and ball game in which players run between posts after hitting the ball.

Roundhead *n English history* a supporter of Parliament against Charles I during the Civil War. ▷ HISTORY referring to their short-cut hair

roundly *adv* bluntly or thoroughly: *the Church roundly criticized the bill.*

round on *vb* to attack or reply to (someone) with sudden irritation or anger.

round robin *n* **1** a petition with the signatures in a circle to disguise the order of signing. **2** a tournament in which each player plays against every other player.

round-shouldered *adj* denoting poor posture with drooping shoulders and a slight forward bending of the back.

round table *n* a meeting of people on equal terms for discussion.

Round Table *n* **1** (in Arthurian legend) the table of King Arthur, shaped so that his knights could sit around as equals. **2** one of an organization of clubs of young business and professional men who meet in order to further charitable work.

round-the-clock *adj* throughout the day and night.

round trip *n* a journey to a place and back again.

round up *vb* **1** to gather together: *the police had rounded up a circle of drug users.* **2** to raise (a number) to the nearest whole number or ten, hundred, or thousand above it. ✧ *n* **roundup 3** a summary or discussion of news and information. **4** the act of gathering together livestock or people.

roundworm *n* a worm that is a common intestinal parasite of man.

rouse[1] *vb* **rousing, roused 1** to wake up. **2** to provoke or excite: *his temper was roused and he had a gun.* **3 rouse oneself** to become energetic. ▷ **HISTORY** origin unknown

rouse[2] (rhymes with **mouse**) *vb* (foll. by *on*) *Austral* to scold or rebuke.

rouseabout *n Austral & NZ* a labourer in a shearing shed.

rousing *adj* lively or vigorous: *a rousing speech.*

roustabout *n* **1** an unskilled labourer on an oil rig. **2** *Austral & NZ* another word for **rouseabout**.

rout[1] *n* **1** an overwhelming defeat. **2** a disorderly retreat. **3** a noisy rabble. ✧ *vb* **4** to defeat and put to flight. ▷ **HISTORY** Anglo-Norman *rute*

rout[2] *vb* **1** to find by searching. **2** to drive out: *the dissidents had been routed out.* **3** to dig (something) up. ▷ **HISTORY** variant of ROOT[2]

route *n* **1** the choice of roads taken to get to a place. **2** a fixed path followed by buses, trains, etc. between two places. **3** a chosen way or method: *the route to prosperity.* ✧ *vb* **routeing, routed 4** to send by a particular route. ▷ **HISTORY** Old French *rute*

> ☑ **WORD TIP**
> When forming the present participle or verbal noun from the verb *to route* it is preferable to retain the *e* in order to distinguish the word from *routing,* the present participle or verbal noun from *rout*[1], to defeat or *rout*[2], to dig, rummage: *the routeing of buses from the city centre to the suburbs.* The spelling *routing* in this sense is, however, sometimes encountered, esp. in American English.

routemarch *n Mil* a long training march.

router *n Computers* a device that allows data to be moved efficiently between two points on a network.

routine *n* **1** a usual or regular method of procedure. **2** the boring repetition of tasks: *mindless routine.* **3** a set sequence of dance steps. **4** *Computers* a program or part of a program performing a specific function: *an input routine.* ✧ *adj* **5** relating to or characteristic of routine. ▷ **HISTORY** Old French *route* a customary way

roux (**roo**) *n* a cooked mixture of fat and flour used as a basis for sauces. ▷ **HISTORY** French: brownish

rove *vb* **roving, roved 1** to wander about (a place). **2** (of the eyes) to look around. ▷ **HISTORY** probably from Old Norse ▸ **rover** *n*

row[1] (rhymes with **know**) *n* **1** an arrangement of people or things in a line: *a row of shops.* **2** a line of seats in a cinema or theatre. **3** *Brit* a street lined with identical houses. **4** *Maths* a horizontal line of numbers. **5 in a row** in succession: *five championships in a row.* ▷ **HISTORY** Old English *rāw, rǣw*

row[2] (rhymes with **know**) *vb* **1** to propel (a boat) by using oars. **2** to carry (people or goods) in a rowing boat. **3** to take part in the racing of rowing boats as a sport. ✧ *n* **4** an act or spell of rowing. **5** an excursion in a rowing boat. ▷ **HISTORY** Old English *rōwan* ▸ **rowing** *n*

row[3] (rhymes with **cow**) *Informal* ✧ *n* **1** a noisy quarrel. **2** a controversy or dispute: *the row over Europe.* **3** a noisy disturbance: *go to the insurance offices and kick up a row about your money.* **4** a reprimand. ✧ *vb* **5** to quarrel noisily. ▷ **HISTORY** origin unknown

rowan *n* a European tree with white flowers and red berries; mountain ash. ▷ **HISTORY** Scandinavian

rowdy *adj* **-dier, -diest 1** rough, noisy, or disorderly. ✧ *n, pl* **-dies 2** a person like this. ▷ **HISTORY** origin unknown ▸ **rowdily** *adv*

rowel (rhymes with **towel**) *n* a small spiked wheel at the end of a spur. ▷ **HISTORY** Old French *roel* a little wheel

rowing boat *n* a small pleasure boat propelled by oars. Usual US and Canad word: **rowboat**

rowlock (**rol**-luk) *n* a swivelling device attached to the top of the side of a boat that holds an oar in place.

royal *adj* **1** of or relating to a king or queen or a member of his or her family: *the royal yacht.* **2 Royal** supported by or in the service of royalty: *the Royal Society of Medicine.* **3** very grand: *royal treatment.* ✧ *n* **4** *Informal* a king or queen or a member of his or her family. ▷ **HISTORY** Old French *roial* ▸ **royally** *adv*

Royal Air Force *n* the air force of the United Kingdom.

royal assent *n Law* (in Britain) the formal signing of an Act of Parliament by the sovereign, by which it becomes law.

royalist *n* **1** a supporter of a monarch or monarchy. ✧ *adj* **2** of or relating to royalists. ▸ **royalism** *n*

royal jelly *n* a substance secreted by worker bees and fed to all larvae when very young and to larvae destined to become queens throughout their growth.

Royal Marines *pl n Brit* a corps of soldiers specially trained in amphibious warfare.

royalty *n, pl* **-ties 1** royal people. **2** the rank or power of a king or queen. **3** a percentage of the revenue from the sale of a book, performance of a work, use of a patented invention or of land, paid to the author, inventor, or owner.

royal warrant *n* an authorization to a tradesman to supply goods to a royal household.

RPI (in Britain) retail price index: a measure of the changes in the average level of retail prices of selected goods.

rpm revolutions per minute.

RR 1 Right Reverend. **2** *US & Canad* rural route.

RSA 1 Republic of South Africa. **2** (in New Zealand) Returned Services Association. **3** Royal Scottish Academy. **4** Royal Society of Arts.

RSI repetitive strain injury: pain in the arm caused by repeated awkward movements, such as in typing.

RSM (in Britain) regimental sergeant major.

RSPCA (in Britain) Royal Society for the Prevention of Cruelty to Animals.

RSVP please reply. ▷ **HISTORY** French *répondez s'il vous plaît*

Rt Hon. Right Honourable: a title of respect for a Privy Councillor, certain peers, and the Lord Mayor or Lord Provost of certain cities.

Ru *Chem* ruthenium.

RU486 *n* the technical name for **abortion pill**.

rub *vb* **rubbing, rubbed 1** to apply pressure and friction to (something) with a circular or backwards-and-forwards movement. **2** to move (something) with pressure along or against (a surface). **3** to clean, polish, or dry by rubbing. **4** to spread with pressure, esp. so that it can be absorbed: *rub beeswax into all polishable surfaces.* **5** to chafe or fray through rubbing. **6** to mix (fat) into flour with the fingertips, as in making pastry. **7 rub it in** to emphasize an unpleasant fact. **8 rub up the wrong way** to annoy. ✧ *n* **9** the act of rubbing. **10 the rub** the obstacle or difficulty: *there's the rub.* ✧ See also **rub along**. ▷ **HISTORY** origin unknown

rub along *vb* **1** to have a friendly relationship. **2** to continue in spite of difficulties.

rubato *Music* ✧ *n, pl* **-tos 1** flexibility of tempo in performance: *his playing brought much beautifully felt but never sentimental rubato to the music.* ✧ *adj, adv* **2** to be played with a flexible tempo. ▷ **HISTORY** Italian, literally: robbed

rubber[1] *n* **1** an elastic material obtained from the latex of certain plants, such as the rubber tree. **2** a similar substance produced synthetically. **3** a piece of rubber used for erasing something written. **4** *US slang* a condom. **5 rubbers** *US* rubber-coated waterproof overshoes. ✧ *adj* **6** made of or producing rubber. ▷ **HISTORY** the tree was so named because its product was used for rubbing out writing ▸ **rubbery** *adj*

rubber[2] *n* **1** *Bridge, whist* a match of three games. **2** a series of matches or games in various sports. ▷ **HISTORY** origin unknown

rubberize *or* **-ise** *vb* **-izing, -ized** *or* **-ising, -ised** to coat or treat with rubber.

rubberneck *US & NZ slang* ✧ *vb* **1** to stare in a naive or foolish manner. ✧ *n* **2** a person who stares inquisitively. **3** a sightseer or tourist.

rubber plant *n* **1** a large house plant with glossy leathery leaves. **2** same as **rubber tree**.

rubber stamp *n* **1** a device used for imprinting dates or signatures on forms or invoices. **2** automatic authorization of something. **3** a person or body that gives official approval to decisions taken elsewhere but has no real power. ✧ *vb* **rubber-stamp 4** *Informal* to approve automatically.

rubber tree *n* a tropical tree cultivated for its latex, which is the major source of commercial rubber.

rubbish *n* **1** discarded or waste matter. **2** anything worthless or of poor quality: *the rubbish on television.* **3** foolish words or speech. ✧ *vb* **4** *Informal* to criticize. ▷ **HISTORY** origin unknown ▸ **rubbishy** *adj*

rubble *n* **1** debris from ruined buildings. **2** pieces of broken stones or bricks. ▷ **HISTORY** origin unknown

rubella (roo-**bell**-a) *n* a mild contagious viral disease characterized by cough, sore throat, and skin rash. Also called: **German measles** ▷ **HISTORY** Latin *rubellus* reddish

Rubicon (**roo**-bik-on) *n* **cross the Rubicon** to commit oneself to a course of action which cannot be altered. ▷ **HISTORY** a stream in N Italy: by leading his army across it, Julius Caesar caused civil war in Rome in 49 BC

rubicund (**roo**-bik-kund) *adj Old-fashioned* of a reddish colour. ▷ **HISTORY** Latin *rubicundus*

rubidium (roo-**bid**-ee-um) *n Chem* a soft highly reactive radioactive metallic element used in electronic valves, photocells, and special glass. Symbol: Rb. ▷ **HISTORY** Latin *rubidus* red

rub off *vb* **1** to remove or be removed by rubbing: *rub the skins off the hazelnuts.* **2** to have an effect through close association: *glamour can rub off on you by association.*

rub out *vb* **1** to remove or be removed with a rubber. **2** *US slang* to murder.

rubric (**roo**-brik) *n* **1** a set of rules of conduct or procedure, esp. one for the conduct of Christian church services. **2** a title or heading in a book. ▷ **HISTORY** Latin *ruber* red

ruby *n, pl* **-bies 1** a deep red transparent precious gemstone. ✧ *adj* **2** deep red. **3** denoting a fortieth anniversary: *a ruby wedding.* ▷ **HISTORY** Latin *ruber* red

ruche *n* a strip of pleated or frilled lace or ribbon used to decorate clothes. ▷ **HISTORY** French, literally: beehive

ruck[1] *n* **1 the ruck** ordinary people, often in a crowd. **2** *Rugby* a loose scrum that forms around the ball when it is on the ground. ▷ **HISTORY** probably from Old Norse

ruck[2] *n* **1** a wrinkle or crease. ✧ *vb* **2** to wrinkle or crease: *the toe of his shoe had rucked up one corner of the pale rug.* ▷ **HISTORY** Scandinavian

rucksack *n Brit, Austral & S African* a large bag, with two straps, carried on the back. ▷ **HISTORY** from German

rudder *n* **1** *Naut* a vertical hinged piece that projects into the water at the stern, used to steer a boat. **2** a vertical control surface attached to the rear of the fin used to steer an aircraft. ▷ **HISTORY** Old English *rōther* ▸ **rudderless** *adj*

ruddy *adj* **-dier, -diest 1** (of the complexion) having a healthy reddish colour. **2** red or pink: *a ruddy glow.* ✧ *adv, adj* **3** *Informal* bloody: *too ruddy slow; I just went through the ruddy ceiling.* ▷ **HISTORY** Old English *rudig*

rude *adj* **1** insulting or impolite. **2** vulgar or obscene: *rude words.* **3** unexpected and unpleasant: *we received a rude awakening.* **4** roughly or crudely made: *the rude hovels.* **5** robust or sturdy: *the very picture of rude health.* **6** lacking refinement. ▷ **HISTORY** Latin *rudis* ▸ **rudely** *adv* ▸ **rudeness** *n*

rudiment *n* **1 rudiments a** the simplest and most basic stages of a subject: *the rudiments of painting.* **b** a partially developed version of something: *the rudiments of a democratic society.* **2** *Biol* an organ or part that is incompletely

A B C D E F G H I J K L M N O P Q R S T U V W X Y Z

developed or no longer functions. ▷ **HISTORY** Latin *rudimentum* ▶ **rudimentary** *adj*

rue[1] *vb* **ruing, rued** *Literary* to feel regret for. ▷ **HISTORY** Old English *hrēowan*

rue[2] *n* an aromatic shrub with bitter evergreen leaves formerly used in medicine. ▷ **HISTORY** Greek *rhutē*

rueful *adj* feeling or expressing sorrow or regret: *a rueful smile.* ▶ **ruefully** *adv*

ruff[1] *n* **1** a circular pleated or fluted cloth collar. **2** a natural growth of long or coloured hair or feathers around the necks of certain animals or birds. **3** a bird of the sandpiper family. ▷ **HISTORY** from *ruffle*

ruff[2] *n, vb Cards* same as **trump**[1] (senses 1, 2). ▷ **HISTORY** Old French *roffle*

ruffian *n* a violent lawless person. ▷ **HISTORY** Old French *rufien*

Ruffini's organs *pl n Anat* a sensory nerve ending that is sensitive to heat. ▷ **HISTORY** from Angelo *Ruffini*, Italian anatomist

ruffle *vb* **-fling, -fled 1** to disturb the smoothness of: *the wind was ruffling Dad's hair.* **2** to annoy or irritate. **3** (of a bird) to erect (its feathers) in anger or display. **4** to flick (cards or pages) rapidly. ✧ *n* **5** a strip of pleated material used as a trim. ▷ **HISTORY** Germanic

rufous *adj* (of birds or animals) reddish-brown. ▷ **HISTORY** Latin *rufus*

rug *n* **1** a small carpet. **2** a thick woollen blanket. **3** *Slang* a wig. **4 pull the rug out from under** to betray or leave defenceless. ▷ **HISTORY** Scandinavian

rugby *or* **rugby football** *n* a form of football played with an oval ball in which the handling and carrying of the ball is permitted. ▷ **HISTORY** after the public school at *Rugby,* where it was first played

rugby league *n* a form of rugby played between teams of 13 players.

rugby union *n* a form of rugby played between teams of 15 players.

rugged (**rug**-gid) *adj* **1** rocky or steep: *the rugged mountains of Sicily's interior.* **2** with an uneven or jagged surface. **3** (of the face) strong-featured. **4** rough, sturdy, or determined in character. **5** (of equipment or machines) designed to withstand rough treatment or use in rough conditions. ▷ **HISTORY** probably from Old Norse

rugger *n Chiefly Brit informal* rugby.

ruin *vb* **1** to destroy or spoil completely: *the suit was ruined.* **2** to cause (someone) to lose money: *the first war ruined him.* ✧ *n* **3** the state of being destroyed or decayed. **4** loss of wealth or position. **5** a destroyed or decayed building or town. **6** something that is severely damaged: *my heart was an aching ruin.* ▷ **HISTORY** Latin *ruina* a falling down

ruination *n* **1** the act of ruining or the state of being ruined. **2** something that causes ruin.

ruinous *adj* **1** causing ruin or destruction. **2** more expensive than can reasonably be afforded: *ruinous rates of exchange.* ▶ **ruinously** *adv*

rule *n* **1** a statement of what is allowed, for example in a game or procedure. **2** a customary form or procedure: *he has his own rule: be firm, be clear, but never be rude.* **3 the rule** the common order of things: *humanitarian gestures were more the exception than the rule.* **4** the exercise of governmental authority or control: *the rule of President Marcos.* **5** the period of time in which a monarch or government has power: *four decades of Communist rule.* **6** a device with a straight edge for guiding or measuring: *a slide rule.* **7** *Printing* a long thin line or dash. **8** *Christianity* a systematic body of laws and customs followed by members of a religious order. **9** *Law* an order by a court or judge. **10 as a rule** usually. ✧ *vb* **ruling, ruled 11** to govern (people or a political unit). **12** to be pre-eminent or superior. **13** to be customary or prevalent: *chaos ruled as the scene turned into one of total confusion.* **14** to decide authoritatively: *the judges ruled that men could be prosecuted for rape offences against their wives.* **15** to mark with straight parallel lines or one straight line. **16** to restrain or control. ▷ **HISTORY** Old French *riule*

rule of law *n Law* the principle that everyone is subject to the law.

rule of thumb *n* a rough and practical approach, based on experience, rather than theory.

rule out *vb* **1** to dismiss from consideration. **2** to make impossible.

ruler *n* **1** a person who rules or commands. **2** a strip of wood, metal, or plastic, with straight edges, used for measuring and drawing straight lines.

ruling *adj* **1** controlling or exercising authority. **2** predominant. ✧ *n* **3** a decision of someone in authority.

rum[1] *n* alcoholic drink made from sugar cane. ▷ **HISTORY** origin unknown

rum[2] *adj* **rummer, rummest** *Brit slang* strange or unusual. ▷ **HISTORY** origin unknown

Rumanian *adj, n* same as **Romanian**.

rumba *n* **1** a rhythmic and syncopated dance of Cuban origin. **2** music for this dance. ▷ **HISTORY** Spanish

rumble *vb* **-bling, -bled 1** to make or cause to make a deep echoing sound: *thunder rumbled overhead.* **2** to move with such a sound: *a slow freight train rumbled past.* **3** *Brit slang* to find out about (someone or something): *his real identity was rumbled.* ✧ *n* **4** a deep resonant sound. **5** *Slang* a gang fight. ▷ **HISTORY** probably from Middle Dutch *rummelen* ▶ **rumbling** *adj, n*

rumbustious *adj* boisterous or unruly. ▷ **HISTORY** probably variant of *robustious*

ruminant *n* **1** a mammal that chews the cud, such as cattle, sheep, deer, goats, and camels. ✧ *adj* **2** of ruminants. **3** meditating or contemplating in a slow quiet way.

ruminate *vb* **-nating, -nated 1** (of ruminants) to chew (the cud). **2** to meditate or ponder. ▷ **HISTORY** Latin *ruminare* to chew the cud ▶ **rumination** *n* ▶ **ruminative** *adj*

rummage *vb* **-maging, -maged 1** to search untidily. ✧ *n* **2** an untidy search through a collection of things. ▷ **HISTORY** Old French *arrumage* to stow cargo

rummy *n* a card game based on collecting sets and sequences. ▷ **HISTORY** origin unknown

rumour *or US* **rumor** *n* **1** information, often a mixture of truth and untruth, told by one person to another. **2** gossip or common talk. ✧ *vb* **3 be rumoured** to be circulated as a rumour: *he is rumoured to have at least 53 yachts.* ▷ **HISTORY** Latin *rumor*

rump *n* **1** a person's buttocks. **2** the rear part of an animal's or bird's body. **3** Also called: **rump steak** a cut of beef from the rump. **4** a small core of members within a group who remain loyal to it: *the rump of the once-influential communist party.* ▷ **HISTORY** probably from Old Norse

rumple *vb* **-pling, -pled** to make or become crumpled or dishevelled. ▷ **HISTORY** Middle Dutch *rompelen*

rumpus *n, pl* **-puses** a noisy or confused commotion. ▷ **HISTORY** origin unknown

run *vb* **running, ran, run 1** to move on foot at a rapid pace. **2** to pass over (a distance or route) in running: *being a man isn't about running the fastest mile.* **3** to take part in (a race): *I ran a decent race.* **4** to carry out as if by running: *he is running errands for his big brother.* **5** to flee. **6** to travel somewhere in a vehicle. **7** to give a lift to (someone) in a vehicle: *one wet day I ran her down to the service.* **8** to drive or maintain and operate (a vehicle). **9** to travel regularly between places on a route: *trains running through the night.* **10** to move or pass quickly: *he ran his hand across his forehead.* **11** to function or cause to function: *run the video tape backwards.* **12** to manage: *he ran a small hotel.* **13** to continue in a particular direction or for a particular time or distance: *a road running alongside the Nile; a performing arts festival running in the city for six weeks.* **14** *Law* to have legal force or effect: *the club's lease runs out next May.* **15** to be subjected to or affected by: *she ran a high risk of losing her hair.* **16** to tend or incline: *he was of medium height and running to fat.* **17** to recur persistently or be inherent: *the capacity for infidelity ran in the genes.* **18** to flow or cause (liquids) to flow: *sweat ran down her face.* **19** to dissolve and spread: *the soles of the shoes peeled off and the colours ran.* **20** (of stitches) to unravel. **21** to spread or circulate: *rumours ran around quickly.* **22** to publish or be published in a newspaper or magazine: *our local newspaper ran a story on the appeal.* **23** *Chiefly US & Canad* to stand as a candidate for political or other office: *he has formally announced his decision to run for the office of President.* **24** to get past or through: *the oil tanker was hit as it tried to run the blockade.* **25** to smuggle (goods, esp. arms). **26** (of fish) to migrate upstream from the sea, esp. in order to spawn. **27** *Cricket* to score (a run or number of runs) by hitting the ball and running between the wickets. ✧ *n* **28** the act or an instance of running: *he broke into a run.* **29** a distance covered by running or a period of running: *it's a short run of about 20 km.* **30** a trip in a vehicle, esp. for pleasure: *our only treat is a run in the car to Dartmoor.* **31** free and unrestricted access: *he had the run of the house.* **32 a** a period of time during which a machine or computer operates. **b** the amount of work performed in such a period. **33** a continuous or sustained period: *a run of seven defeats.* **34** a continuous sequence of performances: *the play had a long run.* **35** *Cards* a sequence of winning cards in one suit: *a run of spades.* **36** type, class, or category: *he had nothing in common with the usual run of terrorists.* **37** a continuous and urgent demand: *a run on the pound.* **38** a series of unravelled stitches, esp. in tights. **39** a steeply inclined course, esp. a snow-covered one used for skiing. **40** an enclosure for domestic fowls or other animals: *the chicken run.* **41** (esp. in Australia and New Zealand) a tract of land for grazing livestock. **42** the migration of fish upstream in order to spawn. **43** *Music* a rapid scalelike passage of notes. **44** *Cricket* a score of one, normally achieved by both batsmen running from one end of the wicket to the other after one of them has hit the ball. **45** *Baseball* an instance of a batter touching all four bases safely, thereby scoring. **46 a run for one's money** *Informal* **a** a close competition. **b** pleasure or success from an activity. **47 in the long run** as an eventual outcome. **48 on the run** escaping from arrest. **49 the runs** *Slang* diarrhoea. ✧ See also **runabout, run across**, etc. ▷ **HISTORY** Old English *runnen*

runabout *n* **1** a small car used for short journeys. ✧ *vb* **run about 2** to move busily from place to place.

run across *vb* to meet unexpectedly by chance.

run away *vb* **1** to go away. **2** to escape. **3** (of a horse) to gallop away uncontrollably: *the horse ran away with him.* **4 run away with a** to abscond or elope with: *I ran away with David.* **b** to escape from the control of: *he let his imagination run away with him.* **c** to win easily or be certain of victory in (a competition): *the Spaniards at one stage seemed to be running away with the match.* ✧ *n* **runaway 5** a person or animal that runs away. ✧ *adj* **runaway 6** no longer under control: *a runaway train.* **7** (of a race or victory) easily won.

run down *vb* **1** to be rude about: *he is busy running us down and insulting other Europeans.* **2** to reduce in number or size: *it should be possible to run down the existing hospitals almost entirely.* **3** (of a device such as a clock or battery) to lose power gradually and cease to function. **4** to hit and knock to the ground with a moving vehicle. **5** to pursue and find or capture: *while I was there, Moscow ran me down, convinced I was ready to defect.* ✧ *adj* **run-down 6** tired or ill. **7** shabby or dilapidated. ✧ *n* **rundown 8** a reduction in number or size. **9** a brief review or summary.

rune *n* **1** any of the characters of the earliest Germanic alphabet. **2** an obscure piece of writing using mysterious symbols. ▷ **HISTORY** Old Norse *rūn* secret ▶ **runic** *adj*

rung[1] *n* **1** one of the bars forming the steps of a ladder. **2** a crosspiece between the legs of a chair. ▷ **HISTORY** Old English *hrung*

rung[2] *vb* the past participle of **ring**[1].

run-holder *n Austral & NZ* the owner or manager of a sheep or cattle station.

run in *vb* **1** to run (an engine) gently, usually when it is new. **2** *Informal* to arrest. ✧ *n* **run-in** **3** *Informal* an argument or quarrel. **4** an approach to the end of an event: *the run-in for the championship.*

run into *vb* **1** to be beset by: *the mission has run into difficulty.* **2** to meet unexpectedly. **3** to extend to: *businessmen denied losses running into the thousands.* **4** to collide with.

runnel *n Literary* a small stream. ▷ **HISTORY** Old English *rynele*

runner *n* **1** a competitor in a race. **2** a messenger for a firm. **3** a person involved in smuggling. **4 a** either of the strips of metal or wood on which a sledge runs. **b** the blade of an ice skate. **5** *Bot* a slender horizontal stem of a plant, such as the strawberry, that grows along the surface of the soil and produces new roots and shoots. **6** a long strip of cloth used to decorate a table or as a rug. **7** a roller or guide for a sliding component. **8 do a runner** *Slang* to run away to escape trouble or to avoid paying for something.

runner bean *n* the edible pod and seeds of a type of climbing bean plant.

runner-up *n, pl* **runners-up** a person who comes second in a competition.

running *adj* **1** maintained continuously: *a running battle.* **2** without interruption: *for the third day running.* **3 a** flowing: *rinse them under cold running water.* **b** supplied through a tap: *there is no electricity, no running water, and no telephone.* **4** operating: *running costs.* **5** discharging pus: *a running sore.* **6** accomplished at a run: *a running jump.* **7** moving or slipping easily, as a rope or a knot. ✧ *n* **8** the act of moving or flowing quickly. **9** management or organization: *the running of the farm.* **10** the operation or maintenance of a machine. **11 in** *or* **out of the running** having *or* not having a good chance in a competition. **12 make the running** to set the pace in a competition or race.

running board *n* a board along the side of a vehicle, for help in stepping into it.

running head *n Printing* a heading printed at the top of every page of a book.

running mate *n* **1** *US* a candidate for the lesser of two linked positions, esp. a candidate for the vice-presidency. **2** a horse that pairs another in a team.

running repairs *pl n* repairs that are done without greatly disrupting operations.

runny *adj* **-nier, -niest 1** tending to flow: *a runny egg.* **2** producing moisture: *a runny nose.*

run off *vb* **1** to leave quickly. **2 run off with a** to run away with in order to marry or live with. **b** to steal. **3** to produce (copies of a document) on a machine. **4** to drain (liquid) or (of liquid) to be drained. ✧ *n* **run-off 5** an extra race or contest to decide the winner after a tie. **6** *Geog* that portion of rainfall that runs into streams as surface water rather than being absorbed into ground water or evaporating. **7** *NZ* grazing land for cattle.

run-of-the-mill *adj* ordinary or average.

run-on line *n Prosody* a line that is not complete at the end of a line of poetry but continues onto the next line without a pause.

run out *vb* **1** to use up or (of a supply) to be used up: *we soon ran out of gas.* **2** to become invalid: *my passport has run out.* **3 run out on** *Informal* to desert or abandon. **4** *Cricket* to dismiss (a running batsman) by breaking the wicket with the ball while he is running between the wickets. ✧ *n* **run-out 5** *Cricket* dismissal of a batsman by running him out.

run over *vb* **1** to knock down (a person) with a moving vehicle. **2** to overflow. **3** to examine hastily.

runt *n* **1** the smallest and weakest young animal in a litter. **2** an undersized or inferior person. ▷ **HISTORY** origin unknown

run up *vb* **1** to amass: *running up massive debts.* **2** to make by sewing together quickly. **3 run up against** to experience (difficulties). ✧ *n* **run-up** **4** the time just before an event: *the run-up to the elections.*

runway *n* a hard level roadway where aircraft take off and land.

rupee *n* the standard monetary unit of a number of countries including India and Pakistan. ▷ **HISTORY** Hindi *rupaīyā*

rupture *n* **1** the act of breaking or the state of being broken. **2** a breach of peaceful or friendly relations. **3** *Pathol* a hernia. ✧ *vb* **-turing, -tured** **4** to break or burst. **5** to cause a breach in relations or friendship. **6** to affect or be affected with a hernia. ▷ **HISTORY** Latin *rumpere* to burst forth

rural *adj* in or of the countryside. ▷ **HISTORY** Latin *ruralis*

rural dean *n Chiefly Brit* a clergyman with authority over a group of parishes.

rural urban fringe *n Geog* the area around the very edge of a town or city.

ruse (**rooz**) *n* an action or plan intended to mislead someone. ▷ **HISTORY** Old French

rush[1] *vb* **1** to move or do very quickly. **2** to force (someone) to act hastily. **3** to make a sudden attack upon (a person or place): *scores of pubescent girls rushed the stage.* **4** to proceed or approach in a reckless manner. **5** to come or flow quickly or suddenly: *the water rushed in, and the next instant the boat was swamped.* ✧ *n* **6** a sudden quick or violent movement. **7** *Brit, Austral & NZ* a sudden demand or need. **8** a sudden surge towards someone or something: *the gold rush.* **9** a sudden surge of sensation. **10** a sudden flow of air or liquid. **11 rushes** (in film-making) the initial prints of a scene before editing. ✧ *adj* **12** done with speed or urgency: *a rush job.* ▷ **HISTORY** Old French *ruser* to put to flight

rush[2] *n* a plant which grows in wet places and has a slender pithy stem. ▷ **HISTORY** Old English *risce, rysce* ▶ **rushy** *adj*

rush hour *n* a period at the beginning and end of the working day when large numbers of people are travelling to or from work.

rusk *n* a hard brown crisp biscuit, often used for feeding babies. ▷ **HISTORY** Spanish or Portuguese *rosca* screw, bread shaped in a twist

russet *adj* **1** *Literary* reddish-brown: *a disarray of russet curls.* ✧ *n* **2** an apple with a rough reddish-brown skin. ▷ **HISTORY** Latin *russus*

Russian *adj* **1** of Russia. ✧ *n* **2** a person from Russia. **3** the official language of Russia and, formerly, of the Soviet Union.

Russian roulette *n* an act of bravado in which a person spins the cylinder of a revolver loaded with only one cartridge and presses the trigger with the barrel against his or her own head.

rust *n* **1** a reddish-brown oxide coating formed on iron or steel by the action of oxygen and moisture. **2** a fungal disease of plants which produces a reddish-brown discolouration. ✧ *adj* **3** reddish-brown. ✧ *vb* **4** to become coated with a layer of rust. **5** to deteriorate through lack of use: *my brain had rusted up.* ▷ **HISTORY** Old English *rūst*

rustic *adj* **1** of or resembling country people. **2** of or living in the country. **3** crude, awkward, or uncouth. **4** made of untrimmed branches: *rustic furniture.* ✧ *n* **5** a person from the country. ▷ **HISTORY** Latin *rusticus* ▶ **rusticity** *n*

rusticate *vb* **-cating, -cated 1** *Brit* to send (a student) down from university for a specified time as a punishment. **2** to retire to the country. **3** to make or become rustic. ▷ **HISTORY** Latin *rus* the country

rustle[1] *vb* **-tling, -tled 1** to make a low crisp whispering sound: *the leaves rustled in the breeze.* ✧ *n* **2** this sound. ▷ **HISTORY** Old English *hrūxlian*

rustle[2] *vb* **-tling, -tled** *Chiefly US & Canad* to steal (livestock). ▷ **HISTORY** probably from RUSTLE[1] (in the sense: to move with a quiet sound) ▶ **rustler** *n*

rustle up *vb Informal* to prepare or find at short notice: *Bob rustled up a meal.*

rusty *adj* **rustier, rustiest 1** affected by rust: *a rusty old freighter.* **2** reddish-brown. **3** out of practice in a skill or subject: *your skills may be a little rusty, but your past experience will more than make up for that.* ▶ **rustily** *adv* ▶ **rustiness** *n*

rut[1] *n* **1** a groove or furrow in a soft road, caused by wheels. **2** dull settled habits or way of living: *his career was in a rut.* ▷ **HISTORY** probably from French *route* road

rut[2] *n* **1** a recurrent period of sexual excitement in certain male ruminants. ✧ *vb* **rutting, rutted 2** (of male ruminants) to be in a period of sexual excitement. ▷ **HISTORY** Old French *rut* noise, roar

ruthenium *n Chem* a rare hard brittle white metallic element. Symbol: Ru. ▷ **HISTORY** Medieval Latin *Ruthenia* Russia, where it was discovered

rutherfordium *n chem* an artificially produced radioactive element. Symbol: Rf. ▷ **HISTORY** after E. *Rutherford,* physicist

ruthless *adj* **1** feeling or showing no mercy. **2** thorough and forceful, regardless of effect: *the ruthless pursuit of cost-effectiveness.* ▷ **HISTORY** *ruth* pity ▶ **ruthlessly** *adv* ▶ **ruthlessness** *n*

RV Revised Version (of the Bible).

rye *n* **1** a tall grasslike cereal grown for its light brown grain. **2** the grain of this plant. **3** Also called: **rye whiskey** whisky distilled from rye. ▷ **HISTORY** Old English *ryge*

rye-grass *n* any of several grasses grown for fodder.

S s

A
B
C
D
E
F
G
H
I
J
K
L
M
N
O
P
Q
R
S
T
U
V
W
X
Y
Z

s second (of time).
S **1** South(ern). **2** *Chem* sulphur. **3** *Physics* siemens.
-'s *suffix* **1** forming the possessive singular of nouns and some pronouns: *woman's; one's.* **2** forming the possessive plural of nouns whose plurals do not end in *-s*: *children's.* **3** forming the plural of numbers, letters, or symbols: *20's.* **4** *Informal* contraction of *is* or *has*: *it's over.* **5** *Informal* contraction of *us* with *let*: *let's go.*
SA **1** Salvation Army. **2** South Africa. **3** South America. **4** South Australia.
SAA South African Airways.
Sabbath *n* **1** Saturday, observed by Jews as the day of worship and rest. **2** Sunday, observed by Christians as the day of worship and rest. ▷ **HISTORY** Hebrew *shābath* to rest
sabbatical *adj* **1** denoting a period of leave granted at intervals to university teachers for rest, study, or travel: *a sabbatical year.* ✧ *n* **2** a sabbatical period. ▷ **HISTORY** see SABBATH
SABC South African Broadcasting Corporation.
sable *n, pl* **-bles** *or* **-ble** **1** a marten of N Asia, N Europe, and America, with dark brown luxuriant fur. **2** the highly valued fur of this animal, used to make coats and hats. ✧ *adj* **3** dark brown-to-black. ▷ **HISTORY** Slavic
sable antelope *n* a large black African antelope with stout backward-curving horns.
sabot (**sab**-oh) *n* a heavy wooden or wooden-soled shoe; clog. ▷ **HISTORY** French
sabotage *n* **1** the deliberate destruction or damage of equipment, for example by enemy agents or dissatisfied employees. **2** deliberate obstruction of or damage to a cause or effort. ✧ *vb* **-taging, -taged** **3** to destroy or disrupt by sabotage. ▷ **HISTORY** French
saboteur *n* a person who commits sabotage. ▷ **HISTORY** French
sabre *or US* **saber** *n* **1** a heavy single-edged cavalry sword with a curved blade. **2** a light sword used in fencing, with a narrow V-shaped blade. ▷ **HISTORY** German (dialect) *Sabel*
sac *n* a pouch or pouchlike part in an animal or plant. ▷ **HISTORY** Latin *saccus*
saccharin *n* an artificial sweetener. ▷ **HISTORY** Greek *sakkharon* sugar
saccharine *adj* **1** excessively sweet or sentimental: *saccharine ballads.* **2** like or containing sugar or saccharin.
sacerdotal *adj Formal* of priests or the priesthood. ▷ **HISTORY** Latin *sacerdos* priest
sachet *n* **1** a small sealed usually plastic envelope containing a small portion of a substance such as shampoo. **2** a small soft bag of perfumed powder, placed in drawers to scent clothing. ▷ **HISTORY** French
sack¹ *n* **1** a large bag made of coarse cloth or thick paper and used for carrying or storing goods. **2** the amount contained in a sack. **3** **the sack** *Informal* dismissal from employment. **4** *Slang* bed. **5** **hit the sack** *Slang* to go to bed. ✧ *vb* **6** *Informal* to dismiss from employment. ▷ **HISTORY** Greek *sakkos* ▶ **sacklike** *adj*
sack² *n* **1** the plundering of a captured town or city by an army or mob. ✧ *vb* **2** to plunder and partially destroy (a town or city). ▷ **HISTORY** French *mettre à sac* to put (loot) in a sack
sackcloth *n* **1** same as **sacking**. **2** garments made of such cloth, worn formerly to indicate mourning. **3** **sackcloth and ashes** an exaggerated attempt to apologize or compensate for a mistake or wrongdoing.
sacking *n* coarse cloth woven from flax, hemp, or jute, and used to make sacks.
sacrament *n* **1** a symbolic religious ceremony in the Christian Church, such as baptism or communion. **2** Holy Communion. **3** something regarded as sacred. ▷ **HISTORY** Latin *sacrare* to consecrate ▶ **sacramental** *adj*
sacred *adj* **1** exclusively devoted to a god or gods; holy. **2** connected with religion or intended for religious use: *sacred music.* **3** regarded as too important to be changed or interfered with: *sacred principles of free speech.* **4** **sacred to** dedicated to: *the site is sacred to Vishnu.* ▷ **HISTORY** Latin *sacer* holy
sacred cow *n Informal* a person, custom, belief, or institution regarded as being beyond criticism. ▷ **HISTORY** alluding to the Hindu belief that cattle are sacred
sacrifice *n* **1** a surrender of something of value in order to gain something more desirable or prevent some evil. **2** a ritual killing of a person or animal as an offering to a god. **3** a symbolic offering of something to a god. **4** the person or animal killed or offered. ✧ *vb* **-ficing, -ficed** **5** to make a sacrifice (of). **6** *Chess* to permit or force one's opponent to capture (a piece) as a tactical move. ▷ **HISTORY** Latin *sacer* holy + *facere* to make ▶ **sacrificial** *adj*
sacrilege *n* **1** the misuse of or disrespect shown to something sacred. **2** disrespect for a person who is widely admired or a belief that is widely accepted: *it is a sacrilege to offend democracy.* ▷ **HISTORY** Latin *sacrilegus* temple robber ▶ **sacrilegious** *adj*
sacristan *n* a person in charge of the contents of a church; sexton. ▷ **HISTORY** Latin *sacer* holy
sacristy *n, pl* **-ties** a room attached to a church or chapel where the sacred objects are kept.
sacrosanct *adj* regarded as too important to be criticized or changed: *weekend rest days were considered sacrosanct by staff.* ▷ **HISTORY** Latin *sacer* holy + *sanctus* hallowed ▶ **sacrosanctity** *n*
sacrum (**say**-krum) *n, pl* **-cra** *Anat* the large wedge-shaped bone in the lower part of the back. ▷ **HISTORY** Latin *os sacrum* holy bone, because it was used in sacrifices
sad *adj* **sadder, saddest** **1** feeling sorrow; unhappy. **2** causing, suggesting, or expressing sorrow: *a sad story.* **3** deplorably bad: *the garden*

was in a sad state. **4** regrettable: *it's rather sad he can't be with us.* **5** *Brit informal* ridiculously pathetic: *a sad, boring little wimp.* ✧ *vb* **6 pack a sad** *NZ slang* to express sadness or displeasure strongly. ▷ **HISTORY** Old English *sæd* weary ▶ **sadly** *adv* ▶ **sadness** *n*

sadden *vb* to make (someone) sad.

saddle *n* **1** a seat for a rider, usually made of leather, placed on a horse's back and secured under its belly. **2** a similar seat on a bicycle, motorcycle, or tractor. **3** a cut of meat, esp. mutton, consisting of both loins. **4 in the saddle** in a position of control. ✧ *vb* **-dling, -dled 5** to put a saddle on (a horse): *we saddled up at dawn.* **6 saddle with** to burden with (a responsibility): *he was also saddled with debt.* ▷ **HISTORY** Old English *sadol, sadul*

saddleback *n* **1** an animal with a marking resembling a saddle on its back. **2** a hill with a concave outline at the top. ▶ **saddle-backed** *adj*

saddlebag *n* a pouch or small bag attached to the saddle of a horse, bicycle, or motorcycle.

saddler *n* a person who makes, deals in, or repairs saddles and other leather equipment for horses.

saddlery *n, pl* **-dleries 1** saddles and harness for horses collectively. **2** the work or place of work of a saddler.

saddo *n, pl* **-dos, -does** *Brit informal* a socially inadequate or pathetic person.

Sadducee (**sad**-yew-see) *n Judaism* a member of an ancient Jewish sect that denied the resurrection of the dead and accepted only the traditional written law.

sadhu (**sah**-doo) *n* a Hindu wandering holy man. ▷ **HISTORY** Sanskrit

sadism (**say**-diz-zum) *n* the gaining of pleasure, esp. sexual pleasure, from infliction of suffering on another person. ▶ **sadist** *n* ▶ **sadistic** *adj* ▶ **sadistically** *adv*

WORD HISTORY

The sexual debauchery and scandalous erotic novels of the French writer and soldier the Marquis de Sade (1740-1814) gave rise to this word. The Marquis suffered long periods of imprisonment as punishment for his behaviour and was an infamous figure of his day.

sadomasochism *n* **1** the combination of sadistic and masochistic elements in one person, characterized by both submissive and aggressive periods in relationships with others. **2** a sexual practice in which one partner adopts a masochistic role and the other a sadistic one. ▶ **sadomasochist** *n* ▶ **sadomasochistic** *adj*

s.a.e. *Brit, Austral & NZ* stamped addressed envelope.

safari *n, pl* **-ris** an overland expedition for hunting or observing animals, esp. in Africa. ▷ **HISTORY** Swahili: journey

safari park *n* an enclosed park in which wild animals are kept uncaged in the open and can be viewed by the public from cars or buses.

safe *adj* **1** giving security or protection from harm: *a safe environment.* **2** free from danger: *she doesn't feel safe.* **3** taking or involving no risks: *a safe bet.* **4** not dangerous: *the beef is safe to eat.* **5 on the safe side** as a precaution. ✧ *n* **6** a strong metal container with a secure lock, for storing money or valuables. ▷ **HISTORY** Old French *salf* ▶ **safely** *adv*

safe-conduct *n* **1** a document giving official permission to travel through a dangerous region, esp. in time of war. **2** the protection given by such a document.

safeguard *vb* **1** to protect (something) from being harmed or destroyed. ✧ *n* **2** a person or thing that ensures protection against danger or harm: *safeguards to prevent air collisions.*

safekeeping *n* protection from theft or damage: *I put my money in a bank for safekeeping.*

safe sex *or* **safer sex** *n* nonpenetrative sex, or intercourse using a condom, intended to prevent the spread of AIDS.

safety *n* **1** the quality or state of being free from danger. **2** shelter: *they swam to safety.*

safety belt *n* same as **seat belt**.

safety curtain *n* a fireproof curtain that can be lowered to separate the auditorium from the stage in a theatre to prevent the spread of a fire.

safety lamp *n* a miner's oil lamp designed to prevent it from igniting combustible gas.

safety net *n* **1** a large net under a trapeze or high wire to catch performers if they fall. **2** something that can be relied on for help in the event of difficulties: *the social security safety net.*

safety pin *n* a pin bent back on itself so that it forms a spring, with the point shielded by a guard when closed.

safety valve *n* **1** a valve in a boiler or machine that allows fluid or gases to escape at excess pressure. **2** an outlet that allows one to express strong feelings without harming or offending other people: *sport acted as a safety valve for his pent-up frustrations.*

safflower *n* a thistle-like plant with orange-yellow flowers, which yields a dye and an oil used in paints, medicines, and cooking. ▷ **HISTORY** Old French *saffleur*

saffron *n* **1** a type of crocus with purple or white flowers with orange stigmas. **2** the dried orange-coloured stigmas of this plant, used for colouring or flavouring. ✧ *adj* **3** orange-yellow. ▷ **HISTORY** Arabic *za'farān*

sag *vb* **sagging, sagged 1** to sink in the middle, under weight or pressure: *the bed sagged nearly to the floor.* **2** (of courage or spirits) to weaken or tire. **3** (of clothes) to hang loosely or unevenly. **4** to fall in value: *the stock market sagged.* ✧ *n* **5** the act or state of sagging. ▷ **HISTORY** from Old Norse ▶ **saggy** *adj*

saga (**sah**-ga) *n* **1** a medieval Scandinavian legend telling the adventures of a hero or a family. **2** *Informal* a long story or series of events: *the long-running saga of the hostage issue.* ▷ **HISTORY** Old Norse

sagacious *adj Formal* wise or sensible. ▷ **HISTORY** Latin *sagax* ▶ **sagaciously** *adv* ▶ **sagacity** *n*

sage[1] *n* **1** a person, esp. an old man, regarded as being very wise. ✧ *adj* **2** very wise or knowledgeable, esp. as the result of age or experience.

> **WORD HISTORY**
> In this sense, 'sage' comes via French from Latin *sapere*, meaning 'to be wise'.

sage[2] *n* **1** a Mediterranean plant with grey-green leaves which are used in cooking for flavouring. **2** short for **sagebrush**

> **WORD HISTORY**
> In this sense, 'sage' comes from Latin *salvus*, meaning 'healthy', because of the supposed medicinal properties of the plant.

sagebrush *n* an aromatic plant of W North America, with silver-green leaves and large clusters of small white flowers.

Sagittarius *n Astrol* the ninth sign of the zodiac; the Archer. ▷ **HISTORY** Latin

sago *n* an edible starch from the powdered pith of the sago palm tree, used for puddings and as a thickening agent. ▷ **HISTORY** Malay *sāgū*

sahib *n* an Indian term of address equivalent to *sir*, formerly used as a mark of respect to a European man. ▷ **HISTORY** Urdu

said *adj* **1** named or mentioned already: *she had heard that the said lady was also a medium.* ✧ *vb* **2** the past of **say**.

sail *n* **1** a sheet of canvas or other fabric, spread on rigging to catch the wind and move a ship over water. **2** a voyage on such a ship: *a relaxing sail across the lake.* **3** a ship or ships with sails: *to travel by sail.* **4** one of the revolving arms of a windmill. **5 set sail** to begin a voyage by water. **6 under sail a** under way. **b** with sail hoisted. ✧ *vb* **7** to travel in a boat or ship: *to sail around the world.* **8** to begin a voyage: *he hoped to sail at eleven.* **9** (of a ship) to move over the water. **10** to navigate (a ship): *she sailed the schooner up the channel.* **11** to sail over: *he had already sailed the Pacific.* **12** to move along smoothly. **13 sail into** *Informal* to make a violent attack on. **14 sail through** to progress quickly or effortlessly: *the top seed sailed through to the second round.* ▷ **HISTORY** Old English *segl*

sailboard *n* a board with a mast and a single sail, used for windsurfing.

sailcloth *n* **1** the fabric used for making sails. **2** a canvas-like cloth used for clothing.

sailfish *n, pl* **-fish** *or* **-fishes** a large tropical game fish, with a long sail-like fin on its back.

sailor *n* **1** any member of a ship's crew, esp. one below the rank of officer. **2** a person considered as liable or not liable to seasickness: *a good sailor.*

sainfoin (**san**-foin) *n* a Eurasian plant with pink flowers, widely grown as feed for grazing farm animals. ▷ **HISTORY** Medieval Latin *sanum faenum* wholesome hay

saint *n* **1** a person who after death is formally recognized by a Christian Church as deserving special honour because of having lived a very holy life. **2** an exceptionally good person. ▷ **HISTORY** Latin *sanctus* holy ▶ **sainthood** *n* ▶ **saintlike** *adj*

Saint Bernard *n* a very large dog with a dense red-and-white coat, formerly used as a mountain-rescue dog.

Saint John's wort *n* a plant with yellow flowers.

saintly *adj* behaving in a very good, patient, or holy way. ▶ **saintliness** *n*

Saint Vitus's dance *n Pathol* a nontechnical name for **chorea**.

saithe *n Brit* a dark-coloured food fish found in northern seas. ▷ **HISTORY** Old Norse *seithr* coalfish

sake[1] *n* **1 for someone's** *or* **one's own sake** for the benefit or interest of someone *or* oneself. **2 for the sake of something** for the purpose of obtaining or achieving something. **3 for its own sake** for the enjoyment obtained by doing something. **4** used in various exclamations of annoyance, impatience, or urgency: *for God's sake.* ▷ **HISTORY** Old English *sacu* lawsuit (hence, a cause)

sake[2] *or* **saki** (**sah**-kee) *n* a Japanese alcoholic drink made from fermented rice. ▷ **HISTORY** Japanese

salaam (sal-**ahm**) *n* **1** a Muslim greeting consisting of a deep bow with the right palm on the forehead. **2** a greeting signifying peace. ✧ *vb* **3** to make a salaam (to). ▷ **HISTORY** Arabic *salām* peace

salacious *adj* **1** having an excessive interest in sex. **2** (of books, films, or jokes) concerned with sex in an unnecessarily detailed way. ▷ **HISTORY** Latin *salax* fond of leaping ▶ **salaciousness** *n*

salad *n* a dish of raw vegetables, often served with a dressing, eaten as a separate course or as part of a main course. ▷ **HISTORY** Old French *salade*

salad days *pl n* a period of youth and inexperience.

salad dressing *n* a sauce for salad, such as oil and vinegar or mayonnaise.

salamander *n* **1** a tailed amphibian which looks like a lizard. **2** a mythical creature supposed to live in fire. ▷ **HISTORY** Greek *salamandra*

salami *n* a highly spiced sausage, usually flavoured with garlic. ▷ **HISTORY** Italian

salaried *adj* earning or providing a salary: *a salaried employee; a salaried position.*

salary *n, pl* **-ries** a fixed regular payment made by an employer, usually monthly, for professional or office work. ▷ **HISTORY** Latin *salarium* the sum given to Roman soldiers to buy salt

sale *n* **1** the exchange of goods or property for an agreed sum of money. **2** the amount sold. **3** an event at which goods are sold at reduced prices. **4** an auction. **5 sales** the department dealing with selling its company's products. ▷ **HISTORY** Old English *sala*

saleable *or US* **salable** *adj* fit for selling or capable of being sold. ▶ **saleability** *or US* ▶ **salability** *n*

saleroom *n Chiefly Brit* a room where objects are displayed for sale by auction.

salesman *n, pl* **-men** a man who sells goods in a shop.

salesmanship *n* the technique of or skill in selling.

salesperson *n, pl* **-people** *or* **-persons** a person who sells goods in a shop.

sales pitch *or* **talk** *n* persuasive talk used by a salesperson in persuading a customer to buy something.

saleswoman *n, pl* **-women** a woman who sells goods in a shop.

saleyard *n Austral & NZ* an area with pens for holding animals before auction.

salicylic acid (sal-liss-**ill**-ik) *n* a white crystalline substance used to make aspirin and as a fungicide. ▷ **HISTORY** Latin *salix* willow

salient (**say**-lee-ent) *adj* **1** (of points or facts) most important: *the salient points of his speech.* ✧ *n* **2** *Mil* a projection of the forward line of an army into enemy-held territory. ▷ **HISTORY** Latin *salire* to leap

saline (**say**-line) *adj* **1** of or containing salt: *a saline flavour.* **2** *Med* of or relating to a saline: *a saline drip.* ✧ *n* **3** *Med* a solution of sodium chloride and water. ▷ **HISTORY** Latin *sal* salt

salinity *n Chem* the condition of containing salt or the degree to which something contains salt.

saliva (sal-**lie**-va) *n* the watery fluid secreted by glands in the mouth, which aids digestion. ▷ **HISTORY** Latin ▶ **salivary** *adj*

salivate *vb* **-vating, -vated** to produce saliva, esp. an excessive amount. ▶ **salivation** *n*

sallee *n Austral* **1** a SE Australian eucalyptus with a pale grey bark. **2** an acacia tree. Also: **snow gum**

sallow *adj* (of human skin) of an unhealthy pale or yellowish colour. ▷ **HISTORY** Old English *salu* ▶ **sallowness** *n*

sally *n, pl* **-lies 1** a witty remark. **2** a sudden brief attack by troops. **3** an excursion. ✧ *vb* **-lies, -lying, -lied 4 sally forth a** to set out on a journey. **b** to set out in an energetic manner. ▷ **HISTORY** Latin *salire* to leap

salmon *n, pl* **-ons** *or* **-on** a large pink-fleshed fish which is highly valued for food and sport: salmon live in the sea but return to fresh water to spawn. ▷ **HISTORY** Latin *salmo*

salmonella (sal-mon-**ell**-a) *n* a kind of bacteria that can cause food poisoning. ▷ **HISTORY** after Daniel E. *Salmon,* veterinary surgeon

salon *n* **1** a commercial establishment in which hairdressers or fashion designers carry on their business. **2** an elegant room in a large house in which guests are received. **3** an informal gathering, esp. in the 18th, 19th, and early 20th centuries, of major literary, artistic, and political figures in a fashionable household. **4** an art exhibition. ▷ **HISTORY** French

saloon *n* **1** a two-door or four-door car with a fixed roof. **2** a comfortable but more expensive bar in a pub or hotel. **3** a large public room on a passenger ship. **4** *Chiefly US & Canad* a place where alcoholic drink is sold and consumed. ▷ **HISTORY** from *salon*

salsa *n* **1** a lively Puerto Rican dance. **2** big-band music accompanying this dance. ▷ **HISTORY** Spanish, literally: sauce

salsify *n, pl* **-fies** a Mediterranean plant with a long white edible root. ▷ **HISTORY** Italian *sassefrica*

salt *n* **1** sodium chloride, a white crystalline substance, used for seasoning and preserving food. **2** *Chem* a crystalline solid compound formed from an acid by replacing its hydrogen with a metal. **3** lively wit: *his humour added salt to the discussion.* **4 old salt** an experienced sailor. **5 rub salt into someone's wounds** to make an unpleasant situation even worse for someone. **6 salt of the earth** a person or people regarded as the finest of their kind. **7 take something with a pinch of salt** to refuse to believe something is completely true or accurate. **8 worth one's salt** worthy of one's pay; efficient. ✧ *vb* **9** to season or preserve with salt. **10** to scatter salt over (an iced road or path) to melt the ice. ✧ *adj* **11** preserved in or tasting of salt: *salt beef.* ✧ See also **salt away, salts**. ▷ **HISTORY** Old English *sealt* ▶ **salted** *adj*

SALT Strategic Arms Limitation Talks *or* Treaty.

saltation *n* **1** *Biol* an abrupt variation in the appearance of an organism, species, etc. **2** *Geog* the leaping movement of sand or soil particles carried in water or by the wind. **3** a sudden abrupt movement. ▷ **HISTORY** Latin *saltātiō* a dance, from *saltāre* to leap about

salt away *vb* to hoard or save (money) for the future.

saltbush *n Bot* any of several shrubs found in alkaline desert regions.

saltire *n* **1** *Heraldry* a diagonal cross on a shield. **2** the national flag of Scotland, a white diagonal cross on a blue background.

salt lake *n Geog* a highly saline inland lake.

salt lick *n* **1** a place where wild animals go to lick salt deposits. **2** a block of salt given to domestic animals to lick.

saltpan *n Geog* a shallow basin, usually in a desert region, containing salt, gypsum, etc., that was deposited from an evaporated salt lake.

saltpetre *or US* **saltpeter** *n* same as **potassium nitrate**. ▷ **HISTORY** Latin *sal petrae* salt of rock

salts *pl n* **1** *Med* mineral salts used as a medicine. **2 like a dose of salts** *Informal* very quickly.

saltwater *adj* of or inhabiting salt water, esp. the sea: *saltwater fish.*

salty *adj* **saltier, saltiest 1** of, tasting of, or containing salt. **2** (esp. of humour) sharp and witty. ▶ **saltiness** *n*

salubrious *adj* favourable to health. ▷ **HISTORY** Latin *salus* health ▶ **salubrity** *n*

Saluki *n* a tall hound with a smooth coat and long fringes on the ears and tail. ▷ **HISTORY** from *Saluq,* ancient Arabian city

salutary *adj* **1** (of an experience) producing a beneficial result despite being unpleasant: *a* *salutary reminder.* **2** promoting health. ▷ **HISTORY** Latin *salutaris* wholesome

salutation *n Formal* a greeting by words or actions. ▷ **HISTORY** Latin *salutare* to greet

salute *vb* **-luting, -luted 1** to greet with friendly words or gestures of respect, such as bowing. **2** to acknowledge with praise: *the statement salutes the changes of the past year.* **3** *Mil* to pay formal respect to (someone) by raising the right hand to the forehead. ✧ *n* **4** the act of saluting as a formal military gesture of respect. **5** the act of firing guns as a military greeting of honour. ▷ **HISTORY** Latin *salutare* to greet

salvage *n* **1** the rescue of a ship or its cargo from loss at sea. **2** the saving of any goods or property from destruction or waste. **3** the goods or property so saved. **4** compensation paid for the salvage of a ship or its cargo. ✧ *vb* **-vaging, -vaged 5** to save (goods or property) from shipwreck, destruction, or waste. **6** to gain (something beneficial) from a failure: *it's too late to salvage anything from the whole dismal display.* ▷ **HISTORY** Latin *salvare* to save ▶ **salvageable** *adj*

salvation *n* **1** the act of preserving someone or something from harm. **2** a person or thing that preserves from harm. **3** *Christianity* the fact or state of being saved from the influence or consequences of sin. ▷ **HISTORY** Latin *salvatus* saved

Salvation Army *n* a Christian body organized on military lines for working among the poor and spreading the Christian faith.

salve *n* **1** an ointment for wounds. **2** anything that heals or soothes. ✧ *vb* **salving, salved 3 salve one's conscience** to do something in order to feel less guilty. ▷ **HISTORY** Old English *sealf*

salver *n* a tray, usually a silver one, on which something is presented. ▷ **HISTORY** Spanish *salva* tray from which the king's taster sampled food

salvia *n* any small plant or shrub of the sage genus. ▷ **HISTORY** Latin

salvo *n, pl* **-vos** *or* **-voes 1** a simultaneous discharge of guns in battle or on a ceremonial occasion. **2** an outburst of applause or questions. ▷ **HISTORY** Italian *salva,* from Latin *salve!* greetings!

sal volatile (**sal** vol-**at**-ill-ee) *n* a solution of ammonium carbonate, used as smelling salts. ▷ **HISTORY** New Latin: volatile salt

SAM surface-to-air missile.

Samaritan *n* **1** short for **Good Samaritan**. **2** a member of a voluntary organization (**the Samaritans**) which offers counselling to people in despair, esp. by telephone.

samarium *n Chem* a silvery metallic element of the rare-earth series. Symbol: Sm. ▷ **HISTORY** after Col. von *Samarski,* Russian inspector of mines

samba *n, pl* **-bas 1** a lively Brazilian dance. **2** music for this dance. ▷ **HISTORY** Portuguese

same *adj* (usually preceded by *the*) **1** being the very one: *she is wearing the same hat.* **2** being the one previously referred to: *it causes problems for the same reason.* **3** alike in kind or quantity: *the same age.* **4** unchanged in character or nature: *his attitude is the same as ever.* **5 all the same** *or* **just the same** nevertheless; even so. **6 be all the same** to be a matter of indifference: *it was all the same to me.* ✧ *adv* **7** in the same way; similarly: *I felt much the same.* ✧ *n* **8 the same** something that is like something else in kind or quantity: *this is basically much more of the same.* ▷ **HISTORY** Old Norse *samr* ▶ **sameness** *n*

> **WORD TIP**
> The use of *same* exemplified in *if you send us your order for the materials, we will deliver same tomorrow* is common in business and official English. In general English, however, this use of the word is avoided: *may I borrow your book? I'll return it* (not *same*) *tomorrow.*

samizdat *n* (in the former Soviet Union) a system of secret printing and distribution of banned literature. ▷ **HISTORY** Russian

samovar *n* a Russian metal tea urn in which the water is heated by an inner container. ▷ **HISTORY** Russian

Samoyed *n* a dog with a thick white coat and a tightly curled tail. ▷ **HISTORY** Russian *Samoed*

sampan *n* a small flat-bottomed boat with oars, used esp. in China. ▷ **HISTORY** Chinese *san* three + *pan* board

samphire *n* a plant found on rocks by the seashore. ▷ **HISTORY** French *herbe de Saint Pierre* Saint Peter's herb

sample *n* **1** a small part of anything, taken as being representative of a whole. ✧ *vb* **-pling, -pled 2** to take a sample or samples of. **3** *Music* **a** to take a short extract from (one record) and mix it into a different backing track. **b** to record (a sound) and feed it into a computerized synthesizer so that it can be reproduced at any pitch. ▷ **HISTORY** Latin *exemplum*

sampler *n* **1** a piece of embroidery done to show the embroiderer's skill in using many different stitches. **2** *Music* a piece of electronic equipment used for sampling.

sampling *n* **1** *Statistics* the process of selecting a small random group and assuming that it is a representative sample of a much bigger group. **2** *Music* the process of taking a short musical extract and mixing it into a different backing track.

Samson *n* a man of outstanding physical strength. ▷ **HISTORY** from the biblical character who was renowned for his strength

samurai *n, pl* **-rai** a member of the aristocratic warrior caste of feudal Japan. ▷ **HISTORY** Japanese

sanatorium *or US* **sanitarium** *n, pl* **-riums** *or* **-ria 1** an institution providing medical treatment and rest for invalids or convalescents. **2** *Brit* a room in a boarding school where sick pupils may be treated. ▷ **HISTORY** Latin *sanare* to heal

sanctify *vb* **-fies, -fying, -fied 1** to make holy. **2** to free from sin. **3** to approve (an action or practice) as religiously binding: *she is trying to make amends for her marriage not being sanctified.* ▷ **HISTORY** Latin *sanctus* holy + *facere* to make ▶ **sanctification** *n*

sanctimonious *adj* pretending to be very religious and virtuous. ▷ HISTORY Latin *sanctimonia* sanctity

sanction *n* **1** permission granted by authority: *official sanction.* **2** support or approval: *they could not exist without his sanction.* **3** something that gives binding force to a law, such as a penalty for breaking it or a reward for obeying it. **4 sanctions** coercive measures, such as boycotts and trade embargoes, taken by one or more states against another guilty of violating international law. ✧ *vb* **5** to officially approve of or allow: *they do not want to sanction direct payments.* **6** to confirm or ratify. ▷ HISTORY Latin *sancire* to decree

sanctity *n* the quality of something considered so holy or important it must be respected totally: *the sanctity of the Sabbath; the sanctity of marriage.*

sanctuary *n, pl* **-aries 1** a holy place, such as a consecrated building or shrine. **2** the part of a church nearest the main altar. **3** a place of refuge or protection for someone who is being chased or hunted. **4** refuge or safety: *the sanctuary of your own home.* **5** a place, protected by law, where animals can live and breed without interference. ▷ HISTORY Latin *sanctus* holy

sanctum *n, pl* **-tums** *or* **-ta 1** a sacred or holy place. **2** a room or place of total privacy. ▷ HISTORY Latin

sand *n* **1** a powdery substance consisting of very small rock or mineral grains, found on the seashore and in deserts. **2 sands** a large sandy area, esp. on the seashore or in a desert. ✧ *vb* **3** to smooth or polish the surface of (something) with sandpaper or a sander. **4** to fill with sand: *the channel sanded up.* ▷ HISTORY Old English

sandal *n* a light shoe consisting of a sole held on the foot by thongs or straps. ▷ HISTORY Greek *sandalon* ▶ **sandalled** *or US* **sandaled** *adj*

sandalwood *n* **1** the hard light-coloured wood of a S Asian or Australian tree, which is used for carving and for incense, and which yields an aromatic oil used in perfumes. **2** a tree yielding this wood. ▷ HISTORY Sanskrit *candana*

sandbag *n* **1** a sack filled with sand used to make a temporary defence against gunfire or flood water. ✧ *vb* **-bagging, -bagged 2** to protect or strengthen with sandbags.

sandbank *or* **sand bar** *n* a bank of sand in a sea or river, that may be exposed at low tide.

sandblast *n* **1** a jet of sand blown from a nozzle under air or steam pressure. ✧ *vb* **2** to clean or decorate (a surface) with a sandblast. ▶ **sandblaster** *n*

sand castle *n* a model of a castle made from sand.

sander *n* a power-driven tool for smoothing surfaces, removing layers of paint from walls, etc.

sand martin *n* a small brown European songbird which nests in tunnels bored in sand or river banks.

sandpaper *n* **1** a strong paper coated with sand or other abrasive material for smoothing or polishing a surface. ✧ *vb* **2** to smooth or polish (a surface) with sandpaper.

sandpiper *n* a wading shore bird with a long bill and slender legs.

sandshoes *pl n* light canvas shoes with rubber soles.

sandstone *n* a sedimentary rock consisting mainly of sand grains, much used in building.

sandstorm *n* a strong wind that whips up clouds of sand, esp. in a desert.

sandwich *n* **1** two or more slices of bread, usually buttered, with a layer of food between them. ✧ *vb* **2** to place between two other things: *shops sandwiched between flats.*

> **WORD HISTORY**
> Sandwiches are named after John Montagu (1718–1792), the 4th Earl of Sandwich, who was in the habit of spending whole days at gambling tables. Since he did not want to leave the tables to eat, he asked waiters to bring him meals in the form of meat placed between two slices of bread.

sandwich board *n* one of two connected boards that are hung over the shoulders in front of and behind a person to display advertisements.

sandwich course *n Brit* an educational course consisting of alternate periods of study and industrial work.

sandy *adj* **sandier, sandiest 1** resembling, containing, or covered with sand. **2** (of hair) reddish-yellow. ▶ **sandiness** *n*

sane *adj* **1** having a normal healthy mind. **2** sensible or well-judged: *sane advice.* ▷ HISTORY Latin *sanus* healthy

sang *vb* the past tense of **sing**.

> **WORD TIP**
> See at **ring**[1].

sang-froid (sahng-**frwah**) *n* composure and calmness in a difficult situation. ▷ HISTORY French, literally: cold blood

sangoma (sang-**go**-ma) *n S African* a witch doctor. ▷ HISTORY Nguni (language group of southern Africa) *isangoma* a diviner

sangria *n* a Spanish drink of red wine, sugar, and orange or lemon juice. ▷ HISTORY Spanish: a bleeding

sanguinary *adj Formal* **1** (of a battle or fight) involving much violence and bloodshed. **2** (of a person) eager to see violence and bloodshed. **3** of or stained with blood. ▷ HISTORY Latin *sanguinarius*

sanguine *adj* **1** cheerful and confident. **2** (of the complexion) ruddy. ▷ HISTORY Latin *sanguineus* bloody

Sanhedrin (**san**-id-rin) *n Judaism* the highest court and supreme council of the ancient Jewish nation.

sanitary *adj* **1** promoting health by getting rid of dirt and germs. **2** free from dirt or germs; hygienic. ▷ HISTORY Latin *sanitas* health

sanitary towel *or esp US* **napkin** *n* a pad worn externally by women during menstruation to absorb the flow of blood.

sanitation *n* **1** the use of sanitary measures to maintain public health. **2** the drainage and disposal of sewage.

sanity *n* **1** the state of having a normal healthy mind. **2** good sense or soundness of judgment. ▷ **HISTORY** Latin *sanitas* health

sank *vb* the past tense of **sink**.

sans-culotte (sanz-kew-**lot**) *n* a revolutionary extremist. ▷ **HISTORY** French, literally: without knee breeches, because during the French Revolution the revolutionaries wore trousers

Sanskrit *n* the classical literary language of India, used since ancient times for religious purposes. ▷ **HISTORY** Sanskrit *samskrta* perfected ▶ **Sanskritic** *adj*

Santa Claus *n* the legendary patron saint of children, who brings presents to children on Christmas Eve, commonly identified with Saint Nicholas.

sap¹ *n* **1** a thin liquid that circulates in a plant, carrying food and water. **2** *Slang* a gullible person. ✧ *vb* **sapping, sapped 3** to drain of sap. ▷ **HISTORY** Old English *sæp*

sap² *vb* **sapping, sapped 1** to weaken or exhaust the strength or confidence of. **2** to undermine (an enemy position) by digging saps. ✧ *n* **3** a deep and narrow trench used to approach or undermine an enemy position. ▷ **HISTORY** Italian *zappa* spade

sapient (**say**-pee-ent) *adj Often used ironically* having great wisdom or sound judgment. ▷ **HISTORY** Latin *sapere* to taste, know ▶ **sapience** *n*

sapling *n* a young tree.

saponify *vb* **-fies, -fying, -fied** *Chem* to convert (a fat) into a soap by treatment with alkali. ▷ **HISTORY** Latin *sapo* soap ▶ **saponification** *n*

sapper *n* **1** a soldier who digs trenches. **2** (in the British Army) a private of the Royal Engineers.

sapphire *n* **1** a transparent blue precious stone. ✧ *adj* **2** deep blue. ▷ **HISTORY** Greek *sappheiros*

sappy *adj* **-pier, -piest** (of plants) full of sap.

saprophyte *n Biol* any plant, such as a fungus, that lives and feeds on dead organic matter. ▷ **HISTORY** Greek *sapros* rotten + *phuton* plant

sarabande *or* **saraband** *n* **1** a stately slow Spanish dance. **2** music for this dance. ▷ **HISTORY** Spanish *zarabanda*

Saracen *n* **1** an Arab or Muslim who opposed the Crusades. ✧ *adj* **2** of the Saracens. ▷ **HISTORY** Late Greek *Sarakēnos*

sarcasm *n* **1** mocking or ironic language intended to insult someone. **2** the use or tone of such language. ▷ **HISTORY** Greek *sarkazein* to rend the flesh

sarcastic *adj* **1** full of or showing sarcasm. **2** tending to use sarcasm: *a sarcastic critic.* ▶ **sarcastically** *adv*

sarcoma *n Pathol* a malignant tumour beginning in connective tissue. ▷ **HISTORY** Greek *sarkōma* fleshy growth

sarcophagus (sahr-**koff**-a-guss) *n, pl* **-gi** (-guy) *or* **-guses** a stone or marble coffin or tomb, esp. one bearing sculpture or inscriptions. ▷ **HISTORY** Greek *sarkophagos* flesh-devouring

sardine *n, pl* **-dines** *or* **-dine 1** a small fish of the herring family, often preserved in tightly packed tins. **2 like sardines** very closely crowded together. ▷ **HISTORY** Latin *sardina*

sardonic *adj* (of behaviour) mocking or scornful. ▷ **HISTORY** Greek *sardonios* ▶ **sardonically** *adv*

sardonyx *n* a type of gemstone with alternating reddish-brown and white parallel bands. ▷ **HISTORY** Greek *sardonux*

sargassum *n* a floating brown seaweed with long stringy fronds containing air sacs. ▷ **HISTORY** Portuguese *sargaço*

sarge *n Informal* sergeant.

sari *or* **saree** *n, pl* **-ris** *or* **-rees** the traditional dress of Hindu women, consisting of a very long piece of cloth swathed around the body with one end over the shoulder. ▷ **HISTORY** Hindi

sarking *n Scot, N English, Austral & NZ* flat planking supporting the roof cladding of a building. ▷ **HISTORY** Scots *sark* shirt

sarky *adj* **-kier, -kiest** *Brit & NZ informal* sarcastic.

sarmie *n S African children's slang* a sandwich.

sarong *n* a garment worn by Malaysian men and women, consisting of a long piece of cloth tucked around the waist or under the armpits. ▷ **HISTORY** Malay

sarsaparilla *n* a nonalcoholic drink prepared from the roots of a tropical American climbing plant. ▷ **HISTORY** Spanish *sarzaparrilla*

sartorial *adj Formal* of men's clothes or tailoring: *sartorial elegance.* ▷ **HISTORY** Latin *sartor* a tailor

SAS (in Britain) Special Air Service.

sash¹ *n* a long piece of cloth worn around the waist or over one shoulder, usually as a symbol of rank. ▷ **HISTORY** Arabic *shāsh* muslin

sash² *n* **1** a frame that contains the panes of a window or door. **2** a complete frame together with panes of glass. ▷ **HISTORY** French *châssis* a frame

sash window *n* a window consisting of two sashes placed one above the other so that the window can be opened by sliding one frame over the front of the other.

sassafras *n* a tree of North America, with aromatic bark used medicinally and as a flavouring. ▷ **HISTORY** Spanish *sasafras*

Sassenach *n Scot & occasionally Irish* an English person. ▷ **HISTORY** Gaelic *Sassunach*

sat *vb* the past of **sit**.

Sat. Saturday.

Satan *n* the Devil. ▷ **HISTORY** Hebrew: plotter

satanic *adj* **1** of Satan. **2** supremely evil or wicked.

Satanism *n* the worship of Satan. ▶ **Satanist** *n, adj*

satchel *n* a small bag, usually with a shoulder strap. ▷ **HISTORY** Old French *sachel*

sate *vb* **sating, sated** to satisfy (a desire or appetite) fully. ▷ **HISTORY** Old English *sadian*

satellite *n* **1** a man-made device orbiting the earth or another planet, used in communications or to collect scientific information. **2** a heavenly body orbiting a planet or star: *the earth is a satellite of the*

A B C D E F G H I J K L M N O P Q R S T U V W X Y Z

sun. **3** a country controlled by or dependent on a more powerful one. ✧ *adj* **4** of, used in, or relating to the transmission of television signals from a satellite to the home: *satellite TV; a satellite dish.* ▷ **HISTORY** Latin *satelles* an attendant

satellite imagery *n* pictures of earth taken and transmitted from space.

satellite town *n* a subordinate community dependent upon a larger adjacent city.

satiate (**say**-she-ate) *vb* **-ating, -ated** to provide with more than enough, so as to disgust or weary: *enough cakes to satiate several children.* ▷ **HISTORY** Latin *satiare* ▶ **satiable** *adj* ▶ **satiation** *n*

satiety (sat-**tie**-a-tee) *n Formal* the feeling of having had too much.

satin *n* **1** a fabric, usually made from silk or rayon, closely woven to give a smooth glossy surface on one side. ✧ *adj* **2** like satin in texture: *satin polyurethane varnish.* ▷ **HISTORY** Arabic *zaitūnī* ▶ **satiny** *adj*

satinwood *n* **1** a hard wood with a satiny texture, used in fine furniture. **2** the East Indian tree yielding this wood.

satire *n* **1** the use of ridicule to expose incompetence, evil, or corruption. **2** a play, novel, or poem containing satire. ▷ **HISTORY** Latin *satira* a mixture ▶ **satirical** *adj*

satirist *n* **1** a writer of satire. **2** a person who uses satire.

satirize *or* **-rise** *vb* **-rizing, -rized** *or* **-rising, -rised** to ridicule (a person or thing) by means of satire. ▶ **satirization** *or* **-risation** *n*

satisfaction *n* **1** the pleasure obtained from the fulfilment of a desire. **2** something that brings fulfilment: *craft workers get satisfaction from their work.* **3** compensation or an apology for a wrong done: *consumers unable to get satisfaction from the gas board.*

satisfactory *adj* **1** adequate or acceptable. **2** giving satisfaction. ▶ **satisfactorily** *adv*

satisfy *vb* **-fies, -fying, -fied 1** to fulfil the desires or needs of (a person): *his answer didn't satisfy me.* **2** to provide sufficiently for (a need or desire): *to satisfy public demand.* **3** to convince: *that trip did seem to satisfy her that he was dead.* **4** to fulfil the requirements of: *unable to satisfy the conditions set by the commission.* ▷ **HISTORY** Latin *satis* enough + *facere* to make ▶ **satisfiable** *adj* ▶ **satisfying** *adj*

satnav *n Motoring informal* satellite navigation.

satrap *n* (in ancient Persia) a provincial governor or subordinate ruler. ▷ **HISTORY** Old Persian *khshathrapāvan,* literally: protector of the land

SATs *Brit* standard assessment tasks.

satsuma *n* a small loose-skinned variety of orange with easily separable segments. ▷ **HISTORY** *Satsuma,* former province of Japan

saturate *vb* **-rating, -rated 1** to soak completely. **2** to fill so completely that no more can be added: *saturating the area with their men.* **3** *Chem* to combine (a substance) or (of a substance) to be combined with the greatest possible amount of another substance. ▷ **HISTORY** Latin *saturare*

saturated solution *n Chem* a solution containing the maximum amount of solute that can normally be dissolved in it at a particular temperature and pressure.

saturation *n* **1** the process or state that occurs when one substance is filled so full of another substance that no more can be added. **2** *Mil* the use of very heavy force, esp. bombing, against an area.

saturation point *n* **1** the point at which the maximum amount of a substance has been absorbed. **2** the point at which some capacity is at its fullest; limit: *the market is close to saturation point.*

Saturday *n* the seventh day of the week. ▷ **HISTORY** Latin *Saturni dies* day of Saturn

Saturn *n* **1** the Roman god of agriculture and vegetation. **2** the sixth planet from the sun, second largest in the solar system, around which revolve concentric rings.

Saturnalia *n, pl* **-lia** *or* **-lias 1** the ancient Roman festival of Saturn, renowned for its unrestrained revelry. **2 saturnalia** a wild party or orgy. ▷ **HISTORY** Latin *Saturnalis* relating to Saturn

saturnine *adj* having a gloomy temperament or appearance. ▷ **HISTORY** Latin *Saturnus* Saturn, from the gloomy influence attributed to the planet

satyr *n* **1** *Greek myth* a woodland god represented as having a man's body with the ears, horns, tail, and legs of a goat. **2** a man who has strong sexual desires. ▷ **HISTORY** Greek *saturos*

sauce *n* **1** a liquid added to food to enhance its flavour. **2** anything that adds interest or zest. **3** *Chiefly Brit informal* impudent language or behaviour. ▷ **HISTORY** Latin *salsus* salted

saucepan *n* a metal pan with a long handle and often a lid, used for cooking food.

saucer *n* **1** a small round dish on which a cup is set. **2** something shaped like a saucer. ▷ **HISTORY** Old French *saussier* container for sauce ▶ **saucerful** *n*

saucy *adj* **saucier, sauciest 1** cheeky or slightly rude in an amusing and light-hearted way. **2** jaunty and boldly smart: *a saucy hat.* ▶ **sauciness** *n*

sauerkraut *n* a German dish of finely shredded pickled cabbage. ▷ **HISTORY** German *sauer* sour + *Kraut* cabbage

sauna *n* **1** a Finnish-style hot steam bath, usually followed by a cold plunge. **2** the place in which such a bath is taken. ▷ **HISTORY** Finnish

saunter *vb* **1** to walk in a leisurely manner; stroll. ✧ *n* **2** a leisurely pace or stroll. ▷ **HISTORY** origin unknown

saurian *adj* of or resembling a lizard. ▷ **HISTORY** Greek *sauros* lizard

sausage *n* **1** finely minced meat mixed with fat, cereal, and seasonings, in a tube-shaped casing. **2** an object shaped like a sausage. **3 not a sausage** *Informal* nothing at all. ▷ **HISTORY** Old French *saussiche*

sausage dog *n Informal* same as **dachshund**.

sausage roll *n* a roll of sausage meat in pastry.

sausage sizzle *n Austral & NZ* an event at which sausages are barbecued, often to raise money for a school or other organization.

sauté (**so**-tay) *vb* **-téing** *or* **-téeing, -téed 1** to fry (food) quickly in a little fat. ✧ *n* **2** a dish of sautéed food. ✧ *adj* **3** sautéed until lightly brown: *sauté potatoes.* ▷ **HISTORY** French: tossed

savage *adj* **1** wild and untamed: *savage tigers.* **2** fierce and cruel: *savage cries.* **3** (of peoples) uncivilized or primitive: *savage tribes.* **4** rude, crude, and violent: *savage behaviour on the terraces.* **5** (of terrain) wild and uncultivated. ✧ *n* **6** a member of an uncivilized or primitive society. **7** a fierce or vicious person. ✧ *vb* **-aging, -aged 8** to attack ferociously and wound: *savaged by a wild dog.* **9** to criticize extremely severely: *savaged by the press for incompetence.* ▷ **HISTORY** Latin *silvaticus* belonging to a wood ▶ **savagely** *adv*

savagery *n, pl* **-ries** viciousness and cruelty.

savannah *or* **savanna** *n Geog* (in Africa) open grasslands, usually with scattered bushes or trees. ▷ **HISTORY** Spanish *zavana*

savant *n* a very wise and knowledgeable man. ▷ **HISTORY** French ▶ **savante** *fem n*

save[1] *vb* **saving, saved 1** to rescue or preserve (a person or thing) from danger or harm. **2** to avoid the spending, waste, or loss of (something): *an appeal on television for the public to save energy.* **3** to set aside or reserve (money or goods) for future use: *I'm saving for a vintage Mercedes.* **4** to treat with care so as to preserve. **5** to prevent the necessity for: *a chance saved him from having to make up his mind.* **6** *Sport* to prevent (a goal) by stopping (a ball or puck). **7** *Christianity* to free (someone) from the influence or consequences of sin. ✧ *n* **8** *Sport* the act of saving a goal. **9** *Computers* an instruction to write information from the memory onto a tape or disk. ▷ **HISTORY** Old French *salver* ▶ **savable** *or* **saveable** *adj* ▶ **saver** *n*

save[2] *Old-fashioned* ✧ *prep* **1** (often foll. by *for*) with the exception of: *the stage was empty save for a single chair.* ✧ *conj* **2** but. ▷ **HISTORY** Middle English *sauf*

save as you earn *n* (in Britain) a savings scheme operated by the government, in which regular deposits are made into a savings account from a salary.

saveloy *n Brit, Austral & NZ* a highly seasoned smoked sausage made from salted pork. ▷ **HISTORY** Italian *cervellato*

saving *n* **1** preservation from destruction or danger. **2** a reduction in the amount of time or money used. **3 savings** money saved for future use. ✧ *adj* **4** tending to rescue or preserve. ✧ *prep* **5** with the exception of.

saving grace *n* a good quality in a person that prevents him or her from being entirely bad or worthless.

saviour *or US* **savior** *n* a person who rescues another person or a thing from danger or harm. ▷ **HISTORY** Church Latin *Salvator* the Saviour

Saviour *or US* **Savior** *n Christianity* Jesus Christ, regarded as the saviour of people from sin.

savoir-faire (**sav**-wahr-**fair**) *n* the ability to say and do the right thing in any situation. ▷ **HISTORY** French

savory *n, pl* **-vories** an aromatic plant whose leaves are used in cooking. ▷ **HISTORY** Latin *satureia*

savour *or US* **savor** *vb* **1** to enjoy and appreciate (food or drink) slowly. **2** to enjoy (a pleasure) for as long as possible: *an experience to be savoured.* **3 savour of a** to have a suggestion of: *that could savour of ostentation.* **b** to possess the taste or smell of: *the vegetables savoured of coriander.* ✧ *n* **4** the taste or smell of something. **5** a slight but distinctive quality or trace. ▷ **HISTORY** Latin *sapor* taste

savoury *or US* **savory** *adj* **1** salty or spicy: *savoury foods.* **2** attractive to the sense of taste or smell. **3** pleasant or acceptable: *one of the book's less savoury characters.* ✧ *n, pl* **-ries 4** *Chiefly Brit* a savoury dish served before or after a meal. ▶ **savouriness** *or US* **savoriness** *n*

savoy *n* a cabbage with a compact head and wrinkled leaves. ▷ **HISTORY** after the *Savoy* region in France

savvy *Slang* ✧ *vb* **-vies, -vying, -vied 1** to understand. ✧ *n* **2** understanding or common sense. ▷ **HISTORY** corruption of Spanish *sabe (usted)* (you) know

saw[1] *n* **1** a cutting tool with a toothed metal blade or edge, either operated by hand or powered by electricity. ✧ *vb* **sawing, sawed; sawed** *or* **sawn 2** to cut with or as if with a saw. **3** to form by sawing. **4** to move (an object) from side to side as if moving a saw. ▷ **HISTORY** Old English *sagu*

saw[2] *vb* the past tense of **see**[1].

saw[3] *n Old-fashioned* a wise saying or proverb. ▷ **HISTORY** Old English *sagu* a saying

saw doctor *n NZ* a sawmill specialist who sharpens and services saw blades.

sawdust *n* particles of wood formed by sawing.

sawfish *n, pl* **-fish** *or* **-fishes** a sharklike ray with a long toothed snout resembling a saw.

sawhorse *n Austral & NZ* a structure for supporting wood that is being sawn.

sawmill *n* a factory where timber is sawn into planks.

sawyer *n* a person who saws timber for a living.

sax *n Informal* short for **saxophone**.

saxifrage *n* an alpine rock plant with small white, yellow, purple, or pink flowers. ▷ **HISTORY** Late Latin *saxifraga,* literally: rock breaker

Saxon *n* **1** a member of a West Germanic people who raided and settled parts of Britain in the fifth and sixth centuries AD. **2** any of the West Germanic dialects spoken by the ancient Saxons. ✧ *adj* **3** of the ancient Saxons or their language. ▷ **HISTORY** Late Latin *Saxon-, Saxo*

saxophone *n* a brass wind instrument with keys and a curved metal body. ▶ **saxophonist** *n*

> **WORD HISTORY**
> The saxophone is named after its inventor Adolphe Sax (1814-1894), a French musical-instrument maker. Sax invented a number of other musical instruments, including the saxhorn, the sax-tromba, and the saxtuba.

say *vb* **saying, said 1** to speak or utter. **2** to express (an idea) in words: *I can't say what I feel.* **3** to state (an opinion or fact) positively: *I say you are wrong.* **4** to indicate or show: *the clock says ten to nine.* **5** to recite: *to say grace.* **6** to report or allege: *they say we shall have rain today.* **7** to suppose as an example or possibility: *let us say that he is lying.* **8** to convey by means of artistic expression: *what does the artist have to say in this picture?* **9** to make a case for: *there is much to be said for it.* **10 go without saying** to be so obvious as to need no explanation. **11 to say the least** at the very least. ✧ *adv* **12** approximately: *there were, say, 20 people present.* **13** for example: *choose a number, say, four.* ✧ *n* **14** the right or chance to speak: *the opposition has hardly had a say in these affairs.* **15** authority, esp. to influence a decision: *he has a lot of say.* ▷ **HISTORY** Old English *secgan*

SAYE (in Britain) save as you earn.

saying *n* a well-known phrase or sentence expressing a belief or a truth.

Sb *Chem* antimony. ▷ **HISTORY** New Latin *stibium*

Sc *Chem* scandium.

SC South Carolina.

scab *n* **1** the dried crusty surface of a healing skin wound or sore. **2** *Disparaging* a person who refuses to support a trade union's actions, and continues to work during a strike. **3** a contagious disease of sheep, caused by a mite. **4** a fungal disease of plants. ✧ *vb* **scabbing, scabbed 5** to become covered with a scab. **6** *Disparaging* to work as a scab. ▷ **HISTORY** Old English *sceabb*

scabbard *n* a holder for a sword or dagger. ▷ **HISTORY** Middle English *scauberc*

scabby *adj* **-bier, -biest 1** *Pathol* covered with scabs. **2** *Informal* mean or despicable. ▶ **scabbiness** *n*

scabies (**skay**-beez) *n* a contagious skin infection caused by a mite, characterized by intense itching. ▷ **HISTORY** Latin *scabere* to scratch

scabious (**skay**-bee-uss) *n* a plant with showy blue, red, or whitish dome-shaped flower heads. ▷ **HISTORY** Medieval Latin *scabiosa herba* the scabies plant

scabrous (**skay**-bruss) *adj* **1** rough and scaly. **2** indecent or crude: *scabrous stand-up comedy.* ▷ **HISTORY** Latin *scaber* rough

scaffold *n* **1** a temporary framework used to support workmen and materials during the construction or repair of a building. **2** a raised wooden platform on which criminals are hanged; gallows. ▷ **HISTORY** Old French *eschaffaut*

scaffolding *n* **1** a scaffold or scaffolds. **2** the building materials used to make scaffolds.

scalar *Maths* ✧ *n* **1** a quantity, such as time or temperature, that has magnitude but not direction. ✧ *adj* **2** having magnitude but not direction. ▷ **HISTORY** Latin *scala* ladder

scald *vb* **1** to burn with hot liquid or steam. **2** to sterilize with boiling water. **3** to heat (a liquid) almost to boiling point. ✧ *n* **4** a burn caused by scalding. ▷ **HISTORY** Late Latin *excaldare* to wash in warm water

scale[1] *n* **1** one of the thin flat overlapping plates covering the bodies of fishes and reptiles. **2** a thin flat piece or flake. **3** a coating which sometimes forms in kettles and hot-water pipes in areas where the water is hard. **4** tartar formed on the teeth. ✧ *vb* **scaling, scaled 5** to remove the scales or coating from. **6** to peel off in flakes or scales. **7** to cover or become covered with scales. ▷ **HISTORY** Old French *escale* ▶ **scaly** *adj*

scale[2] *n* **1** (*often pl*) a machine or device for weighing. **2** one of the pans of a balance. **3 tip the scales** to have a decisive influence. **4 tip the scales at** to amount in weight to. ▷ **HISTORY** Old Norse *skāl* bowl

scale[3] *n* **1** a sequence of marks at regular intervals, used as a reference in making measurements. **2** a measuring instrument with such a scale. **3** the ratio between the size of something real and that of a representation of it: *the map has a scale of 1:10 000.* **4** a series of degrees or graded system of things: *the Western wage scale for the same work.* **5** a relative degree or extent: *growing flowers on a very small scale.* **6** *Music* a sequence of notes taken in ascending or descending order, esp. within one octave. **7** *Maths* the notation of a given number system: *the decimal scale.* ✧ *vb* **scaling, scaled 8** to climb to the top of (an object or height): *the men scaled a wall.* **9 scale up** *or* **down** to increase *or* reduce proportionately in size: *the design can easily be scaled up; after five days the search was scaled down.* ▷ **HISTORY** Latin *scala* ladder

scalene *adj Maths* (of a triangle) having all sides of unequal length. ▷ **HISTORY** Greek *skalēnos*

scallion *n* a spring onion. ▷ **HISTORY** Anglo-French *scalun*

scallop *n* **1** an edible marine mollusc with two fluted fan-shaped shells. **2** a single shell of this mollusc. **3** one of a series of small curves along an edge. ▷ **HISTORY** Old French *escalope* shell ▶ **scalloping** *n*

scalloped *adj* decorated with small curves along the edge.

scallywag *n Informal* a badly behaved but likeable person; rascal. ▷ **HISTORY** origin unknown

scalp *n* **1** *Anat* the skin and hair covering the top of the head. **2** (formerly among Native Americans of N America) a part of this removed as a trophy from a slain enemy. ✧ *vb* **3** to cut the scalp from. **4** *Informal, chiefly US* to buy and resell so as to make a high or quick profit. ▷ **HISTORY** probably from Old Norse *skālpr* sheath

scalpel *n* a small surgical knife with a very sharp thin blade. ▷ **HISTORY** Latin *scalper* a knife

scam *n Slang* a stratagem for gain; a swindle.

A B C D E F G H I J K L M N O P Q R S T U V W X Y Z

scamp *n* a mischievous person, esp. a child. ▷ **HISTORY** probably from Middle Dutch *schampen* to decamp

scamper *vb* **1** to run about hurriedly or quickly. ✧ *n* **2** the act of scampering. ▷ **HISTORY** see SCAMP

scampi *n* large prawns, usually eaten fried in breadcrumbs. ▷ **HISTORY** Italian

scan *vb* **scanning, scanned 1** to scrutinize carefully. **2** to glance over quickly. **3** *Prosody* to analyse (verse) by examining its rhythmic structure. **4** *Prosody* (of a line or verse) to be metrically correct. **5** to examine or search (an area) by systematically moving a beam of light or electrons, or a radar or sonar beam over it. **6** *Med* to obtain an image of (a part of the body) by means of ultrasound or a scanner. ✧ *n* **7** an instance of scanning. ▷ **HISTORY** Latin *scandere* to climb

scandal *n* **1** a disgraceful action or event: *the chairman resigned after a loans scandal.* **2** shame or outrage arising from a disgraceful action or event: *the figures were a national scandal.* **3** malicious gossip. ▷ **HISTORY** Greek *skandalon* a trap ▸ **scandalous** *adj* ▸ **scandalously** *adv*

scandalize *or* **-ise** *vb* **-izing, -ized** *or* **-ising, -ised** to shock or be shocked by improper behaviour.

scandalmonger *n* a person who spreads or enjoys scandal or gossip.

Scandinavian *adj* **1** of Scandinavia (Norway, Sweden, Denmark, and often Finland, Iceland, and the Faeroe Islands). ✧ *n* **2** a person from Scandinavia. **3** the northern group of Germanic languages, consisting of Swedish, Danish, Norwegian, Icelandic, and Faeroese.

scandium *n Chem* a rare silvery-white metallic element. Symbol: Sc. ▷ **HISTORY** Latin *Scandia* Scandinavia, where discovered

scanner *n* **1** an aerial or similar device designed to transmit or receive signals, esp. radar signals. **2** a device used in medical diagnosis to obtain an image of an internal organ or part. **3** *Computing* a device connected to a computer, which enables printed material, including text and pictures, to be scanned and converted into a form that can be stored in a computer.

scansion *n* the metrical scanning of verse.

scant *adj* scarcely sufficient: *some issues will get scant attention.* ▷ **HISTORY** Old Norse *skamt* short

scanty *adj* **scantier, scantiest** barely sufficient or not sufficient. ▸ **scantily** *adv* ▸ **scantiness** *n*

scapegoat *n* **1** a person made to bear the blame for others. ✧ *vb* **2** to make a scapegoat of. ▷ **HISTORY** *escape + goat,* coined to translate Biblical Hebrew *azāzēl,* probably goat for Azazel, mistakenly thought to mean 'goat that escapes'

scapula (**skap**-pew-la) *n, pl* **-lae** (-lee) the technical name for **shoulder blade**. ▷ **HISTORY** Late Latin: shoulder

scapular *adj* **1** *Anat* of the scapula. ✧ *n* **2** a loose sleeveless garment worn by monks over their habits.

scar¹ *n* **1** a mark left on the skin following the healing of a wound. **2** a permanent effect on a person's character resulting from emotional distress. **3** a mark on a plant where a leaf was formerly attached. **4** a mark of damage. ✧ *vb* **scarring, scarred 5** to mark or become marked with a scar. ▷ **HISTORY** Greek *eskhara* scab

scar² *n* a bare craggy rock formation. ▷ **HISTORY** Old Norse *sker* low reef

scarab *n* **1** the black dung-beetle, regarded by the ancient Egyptians as divine. **2** an image or carving of this beetle. ▷ **HISTORY** Latin *scarabaeus*

scarce *adj* **1** insufficient to meet the demand: *scarce water resources.* **2** not common; rarely found. **3 make oneself scarce** *Informal* to go away. ✧ *adv* **4** *Archaic or literary* scarcely. ▷ **HISTORY** Old French *scars*

scarcely *adv* **1** hardly at all. **2** *Often used ironically* probably or definitely not: *that is scarcely justification for your actions.*

> ☑ **WORD TIP**
> See at **hardly.**

scarcity *n, pl* **-ties** an inadequate supply.

scare *vb* **scaring, scared 1** to frighten or be frightened. **2 scare away** *or* **off** to drive away by frightening. ✧ *n* **3** a sudden attack of fear or alarm: *you gave me a scare.* **4** a period of general fear or alarm: *the latest AIDS scare.* ▷ **HISTORY** Old Norse *skirra*

scarecrow *n* **1** an object, usually in the shape of a man, made out of sticks and old clothes, to scare birds away from crops. **2** *Informal* a raggedly dressed person.

scaremonger *n* a person who starts or spreads rumours of disaster to frighten people. ▸ **scaremongering** *n*

scarf¹ *n, pl* **scarves** *or* **scarfs** a piece of material worn around the head, neck, or shoulders. ▷ **HISTORY** origin unknown

scarf² *n, pl* **scarfs 1** a joint between two pieces of timber made by notching the ends and strapping or gluing the two pieces together. ✧ *vb* **2** to join (two pieces of timber) by means of a scarf. ▷ **HISTORY** probably from Old Norse

scarify *vb* **-fies, -fying, -fied 1** *Surgery* to make slight incisions in (the skin). **2** *Agriculture* to break up and loosen (topsoil). **3** to criticize without mercy. ▷ **HISTORY** Latin *scarifare* to scratch open ▸ **scarification** *n*

> ☑ **WORD TIP**
> *Scarify* is sometimes wrongly thought to mean the same as *scare: a frightening* (not *scarifying*) *film.*

scarlatina *n* the technical name for **scarlet fever**. ▷ **HISTORY** Italian *scarlatto* scarlet

scarlet *adj* bright red. ▷ **HISTORY** Old French *escarlate* fine cloth

scarlet fever *n* an acute contagious disease characterized by fever, a sore throat, and a red rash on the body.

scarp *n* **1** a steep slope or ridge of rock. **2** *Fortifications* the side of a ditch cut nearest to a rampart. ▷ **HISTORY** Italian *scarpa*

scarper *vb Chiefly Brit slang* to run away or escape. ▷ **HISTORY** origin unknown

Scart *or* **SCART** *n Electronics* a plug-and-socket system which carries pictures and sound, used in home entertainment systems.

scary *adj* **scarier, scariest** *Informal* quite frightening.

scat[1] *vb* **scatting, scatted** *Informal* to go away in haste. ▷ **HISTORY** origin unknown

scat[2] *n* **1** a type of jazz singing using improvised vocal sounds instead of words. ✧ *vb* **scatting, scatted 2** to sing jazz in this way. ▷ **HISTORY** perhaps imitative

scathing *adj* harshly critical: *there was a scathing review of the play in the paper.* ▷ **HISTORY** Old Norse *skathi* harm ▶ **scathingly** *adv*

scatology *n* preoccupation with obscenity, esp. with references to excrement. ▷ **HISTORY** Greek *skat-* excrement + -LOGY ▶ **scatological** *adj*

scatter *vb* **1** to throw about in various directions: *scatter some oatmeal on top of the cake.* **2** to separate and move in various directions; disperse: *the infantry were scattering.* ✧ *n* **3** the act of scattering. **4** a number of objects scattered about. ▷ **HISTORY** probably variant of *shatter*

scatterbrain *n* a person who is incapable of serious thought or concentration. ▶ **scatterbrained** *adj*

scatter diagram *n Statistics* a graph with points plotted along two axes at right angles to each other to show the relationship between two variable quantities.

scatty *adj* **-tier, -tiest** *Informal* rather absent-minded. ▷ **HISTORY** from *scatterbrained* ▶ **scattiness** *n*

scavenge *vb* **-enging, -enged** to search for (anything usable) among discarded material.

scavenger *n* **1** a person who collects things discarded by others. **2** any animal that feeds on discarded or decaying matter. ▷ **HISTORY** Old French *escauwer* to scrutinize

SCE (in Scotland) Scottish Certificate of Education.

scenario *n, pl* **-narios 1** a summary of the plot and characters of a play or film. **2** an imagined sequence of future events: *the likeliest scenario is another general election.* ▷ **HISTORY** Italian

scene *n* **1** the place where an action or event, real or imaginary, occurs. **2** an incident or situation, real or imaginary, esp. as described or represented. **3** a division of an act of a play, in which the setting is fixed and the action is continuous. **4** *Films* a shot or series of shots that constitutes a unit of the action. **5** the backcloths or screens used to represent a location in a play or film set. **6** the view of a place or landscape. **7** a display of emotion or loss of temper in public: *you do not want to cause a scene.* **8** *Informal* a particular activity or aspect of life, and all the things associated with it: *the club scene.* **9 behind the scenes a** backstage. **b** in secret or in private. ▷ **HISTORY** Greek *skēnē* tent, stage

scenery *n* **1** the natural features of a landscape. **2** *Theatre* the painted backcloths or screens used to represent a location in a theatre or studio.

scenic *adj* **1** of or having beautiful natural scenery: *untouched scenic areas.* **2** of the stage or stage scenery: *scenic artists.*

scent *n* **1** a distinctive smell, esp. a pleasant one. **2** a smell left in passing, by which a person or animal may be traced. **3** a trail or series of clues by which something is followed: *he must have got on to the scent of the story through you.* **4** perfume. ✧ *vb* **5** to become aware of by smelling. **6** to suspect: *he scented the beginnings of irritation in the car.* **7** to fill with odour or fragrance. ▷ **HISTORY** Old French *sentir* to sense ▶ **scented** *adj*

sceptic *or US* **skeptic** (**skep**-tik) *n* **1** a person who habitually doubts generally accepted beliefs. **2** a person who doubts the truth of a religion. ▶ **sceptical** *or US* **skeptical** *adj* ▶ **sceptically** *or US* **skeptically** *adv* ▶ **scepticism** *or US* **skepticism** *n*

WORD HISTORY

The Sceptics were a school of philosophers in ancient Greece who believed that nothing could be known for certain. The word 'sceptic' comes from the Greek word *skeptikos*, meaning 'someone who considers', from the verb *skeptesthai* meaning 'to consider'.

sceptre *or US* **scepter** *n* an ornamental rod symbolizing royal power. ▷ **HISTORY** Greek *skeptron* staff ▶ **sceptred** *or US* **sceptered** *adj*

Schadenfreude (**shah**-den-froy-da) *n* one person's delight in another's misfortune. ▷ **HISTORY** German *Schaden* harm + *Freude* joy

schedule *n* **1** a timed plan of procedure for a project. **2** a list of details or items: *the schedule of priorities.* **3** a timetable. ✧ *vb* **-uling, -uled 4** to plan and arrange (something) to happen at a certain time. **5** to make a schedule or include in a schedule. ▷ **HISTORY** Latin *scheda* sheet of paper

schema *n, pl* **-mata** an outline of a plan or theory. ▷ **HISTORY** Greek: form

schematic *adj* presented as a diagram or plan. ▶ **schematically** *adv*

schematize *or* **-tise** *vb* **-tizing, -tized** *or* **-tising, -tised** to form into or arrange in a systematic arrangement or plan.

scheme *n* **1** a systematic plan for a course of action. **2** a systematic arrangement of parts or features: *colour scheme.* **3** a secret plot. **4** a chart, diagram, or outline. **5** a plan formally adopted by a government or organization: *a pension scheme.* ✧ *vb* **scheming, schemed 6** to plan in an underhand manner. ▷ **HISTORY** Greek *skhēma* form ▶ **schemer** *n* ▶ **scheming** *adj, n*

scherzo (**skairt**-so) *n, pl* **-zos** a quick lively piece of music, often the second or third movement in a sonata or symphony. ▷ **HISTORY** Italian: joke

schilling *n* a former monetary unit of Austria. ▷ **HISTORY** from German: shilling

schism (**skizz**-um) *n* the division of a group, esp. a religious group, into opposing factions, due to differences in doctrine. ▷ **HISTORY** Greek *skhizein* to split ▸ **schismatic** *adj*

schist (**skist**) *n* a crystalline rock which splits into thin layers. ▷ **HISTORY** Greek *skhizein* to split

schistosomiasis (shiss-ta-so-**my**-a-siss) *n* same as **bilharzia**.

schizo (**skit**-so) *Offensive* ✧ *adj* **1** schizophrenic. ✧ *n, pl* **-os 2** a schizophrenic person.

schizoid *adj* **1** *Psychol* having a personality disorder characterized by extreme shyness and extreme sensitivity. **2** *Informal* characterized by conflicting or contradictory ideas or attitudes. ✧ *n* **3** a person who has a schizoid personality.

schizophrenia *n* **1** a psychotic disorder characterized by withdrawal from reality, hallucinations, or emotional instability. **2** *Informal* behaviour that seems to be motivated by contradictory or conflicting principles. ▷ **HISTORY** Greek *skhizein* to split + *phrēn* mind ▸ **schizophrenic** *adj, n*

Schlieffen Plan (**shlee**-fen) *n History* a plan devised in 1905 by Count von Schlieffen, intended to ensure German victory over a Franco-Russian alliance by holding off Russia with minimal strength and swiftly defeating France by a massive flanking movement through the Low Countries.

schmaltz *n* excessive sentimentality, esp. in music. ▷ **HISTORY** Yiddish: melted fat ▸ **schmaltzy** *adj*

schnapps *n* a strong dry alcoholic drink distilled from potatoes. ▷ **HISTORY** German *Schnaps*

schnitzel *n* a thin slice of meat, esp. veal. ▷ **HISTORY** German: cutlet

scholar *n* **1** a person who studies an academic subject. **2** a student who has a scholarship. **3** a pupil. ▷ **HISTORY** Latin *schola* school ▸ **scholarly** *adj*

scholarship *n* **1** academic achievement; learning gained by serious study. **2** financial aid provided for a scholar because of academic merit.

scholastic *adj* **1** of schools, scholars, or education. **2** of or relating to scholasticism. ✧ *n* **3** a scholarly person. **4** a disciple or adherent of scholasticism. ▷ **HISTORY** Greek *skholastikos* devoted to learning

scholasticism *n* the system of philosophy, theology, and teaching that dominated medieval Europe and was based on the writings of Aristotle.

school[1] *n* **1** a place where children are educated. **2** the staff and pupils of a school. **3** a regular session of instruction in a school: *we stayed behind after school.* **4** a faculty or department specializing in a particular subject: *the dental school.* **5** a place or sphere of activity that instructs: *the school of hard knocks.* **6** a group of artists, writers, or thinkers, linked by the same style, teachers, or methods. **7** *Informal* a group assembled for a common purpose, such as gambling: *a card school.* ✧ *vb* **8** to educate or train: *she schooled herself to be as ambitious as her sister.* ▷ **HISTORY** Greek *skholē* leisure spent in the pursuit of knowledge

school[2] *n* a group of sea-living animals that swim together, such as fish, whales, or dolphins. ▷ **HISTORY** Old English *scolu* shoal

schoolboy *n* a boy attending school.

schooling *n* the education a person receives at school.

schoolmaster *or fem* **schoolmistress** *n* a person who teaches in or runs a school.

schoolteacher *n* a person who teaches in a school.

school year *n* **1** a twelve-month period, usually of three terms, during which pupils remain in the same class. **2** the time during this period when the school is open.

schooner *n* **1** a sailing ship with at least two masts, one at the back and one at the front. **2** *Brit* a large glass for sherry. **3** *US, Canad, Austral, & NZ* a large glass for beer. ▷ **HISTORY** origin unknown

schottische *n* **1** a 19th-century German dance resembling a slow polka. **2** music for this dance. ▷ **HISTORY** German *der schottische Tanz* the Scottish dance

schuss (**shooss**) *n Skiing* a straight high-speed downhill run. ▷ **HISTORY** from German

sciatic *adj* **1** *Anat* of the hip or the hipbone. **2** of or afflicted with sciatica: *a sciatic injury.* ▷ **HISTORY** Greek *iskhia* hip joint

sciatica *n* severe pain in the large nerve in the back of the leg.

sciatic nerve *n Anat* the long nerve from the back of the thigh down to the calf.

science *n* **1** the study of the nature and behaviour of the physical universe, based on observation, experiment, and measurement. **2** the knowledge obtained by these methods. **3** any particular branch of this knowledge: *medical science.* **4** any body of knowledge organized in a way resembling that of the physical sciences but concerned with other subjects: *political science.* ▷ **HISTORY** Latin *scientia* knowledge

science fiction *n* stories and films that make imaginative use of scientific knowledge or theories.

science park *n* an area where scientific research and commercial development are carried on in cooperation.

scientific *adj* **1** relating to science or a particular science: *scientific discovery.* **2** done in a systematic way, using experiments or tests. ▸ **scientifically** *adv*

scientific method *n Science* a system of understanding and gaining knowledge in which some aspect of the universe is observed, and a description, called a hypothesis, is made and used to make predictions. Those predictions are then tested by experiments the hypothesis is adjusted in the light of the results.

scientist *n* a person who studies or practises a science.

sci-fi *n* short for **science fiction**.

scimitar *n* a curved oriental sword. ▷ **HISTORY** probably from Persian *shimshīr*

scintillate *vb* **-lating, -lated** to give off (sparks); sparkle. ▷ **HISTORY** Latin *scintilla* a spark ▸ **scintillation** *n*

scintillating *adj* (of conversation or humour) very lively and amusing.

scion (**sy**-on) *n* **1** a descendant or young member of a family. **2** a shoot of a plant for grafting onto another plant. ▷ HISTORY Old French *cion*

sciophyte *n Bot* any plant that grows best in the shade. ▷ HISTORY via Latin from Greek *skia* shade + -PHYTE

scissors *pl n* a cutting instrument held in one hand, with two crossed blades pivoted so that they close together on what is to be cut. ▷ HISTORY Old French *cisoires*

sclera (**skleer**-a) *n Biol* the tough white substance that forms the outer covering of the eyeball. ▷ HISTORY Greek *sklēros* hard

sclerosis (skleer-**oh**-siss) *n, pl* **-ses** (-seez) *Pathol* an abnormal hardening or thickening of body tissues, esp. of the nervous system or the inner wall of arteries. ▷ HISTORY Greek *sklērōsis* a hardening

sclerotic (skleer-**rot**-ik) *adj* **1** of or relating to the sclera. **2** of, relating to, or having sclerosis.

scoff[1] *vb* **1** (often foll. by *at*) to speak in a scornful and mocking way about (something). ✧ *n* **2** a mocking expression; jeer. ▷ HISTORY probably from Old Norse ▶ **scoffing** *adj, n*

scoff[2] *vb Informal* to eat (food) fast and greedily. ▷ HISTORY variant of *scaff* food

scold *vb* **1** to find fault with or rebuke (a person) harshly. **2** *Old-fashioned* to use harsh or abusive language. ✧ *n* **3** a person, esp. a woman, who constantly scolds. ▷ HISTORY from Old Norse *skāld* ▶ **scolding** *n*

scollop *n, vb* same as **scallop**.

sconce *n* a bracket fixed to a wall for holding candles or lights. ▷ HISTORY Late Latin *absconsa* dark lantern

scone *n* a small plain cake baked in an oven or on a griddle. ▷ HISTORY Scots

scoop *n* **1** a spoonlike tool with a deep bowl, used for handling loose or soft materials such as flour or ice cream. **2** the deep shovel of a mechanical digger. **3** the amount taken up by a scoop. **4** the act of scooping or dredging. **5** a news story reported in one newspaper before all the others. ✧ *vb* **6** (often foll. by *up*) to take up and remove (something) with or as if with a scoop. **7 scoop out** to hollow out with or as if with a scoop. **8** to beat (rival newspapers) in reporting a news item. ▷ HISTORY Germanic

scoot *vb* to leave or move quickly. ▷ HISTORY origin unknown

scooter *n* **1** a child's small cycle which is ridden by pushing the ground with one foot. **2** a light motorcycle with a small engine.

scope *n* **1** opportunity for using abilities: *ample scope for creative work.* **2** range of view or grasp: *that is outside my scope.* **3** the area covered by an activity or topic: *the scope of his essay was vast.* ▷ HISTORY Greek *skopos* target

scorbutic (score-**byewt**-ik) *adj* of or having scurvy. ▷ HISTORY Medieval Latin *scorbutus*

scorch *vb* **1** to burn or become burnt slightly on the surface. **2** to parch or shrivel from heat. **3** *Informal* to criticize harshly. ✧ *n* **4** a slight burn. **5** a mark caused by the application of excessive heat. ▷ HISTORY probably from Old Norse *skorpna* to shrivel up ▶ **scorching** *adj*

scorcher *n Informal* a very hot day.

score *n* **1** the total number of points made by a side or individual in a game. **2** the act of scoring a point or points: *there was no score and three minutes remained.* **3 the score** *Informal* the actual situation: *what's the score on this business?* **4** *Old-fashioned* a group or set of twenty: *three score years and ten.* **5 scores of** lots of: *we received scores of letters.* **6** *Music* a written version of a piece of music showing parts for each musician. **7 a** the incidental music for a film or play. **b** the songs and music for a stage or film musical. **8** a mark or scratch. **9** a record of money due: *what's the score for the drinks?* **10** an amount recorded as due. **11** a reason: *some objections were made on the score of sentiment.* **12** a grievance: *a score to settle.* **13 over the score** *Informal* excessive or unfair. ✧ *vb* **scoring, scored** **14** to gain (a point or points) in a game or contest. **15** to make a total score of. **16** to keep a record of the score (of). **17** to be worth (a certain number of points) in a game: *red aces score twenty.* **18** to make cuts or lines in or on. **19** *Slang* to purchase an illegal drug. **20** *Slang* to succeed in finding a sexual partner. **21** to arrange (a piece of music) for specific instruments or voices. **22** to write the music for (a film or play). **23** to achieve (success or an advantage): *your idea scored with the boss.* ▷ HISTORY Old English *scora*

scoreboard *n Sport* a board for displaying the score of a game or match.

score off *vb* to make a clever or insulting reply to what someone has just said: *they spent the evening scoring off each other.*

scorer *n* **1** a player of a sport who scores a goal, run, or point: *Ireland's record goal scorer has announced his retirement.* **2** a person who keeps note of the score of a match or competition as it is being played.

scoria (**score**-ee-a) *n* **1** *Geol* a mass of solidified lava containing many cavities. **2** refuse left after ore has been smelted. ▷ HISTORY Latin: dross

scorn *n* **1** open contempt for a person or thing. ✧ *vb* **2** to treat with contempt: *she attacked the government for scorning her profession.* **3** to refuse to have or do (something) because it is felt to be undesirable or wrong: *youths who scorn traditional morals.* ▷ HISTORY Old French *escharnir* ▶ **scornful** *adj* ▶ **scornfully** *adv*

Scorpio *n Astrol* the eighth sign of the zodiac; the Scorpion. ▷ HISTORY Latin

scorpion *n* a small lobster-shaped animal with a sting at the end of a jointed tail. ▷ HISTORY Greek *skorpios*

Scot *n* a person from Scotland.

scotch *vb* **1** to put an end to: *she had scotched the idea of bingo in the church.* **2** to wound without killing. ▷ HISTORY origin unknown

a b c d e f g h i j k l m n o p q r s t u v w x y z

Scotch[1] *Not universally accepted* ✧ *adj* **1** same as **Scottish**. ✧ *pl n* **2 the Scotch** the Scots.

> **WORD TIP**
> In the north of England and in Scotland, *Scotch* is not used outside fixed expressions such as *Scotch whisky*. The use of *Scotch* for *Scots* or *Scottish* is otherwise felt to be incorrect, esp. when applied to people.

Scotch[2] *n* whisky distilled in Scotland from fermented malted barley.

Scotch broth *n Brit* a thick soup made from mutton or beef stock, vegetables, and pearl barley.

Scotch egg *n Brit & NZ* a hard-boiled egg encased in sausage meat and breadcrumbs, and fried.

Scotch mist *n* a heavy wet mist or drizzle.

scot-free *adv, adj* without harm or punishment: *the real crooks got off scot-free.* ▷ **HISTORY** obsolete *scot* a tax

Scotland Yard *n* the headquarters of the police force of metropolitan London.

Scots *adj* **1** of Scotland. ✧ *n* **2** any of the English dialects spoken or written in Scotland.

Scotsman *or fem* **Scotswoman** *n, pl* **-men** *or* **-women** a person from Scotland.

Scots pine *n* **1** a coniferous tree found in Europe and Asia, with needle-like leaves and brown cones. **2** the wood of this tree.

Scotticism *n* a Scottish expression or word.

Scottish *adj* of Scotland.

scoundrel *n Old-fashioned* a person who cheats and deceives. ▷ **HISTORY** origin unknown

scour[1] *vb* **1** to clean or polish (a surface) by rubbing with something rough. **2** to clear (a channel) by the force of water. ✧ *n* **3** the act of scouring. ▷ **HISTORY** Old French *escurer* ▶ **scourer** *n*

scour[2] *vb* **1** to search thoroughly and energetically: *he had scoured auction salerooms.* **2** to move quickly over (land) in search or pursuit. ▷ **HISTORY** probably from Old Norse *skūr* shower

scourge *n* **1** a person who or thing that causes affliction or suffering. **2** a whip formerly used for punishing people. ✧ *vb* **scourging, scourged 3** to cause severe suffering to. **4** to whip. ▷ **HISTORY** Latin *excoriare* to whip

Scouse *Brit informal* ✧ *n* **1** Also called: **Scouser** a person from Liverpool. **2** the Liverpool dialect. ✧ *adj* **3** of Liverpool, its people, or their dialect. ▷ **HISTORY** from *lobscouse* a sailor's stew

scout *n* **1** *Mil* a person sent to find out the position of the enemy. **2** same as **talent scout**. **3** the act or an instance of scouting. ✧ *vb* **4** to examine or observe (something) in order to obtain information. **5 scout about** *or* **around** to go in search of. ▷ **HISTORY** Old French *ascouter* to listen to

Scout *or* **scout** *n* a member of the Scout Association, an organization for boys and girls, which aims to develop character and promote outdoor activities. ▶ **Scouting** *n*

scowl *vb* **1** to have an angry or bad-tempered facial expression. ✧ *n* **2** an angry or bad-tempered facial expression. ▷ **HISTORY** probably from Old Norse

scrabble *vb* **-bling, -bled 1** to scrape at or grope for something with hands, feet, or claws: *scrabbling with his feet to find a foothold.* **2** to move one's hands about in order to find something one cannot see: *scrabbling in her handbag for a comb.* ▷ **HISTORY** Middle Dutch *schrabbelen*

scrag *n* **1** the thin end of a neck of veal or mutton. **2** a thin or scrawny person or animal. ▷ **HISTORY** perhaps variant of *crag*

scraggy *adj* **-gier, -giest** unpleasantly thin and bony. ▶ **scragginess** *n*

scram[1] *vb* **scramming, scrammed** *Informal* to leave very quickly. ▷ **HISTORY** from *scramble*

scram[2] *n* **1** an emergency shutdown of a nuclear reactor. ✧ *vb* **scramming, scrammed 2** (of a nuclear reactor) to shut down or be shut down in an emergency. ▷ **HISTORY** perhaps from SCRAM[1]

scramble *vb* **-bling, -bled 1** to climb or crawl hurriedly by using the hands to aid movement. **2** to go hurriedly or in a disorderly manner. **3** to compete with others in a rough and undignified way: *spectators scrambled for the best seats.* **4** to jumble together in a haphazard manner. **5** to cook (eggs that have been whisked up with milk) in a pan. **6** *Mil* (of a crew or aircraft) to take off quickly in an emergency. **7** to make (transmitted speech) unintelligible by the use of an electronic scrambler. ✧ *n* **8** the act of scrambling. **9** a climb or trek over difficult ground. **10** a rough and undignified struggle to gain possession of something. **11** *Mil* an immediate takeoff of crew or aircraft in an emergency. **12** *Brit* a motorcycle race across rough open ground. ▷ **HISTORY** blend of SCRABBLE + RAMP

scrambler *n* an electronic device that makes broadcast or telephone messages unintelligible without a special receiver.

scrap[1] *n* **1** a small piece of something larger; fragment. **2** waste material or used articles, often collected and reprocessed. **3 scraps** pieces of leftover food. ✧ *vb* **scrapping, scrapped 4** to discard as useless. ▷ **HISTORY** Old Norse *skrap*

scrap[2] *Informal* ✧ *n* **1** a fight or quarrel. ✧ *vb* **scrapping, scrapped 2** to quarrel or fight. ▷ **HISTORY** perhaps from *scrape*

scrapbook *n* a book of blank pages in which newspaper cuttings or pictures are stuck.

scrape *vb* **scraping, scraped 1** to move (a rough or sharp object) across (a surface). **2** (often foll. by *away* or *off*) to remove (a layer) by rubbing. **3** to produce a grating sound by rubbing against (something else). **4** to injure or damage by scraping: *he had scraped his knees.* **5 scrimp and scrape** See **scrimp** (sense 2). ✧ *n* **6** the act or sound of scraping. **7** a scraped place: *a scrape on the car door.* **8** *Informal* an awkward or embarrassing situation. **9** *Informal* a conflict or struggle. ▷ **HISTORY** Old English *scrapian* ▶ **scraper** *n*

scrape through *vb* to succeed in or survive with difficulty: *both teams had scraped through their semifinals.*

scrappy *adj* **-pier, -piest** badly organized or done: *a scrappy draft of a chapter of my thesis.*

scratch *vb* **1** to mark or cut (the surface of something) with a rough or sharp instrument. **2** (often foll. by *at, out*) to tear or dig with the nails or claws. **3** to scrape (the surface of the skin) with the nails to relieve itching. **4** to rub against (the skin) causing a slight cut. **5** to make or cause to make a grating sound. **6** (sometimes foll. by *out*) to erase or cross out. **7** to withdraw from a race or (in the US) an election. ✧ *n* **8** the act of scratching. **9** a slight cut on a person's or an animal's body. **10** a mark made by scratching. **11** a slight grating sound. **12 from scratch** *Informal* from the very beginning. **13 not up to scratch** *Informal* not up to standard. ✧ *adj* **14** put together at short notice: *a scratch team.* **15** *Sport* with no handicap allowed: *a scratch golfer.* ▷ **HISTORY** Germanic ▶ **scratchy** *adj*

scratchcard *n* a ticket that reveals whether or not the holder is eligible for a prize when the surface is removed by scratching.

scratching *n Music* a sound produced when the record groove in contact with the stylus of a record player is moved back and forth by hand.

scrawl *vb* **1** to write carelessly or hastily. ✧ *n* **2** careless or scribbled writing. ▷ **HISTORY** perhaps blend of SPRAWL + CRAWL ▶ **scrawly** *adj*

scrawny *adj* **scrawnier, scrawniest** very thin and bony. ▷ **HISTORY** dialect *scranny* ▶ **scrawniness** *n*

scream *vb* **1** to make a sharp piercing cry or sound because of fear or pain. **2** (of a machine) to make a high-pitched noise. **3** to laugh wildly. **4** to utter with a scream: *he screamed abuse up into the sky.* **5** to be unpleasantly conspicuous: *bad news screaming out from the headlines.* ✧ *n* **6** a sharp piercing cry or sound, esp. of fear or pain. **7** *Informal* a very funny person or thing. ▷ **HISTORY** Germanic

scree *n* a pile of rock fragments at the foot of a cliff or hill, often forming a sloping heap. ▷ **HISTORY** Old English *scrīthan* to slip

screech[1] *n* **1** a shrill or high-pitched sound or cry. ✧ *vb* **2** to utter a shrill cry. ▷ **HISTORY** earlier *scritch,* imitative ▶ **screechy** *adj*

screech[2] *n Canad* a dark rum. ▷ **HISTORY** origin unknown

screech owl *n* **1** *Brit* same as **barn owl**. **2** a small North American barn owl.

screed *n* a long tiresome speech or piece of writing. ▷ **HISTORY** probably from Old English *scrēade* shred

screen *n* **1** the blank surface of a television set, VDU, or radar receiver, on which a visible image is formed. **2** the white surface on which films or slides are projected. **3 the screen** the film industry or films collectively. **4** a light movable frame, panel, or partition used to shelter, divide, or conceal. **5** anything that shelters, protects, or conceals: *a screen of leaves blocking out the sun.* **6** a frame containing a mesh that is used to keep out insects. ✧ *vb* **7** (sometimes foll. by *off*) to shelter, protect, or conceal with or as if with a screen. **8** to test or check (an individual or group) so as to assess suitability for a task or to detect the presence of a disease or weapons: *women screened for breast cancer.* **9** to show (a film) in the cinema or show (a programme) on television. ▷ **HISTORY** Old French *escren*

screenplay *n* the script for a film, including instructions for sets and camera work.

screen saver *n Computers* software that produces changing images on a monitor when the computer is operating but idle.

screenwriter *n* a person who writes screenplays.

screw *n* **1** a metal pin with a spiral ridge along its length, twisted into materials to fasten them together. **2** a threaded cylindrical rod that engages with a similarly threaded cylindrical hole. **3** a thread in a cylindrical hole corresponding with the one on the screw with which it is designed to engage. **4** anything resembling a screw in shape. **5** *Slang* a prison guard. **6** *Taboo slang* an act of or partner in sexual intercourse. **7 have a screw loose** *Informal* to be insane. **8 put the screws on** *Slang* to use force on or threatening behaviour against. ✧ *vb* **9** to rotate (a screw or bolt) so as to drive it into or draw it out of a material. **10** to twist or turn: *she screwed up the sheet of paper.* **11** to attach or fasten with or as if with a screw or screws. **12** *Informal* to take advantage of, esp. illegally: *screwed by big business.* **13** *Informal* to distort or contort: *his face was screwed up in pain.* **14** (often foll. by *out of*) *Informal* to force out of; extort. **15** *Taboo slang* to have sexual intercourse (with). **16 have one's head screwed on the right way** *Informal* to be sensible. ✧ See also **screw up**. ▷ **HISTORY** French *escroe*

screwdriver *n* **1** a tool used for turning screws, consisting of a long thin metal rod with a flattened tip that fits into a slot in the head of the screw. **2** a drink consisting of orange juice and vodka.

screw up *vb* **1** *Informal* to mishandle or spoil (something): *that screws up all my arrangements.* **2** to twist out of shape or distort. **3 screw up one's courage** to force oneself to be brave. ▶ **screwed-up** *adj*

screwy *adj* **screwier, screwiest** *Informal* crazy or eccentric.

scribble *vb* **-bling, -bled 1** to write or draw quickly and roughly. **2** to make meaningless or illegible marks (on). ✧ *n* **3** something written or drawn quickly or roughly. **4** meaningless or illegible marks. ▷ **HISTORY** Latin *scribere* to write ▶ **scribbler** *n* ▶ **scribbly** *adj*

scribe *n* **1** a person who made handwritten copies of manuscripts or documents before the invention of printing. **2** *Bible* a recognized scholar and teacher of the Jewish Law. ▷ **HISTORY** Latin *scriba* clerk

scrimmage *n* **1** a rough or disorderly struggle. ✧ *vb* **-maging, -maged 2** to take part in a scrimmage. ▷ **HISTORY** earlier *scrimish*

scrimp *vb* **1** to be very sparing in the use of something: *they were scrimping by on the last of the potatoes.* **2 scrimp and save** *or* **scrape** to spend as little money as possible. ▷ **HISTORY** Scots

scrip[1] *n Finance* a certificate representing a claim to shares or stocks. ▷ **HISTORY** short for *subscription receipt*

scrip² *or* **script** *n Informal* a medical prescription. ▷ **HISTORY** from PRESCRIPTION

script *n* **1** the text of a play, TV programme, or film for the use of performers. **2** an alphabet or system of writing: *Cyrillic script.* **3** a candidate's answer paper in an examination. **4** handwriting. **5** a typeface which looks like handwriting. ✧ *vb* **6** to write a script for. ▷ **HISTORY** Latin *scriptum* something written

scripture *n* the sacred writings of a religion. ▷ **HISTORY** Latin *scriptura* written material ▶ **scriptural** *adj*

Scripture *n Christianity* the Old and New Testaments.

scriptwriter *n* a person who writes scripts, esp. for a film or TV programme. ▶ **scriptwriting** *n*

scrofula *n No longer in technical use* tuberculosis of the lymphatic glands. ▷ **HISTORY** Medieval Latin ▶ **scrofulous** *adj*

scroggin *n NZ* a mixture of nuts and dried fruits.

scroll *n* **1** a roll of parchment or paper, usually inscribed with writing. **2** an ancient book in the form of a roll of parchment, papyrus, or paper. **3** a decorative carving or moulding resembling a scroll. ✧ *vb* **4** *Computers* to move (text) on a screen in order to view a section that cannot be fitted into a single display. ▷ **HISTORY** Middle English *scrowle*

Scrooge *n* a mean or miserly person. ▷ **HISTORY** after a character in Dickens' story *A Christmas Carol*

scrotum *n* the pouch of skin containing the testicles in most male mammals. ▷ **HISTORY** Latin

scrounge *vb* **scrounging, scrounged** *Informal* to get (something) by asking for it rather than buying it or working for it. ▷ **HISTORY** dialect *scrunge* to steal ▶ **scrounger** *n*

scrub¹ *vb* **scrubbing, scrubbed 1** to rub (something) hard in order to clean it. **2** to remove (dirt) by rubbing with a brush and water. **3 scrub up** (of a surgeon) to wash the hands and arms thoroughly before operating. **4** *Informal* to delete or cancel (an idea or plan). ✧ *n* **5** the act of scrubbing. ▷ **HISTORY** Middle Low German *schrubben* or Middle Dutch *schrobben*

scrub² *n* **1** vegetation consisting of stunted trees or bushes growing in a dry area. **2** an area of dry land covered with such vegetation. ✧ *adj* **3** stunted or inferior: *scrub pines.* ▷ **HISTORY** variant of *shrub*

scrubber *n* **1** *Brit & Austral offensive slang* a woman who has many sexual partners. **2** a device that removes pollutants from the gases that are produced when coal is burned industrially.

scrubby *adj* **-bier, -biest 1** (of land) rough, dry, and covered with scrub. **2** (of plants) stunted. **3** *Brit informal* shabby or untidy.

scruff¹ *n* the nape of the neck: *the sergeant had him by the scruff of the neck.* ▷ **HISTORY** perhaps from Old Norse *skoft* hair

scruff² *n Informal* a very untidy person.

scruffy *adj* **scruffier, scruffiest** dirty and untidy in appearance.

scrum *n* **1** *Rugby* a formation in which players from each side form a tight pack and push against each other in an attempt to get the ball which is thrown on the ground between them. **2** *Informal* a disorderly struggle. ✧ *vb* **scrumming, scrummed 3** (usually foll. by *down*) *Rugby* to form a scrum. ▷ **HISTORY** from *scrummage*

scrum half *n Rugby* a player who puts in the ball at scrums and tries to regain its possession in order to pass it to his team's backs.

scrummage *n, vb* **-maging, -maged 1** *Rugby* same as **scrum. 2** same as **scrimmage.** ▷ **HISTORY** variant of *scrimmage*

scrump *vb Brit dialect* to steal (apples) from an orchard or garden. ▷ **HISTORY** variant of *scrimp*

scrumptious *adj Informal* delicious or very attractive. ▷ **HISTORY** probably changed from *sumptuous*

scrumpy *n Brit* a rough dry cider brewed in the West Country of England. ▷ **HISTORY** dialect *scrump* withered apples

scrunch *vb* **1** to press or crush noisily or be pressed or crushed noisily. ✧ *n* **2** the act or sound of scrunching: *the scrunch of tyres on gravel.* ▷ **HISTORY** variant of *crunch*

scrunchie *n* a loop of elastic covered loosely with fabric, used to hold the hair in a ponytail.

scruple *n* **1** a doubt or hesitation as to what is morally right in a certain situation: *he had no scruples about the drug trade.* ✧ *vb* **-pling, -pled 2** to have doubts (about), esp. on moral grounds. ▷ **HISTORY** Latin *scrupulus* a small weight

scrupulous *adj* **1** taking great care to do what is fair, honest, or morally right. **2** very careful or precise: *scrupulous attention to detail.* ▷ **HISTORY** Latin *scrupulosus* ▶ **scrupulously** *adv*

scrutineer *n* a person who examines, esp. one who scrutinizes the conduct of an election poll.

scrutinize *or* **-nise** *vb* **-nizing, -nized** *or* **-nising, -nised** to examine carefully or in minute detail.

scrutiny *n, pl* **-nies 1** very careful study or observation. **2** a searching look. ▷ **HISTORY** Late Latin *scrutari* to search

scuba (**skew**-ba) *n* an apparatus used in skin diving, consisting of cylinders containing compressed air attached to a breathing apparatus. ▷ **HISTORY** *s(elf-)c(ontained) u(nderwater) b(reathing) a(pparatus)*

scud *vb* **scudding, scudded 1** (esp. of clouds) to move along quickly. **2** *Naut* to run before a gale. ✧ *n* **3** the act of scudding. **4** spray, rain, or clouds driven by the wind. ▷ **HISTORY** probably Scandinavian

scuff *vb* **1** to drag (the feet) while walking. **2** to scrape (one's shoes) by doing so. ✧ *n* **3** a mark caused by scuffing. **4** the act or sound of scuffing. ▷ **HISTORY** probably imitative

scuffle *vb* **-fling, -fled 1** to fight in a disorderly manner. ✧ *n* **2** a short disorganized fight. **3** a scuffling sound. ▷ **HISTORY** Scandinavian

scull *n* **1** a single oar moved from side to side over the back of a boat. **2** one of a pair of small oars, both of which are pulled by one oarsman. **3** a racing boat rowed by one oarsman pulling two oars. ✧ *vb* **4** to row (a boat) with a scull. ▷ **HISTORY** origin unknown ▶ **sculler** *n*

scullery *n, pl* **-leries** *Chiefly Brit* a small room where washing-up and other kitchen work is done. ▷ **HISTORY** Anglo-Norman *squillerie*

sculpt *vb* same as **sculpture**.

sculptor *or fem* **sculptress** *n* a person who makes sculptures.

sculpture *n* **1** the art of making figures or designs in wood, plaster, stone, or metal. **2** works or a work made in this way. ✧ *vb* **-turing, -tured 3** to carve (a material) into figures or designs. **4** to represent (a person or thing) in sculpture. **5** to form or be formed in the manner of sculpture: *limestone sculptured by fast-flowing streams.* ▷ **HISTORY** Latin *sculptura* a carving ▶ **sculptural** *adj*

scum *n* **1** a layer of impure or waste matter that forms on the surface of a liquid: *the build-up of soap scum.* **2** a person or people regarded as worthless or criminal. ✧ *vb* **scumming, scummed 3** to remove scum from. **4** *Rare* to form a layer of or become covered with scum. ▷ **HISTORY** Germanic ▶ **scummy** *adj*

scungy (**skun**-jee) *adj* **scungier, scungiest** *Austral & NZ slang* miserable, sordid, or dirty. ▷ **HISTORY** origin unknown

scupper[1] *n Naut* a drain or spout in a ship's side allowing water on the deck to flow overboard. ▷ **HISTORY** origin unknown

scupper[2] *vb* **1** *Brit & NZ slang* to defeat or ruin: *a deliberate attempt to scupper the peace talks.* **2** to sink (one's ship) deliberately. ▷ **HISTORY** origin unknown

scurf *n* **1** same as **dandruff**. **2** any flaky or scaly matter sticking to or peeling off a surface. ▷ **HISTORY** Old English ▶ **scurfy** *adj*

scurrilous *adj* untrue or unfair, insulting, and designed to damage a person's reputation: *scurrilous allegations.* ▷ **HISTORY** Latin *scurra* buffoon ▶ **scurrility** *n*

scurry *vb* **-ries, -rying, -ried 1** to run quickly with short steps. ✧ *n, pl* **-ries 2** a quick hurrying movement or the sound of this movement. **3** a short shower of rain or snow. ▷ **HISTORY** probably from *hurry-scurry*

scurvy *n* **1** a disease caused by a lack of vitamin C, resulting in weakness, spongy gums, and bleeding beneath the skin. ✧ *adj* **-vier, -viest 2** *Old-fashioned* deserving contempt. ▷ **HISTORY** from *scurf* ▶ **scurviness** *n*

scut *n* the short tail of animals such as the deer and rabbit. ▷ **HISTORY** probably from Old Norse

scuttle[1] *n* same as **coal scuttle**. ▷ **HISTORY** Latin *scutella* bowl

scuttle[2] *vb* **-tling, -tled 1** to run with short quick steps. ✧ *n* **2** a hurried pace or run. ▷ **HISTORY** probably from *scud*

scuttle[3] *vb* **-tling, -tled 1** *Naut* to cause (a ship) to sink by making holes in the sides or bottom. **2** to ruin (hopes or plans) or have them ruined: *a new policy scuttled by popular resistance.* ✧ *n* **3** *Naut* a small hatch in a ship's deck or side. ▷ **HISTORY** Spanish *escotilla* a small opening

scythe *n* **1** a long-handled tool for cutting grass or grain, with a curved sharpened blade that is swung parallel to the ground. ✧ *vb* **scything, scythed 2** to cut (grass or grain) with a scythe. ▷ **HISTORY** Old English *sigthe*

SD South Dakota.

SDI Strategic Defense Initiative.

SDLP (in Northern Ireland) Social Democratic and Labour Party.

Se *Chem* selenium.

SE southeast(ern).

sea *n* **1 the sea** the mass of salt water that covers three-quarters of the earth's surface. **2 a** one of the smaller areas of this: *the Irish Sea.* **b** a large inland area of water: *the Caspian Sea.* **3** the area on or close to the edge of the sea, esp. as a place where holidays are taken: *a day by the sea.* **4** strong and uneven swirling movement of waves: *rough seas.* **5** anything resembling the sea in size or movement: *a sea of red and yellow flags.* **6 at sea a** on the ocean. **b** in a state of confusion or uncertainty. **7 go to sea** to become a sailor. **8 put out to sea** to start a sea voyage. ▷ **HISTORY** Old English *sǣ*

sea anchor *n Naut* a canvas-covered frame, dragged in the water behind a ship to slow it down or reduce drifting.

sea anemone *n* a marine animal with a round body and rings of tentacles which trap food from the water.

sea bird *n* a bird that lives on or near the sea.

seaboard *n* land bordering on the sea.

seaborgium *n Chem* a synthetic element. Symbol: Sg. ▷ **HISTORY** after Glenn *Seaborg,* physicist and chemist

sea breeze *n Meteorol* a breeze blowing inland from the sea, usually during the day, caused by the land heating faster than the sea and cooler air from the sea flowing to replace rising warmer air from the land. Compare **land breeze**.

sea cow *n* **1** a whalelike mammal such as a dugong or manatee. **2** *Archaic* a walrus.

sea dog *n* an experienced or old sailor.

seafaring *adj* **1** travelling by sea. **2** working as a sailor. ✧ *n* **3** the act of travelling by sea. **4** the work of a sailor.

seafloor spreading *n Geol* a series of processes in which new oceanic lithosphere is created at oceanic ridges, spreads away from the ridges, and returns to the earth's interior.

seafood *n* edible saltwater fish or shellfish.

seafront *n* a built-up area facing the sea.

seagoing *adj* built for travelling on the sea.

seagull *n* same as **gull**.

sea horse *n* a small marine fish with a horselike head, which swims upright.

sea kale *n* a European coastal plant with broad fleshy leaves and asparagus-like shoots that can be eaten.

seal[1] *n* **1** a special design impressed on a piece of wax, lead, or paper, fixed to a letter or document as a mark of authentication. **2** a stamp or signet ring engraved with a design to form such an impression. **3** a substance placed over an envelope or container, so that it cannot be opened without the seal being broken. **4** something that serves as an official confirmation of approval: *seal of approval.* **5** any substance or device used to close an opening tightly. **6 set the seal on** to confirm something: *the experience set the seal on their friendship.* ✧ *vb* **7** to close or secure with or as if with a seal: *once the manuscripts were sealed up, they were forgotten about.* **8 seal off** to enclose or isolate (a place) completely. **9** to close tightly so as to make airtight or watertight. **10** to inject a compound around the edges of something to make it airtight or watertight. **11** to attach a seal to or stamp with a seal. **12** to finalize or authorize. **13 seal one's fate** to make sure one dies or fails. **14 seal one's lips** to promise not to reveal a secret. ▷ HISTORY Latin *signum* a sign ▶ **sealable** *adj*

seal[2] *n* **1** a fish-eating mammal with four flippers, which lives in the sea but comes ashore to breed. **2** sealskin. ✧ *vb* **3** to hunt seals. ▷ HISTORY Old English *seolh*

sealant *n* any substance, such as wax, used for sealing, esp. to make airtight or watertight.

sea legs *pl n Informal* the ability to maintain one's balance on board ship and to avoid being seasick.

sea level *n Geog* the average level of the sea's surface in relation to the land.

sealing wax *n* a hard material made of shellac and turpentine, which softens when heated and which is used to make a seal.

sea lion *n* a type of large seal found in the Pacific Ocean.

Sea Lord *n* (in Britain) a naval officer on the admiralty board of the Ministry of Defence.

sealskin *n* the skin or prepared fur of a seal, used to make coats.

seam *n* **1** the line along which pieces of fabric are joined by stitching. **2** a ridge or line made by joining two edges: *the seam between the old and the new buildings.* **3** a long narrow layer of coal, marble, or ore formed between layers of other rocks. **4** a mark or line like a seam, such as a wrinkle or scar. ✧ *adj* **5** *Cricket* of a style of bowling in which the bowler uses the stitched seam round the ball in order to make it swing in flight and after touching the ground: *a seam bowler.* ✧ *vb* **6** to join together by or as if by a seam. **7** to mark with furrows or wrinkles. ▷ HISTORY Old English *sēam*

seaman *n, pl* **-men 1** a man ranking below an officer in a navy. **2** a sailor.

seamer *or* **seam bowler** *n Cricket* a fast bowler who makes the ball bounce on its seam so that it will change direction.

seamless *adj* **1** (of a garment) without seams. **2** continuous or flowing: *a seamless performance.* ▶ **seamlessness** *n*

seamstress *n* a woman who sews, esp. professionally.

seamy *adj* **seamier, seamiest** involving the sordid and unpleasant aspects of life, such as crime, prostitution, poverty, and violence. ▶ **seaminess** *n*

seance *or* **séance** (**say**-onss) *n* a meeting at which a spiritualist attempts to communicate with the spirits of the dead. ▷ HISTORY French

seaplane *n* an aircraft that is designed to land on and take off from water.

sear *vb* **1** to scorch or burn the surface of. **2** to cause to wither. ▷ HISTORY Old English *sēarian* to become withered

search *vb* **1** to look through (a place) thoroughly in order to find someone or something. **2** to examine (a person) for hidden objects. **3** to look at or examine (something) closely: *I searched my heart for one good thing she had done.* **4 search out** to find by searching. **5** to make a search. **6 search me** *Informal* I don't know. ✧ *n* **7** an attempt to find something by looking somewhere. ▷ HISTORY Old French *cerchier*

search engine *n Computers* an Internet service enabling users to search for items of interest.

searching *adj* keen or thorough: *a searching analysis.* ▶ **searchingly** *adv*

searchlight *n* **1** a light with a powerful beam that can be shone in any direction. **2** the beam of light produced by this device.

search warrant *n* a legal document allowing a policeman to enter and search premises.

seascape *n* a drawing, painting, or photograph of a scene at sea.

seashell *n* the empty shell of a marine mollusc.

seashore *n* land bordering on the sea.

seasick *adj* suffering from nausea and dizziness caused by the movement of a ship at sea. ▶ **seasickness** *n*

seaside *n* an area, esp. a holiday resort, bordering on the sea.

season *n* **1** one of the four divisions of the year (spring, summer, autumn, and winter), each of which has characteristic weather conditions. **2** a period of the year characterized by particular conditions or activities: *the typhoon season; the football season.* **3** the period during which any particular species of animal, bird, or fish is legally permitted to be caught or killed: *the deer season.* **4** any definite or indefinite period: *the busy season.* **5** any period during which a show or play is performed at one venue: *the show ran for three seasons.* **6 in season a** (of game) permitted to be killed. **b** (of fresh food) readily available. **c** (of animals) ready to mate. ✧ *vb* **7** to add herbs, salt, pepper, or spice to (food) in order to enhance the flavour. **8** (in the preparation of timber) to dry and harden. **9** to make experienced: *old men seasoned by living.* ▷ HISTORY Latin *satio* a sowing ▶ **seasoned** *adj*

seasonable *adj* **1** suitable for the season: *a seasonable Christmas snow scene.* **2** coming or happening just at the right time: *seasonable advice.*

seasonal *adj* of or depending on a certain season or seasons of the year: *seasonal employment.* ▶ **seasonally** *adv*

seasoning *n* something that is added to food to enhance the flavour.

season ticket *n* a ticket for a series of events or number of journeys, usually bought at a reduced rate.

seat *n* **1** a piece of furniture designed for sitting on, such as a chair. **2** the part of a chair or other piece of furniture on which one sits. **3** a place to sit in a theatre, esp. one that requires a ticket: *there were two empty front-row seats at the pageant.* **4** the buttocks. **5** the part of a garment covering the buttocks. **6** the part or surface on which an object rests. **7** the place or centre in which something is based: *the seat of government.* **8** *Brit* a country mansion. **9** a membership or the right to membership of a legislative or administrative body: *a seat on the council.* **10** *Chiefly Brit* a parliamentary constituency. **11** the manner in which a rider sits on a horse. ✧ *vb* **12** to bring to or place on a seat. **13** to provide seats for: *the dining hall seats 150 people.* **14** to set firmly in place. ▷ **HISTORY** Old English *gesete*

seat belt *n* a strap attached to a car or aircraft seat, worn across the body to prevent a person being thrown forward in the event of a collision.

seating *n* **1** seats which are provided somewhere, esp. in a public place: *the grandstand has seating for 10 000; hard plastic seating.* ✧ *adj* **2** of or relating to the provision of places to sit: *the delegation leader complained about the seating arrangements.*

sea urchin *n* a small sea animal with a round body enclosed in a spiny shell.

seaweed *n* any plant growing in the sea or on the seashore.

seaworthy *adj* (of a ship) in a fit condition for a sea voyage. ▶ **seaworthiness** *n*

sebaceous *adj* of, like, or secreting fat. ▷ **HISTORY** Latin *sebum* tallow

sebaceous glands *pl n* the small glands in the skin that secrete oil into hair follicles and onto most of the body surface.

sebum (**see**-bum) *n* the oily substance secreted by the sebaceous glands. ▷ **HISTORY** Latin: tallow

sec[1] *adj* (of wines) dry. ▷ **HISTORY** French

sec[2] *n Informal* a second (of time): *hang on a sec.*

sec[3] secant.

sec. **1** second (of time). **2** secondary. **3** secretary.

secant (**seek**-ant) *n* **1** (in trigonometry) the ratio of the length of the hypotenuse to the length of the adjacent side in a right-angled triangle; the reciprocal of cosine. **2** a straight line that intersects a curve. ▷ **HISTORY** Latin *secare* to cut

secateurs *pl n* a small pair of gardening shears for pruning. ▷ **HISTORY** French

secede *vb* **-ceding, -ceded** to make a formal withdrawal of membership from a political alliance, federation, or group: *it will secede from the federation within six months.* ▷ **HISTORY** Latin *se-* apart + *cedere* to go

secession *n* the act of seceding. ▶ **secessionism** *n* ▶ **secessionist** *n, adj*

seclude *vb* **-cluding, -cluded 1** to remove from contact with others. **2** to shut off or screen from view. ▷ **HISTORY** Latin *secludere*

secluded *adj* **1** kept apart from the company of others: *a secluded private life.* **2** private and sheltered: *a secluded cottage.*

seclusion *n* the state of being secluded; privacy: *the seclusion of his winter retreat.*

second[1] *adj* **1** coming directly after the first in order. **2** rated, graded, or ranked between the first and third levels. **3** alternate: *every second Saturday.* **4** another of the same kind; additional: *a second chance.* **5** resembling or comparable to a person or event from the past: *a second Virgin Mary.* **6** of lesser importance or position; inferior. **7** denoting the second lowest forward gear in a motor vehicle. **8** *Music* denoting a musical part, voice, or instrument subordinate to or lower in pitch than another (the first): *the second tenors.* **9 at second hand** by hearsay. ✧ *n* **10** a person or thing that is second. **11** *Brit education* an honours degree of the second class. **12** the second lowest forward gear in a motor vehicle. **13** (in boxing or duelling) an attendant who looks after a boxer or duellist. **14 seconds a** *Informal* a second helping of food or the second course of a meal. **b** goods that are sold cheaply because they are slightly faulty. ✧ *vb* **15** to give aid or backing to. **16** (in boxing or duelling) to act as second to (a boxer or duellist). **17** to express formal support for (a motion proposed in a meeting). ✧ *adv* **18** Also: **secondly** in the second place. ▷ **HISTORY** Latin *secundus* next in order

second[2] *n* **1** the basic SI unit of time, equal to $^1/_{60}$ of a minute. **2** $^1/_{60}$ of a minute of angle. **3** a very short period of time. ▷ **HISTORY** Latin *pars minuta secunda* the second small part (a minute being the first small part of an hour)

second[3] (sik-**kond**) *vb Brit & NZ* to transfer (a person) temporarily to another job. ▷ **HISTORY** French *en second* in second rank ▶ **secondment** *n*

secondary *adj* **1** below the first in rank or importance: *a secondary consideration.* **2** coming next after the first: *secondary cancers.* **3** derived from or depending on what is primary or first: *a secondary source.* **4** of or relating to the education of people between the ages of 11 and 18 or, in New Zealand, between 13 and 18: *secondary education.* **5** (of an industry) involving the manufacture of goods from raw materials. ✧ *n, pl* **-aries 6** a person or thing that is secondary.

secondary consumer *n Biol* an animal that eats herbivores. Compare **primary consumer, tertiary consumer**.

secondary industry *n Econ, business* an industry concerned with manufacturing and the processing of raw materials. Compare **primary industry, tertiary industry**.

secondary production *n Econ* the process of converting raw materials into products for consumers.

secondary source *n* a description, commentary, or analysis of something not experienced personally but which is based on someone else's experiences, descriptions, work, etc. Compare **primary source**.

second-best *adj* **1** next to the best. ✧ *adv* **second best 2 come off second best** *Informal* to fail to win against someone. ✧ *n* **second best 3** an inferior alternative.

second chamber *n* the upper house of a two-chamber system of government.

second class *n* **1** the class or grade next in value, rank, or quality to the first. ✧ *adj* **second-class 2** of the class or grade next to the best in value, rank, or quality. **3** shoddy or inferior. **4** denoting the class of accommodation in a hotel or on a train, aircraft, or ship, lower in quality and price than first class. **5** (of mail) sent by a cheaper type of postage and taking slightly longer to arrive than first-class mail. ✧ *adv* **6** by second-class mail, transport, etc.

Second Coming *n* the prophesied return of Christ to earth at the Last Judgment.

second-degree burn *n* a burn in which blisters appear on the skin.

second fiddle *n Informal* a person who has a secondary status.

second-hand *adj* **1** previously owned or used. **2** not from an original source or one's own experience: *second-hand opinions.* **3** dealing in or selling goods that are not new: *second-hand furniture shops.* ✧ *adv* **4** from a source of previously owned or used goods: *they preferred to buy second-hand.* **5** not directly or from one's own experience: *his knowledge had been gleaned second-hand.*

second lieutenant *n* an officer holding the lowest commissioned rank in an army or navy.

secondly *adv* same as **second**[1] (sense 18).

second nature *n* a habit or characteristic practised for so long that it seems to be part of one's character.

second person *n Grammar* the form of a pronoun or verb used to refer to the person or people being addressed, as in *you see.*

second-rate *adj* **1** not of the highest quality; mediocre. **2** second in importance or rank: *a second-rate citizen.*

second sight *n* the supposed ability to foresee the future or see actions taking place elsewhere.

second-strike *adj Mil* (of a nuclear weapon) to be used in a counterattack in response to a nuclear attack.

second thoughts *pl n* a revised opinion or idea on a matter already considered.

second wind *n* **1** the return of comfortable breathing following difficult or strenuous exercise. **2** renewed ability to continue in an effort.

secrecy *n, pl* **-cies 1** the state of being secret. **2** the ability or tendency to keep things secret.

secret *adj* **1** kept hidden or separate from the knowledge of all or all but a few others. **2** secretive: *she had become a secret drinker.* **3** operating without the knowledge of outsiders: *secret organizations.* ✧ *n* **4** something kept or to be kept hidden. **5** something unrevealed; a mystery: *the secrets of nature.* **6** an underlying explanation or reason: *the secret of great-looking hair.* **7 in secret** without the knowledge of others. ▷ **HISTORY** Latin *secretus* concealed ▶ **secretly** *adv*

secret agent *n* a person employed by a government to find out the military and political secrets of other governments.

secretariat *n* **1 a** an office responsible for the secretarial, clerical, and administrative affairs of a legislative body or international organization. **b** the staff of such an office or department. **2** the premises of a secretariat. ▷ **HISTORY** French

secretary *n, pl* **-taries 1** a person who handles correspondence, keeps records, and does general clerical work for an individual or organization. **2** the official manager of the day-to-day business of a society, club, or committee. **3** (in Britain) a senior civil servant who assists a government minister. **4** (in the US) the head of a government administrative department. ▷ **HISTORY** Medieval Latin *secretarius* someone entrusted with secrets ▶ **secretarial** *adj*

secretary bird *n* a large long-legged African bird of prey.

secretary-general *n, pl* **secretaries-general** the chief administrative official of a legislative body or international organization.

secretary of state *n* **1** (in Britain) the head of a major government department. **2** (in the US) the head of the government department in charge of foreign affairs.

secrete[1] *vb* **-creting, -creted** (of a cell, organ, or gland) to produce and release (a substance). ▶ **secretory** (sik-**reet**-or-ee) *adj*

secrete[2] *vb* **-creting, -creted** to put in a hiding place. ▷ **HISTORY** variant of obsolete *secret* to hide away

secretin (sick-**ree**-tin) *n Biochem* a peptic hormone secreted in the duodenum and jejunum when food passes to the stomach.

secretion *n* **1** a substance that is released from a cell, organ, or gland. **2** the process involved in producing and releasing such a substance. ▷ **HISTORY** Latin *secretio* a separation

secretive *adj* hiding feelings and intentions. ▶ **secretively** *adv*

secret police *n* a police force that operates secretly to suppress opposition to the government.

secret service *n* a government agency or department that conducts intelligence or counterintelligence operations.

sect *n* **1** a subdivision of a larger religious or political group, esp. one regarded as extreme in its beliefs or practices. **2** a group of people with a common interest or philosophy. ▷ **HISTORY** Latin *secta* faction

sectarian *adj* **1** of or belonging to a sect. **2** narrow-minded as a result of supporting a particular sect. ✧ *n* **3** a member of a sect. ▶ **sectarianism** *n*

section *n* **1** a part cut off or separated from the main body of something: *a non-smoking section.* **2** a part or subdivision of a piece of writing or a book: *the business section.* **3** a distinct part of a country or community: *the Arabic section.* **4** *Surgery* the act or process of cutting or separating by cutting. **5** *Geom* a plane surface formed by cutting through a solid. **6** short for **Caesarean section**. **7** *NZ* a plot of land for building on. **8** *Austral & NZ* a fare stage on a bus. ✧ *vb* **9** to cut or divide into sections. **10** to commit (a mentally disturbed person) to a mental hospital. ▷ **HISTORY** Latin *secare* to cut

sectional *adj* **1** concerned with a particular area or group within a country or community, esp. to the exclusion of others: *narrow sectional interests.* **2** made of sections. **3** of a section.

sector *n* **1** a part or subdivision, esp. of a society or an economy: *the public sector.* **2** *Geom* either portion of a circle bounded by two radii and the arc cut off by them. **3** a portion into which an area is divided for military operations. ▷ **HISTORY** Latin: a cutter

secular *adj* **1** relating to worldly as opposed to sacred things. **2** not connected with religion or the church. **3** (of clerics) not bound by religious vows to a monastic or other order. ▷ **HISTORY** Late Latin *saecularis*

secularism *n* the belief that religion should have no place in civil affairs. ▸ **secularist** *n, adj*

secularize *or* **-ise** *vb* **-izing, -ized** *or* **-ising, -ised** to change (something, such as education) so that it is no longer connected with religion or the Church. ▸ **secularization** *or* **-isation** *n*

secure *adj* **1** free from danger or damage. **2** free from fear, doubt, or care. **3** tightly locked or well protected. **4** fixed or tied firmly in position. **5** able to be relied on: *secure profits.* ✧ *vb* **-curing, -cured** **6** to obtain: *to secure a change in German policy.* **7** to make or become free from danger or fear. **8** to make safe from loss, theft, or attack. **9** to guarantee (payment of a loan) by giving something as security. ▷ **HISTORY** Latin *securus* free from care ▸ **securely** *adv*

security *n, pl* **-ties** **1** precautions taken to ensure against theft, espionage, or other danger. **2** the state of being free from danger, damage, or worry. **3** assured freedom from poverty: *the security of a weekly pay cheque.* **4** a certificate of ownership, such as a share, stock, or bond. **5** something given or pledged to guarantee payment of a loan.

security risk *n* someone or something thought to be a threat to state security.

sedan *n US, Canad, Austral & NZ* a saloon car. ▷ **HISTORY** origin unknown

sedan chair *n* an enclosed chair for one passenger, carried on poles by two bearers, commonly used in the 17th and 18th centuries.

sedate[1] *adj* **1** quiet, calm, and dignified. **2** slow or unhurried: *a sedate walk to the beach.* ▷ **HISTORY** Latin *sedare* to soothe ▸ **sedately** *adv*

sedate[2] *vb* **-dating, -dated** to calm down or make sleepy by giving a sedative drug to.

sedation *n* **1** a state of calm, esp. when brought about by sedatives. **2** the administration of a sedative.

sedative *adj* **1** having a soothing or calming effect. ✧ *n* **2** *Med* a sedative drug or agent that makes people sleep or calm down. ▷ **HISTORY** Latin *sedatus* assuaged

sedentary (**sed**-en-tree) *adj* **1** done sitting down and involving very little exercise: *a sedentary job.* **2** tending to sit about without taking much exercise. ▷ **HISTORY** Latin *sedere* to sit

sedge *n* a coarse grasslike plant growing on wet ground. ▷ **HISTORY** Old English *secg* ▸ **sedgy** *adj*

sedge warbler *n* a European songbird living in marshy areas.

sediment *n* **1** matter that settles to the bottom of a liquid. **2** material that has been deposited by water, ice, or wind. ▷ **HISTORY** Latin *sedimentum* a settling

sedimentary layer *n Geol* a layer within a sedimentary rock.

sedimentary rock *n Geol* rock that forms as mineral and organic materials, deposited by wind, water, and ice, and gradually built up in layers.

sedimentation *n Geol* the process in which layers of mineral and organic materials are deposited by water, ice, or wind.

sedition *n* speech, writing, or behaviour intended to encourage rebellion or resistance against the government. ▷ **HISTORY** Latin *seditio* discord ▸ **seditionary** *n, adj* ▸ **seditious** *adj*

seduce *vb* **-ducing, -duced** **1** to persuade to have sexual intercourse. **2** to tempt into wrongdoing. ▷ **HISTORY** Latin *seducere* to lead apart ▸ **seduction** *n*

seductive *adj* **1** (of a woman) sexually attractive. **2** very attractive or tempting: *a seductive argument.* ▸ **seductively** *adv* ▸ **seductiveness** *n*

sedulous *adj* diligent or painstaking: *a sedulous concern with the achievements of western thought.* ▷ **HISTORY** Latin *sedulus* ▸ **sedulously** *adv*

sedum *n* a rock plant with thick clusters of white, yellow, or pink flowers. ▷ **HISTORY** Latin

see[1] *vb* **seeing, saw, seen** **1** to look at or recognize with the eyes. **2** to understand: *I explained the problem but he could not see it.* **3** to perceive or be aware of: *she had never seen him so angry.* **4** to view, watch, or attend: *we had barely seen a dozen movies in our lives.* **5** to foresee: *they could see what their fate was to be.* **6** to find out (a fact): *I was ringing to see whether you'd got it.* **7** to make sure (of something) or take care (of something): *see that he is never in a position to do these things again; you must see to it.* **8** to consider or decide: *see if you can come next week.* **9** to have experience of: *he had seen active service in the revolution.* **10** to meet or pay a visit to: *I see my specialist every three months.* **11** to receive: *the Prime Minister will see the deputation now.* **12** to frequent the company of: *we've been seeing each other since then.* **13** to accompany: *she saw him to the door.* **14** to refer to or look up: *see page 35.* **15** (in gambling, esp. in poker) to match (another player's bet) or match the bet of (another player) by staking an equal sum. **16** **see fit** to consider it proper (to do something): *I did not see fit to send them home.* **17** **see you, see you later** *or* **be seeing you** an expression of farewell. ✧ See also **see about**. ▷ **HISTORY** Old English *sēon*

A B C D E F G H I J K L M N O P Q R S T U V W X Y Z

see² *n* the diocese of a bishop or the place within it where his cathedral is situated. ▷ **HISTORY** Latin *sedes* a seat

see about *vb* **1** to take care of: *I'll see about some coffee.* **2** to investigate: *to see about a new car.*

seed *n* **1** *Bot* the mature fertilized grain of a plant, containing an embryo ready for germination. RELATED ADJECTIVE ▸ **seminal 2** such seeds used for sowing. **3** the source, beginning, or origin of anything: *the seeds of dissent.* **4** *Chiefly Bible* descendants; offspring: *the seed of David.* **5** *Sport* a player ranked according to his or her ability. **6 go** *or* **run to seed a** (of plants) to produce and shed seeds after flowering. **b** to lose strength or usefulness. ✧ *vb* **7** to plant (seeds) in (soil). **8** (of plants) to produce or shed seeds. **9** to remove the seeds from (fruit or plants). **10** to scatter silver iodide in (clouds) in order to cause rain. **11** to arrange (the draw of a tournament) so that outstanding teams or players will not meet in the early rounds. ▷ **HISTORY** Old English *sǣd* ▶ **seedless** *adj*

seedbed *n* **1** an area of soil prepared for the growing of seedlings before they are transplanted. **2** the place where something develops: *a seedbed of immorality.*

seedling *n* a plant produced from a seed, esp. a very young plant.

seed pod *n Bot* a carpel or pistil enclosing the seeds of a plant, esp. a flowering plant.

seedy *adj* **seedier, seediest 1** shabby in appearance: *a seedy cinema.* **2** *Informal* physically unwell. **3** (of a plant) at the stage of producing seeds. ▶ **seediness** *n*

seeing *n* **1** the sense or faculty of sight. ✧ *conj* **2** (often foll. by *that*) in light of the fact (that).

> **WORD TIP**
> The use of *seeing as how* as in *seeing as (how) the bus is always late, I don't see any reason to hurry* is generally thought to be incorrect or non-standard.

seek *vb* **seeking, sought 1** to try to find by searching: *to seek employment.* **2** to try to obtain: *to seek a diplomatic solution.* **3** to try (to do something): *we seek to establish a stable relationship.* ▷ **HISTORY** Old English *sēcan*

seem *vb* **1** to appear to the mind or eye; give the impression of: *the car seems to be running well.* **2** to appear to be: *there seems no need for all this nonsense.* **3** to have the impression: *I seem to remember you were there too.* ▷ **HISTORY** Old Norse *sōma* to be suitable

> **WORD TIP**
> See at **like.**

seeming *adj* apparent but not real: *his seeming willingness to participate.* ▶ **seemingly** *adv*

seemly *adj* **-lier, -liest** *Formal* proper or fitting.

seen *vb* the past participle of **see**¹.

see off *vb* **1** to be present at the departure of (a person going on a journey): *your sisters came to see you off.* **2** *Informal* to cause to leave or depart, esp. by force.

seep *vb* to leak through slowly; ooze. ▷ **HISTORY** Old English *sīpian* ▶ **seepage** *n*

seer *n* a person who can supposedly see into the future.

seersucker *n* a light cotton fabric with a slightly crinkled surface. ▷ **HISTORY** Hindi *´sīr´sakar*

seesaw *n* **1** a plank balanced in the middle so that two people seated on the ends can ride up and down by pushing on the ground with their feet. **2** an up-and-down or back-and-forth movement. ✧ *vb* **3** to move up and down or back and forth alternately. ▷ **HISTORY** reduplication of *saw,* alluding to the movement from side to side, as in sawing

seethe *vb* **seething, seethed 1** to be in a state of extreme anger or indignation without publicly showing these feelings. **2** (of a liquid) to boil or foam. ▷ **HISTORY** Old English *sēothan* ▶ **seething** *adj*

see through *vb* **1** to perceive the true nature of: *it was difficult to see through people.* **2** to remain with until the end or completion: *not all of them saw it through.* **3** to help out in a time of need or trouble: *he helped see her through her divorce.* ✧ *adj* **see-through 4** (of clothing) made of thin cloth so that the wearer's body or underclothes are visible.

segment *n* **1** one of several parts or sections into which an object is divided. **2** *Maths* **a** a part of a circle cut off by an intersecting line. **b** a part of a sphere cut off by an intersecting plane or planes. ✧ *vb* **3** to cut or divide into segments. ▷ **HISTORY** Latin *segmentum* ▶ **segmental** *adj* ▶ **segmentation** *n*

segregate *vb* **-gating, -gated 1** to set apart from others or from the main group. **2** to impose segregation on (a racial or minority group). ▷ **HISTORY** Latin *se-* apart + *grex* a flock

segregation *n* **1** the practice or policy of creating separate facilities within the same society for the use of a racial or minority group. **2** the act of segregating. ▶ **segregational** *adj* ▶ **segregationist** *n*

seigneur *n* a feudal lord, esp. in France. ▷ **HISTORY** Old French ▶ **seigneurial** *adj*

seine (**sane**) *n* **1** a large fishing net that hangs vertically in the water by means of floats at the top and weights at the bottom. ✧ *vb* **seining, seined 2** to catch (fish) using this net. ▷ **HISTORY** Old English *segne*

seismic *adj* relating to or caused by earthquakes. ▷ **HISTORY** Greek *seismos* earthquake

seismic wave *n Physics* an earth vibration caused by an earthquake or explosion.

seismograph *n* an instrument that records the intensity and duration of earthquakes. ▷ **HISTORY** Greek *seismos* earthquake + -GRAPH ▶ **seismographer** *n* ▶ **seismography** *n*

seismology *n* the branch of geology concerned with the study of earthquakes. ▷ **HISTORY** Greek *seismos* earthquake + -LOGY ▶ **seismologist** *n*

seismometer *n* same as **seismograph**.

seize *vb* **seizing, seized 1** to take hold of forcibly or quickly; grab. **2** to take immediate advantage of: *real journalists would have seized the opportunity.* **3** to take legal possession of. **4** (sometimes foll. by *on* or *upon*) to understand quickly: *she immediately seized his idea.* **5** to affect or fill the mind of suddenly: *a wild frenzy seized her.* **6** to take by force or capture: *the rebels seized a tank factory.* **7** (often foll. by *up*) (of mechanical parts) to become jammed through overheating. ▷ HISTORY Old French *saisir*

seizure *n* **1** *Pathol* a sudden violent attack of an illness, such as an epileptic convulsion. **2** the act of seizing: *a seizure of drug traffickers' assets.*

seldom *adv* rarely; not often. ▷ HISTORY Old English *seldon*

select *vb* **1** to choose (someone or something) in preference to another or others. ✧ *adj* **2** chosen in preference to others. **3** restricted to a particular group; exclusive: *a select audience.* ▷ HISTORY Latin *seligere* to sort ▶ **selector** *n*

select committee *n Government* a small committee of Members of Parliament, set up to investigate and report on a specified matter.

selection *n* **1** a selecting or being selected. **2** a thing or number of things that have been selected. **3** a range from which something may be selected: *a good selection of reasonably priced wines.* **4** *Biol* the process by which certain organisms or individuals are reproduced and survive in preference to others.

selective *adj* **1** tending to choose carefully or characterized by careful choice: *they were selective in their reading.* **2** of or characterized by selection. ▶ **selectively** *adv* ▶ **selectivity** *n*

selective breeding *n Agriculture, horticulture* the practice of producing animals or plants from particular specimens or individuals with particular inherited characteristics.

selenium *n Chem* a nonmetallic element used in photocells, solar cells, and in xerography. Symbol: Se. ▷ HISTORY Greek *selēnē* moon

self *n, pl* **selves 1** the distinct individuality or identity of a person or thing. **2** a person's typical bodily make-up or personal characteristics: *back to my old self after the scare.* **3** one's own welfare or interests: *he only thinks of self.* **4** an individual's consciousness of his or her own identity or being. ✧ *pron* **5** *Not standard* myself, yourself, himself, or herself: *setting goals for self and others.* ▷ HISTORY Old English

self- *combining form* used with many main words to mean: **1** of oneself or itself: *self-defence.* **2** by, to, in, due to, for, or from the self: *self-employed; self-respect.* **3** automatic or automatically: *self-propelled.*

self-absorption *n* preoccupation with oneself to the exclusion of others. ▶ **self-absorbed** *adj*

self-addressed *adj* addressed for return to the sender.

self-assertion *n* the act of putting forward one's own opinions or demanding one's rights, esp. in an aggressive or confident manner. ▶ **self-assertive** *adj*

self-catering *adj* (of accommodation) for tenants providing and preparing their own food.

self-centred *or US* **self-centered** *adj* totally preoccupied with one's own concerns.

self-coloured *or US* **self-colored** *adj* **1** having only a single and uniform colour: *a self-coloured tie.* **2** (of cloth or wool) having the natural or original colour.

self-confessed *adj* according to one's own admission: *a self-confessed addict.*

self-confidence *n* confidence in oneself, one's abilities, or one's judgment. ▶ **self-confident** *adj*

self-conscious *adj* embarrassed or ill at ease through being unduly aware of oneself as the object of the attention of others. ▶ **self-consciously** *adv* ▶ **self-consciousness** *n*

self-contained *adj* **1** containing within itself all parts necessary for completeness. **2** (of a flat) having its own kitchen, bathroom, and toilet not shared by others.

self-control *n* the ability to control one's feelings, emotions, or reactions. ▶ **self-controlled** *adj*

self-defence *or US* **self-defense** *n* **1** the act or skill of defending oneself against physical attack. **2** the act of defending one's actions, ideas, or rights.

self-determination *n* **1** the ability to make a decision for oneself without influence from outside. **2** the right of a nation or people to determine its own form of government. ▶ **self-determined** *adj*

self-employed *adj* earning one's living in one's own business, rather than as the employee of another.

self-esteem *n* respect for or a favourable opinion of oneself.

self-evident *adj* so obvious that no proof or explanation is needed. ▶ **self-evidently** *adv*

self-government *n* the government of a country, nation, or community by its own people. ▶ **self-governing** *adj*

self-help *n* **1** the use of one's own abilities and resources to help oneself without relying on the assistance of others. **2** the practice of solving one's problems within a group of people with similar problems.

self-important *adj* having an unduly high opinion of one's own importance. ▶ **self-importance** *n*

self-indulgent *adj* tending to allow oneself to have or do things that one enjoys. ▶ **self-indulgence** *n*

self-interest *n* **1** one's personal interest or advantage. **2** the pursuit of one's own interest. ▶ **self-interested** *adj*

selfish *adj* **1** caring too much about oneself and not enough about others. **2** (of behaviour or attitude) motivated by self-interest. ▶ **selfishly** *adv* ▶ **selfishness** *n*

selfless *adj* putting other people's interests before one's own. ▶ **selflessly** *adv* ▶ **selflessness** *n*

self-made *adj* having achieved wealth or status by one's own efforts.

self-opinionated *adj* clinging stubbornly to one's own opinions.

self-pollination *n Bot* the transfer of pollen from the anthers to the stigma of the same flower.

self-possessed *adj* having control of one's emotions or behaviour, esp. in difficult situations. ▶ **self-possession** *n*

self-propelled *adj* **1** (of a vehicle) driven by its own engine rather than drawn by a locomotive, horse, etc. **2** (of a rocket launcher or artillery piece) mounted on a motor vehicle. ▶ **self-propelling** *adj*

self-raising *adj* (of flour) having a raising agent, such as baking powder, already added.

self-respect *n* a feeling of confidence and pride in one's own abilities and worth. ▶ **self-respecting** *adj*

self-righteous *adj* thinking oneself more virtuous than others. ▶ **self-righteousness** *n*

selfsame *adj* the very same: *this was the selfsame woman I'd met on the train.*

self-satisfied *adj* smug and complacently satisfied with oneself or one's own actions. ▶ **self-satisfaction** *n*

self-seeking *n* **1** the act or an instance of seeking one's own profit or interests. ✧ *adj* **2** inclined to promote only one's own profit or interests: *self-seeking politicians.* ▶ **self-seeker** *n*

self-service *adj* **1** of or denoting a shop or restaurant where the customers serve themselves and then pay a cashier. ✧ *n* **2** the practice of serving oneself and then paying a cashier.

self-starter *n* **1** an electric motor used to start an internal-combustion engine. **2** a person who is strongly motivated and shows initiative at work.

self-styled *adj* using a title or name that one has given oneself, esp. without right or justification; so-called: *the self-styled leader of the rebellion.*

self-sufficient *adj* able to provide for or support oneself without the help of others. ▶ **self-sufficiency** *n*

self-willed *adj* stubbornly determined to have one's own way, esp. at the expense of others.

sell *vb* **selling, sold 1** to exchange (something) for money. **2** to deal in (objects or property): *he sells used cars.* **3** to give up or surrender for a price or reward: *to sell one's honour.* **4 sell for** to have a specified price: *they sell for 10 pence each.* **5** to promote the sale of (objects or property): *sex sells cigarettes.* **6** to gain acceptance of: *he'll sell an idea to a producer.* **7** to be in demand on the market: *his books did not sell well enough.* **8 sell down the river** *Informal* to betray. **9 sell oneself a** to convince someone else of one's potential or worth. **b** to give up one's moral standards for a price or reward. **10 sell someone short** *Informal* to undervalue someone. ✧ *n* **11** the act or an instance of selling: *the hard sell.* ✧ See also **sell off, sell out, sell up.** ▷ **HISTORY** Old English *sellan* to give, deliver ▶ **seller** *n*

sell-by date *n* **1** *Brit* the date printed on packaged food specifying the date after which the food should not be sold. **2 past one's sell-by date** beyond one's prime.

sell off *vb* to sell (remaining items) at reduced prices.

Sellotape *n* **1** *Trademark* a type of transparent adhesive tape. ✧ *vb* **-taping, -taped 2** to seal or stick using adhesive tape.

sell out *vb* **1** to dispose of (something) completely by selling. **2** *Informal* to betray in order to gain an advantage or benefit. ✧ *n* **sellout 3** *Informal* a performance of a show etc. for which all tickets are sold. **4** a commercial success. **5** *Informal* a betrayal.

sell-through *adj* of the sale of prerecorded video cassettes, without their first being for hire only.

sell up *vb Chiefly Brit & Austral* to sell all one's goods or property.

selvage *or* **selvedge** *n* a specially woven edge on a length of fabric to prevent it from unravelling. ▷ **HISTORY** SELF + EDGE ▶ **selvaged** *adj*

selves *n* the plural of **self**.

semantic *adj* **1** of or relating to the meanings of words. **2** of or relating to semantics. ▷ **HISTORY** Greek *sēma* a sign ▶ **semantically** *adv*

semantics *n* the branch of linguistics that deals with the study of meaning.

semaphore *n* **1** a system of signalling by holding two flags in different positions to represent letters of the alphabet. ✧ *vb* **-phoring, -phored 2** to signal (information) by semaphore. ▷ **HISTORY** Greek *sēma* a signal + *-phoros* carrying

semblance *n* outward or superficial appearance: *some semblance of order had been established.* ▷ **HISTORY** Old French *sembler* to seem

semen *n* the thick whitish fluid containing spermatozoa that is produced by the male reproductive organs and ejaculated from the penis. ▷ **HISTORY** Latin: seed

semester *n* either of two divisions of the academic year. ▷ **HISTORY** Latin *semestris* half-yearly

semi *n Brit, Austral & S African informal* short for **semidetached** (sense 2).

semi- *prefix* used with many main words to mean: **1** half: *semicircle.* **2** partly or almost: *semiprofessional.* **3** occurring twice in a specified period: *semiweekly.* ▷ **HISTORY** Latin

semiarid *adj* denoting land that lies on the edges of a desert but has a slightly higher rainfall (above 300 mm) so that some farming is possible.

semibreve *n Music* a note, now the longest in common use, with a time value that may be divided by any power of 2 to give all other notes.

semicircle *n* **1** one half of a circle. **2** anything having the shape or form of half a circle. ▶ **semicircular** *adj*

semicolon *n* the punctuation mark (;) used to separate clauses or items in a list, or to indicate a pause longer than that of a comma and shorter than that of a full stop.

semiconductor *n Physics* a substance, such as silicon, which has an electrical conductivity that increases with temperature.
semidetached *adj* **1** (of a house) joined to another house on one side by a common wall. ✧ *n* **2** *Brit* a semidetached house: *the mock Georgian semidetached.*
semifinal *n* the round before the final in a competition. ▶ **semifinalist** *n*
seminal *adj* **1** highly original and influential: *seminal thinkers.* **2** potentially capable of development. **3** of semen: *seminal fluid.* **4** *Biol* of seed. ▷ HISTORY Latin *semen* seed
seminar *n* **1** a small group of students meeting regularly under the guidance of a tutor for study and discussion. **2** one such meeting. ▷ HISTORY Latin *seminarium* a nursery garden
seminary *n, pl* **-naries** a college for the training of priests. ▷ HISTORY Latin *seminarium* a nursery garden ▶ **seminarian** *n*
seminiferous *n Biol* containing, conveying, or producing semen: *seminiferous tubules.*
semiotics *n* the study of human communication, esp. communication using signs and symbols. ▷ HISTORY Greek *sēmeion* a sign ▶ **semiotic** *adj*
semipermeable *adj* (of a cell membrane) allowing small molecules to pass through but not large ones.
semiprecious *adj* (of certain stones) having less value than a precious stone.
semiquaver *n Music* a note having the time value of one-sixteenth of a semibreve.
semirigid *adj* (of an airship) maintaining shape by means of a main supporting keel and internal gas pressure.
semiskilled *adj* partly skilled or trained but not sufficiently so to perform specialized work.
Semite *n* a member of the group of peoples who speak a Semitic language, such as the Jews and Arabs. ▷ HISTORY New Latin *semita* descendant of Shem, eldest of Noah's sons
Semitic *n* **1** a group of languages that includes Arabic, Hebrew, and Aramaic. ✧ *adj* **2** of this group of languages. **3** of any of the peoples speaking a Semitic language, esp. the Jews or the Arabs. **4** same as **Jewish**.
semitone *n* the smallest interval between two notes in Western music represented on a piano by the difference in pitch between any two adjacent keys. ▶ **semitonic** *adj*
semitrailer *n Austral* a large truck in two separate sections joined by a pivoted bar. Also called: **semi**
semitropical *adj* bordering on the tropics; nearly tropical. ▶ **semitropics** *pl n*
semivowel *n Phonetics* a vowel-like sound that acts like a consonant, such as the sound *w* in *well.*
semolina *n* the large hard grains of wheat left after flour has been milled, used for making puddings and pasta. ▷ HISTORY Italian *semolino*
SEN (in Britain) State Enrolled Nurse.
Sen. *or* **sen. 1** senate. **2** senator. **3** senior.
senate *n* the main governing body at some universities. ▷ HISTORY Latin *senatus* council of the elders
Senate *n* the upper chamber of the legislatures of Australia, the US, Canada, and many other countries.
senator *n* a member of a Senate. ▶ **senatorial** *adj*
send *vb* **sending, sent 1** to cause (a person or thing) to go or be taken or transmitted to another place: *send a cheque or postal order.* **2 send for** to dispatch a request or command for (someone or something): *she had sent for me.* **3** to cause to go to a place or point: *the bullet sent him flying into the air.* **4** to bring to a state or condition: *his schemes to send her mad.* **5** to cause to happen or come: *the thunderstorm sent by the gods.* **6** *Old-fashioned, slang* to move to excitement or rapture: *this music really sends me.* ▷ HISTORY Old English *sendan* ▶ **sender** *n*
send down *vb* **1** *Brit* to expel from a university. **2** *Informal* to send to prison.
sendoff *n* **1** *Informal* a show of good wishes to a person about to set off on a journey or start a new career. ✧ *vb* **send off 2** to dispatch (something, such as a letter). **3** *Sport* (of a referee) to dismiss (a player) from the field of play for some offence.
send up *Informal* ✧ *vb* **1** to make fun of by doing an imitation or parody. ✧ *n* **send-up 2** a parody or imitation.
senescent *adj Formal* growing old. ▷ HISTORY Latin *senescere* to grow old ▶ **senescence** *n*
seneschal (**sen**-ish-al) *n History* a steward of the household of a medieval prince or nobleman. ▷ HISTORY Old French
senile *adj* mentally or physically weak or infirm on account of old age. ▷ HISTORY Latin *senex* an old man ▶ **senility** *n*
senior *adj* **1** higher in rank or length of service. **2** older in years: *senior citizens.* **3** *Education* of or designating more advanced or older pupils or students. ✧ *n* **4** a senior person. ▷ HISTORY Latin: older
senior aircraftman *n* an ordinary rank in the Royal Air Force.
senior citizen *n* an old person, esp. a pensioner.
seniority *n, pl* **-ties 1** the state of being senior. **2** degree of power or importance in an organization from length of continuous service.
senior service *n Brit* the Royal Navy.
senna *n* **1** a tropical plant with yellow flowers and long pods. **2** the dried leaves and pods of this plant, used as a laxative. ▷ HISTORY Arabic *sanā*
señor (sen-**nyor**) *n* a Spanish form of address equivalent to *sir* or *Mr.*
señora (sen-**nyor**-a) *n* a Spanish form of address equivalent to *madam* or *Mrs.*
señorita (sen-nyor-**ee**-ta) *n* a Spanish form of address equivalent to *madam* or *Miss.*
sensation *n* **1** the power of feeling things physically: *I lose all sensation in my hands.* **2** a physical feeling: *a burning sensation in the throat.*

a b c d e f g h i j k l m n o p q r s t u v w x y z

3 a general feeling or awareness: *a sensation of vague resentment.* **4** a state of excitement: *imagine the sensation in Washington!* **5** an exciting person or thing: *you'll be a sensation.* ▷ **HISTORY** Late Latin *sensatus* endowed with feelings

sensational *adj* **1** causing intense feelings of shock, anger, or excitement: *sensational allegations.* **2** *Informal* extremely good: *the views are sensational.* **3** of the senses or sensation. ▶ **sensationally** *adv*

sensationalism *n* the deliberate use of sensational language or subject matter to arouse feelings of shock, anger, or excitement. ▶ **sensationalist** *adj, n*

sense *n* **1** any of the faculties (sight, hearing, touch, taste, and smell) by which the mind receives information about the external world or the state of the body. **2** the ability to perceive. **3** a feeling perceived through one of the senses: *a sense of warmth.* **4** a mental perception or awareness: *a sense of security.* **5** an ability to make moral judgments: *a sense of honour.* **6** (*usually pl*) sound practical judgment or intelligence: *a man lost his senses and killed his wife.* **7** a reason or purpose: *no sense in continuing.* **8** a general meaning: *he couldn't understand every word but he got the sense of what they were saying.* **9** a specific meaning; definition: *the three senses of the word.* **10 make sense** to be understandable or practical. ✧ *vb* **sensing, sensed 11** to perceive without the evidence of the senses: *he sensed that she was impressed.* **12** to perceive through the senses. ▷ **HISTORY** Latin *sentire* to feel

senseless *adj* **1** having no meaning or purpose: *a senseless act of violence.* **2** unconscious. ▶ **senselessly** *adv* ▶ **senselessness** *n*

sense organ *n* a part of the body that receives stimuli and transmits them as sensations to the brain.

sensibility *n, pl* **-ties 1** (*often pl*) the ability to experience deep feelings. **2** (*usually pl*) the tendency to be influenced or offended: *its sheer callousness offended her sensibilities.* **3** the ability to perceive or feel.

sensible *adj* **1** having or showing good sense or judgment. **2** (of clothing and footwear) practical and hard-wearing. **3** capable of receiving sensation. **4** capable of being perceived by the senses. **5** perceptible to the mind. **6** *Literary* aware: *sensible of your kindness.* ▷ **HISTORY** Latin *sentire* to feel ▶ **sensibly** *adv*

sensitive *adj* **1** easily hurt; tender. **2** responsive to feelings and moods. **3** responsive to external stimuli or impressions. **4** easily offended or shocked. **5** (of a subject or issue) liable to arouse controversy or strong feelings. **6** (of an instrument) capable of registering small differences or changes in amounts. **7** *Photog* responding readily to light: *a sensitive emulsion.* **8** *Chiefly US* connected with matters affecting national security. ▷ **HISTORY** Latin *sentire* to feel ▶ **sensitively** *adv* ▶ **sensitivity** *n*

sensitize *or* **-tise** *vb* **-tizing, -tized** *or* **-tising, -tised** to make sensitive. ▶ **sensitization** *or* **-tisation** *n*

sensor *n* a device that detects or measures a physical property, such as radiation.

sensory *adj* relating to the physical senses.

sensual *adj* **1** giving pleasure to the body and senses rather than the mind: *soft sensual music.* **2** having a strong liking for physical, esp. sexual, pleasures. **3** of the body and senses rather than the mind or soul. ▷ **HISTORY** Latin *sensus* feeling ▶ **sensualist** *n*

sensuality *n* **1** the quality or state of being sensual. **2** enjoyment of physical, esp. sexual, pleasures.

sensuous *adj* **1** pleasing to the senses of the mind or body: *the sensuous rhythms of the drums.* **2** (of a person) appreciating qualities perceived by the senses. ▶ **sensuously** *adv*

sent *vb* the past of **send**.

sentence *n* **1** a sequence of words constituting a statement, question, or a command that begins with a capital letter and ends with a full stop when written down. **2 a** the decision of a law court as to what punishment is passed on a convicted person. **b** the punishment passed on a convicted person. ✧ *vb* **-tencing, -tenced 3** to pronounce sentence on (a convicted person) in a lawcourt. ▷ **HISTORY** Latin *sententia* a way of thinking ▶ **sentential** *adj*

sententious *adj Formal* **1** trying to sound wise. **2** making pompous remarks about morality. ▷ **HISTORY** Latin *sententiosus* full of meaning ▶ **sententiously** *adv*

sentient (**sen**-tee-ent, **sen**-shent) *adj* capable of perception and feeling. ▷ **HISTORY** Latin *sentiens* feeling ▶ **sentience** *n*

sentiment *n* **1** a mental attitude based on a mixture of thoughts and feelings: *anti-American sentiment.* **2** (*often pl*) a thought, opinion, or attitude expressed in words: *his sentiments were echoed by subsequent speakers.* **3** feelings such as tenderness, romance, and sadness, esp. when exaggerated: *a man without the softness of sentiment.* ▷ **HISTORY** Latin *sentire* to feel

sentimental *adj* **1** feeling or expressing tenderness, romance, or sadness to an exaggerated extent. **2** appealing to the emotions, esp. to romantic feelings: *she kept the ring for sentimental reasons.* ▶ **sentimentalism** *n* ▶ **sentimentalist** *n* ▶ **sentimentality** *n* ▶ **sentimentally** *adv*

sentimentalize *or* **-ise** *vb* **-izing, -ized** *or* **-ising, -ised** to make sentimental or behave sentimentally.

sentinel *n Old-fashioned* a sentry. ▷ **HISTORY** Old French *sentinelle*

sentry *n, pl* **-tries** a soldier who keeps watch and guards a camp or building. ▷ **HISTORY** perhaps from obsolete *centrinel* sentinel

sentry box *n* a small shelter with an open front in which a sentry stands during bad weather.

sepal *n Bot* a leaflike division of the calyx of a flower. ▷ **HISTORY** New Latin *sepalum*

separable *adj* able to be separated.

separate *vb* **-rating, -rated 1** to act as a barrier between: *the narrow stretch of water which* *separates Europe from Asia.* **2** to part or be parted from a mass or group. **3** to distinguish: *it's what separates the women from the boys.* **4** to divide or be divided into component parts. **5** to sever or be severed. **6** (of a couple) to stop living together. ✧ *adj* **7** existing or considered independently: *a separate issue.* **8** set apart from the main body or mass. **9** distinct or individual. ▷ **HISTORY** Latin *separare* ▶ **separately** *adv* ▶ **separateness** *n* ▶ **separator** *n*

separates *pl n Brit, Austral & NZ* clothes, such as skirts, blouses, and trousers, that only cover part of the body and are designed to be worn together or separately.

separate school *n* (in certain Canadian provinces) a school for a large religious minority financed by provincial grants in addition to the education tax.

separation *n* **1** the act of separating: *the separation of child from mother.* **2** *Family law* the living apart of a married couple without divorce. **3** a mark, line, or object that separates one thing from another.

separation of powers *n Law* the doctrine that power should be separated rather than concentrated to safeguard individual rights, as in the separate branches for executive, legislative, and judicial powers.

separatist *n* a person who advocates the separation of his or her own group from an organization or country. ▶ **separatism** *n*

sepia *adj* dark reddish-brown, like the colour of very old photographs. ▷ **HISTORY** Latin: a cuttlefish

sepoy *n* (formerly) an Indian soldier in the service of the British. ▷ **HISTORY** Urdu *sipāhī*

sepsis *n* poisoning caused by the presence of pus-forming bacteria in the body. ▷ **HISTORY** Greek: a rotting

sept *n* a clan, esp. in Ireland or Scotland. ▷ **HISTORY** perhaps variant of *sect*

Sept. September.

September *n* the ninth month of the year. ▷ **HISTORY** Latin: the seventh (month)

septet *n* **1** a group of seven performers. **2** a piece of music for seven performers. ▷ **HISTORY** Latin *septem* seven

septic *adj* of or caused by harmful bacteria. ▶ **septicity** *n*

septicaemia *or* **septicemia** (sep-tis-**see**-mee-a) *n* an infection of the blood which develops in a wound. ▷ **HISTORY** Greek *sēptos* decayed + *haima* blood

septic tank *n* a tank in which sewage is decomposed by the action of bacteria.

septuagenarian *n* **1** a person who is between 70 and 79 years old. ✧ *adj* **2** between 70 and 79 years old. ▷ **HISTORY** Latin *septuaginta* seventy

Septuagint (**sept**-yew-a-jint) *n* the ancient Greek version of the Old Testament, including the Apocrypha. ▷ **HISTORY** Latin *septuaginta* seventy

septum *n, pl* **-ta** *Biol, anat* a dividing partition between two tissues or cavities, such as in the nose. ▷ **HISTORY** Latin *saeptum* wall

septuple *vb* **-pling, -pled 1** to multiply by seven. ✧ *adj* **2** seven times as much or as many. **3** consisting of seven parts. ✧ *n* **4** a quantity or number seven times as great as another. ▷ **HISTORY** Latin *septem* seven

sepulchral (sip-**pulk**-ral) *adj* **1** gloomy and solemn, like a tomb or grave. **2** of a sepulchre.

sepulchre *or US* **sepulcher** (**sep**-pulk-er) *n* **1** a burial vault, tomb, or grave. ✧ *vb* **-chring, -chred** *or* **-chering, -chered 2** to bury in a sepulchre. ▷ **HISTORY** Latin *sepulcrum*

sequel *n* **1** a novel, play, or film that continues the story of an earlier one. **2** anything that happens after or as a result of something else: *there was an amusing sequel to this incident.* ▷ **HISTORY** Latin *sequi* to follow

sequence *n* **1** an arrangement of two or more things in a successive order. **2** the successive order of two or more things: *chronological sequence.* **3** an action or event that follows another or others. **4** *Maths* an ordered set of numbers or other quantities in one-to-one correspondence with the integers 1 to *n*. **5** a section of a film forming a single uninterrupted episode. ✧ *vb* **6** to arrange in a sequence. ▷ **HISTORY** Latin *sequi* to follow

sequence of events *n* the order in which several related things happen.

sequential *adj* happening in a fixed order or sequence.

sequester *vb* **1** to seclude: *he could sequester himself in his own home.* **2** *Law* same as **sequestrate**. ▷ **HISTORY** Late Latin *sequestrare* to surrender for safekeeping

sequestrate *vb* **-trating, -trated** *Law* to confiscate (property) temporarily until creditors are satisfied or a court order is complied with. ▶ **sequestrator** *n*

sequestration *n* **1** the act of sequestering or the state of being sequestered. **2** *Law* the sequestering of property. **3** *Chem* the effective removal of ions from a solution by coordination with another type of ion or molecule to form complexes.

sequin *n* a small piece of shiny metal foil used to decorate clothes. ▷ **HISTORY** Italian *zecchino* ▶ **sequined** *adj*

sequoia *n* a giant Californian coniferous tree. ▷ **HISTORY** after *Sequoya,* a Native American scholar

seraglio (sir-**ah**-lee-oh) *n, pl* **-raglios 1** the part of a Muslim house or palace where the owner's wives live. **2** a Turkish sultan's palace. ▷ **HISTORY** Italian *serraglio* animal cage

seraph *n, pl* **-aphim** *Theol* a member of the highest order of angels. ▷ **HISTORY** from Hebrew ▶ **seraphic** *adj*

Serb *adj, n* same as **Serbian**.

Serbian *adj* **1** of Serbia. ✧ *n* **2** a person from Serbia. **3** the dialect of Serbo-Croat spoken in Serbia.

Serbo-Croat *or* **Serbo-Croatian** *n* **1** the chief official language of Serbia and Croatia. ✧ *adj* **2** of this language.

A B C D E F G H I J K L M N O P Q R S T U V W X Y Z

serenade *n* **1** a piece of music played or sung to a woman by a lover. **2** a piece of music suitable for this. **3** an orchestral suite for a small ensemble. ✧ *vb* **-nading, -naded 4** to sing or play a serenade to (someone). ▷ **HISTORY** French

serendipity *n* the gift of making fortunate discoveries by accident. ▷ **HISTORY** from the fairy tale *The Three Princes of Serendip,* in which the heroes possess this gift

serene *adj* **1** peaceful or calm. **2** (of the sky) clear or bright. ▷ **HISTORY** Latin *serenus* ▶ **serenely** *adv* ▶ **serenity** *n*

serf *n* (esp. in medieval Europe) a labourer who could not leave the land on which he worked. ▷ **HISTORY** Latin *servus* a slave ▶ **serfdom** *n*

serge *n* a strong fabric made of wool, cotton, silk, or rayon, used for clothing. ▷ **HISTORY** Old French *sarge*

sergeant *n* **1** a noncommissioned officer in the armed forces. **2** (in Britain and Australia) a police officer ranking between constable and inspector. ▷ **HISTORY** Old French *sergent*

sergeant at arms *n* a parliamentary or court officer responsible for keeping order.

sergeant major *n* a noncommissioned officer of the highest rank in the army.

serial *n* **1** a story published or broadcast in instalments at regular intervals. **2** a publication that is regularly issued and consecutively numbered. ✧ *adj* **3** of, in, or forming a series: *serial pregnancies.* **4** published or presented as a serial. ▷ **HISTORY** Latin *series* series ▶ **serially** *adv*

serialize *or* **-ise** *vb* **-izing, -ized** *or* **-ising, -ised** to publish or present in the form of a serial. ▶ **serialization** *or* **-isation** *n*

serial killer *n* a person who commits a number of murders.

series *n, pl* **-ries 1** a group or succession of related things. **2** a set of radio or television programmes dealing with the same subject, esp. one having the same characters but different stories. **3** *Maths* the sum of a finite or infinite sequence of numbers or quantities. **4** *Electronics* an arrangement of two or more components connected in a circuit so that the same current flows in turn through each of them: *a number of resistors in series.* **5** *Geol* a set of layers that represent the rocks formed during an epoch. ▷ **HISTORY** Latin: a row

series circuit *n Electronics* an electrical circuit in which two or more components are connected in such a way that the same current can flow through each of them in turn.

serious *adj* **1** giving cause for concern: *the situation is serious.* **2** concerned with important matters: *there are some serious questions that need to be answered.* **3** not cheerful; grave: *I am a serious person.* **4** in earnest; sincere: *he believes we are serious.* **5** requiring concentration: *a serious book.* **6** *Informal* impressive because of its substantial quantity or quality: *serious money.* ▷ **HISTORY** Latin *serius* ▶ **seriously** *adv* ▶ **seriousness** *n*

serjeant *n* same as **sergeant**.

sermon *n* **1** a speech on a religious or moral subject given by a clergyman as part of a church service. **2** *Disparaging* a serious talk on behaviour, morals, or duty, esp. a long and tedious one. ▷ **HISTORY** Latin *sermo* discourse

seropositive (seer-oh-**poz**-zit-iv) *adj* (of a person whose blood has been tested for a specific disease, such as AIDS) showing a significant level of serum antibodies, indicating the presence of the disease.

serous (**seer**-uss) *adj* of, containing, or like serum.

serpent *n* **1** *Literary* a snake. **2** a devious person. ▷ **HISTORY** Latin *serpens* a creeping thing

serpentine[1] *adj* twisting like a snake.

serpentine[2] *n* a soft green or brownish-red mineral. ▷ **HISTORY** so named from its snakelike patterns

serrated *adj* having a notched or sawlike edge. ▷ **HISTORY** Latin *serratus* saw-shaped ▶ **serration** *n*

serried *adj Literary* in close formation: *the serried ranks of fans.* ▷ **HISTORY** Old French *serré* close-packed

serum (**seer**-um) *n* **1** the yellowish watery fluid left after blood has clotted. **2** this fluid from the blood of immunized animals used for inoculation or vaccination. **3** *Physiol, zool* any clear watery animal fluid. ▷ **HISTORY** Latin: whey

serval *n* a slender African wild cat with black-spotted tawny fur.

servant *n* **1** a person employed to do household work for another person. **2** a person or thing that is useful or provides a service: *a distinguished servant of this country.* ▷ **HISTORY** Old French: serving

serve *vb* **serving, served 1** to be of service to (a person, community, or cause); help. **2** to perform an official duty or duties: *he served on several university committees.* **3** to attend to (customers) in a shop. **4** to provide (guests) with food or drink: *he served dinner guests German wine.* **5** to provide (food or drink) for customers: *breakfast is served from 7 a.m.* **6** to provide with something needed by the public: *the community served by the school.* **7** to work as a servant for (a person). **8** to go through (a period of police or military service, apprenticeship, or imprisonment). **9** to meet the needs of: *they serve a purpose.* **10** to perform a function: *the attacks only served to strengthen their resolve.* **11** (of a male animal) to mate with (a female animal). **12** *Tennis, squash, etc.* to put (the ball) into play. **13** to deliver (a legal document) to (a person). **14 serve someone right** *Informal* to be what someone deserves, esp. for doing something stupid or wrong. ✧ *n* **15** *Tennis, squash, etc.* short for **service** (sense 12). ▷ **HISTORY** Latin *servus* a slave

server *n* **1** a person who serves. **2** *Computers* a computer or program that supplies data to other machines on a network.

service *n* **1** an act of help or assistance. **2** an organization or system that provides something needed by the public: *a consumer information service.* **3** a department of public employment and its employees: *the diplomatic service.* **4** the installation or maintenance of goods provided by a

dealer after a sale. **5** availability for use by the public: *the new plane could be in service within fifteen years.* **6** a regular check made on a machine or vehicle in which parts are tested, cleaned, or replaced if worn. **7** the serving of guests or customers: *service is included on the wine list.* **8** one of the branches of the armed forces. **9** the serving of food: *silver service.* **10** a set of dishes, cups, and plates for use at table. **11** a formal religious ceremony. **12** *Tennis, squash, etc.* **a** the act, manner, or right of serving the ball. **b** the game in which a particular player serves: *she dropped only one point on her service.* ✧ *adj* **13** of or for the use of servants or employees: *a service elevator.* **14** serving the public rather than producing goods: *the service sector.* ✧ *vb* **-vicing, -viced 15** to provide service or services to. **16** to check and repair (a vehicle or machine). **17** (of a male animal) to mate with (a female animal). ✧ See also **services**.
▷ HISTORY Latin *servitium* condition of a slave

serviceable *adj* **1** performing effectively: *serviceable boots.* **2** able or ready to be used: *five remaining serviceable aircraft.* ▶ **serviceability** *n*

service area *n* a place on a motorway with a garage, restaurants, and toilets.

service charge *n* a percentage added to a bill in a hotel or restaurant to pay for service.

service flat *n* a flat where domestic services are provided by the management.

service industry *n Econ, business* an industry that serves the public rather than producing goods.

serviceman *n, pl* **-men 1** a person in the armed services. **2** a man employed to service and maintain equipment. ▶ **servicewoman** *fem n*

service road *n Brit & Austral* a narrow road running parallel to a main road that provides access to houses and shops situated along its length.

services *pl n* **1** work performed in a job: *the OBE for her services to the community.* **2 the services** the armed forces. **3** a system of providing the public with something it needs, such as gas or water.

service station *n* **1** a place that sells fuel, oil, and spare parts for motor vehicles. **2** same as **service area**.

serviette *n* a table napkin. ▷ HISTORY Old French

servile *adj* **1** too eager to obey people; fawning. **2** of or suitable for a slave. ▷ HISTORY Latin *servus* slave ▶ **servility** *n*

serving *n* a portion of food.

servitude *n Formal* **1** slavery or bondage. **2** the state or condition of being completely dominated.
▷ HISTORY Latin *servus* a slave

servomechanism *n* a device which converts a small force into a larger force, used esp. in steering mechanisms.

sesame (**sess**-am-ee) *n* a plant of the East Indies, grown for its seeds and oil, which are used in cooking. ▷ HISTORY Greek

sessile *adj* **1** (of flowers or leaves) having no stalk. **2** (of animals such as the barnacle) fixed in one position. ▷ HISTORY Latin *sessilis* concerning sitting

session *n* **1** any period devoted to a particular activity. **2** a meeting of a court, parliament, or council. **3** a series or period of such meetings. **4** a school or university term or year. ▷ HISTORY Latin *sessio* a sitting ▶ **sessional** *adj*

sestet *n* **1** *Prosody* the last six lines of a sonnet. **2** same as **sextet** (sense 1). ▷ HISTORY Italian *sesto* sixth

set[1] *vb* **setting, set 1** to put in a specified position or state: *I set him free.* **2 set to** *or* **on** to bring (something) into contact with (something else): *three prisoners set fire to their cells.* **3** to put into order or make ready: *set the table.* **4** to make or become firm or rigid: *before the eggs begin to set.* **5** to put (a broken bone) or (of a broken bone) to be put into a normal position for healing. **6** to adjust (a clock or other instrument) to a particular position. **7** to arrange or establish: *to set a date for diplomatic talks; it set the standards of performance.* **8** to prescribe or assign (a task or material for study): *the examiners have set 'Paradise Lost'.* **9** to arrange (hair) while wet, so that it dries in position. **10** to place a jewel in (a setting): *a ring set with diamonds.* **11** to provide music for (a poem or other text to be sung). **12** *Printing* **a** to arrange (type) for printing. **b** to put (text) into type. **13** to arrange (a stage or television studio) with scenery and props. **14 set to** *or* **on** to value (something) at a specified price or worth: *he set a high price on his services.* **15** (of the sun or moon) to disappear beneath the horizon. **16** (of plants) to produce (fruits or seeds) or (of fruits or seeds) to develop. **17** to place (a hen) on (eggs) to incubate them. **18** (of a gun dog) to turn in the direction of game birds. ✧ *n* **19** the act of setting. **20** a condition of firmness or hardness. **21** manner of standing; posture: *the set of his shoulders.* **22** the scenery and other props used in a play or film. **23** same as **sett**. ✧ *adj* **24** fixed or established by authority or agreement: *set hours of work.* **25** rigid or inflexible: *she is set in her ways.* **26** unmoving; fixed: *a set expression on his face.* **27** conventional or stereotyped: *she made her apology in set phrases.* **28 set in** (of a scene or story) represented as happening at a certain time or place: *a European film set in Africa.* **29 set on** *or* **upon** determined to (do or achieve something): *why are you so set upon avoiding me?* **30** ready: *all set to go.* **31** (of material for study) prescribed for students' preparation for an examination. ▷ HISTORY Old English *settan*

set[2] *n* **1** a number of objects or people grouped or belonging together: *a set of slides.* **2** a group of people who associate with each other or have similar interests: *the tennis set.* **3** *Maths* a collection of numbers or objects that satisfy a given condition or share a property. **4** a television or piece of radio equipment. **5** *Sport* a group of games or points in a match, of which the winner must win a certain number. **6** a series of songs or tunes performed by a musician or group on a given occasion: *the front row spent the rest of the set craning their necks.*
▷ HISTORY Old French *sette*

set back *vb* **1** to delay or hinder. **2** *Informal* to cost (a person) a specified amount. ✧ *n* **setback** **3** anything that delays progress.

set off *vb* **1** to start a journey. **2** to cause (a person) to act or do something, such as laugh. **3** to cause to explode. **4** to act as a contrast to: *blue suits you, sets off the colour of your hair.*

set piece *n* **1** a work of literature, music, or art, intended to create an impressive effect. **2** *Football, hockey, etc.* an attacking move from a corner or free kick.

set square *n* a thin flat piece of plastic or metal in the shape of a right-angled triangle, used in technical drawing.

sett *or* **set** *n* **1** a badger's burrow. **2** a small rectangular paving block made of stone. ▷ HISTORY variant of SET[1] (noun)

settee *n* a seat, for two or more people, with a back and usually with arms; couch. ▷ HISTORY from SETTLE[2]

setter *n* a large long-haired dog originally bred for hunting.

set theory *n Maths* the branch of mathematics concerned with the properties and interrelationships of sets.

setting *n* **1** the surroundings in which something is set. **2** the scenery, properties, or background used to create the location for a stage play or film. **3** a piece of music written for the words of a text. **4** the decorative metalwork in which a gem is set. **5** the plates and cutlery for a single place at a table. **6** one of the positions or levels to which the controls of a machine can be adjusted.

settle[1] *vb* **-tling, -tled 1** to put in order: *he settled his affairs before he died.* **2** to arrange or be arranged firmly or comfortably: *he settled into his own chair by the fire.* **3** to come down to rest: *a bird settled on top of the hedge.* **4** to establish or become established as a resident: *they eventually settled in Glasgow.* **5** to establish or become established in a way of life or a job. **6** to migrate to (a country) and form a community; colonize. **7** to make or become quiet, calm, or stable. **8** to cause (sediment) to sink to the bottom in a liquid or (of sediment) to sink thus. **9** to subside: *the dust settled.* **10** (sometimes foll. by *up*) to pay off (a bill or debt). **11** to decide or dispose of: *to settle an argument.* **12** (often foll. by *on* or *upon*) to agree or fix: *they settled on an elementary code.* **13** (usually foll. by *on* or *upon*) to give (a title or property) to a person by gift or legal deed: *he settled his property on his wife.* **14** to decide (a legal dispute) by agreement without court action: *they settled out of court.* ▷ HISTORY Old English *setlan*

settle[2] *n* a long wooden bench with a high back and arms, sometimes having a storage space under the seat. ▷ HISTORY Old English *setl*

settle down *vb* **1** to make or become quiet and orderly. **2 settle down to** to remove all distractions and concentrate on: *we settled down to a favourite movie.* **3** to adopt an orderly and routine way of life, esp. after marriage.

settle for *vb* to accept or agree to in spite of dissatisfaction.

settlement *n* **1** an act of settling. **2** a place newly settled; colony. **3** subsidence of all or part of a building. **4** an official agreement ending a dispute. **5** *Law* **a** an arrangement by which property is transferred to a person's possession. **b** the deed transferring such property.

settler *n* a person who settles in a new country or a colony.

set to *vb* **1** to begin working. **2** to start fighting. ✧ *n* **set-to 3** *Informal* a brief disagreement or fight.

set-top box *n* a device which converts the signals from a digital television broadcast into a form which can be viewed on a standard television set.

set up *vb* **1** to build or construct: *the soldiers had actually set up a munitions factory.* **2** to put into a position of power or wealth. **3** to begin or enable (someone) to begin (a new venture): *he set up a small shop.* **4** to begin or produce: *to set up a nuclear chain reaction.* **5** to establish: *Broad set up a world record.* **6** *Informal* to cause (a person) to be blamed or accused. **7** to restore the health of: *a pub lunch set me up nicely.* ✧ *n* **setup 8** *Informal* the way in which anything is organized or arranged. **9** *Slang* an event the result of which is prearranged.

seven *n* **1** the cardinal number that is the sum of one and six. **2** a numeral, 7 or VII, representing this number. **3** something representing or consisting of seven units. ✧ *adj* **4** amounting to seven: *seven weeks.* ▷ HISTORY Old English *seofon* ▶ **seventh** *adj, n*

seven seas *pl n Old-fashioned* all the oceans of the world.

seventeen *n* **1** the cardinal number that is the sum of ten and seven. **2** a numeral, 17 or XVII, representing this number. **3** something representing or consisting of seventeen units. ✧ *adj* **4** amounting to seventeen: *seventeen children.* ▶ **seventeenth** *adj, n*

seventh heaven *n* a state of supreme happiness.

seventy *n, pl* **-ties 1** the cardinal number that is the product of ten and seven. **2** a numeral, 70 or LXX, representing this number. **3** something representing or consisting of seventy units. ✧ *adj* **4** amounting to seventy: *seventy countries.* ▶ **seventieth** *adj, n*

sever *vb* **1** to cut right through or cut off (something): *it accidentally severed the electrical cable.* **2** to break off (a tie or relationship). ▷ HISTORY Latin *separare* to separate ▶ **severable** *adj* ▶ **severance** *n*

several *adj* **1** more than a few: *I spoke to several doctors.* **2** *Formal* various or separate: *the members with their several occupations.* **3** *Formal* distinct or different: *misfortune visited her three several times.* ▷ HISTORY Medieval Latin *separalis*

severally *adv Formal* individually or separately: *the Western nations severally rather than jointly decided that they would have to act without Russia.*

severance pay *n* compensation paid by a firm to an employee who has to leave because the job he or she was appointed to do no longer exists.

severe *adj* **1** strict or harsh in the treatment of others: *a severe parent.* **2** serious in appearance or manner: *a severe look; a severe hairdo.* **3** very intense or unpleasant: *severe chest pains; the punishments*

are severe. **4** causing discomfort by its harshness: *severe frost.* **5** hard to perform or accomplish: *a severe challenge.* ▷ **HISTORY** Latin *severus*
▸ **severely** *adv* ▸ **severity** *n*

Seville orange *n* a bitter orange used to make marmalade. ▷ **HISTORY** after *Seville* in Spain

sew *vb* **sewing, sewed; sewn** *or* **sewed 1** to join with thread repeatedly passed through with a needle. **2** to attach, fasten, or close by sewing. ▷ **HISTORY** Old English *sēowan*

sewage *n* waste matter or excrement carried away in sewers or drains.

sewage farm *n* a place where sewage is treated so that it can be used as manure or disposed of safely.

sewer *n* a drain or pipe, usually underground, used to carry away surface water or sewage. ▷ **HISTORY** Old French *essever* to drain

sewerage *n* **1** a system of sewers. **2** the removal of surface water or sewage by means of sewers.

sewn *vb* a past participle of **sew**.

sex *n* **1** the state of being either male or female. **2** either of the two categories, male or female, into which organisms are divided. **3** sexual intercourse. **4** feelings or behaviour connected with having sex or the desire to have sex. **5** sexual matters in general. ✧ *adj* **6** of sexual matters: *sex education.* **7** based on or resulting from the difference between the sexes: *sex discrimination.* ✧ *vb* **8** to find out the sex of (an animal). ▷ **HISTORY** Latin *sexus*

sexagenarian *n* **1** a person who is between 60 and 69 years old. ✧ *adj* **2** between 60 and 69 years old. ▷ **HISTORY** Latin *sexaginta* sixty

sex-and-shopping *adj* (of a novel) of the genre in which the central character has a number of sexual encounters which are graphically described, and the author mentions the name of many upmarket products: *a sex-and-shopping blockbuster.*

sex cell *n, Biol* a cell that can begin a reproductive process.

sex chromosome *n* either of the chromosomes that determine the sex of an animal.

sexism *n* discrimination against the members of one sex, usually women. ▸ **sexist** *n, adj*

sexless *adj* **1** neither male nor female. **2** having no sexual desires. **3** sexually unattractive.

sextant *n* an instrument used in navigation for measuring angular distance, for example between the sun and the horizon, to calculate the position of a ship or aircraft. ▷ **HISTORY** Latin *sextans* one sixth of a unit

sextet *n* **1** a group of six performers. **2** a piece of music for six performers. **3** a group of six people or things. ▷ **HISTORY** variant of *sestet*

sexton *n* a person employed to look after a church and its churchyard. ▷ **HISTORY** Medieval Latin *sacristanus* sacristan

sextuplet *n* one of six children born at one birth.

sexual *adj* **1** of or characterized by sex. **2** (of reproduction) characterized by the union of male and female reproductive cells. **3** of or relating to the differences between males and females.
▸ **sexuality** *n* ▸ **sexually** *adv*

sexual harassment *n* the unwelcome directing of sexual remarks, looks, or advances, usually at a woman in the workplace.

sexual intercourse *n* the sexual act in which the male's erect penis is inserted into the female's vagina, usually followed by the ejaculation of semen.

sex up *vb Informal* to make (something) more exciting.

sexy *adj* **sexier, sexiest** *Informal* **1** sexually exciting or attractive: *a sexy voice.* **2** interesting, exciting, or trendy: *a sexy project; a sexy new car.*
▸ **sexiness** *n*

SF *or* **sf** science fiction.

SFA Scottish Football Association.

SFO (in Britain) Serious Fraud Office.

Sg *Chem* seaborgium.

Sgt. Sergeant.

sh *interj* be quiet!

shabby *adj* **-bier, -biest 1** old and worn in appearance. **2** wearing worn and dirty clothes. **3** behaving in a mean or unfair way: *shabby manoeuvres.* ▷ **HISTORY** Old English *sceabb* scab
▸ **shabbily** *adv* ▸ **shabbiness** *n*

shack *n* **1** a roughly built hut. ✧ *vb* **2 shack up with** *Slang* to live with (a lover). ▷ **HISTORY** perhaps from dialect *shackly* ramshackle

shackle *n* **1** one of a pair of metal rings joined by a chain for securing someone's wrists or ankles. **2 shackles** anything that confines or restricts freedom: *free from the shackles of its feudal past.* **3** a metal loop or link closed by a bolt, used for securing ropes or chains. ✧ *vb* **-ling, -led 4** to fasten with shackles. **5** to restrict or hamper: *an economy shackled by central control.* ▷ **HISTORY** Old English *sceacel*

shad *n, pl* **shad** *or* **shads** a herring-like food fish. ▷ **HISTORY** Old English *sceadd*

shade *n* **1** relative darkness produced by blocking out sunlight. **2** a place sheltered from the sun by trees, buildings, etc. **3** something used to provide a shield or protection from a direct source of light, such as a lamp shade. **4** a shaded area in a painting or drawing. **5** any of the different hues of a colour: *a much darker shade of grey.* **6** a slight amount: *a shade of reluctance.* **7 put someone** *or* **something in the shade** to be so impressive as to make another person or thing seem unimportant by comparison. **8** *Literary* a ghost. ✧ *vb* **shading, shaded 9** to screen or protect from heat or light. **10** to make darker or dimmer. **11** to represent (a darker area) in (a painting or drawing), by graded areas of tone, lines, or dots. **12** to change slightly or by degrees. ▷ **HISTORY** Old English *sceadu*

shades *pl n* **1** *Slang* sunglasses. **2 shades of** a reminder of: *shades of Margaret Thatcher.*

shading *n* the graded areas of tone, lines, or dots, indicating light and dark in a painting or drawing.

shadow *n* **1** a dark image or shape cast on a surface when something stands between a light and the surface. **2** a patch of shade. **3** the dark

A B C D E F G H I J K L M N O P Q R S T U V W X Y Z

portions of a picture. **4** a hint or faint trace: *a shadow of a doubt.* **5** a person less powerful or vigorous than his or her former self. **6** a threatening influence: *news of the murder cast a shadow over the village.* **7** a person who always accompanies another. **8** a person who trails another in secret, such as a detective. ✧ *adj* **9** *Brit & Austral* designating a member or members of the main opposition party in Parliament who would hold ministerial office if their party were in power: *the shadow chancellor.* ✧ *vb* **10** to cast a shade or shadow over. **11** to make dark or gloomy. **12** to follow or trail secretly. ▷ **HISTORY** Old English *sceadwe*

shadow-box *vb Boxing* to box against an imaginary opponent for practice. ▸ **shadow-boxing** *n*

shadowy *adj* **1** (of a place) full of shadows; shady. **2** faint or dark like a shadow: *a shadowy figure.* **3** mysterious or not well known: *the shadowy world of espionage.*

shady *adj* **shadier, shadiest 1** full of shade; shaded. **2** giving or casting shade. **3** *Informal* of doubtful honesty or legality: *shady business dealings.* ▸ **shadiness** *n*

shaft *n* **1 a** a spear or arrow. **b** its long narrow stem. **2 shaft of wit** *or* **humour** a clever or amusing remark. **3** a ray or streak of light. **4** the long straight narrow handle of a tool or golf club. **5** a revolving rod in a machine that transmits motion or power. **6** one of the bars between which an animal is harnessed to a vehicle. **7** *Archit* the middle part of a column or pier, between the base and the capital. **8** a vertical passageway through a building for a lift. **9** a vertical passageway into a mine. ▷ **HISTORY** Old English *sceaft*

shag[1] *n* **1** coarse shredded tobacco. **2** a matted tangle of hair or wool. ✧ *adj* **3** (of a carpet) having long thick woollen threads. ▷ **HISTORY** Old English *sceacga*

shag[2] *n* a kind of cormorant. ▷ **HISTORY** special use of SHAG[1] (with reference to its crest)

shag[3] *vb* **shagging, shagged** *Brit, Austral & NZ slang* **1** *Taboo* to have sexual intercourse with (a person). **2 shagged out** exhausted. ▷ **HISTORY** origin unknown

shaggy *adj* **-gier, -giest 1** having or covered with rough unkempt fur, hair, or wool: *shaggy cattle.* **2** rough and untidy. ▸ **shagginess** *n*

shagreen *n* **1** the skin of a shark, used as an abrasive. **2** a rough grainy leather made from certain animal hides. ▷ **HISTORY** French *chagrin*

shah *n* a ruler of certain Middle Eastern countries, esp. (formerly) Iran. ▷ **HISTORY** Persian: king

shake *vb* **shaking, shook, shaken 1** to move up and down or back and forth with short quick movements. **2** to be or make unsteady. **3** (of a voice) to tremble because of anger or nervousness. **4** to clasp or grasp (the hand) of (a person) in greeting or agreement: *they shook hands.* **5 shake on it** *Informal* to shake hands in agreement or reconciliation. **6** to wave vigorously and angrily: *he shook his fist.* **7** (often foll. by *up*) to frighten or unsettle. **8** to shock, disturb, or upset: *he was badly shaken but unharmed.* **9** to undermine or weaken: *a team whose morale had been badly shaken.* **10** *US & Canad informal* to get rid of. **11** *Music* to perform a trill on (a note). **12 shake one's head** to indicate disagreement or disapproval by moving the head from side to side. ✧ *n* **13** the act or an instance of shaking. **14** a tremor or vibration. **15 the shakes** *Informal* a state of uncontrollable trembling. **16** *Informal* a very short period of time: *in half a shake.* **17** *Music* same as **trill** (sense 1) ✧ See also **shake down, shake off, shake up.** ▷ **HISTORY** Old English *sceacan*

shake down *vb* **1** to go to bed, esp. in a makeshift bed. ✧ *n* **shakedown 2** a makeshift bed.

shake off *vb* **1** to remove or get rid of: *I have been trying to shake off the stigma for some time.* **2** to escape from; get away from: *they switched to a blue car in a bid to shake off reporters.*

shaker *n* **1** a container used for shaking a powdered substance onto something: *a flour shaker.* **2** a container in which the ingredients of alcoholic drinks are shaken together.

Shakespearean *or* **Shakespearian** *adj* **1** of William Shakespeare, English dramatist and poet, or his works. ✧ *n* **2** a student of or specialist in Shakespeare's works.

shake up *vb* **1** to mix by shaking. **2** to reorganize drastically. **3** *Informal* to shock mentally or physically: *the thunderstorm really shook me up.* ✧ *n* **shake-up 4** *Informal* a radical reorganization, such as the reorganization of employees in a company.

shaky *adj* **shakier, shakiest 1** weak and unsteady, esp. due to illness or shock. **2** uncertain or doubtful: *their prospects are shaky.* **3** tending to shake or tremble. ▸ **shakily** *adv*

shale *n* a flaky sedimentary rock formed by compression of successive layers of clay. ▷ **HISTORY** Old English *scealu* shell

shall *vb, past* **should** used as an auxiliary: **1** (esp. with *I* or *we* as subject) to make the future tense: *we shall see you tomorrow.* **2** (with *you, he, she, it, they,* or a noun as subject) **a** to indicate determination on the part of the speaker: *you shall pay for this!* **b** to indicate compulsion or obligation, now esp. in official documents. **3** (with *I* or *we* as subject) in questions asking for advice or agreement: *what shall we do now?; shall I shut the door?* ▷ **HISTORY** Old English *sceal*

WORD TIP

The usual rule given for the use of *shall* and *will* is that where the meaning is one of simple futurity, *shall* is used for the first person of the verb and *will* for the second and third: *I shall go tomorrow; they will be there now.* Where the meaning involves command, obligation, or determination, the positions are reversed: *it shall be done; I will definitely go.* However, *shall* has come to be largely neglected in favour of *will,* which has become the commonest form of the future in all three persons.

shallot (shal-**lot**) *n* a small, onion-like plant used in cooking for flavouring. ▷ **HISTORY** Old French *eschaloigne*

shallow *adj* **1** having little depth. **2** not involving sincere feelings or serious thought. **3** (of breathing) consisting of short breaths. ✧ *n* **4** (*often pl*) a shallow place in a body of water. ▷ **HISTORY** Middle English *shalow* ▶ **shallowness** *n*

sham *n* **1** anything that is not genuine or is not what it appears to be. **2** a person who pretends to be something other than he or she is. ✧ *adj* **3** not real or genuine. ✧ *vb* **shamming, shammed 4** to fake or feign (something); pretend: *he made a point of shamming nervousness.* ▷ **HISTORY** origin unknown

shaman (**sham**-man) *n* **1** a priest of shamanism. **2** a medicine man or witch doctor of a similar religion. ▷ **HISTORY** Russian

shamanism (**sham**-man-iz-zum) *n* a religion of northern Asia, based on a belief in good and evil spirits who can be influenced or controlled only by the shamans. ▶ **shamanist** *n, adj*

shamble *vb* **-bling, -bled 1** to walk or move along in an awkward shuffling way. ✧ *n* **2** an awkward or shuffling walk. ▷ **HISTORY** perhaps from *shambles,* referring to legs of a meat vendor's table ▶ **shambling** *adj, n*

shambles *n* **1** a disorderly or badly organized event or place: *the bathroom was a shambles.* **2** *Chiefly Brit* a butcher's slaughterhouse. **3** *Old-fashioned* any scene of great slaughter. ▷ **HISTORY** Middle English *shamble* table used by meat vendors

shambolic *adj Informal* completely disorganized.

shame *n* **1** a painful emotion resulting from an awareness of having done something wrong or foolish. **2** capacity to feel such an emotion: *have they no shame?* **3** loss of respect; disgrace. **4** a person or thing that causes this. **5** a cause for regret or disappointment: *it's a shame to rush back.* **6 put to shame** to show up as being inferior by comparison: *his essay put mine to shame.* ✧ *interj* **7** *S African informal* **a** an expression of sympathy. **b** an expression of pleasure or endearment. ✧ *vb* **shaming, shamed 8** to cause to feel shame. **9** to bring shame on. **10** (often foll. by *into*) to force someone to do something by making him or her feel ashamed not to: *he was finally shamed into paying the bill.* ▷ **HISTORY** Old English *scamu*

shamefaced *adj* embarrassed or guilty. ▷ **HISTORY** earlier *shamefast* ▶ **shamefacedly** *adv*

shameful *adj* causing or deserving shame: *a shameful lack of concern.* ▶ **shamefully** *adv*

shameless *adj* **1** having no sense of shame: *a shameless manipulator.* **2** without decency or modesty: *a shameless attempt to stifle democracy.* ▶ **shamelessly** *adv*

shammy *n, pl* **-mies** *Informal* a piece of chamois leather. ▷ **HISTORY** variant of *chamois*

shampoo *n* **1** a soapy liquid used to wash the hair. **2** a similar liquid for washing carpets or upholstery. **3** the process of shampooing. ✧ *vb* **-pooing, -pooed 4** to wash (the hair, carpets, or upholstery) with shampoo.

WORD HISTORY
A shampoo was originally a massage rather than a wash. The word 'shampoo' is derived from the Hindi verb *chāmpnā*, meaning 'to press, knead, or massage'.

shamrock *n* a small clover-like plant with three round leaves on each stem: the national emblem of Ireland. ▷ **HISTORY** Irish Gaelic *seamrōg*

shandy *n, pl* **-dies** a drink made of beer and lemonade. ▷ **HISTORY** origin unknown

shanghai *Slang* ✧ *vb* **-haiing, -haied 1** to force or trick (someone) into doing something. **2** *History* to kidnap (a man) and force him to serve at sea. **3** *Austral & NZ* to shoot with a catapult. ✧ *n* **4** *Austral & NZ* a catapult. ▷ **HISTORY** senses 1 and 2 after the city of *Shanghai*; senses 3 and 4 from Scots dialect *shangie, shangan* cleft stick

shank *n* **1** the part of the leg between the knee and the ankle. **2** a cut of meat from the top part of an animal's shank. **3** the long narrow part of a tool, key, spoon, etc. ▷ **HISTORY** Old English *scanca*

shan't shall not.

shantung *n* a heavy Chinese silk with a knobbly surface. ▷ **HISTORY** after province of NE China

shanty[1] *n, pl* **-ties** a small rough hut; crude dwelling. ▷ **HISTORY** Canadian French *chantier* cabin built in a lumber camp

shanty[2] *or* **chanty** *n, pl* **-ties** a rhythmic song originally sung by sailors when working. ▷ **HISTORY** French *chanter* to sing

shantytown *n* a town of poor people living in shanties.

shape *n* **1** the outward form of an object, produced by its outline. **2** the figure or outline of the body of a person. **3** organized or definite form: *to preserve the union in its present shape.* **4** the specific form that anything takes on: *a gold locket in the shape of a heart.* **5** pattern or mould. **6** condition or state of efficiency: *in poor shape.* **7 take shape** to assume a definite form. ✧ *vb* **shaping, shaped 8** (often foll. by *into* or *up*) to receive or cause to receive shape or form: *spinach shaped into a ball.* **9** to mould into a particular pattern or form. **10** to devise or develop: *to shape a system of free trade.* ✧ See also **shape up**. ▷ **HISTORY** Old English *gesceap*, literally: that which is created

shapeless *adj* **1** (of a person or object) lacking a pleasing shape: *a shapeless dress.* **2** having no definite shape or form: *a shapeless mound.* ▶ **shapelessness** *n*

shapely *adj* **-lier, -liest** (esp. of a woman's body or legs) pleasing or attractive in shape. ▶ **shapeliness** *n*

shape up *vb Informal* **1** to progress or develop satisfactorily. **2** to develop a definite or proper form. **3** to start working efficiently or behaving properly: *shape up or face the sack.*

shard *n* a broken piece or fragment of pottery, glass, or metal. ▷ **HISTORY** Old English *sceard*

share[1] *n* **1** a part or portion of something that belongs to or is contributed by a person or group. **2** (*often pl*) any of the equal parts into which the capital stock of a company is divided. ✧ *vb* **sharing, shared 3** (often foll. by *out*) to divide and distribute. **4** to receive or contribute a portion of: *we shared a bottle of mineral water.* **5** to join with another or others in the use of (something): *a programme about four women sharing a house.* **6** to go through (a similar experience) as others: *we have all shared the nightmare of toothache.* **7** to tell others about (something). **8** to have the same (beliefs or opinions) as others: *universal values shared by both east and west.* ▷ HISTORY Old English *scearu*

share[2] *n* short for **ploughshare.** ▷ HISTORY Old English *scear*

shareholder *n* the owner of one or more shares in a company.

sharemilker *n NZ* a person who works on a dairy farm belonging to someone else and gets a share of the proceeds from the sale of the milk.

shark *n* **1** a large, usually predatory fish with a long body, two dorsal fins, and rows of sharp teeth. **2** *Disparaging* a person who swindles or extorts money from other people. ▷ HISTORY origin unknown

sharkskin *n* a smooth glossy fabric used for sportswear.

sharp *adj* **1** having a keen cutting edge. **2** tapering to an edge or point. **3** involving a sudden change in direction: *a sharp bend on a road; a sharp rise in prices.* **4** moving, acting, or reacting quickly: *sharp reflexes.* **5** clearly defined: *a sharp contrast.* **6** quick to notice or understand things; keen-witted. **7** clever in an underhand way: *sharp practices.* **8** bitter or harsh: *a sharp response.* **9** shrill or penetrating: *a sharp cry of horror.* **10** having a bitter or sour taste. **11** (of pain or cold) acute or biting: *a sharp gust of wind.* **12** *Music* **a** (of a note) raised in pitch by one semitone: *F sharp.* **b** (of an instrument or voice) out of tune by being too high in pitch. **13** *Informal* neat and stylish: *a sharp dresser.* ✧ *adv* **14** promptly. **15** exactly: *at ten o'clock sharp.* **16** *Music* **a** higher than a standard pitch. **b** out of tune by being too high in pitch: *she sings sharp.* ✧ *n* **17** *Music* **a** an accidental that raises the pitch of a note by one semitone. Symbol: ♯. **b** a note affected by this accidental. **18** *Informal* a cheat; a cardsharp. ▷ HISTORY Old English *scearp* ▶ **sharpish** *adj* ▶ **sharply** *adv* ▶ **sharpness** *n*

sharpen *vb* to make or become sharp or sharper. ▶ **sharpener** *n*

sharper *n* a person who cheats or swindles; fraud.

sharpshooter *n* a skilled marksman.

shatter *vb* **1** to break suddenly into many small pieces. **2** to damage badly or destroy: *to shatter American confidence.* **3** to upset (someone) greatly: *the whole experience shattered me.* ▷ HISTORY origin unknown ▶ **shattering** *adj*

shattered *adj Informal* **1** completely exhausted. **2** badly upset: *he was shattered by the separation.*

shave *vb* **shaving, shaved; shaved** *or* **shaven 1** to remove (the beard or hair) from (the face, head, or body) by using a razor or shaver. **2** to remove thin slices from (wood or other material) with a sharp cutting tool. **3** to touch (someone or something) lightly in passing. ✧ *n* **4** the act or an instance of shaving. **5** the removal of hair from a man's face by a razor. **6** a tool for cutting off thin slices. **7 close shave** *Informal* a narrow escape. ▷ HISTORY Old English *sceafan*

shaver *n* **1** an electrically powered razor. **2** *Old-fashioned* a young boy.

Shavian (**shave**-ee-an) *adj* **1** of or like George Bernard Shaw, Irish dramatist noted for his sharp wit, or his works. ✧ *n* **2** an admirer of Shaw or his works.

shawl *n* a piece of woollen cloth worn over the head or shoulders by a woman or wrapped around a baby. ▷ HISTORY Persian *shāl*

she *pron* refers to: **1** the female person or animal previously mentioned or in question: *she is my sister.* **2** something regarded as female, such as a car, ship, or nation. ✧ *n* **3** a female person or animal. ▷ HISTORY Old English *sīe*

sheaf *n, pl* **sheaves 1** a bundle of papers tied together. **2** a bundle of reaped corn tied together. ✧ *vb* **3** to bind or tie into a sheaf. ▷ HISTORY Old English *scēaf*

shear *vb* **shearing, sheared** *or Austral & NZ sometimes* **shore; sheared** *or* **shorn 1** to remove (the fleece) of (a sheep) by cutting or clipping. **2** to cut or cut through (something) with shears or a sharp instrument. **3** *Engineering* to cause (a part) to break or (of a part) to break through strain or twisting. ✧ *n* **4** breakage caused through strain or twisting. ✧ See also **shears.** ▷ HISTORY Old English *sceran* ▶ **shearer** *n*

shearing shed *n Austral & NZ* a farm building with equipment for shearing sheep.

shears *pl n* **a** large scissors, used for sheep shearing. **b** a large scissor-like cutting tool with flat blades, used for cutting hedges.

sheath *n, pl* **sheaths 1** a case or covering for the blade of a knife or sword. **2** *Biol* a structure that encloses or protects. **3** *Brit, Austral & NZ* same as **condom. 4** a close-fitting dress. ▷ HISTORY Old English *scēath*

sheathe *vb* **sheathing, sheathed 1** to insert (a knife or sword) into a sheath. **2** to cover with a sheathe or sheathing.

sheaves *n* the plural of **sheaf.**

shebeen *or* **shebean** *n Scot, Irish, & S African* a place where alcoholic drink is sold illegally. ▷ HISTORY Irish Gaelic *sībīn* beer of poor quality

shed[1] *n* **1** a small, roughly made building used for storing garden tools, etc. **2** a large barnlike building used for various purposes at factories, train stations, etc.: *a locomotive shed.* ▷ HISTORY Old English *sced*

shed[2] *vb* **shedding, shed 1** to get rid of: *250 workers shed by the company.* **2 shed tears** to cry. **3 shed light on** to make (a problem or situation) easier to understand. **4** to cast off (skin, hair, or leaves): *the trees were already beginning to shed their* *leaves.* **5** to cause to flow off: *this coat sheds water.* **6** to separate or divide (a group of sheep). ▷ HISTORY Old English *sc(e)ādan*

sheen *n* a glistening brightness on the surface of something: *grass with a sheen of dew on it.* ▷ HISTORY Old English *sciēne*

sheep *n, pl* **sheep 1** a cud-chewing mammal with a thick woolly coat, kept for its wool or meat. RELATED ADJECTIVE ▸ **ovine 2** a timid person. **3 like sheep** (of a group of people) allowing a single person to dictate their actions or beliefs. **4 separate the sheep from the goats** to pick out the members of a group who are superior in some respects. ▷ HISTORY Old English *scēap* ▶ **sheeplike** *adj*

sheep-dip *n* **1** a liquid disinfectant and insecticide in which sheep are immersed. **2** a deep trough containing such a liquid.

sheepdog *n* **1** a dog used for herding sheep. **2** a breed of dog reared originally for herding sheep.

sheepfold *n* a pen or enclosure for sheep.

sheepish *adj* embarrassed because of feeling foolish. ▶ **sheepishly** *adv*

sheepskin *n* the skin of a sheep with the wool still attached, used to make clothing and rugs.

sheer[1] *adj* **1** absolute; complete: *sheer amazement.* **2** perpendicular; very steep: *the sheer rock face.* **3** (of textiles) light, delicate, and see-through. ✧ *adv* **4** steeply: *the cliff drops sheer to the sea.* ▷ HISTORY Old English *scīr*

sheer[2] *vb* **sheer off** *or* **away (from) a** to change course suddenly. **b** to avoid an unpleasant person, thing, or topic. ▷ HISTORY origin unknown

sheet[1] *n* **1** a large rectangular piece of cloth used as an inner bed cover. **2** a thin piece of material such as paper or glass, usually rectangular. **3** a broad continuous surface or layer: *a sheet of ice.* **4** a newspaper. ✧ *vb* **5** to provide with, cover, or wrap in a sheet. **6** (often foll. by *down*) to rain very heavily. ▷ HISTORY Old English *scīete*

sheet[2] *n Naut* a line or rope for controlling the position of a sail. ▷ HISTORY Old English *scēata* corner of a sail

sheet anchor *n* **1** *Naut* a large strong anchor for use in an emergency. **2** a person or thing that can always be relied on.

sheet erosion *n Geol* the wearing away of a layer of surface soil due to rainwater run-off.

sheeting *n* any material from which sheets are made.

sheet lightning *n Meteorol* lightning that appears as a broad sheet, caused by the reflection of more distant lightning.

sheet metal *n* metal formed into a thin sheet by rolling or hammering.

sheikh *or* **sheik** (**shake**) *n* (in Muslim countries) **a** the head of an Arab tribe, village, or family. **b** a religious leader. ▷ HISTORY Arabic *shaykh* old man ▶ **sheikhdom** *or* **sheikdom** *n*

sheila *n Austral & NZ old-fashioned informal* a girl or woman. ▷ HISTORY from the girl's name *Sheila*

shekel *n* **1** the monetary unit of Israel. **2 shekels** *Informal* money. ▷ HISTORY Hebrew *sheqel*

shelduck *or masc* **sheldrake** *n, pl* **-ducks, -duck** *or* **-drakes, -drake** a large brightly coloured wild duck of Europe and Asia. ▷ HISTORY probably from dialect *sheld* pied

shelf *n, pl* **shelves 1** a board fixed horizontally against a wall or in a cupboard, for holding things. **2** a projecting layer of ice or rock on land or in the sea. **3 off the shelf** (of products in shops) sold as standard. **4 on the shelf** put aside or abandoned; used esp. of unmarried women considered to be past the age of marriage. ▷ HISTORY Old English *scylfe* ship's deck

shelf life *n* the length of time a packaged product will remain fresh or usable.

shell *n* **1** the protective outer layer of an egg, fruit, or nut. **2** the hard outer covering of an animal such as a crab or tortoise. **3** any hard outer case. **4** the external structure of a building, car, or ship, esp. one that is unfinished or gutted by fire. **5** an explosive artillery projectile that can be fired from a large gun. **6** a small-arms cartridge. **7** *Rowing* a very light narrow racing boat. **8 come** *or* **bring out of one's shell** to become *or* help to become less shy and reserved. ✧ *vb* **9** to remove the shell or husk from. **10** to attack with artillery shells. ✧ See also **shell out**. ▷ HISTORY Old English *sciell* ▶ **shell-like** *adj*

shellac *n* **1** a yellowish resin used in varnishes and polishes. **2** a varnish made by dissolving shellac in alcohol. ✧ *vb* **-lacking, -lacked 3** to coat with shellac. ▷ HISTORY *shell* + *lac*

shellfish *n, pl* **-fish** *or* **-fishes** a sea-living animal, esp. one that can be eaten, having a shell.

shell out *vb Informal* to pay out or hand over (money).

shell shock *n* a nervous disorder characterized by anxiety and depression that occurs as a result of lengthy exposure to battle conditions. ▶ **shell-shocked** *adj*

shell suit *n Brit* a lightweight tracksuit made of a waterproof nylon layer over a cotton layer.

Shelta *n* a secret language based on Gaelic, used by some travelling people in Ireland and Britain. ▷ HISTORY origin unknown

shelter *n* **1** something that provides cover or protection from weather or danger. **2** the protection given by such a cover. ✧ *vb* **3** to take cover from bad weather. **4** to provide with a place to live or a hiding place: *dissidents sheltering in foreign embassies.* ▷ HISTORY origin unknown

sheltered *adj* **1** protected from wind and rain. **2** protected from unpleasant or upsetting experiences: *a sheltered childhood.* **3** specially designed to provide a safe environment for the elderly, handicapped, or disabled: *sheltered housing.*

shelve[1] *vb* **shelving, shelved 1** to put aside or postpone: *to shelve a project.* **2** to place (something, such as a book) on a shelf. **3** to provide with shelves: *to shelve a cupboard.* **4** to dismiss (someone) from active service. ▷ HISTORY from *shelves*, plural of *shelf*

shelve[2] *vb* **shelving, shelved** to slope away gradually. ▷ HISTORY origin unknown

A B C D E F G H I J K L M N O P Q R S T U V W X Y Z

shelves *n* the plural of **shelf**.

shelving *n* **1** material for shelves. **2** shelves collectively.

shenanigans *pl n Informal* **1** mischief or nonsense. **2** trickery or deception. ▷ **HISTORY** origin unknown

shepherd *n* **1** a person employed to tend sheep. **2** *Christianity* a clergyman when considered as the moral and spiritual guide of the people in the parish. ✧ *vb* **3** to guide or watch over (people). ▷ **HISTORY** SHEEP + HERD ▶ **shepherdess** *fem n*

shepherd's pie *n* a baked dish of minced meat covered with mashed potato.

sherbet *n* **1** *Brit, Austral & NZ* a fruit-flavoured slightly fizzy powder, eaten as a sweet or used to make a drink. **2** *US, Canad & S African* same as **sorbet**. ▷ **HISTORY** Turkish *şerbet*

sheriff *n* **1** (in the US) the chief elected law-enforcement officer in a county. **2** (in Canada) a municipal officer who enforces court orders and escorts convicted criminals to prison. **3** (in England and Wales) the chief executive officer of the Crown in a county, having chiefly ceremonial duties. **4** (in Scotland) a judge in a sheriff court. **5** *(in Australia) an officer of the Supreme Court.* ▷ **HISTORY** Old English *scīrgerēfa*

sheriff court *n* (in Scotland) a court having powers to try all but the most serious crimes and to deal with most civil actions.

Sherpa *n, pl* **-pas** *or* **-pa** a member of a Tibetan people living on the southern slopes of the Himalayas.

sherry *n, pl* **-ries** a pale or dark brown fortified wine, originally from southern Spain.

> **WORD HISTORY**
> 'Sherry' is named after the town of *Jerez de la Frontera* in southwestern Spain, where it was first made.

Shetland pony *n* a very small sturdy breed of pony with a long shaggy mane and tail.

shibboleth *n* **1** a slogan or catch phrase, usually considered outworn, that characterizes a particular party or sect: *the shibboleth of Western strategy.* **2** a custom, phrase, or use of language that reliably distinguishes a member of one group or class from another. ▷ **HISTORY** word used in the Old Testament by the Gileadites as a test word for the Ephraimites, who could not pronounce *sh*

shickered *adj Austral & NZ old-fashioned, slang* drunk. ▷ **HISTORY** Yiddish *shicker* liquor

shied *vb* the past of **shy**[1], **shy**[2].

shield *n* **1** a piece of defensive armour carried in the hand or on the arm to protect the body from blows or missiles. **2** any person or thing that protects, hides, or defends: *a wind shield.* **3** *Heraldry* a representation of a shield used for displaying a coat of arms. **4** anything that resembles a shield in shape, such as a trophy in a sports competition. ✧ *vb* **5** to protect, hide, or defend (someone or something) from danger or harm: *an industry shielded from competition.* ▷ **HISTORY** Old English *scield*

shield volcano *n Geol* a broad volcano built up from the repeated nonexplosive eruption of basalt to form a low dome or shield, usually having a large crater at the summit.

shift *vb* **1** to move from one place or position to another. **2** to pass (blame or responsibility) onto someone else: *he was trying to shift the blame to me.* **3** to change (gear) in a motor vehicle. **4** to remove or be removed: *no detergent can shift these stains.* **5** *US* to change for another or others. **6** *Slang* to move quickly. ✧ *n* **7** the act or an instance of shifting. **8 a** a group of workers who work during a specific period. **b** the period of time worked by such a group. **9** a method or scheme. **10** a loose-fitting straight underskirt or dress. ▷ **HISTORY** Old English *sciftan*

shifting cultivation *n Agriculture* **1** a cultivation system based on the rotations of fields rather than of crops, allowing land to lie fallow and regain fertility. **2** a cultivation system which entails moving to and clearing new land once the fertility of the current land is exhausted.

shiftless *adj* lacking in ambition or initiative.

shifty *adj* **shiftier, shiftiest** looking deceitful and not to be trusted. ▶ **shiftiness** *n*

shillelagh (shil-**lay**-lee) *n* (in Ireland) a heavy club. ▷ **HISTORY** Irish Gaelic *sail* cudgel + *éille* thong

shilling *n* **1** a former British coin worth one twentieth of a pound, replaced by the 5p piece in 1970. **2** a former Australian coin, worth one twentieth of a pound. **3** the standard monetary unit in several E African countries. ▷ **HISTORY** Old English *scilling*

shillyshally *vb* **-shallies, -shallying, -shallied** *Informal* to be indecisive. ▷ **HISTORY** *shill I shall I,* reduplication of *shall I*

shim *n* **1** a thin strip of material placed between two close surfaces to fill a gap. ✧ *vb* **shimming, shimmed 2** to fit or fill up with a shim. ▷ **HISTORY** origin unknown

shimmer *vb* **1** to shine with a faint unsteady light. ✧ *n* **2** a faint unsteady light. ▷ **HISTORY** Old English *scimerian* ▶ **shimmering** *or* **shimmery** *adj*

shin *n* **1** the front part of the lower leg. **2** a cut of beef including the lower foreleg. ✧ *vb* **shinning, shinned 3 shin up** to climb (something, such as a rope or pole) by gripping with the hands or arms and the legs and hauling oneself up. ▷ **HISTORY** Old English *scinu*

shinbone *n* the nontechnical name for **tibia.**

shindig *or* **shindy** *n, pl* **-digs** *or* **-dies** *Slang* **1** a noisy party or dance. **2** a quarrel or brawl. ▷ **HISTORY** variant of *shinty*

shine *vb* **shining, shone 1** to give off or reflect light. **2** to direct the light of (a lamp or torch): *I shone a torch at the ceiling.* **3** (*pt & pp* **shined**) to make clean and bright by polishing: *they earned money by shining shoes.* **4** to be very good at something: *she shone in most subjects; she shone at school.* **5** to appear very bright and clear: *her hair shone like gold.* ✧ *n* **6** brightness or lustre. **7 take a shine to someone** *Informal* to take a liking to someone. ▷ **HISTORY** Old English *scīnan*

shiner *n Informal* a black eye.

shingle[1] *n* **1** a thin rectangular tile laid with others in overlapping rows to cover a roof or a wall. **2** a woman's short-cropped hairstyle. ✧ *vb* **-gling, -gled 3** to cover (a roof or a wall) with shingles. **4** to cut (the hair) in a short-cropped style.
▷ **HISTORY** Latin *scindere* to split

shingle[2] *n* coarse gravel found on beaches.
▷ **HISTORY** Scandinavian

shingles *n* a disease causing a rash of small blisters along a nerve. ▷ **HISTORY** Medieval Latin *cingulum* girdle

shingle slide *n NZ* the loose stones on a steep slope.

Shinto *n* a Japanese religion in which ancestors and nature spirits are worshipped.
▷ **HISTORY** Japanese: the way of the gods
▶ **Shintoism** *n* ▶ **Shintoist** *n, adj*

shinty *n Scot* **1** a game like hockey but with taller goals. **2** (*pl* **-ties**) the stick used in this game.
▷ **HISTORY** perhaps Scottish Gaelic *sinteag* a pace

shiny *adj* **shinier, shiniest 1** bright and polished. **2** (of clothes or material) worn to a smooth and glossy state by continual wear or rubbing.

ship *n* **1** a large seagoing vessel with engines or sails. **2** short for **airship, spaceship**. **3 when one's ship comes in** when one has become successful. ✧ *vb* **shipping, shipped 4** to send or transport by any carrier, esp. a ship. **5** *Naut* to take in (water) over the side. **6** to bring or go aboard a vessel: *to ship oars.* **7** (often foll. by *off*) *Informal* to send away: *they were shipped off to foreign countries.* **8** to be hired to serve aboard a ship: *I shipped aboard a Liverpool liner.* ▷ **HISTORY** Old English *scip*

shipmate *n* a sailor who serves on the same ship as another.

shipment *n* **1** goods shipped together as part of the same lot: *a shipment of arms.* **2** the act of shipping cargo.

shipping *n* **1** the business of transporting freight, esp. by ship. **2** ships collectively: *all shipping should stay clear of the harbour.*

shipshape *adj* **1** neat or orderly. ✧ *adv* **2** in a neat and orderly manner.

shipwreck *n* **1** the destruction of a ship at sea. **2** the remains of a wrecked ship. **3** ruin or destruction: *the shipwreck of the old science.* ✧ *vb* **4** to wreck or destroy (a ship). **5** to bring to ruin or destruction.

shipyard *n* a place where ships are built and repaired.

shire *n* **1** *Brit* a county. **2** *Austral* a rural area with an elected council. **3 the Shires** the Midland counties of England. ▷ **HISTORY** Old English *scīr* office

shire horse *n* a large powerful breed of working horse.

shirk *vb* to avoid doing (work or a duty).
▷ **HISTORY** probably from German *Schurke* rogue
▶ **shirker** *n*

shirt *n* **1** an item of clothing worn on the upper part of the body, usually with a collar and sleeves and buttoning up the front. **2 keep your shirt on** *Informal* keep your temper. **3 put one's shirt on something** *Informal* to bet all one has on something. ▷ **HISTORY** Old English *scyrte*

shirty *adj* **shirtier, shirtiest** *Slang, chiefly Brit & NZ* bad-tempered or annoyed.

shish kebab *n* a dish of small pieces of meat and vegetables grilled on a skewer. ▷ **HISTORY** Turkish *şiş kebab*

shit *Taboo* ✧ *vb* **shitting, shitted, shit** *or* **shat 1** to defecate. ✧ *n* **2** faeces; excrement. **3** *Slang* rubbish; nonsense. **4** *Slang* a worthless person. ✧ *interj* **5** *Slang* an exclamation of anger or disgust. ▷ **HISTORY** Old English *scītan* to defecate ▶ **shitty** *adj*

shiver[1] *vb* **1** to tremble from cold or fear. ✧ *n* **2** a tremble caused by cold or fear. **3 the shivers** a fit of shivering through fear or illness. ▷ **HISTORY** Middle English *chiveren* ▶ **shivering** *n, adj* ▶ **shivery** *adj*

shiver[2] *vb* **1** to break into fragments. ✧ *n* **2** a splintered piece. ▷ **HISTORY** Germanic

shoal[1] *n* **1** a large group of fish swimming together. **2** a large group of people or things.
▷ **HISTORY** Old English *scolu*

shoal[2] *n* **1** a stretch of shallow water. **2** a sandbank or rocky area, esp. one that can be seen at low water. ✧ *vb* **3** to make or become shallow.
▷ **HISTORY** Old English *sceald* shallow

shock[1] *vb* **1** to cause (someone) to experience extreme horror, disgust, or astonishment: *the similarity shocked me.* **2** to cause a state of shock in (a person). ✧ *n* **3** a sudden and violent blow or impact. **4 a** a sudden and violent emotional disturbance. **b** something causing this. **5** *Pathol* a condition in which a person's blood cannot flow properly because of severe injury, burns, or fright. **6** pain and muscular spasm caused by an electric current passing through a person's body.
▷ **HISTORY** Old French *choc* ▶ **shocker** *n*

shock[2] *n* **1** a number of grain sheaves set on end in a field to dry. ✧ *vb* **2** to set up (sheaves) in shocks.
▷ **HISTORY** probably Germanic

shock[3] *n* a thick bushy mass of hair.
▷ **HISTORY** origin unknown

shock absorber *n* any device designed to absorb mechanical shock, esp. one fitted to a motor vehicle to reduce the effects of travelling over bumpy surfaces.

shocking *adj* **1** *Informal* very bad or terrible: *a shocking match at Leicester.* **2** causing dismay or disgust: *a shocking lack of concern.* **3 shocking pink** (of) a very bright shade of pink.

shock jock *n* a radio disc jockey who is deliberately controversial or provocative.

shock therapy *or* **treatment** *n* the treatment of certain mental conditions by passing an electric current through the patient's brain.

shod *vb* past tense and past participle of **shoe**.

shoddy *adj* **-dier, -diest 1** made or done badly or carelessly: *shoddy goods.* **2** of poor quality; shabby.
▷ **HISTORY** origin unknown ▶ **shoddily** *adv*
▶ **shoddiness** *n*

shoe *n* **1** one of a matching pair of coverings shaped to fit the foot, made of leather or other strong material and ending below the ankle.

2 anything resembling a shoe in shape, function, or position. **3** short for **horseshoe**. **4 be in a person's shoes** *Informal* to be in another person's situation. ✧ *vb* **shoeing, shod 5** to fit (a horse) with horseshoes. ▷ **HISTORY** Old English *scōh*

shoehorn *n* a smooth curved piece of metal or plastic inserted at the heel of a shoe to ease the foot into it.

shoelace *n* a cord for fastening shoes.

shoestring *n* **1** same as **shoelace**. **2** *Informal* a very small amount of money: *the theatre will be run on a shoestring.*

shoetree *n* a long piece of metal, plastic, or wood, put into a shoe or boot to keep its shape.

shogun (**show**-gun) *n History* **1** (in Japan from the 8th century A.D.) a chief military commander. **2** (in Japan from the late 12th to the late 19th century) any of a line of hereditary military dictators who relegated the emperors to a position of purely theoretical supremacy. ▷ **HISTORY** Japanese, from Chinese *chiang chün* general, from *chiang* to lead + *chün* army

shone *vb* a past of **shine**.

shonky *adj* **-kier, -kiest** *Austral & NZ informal* unreliable or unsound.

shoo *interj* **1** go away!: used to drive away unwanted or annoying animals or people. ✧ *vb* **shooing, shooed 2** to drive away by crying 'shoo'. ▷ **HISTORY** imitative

shook *vb* the past tense of **shake**.

shoot *vb* **shooting, shot 1** to hit, wound, or kill with a missile fired from a weapon. **2** to fire (a missile or missiles) from a weapon. **3** to fire (a weapon). **4** to hunt game with a gun for sport. **5** to send out or be sent out quickly and aggressively: *he shot questions at her.* **6** to move very rapidly: *the car shot forward.* **7** to go or pass quickly over or through: *he was trying to shoot the white water.* **8** to slide or push into or out of a fastening: *she shot the bolt quickly.* **9** (of a plant) to sprout (a new growth). **10** to photograph or film. **11** *Sport* to hit or kick the ball at goal. ✧ *n* **12** the act of shooting. **13** a new growth or sprout of a plant. **14** *Chiefly Brit* a meeting or party organized for hunting game with guns. **15** an area where game can be hunted with guns. **16** *Informal* a photographic assignment: *a fashion shoot in New York.* ▷ **HISTORY** Old English *sceōtan*

shooting star *n Informal* a meteor.

shooting stick *n* a walking stick with a spike at one end and a folding seat at the other.

shop *n* **1** a place for the sale of goods and services. **2** a place where a specified type of work is done; workshop: *a repair shop.* **3 all over the shop** *Informal* scattered everywhere: *his papers were all over the shop.* **4 shut up shop** to close business at the end of the day or permanently. **5 talk shop** *Informal* to discuss one's business or work on a social occasion. ✧ *vb* **shopping, shopped 6** (often foll. by *for*) to visit a shop or shops in order to buy (goods). **7** *Brit, Austral & NZ slang* to inform on (someone), esp. to the police. ▷ **HISTORY** Old English *sceoppa* stall ▶ **shopper** *n*

shop around *vb Informal* **1** to visit a number of shops or stores to compare goods and prices. **2** to consider a number of possibilities before making a choice.

shop assistant *n* a person who serves in a shop.

shop floor *n* **1** the production area of a factory. **2** workers, esp. factory workers, as opposed to management.

shopkeeper *n* a person who owns or manages a shop. ▶ **shopkeeping** *n*

shoplifter *n* a customer who steals goods from a shop. ▶ **shoplifting** *n*

shopping *n* **1** the act of going to shops and buying things. **2** things that have been bought in shops.

shopping centre *n* **1** a complex of stores, restaurants, and sometimes banks, usually under the same roof. **2** the area of a town where most of the shops are situated.

shopping mall *n* a large enclosed shopping centre.

shopping plaza *n Chiefly US, Canad & Austral* a shopping centre, usually a small group of stores built as a strip.

shop steward *n* a trade-union official elected by his or her fellow workers to be their representative in dealing with their employer.

shopwalker *n Brit* (esp. formerly) a person employed by a department store to assist sales personnel and help customers.

shore[1] *n* **1** the land along the edge of a sea, lake, or wide river. RELATED ADJECTIVE ▶ **littoral 2** land, as opposed to water: *150 yards from shore.* **3 shores** a country: *foreign shores.* ▷ **HISTORY** probably from Middle Low German, Middle Dutch *schōre*

shore[2] *n* **1** a prop placed under or against something as a support. ✧ *vb* **shoring, shored 2 shore up a** to prop up (an unsteady building or wall) with a strong support. **b** to strengthen or support (something weak): *lower interest rates to shore up the economy.* ▷ **HISTORY** Middle Dutch *schōre*

shoreline *n* the edge of a sea, lake, or wide river.

shorn *vb* a past participle of **shear**.

short *adj* **1** of little length; not long. **2** of little height; not tall. **3** not lasting long. **4** not enough: *the number of places laid at the table was short by four.* **5 short of** *or* **on** lacking in: *short of cash; short on detail.* **6** concise: *a short book.* **7** (of drinks) consisting chiefly of a spirit, such as whisky. **8** (of someone's memory) lacking the ability to retain a lot of facts. **9** (of a person's manner) abrupt and rather rude: *Kemp was short with her.* **10** (of betting odds) almost even. **11** *Finance* **a** not possessing at the time of sale the stocks or commodities one sells. **b** relating to such sales, which depend on falling prices for profit. **12** *Phonetics* (of a vowel) of relatively brief duration. **13** (of pastry) crumbly in texture. **14 in short supply** scarce. **15 short and sweet** brief and to the point. **16 short for** a shortened form of. ✧ *adv* **17** abruptly: *to stop short.* **18 be caught short** to have a sudden need to go to the toilet. **19 go short** not to have enough.

20 short of except: *they want nothing short of his removal from power.* ✧ *n* **21** a drink of spirits. **22** a short film shown before the main feature in a cinema. **23** same as **short circuit**. **24 for short** *Informal* as a shortened form: *cystic fibrosis, CF for short.* **25 in short** briefly. ✧ *vb* **26** to short-circuit. ✧ See also **shorts**. ▷ HISTORY Old English *sceort* ▶ **shortness** *n*

shortage *n* not enough of something needed.

shortbread *n* a rich crumbly biscuit made with butter.

shortcake *n* **1** shortbread. **2** a dessert made of layers of biscuit or cake filled with fruit and cream.

short-change *vb* **-changing, -changed 1** to give (someone) less than the correct change. **2** *Slang* to treat (someone), unfairly, esp. by giving less than is expected.

short circuit *n* **1** a faulty or accidental connection in an electric circuit, which deflects current through a path of low resistance, usually causing the failure of the circuit. ✧ *vb* **short-circuit 2** to develop a short circuit. **3** to bypass (a procedure): *she wrote to them direct and short-circuited the job agency.* **4** to hinder or frustrate (a plan).

shortcoming *n* a fault or weakness.

short cut *n* **1** a route that is shorter than the usual one. **2** a way of saving time or effort.

shorten *vb* to make or become short or shorter.

shortfall *n* **1** a failure to meet a requirement. **2** the amount of such a failure; deficit.

shorthand *n* a system of rapid writing using simple strokes and other symbols to represent words or phrases.

short-handed *adj* (of a company or organization) lacking enough staff to do the required work.

shorthand typist *n Brit & Austral* a person skilled in the use of shorthand and in typing.

shorthorn *n* a member of a breed of cattle with short horns.

short list *n* **1** Also called (Scot): **short leet** a list of suitable candidates for a job or prize, from which the successful candidate will be selected. ✧ *vb* **short-list 2** to put (someone) on a short list.

short-lived *adj* lasting only for a short time: *his authority was short-lived.*

shortly *adv* **1** in a short time; soon. **2** spoken in a cross and impatient manner.

shorts *pl n* **1** trousers reaching the top of the thigh or partway to the knee. **2** *Chiefly US & Canad* men's underpants.

short shrift *n* brief and unsympathetic treatment.

short-sighted *adj* **1** unable to see faraway things clearly. **2** not taking likely future developments into account: *a short-sighted approach to the problem.* ▶ **short-sightedness** *n*

short story *n Literature* a fictional narrative of shorter length than the novel.

short-tempered *adj* easily angered.

short-term *adj* of, for, or lasting a short time.

short-termism *n* the tendency to concentrate on short-term gains, often at the expense of long-term success.

short wave *n* a radio wave with a wavelength in the range 10–100 metres.

shot[1] *n* **1** the act or an instance of firing a gun or rifle. **2** *Sport* the act or an instance of hitting, kicking, or throwing the ball. **3** small round lead pellets used in shotguns. **4** a person with specified skill in shooting: *my father was quite a good shot.* **5** *Informal* an attempt: *a second shot at writing a better treaty.* **6** *Informal* a guess. **7 a** a single photograph. **b** an uninterrupted sequence of film taken by a single camera. **8** *Informal* an injection of a vaccine or narcotic drug. **9** *Informal* a drink of spirits. **10** the launching of a rocket or spacecraft to a specified destination: *a moon shot.* **11** *Sport* a heavy metal ball used in the shot put. **12 like a shot** without hesitating. **13 shot in the arm** *Informal* something that brings back energy or confidence. **14 shot in the dark** a wild guess. ▷ HISTORY Old English *scot*

shot[2] *vb* **1** the past of **shoot**. ✧ *adj* **2** (of textiles) woven to give a changing colour effect. **3** streaked with colour: *dark hair shot with streaks of grey.*

shotgun *n* a gun for firing a charge of shot at short range.

shot length *n Films, television* the time that a particular camera shot remains on view.

shot put *n* an athletic event in which contestants hurl a heavy metal ball called a shot as far as possible. ▶ **shot-putter** *n*

should *vb* the past tense of **shall:** used to indicate that an action is considered by the speaker to be obligatory (*you should go*) or to form the subjunctive mood (*I should like to see you; if I should die; should I be late, start without me*). ▷ HISTORY Old English *sceolde*

> **☑ WORD TIP**
> *Should* has, as its most common meaning in modern English, the sense *ought* as in *I should go to the graduation, but I don't see how I can.* However, the older sense of the subjunctive of *shall* is often used with *I* or *we* to indicate a more polite form than *would: I should like to go, but I can't.* In much speech and writing, *should* has been replaced by *would* in contexts of this kind, but it remains in formal English when a conditional subjunctive is used: *should he choose to remain, he would be granted asylum.*

shoulder *n* **1** the part of the body where the arm, wing, or foreleg joins the trunk. **2** a cut of meat including the upper part of the foreleg. **3** the part of an item of clothing that covers the shoulder. **4** the strip of unpaved land that borders a road. **5 a shoulder to cry on** a person one turns to for sympathy with one's troubles. **6 put one's shoulder to the wheel** *Informal* to work very hard. **7 rub shoulders with someone** *Informal* to mix with someone socially. **8 shoulder to shoulder a** side by side. **b** working together. ✧ *vb* **9** to accept (blame or responsibility). **10** to push with one's shoulder: *he shouldered his way through the crowd.*

A B C D E F G H I J K L M N O P Q R S T U V W X Y Z

11 to lift or carry on one's shoulders. **12 shoulder arms** *Mil* to bring one's rifle vertically close to one's right side. ▷ **HISTORY** Old English *sculdor*

shoulder blade *n* either of two large flat triangular bones one on each side of the back part of the shoulder.

shouldn't should not.

shout *n* **1** a loud call or cry. **2** *Informal* one's turn to buy a round of drinks. ✧ *vb* **3** to cry out loudly. **4** *Austral & NZ informal* to treat (someone) to (something, such as a drink). ▷ **HISTORY** probably from Old Norse *skūta* taunt

shout down *vb* to silence (someone) by talking loudly.

shove *vb* **shoving, shoved 1** to give a violent push to. **2** to push (one's way) roughly. **3** *Informal* to put (something) somewhere quickly and carelessly: *shove it into the boot.* ✧ *n* **4** a rough push. ▷ **HISTORY** Old English *scūfan*

shovel *n* **1** a tool for lifting or moving loose material, consisting of a broad blade attached to a large handle. **2** a machine or part of a machine resembling a shovel in function. ✧ *vb* **-elling, -elled** *or US* **-eling, -eled 3** to lift or move (loose material) with a shovel. **4** to put away large quantities of (something) quickly: *shovelling food into their mouths.* ▷ **HISTORY** Old English *scofl*

shove off *vb Informal* to go away; depart.

show *vb* **showing, showed; shown** *or* **showed 1** to make, be, or become visible or noticeable: *to show an interest; excitement showed on everyone's face.* **2** to present for inspection: *someone showed me the plans.* **3** to demonstrate or prove: *evidence showed that this was the most economical way.* **4** to instruct by demonstration: *she showed me how to feed the pullets.* **5** to indicate: *the device shows changes in the pressure.* **6** to behave towards (someone) in a particular way: *to show mercy.* **7** to exhibit or display (works of art): *three artists are showing at the gallery.* **8** to present (a film or play) or (of a film or play) to be presented. **9** to guide or escort: *he offered to show me around.* **10** *Informal* to arrive. ✧ *n* **11** a theatrical or other entertainment: *a magic show.* **12** a display or exhibition: *a show of paintings.* **13** something done to create an impression: *a show of indignation.* **14** vain and conspicuous display: *it was nothing but mere show.* **15** *Slang, chiefly Brit* a thing or affair: *jolly good show.* ✧ See also **show off, show up**. ▷ **HISTORY** Old English *scēawian*

show business *n* the entertainment industry. Also (informal): **show biz**

showcase *n* **1** a setting in which something is displayed to best advantage: *a showcase for young opera singers.* **2** a glass case used to display objects in a museum or shop.

showdown *n Informal* a major confrontation that settles a dispute.

shower *n* **1 a** a kind of bathing in which a person stands upright and is sprayed with water from a nozzle. **b** a device, room, or booth for such bathing. **2** a brief period of rain, hail, sleet, or snow. **3** a sudden fall of many small light objects: *a shower of loose gravel.* **4** *Brit slang* a worthless or contemptible group of people. **5** *US, Canad, Austral & NZ* a party held to honour and present gifts to a prospective bride or prospective mother. ✧ *vb* **6** to take a shower. **7** to sprinkle with or as if with a shower: *the walkers were showered by volcanic ash.* **8** to present (someone) with things liberally: *he showered her with presents.* ▷ **HISTORY** Old English *scūr* ▶ **showery** *adj*

showing *n* **1** a presentation, exhibition, or display. **2** manner of presentation.

showjumping *n* the sport of riding horses in competitions to demonstrate skill in jumping. ▶ **showjumper** *n*

showman *n, pl* **-men 1** a person skilled at presenting anything in an effective manner. **2** a person who presents or produces a show. ▶ **showmanship** *n*

shown *vb* a past participle of **show**.

show off *vb* **1** to exhibit or display (something) so as to invite admiration: *he was eager to show off his new car.* **2** *Informal* to flaunt skills, knowledge, or looks in order to attract attention or impress people. ✧ *n* **show-off 3** *Informal* a person who flaunts his or her skills, knowledge, or looks in order to attract attention or impress people.

showpiece *n* **1** anything displayed or exhibited. **2** something admired as a fine example of its type: *an orchestral showpiece.*

showroom *n* a room in which goods for sale, esp. cars or electrical or gas appliances, are on display.

show trial *n* a trial conducted primarily to make a particular impression on the public or on other nations.

show up *vb* **1** to reveal or be revealed clearly. **2** to expose the faults or defects of (someone or something) by comparison. **3** *Informal* to put (someone) to shame; embarrass. **4** *Informal* to arrive.

showy *adj* **showier, showiest 1** colourful, bright in appearance, and very noticeable, and perhaps rather vulgar: *showy jewellery.* **2** making an imposing display. ▶ **showily** *adv* ▶ **showiness** *n*

shrank *vb* a past tense of **shrink**.

shrapnel *n* **1** an artillery shell containing a number of small pellets or bullets which it is designed to scatter on explosion. **2** fragments from this type of shell.

> **WORD HISTORY**
> 'Shrapnel' is named after Henry *Shrapnel* (1761-1842), the English artillery officer who invented it.

shred *n* **1** a long narrow piece torn off something. **2** a very small amount: *not a shred of truth.* ✧ *vb* **shredding, shredded** *or* **shred 3** to tear into shreds. ▷ **HISTORY** Old English *scrēad* ▶ **shredder** *n*

shrew *n* **1** a small mouselike animal with a long snout. **2** a bad-tempered nagging woman. ▷ **HISTORY** Old English *scrēawa* ▶ **shrewish** *adj*

shrewd *adj* intelligent and making good judgments. ▷ **HISTORY** from *shrew* (obsolete verb) to curse, from *shrew* ▶ **shrewdly** *adv* ▶ **shrewdness** *n*

shriek *n* **1** a high-pitched scream. ✧ *vb* **2** to utter (words or sounds) in a high-pitched tone.
▷ **HISTORY** probably from Old Norse *skrækja* to screech

shrike *n* a bird with a heavy hooked bill, which kills small animals by dashing them on thorns.
▷ **HISTORY** Old English *scrīc* thrush

shrill *adj* **1** (of a sound) sharp and high-pitched. ✧ *vb* **2** to utter (words or sounds) in a shrill tone.
▷ **HISTORY** origin unknown ▶ **shrillness** *n* ▶ **shrilly** *adv*

shrimp *n* **1** a small edible shellfish with a long tail and a pair of pincers. **2** *Informal* a small person. ✧ *vb* **3** to fish for shrimps. ▷ **HISTORY** probably Germanic

shrine *n* **1** a place of worship associated with a sacred person or object. **2** a container for sacred relics. **3** the tomb of a saint or other holy person. **4** a place that is visited and honoured because of its association with a famous person or event: *he'd come to worship at the shrine of Mozart.*
▷ **HISTORY** Latin *scrinium* bookcase

shrink *vb* **shrinking, shrank** *or* **shrunk; shrunk** *or* **shrunken 1** to become or cause to become smaller, sometimes because of wetness, heat, or cold. **2 shrink from a** to withdraw or move away through fear: *they didn't shrink from danger.* **b** to feel great reluctance (to perform a task or duty). ✧ *n* **3** *Slang* a psychiatrist. ▷ **HISTORY** Old English *scrincan*

shrinkage *n* **1** the fact of shrinking. **2** the amount by which anything decreases in size, value, or weight.

shrink-wrap *vb* **-wrapping, -wrapped** to package (a product) in a flexible plastic wrapping which shrinks about its contours to seal it.

shrivel *vb* **-elling, -elled** *or US* **-eling, -eled** to become dry and withered. ▷ **HISTORY** probably Scandinavian

shroud *n* **1** a piece of cloth used to wrap a dead body. **2** anything that hides things: *a shroud of smoke.* ✧ *vb* **3** to hide or obscure (something): *shrouded in uncertainty; shrouded by smog.*
▷ **HISTORY** Old English *scrūd* garment

Shrove Tuesday *n* the day before Ash Wednesday. ▷ **HISTORY** Old English *scrīfan* to confess one's sins

shrub *n* a woody plant, smaller than a tree, with several stems instead of a trunk. ▷ **HISTORY** Old English *scrybb* ▶ **shrubby** *adj*

shrubbery *n, pl* **-beries 1** an area planted with shrubs. **2** shrubs collectively.

shrug *vb* **shrugging, shrugged 1** to draw up and drop (the shoulders) as a sign of indifference or doubt. ✧ *n* **2** the action of shrugging.
▷ **HISTORY** origin unknown

shrug off *vb* **1** to treat (a matter) as unimportant. **2** to get rid of (someone).

shrunk *vb* a past tense and past participle of **shrink**.

shrunken *vb* **1** a past participle of **shrink**. ✧ *adj* **2** reduced in size.

shudder *vb* **1** to shake or tremble suddenly and violently from horror or fear. **2** (of a machine) to shake violently. ✧ *n* **3** a shiver of fear or horror.
▷ **HISTORY** Middle Low German *schōderen*

shuffle *vb* **-fling, -fled 1** to walk or move (the feet) with a slow dragging motion. **2** to mix together in a jumbled mass: *the chairman shuffled his papers.* **3** to mix up (playing cards) so as to change their order. ✧ *n* **4** an instance of shuffling. **5** a rearrangement: *a shuffle of top management.* **6** a dance with short dragging movements of the feet.
▷ **HISTORY** probably from Low German *schüffeln*

shun *vb* **shunning, shunned** to avoid deliberately. ▷ **HISTORY** Old English *scunian*

shunt *vb* **1** to move (objects or people) to a different position. **2** *Railways* to transfer (engines or carriages) from track to track. ✧ *n* **3** the act of shunting. **4** a railway point. **5** *Electronics* a conductor connected in parallel across a part of a circuit to divert a known fraction of the current. **6** *Informal* a collision where one vehicle runs into the back of another. ▷ **HISTORY** perhaps from Middle English *shunen* to shun

shush *interj* **1** be quiet! hush! ✧ *vb* **2** to quiet (someone) by saying 'shush'. ▷ **HISTORY** imitative

shut *vb* **shutting, shut 1** to move (something) so as to cover an opening: *shut the door.* **2** to close (something) by bringing together the parts: *Ridley shut the folder.* **3 shut up** to close or lock the doors of: *let's shut up the shop.* **4 shut in** to confine or enclose. **5 shut out** to prevent from entering. **6** (of a shop or other establishment) to stop operating for the day: *the late-night rush after the pubs shut.* ✧ *adj* **7** closed or fastened. ✧ See also **shutdown**.
▷ **HISTORY** Old English *scyttan*

shutdown *n* **1** the closing of a factory, shop, or other business. ✧ *vb* **shut down 2** to discontinue operations permanently.

shuteye *n Slang* sleep.

shutter *n* **1** a hinged doorlike cover, usually one of a pair, for closing off a window. **2 put up the shutters** to close business at the end of the day or permanently. **3** *Photog* a device in a camera that opens to allow light through the lens so as to expose the film when a photograph is taken. ✧ *vb* **4** to close or equip with a shutter or shutters.

shuttle *n* **1** a bus, train, or aircraft that makes frequent journeys between two places which are fairly near to each other. **2** a bobbin-like device used in weaving to pass the weft thread between the warp threads. **3** a small bobbin-like device used to hold the thread in a sewing machine. ✧ *vb* **-tling, -tled 4** to travel back and forth. ▷ **HISTORY** Old English *scytel* dart, arrow

shuttlecock *n* a rounded piece of cork or plastic with feathers stuck in one end, struck to and fro in badminton.

shut up *vb* **1** *Informal* to stop talking or cause (someone) to stop talking: often used in commands. **2** to confine or imprison (someone).

shy[1] *adj* **1** not at ease in the company of others. **2** easily frightened; timid. **3 shy of** cautious or wary of. **4** reluctant or unwilling: *camera-shy; workshy.* ✧ *vb* **shies, shying, shied 5** to move back or aside suddenly from fear: *with a terrified whinny the horse shied.* **6 shy away from** to draw back from (doing something), through lack of confidence. ✧ *n, pl* **shies 7** a sudden movement back or aside from fear. ▷ **HISTORY** Old English *scēoh* ▶ **shyly** *adv* ▶ **shyness** *n*

shy[2] *vb* **shies, shying, shied 1** to throw (something). ✧ *n, pl* **shies 2** a quick throw. ▷ **HISTORY** Germanic

Shylock *n* an unsympathetic and demanding person to whom one owes money. ▷ **HISTORY** after the heartless usurer in Shakespeare's *The Merchant of Venice*

si *n Music* same as **te**.

Si *Chem* silicon.

SI See **SI unit**.

Siamese *n, pl* **-mese 1** same as **Siamese cat**. ✧ *adj, n, pl* **-mese 2** (formerly) same as **Thai**.

Siamese cat *n* a breed of cat with cream fur, dark ears and face, and blue eyes.

Siamese twins *pl n* twins born joined together at some part of the body. Technical name: **conjoined twins**

sibilant *adj* **1** having a hissing sound. ✧ *n* **2** *Phonetics* a consonant, such as *s* or *z*, that is pronounced with a hissing sound. ▷ **HISTORY** Latin *sibilare* to hiss

sibling *n* a brother or sister. ▷ **HISTORY** Old English: a relative

sibyl *n* (in ancient Greece and Rome) a prophetess. ▷ **HISTORY** Greek *Sibulla* ▶ **sibylline** *adj*

sic[1] *adv* thus: inserted in brackets in a text to indicate that an odd spelling or reading is in fact what was written, even though it is or appears to be wrong. ▷ **HISTORY** Latin

sic[2] *vb* **sicking, sicked 1** to attack: used only in commands to a dog. **2** to urge (a dog) to attack (someone). ▷ **HISTORY** dialect variant of *seek*

sick *adj* **1** vomiting or likely to vomit. **2** physically or mentally unwell. **3** of or for ill people: *sick pay.* **4** deeply affected with mental or spiritual distress: *sick at heart.* **5** mentally disturbed. **6** *Informal* making fun of death, illness, or misfortune: *a sick joke.* **7 sick of** *or* **sick and tired of** *Informal* disgusted by or weary of: *I'm sick of this town.* ✧ *n, vb* **8** *Informal* same as **vomit**. ▷ **HISTORY** Old English *sēoc*

sickbay *n* a room for the treatment of sick people, for example on a ship.

sicken *vb* **1** to make (someone) feel nauseated or disgusted. **2 sicken for** to show symptoms of (an illness).

sickle *n* a tool for cutting grass and grain crops, with a curved blade and a short handle. ▷ **HISTORY** Old English *sicol*

sickly *adj* **-lier, -liest 1** weak and unhealthy. **2** (of a person) looking pale and unwell: *sickly pallor.* **3** unpleasant to smell, taste, or look at. **4** showing excessive emotion in a weak and rather pathetic way: *a sickly tune.* ✧ *adv* **5** suggesting sickness: *sickly pale.* ▶ **sickliness** *n*

sickness *n* **1** a particular illness or disease: *sleeping sickness.* **2** the state of being ill or unhealthy: *absent from work due to sickness.* **3** a feeling of queasiness in the stomach followed by vomiting.

side *n* **1** a line or surface that borders anything. **2** *Geom* a line forming part of the perimeter of a plane figure: *a square has four sides.* **3** either of two parts into which an object, surface, or area can be divided: *the right side and the left side.* **4** either of the two surfaces of a flat object: *write on both sides of the page.* **5** the sloping part of a hill or bank. **6** either the left or the right half of the body, esp. the area around the waist: *he took a nine millimetre bullet in the side.* **7** the area immediately next to a person or thing: *at the side of my bed.* **8** a place within an area identified by reference to a central point: *the south side of the island.* **9** the area at the edge of something, as opposed to the centre: *the far side of the square.* **10** aspect or part: *there is a positive side to truancy.* **11** one of two or more contesting groups or teams: *the two sides will meet in the final.* **12** a position held in opposition to another in a dispute. **13** a line of descent through one parent: *a relative on his father's side.* **14** *Informal* a television channel. **15** *Brit slang* conceit or cheek: *to put on side.* **16 on one side** apart from the rest. **17 on the side** in addition to a person's main work: *she did a little public speaking on the side.* **18 side by side** close together. **19 side by side with** beside or near to. **20 take sides** to support one party in a dispute against another. ✧ *adj* **21** situated at the side: *the side entrance.* **22** less important: *a side issue.* ✧ *vb* **siding, sided 23 side with** to support (one party in a dispute). ▷ **HISTORY** Old English *sīde*

sideboard *n* a piece of furniture for a dining room, with drawers, cupboards, and shelves to hold tableware.

sideboards *or esp US & Canad* **sideburns** *pl n* a man's whiskers grown down either side of the face in front of the ears.

sidecar *n* a small passenger car attached to the side of a motorcycle.

side effect *n* **1** a usually unwanted effect caused by a drug in addition to its intended one. **2** any additional effect, usually an undesirable one: *the unforeseen side effects of the end of the Cold War.*

sidekick *n Informal* a close friend or associate.

sidelight *n* **1** *Brit* either of two small lights at the front of a motor vehicle. **2** either of the two navigational lights used by ships at night.

sideline *n* an extra job in addition to one's main job.

sidelines *pl n* **1** *Sport* **a** the lines that mark the side boundaries of a playing area. **b** the area just outside the playing area, where substitute players sit. **2 on the sidelines a** only passively involved: *on the sidelines of the modern world.* **b** waiting to join in an activity.

sidelong *adj* **1** directed to the side; oblique. ✧ *adv* **2** from the side; obliquely.

sidereal (side-**eer**-ee-al) *adj* of or determined with reference to the stars: *the sidereal time.* ▷ **HISTORY** Latin *sidus* a star

side-saddle *n* **1** a riding saddle originally designed for women in skirts, allowing the rider to sit with both legs on the same side of the horse. ✧ *adv* **2** on a side-saddle.

sideshow *n* **1** an event or incident considered less important than another: *a mere sideshow compared to the war on the Russian front.* **2** a small show or entertainment offered along with the main show at a circus or fair.

sidestep *vb* **-stepping, -stepped 1** to step out of the way of (something). **2** to dodge (an issue). ✧ *n* **side step 3** a movement to one side, such as in dancing or boxing.

sidetrack *vb* to distract (someone) from a main subject.

sidewalk *n US & Canad* a raised space alongside a road, for pedestrians.

sideways *adv* **1** moving, facing, or inclining towards one side. **2** from one side; obliquely. **3** with one side forward. ✧ *adj* **4** moving or directed to or from one side.

siding *n* a short stretch of railway track connected to a main line, used for loading and unloading freight and storing engines and carriages.

sidle *vb* **-dling, -dled** to walk slowly and carefully, not wanting to be noticed. ▷ **HISTORY** obsolete *sideling* sideways

SIDS sudden infant death syndrome; cot death.

siege *n* **1** a military operation carried out to capture a place by surrounding and blockading it. **2** a similar operation carried out by police, for example to force people out of a place. **3 lay siege to** to subject (a place) to a siege. ▷ **HISTORY** Old French *sege* a seat

Siegfried line (**seeg**-freed) *n History* the line of fortifications built by Germany prior to and during World War II opposite the Maginot line in France.

siemens *n, pl* **siemens** the SI unit of electrical conductance. ▷ **HISTORY** after E. W. von *Siemens*, engineer

sienna *n* **1** a natural earth used as a reddish-brown or yellowish-brown pigment. ✧ *adj* **2 burnt sienna** reddish-brown. **3 raw sienna** yellowish-brown. ▷ **HISTORY** after *Siena*, Italian city

sierra *n* a range of mountains with jagged peaks in Spain or America. ▷ **HISTORY** Spanish, literally: saw

sies (**siss**) *interj S African informal* same as **sis**[2].

siesta *n* an afternoon nap, taken in hot countries. ▷ **HISTORY** Spanish

sieve (**siv**) *n* **1** a utensil with a mesh through which a substance is sifted or strained. ✧ *vb* **sieving, sieved 2** to sift or strain through a sieve. ▷ **HISTORY** Old English *sife*

sift *vb* **1** to sieve (a powdery substance) in order to remove the coarser particles. **2** to examine (information or evidence) carefully to select what is important. ▷ **HISTORY** Old English *siftan*

sigh *vb* **1** to draw in and audibly let out a deep breath as an expression of sadness, tiredness, longing, or relief. **2** to make a sound resembling this. **3 sigh for** to long for. **4** to say (something) with a sigh. ✧ *n* **5** the act or sound of sighing. ▷ **HISTORY** Old English *sīcan*

sight *n* **1** the ability to see; vision. RELATED ADJECTIVE ▸ **visual 2** an instance of seeing. **3** the range of vision: *the cemetery was out of sight.* **4** anything that is seen. **5** point of view; judgment: *nothing has changed in my sight.* **6** *Informal* anything unpleasant to see: *she looked a sight in the streetlamps.* **7** a device for guiding the eye in aiming a gun or making an observation with an optical instrument. **8** an aim or observation made with such a device. **9 sights** anything worth seeing: *the great sights of Barcelona.* **10 a sight** *Informal* a great deal: *it's a sight warmer than in the hall.* **11 a sight for sore eyes** a welcome sight. **12 catch sight of** to glimpse. **13 know someone by sight** to be able to recognize someone without having ever been introduced. **14 lose sight of a** to be unable to see (something) any longer. **b** to forget: *we lose sight of priorities.* **15 on sight** as soon as someone or something is seen. **16 set one's sights on** to have (a specified goal) in mind. **17 sight unseen** without having seen the object concerned: *he would have taken it sight unseen.* ✧ *vb* **18** to see (someone or something) briefly or suddenly: *the two suspicious vessels were sighted.* **19** to aim (a firearm) using the sight. ▷ **HISTORY** Old English *sihth*

sighted *adj* not blind.

sightless *adj* blind.

sight-read *vb* **-reading, -read** to sing or play (music in a printed form) without previous preparation. ▶ **sight-reading** *n*

sightscreen *n Cricket* a large white screen placed near the boundary behind the bowler, which helps the batsman see the ball.

sightseeing *n Informal* visiting famous or interesting sights in a place. ▶ **sightseer** *n*

sigma *n* **1** the 18th letter in the Greek alphabet (Σ, σ). **2** *Maths* the symbol Σ, indicating summation.

sign *n* **1** something that indicates a fact or condition that is not immediately or outwardly observable: *a sign of tension.* **2** a gesture, mark, or symbol intended to convey an idea or information. **3** a board or placard displayed in public and intended to advertise, inform, or warn. **4** a conventional mark or symbol that has a specific meaning, for example £ for pounds. **5** *Maths* **a** any symbol used to indicate an operation: *a minus sign.* **b** a symbol used to indicate whether a number or expression is positive or negative. **6** a visible indication: *no sign of the enemy.* **7** an omen. **8** *Med* any evidence of the presence of a disease or disorder. **9** *Astrol* short for **sign of the zodiac**. ✧ *vb* **10** to write (one's name) on (a document or letter) to show its authenticity or one's agreement. **11** to communicate using sign language. **12** to make a sign to someone so as to convey an idea or information. **13** to engage or be engaged by signing a contract: *he signed for another team.* ▷ **HISTORY** Latin *signum*

signal *n* **1** any sign, gesture, sound, or action used to communicate information. **2** anything that causes immediate action: *this is the signal for a detailed examination of the risk.* **3 a** a variable voltage, current, or electromagnetic wave, by which information is conveyed through an electronic circuit. **b** the information so conveyed.

✧ *adj* **4** *Formal* very important: *a signal triumph for the government.* ✧ *vb* **-nalling, -nalled** *or US* **-naling, -naled 5** to communicate (information) by signal. ▷ **HISTORY** Latin *signum* sign ▶ **signally** *adv*

signal box *n* a building from which railway signals are operated.

signalman *n, pl* **-men** a railwayman in charge of the signals and points within a section.

signatory (**sig**-na-tree) *n, pl* **-ries 1** a person, organization, or state that has signed a document such as a treaty. ✧ *adj* **2** having signed a document or treaty.

signature *n* **1** a person's name written by himself or herself, used in signing something. **2** a distinctive characteristic that identifies a person or animal. **3** *Music* a sign at the beginning of a piece to show key or time. **4** *Printing* a sheet of paper printed with several pages, which when folded becomes a section of a book. ▷ **HISTORY** Latin *signare* to sign

signature tune *n* a piece of music used to introduce a particular television or radio programme.

signboard *n* a board carrying a sign or notice, often to advertise a business or product.

signet *n* a small seal used to make documents official. ▷ **HISTORY** Medieval Latin *signetum*

signet ring *n* a finger ring engraved with an initial or other emblem.

significance *n* **1** the effect something is likely to have on other things: *an event of important significance in British history.* **2** meaning: *the occult significance of the symbol.*

significant *adj* **1** very important. **2** having or expressing a meaning. ▶ **significantly** *adv*

significant figures *pl n Maths* **1** the figures of a number that express a magnitude to a specified degree of accuracy: *3.141 59 to four significant figures is 3.142.* **2** the number of such figures: *3.142 has four significant figures.*

signify *vb* **-fies, -fying, -fied 1** to indicate or suggest. **2** to stand as a symbol or sign for: *a blue line on the map signified a river.* **3** to be important. ▷ **HISTORY** Latin *signum* a mark + *facere* to make

signing *n* a system of communication using hand and arm movements, such as one used by deaf people. Also called: **sign language**

sign off *vb* to announce the end of a radio or television programme.

sign of the zodiac *n Astrol* any of the 12 areas into which the zodiac is divided.

sign on *vb* **1** *Brit & Austral* to register and report regularly at an unemployment-benefit office. **2** to commit oneself to a job or activity by signing a form or contract.

signor (see-**nyor**) *n* an Italian form of address equivalent to *sir* or *Mr.*

signora (see-**nyor**-a) *n* an Italian form of address equivalent to *madam* or *Mrs.*

signorina (see-nyor-**ee**-na) *n* an Italian form of address equivalent to *madam* or *Miss.*

signpost *n* **1** a road sign displaying information, such as the distance to the next town. **2** an indication as to how an event is likely to develop or advice on what course of action should be taken. ✧ *vb* **3** to mark (the way) with signposts.

Sikh (**seek**) *n* **1** a member of an Indian religion that teaches that there is only one God. ✧ *adj* **2** of the Sikhs or their religious beliefs or customs. ▷ **HISTORY** Hindi: disciple ▶ **Sikhism** *n*

silage (**sile**-ij) *n* a fodder crop harvested while green and partially fermented in a silo.

silence *n* **1** the state or quality of being silent. **2** the absence of sound. **3** refusal or failure to speak or communicate when expected: *he's broken his silence on the issue.* ✧ *vb* **-lencing, -lenced 4** to cause (someone or something) to become silent. **5** to put a stop to: *a way of silencing criticism.*

silencer *n* any device designed to reduce noise, for example one fitted to the exhaust system of a motor vehicle or one fitted to the muzzle of a gun.

silent *adj* **1** tending to speak very little. **2** failing to speak or communicate when expected: *they remained silent as minutes passed.* **3** producing no noise: *the silent room.* **4** not spoken: *silent reproach.* **5** (of a letter) used in the spelling of a word but not pronounced, such as the *k* in *know*. **6** (of a film) having no soundtrack. ▷ **HISTORY** Latin *silere* to be quiet ▶ **silently** *adv*

silent partner *n Business Chiefly US & Canad* same as **sleeping partner**.

silhouette *n* **1** the outline of a dark shape seen against a light background. **2** an outline drawing, often a profile portrait, filled in with black. ✧ *vb* **-etting, -etted 3** to show (something) in silhouette. ▷ **HISTORY** after E. de *Silhouette,* politician

silica *n* a hard glossy mineral, silicon dioxide, which occurs naturally as quartz and is used in the manufacture of glass. ▷ **HISTORY** Latin *silex* hard stone

silicate *n Mineral* a compound of silicon, oxygen, and a metal.

silicon *n* **1** *Chem* a brittle non-metallic element: used in transistors, solar cells, and alloys. Symbol: Si. ✧ *adj* **2** denoting an area of a country that contains much high-technology industry: *the Silicon Glen.* ▷ **HISTORY** from *silica*

silicon chip *n* same as **chip** (sense 3).

silicone *n Chem* a tough synthetic material made from silicon and used in lubricants, paints, and resins.

silicosis *n Pathol* a lung disease caused by breathing in silica dust.

silk *n* **1** the fine soft fibre produced by a silkworm. **2** thread or fabric made from this fibre. **3 silks** clothing made of this. **4** *Brit* **a** the gown worn by a Queen's (or King's) Counsel. **b** *Informal* a Queen's (or King's) Counsel. **c take silk** to become a Queen's (or King's) Counsel. ▷ **HISTORY** Old English *sioloc*

silken *adj* **1** made of silk. **2** *Literary* smooth and soft: *her silken hair.*

silkworm *n* a caterpillar that spins a cocoon of silk.

silky *adj* **silkier, silkiest 1** soft, smooth, and shiny. **2** (of a voice or manner) smooth and elegant. ▶ **silkiness** *n*

sill *n* **1** a shelf at the bottom of a window, either inside or outside a room. **2** the lower horizontal part of a window or door frame. ▷ **HISTORY** Old English *syll*

silly *adj* **-lier, -liest 1** behaving in a foolish or childish way. **2** *Old-fashioned* unable to think sensibly, as if from a blow. **3** *Cricket* (of a fielding position) near the batsman's wicket: *silly mid-off.* ✧ *n, pl* **-lies 4** *Informal* a foolish person. ▷ **HISTORY** Old English *sælig* (unattested) happy ▶ **silliness** *n*

silo *n, pl* **-los 1** an airtight pit or tower in which silage or grain is made and stored. **2** an underground structure in which missile systems are sited for protection. ▷ **HISTORY** Spanish

silt *n* **1** a fine sediment of mud or clay deposited by moving water. ✧ *vb* **2 silt up** to fill or choke up with silt: *the channels have been silted up.* ▷ **HISTORY** probably Old Norse

Silurian (sile-**yoor**-ee-an) *adj Geol* of the period of geological time about 425 million years ago, during which fishes first appeared. ▷ **HISTORY** after *Silures,* a Welsh tribe who opposed the Romans

silvan *adj* same as **sylvan**.

silver *n* **1** a precious greyish-white metallic element: used in jewellery, tableware, and coins. Symbol: Ag. **2** a coin or coins made of silver. **3** any household articles made of silver. **4** short for **silver medal**. ✧ *adj* **5** greyish-white: *silver hair.* **6** (of anniversaries) the 25th in a series: *Silver Jubilee; silver wedding.* ✧ *vb* **7** to coat with silver or a silvery substance: *a company that silvers their own mirrors.* **8** to cause (something) to become silvery in colour: *the sun silvered the tarmac.* ▷ **HISTORY** Old English *siolfor*

silverbeet *n Austral & NZ* a beet of Australia and New Zealand with edible spinach-like leaves.

silver birch *n* a tree with silvery-white peeling bark.

silverfish *n, pl* **-fish** *or* **-fishes 1** a small wingless silver-coloured insect. **2** a silver-coloured fish.

silver medal *n* a medal of silver awarded to a competitor who comes second in a contest or race.

silver plate *n* **1** a thin layer of silver deposited on a base metal. **2** articles, such as tableware, made of silver plate. ▶ **silver-plate** *vb*

silver screen *n Informal* films collectively or the film industry.

silverside *n* a cut of beef from below the rump and above the leg.

silversmith *n* a craftsman who makes or repairs items made of silver.

silver thaw *n Canad* **1** a freezing rainstorm. **2** same as **glitter** (sense 7).

silvery *adj* **1** having the appearance or colour of silver: *her silvery eyes.* **2** having a clear ringing sound: *a cascade of silvery notes.*

silviculture *n* the cultivation of forest trees. ▷ **HISTORY** Latin *silva* woodland + CULTURE

sim *n* a computer game that simulates an activity such as flying or playing a sport.

simian *adj* **1** of or resembling a monkey or ape. ✧ *n* **2** a monkey or ape. ▷ **HISTORY** Latin *simia* an ape

similar *adj* **1** alike but not identical. **2** *Geom* (of two or more figures) different in size or position, but with exactly the same shape. ▷ **HISTORY** Latin *similis* ▶ **similarity** *n* ▶ **similarly** *adv*

> ☑ **WORD TIP**
> *As* should not be used after *similar: Wilson held a similar position to Jones* (not *a similar position as Jones*); *the system is similar to the one in France* (not *similar as in France*).

simile (**sim**-ill-ee) *n* a figure of speech that likens one thing to another of a different category, introduced by *as* or *like*. ▷ **HISTORY** Latin: something similar

similitude *n Formal* likeness; similarity.

simmer *vb* **1** to cook (food) gently at just below boiling point. **2** (of violence or conflict) to threaten to break out: *revolt simmering among rural MPs.* ✧ *n* **3** the state of simmering. ▷ **HISTORY** perhaps imitative

simmer down *vb Informal* to calm down after being angry.

simnel cake *n Brit* a fruit cake with marzipan, traditionally eaten during Lent or at Easter. ▷ **HISTORY** Latin *simila* fine flour

simony (**sime**-on-ee) *n Christianity* the practice of buying or selling Church benefits such as pardons. ▷ **HISTORY** after *Simon Magus,* a biblical sorcerer who tried to buy magical powers

simoom *n* a hot suffocating sand-laden desert wind. ▷ **HISTORY** Arabic *samūm* poisonous

simper *vb* **1** to smile in a silly and mannered way. **2** to say (something) with a simper. ✧ *n* **3** a simpering smile. ▷ **HISTORY** origin unknown ▶ **simpering** *adj*

simple *adj* **1** easy to understand or do: *in simple English; simple exercises.* **2** plain and not elaborate: *a simple red skirt; a simple answer.* **3** not combined or complex: *simple diagnostic equipment.* **4** leading an uncomplicated life: *I am a simple man myself.* **5** sincere or frank: *a simple apology.* **6** of humble background: *the simple country girl.* **7** *Informal* mentally retarded. **8** straightforward: *a simple matter of choice.* **9** *Music* denoting a time where the number of beats per bar may be two, three, or four. ▷ **HISTORY** Latin *simplex* plain ▶ **simplicity** *n*

simple fraction *n Maths* a fraction in which the numerator and denominator are both whole numbers.

simple fracture *n* a fracture in which the broken bone does not pierce the skin.

simple interest *n Finance* interest paid only on the original amount of a debt.

simple-minded *adj* **1** (of people) naive and unsophisticated. **2** (of opinions or explanations) not taking the complexity of an issue or subject into account. ▶ **simple-mindedness** *n*

A B C D E F G H I J K L M N O P Q R S T U V W X Y Z

simple sentence *n Grammar* a sentence consisting of a single main clause.

simpleton *n* a foolish or stupid person.

simplify *vb* **-fies, -fying, -fied 1** to make (something) less complicated. **2** *Maths* to reduce (an equation or fraction) to its simplest form. ▷ **HISTORY** Latin *simplus* simple + *facere* to make ▶ **simplification** *n*

simplistic *adj* (of an opinion or interpretation) too simple or naive.

> ☑ **WORD TIP**
> Since *simplistic* already has *too* as part of its meaning, it is tautologous to talk about something being *too simplistic* or *over-simplistic*.

simply *adv* **1** in a simple manner: *an interesting book, simply written.* **2** merely; just: *he's simply too slow.* **3** absolutely: *a simply enormous success.*

simulate *vb* **-lating, -lated 1** to pretend to feel or perform (an emotion or action); imitate: *I tried to simulate anger.* **2** to imitate the conditions of (a situation), as in carrying out an experiment: *we can then simulate global warming.* **3** to have the appearance of: *the wood had been painted to simulate stone.* ▷ **HISTORY** Latin *simulare* to copy ▶ **simulated** *adj* ▶ **simulation** *n*

simulator *n* a device that simulates specific conditions for the purposes of research or training: *a flight simulator.*

simultaneous *adj* occurring or existing at the same time. ▷ **HISTORY** Latin *simul* at the same time ▶ **simultaneously** *adv* ▶ **simultaneity** *n*

simultaneous equations *pl n Maths* a set of equations that are all satisfied by the same values of the variables, the number of variables being equal to the number of equations.

sin[1] *n* **1** the breaking of a religious or moral law. **2** any offence against a principle or standard. **3 live in sin** *Old-fashioned, informal* (of an unmarried couple) to live together. ✧ *vb* **sinning, sinned 4** to commit a sin. ▷ **HISTORY** Old English *synn* ▶ **sinner** *n*

sin[2] *Maths* sine.

sin bin *n Slang* (in ice hockey etc.) the area in which players must sit for a specified period after committing a serious foul.

since *prep* **1** during the period of time after: *one of their worst winters since 1945.* ✧ *conj* **2** continuously from the time given: *they've been standing in line ever since she arrived.* **3** for the reason that; because. ✧ *adv* **4** from that time: *I have often been asked since.* ▷ **HISTORY** Old English *siththan*

> ☑ **WORD TIP**
> See at **ago.**

sincere *adj* genuine and honest: *sincere concern.* ▷ **HISTORY** Latin *sincerus* ▶ **sincerely** *adv* ▶ **sincerity** *n*

sine *n* (in trigonometry) the ratio of the length of the opposite side to that of the hypotenuse in a right-angled triangle. ▷ **HISTORY** Latin *sinus* a bend

sinecure (**sin**-ee-cure) *n* a paid job that involves very little work or responsibility. ▷ **HISTORY** Latin *sine* without + *cura* care

sine die (**sin**-ay **dee**-ay) *adv* without fixing a day for future action or meeting. ▷ **HISTORY** Latin, literally: without a day

sine qua non (**sin**-ay kwah **non**) *n* an essential requirement. ▷ **HISTORY** Latin, literally: without which not

sinew *n* **1** *Anat* a tough fibrous cord connecting muscle to bone. **2** *Literary* physical strength. ▷ **HISTORY** Old English *sinu, seonu*

sinewy *adj* lean and muscular.

sinful *adj* **1** having committed or tending to commit sin: *I am a sinful man.* **2** being a sin; wicked: *sinful acts.*

sing *vb* **singing, sang, sung 1** to produce musical sounds with the voice. **2** to perform (a song). **3** (of certain birds and insects) to make musical calls. **4 sing of** to tell a story in song about: *the minstrels sang of courtly love.* **5** to make a humming, ringing, or whistling sound: *the arrow sang past his ear.* **6** (of one's ears) to be filled with a continuous ringing sound. **7** to bring (someone) to a given state by singing: *I sang him to sleep.* **8** *Slang, chiefly US* to act as an informer. ▷ **HISTORY** Old English *singan* ▶ **singer** *n* ▶ **singing** *adj, n*

> ☑ **WORD TIP**
> See at **ring**[1].

singe *vb* **singeing, singed 1** to burn slightly without setting alight; scorch: *it singed his sheepskin.* ✧ *n* **2** a slight burn. ▷ **HISTORY** Old English *sengan*

Singhalese *n, pl* **-lese**, *adj* same as **Sinhalese**.

singing telegram *n* **1** a service by which a person is employed to present greetings to someone on a special occasion by singing. **2** the greetings presented in this way. **3** the person who presents the greetings.

single *adj* **1** existing alone; solitary: *the cottage's single chimney.* **2** distinct from others of the same kind: *every single housing society.* **3** designed for one user: *a single room.* **4** unmarried. **5** even one: *there was not a single bathroom.* **6** (of a flower) having only one circle of petals. **7 single combat** a duel or fight involving two individuals. ✧ *n* **8** a hotel bedroom for one person. **9** a gramophone record, CD, or cassette with a short recording of music on it. **10** *Cricket* a hit from which one run is scored. **11 a** *Brit* a pound note or coin. **b** *US & Canad* a dollar bill. **12** a ticket valid for a one-way journey only. ✧ *vb* **-gling, -gled 13 single out** to select from a group of people or things: *the judge had singled him out for praise.* ✧ See also **singles**. ▷ **HISTORY** Old French *sengle*

single-breasted *adj* (of a jacket or coat) having the fronts overlapping only slightly and with one row of buttons.

single-decker *n Brit informal* a bus with only one passenger deck.

single entry *n* a book-keeping system in which all transactions are entered in one account only.

single file *n* a line of people, one behind the other.

single-handed *adj, adv* unaided or working alone: *the first single-handed sail in my boat; she had to take on the world single-handed.*
▶ **single-handedly** *adv*

single-minded *adj* having one purpose or aim only; dedicated. ▶ **single-mindedly** *adv*
▶ **single-mindedness** *n*

single-parent family *n* a family consisting of one parent and his or her child or children living together, the other parent being dead or permanently absent.

singles *pl n Sport* a match played with one person on each side.

singles bar *n* a bar that is a social meeting place for single people.

singlet *n Brit & NZ* a man's sleeveless vest.

singleton *n Cards* the only card of a particular suit held by a player.

singly *adv* one at a time; one by one.

singsong *n* **1** *Brit & NZ* an informal group singing session. ✧ *adj* **2** (of a voice) having a repetitive rise and fall in tone.

singular *adj* **1** *Grammar* (of a word or form) denoting only one person or thing: *a singular noun.* **2** remarkable; extraordinary: *one of the singular achievements.* **3** unusual; odd: *a lovable but very singular old woman.* ✧ *n* **4** *Grammar* the singular form of a word. ▷ **HISTORY** Latin *singularis* single
▶ **singularity** *n* ▶ **singularly** *adv*

Sinhalese *or* **Singhalese** *n* **1** (*pl* **-lese**) a member of a people living mainly in Sri Lanka. **2** the language of this people. ✧ *adj* **3** of this people.
✧ See also **Sri Lankan**.

sinister *adj* **1** threatening or suggesting evil or harm: *a sinister conspiracy.* **2** *Heraldry* of, on, or starting from the bearer's left side.

> **WORD HISTORY**
> In Latin *sinister* means 'left' or 'on the left-hand side'. The word came to have its 'sinister' meaning because the left side was considered unlucky.

sink *vb* **sinking, sank, sunk** *or* **sunken 1** to submerge (in liquid). **2** to cause (a ship) to submerge by attacking it with bombs, torpedoes, etc. **3** to appear to descend towards or below the horizon. **4** to make or become lower in amount or value: *sterling sank to a record low against the Deutschmark.* **5** to move or fall into a lower position, esp. due to tiredness or weakness: *she sank back in her chair.* **6 sink into** to pass into a lower state or condition, esp. an unpleasant one: *to sink into debt.* **7** (of a voice) to become quieter. **8** to become weaker in health. **9** to dig (something sharp) into a solid object: *she sank her teeth into the steak.* **10** *Informal* to drink (a number of alcoholic drinks). **11** to dig, drill, or excavate (a hole or shaft). **12** to drive (a stake) into the ground. **13 sink in** *or* **into** to invest (money) in (a venture). **14** *Golf, snooker* to hit (the ball) into the hole or pocket: *he finally sank the shot for a bogey.* ✧ *n* **15** a fixed basin in a kitchen or bathroom, with a water supply and drainpipe. ✧ *adj* **16** *Informal* (of a housing estate or school) deprived or having low standards of achievement. ▷ **HISTORY** Old English *sincan*

sinker *n* a weight attached to a fishing line or net to cause it to sink in water.

sinkhole *n Geol* Also called (esp. Brit): **swallow hole** a depression in the ground surface, esp. in limestone, where a surface stream disappears underground.

sink in *vb* (of a fact) to become fully understood: *the euphoria started to wear off as the implications of it all sank in.*

sinking fund *n* a fund set aside to repay a long-term debt.

Sinn Féin (shin **fane**) *n* an Irish Republican political movement linked to the IRA.
▷ **HISTORY** Irish Gaelic: we ourselves

Sino- *combining form* Chinese: *Sino-European; Sinology.* ▷ **HISTORY** Late Latin *Sinae* the Chinese

Sinology (sine-**ol**-a-jee) *n* the study of Chinese history, language, and culture. ▶ **Sinologist** *n*

SI notation *n Maths* scientific notation: a standard system for the representation of numbers or quantities.

sinuous *adj Literary* **1** full of curves. **2** having smooth twisting movements: *sinuous dances.*
▷ **HISTORY** Latin *sinuosus* winding ▶ **sinuosity** *n*

sinus (**sine**-uss) *n Anat* a hollow space in bone, such as one in the skull opening into a nasal cavity.
▷ **HISTORY** Latin: a curve

sinusitis *n* inflammation of the membrane lining a sinus, esp. a nasal sinus.

Sioux (**soo**) *n* **1** (*pl* **Sioux**) a member of a group of Native American peoples, formerly living over a wide area from Lake Michigan to the Rocky Mountains. **2** any of the languages of these peoples.

sip *vb* **sipping, sipped 1** to drink (a liquid) in small mouthfuls. ✧ *n* **2** an amount sipped. **3** an instance of sipping. ▷ **HISTORY** probably from Low German *sippen*

siphon *or* **syphon** *n* **1** a tube which uses air pressure to draw liquid from a container. ✧ *vb* **2 siphon off a** to draw (liquid) off through a siphon. **b** to redirect (resources or money), esp. dishonestly, into other projects or bank accounts.
▷ **HISTORY** Greek

sir *n* a polite term of address for a man.
▷ **HISTORY** variant of SIRE

Sir *n* a title placed before the name of a knight or baronet: *Sir David Attenborough.*

sire *n* **1** a male parent of a horse or other domestic animal. **2** *Archaic* a respectful form of address used to a king. ✧ *vb* **siring, sired 3** to father.
▷ **HISTORY** Old French

siren *n* **1** a device that gives out a loud wailing sound as a warning or signal. **2 Siren** *Greek myth* a sea nymph whose singing lured sailors to

A B C D E F G H I J K L M N O P Q R S T U V W X Y Z

destruction on the rocks. **3** a woman who is attractive but dangerous to men.

> **WORD HISTORY**
> The Sirens in Greek mythology were sea nymphs who had beautiful voices and sang in order to lure sailors to their deaths on the rocks where the nymphs lived.

sirloin *n* a prime cut of beef from the upper part of the loin. ▷ **HISTORY** Old French *surlonge*

sirocco *n, pl* **-cos** a hot stifling wind blowing from N Africa into S Europe. ▷ **HISTORY** Italian

sis[1] *n Informal* short for **sister**.

sis[2] *or* **sies** (**siss**) *interj S African informal* an exclamation of disgust. ▷ **HISTORY** Afrikaans

SIS Secret Intelligence Service: same as **MI6**.

sisal (**size**-al) *n* a stiff fibre obtained from a Mexican plant and used for making rope. ▷ **HISTORY** after *Sisal,* a port in Mexico

siskin *n* a yellow-and-black finch. ▷ **HISTORY** Middle Dutch *sīseken*

sissy *or* **cissy** *n, pl* **-sies 1** an effeminate, weak, or cowardly person. ✧ *adj* **2** effeminate, weak, or cowardly. ▷ **HISTORY** from SIS[1]

sister *n* **1** a woman or girl having the same parents as another person. **2** a female fellow member of a group, race, or profession. **3** a female nurse in charge of a ward. **4** *Chiefly RC Church* a nun. ✧ *adj* **5** of the same class, origin, or design, as another: *its sister paper.* ▷ **HISTORY** Old English *sweostor*

sisterhood *n* **1** the state of being sisters or like sisters. **2** a religious group of women. **3** a group of women united by a common interest or belief.

sister-in-law *n, pl* **sisters-in-law 1** the sister of one's husband or wife. **2** one's brother's wife.

sisterly *adj* of or like a sister; affectionate.

Siswati *n* a language of Swaziland.

sit *vb* **sitting, sat 1** to rest one's body upright on the buttocks: *she had to sit on the ground.* **2** to cause (someone) to rest in such a position: *they sat their grandfather in the shade.* **3** (of an animal) to rest with the rear part of its body lowered to the ground. **4** (of a bird) to perch or roost. **5 sit on** (of a bird) to cover its eggs so as to hatch them. **6** to be located: *the bank sits in the middle of the village.* **7** to pose for a painting or photograph. **8** to occupy a seat in some official capacity: *no police representatives will sit on the committee.* **9** (of a parliament or court) to be in session. **10** to remain unused: *his car sat in the garage.* **11** (of clothes) to fit or hang in a certain way: *that dress sits well on you.* **12** to take (an examination): *he's sitting his finals.* **13** (*in combination*) to look after a specified person or thing for someone else: *is someone going to dog-sit for you?* **14 sit for** *Chiefly Brit* to be a candidate for (a qualification): *he sat for a degree in medicine.* **15 sit tight** *Informal* **a** to wait patiently. **b** to maintain one's position firmly. ✧ See also **sit down**. ▷ **HISTORY** Old English *sittan*

sitar *n* an Indian stringed musical instrument with a long neck and a rounded body. ▷ **HISTORY** Hindi

sitcom *n Informal* (on television or radio) a comedy series involving the same characters in various everyday situations: *yet another unfunny sitcom set in Liverpool.*

sit down *vb* **1** to adopt or cause (someone) to adopt a sitting position. **2 sit down under** to suffer (insults or humiliations) without resistance. ✧ *n* **sit-down 3** a short rest sitting down. ✧ *adj* **sit-down 4** (of a meal) eaten while sitting down at a table.

site *n* **1** the piece of ground where something was, is, or is intended to be located: *a building site; a car park is to be built on the site of a Roman fort.* **2** same as **website**. ✧ *vb* **siting, sited 3** to locate (something) on a specific site. ▷ **HISTORY** Latin *situs* position

sit-in *n* **1** a protest in which the demonstrators sit in a public place and refuse to move. ✧ *vb* **sit in 2 sit in for** to stand in as a substitute for (someone). **3 sit in on** to be present at (a meeting) as an observer.

sitka spruce *n* a tall North American spruce tree, now often grown in Britain. ▷ **HISTORY** after *Sitka,* a town in Alaska

sit on *vb Informal* to delay action on: *they are sitting on their information.*

sit out *vb* **1** to endure to the end: *just sit it out, and it will pass eventually.* **2** to take no part in (a dance or game).

sitter *n* **1** a person posing for his or her portrait or photograph. **2** same as **baby-sitter**. **3** (*in combination*) a person who looks after a specified person or thing for someone else: *a house-sitter.*

sitting *n* **1** a continuous period of being seated at some activity: *you may not be able to complete it in one sitting.* **2** one of the times when a meal is served, when there is not enough space for everyone to eat at the same time: *the second sitting.* **3** a period of posing for a painting or photograph. **4** a meeting of an official body to conduct business. ✧ *adj* **5** current: *a sitting member of Congress.* **6** seated: *a sitting position.*

sitting room *n* a room in a house or flat where people sit and relax.

sitting tenant *n* a tenant occupying a house or flat.

situate *vb* **-ating, -ated** *Formal* to place. ▷ **HISTORY** Late Latin *situare* to position

situation *n* **1 a** state of affairs. **b** a complex or critical state of affairs. **2** location and surroundings. **3** social or financial circumstances. **4** a position of employment.

> **WORD TIP**
> *Situation* is often used in contexts in which it is redundant or imprecise. Typical examples are: *the company is in a crisis situation* or *people in a job situation.* In the first example, *situation* does not add to the meaning and should be omitted. In the second example, it would be clearer and more concise to substitute a phrase such as *people at work.*

situation comedy *n* same as **sitcom**.

SI unit *n* any of the units (metre, kilogram, second, ampere, kelvin, candela, mole, and those derived from them) adopted for international use under the Système International d'Unités, now employed for all scientific and most technical purposes.

Siva *n* a Hindu god, the Destroyer.

six *n* **1** the cardinal number that is the sum of one and five. **2** a numeral, 6 or VI, representing this number. **3** something representing or consisting of six units. **4** *Cricket* a score of six runs, obtained by hitting the ball so that it crosses the boundary without bouncing. **5 at sixes and sevens** in a state of confusion. **6 knock someone for six** *Informal* to upset or overwhelm someone completely. **7 six of one and half a dozen of the other** a situation in which there is no real difference between the alternatives. ✧ *adj* **8** amounting to six: *six days.* ▷ **HISTORY** Old English *siex* ▶ **sixth** *adj, n*

sixfold *adj* **1** having six times as many or as much. **2** composed of six parts. ✧ *adv* **3** by six times as many or as much.

six-pack *n Informal* **1** a package containing six units, esp. six cans of beer. **2** a highly developed set of abdominal muscles in a man.

sixpence *n* (formerly) a small British, Australian & New Zealand coin worth six old pennies, or $2^1/_2$ pence.

sixteen *n* **1** the cardinal number that is the sum of ten and six. **2** a numeral, 16 or XVI, representing this number. **3** something representing or consisting of sixteen units. ✧ *adj* **4** amounting to sixteen: *sixteen years.* ▶ **sixteenth** *adj, n*

sixth form *n* (in England and Wales) the most senior form in a secondary school, in which pupils over sixteen may take A levels or retake GCSEs. ▶ **sixth-former** *n*

sixth sense *n* the supposed ability of knowing something instinctively without having any evidence for it.

sixty *n, pl* **-ties 1** the cardinal number that is the product of ten and six. **2** a numeral, 60 or LX, representing this number. **3** something representing or consisting of sixty units. ✧ *adj* **4** amounting to sixty: *sixty seconds.* ▶ **sixtieth** *adj, n*

sizable *or* **sizeable** *adj* quite large.

size¹ *n* **1** the dimensions, amount, or extent of something. **2** large dimensions, amount, or extent: *I was overwhelmed by the sheer size of the city.* **3** one of a series of standard measurements for goods: *he takes size 11 shoes.* **4** *Informal* state of affairs as summarized: *that's about the size of it.* ✧ *vb* **sizing, sized 5** to sort (things) according to size. ▷ **HISTORY** Old French *sise*

> **WORD TIP**
>
> The use of *-size* and *-sized* after *large* or *small* is redundant, except when describing something which is made in specific sizes: *a large* (not *large-size*) *organization.* Similarly, *in size* is redundant in the expressions *large in size* and *small in size.*

size² *n* **1** a thin gluey substance that is used as a sealer. ✧ *vb* **sizing, sized 2** to treat (a surface) with size. ▷ **HISTORY** origin unknown

size up *vb Informal* to make an assessment of (a person or situation).

sizzle *vb* **-zling, -zled 1** to make a hissing sound like the sound of frying fat. **2** *Informal* to be very hot: *the city was sizzling in a hot summer spell.* **3** *Informal* to be very angry. ✧ *n* **4** a hissing sound. ▷ **HISTORY** imitative ▶ **sizzling** *adj*

sjambok (**sham**-bock) *S African* ✧ *n* **1** a whip or riding crop made of hide. ✧ *vb* **-bokking, -bokked 2** to beat with a sjambok. ▷ **HISTORY** Malay *tjambok*

SK Saskatchewan.

skanky *adj Slang* **1** dirty or unnattractive. **2** promiscuous.

skate¹ *n* **1** same as **ice skate, roller skate**. **2 get one's skates on** *Informal* to hurry. ✧ *vb* **skating, skated 3** to glide on or as if on skates. **4 skate on thin ice** to place oneself in a dangerous situation. ▷ **HISTORY** Old French *éschasse* stilt ▶ **skater** *n* ▶ **skating** *n*

skate² *n, pl* **skate** *or* **skates** a large edible marine fish with a broad flat body. ▷ **HISTORY** Old Norse *skata*

skateboard *n* **1** a narrow board mounted on roller-skate wheels, usually ridden while standing up. ✧ *vb* **2** to ride on a skateboard. ▶ **skateboarding** *n*

skean-dhu (**skee**-an-**doo**) *n* a dagger worn in the sock as part of Highland dress. ▷ **HISTORY** Gaelic *sgian* knife + *dhu* black

skedaddle *vb* **-dling, -dled** *Informal* to run off hastily. ▷ **HISTORY** origin unknown

skein *n* **1** a length of yarn or thread wound in a loose coil. **2** a flock of geese in flight. ▷ **HISTORY** Old French *escaigne*

skeleton *n* **1** the hard framework of bones that supports and protects the organs and muscles of the body. **2** the essential framework of any structure: *a metal skeleton supporting the roof and floors.* **3** *Informal* an extremely thin person or animal. **4** an outline consisting of bare essentials: *the mere skeleton of a script.* **5 skeleton in the cupboard** *or* **closet** an embarrassing or scandalous fact from the past that is kept secret. ✧ *adj* **6** reduced to a minimum: *a skeleton staff.* ▷ **HISTORY** Greek: something dried up ▶ **skeletal** *adj*

skeleton key *n* a key designed so that it can open many different locks.

skelm *n S African informal* a villain or crook. ▷ **HISTORY** Afrikaans

skerry *n, pl* **-ries** *Scot* a rocky island or reef. ▷ **HISTORY** Old Norse *sker*

sketch *n* **1** a quick rough drawing. **2** a brief descriptive piece of writing. **3** a short funny piece of acting forming part of a show. **4** any brief outline. ✧ *vb* **5** to make a quick rough drawing (of). **6 sketch out** to make a brief description of: *they sketched out plans for the invasion.* ▷ **HISTORY** Greek *skhedios* unprepared

sketchbook *n* a book of blank pages for sketching on.

sketchy *adj* **sketchier, sketchiest** giving only a rough or incomplete description. ▶ **sketchily** *adv*

skew *adj* **1** having a slanting position. ✧ *n* **2** a slanting position. ✧ *vb* **3** to take or cause to take a slanting position: *our boat skewed off course.* ▷ **HISTORY** Old French *escuer* to shun

skewbald *adj* **1** marked with patches of white and another colour. ✧ *n* **2** a horse with this marking. ▷ **HISTORY** origin unknown

skewed *adj* distorted or biased because of prejudice or lack of information: *a skewed conception of religion.*

skewer *n* **1** a long pin for holding meat together during cooking. ✧ *vb* **2** to fasten or pierce with or as if with a skewer. ▷ **HISTORY** probably from dialect *skiver*

ski *n, pl* **skis** *or* **ski 1** one of a pair of long runners that are used, fastened to boots, for gliding over snow. ✧ *vb* **skiing, skied** *or* **ski'd 2** to travel on skis. ▷ **HISTORY** Norwegian ▶ **skier** *n* ▶ **skiing** *n*

skid *vb* **skidding, skidded 1** (of a vehicle or person) to slide sideways while in motion. ✧ *n* **2** an instance of skidding. ▷ **HISTORY** origin unknown

skid row *n Slang, chiefly US & Canad* a poor and neglected area of a city, inhabited by down-and-outs.

skiff *n* a small narrow boat for one person. ▷ **HISTORY** French *esquif*

skilful *or US* **skillful** *adj* having or showing skill. ▶ **skilfully** *or US* **skillfully** *adv*

skill *n* **1** special ability or expertise enabling one to perform an activity very well. **2** something, such as a trade, requiring special training or expertise. ▷ **HISTORY** Old Norse *skil* distinction ▶ **skilled** *adj*

skillet *n* **1** a small frying pan. **2** *Chiefly Brit* a long-handled cooking pot. ▷ **HISTORY** origin unknown

skim *vb* **skimming, skimmed 1** to remove floating material from the surface of (a liquid): *skim any impurities off the surface.* **2** to glide smoothly over (a surface). **3** to throw (a flat stone) across a surface, so that it bounces: *two men skimmed stones on the surface of the sea.* **4** (often foll. by *through*) to read (a piece of writing) quickly and without taking in the details. ▷ **HISTORY** Middle English *skimmen*

skimp *vb* **1** to be extremely sparing or supply (someone) sparingly. **2** to do (something) carelessly or with inadequate materials. ▷ **HISTORY** perhaps a combination of SCANT + SCRIMP

skimpy *adj* **skimpier, skimpiest** inadequate in amount or size; scant.

skin *n* **1** the tissue forming the outer covering of the body. **2** a person's complexion: *sallow skin.* **3** any outer layer or covering: *potato skin.* **4** a thin solid layer on the surface of a liquid: *custard with a thick skin on it.* **5** the outer covering of a furry animal, removed and prepared for use. **6** a container for liquids, made from animal skin. **7 by the skin of one's teeth** by a narrow margin. **8 get under one's skin** *Informal* to annoy one. **9 no skin off one's nose** *Informal* not a matter that concerns one. **10 save one's skin** to save one from death or harm. **11 skin and bone** extremely thin. **12 thick** *or* **thin skin** an insensitive *or* sensitive nature. ✧ *vb* **skinning, skinned 13** to remove the outer covering from (a dead animal). **14** to injure (a part of the body) by scraping some of the skin off: *I had skinned my knuckles.* **15** *Slang* to swindle. ▷ **HISTORY** Old English *scinn* ▶ **skinless** *adj*

skin-deep *adj* not of real importance; superficial: *beauty is only skin-deep.*

skin diving *n* underwater swimming using only light breathing apparatus and without a special diving suit. ▶ **skin-diver** *n*

skin flick *n Slang* a pornographic film.

skinflint *n* a very mean person. ▷ **HISTORY** referring to a person so greedy that he or she would skin (swindle) a flint

skin graft *n* a piece of skin removed from one part of the body and surgically grafted at the site of a severe burn or other injury.

skinhead *n* **1** a member of a group of White youths, noted for their closely cropped hair, aggressive behaviour, and overt racism. **2** a closely cropped hairstyle.

skinny *adj* **-nier, -niest** extremely thin.

skint *adj Slang* without money, esp. only temporarily. ▷ **HISTORY** variant of *skinned*

skintight *adj* (of garments) fitting tightly over the body; clinging.

skip[1] *vb* **skipping, skipped 1** to move lightly by hopping from one foot to the other. **2** to jump over a skipping-rope. **3** to cause (a stone) to skim over a surface or (of a stone) to move in this way. **4** to pass over or miss out; omit: *I skipped a few paragraphs.* **5 skip through** *Informal* to read or deal with (something) quickly or without great effort or concentration. **6 skip it!** *Informal* it doesn't matter! **7** *Informal* to miss deliberately: *she skipped the class.* **8** *Informal, chiefly US, Canad & Austral* to leave (a place) in a hurry: *he skipped town three years later.* ✧ *n* **9** a skipping movement or action. ▷ **HISTORY** probably from Old Norse

skip[2] *n* **1** a large open container for transporting building materials or rubbish. **2** a cage used as a lift in mines. ▷ **HISTORY** variant of *skep* a beehive

skipper *n* **1** the captain of a ship or aircraft. **2** the captain of a sporting team. ✧ *vb* **3** to be the captain of. ▷ **HISTORY** Middle Low German, Middle Dutch *schipper* shipper

skipping *n* the act of jumping over a rope held either by the person jumping or by two other people, as a game or for exercise.

skirl *Scot & N English dialect* ✧ *n* **1** the sound of bagpipes. ✧ *vb* **2** (of bagpipes) to give out a shrill sound. ▷ **HISTORY** probably from Old Norse

skirmish *n* **1** a brief or minor fight or argument. ✧ *vb* **2** to take part in a skirmish. ▷ **HISTORY** Old French *eskirmir*

skirt *n* **1** a woman's or girl's garment hanging from the waist. **2** the part of a dress or coat below the waist. **3** a circular hanging flap, for example round the base of a hovercraft. **4** *Brit & NZ* a cut of beef from the flank. **5 bit of skirt** *Offensive slang* a girl or woman. ✧ *vb* **6** to lie along or form the edge of (something): *a track skirting the foot of the mountain.* **7** to go around the outer edge of (something): *we skirted the township.* **8** to avoid dealing with (an issue): *I was skirting around the real issues.* ▷ HISTORY Old Norse *skyrta* shirt

skirting board *n* a narrow board round the bottom of an interior wall where it joins the floor.

skit *n* a short funny or satirical sketch. ▷ HISTORY probably Scandinavian

skite *Austral & NZ* ✧ *vb* **1** to boast. ✧ *n* **2** a boast.

skittish *adj* **1** playful or lively. **2** (of a horse) excitable and easily frightened. ▷ HISTORY probably from Old Norse

skittle *n* **1** a bottle-shaped object used as a target in a game of skittles. **2 skittles** a bowling game in which players knock over as many skittles as possible by rolling a wooden ball at them. ▷ HISTORY origin unknown

skive *vb* **skiving, skived** (often foll. by *off*) *Brit informal* to avoid work or responsibility. ▷ HISTORY origin unknown ▶ **skiver** *n*

skivvy *n, pl* **-vies 1** *Chiefly Brit often disparaging* a female servant who does menial work; drudge. **2** *Austral & NZ* a garment resembling a sweater with long sleeves and a polo neck. ✧ *vb* **-vies, -vying, -vied 3** to work as a skivvy. ▷ HISTORY origin unknown

skolly *or* **skollie** *n, pl* **-lies** *S African* a hooligan, usually one of a gang. ▷ HISTORY origin unknown

skua *n* a large predatory gull living in cold marine regions. ▷ HISTORY Faeroese *skūgvur*

skulduggery *or US* **skullduggery** *n Informal* underhand dealing to achieve an aim. ▷ HISTORY origin unknown

skulk *vb* **1** to move stealthily, so as to avoid notice. **2** to lie in hiding; lurk. ▷ HISTORY from Old Norse

skull *n* **1** the bony framework of the head. **2** *Informal* the head or mind: *that would have penetrated even your thick skull.* ▷ HISTORY probably from Old Norse

skullcap *n* a closely fitting brimless cap.

skunk *n, pl* **skunks** *or* **skunk 1** a mammal with a black-and-white coat and bushy tail, which gives out a foul-smelling fluid when attacked. **2** *Informal* an unpleasant or unfair person. ▷ HISTORY from a Native American language

sky *n, pl* **skies 1** the upper atmosphere as seen from earth. **2 praise to the skies** praise rather excessively. ✧ *vb* **skies, skying, skied 3** *Informal* to hit (a ball) high in the air: *the blond-haired forward skied the ball high over the bar.* ▷ HISTORY Old Norse *skȳ* cloud

skydiving *n* the sport of jumping from an aircraft and falling freely or performing manoeuvres before opening the parachute. ▶ **skydiver** *n*

skyjack *vb* to hijack (an aircraft). ▷ HISTORY SKY + HIJACK

skylark *n* **1** a lark that sings while soaring at a great height. ✧ *vb* **2** *Old-fashioned* to play or frolic.

skylight *n* a window placed in a roof or ceiling to let in daylight.

skyline *n* **1** the line at which the earth and sky appear to meet. **2** the outline of buildings, trees, or hills, seen against the sky.

skyrocket *n* **1** same as **rocket** (sense 1). ✧ *vb* **2** *Informal* to rise very quickly.

skyscraper *n* a very tall building.

slab *n* a broad flat thick piece of wood, stone, or other material. ▷ HISTORY origin unknown

slack[1] *adj* **1** not tight, tense, or taut: *the slack jaw hung open.* **2** careless in one's work. **3** (esp. of water) moving slowly. **4** (of trade) not busy. ✧ *n* **5** a part that is slack or hangs loose: *take up the slack.* **6** a period of less busy activity. ✧ *vb* **7** to neglect (one's work or duty). **8** (often foll. by *off*) to loosen or slacken. ✧ See also **slacks.** ▷ HISTORY Old English *slæc, sleac* ▶ **slackness** *n*

slack[2] *n* small pieces of coal with a high ash content. ▷ HISTORY probably Middle Low German *slecke*

slacken *vb* (often foll. by *off*) **1** to make or become looser. **2** to make or become slower or less intense: *to slacken the pace of reform.*

slacker *n* a person who evades work or duty; shirker.

slacks *pl n Old-fashioned* casual trousers.

slag *n* **1** the waste material left after metal has been smelted. **2** *Brit & NZ, slang* a sexually immoral woman. ✧ *vb* **slagging, slagged 3** *Brit, Austral & NZ slang* to criticize in an unpleasant way: *I don't think anyone can slag it off.* ▷ HISTORY Middle Low German *slagge* ▶ **slagging** *n* ▶ **slaggy** *adj*

slag heap *n* a pile of waste matter from metal smelting or coal mining.

slain *vb* the past participle of **slay.**

slake *vb* **slaking, slaked 1** *Literary* to satisfy (thirst or desire). **2** to add water to (lime) to produce calcium hydroxide. ▷ HISTORY Old English *slacian*

slalom *n Skiing, canoeing* a race over a winding course marked by artificial obstacles. ▷ HISTORY Norwegian

slam[1] *vb* **slamming, slammed 1** to close violently and noisily. **2** to throw (something) down violently. **3** *Slang* to criticize harshly: *his new proposals were slammed by the opposition.* **4** to strike with violent force: *he slammed the ball into the back of the net.* ✧ *n* **5** the act or noise of slamming. ▷ HISTORY Scandinavian

slam[2] *n* the winning of all (**grand slam**) or all but one (**little slam**) of the 13 tricks at bridge. ▷ HISTORY origin unknown

slammer *n* **the slammer** *Slang* prison.

slander *n* **1** *Law* a false and damaging statement about a person. **2** the crime of making such a statement. ✧ *vb* **3** to utter slander (about). ▷ HISTORY Old French *escandle* ▶ **slanderous** *adj*

slang *n* **1** informal language not used in formal speech or writing and often restricted to a particular social group or profession. ✧ *vb* **2** to use insulting language to (someone). ▷ HISTORY origin unknown ▶ **slangy** *adj*

slanging match *n* an angry quarrel in which people trade insults.

slant *vb* **1** to lean at an angle; slope. **2** to write or present (information) in a biased way. ✧ *n* **3** a sloping line or position. **4** a point of view, esp. a biased one: *a right-wing slant on the story.* **5 on a** *or* **the slant** sloping. ✧ *adj* **6** oblique; sloping. ▷ HISTORY Scandinavian ▶ **slanting** *adj* ▶ **slantwise** *adv*

slap *n* **1** a sharp blow or smack with something flat, such as the open hand. **2** the sound made by or as if by such a blow. **3 slap and tickle** *Brit old-fashioned informal* sexual play. **4 a slap in the face** an unexpected rejection or insult. **5 a slap on the back** congratulations. ✧ *vb* **slapping, slapped 6** to strike sharply with something flat, such as the open hand. **7** to bring (something) down forcefully: *he slapped down a fiver.* **8** (usually foll. by *against*) to strike (something) with a slapping sound. **9** *Informal, chiefly Brit & NZ* to cover with quickly or carelessly: *she slapped on some make-up.* **10 slap on the back** to congratulate. ✧ *adv Informal* **11** exactly: *slap in the middle.* **12 slap into** forcibly or abruptly into: *he ran slap into the guard.* ▷ HISTORY Low German *slapp*

slap-bang *adv Informal, chiefly Brit & Austral* **1** directly or exactly: *he's on holiday in LA and has run slap-bang into a famous face.* **2** forcefully and abruptly: *he'd gone and run slap-bang into the watchman.*

slapdash *adv* **1** carelessly or hastily. ✧ *adj* **2** careless or hasty.

slap-happy *adj* **-pier, -piest** *Informal* cheerfully careless.

slapstick *n* rough and high-spirited comedy in which the characters behave childishly.

slap-up *adj Brit informal* (esp. of meals) large and expensive.

slash *vb* **1** to cut (a person or thing) with sharp sweeping strokes. **2** to make large gashes in: *I slashed the tyres of his van.* **3** to reduce drastically: *to slash costs.* **4** to criticize harshly. ✧ *n* **5** a sharp sweeping stroke. **6** a cut made by such a stroke. **7** same as **solidus**. **8** *Brit slang* the act of urinating. ▷ HISTORY origin unknown

slasher *n Austral & NZ* a tool or tractor-drawn machine used for cutting scrub or undergrowth in the bush.

slat *n* a narrow thin strip of wood or metal, such as used in a Venetian blind. ▷ HISTORY Old French *esclat* splinter

slate[1] *n* **1** a dark grey rock that can be easily split into thin layers and is used as a roofing material. **2** a roofing tile of slate. **3** (formerly) a writing tablet of slate. **4** *Chiefly US & Canad* a list of candidates in an election. **5 wipe the slate clean** to forget about past mistakes or failures and start afresh. **6 on the slate** *Brit & Austral informal* on credit. ✧ *vb* **slating, slated 7** to cover (a roof) with slates. **8** *Chiefly US* to plan or schedule: *another exercise is slated for tomorrow.* ▷ HISTORY Old French *esclate* fragment ▶ **slaty** *adj*

slate[2] *vb* **slating, slated** *Informal, chiefly Brit & Austral* to criticize harshly: *the new series was slated by the critics.* ▷ HISTORY probably from Old French *esclate* fragment ▶ **slating** *n*

slattern *n Old-fashioned* a dirty and untidy woman. ▷ HISTORY probably from dialect *slatter* to slop ▶ **slatternliness** *n* ▶ **slatternly** *adj*

slaughter *n* **1** the indiscriminate or brutal killing of large numbers of people. **2** the savage killing of a person. **3** the killing of animals for food. ✧ *vb* **4** to kill indiscriminately or in large numbers. **5** to kill brutally. **6** to kill (animals) for food. **7** *Informal* (in sport) to defeat easily. ▷ HISTORY Old English *sleaht*

slaughterhouse *n* a place where animals are killed for food.

Slav *n* a member of any of the peoples of E Europe or the former Soviet Union who speak a Slavonic language. ▷ HISTORY Medieval Latin *Sclavus* a captive Slav

slave *n* **1** a person legally owned by another for whom he or she has to work without freedom, pay, or rights. **2** a person under the domination of another or of some habit or influence: *a slave to party doctrine.* **3** *Informal* a badly-paid person doing menial tasks. ✧ *vb* **slaving, slaved 4** (often foll. by *away* or *over*) to work very hard for little or no money.

WORD HISTORY

'Slave' is derived from Latin *Sclavus*, meaning 'a Slav', because the Slavonic races were frequently conquered and enslaved during the Middle Ages.

slave-driver *n* **1** a person who makes people work very hard. **2** (esp. formerly) a person forcing slaves to work.

slaver[1] (**slay**-ver) *n* **1** (esp. formerly) a dealer in slaves. **2** *History* a ship used in the slave trade.

slaver[2] (**slav**-ver) *vb* **1** to dribble saliva. **2** (often foll. by *over*) to drool (over someone), making flattering remarks. ✧ *n* **3** saliva dribbling from the mouth. **4** *Informal* nonsense. ▷ HISTORY probably from Low German

slavery *n* **1** the state or condition of being a slave. **2** the practice of owning slaves. **3** hard work with little reward.

slave trade *n* the buying and selling of slaves, esp. the transportation of Black Africans to America and the Caribbean from the 16th to the 19th centuries.

slavish *adj* **1** of or like a slave. **2** imitating or copying exactly without any originality: *a slavish adherence to the conventions of Italian opera.* ▶ **slavishly** *adv*

Slavonic *or esp US* **Slavic** *n* **1** a group of languages including Bulgarian, Russian, Polish, and Czech. ✧ *adj* **2** of this group of languages. **3** of the people who speak these languages.

slay *vb* **slaying, slew, slain** *Archaic or literary* to kill, esp. violently. ▷ HISTORY Old English *slēan* ▶ **slayer** *n*

sleaze *n Informal* behaviour in public life considered immoral, dishonest, or disreputable: *political sleaze.*

sleazy *adj* **-zier, -ziest** dirty, run-down, and not respectable: *a sleazy hotel.* ▷ HISTORY origin unknown ▶ **sleaziness** *n*

sledge[1] *or esp US & Canad* **sled** *n* **1** a vehicle mounted on runners, drawn by horses or dogs, for transporting people or goods over snow. **2** a light wooden frame used, esp. by children, for sliding over snow. ✧ *vb* **sledging, sledged 3** to travel by sledge. ▷ **HISTORY** Middle Dutch *sleedse*

sledge[2] *n* short for **sledgehammer**.

sledgehammer *n* **1** a large heavy hammer with a long handle, used for breaking rocks and concrete. ✧ *adj* **2** crushingly powerful: *the sledgehammer approach.* ▷ **HISTORY** Old English *slecg* a large hammer

sleek *adj* **1** smooth, shiny, and glossy: *sleek blond hair.* **2** (of a person) elegantly dressed. ▷ **HISTORY** variant of *slick*

sleep *n* **1** a state of rest during which the eyes are closed, the muscles and nerves are relaxed, and the mind is unconscious. **2** a period spent sleeping. **3** the substance sometimes found in the corner of the eyes after sleep. **4** a state of inactivity, like sleep. **5** *Poetic* death. ✧ *vb* **sleeping, slept 6** to be in or as in the state of sleep. **7** to be inactive or unaware: *their defence slept as we scored another try.* **8** to have sleeping accommodation for (a certain number): *the villa sleeps ten.* **9** *Poetic* to be dead. **10 sleep on it** to delay making a decision about (something) until the next day, in order to think about it. ✧ See also **sleep in**. ▷ **HISTORY** Old English *slǣpan*

sleeper *n* **1** a railway sleeping car or compartment. **2** one of the blocks supporting the rails on a railway track. **3** a small plain gold ring worn in a pierced ear lobe to prevent the hole from closing up. **4** *Informal* a person or thing that achieves success after an initial period of obscurity.

sleep in *vb* to sleep longer than usual.

sleeping bag *n* a large well-padded bag for sleeping in, esp. outdoors.

sleeping partner *n* a partner in a business who shares in the financing but does not take part in its management.

sleeping pill *n* a pill containing a drug that induces sleep.

sleeping policeman *n Brit* a bump built across a road to prevent motorists from driving too fast.

sleeping sickness *n* an infectious, usually fatal, African disease transmitted by the bite of the tsetse fly, causing fever and sluggishness.

sleepless *adj* **1** (of a night) one during which one does not sleep. **2** unable to sleep. **3** *Chiefly poetic* always active. ▶ **sleeplessness** *n*

sleepout *n NZ* a small building for sleeping in.

sleepover *n* an occasion when a person, esp. a child, stays over night at a friend's house.

sleepwalk *vb* to walk while asleep.
▶ **sleepwalker** *n* ▶ **sleepwalking** *n*

sleep with *vb* to have sexual intercourse and, usually, spend the night with.

sleepy *adj* **sleepier, sleepiest 1** tired and ready for sleep. **2** (of a place) without activity or excitement: *a sleepy little town.* ▶ **sleepily** *adv*

sleet *n* **1** partly melted falling snow or hail or (esp. US) partly frozen rain. ✧ *vb* **2** to fall as sleet. ▷ **HISTORY** Germanic

sleeve *n* **1** the part of a garment covering the arm. **2** a tubelike part which fits over or completely encloses another part. **3** a flat cardboard container to protect a gramophone record. **4 up one's sleeve** secretly ready: *he has a few more surprises up his sleeve.* ▷ **HISTORY** Old English *slīefe, slēfe*
▶ **sleeveless** *adj*

sleigh *n* **1** same as **sledge**[1] (sense 1). ✧ *vb* **2** to travel by sleigh. ▷ **HISTORY** Dutch *slee*

sleight of hand *n* **1** the skilful use of the hands when performing magic tricks. **2** the performance of such tricks.

slender *adj* **1** (esp. of a person's figure) slim and graceful. **2** of small width relative to length or height. **3** small or inadequate in amount or size: *a slender advantage.* ▷ **HISTORY** origin unknown

slept *vb* the past of **sleep**.

sleuth (rhymes with **tooth**) *n Informal* a detective.

> **WORD HISTORY**
> 'Sleuth' is a shortened form of *sleuthhound,*, meaning a 'tracker dog'. It denoted a dog, such as a bloodhound, that can follow trails. The 'sleuth' part of the word comes from Old Norse *sloth*, meaning 'track'.

slew[1] *vb* the past tense of **slay**.

slew[2] *or esp US* **slue** *vb* **1** to slide or skid sideways: *the bus slewed across the road.* ✧ *n* **2** the act of slewing. ▷ **HISTORY** origin unknown

slice *n* **1** a thin flat piece or wedge cut from something: *a slice of tomato.* **2** a share or portion: *the biggest slice of their income.* **3** a kitchen tool having a broad flat blade: *a fish slice.* **4** *Sport* a shot that causes the ball to go to one side, rather than straight ahead. ✧ *vb* **slicing, sliced 5** to cut (something) into slices. **6** (usually foll. by *through*) to cut through cleanly and effortlessly, with or as if with a knife. **7** (usually foll. by *off, from* or *away*) to cut or be cut (from) a larger piece. **8** *Sport* to play (a ball) with a slice. ▷ **HISTORY** Old French *esclice* a piece split off

slick *adj* **1** (esp. of speech) easy and persuasive: *a slick answer.* **2** skilfully devised or executed: *a slick marketing effort.* **3** *Informal, chiefly US & Canad* shrewd; sly. **4** *Informal* well-made and attractive, but superficial: *a slick publication.* **5** *Chiefly US & Canad* slippery. ✧ *n* **6** a slippery area, esp. a patch of oil floating on water. ✧ *vb* **7** to make smooth or shiny: *long hair slicked back with gel.* ▷ **HISTORY** probably from Old Norse

slide *vb* **sliding, slid, slid 1** to move smoothly along a surface in continual contact with it: *doors that slide open.* **2** to slip: *he slid on his back.* **3** (usually foll. by *into, out of* or *away from*) to pass or move smoothly and quietly: *she slid out of her seat.* **4** (usually foll. by *into*) to go (into a specified condition) gradually: *the republic will slide into political anarchy.* **5** (of a currency) to lose value gradually. **6 let slide** to allow to change to a worse state by neglect: *past chairmen have undoubtedly let things slide.* ✧ *n* **7** the act or an instance of sliding. **8** a small glass plate on which specimens are placed for study under a microscope. **9** a photograph on a transparent base, mounted in a frame, that can be viewed by means of a projector. **10** a smooth surface, such as ice, for sliding on. **11** a structure with a steep smooth slope for sliding down in playgrounds. **12** *Chiefly Brit* an ornamental clip to hold hair in place. **13** the sliding curved tube of a trombone that is moved in and out to allow different notes to be played. ▷ **HISTORY** Old English *slīdan*

slide rule *n* a device formerly used to make mathematical calculations consisting of two strips, one sliding along a central groove in the other, each strip graduated in two or more logarithmic scales of numbers.

sliding scale *n* a variable scale according to which things such as wages or prices alter in response to changes in other factors.

slight *adj* **1** small in quantity or extent: *a slight improvement.* **2** not very important or lacking in substance: *her political career was honourable but relatively slight.* **3** slim and delicate. ✧ *vb* **4** to insult (someone) by behaving rudely; snub. ✧ *n* **5** an act of snubbing (someone). ▷ **HISTORY** Old Norse *slēttr* smooth ▸ **slightly** *adv*

slim *adj* **slimmer, slimmest 1** (of a person) attractively thin. **2** small in width relative to height or length: *a slim book.* **3** poor; meagre: *a slim chance of progress.* ✧ *vb* **4** to make or become slim by diets and exercise. **5** to reduce in size: *that would slim the overheads.* ▷ **HISTORY** Dutch: crafty ▸ **slimmer** *n* ▸ **slimming** *n*

Slim *n* the E African name for **AIDS**. ▷ **HISTORY** from its wasting effects

slime *n* **1** soft runny mud or any sticky substance esp. when disgusting or unpleasant. **2** a thick, sticky substance produced by some fish, slugs, and fungi. ▷ **HISTORY** Old English *slīm*

slimy *adj* **slimier, slimiest 1** of, like, or covered with slime. **2** pleasant and friendly in an insincere way.

sling[1] *n* **1** *Med* a wide piece of cloth suspended from the neck for supporting an injured hand or arm. **2** a rope or strap by which something may be lifted. **3** a simple weapon consisting of a strap tied to cords, in which a stone is whirled and then released. ✧ *vb* **slinging, slung 4** *Informal* to throw. **5** to carry or hang loosely from or as if from a sling: *her shoulder bag was slung across her chest.* **6** to hurl with or as if with a sling. ▷ **HISTORY** probably from Old Norse

sling[2] *n* a sweetened mixed drink with a spirit base: *gin sling.* ▷ **HISTORY** origin unknown

slingback *n* a shoe with a strap instead of a complete covering for the heel.

sling off at *vb Austral & NZ informal* to mock and jeer.

slink *vb* **slinking, slunk** to move or act in a quiet and secretive way from fear or guilt. ▷ **HISTORY** Old English *slincan*

slinky *adj* **slinkier, slinkiest** *Informal* **1** (of clothes) figure-hugging. **2** moving in an alluring way.

slip[1] *vb* **slipping, slipped 1** to lose balance and slide unexpectedly: *he slipped on some leaves.* **2** to let loose or be let loose: *the rope slipped from his fingers.* **3** to move smoothly and easily: *small enough to slip into a pocket.* **4** to place quickly or stealthily: *he slipped the pistol back into his holster.* **5** to put on or take off easily or quickly: *we had slipped off our sandals.* **6** to pass out of (the mind or memory). **7** to move or pass quickly and without being noticed: *we slipped out of the ballroom.* **8** to make a mistake. **9** to decline in health or mental ability. **10** to become worse or lower: *sales had slipped below the level for June of last year.* **11** to dislocate (a disc in the spine). **12** to pass (a stitch) from one needle to another without knitting it. **13 let slip a** to allow to escape. **b** to say unintentionally. ✧ *n* **14** a slipping. **15** a mistake or oversight: *one slip in concentration that cost us the game.* **16** a woman's sleeveless undergarment, worn under a dress. **17** same as **slipway**. **18** *Cricket* a fielding position a little behind and to the offside of the wicketkeeper. **19 give someone the slip** to escape from someone. ✧ See also **slip up**. ▷ **HISTORY** Middle Low German or Dutch *slippen*

slip[2] *n* **1** a small piece of paper: *the registration slip.* **2** a cutting taken from a plant. **3** a young slim person: *a slip of a girl.* ▷ **HISTORY** probably Middle Low German, Middle Dutch *slippe* to cut

slip[3] *n* clay mixed with water to a thin paste, used for decorating or patching a ceramic piece. ▷ **HISTORY** Old English *slyppe* slime

slipe *n NZ* wool removed from the pelt of a slaughtered sheep by immersion in a chemical bath. ▷ **HISTORY** Middle English *slype* to skin

slipknot *n* a nooselike knot tied so that it will slip along the rope round which it is made.

slip-off slope *n Geol* the gently sloping inside bank of a meandering stream that builds up as a result of sedimentary deposits from slower-moving water on this side.

slip-on *adj* **1** (of a garment or shoe) without laces or buttons so as to be easily and quickly put on. ✧ *n* **2** a slip-on garment or shoe.

slipped disc *n Pathol* a painful condition in which one of the discs which connects the bones of the spine becomes displaced and presses on a nerve.

slipper *n* a light soft shoe for indoor wear. ▸ **slippered** *adj*

slippery *adj* **1** liable or tending to cause objects to slip: *the road was slippery.* **2** liable to slip from one's grasp: *a bar of slippery soap.* **3** not to be trusted: *slippery politicians.* ▸ **slipperiness** *n*

slippy *adj* **-pier, -piest** *Informal or dialect* same as **slippery** (senses 1, 2). ▸ **slippiness** *n*

slip road *n Brit* a short road connecting a motorway to another road.

slipshod *adj* **1** (of an action) done in a careless way without attention to detail: *a slipshod piece of research.* **2** (of a person's appearance) untidy and slovenly.

slip-slop *n S African* same as **flip-flop**.

slipstream *n* the stream of air forced backwards by an aircraft or car.

slip up *Informal* ✧ *vb* **1** to make a mistake. ✧ *n* **slip-up 2** a mistake.

slipway *n* a large ramp that slopes down from the shore into the water, on which a ship is built or repaired and from which it is launched.

slit *n* **1** a long narrow cut or opening. ✧ *vb* **slitting, slit 2** to make a straight long cut in (something). ▷ **HISTORY** Old English *slītan* to slice

slither *vb* **1** to move or slide unsteadily, such as on a slippery surface. **2** to move along the ground in a twisting way: *a snake slithered towards the tree.* ✧ *n* **3** a slithering movement. ▷ **HISTORY** Old English *slid(e)rian* ▶ **slithery** *adj*

sliver (**sliv**-ver) *n* **1** a small thin piece that is cut or broken off lengthwise. ✧ *vb* **2** to cut into slivers. ▷ **HISTORY** obsolete *sliven* to split

Sloane Ranger *n Informal* (in Britain) a young upper-class woman having a home in London and in the country, characterized as wearing expensive informal clothes. ▷ **HISTORY** from *Sloane* Square, London + *Lone Ranger,* cowboy hero

slob *n Informal* a lazy and untidy person. ▷ **HISTORY** Irish Gaelic *slab* mud ▶ **slobbish** *adj*

slobber *vb* **1** to dribble (liquid or saliva) from the mouth. **2 slobber over** to behave in an excessively sentimental way towards (someone). ✧ *n* **3** liquid or saliva spilt from the mouth. ▷ **HISTORY** Middle Low German, Middle Dutch *slubberen* ▶ **slobbery** *adj*

slob ice *n Canad* sludgy masses of floating sea ice.

sloe *n* **1** the small sour blue-black fruit of the blackthorn. **2** same as **blackthorn**. ▷ **HISTORY** Old English *slāh*

slog *vb* **slogging, slogged 1** to work hard and steadily. **2** to make one's way with difficulty: *we slogged our way through the snow.* **3** to hit hard. ✧ *n* **4** long exhausting work. **5** a long and difficult walk: *a slog through heather and bracken.* **6** a heavy blow. ▷ **HISTORY** origin unknown

slogan *n* a catchword or phrase used in politics or advertising.

> **WORD HISTORY**
> 'Slogan' is derived from Gaelic *sluagh-ghairm*, which means 'war cry'.

sloop *n* a small sailing ship with a single mast. ▷ **HISTORY** Dutch *sloep*

slop *vb* **slopping, slopped 1** (often foll. by *about*) to splash or spill (liquid). **2 slop over** *Informal, chiefly US & Canad* to be excessively sentimental. ✧ *n* **3** a puddle of spilt liquid. **4 slops** liquid refuse and waste food used to feed animals, esp. pigs. **5** (*often pl*) *Informal* liquid food. ▷ **HISTORY** Old English *-sloppe*

slope *n* **1** a stretch of ground where one end is higher than the other. **2 slopes** hills or foothills. **3** any slanting surface. **4** the angle of such a slant. ✧ *vb* **sloping, sloped 5** to slant or cause to slant. **6** (esp. of natural features) to have one end or part higher than another: *the bank sloped sharply down to the river.* **7 slope off** *or* **away** *Informal* to go quietly and quickly in order to avoid something or someone. **8 slope arms** *Mil* (formerly) to hold (a rifle) in a sloping position against the shoulder. ▷ **HISTORY** origin unknown

slop out *vb* (of prisoners) to empty chamber pots and collect water.

sloppy *adj* **-pier, -piest 1** *Informal* careless or untidy: *sloppy workmanship.* **2** *Informal* excessively sentimental and romantic. **3** wet; slushy. ▶ **sloppily** *adv* ▶ **sloppiness** *n*

slosh *n, vb* **1** *Informal* to throw or pour (liquid) carelessly. **2** (often foll. by *about* or *around*) *Informal* **a** to shake or stir (something) in a liquid. **b** (of a person) to splash (around) in water or mud. **3** (usually foll. by *about* or *around*) *Informal* to shake (a container of liquid) or (of liquid in a container) to be shaken. **4** *Brit slang* to deal a heavy blow to. ✧ *n* **5** the sound of splashing liquid. **6** slush. **7** *Brit slang* a heavy blow. ▷ **HISTORY** variant of SLUSH ▶ **sloshy** *adj*

sloshed *adj Slang, chiefly Brit & Austral* drunk.

slot *n* **1** a narrow opening or groove, such as one in a vending machine for inserting a coin. **2** *Informal* a place in a series or scheme: *the late-night slot when people stop watching TV.* ✧ *vb* **slotting, slotted 3** to make a slot or slots in. **4** (usually foll. by *in* or *into*) to fit or be fitted into a slot: *I slotted my card into the machine.* ▷ **HISTORY** Old French *esclot* the depression of the breastbone

sloth (rhymes with **both**) *n* **1** a slow-moving shaggy-coated animal of Central and South America, which hangs upside down in trees by its long arms and feeds on vegetation. **2** *Formal* laziness, esp. regarding work. ▷ **HISTORY** Old English *slǣwth*

slothful *adj* lazy and unwilling to work.

slot machine *n* a machine, esp. for vending food and cigarettes or featuring an electronic game on which to gamble, worked by placing a coin in a slot.

slouch *vb* **1** to sit, stand, or move with a drooping posture. ✧ *n* **2** a drooping posture. **3 be no slouch** *Informal* be very good or talented: *he was no slouch himself as a negotiator.* ▷ **HISTORY** origin unknown

slough[1] (rhymes with **now**) *n* **1** a swamp or marshy area. **2** (rhymes with **blue**) *US & Canad* a large hole where water collects. **3** despair or hopeless depression. ▷ **HISTORY** Old English *slōh*

slough[2] (**sluff**) *n* **1** any outer covering that is shed, such as the dead outer layer of the skin of a snake. ✧ *vb* **slough off 2** to shed (an outer covering) or (of an outer covering) to be shed: *the dead cells would slough off.* **3** to get rid of (something unwanted or unnecessary): *she tried hard to slough off her old personality.* ▷ **HISTORY** Germanic

Slovak *adj* **1** of Slovakia. ✧ *n* **2** a person from Slovakia. **3** the language of Slovakia.

sloven *n* a person who is always untidy or careless in appearance or behaviour. ▷ **HISTORY** origin unknown

Slovene *adj also* **Slovenian 1** of Slovenia. ✧ *n* **2** Also: **Slovenian** a person from Slovenia. **3** the language of Slovenia.

slovenly *adj* **1** always unclean or untidy. **2** negligent and careless: *to write in such a slovenly style.* ✧ *adv* **3** in a slovenly manner. ▸ **slovenliness** *n*

slow *adj* **1** taking a longer time than is usual or expected. **2** lacking speed: *slow movements.* **3** adapted to or producing slow movement: *the slow lane.* **4** (of a clock or watch) showing a time earlier than the correct time. **5** not quick to understand: *slow on the uptake.* **6** dull or uninteresting: *the play was very slow.* **7** not easily aroused: *he is slow to anger.* **8** (of business) not busy; slack. **9** (of a fire or oven) giving off low heat. **10** *Photog* requiring a relatively long time of exposure: *a slow film.* ✧ *adv* **11** in a slow manner. ✧ *vb* **12** (often foll. by *up* or *down*) to decrease or cause to decrease in speed or activity. ▷ **HISTORY** Old English *slāw* sluggish ▸ **slowly** *adv*

slowcoach *n Informal* a person who moves or works slowly.

slow motion *n* **1** *Films, television* action that is made to appear slower than normal by filming at a faster rate or by replaying a video recording more slowly. ✧ *adj* **slow-motion 2** of or relating to such action. **3** moving at considerably less than usual speed.

slow virus *n* a type of virus that is present in the body for a long time before it becomes active or infectious.

slowworm *n* a legless lizard with a brownish-grey snakelike body.

sludge *n* **1** soft mud or snow. **2** any muddy or slushy sediment. **3** sewage. ▷ **HISTORY** probably related to SLUSH ▸ **sludgy** *adj*

slug[1] *n* a mollusc like a snail but without a shell. ▷ **HISTORY** probably from Old Norse

slug[2] *n* **1** a bullet. **2** *Printing* a line of type produced by a Linotype machine. **3** *Informal* a mouthful of alcoholic drink, esp. spirits: *he poured out a large slug of Scotch.* ▷ **HISTORY** probably from SLUG[1] (with allusion to the shape of the animal)

slug[3] *vb* **slugging, slugged 1** *Chiefly US & Canad* to hit very hard. ✧ *n* **2** *US & Canad* a heavy blow. ▷ **HISTORY** probably from SLUG[2] (bullet)

sluggard *n Old-fashioned* a very lazy person. ▷ **HISTORY** Middle English *slogarde*

sluggish *adj* **1** lacking energy. **2** moving or working at slower than the normal rate: *the sluggish waters of the canal.*

sluice *n* **1** a channel that carries a rapid current of water, with a sluicegate to control the flow. **2** the water controlled by a sluicegate. **3** same as **sluicegate**. **4** *Mining* a sloping trough for washing ore. ✧ *vb* **sluicing, sluiced 5** to draw off or drain with a sluice. **6** to wash with a stream of water. **7** (often foll. by *away* or *out*) (of water) to run or flow from or as if from a sluice. ▷ **HISTORY** Old French *escluse*

sluicegate *n* a valve or gate fitted to a sluice to control the rate of flow of water.

slum *n* **1** an overcrowded and badly maintained house. **2** (*often pl*) a poor rundown overpopulated section of a city. ✧ *vb* **slumming, slummed 3** to visit slums, esp. for curiosity. **4 slum it** to temporarily and deliberately experience poorer places or conditions. ▷ **HISTORY** origin unknown ▸ **slummy** *adj*

slumber *Literary* ✧ *vb* **1** to sleep. ✧ *n* **2** sleep. ▷ **HISTORY** Old English *slūma* ▸ **slumbering** *adj*

slump *vb* **1** (of commercial activity or prices) to decline suddenly. **2** to sink or fall heavily and suddenly: *she slumped back with exhaustion.* ✧ *n* **3** a severe decline in commercial activity or prices; depression. **4** a sudden or marked decline or failure: *a slump in demand for oil.* ▷ **HISTORY** probably Scandinavian

slung *vb* the past of **sling[1]**.

slunk *vb* the past of **slink**.

slur *vb* **slurring, slurred 1** to pronounce or say (words) unclearly. **2** to make insulting remarks about. **3** *Music* to sing or play (successive notes) smoothly by moving from one to the other without a break. **4** (often foll. by *over*) to treat hastily or carelessly. ✧ *n* **5** an insulting remark intended to damage someone's reputation. **6** a slurring of words. **7** *Music* **a** a slurring of successive notes. **b** the curved line (⌒ or ‿) indicating this. ▷ **HISTORY** probably from Middle Low German

slurp *Informal* ✧ *vb* **1** to eat or drink (something) noisily. ✧ *n* **2** a slurping sound. ▷ **HISTORY** Middle Dutch *slorpen* to sip

slurry *n, pl* **-ries** a thin watery mixture of something such as cement or mud. ▷ **HISTORY** Middle English *slory*

slush *n* **1** any watery muddy substance, esp. melting snow. **2** *Informal* sloppily sentimental language or writing. ▷ **HISTORY** origin unknown ▸ **slushy** *adj*

slush fund *n* a fund for financing political or commercial corruption.

slut *n Offensive* a promiscuous woman. ▷ **HISTORY** origin unknown ▸ **sluttish** *adj*

sly *adj* **slyer, slyest** *or* **slier, sliest 1** (of a person's remarks or gestures) indicating that he or she knows something of which other people may be unaware: *she had the feeling they were poking sly fun at her.* **2** secretive and skilled at deception: *a sly trickster.* **3** roguish: *sly comedy.* **4 on the sly** secretively: *they were smoking on the sly behind the shed.* ▷ **HISTORY** Old Norse *slœgr* clever ▸ **slyly** *adv*

Sm *Chem* samarium.

smack[1] *vb* **1** to slap sharply. **2** to strike loudly or to be struck loudly. **3** to open and close (the lips) loudly to show pleasure or anticipation. ✧ *n* **4** a sharp loud slap, or the sound of such a slap. **5** a loud kiss. **6** a sharp sound made by the lips in enjoyment. **7 smack in the eye** *Informal* a snub or rejection. ✧ *adv Informal* **8** directly; squarely: *smack in the middle.* **9** sharply and unexpectedly: *he ran smack into one of the men.* ▷ **HISTORY** probably imitative

smack[2] *n* **1** a slight flavour or suggestion (of something): *the smack of loss of self-control.* **2** *Slang* heroin. ✧ *vb* **3 smack of a** to have a slight smell or flavour (of something). **b** to have a suggestion (of something): *it smacks of discrimination.* ▷ **HISTORY** Old English *smæc*

smack[3] *n* a small single-masted fishing vessel. ▷ **HISTORY** Dutch *smak*

smacker *n Slang* **1** a loud kiss. **2** a pound note or dollar bill.

small *adj* **1** not large in size or amount. **2** of little importance or on a minor scale: *a small detail.* **3** mean, ungenerous, or petty: *a small mind.* **4** modest or humble: *small beginnings.* **5 feel small** to be humiliated. **6** (of a child or animal) young; not mature. **7** unimportant or trivial: *a small matter.* **8** (of a letter) written or printed in lower case rather as a capital. ✧ *adv* **9** into small pieces: *cut it small.* ✧ *n* **10** the small narrow part of the back. **11 smalls** *Informal, chiefly Brit* underwear. ▷ **HISTORY** Old English *smæl* ▶ **smallish** *adj* ▶ **smallness** *n*

small change *n* coins of low value.

small fry *pl n* **1** people regarded as unimportant. **2** young children.

small goods *pl n Austral & NZ* meats bought from a delicatessen, such as sausages.

smallholding *n* a piece of agricultural land smaller than a farm. ▶ **smallholder** *n*

small hours *pl n* the early hours of the morning, after midnight and before dawn.

small intestine *n Anat* the narrow, longer part of the alimentary canal, in which digestion is completed.

small-minded *adj* having narrow selfish attitudes; petty.

smallpox *n* a contagious disease causing fever, a rash, and blisters which usually leave permanent scars.

small print *n* details in a contract or document printed in small type, esp. when considered as containing important information that people may regret not reading.

small-scale *adj* of limited size or scope.

small talk *n* light conversation for social occasions.

small-time *adj Informal* operating on a limited scale; minor: *a small-time smuggler.*

smarmy *adj* **smarmier, smarmiest** unpleasantly flattering or polite.

smart *adj* **1** clean and neatly dressed. **2** intelligent and shrewd. **3** quick and witty in speech: *a smart talker.* **4** (of places or events) fashionable; chic: *smart restaurants.* **5** vigorous or brisk: *a smart pace.* **6** causing a sharp stinging pain. **7** (of a weapon) containing an electronic device which enables it to be guided to its target: *a smart bomb.* ✧ *vb* **8** to feel or cause a sharp stinging physical or mental pain: *I was still smarting from the insult.* ✧ *n* **9** a stinging pain or feeling. ✧ *adv* **10** in a smart manner. ▷ **HISTORY** Old English *smeortan* be painful ▶ **smartly** *adv* ▶ **smartness** *n*

smart aleck *n Informal* a person who thinks he or she is an expert on every subject; know-all.

smart card *n* a plastic card with integrated circuits used for storing and processing computer data.

smarten *vb* (usually foll. by *up*) to make or become smart.

smash *vb* **1** to break into pieces violently and noisily. **2** (often foll. by *against, through* or *into*) to throw or crash (against) violently, causing shattering: *his head smashed against a window.* **3** to hit or collide forcefully and suddenly. **4** *Racket sports* to hit (the ball) fast and powerfully with an overhead stroke. **5** to defeat or destroy: *the police had smashed a major drug ring.* ✧ *n* **6** an act or sound of smashing. **7** a violent collision of vehicles. **8** *Racket sports* a fast and powerful overhead stroke. **9** *Informal* a show, record or film which is very popular with the public. ✧ *adv* **10** with a smash. ▷ **HISTORY** probably imitative

smasher *n Informal, chiefly Brit* a person or thing that is very attractive or outstanding.

smashing *adj Informal, chiefly Brit* excellent or first-rate.

smash-up *Informal* ✧ *n* **1** a bad collision or crash involving motor vehicles. ✧ *vb* **smash up 2** to damage to the point of complete destruction: *two men smashed up a bar.*

smattering *n* a slight or superficial knowledge: *I knew a smattering of Russian.*

smear *vb* **1** to spread with a greasy or sticky substance. **2** to apply (a greasy or sticky substance) thickly. **3** to rub so as to produce a smudge. **4** to spread false and damaging rumours (about). ✧ *n* **5** a dirty mark or smudge. **6** a false but damaging rumour spread by a rival or enemy. **7** *Med* a small amount of a substance smeared onto a glass slide for examination under a microscope. ▷ **HISTORY** Old English *smeoru* a smear ▶ **smeary** *adj*

smear test *n Med* same as **Pap test**.

smell *vb* **smelling, smelt** *or* **smelled 1** to perceive the scent of (a substance) with the nose. **2** to have a specified kind of smell: *it smells fruity; your supper smells good.* **3** (often foll. by *of*) to emit an odour (of): *the place smells of milk and babies.* **4** to give off an unpleasant odour. **5** (often foll. by *out*) to detect through instinct: *I smell trouble.* **6** to use the sense of smell; sniff. **7 smell of** to indicate or suggest: *anything that smells of devaluation.* ✧ *n* **8** the sense by which scents or odours are perceived. RELATED ADJECTIVE ➔ **olfactory 9** an odour or scent. **10** the act of smelling. ▷ **HISTORY** origin unknown

smelling salts *pl n* a preparation containing crystals of ammonium carbonate, used to revive a person feeling faint.

smelly *adj* **smellier, smelliest** having a nasty smell. ▶ **smelliness** *n*

smelt[1] *vb* to extract (a metal) from (an ore) by heating. ▷ **HISTORY** Middle Low German, Middle Dutch *smelten*

smelt[2] *n, pl* **smelt** *or* **smelts** a small silvery food fish. ▷ **HISTORY** Old English *smylt*

smelt[3] *vb* a past tense and past participle of **smell**.

smelter *n* an industrial plant in which smelting is carried out.

smile *n* **1** a facial expression in which the corners of the mouth are turned up, showing amusement or friendliness. ✧ *vb* **smiling, smiled 2** to give a smile. **3 smile at a** to look at with a kindly

A B C D E F G H I J K L M N O P Q R S T U V W X Y Z

expression. **b** to look with amusement at. **4 smile on** *or* **upon** to regard favourably: *fortune smiled on us today.* **5** to express by a smile: *he smiled a comrade's greeting.* ▷ **HISTORY** probably from Old Norse

smiley *adj* **1** cheerful. **2** depicting a smile. ✧ *n* **3** a group of symbols depicting a smile, or other facial expression, used in e-mail.

smirch *vb* **1** to disgrace. **2** to dirty or soil. ✧ *n* **3** a disgrace. **4** a smear or stain. ▷ **HISTORY** origin unknown

smirk *n* **1** a smug smile. ✧ *vb* **2** to give such a smile. ▷ **HISTORY** Old English *smearcian*

smite *vb* **smiting, smote; smitten** *or* **smit** *Archaic biblical* **1** to strike with a heavy blow. **2** to affect severely: *hunger smites him again.* **3** to burden with an affliction in order to punish: *God smote the enemies of the righteous.* **4 smite on** to strike abruptly and with force: *the sun smote down on him.* ▷ **HISTORY** Old English *smītan*

smith *n* **1** a person who works in metal: *goldsmith.* **2** See **blacksmith**. ▷ **HISTORY** Old English

smithereens *pl n* shattered fragments. ▷ **HISTORY** Irish Gaelic *smidirīn*

smithy *n, pl* **smithies** the workshop of a blacksmith; forge.

smitten *vb* **1** a past participle of **smite**. ✧ *adj* **2** deeply affected by love (for).

smock *n* **1** a loose overall worn to protect the clothes. **2** a loose blouselike garment worn by women. **3** a loose protective overgarment decorated with smocking, worn formerly by farm workers. ✧ *vb* **4** to gather (material) by sewing in a honeycomb pattern. ▷ **HISTORY** Old English *smocc*

smocking *n* ornamental needlework used to gather material.

smog *n* a mixture of smoke and fog that occurs in some industrial areas. ▷ **HISTORY** SMOKE + FOG ▶ **smoggy** *adj*

smoke *n* **1** the cloudy mass that rises from something burning. **2** the act of smoking tobacco. **3** *Informal* a cigarette or cigar. **4 go up in smoke a** to come to nothing. **b** to burn up vigorously. ✧ *vb* **smoking, smoked 5** to give off smoke: *a smoking fireplace.* **6 a** to draw the smoke of (burning tobacco) into the mouth and exhale it again. **b** to do this habitually. **7** to cure (meat, cheese, or fish) by treating with smoke. ▷ **HISTORY** Old English *smoca*

smokeless *adj* having or producing little or no smoke: *smokeless fuel.*

smokeless zone *n* an area where only smokeless fuels may be used.

smoke out *vb* **1** to drive (a person or animal) out of a hiding place by filling it with smoke. **2** to bring (someone) out of secrecy and into the open: *they smoked out the plotters.*

smoker *n* **1** a person who habitually smokes tobacco. **2** a train compartment where smoking is permitted.

smoke screen *n* **1** something said or done to hide the truth. **2** *Mil* a cloud of smoke used to provide cover for manoeuvres.

smokestack *n* a tall chimney that carries smoke away from a factory.

smoko *or* **smokeho** (**smoke**-oh) *n, pl* **-kos** *or* **-hos** *Austral & NZ informal* **1** a short break from work for tea or a cigarette. **2** refreshment taken during this break.

smoky *adj* **smokier, smokiest 1** filled with or giving off smoke, sometimes excessively: *smoky coal or wood fires.* **2** having the colour of smoke. **3** having the taste or smell of smoke. **4** made dirty or hazy by smoke. ▶ **smokiness** *n*

smolt *n* a young salmon at the stage when it migrates from fresh water to the sea. ▷ **HISTORY** Scots

smooch *Slang* ✧ *vb* **1** (of two people) to kiss and cuddle. **2** *Brit* to dance very slowly with one's arms around another person or (of two people) to dance together in such a way. ✧ *n* **3** the act of smooching. ▷ **HISTORY** dialect *smouch,* imitative

smoodge *or* **smooge** *vb* **smoodging, smoodged** *or* **smooging, smooged** *Austral & NZ* **1** same as **smooch** (sense 1). **2** to attempt to gain favour through flattery.

smooth *adj* **1** having an even surface with no roughness, bumps, or holes. **2** without obstructions or difficulties: *smooth progress towards an agreement.* **3** without lumps: *a smooth paste.* **4** free from jolts and bumps: *a smooth landing.* **5** not harsh in taste; mellow: *an excellent smooth wine.* **6** charming or persuasive but possibly insincere. ✧ *adv* **7** in a smooth manner. ✧ *vb* **8** (often foll. by *down*) to make or become even or without roughness. **9** (often foll. by *out* or *away*) to remove in order to make smooth: *smoothing out the creases.* **10** to make calm; soothe. **11** to make easier: *Moscow smoothed the path to democracy.* ✧ *n* **12** the smooth part of something. **13** the act of smoothing. ▷ **HISTORY** Old English *smōth* ▶ **smoothly** *adv*

smoothie *n* **1** *Slang* a man who is so confident, well-dressed, and charming that one is suspicious of his motives and doubts his honesty. **2** a smooth thick drink made from fresh fruit and yoghurt, ice cream, or milk.

smorgasbord *n* a variety of savoury dishes served as hors d'oeuvres or as a buffet meal. ▷ **HISTORY** Swedish

smote *vb* the past tense of **smite**.

smother *vb* **1** to extinguish (a fire) by covering so as to cut it off from the air. **2** to suffocate. **3** to surround or overwhelm (with): *she smothered him with her idea of affection.* **4** to suppress or stifle: *he smothered an ironic chuckle.* **5** to cover over thickly: *ice cream smothered with sauce.* ▷ **HISTORY** Old English *smorian* to suffocate

smoulder *or US* **smolder** *vb* **1** to burn slowly without flames, usually giving off smoke. **2** (of emotions) to exist in a suppressed state without being released. ▷ **HISTORY** origin unknown

SMS short message system: used for sending data to mobile phones.

smudge *vb* **smudging, smudged 1** to make or become smeared or soiled. ✧ *n* **2** a smear or dirty mark. **3** a blurred form or area: *the dull smudge of a ship.* ▷ **HISTORY** origin unknown ▶ **smudgy** *adj*

smug *adj* **smugger, smuggest** very pleased with oneself; self-satisfied. ▷ **HISTORY** Germanic ▶ **smugly** *adv* ▶ **smugness** *n*

smuggle *vb* **-gling, -gled 1** to import or export (goods that are prohibited or subject to taxation) secretly. **2** (often foll. by *into* or *out of*) to bring or take secretly: *he was smuggled out of the country unnoticed.* ▷ **HISTORY** Low German *smukkelen* ▶ **smuggler** *n* ▶ **smuggling** *n*

smut *n* **1** stories, pictures, or jokes relating to sex or nudity. **2** a speck of soot or a dark mark left by soot. **3** a disease of cereals, in which black sooty masses cover the affected parts. ▷ **HISTORY** Old English *smitte* ▶ **smutty** *adj*

Sn *Chem* tin. ▷ **HISTORY** New Latin *stannum*

snack *n* a light quick meal eaten between or in place of main meals. ▷ **HISTORY** probably from Middle Dutch *snacken*

snack bar *n* a place where light meals or snacks are sold.

snaffle *n* **1** a mouthpiece for controlling a horse. ✧ *vb* **-fling, -fled 2** *Brit, Austral & NZ informal* to steal or take. **3** to fit or control (a horse) with a snaffle. ▷ **HISTORY** origin unknown

snafu (snaf-**foo**) *Chiefly mil slang* ✧ *n* **1** confusion or chaos regarded as the normal state. ✧ *adj* **2** confused or muddled up, as usual. ▷ **HISTORY** *s(ituation) n(ormal): a(ll) f(ucked) u(p)*

snag *n* **1** a small problem or difficulty: *one possible snag in his plans.* **2** a sharp projecting point that may catch on things. **3** a small hole in a fabric caused by a sharp object. **4** a tree stump in a river bed that is a danger to navigation. ✧ *vb* **snagging, snagged 5** to tear or catch on a snag. ▷ **HISTORY** Scandinavian

snail *n* a slow-moving mollusc with a spiral shell. ▷ **HISTORY** Old English *snæg(e)l*

snail mail *Informal* ✧ *n* **1** conventional post, as opposed to e-mail. **2** the conventional postal system. ✧ *vb* **snail-mail 3** to send by the conventional postal system, rather than by e-mail.

snail's pace *n* a very slow speed.

snake *n* **1** a long scaly limbless reptile. **2** Also: **snake in the grass** a person, esp. a colleague or friend, who secretly acts against one. ✧ *vb* **snaking, snaked 3** to glide or move in a winding course, like a snake. ▷ **HISTORY** Old English *snaca*

snakebite *n* **1** the bite of a snake. **2** a drink of cider and lager.

snake charmer *n* an entertainer who appears to hypnotize snakes by playing music.

snaky *adj* **snakier, snakiest 1** twisting or winding. **2** treacherous.

snap *vb* **snapping, snapped 1** to break suddenly, esp. with a sharp sound. **2** to make or cause to make a sudden sharp cracking sound: *he snapped his fingers.* **3** to move or close with a sudden sharp sound: *I snapped the lid shut.* **4** to move in a sudden or abrupt way. **5** to give way or collapse suddenly under strain: *one day someone's temper will snap.* **6** to panic when a situation becomes too difficult to cope with: *he could snap at any moment.* **7** (often foll. by *at* or *up*) to seize suddenly or quickly. **8** (often foll. by *at*) (of animals) to bite at suddenly. **9** to speak (words) sharply and angrily. **10** to take a photograph of. **11 snap one's fingers at** *Informal* to defy or dismiss contemptuously. **12 snap out of it** *Informal* to recover quickly, esp. from depression or anger. ✧ *n* **13** the act of breaking suddenly or the sound of a sudden breakage. **14** a sudden sharp sound. **15** a clasp or fastener that closes with a snapping sound. **16** a sudden grab or bite. **17** a thin crisp biscuit: *brandy snaps.* **18** *Informal* an informal photograph taken with a simple camera. **19** See **cold snap**. **20** *Brit & NZ* a card game in which the word *snap* is called when two similar cards are turned up. ✧ *adj* **21** done on the spur of the moment: *snap judgments.* ✧ *adv* **22** with a snap. ✧ *interj* **23 a** *Cards* the word called while playing snap. **b** a cry used to draw attention to the similarity of two things. ✧ See also **snap up**. ▷ **HISTORY** Middle Dutch *snappen* to seize

snapdragon *n* a plant with spikes of colourful flowers that can open and shut like a mouth; antirrhinum.

snapper *n* a food fish of Australia and New Zealand with a pinkish body covered with blue spots.

snappy *adj* **-pier, -piest 1** smart and fashionable: *snappy designs.* **2** Also: **snappish** (of someone's behaviour) irritable, unfriendly, and cross. **3** brisk or lively: *short snappy movements.* **4 make it snappy** *Slang* hurry up! ▶ **snappiness** *n*

snapshot *n* same as **snap** (sense 18).

snap up *vb* to take advantage of eagerly and quickly: *the tickets have been snapped up.*

snare[1] *n* **1** a trap for birds or small animals, usually a flexible loop that is drawn tight around the prey. **2** anything that traps someone or something unawares. ✧ *vb* **snaring, snared 3** to catch in or as if in a snare. ▷ **HISTORY** Old English *sneare*

snare[2] *n Music* a set of strings fitted against the lower head of a snare drum, which produces a rattling sound when the drum is beaten. ▷ **HISTORY** Middle Dutch *snaer* or Middle Low German *snare* string

snare drum *n Music* a small drum fitted with a snare.

snarl[1] *vb* **1** (of an animal) to growl fiercely with bared teeth. **2** to speak or say (something) fiercely: *he snarled out a command to a subordinate.* ✧ *n* **3** a fierce growl or facial expression. **4** the act of snarling. ▷ **HISTORY** Germanic

snarl[2] *n* **1** a complicated or confused state. **2** a tangled mass. ✧ *vb* **3 snarl up** to become, be, or make confused or complicated: *the postal service was snarled up at Christmas.* ▷ **HISTORY** from Old Norse

snarl-up *n Informal* a confused, disorganized situation such as a traffic jam.

snatch *vb* **1** to seize or grasp (something) suddenly: *she snatched the paper.* **2** (usually foll. by at) to attempt to seize suddenly. **3** to take hurriedly: *these players had snatched a few hours sleep.* **4** to remove suddenly: *she snatched her hand away.* ✧ *n* **5** an act of snatching. **6** a small piece or incomplete part: *snatches of song.* **7** a brief spell: *snatches of sleep.* **8** *Slang, chiefly US* an act of kidnapping. **9** *Brit slang* a robbery: *a wages snatch.* ▷ **HISTORY** Middle English *snacchen*

snazzy *adj* **-zier, -ziest** *Informal* (esp. of clothes) stylish and flashy. ▷ **HISTORY** origin unknown

sneak *vb* **1** to move quietly, trying not be noticed. **2** to behave in a cowardly or underhand manner. **3** to bring, take, or put secretly: *we sneaked him over the border.* **4** *Informal, chiefly Brit & NZ* (esp. in schools) to tell tales. ✧ *n* **5** a person who acts in an underhand or cowardly manner. ✧ *adj* **6** without warning: *a sneak attack.* ▷ **HISTORY** Old English *snīcan* to creep ▸ **sneaky** *adj*

sneakers *pl n US, Canad, Austral & NZ* canvas shoes with rubber soles.

sneaking *adj* **1** slight but nagging: *a sneaking suspicion.* **2** secret: *a sneaking admiration.* **3** acting in a cowardly and furtive way.

sneak thief *n* a burglar who sneaks into houses through open doors and windows.

sneer *n* **1** a facial expression showing distaste or contempt, typically with a curled upper lip. **2** a remark showing distaste or contempt. ✧ *vb* **3** to make a facial expression of scorn or contempt. **4** to say (something) in a scornful manner. ▷ **HISTORY** origin unknown ▸ **sneering** *adj, n*

sneeze *vb* **sneezing, sneezed 1** to expel air from the nose suddenly and without control, esp. as the result of irritation in the nostrils. ✧ *n* **2** the act or sound of sneezing. ▷ **HISTORY** Old English *fnēosan* (unattested)

sneeze at *vb Informal* to ignore or dismiss lightly: *the money's not to be sneezed at.*

snib *n Scot & NZ* the catch of a door or window.

snick *n* **1** a small cut in something; notch. **2** *Cricket* a glancing blow off the edge of the bat. ✧ *vb* **3** to make a small cut or notch in (something). **4** *Cricket* to hit (the ball) with a snick. ▷ **HISTORY** probably Scandinavian

snicker *n, vb Chiefly US & Canad* same as **snigger**. ▷ **HISTORY** probably imitative

snide *or* **snidey** *adj* (of comments) critical in an unfair and nasty way. ▷ **HISTORY** origin unknown

sniff *vb* **1** to inhale through the nose in short audible breaths. **2** (often foll. by *at*) to smell by sniffing. ✧ *n* **3** the act or sound of sniffing. ▷ **HISTORY** imitative ▸ **sniffer** *n*

sniff at *vb* to express contempt or dislike for.

sniffer dog *n* a police dog trained to locate drugs or explosives by smell.

sniffle *vb* **-fling, -fled 1** to sniff repeatedly when the nasal passages are blocked up. ✧ *n* **2** the act or sound of sniffling.

sniffles *or* **snuffles** *pl n* **the sniffles** *Informal* a cold in the head.

snifter *n* **1** *Informal* a small quantity of alcoholic drink. **2** a pear-shaped brandy glass. ▷ **HISTORY** origin unknown

snig *vb* **snigging, snigged** *Austral & NZ* to drag (a felled log) by a chain or cable. ▷ **HISTORY** English dialect

snigger *n* **1** a quiet and disrespectful laugh kept to oneself. ✧ *vb* **2** to utter such a laugh. ▷ **HISTORY** variant of *snicker*

snip *vb* **snipping, snipped 1** to cut with small quick strokes with scissors or shears. ✧ *n* **2** *Informal, chiefly Brit* a bargain. **3** the act or sound of snipping. **4** a small piece snipped off. **5** a small cut made by snipping. ▷ **HISTORY** Low German, Dutch *snippen*

snipe *n, pl* **snipe** *or* **snipes 1** a wading bird with a long straight bill. ✧ *vb* **sniping, sniped 2** (often foll. by *at*) to shoot (someone) from a place of hiding. **3** (often foll. by *at*) to make critical remarks about. ▷ **HISTORY** Old Norse *snīpa* ▸ **sniper** *n*

snippet *n* a small scrap or fragment: *the odd snippet of knowledge.*

snitch *Slang* ✧ *vb* **1** to act as an informer. **2** to steal small amounts. ✧ *n* **3** an informer. ▷ **HISTORY** origin unknown

snitchy *adj* **snitchier, snitchiest** *NZ informal* bad-tempered or irritable.

snivel *vb* **-elling, -elled** *or US* **-eling, -eled 1** to cry and sniff in a self-pitying way. **2** to say (something) tearfully; whine. **3** to have a runny nose. ✧ *n* **4** the act of snivelling. ▷ **HISTORY** Middle English *snivelen*

snob *n* **1** a person who tries to associate with those of higher social status and who hates those of a lower social status. **2** a person who feels smugly superior with regard to his or her tastes or interests: *a cultural snob.* ▷ **HISTORY** origin unknown ▸ **snobbery** *n* ▸ **snobbish** *adj*

snoek (**snook**) *n* a South African edible marine fish. ▷ **HISTORY** Afrikaans, from Dutch: pike

snoep (**snoop**) *adj S African informal* mean or tight-fisted. ▷ **HISTORY** Afrikaans: greedy

snog *Brit, NZ & S African slang* ✧ *vb* **snogging, snogged 1** to kiss and cuddle. ✧ *n* **2** the act of kissing and cuddling. ▷ **HISTORY** origin unknown

snood *n* a pouchlike hat loosely holding a woman's hair at the back. ▷ **HISTORY** Old English *snōd*

snook *n* **cock a snook at** *Brit* **a** to make a rude gesture at (someone) by putting one thumb to the nose with the fingers of the hand outstretched. **b** to show contempt for (someone in authority) without fear of punishment. ▷ **HISTORY** origin unknown

snooker *n* **1** a game played on a billiard table with 15 red balls, six balls of other colours, and a white cue ball. **2** a shot in which the cue ball is left in a position such that another ball blocks the target ball. ✧ *vb* **3** to leave (an opponent) in an unfavourable position by playing a snooker. **4** to put someone in a position where he or she can do nothing. ▷ **HISTORY** origin unknown

snoop *Informal* ✧ *vb* **1** (often foll. by *about* or *around*) to pry into the private business of others. ✧ *n* **2** the act of snooping. ▷ **HISTORY** Dutch *snoepen* to eat furtively ▸ **snooper** *n* ▸ **snoopy** *adj*

snooty *adj* **snootier, snootiest** *Informal* behaving as if superior to other people; snobbish. ▷ **HISTORY** from *snoot* nose

snooze *Informal* ✧ *vb* **snoozing, snoozed 1** to take a brief light sleep. ✧ *n* **2** a nap.
▷ **HISTORY** origin unknown

snore *vb* **snoring, snored 1** to breathe with snorting sounds while asleep. ✧ *n* **2** the act or sound of snoring. ▷ **HISTORY** imitative

snorkel *n* **1** a tube allowing a swimmer to breathe while face down on the surface of the water. **2** a device supplying air to a submarine when under water. ✧ *vb* **-kelling, -kelled** *or US* **-keling, -keled 3** to swim with a snorkel.
▷ **HISTORY** German *Schnorchel*

snort *vb* **1** to exhale air noisily through the nostrils. **2** to express contempt or annoyance by snorting. **3** to say with a snort. **4** *Slang* to inhale a powdered drug through the nostrils. ✧ *n* **5** a loud exhalation of air through the nostrils to express contempt or annoyance: *Clare gave a snort of disgust.* ▷ **HISTORY** Middle English *snorten*

snot *n Usually considered vulgar* **1** mucus from the nose. **2** *Slang* an annoying or disgusting person.
▷ **HISTORY** Old English *gesnot*

snotty *adj* **-tier, -tiest** *Considered vulgar* **1** dirty with nasal discharge. **2** having a proud and superior attitude. **3** *Slang* contemptible; nasty.
▶ **snottiness** *n*

snout *n* **1** the projecting nose and jaws of an animal. **2** anything projecting like a snout: *the snout of a gun.* **3** *Slang* a person's nose.
▷ **HISTORY** Germanic

snow *n* **1** frozen vapour falling from the sky in flakes. **2** a layer of snow on the ground. **3** a falling of snow. **4** *Slang* cocaine. ✧ *vb* **5** (with *it* as subject) to be the case that snow is falling: *it's snowing today.* **6** (usually passive, foll. by *over, under, in* or *up*) to cover or confine with a heavy fall of snow. **7** to fall as or like snow. **8 be snowed under** to be overwhelmed, esp. with paperwork. ▷ **HISTORY** Old English *snāw* ▶ **snowy** *adj*

snowball *n* **1** snow pressed into a ball for throwing. ✧ *vb* **2** to increase rapidly in size or importance: *production snowballed between 1950 and 1970.* **3** to throw snowballs at.

snowberry *n, pl* **-ries** a shrub grown for its white berries.

snow-blind *adj* blinded for a short time by the intense reflection of sunlight from snow. ▶ **snow blindness** *n*

snowboard *n* a shaped board, like a skateboard without wheels, on which a person stands to slide across the snow. ▶ **snowboarding** *n*

snowbound *adj* shut in or blocked off by snow.

snowcap *n* a cap of snow on top of a mountain.
▶ **snowcapped** *adj*

snowdrift *n* a bank of deep snow driven together by the wind.

snowdrop *n* a plant with small drooping white bell-shaped flowers.

snowfall *n* **1** a fall of snow. **2** *Meteorol* the amount of snow that falls in a specified place and time.

snowflake *n* a single crystal of snow.

snow goose *n* a North American goose with white feathers and black wing tips.

snow gum *n* same as **sallee**.

snow line *n Geog* (on a mountain) the altitude above which there is permanent snow.

snowman *n, pl* **-men** a figure like a person, made of packed snow.

snowmobile *n* a motor vehicle for travelling on snow, esp. one with caterpillar tracks and front skis.

snowplough *or esp US* **snowplow** *n* a vehicle for clearing away snow.

snowstorm *n* a storm with heavy snow.

SNP Scottish National Party.

snub *vb* **snubbing, snubbed 1** to insult (someone) deliberately. ✧ *n* **2** a deliberately insulting act or remark. ✧ *adj* **3** (of a nose) short and turned up. ▷ **HISTORY** Old Norse *snubba* to scold

snub-nosed *adj* having a short turned-up nose.

snuff[1] *vb* **1** to inhale through the nose. **2** (esp. of an animal) to examine by sniffing. ✧ *n* **3** a sniff.
▷ **HISTORY** probably Middle Dutch *snuffen* to snuffle

snuff[2] *n* finely powdered tobacco for sniffing up the nostrils. ▷ **HISTORY** Dutch *snuf*

snuff[3] *vb* **1** (often foll. by *out*) to put out (a candle). **2** to cut off the charred part of (a candle wick). **3** (usually foll. by *out*) *Informal* to put an end to. **4 snuff it** *Brit & Austral informal* to die. ✧ *n* **5** the burned portion of the wick of a candle.
▷ **HISTORY** origin unknown

snuffle *vb* **-fling, -fled 1** to breathe noisily or with difficulty. **2** to say or speak through the nose. **3** to cry and sniff in a self-pitying way. ✧ *n* **4** an act or the sound of snuffling. ▷ **HISTORY** Low German or Dutch *snuffelen* ▶ **snuffly** *adj*

snug *adj* **snugger, snuggest 1** comfortably warm and well protected; cosy: *safe and snug in their homes.* **2** small but comfortable: *a snug office.* **3** fitting closely and comfortably. ✧ *n* **4** (in Britain and Ireland) a small room in a pub.
▷ **HISTORY** Swedish *snygg* tidy ▶ **snugly** *adv*

snuggle *vb* **-gling, -gled** to nestle into (a person or thing) for warmth or from affection.
▷ **HISTORY** from SNUG

so[1] *adv* **1** to such an extent: *the river is so dirty that it smells.* **2** to the same extent as: *she is not so old as you.* **3** extremely: *it's so lovely.* **4** also: *I can speak Spanish and so can you.* **5** thereupon: *and so we ended up in France.* **6** in the state or manner expressed or implied: *they're happy and will remain so.* **7 and so on** *or* **forth** and continuing similarly. **8 or so** approximately: *fifty or so people came to see me.* **9 so be it** an expression of agreement or resignation. **10 so much a** a certain degree or amount (of). **b** a lot (of): *it's just so much nonsense.* **11 so much for a** no more need be said about. **b** used to express contempt for something that has failed: *so much for all our plans.* ✧ *conj* (often foll. by *that*) **12** in order (that): *to die so that you might live.* **13** with the consequence (that): *he was late home, so that there was trouble.* **14 so as** in order (to): *to diet so as to lose weight.* **15** *Not universally accepted* in consequence: *she wasn't needed, so she left.* **16 so what!** *Informal* that is unimportant. ✧ *pron* **17** used to substitute for a clause or sentence, which may be understood: *you'll stop because I said so.* ✧ *adj* **18** true: *it can't be so.* ✧ *interj* **19** an exclamation of surprise or triumph. ▷ **HISTORY** Old English *swā*

> **WORD TIP**
> In formal English, *so* is not used as a conjunction to indicate either purpose (*he left by a back door so he could avoid photographers*) or result (*the project was abandoned so his services were no longer needed*). In the former case *to* or *in order to* should be used instead, and in the latter case *and so* or *and therefore* would be more acceptable. The expression *so therefore* should not be used.

so² *n Music* same as **soh**.

soak *vb* **1** to put or lie in a liquid so as to become thoroughly wet. **2** (usually foll. by *in* or *into*) (of a liquid) to penetrate or permeate. **3** (usually foll. by *in* or *up*) to take in; absorb: *white clay soaks up excess oil.* ✧ *n* **4** a soaking or being soaked. **5** *Slang* a person who drinks very heavily. ▷ **HISTORY** Old English *sōcian* ▶ **soaking** *n, adj*

so-and-so *n, pl* **so-and-sos** *Informal* **1** a person whose name is not specified. **2** *Euphemistic* a person regarded as unpleasant; a name used in place of a swear word: *you're a dirty so-and-so.*

soap *n* **1** a compound of alkali and fat, used with water as a cleaning agent. **2** *Informal* short for **soap opera**. ✧ *vb* **3** to apply soap to. ▷ **HISTORY** Old English *sāpe*

soapbox *n* a crate used as a platform for making speeches.

soap opera *n* an on-going television or radio serial about the daily lives of a group of people. ▷ **HISTORY** so called because manufacturers of soap were typical sponsors

soapstone *n* a soft mineral used for making table tops and ornaments.

soapsuds *pl n* foam or lather produced when soap is mixed with water.

soapy *adj* **soapier, soapiest 1** containing or covered with soap: *a soapy liquid.* **2** like soap in texture, smell, or taste: *the cheese had a soapy taste.* **3** *Slang* flattering or persuasive. ▶ **soapiness** *n*

soar *vb* **1** to rise or fly upwards into the air. **2** (of a bird or aircraft) to glide while maintaining altitude. **3** to rise or increase suddenly above the usual level: *television ratings soared.* ▷ **HISTORY** Old French *essorer*

sob *vb* **sobbing, sobbed 1** to cry noisily, breathing in short gasps. **2** to speak with sobs. ✧ *n* **3** the act or sound of sobbing. ▷ **HISTORY** probably from Low German

sober *adj* **1** not drunk. **2** tending to drink only moderate quantities of alcohol. **3** serious and thoughtful: *a sober and serious fellow.* **4** (of colours) plain and dull. **5** free from exaggeration: *a fairly sober version of what happened.* ✧ *vb* **6** (usually foll. by *up*) to make or become less drunk. ▷ **HISTORY** Latin *sobrius* ▶ **sobering** *adj*

sobriety *n* the state of being sober.

sobriquet *or* **soubriquet** (**so**-brik-ay) *n* a nickname. ▷ **HISTORY** French *soubriquet*

sob story *n* a tale of personal misfortune or bad luck intended to arouse sympathy.

Soc. *or* **soc. 1** socialist. **2** society.

so-called *adj* called (in the speaker's opinion, wrongly) by that name: *so-called military experts.*

soccer *n* a game in which two teams of eleven players try to kick or head a ball into their opponents' goal, only the goalkeeper on either side being allowed to touch the ball with his hands.

> **WORD HISTORY**
> 'Soccer' is formed from *Association Football.*

sociable *adj* **1** friendly and enjoying other people's company. **2** (of an occasion) providing the opportunity for relaxed and friendly companionship. ▶ **sociability** *n* ▶ **sociably** *adv*

social *adj* **1** living or preferring to live in a community rather than alone. **2** of or relating to human society or organization. **3** of the way people live and work together in groups: *social organization.* **4** of or for companionship or communal activities: *social clubs.* **5** of or engaged in social services: *a social worker.* **6** relating to a certain class of society: *social misfits.* **7** (of certain species of insects) living together in organized colonies: *social bees.* ✧ *n* **8** an informal gathering. ▷ **HISTORY** Latin *socius* a comrade ▶ **socially** *adv*

Social Charter *n* a proposed declaration of the rights, minimum wages, etc. of workers in the European Union.

social climber *n* a person who tries to associate with people from a higher social class in the hope that he or she will be thought also to be upper-class.

social contract *or* **compact** *n* an agreement among individuals to cooperate for greater security, which results in the loss of some personal liberties.

social democrat *n* **1** a person who is in favour of a market or mixed economy but believes the State must play an active role in ensuring social justice and equality of opportunity. **2** (formerly) a person who believed in the gradual transformation of capitalism into democratic socialism. ▶ **social democracy** *n*

social exclusion *n Sociol* the failure of society to provide certain people with those rights normally available to its members, such as employment, health care, education, etc.

social fund *n* (in Britain) a social security fund from which loans or payments may be made to people in cases of extreme need.

social inclusion *n Sociol* the provision of certain rights to all people in society, such as employment, health care, education, etc.

socialism *n* a political and economic theory or system in which the means of production, distribution, and exchange are owned by the community collectively, usually through the state. ▶ **socialist** *n, adj*

socialite *n* a person who goes to many events attended by the rich, famous, and fashionable.

socialize *or* **-ise** *vb* **-izing, -ized** *or* **-ising, -ised** **1** to meet others socially. **2** to prepare for life in society. **3** *Chiefly US* to organize along socialist principles. ▶ **socialization** *or* **-isation** *n*

social market *n* an economic system in which industry and commerce are run by private enterprise within limits set by the government to ensure equality of opportunity and social responsibility.

social science *n* the systematic study of society and of human relationships within society. ▶ **social scientist** *n*

social security *n* state provision for the welfare of the elderly, unemployed, or sick, through pensions and other financial aid.

social services *pl n* welfare services provided by local authorities or a state agency for people with particular social needs.

social studies *n* the study of how people live and organize themselves in society.

social welfare *n* **1** social services provided by a state for the benefit of its citizens. **2** (in New Zealand) a government department concerned with pensions and benefits for the elderly, the sick, etc.

social work *n* social services that give help and advice to the poor, the elderly, and families with problems. ▶ **social worker** *n*

society *n, pl* **-ties** **1** human beings considered as a group. **2** a group of people forming a single community with its own distinctive culture and institutions. **3** the structure, culture, and institutions of such a group. **4** an organized group of people sharing a common aim or interest: *a dramatic society.* **5** the rich and fashionable class of society collectively. **6** *Old-fashioned* companionship: *I enjoy her society.* ▷ **HISTORY** Latin *societas*

Society of Jesus *n* the religious order of the Jesuits.

socioeconomic *adj* of or involving economic and social factors.

sociology *n* the study of the development, organization, functioning, and classification of human societies. ▶ **sociological** *adj* ▶ **sociologist** *n*

sociopolitical *adj* of or involving political and social factors.

sock[1] *n* **1** a cloth covering for the foot, reaching to between the ankle and knee and worn inside a shoe. **2 pull one's socks up** *Brit & NZ informal* to make a determined effort to improve. **3 put a sock in it** *Slang* be quiet! ▷ **HISTORY** Greek *sukkhos* a light shoe

sock[2] *Slang* ✧ *vb* **1** to hit hard. ✧ *n* **2** a hard blow. ▷ **HISTORY** origin unknown

socket *n* **1** a device into which an electric plug can be inserted in order to make a connection in a circuit. **2** *Anat* a bony hollow into which a part or structure fits: *the hip socket.* ▷ **HISTORY** Anglo-Norman *soket* a little ploughshare

Socratic *adj* of the Greek philosopher Socrates, or his teachings.

Socratic method *n Philosophy* the method of instruction used by Socrates, in which a series of questions and answers lead to a logical conclusion.

sod[1] *n* **1** a piece of grass-covered surface soil; turf. **2** *Poetic* the ground. ▷ **HISTORY** Low German

sod[2] *Slang, chiefly Brit* ✧ *n* **1** an unpleasant person. **2** *Jocular* a person, esp. an unlucky one: *the poor sod hasn't been out for weeks.* **3 sod all** *Slang* nothing. ✧ *interj* **4 sod it** an exclamation of annoyance. ▷ **HISTORY** from *sodomite* ▶ **sodding** *adj*

soda *n* **1** a simple compound of sodium, such as sodium carbonate or sodium bicarbonate. **2** same as **soda water**. **3** *US & Canad* a sweet fizzy drink. ▷ **HISTORY** perhaps from Arabic

soda fountain *n US & Canad* **1** a counter that serves soft drinks and snacks. **2** a device dispensing soda water.

soda lime *n Chem* a solid mixture of sodium and calcium hydroxides used to absorb carbon dioxide and dry gases.

soda water *n* a fizzy drink made by charging water with carbon dioxide under pressure.

sodden *adj* **1** soaking wet. **2** (of someone's senses) dulled, esp. by excessive drinking. ▷ **HISTORY** *soden,* obsolete past participle of *seethe*

sodium *n Chem* a very reactive soft silvery-white metallic element. Symbol: Na. ▷ **HISTORY** from SODA

sodium bicarbonate *n* a white soluble crystalline compound used in fizzy drinks, baking powder, and in medicine as an antacid.

sodium carbonate *n* a colourless or white soluble crystalline compound used in the manufacture of glass, ceramics, soap, and paper, and as a cleansing agent.

sodium chlorate *n* a colourless crystalline compound used as a bleaching agent, antiseptic, and weedkiller.

sodium chloride *n* common table salt; a soluble colourless crystalline compound widely used as a seasoning and preservative for food and in the manufacture of chemicals, glass, and soap.

sodium hydroxide *n* a white strongly alkaline solid used in the manufacture of rayon, paper, aluminium, and soap.

sodomite *n* a person who practises sodomy.

sodomy *n* anal intercourse committed by a man with another man or a woman. ▷ **HISTORY** after *Sodom,* Biblical city, noted for its depravity

sofa *n* a long comfortable seat with back and arms for two or more people.

> **WORD HISTORY**
> 'Sofa' comes from Arabic *suffah*, meaning 'an upholstered raised platform'.

soft *adj* **1** easy to dent, shape, or cut: *soft material.* **2** not hard; giving way easily under pressure: *a soft bed.* **3** fine, smooth, or fluffy to the touch: *soft fur.* **4** (of music or sounds) quiet and pleasing. **5** (of light or colour) not excessively bright or harsh. **6** (of a breeze or climate) temperate, mild, or pleasant. **7** with smooth curves rather than sharp edges: *soft focus.* **8** kind or lenient, often to excess. **9** easy to influence or make demands on: *he's a soft touch.* **10** *Informal* feeble or silly; simple: *soft in the head.* **11** not strong or able to endure hardship. **12** (of a drug) nonaddictive. **13** *Informal* requiring little effort; easy: *a soft option.* **14** *Chem* (of water) relatively free of mineral salts and therefore easily able to make soap lather. **15** loving and tender: *soft words.* **16** *Phonetics* denoting the consonants *c* and *g* when they are pronounced sibilantly, as in *cent* and *germ.* **17 soft on a** lenient towards: *he was accused of being soft on criminals.* **b** experiencing romantic love for. ✧ *adv* **18** softly: *to speak soft.* ✧ *interj* **19** *Archaic* quiet! ▷ **HISTORY** Old English *sōfte* ▶ **softly** *adv*

softball *n* a game similar to baseball, played using a larger softer ball.

soft coal *n* same as **bituminous coal**.

soft drink *n* a nonalcoholic drink.

soften *vb* **1** to make or become soft or softer. **2** to make or become more sympathetic and less critical: *the farmers softened their opposition to the legislation.* **3** to lessen the severity or difficulty of: *foreign relief softened the hardship of a terrible winter.* ▶ **softener** *n*

soft furnishings *pl n* curtains, hangings, rugs, and covers.

softie *or* **softy** *n, pl* **softies** *Informal* a person who is easily hurt or upset.

soft news *n* news stories based on analysis and interpretation rather than substance and real events, or entertaining stories dealing human-interest topics and events of local interest. Compare **hard news**.

soft option *n* the easiest of a number of choices.

soft palate *n* the fleshy part at the back of the roof of the mouth.

soft-pedal *vb* **-alling, -alled** *or US* **-aling, -aled** **1** to deliberately avoid emphasizing (something): *he was soft-pedalling the question of tax increases.* ✧ *n* **soft pedal 2** a pedal on a piano that softens the tone.

soft sell *n* a method of selling based on subtle suggestion and gentle persuasion.

soft-soap *vb Informal* to flatter (a person).

soft touch *n Informal* a person who is easily persuaded to perform favours for, or lend money to, other people.

software *n Computers* the programs used with a computer.

softwood *n* the wood of coniferous trees.

soggy *adj* **-gier, -giest 1** soaked with liquid: *a soggy running track.* **2** moist and heavy: *a soggy sandwich.* ▷ **HISTORY** probably from dialect *sog* marsh ▶ **sogginess** *n*

soh *n Music* the fifth note of any ascending major scale.

soigné *or fem* **soignée** (**swah**-nyay) *adj* neat, elegant, and well-dressed: *the soignée deputy editor of Vogue.* ▷ **HISTORY** French

soil[1] *n* **1** the top layer of the land surface of the earth. **2** a specific type of this material: *sandy soil.* **3** land, country, or region: *the first US side to lose on home soil.* ▷ **HISTORY** Latin *solium* a seat, confused with *solum* the ground

soil[2] *vb* **1** to make or become dirty or stained. **2** to bring disgrace upon: *he's soiled our reputation.* ✧ *n* **3** a soiled spot. **4** refuse, manure, or excrement. ▷ **HISTORY** Old French *soillier*

soil creep *n Geol* the gradual downhill movement of soil and loose rock material on a slope.

soil profile *n Geol* the layers of soil between the surface and the bedrock seen in cross section.

soil texture *n Geol, agriculture* the texture of soil to the touch, dependent on the relative amounts of clay, sand, etc. in it.

soiree (**swah**-ray) *n* an evening social gathering. ▷ **HISTORY** French

sojourn (**soj**-urn) *Literary* ✧ *n* **1** a short stay in a place. ✧ *vb* **2** to stay temporarily: *he sojourned in Basle during a short illness.* ▷ **HISTORY** Old French *sojorner*

sol[1] *n Music* same as **soh**.

sol[2] *n Chem* a liquid colloidal solution.

solace (**sol**-iss) *n* **1** comfort in misery or disappointment: *it drove him to seek increasing solace in alcohol.* **2** something that gives comfort or consolation: *his music was a solace to me during my illness.* ✧ *vb* **-acing, -aced 3** to give comfort or cheer to (a person) in time of sorrow or distress. ▷ **HISTORY** Old French *solas*

solar *adj* **1** of the sun: *a solar eclipse.* **2** operating by or using the energy of the sun: *solar cell.* ▷ **HISTORY** Latin *sol* the sun

solarium *n, pl* **-lariums** *or* **-laria** a place with beds equipped with ultraviolet lights used for giving people an artificial suntan. ▷ **HISTORY** Latin: a terrace

solar plexus *n* **1** *Anat* a network of nerves behind the stomach. **2** *Not in technical use* the vulnerable part of the stomach beneath the diaphragm.

solar power *n Science* heat radiation from the sun converted into electrical power.

solar system *n* the system containing the sun and the planets, comets, and asteroids that go round it.

sold *vb* **1** the past of **sell**. ✧ *adj* **2 sold on** *Slang* enthusiastic and uncritical about.

solder *n* **1** an alloy used for joining two metal surfaces by melting the alloy so that it forms a thin layer between the surfaces. ✧ *vb* **2** to join or mend or be joined or mended with solder. ▷ **HISTORY** Latin *solidare* to strengthen

soldering iron *n* a hand tool with a copper tip that is heated and used to melt and apply solder.

soldier *n* **1 a** a person who serves or has served in an army. **b** a person who is not an officer in an army. ✧ *vb* **2** to serve as a soldier. ▷ **HISTORY** Old French *soudier* ▶ **soldierly** *adj*

soldier of fortune *n* a man who seeks money or adventure as a soldier; mercenary.

soldier on *vb* to continue one's efforts despite difficulties or pressure.

sole[1] *adj* **1** being the only one; only. **2** not shared; exclusive: *sole ownership.* ▷ HISTORY Latin *solus* alone

sole[2] *n* **1** the underside of the foot. **2** the underside of a shoe. **3** the lower surface of an object. ✧ *vb* **soling, soled 4** to provide (a shoe) with a sole. ▷ HISTORY Latin *solea* sandal

sole[3] *n, pl* **sole** *or* **soles** an edible marine flatfish. ▷ HISTORY Latin *solea* a sandal (from the fish's shape)

sole charge school *n NZ* a country school with only one teacher.

solecism (**sol**-iss-iz-zum) *n Formal* **1** a minor grammatical mistake in speech or writing. **2** an action considered not to be good manners. ▷ HISTORY Greek *soloikos* speaking incorrectly ▶ **solecistic** *adj*

solely *adv* **1** only; completely: *an action intended solely to line his own pockets.* **2** without others.

solemn *adj* **1** very serious; deeply sincere: *my solemn promise.* **2** marked by ceremony or formality: *a solemn ritual.* **3** serious or glum: *a solemn look on her face.* ▷ HISTORY Latin *sollemnis* appointed ▶ **solemnly** *adv*

solemnity *n, pl* **-ties 1** the state or quality of being solemn. **2** a solemn ceremony or ritual.

solemnize *or* **-nise** *vb* **-nizing, -nized** *or* **-nising, -nised 1** to celebrate or perform (a ceremony, esp. of marriage). **2** to make solemn or serious. ▶ **solemnization** *or* **-nisation** *n*

solenoid (**sole**-in-oid) *n* a coil of wire, usually cylindrical, in which a magnetic field is set up by passing a current through it. ▷ HISTORY French *solénoïde* ▶ **solenoidal** *adj*

sol-fa *n* short for **tonic sol-fa**.

solicit *vb* **1** *Formal* to seek or request, esp. formally: *she was brushed aside when soliciting his support for the vote.* **2** to approach (a person) with an offer of sex in return for money. ▷ HISTORY Latin *sollicitare* to harass ▶ **solicitation** *n*

solicitor *n Brit, Austral & NZ* a lawyer who advises clients on matters of law, draws up legal documents, and prepares cases for barristers.

Solicitor General *n, pl* **Solicitors General** (in Britain) the law officer of the Crown ranking next to the Attorney General (in Scotland to the Lord Advocate) and acting as his assistant.

solicitous *adj Formal* **1** anxious about someone's welfare. **2** eager. ▷ HISTORY Latin *sollicitus* anxious ▶ **solicitousness** *n*

solicitude *n Formal* anxiety or concern for someone's welfare.

solid *adj* **1** (of a substance) in a physical state in which it resists changes in size and shape; not liquid or gaseous. **2** consisting of matter all through; not hollow. **3** of the same substance all through: *solid gold.* **4** firm, strong, or substantial: *the solid door of a farmhouse.* **5** proved or provable: *solid evidence.* **6** law-abiding and respectable: *solid family men.* **7** (of a meal or food) substantial. **8** without interruption; continuous or unbroken: *solid bombardment.* **9** financially sound: *a solid institution.* **10** strongly united or established: *a solid marriage.* **11** *Geom* having or relating to three dimensions. **12** adequate; sound, but not brilliant: *a solid career.* **13** of a single uniform colour or tone. ✧ *n* **14** *Geom* a three-dimensional shape. **15** a solid substance. ▷ HISTORY Latin *solidus* firm ▶ **solidity** *n* ▶ **solidly** *adv*

solidarity *n, pl* **-ties** agreement in interests or aims among members of a group; total unity.

solid geometry *n* the branch of geometry concerned with three-dimensional figures.

solidify *vb* **-fies, -fying, -fied 1** to make or become solid or hard. **2** to make or become strong or unlikely to change: *a move that solidified the allegiance of our followers.* ▶ **solidification** *n*

solid-state *adj* (of an electronic device) using a semiconductor component, such as a transistor or silicon chip, in which current flow is through solid material, rather than a valve or mechanical part, in which current flow is through a vacuum.

solidus *n, pl* **-di** a short oblique stroke used in text to separate items, such as *and/or.*

soliloquize *or* **-quise** *vb* **-quizing, -quized** *or* **-quising, -quised** to say a soliloquy.

soliloquy *n, pl* **-quies** a speech made by a person while alone, esp. in a play. ▷ HISTORY Latin *solus* sole + *loqui* to speak

WORD TIP
Soliloquy is sometimes wrongly used where *monologue* is meant. Both words refer to a long speech by one person, but a *monologue* can be addressed to other people, whereas in a *soliloquy* the speaker is always talking to himself or herself.

solipsism *n Philosophy* the doctrine that the self is the only thing known to exist. ▷ HISTORY Latin *solus* alone + *ipse* self ▶ **solipsist** *n*

solitaire *n* **1** a game played by one person, involving moving and taking pegs in a pegboard with the object of being left with only one. **2** a gem, esp. a diamond, set alone in a ring. **3** *Chiefly US* patience (the card game). ▷ HISTORY French

solitary *adj* **1** experienced or performed alone: *a solitary dinner.* **2** living a life of solitude: *a solitary child.* **3** single; alone: *the solitary cigarette in the ashtray.* **4** having few friends; lonely. **5** (of a place) without people; empty. ✧ *n, pl* **-taries 6** a person who lives on his or her own; hermit. **7** *Informal* short for **solitary confinement:** *I can't put him back in solitary.* ▷ HISTORY Latin *solitarius* ▶ **solitariness** *n*

solitary confinement *n* isolation of a prisoner in a special cell.

solitude *n* the state of being alone.

solo *n, pl* **-los 1** a piece of music or section of a piece of music for one performer: *a trumpet solo.* **2** any performance by an individual without assistance. ✧ *adj* **3** performed by an individual without assistance: *a solo dance.* **4** Also: **solo whist** a card game in which each person plays on his or her own. ✧ *adv* **5** by oneself; alone: *to fly solo across the Atlantic.* ▷ HISTORY Latin *solus* alone ▶ **soloist** *n*

Solomon *n* any person considered to be very wise. ▷ HISTORY after 10th-century BC king of Israel

A B C D E F G H I J K L M N O P Q R S T U V W X Y Z

Solomon's seal *n* a plant with greenish flowers and long waxy leaves.

so long *interj* **1** *Informal* farewell; goodbye. ✧ *adv* **2** *S African slang* for the time being; meanwhile.

solo parent *n NZ* a parent bringing up a child or children alone.

solstice *n* either the shortest day of the year (**winter solstice**) or the longest day of the year (**summer solstice**). ▷ **HISTORY** Latin *solstitium* the standing still of the sun

soluble *adj* **1** (of a substance) capable of being dissolved. **2** (of a mystery or problem) capable of being solved. ▸ **solubility** *n*

solute *n Chem* the substance in a solution that is dissolved. ▷ **HISTORY** Latin *solutus* free

solution *n* **1** a specific answer to or way of answering a problem. **2** the act or process of solving a problem. **3** *Chem* a mixture of two or more substances in which the molecules or atoms of the substances are completely dispersed. **4** the act or process of forming a solution. **5** the state of being dissolved: *the sugar is held in solution.* ▷ **HISTORY** Latin *solutio* an unloosing

solve *vb* **solving, solved** to find the explanation for or solution to (a mystery or problem). ▷ **HISTORY** Latin *solvere* to loosen ▸ **solvable** *adj*

solvent *adj* **1** having enough money to pay off one's debts. **2** (of a liquid) capable of dissolving other substances. ✧ *n* **3** a liquid capable of dissolving other substances. ▷ **HISTORY** Latin *solvens* releasing ▸ **solvency** *n*

solvent abuse *n* the deliberate inhaling of intoxicating fumes from certain solvents.

somatic *adj* of or relating to the body as distinct from the mind: *somatic symptoms.* ▷ **HISTORY** Greek *sōma* the body

sombre *or US* **somber** *adj* **1** serious, sad, or gloomy: *a sombre message.* **2** (of a place) dim or gloomy. **3** (of colour or clothes) dull or dark. ▷ **HISTORY** Latin *sub* beneath + *umbra* shade ▸ **sombrely** *or US* **somberly** *adv*

sombrero *n, pl* **-ros** a wide-brimmed Mexican hat. ▷ **HISTORY** Spanish

some *adj* **1** unknown or unspecified: *some man called for you.* **2** an unknown or unspecified quantity or number of: *I've got some money.* **3 a** a considerable number or amount of: *he lived some years afterwards.* **b** a little: *show some respect.* **4** *Informal* an impressive or remarkable: *that was some game!* ✧ *pron* **5** certain unknown or unspecified people or things: *some can teach and others can't.* **6** an unknown or unspecified quantity of something or number of people or things: *he will sell some in his pub.* ✧ *adv* **7** approximately: *some thirty pounds.* ▷ **HISTORY** Old English *sum*

somebody *pron* **1** some person; someone. ✧ *n, pl* **-bodies 2** a person of great importance: *he was a somebody.*

> ☑ **WORD TIP**
> See at **everyone.**

somehow *adv* **1** in some unspecified way. **2** for some unknown reason: *somehow I can't do it.*

someone *pron* some person; somebody.

> ☑ **WORD TIP**
> See at **everyone.**

somersault *n* **1** a leap or roll in which the head is placed on the ground and the trunk and legs are turned over it. ✧ *vb* **2** to perform a somersault. ▷ **HISTORY** Old French *soubresault*

something *pron* **1** an unspecified or unknown thing; some thing: *there was something wrong.* **2** an unspecified or unknown amount: *something less than a hundred.* **3** an impressive or important person, thing, or event: *isn't that something?* **4 something else** *Slang, chiefly US* a remarkable person or thing. ✧ *adv* **5** to some degree; somewhat: *he looks something like me.*

-something *n combining form* a person whose age can approximately expressed by a specific decade: *twentysomethings.* ▷ **HISTORY** from the US television series *thirtysomething*

sometime *adv* **1** at some unspecified point of time. ✧ *adj* **2** former: *a sometime actress.*

> ☑ **WORD TIP**
> The form *sometime* should not be used to refer to a fairly long period of time: *he has been away for some time* (not *for sometime*).

sometimes *adv* now and then; from time to time.

somewhat *adv* rather; a bit: *somewhat surprising.*

somewhere *adv* **1** in, to, or at some unknown or unspecified place, point, or amount: *somewhere down south; somewhere between 35 and 45 per cent.* **2 getting somewhere** *Informal* making progress.

somnambulism *n Formal* the condition of walking in one's sleep. ▷ **HISTORY** Latin *somnus* sleep + *ambulare* to walk ▸ **somnambulist** *n*

somnolent *adj Formal* drowsy; sleepy. ▷ **HISTORY** Latin *somnus* sleep ▸ **somnolence** *n*

son *n* **1** a male offspring. **2** a form of address for a man or boy who is younger than the speaker. **3** a male who comes from a certain place or one closely connected with a certain thing: *a good son of the church.* RELATED ADJECTIVE ▸ **filial** ▷ **HISTORY** Old English *sunu*

Son *n Christianity* the second member of the Trinity, Jesus Christ.

sonar *n* a device that locates objects by the reflection of sound waves: used in underwater navigation and target detection. ▷ **HISTORY** *so(und) na(vigation and) r(anging)*

sonata *n* a piece of classical music, usually in three or more movements, for piano or for another instrument with or without piano. ▷ **HISTORY** Italian

son et lumière (**sonn** ay **loom**-yair) *n* an entertainment staged at night at a famous building or historical site, at which its history is described by a speaker accompanied by lighting effects and music. ▷ **HISTORY** French, literally: sound and light

song *n* **1** a piece of music with words, composed for the voice. **2** the tuneful call made by certain birds or insects. **3** the act or process of singing: *he broke into song.* **4 for a song** at a bargain price. **5 make a song and dance** *Brit & NZ informal* to make an unnecessary fuss. ▷ **HISTORY** Old English *sang*

songbird *n* any bird that has a musical call.

songololo (song-gol-**loll**-o) *n, pl* **-los** *S African* a kind of millipede. ▷ **HISTORY** Nguni (language group of southern Africa) *ukusonga* to roll up

songstress *n* a female singer of popular songs.

song thrush *n* a common thrush that repeats each note of its song.

sonic *adj* of, involving, or producing sound. ▷ **HISTORY** Latin *sonus* sound

sonic barrier *n* same as **sound barrier**.

sonic boom *n* a loud explosive sound caused by the shock wave of an aircraft travelling at supersonic speed.

son-in-law *n, pl* **sons-in-law** the husband of one's daughter.

sonnet *n Prosody* a verse form consisting of 14 lines with a fixed rhyme scheme and rhythm pattern. ▷ **HISTORY** Old Provençal *sonet* a little poem

sonny *n Often patronizing* a familiar term of address to a boy or man.

sonorous *adj* **1** (of a sound) deep or rich. **2** (of speech) using language that is unnecessarily complicated and difficult to understand; pompous. ▷ **HISTORY** Latin *sonor* a noise ▶ **sonority** *n*

soon *adv* **1** in or after a short time; before long. **2 as soon as** at the very moment that: *as soon as he had closed the door.* **3 as soon ... as** used to indicate that the first alternative is slightly preferable to the second: *they'd just as soon die for him as live.* ▷ **HISTORY** Old English *sōna*

sooner *adv* **1** the comparative of **soon:** *I only wish I'd been back sooner.* **2** rather; in preference: *he would sooner leave the party than break with me.* **3 no sooner ... than** immediately after or when: *no sooner had he spoken than the stench drifted up.* **4 sooner or later** eventually.

> ☑ **WORD TIP**
> *When* is sometimes used instead of *than* after *no sooner,* but this use is generally regarded as incorrect: *no sooner had he arrived than* (not *when*) *the telephone rang.*

soot *n* a black powder formed by the incomplete burning of organic substances such as coal. ▷ **HISTORY** Old English *sōt* ▶ **sooty** *adj*

soothe *vb* **soothing, soothed 1** to make (a worried or angry person) calm and relaxed. **2** (of an ointment or cream) to relieve (pain). ▷ **HISTORY** Old English *sōthian* to prove ▶ **soothing** *adj*

soothsayer *n* a person who makes predictions about the future; prophet.

sop *n* **1** a small bribe or concession given or made to someone to keep them from causing trouble: *a sop to her conscience.* **2** *Informal* a stupid or weak person. **3 sops** food soaked in a liquid before being eaten. ✧ *vb* **sopping, sopped 4 sop up** to soak up or absorb (liquid). ▷ **HISTORY** Old English *sopp*

sophism *n* an argument that seems reasonable but is actually false and misleading. ▷ **HISTORY** Greek *sophisma* ingenious trick

sophist *n* a person who uses clever but false arguments. ▷ **HISTORY** Greek *sophistēs* a wise man ▶ **sophistic** *adj*

sophisticate *vb* **-cating, -cated 1** to make (someone) less natural or innocent, such as by education. **2** to make (a machine or method) more complex or refined. ✧ *n* **3** a sophisticated person. ▷ **HISTORY** Latin *sophisticus* sophistic ▶ **sophistication** *n*

sophisticated *adj* **1** having or appealing to fashionable and refined tastes and habits: *a sophisticated restaurant.* **2** intelligent, knowledgeable, or able to appreciate culture and the arts: *a sophisticated concert audience.* **3** (of machines or methods) complex and using advanced technology.

sophistry *n* **1** the practice of using arguments which seem clever but are actually false and misleading. **2** (*pl* **-ries**) an instance of this.

sophomore *n Chiefly US & Canad* a second-year student at a secondary (high) school or college. ▷ **HISTORY** probably from earlier *sophum,* variant of *sophism*

soporific *adj* **1** causing sleep. ✧ *n* **2** a drug that causes sleep. ▷ **HISTORY** Latin *sopor* sleep

sopping *adj* completely soaked; wet through. Also: **sopping wet**

soppy *adj* **-pier, -piest** *Informal* foolishly sentimental: *a soppy love song.* ▶ **soppily** *adv*

soprano *n, pl* **-pranos 1** the highest adult female voice. **2** the voice of a young boy before puberty. **3** a singer with such a voice. **4** the highest or second highest instrument in a family of instruments. ✧ *adj* **5** denoting a musical instrument that is the highest or second highest pitched in its family: *the soprano saxophone.* **6** of or relating to the highest female voice, or the voice of a young boy: *the part is quite possibly the most demanding soprano role Wagner ever wrote.* ▷ **HISTORY** Italian

sorbet *n* a flavoured water ice. ▷ **HISTORY** French, from Arabic *sharbah* a drink

sorcerer *or fem* **sorceress** *n* a person who uses magic powers; a wizard. ▷ **HISTORY** Old French *sorcier*

sorcery *n, pl* **-ceries** witchcraft or magic. ▷ **HISTORY** Old French *sorcerie*

sordid *adj* **1** dirty, depressing, and squalid: *a sordid backstreet in a slum area.* **2** relating to sex in a crude or unpleasant way: *the sordid details of his affair.* **3** involving immoral and selfish behaviour: *the sordid history of the slave trade.* ▷ **HISTORY** Latin *sordidus*

sore *adj* **1** (of a wound, injury, etc.) painfully sensitive; tender. **2** causing annoyance and resentment: *a sore point.* **3** upset and angered: *she's still sore about last night.* **4** *Literary* urgent; pressing: *in sore need of firm government.* ✧ *n* **5** a painful or sensitive wound or injury. ✧ *adv* **6 sore afraid** *Archaic* greatly frightened. ▷ **HISTORY** Old English *sār*

sorely *adv* greatly: *sorely disappointed.*

sorghum *n* a grass grown for grain and as a source of syrup. ▷ **HISTORY** Italian *sorgo*

sorority *n, pl* **-ties** *Chiefly US* a society of female students. ▷ **HISTORY** Latin *soror* sister

sorrel *n* a plant with bitter-tasting leaves which are used in salads and sauces. ▷ **HISTORY** Old French *surele*

sorrow *n* **1** deep sadness or regret, associated with death or sympathy for another's misfortune. **2** a particular cause of this. ✧ *vb* **3** *Literary* to feel deep sadness about (death or another's misfortunes); mourn. ▷ **HISTORY** Old English *sorg* ▶ **sorrowful** *adj* ▶ **sorrowfully** *adv*

sorry *adj* **-rier, -riest 1** (often foll. by *for* or *about*) feeling or expressing pity, sympathy, grief, or regret: *I'm sorry about this.* **2** in bad mental or physical condition: *a sorry state.* **3** poor: *a sorry performance.* ✧ *interj* **4** an exclamation expressing apology or asking someone to repeat what he or she has said. ▷ **HISTORY** Old English *sārig*

sort *n* **1** a class, group, or kind sharing certain characteristics or qualities. **2** *Informal* a type of character: *she was a good sort.* **3** a more or less adequate example: *a sort of dream machine.* **4 of sorts** *or* **of a sort a** of a poorer quality: *she was wearing a uniform of sorts.* **b** of a kind not quite as intended or desired: *it was a reward, of sorts, for my efforts.* **5 out of sorts** not in normal good health or temper. **6 sort of** as it were; rather: *I sort of quit; sort of insensitive.* ✧ *vb* **7** to arrange (things or people) according to class or type. **8** to put (something) into working order; fix. **9** to arrange (computer information) by machine in an order the user finds convenient. ▷ **HISTORY** Latin *sors* fate

> **WORD TIP**
> See at **kind**[2].

sortie *n* **1** a short or relatively short return trip. **2** (of troops) a raid into enemy territory. **3** an operational flight made by a military aircraft. ✧ *vb* **-tieing, -tied 4** to make a sortie. ▷ **HISTORY** French

sort out *vb* **1** to find a solution to (a problem): *did they sort out the mess?* **2** to take or separate (things or people) from a larger group: *to sort out the wheat from the chaff.* **3** to organize (things or people) into an orderly and disciplined group. **4** *Informal* to punish or tell off (someone).

SOS *n* **1** an international code signal of distress in which the letters SOS are repeatedly spelt out in Morse code. **2** *Informal* any call for help.

so-so *Informal* ✧ *adj* **1** neither good nor bad. ✧ *adv* **2** in an average or indifferent way.

sot *n* a person who is frequently drunk. ▷ **HISTORY** Old English *sott* ▶ **sottish** *adj*

sotto voce (**sot**-toe **voe**-chay) *adv* with a soft voice. ▷ **HISTORY** Italian

sou *n* **1** a former French coin of low value. **2** *Old-fashioned* a very small amount of money: *the tax man never saw a sou from this income.* ▷ **HISTORY** French

soubrette (soo-**brett**) *n* a minor female role in comedy, often that of a pert maid. ▷ **HISTORY** French

soubriquet *n* same as **sobriquet**.

soufflé (**soo**-flay) *n* a light fluffy dish made with beaten egg whites and other ingredients such as cheese or chocolate. ▷ **HISTORY** French

sough (rhymes with **now**) *vb Literary* (of the wind) to make a sighing sound. ▷ **HISTORY** Old English *swōgan*

sought (**sawt**) *vb* the past of **seek**.

souk (**sook**) *n* an open-air marketplace in Muslim countries. ▷ **HISTORY** Arabic *sūq*

soul *n* **1** the spiritual part of a person, regarded as the centre of personality, intellect, will, and emotions: believed by many to survive the body after death. **2** the essential part or fundamental nature of anything: *the soul of contemporary America.* **3** deep and sincere feelings: *you've got no soul.* **4** Also called: **soul music** a type of Black music using blues and elements of jazz, gospel, and pop. **5** a person regarded as a good example of some quality: *the soul of prudence.* **6** a person: *there was hardly a soul there.* **7 the life and soul** *Informal* a person who is lively, entertaining, and fun to be with: *the life and soul of the campus.* ▷ **HISTORY** Old English *sāwol*

soul-destroying *adj* (of an occupation or situation) very boring and repetitive.

soulful *adj* expressing deep feelings: *a soulful performance of one of Tchaikovsky's songs.*

soulless *adj* **1** lacking human qualities; mechanical: *soulless materialism.* **2** (of a person) lacking in sensitivity or emotion.

soul-searching *n* deep examination of one's actions and feelings.

sound[1] *n* **1** anything that can be heard; noise. **2** *Physics* mechanical vibrations that travel in waves through the air, water, etc. **3** the sensation produced by such vibrations in the organs of hearing. **4** the impression one has of something: *I didn't really like the sound of it.* **5 sounds** *Slang* music, esp. rock, jazz, or pop. ✧ *vb* **6** to make or cause (an instrument, etc.) to make a sound. **7** to announce (something) by a sound: *guns sound the end of the two minutes silence.* **8** to make a noise with a certain quality: *her voice sounded shrill.* **9** to suggest (a particular idea or quality): *his argument sounded false.* **10** to pronounce (something) clearly: *to sound one's r's.* ▷ **HISTORY** Latin *sonus*

sound[2] *adj* **1** free from damage, injury, or decay; in good condition. **2** firm or substantial: *sound documentary evidence.* **3** financially safe or stable: *a sound investment.* **4** showing good judgment or reasoning; wise: *sound advice.* **5** morally correct; honest. **6** (of sleep) deep and uninterrupted. **7** thorough: *a sound defeat.* ✧ *adv* **8 sound asleep** in a deep sleep. ▷ **HISTORY** Old English *sund* ▶ **soundly** *adv*

sound[3] *vb* **1** to measure the depth of (a well, the sea, etc.). **2** *Med* to examine (a part of the body) by tapping or with a stethoscope. ▷ **HISTORY** Old French *sonder*

sound[4] *n* a channel between two larger areas of sea or between an island and the mainland. ▷ HISTORY Old English *sund*

sound barrier *n* a sudden increase in the force of air against an aircraft flying at or above the speed of sound.

sound bite *n* a short pithy sentence or phrase extracted from a longer speech for use on television or radio: *complicated political messages cannot be properly reduced to fifteen-second sound bites.*

sound effects *pl n* sounds artificially produced to make a play, esp. a radio play, more realistic.

sounding board *n* a person or group used to test a new idea or policy.

soundings *pl n* **1** measurements of the depth of a river, lake, or sea. **2** questions asked of someone in order to find out his or her opinion: *soundings among colleagues had revealed enthusiasm for the plan.*

sound mixer *n* **1** (in cinema and television) an audio engineer responsible for the overall sound mix, including dialogue, music and sound effects. **2** an electronic device for mixing sounds.

soundproof *adj* **1** (of a room) built so that no sound can get in or out. ✧ *vb* **2** to make (a room) soundproof.

sound recordist *n* (in cinema and television) the person who operates the audio recording equipment.

soundtrack *n* the recorded sound accompaniment to a film.

sound wave *n* a wave that carries sound.

soup *n* **1** a food made by cooking meat, fish, or vegetables in a stock. **2 in the soup** *Slang* in trouble or difficulties. ▷ HISTORY Old French *soupe* ▶ **soupy** *adj*

soupçon (**soop**-sonn) *n* a slight amount; dash. ▷ HISTORY French

souped-up *adj Slang* (of a car, motorbike, or engine) adjusted so as to be faster or more powerful than normal.

soup kitchen *n* a place where food and drink are served to needy people.

sour *adj* **1** having a sharp biting taste like the taste of lemon juice or vinegar. **2** made acid or bad, such as when milk ferments. **3** (of a person's mood) bad-tempered and unfriendly. **4 go** *or* **turn sour** to become less enjoyable or happy: *the dream has turned sour.* ✧ *vb* **5** to make or become less enjoyable or friendly: *relations soured shortly after the war.* ▷ HISTORY Old English *sūr* ▶ **sourly** *adv*

source *n* **1** the origin or starting point: *the source of discontent among fishermen.* **2** any person, book, or organization that provides information for a news report or for research. **3** the area or spring where a river or stream begins. ✧ *vb* **4** (foll. by *from*) to originate from. ▷ HISTORY Latin *surgere* to rise

sour cream *n* cream soured by bacteria for use in cooking.

sour grapes *n* the attitude of pretending to hate something because one cannot have it oneself.

souse *vb* **sousing, soused 1** to plunge (something) into water or other liquid. **2** to drench. **3** to steep or cook (food) in a marinade. ✧ *n* **4** the liquid used in pickling. **5** the act or process of sousing. ▷ HISTORY Old French *sous*

soused *adj Slang* drunk.

soutane (soo-**tan**) *n RC Church* a priest's robe. ▷ HISTORY French

south *n* **1** one of the four cardinal points of the compass, at 180° from north. **2** the direction along a line of latitude towards the South Pole. **3 the south** any area lying in or towards the south. ✧ *adj* **4** situated in, moving towards, or facing the south. **5** (esp. of the wind) from the south. ✧ *adv* **6** in, to, or towards the south. ▷ HISTORY Old English *sūth*

South *n* **1 the South a** the southern part of England. **b** (in the US) the Southern states that formed the Confederacy during the Civil War. **c** the countries of the world that are not technically and economically advanced. ✧ *adj* **2** of or denoting the southern part of a country, area, etc.

South African *adj* **1** of the Republic of South Africa. ✧ *n* **2** a person from the Republic of South Africa.

southeast *n* **1** the direction midway between south and east. **2 the southeast** any area lying in or towards the southeast. ✧ *adj also* **southeastern 3** of or denoting that part of a country or area which lies in the southeast. **4** situated in, moving towards, or facing the southeast. **5** (esp. of the wind) from the southeast. ✧ *adv* **6** in, to, or towards the southeast. ▶ **southeasterly** *adj, adv, n*

southeaster *n* a strong wind or storm from the southeast.

southerly *adj* **1** of or in the south. ✧ *adv, adj* **2** towards the south. **3** from the south: *light southerly winds.*

southern *adj* **1** situated in or towards the south. **2** facing or moving towards the south. **3** (*sometimes cap*) of or characteristic of the south or South. ▶ **southernmost** *adj*

southern hemisphere *n Geog* that half of the globe lying south of the equator.

southern lights *pl n* same as **aurora australis**.

southern oscillation *n Meteorol* a regularly occurring alternation in atmospheric pressures between the Indonesian region and the eastern tropical Pacific which gives rise to *El Niño* and *La Niña*.

southpaw *Informal* ✧ *n* **1** any left-handed person, esp. a boxer. ✧ *adj* **2** left-handed.

South Pole *n* the southernmost point on the earth's axis, at a latitude of 90°S, which has very low temperatures.

South Seas *pl n* the seas south of the equator.

southward *adj, adv also* **southwards 1** towards the south. ✧ *n* **2** the southward part or direction.

southwest *n* **1** the direction midway between west and south. **2 the southwest** any area lying in or towards the southwest. ✧ *adj also* **southwestern 3** of or denoting that part of a country or area which lies in the southwest. **4** situated in, moving towards, or facing the southwest. **5** (esp. of the wind) from the southwest. ✧ *adv* **6** in, to, or towards the southwest. ▶ **southwesterly** *adj, adv, n*

southwester *n* a strong wind or storm from the southwest.

souvenir *n* an object that reminds one of a certain place, occasion, or person; memento. ▷ **HISTORY** French

sou'wester *n* **1** a seaman's hat with a broad brim that covers the back of the neck. **2** same as **southwester**. ▷ **HISTORY** a contraction of SOUTHWESTER

sovereign *n* **1** the Royal ruler of a country. **2** a former British gold coin worth one pound sterling. ✧ *adj* **3** independent of outside authority; not governed by another country: *a sovereign nation.* **4** supreme in rank or authority: *a sovereign queen.* **5** *Old-fashioned* excellent or outstanding: *a sovereign remedy for epilepsy.* ▷ **HISTORY** Old French *soverain*

sovereignty *n, pl* **-ties 1** the political power a nation has to govern itself. **2** the position or authority of the most powerful institution in a country. **3** the position or authority of a sovereign.

soviet *n* (in the former Soviet Union) an elected government council at the local, regional, and national levels. ▷ **HISTORY** Russian *sovyet*

Soviet *adj* **1** of the former Soviet Union. ✧ *n* **2** a person from the former Soviet Union.

sow[1] *vb* **sowing, sowed; sown** *or* **sowed 1** to scatter or plant (seed) in or on (the ground) so that it may grow: *sow sweet peas in pots; farmers sow their fields with fewer varieties.* **2** to implant or introduce: *to sow confusion among the other members.* ▷ **HISTORY** Old English *sāwan*

sow[2] *n* a female adult pig. ▷ **HISTORY** Old English *sugu*

soya bean *or US & Canad* **soybean** *n* a plant whose bean is used for food and as a source of oil. ▷ **HISTORY** Japanese *shōyu*

soy sauce *n* a salty dark brown sauce made from fermented soya beans, used in Chinese cookery.

sozzled *adj Brit, Austral & NZ informal* drunk. ▷ **HISTORY** origin unknown

spa *n* a mineral-water spring or a resort where such a spring is found. ▷ **HISTORY** after *Spa,* a watering place in Belgium

space *n* **1** the unlimited three-dimensional expanse in which all objects exist. **2** an interval of distance or time between two points, objects, or events. **3** a blank portion or area. **4** unoccupied area or room: *barely enough space to walk around.* **5** the region beyond the earth's atmosphere containing other planets, stars, and galaxies; the universe. ✧ *vb* **spacing, spaced 6** to place or arrange (things) at intervals or with spaces between them. ▷ **HISTORY** Latin *spatium*

space age *n* **1** the period in which the exploration of space has become possible. ✧ *adj* **space-age 2** very modern, futuristic, or using the latest technology: *a space-age helmet.*

space-bar *n* a bar on a typewriter that is pressed in order to leave a space between words or letters.

space capsule *n* the part of a spacecraft in which the crew live and work.

spacecraft *n* a vehicle that can be used for travel in space.

spaceman *or fem* **spacewoman** *n, pl* **-men** *or fem* **-women** a person who travels in space.

space probe *n* a small vehicle equipped to gather scientific information, normally transmitted back to earth by radio, about a planet or conditions in space.

spaceship *n* (in science fiction) a spacecraft used for travel between planets and galaxies.

space shuttle *n* a manned reusable spacecraft designed for making regular flights.

space station *n* a large manned artificial satellite used as a base for scientific research in space and for people travelling in space.

spacesuit *n* a sealed protective suit worn by astronauts.

space-time *or* **space-time continuum** *n Physics* the four-dimensional continuum having three space coordinates and one time coordinate that together completely specify the location of an object or an event.

spacious *adj* having or providing a lot of space; roomy. ▶ **spaciousness** *n*

spade[1] *n* **1** a tool for digging, with a flat steel blade and a long wooden handle. **2 call a spade a spade** to speak plainly and frankly. ▷ **HISTORY** Old English *spadu*

spade[2] *n* **1 a spades** the suit of playing cards marked with a black leaf-shaped symbol. **b** a card with one or more of these symbols on it. **2** *Offensive* a Black person. **3 in spades** *Informal* in plenty: *all you need is talent in spades.* ▷ **HISTORY** Italian *spada* sword, used as an emblem on playing cards

spadework *n* dull or routine work done as preparation for a project or activity.

spadix (**spade**-ix) *n, pl* **spadices** (spade-**ice**-eez) *Bot* a spike of small flowers on a fleshy stem. ▷ **HISTORY** Greek: torn-off frond

spaghetti *n* pasta in the form of long strings. ▷ **HISTORY** Italian

spaghetti junction *n* a junction between motorways with a large number of intersecting roads. ▷ **HISTORY** from the nickname of the Gravelly Hill Interchange, Birmingham

spaghetti western *n* a cowboy film made in Europe by an Italian director.

spam *vb* **spamming, spammed** *Computers slang* to send unsolicited e-mail simultaneously to a number of newsgroups on the Internet. ▷ **HISTORY** from the repeated use of the word *Spam* in a popular sketch from the British television show *Monty Python's Flying Circus*

span *n* **1** the interval or distance between two points, such as the ends of a bridge. **2** the complete extent: *that span of time.* **3** short for **wingspan**. **4** a unit of length based on the width of a stretched hand, usually taken as nine inches (23 cms). ✧ *vb* **spanning, spanned 5** to stretch or extend across, over, or around: *her career spanned fifty years; to span the Danube.* ▷ **HISTORY** Old English *spann*

A B C D E F G H I J K L M N O P Q R S T U V W X Y Z

spangle *n* **1** a small piece of shiny material used as a decoration on clothes or hair; sequin. ✧ *vb* **-gling, -gled 2** to cover or decorate (something) with spangles. ▷ **HISTORY** Middle English *spange* clasp

Spaniard *n* a person from Spain.

spaniel *n* a dog with long drooping ears and a silky coat. ▷ **HISTORY** Old French *espaigneul* Spanish (dog)

Spanish *adj* **1** of Spain. ✧ *n* **2** the official language of Spain, Mexico, and most countries of South and Central America. ✧ *pl n* **3 the Spanish** the people of Spain.

Spanish fly *n* a beetle, the dried body of which is used in medicine.

Spanish Main *n* **1** the N coast of South America. **2** the Caribbean Sea, the S part of which was frequented by pirates.

spank *vb* **1** to slap (someone) with the open hand, on the buttocks or legs. ✧ *n* **2** such a slap. ▷ **HISTORY** probably imitative

spanking[1] *n* a series of spanks, usually as a punishment for children.

spanking[2] *adj* **1** *Informal* outstandingly fine or smart: *spanking new uniforms.* **2** very fast: *a spanking pace.*

spanner *n* **1** a tool for gripping and turning a nut or bolt. **2 throw a spanner in the works** *Brit & NZ informal* to cause a problem that prevents things from running smoothly. ▷ **HISTORY** German *spannen* to stretch

span of control *n Business* the area of responsibility or activity of a particular person or organization.

spanspek *n S African* a cantaloupe melon. ▷ **HISTORY** Afrikaans

spar[1] *n* a pole used as a ship's mast, boom, or yard. ▷ **HISTORY** Old Norse *sperra* beam

spar[2] *vb* **sparring, sparred 1** *Boxing, martial arts* to fight using light blows for practice. **2** to argue with someone. ✧ *n* **3** an argument. ▷ **HISTORY** Old English

spar[3] *n* a light-coloured, crystalline, easily split mineral. ▷ **HISTORY** Middle Low German

spare *adj* **1** extra to what is needed: *there are some spare chairs at the back.* **2** able to be used when needed: *a spare parking space.* **3** (of a person) tall and thin. **4** (of a style) plain and without unnecessary decoration or details; austere: *a spare but beautiful novel.* **5** *Brit slang* frantic with anger or worry: *the boss went spare.* ✧ *n* **6** an extra thing kept in case it is needed. ✧ *vb* **sparing, spared 7** to stop from killing, punishing, or injuring (someone). **8** to protect (someone) from (something) unpleasant: *spare me the sermon.* **9** to be able to afford or give: *can you spare me a moment to talk?* **10 not spare oneself** to try one's hardest. **11 to spare** more than is required: *a few hours to spare.* ▷ **HISTORY** Old English *sparian*

spare tyre *n* **1** an additional tyre kept in a motor vehicle in case of puncture. **2** *Slang* a roll of fat just above the waist.

sparing *adj* (sometimes foll. by *of*) economical (with): *she was mercifully sparing in her use of jargon.* ▸ **sparingly** *adv*

spark *n* **1** a fiery particle thrown out from a fire or caused by friction. **2** a short flash of light followed by a sharp crackling noise, produced by a sudden electrical discharge through the air. **3** a trace or hint: *a spark of goodwill.* **4** liveliness, enthusiasm, or humour: *that spark in her eye.* ✧ *vb* **5** to give off sparks. **6** to cause to start; trigger: *the incident sparked off an angry exchange.* ▷ **HISTORY** Old English *spearca*

sparkie *n NZ informal* electrician.

sparkle *vb* **-kling, -kled 1** to glitter with many bright points of light. **2** (of wine or mineral water) to be slightly fizzy. **3** to be lively, witty, and intelligent. ✧ *n* **4** a small bright point of light. **5** liveliness and wit. ▷ **HISTORY** Middle English *sparklen*

sparkler *n* **1** a type of hand-held firework that throws out sparks. **2** *Informal* a sparkling gem; esp. a diamond.

spark plug *n* a device in an internal-combustion engine that ignites the fuel by producing an electric spark.

sparrow *n* a very common small brown or grey bird which feeds on seeds and insects. ▷ **HISTORY** Old English *spearwa*

sparrowhawk *n* a small hawk which preys on smaller birds.

sparse *adj* small in amount and spread out widely: *a sparse population.* ▷ **HISTORY** Latin *sparsus* ▸ **sparsely** *adv*

Spartan *adj* **1** of or relating to the ancient Greek city of Sparta. **2** (of a way of life) strict or simple and with no luxuries: *Spartan accommodation.* ✧ *n* **3** a citizen of Sparta. **4** a person who leads a strict or simple life without luxuries.

WORD HISTORY

'Spartan' means 'belonging to *Sparta*', a city in ancient Greece whose inhabitants were famous for their discipline, military skill, and stern and plain way of life. Compare the word history for **laconic**.

spasm *n* **1** a sudden tightening of the muscles, over which one has no control. **2** a sudden burst of activity or feeling: *a spasm of applause; sudden spasms of anger.* ▷ **HISTORY** Greek *spasmos* a cramp

spasmodic *adj* taking place in sudden short spells: *spasmodic bouts of illness.* ▸ **spasmodically** *adv*

spastic *n* **1** a person who has cerebral palsy, and therefore has difficulty controlling his or her muscles. ✧ *adj* **2** affected by involuntary muscle contractions: *a spastic colon.* **3** suffering from cerebral palsy. ▷ **HISTORY** Greek *spasmos* a cramp

spat[1] *n* a slight quarrel. ▷ **HISTORY** probably imitative

spat[2] *vb* a past of **spit**[1].

spate *n* **1** a large number of things happening within a period of time: *a spate of bombings.* **2** a fast flow or outpouring: *an incomprehensible spate of* *words.* **3 in spate** *Chiefly Brit* (of a river) flooded. ▷ HISTORY origin unknown

spathe *n Bot* a large leaf that surrounds the base of a flower cluster. ▷ HISTORY Greek *spathē* a blade

spatial *adj* of or relating to size, area, or position: *spatial dimensions.* ▶ **spatially** *adv*

spatial analysis *n Geog* analytical processes that use geographical data for modelling, looking at the suitability of areas for particular purposes, and making predictions about the future.

spatial patterns *pl n Geog* the distribution and arrangement of given elements in an area and how they interrelate.

spats *pl n* cloth or leather coverings formerly worn by men over the ankle and instep. ▷ HISTORY obsolete *spatterdash* a long gaiter

spatter *vb* **1** to scatter or splash (a substance, esp. a liquid) in scattered drops: *spattering mud in all directions.* **2** to sprinkle (an object or a surface) with a liquid. ✧ *n* **3** the sound of spattering. **4** something spattered, such as a spot or splash. ▷ HISTORY imitative

spatula *n* a utensil with a broad flat blade, used in cooking and by doctors. ▷ HISTORY Latin: a broad piece

spawn *n* **1** the jelly-like mass of eggs laid by fish, amphibians, or molluscs. ✧ *vb* **2** (of fish, amphibians, or molluscs) to lay eggs. **3** to cause (something) to be created: *the depressed economy spawned the riots.* ▷ HISTORY Anglo-Norman *espaundre*

spay *vb* to remove the ovaries from (a female animal). ▷ HISTORY Old French *espeer* to cut with the sword

speak *vb* **speaking, spoke, spoken 1** to say words; talk. **2** to communicate or express (something) in words. **3** to give a speech or lecture. **4** to know how to talk in (a specified language): *I don't speak French.* **5 on speaking terms** on good terms; friendly. **6 so to speak** as it were. **7 speak one's mind** to express one's opinions honestly and plainly. **8 to speak of** of a significant nature: *no licensing laws to speak of.* ▷ HISTORY Old English *specan*

speaker *n* **1** a person who speaks, esp. someone making a speech. **2** a person who speaks a particular language: *a fluent Tibetan and English speaker.* **3** same as **loudspeaker**.

Speaker *n* the official chairman of a law-making body.

spear[1] *n* **1** a weapon consisting of a long pole with a sharp point. ✧ *vb* **2** to pierce (someone or something) with a spear or other pointed object: *she took her fork and speared an oyster from its shell.* ▷ HISTORY Old English *spere*

spear[2] *n* **1** a slender shoot, such as of grass. **2** a single stalk of broccoli or asparagus. ▷ HISTORY probably variant of *spire*

spearhead *vb* **1** to lead (an attack or a campaign). ✧ *n* **2** the leading force in an attack or campaign.

spearmint *n* a minty flavouring used for sweets and toothpaste, which comes from a purple-flowered plant.

spec *n* **on spec** *Informal* as a risk or gamble: *I still tend to buy on spec.*

special *adj* **1** distinguished from or better than others of its kind: *a special occasion.* **2** designed or reserved for a specific purpose: *special equipment.* **3** not usual; different from normal: *a special case.* **4** particular or primary: *a special interest in gifted children.* **5** relating to the education of children with disabilities: *a special school.* ✧ *n* **6** a product, TV programme, etc., which is only available or shown at a certain time: *a two-hour Christmas special live from Hollywood.* **7** a meal, usually at a low price, in a bar or restaurant. **8** short for **special constable**. ▷ HISTORY Latin *specialis* ▶ **specially** *adv*

> ☑ **WORD TIP**
> See at **especial**.

Special Branch *n* (in Britain and S Africa) the department of the police force that is concerned with political security.

special constable *n* (in Britain) a person recruited for occasional police duties, such as in an emergency.

special delivery *n* the delivery of a piece of mail outside the time of a scheduled delivery, for an extra fee.

special effects *pl n Films* techniques used in the production of scenes that cannot be achieved by normal methods: *the special effects and make-up are totally convincing.*

specialist *n* **1** a person who is an expert in a particular activity or subject. **2** a doctor who concentrates on treating one particular category of diseases or the diseases of one particular part of the body: *an eye specialist.* ✧ *adj* **3** particular to or concentrating on one subject or activity: *a specialist comic shop.*

speciality *or esp US & Canad* **specialty** *n, pl* **-ties 1** a special interest or skill. **2** a service, product, or type of food specialized in.

specialize *or* **-ise** *vb* **-izing, -ized** *or* **-ising, -ised 1** to concentrate all one's efforts on studying a particular subject, occupation, or activity: *an expert who specializes in transport.* **2** to modify (something) for a special use or purpose: *plants have evolved and specialized in every type of habitat.* ▶ **specialization** *or* **-isation** *n*

special licence *n Brit* a licence allowing a marriage to take place without following all the usual legal procedures.

specialty *n, pl* **-ties** *Chiefly US & Canad* same as **speciality**.

specie *n* coins as distinct from paper money. ▷ HISTORY Latin *in specie* in kind

species *n, pl* **-cies** *Biol* one of the groups into which a genus is divided, the members of which are able to interbreed. ▷ HISTORY Latin: appearance

specific *adj* **1** particular or definite: *a specific area of economic policy.* **2** precise and exact: *try and be* *more specific.* ✧ *n* **3 specifics** particular qualities or aspects of something: *the specifics of the situation.* **4** *Med* any drug used to treat a particular disease. ▷ **HISTORY** Latin *species* kind + *facere* to make ▶ **specifically** *adv* ▶ **specificity** *n*

specification *n* **1** a detailed description of features in the design of something: *engines built to racing specification.* **2** a requirement or detail which is clearly stated: *the main specification was that a good degree was required.* **3** the specifying of something.

specific gravity *n Physics* the ratio of the density of a substance to the density of water.

specific heat capacity *n Physics* the quantity of heat required to raise the temperature of unit mass of a substance by one degree centigrade.

specific performance *n Law* a remedy awarded by a court requiring a person to fulfil obligations under a contract where damages are an insufficient remedy.

specify *vb* **-fies, -fying, -fied 1** to state or describe (something) clearly. **2** to state (something) as a condition: *the rules specify the number of prisoners to be kept in each cell.* ▷ **HISTORY** Medieval Latin *specificare* to describe

specimen *n* **1** an individual or part regarded as typical of its group or class. **2** *Med* a sample of tissue, blood, or urine taken for analysis. **3** *Informal* a person: *I'm quite a healthy specimen.* ▷ **HISTORY** Latin: mark, proof

specious (**spee**-shuss) *adj* apparently correct or true, but actually wrong or false. ▷ **HISTORY** Latin *species* outward appearance

speck *n* **1** a very small mark or spot. **2** a small or tiny piece of something: *a speck of fluff.* ▷ **HISTORY** Old English *specca*

speckle *vb* **-ling, -led 1** to mark (something) with speckles. ✧ *n* **2** a small mark or spot, such as on the skin or on an egg. ▷ **HISTORY** Middle Dutch *spekkel* ▶ **speckled** *adj*

specs *pl n Informal* short for **spectacles**.

spectacle *n* **1** a strange, interesting, or ridiculous scene. **2** an impressive public show: *the opening ceremony of the Olympics was an impressive spectacle.* **3 make a spectacle of oneself** to draw attention to oneself by behaving foolishly. ▷ **HISTORY** Latin *spectare* to watch

spectacles *pl n* a pair of glasses for correcting faulty vision.

spectacular *adj* **1** impressive, grand, or dramatic. ✧ *n* **2** a spectacular show. ▶ **spectacularly** *adv*

spectate *vb* **-tating, -tated** to be a spectator; watch.

spectator *n* a person viewing anything; onlooker. ▷ **HISTORY** Latin *spectare* to watch

spectator ion *n Chem* an ion which is present in a mixture but plays no part in a reaction.

spectre *or US* **specter** *n* **1** a ghost. **2** an unpleasant or menacing vision in one's imagination: *the spectre of famine.* ▷ **HISTORY** Latin *spectrum* ▶ **spectral** *adj*

spectrometer (speck-**trom**-it-er) *n Physics* an instrument for producing a spectrum, usually one in which wavelength, energy, or intensity can be measured.

spectroscope *n Physics* an instrument for forming or recording a spectrum by passing a light ray through a prism or grating.

spectrum *n, pl* **-tra 1** *Physics* the distribution of colours produced when white light is dispersed by a prism or grating: violet, indigo, blue, green, yellow, orange, and red. **2** *Physics* the whole range of electromagnetic radiation with respect to its wavelength or frequency. **3** a range or scale of anything such as opinions or emotions. ▷ **HISTORY** Latin: image

speculate *vb* **-lating, -lated 1** to form opinions about something, esp. its future consequences, based on the information available; conjecture: *it is too early to speculate about Jackie getting married.* **2** to buy securities or property in the hope of selling them at a profit. ▷ **HISTORY** Latin *speculari* to spy out ▶ **speculation** *n* ▶ **speculative** *adj* ▶ **speculator** *n*

speculative buying *n Commerce* the practice of buying in materials in a greater quantity than current requirements demand while prices are low, with the expectation of a future rise in prices.

sped *vb* a past of **speed**.

speech *n* **1** the ability to speak: *the loss of speech.* **2** spoken language: *Doran's lack of coherent speech.* **3** a talk given to an audience: *a speech to parliament.* **4** a person's manner of speaking: *her speech was extremely slow.* **5** a national or regional language or dialect: *Canadian speech.* ▷ **HISTORY** Old English *spēc*

speech bubble *n* an area in the main body of a cartoon where the words of a character are written; this area is shaped so that the words appear to come from the character's mouth.

speech day *n Brit & Austral* (in schools) an annual day on which prizes are presented and speeches are made by guest speakers.

speechify *vb* **-fies, -fying, -fied** to make a dull or pompous speech.

speechless *adj* **1** unable to speak for a short time because of great emotion or shock. **2** unable to be expressed in words: *speechless disbelief.*

speech therapy *n* the treatment of people with speech problems.

speed *n* **1** the quality of acting or moving fast; swiftness. **2** the rate at which something moves or happens. **3** a gear ratio in a motor vehicle or bicycle: *five-speed gearbox.* **4** *Photog* a measure of the sensitivity to light of a particular type of film. **5** *Slang* amphetamine. **6 at speed** quickly. **7 up to speed a** operating at an acceptable level. **b** in possession of all the necessary information. ✧ *vb* **speeding, sped** *or* **speeded 8** to move or go somewhere quickly. **9** to drive a motor vehicle faster than the legal limit. ✧ See also **speed up**. ▷ **HISTORY** Old English *spēd* (originally: success)

speedboat *n* a high-speed motorboat.

speed camera *Brit, Austral & NZ* a camera for photographing vehicles breaking the speed limit.

a b c d e f g h i j k l m n o p q r s t u v w x y z

A B C D E F G H I J K L M N O P Q R S T U V W X Y Z

speed limit *n* the maximum speed at which a vehicle may legally travel on a particular road.
speedo *n, pl* **speedos** *Informal* a speedometer.
speedometer *n* a dial in a vehicle which shows the speed of travel.
speed up *vb* to accelerate.

> **WORD TIP**
> The past tense and past participle of *speed up* is *speeded up* not *sped up*.

speedway *n* **1** the sport of racing on light powerful motorcycles round cinder tracks. **2** *US, Canad & NZ* the track or stadium where such races are held.
speedwell *n* a small blue or pinkish-white flower.
speedy *adj* **speedier, speediest 1** done without delay. **2** (of a vehicle) able to travel fast. ▶ **speedily** *adv*
speleology *n* the scientific study of caves. ▷ **HISTORY** Latin *spelaeum* cave
spell[1] *vb* **spelling, spelt** *or* **spelled 1** to write or name in correct order the letters that make up (a word): *how do you spell that name?* **2** (of letters) to make up (a word): *c-a-t spells cat.* **3** to indicate (a particular result): *share price slump spells disaster.* ✧ See also **spell out**. ▷ **HISTORY** Old French *espeller*
spell[2] *n* **1** a sequence of words used to perform magic. **2** the effect of a spell: *the wizard's spell was broken.* **3 under someone's spell** fascinated by someone. ▷ **HISTORY** Old English *spell* speech
spell[3] *n* **1** a period of time of weather or activity: *the dry spell; a short spell in prison.* **2** a period of duty after which one person or group relieves another. **3** *Scot, Austral & NZ* a period of rest. ▷ **HISTORY** Old English *spelian* to take the place of
spellbound *adj* completely fascinated; as if in a trance.
spellchecker *n Computers* a program that highlights any word in a word-processed document that is not recognized as being correctly spelt.
spelling *n* **1** the way a word is spelt: *the British spelling of 'theatre'.* **2** a person's ability to spell: *my spelling used to be excellent.*
spell out *vb* **1** to make (something) as easy to understand as possible: *to spell out the implications.* **2** to read with difficulty, working out each word letter by letter.
spelt *vb* a past of **spell**[1].
spend *vb* **spending, spent 1** to pay out (money). **2** to pass (time) in a specific way or place: *I spent a year in Budapest.* **3** to concentrate (effort) on an activity: *a lot of energy was spent organizing the holiday.* **4** to use up completely: *the hurricane spent its force.* ▷ **HISTORY** Latin *expendere* ▶ **spending** *n*
spendthrift *n* **1** a person who spends money wastefully. ✧ *adj* **2** of or like a spendthrift: *a spendthrift policy.*
spent *vb* **1** the past of **spend**. ✧ *adj* **2** used up or exhausted.
sperm *n* **1** (*pl* **sperms** *or* **sperm**) one of the male reproductive cells released in the semen during ejaculation. **2** same as **semen**. ▷ **HISTORY** Greek *sperma*
spermaceti (sper-ma-**set**-ee) *n* a white waxy substance obtained from the sperm whale. ▷ **HISTORY** Medieval Latin *sperma ceti* whale's sperm
spermatogenesis *n Biol* the formation and development of spermatozoa in the testis.
spermatozoid (spur-mat-o-**zoh**-id) *n Bot* a small male gamete produced by a lower plant.
spermatozoon (sper-ma-toe-**zoe**-on) *n, pl* **-zoa** same as **sperm** (sense 1). ▷ **HISTORY** Greek *sperma* seed + *zōion* animal
spermicide *n* a substance, esp. a cream or jelly, that kills sperm, used as a means of contraception. ▷ **HISTORY** SPERM + Latin *caedere* to kill ▶ **spermicidal** *adj*
sperm oil *n* an oil obtained from the head of the sperm whale, used as a lubricant.
sperm whale *n* a large whale which is hunted for spermaceti and ambergris. ▷ **HISTORY** short for SPERMACETI WHALE
spew *vb* **1** to vomit. **2** to send or be sent out in a stream: *the hydrant spewed a tidal wave of water.* ▷ **HISTORY** Old English *spīwan*
sphagnum *n* a moss which is found in bogs and which decays to form peat. ▷ **HISTORY** Greek *sphagnos*
sphere *n* **1** *Geom* a round solid figure in which every point on the surface is equally distant from the centre. **2** an object having this shape, such as a planet. **3** a particular field of activity. **4** people of the same rank or with shared interests: *a humbler social sphere.* ▷ **HISTORY** Greek *sphaira*
spherical *adj* shaped like a sphere.
spheroid *n Geom* a solid figure that is almost but not exactly a sphere.
sphincter *n Anat* a ring of muscle surrounding the opening of a hollow organ and contracting to close it. ▷ **HISTORY** Greek *sphingein* to grip tightly
sphinx *n* **1** one of the huge statues built by the ancient Egyptians, with the body of a lion and the head of a man. **2** a mysterious person.
Sphinx *n* **1** the huge statue of a sphinx near the pyramids at El Gîza in Egypt. **2** *Greek myth* a monster with a woman's head and a lion's body, who set a riddle for travellers, killing them when they failed to answer it. Oedipus answered the riddle and the Sphinx then killed herself. ▷ **HISTORY** Greek
spice *n* **1 a** an aromatic substance, such as ginger or cinnamon, used as flavouring. **b** such substances collectively. **2** something that makes life or an activity more exciting. ✧ *vb* **spicing, spiced 3** to flavour (food) with spices. **4** to add excitement or interest to (something): *they spiced their letters with pointed demands.* ▷ **HISTORY** Old French *espice*
spick-and-span *adj* very neat and clean. ▷ **HISTORY** obsolete *spick* spike + *span-new* absolutely new, like a freshly cut spike
spicy *adj* **spicier, spiciest 1** strongly flavoured with spices. **2** *Informal* slightly scandalous: *spicy new story lines.*

spider *n* a small eight-legged creature, many species of which weave webs in which to trap insects for food. ▷ HISTORY Old English *spīthra* ▶ **spidery** *adj*

spider monkey *n* a tree-living monkey with very long legs, a long tail, and a small head.

spiel *n* a prepared speech made to persuade someone to buy or do something. ▷ HISTORY German *Spiel* play

spigot *n* **1** a stopper for the vent hole of a cask. **2** a wooden tap fitted to a cask. ▷ HISTORY probably from Latin *spica* a point

spike[1] *n* **1** a sharp-pointed metal object: *a high fence with iron spikes.* **2** anything long and pointed: *a hedgehog bristling with spikes.* **3** a long metal nail. **4 spikes** sports shoes with metal spikes on the soles for greater grip. ✧ *vb* **spiking, spiked 5** to secure or supply (something) with spikes: *spiked shoes.* **6** to drive a spike or spikes into. **7** to add alcohol to (a drink). ▷ HISTORY Middle English *spyk* ▶ **spiky** *adj*

spike[2] *n Bot* **1** an arrangement of flowers attached at the base to a long stem. **2** an ear of grain. ▷ HISTORY Latin *spica* ear of corn

spikenard *n* **1** a fragrant Indian plant with rose-purple flowers. **2** an ointment obtained from this plant. ▷ HISTORY Medieval Latin *spica nardi*

spill[1] *vb* **spilling, spilt** *or* **spilled 1** to pour from or as from a container by accident. **2** (of large numbers of people) to come out of a place: *rival groups spilled out from the station.* **3** to shed (blood). **4 spill the beans** *Informal* to give away a secret. ✧ *n* **5** *Informal* a fall from a motorbike, bike, or horse, esp. in a competition. **6** an amount of liquid spilt. ▷ HISTORY Old English *spillan* to destroy ▶ **spillage** *n*

spill[2] *n* a splinter of wood or strip of paper for lighting pipes or fires. ▷ HISTORY Germanic

spin *vb* **spinning, spun 1** to revolve or cause to revolve quickly. **2** to draw out and twist (fibres, such as silk or cotton) into thread. **3** (of a spider or silkworm) to form (a web or cocoon) from a silky fibre that comes out of the body. **4 spin a yarn** to tell an unlikely story. **5** *Sport* to throw, hit, or kick (a ball) so that it spins and changes direction or changes speed on bouncing. **6** same as **spin-dry**. **7** to grow dizzy: *her head was spinning.* **8** *Informal* to present information in a way that creates a favourable impression. ✧ *n* **9** a fast rotating motion. **10** a flight manoeuvre in which an aircraft flies in a downward spiral. **11** *Sport* a spinning motion given to a ball. **12** *Informal* a short car drive taken for pleasure. **13** *Informal* the presenting of information in a way that creates a favourable impression. ✧ See also **spin out**. ▷ HISTORY Old English *spinnan* ▶ **spinning** *n*

spina bifida *n* a condition in which part of the spinal cord protrudes through a gap in the backbone, sometimes causing paralysis. ▷ HISTORY New Latin: split spine

spinach *n* a dark green leafy vegetable. ▷ HISTORY Arabic *isfānākh*

spinal column *n* same as **spine** (sense 1).

spinal cord *n* the thick cord of nerve tissue within the spine, which connects the brain to the nerves of the body.

spin bowler *n Cricket* same as **spinner** (1a).

spindle *n* **1** a rotating rod that acts as an axle. **2** a rod with a notch in the top for drawing out, twisting and winding the thread in spinning. ▷ HISTORY Old English *spinel*

spindly *adj* **-dlier, -dliest** tall, thin, and frail.

spin doctor *n Informal* a person who provides a favourable slant to a news item or policy on behalf of a political personality or party. ▷ HISTORY from the spin given to a ball in sport to make it go in the desired direction

spindrift *n* spray blown up from the sea. ▷ HISTORY Scots variant of *spoondrift,* from *spoon* to scud + DRIFT

spin-dry *vb* **-dries, -drying, -dried** to dry (clothes) in a spin-dryer.

spin-dryer *n* a device that removes water from washed clothes by spinning them in a perforated drum.

spine *n* **1** the row of bony segments that surround and protect the spinal cord. **2** the back of a book, record sleeve, or video-tape box. **3** a sharp point on the body of an animal or on a plant. ▷ HISTORY Latin *spina* thorn ▶ **spinal** *adj*

spine-chiller *n* a frightening film or story. ▶ **spine-chilling** *adj*

spineless *adj* **1** behaving in a cowardly way. **2** (of an animal) having no spine.

spinet *n* a small harpsichord. ▷ HISTORY Italian *spinetta*

spinifex *n* a coarse spiny Australian grass.

spinnaker *n* a large triangular sail on a racing yacht. ▷ HISTORY probably from *spin,* but traditionally from Sphinx, the yacht that first used this type of sail

spinner *n* **1** *Cricket* **a** a bowler who specializes in spinning the ball with his or her fingers to make it change direction when it bounces or strikes the batsman's bat. **b** a ball that is bowled with a spinning motion. **2** a small round object used in angling to attract fish to the bait by spinning in the water. **3** a person who makes thread by spinning.

spinneret *n* an organ through which silk threads come out of the body of a spider or insect.

spinney *n Chiefly Brit* a small wood: *the hollow tree in the spinney.* ▷ HISTORY Old French *espinei*

spinning jenny *n* an early type of spinning frame with several spindles.

spinning wheel *n* a wheel-like machine for spinning at home, having one hand- or foot-operated spindle.

spin-off *n* **1** a product or development that unexpectedly results from activities designed to achieve something else: *new energy sources could occur as a spin-off from the space effort.* **2** a television series involving some of the characters from an earlier successful series.

spin out *vb* **1** to take longer than necessary to do (something). **2** to make (money) last as long as possible.

spinster *n* an unmarried woman. ▶ **spinsterish** *adj*

WORD HISTORY

A 'spinster' was originally a spinner, that is, a person - not necessarily a woman - whose occupation was spinning. It is said that a young woman was not considered fit to be a wife until she had spun a certain amount of household linen. Hence, the word came to designate an unmarried woman.

spiny *adj* **spinier, spiniest** (of animals or plants) covered with spines.

spiracle (**spire**-a-kl) *n Zool* a small blowhole for breathing through, such as that of a whale. ▷ **HISTORY** Latin *spiraculum* vent

spiraea *or esp US* **spirea** (spire-**ee**-a) *n* a plant with small white or pink flowers. ▷ **HISTORY** Greek *speiraia*

spiral *n* **1** *Geom* a plane curve formed by a point winding about a fixed point at an ever-increasing distance from it. **2** something that follows a winding course or that has a twisting form. **3** *Econ* a continuous upward or downward movement in economic activity or prices. ✧ *adj* **4** having the shape of a spiral: *a spiral staircase.* ✧ *vb* **-ralling, -ralled** *or US* **-raling, -raled 5** to follow a spiral course or be in the shape of a spiral. **6** to increase or decrease with steady acceleration: *oil prices continue to spiral.* ▷ **HISTORY** Latin *spira* a coil ▶ **spirally** *adv*

spire *n* the tall cone-shaped structure on the top of a church. ▷ **HISTORY** Old English *spīr* blade

spirillum *n, pl* **-la** *Biol* a bacterium with a curved or spirally twisted body.

spirit[1] *n* **1** the nonphysical aspect of a person concerned with profound thoughts and emotions. **2** the nonphysical part of a person believed to live on after death. **3** a shared feeling: *a spirit of fun and adventure.* **4** mood or attitude: *fighting spirit.* **5** a person's character or temperament: *the indomitable spirit of the Polish people.* **6** liveliness shown in what a person does: *it has been undertaken with spirit.* **7** the feelings that motivate someone to survive in difficult times or live according to his or her beliefs: *someone had broken his spirit.* **8 spirits** an emotional state: *in good spirits.* **9** the way in which something, such as a law or an agreement, was intended to be interpreted: *they acted against the spirit of the treaty.* **10** a supernatural being, such as a ghost. ✧ *vb* **-iting, -ited 11 spirit away** *or* **off** to carry (someone or something) off mysteriously or secretly. ▷ **HISTORY** Latin *spiritus* breath, spirit

spirit[2] *n* **1** (*usually pl*) distilled alcoholic liquor, such as whisky or gin. **2** *Chem* **a** a solution of ethanol obtained by distillation. **b** the essence of a substance, extracted as a liquid by distillation. **3** *Pharmacol* a solution of a volatile oil in alcohol. ▷ **HISTORY** special use of SPIRIT[1]

spirited *adj* **1** showing liveliness or courage: *a spirited rendition of Schubert's ninth symphony; a spirited defence of the government's policy.* **2** characterized by the mood as specified: *high-spirited; mean-spirited.*

spirit lamp *n* a lamp that burns methylated or other spirits instead of oil.

spirit level *n* a device for checking whether a surface is level, consisting of a block of wood or metal containing a tube partially filled with liquid set so that the air bubble in it rests between two marks on the tube when the block is level.

spiritual *adj* **1** relating to a person's beliefs as opposed to his or her physical or material needs. **2** relating to religious beliefs. **3 one's spiritual home** the place where one feels one belongs. ✧ *n* **4** Also called: **Negro spiritual** a type of religious folk song originally sung by Black slaves in the American South. ▶ **spirituality** *n* ▶ **spiritually** *adv*

spiritualism *n* the belief that the spirits of the dead can communicate with the living. ▶ **spiritualist** *n*

spirituous *adj* containing alcohol.

spirogyra (spire-oh-**jire**-a) *n* a green freshwater plant that floats on the surface of ponds and ditches. ▷ **HISTORY** Greek *speira* a coil + *guros* a circle

spit[1] *vb* **spitting, spat** *or* **spit 1** to force saliva out of one's mouth. **2** to force (something) out of one's mouth: *he spat tobacco into an old coffee can.* **3** (of a fire or hot fat) to throw out sparks or particles violently and explosively. **4** to rain very lightly. **5** (often foll. by *out*) to say (words) in a violent angry way. **6** to show contempt or hatred by spitting. **7 spit it out!** *Informal* a command given to someone to say what is on his or her mind. ✧ *n* **8** same as **spittle. 9** *Informal, chiefly Brit* same as **spitting image.** ▷ **HISTORY** Old English *spittan*

spit[2] *n* **1** a pointed rod for skewering and roasting meat over a fire or in an oven. **2** a long narrow strip of land jutting out into the sea. ▷ **HISTORY** Old English *spitu*

spite *n* **1** deliberate nastiness. **2 in spite of** regardless of: *he loved them in spite of their shortcomings.* ✧ *vb* **spiting, spited 3** to annoy (someone) deliberately, out of spite: *it was to spite his father.* ▷ **HISTORY** variant of DESPITE ▶ **spiteful** *adj* ▶ **spitefully** *adv*

spitfire *n* a woman or girl who is easily angered.

spitting image *n Informal* a person who looks very like someone else. ▷ **HISTORY** from *spit* likeness

spittle *n* the fluid that is produced in the mouth; saliva. ▷ **HISTORY** Old English *spǣtl* saliva

spittoon *n* a bowl for people to spit into.

spitz *n* a stockily built dog with a pointed face, erect ears, and a tightly curled tail. ▷ **HISTORY** from German

spiv *n Brit, Austral & NZ slang* a smartly dressed man who makes a living by underhand dealings; black marketeer. ▷ **HISTORY** dialect *spiving* smart

splash *vb* **1** to scatter (liquid) on (something). **2** to cause (liquid) to fall or (of liquid) to be scattered in drops. **3** to display (a photograph or story) prominently in a newspaper. ✧ *n* **4** a splashing sound. **5** an amount splashed. **6** a patch (of colour or light). **7 make a splash** *Informal* to attract a lot of attention. **8** a small amount of liquid added to a drink. ▷ **HISTORY** alteration of *plash*

splashdown *n* **1** the landing of a spacecraft on water at the end of a flight. ✧ *vb* **splash down 2** (of a spacecraft) to make a splashdown.

splash out *n* to spend a lot of money on a treat or luxury: *she planned to splash out on a good holiday.*

splatter *vb* **1** to splash (something or someone) with small blobs. ✧ *n* **2** a splash of liquid.

splatter movie *n Slang* a film in which the main feature is the graphic and gory murder of numerous victims.

splay *vb* to spread out, with ends spreading out in different directions: *her hair splayed over the pillow.* ▷ **HISTORY** short for DISPLAY

spleen *n* **1** a spongy organ near the stomach, which filters bacteria from the blood. **2** spitefulness or bad temper: *we vent our spleen on drug barons.* ▷ **HISTORY** Greek *splēn*

spleenwort *n* a kind of fern that grows on walls.

splendid *adj* **1** very good: *a splendid match.* **2** beautiful or impressive: *a splendid palace.* ▷ **HISTORY** Latin *splendere* to shine ▶ **splendidly** *adv*

splendour *or US* **splendor** *n* **1** beauty or impressiveness. **2 splendours** the impressive or beautiful features of something: *the splendours of the Emperor's Palace.*

splenetic *adj Literary* irritable or bad-tempered. ▷ **HISTORY** from SPLEEN

splice *vb* **splicing, spliced 1** to join up the trimmed ends of (two pieces of wire, film, or tape) with an adhesive material. **2** to join (two ropes) by interweaving the ends. **3 get spliced** *Informal* to get married. ▷ **HISTORY** probably from Middle Dutch *splissen*

splint *n* a piece of wood used to support a broken bone. ▷ **HISTORY** Middle Low German *splinte*

splinter *n* **1** a small thin sharp piece broken off, esp. from wood. ✧ *vb* **2** to break or be broken into small sharp fragments. ▷ **HISTORY** Middle Dutch

splinter group *n* a number of members of an organization, who split from the main body and form an independent group of their own.

split *vb* **splitting, split 1** to break or cause (something) to break into separate pieces. **2** to separate (a piece) or (of a piece) to be separated from (something). **3** (of a group) to separate into smaller groups, through disagreement: *the council is split over rent increases.* **4** (often foll. by *up*) to divide (something) among two or more people. **5** *Slang* to leave a place. **6 split on** *Slang* to betray; inform: *he didn't tell tales or split on him.* **7 split one's sides** to laugh a great deal. ✧ *n* **8** a gap or rift caused by splitting. **9** a division in a group or the smaller group resulting from such a division. **10** a dessert of sliced fruit and ice cream, covered with whipped cream and nuts: *banana split.* ✧ *adj* **11** having a split or splits: *split ends.* ✧ See also **splits.** ▷ **HISTORY** Middle Dutch *splitten*

split infinitive *n* (in English grammar) an infinitive used with another word between *to* and the verb, as in *to really finish it*. This is often thought to be incorrect.

> **☑ WORD TIP**
>
> The traditional rule against placing an adverb between *to* and its verb is gradually disappearing. Although it is true that a split infinitive may result in a clumsy sentence (*he decided to firmly and definitively deal with the problem*), this is not enough to justify the absolute condemnation that this practice has attracted. Indeed, very often the most natural position of the adverb is between *to* and the verb (*he decided to really try next time*) and to change it would result in an artificial and awkward construction (*he decided really to try next time*). The current view is therefore that the split infinitive is not a grammatical error. Nevertheless, many writers prefer to avoid splitting infinitives in formal written English, since readers with a more traditional point of view are likely to interpret this type of construction as incorrect.

split-level *adj* (of a house or room) having the floor level of one part about half a storey above that of the other.

split personality *n* **1** the tendency to change mood very quickly. **2** a disorder in which a person's mind appears to have separated into two or more personalities.

splits *n* (in gymnastics and dancing) the act of sitting with both legs outstretched, pointing in opposite directions, and at right angles to the body.

split second *n* **1** an extremely short period of time; instant. ✧ *adj* **split-second 2** made in an extremely short time: *split-second timing.*

splitting *adj* (of a headache) extremely painful.

splodge *or US* **splotch** *n* **1** a large uneven spot or stain. ✧ *vb* **splodging, splodged 2** to mark (something) with a splodge or splodges. ▷ **HISTORY** alteration of earlier *splotch*

splurge *n* **1** a bout of spending money extravagantly. ✧ *vb* **splurging, splurged 2** (foll. by *on*) to spend (money) extravagantly: *they rushed out to splurge their pocket money on chocolate.* ▷ **HISTORY** origin unknown

splutter *vb* **1** to spit out (something) from the mouth when choking or laughing. **2** to say (words) with spitting sounds when choking or in a rage. **3** to throw out or to be thrown out explosively: *sparks spluttered from the fire.* ✧ *n* **4** the act or noise of spluttering. ▷ **HISTORY** variant of SPUTTER

spoil *vb* **spoiling, spoilt** *or* **spoiled 1** to make (something) less valuable, beautiful, or useful. **2** to weaken the character of (a child) by giving it all it wants. **3** (of yourself) to indulge one's desires: *go ahead and spoil yourself.* **4** (of food) to become unfit for consumption. **5 be spoiling for** to have an aggressive urge for: *he is spoiling for a fight.* ✧ See also **spoils.** ▷ **HISTORY** Latin *spolium* booty

spoiler *n* **1** a device fitted to an aircraft wing to increase drag and reduce lift. **2** a similar device fitted to a car.

spoils *pl n* **1** valuables seized during war. **2** the rewards and benefits of having political power.

spoilsport *n Informal* a person who spoils the enjoyment of other people.

spoke[1] *vb* the past tense of **speak**.

spoke[2] *n* **1** a bar joining the centre of a wheel to the rim. **2 put a spoke in someone's wheel** *Brit & NZ* to create a difficulty for someone. ▷ HISTORY Old English *spāca*

spoken *vb* **1** the past participle of **speak**. ✧ *adj* **2** said in speech: *spoken commands.* **3** having speech as specified: *quiet-spoken.* **4 spoken for** engaged or reserved.

spokesman, spokesperson, *or* **spokeswoman** *n, pl* **-men, -people** *or* **-women** a person chosen to speak on behalf of another person or group.

spoliation *n* the act or an instance of plundering: *the spoliation of the countryside.* ▷ HISTORY Latin *spoliare* to plunder

spondee *n Prosody* a metrical foot of two long syllables. ▷ HISTORY Greek *spondē* ritual offering of drink ▸ **spondaic** *adj*

sponge *n* **1** a sea animal with a porous absorbent elastic skeleton. **2** the skeleton of a sponge, or a piece of artificial sponge, used for bathing or cleaning. **3** a soft absorbent material like a sponge. **4** Also called: **sponge cake** a light cake made of eggs, sugar, and flour. **5** Also called: **sponge pudding** *Brit & Austral* a light steamed or baked spongy pudding. **6** a rub with a wet sponge. ✧ *vb* **sponging, sponged 7** (often foll. by *down*) to clean (something) by rubbing it with a wet sponge. **8** to remove (marks) by rubbing them with a wet sponge. **9** (usually foll. by *off* or *on*) to get (something) from someone by taking advantage of his or her generosity: *stop sponging off the rest of us!* ▷ HISTORY Greek *spongia* ▸ **spongy** *adj*

sponge bag *n* a small waterproof bag for holding toiletries when travelling.

sponger *n Informal, offensive* a person who lives off other people by continually taking advantage of their generosity.

sponsor *n* **1** a person or group that promotes another person or group in an activity or the activity itself, either for profit or for charity. **2** *Chiefly US & Canad* a person or firm that pays the costs of a radio or television programme in return for advertising time. **3** a person who presents and supports a proposal or suggestion. **4** a person who makes certain promises on behalf of a person being baptized and takes responsibility for his or her Christian upbringing. ✧ *vb* **5** to act as a sponsor for (someone or something). ▷ HISTORY Latin *spondere* to promise solemnly ▸ **sponsored** *adj* ▸ **sponsorship** *n*

spontaneous *adj* **1** not planned or arranged; impulsive: *a spontaneous celebration.* **2** occurring through natural processes without outside influence: *a spontaneous explosion.* ▷ HISTORY Latin *sponte* voluntarily ▸ **spontaneously** *adv* ▸ **spontaneity** *n*

spontaneous combustion *n Chem* the bursting into flame of a substance as a result of internal oxidation processes, without heat from an outside source.

spoof *Informal* ✧ *n* **1** an imitation of a film, TV programme, etc., that exaggerates in an amusing way the most memorable features of the original. **2** a good-humoured trick or deception. ✧ *vb* **3** to fool (a person) with a trick or deception. ▷ HISTORY made-up word

spook *Informal* ✧ *n* **1** a ghost. **2** a strange and frightening person. ✧ *vb US, Canad & Austral* **3** to frighten: *it was the wind that spooked her.* ▷ HISTORY Dutch ▸ **spooky** *adj*

spool *n* a cylinder around which film, thread, or tape can be wound. ▷ HISTORY Germanic

spoon *n* **1** a small shallow bowl attached to a handle, used for eating, stirring, or serving food. **2 be born with a silver spoon in one's mouth** to be born into a very rich and respected family. ✧ *vb* **3** to scoop up (food or liquid) with a spoon. **4** *Old-fashioned slang* to kiss and cuddle. ▷ HISTORY Old English *spōn* splinter

spoonbill *n* a wading bird with a long flat bill.

spoonerism *n* the accidental changing over of the first sounds of a pair of words, often with an amusing result, such as *hush my brat* for *brush my hat.* ▷ HISTORY after W. A. *Spooner,* clergyman

spoon-feed *vb* **-feeding, -fed 1** to feed (someone, usually a baby) using a spoon. **2** to give (someone) too much help.

spoor *n* the trail of an animal. ▷ HISTORY Afrikaans

sporadic *adj* happening at irregular intervals; intermittent: *sporadic bursts of gunfire.* ▷ HISTORY Greek *sporas* scattered ▸ **sporadically** *adv*

spore *n* a reproductive body, produced by nonflowering plants and bacteria, that develops into a new individual. ▷ HISTORY Greek *spora* a sowing

sporran *n* a large pouch worn hanging from a belt in front of the kilt in Scottish Highland dress. ▷ HISTORY Scottish Gaelic *sporan* purse

sport *n* **1** an activity for exercise, pleasure, or competition: *your favourite sport.* **2** such activities collectively: *the minister for sport.* **3** the enjoyment gained from a pastime: *just for the sport of it.* **4** playful or good-humoured joking: *I only did it in sport.* **5** *Informal* a person who accepts defeat or teasing cheerfully. **6 make sport of someone** to make fun of someone. **7** an animal or plant that is very different from others of the same species, usually because of a mutation. **8** *Austral & NZ informal* a term of address between males. ✧ *vb* **9** *Informal* to wear proudly: *sporting a pair of bright yellow shorts.* ✧ See also **sports**. ▷ HISTORY variant of Middle English *disporten* to disport

sporting *adj* **1** of sport. **2** behaving in a fair and decent way. **3 a sporting chance** a reasonable likelihood of happening: *a sporting chance of winning.*

sportive *adj* playful or high-spirited.

sports *adj* **1** of or used in sports: *a sports arena.* ✧ *n* **2** Also called: **sports day** *Brit* a meeting held at a school or college for competitions in athletic events.

sports car *n* a fast car with a low body and usually seating only two people.

sports jacket *n* a man's casual jacket, usually made of tweed. Also called: *US, Austral, & NZ* **sports coat**

sportsman *n, pl* **-men 1** a man who plays sports. **2** a person who plays by the rules, is fair, and accepts defeat with good humour. ▶ **sportsman-like** *adj* ▶ **sportsmanship** *n*

sportswoman *n, pl* **-women** a woman who plays sports.

sporty *adj* **sportier, sportiest 1** (of a person) interested in sport. **2** (of clothes) suitable for sport. **3** (of a car) small and fast. ▶ **sportily** *adv* ▶ **sportiness** *n*

spot *n* **1** a small mark on a surface, which has a different colour or texture from its surroundings. **2** a location: *a spot where they could sit.* **3** a small mark or pimple on the skin. **4** a feature of something that has the attribute mentioned: *the one bright spot in his whole day; the high spot of our trip.* **5** *Informal, chiefly Brit, Austral & NZ* a small amount: *a spot of bother.* **6** *Informal* an awkward situation: *I'm sometimes in a spot.* **7** a part of a show, TV programme, etc., reserved for a specific performer or type of entertainment. **8** short for **spotlight** (sense 1). **9 in a tight spot** in a difficult situation. **10 knock spots off someone** to be much better than someone. **11 on the spot a** immediately: *he decided on the spot to fly down.* **b** at the place in question: *the expert weapons man on the spot.* **c** in an awkward situation: *the British government will be put on the spot.* **12 soft spot** a special affection for someone: *a soft spot for older men.* ✧ *vb* **spotting, spotted 13** to see (something or someone) suddenly. **14** to put stains or spots on (something). **15** (of some fabrics) to be prone to marking by liquids: *silk spots easily.* **16** to take note of (the numbers of trains or planes observed). **17** (of scouts, agents, etc.) to look out for (talented but unknown actors, sportspersons, etc.). **18** *Brit* to rain lightly. ▷ **HISTORY** from German

spot check *n* a quick unplanned inspection.

spot height *n Geog* a mark on a map indicating the height of a hill, mountain, etc.

spotless *adj* **1** perfectly clean. **2** free from moral flaws: *a spotless reputation.* ▶ **spotlessly** *adv*

spotlight *n* **1** a powerful light focused so as to light up a small area. **2 the spotlight** the centre of attention: *the spotlight moved to the president.* ✧ *vb* **-lighting, -lit** *or* **-lighted 3** to direct a spotlight on (something). **4** to focus attention on (something).

spot-on *adj Informal* absolutely correct; very accurate: *they're spot-on in terms of style.*

spotted *adj* **1** having a pattern of spots. **2** marked with stains.

spotter *n* a person whose hobby is watching for and noting numbers or types of trains or planes.

spotty *adj* **-tier, -tiest 1** covered with spots or pimples. **2** not consistent; irregular in quality: *a rather spotty performance.* ▶ **spottiness** *n*

spouse *n* a person's partner in marriage. ▷ **HISTORY** Latin *sponsus, sponsa* betrothed man or woman

spout *vb* **1** (of a liquid or flames) to pour out in a stream or jet. **2** *Informal* to talk about (something) in a boring way or without much thought. ✧ *n* **3** a projecting tube or lip for pouring liquids. **4** a stream or jet of liquid: *a spout of steaming water.* **5 up the spout** *Slang* **a** ruined or lost: *the motor industry is up the spout.* **b** pregnant. ▷ **HISTORY** Middle English *spouten*

spouting *n NZ* **a** a rainwater downpipe on the outside of a building. **b** such pipes collectively.

sprain *vb* **1** to injure (a joint) by a sudden twist. ✧ *n* **2** this injury, which causes swelling and temporary disability. ▷ **HISTORY** origin unknown

sprang *vb* a past tense of **spring**.

sprat *n* a small edible fish like a herring. ▷ **HISTORY** Old English *sprott*

sprawl *vb* **1** to sit or lie with one's arms and legs spread out. **2** to spread out untidily over a large area: *the pulp mill sprawled over the narrow flats.* ✧ *n* **3** the part of a city or town that has not been planned and spreads out untidily over a large area: *the huge Los Angeles sprawl.* ▷ **HISTORY** Old English *spreawlian* ▶ **sprawling** *adj*

spray[1] *n* **1** fine drops of a liquid. **2 a** a liquid under pressure designed to be discharged in fine drops from an aerosol or atomizer: *hair spray.* **b** the aerosol or atomizer itself. **3** a number of small objects flying through the air: *a spray of bullets.* ✧ *vb* **4** to scatter in fine drops. **5** to squirt (a liquid) from an aerosol or atomizer. **6** to cover with a spray: *spray the crops.* ▷ **HISTORY** Middle Dutch *sprāien* ▶ **sprayer** *n*

spray[2] *n* **1** a sprig or branch with buds, leaves, flowers, or berries. **2** an ornament or design like this. ▷ **HISTORY** Germanic

spray gun *n* a device for spraying fine drops of paint, etc.

spread *vb* **spreading, spread 1** to open out or unfold to the fullest width: *spread the material out.* **2** to extend over a larger expanse: *the subsequent unrest spread countrywide.* **3** to apply as a coating: *spread the paste evenly over your skin.* **4** to be displayed to its fullest extent: *the shining bay spread out below.* **5** to send or be sent out in all directions or to many people: *the news spread quickly; the sandflies that spread the disease.* **6** to distribute or be distributed evenly: *we were advised to spread the workload over the whole year.* ✧ *n* **7** a spreading; distribution, dispersion, or expansion: *the spread of higher education.* **8** *Informal* a large meal. **9** *Informal* the wingspan of an aircraft or bird. **10** *Informal, chiefly US & Canad* a ranch or other large area of land. **11** a soft food which can be spread: *cheese spread.* **12** two facing pages in a book or magazine. **13** a widening of the hips and waist: *middle-age spread.* ▷ **HISTORY** Old English *sprǣdan*

spread-eagled *adj* with arms and legs outstretched.

spreadsheet *n* a computer program for manipulating figures, used for financial planning.

spree *n* a session of overindulgence, usually in drinking or spending money. ▷ **HISTORY** Scots *spreath* plundered cattle

sprig *n* **1** a shoot, twig, or sprout. **2** an ornamental device like this. **3** *NZ* a stud on the sole of a soccer or rugby boot. ▷ **HISTORY** Germanic ▶ **sprigged** *adj*

sprightly *adj* **-lier, -liest** lively and active. ▷ **HISTORY** obsolete *spright,* variant of SPRITE ▶ **sprightliness** *n*

spring *vb* **springing, sprang** *or* **sprung; sprung** **1** to jump suddenly upwards or forwards. **2** to return or be returned into natural shape from a forced position by elasticity: *the coil sprang back.* **3** to cause (something) to happen unexpectedly: *the national coach sprang a surprise.* **4** (usually foll. by *from*) to originate; be descended: *this motivation springs from their inborn curiosity; Truman sprang from ordinary people.* **5** (often foll. by *up*) to come into being or appear suddenly: *new courses will spring up.* **6** to provide (something, such as a mattress) with springs. **7** *Informal* to arrange the escape of (someone) from prison. ✧ *n* **8** the season between winter and summer. **9** a leap or jump. **10** a coil which can be compressed, stretched, or bent and then return to its original shape when released. **11** a natural pool forming the source of a stream. **12** elasticity. ▷ **HISTORY** Old English *springan* ▶ **springlike** *adj*

spring balance *or esp US* **spring scale** *n* a device that indicates the weight of an object by the extension of a spring to which the object is attached.

springboard *n* **1** a flexible board used to gain height or momentum in diving or gymnastics. **2** anything that makes it possible for an activity to begin: *the meeting acted as a springboard for future negotiations.*

springbok *n, pl* **-bok** *or* **-boks** **1** a S African antelope which moves in leaps. **2** a person who has represented S Africa in a national sports team. ▷ **HISTORY** Afrikaans

spring chicken *n* **1** *Chiefly US & S African* a young chicken, which is tender for cooking. **2 he** *or* **she is no spring chicken** *Informal* he *or* she is no longer young.

spring-clean *vb* **1** to clean (a house) thoroughly, traditionally at the end of winter. ✧ *n* **2** an instance of this. ▶ **spring-cleaning** *n*

spring onion *n* a small onion with a tiny bulb and long green leaves, eaten in salads.

spring tide *n* either of the two tides at or just after new moon and full moon: the greatest rise and fall in tidal level.

springtime *n* the season of spring.

springy *adj* **springier, springiest** (of an object) having the quality of returning to its original shape after being pressed or pulled. ▶ **springiness** *n*

sprinkle *vb* **-kling, -kled** **1** to scatter (liquid or powder) in tiny drops over (something). **2** to distribute over (something): *a dozen mud huts sprinkled around it.* ▷ **HISTORY** probably from Middle Dutch *sprenkelen* ▶ **sprinkler** *n*

sprinkling *n* a small quantity or amount: *a sprinkling of diamonds.*

sprint *n* **1** *Athletics* **a** a short race run at top speed. **b** a fast run at the end of a longer race. **2** any quick run. ✧ *vb* **3** to run or cycle a short distance at top speed. ▷ **HISTORY** Scandinavian ▶ **sprinter** *n*

sprit *n Naut* a light pole set diagonally across a sail to extend it. ▷ **HISTORY** Old English *sprēot*

sprite *n* **1** (in folklore) a fairy or elf. **2** an icon in a computer game which can be manoeuvred around the screen. ▷ **HISTORY** Latin *spiritus* spirit

spritsail *n Naut* a sail mounted on a sprit.

sprocket *n* **1** Also called: **sprocket wheel** a wheel with teeth on the rim, that drives or is driven by a chain. **2** a cylindrical wheel with teeth on one or both rims for pulling film through a camera or projector. ▷ **HISTORY** origin unknown

sprout *vb* **1** (of a plant or seed) to produce (new leaves or shoots). **2** (often foll. by *up*) to begin to grow or develop. ✧ *n* **3** a new shoot or bud. **4** same as **Brussels sprout**. ▷ **HISTORY** Old English *sprūtan*

spruce[1] *n* **1** an evergreen pyramid-shaped tree with needle-like leaves. **2** the light-coloured wood of this tree. ▷ **HISTORY** obsolete *Spruce* Prussia

spruce[2] *adj* neat and smart. ▷ **HISTORY** perhaps from *Spruce leather;* see SPRUCE[1]

spruce up *vb* **sprucing, spruced** to make neat and smart.

sprung *vb* a past tense and the past participle of **spring**.

spry *adj* **spryer, spryest** *or* **sprier, spriest** active and lively; nimble. ▷ **HISTORY** origin unknown

spud *n Informal* a potato. ▷ **HISTORY** obsolete *spudde* short knife

spume *n Literary* **1** foam or froth on the sea. ✧ *vb* **spuming, spumed** **2** (of the sea) to foam or froth. ▷ **HISTORY** Latin *spuma*

spun *vb* **1** the past of **spin**. ✧ *adj* **2** made by spinning: *spun sugar; spun silk.*

spunk *n Old-fashioned, informal* courage or spirit. ▷ **HISTORY** Scottish Gaelic *spong* tinder, sponge ▶ **spunky** *adj*

spur *n* **1** an incentive to get something done. **2** a sharp spiked wheel on the heel of a rider's boot used to urge the horse on. **3** a sharp horny part sticking out from a cock's leg. **4** a ridge sticking out from a mountain side. **5 on the spur of the moment** suddenly and without planning; on impulse. **6 win one's spurs** to prove one's ability. ✧ *vb* **spurring, spurred** **7** (often foll. by *on*) to encourage (someone). ▷ **HISTORY** Old English *spura*

spurge *n* a plant with milky sap and small flowers. ▷ **HISTORY** Latin *expurgare* to cleanse

spurious *adj* not genuine or real. ▷ **HISTORY** Latin *spurius* of illegitimate birth

spurn *vb* to reject (a person or thing) with contempt. ▷ **HISTORY** Old English *spurnan*

spurt *vb* **1** to gush or cause (something) to gush out in a sudden powerful stream or jet. **2** to make a sudden effort. ✧ *n* **3** a short burst of activity, speed, or energy. **4** a sudden powerful stream or jet. ▷ **HISTORY** origin unknown

sputnik *n* a Russian artificial satellite. ▷ **HISTORY** Russian, literally: fellow traveller

sputter *vb, n* same as **splutter**. ▷ **HISTORY** Dutch *sputteren,* imitative

sputum *n, pl* **-ta** saliva, usually mixed with mucus. ▷ HISTORY Latin

spy *n, pl* **spies 1** a person employed to find out secret information about other countries or organizations. **2** a person who secretly keeps watch on others. ✧ *vb* **spies, spying, spied 3** (foll. by *on*) to keep a secret watch on someone. **4** to work as a spy. **5** to catch sight of (someone or something); notice. ▷ HISTORY Old French *espier*

spyglass *n* a small telescope.

sq. square.

SQL *n* a computer programming language that is used for database management. ▷ HISTORY *s*tructured *q*uery *l*anguage

squab *n, pl* **squabs** *or* **squab** a young bird yet to leave the nest. ▷ HISTORY probably Germanic

squabble *vb* **-bling, -bled 1** to quarrel over a small matter. ✧ *n* **2** a petty quarrel. ▷ HISTORY probably Scandinavian

squad *n* **1** the smallest military formation, usually a dozen soldiers. **2** any small group of people working together: *the fraud squad.* **3** *Sport* a number of players from which a team is to be selected. ▷ HISTORY Old French *esquade*

squadron *n* the basic unit of an air force. ▷ HISTORY Italian *squadrone* soldiers drawn up in square formation

squadron leader *n* a fairly senior commissioned officer in the air force; the rank above flight lieutenant.

squalid *adj* **1** dirty, untidy, and in bad condition. **2** unpleasant, selfish, and often dishonest: *this squalid affair.* ▷ HISTORY Latin *squalidus*

squall[1] *n* a sudden strong wind or short violent storm. ▷ HISTORY perhaps a special use of SQUALL[2]

squall[2] *vb* **1** to cry noisily; yell. ✧ *n* **2** a noisy cry or yell. ▷ HISTORY probably Scandinavian

squalor *n* **1** dirty, poor, and untidy physical conditions. **2** the condition of being squalid. ▷ HISTORY Latin

squander *vb* to waste (money or resources). ▷ HISTORY origin unknown

square *n* **1** a geometric figure with four equal sides and four right angles. **2** anything of this shape. **3** an open area in a town bordered by buildings or streets. **4** *Maths* the number produced when a number is multiplied by itself: *9 is the square of 3, written* 3^2. **5** *Informal* a person who is dull or unfashionable. **6 go back to square one** to return to the start because of failure or lack of progress. ✧ *adj* **7** being a square in shape. **8 a** having the same area as that of a square with sides of a specified length: *2,500 square metres of hillside.* **b** denoting a square having a specified length on each side: *a cell of only four square metres.* **9** straight or level: *I don't think that painting is square.* **10** fair and honest: *a square deal.* **11** *Informal* dull or unfashionable. **12** having all debts or accounts settled: *if I give you 50 pence, then we'll be square.* **13 all square** on equal terms; even in score. **14 square peg in a round hole** *Informal* a misfit. ✧ *vb* **squaring, squared 15** *Maths* to multiply (a number or quantity) by itself. **16** to position so as to be straight or level: *bravely he squared his shoulders.* **17** to settle (a debt or account). **18** to level the score in (a game). **19** to be or cause to be consistent: *it would not have squared with her image.* ✧ *adv* **20** *Informal* same as **squarely**. ✧ See also **square up**. ▷ HISTORY Old French *esquare*

square-bashing *n Brit mil slang* marching and other drill on a parade ground.

square bracket *n* either of a pair of characters [ ], used to separate a section of writing or printing from the main text.

square dance *n* a country dance in which the couples are arranged in squares.

square leg *n Cricket* a fielding position on the on side, at right angles to the batsman.

squarely *adv* **1** directly; straight: *he looked her squarely in the eye.* **2** in an honest and frank way: *you should face squarely anything that worries you.*

square meal *n* a meal which is large enough to leave the eater feeling full: *we gave him his first square meal in days.*

square proportion *n Maths* a relationship between two variables in which one is proportional to the square of the other.

square-rigged *adj Naut* having sails set at right angles to the keel.

square root *n* a number that when multiplied by itself gives a given number: *the square roots of 4 are 2 and –2.*

square up *vb* **1** to settle bills or debts. **2 square up to** to prepare to confront (a problem or a person).

squash[1] *vb* **1** to press or squeeze (something) so as to flatten it. **2** to overcome (a difficult situation), often with force. **3 squash in** *or* **into** to push or force (oneself or a thing) into a confined space. **4** to humiliate (someone) with a sarcastic reply. ✧ *n* **5** *Brit & Austral* a drink made from fruit juice or fruit syrup diluted with water. **6** a crowd of people in a confined space. **7** Also called: **squash rackets** a game for two players played in an enclosed court with a small rubber ball and long-handled rackets. ▷ HISTORY Old French *esquasser*

squash[2] *n, pl* **squashes** *or* **squash** *US & Canad* a marrow-like vegetable. ▷ HISTORY from a Native American language

squashy *adj* **squashier, squashiest** soft and easily squashed.

squat *vb* **squatting, squatted 1** to crouch with the knees bent and the weight on the feet. **2** *Law* to occupy an unused building to which one has no legal right. ✧ *adj* **3** short and thick. ✧ *n* **4** a building occupied by squatters. ▷ HISTORY Old French *esquater*

squatter *n* an illegal occupier of an unused building.

squaw *n Offensive* a Native American woman of N America. ▷ HISTORY from a Native American language

squawk *n* **1** a loud harsh cry, esp. one made by a bird. **2** *Informal* a loud complaint. ✧ *vb* **3** to make a squawk. ▷ HISTORY imitative

squeak *n* **1** a short high-pitched cry or sound. **2 a narrow squeak** *Informal* a narrow escape or success. ✧ *vb* **3** to make a squeak. **4 squeak through** *or* **by** to pass (an examination), but only just. ▷ **HISTORY** probably Scandinavian ▶ **squeaky** *adj* ▶ **squeakiness** *n*

squeal *n* **1** a long high-pitched yelp. ✧ *vb* **2** to make a squeal. **3** *Slang* to inform on someone to the police. **4** *Informal, chiefly Brit* to complain loudly. ▷ **HISTORY** Middle English *squelen,* imitative ▶ **squealer** *n*

squeamish *adj* easily shocked or upset by unpleasant sights or events. ▷ **HISTORY** Anglo-French *escoymous*

squeegee *n* a tool with a rubber blade used for wiping away excess water from a surface. ▷ **HISTORY** probably imitative

squeeze *vb* **squeezing, squeezed 1** to grip or press (something) firmly. **2** to crush or press (something) so as to extract (a liquid): *squeeze the tomato and strain the juice; freshly squeezed lemon juice.* **3** to push (oneself or a thing) into a confined space. **4** to hug (someone) closely. **5** to obtain (something) by great effort or force: *to squeeze the last dollar out of every deal.* ✧ *n* **6** a squeezing. **7** a hug. **8** a crush of people in a confined space. **9** *Chiefly Brit & NZ* a restriction on borrowing made by a government to control price inflation. **10** an amount extracted by squeezing: *a squeeze of lime.* **11 put the squeeze on someone** *Informal* to put pressure on someone in order to obtain something. ▷ **HISTORY** Old English *cwȳsan*

squelch *vb* **1** to make a wet sucking noise, such as by walking through mud. **2** *Informal* to silence (someone) with a sarcastic or wounding reply. ✧ *n* **3** a squelching sound. ▷ **HISTORY** imitative ▶ **squelchy** *adj*

squib *n* **1** a firework that burns with a hissing noise before exploding. **2 damp squib** something expected to be exciting or successful but turning out to be a disappointment. ▷ **HISTORY** probably imitative of a light explosion

squid *n, pl* **squid** *or* **squids** a sea creature with ten tentacles and a long soft body. ▷ **HISTORY** origin unknown

squiffy *adj* **-fier, -fiest** *Brit informal* slightly drunk: *a bit squiffy.* ▷ **HISTORY** origin unknown

squiggle *n* a wavy line. ▷ **HISTORY** perhaps SQUIRM + WIGGLE ▶ **squiggly** *adj*

squill *n* a Mediterranean plant of the lily family. ▷ **HISTORY** Greek *skilla*

squint *vb* **1** to have eyes which face in different directions. **2** to glance sideways. ✧ *n* **3** an eye disorder in which one or both eyes turn inwards or outwards from the nose. **4** *Informal* a quick look; glance: *take a squint at the map.* ✧ *adj* **5** *Informal* not straight; crooked. ▷ **HISTORY** short for *asquint*

squire *n* **1** a country gentleman in England, usually the main landowner in a country community. **2** *Informal, chiefly Brit* a term of address used by one man to another. **3** *History* a knight's young attendant. ✧ *vb* **squiring, squired 4** *Old-fashioned* (of a man) to escort (a woman). ▷ **HISTORY** Old French *esquier*

squirm *vb* **1** to wriggle. **2** to feel embarrassed or guilty. ✧ *n* **3** a wriggling movement. ▷ **HISTORY** imitative

squirrel *n* a small bushy-tailed animal that lives in trees. ▷ **HISTORY** Greek *skiouros,* from *skia* shadow + *oura* tail

squirt *vb* **1** to force (a liquid) or (of a liquid) to be forced out of a narrow opening. **2** to cover or spatter (a person or thing) with liquid in this way. ✧ *n* **3** a jet of liquid. **4** a squirting. **5** *Informal* a small or insignificant person. ▷ **HISTORY** imitative

squish *vb* **1** to crush (something) with a soft squelching sound. **2** to make a squelching sound. ✧ *n* **3** a soft squelching sound. ▷ **HISTORY** imitative ▶ **squishy** *adj*

Sr **1** (after a name) senior. **2** Señor. **3** *Chem* strontium.

Sri Lankan *adj* **1** of Sri Lanka. ✧ *n* **2** a person from Sri Lanka.

SRN (formerly in Britain) State Registered Nurse.

SS **1** an organization in the Nazi party that provided Hitler's bodyguard, security forces, and concentration-camp guards. ▷ **HISTORY** German *Schutzstaffel* protection squad **2** steamship.

St **1** Saint. **2** Street.

st. stone.

stab *vb* **stabbing, stabbed 1** to pierce with a sharp pointed instrument. **2** (often foll. by *at*) to make a thrust (at); jab. **3 stab someone in the back** to do harm to someone by betraying him or her. ✧ *n* **4** a stabbing. **5** a sudden, usually unpleasant, sensation: *a stab of jealousy.* **6** *Informal* an attempt: *you've got to have a stab at it.* **7 stab in the back** an act of betrayal that harms a person. ▷ **HISTORY** Middle English *stabbe* stab wound ▶ **stabbing** *n*

stability *n* the quality of being stable: *the security and stability of married life.*

stabilize *or* **-lise** *vb* **-lizing, -lized** *or* **-lising, -lised** to make or become stable or more stable. ▶ **stabilization** *or* **-lisation** *n*

stabilizer *or* **-liser** *n* **1** a device for stabilizing a child's bicycle, an aircraft, or a ship. **2** a substance added to food to preserve its texture.

stable[1] *n* **1** a building where horses are kept. **2** an organization that breeds and trains racehorses. **3** an organization that manages or trains several entertainers or athletes. ✧ *vb* **-bling, -bled 4** to put or keep (a horse) in a stable. ▷ **HISTORY** Latin *stabulum* shed

stable[2] *adj* **1** steady in position or balance; firm. **2** lasting and not likely to experience any sudden changes: *a stable environment.* **3** having a calm personality; not moody. **4** *Physics* (of an elementary particle) not subject to decay. **5** *Chem* (of a chemical compound) not easily decomposed. ▷ **HISTORY** Latin *stabilis* steady

staccato (stak-**ah**-toe) *adj* **1** *Music* (of notes) short and separate. **2** consisting of short abrupt sounds: *the staccato sound of high-heels on the stairs.* ✧ *adv* **3** in a staccato manner. ▷ **HISTORY** Italian

stack *n* **1** a pile of things, one on top of the other. **2** a large neat pile of hay or straw. **3 stacks** a large amount: *there's still stacks for us to do.* **4** same as **smokestack**. **5** an area in a computer memory for temporary storage. ✧ *vb* **6** to place (things) in a stack. **7** to load or fill (something) up with piles of objects: *Henry was watching her stack the dishwasher.* **8** to control (a number of aircraft) waiting to land at an airport so that each flies at a different altitude. ▷ **HISTORY** Old Norse *stakkr* haystack

stadium *n, pl* **-diums** *or* **-dia** a large sports arena with tiered rows of seats for spectators. ▷ **HISTORY** Greek *stadion*

staff *n, pl for senses 1 & 2* **staffs;** *for senses 3 & 4* **staffs** *or* **staves 1** the people employed in a company, school, or organization. **2** *Mil* the officers appointed to assist a commander. **3** a stick with some special use, such as a walking stick or an emblem of authority. **4** *Music* a set of five horizontal lines on which music is written and which, along with a clef, indicates pitch. ✧ *vb* **5** to provide (a company, school, or organization) with a staff. ▷ **HISTORY** Old English *stæf*

staff nurse *n* (in Britain) a qualified nurse ranking just below a sister or charge nurse.

staff sergeant *n Mil* a noncommissioned officer in an army or in the US Air Force or Marine Corps.

staff turnover *n Business* the number of workers employed by a firm in a given period to replace those who have left.

stag *n* the adult male of a deer. ▷ **HISTORY** Old English *stagga*

stag beetle *n* a beetle with large branched jaws.

stage *n* **1** a step or period of development, growth, or progress. **2** the platform in a theatre where actors perform. **3 the stage** the theatre as a profession. **4** the scene of an event or action. **5** a part of a journey: *the last stage of his tour around France.* **6** short for **stagecoach**. **7** *Brit & Austral* a division of a bus route for which there is a fixed fare. ✧ *vb* **staging, staged 8** to present (a dramatic production) on stage: *to stage 'Hamlet'.* **9** to organize and carry out (an event). ▷ **HISTORY** Old French *estage* position

stagecoach *n* a large four-wheeled horse-drawn vehicle formerly used to carry passengers and mail on a regular route.

stage direction *n* an instruction to an actor, written into the script of a play.

stage door *n* a door at a theatre leading backstage.

stage fright *n* feelings of fear and nervousness felt by a person about to appear in front of an audience.

stagehand *n* a person who sets the stage and moves props in a theatre.

stage-manage *vb* **-managing, -managed** to arrange (an event) from behind the scenes.

stage manager *n* a person who supervises the stage arrangements of a production at a theatre.

stage-struck *adj* having a great desire to act.

stage whisper *n* **1** a loud whisper from an actor, intended to be heard by the audience. **2** any loud whisper that is intended to be overheard.

stagflation *n* inflation combined with stagnant or falling output and employment. ▷ **HISTORY** STAGNATION + INFLATION

stagger *vb* **1** to walk unsteadily. **2** to amaze or shock (someone): *it staggered her that there was any liaison between them.* **3** to arrange (events) so as not to happen at the same time: *staggered elections.* ✧ *n* **4** a staggering. ▷ **HISTORY** dialect *stacker* ▶ **staggering** *adj* ▶ **staggeringly** *adv*

staggers *n* a disease of horses and other domestic animals that causes staggering.

stagnant *adj* **1** (of water) stale from not moving. **2** unsuccessful or dull from lack of change or development. ▷ **HISTORY** Latin *stagnans*

stagnate *vb* **-nating, -nated** to become inactive or unchanging: *people in old age only stagnate when they have no interests.* ▶ **stagnation** *n*

stagy *or US* **stagey** *adj* **stagier, stagiest** too theatrical or dramatic.

staid *adj* serious, rather dull, and old-fashioned in behaviour or appearance. ▷ **HISTORY** obsolete past participle of STAY

stain *vb* **1** to discolour (something) with marks that are not easily removed. **2** to dye (something) with a lasting pigment. ✧ *n* **3** a mark or discoloration that is not easily removed. **4** an incident in someone's life that has damaged his or her reputation: *a stain on his character.* **5** a liquid used to penetrate the surface of a material, such as wood, and colour it without covering up the surface or grain. ▷ **HISTORY** Middle English *steynen*

stainless steel *n* a type of steel that does not rust, as it contains large amounts of chromium.

stair *n* **1** one step in a flight of stairs. **2** a series of steps: *he fled down the back stair.* ✧ See also **stairs**. ▷ **HISTORY** Old English *stǣger*

staircase *n* a flight of stairs, usually with a handrail or banisters.

stairs *pl n* a flight of steps going from one level to another, usually indoors.

stairway *n* a staircase.

stake[1] *n* **1** a stick or metal bar driven into the ground as part of a fence or as a support or marker. **2 be burned at the stake** to be executed by being tied to a stake in the centre of a pile of wood that is then set on fire. ✧ *vb* **staking, staked 3** to lay (a claim) to land or rights. **4** to support (something, such as a plant) with a stake. ▷ **HISTORY** Old English *staca* stake, post

stake[2] *n* **1** the money that a player must risk in order to take part in a gambling game or make a bet. **2** an interest, usually financial, held in something: *a 50% stake in a new consortium.* **3 at stake** at risk. **4 stakes a** the money that a player has available for gambling. **b** a prize in a race or contest. **c** a horse race in which all owners of competing horses contribute to the prize. ✧ *vb* **staking, staked 5** to risk (something, such as money) on a result. **6** to give financial support to (a business). ▷ **HISTORY** origin unknown

A B C D E F G H I J K L M N O P Q R S T U V W X Y Z

stakeholder *n* **1** a person or group not owning shares in an enterprise but having an interest in its operations, such as the employees, customers, or local community. ✧ *adj* **2** relating to policies intended to allow people to participate in decisions made by enterprises in which they have a stake: *stakeholder economy.*

stakeout *n* **1** *Slang, chiefly US & Canad* a police surveillance of an area or house. ✧ *vb* **stake out** **2** *Slang, chiefly US & Canad* to keep an area or house under surveillance. **3** to surround (a piece of land) with stakes.

stalactite *n* an icicle-shaped mass of calcium carbonate hanging from the roof of a cave: formed by continually dripping water. ▷ **HISTORY** Greek *stalaktos* dripping

stalagmite *n* a large pointed mass of calcium carbonate sticking up from the floor of a cave: formed by continually dripping water from a stalactite. ▷ **HISTORY** Greek *stalagmos* dripping

stale *adj* **1** (esp. of food) no longer fresh, having being kept too long. **2** (of air) stagnant and having an unpleasant smell. **3** lacking in enthusiasm or ideas through overwork or lack of variety. **4** uninteresting from having been done or seen too many times: *such achievements now seem stale today.* **5** no longer new: *her war had become stale news.* ▷ **HISTORY** probably from Old French *estale* motionless ▶ **staleness** *n*

stalemate *n* **1** a chess position in which any of a player's moves would place his king in check: in this position the game ends in a draw. **2** a situation in which further action by two opposing forces is impossible or will not achieve anything; deadlock. ▷ **HISTORY** obsolete *stale* standing place + CHECKMATE

Stalinism *n* the policies associated with Joseph Stalin, general secretary of the Communist Party of the Soviet Union 1922–53, which resulted in rapid industrialization, state terror as a means of political control, and the abolition of collective leadership. ▶ **Stalinist** *n, adj*

stalk[1] *n* **1** the main stem of a plant. **2** a stem that joins a leaf or flower to the main stem of a plant. ▷ **HISTORY** probably from Old English *stalu* upright piece of wood

stalk[2] *vb* **1** to follow (an animal or person) quietly and secretly in order to catch or kill them. **2** to pursue persistently and, sometimes, attack (a person with whom one is obsessed, often a celebrity). **3** to spread over (a place) in a menacing way: *danger stalked the streets.* **4** to walk in an angry, arrogant, or stiff way. ▷ **HISTORY** Old English *bestealcian* ▶ **stalker** *n*

stalking-horse *n* something or someone used to hide a true purpose; pretext.

stall[1] *n* **1** a small stand for the display and sale of goods. **2** a compartment in a stable or shed for a single animal. **3** any small room or compartment: *a shower stall.* ✧ *vb* **4** to stop (a motor vehicle or its engine) or (of a motor vehicle or its engine) to stop, by incorrect use of the clutch or incorrect adjustment of the fuel mixture. ▷ **HISTORY** Old English *steall* a place for standing

stall[2] *vb* to employ delaying tactics towards (someone); be evasive. ▷ **HISTORY** Anglo-French *estale* bird used as a decoy

stallion *n* an uncastrated male horse, usually used for breeding. ▷ **HISTORY** Old French *estalon*

stalls *n* **1** the seats on the ground floor of a theatre or cinema. **2** (in a church) a row of seats, divided by armrests or a small screen, for the choir or clergy.

stalwart (**stawl**-wart) *adj* **1** strong and sturdy. **2** loyal and reliable. ✧ *n* **3** a hard-working and loyal supporter: *local party stalwarts.* ▷ **HISTORY** Old English *stǣlwirthe* serviceable

stamen *n* the part of a flower that produces pollen. ▷ **HISTORY** Latin: the warp in an upright loom

stamina *n* energy and strength sustained while performing an activity over a long time. ▷ **HISTORY** Latin: the threads of life spun out by the Fates, hence energy

stammer *vb* **1** to speak or say (something) with involuntary pauses or repetition, as a result of a speech disorder or through fear or nervousness. ✧ *n* **2** a speech disorder characterized by involuntary repetitions and pauses. ▷ **HISTORY** Old English *stamerian*

stamp *n* **1** a printed paper label attached to a piece of mail to show that the required postage has been paid. **2** a token issued by a shop or business after a purchase that can be saved and exchanged for other goods sold by that shop or business. **3** the action or an act of stamping. **4** an instrument for stamping a design or words. **5** a design, device, or mark that has been stamped. **6** a characteristic feature: *the stamp of inevitability.* **7** *Brit informal* a national insurance contribution, formerly recorded by a stamp on an official card. **8** type or class: *men of his stamp.* ✧ *vb* **9** (often foll. by *on*) to bring (one's foot) down heavily. **10** to walk with heavy or noisy footsteps. **11** to characterize: *a performance that stamped him as a star.* **12** **stamp on** to subdue or restrain: *all of which have stamped on dissent.* **13** to impress or mark (a pattern or sign) on. **14** to mark (something) with an official seal or device. **15** to have a strong effect on: *a picture vividly stamped on memory.* **16** to stick a stamp on (an envelope or parcel). ▷ **HISTORY** probably from Old English *stampian*

stampede *n* **1** a sudden rush of frightened animals or of a crowd. ✧ *vb* **-peding, -peded** **2** to run away in a stampede. ▷ **HISTORY** Spanish *estampar* to stamp

stamping ground *n* a favourite meeting place.

stamp out *vb* **1** to put an end to (something) by force; suppress: *an attempt to stamp out democracy.* **2** to put out by stamping: *I stamped out my cigarette.*

stance *n* **1** an attitude towards a particular matter: *a tough stance in the trade talks.* **2** the manner and position in which a person stands. **3** *Sport* the position taken when about to play the ball. ▷ **HISTORY** Latin *stare* to stand

stanch (**stahnch**) *vb* same as **staunch**[2]. ▷ **HISTORY** Old French *estanchier*

stanchion *n* a vertical pole or bar used as a support. ▷ HISTORY Old French *estanchon*

stand *vb* **standing, stood 1** to be upright. **2** to rise to an upright position. **3** to place (something) upright. **4** to be situated: *the property stands in a prime position.* **5** to have a specified height when standing: *the structure stands sixty feet above the river.* **6** to be in a specified position: *Turkey stands to gain handsomely.* **7** to be in a specified state or condition: *how he stands in comparison to others.* **8** to remain unchanged or valid: *the Conservatives were forced to let much of the legislation stand.* **9 stand at** (of a score or an account) to be in the specified position: *now the total stands at nine.* **10** to tolerate or bear: *Christopher can't stand him.* **11** to survive: *stand the test of time.* **12** (often foll. by *for*) to be a candidate: *to stand for president.* **13** *Informal* to buy: *to stand someone a drink.* **14 stand a chance** to have a chance of succeeding. **15 stand one's ground** to face a difficult situation bravely. **16 stand trial** to be tried in a law court. ✧ *n* **17** a stall or counter selling goods: *the hot dog stand.* **18** a structure at a sports ground where people can sit or stand. **19** the act or an instance of standing. **20** a firmly held opinion: *its firm stand on sanctions.* **21** *US & Austral* a place in a law court where a witness stands. **22** a rack on which coats and hats may be hung. **23** a small table or piece of furniture where articles may be placed or stored: *an umbrella stand.* **24** an effort to defend oneself or one's beliefs against attack or criticism: *a last stand against superior forces.* **25** *Cricket* a long period at the wicket by two batsmen. **26** See **one-night stand.** ✧ See also **stand by, stand down**, etc. ▷ HISTORY Old English *standan*

standard *n* **1** a level of quality: *cuisine of a high standard.* **2** an accepted example of something against which others are judged or measured: *the work was good by any standard.* **3** a moral principle of behaviour. **4** a flag of a nation or cause. **5** an upright pole or beam used as a support: *a lamp standard.* **6** a song that has remained popular for many years. ✧ *adj* **7** of a usual, medium, or accepted kind: *a standard cost.* **8** of recognized authority: *a standard reference book.* **9** denoting pronunciations or grammar regarded as correct and acceptable by educated native speakers. ▷ HISTORY Old French *estandart* gathering place

standard assessment tasks *pl n* (in Britain) national standardized tests for assessing school pupils.

standard-bearer *n* **1** a leader of a movement or party. **2** a person who carries a flag in battle or in a march.

standard form *n Maths* the expression of numbers as multiples of suitable powers of the base of the counting system and so not always employing the decimal point strictly between the integral and fractional parts of the number: *123.45 can be written in standard form as* 1.2345×10^2.

Standard Grade *n* (in Scotland) **1** an examination designed to test skills and application of knowledge, replacing the O Grade. **2** a pass in an examination at this level.

standardize *or* **-ise** *vb* **-izing, -ized** *or* **-ising, -ised** to make (things) standard: *to standardize the preparation process.* ▶ **standardization** *or* **-isation** *n*

standard lamp *n* a tall electric lamp that has a shade and stands on a base.

standard of living *n* the level of comfort and wealth of a person, group, or country.

standard of proof *n Law* the degree of proof required for a case to be proved; in a criminal case, the standard is *beyond reasonable doubt*, while in a civil case, the standard is the lower *balance of probabilities*.

standard time *n* the official local time of a region or country determined by the distance from Greenwich of a line of longitude passing through the area.

stand by *vb* **1** to be available and ready to act if needed: *stand by for firing.* **2** to be present as an onlooker or without taking any action: *the military police stood by watching idly.* **3** to be faithful to: *his wife will stand by him.* ✧ *n* **stand-by 4** a person or thing that is ready for use or can be relied on in an emergency. **5 on stand-by** ready for action or use. ✧ *adj* **stand-by 6** not booked in advance but subject to availability: *stand-by planes.*

stand down *vb* to resign or withdraw, often in favour of another.

stand for *vb* **1** to represent: *AIDS stands for Acquired Immune Deficiency Syndrome.* **2** to support and represent (an idea or a belief): *to stand for liberty and truth.* **3** *Informal* to tolerate or bear: *I won't stand for this!*

stand in *vb* **1** to act as a substitute: *she stood in for her father.* ✧ *n* **stand-in 2** a person who acts as a substitute for another.

standing *adj* **1** permanent, fixed, or lasting: *it was a standing joke.* **2** used to stand in or on: *standing room only.* **3** *Athletics* (of a jump or the start of a race) begun from a standing position. ✧ *n* **4** social or financial status or reputation: *her international standing.* **5** duration: *a friendship of at least ten years' standing.*

standing committee *n Government* a permanent committee appointed to deal with a specified subject.

standing order *n* **1** an instruction to a bank to pay a fixed amount to a person or organization at regular intervals. **2** a rule or order governing the procedure of an organization.

standoffish *adj* behaving in a formal and unfriendly way.

stand out *vb* **1** to be more impressive or important than others of the same kind: *his passing ability stood out in this game.* **2** to be noticeable because of looking different: *her long fair hair made her stand out from the rest.* **3** to refuse to agree or comply: *a hero who stood out against foreign domination.*

standpipe *n Chiefly Brit* a temporary vertical pipe installed in a street and supplying water when household water supplies are cut off.

standpoint *n* a point of view from which a matter is considered.

standstill *n* a complete stoppage or halt: *all traffic came to a standstill.*

stand to *vb* **1** *Mil* to take up positions in order to defend against attack. **2 stand to reason** to be obvious or logical: *it stands to reason you will play better.*

stand up *vb* **1** to rise to one's feet. **2** *Informal* to fail to keep a date with (a boyfriend or girlfriend): *sometimes he would stand me up.* **3** to be accepted as satisfactory or true: *the decision would not stand up in court.* **4 stand up for** to support or defend. **5 stand up to a** to confront or resist (someone) bravely. **b** to withstand and endure (something, such as criticism). ✧ *adj* **stand-up 6** (of a comedian) telling jokes alone to an audience. **7** done while standing: *a stand-up breakfast.* **8** (of a fight or row) angry and unrestrained. ✧ *n* **9** stand-up comedy or a stand-up comedian.

stank *vb* a past tense of **stink**.

Stanley knife *n Trademark* a type of knife with a thick metal handle with a short, very sharp, replaceable blade. ▷ HISTORY after F. T. *Stanley*, businessman

stanza *n Prosody* a verse of a poem. ▷ HISTORY Italian: halting place

staphylococcus (staff-ill-oh-**kok**-uss) *n, pl* **-cocci** (-**kok**-eye) a bacterium occurring in clusters and including many species that cause disease. ▷ HISTORY Greek *staphulē* bunch of grapes + *kokkos* berry

staple[1] *n* **1** a short length of wire bent into a square U-shape, used to fasten papers or secure things. ✧ *vb* **-pling, -pled 2** to secure (things) with staples. ▷ HISTORY Old English *stapol* prop

staple[2] *adj* **1** of prime importance; principal: *the staple diet of a country.* ✧ *n* **2** something that forms a main part of the product, consumption, or trade of a region. **3** a main constituent of anything: *the personal reflections which make up the staple of the book.* ▷ HISTORY Middle Dutch *stapel* warehouse

stapler *n* a device used to fasten things together with a staple.

star *n* **1** a planet or meteor visible in the clear night sky as a point of light. **2** a hot gaseous mass, such as the sun, that radiates energy as heat and light, or in some cases as radio waves and X-rays. *RELATED ADJECTIVES* ▸ **astral, sidereal, stellar 3 stars** same as **horoscope** (sense 1). **4** an emblem with five or more radiating points, often used as a symbol of rank or an award: *the RAC awarded the hotel three stars.* **5** same as **asterisk**. **6** a famous person from the sports, acting, or music professions. **7 see stars** to see flashes of light after a blow on the head. ✧ *vb* **starring, starred 8** to feature (an actor or actress) or (of an actor or actress) to be featured as a star: *he's starred in dozens of films.* **9** to mark (something) with a star or stars. ▷ HISTORY Old English *steorra*

starboard *n* **1** the right side of an aeroplane or ship when facing forwards. ✧ *adj* **2** of or on the starboard.

> **WORD HISTORY**
> 'Starboard' comes from Old English *steorbord*, which means 'steering side'. This is because boats were formerly steered with a paddle held over the right-hand side of the boat.

starch *n* **1** a carbohydrate forming the main food element in bread, potatoes, and rice: in solution with water it is used to stiffen fabric. **2** food containing a large amount of starch. ✧ *vb* **3** to stiffen (cloth) with starch. ▷ HISTORY Old English *sterced* stiffened

starchy *adj* **starchier, starchiest 1** of or containing starch. **2** (of a person's behaviour) very formal and humourless.

stardom *n* the status of a star in the entertainment or sport world.

stare *vb* **staring, stared 1** (often foll. by *at*) to look at for a long time. **2 stare one in the face** to be glaringly obvious. ✧ *n* **3** a long fixed look. ▷ HISTORY Old English *starian*

starfish *n, pl* **-fish** *or* **-fishes** a star-shaped sea creature with a flat body and five limbs.

star fruit *n* same as **carambola**.

stark *adj* **1** harsh, unpleasant, and plain: *a stark choice.* **2** grim, desolate, and lacking any beautiful features: *the stark landscapes.* **3** utter; absolute: *in stark contrast.* ✧ *adv* **4** completely: *stark staring bonkers.* ▷ HISTORY Old English *stearc* stiff ▸ **starkly** *adv* ▸ **starkness** *n*

stark-naked *adj* completely naked. Also (informal): **starkers** ▷ HISTORY Middle English *stert naket*, literally: tail naked

starlet *n* a young actress who has the potential to become a star.

starlight *n* the light that comes from the stars.

starling *n* a common songbird with shiny blackish feathers and a short tail. ▷ HISTORY Old English *stærlinc*

Star of David *n* a symbol of Judaism, consisting of a star formed by two interlaced equilateral triangles.

starry *adj* **-rier, -riest 1** (of a sky or night) full of or lit by stars. **2** of or like a star or stars: *a starry cast.*

starry-eyed *adj* full of unrealistic hopes and dreams; naive.

Stars and Stripes *n* the national flag of the United States of America.

star sign *n Astrol* the sign of the zodiac under which a person was born.

star-studded *adj* featuring many well-known performers: *a star-studded premiere.*

start *vb* **1** to begin (something or to do something): *to start a war; we've already started building.* **2** to set or be set in motion: *he started the van.* **3** to make a sudden involuntary movement from fright or surprise; jump. **4** to establish; set up: *to start a state lottery.* **5** to support (someone) in the first part of a career or activity. **6** *Brit informal* to begin quarrelling or causing a disturbance: *don't start with me.* **7 to start with** in the first place. ✧ *n* **8** the first part of something. **9** the place or time at which something begins. **10** a signal to begin, such as in a race. **11** a lead or advantage, either in time or distance, in a competitive activity: *he had an hour's start on me.* **12** a slight involuntary movement from fright or surprise: *I awoke with a start.* **13** an opportunity to enter a career or begin a project. **14 for a start** in the first place. ▷ **HISTORY** Old English *styrtan*

starter *n* **1** *Chiefly Brit* the first course of a meal. **2 for starters** *Slang* in the first place. **3** a device for starting an internal-combustion engine. **4** a person who signals the start of a race. **5** a competitor in a race or contest. **6 under starter's orders** (of competitors in a race) waiting for the signal to start.

startle *vb* **-tling, -tled** to slightly surprise or frighten someone. ▷ **HISTORY** Old English *steartlian* to kick, struggle ▶ **startling** *adj*

start up *vb* **1** to come or cause (something, such as a business) to come into being; found. **2** to set (something) in motion: *she started up the car.*

starve *vb* **starving, starved 1** to die from lack of food. **2** to deliberately prevent (a person or animal) from having any food. **3** *Informal* to be very hungry: *we're both starving.* **4 starve of** to deprive (someone) of something needed: *the heart is starved of oxygen.* **5 starve into** to force someone into a specified state by starving: *an attempt to starve him into submission.* ▷ **HISTORY** Old English *steorfan* to die ▶ **starvation** *n*

Star Wars *n* (in the US) a proposed system of artificial satellites armed with lasers to destroy enemy missiles in space.

stash *Informal* ✧ *vb* **1** (often foll. by *away*) to store (money or valuables) in a secret place for safekeeping. ✧ *n* **2** a secret store, usually of illegal drugs, or the place where this is hidden. ▷ **HISTORY** origin unknown

state *n* **1** the condition or circumstances of a person or thing. **2** *Physics* the structure, form, or constitution of something: *a solid state.* **3** a sovereign political power or community. **4** the territory of such a community. **5** the sphere of power in such a community: *matters of state.* **6** (*often cap*) one of a number of areas or communities having their own governments and forming a federation under a sovereign government, such as in the US or Australia. **7** (*often cap*) the government, civil service, and armed forces. **8 in a state** *Informal* in an emotional or very worried condition. **9 lie in state** (of a body) to be placed on public view before burial. **10 state of affairs** circumstances or condition: *this wonderful state of affairs.* **11** grand and luxurious lifestyle, as enjoyed by royalty, aristocrats, or the wealthy: *living in state.* ✧ *adj* **12** controlled or financed by a state: *state ownership.* **13** of or concerning the State: *state secrets.* **14** involving ceremony: *a state visit.* ✧ *vb* **stating, stated 15** to express (something) in words. ▷ **HISTORY** Latin *stare* to stand

State Enrolled Nurse *n* (in Britain) a nurse who has completed a two-year training course.

statehouse *n NZ* a rented house built by the government.

stateless *adj* not belonging to any country: *stateless refugees.*

stately *adj* **-lier, -liest** having a dignified, impressive, and graceful appearance or manner: *the Rolls-Royce approached him at a stately speed.* ▶ **stateliness** *n*

statement *n* **1** something stated, usually a formal prepared announcement or reply. **2** an account prepared by a bank at regular intervals for a client to show all credits and debits and the balance at the end of the period. **3** an account containing a summary of bills or invoices and showing the total amount due. **4** the act of stating.

statement of claim *n Law* (in a civil case) the formal written statement made by a plaintiff setting out his or her allegations and the remedy sought.

State Registered Nurse *n* (formerly in Britain) a nurse who has completed an extensive three-year training course.

stateroom *n* **1** a private room on a ship. **2** *Chiefly Brit* a large room in a palace, etc., used on ceremonial occasions.

States *pl n* **the States** *Informal* the United States of America.

state school *n* a school funded by the state, in which education is free.

statesman *n, pl* **-men** an experienced and respected political leader. ▶ **statesmanship** *n*

static *adj* **1** not active, changing, or moving; stationary. **2** *Physics* (of a weight, force, or pressure) acting but causing no movement. **3** *Physics* of forces that do not produce movement. ✧ *n* **4** hissing or crackling or a speckled picture caused by interference in the reception of radio or television transmissions. **5** electric sparks or crackling produced by friction. ▷ **HISTORY** Greek *statikos* causing to stand

statics *n* the branch of mechanics concerned with the forces producing a state of equilibrium.

station *n* **1** a place along a route or line at which a bus or train stops to pick up passengers or goods. **2** the headquarters of an organization such as the police or fire service. **3** a building with special equipment for some particular purpose: *power station; a filling station.* **4** a television or radio channel. **5** *Mil* a place of duty. **6** position in society: *he had ideas above his station.* **7** *Austral & NZ* a large sheep or cattle farm. **8** the place or position where a person is assigned to stand: *every man stood at his station.* ✧ *vb* **9** to assign (someone) to a station. ▷ **HISTORY** Latin *statio* a standing still

stationary *adj* not moving: *a line of stationary traffic.* ▷ **HISTORY** Latin *stationarius*

> ☑ **WORD TIP**
> Avoid confusion with **stationery.**

stationer *n* a person or shop selling stationery. ▷ **HISTORY** Medieval Latin *stationarius* a person having a regular station, hence a shopkeeper

stationery *n* writing materials, such as paper, envelopes, and pens.

> ☑ **WORD TIP**
> Avoid confusion with **stationary.**

stationmaster *n* the senior official in charge of a railway station.

Stations of the Cross *pl n RC Church* **1** a series of 14 crosses with pictures or carvings, arranged around the walls of a church, to commemorate 14 stages in Christ's journey to Calvary. **2** a series of 14 prayers relating to each of these stages.

station wagon *n US, Austral & NZ* an estate car.

statistic *n* a numerical fact collected and classified systematically. ▶ **statistical** *adj* ▶ **statistically** *adv* ▶ **statistician** *n*

statistics *n* **1** the science dealing with the collection, classification, and interpretation of numerical information. ✧ *pl n* **2** numerical information which has been collected, classified, and interpreted. ▷ **HISTORY** originally: science dealing with facts of a state, from New Latin *statisticus* concerning state affairs

statuary *n* statues collectively.

statue *n* a sculpture of a human or animal figure, usually life-size or larger. ▷ **HISTORY** Latin *statuere* to set up

statuesque (stat-yoo-**esk**) *adj* (of a woman) tall and well-proportioned; like a classical statue.

statuette *n* a small statue.

stature *n* **1** height and size of a person. **2** the reputation of a person or their achievements: *a batsman of international stature.* **3** moral or intellectual distinction. ▷ **HISTORY** Latin *stare* to stand

status *n* **1** a person's position in society. **2** the esteem in which people hold a person: *priests feel they have lost some of their status in society.* **3** the legal or official standing or classification of a person or country: *the status of refugees; Ireland's non-aligned status.* **4** degree of importance. ▷ **HISTORY** Latin: posture

status quo *n* the existing state of affairs. ▷ **HISTORY** literally: the state in which

status symbol *n* a possession regarded as a mark of social position or wealth.

statute *n* **1** a law made by a government and expressed in a formal document. **2** a permanent rule made by a company or other institution. ▷ **HISTORY** Latin *statuere* to set up, decree

statute law *n* **1** a law made by a government. **2** such laws collectively.

statutory *adj* **1** required or authorized by law. **2** (of an offence) declared by law to be punishable.

staunch[1] *adj* strong and loyal: *a staunch supporter.* ▷ **HISTORY** Old French *estanche* ▶ **staunchly** *adv*

staunch[2] *or* **stanch** *vb* to stop the flow of (blood) from someone's body.

stave *n* **1** one of the long strips of wood joined together to form a barrel or bucket. **2** a stick carried as a symbol of office. **3** a verse of a poem. **4** *Music* same as **staff.** ✧ *vb* **staving, stove 5 stave in** to burst a hole in something. ▷ **HISTORY** from *staves,* plural of STAFF

stave off *vb* **staving, staved** to delay (something) for a short time: *to stave off political rebellion.*

staves *n* a plural of **staff, stave.**

stay[1] *vb* **1** to continue or remain in a place, position, or condition: *to stay away; to stay inside.* **2** to lodge as a guest or visitor temporarily: *we stay with friends.* **3** *Scot & S African* to reside permanently; live. **4** to endure (something testing or difficult): *you have stayed the course this long.* ✧ *n* **5** the period spent in one place. **6** the postponement of an order of a court of law: *a stay of execution.* ▷ **HISTORY** Old French *ester*

stay[2] *n* something that supports or steadies something, such as a prop or buttress. ▷ **HISTORY** Old French *estaye*

stay[3] *n* a rope or chain supporting a ship's mast or funnel. ▷ **HISTORY** Old English *stæg*

stay-at-home *adj* **1** (of a person) enjoying a quiet, settled, and unadventurous life. ✧ *n* **2** a stay-at-home person.

staying power *n* endurance to complete something undertaken; stamina.

STD **1** sexually transmitted disease. **2** *Brit, Austral & S African* subscriber trunk dialling. **3** *NZ* subscriber toll dialling.

STD code *n Brit* a code preceding a local telephone number, allowing a caller to dial direct without the operator's help. ▷ **HISTORY** *s(ubscriber) t(runk) d(ialling)*

stead *n* **1 stand someone in good stead** to be useful to someone in the future. **2** *Rare* the function or position that should be taken by another: *I cannot let you rule in my stead.* ▷ **HISTORY** Old English *stede*

steadfast *adj* dedicated and unwavering. ▶ **steadfastly** *adv* ▶ **steadfastness** *n*

steady *adj* **steadier, steadiest 1** firm and not shaking. **2** without much change or variation: *we're on a steady course.* **3** continuous: *a steady decline.* **4** not easily excited; sober. **5** regular; habitual: *the steady drinking of alcohol.* ✧ *vb* **steadies, steadying, steadied 6** to make or become steady. ✧ *adv* **7** in a steady manner. **8 go steady** *Informal* to date one person regularly. ✧ *n, pl* **steadies 9** *Informal* one's regular boyfriend or girlfriend. ✧ *interj* **10** a warning to keep calm or be careful. ▷ **HISTORY** from *stead* ▶ **steadily** *adv* ▶ **steadiness** *n*

steady state *n Physics* the condition of a system when all or most changes or disturbances have been eliminated from it.

steak *n* **1** a lean piece of beef for grilling or frying. **2** a cut of beef for braising or stewing. **3** a thick slice of pork, veal, or fish. ▷ **HISTORY** Old Norse *steik* roast

steakhouse *n* a restaurant that specializes in steaks.

steal *vb* **stealing, stole, stolen 1** to take (something) from someone without permission or unlawfully. **2** to use (someone else's ideas or work) without acknowledgment. **3** to move quietly and carefully, not wanting to be noticed: *my father stole up behind her.* **4 steal the show** (of a performer) to draw the audience's attention to oneself and away from the other performers. **5** to obtain or do (something) stealthily: *I stole a glance behind.* ✧ *n* **6** *US, Canad & NZ informal* something acquired easily or at little cost. ▷ **HISTORY** Old English *stelan*

stealth *n* **1** moving carefully and quietly, so as to avoid being seen. **2** cunning or underhand behaviour. ▷ **HISTORY** Old English *stelan* to steal ▶ **stealthy** *adj* ▶ **stealthily** *adv*

stealth tax *n Brit & Austral* an indirect tax, such as a tax on fuel or pension plans, esp. one of which people are unaware or one that is felt to be unfair.

steam *n* **1** the vapour into which water changes when boiled. **2** the mist formed when such vapour condenses in the atmosphere. **3** *Informal* power, energy, or speed. **4 let off steam** *Informal* to release pent-up energy or feelings. **5 pick up steam** *Informal* to gather momentum. ✧ *adj* **6** operated, heated, or powered by steam: *a steam train.* ✧ *vb* **7** to give off steam. **8** (of a vehicle) to move by steam power. **9** *Informal* to proceed quickly and often forcefully. **10** to cook (food) in steam. **11** to treat (something) with steam, such as in cleaning or pressing clothes. **12 steam open** *or* **off** to use steam in order to open or remove (something): *let me steam open this letter.* ▷ **HISTORY** Old English *stēam*

steam engine *n* an engine worked by steam.

steamer *n* **1** a boat or ship driven by steam engines. **2** a container with holes in the bottom, used to cook food by steam.

steam iron *n* an electric iron that uses steam to take creases out of clothes.

steamroller *n* **1** a steam-powered vehicle with heavy rollers used for flattening road surfaces during road-making. ✧ *vb* **2** to make (someone) do what one wants by overpowering force.

steamy *adj* **steamier, steamiest 1** full of steam. **2** *Informal* (of books, films, etc.) erotic.

steatite (**stee**-a-tite) *n* same as **soapstone**. ▷ **HISTORY** Greek *stear* fat

steed *n Archaic or literary* a horse. ▷ **HISTORY** Old English *stēda* stallion

steel *n* **1** an alloy of iron and carbon, often with small quantities of other elements. **2** a steel rod used for sharpening knives. **3** courage and mental toughness. ✧ *vb* **4** to prepare (oneself) for coping with something unpleasant: *he had steeled himself to accept the fact.* ▷ **HISTORY** Old English *stēli* ▶ **steely** *adj*

steel band *n Music* a band of people playing on metal drums, popular in the West Indies.

steel wool *n* a mass of fine steel fibres, used for cleaning metal surfaces.

steelworks *n* a factory where steel is made. ▶ **steelworker** *n*

steep[1] *adj* **1** having a sharp slope. **2** *Informal* (of a fee, price, or demand) unreasonably high; excessive. ▷ **HISTORY** Old English *stēap* ▶ **steeply** *adv* ▶ **steepness** *n*

steep[2] *vb* **1** to soak or be soaked in a liquid in order to soften or cleanse. **2 steeped in** filled with: *an industry steeped in tradition.* ▷ **HISTORY** Old English *stēpan*

steeple *n* a tall ornamental tower on a church roof. ▷ **HISTORY** Old English *stēpel*

steeplechase *n* **1** a horse race over a course with fences to be jumped. **2** a track race in which the runners have to leap hurdles and a water jump. ✧ *vb* **-chasing, -chased 3** to race in a steeplechase.

> **WORD HISTORY**
> A 'steeplechase' was originally a horse race across country using a distant church steeple as the landmark to aim for as the finishing point of the race.

steeplejack *n* a person who repairs steeples and chimneys.

steer[1] *vb* **1** to direct the course of (a vehicle or vessel) with a steering wheel or rudder. **2** to direct the movements or course of (a person, conversation, or activity). **3** to follow (a specified course): *the Dutch government steered a middle course.* **4 steer clear of** to avoid. ▷ **HISTORY** Old English *stīeran*

steer[2] *n* a castrated male ox or bull. ▷ **HISTORY** Old English *stēor*

steerage *n* **1** the cheapest accommodation on a passenger ship. **2** steering.

steering committee *n* a committee set up to prepare and arrange topics to be discussed, and the order of business, for a government, etc.

steering wheel *n* a wheel turned by the driver of a vehicle in order to change direction.

stein (**stine**) *n* an earthenware beer mug. ▷ **HISTORY** German *Stein,* literally: stone

stela (**steal**-a) *or* **stele** (**steal**-ee) *n, pl* **stelae** (**steal**-ee) *or* **steles** an upright stone slab or column decorated with figures or inscriptions, common in prehistoric times. ▷ **HISTORY** Greek *stēlē*

stellar *adj* **1** relating to the stars. **2** *Informal* outstanding or immense: *stellar profits.* ▷ **HISTORY** Latin *stella* star

stem[1] *n* **1** the long thin central part of a plant. **2** a stalk that bears a flower, fruit, or leaf. **3** the long slender part of anything, such as a wineglass. **4** *Linguistics* the form of a word that remains after removal of all inflectional endings. ✧ *vb* **stemming, stemmed 5 stem from** originate from: *this tradition stems from pre-Christian times.* ▷ **HISTORY** Old English *stemn*

stem[2] *vb* **stemming, stemmed** to stop or hinder the spread of (something): *to stem the flow of firearms.* ▷ **HISTORY** Old Norse *stemma*

stem cell *n Histology* an undifferentiated embryonic cell that gives rise to specialized cells, such as blood, bone, etc.

stench *n* a strong and very unpleasant smell. ▷ **HISTORY** Old English *stenc*

stencil *n* **1** a thin sheet with a cut-out pattern through which ink or paint passes to form the pattern on the surface below. **2** a design or letters made in this way. ✧ *vb* **-cilling, -cilled** *or US* **-ciling,**

-ciled 3 to make (a design or letters) with a stencil. ▷ **HISTORY** Old French *estenceler* to decorate brightly

Sten gun *n* a light sub-machine-gun. ▷ **HISTORY** *S* & *T* (initials of the inventors) + *-en*, as in *Bren gun*

stenographer *n US & Canad* a shorthand typist. ▷ **HISTORY** Greek *stenos* narrow + *graphein* to write

stent *n* a surgical implant used to keep an artery open.

stentorian *adj* (of the voice) very loud: *a stentorian tone.* ▷ **HISTORY** after *Stentor*, a herald in Greek mythology

step *n* **1** the act of moving and setting down one's foot, such as when walking. **2** the distance covered by such a movement. **3** the sound made by such a movement. **4** one of a sequence of foot movements that make up a dance. **5** one of a sequence of actions taken in order to achieve a goal. **6** a degree or rank in a series or scale. **7** a flat surface for placing the foot on when going up or down. **8** manner of walking: *he moved with a purposeful step.* **9 steps a** a flight of stairs, usually out of doors. **b** same as **stepladder**. **10** a short easily travelled distance: *Mexico and Brazil were only a step away.* **11 break step** to stop marching in step. **12 in step a** marching or dancing in time or at the same pace as other people. **b** *Informal* in agreement: *in step with the West on this issue.* **13 out of step a** not marching or dancing in time or at the same pace as other people. **b** *Informal* not in agreement: *out of step with the political mood.* **14 step by step** gradually. **15 take steps** to do what is necessary (to achieve something). **16 watch one's step a** *Informal* to behave with caution. **b** to walk carefully. ✧ *vb* **stepping, stepped 17** to move by taking a step, such as in walking. **18** to walk a short distance: *please step this way.* **19 step into** to enter (a situation) apparently without difficulty: *she stepped into a life of luxury.* ✧ See also **step down, step in**, etc. ▷ **HISTORY** Old English *stepe, stæpe*

stepbrother *n* a son of one's stepmother or stepfather.

stepchild *n, pl* **-children** a stepson or stepdaughter.

stepdaughter *n* a daughter of one's husband or wife by an earlier relationship.

step down *vb Informal* to resign from a position.

step-down transformer *n Electronics* a transformer that reduces voltage.

stepfather *n* a man who has married one's mother after the death or divorce of one's father.

stephanotis (stef-fan-**note**-iss) *n* a tropical climbing shrub with sweet-smelling white flowers. ▷ **HISTORY** Greek: fit for a crown

step in *vb Informal* to intervene (in a quarrel or difficult situation).

stepladder *n* a small folding portable ladder with a supporting frame.

stepmother *n* a woman who has married one's father after the death or divorce of one's mother.

step-parent *n* a stepfather or stepmother.

steppes *pl n Geog* wide grassy plains without trees. ▷ **HISTORY** Old Russian *step* lowland

stepping stone *n* **1** one of a series of stones acting as footrests for crossing a stream. **2** a stage in a person's progress towards a goal: *it was a big stepping stone in his career.*

stepsister *n* a daughter of one's stepmother or stepfather.

stepson *n* a son of one's husband or wife by an earlier relationship.

step up *vb Informal* to increase (something) by stages; accelerate.

step-up transformer *n Electronics* a transformer that raises voltage.

stereo *adj* **1** (of a sound system) using two or more separate microphones to feed two or more loudspeakers through separate channels. ✧ *n, pl* **stereos 2** a music system in which sound is directed through two speakers. **3** sound broadcast or played in stereo.

stereophonic *adj* same as **stereo** (sense 1). ▷ **HISTORY** Greek *stereos* solid + *phōnē* sound

stereoscopic *adj* having a three-dimensional effect: *stereoscopic vision.*

stereotype *n* **1** a set of characteristics or a fixed idea considered to represent a particular kind of person. **2** an idea or convention that has grown stale through fixed usage. ✧ *vb* **-typing, -typed 3** to form a standard image or idea of (a type of person). ▷ **HISTORY** Greek *stereos* solid + TYPE

sterile *adj* **1** free from germs. **2** unable to produce offspring. **3** (of plants) not producing or bearing seeds. **4** lacking inspiration or energy; unproductive. ▷ **HISTORY** Latin *sterilis* ▶ **sterility** *n*

sterilize *or* **-lise** *vb* **-lizing, -lized** *or* **-lising, -lised** to make sterile. ▶ **sterilization** *or* **-lisation** *n*

sterling *n* **1** British money: *sterling fell by almost a pfennig.* ✧ *adj* **2** genuine and reliable: first-class: *he has a reputation for sterling honesty.* ▷ **HISTORY** probably Old English *steorra* star, referring to a small star on early Norman pennies

sterling silver *n* **1** an alloy containing at least 92.5 per cent of silver. **2** articles made of sterling silver.

stern[1] *adj* **1** strict and serious: *he's a very stern taskmaster.* **2** difficult and often unpleasant: *the stern demands of the day.* **3** (of a facial expression) severe and disapproving. ▷ **HISTORY** Old English *styrne* ▶ **sternly** *adv*

stern[2] *n* the rear part of a boat or ship. ▷ **HISTORY** Old Norse *stjörn* steering

sternum *n, pl* **-na** *or* **-nums** a long flat bone in the front of the body, to which the collarbone and most of the ribs are attached. ▷ **HISTORY** Greek *sternon*

steroid *n Biochem* an organic compound containing a carbon ring system, such as sterols and many hormones.

sterol *n Biochem* a natural insoluble alcohol such as cholesterol and ergosterol. ▷ **HISTORY** shortened from *cholesterol, ergosterol,* etc.

stertorous *adj* (of breathing) laboured and noisy. ▷ **HISTORY** Latin *stertere* to snore

stet *vb* **stetting, stetted 1** used as an instruction to indicate to a printer that certain deleted matter is to be kept. **2** to mark (matter) in this way. ▷ **HISTORY** Latin, literally: let it stand

stethoscope *n Med* an instrument for listening to the sounds made inside the body, consisting of a hollow disc that transmits the sound through hollow tubes to earpieces. ▷ **HISTORY** Greek *stēthos* breast + *skopein* to look at

Stetson *n Trademark* a felt hat with a broad brim and high crown, worn mainly by cowboys. ▷ **HISTORY** after John *Stetson*, American hat maker

stevedore *n Chiefly US* a person employed to load or unload ships. ▷ **HISTORY** Spanish *estibador* a packer

stew *n* **1** a dish of meat, fish, or other food, cooked slowly in a closed pot. **2 in a stew** *Informal* in a troubled or worried state. ✧ *vb* **3** to cook by long slow simmering in a closed pot. **4** *Informal* (of a person) to be too hot. **5** to cause (tea) to become bitter or (of tea) to become bitter through infusing for too long. **6 stew in one's own juice** to suffer, without help, the results of one's actions. ▷ **HISTORY** Middle English *stuen* to take a very hot bath

steward *n* **1** a person who looks after passengers and serves meals on a ship or aircraft. **2** an official who helps to supervise a public event, such as a race. **3** a person who administers someone else's property. **4** a person who manages the eating arrangements, staff, or service at a club or hotel. **5** See **shop steward.** ✧ *vb* **6** to act as a steward (of). ▷ **HISTORY** Old English *stigweard* hall keeper

stewardess *n* a female steward on an aircraft or ship.

stick[1] *n* **1** a small thin branch of a tree. **2 a** a long thin piece of wood. **b** such a piece of wood shaped for a special purpose: *a walking stick; a hockey stick.* **3** a piece of something shaped like a stick: *a stick of cinnamon.* **4** *Slang* verbal abuse, criticism: *they gave me a lot of stick.* **5 the sticks** a country area considered backward or unsophisticated: *places out in the sticks.* **6 sticks** pieces of furniture: *these few sticks are all I have.* **7** *Informal* a person: *not a bad old stick.* **8 get hold of the wrong end of the stick** to misunderstand a situation or an explanation completely. ▷ **HISTORY** Old English *sticca*

stick[2] *vb* **sticking, stuck 1** to push (a pointed object) or (of a pointed object) to be pushed into another object. **2** to fasten (something) in position by pins, nails, or glue: *she just stuck the label on.* **3** to extend beyond something else; protrude: *he stuck his head out of the door.* **4** *Informal* to place (something) in a specified position: *stick it in the oven.* **5** to fasten or be fastened by or as if by an adhesive. **6** to come or be brought to a standstill: *stuck in a rut; two army lorries stuck behind us.* **7** to remain for a long time: *the room that sticks in my mind the most.* **8** *Slang, chiefly Brit* to tolerate; abide: *you couldn't stick it for more than two days.* **9 be stuck** *Informal* to be at a loss for; to be baffled or puzzled: *I'm stuck; stuck for words.* ✧ See also **stick around.** ▷ **HISTORY** Old English *stician*

stick around *vb Informal* to remain in a place, often when waiting for something.

sticker *n* a small piece of paper with a picture or writing on it that can be stuck to a surface.

sticking plaster *n* a piece of adhesive material used for covering slight wounds.

stick insect *n* a tropical insect with a long thin body and legs, which looks like a twig.

stick-in-the-mud *n Informal* a person who is unwilling to try anything new or do anything exciting.

stickleback *n* a small fish with sharp spines along its back. ▷ **HISTORY** Old English *sticel* prick, sting + BACK

stickler *n* a person who insists on something: *a stickler for punctuality.*

stick-up *n Slang, chiefly US* a robbery at gunpoint; hold-up.

stick up for *vb Informal* to support or defend (oneself, another person, or a principle).

sticky *adj* **stickier, stickiest 1** covered with a substance that sticks to other things: *sticky little fingers.* **2** intended to stick to a surface: *sticky labels.* **3** *Informal* difficult or painful: *a sticky meeting.* **4** (of weather) unpleasantly warm and humid. ▸ **stickiness** *n*

stiff *adj* **1** firm and not easily bent. **2** moving with pain or difficulty: *stiff and aching joints.* **3** not moving easily: *the door is stiff.* **4** difficult or severe: *a stiff challenge; stiff penalties.* **5** formal and not relaxed. **6** fairly firm in consistency; thick. **7** powerful: *a stiff breeze.* **8** (of a drink) containing a lot of alcohol. ✧ *n* **9** *Slang* a corpse. ✧ *adv* **10** completely or utterly: *I was bored stiff.* ▷ **HISTORY** Old English *stīf* ▸ **stiffly** *adv* ▸ **stiffness** *n*

stiffen *vb* to make or become stiff or stiffer.

stiff-necked *adj* proud and stubborn.

stifle *vb* **-fling, -fled 1** to stop oneself from expressing (a yawn or cry). **2** to stop (something) from continuing: *the new leadership stifled all internal debate.* **3** to feel discomfort and difficulty in breathing. **4** to kill (someone) by preventing him or her from breathing. ▷ **HISTORY** probably from Old French *estouffer* to smother

stifling *adj* uncomfortably hot and stuffy.

stigma *n, pl* **stigmas** *or* **stigmata 1** a mark of social disgrace: *a stigma attached to being redundant.* **2** *Bot* the part of a flower that receives pollen. **3 stigmata** *Christianity* marks resembling the wounds of the crucified Christ, believed to appear on the bodies of certain people. ▷ **HISTORY** Greek: brand

stigmatize *or* **-tise** *vb* **-tizing, -tized** *or* **-tising, -tised** to regard as being shameful.

stile *n* a set of steps in a wall or fence to allow people, but not animals, to pass over. ▷ **HISTORY** Old English *stigel*

stiletto *n, pl* **-tos 1** Also called: **spike heel, stiletto heel** a high narrow heel on a woman's shoe or a shoe with such a heel. **2** a small dagger with a slender tapered blade. ▷ **HISTORY** Italian: little dagger

A B C D E F G H I J K L M N O P Q R S T U V W X Y Z

still[1] *adv* **1** continuing now or in the future as in the past: *she still loved the theatre.* **2** up to this or that time; yet. **3** even or yet: *still more pressure on the government.* **4** even then; nevertheless: *the baby has been fed and still cries.* **5** quietly or without movement: *keep still.* ✧ *adj* **6** motionless; stationary. **7** undisturbed; silent and calm. **8** (of a soft drink) not fizzy. ✧ *n* **9** *Poetic* silence or tranquillity: *the still of night.* **10** a still photograph from a film. ✧ *vb* **11** to make or become quiet or calm. **12** to relieve or end: *Fowler stilled his conscience.* ▷ HISTORY Old English *stille* ▶ **stillness** *n*

still[2] *n* an apparatus for distilling spirits. ▷ HISTORY Latin *stilla* a drip

stillborn *adj* **1** (of a baby) dead at birth. **2** (of an idea or plan) completely unsuccessful. ▶ **stillbirth** *n*

still life *n, pl* **still lifes 1** a painting or drawing of objects such as fruit or flowers. **2** this kind of painting or drawing.

stilt *n* **1** either of a pair of long poles with footrests for walking raised from the ground. **2** a long post or column used with others to support a building above ground level. ▷ HISTORY Middle English *stilte*

stilted *adj* (of speech, writing, or behaviour) formal or pompous; not flowing continuously or naturally.

Stilton *n Trademark* a strong-flavoured blue-veined cheese. ▷ HISTORY named after *Stilton*, Cambridgeshire

stimulant *n* **1** a drug, food, or drink that makes the body work faster, increases heart rate, and makes sleeping difficult. **2** any stimulating thing. ✧ *adj* **3** stimulating.

stimulate *vb* **-lating, -lated 1** to encourage to start or progress further: *a cut in interest rates should help stimulate economic recovery.* **2** to fill (a person) with ideas or enthusiasm: *books satisfy a part of the intellect that needs to be stimulated.* **3** *Physiol* to excite (a nerve or organ) with a stimulus. ▷ HISTORY Latin *stimulare* ▶ **stimulation** *n*

stimulus (**stim**-myew-luss) *n, pl* **-li** (-lie) **1** something that acts as an incentive to (someone). **2** something, such as a drug or electrical impulse, that is capable of causing a response in a person or an animal. ▷ HISTORY Latin: a cattle goad

sting *vb* **stinging, stung 1** (of certain animals and plants) to inflict a wound on (someone) by the injection of poison. **2** to cause (someone) to feel a sharp physical pain: *her hand was stinging.* **3** to offend or upset (someone) with a critical remark: *I was stung by what he said.* **4** to provoke (a response) by angering: *the consulate would be stung into convulsive action.* **5** *Informal* to cheat (someone) by overcharging. ✧ *n* **6** a skin wound caused by stinging. **7** pain caused by or as if by a sting. **8** a mental pain: *the sting of memory.* **9** the sharp pointed organ of certain animals or plants used to inject poison. **10** *Slang* a deceptive trick. **11** *Slang* a trap set up by the police to entice a person to commit a crime, thereby producing evidence. ▷ HISTORY Old English *stingan* ▶ **stinging** *adj*

stinging nettle *n* same as **nettle** (sense 1).

stingray *n* a flat fish with a jagged whiplike tail capable of inflicting painful wounds.

stingy *adj* **-gier, -giest** very mean. ▷ HISTORY perhaps from *stinge*, dialect variant of STING ▶ **stinginess** *n*

stink *n* **1** a strong unpleasant smell. **2 make, create** *or* **kick up a stink** *Slang* to make a fuss. ✧ *vb* **stinking, stank** *or* **stunk; stunk 3** to give off a strong unpleasant smell. **4** *Slang* to be thoroughly bad or unpleasant: *the script stinks, the casting stinks.* ▷ HISTORY Old English *stincan* ▶ **stinky** *adj*

stink bomb *n* a small glass globe used by practical jokers: it releases a liquid with a strong unpleasant smell when broken.

stinker *n Slang* a difficult or very unpleasant person or thing.

stinking *adj* **1** having a strong unpleasant smell. **2** *Informal* unpleasant or disgusting. ✧ *adv* **3 stinking rich** *Informal* very wealthy.

stink out *vb* **1** to drive (people) away by a foul smell. **2** *Brit & NZ* to cause (a place) to stink: *I won't have it stinking the car out!*

stint *vb* **1** to be miserly with (something): *don't stint on paper napkins.* ✧ *n* **2** a given amount of work. ▷ HISTORY Old English *styntan* to blunt

stipend (**sty**-pend) *n* a regular salary or allowance, esp. that paid to a member of the clergy. ▷ HISTORY Latin *stipendium* tax ▶ **stipendiary** *adj*

stipple *vb* **-pling, -pled** to draw, engrave, or paint (something) using dots or flecks. ▷ HISTORY Dutch *stippelen*

stipulate *vb* **-lating, -lated** to specify (something) as a condition of an agreement. ▷ HISTORY Latin *stipulari* ▶ **stipulation** *n*

stir[1] *vb* **stirring, stirred 1** to mix up (a liquid) by moving a spoon or stick around in it. **2** to move slightly. **3 stir from** to depart (from one's usual or preferred place). **4** to get up after sleeping. **5** to excite or move (someone) emotionally. **6** to move (oneself) quickly or vigorously; exert (oneself). **7** to wake up: *to stir someone from sleep.* ✧ *n* **8** a stirring. **9** a strong reaction, usually of excitement: *she created a stir wherever she went.* ✧ See also **stir up**. ▷ HISTORY Old English *styrian*

stir[2] *n Chiefly US slang* prison: *in stir.* ▷ HISTORY Romany *stariben* prison

stir-crazy *adj Slang* mentally disturbed as a result of being in prison.

stir-fry *vb* **-fries, -frying, -fried 1** to cook (food) quickly by stirring it in a wok or frying pan over a high heat. ✧ *n, pl* **-fries 2** a dish cooked in this way.

stirrer *n Informal* a person who deliberately causes trouble.

stirrup *n* a metal loop attached to a saddle for supporting a rider's foot. ▷ HISTORY Old English *stig* step + *rāp* rope

stirrup pump *n* a hand-operated pump, the base of which is placed in a bucket of water: used in fighting fires.

stir up *vb* **1** to cause (leaves or dust) to rise up and swirl around. **2** to set (something) in motion: *that fact has stirred up resentment.*

stitch *n* **1** a link made by drawing a thread through material with a needle. **2** a loop of yarn formed around a needle or hook in knitting or crocheting. **3** a particular kind of stitch. **4** *Informal* a link of thread joining the edges of a wound together. **5** a sharp pain in the side caused by running or exercising. **6 in stitches** *Informal* laughing uncontrollably. **7 not a stitch** *Informal* no clothes at all. ✧ *vb* **8** to sew or fasten (something) with stitches. ▷ **HISTORY** Old English *stice* sting ▶ **stitching** *n*

stitch up *vb* **1** to join by stitching. **2** *Slang* to incriminate by manufacturing evidence. **3** *Slang* to prearrange in a clandestine manner. ✧ *n* **stitch-up** **4** *Slang* a matter that has been prearranged clandestinely.

stoat *n* a small brown N European mammal related to the weasel: in winter it has a white coat and is then known as an ermine. ▷ **HISTORY** origin unknown

stock *n* **1** the total amount of goods kept on the premises of a shop or business. **2** a supply of something stored for future use. **3** *Finance* **a** the money raised by a company through selling shares entitling their holders to dividends, partial ownership, and usually voting rights. **b** the proportion of this money held by an individual shareholder. **c** the shares of a specified company or industry. **4** farm animals bred and kept for their meat, skins, etc. **5** the original type from which a particular race, family, or group is descended. **6** the handle of a rifle, held by the firer against the shoulder. **7** a liquid produced by simmering meat, fish, bones, or vegetables, and used to make soups and sauces. **8** a kind of plant grown for its brightly coloured flowers. **9** *Old-fashioned* the degree of status a person has. **10** See **laughing stock**. **11 in stock** stored on the premises or available for sale or use. **12 out of stock** not immediately available for sale or use. **13 take stock** to think carefully about a situation before making a decision. ✧ *adj* **14** staple; standard: *stock sizes in clothes.* **15** being a cliché; hackneyed: *the stock answer.* ✧ *vb* **16** to keep (goods) for sale. **17** to obtain a store of (something) for future use or sale: *to stock up on food.* **18** to supply (a farm) with animals or (a lake or stream) with fish. ✧ See also **stocks**. ▷ **HISTORY** Old English *stocc* tree trunk

stockade *n* an enclosure or barrier of large wooden posts. ▷ **HISTORY** Spanish *estacada*

stockbreeder *n* a person who breeds or rears farm animals.

stockbroker *n* a person who buys and sells stocks and shares for customers and receives a percentage of their profits. ▶ **stockbroking** *n*

stock car *n* a car that has been strengthened and modified for a form of racing in which the cars often collide.

stock exchange *n* **1 a** a highly organized market for the purchase and sale of stocks and shares, operated by professional stockbrokers and market makers according to fixed rules. **b** a place where stocks and shares are traded. **2** the prices or trading activity of a stock exchange: *the stock exchange has been rising.*

stockholder *n* an owner of some of a company's stock.

stockinette *n* a machine-knitted elastic fabric. ▷ **HISTORY** perhaps from *stocking-net*

stocking *n* a long piece of close-fitting nylon or knitted yarn covering the foot and part or all of a woman's leg. ▷ **HISTORY** dialect *stock* stocking

stocking stitch *n* alternate rows of plain and purl in knitting.

stock in trade *n* a person's typical behaviour or usual work: *practicality is the farmer's stock in trade.*

stockist *n Commerce Brit* a dealer who stocks a particular product.

stock market *n* same as **stock exchange**.

stockpile *vb* **-piling, -piled** **1** to store a large quantity of (something) for future use. ✧ *n* **2** a large store gathered for future use.

stockpot *n Brit & NZ* a pot in which stock for soup is made.

stockroom *n* a room in which a stock of goods is kept in a shop or factory.

stock route *n Austral & NZ* a route designated for droving farm animals, so as to avoid traffic.

stocks *pl n History* an instrument of punishment consisting of a heavy wooden frame with holes in which the feet, hands, or head of an offender were locked.

stock-still *adv* absolutely still; motionlessly.

stocktaking *n* **1** the counting and valuing of goods in a shop or business. **2** a reassessment of a person's current situation and prospects.

stocky *adj* **stockier, stockiest** (of a person) short but well-built. ▶ **stockily** *adv* ▶ **stockiness** *n*

stockyard *n* a large yard with pens or covered buildings where farm animals are sold.

stodge *n Brit, Austral & NZ informal* heavy and filling starchy food. ▷ **HISTORY** perhaps blend of STUFF + *podge* a short plump person

stodgy *adj* **stodgier, stodgiest** **1** (of food) full of starch and very filling. **2** (of a person) dull, serious, or excessively formal. ▷ **HISTORY** from STODGE ▶ **stodginess** *n*

stoep (**stoop**) *n* (in South Africa) a verandah. ▷ **HISTORY** Afrikaans

stoic (**stow**-ik) *n* **1** a person who suffers great difficulties without showing his or her emotions. ✧ *adj* **2** same as **stoical**

WORD HISTORY

'Stoic' behaviour mirrors that advocated by the Stoics.

Stoic *n* **1** a member of the ancient Greek school of philosophy which believed that virtue and happiness could be achieved only by calmly accepting Fate. ✧ *adj* **2** of or relating to the Stoics. ▷ **HISTORY** Greek *stoa* porch ▶ **Stoicism** *n*

stoke *vb* **stoking, stoked** **1** to feed and tend (a fire or furnace). **2** to excite or encourage (a strong emotion) in oneself or someone else. ▷ **HISTORY** from STOKER

stokehold *n Naut* the hold for a ship's boilers; fire room.

stoker *n* a person employed to tend a furnace on a ship or train powered by steam. ▷ HISTORY Dutch *stoken* to stoke

stole[1] *vb* the past tense of **steal**.

stole[2] *n* a long scarf or shawl, worn by women. ▷ HISTORY Greek *stolē* clothing

stolen *vb* the past participle of **steal**.

stolid *adj* showing little or no emotion or interest in anything. ▷ HISTORY Latin *stolidus* dull ▶ **stolidity** *n* ▶ **stolidly** *adv*

stolon *n Bot* same as **runner** (sense 5).

stoma (**stow**-ma) *n, pl* **stomata** (**stow**-ma-ta) **1** *Bot* a pore in a plant leaf that controls the passage of gases into and out of the plant. **2** *Zool* a mouth or mouthlike part. ▷ HISTORY Greek: mouth

stomach *n* **1** an organ inside the body in which food is stored until it has been partially digested. **2** the front of the body around the waist. **3** desire or appetite: *he still has the stomach for a fight.* ✧ *vb* **4** to put up with: *liberals could not stomach the rest of the package.* ▷ HISTORY Greek *stoma* mouth

stomachache *n* pain in the stomach, such as from indigestion. Also called: **stomach upset, upset stomach**

stomacher *n History* a decorative V-shaped panel of stiff material worn over the chest and stomach mainly by women.

stomach pump *n Med* a pump with a long tube used for removing the contents of a person's stomach, for instance after he or she has swallowed poison.

stomp *vb* to tread or stamp heavily. ▷ HISTORY variant of STAMP

stompie *n S African slang* **1** a cigarette butt. **2** a short man. ▷ HISTORY Afrikaans *stomp* stump

stone *n* **1** the hard nonmetallic material of which rocks are made. **2** a small lump of rock. **3** Also called: **gemstone** a precious or semiprecious stone that has been cut and polished. **4** a piece of rock used for some particular purpose: *gravestone; millstone.* **5** the hard central part of fruits such as the peach or date. **6** (*pl* **stone**) *Brit* a unit of weight equal to 14 pounds or 6.350 kilograms. **7** *Pathol* a hard deposit formed in the kidney or bladder. **8 heart of stone** a hard or unemotional personality. **9 leave no stone unturned** to do everything possible to achieve something. ✧ *adj* **10** made of stoneware: *the polished stone planter.* ✧ *vb* **stoning, stoned 11** to throw stones at (someone), for example as a punishment. **12** to remove the stones from (a fruit). ▷ HISTORY Old English *stān*

Stone Age *n* a phase of human culture identified by the use of tools made of stone.

stonechat *n* a songbird that has black feathers and a reddish-brown breast. ▷ HISTORY from its cry, which sounds like clattering pebbles

stone-cold *adj* **1** completely cold. ✧ *adv* **2 stone-cold sober** completely sober.

stoned *adj Slang* under the influence of drugs or alcohol.

stone-deaf *adj* completely deaf.

stone fruit *n* same as **drupe**.

stonewall *vb* **1** to deliberately prolong a discussion by being long-winded or evasive. **2** *Cricket* (of a batsman) to play defensively.

stoneware *n* a hard type of pottery, fired at a very high temperature.

stonework *n* any structure or part of a building made of stone.

stonkered *adj NZ slang* completely exhausted or beaten; whacked. ▷ HISTORY from *stonker* to beat, of unknown origin

stony *or* **stoney** *adj* **stonier, stoniest 1** (of ground) rough and covered with stones: *the stony path.* **2** (of a face, voice, or attitude) unfriendly and unsympathetic. ▶ **stonily** *adv*

stony-broke *adj Slang* completely without money.

stood *vb* the past of **stand**.

stooge *n* **1** an actor who feeds lines to a comedian or acts as the butt of his jokes. **2** *Slang* someone who is taken advantage of by someone in a superior position. ▷ HISTORY origin unknown

stool *n* **1** a seat with legs but no back. **2** waste matter from the bowels. ▷ HISTORY Old English *stōl*

stool pigeon *n* an informer for the police.

stoop[1] *vb* **1** to bend (the body) forward and downward. **2** to stand or walk with head and shoulders habitually bent forward. **3 stoop to** to lower one's normal standards of behaviour; degrade oneself: *no real journalist would stoop to faking.* ✧ *n* **4** the act, position, or habit of stooping. ▷ HISTORY Old English *stūpian* ▶ **stooping** *adj*

stoop[2] *n US* an open porch or small platform with steps leading up to it at the entrance to a building. ▷ HISTORY Dutch *stoep*

stop *vb* **stopping, stopped 1** to cease doing (something); discontinue. **2** to cause (something moving) to halt or (of something moving) to come to a halt. **3** to prevent the continuance or completion of (something). **4** (often foll. by *from*) to prevent or restrain: *I stopped her from going on any further.* **5** to keep back: *no agreement to stop arms supplies.* **6 stop up** to block or plug: *to stop up a pipe.* **7** to stay or rest: *we stopped at a camp site for a change.* **8** to instruct a bank not to honour (a cheque). **9** to deduct (money) from pay. **10** *Informal* to receive (a blow or hit). **11** *Music* to alter the vibrating length of (a string on a violin, guitar, etc.) by pressing down on it at some point with the finger. **12 stop at nothing** to be prepared to do anything; be ruthless. ✧ *n* **13** prevention of movement or progress: *you can put a stop to it quite easily.* **14** the act of stopping or the state of being stopped: *the car lurched to a stop.* **15** a place where something halts or pauses: *a bus stop.* **16** the act or an instance of blocking or obstructing. **17** a device that prevents, limits, or ends the motion of a mechanism or moving part. **18** *Brit* a full stop. **19** *Music* a knob on an organ that is operated to allow sets of pipes to sound. **20 pull out all the stops** to make a great effort. ▷ HISTORY Old English *stoppian* (unattested)

stopbank *n NZ* an embankment to prevent flooding.

stopcock *n* a valve used to control or stop the flow of a fluid in a pipe.

stopgap *n* a thing that serves as a substitute for a short time until replaced by something more suitable.

stopover *n* **1** a break in a journey. ✧ *vb* **stop over 2** to make a stopover.

stoppage *n* **1** the act of stopping something or the state of being stopped: *a heart stoppage.* **2** a deduction of money, such as taxation, from pay. **3** an organized stopping of work during industrial action.

stoppage time *n Chiefly Brit* same as **injury time**.

stopper *n* a plug for closing a bottle, pipe, etc.

stop press *n* news items inserted into a newspaper after the printing has been started.

stopwatch *n* a watch which can be stopped instantly for exact timing of a sporting event.

storage *n* **1** the act of storing or the state of being stored. **2** space for storing. **3** *Computers* the process of storing information in a computer.

storage device *n* a piece of computer equipment, such as a magnetic tape or a disk in or on which information can be stored.

storage heater *n* an electric device that accumulates and radiates heat generated by cheap off-peak electricity.

store *vb* **storing, stored 1** to keep, set aside, or gather (things) for future use. **2** to place furniture or other possessions in a warehouse for safekeeping. **3** to supply or stock (certain goods). **4** *Computers* to enter or keep (information) in a storage device. ✧ *n* **5** a shop (in Britain usually a large one). **6** a large supply or stock kept for future use. **7** short for **department store**. **8** a storage place, such as a warehouse. **9** *Computers chiefly Brit* same as **memory** (sense 7). **10 in store** about to happen; forthcoming: *you've got a treat in store.* **11 set great store by something** to value something as important. ✧ See also **stores**. ▷ HISTORY Old French *estor*

stores *pl n* supply or stock of food and other essentials for a journey.

storey *or esp US* **story** *n, pl* **-reys** *or* **-ries** a floor or level of a building. ▷ HISTORY Anglo-Latin *historia* picture, probably from the pictures on medieval windows

stork *n* a large wading bird with very long legs, a long bill, and white-and-black feathers. ▷ HISTORY Old English *storc*

storm *n* **1** a violent weather condition of strong winds, rain, hail, thunder, lightning, etc. **2** a violent disturbance or quarrel: *a storm of protest from the opposition.* **3** (usually foll. by *of*) a heavy discharge of bullets or missiles. **4 take a place by storm a** to capture or overrun a place by a violent attack. **b** to surprise people, but receive their praise, by being extremely successful at something. ✧ *vb* **5** to attack or capture (a place) suddenly and violently. **6** to shout angrily. **7** to move or rush violently or angrily: *she stormed into the study.* ▷ HISTORY Old English

storm centre *n* **1** the centre of a storm, where pressure is lowest. **2** the centre of any disturbance or trouble.

storm surge *n Geog* an occasion when ocean water is driven inland due to extreme weather conditions and significant flooding occurs.

storm trooper *n* a member of the paramilitary wing of the Nazi Party.

stormy *adj* **stormier, stormiest 1** (of weather) violent with dark skies, heavy rain or snow, and strong winds. **2** involving violent emotions: *a stormy affair.*

stormy petrel *or* **storm petrel** *n* **1** a small sea bird with dark feathers and paler underparts. **2** a person who brings trouble.

story[1] *n, pl* **-ries 1** a description of a chain of events told or written in prose or verse. **2** Also called: **short story** a piece of fiction, shorter and usually less detailed than a novel. **3** Also called: **story line** the plot of a book or film. **4** a news report. **5** the event or material for such a report. **6** *Informal* a lie. ▷ HISTORY Latin *historia*

story[2] *n, pl* **-ries** *Chiefly US* same as **storey**.

storyboard *n Films, television* a series of sketches or photographs showing the sequence of shots or images planned for a film.

storybook *n* **1** a book containing stories for children. ✧ *adj* **2** better or happier than in real life: *a storybook romance.*

storyteller *n* a person who tells stories.

stoup *or* **stoop** (**stoop**) *n* a small basin in a church for holy water. ▷ HISTORY from Old Norse

stoush *Austral & NZ slang* ✧ *vb* **1** to hit or punch (someone). ✧ *n* **2** fighting or violence. ▷ HISTORY origin unknown

stout *adj* **1** solidly built or fat. **2** strong and sturdy: *stout footwear.* **3** brave or determined: *we met unexpectedly stout resistance.* ✧ *n* **4** strong dark beer. ▷ HISTORY Old French *estout* bold ▶ **stoutly** *adv*

stove[1] *n* **1** same as **cooker** (sense 1). **2** any apparatus for heating, such as a kiln. ▷ HISTORY Old English *stofa* bathroom

stove[2] *vb* a past tense and past participle of **stave**.

stovepipe *n* a pipe that takes fumes and smoke away from a stove.

stow *vb* (often foll. by *away*) to pack or store (something). ▷ HISTORY Old English *stōwian* to keep

stowage *n* **1** space, room, or a charge for stowing goods. **2** the act of stowing.

stowaway *n* **1** a person who hides aboard a ship or aircraft in order to travel free. ✧ *vb* **stow away 2** to travel in such a way: *he stowed away on a ferry.*

strabismus *n Pathol* same as **squint** (sense 3). ▷ HISTORY Greek *strabismos*

straddle *vb* **-dling, -dled 1** to have one leg or part on each side of (something). **2** *US & Canad informal* to be in favour of both sides of (an issue or argument). ▷ HISTORY from *stride*

strafe *vb* **strafing, strafed** to machine-gun (an enemy) from the air. ▷ HISTORY German *strafen* to punish

straggle *vb* **-gling, -gled 1** to spread out in an untidy and rambling way: *the town straggled off to the east.* **2** to linger behind or wander from a main line or part. ▷ **HISTORY** origin unknown ▶ **straggler** *n* ▶ **straggly** *adj*

straight *adj* **1** continuing in the same direction without bending; not curved or crooked. **2** even, level, or upright. **3** in keeping with the facts; accurate. **4** outright or candid: *a straight rejection.* **5** in continuous succession. **6** (of an alcoholic drink) undiluted. **7** not wavy or curly: *straight hair.* **8** in good order. **9** (of a play or acting style) straightforward or serious. **10** honest, respectable, or reliable. **11** *Slang* heterosexual. **12** *Slang* conventional in views, customs, or appearance. **13** *Informal* no longer owing or being owed something: *if you buy the next round we'll be straight.* ✧ *adv* **14** in a straight line or direct course. **15** immediately; at once: *get straight back here.* **16** in a level or upright position: *he sat up straight.* **17** continuously; uninterruptedly: *we waited for three hours straight.* **18** (often foll. by *out*) frankly; candidly: *she asked me straight out.* **19 go straight** *Informal* to reform after having been a criminal. **20 straight away** *or* **straightaway** at once. ✧ *n* **21** a straight line, form, part, or position. **22** *Brit* a straight part of a racetrack. **23** *Slang* a heterosexual person. ▷ **HISTORY** Old English *streccan* to stretch

straighten *vb* (sometimes foll. by *up* or *out*) **1** to make or become straight. **2** to make (something) neat or tidy.

straight face *n* a serious facial expression which hides a desire to laugh. ▶ **straight-faced** *adj*

straightforward *adj* **1** (of a person) honest, frank, and open. **2** *Brit & NZ* (of a task) easy to do.

straight man *n* an actor who acts as the butt of a comedian's jokes.

strain¹ *n* **1** tension or tiredness resulting from overwork or worry. **2** tension between people or organizations: *there are signs of strain between the economic superpowers.* **3** an intense physical or mental effort. **4** the damage resulting from excessive physical exertion. **5** a great demand on the emotions, strength, or resources. **6** a way of speaking: *he would have gone on in this strain for some time.* **7** *Physics* the change in dimension of a body caused by outside forces. **8 strains** *Music* a theme, melody, or tune. ✧ *vb* **9** to subject (someone) to mental tension or stress. **10** to make an intense effort: *the rest were straining to follow the conversation.* **11** to use (resources) to, or beyond, their limits. **12** to injure or damage (oneself or a part of one's body) by overexertion: *he appeared to have strained a muscle.* **13** to pour (a substance) through a sieve or filter. **14 strain at** to push, pull, or work with violent effort (on something). **15** to draw (something) taut or be drawn taut. ▷ **HISTORY** Latin *stringere* to bind tightly

strain² *n* **1** a group of animals or plants within a species or variety, distinguished by one or more minor characteristics. **2** a trace or streak: *a strain of ruthlessness in their play.* ▷ **HISTORY** Old English *strēon*

strained *adj* **1** (of an action, expression, etc.) not natural or spontaneous. **2** (of an atmosphere, relationship, etc.) not relaxed; tense.

strainer *n* a sieve used for straining sauces, vegetables, or tea.

strait *n* **1** (*often pl*) a narrow channel of the sea linking two larger areas of sea. **2 straits** a position of extreme difficulty: *in desperate straits.* ▷ **HISTORY** Old French *estreit* narrow

straitened *adj* **in straitened circumstances** not having much money.

straitjacket *n* **1** a strong canvas jacket with long sleeves used to bind the arms of a violent person. **2** anything which holds back or restricts development or freedom: *exporters are wrapped in a straitjacket of regulations.*

strait-laced *or* **straight-laced** *adj* having a strict code of moral standards; puritanical.

strand¹ *vb* **1** to leave or drive (ships or fish) ashore. **2** to leave (someone) helpless, for example without transport or money. ✧ *n* **3** *Chiefly poetic* a shore or beach. ▷ **HISTORY** Old English

strand² *n* **1** one of the individual fibres of string or wire that form a rope, cord, or cable. **2** a single length of string, hair, wool, or wire. **3** a string of pearls or beads. **4** a part of something; element: *the many disparate strands of the Anglican Church.* ▷ **HISTORY** origin unknown

strange *adj* **1** odd or unexpected. **2** not known, seen, or experienced before; unfamiliar. **3 strange to** inexperienced (in) or unaccustomed (to): *they are in some degree strange to it.* ▷ **HISTORY** Latin *extraneus* foreign ▶ **strangely** *adv* ▶ **strangeness** *n*

stranger *n* **1** any person whom one does not know. **2** a person who is new to a particular place. **3 stranger to** a person who is unfamiliar with or new to something: *Paul is no stranger to lavish spending.*

strangle *vb* **-gling, -gled 1** to kill (someone) by pressing his or her windpipe; throttle. **2** to prevent the growth or development of: *another attempt at strangling national identity.* **3** to stifle (a voice, cry, or laugh) by swallowing suddenly: *the words were strangled by sobs.* ▷ **HISTORY** Greek *strangalē* a halter ▶ **strangler** *n*

stranglehold *n* **1** a wrestling hold in which a wrestler's arms are pressed against his opponent's windpipe. **2** complete power or control over a person or situation.

strangulate *vb* **-lating, -lated 1** *Pathol* to constrict (a hollow organ or vessel) so as to stop the flow of air or blood through it: *a badly strangulated hernia.* **2** same as **strangle.** ▶ **strangulation** *n*

strap *n* **1** a strip of strong flexible material used for carrying, lifting, fastening, or holding things in place. **2** a loop of leather or rubber, hanging from the roof in a bus or train for standing passengers to hold on to. **3 the strap** a beating with a strap as a punishment. ✧ *vb* **strapping, strapped 4** to tie or bind (something) with a strap. ▷ **HISTORY** variant of STROP

strapping *adj* tall, strong, and healthy-looking: *a strapping young lad.* ▷ **HISTORY** from *strap* (in the archaic sense: to work vigorously)

strata *n* the plural of **stratum**.

> **WORD TIP**
> *Strata* is sometimes wrongly used as a singular noun: *this stratum* (not *strata*) *of society is often disregarded.*

stratagem *n* a clever plan to deceive an enemy. ▷ **HISTORY** Greek *stratēgos* a general

strata title *n Austral Law* a system of registered ownership of space in multistorey buildings, to be equivalent to the ownership of the land of a single-storey building. NZ equivalent: **stratum title**

strategic (strat-**ee**-jik) *adj* **1** planned to achieve an advantage; tactical. **2** (of weapons, esp. missiles) directed against an enemy's homeland rather than used on a battlefield. ▶ **strategically** *adv*

strategy *n, pl* **-gies 1** a long-term plan for success, such as in politics or business. **2** the art of the planning and conduct of a war. ▷ **HISTORY** Greek *stratēgia* function of a general ▶ **strategist** *n*

strath *n Scot* a flat river valley. ▷ **HISTORY** Scottish & Irish Gaelic *srath*

strathspey *n* **1** a Scottish dance with gliding steps, slower than a reel. **2** music for this dance. ▷ **HISTORY** after *Strathspey*, valley of the River Spey

stratified *adj* **1** (of rocks) formed in horizontal layers of different materials. **2** *Sociol* (of a society) divided into different classes or groups. ▷ **HISTORY** New Latin *stratificare* to form in layers ▶ **stratification** *n*

stratocumulus (strat-oh-**kew**-myew-luss) *n, pl* **-li** (-lie) *Meteorol* an unbroken stretch of dark grey cloud.

stratosphere *n* the atmospheric layer between about 15 and 50 km above the earth.

strato-volcano *n, pl* **-noes** *or* **-nos** *Geol* Also: **composite cone** a steep cone-shaped volcano composed of alternate layers of viscous lava and pyroclastic material.

stratum (**strah**-tum) *n, pl* **-ta** (-ta) **1** any of the distinct layers into which certain rocks are divided. **2** a layer of ocean or atmosphere marked off naturally or decided arbitrarily by man. **3** a social class. ▷ **HISTORY** Latin: something strewn

stratus (**stray**-tuss) *n, pl* **-ti** (-tie) a grey layer cloud. ▷ **HISTORY** Latin: strewn

straw *n* **1** dried stalks of threshed grain, such as wheat or barley. **2** a single stalk of straw. **3** a long thin hollow paper or plastic tube, used for sucking up liquids into the mouth. **4 clutch at straws** to turn in desperation to something with little chance of success. **5 draw the short straw** to be the person chosen to perform an unpleasant task. ✧ *adj* **6** made of straw: *straw baskets.* ▷ **HISTORY** Old English *strēaw*

strawberry *n, pl* **-ries** a sweet fleshy red fruit with small seeds on the outside. ▷ **HISTORY** Old English *strēawberige*

strawberry mark *n* a red birthmark.

straw-coloured *adj* pale yellow: *straw-coloured hair.*

straw poll *or* **vote** *n* an unofficial poll or vote taken to find out the opinion of a group or the public on some issue.

stray *vb* **1** to wander away from the correct path or from a given area. **2** to move away from the point or lose concentration. **3** to fail to live up to certain moral standards: *her man had strayed.* ✧ *n* **4** a domestic animal that has wandered away from its home. **5** *Old-fashioned* a lost or homeless child. ✧ *adj* **6** (of a domestic animal) having wandered away from its home. **7** random or separated from the main group of things of their kind: *stray bombs and rockets.* ▷ **HISTORY** Old French *estraier*

streak *n* **1** a long thin stripe or trace of some contrasting colour. **2** (of lightning) a sudden flash. **3** a quality or characteristic: *a nasty streak.* **4** a short stretch of good or bad luck: *a losing streak.* **5** *Informal* an instance of running naked through a public place. ✧ *vb* **6** to mark (something) with a streak or streaks: *sweat streaking the grime of his face.* **7** to move quickly in a straight line. **8** *Informal* to run naked through a public place. ▷ **HISTORY** Old English *strica* ▶ **streaked** *or* **streaky** *adj* ▶ **streaker** *n*

stream *n* **1** a small river. **2** any steady flow of water or other liquid. **3** something that resembles a stream in moving continuously in a line or particular direction: *the stream of traffic.* **4** a fast and continuous flow of speech: *the constant stream of jargon.* **5** *Brit, Austral, & NZ* a class of school children grouped together because of similar ability. ✧ *vb* **6** to pour in a continuous flow: *rain streamed down her cheeks.* **7** (of a crowd of people or traffic or a herd of animals) to move in unbroken succession. **8** to float freely or with a waving motion: *a flimsy pink dress that streamed out behind her.* **9** *Brit & NZ* to group (school children) in streams. ▷ **HISTORY** Old English *strēam* ▶ **streaming** *n* ▶ **streamlet** *n*

streamer *n* **1** a long coiled ribbon of coloured paper that unrolls when tossed. **2** a long narrow flag.

streamline *vb* **-lining, -lined 1** to improve (something) by removing the parts that are least useful or profitable. **2** to make (an aircraft, boat, or vehicle) less resistant to flowing air or water by improving its shape. ▶ **streamlined** *adj*

stream of consciousness *n Literature* a literary technique that reveals the flow of thoughts and feelings of characters through long passages of soliloquy.

stream order *n Geog* a system for classifying streams in a drainage basin whereby streams without tributaries are classified as *first order*, the streams they flow into, *second order*, and the streams these flow into, *third order*, etc.

street *n* **1** a public road that is usually lined with buildings, esp. in a town: *Sauchiehall Street.* **2** the part of the road between the pavements, used by vehicles. **3** the people living in a particular street. **4 on the streets** homeless. **5 right up one's street** *Informal* just what one knows or likes best.

6 streets ahead of *Informal* superior to or more advanced than. ▷ **HISTORY** Old English *strǣt*

streetcar *n US & Canad* a tram.

street furniture *n* equipment, such as street lights and pillar boxes, placed in the street for the benefit of the public.

street theatre *n* dramatic entertainments performed in shopping precincts.

street value *n* the price that would be paid for goods, esp. illegal ones such as drugs, by the final user: *cocaine with a street value of £2m was seized at Heathrow airport.*

streetwalker *n* a prostitute who tries to find customers in the streets.

streetwise *adj* knowing how to survive or succeed in poor and often criminal sections of big cities.

strength *n* **1** the state or quality of being physically or mentally strong. **2** the ability to withstand great force, stress, or pressure. **3** something regarded as valuable or a source of power: *his chief strength is rocketry.* **4** potency or effectiveness, such as of a drink or drug. **5** power to convince: *the strength of this argument.* **6** degree of intensity or concentration of colour, light, sound, or flavour: *a strong cheese.* **7** the total number of people in a group: *at full strength; 50 000 men below strength.* **8 go from strength to strength** to have ever-increasing success. **9 on the strength of** on the basis of or relying upon. ▷ **HISTORY** Old English *strengthu*

strengthen *vb* to make (something) stronger or become stronger.

strength of evidence *n Science* a measure of how strongly a hypothesis is supported by the results of experiments or tests.

strenuous *adj* requiring or involving the use of great energy or effort. ▷ **HISTORY** Latin *strenuus* brisk ▸ **strenuously** *adv*

streptococcus (strep-toe-**kok**-uss) *n, pl* **-cocci** (-**kok**-eye) a bacterium occurring in chains and including many species that cause disease. ▷ **HISTORY** Greek *streptos* crooked + *kokkos* berry

streptomycin *n Med* an antibiotic used in the treatment of tuberculosis and other bacterial infections. ▷ **HISTORY** Greek *streptos* crooked + *mukēs* fungus

stress *n* **1** mental, emotional, or physical strain or tension. **2** special emphasis or significance. **3** emphasis placed upon a syllable by pronouncing it more loudly than those that surround it. **4** *Physics* force producing a change in shape or volume. ✧ *vb* **5** to give emphasis to (a point or subject): *she stressed how difficult it had been.* **6** to pronounce (a word or syllable) more loudly than those surrounding it. ▷ **HISTORY** shortened from *distress* ▸ **stressful** *adj*

stressed-out *adj Informal* suffering from anxiety or tension.

stretch *vb* **1 stretch over** *or* **for** to extend or spread over (a specified distance): *the flood barrier stretches for several miles.* **2** to draw out or extend (something) or to be drawn out or extended in length or area. **3** to distort or lengthen (something) or to be distorted or lengthened permanently. **4** to extend (the limbs or body), for example when one has just woken up. **5** (often foll. by *out, forward*) to reach or hold out (a part of one's body). **6** to reach or suspend (a rope, etc.) from one place to another. **7** to draw (something) tight; tighten. **8** (usually foll. by *over*) to extend in time: *a dinner which stretched over three consecutive evenings.* **9** to put a great strain upon (one's money or resources). **10** to make do with (limited resources): *the Walkers decided to stretch their budget.* **11** to extend (someone) to the limit of his or her abilities. **12** to extend (someone) to the limit of his or her tolerance. **13 stretch a point** to make an exception not usually made. ✧ *n* **14** the act of stretching. **15** a large or continuous expanse or distance: *this stretch of desert.* **16** extent in time. **17** a term of imprisonment. **18 at a stretch** *Chiefly Brit & NZ* **a** with some difficulty; by making a special effort. **b** at one time: *for hours at a stretch they had no conversation.* ✧ *adj* **19** (of clothes) able to be stretched without permanently losing shape: *a stretch suit.* ▷ **HISTORY** Old English *streccan* ▸ **stretchy** *adj*

stretcher *n* a frame covered with canvas, on which an ill or injured person is carried.

stretcher-bearer *n* a person who helps to carry a stretcher.

strew *vb* **strewing, strewed, strewn** to scatter (things) over a surface. ▷ **HISTORY** Old English *streowian*

strewth *interj Informal* an expression of surprise or alarm. ▷ **HISTORY** alteration of *God's truth*

stria (**strye**-a) *n, pl* **striae** (**strye**-ee) *Geol* a scratch or groove on the surface of a rock crystal. ▷ **HISTORY** Latin: a groove

striation *n* **1** an arrangement or pattern of striae. **2** same as **stria.** ▸ **striated** *adj*

stricken *adj* badly affected by disease, pain, grief, etc.: *flood-stricken areas.* ▷ **HISTORY** past participle of STRIKE

strict *adj* **1** severely correct in attention to behaviour or morality: *a strict disciplinarian.* **2** following carefully and exactly a set of rules: *she is a strict vegetarian.* **3** (of a rule or law) very precise and requiring total obedience: *a strict code of practice.* **4** (of a meaning) exact: *this is not, in the strictest sense, a biography.* **5** (of a punishment, etc.) harsh or severe. **6** complete; absolute: *strict obedience.* ▷ **HISTORY** Latin *strictus* drawn tight ▸ **strictly** *adv* ▸ **strictness** *n*

strict liability offence *n Law* an offence in which the prosecution need only prove *actus reus* but not *mens rea.*

stricture *n Formal* a severe criticism. ▷ **HISTORY** Latin *strictura* contraction

stride *n* **1** a long step or pace. **2** the length of such a step. **3** a striding walk. **4** progress or development: *he has made great strides in regaining his confidence.* **5** a regular pace or rate of progress: *it put me off my stride.* **6 take something in one's stride** to do something without difficulty or effort. ✧ *vb* **striding, strode, stridden 7** to walk with long steps or paces. **8 stride over** *or* **across** to cross (over a space or an obstacle) with a stride. ▷ **HISTORY** Old English *strīdan*

strident *adj* **1** (of a voice or sound) loud and harsh. **2** loud, persistent, and forceful: *a strident critic of the establishment.* ▷ **HISTORY** Latin *stridens* ▶ **stridency** *n*

strife *n* angry or violent struggle; conflict. ▷ **HISTORY** Old French *estrif*

strike *vb* **striking, struck 1** (of employees) to stop work collectively as a protest against working conditions, low pay, etc. **2** to hit (someone). **3** to cause (something) to come into sudden or violent contact with something. **4 strike at** to attack (someone or something). **5** to cause (a match) to light by friction. **6** to sound (a specific note) on a musical instrument. **7** (of a clock) to indicate (a time) by the sound of a bell. **8** to affect (someone) deeply in a particular way: *he never struck me as the supportive type.* **9** to enter the mind of: *a brilliant thought struck me.* **10** (of a poisonous snake) to injure by biting. **11** (*past participle* **struck** *or* **stricken**) to change into (a different state): *struck blind.* **12** to be noticed by; catch: *the heavy smell of incense struck my nostrils.* **13** to arrive at (something) suddenly or unexpectedly: *to strike on a solution.* **14** to afflict (someone) with a disease: *she has been struck down by breast cancer.* **15** to discover a source of (gold, oil, etc.). **16** to reach (something) by agreement: *to strike a deal.* **17** to take up (a posture or an attitude). **18** to take apart or pack up: *to strike camp.* **19** to make (a coin) by stamping it. **20 strike home** to achieve the desired effect. **21 strike it rich** *Informal* to have an unexpected financial success. ✧ *n* **22** a stopping of work, as a protest against working conditions, low pay, etc.: *a one-day strike.* **23** an act or instance of striking. **24** a military attack, esp. an air attack on a target on land or at sea: *a pre-emptive strike.* **25** *Baseball* a pitched ball swung at and missed by the batter. **26** *Tenpin bowling* the knocking down of all the pins with one bowl. **27** the discovery of a source of gold, oil, etc. **28** *Geol* the horizontal direction of a fault, rock stratum, etc. ✧ See also **strike up**. ▷ **HISTORY** Old English *strīcan*

strikebreaker *n* a person who tries to make a strike fail by working or by taking the place of those on strike.

striker *n* **1** a person who is on strike. **2** *Soccer* an attacking player.

strike-slip fault *n Geol* a fault in which rock on one side or on both sides of a fault scrapes along sideways in relation to the other.

strike up *vb* **1** to begin (a conversation or friendship). **2** (of a band or an orchestra) to begin to play.

striking *adj* **1** attracting attention; impressive: *her striking appearance.* **2** very noticeable: *a striking difference.* ▶ **strikingly** *adv*

Strimmer *n Trademark* an electrical tool for trimming the edges of lawns.

Strine *n* a humorous transliteration of Australian pronunciation, as in *Gloria Soame* for *glorious home.* ▷ **HISTORY** a jocular rendering of the Australian pronunciation of *Australian*

string *n* **1** thin cord or twine used for tying, hanging, or binding things. **2** a group of objects threaded on a single strand: *a string of pearls.* **3** a series of things or events: *a string of wins.* **4** a tightly stretched wire or cord on a musical instrument, such as the guitar, violin, or piano, that produces sound when vibrated. **5 the strings** *Music* **a** violins, violas, cellos, and double basses collectively. **b** the section of an orchestra consisting of such instruments. **6** a group of characters that can be treated as a unit by a computer program. **7 with no strings attached** (of an offer) without complications or conditions. **8 pull strings** *Informal* to use one's power or influence, esp. secretly or unofficially. ✧ *adj* **9** composed of stringlike strands woven in a large mesh: *a string bag.* ✧ *vb* **stringing, strung 10** to hang or stretch (something) from one point to another. **11** to provide (something) with a string or strings. **12** to thread (beads) on a string. **13** to extend in a line or series: *towns strung out along the valley.* ▷ **HISTORY** Old English *streng* ▶ **stringlike** *adj*

string along *vb Informal* **1 string along with** to accompany: *I'll string along with you.* **2** to deceive (someone) over a period of time: *she had only been stringing him along.*

string bean *n* same as **runner bean**.

string course *n Archit* an ornamental projecting band along a wall.

stringed *adj* (of musical instruments) having strings.

stringent (**strin**-jent) *adj* requiring strict attention to rules or detail: *all have particularly stringent environmental laws.* ▷ **HISTORY** Latin *stringere* to bind ▶ **stringency** *n*

stringer *n* **1** *Archit* a long horizontal timber beam that connects upright posts. **2** a journalist employed by a newspaper on a part-time basis to cover a particular town or area.

string quartet *n Music* **1** a group of musicians consisting of two violins, one viola, and one cello. **2** a piece of music composed for such a group.

string up *vb Informal* to kill (a person) by hanging.

stringy *adj* **stringier, stringiest 1** thin and rough: *stringy hair.* **2** (of meat or other food) tough and fibrous.

stringy-bark *n* an Australian eucalyptus with a fibrous bark.

strip[1] *vb* **stripping, stripped 1** to take (the covering or clothes) off (oneself, another person, or thing). **2 a** to undress completely. **b** to perform a striptease. **3** to empty (a building) of all furniture. **4** to take something away from (someone): *they were stripped of their possessions.* **5** to remove (paint) from (a surface or furniture): *she stripped the plaster from the kitchen walls.* **6** (often foll. by *down*) to dismantle (an engine or a mechanism) into individual parts. ✧ *n* **7** the act or an instance of undressing or of performing a striptease. ▷ **HISTORY** Old English *bestrīepan* to plunder

strip[2] *n* **1** a long narrow piece of something. **2** short for **airstrip**. **3** *Brit, Austral & NZ* the clothes a sports team plays in. ▷ **HISTORY** Middle Dutch *strīpe* stripe

strip cartoon *n* a sequence of drawings in a newspaper or magazine, telling an amusing story or an adventure.

stripe[1] *n* **1** a long band of colour that differs from the surrounding material. **2** a chevron or band worn on a uniform to indicate rank. ✧ *vb* **striping, striped 3** to mark (something) with stripes. ▷ **HISTORY** probably from Middle Dutch *strīpe* ▸ **striped, stripy** *or* **stripey** *adj*

stripe[2] *n* a stroke from a whip, rod, or cane. ▷ **HISTORY** from Middle Low German *strippe*

strip lighting *n* a method of electric lighting that uses fluorescent lamps in long glass tubes.

stripling *n* a teenage boy or young man.

stripper *n* **1** a person who performs a striptease. **2** a tool or liquid for removing paint or varnish.

strip-search *vb* **1** (of police, customs officials, etc.) to strip (a prisoner or suspect) naked to search him or her for drugs or smuggled goods. ✧ *n* **2** a search that involves stripping a person naked.

striptease *n* an entertainment in which a person gradually undresses to music.

strive *vb* **striving, strove, striven** to make a great effort: *to strive for a peaceful settlement.* ▷ **HISTORY** Old French *estriver*

strobe *n* short for **strobe lighting stroboscope**.

strobe lighting *n* a flashing beam of very bright light produced by a perforated disc rotating in front of a light source.

stroboscope *n* an instrument producing a very bright flashing light which makes moving people appear stationary. ▷ **HISTORY** Greek *strobos* a whirling + *skopein* to look at

strode *vb* the past tense of **stride**.

stroke *vb* **stroking, stroked 1** to touch or brush lightly or gently. ✧ *n* **2** a light touch or caress with the fingers. **3** *Pathol* rupture of a blood vessel in the brain resulting in loss of consciousness, often followed by paralysis and damage to speech. **4** a blow, knock, or hit. **5** an action or occurrence of the kind specified: *a fantastic stroke of luck; a stroke of intuition.* **6 a** the striking of a clock. **b** the hour registered by this: *at the stroke of twelve.* **7** a mark made by a pen or paintbrush. **8** same as **solidus:** used esp. when dictating or reading aloud. **9** the hitting of the ball in sports such as golf or cricket. **10** any one of the repeated movements used by a swimmer. **11** a particular style of swimming, such as the crawl. **12** a single pull on the oars in rowing. **13 at a stroke** with one action. **14 not a stroke (of work)** no work at all. ▷ **HISTORY** Old English *strācian*

stroll *vb* **1** to walk about in a leisurely manner. ✧ *n* **2** a leisurely walk. ▷ **HISTORY** probably from dialect German *strollen*

strong *adj* **stronger, strongest 1** having physical power. **2** not easily broken or injured; solid or robust. **3** great in degree or intensity; not faint or feeble: *a strong voice; a strong smell of explosive.* **4** (of arguments) supported by evidence; convincing. **5** concentrated; not weak or diluted. **6** having a powerful taste or smell: *strong perfume.* **7** (of language) using swear words. **8** (of a person) self-confident: *a strong personality.* **9** committed or fervent: *a strong believer in free trade.* **10** important or having a lot of power or influence: *a strong left-wing tendency within the university.* **11** very competent at a particular activity: *they sent a very strong team to the Olympics.* **12** containing or having a specified number: *the 700-strong workforce.* **13** (of an accent) distinct and indicating where the speaker comes from. **14** (of a relationship) stable and likely to last. **15** having an extreme or drastic effect: *strong discipline.* **16** (of a colour) very bright and intense. **17** (of a wind, current, or earthquake) moving fast or intensely. **18** (of an economy, an industry, a currency, etc.) growing, successful, or increasing in value. ✧ *adv* **19 come on strong** *Informal* **a** to show blatantly that one is sexually attracted to someone. **b** to make a forceful or exaggerated impression. **20 going strong** *Informal* working or performing well; thriving. ▷ **HISTORY** Old English *strang* ▸ **strongly** *adv*

strong-arm *adj Informal* involving physical force or violence: *strong-arm tactics.*

stronghold *n* **1** an area in which a particular belief is shared by many people: *a Labour stronghold.* **2** a place that is well defended; fortress.

strong point *n* something at which one is very good: *diplomacy wasn't his strong point.*

strongroom *n* a specially designed room in which valuables are locked for safety.

strontium *n Chem* a soft silvery-white metallic element: the radioactive isotope **strontium-90** is used in nuclear power sources and is a hazardous nuclear fallout product. Symbol: Sr. ▷ **HISTORY** after *Strontian,* in Scotland, where it was discovered

strop *n* a leather strap for sharpening razors. ▷ **HISTORY** Greek *strophos* cord

strophe *n* **1** *Poetry* the first of two metrical systems used alternately within a poem. **2** *Drama* the movement made by a chorus during the first part of a choral ode in an ancient Greek drama. ✧ See also **antistrophe, epode**.

stroppy *adj* **-pier, -piest** *Informal* bad-tempered or deliberately awkward. ▷ **HISTORY** from *obstreperous*

strove *vb* the past tense of **strive**.

struck *vb* a past of **strike**.

structural *adj* **1** of or having structure or a structure. **2** of or forming part of the structure of a building. **3** *Chem* of or involving the arrangement of atoms in molecules: *a structural formula.* ▸ **structurally** *adv*

structural control *n Geog* the way that underlying geographical features affect drainage and topography.

structuralism *n* an approach to social sciences and to literature which sees changes in the subject as caused and organized by a hidden set of universal rules. ▸ **structuralist** *n, adj*

structure *n* **1** something that has been built or organized. **2** the way the individual parts of something are made, built, or organized into a whole. **3** the pattern of interrelationships within an

organization, society, etc. **4** an organized method of working, thinking, or behaving. **5** *Chem* the arrangement of atoms in a molecule of a chemical compound. **6** *Geol* the way in which a rock is made up of its component parts. ✧ *vb* **-turing, -tured** **7** to arrange (something) into an organized system or pattern: *a structured school curriculum.*
▷ **HISTORY** Latin *structura*

strudel *n* a thin sheet of filled dough rolled up and baked: *apple strudel.* ▷ **HISTORY** from German

struggle *vb* **-gling, -gled** **1** to work or strive: *the old regime struggled for power; he struggled to keep the conversation flowing.* **2** to move about violently in an attempt to escape from something restricting. **3** to fight with someone, often for possession of something. **4** to go or progress with difficulty. **5** **struggle on** to manage to do (something) with difficulty. ✧ *n* **6** something requiring a lot of exertion or effort to achieve. **7** a fight or battle. **8** **the struggle** *S African* the concerted opposition to apartheid.
▷ **HISTORY** origin unknown ▶ **struggling** *adj*

strum *vb* **strumming, strummed** **1** to play (a stringed instrument) by sweeping the thumb or a plectrum across the strings. **2** to play (a tune) in this way. ▷ **HISTORY** probably imitative

strumpet *n Archaic* a prostitute or promiscuous woman. ▷ **HISTORY** origin unknown

strung *vb* the past of **string**.

strut *vb* **strutting, strutted** **1** to walk in a stiff proud way with head high and shoulders back; swagger. ✧ *n* **2** a piece of wood or metal that forms part of the framework of a structure. ▷ **HISTORY** Old English *strūtian* to stand stiffly

strychnine (**strik**-neen) *n* a very poisonous drug formerly used in small quantities as a stimulant.
▷ **HISTORY** Greek *strukhnos* nightshade

Stuart *adj* of or relating to the royal house that ruled Scotland from 1371 to 1714 and England from 1603 to 1714.

stub *n* **1** a short piece remaining after something has been used: *a cigarette stub.* **2** the section of a ticket or cheque which the purchaser keeps as a receipt. ✧ *vb* **stubbing, stubbed** **3** to strike (one's toe or foot) painfully against a hard surface. **4** **stub out** to put out (a cigarette or cigar) by pressing the end against a surface. ▷ **HISTORY** Old English *stubb*

stubble *n* **1** the short stalks left in a field where a crop has been harvested. **2** the short bristly hair on the chin of a man who has not shaved for a while.
▷ **HISTORY** Old French *estuble* ▶ **stubbly** *adj*

stubble-jumper *n Canad slang* a prairie grain farmer.

stubborn *adj* **1** refusing to agree or give in. **2** persistent and determined. **3** difficult to handle, treat, or overcome: *the most stubborn dandruff.*
▷ **HISTORY** origin unknown ▶ **stubbornly** *adv*
▶ **stubbornness** *n*

stubby *adj* **-bier, -biest** short and broad.

stucco *n* **1** plaster used for coating or decorating outside walls. ✧ *vb* **-coing, -coed** **2** to apply stucco to (a building). ▷ **HISTORY** Italian

stuck *vb* **1** the past of **stick**[2]. ✧ *adj* **2** *Informal* baffled by a problem or unable to find an answer to a question. **3** **be stuck on** *Slang* to feel a strong attraction to; be infatuated with. **4** **get stuck in** *Informal* to perform a task with determination.

stuck-up *adj Informal* proud or snobbish.

stud[1] *n* **1** a small piece of metal attached to a surface for decoration. **2** a fastener consisting of two discs at either end of a short bar, usually used with clothes. **3** one of several small round objects attached to the sole of a football boot to give better grip. ✧ *vb* **studding, studded** **4** to decorate or cover (something) with or as if with studs: *apartment houses studded with satellite dishes.*
▷ **HISTORY** Old English *studu*

stud[2] *n* **1** a male animal, esp. a stallion kept for breeding. **2** Also: **stud farm** a place where animals are bred. **3** the state of being kept for breeding purposes. **4** *Slang* a virile or sexually active man.
▷ **HISTORY** Old English *stōd*

student *n* **1** a person following a course of study in a school, college, or university. **2** a person who makes a thorough study of a subject: *a keen student of opinion polls.* ▷ **HISTORY** Latin *studens* diligent

studied *adj* carefully practised or planned: *studied calm.*

studio *n, pl* **-dios** **1** a room in which an artist, photographer, or musician works. **2** a room used to record television or radio programmes or to make films or records. **3** **studios** the premises of a radio, television, record, or film company.
▷ **HISTORY** Italian

studio flat *n Brit* a flat with one main room and, usually, a small kitchen and bathroom. Also called: **studio apartment**

studious (**styoo**-dee-uss) *adj* **1** serious, thoughtful, and hard-working. **2** precise, careful, or deliberate. ▷ **HISTORY** Latin *studiosus* devoted to
▶ **studiously** *adv*

study *vb* **studies, studying, studied** **1** to be engaged in the learning or understanding of (a subject). **2** to investigate or examine (something) by observation and research. **3** to look at (something or someone) closely; scrutinize. ✧ *n, pl* **studies** **4** the act or process of studying. **5** a room used for studying, reading, or writing. **6** (*often pl*) work relating to a particular area of learning: *environmental studies.* **7** an investigation and analysis of a particular subject. **8** a paper or book produced as a result of study. **9** a work of art, such as a drawing, done for practice or in preparation for another work. **10** a musical composition designed to develop playing technique. ▷ **HISTORY** Latin *studium* zeal

stuff *n* **1** substance or material. **2** any collection of unnamed things. **3** the raw material of something. **4** subject matter, skill, etc.: *this journalist knew his stuff.* **5** woollen fabric. **6** **do one's stuff** *Informal* to do what is expected of one. ✧ *vb* **7** to pack or fill (something) completely; cram. **8** to force, shove, or squeeze (something somewhere): *I stuffed it in my briefcase.* **9** to fill (food such as poultry or tomatoes) with a seasoned mixture. **10** to fill (a dead animal's skin) with material so as to restore the shape of the live animal. **11** *Slang* to frustrate or defeat. **12** **get stuffed!** *Brit, Austral & NZ* *slang* an exclamation of anger or annoyance with someone. **13 stuff oneself** *or* **one's face** to eat a large amount of food. ▷ **HISTORY** Old French *estoffe*

stuffing *n* **1** a mixture of ingredients with which poultry or meat is stuffed before cooking. **2** the material used to fill and give shape to soft toys, pillows, furniture, etc.; padding.

stuffy *adj* **-ier, -iest 1** lacking fresh air. **2** old-fashioned and very formal: *an image of stuffy tradition.* ▸ **stuffiness** *n*

stultify *vb* **-fies, -fying, -fied** to dull (the mind) by boring routine. ▷ **HISTORY** Latin *stultus* stupid + *facere* to make ▸ **stultifying** *adj*

stumble *vb* **-bling, -bled 1** to trip and almost fall while walking or running. **2** to walk in an unsteady or unsure way. **3** to make mistakes or hesitate in speech. **4 stumble across, on** *or* **upon** to encounter or discover (someone or something) by accident. ✧ *n* **5** an act of stumbling. ▷ **HISTORY** Middle English *stomble*

stumbling block *n* any obstacle that prevents something from taking place or progressing.

stump *n* **1** the base of a tree trunk left standing after the tree has been cut down or has fallen. **2** the part of something, such as a tooth or limb, that remains after a larger part has been removed. **3** *Cricket* any of three upright wooden sticks that, with two bails laid across them, form a wicket. ✧ *vb* **4** to baffle or confuse (someone). **5** *Cricket* to dismiss (a batsman) by breaking his wicket with the ball. **6** *Chiefly US & Canad* to campaign or canvass (an area), by political speech-making. **7** to walk with heavy steps; trudge. ▷ **HISTORY** Middle Low German

stump up *vb Brit informal* to give (the money required).

stumpy *adj* **stumpier, stumpiest** short and thick like a stump; stubby.

stun *vb* **stunning, stunned 1** to shock or astonish (someone) so that he or she is unable to speak or act. **2** (of a heavy blow or fall) to make (a person or an animal) unconscious. ▷ **HISTORY** Old French *estoner* to daze

stung *vb* the past of **sting**.

stunk *vb* a past of **stink**.

stunner *n Brit, Austral & NZ informal* a person or thing of great beauty.

stunning *adj Informal* very attractive or impressive. ▸ **stunningly** *adv*

stunt[1] *vb* to prevent or slow down (the growth or development) of a plant, animal, or person. ▷ **HISTORY** Old English: foolish ▸ **stunted** *adj*

stunt[2] *n* **1** an acrobatic or dangerous piece of action in a film or television programme. **2** anything spectacular or unusual done to gain publicity. ✧ *adj* **3** of or relating to acrobatic or dangerous pieces of action in films or television programmes: *a stunt man.* ▷ **HISTORY** origin unknown

stupefaction *n* the state of being unable to think clearly because of tiredness or boredom.

stupefy *vb* **-pefies, -pefying, -pefied 1** to make (someone) feel so bored and tired that he or she is unable to think clearly. **2** to confuse or astound (someone). ▷ **HISTORY** Old French *stupefier* ▸ **stupefying** *adj*

stupendous *adj* very large or impressive. ▷ **HISTORY** Latin *stupere* to be amazed ▸ **stupendously** *adv*

stupid *adj* **1** lacking in common sense or intelligence. **2** trivial, silly, or childish: *we got into a stupid quarrel.* **3** unable to think clearly; dazed: *stupid with tiredness.* ▷ **HISTORY** Latin *stupidus* ▸ **stupidity** *n* ▸ **stupidly** *adv*

stupor *n* a state of near unconsciousness in which a person is unable to behave normally or think clearly. ▷ **HISTORY** Latin

sturdy *adj* **-dier, -diest 1** (of a person) healthy, strong, and unlikely to tire or become injured. **2** (of a piece of furniture, shoes, etc.) strongly built or made. ▷ **HISTORY** Old French *estordi* dazed ▸ **sturdily** *adv*

sturgeon *n* a bony fish from which caviar is obtained. ▷ **HISTORY** Old French *estourgeon*

stutter *vb* **1** to speak (a word or phrase) with involuntary repetition of initial consonants. ✧ *n* **2** the tendency to involuntarily repeat initial consonants while speaking. ▷ **HISTORY** Middle English *stutten* ▸ **stuttering** *n*

sty *n, pl* **sties** a pen in which pigs are kept. ▷ **HISTORY** Old English *stīg*

stye *or* **sty** *n, pl* **styes** *or* **sties** inflammation of a gland at the base of an eyelash. ▷ **HISTORY** Old English *stīgend* swelling + *ye* eye

Stygian (**stij**-jee-an) *adj Chiefly literary* dark or gloomy. ▷ **HISTORY** after the *Styx,* a river in Hades

style *n* **1** a form of appearance, design, or production: *I like that style of dress.* **2** the way in which something is done: *a new style of command.* **3** elegance or refinement of manners and dress: *he has bags of style.* **4** a distinctive manner of expression in words, music, painting, etc.: *a painting in the Expressionist style.* **5** popular fashion in dress and looks: *the old ones had gone out of style.* **6** a fashionable or showy way of life: *the newly rich could dine in style.* **7** the particular kind of spelling, punctuation, and design followed in a book, journal, or publishing house. **8** *Bot* the stemlike part of a flower that bears the stigma. ✧ *vb* **styling, styled 9** to design, shape, or tailor: *neatly styled hair.* **10** to name or call: *Walsh, who styled himself the Memory Man.* ▷ **HISTORY** Latin *stilus* writing implement

style manual *n* a manual containing standardized rules and examples of punctuation, typography, etc., for writers, editors, and printers working for an organization or organizations.

stylish *adj* smart, fashionable, and attracting attention. ▸ **stylishly** *adv*

stylist *n* **1** a hairdresser who styles hair. **2** a person who performs, writes, or acts with great attention to the particular style he or she employs.

stylistic *adj* of the techniques used in creating or performing a work of art: *there are many stylistic problems facing the performers of Baroque music.* ▸ **stylistically** *adv*

stylus *n* a needle-like device in the pick-up arm of a record player that rests in the groove in the record and picks up the sound signals. ▷ **HISTORY** Latin *stilus* writing implement

stymie *vb* **-mieing, -mied 1** to hinder or foil (someone): *the President was stymied by a reluctant Congress.* ✧ *n, pl* **-mies 2** *Golf* (formerly) a situation in which an opponent's ball is blocking the line between the hole and the ball about to be played. ▷ **HISTORY** origin unknown

styptic *adj* **1** used to stop bleeding: *a styptic pencil.* ✧ *n* **2** a styptic drug. ▷ **HISTORY** Greek *stuphein* to contract

suave (**swahv**) *adj* (esp. of a man) smooth, confident, and sophisticated. ▷ **HISTORY** Latin *suavis* sweet ▶ **suavely** *adv*

sub *n* **1** short for **subeditor, submarine, subscription, substitute**. **2** *Brit informal* an advance payment of wages or salary. Formal term: **subsistence allowance** ✧ *vb* **subbing, subbed 3** to act as a substitute.

sub- *or before r* **sur-** *prefix* used with many main words to mean: **1** situated under or beneath: *subterranean.* **2** secondary in rank; subordinate: *sublieutenant; surrogate.* **3** falling short of; less than or imperfectly: *subarctic; subhuman.* **4** forming a subdivision or less important part: *subcommittee.* ▷ **HISTORY** Latin

subaltern *n* a British army officer below the rank of captain. ▷ **HISTORY** Latin *sub-* under + *alter* another

subatomic *adj Physics* of, relating to, or being one of the particles making up an atom.

subclavian vein *n Anat* a vein situated below the clavicle.

subclimax *n Biol, geog* a stage in the development of the natural plant community of an area in which progress to climax vegetation is inhibited by factors other than the weather. Compare **climax vegetation**.

subcommittee *n* a small committee consisting of members of a larger committee and which is set up to look into a particular matter.

subconscious *adj* **1** happening or existing without one's awareness. ✧ *n* **2** *Psychol* the part of the mind that contains memories and motives of which one is not aware but which can influence one's behaviour. ▶ **subconsciously** *adv*

subcontinent *n* a large land mass that is a distinct part of a continent, such as India is of Asia.

subcontract *n* **1** a secondary contract by which the main contractor for a job puts work out to another company. ✧ *vb* **2** to let out (work) on a subcontract. ▶ **subcontractor** *n*

subculture *n* a group of people within a society or class with a distinct pattern of behaviour, beliefs, and attitudes.

subcutaneous (sub-cute-**ayn**-ee-uss) *adj Med* beneath the skin.

subdivide *vb* **-viding, -vided** to divide (a part of something) into smaller parts. ▶ **subdivision** *n*

subduction *n Geol* the process of one tectonic plate sliding under another, resulting in earthquakes and volcanic eruptions.

subdue *vb* **-duing, -dued 1** to overcome and bring (a person or people) under control by persuasion or force. **2** to make (feelings, colour, or lighting) less intense. ▷ **HISTORY** Latin *subducere* to remove

subeditor *n* a person who checks and edits text for a newspaper or other publication.

subgroup *n* a small group that is part of a larger group.

subheading *n* the heading of a subdivision of a piece of writing.

subhuman *adj* lacking the intelligence or decency expected of a human being.

subject *n* **1** the person, thing, or topic being dealt with or discussed. **2** any branch of learning considered as a course of study. **3** a person, object, idea, or scene portrayed in a work of art. **4** *Grammar* a word or phrase that represents the person or thing performing the action of the verb in a sentence; for example, *the cat* in the sentence *The cat catches mice.* **5** a person or thing that undergoes an experiment or treatment. **6** a person under the rule of a monarch or government: *Zambian subjects.* ✧ *adj* **7** being under the rule or a monarch or government: *a subject race.* **8 subject to a** showing a tendency towards: *they are expensive and subject to over-runs in cost and time.* **b** exposed or vulnerable to: *subject to ridicule.* **c** conditional upon: *pay is subject to negotiation.* ✧ *adv* **9 subject to** under the condition that something takes place: *my visit was agreed subject to certain conditions.* ✧ *vb* (sub-**ject**) **10 subject to a** to cause (someone) to experience (something unpleasant): *they were subjected to beatings.* **b** to bring under the control or authority (of): *to subject a soldier to discipline.* ▷ **HISTORY** Latin *subjectus* brought under ▶ **subjection** *n*

subjective *adj* **1** of or based on a person's emotions or prejudices. ✧ *n* **2** *Grammar* the grammatical case in certain languages that identifies the subject of a verb. ▶ **subjectively** *adv*

subjective case *n Grammar* a grammatical case in some languages that identifies the subject of a verb.

subjective shot *n Films, television* a camera shot taken from the angle of vision of one of the characters in the scene rather than from a neutral position. Compare **objective shot**.

sub judice (sub **joo**-diss-ee) *adj* before a court of law: *he declined to comment on the case saying it was sub judice.* ▷ **HISTORY** Latin

subjugate *vb* **-gating, -gated** to bring (a group of people) under one's control. ▷ **HISTORY** Latin *sub-* under + *jugum* yoke ▶ **subjugation** *n*

subjunctive *Grammar* ✧ *adj* **1** denoting a mood of verbs used when the content of the clause is being doubted, supposed, or feared true, for example *were* in the sentence *I'd be careful if I were you.* ✧ *n* **2** the subjunctive mood. ▷ **HISTORY** Latin *subjungere* to add to

sublet *vb* **-letting, -let** to rent out (property which one is renting from someone else).

sublieutenant *n* a junior officer in a navy.

sublimate *vb* **-mating, -mated** *Psychol* to direct the energy of (a strong desire, esp. a sexual one) into activities that are socially more acceptable. ▷ **HISTORY** Latin *sublimare* to elevate

sublimation *n* **1** the act of sublimating. **2** *Chem, physics* the process of subliming.

sublime *adj* **1** causing deep emotions and feelings of wonder or joy. **2** without equal; supreme. **3** of great moral, artistic, or spiritual value. ✧ *n* **4 the sublime** something that is sublime. ✧ *vb* **-liming, -limed 5** *Chem, physics* to change directly from a solid to a vapour without first melting. ▷ **HISTORY** Latin *sublimis* lofty ▸ **sublimely** *adv*

subliminal *adj* resulting from or relating to mental processes of which the individual is not aware: *the subliminal message.* ▷ **HISTORY** Latin *sub* below + *limen* threshold

sub-machine-gun *n* a portable automatic or semiautomatic gun with a short barrel.

submarine *n* **1** a vessel which can operate below the surface of the sea. ✧ *adj* **2** existing or located below the surface of the sea: *submarine cables.* ▸ **submariner** *n*

submaxillary *adj Anat* of the lower jaw.

submerge *vb* **-merging, -merged 1** to put or go below the surface of water or another liquid. **2** to involve totally: *she submerged herself in her work.* ▷ **HISTORY** Latin *submergere* ▸ **submersion** *n*

submersible *adj* **1** capable of operating under water. ✧ *n* **2** a small vessel designed to operate under water.

submission *n* **1** an act or instance of submitting. **2** something submitted, such as a proposal. **3** the state in which someone has to accept the control of another person.

submissive *adj* showing quiet obedience. ▸ **submissively** *adv* ▸ **submissiveness** *n*

submit *vb* **-mitting, -mitted 1** to accept the will of another person or a superior force. **2** to send (an application or proposal) to someone for judgment or consideration. **3** to be voluntarily subjected (to medical or psychiatric treatment). ▷ **HISTORY** Latin *submittere* to place under

submucosa *n, pl* **-sae** *Anat* the connective tissue beneath a mucous membrane.

subnormal *adj* **1** less than the normal: *subnormal white blood cells.* **2** *No longer in technical use* having a lower than average intelligence. ✧ *n* **3** *No longer in technical use* a subnormal person.

subordinate *adj* **1** of lesser rank or importance. ✧ *n* **2** a person or thing that is of lesser rank or importance. ✧ *vb* **-nating, -nated 3** (usually foll. by *to*) to regard (something) as less important than another: *the army's interests were subordinated to those of the air force.* ▷ **HISTORY** Latin *sub-* lower + *ordo* rank ▸ **subordination** *n*

subordinate clause *n Grammar* a clause that functions as an adjective, an adverb, or a noun rather than one that functions as a sentence in its own right.

subordinating conjunction *or* **subordinate conjunction** *n Grammar* a conjunction that introduces subordinate clauses, such as *if, because, although,* and *until.*

suborn *vb Formal* to bribe or incite (a person) to commit a wrongful act. ▷ **HISTORY** Latin *subornare*

subplot *n* a secondary plot in a novel, play, or film.

subpoena (sub-**pee**-na) *n* **1** a legal document requiring a person to appear before a court of law at a specified time. ✧ *vb* **-naing, -naed 2** to summon (someone) with a subpoena. ▷ **HISTORY** Latin: under penalty

sub-post office *n* (in Britain) a post office which is run by a self-employed agent for the Post Office.

sub rosa (sub **rose**-a) *adv Literary* in secret. ▷ **HISTORY** Latin, literally: under the rose; in ancient times a rose was hung over a table as a mark of secrecy

subroutine *n* a section of a computer program that is stored only once but can be used at several different points in the program.

sub-Saharan *adj* in or relating to Africa south of the Sahara desert.

subscribe *vb* **-scribing, -scribed 1** (usually foll. by *to*) to pay (money) as a contribution (to a charity, for a magazine, etc.) at regular intervals. **2 subscribe to** to give support or approval: *I do not subscribe to this view.* ▷ **HISTORY** Latin *subscribere* to write underneath ▸ **subscriber** *n*

subscriber trunk dialling *n Brit & Austral* a system allowing telephone users to obtain trunk calls by dialling direct without the help of an operator.

subscript *Printing* ✧ *adj* **1** (of a character) written or printed below the line. ✧ *n* **2** a subscript character.

subscription *n* **1** a payment for issues of a publication over a specified period of time. **2** money paid or promised, such as to a charity or the fund raised in this way. **3** *Brit, Austral & NZ* the membership fees paid to a society. **4** an advance order for a new product.

subsection *n* any of the smaller parts into which a section may be divided.

subsequent *adj* occurring after; succeeding. ▷ **HISTORY** Latin *subsequens* ▸ **subsequently** *adv*

subservient *adj* **1** overeager to carry out someone else's wishes. **2** of less importance or rank: *the subservient role of women in society.* ▷ **HISTORY** Latin *subserviens* ▸ **subservience** *n*

subset *n* a mathematical set contained within a larger set.

subside *vb* **-siding, -sided 1** to become less loud, excited, or violent. **2** to sink to a lower level. **3** (of the surface of the earth) to cave in; collapse. ▷ **HISTORY** Latin *subsidere* to settle down ▸ **subsidence** *n*

subsidiarity *n* the principle of taking political decisions at the lowest practical level.

subsidiary *n, pl* **-aries 1** Also called: **subsidiary company** a company which is at least half owned by another company. **2** a person or thing that is of lesser importance. ✧ *adj* **3** of lesser importance; subordinate. ▷ HISTORY Latin *subsidiarius* supporting

subsidize *or* **-dise** *vb* **-dizing, -dized** *or* **-dising, -dised** to aid or support (an industry, a person, a public service, or a venture) with money.

subsidy *n, pl* **-dies 1** financial aid supplied by a government, for example to industry, or for public welfare. **2** any financial aid, grant, or contribution. ▷ HISTORY Latin *subsidium* assistance

subsist *vb* **subsist on** to manage to live: *to subsist on a diet of sausage rolls.* ▷ HISTORY Latin *subsistere* to stand firm ▶ **subsistence** *n*

subsistence farming *n Agriculture* a type of farming in which most of the produce is consumed by the farmer and his family.

subsoil *n* the layer of soil beneath the surface soil.

subsonic *adj* being or moving at a speed below that of sound.

substance *n* **1** the basic matter of which a thing consists. **2** a specific type of matter with definite or fairly definite chemical composition: *a fatty substance.* **3** the essential meaning of a speech, thought, or written article. **4** important or meaningful quality: *the only evidence of substance against him.* **5** material possessions or wealth: *a woman of substance.* **6 in substance** with regard to the most important points. ▷ HISTORY Latin *substantia*

substantial *adj* **1** of a considerable size or value: *a substantial amount of money.* **2** (of food or a meal) large and filling. **3** solid or strong: *substantial brick pillars.* **4** *Formal* available to the senses; real: *substantial evidence.* **5** of or relating to the basic material substance of a thing. ▶ **substantially** *adv*

substantiate *vb* **-ating, -ated** to establish (a story) as genuine. ▶ **substantiation** *n*

substantive *n* **1** *Grammar* a noun or pronoun used in place of a noun. ✧ *adj* **2** having importance or significance: *substantive negotiations between management and staff.* **3** of or being the essential element of a thing. ▷ HISTORY Latin *substare* to stand beneath

substitute *vb* **-tuting, -tuted 1** (often foll. by *for*) to take the place of or put in place of another person or thing. **2** *Chem* to replace (an atom or group in a molecule) with (another atom or group). ✧ *n* **3** a person or thing that takes the place of another, such as a player who takes the place of a team-mate. ▷ HISTORY Latin *substituere* ▶ **substitution** *n*

> **WORD TIP**
> *Substitute* is sometimes wrongly used where *replace* is meant: *he replaced* (not *substituted*) *the worn tyre with a new one.*

substitution reaction *n Chem* the replacing of an atom or group in a molecule by another atom or group.

substrate *n Biol* the substance upon which an enzyme acts. ▷ HISTORY Latin *substratus* strewn beneath

subsume *vb* **-suming, -sumed** *Formal* to include (something) under a larger classification or group: *an attempt to subsume fascism and communism under a general concept of totalitarianism.* ▷ HISTORY Latin *sub-* under + *sumere* to take

subtenant *n* a person who rents property from a tenant. ▶ **subtenancy** *n*

subtend *vb Geom* to be opposite (an angle or side). ▷ HISTORY Latin *subtendere* to extend beneath

subterfuge *n* a trick or deception used to achieve an objective. ▷ HISTORY Latin *subterfugere* to escape by stealth

subterranean *adj* **1** found or operating below the surface of the earth. **2** existing or working in a concealed or mysterious way: *the resistance movement worked largely by subterranean methods.* ▷ HISTORY Latin *sub* beneath + *terra* earth

subtext *n* **1** an underlying theme in a piece of writing. **2** a message which is not stated directly but can be inferred.

subtitle *n* **1 subtitles** *Films* a written translation at the bottom of the picture in a film with foreign dialogue. **2** a secondary title given to a book or play. ✧ *vb* **-tling, -tled 3** to provide subtitles for (a film) or a subtitle for (a book or play).

subtle *adj* **1** not immediately obvious: *a subtle change in his views.* **2** (of a colour, taste, or smell) delicate or faint: *the subtle aroma.* **3** using shrewd and indirect methods to achieve an objective. **4** having or requiring the ability to make fine distinctions: *a subtle argument.* ▷ HISTORY Latin *subtilis* finely woven ▶ **subtly** *adv*

subtlety *n* **1** (*pl* **-ties**) a fine distinction. **2** the state or quality of being subtle.

subtract *vb* **1** *Maths* to take (one number or quantity) away from another. **2** to remove (a part of something) from the whole. ▷ HISTORY Latin *subtrahere* to draw away from beneath ▶ **subtraction** *n*

subtribe *n Sociol* a subdivision of a tribe.

subtropical *adj* of the region lying between the tropics and temperate lands.

suburb *n* a residential district on the outskirts of a city or town. ▷ HISTORY Latin *sub-* close to + *urbs* a city

suburban *adj* **1** of, in, or inhabiting a suburb. **2** *Mildly disparaging* conventional and unexciting.

suburbanite *n* a person who lives in a suburb.

suburbia *n* suburbs or the people living in them considered as a distinct community or class in society.

subvention *n Formal* a grant or subsidy, for example one from a government. ▷ HISTORY Late Latin *subventio* assistance

subversion *n* the act or an instance of attempting to weaken or overthrow a government or an institution.

subversive *adj* **1** intended or intending to weaken or overthrow a government or an institution. ✧ *n* **2** a person engaged in subversive activities.

subvert *vb* to bring about the downfall of (something existing by a system of law, such as a government). ▷ **HISTORY** Latin *subvertere* to overturn

subway *n* **1** *Brit & Austral* an underground passage for pedestrians to cross a road or railway. **2** an underground railway.

subzero *adj* lower than zero: *subzero temperatures.*

succeed *vb* **1** to achieve an aim. **2** to turn out satisfactorily: *Grandfather's plan succeeded.* **3** to do well in a specified field: *how to succeed in show biz.* **4** to come next in order after (someone or something): *the first shock had been succeeded by a different kind of gloom.* **5** to take over (a position) from (someone): *Henry VIII succeeded to the throne in 1509; he will be succeeded as president by his deputy.* ▷ **HISTORY** Latin *succedere* to follow after ▶ **succeeding** *adj*

success *n* **1** the achievement of something attempted. **2** the attainment of wealth, fame, or position. **3** a person or thing that is successful. ▷ **HISTORY** Latin *successus* an outcome

successful *adj* **1** having a favourable outcome. **2** having attained fame, wealth, or position. ▶ **successfully** *adv*

succession *n* **1** a number of people or things following one another in order. **2** the act or right by which one person succeeds another in a position. **3** *Biol, geog* the change in the types of plant occupying a given area that takes place over time. **4 in succession** one after another: *the third time in succession.*

successive *adj* following another or others without interruption: *eleven successive victories.* ▶ **successively** *adv*

successor *n* a person or thing that follows another, esp. a person who takes over another's job or position.

succinct *adj* brief and clear: *a succinct answer to this question.* ▷ **HISTORY** Latin *succinctus* ▶ **succinctly** *adv*

succour *or US* **succor** *n* **1** help in time of difficulty. ✧ *vb* **2** to give aid to (someone in time of difficulty). ▷ **HISTORY** Latin *succurrere* to hurry to help

succubus *n, pl* **-bi** a female demon fabled to have sex with sleeping men. ▷ **HISTORY** Latin *succubare* to lie beneath

succulent *adj* **1** (of food) juicy and delicious. **2** (of plants) having thick fleshy leaves or stems. ✧ *n* **3** a plant that can exist in very dry conditions by using water stored in its fleshy tissues. ▷ **HISTORY** Latin *sucus* juice ▶ **succulence** *n*

succumb *vb* **succumb to a** to give way to the force of or desire for (something). **b** to die of (a disease). ▷ **HISTORY** Latin *succumbere*

such *adj* **1** of the sort specified or understood: *such places.* **2** so great or so much: *such a mess.* ✧ *adv* **3** extremely: *such a powerful friend.* ✧ *pron* **4** a person or thing of the sort specified or understood: *such is the law of the land; fruitcakes and puddings and such.* **5 as such** in itself or themselves: *the Nordic countries are not lifting sanctions as such.* **6 such as** for example: *other socialist groups, such as the Fabians.* ▷ **HISTORY** Old English *swilc*

suchlike *n* **1** such or similar things: *shampoos, talcs, and suchlike.* ✧ *adj* **2** of such a kind; similar: *astrology and suchlike nonsense.*

suck *vb* **1** to draw (a liquid) into the mouth through pursed lips. **2** to take (something) into the mouth and moisten, dissolve, or roll it around with the tongue: *suck a mint.* **3** to extract liquid from (a solid food): *he sat sucking orange segments.* **4** to draw in (fluid) as if by sucking: *the mussel sucks in water.* **5** to drink milk from (a mother's breast); suckle. **6** (often foll. by *down, in*) to draw (a thing or person somewhere) with a powerful force. **7** *Slang* to be contemptible or disgusting. ✧ *n* **8** a sucking. ▷ **HISTORY** Old English *sūcan*

sucker *n* **1** *Slang* a person who is easily deceived or swindled. **2** *Slang* a person who cannot resist something: *he's a sucker for fast cars.* **3** *Zool* a part of the body of certain animals that is used for sucking or sticking to a surface. **4** a rubber cup-shaped device attached to objects allowing them to stick to a surface by suction. **5** *Bot* a strong shoot coming from a mature plant's root or the base of its main stem.

suckle *vb* **-ling, -led** to give (a baby or young animal) milk from the breast or udder or (of a baby or young animal) to suck milk from its mother's breast or udder.

suckling *n* a baby or young animal that is still sucking milk from its mother's breast or udder.

suck up to *vb Informal* to flatter (a person in authority) in order to get something, such as praise or promotion.

sucrose (**soo**-kroze) *n Chem* sugar. ▷ **HISTORY** French *sucre* sugar

suction *n* **1** the act or process of sucking. **2** the force produced by drawing air out of a space to make a vacuum that will suck in a substance from another space. ▷ **HISTORY** Latin *sugere* to suck

Sudanese *adj* **1** of the Sudan. ✧ *n, pl* **-nese 2** a person from the Sudan.

sudden *adj* **1** occurring or performed quickly and without warning. ✧ *n* **2 all of a sudden** without warning; unexpectedly. ▷ **HISTORY** Latin *subitus* unexpected ▶ **suddenly** *adv* ▶ **suddenness** *n*

sudden death *n Sport* an extra period of play to decide the winner of a tied competition: the first player or team to go into the lead is the winner.

sudden infant death syndrome *n* same as **cot death**.

sudorific (syoo-dor-**if**-ik) *adj* **1** causing sweating. ✧ *n* **2** a drug that causes sweating. ▷ **HISTORY** Latin *sudor* sweat + *facere* to make

suds *pl n* the bubbles on the surface of water in which soap or detergent has been dissolved; lather. ▷ **HISTORY** probably from Middle Dutch *sudse* marsh

sue *vb* **suing, sued** to start legal proceedings (against): *we want to sue the council; he sued for* *custody of the three children.* ▷ **HISTORY** Latin *sequi* to follow

suede *n* a leather with a fine velvet-like surface on one side.

> **WORD HISTORY**
> In French, *gants de Suède* means 'gloves from Sweden'. The gloves were called 'Swedish gloves' because they were first made there.

suet *n* a hard fat obtained from sheep and cattle and used for making pastry and puddings. ▷ **HISTORY** Old French *seu*

suffer *vb* **1** to undergo or be subjected to (physical pain or mental distress). **2 suffer from** to be badly affected by (an illness): *he was suffering from depression.* **3** to become worse in quality; deteriorate: *his work suffered during their divorce.* **4** to tolerate: *he suffers no fools.* **5** to be set at a disadvantage: *the strongest of them suffers by comparison.* ▷ **HISTORY** Latin *sufferre* ▶ **sufferer** *n* ▶ **suffering** *n*

sufferance *n* **on sufferance** tolerated with reluctance: *I was there on sufferance and all knew it.*

suffice (suf-**fice**) *vb* **-ficing, -ficed 1** to be enough or satisfactory for a purpose. **2 suffice it to say ...** it is enough to say ...: *suffice it to say that AIDS is on the increase.* ▷ **HISTORY** Latin *sufficere*

sufficiency *n, pl* **-cies** an adequate amount.

sufficient *adj* enough to meet a need or purpose; adequate. ▷ **HISTORY** Latin *sufficiens* ▶ **sufficiently** *adv*

suffix *Grammar* ✧ *n* **1** a letter or letters added to the end of a word to form another word, such as *-s* and *-ness* in *dogs* and *softness.* ✧ *vb* **2** to add (a letter or letters) to the end of a word to form another word. ▷ **HISTORY** Latin *suffixus* fastened below

suffocate *vb* **-cating, -cated 1** to kill or die through lack of oxygen, such as by blockage of the air passage. **2** to feel uncomfortable from heat and lack of air. ▷ **HISTORY** Latin *suffocare* ▶ **suffocating** *adj* ▶ **suffocation** *n*

suffragan *n* a bishop appointed to assist an archbishop. ▷ **HISTORY** Medieval Latin *suffragium* assistance

suffrage *n* the right to vote in public elections. ▷ **HISTORY** Latin *suffragium*

suffragette *n* (in Britain at the beginning of the 20th century) a woman who campaigned militantly for women to be given the right to vote in public elections.

suffragist *n* (in Britain at the beginning of the 20th century) a person who campaigned for women to be given the right to vote in public elections.

suffuse *vb* **-fusing, -fused** to spread through or over (something): *the dawn suffused the sky with a cold grey wash.* ▷ **HISTORY** Latin *suffusus* overspread with ▶ **suffusion** *n*

sugar *n* **1** a sweet carbohydrate, usually in the form of white or brown crystals, which is found in many plants and is used to sweeten food and drinks. **2** *Informal, chiefly US & Canad* a term of affection. ✧ *vb* **3** to add sugar to (food or drink) to make it sweet. **4** to cover with sugar: *sugared almonds.* **5 sugar the pill** to make something unpleasant more tolerable by adding something pleasant. ▷ **HISTORY** Old French *çucre,* from Sanskrit *śarkarā* ▶ **sugared** *adj*

sugar beet *n* a beet grown for the sugar obtained from its roots.

sugar cane *n* a tropical grass grown for the sugar obtained from its tall stout canes.

sugar daddy *n* an elderly man who gives a young woman money and gifts in return for her company.

sugar glider *n* a common Australian phalanger that glides from tree to tree feeding on insects and nectar.

sugar maple *n* a North American maple tree, grown as a source of sugar, which is extracted from the sap.

sugary *adj* **1** of, like, or containing sugar: *sugary snacks.* **2** (of behaviour or language) very pleasant but probably not sincere: *sugary sentiment.* ▶ **sugariness** *n*

suggest *vb* **1** to put forward (a plan or an idea) for consideration: *he didn't suggest a meeting.* **2** to bring (a person or thing) to the mind by the association of ideas: *a man whose very name suggests blandness.* **3** to give a hint of: *her grey eyes suggesting a livelier mood than usual.* ▷ **HISTORY** Latin *suggerere* to bring up

suggestible *adj* easily influenced by other people's ideas.

suggestion *n* **1** something that is suggested. **2** a hint or indication: *the entire castle gave no suggestion of period.* **3** *Psychol* the process whereby the presentation of an idea to a receptive individual leads to the acceptance of that idea.

suggestive *adj* **1** (of remarks or gestures) causing people to think of sex. **2 suggestive of** communicating a hint of.

suicidal *adj* **1** wanting to commit suicide. **2** likely to lead to danger or death: *a suicidal attempt to rescue her son.* **3** likely to destroy one's own career or future: *it would be suicidal for them to ignore public opinion.*

suicide *n* **1** the act of killing oneself deliberately: *he tried to commit suicide.* **2** a person who kills himself or herself intentionally. **3** the self-inflicted ruin of one's own career or future: *such a cut would be political suicide.* ▷ **HISTORY** Latin *sui* of oneself + *caedere* to kill

suit *n* **1** a set of clothes of the same material designed to be worn together, usually a jacket with matching trousers or skirt. **2** an outfit worn for a specific purpose: *a diving suit.* **3** a legal action taken against someone; lawsuit. **4** any of the four types of card in a pack of playing cards: spades, hearts, diamonds, or clubs. **5** *Slang* a business executive or white-collar worker. **6 follow suit** to act in the same way as someone else. **7 strong suit** *or* **strongest suit** something one excels in. ✧ *vb* **8** to be fit or appropriate for: *that colour suits you.* **9** to be acceptable to (someone). **10 suit oneself** to do what one wants without considering other people.

▷ HISTORY Old French *sieute* set of things ▸ **suited** *adj*

suitable *adj* appropriate for a particular function or occasion; proper. ▸ **suitability** *n* ▸ **suitably** *adv*

suitcase *n* a large portable travelling case for clothing.

suite *n* **1** a set of connected rooms in a hotel. **2** a matching set of furniture, for example two armchairs and a settee. **3** *Music* a composition of several movements in the same key.
▷ HISTORY French

suitor *n* **1** *Old-fashioned* a man who wants to marry a woman. **2** *Law* a person who starts legal proceedings against someone; plaintiff.
▷ HISTORY Latin *secutor* follower

Sukkoth (**sook**-oat) *n* an eight-day Jewish harvest festival, commemorating the period when the Israelites lived in the wilderness.

sulk *vb* **1** to be silent and moody as a way of showing anger or resentment: *I went home and sulked for two days.* ✧ *n* **2** a mood in which one shows anger or resentment by being silent and moody: *he was just in a sulk.*

sulky *adj* **sulkier, sulkiest** moody or silent because of anger or resentment.
▷ HISTORY perhaps from obsolete *sulke* sluggish
▸ **sulkily** *adv* ▸ **sulkiness** *n*

sullen *adj* unwilling to talk or be sociable; sulky.
▷ HISTORY Latin *solus* alone ▸ **sullenly** *adv*
▸ **sullenness** *n*

sully *vb* **-lies, -lying, -lied 1** to ruin (someone's reputation). **2** to spoil or make dirty: *the stream had been sullied by the smelter's pollution.*
▷ HISTORY probably from French *souiller* to soil

sulpha *or US* **sulfa drug** *n Pharmacol* any of a group of sulphonamides that prevent the growth of bacteria: used to treat bacterial infections.

sulphate *or US* **sulfate** *n Chem* a salt or ester of sulphuric acid.

sulphide *or US* **sulfide** *n Chem* a compound of sulphur with another element.

sulphite *or US* **sulfite** *n Chem* any salt or ester of sulphurous acid.

sulphonamide *or US* **sulfonamide** (sulf-**on**-a-mide) *n Pharmacol* any of a class of organic compounds that prevent the growth of bacteria.

sulphur *or US* **sulfur** *n Chem* a light yellow, highly inflammable, nonmetallic element used in the production of sulphuric acid, in the vulcanization of rubber, and in medicine. Symbol: S. ▷ HISTORY Latin *sulfur* ▸ **sulphuric** *or US* **sulfuric** *adj*

sulphur dioxide *n Chem* a strong-smelling colourless soluble gas, used in the manufacture of sulphuric acid and in the preservation of foodstuffs.

sulphureous *or US* **sulfureous** (sulf-**yoor**-ee-uss) *adj* same as **sulphurous** (sense 1).

sulphuric acid *n Chem* a colourless dense oily corrosive liquid used in the manufacture of fertilizers and explosives.

sulphurize *or* **-rise** *or US* **sulfurize** (**sulf**-yoor-rise) *vb* **-rizing, -rized** *or* **-rising, -rised** *Chem* to combine with or treat (something) with sulphur or a sulphur compound.

sulphurous *or US* **sulfurous** *adj Chem* **1** of or resembling sulphur. **2** containing sulphur, esp. with a valence of four.

sultan *n* the sovereign of a Muslim country.
▷ HISTORY Arabic: rule

sultana *n* **1** the dried fruit of a small white seedless grape. **2** a sultan's wife, mother, daughter, or concubine. ▷ HISTORY Italian

sultanate *n* **1** the territory ruled by a sultan. **2** the office or rank of a sultan.

sultry *adj* **-trier, -triest 1** (of weather or climate) very hot and humid. **2** suggesting hidden passion: *a sultry brunette.* ▷ HISTORY obsolete *sulter* to swelter

sum *n* **1** the result of the addition of numbers or quantities. **2** one or more columns or rows of numbers to be added, subtracted, multiplied, or divided. **3** a quantity of money: *they can win enormous sums.* **4 in sum** as a summary; in short: *in sum, it's been a bad week for the government.* ✧ *adj* **5** complete or final: *the sum total.* ✧ *vb* **summing, summed 6** See **sum up**. ▷ HISTORY Latin *summa* the top, sum

summarize *or* **-rise** *vb* **-rizing, -rized** *or* **-rising, -rised** to give a short account of (something).

summary *n, pl* **-maries 1** a brief account giving the main points of something. ✧ *adj* **2** performed quickly, without formality or attention to details: *a summary judgment.* ▷ HISTORY Latin *summarium* ▸ **summarily** *adv*

summary offence *n Law* a minor criminal offence for which the defendant is tried before a magistrate. Compare **indictable offence**.

summation *n* **1** a summary of what has just been done or said. **2** the process of working out a sum; addition. **3** the result of such a process.

summer *n* **1** the warmest season of the year, between spring and autumn. **2** *Literary* a time of youth, success, or happiness. ▷ HISTORY Old English *sumor* ▸ **summery** *adj*

summerhouse *n* a small building in a garden, used for shade in the summer.

summer school *n* an academic course held during the summer.

summer solstice *n* the time at which the sun is at its northernmost point in the sky (southernmost point in the S hemisphere), appearing at noon at its highest altitude above the horizon. It occurs about June 21 (December 22 in the S hemisphere).

summertime *n* the period or season of summer.

summing-up *n* **1** a summary of the main points of an argument, speech, or piece of writing. **2** concluding statements made by a judge to the jury before they retire to consider their verdict.

summit *n* **1** the highest point or part of a mountain or hill. **2** the highest possible degree or state; peak or climax: *the summit of success.* **3** a

A B C D E F G H I J K L M N O P Q R S T U V W X Y Z

meeting of heads of governments or other high officials. ▷ **HISTORY** Old French *somet*

summon *vb* **1** to order (someone) to come. **2** send for (someone) to appear in court. **3** to call upon (someone) to do something: *the authorities had summoned the relatives to be available.* **4** to convene (a meeting). **5** (often foll. by *up*) to call into action (one's strength, courage, etc.); muster. ▷ **HISTORY** Latin *summonere* to give a discreet reminder

summons *n, pl* **-monses 1** a call or an order to attend a specified place at a specified time. **2** an official order requiring a person to attend court, either to answer a charge or to give evidence. ✧ *vb* **3** to order (someone) to appear in court: *three others had been summonsed for questioning.*

sumo *n* the national style of wrestling of Japan, in which two contestants of great height and weight attempt to force each other out of the ring. ▷ **HISTORY** Japanese

sump *n* **1** a container in an internal-combustion engine into which oil can drain. **2** same as **cesspool**. **3** *Mining* a hollow at the bottom of a shaft where water collects. ▷ **HISTORY** Middle Dutch *somp* marsh

sumptuary *adj* controlling expenditure or extravagant use of resources. ▷ **HISTORY** Latin *sumptuarius* concerning expense

sumptuous *adj* magnificent and very expensive; splendid: *sumptuous decoration.* ▷ **HISTORY** Latin *sumptuosus* costly

sum up *vb* **1** to give a short account of (the main points of an argument, speech, or piece of writing). **2** to form a quick opinion of: *how well you have summed me up!*

sun *n* **1** the star that is the source of heat and light for the planets in the solar system. *RELATED ADJECTIVE* ➧ **solar 2** any star around which a system of planets revolves. **3** the heat and light received from the sun; sunshine. **4 catch the sun** to become slightly suntanned. **5 under the sun** on earth; at all: *there are no free lunches under the sun.* ✧ *vb* **sunning, sunned 6 sun oneself** to lie, sit, or walk in the sunshine on a warm day. ▷ **HISTORY** Old English *sunne* ▶ **sunless** *adj*

Sun. Sunday.

sunbathe *vb* **-bathing, -bathed** to lie or sit in the sunshine, in order to get a suntan. ▶ **sunbather** *n* ▶ **sunbathing** *n*

sunbeam *n* a ray of sunlight.

sunburn *n* painful reddening of the skin caused by overexposure to the sun. ▶ **sunburnt** *or* **sunburned** *adj*

sundae *n* ice cream topped with a sweet sauce, nuts, whipped cream, and fruit. ▷ **HISTORY** origin unknown

Sunday *n* the first day of the week and the Christian day of worship. ▷ **HISTORY** Old English *sunnandæg* day of the sun

Sunday school *n* a school for teaching children about Christianity, usually held in a church hall on Sunday.

sundial *n* a device used for telling the time during the hours of sunlight, consisting of a pointer that casts a shadow onto a surface marked in hours.

sundown *n US* sunset.

sundries *pl n* several things of various sorts.

sundry *adj* **1** several or various; miscellaneous. ✧ *pron* **2 all and sundry** everybody. ▷ **HISTORY** Old English *syndrig* separate

sunfish *n, pl* **-fish** *or* **-fishes** a large sea fish with a rounded body.

sunflower *n* **1** a very tall plant with large yellow flowers. **2 sunflower seed oil** the oil extracted from sunflower seeds, used as a salad oil and in margarine.

sung *vb* the past participle of **sing**.

> ☑ **WORD TIP**
> See at **ring**[1].

sunglasses *pl n* glasses with darkened lenses that protect the eyes from bright sunlight.

sunk *vb* a past participle of **sink**.

sunken *vb* **1** a past participle of **sink**. ✧ *adj* **2** (of a person's cheeks, eyes, or chest) curving inward due to old age or bad health. **3** situated at a lower level than the surrounding or usual one: *the sunken garden.* **4** situated under water; submerged: *sunken ships.*

sun lamp *n* a lamp that gives off ultraviolet rays, used for muscular therapy or for giving people an artificial suntan.

sunlight *n* the light that comes from the sun. ▶ **sunlit** *adj*

sunny *adj* **-nier, -niest 1** full of or lit up by sunshine. **2** cheerful and happy.

sunrise *n* **1** the daily appearance of the sun above the horizon. **2** the time at which the sun rises.

sunrise industry *n* any of the fast-developing high-technology industries, such as electronics.

sunroof *n* a panel in the roof of a car that may be opened to let in air or sunshine.

sunset *n* **1** the daily disappearance of the sun below the horizon. **2** the time at which the sun sets.

sunshine *n* **1** the light and warmth from the sun. **2** *Brit* a light-hearted term of address.

sunspot *n* **1** *Informal* a sunny holiday resort. **2** a dark cool patch on the surface of the sun. **3** *Austral* a small area of skin damage caused by exposure to the sun.

sunstroke *n* a condition caused by spending too much time exposed to intensely hot sunlight and producing high fever and sometimes loss of consciousness.

suntan *n* a brownish colouring of the skin caused by exposure to the sun or a sun lamp. ▶ **suntanned** *adj*

sun-up *n US & Austral* sunrise.

sup[1] *vb* **supping, supped 1** to take (liquid) by swallowing a little at a time. ✧ *n* **2** a sip. ▷ **HISTORY** Old English *sūpan*

sup[2] *vb* **supping, supped** *Archaic* to have supper. ▷ **HISTORY** Old French *soper*

A B C D E F G H I J K L M N O P Q R S T U V W X Y Z

super *Informal* ✧ *adj* **1** very good or very nice: *they had a super holiday.* ✧ *n* **2** *Austral & NZ informal* superannuation. **3** *Austral & NZ informal* superphosphate. ▷ **HISTORY** Latin: above

super- *prefix* used with many main words to mean: **1** above or over: *superscript.* **2** outstanding: *superstar.* **3** of greater size, extent, or quality: *supermarket.* ▷ **HISTORY** Latin

superannuated *adj* **1** discharged with a pension, owing to age or illness. **2** too old to be useful; obsolete. ▷ **HISTORY** Medieval Latin *superannatus* aged more than one year

superannuation *n* **a** a regular payment made by an employee into a pension fund. **b** the pension finally paid.

superb *adj* extremely good or impressive. ▷ **HISTORY** Latin *superbus* distinguished ▶ **superbly** *adv*

Super Bowl *n American football* the championship game held annually between the best team of the American Football Conference and that of the National Football Conference.

superbug *n Informal* a bacterium resistant to antibiotics.

supercharge *vb* **-charging, -charged 1** to increase the power of (an internal-combustion engine) with a supercharger. **2** to charge (the atmosphere, a remark, etc.) with an excess amount of (tension, emotion, etc.). **3** to apply pressure to (a fluid); pressurize.

supercharger *n* a device that increases the power of an internal-combustion engine by forcing extra air into it.

supercilious *adj* behaving in a superior and arrogant manner. ▷ **HISTORY** Latin *supercilium* eyebrow ▶ **superciliously** *adv* ▶ **superciliousness** *n*

superconductivity *n Physics* the ability of certain substances to conduct electric current with almost no resistance at very low temperatures. ▶ **superconducting** *adj* ▶ **superconductor** *n*

supercontinent *n* a huge landmass thought to have existed in the geological past and to have split into smaller landmasses and formed the present continents.

superego *n, pl* **-gos** *Psychoanal* that part of the unconscious mind that governs a person's ideas concerning what is right and wrong.

supererogation *n* the act of doing more work than is required. ▷ **HISTORY** Latin *supererogare* to spend over and above

superficial *adj* **1** not careful or thorough: *a superficial analysis.* **2** only outwardly apparent rather than genuine or actual: *those are merely superficial differences.* **3** (of a person) lacking deep emotions or serious interests; shallow. **4** of, near, or forming the surface: *the gash was superficial.* ▷ **HISTORY** Late Latin *superficialis* ▶ **superficiality** *n* ▶ **superficially** *adv*

superfluous (soo-**per**-flew-uss) *adj* more than is sufficient or required. ▷ **HISTORY** Latin *superfluus* overflowing ▶ **superfluity** *n*

superglue *n* an extremely strong and quick-drying glue.

supergrass *n Brit, Austral & NZ* an informer who names a large number of people as terrorists or criminals, esp. one who gives this information in order to avoid being put on trial.

superhuman *adj* beyond normal human ability or experience: *a superhuman effort.*

superimpose *vb* **-posing, -posed** to set or place (something) on or over something else.

superintend *vb* to supervise (a person or an activity). ▷ **HISTORY** Latin *super-* above + *intendere* to give attention to

superintendent *n* **1** a senior police officer. **2** a person who directs and manages an organization or office.

superior *adj* **1** greater in quality, quantity, or usefulness. **2** higher in rank, position, or status: *he was reprimanded by a superior officer.* **3** believing oneself to be better than others. **4** of very high quality or respectability: *superior merchandise.* **5** *Formal* placed higher up: *damage to the superior surface of the wing.* **6** *Printing* (of a character) written or printed above the line. ✧ *n* **7** a person of greater rank or status. **8** See **mother superior**. ▷ **HISTORY** Latin *superus* placed above ▶ **superiority** *n*

> **WORD TIP**
> *Superior* should not be used with *than: he is a better* (not *a superior*) *poet than his brother; his poetry is superior to* (not *superior than*) *his brother's.*

superior court *n Law* **1** a higher court not subject to control by any other court except by way of appeal. **2** *US* (in several states) a court of general jurisdiction ranking above the inferior courts and below courts of last resort.

superlative (soo-**per**-lat-iv) *adj* **1** of outstanding quality; supreme. **2** *Grammar* denoting the form of an adjective or adverb that expresses the highest degree of quality. ✧ *n* **3** the highest quality. **4** *Grammar* the superlative form of an adjective or adverb. ▷ **HISTORY** Old French *superlatif*

superman *n, pl* **-men** any man with great physical or mental powers.

supermarket *n* a large self-service shop selling food and household goods.

supermodel *n* a famous and highly-paid fashion model.

supernatural *adj* **1** of or relating to things that cannot be explained by science, such as clairvoyance, ghosts, etc. ✧ *n* **2 the supernatural** forces, occurrences, and beings that cannot be explained by science.

supernova *n, pl* **-vae** *or* **-vas** a star that explodes and, for a few days, becomes one hundred million times brighter than the sun.

supernumerary *adj* **1** exceeding the required or regular number; extra. **2** employed as a substitute or assistant. ✧ *n, pl* **-aries 3** a person or thing that exceeds the required or regular number. **4** a substitute or assistant. **5** an actor who has no lines to say. ▷ **HISTORY** Latin *super-* above + *numerus* number

superphosphate *n* a chemical fertilizer, esp. one made by treating rock phosphate with sulphuric acid.

superpower *n* a country of very great military and economic power, such as the US.

superscript *Printing* ✧ *adj* **1** (of a character) written or printed above the line. ✧ *n* **2** a superscript character.

supersede *vb* **-seding, -seded 1** to take the place of (something old-fashioned or less appropriate): *cavalry was superseded by armoured vehicles.* **2** to replace (someone) in function or office. ▷ **HISTORY** Latin *supersedere* to sit above

supersonic *adj* being, having, or capable of a speed greater than the speed of sound.

superstar *n* an extremely popular and famous entertainer or sportsperson. ▶ **superstardom** *n*

superstate *n* a large state, esp. one created from a federation of states.

superstition *n* **1** irrational belief in magic and the powers that supposedly bring good luck or bad luck. **2** a belief or practice based on this. ▷ **HISTORY** Latin *superstitio* ▶ **superstitious** *adj*

superstore *n* a large supermarket.

superstructure *n* **1** any structure or concept built on something else. **2** *Naut* any structure above the main deck of a ship.

supertanker *n* a very large fast tanker.

supertax *n* an extra tax on incomes above a certain level.

supervene *vb* **-vening, -vened** to happen as an unexpected development. ▷ **HISTORY** Latin *supervenire* to come upon ▶ **supervention** *n*

supervise *vb* **-vising, -vised 1** to direct the performance or operation of (an activity or a process). **2** to watch over (people) so as to ensure appropriate behaviour. ▷ **HISTORY** Latin *super-* over + *videre* to see ▶ **supervision** *n* ▶ **supervisor** *n* ▶ **supervisory** *adj*

supine (**soo**-pine) *adj* **1** *Formal* lying on one's back. **2** offering no resistance; submissive: *the team's supine surrender to Dunfermline.* ▷ **HISTORY** Latin *supinus*

supper *n* **1** an evening meal. **2** a late evening snack. ▷ **HISTORY** Old French *soper*

supplant *vb* to take the place of (someone or something). ▷ **HISTORY** Latin *supplantare* to trip up

supple *adj* **1** (of a person) moving and bending easily and gracefully. **2** (of a material or object) soft and bending easily without breaking. ▷ **HISTORY** Latin *supplex* bowed ▶ **suppleness** *n*

supplement *n* **1** an addition designed to make something more adequate. **2** a magazine distributed free with a newspaper. **3** a section added to a publication to supply further information or correct errors. **4** (of money) an additional payment to obtain special services. ✧ *vb* **5** to provide an addition to (something), esp. in order to make up for an inadequacy: *a Saturday job to supplement her grant.* ▷ **HISTORY** Latin *supplementum* ▶ **supplementary** *adj*

supplementary angle *n Geom* either of two angles whose sum is 180 degrees.

supplicant *n Formal* a person who makes a humble request. ▷ **HISTORY** Latin *supplicans* beseeching

supplication *n Formal* a humble request for help. ▷ **HISTORY** Latin *supplicare* to beg on one's knees

supply *vb* **-plies, -plying, -plied 1** to provide with something required: *Nigeria may supply them with oil.* ✧ *n, pl* **-plies 2** the act of providing something. **3** an amount available for use; stock: *electricity supply.* **4 supplies** food and equipment needed for a trip or military campaign. **5** *Econ* the amount of a commodity that producers are willing and able to offer for sale at a specified price: *supply and demand.* **6** a person who acts as a temporary substitute. ✧ *adj* **7** acting as a temporary substitute: *supply teachers.* ▷ **HISTORY** Latin *supplere* to complete ▶ **supplier** *n*

support *vb* **1** to carry the weight of (a thing or person). **2** to provide the necessities of life for (a family or person). **3** to give practical or emotional help to (someone). **4** to give approval to (a cause, idea, or political party). **5** to take an active interest in and be loyal to (a particular football or other sport team). **6** to establish the truthfulness or accuracy of (a theory or statement) by providing new facts. **7** to speak in a debate in favour of (a motion). **8** (in a concert) to perform earlier than (the main attraction). **9** *Films, theatre* to play a less important role to (the leading actor or actress). ✧ *n* **10** the act of supporting or the condition of being supported. **11** a thing that bears the weight of an object from below. **12** a person who gives someone practical or emotional help. **13** the means of providing the necessities of life for a family or person. **14** a band or entertainer not topping the bill. ▷ **HISTORY** Latin *supportare* to bring ▶ **supportive** *adj*

supporter *n* a person who supports a sports team, politician, etc.

suppose *vb* **-posing, -posed 1** to presume (something) to be true without certain knowledge: *I suppose it will be in the papers.* **2** to consider (something) as a possible suggestion for the sake of discussion: *suppose you're arrested on a misdemeanour.* **3** (of a theory) to depend on the truth or existence of: *this scenario supposes that he would do so.* ▷ **HISTORY** Latin *supponere* to substitute

supposed *adj* **1 supposed to** expected to: *spies aren't supposed to be nice.* **2** presumed to be true without certain knowledge; doubtful: *the supposed wonders of drug therapy.* ▶ **supposedly** *adv*

supposition *n* **1** an idea or a statement believed or assumed to be true. **2** the act of supposing: *much of it is based on supposition.*

suppository *n, pl* **-ries** *Med* a medicine in solid form that is inserted into the vagina or rectum and left to dissolve. ▷ **HISTORY** Latin *suppositus* placed beneath

suppress *vb* **1** to put an end to (something) by physical or legal force. **2** to prevent the circulation

A B C D E F G H I J K L M N O P Q R S T U V W X Y Z

or publication of (information or books). **3** to hold (an emotion or a response) in check; restrain: *he could barely suppress a groan.* **4** *Electronics* to reduce or eliminate (interference) in a circuit. ▷ **HISTORY** Latin *suppressus* held down
▶ **suppression** *n*

suppressant *n* a drug that suppresses an action: *a cough suppressant.*

suppurate *vb* **-rating, -rated** *Pathol* (of a wound or sore) to produce or leak pus. ▷ **HISTORY** Latin *suppurare*

supremacy *n* **1** supreme power; dominance. **2** the state or quality of being superior.

supreme *adj* **1** of highest status or power: *the Supreme Council.* **2** of highest quality or importance: *a supreme player.* **3** greatest in degree; extreme: *supreme happiness.* ▷ **HISTORY** Latin *supremus* highest ▶ **supremely** *adv*

Supreme Court *n Law* **1** (in the US) the highest Federal court, possessing final appellate jurisdiction and exercising supervisory jurisdiction over the lower courts. **2** (in many states) the highest state court.

supremo *n, pl* **-mos** *Brit & Austral informal* a person in overall authority.

sur-[1] *prefix* over; above; beyond: *surcharge; surrealism.* ▷ **HISTORY** Old French

sur-[2] *prefix* See **sub-**.

surcharge *n* **1** a charge in addition to the usual payment or tax. **2** an excessive sum charged, often unlawfully. ✧ *vb* **-charging, -charged 3** to charge (someone) an additional sum or tax. **4** to overcharge (someone) for something.

surd *Maths* ✧ *n* **1** an irrational number. ✧ *adj* **2** of or relating to a surd. ▷ **HISTORY** Latin *surdus* muffled

sure *adj* **1** free from doubt or uncertainty (in regard to a belief): *she was sure that she was still at home; I am sure he didn't mean it.* **2 sure of** having no doubt, such as of the occurrence of a future state or event: *sure of winning the point.* **3** reliable or accurate: *a sure sign of dry rot.* **4** bound inevitably (to be or do something); certain: *his aggressive style is sure to please the American fans.* **5 sure of** *or* **about** happy to put one's trust in (someone): *I'm still not quite sure about her.* **6 sure of oneself** confident in one's own abilities and opinions. **7** not open to doubt: *sure proof.* **8** bound to be or occur; inevitable: *victory is sure.* **9** physically secure: *a sure footing.* **10 be sure** to be careful or certain: *be sure to label each jar.* **11 for sure** without a doubt. **12 make sure** to make certain: *make sure there is no-one in the car.* **13 sure enough** *Informal* in fact: *sure enough, this is happening.* **14 to be sure** it has to be acknowledged; admittedly. ✧ *adv* **15** *Informal, chiefly US & Canad* without question; certainly: *it sure is bad news.* ✧ *interj* **16** *Informal* willingly; yes. ▷ **HISTORY** Old French *seur*
▶ **sureness** *n*

sure-fire *adj Informal* certain to succeed: *a sure-fire cure.*

sure-footed *adj* **1** unlikely to fall, slip, or stumble. **2** unlikely to make a mistake.

surely *adv* **1** am I not right in thinking that?; I am sure that: *surely you can see that?* **2** without doubt: *without support they will surely fail.* **3 slowly but surely** gradually but noticeably. ✧ *interj* **4** *Chiefly US & Canad* willingly; yes.

surety *n, pl* **-ties 1** a person who takes legal responsibility for the fulfilment of another's debt or obligation. **2** security given as a guarantee that an obligation will be met. ▷ **HISTORY** Latin *securitas* security

surf *n* **1** foam caused by waves breaking on the shore or on a reef. ✧ *vb* **2** to take part in surfing. **3** to move rapidly through a particular medium: *surfing the Internet.* **4** *Informal* to be carried on top of something: *that guy's surfing the audience.* ▷ **HISTORY** probably variant of *sough* ▶ **surfer** *n*

surface *n* **1** the outside or top of an object. **2** the size of such an area. **3** material covering the surface of an object. **4** the outward appearance as opposed to the real or hidden nature of something: *on the surface the idea seems attractive.* **5** *Geom* **a** the complete boundary of a solid figure. **b** something that has length and breadth but no thickness. **6** the uppermost level of the land or sea. **7 come to the surface** to become apparent after being hidden. ✧ *vb* **-facing, -faced 8** to become apparent or widely known. **9** to rise to the surface of water. **10** to give (an area) a particular kind of surface. **11** *Informal* to get up out of bed. ▷ **HISTORY** French

surface area *n Chem* the area that is exposed for a chemical reaction to take place.

surface tension *n Physics* a property of liquids, caused by molecular forces, that leads to the apparent presence of a surface film and to rising and falling in contact with solids.

surfboard *n* a long narrow board used in surfing.

surfeit *n Formal* **1** an excessive amount. **2** excessive eating or drinking. **3** an uncomfortably full or sickened feeling caused by eating or drinking too much. ▷ **HISTORY** French *sourfait*

surfing *n* the sport of riding towards shore on the crest of a wave by standing or lying on a surfboard.

surge *n* **1** a sudden powerful increase: *a surge in spending.* **2** a strong rolling movement of the sea. **3** a heavy rolling motion or sound: *a great surge of people.* ✧ *vb* **surging, surged 4** to move forward strongly and suddenly. **5** (of the sea) to rise or roll with a heavy swelling motion. ▷ **HISTORY** Latin *surgere* to rise

surgeon *n* a medical doctor who specializes in surgery.

surgery *n, pl* **-geries 1** medical treatment in which a person's body is cut open by a surgeon in order to treat or remove the problem part. **2** *Brit* a place where, or time when, a doctor or dentist can be consulted. **3** *Brit* a time when an MP or councillor can be consulted. ▷ **HISTORY** Greek *kheir* hand + *ergon* work

surgical *adj* involving or used in surgery.
▶ **surgically** *adv*

surgical spirit *n* methylated spirit used medically for cleaning wounds and sterilizing equipment.

surly *adj* **-lier, -liest** bad-tempered and rude. ▷ **HISTORY** from obsolete *sirly* haughty

surmise *vb* **-mising, -mised 1** to guess (something) from incomplete or uncertain evidence. ✧ *n* **2** a conclusion based on incomplete or uncertain evidence. ▷ **HISTORY** Old French *surmettre* to accuse

surmount *vb* **1** to overcome (a problem). **2** to be situated on top of (something): *the island is surmounted by a huge black castle.* ▷ **HISTORY** Old French *surmonter* ▶ **surmountable** *adj*

surname *n* a family name as opposed to a first or Christian name. ▷ **HISTORY** Old French *sur-* over + *nom* name

surpass *vb* **1** to be greater in extent than or superior in achievement to (something or someone). **2 surpass oneself** *or* **expectations** to go beyond the limit of what was expected. ▷ **HISTORY** French *surpasser*

surplice *n* a loose knee-length garment with wide sleeves, worn by clergymen and choristers. ▷ **HISTORY** Old French *sourpelis*

surplus *n* **1** a quantity or amount left over in excess of what is required. **2** *Accounting* an excess of income over spending. ✧ *adj* **3** being in excess; extra: *surplus to requirements.* ▷ **HISTORY** Old French

surprise *n* **1** the act of taking someone unawares: *the element of surprise.* **2** a sudden or unexpected event, gift, etc.: *this is a nice surprise.* **3** the feeling of being surprised; astonishment: *to our great surprise.* **4 take someone by surprise** to capture someone unexpectedly or catch someone unprepared. ✧ *adj* **5** causing surprise: *a surprise attack.* ✧ *vb* **-prising, -prised 6** to cause (someone) to feel amazement or wonder. **7** to come upon or discover (someone) unexpectedly or suddenly. **8** to capture or attack (someone) suddenly and without warning. **9 surprise into** to provoke (someone) to unintended action by a trick or deception. ▷ **HISTORY** Old French *surprendre* to overtake ▶ **surprised** *adj* ▶ **surprising** *adj* ▶ **surprisingly** *adv*

surreal *adj* very strange or dreamlike; bizarre.

surrealism *n* a movement in art and literature in the 1920s, involving the combination of images that would not normally be found together, as if in a dream. ▷ **HISTORY** French *surréalisme* ▶ **surrealist** *n, adj* ▶ **surrealistic** *adj*

surrender *vb* **1** to give oneself up physically to an enemy after defeat. **2** to give (something) up to another, under pressure or on demand: *the rebels surrendered their arms.* **3** to give (something) up voluntarily to another: *he was surrendering his own chance for the championship.* **4** to give in to a temptation or an influence. ✧ *n* **5** the act or instance of surrendering. ▷ **HISTORY** Old French *surrendre*

surreptitious *adj* done in secret or without permission: *surreptitious moments of bliss.* ▷ **HISTORY** Latin *surrepticius* furtive ▶ **surreptitiously** *adv*

surrogate *n* **1** a person or thing acting as a substitute. ✧ *adj* **2** acting as a substitute: *a surrogate father.* ▷ **HISTORY** Latin *surrogare* to substitute

surrogate mother *n* a woman who gives birth to a child on behalf of a couple who cannot have a baby themselves, usually by artificial insemination. ▶ **surrogate motherhood** *or* **surrogacy** *n*

surround *vb* **1** to encircle or enclose (something or someone). **2** to exist around (someone or something): *the family members who surround him.* ✧ *n* **3** *Chiefly Brit* a border, such as the area of uncovered floor between the walls of a room and the carpet. ▷ **HISTORY** Old French *suronder* ▶ **surrounding** *adj*

surroundings *pl n* the area and environment around a person, place, or thing.

surtax *n* an extra tax on incomes above a certain level.

surveillance *n* close observation of a person suspected of being a spy or a criminal. ▷ **HISTORY** French

survey *vb* **1** to view or consider (something) as a whole: *she surveyed her purchases anxiously.* **2** to make a detailed map of (an area of land) by measuring or calculating distances and height. **3** *Brit* to inspect (a building) to assess its condition and value. **4** to make a detailed investigation of the behaviour, opinions, etc., of (a group of people). ✧ *n* **5** a detailed investigation of the behaviour, opinions, etc., of a group of people. **6** the act of making a detailed map of an area of land by measuring or calculating distance and height. **7** *Brit* an inspection of a building to assess its condition and value. ▷ **HISTORY** French *surveoir* ▶ **surveying** *n* ▶ **surveyor** *n*

survival *n* **1** the condition of having survived something. **2** a person or thing that continues to exist in the present despite being from an earlier time, such as a custom. ✧ *adj* **3** of, relating to, or assisting the act of surviving: *survival suits.*

survive *vb* **-viving, -vived 1** to continue to live or exist after (a passage of time or a difficult or dangerous experience). **2** to live after the death of (another). ▷ **HISTORY** Old French *sourvivre* ▶ **survivor** *n*

susceptibility *n, pl* **-ties 1** the quality or condition of being easily affected or influenced by something. **2 susceptibilities** emotional feelings.

susceptible *adj* **1 susceptible to a** giving in easily to: *susceptible to political pressure.* **b** vulnerable to (a disease or injury): *susceptible to pneumonia.* **2** easily affected emotionally; impressionable. ▷ **HISTORY** Late Latin *susceptibilis*

sushi (**soo**-shee) *n* a Japanese dish consisting of small cakes of cold rice with a topping of raw fish. ▷ **HISTORY** Japanese

suspect *vb* **1** to believe (someone) to be guilty without having any proof. **2** to think (something) to be false or doubtful: *he suspected her intent.* **3** to believe (something) to be the case; think probable: *I suspect he had another reason.* ✧ *n* **4** a person who is believed guilty of a specified offence. ✧ *adj* **5** not to be trusted or relied upon: *her commitment to the cause has always been suspect.* ▷ **HISTORY** Latin *suspicere* to mistrust

suspend *vb* **1** to hang (something) from a high place. **2** to cause (something) to remain floating or hanging: *a huge orange sun suspended above the horizon.* **3** to cause (something) to stop temporarily: *the discussions have been suspended.* **4** to remove (someone) temporarily from a job or position, usually as a punishment. ▷ **HISTORY** Latin *suspendere*

suspended animation *n* a state in which the body's functions are slowed down to a minimum for a period of time, such as by freezing or hibernation.

suspended sentence *n* a sentence of imprisonment that is not served by an offender unless he or she commits a further offence during a specified time.

suspenders *pl n* **1 a** elastic straps attached to a belt or corset, with fasteners for holding up women's stockings. **b** similar fasteners attached to garters for holding up men's socks. **2** *US & Canad* braces.

suspense *n* **1** a state of anxiety or uncertainty: *Sue and I stared at each other in suspense.* **2** excitement felt at the approach of the climax of a book, film, or play: *action and suspense abound in this thriller.* ▷ **HISTORY** Medieval Latin *suspensum* delay ▶ **suspenseful** *adj*

suspension *n* **1** the delaying or stopping temporarily of something: *the suspension of the talks.* **2** temporary removal from a job or position, usually as a punishment. **3** the act of suspending or the state of being suspended. **4** a system of springs and shock absorbers that supports the body of a vehicle. **5** a device, usually a wire or spring, that suspends or supports something, such as the pendulum of a clock. **6** *Chem* a mixture in which fine solid or liquid particles are suspended in a fluid.

suspension bridge *n* a bridge suspended from cables that hang between two towers and are secured at both ends.

suspicion *n* **1** the act or an instance of suspecting; belief without sure proof that something is wrong. **2** a feeling of mistrust. **3** a slight trace: *the merest suspicion of a threat.* **4 above suspicion** not possibly guilty of anything, through having a good reputation. **5 under suspicion** suspected of doing something wrong. ▷ **HISTORY** Latin *suspicio* distrust

suspicious *adj* **1** causing one to suspect something is wrong: *suspicious activities.* **2** unwilling to trust: *I'm suspicious of his motives.* ▶ **suspiciously** *adv*

suss out *vb Brit, Austral & NZ slang* to work out (a situation or a person's character), using one's intuition. ▷ **HISTORY** from *suspect*

sustain *vb* **1** to maintain or continue for a period of time: *I managed to sustain a conversation.* **2** to keep up the strength or energy of (someone): *one mouthful of water to sustain him; the merest drop of comfort to sustain me.* **3** to suffer (an injury or loss): *he sustained a spinal injury.* **4** to support (something) from below. **5** to support or agree with (a decision or statement): *objection sustained.* ▷ **HISTORY** Latin *sustinere* to hold up ▶ **sustained** *adj*

sustainable *adj* **1** capable of being sustained. **2** (of economic development or energy sources) capable of being maintained at a steady level without exhausting natural resources or causing ecological damage: *sustainable development.*

sustenance *n* means of maintaining health or life; food and drink.

suture (**soo**-tcher) *n Surgery* a stitch made with catgut or silk thread, to join the edges of a wound together. ▷ **HISTORY** Latin *suere* to sew

SUV sport (*or* sports) utility vehicle.

suzerain *n* **1** a state or sovereign that has some degree of control over a dependent state. **2** (formerly) a person who had power over many people. ▷ **HISTORY** French ▶ **suzerainty** *n*

svelte *adj* attractively or gracefully slim; slender. ▷ **HISTORY** French

SW **1** southwest(ern). **2** short wave.

swab *n* **1** *Med* a small piece of cotton wool used for applying medication or cleansing a wound. ✧ *vb* **swabbing, swabbed 2** to clean or apply medication to (a wound) with a swab. **3** to clean (the deck of a ship) with a mop. ▷ **HISTORY** probably from Middle Dutch *swabbe* mop

swaddle *vb* **-dling, -dled** to wrap (a baby) in swaddling clothes. ▷ **HISTORY** Old English *swæthel* swaddling clothes

swaddling clothes *pl n* long strips of cloth formerly wrapped round a newborn baby.

swag *n* **1** *Slang* stolen property. **2** *Austral & NZ informal* (formerly) a swagman's pack containing personal belongings. ▷ **HISTORY** probably Scandinavian

swagger *vb* **1** to walk or behave in an arrogant manner. ✧ *n* **2** an arrogant walk or manner. ▷ **HISTORY** probably from *swag*

swagger stick *n* a short cane carried by army officers.

swagman *n, pl* **-men** *Austral & NZ informal* a labourer who carries his personal possessions in a pack while looking for work.

Swahili (swah-**heel**-ee) *n* a language of E Africa that is an official language of Kenya and Tanzania. ▷ **HISTORY** Arabic *sawāhil* coasts

swain *n Archaic or poetic* **1** a male lover or admirer. **2** a young man from the countryside. ▷ **HISTORY** Old English *swān* swineherd

swallow¹ *vb* **1** to pass (food, drink, etc.) through the mouth and gullet to the stomach. **2** *Informal* to believe (something) trustingly: *I was supposed to swallow the lie.* **3** not to show: *I believe they should swallow their pride.* **4** to make a gulping movement in the throat, such as when nervous. **5** to put up with (an insult) without answering back. **6 be swallowed up** to be taken into and made a part of something: *the old centre was being swallowed up by new estates.* ✧ *n* **7** the act of swallowing. **8** the amount swallowed at any single time; mouthful. ▷ **HISTORY** Old English *swelgan*

swallow² *n* a small migratory bird with long pointed wings and a forked tail. ▷ **HISTORY** Old English *swealwe*

swallow hole *n esp. Brit* same as **sinkhole**.

swallowtail *n* **1** a butterfly with a long tail-like part on each hind wing. **2** the forked tail of a swallow or similar bird.

swam *vb* the past tense of **swim**.

swami (**swah**-mee) *n* a Hindu religious teacher. ▷ **HISTORY** Hindi *svāmī*

swamp *n* **1** an area of permanently waterlogged land; bog. ✧ *vb* **2** *Naut* to cause (a boat) to sink or fill with water. **3** to overwhelm (a person or place) with more than can be dealt with or accommodated. ▷ **HISTORY** probably from Middle Dutch *somp* ▶ **swampy** *adj*

swan *n* **1** a large, usually white, water bird with a long neck. ✧ *vb* **swanning, swanned 2 swan around** *or* **about** *Informal* to wander about without purpose, but with an air of superiority. ▷ **HISTORY** Old English

swank *Informal* ✧ *vb* **1** to show off or boast. ✧ *n* **2** showing off or boasting. ▷ **HISTORY** origin unknown ▶ **swanky** *adj*

swanndri (**swan**-dry) *n Trademark, NZ* a weatherproof woollen shirt or jacket. Also called: **swannie**

swan song *n* the last public act of a person before retirement or death.

swap *or* **swop** *vb* **swapping, swapped 1** to exchange (something) for something else. ✧ *n* **2** an exchange. ▷ **HISTORY** originally, to shake hands on a bargain, strike: probably imitative

SWAPO *or* **Swapo** South-West Africa People's Organization.

sward *n* a stretch of turf or grass. ▷ **HISTORY** Old English *sweard* skin

swarm[1] *n* **1** a group of bees, led by a queen, that has left the hive to make a new home. **2** a large mass of insects or other small animals. **3** a moving mass of people. ✧ *vb* **4** to move quickly and in large numbers. **5** to be overrun: *the place is swarming with cops.* ▷ **HISTORY** Old English *swearm*

swarm[2] *vb* **swarm up** to climb (a ladder or rope) by gripping it with the hands and feet: *the boys swarmed up the rigging.* ▷ **HISTORY** origin unknown

swarthy *adj* **swarthier, swarthiest** having a dark complexion. ▷ **HISTORY** obsolete *swarty*

swash (**swosh**) *n* the rush of water up a beach following each break of the waves. ▷ **HISTORY** probably imitative

swashbuckling *adj* having the exciting manner or behaviour of pirates, esp. those depicted in films. ▶ **swashbuckler** *n*

> **WORD HISTORY**
> *Swashbuckling* originally meant 'making a noise by "swashing" or banging your sword against your "buckler" or shield'.

swastika *n* **1** a primitive religious symbol in the shape of a Greek cross with the ends of the arms bent at right angles. **2** this symbol with clockwise arms as the emblem of Nazi Germany. ▷ **HISTORY** Sanskrit *svastika*

swat *vb* **swatting, swatted 1** to hit sharply: *swatting the ball with confidence.* ✧ *n* **2** a sharp blow. ▷ **HISTORY** dialect variant of *squat*

swatch *n* **1** a sample of cloth. **2** a collection of such samples. ▷ **HISTORY** origin unknown

swath (**swawth**) *n* same as **swathe**. ▷ **HISTORY** Old English *swæth*

swathe *vb* **swathing, swathed 1** to wrap a bandage, garment, or piece of cloth around (a person or part of the body). ✧ *n* **2** a long strip of cloth wrapped around something. **3** the width of one sweep of a scythe or of the blade of a mowing machine. **4** the strip cut in one sweep. **5** the quantity of cut crops left in one sweep. **6** a long narrow strip of land. ▷ **HISTORY** Old English *swathian*

sway *vb* **1** to swing to and fro: *red poppies swayed in the faint breeze.* **2** to lean to one side and then the other: *entire rows swayed in time.* **3** to be unable to decide between two or more opinions. **4** to influence (someone) in his or her opinion or judgment. ✧ *n* **5** power or influence. **6** a swinging or leaning movement. **7 hold sway** to have power or influence. ▷ **HISTORY** probably from Old Norse *sveigja* to bend

swear *vb* **swearing, swore, sworn 1** to use words considered obscene or blasphemous. **2** to promise solemnly on oath; vow: *Sally and Peter swore to love and cherish each other.* **3 swear by** to have complete confidence in (something). **4** to state (something) earnestly: *I swear he was all right.* **5** to give evidence on oath in a law court. ▷ **HISTORY** Old English *swerian*

swear in *vb* to make (someone) take an oath when taking up an official position or entering the witness box to give evidence in court: *a new federal president was sworn in.*

swearword *n* a word considered rude or blasphemous.

sweat *n* **1** the salty liquid that comes out of the skin's pores during strenuous activity in excessive heat or when afraid. **2** the state or condition of sweating: *he worked up a sweat.* **3** *Slang* hard work or effort: *climbing to the crest of Ward Hill was a sweat.* **4 in a sweat** *Informal* in a state of worry. **5 no sweat** *Slang* no problem. ✧ *vb* **sweating, sweat** *or* **sweated 6** to have sweat come through the skin's pores, as a result of strenuous activity, excessive heat, nervousness, or fear. **7** *Informal* to suffer anxiety or distress. **8 sweat blood** *Informal* **a** to work very hard. **b** to be filled with anxiety. ✧ See also **sweats**. ▷ **HISTORY** Old English *swǣtan* ▶ **sweaty** *adj*

sweatband *n* a piece of cloth tied around the forehead or around the wrist to absorb sweat during strenuous physical activity.

sweater *n* a warm knitted piece of clothing covering the upper part of the body.

sweat out *vb* **sweat it out** *Informal* to endure an unpleasant situation for a time, hoping for an improvement.

sweats *pl n* sweatshirts and sweat suit trousers collectively.

sweatshirt *n* a long-sleeved casual top made of knitted cotton or cotton mixture.

sweatshop *n* a workshop where employees work long hours in poor conditions for low pay.

A B C D E F G H I J K L M N O P Q R S T U V W X Y Z

swede *n* a round root vegetable with a purplish-brown skin and yellow flesh. ▷ **HISTORY** introduced from Sweden in the 18th century

Swede *n* a person from Sweden.

Swedish *adj* **1** of Sweden. ✧ *n* **2** the language of Sweden.

sweep *vb* **sweeping, swept 1** to clean (a floor or chimney) with a brush. **2** (often foll. by *up*) to remove or collect (dirt or rubbish) with a brush. **3** to move smoothly and quickly: *the car swept into the drive.* **4** to spread rapidly across or through (a place): *the wave of democracy that had swept through Eastern Europe.* **5** to move in a proud and majestic fashion: *the boss himself swept into the hall.* **6** to direct (one's eyes, line of fire, etc.) over (a place or target). **7 sweep away** *or* **off** to overwhelm (someone) emotionally: *I've been swept away by my fears.* **8** to brush or lightly touch (a surface): *the dress swept along the ground.* **9** to clear away or get rid of (something) suddenly or forcefully: *these doubts were quickly swept aside; bridges have been swept away by the floods.* **10** to stretch out gracefully or majestically, esp. in a wide circle: *the hills swept down into the green valley.* **11** to win overwhelmingly in an election: *the umbrella party which swept these elections.* **12 sweep the board** to win every event or prize in a contest. ✧ *n* **13** the act or an instance of sweeping. **14** a swift or steady movement: *the wide sweep of the shoulders.* **15** a wide expanse: *the whole sweep of the bay.* **16** any curving line or contour, such as a driveway. **17** short for **sweepstake. 18** *Chiefly Brit* same as **chimney sweep. 19 make a clean sweep** to win an overwhelming victory. ▷ **HISTORY** Middle English *swepen*

sweeper *n* **1** a device used to sweep carpets, consisting of a long handle attached to a revolving brush. **2** *Soccer* a defensive player usually positioned in front of the goalkeeper.

sweeping *adj* **1** affecting many people to a great extent: *sweeping financial reforms.* **2** (of a statement) making general assumptions about an issue without considering the details. **3** decisive or overwhelming: *to suffer sweeping losses.* **4** taking in a wide area: *a sweeping view of the area.*

sweepstake *or esp US* **sweepstakes** *n* **1** a lottery in which the stakes of the participants make up the prize. **2** a horse race involving such a lottery. ▷ **HISTORY** originally referring to someone who *sweeps* or takes all the stakes in a game

sweet *adj* **1** tasting of or like sugar. **2** kind and charming: *that was really sweet of you.* **3** attractive and delightful: *a sweet child.* **4** (of a sound) pleasant and tuneful: *sweet music.* **5** (of wine) having a high sugar content; not dry. **6** fresh, clear, and clean: *sweet water; sweet air.* **7 sweet on someone** fond of or infatuated with someone. ✧ *n* **8** *Brit, Austral & NZ* a shaped piece of confectionery consisting mainly of sugar. **9** *Brit, Austral & NZ* a dessert. ▷ **HISTORY** Old English *swēte* ▸ **sweetly** *adv* ▸ **sweetness** *n*

sweetbread *n* the meat obtained from the pancreas of a calf or lamb.

sweetbrier *n* a wild rose with sweet-smelling leaves and pink flowers.

sweet corn *n* **1** a kind of maize with sweet yellow kernels, eaten as a vegetable when young. **2** the sweet kernels removed from the maize cob, cooked as a vegetable.

sweeten *vb* **1** to make (food or drink) sweet or sweeter. **2** to be nice to (someone) in order to ensure cooperation. **3** to make (an offer or a proposal) more acceptable.

sweetener *n* **1** a sweetening agent that does not contain sugar. **2** *Brit, Austral & NZ slang* an inducement offered to someone in order to persuade them to accept an offer or business deal.

sweetheart *n* **1** an affectionate name to call someone. **2** *Old-fashioned* one's boyfriend or girlfriend. **3** *Informal* a lovable or generous person.

sweetie *n Informal* **1** an affectionate name to call someone. **2** *Brit & NZ* same as **sweet** (sense 8). **3** *Chiefly Brit* a lovable or generous person.

sweetmeat *n Old-fashioned* a small delicacy preserved in sugar.

sweet pea *n* a climbing plant with sweet-smelling pastel-coloured flowers.

sweet pepper *n* the large bell-shaped fruit of the pepper plant, which is eaten unripe (**green pepper**) or ripe (**red pepper**) as a vegetable.

sweet potato *n* a root vegetable, grown in the tropics, with pinkish-brown skin and yellow flesh.

sweet spot *n Sport* the centre area of a racquet, club, etc., from which the cleanest shots are made.

sweet-talk *Informal* ✧ *vb* **1** to persuade (someone) by flattery: *I thought I could sweet-talk you into teaching me.* ✧ *n* **sweet talk 2** insincere flattery intended to persuade.

sweet tooth *n* a strong liking for sweet foods.

sweet william *n* a garden plant with clusters of white, pink, red, or purple flowers.

swell *vb* **swelling, swelled; swollen** *or* **swelled 1** (of a part of the body) to grow in size as a result of injury or infection: *his face swelled and became pale.* **2** to increase in size as a result of being filled with air or liquid: *a balloon swells if you force in more air.* **3** to grow or cause (something) to grow in size, numbers, amount, or degree: *Israel's population is swelling.* **4** (of an emotion) to become more intense: *his anger swelled within him.* **5** (of the seas) to rise in waves. **6** (of a sound) to become gradually louder and then die away. ✧ *n* **7** the waving movement of the surface of the open sea. **8** an increase in size, numbers, amount, or degree. **9** a bulge. **10** *Old-fashioned, informal* a person who is wealthy, upper class, and fashionably dressed. **11** *Music* an increase in sound followed by an immediate dying away. ✧ *adj* **12** *Slang, chiefly US* excellent or fine. ▷ **HISTORY** Old English *swellan*

swelling *n* an enlargement of a part of the body as the result of injury or infection.

swelter *vb* **1** to feel uncomfortable under extreme heat. ✧ *n* **2** a hot and uncomfortable condition: *they left the city swelter for the beach.* ▷ **HISTORY** Old English *sweltan* to die

sweltering *adj* uncomfortably hot: *a sweltering summer.*

swept *vb* the past of **sweep**.

swerve *vb* **swerving, swerved 1** to turn aside from a course sharply or suddenly. ✧ *n* **2** the act of swerving. ▷ **HISTORY** Old English *sweorfan* to scour

swift *adj* **1** moving or able to move quickly; fast. **2** happening or performed quickly or suddenly: *a swift glance this way.* **3 swift to** prompt to (do something): *swift to retaliate.* ✧ *n* **4** a small fast-flying insect-eating bird with long wings. ▷ **HISTORY** Old English ▶ **swiftly** *adv* ▶ **swiftness** *n*

swig *Informal* ✧ *n* **1** a large swallow or deep drink, esp. from a bottle. ✧ *vb* **swigging, swigged 2** to drink (some liquid) in large swallows, esp. from a bottle. ▷ **HISTORY** origin unknown

swill *vb* **1** to drink large quantities of (an alcoholic drink). **2** (often foll. by *out*) *Chiefly Brit & NZ* to rinse (something) in large amounts of water. ✧ *n* **3** a liquid mixture containing waste food, fed to pigs. **4** a deep drink, esp. of beer. ▷ **HISTORY** Old English *swilian* to wash out

swim *vb* **swimming, swam, swum 1** to move along in water by movements of the arms and legs, or (in the case of fish) tail and fins. **2** to cover (a stretch of water) in this way: *the first person to swim the Atlantic.* **3** to float on a liquid: *flies swimming on the milk.* **4** to be affected by dizziness: *his head was swimming.* **5** (of the objects in someone's vision) to appear to spin or move around: *the faces of the nurses swam around her.* **6** (often foll. by *in* or *with*) to be covered or flooded with liquid: *a steak swimming in gravy.* ✧ *n* **7** the act, an instance, or a period of swimming. **8 in the swim** *Informal* fashionable or active in social or political activities. ▷ **HISTORY** Old English *swimman* ▶ **swimmer** *n* ▶ **swimming** *n*

swimming bath *n* an indoor swimming pool.

swimming costume *or* **bathing costume** *n Chiefly Brit, Austral & NZ* same as **swimsuit**.

swimmingly *adv* successfully, effortlessly, or well: *everything went swimmingly.*

swimming pool *n* a large hole in the ground, tiled and filled with water for swimming in.

swimsuit *n* a woman's swimming garment that leaves the arms and legs bare.

swindle *vb* **-dling, -dled 1** to cheat (someone) out of money. **2** to obtain (money) from someone by fraud. ✧ *n* **3** an instance of cheating someone out of money. ▷ **HISTORY** German *schwindeln* ▶ **swindler** *n*

swine *n* **1** a mean or unpleasant person. **2** (*pl* **swine**) same as **pig**. ▷ **HISTORY** Old English *swīn* ▶ **swinish** *adj*

swing *vb* **swinging, swung 1** to move backwards and forwards; sway. **2** to pivot or cause (something) to pivot from a fixed point such as a hinge: *the door swung open.* **3** to move in a sweeping curve: *the headlights swung along the street.* **4** to alter one's opinion or mood suddenly. **5** to hang so as to be able to turn freely. **6** *Old-fashioned, slang* to be hanged: *you'll swing for this!* **7** *Informal* to manipulate or influence successfully: *it may help to swing the election.* **8** (often foll. by *at*) to hit out with a sweeping motion. **9** *Old-fashioned* to play (music) in the style of swing. **10** *Old-fashioned, slang* to be lively and modern. ✧ *n* **11** the act of swinging. **12** a sweeping stroke or punch. **13** a seat hanging from two chains or ropes on which a person may swing back and forth. **14** popular dance music played by big bands in the 1930s and 1940s. **15** *Informal* the normal pace at which an activity, such as work, happens: *I'm into the swing of things now.* **16** a sudden or extreme change, for example in some business activity or voting pattern. **17 go with a swing** to go well; be successful. **18 in full swing** at the height of activity. ▷ **HISTORY** Old English *swingan*

swingboat *n* a boat-shaped carriage for swinging in at a fairground.

swing bridge *n* a bridge that can be swung open to let ships pass through.

swingeing (**swin**-jing) *adj Chiefly Brit* severe or causing hardship: *swingeing spending cuts.*

swipe *vb* **swiping, swiped 1** *Informal* to try to hit (someone or something) with a sweeping blow: *he swiped at a boy who ran forward.* **2** *Slang* to steal (something). **3** to pass (a credit or debit card) through a machine which electronically interprets the information stored in the card. ✧ *n* **4** *Informal* a hard blow. ▷ **HISTORY** origin unknown

swirl *vb* **1** to turn round and round with a twisting motion. ✧ *n* **2** a twisting or spinning motion. **3** a twisting shape. ▷ **HISTORY** probably from Dutch *zwirrelen* ▶ **swirling** *adj*

swish *vb* **1** to move with or cause (something) to make a whistling or hissing sound. ✧ *n* **2** a hissing or rustling sound or movement: *she turned with a swish of her skirt.* ✧ *adj* **3** *Informal, chiefly Brit, Austral & NZ* smart and fashionable. ▷ **HISTORY** imitative

Swiss *adj* **1** of Switzerland. ✧ *n, pl* **Swiss 2** a person from Switzerland.

swiss roll *n* a sponge cake spread with jam or cream and rolled up.

switch *n* **1** a device for opening or closing an electric circuit. **2** a sudden quick change. **3** an exchange or swap. **4** a flexible rod or twig, used for punishment. **5** *US & Canad* a pair of movable rails for diverting moving trains from one track to another. ✧ *vb* **6** to change quickly and suddenly. **7** to exchange (places) or swap (something for something else). **8** *Chiefly US & Canad* to transfer (rolling stock) from one railway track to another. ▷ **HISTORY** probably from Middle Dutch *swijch* twig

switchback *n* a steep mountain road, railway, or track which rises and falls sharply many times.

switchboard *n* the place in a telephone exchange or office building where telephone calls are connected.

swivel *vb* **-elling, -elled** *or US* **-eling, -eled 1** to turn on or swing round on a central point. ✧ *n* **2** a coupling device which allows an attached object to turn freely. ▷ **HISTORY** Old English *swīfan* to turn

swizz *n Brit, NZ & S African informal* a swindle or disappointment. ▷ **HISTORY** origin unknown

swizzle stick *n* a small stick used to stir cocktails.

swollen *vb* **1** a past participle of **swell**. ✧ *adj* **2** enlarged by swelling.

swoon *vb* **1** *Literary* to faint because of shock or strong emotion. **2** to be deeply affected by passion for (someone): *you've swooned over a string of rotten men.* ✧ *n* **3** *Literary* a faint. ▷ **HISTORY** Old English *geswōgen* insensible ▶ **swooning** *adj*

swoop *vb* **1** (usually foll. by *down*) to move quickly through the air in a downward curve: *an owl swooped down from its perch.* **2** (usually foll. by *on*) to move suddenly and quickly towards (a place) in order to attack, arrest, or question the people inside: *nine police cars and vans swooped on the premises.* ✧ *n* **3** the act of swooping. ▷ **HISTORY** Old English *swāpan* to sweep

swop *vb* **swopping, swopped**, *n* same as **swap**.

sword *n* **1** a weapon with a long sharp blade and a short handle. **2 the sword a** military power. **b** death; destruction: *we will put them to the sword.* **3 cross swords** to have a disagreement with someone. ▷ **HISTORY** Old English *sweord*

sword dance *n* a dance in which the performer dances over swords on the ground.

swordfish *n, pl* **-fish** *or* **-fishes** a large fish with a very long upper jaw that resembles a sword.

swordsman *n, pl* **-men** a person who is skilled in the use of a sword. ▶ **swordsmanship** *n*

swore *vb* the past tense of **swear**.

sworn *vb* **1** the past participle of **swear**. ✧ *adj* **2** bound by or as if by an oath: *a sworn enemy.*

swot[1] *Informal* ✧ *vb* **swotting, swotted 1** (often foll. by *up*) to study (a subject) very hard, esp. for an exam; cram. ✧ *n* **2** a person who works or studies hard. ▷ **HISTORY** variant of *sweat*

swot[2] *vb* **swotting, swotted**, *n* same as **swat**.

swum *vb* the past participle of **swim**.

swung *vb* the past of **swing**.

sybarite (**sib**-bar-ite) *n* **1** a lover of luxury and pleasure. ✧ *adj* **2** luxurious or sensuous. ▷ **HISTORY** after *Sybaris,* ancient Greek colony in S Italy, famed for its luxury ▶ **sybaritic** *adj*

sycamore *n* **1** a tree with five-pointed leaves and two-winged fruits. **2** *US & Canad* an American plane tree. ▷ **HISTORY** Latin *sycomorus*

sycophant *n* a person who uses flattery to win favour from people with power or influence. ▷ **HISTORY** Greek *sukophantēs* ▶ **sycophancy** *n* ▶ **sycophantic** *adj*

syllabic *adj* of or relating to syllables.

syllabify *vb* **-fies, -fying, -fied** to divide (a word) into syllables. ▶ **syllabification** *n*

syllable *n* **1** a part of a word which is pronounced as a unit, which contains a single vowel sound, and which may or may not contain consonants: for example, 'paper' has two syllables. **2** the least mention: *without a syllable about what went on.* **3 in words of one syllable** simply and plainly. ▷ **HISTORY** Greek *sullabē*

syllabub *n Brit & Austral* a dessert made from milk or cream beaten with sugar, wine, and lemon juice. ▷ **HISTORY** origin unknown

syllabus (**sill**-lab-buss) *n, pl* **-buses** *or* **-bi** (-bye) **a** the subjects studied for a particular course. **b** a list of these subjects. ▷ **HISTORY** Late Latin

syllogism *n* a form of reasoning consisting of two premises and a conclusion, for example *some temples are in ruins; all ruins are fascinating; so some temples are fascinating.* ▷ **HISTORY** Greek *sullogismos* ▶ **syllogistic** *adj*

sylph *n* **1** a slender graceful girl or young woman. **2** an imaginary creature believed to live in the air. ▷ **HISTORY** New Latin *sylphus* ▶ **sylphlike** *adj*

sylvan *or* **silvan** *adj Chiefly poetic* of or consisting of woods or forests. ▷ **HISTORY** Latin *silva* forest

symbiosis *n* **1** *Biol* a close association of two different animal or plant species living together to their mutual benefit. **2** a similar relationship between different individuals or groups: *the symbiosis of the coal and railway industries.* ▷ **HISTORY** Greek: a living together ▶ **symbiotic** *adj*

symbol *n* **1** something that represents or stands for something else, usually an object used to represent something abstract. **2** a letter, figure, or sign used in mathematics, music, etc., to represent a quantity, operation, function, etc. ▷ **HISTORY** Greek *sumbolon* sign

symbolic *adj* **1** of or relating to a symbol or symbols. **2** being a symbol of something. ▶ **symbolically** *adv*

symbolism *n* **1** the representation of something by the use of symbols. **2** an art movement involving the use of symbols to express mystical or abstract ideas. ▶ **symbolist** *adj, n*

symbolize *or* **-ise** *vb* **-izing, -ized** *or* **-ising, -ised** **1** to be a symbol of (something). **2** to represent with a symbol. ▶ **symbolization** *or* **-isation** *n*

symmetry *n, pl* **-tries 1** the state of having two halves that are mirror images of each other. **2** beauty resulting from a balanced arrangement of parts. ▷ **HISTORY** Greek *summetria* proportion ▶ **symmetrical** *adj* ▶ **symmetrically** *adv*

sympathetic *adj* **1** feeling or showing kindness and understanding. **2** (of a person) likeable and appealing: *the film's only sympathetic character.* **3 sympathetic to** showing agreement with or willing to lend support to: *sympathetic to the movement.* ▶ **sympathetically** *adv*

sympathize *or* **-thise** *vb* **-thizing, -thized** *or* **-thising, -thised sympathize with a** to feel or express sympathy for: *I sympathized with this fear.* **b** to agree with or support: *Pitt sympathized with these objectives.* ▶ **sympathizer** *or* **-thiser** *n*

sympathy *n, pl* **-thies 1** (often foll. by *for*) understanding of other people's problems; compassion. **2 sympathy with** agreement with someone's feelings or interests: *we have every sympathy with how she felt.* **3** (*often pl*) feelings of loyalty or support for an idea or a cause: *was this where her sympathies lay?* **4** mutual affection or understanding between two people or a person and an animal. ▷ **HISTORY** Greek *sympatheia*

symphony *n, pl* **-nies 1** a large-scale orchestral composition with several movements. **2** an orchestral movement in a vocal work such as an oratorio. **3** short for **symphony orchestra**.

4 anything that has a pleasing arrangement of colours or shapes: *the garden was a symphony of coloured bunting.* ▷ **HISTORY** Greek *sun-* together + *phōnē* sound ▶ **symphonic** *adj*

symphony orchestra *n Music* a large orchestra that performs symphonies.

symposium *n, pl* **-sia** *or* **-siums 1** a conference at which experts or academics discuss a particular subject. **2** a collection of essays on a particular subject. ▷ **HISTORY** Greek *sumposion* a drinking party

symptom *n* **1** *Med* a sign indicating the presence of an illness or disease. **2** anything that is taken as an indication that something is wrong: *a growing symptom of grave social injustice.* ▷ **HISTORY** Greek *sumptōma* chance ▶ **symptomatic** *adj*

synagogue *n* a building for Jewish religious services and religious instruction. ▷ **HISTORY** Greek *sunagōgē* a gathering

synapse *n Anat* a gap where nerve impulses pass between two nerve cells. ▷ **HISTORY** Greek *sunapsis* junction

sync *or* **synch** *Films, television, computers informal* ✧ *vb* **1** to synchronize. ✧ *n* **2** synchronization: *the film and sound are in sync.*

synchromesh *adj* **1** (of a gearbox) having a system of clutches that synchronizes the speeds of the gearwheels before they engage. ✧ *n* **2** a gear system having these features. ▷ **HISTORY** *synchronized mesh*

synchronism *n* the quality or condition of occurrence at the same time or rate.

synchronize *or* **-nise** *vb* **-nizing, -nized** *or* **-nising, -nised 1** (of two or more people) to perform (an action) at the same time: *a synchronized withdrawal of Allied forces.* **2** to cause (two or more clocks or watches) to show the same time. **3** *Films* to match (the soundtrack and the action of a film) precisely. ▶ **synchronization** *or* **-nisation** *n*

synchronous *adj* occurring at the same time and rate. ▷ **HISTORY** Greek *sun-* together + *khronos* time ▶ **synchrony** *n*

synclinal *adj Geol* (of folds, structures) dipping towards each other.

syncline *n Geol* a downward slope of stratified rock in which the layers dip towards each other from either side.

syncopate *vb* **-pating, -pated** *Music* to stress the weak beats in (a rhythm or a piece of music) instead of the strong beats. ▷ **HISTORY** Medieval Latin *syncopare* to omit a letter or syllable ▶ **syncopation** *n*

syncope (**sing**-kop-ee) *n* **1** *Med* a faint. **2** *Linguistics* the omission of sounds or letters from the middle of a word, as in *ne'er* for *never.* ▷ **HISTORY** Greek *sunkopē* a cutting off

syndic *n Brit* a business or legal agent of some universities or other institutions. ▷ **HISTORY** Greek *sundikos* defendant's advocate

syndicalism *n* a movement advocating seizure of economic and political power by the industrial working class by means of industrial action, esp. general strikes. ▶ **syndicalist** *n*

syndicate *n* **1** a group of people or firms organized to undertake a joint project. **2** an association of individuals who control organized crime. **3** a news agency that sells articles and photographs to a number of newspapers for simultaneous publication. ✧ *vb* **-cating, -cated 4** to sell (articles and photographs) to several newspapers for simultaneous publication. **5** to form a syndicate of (people). ▷ **HISTORY** Old French *syndicat* ▶ **syndication** *n*

syndrome *n* **1** *Med* a combination of signs and symptoms that indicate a particular disease. **2** a set of characteristics indicating the existence of a particular condition or problem. ▷ **HISTORY** Greek *sundromē,* literally: a running together

synecdoche (sin-**neck**-dock-ee) *n* a figure of speech in which a part is substituted for a whole or a whole for a part, as in *50 head of cattle* for *50 cows.* ▷ **HISTORY** Greek *sunekdokhē*

synergy *n* the potential ability for individuals or groups to be more successful working together than on their own. ▷ **HISTORY** Greek *sunergos*

synod *n* a special church council which meets regularly to discuss church affairs. ▷ **HISTORY** Greek *sunodos*

synonym *n* a word that means the same as another word, such as *bucket* and *pail.* ▷ **HISTORY** Greek *sun-* together + *onoma* name

synonymous *adj* **synonymous with a** having the same meaning. **b** closely associated with: *a family whose name had been synonymous with fine jewellery.*

synopsis (sin-**op**-siss) *n, pl* **-ses** (-seez) a brief review or outline of a subject; summary: *they have sent me a monthly synopsis of the plot.* ▷ **HISTORY** Greek *sunopsis*

synoptic *adj* **1** of or relating to a synopsis. **2** *Bible* of or relating to the Gospels of Matthew, Mark, and Luke. ▶ **synoptically** *adv*

synoptic chart *n Meteorol* a weather chart showing the distribution of meteorological conditions over a wide area at a given time.

synovia (sine-**oh**-vee-a) *n Med* a clear thick fluid that lubricates the body joints. ▷ **HISTORY** New Latin ▶ **synovial** *adj*

syntax *n* the grammatical rules of a language and the way in which words are arranged to form phrases and sentences. ▷ **HISTORY** Greek *suntassein* to put in order ▶ **syntactic** *or* **syntactical** *adj*

synthesis (**sinth**-iss-siss) *n, pl* **-ses** (-seez) **1** the process of combining objects or ideas into a complex whole. **2** the combination produced by such a process. **3** *Chem* the process of producing a compound by one or more chemical reactions, usually from simpler starting materials. ▷ **HISTORY** Greek *sunthesis*

synthesize *or* **-sise** *vb* **-sizing, -sized** *or* **-sising, -sised 1** to combine (objects or ideas) into a complex whole. **2** to produce (a compound) by synthesis.

synthesizer *n* a keyboard instrument in which speech, music, or other sounds are produced electronically.

synthetic *adj* **1** (of a substance or material) made artificially by chemical reaction. **2** not sincere or genuine: *synthetic compassion.* ✧ *n* **3** a synthetic substance or material. ▷ HISTORY Greek *sunthetikos* expert in putting together ▶ **synthetically** *adv*

syphilis *n* a sexually transmitted disease that causes sores on the genitals and eventually on other parts of the body. ▷ HISTORY *Syphilis,* hero of a 16th-century Latin poem ▶ **syphilitic** *adj*

syphon *n, vb* same as **siphon**.

Syrian *adj* **1** of Syria. ✧ *n* **2** a person from Syria.

syringa *n* same as **mock orange lilac**. ▷ HISTORY Greek *surinx* tube (its hollow stems were used for pipes)

syringe *n* **1** *Med* a device used for withdrawing or injecting fluids, consisting of a hollow cylinder of glass or plastic, a tightly fitting piston, and a hollow needle. ✧ *vb* **-ringing, -ringed 2** to wash out, inject, or spray with a syringe: *a harmless blue dye is syringed into the uterus.* ▷ HISTORY Greek *surinx* tube

syrup *n* **1** a solution of sugar dissolved in water and often flavoured with fruit juice: used for sweetening fruit, etc. **2** a thick sweet liquid food made from sugar or molasses: *maple syrup.* **3** a liquid medicine containing a sugar solution: *cough syrup.* ▷ HISTORY Arabic *sharāb* a drink

syrupy *adj* **1** (of a liquid) thick or sweet. **2** excessively sentimental: *a soundtrack of syrupy violins.*

system *n* **1** a method or set of methods for doing or organizing something: *a new system of production or distribution.* **2** orderliness or routine; an ordered manner: *there is no system in his work.* **3** the manner in which an institution or aspect of society has been arranged: *the Scottish legal system.* **4 the system** the government and state regarded as exploiting, restricting, and repressing individuals. **5** the manner in which the parts of something fit or function together; structure: *disruption of the earth's weather system.* **6** any scheme or set of rules used to classify, explain, or calculate: *the Newtonian system of physics.* **7** a network of communications, transportation, or distribution. **8** *Biol* an animal considered as a whole. **9** *Biol* a set of organs or structures that together perform some function: *the immune system.* **10** one's physical or mental constitution: *the intrusion of the ME virus into my system; to get the hate out of my system.* **11** an assembly of electronic or mechanical parts forming a self-contained unit: *an alarm system.* ▷ HISTORY Greek *sustēma*

systematic *adj* following a fixed plan and done in an efficient and methodical way: *a systematic approach to teaching.* ▶ **systematically** *adv*

systematize *or* **-tise** *vb* **-tizing, -tized** *or* **-tising, -tised** to arrange (information) in a system. ▶ **systematization** *or* **-tisation** *n*

systemic *adj Biol* (of a poison, disease, etc.) affecting the entire animal or body. ▶ **systemically** *adv*

systems analysis *n* the analysis of the requirements of a task and the expression of these in a form that enables a computer to perform the task. ▶ **systems analyst** *n*

systole (**siss**-tol-ee) *n Physiol* contraction of the heart, during which blood is pumped into the arteries. ▷ HISTORY Greek *sustolē* ▶ **systolic** *adj*

T t

t *or* **T** *n, pl* **t's, T's** *or* **Ts 1** the 20th letter of the English alphabet. **2 to a T a** in every detail: *that's her to a T.* **b** perfectly: *that dress suits you to a T.*
t tonne(s).
T 1 *Chem* tritium. **2** tera-.
t. 1 temperature. **2** ton(s).
ta *interj Brit, Austral & NZ informal* thank you. ▷ HISTORY imitative of baby talk
Ta *Chem* tantalum.
TA (in Britain) Territorial Army.
tab¹ *n* **1** a small flap of material, esp. one on a garment for decoration or for fastening to a button. **2** any similar flap, such as a piece of paper attached to a file for identification. **3** *Chiefly US & Canad* a bill, esp. for a meal or drinks. **4 keep tabs on** *Informal* to keep a watchful eye on. ▷ HISTORY origin unknown
tab² *n* short for **tabulator**.
TAB (in New Zealand) Totalisator Agency Board.
tabard *n* **1** a sleeveless jacket, esp. one worn by a medieval knight over his armour. **2** a short coat bearing the coat of arms of the sovereign, worn by a herald. ▷ HISTORY Old French *tabart*
Tabasco *n Trademark* a very hot red sauce made from peppers.
tabby *n, pl* **-bies 1** a cat whose fur has dark stripes or wavy markings on a lighter background. ✧ *adj* **2** having dark stripes or wavy markings on a lighter background. ▷ HISTORY from the girl's name *Tabitha,* influenced by *tabby,* old kind of striped silk
tabernacle *n* **1 the Tabernacle** *Bible* the portable sanctuary in which the ancient Israelites carried the Ark of the Covenant. **2** any place of Christian worship that is not called a church. **3** *RC Church* a receptacle in which the Blessed Sacrament is kept. ▷ HISTORY Latin *tabernaculum* a tent
tabla *n, pl* **-bla** *or* **-blas** one of a pair of Indian drums played with the hands. ▷ HISTORY Hindi, from Arabic: drum
table *n* **1** a piece of furniture consisting of a flat top supported by legs: *a coffee table.* **2** a set of facts or figures arranged in rows and columns: *a league table.* **3** a group of people sitting round a table for a meal, game, etc.: *the whole table laughed.* **4** *Formal* the food provided at a meal or in a particular house: *he keeps a good table.* **5 turn the tables** to cause a complete reversal of circumstances. ✧ *vb* **-bling, -bled 6** *Brit & Austral* to submit (a motion) for discussion by a meeting. **7** *US* to suspend discussion of (a proposal) indefinitely. ▷ HISTORY Latin *tabula* a writing tablet
tableau (**tab**-loh) *n, pl* **-leaux** (-loh) a silent motionless group of people arranged to represent a scene from history, legend, or literature. ▷ HISTORY French
tablecloth *n* a cloth for covering the top of a table, esp. during meals.
table d'hôte (**tah**-bla **dote**) *adj* **1** (of a meal) consisting of a set number of courses with a limited choice of dishes offered at a fixed price. ✧ *n, pl* **tables d'hôte** (**tah**-bla **dote**) **2** a table d'hôte meal or menu. ▷ HISTORY French: the host's table
tableland *n* a flat area of high ground; plateau.
tablespoon *n* **1** a spoon, larger than a dessertspoon, used for serving food. **2** Also called: **tablespoonful** the amount contained in such a spoon. **3** a unit of capacity used in cooking, equal to half a fluid ounce.
tablet *n* **1** a pill consisting of a compressed medicinal substance. **2** a flattish cake of some substance, such as soap. **3** a slab of stone, wood, etc., used for writing on before the invention of paper. **4** an inscribed piece of stone, wood, etc., that is fixed to a wall as a memorial: *a tablet in memory of those who died.* ▷ HISTORY Latin *tabula* a board
table tennis *n* a game resembling a miniature form of tennis played on a table with bats and a small light ball.
tabloid *n* a newspaper with fairly small pages, usually with many photographs and a concise and often sensational style. ▷ HISTORY from *tablet*
taboo *or* **tabu** *n, pl* **-boos** *or* **-bus 1** a restriction or prohibition resulting from social or other conventions. **2** a ritual prohibition, esp. of something that is considered holy or unclean. ✧ *adj* **3** forbidden or disapproved-of: *a taboo subject.* ▷ HISTORY Tongan *tapu*
tabor *n* a small drum used esp. in the Middle Ages, struck with one hand while the other held a pipe. ▷ HISTORY Old French *tabour*
tabular *adj* arranged in parallel columns so as to form a table. ▷ HISTORY Latin *tabula* a board
tabulate *vb* **-lating, -lated** to arrange (information) in rows and columns. ▶ **tabulation** *n*
tabulator *n* a key on a typewriter or word processor that sets stops so that data can be arranged and presented in columns.
tachograph *n* a device that measures the speed of a vehicle and the distance that it covers, and produces a record (**tachogram**) of its readings. ▷ HISTORY Greek *takhos* speed + -GRAPH
tachometer *n* a device for measuring speed, esp. that of a revolving shaft. ▷ HISTORY Greek *takhos* speed + -METER
tacit (**tass**-it) *adj* understood or implied without actually being stated: *tacit support.* ▷ HISTORY Latin *tacitus* silent
taciturn (**tass**-it-turn) *adj* habitually silent, reserved, or uncommunicative. ▷ HISTORY Latin *tacere* to be silent ▶ **taciturnity** *n*
tack¹ *n* **1** a short sharp-pointed nail with a large flat head. **2** *Brit & NZ* a long loose temporary stitch used in dressmaking. ✧ *vb* **3** to fasten (something) with a tack or tacks: *the carpet needs to be tacked down.* **4** *Brit & NZ* to sew (something) with long loose temporary stitches. ✧ See also **tack on**. ▷ HISTORY Middle English *tak* fastening, nail
tack² *n* **1** *Naut* the course of a boat sailing obliquely into the wind, expressed in terms of the

side of the boat against which the wind is blowing: *on the port tack.* **2** a course of action or a policy: *telling her to get off my back hadn't worked, so I took a different tack.* ✧ *vb* **3** *Naut* to steer (a boat) on a zigzag course, so as to make progress against the wind. ▷ HISTORY from *tack* rope used to secure a sail

tack³ *n* riding harness for horses, including saddles and bridles. ▷ HISTORY from *tackle*

tackies *or* **takkies** *pl n, sing* **tacky** *S African informal* tennis shoes or plimsolls. ▷ HISTORY origin unknown

tackle *vb* **-ling, -led 1** to deal with (a problem or task) in a determined way. **2** to confront (someone) about something: *I intend to tackle both management and union on this issue.* **3** to attack and fight (a person or animal). **4** *Sport* to attempt to get the ball away from (an opposing player). ✧ *n* **5** *Sport* an attempt to get the ball away from an opposing player. **6** the equipment required for a particular sport or occupation: *fishing tackle.* **7** a set of ropes and pulleys for lifting heavy weights. **8** *Naut* the ropes and other rigging aboard a ship. ▷ HISTORY Middle English

tack on *vb* to attach or add (something) to something that is already complete: *an elegant mansion with a modern extension tacked on at the back.*

tacky¹ *adj* **tackier, tackiest** slightly sticky. ▷ HISTORY earlier *tack* stickiness ▶ **tackiness** *n*

tacky² *adj* **tackier, tackiest** *Informal* **1** vulgar and tasteless: *tacky commercialism.* **2** shabby or shoddy: *tacky streets.* ▷ HISTORY origin unknown ▶ **tackiness** *n*

taco (**tah**-koh) *n, pl* **tacos** *Mexican cookery* a tortilla folded into a roll with a filling and usually fried. ▷ HISTORY from Mexican Spanish, from Spanish: literally, a bite to eat

tact *n* **1** a sense of the best and most considerate way to deal with people so as not to upset them. **2** skill in handling difficult situations. ▷ HISTORY Latin *tactus* a touching ▶ **tactful** *adj* ▶ **tactfully** *adv* ▶ **tactless** *adj* ▶ **tactlessly** *adv* ▶ **tactlessness** *n*

tactic *n* a move or method used to achieve an aim or task: *he has perfected dissent as a tactic to further his career.* See also **tactics**.

tactical *adj* **1** of or employing tactics: *a tactical advantage.* **2** (of missiles, bombing, etc.) for use in limited military operations. ▶ **tactically** *adv*

tactical voting *n* (in an election) the practice of voting for a candidate or party one would not normally support in an attempt to prevent an even less acceptable candidate or party being elected.

tactics *n* **1** *Mil* the science of the detailed direction of forces in battle to achieve an aim or task. ✧ *pl n* **2** the plans and methods used to achieve a particular short-term aim. ▷ HISTORY Greek *tassein* to arrange ▶ **tactician** *n*

tactile *adj* of or having a sense of touch: *the tactile sense.* ▷ HISTORY Latin *tactilis*

tadpole *n* the aquatic larva of a frog or toad, which develops from a limbless tailed form with external gills into a form with internal gills, limbs, and a reduced tail. ▷ HISTORY Middle English *tadde* toad + *pol* head

TAFE (in Australia) Technical and Further Education.

taffeta *n* a thin shiny silk or rayon fabric used esp. for women's clothes. ▷ HISTORY Persian *tāftah* spun

taffrail *n Naut* a rail at the back of a ship or boat. ▷ HISTORY Dutch *taffereel* panel

tag¹ *n* **1** a piece of paper, leather, etc., for attaching to something as a mark or label: *the price tag.* **2** a point of metal or plastic at the end of a cord or lace. **3** a brief trite quotation. **4** an electronic device worn by a prisoner under house arrest so that his or her movements can be monitored. **5** *Slang* a graffito consisting of a nickname or personal symbol. ✧ *vb* **tagging, tagged 6** to mark with a tag. ✧ See also **tag along**. ▷ HISTORY origin unknown

tag² *n* **1** a children's game in which one player chases the others in an attempt to touch one of them, who will then become the chaser. ✧ *vb* **tagging, tagged 2** to catch and touch (another child) in the game of tag. ✧ Also: **tig** ▷ HISTORY origin unknown

Tagalog (tag-**gah**-log) *n* a language spoken in the Philippines.

tag along *vb* to accompany someone, esp. when uninvited: *I tagged along behind the gang.*

tagetes (taj-**eat**-eez) *n, pl* **-tes** any of a genus of plants with yellow or orange flowers, including the French and African marigolds. ▷ HISTORY Latin *Tages,* a god of ancient Etruria

tagliatelle (tal-yat-**tell**-ee) *n* a form of pasta made in narrow strips. ▷ HISTORY Italian

taiga (**tie**-ga) *n* the belt of coniferous forest extending across much of subarctic North America, Europe, and Asia.

tail¹ *n* **1** the rear part of an animal's body, usually forming a long thin flexible part attached to the trunk. RELATED ADJECTIVE ➧ **caudal 2** any long thin part projecting or hanging from the back or end of something: *the waiter produced menus from beneath the tail of his coat.* **3** the last part: *the tail of the procession.* **4** the rear part of an aircraft. **5** *Astron* the luminous stream of gas and dust particles driven from the head of a comet when it is close to the sun. **6** *Informal* a person employed to follow and spy upon another. **7 turn tail** to run away. **8 with one's tail between one's legs** completely defeated and demoralized. ✧ *adj* **9** at the back: *tail feathers.* ✧ *vb* **10** *Informal* to follow (someone) stealthily. ✧ See also **tail off, tails**. ▷ HISTORY Old English *tægel* ▶ **tailless** *adj*

tail² *n Law* the limitation of an estate or interest to a person and his or her descendants. ▷ HISTORY Old French *taille* a division

tailback *n Brit* a queue of traffic stretching back from an obstruction.

tailboard *n* a removable or hinged rear board on a lorry or trailer.

tail coat *n* a man's black coat which stops at the hips at the front and has a long back split into two below the waist.

tailgate *n* **1** same as **tailboard**. **2** a door at the rear of a hatchback vehicle. ✧ *vb* **3** to drive very close behind (a vehicle). ▶ **tailgater** *n*

tail-light *or* **tail lamp** *n* same as **rear light**.

tail off *or* **away** *vb* **1** to decrease gradually: *orders tailed off.* **2** (of someone's voice) to become gradually quieter and then silent.

tailor *n* **1** a person who makes, repairs, or alters outer garments, esp. menswear. RELATED ADJECTIVE ▸ **sartorial** ✧ *vb* **2** to cut or style (a garment) to satisfy specific requirements. **3** to adapt (something) so as to make it suitable: *activities are tailored to participants' capabilities.* ▷ **HISTORY** Old French *taillier* to cut ▶ **tailored** *adj*

tailorbird *n* a tropical Asian warbler that builds a nest by sewing together large leaves using plant fibres.

tailor-made *adj* **1** (of clothing) made by a tailor to fit exactly. **2** perfect for a particular purpose: *I'm tailor-made for the role.*

tailpipe *n* a pipe from which exhaust gases are discharged, esp. in a motor vehicle.

tailplane *n* a small horizontal wing at the tail of an aircraft to help keep it stable.

tails *pl n* **1** *Informal* same as **tail coat**. ✧ *interj, adv* **2** with the side of a coin uppermost that does not have a portrait of a head on it.

tailspin *n* **1** *Aeronautics* same as **spin** (sense 10). **2** *Informal* a state of confusion or panic.

tailwind *n* a wind blowing from behind an aircraft or vehicle.

taint *vb* **1** to spoil or contaminate by an undesirable quality: *tainted by corruption.* ✧ *n* **2** a defect or flaw. **3** a trace of contamination or infection. ▷ **HISTORY** Old French *teindre* to dye ▶ **tainted** *adj*

taipan *n* a large poisonous Australian snake. ▷ **HISTORY** Aboriginal

take *vb* **taking, took, taken 1** to remove from a place, usually by grasping with the hand: *he took a fifty-dollar note from his wallet.* **2** to accompany or escort: *he took me home.* **3** to use as a means of transport: *we took a taxi.* **4** to conduct or lead: *that road takes you to Preston.* **5** to obtain possession of (something), often dishonestly: *they had taken everything most precious to us.* **6** to seize or capture: *her husband had been taken by the rebels.* **7** (in games such as chess or cards) to win or capture (a piece, trick, etc.). **8** to choose or select (something to use or buy): *I'll take the green one, please.* **9** to put an end to: *he took his own life.* **10** to require (time, resources, or ability): *this would have taken years to set up.* **11** to use as a particular case: *take a friend of mine for example.* **12** to find and make use of (a seat, flat, etc.). **13** to accept the duties of: *the legitimate government will take office.* **14** to receive in a specified way: *my mother took it calmly.* **15** to receive and make use of: *she took the opportunity to splash her heated face.* **16** to eat or drink: *all food substances are toxic if taken in excess.* **17** to perform (an action, esp. a beneficial one): *she took a deep breath.* **18** to accept (something that is offered or given): *she took a job as a waitress.* **19** to put into effect: *taking military action simply.* **20** to make (a photograph). **21** to write down or copy: *taking notes.* **22** to work at or study: *taking painting lessons.* **23** to do or sit (a test, exam, etc.). **24** to begin to experience or feel: *he took an interest in psychoanalysis.* **25** to accept (responsibility, blame, or credit). **26** to accept as valid: *I take your point.* **27** to stand up to or endure: *I can't take this harassment any more.* **28** to wear a particular size of shoes or clothes: *what size of shoes do you take?* **29** to have a capacity of or room for: *the Concert Hall can take about 2500 people.* **30** to ascertain by measuring: *she comes after breakfast to take her pulse and temperature.* **31** to subtract or deduct: *take seven from eleven.* **32** to aim or direct: *he took a few steps towards the door.* **33** (of a shop, club, etc.) to make (a specified amount of money) from sales, tickets, etc.: *films that take no money at the box office.* **34** to have or produce the intended effect: *the dye hasn't taken on your shoes.* **35** (of seedlings) to start growing successfully. **36 take account of** *or* **take into account** See **account** (sense 9). **37 take advantage of** See **advantage** (sense 4). **38 take care** See **care** (sense 10). **39 take care of** See **care** (sense 11). **40 take it** to assume or believe: *I take it that means they don't want to leave.* **41 take part in** See **part** (sense 17). **42 take place** See **place** (sense 20). **43 take upon oneself** to assume the right or duty (to do something). **44 take your time** use as much time as you need. ✧ *n* **45** *Films, music* one of a series of recordings from which the best will be selected. **46** *Informal, chiefly US* a version or interpretation: *Minnelli's bleak take on the story.* ✧ See also **take after, take against**, etc. ▷ **HISTORY** Old English *tacan*

take after *vb* to resemble in appearance or character: *he takes after his grandfather.*

take against *vb Informal* to start to dislike, esp. for no good reason: *I took against her right from the start.*

take away *vb* **1** to remove or subtract: *the lymph glands are taken away and examined under a microscope.* **2** to detract from or lessen the value of (something): *the fact that he beat his wife doesn't take away from his merits as a writer.* ✧ *prep* **3** minus: *six take away two is four.* ✧ *adj* **takeaway 4** *Brit, Austral, & NZ* sold for consumption away from the premises: *takeaway food.* ✧ *n* **takeaway** *Brit, Austral, & NZ* **5** a shop or restaurant that sells such food. **6** a meal sold for consumption away from the premises.

take-home pay *n* the remainder of one's pay after income tax and other compulsory deductions have been made.

take in *vb* **1** to understand: *I was too tired to take in all of what was being said.* **2** *Informal* to cheat or deceive: *don't be taken in by his charming manner.* **3** to include: *this tour takes in the romance and history of Salzburg, Vienna, and Munich.* **4** to receive into one's house: *his widowed mother lived by taking in boarders.* **5** to make (clothing) smaller by altering the seams. **6** *Biol* to absorb (a substance). **7** to go to: *taking in a movie.*

take off *vb* **1** to remove (a garment). **2** (of an aircraft) to become airborne. **3** *Informal* to set out on a journey: *taking off for the Highlands.* **4** *Informal*

a b c d e f g h i j k l m n o p q r s t u v w x y z

A B C D E F G H I J K L M N O P Q R S T U V W X Y Z

to become successful or popular: *the record took off after being used in a film.* **5** to deduct (an amount) from a price or total. **6** to withdraw or put an end to: *the bus service has been taken off because of lack of demand.* **7** *Informal* to mimic (someone). ✧ *n* **takeoff 8** the act or process of making an aircraft airborne. **9** *Informal* an act of mimicry.

take up *vb* **1** to occupy or fill (space or time): *looking after the baby takes up most of my time.* **2** to adopt the study, practice, or activity of: *I took up architecture.* **3** to shorten (a garment). **4** to accept (an offer): *I'd like to take up your offer of help.* **5 take up on a** to accept what is offered by (someone): *I might just take you up on that offer.* **b** to discuss (something) further with (someone): *I'd like to take you up on that last point.* **6 take up with a** to discuss (an issue) with (someone): *take up the matter with the District Council more seriously.* **b** to begin to be friendly and spend time with (someone): *he's already taken up with the woman he would marry.*

taking *adj* charming, fascinating, or intriguing.

takings *pl n* receipts; earnings.

talc *or* **talcum** *n* **1** same as **talcum powder**. **2** a soft mineral, consisting of magnesium silicate, used in the manufacture of ceramics, paints, and talcum powder. ▷ **HISTORY** Persian *talk*

talcum powder *n* a powder made of purified talc, usually scented, used to dry or perfume the body.

tale *n* **1** a report, account, or story: *everyone had their own tale to tell about the flood.* **2** a malicious piece of gossip. **3 tell tales a** to tell fanciful lies. **b** to report malicious stories or trivial complaints, esp. to someone in authority. **4 tell a tale** to reveal something important. **5 tell its own tale** to be self-evident. ▷ **HISTORY** Old English *talu*

talent *n* **1** a natural ability to do something well: *the boy has a real talent for writing.* **2** a person or people with such ability: *he is the major talent in Italian fashion.* **3** *Informal* attractive members of the opposite sex collectively: *there's always lots of talent in that pub.* **4** any of various ancient units of weight and money. ▷ **HISTORY** Greek *talanton* unit of money ▶ **talented** *adj*

talent scout *n* a person whose occupation is the search for talented people, such as sportsmen or performers, for work as professionals.

talisman *n, pl* **-mans** a stone or other small object, usually inscribed or carved, believed to protect the wearer from evil influences. ▷ **HISTORY** Medieval Greek *telesma* ritual ▶ **talismanic** *adj*

talk *vb* **1** to express one's thoughts or feelings by means of spoken words. **2** to exchange ideas or opinions about something: *they were talking about where they would go on holiday.* **3** to give voice to; utter: *he was talking rubbish.* **4** to discuss: *the political leaders were talking peace.* **5** to reveal information: *she was ready to talk.* **6** to be able to speak (a language or style) in conversation: *the ferry was full of people talking French.* **7** to spread rumours or gossip. **8** to be effective or persuasive: *money talks.* **9** to get into a particular condition or state of mind by talking: *I had talked myself hoarse.* **10 now you're talking** *Informal* at last you're saying something agreeable. **11 you can** *or* **can't talk** *Informal* you are in no position to comment or criticize. ✧ *n* **12** a speech or lecture: *a talk on local government reform.* **13** an exchange of ideas or thoughts: *we had a talk about our holiday plans.* **14** idle chatter, gossip, or rumour. **15** (*often pl*) a conference, discussion, or negotiation. ✧ See also **talk back, talk down**, etc. ▷ **HISTORY** Middle English *talkien* ▶ **talker** *n*

talkative *adj* given to talking a great deal.

talkback *n NZ* a broadcast in which telephone comments or questions from the public are transmitted live.

talk back *vb* to answer (someone) rudely or cheekily.

talk down *vb* **1 talk down to** to speak to (someone) in a patronizing manner. **2** to give instructions to (an aircraft) by radio to enable it to land.

talkie *n Informal* an early film with a soundtrack.

talking-to *n Informal* a scolding or telling-off.

talk into *vb* to persuade (someone) to do something by talking to him or her: *don't let anyone talk you into buying things you don't want.*

talk out *vb* **1** to resolve (a problem) by talking: *we won't reach a compromise unless we can talk out our differences.* **2** *Brit* to block (a bill) in parliament by discussing it for so long that there is no time to vote on it. **3 talk out of** to dissuade (someone) from doing something by talking to him or her.

tall *adj* **1** of greater than average height. **2** having a specified height: *five feet tall.* ▷ **HISTORY** Middle English

tallboy *n Brit* a high chest of drawers made in two sections placed one on top of the other.

tall order *n Informal* a difficult or unreasonable request.

tallow *n* a hard fatty animal fat used in making soap and candles.

tall poppy syndrome *n Austral & NZ informal* a tendency to disparage any person who is conspicuously successful.

tall story *n Informal* an unlikely and probably untrue tale.

tally *vb* **-lies, -lying, -lied 1** to agree with or be consistent with something else: *this description didn't seem to me to tally with what we saw.* **2** to keep score. ✧ *n, pl* **-lies 3** any record of debit, credit, the score in a game, etc. **4** an identifying label or mark. **5** a stick used (esp. formerly) as a record of the amount of a debt according to the notches cut in it. ▷ **HISTORY** Latin *talea* a stick

tally-ho *interj* the cry of a participant at a hunt when the quarry is sighted.

tally table *n Maths* a table where data is recorded as a series of marks that each represent a certain number.

Talmud *n Judaism* the primary source of Jewish religious law. ▷ **HISTORY** Hebrew *talmūdh* instruction ▶ **Talmudic** *adj* ▶ **Talmudist** *n*

talon *n* a sharply hooked claw, such as that of a bird of prey. ▷ **HISTORY** Latin *talus* ankle

tamarillo *n, pl* **-los** a shrub with a red oval edible fruit.

tamarind *n* a tropical evergreen tree with fruit whose acid pulp is used as a food and to make beverages and medicines. ▷ HISTORY Arabic *tamr hindī* Indian date

tamarisk *n* a tree or shrub of the Mediterranean region and S Asia, with scalelike leaves, slender branches, and feathery flower clusters. ▷ HISTORY Latin *tamarix*

tambourine *n Music* a percussion instrument consisting of a single drum skin stretched over a circular wooden frame with pairs of metal discs that jingle when it is struck or shaken. ▷ HISTORY from Old French

tame *adj* **1** (of an animal) **a** changed by humans from a wild state into a domesticated state. **b** not afraid of or aggressive towards humans. **2** (of a person) tending to do what one is told without questioning or criticizing it. **3** mild and unexciting: *the love scenes are fairly tame by modern standards.* ✧ *vb* **taming, tamed 4** to make (an animal) tame; domesticate. **5** to bring under control; make less extreme or dangerous: *many previously deadly diseases have been tamed by antibiotics.* ▷ HISTORY Old English *tam*

Tamil *n* **1** (*pl* **-ils** *or* **-il**) a member of a people of S India and Sri Lanka. **2** the language of the Tamils. ✧ *adj* **3** of the Tamils.

tam-o'-shanter *n* a Scottish brimless woollen cap with a bobble in the centre. ▷ HISTORY after the hero of Burns's poem *Tam o' Shanter*

tamp *vb* to force or pack (something) down by tapping it several times: *he tamped the bowl of his pipe.* ▷ HISTORY probably from obsolete *tampin* plug for gun's muzzle

tamper *vb* (foll. by *with*) **1** to interfere or meddle with without permission: *someone has been tampering with the locks.* **2** to attempt to influence someone, esp. by bribery: *an attempt to tamper with the jury.* ▷ HISTORY alteration of *temper* (verb)

tampon *n* an absorbent plug of cotton wool inserted into the vagina during menstruation. ▷ HISTORY French

tan[1] *n* **1** a brown coloration of the skin caused by exposure to ultraviolet rays, esp. those of the sun. ✧ *vb* **tanning, tanned 2** (of a person or his or her skin) to go brown after exposure to ultraviolet rays. **3** to convert (a skin or hide) into leather by treating it with a tanning agent. **4** *Slang* to beat or flog. ✧ *adj* **5** yellowish-brown. ▷ HISTORY Medieval Latin *tannare*

tan[2] *Maths* tangent.

tandem *n* **1** a bicycle with two sets of pedals and two saddles, arranged one behind the other for two riders. **2 in tandem** together or in conjunction: *the two drugs work in tandem to combat the disease.* ✧ *adv* **3** one behind the other: *Jim and Ruth arrived, riding tandem.* ▷ HISTORY Latin *tandem* at length

tandoori *adj* cooked in a tandoor: *tandoori chicken.*

tang *n* **1** a strong sharp taste or smell: *we could already smell the tang of the distant sea.* **2** a trace or hint of something: *there was a tang of cloves in the apple pie.* **3** the pointed end of a tool, such as a knife or chisel, which fits into the handle. ▷ HISTORY Old Norse *tangi* point ▶ **tangy** *adj*

tangata whenua (**tang**-ah-tah **fen**-noo-ah) *pl n NZ* **1** the original Polynesian settlers in New Zealand. **2** descendents of the original Polynesian settlers. ▷ HISTORY Maori: people of the land

tangent *n* **1** a line, curve, or plane that touches another curve or surface at one point but does not cross it. **2** (in trigonometry) the ratio of the length of the opposite side to that of the adjacent side of a right-angled triangle. **3 go off at a tangent** suddenly take a completely different line of thought or action. ✧ *adj* **4** of or involving a tangent. **5** touching at a single point. ▷ HISTORY Latin *linea tangens* the touching line

tangential *adj* **1** only having an indirect or superficial relevance: *Hitler's vegetarianism only has a tangential link with the policies of the Nazis.* **2** of or being a tangent: *a street tangential to the market square.* ▶ **tangentially** *adv*

tangerine *n* **1** the small orange-like fruit, with a sweet juicy flesh, of an Asian tree. ✧ *adj* **2** reddish-orange. ▷ HISTORY *Tangier,* a port in Morocco

tangi (**tang**-ee) *n NZ* **1** a Maori funeral ceremony. **2** *Informal* a lamentation.

tangible *adj* **1** able to be touched; material or physical. **2** real or substantial: *tangible results.* ▷ HISTORY Latin *tangere* to touch ▶ **tangibility** *n* ▶ **tangibly** *adv*

tangle *n* **1** a confused or complicated mass of things, such as hair or fibres, knotted or coiled together: *a tangle of wires.* **2** a complicated problem or situation. ✧ *vb* **-gling, -gled 3** to twist (things, such as hair or fibres) together in a confused mass. **4** to come into conflict: *the last thing she wanted was to tangle with the police.* **5** to catch or trap in a net, ropes, etc.: *the string of the kite had got tangled in the branches.* ▷ HISTORY Middle English *tangilen* ▶ **tangled** *adj*

tango *n, pl* **-gos 1** a Latin-American dance characterized by long gliding steps and sudden pauses. **2** music for this dance. ✧ *vb* **-going, -goed 3** to perform this dance. ▷ HISTORY American Spanish

taniwha (**tun**-ee-fah) *n NZ* a mythical Maori monster that lives in rivers and lakes. ▷ HISTORY Maori

tank *n* **1** a large container for storing liquids or gases. **2** an armoured combat vehicle moving on tracks and armed with guns. **3** Also called: **tankful** the quantity contained in a tank. ▷ HISTORY Gujarati (language of W India) *tānkh* artificial lake

tankard *n* a large one-handled beer-mug, sometimes fitted with a hinged lid. ▷ HISTORY Middle English

tanker *n* a ship or lorry for carrying liquid in bulk: *an oil tanker.*

tank farming *n* same as **hydroponics.** ▶ **tank farmer** *n*

tannery *n, pl* **-neries** a place or building where skins and hides are tanned.

tannic *adj* of, containing, or produced from tannin or tannic acid.

tannie (**tun**-nee) *n S African* a title of respect used to refer to an elderly woman. ▷ **HISTORY** Afrikaans, literally: aunt

tannin *n* a yellowish compound found in many plants, such as tea and grapes, and used in tanning and dyeing. Also called: **tannic acid**

Tannoy *n Trademark, Brit* a type of public-address system.

tansy *n, pl* **-sies** a plant with yellow flowers in flat-topped clusters. ▷ **HISTORY** Greek *athanasia* immortality

tantalize *or* **-lise** *vb* **-lizing, -lized** *or* **-lising, -lised** to tease or make frustrated, for example by tormenting (someone) with the sight of something that he or she wants but cannot have. ▷ **HISTORY** after *Tantalus,* a mythological king condemned to stand in water that receded when he tried to drink it and under fruit that moved away when he reached for it ▶ **tantalizing** *or* **-lising** *adj* ▶ **tantalizingly** *or* **-lisingly** *adv*

tantalum *n Chem* a hard greyish-white metallic element that resists corrosion. Symbol: Ta. ▷ **HISTORY** after *Tantalus* (see TANTALIZE), from the metal's incapacity to absorb acids

tantamount *adj* **tantamount to** equivalent in effect to: *the raid was tantamount to a declaration of war.* ▷ **HISTORY** Anglo-French *tant amunter* to amount to as much

tantrum *n* a childish outburst of bad temper. ▷ **HISTORY** origin unknown

Taoiseach (**tee**-shack) *n* the Prime Minister of the Irish Republic.

Taoism (rhymes with **Maoism**) *n* a Chinese system of religion and philosophy advocating a simple honest life and noninterference with the course of natural events. ▶ **Taoist** *n, adj*

tap[1] *vb* **tapping, tapped 1** to knock lightly and usually repeatedly: *she tapped gently on the door.* **2** to make a rhythmic sound with the hands or feet by lightly and repeatedly hitting a surface with them: *he was tapping one foot to the music.* ✧ *n* **3** a light blow or knock, or the sound made by it. **4** the metal piece attached to the toe or heel of a shoe used for tap-dancing. **5** same as **tap-dancing**. ▷ **HISTORY** Middle English *tappen*

tap[2] *n* **1** *Brit, Austral & NZ* a valve by which the flow of a liquid or gas from a pipe can be controlled. Usual US word: **faucet 2** a stopper to plug a cask or barrel. **3** a concealed listening or recording device connected to a telephone. **4** *Med* the withdrawal of fluid from a bodily cavity: *a spinal tap.* **5 on tap a** *Informal* ready for use. **b** (of drinks) on draught rather than in bottles. ✧ *vb* **tapping, tapped 6** to listen in on (a telephone conversation) secretly by making an illegal connection. **7** to obtain something useful or desirable from (something): *a new way of tapping the sun's energy.* **8** to withdraw liquid from (something) as if through a tap: *to tap a cask of wine.* **9** to cut into (a tree) and draw off sap from it. **10** *Brit, Austral & NZ informal* to obtain (money or information) from (someone). **11** *Informal* to make an illicit attempt to recruit (a player or employee bound by an existing contract). ▷ **HISTORY** Old English *tæppa*

tap-dancing *n* a style of dancing in which the performer wears shoes with metal plates on the heels and toes that make a rhythmic sound on the stage as he or she dances. ▶ **tap-dancer** *n* ▶ **tap dance** *n*

tape *n* **1** a long thin strip of cotton or linen used for tying or fastening: *a parcel tied with pink tape.* **2 a** short for **magnetic tape**. **b** a spool or cassette containing magnetic tape, and used for recording or playing sound or video signals: *he put a tape into his stereo.* **c** the music, speech, or pictures which have been recorded on a particular cassette or spool of magnetic tape. **3** a narrow strip of plastic which has one side coated with an adhesive substance and is used to stick paper, etc., together: *sticky tape.* **4** a string stretched across the track at the end of a race course. **5** short for **tape measure**. ✧ *vb* **taping, taped 6** Also: **tape-record** to record (speech, music, etc.) on magnetic tape. **7** to bind or fasten with tape. **8 have a person** *or* **situation taped** *Brit & Austral informal* to have full understanding and control of a person *or* situation. ▷ **HISTORY** Old English *tæppe*

tape deck *n* **1** the part of a tape recorder which supports the spools or cassettes, and contains the motor and the playback, recording, and erasing heads. **2** the unit in a hi-fi system which fulfils the same function.

tape measure *n* a tape or length of metal marked off in centimetres or inches, used for measuring.

taper *vb* **1** to become narrower towards one end. **2 taper off** to become gradually less: *treatment should be tapered off gradually.* ✧ *n* **3** a long thin fast-burning candle. **4** a narrowing. ▷ **HISTORY** Old English *tapor*

tape recorder *n* an electrical device used for recording and reproducing sounds on magnetic tape.

tape recording *n* **1** the act of recording sounds on magnetic tape. **2** the magnetic tape used for this: *a tape recording of the interview.* **3** the sounds so recorded.

tape streamer *n Computers* a device that enables data to be copied byte by byte from a hard disk onto magnetic tape for storage.

tapestry *n, pl* **-tries 1** a heavy woven fabric, often in the form of a picture, used for wall hangings or furnishings. **2** same as **needlepoint** (sense 1). **3** a colourful and complicated situation that is made up of many different kinds of things: *the rich tapestry of Hindustani music.* ▷ **HISTORY** Old French *tapisserie* carpeting

tapeworm *n* a long flat parasitic worm that inhabits the intestines of vertebrates, including man.

tapioca *n* a beadlike starch made from cassava root, used in puddings. ▷ **HISTORY** S American Indian *tipioca* pressed-out juice

tapir (**tape**-er) *n* a piglike mammal of South and Central America and SE Asia, with a long snout, three-toed hind legs, and four-toed forelegs. ▷ **HISTORY** S American Indian *tapiira*

tappet *n* a short steel rod in an engine which moves up and down transferring movement from one part of the machine to another. ▷ **HISTORY** from TAP[1]

taproot *n* the main root of plants such as the dandelion, which grows straight down and bears smaller lateral roots.

tar[1] *n* **1** a dark sticky substance obtained by distilling organic matter such as coal, wood, or peat. **2** same as **coal tar**. ✧ *vb* **tarring, tarred 3** to coat with tar. **4 tar and feather** to cover (someone) with tar and feathers as a punishment. **5 tarred with the same brush** having, or regarded as having, the same faults. ▷ **HISTORY** Old English *teoru* ▶ **tarry** *adj*

tar[2] *n Informal* a seaman. ▷ **HISTORY** short for *tarpaulin*

tarakihi (**tarr**-a-kee-hee) *or* **terakihi** (**terr**-a-kee-hee) *n* a common edible sea fish of New Zealand waters. ▷ **HISTORY** Maori

taramasalata *n* a creamy pale pink pâté, made from the eggs of fish, esp. smoked cod's roe, and served as an hors d'oeuvre. ▷ **HISTORY** Modern Greek

tarantella *n* **1** a peasant dance from S Italy. **2** music for this dance. ▷ **HISTORY** Italian

tarantula *n* **1** a large hairy spider of tropical America with a poisonous bite. **2** a large hairy spider of S Europe. ▷ **HISTORY** Medieval Latin

tardy *adj* **-dier, -diest 1** occurring later than it is expected to or than it should: *he spent the weekend writing tardy thank-you letters.* **2** slow in progress, growth, etc.: *we made tardy progress across the ice.* ▷ **HISTORY** Latin *tardus* slow ▶ **tardily** *adv* ▶ **tardiness** *n*

tare[1] *n* **1** the weight of the wrapping or container in which goods are packed. **2** the weight of a vehicle without its cargo or passengers. ▷ **HISTORY** Arabic *tarhah* something discarded

tare[2] *n* **1** any of various vetch plants of Eurasia and N Africa. **2** *Bible* a weed, thought to be the darnel. ▷ **HISTORY** origin unknown

target *n* **1** the object or person that a weapon, ball, etc., is aimed at: *the station was an easy target for an air attack.* **2** an object at which an archer or marksman aims, usually a round flat surface marked with circles. **3** a fixed goal or objective: *our sales figures are well below target.* **4** a person or thing at which criticism or ridicule is directed: *the Chancellor has been the target of much of the criticism.* ✧ *vb* **-geting, -geted 5** to direct: *an advertising campaign targeted at gay men.* **6** to aim (a missile). ▷ **HISTORY** Old French *targette* a little shield

target audience *n* the group of people at whom a particular film, show, or advertisement is aimed.

tariff *n* **1 a** a tax levied by a government on imports or occasionally exports. **b** a list of such taxes. **2** a list of fixed prices, for example in a hotel. **3** *Chiefly Brit* a method of charging for services such as gas and electricity by setting a price per unit. ▷ **HISTORY** Arabic *ta'rīfa* to inform

Tarmac *n* **1** *Trademark* a paving material made of crushed stone bound with a mixture of tar and bitumen, used for a road or airport runway. **2 the tarmac** the area of an airport where planes wait, taxi, and take off or land: *we had to wait for an hour on the tarmac.* ✧ *vb* **tarmac, -macking, -macked 3** to apply Tarmac to (a surface).

WORD HISTORY

'Tarmac' is short for *tarmacadam*, from the surname of John McAdam (1756-1836), the Scottish road engineer who greatly improved the state of British roads and invented the process of making road surfaces from a layer of small stones on top of larger stones.

tarn *n Chiefly Brit* a small mountain lake. ▷ **HISTORY** from Old Norse

tarnish *vb* **1** (of a metal) to become stained or less bright, esp. by exposure to air or moisture. **2** to damage or taint: *the affair could tarnish the reputation of the prime minister.* ✧ *n* **3** a tarnished condition, surface, or film on a surface. ▷ **HISTORY** Old French *ternir* to make dull ▶ **tarnished** *adj*

taro *n, pl* **-ros** a plant with a large edible rootstock. ▷ **HISTORY** Tahitian & Polynesian

tarot (**tarr**-oh) *n* **1** a special pack of cards, now used mainly for fortune-telling. **2** a card in a tarot pack with a distinctive symbolic design. ▷ **HISTORY** French

tarpaulin *n* **1** a heavy waterproof canvas coated with tar, wax, or paint. **2** a sheet of this canvas, used as a waterproof covering. ▷ **HISTORY** probably from TAR[1] + PALL[1]

tarragon *n* a European herb with narrow leaves, which are used as seasoning in cooking. ▷ **HISTORY** Old French *targon*

tarry *vb* **-ries, -rying, -ried** *Old-fashioned* **1** to delay or linger: *I have no plans to tarry longer than necessary.* **2** to stay briefly: *most people tarried only a few hours before moving on.* ▷ **HISTORY** origin unknown

tarsal *Anat* ✧ *adj* **1** of the tarsus or tarsi. ✧ *n* **2** a tarsal bone.

tarseal *n NZ* **1** the bitumen surface of a road. **2 the tarseal** the main highway.

tarsier *n* a small nocturnal primate of the E Indies, which has very large eyes.

tarsus *n, pl* **-si 1** the bones of the ankle and heel collectively. **2** the corresponding part in other mammals and in amphibians and reptiles. ▷ **HISTORY** Greek *tarsos* flat surface, instep

tart[1] *n* **1** a pastry case, often having no top crust, with a sweet filling, such as jam or custard. **2** *Chiefly US* a small open pie with a fruit filling. ▷ **HISTORY** Old French *tarte*

tart[2] *adj* **1** (of a flavour) sour or bitter. **2** sharp and hurtful: *he made a rather tart comment.* ▷ **HISTORY** Old English *teart* rough ▶ **tartly** *adv* ▶ **tartness** *n*

tart[3] *n Informal* a sexually provocative or promiscuous woman: *you look like a tart.* See also **tart up**. ▷ HISTORY from *sweetheart*

tartan *n* **1** a design of straight lines, crossing at right angles to give a chequered appearance, esp. one associated with a Scottish clan. **2** a fabric with this design. ▷ HISTORY origin unknown

tartar[1] *n* **1** a hard deposit on the teeth. **2** a brownish-red substance deposited in a cask during the fermentation of wine. ▷ HISTORY Medieval Greek *tartaron*

tartar[2] *n* a fearsome or formidable person. ▷ HISTORY from *Tartar*

Tartar *or* **Tatar** *n* **1** a member of a Mongoloid people who established a powerful state in central Asia in the 13th century, now scattered throughout Russia and central Asia. ✧ *adj* **2** of the Tartars. ▷ HISTORY Persian *Tātār*

tartaric *adj* of or derived from tartar or tartaric acid.

tartaric acid *n* a colourless crystalline acid which is found in many fruits.

tartrazine (**tar**-traz-zeen) *n* an artificial yellow dye used as a food additive.

tart up *vb Brit informal* **1** to decorate in a cheap and flashy way: *the shops were tarted up for Christmas.* **2** to try to make (oneself) look smart and attractive.

task *n* **1** a specific piece of work required to be done. **2** an unpleasant or difficult job or duty. **3 take to task** to criticize or rebuke. ▷ HISTORY Old French *tasche*

task force *n* **1** a temporary grouping of military units formed to undertake a specific mission. **2** any organization set up to carry out a continuing task.

taskmaster *n* a person who enforces hard or continuous work.

Tasmanian devil *n* a small flesh-eating marsupial of Tasmania.

Tasmanian tiger *n* same as **thylacine**.

Tass *n* (formerly) the principal news agency of the Soviet Union.

tassel *n* a tuft of loose threads secured by a knot or knob, used to decorate a cushion, piece of clothing, etc. ▷ HISTORY Old French

taste *n* **1** the sense by which the flavour of a substance is distinguished by the taste buds. **2** the sensation experienced by means of the taste buds. **3** a small amount eaten, sipped, or tried on the tongue. **4** a brief experience of something: *a taste of the planter's life.* **5** a liking for something: *a taste for puns.* **6** the ability to appreciate what is beautiful and excellent: *she's got very good taste in clothes.* **7** a person's typical preferences as displayed by what they choose to buy, enjoy, etc.: *the film was good but a bit violent for my taste.* **8** the quality of not being offensive or bad-mannered: *that remark was in rather poor taste.* ✧ *vb* **tasting, tasted 9** to distinguish the taste of (a substance) by means of the taste buds: *I've got a stinking cold and can't taste anything.* **10** to take a small amount of (a food or liquid) into the mouth, esp. in order to test the flavour. **11** to have a flavour or taste as specified: *the pizza tastes delicious.* **12** to have a brief experience of (something): *they have tasted democracy and they won't let go.* ▷ HISTORY Old French *taster*

taste bud *n* any of the cells on the surface of the tongue, by means of which the sensation of taste is experienced.

tasteful *adj* having or showing good social or aesthetic taste: *tasteful decor.* ▶ **tastefully** *adv*

tasteless *adj* **1** lacking in flavour: *the canteen serves cold, tasteless pizzas.* **2** lacking social or aesthetic taste: *a room full of tasteless ornaments; a tasteless remark.* ▶ **tastelessly** *adv* ▶ **tastelessness** *n*

taster *n* **1** a person employed to test the quality of food or drink by tasting it. **2** a sample of something intended to indicate what the entire thing is like: *the entrance hall was filled with flowers, giving a taster of the splendours in the main exhibition.*

tasty *adj* **tastier, tastiest** having a pleasant flavour.

tat *n Brit* tatty or tasteless articles.

Tatar *n, adj* same as **Tartar**.

tater *n Brit dialect* a potato.

tattered *adj* **1** ragged or torn: *a tattered old book.* **2** wearing ragged or torn clothing: *the tattered refugees.*

tatters *pl n* **1** torn ragged clothing. **2 in tatters a** (of clothing) torn in several places. **b** (of an argument, plan, etc.) completely destroyed.

tattle *vb* **-tling, -tled 1** to gossip or chatter. ✧ *n* **2** gossip or chatter. ▷ HISTORY Middle Dutch *tatelen* ▶ **tattler** *n*

tattoo[1] *n, pl* **-toos 1** a picture or design made on someone's body by pricking small holes in the skin and filling them with indelible dye. ✧ *vb* **-tooing, -tooed 2** to make pictures or designs on (a person's skin) by pricking and staining it with indelible colours. ▷ HISTORY Tahitian *tatau* ▶ **tattooed** *adj* ▶ **tattooist** *n*

tattoo[2] *n, pl* **-toos 1** (formerly) a signal by drum or bugle ordering soldiers to return to their quarters. **2** a military display or pageant. **3** any drumming or tapping. ▷ HISTORY Dutch *taptoe*

tatty *adj* **-tier, -tiest** worn out, shabby, or unkempt. ▷ HISTORY Scots

taught *vb* the past of **teach**.

taunt *vb* **1** to tease or provoke (someone) with jeering remarks. ✧ *n* **2** a jeering remark. ▷ HISTORY French *tant pour tant* like for like ▶ **taunting** *adj*

Taurus *n Astrol* the second sign of the zodiac; the Bull. ▷ HISTORY Latin

taut *adj* **1** stretched tight: *the cable must be taut.* **2** showing nervous strain: *he was looking taut and anxious.* **3** (of a film or piece of writing) having no unnecessary or irrelevant details: *a taut thriller.* ▷ HISTORY Middle English *tought*

tauten *vb* to make or become taut.

tautology *n, pl* **-gies** the use of words which merely repeat something already stated, as in *reverse back.* ▷ **HISTORY** Greek *tautologia* ▶ **tautological** *or* **tautologous** *adj*

tavern *n* **1** *Old-fashioned* a pub. **2** *US, Canad, Austral & NZ* a place licensed for the sale and consumption of alcoholic drink. ▷ **HISTORY** Latin *taberna* hut

tawdry *adj* **-drier, -driest** cheap, showy, and of poor quality: *tawdry Christmas decorations.* ▷ **HISTORY** Middle English *seynt Audries lace,* finery sold at the fair of St *Audrey*

tawny *adj* brown to brownish-orange. ▷ **HISTORY** Old French *tané*

tawny owl *n* a European owl having a reddish-brown plumage and a round head.

tawse *n Scot* a leather strap with one end cut into thongs, formerly used by schoolteachers to hit children who had misbehaved. ▷ **HISTORY** probably plural of obsolete *taw* strip of leather

tax *n* **1** a compulsory payment to a government to raise revenue, levied on income, property, or goods and services. ✧ *vb* **2** to levy a tax on (people, companies, etc.). **3** to make heavy demands on: *the task taxed his ingenuity and patience.* **4 tax someone with** to accuse someone of: *he was taxed with parochialism and meanness.* ▷ **HISTORY** Latin *taxare* to appraise ▶ **taxable** *adj* ▶ **taxing** *adj*

taxation *n* the levying of taxes or the condition of being taxed.

tax avoidance *n* reduction of tax liability by lawful methods.

tax-deductible *adj* legally deductible from income or wealth before tax assessment.

tax evasion *n* reduction of tax liability by illegal methods.

tax-free *adj* not needing to have tax paid on it: *a tax-free lump sum.*

tax haven *n* a country or state having a lower rate of taxation than elsewhere.

taxi *n, pl* **taxis 1** Also called: **cab, taxicab** a car that may be hired, along with its driver, to carry passengers to any specified destination. ✧ *vb* **taxiing, taxied 2** (of an aircraft) to move along the ground, esp. before takeoff and after landing. ▷ **HISTORY** *taximeter cab*

taxidermy *n* the art of preparing, stuffing, and mounting animal skins so that they have a lifelike appearance. ▷ **HISTORY** Greek *taxis* arrangement + *derma* skin ▶ **taxidermist** *n*

taxi rank *n* a place where taxis wait to be hired.

taxman *n, pl* **-men 1** a collector of taxes. **2** *Informal* a tax-collecting body personified: *he was convicted of conspiring to cheat the taxman.*

taxonomic group *n Biol* a group of organisms that have been classified according to their structure, origin, etc.

taxonomy *n* **1** the branch of biology concerned with the classification of plants and animals into groups based on their similarities and differences. **2** the science or practice of classification. ▷ **HISTORY** Greek *taxis* order + *nomia* law ▶ **taxonomic** *adj* ▶ **taxonomist** *n*

taxpayer *n* a person or organization that pays taxes.

tax relief *n* a reduction in the amount of tax a person or company has to pay.

tax return *n* a declaration of personal income used as a basis for assessing an individual's liability for taxation.

tax year *n* a period of twelve months used by a government as a basis for calculating taxes.

Tb *Chem* terbium.

TB tuberculosis.

T-bone steak *n* a large choice steak cut from the sirloin of beef, containing a T-shaped bone.

tbs. *or* **tbsp.** tablespoon(ful).

Tc *Chem* technetium.

te *n Music* (in tonic sol-fa) the seventh note of any ascending major scale.

Te *Chem* tellurium.

tea *n* **1 a** a drink made by infusing the dried chopped leaves of an Asian shrub in boiling water: *would you like a cup of tea?* **b** the dried chopped leaves of an Asian shrub used to make this drink: *could you get some tea at the grocer's?* **c** the Asian shrub on which these leaves grow. **2** *Brit, Austral, & NZ* the main evening meal. **3** *Chiefly Brit* a light meal eaten in mid-afternoon, usually consisting of tea and cakes, sometimes with sandwiches. **4** a drink like tea made from other plants: *mint tea.* ▷ **HISTORY** Ancient Chinese *d'a*

tea bag *n* a small bag containing tea leaves, infused in boiling water to make tea.

teach *vb* **teaching, taught 1** to tell or show (someone) how to do something. **2** to give instruction or lessons in (a subject) to (students). **3** to cause to learn or understand: *life has taught me to seize the day.* **4 teach someone a lesson** to warn or punish someone: *a bully has to be taught a lesson.* ▷ **HISTORY** Old English *tǣcan* ▶ **teachable** *adj*

teacher *n* a person whose job is to teach others, esp. children.

teaching *n* **1** the art or profession of a teacher. **2 teachings** the ideas and principles taught by a person, school of thought, etc.: *the teachings of the Catholic Church.*

teaching hospital *n* a hospital attached to a medical school, in which students are taught and given supervised practical experience.

tea cloth *n* same as **tea towel**.

tea cosy *n* a covering for a teapot to keep the contents hot.

teacup *n* **1** a cup out of which tea may be drunk. **2** Also called: **teacupful** the amount a teacup will hold.

teahouse *n* a restaurant, esp. in Japan or China, where tea and light refreshments are served.

teak *n* the hard yellowish-brown wood of an East Indian tree, used for furniture making. ▷ **HISTORY** Malayalam (a language of S India) *tēkka*

teal *n, pl* **teals** *or* **teal** a small freshwater duck related to the mallard. ▷ **HISTORY** Middle English *tele*

team *n* **1** a group of players forming one of the sides in a sporting contest. **2** a group of people organized to work together: *a team of scientists.* **3** two or more animals working together: *a sledge* *pulled by a team of dogs.* ✧ *vb* **4 team up with** to join with (someone) in order to work together. **5 team with** to match (something) with something else: *navy skirts teamed with various coloured blouses.* ▷ **HISTORY** Old English *tēam* offspring

team spirit *n* willingness to cooperate as part of a team.

teamster *n* **1** *US & Canad* a truck driver. **2** (formerly) a driver of a team of horses.

teamwork *n* the cooperative work done by a team.

teapot *n* a container with a lid, spout, and handle, in which tea is made and from which it is served.

tear[1] *n* **1** Also called: **teardrop** a drop of salty fluid appearing in and falling from the eye. *RELATED ADJECTIVES* ➔ **lacrimal, lachrymal, lacrymal 2 in tears** weeping. ▷ **HISTORY** Old English *tēar*

tear[2] *vb* **tearing, tore, torn 1** to rip a hole in (something): *I tore my jumper on a nail.* **2** to pull apart or to pieces: *eagles have powerful beaks for tearing flesh.* **3** to hurry or rush. **4** to remove or take by force: *the sacred things torn from the temples of Inca worshippers.* **5 tear at someone's heartstrings** to cause someone distress or anguish. **6** to injure (a muscle or ligament) by moving or twisting it violently. ✧ *n* **7** a hole or split. ▷ **HISTORY** Old English *teran*

tear duct *n* a short tube in the inner corner of the eyelid, through which tears drain into the nose.

tearful *adj* weeping or about to weep. ▶ **tearfully** *adv*

tear gas *n* a gas that stings the eyes and causes temporary blindness, used in warfare and to control riots.

tear-jerker *n Informal* an excessively sentimental film or book.

tearoom *n* **1** *Chiefly Brit* a restaurant where tea and light refreshments are served. **2** *NZ* a room in a school or university where hot drinks are served.

tease *vb* **teasing, teased 1** to make fun of (someone) in a provocative and often playful manner. **2** to arouse sexual desire in (someone) with no intention of satisfying it. **3** to raise the nap of (a fabric) with a teasel. ✧ *n* **4** a person who teases. **5** a piece of teasing behaviour. ▷ **HISTORY** Old English *tǣsan* ▶ **teasing** *adj*

teasel, teazel, *or* **teazle** *n* **1** a plant of Eurasia and N Africa, with prickly heads of yellow or purple flowers. **2** the dried flower head of a teasel, used, esp. formerly, for raising the nap of cloth. ▷ **HISTORY** Old English *tǣsel*

tease out *vb* **1** to comb (hair, flax, or wool) so as to remove any tangles. **2** to extract information with difficulty: *it's not easy to tease out the differences between anxiety and depression.*

teaser *n* **1** a difficult question. **2** a preliminary advertisement in a campaign that makes people curious to know what product is being advertised.

teaspoon *n* **1** a small spoon used for stirring tea or coffee. **2** Also called: **teaspoonful** the amount contained in such a spoon. **3** a unit of capacity used in cooking etc., equal to 5 ml.

teat *n* **1** the nipple of a breast or udder. **2** something resembling a teat such as the rubber mouthpiece of a feeding bottle. ▷ **HISTORY** Old French *tete*

tea towel *or* **tea cloth** *n* a towel for drying dishes.

tea tree *n* a tree of Australia and New Zealand that yields an oil used as an antiseptic.

tech *n Informal* a technical college.

techie *Informal* ✧ *n* **1** a person who is skilled in the use of technology. ✧ *adj* **2** relating to or skilled in the use of technology.

technetium (tek-**neesh**-ee-um) *n Chem* a silvery-grey metallic element, produced artificially, esp. by the fission of uranium. Symbol: Tc. ▷ **HISTORY** Greek *tekhnētos* man-made

technical *adj* **1** of or specializing in industrial, practical, or mechanical arts and applied sciences: *a technical school.* **2** skilled in practical activities rather than abstract thinking. **3** relating to a particular field of activity: *technical jargon.* **4** according to the letter of the law: *a last-minute penalty awarded to the Irish for a technical offence.* **5** showing technique: *technical perfection.* ▶ **technically** *adv*

technical college *n Brit & Austral* an institution for further education that provides courses in art and technical subjects.

technical drawing *n* drawing done by a draughtsman with compasses, T-squares, etc.

technicality *n, pl* **-ties 1** a petty formal point arising from a strict interpretation of the law or a set of rules: *the case was dismissed on a legal technicality.* **2** a detail of the method used to do something: *the technicalities of making a recording.*

technical knockout *n Boxing* a judgment of a knockout given when a boxer is, in the referee's opinion, too badly beaten to continue without risk of serious injury.

technician *n* a person skilled in a particular technical field: *oil technicians.*

Technicolor *n Trademark* a process of producing colour film for the cinema by superimposing synchronized films of the same scene, each having a different colour filter.

technikon *n S African* a technical college.

technique *n* **1** a method or skill used for a particular task: *modern management techniques.* **2** proficiency in a practical or mechanical skill: *he lacks the technique to be a good player.* ▷ **HISTORY** Greek *tekhnē* skill

techno *n* a type of very fast disco music, using electronic sounds and having a strong technological influence.

techno- *combining form* of or relating to technology: *technocrat.* ▷ **HISTORY** Greek *tekhnē* skill

technocracy *n, pl* **-cies** government by scientists, engineers, and other experts. ▷ **HISTORY** Greek *tekhnē* skill + *kratos* power ▶ **technocrat** *n* ▶ **technocratic** *adj*

technology *n, pl* **-gies 1** the application of practical or mechanical sciences to industry or commerce. **2** the scientific methods or devices used in a particular field: *the latest aircraft technology.* ▷ **HISTORY** Greek *tekhnologia* systematic treatment ▶ **technological** *adj* ▶ **technologist** *n*

technophobia *n* fear of using technological devices, such as computers. ▶ **technophobe** *n* ▶ **technophobic** *adj*

tectonic *adj* **1** denoting or relating to building. **2** *Geol* **a** (of landforms, etc.) resulting from distortion of the earth's crust due to forces within it. **b** (of processes, movements, etc.) occurring within the earth's crust and causing structural deformation. ▷ **HISTORY** Late Latin *tectonicus,* from Greek *tektonikos* belonging to carpentry, from *tektōn* a builder

tectonic plate *n Geol* a large section of the earth's crust.

tectonics *n Geol* the study of the earth's crust and the forces that produce changes in it. ▷ **HISTORY** Greek *tektōn* a builder

ted[1] *vb* **tedding, tedded** to shake out (hay), so as to dry it. ▷ **HISTORY** Old Norse *tethja*

ted[2] *n Brit informal* short for **teddy boy**.

teddy[1] *n, pl* **-dies** short for **teddy bear**.

teddy[2] *n, pl* **-dies** a woman's one-piece undergarment incorporating a camisole top and French knickers. ▷ **HISTORY** origin unknown

teddy bear *n* a stuffed toy bear.

> **WORD HISTORY**
> 'Teddy bears' are named after the American president Theodore (Teddy) Roosevelt (1859-1919), who was keen on bear-hunting.

teddy boy *n* (in Britain, esp. in the mid-1950s) a youth who wore mock Edwardian fashions. ▷ **HISTORY** *Teddy,* from *Edward*

Te Deum (tee **dee**-um) *n Christianity* an ancient Latin hymn beginning Te Deum Laudamus (we praise thee, O God).

tedious *adj* boring and uninteresting. ▶ **tediously** *adv* ▶ **tediousness** *n*

tedium *n* the state of being bored or the quality of being boring: *the tedium of a nine-to-five white-collar job.* ▷ **HISTORY** Latin *taedium*

tee *n* **1** a support for a golf ball, usually a small wooden or plastic peg, used when teeing off. **2** an area on a golf course from which the first stroke of a hole is made. **3** a mark used as a target in certain games such as curling and quoits. ✧ See also **tee off**. ▷ **HISTORY** origin unknown

teem[1] *vb* **teem with** to have a great number of: *the woods were teeming with snakes and bears.* ▷ **HISTORY** Old English *tēman* to produce offspring

teem[2] *vb* (of rain) to pour down in torrents. ▷ **HISTORY** Old Norse *tœma*

teenage *adj* **1** (of a person) aged between 13 and 19. **2** typical of or designed for people aged between 13 and 19: *teenage fashions.*

teenager *n* a person between the ages of 13 and 19.

teens *pl n* **1** the years of a person's life between the ages of 13 and 19. **2** all the numbers that end in *-teen.*

teeny *adj* **-nier, -niest** *Informal* extremely small. ▷ **HISTORY** variant of *tiny*

tee off *vb* **teeing, teed** *Golf* to hit (the ball) from a tee at the start of a hole.

teepee *n* same as **tepee**.

teeter *vb* to wobble or move unsteadily. ▷ **HISTORY** Middle English *titeren*

teeth *n* **1** the plural of **tooth**. **2** the power to produce a desired effect: *resolution 672 had no teeth.* **3 armed to the teeth** very heavily armed. **4 get one's teeth into** to become engrossed in. **5 in the teeth of** in spite of: *trying to run a business in the teeth of the recession.*

teethe *vb* **teething, teethed** (of a baby) to grow his or her first teeth.

teething troubles *pl n* problems arising during the early stages of a project.

teetotal *adj* never drinking alcohol. ▷ **HISTORY** reduplication of *t* + *total* ▶ **teetotaller** *n*

TEFL Teaching of English as a Foreign Language.

Teflon *n Trademark* a substance used for nonstick coatings on saucepans etc.

tel. telephone.

tele- *combining form* **1** at or over a distance: *telecommunications.* **2** television: *telegenic.* **3** via telephone or television: *teleconference.* ▷ **HISTORY** Greek *tele* far

telecommunications *n* communications using electronic equipment, such as telephones, radio, and television.

telecommuting *n* same as **teleworking**.

telegram *n* (formerly) a message transmitted by telegraph.

telegraph *n* **1** (formerly) a system by which information could be transmitted over a distance, using electrical signals sent along a cable. ✧ *vb* **2** (formerly) to send (a message) by telegraph. **3** to give advance notice of (something), esp. unintentionally: *the twist in the plot was telegraphed long in advance.* **4** *Canad informal* to cast (a vote) illegally by impersonating a registered voter. ▶ **telegraphist** *n* ▶ **telegraphic** *adj*

telegraphy *n* (formerly) the science or use of a telegraph.

telekinesis *n* movement of a body by thought or willpower, without the application of a physical force. ▶ **telekinetic** *adj*

Telemessage *n Trademark, Brit* a message sent by telephone or telex and delivered in printed form.

telemetry *n* the use of electronic devices to record or measure a distant event and transmit the data to a receiver. ▶ **telemetric** *adj*

teleology *n* **1** *Philosophy* the doctrine that there is evidence of purpose or design in the universe. **2** *Biol* the belief that natural phenomena have a predetermined purpose and are not determined by mechanical laws. ▷ **HISTORY** Greek *telos* end + -LOGY ▶ **teleological** *adj* ▶ **teleologist** *n*

a b c d e f g h i j k l m n o p q r s t u v w x y z

telepathy *n* the direct communication of thoughts and feelings between minds without the need to use normal means such as speech, writing, or touch. ▷ HISTORY Greek *tele* far + *pathos* suffering ▶ **telepathic** *adj* ▶ **telepathically** *adv*

telephone *n* **1** a piece of equipment for transmitting speech, consisting of a microphone and receiver mounted on a handset: *the telephone was ringing.* **2** the worldwide system of communications using telephones: *reports came in by telephone.* ✧ *vb* **-phoning, -phoned 3** to call or talk to (a person) by telephone. ✧ *adj* **4** of or using a telephone: *a telephone call.* ▷ HISTORY Greek *tele* far + *phōnē* voice ▶ **telephonic** *adj*

telephone box *n* an enclosure from which a paid telephone call can be made.

telephone directory *n* a book listing the names, addresses, and telephone numbers of subscribers in a particular area.

telephonist *n* a person who operates a telephone switchboard.

telephony *n* a system of telecommunications for the transmission of speech or other sounds.

telephoto lens *n* a lens fitted to a camera to produce a magnified image of a distant object.

teleprinter *n Brit* an apparatus, similar to a typewriter, by which typed messages are sent and received by wire.

Teleprompter *n Trademark* a device for displaying a script under a television camera, so that a speaker can read it while appearing to look at the camera.

telesales *n* the selling of a commodity or service by telephone.

telescope *n* **1** an optical instrument for making distant objects appear closer by use of a combination of lenses. **2** See **radio telescope.** ✧ *vb* **-scoping, -scoped 3** to shorten (something) while still keeping the important parts: *a hundred years of change has been telescoped into five years.* ▷ HISTORY New Latin *telescopium* far-seeing instrument ▶ **telescopic** *adj*

Teletext *n Trademark* a Videotex service in which information is broadcast by a television station and received on a specially equipped television set.

Teletype *n Trademark* a type of teleprinter.

televangelist *n US* an evangelical preacher who appears regularly on television, preaching the gospel and appealing for donations from viewers. ▷ HISTORY *tele(vision)* + *(e)vangelist*

televise *vb* **-vising, -vised** to show (a programme or event) on television.

television *n* **1** the system or process of producing a moving image with accompanying sound on a distant screen. **2** Also called: **television set** a device for receiving broadcast signals and converting them into sound and pictures. **3** the content of television programmes: *some people think that television is too violent nowadays.* ✧ *adj* **4** of or relating to television: *a television interview.* ▶ **televisual** *adj*

teleworking *n* the use of home computers, telephones, etc., to enable a person to work from home while maintaining contact with colleagues or customers. ▶ **teleworker** *n*

telex *n* **1** an international communication service which sends messages by teleprinter. **2** a teleprinter used in such a service. **3** a message sent by telex. ✧ *vb* **4** to transmit (a message) by telex. ▷ HISTORY *tel(eprinter) ex(change)*

tell *vb* **telling, told 1** to make known in words; notify: *I told her what had happened.* **2** to order or instruct (someone to do something): *he had been told to wait in the lobby.* **3** to give an account (of an event or situation): *the President had been told of the developments.* **4** to communicate by words: *he was woken at 5 a.m. to be told the news.* **5** to discover, distinguish, or discern: *she could tell that he was not sorry.* **6** to have or produce an impact or effect: *the pressure had begun to tell on him.* **7** *Informal* to reveal secrets or gossip. **8 tell the time** to read the time from a clock. **9 you're telling me** *Slang* I know that very well. ▷ HISTORY Old English *tellan*

teller *n* **1** a narrator. **2** a bank cashier. **3** a person appointed to count votes.

telling *adj* having a marked effect or impact: *to inflict telling damage on the enemy.*

tell off *vb Informal* to reprimand or scold (someone). ▶ **telling-off** *n*

telltale *n* **1** a person who tells tales about others. ✧ *adj* **2** giving away information: *examining the hands for telltale signs of age.*

tellurian *adj* of the earth. ▷ HISTORY Latin *tellus* the earth

tellurium *n Chem* a brittle silvery-white nonmetallic element. Symbol: Te. ▷ HISTORY Latin *tellus* the earth

telly *n, pl* **-lies** *informal* short for **television.**

TEM *Science* transmission electron microscope.

temazepam (ti-**maz**-i-pam) *n* (*sometimes cap*) a sedative in the form of a gel-like capsule, which is taken orally or melted and injected by drug users.

temerity (tim-**merr**-it-tee) *n* boldness or audacity. ▷ HISTORY Latin *temere* at random

temp *Brit informal* ✧ *n* **1** a person, esp. a secretary, employed on a temporary basis. ✧ *vb* **2** to work as a temp.

temp. 1 temperature. **2** temporary.

temper *n* **1** a sudden outburst of anger: *she stormed out in a temper.* **2** a tendency to have sudden outbursts of anger: *you've got a temper all right.* **3** a mental condition of moderation and calm: *he lost his temper.* **4** a person's frame of mind: *he was in a bad temper.* ✧ *vb* **5** to modify so as to make less extreme or more acceptable: *past militancy has been tempered with compassion and caring.* **6** to reduce the brittleness of (a hardened metal) by reheating it and allowing it to cool. **7** *Music* to adjust the frequency differences between the notes of a scale on (a keyboard instrument). ▷ HISTORY Latin *temperare* to mix

tempera *n* a painting medium for powdered pigments, consisting usually of egg yolk and water. ▷ HISTORY Italian *temperare* to mingle

temperament *n* a person's character or disposition. ▷ **HISTORY** Latin *temperamentum* a mixing

temperamental *adj* **1** (of a person) tending to be moody and have sudden outbursts of anger. **2** *Informal* working erratically and inconsistently; unreliable: *the temperamental microphone.* **3** of or relating to a person's temperament: *we discussed temperamental and developmental differences.* ▶ **temperamentally** *adv*

temperance *n* **1** restraint or moderation, esp. in yielding to one's appetites or desires. **2** abstinence from alcoholic drink. ▷ **HISTORY** Latin *temperare* to regulate

temperate *adj* **1** of a climate which is never extremely hot or extremely cold. **2** mild or moderate in quality or character: *try to be more temperate in your statements.* ▷ **HISTORY** Latin *temperatus*

Temperate Zone *n Geog* those parts of the earth's surface lying between the Arctic Circle and the tropic of Cancer and between the Antarctic Circle and the tropic of Capricorn. Compare **Frigid Zone, Torrid Zone.**

temperature *n* **1** the hotness or coldness of something, as measured on a scale that has one or more fixed reference points. **2** *Chem* the average kinetic energy of the atoms or molecules of a substance. **3** *Informal* an abnormally high body temperature. **4** the strength of feeling among a group of people: *his remarks are likely to raise the political temperature considerably.* ▷ **HISTORY** Latin *temperatura* proportion

temperature inversion *n Meteorol* the condition in which layers of warmer air lie above cooler air.

tempest *n Literary* a violent wind or storm. ▷ **HISTORY** Latin *tempestas*

tempestuous *adj* **1** violent or stormy. **2** extremely emotional or passionate: *a tempestuous relationship.* ▶ **tempestuously** *adv*

template *n* a wood or metal pattern, used to help cut out shapes accurately. ▷ **HISTORY** from *temple* a part in a loom that keeps the cloth stretched

temple[1] *n* a building or place used for the worship of a god or gods. ▷ **HISTORY** Latin *templum*

temple[2] *n* the region on each side of the head in front of the ear and above the cheek bone. ▷ **HISTORY** Latin *tempus*

tempo (**tem**-po) *n, pl* **-pi** (-pee) *or* **-pos 1** rate or pace: *the slow tempo of change in an overwhelmingly rural country.* **2** the speed at which a piece of music is played or meant to be played. ▷ **HISTORY** Italian

temporal[1] *adj* **1** of or relating to time. **2** of secular as opposed to spiritual or religious affairs: *in the Middle Ages the Pope had temporal as well as spiritual power.* **3** not permanent or eternal: *a temporal view of drugs as the No. 1 social problem.* ▷ **HISTORY** Latin *tempus* time

temporal[2] *adj Anat* of or near the temple or temples.

temporal bone *n* either of two compound bones forming the sides of the skull.

temporary *adj* lasting only for a short time; not permanent: *temporary accommodation.* ▷ **HISTORY** Latin *temporarius* ▶ **temporarily** *adv*

temporary deafness *n Pathol* an inability to hear which is not permanent.

temporary magnet *n Physics* a magnet that loses its magnetization after the magnetic field producing it has been removed.

temporize *or* **-rise** *vb* **-rizing, -rized** *or* **-rising, -rised 1** to delay, act evasively, or protract a negotiation in order to gain time or avoid making a decision: *'Well,' I temporized, 'I'll have to ask your mother'.* **2** to adapt oneself to circumstances, as by temporary or apparent agreement. ▷ **HISTORY** Latin *tempus* time

tempt *vb* **1** to entice (someone) to do something, esp. something morally wrong or unwise: *can I tempt you to have another whisky?* **2** to allure or attract: *she was tempted by the glamour of a modelling career.* **3 be tempted** to want to do something while knowing it would be wrong or inappropriate to do so: *many youngsters are tempted to experiment with drugs.* **4 tempt fate** *or* **providence** to take foolish or unnecessary risks. ▷ **HISTORY** Latin *temptare* to test ▶ **tempter** *n* ▶ **temptress** *fem n*

temptation *n* **1** the act of tempting or the state of being tempted. **2** a person or thing that tempts.

tempting *adj* attractive or inviting: *it's tempting to say I told you so.* ▶ **temptingly** *adv*

ten *n* **1** the cardinal number that is the sum of one and nine. **2** a numeral, 10 or X, representing this number. **3** something representing or consisting of ten units. ✧ *adj* **4** amounting to ten: *ten years.* ▷ **HISTORY** Old English *tēn* ▶ **tenth** *adj, n*

tenable *adj* **1** able to be upheld or maintained: *a tenable strategy.* **2** (of a job) intended to be held by a person for a particular length of time: *the post will be tenable for three years in the first instance.* ▷ **HISTORY** Latin *tenere* to hold ▶ **tenability** *n* ▶ **tenably** *adv*

tenacious *adj* **1** holding firmly: *a tenacious grasp.* **2** stubborn or persistent: *tenacious support.* ▷ **HISTORY** Latin *tenere* to hold ▶ **tenaciously** *adv* ▶ **tenacity** *n*

tenancy *n, pl* **-cies 1** the temporary possession or use of lands or property owned by somebody else, in return for payment. **2** the period of holding or occupying such property.

tenant *n* **1** a person who pays rent for the use of land or property. **2** any holder or occupant. ▷ **HISTORY** Old French: one who is holding

tenant farmer *n* a person who farms land rented from somebody else.

tenantry *n Old-fashioned* tenants collectively.

tench *n* a European freshwater game fish of the carp family. ▷ **HISTORY** Old French *tenche*

Ten Commandments *pl n Bible* the commandments given by God to Moses on Mount Sinai, summarizing the basic obligations of people towards God and their fellow humans.

A B C D E F G H I J K L M N O P Q R S T U V W X Y Z

tend[1] *vb* to be inclined (to take a particular kind of action or to be in a particular condition) as a rule: *she tends to be rather absent-minded.* ▷ **HISTORY** Latin *tendere* to stretch

tend[2] *vb* **1** to take care of: *it is she who tends his wounds.* **2 tend to** to attend to: *excuse me, I have to tend to the other guests.* ▷ **HISTORY** variant of *attend*

tendency *n, pl* **-cies 1** an inclination to act in a particular way. **2** the general course or drift of something. **3** a faction, esp. within a political party. ▷ **HISTORY** Latin *tendere* to stretch

tendentious *adj* expressing a particular viewpoint or opinion, esp. a controversial one, in very strong terms: *a somewhat tendentious reading of French history.* ▶ **tendentiously** *adv*

tender[1] *adj* **1** (of cooked food) having softened and become easy to chew or cut. **2** gentle and kind: *tender loving care.* **3** vulnerable or sensitive: *at the tender age of 9.* **4** painful when touched: *his wrist was swollen and tender.* ▷ **HISTORY** Old French *tendre* ▶ **tenderly** *adv* ▶ **tenderness** *n*

tender[2] *vb* **1** to present or offer: *he tendered his resignation.* **2** to make a formal offer or estimate for a job or contract: *contractors tendering for government work.* ✧ *n* **3** a formal offer to supply specified goods or services at a stated cost or rate: *the government invited tenders to run television and radio services.* ▷ **HISTORY** Latin *tendere* to extend ▶ **tenderer** *n* ▶ **tendering** *n*

tender[3] *n* **1** a small boat that brings supplies to larger vessels in a port. **2** a wagon attached to the rear of a steam locomotive that carries the fuel and water. ▷ **HISTORY** variant of *attender*

tenderize *or* **-ise** *vb* **-izing, -ized** *or* **-ising, -ised** to make (meat) tender, by pounding it or adding a substance to break down the fibres. ▶ **tenderizer** *or* **-iser** *n*

tenderloin *n* a tender cut of pork from between the sirloin and ribs.

tendon *n* a band of tough tissue that attaches a muscle to a bone. ▷ **HISTORY** Medieval Latin *tendo*

tendril *n* a threadlike leaf or stem by which a climbing plant attaches itself to a support. ▷ **HISTORY** probably from Old French *tendron*

tenement *n* a large building divided into several different flats. ▷ **HISTORY** Latin *tenere* to hold

tenet (**ten**-nit) *n* a principle on which a belief or doctrine is based. ▷ **HISTORY** Latin, literally: he (it) holds

tenfold *adj* **1** having ten times as many or as much. **2** composed of ten parts. ✧ *adv* **3** by ten times as many or as much.

tenner *n Brit, Austral & NZ informal* **1** a ten-pound or ten-dollar note. **2** the sum of ten pounds or ten dollars: *it's worth a tenner at least.*

tennis *n* a game played between two players or pairs of players who use a racket to hit a ball to and fro over a net on a rectangular court. ✧ See also **lawn tennis, real tennis, table tennis.** ▷ **HISTORY** probably from Anglo-French *tenetz* hold!

tennis elbow *n* inflammation of the elbow, typically caused by exertion in playing tennis.

tenon *n* a projecting end of a piece of wood, formed to fit into a corresponding slot in another piece. ▷ **HISTORY** Old French

tenor *n* **1 a** the second highest male voice, between alto and baritone. **b** a singer with such a voice. **c** a saxophone, horn, or other musical instrument between the alto and baritone or bass. **2** a general meaning or character: *it was clear from the tenor of the meeting that the chairman's actions are very unpopular.* ✧ *adj* **3** denoting a musical instrument between alto and baritone: *a tenor saxophone.* **4** of or relating to the second highest male voice: *his voice lacks the range needed for the tenor role.* ▷ **HISTORY** Old French *tenour*

tenpin bowling *n* a game in which players try to knock over ten skittles by rolling a ball at them.

tense[1] *adj* **1** having, showing, or causing mental or emotional strain: *the tense atmosphere.* **2** stretched tight: *tense muscles.* ✧ *vb* **tensing, tensed 3** Also: **tense up** to make or become tense. ▷ **HISTORY** Latin *tensus* taut ▶ **tensely** *adv* ▶ **tenseness** *n*

tense[2] *n Grammar* the form of a verb that indicates whether the action referred to in the sentence is located in the past, the present, or the future: *'ate' is the past tense of 'to eat'.* ▷ **HISTORY** Old French *tens* time

tensile *adj* of or relating to tension or being stretched: *the addition of linseed oil improved the tensile strength of the cricket bat.*

tensile strength *n* a measure of the ability of a material to withstand lengthwise stress, expressed as the greatest stress that the material can stand without breaking.

tension *n* **1** a situation or condition of hostility, suspense, or uneasiness: *a renewed state of tension between old enemies.* **2** mental or emotional strain: *nervous tension.* **3** a force that stretches or the state or degree of being stretched tight: *keep tension on the line until the fish comes within range of the net.* **4** *Physics* a force that tends to produce an elongation of a body or structure. **5** *Physics* voltage, electromotive force, or potential difference. ▷ **HISTORY** Latin *tensio*

tensional plate boundary *n Geol* a place where the edges of two tectonic plates move away from each other.

tent *n* **1** a portable shelter made of canvas or other fabric supported on poles, stretched out, and fastened to the ground by pegs and ropes. **2** See **oxygen tent**. ▷ **HISTORY** Old French *tente*

tentacle *n* **1** a flexible organ that grows near the mouth in many invertebrates and is used for feeding, grasping, etc. **2 tentacles** the unseen methods by which an organization or idea, esp. a sinister one, influences people and events: *the tentacles of the secret police.* ▷ **HISTORY** Latin *tentare* to feel ▶ **tentacled** *adj*

tentative *adj* **1** provisional or unconfirmed: *a tentative agreement.* **2** hesitant, uncertain, or cautious: *their rather tentative approach.* ▷ **HISTORY** Latin *tentare* to test ▶ **tentatively** *adv* ▶ **tentativeness** *n*

tenterhooks *pl n* **on tenterhooks** in a state of tension or suspense. ▷ **HISTORY** Latin *tentus* stretched + HOOK

tenth *adj, n* See **ten**.

tenuous *adj* insignificant or flimsy: *there is only the most tenuous evidence for it.* ▷ **HISTORY** Latin *tenuis* ▶ **tenuously** *adv*

tenure *n* **1** the holding of an office or position. **2** the length of time an office or position lasts. **3** the holding of a teaching position at a university on a permanent basis. **4** the legal right to live in a place or to use land or buildings for a period of time. ▷ **HISTORY** Latin *tenere* to hold

tepee *or* **teepee** (**tee**-pee) *n* a cone-shaped tent of animal skins, formerly used by American Indians. ▷ **HISTORY** Sioux *tīpī*

tepid *adj* **1** slightly warm. **2** lacking enthusiasm: *tepid applause.* ▷ **HISTORY** Latin *tepidus* ▶ **tepidity** *n* ▶ **tepidly** *adv*

tequila *n* a Mexican alcoholic spirit distilled from the agave plant. ▷ **HISTORY** after *Tequila,* district in Mexico

tera- *combining form* denoting one million million (10^{12}): *terameter.* ▷ **HISTORY** Greek *teras* monster

teratology (terr-a-**tol**-a-jee) *n* the branch of medicine concerned with the development of physical abnormalities during the fetal or early embryonic stage. ▷ **HISTORY** Greek *teras* monster + -LOGY

terbium *n Chem* a soft silvery-grey element of the lanthanide series of metals. Symbol: Tb. ▷ **HISTORY** after *Ytterby,* Sweden, where discovered

tercentenary *or* **tercentennial** *adj* **1** marking a 300th anniversary. ✧ *n, pl* **-tenaries** *or* **-tennials 2** a 300th anniversary. ▷ **HISTORY** Latin *ter* three times + CENTENARY

teredo (ter-**ree**-doh) *n, pl* **-dos** *or* **-dines** (-din-eez) a marine mollusc that bores into and destroys submerged timber. ▷ **HISTORY** Greek *terēdōn* wood-boring worm

term *n* **1** a word or expression, esp. one used in a specialized field of knowledge: *he coined the term 'inferiority complex'.* **2** a period of time: *a four-year prison term.* **3** one of the periods of the year when a school, university, or college is open or a lawcourt holds sessions. **4** the period of pregnancy when childbirth is imminent. **5** *Maths* any distinct quantity making up a fraction or proportion, or contained in a sequence, series, etc. **6** *Logic* any of the three subjects or predicates occurring in a syllogism. **7 full term** the end of a specific period of time: *the agony of carrying the child to full term.* ✧ *vb* **8** to name, call, or describe as being: *social workers tend to be termed lefties.* ✧ See also **terms**. ▷ **HISTORY** Latin *terminus* end

termagant *n Literary* an unpleasant, aggressive, and overbearing woman. ▷ **HISTORY** earlier *Tervagaunt,* after an arrogant character in medieval mystery plays

terminable *adj* capable of being terminated: *his terminable interest in the property.* ▶ **terminability** *n*

terminal *adj* **1** (of an illness) ending in death. **2** situated at an end, terminus, or boundary: *the terminal joints of the fingers.* **3** *Informal* extreme or severe: *terminal boredom.* ✧ *n* **4** a place where vehicles, passengers, or goods begin or end a journey: *the ferry terminal.* **5** a point at which current enters or leaves an electrical device. **6** *Computers* a device, usually a keyboard and a visual display unit, having input/output links with a computer. ▷ **HISTORY** Latin *terminus* end ▶ **terminally** *adv*

terminal velocity *n Physics* the maximum velocity reached by a body falling under gravity through a liquid or gas, esp. the atmosphere.

terminate *vb* **-nating, -nated 1** to bring or come to an end: *his flying career was terminated by this crash.* **2** to put an end to (a pregnancy) by inducing an abortion. **3** (of the route of a train, bus, etc.) to stop at a particular place and not go any further: *this train terminates at Leicester.* ▷ **HISTORY** Latin *terminare* to set boundaries ▶ **termination** *n*

terminology *n, pl* **-gies** the specialized words and expressions relating to a particular subject. ▶ **terminological** *adj* ▶ **terminologist** *n*

terminus (**term**-in-nuss) *n, pl* **-ni** (-nye) *or* **-nuses** the station or town at one end of a railway line or bus route: *Vienna's Westbahnhof is the terminus for trains to France.* ▷ **HISTORY** Latin: end

termite *n* a whitish antlike insect of warm and tropical regions that destroys timber. ▷ **HISTORY** New Latin *termites* white ants

terms *pl n* **1** the actual language or mode of presentation used: *the test is carried out in plain non-engineering terms.* **2** the conditions of an agreement. **3** mutual relationship or standing of a specified nature: *he is on first-name terms with many of the directors.* **4 come to terms with** to learn to accept (an unpleasant or difficult situation). **5 in terms of** as expressed by; with regard to: *he is the best cricketer we have got in fact in terms of pure ability.*

tern *n* a gull-like sea bird with a forked tail and long narrow wings. ▷ **HISTORY** Old Norse *therna*

ternary *adj* **1** consisting of three items or groups of three items. **2** *Maths* (of a number system) to the base three. ▷ **HISTORY** Latin *ternarius*

Terpsichore (turp-**sick**-or-ee) *n Greek myth* the Muse of dance.

Terpsichorean (turp-sick-or-**ee**-an) *adj Often used facetiously* of or relating to dancing. ▷ **HISTORY** from *Terpsichore,* the Muse of dance in Greek mythology

terrace *n* **1** a row of houses, usually identical and joined together by common dividing walls, or the street onto which they face. **2** a paved area alongside a building. **3** a horizontal flat area of ground, often one of a series in a slope. **4 the terraces** *or* **terracing** *Brit & NZ* a tiered area in a stadium where spectators stand. ✧ *vb* **-racing, -raced 5** to make into terraces. ▷ **HISTORY** Latin *terra* earth

terracotta *n* **1** a hard unglazed brownish-red earthenware used for pottery. ✧ *adj* **2** made of

A B C D E F G H I J K L M N O P Q R S T U V W X Y Z

terracotta. **3** brownish-orange. ▷ **HISTORY** Italian, literally: baked earth

terra firma *n* the ground, as opposed to the sea. ▷ **HISTORY** Latin

terrain *n* an area of ground, esp. with reference to its physical character: *mountainous terrain.* ▷ **HISTORY** Latin *terra* earth

terra nullius *n International law* land belonging to nobody, and therefore available to an occupier; used in the past to justify land acquisition in Australia. ▷ **HISTORY** Latin See also **Mabo decision.**

terrapin *n* a small turtle-like reptile of N America that lives in fresh water and on land. ▷ **HISTORY** from a Native American language

terrarium *n* **1** an enclosed area or container where small land animals are kept. **2** a glass container in which plants are grown. ▷ **HISTORY** Latin *terra* earth

terrazzo *n, pl* **-zos** a floor made by setting marble chips into a layer of mortar and polishing the surface. ▷ **HISTORY** Italian: terrace

terrestrial *adj* **1** of the planet earth. **2** of the land as opposed to the sea or air. **3** (of animals and plants) living or growing on the land. **4** *Television* denoting or using a signal sent over land from a transmitter on land, rather than by satellite. ▷ **HISTORY** Latin *terra* earth

terrible *adj* **1** very serious or extreme: *war is a terrible thing.* **2** *Informal* very bad, unpleasant, or unsatisfactory: *terrible books.* **3** causing fear. ▷ **HISTORY** Latin *terribilis* ▶ **terribly** *adv*

terrier *n* any of several small active breeds of dog, originally trained to hunt animals living underground. ▷ **HISTORY** Old French *chien terrier* earth dog

terrific *adj* **1** very great or intense: *a terrific blow on the head.* **2** *Informal* very good; excellent: *a terrific book.* ▷ **HISTORY** Latin *terrere* to frighten ▶ **terrifically** *adv*

terrify *vb* **-fies, -fying, -fied** to frighten greatly. ▷ **HISTORY** Latin *terrificare* ▶ **terrified** *adj* ▶ **terrifying** *adj* ▶ **terrifyingly** *adv*

terrine (terr-**reen**) *n* **1** an oval earthenware cooking dish with a tightly fitting lid. **2** the food cooked or served in such a dish, esp. pâté. ▷ **HISTORY** earlier form of *tureen*

territorial *adj* **1** of or relating to a territory or territories. **2** of or concerned with the ownership and control of an area of land or water: *a territorial dispute.* **3** (of an animal or bird) establishing and defending an area which it will not let other animals or birds into: *the baboon is a territorial species.* **4** of or relating to a territorial army. ▶ **territorially** *adv* ▶ **territoriality** *n*

Territorial *n* a member of a Territorial Army.

Territorial Army *n* (in Britain) a reserve army whose members are not full-time soldiers but undergo military training in their spare time so that they can be called upon in an emergency.

territorial waters *pl n* the part of the sea near to a country's coast, which is under the control of the government of that country.

territory *n, pl* **-ries 1** any tract of land; district: *mountainous territory.* **2** the geographical area under the control of a particular government: *the islands are Japanese territory.* **3** an area inhabited and defended by a particular animal or pair of animals. **4** an area of knowledge or experience: *all this is familiar territory to readers of her recent novels.* **5** a country or region under the control of a foreign country: *a French Overseas Territory.* **6** a region of a country, esp. of a federal state, that enjoys less autonomy and a lower status than most constituent parts of the state. ▷ **HISTORY** Latin *territorium* land surrounding a town

terror *n* **1** very great fear, panic, or dread. **2** a person or thing that inspires great dread. **3** *Brit, Austral & NZ informal* a troublesome person, esp. a child. ▷ **HISTORY** Latin

terrorism *n* the systematic use of violence and intimidation to achieve political ends. ▶ **terrorist** *n, adj*

terrorize *or* **-ise** *vb* **-izing, -ized** *or* **-ising, -ised** **1** to control or force (someone) to do something by violence, fear, threats, etc.: *he was terrorized into withdrawing his accusations.* **2** to make (someone) very frightened. ▶ **terrorization** *or* **-isation** *n* ▶ **terrorizer** *or* **-iser** *n*

terry *n* a fabric covered on both sides with small uncut loops, used for towelling and nappies. ▷ **HISTORY** origin unknown

terse *adj* **1** neatly brief and concise. **2** curt or abrupt. ▷ **HISTORY** Latin *tersus* precise ▶ **tersely** *adv* ▶ **terseness** *n*

tertiary (**tur**-shar-ee) *adj* **1** third in degree, order, etc. **2** (of education) at university or college level. **3** (of an industry) involving services, such as transport and financial services, as opposed to manufacture. ▷ **HISTORY** Latin *tertius*

Tertiary *adj Geol* of the period of geological time lasting from about 65 million years ago to 600 000 years ago.

tertiary consumer *n Biol* an animal that eats other carnivores. Compare **primary consumer, secondary consumer.**

tertiary industry *n Econ, business* an industry concerned with providing a service. Compare **primary industry, secondary industry.**

tertiary production *n Econ* the provision of services which help to support the primary and secondary sectors. Tertiary production includes administration, transportation, financial services, education, health care, etc.

Terylene *n Trademark* a synthetic polyester fibre or fabric.

TESL Teaching of English as a Second Language.

tessellated *adj* paved or inlaid with a mosaic of small tiles. ▷ **HISTORY** Latin *tessellatus* checked

tessellation *n Maths* the fitting together exactly of identical shapes.

tessera *n, pl* **-serae** a small square tile used in mosaics. ▷ **HISTORY** Latin

test[1] *vb* **1** to try (something) out to ascertain its worth, safety, or endurance: *the company has never tested its products on animals.* **2** to carry out an examination on (a substance, material, or system) in order to discover whether a particular substance, component, or feature is present: *baby foods are regularly tested for pesticides.* **3** to put under severe strain: *the long delay tested my patience.* **4** to achieve a result in a test which indicates the presence or absence of something: *he tested positive for cocaine.* ✧ *n* **5** a method, practice, or examination designed to test a person or thing. **6** a series of questions or problems designed to test a specific skill or knowledge: *a spelling test.* **7** a chemical reaction or physical procedure for testing the composition or other qualities of a substance. **8** *Sport* short for **Test match**. **9 put to the test** to use (something) in order to gauge its usefulness or effectiveness. ▷ **HISTORY** Latin *testum* earthen vessel ▶ **testable** *adj* ▶ **testing** *adj*

test² *n* the hard outer covering of certain invertebrates. ▷ **HISTORY** Latin *testa* shell

testa (**tess**-ta) *n, pl* **-tae** (-tee) the hard outer layer of a seed. ▷ **HISTORY** Latin: shell

testaceous (test-**ay**-shuss) *adj Biol* of or having a hard continuous shell. ▷ **HISTORY** Latin *testacens,* from TESTA

testament *n* **1** something which provides proof of a fact about someone or something: *the size of the audience was an immediate testament to his appeal.* **2** *Law* a formal statement of how a person wants his or her property to be disposed of after his or her death: *last will and testament.* ▷ **HISTORY** Latin *testis* a witness ▶ **testamentary** *adj*

Testament *n* either of the two main parts of the Bible, the Old Testament or the New Testament.

testate *Law* ✧ *adj* **1** having left a legally valid will at death. ✧ *n* **2** a person who dies and leaves a legally valid will. ▷ **HISTORY** Latin *testari* to make a will ▶ **testacy** *n*

testator (test-**tay**-tor) *or fem* **testatrix** (test-**tay**-triks) *n Law* a person who has made a will, esp. one who has died testate.

test case *n* a legal action that serves as a precedent in deciding similar succeeding cases.

testicle *n* either of the two male reproductive glands, in most mammals enclosed within the scrotum, that produce spermatozoa. ▷ **HISTORY** Latin *testis* a witness (to masculinity)

testify *vb* **-fies, -fying, -fied 1** *Law* to declare or give evidence under oath, esp. in court. **2 testify to** to be evidence of: *a piece of paper testifying to their educational qualifications.* ▷ **HISTORY** Latin *testis* witness

testimonial *n* **1** a recommendation of the character or worth of a person or thing. **2** a tribute given for services or achievements. ✧ *adj* **3** of a testimony or testimonial: *a testimonial match.*

> ☑ **WORD TIP**
> *Testimonial* is sometimes wrongly used where *testimony* is meant: *his re-election is a testimony* (not *a testimonial*) *to his popularity with his constituents.*

testimony *n, pl* **-nies 1** a declaration of truth or fact. **2** *Law* evidence given by a witness, esp. in court under oath. **3** evidence proving or supporting something: *that they are still talking is a testimony to their 20-year friendship.* ▷ **HISTORY** Latin *testimonium*

testis *n, pl* **-tes** same as **testicle**.

Test match *n* (in various sports, esp. cricket) an international match, esp. one of a series.

testosterone *n* a steroid male sex hormone secreted by the testes.

test paper *n* **1** the question sheet of a test. **2** *Chem* paper impregnated with an indicator for use in chemical tests.

test pilot *n* a pilot who flies aircraft of new design to test their performance in the air.

test tube *n* a cylindrical round-bottomed glass tube open at one end, which is used in scientific experiments.

test-tube baby *n* **1** a fetus that has developed from an ovum fertilized in an artificial womb. **2** a baby conceived by artificial insemination.

testy *adj* **-tier, -tiest** irritable or touchy. ▷ **HISTORY** Anglo-Norman *testif* headstrong ▶ **testily** *adv* ▶ **testiness** *n*

tetanus *n* an acute infectious disease in which toxins released from a bacterium cause muscular spasms and convulsions. ▷ **HISTORY** Greek *tetanos*

tetchy *adj* **tetchier, tetchiest** cross, irritable, or touchy. ▷ **HISTORY** probably from obsolete *tetch* defect ▶ **tetchily** *adv* ▶ **tetchiness** *n*

tête-à-tête *n, pl* **-têtes** *or* **-tête 1** a private conversation between two people. ✧ *adv* **2** together in private: *they dined tête-à-tête.* ▷ **HISTORY** French, literally: head to head

tether *n* **1** a rope or chain for tying an animal to a fence, post, etc., so that it cannot move away from a particular place. **2 at the end of one's tether** at the limit of one's patience or endurance. ✧ *vb* **3** to tie with a tether. ▷ **HISTORY** Old Norse *tjōthr*

tetra- *combining form* four: *tetrapod.*

tetrad *n* a group or series of four. ▷ **HISTORY** Greek *tetras*

tetraethyl lead *n* a colourless oily insoluble liquid used in petrol to prevent knocking.

tetragon *n* a shape with four angles and four sides. ▷ **HISTORY** Greek *tetragōnon* ▶ **tetragonal** *adj*

tetrahedron (tet-ra-**heed**-ron) *n, pl* **-drons** *or* **-dra** a solid figure with four triangular plane faces. ▷ **HISTORY** Late Greek *tetraedron* ▶ **tetrahedral** *adj*

tetralogy *n, pl* **-gies** a series of four related books, dramas, operas, etc. ▷ **HISTORY** Greek *tetralogia*

tetrameter (tet-**tram**-it-er) *n* **1** *Prosody* a line of verse consisting of four metrical feet. **2** verse consisting of such lines. ▷ **HISTORY** Greek *tetra-* four + METER

Teuton (**tew**-tonn) *n* **1** a member of an ancient Germanic people of N Europe. **2** a member of any people speaking a Germanic language, esp. a German. ✧ *adj* **3** Teutonic. ▷ **HISTORY** Latin *Teutoni* the Teutons

Teutonic (tew-**tonn**-ik) *adj* **1** characteristic of or relating to the Germans. **2** of the ancient Teutons.

text *n* **1** the main body of a printed or written work as distinct from items such as notes or illustrations. **2** any written material, such as words displayed on a visual display unit. **3** the written version of the words of a speech, broadcast or recording: *an advance text of the remarks the president will deliver tonight.* **4** a short passage of the Bible used as a starting point for a sermon. **5** a book required as part of a course of study: *shelves full of sociology texts.* ✧ *vb* **6** to send (a text message) by mobile phone. **7** to contact (a person) by means of a text message. ▷ **HISTORY** Latin *texere* to compose

textbook *n* **1** a book of facts about a subject used by someone who is studying that subject. ✧ *adj* **2** perfect or exemplary: *a textbook example of an emergency descent.*

textile *n* **1** any fabric or cloth, esp. a woven one. ✧ *adj* **2** of or relating to fabrics or their production: *the world textile market.* ▷ **HISTORY** Latin *textilis* woven

text message *n* **1** a message sent in text form, esp. by means of a mobile phone. **2** a message appearing on a computer screen. ▶ **text messaging** *n*

text type *n* one of the categories according to which texts can typically be grouped.

textual *adj* of, based on, or relating to, a text or texts. ▶ **textually** *adv*

texture *n* **1** the structure, appearance, and feel of a substance: *curtains of many textures and colours.* **2** the overall sound of a piece of music, resulting from the way the different instrumental parts in it are combined: *a big orchestra weaving rich textures.* ✧ *vb* **-turing, -tured 3** to give a distinctive texture to (something). ▷ **HISTORY** Latin *texere* to weave ▶ **textural** *adj*

Th *Chem* thorium.

Thai *adj* **1** of Thailand. ✧ *n* **2** (*pl* **Thais** *or* **Thai**) a person from Thailand. **3** the main language of Thailand.

Thalia *n Greek myth* the Muse of comedy.

thalidomide (thal-**lid**-oh-mide) *n* a drug formerly used as a sedative and hypnotic but withdrawn from use when found to cause abnormalities in developing fetuses. ▷ **HISTORY** *thali(mi)do(glutari)mide*

thallium *n Chem* a soft highly toxic white metallic element. Symbol: Tl. ▷ **HISTORY** Greek *thallos* a green shoot; from the green line in its spectrum

than *conj, prep* **1** used to introduce the second element of a comparison, the first element of which expresses difference: *men are less observant than women and children.* **2** used to state a number, quantity, or value in approximate terms by contrasting it with another number, quantity, or value: *temperatures lower than 25 degrees.* **3** used after the adverbs *rather* and *sooner* to introduce a rejected alternative: *fruit is examined by hand, rather than by machine.* ▷ **HISTORY** Old English *thanne*

> **WORD TIP**
> In formal English, *than* is usually regarded as a conjunction governing an unexpressed verb: *he does it far better than I (do).* The case of any pronoun therefore depends on whether it is the subject or object of the unexpressed verb: *she likes him more than I (like him); she likes him more than (she likes) me.* However in ordinary speech and writing *than* is usually treated as a preposition and is followed by the object form of a pronoun: *my brother is younger than me.*

thane *n* **1** (in Anglo-Saxon England) a nobleman who held land from the king or from a superior nobleman in return for certain services. **2** (in medieval Scotland) a person of rank holding land from the king. ▷ **HISTORY** Old English *thegn*

thank *vb* **1** to convey feelings of gratitude to: *he thanked the nursing staff for saving his life.* **2** to hold responsible: *he has his father to thank for his familiarity with the film world.* **3 thank you** a polite response or expression of gratitude. **4 thank goodness, thank heavens** *or* **thank God** an exclamation of relief. ▷ **HISTORY** Old English *thancian*

thankful *adj* grateful and appreciative. ▶ **thankfully** *adv*

thankless *adj* unrewarding or unappreciated: *she took on the thankless task of organizing the office Xmas lunch.* ▶ **thanklessly** *adv* ▶ **thanklessness** *n*

thanks *pl n* **1** an expression of appreciation or gratitude. **2 thanks to** because of: *the birth went very smoothly, thanks to the help of the GHQ medical officer.* ✧ *interj* **3** *Informal* an exclamation expressing gratitude.

thanksgiving *n* a formal public expression of thanks to God.

Thanksgiving Day *n* (in North America) an annual holiday celebrated on the fourth Thursday of November in the United States and on the second Monday of October in Canada.

that *adj* **1** used preceding a noun that has been mentioned or is already familiar: *he'd have to give up on that idea.* **2** used preceding a noun that denotes something more remote: *that book on the top shelf.* ✧ *pron* **3** used to denote something already mentioned or understood: *that's right.* **4** used to denote a more remote person or thing: *is that him over there?* **5** used to introduce a restrictive relative clause: *a problem that has to be overcome.* **6 and all that** *or* **and that** *Informal* and similar or related things: *import cutting and all that.* **7 that is a** to be precise. **b** in other words. **8 that's that** there is no more to be said or done. ✧ *conj* **9** used to introduce a noun clause: *he denied that the country was suffering from famine.* **10** used, usually after *so,* to introduce a clause of purpose: *he turns his face away from her so that she shall not see his tears.* **11** used to introduce a clause of result: *a scene so sickening and horrible that it is impossible to describe it.* ✧ *adv* **12** Also: **all that** *Informal* very or particularly: *the*

A B C D E F G H I J K L M N O P Q R S T U V W X Y Z

fines imposed have not been that large.
▷ **HISTORY** Old English *thæt*

> **WORD TIP**
> Precise writers maintain a distinction between *that* and *which*: *that* is used as a relative pronoun in restrictive clauses and *which* in nonrestrictive clauses. In *the book that is on the table is mine,* the clause *that is on the table* is used to distinguish one particular book (the one on the table) from another or others (which may be anywhere, but not on the table). In *the book, which is on the table, is mine,* the *which* clause is merely descriptive or incidental. The more formal the level of language, the more important it is to preserve the distinction between the two relative pronouns; but in informal or colloquial usage, the words are often used interchangeably.

thatch *n* **1** Also called: **thatching** a roofing material that consists of straw or reeds. **2** a roof made of such a material. **3** a mass of thick untidy hair on someone's head. ✧ *vb* **4** to cover with thatch. ▷ **HISTORY** Old English *theccan* to cover ▸ **thatched** *adj* ▸ **thatcher** *n*

thaw *vb* **1** to melt or cause to melt: *snow thawing in the gutter.* **2** (of frozen food) to become or cause to become unfrozen; defrost. **3** (of weather) to be warm enough to cause ice or snow to melt: *it's not freezing, it's thawing again.* **4** to become more relaxed or friendly: *only with Llewelyn did he thaw, let his defences down.* ✧ *n* **5** the act or process of thawing. **6** a spell of relatively warm weather, causing snow or ice to melt. ▷ **HISTORY** Old English *thawian*

the[1] *adj* (*definite article*) **1** used preceding a noun that has been previously specified or is a matter of common knowledge: *those involved in the search.* **2** used to indicate a particular person or object: *the man called Frank turned to look at it.* **3** used preceding certain nouns associated with one's culture, society, or community: *to comply with the law.* **4** used preceding an adjective that is functioning as a collective noun: *the unemployed.* **5** used preceding titles and certain proper nouns: *the Middle East.* **6** used preceding an adjective or noun in certain names or titles: *Alexander the Great.* **7** used preceding a noun to make it refer to its class as a whole: *cultivation of the coca plant.* **8** used instead of *my, your, her,* etc., with parts of the body: *swelling of tissues in the brain.* **9** the best or most remarkable: *it's THE place in town for good Mexican food.* ▷ **HISTORY** Old English *thē*

the[2] *adv* used in front of each of two things which are being compared to show how they increase or decrease in relation to each other: *the smaller the baby, the lower its chances of survival.* ▷ **HISTORY** Old English *thē, thȳ*

theatre *or US* **theater** *n* **1** a building designed for the performance of plays, operas, etc. **2** a large room or hall with tiered seats for an audience: *a lecture theatre.* **3** a room in a hospital equipped for surgical operations. **4 the theatre** drama and acting in general. **5** a region in which a war or conflict takes place: *a potential theatre of war close to Russian borders.* **6** *US, Austral, & NZ* same as **cinema** (sense 1). ▷ **HISTORY** Greek *theatron*

theatre in the round *n, pl* **theatres in the round** a theatre with seats arranged around a central acting area.

theatre of the absurd *n Drama* drama in which normal conventions and dramatic structure are ignored or modified in order to present life as irrational or meaningless.

Theatresports *n Trademark* competitive improvised theatre involving teams.

theatrical *adj* **1** of or relating to the theatre or dramatic performances. **2** exaggerated and affected in manner or behaviour. ▸ **theatricality** *n* ▸ **theatrically** *adv*

theatricals *pl n* dramatic performances, esp. as given by amateurs.

thee *pron Old-fashioned* the objective form of **thou**[1].

theft *n* **1** the act or an instance of stealing: *he reported the theft of his passport.* **2** the crime of stealing: *he had a number of convictions for theft.* ▷ **HISTORY** Old English *thēofth*

their *adj* of or associated with them: *owning their own land; two girls on their way to school.* ▷ **HISTORY** Old Norse *theira*

> **WORD TIP**
> See at **they.**

theirs *pron* **1** something or someone belonging to or associated with them: *it was his fault, not theirs.* **2 of theirs** belonging to them.

theism (**thee**-iz-zum) *n* **1** belief in one God as the creator of everything in the universe. **2** belief in the existence of a God or gods. ▷ **HISTORY** Greek *theos* god ▸ **theist** *n, adj* ▸ **theistic** *adj*

them *pron* (*objective*) refers to things or people other than the speaker or people addressed: *I want you to give this to them.* ▷ **HISTORY** Old English *thǣm*

> **WORD TIP**
> See at **me, they.**

theme *n* **1** the main idea or topic in a discussion or lecture. **2** (in literature, music, or art) an idea, image, or motif, repeated or developed throughout a work or throughout an artist's career. **3** *Music* a group of notes forming a recognizable melodic unit, used as the basis of part or all of a composition. **4** a short essay, esp. one set as an exercise for a student. **5** *Grammar* the first major constituent of a sentence, usually but not necessarily the subject. Compare **rheme.** ▷ **HISTORY** Greek *thema* ▸ **thematic** *adj* ▸ **thematically** *adv*

theme park *n* an area planned as a leisure attraction in which all the displays and activities are based on a particular theme, story, or idea: *a Wild West theme park.*

themselves *pron* **1 a** the reflexive form of *they* or *them*: *two men barricaded themselves into a cell.*

A B C D E F G H I J K L M N O P Q R S T U V W X Y Z

b used for emphasis: *among the targets were police officers themselves.* **2** their normal or usual selves: *they don't seem themselves these days.*

then *adv* **1** at that time: *he was then at the height of his sporting career.* **2** after that: *let's eat first and then we can explore the town.* **3** in that case: *then why did he work for you?* ✧ *pron* **4** that time: *since then the list of grievances has steadily grown.* ✧ *adj* **5** existing or functioning at that time: *the then Defence Minister.* ▷ HISTORY Old English *thænne, thanne*

thence *adv Formal* **1** from that place: *the train went south into Switzerland, and thence on to Italy.* **2** for that reason; therefore. ▷ HISTORY Middle English *thannes*

theocracy *n, pl* **-cies 1** government by a god or by priests. **2** a community under such government. ▷ HISTORY Greek *theos* god + *kratos* power ▶ **theocrat** *n* ▶ **theocratic** *adj* ▶ **theocratically** *adv*

theodolite (thee-**odd**-oh-lite) *n* an instrument used in surveying for measuring horizontal and vertical angles. ▷ HISTORY origin unknown

theologian *n* a person versed in the study of theology.

theology *n, pl* **-gies 1** the systematic study of religions and religious beliefs. **2** a specific system, form, or branch of this study: *Muslim theology.* ▷ HISTORY Greek *theos* god + -LOGY ▶ **theological** *adj* ▶ **theologically** *adv*

theorem *n* a proposition, esp. in maths, that can be proved by reasoning from the basic principles of a subject. ▷ HISTORY Greek *theōrein* to view

theoretical *or* **theoretic** *adj* **1** based on or concerned with the ideas and abstract principles relating to a particular subject rather than its practical uses: *theoretical physics.* **2** existing in theory but perhaps not in reality: *the secret service is under the theoretical control of the government.* ▶ **theoretically** *adv*

theorize *or* **-rise** *vb* **-rizing, -rized** *or* **-rising, -rised** to produce or use theories; speculate. ▶ **theorist** *n*

theory *n, pl* **-ries 1** a set of ideas, based on evidence and careful reasoning, which offers an explanation of how something works or why something happens, but has not been completely proved: *the theory of cosmology.* **2** the ideas and abstract knowledge relating to something: *political theory.* **3** an idea or opinion: *it's only a theory, admittedly, but I think it's worth pursuing.* **4 in theory** in an ideal or hypothetical situation: *in theory, the tax is supposed to limit inflation.* ▷ HISTORY Greek *theōria* a sight

theosophy *n* a religious or philosophical system claiming to be based on an intuitive insight into the divine nature. ▷ HISTORY Greek *theos* god + *sophia* wisdom ▶ **theosophical** *adj* ▶ **theosophist** *n*

therapeutic (ther-rap-**pew**-tik) *adj* of or relating to the treatment and cure of disease. ▷ HISTORY Greek *therapeuein* to minister to ▶ **therapeutically** *adv*

therapeutics *n* the branch of medicine concerned with the treatment of disease.

therapy *n, pl* **-pies** the treatment of physical, mental, or social disorders or disease. ▷ HISTORY Greek *therapeia* attendance ▶ **therapist** *n*

there *adv* **1** in, at, or to that place or position: *he won't be there.* **2** in that respect: *you're right there.* **3 there and then** immediately and without delay: *he walked out there and then.* ✧ *adj* **4 not all there** *Informal* mentally defective or silly. ✧ *pron* **5** that place: *to return from there.* **6** used as a grammatical subject when the true subject follows the verb, esp. the verb 'to be': *there are no children in the house.* **7 so there!** an exclamation, used esp. by children, that usually follows a declaration of refusal or defiance: *you can't come, so there!* **8 there you are** *or* **go a** an expression used when handing a person something. **b** an exclamation of satisfaction or vindication. ✧ *interj* **9** an expression of sympathy, for example when consoling a child: *there, there, pet!* ▷ HISTORY Old English *thǣr*

> **☑ WORD TIP**
>
> In correct usage, the verb should agree with the number of the subject in such constructions as *there is a man waiting* and *there are several people waiting.* However, where the subject is compound, it is common in speech to use the singular as in *there's a police car and an ambulance outside.*

thereabouts *or US* **thereabout** *adv* near that place, time, amount, etc.: *meet me at three o'clock or thereabouts; Methuselah lived 900 years or thereabouts.*

thereafter *adv Formal* from that time onwards.

thereby *adv Formal* by that means or consequently.

therefore *adv* for that reason: *the training is long, and therefore expensive.*

therein *adv Formal* in or into that place or thing.

thereof *adv Formal* of or concerning that or it.

thereto *adv Formal* **1** to that or it. **2** Also: **thereunto** in addition to that.

thereupon *adv Formal* immediately after that; at that point.

therm *n Brit* a unit of heat equal to $1.055\,056 \times 10^8$ joules. ▷ HISTORY Greek *thermē* heat

thermal *adj* **1** of, caused by, or generating heat. **2** hot or warm: *thermal springs.* **3** (of garments) specially made so as to have exceptional heat-retaining qualities: *thermal underwear.* ✧ *n* **4** a column of rising air caused by uneven heating of the land surface, and used by gliders and birds to gain height.

thermal conductivity *n Physics* a measure of the ability of a substance to conduct heat.

thermionic valve *or esp US & Canad* **thermionic tube** *n* an electronic valve in which electrons are emitted from a heated rather than a cold cathode.

thermistor (therm-**mist**-or) *n Physics* a metal-oxide rod whose resistance falls as temperature rises, used in electronic circuits and as a thermometer.

thermocouple *n* a device for measuring temperature, consisting of a pair of wires of different metals joined at both ends.

thermodynamics *n* the branch of physical science concerned with the relationship between heat and other forms of energy.

thermoelectric *or* **thermoelectrical** *adj* of or relating to the conversion of heat energy to electrical energy.

thermometer *n* an instrument used to measure temperature, esp. one in which a thin column of liquid, such as mercury, expands and contracts within a sealed tube marked with a temperature scale.

thermonuclear *adj* **1** (of a nuclear reaction) involving a nuclear fusion reaction of a type which occurs at very high temperatures. **2** (of a weapon) giving off energy as the result of a thermonuclear reaction. **3** involving thermonuclear weapons.

thermoplastic *adj* **1** (of a material, esp. a synthetic plastic) becoming soft when heated and rehardening on cooling. ✧ *n* **2** a synthetic plastic or resin, such as polystyrene.

Thermos *or* **Thermos flask** *n Trademark* a type of stoppered vacuum flask used to preserve the temperature of its contents.

thermosetting *adj* (of a material, esp. a synthetic plastic) hardening permanently after one application of heat and pressure.

thermosphere *n Geog* an atmospheric layer lying between the mesosphere and the exosphere.

thermostat *n* a device which automatically regulates the temperature of central heating, an oven, etc., by switching it off or on when it reaches or drops below a particular temperature.
▶ **thermostatic** *adj* ▶ **thermostatically** *adv*

thesaurus (thiss-**sore**-uss) *n, pl* **-ruses** *or* **-ri** a book containing lists of synonyms and related words. ▷ **HISTORY** Greek *thēsauros* a treasury

these *adj, pron* the plural of **this**.

thesis (**theess**-siss) *n, pl* **-ses** (-seez) **1** a written work resulting from original research, esp. one submitted for a higher degree in a university. **2** an opinion supported by reasoned argument: *it is the author's thesis that Britain has yet to come to terms with the loss of its Empire.* **3** *Logic* an unproved statement put forward as a premise in an argument. ▷ **HISTORY** Greek: a placing

Thespian *n* **1** *Often facetious* an actor or actress. ✧ *adj* **2** of or relating to drama and the theatre. ▷ **HISTORY** after *Thespis,* a Greek poet

they *pron* (*subjective*) refers to: **1** people or things other than the speaker or people addressed: *they both giggled.* **2** people in general: *they say he beats his wife.* **3** *Informal* an individual person, whose sex is either not known or not regarded as important: *someone could have a nasty accident if they tripped over that.* ▷ **HISTORY** Old Norse *their*

> **☑ WORD TIP**
> It was formerly considered correct to use *he, him,* or *his* after pronouns such as *everyone, no-one, anyone,* or *someone* as in *everyone did his best,* but it is now more common to use *they, them,* or *their,* and this use has become acceptable in all but the most formal contexts: *everyone did their best.*

thiamine *or* **thiamin** *n* vitamin B_1, a vitamin found in the outer coat of rice and other grains, a deficiency of which leads to nervous disorders and beriberi. ▷ **HISTORY** Greek *theion* sulphur + VITAMIN

thick *adj* **1** having a relatively great distance between opposite surfaces: *thick slices.* **2** having a specified distance between opposite surfaces: *fifty metres thick.* **3** having a dense consistency: *thick fog.* **4** consisting of a lot of things grouped closely together: *thick forest.* **5** (of clothes) made of heavy cloth or wool: *a thick jumper.* **6** *Informal* stupid, slow, or insensitive. **7** (of an accent) very noticeable: *each word was pronounced in a thick Dutch accent.* **8** Also: **thick as thieves** *Informal* very friendly. **9 a bit thick** *Brit informal* unfair or unreasonable: *£2 an hour, that's a bit thick!* **10 thick with a** covered with a lot of: *glass panels thick with dust.* **b** (of a voice) throaty and hard to make out: *his voice was thick with emotion.* ✧ *adv* **11** in order to produce something thick: *the machine sliced the potatoes too thick.* **12 lay it on thick** *Informal* **a** to exaggerate a story. **b** to flatter someone excessively. **13 thick and fast** quickly and in large numbers: *theories were flying thick and fast.* ✧ *n* **14 the thick** the most intense or active part: *in the thick of the fighting.* **15 through thick and thin** in good times and bad. ▷ **HISTORY** Old English *thicce*
▶ **thickly** *adv*

thicken *vb* **1** to make or become thick or thicker. **2** to become more complicated: *the plot thickens.*
▶ **thickener** *n*

thicket *n* a dense growth of small trees or shrubs. ▷ **HISTORY** Old English *thiccet*

thickhead *n Slang* a stupid or ignorant person.
▶ **thickheaded** *adj*

thickness *n* **1** the state or quality of being thick. **2** the dimension through an object, as opposed to length or width. **3** a layer: *several thicknesses of brown paper.*

thickset *adj* **1** stocky in build. **2** planted or placed close together.

thick-skinned *adj* insensitive to criticism or hints; not easily upset.

thief *n, pl* **thieves** a person who steals something from another. ▷ **HISTORY** Old English *thēof*
▶ **thievish** *adj*

thieve *vb* **thieving, thieved** to steal other people's possessions. ▷ **HISTORY** Old English *thēofian* ▶ **thieving** *adj*

thigh *n* the part of the human leg between the hip and the knee. ▷ **HISTORY** Old English *thēh*

thighbone *n* same as **femur**.

A B C D E F G H I J K L M N O P Q R S T U V W X Y Z

thimble *n* a small metal or plastic cap used to protect the end of the finger from the needle when sewing. ▷ HISTORY Old English *thȳmel* thumbstall

thin *adj* **thinner, thinnest 1** having a relatively small distance between opposite surfaces: *a thin mattress.* **2** much narrower than it is long: *push a thin stick up the pipe in order to clear it.* **3** (of a person or animal) having no excess body fat. **4** made up of only a few, widely separated, people or things: *thin hair.* **5** not dense: *a thin film of dust.* **6** unconvincing because badly thought out or badly presented: *the evidence against him was extremely thin.* **7** (of a voice) high-pitched and not very loud: *a thin squeaky voice.* ✧ *adv* **8** in order to produce something thin: *roll the dough very thin.* ✧ *vb* **thinning, thinned 9** to make or become thin or sparse. ▷ HISTORY Old English *thynne* ▶ **thinly** *adv* ▶ **thinness** *n*

thine *Old-fashioned* ✧ *adj* **1** (*preceding a vowel*) of or associated with you (thou): *if thine eye offend thee, pluck it out!* ✧ *pron* **2** something belonging to you (thou): *the victory shall be thine.* ▷ HISTORY Old English *thīn*

thing *n* **1** any physical object that is not alive: *there are very few jobs left where people actually make things.* **2** an object, fact, circumstance, or concept considered as being a separate entity: *that would be a terrible thing to do.* **3** an object or entity that cannot or need not be precisely named: *squares and circles and things.* **4** *Informal* a person or animal: *pretty little thing, isn't she?* **5** a possession, article of clothing, etc.: *have you brought your swimming things?* **6** *Informal* a preoccupation or obsession: *they have this thing about policemen.* **7 do one's own thing** to engage in an activity or mode of behaviour satisfying to one's personality. **8 make a thing of** to exaggerate the importance of. **9 the thing** the latest fashion. ▷ HISTORY Old English: assembly

think *vb* **thinking, thought 1** to consider, judge, or believe: *I think that it is scandalous.* **2** to make use of the mind, for example in order to make a decision: *I'll need to think about what I'm going to do.* **3** to engage in conscious thought: *that made me think.* **4** to be considerate enough or remember (to do something): *no other company had thought to bring high tech down to the user.* **5 think much** *or* **a lot of** to have a favourable opinion of: *I don't think much of the new design.* **6 think of a** to remember or recollect: *I couldn't think of your surname.* **b** to conceive of or formulate: *for a long time he couldn't think of a response.* **7 think twice** to consider something carefully before making a decision. ✧ *n* **8** *Informal* a careful open-minded assessment: *she had a long hard think.* ▷ HISTORY Old English *thencan* ▶ **thinker** *n*

thinking *n* **1** opinion or judgment: *contrary to all fashionable thinking.* **2** the process of thought. ✧ *adj* **3** using intelligent thought: *the thinking man's sport.*

think-tank *n Informal* a group of experts employed to study specific problems.

think up *vb* to invent or devise.

thinner *n* a solvent, such as turpentine, added to paint or varnish to dilute it.

thin-skinned *adj* sensitive to criticism or hints; easily upset.

third *adj* **1** of or being number three in a series. **2** rated, graded, or ranked below the second level. **3** denoting the third from lowest forward gear in a motor vehicle. ✧ *n* **4** one of three equal parts of something. **5** the fraction equal to one divided by three ($^1/_3$). **6** the third from lowest forward gear in a motor vehicle. **7** *Brit* an honours degree of the third and usually the lowest class. **8** *Music* the interval between one note and the note four semitones (**major third**) or three semitones (**minor third**) higher or lower than it. ✧ *adv* **9** Also: **thirdly** in the third place. ▷ HISTORY Old English *thirda*

third class *n* **1** the class or grade next in value, rank, or quality to the second. ✧ *adj* **third-class 2** of the class or grade next in value, rank, or quality to the second.

third degree *n Informal* torture or bullying, esp. as used to extort confessions or information.

third-degree burn *n* a burn in which both the surface and the underlying layers of the skin are destroyed.

third man *n Cricket* a fielding position on the off side, near the boundary behind the batsman's wicket.

third party *n* **1** a person who is involved in an event, legal proceeding, agreement, or other transaction only by chance or indirectly. ✧ *adj* **third-party 2** *Insurance* providing protection against liability caused by accidental injury or death of other people: *third-party cover.*

third person *n* the form of a pronoun or verb used to refer to something or someone other than the speaker or the person or people being addressed, as in *he understands* or *they understand.*

Third Reich *n* See **Reich.**

Third World *n* the developing countries of Africa, Asia, and Latin America collectively.

thirst *n* **1** a desire to drink, accompanied by a feeling of dryness in the mouth and throat. **2** a craving or yearning: *a thirst for knowledge.* ✧ *vb* **3** to feel a thirst. ▷ HISTORY Old English *thurst*

thirsty *adj* **thirstier, thirstiest 1** feeling a desire to drink. **2** causing thirst: *morris dancing is thirsty work.* **3 thirsty for** feeling an eager desire for: *thirsty for information.* ▶ **thirstily** *adv*

thirteen *n* **1** the cardinal number that is the sum of ten and three. **2** a numeral, 13 or XIII, representing this number. **3** something representing or consisting of thirteen units. ✧ *adj* **4** amounting to thirteen: *thirteen people.* ▶ **thirteenth** *adj, n*

thirty *n, pl* **-ties 1** the cardinal number that is the product of ten and three. **2** a numeral, 30 or XXX, representing this number. **3** something representing or consisting of thirty units. ✧ *adj* **4** amounting to thirty: *thirty miles.* ▶ **thirtieth** *adj, n*

Thirty-nine Articles *pl n* a set of formulas defining the doctrinal position of the Church of England.

this *adj* **1** used preceding a noun referring to something or someone that is closer: *on this side of the Channel.* **2** used preceding a noun that has just been mentioned or is understood: *this text has two chief goals.* **3** used to refer to something about to be mentioned: *NPR's Anne Garrels has this report.* **4** used to refer to the present time or occasion: *this week's edition of the newspaper.* **5** *Informal* used instead of *a* or *the* in telling a story: *see, it's about this bird who fancies you.* ✧ *pron* **6** used to denote a person or thing that is relatively close: *black coral like this.* **7** used to denote something already mentioned or understood: *this didn't seem fair to me.* **8** used to denote something about to be mentioned: *just say this: collect Standish from the top of the fire escape.* **9** the present time or occasion: *after this it was impossible to talk to him about his feelings.* **10 this and that** various unspecified and trivial events or facts. ▷ HISTORY Old English *thes, thēos, this* (masculine, feminine, and neuter singular)

thistle *n* a plant with prickly-edged leaves, dense flower heads, and feathery hairs on the seeds. ▷ HISTORY Old English *thīstel* ▶ **thistly** *adj*

thistledown *n* the mass of feathery plumed seeds produced by a thistle.

thither *adv Formal* to or towards that place. ▷ HISTORY Old English *thider*

tho' *or* **tho** *conj, adv US or poetic* same as **though**.

thole[1] *or* **tholepin** *n* one of a pair of wooden pins set upright in the gunwale on either side of a rowing boat to serve as a fulcrum in rowing. ▷ HISTORY Old English *tholl*

thole[2] *vb* **tholing, tholed** *Scot & N English* to bear or put up with.

thong *n* **1** a thin strip of leather or other material. **2** *US, Canad, & Austral* same as **flip-flop**. **3** a skimpy article of beachwear consisting of thin strips of leather or cloth attached to a piece of material that covers the genitals while leaving the buttocks bare. ▷ HISTORY Old English *thwang*

Thor *n Norse myth* the god of thunder.

thorax (**thaw**-racks) *n, pl* **thoraxes** *or* **thoraces** (**thaw**-rass-seez) **1** the part of the human body enclosed by the ribs. **2** the part of an insect's body between the head and abdomen. ▷ HISTORY Greek: breastplate, chest ▶ **thoracic** *adj*

thorium *n Chem* a silvery-white radioactive metallic element. It is used in electronic equipment and as a nuclear power source. Symbol: Th. ▷ HISTORY after *Thor,* Norse god of thunder

thorn *n* **1** a sharp pointed woody projection from a stem or leaf. **2** any of various trees or shrubs having thorns, esp. the hawthorn. **3 a thorn in one's side** *or* **flesh** a source of irritation: *he was sufficiently bright at school to become a thorn in the side of his maths teacher.* ▷ HISTORY Old English ▶ **thornless** *adj*

thorny *adj* **thornier, thorniest 1** covered with thorns. **2** difficult or unpleasant: *a thorny issue.*

thorough *adj* **1** carried out completely and carefully: *he needs a thorough checkup by the doctor.* **2** (of a person) painstakingly careful: *he is very thorough if rather unimaginative.* **3** great in extent or degree; utter: *a thorough disgrace.* ▷ HISTORY Old English *thurh* through ▶ **thoroughly** *adv* ▶ **thoroughness** *n*

thoroughbred *adj* **1** obtained through successive generations of selective breeding: *thoroughbred horses.* ✧ *n* **2** a pedigree animal, esp. a horse.

thoroughfare *n* a way through from one place to another: *the great thoroughfare from the Castle to the Palace of Holyrood.*

thoroughgoing *adj* **1** extremely thorough. **2** absolute or complete: *a thoroughgoing hatred.*

those *adj, pron* the plural of **that**. ▷ HISTORY Old English *thās*, plural of *this*

thou[1] *pron Old-fashioned* same as **you:** used when talking to one person. ▷ HISTORY Old English *thū*

thou[2] *n, pl* **thou** *Informal* **1** one thousandth of an inch. **2** a thousand.

though *conj* **1** despite the fact that: *he was smiling with relief and happiness though the tears still flowed down his cheeks.* ✧ *adv* **2** nevertheless or however: *he can't dance – he sings well, though.* ▷ HISTORY Old English *thēah*

thought *vb* **1** the past of **think**. ✧ *n* **2** the act or process of thinking. **3** a concept or idea. **4** ideas typical of a particular time or place: *the development of Western intellectual thought.* **5** detailed consideration: *he appeared to give some sort of thought to the question.* **6** an intention, hope, or reason for doing something: *his first thought was to call the guard and have the man arrested.* ▷ HISTORY Old English *thōht*

thoughtful *adj* **1** considerate in the treatment of other people. **2** showing careful thought: *a thoughtful and scholarly book.* **3** quiet, serious, and deep in thought. ▶ **thoughtfully** *adv* ▶ **thoughtfulness** *n*

thoughtless *adj* not considerate of the feelings of other people. ▶ **thoughtlessly** *adv* ▶ **thoughtlessness** *n*

thousand *n, pl* **-sands** *or* **-sand 1** the cardinal number that is the product of ten and one hundred. **2** a numeral, 1000 or 10^3, representing this number. **3** a very large but unspecified number: *thousands of bees swarmed out of the hive.* **4** something representing or consisting of 1000 units. ✧ *adj* **5** amounting to a thousand: *a thousand members.* ▷ HISTORY Old English *thūsend* ▶ **thousandth** *adj, n*

thrall *n* the state of being completely in the power of, or spellbound by, a person or thing: *he was held in thrall by her almost supernatural beauty.* ▷ HISTORY Old English *thræl* slave

thrash *vb* **1** to beat (someone), esp. with a stick or whip. **2** to defeat totally: *the All Blacks thrashed England 24-3.* **3** to move about in a wild manner: *his legs stuck and he fell sideways, thrashing about wildly.* **4** same as **thresh**. ✧ *n* **5** *Informal* a party. ✧ See also **thrash out**. ▷ HISTORY Old English *therscan*

thrashing *n* a severe beating.

thrash out *vb* to discuss (a problem or difficulty) fully in order to come to an agreement or decision about it: *we must arrange a meeting to thrash out the details of the scheme.*

thread *n* **1** a fine strand or fibre of some material. **2** a fine cord of twisted yarns, esp. of cotton, used in sewing or weaving. **3** something acting as the continuous link or theme of a whole: *the thread of the story.* **4** the spiral ridge on a screw, bolt, or nut. **5** a very small amount (of something): *there was a thread of nervousness in his voice.* **6** a very thin seam of coal or vein of ore. ✧ *pl n* **threads 7** *Chiefly US slang* clothes. ✧ *vb* **8** to pass thread through the eye of (a needle) before sewing with it. **9** to string together: *plastic beads threaded on lengths of nylon line.* **10** to make (one's way) through a crowd of people or group of objects: *she threaded and pushed her way through the crowds.* ▷ **HISTORY** Old English *thrǣd* ▸ **threadlike** *adj*

threadbare *adj* **1** (of cloth, clothing, or a carpet) having the nap worn off so that the threads are exposed. **2** having been used or expressed so often as to be no longer interesting: *threadbare ideas.* **3** wearing shabby worn-out clothes.

threadworm *n* a small threadlike worm that is a parasite of humans.

threat *n* **1** a declaration of an intention to inflict harm: *they carried out their threat to kill the hostages.* **2** a strong possibility of something dangerous or unpleasant happening: *the wet weather will bring a threat of flooding.* **3** a person or thing that is regarded as dangerous and likely to inflict harm: *unemployment is a serious threat to the social order.* ▷ **HISTORY** Old English *thrēat*

threaten *vb* **1** to express a threat to (someone): *he threatened John with the sack.* **2** to be a threat to: *he was worried about anything that might threaten the health of his child.* **3** to be a menacing indication of (something): *the early summer threatened drought.* ▸ **threatening** *adj* ▸ **threateningly** *adv*

three *n* **1** the cardinal number that is the sum of one and two. **2** a numeral, 3 or III, representing this number. **3** something representing or consisting of three units. ✧ *adj* **4** amounting to three: *three days.* ▷ **HISTORY** Old English *thrēo*

three-decker *n* **1** a warship with guns on three decks. **2** anything that has three levels, layers, or tiers.

three-dimensional *or* **3-D** *adj* **1** having three dimensions. **2** lifelike or realistic: *all the characters are three-dimensional.*

threefold *adj* **1** having three times as many or as much. **2** composed of three parts. ✧ *adv* **3** by three times as many or as much.

three-ply *adj* made of three thicknesses, layers, or strands.

three-point turn *n* a complete turn of a motor vehicle using forward and reverse gears alternately, and completed after only three movements.

three-quarter *adj* **1** amounting to three out of four equal parts of something. **2** being three quarters of the normal length: *a three-quarter-length coat.* ✧ *n* **3** *Rugby* any of the four players between the fullback and the halfbacks.

three Rs *pl n* reading, writing, and arithmetic regarded as the three fundamental skills to be taught in primary schools. ▷ **HISTORY** humorous spelling of *reading, 'riting, and 'rithmetic*

threesome *n* a group of three people.

threnody *n, pl* **threnodies** *Formal* a lament for the dead. ▷ **HISTORY** Greek *thrēnōidia* ▸ **threnodic** *adj* ▸ **threnodist** *n*

thresh *vb* **1** to beat (stalks of ripe corn, rice, etc.), either with a hand tool or by machine to separate the grain from the husks and straw. **2 thresh about** to toss and turn. ▷ **HISTORY** Old English *therscan*

thresher *n* any of a genus of large sharks occurring in tropical and temperate seas. They have a very long whiplike tail.

threshold *n* **1** the lower horizontal part of an entrance or doorway, esp. one made of stone or hardwood. **2** any doorway or entrance: *he had never been over the threshold of a pub before.* **3** the starting point of an experience, event, or venture: *she was on the threshold of a glorious career.* **4** the point at which something begins to take effect or be noticeable: *the threshold for basic rate tax; he has a low boredom threshold.* ▷ **HISTORY** Old English *therscold*

threw *vb* the past tense of **throw**.

thrice *adv Literary* **1** three times: *twice or thrice in a lifetime.* **2** three times as big, much, etc.: *his vegetables are thrice the size of mine.* ▷ **HISTORY** Old English *thrīwa, thrīga*

thrift *n* **1** wisdom and caution with money. **2** a low-growing plant of Europe, W Asia, and North America, with narrow leaves and round heads of pink or white flowers. ▷ **HISTORY** Old Norse: success ▸ **thriftless** *adj*

thrifty *adj* **thriftier, thriftiest** not wasteful with money. ▸ **thriftily** *adv* ▸ **thriftiness** *n*

thrill *n* **1** a sudden sensation of excitement and pleasure: *he felt a thrill of excitement.* **2** a situation producing such a sensation: *all the thrills of rafting the meandering Dordogne.* **3** a sudden trembling sensation caused by fear or emotional shock. ✧ *vb* **4** to feel or cause to feel a thrill. **5** to vibrate or quiver. ▷ **HISTORY** Old English *thȳrlian* to pierce ▸ **thrilling** *adj*

thriller *n* a book, film, or play depicting crime, mystery, or espionage in an atmosphere of excitement and suspense.

thrips *n, pl* **thrips** a small slender-bodied insect with piercing mouthparts that feeds on plant sap. ▷ **HISTORY** Greek: woodworm

thrive *vb* **thriving; thrived** *or* **throve; thrived** *or* **thriven 1** to do well; be successful: *Munich has thrived as a centre of European commerce.* **2** to grow strongly and vigorously: *the vine can thrive in the most unlikely soils.* ▷ **HISTORY** Old Norse *thrīfask* to grasp for oneself

throat *n* **1** the passage from the mouth and nose to the stomach and lungs. **2** the front part of the neck. **3 at each other's throats** quarrelling or fighting with each other. **4 cut one's own throat** to bring about one's own ruin. **5 cut someone's throat** to kill someone. **6 ram** *or* **force something down someone's throat** to insist that someone listen to or accept something. **7 stick in one's**

throat to be hard to accept: *his arrogance really sticks in my throat.* ▷ HISTORY Old English *throtu*

throaty *adj* **throatier, throatiest 1** hoarse and suggestive of a sore throat: *a throaty 40 fags-a-day bark.* **2** deep, husky, or guttural: *she gives a deliciously throaty laugh.*

throb *vb* **throbbing, throbbed 1** to pulsate or beat repeatedly, esp. with abnormally strong force: *her eardrums were throbbing with pain.* **2** (of engines, drums, etc.) to have a strong rhythmic vibration or beat. ✧ *n* **3** the act or sensation of throbbing: *he felt a throb of fear; the throb of the engines.* ▷ HISTORY imitative ▶ **throbbing** *adj, n*

throes *pl n* **1** violent pangs, pain, or convulsions: *an animal in its death throes.* **2 in the throes of** struggling to cope with (something difficult or disruptive): *in the throes of a civil war.* ▷ HISTORY Old English *thrāwu* threat

thrombosis (throm-**boh**-siss) *n, pl* **-ses** (-seez) coagulation of the blood in the heart or in a blood vessel, forming a blood clot. ▷ HISTORY Greek: curdling

throne *n* **1** the ceremonial seat occupied by a monarch or bishop on occasions of state. **2** the rank or power of a monarch: *she came to the throne after her father was murdered.* ▷ HISTORY Greek *thronos*

throng *n* **1** a great number of people or things crowded together. ✧ *vb* **2** to gather in or fill (a place) in large numbers: *streets thronged with shoppers.* ▷ HISTORY Old English *gethrang*

throstle *n Poetic* a song thrush. ▷ HISTORY Old English

throttle *n* **1** a device that controls the fuel-and-air mixture entering an engine. ✧ *vb* **-tling, -tled 2** to kill or injure (someone) by squeezing his or her throat. **3** to suppress or censor: *the government is trying to throttle dissent.* ▷ HISTORY Middle English *throtel* throat

through *prep* **1** going in at one side and coming out at the other side of: *he drove through the West of the city.* **2** occupying or visiting several points scattered around in (an area): *a journey through the Scottish Highlands.* **3** as a result of: *diminished responsibility through temporary insanity.* **4** during: *driving for five hours through the night.* **5** for all of (a period): *it rained all through that summer.* **6** *Chiefly US* up to and including: *from Monday through Saturday.* ✧ *adj* **7** finished: *I'm through with history.* **8** having completed a specified amount of an activity: *he tried to stop the investigation halfway through.* **9** (on a telephone line) connected. **10** no longer able to function successfully in some specified capacity: *they are through, they haven't got a chance.* **11** (of a train, plane flight, etc.) going directly to a place, so that passengers do not have to change: *the first ever through train between Singapore and Bangkok.* ✧ *adv* **12** through a thing, place, or period of time: *the script gives up around halfway through.* **13** extremely or absolutely: *I'm soaked through.* **14 through and through** to the greatest possible extent: *the boards are rotten through and through.* ▷ HISTORY Old English *thurh*

throughout *prep* **1** through the whole of (a place or a period of time): *radio stations throughout the UK.* ✧ *adv* **2** through the whole of a place or a period of time: *I led both races throughout.*

throughput *n* the amount of material processed in a given period, esp. by a computer.

throve *vb* a past tense of **thrive**.

throw *vb* **throwing, threw, thrown 1** to hurl (something) through the air, esp. with a rapid motion of the arm. **2** to put or move suddenly, carelessly, or violently: *she threw her arms round his neck.* **3** to bring into a specified state or condition, esp. suddenly: *the invasion threw the region into turmoil.* **4** to move (a switch or lever) so as to engage or disengage a mechanism. **5** to cause (someone) to fall: *I'm riding the horse that threw me.* **6 a** to tip (dice) out onto a flat surface. **b** to obtain (a specified number) in this way: *one throws a 3 and the other throws a 5.* **7** to shape (clay) on a potter's wheel. **8** to give (a party). **9** *Informal* to confuse or disconcert: *the question threw me.* **10** to direct or cast (a look, light, etc.): *the lamp threw a shadow on the ceiling.* **11** to project (the voice) so as to make it appear to come from somewhere else. **12** *Informal* to lose (a contest) deliberately. **13 throw a punch** to strike, or attempt to strike, someone with one's fist. **14 throw oneself at** to behave in a way which makes it clear that one is trying to win the affection of (someone). **15 throw oneself into** to involve oneself enthusiastically in. **16 throw oneself on** to rely entirely upon (someone's goodwill, etc.): *the president threw himself on the mercy of the American people.* ✧ *n* **17** the act or an instance of throwing. **18** the distance thrown: *a throw of 90 metres.* **19** (in sports such as wrestling or judo) a move which causes one's opponent to fall to the floor. **20** a decorative blanket or cover. **21 a throw** each: *we drank our way through a couple of bottles of claret at £12.50 a throw.* ✧ See also **throwaway, throwback**, etc. ▷ HISTORY Old English *thrāwan* to turn, torment

throwaway *adj* **1** *Chiefly Brit & NZ* said or done incidentally: *a throwaway line.* **2** designed to be discarded after use: *throwaway cups.* ✧ *vb* **throw away 3** to get rid of or discard: *try to recycle glass bottles instead of simply throwing them away.* **4** to fail to make good use of: *she threw away the chance of a brilliant career when she got married.*

throwback *n* **1** a person or thing that is like something that existed or was common long ago: *his ideas were a throwback to old colonial attitudes.* ✧ *vb* **throw back 2** to remind someone of (something he or she said or did previously) in order to upset him or her: *he threw back at me everything I'd said the week before.*

throw in *vb* **1** to add at no additional cost: *he'd got good at bargaining them down, making them throw in variations for free.* **2** to contribute (a remark) in a discussion. **3 throw in the towel** *Informal* to give in; accept defeat. ✧ *n* **throw-in 4** *Soccer etc.* the act of putting the ball back into play when it has gone over one of the sidelines, by throwing it over one's head with both hands.

throw up *vb* **1** *Informal* to vomit. **2** to give up or abandon: *he would threaten to throw up his job.* **3** to construct (a building or structure) hastily. **4** to

A B C D E F G H I J K L M N O P Q R S T U V W X Y Z

produce: *these links are throwing up fresh opportunities.*

thrum *vb* **thrumming, thrummed 1** to strum rhythmically but without expression on (a musical instrument). **2** to make a low beating or humming sound: *the air conditioner thrummed.* ✧ *n* **3** a repetitive strumming. ▷ **HISTORY** imitative

thrush[1] *n* any of a large group of songbirds, esp. one having a brown plumage with a spotted breast, such as the mistle thrush and song thrush. ▷ **HISTORY** Old English *thrȳsce*

thrush[2] *n* **1** a fungal disease, esp. of infants, in which whitish spots form on the mouth, throat, and lips. **2** a genital infection caused by the same fungus. ▷ **HISTORY** origin unknown

thrust *vb* **thrusting, thrust 1** to push (someone or something) with force: *he took him by the arm and thrust him towards the door.* **2** to force (someone) into some condition or situation: *the unemployed have been thrust into the front line of politics.* **3** to force (one's way) through a crowd, forest, etc.: *Edward thrust his way towards them.* **4** to stick out or up: *she thrust out her lower lip.* ✧ *n* **5** a forceful drive, push, stab, or lunge: *the thrust of his spear.* **6** a force, esp. one that produces motion. **7** the propulsive force produced by the pressure of air and gas forced out of a jet engine or rocket engine. **8** the essential or most forceful part: *the main thrust of the report.* **9** *Physics* a continuous pressure exerted by one part of an object against another. **10** *Informal* intellectual or emotional drive; forcefulness: *thanks to the ingenuity and enterprising thrust of this company.* ▷ **HISTORY** Old Norse *thrȳsta*

thud *n* **1** a dull heavy sound. **2** a blow or fall that causes such a sound. ✧ *vb* **thudding, thudded 3** to make or cause to make such a sound. ▷ **HISTORY** Old English *thyddan* to strike

thug *n* a tough and violent man, esp. a criminal. ▷ **HISTORY** Hindi *thag* thief ▶ **thuggery** *n* ▶ **thuggish** *adj*

thulium *n Chem* a silvery-grey element of the lanthanide series. Symbol: Tm. ▷ **HISTORY** after *Thule,* a region thought by ancient geographers to be northernmost in the world

thumb *n* **1** the short thick finger of the hand set apart from the others. **2** the part of a glove shaped to fit the thumb. **3 all thumbs** very clumsy. **4 thumbs down** an indication of refusal or disapproval. **5 thumbs up** an indication of encouragement or approval. **6 under someone's thumb** completely under someone else's control. ✧ *vb* **7** to touch, mark, or move with the thumb: *he thumbed the volume switch to maximum.* **8** to attempt to obtain (a lift in a motor vehicle) by signalling with the thumb: *he thumbed a lift to the station.* **9 thumb one's nose at** to behave in a way that shows one's contempt or disregard for: *her mother had always thumbed her nose at convention.* **10 thumb through** to flip the pages of (a book or magazine) in order to glance at the contents. ▷ **HISTORY** Old English *thūma*

thumb index *n* a series of notches cut into the fore-edge of a book to facilitate quick reference.

thumbnail *n* **1** the nail of the thumb. ✧ *adj* **2** concise and brief: *a thumbnail sketch.*

thumbscrew *n* (formerly) an instrument of torture that pinches or crushes the thumbs.

thump *n* **1** the sound of something heavy hitting a comparatively soft surface. **2** a heavy blow with the hand. ✧ *vb* **3** to place (something) on or bang against (something) with a loud dull sound: *thumping the table is aggressive.* **4** to hit or punch (someone): *stop that at once or I'll thump you!* **5** to throb or beat violently: *he could feel his heart thumping.* ▷ **HISTORY** imitative

thumping *adj Slang* huge or excessive: *a thumping majority.*

thunder *n* **1** a loud cracking or deep rumbling noise caused by the rapid expansion of atmospheric gases that are suddenly heated by lightning. **2** any loud booming sound: *the thunder of heavy gunfire.* **3 steal someone's thunder** to lessen the effect of someone's idea or action by anticipating it. ✧ *vb* **4** to make a loud noise like thunder: *an explosion thundered through the shaft.* **5** to speak in a loud, angry manner: *'Get out of here this instant!' he thundered.* **6** to move fast, heavily, and noisily: *a lorry thundered by.* ▷ **HISTORY** Old English *thunor* ▶ **thundery** *adj*

thunderbolt *n* **1** a flash of lightning accompanying thunder. **2** something sudden and unexpected: *his career has been no thunderbolt.* **3** *Myth* a weapon thrown to earth by certain gods. **4** *Sport* a very fast-moving shot or serve.

thunderclap *n* **1** a loud outburst of thunder. **2** something as violent or unexpected as a clap of thunder.

thundercloud *n* a large dark electrically charged cloud associated with thunderstorms.

thunderous *adj* **1** resembling thunder in loudness: *thunderous applause.* **2** threatening or angry: *a thunderous scowl.*

thunderstorm *n* a storm with thunder and lightning and usually heavy rain or hail.

thunderstruck *adj* amazed or shocked.

thurible (**thyoor**-rib-bl) *n* same as **censer**. ▷ **HISTORY** Latin *turibulum*

Thurs. Thursday.

Thursday *n* the fifth day of the week. ▷ **HISTORY** Old English *Thursdæg* Thor's day

thus *adv* **1** as a result or consequence: *the platforms provided a new floor and thus improved and enlarged the premises.* **2** in this manner: *I sat thus for nearly half an hour.* **3** to such a degree: *the competition has been almost bereft of surprise thus far.* ▷ **HISTORY** Old English

thwack *vb* **1** to beat with something flat. ✧ *n* **2 a** a blow with something flat. **b** the sound made by it. ▷ **HISTORY** imitative

thwart *vb* **1** to prevent or foil: *they inflicted such severe losses that they thwarted the invasion.* ✧ *n* **2** the seat across a boat where the rower sits. ▷ **HISTORY** Old Norse *thvert* across

thy *adj Old-fashioned* belonging to or associated in some way with you (thou): *love thy neighbour.* ▷ **HISTORY** variant of *thine*

thylacine *n* an extinct doglike Tasmanian marsupial.

thyme (**time**) *n* a small shrub with white, pink, or red flowers and scented leaves used for seasoning food. ▷ HISTORY Greek *thumon*

thymine *n Biochem* a white crystalline pyrimidine base found in DNA.

thymol *n* a white crystalline substance obtained from thyme, used as a fungicide and an antiseptic.

thymus (**thigh**-muss) *n, pl* **-muses** *or* **-mi** (-my) *Anat* a small gland situated near the base of the neck. ▷ HISTORY Greek *thumos* sweetbread

thyroid *Anat* ✧ *adj* **1** of or relating to the thyroid gland. **2** of or relating to the largest cartilage of the larynx, which forms the Adam's apple in men. ✧ *n* **3** the thyroid gland. ▷ HISTORY Greek *thureos* oblong shield

thyroid gland *n Anat* an endocrine gland that secretes hormones that control metabolism and body growth.

thyself *pron Archaic* the reflexive form of **thou**[1].

ti *n Music* same as **te**.

Ti *Chem* titanium.

tiara *n* **1** a semicircular jewelled headdress worn by some women on formal occasions. **2** the triple-tiered crown sometimes worn by the pope. ▷ HISTORY Greek

tibia (**tib**-ee-a) *n, pl* **tibiae** (**tib**-ee-ee) *or* **tibias** the inner and thicker of the two bones of the human leg below the knee; shinbone. ▷ HISTORY Latin: leg, pipe ▶ **tibial** *adj*

tic *n* a spasmodic muscular twitch. ▷ HISTORY French

tick[1] *n* **1** a mark (✓) used to check off or indicate the correctness of something. **2** a recurrent metallic tapping or clicking sound, such as that made by a clock. **3** *Informal* a moment or instant: *won't be a tick.* ✧ *vb* **4** to mark or check with a tick. **5** to produce a recurrent tapping sound or indicate by such a sound: *the clock ticked away.* **6 what makes someone tick** *Informal* the basic motivation of a person. ✧ See also **tick off, tick over**. ▷ HISTORY Low German *tikk* touch

tick[2] *n* a small parasitic creature typically living on the skin of warm-blooded animals and feeding on the blood and tissues of their hosts: *a sheep tick.* ▷ HISTORY Old English *ticca*

tick[3] *n Brit & NZ informal* account or credit: *a spending spree that was financed on tick.* ▷ HISTORY from *ticket*

ticker *n Slang* the heart.

ticker tape *n* (formerly) a continuous paper tape on which current stock quotations were printed by machine.

ticket *n* **1** a printed piece of paper or cardboard showing that the holder is entitled to certain rights, such as travel on a train or bus or entry to a place of public entertainment. **2** a label or tag attached to an article showing information such as its price and size. **3** an official notification of a parking or traffic offence. **4** the declared policy of a political party. **5 that's (just) the ticket** *Informal* that's the right or appropriate thing. ✧ *vb* **-eting, -eted 6** to issue or attach a ticket or tickets to. ▷ HISTORY Old French *etiquet*

tickets *pl n S African informal* death or ruin; the end.

ticking *n* a strong cotton fabric, often striped, used esp. for mattress and pillow covers. ▷ HISTORY probably from Middle Dutch *tīke*

tickle *vb* **-ling, -led 1** to touch or stroke (someone), so as to produce laughter or a twitching sensation. **2** to itch or tingle. **3** to amuse or please. **4 tickled pink** *or* **to death** *Informal* greatly pleased. **5 tickle someone's fancy** to appeal to or amuse someone. ✧ *n* **6** a sensation of light stroking or itching: *a tickle in the throat.* **7** the act of tickling. **8** *Canad* (in the Atlantic Provinces) a narrow strait. ▷ HISTORY Middle English *titelen*

ticklish *adj* **1** sensitive to being tickled. **2** delicate or difficult: *a ticklish problem.*

tick off *vb* **1** to mark with a tick, esp. to show that an item on a list has been dealt with. **2** *Informal* to reprimand or scold (someone). ▶ **ticking-off** *n*

tick over *vb* **1** (of an engine) to run at low speed with the transmission disengaged. **2** to run smoothly without any major changes: *the business is just ticking over.*

ticktack *n Brit & Austral* a system of sign language, mainly using the hands, by which bookmakers transmit their odds to each other at race courses.

tidal *adj* **1** (of a river, lake, or sea) having tides. **2** of or relating to tides: *a tidal surge.*

tidal energy *n Physics* energy obtained by harnessing tidal power.

tidal flat *n* a level area that is covered with water at high tide.

tidal wave *n* **1** *Not in technical use* same as **tsunami**. **2** an unusually large incoming wave, often caused by high winds and spring tides. **3** a forceful and widespread movement in public opinion, action, etc.: *a tidal wave of scandals and embezzlement.*

tiddler *n Informal* **1** a very small fish, esp. a stickleback. **2** a small child. ▷ HISTORY perhaps from TIDDLY[1]

tiddly[1] *adj* **-dlier, -dliest** *Brit* very small. ▷ HISTORY childish variant of *little*

tiddly[2] *adj* **-dlier, -dliest** *Informal, chiefly Brit* slightly drunk. ▷ HISTORY origin unknown

tiddlywinks *n* a game in which players try to flick discs of plastic into a cup. ▷ HISTORY origin unknown

tide *n* **1** the alternate rise and fall of sea level caused by the gravitational pull of the sun and moon. **2** the current caused by these changes in level: *I got caught by the tide and almost drowned.* **3** a widespread tendency or movement: *the rising tide of nationalism.* **4** *Literary or old-fashioned* a season or time: *Yuletide.* ▷ HISTORY Old English *tīd* time

tideline *n* the mark or line left by the tide when it retreats from its highest point.

tidemark *n* **1** a mark left by the highest or lowest point of a tide. **2** *Chiefly Brit & NZ* a line of dirt left

A B C D E F G H I J K L M N O P Q R S T U V W X Y Z

round a bath after the water has been drained away. **3** *Informal, chiefly Brit* a dirty mark on the skin, indicating the extent to which someone has washed.

tide over *vb* **tiding, tided** to help (someone) to get through a period of difficulty or distress: *they need some form of Social Security to tide them over.*

tidings *pl n* information or news. ▷ **HISTORY** Old English *tīdung*

tidy *adj* **-dier, -diest 1** neat and orderly. **2** *Brit, Austral & NZ informal* quite large: *a tidy sum of money.* ✧ *vb* **-dies, -dying, -died 3** to put (things) in their proper place; make neat: *I've tidied up the toys under the bed.* ✧ *n, pl* **-dies 4** a small container for odds and ends. ▷ **HISTORY** (originally: timely, excellent) from *tide* ▶ **tidily** *adv* ▶ **tidiness** *n*

tie *vb* **tying, tied 1** to fasten or be fastened with string, rope, etc.: *a parcel tied with string.* **2** to make a knot or bow in (something): *hang on while I tie my laces.* **3** to restrict or limit: *they had children and were consequently tied to the school holidays.* **4** to equal the score of a competitor or fellow candidate: *three players tied for second place.* ✧ *n* **5** a long narrow piece of material worn, esp. by men, under the collar of a shirt, tied in a knot close to the throat with the ends hanging down the front. **6** a bond or link: *he still has close ties to the town where he grew up.* **7** a string, wire, etc., with which something is tied. **8** *Brit sport* a match in a knockout competition: *whoever wins the tie will play Australia in the semifinals.* **9 a** a result in a match or competition in which the scores or times of some of the competitors are the same: *a tie for second place.* **b** the match or competition in which the scores or results are equal. **10** a regular commitment that limits a person's freedom: *it's a bit of a tie having to visit him every day.* **11** something which supports or links parts of a structure. **12** *US & Canad* a sleeper on a railway track. **13** *Music* a curved line connecting two notes of the same pitch indicating that the sound is to be prolonged for their joint time value. ✧ See also **tie in, tie up**. ▷ **HISTORY** Old English *tīgan*

tie-break *or* **tie-breaker** *n* an extra game or question that decides the result of a contest that has ended in a draw.

tied *adj Brit* **1** (of a public house) allowed to sell beer from only one particular brewery. **2** (of a house) rented out to the tenant for as long as he or she is employed by the owner.

tie in *vb* **1** to have or cause to have a close link or connection: *there's no evidence to tie this killing in with the murder of Mrs McGowan.* ✧ *n* **tie-in 2** a link or connection. **3** a book or other product that is linked with a film or TV programme.

tier *n* one of a set of rows placed one above and behind the other, such as theatre seats. ▷ **HISTORY** Old French *tire*

tie up *vb* **1** to bind (someone or something) securely with string or rope. **2** to moor (a vessel). **3** to commit (money etc.) so that it is unavailable for other uses: *people don't want to tie up their savings for a long period.* ✧ *n* **tie-up 4** a link or connection.

tiff *n* a minor quarrel. ▷ **HISTORY** origin unknown

tiger *n* **1** a large Asian mammal of the cat family which has a tawny yellow coat with black stripes. **2** a dynamic, forceful, or cruel person. **3** a country, esp. in E Asia, that is achieving rapid economic growth. ▷ **HISTORY** Greek *tigris*

tiger lily *n* a lily of China and Japan with black-spotted orange flowers.

tiger moth *n* a moth with conspicuously striped and spotted wings.

tiger snake *n* a highly venomous brown-and-yellow Australian snake.

tight *adj* **1** stretched or drawn taut: *loosening-up of tight muscles.* **2** closely fitting: *wearing a jacket that was too tight for him.* **3** made, fixed, or closed firmly and securely: *a tight band.* **4** constructed so as to prevent the passage of water, air, etc.: *watertight; airtight.* **5** cramped and allowing very little room for movement: *they squeezed him into the tight space.* **6** unyielding or stringent: *tight security.* **7** (of a situation) difficult or dangerous. **8** allowing only the minimum time or money for doing something: *we have been working to a tight schedule.* **9** *Brit, Austral & NZ informal* mean or miserly. **10** (of a match or game) very close or even. **11** *Informal* drunk. **12** (of a corner or turn) turning through a large angle in a short distance: *the boat skidded round in a tight turn.* ✧ *adv* **13** in a close, firm, or secure way: *they held each other tight.* ▷ **HISTORY** Old Norse *thēttr* of close texture ▶ **tightly** *adv* ▶ **tightness** *n*

tighten *vb* to make or become tight or tighter.

tight-lipped *adj* **1** unwilling to give any information; secretive: *the Minister remained tight-lipped when it came to answering the press's questions.* **2** with the lips pressed tightly together, as through anger: *tight-lipped determination.*

tightrope *n* a rope stretched taut on which acrobats perform.

tights *pl n* a one-piece clinging garment covering the body from the waist to the feet, worn by women and also by acrobats, dancers, etc.

tigress *n* **1** a female tiger. **2** a fierce, cruel, or passionate woman.

tiki (**tee**-kee) *n* a Maori greenstone neck ornament in the form of a fetus. ▷ **HISTORY** Maori

tikka *adj Indian cookery* (of meat) marinated in spices and then dry-roasted: *chicken tikka.*

tilde *n* a mark (~) used in some languages to indicate that the letter over which it is placed is pronounced in a certain way, as in Spanish *señor.* ▷ **HISTORY** Spanish

tile *n* **1** a thin piece of ceramic, plastic, etc., used with others to cover a surface, such as a floor or wall. **2** a rectangular block used as a playing piece in mah jong and other games. **3 on the tiles** *Informal* out having a good time and drinking a lot. ✧ *vb* **tiling, tiled 4** to cover (a surface) with tiles. ▷ **HISTORY** Latin *tegula* ▶ **tiled** *adj* ▶ **tiler** *n*

tiling *n* **1** tiles collectively. **2** something made of or surfaced with tiles.

till[1] *conj, prep* same as **until.** ▷ HISTORY Old English *til*

WORD TIP
Till is a variant of *until* that is acceptable at all levels of language. *Until* is, however, often preferred at the beginning of a sentence in formal writing: *until his behaviour improves, he cannot become a member.*

till[2] *vb* to cultivate (land) for the raising of crops: *a constant round of sowing, tilling and harvesting.* ▷ HISTORY Old English *tilian* to try, obtain ▶ **tillable** *adj* ▶ **tiller** *n*

till[3] *n* a box or drawer into which money taken from customers is put, now usually part of a cash register. ▷ HISTORY origin unknown

tillage *n* **1** the act, process, or art of tilling. **2** tilled land.

tiller *n Naut* a handle used to turn the rudder when steering a boat. ▷ HISTORY Anglo-French *teiler* beam of a loom

tillite *n Geol* sedimentary rock composed of consolidated glacial sediment.

tilt *vb* **1** to move into a sloping position with one end or side higher than the other: *Dave tilted his chair back on two legs.* **2** to move (part of the body) slightly upwards or to the side: *Marie tilted her head back.* **3** to become more influenced by a particular idea or group: *the party is tilting more and more to the right.* **4** to compete against someone in a jousting contest. ✧ *n* **5** a slope or angle: *a tilt to one side.* **6** the act of tilting. **7** (esp. in medieval Europe) **a** a jousting contest. **b** a thrust with a lance delivered during a tournament. **8** an attempt to win a contest: *a tilt at the world title.* **9 at full tilt** at full speed or force. ▷ HISTORY Old English *tealtian*

tilth *n* **1** the tilling of land. **2** the condition of land that has been tilled.

timber *n* **1** wood as a building material. **2** trees collectively. **3** a wooden beam in the frame of a house, boat, etc. ✧ *adj* **4** made out of timber: *timber houses.* **5** of or involved in the production or sale of wood as a building material: *a timber merchant.* ▷ HISTORY Old English ▶ **timbered** *adj* ▶ **timbering** *n*

timber line *n* the geographical limit beyond which trees will not grow.

timbre (**tam**-bra) *n* the distinctive quality of sound produced by a particular voice or musical instrument. ▷ HISTORY French

timbrel *n Chiefly biblical* a tambourine. ▷ HISTORY Old French

time *n* **1** the past, present, and future regarded as a continuous whole. *RELATED ADJECTIVE* ➧ **temporal** **2** *Physics* a quantity measuring duration, measured with reference to the rotation of the earth or from the vibrations of certain atoms. **3** a specific point in time expressed in hours and minutes: *what time are you going?* **4** a system of reckoning for expressing time: *the deadline is 5:00 Eastern Time today.* **5** an unspecified interval; a while: *some recover for a time and then relapse.* **6** an instance or occasion: *when was the last time you saw it?* **7** a sufficient interval or period: *I need time to think.* **8** an occasion or period of specified quality: *they'd had a lovely time.* **9** a suitable moment: *the time has come to make peace.* **10** a period or point marked by specific attributes or events: *in Victorian times.* **11** *Brit* the time at which licensed premises are required by law to stop selling alcoholic drinks. **12** the rate of pay for work done in normal working hours: *you get double time for working on a Sunday.* **13 a** the system of combining beats in music into successive groupings by which the rhythm of the music is established. **b** a specific system having a specific number of beats in each grouping or bar: *duple time.* **14 against time** in an effort to complete something in a limited period. **15 ahead of time** before the deadline. **16 at one time a** once or formerly. **b** simultaneously. **17 at the same time a** simultaneously. **b** nevertheless or however. **18 at times** sometimes. **19 beat time** to indicate the tempo of a piece of music by waving a baton, hand, etc. **20 do time** *Informal* to serve a term in jail. **21 for the time being** for the moment; temporarily. **22 from time to time** at intervals; occasionally. **23 have no time for** to have no patience with. **24 in no time** very quickly. **25 in one's own time a** outside paid working hours. **b** at the speed of one's choice. **26 in time a** early or at the appointed time: *he made it to the hospital in time for the baby's arrival.* **b** eventually: *in time, the children of intelligent parents will come to dominate.* **c** *Music* at a correct metrical or rhythmic pulse. **27 make time** to find an opportunity. **28 on time** at the expected or scheduled time. **29 pass the time** to occupy oneself when there is nothing else to do: *they pass their time watching game shows on television.* **30 pass the time of day** to have a short casual conversation (with someone). **31 time and again** frequently. **32 time of one's life** a memorably enjoyable time. **33 time out of mind** from long before anyone can remember. ✧ *vb* **timing, timed 34** to measure the speed or duration of: *my Porsche was timed at 128 mph.* **35** to set a time for: *the attack was timed for 6 a.m.* **36** to do (something) at a suitable time: *her entry could not have been better timed.* ✧ *adj* **37** operating automatically at or for a set time: *an electrical time switch.* ✧ *interj* **38** the word called out by a publican signalling that it is closing time. ✧ See also **times.** ▷ HISTORY Old English *tīma*

time-and-motion study *n* the analysis of work procedures to work out the most efficient methods of operation.

time capsule *n* a container holding articles representative of the current age, buried for discovery in the future.

time exposure *n* a photograph produced by exposing film for a relatively long period, usually a few seconds.

time-honoured *adj* having been used or done for a long time and established by custom.

time-lapse photography *n Photog* the technique of photographing a slow process, such as a flower opening, by taking pictures at regular intervals and then viewing them as a film at normal speed.

a b c d e f g h i j k l m n o p q r s t u v w x y z

A B C D E F G H I J K L M N O P Q R S T U V W X Y Z

timeless *adj* **1** unaffected by time or by changes in fashion, society, etc.: *the timeless appeal of tailored wool jackets.* **2** eternal and everlasting: *the timeless universal reality behind all religions.* ▶ **timelessness** *n*

timely *adj* **-lier, -liest,** *adv* at the right or an appropriate time.

time-out *n* **1** *Sport chiefly US, Canad & Austral* an interruption in play during which players rest, discuss tactics, etc. **2 take time out** to take a break from a job or activity.

timepiece *n* a device, such as a clock or watch, which measures and indicates time.

timer *n* a device for measuring time, esp. a switch or regulator that causes a mechanism to operate at a specific time.

times *prep* multiplied by: *ten times four is forty.*

timescale *n* the period of time within which events occur or are due to occur.

timeserver *n* a person who changes his or her views in order to gain support or favour.

time sharing *n* **1** a system of part ownership of a property for use as a holiday home whereby each participant owns the property for a particular period every year. **2** a system by which users at different terminals of a computer can communicate with it at the same time.

time signature *n Music* a sign, usually consisting of two figures placed after the key signature, that indicates the number and length of beats in the bar.

timetable *n* **1** a plan of the times when a job or activity should be done: *the timetable for the Royal Visit.* **2** a list of departure and arrival times of trains or buses: *a timetable hung on the wall beside the ticket office.* **3** a plan of the times when different subjects or classes are taught in a school or college: *a heavy timetable of lectures and practical classes.* ✧ *vb* **-tabling, -tabled 4** to set a time when a particular thing should be done: *the meeting is timetabled for 3 o'clock.*

time value *n Music* the duration of a note relative to other notes in a composition and considered in relation to the basic tempo.

time warp *n* an imagined distortion of the progress of time, so that, for instance, events from the past seem to be happening in the present.

time zone *n Geog* a region throughout which the same standard time is used.

timid *adj* **1** lacking courage or self-confidence: *a timid youth.* **2** indicating shyness or fear: *a timid and embarrassed smile.* ▷ **HISTORY** Latin *timere* to fear ▶ **timidity** *n* ▶ **timidly** *adv*

timing *n* the ability to judge when to do or say something so as to make the best effect, for instance in the theatre, in playing an instrument, or in hitting a ball in sport.

timorous (**tim**-mor-uss) *adj Literary* lacking courage or self-confidence: *a reclusive timorous creature.* ▷ **HISTORY** Latin *timor* fear ▶ **timorously** *adv*

timpani *or* **tympani** (**tim**-pan-ee) *pl n* a set of kettledrums. ▷ **HISTORY** Italian ▶ **timpanist** *or* **tympanist** *n*

tin *n* **1** a soft silvery-white metallic element. Symbol: Sn. **2** a sealed airtight metal container used for preserving and storing food or drink: *a cupboard full of packets and tins.* **3** any metal container: *a tin of paint.* **4** the contents of a tin. **5** *Brit, Austral, & NZ* galvanized iron, used to make roofs. ✧ *vb* **tinning, tinned 6** to put (food) into tins. ▷ **HISTORY** Old English

tincture *n* a medicine consisting of a small amount of a drug dissolved in alcohol. ▷ **HISTORY** Latin *tinctura* a dyeing

tinder *n* dry wood or other easily-burning material used to start a fire. ▷ **HISTORY** Old English *tynder* ▶ **tindery** *adj*

tinderbox *n* (formerly) a small box for tinder, esp. one fitted with a flint and steel which could be used to make a spark.

tine *n* a slender prong of a fork or a deer's antler. ▷ **HISTORY** Old English *tind* ▶ **tined** *adj*

tinfoil *n* a paper-thin sheet of metal, used for wrapping foodstuffs.

ting *n* a high metallic sound such as that made by a small bell. ▷ **HISTORY** imitative

tinge *n* **1** a slight tint or colouring: *his skin had an unhealthy greyish tinge.* **2** a very small amount: *both goals had a tinge of fortune.* ✧ *vb* **tingeing** *or* **tinging, tinged 3** to colour or tint faintly: *the sunset tinged the lake with pink.* **4 tinged with** having a small amount of a particular quality: *the victory was tinged with sadness.* ▷ **HISTORY** Latin *tingere* to colour

tingle *vb* **-gling, -gled 1** to feel a mild prickling or stinging sensation, as from cold or excitement. ✧ *n* **2** a mild prickling or stinging feeling. ▷ **HISTORY** probably a variant of *tinkle* ▶ **tingling** *adj* ▶ **tingly** *adj*

tinker *n* **1** (esp. formerly) a travelling mender of pots and pans. **2** *Scot & Irish* a Gypsy. **3** a mischievous child. ✧ *vb* **4 tinker with** to try to repair or improve (something) by making lots of minor adjustments. ▷ **HISTORY** origin unknown

tinkle *vb* **-kling, -kled 1** to ring with a high tinny sound like a small bell. ✧ *n* **2** a high clear ringing sound. **3** *Brit informal* a telephone call. ▷ **HISTORY** imitative ▶ **tinkly** *adj*

tinned *adj* (of food) preserved by being sealed in a tin.

tinny[1] *adj* **-nier, -niest 1** (of a sound) high, thin, and metallic: *the tinny sound of a transistor radio.* **2** cheap or shoddy: *a tinny East European car.*

tinny[2] *adj* **-nier, -niest** *Austral & NZ slang* lucky.

tin-opener *n* a small tool for opening tins.

tin plate *n* thin steel sheet coated with a layer of tin to protect it from corrosion.

tinpot *adj Informal* worthless or unimportant: *a tinpot dictator.*

tinsel *n* **1** a decoration consisting of a piece of metallic thread with thin strips of metal foil attached along its length. **2** anything cheap, showy, and gaudy: *all their tinsel and show counts* *for nothing.* ✧ *adj* **3** made of or decorated with tinsel. **4** cheap, showy, and gaudy. ▷ **HISTORY** Latin *scintilla* a spark ▶ **tinselly** *adj*

tint *n* **1** a shade of a colour, esp. a pale one: *his eyes had a yellow tint.* **2** a colour that is softened by the addition of white: *a room decorated in pastel tints.* **3** a dye for the hair. ✧ *vb* **4** to give a tint to (something, such as hair). ▷ **HISTORY** Latin *tingere* to colour

tintinnabulation *n* the ringing or pealing of bells. ▷ **HISTORY** Latin *tintinnare* to tinkle

tiny *adj* **tinier, tiniest** very small. ▷ **HISTORY** origin unknown

tip[1] *n* **1** a narrow or pointed end of something: *the northern tip of Japan.* **2** a small piece attached to the end or bottom of something: *boot tips keep boots from getting scuffed.* ✧ *vb* **tipping, tipped 3** to make or form a tip on: *the long strips that hang down are tipped with silver cones.* ▷ **HISTORY** Old Norse *typpi* ▶ **tipped** *adj*

tip[2] *n* **1** an amount of money given to someone, such as a waiter, in return for service. **2** a helpful hint or warning: *here are some sensible tips to help you avoid sunburn.* **3** a piece of inside information, esp. in betting or investing. ✧ *vb* **tipping, tipped 4** to give a tip to. ▷ **HISTORY** origin unknown

tip[3] *vb* **tipping, tipped 1** to tilt: *he tipped back his chair.* **2 tip over** to tilt so as to overturn or fall: *the box tipped over and the clothes in it spilled out.* **3** *Brit* to dump (rubbish). **4** to pour out (the contents of a container): *he tipped the water from the basin down the sink.* ✧ *n* **5** a rubbish dump. ▷ **HISTORY** origin unknown

tippet *n* a scarflike piece of fur, often made from a whole animal skin, worn, esp. formerly, round a woman's shoulders. ▷ **HISTORY** probably from TIP[1]

tipple *vb* **-pling, -pled 1** to drink alcohol regularly, esp. in small quantities. ✧ *n* **2** an alcoholic drink. ▷ **HISTORY** origin unknown ▶ **tippler** *n*

tipstaff *n* **1** a court official. **2** a metal-tipped staff formerly used as a symbol of office.

tipster *n* a person who sells tips to people betting on horse races or speculating on the stock market.

tipsy *adj* **-sier, -siest** slightly drunk. ▷ **HISTORY** from TIP[3] ▶ **tipsiness** *n*

tiptoe *vb* **-toeing, -toed 1** to walk quietly with the heels off the ground. ✧ *n* **2 on tiptoe** on the tips of the toes or on the ball of the foot and the toes: *I stood on tiptoe.*

tiptop *adj, adv* of the highest quality or condition.

TIR International Road Transport. ▷ **HISTORY** French *Transports Internationaux Routiers*

tirade *n* a long angry speech or denunciation. ▷ **HISTORY** French

tire[1] *vb* **tiring, tired 1** to reduce the energy of, as by exertion: *she could still do things that would tire women half her age.* **2** to become wearied or bored: *he simply stopped talking when he tired of my questions.* ▷ **HISTORY** Old English *tēorian* ▶ **tiring** *adj*

tire[2] *n US* same as **tyre**.

tired *adj* **1** weary or exhausted: *they were tired after their long journey.* **2** bored with or no longer interested in something: *I'm tired of staying in watching TV every night.* **3** having been used so often as to be no longer interesting: *you haven't fallen for that tired old line, have you?* ▶ **tiredness** *n*

tireless *adj* energetic and determined: *a tireless worker for charity.* ▶ **tirelessly** *adv*

tiresome *adj* boring and irritating.

tissue *n* **1** a group of cells in an animal or plant with a similar structure and function: *muscular tissue forms 42% of the body tissue.* **2** a thin piece of soft absorbent paper used as a disposable handkerchief, towel, etc. **3** an interwoven series: *a tissue of lies.* ▷ **HISTORY** Old French *tissu* woven cloth

tit[1] *n* any of various small European songbirds, such as the bluetit, that feed on insects and seeds. ▷ **HISTORY** Middle English *tite* little

tit[2] *n* **1** *Slang* a female breast. **2** a teat or nipple. ▷ **HISTORY** Old English *titt*

titan *n* a person of great strength, importance, or size: *one of the titans of the computer industry.* ▷ **HISTORY** after the *Titans,* a family of gods in Greek mythology

titanic *adj* having or requiring colossal strength: *a titanic struggle.*

> **WORD HISTORY**
> In Greek mythology, the *Titans* were a family of twelve giants, the children of Uranus and Gaia.

titanium *n Chem* a strong white metallic element used in the manufacture of strong lightweight alloys, esp. aircraft parts. Symbol: Ti. ▷ **HISTORY** from *titan*

titbit *or esp US* **tidbit** *n* **1** a tasty small piece of food. **2** a pleasing scrap of scandal: *an interesting titbit of gossip.* ▷ **HISTORY** origin unknown

tit-for-tat *adj* done in return or retaliation for a similar act: *a spate of tit-for-tat killings.* ▷ **HISTORY** earlier *tip for tap*

tithe *n* **1** one tenth of one's income or produce paid to the church as a tax. **2** a tenth or very small part of anything: *he had accomplished only a tithe of his great dream.* ✧ *vb* **tithing, tithed 3** to demand a tithe from. **4** to pay a tithe or tithes. ▷ **HISTORY** Old English *teogotha* ▶ **tithable** *adj*

tithe barn *n* a large barn where, formerly, the agricultural tithe of a parish was stored.

Titian (**tish**-un) *adj* (of hair) reddish-yellow. ▷ **HISTORY** from *Titian,* Italian painter, because he often used this hair colour in his paintings

titillate *vb* **-lating, -lated** to arouse or excite pleasurably, esp. in a sexual way. ▷ **HISTORY** Latin *titillare* ▶ **titillating** *adj* ▶ **titillation** *n*

titivate *vb* **-vating, -vated** to make smarter or neater. ▷ **HISTORY** perhaps from *tidy* + *cultivate* ▶ **titivation** *n*

title *n* **1** the distinctive name of a book, film, record, etc.: *his first album bore the title 'Safe as Milk'.* **2** a descriptive name or heading of a section of a book, speech, etc. **3** a book or periodical: *publishers were averaging a total of 500 new titles annually.* **4** a name or epithet signifying rank, office, or function: *the job bears the title Assistant Divisional Administrator.* **5** a formal designation, such as *Mrs* or *Dr.* **6** *Sport* a championship: *the Italians have won the title.* **7** *Law* the legal right to possession of property. ▷ **HISTORY** Latin *titulus*

titled *adj* having a title such as 'Lady' or 'Sir' which indicates a high social rank.

title deed *n* a document containing evidence of a person's legal right or title to property, esp. a house or land.

titleholder *n* a person who holds a title, esp. a sporting championship.

title role *n* the role of the character after whom a play or film is named.

titmouse *n, pl* **-mice** same as **tit**[1].
▷ **HISTORY** Middle English *tite* little + MOUSE

titrate (**tite**-rate) *vb* **-trating, -trated** *Chem* to measure the volume or concentration of (a solution) by titration. ▷ **HISTORY** French *titrer*

titration *n Chem* an operation in which a measured amount of one solution is added to a known quantity of another solution until the reaction between the two is complete. If the concentration of one solution is known, that of the other can be calculated.

titter *vb* **1** to snigger, esp. derisively or in a suppressed way. ✧ *n* **2** a suppressed laugh or snigger. ▷ **HISTORY** imitative

tittle-tattle *n* **1** idle chat or gossip. ✧ *vb* **-tattling, -tattled 2** to chatter or gossip.

titular *adj* **1** in name only: *titular head of state.* **2** of or having a title.

tizzy *n, pl* **-zies** *Informal* a state of confusion or excitement. ▷ **HISTORY** origin unknown

T-junction *n* a junction where one road joins another at right angles but does not cross it.

Tl *Chem* thallium.

Tm *Chem* thulium.

TN Tennessee.

TNT *n* 2,4,6-trinitrotoluene: a type of powerful explosive.

to *prep* **1** used to indicate the destination of the subject or object of an action: *he went to the theatre.* **2** used to introduce the indirect object of a verb: *talk to him.* **3** used to introduce the infinitive of a verb: *I'm going to lie down.* **4** as far as or until: *from September 11 to October 25.* **5** used to indicate that two things have an equivalent value: *there are 16 ounces to the pound.* **6** against or onto: *I put my ear to the door.* **7** before the hour of: *17 minutes to midnight.* **8** accompanied by: *dancing to a live band.* **9** as compared with: *four goals to nil.* **10** used to indicate a resulting condition: *burnt to death.* **11** working for or employed by: *Chaplain to the Nigerian Chaplaincy in Britain.* **12** in commemoration of: *a memorial to the victims of the disaster.* ✧ *adv* **13** towards a closed position: *push the door to.* ▷ **HISTORY** Old English *tō*

toad *n* **1** an amphibian which resembles a frog, but has a warty skin and spends more time on dry land. **2** a loathsome person. ▷ **HISTORY** Old English *tādige*

toadflax *n* a plant with narrow leaves and yellow-orange flowers.

toad-in-the-hole *n Brit & NZ* a dish made of sausages baked in a batter.

toadstool *n* any of various poisonous funguses consisting of a caplike top on a stem.

toady *n, pl* **toadies 1** a person who flatters and ingratiates himself or herself in a fawning way: *a spineless political toady.* ✧ *vb* **toadies, toadying, toadied 2** to fawn on and flatter (someone).
▷ **HISTORY** shortened from *toadeater,* originally a quack's assistant who pretended to eat toads, hence a flatterer ▶ **toadyism** *n*

to and fro *adv, adj also* **to-and-fro 1** back and forth: *he moved his head to and fro as if dodging blows.* **2** from one place to another then back again: *the ferry sailed to and fro across the river.* ▶ **toing and froing** *n*

toast[1] *n* **1** sliced bread browned by exposure to heat. ✧ *vb* **2** to brown (bread) under a grill or over a fire. **3** to warm or be warmed: *toasting his feet at the fire.* ▷ **HISTORY** Latin *tostus* parched

toast[2] *n* **1** a proposal of health or success given to a person or thing and marked by people raising glasses and drinking together. **2** a person or thing that is honoured: *his success made him the toast of the British film industry.* ✧ *vb* **3** to propose or drink a toast to (a person or thing). ▷ **HISTORY** from the spiced toast formerly put in wine

toaster *n* an electrical device for toasting bread.

tobacco *n, pl* **-cos** *or* **-coes** an American plant with large leaves which are dried for smoking, or chewing, or made into snuff. ▷ **HISTORY** Spanish *tabaco*

tobacconist *n Brit & Austral* a person or shop that sells tobacco, cigarettes, pipes, etc.

toboggan *n* **1** a long narrow sledge used for sliding over snow and ice. ✧ *vb* **2** to ride on a toboggan. ▷ **HISTORY** from a Native American language

toby *n, pl* **-bies** *NZ* a water stopcock at the boundary of a street and house section.
▷ **HISTORY** origin unknown

toby jug *n Chiefly Brit* a beer mug or jug in the form of a stout seated man wearing a three-cornered hat and smoking a pipe.
▷ **HISTORY** from the name *Tobias*

toccata (tok-**kah**-ta) *n* a piece of fast music for the organ, harpsichord, or piano, usually in a rhythmically free style. ▷ **HISTORY** Italian

Toc H *n* a society formed after World War I to encourage Christian comradeship. ▷ **HISTORY** from initials of *Talbot House,* Poperinge, Belgium, its original headquarters

tod *n* **on one's tod** *Brit slang* by oneself; alone.
▷ **HISTORY** rhyming slang *Tod Sloan/own*

today *n* **1** this day, as distinct from yesterday or tomorrow. **2** the present age: *in today's world.* ✧ *adv* **3** during or on this day: *I hope you're feeling better today.* **4** nowadays: *this is one of the most reliable cars available today.* ▷ **HISTORY** Old English *tō dæge,* literally: on this day

A B C D E F G H I J K L M N O P Q R S T U V W X Y Z

toddle *vb* **-dling, -dled 1** to walk with short unsteady steps, like a young child. **2 toddle off** *Jocular* to depart: *he toddled off to bed.* ✧ *n* **3** the act or an instance of walking with short unsteady steps. ▷ **HISTORY** origin unknown

toddler *n* a young child who has only just learned how to walk.

toddy *n, pl* **-dies** a drink made from spirits, esp. whisky, hot water, sugar, and usually lemon juice. ▷ **HISTORY** Hindi *tārī* juice of the palmyra palm

to-do *n, pl* **-dos** *Brit, Austral & NZ* a commotion, fuss, or quarrel.

toe *n* **1** any one of the digits of the foot. **2** the part of a shoe or sock covering the toes. **3 on one's toes** alert. **4 tread on someone's toes** to offend a person, esp. by trespassing on his or her field of responsibility. ✧ *vb* **toeing, toed 5** to touch or kick with the toe. **6 toe the line** to conform to expected attitudes or standards. ▷ **HISTORY** Old English *tā*

toecap *n* a reinforced covering for the toe of a boot or shoe.

toehold *n* **1** a small space on a rock, mountain, etc., which can be used to support the toe of the foot in climbing. **2** any means of gaining access or advantage: *the French car industry has lost its last toehold in America.*

toenail *n* a thin hard clear plate covering part of the upper surface of the end of each toe.

toerag *n Brit slang* a contemptible or despicable person.

toff *n Brit slang* a well-dressed or upper-class person. ▷ **HISTORY** perhaps from *tuft,* nickname for a titled student at Oxford University wearing a cap with a gold tassel

toffee *n* **1** a sticky chewy sweet made by boiling sugar with water and butter. **2 can't (do something) for toffee** *Informal* is not competent or talented at (doing something): *she couldn't dance for toffee.* ▷ **HISTORY** earlier *taffy*

toffee-apple *n* an apple fixed on a stick and coated with a thin layer of toffee.

toffee-nosed *adj Slang* snobbish or conceited.

tofu *n* a food with a soft cheeselike consistency made from unfermented soya-bean curd. ▷ **HISTORY** Japanese

tog *n* unit for measuring the insulating power of duvets.

toga (**toe**-ga) *n* a garment worn by citizens of ancient Rome, consisting of a piece of cloth draped around the body. ▷ **HISTORY** Latin ▶ **togaed** *adj*

together *adv* **1** with cooperation between people or organizations: *we started a company together.* **2** in or into contact with each other: *he clasped his hands together.* **3** in or into one place: *the family gets together to talk.* **4** at the same time: *'Disgusting,' said Julie and Alice together.* **5** considered collectively: *the properties together were worth more as a unit.* **6** *Old-fashioned* continuously: *working for eight hours together.* **7 together with** in addition to. ✧ *adj* **8** *Slang* self-possessed, competent, and well-organized. ▷ **HISTORY** Old English *tōgædere*

> **☑ WORD TIP**
> See at **plus.**

toggle *n* **1** a bar-shaped button inserted through a loop for fastening coats etc. **2** *Computers* a key on a keyboard which, when pressed, will turn a function or feature on if it is currently off, and turn it off if it is currently on. **3** short for **toggle switch** (sense 1). ▷ **HISTORY** origin unknown

toggle switch *n* **1** an electric switch with a projecting lever that is moved in a particular way to open or close a circuit. **2** same as **toggle** (sense 2).

togs *pl n* **1** *Brit, Austral & NZ informal* clothes. **2** *Austral, NZ & Irish* a swimming costume. ▷ **HISTORY** probably from *toga*

toheroa (toe-a-**roe**-a) *n* a large edible mollusc of New Zealand with a distinctive flavour. ▷ **HISTORY** Maori

tohunga (**toe**-hung-a) *n NZ* a Maori priest. ▷ **HISTORY** Maori

toil *n* **1** hard or exhausting work: *hours of toil beneath the Catalan sun.* ✧ *vb* **2** to work hard: *workers toiling in the fields to produce tea for westerners to drink.* **3** to move slowly and with difficulty, for instance because of exhaustion or the steepness of a slope: *Joanna toiled up the steps to the church.* ▷ **HISTORY** Anglo-French *toiler* to struggle

toilet *n* **1 a** a bowl fitted with a water-flushing device and connected to a drain, for receiving and disposing of urine and faeces. **b** a room with such a fitment. **2** *Old-fashioned* the act of dressing and preparing oneself. ▷ **HISTORY** French *toilette* dress

toilet paper *n* thin absorbent paper used for cleaning oneself after defecation or urination.

toiletry *n, pl* **-ries** an object or cosmetic used in making up, dressing, etc.

toilet water *n* liquid perfume lighter than cologne.

token *n* **1** a symbol, sign, or indication of something: *as a token of respect.* **2** a gift voucher that can be used as payment for goods of a specified value. **3** a metal or plastic disc, such as a substitute for currency for use in a slot machine. **4 by the same token** in the same way as something mentioned previously. ✧ *adj* **5** intended to create an impression but having no real importance: *as a token gesture of goodwill.* ▷ **HISTORY** Old English *tācen*

tokenism *n* the practice of making only a token effort or doing no more than the minimum, esp. in order to comply with a law. ▶ **tokenist** *adj*

told *vb* the past of **tell.**

tolerable *adj* **1** able to be put up with; bearable. **2** *Informal* fairly good. ▶ **tolerably** *adv*

tolerance *n* **1** the quality of accepting other people's rights to their own opinions, beliefs, or actions. **2** capacity to endure something, esp. pain or hardship. **3** the ability of a substance to withstand heat, stress, etc., without damage. **4** *Med* the capacity to endure the effects of a continued or increasing dose of a drug, poison, etc. **5** an acceptable degree of variation in a measurement or value: *the bodywork of the car is precision-engineered with a tolerance of 0.01 millimetres.*

tolerant *adj* **1** accepting of the beliefs, actions, etc., of other people. **2 tolerant of** able to withstand (heat, stress, etc.) without damage.

tolerate *vb* **-ating, -ated 1** to allow something to exist or happen, even although one does not approve of it: *you must learn to tolerate opinions other than your own.* **2** to put up with (someone or something): *he found the pain hard to tolerate.* ▷ HISTORY Latin *tolerare* to sustain ▶ **toleration** *n*

toll[1] *vb* **1** to ring (a bell) slowly and regularly. **2** to announce by tolling: *the bells tolled the Queen's death.* ✧ *n* **3** the slow regular ringing of a bell. ▷ HISTORY origin unknown

toll[2] *n* **1** a charge for the use of certain roads and bridges: *the Skye bridge toll.* **2** loss or damage from a disaster: *the annual death toll on the roads is about 4500.* **3 take a** *or* **its toll** to have a severe and damaging effect: *the continued stress had taken a toll on her health.* ▷ HISTORY Old English *toln*

tolu (tol-**loo**) *n* a sweet-smelling balsam obtained from a South American tree, used in medicine and perfume. ▷ HISTORY after *Santiago de Tolu,* Colombia

toluene *n* a flammable liquid obtained from petroleum and coal tar and used as a solvent and in the manufacture of dyes, explosives, etc. ▷ HISTORY previously obtained from tolu

tom *n* **1** a male cat. ✧ *adj* **2** (of an animal) male: *a tom turkey.* ▷ HISTORY from *Thomas*

tomahawk *n* a fighting axe used by the Native Americans of N America. ▷ HISTORY from a Native American language

tomato *n, pl* **-toes 1** a red fleshy juicy fruit with many edible seeds, eaten in salads, as a vegetable, etc. **2** the plant, originally from South America, on which this fruit grows. ▷ HISTORY S American Indian *tomatl*

tomb *n* **1** a place for the burial of a corpse. **2** a monument over a grave. **3 the tomb** *Poetic* death. ▷ HISTORY Greek *tumbos*

tombola *n Brit* a type of lottery, in which tickets are drawn from a revolving drum. ▷ HISTORY Italian

tombolo *n, pl* **-los** *Geog* a narrow sand or shingle bar linking a small island with another island or the mainland. ▷ HISTORY Italian, from Latin *tumulus* mound

tomboy *n* a girl who behaves or dresses like a boy.

tombstone *n* a gravestone.

tome *n* a large heavy book. ▷ HISTORY Greek *tomos* a slice

tomfoolery *n* foolish behaviour.

Tommy *n, pl* **-mies** *Brit old-fashioned, informal* a private in the British Army. ▷ HISTORY originally *Thomas Atkins,* name used in specimen copies of official forms

Tommy gun *n* a type of light sub-machine-gun. ▷ HISTORY in full *Thompson sub-machine-gun,* from the name of the manufacturer

tomorrow *n* **1** the day after today: *tomorrow's meeting has been cancelled.* **2** the future: *the struggle to build a better tomorrow.* ✧ *adv* **3** on the day after today: *the festival starts tomorrow.* **4** at some time in the future: *they live today as millions more will live tomorrow.* ▷ HISTORY Old English *tō morgenne*

tomtit *n Brit* a small European bird that eats insects and seeds.

tom-tom *n* a long narrow drum beaten with the hands. ▷ HISTORY Hindi *tamtam*

ton[1] *n* **1** *Brit* a unit of weight equal to 2240 pounds or 1016.046 kilograms. **2** *US & Canad* a unit of weight equal to 2000 pounds or 907.184 kilograms. **3** See **metric ton. 4 come down on someone like a ton of bricks** to scold someone very severely. ✧ *adv* **5 tons** a lot: *I've got tons of things to do before going on holiday.* ▷ HISTORY variant of *tun*

ton[2] *n Slang, chiefly Brit* a hundred miles per hour. ▷ HISTORY special use of TON[1]

tonal *adj* **1** *Music* written in a key. **2** of or relating to tone or tonality.

tonality *n, pl* **-ties 1** *Music* the presence of a musical key in a composition. **2** the overall scheme of colours and tones in a painting.

tone *n* **1** sound with reference to its pitch, timbre, or volume. **2** *US & Canad* same as **note** (sense 6). **3** *Music* an interval of two semitones, such as that between doh and ray in tonic sol-fa. **4** the quality or character of a sound: *her tone was angry.* **5** general aspect, quality, or style: *the tone of the conversation made him queasy.* **6** high quality or style: *my car with its patches of rust lowered the tone of the neighbourhood.* **7** the quality of a given colour, as modified by mixture with white or black; shade or tint. **8** *Physiol* the natural firmness of the tissues and normal functioning of bodily organs in health. ✧ *vb* **toning, toned 9** to be of a matching or similar tone. **10** to give a tone to or correct the tone of. ▷ HISTORY Greek *tonos* ▶ **toneless** *adj* ▶ **tonelessly** *adv*

tone-deaf *adj* unable to distinguish subtle differences in musical pitch.

tone down *vb* to moderate in tone: *I sensed some reserve in his manner, so I toned down my enthusiasm.*

tone poem *n Music* an extended orchestral composition based on nonmusical material, such as a work of literature or a fairy tale.

toner *n* **1** a cosmetic applied to the skin to reduce oiliness. **2** a powdered chemical that forms the image produced by a photocopier.

tone up *vb* to make or become more vigorous, healthy, etc.: *muscle tissue can be toned up.*

tong *n* (formerly) a secret society of Chinese Americans. ▷ HISTORY Chinese (Cantonese) *t'ong* meeting place

tongs *pl n* a tool for grasping or lifting, consisting of two long metal or wooden arms, joined with a hinge or flexible metal strip at one end. ▷ HISTORY Old English *tange*

A B C D E F G H I J K L M N O P Q R S T U V W X Y Z

tongue *n* **1** a movable mass of muscular tissue attached to the floor of the mouth, used for tasting, eating, and speaking. **2** a language, dialect, or idiom: *the Scots tongue.* **3** the ability to speak: *taken aback, she could not find her tongue.* **4** a manner of speaking: *a sharp tongue.* **5** the tongue of certain animals used as food. **6** a narrow strip of something that extends outwards: *a narrow tongue of flame.* **7** a flap of leather on a shoe. **8** the clapper of a bell. **9** a projecting strip along an edge of a board that is made to fit a groove in another board. **10 hold one's tongue** to keep quiet. **11 on the tip of one's tongue** about to come to mind. **12 with (one's) tongue in one's cheek** with insincere or ironical intent. ▷ HISTORY Old English *tunge*

tongue-tie *n* a congenital condition in which movement of the tongue is limited as the result of the fold of skin under the tongue extending too close to the front of the tongue.

tongue-tied *adj* speechless, esp. with embarrassment or shyness.

tongue twister *n* a sentence or phrase that is difficult to say clearly and quickly, such as *the sixth sick sheikh's sixth sheep's sick.*

tonguing *n* a technique of playing a wind instrument by obstructing and uncovering the air passage through the lips with the tongue.

tonic *n* **1** a medicine that improves the functioning of the body or increases the feeling of wellbeing. **2** anything that enlivens or strengthens: *his dry humour was a stimulating tonic.* **3** Also called: **tonic water** a carbonated beverage containing quinine and often mixed with alcoholic drinks: *gin and tonic.* **4** *Music* the first note of a major or minor scale and the tonal centre of a piece composed in a particular key. ✧ *adj* **5** having an invigorating or refreshing effect: *a tonic bath.* **6** *Music* of the first note of a major or minor scale. ▷ HISTORY Greek *tonikos* concerning tone

tonic sol-fa *n* a method of teaching music, by which syllables are used as names for the notes of the major scale in any key.

tonight *n* **1** the night or evening of this present day: *tonight's programme examines the rise of poverty in the 1990s.* ✧ *adv* **2** in or during the night or evening of this day: *I want to go out dancing tonight.* ▷ HISTORY Old English *tōniht*

toning table *n* an exercise table, parts of which move mechanically to exercise specific parts of the body of the person lying on it.

tonnage *n* **1** the capacity of a merchant ship expressed in tons. **2** the weight of the cargo of a merchant ship. **3** the total amount of shipping of a port or nation.

tonne (**tunn**) *n* a unit of mass equal to 1000 kg or 2204.6 pounds. ▷ HISTORY French

tonoplast *n Bot* the membrane that encloses a vacuole in a plant cell.

tonsil *n* either of two small oval lumps of spongy tissue situated one on each side of the back of the mouth. ▷ HISTORY Latin *tonsillae* tonsils ▶ **tonsillar** *adj*

tonsillectomy *n, pl* **-mies** surgical removal of the tonsils. ▷ HISTORY TONSIL + Greek *tomē* a cutting

tonsillitis *n* inflammation of the tonsils, causing a sore throat and fever.

tonsure *n* **1** (in certain religions and monastic orders) **a** the shaving of the head or the crown of the head only. **b** the part of the head left bare by shaving. ✧ *vb* **-suring, -sured 2** to shave the head of. ▷ HISTORY Latin *tonsura* a clipping ▶ **tonsured** *adj*

too *adv* **1** as well or also: *I'll miss you, too.* **2** in or to an excessive degree: *it's too noisy in here.* **3** extremely: *you're too kind.* **4** *US, Canad & Austral informal* used to emphasize contradiction of a negative statement: *You didn't! – I did too!* ▷ HISTORY Old English *tō*

> ☑ **WORD TIP**
> See at **very.**

took *vb* the past tense of **take**.

tool *n* **1 a** an implement, such as a hammer, saw, or spade, that is used by hand to help do a particular type of work. **b** a power-driven instrument: *machine tool.* **2** the cutting part of such an instrument. **3** a person used to perform dishonourable or unpleasant tasks for another: *the government is acting as a tool of big business.* **4** any object, skill, etc., used for a particular task or in a particular job: *a skilled therapist can use photographs as tools.* ✧ *vb* **5** to work, cut, or form (something) with a tool. ▷ HISTORY Old English *tōl*

toot *n* **1** a short hooting sound. ✧ *vb* **2** to give or cause to give a short blast, hoot, or whistle: *motorists tooted their car horns.* ▷ HISTORY imitative

tooth *n, pl* **teeth 1** one of the bonelike projections in the jaws of most vertebrates that are used for biting, tearing, or chewing. **2** one of the sharp projections on the edge of a comb, saw, zip, etc. **3 long in the tooth** old or ageing. **4 a sweet tooth** a liking for sweet food. **5 tooth and nail** with great vigour and determination: *the union would oppose compulsory redundancies tooth and nail.* ✧ See also **teeth**. ▷ HISTORY Old English *tōth*

toothless *adj* **1** having no teeth. **2** having no real power: *the proposed Commission will not be as toothless as scoffers suggest.*

toothpaste *n* a paste used for cleaning the teeth, applied with a toothbrush.

toothpick *n* a small wooden or plastic stick used for extracting pieces of food from between the teeth.

tooth powder *n* a powder used for cleaning the teeth, applied with a toothbrush.

top[1] *n* **1** the highest point or part of anything: *the top of the stairs.* **2** the most important or successful position: *at the top of the agenda.* **3** a lid or cap that fits on to one end of something, esp. to close it: *he unscrewed the top from a quart of ale.* **4** the highest degree or point: *the two people at the top of the Party.* **5** the most important person or people in an organization: *the top of the military establishment.* **6** the loudest or highest pitch: *she cheered and sang at the top of her voice.* **7** a garment, esp. for a woman, that extends from the shoulders to the waist or hips. **8** the part of a plant that is above ground: *nettle tops.* **9** same as **top gear**. **10 off the top of one's head** without previous preparation or careful thought. **11 on top of a** in addition to: *the average member of staff will get 25% on top of salary.* **b** *Informal* in complete control of: *we're on top of our costs and expenses and looking for other opportunities.* **12 over the top a** lacking restraint or a sense of proportion: *you went over the top when you called her a religious maniac.* **b** *Mil* over the edge of a trench. ✧ *adj* **13** at, of, or being the top: *men still hold most of the top jobs in industry.* ✧ *vb* **topping, topped 14** to put on top of (something): *top your salad with a mild dressing.* **15** to reach or pass the top of. **16** to be at the top of: *her biggest hit topped the charts for six weeks.* **17** to exceed or surpass: *his estimated fortune tops £2 billion.* **18 top and tail a** to trim off the ends of (fruit or vegetables) before cooking. **b** to wash only a baby's face and bottom. ▷ **HISTORY** Old English *topp*

top² *n* **1** a toy that is spun on its pointed base. **2 sleep like a top** to sleep very soundly. ▷ **HISTORY** Old English

topaz (**toe**-pazz) *n* a hard glassy yellow, pink, or colourless mineral used in making jewellery. ▷ **HISTORY** Greek *topazos*

top brass *pl n* the most important or high-ranking officials or leaders.

top-down reading *n* an approach to reading and understanding involving using historical or other background clues as well as reading for gist to gain an overview of a text. Compare **bottom-up reading**.

top dressing *n* a layer of fertilizer or manure spread on the surface of land. ▶ **top-dress** *vb*

tope¹ *vb* **toping, toped** to drink (alcohol), usually in large quantities. ▷ **HISTORY** perhaps from French *toper* to take a bet ▶ **toper** *n*

tope² *n* a small grey shark of European coastal waters. ▷ **HISTORY** origin unknown

topee *or* **topi** (**toe**-pee) *n* same as **pith helmet**. ▷ **HISTORY** Hindi *topī* hat

top gear *n* the highest forward ratio of a gearbox in a motor vehicle.

top hat *n* a man's hat with a tall cylindrical crown and narrow brim, now only worn for some formal occasions.

top-heavy *adj* unstable through being overloaded at the top.

topiary (**tope**-yar-ee) *n* **1** the art of trimming trees or bushes into artificial decorative shapes. **2** trees or bushes trimmed into decorative shapes. ✧ *adj* **3** of or relating to topiary. ▷ **HISTORY** Latin *topia* decorative garden work ▶ **topiarist** *n*

topic *n* a subject of a speech, book, conversation, etc. ▷ **HISTORY** Greek *topos* place

topical *adj* of or relating to current affairs. ▶ **topicality** *n* ▶ **topically** *adv*

topknot *n* a crest, tuft, decorative bow, etc., on the top of the head.

topless *adj* of or relating to women wearing costumes that do not cover the breasts: *topless bars.*

topmost *adj* at or nearest the top.

top-notch *adj Informal* excellent or superb: *top-notch entertainment.*

topographic map *n* a map that shows natural and significant features of the landscape and uses contour lines to show elevations.

topography *n, pl* **-phies 1** the surface features of a region, such as its hills, valleys, or rivers: *the islands are fragile, with a topography constantly changed by wind and wave.* **2** the study or description of such surface features. **3** the representation of these features on a map. ▷ **HISTORY** Greek *topos* a place + -GRAPHY ▶ **topographer** *n* ▶ **topographical** *adj*

topology *n* a branch of geometry describing the properties of a figure that are unaffected by continuous distortion. ▷ **HISTORY** Greek *topos* a place + -LOGY ▶ **topological** *adj*

topping *n* a sauce or garnish for food.

topple *vb* **-pling, -pled 1** to fall over or cause (something) to fall over, esp. from a height: *he staggered back against the railing and toppled over into the river.* **2** to overthrow or oust: *few believe the scandal will topple the government.* ▷ **HISTORY** from TOP¹ (verb)

top-secret *adj* (of military or government information) classified as needing the highest level of secrecy and security.

top slicing *n* the act of using a specific part of a sum of money for a special purpose, such as assessing a taxable gain.

topsoil *n* the surface layer of soil.

topsy-turvy *adj* **1** upside down. **2** in a state of confusion. ✧ *adv* **3** in a topsy-turvy manner. ▷ **HISTORY** probably *top* + obsolete *tervy* to turn upside down

top up *vb* **1** to refill (a container), usually to the brim: *I topped up his glass.* **2** to add to (an amount) in order to make it sufficient: *the grant can be topped up by a student loan.* ✧ *n* **top-up 3** another serving of a drink in the glass that was used for the first one: *anyone want a top-up?* ✧ *adj* **top-up 4** serving to top something up: *a top-up loan.*

toque (**toke**) *n* **1** a woman's small round brimless hat. **2** *Canad* same as **tuque** (sense 2). ▷ **HISTORY** French

tor *n Chiefly Brit* a high hill, esp. a bare rocky one. ▷ **HISTORY** Old English *torr*

Torah *n* the whole body of traditional Jewish teaching, including the Oral Law. ▷ **HISTORY** Hebrew: precept

torch *n* **1** a small portable electric lamp powered by batteries. **2** a wooden shaft dipped in wax or tallow and set alight. **3** anything regarded as a source of enlightenment, guidance, etc.: *a torch of hope.* **4 carry a torch for** to be in love with (someone), esp. unrequitedly. ✧ *vb* **5** *Informal* to deliberately set (a building) on fire. ▷ **HISTORY** Old French *torche* handful of twisted straw

tore *vb* the past tense of **tear²**.

toreador (**torr**-ee-a-dor) *n* a bullfighter, esp. one on horseback. ▷ **HISTORY** Spanish

torment *vb* **1** to cause (someone) great pain or suffering. **2** to tease or pester (a person or animal) in an annoying or cruel way. ✧ *n* **3** physical or mental pain. **4** a source of pain or suffering. ▷ **HISTORY** Latin *tormentum* ▶ **tormentor** *n*

tormentil *n* a creeping plant with yellow four-petalled flowers. ▷ **HISTORY** Old French *tormentille*

torn *vb* **1** the past participle of **tear**[2]. ✧ *adj* **2** split or cut. **3** divided or undecided, as in preference: *torn between two lovers.*

tornado *n, pl* **-dos** *or* **-does** a rapidly whirling column of air, usually characterized by a dark funnel-shaped cloud causing damage along its path. ▷ **HISTORY** Spanish *tronada* thunderstorm

torpedo *n, pl* **-does 1** a cylindrical self-propelled weapon carrying explosives that is launched from aircraft, ships, or submarines and follows an underwater path to hit its target. ✧ *vb* **-doing, -doed 2** to attack or hit (a ship) with one or a number of torpedoes. **3** to destroy or wreck: *the Prime Minister warned his party against torpedoing the bill.* ▷ **HISTORY** Latin: crampfish (whose electric discharges can cause numbness)

torpedo boat *n* (formerly) a small high-speed warship for torpedo attacks.

torpid *adj* **1** sluggish or dull: *he has a rather torpid intellect.* **2** (of a hibernating animal) dormant. ▷ **HISTORY** Latin *torpere* to be numb

torpor *n* drowsiness and apathy.

torque (**tork**) *n* **1** a force that causes rotation around a central point such as an axle. **2** an ancient Celtic necklace or armband made of twisted metal. ▷ **HISTORY** Latin *torques* necklace + *torquere* to twist

torr *n, pl* **torr** a unit of pressure equal to one millimetre of mercury (133.3 newtons per square metre). ▷ **HISTORY** after E. *Torricelli,* physicist

Torrens title *n Austral Law* legal title to land based on record of registration rather than on title deeds. ▷ **HISTORY** from Sir Robert Richard *Torrens* (1814—84), who introduced the system as premier of South Australia in 1857

torrent *n* **1** a fast or violent stream, esp. of water. **2** a rapid flow of questions, abuse, etc. ▷ **HISTORY** Latin *torrens*

torrential *adj* (of rain) very heavy.

torrid *adj* **1** (of weather) so hot and dry as to parch or scorch. **2** (of land) arid or parched. **3** highly charged emotionally: *a torrid affair.* ▷ **HISTORY** Latin *torrere* to scorch

Torrid Zone *n Geog* those parts of the earth's surface lying between the tropics of Cancer and Capricorn. Compare **Frigid Zone, Temperate Zone**.

torsion *n* the twisting of a part by equal forces being applied at both ends but in opposite directions. ▷ **HISTORY** Latin *torquere* to twist ▶ **torsional** *adj*

torso *n, pl* **-sos 1** the trunk of the human body. **2** a statue of a nude human trunk, esp. without the head or limbs. ▷ **HISTORY** Italian: stalk, stump

tort *n Law* a civil wrong or injury, for which an action for damages may be brought. ▷ **HISTORY** Latin *torquere* to twist

tortilla *n Mexican cookery* a kind of thin pancake made from corn meal. ▷ **HISTORY** Spanish: little cake

tortoise *n* a land reptile with a heavy dome-shaped shell into which it can withdraw its head and legs. ▷ **HISTORY** Medieval Latin *tortuca*

tortoiseshell *n* **1** the horny yellow-and-brown mottled shell of a sea turtle, used for making ornaments and jewellery. **2** a domestic cat with black, cream, and brownish markings. **3** a butterfly which has orange-brown wings with black markings. ✧ *adj* **4** made of tortoiseshell.

tortuous *adj* **1** twisted or winding: *a tortuous route.* **2** devious or cunning: *months of tortuous negotiations.*

> **WORD TIP**
> See at **torture**.

torture *vb* **-turing, -tured 1** to cause (someone) extreme physical pain, esp. to extract information, etc.: *suspects were regularly tortured and murdered by the secret police.* **2** to cause (someone) mental anguish. ✧ *n* **3** physical or mental anguish. **4** the practice of torturing a person. **5** something which causes great mental distress: *she was going through the torture of a collapsing marriage.* ▷ **HISTORY** Latin *torquere* to twist ▶ **tortured** *adj* ▶ **torturer** *n* ▶ **torturous** *adj*

> **WORD TIP**
> The adjective *torturous* is sometimes confused with *tortuous*. One speaks of a *torturous* experience, i.e. one that involves pain or suffering, but of a *tortuous* road, i.e. one that winds or twists.

Tory *n, pl* **-ries 1** a member or supporter of the Conservative Party in Great Britain or Canada. **2** *History* a member of the English political party that supported the Church and Crown and traditional political structures and opposed the Whigs. ✧ *adj* **3** of or relating to a Tory or Tories. ▶ **Toryism** *n*

> **WORD HISTORY**
> 'Tory' comes from Irish *toraidhe* or *toiridhe*, meaning 'outlaw' or 'robber'. The name was first given to Irish outlaws who harassed the English in Ireland, and then came to be applied to members of the English political faction that opposed the exclusion of the Roman Catholic James, Duke of York, from succession to the throne. Thereafter 'Tory' remained as a political label for those of a conservative outlook, as opposed to the more reformist Whigs.

tosa (**toe**-za) *n* a large reddish dog, originally bred for fighting. ▷ **HISTORY** after a province on the Japanese island of Skikoku

toss *vb* **1** to throw (something) lightly. **2** to fling or be flung about, esp. in a violent way: *the salty sea breeze tossing the branches of the palms.* **3** to coat (food) with a dressing by gentle stirring or mixing: *her technique for tossing Caesar salad.* **4** (of a horse) to throw (its rider). **5** to move (one's head) suddenly backwards, as in impatience. **6** to throw up (a coin) to decide between alternatives by guessing which side will land uppermost. **7 toss and turn** to be

A B C D E F G H I J K L M N O P Q R S T U V W X Y Z

restless when trying to sleep. ✧ *n* **8** the act or an instance of tossing. **9** the act of deciding between alternatives by throwing up a coin and guessing which side will land uppermost: *Essex won the toss and decided to bat first.* **10 argue the toss** to waste time and energy arguing about an unimportant point. **11 not give a toss** *Informal* not to care at all. ▷ HISTORY Scandinavian

toss up *vb* **1** to spin (a coin) in the air in order to decide between alternatives by guessing which side will land uppermost. ✧ *n* **toss-up 2** an instance of tossing up a coin. **3** *Informal* an even chance or risk: *if it's a toss-up for a top position, he gives it to the woman.*

tot *n* **1** a very young child. **2** a small drink of spirits. ▷ HISTORY origin unknown

total *n* **1** the whole, esp. regarded as the sum of a number of parts. **2 in total** overall: *the company employs over 700 people in total.* ✧ *adj* **3** complete: *a total ban on alcohol.* **4** being or related to a total: *the total number of deaths.* ✧ *vb* **-talling, -talled** *or US* **-taling, -taled 5** to amount to: *the firm's losses totalled more than $2 billion.* **6** to add up: *purchases are totalled with a pencil and a notepad.* ▷ HISTORY Latin *totus* all ▶ **totally** *adv*

total internal reflection *n Physics* the complete reflection of a light ray at the boundary of two media, when the ray is in the medium with greater refractive index.

totalitarian *adj* **1** of a political system in which there is only one party, which allows no opposition and attempts to control everything: *a totalitarian state.* ✧ *n* **2** a person who is in favour of totalitarian policies. ▶ **totalitarianism** *n*

totality *n, pl* **-ties 1** the whole amount. **2** the state of being total.

totalizator, totalizer, *or* **totalisator, totaliser** *n* a machine to operate a system of betting on a racecourse in which money is paid out to the winners in proportion to their stakes.

total war *n* a war in which all economic and military resources are mobilized as part of the war effort and in which the whole of the population is involved.

tote[1] *vb* **toting, toted** *Informal* **1** to carry or wear (a gun). **2** to haul or carry. ▷ HISTORY origin unknown

tote[2] *n* **the tote** *Informal* short for **totalizator**.

totem *n* **1** (esp. among Native Americans) an object or animal symbolizing a clan or family. **2** a representation of such an object. ▷ HISTORY from a Native American language ▶ **totemic** *adj* ▶ **totemism** *n*

totem pole *n* a pole carved or painted with totemic figures set up by certain Native Americans as a tribal symbol.

totter *vb* **1** to move in an unsteady manner. **2** to sway or shake as if about to fall. **3** to be failing, unstable, or precarious: *the world was tottering on the edge of war.* ▷ HISTORY origin unknown

toucan *n* a tropical American fruit-eating bird with a large brightly coloured bill. ▷ HISTORY Portuguese *tucano*

touch *vb* **1** to cause or permit a part of the body to come into contact with (someone or something): *the baking tin is too hot to touch.* **2** to tap, feel, or strike (someone or something): *he touched me on the shoulder.* **3** to come or bring (something) into contact with (something else): *the plane's wheels touched the runway.* **4** to move or disturb by handling: *we shouldn't touch anything before the police arrive.* **5** to have an effect on: *millions of people's lives had been touched by the music of the Beatles.* **6** to produce an emotional response in: *the painful truth of it touched her.* **7** to eat or drink: *she hardly ever touched alcohol.* **8** to compare to in quality or attainment; equal or match: *nothing can touch them for scope and detail.* **9** *Brit, Austral & NZ slang* to ask (someone) for a loan or gift of money. **10** to fondle in a sexual manner: *I wouldn't let him touch me unless I was in the mood.* **11** to strike, harm, or molest: *I never touched him!* **12 touch on** *or* **upon** to allude to briefly or in passing: *these two issues may be touched upon during the talks.* ✧ *n* **13** the sense by which the texture and other qualities of objects can be experienced when they come in contact with a part of the body surface, esp. the tips of the fingers. RELATED ADJECTIVE ▶ **tactile 14** the feel or texture of an object as perceived by this sense: *she enjoyed the touch of the damp grass on her feet.* **15** the act or an instance of something coming into contact with the body: *he remembered the touch of her hand.* **16** a gentle push, tap, or caress: *the switch takes only the merest touch to operate.* **17** a small amount; trace: *a touch of luxury.* **18** a particular manner or style of doing something: *his songs always reveal his keen melodic touch.* **19** a detail of some work: *final touches were now being put to the plans.* **20** a slight attack: *a touch of dysentery.* **21** (in sports such as football or rugby) the area outside the lines marking the side of the pitch: *he kicked the ball into touch.* **22** the technique of fingering a keyboard instrument. **23 a touch** slightly or marginally: *it's nice, but a touch expensive.* **24 in touch a** regularly speaking to, writing to, or visiting someone. **b** having up-to-date knowledge or understanding of a situation or trend. **25 lose touch a** to gradually stop speaking to, writing to, or visiting someone. **b** to stop having up-to-date knowledge or understanding of a situation or trend. **26 out of touch a** no longer speaking to, writing to, or visiting someone. **b** no longer having up-to-date knowledge or understanding of a situation or trend. ✧ See also **touchdown**. ▷ HISTORY Old French *tochier*

touch and go *adj* risky or critical: *it was touch and go whether the mission would succeed.*

touchdown *n* **1** the moment at which a landing aircraft or spacecraft comes into contact with the landing surface. **2** *American football* a scoring move in which an attacking player takes the ball into the area behind his opponents' goal. ✧ *vb* **touch down 3** (of an aircraft or spacecraft) to land.

touché (too-**shay**) *interj* **1** an acknowledgment that a remark or witty reply has been effective. **2** an acknowledgment of a scoring hit in fencing. ▷ HISTORY French, literally: touched

touched *adj* **1** moved to sympathy or emotion: *I was touched by her understanding.* **2** slightly mad: *she's a bit touched.*

touching *adj* **1** arousing tender feelings. ✧ *prep* **2** relating to or concerning: *she might talk about matters touching both of them.*

touchline *n* either of the lines marking the side of the playing area in certain games, such as rugby.

touchstone *n* a standard by which judgment is made: *this restaurant is the touchstone for genuine Italian cookery in Leeds.*

touch-type *vb* **-typing, -typed** to type without looking at the keyboard. ▶ **touch-typist** *n*

touchy *adj* **touchier, touchiest 1** easily upset or irritated: *he is a touchy and quick-tempered man.* **2** requiring careful and tactful handling: *a touchy subject.* ▶ **touchiness** *n*

touchy-feely *adj Informal, sometimes offensive* sensitive and caring.

tough *adj* **1** strong and difficult to break, cut, or tear: *this fabric is tough and water-resistant.* **2** (of meat or other food) difficult to cut and chew; not tender. **3** physically or mentally strong and able to cope with hardship: *a tough uncompromising woman, unwilling to take no for an answer.* **4** rough or violent: *a tough and ruthless mercenary.* **5** strict and firm: *the country's tough drugs laws.* **6** difficult or troublesome to do or deal with: *a tough task.* **7 tough luck!** *Informal* an expression of lack of sympathy for someone else's problems. ✧ *n* **8** a rough, vicious, or violent person. ✧ *vb* **9 tough it out** *Informal* to endure a difficult situation until it improves: *criticism of his performance has reinforced his desire to tough it out.* ▷ **HISTORY** Old English *tōh* ▶ **toughness** *n*

toughen *vb* to make or become tough or tougher.

toupee (**too**-pay) *n* a hairpiece worn by men to cover a bald place. ▷ **HISTORY** French *toupet* forelock

tour *n* **1** an extended journey visiting places of interest along the route. **2** a trip, by a band, theatre company, etc., to perform in several places. **3** an overseas trip made by a cricket team, rugby team, etc., to play in several places. **4** *Mil* a period of service, esp. in one place: *the regiment has served several tours in Northern Ireland.* ✧ *vb* **5** to make a tour of (a place). ▷ **HISTORY** Old French: a turn

tour de force *n, pl* **tours de force** a masterly or brilliant stroke or achievement. ▷ **HISTORY** French, literally: feat of skill or strength

tourism *n* tourist travel, esp. when regarded as an industry.

tourist *n* **1** a person who travels for pleasure, usually sightseeing and staying in hotels. **2** a member of a sports team which is visiting a country to play a series of matches: *the tourists were bowled out for 135.* **3** the lowest class of accommodation on a passenger ship. ✧ *adj* **4** of or relating to tourists or tourism: *a popular tourist attraction.* **5** of the lowest class of accommodation on a passenger ship or aircraft.

touristy *adj Informal, often disparaging* full of tourists or tourist attractions.

tourmaline *n* a hard crystalline mineral used in jewellery and electrical equipment. ▷ **HISTORY** German *Turmalin*

tournament *n* **1** a sporting competition in which contestants play a series of games to determine an overall winner. **2** Also: **tourney** *Medieval history* a contest in which mounted knights fought for a prize. ▷ **HISTORY** Old French *torneiement*

tourniquet (**tour**-nick-kay) *n Med* a strip of cloth tied tightly round an arm or leg to stop bleeding from an artery. ▷ **HISTORY** French

tout (rhymes with **shout**) *vb* **1** to seek (business, customers, etc.) or try to sell (goods), esp. in a persistent or direct manner: *he went from door to door touting for business.* **2** to put forward or recommend (a person or thing) as a good or suitable example or candidate: *the plant was once touted as a showcase factory.* ✧ *n* **3** a person who sells tickets for a heavily booked event at inflated prices. ▷ **HISTORY** Old English *tȳtan* to peep

tow¹ *vb* **1** to pull or drag (a vehicle), esp. by means of a rope or cable. ✧ *n* **2** the act or an instance of towing. **3 in tow** *Informal* in one's company or one's charge or under one's influence: *she had an older man in tow.* **4 on tow** (of a vehicle) being towed. ▷ **HISTORY** Old English *togian*

tow² *n* fibres of hemp, flax, jute, etc., prepared for spinning. ▷ **HISTORY** Old English *tōw*

towards *or US* **toward** *prep* **1** in the direction of: *towards the lake.* **2** with regard to: *hostility towards the President.* **3** as a contribution to: *the profits will go towards three projects.* **4** just before: *towards evening.*

towbar *n* a rigid metal bar attached to the back of a vehicle, from which a trailer or caravan can be towed.

towel *n* **1** a piece of absorbent cloth or paper used for drying things. **2 throw in the towel** See **throw in** (sense 3). ✧ *vb* **-elling, -elled** *or US* **-eling, -eled 3** to dry or wipe with a towel. ▷ **HISTORY** Old French *toaille*

towelling *or US* **toweling** *n* a soft, fairly thick fabric used to make towels and dressing gowns.

tower *n* **1** a tall, usually square or circular structure, sometimes part of a larger building and usually built for a specific purpose. **2 tower of strength** a person who supports or comforts someone else at a time of difficulty. ✧ *vb* **3 tower over** to be much taller than: *sheer walls of limestone towered over us.* ▷ **HISTORY** Latin *turris*

tower block *n Brit* a very tall building divided into flats or offices.

towering *adj* **1** very tall. **2** very impressive or important: *his towering presence on stage.* **3** very intense: *in a towering rage.*

town *n* **1** a large group of houses, shops, factories, etc., smaller than a city and larger than a village. *RELATED ADJECTIVE* ▶ **urban 2** the nearest town or the chief town of an area: *people from town rarely went out to the farm.* **3** the central area of a town where most of the shops and offices are: *we're going to a pub in town tonight.* **4** the people of a town: *the town is split over the plans for a bypass.* **5** built-up areas in general, as opposed to the countryside: *migration from the country to the town.* **6 go to town** to make a supreme or unrestricted effort. **7 on the town** visiting nightclubs, restaurants, etc.: *we'd a night on the town to celebrate her promotion.* ▷ HISTORY Old English *tūn* village

town clerk *n* (currently in Australia and in Britain until 1974) the chief administrative officer of a town.

town crier *n* (formerly) a person employed to make public announcements in the streets.

town hall *n* a large building in a town often containing the council offices and a hall for public meetings.

town house *n* **1** a terraced house in an urban area, esp. an up-market one. **2** a person's town residence as distinct from his or her country residence.

town planning *n* the comprehensive planning of the physical and social development of a town.

township *n* **1** a small town. **2** (in South Africa) a planned urban settlement of Black Africans or Coloureds. **3** (in the US and Canada) a small unit of local government, often consisting of a town and the area surrounding it. **4** (in Canada) a land-survey area, usually 36 square miles (93 square kilometres).

townsman *n, pl* **-men** an inhabitant of a town. ▶ **townswoman** *fem n*

townspeople *or* **townsfolk** *pl n* the people who live in a town.

towpath *n* a path beside a canal or river, formerly used by horses pulling barges.

towrope *n* a rope or cable used for towing a vehicle or vessel.

toxaemia *or US* **toxemia** (tox-**seem**-ya) *n* **1** a form of blood poisoning caused by toxins released by bacteria at a wound or other site of infection. **2** a condition in pregnant women characterized by high blood pressure. ▷ HISTORY Latin *toxicum* poison + *haima* blood ▶ **toxaemic** *or US* **toxemic** *adj*

toxic *adj* **1** poisonous: *toxic fumes.* **2** caused by poison: *toxic effects.* ▷ HISTORY Greek *toxikon (pharmakon)* (poison) used on arrows ▶ **toxicity** *n*

toxicology *n* the branch of science concerned with poisons and their effects. ▶ **toxicological** *adj* ▶ **toxicologist** *n*

toxin *n* **1** any of various poisonous substances produced by microorganisms and causing certain diseases. **2** any other poisonous substance of plant or animal origin.

toy *n* **1** an object designed for children to play with, such as a doll or model car. **2** an object that adults use for entertainment rather than for a serious purpose: *I do use my computer: it's not just a toy.* ✧ *adj* **3** being an imitation or model of something for children to play with: *a toy aeroplane.* **4** (of a dog) of a variety much smaller than is normal for that breed: *a toy poodle.* ▷ HISTORY origin unknown

toy-toy *or* **toyi-toyi** *S African* ✧ *n* **1** a dance expressing defiance and protest. ✧ *vb* **2** to dance in this way. ▷ HISTORY origin uncertain

toy with *vb* **1** to consider an idea without being serious about it or being able to decide about it: *I've been toying with the idea of setting up my own firm.* **2** to keep moving (an object) about with one's fingers, esp. when thinking about something else: *Jessica sat toying with her glass.*

trace *vb* **tracing, traced 1** to locate or work out (the cause or source of something): *he traced the trouble to a faulty connection.* **2** to find (something or someone that was missing): *the police were unable to trace her missing husband.* **3** to discover or describe the progress or development of (something): *throughout the 19th century we can trace the development of more complex machinery.* **4** to copy (a design, map, etc.) by putting a piece of transparent paper over it and following the lines which show through the paper with a pencil. **5** to make the outline of (a shape or pattern): *his index finger was tracing circles on the arm of the chair.* ✧ *n* **6** a mark, footprint, or other sign that shows that a person, animal, or thing has been in a particular place: *the police could find no trace of the missing van.* **7** an amount of something so small that it is barely noticeable: *I detected a trace of jealousy in her voice.* **8** a remnant of something: *traces of an Iron-Age fort remain visible.* **9** a pattern made on a screen or a piece of paper by a device that is measuring or detecting something: *a baffling radar trace.* ▷ HISTORY French *tracier* ▶ **traceable** *adj*

trace element *n* a chemical element that occurs in very small amounts in soil, water, etc. and is essential for healthy growth.

tracer *n* **1** a projectile that can be observed when in flight by the burning of chemical substances in its base. **2** *Med* an element or other substance introduced into the body to study metabolic processes.

tracery *n, pl* **-eries 1** a pattern of interlacing lines, esp. one in a stained glass window. **2** any fine lacy pattern resembling this.

traces *pl n* **1** the two side straps that connect a horse's harness to the vehicle being pulled. **2 kick over the traces** to escape or defy control. ▷ HISTORY Old French *trait*

trachea (track-**kee**-a) *n, pl* **-cheae** (-**kee**-ee) *Anat, zool* the tube that carries inhaled air from the throat to the lungs. ▷ HISTORY Greek

tracheotomy (track-ee-**ot**-a-mee) *n, pl* **-mies** surgical incision into the trachea, as performed when the air passage has been blocked. ▷ HISTORY TRACHEA + Greek *tomē* a cutting

trachoma (track-**oh**-ma) *n* a chronic contagious disease of the eye characterized by inflammation of the inner surface of the lids and the formation of scar tissue. ▷ HISTORY Greek *trakhōma* roughness

tracing *n* **1** a copy of something, such as a map, made by tracing. **2** a line traced by a recording instrument.

track *n* **1** a rough road or path: *a farm track.* **2** the mark or trail left by something that has passed by: *the fox didn't leave any tracks.* **3** a rail or pair of parallel rails on which a vehicle, such as a train, runs. **4** a course for running or racing on: *a running track.* **5** a separate song or piece of music on a record, tape, or CD: *Dolphy switches back to bass clarinet for the final track.* **6** a course of action, thought, etc.: *I don't think you're on the right track at all.* **7** an endless band on the wheels of a tank, bulldozer, etc. to enable it to move across rough ground. **8 keep** *or* **lose track of** to follow *or* fail to follow the course or progress of. **9 off the beaten track** in an isolated location: *the village where she lives is a bit off the beaten track.* ✧ *vb* **10** to follow the trail of (a person or animal). **11** to follow the flight path of (a satellite etc.) by picking up signals transmitted or reflected by it. **12** *Films* to follow (a moving object) while filming. ✧ See also **tracks**. ▷ HISTORY Old French *trac* ▶ **tracker** *n*

track down *vb* to find (someone or something) by tracking or pursuing.

tracker dog *n* a dog specially trained to search for missing people.

track event *n* a competition in athletics, such as sprinting, that takes place on a running track.

track record *n Informal* the past record of the accomplishments and failures of a person or organization.

tracks *pl n* **1** marks, such as footprints, left by someone or something that has passed. **2 in one's tracks** on the very spot where one is standing: *those words stopped her in her tracks.* **3 make tracks** to leave or depart: *it was time to start making tracks.*

track shoe *n* a light running shoe fitted with steel spikes for better grip.

tracksuit *n* a warm loose-fitting suit worn by athletes etc., esp. during training.

tract[1] *n* **1** a large area, esp. of land: *an extensive tract of moorland.* **2** *Anat* a system of organs or glands that has a particular function: *the urinary tract.* ▷ HISTORY Latin *tractus* a stretching out

tract[2] *n* a pamphlet, esp. a religious one. ▷ HISTORY Latin *tractatus*

tractable *adj Formal* easy to control, manage, or deal with: *he could easily manage his tractable and worshipping younger brother.* ▷ HISTORY Latin *tractare* to manage ▶ **tractability** *n*

traction *n* **1** pulling, esp. by engine power: *the increased use of electric traction.* **2** *Med* the application of a steady pull on an injured limb using a system of weights and pulleys or splints: *he was in traction for weeks following the accident.* **3** the grip that the wheels of a vehicle have on the ground: *four-wheel drive gives much better traction in wet or icy conditions.* ▷ HISTORY Latin *tractus* dragged

traction engine *n* a heavy steam-powered vehicle used, esp. formerly, for drawing heavy loads along roads or over rough ground.

traction load *n Geol* the solid material that is carried along the bed of a river.

tractor *n* a motor vehicle with large rear wheels, used to pull heavy loads, esp. farm machinery. ▷ HISTORY Late Latin: one who pulls

trade *n* **1** the buying and selling of goods and services. **2** a person's job, esp. a craft requiring skill: *he's a plumber by trade.* **3** the people and practices of an industry, craft, or business. **4** amount of custom or commercial dealings: *a brisk trade in second-hand weapons.* **5** a specified market or business: *the wool trade.* **6 trades** the trade winds. ✧ *vb* **trading, traded 7** to buy and sell (goods). **8** to exchange: *he traded a job in New York for a life as a cowboy.* **9** to engage in trade. **10** to deal or do business (with). ▷ HISTORY Low German: track, hence a regular business ▶ **tradable** *or* **tradeable** *adj* ▶ **trading** *n* ▶ **trader** *n*

trade-in *n* **1** a used article given in part payment for the purchase of a new article. ✧ *vb* **trade in 2** to give (a used article) as part payment for a new article.

trade magazine *n Publishing* a periodical containing new articles and information specific to a trade or profession.

trademark *n* **1 a** the name or other symbol used by a manufacturer to distinguish his or her products from those of competitors. **b Registered Trademark** one that is officially registered and legally protected. **2** any distinctive sign or mark of a person or thing: *the designer bars which have become the trademark of the city.*

trade name *n* **1** the name used by a trade to refer to a product or range of products. **2** the name under which a commercial enterprise operates in business.

trade-off *n* an exchange, esp. as a compromise: *there is often a trade-off between manpower costs and computer costs.*

tradescantia (trad-dess-**kan**-shee-a) *n* a widely cultivated plant with striped leaves. ▷ HISTORY after John *Tradescant,* botanist

trade secret *n* a secret formula, technique, or process known and used to advantage by only one manufacturer.

tradesman *n, pl* **-men 1** a skilled worker, such as an electrician or painter. **2** a shopkeeper. ▶ **tradeswoman** *fem n*

Trades Union Congress *n* (in Britain and S Africa) the major association of trade unions, which includes all the larger unions.

trade union *or* **trades union** *n* a society of workers formed to protect and improve their working conditions, pay, etc. ▶ **trade unionism** *or* **trades unionism** *n* ▶ **trade unionist** *or* **trades unionist** *n*

trade wind *n Meteorol* a wind blowing steadily towards the equator either from the northeast in the N hemisphere or the southeast in the S hemisphere.

trading estate *n Chiefly Brit* a large area in which a number of commercial or industrial firms are situated.

tradition *n* **1** the handing down from generation to generation of customs, beliefs, etc. **2** the unwritten body of beliefs, customs, etc. handed down from generation to generation. **3** a custom or practice of long standing. **4 in the tradition of** having many features similar to those of a person or thing in the past: *a thriller writer in the tradition of Chandler.* ▷ HISTORY Latin *traditio* a handing down

A B C D E F G H I J K L M N O P Q R S T U V W X Y Z

traditional *adj* of, relating to, or being a tradition. ▶ **traditionally** *adv*

traditional grammar *n* rules and terminology for language analysis based on parts of speech. Compare **functional grammar**.

traditionalist *n* a person who supports established customs or beliefs. ▶ **traditionalism** *n*

traduce *vb* **-ducing, -duced** *Formal* to speak badly of (someone). ▷ **HISTORY** Latin *traducere* to lead over, disgrace ▶ **traducement** *n* ▶ **traducer** *n*

traffic *n* **1** the vehicles travelling on roads. **2** the movement of vehicles or people in a particular place or for a particular purpose: *air traffic.* **3** trade, esp. of an illicit kind: *drug traffic.* **4** the exchange of ideas between people or organizations: *a lively traffic in ideas.* ✧ *vb* **-ficking, -ficked 5** to carry on trade or business, esp. of an illicit kind: *he confessed to trafficking in gold and ivory.* ▷ **HISTORY** Old French *trafique* ▶ **trafficker** *n*

traffic calming *n Chiefly Brit* the use of devices, such as bends and humps in the road, designed to slow down traffic, esp. in residential areas.

traffic island *n* a raised area in the middle of a road designed as a guide for traffic flow and to provide a stopping place for pedestrians crossing.

traffic warden *n Brit* a person employed to supervise road traffic and report traffic offences.

tragedian (traj-**jee**-dee-an) *or fem* **tragedienne** (traj-jee-dee-**enn**) *n* **1** an actor who specializes in tragic roles. **2** a writer of tragedy.

tragedy *n, pl* **-dies 1** a shocking or sad event. **2** a serious play, film, or opera in which the main character is destroyed by a combination of a personal failing and adverse circumstances. ▷ **HISTORY** Greek *tragōidia*

tragic *adj* **1** sad and distressing because it involves death or suffering: *she was blinded in a tragic accident.* **2** of or like a tragedy: *a tragic hero.* **3** sad or mournful: *a tragic melody.* ▶ **tragically** *adv*

tragic flaw *adj Theatre* the character failing in a tragic hero that brings about his downfall.

tragicomedy *n, pl* **-dies** a play or other written work having both comic and tragic elements. ▶ **tragicomic** *adj*

trail *n* **1** a rough path across open country or through a forest. **2** a route along a series of roads or paths that has been specially planned to let people see or do particular things: *a nature trail through the woods.* **3** a print, mark, or scent left by a person, animal, or object: *a trail of blood was found down three flights of stairs.* **4** something that trails behind: *a vapour trail.* **5** a sequence of results from an event: *a trail of mishaps.* ✧ *vb* **6** to drag or stream along the ground or through the air behind someone or something: *part of her sari trailed behind her on the floor.* **7** to lag behind (a person or thing): *Max had arrived as well, trailing behind the others.* **8** to follow or hunt (an animal or person), usually secretly, by following the marks or tracks he, she, or it has made: *the police had trailed him the length and breadth of the country.* **9** to be falling behind in a race, match or competition: *they trailed 2-1 at half-time.* **10** to move wearily or slowly: *we spent the afternoon trailing round the shops.* ▷ **HISTORY** Old French *trailler* to tow

trailer *n* **1** a road vehicle, usually two-wheeled, towed by a motor vehicle and used for carrying goods, transporting boats, etc.: *ahead of us was a tractor, drawing a trailer laden with dung.* **2** the rear section of an articulated lorry. **3** an extract or series of extracts from a film, TV or radio programme, used to advertise it. **4** *US & Canad* same as **caravan** (sense 1).

trailer trash *n Derogatory* poor people living in trailer parks in the US.

trailing *adj* (of a plant) having a long stem which spreads over the ground or hangs loosely: *trailing ivy.*

train *vb* **1** to instruct (someone) in a skill: *soldiers are trained to obey orders unquestioningly.* **2** to learn the skills needed to do a particular job or activity: *she was training to be a computer programmer.* **3** to do exercises and prepare for a specific purpose: *he was training for a marathon.* **4** to focus on or aim at (something): *the warship kept its guns trained on the trawler.* **5** to discipline (an animal) to obey commands or perform tricks. **6** to tie or prune (a plant) so that it grows in a particular way: *he had trained the roses to grow up the wall.* ✧ *n* **7** a line of railway coaches or wagons coupled together and drawn by a engine. **8** a sequence or series: *following an earlier train of thought.* **9** the long back section of a dress that trails along the floor. **10 in its train** as a consequence: *economic mismanagement brought unemployment and inflation in its train.* **11 in train** actually happening or being done: *the programme of reforms set in train by the new government.* ✧ *adj* **12** of or by a train: *the long train journey North.* ▷ **HISTORY** Old French *trahiner*

trainee *n* **1** a person undergoing training. ✧ *adj* **2** (of a person) undergoing training: *a trainee journalist.*

trainer *n* **1** a person who coaches a person or team in a sport. **2** a person who trains racehorses. **3** an aircraft used for training pilots. **4** *Brit* a flat-soled sports shoe of the style used by athletes when training.

training *n* the process of bringing a person to an agreed standard of proficiency by practice and instruction.

train spotter *n Brit* **1** a person who collects the numbers of railway locomotives. **2** *Informal* a person who is obsessed with trivial details, esp. of a subject generally considered uninteresting.

traipse *Informal* ✧ *vb* **traipsing, traipsed 1** to walk heavily or tiredly. ✧ *n* **2** a long or tiring walk. ▷ **HISTORY** origin unknown

trait *n* a characteristic feature or quality of a person or thing. ▷ **HISTORY** French

traitor *n* a person who betrays friends, country, a cause, etc. ▷ **HISTORY** Latin *tradere* to hand over ▶ **traitorous** *adj* ▶ **traitress** *fem n*

trajectory *n, pl* **-ries** the path described by an object moving in air or space, esp. the curved path of a projectile. ▷ **HISTORY** Latin *trajectus* cast over

tram *n* an electrically driven public transport vehicle that runs on rails laid into the road and takes its power from an overhead cable. ▷ HISTORY probably from Low German *traam* beam

tramlines *pl n* **1** the tracks on which a tram runs. **2** the outer markings along the sides of a tennis or badminton court.

trammel *vb* **-elling, -elled** *or US* **-eling, -eled 1** to hinder or restrict: *trammelled by family responsibilities.* ✧ *n* **2 trammels** things that hinder or restrict someone: *the trammels of social respectability.* ▷ HISTORY Old French *tramail* three-mesh net

tramp *vb* **1** to walk long and far; hike. **2** to walk heavily or firmly across or through (a place): *she tramped slowly up the beach.* ✧ *n* **3** a homeless person who travels about on foot, living by begging or doing casual work. **4** a long hard walk; hike: *we went for a long tramp over the downs.* **5** the sound of heavy regular footsteps: *we could hear the tramp of the marching soldiers.* **6** a small cargo ship that does not run on a regular schedule. **7** *US, Canad, Austral & NZ slang* a promiscuous woman. ▷ HISTORY probably from Middle Low German *trampen*

tramping *n NZ* the leisure activity of walking in the bush. ▶ **tramper** *n*

trample *vb* **-pling, -pled 1** Also: **trample on** to tread on and crush: *three children were trampled to death when the crowd panicked and ran.* **2 trample on** to treat (a person or his or her rights or feelings) with disregard or contempt. ▷ HISTORY from *tramp*

trampoline *n* **1** a tough canvas sheet suspended by springs or cords from a frame, which acrobats, gymnasts, etc., bounce on. ✧ *vb* **-lining, -lined 2** to exercise on a trampoline. ▷ HISTORY Italian *trampolino*

trance *n* **1** a hypnotic state resembling sleep in which a person is unable to move or act of his or her own will. **2** a dazed or stunned state. ▷ HISTORY Latin *transire* to go over

tranche (**trahnsh**) *n* an instalment or portion, esp. of a loan or share issue: *the new shares will be offered in four tranches around the world.*

trannie *or* **tranny** *n, pl* **-nies** *Informal, chiefly Brit* a transistor radio.

tranquil *adj* calm, peaceful, or quiet. ▷ HISTORY Latin *tranquillus* ▶ **tranquilly** *adv*

tranquillity *or US sometimes* **tranquility** *n* a state of calmness or peace.

tranquillize, -lise *or US* **tranquilize** *vb* **-lizing, -lized** *or* **-lising, -lised 1** to make or become calm or calmer. **2** to give (someone) a drug to make them calm or calmer. ▶ **tranquillization, -lisation** *or US* **tranquilization** *n* ▶ **tranquillizing, -lising** *or US* **tranquilizing** *adj*

tranquillizer, -liser *or US* **tranquilizer** *n* a drug that calms someone suffering from anxiety, tension, etc.

trans. **1** transitive. **2** translated.

trans- *prefix* **1** across, beyond, crossing, or on the other side of: *transnational.* **2** changing thoroughly: *transliterate.* ▷ HISTORY Latin

transact *vb* to do, conduct, or negotiate (a business deal). ▷ HISTORY Latin *transigere* to drive through

transaction *n* **1** something that is transacted, esp. a business deal. **2 transactions** the records of the proceedings of a society etc.: *an article on land use in the Niagara area taken from the 'Transactions of the Royal Canadian Institute'.*

transalpine *adj* beyond the Alps, esp. as viewed from Italy.

transatlantic *adj* **1** on or from the other side of the Atlantic. **2** crossing the Atlantic.

transceiver *n* a device which transmits and receives radio or electronic signals. ▷ HISTORY *trans(mitter) + (re)ceiver*

transcend *vb* **1** to go above or beyond what is expected or normal: *a vital party issue that transcends traditional party loyalties.* **2** to overcome or be superior to: *to transcend all difficulties.* ▷ HISTORY Latin *transcendere* to climb over

transcendent *adj* **1** above or beyond what is expected or normal. **2** *Theol* (of God) having existence outside the created world. ▶ **transcendence** *n*

transcendental *adj* **1** above or beyond what is expected or normal. **2** *Philosophy* based on intuition or innate belief rather than experience. **3** supernatural or mystical. ▶ **transcendentally** *adv*

transcendentalism *n* any system of philosophy that seeks to discover the nature of reality by examining the processes of thought rather than the things thought about, or that emphasizes intuition as a means to knowledge. ▶ **transcendentalist** *n, adj*

transcendental meditation *n Trademark* a technique, based on Hindu traditions, for relaxing and refreshing the mind and body through the silent repetition of a special formula of words.

transcribe *vb* **-scribing, -scribed 1** to write, type, or print out (a text) fully from a speech or notes. **2** to make an electrical recording of (a programme or speech) for a later broadcast. **3** *Music* to rewrite (a piece of music) for an instrument other than that originally intended. ▷ HISTORY Latin *transcribere* ▶ **transcriber** *n*

transcript *n* **1** a written, typed, or printed copy made by transcribing. **2** *Chiefly US & Canad* an official record of a student's school progress.

transducer *n* any device, such as a microphone or electric motor, that converts one form of energy into another. ▷ HISTORY Latin *transducere* to lead across

transect *n Biol* a sample strip of land used to monitor plant distribution and animal populations within a given area.

transept *n* either of the two shorter wings of a cross-shaped church. ▷ HISTORY Latin *trans-* across + *saeptum* enclosure

transfer *vb* **-ferring, -ferred 1** to change or move from one thing, person, place, etc., to another: *he was transferred from prison to hospital.* **2** to move (money or property) from the control of one person or organization to that of another: *the* *money has been transferred into your account.* **3** (of a football club) to sell or release (a player) to another club: *he was transferred to Juventus for a world record fee.* **4** to move (a drawing or design) from one surface to another. ✧ *n* **5** the act, process, or system of transferring, or the state of being transferred. **6** a person or thing that transfers or is transferred. **7** a design or drawing that is transferred from one surface to another. **8** the moving of (money or property) from the control of one person or organization to that of another. ▷ HISTORY Latin *trans* across + *ferre* to carry ▶ **transferable** *or* **transferrable** *adj* ▶ **transference** *n*

transfer station *n NZ* a depot where rubbish is sorted for recycling.

transfiguration *n* a transfiguring or being transfigured.

Transfiguration *n* **1** *New Testament* the change in the appearance of Christ on the mountain. **2** the Church festival held in commemoration of this on August 6.

transfigure *vb* **-uring, -ured 1** to change or cause to change in appearance. **2** to become or cause to become more exalted. ▷ HISTORY Latin *trans-* beyond + *figura* appearance

transfix *vb* **-fixing, -fixed** *or* **-fixt 1** to make (someone) motionless, esp. with horror or shock: *they stood transfixed and revolted by what they saw.* **2** to pierce (a person or animal) through with a pointed object: *the Pharaoh is shown transfixing enemies with arrows from a moving chariot.* ▷ HISTORY Latin *transfigere* to pierce through

transform *vb* **1** to change completely in form or function: *the last forty years have seen the country transformed from a peasant economy to a major industrial power.* **2** to change so as to make better or more attractive: *most religions claim to be able to transform people's lives.* **3** to convert (one form of energy) to another. **4** *Maths* to change the form of (an equation, expression, etc.) without changing its value. **5** to change (an alternating current or voltage) using a transformer. ▷ HISTORY Latin *transformare*

transformation *n* **1** a change or alteration, esp. a radical one. **2** the act of transforming or the state of being transformed. **3** *S African* a political slogan for demographic change in the power struggle. **4** *n Geom* the mapping, or movement, of all the points of a figure in a plane according to a common operation. Some transformations, like dilation, affect the size of the figure, while others, called isometries, preserve the size of the figure.

transformer *n* a device that transfers an alternating current from one circuit to one or more other circuits, usually with a change of voltage.

transfuse *vb* **-fusing, -fused 1** to inject (blood or other fluid) into a blood vessel. **2** *Literary* to transmit or instil. ▷ HISTORY Latin *transfundere* to pour out

transfusion *n* **1** the injection of blood, blood plasma, etc., into the blood vessels of a patient. **2** the act of transferring something: *a transfusion of new funds.*

transgress *vb Formal* **1** to break (a law or rule). **2** to overstep (a limit): *he had never before been known to transgress the very slowest of walks.* ▷ HISTORY Latin *trans* beyond + *gradi* to step ▶ **transgression** *n* ▶ **transgressor** *n*

transhumance *n Agriculture* the seasonal migration of livestock to suitable grazing grounds. ▷ HISTORY French *transhumer* to change one's pastures, from Spanish *trashumar,* from Latin TRANS- + *humus* ground

transient *adj* **1** lasting for a short time only: *she had a number of transient relationships with fellow students.* **2** (of a person) not remaining in a place for a long time: *the transient population of the inner city.* ✧ *n* **3** a transient person or thing. ▷ HISTORY Latin *transiens* going over ▶ **transience** *n*

transistor *n* **1** a semiconductor device used to amplify and control electric currents. **2** *Informal* a small portable radio containing transistors. ▷ HISTORY *transfer* + *resistor*

transistorized *or* **-ised** *adj* (of an electronic device) using transistors.

transit *n* **1** the moving or carrying of goods or people from one place to another. **2** a route or means of transport: *transit by road.* **3** *Astron* the apparent passage of a celestial body across the meridian. **4 in transit** while travelling or being taken from one place to another: *in transit the fruit can be damaged.* ✧ *adj* **5** indicating a place or building where people wait or goods are kept between different stages of a journey: *a transit lounge for passengers who are changing planes.* ▷ HISTORY Latin *transitus* a going over

transition *n* **1** the process of changing from one state or stage to another: *the transition from dictatorship to democracy.* **2** *Music* a movement from one key to another. ▷ HISTORY Latin *transitio* a going over ▶ **transitional** *adj*

transition element *or* **metal** *n Chem* any element belonging to one of three series of elements with atomic numbers between 21 and 30, 39 and 48, and 57 and 80 (**transition series**). They tend to have more than one valency and to form complexes.

transitive *adj Grammar* denoting a verb which takes a direct object: *'to find' is a transitive verb.*

transitive verb *n Grammar* a verb which takes a direct object: *'to raise' is a transitive verb.* Compare **intransitive verb**.

transitory *adj* lasting only for a short time.

translate *vb* **-lating, -lated 1 a** to change (something spoken or written in one language) into another. **b** to be capable of being changed from one language into another: *puns do not translate well.* **2** to express (something) in a different way, for instance by using a different measurement system or less technical language: *the temperature is 30° Celsius, or if we translate into Fahrenheit, 86°.* **3** to transform or convert, for instance by putting an idea into practice: *cheap crops translate into lower feed prices.* **4** to interpret the significance of (a gesture, action, etc.): *I gave him what I hoped would be translated as a thoughtful look.* **5** to act as a translator: *I had to translate for a* *party of visiting Greeks.* ▷ HISTORY Latin *translatus* carried over ▶ **translatable** *adj* ▶ **translator** *n*

translation *n* **1** a piece of writing or speech that has been translated into another language. **2** the act of translating something. **3** the expression of something in a different way or form: *the book's plot was radically altered during its translation to film.* **4** *Maths* a transformation in which the origin of a coordinate system is moved to another position so that each axis retains the same direction. ▶ **translational** *adj*

transliterate *vb* **-ating, -ated** to write or spell (a word etc.) into corresponding letters of another alphabet. ▷ HISTORY Latin *trans-* across + *littera* letter ▶ **transliteration** *n*

translucent *adj* allowing light to pass through, but not transparent. ▷ HISTORY Latin *translucere* to shine through ▶ **translucency** *or* **translucence** *n*

transmigrate *vb* **-grating, -grated** (of a soul) to pass from one body into another at death. ▶ **transmigration** *n*

transmission *n* **1** the sending or passing of something, such as a message or disease from one place or person to another. **2** something that is transmitted, esp. a radio or television broadcast. **3** a system of shafts and gears that transmits power from the engine to the driving wheels of a motor vehicle.

transmit *vb* **-mitting, -mitted 1** to pass (something, such as a message or disease) from one place or person to another. **2 a** to send out (signals) by means of radio waves. **b** to broadcast (a radio or television programme). **3** to allow the passage of (particles, energy, etc.): *water transmits sound better than air.* **4** to transfer (a force, motion, etc.) from one part of a mechanical system to another: *the chain of the bike transmits the motion of the pedals to the rear wheel.* ▷ HISTORY Latin *transmittere* to send across ▶ **transmittable** *adj*

transmitter *n* **1** a piece of equipment used for broadcasting radio or television programmes. **2** a person or thing that transmits something.

transmogrify *vb* **-fies, -fying, -fied** *Jocular* to change or transform (someone or something) into a different shape or appearance, esp. a grotesque or bizarre one. ▷ HISTORY origin unknown ▶ **transmogrification** *n*

transmute *vb* **-muting, -muted** to change the form or nature of: *self-contempt is transmuted into hatred of others.* ▷ HISTORY Latin *transmutare* to shift ▶ **transmutation** *n*

transom *n* **1** a horizontal bar across a window. **2** a horizontal bar that separates a door from a window over it. ▷ HISTORY Old French *traversin*

transparency *n, pl* **-cies 1** the state of being transparent. **2** a positive photograph on transparent film, usually mounted in a frame or between glass plates, which can be viewed with the use of a slide projector.

transparent *adj* **1** able to be seen through; clear. **2** easy to understand or recognize; obvious: *transparent honesty.* ▷ HISTORY Latin *trans-* through + *parere* to appear ▶ **transparently** *adv*

transpiration *n Bot* (in plants) water loss through pores known as *stomata.*

transpire *vb* **-spiring, -spired 1** to come to light; become known. **2** *Not universally accepted* to happen or occur. **3** *Physiol* to give off (water or vapour) through the pores of the skin, etc. **4** (of plants) to lose (water vapour) through the stomata. ▷ HISTORY Latin *trans-* through + *spirare* to breathe

> ☑ **WORD TIP**
> It is often maintained that *transpire* should not be used to mean happen or occur, as in *the event transpired late in the evening,* and that the word is properly used to mean become known, as in *it transpired later that the thief had been caught.* The word is, however, widely used in the former sense, esp. in spoken English.

transplant *vb* **1** *Surgery* to transfer (an organ or tissue) from one part of the body or from one person to another. **2** to remove or transfer (esp. a plant) from one place to another. ✧ *n* **3** *Surgery* **a** the procedure involved in transferring an organ or tissue. **b** the organ or tissue transplanted. ▶ **transplantation** *n*

transponder *n* a type of radio or radar transmitter-receiver that transmits signals automatically when it receives predetermined signals. ▷ HISTORY *transmitter* + *responder*

transport *vb* **1** to carry or move (people or goods) from one place to another, esp. over some distance. **2** *History* to exile (a criminal) to a penal colony. **3** to have a strong emotional effect on: *transported by joy.* ✧ *n* **4** the business or system of transporting goods or people: *public transport.* **5** *Brit* freight vehicles generally. **6** a vehicle used to transport troops. **7** a transporting or being transported. **8** ecstasy or rapture: *transports of delight.* ▷ HISTORY Latin *trans-* across + *portare* to carry ▶ **transportable** *adj*

transportation *n* **1** a means or system of transporting. **2** the act of transporting or the state of being transported. **3** *History* deportation to a penal colony.

transporter *n* a large vehicle used for carrying cars from the factory to garages for sale.

transpose *vb* **-posing, -posed 1** to change the order of (letters, words, or sentences). **2** *Music* to play (notes, music, etc.) in a different key. **3** *Maths* to move (a term) from one side of an equation to the other with a corresponding reversal in sign: *transposing 3 in* $x - 3 = 6$ *gives* $x = 6 + 3$. ▷ HISTORY Old French *transposer* ▶ **transposition** *n*

transsexual *or* **transexual** *n* **1** a person who believes that his or her true identity is of the opposite sex. **2** a person who has had medical treatment to alter his or her sexual characteristics to those of the opposite sex.

transubstantiation *n Christianity* the doctrine that the bread and wine consecrated in Communion changes into the substance of Christ's body and blood. ▷ HISTORY Latin *trans-* over + *substantia* substance

transuranic (tranz-yoor-**ran**-ik) *adj Chem* (of an element) having an atomic number greater than that of uranium.

transversal *n Geom* a line intersecting two or more other lines.

transverse *adj* crossing from side to side: *the transverse arches in the main hall of the college.* ▷ HISTORY Latin *transvertere* to turn across

transverse dune *n Geog* a dune that lies at right angles to the direction of the prevailing wind with a gentle slope facing the wind and a steeper slope on the other side.

transverse wave *n Physics* a wave that is propagated at right angles to the direction of displacement of the transmitting field or medium.

transvestite *n* a person, esp. a man, who seeks sexual pleasure from wearing clothes of the opposite sex. ▷ HISTORY Latin *trans-* across + *vestitus* clothed ▶ **transvestism** *n*

trap *n* **1** a device or hole in which something, esp. an animal, is caught: *a fox trap.* **2** a plan for tricking a person into being caught unawares. **3** a situation from which it is difficult to escape: *caught in the poverty trap.* **4** a bend in a pipe that contains standing water to prevent the passage of gases. **5** a boxlike stall in which greyhounds are enclosed before the start of a race. **6** a device that hurls clay pigeons into the air to be fired at. **7** a light two-wheeled carriage: *a pony and trap.* **8** *Brit, Austral & NZ slang* the mouth: *shut your trap!* ✧ *vb* **trapping, trapped 9** to catch (an animal) in a trap. **10** to catch (someone) by a trick: *the police trapped the drug dealers by posing as potential customers.* **11** to hold or confine in an unpleasant situation from which it is difficult to escape: *trapped in the rubble of collapsed buildings.* ▷ HISTORY Old English *træppe*

trap-door spider *n* a spider that builds a silk-lined hole in the ground closed by a hinged door of earth and silk.

trapeze *n* a horizontal bar suspended from two ropes, used by circus acrobats. ▷ HISTORY French

trapezium *n, pl* **-ziums** *or* **-zia 1** a quadrilateral having two parallel sides of unequal length. **2** *Chiefly US & Canad* a quadrilateral having neither pair of sides parallel. ▷ HISTORY Greek *trapeza* table ▶ **trapezial** *adj*

trapezoid (**trap**-piz-zoid) *n* **1** a quadrilateral having neither pair of sides parallel. **2** *US & Canad* same as **trapezium** (sense 1). ▷ HISTORY Greek *trapeza* table

trapper *n* a person who traps animals, esp. for their furs or skins.

trappings *pl n* **1** the accessories that symbolize a condition, office, etc.: *the trappings of power.* **2** ceremonial harness for a horse or other animal. ▷ HISTORY probably from Old French *drap* cloth

Trappist *n* a member of an order of Christian monks who follow a rule of strict silence.

trash *n* **1** foolish ideas or talk; nonsense. **2** *US, Canad, NZ & S African* unwanted objects; rubbish. **3** *Chiefly US, Canad & NZ* a worthless person or group of people. ✧ *vb* **4** *Slang* to attack or destroy maliciously: *we've never trashed a hotel room.* ▷ HISTORY origin unknown ▶ **trashy** *adj*

trauma (**traw**-ma) *n* **1** *Psychol* an emotional shock that may have long-lasting effects. **2** *Pathol* any bodily injury or wound. ▷ HISTORY Greek: a wound ▶ **traumatic** *adj* ▶ **traumatically** *adv* ▶ **traumatize** *or* **-ise** *vb*

travail *n Literary* painful or exceptionally hard work. ▷ HISTORY Old French *travaillier*

travel *vb* **-elling, -elled** *or US* **-eling, -eled 1** to go or move from one place to another. **2** to go or journey through or across (an area, region, etc.): *Margaret travelled widely when she was in New Zealand.* **3** to go at a specified speed or for a specified distance: *the car was travelling at 30 mph.* **4** to go from place to place as a salesman. **5** (of perishable goods) to withstand a journey: *not all wines travel well.* **6** (of light or sound) to be transmitted or carried from one place to another: *sound travels a long distance in these conditions.* **7** (of a machine or part) to move in a fixed path. **8** (of a vehicle) *Informal* to move rapidly. ✧ *n* **9** the act or a means of travelling: *air travel has changed the way people live.* **10** a tour or journey: *his travels took him to Dublin.* **11** the distance moved by a mechanical part, such as the stroke of a piston. ▷ HISTORY Old French *travaillier* to travail

travel agency *n* an agency that arranges flights, hotel accommodation, etc., for tourists. ▶ **travel agent** *n*

traveller *n* **1** a person who travels, esp. habitually. **2** a travelling salesman. **3** a Gypsy.

traveller's cheque *n* a cheque sold by a bank, travel agency, etc., which the buyer signs on purchase and can cash abroad by re-signing it.

travelogue *or US* **travelog** *n* a film or lecture on travels and travelling.

traverse *vb* **-ersing, -ersed 1** to move over or back and forth over; cross: *he once traversed San Francisco harbour in a balloon.* **2** to reach across. **3** to walk, climb, or ski diagonally up or down a slope. ✧ *n* **4** something being or lying across, such as a crossbar. **5** the act or an instance of traversing or crossing. **6** a path or road across. ✧ *adj* **7** being or lying across. ▷ HISTORY Latin *transversus* turned across ▶ **traversal** *n*

travesty *n, pl* **-ties 1** a grotesque imitation or mockery: *a travesty of justice.* ✧ *vb* **-ties, -tying, -tied 2** to make or be a travesty of. ▷ HISTORY French *travesti* disguised

travois (trav-**voy**) *n, pl* **-vois** (**-voyz**) *Canad* a sled used for dragging logs. ▷ HISTORY Canadian French

trawl *n* **1** a large net, usually in the shape of a sock or bag, dragged at deep levels behind a fishing boat. ✧ *vb* **2** to fish using such a net. ▷ HISTORY Middle Dutch *traghelen* to drag

trawler *n* a ship used for trawling.

tray *n* **1** a flat board of wood, plastic, or metal, usually with a rim, on which things can be carried. **2** an open receptacle for office correspondence. ▷ HISTORY Old English *trieg*

TRC *n* (in S Africa) Truth and Reconciliation Commission: a commission which encourages people who committed human rights abuses or acts of terror during the apartheid era to reveal the truth about their crimes in return for immunity from prosecution.

treacherous *adj* **1** disloyal and untrustworthy: *he was cruel, treacherous, and unscrupulous.* **2** unreliable or dangerous, esp. because of sudden changes: *the tides here can be very treacherous.* ▸ **treacherously** *adv*

treachery *n, pl* **-eries** the act or an instance of wilful betrayal. ▷ HISTORY Old French *trecherie*

treacle *n* a thick dark syrup produced during the refining of sugar. ▷ HISTORY Latin *theriaca* antidote to poison ▸ **treacly** *adj*

tread *vb* **treading, trod; trodden** *or* **trod 1** to set one's foot down on or in something: *he trod on some dog's dirt.* **2** to crush or squash by treading (on): *treading on a biscuit.* **3** to walk along (a path or road). **4 tread carefully** *or* **warily** to proceed in a delicate or tactful manner. **5 tread water** to stay afloat in an upright position by moving the legs in a walking motion. ✧ *n* **6** a way of walking or the sound of walking: *he walked, with a heavy tread, up the stairs.* **7** the top surface of a step in a staircase. **8** the pattern of grooves in the outer surface of a tyre that helps it grip the road. **9** the part of a shoe that is generally in contact with the ground. ▷ HISTORY Old English *tredan*

treadle (**tred**-dl) *n* a lever operated by the foot to turn a wheel. ▷ HISTORY Old English *tredan* to tread

treadmill *n* **1** (formerly) an apparatus turned by the weight of men or animals climbing steps on a revolving cylinder or wheel. **2** a dreary routine: *they are chained to the treadmill of a job.* **3** an exercise machine that consists of a continuous moving belt on which to walk or jog.

treason *n* **1** betrayal of one's sovereign or country, esp. by attempting to overthrow the government. **2** any treachery or betrayal. ▷ HISTORY Latin *traditio* a handing over ▸ **treasonable** *adj* ▸ **treasonous** *adj*

treasure *n* **1** a collection of wealth, esp. in the form of money, precious metals, or gems. **2** a valuable painting, ornament, or other object: *the museum has many art treasures.* **3** *Informal* a person who is highly valued: *she can turn her hand to anything, she's a perfect treasure.* ✧ *vb* **-uring, -ured 4** to cherish (someone or something). ▷ HISTORY Greek *thēsauros*

treasurer *n* a person appointed to look after the funds of a society or other organization.

treasure-trove *n Law* any articles, such as coins or valuable objects found hidden and without any evidence of ownership. ▷ HISTORY Anglo-French *tresor trové* treasure found

treasury *n, pl* **-uries 1** a storage place for treasure. **2** the revenues or funds of a government or organization.

Treasury *n* (in various countries) the government department in charge of finance.

treat *vb* **1** to deal with or regard in a certain manner: *her love for a man who treats her abominably.* **2** to attempt to cure or lessen the symptoms of (an illness or injury or a person suffering from it): *the drug is prescribed to treat asthma.* **3** to subject to a chemical or industrial process: *the wood should be treated with a preservative.* **4** to provide (someone) with something as a treat: *I'll treat you to an ice cream.* **5 treat of** to deal with (something) in writing or speaking: *this book treats of a most abstruse subject.* ✧ *n* **6** a celebration, entertainment, gift, or meal given for or to someone and paid for by someone else. **7** any delightful surprise or specially pleasant occasion. ▷ HISTORY Old French *tretier* ▸ **treatable** *adj*

treatise (**treat**-izz) *n* a formal piece of writing that deals systematically with a particular subject. ▷ HISTORY Anglo-French *tretiz*

treatment *n* **1** the medical or surgical care given to a patient. **2** a way of handling a person or thing: *the party has had unfair treatment in the press.*

treaty *n, pl* **-ties 1** a formal written agreement between two or more states, such as an alliance or trade arrangement: *the Treaty of Rome established the Common Market.* **2** an agreement between two parties concerning the purchase of property. ▷ HISTORY Old French *traité*

Treaty of Versailles (ver-**sigh**) *n History* the treaty of 1919 imposed upon Germany by the Allies, except for the USA and the Soviet Union.

treble *adj* **1** three times as much or as many. **2** of or denoting a soprano voice or part or a high-pitched instrument. ✧ *n* **3** a soprano voice or part or a high-pitched instrument. **4** of the highest range of musical notes: *these loudspeakers give excellent treble reproduction.* ✧ *vb* **-bling, -bled 5** to make or become three times as much or as many: *sales have trebled in three years.* ▷ HISTORY Latin *triplus* threefold ▸ **trebly** *adv*

treble clef *n Music* the clef that establishes G a fifth above middle C as being on the second line of the staff.

tree *n* **1** any large woody perennial plant with a distinct trunk and usually having leaves and branches. *RELATED ADJECTIVE* ▸ **arboreal 2** See **family tree, shoetree**. **3 at the top of the tree** in the highest position of a profession. ▷ HISTORY Old English *trēow* ▸ **treeless** *adj*

tree creeper *n* a small songbird of the N hemisphere that creeps up trees to feed on insects.

tree diagram *n Maths* a branching diagram showing the probability of various events.

tree fern *n* any of numerous large tropical ferns with a trunklike stem.

tree kangaroo *n* a tree-living kangaroo of New Guinea and N Australia.

tree line *n* same as **timber line**.

tree surgery *n* the treatment of damaged trees by filling cavities, applying braces, etc. ▸ **tree surgeon** *n*

tree tomato *n* same as **tamarillo**.

trefoil (**tref**-foil) *n* **1** a plant, such as clover, with leaves divided into three smaller leaves. **2** *Archit* a carved ornament with a shape like such leaves. ▷ HISTORY Latin *trifolium* three-leaved herb ▸ **trefoiled** *adj*

trek *n* **1** a long and often difficult journey, esp. on foot. **2** *S African* a journey or stage of a journey, esp. a migration by ox wagon. ✧ *vb* **trekking, trekked 3** to make a trek. ▷ HISTORY Afrikaans

trellis *n* a frame made of vertical and horizontal strips of wood, esp. one used to support climbing plants. ▷ HISTORY Old French *treliz* fabric of open texture ▸ **trelliswork** *n*

tremble *vb* **-bling, -bled 1** to shake with short slight movements: *her hands trembled uncontrollably; he felt the ground trembling beneath him.* **2** to experience fear or anxiety: *his parents trembled with apprehension about his future.* **3** (of the voice) to sound uncertain or unsteady, for instance through pain or emotion. ✧ *n* **4** the act or an instance of trembling. ▷ HISTORY Latin *tremere* ▸ **trembling** *adj*

tremendous *adj* **1** very large or impressive: *a tremendous amount of money.* **2** very exciting or unusual: *a tremendous feeling of elation.* **3** very good or pleasing: *my wife has given me tremendous support.* ▷ HISTORY Latin *tremendus* terrible ▸ **tremendously** *adv*

tremolo *n, pl* **-los** *Music* **1** (in playing the violin or other stringed instrument) the rapid repetition of a note or notes to produce a trembling effect. **2** (in singing) a fluctuation in pitch. ▷ HISTORY Italian: quavering

tremor *n* **1** an involuntary shudder or vibration: *the slight tremor of excitement.* **2** a minor earthquake. ▷ HISTORY Latin

tremulous *adj Literary* trembling, as from fear or excitement: *I managed a tremulous smile.* ▷ HISTORY Latin *tremere* to shake ▸ **tremulously** *adv*

trench *n* **1** a long narrow ditch in the ground, such as one for laying a pipe in. **2** a long deep ditch used by soldiers for protection in a war: *my grandfather fought in the trenches in the First World War.* ✧ *adj* **3** of or involving military trenches: *trench warfare.* ▷ HISTORY Old French *trenche* something cut

trenchant *adj* **1** keen or incisive: *a trenchant screenplay.* **2** vigorous and effective: *the prime minister's trenchant adoption of this issue.* ▷ HISTORY Old French: cutting ▸ **trenchancy** *n*

trench coat *n* a belted raincoat similar in style to a military officer's coat.

trencher *n History* a wooden board on which food was served or cut. ▷ HISTORY Old French *trencheoir*

trencherman *n, pl* **-men** a person who enjoys food; hearty eater.

trench warfare *n* a type of warfare in which opposing armies face each other in entrenched positions.

trend *n* **1** general tendency or direction: *an accelerating trend towards the use of mobile phones.* **2** fashionable style: *she set a trend for wearing lingerie as outer garments.* ✧ *vb* **3** to take a certain trend. ▷ HISTORY Old English *trendan* to turn

trendsetter *n* a person or thing that creates, or may create, a new fashion. ▸ **trendsetting** *adj*

trendy *Informal* ✧ *adj* **trendier, trendiest 1** consciously fashionable: *a flat in Glasgow's trendy West End.* ✧ *n, pl* **trendies 2** a trendy person: *a media trendy.* ▸ **trendily** *adv* ▸ **trendiness** *n*

trepidation *n Formal* a state of fear or anxiety. ▷ HISTORY Latin *trepidatio*

trespass *vb* **1** to go onto somebody else's property without permission. ✧ *n* **2** the act or an instance of trespassing. **3** *Old-fashioned* a sin or wrong-doing. ▷ HISTORY Old French *trespas* a passage ▸ **trespasser** *n*

trespass on *or* **upon** *vb Formal* to take unfair advantage of (someone's friendship, patience, etc.): *I won't trespass upon your hospitality any longer.*

tresses *pl n* a woman's long flowing hair. ▷ HISTORY Old French *trece*

trestle *n* **1** a support for one end of a table or beam, consisting of two rectangular frameworks or sets of legs which are joined at the top but not the bottom. **2** Also called: **trestle table** a table consisting of a board supported by a trestle at each end. ▷ HISTORY Old French *trestel*

trevally (trih-**val**-lee) *n, pl* **-lies** *Austral & NZ* any of various food and game fishes. ▷ HISTORY probably alteration of *cavalla,* species of tropical fish

trews *pl n Chiefly Brit* close-fitting trousers of tartan cloth. ▷ HISTORY Scottish Gaelic *triubhas*

tri- *combining form* **1** three or thrice: *trilingual.* **2** occurring every three: *triweekly.* ▷ HISTORY Latin *tres*

triad *n* **1** a group of three. **2** *Music* a three-note chord consisting of a note and the third and fifth above it. ▷ HISTORY Greek *trias* ▸ **triadic** *adj*

Triad *n* a Chinese secret society involved in criminal activities, such as drug trafficking.

trial *n* **1** *Law* an investigation of a case in front of a judge to decide whether a person is innocent or guilty of a crime by questioning him or her and considering the evidence. **2** the act or an instance of trying or proving; test or experiment: *the new drug is undergoing clinical trials.* **3** an annoying or frustrating person or thing: *young children can be a great trial at times.* **4** a motorcycling competition in which the skills of the riders are tested over rough ground. **5 trials** a sporting competition for individual people or animals: *horse trials.* **6 on trial a** undergoing trial, esp. before a court of law. **b** being tested, for example before a commitment to purchase: *I only have the car out on trial.* ✧ *adj* **7** on a temporary basis while being tried out or tested: *a trial run.* ✧ *vb* **trialling, trialled 8** to test or make experimental use of: *the idea has been trialled in several schools.* ▷ HISTORY Anglo-French *trier* to try

trial and error *n* a method of discovery based on practical experiment and experience rather than on theory: *raising her children has been a matter of trial and error.*

trial balance *n Book-keeping* a statement of all the debit and credit balances in the double-entry ledger.

triallist *or* **trialist** *n* **1** a person who takes part in a competition. **2** *Sport* a person who takes part in a preliminary match or heat held to determine selection for a team or event.

triangle *n* **1** a geometric figure with three sides and three angles. **2** any object shaped like a triangle: *a triangle of streets running up from the river.* **3** *Music* a percussion instrument that consists of a metal bar bent into a triangular shape, played by striking it with a metal stick. **4** any situation involving three people or points of view: *a torrid sex triangle.* ▷ **HISTORY** TRI- + Latin *angulus* corner ▶ **triangular** *adj*

triangulate *vb* **-lating, -lated** to survey (an area) by dividing it into triangles.

triangulation *n* a method of surveying in which an area is divided into triangles, one side (the base line) and all angles of which are measured and the lengths of the other lines calculated by trigonometry.

Triassic *adj Geol* of the period of geological time about 230 million years ago. ▷ **HISTORY** Latin *trias* triad

tribalism *n* loyalty to a tribe, esp. as opposed to a modern political entity such as a state.

tribe *n* **1** a group of families or clans believed to have a common ancestor. **2** *Informal* a group of people who do the same type of thing: *a tribe of German yachtsmen.* ▷ **HISTORY** Latin *tribus* ▶ **tribal** *adj*

tribesman *n, pl* **-men** a member of a tribe.

tribulation *n* great distress: *the tribulations of a deserted wife.* ▷ **HISTORY** Latin *tribulare* to afflict

tribunal *n* **1** a special court or committee that is appointed to deal with a particular problem: *an industrial tribunal investigating allegations of unfair dismissal.* **2** a court of justice. ▷ **HISTORY** Latin *tribunus* tribune

tribune *n* **1** a person who upholds public rights. **2** (in ancient Rome) an officer elected by the plebs to protect their interests. ▷ **HISTORY** Latin *tribunus*

tributary *n, pl* **-taries 1** a stream or river that flows into a larger one: *Frankfurt lies on the River Main, a tributary of the Rhine.* **2** a person, nation, or people that pays tribute. ✧ *adj* **3** (of a stream or river) flowing into a larger stream. **4** paying tribute: *Egypt was formerly a tributary province of the Turkish Empire.*

tribute *n* **1** something given, done, or said as a mark of respect or admiration. **2** a payment by one ruler or state to another, usually as an acknowledgment of submission. **3** something that shows the merits of a particular quality of a person or thing: *the car's low fuel consumption is a tribute to the quality of its engine.* ▷ **HISTORY** Latin *tributum*

trice *n* **in a trice** in a moment: *she was back in a trice.* ▷ **HISTORY** originally, at one tug, from *trice* to haul up

triceps *n* the muscle at the back of the upper arm. ▷ **HISTORY** Latin

trichology (trick-**ol**-a-jee) *n* the branch of medicine concerned with the hair and its diseases. ▷ **HISTORY** Greek *thrix* hair ▶ **trichologist** *n*

trichromatic *or* **trichromic** *adj* **1** having or involving three colours. **2** of or having normal colour vision. ▶ **trichromatism** *n*

trick *n* **1** a deceitful or cunning action or plan: *she was willing to use any dirty trick to get what she wanted.* **2** a joke or prank: *he loves playing tricks on his sister.* **3** a clever way of doing something, learned from experience: *an old campers' trick is to use three thin blankets rather than one thick one.* **4** an illusory or magical feat or device. **5** a simple feat learned by an animal or person. **6** a deceptive illusion: *a trick of the light.* **7** a habit or mannerism: *she had a trick of saying 'oh dear'.* **8** *Cards* a batch of cards played in turn and won by the person playing the highest card. **9 do the trick** *Informal* to produce the desired result. **10 how's tricks?** *Slang* how are you? ✧ *vb* **11** to defraud, deceive, or cheat (someone). ▷ **HISTORY** Old French *trique* ▶ **trickery** *n*

trickle *vb* **-ling, -led 1** to flow or cause to flow in a thin stream or drops: *tears trickled down her cheeks.* **2** to move slowly or in small groups: *voters trickled to the polls.* ✧ *n* **3** a thin, irregular, or slow flow of something: *a trickle of blood.* ▷ **HISTORY** probably imitative

trickle-down *adj* of the theory that granting concessions like tax cuts to the rich will benefit all levels of society by stimulating the economy.

trickster *n* a person who deceives or plays tricks.

tricky *adj* **trickier, trickiest 1** involving snags or difficulties: *a tricky task.* **2** needing careful handling: *a tricky situation.* **3** sly or wily: *a tricky customer.* ▶ **trickily** *adv* ▶ **trickiness** *n*

tricolour *or US* **tricolor** (**trick**-kol-lor) *n* a flag with three equal stripes in different colours, esp. the French or Irish national flags.

tricuspid *adj Anat* having three points, cusps, or segments: *a tricuspid valve.*

tricycle *n* a three-wheeled cycle. ▶ **tricyclist** *n*

trident *n* a three-pronged spear. ▷ **HISTORY** Latin *tridens* three-pronged

triennial *adj* occurring every three years. ▷ **HISTORY** TRI- + Latin *annus* year ▶ **triennially** *adv*

trifle[1] *n* **1** a thing of little or no value or significance. **2** *Brit, Austral & NZ* a cold dessert made of sponge cake spread with jam or fruit, soaked in sherry, covered with custard and cream. **3 a trifle** to a small extent or degree; slightly: *he is a trifle eccentric.* ▷ **HISTORY** Old French *trufle* mockery

trifle[2] *vb* **trifling, trifled trifle with** to treat (a person or his or her feelings) with disdain or disregard.

trifling *adj* insignificant, petty, or frivolous: *a trifling misunderstanding.*

trig. trigonometry.

trigger *n* **1** a small lever that releases a catch on a gun or machine. **2** any event that sets a course of action in motion: *his murder was the trigger for a night of rioting.* ✧ *vb* **3** Also: **trigger off** to set (an action or process) in motion: *various factors can trigger off a migraine.* ▷ **HISTORY** Dutch *trekker*

a b c d e f g h i j k l m n o p q r s t u v w x y z

trigger-happy *adj Informal* too ready or willing to use guns or violence: *trigger-happy border guards.*

trigonometric function *n Maths* a function of an angle expressed as a ratio of two of the sides of a right-angled triangle containing the angle.

trigonometry *n* the branch of mathematics concerned with the relations of sides and angles of triangles, which is used in surveying, navigation, etc. ▷ **HISTORY** Greek *trigōnon* triangle

trig point *n* a point on a hilltop etc., used for triangulation by a surveyor.

trike *n Informal* a tricycle.

trilateral *adj* having three sides.

trilby *n, pl* **-bies** a man's soft felt hat with an indented crown. ▷ **HISTORY** after *Trilby,* the heroine of a novel by George Du Maurier

trill *n* **1** *Music* a rapid alternation between a note and the note above it. **2** a shrill warbling sound made by some birds: *the canary's high trills.* ✧ *vb* **3** (of a bird) to make a shrill warbling sound. **4** (of a person) to talk or laugh in a high-pitched musical voice. ▷ **HISTORY** Italian *trillo*

trillion *n* **-lions** *or* **-lion 1** the number represented as one followed by twelve zeros (10^{12}); a million million. **2** (in Britain, originally) the number represented as one followed by eighteen zeros (10^{18}); a million million million. ✧ *adj* **3** amounting to a trillion: *a trillion dollars.* ▷ **HISTORY** French ▶ **trillionth** *n, adj*

trillium *n* a plant of Asia and North America that has three leaves at the top of the stem with a single white, pink, or purple three-petalled flower. ▷ **HISTORY** New Latin

trilobite (**trile**-oh-bite) *n* a small prehistoric marine arthropod, found as a fossil. ▷ **HISTORY** Greek *trilobos* having three lobes

trilogy (**trill**-a-jee) *n, pl* **-gies** a series of three books, plays, etc., which form a related group but are each complete works in themselves. ▷ **HISTORY** Greek *trilogia*

trim *adj* **trimmer, trimmest 1** neat and spruce in appearance: *trim lace curtains.* **2** attractively slim: *his body was trim and athletic.* ✧ *vb* **trimming, trimmed 3** to make (something) neater by cutting it slightly without changing its basic shape: *his white beard was neatly trimmed.* **4** to adorn or decorate (something, such as a garment) with lace, ribbons, etc.: *a cotton camisole neatly trimmed with lace.* **5 a** to adjust the balance of (a ship or aircraft) by shifting cargo etc. **b** to adjust (a ship's sails) to take advantage of the wind. **6** to reduce or lower the size of: *the company has trimmed its pretax profits forecast by $2.3 million.* **7** to alter (a plan or policy) by removing parts which seem unnecessary or unpopular: *the government would rather trim its policies than lose the election.* **8 trim off** *or* **away** to cut so as to remove: *trim off most of the fat before cooking the meat.* ✧ *n* **9** a decoration or adornment: *a black suit with scarlet trim.* **10** the upholstery and decorative facings of a car's interior. **11** good physical condition: *he had always kept himself in trim.* **12** a haircut that neatens but does not alter the existing hairstyle. ▷ **HISTORY** Old English *trymman* to strengthen

trimaran (**trime**-a-ran) *n* a boat with one smaller hull on each side of the main hull. ▷ **HISTORY** *tri-* + *(cata)maran*

trimeter *n Poetry* a verse line consisting of three metrical feet.

trimming *n* **1** an extra piece added to a garment for decoration: *a pink nightie with lace trimming.* **2 trimmings** usual or traditional accompaniments: *bacon and eggs with all the trimmings.*

Trinitarian *n* **1** a person who believes in the doctrine of the Trinity. ✧ *adj* **2** of or relating to the Trinity. ▶ **Trinitarianism** *n*

trinitrotoluene *n* the full name for **TNT**.

trinity *n, pl* **-ties** a group of three people or things. ▷ **HISTORY** Latin *trinus* triple

Trinity *n Christianity* the union of three persons, the Father, Son, and Holy Spirit, in one God.

trinket *n* a small or worthless ornament or piece of jewellery. ▷ **HISTORY** origin unknown

trio *n, pl* **trios 1** a group of three people or things. **2** a group of three instrumentalists or singers. **3** a piece of music for three performers. ▷ **HISTORY** Italian

trip *n* **1** a journey to a place and back, esp. for pleasure: *they took a coach trip round the island.* **2** a false step; stumble. **3** the act of causing someone to stumble or fall by catching his or her foot with one's own. **4** *Informal* a hallucinogenic drug experience. **5** a catch on a mechanism that acts as a switch. ✧ *vb* **tripping, tripped 6** Also: **trip up** to stumble or cause (someone) to stumble. **7** Also: **trip up** to trap or catch (someone) in a mistake. **8** to walk lightly and quickly, with a dancelike motion: *I could see Amelia tripping along beside him.* **9** *Informal* to experience the effects of a hallucinogenic drug. ▷ **HISTORY** Old French *triper* to tread

tripartite *adj* involving or composed of three people or parts. ▶ **tripartism** *n*

tripe *n* **1** the stomach lining of a cow or pig used as a food. **2** *Brit, Austral & NZ informal* nonsense or rubbish. ▷ **HISTORY** Old French

tripeptide *n Biochem* a protein consisting of three linked amino acids.

Tripitaka (trip-it-**tah**-ka) *n* the three collections of books making up the Buddhist scriptures. ▷ **HISTORY** Pali (an ancient language of India) *tri* three + *pitaka* basket

triple *adj* **1** made up of three parts or things: *a triple murder.* **2** (of musical time or rhythm) having three beats in each bar. **3** three times as great or as much: *a triple brandy.* ✧ *vb* **-pling, -pled 4** to make or become three times as much or as many: *the company has tripled its sales over the past five years.* ✧ *n* **5** something that is, or contains, three times as much as normal. **6** a group of three. ▷ **HISTORY** Latin *triplus* ▶ **triply** *adv*

Triple Entente *n History* the understanding between Britain, France, and Russia that developed between 1894 and 1907, which became a formal alliance on the outbreak of World War I.

triple jump *n* an athletic event in which the competitor has to perform a hop, a step, and a jump in a continuous movement.

triple point *n Chem* the temperature and pressure at which a substance can exist as a solid, liquid, and gas.

triplet *n* **1** one of three children born at one birth. **2** a group of three musical notes played in the time that two would normally take. **3** a group or set of three similar things.

triplicate *adj* **1** triple. ✧ *vb* **-cating, -cated 2** to multiply or be multiplied by three. ✧ *n* **3 in triplicate** written out three times: *my request to interview the commander had to be made in triplicate.* ▷ **HISTORY** Latin *triplicare* to triple ▶ **triplication** *n*

tripod (**tripe**-pod) *n* **1** a three-legged stand to which a camera can be attached to hold it steady. **2** a three-legged stool, table, etc. ▷ **HISTORY** TRI- + Greek *pous* a foot

tripos (**tripe**-poss) *n Brit* the final honours degree examinations at Cambridge University. ▷ **HISTORY** Latin *tripus* tripod

tripper *n Chiefly Brit* a tourist.

triptych (**trip**-tick) *n* a set of three pictures or panels, usually hinged together and often used as an altarpiece. ▷ **HISTORY** TRI- + Greek *ptux* plate

trireme (**try**-ream) *n* an ancient Greek warship with three rows of oars on each side. ▷ **HISTORY** TRI- + Latin *remus* oar

trismus *n Pathol* the state of being unable to open the mouth because of sustained contractions of the jaw muscles, caused by tetanus. Nontechnical name: **lockjaw** ▷ **HISTORY** Greek *trismos* a grinding

trite *adj* (of a remark or idea) commonplace and unoriginal. ▷ **HISTORY** Latin *tritus* worn down

tritium *n* a radioactive isotope of hydrogen. Symbol: T or ^{3}H. ▷ **HISTORY** Greek *tritos* third

triumph *n* **1** the feeling of great happiness resulting from a victory or major achievement. **2** an outstanding success, achievement, or victory: *the concert was a musical triumph.* **3** (in ancient Rome) a procession held in honour of a victorious general. ✧ *vb* **4** to gain control or success: *triumphing over adversity.* **5** to rejoice over a victory. ▷ **HISTORY** Latin *triumphus* ▶ **triumphal** *adj*

triumphant *adj* **1** feeling or displaying triumph: *her smile was triumphant.* **2** celebrating a victory or success: *the general's triumphant tour round the city.* ▶ **triumphantly** *adv*

triumvir (try-**umm**-vir) *n* (esp. in ancient Rome) a member of a triumvirate. ▷ **HISTORY** Latin

triumvirate (try-**umm**-vir-rit) *n* **1** a group of three people in joint control of something: *the triumvirate of great orchestras which dominates classical music in Europe.* **2** (in ancient Rome) a board of three officials jointly responsible for some task.

trivalent *adj Chem* **1** having a valency of three. **2** having three valencies. ▶ **trivalency** *n*

trivet (**triv**-vit) *n* **1** a three-legged stand for holding a pot, kettle, etc., over a fire. **2** a short metal stand on which hot dishes are placed on a table. ▷ **HISTORY** Old English *trefet*

trivia *n* petty and unimportant things or details.

trivial *adj* of little importance: *a trivial matter.* ▷ **HISTORY** Latin *trivialis* common ▶ **triviality** *n* ▶ **trivially** *adv*

trivialize *or* **-ise** *vb* **-izing, -ized** *or* **-ising, -ised** to make (something) seem less important or complex than it is.

trochee (**troke**-ee) *n Prosody* a metrical foot of one long and one short syllable. ▷ **HISTORY** Greek *trekhein* to run ▶ **trochaic** *adj*

trod *vb* the past tense and a past participle of **tread**.

trodden *vb* a past participle of **tread**.

troglodyte *n* a person who lives in a cave. ▷ **HISTORY** Greek *trōglodutēs* one who enters caves

troika *n* **1** a Russian coach or sleigh drawn by three horses abreast. **2** a group of three people in authority: *a troika of European foreign ministers.* ▷ **HISTORY** Russian

Trojan *adj* **1** of ancient Troy or its people. ✧ *n* **2** a person from ancient Troy. **3** a hard-working person.

Trojan Horse *n* **1** *Greek myth* the huge wooden hollow figure of a horse used by the Greeks to enter Troy. **2** a trap or trick intended to undermine an enemy.

troll[1] *n* (in Scandinavian folklore) a supernatural dwarf or giant that dwells in a cave or mountain. ▷ **HISTORY** Old Norse: demon

troll[2] *vb Angling* to fish by dragging a lure through the water. ▷ **HISTORY** Old French *troller* to run about

trolley *n* **1** a small table on casters used for carrying food or drink. **2** a wheeled cart or stand used for moving heavy items, such as shopping in a supermarket or luggage at a railway station. **3** *Brit* See **trolley bus. 4** *US & Canad* See **trolley car. 5** a device, such as a wheel that collects the current from an overhead wire, to drive the motor of an electric vehicle. **6** *Brit & Austral* a low truck running on rails, used in factories, mines, etc. ▷ **HISTORY** probably from TROLL[2]

trolley bus *n* a bus powered by electricity from two overhead wires but not running on rails.

trolley car *n US & Canad* same as **tram**.

trollop *n Derogatory* a promiscuous or slovenly woman. ▷ **HISTORY** origin unknown

trombone *n* a brass musical instrument with a sliding tube which is moved in or out to alter the note played. ▷ **HISTORY** Italian ▶ **trombonist** *n*

trompe l'oeil (tromp **luh**-ee) *n, pl* **trompe l'oeils** (tromp **luh**-ee) **1** a painting etc. giving a convincing illusion that the objects represented are real. **2** an effect of this kind. ▷ **HISTORY** French, literally: deception of the eye

troop *n* **1** a large group: *a troop of dogs.* **2 troops** soldiers: *troops have been maintaining an unusually high profile.* **3** a subdivision of a cavalry or armoured regiment. **4** a large group of Scouts made up of several patrols. ✧ *vb* **5** to move in a crowd: *we trooped into the room after her.* **6** *Mil chiefly Brit & Austral* to parade (a flag or banner) ceremonially: *trooping the colour.* ▷ **HISTORY** French *troupe*

trooper *n* **1** a soldier in a cavalry regiment. **2** *US & Austral* a mounted policeman. **3** *US* a state policeman. **4** a cavalry horse. **5** *Informal, chiefly Brit* a troopship.

troopship *n* a ship used to transport military personnel.

trope *n* a word or expression used in a figurative sense. ▷ **HISTORY** Greek *tropos* style, turn

trophic *adj Biol* of or relating to nutrition. ▷ **HISTORY** Greek *trophikos,* from *trophē* food, from *trephein* to feed

trophic level *n Biol* position (of an organism) in the food chain, as determined by whether it is a primary producer, a primary consumer, a secondary consumer, or a tertiary consumer.

trophy *n, pl* **-phies 1** a cup, shield, etc., given as a prize. **2** a memento of success, esp. one taken in war or hunting: *stuffed animal heads and other hunting trophies.* ✧ *adj* **3** *Informal* regraded as a highly desirable symbol of wealth or success: *a trophy wife.* ▷ **HISTORY** Greek *tropaion*

tropic *n* **1** either of the lines of latitude at about 23½°N (**tropic of Cancer**) and 23½°S (**tropic of Capricorn**) of the equator. **2 the tropics** that part of the earth's surface between the tropics of Cancer and Capricorn: *the intense heat and humidity of the tropics.* ▷ **HISTORY** Greek *tropos* a turn; from the belief that the sun turned back at the solstices

-tropic *combining form Physiol* turning or developing in response to a certain stimulus: *heliotropic.*

tropical *adj* belonging to, typical of, or located in, the tropics: *tropical rainforests.* ▶ **tropically** *adv*

tropism *n* the tendency of a plant or animal to turn or curve in response to an external stimulus. ▷ **HISTORY** Greek *tropos* a turn

troposphere *n* the lowest layer of the earth's atmosphere, about 18 kilometres (11 miles) thick at the equator to about 6 km (4 miles) at the Poles. ▷ **HISTORY** Greek *tropos* a turn + SPHERE

trot *vb* **trotting, trotted 1** (of a horse) to move in a manner faster than a walk but slower than a gallop, in which diagonally opposite legs come down together. **2** (of a person) to move fairly quickly, with small quick steps. ✧ *n* **3** a medium-paced gait of a horse, in which diagonally opposite legs come down together. **4** a steady brisk pace. **5 on the trot** *Informal* one after the other: *ten years on the trot.* **6 the trots** *Slang* diarrhoea. ▷ **HISTORY** Old French

Trot *n Chiefly Brit informal* a follower of Trotsky.

troth (rhymes with **growth**) *n Archaic* **1** a pledge of fidelity, esp. a betrothal. **2 in troth** truly. ▷ **HISTORY** Old English *trēowth*

trot out *vb Informal* to repeat (old information or ideas) without fresh thought: *the government trots out the same excuse every time.*

Trotskyist *or* **Trotskyite** *adj* **1** of the theories of Leon Trotsky (1879–1940), Russian Communist, which call for a worldwide revolution by the proletariat. ✧ *n* **2** a supporter of Trotsky or his theories. ▶ **Trotskyism** *n*

trotter *n* **1** the foot of a pig. **2** a horse that is specially trained to trot fast.

troubadour (**troo**-bad-oor) *n* a travelling poet and singer in S France or N Italy from the 11th to the 13th century who wrote chiefly on courtly love. ▷ **HISTORY** French

trouble *n* **1** difficulties or problems: *I'd trouble finding somewhere to park.* **2** a cause of distress, disturbance, or pain: *we must be sensitive to the troubles of other people.* **3** disease or a problem with one's health: *ear trouble.* **4** a state of disorder, ill-feeling, or unrest: *the police had orders to intervene at the first sign of trouble.* **5** effort or exertion to do something: *they didn't even take the trouble to see the film before banning it.* **6** a personal weakness or cause of annoyance: *his trouble is that he's constitutionally jealous.* **7 in trouble a** likely to be punished for something one has done: *in trouble with the public prosecutor.* **b** pregnant when not married. **8 more trouble than it's worth** involving a lot of time or effort for very little reward: *making your own pasta is more trouble than it's worth.* ✧ *vb* **-bling, -bled 9** to cause trouble to. **10** to make an effort or exert oneself: *he dismissed the letters as forgeries without troubling to examine them.* **11** to cause inconvenience or discomfort to: *sorry to trouble you!* ▷ **HISTORY** Old French *troubler* ▶ **troubled** *adj*

troublemaker *n* a person who causes trouble, esp. between people. ▶ **troublemaking** *adj, n*

troubleshooter *n* a person employed to locate and deal with faults or problems. ▶ **troubleshooting** *n, adj*

troublesome *adj* causing trouble.

trouble spot *n* a place where there is frequent fighting or violence: *the Balkans have long been one of the major European trouble spots.*

troublous *adj Literary* unsettled or agitated.

trough (**troff**) *n* **1** a long open container, esp. one for animals' food or water. **2** a narrow channel between two waves or ridges. **3** a low point in a pattern that has regular high and low points: *the trough of the slump in pupil numbers was in 1985.* **4** *Meteorol* a long narrow area of low pressure. **5** a narrow channel or gutter. ▷ **HISTORY** Old English *trōh*

trounce *vb* **trouncing, trounced** to defeat (someone) utterly. ▷ **HISTORY** origin unknown

troupe (**troop**) *n* a company of actors or other performers. ▷ **HISTORY** French

trouper *n* **1** a member of a troupe. **2** an experienced person: *Bette plays a showbiz trouper.*

trouser *adj* **1** of or relating to trousers: *trouser legs.* ✧ *vb* **2** *Brit slang* to take (something, esp. money), often surreptitiously or unlawfully.

trousers *pl n* a garment that covers the body from the waist to the ankles or knees with a separate tube-shaped section for each leg. ▷ **HISTORY** Scottish Gaelic *triubhas* trews

trousseau (**troo**-so) *n, pl* **-seaux** (-so) the clothes, linen, and other possessions collected by a bride for her marriage. ▷ **HISTORY** Old French

trout *n, pl* **trout** *or* **trouts** any of various game fishes related to the salmon and found chiefly in fresh water in northern regions. ▷ **HISTORY** Old English *trūht*

trowel *n* **1** a hand tool resembling a small spade with a curved blade, used by gardeners for lifting plants, etc. **2** a similar tool with a flat metal blade, used for spreading cement or plaster on a surface. ▷ **HISTORY** Latin *trulla* a scoop

troy weight *or* **troy** *n* a system of weights used for precious metals and gemstones in which one pound equals twelve ounces. ▷ **HISTORY** after the city of *Troyes,* France, where first used

truant *n* **1** a pupil who stays away from school without permission. **2 play truant** to stay away from school without permission. ✧ *adj* **3** being or relating to a truant: *a truant schoolkid.* ▷ **HISTORY** Old French: vagabond ▶ **truancy** *n*

truce *n* a temporary agreement to stop fighting or quarrelling. ▷ **HISTORY** plural of Old English *trēow* pledge

truck[1] *n* **1** *Brit* a railway wagon for carrying freight. **2** a large motor vehicle for transporting heavy loads. **3** any wheeled vehicle used to move goods. ✧ *vb* **4** *Chiefly US* to transport goods in a truck. ▷ **HISTORY** perhaps from *truckle* a small wheel

truck[2] *n* **1** *History* the payment of wages in goods rather than in money. **2 have no truck with** to refuse to be involved with: *the opposition will have no truck with the planned cut in pensions.* ▷ **HISTORY** Old French *troquer* (unattested) to barter

truckie *n Austral & NZ informal* a truck driver.

truckle bed *n Chiefly Brit* a low bed on wheels, stored under a larger bed.

truculent (**truck**-yew-lent) *adj* defiantly aggressive or bad-tempered. ▷ **HISTORY** Latin *trux* fierce ▶ **truculence** *n* ▶ **truculently** *adv*

trudge *vb* **trudging, trudged 1** to walk or plod heavily or wearily. ✧ *n* **2** a long tiring walk. ▷ **HISTORY** origin unknown

true *adj* **truer, truest 1** in accordance with the truth or facts; factual: *not all of the stories about her are true.* **2** real or genuine: *he didn't want to reveal his true feelings.* **3** faithful and loyal: *a true friend.* **4** accurate or precise: *he looked through the telescopic sight until he was convinced his aim was true.* **5** (of a compass bearing) according to the earth's geographical rather than magnetic poles: *true north.* **6 come true** to actually happen: *fortunately his gloomy prediction didn't come true.* **7 in** *or* **out of true** in *or* not in correct alignment. ✧ *adv* **8** truthfully or rightly: *I'd like to move to Edinburgh, true, but I'd need to get a job there first.* ▷ **HISTORY** Old English *trīewe*

true-blue *adj* **1** staunchly loyal. ✧ *n* **true blue 2** *Chiefly Brit & Austral* a staunch royalist or Conservative.

truelove *n* the person that one loves.

true north *n* the direction from any point along a meridian towards the North Pole.

truffle *n* **1** a round fungus which grows underground and is regarded as a delicacy. **2** Also called: **rum truffle** a sweet flavoured with chocolate or rum. ▷ **HISTORY** French *truffe*

trug *n Brit* a long shallow basket for carrying garden tools, flowers, etc. ▷ **HISTORY** perhaps variant of *trough*

truism *n* a statement that is clearly true and well known.

truly *adv* **1** in a true, just, or faithful manner. **2** really: *a truly awful poem.*

trump[1] *n* **1** same as **trump card**. ✧ *vb* **2** *Cards* to beat a card by playing a card which belongs to a suit which outranks it. **3** to outdo or surpass: *she trumped his news by announcing that she had been picked for the Olympic team.* ✧ See also **trumps**. ▷ **HISTORY** variant of *triumph*

trump[2] *n Archaic or literary* **1** a trumpet or the sound produced by one. **2 the last trump** the final trumpet call on the Day of Judgment. ▷ **HISTORY** Old French *trompe*

trump card *n* **1** any card from the suit that ranks higher than any other suit in one particular game. **2** an advantage, weapon, etc., that is kept in reserve until needed: *the President hoped to use his experience of foreign affairs as a trump card in the election.*

trumped up *adj* (of charges, excuses, etc.) made up in order to deceive.

trumpery *n, pl* **-eries 1** something useless or worthless. ✧ *adj* **2** useless or worthless. ▷ **HISTORY** Old French *tromperie* deceit

trumpet *n* **1** a valved brass musical instrument consisting of a narrow tube ending in a flare. **2** a loud sound such as that of a trumpet: *the elephant gave a loud trumpet.* **3 blow one's own trumpet** to boast about one's own skills or good qualities. ✧ *vb* **-peting, -peted 4** to proclaim or state forcefully: *almost every one of the party's loudly trumpeted election claims is untrue.* **5** (of an elephant) to make a loud cry. ▷ **HISTORY** Old French *trompette* ▶ **trumpeter** *n*

trumps *pl n* **1** *Cards* any one of the four suits that outranks all the other suits for the duration of a deal or game. **2 turn up trumps** (of a person) to bring about a happy or successful conclusion, esp. unexpectedly.

truncate *vb* **-cating, -cated** to shorten by cutting. ▷ **HISTORY** Latin *truncare* ▶ **truncated** *adj* ▶ **truncation** *n*

truncheon *n Chiefly Brit* a stick carried by a policeman as a weapon. ▷ **HISTORY** Old French *tronchon* stump

trundle *vb* **-dling, -dled** to move heavily on or as if on wheels: *a bus trundled along the drive.* ▷ **HISTORY** Old English *tryndel* circular or spherical object

trundle bed *n US, Canad & NZ* a low bed on wheels, stored under a larger bed.

trundler *n* **1** *NZ* a golf or shopping trolley. **2** a child's pushchair.

trunk *n* **1** the main stem of a tree. **2** a large strong case or box used to contain clothes when travelling and for storage. **3** a person's body excluding the head, neck, and limbs; torso. **4** the long nose of an elephant. **5** *US* the boot of a car. ✧ See also **trunks**. ▷ **HISTORY** Latin *truncus*

trunk call *n Chiefly Brit & Austral* a long-distance telephone call.

trunk line *n* **1** a direct link between two distant telephone exchanges or switchboards. **2** the main route or routes on a railway.

trunk road *n Brit* a main road, esp. one maintained by the central government.

trunks *pl n* shorts worn by a man for swimming.

trunk stream *n Geog* the main stream in a drainage basin.

truss *vb* **1** to tie or bind (someone) up. **2** to bind the wings and legs of (a fowl) before cooking. ✧ *n* **3** *Med* a device for holding a hernia in place. **4** a framework of wood or metal used to support a roof, bridge, etc. **5** a cluster of flowers or fruit growing at the end of a single stalk. ▷ **HISTORY** Old French *trousse*

trust *vb* **1** to believe that (someone) is honest and means no harm: *my father warned me never to trust strangers.* **2** to feel that (something) is safe and reliable: *I don't trust those new gadgets.* **3** to entrust (someone) with important information or valuables: *she's not somebody I would trust with this sort of secret.* **4** to believe that (someone) is likely to do something safely and reliably: *I wouldn't trust anyone else to look after my child properly.* **5** to believe (a story, account, etc.). **6** to expect, hope, or suppose: *I trust you've made your brother welcome here.* ✧ *n* **7** confidence in the truth, worth, reliability, etc., of a person or thing; faith: *he knew that his father had great trust in him.* **8** the obligation of someone in a responsible position: *he was in a position of trust as her substitute father.* **9 a** a legal arrangement whereby one person looks after property, money, etc., on another's behalf. **b** property that is the subject of such an arrangement. **10** (in Britain) a self-governing hospital, group of hospitals, or other body that operates as an independent commercial unit within the National Health Service. **11** *Chiefly US & Canad* a group of companies joined together to control the market for any commodity. ✧ *adj* **12** of or relating to a trust or trusts: *trust status.* ▷ **HISTORY** Old Norse *traust* help, support, confidence

trustee *n* **1** a person who administers property on someone else's behalf. **2** a member of a board that manages the affairs of an institution or organization.

trustful *or* **trusting** *adj* characterized by a readiness to trust others. ▶ **trustfully** *or* **trustingly** *adv*

trust fund *n* money, securities, etc., held in trust.

trustworthy *adj* (of a person) honest, reliable, or dependable.

trusty *adj* **trustier, trustiest 1** faithful or reliable: *his trusty steed.* ✧ *n, pl* **trusties 2** a trustworthy convict to whom special privileges are granted.

truth *n* **1** the quality of being true, genuine, or factual: *there is no truth in the allegations.* **2** something that is true: *he finally learned the truth about his parents' marriage.* **3** a proven or verified fact, principle, etc.: *some profound truths about biology have come to light.* ▷ **HISTORY** Old English *trīewth*

truthful *adj* **1** telling the truth; honest. **2** true; based on facts: *a truthful answer.* ▶ **truthfully** *adv* ▶ **truthfulness** *n*

try *vb* **tries, trying, tried 1** to make an effort or attempt: *you must try to understand.* **2** to sample or test (something) to see how enjoyable, good, or useful it is: *I tried smoking once but didn't like it.* **3** to put strain or stress on (someone's patience). **4** to give pain, affliction, or vexation to: *sometimes when I've been sorely tried, my temper gets a little out of hand.* **5 a** to investigate (a case) in a court of law. **b** to hear evidence in order to determine the guilt or innocence of (a person). ✧ *n, pl* **tries 6** an attempt or effort. **7** *Rugby* a score made by placing the ball down behind the opposing team's goal line. ▷ **HISTORY** Old French *trier* to sort

> **☑ WORD TIP**
> The use of *and* instead of *to* after *try* is very common, but should be avoided in formal writing: *we must try to prevent* (not *try and prevent*) *this happening.*

trying *adj* upsetting, difficult, or annoying.

tryst *n Archaic or literary* **1** an arrangement to meet, esp. secretly. **2** a meeting, esp. a secret one with a lover, or the place where such a meeting takes place. ▷ **HISTORY** Old French *triste* lookout post

tsar *or* **czar** (**zahr**) *n* (until 1917) the emperor of Russia. Also: **tzar** ▷ **HISTORY** Russian, ultimately from CAESAR ▶ **tsarist** *or* **czarist** *n*

tsarevitch *or* **czarevitch** (**zahr**-rev-itch) *n* the eldest son of a Russian tsar.

tsarina *or* **czarina** (zahr-**een**-a) *n* the wife of a Russian tsar.

tsetse fly *or* **tzetze fly** (**tset**-see) *n* a bloodsucking African fly whose bite transmits disease, esp. sleeping sickness. ▷ **HISTORY** Tswana (language of southern Africa) *tse tse*

T-shirt *or* **tee-shirt** *n* a short-sleeved casual shirt or top. ▷ **HISTORY** T-shape formed when laid flat

tsotsi (**tsot**-see) *n S African* a Black street thug or gang member. ▷ **HISTORY** perhaps from Nguni (language group of southern Africa) *tsotsa* to dress flashily

tsp. teaspoon.

T-square *n* a T-shaped ruler used for drawing horizontal lines and to support set squares when drawing vertical and inclined lines.

tsunami *n* a large, often destructive, sea wave, usually caused by an earthquake under the sea. ▷ **HISTORY** Japanese

TT 1 teetotal. **2** teetotaller. **3** tuberculin-tested.

tuatara (too-ah-**tah**-rah) *n* a large lizard-like New Zealand reptile. ▷ **HISTORY** Maori *tua* back + *tara* spine

tub *n* **1** a low, wide, usually round container. **2** a small plastic or cardboard container for ice cream etc. **3** *Chiefly US* same as **bath** (sense 1). **4** Also called: **tubful** the amount a tub will hold. **5** a slow and uncomfortable boat or ship. ▷ **HISTORY** Middle Dutch *tubbe*

tuba (**tube**-a) *n* a low-pitched brass musical instrument with valves. ▷ **HISTORY** Latin

tubby *adj* **-bier, -biest** (of a person) fat and short. ▶ **tubbiness** *n*

tube *n* **1** a long hollow cylindrical object, used for the passage of fluids or as a container. **2** a flexible cylinder of soft metal or plastic closed with a cap, used to hold substances such as toothpaste. **3** *Anat* any hollow cylindrical structure: *the Fallopian tubes.* **4 the tube** *Brit* the underground railway system in London. **5** *Electronics* See **cathode-ray tube**. **6** *Slang, chiefly US* a television set. ▷ **HISTORY** Latin *tubus* ▶ **tubeless** *adj*

tuber (**tube**-er) *n* a fleshy underground root of a plant such as a potato. ▷ **HISTORY** Latin: hump

tubercle (**tube**-er-kl) *n* **1** a small rounded swelling. **2** any abnormal hard swelling, esp. one characteristic of tuberculosis. ▷ **HISTORY** Latin *tuberculum* a little swelling

tubercular (tube-**berk**-yew-lar) *or* **tuberculous** *adj* **1** of or symptomatic of tuberculosis. **2** of or relating to a tubercle.

tuberculin (tube-**berk**-yew-lin) *n* a sterile liquid prepared from cultures of the tubercle bacillus and used in the diagnosis of tuberculosis.

tuberculin-tested *adj* (of milk) produced by cows that have been certified as free of tuberculosis.

tuberculosis (tube-berk-yew-**lohss**-iss) *n* an infectious disease characterized by the formation of tubercles, esp. in the lungs.

tuberous (**tube**-er-uss) *adj* (of plants) forming, bearing, or resembling a tuber or tubers.

tubing (**tube**-ing) *n* **1** a length of tube. **2** a system of tubes.

tubular (**tube**-yew-lar) *adj* **1** having the shape of a tube or tubes. **2** of or relating to a tube or tubing.

tubule (**tube**-yewl) *n* any small tubular structure, esp. in an animal or plant.

TUC (in Britain and S Africa) Trades Union Congress.

tuck *vb* **1** to push or fold into a small space or between two surfaces: *she tucked the letter into her handbag.* **2** to thrust the loose ends or sides of (something) into a confining space, so as to make it neat and secure: *he tucked his shirt back into his trousers.* **3** to make a tuck or tucks in (a garment). ✧ *n* **4** a pleat or fold in a part of a garment, usually stitched down. **5** *Brit informal* food, esp. cakes and sweets. ▷ **HISTORY** Old English *tūcian* to torment

tuck away *vb Informal* **1** to eat (a large amount of food). **2** to store (something) in a safe place: *we knew he had some money tucked away somewhere.* **3** to have a quiet, rarely disturbed or visited location: *the chapel is tucked away in a side street.*

tucker *n* **1** a detachable yoke of lace, linen, etc., formerly worn over the breast of a low-cut dress. **2** *Austral & NZ informal* food. **3 one's best bib and tucker** *Informal* one's best clothes.

Tudor *adj* **1** of or in the reign of the English royal house ruling from 1485 to 1603. **2** denoting a style of architecture characterized by half-timbered houses: *a Tudor cottage.*

Tues. Tuesday.

Tuesday *n* the third day of the week. ▷ **HISTORY** Old English *tīwesdæg* day of Tyr, Norse god

tufa (**tew**-fa) *n* a porous rock formed of calcium carbonate deposited from springs. ▷ **HISTORY** Italian *tufo*

tuff *n Geol* a porous rock formed from volcanic dust or ash. ▷ **HISTORY** Old French *tuf*

tuffet *n* a small mound or low seat. ▷ **HISTORY** from *tuft*

tuft *n* a bunch of feathers, grass, hair, threads, etc., held together at the base. ▷ **HISTORY** probably from Old French *tufe* ▶ **tufted** *adj* ▶ **tufty** *adj*

tug *vb* **tugging, tugged 1** to pull or drag with a sharp or powerful movement: *she tugged at my arm.* **2** to tow (a ship or boat) by means of a tug. ✧ *n* **3** a strong pull or jerk. **4** Also called: **tugboat** a boat with a powerful engine, used for towing barges, ships, etc. ▷ **HISTORY** Middle English *tuggen*

tuition *n* **1** instruction, esp. that received individually or in a small group. **2** the payment for instruction, esp. in colleges or universities. ▷ **HISTORY** Latin *tueri* to watch over

tulip *n* **1** a plant which produces bright cup-shaped flowers in spring. **2** the flower or bulb.

> **WORD HISTORY**
> 'Tulip' comes from Turkish *tulbend*, meaning 'turban', because of the shape of the flowers.

tulip tree *n* a North American tree with tulip-shaped greenish-yellow flowers and long conelike fruits.

tulle (**tewl**) *n* a fine net fabric of silk, rayon, etc., used to make evening dresses. ▷ **HISTORY** French

tumble *vb* **-bling, -bled 1** to fall or cause to fall, esp. awkwardly or violently: *chairs tumbled over.* **2** to roll or twist, esp. in playing: *they rolled and tumbled as wild beasts.* **3** to decrease in value suddenly: *interest rates tumbled.* **4** to move in a quick and uncontrolled manner: *the crowd tumbled down the stairs.* **5** to disturb, rumple, or toss around: *she was all tumbled by the fall.* **6** to perform leaps or somersaults. ✧ *n* **7** a fall, esp. an awkward or violent one: *he took a tumble down the stairs.* **8** a somersault. ▷ **HISTORY** Old English *tumbian* dance, jump ▶ **tumbled** *adj*

tumbledown *adj* (of a building) falling to pieces; dilapidated.

tumbler *n* **1 a** a flat-bottomed drinking glass with no handle or stem. **b** the amount a tumbler will hold. **2** a person who performs somersaults and other acrobatic feats. **3** a part of the mechanism of a lock.

tumble to *vb* to understand or become aware of: *how did he tumble to this?*

tumbril *n* a farm cart that tilts backwards to empty its load, which was used to take condemned prisoners to the guillotine during the French Revolution. ▷ **HISTORY** Old French *tumberel*

tumescent (tew-**mess**-ent) *adj* swollen or becoming swollen.

tumid (**tew**-mid) *adj Rare* **1** (of an organ or part of the body) enlarged or swollen. **2** pompous or fulsome in style: *a tumid tome.* ▷ HISTORY Latin *tumere* to swell ▸ **tumidity** *n*

tummy *n, pl* **-mies** an informal or childish word for **stomach**.

tumour *or US* **tumor** (**tew**-mer) *n Pathol* **a** any abnormal swelling. **b** a mass of tissue formed by a new growth of cells. ▷ HISTORY Latin *tumere* to swell ▸ **tumorous** *adj*

tumult (**tew**-mult) *n* **1** a loud confused noise, such as one produced by a crowd. **2** a state of confusion and excitement: *a tumult of emotions.* ▷ HISTORY Latin *tumultus*

tumultuous (tew-**mull**-tew-uss) *adj* **1** exciting, confused, or turbulent: *this week's tumultuous events.* **2** unruly, noisy, or excited: *a tumultuous welcome.*

tumulus (**tew**-myew-luss) *n, pl* **-li** (-lie) *Archaeol no longer in technical usage* a burial mound. ▷ HISTORY Latin: a hillock

tun *n* a large beer cask. ▷ HISTORY Old English *tunne*

tuna (**tune**-a) *n, pl* **-na** *or* **-nas** **1** a large marine spiny-finned fish. **2** the flesh of this fish, often tinned for food. ▷ HISTORY American Spanish

tundra *n* a vast treeless Arctic region with permanently frozen subsoil. ▷ HISTORY Russian

tune *n* **1** a melody, esp. one for which harmony is not essential. **2** the correct musical pitch: *many of the notes are out of tune.* **3 call the tune** to be in control of the proceedings. **4 change one's tune** to alter one's attitude or tone of speech. **5 in** *or* **out of tune with** in *or* not in agreement or sympathy with: *in tune with public opinion.* **6 to the tune of** *Informal* to the amount or extent of. ✧ *vb* **tuning, tuned 7** to adjust (a musical instrument) so each string, key, etc., produces the right note. **8** to make small adjustments to (an engine, machine, etc.) to obtain the proper or desired performance. **9** to adjust (a radio or television) to receive a particular station or programme: *the radio was tuned to the local station.* ▷ HISTORY variant of *tone* ▸ **tuner** *n*

tuneful *adj* having a pleasant tune. ▸ **tunefully** *adv*

tune in *vb* **1** to adjust (a radio or television) to receive (a station or programme). **2 tuned in to** *Slang* aware of or knowledgeable about: *tuned in to European cinema.*

tuneless *adj* having no melody or tune.

tune up *vb* **1** to adjust (a musical instrument) to a particular pitch. **2** to adjust the engine of a car, etc., to improve its performance.

tungsten *n Chem* a hard greyish-white metallic element. Symbol: W. ▷ HISTORY Swedish *tung* heavy + *sten* stone

tunic *n* **1** a close-fitting jacket forming part of some uniforms. **2** a loose-fitting knee-length garment. ▷ HISTORY Latin *tunica*

tuning fork *n* a two-pronged metal fork that when struck produces a pure note of constant specified pitch.

tunnel *n* **1** an underground passageway, esp. one for trains or cars. **2** any passage or channel through or under something: *the carpal tunnel.* ✧ *vb* **-nelling, -nelled** *or US* **-neling, -neled 3** to make one's way through or under (something) by digging a tunnel: *ten men succeeded in tunnelling out of the prisoner-of-war camp.* **4** to dig a tunnel (through or under something): *the idea of tunnelling under the English Channel has been around for a long time.* ▷ HISTORY Old French *tonel* cask

tunnel vision *n* **1** a condition in which a person is unable to see things that are not straight in front. **2** narrowness of viewpoint resulting from concentration on only one aspect of a subject or situation.

tunny *n, pl* **-nies** *or* **-ny** same as **tuna**. ▷ HISTORY Latin *thunnus*

tup *n Chiefly Brit* a male sheep. ▷ HISTORY origin unknown

tupik (**too**-pick) *n* a tent of seal or caribou skin used for shelter by the Inuit in summer. ▷ HISTORY Inuit *tupiq*

tuque *n Canad* **1** a knitted cap with a long tapering end. **2** a close-fitting knitted hat often with a tassel or pompom.

turban *n* **1** a head-covering worn by a Muslim, Hindu, or Sikh man, consisting of a long piece of cloth wound round the head. **2** any head-covering resembling this. ▷ HISTORY Turkish *tülbend* ▸ **turbaned** *adj*

turbid *adj Literary* (of water or air) full of mud or dirt, and frequently swirling around: *the turbid stream of the Loire.* ▷ HISTORY Latin *turbare* to agitate ▸ **turbidity** *n*

turbine *n* a machine in which power is produced by a stream of water, air, etc., that pushes the blades of a wheel and causes it to rotate. ▷ HISTORY Latin *turbo* whirlwind

turbocharger *n* a device that increases the power of an internal-combustion engine by using the exhaust gases to drive a turbine. ▸ **turbocharged** *adj*

turbofan *n* a type of engine in which a large fan driven by a turbine forces air rearwards to increase the propulsive thrust.

turbojet *n* **1** a gas turbine in which the exhaust gases provide the propulsive thrust to drive an aircraft. **2** an aircraft powered by turbojet engines.

turboprop *n* an aircraft propulsion unit where the propeller is driven by a gas turbine.

turbot *n, pl* **-bot** *or* **-bots** a European flatfish, highly valued as a food fish. ▷ HISTORY Old French *tourbot*

turbulence *n* **1** a state or condition of confusion, movement, or agitation. **2** *Meteorol* instability in the atmosphere causing gusty air currents.

turbulent *adj* **1** involving a lot of sudden changes and conflicting elements: *the city has had a turbulent history.* **2** (of people) wild and unruly: *a harsh mountain land inhabited by a score of* *turbulent tribes.* **3** (of water or air) full of violent unpredictable currents: *the turbulent ocean.* ▷ HISTORY Latin *turba* confusion

tureen *n* a large deep dish with a lid, used for serving soups. ▷ HISTORY French *terrine* earthenware vessel

turf *n, pl* **turfs** *or* **turves 1** a layer of thick even grass with roots and soil attached: *a short turf rich in wild flowers.* **2** a piece cut from this layer: *we spent the afternoon digging turves.* **3** *Informal* **a** the area where a person lives and feels at home: *my boyhood turf of east Cork.* **b** a person's area of knowledge or influence: *when Kate is at work, she's on her own turf.* **4 the turf a** a track where horse races are run. **b** horse racing as a sport or industry. **5** same as **peat.** ✧ *vb* **6** to cover (an area of ground) with pieces of turf. ▷ HISTORY Old English

turf accountant *n Brit* same as **bookmaker.**

turf out *vb Informal* to throw (someone or something) out: *the residents fear a new landlord might push up rents and turf them out of their homes.*

turgid (**tur**-jid) *adj* **1** (of language) pompous, boring, and hard to understand. **2** (of water or mud) unpleasantly thick and brown. ▷ HISTORY Latin *turgere* to swell ▶ **turgidity** *n*

turgor *n Biol* the normal rigid state of a cell, caused by pressure of the cell contents against the cell wall or membrane.

Turk *n* a person from Turkey.

turkey *n, pl* **-keys** *or* **-key 1** a large bird of North America bred for its meat. **2** *Informal, chiefly US & Canad* something, esp. a theatrical production, that fails. **3 cold turkey** *Slang* a method of curing drug addiction by abrupt withdrawal of all doses. **4 talk turkey** *Informal, chiefly US & Canad* to discuss, esp. business, frankly and practically. ▷ HISTORY used at first of the African guinea fowl (because it was brought through Turkish territory), later applied by mistake to the American bird

Turkic *n* a family of Asian languages including Turkish and Azerbaijani.

Turkish *adj* **1** of Turkey. ✧ *n* **2** the language of Turkey.

Turkish bath *n* **1** a type of bath in which the bather sweats freely in hot dry air, is then washed, often massaged, and has a cold plunge or shower. **2 Turkish baths** an establishment for such baths.

Turkish delight *n* a jelly-like sweet flavoured with flower essences, usually cut into cubes and covered in icing sugar.

turmeric *n* **1** a tropical Asian plant with yellow flowers and an aromatic underground stem. **2** a yellow spice obtained from the root of this plant. ▷ HISTORY Old French *terre merite* meritorious earth

turmoil *n* disorder, agitation, or confusion: *a period of political turmoil and uncertainty.* ▷ HISTORY origin unknown

turn *vb* **1** to move to face in another direction. **2** to rotate or move round. **3** to operate (a switch, key, etc.) by twisting it. **4** to aim or point (something) in a particular direction: *they turned their guns on the crowd.* **5** to change in course or direction: *the van turned right into Victoria Road.* **6** (of a road, river, etc.) to have a bend or curve in it. **7** to perform or do (something) with a rotating movement: *a small boy was turning somersaults.* **8** to change so as to become: *he turned pale.* **9** to reach, pass, or progress beyond in age, time, etc.: *she had just turned fourteen.* **10** to find (a particular page) in a book: *turn to page 78.* **11** to look at the other side of: *turning the pages of a book.* **12** to shape (wood, metal, etc.) on a lathe. **13** (of leaves) to change colour in autumn. **14** to make or become sour: *the milk is starting to turn.* **15** to affect or be affected with nausea or giddiness: *that would turn the strongest stomach.* **16** (of the tide) to start coming in or going out. **17 turn against** to stop liking (something or someone one previously liked): *people turned against her because she became so dictatorial.* **18 turn into** to become or change into: *my mother turned our house into four apartments.* **19 turn loose** to set (an animal or a person) free. **20 turn someone's head** to affect someone mentally or emotionally. **21 turn to a** to direct or apply (one's attention or thoughts) to. **b** to stop doing or using one thing and start doing or using (another): *I turned to photography from writing.* **c** to appeal or apply to (someone) for help, advice, etc. ✧ *n* **22** the act of turning. **23** a movement of complete or partial rotation: *a turn of the dial.* **24** a change of direction or position. **25** same as **turning** (sense 1). **26** the right or opportunity to do something in an agreed order or succession: *it was her turn to play next.* **27** a change in something that is happening or being done: *events took an unhappy turn.* **28** a period of action, work, etc. **29** a short walk, ride, or excursion. **30** natural inclination: *a liberal turn of mind.* **31** distinctive form or style: *she'd a nice turn of phrase.* **32** a deed that helps or hinders someone: *I'm trying to do you a good turn.* **33** a twist, bend, or distortion in shape. **34** a slight attack of an illness: *she's just having one of her turns.* **35** *Music* a melodic ornament that alternates the main note with the notes above and below it, beginning with the note above, in a variety of sequences. **36** a short theatrical act: *tonight's star turn.* **37** *Informal* a shock or surprise: *you gave me rather a turn.* **38 done to a turn** *Informal* cooked perfectly. **39 turn and turn about** one after another; alternately. ✧ See also **turn down, turn in**, etc. ▷ HISTORY Old English *tyrnan* ▶ **turner** *n*

turnaround *or* **turnabout** *n* a complete change or reversal: *a prompt economic turnaround.*

turncoat *n* a person who deserts one cause or party to join an opposing one.

turn down *vb* **1** to reduce (the volume, brightness, or temperature of something): *turn the heat down.* **2** to reject or refuse: *the invitation was turned down.* **3** to fold down (sheets, etc.).

turn in *vb Informal* **1** to go to bed for the night. **2** to hand in: *turning in my essay.* **3** to hand (a suspect or criminal) over to the police: *his own brother turned him in.*

turning *n* **1** a road, river, or path that turns off the main way. **2** the point where such a way turns off. **3** the process of turning objects on a lathe.

turning circle *n* the smallest circle in which a vehicle can turn.

A B C D E F G H I J K L M N O P Q R S T U V W X Y Z

turning effect *n Physics* a tendency to produce motion, esp. rotation about a point or axis. Also called **moment**.

turning point *n* a moment when a decisive change occurs.

turnip *n* a vegetable with a large yellow or white edible root. ▷ **HISTORY** Latin *napus*

turnkey *n Old-fashioned* a jailer.

turn off *vb* **1** to leave (a road or path): *turning off the main road.* **2** (of a road or path) to lead away from (another road or path): *a main street with alleys twisting and turning off it.* **3** to cause (something) to stop operating by turning a knob, pushing a button, etc. **4** *Informal* to cause disgust or disinterest in (someone): *keeping kids from getting turned off by mathematics.* ✧ *n* **turn-off 5** a road or other way branching off from the main thoroughfare. **6** *Informal* a person or thing that causes dislike.

turn on *vb* **1** to cause (something) to operate by turning a knob, pushing a button, etc.: *turn on the radio, please.* **2** to attack (someone), esp. without warning: *the Labrador turned on me.* **3** *Informal* to produce suddenly or automatically: *turning on that bland smile.* **4** *Slang* to arouse emotionally or sexually. **5** to depend or hinge on: *the match turned on three double faults by Sampras.* ✧ *n* **turn-on 6** *Slang* a person or thing that causes emotional or sexual arousal.

turn out *vb* **1** to cause (something, esp. a light) to stop operating by moving a switch. **2** to produce or create: *turning out two hits a year.* **3** to force (someone) out of a place or position: *turned out of office.* **4** to empty the contents of (something): *the police ordered him to turn out his pockets.* **5** to be discovered or found (to be or do something): *he turned out to be a Finn.* **6** to end up or result: *how interesting to see how it all turned out!* **7** to dress and groom: *she is always very well turned out.* **8** to assemble or gather: *crowds turned out to see him.* **9 turn out for** *Informal* to make an appearance, esp. in a sporting competition: *he was asked to turn out for Liverpool.* ✧ *n* **turnout 10** a number of people attending an event: *there has been a high turnout of voters in elections in Bulgaria.* **11** the quantity or amount produced.

turn over *vb* **1** to change position, esp. so as to reverse top and bottom. **2** to shift position, for instance by rolling onto one's side: *he turned over and went straight to sleep.* **3** to consider carefully: *as I walked, I turned her story over.* **4** to give (something) to someone who has a right to it or to the authorities: *the police ordered him to turn over the files to them.* **5** (of an engine) to start or function correctly: *when he pressed the starter button, the engine turned over at once.* **6** *Slang* to rob: *the house had been turned over while they were out.* ✧ *n* **turnover 7 a** the amount of business done by a company during a specified period. **b** the rate at which stock in trade is sold and replenished. **8** a small pastry case filled with fruit or jam: *an apple turnover.* **9** the number of workers employed by a firm in a given period to replace those who have left.

turnpike *n* **1** *History* a barrier across a road to prevent vehicles or pedestrians passing until a charge (toll) had been paid. **2** *US* a motorway for use of which a toll is charged. ▷ **HISTORY** *turn* + *pike* a spike

turnstile *n* a mechanical barrier with arms that are turned to admit one person at a time.

turntable *n* **1** the circular platform in a record player that rotates the record while it is being played. **2** a circular platform used for turning locomotives and cars.

turn up *vb* **1** to arrive or appear: *few people turned up.* **2** to find or discover or be found or discovered: *a medical checkup has only turned up a sinus infection.* **3** to increase the flow, volume, etc., of: *he turned up the radio.* ✧ *n* **turn-up 4** *Brit* the turned-up fold at the bottom of some trouser legs. **5 a turn-up for the books** *Informal* an unexpected happening.

turpentine *n* **1** a strong-smelling colourless oil distilled from the resin of some coniferous trees, and used for thinning paint, for cleaning, and in medicine. **2** a semisolid mixture of resin and oil obtained from various conifers, which is the main source of commercial turpentine. **3** *Not in technical usage* any one of a number of thinners for paints and varnishes, consisting of fractions of petroleum. ▷ **HISTORY** Latin *terebinthina*

turpitude *n Formal* depravity or wickedness: *newspapers owned by proprietors whose moral turpitude far exceeded anything chronicled in their pages.* ▷ **HISTORY** Latin *turpitudo* ugliness

turps *n* short for **turpentine** (senses 1, 3).

turquoise *adj* **1** greenish-blue. ✧ *n* **2** a greenish-blue precious stone. ▷ **HISTORY** Old French *turqueise* Turkish (stone)

turret *n* **1** a small tower that projects from the wall of a building, esp. a castle. **2** (on a tank or warship) a rotating structure on which guns are mounted. **3** (on a machine tool) a turret-like steel structure with tools projecting from it that can be rotated to bring each tool to bear on the work. ▷ **HISTORY** Latin *turris* tower ▶ **turreted** *adj*

turtle *n* **1** an aquatic reptile with a flattened shell enclosing the body and flipper-like limbs adapted for swimming. **2 turn turtle** (of a boat) to capsize. ▷ **HISTORY** French *tortue* tortoise

turtledove *n* an Old World dove noted for its soft cooing and devotion to its mate. ▷ **HISTORY** Old English *turtla*

turtleneck *n* a round high close-fitting neck on a sweater or a sweater with such a neck.

Tuscan *adj* of a style of classical architecture characterized by unfluted columns. ▷ **HISTORY** from *Tuscany*, a region in central Italy

tusk *n* a long pointed tooth in the elephant, walrus, and certain other mammals. ▷ **HISTORY** Old English *tūsc* ▶ **tusked** *adj*

tussle *n* **1** an energetic fight, struggle, or argument: *she resigned following a protracted boardroom tussle.* ✧ *vb* **-sling, -sled 2** to fight or struggle energetically. ▷ **HISTORY** Middle English *tusen* to pull

tussock *n* a dense tuft of grass or other vegetation. ▷ **HISTORY** origin unknown ▶ **tussocky** *adj*

tutelage (**tew**-till-lij) *n Formal* **1** instruction or guidance, esp. by a tutor. **2** the state of being supervised by a guardian or tutor. ▷ **HISTORY** Latin *tueri* to watch over

tutelary (**tew**-till-lar-ee) *adj Literary* **1** having the role of guardian or protector. **2** of a guardian.

tutor *n* **1** a teacher, usually one instructing individual pupils. **2** (at a college or university) a member of staff responsible for the teaching and supervision of a certain number of students. ✧ *vb* **3** to act as a tutor to (someone). ▷ **HISTORY** Latin: a watcher ▶ **tutorship** *n*

tutorial *n* **1** a period of intensive tuition given by a tutor to an individual student or to a small group of students. ✧ *adj* **2** of or relating to a tutor.

tutti *adj, adv Music* to be performed by the whole orchestra, choir, etc. ▷ **HISTORY** Italian

tutti-frutti *n, pl* **-fruttis** an ice cream or other sweet food containing small pieces of candied or fresh fruits. ▷ **HISTORY** Italian, literally: all the fruits

tutu *n* a very short skirt worn by ballerinas, made of projecting layers of stiffened material. ▷ **HISTORY** French

tuxedo *n, pl* **-dos** *US, Canad & Austral* a dinner jacket. ▷ **HISTORY** after a country club in *Tuxedo Park,* New York

TV television.

TVEI *Brit* technical and vocational educational initiative: a national educational scheme in which pupils gain practical experience in technology and industry, often through work placement.

twaddle *n* **1** silly, trivial, or pretentious talk or writing. ✧ *vb* **-dling, -dled 2** to talk or write in a silly or pretentious way. ▷ **HISTORY** earlier *twattle*

twain *adj, n Archaic* two. ▷ **HISTORY** Old English *twēgen*

twang *n* **1** a sharp ringing sound produced by or as if by the plucking of a taut string. **2** a strongly nasal quality in a person's speech: *a high-pitched Texas twang.* ✧ *vb* **3** to make or cause to make a twang: *a bunch of angels twanging harps.* ▷ **HISTORY** imitative ▶ **twangy** *adj*

twat *n Brit, Austral & NZ taboo slang* **1** the female genitals. **2** a foolish person. ▷ **HISTORY** origin unknown

tweak *vb* **1** to twist or pinch with a sharp or sudden movement: *she tweaked his ear.* **2** *Informal* to make a minor alteration. ✧ *n* **3** the act of tweaking. **4** *Informal* a minor alteration. ▷ **HISTORY** Old English *twiccian*

twee *adj Informal* excessively sentimental, sweet, or pretty. ▷ **HISTORY** from *tweet,* affected pronunciation of *sweet*

tweed *n* **1** a thick woollen cloth produced originally in Scotland. **2 tweeds** a suit made of tweed. ▷ **HISTORY** probably from *tweel,* Scots variant of *twill*

tweedy *adj* **tweedier, tweediest 1** of, made of, or resembling tweed. **2** showing a fondness for a hearty outdoor life, often associated with wearers of tweeds.

tweet *interj* **1** an imitation of the thin chirping sound made by small birds. ✧ *vb* **2** to make this sound. ▷ **HISTORY** imitative

tweeter *n* a loudspeaker used in high-fidelity systems for the reproduction of high audio frequencies.

tweezers *pl n* a small pincer-like tool used for tasks such as handling small objects or plucking out hairs. ▷ **HISTORY** obsolete *tweeze* case of instruments

twelfth *adj* **1** of or being number twelve in a series. ✧ *n* **2** number twelve in a series. **3** one of twelve equal parts of something.

Twelfth Day *n* Jan 6, the twelfth day after Christmas and the feast of the Epiphany.

Twelfth Night *n* **a** the evening of Jan 5, the eve of Twelfth Day. **b** the evening of Twelfth Day itself.

twelve *n* **1** the cardinal number that is the sum of ten and two. **2** a numeral, 12 or XII, representing this number. **3** something representing or consisting of twelve units. ✧ *adj* **4** amounting to twelve: *twelve months.* ▷ **HISTORY** Old English *twelf*

twenty *n, pl* **-ties 1** the cardinal number that is the product of ten and two. **2** a numeral, 20 or XX, representing this number. **3** something representing or consisting of twenty units. ✧ *adj* **4** amounting to twenty: *twenty minutes.* ▶ **twentieth** *adj, n*

twenty-four-seven *or* **24/7** *adv US & Brit informal* constantly or all the time: *consultants would no longer be available 24/7.* ▷ **HISTORY** from twenty-four hours a day, seven days a week

twerp *or* **twirp** *n Informal* a silly, stupid, or contemptible person. ▷ **HISTORY** origin unknown

twice *adv* **1** two times; on two occasions or in two cases: *I've met her only twice.* **2** double in degree or quantity: *twice as big.* ▷ **HISTORY** Old English *twiwa*

twiddle *vb* **-dling, -dled 1** to twirl or fiddle, often in an idle way: *twiddling the knobs of a radio.* **2 twiddle one's thumbs a** to rotate one's thumbs around one another, when bored or impatient. **b** to be bored, with nothing to do. ✧ *n* **3** an unnecessary decoration, esp. a curly one. ▷ **HISTORY** probably *twirl* + *fiddle*

twig[1] *n* a small branch or shoot of a tree. ▷ **HISTORY** Old English *twigge* ▶ **twiggy** *adj*

twig[2] *vb* **twigging, twigged** *Informal* to realize or understand: *I should have twigged it earlier.* ▷ **HISTORY** origin unknown

twilight *n* **1** the soft dim light that occurs when the sun is just below the horizon after sunset. **2** the period in which this light occurs: *soon after twilight we started marching again.* **3** a period in which strength, importance, etc., is gradually declining: *the twilight of his political career.* ✧ *adj* **4** of or relating to the period towards the end of the day: *the twilight shift.* **5** of or being a period of decline: *he spent most of his twilight years working on a history of France.* **6** denoting irregularity and obscurity: *a twilight existence.* ▷ **HISTORY** Old English *twi-* half + LIGHT ▶ **twilit** *adj*

twilight zone *n* any indefinite or intermediate condition or area: *the twilight zone between sleep and wakefulness.*

twill *n* a fabric woven to produce an effect of parallel diagonal lines or ribs in the cloth. ▷ HISTORY Old English *twilic* having a double thread

twin *n* **1** one of a pair of people or animals conceived at the same time. **2** one of a pair of people or things that are identical or very similar. ✧ *vb* **twinning, twinned 3** to pair or be paired together. ▷ HISTORY Old English *twinn*

twine *n* **1** string or cord made by twisting fibres together. ✧ *vb* **twining, twined 2** to twist or wind together: *she twined the flowers into a garland.* **3 twine round** *or* **around** to twist or wind around: *she twined her arms around her neck.* ▷ HISTORY Old English *twīn*

twinge *n* **1** a sudden brief darting or stabbing pain. **2** a sharp emotional pang: *a twinge of conscience.* ▷ HISTORY Old English *twengan* to pinch

twinkle *vb* **-kling, -kled 1** to shine brightly and intermittently; sparkle. **2** (of the eyes) to sparkle, esp. with amusement or delight. ✧ *n* **3** a flickering brightness; sparkle. ▷ HISTORY Old English *twinclian*

twin town *n* a town that has cultural and social links with a foreign town: *Nuremberg is one of Glasgow's twin towns.*

twirl *vb* **1** to move around rapidly and repeatedly in a circle. **2** to twist, wind, or twiddle, often idly: *twirling the glass in her hand.* ✧ *n* **3** a whirl or twist. **4** a written flourish. ▷ HISTORY origin unknown

twist *vb* **1** to turn one end or part while the other end or parts remain still or turn in the opposite direction: *never twist or wring woollen garments.* **2** to distort or be distorted. **3** to wind or twine: *the wire had been twisted twice.* **4** to force or be forced out of the natural form or position: *I twisted my knee.* **5** to change the meaning of; distort: *he'd twisted the truth to make himself look good.* **6** to revolve or rotate: *he twisted the switch to turn the radio off.* **7** to wrench with a turning action: *he twisted the wheel sharply.* **8** to follow a winding course: *the road twisted as it climbed.* **9** to dance the twist. **10 twist someone's arm** to persuade or coerce someone. ✧ *n* **11** the act of twisting: *she gave a dainty little twist to her parasol.* **12** something formed by or as if by twisting: *there's a twist in the cable.* **13** a decisive change of direction, aim, meaning, or character: *the latest revelations give a new twist to the company's boardroom wranglings.* **14** an unexpected development in a story, play, or film. **15** a bend: *a twist of the mountain road.* **16** a distortion of the original shape or form. **17** a jerky pull, wrench, or turn. **18 the twist** a dance popular in the 1960s, in which dancers vigorously twist the hips. **19 round the twist** *Slang* mad or eccentric. ▷ HISTORY Old English ▶ **twisty** *adj*

twisted *adj* (of a person) cruel or perverted.

twister *n Brit* a swindling or dishonest person.

twit[1] *vb* **twitting, twitted** *Brit* to poke fun at (someone). ▷ HISTORY Old English *ætwītan*

twit[2] *n Informal* a foolish or stupid person. ▷ HISTORY from TWIT[1]

twitch *vb* **1** (of a person or part of a person's body) to move in a jerky spasmodic way: *his left eyelid twitched involuntarily.* **2** to pull (something) with a quick jerky movement: *she twitched the curtains shut.* ✧ *n* **3** a sharp jerking movement, esp. one caused by a nervous condition. ▷ HISTORY Old English *twiccian* to pluck

twitter *vb* **1** (esp. of a bird) to utter a succession of chirping sounds. **2** to talk rapidly and nervously in a high-pitched voice: *novelists who twittered about how much they admired him.* ✧ *n* **3** the act or sound of twittering. **4 in a twitter** in a state of nervous excitement. ▷ HISTORY imitative ▶ **twittering** *n* ▶ **twittery** *adj*

two *n* **1** the cardinal number that is the sum of one and one. **2** a numeral, 2 or II, representing this number. **3** something representing or consisting of two units. **4 in two** in or into two parts: *cut the cake in two and take a bit each.* **5 put two and two together** to reach an obvious conclusion by considering the evidence available. **6 that makes two of us** the same applies to me. ✧ *adj* **7** amounting to two: *two years.* ▷ HISTORY Old English *twā*

twoccing *or* **twocking** *n Brit slang* the act of breaking into a motor vehicle and driving it away. ▷ HISTORY from *T(aking) W(ithout) O(wner's) C(onsent),* the legal offence ▶ **twoccer** *or* **twocker** *n*

two-dimensional *adj* **1** having two dimensions. **2** somewhat lacking in depth or complexity: *a modern audience is unable to tolerate two-dimensional characters.*

two-edged *adj* **1** (of a remark) having both a favourable and an unfavourable interpretation, such as *she looks nice when she smiles.* **2** (of a knife, saw, etc.) having two cutting edges.

two-faced *adj* deceitful or hypocritical: *he's a two-faced liar and opportunist.*

twofold *adj* **1** having twice as many or as much. **2** composed of two parts. ✧ *adv* **3** by twice as many or as much.

twopence *or* **tuppence** (**tup**-pence) *n Brit* **1** the sum of two pennies. **2** the slightest amount: *I don't care twopence who your father is.*

two-ply *adj* made of two thicknesses, layers, or strands.

two-stroke *adj* of an internal-combustion engine whose piston makes two strokes for every explosion.

two-time *vb* **-timing, -timed** *Informal* to deceive (a lover) by having an affair with someone else. ▶ **two-timer** *n*

two-way *adj* **1** moving in, or allowing movement in, two opposite directions: *two-way traffic.* **2** involving mutual involvement or cooperation: *two-way communication.* **3** (of a radio or transmitter) capable of both transmission and reception of messages.

TX Texas.

tycoon *n* a businessman of great wealth and power.

> **WORD HISTORY**
> 'Tycoon' comes from Japanese *taikun*, meaning 'great lord'. It was a term of respect given to the Japanese shoguns, the hereditary military commanders who were for centuries the real rulers of Japan although nominally subordinate to the emperors.

tyke *or* **tike** *n* **1** *Brit, Austral & NZ informal* a small or cheeky child. **2** *Brit dialect* a rough ill-mannered person. ▷ **HISTORY** Old Norse *tīk* bitch

tympanic membrane *n Anat* the thin membrane separating the external ear from the middle ear; eardrum.

tympanum *n, pl* **-nums** *or* **-na 1** *Anat* **a** the cavity of the middle ear. **b** same as **tympanic membrane**. **2** *Archit* the recessed space between the arch and the lintel above a door. ▷ **HISTORY** Greek *tumpanon* drum ▶ **tympanic** *adj*

Tynwald (**tin**-wold) *n* the Parliament of the Isle of Man. ▷ **HISTORY** Old Norse *thing* assembly + *vollr* field

type *n* **1** a kind, class, or category of things, all of which have something in common. **2** a subdivision of a particular class; sort: *it is more alcoholic than most wines of this type.* **3** the general characteristics distinguishing a particular group: *the old-fashioned type of nanny.* **4** *Informal* a person, esp. of a specified kind: *a seagoing type.* **5** a block with a raised character on it used for printing. **6** text printed from type; print. ✧ *vb* **typing, typed 7** to write using a typewriter or word processor. **8** to be a symbol of or typify. **9** to decide the type of; classify. ▷ **HISTORY** Greek *tupos* image

typecast *vb* **-casting, -cast** to cast (an actor or actress) in the same kind of role continually.

typeface *n* the size and style of printing used in a book, magazine, etc.

typescript *n* any typewritten document.

typeset *vb* **-setting, -set** *Printing* to set (text for printing) in type.

typewriter *n* a machine which prints a letter or other character when the appropriate key is pressed.

typhoid *Pathol* ✧ *n* **1** short for **typhoid fever**. ✧ *adj* **2** of or relating to typhoid fever: *typhoid vaccines.*

typhoid fever *n* an acute infectious disease characterized by high fever, spots, abdominal pain, etc. It is spread by contaminated food or water.

typhoon *n* a violent tropical storm, esp. one in the China Seas or W Pacific. ▷ **HISTORY** Chinese *tai fung* great wind

typhus *n* an acute infectious disease transmitted by lice or mites and characterized by high fever, skin rash, and severe headache. ▷ **HISTORY** Greek *tuphos* fever

typical *adj* **1** being or serving as a representative example of a particular type; characteristic: *a typical working day.* **2** considered to be an example of some undesirable trait: *it was typical that he should start talking almost before he was inside the room.* ▷ **HISTORY** Greek *tupos* image ▶ **typically** *adv*

typify *vb* **-fies, -fying, -fied 1** to be typical of or characterize: *the beers made here typify all that is best about the independent brewing sector.* **2** to symbolize or represent: *a number of dissident intellectuals, typified by Andrei Sakharov.*

typing *n* **1** the work or activity of using a typewriter or word processor. **2** the skill of using a typewriter quickly and accurately.

typist *n* a person who types letters, reports, etc., esp. for a living.

typography *n* **1** the art or craft of printing. **2** the style or quality of printing and layout in a book, magazine, etc. ▶ **typographical** *adj* ▶ **typographically** *adv*

tyrannical *adj* of or like a tyrant; unjust and oppressive.

tyrannize *or* **-ise** *vb* **-nizing, -nized** *or* **-nising, -nised** to rule or exercise power (over) in a cruel or oppressive manner: *he dominated and tyrannized his younger brother.*

tyrannosaurus *or* **tyrannosaur** (tirr-ran-oh-**sore**-uss) *n* a large two-footed flesh-eating dinosaur common in North America in Cretaceous times. ▷ **HISTORY** Greek *turannos* tyrant + *sauros* lizard

tyranny *n, pl* **-nies 1 a** government by a tyrant. **b** oppressive and unjust government by more than one person. **2** the condition or state of being dominated or controlled by something that makes unpleasant or harsh demands: *the tyranny of fashion drives many women to diet although they are not overweight.* ▶ **tyrannous** *adj*

tyrant *n* **1** a person who governs oppressively, unjustly, and arbitrarily. **2** any person who exercises authority in a tyrannical manner: *a domestic tyrant.* ▷ **HISTORY** Greek *turannos*

tyre *or US* **tire** *n* a ring of rubber, usually filled with air but sometimes solid, fitted round the rim of a wheel of a road vehicle to grip the road. ▷ **HISTORY** earlier *tire*, probably archaic variant of *attire*

tyro *n, pl* **-ros** a novice or beginner. ▷ **HISTORY** Latin *tiro* recruit

tzar *n* same as **tsar**.

tzetze fly *n* same as **tsetse fly**.

U u

A B C D E F G H I J K L M N O P Q R S T U V W X Y Z

U 1 (in Britain) universal (used to describe a film certified as suitable for viewing by anyone). **2** *Chem* uranium. ✧ *adj* **3** *Brit informal* (of language or behaviour) characteristic of the upper class.

UB40 *n* (in Britain) **1** a registration card issued to an unemployed person. **2** *Informal* a person registered as unemployed.

ubiquitous (yew-**bik**-wit-uss) *adj* being or seeming to be everywhere at once. ▷ HISTORY Latin *ubique* everywhere ▶ **ubiquity** *n*

U-boat *n* a German submarine. ▷ HISTORY German *Unterseeboot* undersea boat

Ubuntu *n S African* humanity or fellow feeling; kindness. ▷ HISTORY Nguni (language group of southern Africa)

uc *Printing* upper case.

UCAS (in Britain) Universities and Colleges Admissions Service.

UCCA (formerly, in Britain) Universities Central Council on Admissions.

udder *n* the large baglike milk-producing gland of cows, sheep, or goats, with two or more teats. ▷ HISTORY Old English *ūder*

UDI Unilateral Declaration of Independence.

UEFA Union of European Football Associations.

UFO unidentified flying object.

ugh (**uhh**) *interj* an exclamation of disgust, annoyance, or dislike.

UGLI *n, pl* **-LIS** *or* **-LIES** *Trademark* a yellow citrus fruit: a cross between a tangerine, grapefruit, and orange. ▷ HISTORY probably an alteration of *ugly*, from its wrinkled skin

ugly *adj* **uglier, ugliest 1** so unattractive as to be unpleasant to look at. **2** very unpleasant and involving violence or aggression: *an ugly incident in which one man was stabbed.* **3** repulsive or displeasing: *ugly rumours.* **4** bad-tempered or sullen: *an ugly mood.* ▷ HISTORY Old Norse *uggligr* dreadful ▶ **ugliness** *n*

UHF *Radio* ultrahigh frequency.

UHT ultra-heat-treated (milk or cream).

UK United Kingdom.

ukase (yew-**kaze**) *n* (in imperial Russia) a decree from the tsar. ▷ HISTORY Russian *ukaz*

Ukrainian *adj* **1** of the Ukraine. ✧ *n* **2** a person from the Ukraine. **3** the language of the Ukraine.

ukulele *or* **ukelele** (yew-kal-**lay**-lee) *n* a small four-stringed guitar. ▷ HISTORY Hawaiian, literally: jumping flea

ulcer *n* an open sore on the surface of the skin or a mucous membrane. ▷ HISTORY Latin *ulcus*

ulcerated *adj* made or becoming ulcerous. ▶ **ulceration** *n*

ulcerous *adj* of, like, or characterized by ulcers.

ulna *n, pl* **-nae** *or* **-nas** the inner and longer of the two bones of the human forearm or of the forelimb in other vertebrates. ▷ HISTORY Latin: elbow ▶ **ulnar** *adj*

ulnar nerve *n Anat* a nerve situated along the inner side of the arm and passing close to the surface of the skin near the elbow.

ulster *n* a man's heavy double-breasted overcoat. ▷ HISTORY *Ulster,* the northernmost province of Ireland

Ulsterman *or fem* **Ulsterwoman** *n, pl* **-men** *or* **-women** a person from Ulster.

ulterior (ult-**ear**-ee-or) *adj* (of an aim, reason, etc.) concealed or hidden: *an ulterior motive.* ▷ HISTORY Latin: further

ultimate *adj* **1** final in a series or process: *predictions about the ultimate destination of modern art.* **2** highest, supreme, or unchallengeable: *he has the ultimate power to dismiss the Prime Minister.* **3** fundamental or essential: *a believer in the ultimate goodness of man.* **4** most extreme: *genocide is the ultimate abuse of human rights.* **5** final or total: *she should be able to estimate the ultimate cost.* ✧ *n* **6 the ultimate in** the best example of: *the ultimate in luxury holidays.* ▷ HISTORY Latin *ultimus* last, distant ▶ **ultimately** *adv*

ultimatum (ult-im-**may**-tum) *n* a final warning to someone that they must agree to certain conditions or requirements, or else action will be taken against them: *Britain declared war after the Nazis rejected the ultimatum to withdraw from Poland.*

ultra *n* a person who has extreme or immoderate beliefs or opinions. ▷ HISTORY Latin: beyond

ultra- *prefix* **1** beyond a specified extent, range, or limit: *ultrasonic.* **2** extremely: *ultraleftist.* ▷ HISTORY Latin

ultraconservative *adj* **1** highly reactionary. ✧ *n* **2** a reactionary person.

ultrahigh frequency *n* a radio frequency between 3000 and 300 megahertz.

ultramarine *n* **1** a blue pigment originally made from lapis lazuli. ✧ *adj* **2** vivid blue.

WORD HISTORY

'Ultramarine' comes from Latin *ultramarinus*, meaning 'from beyond the sea'. It was given this name because the blue mineral, lapis lazuli, that the pigment was made from was imported from Asia.

ultramontane *adj* **1** on the other side of the mountains, usually the Alps, from the speaker or writer. **2** of a movement in the Roman Catholic Church which favours supreme papal authority. ✧ *n* **3** a person from beyond the Alps. **4** a member of the ultramontane party of the Roman Catholic Church.

ultrasonic *adj* of or producing sound waves with higher frequencies than humans can hear. ▶ **ultrasonically** *adv*

ultrasonics *n* the branch of physics concerned with ultrasonic waves.

ultrasound *n* ultrasonic waves, used in echo sounding, medical diagnosis, and therapy.

ultrasound scan *n* an examination of an internal bodily structure by the use of ultrasonic waves, esp. for diagnosing abnormality in a fetus.

ultraviolet *n* **1** the part of the electromagnetic spectrum with wavelengths shorter than light but longer than X-rays. ✧ *adj* **2** of or consisting of radiation lying in the ultraviolet: *ultraviolet light.*

ultraviolet radiation *n Science* the damaging ultraviolet light waves from the sun that can cause sunburn in humans.

ultra vires (**ul**-tra-**vire**-reez) *adv, adj Law* beyond the legal power of a person or organization. ▷ **HISTORY** Latin, literally: beyond strength

ululate (**yewl**-yew-late) *vb Literary* **-lating, -lated** to howl or wail. ▷ **HISTORY** Latin *ululare* ▶ **ululation** *n*

umbel *n* a type of compound flower in which the flowers arise from the same point in the main stem and have stalks of the same length, to give a cluster with the youngest flowers at the centre. ▷ **HISTORY** Latin *umbella* a sunshade ▶ **umbellate** *adj*

umbelliferous *adj* of or denoting a plant with flowers in umbels, such as fennel, parsley, carrot, or parsnip. ▷ **HISTORY** Latin *umbella* a sunshade + *ferre* to bear

umber *n* **1** a type of dark brown earth containing ferric oxide (rust). ✧ *adj* **2** dark brown to reddish-brown. ▷ **HISTORY** French *(terre d')ombre* or Italian *(terra di) ombra* shadow (earth)

umbilical (um-**bill**-ik-kl) *adj* of or like the navel or the umbilical cord.

umbilical cord *n* the long flexible cordlike structure that connects a fetus to the placenta.

umbilicus (um-**bill**-ik-kuss) *n Anat* the navel. ▷ **HISTORY** Latin: navel, centre

umbra *n, pl* **-brae** *or* **-bras** a shadow, usually the shadow cast by the moon onto the earth during a solar eclipse. ▷ **HISTORY** Latin: shade

umbrage *n* **take umbrage** to take offence. ▷ **HISTORY** Latin *umbra* shade

umbrella *n* **1** a portable device used for protection against rain, consisting of a light canopy supported on a collapsible metal frame mounted on a central rod. **2** a single organization, idea, etc., that contains or covers many different organizations or ideas. **3** anything that has the effect of a protective screen or general cover: *under the umbrella of the Helsinki security conference.* ✧ *adj* **4** containing or covering many different organizations, ideas, etc.: *an umbrella group of nationalists and anti-communists.* ▷ **HISTORY** Italian *ombrella,* from *ombra* shade ▶ **umbrella-like** *adj*

umiak, oomiak, *or* **oomiac** (**oo**-mee-ak) *n* a large open boat made of stretched skins, used by Eskimos. ▷ **HISTORY** Inuit

umlaut (**oom**-lout) *n* **1** the mark (¨) placed over a vowel, esp. in German, indicating a change in its sound. **2** (esp. in Germanic languages) the change of a vowel brought about by the influence of a vowel in the next syllable. ▷ **HISTORY** German, from *um* around + *Laut* sound

umlungu (oom-**loong**-goo) *n S African* a White man: used esp. as a term of address. ▷ **HISTORY** Nguni (language group of southern Africa)

umpire *n* **1** an official who ensures that the people taking part in a game follow the rules; referee. ✧ *vb* **-piring, -pired 2** to act as umpire in a game. ▷ **HISTORY** Old French *nomper* not one of a pair

umpteen *adj Informal* very many: *the centre of umpteen scandals.* ▷ **HISTORY** *umpty* a great deal + *-teen* ten ▶ **umpteenth** *n, adj*

UN United Nations.

un-[1] *prefix (freely used with adjectives, participles, and their derivative adverbs and nouns: less frequently used with certain other nouns)* not; contrary to; opposite of: *uncertain; untidiness; unbelief; untruth.* ▷ **HISTORY** Old English *on-, un-*

un-[2] *prefix forming verbs* **1** denoting reversal of an action or state: *uncover; untie.* **2** denoting removal from, release, or deprivation: *unharness.* ▷ **HISTORY** Old English *un-, on-*

unabated *adv* without any reduction in force: *the storm continued unabated.*

unable *adj* **unable to** not having the power, ability, or authority to; not able to.

unaccented syllable *n* see **unstressed syllable**.

unaccountable *adj* **1** without any sensible explanation: *for some unaccountable reason I got on the wrong bus.* **2** not having to justify or answer for one's actions to other people: *the secret service remains unaccountable to the public.* ▶ **unaccountably** *adv*

unadulterated *adj* **1** completely pure, with nothing added: *fresh unadulterated spring water.* **2** (of an emotion) not mixed with anything else: *a look of unadulterated terror.*

unaffected[1] *adj* unpretentious, natural, or sincere.

unaffected[2] *adj* not influenced or changed.

unalienable *adj Law* same as **inalienable**.

unanimous (yew-**nan**-im-uss) *adj* **1** in complete agreement. **2** characterized by complete agreement: *unanimous approval.* ▷ **HISTORY** Latin *unus* one + *animus* mind ▶ **unanimity** *n* ▶ **unanimously** *adv*

unannounced *adv* without warning: *she turned up unannounced.*

unapproachable *adj* discouraging friendliness; aloof.

unarmed *adj* **1** not carrying any weapons: *they were shooting unarmed peasants.* **2** not using any weapons: *unarmed combat.*

unassailable *adj* not able to be destroyed or overcome: *an unassailable lead.*

unassuming *adj* modest or unpretentious.

unattached *adj* **1** not connected with any specific body or group. **2** not engaged or married.

unavailing *adj* useless or futile.

unavoidable *adj* unable to be avoided or prevented. ▶ **unavoidably** *adv*

unaware *adj* **1** not aware or conscious: *unaware of my surroundings.* ✧ *adv* **2** *Not universally accepted* same as **unawares**.

unawares *adv* **1** by surprise: *death had taken him unawares.* **2** without knowing: *had he passed her, all unawares?*

unbalanced *adj* **1** lacking balance. **2** mentally deranged. **3** biased; one-sided: *his unbalanced summing-up.*

unbearable *adj* not able to be endured. ▸ **unbearably** *adv*

unbecoming *adj* **1** unattractive or unsuitable: *unbecoming garments.* **2** not proper or appropriate to a person or position: *acts unbecoming of university students.*

unbeknown *adv* (foll. by *to*) without the knowledge of (a person): *unbeknown to her family she had acquired modern ways.* Also (esp. Brit): **unbeknownst** ▷ **HISTORY** archaic *beknown* known

unbelievable *adj* **1** too unlikely to be believed. **2** extremely impressive; marvellous. **3** *Informal* terrible or shocking. ▸ **unbelievably** *adv*

unbeliever *n* a person who does not believe in a religion.

unbend *vb* **-bending, -bent** to become less strict or more informal in one's attitudes or behaviour.

unbending *adj* rigid or inflexible: *an unbending routine.*

unbiased *adj* not having or showing prejudice or favouritism; impartial.

unbidden *adj Literary* not ordered or asked; voluntary or spontaneous: *unbidden thoughts came into Catherine's mind.*

unborn *adj* not yet born.

unbosom *vb* to relieve oneself of secrets or feelings by telling someone. ▷ **HISTORY** UN-[2] + *bosom* (in the sense: centre of the emotions)

unbridled *adj* (of feelings or behaviour) not restrained or controlled in any way: *unbridled passion.*

unbroken *adj* **1** complete or whole. **2** continuous: *I slept for eight unbroken hours.* **3** not disturbed or upset: *an unbroken night.* **4** (of a record) not improved upon. **5** (of animals, esp. horses) not tamed.

unburden *vb* to relieve one's mind or oneself of a worry or trouble by telling someone about it.

uncalled-for *adj* unnecessary or unwarranted: *uncalled-for comments.*

uncanny *adj* **1** weird or mysterious: *an uncanny silence.* **2** beyond what is normal: *an uncanny eye for detail.* ▸ **uncannily** *adv* ▸ **uncanniness** *n*

unceremonious *adj* **1** relaxed and informal: *she greeted him with unceremonious friendliness.* **2** abrupt or rude: *the answer was an unceremonious 'no'.* ▸ **unceremoniously** *adv*

uncertain *adj* **1** not able to be accurately known or predicted: *an uncertain future.* **2** not definitely decided: *they are uncertain about the date.* **3** not to be depended upon: *an uncertain career.* **4** changeable: *an uncertain sky.* ▸ **uncertainty** *n*

uncharacteristic *adj* not typical. ▸ **uncharacteristically** *adv*

uncharitable *adj* unkind or harsh. ▸ **uncharitably** *adv*

uncharted *adj* **1** (of an area of sea or land) not having had a map made of it, esp. because it is unexplored. **2** unknown or unfamiliar: *a whole uncharted universe of emotions.*

unchristian *or* **un-Christian** *adj* not in accordance with Christian principles.

uncial (**un**-see-al) *adj* **1** of or written in letters that resemble modern capitals, as used in Greek and Latin manuscripts of the third to ninth centuries. ✧ *n* **2** an uncial letter or manuscript. ▷ **HISTORY** Late Latin *unciales litterae* letters an inch long

uncivilized *or* **-ised** *adj* **1** (of a tribe or people) not yet civilized. **2** lacking culture or sophistication.

unclassified *adj* **1** not arranged in any specific order or grouping. **2** (of official information) not secret.

uncle *n* **1** a brother of one's father or mother. **2** the husband of one's aunt. **3** a child's term of address for a male friend of its parents. **4** *Slang* a pawnbroker. ▷ **HISTORY** Latin *avunculus*

unclean *adj* lacking moral, spiritual, or physical cleanliness.

Uncle Sam *n* a personification of the government of the United States. ▷ **HISTORY** apparently a humorous interpretation of the letters stamped on army supply boxes during the War of 1812: *US*

uncomfortable *adj* **1** not physically relaxed: *he was forced to sit in an uncomfortable cross-legged position.* **2** not comfortable to be in or use: *an uncomfortable chair.* **3** causing discomfort or unease: *the uncomfortable truth.* ▸ **uncomfortably** *adv*

uncommon *adj* **1** not happening or encountered often. **2** in excess of what is normal: *an uncommon amount of powder.*

uncommonly *adv* **1** in an unusual manner or degree. **2** extremely: *an uncommonly good humour.*

uncompromising *adj* not prepared to compromise; inflexible. ▸ **uncompromisingly** *adv*

unconcerned *adj* **1** not interested in something and not wanting to become involved. **2** not worried or troubled. ▸ **unconcernedly** (un-kon-**sern**-id-lee) *adv*

unconditional *adj* without conditions or limitations: *an unconditional ceasefire.* ▸ **unconditionally** *adv*

unconscionable *adj* **1** unscrupulous or unprincipled: *an unconscionable charmer.* **2** excessive in amount or degree: *unconscionable number of social obligations.*

unconscious *adj* **1** unable to notice or respond to things which one would normally be aware of through the senses; insensible or comatose. **2** not aware of one's actions or behaviour: *unconscious of his failure.* **3** not realized or intended: *unconscious duplicity.* **4** coming from or produced by the unconscious: *unconscious mental processes.* ✧ *n* **5** *Psychoanal* the part of the mind containing instincts, impulses, and ideas that are not available for direct examination. ▶ **unconsciously** *adv* ▶ **unconsciousness** *n*

unconstitutional *adj* forbidden by the rules or laws which state how an organization or country must function.

unconventional *adj* not conforming to accepted rules or standards.

uncooperative *adj* not willing to help other people with what they are trying to do.

uncoordinated *adj* **1** not joining or functioning together properly to form a whole. **2** (of a person) not able to control his or her movements properly; clumsy.

uncountable *adj* existing in such large numbers that it is impossible to say how many there are: *uncountable millions.*

uncouth *adj* lacking in good manners, refinement, or grace. ▷ **HISTORY** Old English *un-* not + *cūth* familiar

uncover *vb* **1** to remove the cover or top from. **2** to reveal or disclose: *they have uncovered a plot to overthrow the government.* ▶ **uncovered** *adj*

uncrowned *adj* **1** having the powers, but not the title, of royalty. **2** (of a king or queen) not yet crowned.

UNCTAD *Econ* United Nations Conference on Trade and Development.

unction *n* **1** *Chiefly RC & Eastern Churches* the act of anointing with oil in sacramental ceremonies. **2** oily charm. **3** an ointment. **4** anything soothing. ▷ **HISTORY** Latin *unguere* to anoint

unctuous *adj* pretending to be kind and concerned but obviously not sincere. ▷ **HISTORY** Latin *unctum* ointment

undecided *adj* **1** not having made up one's mind. **2** (of an issue or problem) not agreed or decided upon.

undeniable *adj* **1** unquestionably true. **2** of unquestionable excellence: *of undeniable character.* ▶ **undeniably** *adv*

under *prep* **1** directly below; on, to, or beneath the underside or base of: *under the bed.* **2** less than: *in just under an hour.* **3** lower in rank than: *under a general.* **4** subject to the supervision, control, or influence of: *under communism for 45 years.* **5** in or subject to certain circumstances or conditions: *the bridge is still under construction; under battle conditions.* **6** in (a specified category): *he had filed Kafka's 'The Trial' under crime stories.* **7** known by: *under their own names.* **8** planted with: *a field under corn.* **9** powered by: *under sail.* ✧ *adv* **10** below; to a position underneath. ▷ **HISTORY** Old English

under- *prefix* **1** below or beneath: *underarm; underground.* **2** insufficient or insufficiently: *underemployed.* **3** of lesser importance or lower rank: *undersecretary.* **4** indicating secrecy or deception: *underhand.*

underachieve *vb* **-achieving, -achieved** to fail to achieve a performance appropriate to one's age or talents. ▶ **underachiever** *n*

underactive *adj* less active than is normal or desirable: *an underactive thyroid gland.*

underage *adj* below the required or standard age, usually below the legal age for voting or drinking: *underage sex.*

underarm *adj* **1** *Sport* denoting a style of throwing, bowling, or serving in which the hand is swung below shoulder level. **2** below the arm. ✧ *adv* **3** in an underarm style.

underbelly *n, pl* **-lies 1** the part of an animal's belly nearest the ground. **2** a vulnerable or unprotected part, aspect, or region.

underbrush *n US, Canad, & Austral* same as **undergrowth**.

undercarriage *n* **1** the wheels, shock absorbers, and struts that support an aircraft on the ground and enable it to take off and land. **2** the framework supporting the body of a vehicle.

undercharge *vb* **-charging, -charged** to charge too little for something.

underclass *n* a class beneath the usual social scale consisting of the most disadvantaged people, such as the long-term unemployed.

underclothes *pl n* same as **underwear**. Also called: **underclothing**

undercoat *n* **1** a coat of paint applied before the top coat. **2** *Zool* a layer of soft fur beneath the outer fur of animals such as the otter. ✧ *vb* **3** to apply an undercoat to a surface.

undercover *adj* done or acting in secret: *an undercover investigation.*

undercurrent *n* **1** a current that is not apparent at the surface. **2** an underlying opinion or emotion.

undercut *vb* **-cutting, -cut 1** to charge less than a competitor in order to obtain trade. **2** to undermine or render less effective: *the latest fighting undercuts diplomatic attempts to find a peaceful solution.* **3** to cut away the under part of something.

underdeveloped *adj* **1** immature or undersized. **2** (of a country or its economy) lacking the finance, industries, and organization necessary to advance.

underdog *n* a person or team in a weak or underprivileged position.

underdone *adj* insufficiently or lightly cooked.

underestimate *vb* **-mating, -mated 1** to make too low an estimate of: *the trust had underestimated the cost of work.* **2** to not be aware or take account of the full abilities or potential of: *the police had underestimated him.* ✧ *n* **3** too low an estimate. ▶ **underestimation** *n*

> ☑ **WORD TIP**
> *Underestimate* is sometimes wrongly used where *overestimate* is meant: *the importance of his work cannot be overestimated* (not *cannot be underestimated*).

underexpose *vb* **-posing, -posed** *Photog* to expose (a film, plate, or paper) for too short a time or with insufficient light. ▶ **underexposure** *n*

underfelt *n* thick felt laid under a carpet to increase insulation.

underfoot *adv* **1** underneath the feet; on the ground. **2 trample** *or* **crush underfoot a** to

a b c d e f g h i j k l m n o p q r s t u v w x y z

A B C D E F G H I J K L M N O P Q R S T U V W X Y Z

damage or destroy by stepping on. **b** to treat with contempt.

undergarment *n* a garment worn under clothes.

undergo *vb* **-going, -went, -gone** to experience, endure, or sustain: *he underwent a three-hour operation.* ▷ HISTORY Old English *undergān*

undergraduate *n* a person studying in a university for a first degree.

underground *adj, adv* **1** occurring, situated, used, or going below ground level. **2** secret or secretly: *an underground organization; several political parties had to operate underground for many years.* **3** (of art, film, music, etc.) avant-garde, experimental, or subversive. ✧ *n* **4** a movement dedicated to overthrowing a government or occupation forces. **5** (often preceded by *the*) an electric passenger railway operated in underground tunnels.

undergrowth *n* small trees and bushes growing beneath taller trees in a wood or forest.

underhand *adj also* **underhanded 1** sly, deceitful, and secretive. **2** *Sport* same as **underarm**. ✧ *adv* **3** in an underhand manner or style.

underinsurance *n Insurance* inadequate insurance cover.

underlay *n* felt or rubber laid under a carpet to increase insulation and resilience.

underlie *vb* **-lying, -lay, -lain 1** to lie or be placed under. **2** to be the foundation, cause, or basis of: *the basic unity which underlies all religion.*

underline *vb* **-lining, -lined 1** to put a line under. **2** to emphasize.

underling *n Derogatory* a subordinate.

underlying *adj* **1** not obvious but detectable: *the deeper and underlying aim of her travels.* **2** fundamental; basic: *an underlying belief.* **3** lying under: *the underlying layers of the skin.*

undermine *vb* **-mining, -mined 1** to weaken gradually or insidiously: *morphia had undermined his grasp of reality.* **2** (of the sea or wind) to wear away the base of cliffs.

WORD HISTORY

'Undermining' is originally a military term, denoting the practice in warfare of digging mines or tunnels under enemy fortifications in order to make them collapse.

underneath *prep, adv* **1** under or beneath. ✧ *adj* **2** lower. ✧ *n* **3** a lower part or surface. ▷ HISTORY Old English *underneothan*

underpants *pl n* a man's undergarment covering the body from the waist or hips to the thighs.

underpass *n* **1** a section of a road that passes under another road or a railway line. **2** a subway for pedestrians.

underpin *vb* **-pinning, -pinned 1** to give strength or support to: *the principles that underpin his political convictions.* **2** to support from beneath with a prop: *to underpin a wall.* ▶ **underpinning** *n*

underplay *vb* to achieve (an effect) by deliberate lack of emphasis.

underprivileged *adj* **1** lacking the rights and advantages of other members of society; deprived. ✧ *n* **2 the underprivileged** underprivileged people regarded as a group.

underrate *vb* **-rating, -rated** to not be aware or take account of the full abilities or potential of. ▶ **underrated** *adj*

undersea *adj, adv* below the surface of the sea.

underseal *n* **1** a special coating applied to the underside of a motor vehicle to prevent corrosion. ✧ *vb* **2** to apply such a coating to a motor vehicle.

undersecretary *n, pl* **-taries** a senior civil servant or junior minister in a government department.

undersell *vb* **-selling, -sold** to sell at a price lower than that of another seller.

undersexed *adj* having weaker sexual urges than is considered normal.

undershoot *vb* **-shooting, -shot** *Aviation* to land an aircraft short of a runway.

underside *n* the bottom or lower surface.

undersized *adj* smaller than normal.

underskirt *n* a skirtlike garment worn under a skirt or dress; petticoat.

understand *vb* **-standing, -stood 1** to know and comprehend the nature or meaning of: *I understand what you are saying.* **2** to know what is happening or why it is happening: *in order to understand the problems that can occur.* **3** to assume, infer, or believe: *I understand he is based in this town.* **4** to know how to translate or read: *don't you understand Russian?* **5** to be sympathetic to or compatible with: *she needed him to understand her completely.* ▷ HISTORY Old English *understandan* ▶ **understandable** *adj* ▶ **understandably** *adv*

understanding *n* **1** the ability to learn, judge, or make decisions. **2** personal opinion or interpretation of a subject: *my understanding of what he said.* **3** a mutual agreement, usually an informal or private one. ✧ *adj* **4** kind, sympathetic, or tolerant towards people.

understate *vb* **-stating, -stated 1** to describe or portray something in restrained terms, often to obtain an ironic effect. **2** to state that something, such as a number, is less than it is. ▶ **understatement** *n*

understudy *n, pl* **-studies 1** an actor who studies a part so as to be able to replace the usual actor if necessary. **2** anyone who is trained to take the place of another if necessary. ✧ *vb* **-studies, -studying, -studied 3** to act as an understudy to.

undertake *vb* **-taking, -took, -taken 1** to agree to or commit oneself to something or to do something: *I undertook the worst job in gardening.* **2** to promise to do something.

undertaker *n* a person whose job is to look after the bodies of people who have died and to organize funerals.

undertaking *n* **1** a task or enterprise. **2** an agreement to do something. **3** *Informal* the practice of overtaking on an inner lane a vehicle which is travelling in an outer lane.

undertone *n* **1** a quiet tone of voice. **2** something which suggests an underlying quality or feeling: *an undertone of anger.*

undertow *n* a strong undercurrent flowing in a different direction from the surface current, such as in the sea.

undervalue *vb* **-valuing, -valued** to value a person or thing at less than the true worth or importance.

underwater *adj* **1** situated, occurring, or for use under the surface of the sea, a lake, or a river. ✧ *adv* **2** beneath the surface of the sea, a lake, or a river.

under way *adj* **1** in progress; taking place: *this test is already under way.* **2** *Naut* in motion in the direction headed.

underwear *n* clothing worn under other garments, usually next to the skin.

underweight *adj* weighing less than is average, expected, or healthy.

underworld *n* **1** criminals and their associates. **2** *Greek & Roman myth* the regions below the earth's surface regarded as the abode of the dead.

underwrite *vb* **-writing, -wrote, -written 1** to accept financial responsibility for a commercial project or enterprise. **2** to sign and issue an insurance policy, thus accepting liability. **3** to support. ▶ **underwriter** *n*

undesirable *adj* **1** not desirable or pleasant; objectionable. ✧ *n* **2** a person considered undesirable.

undies *pl n Brit, Austral & NZ informal* women's underwear.

undiluted *adj* **1** (of a liquid) not having any water added to it; concentrated. **2** not mixed with any other feeling or quality: *undiluted hatred.*

undistinguished *adj* not particularly good or bad; mediocre.

undo *vb* **-doing, -did, -done 1** to open, unwrap or untie. **2** to reverse the effects of: *all the work of the congress would be undone.* **3** to cause the downfall of.

undoing *n* **1** ruin; downfall. **2** the cause of someone's downfall: *his confidence was his undoing.*

undone[1] *adj* not done or completed; unfinished.

undone[2] *adj* **1** ruined; destroyed. **2** unfastened; untied.

undoubted *adj* beyond doubt; certain or indisputable. ▶ **undoubtedly** *adv*

undress *vb* **1** to take off the clothes of oneself or another. ✧ *n* **2 in a state of undress** naked or nearly naked. **3** informal or ordinary working clothes or uniform. ▶ **undressed** *adj*

undue *adj* greater than is reasonable; excessive: *undue attention.*

> **WORD TIP**
> The use of *undue* in sentences such as *there is no cause for undue alarm* is redundant and should be avoided.

undulate *vb* **-lating, -lated 1** to move gently and slowly from side to side or up and down. **2** to have a wavy shape or appearance. ▷ **HISTORY** Latin *unda* a wave ▶ **undulation** *n*

unduly *adv* excessively.

undying *adj* never ending; eternal.

unearned income *n* income from property or investments rather than work.

unearth *vb* **1** to discover by searching. **2** to dig up out of the earth.

unearthly *adj* **1** strange, unnatural, or eerie: *unearthly beauty.* **2** ridiculous or unreasonable: *the unearthly hour of seven in the morning.* ▶ **unearthliness** *n*

unease *n* **1** anxiety or nervousness: *my unease grew when she was not back by midnight.* **2** dissatisfaction or tension: *unease about the government's handling of the affair.*

uneasy *adj* **1** (of a person) anxious or apprehensive. **2** (of a condition) precarious or insecure: *an uneasy peace.* **3** (of a thought or feeling) disquieting. ▶ **uneasily** *adv* ▶ **uneasiness** *n*

uneatable *adj* (of food) so rotten or unattractive as to be unfit to eat.

uneconomic *adj* not producing enough profit.

unemployed *adj* **1** without paid employment; out of work. **2** not being used; idle. ✧ *pl n* **3** people who are out of work: *the long-term unemployed.*

unemployment *n* **1** the condition of being unemployed. **2** the number of unemployed workers: *unemployment rose again last month.*

unemployment benefit *n* (formerly, in the British National Insurance scheme, and currently, in New Zealand) a regular payment to an unemployed person.

unequivocal *adj* completely clear in meaning; unambiguous. ▶ **unequivocally** *adv*

unerring *adj* never mistaken; consistently accurate.

UNESCO United Nations Educational, Scientific, and Cultural Organization.

uneven *adj* **1** (of a surface) not level or flat. **2** not consistent in quality: *an uneven performance.* **3** not parallel, straight, or horizontal. **4** not fairly matched: *the uneven battle.*

unexceptionable *adj* not likely to be criticized or objected to.

unexceptional *adj* usual, ordinary, or normal.

unexpected *adj* surprising or unforeseen. ▶ **unexpectedly** *adv*

unexpurgated *adj* (of a piece of writing) not censored by having allegedly offensive passages removed.

unfailing *adj* continuous or reliable: *his unfailing enthusiasm.* ▶ **unfailingly** *adv*

unfair *adj* **1** unequal or unjust. **2** dishonest or unethical. ▶ **unfairly** *adv* ▶ **unfairness** *n*

unfaithful *adj* **1** having sex with someone other than one's regular partner. **2** not true to a promise or vow. ▶ **unfaithfulness** *n*

unfathomable *adj* too strange or complicated to be understood: *pugs exert a powerful, unfathomable hold over their owners.*

unfavourable *or US* **unfavorable** *adj* **1** making a successful or positive outcome unlikely: *unfavourable weather conditions.* **2** disapproving: *an unfavourable opinion.* ▸ **unfavourably** *or US* ▸ **unfavorably** *adv*

unfeeling *adj* without sympathy; callous.

unfit *adj* **1** unqualified for or incapable of a particular role or task: *an unfit mother; he was unfit to drive.* **2** unsuitable: *this meat is unfit for human consumption.* **3** in poor physical condition.

unflappable *adj Informal* (of a person) not easily upset. ▸ **unflappability** *n*

unfledged *adj* **1** (of a young bird) not having developed adult feathers. **2** immature and inexperienced.

unfold *vb* **1** to open or spread out from a folded state. **2** to reveal or be revealed: *a terrible truth unfolds.* **3** to develop or be developed: *the novel unfolds through their recollections.*

unforeseen *adj* surprising because not expected.

unforgettable *adj* making such a strong impression that it is impossible to forget. ▸ **unforgettably** *adv*

unfortunate *adj* **1** caused or accompanied by bad luck: *an unfortunate coincidence.* **2** having bad luck: *my unfortunate daughter.* **3** regrettable or unsuitable: *an unfortunate choice of phrase.* ✧ *n* **4** an unlucky person. ▸ **unfortunately** *adv*

unfounded *adj* (of ideas, fears, or allegations) not based on facts or evidence.

unfreeze *vb* **-freezing, -froze, -frozen 1** to thaw or cause to thaw. **2** to relax restrictions or controls on (trade, the transfer of money, etc.): *Congress is considering unfreezing US aid to Jordan.*

unfrock *vb* to deprive a person in holy orders of the status of a priest.

unfurl *vb* to unroll or spread out (an umbrella, flag, or sail) or (of an umbrella, flag, or sail) to be unrolled or spread out.

ungainly *adj* **-lier, -liest** lacking grace when moving. ▷ HISTORY dialect *gainly* graceful ▸ **ungainliness** *n*

ungodly *adj* **-lier, -liest 1** wicked or sinful. **2** *Informal* unreasonable or outrageous: *at this ungodly hour.* ▸ **ungodliness** *n*

ungovernable *adj* **1** (of an emotion) not able to be controlled or restrained: *an ungovernable rage.* **2** (of a country or area) not able to be effectively governed, esp. because of unrest or violence: *years of religious conflict had made much of the island ungovernable.*

ungrammatical *adj* not following the rules of grammar.

ungrateful *adj* not showing or offering thanks for a favour or compliment.

unguarded *adj* **1** unprotected. **2** open or frank: *one unguarded briefing.* **3** incautious or careless: *an unguarded moment.*

unguent (**ung**-gwent) *n Literary* an ointment. ▷ HISTORY Latin *unguere* to anoint

ungulate (**ung**-gyew-lit) *n* a hoofed mammal. ▷ HISTORY Latin *ungula* hoof

unhallowed *adj* **1** not consecrated or holy: *unhallowed ground.* **2** sinful or wicked.

unhand *vb Old-fashioned or literary* to release from one's grasp.

unhappy *adj* **-pier, -piest 1** sad or depressed. **2** unfortunate or wretched. ▸ **unhappily** *adv* ▸ **unhappiness** *n*

unhealthy *adj* **-healthier, -healthiest 1** likely to cause illness or poor health: *unhealthy foods such as hamburger and chips.* **2** not very fit or well. **3** caused by or looking as if caused by poor health: *a thin unhealthy look about him.* **4** morbid or unwholesome: *an unhealthy interest in computer fraud.* ▸ **unhealthiness** *n*

unheard-of *adj* **1** without precedent: *an unheard-of phenomenon.* **2** highly offensive: *unheard-of behaviour.*

unhinge *vb* **-hinging, -hinged** to make a person mentally deranged or unbalanced. ▸ **unhinged** *adj*

unholy *adj* **-lier, -liest 1** immoral or wicked. **2** *Informal* outrageous or unnatural: *this unholy mess.* ▸ **unholiness** *n*

uni *n Brit, Austral & NZ informal* short for **university**.

uni- *combining form* of, consisting of, or having only one: *unilateral.* ▷ HISTORY Latin *unus* one

unicameral *adj* of or having a single legislative chamber: *Denmark's unicameral parliament, known as the Folketing.*

UNICEF United Nations Children's Fund.

unicellular *adj* (of organisms) consisting of a single cell.

unicorn *n* a legendary creature resembling a white horse with one horn growing from its forehead. ▷ HISTORY Latin *unus* one + *cornu* a horn

unicycle *n* a one-wheeled vehicle driven by pedals, used in a circus. ▸ **unicyclist** *n*

uniform *n* **1** a special identifying set of clothes for the members of an organization, such as soldiers. ✧ *adj* **2** regular and even throughout: *the mixture must be beaten to a uniform consistency.* **3** alike or like: *uniform green metal filing cabinets.* ▷ HISTORY Latin *unus* one + *forma* shape ▸ **uniformity** *n* ▸ **uniformly** *adv*

unify *vb* **-fies, -fying, -fied** to make or become one; unite. ▷ HISTORY Latin *unus* one + *facere* to make ▸ **unification** *n*

unilateral *adj* made or done by only one person or group: *unilateral action.* ▸ **unilateralism** *n*

unimpeachable *adj* completely honest and reliable.

uninsurable *adj Insurance* considered to be too great a risk for insurance cover.

uninterested *adj* having or showing no interest in someone or something.

> ✔ **WORD TIP**
> See at **disinterested.**

union *n* **1** the act of merging two or more things to become one, or the state of being merged in such a way. **2** short for **trade union**. **3** an association of individuals or groups for a common purpose: *the Scripture Union.* **4 a** an association or society: *the Students' union.* **b** the buildings of such an organization. **5** marriage or sexual intercourse. **6** *Maths* a set containing all the members of two given sets. **7** (in 19th-century England) a workhouse maintained by a number of parishes. ✧ *adj* **8** of a trade union. ▷ **HISTORY** Latin *unus* one

unionism *n* **1** the principles of trade unions. **2** adherence to the principles of trade unions. ▶ **unionist** *n, adj*

Unionist *n* a supporter of union between Britain and Northern Ireland.

unionize *or* **-ise** *vb* **-izing, -ized** *or* **-ising, -ised** to organize workers into a trade union. ▶ **unionization** *or* **-isation** *n*

Union Jack *or* **Union flag** *n* the national flag of the United Kingdom, combining the crosses of Saint George, Saint Andrew, and Saint Patrick.

unique (yew-**neek**) *adj* **1** being the only one of a particular type. **2 unique to** concerning or belonging to a particular person, thing, or group: *certain dishes are unique to this restaurant.* **3** without equal or like. **4** *Informal* remarkable. ▷ **HISTORY** Latin *unicus* unparalleled ▶ **uniquely** *adv*

> ☑ **WORD TIP**
> *Unique* is normally taken to describe an absolute state, i.e. one that cannot be qualified; thus something is either *unique* or *not unique;* it cannot be *rather unique* or *very unique*. However *unique* is sometimes used informally to mean remarkable or unusual, and this makes it possible to use comparatives or intensifiers with it, although many people object to this use.

unisex *adj* (of clothing, a hairstyle, or hairdressers) designed for both sexes.

unisexual *adj* **1** of one sex only. **2** (of an organism) having either male or female reproductive organs but not both.

unison *n* **1 in unison** at the same time as another person or other people: *smiling and nodding in unison.* **2** complete agreement: *to act in unison.* **3** *Music* a style, technique, or passage in which all the performers sing or play the same notes at the same time. ▷ **HISTORY** Latin *unus* one + *sonus* sound

UNISON *n* a British trade union consisting mainly of council and hospital workers.

unit *n* **1** a single undivided entity or whole. **2** a group or individual regarded as a basic element of a larger whole: *the clan was the basic unit of Highland society.* **3** a mechanical part or small device that does a particular job: *a waste disposal unit.* **4** a team of people that performs a specific function, and often also their buildings and equipment: *a combat unit.* **5** a standard amount of a physical quantity, such as length or energy, used to express magnitudes of that quantity: *the year as a unit of time.* **6** *Maths* the digit or position immediately to the left of the decimal point. **7** a piece of furniture designed to be fitted with other similar pieces: *bedroom units.* **8** *NZ* a self-propelled railcar. **9** *Austral & NZ* short for **home unit**. ▷ **HISTORY** from *unity*

Unitarian *n* **1** a person who believes that God is one being and rejects the Trinity. ✧ *adj* **2** of Unitarians or Unitarianism. ▶ **Unitarianism** *n*

unitary *adj* **1** consisting of a single undivided whole: *a unitary state.* **2** of a unit or units.

unit cost *n* the actual cost of producing one article.

unite *vb* **uniting, united 1** to make or become an integrated whole: *conception occurs when a sperm unites with the egg.* **2** to form an association or alliance: *the opposition parties united to fight against privatization.* **3** to possess (a combination of qualities) at the same time: *he manages to unite charm and ruthlessness.* ▷ **HISTORY** Latin *unus* one

united *adj* **1** produced by two or more people or things in combination: *a united effort.* **2** in agreement: *we are united in our opposition to these proposals.* **3** in association or alliance.

United Kingdom *n* a kingdom of NW Europe, consisting of the island of Great Britain together with Northern Ireland.

United Nations *n* an international organization of independent states, formed to promote peace and international security.

unit price *n* the price charged per unit.

unit trust *n Brit & Austral* an investment trust that issues units for public sale and invests the money in many different businesses.

unity *n, pl* **-ties 1** the state of being one. **2** mutual agreement: *unity of intention.* **3** the state of being a single thing that is composed of separate parts, organizations, etc.: *moves towards church unity.* **4** *Maths* the number or numeral one. ▷ **HISTORY** Latin *unus* one

Univ. University.

univalent *adj Chem* same as **monovalent**.

universal *adj* **1** of or relating to everyone in the world or everyone in a particular place or society: *the introduction of universal primary education.* **2** of, relating to, or affecting the entire world or universe: *the universal laws of physics.* **3** true and relevant at all times and in all situations: *there may be no single universal solution.* ✧ *n* **4** something which exists or is true in all places and all situations: *universals such as beauty and justice.* ▶ **universality** *n* ▶ **universally** *adv*

> ☑ **WORD TIP**
> The use of *more universal* as in *his writings have long been admired by fellow scientists, but his latest book should have more universal appeal* is acceptable in modern English usage.

universal joint *or* **coupling** *n* a form of coupling between two rotating shafts allowing freedom of movement in all directions.

universe *n* **1** the whole of all existing matter, energy, and space. **2** the world. ▷ **HISTORY** Latin *universum* the whole world

university *n, pl* **-ties 1** an institution of higher education with authority to award degrees. **2** the buildings, members, staff, or campus of a university. ▷ **HISTORY** Medieval Latin *universitas* group of scholars

Unix (**yew**-nicks) *n Trademark* an operating system found on many types of computer.

unkempt *adj* **1** (of the hair) uncombed or dishevelled. **2** untidy or slovenly: *an unkempt appearance.* ▷ **HISTORY** Old English *uncembed,* from *cemban* to comb

unkind *adj* unsympathetic or cruel. ▶ **unkindly** *adv* ▶ **unkindness** *n*

unknown *adj* **1** not known, understood, or recognized. **2** not famous: *a young and then unknown actor.* **3 unknown quantity** a person or thing whose action or effect is unknown or unpredictable. ✧ *n* **4** an unknown person, quantity, or thing. **5** *Maths* a variable whose value is to be discovered by solving an equation. ✧ *adv* **6 unknown to someone** without someone being aware: *unknown to him, the starboard engine had dropped off.*

unlawful *adj* not permitted by law; illegal.

unleaded *adj* (of petrol) containing less tetraethyl lead, in order to reduce environmental pollution.

unleash *vb* to set loose or cause (something bad): *to unleash war.*

unleavened (un-**lev**-vend) *adj* (of bread) made without yeast or leavening.

unless *conj* except under the circumstances that; except on the condition that: *you can't get in unless you can prove you're over eighteen.*

unlettered *adj* uneducated or illiterate.

unlike *adj* **1** not similar; different. ✧ *prep* **2** not like or typical of: *unlike his brother, he could not control his weight.* ▶ **unlikeness** *n*

unlikely *adj* not likely; improbable. ▶ **unlikeliness** *n*

unlikely outcome *n Statistics* an outcome which falls at the opposite end of a likelihood scale from a certain chance.

unlimited *adj* **1** apparently endless: *there was unlimited coffee.* **2** not restricted or limited: *unlimited access to the rest of the palace.*

unlisted *adj* **1** not entered on a list. **2** (of securities) not quoted on a stock exchange. **3** *Austral, US & Canad* not listed in a telephone directory by request.

unload *vb* **1** to remove cargo from a ship, lorry, or plane. **2** to express worries or problems by telling someone about them. **3** to remove the ammunition from a gun.

unlooked-for *adj* unexpected or unforeseen.

unlucky *adj* **1** having bad luck or misfortune: *an unlucky man.* **2** caused by bad luck or misfortune: *an unlucky coincidence.* **3** regarded as likely to bring about bad luck: *an unlucky number.* ▶ **unluckily** *adv*

unman *vb* **-manning, -manned 1** to cause to lose courage or nerve. **2** to make effeminate.

unmanned *adj* **1** having no personnel or crew: *the border posts were unmanned.* **2** (of an aircraft or spacecraft) operated by automatic or remote control.

unmarried *adj* not married.

unmask *vb* **1** to remove the mask or disguise from. **2** to expose or reveal the true nature or character of.

unmentionable *adj* unsuitable as a topic of conversation.

unmistakable *or* **unmistakeable** *adj* clear or unambiguous. ▶ **unmistakably** *or* **unmistakeably** *adv*

unmitigated *adj* **1** not reduced or lessened in severity or intensity. **2** total and complete: *unmitigated boredom.*

unmoved *adj* not affected by emotion; indifferent.

unnatural *adj* **1** strange and slightly frightening because it is not usual; abnormal: *an unnatural silence.* **2** not in accordance with accepted standards of behaviour: *an unnatural relationship.* **3** affected or forced: *a determined smile which seemed unnatural.* **4** inhuman or monstrous: *unnatural evils.* ▶ **unnaturally** *adv*

unnecessary *adj* not essential, or more than is essential. ▶ **unnecessarily** *adv*

unnerve *vb* **-nerving, -nerved** to cause to lose courage, confidence, or self-control: *he unnerves me.* ▶ **unnerving** *adj*

unnumbered *adj* **1** countless; too many to count. **2** not counted or given a number.

UNO United Nations Organization.

unobtrusive *adj* not drawing attention to oneself or itself; inconspicuous.

unoccupied *adj* **1** (of a building) without occupants. **2** unemployed or idle. **3** (of an area or country) not overrun by foreign troops.

unofficial *adj* **1** not authorized or approved by the relevant organization or person: *an unofficial strike.* **2** not confirmed officially: *unofficial reports of the minister's resignation.*

unorganized *or* **-nised** *adj* **1** not arranged into an organized system or structure. **2** (of workers) not unionized.

unorthodox *adj* **1** (of ideas, methods, etc.) unconventional and not generally accepted. **2** (of a person) not conventional in beliefs, behaviour, etc.

unpack *vb* **1** to remove the packed contents of a case. **2** to take something out of a packed container.

unpaid *adj* **1** without a salary or wage: *unpaid overtime.* **2** still to be paid: *unpaid bills.*

unpalatable *adj* **1** (of food) unpleasant to taste. **2** (of a fact, idea, etc.) unpleasant and hard to accept.

unparalleled *adj* not equalled; supreme.

unparliamentary *adj* not consistent with parliamentary procedure or practice.

unpick *vb* to undo the stitches of a piece of sewing.

unplayable *adj Sport* **1** (of a ball) thrown too fast or too skilfully to be hit. **2** (of a pitch or course) too badly affected by rain or frost to be used.

unpleasant *adj* not pleasant or agreeable. ▶ **unpleasantly** *adv* ▶ **unpleasantness** *n*

unplug *vb* **-plugging, -plugged** to disconnect a piece of electrical equipment by taking the plug out of the socket.

unpopular *adj* generally disliked or disapproved of. ▶ **unpopularity** *n*

unprecedented *adj* never having happened before: *an unprecedented decision.*

unprepossessing *adj* not very attractive or appealing.

unpretentious *adj* modest, unassuming, and down-to-earth.

unprincipled *adj* lacking moral principles; unscrupulous.

unprintable *adj* unsuitable for printing for reasons of obscenity, libel, or indecency.

unproductive *adj* not producing any worthwhile results: *unproductive talks.*

unprofessional *adj* not behaving according to the standards expected of a member of a particular profession.

unprofitable *adj* **1** not making a profit. **2** not producing any worthwhile results: *an unprofitable line of thinking.*

unputdownable *adj* (of a book, usually a novel) so gripping that one wants to read it at one sitting.

unqualified *adj* **1** lacking the necessary qualifications. **2** having no conditions or limitations: *an unqualified denial.* **3** total or complete: *unqualified admiration.*

unquestionable *adj* not to be doubted; indisputable. ▶ **unquestionably** *adv*

unquote *interj* an expression used to indicate the end of a quotation that was introduced with the word 'quote'.

unravel *vb* **-elling, -elled** *or US* **-eling, -eled 1** to separate something knitted or woven into individual strands. **2** to become separated into individual strands. **3** to explain or solve: *we unravelled the secrets.*

unreactive *adj* (of a substance) not readily partaking in chemical reactions.

unreadable *adj* **1** unable to be read or deciphered; illegible. **2** too difficult or dull to read.

unreal *adj* **1** existing only in the imagination or giving the impression of doing so: *an unreal quality.* **2** insincere or artificial. ▶ **unreality** *n*

unreasonable *adj* **1** unfair and excessive: *an unreasonable request.* **2** refusing to listen to reason. ▶ **unreasonably** *adv*

unrecognized *or* **-ised** *adj* not properly identified or acknowledged: *her talents went unrecognized during her lifetime.*

unremitting *adj* never slackening or stopping.

unrequited *adj* (of love) not returned.

unreserved *adj* **1** complete and without holding back any doubts: *unreserved support.* **2** open and forthcoming in manner. **3** not booked or not able to be booked: *all the seats are unreserved.* ▶ **unreservedly** (un-riz-**zerv**-id-lee) *adv*

unrest *n* **1** a rebellious state of discontent. **2** an uneasy or troubled state.

unrighteous *adj* sinful or wicked.

unrivalled *or US* **unrivaled** *adj* having no equal; matchless.

unroll *vb* **1** to open out or unwind: *I unrolled the map.* **2** (of a series of events or period of time) to happen or be revealed or remembered one after the other.

unruffled *adj* **1** calm and unperturbed. **2** smooth and still: *unruffled ponds.*

unruly *adj* **-lier, -liest** difficult to control or organize; disobedient or undisciplined. ▶ **unruliness** *n*

unsafe *adj* **1** dangerous. **2** (of a criminal conviction) based on inadequate or false evidence.

unsaturated *adj* **1** *Chem* (of an organic compound) containing a double or triple bond and therefore capable of combining with other substances. **2** (of a fat, esp. a vegetable fat) containing a high proportion of fatty acids with double bonds.

unsavoury *or US* **unsavory** *adj* objectionable or distasteful: *an unsavoury divorce.*

unscathed *adj* not harmed or injured.

unscrupulous *adj* prepared to act in a dishonest or immoral manner.

unseasonable *adj* **1** (of the weather) inappropriate for the season. **2** inappropriate or unusual for the time of year: *an unseasonable dip in the sea.*

unseat *vb* **1** to throw or displace from a seat or saddle. **2** to depose from office or position.

unseemly *adj* not according to expected standards of behaviour. ▶ **unseemliness** *n*

unseen *adj* **1** hidden or invisible: *an unseen organist was practising.* **2** mysterious or supernatural: *unseen powers.* ✧ *adv* **3** without being seen; unnoticed: *the thief entered unseen.* ✧ *n* **4** a passage which is given to students for translation without them having seen it in advance.

unsettled *adj* **1** lacking order or stability: *an unsettled time.* **2** disturbed and restless: *your child will feel unsettled and insecure.* **3** constantly changing or moving from place to place: *his wandering unsettled life.* **4** (of an argument or dispute) not resolved. **5** (of a debt or bill) not yet paid.

unshakable *or* **unshakeable** *adj* (of beliefs) utterly firm and unwavering.

unsightly *adj* unpleasant to look at; ugly. ▶ **unsightliness** *n*

unsigned *adj* (of a letter etc.) anonymous.

unsocial *adj* **1** not fond of the company of other people. **2** (of the hours of work of a job) falling outside the normal working day.

unsound *adj* **1** unhealthy or unstable: *of unsound mind.* **2** based on faulty ideas: *unsound judgment.* **3** not firm: *unsound foundations.* **4** not financially reliable: *his business plan was unsound.*

A B C D E F G H I J K L M N O P Q R S T U V W X Y Z

unspeakable *adj* **1** incapable of expression in words: *unspeakable gratitude.* **2** indescribably bad or evil: *unspeakable atrocities.* ▶ **unspeakably** *adv*

unstable *adj* **1** not firmly fixed and likely to wobble or fall: *an unstable pile of books.* **2** likely to change suddenly and create difficulties or danger: *the unstable political climate.* **3** (of a person) having abrupt changes of mood or behaviour. **4** *Chem, physics* readily decomposing.

unsteady *adj* **1** not securely fixed: *unsteady metal posts.* **2** (of a manner of walking, standing, or holding) shaky or staggering. ▶ **unsteadily** *adv* ▶ **unsteadiness** *n*

unstinting *adj* generous and gladly given: *unstinting praise.*

unstressed syllable *n Linguistics* a part of a word that is not stressed when it is pronounced.

unstructured *adj* without formal or systematic organization.

unstuck *adj* **1** freed from being stuck, glued, or fastened. **2 come unstuck** to suffer failure or disaster.

unstudied *adj* natural or spontaneous: *her unstudied elegance and grace.*

unsuccessful *adj* not achieving success.

unsuitable *adj* not right or appropriate for a particular purpose.

unsuited *adj* **1** not appropriate for a particular task or situation: *a likeable man unsuited to a military career.* **2** (of a couple) having different personalities or tastes and unlikely to form a lasting relationship: *they are totally unsuited to each other.*

unsung *adj* not appreciated or honoured: *an unsung hero.*

unswerving *adj* not turning aside; constant.

unsympathetic *adj* **1** not feeling or showing sympathy. **2** unpleasant and unlikeable. **3** (foll. by *to*) opposed or hostile to.

untapped *adj* not yet used or exploited: *untapped mineral reserves.*

untaught *adj* **1** without training or education. **2** acquired without instruction.

untenable *adj* (of a theory, idea, etc.) impossible to defend in an argument.

unthinkable *adj* **1** so shocking or unpleasant that one cannot believe it to be true. **2** unimaginable or inconceivable.

untidy *adj* **-dier, -diest** not neat; messy and disordered. ▶ **untidily** *adv* ▶ **untidiness** *n*

untie *vb* **-tying, -tied** to unfasten or free something that is tied.

until *conj* **1** up to a time that: *he lifted the wire until it was taut.* **2** before (a time or event): *until the present crisis, they weren't allowed into the country.* ✧ *prep* **3** (often preceded by *up*) in or throughout the period before: *up until then I'd never thought about having kids.* **4** before: *Baker does not get to Israel until Sunday.* ▷ **HISTORY** earlier *untill*

> ☑ **WORD TIP**
> The use of *until such time as* (as in *industrial action will continue until such time as our demands are met*) is unnecessary and should be avoided: *industrial action will continue until our demands are met.* See also at **till**.

untimely *adj* **1** occurring before the expected or normal time: *his untimely death.* **2** inappropriate to the occasion or time: *an untimely idea to raise at the United Nations.* ▶ **untimeliness** *n*

unto *prep Archaic* to. ▷ **HISTORY** from Old Norse

untold *adj* **1** incapable of description: *untold misery.* **2** incalculably great in number or quantity: *untold millions.* **3** not told.

untouchable *adj* **1** above criticism, suspicion or punishment. **2** unable to be touched. ✧ *n* **3** a member of the lowest class in India, whose touch was formerly regarded as defiling to the four main castes.

untoward *adj* **1** causing misfortune or annoyance. **2** unfavourable: *untoward reactions.* **3** out of the ordinary; out of the way: *nothing untoward had happened.*

untried *adj* **1** not yet used, done, or tested. **2** (of a prisoner) not yet put on trial.

untrue *adj* **1** incorrect or false. **2** disloyal or unfaithful.

untruth *n* a statement that is not true; lie.

untruthful *adj* **1** (of a person) given to lying. **2** (of a statement) not true. ▶ **untruthfully** *adv*

untutored *adj* **1** without formal education. **2** lacking sophistication or refinement.

unusual *adj* uncommon or extraordinary. ▶ **unusually** *adv*

unutterable *adj* incapable of being expressed in words. ▶ **unutterably** *adv*

unvarnished *adj* not elaborated upon; plain: *an unvarnished account of literary life.*

unveil *vb* **1** to ceremonially remove the cover from a new picture, statue, plaque, etc. **2** to make public a secret. **3** to remove the veil from one's own or another person's face.

unveiling *n* **1** a ceremony involving the removal of a veil covering a statue. **2** the presentation of something for the first time.

unvoiced *adj* **1** not expressed or spoken. **2** *Phonetics* voiceless.

unwarranted *adj* not justified or necessary.

unwell *adj* not healthy; ill.

unwieldy *adj* too heavy, large, or awkward to be easily handled.

unwilling *adj* **1** reluctant. **2** done or said with reluctance. ▶ **unwillingly** *adv* ▶ **unwillingness** *n*

unwind *vb* **-winding, -wound 1** to slacken, undo, or unravel: *Paul started to unwind the bandage.* **2** to relax after a busy or tense time: *we go out to unwind after work.*

unwitting *adj* **1** not intentional. **2** not knowing or conscious. ▷ HISTORY Old English *unwitende* ▶ **unwittingly** *adv*

unwonted *adj* out of the ordinary; unusual.

unworthy *adj* **1** not deserving or meriting: *a person deemed unworthy of membership.* **2** (often foll. by *of*) beneath the level considered befitting (to): *unworthy of a prime minister.* **3** lacking merit or value. ▶ **unworthiness** *n*

unwrap *vb* **-wrapping, -wrapped** to remove the wrapping from something or (of something wrapped) to have the covering removed.

unwritten *adj* **1** not printed or in writing. **2** operating only through custom: *an unwritten code of conduct.*

up *prep* **1** indicating movement to a higher position: *go up the stairs.* **2** at a higher or further level or position in or on: *a shop up the road.* ✧ *adv* **3** to an upward, higher, or erect position: *the men straightened up from their digging.* **4** indicating readiness for an activity: *up and about.* **5** indicating intensity or completion of an action: *he tore up the cheque.* **6** to the place referred to or where the speaker is: *a man came up to me.* **7 a** to a more important place: *up to the city.* **b** to a more northerly place: *pensioners who were going up to Norway.* **c** to or at university. **8** above the horizon: *the sun came up.* **9** appearing for trial: *up before the judge.* **10** having gained: *ten pounds up on the deal.* **11** higher in price: *beer has gone up again.* **12 all up with someone** *Informal* over for or hopeless for someone. **13 something's up** *Informal* something strange is happening. **14 up against** having to cope with: *look what we're up against now.* **15 up for** being a candidate or applicant for: *he's up for the job.* **16 up to a** occupied with; scheming: *she's up to no good.* **b** dependent upon: *the decision is up to you.* **c** equal to or capable of: *are you up to playing in the final?* **d** as far as: *up to his neck in mud.* **e** as many as: *up to two years' credit.* **f** comparable with: *not up to my usual standard.* **17 what's up?** *Informal* **a** what is the matter? **b** what is happening? ✧ *adj* **18** of a high or higher position. **19** out of bed: *aren't you up yet?* **20** (of a period of time) over or completed: *the examiner announced that their time was up.* **21** of or relating to a train going to a more important place: *the up platform.* ✧ *vb* **upping, upped 22** to increase or raise. **23 up and** *Informal* to do something suddenly: *he upped and left her.* ✧ *n* **24** a high point: *every couple has ups and downs.* **25 on the up and up a** *Brit* trustworthy or honest. **b** *Brit, Austral & NZ* on an upward trend: *our firm's on the up and up.* ▷ HISTORY Old English *upp*

> **☑ WORD TIP**
> The use of *up* before *until* is redundant and should be avoided: *the talks will continue until* (not *up until*) *23rd March.*

up-and-coming *adj* likely to be successful in the future; promising.

upbeat *adj* **1** *Informal* cheerful and optimistic: *the upbeat atmosphere of a thriving metropolis.* ✧ *n* **2** *Music* **a** an unaccented beat. **b** the upward gesture of a conductor's baton indicating this.

upbraid *vb* to scold or reproach. ▷ HISTORY Old English *upbrēdan*

upbringing *n* the education of a person during his or her formative years.

upcountry *adj* **1** of or from the interior of a country. ✧ *adv* **2** towards or in the interior of a country.

update *vb* **-dating, -dated** to bring up to date.

upend *vb* to turn or set or become turned or set on end.

upfront *adj* **1** open and frank. ✧ *adv, adj* **2** (of money) paid out at the beginning of a business arrangement.

upgrade *vb* **-grading, -graded 1** to promote a person or job to a higher rank. **2** to raise in value, importance, or esteem.

upheaval *n* a strong, sudden, or violent disturbance.

uphill *adj* **1** sloping or leading upwards. **2** requiring a great deal of effort: *an uphill struggle.* ✧ *adv* **3** up a slope. ✧ *n* **4** *S African* a difficulty.

uphold *vb* **-holding, -held 1** to maintain or defend against opposition. **2** to give moral support to. ▶ **upholder** *n*

upholster *vb* to fit chairs or sofas with padding, springs, and covering. ▶ **upholstered** *adj* ▶ **upholsterer** *n*

upholstery *n* the padding, springs, and covering of a chair or sofa.

upkeep *n* **1** the act or process of keeping something in good repair. **2** the cost of maintenance.

upland *adj* of or in an area of high or relatively high ground: *an upland wilderness.*

uplands *pl n* an area of high or relatively high ground: *the uplands of Nepal.*

uplift *vb* **1** to raise or lift up. **2** to raise morally or spiritually. **3** *Scot* to collect or pick up. ✧ *n* **4** the act or process of bettering moral, social, or cultural conditions. ✧ *adj* **5** (of a bra) designed to lift and support the breasts. ▶ **uplifting** *adj*

upload *v* to transfer (data or a program) from one's own computer into the memory of another computer.

up-market *adj* expensive and of superior quality.

upon *prep* **1** on. **2** up and on: *they climbed upon his lap for comfort.* ▷ HISTORY *up* + *on*

upper *adj* **1** higher or highest in physical position, wealth, rank, or status. **2 Upper** *Geol* denoting the late part of a period or formation: *Upper Cretaceous.* ✧ *n* **3** the part of a shoe above the sole. **4 on one's uppers** *Brit, Austral & NZ* very poor; penniless.

upper-case *adj* denoting capital letters as used in printed or typed matter.

upper class *n* **1** the highest social class; aristocracy. ✧ *adj* **upper-class 2** of the upper class.

upper crust *n Brit, Austral & NZ informal* the upper class.

uppercut *n* a short swinging upward punch delivered to the chin.

A B C D E F G H I J K L M N O P Q R S T U V W X Y Z

upper hand *n* the position of control: *the hardliners have gained the upper hand.*

Upper House *n* the smaller and less representative chamber of a two-chamber parliament, for example the House of Lords or a Senate.

uppermost *adj* **1** highest in position, power, or importance. ✧ *adv* **2** in or into the highest place or position.

uppish *adj Brit informal* uppity.

uppity *adj Informal* snobbish, arrogant, or presumptuous. ▷ HISTORY *up* + fanciful ending

upright *adj* **1** vertical or erect. **2** honest or just. ✧ *adv* **3** vertically or in an erect position. ✧ *n* **4** a vertical support, such as a post. **5** the state of being vertical. ▶ **uprightness** *n*

uprising *n* a revolt or rebellion.

uproar *n* **1** a commotion or disturbance characterized by loud noise and confusion. **2** angry public criticism or debates: *the decision to close the railway led to an uproar.*

uproarious *adj* **1** very funny. **2** (of laughter) loud and boisterous.

uproot *vb* **1** to pull up by or as if by the roots. **2** to displace (a person or people) from their native or usual surroundings. **3** to remove or destroy utterly: *we must uproot all remnants of feudalism.*

ups and downs *pl n* alternating periods of good and bad luck or high and low spirits.

upset *adj* **1** emotionally or physically disturbed or distressed. ✧ *vb* **-setting, -set 2** to turn or tip over. **3** to disrupt the normal state or progress of: *bad weather upset their plans.* **4** to disturb mentally or emotionally. **5** to make physically ill: *it still seems to upset my stomach.* ✧ *n* **6** an unexpected defeat or reversal, as in a contest or plans. **7** a disturbance or disorder of the emotions, mind, or body.
▶ **upsetting** *adj*

upset price *n Chiefly Scot, US, & Canad* the lowest price acceptable for something that is for sale by auction, usually a house.

upshot *n* the final result or conclusion; outcome. ▷ HISTORY *up* + *shot*

upside down *adj* **1** with the bottom where the top would normally be; inverted. **2** *Informal* confused or jumbled. ✧ *adv* **3** in an inverted fashion. **4** in a chaotic manner or into a chaotic state: *recent events have changed many people's lives upside down.* ▷ HISTORY by folk etymology, from *upsodown*

upstage *adv* **1** on, at, or to the rear of the stage. ✧ *adj* **2** at the back half of the stage. ✧ *vb* **-staging, -staged 3** to move upstage of another actor, forcing him or her to turn away from the audience. **4** *Informal* to draw attention to oneself and away from someone else.

upstairs *adv* **1** to or on an upper floor of a building. **2** *Informal* to or into a higher rank or office. ✧ *n* **3** an upper floor. ✧ *adj* **4** situated on an upper floor: *an upstairs bedroom.*

upstanding *adj* **1** of good character. **2** upright and vigorous in build.

upstart *n* a person who has risen suddenly to a position of power and behaves arrogantly.

upstream *adv, adj* in or towards the higher part of a stream; against the current.

upsurge *n* a rapid rise or swell.

upswing *n* **1** *Econ* a recovery period in the trade cycle. **2** any increase or improvement.

uptake *n* **1 quick** *or* **slow on the uptake** *Informal* quick *or* slow to understand or learn. **2** the use or consumption of something by a machine or part of the body: *the uptake of oxygen into the blood.*

upthrust *n* **1** an upward push. **2** *Geol* a violent upheaval of the earth's surface.

uptight *adj Informal* **1** nervously tense, irritable, or angry. **2** unable to express one's feelings.

up-to-date *adj* modern or fashionable: *an up-to-date kitchen.*

upturn *n* **1** an upward trend or improvement. ✧ *vb* **2** to turn or cause to turn over or upside down.

UPVC unplasticized polyvinyl chloride.

upward *adj* **1** directed or moving towards a higher place or level. ✧ *adv also* **upwards 2** from a lower to a higher place, level, or condition.
3 upward *or* **upwards of** more than (the stated figure): *a crowd estimated at upward of one hundred thousand people.*

upward mobility *n* movement from a lower to a higher economic and social status.

upwind *adv* **1** into or against the wind. **2** towards or on the side where the wind is blowing. ✧ *adj* **3** going against the wind. **4** on the windward side.

Urania *n Greek myth* the Muse of astronomy.

uranium (yew-**rain**-ee-um) *n Chem* a radioactive silvery-white metallic element of the actinide series. It is used chiefly as a source of nuclear energy by fission of the radioisotope **uranium 235**. Symbol: U. ▷ HISTORY from *Uranus,* from the fact that the element was discovered soon after the planet

Uranus *n* **1** *Greek myth* a god; the personification of the sky. **2** the seventh planet from the sun. ▷ HISTORY Greek *Ouranos* heaven

urban *adj* **1** of or living in a city or town. **2** relating to modern pop music of African-American origin, such as hip-hop. ▷ HISTORY Latin *urbs* city

urban decay *n* deterioration in an area of a town or city characterized by lack of maintenance, poor infrastucture, vandalism, etc.

urbane *adj* polite, elegant, and sophisticated in manner. ▷ HISTORY Latin *urbanus* of the town

urban heat island *n Geog* an area of heat intensification in a city caused by ultra-violet light rays becoming trapped by atmospheric pollution.

urban hierarchy *n* the ranking of cities, towns, and villages by size and provision of services.

urbanity *n* the quality of being urbane.

urbanize *or* **-ise** *vb* **-izing, -ized** *or* **-ising, -ised 1** to make a rural area more industrialized and urban. **2** *Geog* to cause people to move out of rural areas and settle in cities. ▶ **urbanization** *or* **-isation** *n*

urban morphology *n Geog, civil engineering* the shape and structure of a town or city.

urban renewal *n Civil engineering* the process of redeveloping dilapidated or no longer functional urban areas.

urban sprawl *n Civil engineering* the part of a city or town that has not been planned and spreads out untidily over a large area.

urchin *n* **1** a mischievous child. **2** See **sea urchin**. ▷ **HISTORY** Latin *ericius* hedgehog

Urdu (**oor**-doo) *n* an Indic language of the Indo-European family which is an official language of Pakistan and is also spoken in India. ▷ **HISTORY** Hindustani *(zabāni) urdū* (language of the) camp

urea (**yew**-ree-a) *n* a white soluble crystalline compound found in urine. ▷ **HISTORY** Greek *ouron* urine

ureter (yew-**reet**-er) *n* the tube that carries urine from the kidney to the bladder. ▷ **HISTORY** Greek *ourein* to urinate

urethra (yew-**reeth**-ra) *n* the tube that in most mammals carries urine from the bladder out of the body. ▷ **HISTORY** Greek *ourein* to urinate

urethritis (yew-rith-**rite**-iss) *n* inflammation of the urethra causing a discharge and painful urination. ▶ **urethritic** *adj*

urge *n* **1** a strong impulse, inner drive, or yearning. ✧ *vb* **urging, urged 2** to plead with or press someone to do something: *he urged his readers to do the same.* **3** to advocate earnestly and persistently: *I have long urged this change.* **4** to force or hasten onwards: *something very powerful urged him on.* ▷ **HISTORY** Latin *urgere*

urgent *adj* **1** requiring speedy action or attention: *an urgent inquiry.* **2** earnest and forceful: *she heard loud urgent voices in the corridor.* ▷ **HISTORY** Latin *urgere* to urge ▶ **urgency** *n* ▶ **urgently** *adv*

uric (**yew**-rik) *adj* of or derived from urine.

uric acid *n* a white odourless crystalline acid present in the blood and urine.

urinal *n* **1** a sanitary fitting, used by men for urination. **2** a room containing urinals.

urinary *adj Anat* of urine or the organs that secrete and pass urine.

urinary bladder *n* a membranous sac that can expand in which urine excreted from the kidneys is stored.

urinate *vb* **-nating, -nated** to excrete urine. ▶ **urination** *n*

urine *n* the pale yellow fluid excreted by the kidneys, containing waste products from the blood. It is stored in the bladder and discharged through the urethra. ▷ **HISTORY** Latin *urina*

urinogenital (yew-rin-oh-**jen**-it-al) *adj* same as **urogenital**.

URL uniform resource locator: a standardized address of a location on the Internet.

urn *n* **1** a vaselike container, usually with a foot and a rounded body. **2** a vase used as a container for the ashes of the dead. **3** a large metal container, with a tap, used for making and holding tea or coffee. ▷ **HISTORY** Latin *urna*

urogenital (yew-roh-**jen**-it-al) *or* **urinogenital** *adj* of the urinary and genital organs and their functions. Also: **genitourinary**

urology (yew-**rol**-a-jee) *n* the branch of medicine concerned with the urinary system and its diseases.

ursine *adj* of or like a bear. ▷ **HISTORY** Latin *ursus* a bear

us *pron (objective)* **1** refers to the speaker or writer and another person or other people: *the bond between us.* **2** refers to all people or people in general: *this table shows us the tides.* **3** *Informal* me: *give us a kiss!* **4** *Formal* same as **me:** used by monarchs. ▷ **HISTORY** Old English *ūs*

> ☑ **WORD TIP**
> See at **me.**

US *or* **U.S.** United States.

USA *or* **U.S.A.** United States of America.

usable *adj* able to be used. ▶ **usability** *n*

usage *n* **1** regular or constant use: *a move to reduce pesticide usage.* **2** the way in which a word is actually used in a language. **3** a particular meaning or use that a word can have. ▷ **HISTORY** Latin *usus* a use

use *vb* **using, used 1** to put into service or action; employ for a given purpose: *use a garden fork to mix them together.* **2** to choose or employ regularly: *what sort of toothpaste do you use?* **3** to take advantage of; exploit: *I used Jason and he used me.* **4** to consume or expend: *a manufacturing plant uses 1000 tonnes of steel a month.* ✧ *n* **5** the act or fact of using or being used: *large-scale use of pesticides.* **6** the ability or permission to use. **7** need or opportunity to use: *the Colombian government had no use for them.* **8** usefulness or advantage: *there is no use in complaining.* **9** the purpose for which something is used. **10 have no use for a** to have no need of. **b** to have a contemptuous dislike for. **11 make use of a** to employ; use. **b** to exploit (a person). ▷ **HISTORY** Latin *usus* having used ▶ **user** *n*

use-by date *n Austral, NZ & S African* the date on packaged food after which it should not be sold.

used *adj* second-hand: *it was a used car.*

used to *adj* **1** accustomed to: *I am used to being a medical guinea pig.* ✧ *vb* **2** used as an auxiliary to express habitual or accustomed actions or states taking place in the past but not continuing to be the case in the present: *he used to vanish into his studio for days.*

> ☑ **WORD TIP**
> The most common negative form of *used to* is *didn't used to* (or *didn't use to*), but in formal contexts *used not to* is preferred.

useful *adj* **1** able to be used advantageously or for several purposes. **2** *Informal* commendable or capable: *a useful hurdler.* ▶ **usefully** *adv* ▶ **usefulness** *n*

A B C D E F G H I J K L M N O P Q R S T U V W X Y Z

useless *adj* **1** having no practical use. **2** *Informal* ineffectual, weak, or stupid: *I'm useless at most things.* ▶ **uselessly** *adv* ▶ **uselessness** *n*

user-friendly *adj* easy to familiarize oneself with, understand, and use.

U-shaped valley *n* a steep-sided valley caused by glacial erosion.

usher *n* **1** an official who shows people to their seats, as in a church. **2** a person who acts as doorkeeper in a court of law. ✧ *vb* **3** to conduct or escort. **4** (foll. by *in*) to happen immediately before something or cause it to happen; herald: *the French Revolution ushered in a new age.* ▷ **HISTORY** Old French *huissier* doorkeeper

usherette *n* a woman assistant in a cinema, who shows people to their seats.

USSR Union of Soviet Socialist Republics: a former state in E Europe and N Asia, covering the area now composed of Russia, the Ukraine, Kazakhstan and a number of smaller states.

usual *adj* **1** of the most normal, frequent, or regular type: *the usual assortment of stories.* ✧ *n* **2** ordinary or commonplace events: *the dirt was nothing out of the usual.* **3 as usual** as happens normally. **4 the usual** *Informal* the habitual or usual drink. ▷ **HISTORY** Latin *usus* use ▶ **usually** *adv*

usurp (yewz-**zurp**) *vb* to seize a position or power without authority. ▷ **HISTORY** Latin *usurpare* to take into use ▶ **usurpation** *n* ▶ **usurper** *n*

usury (**yewz**-yoor-ree) *n, pl* **-ries** *Old-fashioned* **1** the practice of loaning money at an exorbitant rate of interest. **2** an unlawfully high rate of interest. ▷ **HISTORY** Latin *usura* usage ▶ **usurer** *n*

UT Utah.

ute *n Austral & NZ informal* utility truck.

utensil *n* a tool or container for practical use: *cooking utensils.* ▷ **HISTORY** Latin *utensilia* necessaries

uterine *adj* of or affecting the womb.

uterus (**yew**-ter-russ) *n, pl* **uteri** (**yew**-ter-rye) *Anat* a hollow muscular organ in the pelvic cavity of female mammals, which houses the developing fetus; womb. ▷ **HISTORY** Latin

utilitarian *adj* **1** useful rather than beautiful. **2** of utilitarianism. ✧ *n* **3** an advocate of utilitarianism.

utilitarianism *n Ethics* the doctrine that the right thing to do is that which brings about the greatest good for the greatest number.

utility *n, pl* **-ties 1** usefulness. **2** something useful. **3** a public service, such as water or electricity. ✧ *adj* **4** designed for use rather than beauty: *utility fabrics.* ▷ **HISTORY** Latin *utilitas* usefulness, from *uti* to use

utility room *n* a room with equipment for domestic work like washing and ironing.

utility truck *n Austral & NZ* a small truck with an open body and low sides.

utilize *or* **-lise** *vb* **-lizing, -lized** *or* **-lising, -lised** to make practical or worthwhile use of. ▶ **utilization** *or* **-lisation** *n*

utmost *adj* **1** of the greatest possible degree or amount: *the utmost seriousness.* **2** at the furthest limit: *the utmost point.* ✧ *n* **3** the greatest possible degree or amount: *I was doing my utmost to comply.* ▷ **HISTORY** Old English *ūtemest*

utmost good faith *n Insurance* a principle used in insurance contracts, legally obliging all parties to reveal to the others any information that might influence the others' decision to enter into the contract.

Utopia (yew-**tope**-ee-a) *n* any real or imaginary society, place, or state considered to be perfect or ideal. ▷ **HISTORY** coined by Sir Thomas More in 1516 as the title of his book that described an imaginary island representing the perfect society, literally: no place, from Greek *ou* not + *topos* a place ▶ **Utopian** *adj*

utter[1] *vb* **1** to express something in sounds or words: *she hadn't uttered a single word.* **2** *Criminal law* to put counterfeit money or forged cheques into circulation. ▷ **HISTORY** Middle Dutch *ūteren* to make known

utter[2] *adj* total or absolute: *utter amazement.* ▷ **HISTORY** Old English *ūtera* outer ▶ **utterly** *adv*

utterance *n* **1** something expressed in speech or writing. **2** the expression in words of ideas, thoughts, or feelings.

uttermost *adj, n* same as **utmost**.

U-turn *n* **1** a turn, made by a vehicle, in the shape of a U, resulting in a reversal of direction. **2** a complete change in policy.

UV ultraviolet.

UV-A *or* **UVA** *n* ultraviolet radiation with a range of 320-380 nanometres.

UV-B *or* **UVB** *n* ultraviolet radiation with a range of 280-320 nanometres.

uvula (**yew**-view-la) *n* the small fleshy part of the soft palate that hangs in the back of the throat. ▷ **HISTORY** Medieval Latin, literally: a little grape ▶ **uvular** *adj*

uxorious (ux-**or**-ee-uss) *adj* excessively fond of or dependent on one's wife. ▷ **HISTORY** Latin *uxor* wife

V v

V 1 *Chem* vanadium. 2 volt. 3 the Roman numeral for five.

v. 1 verb. 2 verse. 3 versus. 4 volume.

VA Virginia.

vacancy *n, pl* **-cies** 1 an unoccupied job or position: *he had heard of a vacancy for a librarian.* 2 an unoccupied room in a hotel or guesthouse: *the last hotel we tried had a vacancy.* 3 the state of being unoccupied.

vacant *adj* 1 (of a toilet, room, etc.) unoccupied or not being used: *I sat down in a vacant chair.* 2 (of a job or position) unfilled at the present time. 3 having or suggesting a lack of interest or understanding: *he sat there staring at me with a vacant look.* 4 (of a period of time) not set aside for any particular activity: *two slots in his programme have been left vacant.* ▷ HISTORY Latin *vacare* to be empty ▶ **vacantly** *adv*

vacate *vb* **-cating, -cated** 1 to cause (something) to be empty by leaving: *do you wish us to vacate the room?* 2 to give up (a job or position).

vacation *n* 1 *Brit & S African* a time of the year when the universities or law courts are closed. 2 *US, Canad & Austral* same as **holiday** (sense 2). ▷ HISTORY Latin *vacatio* freedom

vaccinate *vb* **-nating, -nated** to inject (someone) with a vaccine in order to protect them against a disease: *children vaccinated against meningitis.* ▶ **vaccination** *n*

vaccine *n* 1 *Med* a substance made from the germs that cause a disease which is given to people to prevent them getting the disease. 2 *Computers* a piece of software that detects and removes computer viruses from a system.

WORD HISTORY

'Vaccine' comes from Latin *vacca*, meaning 'a cow'. At a time when many people were dying of smallpox, the English surgeon Edward Jenner (1749-1823) noted that people who had contracted cowpox, a relatively mild disease caught from cattle, were immune to smallpox. He therefore advocated inoculation with the cowpox virus as a means of immunizing against smallpox.

vacillate (**vass**-ill-late) *vb* **-lating, -lated** to keep changing one's mind or opinions about something: *he vacillated between republican and monarchist sentiments.* ▷ HISTORY Latin *vacillare* to sway ▶ **vacillation** *n*

vacuity *n* an absence of intelligent thought or ideas: *I suggested to one of his advisers that his vacuity was a handicap in these debates.*

vacuole (**vack**-yew-ohl) *n Biol* a fluid-filled cavity in the cytoplasm of a cell.

vacuous *adj* 1 lacking in intelligent ideas. 2 showing no sign of intelligence or understanding: *her smile was vacuous but without malice.* ▷ HISTORY Latin *vacuus* empty

vacuum *n, pl* **vacuums** *or* **vacua** 1 a space which contains no air or other gas. 2 a vacant place or position that needs to be filled by someone or something else: *the army moved in to fill the power vacuum.* 3 short for **vacuum cleaner**. ✧ *vb* 4 to clean (something) with a vacuum cleaner. ▷ HISTORY Latin *vacuus* empty

vacuum cleaner *n* an electric machine which sucks up dust and dirt from carpets and upholstery. ▶ **vacuum cleaning** *n*

vacuum flask *n* a double-walled flask with a vacuum between the walls that keeps drinks hot or cold.

vacuum-packed *adj* (of food) packed in an airtight container in order to preserve freshness.

vacuum tube *or* **valve** *n* same as **valve** (sense 3).

vagabond *n* a person who travels from place to place and has no fixed home or job. ▷ HISTORY Latin *vagari* to roam

vagary (**vaig**-a-ree) *n, pl* **-garies** an unpredictable change in a situation or in someone's behaviour: *I was unused to the vagaries of the retailer's world.* ▷ HISTORY probably from Latin *vagari* to roam

vagina (vaj-**jine**-a) *n* the passage in most female mammals that extends from the neck of the womb to the external genitals. ▷ HISTORY Latin: sheath ▶ **vaginal** *adj*

vagrant (**vaig**-rant) *n* 1 a person who moves from place to place and has no regular home or job. ✧ *adj* 2 wandering about. ▷ HISTORY probably from Old French *waucrant* ▶ **vagrancy** *n*

vague *adj* 1 not expressed or explained clearly: *he thought of his instructions, so vague and imprecise.* 2 deliberately withholding information: *he was rather vague about the whole deal.* 3 (of a sound or shape) unable to be heard or seen clearly: *he heard some vague sound from downstairs.* 4 (of a person) not concentrating or thinking clearly: *she was mumbling to herself in a vague way.* 5 not clearly established or known: *it was a vague rumour which would fade away and be forgotten.* ▷ HISTORY Latin *vagus* wandering ▶ **vaguely** *adv* ▶ **vagueness** *n*

vain *adj* 1 excessively proud of one's appearance or achievements. 2 senseless or unsuccessful: *he made a vain attempt to lighten the atmosphere.* ✧ *n* 3 **in vain** without achieving the desired effects or results: *the old man searched in vain for his son.* ▷ HISTORY Latin *vanus* ▶ **vainly** *adv*

vainglorious *adj* boastful or proud: *his vainglorious posturing had earned him numerous powerful enemies.*

valance (**val**-lenss) *n* a short piece of decorative material hung round the edge of a bed or above a window. ▷ HISTORY perhaps after *Valence* in SE France

vale *n Literary* a valley. ▷ HISTORY Latin *vallis* valley

valediction (val-lid-**dik**-shun) *n* a farewell speech. ▷ HISTORY Latin *vale* farewell + *dicere* to say ▶ **valedictory** *adj*

valence (**vale**-enss) *n Chem* the ability of atoms and chemical groups to form compounds.

valency *or esp US & Canad* **valence** *n, pl* **-cies** *or* **-ces** *Chem* the number of atoms of hydrogen that an atom or chemical group is able to combine with in forming compounds. ▷ **HISTORY** Latin *valere* to be strong

valentine *n* **1** a card sent, often anonymously, as an expression of love on Saint Valentine's Day, February 14. **2** the person to whom one sends such a card. ▷ **HISTORY** after Saint *Valentine*

valerian *n* a plant with small white or pinkish flowers and a medicinal root. ▷ **HISTORY** Medieval Latin *valeriana (herba)* (herb) of Valerius

valet *n* **1** a male servant employed to look after another man. ✧ *vb* **-eting, -eted 2** to act as a valet (for). **3** to clean the bodywork and interior of (a car) as a professional service. ▷ **HISTORY** Old French *vaslet* page

valetudinarian (val-lit-yew-din-**air**-ee-an) *n* **1** a person who is chronically sick. **2** a person who continually worries about his or her health. ▷ **HISTORY** Latin *valetudo* state of health ▶ **valetudinarianism** *n*

Valhalla *n Norse myth* the great hall of Odin where warriors who die as heroes in battle dwell eternally. ▷ **HISTORY** Old Norse *valr* slain warriors + *höll* hall

valiant *adj* very brave: *it was a valiant attempt to rescue the struggling victim.* ▷ **HISTORY** Latin *valere* to be strong ▶ **valiantly** *adv*

valid *adj* **1** based on sound reasoning: *I think that's a very valid question.* **2** legally acceptable: *she must produce a valid driving licence.* **3** important or serious enough to say or do: *religious broadcasting has a valid purpose.* ▷ **HISTORY** Latin *validus* robust ▶ **validity** *n*

validate *vb* **-dating, -dated 1** to prove (a claim or statement) to be true or correct. **2** to give legal force or official confirmation to. ▶ **validation** *n*

valise (val-**leez**) *n Old-fashioned* a small suitcase. ▷ **HISTORY** Italian *valigia*

Valium *n Trademark* a drug used as a tranquillizer.

Valkyrie (**val**-keer-ee) *n Norse myth* any of the beautiful maidens who take the dead heroes to Valhalla. ▷ **HISTORY** Old Norse *valr* slain warriors + *kyrja* chooser

valley *n* a long stretch of land between hills, often with a river flowing through it. ▷ **HISTORY** Latin *vallis*

valour *or US* **valor** *n Literary* great bravery, esp. in battle. ▷ **HISTORY** Latin *valere* to be strong ▶ **valorous** *adj*

valuable *adj* **1** worth a large amount of money: *his house was furnished with valuable antique furniture.* **2** of great use or importance: *the investigations will provide valuable information.* ✧ *n* **3 valuables** valuable articles of personal property, such as jewellery.

valuation *n* **1** a formal assessment of how much something is worth: *they will arrange a valuation on your house.* **2** the price arrived at by the process of valuing.

value *n* **1** the desirability of something, often in terms of its usefulness or exchangeability. **2** an amount of money considered to be a fair exchange for something: *50 kilos of cocaine with a high street value.* **3** something worth the money it cost: *the set meal was value for money.* **4 values** the moral principles and beliefs of a person or group. **5** *Maths* a particular number or quantity represented by a figure or symbol. **6** *Music* short for **time value.** ✧ *vb* **-uing, -ued 7** to assess the worth or desirability of (something). **8** to hold (someone or something) in high regard. ▷ **HISTORY** Latin *valere* to be worth ▶ **valued** *adj* ▶ **valueless** *adj* ▶ **valuer** *n*

value-added tax *n Brit & S African* See **VAT**.

value judgment *n* a personal opinion about something based on an individual's beliefs and not on facts which can be checked or proved.

valve *n* **1** a part attached to a pipe or tube which controls the flow of gas or liquid. **2** *Anat* a small flap in a hollow organ, such as the heart, that controls the flow and direction of blood. **3** a closed tube through which electrons move in a vacuum. **4** *Zool* one of the hinged shells of an oyster or clam. **5** *Music* a device on some brass instruments by which the effective length of the tube may be varied. ▷ **HISTORY** Latin *valva* a folding door

valvular *adj* of or relating to valves: *valvular heart disease.*

vamp¹ *Informal* ✧ *n* **1** a sexually attractive woman who seduces men. ✧ *vb* **2** (of a woman) to seduce (a man). ▷ **HISTORY** short for *vampire*

vamp² *vb* **vamp up** to make (a story, piece of music, etc.) seem new by inventing additional parts. ▷ **HISTORY** Old French *avantpié* the front part of a shoe

vampire *n* (in European folklore) a corpse that rises nightly from its grave to drink the blood of living people. ▷ **HISTORY** from Magyar

vampire bat *n* a bat of Central and South America that feeds on the blood of birds and mammals.

van¹ *n* **1** a road vehicle with a roof and no side windows used to transport goods. **2** *Brit* a closed railway wagon used to transport luggage, goods, or mail. ▷ **HISTORY** shortened from *caravan*

van² *n* short for **vanguard**.

vanadium *n Chem* a silvery-white metallic element used to toughen steel. Symbol: V. ▷ **HISTORY** Old Norse *Vanadīs*, epithet of the goddess Freya

Van Allen belt *n* either of two belts of charged particles which surround the Earth. ▷ **HISTORY** after J. A. *Van Allen*, physicist

vandal *n* someone who deliberately causes damage to personal or public property. ▷ **HISTORY** from the name of a Germanic tribe of the 3rd and 4th centuries AD ▶ **vandalism** *n*

vandalize *or* **-ise** *vb* **-izing, -ized** *or* **-ising, -ised** to cause damage to (personal or public property) deliberately.

Van de Graaf generator *n Physics* a device for producing high electrostatic potentials (up to 15 million volts), consisting of a hollow metal sphere on which a charge is accumulated from a continuous moving belt of insulating material. ▷ **HISTORY** after R. J. *Van de Graaf*, US physicist

Van der Hum *n S African* a liqueur made from tangerines. ▷ **HISTORY** origin uncertain but possibly derived from the humorous uncertainty of the name, equivalent of *whatshisname*

vane *n* **1** one of the blades forming part of the wheel of a windmill, a screw propeller, etc. **2** short for **weather vane**. ▷ **HISTORY** Old English *fana*

vanguard *n* **1** the leading division or units of an army. **2** the most advanced group or position in scientific research, a movement, etc.: *a distinguished architect in the vanguard of his profession.* ▷ **HISTORY** Old French *avant-garde* advance guard

vanilla *n* **1** a flavouring for food such as ice cream, which comes from the pods of a tropical plant. **2** a flavouring extract prepared from the beans of this plant and used in cooking. ✧ *adj* **3** flavoured with vanilla: *vanilla essence.* **4** *Slang* ordinary or conventional: *a vanilla kind of guy.* ▷ **HISTORY** Spanish *vainilla* pod

vanish *vb* **1** to disappear suddenly: *the choppers vanished from radar screens at dawn yesterday.* **2** to cease to exist: *the old landmarks had vanished.* ▷ **HISTORY** Latin *evanescere* to evaporate

vanishing point *n* the point in the distance where parallel lines appear to meet.

vanity *n* **1** a feeling of pride about one's appearance or ability. **2** (*pl* **-ties**) something about which one is vain: *it's one of my vanities that I can guess scents.* ▷ **HISTORY** Latin *vanitas* emptiness

vanity case *n* a small bag for holding cosmetics.

vanquish *vb Literary* to defeat (someone) in a battle, contest, or argument. ▷ **HISTORY** Latin *vincere*

vantage *n* a state, position, or opportunity offering advantage. ▷ **HISTORY** Old French *avantage* advantage

vapid *adj* dull and uninteresting: *their publications were vapid and amateurish.* ▷ **HISTORY** Latin *vapidus* ▶ **vapidity** *n*

vapor *n US* same as **vapour**.

vaporize *or* **-ise** *vb* **-izing, -ized** *or* **-ising, -ised** (of a liquid or solid) to change into vapour. ▶ **vaporization** *or* **-isation** *n*

vaporous *adj* resembling or full of vapour.

vapour *or US* **vapor** *n* **1** a mass of tiny drops of water or other liquids in the air, which appear as a mist. **2** the gaseous form of a substance that is usually a liquid or a solid. **3 the vapours** *Old-fashioned* a feeling of faintness, dizziness, and depression. ▷ **HISTORY** Latin *vapor*

variable *adj* **1** likely to change at any time: *variable weather.* **2** *Maths* having a range of possible values. ✧ *n* **3** something that is subject to variation. **4** *Maths* an expression that can be assigned any of a set of values. ▷ **HISTORY** Latin *variare* to diversify ▶ **variability** *n* ▶ **variably** *adv*

variance *n* **at variance** not in agreement: *the real record is at variance with the public record.*

variant *adj* **1** differing from a standard or type: *variant spellings.* ✧ *n* **2** something that differs from a standard or type.

variation *n* **1** something presented in a slightly different form: *his books are all variations on a basic theme.* **2** a change in level, amount, or quantity: *there was a variation in the figures.* **3** *Music* the repetition of a simple tune with the addition of new harmonies or a change in rhythm: *Variations on a Hussar's Song.*

varicose *adj* of or resulting from varicose veins: *a varicose ulcer.* ▷ **HISTORY** Latin *varix* a swollen vein

varicose veins *pl n* veins, usually in the legs, which have become knotted, swollen, and sometimes painful.

varied *adj* of different types, sizes, or quantities: *these young men and women would be of varied backgrounds.*

variegated *adj* having patches or streaks of different colours: *variegated holly.* ▶ **variegation** *n*

variety *n, pl* **-ties 1** the state of being diverse or various. **2** different things of the same kind: *I'm cooking the mince with a variety of vegetables.* **3** a particular type of something in the same general category: *this variety of pear is extremely juicy.* **4** *Taxonomy* a race whose distinct characters do not justify classification as a separate species. **5** a type of entertainment consisting of short unrelated acts, such as singing, dancing, and comedy. ▷ **HISTORY** Latin *varietas*

varifocal *adj* of a lens that is gradated to permit any length of vision between near and distant.

varifocals *pl n* a pair of spectacles with varifocal lenses.

various *adj* **1** several different: *there are various possible answers to this question.* **2** of different kinds: *the causes of high blood pressure are various and complicated.* ▷ **HISTORY** Latin *varius* changing ▶ **variously** *adv*

> ☑ **WORD TIP**
> The use of *different* after *various* should be avoided: *the disease exists in various forms* (not *in various different forms*).

varlet *n Old-fashioned* **1** a menial servant. **2** a rascal. ▷ **HISTORY** Old French *vaslet*

varnish *n* **1** a liquid painted onto a surface to give it a hard glossy finish. **2** a smooth surface, coated with or as if with varnish. **3** an artificial, superficial, or deceptively pleasing manner or appearance: *those who aspired to become civil servants acquired a varnish of university education.* ✧ *vb* **4** to apply varnish to. **5** to try to make (something unpleasant) appear more attractive: *when did we start equivocating, camouflaging, varnishing the truth?* ▷ **HISTORY** Old French *vernis*

varsity *n, pl* **-ties** *Old-fashioned & informal* short for **university**.

vary *vb* **varies, varying, varied 1** to change in appearance, character, or form. **2** to be different or cause to be different: *the age of appearance of underarm and body hair varies greatly from person to person.* **3** to give variety to: *you can vary the type of* *exercise you do.* **4** to change in accordance with another variable: *an individual's calorie requirement varies with age, sex, and physical activity.* ▷ HISTORY Latin *varius* changing ▶ **varying** *adj*

vas *n, pl* **vasa** *Anat, zool* a vessel or tube that carries a fluid. ▷ HISTORY Latin: vessel

vascular *adj Biol, anat* of or relating to the vessels that conduct and circulate body fluids such as blood or sap. ▷ HISTORY Latin *vas* vessel

vas deferens *n, pl* **vasa deferentia** *Anat* either of the two ducts that convey sperm from the testicles to the penis. ▷ HISTORY Latin *vas* vessel + *deferens* carrying away

vase *n* a glass or pottery jar used as an ornament or for holding cut flowers. ▷ HISTORY Latin *vas* vessel

vasectomy *n, pl* **-mies** surgical removal of all or part of the vas deferens as a method of contraception. ▷ HISTORY VAS + Greek *tomē* a cutting

Vaseline *n Trademark* petroleum jelly, used as an ointment or a lubricant.

vassal *n* **1** (in feudal society) a man who gave military service to a lord in return for protection and often land. **2** a person, nation, or state dominated by another. ▷ HISTORY Medieval Latin *vassus* servant ▶ **vassalage** *n*

vast *adj* unusually large in size, degree, or number. ▷ HISTORY Latin *vastus* deserted ▶ **vastly** *adv* ▶ **vastness** *n*

vat *n* a large container for holding or storing liquids. ▷ HISTORY Old English *fæt*

VAT (in Britain and S Africa) value-added tax: a tax levied on the difference between the cost of materials and the selling price of a commodity or service.

Vatican *n* **1** the Pope's palace, in Rome. **2** the authority of the Pope. ▷ HISTORY Latin *Vaticanus (mons)* Vatican (hill)

vaudeville *n* variety entertainment consisting of short acts such as song-and-dance routines and comic turns. ▷ HISTORY French

vault[1] *n* **1** a secure room where money and other valuables are stored safely. **2** an underground burial chamber. **3** an arched structure that forms a roof or ceiling. **4** a cellar for storing wine. ▷ HISTORY Old French *voute, voulte*

vault[2] *vb* **1** to jump over (something) by resting one's hands on it or by using a long pole. ✧ *n* **2** the act of vaulting. ▷ HISTORY Italian *voltare* to turn ▶ **vaulter** *n*

vaulted *adj* being or having an arched roof: *an atmospheric vaulted dining room.*

vaunt *vb* **1** to describe or display (one's success or possessions) boastfully. ✧ *n* **2** a boast. ▷ HISTORY Latin *vanus* vain ▶ **vaunted** *adj*

vb verb.

VC **1** Vice Chancellor. **2** Victoria Cross. **3** *History* Vietcong: the Communist-led guerrilla force of South Vietnam.

vCJD variant Creutzfeldt-Jakob disease.

VCR video cassette recorder.

VD venereal disease.

VDU visual display unit.

veal *n* the meat from a calf, used as food. ▷ HISTORY Latin *vitulus* calf

vector *n* **1** *Maths* a variable quantity, such as force, that has magnitude and direction. **2** *Pathol* an animal, usually an insect, that carries a disease-producing microorganism from person to person. ▷ HISTORY Latin: carrier

Veda (**vay**-da) *n* any or all of the most ancient sacred writings of Hinduism. ▷ HISTORY Sanskrit: knowledge ▶ **Vedic** *adj*

veer *vb* **1** to change direction suddenly: *the plane veered off the runway and careered through the perimeter fence.* **2** to change from one position or opinion to another: *her feelings veered from tenderness to sudden spurts of genuine love.* ✧ *n* **3** a change of course or direction. ▷ HISTORY Old French *virer*

veg *n Informal* a vegetable or vegetables.

vegan (**vee**-gan) *n* a person who does not eat meat, fish, or any animal products such as cheese, butter, etc.

vegetable *n* **1** a plant, such as potato or cauliflower, with parts that are used as food. **2** *Informal* someone who is unable to move or think, as a result of brain damage. ✧ *adj* **3** of or like plants or vegetables. ▷ HISTORY Late Latin *vegetabilis* animating

vegetable marrow *n* a long green vegetable which can be cooked and eaten.

vegetable oil *n* any of a group of oils that are obtained from plants.

vegetal *adj* of or relating to plant life.

vegetarian *n* **1** a person who does not eat meat or fish. ✧ *adj* **2** excluding meat and fish: *a vegetarian diet.* ▶ **vegetarianism** *n*

vegetate *vb* **-tating, -tated** to live in a dull and boring way with no mental stimulation.

vegetation *n* plant life as a whole.

vegetative *adj* **1** of or relating to plant life or plant growth. **2** (of reproduction) characterized by asexual processes.

vehement *adj* **1** expressing strong feelings or opinions. **2** (of actions or gestures) performed with great force or energy. ▷ HISTORY Latin *vehemens* ardent ▶ **vehemence** *n* ▶ **vehemently** *adv*

vehicle *n* **1** a machine such as a bus or car for transporting people or goods. **2** something used to achieve a particular purpose or as a means of expression: *the newspaper was a vehicle for explaining government policies.* **3** *Pharmacol* an inactive substance mixed with the active ingredient in a medicine. **4** a liquid, such as oil, in which a pigment is mixed before it is applied to a surface. ▷ HISTORY Latin *vehere* to carry ▶ **vehicular** *adj*

veil *n* **1** a piece of thin cloth, usually as part of a hat or headdress, used to cover a woman's face. **2** something that conceals the truth: *a veil of secrecy.* **3** **take the veil** to become a nun. ✧ *vb* **4** to cover or conceal with or as if with a veil. ▷ HISTORY Latin *velum* a covering

veiled *adj* (of a comment or remark) presented in a disguised form: *it was a thinly veiled criticism.*

vein *n* **1** any of the tubes that carry blood to the heart. **2** a thin line in a leaf or in an insect's wing. **3** a clearly defined layer of ore or mineral in rock. **4** an irregular streak of colour in marble, wood, or cheese. **5** a distinctive trait or quality in speech or writing: *critics have exposed a strong vein of moralism in the poem.* **6** a temporary mood: *we're in a very humorous vein tonight.* ▷ **HISTORY** Latin *vena* ▶ **veined** *adj*

Velcro *n Trademark* a type of fastening consisting of one piece of fabric with tiny hooked threads and another with a coarse surface that sticks to it.

veld *or* **veldt** *n* the open country of South Africa including landscapes which are grassy, bushy, or thinly forested. ▷ **HISTORY** Afrikaans: field

veldskoen *n* same as **velskoen.**

vellum *n* **1** a fine calf, kid, or lamb parchment. **2** a strong good-quality paper that resembles vellum. ▷ **HISTORY** Old French *velin* of a calf

velocipede (vel-**loss**-sip-peed) *n* an early form of bicycle. ▷ **HISTORY** Latin *velox* swift + *pes* foot

velocity (vel-**loss**-it-ee) *n, pl* **-ties** the speed at which something is moving in a particular direction. ▷ **HISTORY** Latin *velox* swift

velour *or* **velours** (vel-**loor**) *n* a silk or cotton cloth similar to velvet. ▷ **HISTORY** Latin *villus* shaggy hair

velskoen *or* **veldskoen** (**fell**-skoon) *n S African* a sturdy ankle boot. ▷ **HISTORY** Afrikaans

velvet *n* **1** a fabric with a thick close soft pile on one side. **2** the furry covering of the newly formed antlers of a deer. ✧ *adj* **3** made of velvet. **4** soft or smooth like velvet. **5 an iron fist** *or* **hand in a velvet glove** determination concealed by a gentle manner. ▷ **HISTORY** Old French, from Latin *villus* shaggy hair ▶ **velvety** *adj*

velveteen *n* a cotton fabric that resembles velvet.

vena cava (vee-na **kay**-va) *n, pl* **venae cavae** (vee-nee **kay**-vee) *Anat* either one of the two large veins that convey blood to the heart.

venal (**vee**-nal) *adj* **1** willing to accept bribes in return for acting dishonestly: *venal politicians.* **2** associated with corruption or bribery: *venal greed.* ▷ **HISTORY** Latin *venum* sale ▶ **venality** *n*

vend *vb* to sell (goods). ▷ **HISTORY** Latin *vendere* to sell

Venda *n* **1** (*pl* **-da** *or* **-das**) a member of a Negroid people of southern Africa, living chiefly in NE South Africa. **2** the language of this people.

vendetta *n* **1** a long-lasting quarrel between people or organizations in which they attempt to harm each other: *it's an inexplicable vendetta against the firm and its directors.* **2** a private feud between families in which members of one family kill members of the other family in revenge for earlier murders. ▷ **HISTORY** Italian

vending machine *n* a machine that automatically dispenses food, drinks, or cigarettes when money is inserted.

vendor *n* **1** a person who sells goods such as newspapers or hamburgers from a stall or cart. **2** *Chiefly law* a person who sells property.

veneer *n* **1** a thin layer of wood or plastic used to cover the surface of something made of cheaper material. **2** a deceptive but convincing appearance: *nobody penetrated his veneer of modest charm.* ▷ **HISTORY** Old French *fournir* to furnish

venerable *adj* **1** (of a person) entitled to respect because of great age or wisdom. **2** (of an object) impressive because it is old or important historically. **3** *RC Church* a title given to a dead person who is going to be declared a saint. **4** *Church of England* a title given to an archdeacon. ▷ **HISTORY** Latin *venerari* to venerate

venerate *vb* **-ating, -ated** to hold (someone) in deep respect. ▷ **HISTORY** Latin *venerari* ▶ **venerator** *n*

veneration *n* a feeling of awe or great respect: *George Gershwin is worthy of the veneration accorded his classical counterparts.*

venereal (vin-**ear**-ee-al) *adj* **1** transmitted by sexual intercourse: *venereal infections.* **2** of the genitals: *venereal warts.* ▷ **HISTORY** Latin *venus* sexual love

venereal disease *n* a disease, such as syphilis, transmitted by sexual intercourse.

Venetian *adj* **1** of Venice, a port in NE Italy. ✧ *n* **2** a person from Venice.

Venetian blind *n* a window blind made of thin horizontal slats.

vengeance *n* **1** the act of killing, injuring, or harming someone for revenge. **2 with a vengeance** to a much greater extent or with much greater force than expected: *my career was beginning to take off with a vengeance.* ▷ **HISTORY** Old French, from Latin *vindicare* to punish

vengeful *adj* wanting revenge.

venial (**veen**-ee-al) *adj* easily excused or forgiven: *venial sins.* ▷ **HISTORY** Latin *venia* forgiveness

venison *n* the flesh of a deer, used as food. ▷ **HISTORY** Old French *venaison*

Venn diagram *n Maths* a drawing which uses circles to show the relationships between different sets. ▷ **HISTORY** after John *Venn,* logician

venom *n* **1** a feeling of great bitterness or anger towards someone. **2** the poison that certain snakes and scorpions inject when they bite or sting. ▷ **HISTORY** Latin *venenum* poison, love potion ▶ **venomous** *adj* ▶ **venomously** *adv*

venous (**vee**-nuss) *adj* of or relating to veins. ▷ **HISTORY** Latin *vena* vein

vent[1] *n* **1** a small opening in something through which fresh air can enter and fumes can be released. **2** the shaft of a volcano through which lava and gases erupt. **3** the anal opening of a bird or other small animal. **4 give vent to** to release (an emotion) in an outburst: *she gave vent to her misery and loneliness.* ✧ *vb* **5** to release or express freely: *consumers vented their anger on the group by boycotting its products.* **6** to make vents in. ▷ **HISTORY** Old French *esventer* to blow out

vent[2] *n* a vertical slit in the lower hem of a jacket. ▷ HISTORY Latin *findere* to cleave

ventilate *vb* **-lating, -lated 1** to let fresh air into (a room or building). **2** to discuss (ideas or feelings) openly: *ultra-rightists ventilated anti-Semitic sentiments.* ▷ HISTORY Latin *ventilare* to fan

ventilation *n* **1** the act or process of ventilating. **2** a system in a building that provides a supply of fresh air. **3** *Biol* the process by which oxygen is added to the blood through the lungs.

ventilator *n* an opening or device, such as a fan, used to let fresh air into a room or building.

ventral *adj* relating to the front part of the body. ▷ HISTORY Latin *venter* abdomen ▶ **ventrally** *adv*

ventricle *n Anat* **1** a chamber of the heart that pumps blood to the arteries. **2** any one of the four main cavities of the brain. ▷ HISTORY Latin *ventriculus* ▶ **ventricular** *adj*

ventriloquism *n* the ability to speak without moving the lips so that the words appear to come from another person or from another part of the room. ▷ HISTORY Latin *venter* belly + *loqui* to speak ▶ **ventriloquist** *n*

venture *n* **1** a project or activity that is risky or of uncertain outcome. **2** a business operation in which there is the risk of loss as well as the opportunity for profit. ✧ *vb* **-turing, -tured 3** to do something that involves risk or danger: *I thought it wise to venture into foreign trade.* **4** to dare to express (an opinion). **5** to go to an unknown or dangerous place. **6** to dare (to do something): *you have asked me so often to come to your place that I ventured to drop in.* ▷ HISTORY variant of *adventure* ▶ **venturer** *n*

venturesome *adj* willing to take risks.

venue *n* a place where an organized gathering, such as a concert or a sporting event, is held. ▷ HISTORY Latin *venire* to come

Venus *n* **1** the Roman goddess of love. **2** the planet second nearest to the sun.

Venus's flytrap *or* **Venus flytrap** *n* a plant that traps and digests insects between hinged leaves.

veracious *adj* habitually truthful. ▷ HISTORY Latin *verus* true

veracity *n* **1** habitual truthfulness. **2** accuracy.

verandah *or* **veranda** *n* **1** an open porch attached to a house. **2** *NZ* a continuous overhead canopy outside shops that gives shelter to pedestrians. ▷ HISTORY Portuguese *varanda* railing

verb *n* a word that is used to indicate the occurrence or performance of an action or the existence of a state, for example *run, make,* or *do.* ▷ HISTORY Latin *verbum* word

verbal *adj* **1** of or relating to words: *verbal skills.* **2** spoken rather than written: *a verbal agreement.* **3** *Grammar* of or relating to a verb. ▶ **verbally** *adv*

verbalize *or* **-ise** *vb* **-izing, -ized** *or* **-ising, -ised** to express (an idea or feeling) in words.

verbal noun *n Grammar* a noun derived from a verb, for example *smoking* in the sentence *smoking is bad for you.*

verbal process *n Functional grammar* the process of saying, stating or exclaiming, etc., as specified by a verb group. Compare **material process, mental process, relational process.**

verbatim (verb-**bait**-im) *adv, adj* using exactly the same words: *a verbatim account of events.* ▷ HISTORY Medieval Latin: word by word

verbena *n* a plant with red, white, or purple sweet-smelling flowers. ▷ HISTORY Latin: sacred bough used by the priest in religious acts

verbiage *n* the excessive use of words. ▷ HISTORY Latin *verbum* word

verbose (verb-**bohss**) *adj* using more words than is necessary. ▶ **verbosity** *n*

verdant *adj Literary* covered with green vegetation. ▷ HISTORY from Latin *viridis* green

verdict *n* **1** the decision made by a jury about the guilt or innocence of a defendant. **2** an opinion formed after examining the facts. ▷ HISTORY Latin *vere dictum* truly spoken

verdigris (**ver**-dig-reess) *n* a green or bluish coating which forms on copper, brass, or bronze that has been exposed to damp. ▷ HISTORY Old French *vert de Grice* green of Greece

verdure *n Literary* flourishing green vegetation. ▷ HISTORY from Latin *viridis* green

verge[1] *n* **1** a grass border along a road. **2 on the verge of** having almost reached (a point or condition). **3** an edge or rim. ✧ *vb* **verging, verged 4 verge on** to be near to: *she was verging on hysteria.* ▷ HISTORY Latin *virga* rod

verge[2] *vb* **verging, verged** to move in a specified direction: *verging towards the Irish Sea.* ▷ HISTORY Latin *vergere*

verger *n Chiefly Church of England* **1** a church official who acts as caretaker. **2** an official who carries the rod of office before a bishop or dean in ceremonies and processions. ▷ HISTORY Latin *virga* rod, twig

verify *vb* **-fies, -fying, -fied 1** to check the truth of (something) by investigation. **2** to prove (something) to be true. ▷ HISTORY Latin *verus* true + *facere* to make ▶ **verifiable** *adj* ▶ **verification** *n*

verily *adv Literary* truly: *for verily, this was their destiny.* ▷ HISTORY from *very*

verisimilitude *n* the appearance of truth or reality. ▷ HISTORY Latin *verus* true + *similitudo* similitude

veritable *adj* rightly called; real: *a veritable mine of information.* ▶ **veritably** *adv*

verity *n, pl* **-ties** a true statement or principle. ▷ HISTORY Latin *verus* true

vermicelli (ver-me-**chell**-ee) *n* **1** very fine strands of pasta, used in soups. **2** tiny chocolate strands used as a topping for cakes or ice cream. ▷ HISTORY Italian: little worms

vermiform *adj* shaped like a worm.

vermiform appendix *n Anat* same as **appendix.**

vermilion *adj* **1** orange-red. ✧ *n* **2** mercuric sulphide, used as an orange-red pigment; cinnabar. ▷ HISTORY Late Latin *vermiculus* insect from which red dye was prepared

vermin *pl n* **1** small animals collectively, such as insects and rodents, that spread disease and damage crops. **2** unpleasant people. ▷ **HISTORY** Latin *vermis* worm ▶ **verminous** *adj*

vermouth (**ver**-muth) *n* a wine flavoured with herbs. ▷ **HISTORY** German *Wermut* wormwood

vernacular (ver-**nak**-yew-lar) *n* **1** the commonly spoken language or dialect of a particular people or place. ✧ *adj* **2** in or using the vernacular. ▷ **HISTORY** Latin *vernaculus* belonging to a household slave

vernal *adj* of or occurring in spring. ▷ **HISTORY** Latin *ver* spring ▶ **vernally** *adv*

vernier (**ver**-nee-er) *n* a small movable scale in certain measuring instruments such as theodolites, used to obtain a fractional reading of one of the divisions on the main scale. ▷ **HISTORY** after Paul *Vernier,* mathematician

veronica *n* a plant with small blue, pink, or white flowers. ▷ **HISTORY** perhaps from the name *Veronica*

verruca (ver-**roo**-ka) *n Pathol* a wart, usually on the sole of the foot. ▷ **HISTORY** Latin: wart

versatile *adj* having many different skills or uses. ▷ **HISTORY** Latin *versare* to turn ▶ **versatility** *n*

verse *n* **1** a division of a poem or song. **2** poetry as distinct from prose. **3** one of the short sections into which chapters of the books of the Bible are divided. **4** a poem. ▷ **HISTORY** Latin *versus* furrow, literally: a turning (of the plough)

versify *vb* **-fies, -fying, -fied 1** to put (something) into verse. **2** to write in verse. ▷ **HISTORY** Latin *versus* verse + *facere* to make ▶ **versification** *n* ▶ **versifier** *n*

version *n* **1** a form of something, such as a piece of writing, with some differences from other forms. **2** an account of something from a certain point of view: *so far there's been no official version of the incident.* **3** an adaptation, for example of a book or play into a film. ▷ **HISTORY** Latin *vertere* to turn

verso *n, pl* **-sos 1** the left-hand page of a book. **2** the back of a sheet of printed paper. ▷ **HISTORY** New Latin *verso (folio)* (the leaf) having been turned

versus *prep* **1** (in a sporting competition or lawsuit) against. **2** in opposition to or in contrast with: *man versus machine.* ▷ **HISTORY** Latin: turned (in the direction of), opposite

vertebra (**ver**-tib-bra) *n, pl* **-brae** (-bree) one of the bony segments of the spinal column. ▷ **HISTORY** Latin ▶ **vertebral** *adj*

vertebrate *n* **1** an animal with a backbone, such as a fish, amphibian, reptile, bird, or mammal. ✧ *adj* **2** having a backbone.

vertex (**ver**-tex) *n, pl* **-tices** (-tiss-seez) **1** the highest point. **2** *Maths* **a** the point on a geometric figure where the sides form an angle. **b** the highest point of a triangle. ▷ **HISTORY** Latin: top

vertical *adj* **1** at right angles to the horizon: *the vertical cliff.* **2** straight up and down: *a vertical cut.* **3** *Econ* of or relating to associated or consecutive, though not identical, stages of industrial activity: *the purchase of a chain of travel agents by a leading tour operator will increase vertical integration in the holiday industry.* ✧ *n* **4** a vertical line or direction. ▷ **HISTORY** from Latin *vertex* top, pole of the sky ▶ **vertically** *adv*

vertical exaggeration *n Geog* distortion that occurs on cross section diagrams when the units on the vertical axis showing height are bigger than those on the horizontal axis showing distance, making the highs and lows look disproportionately great.

vertically opposite angles *pl n Geom* the pair of equal angles between a pair of intersecting lines.

vertiginous *adj* producing dizziness.

vertigo *n Pathol* a sensation of dizziness felt because one's balance is disturbed, sometimes experienced when looking down from a high place. ▷ **HISTORY** Latin: a whirling round

vervain *n* a plant with long slender spikes of purple, blue, or white flowers. ▷ **HISTORY** Latin *verbena* sacred bough

verve *n* great enthusiasm or liveliness. ▷ **HISTORY** Latin *verba* words, chatter

very *adv* **1** used to add emphasis to adjectives and adverbs that are able to be graded: *I'm very happy; he'll be home very soon.* ✧ *adj* **2** used with nouns to give emphasis or exaggerated intensity: *the very end of his visit.* ▷ **HISTORY** Old French *verai* true

> **☑ WORD TIP**
>
> In strict usage adverbs of degree such as *very, too, quite, really,* and *extremely* are used only to qualify adjectives: *he is very happy; she is too sad.* By this rule, these words should not be used to qualify past participles that follow the verb *to be,* since they would then be technically qualifying verbs. With the exception of certain participles, such as *tired* or *disappointed,* that have come to be regarded as adjectives, all other past participles are qualified by adverbs such as *much, greatly, seriously,* or *excessively: he has been much* (not *very*) *inconvenienced; she has been excessively* (not *too*) *criticized.*

very high frequency *n* a radio-frequency band lying between 30 and 300 megahertz.

vesicle *n Biol* **1** a small sac or cavity, esp. one filled with fluid. **2** a blister. ▷ **HISTORY** Latin *vesica* bladder, sac

vespers *n* an evening service in some Christian churches. ▷ **HISTORY** Latin *vesper* the evening star

vessel *n* **1** a ship or large boat. **2** an object used as a container for liquid. **3** *Biol* a tubular structure in animals and plants that carries body fluids, such as blood and sap. ▷ **HISTORY** Latin *vas*

vest *n* **1** *Brit* an undergarment covering the top half of the body. **2** *US, Canad, & Austral* a waistcoat. ✧ *vb* **3 vest in** to settle (power or property) on: *by the power vested in me, I pronounce you man and wife.* **4 vest with** to bestow on: *the sponsorship has vested these matches with a new interest.* ▷ **HISTORY** Latin *vestis* clothing

A B C D E F G H I J K L M N O P Q R S T U V W X Y Z

vestal *adj* **1** chaste or pure. ✧ *n* **2** a chaste woman. ▷ **HISTORY** Latin *Vestalis* virgin priestess of the goddess Vesta

vestal virgin *n* (in ancient Rome) one of the virgin priestesses dedicated to the goddess Vesta and to maintaining the sacred fire in her temple.

vested *adj Property law* having an existing right to the immediate or future possession of property.

vested interest *n* **1** a strong personal interest someone has in a matter because he or she might benefit from it. **2** *Property law* an existing right to the immediate or future possession of property.

vestibule *n* a small entrance hall. ▷ **HISTORY** Latin *vestibulum*

vestige (**vest**-ij) *n* **1** a small amount or trace. **2** *Biol* an organ or part that is a small nonfunctional remnant of a functional organ in an ancestor. ▷ **HISTORY** Latin *vestigium* track

vestigial (vest-**ij**-ee-al) *adj* remaining after a larger or more important thing has gone: *a strong seam of vestigial belief.*

vestments *pl n* **1** ceremonial clothes worn by the clergy at religious services. **2** robes that show authority or rank. ▷ **HISTORY** Latin *vestire* to clothe

vestry *n, pl* **-tries** a room in a church used as an office by the priest or minister. ▷ **HISTORY** probably Old French *vestiarie* wardrobe

vet[1] *n* **1** short for **veterinary surgeon.** ✧ *vb* **vetting, vetted 2** to make a careful check of (a person or document) for suitability: *guests have to be vetted and vouched for.*

vet[2] *n US, Canad, Austral & NZ* short for **veteran.**

vetch *n* **1** a climbing plant with blue or purple flowers. **2** the beanlike fruit of the vetch, used as fodder. ▷ **HISTORY** Latin *vicia*

veteran *n* **1** a person who has given long service in some capacity. **2** a soldier who has seen a lot of active service. **3** *US, Canad & Austral* a person who has served in the military forces. ✧ *adj* **4** long-serving: *the veteran American politician.* ▷ **HISTORY** Latin *vetus* old

veteran car *n Brit & Austral* a car built before 1919, esp. before 1905.

veterinarian *n US, Canad & Austral* a veterinary surgeon.

veterinary *adj* relating to veterinary science.

> **WORD HISTORY**
>
> In Latin *veterinae* means 'animals used for pulling carts and ploughs'.

veterinary medicine *or* **science** *n* the branch of medicine concerned with the treatment of animals.

veterinary surgeon *n Brit* a person qualified to practise veterinary medicine.

veto (**vee**-toe) *n, pl* **-toes 1** the power to prevent legislation or action proposed by others: *no single state has a veto.* **2** the exercise of this power. ✧ *vb* **-toing, -toed 3** to refuse consent to (a proposal, such as a government bill). **4** to prohibit or forbid: *the Sports Minister vetoed the appointments.* ▷ **HISTORY** Latin: I forbid

vex *vb* to cause (someone) to feel annoyance or irritation. ▷ **HISTORY** Latin *vexare* to jolt (in carrying) ▶ **vexing** *adj* ▶ **vexation** *n*

vexatious *adj* vexing.

VHF *or* **vhf** *Radio* very high frequency.

VHS Video Home System: a video cassette recorder system using half-inch magnetic tape.

VI Vancouver Island.

via *prep* **1** by way of; through: *he fled to London via Crete.* **2** by means of: *working from home and keeping in touch with office life via a video link-up.* ▷ **HISTORY** Latin

viable *adj* **1** able to be put into practice: *the party has failed to propose a viable alternative.* **2** (of seeds or eggs) capable of growth. **3** (of a fetus) sufficiently developed to survive outside the uterus. ▷ **HISTORY** Latin *vita* life ▶ **viability** *n*

viaduct *n* a bridge for carrying a road or railway across a valley. ▷ **HISTORY** Latin *via* way + *ducere* to bring

Viagra *n Trademark* a drug that allows increased blood flow into the penis, used to treat impotence in men.

vial *n* same as **phial.** ▷ **HISTORY** Greek *phialē* a bowl

viands *pl n Old-fashioned* food. ▷ **HISTORY** Latin *vivenda* things to be lived on

viaticum *n, pl* **-ca** *or* **-cums** *Christianity* Holy Communion given to a person dying or in danger of death. ▷ **HISTORY** Latin *viaticus* belonging to a journey

vibes *pl n Informal* **1** the emotional reactions between people. **2** the atmosphere of a place. **3** short for **vibraphone.**

vibrant (**vibe**-rant) *adj* **1** full of energy and enthusiasm. **2** (of a voice) rich and full of emotion. **3** (of a colour) strong and bright. ▷ **HISTORY** Latin *vibrare* to agitate ▶ **vibrancy** *n*

vibraphone *n* a musical instrument with metal bars that resonate electronically when hit.

vibrate *vb* **-brating, -brated 1** to move backwards and forwards rapidly. **2** to have or produce a quivering or echoing sound. **3** *Physics* to undergo or cause to undergo vibration. ▷ **HISTORY** Latin *vibrare* ▶ **vibratory** *adj*

vibration *n* **1** a vibrating. **2** *Physics* **a** a periodic motion about an equilibrium position, such as in the production of sound. **b** a single cycle of such a motion.

vibrato *n, pl* **-tos** *Music* a slight rapid fluctuation in the pitch of a note.

vibrator *n* a device for producing a vibratory motion, used for massage or as a sex aid.

viburnum (vie-**burn**-um) *n* a subtropical shrub with white flowers and berry-like fruits. ▷ **HISTORY** Latin

Vic. Victoria (Australian state).

vicar *n* **1** *Church of England* a priest who is in charge of a parish. **2** *RC Church* a church officer acting as deputy to a bishop. ▷ **HISTORY** Latin *vicarius* a deputy ▶ **vicarial** *adj*

vicarage *n* the house where a vicar lives.

vicar apostolic *n RC Church* a clergyman with authority in missionary countries.

vicar general *n, pl* **vicars general** an official appointed to assist the bishop in his administrative duties.

vicarious (vik-**air**-ee-uss) *adj* **1** felt indirectly by imagining what another person experiences: *vicarious satisfaction.* **2** undergone or done as the substitute for another: *vicarious adventures.* **3** delegated: *vicarious power.* ▷ **HISTORY** Latin *vicarius* substituted ▶ **vicariously** *adv*

vicarious liability *n Law* liability of one person for the crimes or torts of another, as in the case of an employer being liable for the actions of an employee.

Vicar of Christ *n RC Church* the Pope as Christ's representative on earth.

vice[1] *n* **1** an immoral or evil habit or action: *greed is only one of their vices.* **2** a habit regarded as a weakness in someone's character: *one of his few vices is cigars.* **3** criminal activities involving sex, drugs, or gambling. ▷ **HISTORY** Latin *vitium* a defect

vice[2] *or US* **vise** *n* a tool with a pair of jaws for holding an object while work is done on it. ▷ **HISTORY** Latin *vitis* vine, plant with spiralling tendrils

vice[3] *adj* serving in the place of; being next in importance to: *the vice chairman.* ▷ **HISTORY** Latin *vicis* interchange

vice admiral *n* a senior commissioned officer in certain navies.

vice chancellor *n* the chief executive or administrator at a number of universities.

vicegerent *n* a person appointed to exercise all or some of the authority of another. ▷ **HISTORY** VICE[3] + Latin *gerere* to manage

vice president *n* an officer ranking immediately below a president and serving as his or her deputy. ▶ **vice-presidency** *n*

viceregal *adj* **1** of a viceroy. **2** *Chiefly Austral & NZ* of a governor or governor general.

viceroy *n* a governor of a colony or country who represents the monarch. ▷ **HISTORY** VICE[3] + French *roi* king

vice squad *n* a police division responsible for the enforcement of gaming and prostitution laws.

vice versa *adv* the other way round: *there were attacks on northerners by southerners and vice versa.* ▷ **HISTORY** Latin: relations being reversed

Vichy water (**vee**-shee) *n* a natural mineral water from Vichy in France which is supposed to be good for the health.

vicinity (viss-**in**-it-ee) *n* the area immediately surrounding a place. ▷ **HISTORY** Latin *vicinus* neighbouring

vicious *adj* **1** cruel or violent: *vicious attacks.* **2** forceful or ferocious: *she gave the chair a vicious jerk.* **3** intended to cause hurt or distress: *vicious letters.* **4** (of an animal) fierce or hostile. ▷ **HISTORY** Latin *vitiosus* full of faults ▶ **viciously** *adv* ▶ **viciousness** *n*

vicious circle *n* a situation in which an attempt to resolve one problem creates new problems that recreate the original one.

vicissitudes (viss-**iss**-it-yewds) *pl n* changes in circumstance or fortune. ▷ **HISTORY** Latin *vicis* change

victim *n* **1** a person or thing that suffers harm or death. **2** a person who is tricked or swindled. **3** a living person or animal sacrificed in a religious rite. ▷ **HISTORY** Latin *victima*

victimize *or* **-ise** *vb* **-izing, -ized** *or* **-ising, -ised** to punish or discriminate against (someone) selectively or unfairly. ▶ **victimization** *or* **-isation** *n*

victimless crime *n Law* a type of crime in which there is no obvious victim or in which the supposed victim willingly participates.

victor *n* **1** a person or nation that has defeated an enemy in war. **2** the winner of a contest or struggle. ▷ **HISTORY** Latin, from *vincere* to conquer

victoria *n* **1** a large sweet red-and-yellow plum. **2** a light four-wheeled horse-drawn carriage with a folding hood. ▷ **HISTORY** after Queen *Victoria*

Victoria Cross *n* the highest decoration for bravery in battle awarded to the British and Commonwealth armed forces.

Victorian *adj* **1** of or in the reign of Queen Victoria of Great Britain and Ireland (1837–1901). **2** characterized by prudery or hypocrisy. **3** of or relating to Victoria (the state or any of the cities). ✧ *n* **4** a person who lived during the reign of Queen Victoria. **5** an inhabitant of Victoria (the state or any of the cities).

victorious *adj* **1** having defeated an enemy or opponent: *the victorious allies.* **2** of or characterized by victory: *a victorious smile.*

victory *n, pl* **-ries 1** the winning of a war or battle. **2** success attained in a contest or struggle. ▷ **HISTORY** Latin *victoria*

victual *vb* **-ualling, -ualled** *or US* **-ualing, -ualed** *Old-fashioned* to supply with or obtain victuals. ▷ **HISTORY** Latin *victus* sustenance ▶ **victualler** *or US* **-ualer** *n*

victuals (**vit**-tals) *pl n Old-fashioned* food and drink.

vide (**vie**-dee) see: used to direct a reader to a specified place in a text or in another book. ▷ **HISTORY** Latin

videlicet (vid-**deal**-ee-set) *adv* namely: used to specify items. ▷ **HISTORY** Latin

video *n, pl* **-os 1** the recording and showing of films and events using a television set, video tapes, and a video recorder. **2** short for **video cassette.** **3** short for **video cassette recorder.** ✧ *vb* **videoing, videoed 4** to record (a television programme or an event) on video. ✧ *adj* **5** relating to or used in producing televised images. ▷ **HISTORY** Latin *videre* to see

video cassette *n* a cassette containing video tape.

video cassette recorder *n* a tape recorder for recording and playing back television programmes and films.

a b c d e f g h i j k l m n o p q r s t u v w x y z

A B C D E F G H I J K L M N O P Q R S T U V W X Y Z

video conferencing *n Electronics* a facility that enables participants in distant locations to take part in a conference by means of electronic sound and video communication.

video frequency *n* the frequency of a signal conveying the image and synchronizing pulses in a television broadcasting system.

video game *n* a game that can be played by using an electronic control to move symbols on the screen of a visual display unit.

video nasty *n* a film, usually specially made for video, that is explicitly horrific and pornographic.

videophone *n* a communications device by which people can see and speak to each other.

video tape *n* **1** magnetic tape used mainly for recording the video-frequency signals of a television programme or film. ✧ *vb* **video-tape, -taping, -taped 2** to record (a film or programme) on video tape.

video tape recorder *n* a tape recorder for visual signals, using magnetic tape on open spools: used in television broadcasting.

Videotex *n Trademark* same as **Viewdata**.

videotext *n* a means of providing a written or graphical representation of computerized information on a television screen.

vie *vb* **vying, vied** to compete (with someone): *the sisters vied with each other to care for her.* ▷ **HISTORY** probably Old French *envier* to challenge

Vietnamese *adj* **1** of Vietnam. ✧ *n* **2** (*pl* **-ese**) a person from Vietnam. **3** the language of Vietnam.

view *n* **1** opinion, judgment, or belief: *in my view that doesn't really work.* **2** an understanding of or outlook on something: *a specific view of human history.* **3** everything that can be seen from a particular place or in a particular direction: *there was a beautiful view from the window.* **4** vision or sight, esp. range of vision: *as they turned into the drive, the house came into view.* **5** a picture of a scene. **6** the act of seeing or observing. **7 in view of** taking into consideration. **8 on view** exhibited to the public. **9 take a dim** *or* **poor view of** to regard (something) unfavourably. **10 with a view to** with the intention of. ✧ *vb* **11** to consider in a specified manner: *they viewed the visit with apprehension.* **12** to examine or inspect (a house or flat) carefully with a view to buying it. **13** to look at. **14** to watch (television). ▷ **HISTORY** Latin *videre* to see

Viewdata *n Trademark* a videotext service linking users to a computer by telephone, enabling shopping, etc. to be done from home.

viewer *n* **1** a person who views something, esp. television. **2** a hand-held device for looking at photographic slides.

viewfinder *n* a device on a camera that lets the user see what will be included in the photograph.

vigil (**vij**-ill) *n* **1** a night-time period of staying awake to look after a sick person, pray, etc. **2** *RC Church, Church of England* the eve of certain major festivals. ▷ **HISTORY** Latin: alert

vigilance *n* careful attention.

vigilant *adj* on the watch for trouble or danger. ▷ **HISTORY** Latin *vigilare* to be watchful

vigilante (vij-ill-**ant**-ee) *n* a person who takes it upon himself or herself to enforce the law. ▷ **HISTORY** Spanish, from Latin *vigilare* to keep watch

vignette (vin-**yet**) *n* **1** a short description of the typical features of something. **2** a small decorative illustration in a book. **3** a photograph or drawing with edges that are shaded off. ▷ **HISTORY** French, literally: little vine (often used to embellish a text)

vigorous *adj* **1** having physical or mental energy. **2** displaying or performed with vigour: *vigorous exercise.* ▶ **vigorously** *adv*

vigour *or US* **vigor** *n* **1** physical or mental energy. **2** forcefulness: *the vigour of his invective astonished MPs.* **3** strong healthy growth. ▷ **HISTORY** Latin *vigor*

Viking *n* any of the Scandinavians who raided by sea most of N and W Europe from the 8th to the 11th centuries. ▷ **HISTORY** Old Norse *vīkingr*

vile *adj* **1** morally wicked: *a vile act.* **2** disgusting: *the vile smell.* **3** unpleasant or bad: *a vile day at work.* ▷ **HISTORY** Latin *vilis* cheap ▶ **vilely** *adv* ▶ **vileness** *n*

vilify (**vill**-if-fie) *vb* **-fies, -fying, -fied** to speak very badly of (someone). ▷ **HISTORY** Latin *vilis* worthless + *facere* to make ▶ **vilification** *n*

villa *n* **1** a large house with gardens. **2** *Brit* a house rented to holiday-makers. ▷ **HISTORY** Latin: a farmhouse

village *n* **1** a small group of houses in a country area. **2** the inhabitants of such a community. ▷ **HISTORY** Latin *villa* a farmhouse ▶ **villager** *n*

villain *n* **1** a wicked or evil person. **2** the main wicked character in a novel or play. ▷ **HISTORY** Late Latin *villanus* worker on a country estate

villainous *adj* of or like a villain.

villainy *n, pl* **-lainies** evil or vicious behaviour.

villein (**vill**-an) *n* (in medieval Europe) a peasant who was directly subject to his lord, to whom he paid dues and services in return for his land. ▷ **HISTORY** see VILLAIN ▶ **villeinage** *n*

villus *n, pl* **villi** *Zool, anat* **1** any of the numerous finger-like projections of the mucous membrane lining the small intestine of many vertebrates. **2** any of the finger-like projections formed in the placenta of mammals. ▷ **HISTORY** from Latin: shaggy hair

vim *n Informal* vigour and energy. ▷ **HISTORY** Latin *vis* force

vinaigrette *n* salad dressing made from oil and vinegar with seasonings. ▷ **HISTORY** French

vindicate *vb* **-cating, -cated 1** to clear (someone) of guilt or suspicion. **2** to provide justification for. ▷ **HISTORY** Latin *vindex* claimant ▶ **vindication** *n*

vindictive *adj* **1** maliciously seeking revenge. **2** characterized by spite or ill will. ▷ **HISTORY** Latin *vindicare* to avenge ▶ **vindictively** *adv* ▶ **vindictiveness** *n*

vine *n* **1** a plant, such as the grapevine, with long flexible stems that climb by clinging to a support. **2** the stem of such a plant. ▷ **HISTORY** Latin *vinea* vineyard ▶ **viny** *adj*

vinegar *n* **1** a sour-tasting liquid made by fermentation of beer, wine, or cider, used for salad dressing or for pickling. **2** bad temper or spitefulness. ▷ **HISTORY** French *vin* wine + *aigre* sour ▶ **vinegary** *adj*

vineyard (**vinn**-yard) *n* an area of land where grapes are grown. ▷ **HISTORY** Old English *wingeard*

viniculture *n* the process or business of growing grapes and making wine. ▷ **HISTORY** Latin *vinum* wine + CULTURE ▶ **viniculturist** *n*

vino (**vee**-noh) *n, pl* **-nos** *Informal* wine. ▷ **HISTORY** Spanish or Italian: wine

vintage *n* **1** the wine obtained from a particular harvest of grapes. **2** the harvest from which such a wine is obtained. **3** a time of origin: *an open-necked shirt of uncertain vintage.* ✧ *adj* **4** (of wine) of an outstandingly good year. **5** representative of the best and most typical: *a vintage Saint Laurent dress.* ▷ **HISTORY** Latin *vindemia*

vintage car *n Brit & Austral* a car built between 1919 and 1930.

vintner *n* a wine merchant. ▷ **HISTORY** Latin *vinetum* vineyard

vinyl (**vine**-ill) *n* **1** any of various strong plastics made by the polymerization of vinyl compounds, such as PVC. **2** conventional records made of vinyl as opposed to compact discs. ✧ *adj* **3** *Chem* of or containing the monovalent group of atoms CH_2CH–: *vinyl chloride.* **4** of or made of vinyl: *vinyl tiles.* ▷ **HISTORY** Latin *vinum* wine

viol (**vie**-oll) *n* a stringed musical instrument that preceded the violin. ▷ **HISTORY** Old Provençal *viola*

viola[1] (vee-**oh**-la) *n* a bowed stringed instrument of the violin family, slightly larger and lower in pitch than the violin. ▷ **HISTORY** Italian

viola[2] (**vie**-ol-la) *n* a variety of pansy. ▷ **HISTORY** Latin: violet

violate *vb* **-lating, -lated 1** to break (a law or agreement): *he violated export laws.* **2** to disturb rudely or improperly: *these men who were violating her privacy.* **3** to treat (a sacred place) disrespectfully. **4** to rape. ▷ **HISTORY** Latin *violare* to do violence to ▶ **violation** *n* ▶ **violator** *n*

violence *n* **1** the use of physical force, usually intended to cause injury or destruction. **2** great force or strength in action, feeling, or expression. ▷ **HISTORY** Latin *violentus* violent

violent *adj* **1** using or involving physical force with the intention of causing injury or destruction: *violent clashes with government supporters.* **2** very intense: *I took a violent dislike to him.* **3** sudden and forceful: *a violent explosion.* ▶ **violently** *adv*

violet *n* **1** a plant with bluish-purple flowers. ✧ *adj* **2** bluish-purple. ▷ **HISTORY** Latin *viola*

violin *n* a musical instrument, the highest member of the violin family, with four strings played with a bow. ▷ **HISTORY** Italian *violino* a little viola

violinist *n* a person who plays the violin.

violoncello (vie-oll-on-**chell**-oh) *n, pl* **-los** same as **cello**. ▷ **HISTORY** Italian

VIP very important person.

viper *n* a type of poisonous snake. ▷ **HISTORY** Latin *vipera*

virago (vir-**rah**-go) *n, pl* **-goes** *or* **-gos** an aggressive woman. ▷ **HISTORY** Latin: a manlike maiden

viral (**vie**-ral) *adj* of or caused by a virus.

virgin *n* **1** a person, esp. a woman, who has never had sexual intercourse. **2** a person who is inexperienced in a specified field: *a ski virgin.* ✧ *adj* **3** not having had sexual intercourse. **4** fresh and unused: *a scrap of virgin paper.* **5** not yet cultivated, explored, or exploited by people: *virgin territory.* ▷ **HISTORY** Latin *virgo*

Virgin *n* **1 the Virgin** same as **Virgin Mary**. **2** a statue or picture of the Virgin Mary.

virginal[1] *adj* **1** like a virgin. **2** extremely pure or fresh.

virginal[2] *n* an early keyboard instrument like a small harpsichord. ▷ **HISTORY** probably Latin *virginalis* virginal, perhaps because it was played largely by young ladies

Virgin Birth *n Christianity* the doctrine that Jesus Christ was conceived solely by the direct intervention of the Holy Spirit so that Mary remained a virgin.

Virginia creeper *n* a climbing plant with leaves that turn red in autumn.

virginity *n* the condition or fact of being a virgin.

Virgin Mary *n* **the Virgin Mary** *Christianity* Mary, the mother of Christ.

Virgo *n Astrol* the sixth sign of the zodiac; the Virgin. ▷ **HISTORY** Latin

virile *adj* **1** having the traditional male characteristics of physical strength and a high sex drive. **2** forceful and energetic: *a virile Highland fling.* ▷ **HISTORY** Latin *virilis* manly ▶ **virility** *n*

virology *n* the branch of medicine concerned with the study of viruses. ▶ **virological** *adj*

virtual *adj* **1** having the effect but not the appearance or form of: *the investigation has now come to a virtual standstill.* **2** *Computers* designed so as to extend the potential of a finite system beyond its immediate limits: *virtual memory.* **3** of or relating to virtual reality. ▷ **HISTORY** Latin *virtus* virtue

virtually *adv* almost or nearly: *he is virtually a prisoner in his own palace.*

virtual reality *n* a computer-generated environment that seems real to the user.

virtue *n* **1** moral goodness. **2** a positive moral quality: *the virtue of humility.* **3** an advantage or benefit: *the added virtue of being harmless.* **4** chastity, esp. in women. **5 by virtue of** by reason of; because of: *they escaped execution by virtue of their high rank.* ▷ **HISTORY** Latin *virtus* manliness

virtuoso *n, pl* **-si** *or* **-sos 1** a person with exceptional musical skill. **2** a person with exceptional skill in any area. ✧ *adj* **3** showing exceptional skill or brilliance. ▷ **HISTORY** Italian: skilled ▶ **virtuosity** *n*

virtuous *adj* **1** morally good. **2** (of a woman) chaste. ▶ **virtuously** *adv*

virulent (**vir**-yew-lent) *adj* **1** extremely bitter or hostile. **2 a** (of a microorganism) very infectious.

a b c d e f g h i j k l m n o p q r s t u v w x y z

A B C D E F G H I J K L M N O P Q R S T U V W X Y Z

b (of a disease) having a violent effect. **3** extremely poisonous or harmful: *the most virulent poison known to man.* ▷ HISTORY Latin *virulentus* full of poison ▶ **virulence** *n*

virus *n* **1** a microorganism that is smaller than a bacterium and can cause disease in humans, animals, or plants. **2** *Informal* a disease caused by a virus. **3** *Computers* an unsanctioned and self-replicating program which, when activated, corrupts a computer's data and disables its operating system. ▷ HISTORY Latin: slime, poisonous liquid

visa *n* an official stamp in a passport permitting its holder to travel into or through the country of the government issuing it. ▷ HISTORY Latin: things seen

visage (**viz**-zij) *n Chiefly literary* **1** face. **2** appearance. ▷ HISTORY Latin *visus* appearance

vis-à-vis (**veez**-ah-**vee**) *prep* in relation to. ▷ HISTORY French: face-to-face

viscera (**viss**-er-a) *pl n Anat* the large internal organs of the body collectively. ▷ HISTORY Latin: entrails

visceral *adj* **1** of or affecting the viscera. **2** instinctive rather than rational: *visceral hatred.*

viscid (**viss**-id) *adj* sticky. ▷ HISTORY Latin *viscum* mistletoe, birdlime

viscose *n* **1** a sticky solution obtained by dissolving cellulose. **2** rayon made from this material. ▷ HISTORY Latin *viscum* birdlime

viscosity *n, pl* **-ties 1** the state of being viscous. **2** *Physics* the extent to which a fluid resists a tendency to flow.

viscount (**vie**-count) *n* (in the British Isles) a nobleman ranking below an earl and above a baron. ▷ HISTORY Old French *visconte* ▶ **viscountcy** *n*

viscountess (**vie**-count-iss) *n* **1** a woman holding the rank of viscount. **2** the wife or widow of a viscount.

viscous *adj* (of liquids) thick and sticky.

vise *n US* same as **vice**[2].

Vishnu *n* a Hindu god, the Preserver.

visibility *n* **1** the range or clarity of vision. **2** the condition of being visible.

visible *adj* **1** able to be seen. **2** able to be perceived by the mind: *a visible and flagrant act of aggression.* ▷ HISTORY Latin *visibilis* ▶ **visibly** *adv*

vision *n* **1** the ability to see. **2** a vivid mental image produced by the imagination: *I kept having visions of him being tortured.* **3** a hallucination caused by divine inspiration, madness, or drugs: *visions of God.* **4** great perception of future developments. **5** the image on a television screen. **6** a person or thing of extraordinary beauty. ▷ HISTORY Latin *visio* sight, from *videre* to see

visionary *adj* **1** showing foresight: *a visionary statesman.* **2** idealistic but impractical. **3** given to having visions. **4** of or like visions. ✧ *n, pl* **-aries 5** a visionary person.

visit *vb* **-iting, -ited 1** to go or come to see (a person or place). **2** to stay with (someone) as a guest. **3** *Old-fashioned* (of a disease or disaster) to afflict. **4 visit on** *or* **upon** to inflict (punishment) on. **5 visit with** *US informal* to chat with (someone). ✧ *n* **6** the act or an instance of visiting. **7** a professional or official call. **8** a stay as a guest. ▷ HISTORY Latin *visitare* to go to see

visitant *n* **1** a ghost or apparition. **2** a migratory bird temporarily resting in a particular region.

visitation *n* **1** an official visit or inspection. **2** a punishment or reward from heaven. **3** an appearance of a supernatural being.

Visitation *n* **a** the visit made by the Virgin Mary to her cousin Elizabeth (Luke 1: 39–56). **b** the Church festival commemorating this, held on July 2.

visitor *n* a person who visits a person or place.

visitor's passport *n* a British passport, valid for one year, that grants access to some countries, usually for a restricted period.

visor (**vize**-or) *n* **1** a transparent flap on a helmet that can be pulled down to protect the face. **2** a small movable screen attached above the windscreen in a vehicle, used as protection against the glare of the sun. **3** a peak on a cap. ▷ HISTORY Old French *vis* face

vista *n* **1** an extensive view. **2** a wide range of possibilities or future events. ▷ HISTORY Italian

visual *adj* **1** done by or used in seeing. **2** capable of being seen. ▷ HISTORY Latin *visus* sight ▶ **visually** *adv*

visual aids *pl n* objects to be looked at that help the viewer to understand or remember something.

visual display unit *n Computers* a device with a screen for displaying data held in a computer.

visualize *or* **-ise** *vb* **-izing, -ized** *or* **-ising, -ised** to form a mental image of (something not at that moment visible). ▶ **visualization** *or* **-isation** *n*

visual literacy *n* the ability to interpret and manipulate visual forms of communication.

visual text *n* a combination of written material and images, signs, or symbols.

vital *adj* **1** essential or highly important: *marriage isn't such a vital part of his life.* **2** energetic or lively: *vital youthful manhood.* **3** necessary to maintain life: *the vital organs.* ✧ *n* **4 vitals** the bodily organs, such as the brain and heart, that are necessary to maintain life. ▷ HISTORY Latin *vita* life ▶ **vitally** *adv*

vitality *n* physical or mental energy.

vital statistics *pl n* **1** population statistics, such as the numbers of births, marriages, and deaths. **2** *Informal* the measurements of a woman's bust, waist, and hips.

vitamin *n* one of a group of substances that occur naturally in certain foods and are essential for normal health and growth. ▷ HISTORY from Latin *vita* life + AMINE

vitiate (**vish**-ee-ate) *vb* **-ating, -ated 1** to spoil or weaken the effectiveness of (something). **2** to destroy the legal effect of (a contract). ▷ HISTORY Latin *vitiare* to injure ▶ **vitiation** *n*

viticulture *n* the cultivation of grapevines. ▷ HISTORY Latin *vitis* vine

vitreous *adj* **1** of or like glass. **2** of or relating to the vitreous humour. ▷ HISTORY Latin *vitrum* glass

vitreous humour *or* **body** *n* a transparent gelatinous substance that fills the eyeball between the lens and the retina.

vitrify *vb* **-fies, -fying, -fied** to change into glass or a glassy substance. ▶ **vitrification** *n*

vitriol *n* **1** language expressing bitterness and hatred. **2** sulphuric acid. ▷ **HISTORY** Latin *vitrum* glass, referring to the glossy appearance of the sulphates

vitriolic *adj* (of language) severely bitter or harsh.

vituperative (vite-**tyew**-pra-tiv) *adj* bitterly abusive. ▷ **HISTORY** Latin *vituperare* to blame ▶ **vituperation** *n*

viva[1] *interj* long live (a specified person or thing). ▷ **HISTORY** Italian, literally: may (he) live!

viva[2] *Brit* ✧ *n* **1** an examination in the form of an interview. ✧ *vb* **vivaing, vivaed 2** to examine (a candidate) in a spoken interview. ▷ **HISTORY** from VIVA VOCE

vivace (viv-**vah**-chee) *adj Music* to be performed in a lively manner. ▷ **HISTORY** Italian

vivacious *adj* full of energy and enthusiasm. ▷ **HISTORY** Latin *vivax* lively

vivacity *n* the quality of being vivacious.

vivarium *n, pl* **-iums** *or* **-ia** a place where live animals are kept under natural conditions. ▷ **HISTORY** Latin *vivus* alive

viva voce (**vive**-a **voh**-chee) *adv, adj* **1** by word of mouth. ✧ *n* **2** same as **viva**[2] (sense 1). ▷ **HISTORY** Medieval Latin, literally: with living voice

vivid *adj* **1** very bright: *a vivid blue sky*. **2** very clear and detailed: *vivid memories*. **3** easily forming lifelike images: *a vivid imagination*. ▷ **HISTORY** Latin *vividus* animated ▶ **vividly** *adv* ▶ **vividness** *n*

vivify *vb* **-fies, -fying, -fied 1** to bring to life. **2** to make more vivid or striking. ▷ **HISTORY** Latin *vivus* alive + *facere* to make

viviparous (viv-**vip**-a-russ) *adj* giving birth to living offspring, as most mammals do. ▷ **HISTORY** Latin *vivus* alive + *parere* to bring forth

vivisection *n* the performing of experiments on living animals, involving cutting into or dissecting the body. ▷ **HISTORY** Latin *vivus* living + *sectio* a cutting ▶ **vivisectionist** *n*

vixen *n* **1** a female fox. **2** *Brit, Austral & NZ informal* a spiteful woman. ▷ **HISTORY** related to Old English *fyxe*, feminine of *fox*

vizier (viz-**zeer**) *n* a high official in certain Muslim countries. ▷ **HISTORY** Turkish *vezīr*

vizor *n* same as **visor**.

VLF *or* **vlf** *Radio* very low frequency.

V neck *n* **a** a neck on a garment that comes down to a point, like the letter V. **b** a sweater with a neck like this. ▶ **V-neck** *or* **V-necked** *adj*

vocab *n* short for **vocabulary**.

vocable *n Linguistics* a word regarded simply as a sequence of letters or spoken sounds. ▷ **HISTORY** Latin *vocare* to call

vocabulary *n, pl* **-laries 1** all the words that a person knows. **2** all the words contained in a language. **3** the specialist terms used in a given subject. **4** a list of words in another language with their translations. **5** a range of symbols or techniques as used in any of the arts or crafts. ▷ **HISTORY** Latin *vocabulum* vocable

vocal *adj* **1** of or relating to the voice: *vocal pitch*. **2** expressing one's opinions clearly and openly: *a vocal minority with racist views*. ✧ *n* **3 vocals** the singing part of a piece of jazz or pop music. ▷ **HISTORY** Latin *vox* voice ▶ **vocally** *adv*

vocal cords *pl n* either of two pairs of membranous folds in the larynx, of which the lower pair can be made to vibrate and produce sound by forcing air from the lungs over them.

vocalist *n* a singer with a pop group.

vocalize *or* **-ise** *vb* **-izing, -ized** *or* **-ising, -ised 1** to express with or use the voice. **2** to make vocal or articulate: *vocalize your discontent*. **3** *Phonetics* to articulate (a speech sound) with voice.

vocation *n* **1** a specified profession or trade. **2 a** a special urge to a particular calling or career, esp. a religious one. **b** such a calling or career. ▷ **HISTORY** Latin *vocare* to call

vocational *adj* directed towards a particular profession or trade: *vocational training*.

vocative *n Grammar* a grammatical case used in some languages when addressing a person or thing. ▷ **HISTORY** Latin *vocare* to call

vociferate *vb* **-ating, -ated** to exclaim or cry out about (something) noisily. ▷ **HISTORY** Latin *vox* voice + *ferre* to bear ▶ **vociferation** *n*

vociferous *adj* loud and forceful: *a vociferous minority*. ▶ **vociferously** *adv*

vodka *n* a clear alcoholic spirit originating in Russia, made from potatoes or grain. ▷ **HISTORY** Russian

voetsak *or* **voetsek** (**foot**-sak) *interj S African offensive* an expression of dismissal or rejection. ▷ **HISTORY** Afrikaans, from Dutch *voort se ek* forward, I say, commonly applied to animals

vogue *n* **1** the popular style at a given time. **2 in vogue** fashionable. ✧ *adj* **3** fashionable: *a vogue word*. ▷ **HISTORY** French ▶ **voguish** *adj*

voice *n* **1** the sound made by the vibration of the vocal cords, esp. when modified by the tongue and mouth. **2** a distinctive tone of the speech sounds characteristic of a particular person: *he can recognize her voice*. **3** the ability to speak or sing: *he had at last found his voice*. **4** the condition or quality of a person's voice: *her voice was kind*. **5** the musical sound of a singing voice: *what I have is a good voice and a great love of lyrics*. **6** the expression of feeling or opinion: *dissenting voices*. **7** a right to express an opinion. **8** *Grammar* a category of the verb that expresses whether it is active or passive. **9** *Phonetics* the sound characterizing the articulation of several speech sounds, that is produced when the vocal cords are vibrated by the breath. **10 with one voice** unanimously. ✧ *vb* **voicing, voiced 11** to express verbally: *anyone with an objection has a chance to voice it*. **12** to articulate (a speech sound) with voice. ▷ **HISTORY** Latin *vox*

voiced *adj Phonetics* articulated with accompanying vibration of the vocal cords, for example 'b' in English.

a b c d e f g h i j k l m n o p q r s t u v w x y z

voiceless *adj* **1** without a voice. **2** *Phonetics* articulated without accompanying vibration of the vocal cords, for example 'p' in English.

voice mail *n* an electronic system for the transfer and storage of telephone messages, which can then be dealt with by the user at his or her convenience.

voice-over *n Films, television* the voice of an unseen commentator heard during a film.

void *n* **1** a feeling or condition of loneliness or deprivation. **2** an empty space or area. ✧ *adj* **3** having no official value or authority, because the terms have been broken or have not been fulfilled: *the race was declared void.* **4** *Old-fashioned or literary* empty: *behold, the tomb is void!* **5 void of** devoid of or without: *the fact of being punished becomes void of all moral significance.* ✧ *vb* **6** to make ineffective or invalid. **7** to empty. **8** to discharge the contents of (the bowels or bladder). ▷ HISTORY Latin *vacare* to be empty

voile (**voyl**) *n* a light semitransparent dress fabric. ▷ HISTORY French: veil

vol. volume.

volatile (**voll**-a-tile) *adj* **1** (of circumstances) liable to sudden change. **2** (of people) liable to sudden changes of mood and behaviour. **3** (of a substance) changing quickly from a solid or liquid form to a vapour. ▷ HISTORY Latin *volare* to fly ▸ **volatility** *n*

volatilize *or* **-lise** *vb* **-lizing, -lized** *or* **-lising, -lised** to change from a solid or liquid to a vapour.

vol-au-vent (**voll**-oh-von) *n* a very light puff pastry case with a savoury filling. ▷ HISTORY French, literally: flight in the wind

volcanic *adj* **1** of or relating to volcanoes. **2** displaying sudden violence or anger.

volcanic ash *n Geol* dust produced by a volcano when it erupts.

volcanic plug *n Geol* solidified lava in the vent of a volcano.

volcano *n, pl* **-noes** *or* **-nos 1** an opening in the earth's crust from which molten lava, ashes, dust, and gases are ejected from below the earth's surface. **2** a mountain formed from volcanic material ejected from a vent. ▷ HISTORY Italian, from Latin *Volcanus* Vulcan, Roman god of fire

vole *n* a small rodent with a stocky body and a short tail. ▷ HISTORY short for *volemouse,* from Old Norse *vollr* field + *mus* mouse

volition *n* **1** the ability to decide things for oneself. **2 of one's own volition** through one's own choice. ▷ HISTORY Latin *volo* I will

volley *n* **1** the simultaneous firing of several weapons. **2** the bullets fired. **3** a burst of questions or critical comments. **4** *Sport* a stroke or kick at a moving ball before it hits the ground. ✧ *vb* **5** to fire (weapons) in a volley. **6** *Sport* to hit or kick (a moving ball) before it hits the ground. ▷ HISTORY French *volée* a flight

volleyball *n* a game in which two teams hit a large ball backwards and forwards over a high net with their hands.

volt *n* the SI unit of electric potential; the potential difference between two points on a conductor carrying a current of 1 ampere, when the power dissipated between these points is 1 watt. ▷ HISTORY after Count Alessandro *Volta,* physicist

volta *n Prosody* (in a sonnet) the point where there is a change of mood or argument. ▷ HISTORY Italian *volta* a turn

voltage *n* an electromotive force or potential difference expressed in volts.

voltaic *adj* same as **galvanic** (sense 1).

volte-face (volt-**fass**) *n, pl* **volte-face** a reversal of opinion. ▷ HISTORY Italian *volta* turn + *faccia* face

voltmeter *n* an instrument for measuring voltage.

voluble *adj* talking easily and at length. ▷ HISTORY Latin *volubilis* turning readily ▸ **volubility** *n* ▸ **volubly** *adv*

volume *n* **1** the magnitude of the three-dimensional space enclosed within or occupied by something. **2** an amount or total: *the volume of trade between the two countries.* **3** loudness of sound. **4** the control on a radio etc., for adjusting the loudness of sound. **5** a book: *a slim volume.* **6** one of several books that make up a series. **7** a set of issues of a magazine over a specified period. ▷ HISTORY Latin *volumen* a roll

volumetric *adj* of or using measurement by volume: *a simple volumetric measurement.*

voluminous *adj* **1** (of clothes) large and roomy. **2** (of writings) extensive and detailed.

voluntary *adj* **1** done or undertaken by free choice: *voluntary repatriation.* **2** done or maintained without payment: *voluntary work.* **3** (of muscles) having their action controlled by the will. ✧ *n, pl* **-taries 4** *Music* a composition, usually for organ, played at the beginning or end of a church service. ▷ HISTORY Latin *voluntarius* ▸ **voluntarily** *adv*

volunteer *n* **1** a person who offers voluntarily to do something. **2** a person who freely undertakes military service. ✧ *vb* **3** to offer (oneself or one's services) by choice and without being forced. **4** to enlist voluntarily for military service. **5** to give (information) willingly. **6** to offer the services of (another person).

voluptuary *n, pl* **-aries** a person devoted to luxury and sensual pleasures. ▷ HISTORY Latin *voluptas* pleasure

voluptuous *adj* **1** (of a woman) sexually alluring because of the fullness of her figure. **2** pleasing to the senses: *voluptuous yellow peaches.* ▸ **voluptuously** *adv* ▸ **voluptuousness** *n*

volute *n* a spiral or twisting shape or object, such as a carved spiral scroll on an Ionic capital. ▷ HISTORY Latin *volvere* to roll up

vomit *vb* **-iting, -ited 1** to eject (the contents of the stomach) through the mouth. **2** to eject or be ejected forcefully. ✧ *n* **3** the partly digested food and drink ejected in vomiting. ▷ HISTORY Latin *vomitare* to vomit repeatedly

voodoo *n* **1** a religion involving ancestor worship and witchcraft, practised by Black people in the West Indies, esp. in Haiti. ✧ *adj* **2** of or relating to voodoo. ▷ HISTORY from West African

voorkamer (foor-kahm-er) *n S African* the front room of a house. ▷ **HISTORY** Afrikaans

voracious *adj* **1** eating or craving great quantities of food. **2** very eager or insatiable in some activity: *a voracious collector.* ▷ **HISTORY** Latin *vorare* to devour ▶ **voraciously** *adv* ▶ **voracity** *n*

vortex (vor-tex) *n, pl* **-tices** (-tiss-seez) **1** a whirling mass or motion, such as a whirlpool or whirlwind. **2** a situation which draws people into it against their will. ▷ **HISTORY** Latin: a whirlpool

votary *n, pl* **-ries 1** *RC Church, Eastern Churches* a person who has dedicated himself or herself to religion by taking vows. **2** a person devoted to a cause. ▷ **HISTORY** Latin *votum* a vow

vote *n* **1** a choice made by a participant in a shared decision, esp. in electing a candidate. **2** the right to vote. **3** the total number of votes cast. **4** the opinion of a group of people as determined by voting: *the draft should be put to the vote.* **5** a body of votes or voters collectively: *the youth vote.* ✧ *vb* **voting, voted 6** to make a choice by vote. **7** to authorize or allow by voting. **8** to declare oneself as being (something or in favour of something) by voting: *I've always voted Labour.* **9** *Informal* to declare by common opinion. ▷ **HISTORY** Latin *votum* a solemn promise

vote down *vb* to decide against or defeat in a vote: *a proposed British resolution was voted down.*

voter *n* a person who can or does vote.

votive *adj* done or given to fulfil a vow. ▷ **HISTORY** Latin *votivus* promised by a vow

vouch *vb* **vouch for a** to give personal assurance about. **b** to give supporting evidence for or be proof of. ▷ **HISTORY** Latin *vocare* to call

voucher *n* **1** a ticket or card used instead of money to buy specified goods: *a gift voucher.* **2** a document recording a financial transaction. ▷ **HISTORY** Old French *vo(u)cher* to summon

vouchsafe *vb* **-safing, -safed 1** *Old-fashioned* to give or grant: *she has powers vouchsafed to few.* **2** to offer assurances about; guarantee: *he absolutely vouchsafed your integrity.* ▷ **HISTORY** *vouch + safe*

vow *n* **1** a solemn and binding promise. **2 take vows** to enter a religious order and commit oneself to its rule of life by the vows of poverty, chastity, and obedience. ✧ *vb* **3** to promise or decide solemnly. ▷ **HISTORY** Latin *votum*

vowel *n* **a** a voiced speech sound made with the mouth open and the stream of breath unobstructed by the tongue, teeth, or lips, for example *a* or *e*. **b** a letter representing this. ▷ **HISTORY** Latin *vocalis (littera),* from *vox* voice

vox pop *n Brit* interviews with members of the public on a radio or television programme.

vox populi *n* public opinion. ▷ **HISTORY** Latin: the voice of the people

voyage *n* **1** a long journey by sea or in space. ✧ *vb* **-aging, -aged 2** to go on a voyage. ▷ **HISTORY** Latin *viaticum* provision for travelling ▶ **voyager** *n*

voyageur (voy-ahzh-**ur**) *n* **1** formerly a French or Métis canoeman who transported furs from trading posts in the North American interior. **2** (in Canada) a woodsman, guide, trapper, boatman, or explorer, esp. in the North. ▷ **HISTORY** French: voyager

voyeur *n* a person who obtains sexual pleasure from watching people undressing or having sexual intercourse. ▷ **HISTORY** French, literally: one who sees ▶ **voyeurism** *n* ▶ **voyeuristic** *adj*

VR virtual reality.

vrou (**froh**) *n S African* an Afrikaner woman, esp. a married woman. ▷ **HISTORY** Afrikaans

vs versus.

VSA (in New Zealand) Voluntary Service Abroad.

V-sign *n* **1** (in Britain and Australia) an offensive gesture made by sticking up the index and middle fingers with the palm of the hand inwards. **2** a similar gesture with the palm outwards meaning victory or peace.

VSO (in Britain) Voluntary Service Overseas.

VSOP very special (*or* superior) old pale: used of brandy or port.

VT Vermont.

VTOL vertical takeoff and landing.

VTR video tape recorder.

Vulcan *n* the Roman god of fire.

vulcanite *n* a hard black rubber produced by vulcanizing natural rubber with sulphur.

vulcanize *or* **-ise** *vb* **-izing, -ized** *or* **-ising, -ised** to treat (rubber) with sulphur under heat and pressure to improve elasticity and strength. ▷ **HISTORY** after *Vulcan,* Roman god of fire

vulgar *adj* **1** showing lack of good taste, decency, or refinement. **2** denoting a form of a language spoken by the ordinary people, rather than the literary form. ▷ **HISTORY** Latin *vulgus* the common people ▶ **vulgarly** *adv*

vulgar fraction *n* same as **simple fraction**.

vulgarian *n* a rich vulgar person.

vulgarism *n* a coarse or obscene word or phrase.

vulgarity *n, pl* **-ties 1** the condition of being vulgar. **2** a vulgar action or phrase.

vulgarize *or* **-ise** *vb* **-izing, -ized** *or* **-ising, -ised 1** to make vulgar. **2** to make (something little known or difficult to understand) popular.

Vulgar Latin *n* any of the dialects of Latin spoken in the Roman Empire other than classical Latin.

Vulgate *n* the fourth-century Latin version of the Bible.

vulnerable *adj* **1** able to be physically or emotionally hurt. **2** easily influenced or tempted. **3** *Mil* exposed to attack. **4** financially weak and likely to fail. **5** *Bridge* (of a side that has won one game towards rubber) subject to increased bonuses or penalties. ▷ **HISTORY** Latin *vulnus* a wound ▶ **vulnerability** *n*

vulpine *adj* **1** of or like a fox. **2** clever and cunning. ▷ **HISTORY** Latin *vulpes* fox

vulture *n* **1** a very large bird of prey that feeds on flesh of dead animals. **2** a person who profits from the misfortune and weakness of others. ▷ **HISTORY** Latin *vultur*

vulva *n* the external genitals of human females. ▷ **HISTORY** Latin: covering, womb, matrix

vying *vb* the present participle of **vie**.

a b c d e f g h i j k l m n o p q r s t u v w x y z

A B C D E F G H I J K L M N O P Q R S T U V W X Y Z

W w

w *Cricket* **a** wicket. **b** wide.

W **1** *Chem* tungsten. ▷ **HISTORY** German *Wolfram* **2** watt. **3** West(ern).

WA **1** Washington (state). **2** Western Australia.

wacky *adj* **wackier, wackiest** *Slang* odd, eccentric, or crazy: *a wacky idea.* ▷ **HISTORY** dialect: a fool ▶ **wackiness** *n*

wad *n* **1** a small mass of soft material, such as cotton wool, used for packing or stuffing. **2** a roll or bundle of banknotes or papers. ▷ **HISTORY** Late Latin *wadda*

wadding *n* a soft material used for padding or stuffing.

waddle *vb* **-dling, -dled 1** to walk with short steps, rocking slightly from side to side. ✧ *n* **2** a swaying walk. ▷ **HISTORY** from *wade*

waddy *n, pl* **-dies** a heavy wooden club used by Australian Aborigines.

wade *vb* **wading, waded 1** to walk slowly and with difficulty through water or mud. **2 wade in** *or* **into** to begin doing (something) in an energetic way: *wading into the fray.* **3 wade through** to proceed with difficulty through: *a stack of literature to wade through.* ▷ **HISTORY** Old English *wadan*

wader *n* a long-legged bird, such as the heron or stork, that lives near water and feeds on fish. Also called: **wading bird**

waders *pl n* long waterproof boots which completely cover the legs, worn by anglers for standing in water.

wadi (**wod**-dee) *n, pl* **-dies** a river in N Africa or Arabia, which is dry except in the rainy season. ▷ **HISTORY** Arabic

wafer *n* **1** a thin crisp sweetened biscuit, often served with ice cream. **2** *Christianity* a round thin piece of unleavened bread used at Communion. **3** *Electronics* a small thin slice of germanium or silicon that is separated into numerous individual components or circuits. ▷ **HISTORY** Old French *waufre*

wafer-thin *adj* very thin: *wafer-thin meat.*

waffle[1] *n* a square crisp pancake with a gridlike pattern. ▷ **HISTORY** Dutch *wafel*

waffle[2] *Informal, chiefly Brit, Austral & NZ* ✧ *vb* **-fling, -fled 1** to speak or write in a vague and wordy manner. ✧ *n* **2** vague and wordy speech or writing. ▷ **HISTORY** origin unknown

waft *vb* **1** to move gently through the air as if being carried by the wind: *the scent of summer flowers gently wafting through my window.* ✧ *n* **2** a scent carried on the air. ▷ **HISTORY** Middle Dutch *wachter* guard

wag[1] *vb* **wagging, wagged 1** to move rapidly and repeatedly from side to side or up and down: *Franklin wagged his tail.* ✧ *n* **2** an instance of wagging. ▷ **HISTORY** Old English *wagian*

wag[2] *n Old-fashioned* a humorous or witty person. ▷ **HISTORY** origin unknown ▶ **waggish** *adj*

wage *n* **1** Also: **wages** the money paid in return for a person's work, esp. when paid weekly or daily rather than monthly: *a campaign for higher wages.* ✧ *vb* **waging, waged 2** to engage in (a campaign or war). ▷ **HISTORY** Old French *wagier* to pledge

wager *n* **1** a bet on the outcome of an event or activity. ✧ *vb* **2** to bet (something, esp. money) on the outcome of an event or activity. ▷ **HISTORY** Old French *wagier* to pledge

waggle *vb* **-gling, -gled** to move with a rapid shaking or wobbling motion. ▷ **HISTORY** from WAG[1]

wagon *or* **waggon** *n* **1** a four-wheeled vehicle used for carrying heavy loads, sometimes pulled by a horse or tractor. **2** an open railway freight truck. **3** a lorry. **4 on the wagon** *Informal* abstaining from alcoholic drink. ▷ **HISTORY** Dutch *wagen*
▶ **wagoner** *or* **waggoner** *n*

wagtail *n* a small songbird of Eurasia and Africa with a very long tail that wags up and down when it walks.

wahine (wah-**hee**-nay) *n NZ* a Maori woman, esp. a wife. ▷ **HISTORY** Maori

wahoo *n* a food and game fish of tropical seas.

waif *n* a person, esp. a child, who is, or who looks as if he or she might be, homeless or neglected. ▷ **HISTORY** Anglo-Norman

wail *vb* **1** to utter a prolonged high-pitched cry of pain or sorrow. ✧ *n* **2** a prolonged high-pitched cry of pain or sorrow. ▷ **HISTORY** from Old Norse
▶ **wailing** *n, adj*

wain *n Poetic* a farm cart. ▷ **HISTORY** Old English *wægn*

wainscot *n* a wooden covering on the lower half of the walls of a room. Also: **wainscoting** ▷ **HISTORY** Middle Low German *wagenschot*

waist *n* **1** *Anat* the narrow part of the body between the ribs and the hips. **2** the part of a garment covering the waist. ▷ **HISTORY** origin unknown

waistband *n* a band of material sewn on to the waist of a garment to strengthen it.

waistcoat *n* a sleeveless upper garment which buttons up the front and is usually worn by men over a shirt and under a jacket.

waistline *n* **1** an imaginary line around the body at the narrowest part of the waist. **2** the place where the upper and lower part of a garment are joined together.

wait *vb* **1** to stay in one place or remain inactive in expectation of something: *the delegates have to wait for a reply.* **2** to be temporarily delayed: *the celebrations can wait.* **3** (of a thing) to be ready or be in store: *waiting for her on the library table was the latest Jilly Cooper novel.* ✧ *n* **4** the act or a period of waiting. **5 lie in wait for a** to prepare an ambush for. **b** to be ready or be in store for. ✧ See also **wait on.** ▷ **HISTORY** Old French *waitier*

Waitangi Day *n* February 6th, the national day of New Zealand commemorating the Treaty Of Waitangi in 1840.

waiter *n* a man who serves people with food and drink in a restaurant.

waiting list *n* a list of people waiting for something that is not immediately available: *a long waiting list for heart surgery.*

wait on *vb* **1** to serve (people) with food and drink in a restaurant. **2** to look after the needs of: *they were waited on by a manservant.* ✧ *interj* **3** *NZ* stop! hold on! Also (for senses 1, 2): **wait upon**

waitress *n* **1** a woman who serves people with food and drink in a restaurant. ✧ *vb* **2** to work as a waitress.

waive *vb* **waiving, waived** to refrain from enforcing or claiming (a rule or right). ▷ HISTORY Old French *weyver*

waiver *n* the act or an instance of voluntary giving up a claim or right.

waka *n NZ* a Maori canoe.

wake[1] *vb* **waking, woke, woken 1** Also: **wake up** to become conscious again or bring (someone) to consciousness again after a sleep. **2 wake up** to make (someone) more alert after a period of inactivity. **3 wake up to** to become aware of: *the world did not wake up to this tragedy until many people had died.* **4 waking hours** the time when a person is awake: *he often used his waking hours to write music.* ✧ *n* **5** a watch or vigil held over the body of a dead person during the night before burial. ▷ HISTORY Old English *wacian*

> **☑ WORD TIP**
> Where there is an object and the sense is the literal one *wake (up)* and *waken* are the commonest forms: *I wakened him; I woke him (up).* Both verbs are also commonly used without an object: *I woke up. Awake* and *awaken* are preferred to other forms of *wake* where the sense is a figurative one: *he awoke to the danger.*

wake[2] *n* **1** the track left by a ship moving through water. **2 in the wake of** following soon after: *the arrests come in the wake of the assassination.* ▷ HISTORY Scandinavian

wakeful *adj* **1** unable to sleep. **2** without sleep: *wakeful nights.* **3** alert: *wakeful readiness.* ▶ **wakefulness** *n*

waken *vb* to become conscious again or bring (someone) to consciousness again after a sleep.

> **☑ WORD TIP**
> See at **wake.**

walk *vb* **1** to move on foot at a moderate rate with at least one foot always on the ground. **2** to pass through, on, or over on foot: *to walk a short distance.* **3** to walk somewhere with (a person or a dog). **4 walking on air** very happy and excited. **5 walk the streets** to wander about, esp. when looking for work or when homeless. ✧ *n* **6** a short journey on foot, usually for pleasure. **7** the action of walking rather than running. **8** a manner of walking: *a proud slow walk.* **9** a place or route for walking. **10 walk of life** social position or profession: *people from all walks of life were drawn to her.* ✧ See also **walk into.** ▷ HISTORY Old English *wealcan* ▶ **walker** *n*

walkabout *n* **1** an occasion when royalty, politicians, or other celebrities walk among and meet the public. **2 go walkabout** *Austral* **a** to wander through the bush as a nomad. **b** *Informal* to be lost or misplaced. **c** *Informal* to lose one's concentration.

walkie-talkie *n* a small combined radio transmitter and receiver that can be carried around by one person.

walking stick *n* a stick or cane carried in the hand to assist walking.

walk into *vb* to encounter unexpectedly: *the troop reinforcements had walked into a trap.*

Walkman *n Trademark* a small portable cassette player with headphones.

walk-on *adj* (of a part in a film or play) small and not involving speaking.

walkover *n* **1** *Informal* an easy victory. ✧ *vb* **walk over 2** to mistreat or bully; take advantage of: *if you don't make your mark early, people will walk all over you.*

walkway *n* **1** a path designed for use by pedestrians. **2** a passage or pathway between two buildings.

wall *n* **1** a vertical structure made of stone, brick, or wood, with a length and height much greater than its thickness, used to enclose, divide, or support. *RELATED ADJECTIVE* ▶ **mural 2** anything that suggests a wall in function or effect: *a wall of elm trees; a wall of suspicion.* **3** *Anat* any lining or membrane that encloses a bodily cavity or structure: *cell walls.* **4 drive someone up the wall** *Slang* to make someone angry or irritated. **5 go to the wall** *Informal* to be financially ruined. **6 have one's back to the wall** *Informal* to be in a very difficult situation, with no obvious way out of it. ✧ *vb* **7** to surround or enclose (an area) with a wall. **8 wall in** *or* **up** to enclose (someone or something) completely in a room or place. ▷ HISTORY Old English *weall* ▶ **walled** *adj*

wallaby *n, pl* **-bies** a marsupial of Australia and New Guinea that resembles a small kangaroo. ▷ HISTORY Aboriginal *wolabā*

wallaroo *n* a large stocky Australian kangaroo of rocky regions.

wallet *n* a small folding case, usually of leather, for holding paper money and credit cards. ▷ HISTORY Germanic

walleye *n* a fish with large staring eyes. Also: **dory**

walleyed *adj* having eyes with an abnormal amount of white showing because of a squint. ▷ HISTORY Old Norse *vagleygr*

wallflower *n* **1** a plant grown for its clusters of yellow, orange, red, or purple fragrant flowers. **2** *Informal* a woman who does not join in the dancing at a party or dance because she has no partner.

Walloon (wol-**loon**) *n* **1** a French-speaking person from S Belgium or the neighbouring part of France. **2** the French dialect of Belgium. ✧ *adj* **3** of the Walloons. ▷ HISTORY Germanic

wallop *Informal* ✧ *vb* **1** to hit hard. ✧ *n* **2** a hard blow. ▷ HISTORY Old French *waloper* to gallop

walloping *Informal* ✧ *n* **1** a severe physical beating. ✧ *adj* **2** large or great: *a walloping amount of sodium.*

wallow *vb* **1** to indulge oneself in some emotion: *they wallow in self-pity.* **2** to lie or roll about in mud or water for pleasure. ✧ *n* **3** the act or an instance of wallowing. **4** a muddy place where animals wallow. ▷ **HISTORY** Old English *wealwian* to roll (in mud)

wallpaper *n* **1** a printed or embossed paper for covering the walls of a room. ✧ *vb* **2** to cover (walls) with wallpaper.

Wall Street *n Finance* a street in New York City, where the Stock Exchange and major banks are situated.

wall-to-wall *adj* (of carpeting) completely covering a floor.

wally *n, pl* **-lies** *Brit slang* a stupid or foolish person. ▷ **HISTORY** from the name *Walter*

walnut *n* **1** an edible nut with a hard, wrinkled, light brown shell. **2** a tree on which walnuts grow. **3** the light brown wood of a walnut tree, used for making furniture.

> **WORD HISTORY**
>
> 'Walnut' comes from Old English *walh-hnutu* meaning 'foreign nut'. The walnut is an Asian tree that was not introduced into Britain until the 15th or 16th century, and so walnuts originally were imported from abroad.

walrus *n, pl* **-ruses** *or* **-rus** a mammal of cold northern seas, with two tusks that hang down from the upper jaw, tough thick skin, and coarse whiskers. ▷ **HISTORY** Dutch: whale horse

waltz *n* **1** a ballroom dance in triple time in which couples spin round as they progress round the room. **2** music for this dance. ✧ *vb* **3** to dance a waltz. **4** *Informal* to move in a relaxed and confident way: *he waltzed over to her table to say hello.* ▷ **HISTORY** German *Walzer*

wampum (**wom**-pum) *n* (formerly) money used by Native Americans of N America, made of shells strung or woven together. ▷ **HISTORY** Native American *wampompeag*

wan (rhymes with **swan**) *adj* **wanner, wannest** very pale, as a result of illness or unhappiness. ▷ **HISTORY** Old English *wann* dark ▶ **wanly** *adv*

wand *n* **1** a rod used by a magician when performing a trick or by a fairy when casting a spell. **2** a hand-held electronic device which is pointed at or passed over an item to read the data stored there. ▷ **HISTORY** Old Norse *vǒndr*

wander *vb* **1** to walk about in a place without any definite purpose or destination. **2** to leave a place where one is supposed to stay: *kids wander off.* **3** (of the mind) to lose concentration. ✧ *n* **4** the act or an instance of wandering. ▷ **HISTORY** Old English *wandrian* ▶ **wanderer** *n* ▶ **wandering** *adj, n*

wanderlust *n* a great desire to travel.

wane *vb* **waning, waned 1** to decrease gradually in size, strength, or power: *the influence of the extremists is waning.* **2** (of the moon) to show a gradually decreasing area of brightness from full moon until new moon. ✧ *n* **3 on the wane** decreasing in size, strength, or power: *his fame was on the wane.* ▷ **HISTORY** Old English *wanian* ▶ **waning** *adj*

wangle *vb* **-gling, -gled** *Informal* to get (something) by cunning or devious methods: *I've wangled you both an invitation.* ▷ **HISTORY** origin unknown

want *vb* **1** to feel a need or longing for: *I want a job.* **2** to wish or desire (to do something): *we did not want to get involved.* **3** *Brit, Austral & NZ* to have need of or require (doing or being something): *what will you do when it wants cleaning?* **4** *Informal* should or ought (to do something): *the last person you want to hire is someone who is desperate for a job.* **5 want for** to be lacking or deficient in: *they were convinced I was wealthy and wanted for nothing.* ✧ *n* **6** something that is needed, desired, or lacked: *attempts to satisfy a number of wants.* **7** a lack, shortage, or absence: *for want of opportunity.* **8 in want of** needing or lacking: *the Chinese peasant farmer may be in want of a roof, a job, a doctor nearby.* ▷ **HISTORY** Old Norse *vanta* to be deficient

wanted *adj* being searched for by the police in connection with a crime that has been committed.

wanting *adj* **1** lacking: *I would be wanting in charity if I did not explain the terms.* **2** not meeting requirements or expectations: *she compares herself to her sister and finds herself wanting.*

wanton *adj* **1** without motive, provocation, or justification: *sheer wanton destruction.* **2** (of a person) maliciously and unnecessarily cruel. **3** *Old-fashioned* (of a woman) sexually unrestrained or immodest. ✧ *n* **4** *Old-fashioned* a sexually unrestrained or immodest woman. ▷ **HISTORY** Middle English *wantowen* unruly

WAP Wireless Application Protocol: a system that allows mobile phone users to access the Internet and other information services.

wapiti (**wop**-pit-tee) *n, pl* **-tis** a large North American deer, now also found in New Zealand. ▷ **HISTORY** from a Native American language

war *n* **1** open armed conflict between two or more countries or groups: *this international situation led to war.* **2** a particular armed conflict: *the American war in Vietnam.* **3** any conflict or contest: *a trade war.* **4 have been in the wars** *Informal* to look as if one has been in a fight. ✧ *adj* **5** relating to war or a war: *the war effort; a war correspondent.* ✧ *vb* **warring, warred 6** to conduct a war. ▷ **HISTORY** Old Northern French *werre* ▶ **warring** *adj*

waratah *n* an Australian shrub with crimson flowers.

warble *vb* **-bling, -bled** to sing in a high-pitched trilling voice. ▷ **HISTORY** Old French *werbler*

warbler *n* any of various small songbirds.

War Communism *n History* the economic policies of the Bolsheviks in the aftermath of the 1917 Russian revolution, consisting of the abolition of private trade, the nationalization of industry, and the forced acquisition of almost all agricultural produce.

war crime *n* a crime committed in wartime in violation of the accepted customs, such as ill-treatment of prisoners. ▶ **war criminal** *n*

war cry *n* **1** a rallying cry used by combatants in battle. **2** a slogan used to rally support for a cause.

ward *n* **1** a room in a hospital for patients requiring similar kinds of care: *the maternity ward.* **2** one of the districts into which a town, parish, or other area is divided for administration or elections. **3** *Law* Also called: **ward of court** a person, esp. a child whose parents are dead, who is placed under the control or protection of a guardian or of a court. ✧ See also **ward off**. ▷ **HISTORY** Old English *weard* protector ▶ **wardship** *n*

-ward *suffix* **1** *(forming adjectives)* indicating direction towards: *a backward step.* **2** *(forming adverbs) Chiefly US & Canad* same as **-wards**. ▷ **HISTORY** Old English *-weard*

warden *n* **1** a person who is in charge of a building, such as a youth hostel, and its occupants. **2** a public official who is responsible for the enforcement of certain regulations: *a game warden.* **3** the chief officer in charge of a prison. ▷ **HISTORY** Old French *wardein*

warder *or fem* **wardress** *n Chiefly Brit* a prison officer. ▷ **HISTORY** Old French *warder* to guard

ward off *vb* to prevent (something unpleasant) from happening or from causing harm: *to ward off the pangs of hunger; to ward off cancer cells.*

wardrobe *n* **1** a tall cupboard, with a rail or hooks on which to hang clothes. **2** the total collection of articles of clothing belonging to one person: *your autumn wardrobe.* **3** the collection of costumes belonging to a theatre or theatrical company. ▷ **HISTORY** Old French *warder* to guard + *robe* robe

wardrobe mistress *n* the woman in charge of the costumes in a theatre or theatrical company. ▶ **wardrobe master** *masc n*

wardroom *n* the quarters assigned to the officers of a warship, apart from the captain.

-wards *or* **-ward** *suffix forming adverbs* indicating direction towards: *a step backwards.* ▷ **HISTORY** Old English *-weardes*

ware *n* articles of the same kind or material: *crystal ware.* See also **wares**. ▷ **HISTORY** Old English *waru*

warehouse *n* a place where goods are stored prior to their sale or distribution.

wares *pl n* goods for sale.

warfare *n* **1** the act of conducting a war. **2** a violent or intense conflict of any kind: *class warfare.*

war game *n* **1** a tactical exercise for training military commanders, in which no military units are actually deployed. **2** a game in which model soldiers are used to create battles in order to study tactics.

warhead *n* the front section of a missile or projectile that contains explosives.

warhorse *n* **1** (formerly) a horse used in battle. **2** *Informal* a veteran soldier or politician.

warlike *adj* **1** of or relating to war: *warlike stores and equipment.* **2** hostile and eager to have a war: *a warlike nation.*

warlock *n* a man who practises black magic. ▷ **HISTORY** Old English *wærloga* oath breaker

warlord *n* a military leader of a nation or part of a nation.

warm *adj* **1** feeling or having a moderate degree of heat. **2** giving heat: *warm clothing.* **3** (of colours) predominantly red or yellow in tone. **4** kindly or affectionate: *warm embraces.* **5** *Informal* near to finding a hidden object or guessing facts, for example in a children's game. ✧ *vb* **6** to make warm. **7 warm to a** to become fonder of: *I warmed to him when he defended me.* **b** to become more excited or enthusiastic about: *he had warmed to his theme.* ✧ See also **warm up**. ▷ **HISTORY** Old English *wearm* ▶ **warmly** *adv* ▶ **warmness** *n*

warm-blooded *adj* **1** (of an animal, such as a mammal or a bird) having a constant body temperature, usually higher than the surrounding temperature. **2** having a passionate nature. ▶ **warm-bloodedness** *n*

warm front *n Meteorol* the boundary between a warm air mass and the cold air it is replacing.

warmonger *n* a person who encourages warlike ideas or advocates war. ▶ **warmongering** *n*

warmth *n* **1** the state of being warm. **2** affection or cordiality: *the warmth of their friendship.*

warm up *vb* **1** to make or become warm or warmer. **2** to prepare for a race, sporting contest, or exercise routine by doing gentle exercises immediately beforehand. **3** (of an engine or machine) to be started and left running until the working temperature is reached. **4** to become more lively: *wait until things warm up.* **5** to reheat (food that has already been cooked). ✧ *n* **warm-up** **6** a preparatory exercise routine.

warn *vb* **1** to make (someone) aware of a possible danger or problem. **2** to inform (someone) in advance: *you'd better warn your girlfriend that you'll be working at the weekend.* **3 warn off** to advise (someone) to go away or not to do something. ▷ **HISTORY** Old English *wearnian*

warning *n* **1** a hint, threat, or advance notice of a possible danger or problem. **2** advice not to do something. ✧ *adj* **3** giving or serving as a warning: *warning signs.* ▶ **warningly** *adv*

warp *vb* **1** (esp. of wooden objects) to be twisted out of shape, for example by heat or damp. **2** to distort or influence in a negative way: *love warps judgment.* ✧ *n* **3** a fault or an irregularity in the shape or surface of an object. **4** a fault or deviation in someone's character. **5** See **time warp**. **6** the yarns arranged lengthways on a loom through which the weft yarns are woven. ▷ **HISTORY** Old English *wearp* a throw ▶ **warped** *adj*

war paint *n* **1** paint applied to the face and body by certain North American Indians before battle. **2** *Informal* cosmetics.

warpath *n* **on the warpath a** preparing to engage in battle. **b** *Informal* angry and looking for a fight or conflict.

warrant *n* **1** an official authorization for some action or decision: *Scotland Yard today issued a warrant for the arrest of this man.* **2** a document that certifies or guarantees something, such as a receipt or licence. ✧ *vb* **3** to make necessary: *we've no hard evidence to warrant a murder investigation.* ▷ **HISTORY** Old French *guarant*

warrant officer *n* an officer in certain armed services with a rank between those of commissioned and noncommissioned officers.

Warrant of Fitness *n NZ* a six-monthly certificate required for a motor vehicle certifying that it is mechanically sound.

warrantor *n* a person or company that provides a warranty.

warranty *n, pl* **-ties** a guarantee or assurance that goods meet a specified standard or that the facts in a legal document are as stated. ▷ **HISTORY** Anglo-French *warantie*

warren *n* **1** a series of interconnected underground tunnels in which rabbits live. **2** an overcrowded building or area of a city with many narrow passages or streets: *a mountainous concrete warren of apartments.* ▷ **HISTORY** Anglo-French *warenne*

warrigal *Austral* ✧ *n* **1** a dingo. ✧ *adj* **2** wild.

warrior *n* a person who is engaged in or experienced in war. ▷ **HISTORY** Old French *werreieor*

Warsaw Pact *n History* a military treaty and association of the Soviet Union and its E European allies, formed in 1955 and dissolved in 1991.

warship *n* a ship designed for naval warfare.

wart *n* **1** a firm abnormal growth on the skin caused by a virus. **2 warts and all** including faults: *she loves him warts and all.* ▷ **HISTORY** Old English *weart(e)* ▶ **warty** *adj*

warthog *n* a wild African pig with heavy tusks, wartlike lumps on the face, and a mane of coarse hair.

wartime *n* **1** a time of war. ✧ *adj* **2** of or in a time of war: *the wartime coalition.*

wary (**ware**-ree) *adj* **warier, wariest** cautious or on one's guard: *be wary of hitchhikers.* ▷ **HISTORY** Old English *wær* aware, careful ▶ **warily** *adv* ▶ **wariness** *n*

was *vb* (used with *I, he, she, it* and with singular nouns) the past tense of **be**. ▷ **HISTORY** Old English *wæs*

wash *vb* **1** to clean (oneself, part of one's body, or a thing) with soap or detergent and water. **2** (of a garment or fabric) to be capable of being washed without damage or loss of colour. **3** to move or be moved in a particular direction by water: *houses may be washed away in floods.* **4** (of waves) to flow or sweep against or over (a surface or object), often with a lapping sound. **5** *Informal* to be acceptable or believable: *the masculine pride argument won't wash now when so many women go out to work.* ✧ *n* **6** the act or process of washing. **7** all the clothes etc. to be washed together on one occasion. **8** a thin layer of paint or ink: *a pale wash of blue.* **9** the disturbance in the air or water produced at the rear of an aircraft, boat, or other moving object: *we were hit by the wash of a large vessel.* **10 come out in the wash** *Informal* to become known or apparent in the course of time. ✧ See also **wash out, wash up**. ▷ **HISTORY** Old English *wæscan, waxan* ▶ **washable** *adj*

washbasin *n* a small sink in a bathroom, used for washing the face and hands. Also: **wash-hand basin**

washed out *adj* **1** exhausted and lacking in energy. **2** faded or colourless.

washed up *adj Informal, chiefly US, Canad, Austral & NZ* no longer as successful or important as previously: *she stands discredited, her career probably washed up.*

washer *n* **1** a flat ring of rubber, felt, or metal used to provide a seal under a nut or bolt or in a tap or valve. **2** *Informal* a washing machine. **3** a person who washes things, esp. as a job: *chief cook and bottle washer.* **4** *Austral* a small piece of towelling cloth used to wash the face.

washing *n* all the clothes etc. to be washed together on one occasion.

washing machine *n* a machine for washing clothes and bed linen in.

washing soda *n* crystalline sodium carbonate, used as a cleansing agent.

washing-up *n* the act of washing used dishes and cutlery after a meal.

wash out *vb* **1** Also: **wash off** to remove or be removed by washing: *the rain washes the red dye out of the cap.* **2** to wash the inside of (a container). ✧ *n* **washout 3** *Informal* a total failure or disaster. **4** *NZ* a part of a road or railway washed away by floodwaters.

wash up *vb* **1** to wash used dishes and cutlery after a meal. **2** *US & Canad* to wash one's face and hands.

wasp *n* a common stinging insect with a slender black-and-yellow striped body. ▷ **HISTORY** Old English *wæsp*

Wasp *or* **WASP** (in the US and Canada) White Anglo-Saxon Protestant: a person descended from N European, usually Protestant stock, forming a group often considered to be the most dominant and privileged in N American society.

waspish *adj* bad-tempered or spiteful: *waspish comments.*

wassail *n* **1** (formerly) a toast drunk to a person during festivities. **2** a festivity involving a lot of drinking. **3** hot spiced beer or mulled wine drunk at such a festivity. ✧ *vb* **4 go wassailing** to go from house to house singing carols at Christmas. ▷ **HISTORY** Old Norse *ves heill* be in good health

wastage *n* **1** the act of wasting something or the state of being wasted: *wastage of raw materials.*

2 reduction in the size of a workforce by retirement, redundancy, etc.

> ☑ **WORD TIP**
> *Waste* and *wastage* are to some extent interchangeable, but many people think that *wastage* should not be used to refer to loss resulting from human carelessness, inefficiency, etc.: *a waste* (not *a wastage*) *of time, money, effort,* etc.

waste *vb* **wasting, wasted 1** to use up thoughtlessly, carelessly, or unsuccessfully. **2** to fail to take advantage of: *let's not waste an opportunity to see the children.* **3 be wasted on** to be too good for; not be appreciated by: *fine brandy is wasted on you.* **4 waste away** to lose one's strength or health: *wasting away from unrequited love.* ✧ *n* **5** the act of wasting something or the state of being wasted: *a waste of time.* **6** something that is left over because it is in excess of requirements. **7** rubbish: *toxic waste.* **8** *Physiol* matter discharged from the body as faeces or urine. **9 wastes** a region that is wild or uncultivated. ✧ *adj* **10** rejected as being useless, unwanted, or worthless: *waste products.* **11** not cultivated or productive: *waste ground.* **12** *Physiol* discharged from the body as faeces or urine: *waste matter.* **13 lay waste** *or* **lay waste to** to devastate or destroy: *the Bikini atoll, laid waste by nuclear tests.* ▷ **HISTORY** Latin *vastare* to lay waste

wasted *adj* **1** unnecessary or unfruitful: *wasted effort.* **2** pale, thin, and unhealthy: *the hunched shoulders and the wasted appearance of his body.*

wasteful *adj* causing waste: *wasteful expenditure.* ▶ **wastefully** *adv*

wasteland *n* **1** a barren or desolate area of land. **2** something that is considered spiritually, intellectually, or aesthetically barren: *the TV wasteland.*

wastepaper basket *n* a container for paper discarded after use.

waster *n Informal* a lazy or worthless person.

wastrel *n Literary* a lazy or worthless person.

watch *vb* **1** to look at or observe closely and attentively. **2** to look after (a child or a pet). **3** to maintain a careful interest in or control over: *it reminds me to watch my diet.* **4 watch for** to be keenly alert to or cautious about: *the vigilant night watchman hired to watch for thieves.* **5 watch it!** be careful! ✧ *n* **6** a small portable timepiece worn strapped to the wrist or in a waistcoat pocket. **7** the act or an instance of watching. **8** *Naut* any of the periods, usually of four hours, during which part of a ship's crew are on duty. **9 keep a close watch on** to maintain a careful interest in or control over: *he keeps a close watch on party opinion.* **10 keep watch** to be keenly alert to danger; keep guard. **11 on the watch** on the lookout. ▷ **HISTORY** Old English *wæccan* ▶ **watcher** *n*

watchable *adj* interesting, enjoyable, or entertaining: *watchable films.*

watchdog *n* **1** a dog kept to guard property. **2** a person or group that acts as a guard against inefficiency or illegality.

watchful *adj* **1** carefully observing everything that happens. **2 under the watchful eye of** being closely observed by. ▶ **watchfully** *adv* ▶ **watchfulness** *n*

watchman *n, pl* **-men** a man employed to guard buildings or property.

watchtower *n* a tower on which a sentry keeps watch.

watchword *n* a slogan or motto: *quality, not quantity, is the watchword.*

water *n* **1** a clear colourless tasteless liquid that is essential for plant and animal life, that falls as rain, and forms seas, rivers, and lakes. *RELATED ADJECTIVES* ➧ **aquatic, aqueous 2** any area of this liquid, such as a sea, river, or lake. **3** the surface of such an area of water: *four-fifths of an iceberg's mass lie below water.* **4** the level of the tide: *at high water.* **5** *Physiol* **a** any fluid discharged from the body, such as sweat, urine, or tears. **b waters** the fluid surrounding a fetus in the womb. **6 hold water** (of an argument or idea) to be believable or reasonable. **7 of the first water** of the highest quality or the most extreme degree: *he's a scoundrel of the first water.* **8 pass water** to urinate. **9 water under the bridge** events that are past and done with. ✧ *vb* **10** to moisten or soak with water: *keep greenhouse plants well watered.* **11** to give (an animal) water to drink. **12** (of the eyes) to fill with tears: *our eyes were watering from the fumes.* **13** (of the mouth) to fill with saliva in anticipation of food. ✧ See also **water down**. ▷ **HISTORY** Old English *wæter* ▶ **waterless** *adj*

water buffalo *n* a large black oxlike draught animal of S Asia, with long backward-curving horns.

water chestnut *n* the edible tuber of a Chinese plant, used in Oriental cookery.

water closet *n Old-fashioned* a toilet. Abbrev: **WC**

watercolour *or US* **watercolor** *n* **1** a kind of paint that is applied with water rather than oil. **2** a painting done in watercolours.

watercourse *n* the channel or bed of a river or stream.

watercress *n* a plant that grows in ponds and streams, with strong-tasting leaves that are used in salads and as a garnish.

water cycle *n Geog* the circulation of the earth's water, in which water from the sea evaporates, forms clouds, falls as rain or snow, and returns to the sea by rivers.

water down *vb* **1** to weaken (a drink or food) with water. **2** to make (a story, plan, or proposal) weaker and less controversial. ▶ **watered-down** *adj*

waterfall *n* a cascade of falling water where there is a vertical or almost vertical step in a river.

waterfowl *n, pl* **-fowl** a bird that swims on water, such as a duck or swan.

waterfront *n* the area of a town or city next to an area of water, such as a harbour or dockyard.

waterhole *n* a pond or pool in a desert or other dry area, used by animals as a drinking place.

water ice *n* ice cream made from frozen fruit-flavoured syrup.

watering can *n* a container with a handle and a spout with a perforated nozzle, used to sprinkle water over plants.

watering hole *n Facetious slang* a pub.

watering place *n* **1** a place where people or animals can find drinking water. **2** *Brit* a spa or seaside resort.

water lily *n* a plant with large leaves and showy flowers that float on the surface of an area of water.

waterlogged *adj* **1** saturated with water: *waterlogged meadows.* **2** (of a boat) having taken in so much water as to be likely to sink.

water main *n* a principal supply pipe in an arrangement of pipes for distributing water to houses and other buildings.

watermark *n* **1** a mark impressed on paper during manufacture, visible when the paper is held up to the light. **2** a line marking the level reached by an area of water.

water meadow *n* a meadow that remains fertile by being periodically flooded by a stream.

watermelon *n* a large round melon with a hard green rind and sweet watery reddish flesh.

water polo *n* a game played in water by two teams of seven swimmers in which each side tries to throw a ball into the opponents' goal.

water power *n* the power of flowing or falling water to drive machinery or generate electricity.

waterproof *adj* **1** not allowing water to pass through: *waterproof trousers.* ✧ *n* **2** *Chiefly Brit* a waterproof garment, such as a raincoat. ✧ *vb* **3** to make waterproof: *the bridge is having its deck waterproofed.*

water rat *n* same as **water vole**.

water rate *n* a charge made for the public supply of water.

watershed *n* **1** *Geog* **a** the dividing line between two adjacent river systems, such as a ridge. **b** *US* same as **drainage basin**. **2** an important period or factor that serves as a dividing line: *a watershed in history.*

waterside *n* the area of land beside a river or lake.

watersider *n NZ* a person employed to load and unload ships.

water-ski *n* **1** a type of ski used for gliding over water. ✧ *vb* **-skiing, -skied** *or* **-ski'd** **2** to ride over water on water-skis while holding a rope towed by a speedboat. ▸ **water-skier** *n* ▸ **water-skiing** *n*

water softener *n* a device or substance that removes the minerals that make water hard.

waterspout *n* a tornado occurring over water, which forms a column of water and mist.

water table *n Geog* the level below which the ground is saturated with water.

watertight *adj* **1** not letting water through: *watertight compartments.* **2** without loopholes or weak points: *a watertight system.*

water tower *n* a storage tank mounted on a tower so that water can be distributed at a steady pressure.

water vapour *n* water in a gaseous state, esp. when due to evaporation at a temperature below the boiling point.

water vole *n* a small ratlike animal that can swim and lives on the banks of streams and ponds.

waterway *n* a river, canal, or other navigable channel used as a means of travel or transport.

water wheel *n* a large wheel with vanes set across its rim, which is turned by flowing water to drive machinery.

water wings *pl n* an inflatable rubber device shaped like a pair of wings, which is placed under the arms of a person learning to swim.

waterworks *n* **1** an establishment for storing, purifying, and distributing water for community supply. ✧ *pl n* **2** *Informal, Chiefly Brit euphemistic* the urinary system. **3 turn on the waterworks** *Informal* to begin to cry deliberately, in order to attract attention or gain sympathy.

watery *adj* **1** of, like, or containing water: *a watery discharge.* **2** (of eyes) filled with tears. **3** insipid, thin, or weak: *a watery sun had appeared.*

watt (**wott**) *n* the SI unit of power, equal to the power dissipated by a current of 1 ampere flowing across a potential difference of 1 amp.
▷ **HISTORY** after J. *Watt,* engineer

wattage *n* the amount of electrical power, expressed in watts, that an appliance uses or generates.

wattle (**wott**-tl) *n* **1** a frame of rods or stakes interwoven with twigs or branches used to make fences. **2** a loose fold of brightly coloured skin hanging from the throat of certain birds and lizards. **3** an Australian acacia with spikes of small brightly coloured flowers and flexible branches formerly used for making fences. ✧ *adj* **4** made of, formed by, or covered with wattle: *a wattle fence.*
▷ **HISTORY** Old English *watol*

wattle and daub *n* a building material consisting of interwoven twigs plastered with a mixture of clay and water.

wave *vb* **waving, waved 1** to move (one's hand) to and fro as a greeting. **2** to direct (someone) to move in a particular direction by waving: *I waved him on.* **3** to hold (something) up and move it from side to side in order to attract attention. **4** to move freely to and fro: *flowers waving in the wind.* ✧ *n* **5** one of a sequence of ridges or undulations that moves across the surface of the sea or a lake. **6** a curve in the hair. **7** a sudden rise in the frequency or intensity of something: *a wave of sympathy.* **8** a widespread movement that advances in a body: *a new wave of refugees.* **9** a prolonged spell of some particular type of weather: *a heat wave.* **10** the act or an instance of waving. **11** *Physics* an energy-carrying disturbance travelling through a medium or space by a series of vibrations without any overall movement of matter. **12 make waves** to cause trouble. ▷ **HISTORY** Old English *wafian*

A B C D E F G H I J K L M N O P Q R S T U V W X Y Z

waveband *n* a range of wavelengths or frequencies used for a particular type of radio transmission.

wave-cut notch *n Geol* a groove under the base of a cliff formed by the erosive action of waves.

wave-cut platform *n Geol* a flat surface at the base of a cliff formed by the erosive action of waves.

wave down *vb* to signal to (the driver of a vehicle) to stop.

wavelength *n* **1** *Physics* the distance between two points of the same phase in consecutive cycles of a wave. **2** the wavelength of the carrier wave used by a particular broadcasting station. **3 on the same wavelength** *Informal* having similar views, feelings, or thoughts.

waver *vb* **1** to hesitate between possibilities; be indecisive. **2** to swing from one thing to another: *she wavered between annoyance and civility.* **3** (of a voice or stare) to become unsteady. **4** to move back and forth or one way and another: *the barrel of the gun began to waver.* ▷ HISTORY Old Norse *vafra* to flicker ▶ **wavering** *adj*

wave refraction *n Geog* the process whereby waves bend as they approach the shore.

wavey *n Canad* a snow goose or other wild goose. ▷ HISTORY from a Native American language

wavy *adj* **wavier, waviest** having curves: *wavy hair; a wavy line.*

wax[1] *n* **1** a solid fatty or oily substance used for making candles and polish, which softens and melts when heated. **2** short for **beeswax sealing wax**. **3** *Physiol* a brownish-yellow waxy substance secreted by glands in the ear. ✧ *vb* **4** to coat or polish with wax. ▷ HISTORY Old English *weax* ▶ **waxed** *adj* ▶ **waxy** *adj*

wax[2] *vb* **1** to increase gradually in size, strength, or power: *trading has waxed and waned with the economic cycle.* **2** (of the moon) to show a gradually increasing area of brightness from new moon until full moon. **3** to become: *he waxed eloquent on the disadvantages of marriage.* ▷ HISTORY Old English *weaxan*

waxen *adj* **1** resembling wax in colour or texture: *his face is waxen and pale.* **2** made of, treated with, or covered with wax: *a waxen image.*

waxeye *n* a small New Zealand bird with a white circle round its eye.

waxwork *n* a life-size lifelike wax figure of a famous person.

way *n* **1** a manner, method, or means: *a new way of life; a tactful way of finding out.* **2** a characteristic style or manner: *we are all special in our own way.* **3 ways** habits or customs: *he had a liking for British ways.* **4** an aspect or detail of something: *the tourist industry is in many ways a success story.* **5** a choice or option, for example in a vote: *he thought it could go either way.* **6** a route or direction: *the shortest way home.* **7** a journey: *you could buy a magazine to read on the way.* **8** distance: *they are a long way from Paris.* **9** space or room for movement or activity: *you won't be in his way.* **10 by the way** incidentally: *by the way, I've decided to leave.* **11 by way of a** serving as: *by way of explanation.* **b** by the route of: *I went by way of my family home.* **12 get one's own way** to have things exactly as one wants them to be. **13 give way a** to collapse or break. **b** to yield or concede: *I tried to make him understand but he did not give way an inch.* **14 give way to a** to be replaced by: *my first feelings of dismay have given way to comparative complacency.* **b** to show (an emotion) unrestrainedly. **c** to slow down or stop when driving to let (another driver) pass. **15 go out of one's way** to take considerable trouble: *he had gone out of his way to reassure me.* **16 have it both ways** to enjoy two things that would normally be mutually exclusive. **17 in a bad way** *Informal* in a poor state of health or a poor financial state. **18 in a way** in some respects. **19 in no way** not at all. **20 make one's way** to proceed or go: *he decided to make his way back in the dark.* **21 on the way out** *Informal* becoming unfashionable. **22 out of the way a** removed or dealt with so as to be no longer a hindrance. **b** remote. **23 under way** having started moving or making progress. ✧ *adv* **24** *Informal* far or by far: *that is way out of line.* ▷ HISTORY Old English *weg*

waybill *n* a document stating the nature, origin, and destination of goods being transported.

wayfarer *n Old-fashioned* a traveller.

waylay *vb* **-laying, -laid 1** to lie in wait for and attack. **2** to intercept (someone) unexpectedly.

way-out *adj Old-fashioned informal* extremely unconventional.

ways and means *pl n* **1** the methods and resources for accomplishing something. **2** the money and the methods of raising the money needed for the functioning of a political unit.

wayside *adj* **1** *Old-fashioned* situated by the side of a road: *wayside shrines.* ✧ *n* **2 fall by the wayside** to be unsuccessful or stop being successful: *thousands of new diets are dreamed up yearly – many fall by the wayside.*

wayward *adj* erratic, selfish, or stubborn. ▷ HISTORY AWAY + -WARD ▶ **waywardness** *n*

Wb *Physics* weber.

WC *or* **wc** *n* a toilet.

we *pron* (*used as the subject of a verb*) **1** the speaker or writer and another person or other people: *we arrived in Calais.* **2** all people or people in general: *it's an unfair world we live in.* **3** *Formal* same as **I**: used by monarchs and editors. ▷ HISTORY Old English *wē*

weak *adj* **1** lacking in physical or mental strength. **2** (of a part of the body) not functioning as well as is normal: *a weak heart.* **3** liable to collapse or break: *weak bridges.* **4** lacking in importance, influence, or strength: *a weak government.* **5** (of a currency or shares) falling in price or characterized by falling prices. **6** lacking in moral strength; easily influenced. **7** not convincing: *weak arguments.* **8** lacking strength or power: *his voice was weak.* **9** not having a strong flavour: *weak coffee.* ▷ HISTORY Old English *wāc* soft ▶ **weakly** *adv*

weaken *vb* to become or make weak or weaker.

weak-kneed *adj Informal* lacking strength, courage, or resolution.

weakling *n* a person who is lacking in physical or mental strength.

weak-minded *adj* **1** lacking willpower. **2** of low intelligence; foolish.

weakness *n* **1** the state of being weak. **2** a failing in a person's character: *his weakness is his impetuosity.* **3** a self-indulgent liking: *a weakness for gin.*

weal[1] *n* a raised mark on the skin produced by a blow. ▷ HISTORY from Old English *walu* ridge

weal[2] *n Old-fashioned* prosperity or wellbeing: *the public weal.* ▷ HISTORY Old English *wela*

wealth *n* **1** the state of being rich. **2** a large amount of money and valuable material possessions: *redistribution of wealth.* **3** a great amount or number: *a wealth of detail.* ▷ HISTORY Middle English *welthe*

wealthy *adj* **wealthier, wealthiest 1** having a large amount of money and valuable material possessions. **2 wealthy in** having a great amount or number of: *a continent exceptionally wealthy in minerals.*

wean *vb* **1** to start giving (a baby or young mammal) food other than its mother's milk. **2** to cause (oneself or someone else) to give up a former habit: *they are unable to wean themselves from the tobacco habit.* ▷ HISTORY Old English *wenian* to accustom ▶ **weaning** *n*

weapon *n* **1** an object used in fighting, such as a knife or gun. **2** anything used to get the better of an opponent: *having a sense of humour is a weapon of self-defence.* ▷ HISTORY Old English *wǣpen*

weaponry *n* weapons regarded collectively.

wear *vb* **wearing, wore, worn 1** to carry or have (a garment or jewellery) on one's body as clothing or ornament. **2** to have (a particular facial expression): *she wore a scowl of frank antagonism.* **3** to style (the hair) in a particular way: *she wears her hair in a braid.* **4** to deteriorate or cause to deteriorate by constant use or action. **5** *Informal* to accept: *he won't be given a top job – the Party wouldn't wear it.* **6 wear thin** to lessen or become weaker: *his patience began to wear thin.* **7 wear well** to remain in good condition for a long time. ✧ *n* **8** clothes that are suitable for a particular time or purpose: *evening wear; beach wear.* **9** deterioration from constant or normal use. **10** the quality of resisting the effects of constant use. ✧ See also **wear off, wear out**. ▷ HISTORY Old English *werian* ▶ **wearable** *adj* ▶ **wearer** *n*

wear and tear *n* damage or loss resulting from ordinary use.

wearing *adj* causing exhaustion and sometimes irritation.

wearisome *adj* causing fatigue and irritation.

wear off *vb* to have a gradual decrease in effect or intensity: *the cocaine injection was beginning to wear off.*

wear out *vb* **1** to make or become unfit for use through wear: *my red trousers are worn out.* **2** *Informal* to exhaust: *the afternoon's races and games had worn him out.*

weary *adj* **-rier, -riest 1** very tired; lacking energy. **2** caused by or suggestive of weariness: *he managed a weary smile.* **3** causing exhaustion: *a long weary struggle.* **4 weary of** discontented or bored with: *he was weary of the war.* ✧ *vb* **-ries, -rying, -ried 5** to make weary. **6 weary of** to become discontented or bored with: *he seems to have wearied of her possessiveness.* ▷ HISTORY Old English *wērig* ▶ **wearily** *adv* ▶ **weariness** *n* ▶ **wearying** *adj*

weasel *n, pl* **-sels** *or* **-sel** a small meat-eating mammal with reddish-brown fur, a long body and neck, and short legs. ▷ HISTORY Old English *wesle*

weather *n* **1** the day-to-day atmospheric conditions, such as temperature, cloudiness, and rainfall, affecting a specific place. **2 make heavy weather of** *Informal* to carry out (a task) with great difficulty or needless effort. **3 under the weather** *Informal* feeling slightly ill. ✧ *vb* **4** to undergo or cause to undergo changes, such as discoloration, due to the action of the weather. **5** to come safely through (a storm, problem, or difficulty). ▷ HISTORY Old English *weder*

weather balloon *n Meteorol* a balloon that carries instruments for collecting meteorological data.

weather-beaten *adj* **1** tanned by exposure to the weather: *a crumpled weather-beaten face.* **2** worn or damaged as a result of exposure to the weather.

weathercock *n* a weather vane in the shape of a cock.

weather eye *n* **keep a weather eye on** to keep a careful watch on: *keep a weather eye on your symptoms.*

weathering *n* the breakdown of rocks by the action of the weather.

weatherman *n, pl* **-men** a man who forecasts the weather on radio or television. ▶ **weather girl** *fem n*

weather ship *n Meteorol* a ship that carries instruments for collecting meteorological data.

weather station *n Meteorol* one of a network of meteorological observation posts where information about the weather is recorded.

weather vane *n* a metal object on a roof that indicates the direction in which the wind is blowing.

weave *vb* **weaving, wove** *or* **weaved, woven** *or* **weaved 1** to form (a fabric) by interlacing yarn on a loom. **2** to make (a garment or a blanket) by this process. **3** to construct (a basket or fence) by interlacing cane or twigs. **4** to compose (a story or plan) by combining separate elements into a whole. **5** to move from side to side while going forward: *to weave in and out of lanes.* **6 get weaving** *Informal* to hurry. ✧ *n* **7** the structure or pattern of a woven fabric: *the rough weave of the cloth.* ▷ HISTORY Old English *wefan* ▶ **weaver** *n* ▶ **weaving** *n*

web *n* **1** a mesh of fine tough threads built by a spider to trap insects. **2** anything that is intricately formed or complex: *a web of relationships.* **3** a membrane connecting the toes of some water birds and water-dwelling animals such as frogs. **4 the web** (*often cap*) short for **World Wide Web**. ✧ *adj* **5** of or situated on the World Wide Web: *a web server; web pages.* ▷ HISTORY Old English *webb* ▶ **webbed** *adj*

webbing *n* a strong fabric that is woven in strips and used under springs in upholstery or for straps.

webcam *n* a camera that transmits still or moving images over the Internet.

webcast *n* a broadcast of an event over the Internet.

weber (**vay**-ber) *n* the SI unit of magnetic flux (the strength of a magnetic field over a given area). ▷ HISTORY after W. E. *Weber,* physicist

web-footed *or* **web-toed** *adj* (of certain animals or birds) having webbed feet that aid swimming.

weblog *n* a person's online journal. Also: **blog**

website *n* a group of connected pages on the World Wide Web containing information on a particular subject.

wed *vb* **wedding, wedded** *or* **wed** **1** *Old-fashioned* to take (a person) as a husband or wife; marry. **2** to unite closely: *to wed folklore and magic.* ▷ HISTORY Old English *weddian*

Wed. Wednesday.

wedded *adj* **1** of marriage: *wedded bliss.* **2** firmly in support of an idea or institution: *wedded to the virtues of capitalism.*

wedding *n* **1** a marriage ceremony. **2** a special wedding anniversary, esp. the 25th (**silver wedding**) or 50th (**golden wedding**).

wedge *n* **1** a block of solid material, esp. wood or metal, that is shaped like a narrow V in cross section and can be pushed or driven between two objects or parts of an object in order to split or secure them. **2** a slice shaped like a wedge: *a wedge of quiche.* **3** *Golf* a club with a wedge-shaped face, used for bunker or pitch shots. **4 drive a wedge between** to cause a split between (people or groups). **5 the thin end of the wedge** anything unimportant in itself that implies the start of something much larger. ✧ *vb* **wedging, wedged 6** to secure (something) with a wedge. **7** to squeeze into a narrow space: *a book wedged between the bed and the table.* ▷ HISTORY Old English *wecg*

wedge-tailed eagle *n* a large brown Australian eagle with a wedge-shaped tail.

wedlock *n* **1** the state of being married. **2 born out of wedlock** born when one's parents are not legally married. ▷ HISTORY Old English *wedlāc*

Wednesday *n* the fourth day of the week. ▷ HISTORY Old English *Wōdnes dæg* Woden's day

wee[1] *adj Brit, Austral & NZ* small or short. ▷ HISTORY Old English *wǣg* weight

wee[2] *Informal* ✧ *n* **1** an instance of urinating. ✧ *vb* **weeing, weed 2** to urinate. Also: **wee-wee** ▷ HISTORY origin unknown

weed *n* **1** any plant that grows wild and profusely, esp. among cultivated plants. **2** *Slang* **a** marijuana. **b the weed** *or* **the evil weed** tobacco. **3** *Informal* a thin weak person. ✧ *vb* **4** to remove weeds from (a garden). ▷ HISTORY Old English *wēod*

weedkiller *n* a chemical or hormonal substance used to kill weeds.

weed out *vb* to separate out, remove, or eliminate (an unwanted element): *to weed out the thugs.*

weedy *adj* **weedier, weediest 1** *Informal* thin or weak: *sick and weedy children.* **2** full of weeds: *weedy patches of garden.*

week *n* **1** a period of seven consecutive days, esp. one beginning with Sunday. **2** a period of seven consecutive days from a specified day: *a week from today.* **3** the period of time within a week that is spent at work. ▷ HISTORY Old English *wice, wicu*

weekday *n* any day of the week other than Saturday or Sunday.

weekend *n* Saturday and Sunday.

weekly *adj* **1** happening once a week or every week: *a weekly column.* **2** determined or calculated by the week: *weekly earnings.* ✧ *adv* **3** once a week or every week: *report to the police weekly.* ✧ *n, pl* **-lies 4** a newspaper or magazine issued every week.

weep *vb* **weeping, wept 1** to shed tears; cry. **2** to ooze liquid: *the skin cracked and wept; the label is weeping black ink in the rain.* ✧ *n* **3** a spell of weeping: *together we had a good weep.* ▷ HISTORY Old English *wēpan*

weeping willow *n* a willow tree with graceful drooping branches.

weepy *Informal* ✧ *adj* **weepier, weepiest 1** liable or tending to weep. ✧ *n, pl* **weepies 2** a sentimental film or book.

weevil *n* a beetle with a long snout that feeds on plants. ▷ HISTORY Old English *wifel*

wee-wee *n, vb* **-weeing, -weed** *Informal, chiefly Brit* same as **wee**[2].

weft *n* the yarns woven across the width of the fabric through the lengthways warp yarns. ▷ HISTORY Old English

weigh *vb* **1** to have weight as specified: *the tree weighs nearly three tons.* **2** to measure the weight of. **3** to consider carefully: *the President now has to weigh his options.* **4** to be influential: *the authorities did not enter my mind or weigh with me.* **5 weigh anchor** to raise a ship's anchor. **6 weigh out** to measure out by weight. ✧ See also **weigh in**. ▷ HISTORY Old English *wegan*

weighbridge *n* a machine for weighing vehicles by means of a metal plate set into a road.

weigh in *vb* **1** (of a boxer or jockey) to be weighed to check that one is of the correct weight for the contest. **2** *Informal* to contribute to a discussion or conversation: *he weighed in with a few sharp comments.* ✧ *n* **weigh-in 3** *Sport* the occasion of checking the competitors' weight before a boxing match or a horse race.

weight *n* **1** the heaviness of an object, substance, or person. **2** *Physics* the vertical force experienced by a mass as a result of gravitation. **3 a** a system of units used to express weight: *metric weight.* **b** a unit used to measure weight: *the kilogram is the weight used in the metric system.* **4 a** an object of known heaviness used for weighing objects, substances,

A B C D E F G H I J K L M N O P Q R S T U V W X Y Z

or people. **b** an object of known heaviness used in weight training or weightlifting to strengthen the muscles. **5** any heavy load: *with a weight of fish on their backs.* **6** force, importance, or influence: *they want their words to carry weight.* **7** an oppressive force: *the weight of expectation.* **8 pull one's weight** *Informal* to do one's full share of a task. **9 throw one's weight about** *Informal* to act in an aggressive authoritarian manner. ✧ *vb* **10** to add weight to; make heavier. **11** to slant (a system) so that it favours one side rather than another. ▷ HISTORY Old English *wiht*

weighting *n Brit* an allowance paid to compensate for higher living costs: *salary includes Inner London weighting.*

weightless *adj* **1** seeming to have very little weight or no weight at all. **2** seeming not to be affected by gravity, as in the case of astronauts in an orbiting spacecraft. ▶ **weightlessness** *n*

weightlifting *n* the sport of lifting barbells of specified weights in a prescribed manner. ▶ **weightlifter** *n*

weight training *n* physical exercise using light or heavy weights in order to strengthen the muscles.

weighty *adj* **weightier, weightiest 1** important or serious: *weighty matters.* **2** very heavy.

Weimar Republic (**vie**-mar) *n History* the German republic that existed from 1919 till Hitler's accession to power in 1933.

weir *n* **1** a low dam that is built across a river to divert the water or control its flow. **2** a fencelike trap built across a stream for catching fish in. ▷ HISTORY Old English *wer*

weird *adj* **1** strange or bizarre. **2** suggestive of the supernatural; uncanny. ▷ HISTORY Old English *(ge)wyrd* destiny ▶ **weirdly** *adv* ▶ **weirdness** *n*

weirdo *n, pl* **-dos** *Informal* a person who behaves in a bizarre or eccentric manner.

welch *vb* same as **welsh**.

welcome *vb* **-coming, -comed 1** to greet the arrival of (a guest) cordially. **2** to receive or accept (something) gladly: *I would welcome a chance to speak to him.* ✧ *n* **3** the act of greeting or receiving someone or something in a specified manner: *the President was given a warm welcome.* ✧ *adj* **4** gladly received or admitted: *I wouldn't want to stay where I'm not welcome.* **5** encouraged or invited: *you are welcome to join us at one of our social events.* **6** bringing pleasure: *a welcome change.* **7 you're welcome** an expression used to acknowledge someone's thanks. ▷ HISTORY Old English *wilcuma* ▶ **welcoming** *adj*

weld *vb* **1** to join (two pieces of metal or plastic) by softening with heat and hammering or by fusion. **2** to unite closely: *the diverse ethnic groups had been welded together by the anti-Fascist cause.* ✧ *n* **3** a joint formed by welding. ▷ HISTORY obsolete *well* to melt, weld ▶ **welder** *n*

welfare *n* **1** health, happiness, prosperity, and general wellbeing. **2** financial and other assistance given, usually by the government, to people in need. ▷ HISTORY WEL(L)[1] + FARE

welfare state *n* a system in which the government undertakes responsibility for the wellbeing of its population, through unemployment insurance, old age pensions, and other social-security measures.

well[1] *adv* **better, best 1** satisfactorily or pleasingly: *well proportioned.* **2** skilfully: *I played well for the last six holes.* **3** thoroughly: *make sure the chicken is well cooked.* **4** comfortably or prosperously: *he has lived well from his various nautical exploits.* **5** suitably or fittingly: *you can't very well refuse.* **6** intimately: *darling Robert, I know him so well.* **7** favourably: *it will go down very well with all the people who support him.* **8** by a considerable margin: *well over half; she left well before tea.* **9** very likely: *the claim may well be true.* **10** *Informal* extremely: *well cool.* **11 all very well** used ironically to express discontent or annoyance: *that's all very well, but I'm left to pick up the pieces.* **12 as well a** in addition. **b** with equal effect: used to express indifference or reluctance: *I might as well go out.* **13 as well as** in addition to. **14 just as well** fortunate or appropriate: *it's just as well I didn't spend all my money.* ✧ *adj* **15** in good health: *I'm not feeling well.* **16** satisfactory or acceptable: *all was well in the aircraft.* ✧ *interj* **17 a** an expression of surprise, indignation, or reproof: *well, what a cheek!* **b** an expression of anticipation in waiting for an answer or remark: *well, what do you think?* ▷ HISTORY Old English *wel*

well[2] *n* **1** a hole or shaft bored into the earth to tap a supply of water, oil, or gas. **2** an open shaft through the floors of a building, used for a staircase. ✧ *vb* **3** to flow upwards or outwards: *tears welled up into my eyes.* ▷ HISTORY Old English *wella*

well-balanced *adj* sensible and emotionally stable.

wellbeing *n* the state of being contented and healthy: *a sense of wellbeing.*

well-bred *adj* having good manners; polite.

well-built *adj* strong and well-proportioned.

well-disposed *adj* inclined to be sympathetic, kindly, or friendly towards a person or idea.

well-done *adj* **1** made or accomplished satisfactorily. **2** (of food, esp. meat) cooked very thoroughly.

well-grounded *adj* having a sound basis in fact: *well-grounded suspicions.*

wellhead *n* **1** the source of a well or stream. **2** a source, fountainhead, or origin.

well-heeled *adj Informal* wealthy.

wellies *pl n Brit & Austral informal* Wellington boots.

Wellington boots *or* **wellingtons** *pl n Brit & Austral* long rubber boots, worn in wet or muddy conditions. ▷ HISTORY after the 1st Duke of *Wellington*, soldier & statesman

well-known *adj* widely known; famous.

well-meaning *adj* having or indicating good intentions, usually with unfortunate results.

well-nigh *adv* almost: *a well-nigh impossible task.*

well-off *adj* **1** moderately wealthy. **2** in a fortunate position: *some people don't know when they are well-off.*

well-read *adj* having read and learned a lot.

well-spoken *adj* having a clear, articulate, and socially acceptable accent and way of speaking.

wellspring *n* a source of abundant supply: *the wellspring of truth.*

well-to-do *adj* moderately wealthy.

well-worn *adj* **1** (of a word or phrase) having lost its meaning or force through being overused. **2** having been used so much as to show signs of wear: *well-worn leather.*

welsh *or* **welch** *vb* **welsh on** to fail to pay (a debt) or fulfil (an obligation). ▷ **HISTORY** origin unknown

Welsh *adj* **1** of Wales. ✧ *n* **2** a Celtic language spoken in some parts of Wales. ✧ *pl n* **3 the Welsh** the people of Wales. ▷ **HISTORY** Old English *Wēlisc, Wælisc*

Welshman *or fem* **Welshwoman** *n, pl* **-men** *or* **-women** a person from Wales.

Welsh rarebit *n* melted cheese, sometimes mixed with milk or seasonings, served on hot toast.

welt *n* **1** a raised mark on the skin produced by a blow. **2** a raised or strengthened seam in a garment. ▷ **HISTORY** origin unknown

welter *n* a confused mass or jumble: *a welter of facts.* ▷ **HISTORY** Middle Low German, Middle Dutch *weltern*

welterweight *n* a professional boxer weighing up to 147 pounds (66.5 kg) or an amateur boxer weighing up to 67 kg.

wen *n Pathol* a cyst on the scalp. ▷ **HISTORY** Old English *wenn*

wench *n Old-fashioned* **1** *Facetious* a girl or young woman. **2** a prostitute or female servant. ▷ **HISTORY** Old English *wencel* child

wend *vb* to make (one's way) in a particular direction: *it's time to wend our way back home.* ▷ **HISTORY** Old English *wendan*

wensleydale *n* a white cheese with a flaky texture. ▷ **HISTORY** after *Wensleydale*, North Yorkshire

went *vb* the past tense of **go**.

wept *vb* the past of **weep**.

were *vb* the form of the past tense of **be:** used after *we, you, they,* or a plural noun, or as a subjunctive in conditional sentences. ▷ **HISTORY** Old English *wēron, wæron*

> ☑ **WORD TIP**
> *Were,* as a remnant of the past subjunctive in English, is used in formal contexts in clauses expressing hypotheses (*if he were to die, she would inherit everything*), suppositions contrary to fact (*if I were you, I would be careful*), and desire (*I wish he were there now*). In informal speech, however, *was* is often used instead.

we're we are.

weren't were not.

werewolf *n, pl* **-wolves** (in folklore) a person who can turn into a wolf. ▷ **HISTORY** Old English *wer* man + *wulf* wolf

west *n* **1** one of the four cardinal points of the compass, at 270° clockwise from north; the direction along a line of latitude towards the sunset. **2 the west** any area lying in or towards the west. ✧ *adj* **3** situated in, moving towards, or facing the west. **4** (esp. of the wind) from the west. ✧ *adv* **5** in, to, or towards the west. ▷ **HISTORY** Old English

West *n* **1 the West a** the western part of the world contrasted historically and culturally with the East. **b** (esp. formerly) the non-Communist countries of Europe and America contrasted with the Communist states of the East. ✧ *adj* **2** of or denoting the western part of a country or region.

westerly *adj* **1** of or in the west. ✧ *adv, adj* **2** towards the west. **3** from the west: *a westerly wind.*

western *adj* **1** situated in or towards the west. **2** facing or moving towards the west. **3** (*sometimes cap*) of or characteristic of the west or West. ✧ *n* **4** a film or book about cowboys in the western states of the US in the 19th century. ▶ **westernmost** *adj*

Western *adj* (esp. formerly) of or characteristic of the Americas and the parts of Europe not under Communist rule.

western hemisphere *n Geog* the half of the globe that contains the Americas.

westernize *or* **-ise** *vb* **-izing, -ized** *or* **-ising, -ised** to influence or make familiar with the customs or practices of the West. ▶ **westernization** *or* **-isation** *n*

West Indian *adj* **1** of the West Indies. ✧ *n* **2** a person from the West Indies.

Westminster *n* the British Houses of Parliament.

westward *adj, adv also* **westwards 1** towards the west. ✧ *n* **2** the westward part or direction.

wet *adj* **wetter, wettest 1** moistened, covered, or soaked with water or some other liquid. **2** not yet dry or solid: *wet paint.* **3** rainy: *the weather was cold and wet.* **4** *Brit & NZ informal* feeble or foolish. **5 wet behind the ears** *Informal* immature or inexperienced. ✧ *n* **6** rainy weather. **7** *Brit informal* a feeble or foolish person. **8** *Brit informal* a Conservative politician who supports moderate policies. ✧ *vb* **wetting, wet** *or* **wetted 9** to make wet: *wet the brush before applying the paint.* **10** to urinate in (one's clothes or bed). **11 wet oneself** to urinate in one's clothes. ▷ **HISTORY** Old English *wæt* ▶ **wetly** *adv* ▶ **wetness** *n*

wet blanket *n Informal* a person whose low spirits or lack of enthusiasm have a depressing effect on others.

wet dream *n* an erotic dream accompanied by an emission of semen.

wether *n* a male sheep, esp. a castrated one. ▷ **HISTORY** Old English

wetland *n Geog* an area of marshy land.

wet nurse *n* (esp. formerly) a woman hired to breast-feed another woman's baby.

wet suit *n* a close-fitting rubber suit used by skin-divers and yachtsmen to retain body heat.

whack *vb* **1** to hit hard: *that lad whacked him over the head with a bottle.* ✧ *n* **2** a hard blow or the sound of one: *a whack with a blunt instrument.* **3** *Informal* a share: *he took his whack of that money.* **4 have a whack** to make an attempt. **5 out of whack** *Informal* out of order or out of condition: *my body is just a little out of whack.* ▷ **HISTORY** imitative

whacked *adj Informal* completely exhausted.

whacking *n* **1** *Old-fashioned* a severe beating. ✧ *adv* **2** *Brit, Austral & NZ informal* extremely: *a whacking great elm.*

whale *n* **1** a very large fishlike sea mammal that breathes through a blowhole on the top of its head. **2 have a whale of a time** *Informal* to enjoy oneself very much. ▷ **HISTORY** Old English *hwæl*

whalebone *n* a thin strip of a horny material that hangs from the upper jaw of some whales, formerly used for stiffening corsets.

whalebone whale *n* any whale with a double blowhole and strips of whalebone between the jaws instead of teeth, including the right whale and the blue whale.

whaler *n* **1** a ship used for hunting whales. **2** a person whose job is to hunt whales.

whaling *n* the activity of hunting and killing whales for food or oil.

wham *interj Informal* an expression indicating suddenness or forcefulness: *suddenly, wham! you are caught up right in the middle of it.* ▷ **HISTORY** imitative

wharepuni (**for**-rep-poon-ee) *n NZ* (in a Maori community) a tall carved building used as a guesthouse. ▷ **HISTORY** Maori

wharf *n, pl* **wharves** *or* **wharfs** a platform along the side of a waterfront for docking, loading, and unloading ships. ▷ **HISTORY** Old English *hwearf*

wharfie *n Austral & NZ* a dock labourer.

what *pron* **1** used in requesting further information about the identity or categorization of something: *what was he wearing?; I knew what would happen.* **2** the person, thing, people, or things that: *all was not what it seemed.* **3** used in exclamations to add emphasis: *what a creep!* **4 what for?** for what reason? **5 what have you** other similar or related things: *qualifications, interests, profession, what have you.* ✧ *adj* **6** used with a noun in requesting further information about the identity or categorization of something: *what difference can it make now?* **7** to any degree or in any amount: *they provided what financial support they could.* ▷ **HISTORY** Old English *hwæt*

> ☑ **WORD TIP**
>
> The use of *are* in sentences such as *what we need are more doctors* is common, although many people think *is* should be used: *what we need is more doctors.*

whatever *pron* **1** everything or anything that: *I can handle whatever comes up.* **2** no matter what: *whatever you do, keep your temper.* **3** *Informal* other similar or related things: *a block of wood, rock, or whatever.* **4** an intensive form of *what,* used in questions: *whatever gave you that impression?* ✧ *adj* **5** an intensive form of *what*: *I can take whatever actions I deem necessary.* **6** at all: *there is no foundation whatever for such opinions.*

whatnot *n Informal* other similar or related things: *groceries, wines, and whatnot.*

whatsoever *adj* at all: used for emphasis after a noun phrase that uses words such as *none* or *any*: *there is nothing whatsoever wrong with your heart; it can be used at any time and under any circumstances whatsoever.*

wheat *n* **1** a kind of grain used in making flour and pasta. **2** the plant from which this grain is obtained. ▷ **HISTORY** Old English *hwǣte*

wheatear *n* a small northern songbird with a white rump. ▷ **HISTORY** from *white* + *arse*

wheaten *adj* made from the grain or flour of wheat: *wheaten bread.*

wheat germ *n* the vitamin-rich middle part of a grain of wheat.

wheatmeal *n* a brown flour intermediate between white flour and wholemeal flour.

wheedle *vb* **-dling, -dled 1** to try to persuade (someone) by coaxing or flattery: *wheedling you into giving them their way.* **2** to obtain (something) in this way: *she wheedled money out of him.* ▷ **HISTORY** origin unknown ▶ **wheedling** *adj, n*

wheel *n* **1** a circular object mounted on a shaft around which it can turn, fixed under vehicles to enable them to move. **2** anything like a wheel in shape or function: *the steering wheel; a spinning wheel.* **3** something that is repeated in cycles: *the wheel of fashion would turn, and the clothes would be back in style.* **4 at** *or* **behind the wheel** driving a vehicle. ✧ *vb* **5** to push (a bicycle, wheelchair, or pram) along. **6** to turn in a circle. **7 wheel and deal** to operate shrewdly and sometimes unscrupulously in order to advance one's own interests. **8 wheel round** to change direction or turn round suddenly. ✧ See also **wheels.** ▷ **HISTORY** Old English *hwēol, hweowol*

wheelbarrow *n* a shallow open box for carrying small loads, with a wheel at the front and two handles.

wheelbase *n* the distance between the front and back axles of a motor vehicle.

wheelchair *n* a special chair on large wheels, for use by people who cannot walk properly.

wheel clamp *n* a device fixed onto one wheel of an illegally parked car to prevent the car being driven off.

wheelie *n* a manoeuvre on a cycle or skateboard in which the front wheel or wheels are raised off the ground.

wheelie bin *n Brit, Austral & NZ* a large container for household rubbish, mounted on wheels so that it can be moved more easily.

wheeling and dealing *n* shrewd and sometimes unscrupulous moves made in order to advance one's own interests. ▶ **wheeler-dealer** *n*

wheels *pl n* **1** *Informal* a car. **2** the main force and mechanism of an organization or system: *the* *wheels of the economy.* **3 wheels within wheels** a series of intricately connected events or plots.

wheelwright *n* a person whose job is to make and mend wheels.

wheeze *vb* **wheezing, wheezed 1** to breathe with a rasping or whistling sound. ✧ *n* **2** a wheezing breath or sound. **3** *Brit old-fashioned slang* a trick or plan: *a glorious tax wheeze.* ▷ **HISTORY** probably from Old Norse *hvæsa* to hiss ▶ **wheezy** *adj*

whelk *n* an edible sea creature with a strong snail-like shell. ▷ **HISTORY** Old English *weoloc*

whelp *n* **1** a young wolf or dog. **2** *Offensive* a youth. ✧ *vb* **3** (of an animal) to give birth. ▷ **HISTORY** Old English *hwelp*

when *adv* **1** at what time?: *when are they leaving?* ✧ *conj* **2** at the time at which: *he was twenty when the war started.* **3** although: *he drives when he could walk.* **4** considering the fact that: *how did you pass the exam when you hadn't studied for it?* ✧ *pron* **5** at which time: *she's at the age when girls get interested in boys.* ▷ **HISTORY** Old English *hwanne, hwænne*

> **☑ WORD TIP**
> *When* should not be used loosely as a substitute for *in which* after a noun which does not refer to a period of time: *paralysis is a condition in which* (not *when*) *parts of the body cannot be moved.*

whence *conj Old-fashioned or poetic* from what place, cause, or origin: *he would then ask them whence they came.* ▷ **HISTORY** Middle English *whannes*

> **☑ WORD TIP**
> The expression *from whence* should be avoided, since *whence* already means from which place: *the tradition whence* (not *from whence*) *such ideas flowed.*

whenever *conj* **1** at every or any time that: *the filly was trained to stop whenever a jockey used a whip.* ✧ *adv* **2** no matter when: *I am eager to come whenever you suggest.* **3** *Informal* at an unknown or unspecified time: *the 16th, 17th, or whenever.* **4** an intensive form of *when*, used in questions: *if we can't exercise restraint now, whenever can we?*

where *adv* **1** in, at, or to what place, point, or position?: *where are we going?; I know where he found it.* ✧ *pron* **2** in, at, or to which place: *he found a sandwich bar where he could get a snack.* ✧ *conj* **3** in the place at which: *he should have stayed where he was doing well.* ▷ **HISTORY** Old English *hwǣr*

whereabouts *pl n* **1** the place, esp. the approximate place, where a person or thing is: *the whereabouts of the president are unknown.* ✧ *adv* **2** approximately where: *whereabouts will you go?*

whereas *conj* but by contrast: *she was crazy about him, whereas for him it was just another affair.*

whereby *pron* by or because of which: *the process whereby pests become resistant to pesticides.*

wherefore *n* **1 the whys and wherefores** the reasons or explanation: *the whys and wherefores of the war.* ✧ *conj* **2** *Old-fashioned or formal* for which reason.

whereupon *conj* at which point: *they sentenced him to death, whereupon he fainted.*

wherever *pron* **1** at, in, or to every place or point which: *I got a wonderful reception wherever I went.* ✧ *conj* **2** in, to, or at whatever place: *wherever they went, the conditions were harsh.* ✧ *adv* **3** no matter where: *we're going to find him, wherever he is.* **4** *Informal* at, in, or to an unknown or unspecified place: *the jungles of Borneo or wherever.* **5** an intensive form of *where*, used in questions: *wherever have you been?*

wherewithal *n* **the wherewithal** the necessary funds, resources, or equipment: *the wherewithal for making chemical weapons.*

whet *vb* **whetting, whetted 1 whet someone's appetite** to increase someone's desire for or interest in something: *she gave him just enough information to whet his appetite.* **2** *Old-fashioned* to sharpen (a knife or other tool). ▷ **HISTORY** Old English *hwettan*

whether *conj* **1** used to introduce an indirect question: *he asked him whether he had seen the hunter.* **2** used to introduce a clause expressing doubt or choice: *you are entitled to the assistance of a lawyer, whether or not you can afford one; we learn from experience, whether good or bad.* ▷ **HISTORY** Old English *hwæther*

whetstone *n* a stone used for sharpening knives or other tools.

whew *interj* an exclamation of relief, surprise, disbelief, or weariness.

whey *n* the watery liquid that separates from the curd when milk is clotted, for example in making cheese. ▷ **HISTORY** Old English *hwǣg*

which *adj* **1** used with a noun in requesting that the particular thing being referred to is further identified or distinguished: *which way had he gone?; a questionnaire to find out which shops local consumers use.* **2** any out of several: *you have to choose which goods and services you want.* ✧ *pron* **3** used in requesting that the particular thing being referred to is further identified or distinguished: *which of these occupations would be suitable for you?* **4** used in relative clauses referring to a thing rather than a person: *a discovery which could have lasting effects.* **5** and that: *her books were all over the dining table, which meant we had to eat in the kitchen.* ▷ **HISTORY** Old English *hwelc*

> **☑ WORD TIP**
> See at **that.**

whichever *adj* **1** any out of several: *choose whichever line you feel more comfortable with.* **2** no matter which: *whichever bridge you take, pause mid-stream for a look up and down the river.* ✧ *pron* **3** any one or ones out of several: *delete whichever is inapplicable.* **4** no matter which one or ones: *whichever you choose, you must be consistent throughout.*

whiff *n* **1** a passing odour: *I got a whiff of her perfume.* **2** a trace or hint: *the first whiff of jealousy.* ✧ *vb* **3** *Brit informal* to have an unpleasant smell. ▷ **HISTORY** imitative ▶ **whiffy** *adj*

A B C D E F G H I J K L M N O P Q R S T U V W X Y Z

Whig *n* **1** a member of a British political party of the 18th–19th centuries that sought limited political and social reform and provided the core of the Liberal Party. ✧ *adj* **2** of or relating to Whigs. ▷ **HISTORY** probably from *whiggamore*, one of a group of 17th-century Scottish rebels ▶ **Whiggism** *n*

while *conj* **1** at the same time that: *anti-inflammatory remedies may be used to alleviate the condition while background factors are investigated.* **2** at some point during the time that: *her father had died while she was gone.* **3** although or whereas: *while she tossed and turned, he fell into a dreamless sleep.* ✧ *n* **4** a period of time: *I'd like to stay a while.* ▷ **HISTORY** Old English *hwīl*

> **WORD TIP**
> It was formerly considered incorrect to use *while* to mean *although* or *whereas*, but these uses have now become acceptable.

while away *vb* **whiling, whiled** to pass (time) idly but pleasantly.

whilst *conj Chiefly Brit* same as **while**.

whim *n* a sudden, passing, and often fanciful idea. ▷ **HISTORY** origin unknown

whimper *vb* **1** to cry, complain, or say (something) in a whining plaintive way. ✧ *n* **2** a soft plaintive whine. ▷ **HISTORY** imitative

whimsical *adj* unusual, playful, and fanciful: *a whimsical story.* ▶ **whimsically** *adv*

whimsy *n* **1** (*pl* **-sies**) a fanciful or playful idea: *they thought sparing the rod a foolish whimsy.* **2** capricious or playful behaviour: *sudden flights of whimsy.* ▷ **HISTORY** from *whim*

whin *n Chiefly Brit* same as **gorse**. ▷ **HISTORY** from Old Norse

whine *n* **1** a long high-pitched plaintive cry or moan. **2** a peevish complaint. ✧ *vb* **whining, whined 3** to utter a whine. ▷ **HISTORY** Old English *hwinan* ▶ **whiner** *n* ▶ **whining** *adj, n*

whinge *Brit, Austral & NZ informal* ✧ *vb* **whingeing, whinged 1** to complain in a moaning manner. ✧ *n* **2** a complaint. ▷ **HISTORY** Old English *hwinsian* to whine ▶ **whinger** *n*

whinny *vb* **-nies, -nying, -nied 1** (of a horse) to neigh softly or gently. ✧ *n, pl* **-nies 2** a gentle or low-pitched neigh. ▷ **HISTORY** imitative

whip *n* **1** a piece of leather or rope attached at one end to a stiff handle, used for hitting people or animals. **2 a** a member of a political party who is responsible for urging members to attend Parliament to vote on an important issue. **b** a notice sent to members of a political party by the whip, urging them to attend Parliament to vote in a particular way on an important issue. **3** a dessert made from egg whites or cream beaten stiff: *raspberry whip.* ✧ *vb* **whipping, whipped 4** to hit with a whip. **5** to hit sharply: *strands of hair whipped across her cheeks.* **6** *Informal* to move or go quickly and suddenly: *machine-gun bullets whipped past him.* **7** to beat (cream or eggs) with a whisk or fork until frothy or stiff. **8** to rouse (someone) into a particular condition: *politicians and businessmen have whipped themselves into a panic about never-ending recession.* **9** *Informal* to steal (something). ✧ See also **whip-round**. ▷ **HISTORY** perhaps from Middle Dutch *wippen* to swing ▶ **whipping** *n*

whip bird *n Austral* a bird with a whistle ending in a whipcrack note.

whip hand *n* **the whip hand** an advantage or dominating position: *buyers have the whip hand over estate agents.*

whiplash *n* **1** a quick lash of a whip. **2** short for **whiplash injury**.

whiplash injury *n* an injury to the neck resulting from the head being suddenly thrust forward and then snapped back, for example in a car crash.

whippet *n* a small slender dog similar to a greyhound. ▷ **HISTORY** perhaps based on *whip it!* move quickly!

whipping boy *n* a person who is expected to take the blame for other people's mistakes or incompetence.

whip-round *n Informal* an impromptu collection of money.

whir *n, vb* **whirring, whirred** same as **whirr**.

whirl *vb* **1** to spin or turn round very fast. **2** to seem to spin from dizziness or confusion: *my mind whirled with half-formed thoughts.* ✧ *n* **3** the act or an instance of whirling: *he grasps her by the waist and gives her a whirl.* **4** a round of intense activity: *the social whirl of Paris.* **5** a confused state: *my thoughts are in a whirl.* **6 give something a whirl** *Informal* to try something new. ▷ **HISTORY** Old Norse *hvirfla* to turn about

whirlpool *n* a powerful circular current of water, into which objects floating nearby are drawn.

whirlwind *n* **1** a column of air whirling violently upwards in a spiral. ✧ *adj* **2** done or happening much more quickly than usual: *a whirlwind tour of France.*

whirr *or* **whir** *n* **1** a prolonged soft whizz or buzz: *the whirr of the fax machine.* ✧ *vb* **whirring, whirred 2** to produce a prolonged soft whizz or buzz. ▷ **HISTORY** probably from Old Norse ▶ **whirring** *n, adj*

whisk *vb* **1** to move or take somewhere swiftly: *I was whisked away in a police car.* **2** to brush away lightly: *the waiter whisked the crumbs away with a napkin.* **3** to beat (cream or eggs) with a whisk or fork until frothy or stiff. ✧ *n* **4** the act or an instance of whisking: *a whisk of a scaly tail.* **5** a utensil for beating cream or eggs until frothy or stiff. ▷ **HISTORY** Old Norse *visk* wisp

whisker *n* **1** any of the long stiff hairs that grow out from the sides of the mouth of a cat or other mammal. **2** any of the hairs growing on a man's face, esp. on the cheeks or chin. **3 by a whisker** by a very small distance or amount: *we missed him by a whisker.* ▷ **HISTORY** Old Norse *visk* wisp ▶ **whiskered** *or* **whiskery** *adj*

whiskey *n* Irish or American whisky.

whisky *n, pl* **-kies** a strong alcoholic drink made by distilling fermented cereals, esp. in Scotland.

> **WORD HISTORY**
> The word 'whisky' comes from Scottish Gaelic *uisge beatha*, meaning 'water of life'. Whisky is not the only alcoholic 'water of life': 'aqua vitae', which means 'water of life' in Latin, is an old name for brandy, and there is also in Scandinavia a strong alcoholic drink called 'aquavit' or 'akvavit'.

whisper *vb* **1** to speak or say (something) very softly, using the breath instead of the vocal cords. **2** to make a low soft rustling sound: *the leaves whispered.* ✧ *n* **3** a low soft voice: *her voice sank to a whisper.* **4** *Informal* a rumour: *I just picked up a whisper on this killing.* **5** a low soft rustling sound: *a whisper of breeze in the shrubbery.* ▷ **HISTORY** Old English *hwisprian* ▶ **whispered** *adj*

whist *n* a card game for two pairs of players. ▷ **HISTORY** perhaps from *whisk,* referring to the whisking up of the tricks

whist drive *n* a social gathering where whist is played.

whistle *vb* **-tling, -tled 1** to produce a shrill sound by forcing breath between pursed lips. **2** to produce (a tune) by making a series of such sounds. **3** to signal (to) by whistling or blowing a whistle: *the doorman whistled a cruising cab.* **4** to move with a whistling sound: *a shell whistled through the upper air.* **5** (of a kettle or train) to produce a shrill sound caused by steam being forced through a small opening. **6** (of a bird) to give a shrill cry. **7 whistle in the dark** to try to keep up one's confidence in spite of being afraid. ✧ *n* **8** the act or sound of whistling: *he gave a whistle of astonishment.* **9** a metal instrument that is blown down its end to produce a tune, signal, or alarm: *he played the tin whistle; the referee's whistle.* **10** a device in a kettle or a train that makes a shrill sound by means of steam under pressure. **11 blow the whistle on** *Informal* to reveal and put a stop to (wrongdoing or a wrongdoer): *to blow the whistle on corrupt top-level officials.* **12 wet one's whistle** *Informal* to have a drink. ▷ **HISTORY** Old English *hwistlian*

whit *n* **not a whit** not at all: *it does not matter a whit.* ▷ **HISTORY** probably variant of obsolete *wight* a person

Whit *n* **1** short for **Whitsuntide.** ✧ *adj* **2** of Whitsuntide: *Whit Monday.*

white *adj* **1** having no hue, owing to the reflection of all or almost all light; of the colour of snow. **2** pale, because of illness, fear, shock, or another emotion: *white with rage.* **3** (of hair) having lost its colour, usually from age. **4** (of coffee or tea) with milk or cream. **5** (of wine) made from pale grapes or from black grapes separated from their skins. **6** denoting flour, or bread made from flour, that has had part of the grain removed. ✧ *n* **7** the lightest colour; the colour of snow. **8** the clear fluid that surrounds the yolk of an egg. **9** *Anat* the white part of the eyeball. **10** anything white, such as white paint or white clothing: *a room decorated all in white.* ✧ See also **whites.** ▷ **HISTORY** Old English *hwīt* ▶ **whiteness** *n* ▶ **whitish** *adj*

White *n* **1** a member of a light-skinned race. ✧ *adj* **2** of or relating to a White or Whites.

whitebait *n* **1** the young of herrings, sprats, or pilchards, cooked and eaten whole. **2** any of various small silvery fishes of Australia and New Zealand and of North American coastal regions of the Pacific.

white blood cell *n* same as **leucocyte.**

white-collar *adj* denoting workers employed in professional and clerical occupations.

white-collar crime *n Law* criminal activities relating to fraud, embezzlement, tax evasion, and other crimes linked to business and finance rather than to violence, drugs, etc.

white dwarf *n* a small, faint, very dense star.

white elephant *n* a possession that is unwanted by its owner.

white fish *n* a sea fish with white flesh that is used for food, such as cod or haddock.

white flag *n* a signal of surrender or to request a truce.

whitefly *n, pl* **-flies** a tiny whitish insect that is harmful to greenhouse plants.

white gold *n* a white lustrous hard-wearing alloy containing gold together with platinum or other metals, used in jewellery.

white goods *pl n* large household appliances, such as refrigerators and cookers.

white heat *n* **1** intense heat that produces a white light. **2** *Informal* a state of intense emotion: *the white heat of hate.*

white-hot *adj* **1** at such a high temperature that white light is produced. **2** *Informal* in a state of intense emotion: *white-hot agony.*

White House *n* the US president and the executive branch of the US government: *the White House reviewed the report.* ▷ **HISTORY** after the official home of the US president in Washington DC

white lie *n* a small lie, usually told to avoid hurting someone's feelings.

white light *n* light that contains all the wavelengths of the visible spectrum, as in sunlight.

white matter *n* the whitish tissue of the brain and spinal cord, consisting mainly of nerve fibres.

whiten *vb* to make or become white or whiter. ▶ **whitener** *n* ▶ **whitening** *n*

white noise *n* noise that has a wide range of frequencies of uniform intensity.

white paper *n Government* an official government report which sets out the government's policy on a specific matter.

White Russian (formerly) *adj* **1** of Byelorussia, an administrative division of the W Soviet Union: now Belarus. ✧ *n* **2** a person from Byelorussia. **3** the language of Byelorussia.

whites *pl n* white clothes, as worn for playing cricket.

white sauce *n* a thick sauce made from flour, butter, seasonings, and milk or stock.

A B C D E F G H I J K L M N O P Q R S T U V W X Y Z

white spirit *n* a colourless liquid obtained from petroleum and used as a substitute for turpentine.

White supremacy *n* the theory or belief that White people are superior to people of other races. ▶ **White supremacist** *n, adj*

white trash *n* poor White people living in the United States, esp. in the South.

whitewash *n* **1** a mixture of lime or chalk in water, for whitening walls and other surfaces. **2** an attempt to conceal the unpleasant truth: *the report was a whitewash.* ✧ *vb* **3** to cover with whitewash. **4** to conceal the unpleasant truth about. ▶ **whitewashed** *adj*

whitewood *n* a light-coloured wood often prepared for staining.

whither *conj Old-fashioned or poetic* to what place or for what purpose: *they knew not whither they went.* ▷ HISTORY Old English *hwider, hwæder*

whiting (**white**-ing) *n* **1** a white-fleshed food fish of European seas. **2** *Austral* any of several marine food fishes.

whitlow *n* an inflamed sore on the end of a finger or toe. ▷ HISTORY originally *white + flaw*

Whitsun *n* **1** short for **Whitsuntide**. ✧ *adj* **2** of Whit Sunday or Whitsuntide.

Whit Sunday *n* the seventh Sunday after Easter. ▷ HISTORY Old English *hwīta sunnandæg* white Sunday

Whitsuntide *n* the week that begins with Whit Sunday.

whittle *vb* **-tling, -tled 1** to make (an object) by cutting or shaving pieces from (a piece of wood) with a small knife. **2 whittle down** *or* **away** to reduce in size or effectiveness gradually: *my self-confidence had been whittled away to almost nothing.* ▷ HISTORY Old English *thwītan* to cut

whizz *or* **whiz** *vb* **whizzing, whizzed 1** to move with a loud humming or buzzing sound: *the bullets whizzed overhead.* **2** *Informal* to move or go quickly: *the wind surfers fairly whizzed along the water.* ✧ *n, pl* **whizzes 3** a loud humming or buzzing sound. **4** *Informal* a person who is extremely good at something: *he's a whizz on finance.* **5** *Slang* amphetamine. ▷ HISTORY imitative

whizz kid *or* **whiz kid** *n Informal* a person who is outstandingly able and successful for his or her age.

who *pron* **1** which person: *who are you?; he didn't know who had started it.* **2** used at the beginning of a relative clause referring to a person or people already mentioned: *he is a man who can effect change.* ▷ HISTORY Old English *hwā*

> ☑ **WORD TIP**
> See at **whom.**

WHO World Health Organization.

whoa *interj* a command used to stop horses or to slow down someone who is moving or talking too fast.

whodunnit *or* **whodunit** (hoo-**dun**-nit) *n Informal* a novel, play, or film about the solving of a murder mystery.

whoever *pron* **1** the person or people who: *whoever bought it for you has to make the claim.* **2** no matter who: *I pity him, whoever he is.* **3** *Informal* other similar or related people or person: *your best friend, your neighbours, or whoever.* **4** an intensive form of *who*, used in questions: *whoever thought of such a thing?*

whole *adj* **1** constituting or referring to all of something: *I'd spent my whole allowance by Saturday afternoon.* **2** unbroken or undamaged. ✧ *adv* **3** in an undivided or unbroken piece: *truffles are cooked whole.* **4** *Informal* completely or entirely: *a whole new theory of treatment.* ✧ *n* **5** all there is of a thing: *the whole of my salary.* **6** a collection of parts viewed together as a unit: *taking Great Britain as a whole.* **7 on the whole a** taking all things into consideration: *on the whole he has worked about one year out of twelve.* **b** in general: *on the whole they were not successful.* ▷ HISTORY Old English *hāl* ▶ **wholeness** *n*

wholefood *n* **1** food that has been refined or processed as little as possible. ✧ *adj* **2** of or relating to wholefood: *a wholefood diet.*

wholehearted *adj* done or given with total sincerity or enthusiasm: *wholehearted support.* ▶ **wholeheartedly** *adv*

wholemeal *adj Brit & Austral* **1** (of flour) made from the entire wheat kernel. **2** made from wholemeal flour: *wholemeal bread.*

whole number *n Maths* a number that does not contain a fraction, such as 0, 1, or 2.

wholesale *adj, adv* **1** of or by the business of selling goods in large quantities and at lower prices to retailers for resale: *wholesale prices; we buy fruit and vegetables wholesale.* **2** on a large scale or indiscriminately: *the wholesale destruction of forests; they were being hunted without mercy and slaughtered wholesale.* ▶ **wholesaler** *n*

wholesome *adj* **1** physically beneficial: *wholesome food.* **2** morally beneficial: *a wholesome attitude of the mind.* ▷ HISTORY from *whole* healthy

wholly *adv* completely or totally.

whom *pron* the objective form of *who*: *whom will you tell?; he was devoted to his wife, whom he married in 1960.* ▷ HISTORY Old English *hwām*

> ☑ **WORD TIP**
> It was formerly considered correct to use *whom* whenever the objective form of *who* was required. This is no longer thought to be necessary and the objective form *who* is now commonly used, even in formal writing: *there were several people there who he had met before. Who* cannot be used directly after a preposition – the preposition is usually displaced, as in *the man (who) he sold his car to.* In formal writing *whom* is preferred in sentences like these: *the man to whom he sold his car.* There are some types of sentence in which *who* cannot be used: *the refugees, many of whom were old and ill, were allowed across the border.*

whoop *vb* **1** to cry out in excitement or joy. **2 whoop it up** *Informal* to indulge in a noisy celebration. ✧ *n* **3** a loud cry of excitement or joy. ▷ **HISTORY** imitative

whoopee *Old-fashioned informal* ✧ *interj* **1** an exclamation of joy or excitement. ✧ *n* **2 make whoopee a** to indulge in a noisy celebration. **b** to make love.

whooping cough *n* an acute infectious disease mainly affecting children, that causes coughing spasms ending with a shrill crowing sound on breathing in.

whoops *interj* an exclamation of mild surprise or of apology.

whopper *n Informal* **1** an unusually large or impressive example of something: *Deauville's beach is a whopper.* **2** a big lie.

whopping *Informal* ✧ *adj* **1** unusually large: *a whopping 40 per cent.* ✧ *adv* **2** extremely: *it's a whopping great gamble.*

whore (**hore**) *n* a prostitute or promiscuous woman: often a term of abuse. ▷ **HISTORY** Old English *hōre*

whorl *n* **1** *Bot* a circular arrangement of leaves or flowers round the stem of a plant. **2** *Zool* a single turn in a spiral shell. **3** anything shaped like a coil. ▷ **HISTORY** probably variant of *whirl*

whose *pron* **1** of whom? belonging to whom?: used in direct and indirect questions: *whose idea was it?; I wondered whose it was.* **2** of whom or of which: used as a relative pronoun: *Gran had sympathy for anybody whose life had gone wrong.* ▷ **HISTORY** Old English *hwæs*, genitive of *hwā* who + *hwæt* what

why *adv* **1** for what reason?: *why did he marry her?; she avoided asking him why he was there.* ✧ *pron* **2** for or because of which: *you can think of all kinds of reasons why you should not believe it.* ✧ *n, pl* **whys 3 the whys and wherefores** See **wherefore** (sense 1). ✧ *interj* **4** an exclamation of surprise, indignation, or impatience: *why, I listen to you on the radio twice a week.* ▷ **HISTORY** Old English *hwȳ, hwī*

WI 1 Wisconsin. **2** *Brit & NZ* Women's Institute.

wick *n* **1** a cord through the middle of a candle, through which the fuel reaches the flame. **2 get on someone's wick** *Brit & Austral slang* to annoy someone. ▷ **HISTORY** Old English *wēoce*

wicked *adj* **1** morally bad: *the wicked queen in 'Snow White'.* **2** playfully mischievous or roguish: *let's be wicked and go skinny-dipping.* **3** dangerous or unpleasant: *there was a wicked cut over his eye.* **4** *Slang* very good. ▷ **HISTORY** Old English *wicca* sorcerer, *wicce* witch ▶ **wickedly** *adv* ▶ **wickedness** *n*

wicker *adj* made of wickerwork: *a wicker chair.* ▷ **HISTORY** from Old Norse

wickerwork *n* a material consisting of slender flexible twigs woven together.

wicket *n Cricket* **1** either of two sets of three stumps stuck in the ground with two wooden bails resting on top, at which the batsman stands. **2** the playing space between these. **3** the act or instance of a batsman being got out. ▷ **HISTORY** Old French *wiket*

wicketkeeper *n Cricket* the fielder positioned directly behind the wicket.

wide *adj* **1** having a great extent from side to side: *the wide main street.* **2** having a specified extent from side to side: *three metres wide.* **3** covering or including many different things: *a wide range of services.* **4** covering a large distance or extent: *the proposal was voted down by a wide margin.* **5** (of eyes) opened fully. ✧ *adv* **6** to a large or full extent: *he swung the door wide.* **7 far and wide** See **far** (sense 7). ✧ *n* **8** *Cricket* a ball bowled outside the batsman's reach, which scores a run for the batting side. ▷ **HISTORY** Old English *wīd* ▶ **widely** *adv*

wide-angle lens *n* a lens on a camera which can cover a wider angle of view than an ordinary lens.

wide-awake *adj* fully awake.

wide-eyed *adj* **1** innocent or naive. ✧ *adv, adj* **2** surprised or frightened: *wide-eyed astonishment.*

widen *vb* to make or become wide or wider.

widespread *adj* affecting an extensive area or a large number of people: *widespread damage; widespread public support.*

widgeon *n* same as **wigeon**.

widget *n* **1** *Informal* any small device, the name of which is unknown or forgotten. **2** a small device in a beer can which, when the can is opened, releases nitrogen gas into the beer, giving it a head. ▷ **HISTORY** changed from GADGET

widow *n* a woman whose husband has died and who has not remarried. ▷ **HISTORY** Old English *widewe* ▶ **widowhood** *n*

widowed *adj* denoting a person, usually a woman, whose spouse has died and who has not remarried.

widower *n* a man whose wife has died and who has not remarried.

width *n* **1** the extent or measurement of something from side to side. **2** the distance across a rectangular swimming bath, as opposed to its length.

wield *vb* **1** to handle or use (a weapon or tool). **2** to exert or maintain (power or influence). ▷ **HISTORY** Old English *wieldan, wealdan*

wife *n, pl* **wives** the woman to whom a man is married. ▷ **HISTORY** Old English *wīf* ▶ **wifely** *adj*

wig *n* an artificial head of hair. ▷ **HISTORY** from *periwig*

wigeon *or* **widgeon** *n* a wild marshland duck. ▷ **HISTORY** origin unknown

wigging *n Brit old-fashioned slang* a reprimand. ▷ **HISTORY** origin unknown

wiggle *vb* **-gling, -gled 1** to move with jerky movements from side to side or up and down: *she wiggled her toes in the cool water.* ✧ *n* **2** a wiggling movement or walk. ▷ **HISTORY** Middle Low German, Middle Dutch *wiggelen*

wigwam *n* a N Native American's tent, made of animal skins. ▷ **HISTORY** Native American *wikwām*

wilco *interj* an expression in signalling and telecommunications, indicating that a message just received will be complied with. ▷ **HISTORY** abbreviation for *I will comply*

wild *adj* **1** (of animals or birds) living in natural surroundings; not domesticated or tame. **2** (of plants) growing in a natural state; not cultivated. **3** uninhabited and desolate: *wild country.* **4** living in a savage or uncivilized way: *a wild mountain man.* **5** lacking restraint or control: *a wild party.* **6** stormy or violent: *a wild windy October morning.* **7** in a state of extreme emotional intensity: *wild with excitement.* **8** without reason or substance: *wild accusations.* **9 wild about** *Informal* very enthusiastic about: *his colleagues aren't all that wild about him.* ✧ *adv* **10 run wild** to behave without restraint: *she was allowed to run completely wild.* ✧ *n* **11 the wild** a free natural state of living: *creatures of the wild.* **12 the wilds** a desolate or uninhabited region: *the wilds of Africa.* ▷ HISTORY Old English *wilde* ▶ **wildly** *adv* ▶ **wildness** *n*

wild card *n* **1** *Sport* a player or team that is allowed to take part in a competition despite not having met the normal qualifying requirements. **2** *Computers* a character that can be substituted for any other in a file.

wildcat *n, pl* **-cats** *or* **-cat 1** a wild European cat that looks like a domesticated cat but is larger and has a bushy tail. **2** *Informal* a quick-tempered person. ✧ *adj* **3** *Chiefly US* risky and financially unsound: *a wildcat operation.*

wildcat strike *n* a strike begun by workers spontaneously or without union approval.

wildebeest *n, pl* **-beests** *or* **-beest** same as **gnu**. ▷ HISTORY Afrikaans

wilderness *n* **1** a wild uninhabited uncultivated region. **2** a confused mass or tangle: *a wilderness of long grass and wild flowers.* **3** a state of being no longer in a prominent position: *a long spell in the political wilderness.* ▷ HISTORY Old English *wildēornes,* from *wildēor* wild beast

wildfire *n* **spread like wildfire** to spread very quickly or uncontrollably.

wild flower *n* any flowering plant that grows in an uncultivated state.

wildfowl *pl n* wild birds, such as grouse and pheasants, that are hunted for sport or food.

wild-goose chase *n* a search that has little or no chance of success.

wildlife *n* wild animals and plants collectively.

wild rice *n* the dark-coloured edible grain of a North American grass that grows on wet ground.

Wild West *n* the western US during its settlement, esp. with reference to its lawlessness.

wiles *pl n* artful or seductive tricks or ploys. ▷ HISTORY from Old Norse *vēl* craft

wilful *or US* **willful** *adj* **1** determined to do things in one's own way: *a wilful and insubordinate child.* **2** deliberate and intentional: *wilful misconduct.* ▶ **wilfully** *adv*

will[1] *vb, past* **would** used as an auxiliary: **1** to make the future tense: *he will go on trial on October 7th.* **2** to express resolution: *they will not consider giving up territories.* **3** to express a polite request: *will you please calm Mummy and Daddy down.* **4** to express ability: *many essential oils will protect clothing from moths.* **5** to express probability or expectation: *his followers will be relieved to hear that.* **6** to express customary practice: *boys will be boys!* **7** to express desire: *go in very small steps, if you will.* ▷ HISTORY Old English *willan*

> **☑ WORD TIP**
> See at **shall.**

will[2] *n* **1** a strong determination: *a fierce will to survive.* **2** desire or wish: *a referendum to determine the will of the people.* **3** a document setting out a person's wishes regarding the disposal of his or her property after death. **4 at will** when and as one chooses: *customers can withdraw money at will.* ✧ *vb* **willing, willed 5** to try to make (something) happen by wishing very hard for it: *she willed herself not to cry.* **6** to wish or desire: *if he wills it, we will meet again.* **7** to leave (property) in one's will: *the farm had been willed to her.* ▷ HISTORY Old English *willa*

willies *pl n* **give someone the willies** *Slang* to make someone nervous or frightened. ▷ HISTORY origin unknown

willing *adj* **1** favourably disposed or inclined: *I'm willing to hear what you have to say.* **2** keen and obliging: *willing volunteers.* ▶ **willingly** *adv* ▶ **willingness** *n*

will-o'-the-wisp *n* **1** someone or something that is elusive or deceptively alluring: *their freedom was just a will-o'-the-wisp.* **2** a pale light that is sometimes seen over marshy ground at night. ▷ HISTORY *Will,* short for *William* + *wisp* twist of hay burning as a torch

willow *n* a tree that grows near water, with thin flexible branches used in weaving baskets and wood used for making cricket bats. ▷ HISTORY Old English *welig*

willowherb *n* a plant with narrow leaves and purplish flowers.

willowy *adj* slender and graceful.

willpower *n* strong self-disciplined determination to do something.

willy *n, pl* **-lies** *Brit, Austral & NZ informal* a childish or jocular word for **penis.**

willy-nilly *adv* whether desired or not. ▷ HISTORY Old English *wile hē, nyle hē* will he or will he not

willy wagtail *n Austral* a black-and-white flycatcher.

willy-willy *n Austral* a small tropical dust storm. ▷ HISTORY from a native Australian language

wilt *vb* **1** (of a flower or plant) to become limp or drooping. **2** (of a person) to lose strength or confidence. ▷ HISTORY perhaps from obsolete *wilk* to wither

wily *adj* **wilier, wiliest** sly or crafty.

wimp *Informal* ✧ *n* **1** a feeble ineffective person. ✧ *vb* **2 wimp out of** to fail to do (something) through lack of courage. ▷ HISTORY origin unknown ▶ **wimpish** *or* **wimpy** *adj*

WIMP *Computers* windows, icons, menus (or mice), pointers: denoting a type of user-friendly screen display used on small computers.

wimple *n* a piece of cloth draped round the head to frame the face, worn by women in the Middle

Ages and now by some nuns. ▷ **HISTORY** Old English *wimpel*

win *vb* **winning, won 1** to achieve first place in (a competition or race). **2** to gain (a prize or first place) in a competition or race. **3** to gain victory in (a battle, argument, or struggle). **4** to gain (sympathy, approval, or support). ✧ *n* **5** *Informal* a success, victory, or triumph: *three consecutive wins.* ✧ See also **win over.** ▷ **HISTORY** Old English *winnan* ▶ **winnable** *adj*

wince *vb* **wincing, winced 1** to draw back slightly, as if in sudden pain. ✧ *n* **2** the act of wincing. ▷ **HISTORY** Old French *wencier, guenchir* to avoid

winch *n* **1** a lifting or hauling device consisting of a rope or chain wound round a barrel or drum. ✧ *vb* **2** to haul or lift using a winch: *two men were winched to safety by a helicopter.* ▷ **HISTORY** Old English *wince* pulley

wind[1] *n* **1** a current of air moving across the earth's surface. **2** a trend or force: *the chill wind of change.* **3** the power to breathe normally, esp. during or after physical exercise: *if you feel tired during the exercise, persevere – you'll soon get a second wind.* **4** gas in the stomach or intestines. **5** *Informal* foolish or empty talk: *political language is designed to give an appearance of solidity to pure wind.* **6 break wind** to release intestinal gas through the anus. **7 get wind of** *Informal* to find out about: *the media finally got wind of her disappearance.* ✧ *adj* **8** *Music* of or relating to wind instruments: *the wind section.* ✧ *vb* **winding, winded 9** to cause (someone) to be short of breath: *he fell with a thud that left him winded.* **10** to cause (a baby) to bring up wind after feeding. ▷ **HISTORY** Old English ▶ **windless** *adj*

wind[2] *vb* **winding, wound 1** to twist (something flexible) round some object: *a sweatband was wound round his head.* **2** to tighten the spring of (a clock or watch) by turning a key or knob. **3** to follow a twisting course: *a narrow path wound through the shrubbery.* ✧ See also **wind down, wind up.** ▷ **HISTORY** Old English *windan* ▶ **winding** *adj, n*

windbag *n Slang* a person who talks a lot but says little of interest.

windblown *adj* blown about by the wind: *windblown hair.*

windbreak *n* a fence or a line of trees that gives protection from the wind by breaking its force.

wind down *vb* **1** to move downwards by turning a handle: *he wound down the rear window.* **2** (of a clock or watch) to slow down before stopping completely. **3** to relax after a stressful or tiring time: *I have not had a chance to wind down from a busy day.* **4** to diminish gradually: *trading wound down for the day.*

winded *adj* temporarily out of breath after physical exercise or a blow to the stomach.

wind energy *n Physics* energy obtained by harnessing wind power.

windfall *n* **1** a piece of unexpected good fortune, esp. financial gain. **2** a fruit blown off a tree by the wind.

windfall tax *n* a tax levied on profits made from the privatization of public utilities.

wind farm *n* a large group of wind-driven generators for electricity supply.

wind gauge *n* same as **anemometer.**

winding sheet *n* a sheet in which a dead person is wrapped before being buried.

wind instrument *n* a musical instrument, such as a flute, that is played by having air blown into it.

windjammer *n History* a large merchant sailing ship.

windlass *n* a machine for lifting heavy objects by winding a rope or chain round a barrel or drum driven by a motor. ▷ **HISTORY** Old Norse *vindāss*

windmill *n* **1** a building containing machinery for grinding corn or for pumping, driven by sails that are turned by the wind. **2** *Brit* a toy consisting of a stick with plastic vanes attached, which revolve in the wind.

window *n* **1** an opening in a building or a vehicle containing glass within a framework, which lets in light and enables people to see in or out. **2** the display area behind a glass window in a shop. **3** a transparent area in an envelope which reveals the address on the letter inside. **4** an area on a computer screen that can be manipulated separately from the rest of the display area, for example so that two or more files can be displayed at the same time. **5** a period of unbooked time in a diary or schedule. ▷ **HISTORY** Old Norse *vindauga* wind eye

window box *n* a long narrow box, placed on a windowsill, in which plants are grown.

window-dressing *n* **1** the art of arranging goods in shop windows in such a way as to attract customers. **2** an attempt to make something seem better than it is by stressing only its attractive features: *do you think that the president's calling for an investigation is window-dressing, or do you think he actually means to do something?* ▶ **window-dresser** *n*

window-shopping *n* looking at goods in shop windows without intending to buy anything.

windowsill *n* a shelf at the bottom of a window, either inside or outside a room.

windpipe *n* a nontechnical name for **trachea.**

wind-pollination *n Bot* pollination by wind-borne pollen.

wind rose *n Geog* a diagram with radiating lines showing the frequency and strength of winds from each direction affecting a specific place.

windscreen *n Brit, Austral & NZ* the sheet of glass that forms the front window of a motor vehicle.

windscreen wiper *n Brit, Austral & NZ* an electrically operated blade with a rubber edge that wipes a windscreen clear of rain.

windshield *n US & Canad* the sheet of glass that forms the front window of a motor vehicle.

windsock *n* a cloth cone mounted on a mast, used esp. at airports to indicate the direction of the wind.

wind speed *n Meteorol* the strength of the wind. See also **Beaufort scale.**

windsurfing *n* the sport of riding on water using a surfboard steered and propelled by an attached sail. ▶ **windsurfer** *n*

windswept *adj* **1** exposed to the wind: *the vast windswept plains.* **2** blown about by the wind: *his hair was looking a bit windswept.*

wind tunnel *n* a chamber through which a stream of air is forced, in order to test the effects of wind on aircraft.

wind up *vb* **1** to bring to a conclusion: *we want to wind this conflict up as quickly as possible.* **2** *Informal* to dissolve (a company) and divide its assets among creditors. **3** to tighten the spring of (a clockwork mechanism) by turning a key or knob. **4** to move (a car window) upwards by turning a handle. **5** *Informal* to end up: *to wind up in the hospital.* **6** *Informal* to make nervous or tense: *as crisis after crisis broke, I became increasingly wound up.* **7** *Brit, Austral & NZ slang* to tease or annoy: *that really used to wind my old man up something rotten.* ✧ *adj* **wind-up 8** operated by clockwork: *a wind-up toy.* ✧ *n* **wind-up 9** the act of winding someone or something up.

windward *Chiefly naut* ✧ *adj* **1** of or in the direction from which the wind blows. ✧ *n* **2** the windward direction. ✧ *adv* **3** towards the wind.

windward side *n Geog* the side towards the wind.

windy *adj* **windier, windiest 1** denoting a time or conditions in which there is a strong wind: *a windy day.* **2** exposed to the wind: *the windy graveyard.* **3** long-winded or pompous: *his speeches are long and windy.* **4** *Old-fashioned slang* frightened.

wine *n* **1 a** an alcoholic drink produced by the fermenting of grapes with water and sugar. **b** an alcoholic drink produced in this way from other fruits or flowers: *dandelion wine.* ✧ *adj* **2** dark purplish-red. ✧ *vb* **wining, wined 3 wine and dine** to entertain (someone) with wine and fine food. ▷ **HISTORY** Latin *vinum*

wine bar *n* a bar that specializes in serving wine and usually food.

wing *n* **1** one of the limbs or organs of a bird, bat, or insect that are used for flying. **2** one of the two winglike supporting parts of an aircraft. **3** a projecting part of a building: *converting the unused east wing into a suitable habitation.* **4** a faction or group within a political party or other organization: *the youth wing of the African National Congress.* **5** *Brit* the part of a car body surrounding the wheels. **6** *Sport* **a** either of the two sides of the pitch near the touchline. **b** same as **winger**. **7 wings** *Theatre* the space offstage to the right or left of the acting area. **8 in the wings** ready to step in when needed. **9 on the wing** flying. **10 spread one's wings** to make fuller use of one's abilities by trying new experiences: *he increasingly spread his wings abroad.* **11 take someone under one's wing** to look after someone. **12 take wing** to fly away. ✧ *vb* **13** to fly: *a lone bird winging its way from the island.* **14** to move through the air: *sending a shower of loose gravel winging towards the house.* **15** to shoot or wound in the wing or arm. **16** to provide with wings. ▷ **HISTORY** Old Norse *vængr* ▶ **winged** *adj* ▶ **wingless** *adj*

wing commander *n* a middle-ranking commissioned officer in an air force.

winger *n Sport* a player positioned on a wing.

wing nut *n* a threaded nut with two flat projections which allow it to be turned by the thumb and forefinger.

wingspan *n* the distance between the wing tips of a bird, insect, bat, or aircraft.

wink *vb* **1** to close and open one eye quickly as a signal. **2** (of a light) to shine brightly and intermittently; twinkle. ✧ *n* **3** the act or an instance of winking, esp. as a signal. **4** a twinkling of light. **5** *Informal* the smallest amount of sleep: *I didn't sleep a wink last night.* **6 tip someone the wink** *Brit, Austral & NZ informal* to give someone a hint or warning. ▷ **HISTORY** Old English *wincian*

winkle *n* **1** an edible shellfish with a spirally coiled shell. ✧ *vb* **-kling, -kled 2 winkle out** *Informal, chiefly Brit* **a** to obtain (information) from someone who is not willing to provide it: *try to winkle the real problem out of them.* **b** to coax or force out: *he somehow managed to winkle him out of his room.*

winner *n* **1** a person or thing that wins. **2** *Informal* a person or thing that seems sure to be successful.

winning *adj* **1** gaining victory: *the winning side.* **2** charming or attractive: *her winning smiles.*

winnings *pl n* the money won in a competition or in gambling.

winnow *vb* **1** to separate (grain) from (chaff) by a current of air. **2** to separate out (an unwanted element): *the committee will need to winnow out the nonsense.* ▷ **HISTORY** Old English *windwian*

win over *vb* to gain the support or consent of: *his robust performance won over his critics.*

winsome *adj Literary* charming or attractive: *a winsome smile.* ▷ **HISTORY** Old English *wynsum*

winter *n* **1** the coldest season of the year, between autumn and spring. ✧ *vb* **2** to spend the winter in a specified place: *wintering in Rome.* ▷ **HISTORY** Old English

wintergreen *n* an evergreen shrub from which is obtained a pleasant-smelling oil that is used medicinally and for flavouring.

winter solstice *n* the time, about December 22, at which the sun is at its southernmost point in the sky.

winter sports *pl n* sports held on snow or ice, such as skiing and skating.

wintertime *n* the period or season of winter.

wintry *adj* **-trier, -triest 1** of or characteristic of winter: *a cold wintry day.* **2** cold or unfriendly: *a wintry smile.*

wipe *vb* **wiping, wiped 1** to rub (a surface or object) lightly with a cloth or the hand, in order to remove dirt or liquid from it. **2** to remove by wiping: *she made a futile attempt to wipe away her tears.* **3** to erase a recording from (a video or audio tape). ✧ *n* **4** the act or an instance of wiping: *a quick wipe.* ▷ **HISTORY** Old English *wīpian*

wipe out *vb* to destroy or get rid of completely: *a hail storm wipes out a wheat crop in five minutes.*

wiper *n* short for **windscreen wiper**.

wire *n* **1** a slender flexible strand of metal. **2** a length of this used to carry electric current in a circuit. **3** a long continuous piece of wire or cable connecting points in a telephone or telegraph system. **4** *Old-fashioned informal* a telegram. ✧ *vb* **wiring, wired 5** to fasten with wire. **6** to equip (an electrical system, circuit, or component) with wires. **7** *Informal* to send a telegram to. **8** to send by telegraph: *they wired the money for a train ticket.* ▷ **HISTORY** Old English *wīr*

wired *adj* **1** *Slang* excitable or edgy, usually from stimulant intake: *I don't want coffee, I'm wired enough as it is.* **2** using computers to send and receive information, esp. via the Internet.

wire-haired *adj* (of a dog) having a rough wiry coat.

wireless *n* **1** *Old-fashioned* same as **radio**. ✧ *adj* **2** communicating without connecting wires: *wireless communications.*

wire netting *n* a net made of wire, used for fencing.

wireworm *n* a destructive wormlike beetle larva.

wiring *n* the network of wires used in an electrical system, device, or circuit.

wiry *adj* **wirier, wiriest 1** (of a person) slim but strong. **2** coarse and stiff: *wiry grass.*

wisdom *n* **1** the ability to use one's experience and knowledge to make sensible decisions or judgments. **2** accumulated knowledge or learning: *the wisdom of Asia and of Africa.* ▷ **HISTORY** Old English *wīsdōm*

wisdom tooth *n* any of the four molar teeth, one at the back of each side of the jaw, that are the last of the permanent teeth to come through.

wise[1] *adj* **1** possessing or showing wisdom: *a wise move.* **2 none the wiser** knowing no more than before: *I left the conference none the wiser.* **3 wise to** *Informal* aware of or informed about: *they'll get wise to our system; he put him wise to the rumour.* ▷ **HISTORY** Old English *wīs* ▸ **wisely** *adv*

wise[2] *n Old-fashioned* way, manner, or respect: *in no wise.* ▷ **HISTORY** Old English *wīse* manner

-wise *adv suffix* **1** indicating direction or manner: *crabwise.* **2** with reference to: *moneywise.* ▷ **HISTORY** Old English *-wisan*

wiseacre *n* a person who wishes to seem wise. ▷ **HISTORY** Middle Dutch *wijsseggher* soothsayer

wisecrack *Informal* ✧ *n* **1** a clever, amusing, sometimes unkind, remark. ✧ *vb* **2** to make such remarks. ▸ **wisecracking** *adj*

wish *vb* **1** to want or desire (something impossible or improbable): *he wished he'd kept quiet.* **2** to desire or prefer to be or do something: *the next person who wished to speak.* **3** to feel or express a hope concerning the welfare, health, or success of: *we wished him well.* **4** to greet as specified: *I wished her a Merry Christmas.* ✧ *n* **5** a desire, often for something impossible or improbable: *a desperate wish to succeed as a professional artist.* **6** something desired or wished for: *your wishes will come true.* **7** the expression of a hope for someone's welfare, health, or success: *give him our best wishes.* ▷ **HISTORY** Old English *wȳscan*

wishbone *n* the V-shaped bone above the breastbone of a chicken or turkey.

wishful *adj* desirous or longing: *she seemed wishful of prolonging the discussion.*

wishful thinking *n* an interpretation of the facts as one would like them to be, rather than as they are: *was it wishful thinking, or had the enemy lost heart?*

wish list *n* a list of things desired by a person or organization: *the government's wish list.*

wishy-washy *adj Informal* lacking in character, force, or colour.

wisp *n* **1** a thin, delicate, or filmy piece or streak: *little wisps of cloud.* **2** a small untidy bundle, tuft, or strand: *a wisp of hair.* **3** a slight trace: *a wisp of a smile.* ▷ **HISTORY** origin unknown

wispy *adj* **wispier, wispiest** thin, fine, or delicate: *grey wispy hair.*

wisteria *n* a climbing plant with large drooping clusters of blue, purple, or white flowers. ▷ **HISTORY** after Caspar *Wistar,* anatomist

wistful *adj* sadly wishing for something lost or unobtainable. ▸ **wistfully** *adv* ▸ **wistfulness** *n*

wit[1] *n* **1** the ability to use words or ideas in a clever, amusing, and imaginative way. **2** a person possessing this ability. **3** practical intelligence: *do credit me with some wit.* ✧ See also **wits**. ▷ **HISTORY** Old English *witt*

wit[2] *vb* **to wit** (used to introduce a statement or explanation) that is to say; namely. ▷ **HISTORY** Old English *witan*

witblits (**vit**-blits) *n S African* an illegally distilled strong alcoholic drink. ▷ **HISTORY** Afrikaans *wit* white + *blits* lightning

witch *n* **1** (in former times) a woman believed to possess evil magic powers. **2** a person who practises magic or sorcery, esp. black magic. **3** an ugly or wicked old woman. ▷ **HISTORY** Old English *wicce*

witchcraft *n* the use of magic, esp. for evil purposes.

witch doctor *n* a man in certain tribal societies who is believed to possess magical powers, which can be used to cure sickness or to harm people.

witchetty grub *n* a wood-boring edible Australian caterpillar.

witch hazel *n* a medicinal solution made from the bark and leaves of a N American shrub, which is put on the skin to treat bruises and inflammation.

witch-hunt *n* a rigorous campaign to expose and discredit people considered to hold unorthodox views on the pretext of safeguarding the public welfare.

with *prep* **1** accompanying; in the company of: *the captain called to the sergeant to come with him.* **2** using; by means of: *unlocking the padlock with a key.* **3** possessing or having: *a woman with black hair; the patient with angina.* **4** concerning or regarding: *be gentle with me.* **5** in a manner characterized by: *I know you will handle it with discretion.* **6** as a result of: *his voice was hoarse with* *nervousness.* **7** following the line of thought of: *are you with me so far?* **8** having the same opinions as; supporting: *are you with us or against us?* ▷ **HISTORY** Old English

withdraw *vb* **-drawing, -drew, -drawn 1** to take out or remove: *he withdrew an envelope from his pocket.* **2** to remove (money) from a bank account or savings account. **3** to leave one place to go to another, usually quieter, place: *he withdrew into his bedroom.* **4** (of troops) to leave or be pulled back from the battleground. **5** to take back (a statement) formally. **6 withdraw from** to give up: *they withdrew from the competition.* ▷ **HISTORY** *with,* in the sense: away from

withdrawal *n* **1** the act or an instance of withdrawing. **2** the period that a drug addict goes through after stopping using drugs, during which he or she may experience symptoms such as tremors, sweating, and vomiting. ✧ *adj* **3** of or relating to withdrawal from an addictive drug: *withdrawal symptoms.*

withdrawn *vb* **1** the past participle of **withdraw**. ✧ *adj* **2** extremely reserved or shy.

wither *vb* **1** to make or become dried up or shrivelled: *the leaves had withered but not fallen.* **2** to fade or waste: *deprived of the nerve supply the muscles wither.* **3** to humiliate (someone) with a scornful look or remark. ▷ **HISTORY** probably variant of *weather* (verb) ► **withered** *adj*

withering *adj* (of a look or remark) extremely scornful.

withers *pl n* the highest part of the back of a horse, between the shoulders. ▷ **HISTORY** earlier *widersones*

withhold *vb* **-holding, -held** to keep back (information or money).

within *prep* **1** in or inside: *within the hospital grounds.* **2** before (a period of time) has passed: *within a month.* **3** not beyond: *within the confines of a low budget; he positioned a low table within her reach.* ✧ *adv* **4** *Formal* inside or internally: *a glimpse of what was hidden within.*

without *prep* **1** not accompanied by: *I can't imagine going through life without him.* **2** not using: *our Jeep drove without lights.* **3** not possessing or having: *four months without a job; a lot of them came across the border without shoes.* **4** in a manner showing a lack of: *without reverence.* **5** while not or after not: *she sat without speaking for some while.* ✧ *adv* **6** *Formal* outside: *seated on the graveyard without.*

withstand *vb* **-standing, -stood** to resist or endure successfully: *our ability to withstand stress.*

witless *adj* **1** *Formal* lacking intelligence or sense. **2 scared witless** extremely frightened.

witness *n* **1** a person who has seen or can give first-hand evidence of some event: *the only witness to a killing.* **2** a person who gives evidence in a court of law: *a witness for the defence.* **3** a person who confirms the genuineness of a document or signature by adding his or her own signature. **4** evidence proving or supporting something: *the Church of England, that historic witness to the power of the Christian faith.* **5 bear witness to** to be evidence or proof of: *the high turn-out bore witness to the popularity of the contest.* ✧ *vb* **6** to see, be present at, or know at first hand: *I have witnessed many motor-racing accidents.* **7** to be the scene or setting of: *the 1970s witnessed an enormous increase in international lending.* **8** to confirm the genuineness of (a document or signature) by adding one's own signature. **9 witness to** *Formal* to confirm: *our aim is to witness to the fact of the empty tomb.* ▷ **HISTORY** Old English *witnes*

witness box *or esp US* **witness stand** *n* the place in a court of law where witnesses stand to give evidence.

wits *pl n* **1** the ability to think and act quickly: *when he was sober his wits were razor-sharp.* **2 at one's wits' end** at a loss to know what to do. **3 have one's wits about one** to be able to think and act quickly. **4 live by** *or* **on one's wits** to gain a livelihood by craftiness rather than by hard work. **5 scared out of one's wits** extremely frightened.

witter *vb Chiefly Brit informal* to chatter or babble pointlessly or at unnecessary length. ▷ **HISTORY** origin unknown

witticism *n* a witty remark.

wittingly *adv* intentionally and knowingly.

witty *adj* **-tier, -tiest** clever and amusing. ► **wittily** *adv*

wives *n* the plural of **wife**.

wizard *n* **1** a man in fairy tales who has magic powers. **2** a person who is outstandingly gifted in some specified field: *a financial wizard.* ▷ **HISTORY** from *wise*

wizardry *n* **1** magic or sorcery. **2** outstanding skill or accomplishment in some specified field: *technological wizardry.*

wizened (**wiz**-zend) *adj* shrivelled, wrinkled, or dried up with age.

WMD weapon(s) of mass destruction.

woad *n* a blue dye obtained from a European plant, used by the ancient Britons as a body dye. ▷ **HISTORY** Old English *wād*

wobbegong *n* an Australian shark with brown-and-white skin.

wobble *vb* **-bling, -bled 1** to move or sway unsteadily. **2** to shake: *she was having difficulty in controlling her voice, which wobbled about.* ✧ *n* **3** a wobbling movement or sound. ▷ **HISTORY** Low German *wabbeln*

wobbly *adj* **-blier, -bliest 1** unsteady. **2** trembling. ✧ *n* **3 throw a wobbly** *Slang* to become suddenly angry or upset.

wodge *n Brit & NZ informal* a thick lump or chunk: *my wodge of Kleenex was a sodden ball.* ▷ **HISTORY** from *wedge*

woe *n* **1** *Literary* intense grief. **2 woes** misfortunes or problems: *economic woes.* **3 woe betide someone** someone will or would experience misfortune: *woe betide anyone who got in his way.* ▷ **HISTORY** Old English *wā, wǣ*

woebegone *adj* sad in appearance. ▷ **HISTORY** *woe* + obsolete *bego* to surround

woeful *adj* **1** extremely sad. **2** pitiful or deplorable: *a woeful lack of understanding.* ▶ **woefully** *adv*

wok *n* a large bowl-shaped metal Chinese cooking pot, used for stir-frying. ▷ HISTORY Chinese (Cantonese)

woke *vb* the past tense of **wake**[1].

woken *vb* the past participle of **wake**[1].

wold *n* a large area of high open rolling country. ▷ HISTORY Old English *weald* wood

wolf *n, pl* **wolves 1** a predatory doglike wild animal which hunts in packs. **2** *Old-fashioned informal* a man who habitually tries to seduce women. **3 cry wolf** to give false alarms repeatedly: *if you cry wolf too often, people will take no notice.* ✧ *vb* **4 wolf down** to eat quickly or greedily: *they will wolf down kidneys but refuse tongue.* ▷ HISTORY Old English *wulf*

wolfhound *n* a very large dog, formerly used to hunt wolves.

wolf whistle *n* **1** a whistle produced by a man to express admiration of a woman's appearance. ✧ *vb* **wolf-whistle, -whistling, -whistled 2** to produce such a whistle.

wolverine *n* a large meat-eating mammal of Eurasia and North America with very thick dark fur. ▷ HISTORY earlier *wolvering,* from *wolf*

wolves *n* the plural of **wolf**.

woman *n, pl* **women 1** an adult female human being. **2** adult female human beings collectively: *the very image of woman pared of the trappings of 'femininity'.* **3** an adult female human being with qualities associated with the female, such as tenderness or maternalism: *she's more woman than you know.* **4** a female servant or domestic help. **5** *Informal* a wife or girlfriend. ✧ *adj* **6** female: *a woman doctor.* ▷ HISTORY Old English *wīfmann*

womanhood *n* **1** the state of being a woman: *young girls approaching womanhood.* **2** women collectively: *Asian womanhood.*

womanish *adj* (of a man) looking or behaving like a woman.

womanizer *or* **-iser** *n* a man who has casual affairs with many women.

womanizing *or* **-ising** *n* (of a man) the practice of indulging in casual affairs with women.

womankind *n* all women considered as a group.

womanly *adj* possessing qualities generally regarded as typical of, or appropriate to, a woman.

womb *n* the nontechnical name for **uterus**. ▷ HISTORY Old English *wamb*

wombat *n* a furry heavily-built plant-eating Australian marsupial. ▷ HISTORY Aboriginal

women *n* the plural of **woman**.

womenfolk *pl n* **1** women collectively. **2** a group of women, esp. the female members of one's family.

Women's Liberation *n* a movement promoting the removal of inequalities based upon the assumption that men are superior to women. Also called: **women's lib**

won *vb* the past of **win**.

wonder *vb* **1** to think about something with curiosity or doubt: *I wonder why she did that.* **2** to be amazed: *I did wonder at her leaving valuable china on the shelves.* ✧ *n* **3** something that causes surprise or awe: *it's a wonder she isn't speechless with fright.* **4** the feeling of surprise or awe caused by something strange: *the wonder of travel.* **5 do** *or* **work wonders** to achieve spectacularly good results. **6 no** *or* **small wonder** it is not surprising: *no wonder you're going broke.* ✧ *adj* **7** causing surprise or awe because of spectacular results achieved: *a new wonder drug for treating migraine.* ▷ HISTORY Old English *wundor* ▶ **wonderingly** *adv* ▶ **wonderment** *n*

wonderful *adj* **1** extremely fine; excellent: *I've been offered a wonderful job.* **2** causing surprise, amazement, or awe: *a strange and wonderful phenomenon.* ▶ **wonderfully** *adv*

wonderland *n* **1** an imaginary land of marvels or wonders. **2** an actual place of great or strange beauty: *the apartment was a wonderland of design and colour.*

wondrous *adj Old-fashioned or literary* causing surprise or awe; marvellous.

wonky *adj* **-kier, -kiest** *Brit, Austral & NZ slang* **1** shaky or unsteady: *wonky wheelbarrows; wonky knees.* **2** insecure or unreliable: *his marriage is looking a bit wonky.* ▷ HISTORY dialect *wanky*

wont (rhymes with **don't**) *Old-fashioned* ✧ *adj* **1** accustomed: *most murderers, his police friends were wont to say, were male.* ✧ *n* **2** a usual practice: *she waded straight in, as was her wont.* ▷ HISTORY Old English *gewunod*

won't will not.

woo *vb* **wooing, wooed 1** to coax or urge: *it will woo people back into the kitchen.* **2** *Old-fashioned* to attempt to gain the love of (a woman). ▷ HISTORY Old English *wōgian* ▶ **wooing** *n*

wood *n* **1** the hard fibrous substance beneath the bark in trees and shrubs, which is used in building and carpentry and as fuel. *RELATED ADJECTIVE* ➧ **ligneous 2** an area of trees growing together that is smaller than a forest: *a track leading into a wood.* *RELATED ADJECTIVE* ➧ **sylvan 3** *Golf* a long-shafted club with a wooden head. ✧ *adj* **4** made of, using, or for use with wood: *wood fires.* ✧ See also **woods**. ▷ HISTORY Old English *widu, wudu*

wood alcohol *n* same as **methanol**.

woodbine *n* a wild honeysuckle with sweet-smelling yellow flowers.

woodcarving *n* **1** a work of art produced by carving wood. **2** the act or craft of carving wood.

woodcock *n* a large game bird with a long straight bill.

woodcut *n* a print made from a block of wood with a design cut into it.

woodcutter *n* a person who cuts down trees or chops wood.

wooded *adj* covered with woods or trees.

wooden *adj* **1** made of wood. **2** lacking spirit or animation: *the man's expression became wooden.* ▶ **woodenly** *adv*

woodland *n* **1** land that is mostly covered with woods or trees. ✧ *adj* **2** living in woods: *woodland birds.*

woodlouse *n, pl* **-lice** a very small grey creature with many legs that lives in damp places.

woodpecker *n* a bird with a strong beak with which it bores into trees for insects.

wood pulp *n* pulp made from wood fibre, used to make paper.

woodruff *n* a plant with small sweet-smelling white flowers and sweet-smelling leaves. ▷ HISTORY Old English *wudurofe*

woods *pl n* closely packed trees forming a forest or wood.

woodsman *n, pl* **-men** a person who lives in a wood or who is skilled at woodwork or carving.

woodwind *Music* ✧ *adj* **1** of or denoting a type of wind instrument, such as the oboe. ✧ *n* **2** the woodwind instruments of an orchestra.

woodwork *n* **1** the parts of a room or house that are made of wood, such as the doors and window frames: *stark white walls and blue woodwork.* **2** the art or craft of making objects from wood. **3 crawl out of the woodwork** to appear suddenly and in large numbers: *intellectuals and environmentalists crawled out of the woodwork.*

woodworm *n* **1** a beetle larva that bores into wooden furniture or beams. **2** the damage caused to wood by these larvae.

woody *adj* **woodier, woodiest 1** (of a plant) having a very hard stem. **2** (of an area) covered with woods or trees.

woof[1] *n* same as **weft**. ▷ HISTORY Old English *ōwef*

woof[2] *n* an imitation of the bark of a dog.

woofer *n* a loudspeaker used in high-fidelity systems for the reproduction of low audio frequencies.

wool *n* **1** the soft curly hair of sheep and some other animals. **2** yarn spun from this, used in weaving and knitting. **3** cloth made from this yarn. **4 pull the wool over someone's eyes** to deceive someone. ▷ HISTORY Old English *wull*

woolgathering *n* idle or absent-minded daydreaming.

woollen *or US* **woolen** *adj* **1** made of wool or of a mixture of wool and another material. **2** relating to wool: *woollen mills.* ✧ *n* **3 woollens** woollen clothes, esp. knitted ones.

woolly *or US* **wooly** *adj* **-lier, -liest 1** made of or like wool. **2** confused or indistinct: *woolly ideas.* ✧ *n, pl* **-lies 3** a woollen garment, such as a sweater.

woolshed *n Austral & NZ* a large building in which sheep shearing takes place.

woomera *n* a notched stick used by Australian Aborigines to aid the propulsion of a spear.

woozy *adj* **woozier, wooziest** *Informal* feeling slightly dizzy. ▷ HISTORY origin unknown

wop-wops *pl n NZ informal* remote rural areas.

word *n* **1** the smallest single meaningful unit of speech or writing. RELATED ADJECTIVE ▸ **lexical 2** a brief conversation: *I would like a word with you.* **3** a brief statement: *a word of warning.* **4** news or information: *let me know if you get word of my wife.* **5** a solemn promise: *he had given his word as a rabbi.* **6** a command or order: *he had only to say the word and they'd hang him.* **7** *Computers* a set of bits used to store, transmit, or operate upon an item of information in a computer. **8 by word of mouth** by spoken rather than by written means: *their reputation spreads by word of mouth.* **9 in a word** briefly or in short: *in a word, we've won.* **10 my word!** Also: **upon my word!** *Old-fashioned* an exclamation of surprise or amazement. **11 take someone at his** *or* **her word** to accept that someone really means what he or she says: *they're willing to take him at his word when he says he'll change.* **12 take someone's word for it** to believe what someone says. **13 the last word** the closing remark of a conversation or argument, often regarded as settling an issue. **14 the last word in** the finest example of: *the last word in comfort.* **15 word for word** using exactly the same words: *he repeated almost word for word what had been said.* **16 word of honour** a solemn promise. ✧ *vb* **17** to state in words: *the questions have to be carefully worded.* ✧ See also **words**. ▷ HISTORY Old English

Word *n* **the Word** the message and teachings contained in the Bible.

-word *n combining form* (preceded by **the** and an initial letter) a euphemistic way of referring to a word by its first letter because it is considered to be unmentionable by the user: *the c-word, meaning cancer.*

word equation *n Chem* the expression of a chemical equation in words rather than using symbols.

wording *n* the way in which words are used to express something: *the exact wording of the regulation has still not been worked out.*

word-perfect *adj* able to repeat from memory the exact words of a text one has learned.

word processing *n* the storage and organization of text by electronic means, esp. for business purposes.

word processor *n* an electronic machine for word processing, consisting of a keyboard, a VDU incorporating a microprocessor, and a printer.

words *pl n* **1** the text of a song, as opposed to the music. **2** the text of an actor's part. **3 have words** to have an argument or disagreement. **4 in other words** expressing the same idea in a different, more understandable, way. **5 put into words** to express in speech or writing: *she was reluctant to put her thoughts into words.*

wordy *adj* **wordier, wordiest** using too many words, esp. long words: *wordy explanations.*

wore *vb* the past tense of **wear**.

work *n* **1** physical or mental effort directed to doing or making something. **2** paid employment at a job, trade, or profession. **3** duties or tasks: *I had to delegate as much work as I could.* **4** something done or made as a result of effort: *a work by a major artist.* **5** the place where a person is employed: *accidents at work.* **6** *Physics old-fashioned* the transfer of energy occurring when a force is applied to move a body. **7 at work** working or in action: *the social* *forces at work in society.* ✧ *adj* **8** of or for work: *work experience.* ✧ *vb* **9** to do work; labour: *no-one worked harder than Arnold.* **10** to be employed: *she worked as a waitress.* **11** to make (a person or animal) labour. **12** to operate (a machine or a piece of equipment). **13** (of a machine or a piece of equipment) to function, esp. effectively: *he doesn't have to know how things work.* **14** (of a plan or system) to be successful. **15** to cultivate (land). **16** to move gradually into a specific condition or position: *he picked up the shovel, worked it under the ice, and levered.* **17** to make (one's way) with effort: *he worked his way to the top.* **18** *Informal* to manipulate to one's own advantage: *they could see an angle and they'd know how to work it.* ✧ See also **work off, works**, etc. ▷ **HISTORY** Old English *weorc*

workable *adj* **1** able to operate efficiently: *a workable solution.* **2** able to be used: *a workable mine.*

workaday *adj* commonplace or ordinary: *workaday surroundings.*

workaholic *n* a person who is obsessed with work.

worker *n* **1** a person who works in a specified way: *a hard worker.* **2** a person who works at a specific job: *a government worker.* **3** an employee, as opposed to an employer. **4** a sterile female bee, ant, or wasp, that works for the colony.

work ethic *n* a belief in the moral value of work.

workforce *n* **1** the total number of workers employed by a company. **2** the total number of people available for work: *the local workforce.*

workhorse *n* a person or thing that does a lot of work, esp. dull or routine work: *this plane is the workhorse of most short-haul airlines.*

workhouse *n* (formerly, in England) a public institution where very poor people did work in return for food and accommodation.

working *adj* **1** having a job: *the working mother.* **2** concerned with, used in, or suitable for work: *working conditions.* **3** capable of being operated or used: *a working mechanism.* ✧ *n* **4** a part of a mine or quarry that is or has been used. **5 workings** the way that something works: *the workings of the human brain.*

working capital *n* the amount of capital that a business has available to meet the day-to-day cash requirements of its operations.

working class *n* **1** the social group that consists of people who earn wages, esp. as manual workers. ✧ *adj* **working-class 2** of or relating to the working class: *a working-class neighbourhood.*

working day *or esp US & Canad* **workday** *n* **1** a day when people normally go to work: *the last working day of the week.* **2** the part of the day allocated to work: *the long working day of twelve to fourteen hours.*

working party *n* a committee established to investigate a problem.

workload *n* the amount of work to be done, esp. in a specified period: *a heavy workload.*

workman *n, pl* **-men** a man who is employed to do manual work.

workmanship *n* the degree of skill with which an object is made: *shoddy workmanship.*

work of art *n* **1** a piece of fine art, such as a painting or sculpture. **2** an object or a piece of work that has been exceptionally skilfully made or produced: *the doll was truly a work of art.*

work off *vb* to get rid of, usually by effort: *he went along to the tennis club and worked off his pique there.*

work out *vb* **1** to solve, find out, or plan by reasoning or calculation: *working out a new budget.* **2** to happen in a particular way: *he decided to wait and see how things worked out.* **3** to be successful or satisfactory: *the dates never worked out.* **4** to take part in physical exercise. **5 work out at** to be calculated at (a certain amount): *the return on capital works out at 15 per cent.* ✧ *n* **workout 6** a session of physical exercise for training or to keep fit.

works *n* **1** a place where something is manufactured: *a chemical works.* ✧ *pl n* **2** the sum total of a writer's or artist's achievements considered together: *the works of Goethe.* **3 the works** *Slang* everything associated with a particular subject or thing: *traditional Indian music, sitars, the works.*

worksheet *n* a sheet of paper containing exercises to be completed by a student.

workshop *n* **1** a room or building where manufacturing or other manual work is carried on. **2** a group of people engaged in intensive study or work in a creative or practical field: *a writers' workshop.*

work station *n* **1** an area in an office where one person works. **2** *Computers* a component of an electronic office system consisting of a VDU and keyboard.

worktop *n* a surface in a kitchen, usually the top of a fitted kitchen unit, which is used for food preparation. Also: **work surface**

work-to-rule *n* a form of industrial action in which employees keep strictly to their employers' rules, with the result of reducing the work rate.

work up *vb* **1** to make angry, excited, or upset: *he worked himself up into a rage.* **2** to build up or develop: *I'd worked up a thirst.* **3** to work on (something) in order to improve it: *there was enough material to be worked up into something publishable.* **4 work one's way up** to make progress: *he worked his way up in the catering trade.* **5 work up to** to develop gradually towards: *the fete worked up to a climax around lunch time.*

world *n* **1** the earth as a planet. **2** the human race; people generally: *providing food for the world.* **3** any planet or moon, esp. one that might be inhabited. **4** a particular group of countries or period of history, or its inhabitants: *the Arab world; the post-Cold War world.* **5** an area, sphere, or realm considered as a complete environment: *the art world; the world of nature.* **6** the total circumstances and experience of a person that make up his or her life: *there may not ever be a place for us in your world.* **7 bring into the world** to deliver or give birth to (a baby). **8 come into the world** to be born. **9 for all**

the world exactly or very much: *they looked for all the world like a pair of newly-weds.* **10 in the world** used to emphasize a statement: *she didn't have a worry in the world.* **11 man** *or* **woman of the world** a man *or* woman who is experienced in social or public life. **12 worlds apart** very different from each other: *this man and I are worlds apart.* ✧ *adj* **13** of or concerning the entire world: *the world championship.* ▷ **HISTORY** Old English *w(e)orold*

worldly *adj* **-lier, -liest 1** not spiritual; earthly or temporal: *as a simple monk he had no interest in politics and other worldly affairs.* **2** of or relating to material things: *all his worldly goods.* **3** wise in the ways of the world; sophisticated: *a suave, worldly, charming Frenchman.* ▶ **worldliness** *n*

world music *n* popular music of a variety of ethnic origins and styles.

World War I *n* the war (1914–18) between the Allies (principally France, Russia, Britain, Italy, Australia, Canada, and the US) and the Central Powers (principally Germany, Austria-Hungary, and Turkey). Also: **First World War**

World War II *n* the war (1939–45) between the Allies (Britain, France, Australia, Canada, the US, and the Soviet Union) and the Axis (Germany, Italy, and Japan). Also: **Second World War**

world-weary *adj* no longer finding pleasure in life.

worldwide *adj* applying or extending throughout the world.

World Wide Web *n Computers* a vast network of hypertext files, stored on computers throughout the world, that can provide a computer user with information on a huge variety of subjects.

worm *n* **1** a small invertebrate animal with a long thin body and no limbs. **2** an insect larva that looks like a worm. **3** a despicable or weak person. **4** a slight trace: *a worm of doubt.* **5** a shaft on which a spiral thread has been cut, for example in a gear arrangement in which such a shaft drives a toothed wheel. **6** *Computers* a type of virus. ✧ *vb* **7** to rid (an animal) of worms in its intestines. **8 worm one's way a** to go or move slowly and with difficulty: *I had to worm my way out sideways from the bench.* **b** to get oneself into a certain situation or position gradually: *worming your way into my good books.* **9 worm out of** to obtain (information) from someone who is not willing to provide it: *it took me weeks to worm the facts out of him.* ✧ See also **worms**. ▷ **HISTORY** Old English *wyrm*

WORM *n Computers* write once read many (times): an optical disk which enables users to store their own data.

wormcast *n* a coil of earth or sand that has been excreted by a burrowing worm.

worm-eaten *adj* eaten into by worms: *worm-eaten beams.*

wormhole *n* a hole made by a worm in timber, plants, or fruit.

worms *n* a disease caused by parasitic worms living in the intestines.

wormwood *n* a plant from which a bitter oil formerly used in making absinthe is obtained. ▷ **HISTORY** Old English *wormōd, wermōd*

wormy *adj* **wormier, wormiest** infested with or eaten by worms.

worn *vb* **1** the past participle of **wear**. ✧ *adj* **2** showing signs of long use or wear: *the worn soles of his boots.* **3** looking tired and ill: *that worn pain-creased face.*

worn-out *adj* **1** worn or used until threadbare, valueless, or useless. **2** completely exhausted: *worn-out by their exertions.*

worried *adj* concerned and anxious about things that may happen. ▶ **worriedly** *adv*

worry *vb* **-ries, -rying, -ried 1** to be or cause to be anxious or uneasy. **2** to annoy or bother: *don't worry yourself with the details.* **3** (of a dog) to frighten (sheep or other animals) by chasing and trying to bite them. **4 worry away at** to struggle with or work on (a problem). ✧ *n, pl* **-ries 5** a state or feeling of anxiety: *he was beside himself with worry.* **6** a cause for anxiety: *having a premature baby is much less of a worry these days.* ▷ **HISTORY** Old English *wyrgan* ▶ **worrier** *n*

worrying *adj* causing concern and anxiety.

worse *adj* **1** the comparative of **bad**. **2 none the worse for** not harmed by (adverse events or circumstances). **3 the worse for wear** *Informal* in a poor condition; not at one's best: *returning the worse for wear from the pub.* ✧ *n* **4 for the worse** into a worse condition: *taking a turn for the worse.* ✧ *adv* **5** the comparative of **badly**. **6 worse off** in a worse condition, esp. financially. ▷ **HISTORY** Old English *wiersa*

worsen *vb* to make or become worse. ▶ **worsening** *adj, n*

worship *vb* **-shipping, -shipped** *or US* **-shiping, -shiped 1** to show profound religious devotion to (one's god), for example by praying. **2** to have intense love and admiration for (a person). ✧ *n* **3** religious adoration or devotion. **4** formal expression of religious adoration, for example by praying. **5** intense love or devotion to a person. ▷ **HISTORY** Old English *weorthscipe* ▶ **worshipper** *n*

Worship *n* **Your, His** *or* **Her Worship** *Chiefly Brit* a title for a mayor or magistrate.

worshipful *adj* feeling or showing reverence or adoration.

worst *adj, adv* **1** the superlative of **bad, badly**. ✧ *n* **2** the least good or the most terrible person, thing, or part: *the worst is yet to come.* **3 at one's worst** in the worst condition or aspect of a thing or person: *the British male is at his worst in July and August.* **4 at worst** in the least favourable interpretation or conditions: *all the questions should ideally be answered 'no', or at worst 'sometimes'.* ✧ *vb* **5** *Old-fashioned* to defeat or beat. ▷ **HISTORY** Old English *wierrest*

worsted (**wooss**-tid) *n* a close-textured woollen fabric used to make jackets and trousers. ▷ **HISTORY** after *Worstead,* a district in Norfolk

worth *prep* **1** having a value of: *the fire destroyed property worth $200 million.* **2** worthy of; meriting or justifying: *if a job is worth doing, it's worth doing well.* **3 worth one's weight in gold** extremely useful or helpful; very highly valued. **4 worth one's while** worthy of spending one's time or effort on something: *they needed a wage of at least £140 a week to make it worth their while returning to work.* ✧ *n* **5** monetary value: *the corporation's net worth.* **6** high quality; value: *the submarine proved its military worth during the Second World War.* **7** the amount of something that can be bought for a specified price: *$10 billion worth of property.* ▷ **HISTORY** Old English *weorth*

worthless *adj* **1** without value or usefulness: *worthless junk bonds.* **2** without merit: *he sees himself as a worthless creature.* ▶ **worthlessness** *n*

worthwhile *adj* sufficiently important, rewarding, or valuable to justify spending time or effort on it.

worthy *adj* **-thier, -thiest 1** deserving of admiration or respect: *motives which were less than worthy.* **2 worthy of** deserving of: *he would practise extra hard to be worthy of such an honour.* ✧ *n, pl* **-thies 3** *Often facetious* an important person. ▶ **worthily** *adv* ▶ **worthiness** *n*

would *vb* used as an auxiliary: **1** to form the past tense or subjunctive mood of **will**[1]: *he asked if she would marry him; that would be delightful.* **2** to express a polite offer or request: *would you like some lunch?* **3** to describe a habitual past action: *sometimes at lunch time I would choose a painting to go and see.*

> ☑ **WORD TIP**
> See at **should.**

would-be *adj* wanting or pretending to be: *would-be brides.*

wouldn't would not.

wound[1] *n* **1** an injury to the body such as a cut or a gunshot injury. **2** an injury to one's feelings or reputation. ✧ *vb* **3** to cause an injury to the body or feelings of. ▷ **HISTORY** Old English *wund* ▶ **wounding** *adj*

wound[2] *vb* the past of **wind**[2].

wove *vb* a past tense of **weave.**

woven *vb* a past participle of **weave.**

wow *interj* **1** an exclamation of admiration or amazement. ✧ *n* **2** *Slang* a person or thing that is amazingly successful: *he would be an absolute wow on the chat shows.* ✧ *vb* **3** *Slang* to be a great success with: *the new Disney film wowed festival audiences.* ▷ **HISTORY** Scots

wowser *n Austral & NZ slang* **1** a fanatically puritanical person. **2** a teetotaller. ▷ **HISTORY** dialect *wow* to complain

WPC (in Britain) woman police constable.

wpm words per minute.

WRAC (in Britain) Women's Royal Army Corps.

wrack[1] *n* same as **rack**[2]. ▷ **HISTORY** Old English *wræc* persecution

> ☑ **WORD TIP**
> The use of the spelling *wrack* rather than *rack* in sentences such as *she was wracked by grief* or *the country was wracked by civil war* is very common but is thought by many people to be incorrect.

wrack[2] *n* seaweed that is floating in the sea or has been washed ashore. ▷ **HISTORY** probably from Middle Dutch *wrak* wreckage

WRAF (in Britain) Women's Royal Air Force.

wraith *n Literary* a ghost. ▷ **HISTORY** Scots ▶ **wraithlike** *adj*

wrangle *vb* **-gling, -gled 1** to argue noisily or angrily. ✧ *n* **2** a noisy or angry argument. ▷ **HISTORY** Low German *wrangeln*

wrap *vb* **wrapping, wrapped 1** to fold a covering round (something) and fasten it securely: *a small package wrapped in brown paper.* **2** to fold or wind (something) round a person or thing: *she wrapped a handkerchief around her bleeding palm.* **3** to fold, wind, or coil: *she wrapped her arms around her mother.* **4** to complete the filming of (a motion picture or television programme). ✧ *n* **5** *Old-fashioned* a garment worn wrapped round the shoulders. **6** (in the filming of a motion picture or television programme) the end of a day's filming or the completion of filming. **7** *Brit slang* a small packet of an illegal drug in powder form: *a wrap of heroin.* **8 keep something under wraps** to keep something secret. ▷ **HISTORY** origin unknown

wraparound *adj* **1** (of a skirt) designed to be worn wrapped round the body. **2** extending in a curve from the front round to the sides: *wraparound shades.*

wrapper *n* a paper, foil, or plastic cover in which a product is wrapped: *a single sweet wrapper.*

wrapping *n* a piece of paper, foil, or other material used to wrap something in.

wrap up *vb* **1** to fold paper, cloth, or other material round (something). **2** to put warm clothes on: *remember to wrap up warmly on cold or windy days.* **3** *Informal* to finish or settle: *he will need 60 to 90 days to wrap up his current business dealings.* **4** *Slang* to stop talking. **5 wrapped up in** giving all one's attention to: *wrapped up in her new baby.*

wrasse *n* a brightly coloured sea fish. ▷ **HISTORY** Cornish *wrach*

wrath (**roth**) *n Old-fashioned or literary* intense anger. ▷ **HISTORY** Old English *wræththu* ▶ **wrathful** *adj*

wreak *vb* **1 wreak havoc** to cause chaos or damage: *this Australian sun will wreak havoc with your complexions.* **2 wreak vengeance on** to take revenge on. ▷ **HISTORY** Old English *wrecan*

> ☑ **WORD TIP**
> See at **wrought.**

wreath *n, pl* **wreaths 1** a ring of flowers or leaves, placed on a grave as a memorial or worn on the head as a garland or a mark of honour. **2** anything circular or spiral: *a wreath of smoke.* ▷ **HISTORY** Old English *writha*

wreck *vb* **1** to break, spoil, or destroy completely. **2** to cause the accidental sinking or destruction of (a ship) at sea. ✧ *n* **3** something that has been destroyed or badly damaged, such as a crashed car or aircraft. **4** a ship that has been sunk or destroyed at sea. **5** a person in a poor mental or physical state. ▷ **HISTORY** from Old Norse

wreckage *n* the remains of something that has been destroyed or badly damaged, such as a crashed car or aircraft.

wrecker *n* **1** a person who destroys or badly damages something: *a marriage wrecker.* **2** (formerly) a person who lured ships on to the rocks in order to plunder them. **3** *Chiefly US, Canad & NZ* a person whose job is to demolish buildings or dismantle cars. **4** *US & Canad* a breakdown van.

wreckers *pl n NZ* a business which sells material from demolished cars or buildings.

wren *n* a very small brown songbird. ▷ **HISTORY** Old English *wrenna*

Wren *n Informal* (in Britain) a member of the former Women's Royal Naval Service. ▷ **HISTORY** from abbreviation *WRNS*

wrench *vb* **1** to twist or pull (something) violently, for example to remove it from something to which it is attached: *he grabbed the cable and wrenched it out of the wall socket.* **2** to move or twist away with a sudden violent effort: *she wrenched free of his embrace.* **3** to injure (a limb or joint) by a sudden twist. ✧ *n* **4** a violent twist or pull. **5** an injury to a limb or joint, caused by twisting it. **6** a feeling of sadness experienced on leaving a person or place: *it would be a wrench to leave Essex after all these years.* **7** a spanner with adjustable jaws. ▷ **HISTORY** Old English *wrencan*

wrest *vb* **1** to take (something) away from someone with a violent pull or twist. **2** to seize forcibly by violent or unlawful means: *she must begin to wrest control of the army and the police.* ▷ **HISTORY** Old English *wrǣstan*

wrestle *vb* **-tling, -tled 1** to fight (someone) by grappling and trying to throw or pin him or her to the ground, often as a sport. **2 wrestle with** to struggle hard with (a person, problem, or thing): *I wrestled with my conscience.* ▷ **HISTORY** Old English *wrǣstlian* ▶ **wrestler** *n*

wrestling *n* a sport in which each contestant tries to overcome the other either by throwing or pinning him or her to the ground or by forcing a submission.

wretch *n Old-fashioned* **1** a despicable person. **2** a person pitied for his or her misfortune. ▷ **HISTORY** Old English *wrecca*

wretched (**retch**-id) *adj* **1** in poor or pitiful circumstances: *a vast wretched slum.* **2** feeling very unhappy. **3** of poor quality: *the wretched state of the cabbages.* **4** *Informal* undesirable or displeasing: *what a wretched muddle.* ▶ **wretchedly** *adv* ▶ **wretchedness** *n*

wriggle *vb* **-gling, -gled 1** to twist and turn with quick movements: *he wriggled on the hard seat.* **2** to move along by twisting and turning. **3 wriggle out of** to avoid (doing something that one does not want to do): *he wriggled out of donating blood.* ✧ *n* **4** a wriggling movement or action. ▷ **HISTORY** Middle Low German *wriggeln*

wring *vb* **wringing, wrung 1** Also: **wring out** to squeeze water from (a cloth or clothing) by twisting it tightly. **2** to twist (a neck) violently. **3** to clasp and twist (one's hands) in anguish. **4** to grip (someone's hand) vigorously in greeting. **5** to obtain by forceful means: *to wring concessions from the army.* **6 wring someone's heart** to make someone feel sorrow or pity. ▷ **HISTORY** Old English *wringan*

wringer *n* same as **mangle**² (sense 1).

wrinkle *n* **1** a slight ridge in the smoothness of a surface, such as a crease in the skin as a result of age. ✧ *vb* **-kling, -kled 2** to develop or cause to develop wrinkles. ▷ **HISTORY** Old English *wrinclian* to wind around ▶ **wrinkled** *or* **wrinkly** *adj*

wrist *n* **1** the joint between the forearm and the hand. **2** the part of a sleeve that covers the wrist. ▷ **HISTORY** Old English

wristwatch *n* a watch worn strapped round the wrist.

writ *n* a formal legal document ordering a person to do or not to do something. ▷ **HISTORY** Old English

write *vb* **writing, wrote, written 1** to draw or mark (words, letters, or numbers) on paper or a blackboard with a pen, pencil, or chalk. **2** to describe or record (something) in writing: *he began to write his memoirs.* **3** to be an author: *he still taught writing, but he didn't write.* **4** to write a letter to or correspond regularly with someone: *don't forget to write!* **5** *Informal, chiefly US & Canad* to write a letter to (someone): *I wrote him several times.* **6** to say or communicate in a letter or a book: *in a recent letter a friend wrote that everything costs more in Russia now.* **7** to fill in the details for (a cheque or document). **8** *Computers* to record (data) in a storage device. **9 write down** to record in writing: *write it down if you find it too embarrassing to talk about.* ▷ **HISTORY** Old English *wrītan*

write off *vb* **1** *Accounting* to cancel (a bad debt) from the accounts. **2** to dismiss from consideration: *he wrote her off as a tense woman.* **3** to send a written request (for something): *he wrote off for leaflets on the subject.* **4** *Informal* to damage (a vehicle) beyond repair. ✧ *n* **write-off 5** *Informal* a vehicle that is damaged beyond repair.

write out *vb* **1** to put into writing or reproduce in full form in writing. **2** to remove (a character) from a television or radio series: *another actress is to be written out of the BBC soap.*

writer *n* **1** a person whose job is writing; author. **2** the person who has written something specified: *the writer of this letter is pretty dangerous.*

write up *vb* **1** to describe fully, complete, or bring up to date in writing: *she would write up her diary in bed.* ✧ *n* **write-up 2** a published account of something, such as a review in a newspaper or magazine: *I see the Herald didn't give you a very good write-up.*

writhe *vb* **writhing, writhed** to twist or squirm in pain: *writhing in agony.* ▷ **HISTORY** Old English *wrīthan*

writing *n* **1** something that has been written: *the writing on the outer flap was faint.* **2** written form: *permission in writing.* **3** short for **handwriting**. **4** a kind or style of writing: *creative writing.* **5** the work of a writer: *Wilde never mentioned chess in his writing.*

written *vb* **1** the past participle of **write**. ✧ *adj* **2** recorded in writing: *written permission.*

WRNS (in Britain, formerly) Women's Royal Naval Service.

wrong *adj* **1** not correct or accurate: *the wrong answers.* **2** acting or judging in error; mistaken: *do correct me if I'm wrong.* **3** not in accordance with correct or conventional rules or standards; immoral: *this group argues that even gently slapping a child is wrong.* **4** not intended or appropriate: *I ordered the wrong things; you've picked the wrong time to ask such questions.* **5** being a problem or trouble: *come on, I know when something's wrong.* **6** not functioning properly: *there's something wrong with the temperature sensor.* **7** denoting the side of cloth that is worn facing inwards. ✧ *adv* **8** in a wrong manner: *I guessed wrong.* **9 get someone wrong** to misunderstand someone: *don't get me wrong, I'm not making threats.* **10 get something wrong** to make a mistake about something: *he had got his body language wrong.* **11 go wrong a** to turn out badly or not as intended. **b** to make a mistake. **c** (of a machine) to stop functioning properly: *pilots must be able to react instantly if the automatic equipment suddenly goes wrong.* ✧ *n* **12** something bad, immoral, or unjust: *how can such a wrong be redressed?* **13 in the wrong** mistaken or guilty. ✧ *vb* **14** to treat (someone) unjustly. **15** to think or speak unfairly of (someone). ▷ HISTORY Old English *wrang* injustice ▶ **wrongly** *adv*

wrongdoing *n* immoral or illegal behaviour. ▶ **wrongdoer** *n*

wrong-foot *vb* **1** *Sport* to play a shot in such a way as to catch (an opponent) off-balance: *he constantly wrong-footed his opponent with fine passing.* **2** to gain an advantage over (someone) by doing something unexpected: *China wrong-footed Vietnam by supporting the peace plan.*

wrongful *adj* unjust or illegal: *wrongful imprisonment.* ▶ **wrongfully** *adv*

wrote *vb* the past tense of **write**.

wrought (**rawt**) *vb* **1** *Old-fashioned* a past of **work**. ✧ *adj* **2** *Metallurgy* shaped by hammering or beating: *wrought copper and brass.*

> **☑ WORD TIP**
>
> *Wrought* is sometimes used as if it were the past tense and past participle of *wreak*, as in *the hurricane wrought havoc in coastal areas.* Many people think this use is incorrect.

wrought iron *n* a pure form of iron with a low carbon content, often used for decorative work.

wrung *vb* the past of **wring**.

WRVS (in Britain) Women's Royal Voluntary Service.

wry *adj* **wrier, wriest** *or* **wryer, wryest 1** drily humorous; sardonic: *wry amusement.* **2** (of a facial expression) produced by twisting one's features to denote amusement or displeasure: *a small wry smile twisted the corner of his mouth.* ▷ HISTORY Old English *wrīgian* to turn ▶ **wryly** *adv*

wrybill *n* a New Zealand plover whose bill is bent to one side enabling it to search for food beneath stones.

wryneck *n* a woodpecker that has a habit of twisting its neck round.

wt. weight.

WTO World Trade Organization.

WV West Virginia.

WWI World War One.

WWII World War Two.

WWW World Wide Web.

WY Wyoming.

wych-elm *or* **witch-elm** *n* a Eurasian elm with long pointed leaves. ▷ HISTORY Old English *wice*

WYSIWYG *n, adj Computers* what you see is what you get: referring to what is displayed on the screen being the same as what will be printed out.

X x

x *Maths* **1** (along with *y* and *z*) an unknown quantity. **2** the multiplication symbol.

X 1 indicating an error, a choice, or a kiss. **2** indicating an unknown, unspecified, or variable factor, person, or thing: *Miss X.* **3** the Roman numeral for ten. **4** (formerly) indicating a film that may not be publicly shown to anyone under 18: since 1982 replaced by symbol 18.

***x*-axis** *n Maths* a reference axis, usually horizontal, of a graph along which the *x*-coordinate is measured.

X-chromosome *n* the sex chromosome that occurs in pairs in the females of many animals, including humans, and as one of a pair with the Y-chromosome in males.

Xe *Chem* xenon.

xenon *n Chem* a colourless odourless gas found in minute quantities in the air. Symbol: Xe. ▷ **HISTORY** Greek: something strange

xenophobia (zen-oh-**fobe**-ee-a) *n* hatred or fear of foreigners or strangers. ▶ **xenophobic** *adj*

> **WORD HISTORY**
> 'Xenophobia' comes from the Greek words *xenos*, meaning 'stranger', and *phobos*, meaning 'fear'.

xerophyte *n Bot* a plant such as a cactus, which is adapted for growing or living in dry surroundings.

Xerox (**zeer**-ox) *n Trademark* **1** a machine for copying printed material. **2** a copy made by a Xerox machine. ✧ *vb* **3** to produce a copy of (a document) using such a machine.

Xhosa (**kawss**-a) *n* **1** (*pl* **-sa** *or* **-sas**) a member of a Black people living in the Republic of South Africa. **2** the language of this people. ▶ **Xhosan** *adj*

Xmas (**eks**-mass) *n Informal* short for **Christmas**. ▷ **HISTORY** from the Greek letter *chi* (X), first letter of *Khristos* Christ

X-rated *adj* **1** (formerly, in Britain) (of a film) considered suitable for viewing by adults only. **2** *Informal* involving bad language, violence, or sex: *an X-rated conversation.*

X-ray *or* **x-ray** *n* **1** a stream of electromagnetic radiation of short wavelength that can pass through some solid materials. **2** a picture produced by exposing photographic film to X-rays: used in medicine as a diagnostic aid, since parts of the body, such as bones, absorb X-rays and so appear as opaque areas on the picture. ✧ *vb* **3** to photograph, treat, or examine using X-rays.

X-ray diffraction *n Physics* the scattering of X-rays on contact with matter, resulting in changes in radiation intensity, which is used for studying atomic structure.

xylem (**zile**-em) *n Bot* a plant tissue that conducts water and mineral salts from the roots to all other parts. ▷ **HISTORY** Greek *xulon* wood

xylene (**zile**-lean) *n Chem* a hydrocarbon existing in three isomeric forms, all three being colourless flammable volatile liquids used as solvents and in the manufacture of synthetic resins, dyes, and insecticides. ▷ **HISTORY** Greek *xulon* wood

xylophone (**zile**-oh-fone) *n Music* a percussion instrument consisting of a set of wooden bars played with hammers. ▷ **HISTORY** Greek *xulon* wood ▶ **xylophonist** *n*

Y y

y *Maths* (along with *x* and *z*) an unknown quantity.
Y **1** an unknown, unspecified, or variable factor, number, person, or thing. **2** *Chem* yttrium.
Y2K *n Informal* name for the year 2000 AD (esp. referring to the millennium bug).
ya *interj S African* yes.
yabby *n, pl* **-bies** *Austral* **1** a small freshwater crayfish. **2** a marine prawn used as bait. ▷ **HISTORY** from a native Australian language
yacht (**yott**) *n* **1** a large boat with sails or an engine, used for racing or pleasure cruising. ✧ *vb* **2** to sail or cruise in a yacht. ▷ **HISTORY** obsolete Dutch *jaghte* ▶ **yachting** *n, adj*
yachtsman *or fem* **yachtswoman** *n, pl* **-men** *or* **-women** a person who sails a yacht.
yahoo *n, pl* **-hoos** a crude, brutish, or obscenely coarse person. ▷ **HISTORY** after the brutish creatures in *Gulliver's Travels*
yahweh *or* **yahveh** *n Bible* a personal name of god. ▷ **HISTORY** Hebrew YHVH, with conjectural vowels
yak[1] *n* a Tibetan ox with long shaggy hair. ▷ **HISTORY** Tibetan *gyag*
yak[2] *Slang* ✧ *n* **1** noisy, continuous, and trivial talk. ✧ *vb* **yakking, yakked 2** to talk continuously about unimportant matters. ▷ **HISTORY** imitative
yakka *n Austral & NZ informal* work. ▷ **HISTORY** from a native Australian language
Yale lock *n Trademark* a type of cylinder lock using a flat serrated key. ▷ **HISTORY** after L. *Yale*, inventor
Yalta Conference *n History* a conference held in 1945, when US, Soviet, and British leaders met to plan the final defeat and occupation of Nazi Germany.
yam *n* **1** a twining plant of tropical and subtropical regions, cultivated for its starchy roots which are eaten as a vegetable. **2** the sweet potato. ▷ **HISTORY** Portuguese *inhame*
yammer *Informal* ✧ *vb* **1** to whine in a complaining manner. ✧ *n* **2** a yammering sound. **3** nonsense or jabber. ▷ **HISTORY** Old English *geōmrian* to grumble
Yang *n* See **Yin and Yang**.
yank *vb* **1** to pull (someone or something) with a sharp movement: *I yanked myself out of the water.* ✧ *n* **2** a sudden pull or jerk. ▷ **HISTORY** origin unknown
Yank *n Slang* a person from the United States.
Yankee *n* **1** *Slang* same as **Yank**. **2** a person from the Northern United States. ✧ *adj* **3** of or characteristic of Yankees. ▷ **HISTORY** perhaps from Dutch *Jan Kees* John Cheese, nickname for English colonists
yap *vb* **yapping, yapped 1** to bark with a high-pitched sound. **2** *Informal* to talk at length in an annoying or stupid way. ✧ *n* **3** a high-pitched bark. **4** *Slang* annoying or stupid speech. ▷ **HISTORY** imitative ▶ **yappy** *adj*
yarborough *n Bridge, whist* a hand in which no card is higher than nine. ▷ **HISTORY** supposedly after the second earl of *Yarborough*, said to have bet a thousand to one against its occurrence
yard[1] *n* **1** a unit of length equal to 3 feet (0.9144 metre). **2** *Naut* a spar slung across a ship's mast to extend the sail. ▷ **HISTORY** Old English *gierd* rod, twig
yard[2] *n* **1** a piece of enclosed ground, often adjoining or surrounded by a building or buildings. **2** an enclosed or open area where a particular type of work is done: *a shipbuilding yard.* **3** *US, Canad, & Austral* the garden of a house. **4** *US & Canad* the winter pasture of deer, moose, and similar animals. ▷ **HISTORY** Old English *geard*
Yard *n* **the Yard** *Brit informal* short for **Scotland Yard**.
yardang *n Geol* (in arid areas) a ridge formed by wind erosion, often parallel to the direction of the prevailing wind.
yardarm *n Naut* the outer end of a ship's yard.
yardstick *n* **1** a measure or standard used for comparison: *there's no yardstick for judging a problem of this sort.* **2** a graduated measuring stick one yard long.
yarmulke (**yar**-mull-ka) *n* a skullcap worn by Jewish men. ▷ **HISTORY** Yiddish
yarn *n* **1** a continuous twisted strand of natural or synthetic fibres, used for knitting or making cloth. **2** *Informal* a long involved story. **3 spin a yarn** *Informal* to tell such a story. ▷ **HISTORY** Old English *gearn*
yarrow *n* a wild plant with flat clusters of white flowers. ▷ **HISTORY** Old English *gearwe*
yashmak *n* a veil worn by a Muslim woman to cover her face in public. ▷ **HISTORY** Arabic
yaw *vb* **1** (of an aircraft or ship) to turn to one side or from side to side while moving. ✧ *n* **2** the act or movement of yawing. ▷ **HISTORY** origin unknown
yawl *n* **1** a two-masted sailing boat. **2** a ship's small boat. ▷ **HISTORY** Dutch *jol* or Middle Low German *jolle*
yawn *vb* **1** to open one's mouth wide and take in air deeply, often when sleepy or bored. **2** to be open wide as if threatening to engulf someone or something: *the doorway yawned blackly open at the end of the hall.* ✧ *n* **3** the act or an instance of yawning. ▷ **HISTORY** Old English *geonian* ▶ **yawning** *adj*
yaws *n* an infectious disease of tropical climates characterized by red skin eruptions. ▷ **HISTORY** Carib
***y*-axis** *n Maths* a reference axis, usually vertical, of a graph along which the *y*-coordinate is measured.
Yb *Chem* ytterbium.
Y-chromosome *n* the sex chromosome that occurs as one of a pair with the X-chromosome in the males of many animals, including humans.
yd yard (measure).

A B C D E F G H I J K L M N O P Q R S T U V W X Y Z

ye[1] (**yee**) *pron Old-fashioned or dialect* you. ▷ **HISTORY** Old English *gē*

ye[2] *adj (definite article) Old-fashioned or jocular* the: *ye olde Rose and Crown pub.* ▷ **HISTORY** a misinterpretation of *the*, written with the old letter thorn (þ), representing *th*

yea *interj* **1** *Old-fashioned* yes. ✧ *adv* **2** *Old-fashioned or literary* indeed or truly: *they wandered about the church, yea, even unto the altar.* ▷ **HISTORY** Old English *gēa*

yeah *interj Informal* same as **yes**.

year *n* **1** the time taken for the earth to make one revolution around the sun, about 365 days. **2** the twelve months from January 1 to December 31. **3** a period of twelve months from any specified date. **4** a specific period of time, usually occupying a definite part or parts of a twelve-month period, used for some particular activity: *the financial year.* **5** a group of people who have started an academic course at the same time. **6 year in, year out** regularly or monotonously, over a long period. **7 years a** a long time: *the legal case could take years to resolve.* **b** age, usually old age: *a man of his years.* ▷ **HISTORY** Old English *gēar*

> **WORD TIP**
> In writing spans of years, it is important to choose a style that avoids ambiguity. The practice adopted in this dictionary is, in four-figure dates, to specify the last two digits of the second date if it falls within the same century as the first: *1801–08; 1850–51; 1899–1901*. In writing three-figure BC dates, it is advisable to give both dates in full: *159–156* BC, not *159–56* BC unless of course the span referred to consists of 103 years rather than three years. It is also advisable to specify BC or AD in years under 1000 unless the context makes this self-evident.

yearbook *n* a reference book published once a year containing details of events of the previous year.

yearling *n* an animal that is between one and two years old.

yearly *adj* **1** occurring, done, or appearing once a year or every year. **2** lasting or valid for a year: *the yearly cycle.* ✧ *adv* **3** once a year.

yearn *vb* **1** to have an intense desire or longing: *he often yearned for life in a country town.* **2** to feel tenderness or affection: *I yearn for you.* ▷ **HISTORY** Old English *giernan* ▶ **yearning** *n, adj*

yeast *n* a yellowish fungus used in fermenting alcoholic drinks and in raising dough for bread. ▷ **HISTORY** Old English *giest* ▶ **yeasty** *adj*

yebo *interj S African informal* yes. ▷ **HISTORY** Zulu *yebo* yes, I agree

yell *vb* **1** to shout, scream, or cheer in a loud or piercing way. ✧ *n* **2** a loud piercing cry of pain, anger, or fear. ▷ **HISTORY** Old English *giellan*

yellow *n* **1** the colour of a lemon or an egg yolk. **2** anything yellow, such as yellow clothing or yellow paint: *painted in yellow.* ✧ *adj* **3** of the colour yellow; of the colour of a lemon or an egg yolk. **4** *Informal* cowardly or afraid. **5** having a yellowish complexion. ✧ *vb* **6** to make or become yellow or yellower. ▷ **HISTORY** Old English *geolu* ▶ **yellowish** *or* **yellowy** *adj*

yellow-belly *n, pl* **-bellies** *Slang* a coward. ▶ **yellow-bellied** *adj*

yellow belly *n Austral* a freshwater food fish with yellow underparts.

yellow card *n Soccer* a piece of yellow pasteboard raised by a referee to indicate that a player has been booked for a serious violation of the rules.

yellow fever *n* an acute infectious tropical disease causing fever and jaundice, caused by certain mosquitoes.

yellowhammer *n* a European songbird with a yellowish head and body. ▷ **HISTORY** origin unknown

Yellow Pages *pl n Trademark* a telephone directory that lists businesses under the headings of the type of business or service they provide.

yelp *vb* **1** to utter a sharp or high-pitched cry of pain. ✧ *n* **2** a sharp or high-pitched cry of pain. ▷ **HISTORY** Old English *gielpan* to boast

yen[1] *n, pl* **yen** the standard monetary unit of Japan. ▷ **HISTORY** Japanese *en*

yen[2] *Informal* ✧ *n* **1** a longing or desire. ✧ *vb* **yenning, yenned 2** to have a longing. ▷ **HISTORY** perhaps from Chinese *yän* a craving

yeoman (**yo**-man) *n, pl* **-men** *History* a farmer owning and farming his own land. ▷ **HISTORY** perhaps from *yongman* young man

yeoman of the guard *n* a member of the ceremonial bodyguard (**Yeomen of the Guard**) of the British monarch.

yeomanry *n* **1** yeomen collectively. **2** (in Britain) a former volunteer cavalry force.

yes *interj* **1** used to express consent, agreement, or approval, or to answer when one is addressed. **2** used to signal someone to speak or keep speaking, enter a room, or do something. ✧ *n* **3** an answer or vote of *yes*. **4** a person who answers or votes *yes*. ▷ **HISTORY** Old English *gēse*

yes man *n* a person who always agrees with his or her superior in order to gain favour.

yesterday *n* **1** the day before today. **2** the recent past. ✧ *adv* **3** on or during the day before today. **4** in the recent past.

yet *conj* **1** nevertheless or still: *I'm too tired to work, yet I have to go on.* ✧ *adv* **2** up until then or now: *this may be her most rewarding book yet.* **3** still: *yet more work to do.* **4** now (as contrasted with later): *not ready for that yet.* **5** eventually in spite of everything: *I'll break your spirit yet!* **6 as yet** up until then or now. ▷ **HISTORY** Old English *gīeta*

yeti *n* same as **abominable snowman**. ▷ **HISTORY** Tibetan

yew *n* an evergreen tree with needle-like leaves, red berries, and fine-grained elastic wood. ▷ **HISTORY** Old English *īw*

Y-fronts *pl n Trademark* men's or boys' underpants that have a front opening within an inverted Y shape.

YHA (in Britain) Youth Hostels Association.

Yiddish *n* **1** a language derived from High German, spoken by Jews in Europe and elsewhere by Jewish emigrants, and usually written in the Hebrew alphabet. ✧ *adj* **2** of this language. ▷ HISTORY German *jüdisch* Jewish

yield *vb* **1** to produce or bear. **2** to give as a return: *some of his policies have yielded large savings.* **3** to give up control of; surrender. **4** to give way, submit, or surrender, through force or persuasion: *the players finally yielded to the weather.* **5** to agree (to): *governments too weak to say no repeatedly yielded to petitions for charters.* **6** to grant or allow: *to yield right of way.* ✧ *n* **7** the amount produced. ▷ HISTORY Old English *gieldan*

yielding *adj* **1** compliant or submissive. **2** soft or flexible: *he landed on a yielding surface rather than rock or board.*

Yin and Yang *n* two complementary principles of Chinese philosophy: Yin is negative, dark, and feminine, Yang is positive, bright, and masculine. ▷ HISTORY Chinese *yin* dark + *yang* bright

yippee *interj* an exclamation of joy, pleasure, or anticipation.

YMCA Young Men's Christian Association.

yob *or* **yobbo** *n, pl* **yobs** *or* **yobbos** *Brit, Austral & NZ slang* a bad-mannered aggressive youth. ▷ HISTORY perhaps back slang for *boy* ▸ **yobbish** *adj*

yodel *vb* **-delling, -delled** *or US* **-deling, -deled** **1** to sing with abrupt changes back and forth between the normal voice and falsetto, as in folk songs of the Swiss Alps. ✧ *n* **2** the act or sound of yodelling. ▷ HISTORY German *jodeln* (imitative) ▸ **yodeller** *or US* ▸ **yodeler** *n*

yoga *n* **1** a Hindu system of philosophy aiming at spiritual, mental, and physical wellbeing by means of deep meditation, prescribed postures, and controlled breathing. **2** a system of exercising involving such meditation, postures, and breathing.

> **WORD HISTORY**
> 'Yoga' comes from Sanskrit *yoga*, meaning 'union'. The practice of yoga was intended to produce a mystical union between the practitioner and the Supreme Being.

yogi *n* a person who practises or is a master of yoga.

yogurt *or* **yoghurt** *n* a slightly sour custard-like food made from milk curdled by bacteria, often sweetened and flavoured with fruit. ▷ HISTORY Turkish

yoke *n, pl* **yokes** *or* **yoke** **1** a wooden frame with a bar put across the necks of two animals to hold them together so that they can be worked as a team. **2** a pair of animals joined by a yoke. **3** a frame fitting over a person's shoulders for carrying buckets. **4** an oppressive force or burden: *people are still suffering under the yoke of slavery.* **5** a fitted part of a garment to which a fuller part is attached. ✧ *vb* **yoking, yoked** **6** to put a yoke on. **7** to unite or link. ▷ HISTORY Old English *geoc*

yokel *n Disparaging* a person who lives in the country, esp. one who appears simple and old-fashioned. ▷ HISTORY perhaps from dialect *yokel* green woodpecker

yolk *n* the yellow part in the middle of an egg that provides food for the developing embryo. ▷ HISTORY Old English *geoloca*

Yom Kippur *n* an annual Jewish holiday celebrated as a day of fasting, with prayers of penitence. ▷ HISTORY Hebrew *yōm* day + *kippūr* atonement

yon *adj* **1** *Chiefly Scot & N English dialect* that: *yon dog.* ✧ *adv* **2** yonder: *he flicked glances hither and yon.* ✧ *pron* **3** that person or thing: *yon was a pretty sight.* ▷ HISTORY Old English *geon*

yonder *adv* **1** over there. ✧ *adj* **2** situated over there: *a tree at yonder waterfall.* ▷ HISTORY Old English *geond*

yonks *pl n Informal* a very long time: *he must have been planning this for yonks.* ▷ HISTORY origin unknown

yoo-hoo *interj* a call to attract a person's attention.

yore *n* **of yore** a long time ago: *in days of yore.* ▷ HISTORY Old English *geāra*

yorker *n Cricket* a ball bowled so as to pitch just under or just beyond the bat. ▷ HISTORY probably after the *Yorkshire* County Cricket Club

Yorkist *English history* ✧ *n* **1** a supporter of the royal House of York, esp. during the Wars of the Roses. ✧ *adj* **2** of or relating to the supporters or members of the House of York.

Yorkshire pudding *n* a baked pudding made from a batter of flour, eggs, and milk, often served with roast beef. ▷ HISTORY from *Yorkshire*, county in NE England

you *pron* refers to: **1** the person or people addressed: *can I get you a drink?* **2** an unspecified person or people in general: *stick to British goods and you can't go wrong.* ✧ *n* **3** *Informal* the personality of the person being addressed: *that hat isn't really you.* ▷ HISTORY Old English *ēow*

> **WORD TIP**
> See at **me.**

young *adj* **1** having lived or existed for a relatively short time. **2** having qualities associated with youth: *their innovative approach and young attitude appealed to him.* **3** of or relating to youth: *he'd been a terrorist himself in France in his young days.* **4** of a group representing the younger members of a larger organization: *Young Conservatives.* ✧ *n* **5** young people in general: *that never seems very important to the young.* **6** offspring, esp. young animals: *a deer suckling her young.* ▷ HISTORY Old English *geong* ▸ **youngish** *adj*

youngster *n* a young person.

your *adj* **1** of, belonging to, or associated with you: *ask your doctor to make the necessary calls.* **2** of, belonging to, or associated with an unspecified person or people in general: *it is not right to take another baby to replace your own.* **3** *Informal* used to indicate all things or people of a certain type: *these* *characters are not your average housebreakers.* ▷ HISTORY Old English *ēower*

yours *pron* **1** something belonging to you: *my reputation is better than yours.* **2** your family: *a blessed Christmas to you and yours.* **3** used in closing phrases at the end of a letter: *yours sincerely; yours faithfully.* **4 of yours** belonging to you: *that husband of yours.*

yourself *pron, pl* **-selves 1 a** the reflexive form of *you.* **b** used for emphasis: *you've stated publicly that you yourself use drugs.* **2** your normal self: *you're not yourself today.*

youth *n* **1** the period between childhood and maturity. **2** the quality or condition of being young, immature, or inexperienced: *his youth told against him in the contest.* **3** a young man or boy. **4** young people collectively: *there is still hope for today's youth.* **5** the freshness, vigour, or vitality associated with being young. ▷ HISTORY Old English *geogoth*

youth club *n* a club that provides leisure activities for young people.

youthful *adj* **1** vigorous or active: *the intermediate section was won by a youthful grandmother.* **2** of, relating to, possessing, or associated with youth: *youthful good looks.* ▸ **youthfully** *adv* ▸ **youthfulness** *n*

youth hostel *n* an inexpensive lodging place for young people travelling cheaply.

yowl *vb* **1** to produce a loud mournful wail or cry. ✧ *n* **2** a wail or howl. ▷ HISTORY Old Norse *gaula*

yo-yo *n, pl* **-yos 1** a toy consisting of a spool attached to a string, the end of which is held while it is repeatedly spun out and reeled in. ✧ *vb* **yo-yoing, yo-yoed 2** to change repeatedly from one position to another. ▷ HISTORY originally a trademark for this type of toy

YT Yukon Territory.

ytterbium (it-**terb**-ee-um) *n Chem* a soft silvery element that is used to improve the mechanical properties of steel. Symbol: Yb. ▷ HISTORY after *Ytterby,* Swedish quarry where discovered

yttrium (**it**-ree-um) *n Chem* a silvery metallic element used in various alloys and in lasers. Symbol: Y. ▷ HISTORY see YTTERBIUM

yuan *n, pl* **-an** the standard monetary unit of the People's Republic of China. ▷ HISTORY Chinese *yüan* round object

yucca *n* a tropical plant with spiky leaves and white flowers. ▷ HISTORY from a Native American language

yucky *or* **yukky** *adj* **yuckier, yuckiest** *or* **yukkier, yukkiest** *Slang* disgusting or nasty. ▷ HISTORY from *yuck,* exclamation of disgust

Yugoslav *adj* **1** of the former Yugoslavia. ✧ *n* **2** a person from the former Yugoslavia.

Yule *n Literary or old-fashioned* Christmas or the Christmas season: *Yuletide.*

> **WORD HISTORY**
> Although 'Yuletide' is an archaic word virtually synonymous with 'Christmas-time', Yule (Old English *geola*) was actually a pagan festival. It went on for twelve days around the time of the winter solstice.

yummy *Slang* ✧ *adj* **-mier, -miest 1** delicious or attractive: *yummy sauces.* ✧ *interj* **2** Also: **yum-yum** an exclamation indicating pleasure or delight, as in anticipation of delicious food. ▷ HISTORY *yum-yum* (imitative)

yuppie *n* **1** a young highly-paid professional person, esp. one who has a fashionable way of life. ✧ *adj* **2** typical of or reflecting the values of yuppies: *a yuppie accessory.* ▷ HISTORY *y(oung) u(rban)* or *u(pwardly mobile) p(rofessional)*

yuppify *vb* **-fies, -fying, -fied** to make yuppie in nature: *Mount Pleasant was being yuppified.* ▸ **yuppification** *n*

YWCA Young Women's Christian Association.

Z z

z *or* **Z** *n, pl* **z's, Z's** *or* **Zs 1** the 26th and last letter of the English alphabet. **2 from A to Z** See **a** (sense 3).
z *Maths* (along with *x* and *y*) an unknown quantity.
Z *Chem* atomic number.
zany (**zane**-ee) *adj* **zanier, zaniest** comical in an endearing way.

> **WORD HISTORY**
> 'Zany' comes from Italian *zanni*, meaning 'clown'. 'Zanni' is the Venetian form of the Italian name *Giovanni*, meaning 'John', and was the name often given to comic characters in medieval Italian plays.

zap *vb* **zapping, zapped** *Slang* **1** to kill, esp. by shooting. **2** to change television channels rapidly by remote control. **3** to move quickly.
▷ HISTORY imitative
zeal *n* great enthusiasm or eagerness, esp. for a religious movement. ▷ HISTORY Greek *zēlos*
zealot (**zel**-lot) *n* a fanatic or an extreme enthusiast. ▶ **zealotry** *n*
zealous (**zel**-luss) *adj* extremely eager or enthusiastic. ▶ **zealously** *adv*
zebra *n, pl* **-ras** *or* **-ra** a black-and-white striped African animal of the horse family. ▷ HISTORY Old Spanish: wild ass
zebra crossing *n Brit* a pedestrian crossing marked by broad black and white stripes: once on the crossing the pedestrian has right of way.
zebu (**zee**-boo) *n* a domesticated ox of Africa and Asia, with a humped back and long horns.
▷ HISTORY French
zed *n* the British and New Zealand spoken form of the letter *z*.
zee *n* the US spoken form of the letter *z*.
Zeitgeist (**tsite**-guyst) *n* the spirit or general outlook of a specific time or period.
▷ HISTORY German, literally: time spirit
Zen *n* a Japanese form of Buddhism that concentrates on learning through meditation and intuition.
Zend-Avesta *n* the Zoroastrian scriptures (the **Avesta**), together with the traditional interpretive commentary known as the **Zend**.
zenith *n* **1** the point in the sky directly above an observer. **2** the highest or most successful point of anything: *he was at the zenith of his military career.*
▷ HISTORY Arabic *samt arrās* path over one's head
▶ **zenithal** *adj*
zephyr (**zef**-fer) *n* a soft gentle breeze.
▷ HISTORY Greek *zephuros* the west wind
zero *n, pl* **-ros** *or* **-roes 1** the cardinal number between +1 and −1. **2** the symbol, 0, representing this number. **3** the line or point on a scale of measurement from which the graduations commence. **4** the lowest point or degree: *my credibility is down to zero.* **5** nothing or nil. **6** the temperature, pressure, etc., that registers a reading of zero on a scale. ✧ *adj* **7** amounting to zero: *zero inflation.* **8** *Meteorol* (of visibility) limited to a very short distance. ✧ *vb* **-roing, -roed 9** to adjust (an instrument or scale) so as to read zero.
▷ HISTORY Arabic *sifr* empty
zero gravity *n* the state of weightlessness.
zero hour *n* **1** *Mil* the time set for the start of an operation. **2** *Informal* a critical time, usually at the beginning of an action.
zero in on *vb* **1** to aim a weapon at (a target). **2** to concentrate one's attention on.
zero population growth *n* the condition in which population numbers remain static since births and immigration do not exceed deaths and emigration.
zero-rated *adj* denoting goods on which the buyer pays no value-added tax.
zest *n* **1** invigorating or keen excitement or enjoyment: *he has a zest for life and a quick intellect.* **2** added interest, flavour, or charm: *he said that she would provide a new zest for his government.* **3** the peel of an orange or lemon, used as flavouring.
▷ HISTORY French *zeste* ▶ **zestful** *adj*
Zeus *n Greek myth* the ruler of the gods.
ziggurat *n* (in ancient Mesopotamia) a temple in the shape of a pyramid. ▷ HISTORY Assyrian *ziqqurati* summit
zigzag *n* **1** a line or course having sharp turns in alternating directions. ✧ *adj* **2** formed in or proceeding in a zigzag. ✧ *adv* **3** in a zigzag manner. ✧ *vb* **-zagging, -zagged 4** to move in a zigzag.
▷ HISTORY German *zickzack*
zilch *n Informal* nothing. ▷ HISTORY origin unknown
Zimmer *n Trademark* a tubular frame with rubber feet, used as a support to help disabled or infirm people walk.
zinc *n Chem* a brittle bluish-white metallic element that is used in alloys such as brass, to form a protective coating on metals, and in battery electrodes. Symbol: Zn. ▷ HISTORY German *Zink*
zinc chloride *n Chem* an odourless soluble poison used in manufacturing parchment paper, preserving wood, for embalming and as a medical astringent and antiseptic
zinc ointment *n* a medicinal ointment consisting of zinc oxide, petroleum jelly, and paraffin.
zinc oxide *n Chem, pharmacol* a white insoluble powder used as a pigment and in making zinc ointment.
zing *n* **1** *Informal* the quality in something that makes it lively or interesting. **2** a short high-pitched buzzing sound, like the sound of a bullet or vibrating string. ▷ HISTORY imitative
zinnia *n* a plant of tropical and subtropical America, with solitary heads of brightly coloured flowers. ▷ HISTORY after J. G. *Zinn*, botanist
Zion *n* **1** the hill on which the city of Jerusalem stands. **2 a** the modern Jewish nation. **b** Israel as

the national home of the Jewish people. **3** *Christianity* heaven.

Zionism *n* a political movement for the establishment and support of a national homeland for Jews in what is now Israel. ▶ **Zionist** *n, adj*

zip *n* **1** Also called: **zip fastener** a fastener with two parallel rows of metal or plastic teeth, one on either side of a closure, which are interlocked by a sliding tab. **2** *Informal* energy or vigour. **3** a short sharp whizzing sound, like the sound of a passing bullet. ✧ *vb* **zipping, zipped 4** (often foll. by *up*) to fasten with a zip. **5** to move with a sharp whizzing sound: *bullets zipped and ricocheted all around us.* **6** to hurry or rush. ▷ **HISTORY** imitative

zircon *n Mineral* a hard mineral consisting of zirconium silicate, used as a gemstone and in industry. ▷ **HISTORY** German *Zirkon*

zirconium *n Chem* a greyish-white metallic element, occurring chiefly in zircon, that is exceptionally corrosion-resistant. Symbol: Zr.

zit *n Slang* a spot or pimple.

zither *n* a musical instrument consisting of numerous strings stretched over a flat box and plucked to produce notes. ▷ **HISTORY** Greek *kithara* ▶ **zitherist** *n*

zloty *n, pl* **-tys** *or* **-ty** the standard monetary unit of Poland. ▷ **HISTORY** Polish: golden

Zn *Chem* zinc.

zodiac *n* **1** an imaginary belt in the sky within which the sun, moon, and planets appear to move, and which is divided into 12 equal areas called **signs of the zodiac,** each named after the constellation which once lay in it. **2** *Astrol* a diagram, usually circular, representing this belt. ▷ **HISTORY** Greek *zōidion* animal sign, from *zōion* animal ▶ **zodiacal** *adj*

zombie *or* **zombi** *n, pl* **-bies** *or* **-bis 1** a person who appears to be lifeless, apathetic, or totally lacking in independent judgment. **2** a corpse brought to life by witchcraft.

WORD HISTORY

'Zombie' comes from an African word *zumbi*, meaning a 'fetish' or 'good-luck charm'.

zone *n* **1** a region, area, or section characterized by some distinctive feature or quality: *a demilitarized zone.* **2** *Geog* one of the divisions of the earth's surface according to temperature. **3** a section on a transport route. **4** *Maths* a portion of a sphere between two parallel lines intersecting the sphere. **5** *NZ* a catchment area for a specific school. ✧ *vb* **zoning, zoned 6** to divide (a place) into zones for different uses or activities. ▷ **HISTORY** Greek *zōnē* girdle ▶ **zonal** *adj* ▶ **zoning** *n*

zonked *adj Brit, Austral & NZ slang* **1** highly intoxicated with drugs or alcohol. **2** exhausted. ▷ **HISTORY** imitative

zoo *n, pl* **zoos** a place where live animals are kept, studied, bred, and exhibited to the public. ▷ **HISTORY** from *zoological garden*

zooid (**zoh**-oid) *n* **1** any independent animal body, such as an individual of a coral colony. **2** a cell or body, produced by an organism and capable of independent motion, such as a gamete. ▷ **HISTORY** Greek *zōion* animal

zool. 1 zoological. **2** zoology.

zoological garden *n* the formal term for **zoo**.

zoology *n* the study of animals, including their classification, structure, physiology, and history. ▷ **HISTORY** Greek *zōion* animal + -LOGY ▶ **zoological** *adj* ▶ **zoologist** *n*

zoom *vb* **1** to move very rapidly: *the first rocket zoomed into the sky.* **2** to increase or rise rapidly: *stocks zoomed on the American exchange.* **3** to move with or make a continuous buzzing or humming sound. ✧ *n* **4** the sound or act of zooming. **5** a zoom lens. ▷ **HISTORY** imitative

zoom in *or* **out** *vb Photog, films, television* to increase or decrease rapidly the magnification of the image of a distant object by means of a zoom lens.

zoom lens *n* a lens system that can make the details of a picture larger or smaller while keeping the picture in focus.

zoophyte (**zoh**-a-fite) *n* any animal resembling a plant, such as a sea anemone. ▷ **HISTORY** Greek *zōion* animal + *phuton* plant

Zoroastrianism (zorr-oh-**ass**-tree-an-iz-zum) *or* **Zoroastrism** *n* the religion founded by the ancient Persian prophet Zoroaster, based on the concept of a continuous struggle between good and evil. ▶ **Zoroastrian** *adj*

Zr *Chem* zirconium.

zucchetto (tsoo-**ket**-toe) *n, pl* **-tos** *RC Church* a small round skullcap worn by clergymen and varying in colour according to the rank of the wearer. ▷ **HISTORY** Italian

zucchini (zoo-**keen**-ee) *n, pl* **-ni** *or* **-nis** *Chiefly US, Canad, & Austral* a courgette. ▷ **HISTORY** Italian

Zulu *n* **1** (*pl* **-lus** *or* **-lu**) a member of a tall Black people of Southern Africa. **2** the language of this people.

zygote *n* the cell resulting from the union of an ovum and a spermatozoon. ▷ **HISTORY** Greek *zugōtos* yoked

SURVIVAL GUIDE TO ENGLISH

CONTENTS

INTRODUCTION

The ability to write and communicate well is one of the keys to success both at school and beyond.
In this supplement, you will find practical guidance on writing for different purposes, making presentations, punctuation, spelling and tips to help you do your best in exams.
Use this supplement whenever and whatever you are writing and you will soon see an improvement in your writing skills.

IMPROVING YOUR WRITING STYLE

- The more you read, the better your writing will become, since you will find it easier to recognize what works and what does not.
- Use a thesaurus to expand your vocabulary and look up words you don't know; precise and thoughtful word choices from a wide-ranging vocabulary make for more stimulating reading.
- Think about the tone of what you are writing. Avoid using informal and slang terms in a formal piece; by the same token, if you are writing a personal letter or an e-mail, a more informal tone may be appropriate.
- Try varying the length of your sentences to make your writing read more interestingly.
- You may find it useful to read your work aloud to check that you have expressed yourself clearly.
- If a sentence does not read well as it is, try rearranging it. Just moving the end of a sentence to the beginning can work wonders.

FINDING THE RIGHT REFERENCE MATERIALS

Before starting on a piece, you will probably already have material from your lessons, reading list and notes. You may want to supplement this, however, with information from:

- a library or family reference books;
- the Internet;
- TV and radio programmes;

- people with first-hand experience of your chosen topic.

If you are new to using the Internet, make sure you know the best ways to refine your searches. Try looking at the search tips provided by the search engines or asking a teacher or an experienced Internet surfer for advice. This will help you avoid wasting time wading through screenfuls of irrelevant hits.

Remember that not all websites are equally reliable; concentrate on academic and other authoritative sites, such as government ones or those of well-known institutions.

PLANNING

If you are writing an essay or report, plan it before you start. This means:

- thinking through your ideas to make sure you have a clear picture of the subject and of how you are going to tackle it;
- thinking about the person or group for whom you are writing, what they need to know and how it should be presented;
- deciding what you are going to include in the introduction, development and conclusion as well as in each paragraph.

Your written plan may consist of just a few key words per heading, or else contain quotations, ideas and sentences to help you stay on track. Include all the ideas you have under each heading at the planning stage even if you reject some afterwards. This will make it less likely that you will forget something vital when you write your piece.

REMEMBER

The more you practise your essay-planning skills, the faster you will become, and the more successful your essays will be.

SOME GOLDEN RULES

General

- Keep checking the title or the question you are answering to ensure that you are keeping to the point.
- Don't lose sight of the person or group for whom you are writing.
- Avoid irrelevant detail.

- Make sure that what you write makes sense and that your argument follows logically.
- Watch that you are not endlessly repeating a particular word or expression.
- Don't try to write in an overcomplicated style.
- Always check what you write in terms of sense, spelling and punctuation (including apostrophes).

Structure and paragraphing

- Don't clutter paragraphs with too many ideas. Aim for one unifying idea per paragraph.
- Sketch out what point each paragraph is covering at or near the start of it.
- Develop the idea logically.
- Try to organize your paragraphs so that they lead on naturally from one another.
- Use signposting words to show the progress of an argument, e.g.:

  firstly, ***finally*** to show progress;
  moreover, ***what is more***, ***in addition*** to provide support for a case;
  however, ***nevertheless*** to introduce a counter-argument;
  in conclusion, ***to summarize*** to round up.

  You may find it useful to make a list of these and other expressions that are used in a similar way for future reference.

Sentences

- Link sentences together logically.
- Avoid sentences that are longer than three lines. If it looks too long, break it up.
- Use short sentences for impact, followed by longer sentences to explore an idea.
- Avoid saying the same thing twice in a sentence. Make every word count.

WRITING FOR DIFFERENT PURPOSES

Giving information

As with any writing, think about the person or group for whom you are writing and what and how much they need to be told. Summarize the facts briefly, clearly, objectively and in a logical order using simple language. If working on a PC, try experimenting with different page layouts and type sizes to help divide up the information and draw the reader's attention to the most important facts.

Explaining

Think about your audience and how much or how little you need to explain. Plan your explanation so that it follows a sensible order and is easy to understand.

Describing

When writing descriptively, your aim is to show the reader how interesting aspects look, taste, sound or feel through the use of carefully chosen words and contrasts. Avoid using too many adjectives at once. It is generally better to pick a strong adjective that captures a feeling or impression rather than using three less punchy ones. It is often useful to use comparison, metaphor and simile.

Persuading

When writing to persuade, you need to sound reasonable and trustworthy. Avoid ranting as it is likely to distance your readers. Think about who you are writing for and get them on your side by appealing to their aspirations and interests. Alternatively, you may be able to shame them into supporting a worthwhile cause by highlighting the differences between their circumstances and those of the less fortunate group for whom you are seeking support.

Advising

Tailor the style of your advice to the person or group for whom it is meant. If it is personal advice, a more informal style may be appropriate. Give the advantages and disadvantages of any options you propose. To make your advice sound well thought out, back it up with facts or an anecdote.

Arguing

When presenting an argument, you need to look at both sides of it, even if you focus more attention on the side you support. Structure your piece logically. Try to sum up the key points and draw conclusions from these. Make sure your line of argument is reasonable and takes all the necessary facts into account. Do justice to the opposing side and never resort to abusive comments or statements you cannot back up.

Analysis, review and comment

Look at a variety of newspapers and magazines to see how journalists analyse, review and comment on current affairs. Note how their approaches and focuses vary to suit their differing readerships.
As when explaining or arguing, you should first establish the main facts and then move on to analysis, review or comment. The essential difference between the three is this:

- analysis: an objective exploration of the facts
- review: a detached presentation of the facts followed by impressions and opinions
- comment: an opinion, either personal or political, on the overall topic

WRITING ESSAYS

Before starting

- Read the question closely, look up any unfamiliar words and, if a quotation is included, make sure you know its context.
- Pay close attention to the verbs used in the title.

Analyse	Break up into parts; investigate
Compare	Look for similarities and differences between
Contrast	Bring out the differences between
Define	Give the meaning of
Describe	Give a detailed account of
Discuss	Investigate, giving reasons for and against
Distinguish	Indicate the differences between
Enumerate	List in order
Evaluate	Give a judgment based on evidence
Examine	Look closely into
Explain	Give reasons for

Explore	Consider from a variety of viewpoints
Illustrate	Make clear by using examples
Interpret	Show the meaning of
Justify	Respond to the most obvious objections concerning
Outline	Give only the main features of
Relate	Tell in order
Relate to	Show how one thing is connected to another
State	Present in a clear form
Summarize	Give a concise account of, omitting details
Trace	Show the development of a topic from a particular point

- Think about the question and note down any ideas that occur to you in rough, including any further questions you might want to raise which are triggered by the essay title.
- Write out a plan of what to include in your introduction, conclusion and development, if not in every paragraph.
- Write any quotations, data and facts that you want to include beside the relevant points in your plan.

Introduction

This should typically be a concise paragraph that includes a short, clear statement of the subject you are going to discuss, your definition of any technical terms used in the question and an indication of how you are going to tackle the question.
Remember to make it interesting to engage your readers.

Development

Keep to your plan, be aware of the question at all times and keep your writing relevant.

Conclusion

Like the introduction, this will be fairly short and should summarize the essence of the essay, bringing together all of the major points and referring back to the question to demonstrate that you have answered it. Don't be afraid to make a bold statement on the subject at this point or to include a choice quotation which supports your conclusion; similarly, if there are further questions that have occurred to you in the course of planning or writing the essay, you could include these here, provided they offer an interesting natural progression from what has gone before.

Word counts

Make sure you keep to the required number of words. Doing otherwise is likely to lose you marks.

WRITING SUMMARIES

Summarizing stories, articles and reports is a skill everyone employs from time to time, whether it is explaining to a friend what happened in the latest episode of a television serial, or whether it is condensing the findings of a long report for the benefit of others.

What are the features of a good summary?

- It is concise and to the point.
- It provides an accurate overview of what was discussed in the original.
- It is objective and therefore does not reveal the views of the summarizer.
- It is written in the summarizer's own words and does not plagiarize.
- From the start, it contains phrases which clarify whose views are being presented – e.g. *Murphy argues that; the writer claims that…*

Tips for summary writing

- Read the text once or twice, mentally identifying the main points.
- Next, jot these down from memory.
- Go through the text highlighting or noting any other key points made by the writer and amending your jottings as necessary.
- Now write the summary in your own words as concisely as you can or as required.
- After you have done this, reread the text to check that you have mentioned all the essential points.
- If a word count has been given, count the words you have used and make sure your summary is the right length. If not, you will need to edit it.
- Once the summary is the right length and contains everything it should, reread it to ensure that it follows on logically and that you have not accidentally cut something vital for it to make sense.

Timing

If you are working under exam conditions, you may need to leave enough time to make a clean copy of your summary. If time is too short, be especially careful to make all alterations neatly and clearly.

WRITING REPORTS

For some subjects, such as geography or sociology, you may need to write a report presenting the results of a field trip or project.

Points to remember

Keep all of the information you gather during the field trip in one place.
Stick to the introduction-development-conclusion model.
Avoid using *I* or *we*; adopt an objective tone instead: *The field trip was… The information gathered showed that… The aim of…*

Clear presentation

Where helpful, use simple graphs, bar and pie charts to represent data. These provide a quick overview of the results and can aid understanding.
Organize the information into different sections, giving each one a clear heading to help the reader navigate the report.
If there are a lot of sections, it may be helpful to number them. If one section is composed of several smaller sections, number them as follows:

1. [*Section heading*]
1.1 [*Subsection heading*]
1.2 [*Subsection heading*]

If you need to include a large amount of data in the report but do not want to interrupt the flow of the text, put it in an appendix.
Be consistent in your presentation; pay attention to the numbering of sections and appendices.

The professional look

To achieve a really professional-looking report, try structuring as follows:

- **Title page**
  This includes the title, author and date.

- **Abstract**
  This is a short summary of the report, including aims, methods and conclusions.
- **Contents**
  This lists the different sections of the report along with the corresponding page numbers.
- **Introduction**
  This explains the purpose of the report and the methods used.
- **Development**
  This contains the information you have collected for the report in a number of clearly headed sections.
- **Conclusion and recommendations**
  This is a brief, easy-to-understand section saying what you have found and what you think needs to be done.
- **Appendices**
  These contain additional information that has been omitted from the main body of the text but which is relevant to the report as a whole.
- **Notes**
  These give details that would be too cumbersome to include in the main text.
- **Bibliography**
  This gives an alphabetical list of books, journals, websites, newspapers, etc., to which you have referred during your investigation or in the text itself. Included with the source is the author, title, publisher and place and date of publication.

WRITING UP EXPERIMENTS

As you will doubtless already be used to writing up experiments in chemistry, physics or biology following the *methods–results–conclusion* model, this section deals with slightly longer experiments.

Be clear, be concise

Explain why and how the experiment was performed, what results were obtained and what conclusions can be drawn.
Imagine your reader has never carried out the experiment and make no assumptions about his or her knowledge of the processes involved.
Explain each step of the experiment fully, logically and concisely.

Avoid using *I* or *we*; adopt an objective tone instead: *The solution was placed… The aim of…*

Clear presentation

Organize the information into different sections, giving each one a clear heading to help the reader navigate.

If there are a lot of sections, it may be helpful to number them. If one section is composed of several smaller sections, number them as follows:

1. [*Section heading*]

1.1 [*Subsection heading*]

1.2 [*Subsection heading*]

Be consistent in your presentation; pay attention to the numbering of sections and figures.

Always include units with quantities, whether in the text, table column headings, graph axes or diagrams (*mm, kg,* cm^3).

The professional look

To achieve a really professional-looking write-up of your experiment, try structuring as follows:

- **Title**
  This indicates what the experiment is about.
- **Aims**
  A brief summary of the aims of the experiment.
- **Introduction**
  This details the theory behind the experiment and any equations to be used in the calculation of results, chemical reaction pathways, and principles behind the methodology. It explains the assumption on which the experiment is based, *e.g. If A is mixed with B, it produces C.*
- **The Experiment**
  This describes what occurred during the experiment: what you did and what happened as a result. Instead of using *I* or *we*; it adopts an objective tone: *The aim of the experiment was… The magnesium ribbon was placed in the flame…* This part of the write-up can be divided up if it helps present the information more clearly, e.g. ***Description of Apparatus*** (with diagrams) or ***Method*** (saying how you did what you did, including any special precautions or techniques used).

Results

Where possible, these are shown in tables and graphs to aid comprehension. Also included are any external factors which may affect the results, e.g. room temperature, pressure.

Discussion

Here, the results of the experiment are compared with the theory or expected behaviour described in the introduction. Also detailed are any calculations based on the results.

Conclusion

This is a summary of the conclusions you draw from the experiment.

WRITING IN EXAMS

If panic strikes because you cannot see any questions you know you can tackle, relax and read the questions again. Provided you have done your revision, there will be a number of questions you are equipped to answer. However, do not be tempted to bend questions to allow you to make use of essay material you have worked on previously.

Top Tips

Revision time

- Revision does not have to be dull. Help motivate yourself by watching any relevant television programmes advised by your teachers and by going on field trips designed to help your studies.
- Read round your subjects as advised by your teachers.
- Look at past papers, noting the kind of questions, the amount of detail required to answer them and so on.
- Get used to sketching out a brief plan to answer each question. You should spend no more than a couple of minutes doing this.
- Practise answering these questions under timed conditions. Be strict with yourself – practising writing against the clock outside the exam room will give you more confidence and focus inside it.
- Revise and learn any mnemonics that will help you remember facts, dates, spellings, etc.
- Don't procrastinate. Decide to do a realistic amount of revision each week and try to keep to it. On the other hand, don't be obsessive about

it; allow some time for relaxation.

- Don't endlessly write out revision plans when you could be revising. Be honest with yourself; these are often a way of putting off doing that all-important revision.

REMEMBER

The best results are likely to be achieved by those who read over their work regularly. Well-planned revision is essential, however, for refreshing your memory and ensuring you do your best in your exams.

Before the exam

- Instead of talking to the other candidates outside the exam room, take the opportunity to collect your thoughts and prepare.
- Have to hand a short list of quotations or any other brief information you need to memorize before entering the exam room. Read it on the way to the exam but do not forget to leave it outside.

During the exam

- Make sure you know how many questions you have to answer, then work out how much time you need to spend on each one, giving the most time to the questions that carry the most marks.
- Read each question slowly and carefully. Make sure that you have understood it properly before you jot down your plan. Sketch out a brief plan for any essay, plus any quotations you wish to include.
- Refer back to the plan as you write, ticking off the points as you go. This way you will know you have included everything you meant to.

In the last few minutes

Try to complete all your answers with a few minutes to spare at the end of the exam; this is to give you time to double-check your spelling and punctuation and to reassure yourself you have answered all the questions or parts of them that are required. If you discover you have missed out a vital point, you will still be able to add it at this stage.

Points to watch

- Read each question carefully. Don't assume it is identical to one you have answered as a practice question.
- To ensure you remember to answer each part of a complex question, underline or highlight the elements that you need to consider.

- If there is a choice of questions, make sure that you pick the ones you can answer best and which allow you the most scope to show off with thorough, focused answers.
- If asked to comment on a piece of writing containing some unlikely views, think about whether it is meant to be taken literally or whether the writer is making use of irony or satire.
- Plan the essay before you start writing. This leads to more focused, relevant answers.
- Keep to the point. Avoid the temptation to go off at a tangent.
- Split your time between the questions. Don't fall into the trap of spending all your time on question 1.
- Make use of paragraphs to show each new idea. This makes it easier for the examiner to follow your argument. If your ideas are clearly presented, there is a greater chance of your gaining good marks.
- Use commas to indicate natural breaks in sentences; if in doubt, insert commas where you would pause for breath.

Common errors

- Spelling mistakes are common in exam scripts. If you often misspell a word, invent a mnemonic to help you remember it correctly.
- Candidates often make silly errors such as writing *there* when they meant *their*, or *by* instead of *buy*, etc. Always check your work carefully to ensure you have not made careless and preventable mistakes.
- Apostrophes are often misused, with the most common problems being a confusion of *it's* and *its* or an inappropriate apostrophe at the end of a word that is merely plural.
- Be careful not to write *should of, could of* and *would of* instead of *should have, could have* and *would have*.

Extra marks

- Use your vocabulary to its fullest extent.
- Show the examiner that you know your subject by including a range of quotations, where appropriate, and briefly mentioning any secondary texts.
- Show you have understood the question by relating points back to it. Clarify any potentially confusing parts of the question.

GIVING A PRESENTATION

As with writing, one of the keys to giving a good presentation is organizing your material. Your topic should be clearly stated, logically thought through and explained interestingly enough to hold the interest of your audience.

Notes

- Don't learn your presentation by heart or write it down word for word. Such strategies make for very boring presentations.
- Make notes to refer to during the presentation in case you dry up. If you write these on index cards, you will be able to put each card to the back of the pile once you have used it and will therefore not lose your place.
- Try practising your presentation in front of a supportive friend or family member. Ask him or her to point out any distracting habits you may have and which you should avoid; for example, fiddling with your hair or saying "you know" too often can be very off-putting to your audience.

Content

- Try to start with something exciting but relevant to make your audience sit up and listen.
- Give an introductory outline of your talk and make sure you stick to it in what follows.
- Avoid introducing a completely new subject later or changing the tone of your presentation halfway through.
- Use linking sentences to lead from one point to the next.
- Give specific examples – this gives the audience something to discuss in a question-and-answer session.
- If you are presenting an argument, build from the weakest to the strongest point.
- Include a few light jokes or puns to entertain your audience, but remember that they should be appropriate to the overall tone.
- Try to bring your own perspective to the presentation material – there may be facts that are known to people in your audience but anything

extra you can add will be of interest.

- Don't be afraid to express your opinions.
- Consider including some aspect of audience participation, provided it is not intimidating and provided you are not dependent on getting a reaction – audiences do not always cooperate. In general, some degree of interaction makes a presentation more interesting.
- Your presentation should end with a quick recap of the main points and a strong, and preferably exciting, conclusion.

Visual aids

- Use visual aids to illustrate your presentation, provided they are simple, useful and clearly visible from the back of the room.
- Do not overdo the number of visual aids; the last thing you want is to overwhelm your audience with too much visual information and to distract them from your talk.
- If you have access to a computer, you might like to use a presentation program such as PowerPoint®. Keep the number of slides to a minimum and have a maximum of four bullet points per slide. Keep each one short and to the point.
- If giving your audience hand-outs, make sure you have enough for everyone. Do not rely on being able to do photocopies at the last minute.

Timing

- Practise giving your presentation in advance, making sure that you tailor it to fit the time you have been given. Failing to complete your talk by the time the next speaker is due to come on can be a disaster. Similarly, finding that there is too much time to fill can be very stressful and look unprofessional.
- When you practise your presentation and when you give it, make sure you do not talk too quickly. Take your time. Don't speak at the same rate as you would when chatting to a friend. Slow down and pause for breath between points. This also helps the audience know when you are moving on to a different subject.

Venue

- If you are going to use a computer or overhead projector in your presentation, make sure you are familiar with how it works beforehand.

Fumbling for an on-switch in front of your audience will not increase your confidence.

- Make sure there are enough seats to accommodate your audience.
- Familiarize yourself with the venue and its acoustics to ensure that you feel comfortable speaking and know how to project your voice into all corners of the room.

You, your body language and your voice

- If you feel nervous before you begin speaking, practise deep breathing and rehearse your opening sentences to yourself.
- Stand up straight and keep your chin up as you talk. Posture says a lot about how you feel and a positive, strong stance will both improve your confidence and convince the audience that you have something interesting to say.
- If you are nervous, standing behind a lectern or table may help you feel less vulnerable, as well as give you something to lean on and to put any notes on.
- Speak sincerely and with warmth.
- Vary your tone of voice. Slightly exaggerate the rising and falling notes to add interest.
- Vary your pace, but do not talk too fast as you will lose your audience.
- Smile from time to time. It will relax you and encourage a link with your audience.
- Look members of your audience very briefly in the eye when you can, though avoid looking at any one individual for too long. Look round the faces with a sweeping glance.
- Allow pauses for audience reaction.
- Don't be put off if you make a mistake during the presentation. Apologize quickly and move on.

WRITTEN CONVENTIONS TO REMEMBER

Abbreviations

There are no set rules about how to write abbreviations, but these guidelines will help:

- Use a full stop after any abbreviation that does not end with the final letter of the word.
  E.g. *Co., Jan., misc.*
- A full stop is unnecessary when the last letter of the abbreviation is the final letter of the word.
  E.g. *Dr, Mr, Mrs, Revd, Mgr*
- Treat as words acronyms and common abbreviations for countries, organizations and institutions formed from initial letters.
  E.g. *NATO, AIDS, UK, EU, VAT*
- Only use abbreviations in formal writing when it would look odd to write the full form of the word.
- The first time you mention an abbreviation that is uncommon in everyday speech and writing, make sure you always explain what it is by giving the full form too.

Capital letters

Use a capital letter in the following cases:

- for the first word in a sentence: *Let's go*
- for the first word in each line of most poems:
  Hence, loathed Melancholy,
  Of Cerberus, and blackest Midnight born…
- to begin each word in a person's name: *Seamus Heaney*
- for official, royal and courtesy titles: *Prime Minister, Prince William*
- to begin all significant words in book and film titles:
  Far from the Madding Crowd, Raiders of the Lost Ark
- for trade names: *Hoover®*
- for the names of countries: *Sri Lanka*
- for the names of peoples and languages: *Spanish, Thai*
- for religions, their gods and their holy books: *Islam, God, Koran*
- for adjectives derived from proper nouns: *Islamic, Russian*

However, use a lower-case letter when referring to points of the compass, the seasons and for the first word after a semicolon:

It was a long hot summer; we were heading north to escape the heat.

Numbers

- Write out numbers from one to ten, use numerals from 11–99, but use common sense to judge if the number should be written in words, e.g. two million, five thousand.
- Hyphenate numbers from 21–99 if written out; again, use common sense to decide. If it will look unwieldy, avoid writing it out in words.
- Use commas when giving figures greater than 999: *1,354; 3,078,000*.

Using quotations and references

- Put " ..." or '...' around quotations if the words are not your own.
- You can include a brief quotation inside a sentence: *Macbeth says life is "a walking shadow".*
- If you are quoting a couple of lines of poetry, show where the line breaks with a slash:

  Macbeth calls life "a walking shadow, a poor player, / That struts and frets his hour upon the stage".
- When quoting a longer piece of poetry, keep the lines and indent the entire section quoted:

  As Macbeth says:
  "Life's but a walking shadow, a poor player,
  That struts and frets his hour upon the stage,
  And then is heard no more".
- Indicate missing words in a quotation with ..., and put square brackets round any words added to make sense: [*he*].
- If quoting the title of a book or film in a handwritten text, underline it. If working on a computer, use italics.
- Indicate your sources, either by using footnotes or briefly in the text immediately after the quotation. Include the title, author's name and, if quoting from a play, the act, scene and line number(s).
- If required, supply a bibliography listing all of your sources, including websites, at the end of the essay. For each source significantly referred to or quoted, you should include: author, title, publisher and place and date of publication. Arrange the sources alphabetically.

PUNCTUATION

Punctuation marks are an essential part of good writing. They help the reader understand what is meant and how something should be read.

Apostrophe 9

Possession

The apostrophe is used to show that something belongs to someone.

- **'s** is added to the end of singular words:
  e.g. *a child'**s** cry* ◆ *Hannah'**s** book*
- **'s** is added to the end of plural words not ending in ***s***:
  e.g. *children'**s** games* ◆ *women'**s** clothes*
- **'** An apostrophe alone is added to plural words ending in ***s***:
  e.g. *worker**s'** rights* ◆ *ladie**s'** fashion*
- **'s** is added to the end of names and singular words ending in ***s***:
  e.g. *James'**s** car* ◆ *the octopus'**s** tentacles*

⚠ But if the word is a classical Greek name, an apostrophe only is sometimes preferred:
e.g. *Socrates' Athens*

To test whether an apostrophe is in the right place, think about who the owner is:
e.g. *the boy's books* [= *the books belonging to the boy*]
the boys' books [= *the books belonging to the boys*]

Missing letters

An apostrophe is used in shortened forms of words where letters have been missed out:
e.g. *it's* [= *it is*] ◆ *he'll* [= *he will*] ◆ *rock'n'roll* [= *rock and roll*]

⚠ An apostrophe is **not** used to form possessive pronouns:
e.g. *Is the responsibility yours or theirs?*

⚠ An apostrophe is **not** used to form the plurals of words:
e.g. *2 kilos of potatoes* ◆ *The girls laughed.*

An apostrophe **can** be used in plurals of letters and numbers to make them more readable:
e.g. *p's and q's* ◆ *His 2's look a bit like 7's.*

REMEMBER

it's = it is e.g. *It's a holiday today.*

its = belonging to it e.g. *The dog was scratching its ear.*

Brackets ( )

- Brackets are used to enclose a word or words which can be left out and still leave a meaningful sentence:
  e.g. *The wooded area (see map below) is approximately 4,000 hectares.*
- Brackets are also used to show alternatives or options:
  e.g. *Any student(s) interested in taking part should e-mail me.*

⚠ Note that when the structure of the sentence as a whole demands punctuation after a bracketed section, the punctuation is given *outside* the brackets.
e.g. I haven't yet spoken to John (I mean John Maple, my boss), but I have a meeting with him on Friday.
Punctuation is given before the closing brackets only when it applies to the bracketed section rather than to the sentence as a whole:
e.g. He's very handsome (positively gorgeous in fact!) and still single.

Colon :

The colon is used to introduce a list, a quotation or an explanation:
e.g. *I used three colours: green, blue and pink.* ◆ *He received a telegram which read: "Return home."* ◆ *I like the room: it is light and airy.*

Comma ,

The comma marks a short pause between elements in a sentence.

- A comma is used between two long main clauses joined by a conjunction:
  e.g. *He was talking quite loudly, but I couldn't hear him.*
- A comma is often used to separate an introductory word or phrase from the main clause in a sentence, or to separate a subordinate clause or short phrase that comes after the main clause:
  e.g. *If we get another goal, we'll have won the league.* ◆ *He'll be there, come what may.* ◆ *In winter, we usually go skiing.*
- When words like *however*, *therefore* and *moreover* are included in a sentence, these words should be marked off by commas:
  e.g. *The forecasters got it wrong. There was no warning, therefore, of the*

heavy rain and flooding that hit the south.

- Commas are also used to separate off a subordinate clause inserted into a main clause:
  e.g. *A new model, which will be made in Spain, is to be introduced.*
- Commas are used to separate the name of a person or group being addressed from the rest of the sentence:
  e.g. *And now, ladies and gentlemen, please raise your glasses in a toast.*
- Commas are also used to separate items in a list or series:
  e.g. *bread, butter and jam*

⚠ Note that the comma is not usually given before the final *and* or *or* in such cases in everyday English:
e.g. *dogs, cats, rabbits and hamsters* ◆ *Jim, Mark, Peter or Eddy*

- A comma is used to separate words in direct speech from the rest of the sentence, if there is no question or exclamation mark after the quotation:
  e.g. *"I don't understand this question," said Peter.*
- Commas are also used after reporting verbs such as *say*, *ask* and *exclaim*, when they are followed by a quotation:
  e.g. *Peter said, "Dream on!"*
- A comma must be used between the day of the month and the year when the two numbers are next to each other:
  e.g. October 29, 1989

Dash –

- The dash is used at the beginning and end of a comment that interrupts the flow of a sentence:
  e.g. *Now children – Kenneth, stop that immediately! – open your books on page 20.*
- The dash (–) also separates off extra information:
  e.g. *Boots and shoes – all shapes, sizes and colours – tumbled out.*
- The dash is also used to indicate a range:
  e.g. *pages 26–42*

Exclamation mark !

The exclamation mark is used after exclamations and emphatic expressions:
e.g. *I can't believe it!* ◆ *Oh, no! Look at this mess!*

SURVIVAL GUIDE TO ENGLISH

⚠ The exclamation mark loses its effect if overused. It is better to use a full stop after a sentence expressing mild excitement or humour:
e.g. *It was such a beautiful day.*

Full stop .

- A full stop is used to mark the end of a statement:
e.g. *Harry loves football.*
- Full stops are used after initials and abbreviations (but see **Abbreviations** under **WRITTEN CONVENTIONS TO REMEMBER**) :
e.g. *George W. Bush* ◆ *etc.* ◆ *Rev. Adams*
- A full stop is used after an indirect question or a polite request:
e.g. *He asked if the bus had left.* ◆ *Will you open your books on page 14.*

Hyphen -

The hyphen joins words or parts of words.

- A hyphen is used to join two or more words that together form an adjective, where this adjective is used *before* the noun it describes:
e.g. *an up-to-date account* ◆ *a last-minute rush* ◆ *a six-year-old boy*
- The hyphen is omitted when the adjective so formed comes after the noun or pronoun it describes:
e.g. *The accounts are up to date.* ◆ *It was all rather last minute.* ◆ *He's six years old.*
- Some common compound nouns are usually written with hyphens:
e.g. mother-in-law
- Hyphens can be used to split words formed by adding a prefix to another word, especially to avoid an awkward combination of letters or confusion with another word:
e.g. *re-elect* ◆ *re-covering furniture*
- Hyphens are used at the ends of lines where a word has been split, to warn the reader that the word continues on the next line:
e.g *He was just leaving the house when he remem-*
bered that he'd left his lunch on the kitchen table.

Question mark ?

The question mark marks the end of a question:
e.g. *When will we be arriving?* ◆ *Not your best effort, eh?*

⚠ A full stop, rather than a question mark, is used after a reported question or a polite request:

e.g. *George asked when we would be arriving.* ◆ *Will you please return the completed forms to me.*

Semicolon ;

- The semicolon marks a stronger break than a comma, but a weaker one than a full stop. It is used to mark a break between two main clauses when there is a balance or contrast between the clauses:

  e.g. *I'm not that interested in jazz; I prefer classical music.*

- The semicolon is used to separate clauses or items of more than one word in a long list:

  e.g. *The holiday was a disaster: the flight was four hours late; the hotel was overbooked; and it rained for the whole fortnight*

Slash, oblique /

The slash separates letters, words or numbers. It is used to indicate alternatives, ratios and ranges, and in website addresses:

e.g. *he/she/it* ◆ *200 km/hr* ◆ *the 2001/02 accounting year* ◆ *http://www.abcdefg.com*

Speech marks, inverted commas, quotation marks “” ‘’

- Speech marks mark the beginning and end of direct speech (a speaker's words written down exactly as they were said):

  e.g. *"I will," said Ian.* ◆ *Jo declared abruptly, "We're leaving."*

- Speech marks can be used to indicate the title of a book, poem, piece of music, film or work of art, although italics and underlining are probably more usual:

  e.g. *Have you read "The Lord of the Rings"?* ◆ *music from "Swan Lake"*

- Speech marks are also used to show that a word is being used in an unusual way, or that the word itself is being discussed:

  e.g. *Braille allows a blind person to "see" with the fingers.* ◆ *What is the French for "egg"?*

⚠ Speech marks are *not* used for indirect or reported speech (what someone has said, but not in their exact words):

e.g. *Ian said that he would.* ◆ *Jo declared abruptly that they were leaving.*

SPELLING RULES

- Most people know the rule ***i* before *e*, except after *c***, when they make the *ee* sound. For example:

ach**ie**ve	br**ie**f	ch**ie**f
gr**ie**ve	n**ie**ce	rel**ie**f
s**ie**ge	th**ie**f	p**ie**ce
c**ei**ling	conc**ei**t	dec**ei**t
dec**ei**ve	rec**ei**pt	rec**ei**ve

but note some common exceptions:

s**ei**ze	prot**ei**n

- Many words can be spelled with either of the endings *–ize* or *–ise* (and *–ization* or *-isation*). Care should be taken, however, because some words can only be spelled with *-ize* and others only with *-ise*.

Verbs (and nouns) only spelled with -ize:

caps**ize**
pr**ize** [= value highly]

Verbs (and nouns) only spelled with -ise:

advert**ise**	desp**ise**	franch**ise**	surpr**ise**
adv**ise**	dev**ise**	improv**ise**	telev**ise**
chast**ise**	disgu**ise**	pr**ise** [= force]	
compr**ise**	exc**ise**	rev**ise**	
comprom**ise**	exerc**ise**	superv**ise**	

- A final silent *e* is dropped when an ending that begins with a vowel is added:

servile + ity	=	servil**ity**
response + ible	=	respons**ible**
tolerate + ing	=	tolerat**ing**
value + able	=	valu**able**
excuse + ed	=	excus**ed**

SURVIVAL GUIDE TO ENGLISH

- But the *e* is kept if an ending beginning with a vowel is added to a word that ends in *-ce* or *-ge* and these letters keep a soft sound:

change + able	=	change**able**
notice + able	=	notice**able**
outrage + ous	=	outrage**ous**
peace + able	=	peace**able**

- When an ending beginning with a vowel is added to a word that ends in a single vowel + a consonant (other than *h, w, x* and *y*), the consonant is doubled if the stress is on the end of the base form:

admit + ance	=	admi**tt**ance
begin + ing	=	begi**nn**ing
occur +ence	=	occu**rr**ence
equip + ed	=	equi**pp**ed
stop +ing	=	sto**pp**ing

- When an ending beginning with a vowel is added to a word that ends in a vowel + *l* or *p*, the *l* or *p* is usually doubled:

cancel + ation	=	cance**ll**ation
dial + ing	=	dia**ll**ing
fulfil + ed	=	fulfi**ll**ed
kidnap + er	=	kidna**pp**er
slip + ing	=	sli**pp**ing

- When the adverb suffix *-ly* is added to an adjective that ends in a consonant followed by *-le*, the *-le* in the adjective is usually dropped:

gentle + ly	=	gent**ly**
idle + ly	=	id**ly**
subtle + ly	=	subt**ly**

- When the adjective suffix *-ous* or *-ary* is added to a word that ends in *-our*, the *u* of the *-our* is dropped:

glamour + ous	=	glam**o**rous
honour + ary	=	hon**o**rary
humour + ous	=	hum**o**rous

- When an ending beginning with *e, i* or *y* is added to a word that ends in *c*, a *k* is added to the *c* to keep its hard sound:

mimic	→	mimic**k**ed	→	mimic**k**ing
picnic	→	picnic**k**ing	→	picnic**k**ed

- When an ending other than *–ing* is added to a word that ends in a consonant + *y*, the *y* usually changes to i:

beauty	→	beaut**i**ful
crazy	→	craz**i**ly
woolly	→	wooll**i**er

- But, with certain short adjectives that end in a consonant + *y*, the *-ly* ending is added after the *y*:

shy	→	shy**ly**
wry	→	wry**ly**

- The plural of a word that ends in a consonant + *y* is made by changing the *y* to *i* and adding *-es*:

memory	→	memor**ies**
whisky	→	whisk**ies**

- The plural of a word that ends in a vowel plus *y* is made by adding *-s*:

donkey	→	donkey**s**
buoy	→	buoy**s**
whiskey	→	whiskey**s**

- The plural of a word that ends in *s, x, z, sh* or *ch* is made by adding *-es*:

bus	→	bus**es**
mass	→	mass**es**
fox	→	fox**es**
buzz	→	buzz**es**
rash	→	rash**es**
match	→	match**es**

- The suffix *-ful* is spelt with one *l*:

grate**ful**	faith**ful**	cup**ful**

- But *-fully* is spelt with two:

grate**fully**	faith**fully**

? WORDS THAT ARE SOMETIMES CONFUSED

accept – VERB – e.g. *Please accept my apologies.*
except – PREPOSITION & VERB – e.g. *every day except Friday / If we except cats, most animals only kill for food.*

advice – NOUN – e.g. *He gave me some good advice.*
advise – VERB – e.g. *You could go that way but I wouldn't advise it.*

affect – VERB – e.g. *Tiredness affects concentration.*
effect – NOUN & VERB – e.g. *the effects of global warming / prospects for effecting real change*

allude – VERB – e.g. *He never alluded to the difficulties he'd had.*
elude – VERB – e.g. *I recognized his face, but his name eluded me.*

altar – NOUN – e.g. *There were some flowers on the altar.*
alter – VERB – e.g. *His tone altered suddenly.*

ascent – NOUN – e.g. *the first ascent of Everest*
assent – NOUN & VERB – e.g. *The king gave his assent. / He assented.*

aural – ADJECTIVE – e.g. *They use music as a kind of aural wallpaper.*
oral – ADJECTIVE & NOUN – e.g. *You'll have to talk in the oral (exam).*

breath – NOUN – e.g. *There wasn't a breath of wind.*
breathe – VERB – e.g. *Breathe deeply a couple of times.*

broach – VERB – e.g. *She didn't dare broach the subject of a pay rise.*
brooch – NOUN – e.g. *a gold brooch set with emeralds and diamonds*

canvas – NOUN – e.g. *a hammock made from heavy canvas*
canvass – VERB – e.g. *pollsters canvassing opinion*

ceiling – NOUN – e.g. *a high domed ceiling*
sealing – VERB & ADJECTIVE – e.g. *sealing the edges with putty / sealing wax*

cent – NOUN – e.g. *four dollars and fifty cents*
scent – NOUN & VERB – e.g. *the scent of roses / He scented victory.*
sent – VERB – e.g. *Have you sent your Christmas cards yet?*

cereal – NOUN – e.g. *corn and other cereals*
serial – NOUN & ADJECTIVE – e.g. *a TV serial / a serial killer*

chute – NOUN – e.g. *a laundry chute to the basement*
shoot – VERB & NOUN – e.g. *Stop or I'll shoot! / a film shoot*

cite – VERB – e.g. *He could cite several examples.*
sight – NOUN & VERB – e.g. *My sight is failing. / He was sighted in a bar.*
site – NOUN & VERB – e.g. *the site of a battle / It will be sited near shops.*

coarse – ADJECTIVE – e.g. *a coarse cloth which scratched the skin*
course – NOUN & VERB – e.g. *the course of the river / Tears coursed down her cheeks.*

compliment – NOUN & VERB – e.g. *My compliments to the chef. / He complimented her on her dress.*
complement – NOUN & VERB – e.g. *a ship with its full complement of men / wine to complement your meal*

council – NOUN – e.g. *the local council / a council of war*
counsel – VERB & NOUN – e.g. *He counsels victims of crime./ give good counsel*

cue – NOUN & VERB – e.g. *the leading lady's cue / billiard cues / I'll cue you in.*
queue – NOUN & VERB – e.g. *a long queue for tickets / We queued for hours.*

curb – VERB & NOUN – e.g. *You must curb your appetite. / price curbs*
kerb – NOUN – e.g. *The taxi drew up at the kerb.*

currant – NOUN – e.g. *raisins, sultanas and currants*
current – NOUN & ADJECTIVE – e.g. *ocean currents / current affairs*

dairy – NOUN – e.g. – *milk from the local dairy*
diary – NOUN – e.g. – *I'll put the date in my diary.*

dependant – NOUN – e.g. *Do you have children or other dependants?*
dependent – ADJECTIVE – e.g. *We are dependent on aid.*

desert – NOUN & VERB – e.g. *the Gobi Desert / The sentry deserted his post.*
dessert – NOUN – e.g. *Would you like ice cream or fresh fruit for dessert?*

device – NOUN – e.g. *a device for slicing vegetables very thinly*
devise – VERB – e.g. *We've devised a cunning plan.*

draft – NOUN & VERB – *a first draft of the report / He's drafting a reply.*
draught – NOUN – e.g. *There's a draught coming under that door.*

dual – ADJECTIVE – e.g. *Their children have dual nationality.*
duel – NOUN & VERB – e.g. *They fought a duel./ an injury sustained while duelling*

dying – VERB – e.g. *The weakest are dying first, of hunger and cold.*
dyeing – VERB – e.g. *Have you been dyeing your hair again?*

eerie – ADJECTIVE – e.g. *an eerie silence*
eyrie – NOUN – e.g. *Two unfledged chicks were in the golden eagle's eyrie.*

envelop – VERB – e.g. *A greenish haze seemed to envelop the landscape.*
envelope – NOUN – e.g. *Send a stamped addressed envelope.*

excerpt – NOUN – e.g. *He played an excerpt from a Mozart opera.*
exert – VERB – e.g. *He is keen to exert his influence.*